STAGES OF DRAMA
Classical to Contemporary Theater

Third Edition

CARL H. KLAUS
University of Iowa

MIRIAM GILBERT
University of Iowa

BRADFORD S. FIELD, JR.
Wayne State University

ST. MARTIN'S PRESS
New York

Editor: Nancy Lyman
Managing editor: Patricia Mansfield Phelan
Project editor: Diana M. Puglisi
Production supervisor: Joe Ford
Art director: Sheree Goodman
Internal art: A. G. Smith
Cover design: Tom McKeveney
Cover photos: Front cover, left to right: Photo courtesy Guthrie Theater; Brigitte Lacombe. *Back cover, left to right:*
Photograph Morris Newcombe, copyright 1994; Douglas Spillane, courtesy of the Stratford Festival; Angus
McBean, Harvard Theatre Collection.

Library of Congress Catalog Card Number: 94-65178

Manufactured in the United States of America.

9 8 7 6 5
f e d c b

For information, write:
St. Martin's Press, Inc.
175 Fifth Avenue
New York, NY 10010

ISBN: 0-312-10135-X

CREDITS

Stages of Drama, third edition, offers a comprehensive one-volume collection of outstanding plays—forty-one in all—from the classical Greek period to the present. The increased size of this edition has enabled us to strengthen the broadly historical and generically representative coverage of the second edition, particularly in the modern and contemporary period, which now includes the work of twenty-six playwrights from twelve different countries, spanning a period of more than 150 years—a range of coverage unmatched among introductory texts for its theatrical variety and cultural diversity. Our modern section has been enriched by the addition of Georg Büchner's *Woyzeck*, Bernard Shaw's *Pygmalion*, and Federico Garcia Lorca's *The House of Bernarda Alba*; and our contemporary section by the addition of Eugène Ionesco's *The Lesson*, Edward Albee's *The Zoo Story*, Imamu Amiri Baraka's *Dutchman*, Maria Irene Fornes's *Fefu and Her Friends*, Ntozake Shange's *spell #7*, Sam Shepard's *Fool for Love*, David Henry Hwang's *M. Butterfly*, and David Mamet's *Oleanna*.

Our extensive introductory material has again been expanded in this edition, so as to provide three distinctive layers of commentary that we hope will contribute to understanding and enjoying drama:

1. A general introduction on reading and witnessing a play, illustrated with a discussion of Wendy Wasserstein's *The Man in a Case*.

2. Introductions to each period of drama, illustrated with detailed line drawings of theaters typical of the period, so that each play can be seen in the context of the stage for which it was originally performed.

3. Introductions to each of the dramatists, surveying their theatrical careers and their major works, as well as discussing issues related not only to understanding but also to staging their plays.

Above all, plays are meant to be staged and witnessed. Given this truth, we have once again provided two special kinds of supplementary materials:

1. Following each play, production photographs from a challenging twentieth-century production of the play; these production photos illustrate important dramatic moments as performed by major actors or repertory groups from the United States, Canada, England, and Europe.

2. Provocative reviews of each illustrated production which collectively exemplify a wide range of approaches to understanding dramatic performance.

A new appendix, "Analyzing a Play: Close Reading for Writing," offers a detailed example of annotating a section of Ionesco's *The Lesson*, together with specific suggestions for kinds of papers that might develop from such analysis. And we have again provided an appendix listing film and video productions of the plays in this collection, including a list of distributors from whom copies of the films and videos may be obtained. Thus from dramatist, to play, to performance, *Stages of Drama*, third edition, constitutes an invitation to experience the richly varied world of theater.

For their detailed reactions to the second edition of *Stages of Drama* and for their suggestions of plays to consider for the third edition, we are grateful to Victor L. Cahn (Skidmore College), Hilda Carey (Boston College), John J. Conlon (Boston University), Verna Foster (Loyola University, Chicago), Ivan Fuller (Augustana College), Tony Gilleran (Santa Barbara City College), Frances L. Helphinstine (Morehead State University), Jeffrey Huberman (Bradley University), Jane Anderson Jones (Manatee Community College), Jerrie Kennedy (Bellevue Community College), Robert C. Liberatore (Kent State University, Tuscarawas Campus), Kevin M. Lynch (Central Connecticut State University), Russ McDonald (University of North Carolina, Greensboro), Anthony Merzlak (Suffolk University), Patrick F. O'Connell (Gannon University), Peggy Poteet (Southern Nazarene University), Estelle M. Raben (Queens College, CUNY), Mark Rocha (California State University, Northridge), Tramble T. Turner (Pennsylvania State University), Sharon Walsh (Loyola University, Chicago), John Watson (University of Oregon), Keith Welsh (Webster University), and Frances Murphy Zauhar (St. Vincent College).

For her excellent research assistance in preparing the apparatus, we are particularly grateful to Kate Moncrief (University of Iowa). For their expert work in bringing this third edition into print, we are grateful to the staff of St. Martin's Press, especially Denise Quirk and editorial assistant Susan Cottenden, who played important roles in manuscript development, and Diana Puglisi, the project editor who coordinated the production process. We owe special thanks to Sandy Cohen for her energetic work in securing permissions for plays, production photographs, and reviews. Above all, we are indebted to Cathy Pusateri, our former editor, for launching this complex revision, and to Nancy Lyman, our current editor, for skillfully guiding it to completion.

CARL H. KLAUS
MIRIAM GILBERT
BRADFORD S. FIELD, JR.

CONTENTS

READING AND WITNESSING A PLAY

The plays in this collection, like most works of drama, are meant to be performed on a stage and witnessed by an audience. The life of drama is, in fact, so intimately connected to stage performance that a single word—"theater"—is often used to refer both to plays and to the place where they are performed and witnessed. The theatrical nature of plays is immediately evident from the fact that they consist largely of dialogue, in which characters are speaking to one another rather than to us, communicating with each other rather than with us as readers. In reading a play, we must infer a great deal more about the plot, the characters, and the significance of their experience than we do in reading a story, where we can rely on a narrator to tell us what is happening, characterize the persons who are involved, detail their thoughts and actions, explain what is at stake, and perhaps even comment on the significance of events as they unfold.

In reading a play rather than witnessing it on stage, we also have to imagine what it might look like in performance, projecting in our mind's eye an image of the setting and the props, as well as the movements, gestures, facial expressions, and vocal intonations of the characters. In other words, we have to recognize that the text of a play is actually a script for production—but a script that contains relatively few explicit stage directions compared to the many implicit staging clues from which the director, set designer, costumer, and actors create the complex spectacle of a theatrical production. And we—like the director, designers, and actors—must develop our understanding of the play and our idea of the play in performance primarily from a careful reading of the dialogue, as well as from whatever stage directions and other information the dramatist might provide about the characters and the setting.

As an example of what you can discover about the imaginative world of a play through close and careful reading, consider the information that Wendy Wasserstein offers at the beginning of her short play, *The Man in a Case*. She lists two characters, Byelinkov and Varinka—presumably a man and a woman, given the sound of their names—but tells us nothing else about them. We do not know who they are, how old they are, how they look, how they are dressed, or how they are related to each other. By the end of the play, however, all of these unknowns—or at least the ones that turn out to be relevant—will be revealed. But it is clear just from the list of characters that this play focuses only on two people, leading us to suppose perhaps that the play is concerned with illuminating an intimate human relationship. Having named the characters, Wasserstein then provides a few hints about the setting: "A small garden in the village of Mironitski, 1898." A reader may think, "But I've never heard of Mironitski," and that is probably the point—it's a small village somewhere in Russia, as the names of the characters would also indicate. But a set designer would look for additional clues about the garden and discover that it is evidently a flower garden, given the later references of both Byelinkov and Varinka to the fact that "the roses are in full bloom." So, one might imagine a set depicting a turn-of-the-century flower garden with white trellis-work panels and old-fashioned climbing roses—a setting evocative of warmth and romance.

Having named the characters and identified the scene, Wasserstein then shows us the characters in action rather than labeling them or describing them: "Byelinkov is pacing. Enter Varinka out of breath." A reader, or an audience member, might well ask "why is he pacing?" The actor who portrays Byelinkov will also want to know exactly *how* he is pacing: Is he walking slowly up and down, as if meditating, or is he walking anxiously back and forth along the same strip of stage, or is he deliberately putting one foot in front of the other, ostentatiously filling up time? And what is he doing while he is pacing? The fact that he begins by saying to Varinka "You are ten minutes late" suggests that he has been looking at his watch—probably a pocket watch suspended from a buttonhole on his vest—or that he looked at his watch just before Varinka came in. In any case, his opening line, far from being romantic or in any way solicitous, makes him appear to be quite stiff, strict, and reproving. Byelinkov's opening line also raises a host of questions about the reasons for his impatience with Varinka as well as about the nature of his relationship to her—questions that can only be answered by the play itself.

To discover what their relationship is like, as well as to try your hand at understanding a play and staging it imaginatively in the theater of your own mind, we suggest that you take a few minutes to read Wasserstein's very brief play, which begins on the next page. Then we will provide a brief commentary that you can compare with your own impressions and that you can use as a source of ideas for reading other plays in this collection.

THE MAN IN A CASE

BY WENDY WASSERSTEIN

CHARACTERS

BYELINKOV
VARINKA

SCENE

A small garden in the village of Mironitski. 1898.

(BYELINKOV *is pacing. Enter* VARINKA *out of breath.*)

BYELINKOV: You are ten minutes late.

VARINKA: The most amazing thing happened on my way over here. You know the woman who runs the grocery store down the road. She wears a black wig during the week, and a blond wig on Saturday nights. And she has the daughter who married an engineer in Moscow who is doing very well thank you and is living, God bless them, in a three-room apartment. But he really is the most boring man in the world. All he talks about is his future and his station in life. Well, she heard we were to be married and she gave me this basket of apricots to give to you.

BYELINKOV: That is a most amazing thing!

VARINKA: She said to me, "Varinka, you are marrying the most honorable man in the entire village. In this village he is the only man fit to speak with my son-in-law."

BYELINKOV: I don't care for apricots. They give me hives.

VARINKA: I can return them. I'm sure if I told her they give you hives she would give me a basket of raisins or a cake.

BYELINKOV: I don't know this woman or her pompous son-in-law. Why would she give me her cakes?

VARINKA: She adores you!

BYELINKOV: She is emotionally loose.

VARINKA: She adores you by reputation. Everyone adores you by reputation. I tell everyone I am to marry Byelinkov, the finest teacher in the county.

BYELINKOV: You tell them this?

VARINKA: If they don't tell me first.

BYELINKOV: Pride can be an imperfect value.

VARINKA: It isn't pride. It is the truth. You are a great man!

BYELINKOV: I am the master of Greek and Latin at a local school at the end of the village of Mironitski.

(VARINKA *kisses him.*)

VARINKA: And I am to be the master of Greek and Latin's wife!

BYELINKOV: Being married requires a great deal of re-sponsibility. I hope I am able to provide you with all that a married man must properly provide a wife.

VARINKA: We will be very happy.

BYELINKOV: Happiness is for children. We are entering into a social contract, an amicable agreement to provide us with a secure and satisfying future.

VARINKA: You are so sweet! You are the sweetest man in the world!

BYELINKOV: I'm a man set in his ways who saw a chance to provide himself with a small challenge.

VARINKA: Look at you! Look at you! Your sweet round spectacles, your dear collar always starched, always raised, your perfectly pressed pants always creasing at right angles perpendicular to the floor, and my most favorite part, the sweet little galoshes, rain or shine, just in case. My Byelinkov, never taken by surprise. Except by me.

BYELINKOV: You speak about me as if I were your pet.

VARINKA: You are my pet! My little school mouse.

BYELINKOV: A mouse?

VARINKA: My sweetest dancing bear with galoshes, my little stale babka.

BYELINKOV: A stale babka?

VARINKA: I am not Pushkin.

BYELINKOV (*Laughs*): That depends what you think of Pushkin.

VARINKA: You're smiling. I knew I could make you smile today.

BYELINKOV: I am a responsible man. Every day I have for breakfast black bread, fruit, hot tea, and every day I smile three times. I am halfway into my trans-lation of the *Aeneid* from classical Greek hexameter into Russian alexandrines. In twenty years I have never been late to school. I am a responsible man, but no dancing bear.

VARINKA: Dance with me.

BYELINKOV: Now? It is nearly four weeks before the wedding!

VARINKA: It's a beautiful afternoon. We are in your garden. The roses are in full bloom.

BYELINKOV: The roses have beetles.

VARINKA: Dance with me!

BYELINKOV: You are a demanding woman.

VARINKA: You chose me. And right. And left. And turn. And right. And left.

BYELINKOV: And turn. Give me your hand. Yo͟ like a school mouse. It's a beautiful af͟ are in my garden. The roses are in fu͟ turn. And turn. (*Twirls* VARINKA *arou͟*

VARINKA: I am the luckiest woman!

(BYELINKOV *stops dancing.*)

Why are you stopping?

BYELINKOV: To place a lilac in your hair. Every year on this day I will place a lilac in your hair.

VARINKA: Will you remember?

BYELINKOV: I will write it down. (*Takes a notebook from his pocket*) Dear Byelinkov, don't forget the day a young lady, your bride, entered your garden, your peace, and danced on the roses. On that day every year you are to place a lilac in her hair.

VARINKA: I love you.

BYELINKOV: It is convenient we met.

VARINKA: I love you.

BYELINKOV: You are a girl.

VARINKA: I am thirty.

BYELINKOV: But you think like a girl. That is an attractive attribute.

VARINKA: Do you love me?

BYELINKOV: We've never spoken about housekeeping.

VARINKA: I am an excellent housekeeper. I kept house for my family on the farm in Gadyatchsky. I can make a beetroot soup with tomatoes and aubergines which is so nice. Awfully, awfully nice.

BYELINKOV: You are fond of expletives.

VARINKA: My beet soup, sir, is excellent!

BYELINKOV: Please don't be cross. I too am an excellent housekeeper. I have a place for everything in the house. A shelf for each pot, a cubby for every spoon, a folder for favorite recipes. I have cooked for myself for twenty years. Though my beet soup is not outstanding, it is sufficient.

VARINKA: I'm sure it's very good.

BYELINKOV: No. It is awfully, awfully not. What I am outstanding in, however, what gives me greatest pleasure, is preserving those things which are left over. I wrap each tomato slice I haven't used in a wet cloth and place it in the coolest corner of the house. I have had my shoes for seven years because I wrap them in the galoshes you are so fond of. And every night before I go to sleep I wrap my bed in quilts and curtains so I never catch a draft.

VARINKA: You sleep with curtains on your bed?

BYELINKOV: I like to keep warm.

VARINKA: I will make you a new quilt.

BYELINKOV: No. No new quilt. That would be hazardous.

VARINKA: It is hazardous to sleep under curtains.

BYELINKOV: Varinka, I don't like change very much. If one works out the arithmetic, the final fraction of improvement is at best less than an eighth of value over the total damage caused by disruption. I never thought of marrying till I saw your eyes dancing among the familiar faces at the headmaster's tea. I assumed I would grow old preserved like those

which are left over, wrapped suitably in my case of curtains and quilts.

VARINKA: Byelinkov, I want us to have dinners with friends and summer country visits. I want people to say, "Have you spent time with Varinka and Byelinkov? He is so happy now that they are married. She is just what he needed."

BYELINKOV: You have already brought me some happiness. But I never was a sad man. Don't ever think I thought I was a sad man.

VARINKA: My sweetest darling, you can be whatever you want! If you are sad, they'll say she talks all the time, and he is soft-spoken and kind.

BYELINKOV: And if I am difficult?

VARINKA: Oh, they'll say he is difficult because he is highly intelligent. All great men are difficult. Look at Lermontov, Tchaikovsky, Peter the Great.

BYELINKOV: Ivan the Terrible.

VARINKA: Yes, him too.

BYELINKOV: Why are you marrying me? I am none of these things.

VARINKA: To me you are.

BYELINKOV: You have imagined this. You have constructed an elaborate romance for yourself. Perhaps you are the great one. You are the one with the great imagination.

VARINKA: Byelinkov, I am a pretty girl of thirty. You're right, I am not a woman. I have not made myself into a woman because I do not deserve that honor. Until I came to this town to visit my brother I lived on my family's farm. As the years passed I became younger and younger in fear that I would never marry. And it wasn't that I wasn't pretty enough or sweet enough, it was just that no man ever looked at me and saw a wife. I was not the woman who would be there when he came home. Until I met you I thought I would lie all my life and say I never married because I never met a man I loved. I will love you, Byelinkov. And I will help you to love me. We deserve the life everyone else has. We deserve not to be different.

BYELINKOV: Yes. We are the same as everyone else.

VARINKA: Tell me you love me.

BYELINKOV: I love you.

VARINKA (*Takes his hands*): We will be very happy. I am very strong. (*Pauses*) It is time for tea.

BYELINKOV: It is too early for tea. Tea is at half past the hour.

VARINKA: Do you have heavy cream? It will be awfully nice with apricots.

BYELINKOV: Heavy cream is too rich for teatime.

VARINKA: But today is special. Today you placed a lilac in my hair. Write in your note pad. Every year we will celebrate with apricots and heavy cream. I will go to my brother's house and get some.

BYELINKOV: But your brother's house is a mile from here.

VARINKA: Today it is much shorter. Today my brother gave me his bicycle to ride. I will be back very soon.

BYELINKOV: You rode to my house by bicycle! Did anyone see you?

VARINKA: Of course. I had such fun. I told you I saw the grocery store lady with the son-in-law who is doing very well thank you in Moscow, and the headmaster's wife.

BYELINKOV: You saw the headmaster's wife!

VARINKA: She smiled at me.

BYELINKOV: Did she laugh or smile?

VARINKA: She laughed a little. She said, "My dear, you are very progressive to ride a bicycle." She said you and your fiancé Byelinkov must ride together sometime. I wonder if he'll take off his galoshes when he rides a bicycle.

BYELINKOV: She said that?

VARINKA: She adores you. We had a good giggle.

BYELINKOV: A woman can be arrested for riding a bicycle. That is not progressive, it is a premeditated revolutionary act. Your brother must be awfully, awfully careful on behalf of your behavior. He has been careless—oh so careless—in giving you the bicycle.

VARINKA: Dearest Byelinkov, you are wrapping yourself under curtains and quilts! I made friends on the bicycle.

BYELINKOV: You saw more than the headmaster's wife and the idiot grocery woman.

VARINKA: She is not an idiot.

BYELINKOV: She is a potato-vending, sausage-armed fool!

VARINKA: Shhhh! My school mouse. Shhh!

BYELINKOV: What other friends did you make on this bicycle?

VARINKA: I saw students from my brother's classes. They waved and shouted, "Anthropos in love! Anthropos in love!!"

BYELINKOV: Where is that bicycle?

VARINKA: I left it outside the gate. Where are you going?

BYELINKOV (Muttering as he exits): Anthropos in love, anthropos in love.

VARINKA: They were cheering me on. Careful, you'll trample the roses.

BYELINKOV (Returning with the bicycle): Anthropos is the Greek singular for man. Anthropos in love translates as the Greek and Latin master in love. Of course they cheered you. Their instructor, who teaches them the discipline and contained beauty of the classics, is in love with a sprite on a bicycle. It is a good giggle, isn't it? A very good giggle! I am returning this bicycle to your brother.

VARINKA: But it is teatime.

BYELINKOV: Today we will not have tea.

VARINKA: But you will have to walk back a mile.

BYELINKOV: I have my galoshes on. (Gets on the bicycle) Varinka, we deserve not to be different. (Begins to pedal. The bicycle doesn't move)

VARINKA: Put the kickstand up.

BYELINKOV: I beg your pardon.

VARINKA (Giggling): Byelinkov, to make the bicycle move, you must put the kickstand up.

(BYELINKOV puts it up and awkwardly falls off the bicycle as it moves.)

(Laughing) Ha ha ha. My little school mouse. You look so funny! You are the sweetest dearest man in the world. Ha ha ha!

(Pause.)

BYELINKOV: Please help me up. I'm afraid my galosh is caught.

VARINKA (Trying not to laugh): Your galosh is caught! (Explodes in laughter again) Oh, you are so funny! I do love you so. (Helps BYELINKOV up) You were right, my pet, as always. We don't need heavy cream for tea. The fraction of improvement isn't worth the damage caused by the disruption.

BYELINKOV: Varinka, it is still too early for tea. I must complete two stanzas of my translation before late afternoon. That is my regular schedule.

VARINKA: Then I will watch while you work.

BYELINKOV: No. You had a good giggle. That is enough.

VARINKA: Then while you work I will work too. I will make lists of guests for our wedding.

BYELINKOV: I can concentrate only when I am alone in my house. Please take your bicycle home to your brother.

VARINKA: But I don't want to leave you. You look so sad.

BYELINKOV: I never was a sad man. Don't ever think I was a sad man.

VARINKA: Byelinkov, it's a beautiful day, we are in your garden. The roses are in bloom.

BYELINKOV: Allow me to help you on to your bicycle. (Takes VARINKA's hand as she gets on the bike)

VARINKA: You are such a gentleman. We will be very happy.

BYELINKOV: You are very strong. Good day, Varinka.

(VARINKA pedals off. BYELINKOV, alone in the garden, takes out his pad and rips up the note about the lilac, strews it over the garden, then carefully picks up each piece of paper and places them all in a small envelope as lights fade to black.)

Reading and Witnessing *The Man in a Case*

The best place to begin reading closely is with the first words of a play, as we did in our commentary on the names of the characters, the setting, the opening stage directions, and Byelinkov's opening line. As you may have noticed, we found ourselves raising more questions than we could answer about Byelinkov and Varinka. At this early point in a play, it is entirely natural to feel oneself bombarded by a host of such questions. Moreover, it is probably best to leave the questions unanswered, allowing the play itself to answer the questions in its own time and its own way. For example, when Varinka responds to Byelinkov's reproof with a long speech explaining why she is late, we find out that she was delayed by the woman who runs the grocery store, but we also find out many more things. Look at the outpouring of details:

> The most amazing thing happened on my way over here. You know the woman who runs the grocery store down the road. She wears a black wig during the week, and a blond wig on Saturday nights. And she has the daughter who married an engineer in Moscow who is doing very well thank you and is living, God bless them, in a three-room apartment. But he really is the most boring man in the world. All he talks about is his future and his station in life. Well, she heard we were to be married and she gave me this basket of apricots to give to you.

The most important information in this speech seems to come in the last sentence, "she heard we were to be married," for it answers the crucial question of how Byelinkov and Varinka are related to each other. The revelation that they are engaged also raises new questions about the status of their engagement and the nature of their feelings for each other, particularly given the sharp contrast between the stern tone of Byelinkov's reproof and the lively manner of Varinka's report about "the woman who runs the grocery store." But the real revelation in this speech is the gossipy, vivacious, and sociable behavior of Varinka. We will never meet the woman who runs the grocery store or her daughter or her son-in-law from Moscow, but to Varinka, at this moment, they seem interesting enough to talk about, so much so that she enlivens her story with bits and pieces of the woman's conversation—"thank you" and "God bless them." Varinka's dialogue here, as elsewhere, is not just a source of information about her relationship to Byelinkov, but also a display of her character and a source of insight into her complex motives. In this case, for example, she is evidently telling Byelinkov about the woman in part to justify her lateness, but also to account for the basket of apricots that she is carrying and to pay court to Byelinkov by flattering him with reports of his local reputation. Thus, when Varinka comes to the final sentence of this speech, we should imagine her buoyantly gesturing as if to give Byelinkov the basket of apricots she is carrying, and, in light of the next few lines, we should imagine Byelinkov making a gesture that indicates his grumpy refusal to accept them—"I don't care for apricots. They give me hives."

Thus the first five speeches of the play reveal a striking contrast between the behavior and inclinations of Byelinkov and Varinka: he characterized by his reliance on the watch, his sternly reproving manner, and his apparent isolation from people, and she by her eager delight in people and in the trivial details of everyday life. But, along with this clear-cut contrast, we should also recognize that choices can be made about the degree of exasperation Byelinkov may be feeling or the amount of interest that Varinka seems to have in the woman with whom she talked. The audience member will perhaps have fewer questions, since the actors will have made choices about how to portray the two characters at this point in the play. But the process by which the choices are made is the same for the actors and for readers: Both will ask, "what do these lines reveal about the characters, their situation, their motives, their actions, their movements on stage, their gestures, their facial expressions, and so on?"

One could work through the entire play in this fashion, asking questions and looking for answers about the implications of almost every line. Indeed, the work of rehearsing a play for the stage, like the work of close reading, inevitably involves just this kind of painstaking analysis. But performing, witnessing, and reading also call upon one to look for the overall shape of the play—to notice where the mood seems to change, where complications in the plot seem to arise or dissipate, where tensions between the characters seem to develop or be resolved, where surprising events occur—and to consider why these changes take place. For example, the opening lines that we have just discussed hardly suggest that only a few pages later Byelinkov and Varinka will be joyously dancing with one another. Yet that moment when they dance around the stage, a moment easily imaginable from Varinka's zestful lines—"And right. And left. And turn. And right. And left."—is one of the major "actions" in the play, growing out of Byelinkov's statement, "I am a responsible man, but no dancing bear." Varinka must hear that line as an implicit challenge, and she surprises both Byelinkov and the audience with her exuberant command—"Dance with me!"—and even more with her success. Perhaps that very success, which she follows up with repeated statements of "I love you," and then with the more frightening question, "Do you love me?," precipitates the next big movement of the play, which shows Byelinkov in retreat, insisting on his ways of doing things and building up to his crucial and withering statement, "Varinka, I don't like change very much."

By now it should become clear to the audience, and to the reader, that change is exactly what Varinka will bring into Byelinkov's life, and that change is perhaps something he cannot accept. The challenge for the playwright is to find a way of showing both the reality of their impending marriage—through the dance—and then the fact that it may not, in fact probably cannot, come to pass. The reciprocal challenge for the reader is to pay close attention to the swiftly changing circumstances that culminate in the apparent unraveling of their engagement. For example, when Varinka asks Byelinkov the apparently harmless question "Do you have heavy cream? It will be awfully nice with apricots" and then impulsively offers to get some from her brother's by cycling a mile to his house, she begins the action that will lead first to Byelinkov's fulminations against a woman riding a bicycle, then to the description of the students she saw while riding and their cries of "Anthropos in love," and finally to the moment when Byelinkov decides that he will ride the bicycle to her brother's and walk back—a decision that leads inexorably to the seeming breakdown of their engagement. Once he gets on the bicycle, it becomes clear that he has never ridden one before, since he doesn't seem to realize that he has to put up the kickstand "to make the bicycle move." Varinka's laughter throughout this slapstick episode, despite her assurance, "I do love you so," is something that Byelinkov obviously cannot accept, since it constitutes a direct challenge to his own strongly felt need for obedience and respect. So in his stiff, proud, and formal way, he helps her onto the bicycle and sends her away.

The development of this play, with its focus on particular moments (the tense opening, the briefly buoyant dance, the conversation about change, the slapstick bicycle episode), seems to unfold quite naturally. Yet when one compares the play to its source—Anton Chekhov's short story, "The Man in a Case"—one sees just how carefully Wasserstein has condensed and reshaped the story for the stage, and thus how radically different a playscript is from a narrative text. For example, whereas Wasserstein portrays only the ending of Byelinkov and Varinka's relationship, Chekhov's narrator sketches the entire life of Byelinkov's counterpart, Belikov. And, whereas Wasserstein depicts the relationship without any kind of explanatory comment about the characters or their situation, Chekhov's narrator pointedly prefaces his account of Belikov with a thematic generalization: "There's so many of these solitary types around, like hermit crabs or snails, they are, always seeking safety in their shells." In fact, Chekhov's narrator spends several pages showing Belikov's repressed and repressive nature before coming to the surprising statement, "and this teacher of Greek, this man in his case, nearly got married once, believe it or not." The lack of

any such explanatory comment in Wasserstein's play continually obliges a reader to make inferences about the characters and their situation from what they say and what they do.

Perhaps the most striking instance of the carefully inferential process one needs to use in reading a dramatic text can be seen in connection with the concluding lines of Wasserstein's play. A casual reading of those last few lines, in which Varinka pedals off on her bicycle and Byelinkov tears up her love note, might lead one to suppose that the engagement has completely and irretrievably broken down—as irretrievably as in Chekhov's narrative version, where Belikov not only breaks off the engagement but turns sick and dies a month later. But, in Wasserstein's play, the resolution is not so clear-cut, as can be seen through a close examination of the text. Byelinkov's tearing up the note and strewing the pieces over the garden does, admittedly, seem to constitute a tangible and visible repudiation of all the affection and joy embodied in their dancing together earlier and in his uncharacteristically spontaneous penning of the note. Indeed, the act of deliberately strewing the pieces of the note over the garden suggests that Byelinkov is trying to disperse even the memory of his attachment to Varinka. But Byelinkov's final gesture, in which he "carefully picks up each piece of paper and places them all in a small envelope," is by contrast a complex and ambiguous theatrical image. One can read this gesture as the ultimate sign of Byelinkov's repression, indicating that he is so encased in his conventional morality that he cannot even allow himself to tear up a note and toss away the pieces without then picking them up and tidying up the garden, much as he has just tidied up his life by sending Varinka away. Yet one can also interpret this final gesture as signaling a sudden change of heart, a desire at least to save the pieces of what he has just torn up, possibly even to put them—and their relationship—back together again. In fact, Varinka, as he knows, is committed to the relationship, for her parting words to him indicate her continuing belief that "we will be very happy."

Wasserstein does not tell us how to interpret Byelinkov's final gesture, for in drama, as in life, the scenes and images we behold are often quite ambiguous. If our reading is to be true to the complexity of the dramatic experience, we must be willing to let the "lights fade to black" as we behold Byelinkov picking up the pieces of paper and putting them "in a small envelope," even if this final image leaves us in a state of uncertainty. Reading a play is thus a dynamic process, as our minds take in words that imply and develop images evocative of the richness and complexity of experience.

CLASSICAL GREEK THEATER

During the fifth century B.C., the age of classical Greek drama, the theater in Athens stood empty almost 360 days a year, and yet the theater has probably never commanded quite so much attention as it did in fifth century Athens, the home of classical Greek drama. Drama occupied a unique place in the culture of ancient Athenians, for it was intimately related to one of their most important religious celebrations, and it was vigorously supported by their most powerful political institution. It was, in fact, produced under the auspices of the Athenian government, and during the greater part of the fifth century it was performed only once a year in connection with the *City Dionysia*, the major festival honoring Dionysus, the Greek god of fertility.

Dionysus had for centuries been worshipped in choric rituals known as *dithyrambs*, and these religious ceremonies are thought to be the principal source from which Greek tragedy emerged sometime in the mid-sixth century. It was during this period that Thespis, reputedly the first playwright, added an actor to the dithyrambic chorus, thereby bringing dramatic impersonation into ritual ceremonies that had previously consisted of narrative hymns chanted by a choric leader together with refrains sung and danced by a chorus. The Dionysian heritage of Greek tragedy probably accounts for the special status it achieved at the City Dionysia in 534 B.C., when the Athenian government established a prize, won appropriately by Thespis, for the best tragedy to be presented at the festival. By 486 B.C., when the contest was expanded to include comedy, the City Dionysia had become the most prestigious of the four annual celebrations of Dionysus. Thousands came from everywhere in the Greek world to attend the festival, which was held in late March or early April to insure a fruitful spring. Obviously, theatrical productions constituted a major event in the rhythm of Athenian life, an event uniting the entire community in an expression of its civic pride and sacred convictions.

The magnitude of that event is revealed by the elaborate arrangements connected with the festival productions. The sole responsibility for supervising the contest was entrusted to a state official chosen by lot from the Athenian public. Dramatists who wished to enter the contest were required to submit their plays to him almost a year in advance of the festival, and he chose the three tragic as well as the three comic playwrights who had the honor of competing for each prize. This official also appointed wealthy citizens to serve as producers for each contestant, and these citizens financed the training and costuming of the chorus, the largest and most complex element of Greek theater. The balance of the costs, such as salaries for the actors and prizes for the winners, was paid by the government of Athens. This dramatic festival was the climax of nearly a year of activity on the part of hundreds of Athenian citizens.

The contest was preceded by a splendid public ceremony, featuring a lengthy procession of officials, priests, theatrical sponsors, and citizens who carried ritual offerings that they presented at the altar of Dionysus located in the theater. Once the contest began, it ran for three days, starting early in the morning and continuing throughout the afternoon. Each tragic dramatist needed almost an entire day to produce the three or four plays he was required to submit, and the remainder of each day was taken up by a single comedy each comic dramatist was required to submit. During those three days, the city of Athens became the center of a spectacular drama festival at which a total of twelve to fifteen new plays were produced.

The climax of the contest, when the prizes were awarded, was a moment of extraordinary honor for the winning dramatist and his producer. This honor was so important that the contest was judged by a panel of citizens chosen according to a very elaborate procedure that prevented bribery or any other form of unfair influence on their decision. The honor was so prestigious, in fact, that the government maintained records of all the contests, and many of the producers in turn commissioned monuments to be built as enduring records of their victories. By the middle of the fifth century, prizes had also been established for actors, and the profession of acting came to be so highly regarded that eminent actors were frequently given special public appointments and privileges. Classical Greek drama was neither a commercial enterprise as it is on Broadway, nor a coterie activity as it so often is off Broadway. It was a major public institution commanding the respect and support of the entire city-state.

The prestige of the dramatic contest was matched by the magnitude of the theater where it took place, the Theater of Dionysus, which was a sanctuary restricted to worship and celebration of the god. The design of this theater (see Figures 1 and 2), like the drama performed there, reflected its ritual origin. Its central element was the *orchestra* (literally, the dancing place), a circular area sixty-four feet in diameter where the dithyrambic choruses had performed their hymns to Dionysus and where the altar of Dionysus, the *thymele*, retained its focal location. The *orchestra* was surrounded by the *theatron* (literally, the seeing place), a semicircular sloping hillside that was terraced and equipped with benches capable of seating approximately 15,000 spectators. Facing the *theatron* was the *skene* (literally, the hut), which probably originated as a temporary dressing room for actors and then developed into a scenic structure possibly one-hundred feet long, with three openings on to the *orchestra,* wings projecting toward the *orchestra,* and a slightly raised stage-like platform extending between the wings. Though the theater was frequently remodelled, its basic three-part structure—*theatron, orchestra,* and *skene*—was never altered and, in fact, served as the pattern for others in the ancient Greek world. The classical simplicity of that structure and the magnitude of its parts are unparalleled in the history of the theater.

The 15,000 people who attended the Theater of Dionysus were treated to a unique dramatic spectacle—a spectacle perfectly suited to the size, shape, and ceremonial heritage of that theater. For example, the typical Greek play whether tragedy or comedy contained not only units of dramatic action, known as episodes, but also choral odes following each episode. The performance included not only dialogue and action, but also song and dance that amplified the mood and significance of the action. The chorus typically made its entrance, the *parados,* after a brief expository episode, the *prologos,* and the *parados* must have been a splendid event, for the members of the chorus, using either the stately

Figure 1. The classical Greek theater.

Figure 2. The classical Greek theater at Epidaurus, in its restored state, during a production of *Agamemnon* by the National Theatre Company of Greece, 1965. (Photograph: D. A. Harissiadis.)

rhythms of tragedy or the burlesque movements of comedy, marched into the *orchestra* through the passageways between the *theatron* and *skene,* then arranged themselves in a rectangular formation and began to perform their choral song and dance to the accompaniment of a flute. Once the chorus had entered the *orchestra,* it remained there throughout the play, performing not only during its odes but also during the episodes, sometimes exchanging dialogue with the characters through its leader, the *choragos,* sometimes making gestures and movements in sympathetic response to the action. The chorus provided a sustained point of reference, a continuous source of mediation between the audience and the actors themselves, who moved back and forth between the *orchestra* and the *skene* as their parts dictated. Although the chorus may strike modern audiences as unrealistic and undramatic, it was in keeping with the expectations of the ancient Greek audience, and it was totally consistent with the ceremonial form of drama required by the design and dimensions of their theater.

This theater required above all a bold and monumental form of drama—both in conception and execution. Nuances of character, complexities of plot, delicacies of gesture, subtleties of inflection—none of these qualities could have made an impact in so large a theater. Such a theater simply did not lend itself to the kinds of detail that produce a modern realistic illusion. Consequently, all the elements of staging were highly conventionalized, formalized, and stylized. Painted scenery, for example, which developed during the second quarter of the fifth century, probably consisted only of a few generalized locales, such as a palace, a temple, a cave, or a forest, represented on the areas between the entrances to the *skene.* Only a few props or machines were available to assist the imagination of the audience, such as a crane by which characters might be suspended as if in flight from the roof of the *skene,* or a tableau wheeled out of the *skene* to suggest offstage action, or a horse-drawn chariot wheeled into the *orchestra* to mark the arrival of a hero, or a torch held up to signify nighttime— props and machines, which, like the painted scenes, were capable of making a clear visual impact.

Actors also required special techniques and equipment. They made large gestures with their arms, for small movements of the hands would have been indetectable by the audience. They also delivered their lines with a clear and strong inflection; no matter how good the acoustics may have been, the actors still had to contend with sounds in the audience, and 15,000 people even when they are trying to be quiet can generate a great deal of noise. Because facial movements would have been invisible to almost everyone in the audience, the actors wore large stylized masks representing basic character types and, as their fortunes and emotions changed, they changed their masks to suit the situation. No doubt their costumes were also designed to accentuate their stature, to make them appear larger than life. In fact, after the fifth century, actors were even equipped with elevated shoes to increase the impression of their height. The chorus also wore masks and probably used lightweight costumes and shoes to facilitate the various dance movements it performed while singing choral odes. Taken as a whole—the choric singing and dancing, the simplified setting, the bold acting—dramatic productions in ancient Greece must have matched the epic dimensions of the theater and of the plays that were written for it by Aeschylus, Sophocles, Euripides, and Aristophanes.

AESCHYLUS

ca. 524–456 B.C.

The tragedies of Aeschylus are the oldest works of Greek drama, and thus of western drama, that have survived. Although they date from the early period of Greek drama, they are by no means primitive either in conception or execution. Aeschylus, in fact, is generally credited with transforming the semidramatic elements he inherited from his predecessors into an authentically dramatic form, and he is, therefore, regarded as having created the structure and style of classical Greek tragedy. He was born near Athens less than ten years after the inauguration of the dramatic contests, which he entered for the first time in 499, but did not win until 484. Subsequently, however, he was so successful and influential a dramatist in Athens that he was honored after his death by an exceptional decree of the state permitting his plays to be revived in the festival contests. He won the contest thirteen times during his life, and after his death he continued to win prizes even though his plays were competing with new works by living dramatists. He reportedly wrote more than ninety plays, and the titles of seventy-nine have been recovered from Athenian records, but only seven of his tragedies have survived.

These seven plays reveal a comprehensive vision of experience, for their action always takes into account not simply the lives of individual men and women but also the destinies of entire families, communities, nations, and sometimes even cosmic forces. In *The Persians* (472), for example, which is the earliest of his extant plays and the only one based completely on historical experience, Aeschylus shows the majestic suffering in defeat of those people who only a few years earlier had invaded Greece and threatened to replace Athenian democracy with Persian tyranny. In *Prometheus Bound* (ca. 460), he dramatizes a cosmic experience, a conflict between the gods, represented by the defiant refusal of Prometheus, though chained to a desolate mountain and threatened with endless torture, to give in to the will of Zeus.

Events and conflicts of a Promethean magnitude could not have been worked out within the limits of a single play. Thus it is not surprising that Aeschylus developed and perfected the trilogy, for its grand scope—three full length plays joined to one another by their treatment of a single subject or theme—was ideally suited to his cosmic view of experience. His only surviving trilogy is *The Oresteia* (458), but it exemplifies the large-scale movements through time and space that are possible within the form. The three plays that make up this trilogy—*Agamemnon, The Libation Bearers,* and *The Eumenides*—dramatize a synoptic history of cultural progress, a history encompassing two generations of a family, during which men and the gods are shown advancing from a barbaric to a civilized form of justice, from the personal vengeance enacted in *Agamemnon* and *The Libation Bearers* to the public trial by jury conducted in *The Eumenides*. Drama so large in scope had not been attempted before Aeschylus, but since his time the trilogy and other multiplay structures have been used by many dramatists, such as Shakespeare in *Henry VI*, Eugene O'Neill in *Mourning Becomes Electra*, which is based on *The Oresteia,* and Ed Bullins in *The Twentieth Century Cycle.*

Aeschylus could never have achieved the dramatic power of his trilogies, or even of the individual plays that constitute them, had he limited himself to the rudimentary theatrical elements he inherited from Thespis: a chorus and a single actor. Given these conditions, tragedy before the time of Aeschylus must have been heavily dominated by the chorus, punctuated occasionally by the single actor impersonating a character and reciting a set speech or exchanging a few lines with the leader of the chorus. But early in his career, as early certainly as *The Persians,* Aeschylus made the revolutionary and dramatically essential innovation of using a second actor. Aeschylus thus made it possible to show characters interacting with one another, as well as with the chorus. He could then dramatize conflict and through conflict show character in action and plot in motion. In his later plays, such as *Agamemnon,* Aeschylus followed the precedent of Sophocles and used three actors.

Once it became possible to represent multiple characters, it was only a matter of time before the actors became as important as the chorus, then more important, then solely important. Aeschylus never went beyond the first stage in this process, for in his plays the chorus continues to have an important dramatic role, not only observing events and meditating on them, but also interacting continuously with the characters, questioning them, prodding them, rebuking them, praising them—taking part in events as they take place. In Aeschylean drama the chorus is not a minor or detachable element. In *Agamemnon,* in fact, the chorus has nearly as many lines as the characters, and without the chorus the play would be only an abbreviated melodrama, consisting of a few sensational incidents from the aftermath of the Trojan War.

Although *Agamemnon* is the first play of a trilogy, it stands alone as a consummately tragic expression of the cultural issues resolved by the remaining two plays. Its plot, as in all the plays of Aeschylus, is remarkably spare and simple, consisting of a few bold events—the return of Agamemnon with Cassandra and the slaying of them by Clytemnestra and Aegisthus. From all the events of the Trojan War, from all the stories about Agamemnon, his ancestors, and his children, Aeschylus chooses to dramatize only the events of a single day. But through the dialogue and lyrical reflections of the chorus, these events are made to symbolize an enduring problem in the life of Agamemnon, his ancestors, his country, and his world—the problem of vengeance, that primitive form of justice, which, rather than ending crime, endlessly renews it. The cyclical nature of revenge is discovered and expressed by the chorus, which repeatedly makes the past vividly present in its recollections—of "hearts howling in boundless bloodlust," of "a war for a runaway wife," of "a virgin's blood upon the altar," of "barbarous building of hates and disloyalties grown on the family." In mingling reflection with memory, the chorus seeks both to justify revenge and to find moral alternatives to it. Through its wavering attitude, its dilemma, its repeated questionings, rememberings, and meditations, the chorus becomes a character in its own right, as dramatically compelling as Agamemnon with all his grandeur and pride, or Clytemnestra with all her bitterness and hate, or Cassandra with all her foresight and all her helplessness.

These characters and the stories about them were, of course, standard items of

Greek legend, readily available to Aeschylus and totally familiar to all the members of his audience. Homer had told about them several hundred years earlier, and his tales had been retold by a long line of Greek poets and storytellers, but those stories took on a strikingly new meaning in the hands of Aeschylus. Just how new (and how different) can be seen by comparing the way that Agamemnon is viewed in Homer's *Odyssey* with the way he is represented in the work of Aeschylus. Whereas Homer had presented Agamemnon as a completely sympathetic character, Aeschylus shows him to be a morally ambiguous character. Their differing conceptions of Agamemnon are, at last, the consequence of their differing ideas of justice. Vengeance, which Homer takes for granted, Aeschylus calls into question.

Because it raises such large questions about the conduct of men, of families, of communities, of nations—and because neither men, nor families, nor communities, nor nations conduct themselves much differently now from the way they have for thousands of years—*Agamemnon* remains a perennially compelling play, a permanently tragic statement about the condition of things. In conjunction with the other two plays that make up *The Oresteia,* it offers actors and directors an extraordinary theatrical challenge, for its grand scope calls for a correspondingly grand form of staging. Grandness, of course, is difficult to achieve within the intimate space of most contemporary theaters, not to mention the naturalistic style of much contemporary acting. But modern productions of *The Oresteia* have sought to meet this challenge either by staging the work in a classical Greek theater (see Figure 2 on p. 11 and Figure 1 on p. 35), or by performing it in costumes, masks, and styles of acting modelled on classical Greek practices (see Figures 2 and 3 on pp. 35–36). Judging from photographs and reviews of these performances, the heroic theater of Aeschylus can be reclaimed, or at least approximated, even in an unheroic age.

AGAMEMNON

BY AESCHYLUS / TRANSLATED BY LOUIS MACNEICE

CHARACTERS*

WATCHMAN
CHORUS OF OLD MEN OF THE CITY
CLYTEMNESTRA
HERALD
AGAMEMNON
CASSANDRA
AEGISTHUS

SCENE

A space in front of the palace of Agamemnon in Argos.
Night. A WATCHMAN *on the roof of the palace.*

WATCHMAN: The gods it is I ask to release me from
    this watch
A year's length now, spending my nights like a dog,
Watching on my elbow on the roof of the sons of
    Atreus
So that I have come to know the assembly of the
    nightly stars

Those which bring storm and those which bring
    summer to men,
The shining Masters riveted in the sky—   10
I know the decline and rising of those stars.
And now I am waiting for the sign of the beacon,
The flame of fire that will carry the report from
    Troy,
News of her taking. Which task has been assigned
    me
By a woman of sanguine heart but a man's mind.
Yet when I take my restless rest in the soaking dew,
My night not visited with dreams—   20
For fear stands by me in the place of sleep
That I cannot firmly close my eyes in sleep—
Whenever I think to sing or hum to myself
As an antidote to sleep, then every time I groan
And fall to weeping for the fortunes of this house
Where not as before are things well ordered now.
But now may a good chance fall, escape from pain,
The good news visible in the midnight fire.

(Pause. A light appears, gradually increasing, the light of
the beacon.)

Ha! I salute you, torch of the night whose light
Is like the day, an earnest of many dances   30
In the city of Argos, celebration of Peace.
I call to Agamemnon's wife; quickly to rise
Out of her bed and in the house to raise
Clamour of joy in answer to this torch
For the city of Troy is taken—
Such is the evident message of the beckoning
    flame.
And I myself will dance my solo first
For I shall count my master's fortune mine
Now that this beacon has thrown me a lucky throw. 40
And may it be when he comes, the master of this
    house,
That I grasp his hand in my hand.
As to the rest, I am silent. A great ox, as they say,
Stands on my tongue. The house itself, if it took
    voice,

---

*THE FAMILY TREE

THE CHAIN OF CRIMES

    The chain of crimes in this play is as follows (see Family Tree above):

Past
    (1) Thyestes seduced Atreus' wife.
    (2) Atreus killed Thyestes' young children and gave him them as meat.
    (3) Helen forsook her husband and went to Troy with Paris.
    (4) Agamemnon, to promote the Trojan War, sacrificed his daughter Iphigeneia.

Present.
    (5) Aegisthus and Clytemnestra murder Agamemnon.

Future.
    (6) Orestes will kill Aegisthus and his mother Clytemnestra.

16

Could tell the case most clearly. But I will only speak
50 To those who know. For the others I remember nothing.

(Enter CHORUS OF OLD MEN. *During the following chorus the day begins to dawn.)*

CHORUS: The tenth year it is since Priam's high
Adversary, Menelaus the king
And Agamemnon, the double-throned and sceptred
Yoke of the sons of Atreus
Ruling in fee from God,
From this land gathered an Argive army
On a mission of war a thousand ships,
Their hearts howling in boundless bloodlust
60 In eagles' fashion who in lonely
Grief for nestlings above their homes hang
Turning in cycles
Beating the air with the oars of their wings,
    Now to no purpose
    Their love and task of attention.

But above there is One,
Maybe Pan, maybe Zeus or Apollo,
Who cries the harsh cries of the birds
Guests in his kingdom,
70 Wherefore, though late, in requital
He sends the Avenger.
Thus Zeus our master
Guardian of guest and of host
Sent against Paris the sons of Atreus
For a woman of many men
Many the dog-tired wrestlings
Limbs and knees in the dust pressed—
    For both the Greeks and Trojans
    An overture of breaking spears.

80 Things are where they are, will finish
In the manner fated and neither
Fire beneath nor oil above can soothe
The stubborn anger of the unburnt offering.
As for us, our bodies are bankrupt,
The expedition left us behind
And we wait supporting on sticks
Our strength—the strength of a child;
For the marrow that leaps in a boy's body
Is no better than that of the old
90 For the War God is not in his body;
While the man who is very old
And his leaf withering away
Goes on the three-foot way
No better than a boy, and wanders
A dream in the middle of the day.

But you, daughter of Tyndareus,
Queen Clytemnestra,

What is the news, what is the truth, what have you learnt,
On the strength of whose word have you thus   100
Sent orders for sacrifice round?
All the gods, the gods of the town,
Of the worlds of Below and Above,
By the door, in the square,
Have their altars ablaze with your gifts,
From here, from there, all sides, all corners,
Sky-high leap the flame-jets fed
By gentle and undeceiving
Persuasion of sacred unguent,
Oil from the royal stores.   110
Of these things tell
That which you can, that which you may,
Be healer of this our trouble
Which at times torments with evil
Though at times by propitiations
A shining hope repels
The insatiable thought upon grief
Which is eating away our hearts.

Of the omen which powerfully speeded
That voyage of strong men, by God's grace even I   120
Can tell, my age can still
Be galvanized to breathe the strength of song,
To tell how the kings of all the youth of Greece
Two-throned but one in mind
Were launched with pike and punitive hand
Against the Trojan shore by angry birds.
Kings of the birds to our kings came,
One with a white rump, the other black,
Appearing near the palace on the spear-arm side
Where all could see them,   130
Tearing a pregnant hare with the unborn young
Foiled of their courses.
    Cry, cry upon Death; but may the good prevail.

But the diligent prophet of the army seeing the sons
Of Atreus twin in temper knew
That the hare-killing birds were the two
Generals, explained it thus—
'In time this expedition sacks the town
Of Troy before whose towers   140
By Fate's force the public
Wealth will be wasted.
Only let not some spite from the gods benight the bulky battalions,
The bridle of Troy, nor strike them untimely;
For the goddess feels pity, is angry
With the winged dogs of her father
Who killed the cowering hare with her unborn young;
Artemis hates the eagles' feast.'   150
    Cry, cry upon Death; but may the good prevail.

'But though you are so kind, goddess,
To the little cubs of lions
And to all the sucking young of roving beasts
In whom your heart delights,
Fulfil us the signs of these things,
The signs which are good but open to blame,
And I call on Apollo the Healer
That his sister raise not against the Greeks
160 Unremitting gales to baulk their ships,
Hurrying on another kind of sacrifice, with no
    feasting,
Barbarous building of hates and disloyalties
Grown on the family. For anger grimly returns
Cunningly haunting the house, avenging the death
    of a child, never forgetting its due.'
So cried the prophet—evil and good together,
Fate that the birds foretold to the king's house.
In tune with this
170   Cry, cry upon Death; but may the good prevail.

Zeus, whoever He is, if this
Be a name acceptable,
By this name I will call him.
There is no one comparable
When I reckon all of the case
Excepting Zeus, if ever I am to jettison
The barren care which clogs my heart.

Not He who formerly was great
With brawling pride and mad for broils
180 Will even be said to have been.
And He who was next has met
His match and is seen no more,
But Zeus is the name to cry in your triumph-song
And win the prize for wisdom.

Who setting us on the road
Made this a valid law—
    'That men must learn by suffering.'
Drop by drop in sleep upon the heart
Falls the laborious memory of pain,
190 Against one's will comes wisdom;
The grace of the gods is forced on us
    Throned inviolably.

So at that time the elder
Chief of the Greek ships
Would not blame any prophet
Nor face the flail of fortune;
For unable to sail, the people
Of Greece were heavy with famine,
Waiting in Aulis where the tides
200   Flow back, opposite Chalcis.

But the winds that blew from the Strymon,
Bringing delay, hunger, evil harbourage,
Crazing men, rotting ships and cables,
By drawing out the time

Were shredding into nothing the flower of Argos,
When the prophet screamed a new
Cure for that bitter tempest
And heavier still for the chiefs,
Pleading the anger of Artemis so that the sons of
    Atreus   210
Beat the ground with their sceptres and shed tears.

Then the elder king found voice and answered:
'Heavy is my fate, not obeying,
And heavy it is if I kill my child, the delight of my
    house,
And with a virgin's blood upon the altar
Make foul her father's hands.
Either alternative is evil.
How can I betray the fleet
And fail the allied army?   220
It is right they should passionately cry for the winds
    to be lulled
By the blood of a girl. So be it. May it be well.'

But when he had put on the halter of Necessity
Breathing in his heart a veering wind of evil
Unsanctioned, unholy, from that moment forward
He changed his counsel, would stop at nothing.
For the heart of man is hardened by infatuation,
A faulty adviser, the first link of sorrow.
Whatever the cause, he brought himself to slay   230
His daughter, an offering to promote the voyage
To a war for a runaway wife.

Her prayers and her cries of father,
Her life of a maiden,
Counted for nothing with those militarists;
But her father, having duly prayed, told the
    attendants
To lift her, like a goat, above the altar
With her robes falling about her,
To lift her boldly, her spirit fainting,   240
And hold back with a gag upon her lovely mouth
By the dumb force of a bridle
The cry which would curse the house.

Then dropping on the ground her saffron dress,
Glancing at each of her appointed
Sacrificers a shaft of pity,
Plain as in a picture she wished
To speak to them by name, for often
At her father's table where men feasted
She had sung in celebration for her father   250
With a pure voice, affectionately, virginally,
The hymn for happiness at the third libation.

The sequel to this I saw not and tell not
But the crafts of Calchas gained their object.
To learn by suffering is the equation of Justice; the
    Future
Is known when it comes, let it go till then.

To know in advance is sorrow in advance.
The facts will appear with the shining of the dawn.

(Enter CLYTEMNESTRA.)

260 But may good, at the least, follow after
As the queen here wishes, who stands
Nearest the throne, the only
    Defence of the land of Argos.

LEADER OF THE CHORUS: I have come, Clytemnestra,
    reverencing your authority.
For it is right to honour our master's wife
When the man's own throne is empty.
But you, if you have heard good news for certain,
    or if
270 You sacrifice on the strength of flattering hopes,
I would gladly hear. Though I cannot cavil at
    silence.
CLYTEMNESTRA: Bearing good news, as the proverb
    says, may Dawn
Spring from her mother Night.
You will hear something now that was beyond your
    hopes.
The men of Argos have taken Priam's city.
LEADER OF THE CHORUS: What! I cannot believe it. It
280   escapes me.
CLYTEMNESTRA: Troy in the hands of the Greeks. Do
    I speak plain?
LEADER OF THE CHORUS: Joy creeps over me, calling
    out my tears.
CLYTEMNESTRA: Yes. Your eyes proclaim your loyalty.
LEADER OF THE CHORUS: But what are your grounds?
    Have you a proof of it?
CLYTEMNESTRA: There is proof indeed—unless God
    has cheated us.
290 LEADER OF THE CHORUS: Perhaps you believe the
    inveigling shapes of dreams?
CLYTEMNESTRA: I would not be credited with a dozing
    brain!
LEADER OF THE CHORUS: Or are you puffed up by
    Rumour, the wingless flyer?
CLYTEMNESTRA: You mock my common sense as if I
    were a child.
LEADER OF THE CHORUS: But at what time was the city
    given to sack?
300 CLYTEMNESTRA: In this very night that gave birth to
    this day.
LEADER OF THE CHORUS: What messenger could come
    so fast?
CLYTEMNESTRA: Hephaestus, launching a fine flame
    from Ida,
Beacon forwarding beacon, despatch-riders of fire,
Ida relayed to Hermes' cliff in Lemnos
And the great glow from the island was taken over
    third
310 By the height of Athos that belongs to Zeus,
And towering then to straddle over the sea
The might of the running torch joyfully tossed

The gold gleam forward like another sun,
Herald of light to the heights of Mount Macistus,
And he without delay, nor carelessly by sleep
Encumbered, did not shirk his intermediary role,
His farflung ray reached the Euripus' tides
And told Messapion's watchers, who in turn
Sent on the message further
Setting a stack of dried-up heather on fire.   320
And the strapping flame, not yet enfeebled, leapt
Over the plain of Asopus like a blazing moon
And woke on the crags of Cithaeron
Another relay in the chain of fire.
The light that was sent from far was not declined
By the look-out men, who raised a fiercer yet,
A light which jumped the water of Gorgopis
And to Mount Aegiplanctus duly come
Urged the reveille of the punctual fire.
So then they kindle it squanderingly and launch   330
A beard of flame big enough to pass
The headland that looks down upon the Saronic
    gulf,
Blazing and bounding till it reached at length
The Arachnaean steep, our neighbouring heights;
And leaps in the latter end on the roof of the sons
    of Atreus
Issue and image of the fire on Ida.
Such was the assignment of my torch-racers,
The task of each fulfilled by his successor,   340
And victor is he who ran both first and last.
Such is the proof I offer you, the sign
My husband sent me out of Troy.
LEADER OF THE CHORUS: To the gods, queen, I shall
    give thanks presently.
But I would like to hear this story further,
To wonder at it in detail from your lips.
CLYTEMNESTRA: The Greeks hold Troy upon this
    day.
The cries in the town I fancy do not mingle.   350
Pour oil and vinegar into the same jar,
You would say they stand apart unlovingly;
Of those who are captured and those who have
    conquered
Distinct are the sounds of their diverse fortunes,
For *these* having flung themselves about the bodies
Of husbands and brothers, or sons upon the bodies
Of aged fathers from a throat no longer
Free, lament the fate of their most loved.
But *those* a night's marauding after battle   360
Sets hungry to what breakfast the town offers
Not billeted duly in any barracks order
But as each man has drawn his lot of luck.
So in the captive homes of Troy already
They take their lodging, free of the frosts
And dews of the open. Like happy men
They will sleep all night without sentry.
But if they respect duly the city's gods,
Those of the captured land and the sanctuaries of
    the gods,
                                                      370

They need not, having conquered, fear reconquest.
But let no lust fall first upon the troops
To plunder what is not right, subdued by gain,
For they must still, in order to come home safe,
Get round the second lap of the doubled course.
So if they return without offence to the gods
The grievance of the slain may learn at last
A friendly talk—unless some fresh wrong falls.
Such are the thoughts you hear from me, a woman.
380   But may the good prevail for all to see.
We have much good. I only ask to enjoy it.
LEADER OF THE CHORUS: Woman, you speak with
    sense like a prudent man.
I, who have heard your valid proofs, prepare
To give the glory to God.
Fair recompense is brought us for our troubles.

(CLYTEMNESTRA *goes back into the palace.*)

CHORUS: O Zeus our king and Night our friend
    Donor of glories;
    Night who cast on the towers of Troy
390   A close-clinging net so that neither the grown
    Nor any of the children can pass
    The enslaving and huge
    Trap of all-taking destruction.
    Great Zeus, guardian and host and guest,
    I honour who has done his work and taken
    A leisured aim at Paris so that neither
    Too short nor yet over the stars
        He might shoot to no purpose.

    From Zeus is the blow they can tell of,
400   This at least can be established,
    They have fared according to his ruling. For some
    Deny that the gods deign to consider those among
        men
    Who trample on the grace of inviolate things;
    It is the impious man says this,
    For Ruin is revealed the child
    Of not to be attempted actions
    When men are puffed up unduly
    And their houses are stuffed with riches.
410   Measure is the best. Let danger be distant,
    This should suffice a man
    With a proper part of wisdom.
        For a man has no protection
        Against the drunkenness of riches
        Once he has spurned from his sight
        The high altar of Justice.

    Sombre Persuasion compels him,
    Intolerable child of calculating Doom;
    All cure is vain, there is no glozing it over
420   But the mischief shines forth with a deadly light
    And like bad coinage
    By rubbings and frictions
    He stands discoloured and black

    Under the test—like a boy
    Who chases a winged bird.
    He has branded his city for ever.
    His prayers are heard by no god.
    Who makes such things his practice
    The gods destroy him.
        This way came Paris   430
        To the house of the sons of Atreus
        And outraged the table of friendship
        Stealing the wife of his host.

Leaving to her countrymen clanging of
Shields and of spears and
Launching of warships
And bringing instead of a dowry destruction to
    Troy
Lightly she was gone through the gates daring
Things undared. Many the groans   440
Of the palace spokesmen on this theme—
'O the house, the house, and its princes,
O the bed and the imprint of her limbs;
One can see him crouching in silence
Dishonoured and unreviling.'
Through desire for her who is overseas, a ghost
Will seem to rule the household.
    And now her husband hates
    The grace of shapely statues;
    In the emptiness of their eyes   450
    All their appeal is departed.

But appearing in dreams persuasive
Images come bringing a joy that is vain,
Vain for when in fancy he looks to touch her—
Slipping through his hands the vision
Rapidly is gone
Following on wings the walks of sleep.
Such are his griefs in his house on his hearth,
Such as these and worse than these,
But everywhere through the land of Greece which   460
    men have left
Are mourning women with enduring hearts
To be seen in all houses; many
Are the thoughts which stab their hearts;
    For those they sent to war
    They know, but in place of men
    That which comes home to them
    Is merely an urn and ashes.

But the money-changer War, changer of bodies,
Holding his balance in the battle   470
Home from Troy refined by fire
Sends back to friends the dust
That is heavy with tears, stowing
A man's worth of ashes
In an easily handled jar.
And they wail speaking well of the men how that
    one

Was expert in battle, and one fell well in the
carnage—
480 But for another man's wife.
Muffled and muttered words;
And resentful grief creeps up against the sons
Of Atreus and their cause.
  But others there by the wall
  Entombed in Trojan ground
  Lie, handsome of limb,
  Holding and hidden in enemy soil.

Heavy is the murmur of an angry people
Performing the purpose of a public curse;
490 There is something cowled in the night
That I anxiously wait to hear.
For the gods are not blind to the
Murderers of many and the black
Furies in time
When a man prospers in sin
By erosion of life reduce him to darkness,
Who, once among the lost, can no more
Be helped. Over-great glory
Is a sore burden. The high peak
500 Is blasted by the eys of Zeus.
  I prefer an unenvied fortune,
  Not to be a sacker of cities
  Nor to find myself living at another's
  Ruling, myself a captive.

AN OLD MAN: From the good news' beacon a swift
Rumour is gone through the town.
Who knows if it be true
Or some deceit of the gods?
ANOTHER OLD MAN: Who is so childish or broken in
510 wit
To kindle his heart at a new-fangled message of
flame
And then be downcast
At a change of report?
ANOTHER OLD MAN: It fits the temper of a woman
To give her assent to a story before it is proved.
ANOTHER OLD MAN: The over-credulous passion of
women expands
In swift conflagration but swiftly declining is gone
520 The news that a woman announced.
LEADER OF THE CHORUS: Soon we shall know about
the illuminant torches,
The beacons and the fiery relays,
Whether they were true or whether like dreams
That pleasant light came here and hoaxed our wits.
Look: I see, coming from the beach, a herald
Shadowed with olive shoots; the dust upon him,
Mud's thirsty sister and colleague, is my witness
That he will not give dumb news nor news by
530 lighting
A flame of fire with the smoke of mountain timber;
In words he will either corroborate our joy—

But the opposite version I reject with horror.
To the good appeared so far may good be added.
ANOTHER SPEAKER: Whoever makes other prayers for
this our city,
May he reap himself the fruits of his wicked heart.

(*Enter the* HERALD, *who kisses the ground before speaking.*)

HERALD: Earth of my fathers, O the earth of Argos,
In the light of the tenth year I reach you thus
After many shattered hopes achieving one, 540
For never did I dare to think that here in Argive
land
I should win a grave in the dearest soil of home;
But now hail, land, and hail, light of the sun,
And Zeus high above the country and the Pythian
king—
May he no longer shoot his arrows at us
(Implacable long enough beside Scamander)
But now be saviour to us and be healer,
King Apollo. And all the Assembly's gods 550
I call upon, and him my patron, Hermes,
The dear herald whom all heralds adore,
And the Heroes who sped our voyage, again with
favour
Take back the army that has escaped the spear.
O cherished dwelling, palace of royalty,
O august thrones and gods facing the sun,
If ever before, now with your bright eyes
Gladly receive your king after much time,
Who comes bringing light to you in the night time, 560
And to all these as well—King Agamemnon.
Give him a good welcome as he deserves,
Who with the axe of judgment-awarding God
Has smashed Troy and levelled the Trojan land;
The altars are destroyed, the seats of the gods,
And the seed of all the land is perished from it.
Having cast this halter round the neck of Troy
The King, the elder son of Atreus, a blessed man,
Comes, the most worthy to have honour of all
Men that are now. Paris nor his guilty city 570
Can boast that the crime was greater than the
atonement.
Convicted in a suit for rape and robbery
He has lost his stolen goods and with consummate
ruin
Mowed down the whole country and his father's
house.
The sons of Priam have paid their account with
interest.
LEADER OF THE CHORUS: Hail and be glad, herald of 580
the Greek army.
HERALD: Yes. Glad indeed! So glad that at the god's
demand
I should no longer hesitate to die.
LEADER OF THE CHORUS: Were you so harrowed by
desire for home?

HERALD: Yes. The tears come to my eyes for joy.

LEADER OF THE CHORUS: Sweet then is the fever which afflicts you.

590 HERALD: What do you mean? Let me learn your drift.

LEADER OF THE CHORUS: Longing for those whose love came back in echo.

HERALD: Meaning the land was homesick for the army?

LEADER OF THE CHORUS: Yes. I would often groan from a darkened heart.

HERALD: This sullen hatred—how did it fasten on you?

LEADER OF THE CHORUS: I cannot say. Silence is my
600 stock prescription.

HERALD: What? In your masters' absence were there some you feared?

LEADER OF THE CHORUS: Yes. In your phrase, death would now be a gratification.

HERALD: Yes, for success is ours. These things have taken time.

Some of them we could say have fallen well,
While some we blame. Yet who except the gods
Is free from pain the whole duration of life?
610 If I were to tell of our labours, our hard lodging,
The sleeping on crowded decks, the scanty blankets,
Tossing and groaning, rations that never reached us—
And the land too gave matter for more disgust,
For our beds lay under the enemy's walls.
Continuous drizzle from the sky, dews from the marshes,
Rotting our clothes, filling our hair with lice.
620 And if one were to tell of the bird-destroying winter
Intolerable from the snows of Ida
Or of the heat when the sea slackens at noon
Waveless and dozing in a depressed calm—
But why make these complaints? The weariness is over;
Over indeed for some who never again
Need even trouble to rise.
Why make a computation of the lost?
630 Why need the living sorrow for the spites of fortune?
I wish to say a long goodbye to disasters.
For us, the remnant of the troops of Argos,
The advantage remains, the pain can not outweigh it;
So we can make our boast to this sun's light,
Flying on words above the land and sea:
'Having taken Troy the Argive expedition
Has nailed up throughout Greece in every temple
640 These spoils, these ancient trophies.'
Those who hear such things must praise the city
And the generals. And the grace of God be honoured

Which brought these things about. You have the whole story.

LEADER OF THE CHORUS: I confess myself convinced by your report.

Old men are always young enough to learn.

(Enter CLYTEMNESTRA *from the palace.)*

This news belongs by right first to the house
And Clytemnestra—though I am enriched also. 650

CLYTEMNESTRA: Long before I shouted at joy's command
At the coming of the first night-messenger of fire
Announcing the taking and capsizing of Troy.
And people reproached me saying, 'Do mere beacons
Persuade you to think that Troy is already down?
Indeed a woman's heart is easily exalted.'
Such comments made me seem to be wandering but yet 660
I began my sacrifices and in the women's fashion
Throughout the town they raised triumphant cries
And in the gods' enclosures
Lulling the fragrant, incense-eating flame.
And now what need is there for you to tell me more?
From the King himself I shall learn the whole story.
But how the best to welcome my honoured lord
I shall take pains when he comes back—For what
Is a kinder light for a woman to see than this, 670
To open the gates to her man come back from war
When God has saved him? Tell this to my husband,

To come with all speed, the city's darling;
May he returning find a wife as loyal
As when he left her, watchdog of the house,
Good to *him* but fierce to the ill-intentioned,
And in all other things as ever, having destroyed
No seal or pledge at all in the length of time,
I know no pleasure with another man, no scandal,
More than I know how to dye metal red. 680
Such is my boast, bearing a load of truth,
A boast that need not disgrace a noble wife.

(Exit.)

LEADER OF THE CHORUS: Thus has she spoken; if you take her meaning,
Only a specious tale to shrewd interpreters.
But do you, herald, tell me; I ask after Menelaus
Whether he will, returning safe preserved,
Come back with you, our land's loved master.

HERALD: I am not able to speak the lovely falsehood
To profit you, my friends, for any stretch of time. 690

LEADER OF THE CHORUS: But if only the true tidings could be also good!
It is hard to hide a division of good and true.

HERALD: The prince is vanished out of the Greek fleet,

Himself and ship. I speak no lie.

LEADER OF THE CHORUS: Did he put forth first in the sight of all from Troy,
Or a storm that troubled all sweep him apart?

700 HERALD: You have hit the target like a master archer,
Told succinctly a long tale of sorrow.

LEADER OF THE CHOURS: Did the rumours current among the remaining ships
Represent him as alive or dead?

HERALD: No one knows so as to tell for sure
Except the sun who nurses the breeds of earth.

LEADER OF THE CHORUS: Tell me how the storm came on the host of ships
Through the divine anger, and how it ended.

710 HERALD: Day of good news should not be fouled by tongue
That tells ill news. To each god his season.
When, despair in his face, a messenger brings to a town
The hated news of a fallen army—
One general wound to the city and many men
Outcast, outcursed, from many homes
By the double whip which War is fond of,
Doom with a bloody spear in either hand,
720 One carrying such a pack of grief could well
Recite this hymn of the Furies at your asking.
But when our cause is saved and a messenger of good
Comes to a city glad with festivity,
How am I to mix good news with bad, recounting
The storm that meant God's anger on the Greeks?
For they swore together, those inveterate enemies,
Fire and sea, and proved their alliance, destroying
The unhappy troops of Argos.
730 In night arose ill-waved evil,
Ships on each other the blasts from Thrace
Crashed colliding, which butting with horns in the violence
Of big wind and rattle of rain were gone
To nothing, whirled all ways by a wicked shepherd.
But when there came up the shining light of the sun
We saw the Aegean sea flowering with corpses
Of Greek men and their ships' wreckage.
740 But for us, our ship was not damaged,
Whether someone snatched it away or begged it off,
Some god, not a man, handling the tiller;
And Saving Fortune was willing to sit upon our ship
So that neither at anchor we took the tilt of waves
Nor ran to splinters on the crag-bound coast.
But then having thus escaped death on the sea,
In the white day, not trusting our fortune,
750 We pastured this new trouble upon our thoughts,
The fleet being battered, the sailors weary,
And now if any of *them* still draw breath,

They are thinking no doubt of us as being lost
And we are thinking of them as being lost.
May the best happen. As for Menelaus
The first guess and most likely is a disaster.
But still—if any ray of sun detects him
Alive, with living eyes, by the plan of Zeus
Not yet resolved to annul the race completely,
There is some hope then that he will return home. 760
So much you have heard. Know that it is the truth.

(Exit.)

CHORUS: Who was it named her thus
In all ways appositely
Unless it was Someone whom we do not see,
Fore-knowing fate
And plying an accurate tongue?
Helen, bride of spears and conflict's
Focus, who as was befitting
Proved a hell to ships and men,
Hell to her country, sailing 770
Away from delicately-sumptuous curtains,
Away on the wind of a giant Zephyr,
And shielded hunters mustered many
On the vanished track of the oars,
Oars beached on the leafy
Banks of a Trojan river
For the sake of bloody war.

But on Troy was thrust a marring marriage
By the Wrath that working to an end exacts
In time a price from guests 780
Who dishonoured their host
And dishonoured Zeus of the Hearth,
From those noisy celebrants
Of the wedding hymn which fell
To the brothers of Paris
To sing upon that day.
But learning this, unlearning that,
Priam's ancestral city now
Continually mourns, reviling
Paris the fatal bridegroom. 790
The city has had much sorrow,
Much desolation in life,
From the pitiful loss of her people.

So in his house a man might rear
A lion's cub caught from the dam
In need of suckling,
In the prelude of its life
Mild, gentle with children,
For old men a playmate,
Often held in the arms 800
Like a new-born child,
Wheedling the hand,
Fawning at belly's bidding.

But matured by time he showed
The temper of his stock and payed
Thanks for his fostering
With disaster of slaughter of sheep
Making an unbidden banquet
And now the house is a shambles,
810 Irremediable grief to its people,
Calamitous carnage;
For the pet they had fostered was sent
By God as a priest of Ruin.

So I would say there came
To the city of Troy
A notion of windless calm,
Delicate adornment of riches,
Soft shooting of the eyes and flower
Of desire that stings the fancy.
820 But swerving aside she achieved
A bitter end to her marriage,
Ill guest and ill companion,
Hurled upon Priam's sons, convoyed
By Zeus, patron of guest and host,
Dark angel dowered with tears.

Long current among men an old saying
Runs that a man's prosperity
When grown to greatness
Comes to the birth, does not die childless—
830 His good luck breeds for his house
Distress that shall not be appeased.
I only, apart from the others,
Hold that the unrighteous action
Breeds true to its kind,
Leaves its own children behind it.
But the lot of a righteous house
Is a fair offspring always.

Ancient self-glory is accustomed
To bear to light in the evil sort of men
840 A new self-glory and madness,
Which sometime or sometime finds
The appointed hour for its birth,
And born therewith is the Spirit, intractable,
    unholy, irresistible,
The reckless lust that brings black Doom upon the
    house,
A child that is like its parents.

But Honest Dealing is clear
Shining in smoky homes,
850 Honours the god-fearing life.
Mansions gilded by filth of hands she leaves,
Turns her eyes elsewhere, visits the innocent
    house,
Not respecting the power
Of wealth mis-stamped with approval,
But guides all to the goal.

(Enter AGAMEMNON *and* CASSANDRA *on chariots.)*

CHORUS: Come then my King, stormer of Troy,
    Offspring of Atreus,
    How shall I hail you, how give you honour
    Neither overshooting nor falling short   860
        Of the measure of homage?
    There are many who honour appearance too much
    Passing the bounds that are right.
    To condole with the unfortunate man
    Each one is ready but the bite of the grief
        Never goes through to the heart.
    And they join in rejoicing, affecting to share it,
    Forcing their face to a smile.
    But he who is shrewd to shepherd his sheep
    Will not fail to notice the eyes of a man   870
    Which seem to be loyal but lie,
        Fawning with watery friendship.
    Even you, in my thought, when you marshalled the
        troops
    For Helen's sake, I will not hide it,
    Made a harsh and ugly picture,
    Holding badly the tiller of reason,
    Paying with the death of men
        Ransom for a willing whore.
    But now, not unfriendly, not superficially,   880
    I offer my service, well-doers' welcome.
    In time you will learn by inquiry
    Who has done rightly, who transgressed
        In the work of watching the city.
AGAMEMNON: First to Argos and the country's gods
    My fitting salutations, who have aided me
    To return and in the justice which I exacted
    From Priam's city. Hearing the unspoken case
    The gods unanimously had cast their vote
    Into the bloody urn for the massacre of Troy;   890
    But to the opposite urn
    Hope came, dangled her hand, but did no more.
    Smoke marks even now the city's capture.
    Whirlwinds of doom are alive, the dying ashes
    Spread on the air the fat savour of wealth.
    For these things we must pay some memorable
        return
    To Heaven, having exacted enormous vengeance
    For wife-rape; for a woman
    The Argive monster ground a city to powder,   900
    Sprung from a wooden horse, shield-wielding folk,
    Launching a leap at the setting of the Pleiads,
    Jumping the ramparts, a ravening lion,
    Lapped its fill of the kingly blood.
    To the gods I have drawn out this overture
    But as for your concerns, I bear them in my mind
    And say the same, you have me in agreement.
    To few of men does it belong by nature
    To congratulate their friends unenviously,
    For a sullen poison fastens on the heart,   910
    Doubling the pain of a man with this disease;

He feels the weight of his own griefs and when
He sees another's prosperity he groans.
I speak with knowledge, being well acquainted
With the mirror of comradeship—ghost of a
    shadow
Were those who seemed to be so loyal to me.
Only Odysseus, who sailed against his will,
Proved, when yoked with me, a ready tracehorse;
920 I speak of him not knowing if he is alive.
But for what concerns the city and the gods
Appointing public debates in full assembly
We shall consult. That which is well already
We shall take steps to ensure it remain well.
But where there is need of medical remedies,
By applying benevolent cautery or surgery
We shall try to deflect the dangers of disease.
But now, entering the halls where stands my
    hearth,
930 First I shall make salutation to the gods
Who sent me a far journey and have brought me
    back.
And may my victory not leave my side.

(Enter CLYTEMNESTRA, followed by women slaves carrying purple tapestries.)

CLYTEMNESTRA: Men of the city, you the aged of
    Argos,
I shall feel no shame to describe to you my love
Towards my husband. Shyness in all of us
Wears thin with time. Here are the facts first hand.
I will tell you of my own unbearable life
940 I led so long as this man was at Troy.
For first that the woman separate from her man
Should sit alone at home is extreme cruelty,
Hearing so many malignant rumours—First
Comes one, and another comes after, bad news to
    worse,
Clamour of grief to the house. If Agamemnon
Had had so many wounds as those reported
Which poured home through the pipes of hearsay,
    then—
950 Then he would be gashed fuller than a net has
    holes!
And if only he had died . . . as often as rumour told
    us,
He would be like the giant in the legend,
Three-bodied. Dying once for every body,
He should have by now three blankets of earth
    above him—
All that above him; I care not how deep the
    mattress under!
960 Such are the malignant rumours thanks to which
They have often seized me against my will and
    undone
The loop of a rope from my neck.
And this is why our son is not standing here,
The guarantee of your pledges and mine,

As he should be, Orestes. Do not wonder;
He is being brought up by a friendly ally and host,
Strophius the Phocian, who warned me in advance
Of dubious troubles, both your risks at Troy
And the anarchy of shouting mobs that might   970
Overturn policy, for it is born in men
To kick the man who is down.
This is not a disingenuous excuse.
For me the outrushing wells of weeping are dried
    up,
There is no drop left in them.
My eyes are sore from sitting late at nights
Weeping for you and for the baffled beacons,
Never lit up. And, when I slept, in dreams
I have been waked by the thin whizz of a buzzing   980
Gnat, seeing more horrors fasten on you
Than could take place in the mere time of my
    dream.
Having endured all this, now, with unsorrowed
    heart
I would hail this man as the watchdog of the farm,
Forestay that saves the ship, pillar that props
The lofty roof, appearance of an only son
To a father or of land to sailors past their hope,
The loveliest day to see after the storm,   990
Gush of well-water for the thirsty traveller.
Such are the metaphors I think befit him,
But envy be absent. Many misfortunes already
We have endured. But now, dear head, come down
Out of that car, not placing upon the ground
Your foot, O King, the foot that trampled Troy.
Why are you waiting, slaves, to whom the task is
    assigned
To spread the pavement of his path with
    tapestries?   1000
At once, at once let his way be strewn with purple
That Justice lead him toward his unexpected
    home.
The rest a mind, not overcome by sleep
Will arrange rightly, with God's help, as destined.
AGAMEMNON: Daughter of Leda, guardian of my
    house,
You have spoken in proportion to my absence.
You have drawn your speech out long. Duly to
    praise me,   1010
That is a duty to be performed by others.
And further—do not by women's methods make
    me
Effeminate nor in barbarian fashion
Gape ground-grovelling acclamations at me
Nor strewing my path with cloths make it invidious.
It is the gods should be honoured in this way.
But being mortal to tread embroidered beauty
For me is no way without fear.
I tell you to honour me as a man, not god.   1020
Footcloths are very well—Embroidered stuffs
Are stuff for gossip. And not to think unwisely

Is the greatest gift of God. Call happy only him
Who has ended his life in sweet prosperity.
I have spoken. This thing I could not do with
confidence.

CLYTEMNESTRA: Tell me now, according to your
judgment.

AGAMEMNON: I tell you you shall not override my
1030 judgment.

CLYTEMNESTRA: Supposing you had feared
something . . .
Could you have vowed to God to do this thing?

AGAMEMNON: Yes. If an expert had prescribed that
vow.

CLYTEMNESTRA: And how would Priam have acted in
your place?

AGAMEMNON: He would have trod the cloths, I think,
for certain.

1040 CLYTEMNESTRA: Then do not flinch before the blame
of men.

AGAMEMNON: The voice of the multitude is very
strong.

CLYTEMNESTRA: But the man none envy is not
enviable.

AGAMEMNON: It is not a woman's part to love
disputing.

CLYTEMNESTRA: But it is a conqueror's part to yield
upon occasion.

1050 AGAMEMNON: You think such victory worth fighting
for?

CLYTEMNESTRA: Give way. Consent to let me have the
mastery.

AGAMEMNON: Well, if such is your wish, let someone
quickly loose
My vassal sandals, underlings of my feet,
And stepping on these sea-purples may no god
Shoot me from far with the envy of his eye.
Great shame it is to ruin my house and spoil
1060 The wealth of costly weavings with my feet.
But of this matter enough. This stranger woman
here
Take in with kindness. The man who is a gentle
master
God looks on from far off complacently.
For no one of his will bears the slave's yoke.
This woman, of many riches being the chosen
Flower, gift of the soldiers, has come with me.
But since I have been prevailed on by your words
1070 I will go to my palace home, treading on purples.

(He dismounts from the chariot and begins to walk up the
tapestried path. During the following speech he enters the
palace.)

CLYTEMNESTRA: There is the sea and who shall drain
it dry? It breeds
Its wealth in silver of plenty of purple gushing
And ever-renewed, the dyeings of our garments.

The house has its store of these by God's grace,
King.
This house is ignorant of poverty
And I would have vowed a pavement of many
garments
Had the palace oracle enjoined that vow   1080
Thereby to contrive a ransom for his life.
For while there is root, foliage comes to the house
Spreading a tent of shade against the Dog Star.
So now that you have reached your hearth and
home
You prove a miracle—advent of warmth in winter;
And further this—even in the time of heat
When God is fermenting wine from the bitter
grape,
Even then it is cool in the house if only   1090
Its master walk at home, a grown man, ripe.
O Zeus the Ripener, ripen these my prayers;
Your part it is to make the ripe fruit fall.

(She enters the palace.)

CHORUS: Why, why at the doors
Of my fore-seeing heart
Does this terror keep beating its wings?
And my song play the prophet
Unbidden, unhired—
Which I cannot spit out
Like the enigmas of dreams   1100
Nor plausible confidence
Sit on the throne of my mind?
It is long time since
The cables let down from the stern
Were chafed by the sand when the seafaring army
started for Troy.

And I learn with my eyes
And witness myself their return;
But the hymn without lyre goes up,
The dirge of the Avenging Fiend,   1110
In the depths of my self-taught heart
Which has lost its dear
Possession of the strength of hope.
But my guts and my heart
Are not idle which seethe with the waves
Of trouble nearing its hour.
But I pray that these thoughts
May fall out not as I think
And not be fulfilled in the end.

Truly when health grows much   1120
It respects not limit; for disease,
Its neighbour in the next door room,
Presses upon it.
A man's life, crowding sail,
Strikes on the blind reef:
But if caution in advance
Jettison part of the cargo

With the derrick of due proportion,
The whole house does not sink,
1130 Though crammed with a weight of woe
The hull does not go under.
The abundant bounty of God
And his gifts from the year's furrows
Drive the famine back.

But when upon the ground there has fallen once
The black blood of a man's death,
Who shall summon it back by incantations?
Even Asclepius who had the art
To fetch the dead to life, even to him
1140 Zeus put a provident end.
But, if of the heaven-sent fates
One did not check the other,
Cancel the other's advantage,
My heart would outrun my tongue
In pouring out these fears.
But now it mutters in the dark,
Embittered, no way hoping
To unravel a scheme in time
    From a burning mind.

(CLYTEMNESTRA *appears in the door of the palace.*)

1150 CLYTEMNESTRA: Go in too, you; I speak to you,
        Cassandra,
    Since God in his clemency has put you in this house
    To share our holy water, standing with many slaves
    Beside the altar that protects the house,
    Step down from the car there, do not be
        overproud.
    Heracles himself they say was once
    Sold, and endured to eat the bread of slavery.
    But should such a chance inexorably fall,
1160 There is much advantage in masters who have long
        been rich.
    Those who have reaped a crop they never expected
    Are in all things hard on their slaves and overstep
        the line.
    From us you will have the treatment of tradition.
LEADER OF THE CHORUS: You, it is you she has
        addressed, and clearly.
    Caught as you are in these predestined toils
    Obey her if you can. But should you disobey . . .
1170 CLYTEMNESTRA: If she has more than the gibberish of
        the swallow,
    An unintelligible barbaric speech,
    I hope to read her mind, persuade her reason.
LEADER OF THE CHORUS: As things now stand for you,
        she says the best.
    Obey her; leave that car and follow her.
CLYTEMNESTRA: I have no leisure to waste out here,
        outside the door.
    Before the hearth in the middle of my house
1180 The victims stand already, wait the knife.
    You, if you will obey me, waste no time.

But if you cannot understand my language—

(*To* CHORUS LEADER)

You make it plain to her with the brute and
    voiceless hand.
LEADER OF THE CHORUS: The stranger seems to need a
    clear interpreter.
    She bears herself like a wild beast newly captured.
CLYTEMNESTRA: The fact is she is mad, she listens to
    evil thoughts,
    Who has come here leaving a city newly captured   1190
    Without experience how to bear the bridle
    So as not to waste her strength in foam and blood.
    I will not spend more words to be ignored.

(*She re-enters the palace.*)

CHORUS: But I, for I pity her, will not be angry.
    Obey, unhappy woman. Leave this car.
    Yield to your fate. Put on the untried yoke.
CASSANDRA: Apollo! Apollo!
CHORUS: Why do you cry like this upon Apollo?
    He is not the kind of god that calls for dirges.
CASSANDRA: Apollo! Apollo!   1200
CHORUS: Once more her funeral cries invoke the god
    Who has no place at the scene of lamentation.
CASSANDRA: Apollo! Apollo!
    God of the Ways! My destroyer!
    Destroyed again—and this time utterly!
CHORUS: She seems about to predict her own
    misfortunes.
    The gift of the god endures, even in a slave's mind.
CASSANDRA: Apollo! Apollo!
    God of the Ways! My destroyer!   1210
    Where? To what house? Where, where have you
    brought me?
CHORUS: To the house of the sons of Atreus. If you
    do not know it,
    I will tell you so. You will not find it false.
CASSANDRA: No, no, but to a god-hated, but to an
    accomplice
    In much kin-killing, murdering nooses,
    Man-shambles, a floor asperged with blood.
CHORUS: The stranger seems like a hound with a   1220
    keen scent,
    Is picking up a trail that leads to murder.
CASSANDRA: Clues! I have clues! Look! They are
    these.
    These wailing, these children, butchery of
    children;
    Roasted flesh, a father sitting to dinner.
CHORUS: Of your prophetic fame we have heard
    before
    But in this matter prophets are not required.   1230
CASSANDRA: What is she doing? What is she
    planning?
    What is this new great sorrow?
    Great crime . . . within here . . . planning

Unendurable to his folk, impossible
Ever to be cured. For help
  Stands far distant.
CHORUS: This reference I cannot catch. But the children
1240 I recognized; that refrain is hackneyed.
CASSANDRA: Damned, damned, bringing this work to completion—
Your husband who shared your bed
To bathe him, to cleanse him, and then—
How shall I tell of the end?
Soon, very soon, it will fall.
  The end comes hand over hand
  Grasping in greed.
CHORUS: Not yet do I understand. After her former
1250 riddles
Now I am baffled by these dim pronouncements.
CASSANDRA: Ah God, the vision! God, God, the vision!
A net, is it? Net of Hell!
But herself is the net; shared bed; shares murder.
O let the pack ever-hungering after the family
Howl for the unholy ritual, howl for the victim.
CHORUS: What black Spirit is this you call upon the house—
1260 To raise aloft her cries? Your speech does not lighten me.
Into my heart runs back the blood
Yellow as when for men by the spear fallen
The blood ebbs out with the rays of the setting life
  And death strides quickly.
CASSANDRA: Quick! Be on your guard! The bull—
Keep him clear of the cow.
Caught with a trick, the black horn's point,
She strikes. He falls; lies in the water.
1270 Murder; a trick in a bath. I tell what I see.
CHORUS: I would not claim to be expert in oracles
But these, as I deduce, portend disaster.
Do men ever get a good answer from oracles?
No. It is only through disaster
That their garrulous craft brings home
  The meaning of the prophet's panic.
CASSANDRA: And for me also, for me, chance ill-destined!
My own now I lament, pour into the cup my own.
1280 Where is this you have brought me in my misery?
Unless to die as well. What else is meant?
CHORUS: You are mad, mad, carried away by the god,
Raising the dirge, the tuneless
Tune, for yourself. Like the tawny
Unsatisfied singer from her luckless heart
Lamenting 'Itys, Itys', the nightingale
  Lamenting a life luxuriant with grief.
CASSANDRA: Oh the lot of the songful nightingale!
The gods enclosed her in a winged body,
1290 Gave her a sweet and tearless passing.
But for me remains the two-edged cutting blade.

CHORUS: From whence these rushing and God-inflicted
Profitless pains?
Why shape with your sinister crying
The piercing hymn—fear-piercing?
How can you know the evil-worded landmarks
  On the prophetic path?
CASSANDRA: Oh the wedding, the wedding of
Paris—death to his people!   1300
O river Scamander, water drunk by my fathers!
When I was young, alas, upon your beaches
I was brought up and cared for.
But now it is the River of Wailing and the banks of Hell
  That shall hear my prophecy soon.
CHORUS: What is this clear speech, too clear?
A child could understand it.
I am bitten with fangs that draw blood
By the misery of your cries,   1310
  Cries harrowing the heart.
CASSANDRA: O trouble on trouble of a city lost, lost utterly!
My father's sacrifices before the towers,
Much killing of cattle and sheep,
No cure—availed not at all
To prevent the coming of what came to Troy,
And I, my brain on fire, shall soon enter the trap.
CHORUS: This speech accords with the former.
What god, malicious, over-heavy, persistently   1320
  pressing,
Drives you to chant of these lamentable
Griefs with death their burden?
  But I cannot see the end.

(CASSANDRA *now steps down from the car.*)

CASSANDRA: The oracle now no longer from behind veils
Will be peeping forth like a newly-wedded bride;
But I can feel it like a fresh wind swoop
And rush in the face of the dawn and, wave-like, wash   1330
Against the sun a vastly greater grief
Than this one. I shall speak no more conundrums.
And bear me witness, pacing me, that I
Am trailing on the scene of ancient wrongs.
For this house here a choir never deserts,
Chanting together ill. For they mean ill,
And to puff up their arrogance they have drunk
Men's blood, this band of revellers that haunts the house,
Hard to be rid of, fiends that attend the family.   1340
Established in its rooms they hymn their hymn
Of that original sin, abhor in turn
The adultery that proved a brother's ruin.
A miss? Or do my arrows hit the mark?
Or am I a quack prophet who knocks at doors, a babbler?

Give me your oath, confess I have the facts,
The ancient history of this house's crimes.
LEADER OF THE CHORUS: And how could an oath's
1350   assurance, however finely assured,
Turn out a remedy? I wonder, though, that you
Being brought up overseas, of another tongue,
Should hit on the whole tale as if you had been
  standing by.
CASSANDRA: Apollo the prophet set me to prophesy.
LEADER OF THE CHORUS: Was he, although a god,
  struck by desire?
CASSANDRA: Till now I was ashamed to tell that story.
LEADER OF THE CHORUS: Yes. Good fortune keeps us
1360   all fastidious.
CASSANDRA: He wrestled hard upon me, panting
  love.
LEADER OF THE CHORUS: And did you come, as they
  do, to child-getting?
CASSANDRA: No. I agreed to him. And I cheated him.
LEADER OF THE CHORUS: Were you already possessed
  by the mystic art?
CASSANDRA: Already I was telling the townsmen all
  their future suffering.
1370 LEADER OF THE CHORUS: Then how did you escape the
  doom of Apollo's anger?
CASSANDRA: I did not escape. No one ever believed
  me.
LEADER OF THE CHORUS: Yet to us your words seem
  worthy of belief.
CASSANDRA: Oh misery, misery!
Again comes on me the terrible labour of true
Prophecy, dizzying prelude; distracts . . .
Do you see these who sit before the house,
1380 Children, like the shapes of dreams?
Children who seem to have been killed by their
  kinsfolk,
Filling their hands with meat, flesh of themselves,
Guts and entrails, handfuls of lament—
Clear what they hold—the same their father tasted.
For this I declare someone is plotting vengeance—
A lion? Lion but coward, that lurks in bed,
Good watchdog truly against the lord's return—
My lord, for I must bear the yoke of serfdom.
1390 Leader of the ships, overturner of Troy,
He does not know what plots the accursed hound
With the licking tongue and the pricked-up ear will
  plan
In the manner of a lurking doom, in an evil hour.
A daring criminal! Female murders male.
What monster could provide her with a title?
An amphisbaena or hag of the sea who dwells
In rocks to ruin sailors—
A raving mother of death who breathes against her
  folk
1400 War to the finish. Listen to her shout of triumph,
Who shirks no horrors, like men in a rout of battle.
And yet she poses as glad at their return.

If you distrust my words, what does it matter?
That which will come will come. You too will soon
  stand here
And admit with pity that I spoke too truly.
LEADER OF THE CHORUS: Thyestes' dinner of his
  children's meat
I understood and shuddered, and fear grips me   1410
To hear the truth, not framed in parables.
But hearing the rest I am thrown out of my course.
CASSANDRA: It is Agamemnon's death I tell you you
  shall witness.
LEADER OF THE CHORUS: Stop! Provoke no evil. Quiet
  your mouth!
CASSANDRA: The god who gives me words is here no
  healer.
LEADER OF THE CHORUS: Not if this shall be so. But
  may some chance avert it.   1420
CASSANDRA: *You* are praying. But others are busy
  with murder.
LEADER OF THE CHORUS: What man is he promotes
  this terrible thing?
CASSANDRA: Indeed you have missed my drift by a
  wide margin!
LEADER OF THE CHORUS: But I do not understand the
  assassin's method.
CASSANDRA: And yet too well I know the speech of
  Greece!   1430
LEADER OF THE CHORUS: So does Delphi but the
  replies are hard.
CASSANDRA: Ah what a fire it is! It comes upon me.
Apollo, Wolf-Destroyer, pity, pity . . .
It is the two-foot lioness who beds
Beside a wolf, the noble lion away,
It is she will kill me. Brewing a poisoned cup
She will mix my punishment too in the angry
  draught
And boasts, sharpening the dagger for her   1440
  husband,
To pay back murder for my bringing here.
Why then do I wear these mockeries of myself,
The wand and the prophet's garland round my
  neck?
My hour is coming—but you shall perish first.
Destruction! Scattered thus you give me my
  revenge;
Go and enrich some other woman with ruin.
See: Apollo himself is stripping me   1450
Of my prophetic gear, who has looked on
When in this dress I have been a laughing-stock
To friends and foes alike, and to no purpose;
They called me crazy, like a fortune-teller,
A poor starved beggar-woman—and I bore it.
And now the prophet undoing his prophetess
Has brought me to this final darkness.
Instead of my father's altar the executioner's block
Waits me the victim, red with my hot blood.
But the gods will not ignore me as I die.   1460

One will come after to avenge my death,
A matricide, a murdered father's champion.
Exile and tramp and outlaw he will come back
To gable the family house of fatal crime;
His father's outstretched corpse shall lead him
    home.
Why need I then lament so pitifully?
For now that I have seen the town of Troy
Treated as she was treated, while her captors
1470   Come to their reckoning thus by the god's verdict,
I will go in and have the courage to die.
Look, these gates are the gates of Death. I greet
    them.
And I pray that I may meet a deft and mortal
    stroke
So that without a struggle I may close
My eyes and my blood ebb in easy death.

LEADER OF THE CHORUS: Oh woman very unhappy
    and very wise,
1480   Your speech was long. But if in sober truth
You know your fate, why like an ox that the gods
Drive, do you walk so bravely to the altar?

CASSANDRA: There is no escape, strangers. No; not by
    postponement.

LEADER OF THE CHORUS: But the last moment has the
    privilege of hope.

CASSANDRA: The day is here. Little should I gain by
    flight.

LEADER OF THE CHORUS: This patience of yours comes
1490   from a brave soul.

CASSANDRA: A happy man is never paid that
    compliment.

LEADER OF THE CHORUS: But to die with credit graces
    a mortal man.

CASSANDRA: Oh my father! You and your noble sons!

(She approaches the door, then suddenly recoils.)

LEADER OF THE CHORUS: What is it? What is the fear
    that drives you back?

CASSANDRA: Faugh.

LEADER OF THE CHORUS: Why faugh? Or is this some
1500   hallucination?

CASSANDRA: These walls breathe out a death that
    drips with blood.

LEADER OF THE CHORUS: Not so. It is only the smell of
    the sacrifice.

CASSANDRA: It is like a breath out of a charnel-house.

LEADER OF THE CHORUS: You think our palace burns
    odd incense then!

CASSANDRA: But I will go to lament among the dead
My lot and Agamemnon's. Enough of life!
1510   Strangers,
I am not afraid like a bird afraid of a bush
But witness you my words after my death
When a woman dies in return for me a woman
And a man falls for a man with a wicked wife.
I ask this service, being about to die.

LEADER OF THE CHORUS: Alas, I pity you for the death
    you have foretold.

CASSANDRA: One more speech I have; I do not wish to
    raise
The dirge for my own self. But to the sun I pray   1520
In face of his last light that my avengers
May make my murderers pay for this my death,
Death of a woman slave, an easy victim.

(She enters the palace.)

LEADER OF THE CHORUS: Ah the fortunes of men!
    When they go well
A shadow sketch would match them, and in
    ill-fortune
The dab of a wet sponge destroys the drawing.
It is not myself but the life of man I pity.

CHORUS: Prosperity in all men cries   1530
For more prosperity. Even the owner
Of the finger-pointed-at palace never shuts
His door against her, saying 'Come no more'.
So to our king the blessed gods had granted
To take the town of Priam, and heaven-favoured
He reaches home. But now if for former bloodshed
    He must pay blood
And dying for the dead shall cause
    Other deaths in atonement
What man could boast he was born   1540
    Secure, who heard this story?

AGAMEMNON:

(Within)

Oh! I am struck a mortal blow—within!

LEADER OF THE CHORUS: Silence! Listen. Who calls
    out, wounded with a mortal stroke?

AGAMEMNON: Again—the second blow—I am struck
    again.

LEADER OF THE CHORUS: You heard the king cry out. I
    think the deed is done.
Let us see if we can concert some sound proposal.   1550

2ND OLD MAN: Well, I will tell you my opinion—
Raise an alarm, summon the folk to the palace.

3RD OLD MAN: I say burst in with all speed possible,
Convict them of the deed while still the sword is wet.

4TH OLD MAN: And I am partner to some such
    suggestion.
I am for taking some course. No time to dawdle.

5TH OLD MAN: The case is plain. This is but the
    beginning.
They are going to set up dictatorship in the state.   1560

6TH OLD MAN: We are wasting time. The assassins
    tread to earth
The decencies of delay and give their hands no
    sleep.

7TH OLD MAN: I do not know what plan I could hit on
   to propose.
   The man who acts is in the position to plan.
8TH OLD MAN: So I think, too, for I am at a loss
   To raise the dead man up again with words.
1570 9TH OLD MAN: Then to stretch out our life shall we
   yield thus
   To the rule of these profaners of the house?
10TH OLD MAN: It is not to be endured. To die is
   better.
   Death is more comfortable than tyranny.
11TH OLD MAN: And are we on the evidence of groans
   Going to give oracle that the prince is dead?
12TH OLD MAN: We must know the facts for sure and
   then be angry.
1580 Guesswork is not the same as certain knowledge.
LEADER OF THE CHORUS: Then all of you back me and
   approve this plan—
   To ascertain how it is with Agamemnon.

(The doors of the palace open, revealing the bodies of
AGAMEMNON *and* CASSANDRA. CLYTEMNESTRA *stands*
above them.)

CLYTEMNESTRA: Much having been said before to fit
   the moment,
   To say the opposite now will not outface me.
   How else could one serving hate upon the hated,
   Thought to be friends, hang high the nets of doom
   To preclude all leaping out?
1590 For me I have long been training for this match,
   I tried a fall and won—a victory overdue.
   I stand here where I struck, above my victims;
   So I contrived it—this I will not deny—
   That he could neither fly nor ward off death;
   Inextricable like a net for fishes
   I cast about him a vicious wealth of raiment
   And struck him twice and with two groans he
   loosed
   His limbs beneath him, and upon him fallen
1600 I deal him the third blow to the God beneath the
   earth,
   To the safe keeper of the dead a votive gift,
   And with that he spits his life out where he lies
   And smartly spouting blood he sprays me with
   The sombre drizzle of bloody dew and I
   Rejoice no less than in God's gift of rain
   The crops are glad when the ear of corn gives
   birth.
   These things being so, you, elders of Argos,
1610 Rejoice if rejoice you will. Mine is the glory.
   And if I could pay this corpse his due libation
   I should be right to pour it and more than right;
   With so many horrors this man mixed and filled
   The bowl—and, coming home, has drained the
   draught himself.
LEADER OF THE CHORUS: Your speech astonishes us.
   This brazen boast

Above the man who was your king and husband!
CLYTEMNESTRA: You challenge me as a woman
   without foresight   1620
   But I with unflinching heart to you who know
   Speak. And you, whether you will praise or blame,
   It makes no matter. Here lies Agamemnon,
   My husband, dead, the work of this right hand,
   An honest workman. There you have the facts.
CHORUS: Woman, what poisoned
   Herb of the earth have you tasted
   Or potion of the flowing sea
   To undertake this killing and the people's curses?
   You threw down, you cut off—The people will cast   1630
   you out,
   Black abomination to the town.
CLYTEMNESTRA: Now your verdict—in my case—is
   exile
   And to have the people's hatred, the public curses,
   Though then in no way you opposed this man
   Who carelessly, as if it were a head of sheep
   Out of the abundance of his fleecy flocks,
   Sacrificed his own daughter, to me the dearest   1640
   Fruit of travail, charm for the Thracian winds.
   He was the one to have banished from this land,
   Pay off the pollution. But when you hear what I
   Have done, you judge severely. But I warn you—
   Threaten me on the understanding that I am ready
   For two alternatives—Win by force the right
   To rule me, but, if God brings about the contrary,
   Late in time you will have to learn self-discipline.
CHORUS: You are high in the thoughts,
   You speak extravagant things,   1650
   After the soiling murder your crazy heart
   Fancies your forehead with a smear of blood.
   Unhonoured, unfriended, you must
   Pay for a blow with a blow.
CLYTEMNESTRA: Listen then to this—the sanction of
   my oaths:
   By the Justice totting up my child's atonement,
   By the Avenging Doom and Fiend to whom I killed
   this man,
   For me hope walks not in the rooms of fear   1660
   So long as my fire is lit upon my hearth
   By Aegisthus, loyal to me as he was before.
   The man who outraged me lies here,
   The darling of each courtesan at Troy,
   And here with him is the prisoner clairvoyante,
   The fortune-teller that he took to bed,
   Who shares his bed as once his bench on shipboard,
   A loyal mistress. Both have their deserts.
   He lies so; and she who like a swan
   Sang her last dying lament   1670
   Lies his lover, and the sight contributes
   An appetiser to my own bed's pleasure.
CHORUS: Ah would some quick death come not
   overpainful,
   Not overlong on the sickbed,

Establishing in us the ever-
Lasting unending sleep now that our guardian
Has fallen, the kindest of men,
Who suffering much for a woman
1680 By a woman has lost his life.
　　O Helen, insane, being one
　　One to have destroyed so many
　　And many souls under Troy,
　　Now is your work complete, blossomed not for
　　　　oblivion,
　　Unfading stain of blood. Here now, if in any
　　　　home,
　　Is Discord, here is a man's deep-rooted ruin.

CLYTEMNESTRA: Do not pray for the portion of death
1690 Weighed down by these things, do not turn
Your anger on Helen as destroyer of men,
One woman destroyer of many
Lives of Greek men,
　　A hurt that cannot be healed.

CHORUS: O Evil Spirit, falling on the family,
On the two sons of Atreus and using
Two sisters in heart as your tools,
A power that bites to the heart—
See on the body
1700 Perched like a raven he gloats
Harshly croaking his hymn.

CLYTEMNESTRA: Ah, now you have amended your
　　lips' opinion,
Calling upon this family's three times gorged
Genius—demon who breeds
Blood-hankering lust in the belly:
Before the old sore heals, new pus collects.

CHORUS: It is a great spirit—great—
You tell of, harsh in anger,
1710 A ghastly tale, alas,
Of unsatisfied disaster
Brought by Zeus, by Zeus,
Cause and worker of all.
For without Zeus what comes to pass among us?
Which of these things is outside Providence?
　　O my king, my king,
　　How shall I pay you in tears,
　　Speak my affection in words?
　　You lie in that spider's web,
1720 In a desecrating death breathe out your life,
　　Lie ignominiously
　　Defeated by a crooked death
　　And the two-edged cleaver's stroke.

CLYTEMNESTRA: You say this is *my* work—mine?
Do not cozen yourself that I am Agamemnon's
　　wife.
Masquerading as the wife
Of the corpse there the old sharp-witted Genius
Of Atreus who gave the cruel banquet
1730 Has paid with a grown man's life
The due for children dead.

CHORUS: That you are not guilty of
This murder who will attest?
No, but you may have been abetted
By some ancestral Spirit of Revenge.
Wading a millrace of the family's blood
The black Manslayer forces a forward path
To make the requital at last
For the eaten children, the blood-clot cold with
　　time.
1740
　　Oh my king, my king,
　　How shall I pay you in tears,
　　Speak my affection in words?
　　You lie in that spider's web,
　　In a desecrating death breathe out your life,
　　Lie ignominiously
　　Defeated by a crooked death
　　And the two-edged cleaver's stroke.

CLYTEMNESTRA: Did he not, too, contrive a crooked
Horror for the house? My child by him, 1750
Shoot that I raised, much-wept-for Iphigeneia,
He treated her like this;
So suffering like this he need not make
Any great brag in Hell having paid with death
Dealt by the sword for work of his own beginning.

CHORUS: I am at a loss for thought, I lack
All nimble counsel as to where
To turn when the house is falling.
I fear the house-collapsing crashing
Blizzard of blood—of which these drops are 1760
　　earnest.
Now is Destiny sharpening her justice
On other whetstones for a new infliction.
　　O earth, earth, if only you had received me
　　Before I saw this man lie here as if in bed
　　　　In a bath lined with silver.
　　Who will bury him? Who will keen him?
　　Will you, having killed your own husband,
　　Dare now to lament him
　　And after great wickedness make 1770
　　　　Unamending amends to his ghost?
　　And who above this godlike hero's grave
　　Pouring praises and tears
　　　　Will grieve with a genuine heart?

CLYTEMNESTRA: It is not your business to attend to
　　that.
By my hand he fell low, lies low and dead,
And I shall bury him low down in the earth,
And his household need not weep him
For Iphigeneia his daughter 1780
Tenderly, as is right,
Will meet her father at the rapid ferry of sorrows,
Put her arms round him and kiss him!

CHORUS: Reproach answers reproach,
It is hard to decide,
The catcher is caught, the killer pays for his kill.
But the law abides while Zeus abides enthroned

That the wrongdoer suffers. That is established.
Who could expel from the house the seed of the
1790   Curse?
The race is soldered in sockets of Doom and
    Vengeance.

CLYTEMNESTRA: In this you say what is right and the
    will of God.
But for my part I am ready to make a contract
With the Evil Genius of the House of Atreus
To accept what has been till now, hard though it is,
But for the future he shall leave this house
And wear away some other stock with deaths
1800 Imposed among themselves. Of my possessions
A small part will suffice if only I
Can rid these walls of the mad exchange of
    murder.

(Enter AEGISTHUS, followed by soldiers.)

AEGISTHUS: O welcome light of a justice-dealing day!
From now on I will say that the gods, avenging
    men,
Look down from above on the crimes of earth,
Seeing as I do in woven robes of the Furies
This man lying here—a sight to warm my heart—
1810 Paying for the crooked violence of his father.
For this father Atreus, when he ruled the country,
Because his power was challenged, hounded out
From state and home his own brother Thyestes.
My father—let me be plain—was this Thyestes,
Who later came back home a suppliant,
There, miserable, found so much asylum
As not to die on the spot, stain the ancestral floor.
But to show his hospitality godless Atreus
Gave him an eager if not a loving welcome,
1820 Pretending a day of feasting and rich meats
Served my father with his children's flesh.
The hands and feet, fingers and toes, he hid
At the bottom of the dish. My father sitting apart
Took unknowing the unrecognizable portion
And ate of a dish that has proved, as you see,
    expensive.
But when he knew he had eaten worse than poison
He fell back groaning, vomiting their flesh,
And invoking a hopeless doom on the sons of
1830   Pelops
Kicked over the table to confirm his curse—
So may the whole race perish!
Result of this—you see this man lie here.
I stitched this murder together; it was my title.
Me the third son he left, an unweaned infant,
To share the bitterness of my father's exile.
But I grew up and Justice brought me back,
I grappled this man while still beyond his door,
Having pieced together the programme of his ruin.
1840 So now would even death be beautiful to me
Having seen Agamemnon in the nets of Justice.

LEADER OF THE CHORUS: Aegisthus. I cannot respect
    brutality in distress.
You claim that you deliberately killed this prince
And that you alone planned this pitiful murder.
Be sure that in your turn your head shall not
    escape
The people's volleyed curses mixed with stones.

AEGISTHUS: Do you speak so who sit at the lower oar
While those on the upper bench control the ship? 1850
Old as you are, you will find it is a heavy load
To go to school when old to learn the lesson of tact.
For old age, too, gaol and hunger are fine
Instructors in wisdom, second-sighted doctors.
You have eyes. Cannot you see?
Do not kick against the pricks. The blow will hurt
    you.

LEADER OF THE CHORUS: You woman waiting in the
    house for those who return from battle
While you seduce their wives! Was it you devised 1860
The death of a master of armies?

AEGISTHUS: And these words, too, prepare the way
    for tears.
Contrast your voice with the voice of Orpheus: he
Led all things after him bewitched with joy, but you
Having stung me with your silly yelps shall be
Led off yourself, to prove more mild when
    mastered.

LEADER OF THE CHORUS: Indeed! So you are now to be
    king of Argos, 1870
You who, when you had plotted the king's death,
Did not even dare to do that thing yourself!

AEGISTHUS: No. For the trick of it was clearly
    woman's work.
I was suspect, an enemy of old.
But now I shall try with Agamemnon's wealth
To rule the people. Any who is disobedient
I will harness in a heavy yoke, no tracehorse work
    for him
Like barley-fed colt, but hateful hunger lodging 1880
Beside him in the dark will see his temper soften.

LEADER OF THE CHORUS: Why with your cowardly soul
    did you yourself
Not strike this man but left that work to a woman
Whose presence pollutes our country and its gods?
But Orestes—does he somewhere see the light
That he may come back here by favour of fortune
And kill this pair and prove the final victor?

AEGISTHUS (summoning his guards): Well, if such is
    your design in deeds and words, you will quickly 1890
    learn—
Here my friends, here my guards, there is work for
    you at hand.

LEADER OF THE CHORUS: Come then, hands on hilts,
    be each and all of us prepared.

(The old men and the guards threaten each other.)

AEGISTHUS: Very well! I too am ready to meet death with sword in hand.

LEADER OF THE CHORUS: We are glad you speak of dying. We accept your words for luck.

1900 CLYTEMNESTRA: No, my dearest, do not so. Add no more to the train of wrong.

To reap these many present wrongs is harvest enough of misery.

Enough of misery. Start no more. Our hands are red.

But do you, and you old men, go home and yield to fate in time,

In time before you suffer. We have tried as we had to act.

1910 If only our afflictions now could prove enough, we should agree—

We who have been so hardly mauled in the heavy claws of the evil god.

So stands my word, a woman's, if any man thinks fit to hear.

AEGISTHUS: But to think that these should thus pluck the blooms of an idle tongue

And should throw out words like these, giving the evil god his chance,

And should miss the path of prudence and insult 1920 their master so!

LEADER OF THE CHORUS: It is not the Argive way to fawn upon a cowardly man.

AEGISTHUS: Perhaps. But I in later days will take further steps with you.

LEADER OF THE CHORUS: Not if the god who rules the family guides Orestes to his home.

AEGISTHUS: Yes. I know that men in exile feed themselves on barren hopes.

LEADER OF THE CHORUS: Go on, grow fat defiling 1930 justice . . . while you have your hour.

AEGISTHUS: Do not think you will not pay me a price for your stupidity.

LEADER OF THE CHORUS: Boast on in your self-assurance, like a cock beside his hen.

CLYTEMNESTRA: Pay no heed, Aegisthus, to these futile barkings. You and I,

Masters of this house, from now shall order all things well.

(They enter the palace.)

Figure 1. Clytemnestra, center, welcomes Agamemnon and Cassandra in the production of *Agamemnon* by the National Theatre Company of Greece, Epidaurus, 1965. (Photograph: D. A. Harissiadis.)

Figure 2. Clytemnestra (Douglas Campbell, *left*) welcomes Agamemnon (Lee Richardson) upon his return from Troy in the Guthrie Theater Company production of *The House of Atreus*, directed by Tyrone Guthrie and designed by Tanya Moiseiwitsch, Minneapolis, 1967/68. (Photograph: the Guthrie Theater.)

Figure 3. Agamemnon (Lee Richardson, *left*) returns from the Trojan war with Cassandra (Robin Gammell) in the Guthrie Theater Company production of *The House of Atreus,* directed by Tyrone Guthrie and designed by Tanya Moiseiwitsch, Minneapolis, 1967/68. (Photograph: the Guthrie Theater.)

Staging of *Agamemnon*

REVIEW OF THE GUTHRIE THEATER
PRODUCTION, 1967, BY RODERICK NORDELL

The Minnesota Theater Company's "House of Atreus" is like an ancient carving freed from stone to tell us about ourselves. Compressing Aeschylus' "Oresteia" trilogy into a single lengthy evening, it is attracting full houses to the Tyrone Guthrie Theater for a rigorous combination of spectacle, psychology, philosophy, and even a kind of God-is-alive theology.

As seen last week, the production tempted one to stay on the level of spectacle—an awesome theatrical representation of the theme familiarly translated as "Men shall learn wisdom, by affliction schooled." For Tyrone Guthrie's monumentally stylized direction is aided by the designing hand of Tanya Moiseiwitsch, as it was in "Oedipus" at Stratford, Ont., some dozen years ago. And the mythic grandeur of their work is heightened by the grotesque but tellingly differentiated masks credited to Carolyn Parker and Dahl Delu.

Cassandra's mask, for example, is vaguely reminiscent of a tragic, dark-lined Rouault portrait. Clytemnestra's is haughty, blank-eyed, with a forbidding version of the "onkos," the high hairdress Aeschylus favored.

The sleeved robes he pioneered for actors are also effectively suggested, though sometimes they seem to have been given an antiquing process recalling a painter's spattered tarpaulin. And, if history is right in saying Aeschylus raised the height of the actors' elevator shoes, "The House of Atreus" must go further than he did.

In this production, only the ordinary people, "like ourselves," are on ground level, as Guthrie has commented. The main characters, "heroic figures," are larger than life. The gods are immense.

The great rings in the massive palace gates almost overwhelm the mortal men who open them. Even the heroic figure of Orestes is dwarfed by the golden, towering Apollo who has set him on the path of vengeance—and by the enormous seated Pallas Athena who seeks to bring rational justice to the primitive situation of blood-will-have-blood.

It takes some effort to wrench oneself from the spectacle; from Dominick Argento's music with its breathy cymbal ending a spoken phrase, its tinkling triangles and more stentorian flourishes; from the sound and sight of the skilled actors, notably Douglas Campbell, who makes Clytemnestra's first silent entrance a chilling image of threat and who—without obvious feminine pitch—speaks the lines with a thoughtful, savage, womanly eloquence.

The display is marvelous in itself; it can be justified both by old tradition and by the new demands of the theater to break out of realism and into its own unique truth. Yet one has at least a passing feeling that the production could have gone in another direction—toward the sparest everyday restraint—in eliciting what Aeschylus says to today, and what is seen in him by his sensitive latter-day adapter, John Lewin, the company's resident playwright.

The feeling does not apply only to such humanizing touches as those derived from Aeschylus' own experience in the army. When a soldier returns from Troy, Mr. Lewin plausibly has him say, "You think it's cold in Greece—this was unbelievable." Is it too human to be spoken through a mask?

One also questions the apparatus when the play gets into Mr. Lewin's stated interpretation of its psychological level, with the unconscious and the "ordering intellect" in conflict and collaboration. The nightmarish Furies and the gleaming Apollo make strong images, but might they not be stronger in street clothes, so to speak? Today's dilemmas tend to be gray.

As it is, the dazzled spectator may not listen closely enough when Orestes challenges his god, Apollo: "You know what it means to do wrong. Do you know what it means to take responsibility?"

But in such lines, in the interplay between "new" and "old" gods, in the emergence of a more sophisticated form of justice, lie the issues that still exercise philosophers and theologians. In the company's "play guide," Minnesota poet Robert Bly finds Aeschylus' exploration of the "inability to forgive" pertinent to such present-day episodes as Eichmann and Vietnam. Guthrie finds a parallel to humanity's growing conception of God: "the vengeful tribal deity, the Jehovah of the earlier books of the Old Testament, becomes God the All-Merciful Father, something very different, very much more humane."

On afterthought, such themes can be pondered in relation to the sheer theater that envelops them. But in the playhouse the weight of effects, as well as that of tragedy, may contribute to the audience's laughing sigh of relief when Orestes' old nurse brings it back to earth with: "It's just one thing after another." The outer and inner drama fuse during moments such as that when the well-deployed chorus says: "The gods that give us sorrows give us tongues to mourn."

SOPHOCLES

496–406 B.C.

Because his life spanned almost the entire fifth century, Sophocles witnessed both the rise and the fall of Athens—a reversal of political fortune as astonishing as the one he dramatized in *Oedipus Rex*. As a young man he lived through the extraordinary growth of Athenian power and culture that followed upon the Persian Wars; as a mature man he served its power and culture in various capacities: as ambassador, dramatist, general, priest, and treasurer; and as an old man he witnessed the collapse of its power and culture under the strains of the Peloponnesian Wars, his death coming only two years before the Athenian surrender to Sparta. In many respects he seems to have been a consummate representative of the best qualities in fifth century Athenian culture, a man who not only was gifted with good looks, great wealth, and even greater talent, but who also made the most of those gifts in his public life, his religious duties, and his artistic career. Through all the distractions of public appointments and religious obligations, he somehow managed to write more than 120 plays.

Although he was a prolific writer, he wrote with great care, and his carefully wrought plays brought him great success in the festival competitions. He won first prize twenty-four times, and he never ranked lower than second. Only seven of his plays have survived, all from the mature period of his life: *Ajax* (ca. 445). *Antigone* (ca. 440), *Trachiniae* (ca. 435), *Oedipus Rex* (ca. 425). *Electra* (ca. 415), *Philoctetes* (409), and *Oedipus at Colonus* (406). All of these show him to have been a painstaking and meticulous dramatist. His plots, however complex, are always clearly worked out, with each event connected by a logic of cause and effect to every other event, so that they never contain any loose ends or improbable outcomes. His characters, though complexly motivated, are always clearly and consistently developed. Because of these qualities, his plays have always been considered the most polished examples of classical Greek tragedy—the perfection of the form.

He completely departed from Aeschylus by abandoning the trilogy, preferring instead to submit three unrelated and self-sufficient plays. Although he sacrificed the comprehensive scope of the trilogy, he was able to develop a far more intense and complete dramatic experience within the limits of a single play—an experience centering on the fate of individuals rather than on the destinies of families and nations. In developing the art of the single play, his most decisive contribution was to increase the number of actors from two to three. He was thus able to create various kinds of highly dramatic episodes out of the triangular interplay among characters that became possible with the third actor. Two such episodes occur in *Oedipus Rex:* the first, when the messenger comes to bring what he thinks is good news to Oedipus and Iocaste, but the news gradually reveals to Iocaste a horrible truth that she seeks to withold from Oedipus; the second, when the shepherd arrives and reluctantly answers the questions of the messenger and Oedipus, providing information that finally reveals the horrible truth to Oedipus.

Once it became possible to stage such theatrically compelling episodes, it was inevitable that the actors would become more important than the chorus, and that is precisely what happened in the plays of Sophocles. Although he increased the size of the chorus from twelve to fifteen members, he actually reduced its functions, confining its activities almost exclusively to choral odes and leaving it little opportunity to interact with the characters. Its odes continued to be relevant to the mood and meaning of the action, but the chorus was no longer a dramatically integral part of that action, as it had been in the plays of Aeschylus. Thus Sophocles moved tragedy further away from its lyric origins and closer to a purely dramatic form.

Sophocles used the sophisticated form of his tragedies to represent and explore the fate of heroic individuals in a moment of moral crisis. All of his protagonists prove to be singularly heroic in their commitment to a moral principle they establish for themselves, even though their commitment brings great suffering to themselves and their loved ones. In *Antigone,* for example, the heroine opposes her uncle Creon, who as ruler of Thebes has decreed that her brother Polyneices is not to be given a burial because he had led an attack on the city. Creon regards his edict as a politically necessary action, whereas Antigone believes the burial of her brother is a sacred obligation. Although Antigone is shown to be coldly, fanatically, and inflexibly devoted to her cause, the events of the play bear out the righteousness of her action. Yet her righteous commitment is not only the source of her dignity; it is also the cause of her undoing. This paradoxical fate repeatedly besets the heroes of Sophocles, and it is one of the qualities that make his plays so compelling. Indeed, his tragedies would not be so terrifying as they are, if his protagonists were so flawed as they are often considered to be.

The disaster experienced by Oedipus is often regarded as a fitting outcome of his pride, but it is difficult to see how the play justifies this interpretation of his fate. Throughout the play he is shown to be nobly unyielding in his attempt to rid Thebes of the plague by discovering and punishing the murderer of its previous king, Laius. Even when the investigation turns into an investigation of himself, he is unflinching in his quest for truth, though he is warned against it by Teiresias and Iocaste. He relentlessly conducts his search until he discovers himself to be the criminal, the source of the city's sickness, and by exposing himself brings about the renewed health of the city. His commitment to the truth thereby proves to be at once his triumph and his disaster. *Oedipus Rex* raises haunting questions about the fate of heroic individuals, questions that it does not finally answer, except through the chorus' concluding reflections on human frailty.

Because its plot and characters are so skillfully conceived and developed, *Oedipus Rex* has come to be the most influential play ever written. The perfection of its form was recognized by Aristotle during the fourth century B.C. when he expounded his theory of tragedy in *The Poetics*. In his discussions of character and plot, Aristotle provides detailed explanations of important dramatic elements, such as "discovery" and "reversal of fortune," repeatedly citing *Oedipus Rex* as the outstanding embodiment of them. Using it as his model play, Aristotle produced a study that has come to be the most influential document in the history of dramatic theory and criticism. In choosing his model Aristotle also had his eye on the audience, for he knew from his own experience of witnessing Greek drama just how strongly an audience can be moved to "pity and fear" by discoveries and reversals of fortune on the part of a tragic hero.

Because it is the consummate embodiment of tragic irony, *Oedipus Rex* continues to be highly successful in the modern theater. But because it is so well known and so often produced, contemporary directors, seeking to renew the interest of their audiences, have often felt compelled to develop alternatives to the traditional way of presenting the play in classical masks and costumes as a study of pride and its influence on the outcome of human beings. Consequently, some directors have staged it in modern dress, either as a suspenseful murder mystery or as a Freudian psychodrama. Yet another approach, taken recently by the Guthrie Theater, has been to stage the play in primitivistic costumes and settings (see Figures 1 and 2) as an exhibition of archetypal fears and powerful taboos. A review of that production, reproduced following the text, suggests both the appeals and the perils of experimental approaches to the play. Still, in any style of performance, the astonishing climax of *Oedipus Rex* continues to bear witness to the dignity and the frailty of human nature.

OEDIPUS REX

BY SOPHOCLES/TRANSLATED BY DUDLEY FITTS AND ROBERT FITZGERALD

CHARACTERS

OEDIPUS
A PRIEST
CREON
TEIRESIAS
IOCASTE
MESSENGER
SHEPHERD OF LAÏOS
SECOND MESSENGER
CHORUS OF THEBAN ELDERS

SCENE

Before the palace of Oedipus, King of Thebes. A central door and two lateral doors open onto a platform which runs the length of the façade. On the platform, right and left, are altars; and three steps lead down into the "orchestra," or chorus-ground. At the beginning of the action these steps are crowded by suppliants who have brought branches and chaplets of olive leaves and who lie in various attitudes of despair. OEDIPUS *enters.*

PROLOGUE

OEDIPUS: My children, generations of the living
　　In the line of Kadmos, nursed at his ancient
　　　　hearth:
　　Why have you strewn yourselves before these altars
　　In supplication, with your boughs and garlands?
　　The breath of incense rises from the city
　　With a sound of prayer and lamentation.
　　Children,
　　I would not have you speak through messengers,
10　　And therefore I have come myself to hear you—
　　I, Oedipus, who bear the famous name.

　　(*To a* PRIEST)

　　You, there, since you are eldest in the company,
　　Speak for them all, tell me what preys upon you,
　　Whether you come in dread, or crave some
　　　　blessing:
　　Tell me, and never doubt that I will help you
　　In every way I can; I should be heartless
　　Were I not moved to find you suppliant here.
PRIEST: Great Oedipus, O powerful King of Thebes!
20　　You see how all the ages of our people
　　Cling to your altar steps: here are boys
　　Who can barely stand alone, and here are priests
　　By weight of age, as I am a priest of God,
　　And young men chosen from those yet unmarried;
　　As for the others, all that multitude,
　　They wait with olive chaplets in the squares,
　　At the two shrines of Pallas, and where Apollo
　　Speaks in the glowing embers.
　　Your own eyes
30　　Must tell you: Thebes is tossed on a murdering sea
　　And can not lift her head from the death surge.
　　A rust consumes the buds and fruits of the earth;
　　The herds are sick; children die unborn,
　　And labor is vain. The god of plague and pyre
　　Raids like detestable lightning through the city,
　　And all the house of Kadmos is laid waste,

All emptied, and all darkened: Death alone
Battens upon the misery of Thebes.

You are not one of the immortal gods, we know;
Yet we have come to you to make our prayer　　40
As to the man surest in mortal ways
And wisest in the ways of God. You saved us
From the Sphinx, that flinty singer, and the tribute
We paid to her so long; yet you were never
Better informed than we, nor could we teach you;
A god's touch, it seems, enabled you to help us.

Therefore, O mighty power, we turn to you:
Find us our safety, find us a remedy,
Whether by counsel of the gods or of men.
A king of wisdom tested in the past　　50
Can act in a time of troubles, and act well.
Noblest of men, restore
Life to your city! Think how all men call you
Liberator for your boldness long ago;
Ah, when your years of kingship are remembered,
Let them not say *We rose, but later fell*—
Keep the State from going down in the storm!
Once, years ago, with happy augury,
You brought us fortune; be the same again!
No man questions your power to rule the land:　　60
But rule over men, not a dead city!
Ships are only hulls, high walls are nothing,
When no life moves in the empty passageways.
OEDIPUS: Poor children! You may be sure I know
　　All that you longed for in your coming here.
　　I know that you are deathly sick; and yet,
　　Sick as you are, not one is as sick as I.
　　Each of you suffers in himself alone
　　His anguish, not another's; but my spirit
　　Groans for the city, for myself, for you.　　70

　　I was not sleeping, you are not waking me.
　　No, I have been in tears for a long while

And in my restless thought walked many ways.
In all my search I found one remedy,
And I have adopted it: I have sent Kreon,
Son of Menoikeus, brother of the Queen,
To Delphi, Apollo's place of revelation,
To learn there, if he can,
What act or pledge of mine may save the city.
80 I have counted the days, and now, this very day,
I am troubled, for he has overstayed his time.
What is he doing? He has been gone too long.
Yet whenever he comes back, I should do ill
Not to take any action the god orders.
PRIEST: It is a timely promise. At this instant
They tell me Kreon is here.
OEDIPUS: O Lord Apollo!
May his news be fair as his face is radiant!
PRIEST: Good news, I gather: he is crowned with bay,
90 The chaplet is thick with berries.
OEDIPUS: We shall soon know;
He is near enough to hear us now.

(Enter KREON.*)*

O Prince:
Brother: son of Menoikeus
What answer do you bring us from the God?
KREON: A strong one. I can tell you, great afflictions
Will turn out well, if they are taken well.
OEDIPUS: What was the oracle? These vague words
Leave me still hanging between hope and fear.
100 KREON: Is it your pleasure to hear me with all these
Gathered around us? I am prepared to speak,
But should we not go in?
OEDIPUS: Speak to them all.
It is for them I suffer, more than for myself.
KREON: Then I will tell you what I heard at Delphi.
In plain words
The god commands us to expel from the land of
Thebes
An old defilement we are sheltering.
110 It is a deathly thing, beyond cure;
We must not let it feed upon us longer.
OEDIPUS: What defilement? How shall we rid
ourselves of it?
KREON: By exile or death, blood for blood. It was
Murder that brought the plague-wind on the city.
OEDIPUS: Murder of whom? Surely the god has
named him?
KREON: My lord: Laïos once ruled this land,
Before you came to govern us.
120 OEDIPUS: I know;
I learned of him from others; I never saw him.
KREON: He was murdered; and Apollo commands us
now
To take revenge upon whoever killed him.

OEDIPUS: Upon whom? Where are they? Where shall
we find a clue
To solve that crime, after so many years?
KREON: Here in this land, he said. Search reveals
Things that escape an inattentive man.
OEDIPUS: Tell me: Was Laïos murdered in his house, 130
Or in the fields, or in some foreign country?
KREON: He said he planned to make a pilgrimage.
He did not come home again.
OEDIPUS: And was there no one,
No witness, no companion, to tell what happened?
KREON: They were all killed but one, and he got away
So frightened that he could remember one thing
only.
OEDIPUS: What was that one thing? One may be the
key   140
To everything, if we resolve to use it.
KREON: He said that a band of highwaymen attacked
them,
Outnumbered them, and overwhelmed the King.
OEDIPUS: Strange, that a highwayman should be so
daring—
Unless some faction here bribed him to do it.
KREON: We thought of that. But after Laïos' death
New troubles arose and we had no avenger.
OEDIPUS: What troubles could prevent your hunting 150
down the killers?
KREON: The riddling Sphinx's song
Made us deaf to all mysteries but her own.
OEDIPUS: Then once more I must bring what is dark
to light.
It is most fitting that Apollo shows,
As you do, this compunction for the dead.
You shall see how I stand by you, as I should,
Avenging this country and the god as well,
And not as though it were for some distant friend, 160
But for my own sake, to be rid of evil.
Whoever killed King Laïos might—who knows?—
Lay violent hands even on me—and soon.
I act for the murdered king in my own interest.

Come, then, my children: leave the altar steps,
Lift up your olive boughs!
One of you go
And summon the people of Kadmos to gather
here.
I will do all that I can; you may tell them that.   170

(Exit a PAGE.*)*

So, with the help of God.
We shall be saved—or else indeed we are lost.
PRIEST: Let us rise, children. It was for this we came,
And now the King has promised it.
Phoibos has sent us an oracle; may he descend
Himself to save us and drive out the plague.

(Exeunt OEDIPUS *and* KREON *into the palace by the central door. The* PRIEST *and the* SUPPLIANTS *disperse right and left. After a short pause the* CHORUS *enters the orchestra.)*

PARADOS

Strophe 1

CHORUS: What is God singing in his profound
Delphi of gold and shadow?
What oracle for Thebes, the sunwhipped city?

180   Fear unjoints me, the roots of my heart tremble.

Now I remember, O Healer, your power and
    wonder:
Will you send doom like a sudden cloud, or weave
    it
Like nightfall of the past?

Speak to me, tell me, O
Child of golden Hope, immortal Voice.

Antistrophe 1

Let me pray to Athene, the immortal daughter of
    Zeus,
190   And to Artemis her sister
Who keeps her famous throne in the market ring,

And to Apollo, archer from distant heaven—

O gods, descend! Like three streams leap against
The fires of our grief, the fires of darkness;
Be swift to bring us rest!

As in the old time from the brilliant house
Of air you stepped to save us, come again!

Strophe 2

Now our afflictions have no end,
Now all our stricken host lies down
200   And no man fights off death with his mind;

The noble plowland bears no grain,
And groaning mothers can not bear—

See, how our lives like birds take wing,
Like sparks that fly when a fire soars,
To the shore of the god of evening.

Antistrophe 2

The plague burns on, it is pitiless,
Though pallid children laden with death
Lie unwept in the stony ways,

And old gray women by every path
210   Flock to the strand about the altars

There to strike their breasts and cry
Worship of Phoibos in wailing prayers:
Be kind, God's golden child!

Strophe 3

There are no swords in this attack by fire,
No shields, but we are ringed with cries.

Send the besieger plunging from our homes
Into the vast sea-room of the Atlantic
Or into the waves that foam eastward of Thrace—

For the day ravages what the night spares—

Destroy our enemy, lord of the thunder!   220
Let him be riven by lightning from heaven!

Antistrophe 3

Phoibos Apollo, stretch the sun's bowstring,
That golden cord, until it sing for us,
Flashing arrows in heaven!
Artemis, Huntress,
Race with flaring lights upon our mountains!

O scarlet god, O golden-banded brow,
O Theban Bacchos in a storm of Maenads,

(Enter OEDIPUS, *center.)*

Whirl upon Death, that all the Undying hate!
Come with blinding torches, come in joy!   230

SCENE I

OEDIPUS: Is this your prayer? It may be answered.
    Come,
Listen to me, act as the crisis demands,
And you shall have relief from all these evils.

Until now I was a stranger to this tale.
As I had been a stranger to the crime.
Could I track down the murderer without a clue?
But now, friends,
As one who became a citizen after the murder,
I make this proclamation to all Thebans: 10

If any man knows by whose hand Laïos, son of
    Labdakos,
Met his death, I direct that man to tell me
    everything,
No matter what he fears for having so long
    withheld it.
Let it stand as promised that no further trouble
Will come to him, but he may leave the land in
    safety.

Moreover: If anyone knows the murderer to be   20
    foreign,
Let him not keep silent: he shall have his reward
    from me.
However, if he does conceal it; if any man

Fearing for his friend or for himself disobeys this
    edict,
Hear what I propose to do:

I solemnly forbid the people of this country,
Where power and throne are mine, ever to receive
30   that man
Or speak to him, no matter who he is, or let him
Join in sacrifice, lustration, or in prayer.
I decree that he be driven from every house,
Being, as he is, corruption itself to us: the Delphic
Voice of Apollo has pronounced this revelation.
Thus I associate myself with the oracle
And take the side of the murdered king.

As for the criminal, I pray to God—
Whether it be a lurking thief, or one of a number—
40   I pray that that man's life be consumed in evil and
    wretchedness.
And as for me, this curse applies no less
If it should turn out that the culprit is my guest
    here,
Sharing my hearth.
You have heard the penalty.

I lay it on you now to attend to this
For my sake, for Apollo's, for the sick
Sterile city that heaven has abandoned.
50   Suppose the oracle had given you no command:
Should this defilement go uncleansed for ever?
You should have found the murderer: your king,
A noble king, had been destroyed!
Now I,
Having the power that he held before me,
Having his bed, begetting children there
Upon his wife, as he would have, had he lived—
Their son would have been my children's brother,
If Läios had had luck in fatherhood!
60   (And now his bad fortune has struck him down)—
I say I take the son's part, just as though
I were his son, to press the fight for him
And see it won! I'll find the hand that brought
Death to Labdakos' and Polydoros' child,
Heir of Kadmos' and Agenor's line.
And as for those who fail me,
May the gods deny them the fruit of the earth,
Fruit of the womb, and may they rot utterly!
Let them be wretched as we are wretched, and
70   worse!

For you, my loyal Thebans, and for all
Who find my actions right, I pray the favor
Of justice, and of all the immortal gods.
CHORAGOS: Since I am under oath, my lord, I swear
I did not do the murder, I can not name
The murderer. Phoibos ordained the search;

Why did he not say who the culprit was?
OEDIPUS: An honest question. But no man in the
    world
Can make the gods do more than the gods will.   80
CHORAGOS: There is an alternative, I think—
OEDIPUS: Tell me.
Any or all, you must not fail to tell me.
CHORAGOS: A lord clairvoyant to the lord Apollo,
As we all know, is the skilled Teiresias.
One might learn much about this from him,
    Oedipus.
OEDIPUS: I am not wasting time:
Kreon spoke of this, and I have sent for him—
Twice, in fact; it is strange that he is not here.   90
CHORAGOS: The other matter—that old
    report—seems useless.
OEDIPUS: What was that? I am interested in all
    reports.
CHORAGOS: The King was said to have been killed by
    highwaymen.
OEDIPUS: I know. But we have no witnesses to that.
CHORAGOS: If the killer can feel a particle of dread,
Your curse will bring him out of hiding!
OEDIPUS: No.   100
The man who dared that act will fear no curse.

(Enter the blind seer TEIRESIAS, *led by a* PAGE*).*

CHORAGOS: But there is one man who may detect the
    criminal.
This is Teiresias, this is the holy prophet
In whom, alone of all men, truth was born.
OEDIPUS: Teiresias: seer: student of mysteries,
Of all that's taught and all that no man tells,
Secrets of Heaven and secrets of the earth:
Blind though you are, you know the city lies
Sick with plague; and from this plague, my lord,   110
We find that you alone can guard or save us.

Possibly you did not hear the messengers?
Apollo, when we sent to him,
Sent us back word that this great pestilence
Would lift, but only if we established clearly
The identity of those who murdered Läios.
They must be killed or exiled.
Can you use
Birdflight or any art of divination
To purify yourself, and Thebes, and me   120
From this contagion? We are in your hands.
There is no fairer duty
Than that of helping others in distress.
TEIRESIAS: How dreadful knowledge of the truth can
    be
When there's no help in truth! I knew this well,
But did not act on it: else I should not have come.
OEDIPUS: What is troubling you? Why are your eyes
    so cold?

130 TEIRESIAS: Let me go home. Bear your own fate, and
   I'll
      Bear mine. It is better so: trust what I say.
   OEDIPUS: What you say is ungracious and unhelpful
      To your native country. Do not refuse to speak.
   TEIRESIAS: When it comes to speech, your own is
      neither temperate
      Nor opportune. I wish to be more prudent.
   OEDIPUS: In God's name, we all beg you—
   TEIRESIAS: You are all ignorant.
140   No; I will never tell you what I know.
      Now it is my misery; then it would be yours.
   OEDIPUS: What! You do know something, and will
      not tell us?
      You would betray us all and wreck the State?
   TEIRESIAS: I do not intend to torture myself, or you.
      Why persist in asking? You will not persuade me.
   OEDIPUS: What a wicked old man you are! You'd try a
      stone's
      Patience! Out with it. Have you no feeling at all?
150 TEIRESIAS: You call me unfeeling. If you could only
      see
      The nature of your own feelings . . .
   OEDIPUS: Why,
      Who would not feel as I do? Who could endure
      Your arrogance toward the city?
   TEIRESIAS: What does it matter?
      Whether I speak or not, it is bound to come.
   OEDIPUS: Then, if 'it' is bound to come, you are
      bound to tell me.
160 TEIRESIAS: No, I will not go on. Rage as you please.
   OEDIPUS: Rage? Why not!
      And I'll tell you what I think:
      You planned it, you had it done, you all but
      Killed him with your own hands: if you had eyes,
      I'd say the crime was yours, and yours alone.
   TEIRESIAS: So? I charge you, then,
      Abide by the proclamation you have made:
      From this day forth
      Never speak again to these men or to me;
170   You yourself are the pollution of this country.
   OEDIPUS: You dare say that! Can you possibly think
      you have
      Some way of going free, after such insolence?
   TEIRESIAS: I have gone free. It is the truth sustains
      me.
   OEDIPUS: Who taught you shamelessness? It was not
      your craft.
   TEIRESIAS: You did. You made me speak. I did not
      want to.
180 OEDIPUS: Speak what? Let me hear it again more
      clearly.
   TEIRESIAS: Was it not clear before? Are you tempting
      me?
   OEDIPUS: I did not understand it. Say it again.
   TEIRESIAS: I say that you are the murderer whom you
      seek.

   OEDIPUS: Now twice you have spat out infamy. You'll
      pay for it!
   TEIRESIAS: Would you care for more? Do you wish to
      be really angry?   190
   OEDIPUS: Say what you will. Whatever you say is
      worthless.
   TEIRESIAS: I say you live in hideous shame with those
      Most dear to you. You can not see the evil.
   OEDIPUS: Can you go on babbling like this for ever?
   TEIRESIAS: I can, if there is power in truth.
   OEDIPUS: There is:
      But not for you, not for you,
      You sightless, witless, senseless, mad old man!
   TEIRESIAS: You are the madman. There is no one   200
      here
      Who will not curse you soon, as you curse me.
   OEDIPUS: You child of total night! I would not touch
      you;
      Neither would any man who sees the sun.
   TEIRESIAS: True: it is not from you my fate will come.
      That lies within Apollo's competence,
      As it is his concern.
   OEDIPUS: Tell me, who made
      These fine discoveries? Kreon? Or someone else?   210
   TEIRESIAS: Kreon is no threat. You weave your own
      doom.
   OEDIPUS: Wealth, power, craft of statesmanship!
      Kingly position, everywhere admired!
      What savage envy is stored up against these,
      If Kreon, whom I trusted, Kreon my friend,
      For this great office which the city once
      Put in my hands unsought—if for this power
      Kreon desires in secret to destroy me!

      He has brought this decrepit fortune-teller, this   220
      Collector of dirty pennies, this prophet fraud—
      Why, he is no more clairvoyant than I am!
      Tell us:
      Has your mystic mummery ever approached the
         truth?
      When that hellcat the Sphinx was performing here,
      What help were you to these people?
      Her magic was not for the first man who came
         along:
      It demanded a real exorcist. Your birds—   230
      What good were they? or the gods, for the matter
         of that?
      But I came by,
      Oedipus, the simple man, who knows nothing—
      I thought it out for myself, no birds helped me!
      And this is the man you think you can destroy,
      That you may be close to Kreon when he's king!
      Well, you and your friend Kreon, it seems to me,
      Will suffer most. If you were not an old man,
      You would have paid already for your plot.   240
   CHORAGOS: We can not see that his words or yours
      Have been spoken except in anger, Oedipus,

And of anger we have no need. How to accomplish
The god's will best: that is what most concerns us.
TEIRESIAS: You are a king. But where argument's
     concerned
I am your man, as much a king as you.
I am not your servant, but Apollo's.
I have no need of Kreon's name.

250   Listen to me. You mock my blindness, do you?
But I say that you, with both your eyes, are blind:
You can not see the wretchedness of your life,
Nor in whose house you live, no, nor with whom.
Who are your father and mother? Can you tell me?
You do not even know the blind wrongs
That you have done them, on earth and in the
     world below.
But the double lash of your parents' curse will whip
     you
260   Out of this land some day, with only night
Upon your precious eyes.
Your cries then—where will they not be heard?
What fastness of Kithairon will not echo them?
And that bridal-descant of yours—you'll know it
     then,
The song they sang when you came here to Thebes
And found your misguided berthing.
All this, and more, that you can not guess at now,
Will bring you to yourself among your children.

270   Be angry, then. Curse Kreon. Curse my words.
I tell you, no man that walks upon the earth
Shall be rooted out more horribly than you.
OEDIPUS: Am I to bear this from him?—Damnation
Take you! Out of this place! Out of my sight!
TEIRESIAS: I would not have come at all if you had not
     asked me.
OEDIPUS: Could I have told that you'd talk nonsense,
     that
You'd come here to make a fool of yourself, and of
280   me?
TEIRESIAS: A fool? Your parents thought me sane
     enough.
OEDIPUS: My parents again!—Wait: who were my
     parents?
TEIRESIAS: This day will give you a father, and break
     your heart.
OEDIPUS: Your infantile riddles! Your damned
     abracadabra!
TEIRESIAS: You were a great man once at solving
290   riddles.
OEDIPUS: Mock me with that if you like; you will find
     it true.
TEIRESIAS: It was true enough. It brought about your
     ruin.
OEDIPUS: But if it saved this town?
TEIRESIAS (to the PAGE): Boy, give me your hand.
OEDIPUS: Yes, boy; lead him away.

—While you are here
We can do nothing. Go; leave us in peace.
TEIRESIAS: I will go when I have said what I have to   300
     say.
How can you hurt me? And I tell you again:
The man you have been looking for all this time,
The damned man, the murderer of Laïos,
That man is in Thebes. To your mind he is
     foreign-born,
But it will soon be shown that he is a Theban,
A revelation that will fail to please.
A blind man,
Who has his eyes now; a penniless man, who is rich   310
     now;
And he will go tapping the strange earth with his
     staff.
To the children with whom he lives now he will be
Brother and father—the very same; to her
Who bore him, son and husband—the very same
Who came to his father's bed, wet with his father's
     blood.

Enough. Go think that over.
If later you find error in what I have said,   320
You may say that I have no skill in prophecy.

(*Exit* TEIRESIAS, *led by his* PAGE. OEDIPUS *goes into the
palace.*)

ODE I

Strophe 1

CHORUS: The Delphic stone of prophecies
Remembers ancient regicide
And a still bloody hand.
That killer's hour of flight has come.
He must be stronger than riderless
Coursers of untiring wind,
For the son of Zeus armed with his father's thunder
Leaps in lightning after him;
And the Furies hold his track, the sad Furies.   330

Antistrophe 1

Holy Parnassos' peak of snow
Flashes and blinds that secret man,
That all shall hunt him down:
Though he may roam the forest shade
Like a bull gone wild from pasture
To rage through glooms of stone.
Doom comes down on him; flight will not avail
     him;
For the world's heart calls him desolate,
And the immortal voices follow, for ever follow.   340

Strophe 2

But now a wilder thing is heard
From the old man skilled at hearing Fate in the
     wingbeat of a bird.

Bewildered as a blown bird, my soul hovers and can
not find
Foothold in this debate, or any reason or rest of
mind.
But no man ever brought—none can bring
Proof of strife between Thebes' royal house,
350 Labdakos' line, and the son of Polybos;
And never until now has any man brought word
Of Laïos' dark death staining Oedipus the King.

Antistrophe 2

Divine Zeus and Apollo hold
Perfect intelligence alone of all tales ever told;
And well though this diviner works, he works in his
own night;
No man can judge that rough unknown or trust in
second sight,
For wisdom changes hands among the wise.
360 Shall I believe my great lord criminal
At a raging word that a blind old man let fall?
I saw him, when the carrion woman faced him of
old,
Prove his heroic mind. These evil words are lies.

SCENE II

KREON: Men of Thebes:
I am told that heavy accusations
Have been brought against me by King Oedipus.

I am not the kind of man to bear this tamely.

If in these present difficulties
He holds me accountable for any harm to him
Through anything I have said or done—why, then,
I do not value life in this dishonor.

It is not as though this rumor touched upon
10 Some private indiscretion. The matter is grave.
The fact is that I am being called disloyal
To the State, to my fellow citizens, to my friends.
CHORAGOS: He may have spoken in anger, not from
his mind.
KREON: But did you not hear him say I was the one
Who seduced the old prophet into lying?
CHORAGOS: The thing was said: I do not know how
seriously.
KREON: But you were watching him! Were his eyes
20 steady?
Did he look like a man in his right mind?
CHORAGOS: I do not know.
I can not judge the behavior of great men.
But here is the King himself.

(Enter OEDIPUS.)

OEDIPUS: So you dared come back.
Why? How brazen of you to come to my house,

You murderer!
Do you think I do not know
That you plotted to kill me, plotted to steal my
throne?   30
Tell me, in God's name: am I coward, a fool,
That you should dream you could accomplish this?
A fool who could not see your slippery game?
A coward, not to fight back when I saw it?
You are the fool, Kreon, are you not? hoping
Without support or friends to get a throne?
Thrones may be won or bought: you could do
neither.
KREON: Now listen to me. You have talked; let me
talk, too.   40
You can not judge unless you know the facts.
OEDIPUS: You speak well: there is one fact; but I find
it hard
To learn from the deadliest enemy I have.
KREON: That above all I must dispute with you.
OEDIPUS: That above all I will not hear you deny.
KREON: If you think there is anything good in being
stubborn
Against all reason, then I say you are wrong.
OEDIPUS: If you think a man can sin against his own   50
kind
And not be punished for it, I say you are mad.
KREON: I agree. But tell me: what have I done to you?
OEDIPUS: You advised me to send for that wizard, did
you not?
KREON: I did. I should do it again.
OEDIPUS: Very well. Now tell me:
How long has it been since Laïos—
KREON: What of Laïos?
OEDIPUS: Since he vanished in that onset by the road?   60
KREON: It was long ago, a long time.
OEDIPUS: And this prophet,
Was he practicing here then?
KREON: He was; and with honor, as now
OEDIPUS: Did he speak of me at that time?
KREON: He never did;
At least, not when I was present.
OEDIPUS: But . . . the enquiry?
I suppose you held one?
KREON: We did, but we learned nothing.   70
OEDIPUS: Why did the prophet not speak against me
then?
KREON: I do not know; and I am the kind of man
Who holds his tongue when he has no facts to go
on.
OEDIPUS: There's one fact that you know, and you
could tell it.
KREON: What fact is that? If I know it, you shall have
it.
OEDIPUS: If he were not involved with you, he could   80
not say
That it was I who murdered Laïos.
KREON: If he says that, you are the one that knows
it!—

But now it is my turn to question you.
OEDIPUS: Put your questions. I am no murderer.
KREON: First, then: You married my sister?
OEDIPUS: I married your sister.
KREON: And you rule the kingdom equally with her?
90 OEDIPUS: Everything that she wants she has from me.
KREON: And I am the third, equal to both of you?
OEDIPUS: That is why I call you a bad friend.
KREON: No. Reason it out, as I have done.
    Think of this first: Would any sane man prefer
    Power, with all a king's anxieties,
    To that same power and the grace of sleep?
    Certainly not I.
    I have never longed for the king's power—only his
      rights.
100   Would any wise man differ from me in this?
    As matters stand, I have my way in everything
    With your consent, and no responsibilities.
    If I were king, I should be a slave to policy.
    How could I desire a sceptre more
    Than what is now mine—untroubled influence?
    No, I have not gone mad; I need no honors,
    Except those with the perquisites I have now.
    I am welcome everywhere; every man salutes me,
    And those who want your favor seek my ear,
110   Since I know how to manage what they ask.
    Should I exchange this ease for that anxiety?
    Besides, no sober mind is treasonable.
    I hate anarchy
    And never would deal with any man who likes it.

    Test what I have said. Go to the priestess
    At Delphi, ask if I quoted her correctly.
    And as for this other thing: If I am found
    Guilty of treason with Teiresias,
    Then sentence me to death. You have my word
120   It is a sentence I should cast my vote for—
    But not without evidence!
    You do wrong
    When you take good men for bad, bad men for
      good.
    A true friend thrown aside—why, life itself
    Is not more precious!
    In time you will know this well:
    For time, and time alone, will show the just man,
    Though scoundrels are discovered in a day.
130 CHORAGOS: This is well said, and a prudent man
      would ponder it.
    Judgments too quickly formed are dangerous.
   OEDIPUS: But is he not quick in his duplicity?
    And shall I not be quick to parry him?
    Would you have me stand still, hold my peace, and
      let
    This man win everything, through my inaction?
KREON: And you want—what is it, then? To banish
    me?
140 OEDIPUS: No, not exile. It is your death I want,
    So that all the world may see what treason means.

KREON: You will persist then? You will not believe
    me?
OEDIPUS: How can I believe you?
KREON: Then you are a fool.
OEDIPUS: To save myself?
KREON: In justice, think of me.
OEDIPUS: You are evil incarnate.
KREON: But suppose that you are wrong?
OEDIPUS: Still I must rule.   150
KREON: But not if you rule badly.
OEDIPUS: O city, city!
KREON: It is my city, too!
CHORAGOS: Now, my lords, be still. I see the Queen,
    Iokastê, coming from her palace chambers;
    And it is time she came, for the sake of you both,
    This dreadful quarrel can be resolved through her.

(Enter IOKASTE.*)*

IOKASTE: Poor foolish men, what wicked din is this?
    With Thebes sick to death, is it not shameful
    That you should rake some private quarrel up?   160

(To OEDIPUS*)*

Come into the house.
And you, Kreon, go now:
Let us have no more of this tumult over nothing.
KREON: Nothing? No, sister: what your husband
    plans for me
    Is one of two great evils: exile or death.
OEDIPUS: He is right.
    Why, woman I have caught him squarely
    Plotting against my life.
KREON: No! Let me die   170
    Accurst if ever I have wished you harm!
IOKASTE: Ah, believe it, Oedipus!
    In the name of the gods, respect this oath of his
    For my sake, for the sake of these people here!

Strophe 1

CHORAGOS: Open your mind to her, my lord. Be
    ruled by her, I beg you!
OEDIPUS: What would you have me do?
CHORAGOS: Respect Kreon's word. He has never
    spoken like a fool,
    And now he has sworn an oath.   180
OEDIPUS: You know what you ask?
CHORAGOS: I do.
OEDIPUS: Speak on, then.
CHORAGOS: A friend so sworn should not be baited
    so,
    In blind malice, and without final proof.
OEDIPUS: You are aware, I hope, that what you say
    Means death for me, or exile at the least.

Strophe 2

CHORAGOS: No, I swear by Helios, first in Heaven!
    May I die friendless and accurst,   190
    The worst of deaths, if ever I meant that!

It is the withering fields
That hurt my sick heart:
Must we bear all these ills,
And now your bad blood as well?

OEDIPUS: Then let him go. And let me die, if I must,
Or be driven by him in shame from the land of
Thebes.
It is your unhappiness, and not his talk,
200 That touches me.
As for him—
Wherever he goes, hatred will follow him.
KREON: Ugly in yielding, as you were ugly in rage!
Natures like yours chiefly torment themselves.
OEDIPUS: Can you not go? Can you not leave me?
KREON: I can.
You do not know me; but the city knows me,
And in its eyes I am just, if not in yours.

(Exit KREON.)

Antistrophe 1

CHORAGOS: Lady Iokastê, did you not ask the King to
210   go to his chambers?
IOKASTE: First tell me what has happened.
CHORAGOS: There was suspicion without evidence;
yet it rankled
As even false charges will.
IOKASTE: On both sides?
CHORAGOS: On both.
IOKASTE: But what was said?
CHORAGOS: Oh let it rest, let it be done with!
Have we not suffered enough?
220 OEDIPUS: You see to what your decency has brought
you:
You have made difficulties where my heart saw
none.

Antistrophe 2

CHORAGOS: Oedipus, it is not once only I have told
you—
You must know I should count myself unwise
To the point of madness, should I now forsake
you—
You, under whose hand,
230   In the storm of another time,
Our dear land sailed out free.
But now stand fast at the helm!

IOKASTE: In God's name, Oedipus, inform your wife
as well:
Why are you so set in this hard anger?
OEDIPUS: I will tell you, for none of these men
deserves
My confidence as you do. It is Kreon's work,
His treachery, his plotting against me.
IOKASTE: Go on, if you can make this clear to me.

OEDIPUS: He charges me with the murder of Laïos.
IOKASTE: Has he some knowledge? Or does he speak
from hearsay?
OEDIPUS: He would not commit himself to such a
charge,
But he has brought in that damnable soothsayer
To tell his story.
IOKASTE: Set your mind at rest.
If it is a question of soothsayers, I tell you
That you will find no man whose craft gives   250
knowledge
Of the unknowable.

Here is my proof:
An oracle was reported to Laïos once
(I will not say from Phoibos himself, but from
His appointed ministers, at any rate)
That his doom would be death at the hands of his
own son—
His son, born of his flesh and of mine!

Now, you remember the story: Laïos was killed   260
By marauding strangers where three highways
meet;
But his child had not been three days in this world
Before the King had pierced the baby's ankles
And left him to die on a lonely mountainside.
Thus, Apollo never caused that child
To kill his father, and it was not Laïos' fate
To die at the hands of his son, as he had feared.
This is what prophets and prophecies are worth!
Have no dread of them.   270
It is God himself
Who can show us what he wills, in his own way.
OEDIPUS: How strange a shadowy memory crossed
my mind,
Just now while you were speaking; it chilled my
heart.
IOKASTE: What do you mean? What memory do you
speak of?
OEDIPUS: If I understand you, Laïos was killed
At a place where three roads meet.   280
IOKASTE: So it was said;
We have no later story.
OEDIPUS: Where did it happen?
IOKASTE: Phokis, it is called: at a place where the
Theban Way
Divides into the roads toward Delphi and Daulia.
OEDIPUS: When?
IOKASTE: We had the news not long before you came
And proved the right to your succession here.
OEDIPUS: Ah, what net has God been weaving for me?   290
IOKASTE: Oedipus! Why does this trouble you?
OEDIPUS: Do not ask me yet.
First, tell me how Laïos looked, and tell me
How old he was.
IOKASTE: He was tall, his hair just touched

With white; his form was not unlike your own.

OEDIPUS: I think that I myself may be accurst
By my own ignorant edict.

IOKASTE: You speak strangely.
300   It makes me tremble to look at you, my King.

OEDIPUS: I am not sure that the blind man can not
see.
But I should know better if you were to tell me—

IOKASTE: Anything—though I dread to hear you ask
it.

OEDIPUS: Was the King lightly escorted, or did he
ride
With a large company, as a ruler should?

IOKASTE: There were five men with him in all: one
310   was a herald;
And a single chariot, which he was driving.

OEDIPUS: Alas, that makes it plain enough!
But who—
Who told you how it happened?

IOKASTE: A household servant,
The only one to escape.

OEDIPUS: And is he still
A servant of ours?

IOKASTE: No; for when he came back at last
320   And found you enthroned in the place of the dead
king,
He came to me, touched my hand with his, and
begged
That I would send him away to the frontier district
Where only the shepherds go—
As far away from the city as I could send him.
I granted his prayer; for although the man was a
slave,
He had earned more than this favor at my hands.

330 OEDIPUS: Can he be called back quickly?

IOKASTE: Easily.
But why?

OEDIPUS: I have taken too much upon myself
Without enquiry; therefore I wish to consult him.

IOKASTE: Then he shall come.
But am I not one also
To whom you might confide these fears of yours?

OEDIPUS: That is your right; it will not be denied you,
Now least of all; for I have reached a pitch
340   Of wild foreboding. Is there anyone
To whom I should sooner speak?

Polybos of Corinth is my father.
My mother is a Dorian: Meropê.
I grew up chief among the men of Corinth
Until a strange thing happened—
Not worth my passion, it may be, but strange.

At a feast, a drunken man maundering in his cups
Cries out that I am not my father's son!
I contained myself that night, though I felt anger
350   And a sinking heart. The next day I visited

My father and mother, and questioned them. They
stormed,
Calling it all the slanderous rant of a fool;
And this relieved me. Yet the suspicion
Remained always aching in my mind;
I knew there was talk; I could not rest;
And finally, saying nothing to my parents,
I went to the shrine at Delphi.

The god dismissed my question without reply;
He spoke of other things.   360
Some were clear,
Full of wretchedness, dreadful, unbearable:
As, that I should lie with my own mother, breed
Children from whom all men would turn their
eyes;
And that I should be my father's murderer.

I heard all this, and fled. And from that day
Corinth to me was only in the stars
Descending in that quarter of the sky,
As I wandered farther and farther on my way   370
To a land where I should never see the evil
Sung by the oracle. And I came to this country
Where, so you say, King Laïos was killed.

I will tell you all that happened there, my lady.

There were three highways
Coming together at a place I passed;
And there a herald came towards me, and a chariot
Drawn by horses, with a man such as you describe
Seated in it. The groom leading the horses
Forced me off the road at his lord's command;   380
But as this charioteer lurched over towards me
I struck him in my rage. The old man saw me
And brought his double goad down upon my head
As I came abreast.
He was paid back, and more!
Swinging my club in this right hand I knocked him
Out of his car, and he rolled on the ground.
I killed him.
I killed them all.
Now if that stranger and Laïos were—kin,   390
Where is a man more miserable than I?
More hated by the gods? Citizen and alien alike
Must never shelter me or speak to me—
I must be shunned by all.
And I myself
Pronounced this malediction upon myself!

Think of it: I have touched you with these hands,
These hands that killed your husband. What
defilement!

Am I all evil, then? It must be so,   400
Since I must flee from Thebes, yet never again

See my own countrymen, my own country,
For fear of joining my mother in marriage
And killing Polybos, my father.
Ah,
If I was created so, born to this fate,
Who could deny the savagery of God?

O holy majesty of heavenly powers!
May I never see that day! Never!
410   Rather let me vanish from the race of men
Than know the abomination destined me!
CHORAGOS: We too, my lord, have felt dismay at this.
But there is hope: you have yet to hear the
shepherd.
OEDIPUS: Indeed, I fear no other hope is left me.
IOKASTE: What do you hope from him when he
comes?
OEDIPUS: This much:
If his account of the murder tallies with yours,
420   Then I am cleared.
IOKASTE: What was it that I said
Of such importance?
OEDIPUS: Why, 'marauders', you said,
Killed the King, according to this man's story.
If he maintains that still, if there were several,
Clearly the guilt is not mine: I was alone.
But if he says one man, singlehanded, did it,
Then the evidence all points to me.
IOKASTE: You may be sure that he said there were
430   several;
And can he call back that story now? He can not.
The whole city heard it as plainly as I.
But suppose he alters some detail of it:
He can not ever show that Laïos' death
Fulfilled the oracle: for Apollo said
My child was doomed to kill him; and my child—
Poor baby!—it was my child that died first.

No. From now on, where oracles are concerned,
I would not waste a second thought on any.
440   OEDIPUS: You may be right.
But come: let someone go
For the shepherd at once. This matter must be
settled.
IOKASTE: I will send for him.
I would not wish to cross you in anything,
And surely not in this.—Let us go in.

(Exeunt into the palace.)

ODE II

Strophe 1

CHORUS: Let me be reverent in the ways of right,
Lowly the paths I journey on;
Let all my words and actions keep
The laws of the pure universe

From highest Heaven handed down.
For Heaven is their bright nurse,
Those generations of the realms of light;
Ah, never of mortal kind were they begot,
Nor are they slaves of memory, lost in sleep:
Their Father is greater than Time, and ages not.

Antistrophe 1

The tyrant is a child of Pride
Who drinks from his great sickening cup
Recklessness and vanity,
Until from his high crest headlong   460
He plummets to the dust of hope.
That strong man is not strong.
But let no fair ambition be denied;
May God protect the wrestler for the State
In government, in comely policy,
Who will fear God, and on His ordinance wait.

Strophe 2

Haughtiness and the high hand of disdain
Tempt and outrage God's holy law;
And any mortal who dares hold
No immortal Power in awe   470
Will be caught up in a net of pain:
The price for which his levity is sold.
Let each man take due earnings, then,
And keep his hands from holy things,
And from blasphemy stand apart—
Else the crackling blast of heaven
Blows on his head, and on his desperate heart.
Though fools will honor impious men,
In their cities no tragic poet sings.

Antistrophe 2

Shall we lose faith in Delphi's obscurities,   480
We who have heard the world's core
Discredited, and the sacred wood
Of Zeus at Elis praised no more?
The deeds and the strange prophecies
Must make a pattern yet to be understood.
Zeus, if indeed you are lord of all,
Throned in light over night and day,
Mirror this in your endless mind:
Our masters call the oracle
Words on the wind, and the Delphic vision blind!   490
Their hearts no longer know Apollo,
And reverence for the gods has died away.

SCENE III

(Enter IOKASTE.)

IOKASTE: Princes of Thebes, it has occurred to me
To visit the altars of the gods, bearing
These branches as a suppliant, and this incense.
Our King is not himself: his noble soul

Is overwrought with fantasies of dread,
Else he would consider
The new prophecies in the light of the old.
He will listen to any voice that speaks disaster,
And my advice goes for nothing.

(She approaches the altar, right.)

10 To you, then, Apollo,
Lycéan lord, since you are nearest, I turn in prayer.

Receive these offerings, and grant us deliverance
From defilement. Our hearts are heavy with fear
When we see our leader distracted, as helpless
    sailors
Are terrified by the confusion of their helmsman.

(Enter MESSENGER.)

MESSENGER: Friends, no doubt you can direct me:
Where shall I find the house of Oedipus,
Or, better still, where is the King himself?
20 CHORAGOS: It is this very place, stranger; he is inside.
This is his wife and mother of his children.
MESSENGER: I wish her happiness in a happy house,
Blest in all the fulfillment of her marriage.
IOKASTE: I wish as much for you: your courtesy
Deserves a like good fortune. But now, tell me:
Why have you come? What have you to say to us?
MESSENGER: Good news, my lady, for your house and
    your husband.
IOKASTE: What news? Who sent you here?
30 MESSENGER: I am from Corinth.
The news I bring ought to mean joy for you,
Though it may be you will find some grief in it.
IOKASTE: What is it? How can it touch us in both
    ways?
MESSENGER: The word is that the people of the
    Isthmus
Intend to call Oedipus to be their king.
IOKASTE: But old King Polybos—is he not reigning
    still?
40 MESSENGER: No. Death holds him in his sepulchre.
IOKASTE: What are you saying? Polybos is dead?
MESSENGER: If I am not telling the truth, may I die
    myself.
IOKASTE *(to a MAIDSERVANT)*: Go in, go quickly; tell
    this to your master.

O riddlers of God's will, where are you now!
This was the man whom Oedipus, long ago,
Feared so, fled so, in dread of destroying him—
But it was another fate by which he died.

(Enter OEDIPUS, center.)

50 OEDIPUS: Dearest Iokaste, why have you sent for me?
IOKASTE: Listen to what this man says, and then tell
    me
What has become of the solemn prophecies.

OEDIPUS: Who is this man? What is his news for me?
IOKASTE: He has come from Corinth to announce
    your father's death!
OEDIPUS: Is it true, stranger? Tell me in your own
    words.
MESSENGER: I can not say it more clearly: the King is
    dead.   60
OEDIPUS: Was it by treason? Or by an attack of illness?
MESSENGER: A little thing brings old men to their rest.
OEDIPUS: It was sickness, then?
MESSENGER: Yes, and his many years.
OEDIPUS: Ah!
Why should a man respect the Pythian hearth, or
Give heed to the birds that jangle above his head?
They prophesied that I should kill Polybos,
Kill my own father; but he is dead and buried,
And I am here—I never touched him, never,   70
Unless he died of grief for my departure,
And thus, in a sense, through me. No. Polybos
Has packed the oracles off with him underground.
They are empty words.
IOKASTE: Had I not told you so?
OEDIPUS: You had; it was my faint heart that betrayed
    me.
IOKASTE: From now on never think of those things
    again.
OEDIPUS: And yet—must I not fear my mother's bed?   80
IOKASTE: Why should anyone in this world be afraid,
Since Fate rules us and nothing can be foreseen?
A man should live only for the present day.

Have no more fear of sleeping with your mother:
How many men, in dreams, have lain with their
    mothers!
No reasonable man is troubled by such things.
OEDIPUS: That is true; only—
If only my mother were not still alive!
But she is alive. I can not help my dread.   90
IOKASTE: Yet this news of your father's death is
    wonderful.
OEDIPUS: Wonderful. But I fear the living woman.
MESSENGER: Tell me, who is this woman that you
    fear?
OEDIPUS: It is Meropê, man; the wife of King
    Polybos.
MESSENGER: Meropê? Why should you be afraid of
    her?
OEDIPUS: An oracle of the gods, a dreadful saying.   100
MESSENGER: Can you tell me about it or are you sworn
    to silence?
OEDIPUS: I can tell you, and I will.
Apollo said through his prophet that I was the man
Who should marry his own mother, shed his
    father's blood
With his own hands. And so, for all these years
I have kept clear of Corinth, and no harm has
    come—

110   Though it would have been sweet to see my parents
            again.
MESSENGER: And is this the fear that drove you out of
            Corinth?
OEDIPUS: Would you have me kill my father?
MESSENGER: As for that
            You must be reassured by the news I gave you.
OEDIPUS: If you could reassure me, I would reward
            you.
MESSENGER: I had that in mind, I will confess: I
120   thought
            I could count on you when you returned to
            Corinth.
OEDIPUS: No: I will never go near my parents again.
MESSENGER: Ah, son, you still do not know what you
            are doing—
OEDIPUS: What do you mean? In the name of God tell
            me!
MESSENGER: —If these are your reasons for not going
            home.
130 OEDIPUS: I tell you, I fear the oracle may come true.
MESSENGER: And guilt may come upon you through
            your parents?
OEDIPUS: That is the dread that is always in my heart.
MESSENGER: Can you not see that all your fears are
            groundless?
OEDIPUS: Groundless? Am I not my parents' son?
MESSENGER: Polybos was not your father.
OEDIPUS: Not my father?
MESSENGER: No more your father than the man
140   speaking to you.
OEDIPUS: But you are nothing to me!
MESSENGER: Neither was he.
OEDIPUS: Then why did he call me son?
MESSENGER: I will tell you:
            Long ago he had you from my hands, as a gift.
OEDIPUS: Then how could he love me so, if I was not
            his?
MESSENGER: He had no children, and his heart
            turned to you.
150 OEDIPUS: What of you? Did you buy me? Did you find
           me by chance?
MESSENGER: I came upon you in the woody vales of
            Kithairon.
OEDIPUS: And what were you doing there?
MESSENGER: Tending my flocks.
OEDIPUS: A wandering shepherd?
MESSENGER: But your savior, son, that day.
OEDIPUS: From what did you save me?
MESSENGER: Your ankles should tell you that.
160 OEDIPUS: Ah, stranger, why do you speak of that
           childhood pain?
MESSENGER: I pulled the skewer that pinned your feet
            together.
OEDIPUS: I have had the mark as long as I can
            remember.

MESSENGER: That was why you were given the name
            you bear.
OEDIPUS: God! Was it my father or my mother who
            did it?
            Tell me!   170
MESSENGER: I do not know. The man who gave you to
            me
            Can tell you better than I.
OEDIPUS: It was not you that found me, but another?
MESSENGER: It was another shepherd gave you to me.
OEDIPUS: Who was he? Can you tell me who he was?
MESSENGER: I think he was said to be one of Laïos'
            people.
OEDIPUS: You mean the Laïos who was king here
           years ago?   180
MESSENGER: Yes; King Laïos; and the man was one of
            his herdsmen.
OEDIPUS: Is he still alive? Can I see him?
MESSENGER: These men here
            Know best about such things.
OEDIPUS: Does anyone here
            Know this shepherd that he is talking about?
            Have you seen him in the fields, or in the town?
            If you have, tell me. It is time things were made
            plain.   190
CHORAGOS: I think the man he means is that same
            shepherd
            You have already asked to see. Iokastê perhaps
            Could tell you something.
OEDIPUS: Do you know anything
            About him, Lady? Is he the man we have
            summoned?
            Is that the man this shepherd means?
IOKASTE: Why think of him?
            Forget this herdsman. Forget it all.   200
            This talk is a waste of time.
OEDIPUS: How can you say that,
            When the clues to my true birth are in my hands?
IOKASTE: For God's love, let us have no more
            questioning!
            Is your life nothing to you?
            My own is pain enough for me to bear.
MESSENGER: You need not worry. Suppose my
            mother a slave,
            And born of slaves: no baseness can touch you. 210
IOKASTE: Listen to me, I beg of you: do not do this
            thing!
OEDIPUS: I will not listen; the truth must be made
            known.
IOKASTE: Everything that I say is for your own good!
OEDIPUS: My own good
            Snaps my patience, then; I want none of it.
IOKASTE: You are fatally wrong! May you never learn
            who you are!
OEDIPUS: Go, one of you, and bring the shepherd   220
            here.

Let us leave this woman to brag of her royal name.

IOKASTE: Ah, miserable!
That is the only word I have for you now.
That is the only word I can ever have.

(Exit into the palace.)

CHORAGOS: Why has she left us, Oedipus? Why has
    she gone
In such a passion of sorrow? I fear this silence:
Something dreadful may come of it.

230 OEDIPUS: Let it come!
However base my birth, I must know about it.
The Queen, like a woman, is perhaps ashamed
To think of my low origin. But I
Am a child of Luck; I can not be dishonored.
Luck is my mother; the passing months, my
    brothers,
Have seen me rich and poor.
If this is so,
How could I wish that I were someone else?
240 How could I not be glad to know my birth?

ODE III

Strophe

CHORUS: If ever the coming time were known
    To my heart's pondering,
Kithairon, now by Heaven I see the torches
At the festival of the next full moon,
And see the dance, and hear the choir sing
A grace to your gentle shade:
Mountain where Oedipus was found,
O mountain guard of a noble race!
May the god who heals us lend his aid,
250 And let that glory come to pass
For our King's cradling-ground.

Antistrophe

Of the nymphs that flower beyond the years,
Who bore you, royal child,
To Pan of the hills or the timberline Apollo,
Cold in delight where the upland clears,
Or Hermês for whom Kyllenês heights are piled?
Or flushed as evening cloud,
Great Dionysos, roamer of mountains,
He—was it he who found you there,
260 And caught you up in his own proud
Arms from the sweet god-ravisher
Who laughed by the Muses' fountains?

SCENE IV

OEDIPUS: Sirs: though I do not know the man,
I think I see him coming, this shepherd we want:
He is old, like our friend here, and the men
Bringing him seem to be servants of my house.

But you can tell, if you have ever seen him.

(Enter SHEPHERD *escorted by servants.)*

CHORAGOS: I know him, he was Laïos' man. You can
    trust him.
OEDIPUS: Tell me first, you from Corinth: is this the
    shepherd
We were discussing?   10
MESSENGER: This is the very man.
OEDIPUS *(to* SHEPHERD*):* Come here. No, look at me.
    You must answer
Everything I ask.—You belonged to Laïos?
SHEPHERD: Yes: born his slave, brought up in his
    house.
OEDIPUS: Tell me: what kind of work did you do for
    him?
SHEPHERD: I was a shepherd of his, most of my life.
OEDIPUS: Where mainly did you go for pasturage?   20
SHEPHERD: Sometimes Kithairon, sometimes the hills
    near-by.
OEDIPUS: Do you remember ever seeing this man out
    there?
SHEPHERD: What would he be doing there? This
    man?
OEDIPUS: This man standing here. Have you ever
    seen him before?
SHEPHERD: No. At least, not to my recollection.
MESSENGER: And that is not strange, my lord. But I'll   30
    refresh
His memory: he must remember when we two
Spent three whole seasons together, March to
    September,
On Kithairon or thereabouts. He had two flocks;
I had one. Each autumn I'd drive mine home
And he would go back with his to Laïos'
    sheepfold.—
Is this not true, just as I have described it?
SHEPHERD: True, yes; but it was all so long ago.   40
MESSENGER: Well, then: do you remember, back in
    those days,
That you gave me a baby boy to bring up as my
    own?
SHEPHERD: What if I did? What are you trying to
    say?
MESSENGER: King Oedipus was once that little child.
SHEPHERD: Damn you, hold your tongue!
OEDIPUS: No more of that!
It is your tongue needs watching, not this man's.   50
SHEPHERD: My King, my Master, what is it I have
    done wrong?
OEDIPUS: You have not answered his question about
    the boy.
SHEPHERD: He does not know . . . He is only making
    trouble . . .
OEDIPUS: Come, speak plainly, or it will go hard with
    you.

SHEPHERD: In God's name, do not torture an old
60   man!
OEDIPUS: Come here, one of you; bind his arms
    behind him.
SHEPHERD: Unhappy king! What more do you wish to
    learn?
OEDIPUS: Did you give this man the child he speaks
    of?
SHEPHERD: I did.
    And I would to God I had died that very day.
OEDIPUS: You will die now unless you speak the truth.
70 SHEPHERD: Yet if I speak the truth, I am worse than
    dead.
OEDIPUS (to ATTENDANT): He intends to draw it out,
    apparently—
SHEPHERD: No! I have told you already that I gave
    him the boy.
OEDIPUS: Where did you get him? From your house?
    From somewhere else?
SHEPHERD: Not from mine, no. A man gave him to
    me.
80 OEDIPUS: Is that man here? Whose house did he
    belong to?
SHEPHERD: For God's love, my King, do not ask me
    any more!
OEDIPUS: You are a dead man if I have to ask you
    again.
SHEPHERD: Then . . . Then the child was from the
    palace of Laïos.
OEDIPUS: A slave child? or a child of his own line?
SHEPHERD: Ah, I am on the brink of dreadful speech!
90 OEDIPUS: And I of dreadful hearing. Yet I must hear.
SHEPHERD: If you must be told, then . . .
    They said it was Laïos' child;
    But it is your wife who can tell you about that.
OEDIPUS: My wife!—Did she give it to you?
SHEPHERD: My lord, she did.
OEDIPUS: Do you know why?
SHEPHERD: I was told to get rid of it.
OEDIPUS: Oh heartless mother!
SHEPHERD: But in dread of prophecies . . .
100 OEDIPUS: Tell me.
SHEPHERD: It was said that the boy would kill his own
    father.
OEDIPUS: Then why did you give him over to this old
    man?
SHEPHERD: I pitied the baby, my King,
    And I thought that this man would take him far
    away
    To his own country.
    He saved him—but for what a fate!
110   For if you are what this man says you are,
    No man living is more wretched than Oedipus.
OEDIPUS: Ah God!
    It was true!
    All the prophecies!
    —Now,

O Light, may I look on you for the last time!
I, Oedipus,
Oedipus, damned in his birth, in his marriage
    damned,
Damned in the blood he shed with his own hand!   120

(*He rushes into the palace.*)

ODE IV

Strophe 1

CHORUS: Alas for the seed of men.

What measure shall I give these generations
That breathe on the void and are void
And exist and do not exist?

Who bears more weight of joy
Than mass of sunlight shifting in images,
Or who shall make his thought stay on
That down time drifts away?

Your splendor is all fallen.

O naked brow of wrath and tears,   130
O change of Oedipus!
I who saw your days call no man blest—
Your great days like ghosts gone.

Antistrophe 1

That mind was a strong bow.

Deep, how deep you drew it then, hard archer,
At a dim fearful range,

And brought dear glory down!

You overcame the stranger—
The virgin with her hooking lion claws—
And though death sang, stood like a tower   140
To make pale Thebes take heart.

Fortress against our sorrow!

True king, giver of laws,
Majestic Oedipus!
No prince in Thebes had ever such renown,
No prince won such grace of power.

Strophe 2

And now of all men ever known
Most pitiful is this man's story:
His fortunes are most changed, his state
Fallen to a low slave's   150
Ground under bitter fate.

O Oedipus, most royal one!
The great door that expelled you to the light

Gave at night—ah, gave night to your glory:
As to the father, to the fathering son.

All understood too late.

How could that queen whom Laïos won,
The garden that he harrowed at his height,
Be silent when that act was done?

Antistrophe 2

160 But all eyes fail before time's eye,
All actions come to justice there.
Your bed, your dread sirings,
Are brought to book at last.

Child by Laïos doomed to die,
Then doomed to lose that fortunate little death,
Would God you never took breath in this air
That with my wailing lips I take to cry:

For I weep the world's outcast.

I was blind, and now I can tell why:
170 Asleep, for you had given ease of breath
To Thebes, while the false years went by.

EXODOS

(Enter, from the palace, SECOND MESSENGER.)

SECOND MESSENGER: Elders of Thebes, most honored
    in this land,
What horrors are yours to see and hear, what
    weight
Of sorrow to be endured, if, true to your birth,
You venerate the line of Labdakos!
I think neither Istros nor Phasis, those great rivers,
Could purify this place of all the evil
180 It shelters now, or soon must bring to light—
Evil not done unconsciously, but willed.

The greatest griefs are those we cause ourselves.
CHORAGOS: Surely, friend, we have grief enough
    already;
What new sorrow do you mean?
SECOND MESSENGER: The Queen is dead.
CHORAGOS: O miserable Queen! But at whose hand?
SECOND MESSENGER: Her own.
The full horror of what happened you can not
190   know,
For you did not see it; but I, who did, will tell you
As clearly as I can how she met her death.

When she had left us,
In passionate silence, passing through the court,
She ran to her apartment in the house,
Her hair clutched by the fingers of both hands.
She closed the doors behind her; then, by that bed

Where long ago the fatal son was conceived—
That son who should bring about his father's
    death—   200
We heard her call upon Laïos, dead so many years,
And heard her wail for the double fruit of her
    marriage,
A husband by her husband, children by her child.

Exactly how she died I do not know:
For Oedipus burst in moaning and would not let us
Keep vigil to the end: it was by him
As he stormed about the room that our eyes were
    caught.
From one to another of us he went, begging a   210
    sword,
Hunting the wife who was not his wife, the mother
Whose womb had carried his own children and
    himself.
I do not know: it was none of us aided him,
But surely one of the gods was in control!
For with a dreadful cry
He hurled his weight, as though wrenched out of
    himself,
At the twin doors: the bolts gave, and he rushed in. 220
And there we saw her hanging, her body swaying
From the cruel cord she had noosed about her
    neck.
A great sob broke from him, heartbreaking to hear,
As he loosed the rope and lowered her to the
    ground.

I would blot out from my mind what happened
    next!
For the King ripped from her gown the golden
    brooches   230
That were her ornament, and raised them, and
    plunged them down
Straight into his own eyeballs, crying, 'No more,
No more shall you look on the misery about me,
The horrors of my own doing! Too long you have
    known
The faces of those whom I should never have seen,
Too long been blind to those for whom I was
    searching!
From this hour, go in darkness!' And as he spoke, 240
He struck at his eyes—not once, but many times;
And the blood spattered his beard,
Bursting from his ruined sockets like red hail.

So from the unhappiness of two this evil has
    sprung,
A curse on the man and woman alike. The old
Happiness of the house of Labdakos
Was happiness enough: where is it today?
It is all wailing and ruin, disgrace, death—all
The misery of mankind that has a name—   250
And it is wholly and for ever theirs.

CHORAGOS: Is he in agony still? Is there no rest for
  him?
SECOND MESSENGER: He is calling for someone to
  open the doors wide
  So that all the children of Kadmos may look upon
  His father's murderer, his mother's—no,
  I can not say it!
  And then he will leave Thebes,
260 Self-exiled, in order that the curse
  Which he himself pronounced may depart from
    the house.
  He is weak, and there is none to lead him,
  So terrible is his suffering.
  But you will see:
  Look, the doors are opening; in a moment
  You will see a thing that would crush a heart of
    stone.

  (*The central door is opened;* OEDIPUS, *blinded, is led in.*)

CHORAGOS: Dreadful indeed for men to see.
270 Never have my own eyes
  Looked on a sight so full of fear.

  Oedipus!
  What madness came upon you, what daemon
  Leaped on your life with heavier
  Punishment than a mortal man can bear?
  No: I can not even
  Look at you, poor ruined one.
  And I would speak, question, ponder,
  If I were able. No.
280 You make me shudder.
OEDIPUS: God. God.
  Is there a sorrow greater?
  Where shall I find harbor in this world?
  My voice is hurled far on a dark wind.
  What has God done to me?
CHORAGOS: Too terrible to think of, or to see.

Strophe 1

OEDIPUS: O cloud of night,
  Never to be turned away: night coming on,
  I can not tell how: night like a shroud!

290 My fair winds brought me here.
  O God. Again
  The pain of the spikes where I had sight,
  The flooding pain
  Of memory, never to be gouged out.
CHORAGOS: This is not strange.
  You suffer it all twice over, remorse in pain,
  Pain in remorse.

Antistrophe 1

OEDIPUS: Ah dear friend
  Are you faithful even yet, you alone?
300 Are you still standing near me, will you stay here,

Patient, to care for the blind?
  The blind man!
  Yet even blind I know who it is attends me,
  By the voice's tone—
  Though my new darkness hide the comforter.
CHORAGOS: Oh fearful act!
  What god was it drove you to rake black
  Night across your eyes?

Strophe 2

OEDIPUS: Apollo. Apollo. Dear
  Children, the god was Apollo. 310
  He brought my sick, sick fate upon me.
  But the blinding hand was my own!
  How could I bear to see
  When all my sight was horror everywhere?
CHORAGOS: Everywhere; that is true.
OEDIPUS: And now what is left?
  Images? Love? A greeting even,
  Sweet to the senses? Is there anything?
  Ah, no, friends: lead me away.
  Lead me away from Thebes. 320
  Lead the great wreck
  And hell of Oedipus, whom the gods hate.
CHORAGOS: Your misery, you are not blind to that.
  Would God you had never found it out!

Antistrophe 2

OEDIPUS: Death take the man who unbound
  My feet on the hillside
  And delivered me from death to life! What life?
  If only I had died,
  This weight of monstrous doom
  Could not have dragged me and my darlings down. 330
CHORAGOS: I would have wished the same.
OEDIPUS: Oh never to have come here
  With my father's blood upon me! Never
  To have been the man they call his mother's
    husband!
  Oh accurst! Oh child of evil,
  To have entered that wretched bed—
  The selfsame one!
  More primal than sin itself, this fell to me.
CHORAGOS: I do not know what words to offer you. 340
  You were better dead than alive and blind.
OEDIPUS: Do not counsel me any more. This
    punishment
  That I have laid upon myself is just.
  If I had eyes,
  I do not know how I could bear the sight
  Of my father, when I came to the house of Death,
  Or my mother: for I have sinned against them both
  So vilely that I could not make my peace
  By strangling my own life. 350
  Or do you think my children,
  Born as they were born, would be sweet to my eyes?
  Ah never, never! Nor this town with its high walls,

Nor the holy images of the gods.
For I,
Thrice miserable!—Oedipus, noblest of all the line
Of Kadmos, have condemned myself to enjoy
These things no more, by my own malediction
360   Expelling that man whom the gods declared
To be a defilement in the house of Laïos.
After exposing the rankness of my own guilt,
How could I look men frankly in the eyes?
No, I swear it,
If I could have stifled my hearing at its source,
I would have done it, and made all this body
A tight cell of misery, blank to light and sound:
So I should have been safe in my dark mind
Beyond external evil.
Ah Kithairon!
370   Why did you shelter me? When I was cast upon
      you,
Why did I not die? Then I should never
Have shown the world my execrable birth.

Ah Polybos! Corinth, city that I believed
The ancient seat of my ancestors: how fair
I seemed, your child! And all the while this evil
Was cancerous within me!
For I am sick
In my own being, sick in my origin,

380   O three roads, dark ravine, woodland and way
Where three roads met: you, drinking my father's
      blood,
My own blood, spilled by my own hand: can you
      remember
The unspeakable things I did there, and the things
I went on from there to do?
O marriage, marriage!
The act that engendered me, and again the act
Performed by the son in the same bed—
390   Ah, the net
Of incest, mingling fathers, brothers, sons,
With brides, wives, mothers: the last evil
That can be known by men: no tongue can say
How evil!
No. For the love of God, conceal me
Somewhere far from Thebes; or kill me; or hurl
     me
Into the sea, away from men's eyes for ever.
Come, lead me. You need not fear to touch me.
400   Of all men, I alone can bear this guilt.

(Enter KREON.)

CHORAGOS: Kreon is here now. As to what you ask,
    He may decide the course to take. He only
    Is left to protect the city in your place.
OEDIPUS: Alas, how can I speak to him? What right
    have I
    To beg his courtesy whom I have deeply wronged?

KREON: I have not come to mock you, Oedipus,
    Or to reproach you, either.

(To ATTENDANTS)

—You, standing there:
If you have lost all respect for man's dignity,   410
At least respect the flame of Lord Helios:
Do not allow this pollution to show itself
Openly here, an affront to the earth
And Heaven's rain and the light of day. No, take
    him
Into the house as quickly as you can.
For it is proper
That only the close kindred see his grief.
OEDIPUS: I pray you in God's name, since your
    courtesy   420
Ignores my dark expectation, visiting
With mercy this man of all men most execrable:
Give me what I ask—for your good, not for mine.
KREON: And what is it that you turn to me begging
    for?
OEDIPUS: Drive me out of this country as quickly as
    may be
To a place where no human voice can ever greet
    me.
KREON: I should have done that before now—only,   430
    God's will had not been wholly revealed to me.
OEDIPUS: But his command is plain: the parricide
    Must be destroyed. I am that evil man.
KREON: That is the sense of it, yes; but as things are,
    We had best discover clearly what is to be done.
OEDIPUS: You would learn more about a man like
    me?
KREON: You are ready now to listen to the god.
OEDIPUS: I will listen. But it is to you
    That I must turn for help. I beg you, hear me.   440

The woman in there—
Give her whatever funeral you think proper:
She is your sister.
—But let me go, Kreon!
Let me purge my father's Thebes of the pollution
Of my living here, and go out to the wild hills,
To Kithairon, that has won such fame with me,
The tomb my mother and father appointed for me,
And let me die there, as they willed I should.
And yet I know   450
Death will not ever come to me through sickness
Or in any natural way: I have been preserved
For some unthinkable fate. But let that be.

As for my sons, you need not care for them.
They are men, they will find some way to live.
But my poor daughters, who have shared my table,
Who never before have been parted from their
    father—
Take care of them, Kreon; do this for me.

460 And will you let me touch them with my hands
A last time, and let us weep together?
Be kind, my lord,
Great prince, be kind!
Could I but touch them.
They would be mine again, as when I had my eyes.

(*Enter* ANTIGONE *and* ISMENE, *attended.*)

Ah, God!
Is it my dearest children I hear weeping?
Has Kreon pitied me and sent my daughters?
KREON: Yes, Oedipus: I knew that they were dear to
470   you
In the old days, and you must love them still.
OEDIPUS: May God bless you for this—and be a
       friendlier
Guardian to you than he has been to me!

Children, where are you?
Come quickly to my hands: they are your
       brother's—
Hands that have brought your father's once clear
       eyes
480 To this way of seeing—
Ah dearest ones,
I had neither sight nor knowledge then, your
       father
By the woman who was the source of his own life!
And I weep for you—having no strength to see
       you—,
I weep for you when I think of the bitterness
That men will visit upon you all your lives.
What homes, what festivals can you attend
490 Without being forced to depart again in tears?
And when you come to marriageable age,
Where is the man, my daughters, who would dare
Risk the bane that lies on all my children?
Is there any evil wanting? Your father killed
His father; sowed the womb of her who bore him;
Engendered you at the fount of his own existence!

That is what they will say of you.

Then, whom
Can you ever marry? There are no bridegrooms
500   for you,
And your lives must wither away in sterile
       dreaming.

O Kreon, son of Menoikeus!
You are the only father my daughters have,

Since we, their parents, are both of us gone for
       ever.
They are your own blood: you will not let them
Fall into beggary and loneliness;
You will keep them from the miseries that are
       mine!   510
Take pity on them; see, they are only children,
Friendless except for you. Promise me this,
Great Prince, and give me your hand in token of it.

(KREON *clasps his right hand.*)

Children:
I could say much, if you could understand me,
But as it is, I have only this prayer for you:
Live where you can, be as happy as you can—
Happier, please God, than God has made your
       father.
KREON: Enough. You have wept enough. Now go   520
       within.
OEDIPUS: I must; but it is hard.
KREON: Time eases all things.
OEDIPUS: You know my mind, then?
KREON: Say what you desire.
OEDIPUS: Send me from Thebes!
KREON: God grant that I may!
OEDIPUS: But since God hates me . . .
KREON: No, he will grant your wish.
OEDIPUS: You promise?   530
KREON: I can not speak beyond my knowledge.
OEDIPUS: Then lead me in.
KREON: Come now, and leave your children.
OEDIPUS: No! Do not take them from me!
KREON: Think no longer
That you are in command here, but rather think
How, when you were, you served your own
       destruction.

(*Exeunt into the house all but the* CHORUS; *the*
CHORAGOS *chants directly to the audience.*)

CHORAGOS: Men of Thebes: look upon Oedipus.

This is the king who solved the famous riddle   540
And towered up, most powerful of men.
No mortal eyes but looked on him with envy,
Yet in the end ruin swept over him.

Let every man in mankind's frailty
Consider his last day; and let none
Presume on his good fortune until he find
Life, at his death, a memory without pain.

Figure 1. The Chorus of Theban Elders and Jocasta (Patricia Conolly, *rear*) plead with Oedipus (Len Cariou, *center*) to spare the life of Kreon (James Blendick, *rear*) in the Guthrie Theater Company production of *Oedipus the King,* directed by Michael Langham and designed by Desmond Heeley, Minneapolis, 1972. (Photograph: the Guthrie Theater.)

Figure 2. The Corinthian Messenger (Paul Ballantyne, *left*) prods the memory of the Shepherd (Bernard Behrens, *right*) to help Oedipus (Len Cariou) discover the circumstances of his birth in the Guthrie Theater Company production of *Oedipus the King,* directed by Michael Langham and designed by Desmond Heeley, Minneapolis, 1972. (Photograph: the Guthrie Theater.)

Staging of *Oedipus Rex*

REVIEW OF THE GUTHRIE THEATER
PRODUCTION, 1972, BY MELVIN MADDOCKS

In the Tyrone Guthrie Theater, approximately 8,000 miles from Thebes as the Furies fly, "Oedipus the King" is being staged by an English director from a new translation written in Rome by an author also engaged on a novel about Napoleon. If all this suggests dizzy and eclectic flights in time and space, it should.

Through a rather remarkable series of letters Michael Langham, the director, and Anthony Burgess, the translator-adaptor, have recorded their dissatisfaction with conventional approaches to Greek tragedy and their search for a style that might do justice both to Sophocles and to 1972.

Traditionally there have been two general approaches to Greek tragedy, roughly parallel to the usual approaches to Shakespeare. The low road—Sophocles without tears—has attempted to sell "Oedipus the King" as a kind of suspense thriller: the first detective story. The high road—again the comparison to Shakespearean productions seems valid—is the way of the purist: the bookman with a history of Dionysian festivals in one hand and Aristotle's "Poetics" in the other.

Not for Mr. Langham either the souped-up "Dial O for Oedipus" popularization or the stately academic pageant, complete with masks and stilts, before which audiences, recognizing a classic when they see one, simultaneously kneel and yawn. Mr. Langham—like Peter Brook and Jan Kott, to name two Shakespearean experimentalists—is trying for a new alternative.

"I have been groping," he writes, "not so much for answers that are purely Greek as for an atmosphere that is primitive in its overwhelming superstitions and timeless in its fears and hidden meanings."

The Guthrie stage is dominated by two giant pieces of steel sculpture, 23 feet high, 2½ tons. Representing portals to the palace, they appear more like the slashed entrance to a cave when Len Cariou's slightly Neanderthal Oedipus first bursts through. At the front of the stage stands an altar smothered by incense smoke. Unseen drums beat.

Mr. Langham has recreated a Thebes in the image of the sacred grove of Nemi, made famous in "The Golden Bough." It is a place where cruel ceremonies are acted out, where primal fears fill the air, where human law operates at the level of taboo.

The chorus, covered by what look like animal skins, sings its speeches as chants, dances to a sort of tom-tom, and frets with talismans and totems.

Since the translator happens to be Mr. Burgess, one is tempted to see all this as "A Clockwork Orange" run backwards through a time machine.

Here is the anthropologist's Sophocles, out of Levi-Strauss—less contemporaneous with fifth-century B.C. Greek tragedy than with the ancient myth from which "Oedipus the King" was drawn. Here is Oedipus less as a king of a sophisticated city-state than as a tribal chieftain, or even a kind of Jungian Everyman, acting out the dark subconscious of the human race.

The drama plays less like a plot than a ritual, a primitive game of riddles and forfeits. Oedipus solves the Sphinx's riddle and saves Thebes from this monster at its gates. Then Oedipus fails to solve in time the riddle of his own identity and becomes the monster within the gates—a violator of the ultimate taboo: incest. The pattern stands out, as stark as a curse.

It is a brilliantly forceful conceit that keeps the Guthrie stage pulsing and throbbing. No pallid Greek revival could survive here—no fake plaster pillars and noble profiles posing like old coins.

But another "Oedipus the King" does fight for its place. Sophocles's play, after all, stands as one of the most subtle studies of human pride in the history of the theater—a profound inquiry into the overintoxication of power. There is nothing primitive or neo-primitive about lines like: "What was your pride must be your ruin." Or: "The shadow of success is always envy."

Mr. Burgess writes a blank verse with a sort of Elizabethan roll:

"Wide night is a labyrinth I tread
With no thread of useful thought to
Lead me to the light."

Inevitable contradictions result. Around that atavistic altar Oedipus and Creon prowl, like two animals, hurling the most literate lines at one another in the most precise English repertory company accents. If Mr. Cariou's Oedipus is a savage, he is a remarkably self-aware one. Patricia Conolly's Jocasta, a collection of sensitive readings, is simply too refined for this barbaric Thebes. The better the acting, the more it is self-defeating.

Furthermore, the translation bears its own internal contradictions. For there is, as well as an Elizabethan Mr. Burgess, a colloquial Mr. Burgess who can come down too abruptly from elegance and have the chorus speak of "beating our brains." Or allow Jocasta to

63

comment folksily on soothsaying: "I would not cross the street to hear any of that nonsense."

Yet, finally, the raw power of Mr. Langham's vision carries the evening. He has restored to Greek tragedy the Dionysian, the religious dread that more correct productions in their fussiness neglect. He has turned his spectators into participants with the cry: "We are all Oedipus." He has brought to his "Oedipus" the one quintessential gift a classic cannot do without—he has made it of the moment, he has made it live.

EURIPIDES

484–406 B.C.

Euripides expressed more directly than any of his contemporaries the anxieties of his age: the growing skepticism in Athens about the dignity of man, the authority of the gods, and the future of Athens itself. But his view of experience was too harsh, his means of expression too unconventional, for the tastes of his audience. Although he wrote more than ninety plays, he won the festival competition only four times. While he was losing, Sophocles must have been winning, for they were nearly exact contemporaries. But they were exact opposites in both their way of life and their view of it. Whereas Sophocles was a very public and genial man, Euripides was reportedly a very private person, so unsociable that he is rumored to have spent long periods of time secluded in a cave, writing his plays in solitary confinement. Wherever he may have written them, his plays bear witness to a much darker view of human nature than those of Sophocles, for they repeatedly seem to deny it the moral heroism exhibited by the heroes and heroines of Sophocles.

Sophocles is reported to have said that Euripides shows human behavior not as it ought to be but as it is. As Euripides depicts it, human behavior is controlled primarily by emotions and passions—emotions and passions that have been crippled by nature, afflicted by circumstance, or distorted by self-indulgence. His fascination with the nature of intense feeling has also been said to explain his special interest in the experience of women, for they figure as protagonists in twelve of his eighteen surviving plays. Wherever they appear, they are either inflicting pain, or having pain inflicted on them—or both. This is the case in his two most famous studies of women in love: *Hippolytus* (428) and *Medea* (431). In *Hippolytus,* he shows the raging spectacle of a frustrated adulterous love, when Phaedra develops a consuming passion for her stepson Hippolytus, who is himself with equal passion committed to a sexless existence. Moved by both frustration and shame, she commits suicide by hanging herself, but before doing so she leaves a message for her husband Theseus accusing Hippolytus of having raped her. The result of her false accusation is that Theseus exiles his son and prays for his destruction, and his prayers are answered when Hippolytus while riding along a shore is dragged to death by his horses after they have been terrified by a bull rising from the sea. In *Medea,* Euripides represents an even more sensational spectacle, in this case the result of an abused marital love, when Medea, having been deserted by Jason, works herself up into so fierce a rage that she murders their two children and then makes her exit by flying off in a dragon-driven chariot to seek refuge in Athens. Truly, hell hath no fury like these women scorned, nor like the men who scorn them. In his study of deranged passions and human depravity, Euripides did not favor either sex.

When he was not representing the terrors of love, he was showing the horrors of war. His temperament did not permit him to remain silent about the cultural tragedy of his age. Living as he did during the Peloponnesian War, witnessing the extraordinary toll it took on Athens and Sparta during the nearly thirty years of its duration, he felt compelled to dramatize its senseless brutality in a series of antiwar plays—the tragic counterparts of the antiwar comedies written during the same period by Aristophanes. In *Hecuba* (ca. 430–415), he showed the brutality of war in its most brutalizing form, when Hecuba, driven mad by the loss of her children in the aftermath of the Trojan War, avenges their deaths by blinding Polymestor, an act whose bestiality is symbolized by her transformation into a raging dog. In *The Trojan Women* (415), the greatest of his antiwar plays, a play attacking the atrocity of his own country, he turned again to Hecuba, this time showing her to be a magnificent image of suffering as she bids farewell to each of her daughters who are being led off to slavery, then buries Hector's young son, her grandson, and then bemoans the climactic spectacle of the play: the city of Troy in flames.

Only in his tragicomedies, a dramatic form he is credited with inventing, does Euripides ever offer an optimistic view of experience. Yet even these plays, *Ion* (ca. 430–415) and *Iphigenia at Tauris* (ca. 415–410), only avoid disaster by miraculous resolutions—sisters recognizing brothers, or sons recognizing mothers, moments before they are about to kill or be killed by another. Thus they offer at best an ironically comforting view of fate. In these plays, the gods are only somewhat less malign than in his tragedies, for in almost all his plays the suffering of human beings turns out to be the work of the gods. The gods themselves rarely figure among the characters in his plays, but they are almost always taken into account in the prologues and epilogues that Euripides used as a means of beginning and ending his plays. Sometimes these prologues and epilogues are spoken by gods, sometimes by human beings, but always they set the specific action of the play in a wider context that refers its events to the past, to the future, and ultimately to the gods.

Euripides has been criticized for using prologues and epilogues, as he has been criticized for a wide range of other elements distinctive to his plays such as sensational episodes, episodic plots, elaborately rhetorical debates, irrelevant choral odes, supernatural events, and melodramatic scenes. Such elements offended Aristotle, as they have always offended exponents of formal symmetry and dramatic probability. But Euripides was largely indifferent to conventions of dramatic regularity, because he was primarily interested in writing emotionally expressive drama, drama that is necessarily as irregular, unpredictable, and convulsive in its makeup as the passions and the experience of human beings living in a malign and unpredictable universe.

That vision of experience is nowhere more eloquently dramatized than in *The Bacchae* (ca. 407). It is a vision at once terrifying and beautiful, as terrifying and beautiful as Dionysus, the Greek god of fertility, who stood for the mysterious and irrepressible forces working throughout nature, sustaining and renewing life in all of its abundance, all of its vitality, and all of its wild and uncontrollable energy. Those who embrace that vision, who worship Dionysus, experience the joy of his followers, the chorus of Bacchantes; those who defy that vision, who seek to repudiate it and repress it, experience the suffering of Pentheus and his mother Agave. Those who neither embrace it nor deny it, but nonetheless acknowledge its mystical power and meaning, as do Kadmos and Teiresias—they at least survive. Understood in this way, *The Bacchae* is a profoundly religious tragedy, as it was probably meant to be, judging from earlier Greek hymns to Dionysus, all of which stress the necessity of obedience to the god.

The Bacchae has also been understood in other ways by other cultures. It has, for example, been considered as a dramatization of the archetypal conflict between passion and reason, symbolized in the struggle between Dionysus and Pentheus. It has also been thought to be an indictment of all peoples and all cultures that forsake reason, abandoning themselves to a senseless and brutally destructive life of sensual experience. During the late 1960s, it came to be seen as a uniquely relevant statement about the countercultural activities of that decade. It has been widely performed in the United States and abroad as an expression of the conflicting lifestyles in contemporary culture. Many of these recent performances, like the Yale Repertory production that is represented here in photographs (see Figures 1 and 2), have deliberately aimed to stage the play in a context of ultramodern sets, electronic sounds, and psychedelic lighting effects. Whether or not the play can be updated to fit the situation of contemporary experience seems to be a debatable issue, judging from reviews of the Yale production. Nonetheless, it continues to be the most powerful revelation in drama of the mysterious forces working through all of nature—and thus all of humanity.

THE BACCHAE

BY EURIPIDES / TRANSLATED BY KENNETH CAVANDER*

CHARACTERS

DIONYSOS
CHORUS *of Asian women, followers of Dionysos*
TEIRESIAS, *a prophet*
KADMOS, *ex-King of Thebes*
PENTHEUS, *King of Thebes, grandson of Kadmos*

GUARD
HERDSMAN
SERVANT
AGAVE, *mother of Pentheus*
GUARDS, SOLDIERS, SERVANTS, PEOPLE OF THEBES

(DIONYSOS *and* CHORUS.)

DIONYSOS: Dionysos has come.
Here, in Thebes, Zeus came swooping down and took
A woman of the earth. Lightning made
Her labour quick, and out of her burning thighs
I was born.
　　Today I walk on the piece of land enclosed
By two rivers—Dirce and Ismenos—
The land they call . . . Thebes.
10　Today I look like a man, but I am more.
　　Here was the lightning blast that killed my mother,
Semele, here was her room and . . .
There's something alive! Smoke in the rubble, the fire
Of Zeus . . . still. So, something alive
Still . . .
　　Yes, Kadmos has said: "On this ground
No man walks!" to remind Thebes
20　Of Semele, his daughter, to keep her alive in the heart
Of Thebes. I am glad. He was right.
The vines that cover that wall are mine. They flush,
And cluster . . .
And swell . . .
　　Behind me—Lebanon and its golden plains,
Iraq, the sun-struck steppes of Persia,
The fortresses of Syria, the harsh country
Where the Afghans live, Arabia drugged,
30　And all the eastern coasts, where Greece and Asia
Merge, and towers fringe the teeming cities;
Behind me—dance swaying bodies, intoxication,
Life.

---

*This version of *The Bacchae* was originally commissioned by the BBC and later rewritten for production at the Mermaid Theatre in London. It is an acting version. In a few places, for the sake of a twentieth-century audience, it is interpretative rather than literal. Nevertheless, the script stays close to Euripides' own words at all times, and the intentions of the lines are invariably based on the suggestive power of the original.—K.C.

Here—Greece. And first in Greece—Thebes.
My own country, where I will be known,
Where I must be known.
There is a reason why Thebes comes first.
I made this city wild with women shrilling
My name, I slung hide on their backs, I stuck
Branches in their hands, spears tipped　　　40
With ivy—for a reason.
Because my mother's sisters denied I was
The son of Zeus; because they said Semele
Lost her virginity to a man here in Thebes,
Then blamed the result on Zeus; because they swore
Kadmos invented it all; because they claimed
Zeus killed Semele for lying about
Her husband.
They shouldn't have said that. They,　　　50
Particularly, should not have said all that.
Because now, they hurtle out of their homes, possessed,
Scatter to the hills, and they all wear my uniform,
They all know how to bring me to life. . . .
　　I willed it, and they must.
Every woman in this city is mine,
Totally.
They have abandoned Thebes, and now they have joined　　　60
My mother's sisters in the green pine shades,
Among the cliffs and hollows. Mad. Bacchae.
This place must find out what it means
To be half-born, to have no
Dionysos, never to have tried me or tasted me,
This place must take account of my birth
In Semele, my descent from Zeus, my presence here,
And my power over man. This place
May wish it did not have to, but it must learn.
　　Kadmos has given way to Pentheus, his grandson.　　　70
Authority, decision, are now all Pentheus,
Who resists me and my power, keeps me
Clear out of thought. When he looks outside
Himself for help, he never looks to me.
I am despised, pushed aside, stamped upon.
And therefore I'll turn him round to face me. Show
Myself in Thebes, show them they are small

68

And I am great.
        This one matter set to rights I pack up
80   And move on, to make myself known
Elsewhere.
If Thebes recklessly tries to bring the women
Back from the hills and their madness by *force*, you
Will see a fight—the army versus Bacchae—
Arranged by me.
        And so I have dressed myself in flesh today.
I have the body and blood of a man, but
My real nature is . . . still my own.
(To CHORUS*)* Friends, you have been loyal, you have
90   followed me
From countries far across the sea, travelled
Beside me, never deserted me. Lift your drums
Now. Let these proud walls of Pentheus,
The king, hear the sound of the east, the creation
Of Earth, my mother, and myself. The beat!
The beat! Let the city open its eyes.
I will go to the heights of Kithairon where
The women are dancing on the slopes, and join
The Bacchae.

        (Exit.)

100 CHORUS: Look—the hills of
The East, where new life leaps—
We came from there.
Our work . . . !
It's easy,
It's singing work,
It's dancing labour,
It's laughing drudgery.
I never stop, I never tire,
Letting myself run free for Dionysos.
110 Clear the streets—
We're here.
Clear the streets—
We've come.
Room! Room! Stay at home, lips closed, because . . .
A word spilled can make a stain.
The only words allowed here are the words for
Dionysos.
And I sing them
Over and over,
120 I sing them . . .
Who is alive? Who is happy?
The one who knows . . .
Knows?
Knows the secret . . .
The secret?
The secret of the night
When his whole life begins again
And he's all one with the friends of Dionysos,
The pure lovers of the mountains,
130 Bedded in the earth's grasp
Plunged in forgetfulness,
Buried

. . . Living!
Like green leaves in winter, woodsap in snow,
Ivy crowns make you King
And from the pine tree stems your power.
Dionysos, my lord,
Dionysos, my dear harsh master.
Run on, run on! Bring him here, fill the streets
With the young life, the new life—   140
Dionysos!
Flood Greece with his fresh blood,
Beat, beat, beat him into the heart like thunder—
Dionysos!
        Burst from fire, gashed by thunderbolt.
He was flung into life by flame.
His mother screamed, the pain rending her,
And let him go to the lightning.
She died then . . .
But he lived! Hatched in a golden clasp,   150
In the storehouse of life in the body of Zeus.
And Hera never knew!
Then out into the world—
When the time was ready for him,
And he for the time.
He had bull horns empowering him.
He had snake hair crowning him.
And we will wear crowns like that—
We'll catch them, and tame them, and wear them—
Snakes!   160
        Thebes—mother land of Semele—
Wear a crown too—coiled-within-coil ivy.
Let the never-dying blossoms,
Flower in you, drench you in greenery, Thebes!
Oak-leaf mad,
Fir-branch crazy,
Fawn-skin clothed,
And white-wool jewelled—
Then you're dressed.
Hold the branch in your hand,   170
Power in the thick wood, feel it pulsing,
The whole land will rock,
The whole land will jump—
He stirs, yes, now—the power Dionysos.
And then we go up to the hills, to the hills,
Where the women who lived indoors at a loom,
Or a spindle, wait for him now
Packed, trembling, his thorn in their blood.
        Crete holds caves where Zeus was nursed,
And there the drum, the drum, the drum was born.   180
When the dance comes over you, and the strain drags
        tight,
The singing woodwind cools
The drum-beat,
The singing wind softens the drum
And together they make the dance, they make it, till
. . .
The mind splits open,
The world falls in—

And Dionysos is glad.
190   Then you're tired of the running, and at last, at last
You fling yourself on the ground—
Your only cover the flakes of sunlight on the skin of a
    fawn;
This is the moment, sacred and secret, in the
    mountains,
When your hands search for the goat,
Hands grope for its blood,
And you drink,
As it comes from the goat,
200 The fresh red juice, the joy of . . .
That's the way Dionysos has led you
In the hills of the east, the morning sun . . .
    (CHORUS makes a sound—of joy, ecstasy, praise.)
        Earth gushing milk
Gushing wine.
Gushing rivers of honey,
You hold the flame
High, it smells like a scent from Syria,
Its pine wood flaring,
Smoke streaming as you hurl your body
210 Down through dances
Shouting, and raving, and reddening the torch
With your speed
Your hair floods down, the wind-gusts flourish it . . .
And among the shrilling, the shouting, the singing a
    voice
Blares,
"Run on, run on,
My Bacchae,
Like a stream of gold from the lavish east
220 Sing, sing, sing!
Let the drum stamp loud,
Shout for him,
Throat, tongue, breath,
Blaze for him,
Let the leaping flute
Lure and tempt,
Calling out the powers of life
To join us, and play
In the hills,
230 In the hills."
Then, freedom!
Joy of a foal
In the meadows with its mother.
Bacchae, dart!
Bacchae, run!
Bacchae, dance!

    (Enter TEIRESIAS.)

TEIRESIAS (knocks at door of palace): Answer the door!
        Answer it! Call Kadmos
        Out, Kadmos, the man from Phoenicia who built
240 A towering city here at Thebes. Go,
        Someone, tell him Teiresias wants him.
        He knows why I've come . . .

    (A GUARD goes.)

We are collaborating and we have
This pact. We take branches, we twist ivy
Leaves round them, we weave more ivy in
Our hair, like crowns, but live, and then we take
Skins of young deer . . . Well, I may
Be old, but he is older . . .

    (Enter KADMOS.)

KADMOS: Teiresias, my dear friend, I knew
    It was you when I heard your voice.   250
    (To GUARDS) Pay attention.
    This is a wise, wise man.
    (To TEIRESIAS) Look, I am ready. I found the
        things. We
    Must give him all we can, build
    Respect for him. He is a power, a wonder,
    And he is the child of my own daughter.
    Do we dance now? Where do we go? (Shaking his
        head.)
    One—two—back! One—two—back!   260
    Is this right, Teiresias? We are both old
    But you know things, you see more.
    All day and all night, I won't
    Need rest—down, down—(He thumps his stick on the
        ground.)
    Forget the years, we are born again, and it's
        beautiful.
TEIRESIAS: Yes, do you feel it? Young again.
    I'll dance too, I can, I'm ready . . .
KADMOS: We climb   270
    To the hills, then, we don't ride there?
TEIRESIAS: No. We need to go simply into the presence
    Of this being.
KADMOS: An old blind prophet
    And I shall take you by the hand like a child . . .
TEIRESIAS: The one who calls us will lead us there. And
        we
    Shall never notice the journey.
KADMOS: Are we the only
    Two in Thebes to worship this way, dancing?   280
TEIRESIAS: We are the only two in Thebes with our
        senses left
    Intact. The rest of the city has fallen apart.
KADMOS: I want to go. Hurry. Take my hand.
TEIRESIAS: Here, hold on to me, don't let me lose you.
KADMOS: I look at the world, the power in it, and I
    Feel lost, mortal, small, small . . .
TEIRESIAS: Yes,
    You feel those forces working in you. To them
    All our intellect is a joke. There are things   290
    Not measured in time, a birthright, an inheritance.
    They exist. You can't reason them away,
    You can't talk them, define them, describe them
        away,
    Yes, I'm old, but I mean to go dancing,

Put vine leaves in my hair, and I'm not ashamed.
This power does not
Tell men apart. When they dance it can't distinguish
Young from old. It needs to be recognized
300 By everyone in the world—that is how
It lives—but it doesn't keep score. No one comes
Before anyone else . . .
KADMOS: Teiresias,
You have sight, but no eyes. You need
Mine to light your way for you. Listen,
Pentheus is here, the youth I gave my power to.
How he drives himself!
What's happened? What is new now?

(*Enter* PENTHEUS *with* SOLDIERS.)

PENTHEUS: I leave my country, I just go away,
310 And the result—chaos, the city in uproar. I hear
All our women have left home, and the new
Fashion is to be Bacchae, to mob
The mountains—more shadows there, of course—
And all in honour of someone, some moving spirit
They've just discovered—Dionysos. Who
Is he? What is Dionysos?
And this dancing . . . ? Dancing! . . . I was told
There are gatherings where they drink so much
You could never see the cups for the wine.
320 The women creep away, one here, one there,
Into the bushes—and there a man is waiting
And they copulate. They say it's all
Part of the service for this divine power.
Service! All they care about is being
Serviced.
I caught a few and my men have them chained
To the wall in the city gaol. The rest escaped,
They're in the hills, but I shall hunt them down.
Yes, that's how they'll end, in a cage,
330 Behind bars. No more drunken
Dancing then, no more orgies,
No more Bacchae!
They say a stranger has come to my country—
Some sorcerer, hypnotist, from the East,
From Lydia or somewhere, all curly blonde
Hair stinking of scent, cheeks hot
With wine, and flashing eyes—a real seducer—
Who spends all his days—and his nights—
With the girls from my city. He calls it initiation.
340 If I get this initiator inside
My palace, I'll finish his thumping, jumping,
Hair-shaking, snaking game, I'll initiate
That head away from that body.
He claims Dionysos still exists,
Never died, got life from eternal
Powers. Very likely—since Dionysos was roasted
In his mother's womb, after she told
Everyone Zeus was father of her child.
That myth was exploded in a blast of lightning.
350 But this new boy has the gall

To foist it back on us. Whoever he is
He deserves a reward for that—a rope around
His neck . . . (*He sees* KADMOS *and* TEIRESIAS.)
No, I can't believe it! My prophet, Teiresias,
In a fawn skin . . . And my own grandfather
playing
With a woolly stick. Ridiculous!
(*To* KADMOS) Grandfather, you disgust me. Look at
you,
An old man, clowning. Throw away   360
That ivy, drop those toys, don't touch them . . .
(*To* TEIRESIAS) Teiresias, this is you. You talked him
into it.
You want to drag this new obsession across
Our lives, so that you can squint up
At a few birds, burn a few sacrifices,
And make yourself more of a profit than ever.
If you weren't already mouldering in senility
You'd be rattling your chains with all the other
Bacchae   370
For smuggling in this pernicious, lecherous gospel.
When women drink, and their eyes light up like the
wine
Itself, then I say, Goodbye to decency,
The animals are out!
CHORUS: You—King of this place, be careful,
You, stranger, you dirty something pure,
That's dangerous.
Remember—you're born out of the earth yourself.
Kadmos planted dragon's teeth in soil, and   380
harvested men.
To those men you are a living insult.
TEIRESIAS: Easy for some to make speeches. They're
clever,
They pick an easy target, and the words sound
good.
Now you—your tongue races along
And makes a plausible sound, which might
Almost be mistaken for sense, except
That you have none. Arrogant, self-confident, with 390
a gift
For phrases—that kind of man is useless, a danger
To his fellows, while his mind stays closed.
This new life in our midst, which you
Sneer at, is going to be so powerful all
Over Greece, so vast, I . . . I can't
Describe it.
You are a young man. Here are two
Principles for you, the two supreme principles
In life.   400
First the principle of earth, Demeter,
Goddess of the soil, or whatever else
You like to call it. This provides the firm
Solid base in man. Second, the opposite
Principle, Dionysos, who found the living
Juice in the grape, and gave it to us all,
To slake our parched, aching souls, wash us

In streams of wine. When living is a struggle
He is the only drug for our pain, he gives us
410 Sleep and oblivion. We drink him down, we
    swallow
His power, and he comes alive in us. Then
We soar, we fly, we are free, and through his
    agency
Man can know some happiness. You laugh at him.
You laugh at the story that he was sewn in the loins
Of Zeus. Let me show you how to interpret
That—it makes sense.
    Zeus snatched the unborn child out
420 Of the blazing thunderbolt, took him back
To where he came from, Olympos. Hera, the bride
Of Zeus, wanted her rival's child to die.
But Zeus, like the wise power he is, found
A way out of the dilemma. He broke off
A part of the earth's envelope, the atmosphere,
And made a *loan* of it to Hera, to protect
The real Dionysos from her jealousy.
In time people confused "loan" with "loin"—
Told some story of how he was sewn in the loins
430 Of Zeus, and made a new version.
    And there is more. The power of Dionysos can
    break
Out of time. When he invades the mind
And puts reason to sleep, we have sight
Of things to come. If he takes full possession
He makes those who give themselves to him
Tell the future . . . What else? . . . War! He is even
There in war, yes . . . An army is in
The field, marching into battle. Then,
440 Before the weapons have touched, panic! That
Is Dionysos . . . Delphi too, home
Of Apollo, sanctuary of reason. But look
Up at the rocks. Who do you see bounding
Over the high plateau between the peaks,
Through the pine forests, shaking winter
Into life with green branches?—Dionysos!
Yes, he is everywhere.
Believe me, Pentheus, never boast
That you have any power to rule your life.
450 You may think you do, but thought is impotent,
Your certainty an illusion. Dionysos is here,
In your country, at work.
Accept him,
Pour wine for him,
Put vine leaves in your hair for him,
Dance for him.
    Dionysos will not restrain desire
In women. Restraint is something they must
    practise
460 For themselves. It cannot be imposed. But those
Who have control already will not lose it
Merely because they lose themselves
To Dionysos.
    Look, you are glad when crowds at the city

Gates cheer, shout, "Pentheus! Pentheus!"
Till every street rings with your name. Well,
Dionysos, too, I imagine, enjoys
Some recognition.
    And so Kadmos and myself—yes,
You can laugh—but we'll take our ivy branches 470
And we shall dance, we shall partner each other,
Old and grey as we are. Nevertheless
Dance we must. We shall not fight this power;
We shall not listen to your talk, which is
The most terrible madness of all. I pity you,
Pentheus. You'll get no relief from medicine,
Nor can you cure yourself.
CHORUS: The old man understands. He leaves reason
    where it is,
Apollo has his place, and so has Dionysos . . . 480
You are safe. Dionysos has power—and you
Have granted it.
KADMOS: Listen to Teiresias. You are still young,
And he is right. Your place is here, beside us.
Don't close doors on the past. This moment
You're nowhere, suspended in a void. Your brain
Works, but only against yourself.
You may be right. Dionysos may have
No special powers, but even so,
Why not pretend he does? It may be a lie, 490
But it's a useful one. If we can say
That Semele gave birth to a superior
Being, to something undying, it will be
A tremendous honour to our family.
Remember how your cousin, Akteon, died.
That was a horrible end. The hounds from his own
Kennels turned man-eater and tore him apart.
He had boasted he was a greater hunter than
    Artemis
Herself. And so he died in a velvet glade. 500
It could happen to you, unless you change! Come
    here,
I'll put some leaves on your head . . . Ivy . . . Be
With us. Acknowledge him. He is a great
Power. Let me . . .
PENTHEUS: Don't touch me!
Go and play Bacchae, but don't smear
Your idiocy onto me! Just don't
Come near me!
    And now, for your teacher, Teiresias, who fed 510
    you this drivel,
Punishment!
(*To* GUARD) One of you, here!
He has a place where he sits hoping for some
Revelation out of birdsong. Go. Take
A crowbar with you, and destroy that place.
Level it to the ground, all of it,
Throw his bits of wool to the winds, and let
The storms have them. *Hurry!*
    This is the one thing I can do to him 520
That will really hurt.

And you, you go into the city
And bring me this foreigner, this thing
Of doubtful gender, spreading his sick notions
Amongst our women, dragging our marriages
Through the filth.
When you find him, chain him up, and fetch him
Here. And then he'll have justice, because we'll
stone him,
530 (*To* GUARDS) Stone him till he's dead. He'll find
Thebes
A hard, hard place for Bacchae!

TEIRESIAS: You fiend! Do you realise what you're
saying?
No, you're mad. You had little enough sense
Before, but now . . . !
(*To* KADMOS) Kadmos, let's go. And let us pray
For him. Yes, he's a monster, but for the sake
Of the rest of us, let us pray this
540 Is overlooked. Bring your ivy branches
And follow me. Try to help me, hold me
Upright, and I'll help you. We are old
But we must stand by ourselves. Take pride in it . . .
Don't think of him!
We have work to do for this great power, this
supreme
Power . . .
Kadmos—in Greek the name Pentheus signifies
Sorrow. Does that mean anything? . . .
550 I hope not.
I don't talk of things to come—this is happening
Now (*meaning to* PENTHEUS) . . . Only a fool blurts
out his folly!

(*Exeunt* KADMOS *and* TEIRESIAS.)

CHORUS: Back!
Keep away!
This is filth—stain—smear—decay—
Keep away! He turns pure gold black.
Did you hear him?
The scorn that drips,
560 From his mouth, fouling Dionysos, child of his own
city.
Doesn't know happiness, or the pure-drained drink
of joy.
But Dionysos is the one
Who sends you dancing out of your mind,
Flings you laughing out of yourself to the
flute-song,
Stops your crying, stops your caring,
And when the bright wine dazes you
570 Life can't end, ivy glows on your brow
And you swallow thick sleep by the mouthful.
When reason forgets its place, wanders, and starts
an invasion,
And words go mad and run away with their master,
The end has come—
The man is doomed.

Live easy, live calm, and the storm can't wreck
you—
That way you stay whole.
There are powers in the world, who oversee life; 580
It's not so wise to be clever.
Life is short, and since it is,
Why chase more, more, more?
Can't you bear what is here?
Let others go mad, draw up the plans for
destruction—
But don't let them take us with them!
I want to go back to Cyprus, island of Aphrodite,
Where desire blows warm and breathes away
thought; 590
I want to lie in the fields of Paphos,
Where the distant Nile feeds a hundred wells
And gives fruit to the land without rain.
I want to see Pieria, because music is first there,
And the slope of Olympos leads straight to the sky.
Take me there, Dionysos, I'm calling you—
Hear me, come and lead me away. . . .
Then I can hand over my seeing,
Hand over my striving
And dance to my heart-beats, 600
And no one can say no.
Dionysos, child of the universe, comes to life in my
laughter.
His great love is Peace,
Lavish with her treasures, careful of youth.
He sends the poor, he sends the rich, his one
gift—wine.
So that the whole world can know
Where pain stops, and where joy starts.
He hates the man who says no. 610
No to the day,
No to the night,
No to life, and no to all love—
Keep away from that kind,
They are too much for you, they will consume you.
There is another way, never named, never
mapped.
But the unheard-of, untalked-of people follow it.
That way I choose—I say yes to it.

(*Enter a* GUARD, *with* DIONYSOS, *chained.*)

GUARD: Pentheus, we caught him. The hunt is over, 620
and here
Is the animal you sent us after . . .
A gentle animal, we found, made
No attempt to escape, handed himself
Over without a murmur, never went pale,
That wine-stain flush never left his cheek, and he
smiled.
He told us to put on the chains and take him away.
He waited for us, making it so simple
I was embarrassed. So I said, "Stranger," I said, 630
"I only obey orders here. I am taking you

Now, on instructions from Pentheus. Pentheus
Sends for you. *Pentheus*. Not me."
But the women you captured and had locked up in
    prison,
The ones who were dancing,
They're out.
They're free, and they're away in the forest,
    running
640   Like deer, calling on Bromios—he's their master,
And governs them completely.
The chains all fell from their limbs of their own
Accord, keys turned, doors opened,
Without a hand touching them. This man
Is an amazing . . .
He is full of . . .
I don't understand what it is he has brought to
    Thebes
But it is your concern now, all of it.
650   PENTHEUS: Let him go. He is inside the cage and he
    can't
Escape from me now. He doesn't move
So fast.
Well, stranger, you're not at all bad-looking,
Are you? At least, to the women . . . Which is why
You have come to Thebes, I suppose . . . Long hair,
Crinkling down your cheeks—you've never
    wrestled,
I presume—very desirable . . . White
660   Skin—you keep out of the sun, you cultivate
The shadows, where you hunt down love
With your handsome profile. Yes?
Who are you? Where do you come from?
DIONYSOS: I am no one . . .
But I will give you an easier answer.
Have you heard of a river called Tmolos? It runs
Through fields of flowers . . .
PENTHEUS: Yes, I know that river, it circles the town
Of Sardis.
670   DIONYSOS: I come from there. My country is Lydia.
PENTHEUS: And these
Activities. How is it you bring them to Greece?
DIONYSOS: Dionysos inspired me. Dionysos . . . He
Is the son of Zeus.
PENTHEUS: So you have a Zeus
Over there, who fathers new powers
On the world.
DIONYSOS: No. Zeus was united
With Semele in Thebes, and gave her the child
680   Here.
PENTHEUS: Did this irresistible urge
Come to you at night, or were you
"Inspired" in the daytime?
DIONYSOS: I saw him.
He saw me. And he gave me the secret
Means to summon his presence.
PENTHEUS: And this secret—
What is it like? can you tell me?

DIONYSOS: It must not
Be revealed to someone in whom Dionysos   690
Has not been born.
PENTHEUS: Those who share this secret—
Do they benefit—and how?
DIONYSOS: I am forbidden to tell.
But it is worth knowing.
PENTHEUS: You're clever, but
You're a fake! You want to make me curious.
DIONYSOS: For a man who is so sure of what he knows
There are no other powers, there is no other
Life. It simply escapes him.   700
PENTHEUS: You say you saw
Dionysos clearly . . . What did he look like?
DIONYSOS: Whatever
He wished. I didn't arrange it.
PENTHEUS: Very good.
But once more you evade the issue,
Your statement was meaningless.
DIONYSOS: The greatest truths often sound like
    babblings
Of madmen—till they are understood.   710
PENTHEUS: Are we
The first to be visited by you and your offer
Of supernatural aid?
DIONYSOS: No. all
The people of the east are awake. They dance.
They live . . .
PENTHEUS: They're out of their minds, we in Greece
Have more sense.
DIONYSOS: No, in this case, less.
Their way is different, that is all.   720
PENTHEUS: And these practices you claim are
    sacred—
Do they take place at night, or in the day?
DIONYSOS: Mostly at night. Darkness has dignity.
PENTHEUS: For women the night hours are
    dangerous,
Lascivious hours . . .
DIONYSOS: People have been known
To sin during the day.
PENTHEUS: You play with words!   730
You'll be punished for that.
DIONYSOS: You soil mysteries
With your ignorant sneers. You'll be punished
For that.
PENTHEUS: He's so sure. The drunken dancer
Has been in training—for argument.
DIONYSOS: Come,
Pronounce sentence. What terrible fate have you
In store for me?
PENTHEUS: First, I'll clip those flowing   40
Locks . . .
DIONYSOS: My hair must not be touched, I grow it
For Dionysos.
PENTHEUS: Next, you will hand over
Your wand, that branch you carry . . .

DIONYSOS: Take it from me
    Yourself. I carry it for Dionysos.
PENTHEUS: Then
    We shall lock you in prison, and you will never get
750   out.
DIONYSOS: Dionysos will free me, when I wish him to.
PENTHEUS: Yes, when you get your followers round
        you and "summon
    His presence."
DIONYSOS: He sees. He's here. This minute he knows
    What is being done to me.
PENTHEUS: Where is he then?
    I can't see him. Why doesn't he show himself?
DIONYSOS: He's here, where I stand. You, being crass
760   And proud, see nothing.
PENTHEUS: You're raving.
    (To GUARDS) He insults me!
    He insults you all!
DIONYSOS: I am sane. You
    Are not. I say to you, set me free.
PENTHEUS: And I say you go to prison, because
    I am master here, I have the power.
DIONYSOS: You don't know what your life is, what
    You are doing, who you are . . .
770 PENTHEUS: I am Pentheus,
    Son of Echion and Agave.
DIONYSOS: Pentheus;
    A very convenient name for a doomed man.
PENTHEUS: Go away, go on! Go!
    (To GUARDS) Lock him up somewhere near—in the
        stables.
    Leave him to stare at the darkness,
    Darkness all the time.
    (To DIONYSOS) Dance in there!
780   And these creatures you have brought here, these
    Accessories,
    We'll either sell them, or we'll give their hands
        work
    To do—not this banging, thumping on pieces of
        skin,
    But work. Spinning. Weaving. They'll belong to us.
DIONYSOS: I leave you now. But I shall not suffer
    What I have no need to suffer. Dionysos
    Will punish you for your gross contempt. You
790   Say he does not exist. But when you send
    Me to prison
    It is you
    Who commit the crime . . .
    Against him.

    (The GUARDS lead DIONYSOS away.)

CHORUS: Gently flowing Dirce,
    Life-stream to these fields,
    Innocent waters,
    Banks that were a cradle for the newborn Dionysos
    The day his father saved him from the blazing
800   thunderbolt,

The day Zeus shouted:
"Welcome, my son, welcome to the world!
My man's loins shall be your womb.
You'll have a name, and Thebes will know you by it
Because I will open their eyes."
    But now this same river they all live by here,
She doesn't want us.
"Don't come near," she cries,
"No ivy crowns on my banks,
No gatherings, no dancing near me!"   810
    Why?
Why turn away from us?
Why say no to us?
Some day you will long for . . . ache for . . .
. . . dry . . .
Ask for . . . parched . . .
Wine.
You'll thirst! Yes, some day,
You'll thirst for Dionysos.
    Never seen such fury like the fury staring out of   820
Pentheus.
That's not a man. It's a beast run wild.
He's one of the crop, the dragon-toothed flowers.
Who gnashed the soil to get spawned in the
    world—
A monster,
A fiend, murderous to the bone.
He means to shut me away,
Rope me in darkness,
But I'm not his. I belong to Dionysos.   830
Already, in there, in a dungeon, a sightless pit,
He buries our leader . . .
Dionysos . . . can you see this?
We can't move,
We can't breathe,
The only ones who speak for you, crushed.
Down . . .
. . . With a tree in one hand . . .
Down . . .
. . . like a tower of gold   840
Down from Olympos . . .
DIONYSOS!
And tame him.
Dionysos—we are calling you
Wherever you are,
Come . . .
Come from the mountain forests,
Glide from the wild beasts' lairs,
Spring from a cruel snow peak,
Leap from a whirlwind dance,   850
Grow from a thousand branches,
Rise from a sleeping valley,
Descend from Olympos,
Tree-leaved and silent,
Fly on the air,
In the grass that Orpheus tamed,
Over animals silenced by his music

Nearer and nearer—
The drumming of feet heralds you—
860 Dance out of mountain torrents,
Swing over eastern rivers,
Surge over waves towards us,
Driving a storm of souls,
Now he's coming, he's coming into Greece!
   He's over the land now,
In the green plains alive with horses,
In the streams that water the fields,
He's coming.
   YES! YES!
870 DIONYSOS! DIONYSOS! DIONYSOS!

(As the CHORUS *ends, the voice of* DIONYSOS *comes from offstage all round.)*

DIONYSOS *(stereo)*: Aaaaaouoooooowah! Hark!
  I got life!
  I have a voice!
  Hark! Aaaaooooouwah! Take me!
  Aaaooouwah! Take me!
CHORUS: Has it come? . . . Hear it? . . . Feel it? . . .
  The call! The call! . . . Where? . . . Is it here?
DIONYSOS *(stereo)*: Yes! Coming to life . . . Yes!
  Coming
880 To life . . . Aaaooowah! . . . Born in the ground,
  born in
  The sky . . . !
CHORUS: Master! Master!
  Come close, come close. Come into us . . . In . . . *In*
  . . .
  NOW . . . Closer, *closer* . . .
DIONYSOS *(stereo)*: The earth—SHAKE.
  Move, nothing stand still, *move!*
CHORUS: Look, the palace of Pentheus bulges,
  quivers . . . It will
890 Fall, fall . . . It's got into the palace . . . It's in,
  It's *in!* . . . See, pillars melt, marble streams,
  Trembles . . . It's inside now, it's taken, it's taken.
DIONYSOS *(stereo)*: Touch off the fire, flames and
  thunder!
  Burn, burn, house of Pentheus.

(During the following speech of CHORUS, *darkness, thunder, flames, roar of collapsing masonry, triumph noise of* DIONYSOS.)

CHORUS: Fire! Watch the fever-fire dance round the
  grave
  Of Semele, charred earth no one walks on, the
  lightning
900 Left a living flame there . . .
  Down, down! Everyone down to the ground . . .
  Dionysos is . . .
  . . . don't move . . .
  In possession of . . .
  . . . don't look . . .

The palace
. . . don't breathe!
DIONYSOS: Afraid, my friends? After all our journeys
  Together . . . ? Look at you, hugging the earth,
  Terrorstruck . . . Yes, you saw the house   910
  Of Pentheus split and sundered by the presence
  Of Dionysos. But now . . . look up at me,
  You're safe . . . don't flinch . . . All is well . . .
CHORUS: You're dawn for us, our life-light, and calm
  rose
  In the depths of the mind . . . The sight of you is
  comfort . . .
  We'd lost you, we were alone.
DIONYSOS: So you surrendered, gave in to despair.
  When I was taken   920
  In there you thought I would be buried in the
  death
  Cells of Pentheus' darkness?
CHORUS: Yes, yes.
  Who was to protect us if you were harmed?
  But now you're free.
DIONYSOS: As always . . .
CHORUS: And safe . . .
DIONYSOS: I saved myself.
CHORUS: How? The man was in a killing mood . . .   930
DIONYSOS: Easy. I had no trouble with him.
CHORUS: But you couldn't move. He lashed your
  hands
  Together.
DIONYSOS: He thought he did, but he never touched
  them, never came near me. He thought he had
  me, but he breakfasted on lies this morning and
  I laughed—because I had him . . . He took me to
  the stables to be locked up, and found a bull
  there. This bull he loaded with chains—on its   940
  knees, on its hooves—gasping with rage, streaming sweat all over his body, chewing his lips . . . I
  waited close beside him, did nothing, said nothing, just sat there and watched. Meanwhile the
  palace quivered. Dionysos had come, and fire
  spurted from Semele's grave . . . When Pentheus
  saw it he decided his house was on fire. He
  rushed from end to end of the palace, screaming
  at his servants to pump water, more water, on
  the flames, till every slave was working—over   950
  nothing. The fire existed only in his mind. All at
  once he left it—snatched up a long steel sword
  and hurled himself indoors—his prisoner, me,
  had escaped. Then Dionysos—or so I think,
  because I only tell you what I think—created a
  phantom figure. Because Pentheus charged at
  something in the courtyard, stabbing and lung-
  ing as if it was me on the end of his blade. But
  there was nothing there, only clear bright air.
  More havoc followed. Dionysos shattered the   960
  palace. Inside now is nothing but a heap of

rubble. My spell in prison was hard on Pentheus. Finally, spent and limp, he threw away his sword . . . Well, he is a man, and he fought a god. He expected too much . . . Quietly I left his house, and came back here to you. Pentheus never troubled me . . . Listen. I hear footsteps. This will be him . . . Watch that door. He'll come out and say . . . but what can he say now? Let him
970　explode—I'll manage him easily anyhow. The secret of life is balance, tolerance . . .

(*Enter* PENTHEUS.)

PENTHEUS: I've been cheated! I had that foreigner. I had him
So trussed up he couldn't move—and still
He got away!

(*Sees* DIONYSOS *and gives a shout.*)

There he is! That's the man. Look,
He stands there, on the doorstep of my palace,
Out in the open . . .
Look at him!
980　DIONYSOS: Stay where you are!
Calm yourself . . .
Anger's going . . . going . . .
Now . . .
PENTHEUS: How did you get out? You were locked in, chained . . .
DIONYSOS: Didn't I tell you—or didn't you hear?—someone
Would free me?
PENTHEUS: Free you? Who? You always produce
990　A new riddle.
DIONYSOS: The grape-gardener, the wine-grower
To mankind.
PENTHEUS: The planter of all drunkenness
And disorder.
DIONYSOS: Insults from you would make him proud.
PENTHEUS (*to* GUARD): Surround the palace, Close every gate in the city.
Shut him in!
DIONYSOS: Come, come, if such powers
1000　Exist, surely they move on a higher plane
Than your city walls.
PENTHEUS: So clever, so
Clever. All that cleverness misused!
DIONYSOS: I use it where I need it most . . . Look,
Someone is coming with a message for you. Listen
To him first . . . Of course we'll wait for you—
We are in no hurry to go . . . You
Hear what he has to say. He comes from the mountains.

(*Enter* HERDSMAN.)

1010　HERDSMAN: Pentheus, I am one of your subjects here

In Thebes. I come from Kithairon. There's still snow
There, it dazzles you, the hills are all white . . .
PENTHEUS: And what is your news? How urgent is it?
HERDSMAN: I have seen
The Bacchae . . . those women, strange women, they fling
Their white limbs like a storm of javelins across
The fields. I came to tell you and everyone here . . .
I want you to know, master, what marvellous things　1020
They do . . . beyond anything you could imagine.
But first I would like your word that I can speak
Freely about what happened there. Or must I
Trim the facts a little . . . ? It's your temper, you see,
Master, your very quick temper, which rules us
All so harshly . . . too harshly.
PENTHEUS: Tell me, I give my word, nothing will happen
To you. Do your duty, and no one will be angry.　1030
The worse you make the Bacchae sound, the more
Firmly shall I crush their ringmaster, as he deserves.
HERDSMAN: Our herds of cattle are topping the rise of the hills,
Grazing as they go, and the sun's rays are just
Beginning to warm the grass, when I see three
Circles of women—the dancers!
One of them is round Autonoë,
The second with Agave, your mother,　1040
And the third is with Ino.
They are all asleep, lying every way,
Some propped against pine-tree trunks,
Others curled up modestly on a pile
Of oak leaves, pillowed on the earth—
None of the drunkenness you talked about,
None of the obscene abandon, or the wild
Music—no love among the bushes.
All at once, your mother stands up. She cries out
And wakes the rest of the women, says she can hear　1050
The lowing of cattle. They shake the sleep petals
From their eyes, and all stand upright,
A marvel of calm and order . . . Young girls,
Old women, maidens who have never slept
With a man. First, they let their hair tumble
Down their shoulders. Then, the ones whose fawn-skins
Have come loose from the brooches pinning them, fasten them
Back on their shoulders, and belt the spotted hides　1060
With snakes—
And those snakes were live—I saw their tongues
Flicker . . .
One of them might carry a fawn, cradled
In her arms, or a wild wolf cub, and give it her own
Milk—

You see, some had left newborn babies at home
And so their breasts were full . . .
They all weave strands of ivy, oak leaves,
1070 Tendrils of flowering briony in their hair.
Then one of them winds ivy on a branch,
Taps a rock, and out of that rock spouts
Water—running water! Fresh as dew!
Another drops her wand, a little twig,
On to the earth, and where she drops it some
        force
Sends up a spring—a wine-spring! Some
Feel they'd like to drink fresh milk.
They scrape the tips of their fingers on the earth
1080 And they have milk—fountains of milk! From all
Their ivy-covered branches sweet honey
Drips, cascades down . . . Oh, if you
Had been there and seen all this, you would have
        been
On your knees, praying—not criticising—but
        praying
For help and guidance.
All we herdsmen and shepherds hold
A meeting, we begin to talk, we compare
1090 Stories—
Because these were fantastic things the women
        were doing,
We could hardly believe our eyes . . .
Someone who knows his way in the city, knows
How they make speeches there, he stands up
And makes one himself:
"You inhabitants of the majestic mountain acres,
        allow me to propose to you that we hunt down
        Agave, mother of Pentheus, from the midst of
1100   her Dionysiac festivities, and thereby do our
        royal master in Thebes . . . a great good turn
        . . ."
Applause!
We decide to lay an ambush for the women
In the undergrowth,
We hide in the leaves,
We wait.
The hour for their rites approaches . . .
The sticks with ivy begin to beat out a rhythm.
It gets in your blood, that rhythm.
1110 "Iacchos!" they howl in unison,
"Bromios!"
"Son of Zeus!"
    The whole mountain sways to that one beat,
        beat, beat:
The wild beasts join in,
Everything moves,
Everything's running, running. Agave is racing
        towards me, she's coming near, nearer, almost
        touches me, I leap out—I wanted to catch her,
1120   you see—I jump from my safe hiding place
        and—
She gives a screech:

"Look, my swift hounds, we are being hunted
By these men. Follow me!
Follow me!
Branches—get branches and arm yourselves!"
    We turn and run—
If we hadn't we would have been torn to shreds
By the Bacchae . . .
    As it is, they descend on our heifers grazing   1130
In the long grass. They have nothing in their
        hands,
Those women—nothing metal. But imagine you
        see
One of them, just with her hands, tearing a young
Well-grown heifer in two, while it screams . . .
Others have found full-grown cows and are
        wrenching them
Limb from limb. Ribs, hooves, toss
Up in the air, drop to the ground. Parts   1140
Of our animals hang from the branches of pine
        trees,
Dripping there, blood spattering the leaves.
Bulls with surging horns, invincible
Till now, are tripped, sprawl full length
On the ground, while a mob of hands, girls'
Hands, rip them apart. Faster than you can
Blink your royal eyes the flesh is peeled
Off their bones.
    Then down, like flocks of birds, so fast   1150
Their feet never touch the ground, they sweep to
        the Valley
Sleeping between the hills. Here, on the banks
Of the Asopos, the grain grows deep in the
        farmlands,
Little towns, Hysiai, Erythrai, snuggle
Beneath the slopes of Kithairon . . .
Like an invading army those women mill
Through the valley, they tear it apart, chaos!
Children   1160
Snatched from their beds . . . Anything they can
        pick up,
And carry on their backs, stays there—nothing
Holds it on, but it never slips to the ground,
Even the bronze, the iron—they put live coals
In their hair—and nothing burns them!
The people are furious, being plundered by these
        women,
And rush to defend themselves. Then what   1170
        happens?
    —It was a terrible sight to see, master . . .
    No spear, no weapon, nothing so much as
        scratches
The Bacchae. But one of those wooden sticks they
        carry
Draws blood at once. They throw them—and men
        run
For their lives—that isn't human, there's some
        other power   1180

At work . . . At last, they go, back to the mountains
Where they came from, back to the springs of
  water
Which Dionysos sent them. They wash away
The blood . . . and the snakes lick off the dirt and
  gore
From the womens' cheeks with their tongues . . .
  This power, master, whoever he is, whatever
He is . . . let him into Thebes! He
1190   Is great. And one thing above all they say
He has done, I've heard that he gave mankind
The grape . . . And the grape is the best grave—for
  grief.
If there were no wine
There would be no love,
There would be no joy in life.
CHORUS: In this king's company, honesty is a
  dangerous pastime
Yet I must speak . . .
1200   . . . Say it, say it . . . !
Of all the powers in life the greatest is Dionysos.
PENTHEUS: Now, I see . . . yes! Nearer . . . nearer!
This insufferable craze is like a fire, and it's
  spreading!
All Greece despises us. But we must
Be firm, not give way . . .
  (To GUARDS) Go to the gates of Electra, get every
  man
Under arms. I want all the cavalry, every
1210   Spearman, every bowman, mobilised.
We attack the Bacchae at once . . .
I have been too patient. But my patience
Is finished, we are being governed by a pack of
  women.
DIONYSOS: I told you, Pentheus, but you never listen.
You have not been good to me. All the same
I am going to warn you. You must not use force
  against
Dionysos.
1220   End the war in yourself. He will not
Allow you to disturb his Bacchae. Leave them
In the mountains where they are happy.
PENTHEUS: Don't preach
To me. You were in prison and you escaped.
Well, look after your freedom or I may remind
Myself that you have been judged and condemned.
DIONYSOS: I
Would sacrifice to him . . . not rage and struggle
And kick. This is an eternal power—
1230   You are a man.
PENTHEUS: I'll sacrifice to him!
A blood sacrifice, a woman sacrifice—
That is all they are fit for. I will be lavish—
There will be carnage in the glades of Kithairon.
DIONYSOS: You'll lose. It will be an ignominious rout.
Your bronze shields won't hold off wooden sticks
And women's hands.

PENTHEUS: Will someone tell me how
To get rid of this man? Extricate me, someone!
Whatever I do to him, whatever he does   1240
To me, it's the same. Talk, talk, talk!
DIONYSOS: Excuse me—but you can settle all this,
No trouble . . . It is still possible.
PENTHEUS: How? What
Do I do? Make myself lower than the lowest
In this country?
DIONYSOS: I will bring the women
Here, without the use of force.
PENTHEUS: Yes,
I see, thank you. This is the great master   1250
Plan—the great deception.
DIONYSOS: How can you call it
That? I want to keep you whole. I work
For nothing else.
PENTHEUS: You arranged this with your friends.
Licence to dance, disorder in perpetuity.
DIONYSOS: Certainly I arranged it, quite true—
With Dionysos
PENTHEUS (to GUARDS): Bring out my armour . . . (To
  DIONYSOS) You—   1260
Keep quiet!
DIONYSOS (to GUARDS): Wait! (To PENTHEUS) Do you
  want to see them . . .
In their nests up there in the hills. See
The women . . . ?
PENTHEUS: Yes, yes, I do. Yes,
I'll pay if I have to. Gold. How much? A thousand?
Ten thousand?
DIONYSOS: You've fallen in love with my idea.
You can't wait. Why?   1270
PENTHEUS: I'll see them drunk,
Hopelessly drunk. It revolts me, but . . . I . . .
DIONYSOS: But you really want to. That disgusting
  sight
Lures you there . . . ?
PENTHEUS: Yes, I told you, it does.
I won't say anything, I'll be quiet, I'll stay
Among the pine-trees.
DIONYSOS: You can try to hide
But they'll pick up your scent.   1280
PENTHEUS: Good point. I'd forgotten.
I'll go openly.
DIONYSOS: I'll take you there. Would you like that?
The way is before you. Will you dare?
PENTHEUS: Now!
Take me there now. I hate every minute
We lose.
DIONYSOS: Then you must be covered. Find a linen
Dress to wear . . .
PENTHEUS: Wait, now what is   1290
This? I'm a man, I don't change places
With any woman. Why should I?
DIONYSOS: In case
They kill you. Suppose you, a *man*, are discovered

There—you die.

PENTHEUS: Right again. I understand.
There is some intelligence in you. I should have seen it
Before.

DIONYSOS: Dionysos came alive in me.
1300   All I know is him.

PENTHEUS: Yes, yes . . .
Now, this good advice of yours, how
Do we carry it out?

DIONYSOS: We go inside, and there
I prepare you for your journey.

PENTHEUS: How—prepare me?
Dress me up as a woman? Oh no, no,
I would be ashamed.

DIONYSOS: Have you lost heart? The sight
1310   Of those possessed and demented women, it no longer
Interests you?

PENTHEUS: What kind of clothing did you say
I have to wear?

DIONYSOS: Long hair to your shoulders.
You must have a wig . . .

PENTHEUS: And then what else? Is there more
To this costume?

DIONYSOS: A full length robe.
1320   And for the head—a scarf.

PENTHEUS: Anything else
You want to drape me in?

DIONYSOS: We'll give you a stick
Covered with ivy to hold, and wrap a spotted
Fawn-skin round you . . .

PENTHEUS: No, I could never put on
Woman's clothing.

DIONYSOS: What will you do—fight them?
It's a waste of your blood.

1330 PENTHEUS: You're right. First we must go
And watch. Nothing more yet.

DIONYSOS: That
Makes better sense than hunting down evil
With more evil.

PENTHEUS: How can I get through the streets
Of Thebes and not be seen?

DIONYSOS: We'll find a secret
Way. I'll lead you.

PENTHEUS: Anything—but I will not
1340   Be entertainment for that herd of females. Let's go
Inside. I want to consider this plan.

DIONYSOS: Decide,
I'm ready for you. Nothing will be too much trouble . . .

PENTHEUS: No, inside . . . I may call out my army
And march up there . . . Or I may follow
Your advice. We shall see.

(Exit.)

DIONYSOS *(to* CHORUS*):* Friends, the man stands in the gate of the trap.
He'll find the Bacchae and he'll answer to them   1350
with his life.
Dionysos, now your work begins.
You are not too far away, I hope. Let us
Reward this man for his attentions. First,
Dislodge his thoughts, make his reason slither.
If he were sane, he would not agree to put on
Woman's clothing. But when he edges out
Of his mind then, yes, then he'll wear it.
I want him to raise a howl of derision all
Through Thebes when he minces along the streets   1360
In skirts. Once he mouthed fearsome threats,
And now . . .
Now to Pentheus, to disguise him, dress him for
His journey into death. His mother's hands
Will caress him roughly to his grave, and he'll see
Dionysos face to face, know that power,
Know its nature, its ferocious gentle nature
Alive in man, an undeniable *god!*

(Exit.)

CHORUS: Night—will it ever come?
And my flying feet,   1370
Flash of white thighs in the hills,
Head flung back,
And the dew-soaked air kissing my throat—
  And running, running—
Oh, when will it come?
  I want to be free and play and be happy again
Like a young deer, swathed in an emerald meadow,
When he runs in stark terror of the hunt,
And the knotted nets close in—
Then he leaps up and over them,   1380
While the hunter shrieks to his hounds to keep racing,
Pacing behind.
But the deer strains his flashing legs taut.
He skims and spurts across open stretches
Where the river winds
Till he comes to a wood,
And the deep shade lulls him,
The green branches soothe him,
And he rests where no man is.   1390
  What does it mean to live a life?
Can you hope for better than to rise above all warring,
Control what threatens you,
Defeat what oppresses you?
To be strong—
No, nothing is better.
I choose that.
There are forces not ruled by us,
And we obey them.   1400
Trust them—though they travel inch by inch,

They arrive.
Self-swollen and calloused,
Soul, tumoured and hard,
All the malignant growths of thought,
They level, and pare, and crop,
They move in the dark with a subtle glitter
So that no one times their work,
But always the hunt goes on—
1410 For the man who has turned his back on them.
Their rules cannot be overruled—
It is your peril, and your death that follows.
But if you grant their power—what does it cost?
Nothing.
Not even a word—because
These forces lack a name.
Call them whatever you like—
Spirits—
Gods—
1420 Principles—
Elements—
Currents—
Laws—
Anything, anything you like.
But they are born in your blood
They have been observed and preserved since
before time.
     What does it mean to live a life?
Can you hope for better than to rise above all
1430   warring,
Control what threatens you,
Defeat what oppresses you?
To be strong—
No, nothing is better
I choose that.
Life is a stormy sea,
Happiness is a harbour.
Finding your harbour is your life-work.
He is truly happy who succeeds in that life-work.
1440 Some end rich, some poor,
Some are strong, some achieve nothing.
There are ten thousand hopes, ten thousand
     dreams,
They may all come true—they may all vanish,
But happiness—
A man finds happiness when he lies every day
With those forces of the world on his side.
All hail to that man!

(*Enter* DIONYSOS.)

DIONYSOS (*into palace*): You! You with a white-hot
1450   wish for a peep
At the forbidden. You, reaching out for the
     out-of-reach,
You—I'm talking to *you*—Pentheus! Come
Out here, in front of your palace, let me
See you, dressed a woman of the wild wine

Nights of Dionysos. Are you ready to spy?
Your mother is there . . .
All the women are there . . .

(*Enter* PENTHEUS.)

Perfect! You are a daughter of Kadmos to the life.
PENTHEUS: No, listen. I think I see two suns,   1460
And two Thebes. The seven-gated city
Has doubled . . . and you, you look
Like a bull, leading me—horns sprout from your
     head . . .
All the time, were you that beast?
Are you the bull now . . . ?
DIONYSOS: Dionysos favours you. He is bound to us
For the wine-gifts we gave him. Before he was not
Pleased. But now he is. And you see
What you ought to see.   1470
PENTHEUS: How do I look to you?
My aunt . . . isn't this how she walks? . . . Or this . . .
     My mother
Agave,—isn't it? Isn't it Agave?
DIONYSOS: It's them! When I look at you it's them I
     see . . .
Wait—a wisp of hair has come away.
It isn't lying where I set it, under the scarf.
PENTHEUS: Inside, I went this way with my head,
That way—back, forward, back—I was being   1480
A woman in a trance. And I made the hair
Come loose . . .
DIONYSOS: We must keep you groomed. I'll put it in
     place
Again. Here . . . lift your head up straight.
PENTHEUS: Look . . . there . . . you do it. Make me
     pretty.
I am yours to play with. Take me.
DIONYSOS: Your sash is loose—
Look. And your dress is wrong. The pleats should   1490
     hang
The same length round your ankles.
PENTHEUS: Yes,
I see . . . a little too long by the right foot.
But on this side it seems all right, touching
My heel just there . . .
DIONYSOS: Who is your best friend?
I am . . . You don't believe me? Wait till you see
Bacchae, how modest they are, how pure, how
     sane—   1500
Astonishing.
PENTHEUS: This branch with ivy—in my right
Hand—or my left? Which makes me
More like a genuine wild woman of the hills?
DIONYSOS: Hold it in your right hand, and raise it
In time with your right foot . . . Very good.
I see a change, a new mind, in you . . .
PENTHEUS: Now I could . . . I could hoist the whole of
     Kithairon

1510 On my shoulder—valleys full of women
Dancing, madness and all! . . . Yes?
DIONYSOS: Of course,
If you will it. Your mood was before most
unhealthy,
Now it is all it should be.
PENTHEUS: Shall we bring iron bars, or shall I delve it
Up with my own bare hands, wedge
One shoulder or one arm under the hill-top . . . ?
DIONYSOS: And destroy the homes of the nymphs?
1520 No, no.
Pan lives there too. Let him go on playing
His pipes.
PENTHEUS: You're right. One should not coerce
women.
I shall hide myself in the boughs of a pine tree.
DIONYSOS: You find
The hiding place that suits you best. You're a spy,
A secret witness of secret rites.
PENTHEUS: Yes,
1530 Imagine, they are nestling like birds in the thick
leaves,
Locked in their lust, enjoying it . . .
DIONYSOS: You must break in
And prevent them. Perhaps you will find them in
the act . . .
Unless they find you first.
PENTHEUS: Take me through Thebes,
Right through the centre. I am the only man
Here who has any courage.
1540 DIONYSOS: Yes, you alone
Make sacrifices for your people, you alone.
And so—the test. It has always been there, waiting
For you. Follow me. I am your
Protector, your escort . . . as far as Kithairon—
Someone else will bring you back.
PENTHEUS: Yes, my mother . . .
DIONYSOS: In full view of everyone . . .
PENTHEUS: That's why I'm going . . .
DIONYSOS: You will be borne back on high.
1550 PENTHEUS: Yes, in triumph, you mean my great
triumph!
DIONYSOS: In the hands of your mother . . .
PENTHEUS: You'll spoil me—all this pampering!
DIONYSOS: Yes, I'll spoil you, I'll spoil you utterly.
PENTHEUS: Still, I deserve it, and I shall have it!

(*Exit.*)

DIONYSOS: Headstrong, headstrong—you go walking
To your headlong end—which will make you
Famous, far beyond this life, beyond
This time.
1560 Agave, fling open your arms.
Prepare, you sisters, daughters of Kadmos.
I bring this young man to you—
Prepare for a great contest.

The victor shall be myself—and Dionysos.
As for the rest—wait, watch, and listen.

(*Exit.*)

CHORUS: Go, track to the mountains
Dogs of madness,
Run, dogs, run,
Find the daughters of Kadmos,
Snap at their dancing heels, sink your fangs in their 1570
brains,
Then turn them loose on the would-be woman,
The spy in the flapping skirts,
Who goes mad for the secret of the possessed.
His mother will see him first,
As he peers from a rock-wall or cliff-steeple.
She'll scream to the women:
"Look! See what creeps sniffing up to our
mountain,
Our mountain, my friends— 1580
This creature crawling across the hillside!
What mothered such a thing?
Not a woman, no—it got life from a lioness
Or a beast heaved up out of African sands."
Now we shall see balance restored.
We shall see it, sharp, clear, a sword
With blood on its edge, driving deep
To the gullet of Pentheus, the blossom of the
dragon's jawbone,
Who enforces his will on the forces of life, 1590
Outlaws law,
Orders all other order out of existence.
And now—
With insane and petty determination,
With intent sick passion,
All his thought corrupted,
All his mind a sewer,
He smells his way to the living heart
Of the mysteries, where Dionysos is born and
re-born. 1600
He wants to master with violence that forever-free
spirit.
The laws of all life admit no excuses,
Live by them, live as a man—
That is the way of no pain.
I don't grudge man his search for knowledge,
I acclaim it, applaud it,
But there is more, there are great things
That must be brought to the daylight,
Made part of our waking and sleeping. 1610
Calmly accept them, peacefully weave them
Into your life—and it will be a good life,
Freeing you.
Now we shall see balance restored,
We shall see it, sharp, clear, a sword
With blood on its edge, driving deep

To the gullet of Pentheus, the blossom of the
   dragon's jawbone,
Who enforces his will on the forces of life,
1620 Outlaws law,
Orders all other order out of existence.
   Now Dionysos, into the open!
Let him see you . . .
As a BULL!
A dragon with swarming heads!
A lion, vomiting flames!
Come, Dionysos, come sweetly smiling
And string your noose round the throat of this
   hunter.
1630 Bring the one-minded women in a pack
To trip him,
Smother him,
Kill him!

(*Enter* PENTHEUS' *own* SERVANT.)

SERVANT: In this house lived people who were the
   envy
Of all Greece . . . once. A family begun
In dragon's teeth, a summer harvest reaped
By Kadmos, the great traveller and merchant
Of the western seas. And I am nothing,
1640 An obscure someone who takes orders. And yet
   I pity *them*.
CHORUS: What is it? Have you news? Have you been
   in the hills?
SERVANT: Pentheus is dead, King Pentheus, son of
   Echion, is dead.
CHORUS: Victory! The first day of Dionysos—now
   they see you, now you live, now you face them
   . . .
SERVANT: What do you mean? How can you say that?
   My master is dead. Are you glad? He is dead, *dead!*
1650 CHORUS: Not my master. I've another home. I've
   another
Life . . . No more fear, no more prison, no more
   terror . . .
Free, free!
SERVANT: There are still men in Thebes who can . . .
CHORUS: Thebes can't touch me, Thebes has no
   power . . . Dionysos, Dionysos comes first for me.
SERVANT: I can forgive the rest, but not this. Terrible
   things have happened, and you gloat. It's ugly.
1660 CHORUS: Terrible things? Describe them, tell us, how
   did the man die, the wrong-headed master-fool
   . . .
SERVANT: Behind us were the last houses of Thebes—
We had come out at the river Asopos. Then
We began to climb, mounting the slopes of
   Kithairon,
Pentheus and I—he was my master, so
I followed him—and this stranger, who
Was to be the guide of our expedition.

Treading very softly, and never speaking,
So that we could see without being seen, we came 1670
First to a glade thick with grass and rested
There . . . It was in a little valley, overhung
On each side with cliffs, and fed by rills
Of water. Pine trees leant over to shade it,
And somewhere in this valley were the women,
The mad women, the Bacchae.
   Then we saw them.
   They're sitting, quietly working and happy.
   Some
Are re-winding the ivy that slipped off 1680
The tips of their branches. Others, like young
   mares
Unharnessed from their painted chariots, are
   playing.
They sing—the tunes sound strange to me, but
   they
Pick them up and echo each other.
   Though they are everywhere, poor Pentheus
     sees nothing,
Not one woman. "Stranger," he says, "from where 1690
I stand I can't get a sight of these whores
Who call themselves Bacchae. Perhaps if I went
Up that slope and climbed the trunk of a pine tree
I could have a direct view of their filthy games."
And then—a miracle. There is a pine-tree there
That tickles heaven. As I watch, the stranger
Takes the topmost branch and . . .
Down . . . down . . . down he draws it towards us
Out of the sunlight, into the deep shade
Where we stand. It bends like a bow—or like 1700
A wheel, when its rim is marked out with a compass
   and traces
A full circle—that's how the stranger, with his bare
Hands, made the mountain pine curve to the
   ground—
Something no man born of woman
Could have done.
He seats Pentheus on the topmost shoots, then
   gently
Lets the trunk uncoil, from his grip, being 1710
Very careful not to shake our king from his new
   throne
Among the leaves, till it towers straight in the air
Again with Pentheus perched astride it . . . Now
It is he who is in view, rather than having
A view himself . . . He is just rising into sight
Above the surrounding trees, when the stranger
   vanishes,
And out of the air a voice comes—
My belief is—Dionysos spoke then. 1720
"Young women, I bring you this man who intends
To amuse himself with me and my deepest
   mysteries.
Punish him!"

While these words still echo in the hills
A pillar of fierce fire is planted between
Earth and heaven . . .
    The air is still now . . .
Silence.
1730 In the cloistered trees not a leaf moves,
The noises of animals cease . . .
The women, not sure what it is they've heard, stand
On tiptoe, glancing this way and that. So,
Once again, he brands the air with his voice.
This time there is no doubt. The daughters
Of Kadmos know their master, and obey.
They begin to run—they dart, they flash, like
    pigeons
In flight, his mother, Agave, all her sisters,
1740 And the rest of the women, Bacchae! Down
    through the glade,
Across the stream,
Over the rocks,
Whirled in the tempest of Dionysos' power
They rush—then they see my master sitting
On the pine-tree. First they clamber onto
A rock face opposite and try pelting him
With volleys of sharp stones and javelins made
From pine branches, while others fling
1750 Their ivy-covered sticks . . . Poor man,
He can only be a target . . . But they can't reach
    him.
Their victim is sitting too high, even for their
Terrible urgency. All the same,
He's trapped. There's nothing he can do. At last
They snap off great oak boughs—a thunderbolt
Could not do it more cleanly, and using the raw
Wood as levers they try to wrench the tree
Up by its roots—and still they can't do it.
1760 They struggle but they can't . . . they can't . . .
"Here," says Agave, "make a circle and take
Hold of the stem, my friends, and we'll catch this
    agile
Beast. He must never betray the secret of our
    dancing
For Dionysos!"
    A flurry of hands reach out to the pine tree and
    tug.
It comes clean out of the earth.
1770 Down from the height where he sits, falling, falling,
Screaming all the time till he dashes against
The rocks, comes Pentheus.
He knows his end is near, knows it will
Be hideous . . .
    His mother is first, chief priestess of the
    slaughter,
She descends on him. He rips off
The scarf around his head, hoping she'll recognize
    him,
1780 And spare him, he touches her cheeks, he says,
    "Mother,

It's your son, Pentheus, the son
You bore in the house of Echion. Mother, pity me,
Have mercy, I have sinned, but don't murder me,
Your own son, for what I've . . ."
    But she can't help herself. There's froth on her
    lips,
Her eyes are rolling, staring, her mind's gone,
She's been seized by a greater power, Dionysos,
And doesn't listen to her son. She grips   1790
His left arm, just below the elbow,
Rams her foot against the poor man's ribs,
And pulls. His arm comes away at the shoulder . . .
That strength didn't come from her—it came
From Dionysos.
    Meanwhile, Ino is gouging the other side,
Rending the flesh from his bones, while Autonoë
And the whole crowd of the Bacchae press down
On him. His shrieking—so long as there's breath
In his lungs—and their howls of triumph merge 1800
Into one great din. One woman carries
An arm, another, one of his feet, with a sandal
Still on it. His ribs are stripped of skin, the flesh
Hangs in rags. They play with it, they toss
Pieces of Pentheus from hand to bloodstained
    hand
Like a ball, until the mountain is strewn with
    fragments
Of his body—some of it under the sheer
Rock-faces, some under the green   1810
Leaves in the depths of the wood. I don't know
How you could find it all again . . .
    His mother was left holding his destroyed head.
She impaled it on a wooden spike, as if
It was some mountain lion she had caught in the
    heart
Of Kithairon, and left her sisters amongst the
    still-dancing
Women. Now, she's running this way, to the city,
Exulting in her terrible kill. She's praising   1820
Dionysos as her fellow huntsman, the one
Who helps her in the chase, the bringer of bright
Victory . . . But she'll thank him with her tears.
    I want to go. I hate suffering. I don't
Want to see Agave come home. The best
And safest thing is to keep a balance in your life,
And acknowledge the great powers around us and
    in us.
I think that is the meaning of wisdom. If you have
That, and can live that way, you really are   1830
A wise man.

(Exit.)

CHORUS: Dance him into life!
  Move like one,
  Shout like one!
  The last of the dragon is dead,
  Pentheus is dead.

He took woman's clothing,
Picked up a twig, made it live with ivy,
He trusted it—
1840 And it killed him.
And heading him into death was a bull.
Daughters of Kadmos—Bacchae—now you are
    famous.
The prize—
—and the price—
Of your victory is tears, mourning.
You won the contest at a cost—
Your hands are slippery with your child's
Flowing life.
1850   *(Looking offstage.)* Look! She's coming . . . Agave
    . . .
. . . His mother . . .
Running home . . . her eyes, look at her eyes . . .
They're staring, they're mad . . .
Take her into our midst . . . she belongs to the god
    . . .
And to his happiness.

(Enter AGAVE, *carrying the head of* PENTHEUS.)

AGAVE: Women of the cast—Bacchae . . .
CHORUS: Why do you use that word? What do you
    want?
1860 AGAVE: I'm bringing this branch with trailing leaves, I
    cut it just now in the mountains, and look—I'm
    bringing it back home—I had to hunt—but I
    tracked it down . . . and now I'm happy . . .
CHORUS: I see . . . join us . . . become one of us . . .
AGAVE: It's a lion cub. I caught it. I didn't need nets.
    You can see—look . . .
CHORUS: Where—where did it happen? Where did
    you find it?
AGAVE: Kithairon . . .
CHORUS: Kithairon?
1870 AGAVE: . . . was the killer.
CHORUS: Who struck first?
AGAVE: I struck first. I. I did it, no one else. When we
    meet in the hills, I am the one they envy—I am
    so lucky.
CHORUS: And who else?
AGAVE: Kadmos, Kadmos . . .
CHORUS: How, Kadmos . . . ?
AGAVE: Had children . . . those children were there,
    Shared the hunt—but I was first, I was first.
1880 Happy . . . chasing the beast . . . Come with me
    Now . . . to the meal . . .
CHORUS: How can we come . . . What meal?
AGAVE: It's a young bull . . . Here, on his
    Cheek, the hair is soft . . .
    Just below the crest . . . It grows . . . so sleek.
CHORUS: Yes, that hair could belong to a beast.
    It looks like an animal.
AGAVE: The hounds were whipped on by Dionysos
    . . .

He sent us hurtling after the prey . . .
He knew its ways, he knows   1890
Us all . . .
CHORUS: Yes, our prince leads the hunt.
AGAVE: You praise him?
CHORUS: I praise him.
AGAVE: Then soon all Thebes will.
CHORUS: Yes . . . and Pentheus? . . . Your son?
AGAVE: Pentheus . . . Yes, he will praise his mother
    because she caught this young wild lion.
CHORUS: But think what it is.
AGAVE: No! Think how I did it.   1900
CHORUS: You're proud?
AGAVE: I'm happy. We did great, great things—as all
    the world will see—when we hunted today.
CHORUS: Then show your trophy, poor woman, show
    it to everyone.
Let people see what you brought home from the
    day's hunting.
AGAVE: Men and women of Thebes, our city of high
    Towers, so well defended, come and see
What I brought home from the wild country for   1910
    you.—
    A beast . . . We tracked him down, we daughters
    of Kadmos.
We used no snares, no traps,
No spears forged in the workshops of Thessaly—
Only our hands we used, our soft, white,
Delicate hands—they were our spears.
And hunters boast of their machines, their useless
Contraptions of steel and wire . . . we caught this
    beast   1920
And tore it limb from limb with only our hands . . .
Where is my father? I want him here. And where
Is Pentheus, where's my son? . . .
    Go, someone, find a ladder, and lean it
Against the palace and nail this trophy against
The beam ends. I want everyone to see
What I have brought home from the hunt . . .

(Enter KADMOS, *helping* SERVANTS *to carry the body of*
PENTHEUS.)

KADMOS: This way . . . Stay close to me . . . This way
    . . .
He seems so heavy . . . like my grief—now,
Lay him down—there . . .   1930
    Pentheus has come home.
    I searched, hoping and looking, hoping and
        looking—
It was so hard to see them, scattered among the
    trees—
No two parts together, all over Kithairon . . .
Those steep paths!—I have no strength left . . .
Well, here is his body, I found it.
    I had just reached the city with Teiresias
After paying our tribute to Dionysos when   1940

I heard of the monstrous thing my daughters had
   done.
Back I went, back, back to the mountainside
To bring home my grandson—or what remained
After the women . . . What was in their minds then?
   . . .
I saw Akteon's mother in the forest,
Autonoë, and Ino with her—it was hideous . . .
Their contorted bodies, writhing, jerking . . .
Then someone told me the same driving force
1950 Had guided Agave here . . . Yes, they were right
   . . .
There she is . . . I see . . .
No, no . . . I don't want to see!
AGAVE: Father, be proud, you should be—especially
   now—
The proudest man alive. You have such daughters
No one, no one in the world, could
Surpass them . . . I speak for us all, but I have gone
Far beyond the others. I don't spin.
And weave now. I have progressed.
1960 Now I hunt—with my bare hands—wild beasts!
And look . . . the pickings of my success.
Here—for you—my newborn glory;
Hang him against your palace wall—take him,
Father—here . . . Can't you feel the joy, the glory
Of my kill too? Tell your friends to come,
To celebrate with you—because you have much
To be thankful for, much to celebrate.
Think of the great things we have done today.
KADMOS: Can I measure hurt like this . . . No, no way
1970 of . . .
I can't even look . . . The great things you've
   done—yes,
The great murders, the blood, the . . . !
Oh, fling your thanksgiving before some deity.
He'll love it!
And you tell the people they must celebrate . . .
You tell me!
Celebrate! . . . (He weeps.)
For you, my child, this is for you . . .
1980 And for me. Oh, Dionysos is right,
But he is not fair!
Being so right, he has broken us . . . But then
He was born here, this is his home . . .
AGAVE: Old men! All they do is grumble.
And they always look so grim. I wish my son
Was happy hunting. I wish he was like his mother.
She goes out and runs with the young women
Of Thebes till they track down an animal. But all
He can do is oppose the forces from which
1990 We draw life. You should speak to him, father,
You should advise him . . . Someone—go and fetch
   him.
I want him to see me in the full flood of my joy.
KADMOS (a cry is wrenched from him): You'll know—you
   must! You'll see

What you've done, and the pain will wring tears
From you . . .
And yet, if you never wake from the dream you're
   in . . .
Well, it won't be happiness—but you'll feel no pain.   2010
AGAVE: Is something wrong? Are you angry with me,
   father?
KADMOS: Look up at the sky.
AGAVE: There . . . What do you expect me to see?
KADMOS: Does it look the same to you, or do you see
A change?
AGAVE: It looks brighter than before,
Not so blurred.
KADMOS: And inside you—
Do you still feel this sense of flying?   2020
AGAVE: I don't . . .
Understand . . . Wait. Something's happening.
My head! . . . There's a change . . . somewhere
Inside, the mind shifts . . . Yes, I feel . . .
KADMOS: Listen to me.
Do you know what I'm saying? Can you answer me?
AGAVE: I've forgotten . . . What were we talking
   about,
Father?
KADMOS: When you were married, do you remember   2030
whose house you came to?
AGAVE: You . . . gave me to . . .
Didn't they say his name was . . . Echion of the
Dragon's seed?
KADMOS: And you had a son.
Your husband gave you a son. What was his name?
AGAVE: Pentheus—child of our true married love.
KADMOS: Now look at the face that lies between your
Hands. Whose is it?
AGAVE: It's a lion . . . You see . . . they . . . they told   2040
me
So—the hunters . . . the women.
KADMOS: Look! Look properly. It won't take long.
It's easy.
AGAVE (obeys, gives a shriek): What is it—this . . . thing!
I'm carrying?
Oh, dear God! What is this?
KADMOS: Open your eyes, and see. You can't mistake
The face.
AGAVE: This foul wound, this foul . . . object!   2050
I can't bear it . . . !
KADMOS: Does it look like a lion
To you?
AGAVE: No . . . It's Pentheus . . . My son . . .
Your head . . . your poor . . .
KADMOS: My tears flowed for him long before
You knew who he was.
AGAVE: Who killed him? How
Did he come here? How am I holding him?
KADMOS: You will have to hear something . . .   2060
abominable.
Perhaps you are not ready . . .

AGAVE: Tell me! I'll choke,
My heart's bursting—I *must* know!

KADMOS: You,
And your sisters with you, murdered him.

AGAVE: Where?
Where did he die? Here in the palace?

KADMOS: No.

2070 You remember where, long ago, Akteon
Was savaged by his hounds . . .

AGAVE: On Kithairon!
But why did the poor fool go there?

KADMOS: He went to jeer at Dionysos, and your
dancing
In his honour.

AGAVE: And we destroyed him . . . But what
happened?

KADMOS: You have no minds left. The whole city

2080 Was convulsed. Dionysos was in possession.

AGAVE: Dionysos took us and laid us waste. Now
I see it.

KADMOS: He was displaced. He was usurped.
You did not believe he had power.

AGAVE: Where
Is my child's body? . . . Father, I loved him . . .
Where is he?

KADMOS: I brought him home. It was hard—but I
found him.

2090 AGAVE: Are the limbs . . . is his body . . . a body . . . or
. . . ?

KADMOS: He lies there.

AGAVE: Pentheus, Pentheus—my only son—my child.

KADMOS: Yes, your son—*and* your heir . . .
Heir to your madness.

AGAVE: But how could that touch Pentheus? How
Could he inherit that from me?

KADMOS: He took
From you his stubbornness. He would not open
Himself to Dionysos—and we all suffered

2100 For his fault. In a sense, he united us,
The whole family, because now we are all, like him,
Shattered fragments.
     And I, who never had a son, only
This grandson, your boy, I'm left with nothing,
Just a carcass, a shamefully mutilated
Corpse . . . *That* was once the hope, the new
Life of my family . . . Pentheus, my child,
You were our centre, you gave us permanence,
Child of my child, and you were strict with them all

2110 In Thebes. I was an old man, but people
Took notice of me, they respected me, so long as
You were there. If they did not, you would pick out
The culprit and punish him. But now I,
Kadmos, Kadmos the great, I'll be banished—
No home, no rights—and I was the man who sowed
The seed of Thebes, and the harvest I reaped was
the greatest
Of our time. Child I loved best—

And now I can no longer say that.
There's nothing left—never again will you touch   2120
My beard, put your arm round me, and say,
"Father
Of my mother, who has hurt you, who denies you
Your rights? Come, grandfather, who troubles you,
Who is unkind to you? Tell me. If anyone
Has done you wrong I will have him whipped!"
     I have only my grief now, and you are a memory.
If anyone thinks that his own mind alone
Can govern the world, he should see Pentheus here
And believe, believe there are other powers,   2130
Ones he does not dominate.

CHORUS: I grieve for you, Kadmos. Your grandson
died for a good reason, but it hurt you.

AGAVE: Father, you see how all my daylight reason
Dawns again in me. I see, I think,
I feel, and as clearly as you,
I know that I am a murderer for my sacrifice
To Dionysos. The victim is dead; the priestess
Lives polluted.
But Pentheus is my son in my heart still,   2140
The son I gave life to and watched over. I want to
Give him one last gift.
I want to arrange his body for the grave,
Though he'll never know of it—the dead feel no
Gratitude for favours to their unfeeling limbs.

KADMOS: He was your child; I can't refuse you. Be
gentle
With his body—you were not before. I have laid
him there
As if he were asleep. Do not disturb him.   2150

AGAVE: Pentheus, my son . . .
My baby . . .
You lay in my arms so often, so helpless,
And now again you need my loving care,
My dear, dear child . . .
I killed you.
No! I will not say that. I was not there. I was . . .
I was in some other place . . .
It was Dionysos. Dionysos took me, Dionysos
Used me, and Dionysos murdered you!   2160

DIONYSOS: No! (DIONYSOS *as a god now becomes visible
above them all.*)
Accuse yourselves, accept the guilt,
You let Pentheus rule you, you were happy being
ruled,
And for his sake you locked me out of your city.
And so Thebes will have new masters,
An army from the east will live in your homes,
Walk your streets, plough your fields.
Agave—you and your sisters have no place here.   2170
Your home now is . . . wherever a murderer
Can find rest or peace—but not in Thebes.
And you—Kadmos—you must begin again. You
must
Forfeit your human shape, and become a dragon.

Your wife, daughter of the spirit of war, Harmony
Will also be transfigured—into a snake. Then,
With your bride, you'll drive in a chariot hauled
By young bulls, at the head of an army from
2180 The east. With countless men at your command
You will plunder city after city. But once they
Have wrecked the sanctuary where Apollo speaks
Of things to come—their luck will change, they
Will be defeated, and then disperse. The war-spirit,
however,
Will rescue you and Harmony, and keep you both
alive
In the world of the undying . . .
This is the universal will of Zeus and
2190 I tell you these things with authority from him. I
am
Dionysos, his son—I will always return to life.
   If you had understood what wholeness is, you
Would now be happy, the son of Zeus would be
Helping you, a friend, an ally.
But you did not want that.
KADMOS: Dionysos, listen to us, we have been wrong
. . .
DIONYSOS: Now you understand, but now is too late.
When you should have seen, you were blind.
2200 KADMOS: We know that.
But you are like a tide that turns and drowns us.
DIONYSOS: Because I was born with dominion over
you
And you dispossessed me.
KADMOS: Then you should not
Be like us, your subjects. You should have no
passions.
DIONYSOS: And I don't. But these are laws of life. I
cannot
2210 Change them.
AGAVE (weeps): It is decided, father. We must leave
And take our sorrow with us.
DIONYSOS: Why delay?
You can change nothing now. (He vanishes.)
KADMOS: My child, we have suffered cruelly, all of
us—
I did not escape . . .
I am an old man, and I must leave my home,
Go to a foreign country. And then, I am told,
2220 My destiny is to lead this strange army
Into Greece.
I shall be a dragon, my wife, a dragon; myself
And Harmony, beasts, no longer human, will bring
War to the calm altars and graves of Greece.

There will be no end to the suffering, not even in
the country
Of the dead; I am to be allowed no peace.
AGAVE: Father, I shall lose you, never see my home
again . . .
KADMOS: No, don't hold me, my poor child . . . Why? 2230
I'm old, a grey, dying swan—the young
Bird can't protect it . . .
AGAVE: Where shall I go?
I have no country. What will happen to me? . . .
KADMOS: I don't know, my daughter, your father is
weak.
He is tired, he is no use.
AGAVE: Goodbye, my home,
Goodbye, my city. I am leaving you. I have no
Place here. I am cursed. 2240
KADMOS: Go now, Agave . . .
AGAVE: Father! Come here! . . . I want to hold you . . .
KADMOS: Look, my tears . . . for you and for your
sisters.
AGAVE: In our lives Dionysos has been a spirit
Of havoc, cruel, relentless . . .
KADMOS: But only because
He was thrust aside, and no one let him in
Here. The cruelty was yours.
AGAVE: Goodbye, father . . . 2250
KADMOS: Goodbye—daughter—though what is there
good in it?
AGAVE (to PEOPLE OF THEBES): Please, my friends, will
you help me?
Take me to my sisters, who will share my exile
And the years of sorrow with me.
I want to be where Kithairon can't shadow my
life—
Where I don't even have to see its distant slopes . . .
Take me where branches wound with ivy 2260
Can't remind me of what has happened.
Let someone else be possessed.
I have withered.
CHORUS: The forces of life are seen in disguise,
A thousand disguises.
They make all things possible,
They guarantee nothing,
What you thought was forgotten, buried,
They conceive, and bring to birth again.
Today you have watched their power at work— 2270
It never ends.

CURTAIN

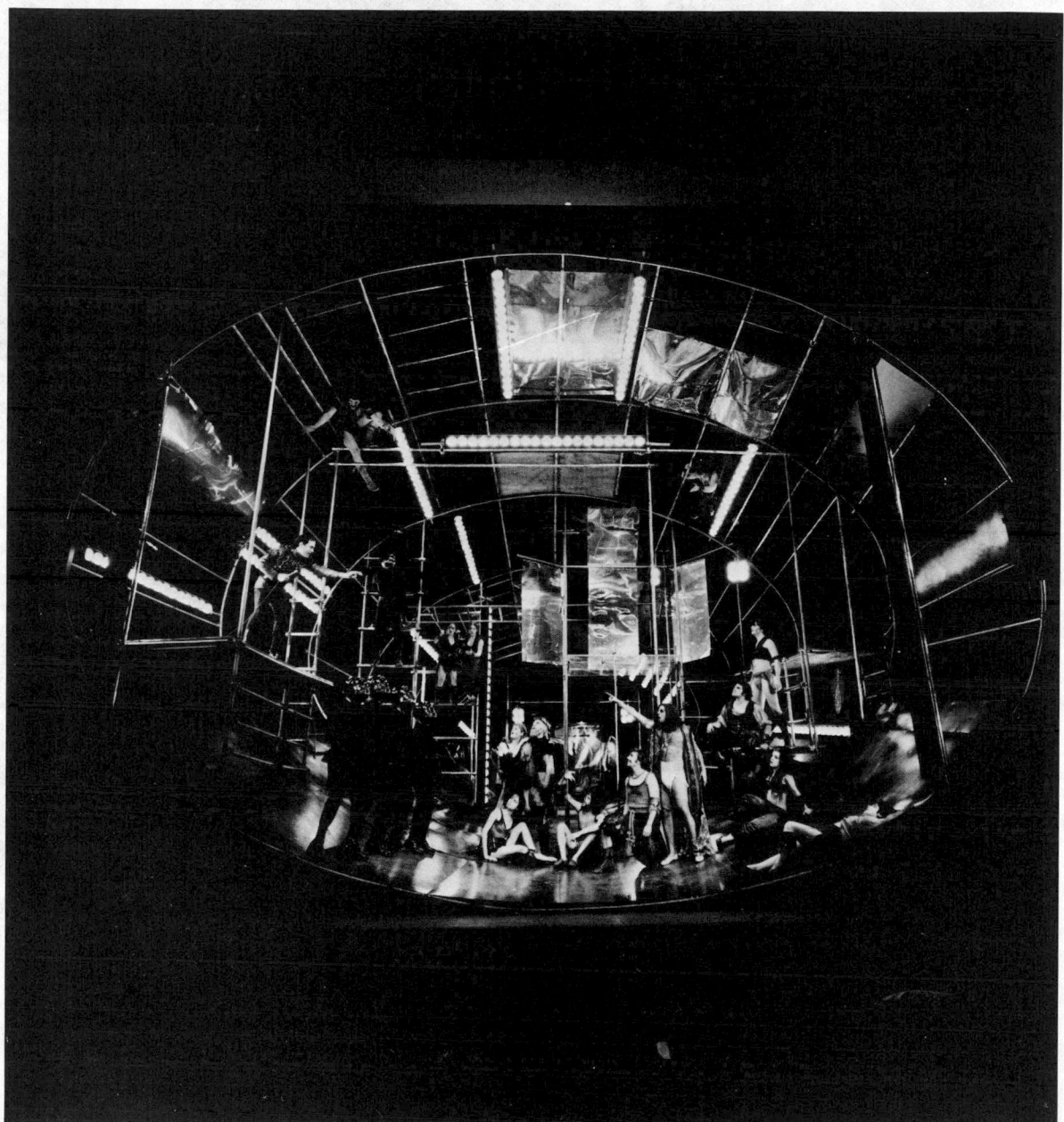

Figure 1. The ultra-modern set designed by Santo Loquasto for the Yale Repertory Theatre production of *The Bacchae*, New Haven, 1969. (Photograph: Yale Joel.)

Figure 2. Dionysos (Alvin Epstein) in the Yale Repertory Theatre production of *The Bacchae,* directed by Andre Gregory, New Haven, 1969. (Photograph: Sean Kernan.)

Staging of *The Bacchae*

REVIEW OF THE YALE REPERTORY THEATRE
PRODUCTION, 1969, BY JACK KROLL

In a disastrous week of a disastrous and dispiriting Broadway season one's anger and depression are relieved by two trips off the Great White Way. At New Haven the Yale School of Drama Repertory Theatre, embattled in recent months by tensions, confrontations and disagreements involving students, some faculty members and its brilliant dean, Robert Brustein, has nonetheless come up with a production that commands attention, that is almost exactly the right activity for a repertory theater connected with a school of drama interested in controlled and intelligent exploration of a beleaguered art.

Kenneth Cavander has written a translation of Euripides' *The Bacchae* that is strong, spare, hard, and that seeks to capture without distorting the shape of the original, resonances of language and idea that will connect the play legitimately to the present. But this production seems in every sense to be a collaboration, a collaboration in which theatrical history itself plays a part. Director Andre Gregory and Brustein have been intensely affected by the recent visit of the Living Theatre to Yale, and this production is the first serious attempt by anybody to assimilate the implications of the Living Theatre's personality, energy and ideas into what was once called the "mainstream" of the theater.

That mainstream may indeed no longer exist. And Yale's attempt under Brustein to stabilize the headlong energies of the avant-garde, to shape them into effective form without diluting their import or impact, is a task which is currently exposing him to the exacerbations of the cultural right and left—but it is certainly the right job for him to do. "The Bacchae" shows both the point and the perils of this task. Under a decisive sculptural hand from Gregory the combined professional and student cast play Euripides' drama of Dionysiac disruption with strong over-all effect and considerable fascinating detail.

Catalyzing the entire production is the remarkable set by Santo Loquasto, Yale '69. Obviously inspired by Julian Beck's wonderful design for the Living Theatre's "Frankenstein," Loquasto achieves his own success with his beautiful oval cage that structures the entire stage into levels, grades and heights that become the public places of Athens, the sequestrations of the Dionysiac forests and the hidden groins and shadows of the mind.

Euripides' play is about the explosive energy system of which human beings are the sentient parts, who forget those energies at their peril. If this description sounds mod and McLuhanesque, it is deliberately so; this "Bacchae" makes no bones about drawing parallels between the ecstatic and lethal revels of the followers of Dionysos and today's subculture of hippies and other glorious human beasts. If the parallel is sometimes too pat (the blind prophet Teiresias comes on like the Maharishi) the attempt to find dramatic shape for the historical continuum between Euripides and us is admirable—and inescapable.

The danger of this type of production is the possibility of a kind of instant academization of the energy of which the Living Theatre is the most notable example. If one questions this energy in some of its moral and esthetic implications, one must be careful not to transmute it into something not healthier but simply tamer. This production bravely confronts the dangers of transmutation and thus sets in motion a process which others must follow. The student chorus (coed) of bacchae does well, and of the professionals who play the central roles, Alvin Epstein as Dionysos—an epicene Olympian super-hoodlum with his snaky blond locks and Mick Jagger mien—and David Spielberg as the doomed Pentheus—torn apart, literally, between his drive for power and his buried passivity—are the best.

The Repertory Theatre's "Bacchae" is good entertainment; it is good spectacle; but it is not necessarily good drama. While the Euripidean tragedy involves the clash of life styles, the tension of fascination, and repulsion of the sensuous grotesque, it is also an intensely emotional human experience. Unfortunately, the present production lacks emotional force. The loss of power is due to several significant factors.

First, and most apparent are the elements of spectacle. Santo Loquasto's brilliant set, which creates a total space on the stage and is the source of numerous surprises and illusions in the play, is simply too overpowering. In the scenes in which it serves as playground equipment for the Bacchae it is most effective. The spirit of gamery and childish abandon is well served by these theatrical monkeybars. But the scenes of personal interplay between Dionysos and Pentheus, and of realization for Agave are needlessly hampered. No depth of emotion can be successfully conveyed when the actors are seen as only a small part of the gymnastic maze of the set. The human experience is minimized at those moments when it should have been most exalted and damned.

As with the set, which both aids and hinders, so too does the music and sound by Richard Peaslee function with ambivalence. When heard alone, without players, lighting and motion, the music offers the purest distillation of the play's themes and conflicts. At no other point is the union of the earthly and the heavenly presented with such lyricism and beauty as it is in Peaslee's intermission music. With some silence in the theater, the intermission can be almost mystic. But the music and sound engineering also subordinate the human voice. After a musical prelude in magnificent stereo encompassing the entire theater, the actors speak in an unavoidable monophony. They seem flat and lifeless in comparison to the rich sounds that precede them. The production fails in integrating effects which work well in isolation into a satisfactory whole. Essentially, "Bacchae" is about people; and it is the people who are drowned in the sea of swampish music and bottomless stages.

The attempt to represent the clash of modi vivendi of the Bacchae against the Thebans by using two directing styles is successful, but also runs into self-imposed difficulties. Director Andre Gregory has worked with Stanley Rosenberg to create a conflict of cultures: freedom versus rigid order, "elect" versus unchosen, hippie versus policeman. The chief failure is the performance of the chorus of revelers. Although they do, at times, convey a real evangelical ecstasy, or drug-induced euphoria, they are frequently as convincing as a group of cheerleaders at a high school football game. Too often, they seem uncomfortable with what they are doing. They offer a less than attractive temptation to a new way of life.

Alvin Epstein, as Dionysos, is the play's outstanding performer. His sinuous movements, glazed-eyed trances, and sagacious slyness make a fine leader, who overcomes the problems of his inadequate and unbelievable followers. His appearance however, is not that of Dionysos. He does look godlike, but the wrong sort. He looks too much like Verrocchio's boyish "David" to be the sly seducer; his godliness is too angelic. He is too innocent; Peter Pan offering Never Never Land.

In contrast to this Huck Finn of a seducer is David Spielberg as an avant garde-mafioso Pentheus. While he expresses wonder and innocence effectively in his delivery, Spielberg too is plagued by appearance. He appears too sinister to be a believable, naive Pentheus.

Michael Lombard (whose occasional bellows project the human voice into the realm of the resonant sounds of the music) as Teiresias, and George Bartenieff, as Kadmos, are properly ridiculous as the oldsters playing with the children.

Unfortunately, Mildred Dunnock's moving portrayal of Agave is lost in the vast scope of attention demanded by the production. For her final, crazed realization that she has killed her son the whole play should become her; the clash and conflict should be heightened by being internalized. Miss Dunnock is, in fact, the focal point on the stage during this climactic scene, but not overwhelmingly so. The set which, by its echoing of every step made on it, had magnified the frolic of the Bacchae chorus, becomes a source of cruel disruption as the audience is distracted by a chorus member shifting his position in the corner, or some other movement on the huge set. By the end of the play, the mind has been trained to view the whole stage, the whole spectacle; insufficient attempt is made to narrow this expanded consciousness for the less spectacular, but emotionally powerful climax.

In short, the present production is one of many fine individual elements that fail to work together properly. In trying to portray the clash of life styles, the styles of production themselves conflict; "Bacchae" has been trapped by the imitative fallacy. Single aspects fight for supremacy and attention; some cannot survive the struggle. "Bacchae" attempts to substitute external turmoil for internal force. In all this chaos, the play loses its humanity, the actors have been squelched. Greater emotional tension will no doubt be found in a tape recording of the performance. It is the people who are lost in the disintegrating world of the stage.

ARISTOPHANES

450–385 B.C.

The plays of Aristophanes are the only surviving examples of fifth century Greek comedy, a form of satiric drama dominated by fantasy—fantasy so outlandish that it has never been surpassed in the history of western drama. Its plot was not really a plot so much as a set of variations on a fantastic situation, a comic idea meant to solve a pressing social or political situation, such as the ingenious scheme of Lysistrata and her cohorts to force their Athenian husbands to make peace by refusing to make love to them until they end the war against Sparta. The fantasy was always designed to make clear the dramatist's satiric object, and what better way to show the absurdity of war than to stage a battle of the sexes, but a battle in the case of *Lysistrata* that threatens to end in sexual frustration instead of fulfillment. The chorus of Greek comedy was often correspondingly fantastic, consisting, for example, of clouds, or in other situations of birds, frogs, and wasps. And even when the chorus itself was not so farfetched, its actions were, as in the knock-down drag-out struggle that takes place between the chorus of old men and the chorus of old women in *Lysistrata*. The fantasy, moreover, was not confined to the play alone, but included the audience too, for the chorus always took the liberty once during each comedy to interrupt the action and deliver a harangue directly to the spectators, as in *Lysistrata* when the chorus of women implores the citizens of Athens "to hear useful words for the state."

Precedents for these extravagant dramatic elements have never been definitely established, although one likely source seems to have been a type of festive masquerade associated with fertility rites, in which participants dressed themselves in outlandish costumes and went throughout the streets, as they do now during Halloween and Mardi Gras, singing, dancing, carousing, and jesting with bystanders. So, too, the actors in Greek comedy would not have limited themselves simply to reciting their lines, but would also have performed ribald dance steps, kicking their buttocks, slapping their thighs, and possibly pummeling one another. Though ancient festivities persist in modern masquerades, ancient Greek comedy has never been matched, for later satiric dramatists have never quite escaped the bounds of ordinary experience and taken off into the free floating world of fantasy. That is the exclusive domain of Aristophanes.

In the comedy of Aristophanes, the world is turned upside down, inside out, and every other way imaginable in a satiric universe where anything is possible. In *The Birds* (414), for example, Peithetaerus, who is disgusted with life in Athens, dreams up the bright idea of creating a new and better city in the sky. Once he is able to convince the birds that they are the original gods, he then gets them to build his Utopia, which in turn enables him to suffocate all of the ruling Greek gods by denying them the smoke of sacrificial offerings. After they give into his power, he becomes ruler of the entire universe, equipped with his own set of wings and a wife whose thunderbolts, like those of Athena, enable him to keep the world justly under control. In *The Frogs* (405), Dionysus, the god whose festival is celebrated by the dramatic competitions, laments the fact that Sophocles and Euripides have recently died, for he fears that their deaths may lead to the death of drama itself. He thus travels to Hades, planning to bring back Euripides, whom he hopes will sustain the vitality of drama. But when Dionysus finally arrives in Hades, he comes upon Aeschylus and Euripides noisily quarreling with one another over who is to be ruler in the world of tragic theater, while Sophocles stands off to the side, reluctant to get involved in the squabble. Dionysus calms them by getting them to agree to a debate in which Aeschylus and Euripides are to criticize one another's tragedies, with the winner determined by Dionysus, and the prize a return to life in Athens. Aeschylus is judged the winner and so is triumphantly led back to Athens to begin again the great age of classical Greek drama. Thus, as in almost all of Aristophanes' plays, fantasy leads to wish-fulfillment and the redemption of the world.

In the process of working out such extravagant fantasies, Aristophanes rarely directs his aim at a single target, but instead scatters his satiric shots in a number of directions, picking off abuses and abusers wherever he finds them. He goes after bad government and bad rulers, bad poetry and bad poets, bad schooling and bad teachers, bad thinking and bad thinkers, freely ridiculing them all, no matter how popular, respected, or powerful they may be. Neither Socrates the philosopher, nor Euripides the dramatist, nor even Cleon the ruling demagogue of Athens escapes the attacks of Aristophanes. But the miraculous quality of his satiric fantasies is that they make it possible for him to solve all the problems of his world—by making a new one, as in *The Birds,* or by going back to an old and better one, as in *The Frogs.* Indeed, the fantasy life of Aristophanes' comedies not only solves all the problems of the world, but also satisfies all the basic desires of men and women. In the free festive air of his plays, anything goes, no matter how lewd or obscene, just as anything went in the phallic fertility rites that gave birth to his plays. Thus, in the process of working out his fantasies, Aristophanes also satisfies the sensual desires of all men and women: for food and drink and comfort and sex.

But the fantasy, no matter how joyous it may be while it is going on, must come to an end. In its ending, as in its very being, the fantasy embodies a very poignant view of experience, for it implies that only through the most fantastic flights of the imagination is it possible, as in *The Birds,* to reclaim a fallen world, and worse still, as it turns out, the new world contains some of the very same problems—the imperial motive and the military might—that made for the misery of the old one. Even when an older and better world is reclaimed, as in *The Frogs,* it necessarily incorporates the one fact of life that is inescapable—death—that even the greatest of persons and the greatest of cultures cannot avoid.

Living as he did during the decline of Athenian culture, Aristophanes could hardly ignore the fact that it was dying, for his coming of age coincided with the beginning of the Peloponnesian Wars in 431 B.C. It is not surprising that three of his eleven surviving comedies are antiwar plays: *Acharnians* (425), *Peace* (421), and *Lysistrata* (411). And two others, *The Birds* and *The Frogs,* although not directly concerned with war, nonetheless deal with the cultural wreckage it produced. *Lysistrata* is unquestionably the most powerful of his antiwar plays, for it reveals, as none of the others do, the absurdity of the war that had gone on for more than twenty years by the time the play was produced. But *Lysistrata* transcends the particular circumstances of the struggle between Athens and Sparta, for it makes a statement about war that has been true for all times; through Lysistrata's scheme, it implicitly urges the audience to make love not war.

Because it makes that plea more boldly than any other antiwar play ever written, *Lysistrata* has been staged more often during the twentieth century than any of Aristophanes' other comedies. But most productions shy away from going all the way back to the theatrical conventions of his times. The large leather phalluses that were worn by the male characters to ridicule their sexual frustration rarely turn up in a modern production. More often, the costuming, stage business, and style of performance are updated, as they were in the Phoenix Theater production (see Figures 1, 2, and 3), where the men wore fig leaves instead, and the women tried to tantalize them with jewelled brassieres. That production, judging from comments of the reviewers, was dominated by raucous activity and risqué routines without actually achieving the sustained sexual fantasy of Aristophanes. However entertaining such productions may be, they lack the nerve that prevailed in the fifth century theater of Aristophanes, and in that respect they are haunting reminders of a similar loss of nerve that took place in Greek comedy after the defeat of Athens in 404 B.C. Although Aristophanes lived on for twenty more years, he gradually turned away from bawdy topical satire to tamer kinds of social comedy, which in turn gave rise to the comedy of Athenian manners that flourished in fourth century Greece and was subsequently imitated in third century Rome by Plautus. When Athens fell so did comedy, and neither Athens nor comedy has ever been quite the same.

LYSISTRATA

BY ARISTOPHANES / TRANSLATED BY WHITNEY OATES AND CHARLES T. MURPHY

CHARACTERS

LYSISTRATA, *an Athenian woman*
CALONICE, *an Athenian woman*
MYRRHINE, *an Athenian woman*
LAMPITO, *a Spartan woman*
LEADER OF CHORUS OF OLD MEN
CHORUS OF OLD MEN
LEADER OF CHORUS OF OLD WOMEN
CHORUS OF OLD WOMEN
ATHENIAN MAGISTRATE
THREE ATHENIAN WOMEN
CINESIAS, *an Athenian, husband of Myrrhine*
SPARTAN HERALD

SPARTAN AMBASSADORS
ATHENIAN AMBASSADORS
TWO ATHENIAN CITIZENS
CHORUS OF ATHENIANS
CHORUS OF SPARTANS

SCENE

In Athens, beneath the Acropolis. In the center of the stage is the propylaea, or gate-way to the Acropolis; to one side is a small grotto, sacred to Pan. The orchestra represents a slope leading up to the gate-way. It is early in the morning. Lysistrata is pacing impatiently up and down.

LYSISTRATA: If they'd been summoned to worship the God of Wine, or Pan, or to visit the Queen of Love, why, you couldn't have pushed your way through the streets for all the timbrels. But now there's not a single woman here—except my neighbour; here she comes.

(Enter CALONICE)

Good day to you, Calonice.

CALONICE: And to you, Lysistrata. *(Noticing LYSISTRATA's impatient air.)* But what ails you? Don't scowl, my dear; it's not becoming to you to knit your brows like that.

LYSISTRATA *(sadly)*: Ah, Calonice, my heart aches; I'm so annoyed at us women. For among men we have a reputation for sly trickery—

CALONICE: And rightly too, on my word!

LYSISTRATA: —but when they were told to meet here to consider a matter of no small importance, they lie abed and don't come.

CALONICE: Oh, they'll come all right, my dear. It's not easy for a woman to get out, you know. One is working on her husband, another is getting up the maid, another has to put the baby to bed, or wash and feed it.

LYSISTRATA: But after all, there are other matters more important than all that.

CALONICE: My dear Lysistrata, just what is this matter you've summoned us women to consider! What's up? Something big?

LYSISTRATA: Very big.

CALONICE *(interested)*: Is it stout, too?

LYSISTRATA *(smiling)*: Yes indeed—both big and stout.

CALONICE: What? And the women still haven't come?

LYSISTRATA: It's not what you suppose; they'd have come soon enough for *that*. But I've worked up something, and for many a sleepless night I've turned it this way and that.

CALONICE *(in mock disappointment)*: Oh, I guess it's pretty fine and slender, if you've turned it this way and that.

LYSISTRATA: So fine that the safety of the whole of Greece lies in us women.

CALONICE: In us women? It depends on a very slender reed then.

LYSISTRATA: Our country's fortunes are in our hands; and whether the Spartans shall perish—

CALONICE: Good! Let them perish, by all means.

LYSISTRATA: —and the Boeotians shall be completely annihilated.

CALONICE: Not completely! Please spare the eels.

LYSISTRATA: As for Athens, I won't use any such unpleasant words. But you understand what I mean. But if the women will meet here—the Spartans, the Boeotians, and we Athenians—then all together we will save Greece.

CALONICE: But what could women do that's clever or distinguished? We just sit around all dolled up in silk robes, looking pretty in our sheer gowns and evening slippers.

LYSISTRATA: These are just the things I hope will save us; these silk robes, perfumes, evening slippers, rouge, and our chiffon blouses.

CALONICE: How so?

LYSISTRATA: So never a man alive will lift a spear against the foe—

CALONICE: I'll get a silk gown at once.

LYSISTRATA: —or take up his shield—

CALONICE: I'll put on my sheerest gown!

LYSISTRATA: —or sword.

CALONICE: I'll buy a pair of evening slippers.

70 LYSISTRATA: Well then, shouldn't the women have come?

CALONICE: Come? Why, they should have *flown* here.

LYSISTRATA: Well, my dear, just watch: they'll act in true Athenian fashion—everything too late! And now there's not a woman here from the shore or from Salamis.

CALONICE: They're coming, I'm sure; at daybreak they were laying—to their oars to cross the straits.

80 LYSISTRATA: And those I expected would be the first to come—the women of Acharnae—they haven't arrived.

CALONICE: Yet the wife of Theagenes means to come; she consulted Hecate about it. *(Seeing a group of women approaching.)* But look! Here come a few. And there are some more over here. Hurrah! Where do they come from?

LYSISTRATA: From Anagyra.

CALONICE: Yes indeed! We've raised up quite a stink
90 from Anagyra anyway.

(Enter MYRRHINE in haste, followed by several other women.)

MYRRHINE *(breathlessly)*: Have we come in time, Lysistrata? What do you say? Why so quiet?

LYSISTRATA: I can't say much for you, Myrrhine, coming at this hour on such important business.

MYRRHINE: Why, I had trouble finding my girdle in the dark. But if it's so important, we're here now; tell us.

LYSISTRATA: No. Let's wait a little for the women from Boeotia and the Peloponnesus.

100 MYRRHINE: That's a much better suggestion. Look! Here comes Lampito now.

(Enter LAMPITO with two other women.)

LYSISTRATA: Greetings, my dear Spartan friend. How pretty you look, my dear. What a smooth complexion and well-developed figure! You could throttle an ox.

LAMPITO: Faith, yes, I think I could. I take exercises and kick my heels against my bum. *(She demonstrates with a few steps of the Spartan "bottom-kicking" dance.)*

110 LYSISTRATA: And what splendid breasts you have.

LAMPITO: La! You handle me like a prize steer.

LYSISTRATA: And who is this young lady with you?

LAMPITO: Faith, she's an Ambassadress from Boeotia.

LYSISTRATA: Oh yes, a Boeotian, and blooming like a garden too.

CALONICE *(lifting up her skirt)*: My word! How neatly her garden's weeded!

LYSISTRATA: And who is the other girl?

LAMPITO: Oh, she's a Corinthian swell.

MYRRHINE *(after a rapid examination)*: Yes indeed. She 120 swells very nicely *(pointing)* here and here.

LAMPITO: Who has gathered together this company of women?

LYSISTRATA: I have.

LAMPITO: Speak up, then. What do you want?

MYRRHINE: Yes, my dear, tell us what this important matter is.

LYSISTRATA: Very well, I'll tell you. But before I speak, let me ask you a little question.

MYRRHINE: Anything you like. 130

LYSISTRATA *(earnestly)*: Tell me: don't you yearn for the fathers of your children, who are away at the wars? I know you all have husbands abroad.

CALONICE: Why, yes; mercy me! my husband's been away for five months in Thrace keeping guard on—Eucrates.

MYRRHINE: And mine for seven whole months in Pylus.

LAMPITO: And mine, as soon as ever he returns from the fray, readjusts his shield and flies out of the 140 house again.

LYSISTRATA: And as for lovers, there's not even a ghost of one left. Since the Milesians revolted from us, I've not even seen an eight-inch dingus to be a leather consolation for us widows. Are you willing, if I can find a way, to help me end the war?

MYRRHINE: Goodness, yes! I'd do it, even if I had to pawn my dress and—get drunk on the spot!

CALONICE: And I, even if I had to let myself be split in 150 two like a flounder.

LAMPITO: I'd climb up Mt. Taygetus if I could catch a glimpse of peace.

LYSISTRATA: I'll tell you, then, in plain and simple words. My friends, if we are going to force our men to make peace, we must do without—

MYRRHINE: Without what? Tell us.

LYSISTRATA: Will you do it?

MYRRHINE: We'll do it, if it kills us.

LYSISTRATA: Well then, we must do without sex al- 160 together. *(General consternation.)* Why do you turn away? Where go you? Why turn so pale? Why those tears? Will you do it or not? What means this hesitation?

MYRRHINE: I won't do it! Let the war go on.

CALONICE: Nor I! Let the war go on.

LYSISTRATA: So, my little flounder? Didn't you say just now you'd split yourself in half?

CALONICE: Anything else you like. I'm willing, even if I have to walk through fire. Anything rather 170 than sex. There's nothing like it, my dear.

LYSISTRATA *(to MYRRHINE)*: What about you?

MYRRHINE *(sullenly)*: I'm willing to walk through fire, too.

LYSISTRATA: Oh vile and cursed breed! No wonder

they make tragedies about us: we're naught but "love-affairs and bassinets." But you, my dear Spartan friend, if you alone are with me, our enterprise might yet succeed. Will you vote with me?

180

LAMPITO: 'Tis cruel hard, by my faith, for a woman to sleep alone without her nooky; but for all that, we certainly do need peace.

LYSISTRATA: O my dearest friend! You're the only real woman here.

CALONICE (wavering): Well, if we do refrain from— (shuddering) what you say (God forbid!), would that bring peace?

190

LYSISTRATA: My goodness, yes! If we sit at home all rouged and powdered, dressed in our sheerest gowns, and neatly depilated, our men will get excited and want to take us; but if you don't come to them and keep away, they'll soon make a truce.

LAMPITO: Aye; Menelaus caught sight of Helen's naked breast and dropped his sword, they say.

CALONICE: What if the men give us up?

LYSISTRATA: "Flay a skinned dog," as Pherecrates says.

200

CALONICE: Rubbish! These make-shifts are not good. But suppose they grab us and drag us into the bedroom?

LYSISTRATA: Hold on to the door.

CALONICE: And if they beat us?

LYSISTRATA: Give in with a bad grace. There's no pleasure in it for them when they have to use violence. And you must torment them in every possible way. They'll give up soon enough; a man gets no joy if he doesn't get along with his wife.

210

MYRRHINE: If this is your opinion, we agree.

LAMPITO: As for our men, we can persuade them to make a just and fair peace; but what about the Athenian rabble? Who will persuade them not to start any more monkey-shines?

LYSISTRATA: Don't worry. We guarantee to convince them.

LAMPITO: Not while their ships are rigged so well and they have that mighty treasure in the temple of Athene.

220

LYSISTRATA: We've taken good care for that too: we shall seize the Acropolis today. The older women have orders to do this, and while we are making our arrangements, they are to pretend to make a sacrifice and occupy the Acropolis.

LAMPITO: All will be well then. That's a very fine idea.

LYSISTRATA: Let's ratify this, Lampito, with the most solemn oath.

LAMPITO: Tell us what oath we shall swear.

230

LYSISTRARA: Well said. Where's our Policewoman? (to a Scythian slave) What are you gaping at? Set a shield upside-down here in front of me, and give me the sacred meats.

CALONICE: Lysistrata, what sort of an oath are we to take?

LYSISTRATA: What oath? I'm going to slaughter a sheep over the shield, as they do in Aeschylus.

CALONICE: Don't, Lysistrata! No oaths about peace over a shield.

LYSISTRATA: What shall the oath be, then?

240

CALONICE: How about getting a white horse somewhere and cutting out its entrails for the sacrifice?

LYSISTRATA: White horse indeed!

CALONICE: Well then, how shall we swear?

MYRRHINE: I'll tell you: let's place a large black bowl upside-down and then slaughter—a flask of Thasian wine. And then let's swear—not to pour in a single drop of water.

LAMPITO: Lord! How I like that oath!

250

LYSISTRATA: Someone bring out a bowl and a flask.

(A slave brings the utensils for the sacrifice.)

CALONICE: Look, my friends! What a big jar! Here's a cup that 'twould give me joy to handle. (She picks up the bowl.)

LYSISTRATA: Set it down and put your hands on our victim. (As CALONICE places her hands on the flask.) O Lady of Persuasion and dear Loving Cup, graciously vouchsafe to receive this sacrifice from us women. (She pours the wine into the bowl.)

260

CALONICE: The blood has a good colour and spurts out nicely.

LAMPITO: Faith, it has a pleasant smell, too.

MYRRHINE: Oh, let me be the first to swear, ladies!

CALONICE: No, by our Lady! Not unless you're allotted the first turn.

LYSISTRATA: Place all your hands on the cup, and one of you repeat on behalf of all what I say. Then all will swear and ratify the oath. I will suffer no man, be he husband or lover,

270

CALONICE: I will suffer no man, be he husband or lover,

LYSISTRATA: To approach me all hot and horny. (As CALONICE hesitates.) Say it!

CALONICE (slowly and painfully): To approach me all hot and horny. O Lysistrata, I feel so weak in the knees!

LYSISTRATA: I will remain at home unmated,

CALONICE: I will remain at home unmated,

LYSISTRATA: Wearing my sheerest gown and carefully adorned,

280

CALONICE: Wearing my sheerest gown and carefully adorned,

LYSISTRATA: That my husband may burn with desire for me,

CALONICE: That my husband may burn with desire for me,

LYSISTRATA: And if he takes me by force against my will,

CALONICE: *And if he takes me by force against my will,*
LYSISTRATA: *I shall do it badly and keep from moving.*
CALONICE: *I shall do it badly and keep from moving.*
LYSISTRATA: *I will not stretch my slippers toward the*
290   *ceiling,*
CALONICE: *I will not stretch my slippers toward the ceiling,*
LYSISTRATA: *Nor will I take the posture of the lioness on the knife-handle.*
CALONICE: *Nor will I take the posture of the lioness on the knife-handle,*
LYSISTRATA: *If I keep this oath, may I be permitted to drink from this cup,*
CALONICE: *If I keep this oath, may I be permitted to drink from this cup,*
300 LYSISTRATA: *But if I break it, may the cup be filled with water.*
CALONICE: *But if I break it, may the cup be filled with water.*
LYSISTRATA: Do you all swear to this?
ALL: I do, so help me!
LYSISTRATA: Come then, I'll just consummate this offering.

(*She takes a long drink from the cup.*)

CALONICE (*snatching the cup away*): Shares, my dear! Let's drink to our continued friendship.

(*A shout is heard from off-stage.*)

310 LAMPITO: What's that shouting?
LYSISTRATA: That's what I was telling you: the women have just seized the Acropolis. Now, Lampito, go home and arrange matters in Sparta; and leave these two ladies here as hostages. We'll enter the Acropolis to join our friends and help them lock the gates.
CALONICE: Don't you suppose the men will come to attack us?
LYSISTRATA: Don't worry about them. Neither threats
320 nor fire will suffice to open the gates, except on the terms we've stated.
CALONICE: I should say not! Else we'd belie our reputation as unmanageable pests.

(LAMPITO *leaves the stage. The other women retire and enter the Acropolis through the Propylaea. Enter the* CHORUS OF OLD MEN, *carrying fire-pots and a load of heavy sticks.*)

LEADER OF MEN: Onward, Draces, step by step, though your shoulder's aching.
    Cursèd logs of olive-wood, what a load you're making!
FIRST SEMI-CHORUS OF OLD MEN (*singing*)
    Aye, many surprises await a man who lives to a ripe
330   old age;
    For who could suppose, Strymodorus my lad, that

the women we've nourished (alas!),
Who sat at home to vex our days,
Would seize the holy image here,
And occupy this sacred shrine,
With bolts and bars, with fell design,
To lock the Propylaea?
LEADER OF MEN: Come with speed, Philourgus, come! to the temple hast'ning.
    There we'll heap these logs about in a circle round 340
    them,
    And whoever has conspired, raising this rebellion,
    Shall be roasted, scorched, and burnt, all without exception,
    Doomed by one unanimous vote—but first the wife of Lycon.
SECOND SEMI-CHORUS (*singing*):
    No, no! by Demeter, while I'm alive, no woman shall mock at me.
    Not even the Spartan Cleomenes, our citadel first 350 to seize,
    Got off unscathed; for all his pride
    And haughty Spartan arrogance;
    He left his arms and sneaked away,
    Stripped to his shirt, unkempt, unshav'd,
With six years' filth still on him.
LEADER OF MEN: I besieged that hero bold, sleeping at my station,
    Marshalled at these holy gates sixteen deep against him. 360
    Shall I not these cursèd pests punish for their daring,
    Burning these Euripides-and-God-detested women?
    Aye! or else may Marathon overturn my trophy.
FIRST SEMI-CHORUS (*singing*): There remains of my road
    Just this brow of the hill;
    There I speed on my way.
    Drag the logs up the hill, though we've got no ass to 370 help.
    (God! my shoulder's bruised and sore!)
    Onward still must we go.
    Blow the fire! Don't let it go out
Now we're near the end of our road.
ALL (*blowing on the fire-pots*): Whew! Whew! Drat the smoke!
SECOND SEMI-CHORUS (*singing*): Lord, what smoke rushing forth
    From the pot, like a dog 380
    Running mad, bites my eyes!
    This must be Lemnos-fire. What a sharp and stinging smoke!
    Rushing onward to the shrine
    Aid the gods. Once for all
    Show your mettle, Laches my boy!
    To the rescue hastening all!

ALL (*blowing on the fire-pots*): Whew! Whew! Drat the smoke!

(*The* CHORUS *has now reached the edge of the Orchestra nearest the stage, in front of the propylaea. They begin laying their logs and fire-pots on the ground.*)

390 LEADER OF MEN: Thank heaven, this fire is still alive. Now let's first put down these logs here and place our torches in the pots to catch; then let's make a rush for the gates with a battering-ram. If the women don't unbar the gate at our summons, we'll have to smoke them out.

Let me put down my load. Ouch! That hurts! (*to the audience*) Would any of the generals in Samos like to lend a hand with this log? (*Throwing down a log.*) Well, *that* won't break my back

400 any more, at any rate. (*Turning to his fire-pot.*) Your job, my little pot, is to keep those coals alive and furnish me shortly with a red-hot torch.

O mistress Victory, be my ally and grant me to rout these audacious women in the Acropolis.

(*While the* MEN *are busy with their logs and fires, the* CHORUS OF OLD WOMEN *enters, carrying pitchers of water.*)

LEADER OF WOMEN: What's this I see? Smoke and flames? Is that a fire ablazing?

Let's rush upon them. Hurry up! They'll find us women ready.

FIRST SEMI-CHORUS OF OLD WOMEN (*singing*):

410 With wingèd foot onward I fly,
Ere the flames consume Neodice;
Lest Critylla be overwhelmed
By a lawless, accurst herd of old men.
I shudder with fear. Am I too late to aid them?
At break of the day filled we our jars with water
Fresh from the spring, pushing our way straight
   through the crowds.
Oh, what a din!
Mid crockery crashing, jostled by slave-girls,

420 Sped we to save them, aiding our neighbours,
Bearing this water to put out the flames.

SECOND SEMI-CHORUS OF OLD WOMEN (*singing*):

Such news I've heard; doddering fools
Come with logs, like furnace-attendants,
Loaded down with three hundred pounds,
Breathing many a vain, blustering threat,
That all these abhorred sluts will be burnt to
  charcoal.
O goddess, I pray never may they be kindled;

430 Grant them to save Greece and our men, madness
  and war help them to end.
With this as our purpose, golden-plumed
  Maiden,
Guardian of Athens, seized we thy precinct.
Be my ally, Warrior-maiden,
'Gainst these old men, bearing water with me.

(*The* WOMEN *have now reached their position in the Orchestra, and their* LEADER *advances toward the* LEADER OF THE MEN.)

LEADER OF WOMEN: Hold on there! What's this, you utter scoundrels? No decent, God-fearing citizens would act like this.

LEADER OF MEN: Oho! Here's something unexpected: 440 a swarm of women have come out to attack us.

LEADER OF WOMEN: What, do we frighten you? Surely you don't think we're too many for you. And yet there are ten thousand times more of us whom you haven't even seen.

LEADER OF MEN: What say, Phaedria? Shall we let these women wag their tongues? Shan't we take our sticks and break them over their backs?

LEADER OF WOMEN: Let's set our pitchers on the ground; then if anyone lays a hand on us, they 450 won't get in our way.

LEADER OF MEN: By God! If someone gave them two or three smacks on the jaw, like Bupalus, they wouldn't talk so much!

LEADER OF WOMEN: Go on, hit me, somebody! Here's my jaw! But no other bitch will bite a piece out of you before me.

LEADER OF MEN: Silence! or I'll knock out your—senility!

LEADER OF WOMEN: Just lay one finger on Stratyllis, I 460 dare you!

LEADER OF MEN: Suppose I dust you off with this fist? What will you do?

LEADER OF WOMEN: I'll tear the living guts out of you with my teeth.

LEADER OF MEN: No poet is more clever than Euripides: "There is no beast so shameless as a woman."

LEADER OF WOMEN: Let's pick up our jars of water, Rhodippe. 470

LEADER OF MEN: Why have you come here with water, you detestable slut?

LEADER OF WOMEN: And why have you come with fire, you funeral vault? To cremate yourself?

LEADER OF MEN: To light a fire and singe your friends.

LEADER OF WOMEN: And I've brought water to put out your fire.

LEADER OF MEN: What? You'll put out my fire?

LEADER OF WOMEN: Just try and see! 480

LEADER OF MEN: I wonder: shall I scorch you with this torch of mine?

LEADER OF WOMEN: If you've got any soap, I'll give you a bath.

LEADER OF MEN: Give *me* a bath, you stinking hag?

LEADER OF WOMEN: Yes—a bridal bath!

LEADER OF MEN: Just listen to her! What crust!

LEADER OF WOMEN: Well, I'm a free citizen.

LEADER OF MEN: I'll put an end to your brawl·ng.

(The MEN *pick up their torches.)*

490 LEADER OF WOMEN: You'll never do jury-duty again.

(The WOMEN *pick up their pitchers.)*

LEADER OF MEN: Singe her hair for her!
LEADER OF WOMEN: Do your duty, water!

(The WOMEN *empty their pitchers on the* MEN.)

LEADER OF MEN: Ow! Ow! For heaven's sake!
LEADER OF WOMEN: Is it too hot?
LEADER OF MEN: What do you mean "hot"? Stop!
What are you doing?
LEADER OF WOMEN: I'm watering you, so you'll be
fresh and green.
LEADER OF MEN: But I'm all withered up with shaking.
500 LEADER OF WOMEN: Well, you've got a fire; why don't
you dry yourself?

(Enter an ATHENIAN MAGISTRATE, *accompanied by*
FOUR SCYTHIAN POLICEMEN.)

MAGISTRATE: Have these wanton women flared up
again with their timbrels and their continual
worship of Sabazius? Is this another Adonis-
dirge upon the roof-tops—which we heard not
long ago in the Assembly? That confounded
Demostratus was urging us to sail to Sicily, and
the whirling women shouted, "Woe for Adonis!"
And then Demostratus said we'd best enroll the
510 infantry from Zacynthus, and a tipsy woman on
the roof shrieked, "Beat your breasts for
Adonis!" And that vile and filthy lunatic forced
his measure through. Such license do our
women take.
LEADER OF MEN: What if you heard of the insolence of
these women here? Besides their other violent
acts, they threw water all over us, and we have to
shake out our clothes just as if we'd leaked in
them.
520 MAGISTRATE: And rightly, too, by God! For we ourselves lead the women astray and teach them to
play the wanton; from these roots such notions
blossom forth. A man goes into the jeweler's
shop and says, "About that necklace you made
for my wife, goldsmith: last night, while she was
dancing, the fastening-bolt slipped out of the
hole. I have to sail over to Salamis today; if
you're free, do come around tonight and fit in a
new bolt for her." Another goes to the shoe-
530 maker, a strapping young fellow with manly
parts, and says, "See here, cobbler, the sandal-
strap chafes my wife's little—toe; it's so tender.
Come around during the siesta and stretch it a
little, so she'll be more comfortable." Now we see
the results of such treatment: here I'm a special
Councillor and need money to procure oars for
the galleys; and I'm locked out of the Treasury
by these women.
    But this is no time to stand around. Bring up
crow-bars there! I'll put an end to their insol- 540
ence *(to one of the policemen.)* What are you gaping at, you wretch! What are you staring at? Got
an eye out for a tavern, eh? Set your crow-bars
here to the gates and force them open. *(Retiring
to a safe distance)* I'll help from over here.

(The gates are thrown open and LYSISTRATA *comes out
followed by several other* WOMEN.)

LYSISTRATA: Don't force the gates; I'm coming out of
my own accord. We don't need crow-bars here.
What we need is good sound common-sense.
MAGISTRATE: Is that so, you strumpet? Where's my
policeman? Officer, arrest her and tie her arms 550
behind her back.
LYSISTRATA: By Artemis, if he lays a finger on me,
he'll pay for it, even if he is a public servant.

(The POLICEMAN *retires in terror.)*

MAGISTRATE: You there, are you afraid? Seize her
round the waist—and you, too. Tie her up, both
of you!
FIRST WOMAN *(as the* SECOND POLICEMAN *approaches*
LYSISTRATA): By Pandrosus, if you but touch her
with your hand, I'll kick the stuffings out of you.

(The SECOND POLICEMAN *retires in terror.)*

MAGISTRATE: Just listen to that: "kick the stuffings 560
out." Where's another policeman? Tie *her* up
first, for her chatter.
SECOND WOMAN: By the Goddess of the Light, if you
lay the tip of your finger on her, you'll soon need
a doctor.

(The THIRD POLICEMAN *retires in terror.)*

MAGISTRATE: What's this? Where's my policeman?
Seize *her* too. I'll soon stop your sallies.
THIRD WOMAN: By the Goddess of Tauros, if you go
near her, I'll tear out your hair until it shrieks
with pain. 570

(The FOURTH POLICEMAN *retires in terror.)*

MAGISTRATE: Oh, damn it all! I've run out of policemen. But women must never defeat us. Officers,
let's charge them all together. Close up your
ranks!

(The POLICEMEN *rally for a mass attack.)*

LYSISTRATA: By heaven, you'll soon find out that we
have four companies of warrior-women, all fully
equipped within!
MAGISTRATE *(advancing)*: Twist their arms off, men!
LYSISTRATA *(shouting)*: To the rescue, my valiant
women! 580

O sellers-of-barley-green-stuffs-and-eggs,
O sellers-of-garlic, ye keepers-of-taverns, and
    vendors-of-bread,
    Grapple! Smite! Smash!
Won't you heap filth on them? Give them a
    tongue-lashing!

(The WOMEN *beat off the* POLICEMEN.)

Halt! Withdraw! No looting on the field.

MAGISTRATE: Damn it! My police-force has put up a
    very poor show.

590 LYSISTRATA: What did you expect? Did you think you
    were attacking slaves?
    Didn't you know that women are filled with pas-
    sion?

MAGISTRATE: Aye, passion enough—for a good
    strong drink!

LEADER OF MEN: O chief and leader of this land, why
    spend your words in vain?
    Don't argue with these shameless beasts. You know
    not how we've fared:

600 A soapless bath they've given us; our clothes are
    soundly soaked.

LEADER OF WOMEN: Poor fool! You never should at-
    tack or strike a peaceful girl.
    But if you do, your eyes must swell. For I am quite
    content
    To sit unmoved, like modest maids, in peace and
    cause no pain;
    But let a man stir up my hive, he'll find me like a
    wasp.

610 CHORUS OF MEN (*singing*):
    O God, whatever shall we do with creatures like
        Womankind?
    This can't be endured by any man alive. Question
        them!
    Let us try to find out what this means.
    To what end have they seized on this shrine,
        This steep and rugged, high and holy,
        Undefiled Acropolis?

LEADER OF MEN: Come, put your questions; don't give
620 in, and probe her every statement.
    For base and shameful it would be to leave this
    plot untested.

MAGISTRATE: Well then, first of all I wish to ask her
    this: for what purpose have you barred us from
    the Acropolis?

LYSISTRATA: To keep the treasure safe, so you won't
    make war on account of it.

MAGISTRATE: What? Do we make war on account of
    the treasure?

630 LYSISTRATA: Yes, and you cause all our other troubles
    for it, too. Peisander and those greedy office-
    seekers keep things stirred up so they can find
    occasions to steal. Now let them do what they
    like: they'll never again make off with any of this
    money.

MAGISTRATE: What will you do?

LYSISTRATA: What a question! We'll administer it
    ourselves.

MAGISTRATE: *You* will administer the treasure?

LYSISTRATA: What's so strange in that? Don't we ad-   640
    minister the household money for you?

MAGISTRATE: That's different.

LYSISTRATA: How is it different?

MAGISTRATE: We've got to make war with this money.

LYSISTRATA: But that's the very first thing: you
    mustn't make war.

MAGISTRATE: How else can we be saved?

LYSISTRATA: We'll save you.

MAGISTRATE: *You?*

LYSISTRATA: Yes, we!   650

MAGISTRATE: God forbid!

LYSISTRATA: We'll save you, whether you want it or
    not.

MAGISTRATE: Oh! This is terrible!

LYSISTRATA: You don't like it, but we're going to do it
    none the less.

MAGISTRATE: Good God! it's illegal!

LYSISTRATA: We *will* save you, my little man!

MAGISTRATE: Suppose I don't want you to?

LYSISTRATA: That's all the more reason.   660

MAGISTRATE: What business have you with war and
    peace?

LYSISTRATA: I'll explain.

MAGISTRATE (*shaking his fist*): Speak up, or you'll
    smart for it.

LYSISTRATA: Just listen, and try to keep your hands
    still.

MAGISTRATE: I can't. I'm so mad I can't stop them.

FIRST WOMAN: Then you'll be the one to smart for it.

MAGISTRATE: Croak to yourself, old hag! (*to* LYSIS-   670
    TRATA) Now then, speak up.

LYSISTRATA: Very well. Formerly we endured the war
    for a good long time with our usual restraint, no
    matter what you men did. You wouldn't let us
    say "boo," although nothing you did suited us.
    But we watched you well, and though we stayed
    at home we'd often hear of some terribly stupid
    measure you'd proposed. Then, though grieving
    at heart, we'd smile sweetly and say, "What was
    passed in the Assembly today about writing on   680
    the treaty-stone?" "What's that to you?" my hus-
    band would say. "Hold your tongue!" And I held
    my tongue.

FIRST WOMAN: But I wouldn't have—not I!

MAGISTRATE: You'd have been soundly smacked, if
    you hadn't kept still.

LYSISTRATA: So I kept still at home. Then we'd hear
    of some plan still worse than the first; we'd say,
    "Husband, how could you pass such a stupid
    proposal!" He'd scowl at me and say, "If you   690
    don't mind your spinning, your head will be sore
    for weeks. *War shall be the concern of men.*"

MAGISTRATE: And he was right, upon my word!

LYSISTRATA: Why right, you confounded fool, when

your proposals were so stupid and we weren't allowed to make any suggestions?

"There's not a *man* left in the country," says one. "No, not one," says another. Therefore all we women have decided in council to make a common effort to save Greece. How long should we have waited? Now, if you're willing to listen to our excellent proposals and keep silence for us in your turn, we still may save you.

MAGISTRATE: We men keep silence for you? That's terrible; I won't endure it!

LYSISTRATA: Silence!

MAGISTRATE: Silence for *you,* you wench, when you're wearing a snood? I'd rather die!

LYSISTRATA: Well, if that's all that bothers you—here! Take my snood and tie it round your head. *(During the following words the* WOMEN *dress up the* MAGISTRATE *in women's garments.)* And *now* keep quiet! Here, take this spinning-basket, too, and card your wool with robes tucked up, munching on beans. *War shall be the concern of Women!*

LEADER OF WOMEN: Arise and leave your pitchers, girls; no time is this to falter.

We too must aid our loyal friends; our turn has come for action.

CHORUS OF WOMEN *(singing):*
I'll never tire of aiding them with song and dance; never may
Faintness keep my legs from moving to and fro endlessly.
For I yearn to do all for my friends;
They have charm, they have wit, they have grace,
With courage, brains, and best of virtues—
Patriotic sapience.

LEADER OF WOMEN: Come, child of manliest ancient dames, offspring of stinging nettles,
Advance with rage unsoftened; for fair breezes speed you onward.

LYSISTRATA: If only sweet Eros and the Cyprian Queen of Love shed charm over our breasts and limbs and inspire our men with amorous longing and priapic spasms, I think we may soon be called Peacemakers among the Greeks.

MAGISTRATE: What will you do?

LYSISTRATA: First of all, we'll stop those fellows who run madly about the Marketplace in arms.

FIRST WOMAN: Indeed we shall, by the Queen of Paphos.

LYSISTRATA: For now they roam about the market, amid the pots and greenstuffs, armed to the teeth like Corybantes.

MAGISTRATE: That's what manly fellows ought to do!

LYSISTRATA: But it's so silly: a chap with a Gorgon-emblazoned shield buying pickled herring.

FIRST WOMAN: Why, just the other day I saw one of those long-haired dandies who command our cavalry ride up on horseback and pour into his

bronze helmet the egg-broth he'd bought from an old dame. And there was a Thracian slinger too, shaking his lance like Tereus; he'd scared the life out of the poor fig-peddler and was gulping down all her ripest fruit.

MAGISTRATE: How can you stop all the confusion in the various states and bring them together?

LYSISTRATA: Very easily.

MAGISTRATE: Tell me how.

LYSISTRATA: Just like a ball of wool, when it's confused and snarled: we take it thus, and draw out a thread here and a thread there with our spindles; thus we'll unsnarl this war, if no one prevents us, and draw together the various states with embassies here and embassies there.

MAGISTRATE: Do you suppose you can stop this dreadful business with balls of wool and spindles, you nit-wits?

LYSISTRATA: Why, if *you* had any wits, you'd manage all affairs of state like our wool-working.

MAGISTRATE: How so?

LYSISTRATA: First you ought to treat the city as we do when we wash the dirt out of a fleece: stretch it out and pluck and thrash out of the city all those prickly scoundrels; aye, and card out those who conspire and stick together to gain office, pulling off their heads. Then card the wool, all of it, into one fair basket of goodwill, mingling in the aliens residing here, any loyal foreigners, and anyone who's in debt to the Treasury; and consider that all our colonies lie scattered round about like remnants; from all of these collect the wool and gather it together here, wind up a great ball, and then weave a good stout cloak for the democracy.

MAGISTRATE: Dreadful! Talking about thrashing and winding balls of wool, when you haven't the slightest share in the war!

LYSISTRATA: Why, you dirty scoundrel, we bear more than twice as much as you. First, we bear children and send off our sons as soldiers.

MAGISTRATE: Hush! Let bygones be bygones!

LYSISTRATA: Then, when we ought to be happy and enjoy our youth, we sleep alone because of your expeditions abroad. But never mind us married women: I grieve most for the maids who grow old at home unwed.

MAGISTRATE: Don't men grow old, too?

LYSISTRATA: For heaven's sake! That's not the same thing. When a man comes home, no matter how grey he is, he soon finds a girl to marry. But woman's bloom is short and fleeting; if she doesn't grasp her chance, no man is willing to marry her and she sits at home a prey to every fortune-teller.

MAGISTRATE *(coarsely):* But if a man can still get it up—

LYSISTRATA: See here, you: what's the matter? Aren't

you dead yet? There's plenty of room for you. Buy yourself a shroud and I'll bake you a honey-cake. (*Handing him a copper coin for his passage across the Styx.*) Here's your fare! Now get yourself a wreath.

(*During the following dialogue the* WOMEN *dress up the* MAGISTRATE *as a corpse.*)

FIRST WOMAN: Here, take these fillets.

SECOND WOMAN: Here, take this wreath.

LYSISTRATA: What do you want? What's lacking? Get moving; off to the ferry! Charon is calling you; don't keep him from sailing.

820

MAGISTRATE: Am I to endure these insults? By God! I'm going straight to the magistrates to show them how I've been treated.

LYSISTRATA: Are you grumbling that you haven't been properly laid out? Well, the day after to-morrow we'll send around all the usual offerings early in the morning.

(*The* MAGISTRATE *goes out still wearing his funeral decorations.* LYSISTRATA *and the* WOMEN *retire into the Acropolis.*)

LEADER OF MEN: Wake, ye sons of freedom, wake! 'Tis no time for sleeping. Up and at them, like a man!

830

Let us strip for action.

(*The* CHORUS OF MEN *remove their outer cloaks.*)

CHORUS OF MEN (*singing*):
Surely there is something here greater than meets the eye;
For without a doubt I smell Hippias' tyrany.
Dreadful fear assails me lest certain bands of Spartan men,
Meeting here with Cleisthenes, have inspired through treachery
All these god-detested women secretly to seize

840

Athens' treasure in the temple, and to stop that pay Whence I live at my ease.

LEADER OF MEN: Now isn't it terrible for them to advise the state and chatter about shields, being mere women?

And they think to reconcile us with the Spartans—men who hold nothing sacred any more than hungry wolves. Surely this is a web of deceit, my friends, to conceal an attempt at tyranny. But they'll never lord it over me; I'll be

850

on my guard from now on,
"The blade I bear, A myrtle spray shall wear."
I'll occupy the market under arms and stand next to Aristogeiton.

Thus I'll stand beside him (*He strikes the pose of the famous statue of the tyrannicides, with one arm raised.*) And here's my chance to take this accurst old hag and—(*striking the* LEADER OF WOMEN) smack her on the jaw!

LEADER OF WOMEN: You'll go home in such a state your Ma won't recognize you!

860

Ladies all, upon the ground let us place these garments.

(*The* CHORUS OF WOMEN *remove their outer garments.*)

CHORUS OF WOMEN (*singing*):
Citizens of Athens, hear useful words for the state.
Rightly; for it nurtured me in my youth royally.
As a child of seven years carried I the sacred box;
Then I was a Miller-maid, grinding at Athene's shrine;
Next I wore the saffron robe and played Brauronia's Bear;

870

And I walked as a Basket-bearer, wearing chains of figs,
As a sweet maiden fair.

LEADER OF WOMEN: Therefore, am I not bound to give good advice to the city?

Don't take it ill that I was born a woman, if I contribute something better than our present troubles. I pay my share; for I contribute MEN. But you miserable old fools contribute nothing, and after squandering our ancestral treasure,

880

the fruit of the Persian Wars, you make no contribution in return. And now, all on account of you, we're facing ruin.

What, muttering, are you? If you annoy me, I'll take this hard, rough slipper and—(*striking the* LEADER OF MEN) smack you on the jaw!

CHORUS OF MEN (*singing*):
This is outright insolence! Things go from bad to worse.
If you're men with any guts, prepare to meet the

890

foe.
Let us strip our tunics off! We need the smell of male
Vigour. And we cannot fight all swaddled up in clothes.

(*They strip off their tunics.*)

Come then, my comrades, on to the battle, ye once to Leipsydrion came;
Then ye were MEN. Now call back your youthful vigour.
With light, wingèd footstep advance,

900

Shaking old age from your frame.

LEADER OF MEN: If any of us give these wenches the slightest hold, they'll stop at nothing; such is their cunning.

They will even build ships and sail against us, like Artemisia. Or if they turn to mounting, I count our Knights as done for: a woman's such a tricky jockey when she gets astraddle, with a good firm seat for trotting. Just look at those Amazons that Micon painted, fighting on horse-

910

back against men!

But we must throw them all in the pillory—
(seizing and choking the LEADER OF WOMEN*)* grabbing hold of yonder neck!

CHORUS OF WOMEN *(singing)*:
'Ware my anger! Like a boar 'twill rush upon you men.
Soon you'll bawl aloud for help, you'll be so soundly trimmed!
920 Come, my friends, let's strip with speed, and lay aside these robes;
Catch the scent of women's rage. Attack with tooth and nail!

(They strip off their tunics.)

Now then, come near me, you miserable man!
You'll never eat garlic or black beans again.
And if you utter a single hard word, in rage I will "nurse" you as once
The beetle requited her foe.
LEADER OF WOMEN: For you don't worry me; no, not
930 so long as my Lampito lives and our Theban friend, the noble Ismenia.
You can't do anything, not even if you pass a dozen—decrees! You miserable fool, all our neighbours hate you. Why, just the other day when I was holding a festival for Hecate, I invited as playmate from our neighbours the Boeotians a charming, wellbred Copaic—eel. But they refused to send me one on account of your decrees.
940 And you'll never stop passing decrees until I grab your foot and—*(tripping up the* LEADER OF MEN*)* toss you down and break your neck!

(Here an interval of five days is supposed to elapse. LYSISTRATA *comes out from the Acropolis.)*

LEADER OF WOMEN *(dramatically)*: Empress of this great emprise and undertaking,
Why come you forth, I pray, with frowning brow?
LYSISTRATA: Ah, these cursèd women! Their deeds and female notions make me pace up and down in utter despair.
LEADER OF WOMEN: Ah, what sayest thou?
950 LYSISTRATA: The truth, alas! the truth.
LEADER OF WOMEN: What dreadful tale hast thou to tell thy friends?
LYSISTRATA: 'Tis shame to speak, and not to speak is hard.
LEADER OF WOMEN: Hide not from me whatever woes we suffer.
LYSISTRATA: Well then, to put it briefly, we want—laying!
LEADER OF WOMEN: O Zeus, Zeus!
960 LYSISTRATA: Why call on Zeus? That's the way things are. I can no longer keep them away from the men, and they're all deserting. I caught one wriggling through a hole near the grotto of Pan,

another sliding down a rope, another deserting her post; and yesterday I found one getting on a sparrow's back to fly off to Orsilochus, and had to pull her back by the hair. They're digging up all sorts of excuses to get home. Look, here comes one of them now.

(A WOMAN *comes hastily out of the Acropolis.)*

Here you! Where are you off to in such a hurry? 970
FIRST WOMAN: I want to go home. My very best wool is being devoured by moths.
LYSISTRATA: Moths? Nonsense! Go back inside.
FIRST WOMAN: I'll come back; I swear it. I just want to lay it out on the bed.
LYSISTRATA: Well, you won't lay it out, and you won't go home, either.
FIRST WOMAN: Shall I let my wool be ruined?
LYSISTRATA: If necessary, yes.

(ANOTHER WOMAN comes out.)

SECOND WOMAN: Oh, dear! Oh dear! My precious 980 flax! I left it at home all unpeeled.
LYSISTRATA: Here's another one, going home for her "flax." Come back here!
SECOND WOMAN: But I just want to work it up a little and then I'll be right back.
LYSISTRATA: No indeed! If you start this, all other women will want to do the same.

(A THIRD WOMAN comes out.)

THIRD WOMAN: O Eilithyia, goddess of travail, stop my labour till I come to a lawful spot!
LYSISTRATA: What's this nonsense? 990
THIRD WOMAN: I'm going to have a baby—right now!
LYSISTRATA: But you weren't even pregnant yesterday.
THIRD WOMAN: Well, I am today. O Lysistrata, do send me home to see a midwife, right away.
LYSISTRATA: What are you talking about? *(Putting her hand on her stomach)* What's this hard lump here?
THIRD WOMAN: A little boy.
LYSISTRATA: My goodness, what have you got there? It seems hollow; I'll just find out. *(Pulling aside* 1000 *her robe)* Why, you silly goose, you've got Athene's sacred helmet there. And you said you were having a baby!
THIRD WOMAN: Well, I *am* having one, I swear!
LYSISTRATA: Then what's this helmet for?
THIRD WOMAN: If the baby starts coming while I'm still in the Acropolis, I'll creep into this like a pigeon and give birth to it there.
LYSISTRATA: Stuff and nonsense! It's plain enough what you're up to. You just wait here for the 1010 christening of this—helmet.
THIRD WOMAN: But I can't sleep in the Acropolis since I saw the sacred snake.

FIRST WOMAN: And I'm dying for lack of sleep: the hooting of owls keep me awake.

LYSISTRATA: Enough of these shams, you wretched creatures. You want your husbands, I suppose. Well, don't you think they want us? I'm sure they're spending miserable nights. Hold out, my 1020 friends, and endure for just a little while. There's an oracle that we shall conquer, if we don't split up. (*Producing a roll of paper.*) Here it is.

FIRST WOMAN: Tell us what it says.

LYSISTRATA: Listen.

"When in the length of time the Swallows shall gather together,

Fleeing the Hoopoe's amorous flight and the Cockatoo shunning,

1030 Then shall your woes be ended and Zeus who thunders in heaven

Set what's below on top—"

FIRST WOMAN: What? Are we going to be on top?

LYSISTRATA: "But if the Swallows rebel and flutter away from the temple,

Never a bird in the world shall seem more wanton and worthless."

FIRST WOMAN: That's clear enough, upon my word!

LYSISTRATA: By all that's holy, let's not give up the 1040 struggle now. Let's go back inside. It would be a shame, my dear friends, to disobey the oracle.

(*The* WOMEN *all retire to the Acropolis again.*)

CHORUS OF MEN (*singing*):
I have a tale to tell,
Which I know full well.
     It was told me
     In the nursery.

Once there was a likely lad,
     Melanion they name him;
The thought of marriage made him mad,
1050   For which I cannot blame him.

So off he went to mountains fair;
     (No women to upbraid him!)
A mighty hunter of the hare,
     He had a dog to aid him.

He never came back home to see
     Detested women's faces.
He showed a shrewd mentality.
     With him I'd fain change places!

ONE OF THE MEN (*to* ONE OF THE WOMEN): Come here,
1060   old dame; give me a kiss.

WOMAN: You'll ne'er eat garlic, if you dare!

MAN: I want to kick you—just like this!

WOMAN: Oh, there's a leg with bushy hair!

MAN: Myronides and Phormio
     Were hairy—and they thrashed the foe.

CHORUS OF WOMEN (*singing*):
I have another tale,
With which to assail
     Your contention
     'Bout Melanion.   1070

Once upon a time a man
     Named Timon left our city,
To live in some deserted land.
     (We thought him rather witty.)

He dwelt alone amidst the thorn;
     In solitude he brooded.
From some grim Fury he was born:
     Such hatred he exuded.

He cursed you men, as scoundrels through
     And through, till life he ended.   1080
He couldn't stand the sight of you!
     But women he befriended.

WOMAN (*to* ONE OF THE MEN): I'll smash your face in, if you like.

MAN: Oh no, please don't! You frighten me.

WOMAN: I'll lift my foot—and thus I'll strike.

MAN: Aha! Look there! What's that I see?

WOMAN: Whate'er you see, you cannot say
     That I'm not neatly trimmed today.

(LYSISTRATA *appears on the wall of the Acropolis.*)

LYSISTRATA: Hello! Hello! Girls, come here quick!   1090

(SEVERAL WOMEN *appear beside her.*)

WOMAN: What is it? Why are you calling?

LYSISTRATA: I see a man coming: he's in a dreadful state. He's mad with passion. O Queen of Cyprus, Cythera, and Paphos, just keep on this way!

WOMAN: Where is the fellow?

LYSISTRATA: There beside the shrine of Demeter.

WOMAN: Oh yes, so he is. Who is he?

LYSISTRATA: Let's see. Do any of you know him?

MYRRHINE: Yes indeed. That's my husband, Cinesias.

LYSISTRATA: It's up to you, now: roast him, rack him,   1100
fool him, love him—and leave him! Do everything, except what our oath forbids.

MYRRHINE: Don't worry; I'll do it.

LYSISTRATA: I'll stay here to tease him and warm him up a bit. Off with you.

(*The* OTHER WOMEN *retire from the wall. Enter* CINESIAS *followed by* A SLAVE *carrying a baby.* CINESIAS *is obviously in great pain and distress.*)

CINESIAS (*groaning*): Oh-h! Oh-h-h! This is killing me! O God, what tortures I'm suffering!

LYSISTRATA (*from the wall*): Who's that within our lines?

CINESIAS: Me.   1110

LYSISTRATA: A *man?*

CINESIAS (*pointing*): A *man*, indeed!

LYSISTRATA: Well, go away!

CINESIAS: Who are you to send me away?

LYSISTRATA: The captain of the guard.

CINESIAS: Oh, for heaven's sake, call out Myrrhine for me.

LYSISTRATA: Call Myrrhine? Nonsense! Who are you?

CINESIAS: Her husband, Cinesias of Paionidai.

1120 LYSISTRATA (*appearing much impressed*): Oh, greetings, friend. Your name is not without honour here among us. Your wife is always talking about you, and whenever she takes an egg or an apple, she says, "Here's to my dear Cinesias!"

CINESIAS (*quivering with excitement*): Oh, ye gods in heaven!

LYSISTRATA: Indeed she does! And whenever our conversations turn to men, your wife immediately says, "All others are mere rubbish
1130 compared with Cinesias."

CINESIAS (*groaning*): Oh! Do call her for me.

LYSISTRATA: Why should I? What will you give me?

CINESIAS: Whatever you want. All I have is yours— and you see what I've got.

LYSISTRATA: Well then, I'll go down and call her. (*She descends.*)

CINESIAS: And hurry up! I've had no joy of life ever since she left home. When I go in the house, I feel awful: everything seems so empty and I can't
1140 enjoy my dinner. I'm in such a state all the time!

MYRRHINE (*from behind the wall*): I *do* love him so. But he won't let me love him. No, no! Don't ask me to see him!

CINESIAS: O my darling, O Myrrhine honey, why do you do this to me?

(MYRRHINE *appears on the wall.*)

Come down here!

MYRRHINE: No, I won't come down.

CINESIAS: Won't you come, Myrrhine, when I call you?

1150 MYRRHINE: No; you don't want me.

CINESIAS: *Don't want you?* I'm in agony!

MYRRHINE: I'm going now.

CINESIAS: Please don't. At least, listen to your baby. (*to the baby*) Here you, call your mamma! (*Pinching the baby.*)

BABY: Ma-ma! Ma-ma! Ma-ma!

CINESIAS (*to Myrrhine*): What's the matter with you? Have you no pity for your child, who hasn't been washed or fed for five whole days?

1160 MYRRHINE: Oh, poor child; your father pays no attention to you.

CINESIAS: Come down then, you heartless wretch, for the baby's sake.

MYRRHINE: Oh, what it is to be a mother! I've got to come down, I suppose.

(*She leaves the wall and shortly reappears at the gate.*)

CINESIAS (*to himself*): She seems much younger, and she has such a sweet look about her. Oh, the way she teases me! And her pretty, provoking ways make me burn with longing.

MYRRHINE (*coming out of the gate and taking the baby*): O 1170 my sweet little angel. Naughty papa! Here, let Mummy kiss you, Mamma's little sweetheart!

(*She fondles the baby lovingly.*)

CINESIAS (*in despair*): You heartless creature, why do you do this? Why follow these other women and make both of us suffer so?

(*He tries to embrace her.*)

MYRRHINE: Don't touch me!

CINESIAS: You're letting all our things at home go to wrack and ruin.

MYRRHINE: I don't care.

CINESIAS: You don't care that your wool is being 1180 plucked to pieces by the chickens?

MYRRHINE: Not in the least.

CINESIAS: And you haven't celebrated the rites of Aphrodite for ever so long. Won't you come home?

MYRRHINE: Not on your life, unless you men make a truce and stop the war.

CINESIAS: Well, then, if that pleases you, we'll do it.

MYRRHINE: Well then, if that pleases *you*, I'll come home—afterwards! Right now I'm on oath not 1190 to.

CINESIAS: Then just lie down here with me for a moment.

MYRRHINE: No—(*in a teasing voice*) and yet I won't say I don't love you.

CINESIAS: You love me? Oh, do lie down here, Myrrhine dear!

MYRRHINE: What, you silly fool! in front of the baby?

CINESIAS (*hastily thrusting the baby at the slave*): Of course not. Here—home! Take him, Manes! (*The* 1200 SLAVE *goes off with the baby.*) See, the baby's out of the way. Now won't you lie down?

MYRRHINE: But where, my dear?

CINESIAS: Where? The grotto of Pan's a lovely spot.

MYRRHINE: How could I purify myself before returning to the shrine?

CINESIAS: Easily: just wash here in the Clepsydra.

MYRRHINE: And then, shall I go back on my oath?

CINESIAS: On my head be it! Don't worry about the oath. 1210

MYRRHINE: All right, then. Just let me bring out a bed.

CINESIAS: No, don't. The ground's all right.

MYRRHINE: Heavens, no! Bad as you are, I won't let you lie on the bare ground.

(*She goes into the Acropolis.*)

CINESIAS: Why, she really loves me; it's plain to see.

MYRRHINE (*returning with a bed*): There! Now hurry

up and lie down. I'll just slip off this dress. But—let's see: oh yes, I must fetch a mattress.

1220 CINESIAS: Nonsense! No mattress for me.

MYRRHINE: Yes indeed! It's not nice on the bare springs.

CINESIAS: Give me a kiss.

MYRRHINE (giving him a hasty kiss): There!

(She goes.)

CINESIAS (in mingled distress and delight): Oh-h! Hurry back!

MYRRHINE (returning with a mattress): Here's the mattress; lie down on it. I'm taking my things off now—but—let's see: you have no pillow.

1230 CINESIAS : I don't want a pillow.

MYRRHINE : But I do.

(She goes.)

CINESIAS: Cheated again, just like Heracles and his dinner!

MYRRHINE (returning with a pillow): Here, lift your head. (to herself, wondering how else to tease him) Is that all?

CINESIAS: Surely that's all! Do come here, precious!

MYRRHINE: I'm taking off my girdle. But remember: don't go back on your promise about the truce.

1240 CINESIAS: I hope to die, if I do.

MYRRHINE: You don't have a blanket.

CINESIAS (shouting in exasperation): I don't want one! I WANT TO—

MYRRHINE: Sh-h! There, there, I'll be back in a minute.

(She goes.)

CINESIAS: She'll be the death of me with these bed-clothes.

MYRRHINE (returning with a blanket): Here, get up.

CINESIAS: I've got this up!

1250 MYRRHINE: Would you like some perfume?

CINESIAS: Good heavens, no! I won't have it!

MYRRHINE: Yes, you shall, whether you want it or not.

(She goes.)

CINESIAS: O lord! Confound all perfumes anyway!

MYRRHINE (returning with a flask): Stretch out your hand and put some on.

CINESIAS (suspiciously): By God, I don't much like this perfume. It smacks of shilly-shallying, and has no scent of the marriage-bed.

MYRRHINE: Oh dear! This is Rhodian perfume I've
1260 brought.

CINESIAS: It's quite all right, dear. Never mind.

MYRRHINE: Don't be silly!

(She goes out with the flask.)

CINESIAS: Damn the man who first concocted perfumes!

MYRRHINE (returning with another flask): Here, try this flask.

CINESIAS: I've got another one all ready for you. Come, you wretch, lie down and stop bringing me things.

MYRRHINE: All right; I'm taking off my shoes. But, 1270 my dear, see that you vote for peace.

CINESIAS (absently): I'll consider it.

(MYRRHINE runs away to the Acropolis.)

I'm ruined! The wench has skinned me and run away! (chanting, in tragic style) Alas! Alas! Deceived, deserted by this fairest of women, whom shall I—lay? Ah, my poor little child, how shall I nurture thee? Where's Cynalopex? I needs must hire a nurse!

LEADER OF MEN (chanting): Ah, wretched man, in dreadful wise beguiled, bewrayed, thy soul is 1280 sore distressed. I pity thee, alas! What soul, what loins, what liver could stand this strain? How firm and unyielding he stands, with naught to aid him of a morning.

CINESIAS: O lord! O Zeus! What tortures I endure!

LEADER OF MEN: This is the way she's treated you, that vile and cursèd wanton.

LEADER OF WOMEN: Nay, not vile and cursèd, but sweet and dear.

LEADER OF MEN: Sweet, you say? Nay, hateful, hate- 1290 ful!

CINESIAS: Hateful indeed! O Zeus, Zeus!
Seize her and snatch her away,
Like a handful of dust, in a mighty,
Fiery tempest! Whirl her aloft, then let her drop
Down to the earth, with a crash, as she falls—
On the point of this waiting
Thingummybob!

(He goes out. Enter a SPARTAN HERALD in an obvious state of excitement, which he is doing his best to conceal.)

HERALD: Where can I find the Senate or the Prytanes? I've got an important message. 1300

(The Athenian MAGISTRATE enters.)

MAGISTRATE: Say there, are you a man or Priapus?

HERALD (in annoyance): I'm a herald, you lout! I've come from Sparta about the truce.

MAGISTRATE: Is that a spear you've got under your cloak?

HERALD: No, of course not!

MAGISTRATE: Why do you twist and turn so? Why hold your cloak in front of you. Did you rupture yourself on the trip?

HERALD: By gum, the fellow's an old fool. 1310

MAGISTRATE (pointing): Why, you dirty rascal, you're excited.

HERALD: Not at all. Stop this tom-foolery.

MAGISTRATE: Well, what's that I see?

HERALD: A Spartan message-staff.

MAGISTRATE: Oh, certainly! That's just the kind of message-staff I've got. But tell me the honest truth: how are things going in Sparta?

HERALD: All the land of Sparta is up in arms—and our allies are up, too. We need Pellene.

MAGISTRATE: What brought this trouble on you? A sudden Panic?

HERALD: No, Lampito started it and then all the other women in Sparta with one accord chased their husbands out of their beds.

MAGISTRATE: How do you feel?

HERALD: Terrible. We walk around the city bent over like men lighting matches in a wind. For our women won't let us touch them until we all agree and make peace throughout Greece.

MAGISTRATE: This is a general conspiracy of the women; I see it now. Well, hurry back and tell the Spartans to send ambassadors here with full powers to arrange a truce. And I'll go tell the Council to choose ambassadors from here; I've got something here that will soon persuade them!

HERALD: I'll fly there; for you've made an excellent suggestion.

(The HERALD and the MAGISTRATE depart on opposite sides of the stage.)

LEADER OF MEN: No beast or fire is harder than womankind to tame,

Nor is the spotted leopard so devoid of shame.

LEADER OF WOMEN: Knowing this, you dare provoke us to attack?

I'd be your steady friend, if you'd but take us back.

LEADER OF MEN: I'll never cease my hatred keen of womankind.

LEADER OF WOMEN: Just as you will. But now just let me help you find

That cloak you threw aside. You look so silly there

Without your clothes. Here, put it on and don't go bare.

LEADER OF MEN: That's very kind, and shows you're not entirely bad.

But I threw off my things when I was good and mad.

LEADER OF WOMEN: At last you seem a man, and won't be mocked, my lad.

If you'd been nice to me, I'd take this little gnat

That's in your eye and pluck it out for you, like that.

LEADER OF MEN: So that's what bothered me and bit my eye so long!

Please dig it out for me. I own that I've been wrong.

LEADER OF WOMEN: I'll do so, though you've been a most ill-natured brat.

Ye gods! See here! A huge and monstrous little gnat!

LEADER OF MEN: Oh, how that helps! For it was digging wells in me.

And now it's out. my tears can roll down hard and free.

LEADER OF WOMEN: Here, let me wipe them off, although you're such a knave,

And kiss me.

LEADER OF MEN: No!

LEADER OF WOMEN: Whate'er you say, a kiss I'll have.

(She kisses him.)

LEADER OF MEN: Oh, confound these women! They've a coaxing way about them.

He was wise and never spoke a truer word, who said,

"We can't live with women, but we cannot live without them."

Now I'll make a truce with you. We'll fight no more; instead,

I will not injure you if you do me no wrong.

And now let's join our ranks and then begin a song.

COMBINED CHORUS *(singing)*:

Athenians, we're not prepared,
To say a single ugly word
About our fellow-citizens.

Quite the contrary: we desire but to say and to do

Naught but good. Quite enough are the ills now on hand.

Men and women, be advised:
If anyone requires
Money—minae two or three—
We've got what he desires.

My purse is yours, on easy terms:
When Peace shall reappear,
Whate'er you've borrowed will be due.
So speak up without fear.

You needn't pay me back, you see,
If you can get a cent from me!

We're about to entertain
Some foreign gentlemen;
We've soup and tender, fresh-killed pork.
Come round to dine at ten.

Come early; wash, and dress with care,
And bring the children, too.
Then step right in, no "by your leave."
We'll be expecting you.

Walk in as if you owned the place.
You'll find the door—shut in your face!

(Enter a group of SPARTAN AMBASSADORS; they are in the same desperate condition as the HERALD in the previous scene.)

LEADER OF CHORUS: Here comes the envoys from Sparta, sprouting long beards and looking for the world as if they were carrying pig-pens in front of them.

Greetings, gentlemen of Sparta. Tell me, in what state have you come?

1420

SPARTAN: Why waste words? You can plainly see what state we've come in!

LEADER OF CHORUS: Wow! You're in a pretty high-strung condition, and it seems to be getting worse.

SPARTAN: It's indescribable. Won't someone please arrange a peace for us—in any way you like.

LEADER OF CHORUS: Here come our own, native ambassadors, crouching like wrestlers and holding their clothes in front of them; this seems an athletic kind of malady.

1430

(Enter several Athenian AMBASSADORS.*)*

ATHENIAN: Can anyone tell us where Lysistrata is? You see our condition.

LEADER OF CHORUS: Here's another case of the same complaint. Tell me, are the attacks worse in the morning?

ATHENIAN: No, we're always afflicted this way. If someone doesn't soon arrange this truce, you'd better not let me get my hands on—Cleisthenes!

1440

LEADER OF CHORUS: If you're smart, you'll arrange your cloaks so none of these fellows who smashed the Hermae can see you.

ATHENIAN: Right you are; a very good suggestion.

SPARTAN: Aye, by all means. Here, let's hitch up our clothes.

ATHENIAN: Greetings, Spartan. We've suffered dreadful things.

SPARTAN: My dear fellow, we'd have suffered still worse if one of those fellows had seen us in this condition.

1450

ATHENIAN: Well, gentlemen, we must get down to business. What's your errand here?

SPARTAN: We're ambassadors about peace.

ATHENIAN: Excellent; so are we. Only Lysistrata can arrange things for us; shall we summon her?

SPARTAN: Aye, and Lysistratus too, if you like.

LEADER OF CHORUS: No need to summon her, it seems. She's coming out of her own accord.

(Enter LYSISTRATA *accompanied by a statue of a nude female figure, which represents Reconciliation.)*

Hail, noblest of women; now must thou be

1460

A judge shrewd and subtle, mild and severe,
Be sweet yet majestic: all manners employ.
The leaders of Hellas, caught by thy love-charms,
Have come to thy judgment, their charges submitting.

LYSISTRATA: This is no difficult task, if one catch them still in amorous passion, before they've re-

sorted to each other. But I'll soon find out. Where's Reconciliation? Go, first bring the Spartans here, and don't seize them rudely and violently, as our tactless husbands used to do, but as befits a woman, like an old, familiar friend; if they won't give you their hands, take them however you can. Then go fetch these Athenians here, taking hold of whatever they offer you. Now then, men of Sparta, stand here beside me, and you Athenians on the other side, and listen to my words.

1470

I am a woman, it is true, but I have a mind; I'm not badly off in native wit, and by listening to my father and my elders, I've had a decent schooling.

1480

Now I intend to give you a scolding which you both deserve. With one common font you worship at the same altars, just like brothers, at Olympia, at Thermopylae, at Delphi—how many more might I name, if time permitted;—and the Barbarians stand by waiting with their armies; yet you are destroying the men and towns of Greece.

ATHENIAN: Oh, this tension is killing me!

1490

LYSISTRATA: And now, men of Sparta,—to turn to you—don't you remember how the Spartan Pericleidas came here once as a suppliant, and sitting at our altar, all pale with fear in his crimson cloak, begged us for an army? For all Messene had attacked you and the god sent an earthquake too? Then Cimon went forth with four thousand hoplites and saved all Lacedaemon. Such was the aid you received from Athens, and now you lay waste the country which once treated you so well.

1500

ATHENIAN *(hotly)*: They're in the wrong, Lysistrata, upon my word, they are!

SPARTAN *(absently, looking at the statue of Reconciliation)*: We're in the wrong. What hips! How lovely they are!

LYSISTRATA: Don't think I'm going to let you Athenians off. Don't you remember how the Spartans came in arms when you were wearing the rough, sheepskin cloak of slaves and slew the host of Thessalians, the comrades and allies of Hippias? Fighting with you on that day, alone of all the Greeks, they set you free and instead of a sheepskin gave your folk a handsome robe to wear.

1510

SPARTAN *(looking at* LYSISTRATA*)*: I've never seen a more distinguished woman.

ATHENIAN *(looking at Reconciliation)*: I've never seen a more voluptuous body!

LYSISTRATA: Why then, with these many noble deeds to think of, do you fight each other? Why don't you stop this villainy? Why not make peace? Tell me, what prevents it?

1520

SPARTAN (*waving vaguely at Reconciliation*): We're willing, if you're willing to give up your position on yonder flank.

LYSISTRATA: What position, my good man?

SPARTAN: Pylus, we've been panting for it for ever so long.

1530 ATHENIAN: No, by God! You shan't have it!

LYSISTRATA: Let them have it, my friend.

ATHENIAN: Then what shall we have to rouse things up?

LYSISTRATA: Ask for another place in exchange.

ATHENIAN: Well, let's see: first of all (*pointing to various parts of Reconciliation's anatomy*) give us Echinus here, this Maliac Inlet in back there, and these two Megarian legs.

SPARTAN: No, by heavens! You can't have *everything*,
1540   you crazy fool!

LYSISTRATA: Let it go. Don't fight over a pair of legs.

ATHENIAN (*taking off his cloak*): I think I'll strip and do a little planting now.

SPARTAN (*following suit*): And I'll just do a little fertilizing, by gosh!

LYSISTRATA: Wait until the truce is concluded. Now if you've decided on this course, hold a conference and discuss the matter with your allies.

ATHENIAN: Allies? Don't be ridiculous. They're in the
1550   same state we are. Won't our allies want the same thing we do—to jump in bed with their women?

SPARTAN: Ours will, I know.

ATHENIAN: Especially the Carystians, by God!

LYSISTRATA: Very well. Now purify yourselves, that your wives may feast and entertain you in the Acropolis; we've provisions by the basketfull. Exchange your oaths and pledges there, and then each of you may take his wife and go home.

ATHENIAN: Let's go at once.

1560 SPARTAN: Come on, where you will.

ATHENIAN: For God's sake, let's hurry!

(*They all go into the Acropolis.*)

CHORUS (*singing*):
    Whate'er I have of coverlets
      And robes of varied hue
    And golden trinkets,—without stint
      I offer them to you.

    Take what you will and bear it home,
      Your children to delight,
    Or if your girl's a Basket-maid;
1570   Just choose whate'er's in sight.

    There's naught within so well secured
      You cannot break the seal
    And bear it off; just help yourselves;
      No hesitation feel.

    But you'll see nothing, though you try,
    Unless you've sharper eyes than I!

    If anyone needs bread to feed
      A growing family,
    I've lots of wheat and full-grown loaves;
1580   So just apply to me.

    Let every poor man who desires
      Come round and bring a sack
    To fetch the grain; my slave is there
      To load it on his back.

    But don't come near my door, I say:
    Beware the dog, and stay away!

(*An* ATHENIAN *enters carrying a torch; he knocks at the gate.*)

ATHENIAN: Open the door! (*to the* CHORUS, *which is clustered around the gate*) Make way, won't you! What are you hanging around for? Want me to singe you with this torch? (*to himself*) No; it's a 1590 stale trick, I won't do it! (*to the audience*) Still if I've got to do it to please *you*, I suppose I'll have to take the trouble.

(*A* SECOND ATHENIAN *comes out of the gate.*)

SECOND ATHENIAN: And I'll help you.

FIRST ATHENIAN (*waving his torch at the* CHORUS): Get out! Go bawl your heads off! Move on there, so the Spartans can leave in peace when the banquet's over.

(*They brandish their torches until the* CHORUS *leaves the Orchestra.*)

SECOND ATHENIAN: I've never seen such a pleasant banquet: the Spartans are charming fellows, in- 1600 deed they are! And we Athenians are very witty in our cups.

FIRST ATHENIAN: Naturally: for when we're sober we're never at our best. If the Athenians would listen to me, we'd always get a little tipsy on our embassies. As things are now, we go to Sparta when we're sober and look around to stir up trouble. And then we don't hear what they say—and as for what they *don't* say, we have all sorts of suspicions. And then we bring back vary- 1610 ing reports about the mission. But this time everything is pleasant; even if a man should sing the Telamon-song when he ought to sing "Cleitagorus," we'd praise him and swear it was excellent.

(*The two* CHORUSES *return, as a* CHORUS OF ATHENIANS *and a* CHORUS OF SPARTANS.*)

Here they come back again. Go to the devil, you scoundrels!

SECOND ATHENIAN: Get out, I say! They're coming out from the feast.

(*Enter the* SPARTAN *and* ATHENIAN ENVOYS, *followed by* LYSISTRATA *and all the* WOMEN.)

1620 SPARTAN (*to one of his fellow-envoys*): My good fellow, take up your pipes; I want to do a fancy two-step and sing a jolly song for the Athenians.

ATHENIAN: Yes, do take your pipes, by all means. I'd love to see you dance.

SPARTAN (*singing and dancing with the* CHORUS OF SPARTANS):
  These youths inspire
To song and dance, O Memory;
Stir up my Muse, to tell how we
1630 And Athens' men, in our galleys clashing
At Artemisium, 'gainst foemen dashing in godlike ire,
Conquered the Persian and set Greece free.

  Leonidas
Led on his valiant warriors
Whetting their teeth like angry boars.
Abundant foam on their lips was flow'ring,
A stream of sweat from their limbs was show'ring.
The Persian was
1640 Numberless as the sand on the shores.

O Huntress who slayest the beasts in the glade,
O Virgin divine, hither come to our truce,
Unite us in bonds which all time will not loose.
Grant us to find in this treaty, we pray,
An unfailing source of true friendship today,
And all of our days, helping us to refrain
From weaseling tricks which bring war in their train.
  Then hither, come hither! O huntress maid.

1650 LYSISTRATA: Come then, since all is fairly done, men of Sparta, lead away your wives, and you, Athenians, take yours. Let every man stand beside his wife, and every wife beside her man, and then, to celebrate our fortune, let's dance. And in the future, let's take care to avoid these misunderstandings.

CHORUS OF ATHENIANS (*singing and dancing*):
  Lead on the dances, your graces revealing.
Call Artemis hither, call Artemis' twin,
1660 Leader of dances, Apollo the Healing,
Kindly God—hither! Let's summon him in!

Nysian Bacchus call,
Who with his Maenads, his eyes flashing fire,
Dances, and last of all
Zeus of the thunderbolt flaming, the Sire,
  And Hera in majesty,
  Queen of prosperity.
Come, ye Powers who dwell above
Unforgetting, our witnesses be
Of Peace with bonds of harmonious love—   1670
The Peace which Cypris has wrought for me.
  Alleluia! Io Paean!
  Leap in joy—hurrah! hurrah!
  'Tis victory—hurrah! hurrah!
  Euoi! Euoi! Euai! Euai!

LYSISTRATA (*to the* SPARTANS): Come now, sing a new song to cap ours.

CHORUS OF SPARTANS (*singing and dancing*):
  Leaving Taygetus fair and renown'd
Muse of Laconia, hither come: 1680
Amyclae's god in hymns resound.
Athene of the Brazen Home,
And Castor and Pollux, Tyndareus' sons,
Who sport where Eurotas murmuring runs.

  On with the dance! Heia! Ho!
    All leaping along,
  Mantles a-swinging as we go!
    Of Sparta our song.
There the holy chorus ever gladdens,
There the beat of stamping feet,   1690
As our winsome fillies, lovely maidens,
Dance, beside Eurotas, banks a-skipping,—
Nimbly go to and fro
Hast'ning, leaping feet in measures tripping,

Like the Bacchae's revels, hair a-streaming.
Leda's child, divine and mild,
Leads the holy dance, her fair face beaming.
  On with the dance! as your hand
    Presses the hair
  Streaming away unconfined.   1700
    Leap in the air
  Light as the deer; footsteps resound
    Aiding our dance, beating the ground.
Praise Athene, Maid divine, unrivalled in her might,
Dweller in the Brazen Home, unconquered in the fight.

(*All go out singing and dancing.*)

Figure 1. Lysistrata and her cohorts taunt the Athenian Magistrate (Patrick Hines) in the Phoenix Theater production of *Lysistrata*, directed by Jean Gascon, New York, 1959. (Photograph: the Joseph Abeles Collection.)

Figure 2. The Chorus of Old Men picket the Acropolis in the Phoenix Theater production of *Lysistrata,* directed by Jean Gascon, New York, 1959. (Photograph: the Joseph Abeles Collection.)

Figure 3. Lysistrata (Nan Martin, *standing*) convinces the Athenians and Spartans to reconcile their differences in the Phoenix Theater production of *Lysistrata,* directed by Jean Gascon, New York, 1959. (Photograph: the Joseph Abeles Collection.)

Staging of *Lysistrata*

REVIEW OF THE PHOENIX THEATER
PRODUCTION, NEW YORK, 1959, BY DONALD
MALCOLM

The production of Aristophanes' "Lysistrata" that opened last week at the Phoenix Theatre is crass, low, vulgar, and enjoyable. To declare that it takes liberties with the play would require an enormous extension of the meaning of the word "liberty." There are moments when the text is all but obliterated by an accompanying orgy of pie-throwing, pratfalls, sandbaggings, and cooch dances. But I suspect that Aristophanes might find it in his heart to applaud the irreverent spirit that animates the proceedings even while suffering an author's natural anguish at some of the results thereby obtained. . . .

There are portions of the text, even in this brisk new rendering, by Dudley Fitts, that doubtless meant a great deal more to ancient Athenians than they can mean to contemporary New Yorkers, and it is chiefly these portions that the director, Jean Gascon, annihilates with horseplay. Several speeches by the women's chorus are delivered in the syncopated rhythm of a revivalist chant, and while this sometimes works violence on the metre of the lines and adds nothing to their intelligibility, it does have a certain rowdy fascination. In a similar spirit, the longer verbal exchanges between the sexes are liberally interlarded with hoots, catcalls, and sufficient rough-housing and shimmy dancing to provide steady employment for a circusful of clowns and a whole troupe of bumpers and grinders. Mr. Gascon does not even hesitate to permit the army of old men to picket the citadel with signs that spell out "UNΦAIR" on one side and "Athens Was a Summer Festival" on the other. I think perhaps he should have hesitated.

The actors' contribution to the performance appears to consist chiefly in doing what Mr. Gascon told them to do, and doing it smartly. Broad comedy flourishes at the expense of characterization. Nan Martin, who portrays Lysistrata, exhibits so intense an awareness of her own charms as to perceptibly diminish the appeal of those charms. But a pudgy young lady named Sasha Von Scherler makes a fine sex-crazy matron, and Patrick Hines, who plays an Athenian magistrate, looks like an indignant beach ball and embellishes his every speech with touches of comic art. A number of other gifted clowns caught my eye, but they invariably vanished in a swirl of arms and legs before I could trace them to the program. I congratulate them, though, whoever they are. The costumes consist largely of flesh-colored tights on which an assortment of jewels, spangles, and doodads are distributed to indicate what learned men call the primary sexual characteristics.

REVIEW OF THE PHOENIX THEATER
PRODUCTION, NEW YORK, 1959, BY BROOKS
ATKINSON

Pooling their taste, talent, education and responsibility for the culture of the community, the good people of the Phoenix have tried to kick a little life into Aristophanes' "Lysistrata," which opened on the home grounds last evening.

Wherever Aristophanes is obscene they have anxiously abetted him. The women appear wearing simulated breasts, tipped with sequins, and the ruttish old men strip down to union suits and glittering fig leaves, looking as roguish as all get out. Under the leering direction of Jean Gascon, of Montreal's Théatre du Nouveau Monde, they wallow in sex like refined people doing their best to make the most of a moral holiday. They hope they are being sufficiently Dionysian.

But they are being dull in a frisky manner. For the Phoenix troupe and its artisans are not burlesque queens or mountebanks. Nan Martin as the rebellious Lysistrata is a fine-looking woman with an excellent voice and enlightened intelligence. She brazens out the grotesque bra device that she is required to flaunt before the audience, and she does give Lysistrata the characterization of a sophisticated woman of the world. Directed never to stand still if she can possibly

115

move on every line of the dialogue, she does rather better than the circumstances permit.

But it is dollars to doughnuts that her heart is not in this sort of barnyard horseplay. Nor are the hearts of Gerry Jedd, Sasha Von Scherler, Patricia Falkenhain and Patricia Ripley, who try to look as desperately amorous as possible. Nor does Patrick Hines really believe that he is funny in the mountainous costume of the magistrate, nor do the actors who play the futile old men think that aping feeble-mindedness is really hilarious.

Granted that the Aristophanes text is ribald, it is possible that Dudley Fitts' new translation has wit, humor and poetry that the performance destroys by being over-eager. Mr. Fitts does not evade Aristophanes' licentiousness, but he tries to express it in terse modern English, without the condescension of the intellectual. His translation is coarse without smirking.

In the modern world we are not likely to reproduce the external circumstances that gave pith to "Lysistrata" when Aristophanes wrote it. In the midst of a stupid, interminable war he advocated making peace with the enemy. Aristophanes would be hustled off to the hoosegow if he tried to undermine the safety of a modern nation by producing a similar comedy.

And when he wrote "Lysistrata" women had no political rights or influence. His notion that women could stop a war had an audacity that we can hardly imagine. On at least two counts "Lysistrata" assaulted public complacence in political areas that no longer exist. It was very timely indeed.

All that is left is the single joke about the women of Athens denying themselves to their men until the men make peace with Sparta. On the stage of the Phoenix the joke becomes progressively monotonous. Will Steven Armstrong has designed a gay, bold setting that includes classical mobiles; and his costumes (barring bras) have attractive drape and color.

From a theatrical point of view the production is not without merit. But the Phoenix management and the Phoenix mummers are not hearty roisterers. Their "Lysistrata" is not so funny as "La Plume de Ma Tante."

MEDIEVAL THEATER

During the fourteenth and fifteenth centuries—the heyday of medieval drama—permanent theaters did not exist anywhere in England or on the continent. None had been built since the fall of Rome, and none were built until the middle of the sixteenth century in France. Yet in medieval communities throughout England and Europe, theatrical productions commanded as much public attention and support as they had in Athens during the age of classical Greek drama. Drama held a privileged place in the culture of those late medieval communities because, as in ancient Greece, most of their plays were expressions of religious belief, and most of their productions were occasioned by religious events. Just as the ancient Athenians had dramatized their myths to celebrate the festival of Dionysus, so cities and towns all over England and everywhere in Europe dramatized episodes from the Old and New Testament, from the Apocrypha, and from saints' lives to celebrate sacred events in the Christian calendar. Some towns favored saints' days, others Easter, still others Whitsuntide, which followed Easter by seven weeks, but the most popular occasion was Corpus Christi Day, which took place eight and one-half weeks after Easter, between the last week in May and the third week in June—an ideal time for open-air theater.

During the tenth and eleventh centuries, when religious drama was just beginning to develop, biblical episodes had been staged indoors exclusively, in cathedrals and monasteries, where they originated as an instructive but subordinate element of the church service. But by the beginning of the thirteenth century, the devotional and instructional purposes of religious drama had already stimulated a vigorous theatrical impulse that gave rise to productions outside of the church as well as inside of it. Authority over production of the plays then passed from the church to the town, from bishops and abbots to mayors and town councils. Responsibility for staging the plays likewise passed from clerics and choir boys to craft guilds, trade guilds, and religious fraternities. Theatrical productions became a very public and communal activity, involving townspeople and clergy alike. In England, for example, town councils commissioned new plays and revisions of old ones, selected plays to be performed, scheduled performances, assigned individual plays to the various guilds responsible for production, set standards for production, and even levied fines for inferior productions. Each guild in turn took care of all the other arrangements for the play it had been assigned by the council: directing, staging, costuming, rehearsing, and acting. In France, as well as other European countries, the town council and a religious fraternity that sponsored the production jointly chose a committee of supervisors who appointed a director and assistants to produce its plays. The productions were thus an expression of civic pride as well as of religious belief.

As medieval communities grew and prospered, so did religious plays; at the height of their popularity they achieved a scope and magnitude unparalleled in the history of drama. Whether they encompassed the entire biblical history of the world from creation to the last judgment, as they usually did in England, or whether they were restricted to the life of Christ, as was customary in France, they were almost always encyclopedic. Less like plays than megaplays—they are often called cycle plays—they consisted of numerous playlets, each one devoted to a separate episode or cluster of related episodes from biblical, apocryphal, or saintly experience. The length of cycles varied according to the resources of the towns where they were produced, but judging from the cycles that have survived they were prodigious undertakings—even the shortest of them. Of the four surviving English cycles, for example, the shortest, from the city of Chester, comprises twenty-five individual playlets; Wakefield's contains thirty-two; Lincoln's contains forty-two; and the longest, from York, totals forty-eight. None of these cycles could be staged in a few hours, or even in an entire day. The Chester cycle, according to records from the period, took three days to perform, and no doubt the York cycle ran for the better part of a week. The French passion cycles were no less time consuming, usually requiring four to six days for performance, though in the exceptional case of a mid-sixteenth-century production at Valenciennes, the complete cycle required twenty-five days.

Given the extraordinary number and variety of episodes they contained, the cycles clearly called for extraordinary methods of staging. With the increasing wealth, resourcefulness, and civic pride of late medieval communities, they were able, and eager, to put on extraordinary theatrical productions, using a variety of theatrical structures. Some communities staged their cycles on fixed platforms, others in the round, and others on movable wagons. But all the methods, however different their external characteristics, embodied the same conception of theatrical space and movement that had governed the earlier staging of plays within the church. Specifically, they all combined a neutral acting area with a group of set-like structures known as "mansions" (literally, dwelling places), and as the action moved from one mansion or specific locale to the next, the acting area was understood to be an extension of one location and then another. Consequently, the various outdoor forms of staging cycle plays were all fundamentally symbolic in their use of space and processional in their movement from one mansion or location to the next.

The procession took different forms according to the different methods of staging. In the fixed method, which prevailed in France, all the mansions for a single day's performance were placed side by side, either in a straight line on a long platform, or in a semicircle on a public square (see Figure 1). Here all of the sets—sometimes as many as 20 to 30 on a platform 100 to 200 feet long, ranging from heaven, which traditionally appeared at the right end, to hell, which was located at the left—were simultaneously visible, creating a dazzling spectacle for the audience. As the cycle unfolded, moving from one location and episode to the next, the audience proceeded from one end of the platform, or square, to the other. Staging in the round (the least common of the methods both in England and on the continent) took place in circular areas 100 to 300 feet in diameter that were designed to include spectators, sets, and actors alike (see Figure 2). The series of mansions was arranged around the perimeter of the circle; the audience sat or stood within the circle of sets; and the actors moved from one location to the next around the perimeter or to the general acting area in the center of the circle. The procession took yet another form, its most distinctive form, in the system of movable wagons that was common both in England and Spain, for with this method each separate playlet, staged

Figure 1. The medieval platform stage.

Figure 2. Medieval staging in the round.

by a different guild, was mounted on a separate wagon. Although the exact design and dimensions of the wagons have never been definitely established, they had to be long enough in some cases to provide space for two or three mansions. Playlets about Noah's flood, for example, required one set to designate heaven, from which God spoke to Noah, and another to designate the ark. The wagons were probably wide enough to provide an acting area in front of the sets, though in some towns they were drawn up along stationary acting platforms. The entire audience, however, was not gathered together in a single place, but stood in separate groups at several specified locations within a town, and at each of these points along the route the individual wagons would stop and the actors would perform their playlet (see Figure 3). With movable wagons, the audience stood still and the cycle, like a modern-day parade or procession of floats, was continually unfolding and taking place for different people.

In all these systems of staging, a rough and ready intimacy existed between actors and audience, quite unlike the distance that separated them in a classical Greek theater, and equally unlike their separation from one another by the proscenium arches of post-renaissance theaters. Not only the physical methods of staging, but also the conventions of performance worked to bring actors and audience together. The actors, for example, were largely amateurs, members of the community, friends and relatives of the spectators who were witnessing them from only a few feet away. Sometimes they were not even separated from one another at all. In the fixed method of staging, for example, actors might sit off to the side or actually stand among the audience before and after they performed their parts. In the movable system, the action sometimes spilled off the wagon into the street, particularly when the situation called for action symbolizing great distances between one place and another, as when Satan and his cohorts fell from heaven to hell, or when Adam and Eve were driven out of paradise. Then the actors performed their parts by moving from the acting platform into the area of the audience. Indeed, in many places it was customary for the devils to mingle playfully with the audience. Conventions of performance were clearly not designed to create or sustain a theatrical illusion.

Costumes and props were also designed to create a symbolic spectacle rather than a theatrical illusion. All the characters except the devils were costumed in some kind of medieval garb—God in the imperial vestments of the Pope, Jewish priests in bishops' robes, the tyrant Herod in a kingly crown, and Roman soldiers in knights' armor. The devils, on the other hand, were made up to look like gargoyles, griffins, and other fabulous beasts of prey. All of the costumes, however farfetched, were vividly symbolic, as was every other aspect of staging. Documents from the period reveal props ranging from a red colored rib for the creation of Eve, to gallows, scourges, and a leather bag filled with blood for the crucifixion of Christ. Other special effects included dummy or live animals for Noah's ark, barrels of water for the flood, fire burning at hell's mouth, pulleys for bringing angels from heaven to earth, and trapdoors for the sudden appearance or disappearance of characters. All in all, the cycles must have created for medieval audiences a marvelous and miraculous spectacle, as marvelous and miraculous as the biblical events they dramatized.

Cycle plays were by no means the only form of medieval drama, but they originated so early and prevailed so widely that the spatial concept governing

Figure 3. Medieval staging on movable wagons.

their staging also influenced the staging of other medieval plays, such as farces and moralities. That concept of theatrical space was not only familiar to medieval audiences, but was also readily adaptable to the production of both farces and moralities, whose length rarely exceeded 1500 lines. Like a playlet in a cycle, they were short and simple in their staging requirements, ordinarily calling for only two or three mansions. Although they were staged according to the same theatical conventions, they were not produced under the same auspices. Farces, for example, which were common largely in France during the fifteenth century, were written and performed by lawyers' guilds and student groups, who produced them to celebrate festivals such as Mardi Gras and May Day, when ribaldry and revelry were appropriate to the occasion. Morality plays, popular chiefly in England during the fifteenth and sixteenth centuries, were performed by small troupes of professional players, who toured the countryside and timed their arrival in a town to coincide with a religious holiday or festival, when the spiritual message of their play was most likely to elicit contributions from their audience. Though moralities were designed primarily to exemplify Christian belief, to show the perils of sin and the rewards of virtue, they often loosened the pockets of spectators by appealing also to their sense of humor. They usually contained a few characters known as Vice figures whose dirty jokes and slapstick stage business were meant not only to show the vulgarity of sin but also to amuse a paying audience. And to capitalize on their vulgarity, the Vice figures usually interrupted the play once or twice to collect money from the audience.

The image of the Vice figure mingling with the audience also sums up the unique qualities of medieval theater. Medieval drama encompassed a variety of plays as different as cycles, farces, and moralities, yet it persistently brought actors and spectators closer to one another than ever before or since. They were drawn together not only by the physical characteristics of the stage and the conventions of performance, but also by the festive purpose of their drama. Whether the festivities were sacred or secular, the actors and spectators were joined in celebration. The plays that appear in this section are embodiments of the most communal stage in the history of western theater.

THE WAKEFIELD MASTER

The unknown author of *The Second Shepherds' Play* has come to be known as the Wakefield Master, a name that fittingly identifies him with both the town for which he wrote and the consummate skill of his writing. Exactly when he lived is uncertain, but the language of his plays suggests that he probably wrote sometime during the first half of the fifteenth century. His plays also reveal that he must have received a thoroughgoing religious education, for they incorporate knowledge of biblical literature, scriptural commentary and Latin liturgy. He was undoubtedly a member of the clergy, but he almost certainly did not lead a cloistered existence, for the five pieces he contributed to the Wakefield cycle are filled with an extraordinary array of characters and situations, some of which he must have witnessed firsthand, others that he probably picked up from current folk tales, and some that he invented—but invented out of a rich storehouse of experience.

The Wakefield cycle itself originated during the second half of the fourteenth century, about fifty years before the time of the Wakefield Master, and it continued to be revised and performed until the late sixteenth century. It is, like the other surviving English cycles, a composite of plays written and rewritten by several authors at several different periods to meet the changing needs of the community. New plays were added as guilds became large and prosperous enough to mount their own productions; old plays were dropped or combined with others when a guild ran into hard times and could no longer afford its own production; or they were revised to satisfy objections of the church or the community. Although it is a patchwork of thirty-two plays, its pieces are unified by the pattern of spiritual history embodied in each play individually and all of them collectively. But the five plays written by the Wakefield Master stand out from the rest of the cycle.

His verse form is his most telling signature. The nine-line stanza he uses throughout his five plays does not occur anywhere else in the cycle except at a few points that bear the signs of his revision. In fact, his nine-line stanza is not to be found anywhere else in any of the other cycles, or anywhere else in medieval literature. Not only is it unique, but it is a remarkably complex harmony of rhymes and rhythms, all of which have been reproduced in Anthony Caputi's modernized version of *The Second Shepherds' Play*. The first four lines combine not only identical end rhymes, but also identical internal rhymes. The last five lines have an entirely different rhyme scheme, for the sixth, seventh, and eighth lines rhyme with one another, while the ninth line rhymes with the fifth to hold the elaborate structure of sounds together. As the rhyme scheme shifts from the first to the last part of each stanza, so does the rhythm. Each of the first four lines contains four beats; the fifth consists of only one stressed syllable; the sixth, seventh, and eighth have three stresses; and the ninth contains two stresses. The conception and execution of such an elaborate verse form is unquestionably the work of a technical virtuoso.

Even more remarkable is the fact that he sustains his verse form throughout all his plays, adapting its harmonies to widely different moods and situations, such as God loftily giving Noah specifications for the ark, or Noah's wife peevishly refusing to board the ark, or the shepherds devoutly presenting their gifts to the newborn child, or the Jewish high priest Annas unctuously expounding legal procedure to Christ, or the tyrant Herod maniacally raging about his political power. Dramatic situations so various as these require not only a flexible verse form but also a flexibility of language, and the Wakefield Master repeatedly displays his versatility, for he draws on an extensive vocabulary, ranging from slang, to colloquial, to formal usage, from one medieval dialect to another, from English to Latin and back. Yet he always finds the right word or expression to suit any character in any situation.

Ultimately, his plays stand out because his characters and his plots are masterfully developed, even within the short scope of several hundred lines. *The Second Shepherds' Play,* the longest of his works, contains only 754 lines, yet it projects a vividly developed world of shepherds and sheep stealers, a world with an imaginative life of its own as well as a relevance to the religious theme of the play. In the opening 190 lines, for example, even before the appearance of the sheep stealer Mak, the dialogue of the three shepherds fully distinguishes them from one another. The first shepherd, Coll, is obsessed by his poverty and outraged by the gentry who exploit him and his fellows; the second shepherd, Gib, is preoccupied by the afflictions of married life; and the third shepherd, Daw, is fed up with his job of tending others' sheep while they rest and he goes hungry. Although their complaints are different, they are united by affliction, by the misery of the weather that accentuates these complaints, and by the rough but good fellowship that sustains them. And their combined suffering dramatically presents the image of a world in need of salvation, a need that anticipates the end of the play and which accounts for the joy they express on learning of the savior.

The sheep stealing episode is the supreme example of the Wakefield Master's skill in turning a good folk story into good theater and ultimately into good religious example. As the farce unfolds, even before the marvelous moment of exposure, it becomes increasingly clear that Mak, and his wife, and the stolen sheep disguised as a newborn child are upside down versions of Joseph, Mary, and Christ. The make-believe birth staged by Mak and his wife provides a dramatically sharp contrast to the nativity scene that follows. Clearly, the Wakefield Master has taken enormous liberties with the brief biblical cue in the *Book of Luke*—"And there were in the same country shepherds abiding in the field, keeping watch over their flocks by night." But it is precisely those liberties that account for both the theatrical and the religious effectiveness of *The Second Shepherds' Play*.

Like all biblical plays, it is relatively easy to stage. The cast is small, the parts are short. Only two specific locations are required, one for Mak's house, the other for the stable at Bethlehem, the area between them standing for the open fields. Likewise, only a few props are needed: a crib, a couple of chairs and a table at Mak's house; a crib and a chair at the stable; and some kind of sheep, dummy or live. Because it is so easy to put on, it has been widely performed, especially during the Christmas season, by amateur student groups at colleges and universities throughout England and America. Though physically easy to stage, it is difficult to perform, for it requires actors to move abruptly yet believably from the rough and tumble antics of the sheep stealing episode to the devotional attitudes of the nativity scene. In this respect, *The Second Shepherds' Play* epitomizes the sharp contrasts of mood and action that are at work throughout the Wakefield cycle—contrasts that were evidently displayed by the Mermaid Company of London in its 1961 production of plays from the cycle (see Figures 1, 2, and 3). Judging from a review of that production, the dramatic contrasts of biblical drama are as moving today as they were in their own time.

THE SECOND SHEPHERDS' PLAY

BY THE WAKEFIELD MASTER / MODERNIZED AND EDITED BY ANTHONY CAPUTI

CHARACTERS

FIRST SHEPHERD, COLL
SECOND SHEPHERD, GIB
THIRD SHEPHERD, DAW
MAK
GILL, *his wife*
ANGEL
MARY

(Enter the FIRST SHEPHERD.*)*

FIRST SHEPHERD: Lord, but it's cold, and I'm
    wretchedly wrapped.
My hands nearly numb, so long have I napped.
My legs creak and fold, my fingers are chapped;
It is not as I would, for I am all lapped
    In sorrow.
In storms and tempest,
Now in the east, now in the west,
Woe is him has never rest
    Midday nor morrow!   10

But we poor shepherds that walk on the moor,
We're like, in faith, to be put out of door;
No wonder, as it stands, if we be poor,
For the tilth of our lands lies fallow as a floor,
    As ye ken.
We are so lamed,
So taxed and shamed,
We are made hand-tamed
    By these gentlery-men.

Thus they rob us of rest. Our Lady them harry!
These men that are lord-fast, they make the plough
    tarry.
Some say it's for the best; but we find it contrary.
Thus are tenants oppressed, in point to miscarry,
    In life.
Thus hold they us under;
Thus they bring us in blunder.
It were a great wonder
    If ever we should thrive.

30   'Gainst a man with painted sleeves, or a brooch,
        now-a-days,
Woe to him that shall grieve, or one word gainsay!
No man dare him reprove, what mastery he has.
Yet no man believes one word that he says,

No letter.
He can make purveyance,
With boast and arrogance;
And all is for maintenance
    Of men that are greater.

There shall come a swain as proud as a po,°   40
He must borrow my wain,° and my plough also,
That I am full fain to grant ere he go.
Thus live we in pain, anger, and woe
    By night and day.
Whatever he has willed
Must at once be fulfilled.
I were better be killed
    Than once say him nay.

It does me good, as I walk round alone,
Of this world for to talk in manner of groan.   50
To my sheep will I stalk, now as I moan;
There abide on a ridge, or sit on a stone,
    Full soon.
For I know, pardie,°
True men if they be,
I'll get more company
    Ere it be noon. *(Moves aside)*

(Enter the SECOND SHEPHERD.*)*

SECOND SHEPHERD: Ben'c'te° and Dominus! What
    may this bemean?
Why fares this world thus; the like has seldom   60
    been.
Lord, the weather is spiteful, and the winds bitter
    keen,
And the frosts so hideous, they water my een.°
    No lie.

---

    po, peacock. *wain,* wagon. *pardie,* Pardieu; By God;
indeed. *Ben'c'te,* Benedicte. *een,* eyes.

Now in dry, now in wet,
Now in snow, now in sleet,
My shoes freeze to my feet,
    And all is awry.

70 But as far as I ken, wherever I go,
We poor wedded men endure much woe,
Crushed again and again, it falls oft so.
And Silly Capel, our hen, both to and fro
    She cackles;
But begin she to croak,
To groan or to choke,
For our cock it's no joke,
    For he's in the shackles.

These men that are wed have never their will.
80 When they're full hard bestead,° they sigh and
        keep still.
God knows they are led full hard and full ill;
In bower nor in bed say they aught until
    Ebb tide.
My part have I found,
And my lesson is sound:
Woe to him that is bound,
    For he must abide.

But now late in our lives—a marvel to me,
90 That I think my heart rives such wonders to see,
What destiny drives that it should so be—
Some men will have two wives, and some men three
    In store.
He has woe that has any;
But so far ken I,
He has moe° that has many,
    For he feels sore.

But young men a'wooing, before you've been
        caught,
100 Be well ware of wedding, and keep in your
        thought,
To moan, "Had I known," is a thing that serves
        naught.
Mickle° mourning has wedding to home often
        brought,
    And griefs,
With many a sharp shower;
You may catch in an hour
What shall seem full sour
110   As long as you live.

For as ever read I epistle° I've one as my dear,
As sharp as a thistle, as rough as a brere;°
She is browed like a bristle, with a sour lenten
        cheer;

Had she once wet her whistle, she could sing full
        clear
    Her paternoster.
She's as great as a whale;
She has a gallon of gall;
By him that died for us all   120
    I would I'd run till I'd lost her.

FIRST SHEPHERD: Gib, look over the row! Full deafly,
        ye stand.
SECOND SHEPHERD: Yea, the devil in your maw—ye
        blow on your hand.
Saw ye anywhere Daw?
FIRST SHEPHERD: Yea, on a lea-land
I heard him blow. He comes here at hand,
    Not far.
Stand still.   130
SECOND SHEPHERD: Why?
FIRST SHEPHERD: I think he comes by.
SECOND SHEPHERD: He'll trick us with a lie
    Unless we beware.

(Enter the THIRD SHEPHERD, a boy.)

THIRD SHEPHERD: Christ's cross me speed, and Saint
        Nicholas!
Thereof had I need; and it's worse than it was.
Whoso can take heed and let the world pass;
It's rank as a weed and brittle as glass,
        And slides.   140
    This world fared never so,
With marvels more and moe,
    Now in weal, now in woe,
        Everything writhes.

Never since Noah's flood were such floods seen,
Winds and rains so rude, and storms so keen;
Some stammered, some stood in doubt, as I
        ween.
Now God turn all to good! I say as I mean,
        Hereunder.   150
These floods so they drown,
Both in fields and in town,
And bear all down,
    They make you wonder.

We that walk in the nights our cattle to keep,
We see queer sights when other men sleep.
Yet methinks my heart lightens; I see my pals
        peep.
They are two tall wights! Now I'll give my sheep
    A turn.   160
O full ill am I bent,
As I walk on this land.
I may lightly repent,
    If my toes I spurn.

---

bestead, situated. moe, more. mickle, much. epis-
tle, in the New Testament. brere, briar.

(to the other two) Ah, sir, God you save, and master
    mine!
A drink would I have, and somewhat to dine.
FIRST SHEPHERD: Christ's curse, my knave, thou'rt a
    lazy swine!
170 SECOND SHEPHERD: The boy likes to rave! Let him
      stand there and whine
    Till we've made it.
    Ill thrift on thy pate!
    Though the fellow came late,
    Yet is he in state
      To dine—if he had it.

THIRD SHEPHERD: Such servants as I, that sweat and
    swink,°
Eat our bread full dry, that's what I think.
180 We're oft wet and weary when master men wink,°
Yet come full late both dinners and drink.
    But neatly
Both our dame and our sire,
When we've run in the mire,
Can nip at our hire,
    And pay us full lately.

But hear a truth, master, for you the fare make:
I shall do, hereafter, work as I take;
I shall do a little, sir, and between times play.
190 For I've never had suppers that heavily weigh
    In fields.
And why should I bray?
I can still run away.
What sells cheap, men say,
    Never yields.

FIRST SHEPHERD: Thou are an ill lad, to ride a-wooing
With a man that had but little of spending.
SECOND SHEPHERD: Peace, boy! I bade; no more
    jangling,
200 Or I shall make thee afraid, by the Heaven's King,
    With thy frauds.
Where are the sheep, boy; lorn?
THIRD SHEPHERD: Sir, this same day at morn
I them left in the corn,
    When they rang lauds.°

They have pasture good; they cannot go wrong.
FIRST SHEPHERD: That's right. Oh, by the rood, these
    nights are long!
Yet I would, ere we go, let's have us a song.
210 SECOND SHEPHERD: So I thought as I stood, to cheer
    us along.
THIRD SHEPHERD: I grant.
FIRST SHEPHERD: The tenor I'll try.
SECOND SHEPHERD: And I the treble so high.

THIRD SHEPHERD: Then the middle am I.
Let's see how ye chant. *(They sing.)*

(Enter MAK *with a cloak over his smock.)*

MAK: Now, Lord, of names seven, that made the
    moon so pale,
And more stars than I can name; Thy good will
    fails;   220
I am so in a whirl that my jogged brain ails
Now would God I were in heaven—where no child
    wails—
    Heaven so still.
FIRST SHEPHERD: Who is it that pipes so poor?
MAK: God knows what I endure,
    Here a'walking on the moor,
    And not my will!

SECOND SHEPHERD: From where do ye come, Mak?
    What news do ye bring?   230
THIRD SHEPHERD: Is he come? Then everyone take
    heed to his things.

(Takes the cloak from MAK.*)*

MAK: What! I am a yeoman (hear me you) of the king,
Make way for me, the Lord's tidings I bring,
    And such.
Fie on you! Go hence!
This is no pretence.
I must have reverence.
    And much!

FIRST SHEPHERD: Why make ye so quaint, Mak? It's 240
    no good to try.
SECOND SHEPHERD: Why play ye the saint, Mak? We
    know that you lie.
THIRD SHEPHERD: We know you can feint, Mak, and
    give the devil the lie.
MAK: I'll make such complaint, 'lack,° I'll make you all
    fry
    At a word.
And tell what ye doth.
FIRST SHEPHERD: But, Mak, is that truth?   250
Go gild that green tooth
    With a turd.

SECOND SHEPHERD: Mak, the devil's in your eye! A
    stroke would I lend you.
THIRD SHEPHERD: Mak, know ye not me? By God, I
    could 'tend you.
MAK: God keep you all three! Perhaps I can mend
    you.
You're a fair company.
FIRST SHEPHERD: Can ye so bend you?   260
SECOND SHEPHERD: Rascal jape!°
    Thus late, as thou goes,

---

swink, toil. **wink,** doze. **lauds,** the early morning
service.

'lack, alack: an expression of surprise or dismay. **jape,**
fool.

What will men suppose?
Sure thou hast an ill nose
For stealing of sheep.

MAK: And I am true as steel, all men say,
But a sickness I feel that takes my health away;
My belly's not well, not at all well today.
THIRD SHEPHERD: "Seldom lies the devil dead by the
270   way."
MAK: Therefore
Full sore am I and ill;
And I'll lie stone still
If I've eat even a quill
This month and more.

FIRST SHEPHERD: How fares thy wife? By my hood,
    tell me true.
MAK: Lies sprawling by the fire, but that's nothing
    new;
280 And a house full of brood. She drinks well, too;
Come ill or good that she'll always do
    But so.
Eats as fast as she can;
And each year gives a man
A hungry bairn° to scan,
And some years two.

And were I more gracious and richer by far,
I were eaten still out of house and of barn.
And just look at her close, if ye come near;
290 There is none that knows what 'tis to fear
    Than ken I.
Will ye see what I proffer—
I'll give all in my coffer
And masses I'll offer
To bid her goodbye.

SECOND SHEPHERD: I am so long wakéd, like none in
    this shire,
I would sleep if I takéd less for my hire.
THIRD SHEPHERD: I am cold and near naked, and
300   would have a fire.
FIRST SHEPHERD: I am weary, for-rakéd,° and run in
    the mire.
Stay awake, you!
SECOND SHEPHERD: Nay, I'll lie down by,
I must sleep must I.
THIRD SHEPHERD: I've as good need to put by
As any of you.

But, Mak, come hither! Between us must you be.
MAK: You're sure you don't want to talk privately?°
310   Indeed?
From my top to my toe,

---

bairn, child. **for-rakéd,** exhausted.

Manus tuas commendo,
Pontio Pilato,°
    Christ's cross me speed!

(Then he rises, the shepherds being asleep, and says.)

Now were time for a man that wants for gold
To stealthily enter into a fold,
And nimbly to work then, yet be not too bold,
For he might pay for the bargain, if it were told,
    At the ending.
Now were time for to spell—   320
But he needs good counsel
That fain would fare well,
    And has little spending.

But about you a circle as round as a moon,
Till I've done what I will, till it be noon,
Ye must lie stone still till I have done.
And I shall say thereto of words a few.
    On height.
Over your heads my hands I lift;
Your eyes go out and senses drift   330
Until I make a better shift
    If it be right.

Lord, how they sleep hard! That may ye all hear.
I never was a shepherd, but now will I learn.
If the flock be scared, when I shall creep near.
How! Draw hitherward! Now mends our cheer
    From sorrow.
A fat sheep, I dare say;
A good fleece, dare I lay!
Pay back when I may,   340
    But this will I borrow.

(MAK crosses the stage to his house.)

How, Gill, art thou in? Get us some light.
WIFE: Who makes such din this time of the night?
I am set for to spin; no hope that I might
Rise a penny to win. I curse them on height.
    So sore
A housewife thus fares,
She always has cares
And all for nothing bears
    All these chores.   350

MAK: Good wife, open the latch! Seest thou not what
    I bring?
WIFE: I'll let thee draw the catch. Ah, come in my
    sweeting!
MAK: Yea, thou dost not reek of my long standing.
WIFE: By thy bare neck for this you're like to swing.
MAK: Go away:
I'm good for something yet,

Manus . . . Pilato, "Into thy hands I commend them,
Pontius Pilate."

For in a pinch can I get
360   More than they that swink and sweat
     All the long day.

Thus it fell to my lot, Gill, I had such grace.
WIFE: It were a foul blot to be hanged for the case.
MAK: But I have escaped, Gill, a far narrower place.
WIFE: Yet so long goes the pot to the water, men say,
   At last
Comes it home broken.
MAK: Well know I the token,
   But let it never be spoken;
370   But come and help fast.

I would he were slain; I want to eat.
This twelvemonth have I not ta'en of one sheep's
   meat.
WIFE: Should they come ere he's slain, and hear the
   sheep bleat—
MAK: Then might I be ta'en! That puts me in a heat!
   Go bar
The gate door.
WIFE: Yes, Mak,
380   For if they come at thy back—
MAK: Then might I pay for the pack!
   May the devil us warn.

WIFE: A good trick have I spied, since thou ken none.
Here shall we him hide till they be gone—
In my cradle abide. Let me alone,
And I shall lie beside in childbed, and groan.
MAK: Thou hast said;
   And I'll say thou was light°
   Of a male child this night.
390 WIFE: It's luck I was born bright,
   And cleverly bred.

For shrewdness this trick can't be surpassed;
Yet a woman's advice always helps at the last!
Before they 'gin to spy, hurry thou fast.
MAK: Unless I come ere they rise, they'll blow a loud
   blast!
   I'll go sleep.

(MAK *returns to the shepherds and resumes his place.*)

Yet sleeps all this company;
And I shall go stalk privily,
400   As it had never been me
     That carried their sheep.

FIRST SHEPHERD: *Resurrex a mortuis!*° Take hold of my
   hand.
   Judas carnas dominus!° I can not well stand;
   My foot sleeps, by Jesus; and I'm dry as sand.
   I thought we had laid us near English land.

SECOND SHEPHERD: Ah, yea!
   I slept so well, I feel
   As fresh as an eel,
   As light on my heel 410
     As leaf on a tree.

THIRD SHEPHERD: Lord bless us all! My body's all
   a-quake!
My heart jumps from my skin, sure and that's no
   fake.
Who makes all this din? So my head aches.
I'll teach him something. Hark, fellows, awake!
   We were four.
See ye aught of Mak now?
FIRST SHEPHERD: We were up ere thou. 420
SECOND SHEPHERD: Man, I give God a vow,
   That he went nowhere.

THIRD SHEPHERD: I dreamed he was lapped in a gray
   wolf's skin.
FIRST SHEPHERD: So many are wrapped
   now—namely, within.
THIRD SHEPHERD: When we had so long napped,
   methought he did begin
A fat sheep to trap; but he made no din.
SECOND SHEPHERD: Be still! 430
   Thy dream makes thee brood;
   It's but fancy, by the rood.
FIRST SHEPHERD: Now God turn all to good,
   If it be his will!

SECOND SHEPHERD: Rise, Mak! For shame! Thou liest
   right long.
MAK: Now Christ's holy name be us among!
   What is this? By Saint James, I may not move
   along!
   I think I be the same. Ah! my neck has lain wrong 440
   Enough (*They help* MAK *up.*)
Mickle thanks! Since yestere'en,
Now, by Saint Stephen,
   I was flayed with a dream
     That my heart did cuff.

I thought Gill began to croak and labor full sad,
Indeed at the first cock had borne a young lad
To increase our flock. Guess whether I'm glad;
I am now more in hock than ever I had.
   Ah, my head! 450
A house full of bairns!
'Devil knock out their brains!
For father is the pains,
   And little bread!

I must go home, by your leave, to Gill, as I thought.
I pray you look in my sleeve that I steal naught;
I am loath you to grieve or from you take aught.

---

   light, delivered.   *Resurrex . . . ; Judas . . . dominus,*
These lines are in mock-Latin.

THIRD SHEPHERD: Go forth; ill might thou live! Now
    would I we sought,
460   This morn,
    That we had all our store.
FIRST SHEPHERD: But I will go before;
    Let us meet.
SECOND SHEPHERD: Where?
THIRD SHEPHERD: At the crooked thorn.

(MAK crosses to his cottage.)

MAK: Undo this door, here! How long shall I stand?
WIFE: Who makes such a stir? Go walk in quicksand!
MAK: Ah, Gill, what cheer? It is I, Mak, your
    husband.
470 WIFE: Then may we see here the devil in a band,
    Sir Guile.
    Lo, he comes with a knot
    At the back of his crop.°
    I'll soon to my cot
    For a very long while.

MAK: Will ye hear what she makes to get her a gloze?°
    She does naught but plays, and wiggles her toes.
WIFE: Why, who wanders? Who wakes? Who comes?
    Who goes?
480 Who brews? Who bakes? What makes me this hose?
    And then,
    It's a pity to behold,
    Now in hot, now in cold,
    Full of woe is the household
    That wants a woman.

    But what end has thou made with the shepherds,
    Mak?
MAK: The last word that they said, when I turned my
    back,
490 They would look that they had their sheep, count
    the pack.
    I'm sure they'll not be glad to find one they lack,
    Pardie.
    But howsoever it goes,
    They will surely suppose,
    From me the trouble 'rose,
    And cry out upon me.
    But thou must do as thou hight.°

WIFE: Of course I will.
500 I shall swaddle him right; you trust in your Gill.
    If it were a worse plight, yet could I help still.
    I will lie down straight. Come, cover me.
MAK: I will.
WIFE: Behind!
    It may be a narrow squeak.
MAK: Yes, if too close they peak,
    Or if the sheep should speak!
WIFE: 'Tis then time to whine.

Hearken when they call; for they will come anon.°
Come and make ready all, and sing on thine own;   510
Sing lullaby thou shall, for I must groan
And cry out by the wall on Mary and John,
    For sore.
Sing a lullaby, fast,
Like thou sang at our last;
If I play a false cast,
    Trust me no more!

(The SHEPHERDS meet at the crooked hawthorn.)

THIRD SHEPHERD: Ah, Coll, good morn! Why sleep
    thou not?
FIRST SHEPHERD: Alas, that ever I was born! We have   520
    a foul blot.
    A fat lamb have we lorn.°
THIRD SHEPHERD: Marry, God forbid!
SECOND SHEPHERD: Who should do us that scorne?
    That were a foul spot.
FIRST SHEPHERD: Some shrew.
    I have sought with my dogs
    All Horbury Bogs,
    And with fifteen hogs
    Found I but one ewe.   530

THIRD SHEPHERD: Now trust me if ye will; by Saint
    Thomas of Kent,
    Either Mak or Gill was at that assent.
FIRST SHEPHERD: Peace, man, be still! I saw when he
    went.
    Thou slanders him ill. Thou ought to repent.
    Good speed.
SECOND SHEPHERD: 'Now if ever I lie,
    If I should even here die,
    I would say it were he   540
    That did that same deed.

THIRD SHEPHERD: Go we thither, I rede,° at a running
    trot.
    I shall never eat bread till the truth I've got.
FIRST SHEPHERD: Nor drink, in my heed, until we
    solve this plot.
SECOND SHEPHERD: Till we know all, indeed, I will
    rest no jot,
    My brother!
    One thing I will plight: 550
    Till I see him in sight
    Shall I never sleep one night
    Where I do another.

(At MAK's house they hear GILL groan and MAK sing a
lullaby.)

THIRD SHEPHERD: Will ye hear how they hack? Our
    sir likes to croon.

---

knot . . . crop, an allusion to hanging. **gloze,** an excuse.
hight, promised.

anon, soon. **lorn,** lost. **rede,** advise.

FIRST SHEPHERD: Heard I never one crack so clear out
    of tune!
    Call on him.
SECOND SHEPHERD: Mak! Undo your door soon.
560 MAK: Who is that spake as it were high noon
    On loft?
    Who is that, I say?
THIRD SHEPHERD: Good fellows, were it day.
MAK: As far as ye may,
    Good, speak soft,

Over a sick woman's head that is ill at ease;
I had rather be dead e'er she had any dis-ease.
WIFE: Go to another place! I may not well wheeze.
    Each foot that ye tread goes to make me sneeze,
570   So "he-e-e-e'."
FIRST SHEPHERD: Tell us, Mak, if ye may,
    How fare ye, I say?
MAK: But are ye in town today?
    Now how fare ye?

Ye have run in the mire, and are all wet yet.
I shall make you a fire, if ye will sit.
A nurse would I hire, and never doubt it.
But at my present hire—well, I hope for a bit
    In season.
580 I've more bairns than ye knew,
    And sure the saying is true,
    "We must drink as we brew,"
    And that's but reason.

I would ye dined ere ye go. Methinks that ye sweat.
SECOND SHEPHERD: Nay, that mends not our mood,
    neither drink nor meat.
MAK: Why, what ails you sir?
THIRD SHEPHERD: Yea, our sheep that we get
    Are stolen as they go. Our loss is not sweet.
590 MAK: Sirs, drink!
    Had I been there,
    Someone had paid full dear.
FIRST SHEPHERD: Some men think that ye were;
    And that makes us think.

SECOND SHEPHERD: Mak, some men say that it should
    be ye.
THIRD SHEPHERD: Either ye or your spouse; who else
    could it be?
MAK: Now, if ye suspect us, either Gill or me,
600   Come and rip our house, and then ye may see
    Who had her.
    If I any sheep got
    Any cow or stott°—
    And Gill, my wife, rose not
    Since here she laid her.

As I am true and leal,° to God here I pray.
That this be the first meal that I shall eat this day.
FIRST SHEPHERD: Mak, as I have weal,° have a care, I
    say:
    "He learned timely to steal that could not say nay." 610
WIFE: I swelt!°
    Out, thieves from my home!
    Ye come to rob us, ye drones!
MAK: Hear ye not how she groans?
    Your heart should melt.

WIFE: Out, thieves, from my bairn! Get out of the
    door!
MAK: Knew ye what she had borne, your hearts
    would be sore.
    Ye do wrong, I you warn, that thus come before 620
    To a woman that has borne. But I say no more.
WIFE: Ah, my middle!
    I pray to God so mild,
    If ever I you beguiled,
    Let me eat this child
    That lies in this cradle.

MAK: Peace, woman, for God's pain and cry not so!
    Thou shalt hurt thy brain, and make me full of
    woe.
SECOND SHEPHERD: I think our sheep be slain. Think 630
    you not so?
THIRD SHEPHERD: All work we in vain; as well may we
    go.
    But, drat it,
    I can find no flesh,
    Hard nor nesh,°
    Salt nor fresh,
    But two empty platters.

There's no cattle but this, neither tame nor wild,
None, as have I bliss, that smells as he smelled. 640
WIFE: No, so God me bless, and give me joy of my
    child!
FIRST SHEPHERD: We have marked amiss; I hold us
    beguiled.
SECOND SHEPHERD: Sir, done.
    Sir, Our Lady him save!
    Is your child a knave?
MAK: Any lord might him crave,
    This child as his son.

When he wakens, he skips, that a joy is to see. 650
THIRD SHEPHERD: In good time be his steps, and
    happy they be!
    Who were his godfathers, tell now to me?
MAK: So fair fall their lips!
FIRST SHEPHERD: Hark now, a lie!
MAK: So God them thank,

---

stott, bullock.

leal, loyal. weal, riches. swelt, faint. nesh, tender.

Parkin and Gibbon Waller, I say,
And gentle John Horn, in good faith,
He gave all the array
660   And promised a great shank.

SECOND SHEPHERD: Mak, friends will we be, for we
   are all one.
MAK: We! Now I hold for me, from you help get I
   none.
Farewell, all three! All glad were ye gone!

(The SHEPHERDS *go out.)*

THIRD SHEPHERD: Fair words may there be, but love
   there is none
This year.
FIRST SHEPHERD: Gave ye the child anything?
670   SECOND SHEPHERD: I trow,° not one farthing!
THIRD SHEPHERD: Fast back will I fling;
   Abide ye me here.

(The SHEPHERDS *re-enter the house.)*

Mak, take it to no grief, if I come to thy bairn.
MAK: Nay, thou does me mischief, and foul has thou
   fared.
THIRD SHEPHERD: The child will not grieve, that little
   day-star.
Mak, with your leave, let me give your bairn
   But sixpence.
680   MAK: Nay, go 'way; he sleeps.
THIRD SHEPHERD: Methinks he peeps.
MAK: When he wakens he weeps!
   I pray you, go hence!

THIRD SHEPHERD: Give me leave him to kiss, and lift
   up the clout.°
What the devil is this? What a monstrous snout!
FIRST SHEPHERD: He is marked amiss. Let's not wait
   about.
SECOND SHEPHERD: "Ill spun cloth," iwis, "aye comes
690   foul out."
   Aye, so!
He is like to our sheep!
THIRD SHEPHERD: How, Gib, may I peep?
FIRST SHEPHERD: I trow, nature will creep
   Where it may not go!

SECOND SHEPHERD: This was a quaint fraud, and a far
   cast!
It should be noised abroad.
THIRD SHEPHERD: Yea, sirs, and classed.
700   Let's burn this bawd, and bind her fast.
Everyone will applaud to hang her at last,
   So shall thou.
Will ye see how they swaddle
His four feet in the middle?

Saw I never in cradle
   A horned lad ere now.

MAK: Peace, peace, I ask. You'll give the child a scare.
For I am his father, and yon woman him bare.
FIRST SHEPHERD: After what devil shall he be called?
   "Mak?" Lo, Mak's heir!   710
SECOND SHEPHERD: Let be all that. Now God give him
   care,
I say.
WIFE: A pretty child is he
To sit on a woman's knee;
A dilly-downe, pardie,
   To make a father gay.

THIRD SHEPHERD: I know him by the ear-mark; that's
   a good token.
MAK: I tell you, sirs, hark! His nose was broken;   720
Later told me a clerk that he was forespoken.°
FIRST SHEPHERD: Liar! You deserve to have your
   noddle broken!
Get a weapon.
WIFE: He was taken by an elf,
I saw it myself;
When the clock struck twelve
   He was misshapen.

SECOND SHEPHERD: Ye two are well made to lie in the
   same bed.   730
THIRD SHEPHERD: Since they maintain their theft, let's
   see them both dead.
MAK: If I do wrong again, cut off my head!
   I'm at your will.
FIRST SHEPHERD: Sirs, take this plan, instead,
   For this trespass:
We'll neither curse nor fight,
Quarrel nor chide,
But seize him tight
   And cast him in canvas.   740

(They toss MAK *in a sheet and go back to the fields.)*

FIRST SHEPHERD: Lord, but I am sore; I feel about to
   burst.
In faith, I may no more; therefore will I rest.
SECOND SHEPHERD: As a sheep of seven score he
   weighed in my fist.
Now to sleep anywhere methinks were the best.
THIRD SHEPHERD: Now I pray you,
   Let's lie down on this green.
FIRST SHEPHERD: Oh, these thieves are so keen.
THIRD SHEPHERD: Let's forget what has been,   750
   So I say you. *(They sleep.)*

(An ANGEL *sings "Gloria in excelsis"; then let him say.)*

ANGEL: Rise, herd-men kind! For now is he born

---

trow, assert as true; admit.   *clout,* cloth.

forespoken, bewitched.

That shall take from the fiend what Adam had
  lorn:
That devil to shame this night is he born;
God is made your friend now at this morn.
  He behests
To Bethlehem go ye,
Where lies the Free;°
760 In a manger he'll be
    Between two beasts.

FIRST SHEPHERD: This was a sweet voice as any I've
  heard.
A wonder enough to make a man scared.
SECOND SHEPHERD: To speak of God's son from on
  high he dared.
All the wood on the moor with lightning glared,
  Everywhere.
THIRD SHEPHERD: He said the babe lay
770 In Bethlehem today.
FIRST SHEPHERD: That star points the way.
    Let us seek him there.

SECOND SHEPHERD: Say, what was his song? Heard ye
  not how he cracked it,
Three briefs to a long?°
THIRD SHEPHERD: Yea, marry, he hacked it;
Was no crotchet° wrong, nor nothing that lacked it.
FIRST SHEPHERD: For to sing us among, right as he
  knacked it°
780 I can.
SECOND SHEPHERD: Let's see how ye croon.
Can ye bark at the moon?
THIRD SHEPHERD: Hold your tongues, have done!
FIRST SHEPHERD: Hark after, then!

SECOND SHEPHERD: To Bethlehem he bade that we
  should go;
I am full afeared that we have been too slow.
THIRD SHEPHERD: Be merry and not sad; for sure this
  we know,
790 This news means joy to us men below,
  Of no joy.
FIRST SHEPHERD: Therefore thither hie we,
Be we wet and weary,
To that child and that lady.
  We must see this boy.

SECOND SHEPHERD: We find by the prophecy—let be
  your din!
Of David and Isaiah and others of their kin,
They prophesied by clergy that in a virgin
800 Should he light and lie, to slacken our sin
    And slake it,
Our Race from woe.

For Isaiah said so:
"Ecce virgo
  Concipiet"° a child that is naked.

THIRD SHEPHERD: Full glad may we be that this is that
  day
Him lovely to see, who rules for aye.
Lord, happy I'd be if I could say
That I knelt on my knee so that I might pray 810
  To that child.
But the angel said,
He was poorly arrayed,
And in a manger laid,
  Both humble and mild.

FIRST SHEPHERD: Patriarchs and prophets of old were
  torn
With yearning to see this child that is born.
They are gone full clean, and their trouble they've
  lorn. 820
But we shall see him, I ween,° ere it be morn,
  To token.
When I see him and feel,
Then know I full well
It is true as steel
  That prophets have spoken:

To so poor as we are that he would appear,
To find us and tell us by his messenger!
SECOND SHEPHERD: Go we now, let us fare, for the
  place is near. 830
THIRD SHEPHERD: I am ready, prepared; let us go
  with good cheer
To that bright
Lord, if thy will be—
We are simple all three—
Grant us some kind of glee
  To comfort thy wight.° (They enter the stable.)

FIRST SHEPHERD: Hail, comely and clean! Hail, young
  child!
Hail, Maker, as I mean, born of maiden so mild! 840
Thou has cursed, I ween, the devil so wild;
The false guiler of men, now goes he beguiled.
  Lo, he merry is!
Look, he laughs, the sweeting!
Well, to this meeting
I bring as my greeting
  A bob of cherries!

SECOND SHEPHERD: Hail, sovereign Savior, our
  ransom thou hast bought!

---

the Free, The Divine One. *Three ... long,* musical
notes. *crotchet,* a quarter note. *knacked it,* did it cleverly.

Ecce ... Concipiet, "Behold, a virgin shall conceive,"
Cf. *Isaiah,* 7, 14; *Luke,* 1, 31; and *Matthew,* 1, 23, *I ween,* I
imagine. *wight,* man.

850 Hail, noble child and flower, that all things has
    wrought!
Hail, full of favor, that made all of naught!
Hail! I kneel and I cower. A bird have I brought
    To my bairn.
Hail, little tiny mop!
Of our creed thou art crop.
I would drink of thy cup,
    Little day-star.

THIRD SHEPHERD: Hail, darling dear, thou art God
860   indeed!
I pray thee be near when that I have need.
Hail! Sweet is thy cheer! My heart would bleed
To see thee lie here in so poor a weed,
    With no pennies.
I would give thee my all,
Though I bring but a ball;
Have and play thee withal,
    And go to the tennis.

MARY: The Father of Heaven, God omnipotent,
870   That set all in seven days, his Son has sent.

My name he has blessed with peace ere he went.
I conceived him through grace as God had meant;
    And now he's born.
I shall pray him so
To keep you all from woe!
Tell this wherever ye go,
    And mind this morn.

FIRST SHEPHERD: Farewell, lady, so fair to behold,
    With thy child on thy knee!
SECOND SHEPHERD: Still he lies full cold.   880
    Lord, how favored I be. Now we go forth, behold.
THIRD SHEPHERD: Forsooth, already this seems a
    thing told
    Full oft.
FIRST SHEPHERD: What grace we have found!
SECOND SHEPHERD: Spread the tidings around!
THIRD SHEPHERD: To sing are we bound:
    Let take aloft! *(They sing.)*

Figure 1. Mak steals the sheep while the three shepherds are sleeping in the Mermaid Theatre production of *The Second Shepherds' Play,* directed by Sally Miles and Colin Ellis, London, 1961. (Photograph: The London Company [International Plays] Limited.)

Figure 2. The three shepherds pay a visit to Mak and Gill in the Mermaid Theatre production of *The Second Shepherds' Play,* directed by Sally Miles and Colin Ellis, London, 1961. (Photograph: The London Company [International Plays] Limited.)

Figure 3. The three shepherds journey to Bethlehem to celebrate the birth of Christ in the Mermaid Theatre production of *The Second Shepherds' Play,* directed by Sally Miles and Colin Ellis, London, 1961. (Photograph: The London Company [International Plays] Limited.)

Staging of *The Wakefield Mystery Plays*

**REVIEW OF THE MERMAID THEATRE
PRODUCTION, 1961, BY BAMBER GASCOIGNE**

The mystery plays now being performed at the Mermaid are over 500 years old—yet they are probably nearer to their present audience than they could have been to any since the sixteenth century. The stressed and alliterative poetry sounds familiar to us because Eliot has stretched back to sink his roots in it, and the theatrical convention is little short of Brechtian.

The excellent Mermaid staging of these Wakefield plays has an authentic medieval flavour. Noah, for example, after receiving the measurements of the ark from God, strips off his coat and sets to. Within a very few lines, muttered to himself as he works, he has erected a splendidly painted boat out of four or five preconstructed pieces. The bow and stern slide into the central hull, then the 'castle' fits neatly on the top. Noah stands back in wonder to admire such God-given progress and the audience burst into delighted applause. Later, when the rain begins, he lets down a flap on the front of the boat to reveal painted waves; and when he is chasing his reluctant wife past these waves they both laboriously gather up their skirts and prance high-stepping through the imagined water. This theatricality, making no attempt at illusion, has endless delights of its own—the sight, for example, of two detachable fig leaves waiting on a painted fig-tree for their moment of glory. And, oddly enough, know-ing the story heightens the suspense rather than dissipates it (this is another of those paradoxes which are at the root of the success of Brecht's theater); knowing that Lazarus will appear from the tomb intensifies the drama because it focuses our attention during the early part of the scene. When he does appear, this Mermaid Lazarus, pale, thin and stiff, he delivers a magnificent *memento mori* which will not lightly be forgotten.

The formalism of the comedy scenes becomes, in the serious parts, an admirable and moving formality—a matter of the deepest simplicity. And always, brilliantly, the poetry changes to define the mood. One witnesses a craftsman's carpentry of dramatic language, something used by Eliot in *Murder in the Cathedral* but never again heard of since he buried his muse in the naturalistic drawing room. Martial Rose, the adaptor, faced with countless Middle English and dialect words in the original, has made a version which is always comprehensible without imposing awkward modern phrases and without, hardest of all, spoiling the intricate rhythms and rhymes. The large cast is admirably led by Daniel Thorndike (Noah and Joseph), Donald Eccles (Satan), Gloria Dolskie (The Virgin) and James Bolam (Jesus). 'Cultural' considerations apart, this pageant is an entertainment which shouldn't be missed.

EVERYMAN

ca. 1485

The author of *Everyman* is unknown, but its haunting dramatization of death and redemption has a remarkable ancestry, which can be traced back at least two thousand years earlier to the well known parables of Buddha (563–483 B.C.). Among these parables is the tale of a man who when summoned by death turns to his four wives for companionship, but is refused by the three he loves most and accepted only by the one he loves least. According to Buddha, the three wives who refuse symbolize the man's friends and relatives, his worldly goods, and his bodily powers; the wife who accepts represents his moral intention. Although the parable is an expression of Buddhist faith, it could easily be revised to illustrate Christian belief, as it was thirteen hundred years later, when John Damascene, an eighth century theologian, told about a man with three friends, two who abandon him and one who remains faithful. According to Damascene, the faithful friend represents "the company of good deeds—faith, hope, charity, alms, kindliness, and the whole band of virtues, that can go before us, when we quit the body, and may plead with the Lord on our behalf." The parable of the man and his three friends subsequently made its way throughout medieval Europe and was translated into English by the great fifteenth century printer, William Caxton, who included it in a collection of tales, *The Golden Legend,* which he published in 1483, at about the same time that *Everyman* was probably written. Caxton's version of the parable tells of a man who is summoned by death to make the ultimate pilgrimage, who seeks worldly companionship on his journey, but discovers he can rely only on his spiritual well-being. *Everyman* may be seen as the dramatic embodiment of a universal parable about the vanity of life, the certainty of death, and the undying power of virtue.

Everyman also embodies the anxieties of its age, for the late medieval period was a time when men seemed more preoccupied with death and the afterlife than with life itself. Surely no other age before or since has been so visibly obsessed with thoughts of death. That obsession manifested itself in a wide variety of art forms—woodcuts, murals, sculptures, poems, and plays—all depicting the same morbid image: a skeletal figure who leads a group of men and women from all social stations, literally every man, in a macabre ceremony, the dance of death. That ghastly image expressed the deepest fears of the age, for it portrayed not only the inevitability but also the horror of death, and the horror was frequently emphasized by showing the skeletal figure covered with sores and postules, grisly reminders of the bubonic plague, the Black Death, which ravaged England and the continent during the fourteenth century. Reminders of death were indeed so widespread that they were unavoidable, for if men had not witnessed the plague or seen the dance, then they heard of the agonies from traveling preachers who toured the countryside, admonishing them to think of death and exhorting them to prepare their souls for life after death. That same lesson—the lesson of how to prepare for a godly Christian death—was also the subject of innumerable handbooks, one of which called *The*

Book of the Craft of Dying was printed by Caxton in 1490. Caxton's manual displays the same Christian view of dying that is dramatized in *Everyman*. It describes the temptation of dying men to turn to "temporal things" and counsels "every man, rightful and sinful, (to) bow himself and submit himself fully unto the mighty hand of God."

Everyman exemplifies that religious vision in the allegorical form of a morality play. Its characters are not particular individuals but personified abstractions—Everyman, Death, Fellowship, Good Deeds, Confession—and its plot represents not a unique experience but a paradigm of experience. In its allegorical form as in its Christian theme, *Everyman* is typical of other early morality plays, such as *The Castle of Perseverance* (ca. 1425) and *Mankind* (ca.1475), but its plot is more focussed and its tone far more somber since it concentrates exclusively on the death of Everyman, whereas they portray the entire life of mankind from birth to death. *Mankind* even includes deliberately comic characters whose sacrilegious and obscene jokes were clearly intended to amuse a paying audience, but *Everyman* makes no such concessions. It has only a few comic touches in the behavior of Fellowship, Kindred, and Goods, and those few comic moments are meant less to entertain than to exemplify types of worldly temptation. *Everyman* and its contemporaneous Dutch counterpart *Elckerlijk* (literally, everyman) stand out as the most austerely unified morality plays of the medieval period.

Although *Everyman* is the product of its age—a medieval Catholic morality play—it speaks to all ages and all faiths. Its characters are abstractions, the abstractions of theology expounded in parables and sermons alike, yet those abstractions take on life through the vivid details by which they are characterized. Fellowship, for example, through his hale and hearty welcome to Everyman and his increasingly outlandish promises of assistance immediately shows himself to be a bag of wind, even before his refusal to accompany Everyman reveals him to be a fair weather friend. Kindred and Cousin, on the other hand, are portrayed as solicitous women of few words who have just as little to offer—not much more than the lame excuse of Cousin who claims to have a cramp in her toe. And Goods, far from offering excuses, turns out to be a cruel jester who maliciously delights in Everyman's predicament. Each of the abstractions is individualized so that they become authentic characters whose interaction is dramatically plausible and compelling. When, for example, Everyman turns for assistance to Good Deeds, his pleading is genuinely motivated, following as it does on the increasingly painful series of rejections he has received from Fellowship, Kindred, Cousin, and Goods. Similarly, when Everyman is rejected at the end of the play by Beauty, Strength, Discretion, and Five Wits, his surprise is also well motivated, for while he has been taken up with confession and penance, with the elaborate routine of his last rites, he has still not faced the inescapable facts of death: the physical decay, the loss of consciousness, the end of being in the world as he has known it.

Ultimately, all the characters derive their motivation from the logic of the human psyche, for their interaction is meant to represent the mental, emotional, and spiritual process that takes place in a representative human being during the process of dying. The stages in that process are clearly and eloquently marked out in the play—from the initial denial, to the wish for postponement, to the bargaining, to the frenzied but futile clinging to life, to the acceptance of death, to the spiritual preparation for it, to the experience itself. That is the process Everyman goes through in the play, and it is remarkably similar to the process described in modern psychological studies of dying. They reveal, as does *Everyman,* that dying is something one does alone. Friends and relatives cannot at last help anyone avoid the loneliness of death. The only possible solace is the knowledge of having lived a decent life.

Because of its timelessness, *Everyman* has been one of the most influential plays in the history of drama. In the contemporary period alone, its allegory of dying has been imitated in Beckett's *Endgame,* adapted in Geraldine Fitzgerald's *Everyman and Roach,* and parodied in Arnold Powell's *The Death of Everymom.* It has been performed often and produced variously—in modern dress, in medieval costumes, on proscenium stages, on bare platforms, and on church altars. In one sense, *Everyman* is relatively easy to stage since it requires only a few props, such as a dart for Death, an account book, a scourge for Confession, a crucifix for Everyman, and sacks, packs, and chests for Goods; likewise it mentions specifically only one location: the house of Salvation. But in another sense, it gives directors a compellingly difficult stylistic problem—how to balance its abstract and concrete elements, how to make its experience at once particular and universal. One solution to that problem is discussed in the interview following the play by the director of a recent production at the University of Chicago. His solution was to combine realistic costumes, props, and details of action within the structure of a highly ritualized performance. That combination of effects is clearly revealed in the contrasting dramatic styles shown in Figures 1, 2, 3, and 4. And the combination was evidently unmistakable to the reviewer whose remarks reprinted following the play comment on "its balance between ritual and realism," a balance that is at last not only true to the play, but also to the act of dying itself.

EVERYMAN

MODERNIZED BY KATE FRANKS

CHARACTERS

MESSENGER
GOD
DEATH
EVERYMAN
FELLOWSHIP
KINDRED
COUSIN
GOODS

DOCTOR
GOOD DEEDS
KNOWLEDGE
CONFESSION
BEAUTY
STRENGTH
DISCRETION
FIVE WITS
ANGEL

(Here beginneth a treatise how the High Father of Heaven sendeth Death to summon every creature to come and give account of their lives in this world, and is in manner of a moral play.)

(Enter MESSENGER.*)*

MESSENGER: I pray you all give your audience
And hear this matter with reverence,
By figure a moral play:
The Summoning of Everyman called it is,
That of our lives and ending shows
How transitory we be all day.
This matter is wondrous precious,
But the intent of it is more gracious
And sweet to bear away.
10 The story saith: Man, in the beginning
Look well, and take good heed to the ending,
Be you never so gay!
Ye think sin in the beginning full sweet,
Which in the end causeth the soul to weep,
When the body lieth in clay.
Here shall you see how Fellowship and Jollity
Both, Strength, Pleasure and Beauty
Will fade from thee as flower in May;
For ye shall hear how our Heaven's King
20 Calleth Everyman to a general reckoning.
Give audience, and hear what he doth say.

(Exit MESSENGER.*)*

*(*GOD *speaks.)*

GOD: I perceive, here in my majesty,
How that all creatures be to me unkind,
Living without dread in worldly prosperity.
Of ghostly sight° the people be so blind,
Drowned in sin, they know me not for their God.
In worldly riches is all their mind;
They fear not my righteousness, the sharp rod.
My law that I showed when I for them died

They forget clean, and shedding of my blood red. 30
I hanged between two thieves, it cannot be denied;
To get them life I suffered to be dead;
I healed their feet, with thorns hurt was my head.
I could do no more than I did, truly;
And now I see the people do clean forsake me.
They use the seven deadly sins damnable,
As pride, covetise, wrath, and lechery
Now in the world be made commendable;
And thus they leave of angels the heavenly
  company. 40
Every man liveth so after his own pleasure,
And yet of their life they be nothing sure.
I see the more that I them forbear
The worse they be from year to year.
All that liveth appaireth° fast;
Therefore I will, in all the haste,
Have a reckoning of every man's person;
For, if I leave the people thus alone
In their life and wicked tempests,
Verily they will become much worse than beasts; 50
For now one would by envy another up eat;
Charity they do all clean forget.
I hoped well that every man
In my glory should make his mansion,
And thereto I had them all elect;
But now I see, like traitors deject,
They thank me not for the pleasure that I to them
  meant,
Nor yet for their being that I them have lent.
I proffered the people great multitude of mercy, 60
And few there be that asketh it heartily.
They be so cumbered with worldly riches
That needs on them I must do justice,
On every man living without fear.
Where art thou, Death, thou mighty messenger?

(Enter DEATH.*)*

---

ghostly sight, spiritual sight; knowledge of God.

appaireth, worsens.

DEATH: Almighty God, I am here at your will,
　Your commandment to fulfill.

GOD: Go thou to Everyman
　And show him, in my name,
70　A pilgrimage he must on him take,
　Which he in no wise may escape;
　And that he bring with him a sure reckoning
　Without delay or any tarrying.

DEATH: Lord, I will in the world go run over all
　And cruelly search out both great and small.
　Every man will I beset that liveth beastly
　Out of God's laws, and dreadeth not folly.
　He that loveth riches I will strike with my dart,
　His sight to blind, and from Heaven to depart—
80　Except that alms be his good friend—
　In hell for to dwell, world without end.

(Enter EVERYMAN.*)*

　Lo, yonder I see Everyman walking.
　Full little he thinketh on my coming;
　His mind is on fleshly lusts and his treasure,
　And great pain it shall cause him to endure
　Before the Lord, Heaven's King.
　Everyman, stand still! Whither art thou going
　Thus gaily? Hast thou thy Maker forgot?

EVERYMAN: Why askest thou?
90　Wouldest thou know?

DEATH: Yea, sir. I will you show:
　In great haste I am sent to thee
　From God out of his majesty.

EVERYMAN: What, sent to me?

DEATH: Yea, certainly.
　Though thou have forgot him here,
　He thinketh on thee in the heavenly sphere,
　As, ere we depart, thou shalt know.

EVERYMAN: What desireth God of me?

100　DEATH: That I shall show to thee:
　A reckoning he will needs have
　Without any longer respite.

EVERYMAN: To give a reckoning longer leisure I
　crave;
　This blind° matter troubleth my wit.

DEATH: On thee thou must take a long journey;
　Therefore thy book of account with thee thou
　bring,
　For turn again thou cannot, by no way.
110　And look thou be sure of thy reckoning,
　For before God thou shalt answer and show
　Thy many bad deeds, and good but a few;
　How thou hast spent thy life, and in what wise,
　Before the Chief Lord of Paradise.
　Have ado that thou were in that way,
　For know thou well, thou shalt make no attorney.°

EVERYMAN: Full unready I am, such reckoning to
　give.
　I know thee not. What messenger art thou?

DEATH: I am Death that no man dreadeth,°　　120
　For every man I rest and no man spareth;
　For it is God's commandment
　That all to me should be obedient.

EVERYMAN: O Death, thou comest when I had thee
　least in mind!
　In thy power it lieth me to save;
　Yet of my goods will I give thee, if thou will be
　kind—
　Yea, a thousand pound shalt thou have!—
　And defer this matter till another day.　　130

DEATH: Everyman, it may not be, by no way.
　I set not by gold, silver, nor riches,
　Nor by pope, emperor, king, duke, nor princes;
　For, if I would receive gifts great,
　All the world I might get;
　But my custom is clean contrary:
　I give thee no respite. Come hence, and not tarry!

EVERYMAN: Alas, shall I have no longer respite?
　I may say Death giveth no warning!
　To think on thee, it maketh my heart sick,　　140
　For all unready is my book of reckoning.
　But twelve years if I might have abiding,
　My accounting book I would make so clear
　That my reckoning I should not need to fear.
　Wherefore, Death, I pray thee, for God's mercy,
　Spare me till I be provided of remedy.

DEATH: Thee availeth not to cry, weep and pray;
　But haste thee lightly° that thou were gone that
　journey,
　And prove thy friends if thou can.　　150
　For know thou well the tide abideth no man,
　And in the world each living creature
　For Adam's sin must die of nature.

EVERYMAN: Death, if I should this pilgrimage take
　And my reckoning surely make,
　Show me, for sainted charity,
　Should I not come again shortly?

DEATH: No, Everyman. If thou be once there
　Thou mayst never more come here,
　Trust me verily.　　160

EVERYMAN: O gracious God in the high seat celestial,
　Have mercy on me in this most need!
　Shall I have no company from this vale terrestial
　Of mine acquaintance, that way me to lead?

DEATH: Yea, if any be so hardy
　That would go with thee and bear thee company.
　Hie thee that thou were gone to God's
　magnificence,
　Thy reckoning to give before his presence.
　What, thinkest thou thy life is given thee　　170

---

blind, unknown, obscure.　**no attorney,** You won't be able to plead your case.

---

no man dreadeth, who fears no man.　**lightly,** quickly.

And thy worldly goods also?
EVERYMAN: I had thought so, verily.
DEATH: Nay, nay, it was but lent thee;
For as soon as thou art gone,
Another a while shall have it and then go
    therefrom,
Even as thou hast done.
Everyman, thou art mad! Thou hast thy wits five
And here on earth will not amend thy life;
180   For suddenly I do come.
EVERYMAN: O wretchéd caitiff, whither shall I flee,
That I might escape this endless sorrow?
Now, gentle Death, spare me till tomorrow,
That I may amend me
With good advisement.
DEATH: Nay, thereto I will not consent,
Nor no man will I respite;
But to the heart suddenly I shall smite
Without any advisement.
190   And now out of thy sight I will me hie.
See thou make thee ready shortly;
For thou mayst say this is the day
That no man living may escape away.

(*Exit* DEATH.)

EVERYMAN: Alas, I may well weep with sighs deep!
Now have I no manner of company
To help me in my journey and me to keep;
And also my writing is full unready.
How shall I do now for to excuse me?
I would to God I had never been begot!
200   To my soul a full great profit it had been;
For now I fear pains huge and great.
The time passeth. Lord, help, that all wrought!
For though I mourn it availeth naught.
The day passeth and is almost ago;
I know not well what for to do.
To whom were I best my complaint to make?
What if I to Fellowship thereof spake
And showed him of this sudden chance?
For in him is all mine affiance,°
210   We have in the world so many a day
Been good friends in sport and play.

(*Enter* FELLOWSHIP.)

I see him yonder, certainly.
I trust that he will bear me company;
Therefore to him will I speak to ease my sorrow.
Well met, good Fellowship, and good morrow!
FELLOWSHIP: Everyman, good morrow, by this day!
Sir, why lookest thou so piteously?
If anything be amiss, I pray thee me say,
That I may help to remedy.
220 EVERYMAN: Yea, good Fellowship, yea,
I am in great jeopardy.

FELLOWSHIP: My true friend, show to me your mind.
I will not forsake thee to my life's end
In the way of good company.
EVERYMAN: That was well spoken and lovingly.
FELLOWSHIP: Sir, I must needs know your heaviness;
I have pity to see you in any distress.
If any have you wronged, ye shall revenged be,
Though I on the ground be slain for thee,
Though that I know before that I should die.   230
EVERYMAN: Verily, Fellowship, gramercy.
FELLOWSHIP: Tush! By thy thanks I set not a straw.
Show me your grief, and say no more.
EVERYMAN: If I my heart should to you break,
And then you to turn your mind from me
And would not me comfort when ye hear me
    speak,
Then should I ten times sorrier be.
FELLOWSHIP: Sir, I say as I will do in deed.
EVERYMAN: Then be you a good friend in need.   240
I have found you true herebefore.
FELLOWSHIP: And so ye shall evermore;
For, in faith, if thou go to hell,
I will not forsake thee by the way.
EVERYMAN: Ye speak like a good friend; I believe you
    well.
I shall deserve it, if I may.
FELLOWSHIP: I speak of no deserving, by this day!
For he that will say and nothing do
Is not worthy with good company to go;   250
Therefore show me the grief of your mind,
As to your friend most loving and kind.
EVERYMAN: I shall show you how it is:
Commanded I am to go a journey,
A long way hard and dangerous,
And give a straight account without delay
Before the high judge, Adonai.°
Wherefore I pray you, bear me company,
As ye have promised, in this journey.
FELLOWSHIP: That is matter indeed! Promise is duty;   260
But if I should take such a voyage on me,
I know it well, it should be to my pain;
Also it maketh me afeared, certain.
But let us take counsel here as well as we can,
For your words would fear a strong man.
EVERYMAN: Why, ye said if I had need
Ye would me never forsake, quick nor dead,
Though it were to hell, truly.
FELLOWSHIP:· So I said, certainly,
But such pleasures be set aside, the sooth to say;   270
And also, if we took such a journey
When should we again come?
EVERYMAN: Nay, never again till the day of doom.
FELLOWSHIP: In faith, then will not I come there!
Who hath you these tidings brought?
EVERYMAN: Indeed, Death was with me here.

---

affiance, faith or trust.

Adonai, Hebrew name for God.

FELLOWSHIP: Now, by God that all hath bought,
  If death were the messenger,
  For no man that is living today
280 I will not go that loath journey—
  Not for the father that begat me!
EVERYMAN: Ye promised otherwise, pardie!
FELLOWSHIP: I know well I said so, truly;
  And yet, if thou wilt eat and drink and make good
    cheer,
  Or haunt to women the lusty company°
  I would not forsake you while the day is clear,
  Trust me verily.
EVERYMAN: Yea, thereto ye would be ready!
290 To go to mirth, solace and play
  Your mind will sooner apply
  Than to bear me company in my long journey.
FELLOWSHIP: Now, in good faith, I will not that way;
  But if thou will murder or any man kill,
  In that I will help thee with a good will.
EVERYMAN: O, that is a simple advice indeed.
  Gentle fellow, help me in my necessity!
  We have loved long, and now I need;
  And now, gentle Fellowship, remember me.
300 FELLOWSHIP: Whether ye have loved me or no,
  By Saint John, I will not with thee go!
EVERYMAN: Yet, I pray thee, take the labor and do so
    much for me
  To bring me forward, for sainted charity,
  And comfort me till I come within the town.
FELLOWSHIP: Nay, if thou would give me a new gown,
  I will not a foot with thee go;
  But if thou had tarried, I would not have left thee
    so.
310 And as now, God speed thee in thy journey,
  For from thee I will depart as fast as I may.
EVERYMAN: Wither away, Fellowship? Will thou
    forsake me?
FELLOWSHIP: Yea, by my faith! To God I betake° thee.
EVERYMAN: Farewell, good Fellowship! For thee my
    heart is sore.
  Adieu forever! I shall see thee no more.
FELLOWSHIP: In faith, Everyman, farewell now at the
    ending!
320 For you I will remember that parting is mourning.

(Exit FELLOWSHIP.)

EVERYMAN: Alack, shall we thus depart indeed—
  Ah, Lady, help!—without any more comfort?
  Lo, Fellowship forsaketh me in my most need.
  For help in this world whither shall I resort?
  Fellowship herebefore with me would merry make,
  And now little sorrow for me doth he take.
  It is said, "In prosperity men friends may find,
  Which in adversity be full unkind."

Now whither for succor shall I flee,
Since that Fellowship hath forsaken me?   330
To my kinsmen I will, truly,
Praying them to help me in my necessity.
I believe that they will do so,
For kind will creep where it may not go.°

(Enter KINDRED and COUSIN.)

I will go say, for yonder I see them.
Where be ye now, my friends and kinsmen?
KINDRED: Here be we now at your commandment.
  Cousin, I pray you show us your intent
  In any wise and not spare.
COUSIN: Yea, Everyman, and to us declare   340
  If ye be disposed to go anywhither;
  For know you well, we will live and die together.
KINDRED: In wealth and woe we will with you hold,
  For over his kin a man may be bold.
EVERYMAN: Gramercy, my friends and kinsmen kind.
  Now shall I show you the grief of my mind:
  I was commanded by a messenger,
  That is a high king's chief officer;
  He bade me go a pilgrimage, to my pain,
  And I know well I shall never come again.   350
  Also I must give a reckoning strait,
  For I have a great enemy that hath me in wait,
  Which intendeth me for to hinder.
KINDRED: What account is that which ye must render?
  That would I know.
EVERYMAN: Of all my works I must show
  How I have lived and my days spent;
  Also of ill deeds that I have used
  In my time, since life was me lent;
  And of all virtues that I have refused.   360
  Therefore, I pray you, go thither with me
  To help to make mine account, for saint charity.
COUSIN: What, to go thither? Is that the matter?
  Nay, Everyman, I had liefer fast bread and water
  All this five years and more.
EVERYMAN: Alas, that ever I was born!
  For now shall I never be merry
  If that you forsake me.
KINDRED: Ah, sir, but ye be a merry man!
  Take good heart to you, and make no moan.   370
  But one thing I warn you, by Saint Anne—
  As for me, ye shall go alone.
EVERYMAN: My Cousin, will you not with me go?
COUSIN: No, by our Lady! I have the cramp in my toe.
  Trust not to me; for, so God me speed,
  I will deceive you in your most need.
KINDRED: It availeth not us to entice.
  Ye shall have my maid with all my heart;
  She loveth to go to feasts, there to be nice,
  And to dance and abroad to start.   380

---

haunt . . . company seek women's company for pleasure;
go a-whoring.

betake, entrust. kind . . . go, one's kin will crawl where
they may not walk; i.e., will do what they can.

I will give her leave to help you in that journey,
If that you and she may agree.
EVERYMAN: Now show me the very effect of your mind:
Will you go with me, or abide behind?
KINDRED: Abide behind? Yea, that will I, if I may!
Therefore farewell till another day.

(*Exit* KINDRED.)

EVERYMAN: How should I be merry or glad?
For fair promises men to me make,
390　But when I have most need they me forsake.
I am deceived; that maketh me sad.
COUSIN: Cousin Everyman, farewell now,
For verily I will not go with you.
Also of mine own an unready reckoning
I have to account; therefore I make tarrying.
Now God keep thee, for now I go.

(*Exit* COUSIN.)

EVERYMAN: Ah, Jesus, is all come hereto?
Lo, fair words maketh fools fain;
They promise and nothing will do, certain.
400　My kinsmen promised me faithfully
For to abide with me steadfastly,
And now fast away do they flee,
Even so Fellowship promised me.
What friend were best me of to provide?
I lose my time here longer to abide.
Yet in my mind a thing there is:
All my life I have loved riches;
If that my Goods now help me might,
He would make my heart full light.
410　I will speak to him in this distress.
Where art thou, my Goods and riches?

(GOODS *revealed in a corner.*)

GOODS: Who calleth me? Everyman? What, hast thou haste?
I lie here in corners, trussed and piled so high,
And in chests I am locked so fast,
Also sacked in bags. Thou mayst see with thine eye
I cannot stir; in packs, low I lie.
What would ye have? Lightly me say.
EVERYMAN: Come hither, Goods, in all the haste thou
420　may,
For of counsel I must desire thee.
GOODS: Sir, if ye in the world have sorrow or adversity,
That can I help you to remedy shortly.
EVERYMAN: It is another disease that grieveth me;
In this world it is not, I tell thee so.
I am sent for, another way to go,
To give a strait account general
Before the highest Jupiter of all;
430　And all my life I have had joy and pleasure in thee.
Therefore, I pray thee, go with me;

For, peradventure, thou mayst before God Almighty
My reckoning help to clean and purify;
For it is said ever among
That "money maketh all right that is wrong."
GOODS: Nay, Everyman, I sing another song.
I follow no man in such voyages;
For if I went with thee,
Thou shouldst fare much the worse for me.　440
For because on me thou did set thy mind,
Thy reckoning I have made blotted and blind,
That thine account thou cannot make truly—
And that hast thou for the love of me!
EVERYMAN: That would grieve me full sore,
When I should come to that fearful answer.
Up, let us go thither together.
GOODS: Nay, not so! I am too brittle, I may not endure.
I will follow no man one foot, be ye sure.　450
EVERYMAN: Alas, I have thee loved, and had great pleasure
All my life-days in goods and treasure.
GOODS: That is to thy damnation, without lying,
For my love is contrary to the love everlasting.
But if thou had loved me moderately during,
As to the poor given part of me,
Then shouldst thou not in this dolor be,
Nor in this great sorrow and care.
EVERYMAN: Lo, now was I deceived ere I was aware,　460
And all I may lay to my spending of time.
GOODS: What, thinkest thou that I am thine?
EVERYMAN: I had thought so.
GOODS: Nay, Everyman, I say no.
As for a while I was lent thee;
A season thou hast had me in prosperity.
My condition is a man's soul to kill;
If I save one, a thousand I do spill.
Thinkest thou that I will follow thee?
Nay, from this world not, verily.　470
EVERYMAN: I had thought otherwise.
GOODS: Therefore to thy soul Goods is a thief;
For when thou art dead, this is my guise—
Another to deceive in this same wise
As I have done thee, and all to his soul's reprief.°
EVERYMAN: O false Goods, cursed thou be,
Thou traitor to God, that hast deceived me
And caught me in thy snare!
GOODS: Marry, thou brought thyself in care,
Whereof I am glad.　480
I must needs laugh; I cannot be sad.
EVERYMAN: Ah, Goods, thou hast had long my hearty love;
I gave thee that which should be the Lord's above.
But wilt thou not go with me indeed?

---

reprief, harm.

I pray thee truth to say.

GOODS: No, so God me speed!
Therefore farewell, and have good day.

(Exit GOODS.)

EVERYMAN: O, to whom shall I make my moan
490   For to go with me in that heavy journey?
First Fellowship said he would with me go;
His words were very pleasant and gay,
But afterward he left me alone.
Then spake I to my kinsmen, all in despair,
And also they gave me words fair;
They lacked no fair speaking,
But all forsook me in the ending.
Then went I to my Goods that I loved best,
In hope to have comfort; but there had I least,
500   For my Goods sharply did me tell
That he bringeth many into Hell.
Then of myself I was ashamed,
And so I am worthy to be blamed;
Thus may I well myself hate.
Of whom shall I now counsel take?
I think that I shall never speed
Til that I go to my Good Deeds.
But, alas, she is so weak
That she can neither go nor speak;
510   Yet will I venture on her now.
My Good Deeds, where be you?

(GOOD DEEDS revealed on the ground.)

GOOD DEEDS: Here I lie, cold in the ground.
Thy sins hath me so sore bound
That I cannot stir.
EVERYMAN: O Good Deeds, I stand in fear!
I must you pray of counsel,
For help now should come right well.
GOOD DEEDS: Everyman, I have understanding
That ye be summoned account to make
520   Before Messiah, of Jerusalem King;
If you do by me, that journey with you will I take.
EVERYMAN: Therefore I come to you my moan to
    make.
I pray you that ye will go with me.
GOOD DEEDS: I would full fain, but I cannot stand,
    verily.
EVERYMAN: Why, is there anything on you fallen?
GOOD DEEDS: Yea, sir, I may thank you of all.
If ye had perfectly cheered me,
530   Your book of account full ready would be.
Look, the books of your works and deeds eke,°
As how they lie under the feet
To your soul's heaviness.
EVERYMAN: Our Lord Jesus help me!
For one letter here I cannot see.

---

eke, also.

GOOD DEEDS: There is a blind reckoning in time of
    distress.
EVERYMAN: Good Deeds, I pray you help me in this
    need,
Or else I am forever damned indeed;   540
Therefore help me to make reckoning
Before the Redeemer of all things,
That King is, and was, and ever shall.
GOOD DEEDS: Everyman, I am sorry of your fall,
And fain would I help you if I were able.
EVERYMAN: Good Deeds, your counsel I pray you give
    me.
GOOD DEEDS: That shall I do verily.
Though that on my feet I may not go,
I have a sister that shall with you also,   550
Called Knowledge, which shall with you abide
To help you to make that dreadful reckoning.

(Enter KNOWLEDGE.)

KNOWLEDGE: Everyman, I will go with thee and be thy
    guide,
In thy most need to go by thy side.
EVERYMAN: In good condition I am now in everything
And am wholly content with this good thing;
Thanked be God my Creator.
GOOD DEEDS: And when she hath brought you there,
Where thou shalt heal thee of thy smart,   560
Then go you with your reckoning and your Good
    Deeds together
For to make you joyful at heart
Before the Blessèd Trinity.
EVERYMAN: My Good Deeds, gramercy!
I am well content, certainly,
With your words sweet.

(EVERYMAN and KNOWLEDGE leave GOOD DEEDS.)

KNOWLEDGE: Now go we together lovingly
To Confession, that cleansing river.
EVERYMAN: For joy I weep; I would we were there!   570
But, I pray you, give me cognition
Where dwelleth that holy man, Confession.
KNOWLEDGE: In the house of salvation;
We shall find him in that place
That shall us comfort, by God's grace.

(KNOWLEDGE leads EVERYMAN to CONFESSION.)

Lo, this is Confession. Kneel down and ask mercy,
For he is in good esteem with God Almighty.
EVERYMAN: O glorious fountain, that all uncleanness
    doth clarify,
Wash from me the spots of vice unclean,   580
That on me no sin may be seen.
I come with Knowledge for my redemption,
Redempt with hearty and full contrition;
For I am commanded a pilgrimage to take
And great accounts before God to make.
Now I pray you, Shrift, mother of salvation,

Help my Good Deeds for my piteous exclamation.
CONFESSION: I know your sorrow well, Everyman.
Because with Knowledge ye come to me,
590 I will you comfort as well as I can,
And a precious jewel I will give thee,
Called penance, voider of adversity;
Therewith shall your body chastised be,
With abstinence and perseverance in God's
serviture.
Here shall you receive that scourge of me
Which is penance strong that ye must endure,
To remember thy Saviour was scourged for thee
With sharp scourges and suffered it patiently;
600 So must thou, ere thou escape that painful
pilgrimage.

(CONFESSION gives scourge to KNOWLEDGE.)

Knowledge, keep him in this voyage,
And by that time Good Deeds will be with thee.
But in any wise be sure of mercy,
For your time draweth fast; if ye will saved be,
Ask God mercy, and he will grant truly.
When with the scourge of penance man doth him
bind,
The oil of forgiveness then shall he find.

(EVERYMAN and KNOWLEDGE leave CONFESSION.)

610 EVERYMAN: Thanked be God for his gracious work!
For now I will my penance begin.
This hath rejoiced and lighted my heart,
Though the knots be painful and hard within.
KNOWLEDGE: Everyman, look your penance that ye
fulfill,
What pain that ever it to you be;
And Knowledge shall give you counsel at will
How your account ye shall make clearly.
EVERYMAN: O eternal God, O heavenly figure,
620 O way of righteousness, O goodly vision,
Which descended down in a virgin pure
Because he would every man redeem,
Which Adam forfeited by his disobedience;
O blessèd Godhead, elect and high divine,
Forgive me my grievous offence!
Here I cry thee mercy in this presence.
O ghostly° treasure, O ransomer and redeemer,
Of all the world hope and conductor,
Mirror of joy, foundation of mercy,
630 Which illumineth Heaven and earth thereby,
Hear my clamorous complaint though it late be;
Receive my prayers unworthy in this heavy life!
Though I be a sinner most abominable,
Yet let my name be written in Moses' table.
O Mary, pray to the Maker of all things,
Me for to help at my ending;

And save me from the power of my enemy,
For Death assaileth me strongly.
And, Lady, that I may by means of thy prayer
Of your Son's glory to be partner, 640
By the means of his passion, I it crave;
I beseech you, help my soul to save.
Knowledge, give me the scourge of penance;
My flesh therewith shall give acquittance.
I will now begin if God give me grace.

(KNOWLEDGE gives scourge to EVERYMAN.)

KNOWLEDGE: Everyman, God give you time and
space!
Thus I bequeath you in the hands of our Saviour;
Now may you make your reckoning sure.
EVERYMAN: In the name of the Holy Trinity, 650
My body sore punishéd shall be:
Take this, body, for the sins of the flesh!
Also thou delightest to go gay and fresh,
And in the way of damnation thou did me bring;
Therefore suffer now strokes of punishing.
Now of penance I will wade the water clear
To save me from Purgatory, that sharp fire.

(GOOD DEEDS rises from the ground.)

GOOD DEEDS: I thank God, now I can walk and go
And am delivered of my sickness and woe.
Therefore with Everyman I will go and not spare; 660
His good works I will help him to declare.
KNOWLEDGE: Now, Everyman, be merry and glad!
Your Good Deeds cometh now; ye may not be sad
Now is your Good Deeds whole and sound,
Going upright upon the ground.
EVERYMAN: My heart is light and shall be evermore;
Now will I smite faster than I did before.
GOOD DEEDS: Everyman, pilgrim, my special friend,
Blessed be thou without end!
For thee is prepared the eternal glory. 670
Ye have me made whole and sound,
Therefore I will bide by thee in every stound.°
EVERYMAN: Welcome, my Good Deeds! Now I hear
thy voice
I weep for very sweetness of love.
KNOWLEDGE: Be no more sad, but ever rejoice;
God seeth thy living in his throne above.

(KNOWLEDGE gives EVERYMAN the garment of contrition.)

Put on this garment to thy behove,°
Which is wet with your tears,
Or else before God you may it miss 680
When you to your journey's end come shall.
EVERYMAN: Gentle knowledge, what do ye it call?
KNOWLEDGE: It is the garment of sorrow;

---

ghostly, spiritual, as in Holy Ghost.

stound, instance, occasion. **behove,** benefit.

From pain it will you borrow.
Contrition it is
That getteth forgiveness;
It pleaseth God passing well.

GOOD DEEDS: Everyman, will you wear it for your heal?°

(EVERYMAN *puts on the garment of contrition.*)

690 EVERYMAN: Now blessèd be Jesu, Mary's Son,
For now have I on true contrition;
And let us go now without tarrying.
Good Deeds, have we clear our reckoning?

GOOD DEEDS: Yea, indeed, I have it here.

EVERYMAN: Then I trust we need not fear.
Now, friends, let us not part in twain.

KNOWLEDGE: Nay, Everyman, that will we not, certain.

GOOD DEEDS: Yet must thou lead with thee
700 Three persons of great might.

EVERYMAN: Who should they be?

GOOD DEEDS: Discretion and Strength they hight°
And thy Beauty may not abide behind.

KNOWLEDGE: Also ye must call to mind
Your Five Wits as for your counsellors.

GOOD DEEDS: You must have them ready at all hours.

EVERYMAN: How shall I get them hither?

KNOWLEDGE: You must call them all together,
And they will hear you incontinent.°

710 EVERYMAN: My friends, come hither and be present:
Discretion, Strength, my Five Wits, and Beauty.

(*Enter* DISCRETION, STRENGTH, FIVE WITS, *and* BEAUTY.)

BEAUTY: Here at your will we be all ready.
What would ye that we should do?

GOOD DEEDS: That ye would with Everyman go
And help him in his pilgrimage.
Advise you, will ye with him or not in that voyage?

STRENGTH: We will bring him all thither
To his help and comfort, ye may believe me.

DISCRETION: So will we go with him all together.

720 EVERYMAN: Almighty God, loved may thou be!
I give thee laud that I have hither brought
Strength, Discretion, Beauty and Five Wits. Lack I naught;
And my Good Deeds, with Knowledge clear,
All be in company at my will here.
I desire no more to my business.

STRENGTH: And I, Strength, will by you stand in distress,
Though thou would in battle fight on the ground.

730 FIVE WITS: And though it were through the world round,
We will not depart for sweet nor sour.

BEAUTY: No more will I unto death's hour,
Whatsoever thereof befall.

DISCRETION: Everyman, advise you first of all;
Go with a good advisement and deliberation.
We all give you virtuous monition
That all shall be well.

EVERYMAN: My friends, hearken what I will tell:
I pray God reward you in his heavenly sphere.   740
Now hearken, all that be here,
For I will make my testament
Here before you all present:
In alms, half of my goods I will give with my hands twain
In the way of charity with good intent,
And the other half still shall remain
In queth,° to be returned where it ought to be.
This I do in despite of the fiend of hell,
To go quite out of his peril   750
Ever after and this day.

KNOWLEDGE: Everyman, hearken what I say:
Go to Priesthood, I you advise,
And receive of him in any wise
The holy sacrament and ointment together;
Then shortly see ye turn again hither.
We will all abide you here.

FIVE WITS: Yea, Everyman, hie you that ye ready were.
There is no emperor, king, duke, nor baron   760
That of God hath commission
As hath the least priest in the world being;
For of the blessèd sacraments pure and benign,
He beareth the keys, and thereof hath the cure
For man's redemption—it is ever sure—
Which God for our soul's medicine
Gave us out of his heart with great pine.°
Here in this transitory life, for thee and me,
The blessed sacraments seven there be:
Baptism, confirmation with priesthood good,   770
And the sacrament of God's precious flesh and blood,
Marriage, the holy extreme unction, and penance.
These seven be good to have in remembrance,
Gracious sacraments of high divinity.

EVERYMAN: Fain would I receive that holy body,
And meekly to my ghostly° father I will go.

FIVE WITS: Everyman, that is the best that ye can do.
God will you to salvation bring,
For priesthood exceedeth all other things: 780
To us holy scripture they do teach
And converteth man from sin, Heaven to reach;
God hath to them more power given

---

heal, salvation. *hight,* are called. *incontinent* at once.

In queth, as a bequest; though the remainder of the line indicates that it is actually a restitution of illegally acquired property. *pine,* anguish, torment. *ghostly,* spiritual.

Than to any angel that is in Heaven.
With five words he may consecrate,
God's body in flesh and blood to make,
And handleth his Maker between his hands.
The priest bindeth and unbindeth all bands,
Both in earth and in Heaven.

790 Thou ministers all the sacraments seven;
Though we kissed thy feet, thou were worthy.
Thou art surgeon that cureth sin deadly;
No remedy we find under God
But all only priesthood.
Everyman, God gave priests that dignity
And setteth them in his stead among us to be;
Thus be they above angels in degree.

(Exit EVERYMAN.)

KNOWLEDGE: If priests be good, it is so, surely.
But when Jesu hanged on the cross with great
800   smart,
There he gave, out of his blesséd heart,
The seven sacraments in great torment;
He sold them not to us, that Lord omnipotent;
Therefore Saint Peter the apostle doth say
That Jesu's curse hath all they
Which God their Saviour do buy or sell,
Or they for any money do take or tell.°
Sinful priests giveth the sinners example bad;
Their children sitteth by other men's fires, I have
810   heard;
And some haunteth women's company
With unclean life, as lusts of lechery;
These be with sin made blind.

FIVE WITS: I trust to God no such may we find;
Therefore let us priesthood honor
And follow their doctrine for our souls' succour.
We be their sheep, and they shepherds be
By whom we all be kept in surety.
Peace! For yonder I see Everyman come,
820 Which hath made true satisfaction.

GOOD DEEDS: Methinks it is he indeed.

(Re-enter EVERYMAN.)

EVERYMAN: Now Jesu be your alder speed!°
I have received the sacrament for my redemption
And then mine extreme unction.
Blesséd be all they that counselled me to take it!
And now, friends, let us go without longer respite.
I thank God that ye have tarried so long.
Now set each of you on this rood your hand
And shortly follow me.
830 I go before where I would be. God be our guide!

(They go toward the grave.)

---

tell, count out, as in bank teller. **your alder speed,** help to all of you.

STRENGTH: Everyman, we will not from you go
Till ye have done this voyage long.

DISCRETION: I, Discretion, will bide by you also.

KNOWLEDGE: And though this pilgrimage be never so
    strong,
I will never part you from.

STRENGTH: Everyman, I will be as sure by thee
As ever I did by Judas Maccabee.°

(They arrive at the grave.)

EVERYMAN: Alas, I am so faint I may not stand;
My limbs under me do fold.   840
Friends, let us not turn again to this land,
Not for all the world's gold;
For into this cave must I creep
And turn to earth, and thereto sleep.

BEAUTY: What, into this grave? Alas!

EVERYMAN: Yea, there shall ye consume, more and
    less.°

BEAUTY: And what, should I smother here?

EVERYMAN: Yea, by my faith, and never more appear.
In this world live no more we shall,   850
But in Heaven before the highest Lord of all.

BEAUTY: I cross out all this. Adieu, by Saint John!
I take my tap in my lap and am gone.°

EVERYMAN: What, Beauty, whither will ye?

BEAUTY: Peace! I am deaf. I look not behind me,
Not if thou wouldest give me all the gold in thy
    chest.

(Exit BEAUTY.)

EVERYMAN: Alas, whereto may I trust?
Beauty goeth fast away from me.
She promised with me to live and die.   860

STRENGTH: Everyman, I will thee also forsake and
    deny;
Thy game liketh me not at all.

EVERYMAN: Why, then, ye will forsake me all?
Sweet Strength, tarry a little space.

STRENGTH: Nay, sir, by the rood of grace!
I will hie me from thee fast,
Though thou weep till thy heart to-brast.°

EVERYMAN: Ye would ever bide by me, ye said.

STRENGTH: Yea, I have you far enough conveyed.   870
Ye be old enough, I understand,
Your pilgrimage to take in hand.
I repent me that I hither came.

EVERYMAN: Strength, you to displease I am to blame;
Yet promise is debt, this ye well wot.°

Maccabee, A Jewish leader of the second century B.C., known for his courage (1 Macc. 3). **shall ye consume,** The grave devours all, both the great and the small. **tap,** an unspun tuft of wool or flax. Hence, like a peasant housewife, Beauty is saying, "I'm pocketing my spinning materials and am off." **to-brast,** bursts in two. **wot,** know.

STRENGTH: In faith, I care not.
　Thou art but a fool to complain;
　You spend your speech and waste your brain.
　Go thrust thee into the ground!

(*Exit* STRENGTH.)

880 EVERYMAN: I had thought surer I should you have
　　found.
　He that trusteth in his Strength,
　She him deceiveth at length.
　Both Strength and Beauty forsaketh me;
　Yet they promised me fair and lovingly.
DISCRETION: Everyman, I will after Strength be gone.
　As for me, I will leave you alone.
EVERYMAN: Why, Discretion, will ye forsake me?
DISCRETION: Yea, in faith, I will go from thee;
890 　For when Strength goeth before,
　I follow after evermore.
EVERYMAN: Yet, I pray thee, for the love of the
　　Trinity,
　Look in my grave once piteously.
DISCRETION: Nay, so nigh will I not come.
　Farewell, everyone!

(*Exit* DISCRETION.)

EVERYMAN: O, all things faileth, save God alone—
　Beauty, Strength and Discretion;
　For when Death bloweth his blast,
900 　They all run from me full fast.
FIVE WITS: Everyman, my leave now of thee I take.
　I will follow the others, for here I thee forsake.
EVERYMAN: Alas, then may I wail and weep,
　For I took you for my best friend.
FIVE WITS: I will no longer thee keep.
　Now farewell, and there an end.

(*Exit* FIVE WITS.)

EVERYMAN: O Jesu, help! All hath forsaken me.
GOOD DEEDS: Nay, Everyman, I will bide with thee.
　I will not forsake thee in deed;
910 　Thou shalt find me a good friend in need.
EVERYMAN: Gramercy, Good Deeds! Now may I true
　　friends see.
　They have forsaken me, every one;
　I loved them better than my Good Deeds alone.
　Knowledge, will ye forsake me also?
KNOWLEDGE: Yea, Everyman, when ye to Death shall
　　go;
　But not yet, for no manner of danger.
EVERYMAN: Gramercy, Knowledge, with all my heart.
920 KNOWLEDGE: Nay, yet I will not from hence depart
　Till I see where ye shall be come.
EVERYMAN: Methinks, alas, that I must be gone
　To make my reckoning and my debts pay,
　For I see my time is nigh spent away.
　Take example, all ye that this do hear or see,
　How they that I loved best do forsake me,

Except my Good Deeds that bideth truly.
GOOD DEEDS: All earthly things is but vanity:
　Beauty, Strength and Discretion do man forsake,
　Foolish friends and kinsmen that fair spake—　930
　All fleeth save Good Deeds, and that am I.
EVERYMAN: Have mercy on me, God most mighty,
　And stand by me, thou mother and maid, Holy
　　Mary!
GOOD DEEDS: Fear not, I will speak for thee.
EVERYMAN: Here I cry God mercy.
GOOD DEEDS: Shorten our end, and diminish our
　　pain;
　Let us go and never come again.

(GOOD DEEDS *leads* EVERYMAN *into grave.*)

EVERYMAN: Into thy hands, Lord, my soul I　940
　　commend;
　Receive it, Lord, that it be not lost.
　As thou me boughtest, so me defend
　And save me from the fiend's boast,
　That I may appear with that blessèd host
　That shall be saved at the day of doom.
　In manus tuas, of mights most
　Forever, *commendo spiritum meum.*°

(*Exeunt* EVERYMAN *and* GOOD DEEDS.)

KNOWLEDGE: Now hath he suffered that we all shall
　　endure;　950
　The Good Deeds shall make all sure.
　Now hath he made ending;
　Methinks that I hear angels sing
　And make great joy and melody
　Where Everyman's soul received shall be.

(*Enter* ANGEL.)

THE ANGEL: Come, excellent elect spouse, to Jesu!
　Here above thou shalt go
　Because of thy singular virtue.
　Now thy soul is taken thy body from,
　Thy reckoning is crystal clear.　960
　Now shalt thou into the heavenly sphere,
　Unto the which all ye shall come
　That liveth well before the day of doom.

(*Exeunt* ANGEL *and* KNOWLEDGE.)

(*Enter* DOCTOR.)

DOCTOR: This moral men may have in mind.
　Ye hearers, take it of worth, old and young,
　And forsake Pride, for he deceiveth you in the end;
　And remember Beauty, Five Wits, Strength, and
　　Discretion,
　They all at the last do Everyman forsake,
　Save his Good Deeds there doth he take.　970

In manus tuas . . . commendo spiritum meum, Into thy
hands I commend my spirit.

But beware, for if they be small,
Before God he hath no help at all:
No excuse may be there for Everyman.
Alas, how shall he do then?
For after death amends may no man make,
For them mercy and pity doth him forsake.
If his reckoning be not clear when he doth come,
God will say, *"Ite, maledicti, in ignem eternum."*°

Ite . . . eternum, Go, sinners, into eternal fire.

And he that hath his account whole and sound,
High in Heaven he shall be crowned;   980
Unto which place God bring us all thither,
That we may live body and soul together.
Thereto help the Trinity!
Amen, say ye, for saint charity.

(Exit DOCTOR.*)*

(Thus endeth this moral play of Everyman.)

Figure 1. The multilevel set for the University of Chicago Theater production of *Everyman*, directed by Nicholas Rudall in the Rockefeller Chapel, 1973. (Photograph: Leslie Travis.)

Figure 2. Everyman (Gordon Cameron, *left*) and Goods (Carl Orland) in the University of Chicago Theater production of *Everyman*, directed by Nicholas Rudall, 1973. (Photograph: Leslie Travis.)

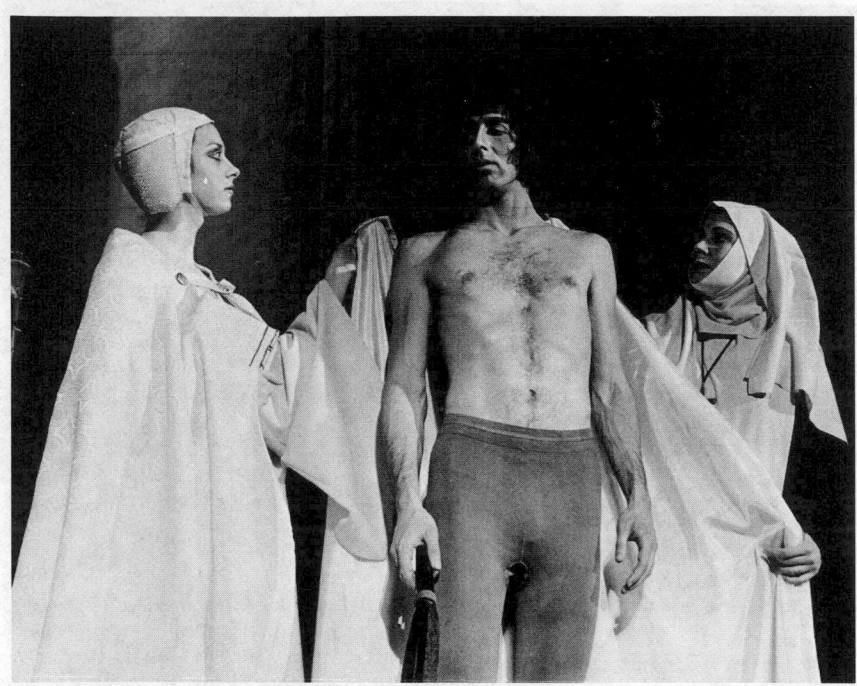

Figure 3. Everyman (Gordon Cameron, *center*) receives the garment of contrition from Good Deeds (Kelly Nespor, *left*) and Knowledge (Ellen Clements) in the University of Chicago Theater production of *Everyman,* directed by Nicholas Rudall, 1973. (Photograph: Leslie Travis.)

Figure 4. Good Deeds (Kelly Nespor, *left*) leads Everyman (Gordon Cameron) into his grave in the University of Chicago Theater production of *Everyman,* directed by Nicholas Rudall, 1973. (Photograph: Leslie Travis.)

Staging of *Everyman*

INTERVIEW WITH NICHOLAS RUDALL, DIRECTOR
OF THE 1973 UNIVERSITY OF CHICAGO
PRODUCTION OF *EVERYMAN*, BY BRADFORD S.
FIELD, JR.

FIELD: What kind of stage does a gothic cathedral like Rockefeller Chapel offer for *Everyman*? Did you do it in the round? Or at the altar?

RUDALL: We placed a large octagon with other levels attached to it right to the center of the chancel. The octagon is raised and raked. It is divided off into a main acting area, which is the octagon, with a sort of inner below at the top of the rake, through which entrances could occur, and through which this sort of tableau that I did at the beginning could be seen. At raked angles away from it, upstage, were separate areas for the individual scenes, especially at the beginning, to take place. That is, Fellowship had his own platform, Kindred had hers, Cousin had hers, Goods had his. Good Deeds was placed on a kind of sarcophagus at the very top of this structure. I conceived the play, not so much as a pilgrimage—where you'd have lots of movement to different mansions all over the church—but rather as a going away, a taking away from Everyman. All these levels were fairly close to him, but they were separate from him. When he goes to a particular area, only that area is lit. When Fellowship, for example, is finished with him, the light in that area goes out. Forever. That area of the stage is black thereafter.

FIELD: Do I get it correctly that Everyman would move to each of their positions . . .

RUDALL: That's right . . .

FIELD: . . . talk to them, and then their exit was a blackout on them, but not on him; he'd move on to the next position?

RUDALL: That's right.

FIELD: Does *Everyman* present any special kinds of problems to a director?

RUDALL: Yes, one stylistic problem, that of the very realistic details in the play, realistic characterizations, coupled with a much higher style within the play. How does one reconcile characters that have cramps in their toes with these reflections about God? How elevated a person should Everyman be? Or how colloquial? How down to earth? What's the right level? He should not be too rich, not too poor . . . not too rustic, not too aristocratic. That was a rather difficult one to solve. I think we hit upon a solution that was partially based upon the fact that it was being done in a huge, almost cathedral-like structure. The play, as it is now performed, has the feeling of a church ritual. The whole building is lit by candlelight

at the beginning and there are monks chanting for the first fifteen minutes as the audience comes in. I have some cross-cutting with contemporary folk song that contrasts between the happy life and the ecclesiastical life, if you like, all before the play starts. The fact that it is in this large structure allows us to have this high-style feeling, this ritual feeling, which I don't think it would have if it were on a small stage. That high style would be impossible; you'd be forced to think of it only as "playing" at that point.

FIELD: If you put it outdoors with a cart.

RUDALL: Right.

FIELD: Or in a playground or in a supermarket parking lot . . .

RUDALL: Exactly. But on this stage it is still possible to play the humanness of Fellowship, the humanness of Kindred and Cousin. I made them very direct, human figures. Fellowship was meant to be a kind of medieval banker, richly dressed, at supper. He's eating chicken and bread and wine while he's talking to Everyman. Kindred is a sort of fifty- or sixty-year-old woman, upper bourgeois, and she's sitting there with her needlepoint, and Cousin is standing, playing with a little bird, very much a young aristocratic lady. And Goods emerges from a chest. Each character I made very specifically medieval characters, not generalizations, but very specific ones.

FIELD: The costumes then were intended to suggest a very particular social level, income level, type of business. . . .

RUDALL: Exactly that. Good Deeds is a young maiden, Knowledge is a young novice, a nun, and Strength a knight, Discretion a lawyer. One other thing, I did find that the play naturally lent itself to doubling. The first four characters to whom he goes, to Fellowship, to Kindred, Cousin and Goods, lend themselves to perfect doubling with the four parts of his personality that come back to him before he goes to the grave, Five-Wits, Beauty, Discretion, and . . .

FIELD: Do they each use the same platforms, or do they come down to him?

RUDALL: I didn't want to repeat the platforms; once their light was out, they had gone forever, I didn't want to return to them. What I had intended to do was have these four characters come back on, but with a life-mask of Everyman on their faces, to show them as four extensions of his own personality. Goods and Fellowship are outside things that he goes to, but the things that he loses at the end are parts of himself—Beauty and Five Wits—so I made life-masks to be placed over their faces, so that there would be five Everymans, as it were, going down toward the grave. But because of the size of the church, that failed. They didn't look like Everyman, even though they were absolutely perfect. At a distance, that effect was lost. So I abandoned it.

FIELD: You did abandon it.

RUDALL: Yes. I did. Only because of the distance. I think in a smaller house, more intimate . . . it would have worked very well.

FIELD: I suppose if they'd all been wearing the same mask, even Everyman, they'd have matched, but then you'd have a hard time telling one from the other. Did the masks create any problem with speech?

RUDALL: Yes, one of the reasons that they failed was that we had to make too large an opening around the mouth and that made it cease to look like the person who was playing Everyman.

FIELD: Everyman was played by a man or a woman?

RUDALL: A man.

FIELD: At the turn of the century there was evidently a famous touring version of *Everyman* in which the title role was played by a—

RUDALL: A woman, yes.

FIELD: Okay . . . What kind of text did you use?

RUDALL: We took what might conveniently be called a translation. But I didn't overly modernize it, and I made adaptations for myself with a couple of professors here at Chicago and we pieced together parts which were obscure.

FIELD: What was obscure?

RUDALL: Somewhere at the beginning the medieval English says, "Thou shalt make no attournay," and we just changed that to "delay." Very simple adaptations like that. We changed many of the "and's" to "if." where there was a modern equivalent.

FIELD: Did you make any cuts in the text?

RUDALL: No. I was sorely tempted, at one particular point. Towards the end, about three-quarters of the way through, there's a long scene about priesthood, where Five-Wits talks at great length about the virtues of priesthood . . . it is self-serving, and honestly written in its time for the priests, but removed from our context. I had no way of solving it for a long, long time. And then I hit upon the idea of—while Five-Wits is discoursing about priesthood—we would actually illustrate it on an upper level, by having two black-robed priest-monks set up the equipment for the last rites. While Five-Wits is giving that long speech, Everyman is supposed to be off-stage getting the last rites. So instead of going off-stage, as is usually suggested, I had them do it in a kind of silhouette against the backdrop of the church, with candles and bread and oil and the chanting of Latin;

while Five-wits is talking about priesthood, we actually see them functioning, we see Everyman go to them, get the last rites, and come back down again. So that the inactivity was filled in that way.

FIELD: Were there any comic moments that you pointed for?

RUDALL: I didn't fight any of them. We pointed them up.

FIELD: Like the cramp in the toe . . .

RUDALL: And by making Kindred a dowager. She was played by a woman with a very thick English accent who sounded somewhat like Edith Evans. One could find comedy in her mere exit lines . . . She suggests too that Everyman take her maid. And that was done with a suggestion of the obscene. As was Fellowship's suggestion that if you want to go off and have fun with women, fine, he'll do that. That was the kind of thing that I didn't resist at all. Obviously the comedy is a very important part of the play.

FIELD: How did you handle Death?

RUDALL: I had Death seated at a kind of banquet. The play opened, as I said, with a chanting, a little tableau in the sort of inner below that we had at the top of the raked platform—a tableau with Death seated at a table with his back to the audience, along with Everyman, Kindred, Fellowship, and a young girl who was singing the secular song. After God spoke to them from the far end of the chapel, He calls upon Death, who just turns around from the feast. I had had Everyman enter with the girl who'd been singing, flirtatiously playing, coming from the feast. That made it very specific when Death asks, "Where are thou going thus gaily," that Everyman's mind is on fleshly lusts, specifically, coming from a feast with a woman.

FIELD: I always notice the bookkeeping imagery in the play. Did you play up any of that?

RUDALL: Yes. There are two notable instances of it. I had made a separate mansion of Everyman's house. Off the main stage, I had a little area that was a corner of his home. When Death comes to him, he runs to the house, looking for the money, the "thousand pounds I will give to you," and his book of accounts. He rifles through his books, looks to see, to offer it to Death, finds that it's not ready, and asks for twelve years . . . The second is that I had Good Deeds placed on a sarcophagus, way, way up; she was there before the audience came in. She was all white, to look like marble. Like a lady laying at rest with a book on her chest. A large pile of books near by. And one main book, carved into the tomb at the bottom. When Everyman goes up and appeals to her she tells him to look in the book there. He takes it from the tomb and looks through it. When he says, "No letter here do I see," that's what he's talking about. And later she brings his book of accounts down to him. So I made three specific uses of the bookkeeping in the action.

FIELD: One other thing that is always interesting about this play—how did the final moment work out? It seems pretty vague when you just read the play . . .

RUDALL: At the base of this octagonal acting area, there's a very steep ramp which leads down right into the audience, and it's absolutely black out there. Whenever Everyman left Fellowship or any of those characters, he would come right to the rim of the octagon, and look out into that blackness, toward the way he was going to go.

FIELD: Toward the audience.

RUDALL: Yes. When his personal attributes leave him at the end, Five-wits and the others, when he starts to walk down that ramp, he says, "Friends, come with me," and he stumbles. "I'm too weak," he says, and he stumbles. That is the first time that the four of them, these attributes, look down into the tomb to see . . . they see him stumble, and then they are for the first time aware of the tomb. They leave him. He's left then with Good Deeds and Knowledge, in a little rim of light above this blackness. There is a line that Knowledge says that ends with the syllable, "come," . . . "where ye shall become," and at that point, I have Death, who made his exit earlier in the play down to the tomb, echo the word "come," from the back of the church.

FIELD: Wow.

RUDALL: She says ". . . become;" "Come!" he says from back there. And then for the first time, Everyman fully realizes Death. It is *the* human moment in the play. While he's acknowleded all these things that he's been going through, penance and that sort of thing, he's been busy at it. Now on these last few lines, very frightened, he asks, "Who'll come with me?" And Good Deeds comforts him. He says his last Latin words, *"In manus tuas. . . ."*, and he walks down with Good Deeds, holding the cross and his book of accounts. He takes the first three steps down that ramp, and then there is a blackout. And there is Death, with a candle, all in black, but he's got an anatomical hand; he turns around and walks out; they follow him, to the chanting of monks. So it's a long death scene before Knowledge starts to speak again. The whole church is black, except for the candle in Death's hand, for about forty-five seconds. Then the lights come back up on Knowledge, and she begins to talk, with some more singing from way back up in the choir loft.

FIELD: Then the doctor comes out?

RUDALL: He's the same character, the prologue and the epilogue, is what I thought for it.

FIELD: The messenger at the beginning and the doctor at the end—

RUDALL: Right, the same character. We made him a monk. Up in the pulpit. He was the one who put out the candles in the church to get the play started. He was able to provide the . . . the solution to the problem of style . . . to acknowledge that this was a church performance. "I am the priest that is telling you to watch this play in my church"—that kind of feeling.

Death, we are told, is increasingly prevalent on TV and in the movies. In fiction it is elaborated at great length. In the newspapers what is lost in detail is made up for by a satisfying sense of authenticity. It would seem that of all the media, the one most unsuited to present the topic to a jaded public is the theatre which has had to content itself with mere psychological decay. Closeups, trick shots and realistic gore are in the province of the cinema. Long verbal accounts, once the messenger's speeches in Greek tragedy, are now exclusively the property of Book of the Month. And to vie with the newspaper for authenticity would create seemingly costly and ticklish casting problems.

Nevertheless, the University Theatre's recent and most ambitious project has been nothing but a revival, so to speak of staged death. *Everyman,* the 15th century Dutch morality play, is a primer on dying that becomes, in the hands of director Nicholas Rudall, both immediate and meaningful. The medieval pageant begins in the traditional *danse macabre* mode as Death, having received instructions from God, puts forth one sinister skeletal claw and touches the terrified and unprepared Everyman. Although Death sternly refused to grant any man respite, Everyman manages to eke nearly 45 minutes which he uses in illustration of the *ars moriendi*—to confess, do penance, receive extreme unction, and make a will leaving half his goods to the poor and half to the church.

Mr. Rudall has taken full advantage of the opportunity for spectacle using to the full the Gothic grandeur of Rockefeller Chapel. The Chapel was lit by candles when the audience entered. These were snuffed out by cowled figures before the prologue. Another monk-like figure paced the center aisle swinging a censer. Gregorian Chant sounded from a choir hidden behind the stage area. The lights dimmed and came up on a tableau of medieval revelers on stage as the priest (Donald Swanton) ascended to the pulpit to deliver the prologue in the form of a sermon to be illustrated by the subsequent action.

God (the inimitable Kenneth Northcott), resplendent in gold and white, held forth from aloft—from the chapel choir left, to be exact—and the bemused audience below craned their necks appropriately to look at him as he made known his displeasure with Everyman. Death (Robert Hoover), in the traditional black with his face also draped in flat black giving the eerie appearance of an empty hood, summons the unsuspecting Everyman (Gordon Cameron) most impressively.

In the expanded moment between Death's initial summons and the descent into the grave at the end, Everyman turns to each of things he has valued in life: fellowship (Joel Cope), Kindred (Anna Gwin Pickens), Cousin (Mary Speers), and Goods (Carl Orland), and later to his faculties: Discretion, Five Wits, Beauty, and Strength who are played by the same actors, doublecast respectively. These players were gorgeously costumed by Judy Fink after Medieval models of bankers and matrons. All that he has held dear fails him now, and his Good Deeds (Kelly Nespor) he finds willing but too weak to assist him. In fact, she had been lying immobile throughout the first half of the play on the top plateau of the many-tiered stage, costumed in marble white, looking like a stone carving on a sarcophagus. When she replies to Everyman's pleas the audience is startled, realizing that they, too, have been ignoring Good Deeds.

Guided by Good Deeds' sister, Knowledge (Ellen Clements), who must be taken as representing not worldly or intellectual knowledge but acknowledgment of past wrong-doing, Everyman is led to confess and do penance in the form of a graphically executed self-flagellation. This revives and strengthens his Good Deeds who is then able to accompany him and plead for him before God.

The difficulties with this brilliantly conceived production were, for the most part, technical ones. The lighting, at best, was barely adequate and was sometimes poor enough to be distracting and break the fragile mood. The stage, an exceptionally interesting design by Michael Gall, was too small for the action and the players did not maneuver on it with ease. Rockefeller Chapel, unexcelled for atmosphere, presents enormous technical problems. The acoustical properties of the vast vault not only include an echo, but also seem to raise the pitch of the speaker's voice, a trick particularly damaging to Gordon Cameron's lovely musical tenor, Mary Speers' soprano, and Anna Gwin Pickens' lilting, high-pitched British.

Mr. Rudall's production, and perhaps every production of a play so far removed from the modern milieu, relies very much on a totality of effect that it suffers disproportionately from minor difficulties that distract the audience's attention. Mr. Rudall's concept also aimed at a balance between ritual and realism, a combination dictated by the stylized, symbolic action, and the delicate characterization revealed in the dialogue. The minor characters lacked a strong sense of this balance and vacillated uncomfortably between the formal and human aspects of their roles. The three main figures, however, Gordon Cameron, Kelly Nespor, and Ellen Clements, had a firm grasp of both the allegorical and realistic aspects of their roles.

The overall achievement is a fine one for the University Theatre and the companion play, T.S. Eliot's *Murder in the Cathedral* also to be staged in Rockefeller in the spring is looked for with great interest.

Figure 1. The Renaissance English theater.

RENAISSANCE ENGLISH THEATER

When James Burbage built the first permanent English public theater in 1576, he called it, simply and boldly, The Theater. Retrospectively, that name takes on emblematic force, signifying not just a single building but the beginning of the greatest period of drama since the Greeks. Burbage was the leader of the Earl of Leicester's Men; his company would later become the Lord Chamberlain's Men and then the King's Men; their principal playwright for twenty years was William Shakespeare. Burbage's theater was so successful that it was quickly followed by others: The Curtain in 1577, The Newington Butts in 1579, The Rose in 1587, The Swan in 1595, The Globe in 1599, The Fortune in 1600, and others in the early seventeenth century.

All these public theaters, though they varied in shape from round to square to octagonal, were designed according to roughly similar principles, and they were all quite large, capable of holding between 2000 and 3000 spectators. The exact origin of their design has never been firmly established, but the basic plan—a yard with a stage jutting into the center of it and three levels of galleries surrounding the yard—suggests that it may well have been modeled on inn-yard or courtyard performances of an earlier period (see Figure 1). The stage itself consisted of two acting levels, and on each level there were several distinct acting areas. In the octagonally shaped Globe, for example, where many of Shakespeare's plays were performed, the primary acting surface on the ground level extended about twenty-seven feet into the yard, which was itself only about fifty-five feet in diameter. Thus the stage occupied about fifty percent of the yard. And at its widest, where it joined with the superstructure of the galleries, the stage was about forty-three feet wide. At the back of the stage on each side were doors and exits, and between the doors was an inner stage that was curtained when not in use (see Figure 1). On the second level there was another set of acting areas: windows above the doors on the lower level, a gallery between the windows, and behind the gallery another inner stage (see Figure 1). Above the second level, there may have been yet another gallery at the back for musicians, but the evidence for one is uncertain. Whatever the case, almost the entire stage was sheltered by a canopy that extended out from the roof of the theater.

The dimensions and design of that stage created a unique theatrical experience, unlike anything else during the Renaissance or at any other time in history. To begin with, the physical proximity of the stage to the surrounding galleries and to the spectators standing in the yard created a much more intimate relationship between actors and audience than the Greek theater provided. That physical intimacy must inevitably have aroused in the audience an immediate and personal involvement with the dramatic experience, much greater certainly than any other staging system provided, except perhaps for the medieval. At the same time, the Renaissance English theater continued to sustain a communal atmosphere, for the yard was open to the sky, and the plays were performed in daylight. The spectators consequently could easily see one another as they sat in the galleries or stood in the yard.

The size and design of the theater also made possible a highly flexible drama. As in the medieval period, the main acting surface was generalized, but unlike the medieval stage, it was not restricted to a limited number of locales established by set pieces. The stage could, in fact, become any number of places simply by the departure of one set of characters and the appearance of another, implying in their dialogue a new location, as in the line, "So this is the forest of Arden." The other acting areas made possible a wide variety of discovery scenes, bedroom scenes, and balcony scenes, not to mention disappearance scenes through a trapdoor on the ground level stage. Only a few props were used to suggest the location of a scene: a bed, a throne, a tree, a rock. Costuming, as in the medieval tradition, followed current rather than historically accurate styles of dress, but since Elizabethan theater managers did not spend much money on sets, they lavished their resources on costumes. The account book of Philip Henslowe, the leader of Worcester's Men and Burbage's chief competitor, records an amount of six pounds, thirteen shillings spent on a black velvet dress to be worn by the title character of *A Woman Killed with Kindness* (1603), while the same accounts tell us that the author, Thomas Heywood, received only six pounds in all for his play.

To these theaters came a rich outpouring of drama, created in part by the opportunities offered on their flexible, nonrealistic, and intimate stages, but growing also out of two different dramatic traditions. Since the mid-fifteenth century, small groups of professional actors had been touring England, setting up their show wherever they could expect to collect enough money or get enough hospitality to make it worth their while. They were highly versatile performers, capable of staging any kind of play in any kind of physical situation—in a banquet room, in a town hall, in an inn-yard, or on a village green. The plays they performed were relatively short pieces known as "Interludes," which combined material from a wide range of sources: biblical tales, classical legends, folk stories, fables, historical events, and fictional narratives. And the range of their sources was matched by the range of activities and moods they often brought together in a single play. Much as *The Second Shepherds' Play* combines the ludicrous sheep-stealing episode with the devotional visit of the shepherds, so the Interludes frequently combined comic and tragic elements, or historical and farcical elements at will. They sustained in England a highly flexible kind of drama that established important precedents for the magnificent multi-plot plays that were to come into being at the end of the sixteenth century.

At the same time that the native tradition was flourishing in the early sixteenth century, the classical influence was beginning to be felt in the grammar schools and universities of England, where Roman plays were being read and performed, and English imitations were being written and performed. During the 1530s, for example, a headmaster at Eton, Nicholas Udall, wrote *Ralph Roister Doister,* which he modelled on a comedy by Plautus, *The Braggart Soldier*. Later, in the 1550s, a comedy by "Mr. S.," *Gammer Gurton's Needle,* which was performed at Cambridge, not only drew on Roman plot devices, but also introduced elements from the native tradition of farce, thus anticipating that distinctive tendency of the great Renaissance drama to unite popular and classical elements in a single play. A similar kind of fusing took place in the first regular English tragedy, *Gorboduc,* which dramatized the story of a legendary king of Britain, who divides his kingdom and thus brings about familial dissension and political disaster. In this instance, pseudo-historical material from English chronicles was treated in the manner both of a Senecan revenge tragedy and a medieval morality play, thus anticipating the history play and the revenge tragedy that were to flourish in the late sixteenth and early seventeenth centuries. The authors of *Gorboduc,* Thomas Sackville and Thomas Norton, were students at the Inner Temple, one of the Inns of Court where young men of the period lived and studied to be lawyers. And, like the grammar schools and the universities, the Inns of Court sustained an active tradition of writing and performing plays that combined classical or Italian neoclassical precedents with native English elements. The Inns of Court performed their plays to celebrate a wide variety of occasions before an audience of the socially elite, the noble, and the educated. In Renaissance England, members of the upper class were being educated in the theater and were themselves creating a theatrical tradition that was to bear fruit in the numerous young men with university training who turned to the public theaters at the end of the sixteenth century.

Once the educated and the professional theater traditions had firmly taken hold, all that remained was for the two to be brought together—in the right way, at the right place, at the right historical moment. The right time had already come when Elizabeth I ascended to the throne in 1558. She brought religious toleration to England, calming the unrest created by her half-sister Mary's attempt to restore Catholicism as the state religion. Elizabeth's political genius stimulated a heady period of exploration and expansion, marked by the voyages of Sir Francis Drake, the commerce of the merchant fleet, the defeat of the Spanish Armada, and the creation of the East India Company. England, under Elizabeth, had become a great naval power, and that power produced great wealth and national pride. The wealth rapidly turned London into a major city, the pride led quickly to a social unity ideal for the life of theater, and The Theater of Burbage gave it a place in which to live.

With the establishment of permanent theaters in London and acting troupes based in London, the golden age of English drama began. The exuberant tendencies of the period were echoed in the richness of dramatic language—for the language, on a stage without sets, had to create the world of the play for its spectators. In *Antony and Cleopatra,* for example, Shakespeare could evoke Rome in one scene and Egypt in the next simply by shifting from the austere language of Caesar to the exotic style of Cleopatra. In *Henry V,* he could evoke the battlefield at Agincourt or the palace of the French king by turning from Henry's military rhetoric to Burgundy's flowing speech of reconciliation. At the same time, the flexibility of this "bare" stage encouraged plays of every kind, and thus Polonius's definition, "comical-tragical-historical-pastoral," is apter than he knew. Because the drama already existing in England combined so many elements, the dramatists were ready for the stage when it finally appeared, almost as if the nature of their art had called it into existence. The drama of Marlowe, Shakespeare, Jonson, Webster, and all their contemporaries, was born from the wedding of fine art and commercial industry—a marriage that we still recognize in the condition of modern theater.

CHRISTOPHER MARLOWE

1564–1593

Marlowe, the earliest of the major English dramatists, wrote all of his plays, except for a youthful college piece, during an extraordinarily productive six-year period between 1587 and his death. Before he turned to the theater, Marlowe had been a scholarship student at Cambridge, where he studied for the clergy, but evidently never took holy orders. Instead, he went off to London and followed the pattern of a number of other young men, most of whom had been to one of the universities and then turned to a career of writing. Usually referred to as the "University Wits," they included Robert Greene, whose double plots and comic heroines established dramatic precedents for Shakespeare's comedies; John Lyly, whose witty and ornate prose style also influenced Shakespeare; and Thomas Kyd, whose sensational revenge play, *The Spanish Tragedy,* established a theatrical precedent for such masterful revenge tragedies as *Hamlet* and John Webster's *The Duchess of Malfi.* Although the "Wits" were writing during the same period as Marlowe, when professional theater was beginning to flourish in London, none of them was so decisively and variously influential as Marlowe, and certainly none was so outstanding a dramatist. Before he was stabbed to death in a tavern quarrel, Marlowe had established the verse form and set major dramatic precedents for English tragedy, heroic drama, and the history play.

In the two parts of *Tamburlaine,* written in 1587 after he left Cambridge, Marlowe turned a fourteenth-century Mongolian warrior whom he had read about in various historical sources into the dramatic archetype of the superhero, the aspiring man of lowly birth who, by force of will and mind and strength, seeks to dominate the entire world—indeed, the entire universe. Though Tamburlaine is undone by the single force he cannot overcome—human mortality—his boldness took the Elizabethan audience by storm, calling forth a whole rash of plays with blood-and-thunder supermen. More influential even than the character of Tamburlaine was his thundering rhetoric, which Marlowe had self-consciously announced in the prologue to the play, inviting his audience to "hear the Scythian Tamburlaine/Threatening the world with high astounding terms." In his brief but polemic prologue, Marlowe deliberately set himself off from what he called the "jigging veins of rhyming mother wits." The poetry of Tamburlaine neither jigs nor rhymes: it roars, and it roars in blank verse, heightened by rhetorical figures, rhythmical patterns, mythological allusions, dramatically suspended sentences, and dazzling imagery, the likes of which had never been heard before on the Elizabethan stage. When Marlowe proved the potency of blank verse, and, in later plays, its flexibility, it quickly became the dominant medium of Elizabethan drama, used in comedies, tragedies, and histories alike.

In subsequent plays, Marlowe continued to be preoccupied with the theme of the aspiring man, a theme that expressed the intense conflict in his own time between the medieval heritage of a divinely ordered hierarchy in religion, government, and society, and the essentially modern world developing out of Protestantism, Machiavellian political theory, and scientific inquiry, all of which opposed medieval authority with Renaissance individualism. In *The Jew of Malta* (ca. 1589), for example, Marlowe created an extraordinarily successful merchant, Barabas the Jew, who regards the wealth he has amassed and the power it brings him as the greatest treasures in the world. Barabas is not the only villain in *The Jew of Malta*: the Christian Knights of Malta exhibit the influence of Machiavellian morality as they lie and cheat and betray their promises. Marlowe's last major play, *Edward II* (ca. 1592), also features an "aspiring man," Young Mortimer, whose opposition to Edward II, England's rightful but incompetent ruler, begins as justifiable anger and ends with an incredibly brutal murder. In true "political" fashion, Mortimer orders that murder in an unpunctuated letter—which can be read either as ordering the King's death or as sparing his life—so that he will not receive any blame if the letter is ever found.

Marlowe ultimately created his most compelling image of the aspiring man in *Dr. Faustus*, which begins with Faustus rejecting Aristotle (philosophy), Galen (medicine), Justinian (law), and the Bible (theology) as subjects of study, choosing instead to turn to magic since he imagines that it will bring him "a world of profit and delight,/Of power, of honor, of omnipotence." He sells his soul to the devil in return for twenty-four years of power, with Mephistophilis as his servant—and seems never to hear the warnings which recur throughout the play, both before and after he makes his bargain. Not only does he ignore clear statements such as Mephistophilis' passionate outcry, "Why, this is hell, nor am I out of it," but he refuses to listen to the Good Angel, who, together with the Bad Angel, appears repeatedly, urging him to repent.

The presence of characters such as the Good Angel, the Bad Angel, the Old Man, and the Seven Deadly Sins explicitly link *Dr. Faustus* with the morality play tradition of the fifteenth century. Indeed, the subject of many of those plays, the *psychomachia,* or conflict between good and evil for the human being's soul, is one of the major themes of Marlowe's play. But Marlowe internalizes that struggle as well, by having Faustus frequently consider the possibility of repentance and then reject it. Even in Faustus's final soliloquy, a speech which takes him and the audience through an hour of time in less than sixty lines, Faustus knows that only one drop of Christ's blood would save his soul, but he is afraid to ask for redemption and resorts instead to bargaining, asking God for a time limit to his damnation.

Marlowe's direct source for the play was a German narrative (published in Frankfurt in 1587) that blended the historical figure of a real Faustus with legends of a scholar who sold his soul to the devil; the English translation appeared in 1592, but if, as some scholars think, the play was written as early as 1588, Marlowe might have seen the translation in manuscript. As with so many details of Marlowe's writing career, the date of *Dr. Faustus* and even the makeup of the text remain open to question, since the play exists in two noticeably different versions: the A-text, published in 1604, and the B-text, which is more than a third longer, published in 1616. The shorter version, the A-text, is quite possibly a touring version of the play, since it lacks some of the scenes requiring complicated technical tricks, which might have been difficult to produce on the road. The longer version (used here) extends the anti-religious tone as well as the comic scenes.

In fact, the comic elements of the play, present in both texts, are closely connected with the problematic nature of magic and how one uses its power. Faustus seems to use his power not for the grand projects he aspires to early on in the play, but for playful, even cheaply funny, conjuring tricks. And, when Orson Welles directed the play in 1937 for the Federal Theater Project, he took a special delight in making the magic as striking and as mystifying as possible. John Houseman, who, as managing producer, collaborated with Welles in staging the play, offers a detailed recollection of Welles's elaborate magical devices in an excerpt from his memoirs (reprinted here following the play). But, as Houseman also makes clear, the magic of the production came not only through the special effects, but through the confrontation of two powerful actors, Welles himself, only twenty-one years old, playing Dr. Faustus (see Figures 1 and 3) and Jack Carter, the black actor who two years earlier had played Macbeth in the famous "voodoo *Macbeth*" staged by Welles and John Houseman, as Mephistophilis (see Figure 2). Houseman's memoirs link the two tall imposing actors, and connect Welles with Faustus himself. All were men of immense talent and immense pride, whose own lives, in some sense, re-enacted the play's central myth and thus underlined *Dr. Faustus*'s timeless relevance for contemporary audiences. We watch a human being grasp for a power beyond human reach, sympathizing perhaps with his desire, but asking if attainment of a dream can ever match the dream itself.

THE TRAGICAL HISTORY OF THE LIFE AND DEATH OF DOCTOR FAUSTUS

BY CHRISTOPHER MARLOWE / TEXT AND NOTES BY IRVING RIBNER

CHARACTERS

THE CHORUS
DOCTOR FAUSTUS
WAGNER, *his student and servant*
VALDES
CORNELIUS
THREE SCHOLARS
AN OLD MAN

POPE ADRIAN
RAYMOND, *King of Hungary*
BRUNO, *the rival Pope*
TWO CARDINALS
THE ARCHBISHOP OF RHEIMS
CHARLES V, *Emperor of Germany*
MARTINO
FREDERICK } *Gentlemen of the Emperor's court*
BENVOLIO
DUKE OF SAXONY
DUKE OF ANHOLT
DUCHESS OF ANHOLT
ROBIN, *the clown, a hostler*
DICK
A VINTNER
A HORSE-COURSER
A CARTER
HOSTESS

GOOD ANGEL
BAD ANGEL
LUCIFER
BEELZEBUB
MEPHISTOPHILIS
PRIDE
COVETOUSNESS
ENVY
WRATH } *The Seven Deadly Sins*
GLUTTONY
SLOTH
LECHERY
ALEXANDER, THE GREAT
HIS PARAMOUR
DARIUS, *King of Persia*
HELEN OF TROY
TWO CUPIDS
DEVILS, BISHOPS, MONKS, FRIARS, SOLDIERS

SCENE

Wittenberg, Rome, the Emperor's court at Innsbruck, court of the Duke of Anholt, and the neighboring country-side.

PROLOGUE

(*Enter* CHORUS.)

CHORUS: Not marching in the fields of Trasimene
Where Mars° did mate° the warlike Carthagens,°
Nor sporting in the dalliance of love
In courts of kings where state° is overturned,
Nor in the pomp of proud audacious deeds

Intends our muse to vaunt his heavenly verse.
Only this, gentles: we must now perform
The form of Faustus' fortunes, good or bad.
And now to patient judgments we appeal,
And speak for Faustus in his infancy.   10
Now is he born, of parents base of stock,
In Germany, within a town called Rhode.
At riper years to Wittenberg he went,
Whereas his kinsmen chiefly brought him up.
So much he profits in divinity,
The fruitful plot of scholarism graced,°
That shortly he was graced with doctor's name,

Note: Material in brackets has been added by the editor.
Trasimene . . . Carthagens, Perhaps an allusion to a lost play about the Carthaginian Hannibal, who achieved one of his greatest victories at Lake Trasimene in 217 B.C. ***Mars,*** Roman god of war; ***mate,*** Rival, meet in battle. ***state,*** Government.

fruitful plot . . . graced, Adorned the university.

Excelling all whose sweet delight disputes°
In th'heavenly matters of theology,
20   Till swoll'n with cunning of a self-conceit,
His waxen wings did mount above his reach,
And melting,° heavens conspired his overthrow;
For, falling to a devilish exercise
And glutted now with learning's golden gifts,
He surfeits upon cursèd necromancy.
Nothing so sweet as magic is to him,
Which he prefers before his chiefest bliss;
And this the man that in his study sits.

ACT 1 / SCENE 1

(FAUSTUS *in his study.*)

FAUSTUS: Settle thy studies, Faustus, and begin
To sound the depth of that thou wilt profess.
Having commenced,° be a divine in show;
Yet level° at the end of every art,
And live and die in Aristotle's works.
Sweet Analytics, 'tis thou hast ravished me!
Bene disserere est finis logices.°
Is to dispute well logic's chiefest end?
Affords this art no greater miracle?
10   Then read no more; thou hast attained that end.
A greater subject fitteth Faustus' wit!
Bid *On cay mae on*° farewell; *Galen*° come.
Seeing *ubi desinit philosophus ibi incipit medicus,*°
Be a physician, Faustus; heap up gold,
And be eternized for some wondrous cure.
Summum bonum medicinae sanitas.°
The end of physic is our body's health.
Why, Faustus, hast thou not attained that end?
Is not thy common talk sound aphorisms?
20   Are not thy bills° hung up as monuments,
Whereby whole cities have escaped the plague,
And divers desperate maladies been cured?
Yet art thou still but Faustus and a man.
Couldst thou make men to live eternally,
Or, being dead, raise them to life again,
Then this profession were to be esteemed.

---

whose sweet delight disputes, Who takes pleasure in
disputing. ***waxen wings . . . melting,*** Metaphor referring
to Icarus's attempt to fly with waxen wings, which melted
when he ignored his father's warning and flew too near the
sun. ***commenced,*** Taken a degree. ***level,*** Aim. ***Bene disserere est finis logices,*** The end of logic is to dispute well. A
tenet of the anti-Aristotelian system introduced at Cambridge when Marlowe was a student there. ***On cay mae on,***
From Aristotle, being or not being; ***Galen,*** Greek physician regarded throughout the Middle Ages as a medical
authority. ***ubi desinit philosophus ibi incipit medicus,***
Where the philosopher stops, the doctor begins. ***Summum
. . . sanitas,*** Health is the highest good of the practice of
medicine. ***bills,*** Medical prescriptions.

Physic, farewell! Where is Justinian?°
Si una eademque res legatus duobus, [*He reads.*]
Alter rem, alter valorem rei, etc.°
A petty case of paltry legacies!   30
Exhaereditare filium non potest pater nisi°—[*He reads.*]
Such is the subject of the Institute
And universal body of the law.
This study fits a mercenary drudge
Who aims at nothing but external trash,
Too servile and illiberal for me.
When all is done, divinity is best.
Jeromè's Bible,° Faustus, view it well:
Stipendium peccati mors est.° Ha! *Stipendium, etc.* [*He
    reads.*]
The reward of sin is death. That's hard.   40
Si pecasse negamus, fallimur [*He reads.*]
Et nulla est in nobis veritas.°
If we say that we have no sin,
We deceive ourselves, and there's no truth in us.
Why then belike we must sin,
And so consequently die.
Ay, we must die an everlasting death.
What doctrine call you this? *Che serà, serà:*
What will be, shall be! Divinity, adieu!
These metaphysics of magicians,   50
And necromantic books are heavenly.
Lines, circles, signs, letters, and characters—
Ay, these are those that Faustus most desires.
O, what a world of profit and delight,
Of power, of honor, of omnipotence
Is promised to the studious artisan!
All things that move between the quiet poles
Shall be at my command. Emperors and kings
Are but obeyed in their several provinces,
Nor can they raise the wind or rend the clouds,   60
But his dominion that exceeds in this
Stretcheth as far as doth the mind of man.
A sound magician is a demi-god.
Here try thy brains to get a deity!
Wagner!

(*Enter* WAGNER.)

          Commend me to my dearest friends,
The German Valdes and Cornelius;
Request them earnestly to visit me.

Justinian, Roman emperor of Constantinople (527–
565), responsible for assembling the Roman law and renowned throughout the Middle Ages as a jurist. ***Si . . .
rei, etc.,*** If the same object is willed to two persons, let one
have the thing itself and the other its value, etc. This is an
incorrect version of one of Justinian's rules. ***Exhaereditare
. . . nisi—,*** The father cannot disinherit the son except—;
another of Justinian's rules roughly paraphrased. ***Jeromè's Bible,*** St. Jerome's Vulgate [Latin] translation of the
Bible. ***Stipendium . . . est,*** Translated in line 40 (Rom.
6:23). ***Si . . . veritas,*** Translated in lines 43–44 (I John
1:8).

WAGNER: I will sir. *(Exit.)*

70 FAUSTUS: Their conference will be a greater help to
me
Than all my labors, plod I ne'er so fast.

(Enter the GOOD ANGEL and the EVIL ANGEL.)

GOOD ANGEL: O, Faustus, lay that damned book aside,
And gaze not on it, lest it tempt thy soul
And heap God's heavy wrath upon thy head.
Read, read the Scriptures. That is blasphemy.

BAD ANGEL: Go forward, Faustus, in that famous art
Wherein all nature's treasury is contained.
Be thou on earth as Jove is in the sky,
80 Lord and commander of these elements.

(Exeunt° ANGELS.)

FAUSTUS: How am I glutted with conceit° of this!
Shall I make spirits fetch me what I please,
Resolve me of° all ambiguities,
Perform what desperate enterprise I will?
I'll have them fly to India for gold,
Ransack the ocean for orient pearl,
And search all corners of the new-found world
For pleasant fruits and princely delicates.
I'll have them read me strange philosophy
90 And tell the secrets of all foreign kings;
I'll have them wall all Germany with brass
And make swift Rhine circle fair Wittenberg.°
I'll have them fill the public schools with silk
Wherewith the students shall be bravely clad.
I'll levy soldiers with the coin they bring
And chase the Prince of Parma from our land
And reign sole king of all the provinces.°
Yea, stranger engines for the brunt of war
Than was the fiery keel at Antwerp's bridge°
100 I'll make my servile spirits to invent.
Come, German Valdes and Cornelius. [*He calls
within.*]
And make me blessed with your sage conference!

(Enter VALDES and CORNELIUS.)

Valdes, sweet Valdes, and Cornelius,
Know that your words have won me at the last
To practice magic and concealed arts;
Yet not your words only, but mine own fantasy
That will receive no object, for my head
But ruminates on necromantic skill.
Philosophy is odious and obscure;
110 Both law and physic are for petty wits;

Divinity is basest of the three,
Unpleasant, harsh, contemptible and vile.
'Tis, magic, magic, that hath ravished me.
Then, gentle friends, aid me in this attempt,
And I, that have with subtle syllogisms
Gravelled° the pastors of the German church,
And made the flowering pride of Wittenberg
Swarm to my problems° as th'infernal spirits
On sweet Musaeus° when he came to hell,
Will be as cunning as Agrippa was,   120
Whose shadows° made all Europe honor him.

VALDES: Faustus, these books, thy wit, and our
experience
Shall make all nations to canonize us.
As Indian Moors° obey their Spanish lords,
So shall the spirits of every element
Be always serviceable to us three.
Like lions shall they guard us when we please,
Like Almain rutters° with their horsemen's staves
Or Lapland giants trotting by our sides,   130
Sometimes like women or unwedded maids,
Shadowing° more beauty in their airy brows
Than in the white breasts of the queen of love.
From Venice shall they drag huge argosies,
And from America the golden fleece
That yearly stuffs old Philip's treasury,
If learnèd Faustus will be resolute.

FAUSTUS: Valdes, as resolute am I in this
As thou to live; therefore object it not.

CORNELIUS: The miracles that magic will perform   140
Will make thee vow to study nothing else.
He that is grounded in astrology,
Enriched with tongues,° well seen in minerals,
Hath all the principles magic doth require.
Then doubt not, Faustus, but to be renowned
And more frequented for this mystery
Than heretofore the Delphian oracle.°
The spirits tell me they can dry the sea
And fetch the treasure of all foreign wracks,
Yea, all the wealth that our forefathers hid   150
Within the massy entrails of the earth.
Then tell me, Faustus, what shall we three want?

FAUSTUS: Nothing, Cornelius. O, this cheers my soul!
Come, show me some demonstrations magical,

Exeunt, Latin for "they go out." *conceit,* The conception of attaining. *Resolve me of,* Explain to me. *Rhine . . .
Wittenberg,* Wittenberg is actually on the Elbe River, not
the Rhine. *provinces,* The Netherlands. *fiery . . . bridge,*
In April 1584 the Dutch used a fireship to destroy a bridge
built across a river by the Prince of Parma in an attempt to
blockade Antwerp.

Gravelled, Puzzled and amazed. *problems,* Public dis-
putations. *Musaeus,* A semimythical Greek poet. Following Virgil, Marlowe has him visit hell like the mythical
Orpheus. *Agrippa . . . shadows,* Cornelius Agrippa
(1486?–1535), a German physician and student of the oc-
cult, was said to have power to raise spirits (shadows) from
the dead. *Indian Moors,* American Indians. *Almain rut-
ters,* German cavalry. *Shadowing,* Harboring, sheltering.
Enriched with tongues, Fluent in Latin, the language used
for communicating with spirits. *Delphian oracle,* The high
priest of Apollo at Delphi who had power to foretell the
future.

That I may conjure in some lusty grove
And have these joys in full possession.
VALDES: Then haste thee to some solitary grove,
And bear wise Bacon's and Abanus' works,°
The Hebrew Psalter, and New Testament;
160   And whatsoever else is requisite
We will inform thee ere our conference cease.
CORNELIUS: Valdes, first let him know the words of
      art,
And then, all other ceremonies learned,
Faustus may try his cunning by himself.
VALDES: First I'll instruct thee in the rudiments,
And then wilt thou be perfecter than I.
FAUSTUS: Then come and dine with me, and after
      meat
We'll canvass every quiddity° thereof,
For ere I sleep I'll try what I can do.
This night I'll conjure, though I die therefore.

(Exeunt.)

ACT 1 / SCENE 2

(Enter two SCHOLARS.)

FIRST SCHOLAR: I wonder what's become of Faustus,
    that was wont to make our schools ring with *sic
    probo.*°

(Enter WAGNER.)

SECOND SCHOLAR: That shall we presently know; here
    comes his boy.
FIRST SCHOLAR: How now sirrah! Where's thy master?
WAGNER: God in heaven knows.
SECOND SCHOLAR: Why, dost not thou know then?
WAGNER: Yes, I know, but that follows not.
10   FIRST SCHOLAR: Go to, sirrah! Leave your jesting and
    tell us where he is.
WAGNER: That follows not by force of argument, which
    you, being licentiates,° should stand upon; there-
    fore acknowledge your error and be attentive.
SECOND SCHOLAR: Then you will not tell us?
WAGNER: You are deceived, for I will tell you. Yet if you
    were not dunces, you would never ask me such a
    question. For is he not *corpus naturale,* and is not
    that *mobile?*° Then wherefore should you ask such
20   a question? But that I am by nature phlegmatic,
    slow to wrath, and prone to lechery—to love, I
    would say—it were not for you to come within forty

Bacon's . . . works, Roger Bacon (1214?–1294) and
Pietro D'Abano (1250–1316) were famous in the Middle
Ages for their feats of magic. **quiddity,** Essential element
(a term from scholastic logic). **sic probo,** Thus I prove
(used in scholastic argument). **licentiates,** Holders of university degrees. **corpus naturale . . . mobile,** The subject
matter of physics, in scholastic terms, was *corpus naturale
seu mobile* (natural body in motion).

foot of the place of execution, although I do not
doubt but to see you both hanged the next sessions.
Thus having triumphed over you, I will set my
countenance like a precisian° and begin to speak
thus: Truly, my dear brethren, my master is within
at dinner with Valdes and Cornelius, as this wine,
if it could speak, would inform your worships. And
so, the Lord bless you, preserve you, and keep you,   30
my dear brethren.

(Exit.)

FIRST SCHOLAR: O Faustus, then I fear that which I
    have long suspected.
That thou art fall'n into that damnèd art
For which they two are infamous through the
    world.
SECOND SCHOLAR: Were he a stranger, not allied to me,
The danger of his soul would make me mourn.
But come, let us go and inform the rector.°
It may be his grave counsel may reclaim him.   40
FIRST SCHOLAR: I fear me nothing will reclaim him now.
SECOND SCHOLAR: Yet let us see what we can do.

(Exeunt.)

ACT 1 / SCENE 3

*(Thunder. Enter [above] LUCIFER and four DEVILS. En-
ter FAUSTUS to conjure.)*

FAUSTUS: Now that the gloomy shadow of the night,
Longing to view Orion's drizzling look,
Leaps from th'Antarctic world unto the sky
And dims the welkin° with her pitchy breath,
Faustus begin thine incantations,
And try if devils will obey thy hest,
Seeing thou hast prayed and sacrificed to them.
Within this circle is Jehovah's name,
Forward and backward anagrammatized,
Th'abbreviated names of holy saints,   10
Figures of every adjunct to the heavens,
And characters of signs and erring° stars,
By which the spirits are enforced to rise.
Then fear not, Faustus, to be resolute,
And try the utmost magic can perform.

(Thunder.)

*Sint mihi Dei Acherontis propitii! Valeat numen triplex
Jehovae. Ignei, aerii, aquatani spiritus, salvete! Orientis
princeps, Beelzebub, inferni ardentis monarcha, et Demogorgon, propitiamus vos, ut appareat et surgat Mephistophilis. Quid tu moraris? Per Jehovam Gehennam, et*   20

---

precisian, Puritan.   **rector,** Head of the university.
welkin, Sky.   **erring,** Wandering.

consecratam aquam quam nunc spargo, signumque crucis
quod nunc facio, et per vota nostra, ipse nunc surgat nobis
dicatus Mephistophilis.°

(Enter [Mephistophilis,] a DEVIL.*)*

I charge thee to return and change thy shape;
Thou art too ugly to attend on me.
Go, and return an old Franciscan friar;
That holy shape becomes a devil best.

(Exit DEVIL.*)*

I see there's virtue in my heavenly words.
Who would not be proficient in this art?
How pliant is this Mephistophilis,   30
Full of obedience and humility.
Such is the force of magic and my spells.
Now Faustus, thou art conjurer laureate,
That canst command great Mephistophilis.
Quin redis Mephistophilis fratris imagine.°

(Enter MEPHISTOPHILIS *[dressed like a Franciscan*
friar].)

MEPHISTOPHILIS: Now Faustus, what wouldst thou
    have me do?
FAUSTUS: I charge thee wait upon me whilst I live,
    To do whatever Faustus shall command,
    Be it to make the moon drop from her sphere   40
    Or the ocean to overwhelm the world.
MEPHISTOPHILIS: I am a servant to great Lucifer
    And may not follow thee without his leave.
    No more than he commands must we perform.
FAUSTUS: Did not he charge thee to appear to me?
MEPHISTOPHILIS: No, I came hither of mine own
    accord.
FAUSTUS: Did not my conjuring speeches raise thee?
    Speak.
MEPHISTOPHILIS: That was the cause, but yet *per*   50
    accidens,°
    For when we hear one rack the name of God,
    Abjure the Scriptures and his Savior Christ,
    We fly in hope to get his glorious soul;
    Nor will we come unless he use such means
    Whereby he is in danger to be damned.
    Therefore the shortest cut for conjuring

Sint . . . Mephistophilis, May the gods of Aceron be
propitious to me. Let the triple name of Jehova [the trinity]
be gone. Hail spirits of fire, air, and water. Prince of the
East, Beelzebub, monarch of burning hell, and Demogorgon, we petition you that Mephistophilis may appear and
rise. Why do you linger? By Jehova, Gehenna and the holy
water which I now sprinkle and the sign of the cross which
I now make and by our vows, let Mephistophilis himself
now rise to serve us. **Quin . . . imagine,** Return, Mephistophilis, in the shape of a friar. **cause . . . per accidens,**
The terms are from scholastic logic.

Is stoutly to abjure the Trinity
And pray devoutly to the prince of hell.
FAUSTUS: So Faustus hath   60
    Already done, and holds this principle:
    There is no chief but only Beelzebub,
    To whom Faustus doth dedicate himself.
    This word "damnation" terrifies not me,
    For I confound hell in Elysium.
    My ghost° be with the old philosophers!
    But leaving these vain trifles of men's souls,
    Tell me what is that Lucifer thy lord?
MEPHISTOPHILIS: Arch-regent and commander of all
    spirits.
FAUSTUS: Was not that Lucifer an angel once?   70
MEPHISTOPHILIS: Yes Faustus, and most dearly loved
    of God.
FAUSTUS: How comes it then that he is prince of
    devils?
MEPHISTOPHILIS: O, by aspiring pride and insolence,
    For which God threw him from the face of heaven.
FAUSTUS: And what are you that live with Lucifer?
MEPHISTOPHILIS: Unhappy spirits that fell with
    Lucifer,
    Conspired against our God with Lucifer,
    And are for ever damned with Lucifer.
FAUSTUS: Where are you damned?
MEPHISTOPHILIS: In hell.   80
FAUSTUS: How comes it then that thou art out of hell?
MEPHISTOPHILIS: Why this is hell, nor am I out of it.
    Think'st thou that I who saw the face of God
    And tasted the eternal joys of heaven
    Am not tormented with ten thousand hells
    In being deprived of everlasting bliss?
    O Faustus, leave these frivolous demands
    Which strike a terror to my fainting soul.
FAUSTUS: What, is great Mephistophilis so passionate
    For being deprivèd of the joys of heaven?   90
    Learn thou of Faustus' manly fortitude,
    And scorn those joys thou never shalt possess.
    Go bear these tidings to great Lucifer:
    Seeing Faustus hath incurred eternal death
    By desperate thoughts against Jove's deity,
    Say he surrenders up to him his soul,
    So he will spare him four and twenty years,
    Letting him live in all voluptuousness,
    Having thee ever to attend on me,
    To give me whatsoever I shall ask,   100
    To tell me whatsoever I demand,
    To slay mine enemies, and aid my friends,
    And always be obedient to my will.
    Go, and return to mighty Lucifer,
    And meet me in my study at midnight,
    And then resolve me of thy master's mind.
MEPHISTOPHILIS: I will, Faustus.

(Exit.)

---

ghost, Spirit.

FAUSTUS: Had I as many souls as there be stars,
I'd give them all for Mephistophilis.
110 By him I'll be great emperor of the world,
And make a bridge thorough the moving air,
To pass the ocean with a band of men.
I'll join the hills that bind° the Afric shore,
And make that country continent to Spain,
And both contributory to my crown.
The Emperor shall not live but by my leave,
Nor any potentate of Germany.
Now that I have obtained what I desire,
I'll live in speculation of this art
Till Mephistophilis return again.

(Exit.)

ACT 1 / SCENE 4

(Enter WAGNER *and [Robin,] the* CLOWN.*)*

WAGNER: Come hither, sirrah boy.
ROBIN: Boy! O disgrace to my person. Zounds, boy in
your face! You have seen many boys with such
pickedevants,° I am sure.
WAGNER: Sirrah, hast thou no comings in?°
ROBIN: Yes, and goings out too, you may see, sir.
WAGNER: Alas, poor slave! See how poverty jests in his
nakedness. I know the villain's out of service, and
so hungry that I know he would give his soul to the
10 devil for a shoulder of mutton, though it were
blood-raw.
ROBIN: Not so neither. I had need to have it well
roasted, and good sauce to it, if I pay so dear, I can
tell you.
WAGNER: Sirrah, wilt thou be my man and wait on me,
and I will make thee go like *Qui mihi discipulus?*°
ROBIN: What, in verse?
WAGNER: No slave; in beaten° silk and staves-acre.°
ROBIN: Staves-acre? That's good to kill vermin. Then,
20 belike, if I serve you I shall be lousy.
WAGNER: Why, so thou shalt be, whether thou dost it or
no; for, sirrah, if thou dost not presently bind thyself to me for seven years, I'll turn all the lice about
thee into familiars° and make them tear thee in
pieces.
ROBIN: Nay sir, you may save yourself a labor, for they
are as familiar with me as if they paid for their meat
and drink, I can tell you.
WAGNER: Well, sirrah, leave your jesting and take these
30 guilders.
ROBIN: Yes, marry sir, and I thank you too.
WAGNER: So, now thou art to be at an hour's warning,

---

bind, Enclose. **pickedevants,** Pointed beards. **comings in,** Earnings. **Qui mihi discipulus,** Who is my disciple
(the opening words of a Latin poem by William Lyly, well
known to Elizabethan schoolboys). **beaten,** Embroidered
with metal; **staves-acre,** A plant used for killing vermin.
familiars, Attendant evil spirits.

whensoever and wheresoever the devil shall fetch
thee.
ROBIN: Here, take your guilders, again. I'll none of 'em.
WAGNER: Not I. Thou art pressed.° Prepare thyself, for
I will presently raise up two devils to carry thee
away. Banio! Belcher!
ROBIN: Belcher? And Belcher come here, I'll belch him.
I am not afraid of a devil.   40

(Enter two DEVILS.*)*

WAGNER: How now, sir? Will you serve me now?
ROBIN: Ay, good Wagner; take away the devil then.
WAGNER: Spirits away! Now, sirrah, follow me.

[Exeunt DEVILS.*]*

ROBIN: I will sir. But hark you, master, will you teach
me this conjuring occupation?
WAGNER: Ay, sirrah. I'll teach thee to turn thyself to a
dog, or a cat, or a mouse, or a rat, or any thing.
ROBIN: A dog, or a cat, or a mouse, or a rat! O brave
Wagner!
WAGNER: Villain, call me Master Wagner, and see that   50
you walk attentively, and let your right eye be always
diametrally° fixed upon my left heel, that thou
may'st *quasi vestigias nostras insistere.*°
ROBIN: Well, sir, I warrant you.

(Exeunt.)

ACT 2 / SCENE 1

(Enter FAUSTUS *in his study.)*

FAUSTUS: Now Faustus must thou needs be damned,
And canst thou not be saved.
What boots° it then to think on God or heaven?
Away with such vain fancies, and despair;
Despair in God, and trust in Beelzebub.
Now go not backward; Faustus, be resolute.
Why waver'st thou? O, something soundeth in mine
ear:
"Abjure this magic; turn to God again."
Ay, and Faustus will turn to God again!
To God? He loves thee not.   10
The God thou serv'st is thine own appetite,
Wherein is fixed the love of Beelzebub.
To him I'll build an altar and a church,
And offer lukewarm blood of new-born babes.

(Enter the two ANGELS.*)*

BAD ANGEL: Go forward, Faustus, in that famous art.
GOOD ANGEL: Sweet Faustus, leave that execrable art.
FAUSTUS: Contrition, prayer, repentance—what of
these?

---

pressed, Enlisted into service in exchange for money.
diametrally, In a straight line. **quasi . . . insistere,** As if to
walk in our tracks. **boots,** Avails.

GOOD ANGEL: O, they are means to bring thee unto
    heaven.
BAD ANGEL: Rather illusions, fruits of lunacy,
20   That make men foolish that do use them most.
GOOD ANGEL: Sweet Faustus, think of heaven and
    heavenly things.
BAD ANGEL: No Faustus; think of honor and wealth.

(Exeunt ANGELS.*)*

FAUSTUS: Wealth? Why, the signory of Emden° shall
    be mine.
    When Mephistophilis shall stand by me,
    What power can hurt me? Faustus thou art safe.
    Cast no more doubts. Mephistophilis, come
    And bring glad tidings from great Lucifer.
    Is't not midnight? Come, Mephistophilis.
    Veni,° veni, Mephistophile.

(Enter MEPHISTOPHILIS.*)*

30   Now tell me what saith Lucifer, thy lord?
MEPHISTOPHILIS: That I shall wait on Faustus whilst
    he lives,
    So he will buy my service with his soul.
FAUSTUS: Already Faustus hath hazarded that for
    thee.
MEPHISTOPHILIS: But now thou must bequeath it
    solemnly
    And write a deed of gift with thine own blood,
    For that security craves great Lucifer.
    If thou deny it, I must back to hell.
FAUSTUS: Stay, Mephistophilis! Tell me what good
    Will my soul do thy lord.
MEPHISTOPHILIS: Enlarge his kingdom.
40 FAUSTUS: Is that the reason why he tempts us thus?
MEPHISTOPHILIS: *Solamen miseris socios habuisse doloris.°*
FAUSTUS: Why, have you any pain that torture others?
MEPHISTOPHILIS: As great as have the human souls of
    men.
    But tell me, Faustus, shall I have thy soul?
    And I will be thy slave and wait on thee
    And give thee more than thou hast wit to ask.
FAUSTUS: Ay, Mephistophilis, I'll give it him.
MEPHISTOPHILIS: Then Faustus, stab thy arm
    courageously,
    And bind thy soul that at some certain day
50   Great Lucifer may claim it as his own,
    And then be thou as great as Lucifer.
FAUSTUS: *[stabbing his arm]* Lo, Mephistophilis, for love
    of thee,
    I cut mine arm, and with my proper° blood
    Assure my soul to be great Lucifer's,
    Chief lord and regent of perpetual night.

Emden, The chief city of East Friesland, near the
mouth of the river Ems, which had considerable trade relations with Elizabethan England. *Veni, veni . . .* Come,
come, Mephistophilis. *Solamen . . . doloris,* It is a consolation in misery to have a fellow sufferer. *proper,* Own.

View here this blood that trickles from mine arm,
And let it be propitious for my wish.
MEPHISTOPHILIS: But Faustus,
    Write it in manner of a deed of gift.
FAUSTUS: Ay, so I do. *[He writes.]* But Mephistophilis, 60
    My blood congeals, and I can write no more.
MEPHISTOPHILIS: I'll fetch thee fire to dissolve it
    straight.

(Exit.)

FAUSTUS: What might the staying of my blood
    portend?
    Is it unwilling I should write this bill?
    Why streams it not that I may write afresh?
    "Faustus gives to thee his soul." Ah, there it stayed.
    Why shouldst thou not? Is not thy soul thine own?
    Then write again: "Faustus gives to thee his soul."

(Enter MEPHISTOPHILIS *with the chafer of fire.)*

MEPHISTOPHILIS: See Faustus, here is fire. Set it on.°
FAUSTUS: So. Now the blood begins to clear again. 70
    Now will I make an end immediately. *[He writes.]*
MEPHISTOPHILIS: *[Aside.]* What will not I do to obtain
    his soul?
FAUSTUS: *Consummatum est;°* this bill is ended,
    And Faustus hath bequeathed his soul to Lucifer.
    But what is this inscription on mine arm?
    Homo fuge!° Whither should I fly?
    If unto God, he'll throw me down to hell.
    My senses are deceived; here's nothing writ.
    O yes, I see it plain. Even here is writ
    Homo fuge! Yet shall not Faustus fly. 80
MEPHISTOPHILIS: *[Aside.]* I'll fetch him somewhat to
    delight his mind.

(Exit.)

(Enter DEVILS, *giving crowns and rich apparel to* FAUS-
TUS. *They dance and then depart. Enter* MEPHISTOPH-
ILIS.*)*

FAUSTUS: What means this show? Speak
    Mephistophilis.
MEPHISTOPHILIS: Nothing, Faustus, but to delight thy
    mind
    And let thee see what magic can perform.
FAUSTUS: But may I raise such spirits when I please?
MEPHISTOPHILIS: Ay Faustus, and do greater things
    than these.
FAUSTUS: Then, Mephistophilis, receive this scroll,
    A deed of gift of body and of soul,
    But yet conditionally that thou perform
    All covenants and articles between us both. 90

Set it on, Set the dish of blood on the fire. **Consummatum est,** It is completed (the words of Jesus at his Crucifixion; John 19:30). **Homo fuge,** Fly, man.

MEPHISTOPHILIS: Faustus, I swear by hell and Lucifer
  To effect all promises between us made.
FAUSTUS: Then hear me read it Mephistophilis.

    On these conditions following:
    First, that Faustus may be a spirit in form and substance;
    Secondly, that Mephistophilis shall be his servant and be at
    his command;
    Thirdly, that Mephistophilis shall do for him and bring him
    whatsoever;
100   *Fourthly, that he shall be in his chamber or house invisible;*
    Lastly, that he shall appear to the said John Faustus at all
    times, in what form or shape soever he please: I, John Faustus,
    of Wittenberg, doctor, by these presents, do give both body and
    soul to Lucifer, Prince of the East, and his minister, Mephis-
    tophilis; and furthermore grant unto them that four and
    twenty years being expired, the articles above written inviolate,
    full power to fetch or carry the said John Faustus, body and
    soul, flesh, blood, or goods, into their habitation wheresoever.
                                     By me, John Faustus.

110 MEPHISTOPHILIS: Speak Faustus. Do you deliver this as
  your deed?
FAUSTUS: Ay, take it, and the devil give thee good of
  it.
MEPHISTOPHILIS: So now, Faustus, ask me what thou
  wilt.
FAUSTUS: First will I question with thee about hell.
  Tell me, where is the place that men call hell?
MEPHISTOPHILIS: Under the heavens.
FAUSTUS: Ay, so are all things else. But whereabouts?
MEPHISTOPHILIS: Within the bowels of these elements,
  Where we are tortured and remain for ever.
  Hell hath no limits, nor is circumscribed
120 In one self place, but where we are is hell,
  And where hell is, there must we ever be.
  And, to be short, when all the world dissolves
  And every creature shall be purified,
  All places shall be hell that is not heaven.
FAUSTUS: I think hell's a fable.
MEPHISTOPHILIS: Ay, think so still, till experience
  change thy mind.
FAUSTUS: Why, dost thou think that Faustus shall be
  damned?
MEPHISTOPHILIS: Ay, of necessity, for here's the scroll
  In which thou hast given thy soul to Lucifer.
130 FAUSTUS: Ay, and body too. But what of that?
  Think'st thou that Faustus is so fond° to imagine
  That after this life there is any pain?
  No, these are trifles and mere old wives' tales.
MEPHISTOPHILIS: But I am an instance to prove the
  contrary,

For I tell thee I am damned and now in hell.
FAUSTUS: Nay, and this be hell, I'll willingly be
  damned.
  What? Sleeping, eating, walking and disputing?
  But, leaving off this, let me have a wife,
  The fairest maid in Germany,
  For I am wanton and lascivious,   140
  And cannot live without a wife.
MEPHISTOPHILIS: I prithee, Faustus, talk not of a wife.
FAUSTUS: Nay, sweet Mephistophilis, fetch me one, for
  I will have one.
MEPHISTOPHILIS: Well, Faustus, thou shalt have a wife.
  Sit there till I come.

(*Enter* [MEPHISTOPHILIS] *with a* DEVIL *dressed like a
woman, with fireworks.*)

FAUSTUS: What sight is this?
MEPHISTOPHILIS: Now Faustus, how dost thou like thy
  wife?
FAUSTUS: Here's a hot whore indeed! No, I'll no wife.
MEPHISTOPHILIS: Marriage is but a ceremonial toy,
  And if thou lovest me, think no more of it.   150
  I'll cull thee out the fairest courtesans
  And bring them every morning to thy bed.
  She whom thine eye shall like, thy heart shall have,
  Were she as chaste as was Penelope,°
  As wise as Saba,° or as beautiful
  As was bright Lucifer before his fall.
  Hold; take this book; peruse it thoroughly.
  The iterating of these lines brings gold;
  The framing of this circle on the ground
  Brings thunder, whirlwinds, storm and lightning.   160
  Pronounce this thrice devoutly to thyself,
  And men in harness° shall appear to thee,
  Ready to execute what thou command'st.
FAUSTUS: Thanks, Mephistophilis, for this sweet book.
  This will I keep as chary as my life.

(*Exeunt.*)

ACT 2 / SCENE 2

(*Enter* FAUSTUS *in his study and* MEPHISTOPHILIS.)

FAUSTUS: When I behold the heavens, then I repent
  And curse thee, wicked Mephistophilis,
  Because thou hast deprived me of those joys.
MEPHISTOPHILIS: 'Twas thine own seeking, Faustus;
  thank thyself.
  But think'st thou heaven is such a glorious thing?
  I tell thee, Faustus, 'tis not half so fair
  As thou, or any man that breathes on earth.
FAUSTUS: How prov'st thou that?

---

fond, Foolish.

Penelope, The faithful wife of Ulysses in Homer's
Odyssey. ***Saba,*** The Queen of Sheba. ***harness,*** Armor.

MEPHISTOPHILIS: 'Twas made for man; then he's more
    excellent.
10 FAUSTUS: If heaven was made for man, 'twas made for
    me.
    I will renounce this magic and repent.

(*Enter the two* ANGELS.)

GOOD ANGEL: Faustus repent; yet God will pity thee.
BAD ANGEL: Thou art a spirit;° God cannot pity thee.
FAUSTUS: Who buzzeth in mine ears I am a spirit?
    Be I a devil, yet God may pity me;
    Yea, God will pity me if I repent.
BAD ANGEL: Ay, but Faustus never shall repent.

(*Exeunt* ANGELS.)

FAUSTUS: My heart is hardened; I cannot repent.
    Scarce can I name salvation, faith, or heaven,
20 But fearful echoes thunder in mine ears:
    "Faustus, thou art damned!" Then swords and
      knives,
    Poison, guns, halters, and envenomed steel
    Are laid before me to dispatch myself;
    And long ere this I should have done the deed,
    Had not sweet pleasure conquered deep despair.
    Have not I made blind Homer sing to me
    Of Alexander's love and Oenone's death?°
    And hath not he, that built the walls of Thebes
    With ravishing sound of his melodious harp,°
30 Made music with my Mephistophilis?
    Why should I die then, or basely despair?
    I am resolved; Faustus shall not repent.
    Come, Mephistophilis, let us dispute again
    And reason of divine astrology.
    Speak; are there many spheres above the moon?
    Are all celestial bodies but one globe,
    As is the substance of this centric earth?
MEPHISTOPHILIS: As are the elements, such are the
    heavens,
    Even from the moon unto the empyreal orb,
40 Mutually folded in each others' spheres,
    And jointly move upon one axle-tree.
    Whose terminè° is termed the world's wide pole;
    Nor are the names of Saturn, Mars, or Jupiter
    Feigned, but are erring stars.°
FAUSTUS: But have they all
    One motion, both *situ et tempore?*°
MEPHISTOPHILIS: All move from east to west in four and
    twenty hours upon the poles of the world, but differ
    in their motions upon the poles of the zodiac.

FAUSTUS: These slender questions Wagner can decide. 50
    Hath Mephistophilis no greater skill?
    Who knows not the double motion of the planets?
    That the first is finished in a natural day?
    The second thus? Saturn in thirty years?
      Jupiter in twelve; Mars in four; the sun, Venus and
      Mercury in a year; the moon in twenty eight days
    These are freshmen's suppositions. But tell me,
    hath every sphere a dominion or *intelligentia?*°
MEPHISTOPHILIS: Ay.
FAUSTUS: How many heavens or spheres are there? 60
MEPHISTOPHILIS: Nine—the seven planets, the firma-
    ment, and the empyreal heaven.
FAUSTUS: But is there not *coelum igneum, et crystallinum?*°
MEPHISTOPHILIS: No, Faustus, they be but fables.
FAUSTUS: Resolve me then in this one question: why are
    not conjunctions, oppositions, aspects, eclipses° all
    at one time, but in some years we have more, in
    some less?
MEPHISTOPHILIS: *Per inaequalem motum respectu totius.*°
FAUSTUS: Well, I am answered. Now tell me who made
    the world.
MEPHISTOPHILIS: I will not. 70
FAUSTUS: Sweet Mephistophilis, tell me.
MEPHISTOPHILIS: Move me not, Faustus.
FAUSTUS: Villain, have not I bound thee to tell me any
    thing?
MEPHISTOPHILIS: Ay, that is not against our kingdom.
    This is. Thou art damned. Think thou of hell.
FAUSTUS: Think, Faustus, upon God that made the
    world.
MEPHISTOPHILIS: Remember this.

(*Exit.*)

FAUSTUS: Ay, go accursèd spirit to ugly hell.
    'Tis thou hast damned distressèd Faustus' soul.
    Is't not too late? 80

(*Enter the two* ANGELS.)

BAD ANGEL: Too late.
GOOD ANGEL: Never too late, if Faustus will repent.
BAD ANGEL: If thou repent, devils will tear thee in
    pieces.
GOOD ANGEL: Repent, and they shall never raze thy
    skin.

(*Exeunt* ANGELS.)

FAUSTUS: O Christ, my Savior, my Savior,
    Help to save distressèd Faustus' soul.

---

spirit, Devil. ***Alexander's . . . death,*** Paris (also called
Alexander) loved the nymph Oenone when he lived as a
shepherd on Mt. Ida. Oenone died of a broken heart when
he left her. ***he . . . harp,*** Amphion, son of Zeus and An-
tiope, caused stones to move and the walls of Thebes to be
built simply by playing on the lyre given to him by Hermes.
terminè, Limit. ***erring stars,*** Planets. ***situ et tempore,*** In
position (direction of movement) and in the time they take
to revolve about the earth.

dominion or intelligentia, Governing angel. ***coelum
. . . crystallinum,*** The fiery heaven and crystalline sphere
of Ptolemaic astronomy. ***conjunctions,*** Seeming proximi-
ties of heavenly bodies; ***oppositions,*** Divergences of heavenly bodies; ***aspects,*** Any other relations of such bodies to
one another; ***eclipses,*** The blottings out of one heavenly
body by another. ***Per : . . totius,*** By their unequal movements in respect to the whole (i.e., the different speeds of
the various planets within the total cosmos).

(Enter LUCIFER, BEELZEBUB, *and* MEPHISTOPHILIS.)

LUCIFER: Christ cannot save thy soul, for he is just.
There's none but I have interest in the same.

FAUSTUS: O, what art thou that look'st so terribly?

90   LUCIFER: I am Lucifer,
And this is my companion prince in hell.

FAUSTUS: O, Faustus, they are come to fetch thy soul.

BEELZEBUB: We are come to tell thee thou dost injure
us.

LUCIFER: Thou call'st on Christ, contrary to thy
promise.

BEELZEBUB: Thou shouldst not think on God.

LUCIFER: Think on the devil.

BEELZEBUB: And his dam too.

FAUSTUS: Nor will I henceforth. Pardon me in this,
And Faustus vows never to look to heaven,
100 Never to name God, or to pray to him,
To burn his Scriptures, slay his ministers,
And make my spirits pull his churches down.

LUCIFER: So shalt thou show thyself an obedient servant,
And we will highly gratify thee for it.

BEELZEBUB: Faustus, we are come from hell in person
to show thee some pastime. Sit down, and thou shalt
behold the Seven Deadly Sins appear to thee in
their own proper shapes and likeness.

FAUSTUS: That sight will be as pleasant to me as Paradise
110   was to Adam the first day of his creation.

LUCIFER: Talk not of Paradise or creation, but mark the
show. Go, Mephistophilis, fetch them in.

[*Exit* MEPHISTOPHILIS.]

(Enter the SEVEN DEADLY SINS *[with* MEPHISTOPHILIS,
led by a* PIPER].)

BEELZEBUB: Now Faustus, question them of their names
and dispositions.

FAUSTUS: That shall I soon. What art thou, the first?

PRIDE: I am Pride. I disdain to have any parents. I am
like to Ovid's flea:° I can creep into every corner of
a wench. Sometimes, like a periwig, I sit upon her
brow. Next, like a necklace, I hang about her neck.
120   Then, like a fan of feathers, I kiss her lips, and
then, turning myself to a wrought smock, do what
I list. But fie, what a smell is here! I'll not speak
another word unless the ground be perfumed and
covered with cloth of Arras.°

FAUSTUS: Thou art a proud knave indeed. What art
thou, the second?

COVETOUSNESS: I am Covetousness, begotten of an old
churl in a leather bag, and might I now obtain my
wish, this house, you and all, should turn to gold,
that I might lock you safe into my chest. O my sweet   130
gold!

FAUSTUS: And what art thou, the third?

ENVY: I am Envy, begotten of a chimney-sweeper and
an oyster-wife. I cannot read and therefore wish all
books burned. I am lean with seeing others eat. O,
that there would come a famine over all the world,
that all might die, and I live alone; then thou
shouldst see how fat I'd be. But must thou sit and
I stand? Come down, with a vengeance.

FAUSTUS: Out envious wretch! But what are thou, the   140
fourth?

WRATH: I am Wrath. I had neither father nor mother.
I leaped out of a lion's mouth when I was scarce an
hour old, and ever since have run up and down the
world with this case of rapiers, wounding myself
when I could get none to fight withal. I was born
in hell, and look to it, for some of you shall be my
father.

FAUSTUS: And what are you, the fifth?

GLUTTONY: I am Gluttony. My parents are all dead, and   150
the devil a penny they have left me but a small
pension, and that buys me thirty meals a day and
ten bevers°—a small trifle to suffice nature. I come
of a royal pedigree. My father was a gammon of
bacon, and my mother was a hogshead of claret
wine. My godfathers were these: Peter Pickled-
herring and Martin Martlemas-beef.° But my godmother, O, she was a jolly gentlewoman, and well
beloved in every good town and city; her name was
Mistress Margery March-beer.° Now Faustus, thou   160
hast heard all my progeny; wilt thou bid me to a
supper.

FAUSTUS: Not I. Thou wilt eat up all my victuals.

GLUTTONY: Then the devil choke thee.

FAUSTUS: Choke thyself, glutton. What art thou, the
sixth?

SLOTH: Heigh ho! I am Sloth. I was begotten on a sunny
bank, where I have lain ever since, and you have
done me great injury to bring me from thence. Let
me be carried thither again by Gluttony and Lech-   170
ery. Heigh ho! I'll not speak a word more for a
king's ransom.

FAUSTUS: And what are you Mistress Minx, the seventh
and last?

LECHERY: Who, I, sir? I am one that loves an inch of
raw mutton° better than an ell of fried stockfish,°
and the first letter of my name begins with lechery.

LUCIFER: Away to hell! Away! On piper!

(Exeunt the SEVEN SINS *[and the* PIPER].)

---

bevers, Light snacks taken between regular meals.
Martlemas-beef, Salted meat hung for the winter on Mar-
tinmas, November 11. **March-beer,** A fine ale made in the
springtime and aged for two years before being drunk.
raw mutton, Common slang for "whore"; **stockfish,** Dried
codfish.

Ovid's flea, The medieval poem *Carmine de Pulice*
(Poem of the Flea) was generally attributed to Ovid. **cloth
of Arras,** Flemish cloth used generally for tapestries.

FAUSTUS: O, how this sight doth delight my soul!

LUCIFER: But Faustus, in hell is all manner of delight.

FAUSTUS: O, might I see hell and return again safe, how
190   happy were I then!

LUCIFER: Faustus, thou shalt. At midnight I will send
        for thee. Meanwhile peruse this book and view it
        thoroughly, and thou shalt turn thyself into what
        shape thou wilt.

FAUSTUS: Thanks, mighty Lucifer.
    This will I keep as chary as my life.

LUCIFER: Now Faustus, farewell.

FAUSTUS: Farewell, great Lucifer. Come, Mephistoph-
        ilis.

(Exeunt, several ways.)

ACT 2 / SCENE 3

(Enter the CLOWN *[Robin, holding a book].)*

ROBIN: What, Dick, look to the horses there till I come
    again. I have gotten one of Doctor Faustus' conjur-
    ing books, and now we'll have such knavery as't
    passes.

(Enter DICK.*)*

DICK: What, Robin, you must come away and walk the
    horses.

ROBIN: I walk the horses? I scorn't, 'faith. I have other
    matters in hand. Let the horses walk themselves
    and they will. [*He reads.*] *A per se a; t, h, e, the; o per*
10 *se o; deny orgon, gorgon.* Keep further from me, O
    thou illiterate and unlearned hostler.

DICK: 'Snails,° what hast thou got there? A book? Why,
    thou canst not tell ne'er a word on't.

ROBIN: That thou shalt see presently. Keep out of the
    circle, I say, lest I send you into the hostry with a
    vengeance.

DICK: That's like, 'faith. You had best leave your fool-
    ery, for an my master come, he'll conjure you, 'faith.

ROBIN: My master conjure me? I'll tell thee what: an my
20 master come here, I'll clap as fair a pair of horns°
    on's head as e'er thou sawest in thy life.

DICK: Thou needst not do that, for my mistress hath
    done it.

ROBIN: Ay, there be of us here that have waded as deep
    into matters as other men, if they were disposed to
    talk.

DICK: A plague take you! I thought you did not sneak
    up and down after her for nothing. But I prithee,
    tell me in good sadness,° Robin, is that a conjuring
30 book?

ROBIN: Do but speak what thou'lt have me to do, and
    I'll do't. If thou'lt dance naked, put off thy clothes,
    and I'll conjure thee about presently. Or if thou'lt
    go but to the tavern with me, I'll give thee white

'*Snails,* By God's nails. *horns,* The common sign of a
cuckold. *sadness,* Seriousness.

wine, red wine, claret wine, sack, muscadine, mal-
mesey and whippincrust.° Hold belly, hold, and
we'll not pay one penny for it.

DICK: O brave! Prithee let's to it presently, for I am as
    dry as a dog.

ROBIN: Come then, let's away.   40

(Exeunt.)

ACT 3 / PROLOGUE

(Enter the CHORUS.*)*

CHORUS: Learnèd Faustus,
    To find the secrets of astronomy
    Graven in the book of Jove's high firmament,
    Did mount him up to scale Olympus' top,
    Where, sitting in a chariot burning bright
    Drawn by the strength of yokèd dragons' necks,
    He views the clouds, the planets, and the stars,
    The tropics, zones, and quarters of the sky,
    From the bright circle of the hornèd moon
    Even to the height of *Primum Mobile*.°   10
    And whirling round with this circumference,
    Within the concave compass of the pole,
    From east to west his dragons swiftly glide
    And in eight days did bring him home again.
    Not long he stayed within his quiet house
    To rest his bones after his weary toil,
    But new exploits do hale him out again,
    And mounted then upon a dragon's back,
    That with his wings did part the subtle air,
    He now is gone to prove cosmography,°   20
    That measures coasts and kingdoms of the earth,
    And, as I guess, will first arrive at Rome
    To see the Pope and manner of his court
    And take some part of holy Peter's feast,
    The which this day is highly solemnized.

(Exit.)

ACT 3 / SCENE 1

(Enter FAUSTUS *and* MEPHISTOPHILIS.*)*

FAUSTUS: Having now, my good Mephistophilis,
    Passed with delight the stately town of Trier,
    Environed round with airy mountain tops,
    With walls of flint, and deep entrenchèd lakes,°
    Not to be won by any conquering prince;
    From Paris next, coasting the realm of France,
    We saw the river Main fall into Rhine,

---

whippincrust, Possibly a corruption of "hippocras," a
highly spiced and sugared wine. *Primum Mobile,* In Ptolemaic astronomy the outermost sphere of creation, which
moves the other nine spheres. *prove cosmography,* Explore
the universe. *entrenchèd lakes,* Castle moats.

Whose banks are set with groves of fruitful vines;
Then up to Naples, rich Campania,
Whose buildings fair and gorgeous to the eye,
The streets straight forth and paved with finest
    brick,
Quarters the town in four equivalents.
There saw we learnèd Maro's° golden tomb,
The way he cut, an English mile in length,
Through a rock of stone in one night's space.°
From thence to Venice, Padua, and the rest,
In midst of which a sumptuous temple stands,
That threats the stars with her aspiring top,
Whose frame is paved with sundry colored stones,
20   And roofed aloft with curious work in gold.°
Thus hitherto hath Faustus spent his time.
But tell me now, what resting-place is this?
Hast thou, as erst I did command,
Conducted me within the walls of Rome?
MEPHISTOPHILIS: I have, my Faustus, and for proof
    thereof
This is the goodly palace of the Pope;
And 'cause we are no common guests,
I choose his privy chamber for our use.
FAUSTUS: I hope his holiness will bid us welcome.
30   MEPHISTOPHILIS: All's one, for we'll be bold with his
    venison.
But now, my Faustus, that thou may'st perceive
What Rome contains for to delight thine eyes,
Know that this city stands upon seven hills
That underprop the groundwork of the same.
Just through the midst runs flowing Tiber's stream,
With winding banks that cut it in two parts,
Over the which four stately bridges lean,
That make safe passage to each part of Rome.
Upon the bridge called Ponte Angelo
40   Erected is a castle passing strong,
Where thou shalt see such store of ordinance
As that the double cannons, forged of brass,
Do match the number of the days contained
Within the compass of one complete year;
Beside the gates and high pyramidès
That Julius Caesar brought from Africa.°
FAUSTUS: Now, by the kingdoms of infernal rule,
Of Styx, of Acheron, and the fiery lake
Of ever-burning Phlegethon, I swear
50   That I do long to see the monuments
And situation of bright-splendent Rome.
Come, therefore, let's away.

Maro, Virgil. *way . . . space,* A tunnel between the bays of Naples and Baiae, through Mt. Posilipo, was said to have been cut by Virgil (regarded as a magician in the Middle Ages) by supernatural art. *In midst . . . gold,* St. Mark's cathedral in Venice. *gates . . . Africa,* Before the gates of St. Peter's there still stands the obelisk that was brought to Rome from Heliopolis by the Emperor Caligula in the first century A.D.

MEPHISTOPHILIS: Nay, stay my Faustus. I know you'd
    see the Pope
And take some part of holy Peter's feast,
The which, in state and high solemnity,
This day is held through Rome and Italy
In honor of the Pope's triumphant victory.
FAUSTUS: Sweet Mephistophilis, thou pleasest me.
Whilst I am here on earth, let me be cloyed
With all things that delight the heart of man.   60
My four and twenty years of liberty
I'll spend in pleasure and in dalliance,
That Faustus' name, whilst this bright frame doth
    stand,
May be admirèd through the furthest land.
MEPHISTOPHILIS: 'Tis well said, Faustus. Come then,
    stand by me
And thou shalt see them come immediately.
FAUSTUS: Nay, stay, my gentle Mephistophilis,
And grant me my request, and then I go.
Thou know'st within the compass of eight days
We viewed the face of heaven, of earth, and hell.   70
So high our dragons soared into the air,
That looking down, the earth appeared to me
No bigger than my hand in quantity.
There did we view the kingdoms of the world,
And what might please mine eye I there beheld.
Then in this show let me an actor be,
That this proud Pope may Faustus' cunning see.
MEPHISTOPHILIS: Let it be so, my Faustus. But, first
    stay
And view their triumphs° as they pass this way,
And then devise what best contents thy mind   80
By cunning in thine art to cross the Pope
Or dash the pride of this solemnity,
To make his monks and abbots stand like apes
And point like antics at his triple crown,
To beat the beads about the friars' pates
Or clap huge horns upon the cardinals' heads,
Or any villainy thou canst devise,
And I'll perform it, Faustus. Hark, they come.
This day shall make thee be admired in Rome.

(Enter the CARDINALS *and* BISHOPS, *some bearing cro-
siers, some the pillars;* MONKS *and* FRIARS *singing their
procession. Then the* POPE, *and* RAYMOND, *King of
Hungary, with* BRUNO, *led in chains.)*

POPE: Cast down our footstool.   90
RAYMOND: Saxon Bruno, stoop,
Whilst on thy back his holiness ascends
Saint Peter's chair and state pontifical.
BRUNO: Proud Lucifer, that state belongs to me,
But thus I fall to Peter, not to thee.
POPE: To me and Peter shalt thou groveling lie
And crouch before the papal dignity.
Sound trumpets then, for thus Saint Peter's heir
From Bruno's back ascends Saint Peter's chair.

---

triumphs, Spectacular displays.

(A flourish while he ascends.)

100 Thus, as the gods creep on with feet of wool
Long ere with iron hands they punish men,
So shall our sleeping vengeance now arise
And smite with death thy hated enterprise.
Lord Cardinals of France and Padua,
Go forthwith to our holy consistory,
And read amongst the Statutes Decretal°
What, by the holy council held at Trent,°
The sacred synod hath decreed for him
That doth assume the papal government
110 Without election and a true consent.
Away, and bring us word with speed.
FIRST CARDINAL: We go my Lord.

(Exeunt CARDINALS.*)*

POPE: Lord Raymond. *[They talk apart.]*
FAUSTUS: Go, haste thee, gentle Mephistophilis,
Follow the cardinals to the consistory,
And as they turn his superstitious books,
Strike them with sloth and drowsy idleness,
And make them sleep so sound that in their shapes
Thyself and I may parley with this Pope,
120 This proud confronter of the Emperor,
And in despite of all his holiness
Restore this Bruno to his liberty
And bear him to the states of Germany.
MEPHISTOPHILIS: Faustus, I go.
FAUSTUS: Dispatch it soon.
The Pope shall curse that Faustus came to Rome.

(Exeunt FAUSTUS *and* MEPHISTOPHILIS.*)*

BRUNO: Pope Adrian,° let me have some right of law.
I was elected by the Emperor.
POPE: We will depose the Emperor for that deed
130 And curse the people that submit to him.
Both he and thou shalt stand excommunicate
And interdict from church's privilege
And all society of holy men.
He grows too proud in his authority,
Lifting his lofty head above the clouds,
And like a steeple overpeers the church.
But we'll pull down his haughty insolence,
And as Pope Alexander, our progenitor,
Trod on the neck of German Frederick,°

Adding this golden sentence to our praise, 140
"That Peter's heirs should tread on emperors
And walk upon the dreadful adder's back,
Treading the lion and the dragon down
And fearless spurn the killing basilisk,"°
So will we quell that haughty schismatic,
And by authority apostolical
Depose him from his regal government.
BRUNO: Pope Julius swore to princely Sigismond,°
For him and the succeeding popes of Rome,
To hold the emperors their lawful lords. 150
POPE: Pope Julius did abuse the church's rites,
And therefore none of his decrees can stand.
Is not all power on earth bestowed on us?
And therefore, though we would, we cannot err.
Behold this silver belt, whereto is fixed
Seven golden keys fast sealed with seven seals
In token of our sevenfold power from heaven,
To bind or loose, lock fast, condemn or judge,
Resign, or seal, or whatso pleaseth us.
Then he and thou and all the world shall stoop, 160
Or be assurèd of our dreadful curse
To light as heavy as the pains of hell.

(Enter FAUSTUS *and* MEPHISTOPHILIS, *like the*
CARDINALS.*)*

MEPHISTOPHILIS: Now tell me, Faustus, are we not
fitted well?
FAUSTUS: Yes, Mephistophilis, and two such cardinals
Ne'er served a holy pope as we shall do.
But whilst they sleep within the consistory,
Let us salute his reverend fatherhood.
RAYMOND: Behold, my lord, the cardinals are
returned.
POPE: Welcome, grave fathers. Answer presently:
What have our holy council there decreed 170
Concerning Bruno and the Emperor,
In quittance of their late conspiracy
Against our state and papal dignity?
FAUSTUS: Most sacred patron of the church of Rome,
By full consent of all the synod
Of priests and prelates it is thus decreed:
That Bruno and the German Emperor
Be held as Lollards° and bold schismatics
And proud disturbers of the church's peace.
And if that Bruno by his own assent, 180
Without enforcement of the German peers,
Did seek to wear the triple diadem

Statutes Decretal, Papal decrees concerning religious doctrine or ecclesiastical law. **council . . . Trent,** The Council of Trent, held by the Church from 1545 to 1563. **Pope Adrian,** Marlowe perhaps means Pope Hadrian IV (1154–1159), who tried to assert his authority over Frederick Barbarossa, the Holy Roman Emperor. What historicity there may be in these scenes at the papal court is badly confused. **Pope Alexander . . . Frederick,** Pope Alexander III (1159–1181), successor to Hadrian IV, continued the struggle against Barbarossa, forcing him to acknowledge the papal supremacy at Canossa.

basilisk, A mythical monster with power to kill by its looks. **Pope Julius . . . Sigismond,** None of the three popes named Julius was contemporary with the Emperor Sigismund (1368–1437). Sigismund did, however, in 1414 summon the Council of Constance, which sought to end the Great Schism (1378–1417), during which the papacy in Rome was challenged by a line of popes in Avignon. **Lollards,** Followers of John Wyclif (1320?–1384), the English reformer.

And by your death to climb Saint Peter's chair,
The Statutes Decretal have thus decreed:
He shall be straight condemned of heresy
And on a pile of fagots burned to death.
POPE: It is enough. Here, take him to your charge,
And bear him straight to Ponte Angelo,
And in the strongest tower enclose him fast.
190 Tomorrow, sitting in our consistory
With all our college of grave cardinals,
We will determine of his life or death.
Here, take his triple crown along with you,
And leave it in the church's treasury.
Make haste again, my good lord cardinals,
And take our blessing apostolical.
MEPHISTOPHILIS: So, so. Was never devil thus blessed
  before.
FAUSTUS: Away, sweet Mephistophilis, be gone.
The cardinals will be plagued for this anon.

(*Exeunt* FAUSTUS *and* MEPHISTOPHILIS [*with* BRUNO].)

200 POPE: Go presently and bring a banquet forth,
That we may solemnize Saint Peter's feast,
And with Lord Raymond, King of Hungary,
Drink to our late and happy victory.

(*Exeunt.*)

ACT 3 / SCENE 2

(*A sennet* [*is sounded*] *while the banquet is brought in;
and then enter* FAUSTUS *and* MEPHISTOPHILIS *in their
own shapes.*)

MEPHISTOPHILIS: Now, Faustus, come, prepare thyself
  for mirth.
The sleepy cardinals are hard at hand
To censure Bruno, that is posted hence,
And on a proud-paced steed, as swift as thought,
Flies o'er the Alps to fruitful Germany,
There to salute the woeful Emperor.
FAUSTUS: The Pope will curse them for their sloth
  today,
That slept both Bruno and his crown away.
But now, that Faustus may delight his mind
10 And by their folly make some merriment,
Sweet Mephistophilis, so charm me here
That I may walk invisible to all
And do whate'er I please unseen of any.
MEPHISTOPHILIS: Faustus, thou shalt. Then kneel
  down presently:

*Whilst on thy head I lay my hand
And charm thee with this magic wand.
First wear this girdle; then appear
Invisible to all are here.
The planets seven, the gloomy air,*

Hell and the Furie's° forkèd hair, 20
*Pluto's blue fire, and Hecate's tree,°
With magic spells so compass thee
That no eye may thy body see.*

So Faustus. Now, for all their holiness,
Do what thou wilt, thou shalt not be discerned.
FAUSTUS: Thanks, Mephistophilis. Now friars take
  heed
Lest Faustus make your shaven crowns to bleed.
MEPHISTOPHILIS: Faustus, no more. See where the
  cardinals come.

(*Enter* POPE *and all the* LORDS. *Enter the* CARDINALS
with a book.)

POPE: Welcome, lord cardinals. Come, sit down.
Lord Raymond, take your seat. Friars attend, 30
And see that all things be in readiness,
As best beseems this solemn festival.
FIRST CARDINAL: First, may it please your sacred
  holiness
To view the sentence of the reverend synod
Concerning Bruno and the Emperor?
POPE: What needs this question? Did I not tell you
Tomorrow we would sit i' th' consistory
And there determine of his punishment?
You brought us word even now; it was decreed
That Bruno and the cursèd Emperor 40
Were by the holy council both condemned
For loathèd Lollards and base schismatics.
Then wherefore would you have me view that
  book?
FIRST CARDINAL: Your grace mistakes. You gave us no
  such charge.
RAYMOND: Deny it not. We all are witnesses
That Bruno here was late delivered you,
With his rich triple crown to be reserved
And put into the church's treasury.
BOTH CARDINALS: By holy Paul, we saw them not.
POPE: By Peter, you shall die 50
Unless you bring them forth immediately.
Hale them to prison. Lade their limbs with gyves.°
False prelates, for this hateful treachery,
Cursed be your souls to hellish misery.

[*Exeunt the two* CARDINALS *with* ATTENDANTS.]

FAUSTUS: So, they are safe. Now, Faustus, to the feast.
The Pope had never such a frolic guest.
POPE: Lord Archbishop of Rheims, sit down with us.
ARCHBISHOP: I thank your holiness.
FAUSTUS: Fall to. The devil choke you an you spare.°

Furies, Spirits called upon to avenge crimes, especially
crimes against kin. **Hecate's tree,** Hecate is the goddess of
witchcraft. **Lade . . . gyves,** Shackle their limbs. **an you
spare,** If you hold back.

60 POPE: Who's that spoke? Friars look about.
FRIAR: Here's nobody, if it like your holiness.
POPE: Lord Raymond, pray fall to. I am beholding
   To the Bishop of Milan for this so rare a present.
FAUSTUS: I thank you, sir. [*He snatches the dish.*]
POPE: How now? Who snatched the meat from me?
   Villains, why speak you not?
   My good Lord Archbishop, here's a most dainty
      dish
   Was sent me from a cardinal in France.
FAUSTUS: I'll have that too. [*He snatches the dish.*]
70 POPE: What Lollards do attend our holiness,
   That we receive such great indignity?
   Fetch me some wine.
FAUSTUS: Ay, pray do, for Faustus is a-dry.
POPE: Lord Raymond, I drink unto your grace.
FAUSTUS: I pledge your grace. [*He snatches the cup.*]
POPE: My wine gone too? Ye lubbers, look about
   And find the man that doth this villainy,
   Or by our sanctitude, you all shall die.
   I pray, my lords, have patience at this
80   Troublesome banquet.
ARCHBISHOP: Please it your holiness, I think it be some
   ghost crept out of purgatory, and now is come unto
   your holiness for his pardon.
POPE: It may be so.
   Go then, command our priests to sing a dirge
   To lay the fury of this same troublesome ghost.

[*Exit an* ATTENDANT.]

Once again, my lord, fall to.

(*The* POPE *crosseth himself.*)

FAUSTUS: How now?
   Must every bit be spicèd with a cross?
90   Nay then, take that. [*He strikes the* POPE.]
POPE: O I am slain. Help me, my lords.
   O come and help to bear my body hence.
   Damned be this soul for ever for this deed.

(*Exeunt the* POPE *and his train.*)

MEPHISTOPHILIS: Now, Faustus, what will you do now?
   For I can tell you you'll be cursed with bell, book,
   and candle.°
FAUSTUS: Bell, book, and candle; candle, book, and
   bell,
   Forward and backward, to curse Faustus to hell.

(*Enter the* FRIARS *with bell, book, and candle for the
dirge.*)

100 FIRST FRIAR: Come, brethren, let's about our business
   with good devotion. [*They chant.*]

Cursed be he that stole his holiness' meat from the
   table.
   Maledicat Dominus!°
Cursed be he that struck his holiness a blow on the
   face.
   Maledicat Dominus!
Cursed be he that struck Friar Sandelo a blow on the
   pate.
   Maledicat Dominus!
Cursed be he that disturbeth our holy dirge.
   Maledicat Dominus!
Cursed be he that took away his holiness' wine.
   Maledicat Dominus! Et omnes sancti.°
Amen.

([FAUSTUS *and* MEPHISTOPHILIS] *beat the* FRIARS, *fling
fireworks among them, and exeunt.*)

ACT 3 / SCENE 3

(*Enter* [ROBIN,] *the* CLOWN, *and* DICK, *with a cup.*)

DICK: Sirrah Robin, we were best look that your devil
   can answer the stealing of this same cup, for the
   vintner's boy follows us at the hard heels.
ROBIN: 'Tis no matter. Let him come. An he follow us,
   I'll so conjure him as he was never conjured in his
   life, I warrant him. Let me see the cup.

(*Enter* VINTNER.)

DICK: Here 'tis. Yonder he comes. Now, Robin, now or
   never show thy cunning.
VINTNER: O, are you here? I am glad I have found you.
   You are a couple of fine companions. Pray, where's
   the cup you stole from the tavern?
ROBIN: How, how? We steal a cup? Take heed what you
   say. We look not like cup stealers, I can tell you.
VINTNER: Never deny't, for I know you have it, and I'll
   search you.
ROBIN: Search me? Ay, and spare not. Hold the cup,
   Dick. [*Aside to* DICK.] Come, come, search me,
   search me.

[*The* VINTNER *searches* ROBIN.]

VINTNER: [*to* DICK] Come on, sirrah, let me search you
   now.
20 DICK: Ay, ay, do, do. Hold the cup, Robin. [*Aside to*
   ROBIN.] I fear not your searching. We scorn to steal
   your cups, I can tell you.

[*The* VINTNER *searches* DICK.]

VINTNER: Never outface me for the matter, for sure the
   cup is between you two.
ROBIN: Nay, there you lie. 'Tis beyond us both.
VINTNER: A plague take you! I thought 'twas your knavery to take it away. Come, give it me again.

---

bell, book, and candle, Used traditionally in the rite of
excommunication.

Maledicat Dominus, May the Lord curse him. **Et
omnes sancti,** And all the saints.

ROBIN: Ay, much. When? Can you tell? Dick, make me
 a circle, and stand close at my back, and stir not for
 thy life. Vintner, you shall have your cup anon. Say
 nothing, Dick, *O per se, O Demogorgon, Belcher and*
 Mephistophilis.

(Enter MEPHISTOPHILIS. *[Exit the* VINTNER, *in fright.*]*)*

MEPHISTOPHILIS: Monarch of hell, under whose black
  survey
 Great potentates do kneel with awful fear,
 Upon whose altars thousand souls do lie,
 How am I vexèd by these villains' charms!
 From Constantinople have they brought me now,
 Only for pleasure of these damnèd slaves.
ROBIN: By Lady, sir, you have had a shrewd journey of
 it. Will it please you to take a shoulder of mutton
 to supper and a tester° in your purse, and go back
 again?
DICK: Ay, I pray you heartily, sir, for we called you but
 in jest, I promise you.
MEPHISTOPHILIS: To purge the rashness of this cursèd
 deed,
 First be thou turnèd to this ugly shape,
 For apish deeds transformèd to an ape.
ROBIN: O brave, an ape! I pray sir, let me have the
 carrying of him about to show some tricks.
MEPHISTOPHILIS: And so thou shalt. Be thou transformed to a dog, and carry him upon thy back.
 Away, be gone!
ROBIN: A dog? That's excellent. Let the maids look well
 to their porridge pots, for I'll into the kitchen pres-
 ently. Come, Dick, come.

*(Exeunt [*ROBIN *and* DICK,*] the two clowns.)*

MEPHISTOPHILIS: Now with the flames of ever-burning
 fire,
 I'll wing myself and forthwith fly amain
 Unto my Faustus, to the great Turk's court.

(Exit.)

ACT 4 / PROLOGUE

(Enter CHORUS.)

CHORUS: When Faustus had with pleasure ta'en the
  view
 Of rarest things and royal courts of kings,
 He stayed his course and so returnèd home;
 Where such as bare his absence but with grief—
 I mean his friends and nearest companions—
 Did gratulate his safety with kind words,
 And in their conference of what befell,
 Touching his journey through the world and air,
 They put forth questions of astrology,
 Which Faustus answered with such learnèd skill

As they admired and wondered at his wit.
Now is his fame spread forth in every land.
Amongst the rest, the Emperor is one—
Carolus the fifth°—at whose palace now
Faustus is feasted 'mongst his noblemen.
What there he did in trial of his art
I leave untold, your eyes shall see performed.

(Exit.)

ACT 4 / SCENE 1

(Enter MARTINO *and* FREDERICK, *at several doors.)*

MARTINO: What ho, officers, gentlemen,
 Hie to the presence° to attend the Emperor.
 Good Frederick, see the rooms be voided straight;
 His majesty is coming to the hall.
 Go back, and see the state° in readiness.
FREDERICK: But where is Bruno, our elected Pope,
 That on a fury's back came post from Rome?
 Will not his grace consort the Emperor?
MARTINO: O yes, and with him comes the German
  conjurer,
 The learnèd Faustus, fame of Wittenberg,
 The wonder of the world for magic art;
 And he intends to show great Carolus
 The race of all his stout progenitors,
 And bring in presence of his majesty
 The royal shapes and warlike semblances
 Of Alexander° and his beauteous paramour.
FREDERICK: Where is Benvolio?
MARTINO: Fast asleep, I warrant you.
 He took his rouse with stoups° of Rhenish wine
 So kindly yesternight to Bruno's health
 That all this day the sluggard keeps his bed.
FREDERICK: See, see, his window's ope. We'll call to
 him.
MARTINO: What ho, Benvolio!

(Enter BENVOLIO *above at a window, in his nightcap,*
buttoning.)

BENVOLIO: What a devil ail you two?
MARTINO: Speak softly, sir, lest the devil hear you,
 For Faustus at the court is late arrived,
 And at his heels a thousand furies wait
 To accomplish whatsoever the doctor please.
BENVOLIO: What of this?
MARTINO: Come, leave thy chamber first, and thou
 shalt see
 This conjurer perform such rare exploits

---

tester, Sixpence.

Carolus the fifth, Charles V, King of Spain (as Charles
I from 1516 to 1556) and Holy Roman Emperor from 1519
to 1556. ***presence,*** Emperor's chamber. **state,** Throne.
Alexander, Alexander the Great. ***took . . . stoups,*** Had a
drinking bout with brimming goblets.

Before the Pope° and royal Emperor
As never yet was seen in Germany.
BENVOLIO: Has not the Pope enough of conjuring yet?
He was upon the devil's back late enough,
And if he be so far in love with him,
I would he would post with him to Rome again.
FREDERICK: Speak, wilt thou come and see this sport?
BENVOLIO: Not I.
40 MARTINO: Wilt thou stand in thy window and see it
then?
BENVOLIO: Ay, and I fall not asleep i' th' meantime.
MARTINO: The Emperor is at hand, who comes to see
What wonders by black spells may compassed be.
BENVOLIO: Well, go you attend the Emperor. I am con-
tent for this once to thrust my head out at a window,
for they say if a man be drunk overnight the devil
cannot hurt him in the morning. If that be true, I
have a charm in my head shall control him as well
as the conjurer, I warrant you.

*(Exit [*FREDERICK, *with* MARTINO. BENVOLIO *remains
at the window above].)*

ACT 4 / SCENE 2

(A sennet [is sounded. Enter] CHARLES, *the German
Emperor,* BRUNO, [*the Duke of*] *Saxony,* FAUSTUS,
MEPHISTOPHILIS, FREDERICK, MARTINO, *and* ATTEN-
DANTS.)

EMPEROR: Wonder of men, renowned magician,
Thrice-learnèd Faustus, welcome to our court.
This deed of thine, in setting Bruno free
From his and our professèd enemy,
Shall add more excellence unto thine art
Than if by powerful necromantic spells
Thou couldst command the world's obedience.
Forever be beloved of Carolus,
And if this Bruno thou hast late redeemed°
10 In peace possess the triple diadem
And sit in Peter's chair despite of chance,
Thou shalt be famous through all Italy
And honored of the German Emperor.
FAUSTUS: These gracious words, most royal Carolus,
Shall make poor Faustus to his utmost power
Both love and serve the German Emperor
And lay his life at holy Bruno's feet.
For proof whereof, if so your grace be pleased,
The doctor stands prepared by power of art
20 To cast his magic charms that shall pierce through
The ebon gates of ever-burning hell,
And hale the stubborn Furies from their caves
To compass whatsoe'er your grace commands.
BENVOLIO: [*above*] Blood, he speaks terribly, but for all
that, I do not greatly believe him. He looks as like

a conjurer as the Pope° to a costermonger.°
EMPEROR: Then, Faustus, as thou late did'st promise
us,
We would behold that famous conqueror,
Great Alexander, and his paramour
In their true shapes and state majestical, 30
That we may wonder at their excellence.
FAUSTUS: Your majesty shall see them presently.
Mephistophilis, away,
And with a solemn noise of trumpets' sound
Present before this royal Emperor,
Great Alexander and his beauteous paramour.
MEPHISTOPHILIS: Faustus, I will.

[*Exit.*]

BENVOLIO: Well, master doctor, an your devils come not
away quickly, you shall have me asleep presently.
Zounds, I could eat myself for anger to think I have 40
been such an ass all this while, to stand gaping after
the devil's governor and can see nothing.
FAUSTUS: I'll make you feel something anon, if my art
fail me not
My lord, I must forewarn your majesty
That when my spirits present the royal shapes
Of Alexander and his paramour,
Your grace demand no questions of the king,
But in dumb silence let them come and go.
EMPEROR: Be it as Faustus please; we are content.
BENVOLIO: Ay, ay, and I am content too. And thou bring 50
Alexander and his paramour before the Emperor,
I'll be Actaeon and turn myself to a stag.
FAUSTUS: And I'll play Diana and send you the horns
presently.

([A] sennet [is sounded]. Enter at one [door] the EM-
PEROR ALEXANDER, *at the other* DARIUS.° *They meet [in
combat].* DARIUS *is thrown down;* ALEXANDER *kills him,
takes off his crown, and, offering to go out, his paramour
meets him. He embraceth her and sets* DARIUS' *crown
upon her head; and coming back, both salute the* EM-
PEROR, *who, leaving his state, offers to embrace them,
which* FAUSTUS *seeing, suddenly stays him. Then trumpets cease and music sounds.)*

My gracious lord, you do forget yourself.
These are but shadows, not substantial.
EMPEROR: O pardon me. My thoughts are so ravishèd
With sight of this renownèd emperor,
That in mine arms I would have compassed him.
But, Faustus, since I may not speak to them,
To satisfy my longing thoughts at full, 60
Let me this tell thee: I have heard it said

---

the Pope, Bruno. *redeemed,* Rescued.

the Pope, Bruno; *costermonger,* Fruit vendor; a term
of contempt. *Darius,* King Darius III of Persia (336–330
B.C.), defeated at Granicus in 334 B.C. by the Greeks under
Alexander the Great.

That this fair lady, whilst she lived on earth,
Had on her neck a little wart or mole;
How may I prove that saying to be true?
FAUSTUS: Your majesty may boldly go and see.
EMPEROR: Faustus, I see it plain,
And in this sight thou better pleasest me
Than if I gained another monarchy.
FAUSTUS: Away! Be gone!

(Exit show.)

70   See, see, my gracious lord, what strange beast is yon,
That thrusts his head out at window?
EMPEROR: O wondrous sight! See, Duke of Saxony,
Two spreading horns most strangely fastenèd
Upon the head of young Benvolio.
SAXONY: What? Is he asleep or dead?
FAUSTUS: He sleeps, my lord, but dreams not of his
horns.
EMPEROR: This sport is excellent. We'll call and wake
him.
What ho, Benvolio!
BENVOLIO: A plague upon you! Let me sleep a while.
EMPEROR: I blame thee not to sleep much, having such
a head of thine own.
SAXONY: Look up, Benvolio; 'tis the Emperor calls.
BENVOLIO: The Emperor? Where? O zounds, my
head!
EMPEROR: Nay, and thy horns hold, 'tis no matter for
thy head, for that's armed sufficiently.
FAUSTUS: Why, how now, sir knight! What, hanged by
the horns? This is most horrible. Fie, fie, pull in
your head for shame. Let not all the world wonder
at you.
BENVOLIO: Zounds, doctor, is this your villainy?
FAUSTUS: O say not so, sir. The doctor has no skill,
No art, no cunning, to present these lords
90   Or bring before this royal Emperor
The mighty monarch, warlike Alexander.
If Faustus do it, you are straight resolved
In bold Actaeon's shape to turn a stag.
And therefore, my lord, so please your majesty,
I'll raise a kennel of hounds shall hunt him so
As all his footmanship shall scarce prevail
To keep his carcass from their bloody fangs.
Ho, Belimote, Argiron, Asterote!
BENVOLIO: Hold, hold! Zounds, he'll raise a kennel
100 of devils, I think, anon. Good, my lord, entreat
for me. 'Sblood, I am never able to endure these
torments.
EMPEROR: Then, good master doctor,
Let me entreat you to remove his horns.
He has done penance now sufficiently.
FAUSTUS: My gracious lord, not so much for injury done
to me, as to delight your majesty with some mirth,
hath Faustus justly requited this injurious° knight;

which being all I desire, I am content to remove his
horns. Mephistophilis, transform him.   110

[MEPHISTOPHILIS *removes the horns.*]

And hereafter, sir, look you speak well of scholars.
BENVOLIO: [*aside.*] Speak well of ye? 'Sblood, and scholars be such cuckold makers to clap horns of honest
men's heads o' this order, I'll ne'er trust smooth
faces and small ruffs° more. But an I be not revenged for this, would I might be turned to a gaping oyster and drink nothing but salt water.

[*Exit* BENVOLIO *above.*]

EMPEROR: Come, Faustus. While the Emperor lives,
In recompense of this thy high desert,
Thou shalt command the state of Germany   120
And lived beloved of mighty Carolus.

(Exeunt.)

ACT 4 / SCENE 3

(Enter BENVOLIO, MARTINO, FREDERICK, *and*
SOLDIERS.)

MARTINO: Nay, sweet Benvolio, let us sway thy
thoughts
From this attempt against the conjurer.
BENVOLIO: Away! You love me not to urge me thus.
Shall I let slip so great an injury,
When every servile groom jests at my wrongs
And in their rustic gambols proudly say,
"Benvolio's head was graced with horns today"?
O, may these eyelids never close again
Till with my sword I have that conjurer slain.
If you will aid me in this enterprise,   10
Then draw your weapons and be resolute.
If not, depart. Here will Benvolio die,
But Faustus' death shall quit° my infamy.
FREDERICK: Nay, we will stay with thee, betide what
may,
And kill that doctor if he come this way.
BENVOLIO: Then, gentle Frederick, hie thee to the
grove,
And place our servants and our followers
Close in an ambush there behind the trees.
By this, I know, the conjurer is near.
I saw him kneel and kiss the Emperor's hand   20
And take his leave, laden with rich rewards.
Then, soldiers, boldly fight. If Faustus die,
Take you the wealth; leave us the victory.
FREDERICK: Come, soldiers. Follow me unto the grove.
Who kills him shall have gold and endless love.

(Exit FREDERICK *with the* SOLDIERS.)

---

injurious, Insulting.   *small ruffs,* Academic gowns.   *quit,* Pay for.

BENVOLIO: My head is lighter than it was by th'horns,
But yet my heart's more ponderous than my head
And pants until I see that conjurer dead.
MARTINO: Where shall we place ourselves, Benvolio?
30 BENVOLIO: Here will we stay to bide the first assault.
O, were that damnèd hell-hound but in place,
Thou soon shouldst see me quit my foul disgrace.

(Enter FREDERICK.*)*

FREDERICK: Close, close, the conjurer is at hand
And all alone comes walking in his gown.
Be ready then, and strike the peasant down.
BENVOLIO: Mine be that honor then. Now, sword,
strike home.
For horns he gave I'll have his head anon.

(Enter FAUSTUS *with the false head.)*

MARTINO: See, see, he comes.
BENVOLIO: No words! This blow ends all.
40 Hell take his soul; his body thus must fall.

[He stabs FAUSTUS.*]*

FAUSTUS: *[falling]* Oh!
FREDERICK: Groan you, master doctor?
BENVOLIO: Break may his heart with groans! Dear
Frederick, see,
Thus will I end his griefs immediately.
MARTINO: Strike with a willing hand. His head is off.

*[*BENVOLIO *strikes off* FAUSTUS' *false head.]*

BENVOLIO: The devil's dead. The Furies now may
laugh.
FREDERICK: Was this that stern aspèct, that awful
frown,
Made the grim monarch of infernal spirits
Tremble and quake at his commanding charms?
50 MARTINO: Was this that damnèd head whose heart
conspired
Benvolio's shame before the Emperor?
BENVOLIO: Ay, that's the head, and here the body lies,
Justly rewarded for his villainies.
FREDERICK: Come, let's devise how we may add more
shame
To the black scandal of his hated name.
BENVOLIO: First, on his head, in quittance of my
wrongs,
I'll nail huge forkèd horns and let them hang
Within the window where he yoked° me first,
That all the world may see my just revenge.
60 MARTINO: What use shall we put his beard to?
BENVOLIO: We'll sell it to a chimney-sweeper. It will wear
out ten birchen brooms, I warrant you.
FREDERICK: What shall his eyes do?
BENVOLIO: We'll put out his eyes, and they shall serve
for buttons to his lips to keep his tongue from
catching cold.
MARTINO: An excellent policy! And now, sirs, having
divided him, what shall the body do?

*[*FAUSTUS *rises.]*

BENVOLIO: Zounds, the devil's alive again.
FREDERICK: Give him his head, for God's sake.   70
FAUSTUS: Nay, keep it. Faustus will have heads and
hands,
Ay, all your hearts, to recompense this deed.
Knew you not, traitors, I was limited
For four-and-twenty years to breathe on earth?
And had you cut my body with your swords,
Or hewed this flesh and bones as small as sand,
Yet in a minute had my spirit returned,
And I had breathed a man made free from harm.
But wherefore do I dally my revenge?
Asteroth, Belimoth, Mephistophilis!   80

(Enter MEPHISTOPHILIS *and other* DEVILS.*)*

Go, horse these traitors on your fiery backs,
And mount aloft with them as high as heaven;
Thence pitch them headlong to the lowest hell.
Yet stay. The world shall see their misery,
And hell shall after plague their treachery.
Go, Belimoth, and take this caitiff° hence,
And hurl him in some lake of mud and dirt.
Take thou this other; drag him through the woods
Amongst the pricking thorns and sharpest briars,
Whilst with my gentle Mephistophilis   90
This traitor flies unto some steepy rock
That, rolling down, may break the villain's bones
As he intended to dismember me.
Fly hence. Dispatch my charge immediately.
FREDERICK: Pity us, gentle Faustus. Save our lives.
FAUSTUS: Away!
FREDERICK: He must needs go that the devil drives.

(Exeunt SPIRITS *with the* KNIGHTS.*)*

(Enter the ambushed SOLDIERS.*)*

FIRST SOLDIER: Come, sirs, prepare yourselves in
readiness.
Make haste to help these noble gentlemen;
I heard them parley with the conjurer.   100
SECOND SOLDIER: See where he comes. Dispatch and
kill the slave.
FAUSTUS: What's here? An ambush to betray my life?
Then, Faustus, try thy skill. Base peasants, stand,
For lo, these trees remove at my command
And stand as bulwarks 'twixt yourselves and me,
To shield me from your hated treachery.
Yet to encounter this your weak attempt,
Behold an army comes incontinent.°

---

yoked, Placed the horns on.   **caitiff,** Despicable wretch.   ***incontinent,*** At once.

(FAUSTUS *strikes the door, and enter a* DEVIL *playing on a drum, after him another bearing an ensign, and divers with weapons,* MEPHISTOPHILIS *with fireworks. They set upon the* SOLDIERS *and drive them out.* [*Exit* FAUSTUS.])

ACT 4 / SCENE 4

(*Enter at several doors* BENVOLIO, FREDERICK, *and* MARTINO, *their heads and faces bloody and besmeared with mud and dirt, all having horns on their heads.*)

MARTINO: What ho, Benvolio!

BENVOLIO: Here! What, Frederick, ho!

FREDERICK: O help me, gentle friend. Where is Martino?

MARTINO: Dear Frederick, here,
Half smothered in a lake of mud and dirt,
Through which the Furies dragged me by the heels.

FREDERICK: Martino, see! Benvolio's horns again.

MARTINO: O misery! How now, Benvolio?

BENVOLIO: Defend me, heaven. Shall I be haunted°
still?

10 MARTINO: Nay, fear not man; we have not power to
kill.

BENVOLIO: My friends transformèd thus! O hellish
spite!
Your heads are all set with horns.

FREDERICK: You hit it right.
It is your own you mean. Feel on your head.

BENVOLIO: Zounds, horns again!

MARTINO: Nay, chafe not man. We all are sped.°

BENVOLIO: What devil attends this damned magician,
That, spite of spite, our wrongs are doublèd?

FREDERICK: What may we do, that we may hide our
shames?

20 BENVOLIO: If we should follow him to work revenge,
He'd join long asses' ears to these huge horns,
And make us laughing-stocks to all the world.

MARTINO: What shall we then do, dear Benvolio?

BENVOLIO: I have a castle joining near these woods,
And thither we'll repair and live obscure
Till time shall alter these our brutish shapes.
Sith black disgrace hath thus eclipsed our fame,
We'll rather die with grief than live with shame.

(*Exeunt omnes.*°)

ACT 4 / SCENE 5°

(*Enter* FAUSTUS *and* MEPHISTOPHILIS.)

---

haunted, (1) Bewitched; (2) hunted, pursued (since he is a stag). **sped,** provided (with horns). ***Exeunt omnes,*** Latin for "All go out." The first eleven lines of [Scene 5] do not appear in all versions of the play, but they provide a transition to the Horse-Courser episode and remind readers of Faustus's impending tragedy.

FAUSTUS: Now, Mephistophilis, the restless course
That time doth run with calm and silent foot,
Shortening my days and thread of vital life,
Calls for the payment of my latest years.
Therefore, sweet Mephistophilis, let us
Make haste to Wittenberg.

MEPHISTOPHILIS: What, will you go on horseback, or
on foot?

FAUSTUS: Nay, till I am past this fair and pleasant
green,
I'll walk on foot.

[*Exit* MEPHISTOPHILIS.]

(*Enter a* HORSE-COURSER.°)

HORSE-COURSER: I have been all this day seeking one   10
Master Fustian.° Mass, see where he is. God save
you, master doctor.

FAUSTUS: What, horse-courser! You are well met.

HORSE-COURSER: I beseech your worship, accept of
these forty dollars.

FAUSTUS: Friend, thou canst not buy so good a horse
for so small a price. I have no great need to sell
him, but if thou likest him for ten dollars more,
take him, because I see thou hast a good mind to
him.   20

HORSE-COURSER: I beseech you, sir, accept of this. I am
a very poor man and have lost very much of late by
horse-flesh, and this bargain will set me up again.

FAUSTUS: Well, I will not stand with thee.° Give me the
money.

[*The* HORSE-COURSER *gives* FAUSTUS *money.*]

Now, sirrah, I must tell you that you may ride him
o'er hedge and ditch, and spare him not. But, do
you hear? In any case, ride him not into the water.

HORSE-COURSER: How sir? Not into the water? Why,
will he not drink of all waters?°   30

FAUSTUS: Yes, he will drink of all waters, but ride him
not into the water—o'er hedge and ditch, or where
thou wilt, but not into the water. Go, bid the hostler
deliver him unto you, and remember what I say.

HORSE-COURSER: I warrant you, sir. O joyful day! Now
am I a man made forever.

(*Exit.*)

FAUSTUS: What art thou, Faustus, but a man
condemned to die?
Thy fatal time draws to a final end.
Despair doth drive distrust into my thoughts.
Confound these passions with a quiet sleep.   40

Horse-Courser, One who deals in horses. **Fustian,** The perversion of Faustus's name is a deliberate attempt at humor. **stand with thee,** Bargain. **drink . . . waters,** Be ready for anything (a common proverb of the time).

Tush! Christ did call the thief upon the cross;
Then rest thee, Faustus, quiet in conceit.°

(He sits to sleep [in his chair].)

(Enter the HORSE-COURSER, *wet.)*

HORSE-COURSER: O what a cozening doctor was this? I
riding my horse into the water, thinking some hidden mystery° had been in the horse, I had nothing
under me but a little straw and had much ado to
escape drowning. Well, I'll go rouse him and make
him give me my forty dollars again. Ho, sirrah
doctor, you cozening scab!° Master doctor, awake
50 and rise, and give me my money again, for your
horse is turned to a bottle° of hay. Master doctor!

(He [tries to wake FAUSTUS, *and in doing so] pulls off
his leg.)*

Alas, I am undone! What shall I do? I have pulled off
his leg.

[FAUSTUS *awakes.*]

FAUSTUS: O, help, help! The villain hath murdered me.
HORSE-COURSER: Murder or not murder, now he has
but one leg, I'll outrun him and cast this leg into
some ditch or other.
FAUSTUS: Stop him, stop him, stop him! Ha, ha, ha,
Faustus hath his leg again, and the horse-courser a
60 bundle of hay for his forty dollars.

(Enter WAGNER.*)*

How now, Wagner, what news with thee?
WAGNER: If it please you, the Duke of Anholt doth
earnestly entreat your company and hath sent some
of his men to attend you with provision fit for your
journey.
FAUSTUS: The Duke of Anholt's an honorable gentleman, and one to whom I must be no niggard of my
cunning. Come away.

(Exeunt.)

ACT 4 / SCENE 6

(Enter [ROBIN, *the*] CLOWN, DICK, [*the*] HORSE-
COURSER, *and a* CARTER.°*)*

CARTER: Come, my masters, I'll bring you to the best
beer in Europe. What ho, hostess! Where be these
whores?

(Enter HOSTESS.*)*

HOSTESS: How now, what lack you? What, my old
guests, welcome.

ROBIN: Sirrah, Dick, dost thou know why I stand so
mute?
DICK: No, Robin; why is't?
ROBIN: I am eighteen pence on the score.° But say noth-
ing; see if she have forgotten me.   10
HOSTESS: Who's this that stands so solemnly by himself?
What, my old guest?
ROBIN: O hostess, how do you? I hope my score stands
still.°
HOSTESS: Ay, there's no doubt of that, for methinks you
make no haste to wipe it out.
DICK: Why, hostess, I say, fetch us some beer.
HOSTESS: You shall presently. Look up into th'hall
there, ho!

(Exit.)

DICK: Come, sirs, what shall we do now till mine hostess   20
come?
CARTER: Marry, sir, I'll tell you the bravest tale how a
conjurer served me. You know Doctor Fauster?
HORSE-COURSER: Ay, a plague take him. Here's some
on's have cause to know him. Did he conjure thee
too?
CARTER: I'll tell you how he served me. As I was going
to Wittenberg t'other day with a load of hay, he met
me and asked me what he should give me for as
much hay as he could eat. Now, sir, I thinking that   30
a little would serve his turn, bade him take as much
as he would for three farthings. So he presently
gave me my money and fell to eating; and as I am
a cursen° man, he never left eating till he had eat
up all my load of hay.
ALL: O monstrous! Eat a whole load of hay!
ROBIN: Yes, yes, that may be, for I have heard of one
that has eat a load of logs.
HORSE-COURSER: Now, sirs, you shall hear how villainously he served me. I went to him yesterday to buy   40
a horse of him, and he would by no means sell him
under forty dollars. So, sir, because I knew him to
be such a horse as would run over hedge and ditch
and never tire, I gave him his money. So when I
had my horse, Doctor Fauster bade me ride him
night and day and spare him no time; but, quoth
he, in any case ride him not into the water. Now sir,
I thinking the horse had had some rare quality that
he would not have me know of, what did I but ride
him into a great river, and when I came just in the   50
midst, my horse vanished away, and I sat straddling
upon a bottle of hay.
ALL: O brave doctor!
HORSE-COURSER: But you shall hear how bravely I
served him for it. I went me home to his house, and

---

conceit, Thoughts. *mystery,* Quality. *cozening scab,*
Deceitful, contemptible rascal. *bottle,* Bundle. *Carter,* A
person who drives a cart.

on the score, In debt. *stands still,* Does not go higher.
cursen, Christened.

there I found him asleep. I kept a hallooing and
whooping in his ears, but all could not wake him. I
seeing that, took him by the leg and never rested
pulling till I had pulled me his leg quite off, and
60   now 'tis at home in mine hostry.

ROBIN: And has the doctor but one leg then? That's
excellent, for one of his devils turned me into the
likeness of an ape's face.

CARTER: Some more drink, hostess.

ROBIN: Hark you, we'll into another room and drink a
while, and then we'll go seek out the doctor.

(*Exeunt.*)

ACT 4 / SCENE 7

(*Enter the* DUKE *of Anholt, his* DUCHESS, FAUSTUS, *and*
MEPHISTOPHILIS [*Servants and Attendants*])

DUKE: Thanks, master doctor, for these pleasant sights.
Nor know I how sufficiently to recompense your
great deserts° in erecting that enchanted castle in
the air, the sight whereof so delighted me, as nothing in the world could please me more.

FAUSTUS: I do think myself, my good lord, highly recompensed in that it pleaseth your grace to think
but well of that which Faustus hath performed. But,
gracious lady, it may be that you have taken no
10   pleasure in those sights. Therefore, I pray you, tell
me what is the thing you most desire to have; be it
in the world, it shall be yours. I have heard that
great-bellied women do long for things are rare
and dainty.

DUCHESS: True, master doctor, and since I find you so
kind, I will make known unto you what my heart
desires to have. And were it now summer, as it is
January, a dead time of the winter, I would request
no better meat than a dish of ripe grapes.

20 FAUSTUS: This is but a small matter. Go, Mephistophilis,
away!

(*Exit* MEPHISTOPHILIS.)

Madam, I will do more than this for your content.

(*Enter* MEPHISTOPHILIS *again with the grapes.*)

Here; now taste ye these. They should be good, for
they come from a far country, I can tell you.

DUKE: This makes me wonder more than all the rest,
that at this time of year, when every tree is barren
of his fruit, from whence you had these ripe grapes.

FAUSTUS: Please it, your grace, the year is divided into
30   two circles over the whole world, so that when it is
winter with us, in the contrary circle it is likewise
summer with them, as in India, Saba,° and such
countries that lie far east, where they have fruit

twice a year. From whence, by means of a swift spirit
that I have, I had these grapes brought, as you see.

DUCHESS: And trust me, they are the sweetest grapes
that e'er I tasted.

(*The* CLOWN[S, ROBIN, DICK, *the* CARTER, *and the*
HORSE-COURSER,] *bounce at the gate within.*)

DUKE: What rude disturbers have we at the gate?
Go, pacify their fury. Set it ope,
And then demand of them what they would have.

[*Exit a* SERVANT.]

(*They knock again and call out to talk with* FAUSTUS.)

[*Enter* SERVANT *to them.*]

SERVANT: Why, how now, masters, what a coil° is   40
there?
What is the reason you disturb the duke.

DICK: We have no reason for it; therefore a fig for
him.

SERVANT: Why, saucy varlets,° dare you be so bold?

HORSE-COURSER: I hope, sir, we have wit enough to be
more bold than welcome.

SERVANT: It appears so. Pray be bold elsewhere,
And trouble not the duke.

DUKE: What would they have?   50

SERVANT: They all cry out to speak with Doctor
Faustus.

CARTER: Ay, and we will speak with him.

DUKE: Will you, sir? Commit the rascals.

DICK: Commit with us! He were as good commit with
his father as commit with us.

FAUSTUS: I do beseech your grace, let them come in;
They are good subject for a merriment.

DUKE: Do as thou wilt, Faustus. I give thee leave.

FAUSTUS: I thank your grace.   60

(*Enter* ROBIN, DICK, CARTER, *and* HORSE-COURSER.)

Why, how now, my good friends?
'Faith you are too outrageous,° but come near;
I have procured your pardons. Welcome all!

ROBIN: Nay, sir, we will be welcome for our money, and
we will pay for what we take. What ho!
Give's half a dozen of beer here, and be hanged.

FAUSTUS: Nay, hark you; can you tell me where you
are?

CARTER: Ay, marry can I: we are under heaven.

SERVANT: Ay, but sir sauce-box, know you in what   70
place?

HORSE-COURSER: Ay, ay, the house is good enough to
drink in. Zouns, fill us some beer, or we'll break all
the barrels in the house and dash out all your brains
with your bottles.

---

deserts, Good deeds.   **Saba,** Sheba.

coil, Disturbance   **varlets,** Knaves, rascals.   **outrageous,** violent.

FAUSTUS: Be not so furious. Come, you shall have
beer.
My lord, beseech you give me leave a while:
I'll gage my credit, 'twill content your grace.

80 DUKE: With all my heart, kind doctor. Please thyself;
Our servants and our court's at thy command.

FAUSTUS: I humbly thank your grace. Then fetch
some beer.

HORSE-COURSER: Ay, marry, there spake a doctor
indeed, and 'faith, I'll drink a health to thy
wooden leg for that word.

FAUSTUS: My wooden leg? What dost thou mean by
that?

CARTER: Ha, ha, ha! Dost hear him, Dick? He has
90 forgot his leg.

HORSE-COURSER: Ay, ay, he does not stand much°
upon that.

FAUSTUS: No, faith; not much upon a wooden leg.

CARTER: Good lord, that flesh and blood should be so
frail with your worship! Do not you remember a
horse-courser you sold a horse to?

FAUSTUS: Yes, I remember I sold one a horse.

CARTER: And do you remember you bid he should not
ride into the water?

100 FAUSTUS: Yes, I do very well remember that.

CARTER: And do you remember nothing of your leg?

FAUSTUS: No, in good sooth.

CARTER: Then, I pray, remember your courtesy.°

FAUSTUS: I thank you, sir.

CARTER: 'Tis not so much worth. I pray you, tell me one
thing.

FAUSTUS: What's that?

CARTER: Be both your legs bedfellows every night
together?

110 FAUSTUS: Wouldst thou make a Colossus° of me, that
thou askest me such questions?

CARTER: No, truly, sir. I would make nothing of you,
but I would fain know that.

(Enter HOSTESS *with drink.)*

FAUSTUS: Then, I assure thee, certainly they are.

CARTER: I thank you; I am fully satisfied.

FAUSTUS: But wherefore dost thou ask?

CARTER: For nothing, sir. But methinks you should
have a wooden bedfellow of one of 'em.

HORSE-COURSER: Why, do you hear, sir; did not I pull
120 off one of your legs when you were asleep?

FAUSTUS: But I have it again, now I am awake. Look
you here, sir.

ALL: O horrible! Had the doctor three legs?

CARTER: Do you remember, sir, how you cozened me
and ate up my load of—

---

stand much, Make much of (with a quibble). **courtesy,**
Curtsy, or leg. **Colossus,** A giant statue said to have stood
with its legs astride at the entrance to the ancient harbor of
Rhodes.

(FAUSTUS charms him dumb.)

DICK: Do you remember how you made me wear an
ape's—

[FAUSTUS *charms him dumb.*]

HORSE-COURSER: You whoreson conjuring scab, do you
remember how you cozened me with a ho—

[FAUSTUS *charms him dumb.*]

ROBIN: Ha' you forgotten me? You think to carry it 130
away° with your *hey-pass* and *re-pass*; do you remember the dog's fa—

[FAUSTUS *charms him dumb.*]

(Exeunt CLOWNS.*)*

HOSTESS: Who pays for the ale? Hear you, master doctor, now you have sent away my guests, I pray who
shall pay me for my a—

[FAUSTUS *charms her dumb.*]

(Exit HOSTESS.*)*

DUCHESS: My lord,
We are much beholding to this learnèd man.

DUKE: So are we, madam, which we will recompense
With all the love and kindness that we may.
His artful sport drives all sad thoughts away. 140

(Exeunt.)

ACT 5 / SCENE 1

(Thunder and lightning. Enter DEVILS *with covered
dishes.* MEPHISTOPHILIS *leads them into* FAUSTUS' *study.
Then enter* WAGNER.*)*

WAGNER: I think my master means to die shortly.
He has made his will and given me his wealth,
His house, his goods, and store of golden plate,
Besides two thousand ducats ready coined.
I wonder what he means. If death were nigh,
He would not frolic thus. He's now at supper
With the scholars, where there's such belly-cheer
As Wagner in his life ne'er saw the like.
And see where they come; belike the feast is done.

(Exit.)

(Enter FAUSTUS, MEPHISTOPHILIS, *and two or three*
SCHOLARS.*)*

FIRST SCHOLAR: Master Doctor Faustus, since our con- 10
ference about fair ladies, which was the beautifulest
in all the world, we have determined with ourselves
that Helen of Greece was the admirablest lady that

---

carry it away, Come off best.

ever lived. Therefore, master doctor, if you will do
us so much favor as to let us see that peerless dame
of Greece, whom all the world admires for majesty,
we should think ourselves much beholding unto
you.

FAUSTUS: Gentlemen,

20 For that I know your friendship is unfeigned,
    And Faustus' custom is not to deny
    The just requests of those that wish him well,
    You shall behold that peerless dame of Greece,
    No otherwise for pomp and majesty
    Than when Sir Paris crossed the seas with her
    And brought the spoils to rich Dardania.°
    Be silent then, for danger is in words.

(Music sounds. MEPHISTOPHILIS *brings in* HELEN; *she
passeth over the stage.)*

SECOND SCHOLAR: Was this fair Helen, whose admirèd
    worth
30 Made Greece with ten years' war afflict poor Troy?
    Too simple is my wit to tell her praise,
    Whom all the world admires for majesty.

THIRD SCHOLAR: No marvel though the angry Greeks
    pursued
    With ten years' war the rape of such a queen,
    Whose heavenly beauty passeth all compare.

FIRST SCHOLAR: Since we have seen the pride of
    nature's works
    And only paragon of excellence,
    We'll take our leaves and for this blessèd sight
    Happy and blest be Faustus evermore.

40 FAUSTUS: Gentlemen, farewell; the same wish I to you.

(Exeunt SCHOLARS.*)*

(Enter an OLD MAN.*)*

OLD MAN: O gentle Faustus, leave this damnèd art,
    This magic that will charm thy soul to hell
    And quite bereave thee of salvation.
    Though thou hast now offended like a man,
    Do not persevere in it like a devil.
    Yet, yet, thou hast an amiable° soul,
    If sin by custom grow not into nature.
    Then, Faustus, will repentance come too late;
    Then thou art banished from the sight of heaven.
50 No mortal can express the pains of hell.
    It may be this my exhortation
    Seems harsh and all unpleasant; let it not,
    For, gentle son, I speak it not in wrath
    Or envy of° thee, but in tender love
    And pity of thy future misery.

And so have hope that this my kind rebuke,
    Checking° thy body, may amend thy soul.

FAUSTUS: Where art thou, Faustus? Wretch, what hast
    thou done?
    Damned art thou, Faustus, damned; despair and
    die!
    Hell claims his right, and with a roaring voice   60
    Says, "Faustus, come; thine hour is almost come";
    And Faustus now will come to do thee right.

*(*MEPHISTOPHILIS *gives him a dagger.)*

OLD MAN: O stay, good Faustus, stay thy desperate
    steps.
    I see an angel hovers o'er thy head,
    And with a vial full of precious grace
    Offers to pour the same into thy soul.
    Then call for mercy and avoid despair.

FAUSTUS: Ah, my sweet friend, I feel thy words
    To comfort my distressèd soul.
    Leave me a while to ponder on my sins.   70

OLD MAN: Faustus, I leave thee, but with grief of
    heart,
    Fearing the enemy of thy hapless soul. *(Exit.)*

FAUSTUS: Accursèd Faustus, where is mercy now?
    I do repent, and yet I do despair.
    Hell strives with grace for conquest in my breast.
    What shall I do to shun the snares of death?

MEPHISTOPHILIS: Thou traitor, Faustus, I arrest thy
    soul
    For disobedience to my sovereign lord.
    Revolt, or I'll in piecemeal tear thy flesh.

FAUSTUS: I do repent I e'er offended him.   80
    Sweet Mephistophilis, entreat thy lord
    To pardon my unjust presumption,
    And with my blood again I will confirm
    The former vow I made to Lucifer.

MEPHISTOPHILIS: Do it then, Faustus, with unfeignèd°
    heart,
    Lest greater dangers do attend thy drift.°

[FAUSTUS *stabs his arm and writes on a paper with his
blood.*]

FAUSTUS: Torment, sweet friend, that base and agèd
    man
    That durst dissuade me from thy Lucifer,
    With greatest torment that our hell affords.

MEPHISTOPHILIS: His faith is great; I cannot touch his   90
    soul,
    But what I may afflict his body with
    I will attempt, which is but little worth.

FAUSTUS: One thing, good servant, let me crave of
    thee
    To glut the longing of my heart's desire—

Peerless dame . . . Dardania, The Greek Helen (the
"peerless dame"), wife of Menelaus, was carried off to Troy
(Dardania) by Paris, sparking the Trojan War. **amiable,**
Worthy of divine love or grace. **envy of,** Ill will toward.

Checking, Admonishing. **unfeignèd,** Honest. **drift,** ose.
Purpose.

That I may have unto my paramour
That heavenly Helen which I saw of late,
Whose sweet embracings may extinguish clear
Those thoughts that do dissuade me from my vow,
And keep mine oath I made to Lucifer.

100 MEPHISTOPHILIS: This, or what else my Faustus shall
        desire,
    Shall be performed in twinkling of an eye.

(Enter HELEN *again, passing over* [the stage] *between
two* CUPIDS.)

FAUSTUS: Was this the face that launched a thousand
        ships
    And burnt the topless towers of Ilium?
    Sweet Helen, make me immortal with a kiss. [*She
        kisses him.*]
    Her lips suck forth my soul. See where it flies!
    Come, Helen, come, give me my soul again.
    Here will I dwell, for heaven is in these lips,
    And all is dross that is not Helena.

[*Enter the* OLD MAN.]

    I will be Paris, and for love of thee
110 Instead of Troy shall Wittenberg be sacked;
    And I will combat with weak Menelaus°
    And wear thy colors on my plumèd crest.
    Yea, I will wound Achilles° in the heel
    And then return to Helen for a kiss.
    O, thou art fairer than the evening's air,
    Clad in the beauty of a thousand stars.
    Brighter art thou than flaming Jupiter°
    When he appeared to hapless Semele,°
    More lovely than the monarch of the sky
120 In wanton Arethusa's azured arms,°
    And none but thou shalt be my paramour.

(Exeunt [all but the OLD MAN].)

OLD MAN: Accursèd Faustus, miserable man,
    That from thy soul exclud'st the grace of heaven
    And fliest the throne of his tribunal seat!

(Enter the DEVILS.)

    Satan begins to sift me with his pride.
    As in this furnace God shall try my faith,
    My faith, vile hell, shall triumph over thee.
    Ambitious fiends, see how the heavens smiles
    At your repulse and laughs your state° to scorn.
130 Hence hell, for hence I fly unto my God.

(Exeunt.)

Menelaus, The husband of Helen of Troy. **Achilles,**
The Greek hero of the Trojan War, wounded in the heel
by Paris. **Jupiter,** Zeus. **Semele,** The daughter of Cadmus
and Harmonia who bore Zeus the child, Dionysus. **monarch . . . arms,** Arethusa was a nymph, one of the Nereids,
who governed a fountain on the isle of Ortygia near Syra-
cuse. **state,** Royal power.

ACT 5 / SCENE 2

(Thunder. Enter [above] LUCIFER, BEELZEBUB, *and*
MEPHISTOPHILIS.)

LUCIFER: Thus from infernal Dis° do we ascend
    To view the subjects of our monarchy,
    Those souls which sin seals the black sons of hell,
    'Mong which as chief, Faustus, we come to thee,
    Bringing with us lasting damnation
    To wait upon thy soul. The time is come
    Which makes it forfeit.
MEPHISTOPHILIS: And this gloomy night,
    Here in this room will wretched Faustus be.
BEELZEBUB: And here we'll stay   10
    To mark him how he doth demean himself.
MEPHISTOPHILIS: How should he, but in desperate
        lunacy?
    Fond worldling, now his heart-blood dries with
        grief;
    His conscience kills it, and his laboring brain
    Begets a world of idle fantasies
    To over-reach the devil. But all in vain;
    His store of pleasures must be sauced° with pain.
    He and his servant, Wagner, are at hand.
    Both come from drawing Faustus' latest will.
    See where they come.   20

(Enter FAUSTUS *and* WAGNER.)

FAUSTUS: Say, Wagner, thou has perused my will;
    How dost thou like it?
WAGNER: Sir, so wondrous well
    As in all humble duty I do yield
    My life and lasting service for your love.

(Enter the SCHOLARS.)

FAUSTUS: Gramercies,° Wagner. Welcome, gentlemen.

[*Exit* WAGNER.]

FIRST SCHOLAR: Now, worthy Faustus, methinks your
    looks are changed.
FAUSTUS: Ah, gentlemen!
SECOND SCHOLAR: What ails Faustus?   30
FAUSTUS: Ah, my sweet chamber-fellow, had I lived with
    thee, then had I lived still, but now must die eter-
    nally. Look, sirs; comes he not? Comes he not?
FIRST SCHOLAR: O my dear Faustus, what imports this
    fear?
SECOND SCHOLAR: Is all our pleasure turned to melan-
    choly?
THIRD SCHOLAR: He is not well with being over-solitary.
SECOND SCHOLAR: If it be so, we'll have physicians, and
    Faustus shall be cured.   40

Dis, Hades, or hell. **sauced,** Paid for. **Gramercies,**
Thanks.

THIRD SCHOLAR: 'Tis but a surfeit sir; fear nothing.

FAUSTUS: A surfeit of deadly sin that hath damned both body and soul.

SECOND SCHOLAR: Yet Faustus, look up to heaven, and remember mercy is infinite.

FAUSTUS: But Faustus' offence can ne'er be pardoned. The serpent that tempted Eve may be saved, but not Faustus. Ah gentlemen, hear me with patience and tremble not at my speeches. Though my heart pants and quivers to remember that I have been a student here these thirty years, O, would I had never seen Wittenberg, never read book. And what wonders I have done, all Germany can witness— yea, all the world—for which Faustus hath lost both Germany and the world, yea heaven itself, heaven the seat of God, the throne of the blessed, the kingdom of joy, and must remain in hell for ever. Hell, ah hell for ever! Sweet friends, what shall become of Faustus, being in hell for ever?

SECOND SCHOLAR: Yet Faustus, call on God.

FAUSTUS: On God, whom Faustus hath abjured? On God, whom Faustus hath blasphemed? Ah, my God, I would weep, but the devil draws in my tears. Gush forth blood instead of tears, yea life and soul. O, he stays my tongue! I would lift up my hands, but see, they hold 'em; they hold 'em.

ALL: Who, Faustus?

FAUSTUS: Why, Lucifer and Mephistophilis. Ah, gentlemen, I gave them my soul for my cunning.

ALL: God forbid!

FAUSTUS: God forbade it indeed, but Faustus hath done it. For the vain pleasure of four and twenty years hath Faustus lost eternal joy and felicity. I writ them a bill with mine own blood. The date is expired. This is the time, and he will fetch me.

FIRST SCHOLAR: Why did not Faustus tell us of this before, that divines might have prayed for thee?

FAUSTUS: Oft have I thought to have done so, but the devil threatened to tear me in pieces if I named God, to fetch me, body and soul, if I once gave ear to divinity. And now 'tis too late. Gentlemen away, lest you perish with me.

SECOND SCHOLAR: O, what may we do to save Faustus?

FAUSTUS: Talk not of me, but save yourselves and depart.

THIRD SCHOLAR: God will strengthen me; I will stay with Faustus.

FIRST SCHOLAR: Tempt not God, sweet friend, but let us into the next room and there pray for him.

FAUSTUS: Ay, pray for me, pray for me; and what noise soever you hear, come not unto me, for nothing can rescue me.

SECOND SCHOLAR: Pray thou, and we will pray that God may have mercy upon thee.

FAUSTUS: Gentlemen, farewell. If I live till morning, I'll visit you; if not, Faustus is gone to hell.

ALL: Faustus, farewell.

(Exeunt SCHOLARS.*)*

MEPHISTOPHILIS: [*above*] Ay, Faustus, now thou hast no hope of heaven;
Therefore despair. Think only upon hell,
For that must be thy mansion, there to dwell.   100

FAUSTUS: O thou bewitching fiend, 'twas thy temptation Hath robbed me of eternal happiness.

MEPHISTOPHILIS: I do confess it, Faustus, and rejoice.
'Twas I, that when thou wert i' the way to heaven,
Damned up thy passage. When thou took'st the book
To view the Scriptures, then I turned the leaves
And led thine eye.
What, weep'st thou? 'Tis too late. Despair! Farewell!
Fools that will laugh on earth must weep in hell.

(Exit.)

(Enter the GOOD ANGEL *and the* BAD ANGEL *at several doors.)*

GOOD ANGEL: Ah, Faustus, if thou hadst given ear to me,   110
Innumerable joys had followed thee;
But thou didst love the world.

BAD ANGEL: Gave ear to me,
And now must taste hell's pains perpetually.

GOOD ANGEL: O what will all thy riches, pleasures, pomps
Avail thee now?

BAD ANGEL: Nothing but vex thee more,
To want in hell, that had on earth such store.

(Music while the throne descends.)

GOOD ANGEL: O, thou hast lost celestial happiness,
Pleasures unspeakable, bliss without end.   120
Hadst thou affected sweet divinity,
Hell or the devil had had no power on thee.
Hadst thou kept on that way, Faustus, behold
In what resplendent glory thou hadst sat
In yonder throne, like those bright shining saints.
And triumphed over hell. That hast thou lost,
And now, poor soul, must thy good angel leave thee.

[*The throne ascends.*]

The jaws of hell are open to receive thee.

(Exit.)

(Hell is discovered.)

BAD ANGEL: Now, Faustus, let thine eyes with horror stare
Into that vast perpetual torture-house.   130
There are the Furies tossing damnèd souls
On burning forks; their bodies boil in lead.
There are live quarters broiling on the coals,

That ne'er can die. This ever-burning chair
Is for o'er-tortured souls to rest them in.
These that are fed with sops of flaming fire
Were gluttons and loved only delicates
And laughed to see the poor starve at their gates.
But yet all these are nothing; thou shalt see

140 Ten thousand tortures that more horrid be.
FAUSTUS: O, I have seen enough to torture me.
BAD ANGEL: Nay, thou must feel them, taste the smart
    of all.
He that loves pleasure must for pleasure fall.
And so I leave thee, Faustus, till anon;
Then wilt thou tumble in confusion.

(Exit.)

([Hell disappears.] The clock strikes eleven.)

FAUSTUS: Ah Faustus,
Now hast thou but one bare hour to live,
And then thou must be damned perpetually.
Stand still, you ever-moving spheres of heaven,

150 That time may cease and midnight never come.
Fair nature's eye, rise, rise again, and make
Perpetual day; or let this hour be but
A year, a month, a week, a natural day,
That Faustus may repent and save his soul.
O lente, lente currite noctis equi!°
The stars move still; time runs; the clock will strike;
The devil will come, and Faustus must be damned.
O, I'll leap up to my God! Who pulls me down?
See, see, where Christ's blood streams in the
    firmament!

160 One drop would save my soul, half a drop! Ah, my
    Christ!
Rend not my heart for naming of my Christ!
Yet will I call on him. O, spare me, Lucifer!
Where is it now? 'Tis gone. And see where God
Stretcheth out his arm and bends his ireful brows.
Mountains and hills, come, come, and fall on me,
And hide me from the heavy wrath of God.
No, no!
Then will I headlong run into the earth.
Earth, gape! O no, it will not harbor me!

170 You stars that reigned at my nativity,
Whose influence hath allotted death and hell.
Now draw up Faustus like a foggy mist
Into the entrails of yon laboring cloud,
That when you vomit forth into the air,
My limbs may issue from your smoky mouths,
So that my soul may but ascend to heaven.

(The watch strikes.)

Ah, half the hour is past; 'twill all be past anon.
O God,

If thou wilt not have mercy on my soul,
Yet for Christ's sake, whose blood hath ransomed   180
    me,
Impose some end to my incessant pain.
Let Faustus live in hell a thousand years,
A hundred thousand, and at last be saved.
O, no end is limited to damnèd souls.
Why wert thou not a creature wanting soul?
Or why is this immortal that thou hast?
Ah, Pythagoras' *metempsychosis*,° were that true,
This soul should fly from me and I be changed
Into some brutish beast. All beasts are happy,
For, when they die   190
Their souls are soon dissolved in elements,
But mine must live still to be plagued in hell.
Cursed be the parents that engendered me!
No, Faustus, curse thyself, curse Lucifer
That hath deprived thee of the joys of heaven.

(The clock strikes twelve.)

O, it strikes, it strikes! Now, body, turn to air,
Or Lucifer will bear thee quick° to hell.
O soul, be changed to little water-drops,
And fall into the ocean, ne'er be found!

(Thunder, and enter the DEVILS.*)*

My God, my God, look not so fierce on me!   200
Adders and serpents, let me breathe a while!
Ugly hell, gape not! Come not, Lucifer!
I'll burn my books! Ah, Mephistophilis!

(Exeunt [FAUSTUS *and* DEVILS].*)*

ACT 5 / SCENE 3

(Enter the SCHOLARS.*)*

FIRST SCHOLAR: Come, gentlemen, let us go visit
    Faustus,
For such a dreadful night was never seen
Since first the world's creation did begin.
Such fearful shrieks and cries were never heard.
Pray heaven the doctor have escaped the danger.
SECOND SCHOLAR: O help us, heaven! See, here are
    Faustus' limbs,
All torn asunder by the hand of death.
THIRD SCHOLAR: The devils whom Faustus served
    have torn him thus;
For 'twixt the hours of twelve and one, methought
I heard him shriek and call aloud for help,   10
At which self time the house seemed all on fire
With dreadful horror of these damnèd fiends.

O . . . equi, O slowly, slowly; run you horses of night
(adapted from Ovid's *Amores*).

metempsychosis, Belief in the transmigration of souls,
associated with the Greek philosopher Pythagoras of Samos. *quick,* Alive.

SECOND SCHOLAR: Well, gentlemen, though Faustus'
    end be such
As every Christian heart laments to think on,
Yet for he was a scholar, once admired
For wondrous knowledge in our German schools,
We'll give his mangled limbs due burial;
And all the students clothed in mourning black,
Shall wait upon° his heavy° funeral.

(Exeunt.)

EPILOGUE

(Enter CHORUS.*)*

CHORUS: Cut is the branch that might have grown full
    straight,

---

wait upon, Be present at; *heavy,* Sorrowful.

And burnèd is Apollo's laurel bough
That sometime grew within this learnèd man.
Faustus is gone. Regard his hellish fall,
Whose fiendful fortune may exhort the wise
Only to wonder at unlawful things,
Whose deepness doth entice such forward wits
To practice more than heavenly power permits.

[Exit.]

    Terminat hora diem; terminat author opus.°

Terminat . . . opus, The hour ends the day; the author
ends his work.

Figure 1. Orson Welles as Faustus, showing the smudge-faced, bearded makeup that he used in the Federal Theater Project production of *The Tragical History of Doctor Faustus,* directed by Orson Welles, 1937. (Photograph: Billy Rose Theatre Collection. The New York Public Library for the Performing Arts. Astor, Lenox, and Tilden Foundations.)

Figure 2. Mephistophilis (Jack Carter) conjures up the Seven Deadly Sins out of one of the magical black cylinders featured in the Federal Theater Project production of *The Tragical History of Doctor Faustus,* directed by Orson Welles, 1937. (Photograph: Billy Rose Theatre Collection. The New York Public Library for the Performing Arts. Astor, Lenox, and Tilden Foundations.)

Figure 3. Orson Welles as Faustus in a scene showing the striking robe and dramatic backlighting that Welles used in the Federal Theater Project production of *The Tragical History of Doctor Faustus,* directed by Orson Welles, 1937. (Photograph: Billy Rose Theatre Collection. The New York Public Library for the Performing Arts. Astor, Lenox, and Tilden Foundations.)

Staging of *Doctor Faustus*

MEMOIR OF THE FEDERAL THEATER PROJECT PRODUCTION, 1937, BY JOHN HOUSEMAN

Of all the shows we did together, *Faustus* looked the simplest and was the most complicated; it was also the most brilliantly executed. In its acting style, its sound patterns, its scenic conception, its costumes (which Orson designed), its props and its magic tricks, it gave unified and vivid expression to Welles's very special theatrical talent.

Marlowe's *Tragical History of Doctor Faustus* (in the form in which it has come down to us) is a curious stage piece in which are to be found, side by side, some of the most noble verse, bombastic rhetoric and earthbound slapstick in English dramatic literature. Orson, with his vast energy and his timeless theatrical instinct, succeeded, as director and actor, in fusing these conflicting elements into a dramatic whole of surprising power. In all his theatrical work (from his schoolboy *Julius Caesar* to the nights, during the Second World War, when he sawed Marlene Dietrich in half at the Hollywood Stage Door Canteen) Orson was always, at heart, a magician. His production of Marlowe's tragedy was designed and executed as a magic show, employing as its basic technique one of the oldest and most effective of stage-magicians' deceptions—the trick professionally known as "black magic." Used for vanishing acts and miraculous appearances, it exploits the absorbent properties of black velvet so that, under certain lighting conditions, not only do black surfaces become totally invisible against each other, but all normal sense of space, depth and perspective becomes lost and confused in the eye of the spectator. Orson, with Feder's assistance, extended and elaborated this device. By using almost no front light and criss-crossing the stage with parallel light curtains and clusters of units carefully focused from the sides and from overhead, he was able to achieve mystifications that would have impressed the great Thurston.

Not the least ingenious and maddening of his inventions was a series of collapsible, forty-foot black velvet cylinders, each carrying in its head one or more 1,000-watt spotlights pointed vertically downward. Hung high up against the grid, these circular curtains were so rigged on large curtain rings along lines of strong, smooth cord, that they could rise or fall, concertina-wise, at high speeds in complete silence. With these cylinders Orson was able to conjure Marlowe's characters out of limbo and, then, equally miraculously, to snuff them out by means that remained quite inexplicable to the audience.

Far away, from depths of darkness, Faustus is disclosed, surrounded by his diabolical books while Mephistophilis is first seen as two gigantic horrible eyes which Faustus conjures into a human head

wrote one perplexed reviewer.

There were other equally magical effects, culminating in Faustus's reception by the Pope in Rome. Here a procession of scarlet and purple princes of the Church and their servants, carrying golden platters piled with roasts and sweetmeats, paraded across the stage to ceremonial music on their way to the banquet hall. Suddenly, under the Pope's nose, a suckling pig was seen to rise from its golden dish, fly straight up to a height of twelve feet, execute a few steps of an obscene dance, then melt into thin air. A haunch of beef followed, then two fat chickens and a gaudy pudding. In consternation, the procession faltered. At that moment, to the accompaniment of subterranean thunder, three Cardinals' hats flew off like giant saucers. When the Pope's own miter rose from his head and a flash box exploded under his skirt amid cries of terror and fiendish laughter, the procession broke up, leaving Faustus alone on a stage that was suddenly and completely bare.

This mystification was accomplished with the aid of eight dancers, dressed from head to foot in black velvet, moving alongside the procession, just far enough upstage to be out of the blaze of the light curtain and thus completely invisible to the audience against the darkness of black velvet. In their black-gloved hands, they held like fishing poles thin, black, flexible steel rods whose ends were affixed to the meats, the pudding and the episcopal headgear that were marked for flight. On cue the boys in black swung those loaded rods up over their heads and brought them down behind them, where their own black costumes formed a screen for them till they were able to leave the stage unobserved in the confusion of the dissolving parade.

Still another form of magic was achieved through trap doors which permitted characters to enter and exit as though they were rising or sinking through the solid black floor of the stage. Among their users was that sinister puppet troupe, the Seven Deadly Sins, who appeared, one by one, through small holes in the apron—obscene, diminutive specimens of evil that flapped and wriggled and squeaked their lewd temptations at the doomed doctor's feet. These, together with the explosions, subterranean rumblings and jagged sheets of lycopodium flame that swept the stage with bursts of hellish brightness, were the gaudy theatrical devices with which Welles adorned his revival. But underneath, at the center of the production, there was deep personal identification which, across a gulf of three and a half centuries, led him to the heart of the work and to its vivid recreation on a contemporary American stage.

The truth is that the legend of the man who sells his soul to the devil in exchange for knowledge and power and who must finally pay for his brief triumph with the agonies of eternal damnation was uncomfortably close to the shape of Welles's own personal myth. Orson really believed in the Devil. (The first time I met him he was writing a play about the Fiend and illustrating it with drawings that were, in fact, grotesque caricatures of himself.) This was not a whimsey but a very real obsession. At twenty-one Orson was sure he was doomed. In his most creative, manic moments, in his wildest transports of love or on the topmost peak of his precocious victories, he was rarely free from a sense of sin and a fear of retribution so intense and immediate that it drove him through long nights of panic to seek refuge in debauchery or work. Quite literally, Orson dared not sleep. No sooner were his eyes closed than, out of the darkness, troupes of demons—the symbols of his sins—surrounded and claimed him, body and soul, in retribution for crimes of which he could not remember the nature, but of which he never for a moment doubted that he was guilty. Neither running nor hiding could save him from their clutches. And when they had seized him with their bleeding claws, they would drag him off into some infernal darkness, there to inflict upon him, through all eternity, those unspeakable torments which he felt he so richly deserved.

Some of this anguish found its way nightly onto the stage of Maxine Elliott's Theatre. Amid the rank fumes and darting flames, there were moments when Faustus seemed to be expressing, through Marlowe's words, some of Orson's personal agony and private terror. This sense of conviction was heightened by Welles's inspired casting of the fiend Mephistophilis, played by the Negro actor Jack Carter, whom Orson had insisted on bringing back onto the project in spite (or perhaps because) of his drunken walk-out from *Macbeth.* Years later, in the *New York Times,* Carter's appearance with Welles was cited as an early and successful example of integrated casting. It was that and far more. Their presence on the stage together was unforgettable: both were around six foot four, both men of abnormal strength capable of sudden, furious violence. Yet their scenes together were played with restraint, verging on tenderness, in which temptation and damnation were treated as acts of love. Welles was brightly garbed, bearded, medieval, ravenous, sweating and human; Carter was in black—a cold, ascetic monk, his face and gleaming bald head moon-white and ageless against the surrounding night. As Orson directed him, he had the beauty, the pride and the sadness of a fallen angel. He watched Faustus sign his deed in blood and, later, officiated at his destruction and listened to his last gasping plea for respite:

> Ah Faustus,
> Now has thou but one bare hour to live
> And then thou must be damned perpetually!

with the contemptuous and elegant calm of a Lucifer who is, himself, more deeply and irrevocably damned than his cringing human victim.

WILLIAM SHAKESPEARE

1564–1616

The story of Othello's life is filled with "most disastrous chances," "moving accidents," and "hair-breadth escapes," but the life of his creator was evidently far more mundane. We know from church registers that Shakespeare married in 1582, that he had a daughter in 1583, and twins, a son and daughter, in 1585. Legal documents tell us that he defaulted several times on paying his taxes, that he bought a large house in Stratford, that, like many of his contemporaries, he engaged in taking others to court. And records from the royal court show him performing for both Elizabeth I and James I. But information about his theatrical career is disappointingly fragmentary. We know that at some point between 1585 and 1592, Shakespeare left Stratford, went to London, and became an actor and playwright, yet we do not know exactly when or how he became involved with the professional theater companies. We know that he was both an actor and shareholder in one of the major theatrical companies, first called the Lord Chamberlain's Men, then the King's Men, but we have no details about their rehearsals and few about their performances, so we do not know anything specific about his day-to-day activities in the company. We do not even know for certain the exact order in which he composed his plays, nor do we know exactly how he occupied himself after 1611, when he appears to have retired almost completely from playwriting and the theatrical world of London.

Although we know little about his personal life in Stratford or his professional activities in London, we can begin to understand his remarkably productive career as a playwright—thirty-seven plays in a period of twenty-three years—by recognizing the numerous literary and dramatic sources that nurtured it, for Shakespeare was not an isolated genius, weaving plots and characters entirely out of the threads of his own imagination. Like his contemporaries, Marlowe, Jonson, and Webster, he was influenced by classical plays available in English translation, as well as numerous French and Italian works, not to mention the rich tradition of native English drama, including cycle plays, morality plays, folk plays from the countryside, and highly formal plays from the University writers of his own time. Throughout his career, in fact, he drew ideas for his plays from a richly varied body of material: Roman comedies, Roman histories, English chronicles, English novellas, and French as well as Italian stories. But he always transformed the material he borrowed. He began his career, for example, by borrowing from the Roman dramatist Plautus (ca. 251–184 B.C.), turning Plautus' *Menaechmi* into his own *The Comedy of Errors* (1590), a farce far more comically confusing than its counterpart because Shakespeare added twin servants to the twin protagonists of Plautus. In history plays, such as *Richard II* (1595), *Henry IV, Part I* (1597), *Henry IV, Part II* (1598), and *Henry V* (1599), he condensed large and cumbersome bodies of material from the English chronicler Holinshed into powerful theatrical experiences, each of which can stand on its own, yet which together embody a coherent political philosophy. In *Twelfth Night* (1600), he drew not only from his own earlier plays (for *Twelfth Night* again features the adventures of twins) but also from Italian comedies based on Plautus and from an English prose narrative (Barnabe Rich's "Apolonius and Silla") based on French and Italian stories. And in *Othello* (1604), he turned a brief but rambling story by the Italian writer Giraldi Cinthio into one of his most tightly constructed tragedies, adding events, creating new characters, such as Roderigo, and endowing the main characters with complex motivations.

In the making of plots, Shakespeare was equally resourceful and experimental. Single plots, double plots, triple plots, framed plots—all kinds of plot construction are found in his plays. In *A Midsummer Night's Dream* (1595), he juggles three wildly different worlds of experience by intertwining the crisscross love entanglements of four young Athenians, with the love jealousy of the King and Queen of the Fairies, with the comically bumbling rehearsal and production of a tragic love story by a group of Athenian workmen—and all these different lines of action are framed by the marriage festivities for Theseus, Duke of Athens, and Hippolyta, Queen of the Amazons. In *Twelfth Night* Shakespeare centers the action around a series of attempts to win the hand of Olivia, a young countess mourning her brother's death; some attempts are comically unsuccessful such as that of the foolish (but rich) knight Sir Andrew and that of the pompous steward Malvolio, while others are comically successful, notably that of the disguised Viola, wooing on behalf of Duke Orsino, but actually winning Olivia's heart for herself. And in *Othello,* he creates a single plot so carefully designed that not a single character or event is irrelevant to the inexorable development of the tragedy.

As in the making of plots, Shakespeare was highly flexible in his use of language. Blank verse is the dominant form for most of his plays, but he tuned that line to the harmonies of every mood and feeling—to the strident rhythms of men at war, as in *Henry V*; to the intoxicated melodies of men and women in love, as in *A Midsummer Night's Dream*; and to the heavenly music of visionaries, as in *The Tempest.* Yet, he did not hesitate to move from the harmonies of verse to the different harmonies of prose—within a play, a scene, or the dialogue of a single character—always suiting the style to the dramatic situation. In act 1, scene 5 of *Twelfth Night,* for example, the disguised Viola begins wooing Olivia in prose, to which Olivia replies with witty banter, still in prose. As the scene progresses, Viola moves into blank verse, and we can hear Olivia fall in love with the disguised woman simply by noting how she too begins speaking blank verse. In act 1, scene 3 and act 2, scene 1 of *Othello*, a prose scene between Roderigo and Iago is followed by a blank verse soliloquy from Iago, and the shift in style subtly reinforces our sense of Iago as a wearer of masks, especially of verbal ones. Thus the shift from one form to another is not tied to specific social classes or emotions. Anyone can speak in rhymed couplets or in blank verse or in prose, and an important clue for an actor's interpretation of a character is to notice when shifts occur and why.

Whatever the form, Shakespeare's language is always tuned to the theatrical situation, implying gestures, movement, tone of voice. Sir Toby's opening line in act 1, scene 3 of *Twelfth Night,* "What a plague means my niece to take the death of her brother thus?," with its casual juxtaposition of "plague" and "death" immediately establishes the character's carefree attitude; Othello's response in act 1, scene 2 to the group of armed men seeking to arrest him—"Keep up your bright swords, for the dew will rust them"—quickly lets us know of the potential fight and of the calm, slightly ironic voice that disarms the men more surely than a blow.

Twelfth Night, coming slightly more than halfway through Shakespeare's career, seems almost a summation of his major comic themes, characters, and plots. Because most of Shakespeare's comedies (with the exception of *The Comedy of Errors* and possibly *The Merry Wives of Windsor*) center around love relationships, the plays constantly invite the audience to reflect on the nature of love, and to see how often "true lovers run into strange capers," as the jester Touchstone puts it in *As You Like It* (1599). To be in love is to fall into foolish behavior, as we see when we watch the quartet of lovers in *A Midsummer Night's Dream* or *The Two Gentlemen of Verona* (1593). But to refuse to admit that one is in love is equally foolish, as the behavior of Berowne in *Love's Labor's Lost* (1594) or Benedick in *Much Ado about Nothing* (1598) makes clear. *Twelfth Night* shows us these "strange capers" in the folly of the lovesick Orsino—so brilliantly parodied by the sighing of the hapless Sir Andrew Aguecheek—and in the folly of the steward, Malvolio, dressing himself up in bright yellow stockings because he thinks Olivia wants him to. It also shows us Olivia's denial of love and then her headlong capitulation to it, a capitulation mocked by the fact that she falls in love with a woman disguised as a man. And it adds yet another kind of love, the unspoken love of the disguised Viola for Orsino, a love made painful both by her disguise and by her employment by Orsino to woo Olivia.

The pain Viola feels reminds us that Shakespeare's comedies deal not just with lovers but with problems of identity and relationships that cannot always be taken lightly. Danger, threats, and malevolence are always present in Shakespeare's comic worlds, whether we think of the destructive power of Shylock in *The Merchant of Venice* (1596) or the scheming of Don John in *Much Ado about Nothing.* Malvolio, whose name means "ill-will," is neither as evil as Don John nor as threatening as Shylock, but he remains a powerful force in the play and will not forgive the jokes that have been played on him. His exit line, "I'll be revenged on the whole pack of you," tells us that he does not take part in the play's general reconciliation, just as the song at the very end of the play reminds us that "the rain it raineth every day."

One of the challenges, then, in producing *Twelfth Night* is to give importance to all the different elements in the play—the hilarious trick of the forged letter placed for Malvolio; the patient sadness of Viola listening to Orsino talk about his love for Olivia; the curious melancholy often created by the songs of Feste, the jester, or by the attempts of Sir Andrew to seem a man of the world; the delaying of the meeting between the twins until the last possible moment and then the further delay as they hesitate to express their joy. But nowhere are the problems more crucial than with the portrayal of Malvolio (see Figure 1, p. 239), who is both comic threat and comic butt. The question becomes, how much do we laugh *at* Malvolio, and how much sympathy do we, or should we, have *for* his predicament?

John Barton's production of *Twelfth Night* in Stratford-upon-Avon, 1969, was notable for the variety of responses it evoked, often for the same character. Donald Sinden's Malvolio was often brilliantly funny, as when he attempted to read the bogus letter which Maria had left for him (see Figure 1, p. 239). But

J. W. Lambert's review describes him as "an almost Ibsenesque figure," and Sinden himself felt that all Malvolio could do at the end of the play was to commit suicide—offstage, of course. Judi Dench, now Dame Judi, was an equally memorable Viola, ranging from the quiet, almost painful lover when she looked at Orsino (see Figure 2, p. 240) to the much more assured "Cesario" who cheekily confronted Olivia (see Figure 3, p. 240). As J. W. Lambert's review suggests, the overriding sense of pain which Barton's production conveyed may be questioned, but it is nonetheless a persistent element of the play itself, inherent in the experience of Malvolio and Viola, as well as in the haunting songs of Feste (see Figure 4, p. 241).

One of the major differences between Shakespeare's comedies and his tragedies is a difference in scale, since the major tragedies—*Hamlet* (1601), *Othello* (1604), *King Lear* (1605), *Macbeth* (1605), and *Antony and Cleopatra* (1606)—are all about imposing figures in extremely trying situations. This emphasis on extremes is the source of the tragedies' special power. The marriage of Othello and Desdemona joins not just a man and a woman, but a middle-aged black Moorish soldier of obscure lineage and a young white Venetian lady of noble birth. This marriage, so hated by Desdemona's father, is for its partners an emblem of perfection. Desdemona tells the senators "My heart's subdued / Even to the very quality of my lord," and Othello repeatedly stresses the extreme value he gives to Desdemona's love, as when he meets her after a dangerous sea voyage and exclaims, "If it were now to die, / 'Twere now to be most happy." Such declarations also imply the possibility of destruction, and the task Shakespeare sets for himself is first to create the reality of this extraordinary relationship and then to destroy it. The marriage of Iago and Emilia, by contrast, with its bitter jests and spiteful remarks, as well as the casual flirtation of Cassio with Bianca, make us see more clearly the special beauty of the love between Othello and Desdemona.

Othello may also be seen as a Shakespearean morality play, with all the forces for good represented by Desdemona's beauty, strength, honesty, and faith balanced by the forces for evil embodied in Iago's hatred of beauty, his cowardice, his lying, and his cynicism. Between them stands Othello, a man outwardly calm when faced by swords, senators, or Turks, but inwardly insecure about his age, his blackness, his status as an outsider in Venetian society. At the beginning of the play we admire his assurance, his eloquence, his military prowess, and the love that he inspires in Desdemona; we watch with horror as that capacity for extreme love is lured into doubts, questions, and finally, murderous jealousy, swinging like a pendulum from total love to total hate. Our helplessness and frustration are increased because Shakespeare does not provide Othello with reliable companions who might convey to him his tragic error. Such characters usually figure in his other tragedies, but here the reasonable commentator on events is also the villain who sets them in motion.

Characters such as Desdemona, Iago, and Othello, given their extremes of good and evil, are not only powerful figures in their own right, but also immensely challenging for actors to portray. An actor playing Iago needs to consider the numerous motives for his action that are spread out through the play, and whether any of these is sufficient for the destruction he seeks and causes. Similarly, Othello must be a believable combination of both the great general and the immature bridegroom, showing both the strength and the vulnerability of the man.

These challenges of the title role are so great that Laurence Olivier, considered by many the greatest Shakespearean actor of our century, waited until he was 57, and had already performed Hamlet, Macbeth, Coriolanus, Lear, and Antony, before finally doing Othello, at the National Theatre in 1964. That production, played on a single set that could be either an outdoor or indoor space (see Figure 1, p. 285) was as concentrated and intense as the play itself. And it produced as much controversy among critics as the play has. The reviews reprinted following the text reflect one principal source of the critics' disagreement about the production, namely, the way it presented the relationship between Othello and Iago—not as that of a deluded victim and a clever victimizer, but as that of a proud lover and a hasty opportunist. Olivier played the role in a way that made him seem to drag the lies out of Iago, and Frank Finlay played Iago with an open face and a slightly bent posture (see Figure 2, p. 285) that seemed to suggest that Iago might, indeed, be harmless. Above all, Olivier's Othello was highly physical and sensual, in his deep black skin and his insinuating smile (see Figure 3, p. 286), as well as in his rolling, barefoot walk and the guttural sounds he used to suggest the voice of a foreigner speaking a new language. But that physicality was at last the key to the animal who tore off his crucifix when he believed that Desdemona had betrayed him, and then who clutched Desdemona's dead body to his own (see Figure 4, p. 286) as he gave his final speech.

TWELFTH NIGHT,
or, What You Will

BY WILLIAM SHAKESPEARE / EDITED BY HERSCEL BAKER

CHARACTERS

ORSINO, *Duke of Illyria*
SEBASTIAN, *brother of* VIOLA
ANTONIO, *a sea captain, friend to* SEBASTIAN
A SEA CAPTAIN, *friend to* VIOLA
VALENTINE }
CURIO } *gentlemen attending on the Duke*
SIR TOBY BELCH, *uncle to* OLIVIA
SIR ANDREW AGUECHEEK
MALVOLIO, *steward to* OLIVIA

FABIAN }
FESTE, *a clown* } *servants to* OLIVIA
OLIVIA, *a countess*
VIOLA, *sister to* SEBASTIAN
MARIA, OLIVIA'S *woman*
LORDS, *a* PRIEST, SAILORS, OFFICERS, MUSICIANS,
and ATTENDANTS

SCENE
Illyria

ACT 1 / SCENE 1 *The* DUKE's *palace.*

(*Enter* ORSINO, *Duke of Illyria,* CURIO, *and other*
LORDS, [*with* MUSICIANS].)

DUKE: If music be the food of love, play on,
Give me excess of it, that, surfeiting,
The appetite° may sicken, and so die.
That strain again! It had a dying fall;°
O, it came o'er my ear like the sweet sound
That breathes upon a bank of violets,
Stealing and giving odor. Enough, no more!
'Tis not so sweet now as it was before.
O spirit of love, how quick and fresh° art thou,
10   That,° notwithstanding thy capacity,
Receiveth as the sea. Nought enters there,°
Of what validity and pitch° soe'er,
But falls into abatement and low price°
Even in a minute. So full of shapes° is fancy°
That it alone is high fantastical.°
CURIO: Will you go hunt, my lord?
DUKE: What, Curio?
CURIO: The hart.
DUKE: Why, so I do, the noblest that I have.
20   O, when mine eyes did see Olivia first,
Methought she purged the air of pestilence.
That instant was I turned into a hart,

And my desires, like fell° and cruel hounds,
E'er since pursue me.°

(*Enter* VALENTINE.)

                    How now? What news from her?
VALENTINE: So please my lord, I might not be
    admitted;
But from her handmaid do return this answer:
The element° itself, till seven years' heat,°
Shall not behold her face at ample view;
But like a cloistress she will veilèd walk,   30
And water once a day her chamber round
With eye-offending brine: all this to season°
A brother's dead love, which she would keep fresh
And lasting in her sad remembrance.°
DUKE: O, she that hath a heart of that fine frame
To pay this debt of love but to a brother,
How will she love when the rich golden shaft°
Hath killed the flock of all affections else°
That live in her; when liver, brain, and heart,°

---

appetite, i.e., the lover's appetite for music. *fall*, cadence. *quick and fresh*, lively and eager. *That*, in that. *there*, i.e., in the lover's "capacity." *validity and pitch*, value and superiority (in falconry, pitch is the highest point of a bird's flight). *price*, esteem. *shapes*, fantasies. *fancy*, love. *high fantastical*, preeminently imaginative.

fell, fierce. *That instant . . . pursue me*, (Orsino's mannered play on "hart-heart"—which exemplified the lover's "high fantastical" wit—derives from the story of Actaeon, a famous hunter who, having seen Diana bathing, was transformed into a stag and torn to pieces by his hounds). *element*, sky. *heat*, course. *season*, preserve (by the salt in her tears). *remembrance*, (pronounced with four syllables, "re-mem-ber-ance"). *golden shaft*, (the shaft, borne by Cupid, that causes love, as distinguished from the leaden shaft, which causes aversion and disdain). *all affections else*, i.e., all other emotions but love. *liver, brain, and heart*, (the seats respectively of sexual desire, thought, and feeling).

40 These sovereign thrones, are all supplied and filled,
    Her sweet perfections,° with one self° king.
    Away before me to sweet beds of flow'rs;
    Love-thoughts lie rich when canopied with bow'rs.

    (*Exeunt.*)

ACT 1 / SCENE 2 *The seacoast.*

(*Enter* VIOLA, *a* CAPTAIN, *and* SAILORS.)

VIOLA: What country, friends, is this?
CAPTAIN: This is Illyria,° lady.
VIOLA: And what should I do in Illyria?
    My brother he is in Elysium.°
    Perchance he is not drowned. What think you,
        sailors?
CAPTAIN: It is perchance that you yourself were saved.
VIOLA: O my poor brother, and so perchance may he
    be.
CAPTAIN: True, madam; and, to comfort you with
        chance,°
    Assure yourself, after our ship did split,
10 When you, and those poor number saved with you,
    Hung on our driving° boat, I saw your brother,
    Most provident in peril, bind himself
    (Courage and hope both teaching him the practice)°
    To a strong mast that lived° upon the sea;
    Where, like Arion° on the dolphin's back,
    I saw him hold acquaintance with the waves
    So long as I could see.
VIOLA: For saying so, there's gold.
    Mine own escape unfoldeth to my hope,°
20 Whereto thy speech serves for authority°
    The like of him. Know'st thou this country?
CAPTAIN: Ay, madam, well, for I was bred and born
    Not three hours' travel from this very place.
VIOLA: Who governs here?
CAPTAIN: A noble duke, in nature as in name.
VIOLA: What is his name?
CAPTAIN: Orsino.
VIOLA: Orsino! I have heard my father name him.
    He was a bachelor then.
30 CAPTAIN: And so is now, or was so very late;
    For but a month ago I went from hence,
    And then 'twas fresh in murmur° (as you know
    What great ones do, the less will prattle of)

    That he did seek the love of fair Olivia.
VIOLA: What's she?
CAPTAIN: A virtuous maid, the daughter of a count
    That died some twelvemonth since, then leaving her
    In the protection of his son, her brother,
    Who shortly also died; for whose dear love,
    They say, she hath abjured the sight   40
    And company of men.
VIOLA: O that I served that lady,
    And might not be delivered° to the world,
    Till I had made mine own occasion mellow,
    What my estate is.°
CAPTAIN: That were hard to compass,°
    Because she will admit no kind of suit,
    No, not° the Duke's.
VIOLA: There is a fair behavior in thee, captain,
    And though that° nature with a beauteous wall   50
    Doth oft close in° pollution, yet of thee
    I will believe thou hast a mind that suits
    With this thy fair and outward character.°
    I prithee (and I'll pay thee bounteously)
    Conceal me what I am, and be my aid
    For such disguise as haply shall become
    The form of my intent.° I'll serve this duke.
    Thou shalt present me as an eunuch to him;
    It may be worth thy pains. For I can sing,
    And speak to him in many sorts of music   60
    That will allow° me very worth his service.
    What else may hap, to time I will commit;
    Only shape thou thy silence to my wit.°
CAPTAIN: Be you his eunuch,° and your mute I'll be;
    When my tongue blabs, then let mine eyes not see.
VIOLA: I thank thee. Lead me on.

    (*Exeunt.*)

ACT 1 / SCENE 3 OLIVIA's *house.*

(*Enter* SIR TOBY *and* MARIA.)

TOBY: What a plague means my niece to take the death
    of her brother thus? I am sure care's an enemy to
    life.
MARIA: By my troth, Sir Toby, you must come in earlier
    a' nights. Your cousin,° my lady, takes great excep-
    tions to your ill hours.
TOBY: Why, let her except before excepted.°

---

perfections, (pronounced with four syllables). **self,**
sole. **Illyria,** region bordering the east coast of the Adri-
atic. **Elysium,** heaven (in classical mythology, the abode of
the happy dead). **chance,** possibility. **driving,** drifting.
practice, procedure. **lived,** i.e., floated. **Arion,** (in classical
mythology, a bard who, having leapt into the sea to escape
from murderous sailors, was borne to shore by a dolphin
that he charmed by his songs). **unfoldeth to my hope,** i.e.,
reinforces my hope for my brother's safety. **serves for
authority,** i.e., tends to justify. **fresh in murmur,** i.e., being
rumored.

delivered, disclosed. **made mine . . . estate is,** found an
appropriate time to reveal my status. **compass,** effect.
not, not even. **though that,** even though. **close in,** conceal.
character, i.e., appearance and demeanor. **become/The
form of my intent,** i.e., suit my purpose. **allow,** certify. **wit,**
i.e., skill in carrying out my plan. **Be you his eunuch,** (this
part of the plan was not carried out). **cousin,** (a term
indicating various degrees of kinship; here, niece). **except
before excepted,** (Sir Toby parodies the legal jargon *exceptis
exceptiendis* ["with the exceptions previously noted"] commonly used in leases and contracts).

MARIA: Ay, but you must confine yourself within the modest limits of order.°

10 TOBY: Confine? I'll confine° myself no finer than I am. These clothes are good enough to drink in, and so be these boots too. And° they be not, let them hang themselves in their own straps.

MARIA: That quaffing and drinking will undo you. I heard my lady talk of it yesterday; and of a foolish knight that you brought in one night here to be her wooer.

TOBY: Who? Sir Andrew Aguecheek?

MARIA: Ay, he.

20 TOBY: He's as tall° a man as any's in Illyria.

MARIA: What's that to th' purpose?

TOBY: Why, he has three thousand ducats a year.

MARIA: Ay, but he'll have but a year in all these ducats. He's a very fool and a prodigal.

TOBY: Fie that you'll say so! He plays o' th' viol-de-gamboys,° and speaks three or four languages word for word without book, and hath all the good gifts of nature.

MARIA: He hath indeed all, most natural;° for, besides
30 that he's a fool, he's a great quarreler; and but that he hath the gift of a coward to allay the gust° he hath in quarreling, 'tis thought among the prudent he would quickly have the gift of a grave.

TOBY: By this hand, they are scoundrels and substractors° that say so of him. Who are they?

MARIA: They that add, moreover, he's drunk nightly in your company.

TOBY: With drinking healths to my niece. I'll drink to her as long as there is a passage in my throat and
40 drink in Illyria. He's a coward and a coistrel° that will not drink to my niece till his brains turn o' th' toe like a parish top.° What, wench? *Castiliano vulgo*;° for here comes Sir Andrew Agueface.

(Enter SIR ANDREW.)

ANDREW: Sir Toby Belch. How now, Sir Toby Belch?

TOBY: Sweet Sir Andrew.

ANDREW: Bless you, fair shrew.

MARIA: And you too, sir.

TOBY: Accost, Sir Andrew, accost.

ANDREW: What's that?

TOBY: My niece's chambermaid.°   50

ANDREW: Good Mistress Accost, I desire better acquaintance.

MARIA: My name is Mary, sir.

ANDREW: Good Mistress Mary Accost.

TOBY: You mistake, knight. "Accost" is front her, board her, woo her, assail her.

ANDREW: By my troth, I would not undertake her in this company. Is that the meaning of "accost"?

MARIA: Fare you well, gentlemen.

TOBY: And thou let part so,° Sir Andrew, would thou   60
mightst never draw sword again.

ANDREW: And you part so, mistress, I would I might never draw sword again! Fair lady, do you think you have fools in hand?°

MARIA: Sir, I have not you by th' hand.

ANDREW: Marry,° but you shall have, and here's my hand.

MARIA: Now, sir, thought is free. I pray you, bring your hand to th' butt'ry° bar and let it drink.

ANDREW: Wherefore, sweetheart? What's your meta-   70
phor?

MARIA: It's dry,° sir.

ANDREW: Why, I think so. I am not such an ass but I can keep my hand dry. But what's your jest?

MARIA: A dry jest, sir.

ANDREW: Are you full of them?

MARIA: Ay, sir, I have them at my finger's ends. Marry, now I let go your hand, I am barren.°

(Exit MARIA.)

TOBY: O knight, thou lack'st a cup of canary!° When   80
did I see thee so put down?

ANDREW: Never in your life, I think, unless you see canary put me down. Methinks sometimes I have no more wit than a Christian or an ordinary man has. But I am a great eater of beef, and I believe that does harm to my wit.

TOBY: No question.

---

modest limits of order, reasonable limits of good behavior. *confine,* i.e., clothe. *And,* if (a common Elizabethan usage). *tall,* i.e., bold and handsome. *viol-de-gamboys,* bass viol. *natural,* i.e., like a natural fool or idiot. *gust,* gusto. *substractors,* slanderers. *coistrel,* knave (literally, a groom who takes care of a knight's horse). *parish top,* (according to George Steevens, a large top "formerly kept in every village, to be whipped in frosty weather, that the peasants might be kept warm by exercise, and out of mischief while they could not work"; however, the allusion may be to the communal top-spinning whose origins are buried in religious ritual). *Castiliano vulgo,* (a phrase of uncertain meaning; perhaps Sir Toby is suggesting that Maria assume a grave and ceremonial manner—like that of the notoriously formal Castilians—for Sir Andrew's benefit).

What's that/My niece's chambermaid, (Sir Andrew asks the meaning of the word "accost," but Sir Toby thinks that he is referring to Maria. Actually, she was not Olivia's chambermaid, but rather her companion, or lady in waiting, as is made clear at Act 1, sc. 5, l. 162). *so,* i.e., without ceremony. *have fools in hand,* i.e., are dealing with fools. *Marry,* indeed (a mild interjection, originally an oath by the Virgin Mary). *butt'ry,* buttery, a storeroom for butts or casks of liquor. *dry,* (1) thirsty (2) indicative of impotence. *barren,* (1) without more jests (2) dull-witted. *canary,* a sweet wine from the Canary Islands.

ANDREW: And I thought that, I'd forswear it. I'll ride home tomorrow, Sir Toby.

TOBY: *Pourquoi,*° my dear knight?

90 ANDREW: What is *"pourquoi"*? Do, or not do? I would I had bestowed that time in the tongues that I have in fencing, dancing, and bearbaiting. O, had I but followed the arts!

TOBY: Then hadst thou had an excellent head of hair.°

ANDREW: Why, would that have mended my hair?

TOBY: Past question, for thou seest it will not curl by nature.

ANDREW: But it becomes me well enough, does't not?

TOBY: Excellent. It hangs like flax on a distaff;° and I

100 hope to see a huswife° take thee between her legs and spin it off.

ANDREW: Faith, I'll home tomorrow, Sir Toby. Your niece will not be seen; or if she be, it's four to one she'll none of me. The Count himself here hard by woos her.

TOBY: She'll none o' th' Count. She'll not match above her degree, neither in estate,° years, nor wit; I have heard her swear't. Tut, there's life in't,° man.

ANDREW: I'll stay a month longer. I am a fellow o' th'

110 strangest mind i' th' world. I delight in masques and revels sometimes altogether.

TOBY: Art thou good at these kickshawses,° knight?

ANDREW: As any man in Illyria, whatsoever he be, under the degree of my betters,° and yet I will not compare with an old° man.

TOBY: What is thy excellence in a galliard,° knight?

ANDREW: Faith, I can cut a caper.°

TOBY: And I can cut the mutton to't.

ANDREW: And I think I have the back-trick° simply as

120 strong as any man in Illyria.

TOBY: Wherefore are these things hid? Wherefore have these gifts a curtain before 'em? Are they like to take° dust, like Mistress Mall's picture? Why dost thou not go to church in a galliard and come home in a coranto?° My very walk should be a jig. I would not so much as make water but in a sink-a-pace.° What dost thou mean? Is it a world to hide virtues°

in? I did think, by the excellent constitution of thy leg, it was formed under the star of a galliard.°

ANDREW: Ay, 'tis strong, and it does indifferent well in   130 a damned-colored stock.° Shall we set about some revels?

TOBY: What shall we do else? Were we not born under Taurus?°

ANDREW: Taurus? That's sides and heart.

TOBY: No, sir; it is legs and thighs. Let me see thee caper. Ha, higher; ha, ha, excellent!

(Exeunt.)

ACT 1 / SCENE 4 *The* DUKE's *palace.*

(Enter VALENTINE, *and* VIOLA *in man's attire.)*

VALENTINE: If the Duke continue these favors towards you, Cesario, you are like to be much advanced. He hath known you but three days and already you are no stranger.

VIOLA: You either fear his humor° or my negligence, that° you call in question the continuance of his love. Is he inconstant, sir, in his favors?

VALENTINE: No, believe me.

(Enter DUKE, CURIO, *and* ATTENDANTS.*)*

VIOLA: I thank you. Here comes the Count.

DUKE: Who saw Cesario, ho?   10

VIOLA: On your attendance, my lord, here.

DUKE: Stand you awhile aloof. Cesario,
Thou know'st no less but all.° I have unclasped
To thee the book even of my secret soul.
Therefore, good youth, address thy gait° unto her;
Be not denied access, stand at her doors,
And tell them there thy fixèd foot shall grow
Till thou have audience.

VIOLA: Sure, my noble lord,
If she be so abandoned to her sorrow   20
As it is spoke, she never will admit me.

DUKE: Be clamorous and leap all civil bounds
Rather than make unprofited° return.

Pourquoi, why (French). **Then hadst thou had an excellent head of hair,** (perhaps Sir Toby is punning on Sir Andrew's "tongues" [line 91] as "tongs" or curling irons). *distaff,* stick used in spinning. *huswife,* housewife. *estate,* fortune. *there's life in't,* i.e., there's hope for you yet. *kickshawses,* trifles (French *quelque chose*). **under the degree of my betters,** i.e., so long as he is not my social superior. *old,* i.e., experienced (?). *galliard,* lively dance in triple time. *caper,* (1) frisky leap (2) spice used to season mutton (hence Sir Toby's remark in the next line). *back-trick,* reverse step in dancing. *take,* gather. *coranto,* quick running dance. *sink-a-pace,* cinquepace (French *cinque pas*), a kind of galliard of five steps (but there is also a scatological pun here). *virtues,* talents, accomplishments.

the star of a galliard, i.e., a dancing star. *damned-colored stock,* (of the many emendations proposed for this stocking of uncertain color—"damasked-colored," "dun-colored," "dove-colored," "damson-colored," and the like—Rowe's "flame-colored" has been most popular). *Taurus,* the Bull (one of the twelve signs of the zodiac, each of which was thought to influence a certain part of the human body. Most authorities assigned Taurus to neither "sides and heart" nor "legs and thighs," but to neck and throat). *humor,* changeable disposition. *that,* in that. *no less but all,* i.e., everything. *address thy gait,* direct your steps. *unprofited,* unsuccessful.

VIOLA: Say I do speak with her, my lord, what then?
DUKE: O, then unfold the passion of my love;
Surprise her with discourse of my dear° faith;
It shall become thee well to act my woes.
She will attend it better in thy youth
Than in a nuncio's° of more grave aspect.°
30 VIOLA: I think not so, my lord.
DUKE: Dear lad, believe it;
For they shall yet belie thy happy years
That say thou art a man. Diana's lip
Is not more smooth and rubious;° thy small pipe°
Is as the maiden's organ, shrill and sound,°
And all is semblative° a woman's part.
I know thy constellation° is right apt°
For this affair. Some four or five attend him,
All, if you will; for I myself am best
40 When least in company. Prosper well in this,
And thou shalt live as freely as thy lord
To call his fortunes thine.
VIOLA: I'll do my best
To woo your lady. (Aside) Yet a barful° strife!
Whoe'er I woo, myself would be his wife.

(Exeunt.)

ACT 1 / SCENE 5 OLIVIA's house.

(Enter MARIA and CLOWN.)

MARIA: Nay, either tell me where thou hast been, or I
will not open my lips so wide as a bristle may enter
in way of thy excuse. My lady will hang thee for thy
absence.
CLOWN: Let her hang me. He that is well hanged in this
world needs to fear no colors.°
MARIA: Make that good.°
CLOWN: He shall see none to fear.
MARIA: A good lenten° answer. I can tell thee where
10   that saying was born, of "I fear no colors."
CLOWN: Where, good Mistress Mary?
MARIA: In the wars; and that may you be bold to say in
your foolery.
CLOWN: Well, God give them wisdom that have it, and
those that are fools, let them use their talents.°

MARIA: Yet you will be hanged for being so long absent,
or to be turned away. Is not that as good as a hanging to you?
CLOWN: Many a good hanging prevents a bad marriage,
and for turning away, let summer bear it out.°   20
MARIA: You are resolute then?
CLOWN: Not so, neither; but I am resolved on two
points.°
MARIA: That if one break, the other will hold; or if both
break, your gaskins° fall.
CLOWN: Apt, in good faith; very apt. Well, go thy way!
If Sir Toby would leave drinking, thou wert as witty
a piece of Eve's flesh° as any in Illyria.
MARIA: Peace, you rogue; no more o' that. Here comes
my lady. Make your excuse wisely, you were best.° 30

(Exit.)

(Enter LADY OLIVIA with MALVOLIO and other ATTEN-
DANTS.)

CLOWN: Wit, and't° be thy will, put me into good fool-
ing. Those wits that think they have thee do very
oft prove fools, and I that am sure I lack thee may
pass for a wise man. For what says Quinapalus?°
"Better a witty fool than a foolish wit." God bless
thee, lady.
OLIVIA: Take the fool away.
CLOWN: Do you not hear, fellows? Take away the lady.
OLIVIA: Go to,° y' are a dry° fool! I'll no more of you.
Besides, you grow dishonest.°   40
CLOWN: Two faults, madonna,° that drink and good
counsel will amend. For give the dry° fool drink,
then is the fool not dry. Bid the dishonest man
mend himself: if he mend, he is no longer dishonest; if he cannot, let the botcher° mend him. Anything that's mended is but patched; virtue that
transgresses is but patched with sin, and sin that
amends is but patched with virtue. If that this simple syllogism will serve, so; if it will not, what remedy? As there is no true cuckold but calamity,° so   50
beauty's a flower. The lady bade take away the fool;
therefore, I say again, take her away.

---

dear, intense. nuncio's, messenger's. aspect, (accent
on second syllable). rubious, ruby-red. pipe, voice. shrill
and sound, high and clear. semblative, like. constellation,
predetermined qualities. apt, suitable. barful, full of impediments. fear no colors, i.e., fear nothing (with a pun
on "color" meaning "flag" and "collar" meaning "hangman's noose"). Make that good, i.e., explain it. lenten,
thin, meager (perhaps an allusion to the colorless, un-
bleached linen that replaced the customary liturgical purple or violet during Lent). talents, native intelligence (with
perhaps a pun on "talons" meaning "claws").

let summer bear it out, i.e., let the warm weather make
it endurable. points, counts (but Maria takes it in the sense
of tagged laces serving as suspenders). gaskins, loose
breeches. thou wert as witty a piece of Eve's flesh, i.e., you
would make as clever a wife. you were best, it would be
best for you. and't, if it. Quinapalus, (a sage of the
Clown's invention). Go to, enough. dry, stupid. dishonest, unreliable. madonna, my lady. dry, thirsty. botcher,
mender of clothes. there is no true cuckold but calamity,
(although the Clown's chatter should not be pressed too
hard for significance, Kittredge's paraphrase of this difficult passage is perhaps the least unsatisfactory: "Every man
is wedded to fortune; hence, when one's fortune is unfaithful, one may in very truth be called a cuckold—the husband
of an unfaithful wife").

OLIVIA: Sir, I bade them take away you.

CLOWN: Misprision in the highest degree.° Lady, *cucullus non facit monachum.*° That's as much to say as, I wear not motley in my brain. Good madonna, give me leave to prove you a fool.

OLIVIA: Can you do it?

CLOWN: Dexteriously,° good madonna.

60 OLIVIA: Make your proof.

CLOWN: I must catechize you for it, madonna. Good my mouse of virtue,° answer me.

OLIVIA: Well, sir, for want of other idleness,° I'll bide your proof.

CLOWN: Good madonna, why mourn'st thou?

OLIVIA: Good fool, for my brother's death.

CLOWN: I think his soul is in hell, madonna.

OLIVIA: I know his soul is in heaven, fool.

CLOWN: The more fool, madonna, to mourn for your
70   brother's soul, being in heaven. Take away the fool, gentlemen.

OLIVIA: What think you of this fool, Malvolio? Doth he not mend?

MALVOLIO: Yes, and shall do till the pangs of death shake him. Infirmity, that decays the wise, doth ever make the better fool.

CLOWN: God send you, sir, a speedy infirmity, for the better increasing your folly. Sir Toby will be sworn that I am no fox,° but he will not pass his word for
80   twopence that you are no fool.

OLIVIA: How say you to that, Malvolio?

MALVOLIO: I marvel your ladyship takes delight in such a barren° rascal. I saw him put down the other day with° an ordinary fool that has no more brain than a stone. Look you now, he's out of his guard° already. Unless you laugh and minister occasion° to him, he is gagged. I protest I take these wise men that crow° so at these set° kind of fools no better than the fools' zanies.°

90 OLIVIA: O, you are sick of self-love, Malvolio, and taste with a distempered appetite. To be generous,° guiltless, and of free disposition, is to take those things for birdbolts° that you deem cannon bullets. There is no slander in an allowed° fool, though he do nothing but rail; nor no railing in a known discreet man, though he do nothing but reprove.

CLOWN: Now Mercury indue thee with leasing,° for thou speak'st well of fools.

(Enter MARIA.)

MARIA: Madam, there is at the gate a young gentleman
100   much desires to speak with you.

OLIVIA: From the Count Orsino, is it?

MARIA: I know not, madam. 'Tis a fair young man, and well attended.

OLIVIA: Who of my people hold him in delay?

MARIA: Sir Toby, madam, your kinsman.

OLIVIA: Fetch him off, I pray you. He speaks nothing but madman. Fie on him! *(Exit MARIA.)* Go you, Malvolio. If it be a suit from the Count, I am sick, or not at home. What you will, to dismiss it. *(Exit
110   MALVOLIO.)* Now you see, sir, how your fooling grows old,° and people dislike it.

CLOWN: Thou hast spoke for us, madonna, as if thy eldest son should be a fool; whose skull Jove° cram with brains, for—here he comes—one of thy kin has a most weak pia mater.°

(Enter SIR TOBY.)

OLIVIA: By mine honor, half drunk. What is he at the gate, cousin?

TOBY: A gentleman.

OLIVIA: A gentleman? What gentleman?

TOBY: 'Tis a gentleman here. A plague o' these pickle-
120   herring!° How now, sot?°

CLOWN: Good Sir Toby.

OLIVIA: Cousin,° cousin, how have you come so early by this lethargy?

TOBY: Lechery? I defy lechery. There's one at the gate.

OLIVIA: Ay, marry, what is he?

TOBY: Let him be the devil and he will, I care not. Give me faith,° say I. Well, it's all one. *(Exit.)*

OLIVIA: What's a drunken man like, fool?

CLOWN: Like a drowned man, a fool, and a madman.
130   One draught above heat° makes him a fool, the second mads him, and a third drowns him.

OLIVIA: Go thou and seek the crowner,° and let him sit o' my coz;° for he's in the third degree of drink— he's drowned. Go look after him.

CLOWN: He is but mad yet, madonna, and the fool shall look to the madman. *(Exit.)*

Misprision in the highest degree, i.e., an egregious error in mistaken identity. *cucullus non facit monachum,* a cowl does not make a monk. *Dexteriously,* dexterously. *Good my mouse of virtue,* my good virtuous mouse (a term of playful affection). *idleness,* trifling. *I am no fox,* i.e., sly and dangerous (like you). *barren,* stupid. *put down . . . with,* bested . . . by. *out of his guard,* defenseless. *minister occasion,* afford opportunity (for his fooling). *crow,* i.e., with laughter. *set,* artificial. *zanies,* inferior buffoons. *generous,* liberal-minded. *birdbolts,* blunt arrows. *allowed,* licensed, privileged.

Mercury indue thee with leasing, may the god of trickery endow you with the gift of deception. *old,* stale, tedious. *Jove,* (if, as is likely, Shakespeare here and elsewhere wrote "God," the printed text reflects the statute of 1606 that prohibited profane stage allusions to the deity). *pia mater,* brain. *pickle-herring,* (to which the drunken Sir Toby attributes his hiccoughing). *sot,* fool. *Cousin,* i.e., uncle (see Act. 1, sc. 3, l. 5). *faith,* (in order to resist the devil). *above heat,* i.e., above what is required to make a man normally warm. *crowner,* coroner. *sit o' my coz,* hold an inquest on my kinsman.

(Enter MALVOLIO.*)*

MALVOLIO: Madam, yond young fellow swears he will
speak with you. I told him you were sick; he takes
on him to understand so much, and therefore
comes to speak with you. I told him you were asleep;
he seems to have a foreknowledge of that too, and
therefore comes to speak with you. What is to be
said to him, lady? He's fortified against any denial.

OLIVIA: Tell him he shall not speak with me.

MALVOLIO: H'as° been told so; and he says he'll stand at
your door like a sheriff's post,° and be the sup-
porter to a bench, but° he'll speak with you.

OLIVIA: What kind o' man is he?

MALVOLIO: Why, of mankind.°

OLIVIA: What manner of man?

MALVOLIO: Of very ill manner. He'll speak with you, will
you or no.

OLIVIA: Of what personage and years is he?

MALVOLIO: Not yet old enough for a man nor young
enough for a boy; as a squash° is before 'tis a peascod, or a codling° when 'tis almost an apple. 'Tis
with him in standing water,° between boy and man.
He is very well-favored and he speaks very shrewishly.° One would think his mother's milk were
scarce out of him.

OLIVIA: Let him approach. Call in my gentlewoman.

MALVOLIO: Gentlewoman, my lady calls. *(Exit.)*

(Enter MARIA.*)*

OLIVIA: Give me my veil; come, throw it o'er my face.
We'll once more hear Orsino's embassy.

(Enter VIOLA.*)*

VIOLA: The honorable lady of the house, which is she?

OLIVIA: Speak to me; I shall answer for her. Your will?

VIOLA: Most radiant, exquisite, and unmatchable
beauty—I pray you tell me if this be the lady of the
house, for I never saw her. I would be loath to cast
away my speech; for, besides that it is excellently
well penned, I have taken great pains to con° it.
Good beauties, let me sustain no scorn. I am very
comptible,° even to the least sinister° usage.

OLIVIA: Whence came you, sir?

VIOLA: I can say little more than I have studied, and
that question's out of my part. Good gentle one,
give me modest° assurance if you be the lady of the
house, that I may proceed in my speech.

OLIVIA: Are you a comedian?°

VIOLA: No, my profound heart;° and yet (by the very
fangs of malice I swear) I am not that° I play. Are
you the lady of the house?

OLIVIA: If I do not usurp° myself, I am.

VIOLA: Most certain, if you are she, you do usurp yourself; for what° is yours to bestow is not yours to
reserve. But this is from my commission.° I will on
with my speech in your praise and then show you
the heart of my message.

OLIVIA: Come to what is important in't. I forgive you°
the praise.

VIOLA: Alas, I took great pains to study it, and 'tis poetical.

OLIVIA: It is the more like to be feigned; I pray you
keep it in. I heard you were saucy at my gates; and
allowed your approach rather to wonder at you
than to hear you. If you be not mad, be gone; if
you have reason, be brief. 'Tis not that time of moon
with me to make one in so skipping a dialogue.°

MARIA: Will you hoist sail, sir? Here lies your way.

VIOLA: No, good swabber; I am to hull° here a little
longer. Some mollification for your giant,° sweet
lady. Tell me your mind. I am a messenger.°

OLIVIA: Sure you have some hideous matter to deliver,
when the courtesy of it is so fearful.° Speak your
office.°

VIOLA: It alone concerns your ear. I bring no overture
of war, no taxation of° homage. I hold the olive° in
my hand. My words are as full of peace as matter.°

OLIVIA: Yet you began rudely. What are you? What
would you?

VIOLA: The rudeness that hath appeared in me have I
learned from my entertainment.° What I am, and
what I would, are as secret as maidenhead:° to your
ears, divinity;° to any other's, profanation.

OLIVIA: Give us the place alone; we will hear this divinity. *(Exit* MARIA *and* ATTENDANTS.*)* Now, sir, what is
your text?

VIOLA: Most sweet lady—

OLIVIA: A comfortable° doctrine, and much may be said
of it. Where lies your text?

H'as, he has. *sheriff's post,* post set up before a sheriff's door for placards, notices, and such. *but,* except. *of
mankind,* i.e., like other men. *squash,* unripe peascod (pea
pod). *codling,* unripe apple. *standing water,* i.e., at the
turning of the tide, between ebb and flood, when it flows
neither way. *shrewishly,* tartly. *con,* learn. *comptible,*
sensitive. *sinister,* discourteous. *modest,* reasonable. *comedian,* actor (because he has had to "con" a "part").

my profound heart, my sagacious lady (a bantering compliment). *that,* that which. *usurp,* counterfeit (but Viola
takes it in the sense "betray," "wrong"). *what,* i.e., your
hand in marriage. *from my commission,* beyond my instructions. *forgive you,* excuse you from repeating. *'Tis
not . . . dialogue,* i.e., I am not in the mood to sustain such
aimless banter. *hull,* lie adrift. *giant,* (an ironical reference to Maria's small size). *Tell me your mind. I am a
messenger.,* (Many editors have divided these sentences,
assigning the first to Olivia and the second to Viola). *when
the courtesy of it is so fearful,* i.e., since your manner is so
truculent. *office,* business. *taxation of,* demand for. *olive,* (the symbol of peace). *matter,* significant content. *entertainment,* reception. *maidenhead,* maidenhood. *divinity,* i.e., a sacred message. *comfortable,* comforting.

VIOLA: In Orsino's bosom.

OLIVIA: In his bosom? In what chapter of his bosom?

VIOLA: To answer by the method,° in the first of his heart.

OLIVIA: O, I have read it; it is heresy. Have you no more to say?

VIOLA: Good madam, let me see your face.

OLIVIA: Have you any commission from your lord to
230   negotiate with my face? You are now out of your text.° But we will draw the curtain and show you the picture. *(Unveils.)* Look you, sir, such a one I was this present.° Is't not well done?

VIOLA: Excellently done, if God did all.

OLIVIA: 'Tis in grain,° sir; 'twill endure wind and weather.

VIOLA: 'Tis beauty truly blent, whose red and white Nature's own sweet and cunning° hand laid on. Lady, you are the cruel'st she alive
240   If you will lead these graces to the grave, And leave the world no copy.

OLIVIA: O, sir, I will not be so hard-hearted. I will give out divers schedules° of my beauty. It shall be inventoried, and every particle and utensil° labeled to my will:° as, item,° two lips, indifferent red; item, two gray eyes, with lids to them; item, one neck, one chin, and so forth. Were you sent hither to praise° me?

250 VIOLA: I see you what you are; you are too proud; But if° you were the devil, you are fair. My lord and master loves you. O, such love Could be but recompensed though you were crowned The nonpareil of beauty.

OLIVIA: How does he love me?

VIOLA: With adorations, with fertile° tears, With groans that thunder love, with sighs of fire.

OLIVIA: Your lord does know my mind; I cannot love him. Yet I suppose him virtuous, know him noble, Of great estate, of fresh and stainless youth;
260 In voices well divulged,° free, learned, and valiant, And in dimension° and the shape of nature A gracious person. But yet I cannot love him. He might have took his answer long ago.

VIOLA: If I did love you in my master's flame, With such a suff'ring, such a deadly° life, In your denial I would find no sense; I would not understand it.

OLIVIA: Why, what would you?

VIOLA: Make me a willow° cabin at your gate And call upon my soul° within the house; 270 Write loyal cantons° of contemnèd° love And sing them loud even in the dead of night; Hallo your name to the reverberate° hills And make the babbling gossip of the air° Cry out "Olivia!" O, you should not rest Between the elements of air and earth But° you should pity me.

OLIVIA: You might do much. What is your parentage?

VIOLA: Above my fortunes, yet my state° is well. I am a gentleman. 280

OLIVIA: Get you to your lord. I cannot love him. Let him send no more, Unless, perchance, you come to me again To tell me how he takes it. Fare you well. I thank you for your pains. Spend this for me.

VIOLA: I am no fee'd post,° lady; keep your purse; My master, not myself, lacks recompense. Love make his heart of flint that you shall love;° And let your fervor, like my master's, be Placed in contempt. Farewell, fair cruelty. *(Exit.)* 290

OLIVIA: "What is your parentage?" "Above my fortunes, yet my state is well. I am a gentleman." I'll be sworn thou art. Thy tongue, thy face, thy limbs, actions, and spirit Do give thee fivefold blazon.° Not too fast; soft,° soft, Unless the master were the man. How now? Even so quickly may one catch the plague? Methinks I feel this youth's perfections With an invisible and subtle stealth To creep in at mine eyes. Well, let it be. 300 What ho, Malvolio!

(Enter MALVOLIO.)

MALVOLIO: Here, madam, at your service.

OLIVIA: Run after that same peevish° messenger, The County's° man. He left this ring behind him, Would I or not. Tell him I'll none of it. Desire him not to flatter with° his lord Nor hold him up with hopes. I am not for him.

---

method, i.e., in the theological style suggested by "divinity," "profanation," "text," and "doctrine." ***You are now out of your text,*** i.e., you have shifted from talking of your master's heart to asking about my face. **this present,** just now (like portrait painters, Olivia gives the age of the subject of the "picture" she has just revealed by drawing the "curtain" of a veil from her face). **in grain,** fast-dyed, indelible. **cunning,** skillful. **schedules,** statements. **utensil,** article. **labeled to my will,** i.e., added as a codicil. **item,** also. **praise,** appraise. **if,** even if. **fertile,** copious. **well divulged,** i.e., of good repute. **dimension,** physique.

deadly, doomed to die. **willow,** (emblem of a disconsolate lover). **my soul,** i.e., Olivia. **cantons,** songs. **contemnèd,** rejected. **reverberate,** reverberating. **babbling gossip of the air,** i.e., echo. **But,** but that. **state,** status. **fee'd post,** i.e., lackey to be tipped. **Love make . . . love,** may Love make the heart of him you love like flint. **blazon,** heraldic insignia. **soft,** i.e., take it slowly. **peevish,** truculent impertinent. **County's,** Count's. **flatter with,** encourage.

If that the youth will come this way tomorrow,
I'll give him reasons for't. Hie thee, Malvolio.

310 MALVOLIO: Madam, I will.

(Exit.)

OLIVIA: I do I know not what, and fear to find
Mine eye too great a flatterer for my mind.°
Fate, show thy force; ourselves we do not owe.°
What is decreed must be—and be this so!

(Exit.)

ACT 2 / SCENE 1 *The seacoast.*

(*Enter* ANTONIO *and* SEBASTIAN.)

ANTONIO: Will you stay no longer? Nor will you not that
I go with you?

SEBASTIAN: By your patience,° no. My stars shine darkly
over me; the malignancy of my fate might perhaps
distemper° yours. Therefore I shall crave of you
your leave, that I may bear my evils alone. It were
a bad recompense for your love to lay any of them
on you.

ANTONIO: Let me yet know of you whither you are
10 bound.

SEBASTIAN: No, sooth,° sir. My determinate° voyage is
mere extravagancy.° But I perceive in you so excellent a touch of modesty that you will not extort
from me what I am willing to keep in; therefore it
charges me in manners the rather to express myself.° You must know of me then, Antonio, my name
is Sebastian, which I called Roderigo. My father was
that Sebastian of Messaline whom I know you have
heard of. He left behind him myself and a sister,
20 both born in an hour.° If the heavens had been
pleased, would we had so ended! But you, sir, altered that, for some hour before you took me from
the breach° of the sea was my sister drowned.

ANTONIO: Alas the day!

SEBASTIAN: A lady, sir, though it was said she much
resembled me, was yet of many accounted beautiful. But though I could not with such estimable
wonder° overfar believe that, yet thus far I will
boldly publish° her: she bore a mind that envy could
30 not but call fair. She is drowned already, sir, with
salt water, though I seem to drown her remembrance again with more.

ANTONIO: Pardon me, sir, your bad entertainment.°

SEBASTIAN: O good Antonio, forgive me your trouble.°

ANTONIO: If you will not murder me° for my love, let
me be your servant.

SEBASTIAN: If you will not undo what you have done,
that is, kill him whom you have recovered,° desire
it not. Fare ye well at once. My bosom is full of
kindness, and I am yet so near the manners of my   40
mother that, upon the least occasion more, mine
eyes will tell tales of me.° I am bound to the Count
Orsino's court. Farewell. (*Exit.*)

ANTONIO: The gentleness of all the gods go with thee.
I have many enemies in Orsino's court,
Else would I very shortly see thee there.
But come what may, I do adore thee so
That danger shall seem sport, and I will go. (*Exit.*)

ACT 2 / SCENE 2 *A street near* OLIVIA's *house.*

(*Enter* VIOLA *and* MALVOLIO *at several° doors.*)

MALVOLIO: Were not you ev'n now with the Countess
Olivia?

VIOLA: Even now, sir. On a moderate pace I have since
arrived but hither.

MALVOLIO: She returns this ring to you, sir. You might
have saved me my pains, to have taken it away
yourself. She adds, moreover, that you should put
your lord into a desperate assurance° she will none
of him. And one thing more, that you be never so
hardy to come again in his affairs, unless it be to   10
report your lord's taking of this. Receive it so.

VIOLA: She took the ring of me.° I'll none of it.

MALVOLIO: Come, sir, you peevishly threw it to her, and
her will is, it should be so returned. If it be worth
stooping for, there it lies, in your eye;° if not, be it
his that finds it. (*Exit.*)

VIOLA: I left no ring with her. What means this lady?
Fortune forbid my outside have not charmed her.
She made good view of me; indeed, so much
That sure methought° her eyes had lost her   20
tongue,°
For she did speak in starts distractedly.
She loves me sure; the cunning° of her passion

Mine eye . . . mind, i.e., my eye, so susceptible to external
attractions, will betray my judgment. *owe,* own. *patience,*
permission. *distemper,* disorder. *sooth,* truly. *determi-
nate,* intended. *extravagancy,* wandering. *it charges me
. . . myself,* i.e., civility requires that I give some account of
myself. *in an hour,* in the same hour. *breach,* breakers.
with such estimable wonder, i.e., with so much esteem in my
appraisal. *publish,* describe. *bad entertainment,* i.e., poor
reception at my hands.

your trouble, the trouble I have given you. *murder me,*
i.e., by forcing me to part from you. *recovered,* saved. *so
near . . . tales of me,* i.e., so overwrought by my sorrow that,
like a woman, I shall weep. *several,* separate. *desperate
assurance,* hopeless certainty. *She took the ring of me,* (of
the various emendations proposed for this puzzling line,
Malone's "She took no ring of me" is perhaps the most
attractive). *eye,* sight. *sure methought,* ("sure," which re-
pairs the defective meter of this line, has been adopted
from the Second Folio. Another common emendation is
"as methought"). *her eyes had lost her tongue,* i.e., her
fixed gaze made her lose the power of speech. *cunning,*
craftiness.

Invites me in this churlish messenger.
None of my lord's ring? Why, he sent her none.
I am the man.° If it be so, as 'tis,
Poor lady, she were better love a dream.
Disguise, I see thou art a wickedness
Wherein the pregnant enemy° does much.
How easy is it for the proper false°
30 In women's waxen hearts to set their forms!
Alas, our frailty is the cause, not we,
For such as we are made of, such we be.
How will this fadge?° My master loves her dearly;
And I (poor monster)° fond° as much on him;
And she (mistaken) seems to dote on me.
What will become of this? As I am man,
My state is desperate° for my master's love.
As I am woman (now alas the day!),
What thriftless° sighs shall poor Olivia breathe?
40 O Time, thou must untangle this, not I;
It is too hard a knot for me t' untie. *(Exit.)*

ACT 2 / SCENE 3 *A room in* OLIVIA'*s house.*

(Enter SIR TOBY *and* SIR ANDREW.*)*

TOBY: Approach, Sir Andrew. Not to be abed after midnight is to be up betimes; and "*Deliculo surgere*,"°
thou know'st.
ANDREW: Nay, by my troth, I know not, but I know to
be up late is to be up late.
TOBY: A false conclusion; I hate it as an unfilled can.°
To be up after midnight, and to go to bed then, is
early; so that to go to bed after midnight is to go to
bed betimes. Does not our lives consist of the four
10 elements?°
ANDREW: Faith, so they say; but I think it rather consists
of eating and drinking.
TOBY: Th' art a scholar! Let us therefore eat and drink.
Marian I say, a stoup° of wine!

(Enter CLOWN.*)*

ANDREW: Here comes the fool, i' faith.
CLOWN: How now, my hearts? Did you never see the
picture of We Three?°
TOBY: Welcome, ass. Now let's have a catch.°

ANDREW: By my troth, the fool has an excellent breast.°
I had rather than forty shillings I had such a leg,° 20
and so sweet a breath to sing, as the fool has. In
sooth, thou wast in very gracious° fooling last night,
when thou spok'st of Pigrogromitus,° of the Vapi-
ans° passing the equinoctial of Queubus.° 'Twas
very good, i' faith. I sent thee sixpence for thy
leman.° Hadst it?
CLOWN: I did impeticos thy gratillity,° for Malvolio's
nose is no whipstock. My lady has a white hand,
and the Myrmidons are no bottle-ale houses.°
ANDREW: Excellent. Why, this is the best fooling, when 30
all is done. Now a song!
TOBY: Come on, there is sixpence for you. Let's have a
song.
ANDREW: There's a testril° of me too. If one knight give
a—°
CLOWN: Would you have a love song, or a song of good
life?°
TOBY: A love song, a love song.
ANDREW: Ay, ay, I care not for good life.

*(*CLOWN *sings.)*

O mistress mine, where are you roaming? 40
O, stay and hear, your true-love's coming,
*   That can sing both high and low.*
Trip no further, pretty sweeting;
Journeys end in lovers meeting,
*   Every wise man's son doth know.*

ANDREW: Excellent good, i' faith.
TOBY: Good, good.

*(*CLOWN *sings.)*

What is love? 'Tis not hereafter;
Present mirth hath present laughter;
*   What's to come is still° unsure:* 50
In delay there lies no plenty;
Then come kiss me, sweet, and twenty,°
*   Youth's a stuff will not endure.*

I am the man, i.e., whom she loves. **pregnant enemy,** crafty fiend (i.e., Satan). **proper false,** attractive but deceitful suitors. **fadge,** turn out. **monster,** (because of her equivocal position as both man and woman). **fond,** dote. **desperate,** hopeless. **thriftless,** unavailing. **Deliculo surgere,** i.e., *Diluculo surgere saluberrimum est,* "it is most healthful to rise early" (a tag from William Lily's Latin grammar, which was widely used in sixteenth-century schools). **can,** tankard. **the four elements,** i.e., air, fire, earth, and water, which were thought to be the basic ingredients of all things. **stoup,** cup. **the picture of We Three,** i.e., a picture of two asses, the spectator making the third. **catch,** round, a simple polyphonic song for several voices.

breast, voice. **leg,** i.e., skill in bowing (?). **gracious,** delightful. **Pigrogromitus, Vapians, Queubus,** (presumably words invented by the Clown as specimens of his "gracious fooling" in mock learning). **leman,** sweetheart. **impeticos thy gratillity,** (more of the Clown's fooling, which perhaps means something like "pocket your gratuity"). **Malvolio's nose . . . bottle-ale houses,** (probably mere nonsense). **testril,** tester, sixpence. **If one knight give a—,** (some editors have tried to supply what seems to be a missing line here, but it is probable that the Clown breaks in without permitting Sir Andrew to finish his sentence). **of good life,** i.e., moral, edifying (?). **still,** always. **Then come kiss me, sweet, and twenty,** i.e., so kiss me, my sweet, and then kiss me twenty times again (some editors, taking "twenty" as an intensive, read the line as "so kiss me then, my very sweet one").

ANDREW: A mellifluous voice, as I am true knight.

TOBY: A contagious breath.°

ANDREW: Very sweet and contagious, i' faith.

TOBY: To hear by the nose, it is dulcet in contagion.° But shall we make the welkin° dance indeed? Shall we rouse the night owl in a catch that will draw three souls out of one weaver?° Shall we do that?

60

ANDREW: And you love me, let's do't. I am dog° at a catch.

CLOWN: By'r Lady, sir, and some dogs will catch well.

ANDREW: Most certain. Let our catch be "Thou knave."

CLOWN: "Hold thy peace, thou knave,"° knight? I shall be constrained in't to call thee knave, knight.

ANDREW: 'Tis not the first time I have constrained one to call me knave. Begin, fool. It begins, "Hold thy peace."

70

CLOWN: I shall never begin if I hold my peace.

ANDREW: Good, i' faith! Come, begin.

(Catch sung. Enter MARIA.)

MARIA: What a caterwauling do you keep here? If my lady have not called up her steward Malvolio and bid him turn you out of doors, never trust me.

TOBY: My lady's a Cataian, we are politicians,° Malvolio's a Peg-a-Ramsey,° and *(sings)* "Three merry men be we."° Am not I consanguineous?° Am I not of her blood? Tilly-vally, lady. *(Sings)* "There dwelt a man in Babylon, lady, lady."

80

CLOWN: Beshrew° me, the knight's in admirable fooling.

ANDREW: Ay, he does well enough if he be disposed, and so do I too. He does it with a better grace, but I do it more natural.°

TOBY: *(Sings)* "O the twelfth day of December."

MARIA: For the love o' God, peace!

(Enter MALVOLIO.)

MALVOLIO: My masters, are you mad? Or what are you? Have you no wit,° manners, nor honesty,° but to gabble like tinkers at this time of night? Do ye make an alehouse of my lady's house, that ye squeak out your coziers'° catches without any mitigation or remorse° of voice? Is there no respect of place, persons, nor time in you?

90

TOBY: We did keep time, sir, in our catches. Sneck up.°

MALVOLIO: Sir Toby, I must be round° with you. My lady bade me tell you that, though she harbors you as her kinsman, she's nothing allied to your disorders. If you can separate yourself and your misdemeanors, you are welcome to the house. If not, and it would please you to take leave of her, she is very willing to bid you farewell.

100

TOBY: *(Sings)* "Farewell, dear heart since I must needs be gone."°

MARIA: Nay, good Sir Toby.

CLOWN: *(Sings)* "His eyes do show his days are almost done."

MALVOLIO: Is't even so?

TOBY: *(Sings)* "But I will never die."

CLOWN: *(Sings)* Sir Toby, there you lie.

MALVOLIO: This is much credit to you.

110

TOBY: *(Sings)* "Shall I bid him go?"

CLOWN: *(Sings)* "What and if you do?"

TOBY: *(Sings)* "Shall I bid him go, and spare not?"

CLOWN: *(Sings)* "O, no, no, no, no, you dare not!"

TOBY: Out o' tune, sir? Ye lie.° Art any more than a steward? Dost thou think, because thou art virtuous, there shall be no more cakes and ale?

CLOWN: Yes, by Saint Anne, and ginger° shall be hot i' th' mouth too.

TOBY: Th' art i' th' right. —Go, sir, rub your chain with crumbs.° A stoup of wine, Maria!

120

MALVOLIO: Mistress Mary, if you prized my lady's favor at anything more than contempt, you would not give means for this uncivil rule.° She shall know of it, by this hand. *(Exit.)*

MARIA: Go shake your ears.°

---

contagious breath, catchy song. *to hear by the nose, it is dulcet in contagion*, i.e., if we could hear through the nose, the Clown's "breath" would be sweet and not malodorous, as "contagious" breaths usually are. *welkin*, sky. *weaver*, (weavers were noted for their singing). *dog*, clever (but in the next line the Clown puns on *dog* i.e., latch, gripping device). *Hold thy peace, thou knave*, (a line from the round proposed by Sir Andrew). *My lady's a Cataian, we are politicians*, (because Sir Toby and his companions are "politicians" [i.e., tricksters, intriguers] they recognize Maria's warning of Olivia's anger as the ruse of a "Cataian" [i.e., native of Cathay, cheater]; hence "Tilly-vally, lady" [line 78], which means something like "Fiddlesticks, lady"). *Peg-a-Ramsey*, (character in an old song whose name Sir Toby uses apparently as a term of contempt). *Three merry men be we*, (like Sir Toby's other snatches, a fragment of an old song). *consanguineous*, related, kin (to Olivia). *Beshrew*, curse. *natural*, (with an unintentional pun on "natural" as a term for fool or idiot; see Act 1, sc. 3, l. 28).

wit, sense. *honesty*, decency. *coziers'*, cobblers'. *mitigation or remorse*, i.e., lowering. *Sneck up*, go hang. *round*, blunt. *Farewell . . . gone*, (what follows, in crude antiphony between Sir Toby and the Clown, is adapted from a ballad, "Corydon's Farewell to Phyllis"). *Out o' tune, sir? Ye lie*, (Sir Toby accuses the Clown of being out of tune, it seems, because he had added an extra "no" and thus an extra note in line 114, and of lying because he had questioned his valor in "you dare not." Then he turns to berating Malvolio). *ginger*, (commonly used to spice ale). *rub your chain with crumbs*, i.e., polish your steward's chain, your badge of office. *give means for this uncivil rule*, i.e., provide liquor for this brawl. *Go shake your ears*, i.e., like the ass you are (?).

ANDREW: 'Twere as good a deed as to drink when a man's ahungry,° to challenge him the field,° and then to break promise with him and make a fool of
130 him.

TOBY: Do't, knight. I'll write thee a challenge; or I'll deliver thy indignation to him by word of mouth.

MARIA: Sweet Sir Toby, be patient for tonight. Since the youth of the Count's was today with my lady, she is much out of quiet. For Monsieur Malvolio, let me alone with him. If I do not gull him into a nayword,° and make him a common recreation, do not think I have wit enough to lie straight in my bed. I know I can do it.

140 TOBY: Possess° us, possess us. Tell us something of him.

MARIA: Marry, sir, sometimes he is a kind of Puritan.°

ANDREW: O, if I thought that, I'd beat him like a dog.

TOBY: What, for being a Puritan? Thy exquisite reason, dear knight.

ANDREW: I have no exquisite reason for't, but I have reason good enough.

MARIA: The devil a Puritan that he is, or anything constantly° but a time-pleaser;° an affectioned° ass, that cons state without book° and utters it by great
150 swarths;° the best persuaded of himself;° so crammed, as he thinks, with excellencies that it is his grounds of faith that all that look on him love him; and on that vice in him will my revenge find notable cause to work.

TOBY: What wilt thou do?

MARIA: I will drop in his way some obscure epistles of love, wherein by the color of his beard, the shape of his leg, the manner of his gait, the expressure° of his eye, forehead, and complexion, he shall find
160 himself most feelingly personated.° I can write very like my lady your niece; on a forgotten matter we can hardly make distinction of our hands.

TOBY: Excellent. I smell a device.

ANDREW: I have't in my nose too.

TOBY: He shall think by the letters that thou wilt drop that they come from my niece, and that she's in love with him.

MARIA: My purpose is indeed a horse of that color.

ANDREW: And your horse now would make him an ass.

170 MARIA: Ass, I doubt not.

ANDREW: O, 'twill be admirable.

MARIA: Sport royal, I warrant you. I know my physic will work with him. I will plant you two, and let the fool make a third,° where he shall find the letter. Observe his construction° of it. For this night, to bed, and dream on the event.° Farewell. *(Exit.)*

TOBY: Good night, Penthesilea.°

ANDREW: Before me,° she's a good wench.

TOBY: She's a beagle° true-bred, and one that adores me. What o' that?   180

ANDREW: I was adored once too.

TOBY: Let's to bed, knight. Thou hadst need send for more money.

ANDREW: If I cannot recover° your niece, I am a foul way out.°

TOBY: Send for money, knight. If thou hast her not i' th' end, call me Cut.°

ANDREW: If I do not, never trust me, take it how you will.

TOBY: Come, come; I'll go burn some sack.° 'Tis too   190
late to go to bed now. Come, knight; come, knight.

(Exeunt.)

ACT 2 / SCENE 4 *The* DUKE'S *palace.*

(Enter DUKE, VIOLA, CURIO, *and others.)*

DUKE: Give me some music. Now good morrow, friends.
Now, good Cesario, but that piece of song,
That old and antic° song we heard last night.
Methought it did relieve my passion° much,
More than light airs and recollected terms°
Of these most brisk and giddy-pacèd times.
Come, but one verse.

CURIO: He is not here, so please your lordship, that should sing it.

DUKE: Who was it?   10

CURIO: Feste the jester, my lord, a fool that the Lady Olivia's father took much delight in. He is about the house.

DUKE: Seek him out, and play the tune the while.

(Exit CURIO. *Music plays.)*

---

ahungry, (characteristically, Sir Andrew confuses hunger and thirst and thus perverts the proverbial expression). **the field,** i.e., to a duel. **nayword,** byword. **Possess,** inform. **Puritan,** i.e., a straight-laced, censorious person (in lines 147–48 Maria makes it clear that she is not using the label in a strict ecclesiastical sense, as Sir Andrew [line 143] thinks). **constantly,** consistently. **time-pleaser,** sycophant. **affectioned,** affected. **cons state without book,** i.e., memorizes stately gestures and turns of phrase. **swarths,** swaths, quantities. **the best persuaded of himself,** i.e., who thinks most highly of himself. **expressure,** expression. **personated,** represented.

let the fool make a third, (like the plan to have Viola present herself to Duke Orsino as a eunuch [Act 1, sc. 2, l. 58], this plot device was abandoned; it is Fabian, not the Clown, who makes the third spectator to Malvolio's exposé). **construction,** interpretation. **event,** outcome. **Penthesilea,** (in classical mythology, the queen of the Amazons). **Before me,** i.e., I swear, with myself as witness. **beagle,** (one of several allusions to Maria's small stature). **recover,** win. **a foul way out,** i.e., badly out of pocket. **Cut,** i.e., a docktailed horse. **burn some sack,** heat and spice some Spanish wine. **antic,** quaint. **passion,** suffering (from unrequited love). **recollected terms,** studied phrases.

Come hither, boy. If ever thou shalt love,
In the sweet pangs of it remember me;
For such as I am all true lovers are,
Unstaid and skittish in all motions° else
Save in the constant image of the creature
20   That is beloved. How dost thou like this tune?
VIOLA: It gives a very echo to the seat°
    Where Love is throned.
DUKE: Thou dost speak masterly.
    My life upon't, young though thou art, thine eye
    Hath stayed upon some favor° that it loves.
    Hath it not, boy?
VIOLA: A little, by your favor.
DUKE: What kind of woman is't?
VIOLA: Of your complexion.°
30   DUKE: She is not worth thee then. What years, i' faith?
VIOLA: About your years, my lord.
DUKE: Too old, by heaven. Let still° the woman take
    An elder than herself: so wears she° to him,
    So sways she level in her husband's heart;°
    For, boy, however we do praise ourselves,
    Our fancies° are more giddy and unfirm,
    More longing, wavering, sooner lost and worn,°
    Than women's are.
VIOLA: I think it well, my lord.
40   DUKE: Then let thy love be younger than thyself,
    Or thy affection cannot hold the bent;°
    For women are as roses, whose fair flow'r,
    Being once displayed, doth fall that very hour.
VIOLA: And so they are; alas, that they are so.
    To die, even when they to perfection grow.

    (Enter CURIO and CLOWN.)

DUKE: O, fellow, come, the song we had last night.
    Mark it, Cesario; it is old and plain.
    The spinsters° and the knitters in the sun,
    And the free° maids that weave their thread with
        bones,°
50   Do use to chant it. It is silly sooth,°
    And dallies° with the innocence of love,
    Like the old age.°
CLOWN: Are you ready, sir?
DUKE: I prithee sing.

    (Music.)

THE SONG

Come away, come away, death,
    And in sad cypress° let me be laid.
Fly away, fly away, breath;
    I am slain by a fair cruel maid.
My shroud of white, stuck all with yew,
    O, prepare it.   60
My part of death, no one so true
    Did share it.

Not a flower, not a flower sweet,
    On my black coffin let there be strown;
Not a friend, not a friend greet
    My poor corpse, where my bones shall be thrown.
A thousand thousand sighs to save,
    Lay me, O, where
Sad true lover never find my grave,
    To weep there.   70

DUKE: There's for thy pains.
CLOWN: No pains, sir. I take pleasure in singing, sir.
DUKE: I'll pay thy pleasure then.
CLOWN: Truly, sir, and pleasure will be paid one time
    or another.
DUKE: Give me now leave to leave thee.
CLOWN: Now the melancholy god protect thee, and the
    tailor make thy doublet of changeable° taffeta, for
    thy mind is a very opal. I would have men of such
    constancy put to sea, that their business might be   80
    everything, and their intent everywhere; for that's
    it that always makes a good voyage of nothing.
    Farewell.

    (Exit.)

DUKE: Let all the rest give place.°

    (Exeunt CURIO and ATTENDANTS.)

                            Once more, Cesario,
    Get thee to yond same sovereign cruelty.°
    Tell her my love, more noble than the world,
    Prizes not quantity of dirty lands;
    The parts° that fortune hath bestowed upon her
    Tell her I hold as giddily° as fortune,   90
    But 'tis that miracle and queen of gems°
    That nature pranks her in° attracts my soul.
VIOLA: But if she cannot love you, sir?
DUKE: I cannot be so answered.
VIOLA: Sooth,° but you must.
    Say that some lady, as perhaps there is,

---

motions, emotions. **seat,** i.e., the heart (see Act 1, sc. 1,
ls. 39–40). **favor,** face. **complexion,** temperament. **still,**
always. **wears she,** she adapts herself. **sways she . . . heart,**
i.e., she keeps steady in her husband's affections. **fancies,**
loves. **worn,** (many editors have adopted the reading
"won" from the Second Folio). **hold the bent,** i.e., maintain
its strength and tension (the image is that of a bent bow).
spinsters, spinners. **free,** carefree. **bones,** i.e., bone bob-
bins. **silly sooth,** simple truth. **dallies,** deals movingly.
the old age, i.e., the good old times.

---

cypress, a coffin made of cypress wood. **changeable,**
i.e., with shifting lights and colors. **give place,** withdraw.
sovereign cruelty, i.e., peerless and disdainful lady. **parts,**
gifts (of wealth and social status). **giddily,** indifferently.
queen of gems, i.e., Olivia's beauty. **pranks her in,** adorns
her with. **Sooth,** truly.

Hath for your love as great a pang of heart
As you have for Olivia. You cannot love her.
You tell her so. Must she not then be answered?
100 DUKE: There is no woman's sides
Can bide° the beating of so strong a passion
As love doth give my heart; no woman's heart
So big to hold so much; they lack retention.°
Alas, their love may be called appetite,
No motion° of the liver° but the palate,
That suffer surfeit, cloyment, and revolt;°
But mine is all as hungry as the sea
And can digest as much. Make no compare
Between that love a woman can bear me
110 And that I owe Olivia.
VIOLA: Ay, but I know—
DUKE: What dost thou know?
VIOLA: Too well what love women to men may owe.
In faith, they are as true of heart as we.
My father had a daughter loved a man
As it might be perhaps, were I a woman,
I should your lordship.
DUKE: And what's her history?
VIOLA: A blank, my lord. She never told her love,
120 But let concealment, like a worm i' th' bud,
Feed on her damask° cheek. She pined in thought;°
And, with a green and yellow melancholy,
She sat like Patience on a monument,
Smiling at grief. Was not this love indeed?
We men may say more, swear more; but indeed
Our shows are more than will;° for still we prove
Much in our vows but little in our love.
DUKE: But died thy sister of her love, my boy?
VIOLA: I am all the daughters of my father's house,
130 And all the brothers too, and yet I know not.°
Sir, shall I to this lady?
DUKE: Ay, that's the theme.
To her in haste. Give her this jewel. Say
My love can give no place,° bide no denay.°

(Exeunt.)

ACT 2 / SCENE 5 OLIVIA'S *garden.*

(Enter SIR TOBY, SIR ANDREW, *and* FABIAN.*)*

TOBY: Come thy ways, Signior Fabian.
FABIAN: Nay, I'll come. If I lose a scruple° of this sport,
let me be boiled° to death with melancholy.

---

bide, endure. **retention,** i.e., the ability to retain. **motion,** stirring, prompting. **liver,** (seat of passion). **revolt,** revulsion. **damask,** i.e., like a pink and white damask rose. **thought,** brooding. ***Our shows are more than will,*** i.e., what we show is greater than the passion that we feel. ***I know not,*** (because she thinks that her brother may be still alive). **can give no place,** cannot yield. **denay,** denial. **scruple,** smallest part. **boiled,** (pronounced "biled," quibbling on "bile," which was thought to be the cause of melancholy).

TOBY: Wouldst thou not be glad to have the niggardly
rascally sheep-biter° come by some notable shame?
FABIAN: I would exult, man. You know he brought me
out o' favor with my lady about a bearbaiting here.
TOBY: To anger him we'll have the bear again, and we
will fool him black and blue. Shall we not, Sir An-   10
drew?
ANDREW: And we do not, it is pity of our lives.

(Enter MARIA.*)*

TOBY: Here comes the little villain. How now, my metal
of India?°
MARIA: Get ye all three into the box tree. Malvolio's
coming down this walk. He has been yonder i' the
sun practicing behavior to his own shadow this half
hour. Observe him, for the love of mockery; for I
know this letter will make a contemplative° idiot of
him. Close,° in the name of jesting. *(The others hide.)*
Lie thou there *(throws down a letter)*; for here comes   20
the trout that must be caught with tickling.° *(Exit.)*

(Enter MALVOLIO.*)*

MALVOLIO: 'Tis but fortune; all is fortune. Maria once
told me she did affect me;° and I have heard herself
come thus near, that, should she fancy,° it should
be one of my complexion. Besides, she uses me with
a more exalted respect than anyone else that fol-
lows° her. What should I think on't?
TOBY: Here's an overweening rogue.
FABIAN: O, peace! Contemplation makes a rare turkey
cock of him. How he jets° under his advanced°   30
plumes!
ANDREW: 'Slight,° I could so beat the rogue.
TOBY: Peace, I say.°
MALVOLIO: To be Count Malvolio.
TOBY: Ah, rogue!
ANDREW: Pistol him, pistol him.
TOBY: Peace, peace.
MALVOLIO: There is example for't. The Lady of the
Strachy° married the yeoman of the wardrobe.
ANDREW: Fie on him, Jezebel.°   40
FABIAN: O, peace! Now he's deeply in. Look how imag-
ination blows him.°

---

sheep-biter, i.e., sneaky dog. **metal of India,** i.e., golden girl. **contemplative,** i.e., self-centered. **Close,** hide. **tickling,** stroking, i.e., flattery. **she did affect me,** i.e., Olivia liked me. **fancy,** love. **follows,** serves. **jets,** struts. **advanced,** uplifted. **'Slight,** by God's light (a mild oath). ***Peace, I say,*** (many editors assign this and line 37 to Fabian on the ground that it is his function throughout the scene to restrain Sir Toby and Sir Andrew). ***The Lady of the Strachy,*** (an unidentified allusion to a great lady who married beneath her). **Jezebel,** (the proud and wicked queen of Ahab, King of Israel, whom Sir Andrew, muddled as usual, regards as Malvolio's prototype in arrogance). ***blows him,*** puffs him up.

MALVOLIO: Having been three months married to her, sitting in my state—

TOBY: O for a stonebow,° to hit him in the eye!

MALVOLIO: Calling my officers about me, in my branched° velvet gown; having come from a daybed,° where I have left Olivia sleeping—

TOBY: Fire and brimstone!

50 FABIAN: O, peace, peace!

MALVOLIO: And then to have the humor of state;° and after a demure travel of regard,° telling them I know my place, as I would they should do theirs, to ask for my kinsman Toby—

TOBY: Bolts and shackles!

FABIAN: O peace, peace, peace, now, now.

MALVOLIO: Seven of my people, with an obedient start, make out for° him. I frown the while, and perchance wind up my watch, or play with my—some

60 rich jewel.° Toby approaches; curtsies there to me—

TOBY: Shall this fellow live?

FABIAN: Though our silence be drawn from us with cars, yet peace.

MALVOLIO: I extend my hand to him thus, quenching my familiar smile with an austere regard of control°—

TOBY: And does not Toby take° you a blow o' the lips then?

70 MALVOLIO: Saying, "Cousin Toby, my fortunes having cast me on your niece, give me this prerogative of speech."

TOBY: What, what?

MALVOLIO: "You must amend your drunkenness."

TOBY: Out, scab!

FABIAN: Nay, patience, or we break the sinews of our plot.

MALVOLIO: "Besides, you waste the treasure of your time with a foolish knight"—

80 ANDREW: That's me, I warrant you.

MALVOLIO: "One Sir Andrew"—

ANDREW: I knew 'twas I, for many do call me fool.

MALVOLIO: What employment° have we here?

(Takes up the letter.)

FABIAN: Now is the woodcock° near the gin.°

TOBY: O, peace, and the spirit of humors intimate reading aloud to him!

MALVOLIO: By my life, this is my lady's hand. These be her very C's, her U's, and her T's; and thus makes she her great P's. It is, in contempt of° question, her hand. 90

ANDREW: Her C's, her U's, and her T's? Why that?

MALVOLIO: *(Reads)* "To the unknown beloved, this, and my good wishes." Her very phrases! By your leave, wax.° Soft,° and the impressure her Lucrece,° with which she uses to seal.° 'Tis my lady. To whom should this be?

FABIAN: This wins him, liver and all.

MALVOLIO: *(Reads)*

"Jove knows I love,
But who?
Lips, do not move; 100
No man must know."

"No man must know." What follows? The numbers altered!° "No man must know." If this should be thee, Malvolio?

TOBY: Marry, hang thee, brock!°

MALVOLIO: *(Reads)*

"I may command where I adore,
But silence, like a Lucrece knife,
With bloodless stroke my heart doth gore.
M. O. A. I. doth sway my life."

FABIAN: A fustian° riddle. 110

TOBY: Excellent wench,° say I.

MALVOLIO: "M. O. A. I. doth sway my life." Nay, but first, let me see, let me see, let me see.

FABIAN: What dish o' poison has she dressed° him!

TOBY: And with what wing the staniel checks at it!°

MALVOLIO: "I may command where I adore." Why, she may command me: I serve her; she is my lady. Why, this is evident to any formal capacity.° There is no obstruction° in this. And the end; what should that alphabetical position portend? If I could make that 120 resemble something in me! Softly, "M. O. A. I."

TOBY: O, ay, make up that. He is now at a cold scent.

---

stonebow, crossbow that shoots stones. *branched,* embroidered. *daybed,* sofa. *to have the humor of state,* i.e., to assume an imperious manner. *after a demure travel of regard,* i.e., having glanced gravely over my retainers. *make out for,* i.e., go to fetch. *play with my—some rich jewel,* (Malvolio automatically reaches for his steward's chain and then catches himself). *an austere regard of control,* i.e., a stern look of authority. *take,* give. *employment,* business. *woodcock,* (a proverbially stupid bird). *gin,* snare.

in contempt of, beyond. *By your leave, wax,* i.e., excuse me for breaking the seal. *Soft,* i.e., take it slowly. *the impressure her Lucrece,* i.e., the seal depicts Lucrece (noble Roman matron who stabbed herself after she was raped by Tarquin, hence a symbol of chastity). *uses to seal,* customarily seals. *The numbers altered,* the meter changed (in the stanza that follows). *brock,* badger. *fustian,* i.e., foolish and pretentious. *wench,* i.e., Maria. *dressed,* prepared for. *with what wing the staniel checks at it,* i.e., with what speed the kestrel (a kind of hawk) turns to snatch at the wrong prey. *formal capacity,* normal intelligence. *obstruction,* difficulty.

FABIAN: Sowter will cry upon't for all this, though it be as rank as a fox.°

MALVOLIO: M.—Malvolio. M.—Why, that begins my name.

FABIAN: Did not I say he would work it out? The cur is excellent at faults.°

130 MALVOLIO: M.—But then there is no consonancy in the sequel.° That suffers under probation.° A should follow, but O does.

FABIAN: And O° shall end, I hope.

TOBY: Ay, or I'll cudgel him, and make him cry O.

MALVOLIO: And then I comes behind.

FABIAN: Ay, and you had any eye behind you, you might see more detraction at your heels than fortunes before you.

MALVOLIO: M, O, A, I. This simulation° is not as the former; and yet, to crush° this a little, it would bow

140 to me, for every one of these letters are in my name. Soft, here follows prose.

(Reads) "If this fall into thy hand, revolve.° In my stars° I am above thee, but be not afraid of greatness. Some are born great, some achieve greatness, and some have greatness thrust upon 'em. Thy Fates open their hands; let thy blood and spirit embrace them; and to inure° thyself to what thou art like to be, cast thy humble slough° and appear fresh. Be opposite with° a kinsman, surly with servants. Let thy tongue tang ar-

150 guments of state;° put thyself into the trick of singularity.° She thus advises thee that sighs for thee. Remember who commended thy yellow stockings and wished to see thee ever cross-gartered.° I say, remember. Go to, thou art made, if thou desir'st to be so. If not, let me see thee a steward still, the fellow of servants, and not worthy to touch Fortune's fingers. Farewell. She that would alter services with thee,

THE FORTUNATE UNHAPPY."

Daylight and champian° discovers° not more. This is open. I will be proud, I will read politic authors,° I

160 will baffle° Sir Toby, I will wash off gross° acquain-
tance, I will be point-devise,° the very man. I do not now fool myself, to let imagination jade° me, for every reason excites to this,° that my lady loves me. She did commend my yellow stockings of late, she did praise my leg being cross-gartered; and in this she manifests herself to my love, and with a kind of injunction drives me to these habits of her liking.° I thank my stars, I am happy. I will be strange,° stout,° in yellow stockings, and cross-gart- 170 ered, even with the swiftness of putting on. Jove and my stars be praised. Here is yet a postscript. (Reads) "Thou canst not choose but know who I am. If thou entertain'st° my love, let it appear in thy smiling. Thy smiles become thee well. Therefore in my presence still smile, dear my sweet, I prithee." Jove, I thank thee. I will smile; I will do everything that thou wilt have me.

(Exit.)

FABIAN: I will not give my part of this sport for a pension of thousands to be paid from the Sophy.°

TOBY: I could marry this wench for this device.

ANDREW: So could I too.

TOBY: And ask no other dowry with her but such another jest.

(Enter MARIA.)

ANDREW: Nor I neither.

FABIAN: Here comes my noble gull-catcher.°

TOBY: Wilt thou set thy foot o' my neck?

ANDREW: Or o' mine either?

TOBY: Shall I play° my freedom at tray-trip° and become thy bondslave?   190

ANDREW: I' faith, or I either?

TOBY: Why, thou hast put him in such a dream that, when the image of it leaves him, he must run mad.

MARIA: Nay, but say true, does it work upon him?

TOBY: Like aqua-vitae° with a midwife.

MARIA: If you will, then, see the fruits of the sport, mark his first approach before my lady. He will come to her in yellow stockings, and 'tis a color she abhors, and cross-gartered, a fashion she detests; and he will smile upon her which will now be so unsuitable 200 to her disposition, being addicted to a melancholy as she is, that it cannot but turn him into a notable contempt. If you will see it, follow me.

Sowter will cry . . . as a fox, i.e., the hound will bay after the false scent even though the deceit is gross and clear. *faults,* breaks in the scent. *consonancy in the sequel,* consistency in what follows. *suffers under probation,* does not stand up under scrutiny. *O,* i.e., sound of lamentation. *simulation,* hidden significance. *crush,* force. *revolve,* reflect. *stars,* fortune. *inure,* accustom. *slough,* skin (of a snake). *opposite with,* hostile to. *tang arguments of state,* i.e., resound with topics of statecraft. *trick of singularity,* affectation of eccentricity. *cross-gartered,* i.e., with garters crossed above and below the knee. *champian,* champaign, open country. *discovers,* reveals. *politic authors,* writers on politics. *baffle,* publicly humiliate. *gross,* low.

---

be point-devise, i.e., follow the advice in the letter in every detail. *jade,* trick. *excites to this,* i.e., enforces this conclusion. *these habits of her liking,* this clothing that she likes. *strange,* haughty. *stout,* proud. *entertain'st,* accept. *Sophy,* Shah of Persia (perhaps with reference to Sir Anthony Shirley's visit to the Persian court in 1599, from which he returned laden with gifts and honors). *gull-catcher,* fool-catcher. *play,* gamble. *tray-trip,* (a dice game). *aqua-vitae,* distilled liquors.

TOBY: To the gates of Tartar,° thou most excellent devil
of wit.

ANDREW: I'll make one° too.

(Exeunt.)

ACT 3 / SCENE 1 OLIVIA's *garden.*

(Enter VIOLA *and* CLOWN *[with a tabor].)*

VIOLA: Save thee,° friend, and thy music. Dost thou live
by° thy tabor?°

CLOWN: No, sir, I live by the church.

VIOLA: Art thou a churchman?

CLOWN: No such matter, sir. I do live by the church; for
I do live at my house, and my house doth stand by
the church.

VIOLA: So thou mayst say, the king lies° by a beggar, if
a beggar dwell near him; or, the church stands by°
10 thy tabor, if thy tabor stand by the church.

CLOWN: You have said, sir. To see this age! A sentence
is but a chev'ril° glove to a good wit. How quickly
the wrong side may be turned outward!

VIOLA: Nay, that's certain. They that dally nicely° with
words may quickly make them wanton.°

CLOWN: I would therefore my sister had had no name,
sir.

VIOLA: Why, man?

CLOWN: Why, sir, her name's a word, and to dally with
20 that word might make my sister wanton. But indeed
words are very rascals since bonds disgraced them.°

VIOLA: Thy reason, man?

CLOWN: Troth,° sir, I can yield you none without words,
and words are grown so false I am loath to prove
reason with them.

VIOLA: I warrant thou art a merry fellow and car'st for
nothing.

CLOWN: Not so, sir; I do care for something; but in my
conscience, sir, I do not care for you. If that be to
30 care for nothing, sir, I would it would make you
invisible.

VIOLA: Art not thou the Lady Olivia's fool?

CLOWN: No, indeed, sir. The Lady Olivia has no folly.
She will keep no fool, sir, till she be married; and
fools are as like husbands as pilchers° are to herrings—the husband's the bigger. I am indeed not
her fool, but her corrupter of words.

Tartar, Tartarus (in classical mythology, the infernal
regions). *make one,* i.e., come. *Save thee,* i.e., God save
you. *live by,* gain a living from (but the Clown takes it in
the sense of "reside near"). *tabor,* (1) drum (2) taborn,
tavern. *lies,* sojourns. *stands by,* (1) stands near (2) up-
holds. *chev'ril,* cheveril (i.e., soft kid leather). *dally nicely,*
play subtly. *wanton,* i.e., equivocal in meaning (but the
Clown takes it in the sense of "unchaste"). *since bonds
disgraced them,* i.e., since it was required that a man's word
be guaranteed by a bond (?). *Troth,* by my troth. *pilchers,*
pilchards (a kind of small herring).

VIOLA: I saw thee late at the Count Orsino's.

CLOWN: Foolery, sir, does walk about the orb° like the
sun; it shines everywhere. I would be sorry, sir, but° 40
the fool should be as oft with your master as with
my mistress. I think I saw your wisdom there.

VIOLA: Nay, and thou pass upon me,° I'll no more with
thee. Hold, there's expenses for thee. *(Gives a coin.)*

CLOWN: Now Jove, in his next commodity° of hair, send
thee a beard.

VIOLA: By my troth, I'll tell thee, I am almost sick for
one, though I would not have it grow on my chin.
Is thy lady within?

CLOWN: Would not a pair of these° have bred, sir? 50

VIOLA: Yes, being kept together and put to use.°

CLOWN: I would play Lord Pandarus of Phrygia, sir, to
bring a Cressida to this Troilus.°

VIOLA: I understand you, sir. 'Tis well begged.

(Gives another coin.)

CLOWN: The matter, I hope, is not great, sir, begging
but a beggar: Cressida was a beggar.° My lady is
within, sir. I will conster° to them whence you come.
Who you are and what you would are out of my
welkin;° I might say "element," but the word is
overworn.° *(Exit.)* 60

VIOLA: This fellow is wise enough to play the fool,
And to do that well craves° a kind of wit.°
He must observe their mood on whom he jests,
The quality of persons, and the time;
And,° like the haggard,° check at° every feather
That comes before his eye. This is a practice°
As full of labor as a wise man's art;
For folly that he wisely shows, is fit;
But wise men, folly-fall'n,° quite taint their wit.°

(Enter SIR TOBY *and* [SIR] ANDREW.)

TOBY: Save you, gentleman. 70

VIOLA: And you, sir.

ANDREW: *Dieu vous garde, monsieur.*

---

orb, earth. *but,* but that. *pass upon me,* i.e., make me
the butt of your witticisms. *commodity,* lot, consignment.
these, i.e., coins of the sort that Viola had just given him.
put to use, put out at interest. *I would play . . . this Troilus,*
(in the story of Troilus and Cressida, which supplied both
Chaucer and Shakespeare the plot for major works, Pandarus was the go-between in the disastrous love affair).
Cressida was a beggar, (in Robert Henryson's *Testament of
Cressida,* a kind of sequel to Chaucer's poem, the faithless
heroine became a harlot and a beggar). *conster,* explain.
welkin, sky. *I might say . . . overworn,* (perhaps a thrust at
Ben Jonson, whose fondness for the word "element" had
been ridiculed by other writers). *craves,* requires. *wit,*
intelligence. *And,* (many editors, following Johnson, have
emended this to "not"). *haggard,* untrained hawk. *check
at,* leave the true course and pursue. *practice,* skill. *folly-
fall'n,* having fallen into folly. *taint their wit,* i.e., betray
their common sense.

VIOLA: *Et vous aussi; votre serviteur.*°
ANDREW: I hope, sir, you are, and I am yours.
TOBY: Will you encounter° the house? My niece is desirous you should enter, if your trade be to° her.
VIOLA: I am bound to° your niece, sir; I mean, she is the list° of my voyage.
TOBY: Taste° your legs, sir; put them to motion.
80 VIOLA: My legs do better understand° me, sir, than I understand what you mean by bidding me taste my legs.
TOBY: I mean, to go, sir, to enter.
VIOLA: I will answer you with gait and entrance.° But we are prevented.°

(Enter OLIVIA and GENTLEWOMAN [MARIA].)

Most excellent accomplished lady, the heavens rain odors on you.
ANDREW: That youth's a rare courtier. "Rain odors"—well!°
90 VIOLA: My matter hath no voice,° lady, but to your own most pregnant and vouchsafed ear.
ANDREW: "Odors," "pregnant," and "vouchsafed"—I'll get 'em all three all ready.
OLIVIA: Let the garden door be shut, and leave me to my hearing. *(Exeunt SIR TOBY, SIR ANDREW, and MARIA.)* Give me your hand, sir.
VIOLA: My duty, madam, and most humble service.
OLIVIA: What is your name?
VIOLA: Cesario is your servant's name, fair princess.
100 OLIVIA: My servant, sir? 'Twas never merry world
Since lowly feigning° was called compliment.
Y' are servant to the Count Orsino, youth.
VIOLA: And he is yours, and his must needs be yours.
Your servant's servant is your servant, madam.
OLIVIA: For° him, I think not on him; for his thoughts,
Would they were blanks, rather than filled with me.
VIOLA: Madam, I come to whet your gentle thoughts
On his behalf.
110 OLIVIA: O, by your leave, I pray you.
I bade you never speak again of him;
But, would you undertake another suit,
I had rather hear you to solicit that
Than music from the spheres.°
VIOLA: Dear lady—

OLIVIA: Give me leave,° beseech you. I did send,
After the last enchantment you did here,
A ring in chase of you. So did I abuse°
Myself, my servant, and, I fear me, you.
Under your hard construction° must I sit,   120
To force that on you in a shameful cunning
Which you knew none of yours. What might you think?
Have you not set mine honor at the stake
And baited it with all th' unmuzzled thoughts°
That tyrannous heart can think? To one of your receiving°
Enough is shown; a cypress,° not a bosom,
Hides my heart. So, let me hear you speak.
VIOLA: I pity you.
OLIVIA: That's a degree° to love.
VIOLA: No, not a grize;° for 'tis a vulgar proof°   130
That very oft we pity enemies.
OLIVIA: Why then, methinks 'tis time to smile again.
O world, how apt the poor are to be proud.
If one should be a prey, how much the better
To fall before the lion than the wolf. *(Clock strikes.)*
The clock upbraids me with the waste of time.
Be not afraid, good youth, I will not have you,
And yet, when wit and youth is come to harvest,°
Your wife is like to reap a proper° man.
There lies your way, due west.°   140
VIOLA: Then westward ho!°
Grace and good disposition° attend your ladyship.
You'll nothing, madam, to my lord by me?
OLIVIA: Stay.
I prithee tell me what thou think'st of me.
VIOLA: That you do think you are not what you are.°
OLIVIA: If I think so, I think the same of you.°
VIOLA: Then think you right. I am not what I am.
OLIVIA: I would you were as I would have you be.
VIOLA: Would it be better, madam, than I am?   150
I wish it might, for now I am your fool.°
OLIVIA: O, what a deal of scorn looks beautiful
In the contempt and anger of his lip.
A murd'rous guilt shows not itself more soon

Dieu vous garde . . . votre serviteur, God protect you, sir./And you also; your servant. *encounter,* approach. *trade be to,* business be with. *bound to,* bound for (carrying on the metaphor in "trade"). *list,* destination. *Taste,* try. *understand,* i.e., stand under, support. *with gait and entrance,* by going and entering (with a pun on "gate"). *prevented,* anticipated. *well,* i.e., well put. *matter hath no voice,* i.e., business must not be revealed. *lowly feigning,* affected humility. *For,* as for. *music from the spheres,* i.e., the alleged celestial harmony of the revolving stars and planets.

Give me leave, i.e., do not interrupt me. *abuse,* deceive. *hard construction,* harsh interpretation. *set mine honor . . . . unmuzzled thoughts,* (the metaphor is from the Elizabethan sport of bearbaiting, in which a bear was tied to a stake and harassed by savage dogs). *receiving,* i.e., perception. *cypress,* gauzelike material. *degree,* step. *grize,* step. *vulgar proof,* i.e., common knowledge. *when wit and youth is come to harvest,* i.e., when you are mature. *proper,* handsome. *due west,* (Olivia is perhaps implying that the sun of her life—Cesario's love—is about to vanish). *westward ho,* (cry of Thames watermen). *good disposition,* i.e., tranquillity of mind. *That you do think you are not what you are,* i.e., that you think you are in love with a man, and are not. *If I think so, I think the same of you,* (Olivia misconstrues Viola's remark to mean that she is out of her mind). *I am your fool,* i.e., you are making a fool of me.

Than love that would seem hid: love's night is
    noon.°
Cesario, by the roses of the spring,
By maidhood,° honor, truth, and everything,
I love thee so that, maugre° all thy pride,
Nor wit nor reason can my passion hide.
160 Do not extort thy reasons from this clause,°
For that° I woo, thou therefore hast no cause;°
But rather reason thus with reason fetter,
Love sought is good, but given unsought is better.
VIOLA: By innocence I swear, and by my youth,
I have one heart, one bosom, and one truth,
And that no woman has; nor never none
Shall mistress be of it, save I alone.
And so adieu, good madam. Never more
Will I my master's tears to you deplore.
170 OLIVIA: Yet come again; for thou perhaps mayst move
That heart which now abhors to like his love.

(Exeunt.)

ACT 3 / SCENE 2 OLIVIA'S *house.*

(Enter SIR TOBY, SIR ANDREW, *and* FABIAN.*)*

ANDREW: No, faith, I'll not stay a jot longer.
TOBY: Thy reason, dear venom; give thy reason.
FABIAN: You must needs yield° your reason, Sir An-
    drew.
ANDREW: Marry, I saw your niece do more favors to the
    Count's servingman than ever she bestowed upon
    me. I saw't i' th' orchard.
TOBY: Did she see thee the while, old boy? Tell me that.
ANDREW: As plain as I see you now.
10 FABIAN: This was a great argument° of love in her to-
    ward you.
ANDREW: 'Slight, will you make an ass o' me?
FABIAN: I will prove it legitimate,° sir, upon the oaths
    of judgment and reason.
TOBY: And they have been grand-jurymen since before
    Noah was a sailor.
FABIAN: She did show favor to the youth in your sight
    only to exasperate you, to awake your dormouse°
    valor, to put fire in your heart and brimstone in
20 your liver. You should then have accosted her, and
    with some excellent jests, fire-new from the mint,
    you should have banged the youth into dumbness.
    This was looked for at your hand, and this was
    balked.° The double gilt° of this opportunity you
    let time wash off, and you are now sailed into the

North of my lady's opinion,° where you will hang
    like an icicle on a Dutchman's beard° unless you do
    redeem it by some laudable attempt either of valor
    or policy.°
ANDREW: And't be any way, it must be with valor; for   30
    policy I hate. I had as lief be a Brownist° as a poli-
    tician.°
TOBY: Why then, build me thy fortunes upon the basis
    of valor. Challenge me the Count's youth to fight
    with him; hurt him in eleven places. My niece shall
    take note of it, and assure thyself there is no love-
    broker in the world can° more prevail in man's
    commendation with woman than report of valor.
FABIAN: There is no way but this, Sir Andrew.
ANDREW: Will either of you bear me a challenge to him?   40
TOBY: Go, write it in a martial hand. Be curst° and brief;
    it is no matter how witty, so it be eloquent and full
    of invention. Taunt him with the license of ink.° If
    thou thou'st° him some thrice, it shall not be amiss;
    and as many lies as will lie in thy sheet of paper,
    although the sheet were big enough for the bed of
    Ware° in England, set 'em down. Go about it. Let
    there be gall enough in thy ink, though thou write
    with a goose-pen, no matter. About it!
ANDREW: Where shall I find you?   50
TOBY: We'll call thee at the cubiculo.° Go.

(Exit SIR ANDREW.*)*

FABIAN: This is a dear manikin° to you, Sir Toby.
TOBY: I have been dear to him,° lad, some two thousand
    strong or so.
FABIAN: We shall have a rare letter from him, but you'll
    not deliver't?
TOBY: Never trust me then; and by all means stir on
    the youth to an answer. I think oxen and wainropes°
    cannot hale them together. For Andrew, if he were
    opened, and you find so much blood in his liver as   60
    will clog the foot of a flea, I'll eat the rest of th'
    anatomy.°
FABIAN: And his opposite,° the youth, bears in his visage
    no great presage of cruelty.

(Enter MARIA.*)*

---

love's night is noon, i.e., love is apparent even when it
is hidden. *maidhood,* maidenhood. *maugre,* despite.
clause, premise. *For that,* that because. *cause,* i.e., to
accept my love. *yield,* give. *great argument,* strong evidence. *legitimate,* valid. *dormouse,* i.e., sleepy. *balked,*
let slip. *gilt,* plating.

the North of my lady's opinion, i.e., her frosty disdain.
an icicle on a Dutchman's beard, (perhaps an allusion to the
arctic voyage [1596–97] of the Dutchman Willem Barents,
an account of which was registered for publication in 1598).
policy, intrigue, trickery. *Brownist,* follower of William
Browne, a reformer who advocated the separation of
church and state. *politician,* schemer. *can,* i.e., that can.
curst, petulant. *the license of ink,* i.e., the freedom that
writing permits. *thou'st,* i.e., use the familiar "thou" instead of the more formal "you." *the bed of Ware,* a famous
bedstead, almost eleven feet square, formerly in an inn at
Ware in Herfordshire. *cubiculo,* little chamber. *manikin,*
puppet. *been dear to him,* i.e., spent his money. *wain-
ropes,* wagon ropes. *anatomy,* cadaver. *opposite,* adversary.

TOBY: Look where the youngest wren° of mine° comes.

MARIA: If you desire the spleen,° and will laugh yourselves into stitches, follow me. Yond gull Malvolio
is turned heathen, a very renegado; for there is no
Christian that means to be saved by believing rightly
70 can ever believe such impossible passages of grossness.° He's in yellow stockings.

TOBY: And cross-gartered?

MARIA: Most villainously; like a pedant that keeps a
school i' th' church. I have dogged him like his
murderer. He does obey every point of the letter
that I dropped to betray him. He does smile his
face into more lines than is in the new map with
the augmentation of the Indies.° You have not seen
such a thing as 'tis. I can hardly forbear hurling
80 things at him. I know my lady will strike him. If she
do, he'll smile, and take't for a great favor.

TOBY: Come bring us, bring us where he is.

(Exeunt omnes.)

ACT 3 / SCENE 3 *A street.*

(Enter SEBASTIAN *and* ANTONIO.)

SEBASTIAN: I would not by my will have troubled you;
But since you make your pleasure of your pains,
I will no further chide you.

ANTONIO: I could not stay behind you. My desire
(More sharp than filèd steel) did spur me forth;
And not all love to see you (though so much
As might have drawn one to a longer voyage)
But jealousy° what might befall your travel,
Being skilless in° these parts; which to a stranger,
10 Unguided and unfriended, often prove
Rough and unhospitable. My willing love,
The rather by these arguments of fear,°
Set forth in your pursuit.

SEBASTIAN: My kind Antonio,
I can no other answer make but thanks,

And thanks, and ever oft good turns°
Are shuffled off with such uncurrent° pay.
But, were my worth° as is my conscience firm,
You should find better dealing. What's to do?
Shall we go see the relics of this town?   20

ANTONIO: Tomorrow, sir; best first go see your
lodging.

SEBASTIAN: I am not weary, and 'tis long to night.
I pray you let us satisfy our eyes
With the memorials and the things of fame
That do renown this city.

ANTONIO: Would you'ld pardon° me.
I do not without danger walk these streets.
Once in a sea-fight 'gainst the Count his galleys°
I did some service; of such note indeed   30
That, were I ta'en here, it would scarce be
answered.°

SEBASTIAN: Belike you slew great number of his
people?

ANTONIO: Th' offense is not of such a bloody nature,
Albeit the quality° of the time and quarrel
Might well have given us bloody argument.°
It might have since been answered° in repaying
What we took from them, which for traffic's° sake
Most of our city did. Only myself stood out;   40
For which, if I be lapsèd° in this place,
I shall pay dear.

SEBASTIAN: Do not then walk too open.

ANTONIO: It doth not fit me. Hold, sir, here's my
purse.
In the south suburbs at the Elephant°
Is best to lodge. I will bespeak our diet,°
Whiles° you beguile the time and feed your
knowledge
With viewing of the town. There shall you have° me.   50

SEBASTIAN: Why I your purse?

ANTONIO: Haply your eye shall light upon some toy°
You have desire to purchase, and your store°
I think is not for idle markets,° sir.

SEBASTIAN: I'll be your purse-bearer, and leave you for
An hour.

ANTONIO: To th' Elephant.

SEBASTIAN: I do remember.

(Exeunt.)

---

youngest wren, i.e., smallest of small birds. **mine,** (most editors adopt Theobald's emendation "nine"). **spleen,** i.e., a fit of laughter. **impossible passages of grossness,** i.e., improbabilities. **the new map with the augmentation of the Indies,** (presumably a map, prepared under the supervision of Richard Hakluyt and others and published about 1600, that employed the principles of projection and showed North America and the East Indies in fuller detail than any earlier map. It was conspicuous for the rhumb lines marking the meridians). **jealousy,** anxiety. **skilless in,** unacquainted with. **The rather by these arguments of fear,** i.e., reinforced by my solicitude for your safety.

And thanks, and ever oft good turns, (the fact that this line is a foot too short has prompted a wide variety of emendations, the most popular of which has been Theobald's "And thanks, and ever thanks; and oft good turns." Later Folios omit this and the following line altogether). **uncurrent,** worthless. **worth,** resources. **pardon,** excuse. **the Count his galleys,** the Count's warships. **answered,** defended. **quality,** circumstances. **argument,** cause. **answered,** compensated. **traffic's,** trade's. **lapsèd,** surprised and apprehended. **Elephant,** an inn. **bespeak our diet,** i.e., arrange for our meals. **Whiles,** while. **have,** find. **toy,** trifle. **store,** wealth. **idle markets,** unnecessary purchases.

ACT 3 / SCENE 4 OLIVIA's *garden.*

(Enter OLIVIA *and* MARIA.*)*

OLIVIA: I have sent after him. He says he'll come:°
How shall I feast him? What bestow of° him?
For youth is bought more oft than begged or
borrowed.
I speak too loud. Where's Malvolio? He is sad and
civil,°
And suits well for a servant with my fortunes.
Where is Malvolio?

MARIA: He's coming, madam, but in very strange manner. He is sure possessed,° madam.

OLIVIA: Why, what's the matter? Does he rave?

MARIA: No, madam, he does nothing but smile. Your
10   ladyship were best to have some guard about you
if he come, for sure the man is tainted in 's wits.

OLIVIA: Go call him hither. I am as mad as he,
If sad and merry madness equal be.

(Enter MALVOLIO.*)*

How now, Malvolio?

MALVOLIO: Sweet lady, ho, ho!

OLIVIA: Smil'st thou? I sent for thee upon a sad° occasion.

MALVOLIO: Sad, lady? I could be sad. This does make
some obstruction in the blood, this cross-gartering;
20   but what of that? If it please the eye of one, it is
with me as the very true sonnet° is, "Please one, and
please all."°

OLIVIA: Why, how dost thou, man? What is the matter
with thee?

MALVOLIO: Not black in my mind, though yellow in my
legs. It did come to his hands, and commands shall
be executed. I think we do know the sweet Roman
hand.°

OLIVIA: Wilt thou go to bed, Malvolio?

30   MALVOLIO: To bed? Ay, sweetheart, and I'll come to
thee.

OLIVIA: God comfort thee. Why dost thou smile so, and
kiss thy hand so oft?

MARIA: How do you, Malvolio?

MALVOLIO: At your request? Yes, nightingales answer
daws!°

MARIA: Why appear you with this ridiculous boldness
before my lady?

MALVOLIO: "Be not afraid of greatness." 'Twas well writ.

OLIVIA: What mean'st thou by that, Malvolio?   40

MALVOLIO: "Some are born great."

OLIVIA: Ha?

MALVOLIO: "Some achieve greatness."

OLIVIA: What say'st thou?

MALVOLIO: "And some have greatness thrust upon
them."

OLIVIA: Heaven restore thee!

MALVOLIO: "Remember who commended thy yellow
stockings."

OLIVIA: Thy yellow stockings?   50

MALVOLIO: "And wished to see thee cross-gartered."

OLIVIA: Cross-gartered?

MALVOLIO: "Go to, thou art made, if thou desir'st to be
so."

OLIVIA: Am I made?

MALVOLIO: "If not, let me see thee a servant still."

OLIVIA: Why, this is very midsummer madness.°

(Enter SERVANT.*)*

SERVANT: Madam, the young gentleman of the Count
Orsino's is returned. I could hardly entreat him
back. He attends your ladyship's pleasure.   60

OLIVIA: I'll come to him. *(Exit* SERVANT.*)* Good Maria,
let this fellow be looked to. Where's my cousin
Toby? Let some of my people have a special care
of him. I would not have him miscarry° for the half
of my dowry.

*(Exit [*OLIVIA, *accompanied by* MARIA*].)*

MALVOLIO: O ho, do you come near me° now? No worse
man than Sir Toby to look to me. This concurs
directly with the letter. She sends him on purpose,
that I may appear stubborn° to him; for she incites
me to that in the letter. "Cast thy humble slough,"
says she; "be opposite with a kinsman, surly with
servants; let thy tongue tang with arguments of
state; put thyself into the trick of singularity." And
consequently sets down the manner how: as, a sad
face, a reverend carriage, a slow tongue, in the
habit° of some sir° of note, and so forth. I have
limed° her; but it is Jove's doing, and Jove make
me thankful. And when she went away now, "Let
this fellow° be looked to." "Fellow." Not "Malvolio,"
nor after my degree,° but "fellow." Why, everything   80

He says he'll come, suppose he says he'll come. *of,* on.
sad and civil, grave and formal. *possessed,* i.e., with a devil,
mad. *sad,* serious. *sonnet,* (any short lyric poem). *Please*
one, and please all, i.e., so long as I please the one I love I
do not care about the rest (from "A prettie newe Ballad,
intytuled: The Crow sits vpon the wall, Please one and
please all"). *the sweet Roman hand,* i.e., italic writing, an
elegant cursive script more fashionable than the crabbed
"secretary hand" commonly used in Shakespeare's time.
At . . . daws, i.e., should I reply to a mere servant like you?
Yes, for sometimes nightingales answer jackdaws.

midsummer madness, extreme folly, Midsummer Eve
(June 23) being traditionally associated with irresponsible
and eccentric behavior. *miscarry,* come to harm. *come*
near me, i.e., begin to understand my importance. *stub-*
born, hostile. *habit,* clothing. *sir,* personage. *limed,*
caught (as birds are caught with sticky birdlime). *fellow,*
(1) menial (2) associate (the sense in which Malvolio takes
the word). *after my degree,* according to my status.

adheres together, that no dram° of a scruple,° no scruple of a scruple, no obstacle, no incredulous or unsafe° circumstance—what can be said?
Nothing that can be can come between me and the
full prospect of my hopes. Well, Jove, not I, is the
doer of this, and he is to be thanked.

*(Enter [*SIR*]* TOBY, FABIAN, *and* MARIA.*)*

TOBY: Which way is he, in the name of sanctity? If all
the devils of hell be drawn in little,° and Legion°
himself possessed him, yet I'll speak to him.

90　FABIAN: Here he is, here he is! How is't with you, sir?

TOBY: How is't with you, man?°

MALVOLIO: Go off; I discard you. Let me enjoy my private.° Go off.

MARIA: Lo, how hollow the fiend speaks within him!
Did not I tell you? Sir Toby, my lady prays you to
have a care of him.

MALVOLIO: Aha, does she so?

TOBY: Go to, go to; peace, peace; we must deal gently
with him. Let me alone. How do you, Malvolio?

100　How is't with you? What, man, defy the devil? Consider, he's an enemy to mankind.

MALVOLIO: Do you know what you say?

MARIA: La you, and you speak ill of the devil, how he
takes it at heart. Pray God he be not bewitched.

FABIAN: Carry his water to th' wise woman.°

MARIA: Marry, and it shall be done tomorrow morning
if I live. My lady would not lose him for more than
I'll say.

MALVOLIO: How now, mistress?

110　MARIA: O Lord.

TOBY: Prithee hold thy peace. This is not the way. Do
you not see you move° him? Let me alone with him.

FABIAN: No way but gentleness; gently, gently. The
fiend is rough° and will not be roughly used.

TOBY: Why, how now, my bawcock?° How dost thou,
chuck?°

MALVOLIO: Sir.

TOBY: Ay, biddy, come with me. What, man, 'tis not for
gravity to play at cherry-pit with Satan.° Hang him,
120　foul collier!°

---

　　dram, (1) minute part (2) apothecary's measure for
one-eighth of an ounce. ***scruple,*** (1) doubt (2) apothecary's
measure for one-third of a dram. ***incredulous or unsafe,***
incredible or doubtful. ***in little,*** in small compass. ***Legion,***
a group of devils (see Mark 5:8–9). ***How is't with you, man,***
(the Folio implausibly assigns this speech to Fabian, but the
contemptuous "man" suggests that the speaker must be
Malvolio's social superior). ***private,*** privacy. ***Carry his
water to th' wise woman,*** i.e., for analysis. ***move,*** agitate.
rough, violent. ***bawcock,*** fine fellow (French *beau coq*).
chuck, chick. ***'tis not for gravity . . . Satan,*** i.e., it is unsuitable for a man of your dignity to play a children's game
with Satan. ***collier,*** vendor of coals.

MARIA: Get him to say his prayers; good Sir Toby, get
him to pray.

MALVOLIO: My prayers, minx?

MARIA: No, I warrant you, he will not hear of godliness.

MALVOLIO: Go hang yourselves all! You are idle° shallow
things; I am not of your element.° You shall know
more hereafter. *(Exit.)*

TOBY: Is't possible?

FABIAN: If this were played upon a stage now, I could
condemn it as an improbable fiction.　　　　　130

TOBY: His very genius° hath taken the infection of the
device, man.

MARIA: Nay, pursue him now, lest the device take air
and taint.°

FABIAN: Why, we shall make him mad indeed.

MARIA: The house will be the quieter.

TOBY: Come, we'll have him in a dark room and bound.
My niece is already in the belief that he's mad. We
may carry it° thus, for our pleasure and his penance, till our very pastime, tired out of breath,　140
prompt us to have mercy on him; at which time we
will bring the device to the bar and crown thee for
a finder of madmen. But see, but see.

(Enter SIR ANDREW.*)*

FABIAN: More matter for a May morning.°

ANDREW: Here's the challenge; read it. I warrant there's
vinegar and pepper in't.

FABIAN: Is't so saucy?°

ANDREW: Ay, is't, I warrant him. Do but read.

TOBY: Give me. *(Reads)* "Youth, whatsoever thou art,
thou art but a scurvy fellow."　　　　　　　　150

FABIAN: Good, and valiant.

TOBY: *(Reads)* "Wonder not nor admire° not in thy
mind why I do call thee so, for I will show thee no
reason for't."

FABIAN: A good note that keeps you from the blow of
the law.

TOBY: *(Reads)* "Thou com'st to the Lady Olivia, and in
my sight she uses thee kindly. But thou liest in thy
throat; that is not the matter I challenge thee for."

FABIAN: Very brief, and to exceeding good sense—less.　160

TOBY: *(Reads)* "I will waylay thee going home; where if
it be thy chance to kill me"—

FABIAN: Good.

TOBY: *(Reads)* "Thou kill'st me like a rogue and a villain."

FABIAN: Still you keep o' th' windy side of the law.°
Good.

---

　　idle, trifling. ***element,*** sphere. ***genius,*** nature, personality. ***take air and taint,*** be exposed and spoiled. ***carry
it,*** i.e., go on with the joke. ***More matter for a May morning,***
i.e., another subject for a May-Day pageant. ***saucy,*** i.e.,
with "vinegar and pepper." ***admire,*** marvel. ***o' th' windy
side of the law,*** i.e., safe from prosecution.

TOBY: (Reads) "Fare thee well, and God have mercy
upon one of our souls. He may have mercy upon
170 mine, but my hope is better, and so look to thyself.
Thy friend, as thou usest him, and thy sworn enemy,   ANDREW AGUECHEEK."
If this letter move him not, his legs cannot. I'll give't
him.
MARIA: You may have very fit occasion for't. He is now
in some commerce° with my lady and will by and
by depart.
TOBY: Go, Sir Andrew. Scout me for him at the corner
of the orchard like a bum-baily.° So soon as ever
180 thou seest him, draw; and as thou draw'st, swear
horrible; for it comes to pass oft that a terrible oath,
with a swaggering accent sharply twanged off, gives
manhood more approbation° than ever proof° itself
would have earned him. Away!
ANDREW: Nay, let me alone for swearing.° (Exit.)
TOBY: Now will not I deliver his letter; for the behavior
of the young gentleman gives him out to be of good
capacity and breeding; his employment between his
lord and my niece confirms no less. Therefore this
190 letter, being so excellently ignorant, will breed no
terror in the youth. He will find it comes from a
clodpoll.° But, sir, I will deliver his challenge by
word of mouth, set upon Aguecheek a notable report of valor, and drive the gentleman (as I know
his youth will aptly receive it) into a most hideous
opinion of his rage, skill, fury, and impetuosity.
This will so fright them both that they will kill one
another by the look, like cockatrices.°

(Enter OLIVIA and VIOLA.)

FABIAN: Here he comes with your niece. Give them way
200 till he take leave, and presently after him.°
TOBY: I will meditate the while upon some horrid message for a challenge.

(Exeunt SIR TOBY, FABIAN, and MARIA.)

OLIVIA: I have said too much unto a heart of stone
And laid mine honor too unchary° on't.
There's something in me that reproves my fault;
But such a headstrong potent fault it is
That it but mocks reproof.
VIOLA: With the same havior° that your passion bears
Goes on my master's griefs.
210 OLIVIA: Here, wear this jewel° for me; 'tis my picture.
Refuse it not; it hath no tongue to vex you.

And I beseech you come again tomorrow.
What shall you ask of me that I'll deny,
That honor, saved, may upon asking give?
VIOLA: Nothing but this: your true love for my master.
OLIVIA: How with mine honor may I give him that
Which I have given to you?
VIOLA: I will acquit you.
OLIVIA: Well, come again tomorrow. Fare thee well.
A fiend like thee° might bear my soul to hell.   220

(Exit.)

(Enter [SIR] TOBY and FABIAN.)

TOBY: Gentleman, God save thee.
VIOLA: And you, sir.
TOBY: That defense thou hast, betake thee to't. Of what
nature the wrongs are thou hast done him, I know
not; but thy intercepter, full of despite,° bloody as
the hunter,° attends° thee at the orchard end. Dismount thy tuck,° be yare° in thy preparation, for
thy assailant is quick, skillful, and deadly.
VIOLA: You mistake, sir. I am sure no man hath any
quarrel to me. My remembrance is very free and   230
clear from any image of offense done to any man.
TOBY: You'll find it otherwise, I assure you. Therefore,
if you hold your life at any price, betake you to your
guard; for your opposite° hath in him what youth,
strength, skill, and wrath can furnish man withal.°
VIOLA: I pray you, sir, what is he?
TOBY: He is knight, dubbed with unhatched° rapier and
on carpet consideration,° but he is a devil in private
brawl. Souls and bodies hath he divorced three;
and his incensement at this moment is so implacable   240
that satisfaction can be none but by pangs of death
and sepulcher. "Hob, nob"° is his word; "give't or
take't."
VIOLA: I will return again into the house and desire
some conduct° of the lady. I am no fighter. I have
heard of some kind of men that put quarrels purposely on others to taste° their valor. Belike this is
a man of that quirk.
TOBY: Sir, no. His indignation derives itself out of a
very competent° injury; therefore get you on and   250
give him his desire. Back you shall not to the house,
unless you undertake that with me which with as
much safety you might answer him. Therefore on,
or strip your sword stark naked; for meddle° you
must, that's certain, or forswear to wear iron about
you.

---

commerce, conversation. **bum-baily,** bailiff, sheriff's
officer. **approbation,** attestation. **proof,** actual trial. **let
me alone for swearing,** i.e., do not worry about my ability at
swearing. **clodpoll,** dunce. **cockatrices,** fabulous serpents
that could kill with a glance. **Give them way . . . after him,**
i.e., do not interrupt them until he goes, and then follow
him at once. **unchary,** carelessly. **havior,** behavior. **jewel,**
i.e., jeweled locket (?).

like thee, i.e., with your attractions. **despite,** defiance.
bloody as the hunter, i.e., bloodthirsty as a hunting dog.
attends, awaits. **Dismount thy tuck,** unsheathe your rapier.
yare, quick, prompt. **opposite,** adversary. **withal,** with.
unhatched, unhacked. **on carpet consideration,** i.e., not
because of his exploits in the field but through connections
at court. **Hob, nob,** have it, or have it not. **conduct,** escort.
taste, test. **competent,** sufficient. **meddle,** engage him,
fight.

VIOLA: This is as uncivil as strange. I beseech you do me this courteous office, as to know of the knight what my offense to him is. It is something of my negligence,° nothing of my purpose.

260

TOBY: I will do so. Signior Fabian, stay you by this gentleman till my return. (*Exit* [SIR] TOBY.)

VIOLA: Pray you, sir, do you know of this matter?

FABIAN: I know the knight is incensed against you, even to a mortal arbitrament;° but nothing of the circumstance more.

VIOLA: I beseech you, what manner of man is he?

FABIAN: Nothing of that wonderful promise, to read him by his form, as you are like to find him in the proof of his valor. He is indeed, sir, the most skillful, bloody, and fatal opposite that you could possibly have found in any part of Illyria. Will you walk towards him? I will make your peace with him if I can.

270

VIOLA: I shall be much bound to you for't. I am one that had rather go with sir priest than sir knight. I care not who knows so much of my mettle.° (*Exeunt.*°)

(*Enter* [SIR] TOBY *and* [SIR] ANDREW.)

TOBY: Why, man, he's a very devil; I have not seen such a firago.° I had a pass° with him, rapier, scabbard, and all, and he gives me the stuck-in° with such a mortal motion° that it is inevitable; and on the answer° he pays you as surely as your feet hits the ground they step on. They say he has been fencer to the Sophy.°

280

ANDREW: Pox on't, I'll not meddle with him.

TOBY: Ay, but he will not now be pacified. Fabian can scarce hold him yonder.

ANDREW: Plague on't, and I thought he had been valiant, and so cunning in fence,° I'd have seen him damned ere I'd have challenged him. Let him let the matter slip, and I'll give him my horse, gray Capilet.

290

TOBY: I'll make the motion.° Stand here; make a good show on't. This shall end without the perdition of souls.° (*Aside*) Marry, I'll ride your horse as well as I ride you.

(*Enter* FABIAN *and* VIOLA.)

I have his horse to take up° the quarrel. I have persuaded him the youth's a devil.

FABIAN: He is as horribly conceited of him,° and pants and looks pale, as if a bear were at his heels.

300

TOBY: There's no remedy, sir; he will fight with you for's oath° sake. Marry, he hath better bethought him of his quarrel,° and he finds that now scarce to be worth talking of. Therefore draw for the supportance of his vow.° He protests he will not hurt you.

VIOLA: (*Aside*) Pray God defend me! A little thing would make me tell them how much I lack of a man.

FABIAN: Give ground if you see him furious.

TOBY: Come, Sir Andrew, there's no remedy. The gentleman will for his honor's sake have one bout with you; he cannot by the duello° avoid it; but he has promised me, as he is a gentleman and a soldier, he will not hurt you. Come on, to't.

310

ANDREW: Pray God he keep his oath! (*Draws.*)

(*Enter* ANTONIO.)

VIOLA: I do assure you 'tis against my will. (*Draws.*)

ANTONIO: Put up your sword. If this young gentleman
Have done offense, I take the fault on me;
If you offend him, I for him defy you.

TOBY: You, sir? Why, what are you?

ANTONIO: (*Draws*) One, sir, that for his love dares yet do more
Than you have heard him brag to you he will.

TOBY: Nay, if you be an undertaker,° I am for you.

320

(*Draws.*)

(*Enter* OFFICERS.)

FABIAN: O good Sir Toby, hold. Here come the officers.

TOBY: (*To* ANTONIO) I'll be with you anon.

VIOLA: (*To* SIR ANDREW) Pray, sir, put your sword up, if you please.

ANDREW: Marry, will I, sir; and for that° I promised you, I'll be as good as my word. He will bear you easily, and reins well.

330

FIRST OFFICER: This is the man; do thy office.°

SECOND OFFICER: Antonio, I arrest thee at the suit
Of Count Orsino.

ANTONIO: You do mistake me, sir.

FIRST OFFICER: No, sir, no jot. I know your favor° well,
Though now you have no sea-cap on your head.
Take him away. He knows I know him well.

ANTONIO: I must obey. (*To* VIOLA) This comes with seeking you.

---

of my negligence, unintentional. **mortal arbitrament,** deadly trial. **mettle,** character, disposition. **Exeunt,** (this stage direction, which leaves the stage empty, properly marks the ending of the scene, but the new scene that opens with the entrance of Sir Toby and Sir Andrew is not indicated as such in the Folio). **firago,** virago (probably a phonetic spelling). **pass,** bout. **stuck-in,** stoccado, thrust. **mortal motion,** deadly pass. **answer,** return. **Sophy,** Shah. **in fence,** at fencing. **motion,** proposal. **perdition of souls,** i.e., loss of life. **take up,** settle.

He is as horribly conceited of him, i.e., Cesario has just as terrifying a notion of Sir Andrew. **oath,** oath's. **his quarrel,** the cause of his resentment. **Therefore draw for the supportance of his vow,** i.e., make a show of valor merely for the satisfaction of his oath. **duello,** duelling code. **an undertaker,** one who takes up a challenge for another (with perhaps a pun on "undertaker" as a government agent, i.e., scoundrel). **for that,** as for what (i.e., his horse, "gray Capilet"). **office,** duty. **favor,** face.

But there's no remedy; I shall answer it.°
What will you do, now my necessity
Makes me to ask you for my purse? It grieves me
Much more for what I cannot do for you
Than what befalls myself. You stand amazed,
But be of comfort.
SECOND OFFICER: Come, sir, away.
ANTONIO: I must entreat of you some of that money.
VIOLA: What money, sir?
350   For the fair kindness you have showed me here,
And part° being prompted by your present trouble,
Out of my lean and low ability
I'll lend you something. My having is not much.
I'll make division of my present° with you.
Hold, there's half my coffer.°
ANTONIO: Will you deny me now?
Is't possible that my deserts to you
Can lack persuasion?° Do not tempt my misery,
Lest that it make me so unsound° a man
360   As to upbraid you with those kindnesses
That I have done for you.
VIOLA: I know of none,
Nor know I you by voice or any feature.
I hate ingratitude more in a man
Than lying, vainness,° babbling, drunkenness,
Or any taint of vice whose strong corruption
Inhabits our frail blood.
ANTONIO: O heavens themselves!
SECOND OFFICER: Come, sir, I pray you go.
370 ANTONIO: Let me speak a little. This youth that you
     see here
I snatched one half out of the jaws of death;
Relieved him with such sanctity of love,
And to his image, which methought did promise
Most venerable° worth, did I devotion.
FIRST OFFICER: What's that to us? The time goes by.
     Away.
ANTONIO: But, O, how vild° an idol proves this god!
Thou hast, Sebastian, done good feature° shame.
380   In nature there's no blemish but the mind;°
None can be called deformed but the unkind.°
Virtue is beauty; but the beauteous evil
Are empty trunks,° o'erflourished° by the devil.
FIRST OFFICER: The man grows mad; away with him!
     Come, come, sir.
ANTONIO: Lead me on. *(Exit [with* OFFICERS].*)*
VIOLA: Methinks his words do from such passion fly

That he believes himself; so do not I.
Prove true, imagination, O, prove true,
That I, dear brother, be now ta'en for you!   390
TOBY: Come hither, knight; come hither, Fabian. We'll
     whisper o'er a couplet or two of most sage saws.°
VIOLA: He named Sebastian. I my brother know
Yet living in my glass.° Even such and so
In favor was my brother, and he went
Still in this fashion, color, ornament,
For him I imitate. O, if it prove,
Tempests are kind, and salt waves fresh in love! *(Exit.)*
TOBY: A very dishonest° paltry boy, and more a cow-
     ard than a hare. His dishonesty appears in leaving   400
     his friend here in necessity and denying him; and
     for his cowardship, ask Fabian.
FABIAN: A coward, a most devout coward; religious in
     it.°
ANDREW: 'Slid,° I'll after him again and beat him.
TOBY: Do; cuff him soundly, but never draw thy sword.
ANDREW: And I do not— *(Exit.)*
FABIAN: Come, let's see the event.°
TOBY: I dare lay any money 'twill be nothing yet.°

(Exit [with SIR ANDREW *and* FABIAN].*)*

ACT 4 / SCENE 1 *Before* OLIVIA's *house.*

(Enter SEBASTIAN *and* CLOWN.*)*

CLOWN: Will you make me believe that I am not sent
     for you?
SEBASTIAN: Go to, go to, thou art a foolish fellow. Let
     me be clear of thee.
CLOWN: Well held out,° i' faith! No, I do not know you;
     nor I am not sent to you by my lady, to bid you
     come speak with her; nor your name is not Master
     Cesario; nor this is not my nose neither. Nothing
     that is so is so.
SEBASTIAN: I prithee vent thy folly somewhere else.   10
     Thou know'st not me.
CLOWN: Vent my folly! He has heard that word of some
     great man, and now applies it to a fool. Vent my
     folly! I am afraid this great lubber,° the world, will
     prove a cockney.° I prithee now, ungird thy strange-
     ness,° and tell me what I shall vent° to my lady. Shall
     I vent to her that thou art coming?
SEBASTIAN: I prithee, foolish Greek,° depart from me.
     There's money for thee. If you tarry longer, I shall
     give worse payment.   20

---

answer it, i.e., try to defend myself against the accusation. *part,* partly. *present,* present resources. *coffer,*
chest, i.e., money. *deserts to you/Can lack persuasion,*
claims on you can fail to be persuasive. *unsound,* weak,
unmanly. *vainness,* (1) falseness (2) boasting. *venerable,*
worthy of veneration. *vild,* vile. *feature,* shape, external
appearance. *mind,* (as distinguished from body or "feature"). *unkind,* unnatural. *trunks,* chests. *o'erflourished,*
decorated with carving and painting.

---

sage saws, wise maxims. *living in my glass,* i.e., staring
at me from my mirror. *dishonest,* dishonorable. *religious
in it,* i.e., dedicated to his cowardice (following "devout").
'Slid, by God's eyelid. *event,* outcome. *yet,* after all. *held
out,* maintained. *lubber,* lout. *cockney,* affected fop. *un-
gird thy strangeness,* i.e., abandon your silly pretense (of
not recognizing me). *vent,* say. *Greek,* buffoon.

30   CLOWN: By my troth, thou hast an open hand. These wise men that give fools money get themselves a good report—after fourteen years' purchase.°

(*Enter* [SIR] ANDREW, [SIR] TOBY, *and* FABIAN.)

ANDREW: Now, sir, have I met you again? There's for you! (*Strikes* SEBASTIAN.)
SEBASTIAN: Why, there's for thee, and there, and there!

(*Strikes* SIR ANDREW.)

Are all the people mad?
TOBY: Hold, sir, or I'll throw your dagger o'er the house.

(*Seizes* SEBASTIAN.)

CLOWN: This will I tell my lady straight.° I would not
40   be in some of your coats for twopence. (*Exit.*)
TOBY: Come on, sir; hold.
ANDREW: Nay, let him alone. I'll go another way to work with him. I'll have an action of battery against him,° if there be any law in Illyria. Though I stroke° him first, yet it's no matter for that.
SEBASTIAN: Let go thy hand.
TOBY: Come, sir, I will not let you go. Come, my young soldier, put up your iron. You are well fleshed.° Come on.
50   SEBASTIAN: I will be free from thee. (*Frees himself.*) What wouldst thou now? If thou dar'st tempt me further, draw thy sword.
TOBY: What, what? Nay then, I must have an ounce or two of this malapert° blood from you. (*Draws.*)

(*Enter* OLIVIA)

OLIVIA: Hold, Toby! On thy life I charge thee hold!
TOBY: Madam.
OLIVIA: Will it be ever thus? Ungracious wretch, Fit for the mountains and the barbarous caves, Where manners ne'er were preached! Out of my
60   sight! Be not offended, dear Cesario. Rudesby,° begone.

(*Exeunt* SIR TOBY, SIR ANDREW, *and* FABIAN.)

               I prithee gentle friend, Let thy fair wisdom, not thy passion, sway° In this uncivil° and unjust extent° Against thy peace. Go with me to my house, And hear thou there how many fruitless pranks This ruffian hath botched up,° that thou thereby Mayst smile at this. Thou shalt not choose but go.

---

after fourteen years' purchase, i.e., after a long delay, at a high price. **straight,** straightaway, at once. **have an action of battery against him,** charge him with assaulting me. **stroke,** struck. **well fleshed,** i.e., made eager for fighting by having tasted blood. **malapert,** saucy. **Rudesby,** ruffian. **sway,** rule. **uncivil,** barbarous. **extent,** display. **botched up,** clumsily contrived.

Do not deny. Beshrew° his soul for me.
He started° one poor heart° of mine, in thee.   70
SEBASTIAN: What relish is in this?° How runs the stream?
Or° I am mad, or else this is a dream.
Let fancy still my sense in Lethe° steep;
If it be thus to dream, still let me sleep!
OLIVIA: Nay, come, I prithee. Would thou'dst be ruled by me!
SEBASTIAN: Madam, I will.
OLIVIA: O, say so, and so be.   80

(*Exeunt.*)

ACT 4 / SCENE 2   OLIVIA's *house.*

(*Enter* MARIA *and* CLOWN.)

MARIA: Nay, I prithee put on this gown and this beard; make him believe thou art Sir Topas° the curate; do it quickly. I'll call Sir Toby the whilst.° (*Exit.*)
CLOWN: Well, I'll put it on, and I will dissemble° myself in't, and I would I were the first that ever dissembled in such a gown. I am not tall enough to become the function° well, nor lean enough to be thought a good student;° but to be said an honest man and a good housekeeper° goes as fairly as to say a careful° man and a great scholar. The competitors°   10 enter.

(*Enter* [SIR] TOBY [*and* MARIA].)

TOBY: Jove bless thee, Master Parson.
CLOWN: *Bonos dies,*° Sir Toby; for, as the old hermit of Prague,° that never saw pen and ink, very wittily said to a niece of King Gorboduc,° "That that is is"; so, I, being Master Parson, am Master Parson; for what is "that" but that, and "is" but is?
TOBY: To him, Sir Topas.
CLOWN: What ho, I say. Peace in this prison!
TOBY: The knave counterfeits well; a good knave.°   20

(MALVOLIO *within.*)

MALVOLIO: Who calls there?
CLOWN: Sir Topas the curate, who comes to visit Malvolio the lunatic.
MALVOLIO: Sir Topas, Sir Topas, good Sir Topas, go to   30 my lady.

Beshrew, curse. **started,** roused. **heart,** (with a pun on "hart"). **What relish is in this?,** i.e., what does this mean?. **Or,** either. **Lethe,** in classical mythology, the river of oblivion in Hades. **Sir Topas,** (the ridiculous hero of Chaucer's *Rime of Sir Thopas,* a parody of chivalric romances). **the whilst,** meanwhile. **dissemble,** disguise. **function,** clerical office. **student,** student. **good housekeeper,** solid citizen. **careful,** painstaking. **competitors,** confederates. **Bonos dies,** good day. **the old hermit of Prague,** (apparently the Clown's nonsensical invention). **King Gorboduc,** (a legendary king of Britain). **knave,** fellow.

CLOWN: Out, hyperbolical° fiend! How vexest thou this man! Talkest thou nothing but of ladies?

TOBY: Well said, Master Parson.

MALVOLIO: Sir Topas, never was man thus wronged. Good Sir Topas, do not think I am mad. They have laid me here in hideous darkness.

CLOWN: Fie, thou dishonest Satan. I call thee by the most modest° terms, for I am one of those gentle
40 ones that will use the devil himself with courtesy. Say'st thou that house° is dark?

MALVOLIO: As hell, Sir Topas.

CLOWN: Why, it hath bay windows transparent as barricadoes,° and the clerestories° toward the south north are as lustrous as ebony; and yet complainest thou of obstruction?

MALVOLIO: I am not mad, Sir Topas. I say to you this house is dark.

CLOWN: Madman, thou errest. I say there is no darkness
50 but ignorance, in which thou art more puzzled than the Egyptians in their fog.°

MALVOLIO: I say this house is as dark as ignorance, though ignorance were as dark as hell; and I say there was never man thus abused. I am no more mad than you are. Make the trial of it in any constant question.°

CLOWN: What is the opinion of Pythagoras° concerning wild fowl?

MALVOLIO: That the soul of our grandam might hap-
60 pily° inhabit a bird.

CLOWN: What think'st thou of his opinion?

MALVOLIO: I think nobly of the soul and no way approve his opinion.

CLOWN: Fare thee well. Remain thou still in darkness. Thou shalt hold th' opinion of Pythagoras ere I will allow of thy wits,° and fear to kill a woodcock,° lest thou dispossess the soul of thy grandam. Fare thee well.

MALVOLIO: Sir Topas, Sir Topas!

70 TOBY: My most exquisite Sir Topas!

CLOWN: Nay, I am for all waters.°

MARIA: Thou mightst have done this without thy beard and gown. He sees thee not.

TOBY: To him in thine own voice, and bring me word how thou find'st him. (To MARIA) I would we were well rid of this knavery. If he may be conveniently

delivered,° I would he were; for I am now so far in offense with my niece that I cannot pursue with any safety this sport to the upshot.° (To the CLOWN) Come by and by to my chamber. (Exit [with MARIA].) 80

CLOWN: (Sings)

"Hey, Robin, jolly Robin,
    Tell me how thy lady does."°

MALVOLIO: Fool.

CLOWN: "My lady is unkind, perdie."°

MALVOLIO: Fool.

CLOWN: "Alas, why is she so?"

MALVOLIO: Fool, I say.

CLOWN: "She loves another." Who calls, ha?

MALVOLIO: Good fool, as ever thou wilt deserve well at 90 my hand, help me to a candle, and pen, ink, and paper. As I am a gentleman, I will live to be thankful to thee for't.

CLOWN: Master Malvolio?

MALVOLIO: Ay, good fool.

CLOWN: Alas, sir, how fell you besides your five wits?°

MALVOLIO: Fool, there was never man so notoriously° abused. I am as well in my wits, fool, as thou art.

CLOWN: But as well? Then you are mad indeed, if you be no better in your wits than a fool. 100

MALVOLIO: They have here propertied° me; keep me in darkness, send ministers to me, asses, and do all they can to face me out of my wits.°

CLOWN: Advise you° what you say. The minister is here.°— Malvolio, Malvolio, thy wits the heavens restore. Endeavor thyself to sleep and leave thy vain bibble babble.

MALVOLIO: Sir Topas.

CLOWN: Maintain no words with him, good fellow.— Who, I, sir? Not I, sir. God buy you,° good Sir 110 Topas.—Marry, amen.—I will, sir, I will.

MALVOLIO: Fool, fool, fool, I say!

CLOWN: Alas, sir, be patient. What say you, sir? I am shent° for speaking to you.

MALVOLIO: Good fool, help me to some light and some paper. I tell thee, I am as well in my wits as any man in Illyria.

CLOWN: Well-a-day that you were,° sir.

---

hyperbolical, boisterous (a term from rhetoric meaning "exaggerated in style"). *most modest,* mildest. *house,* madman's cell. *barricadoes,* barricades. *clerestories,* upper windows. *Egyptians in their fog,* (to plague the Egyptians Moses brought a "thick darkness" that lasted three days; see Exodus 10:21–23). *constant question,* consistent topic, normal conversation. *Pythagoras,* (ancient Greek philosopher who expounded the doctrine of the transmigration of souls). *happily,* haply, perhaps. *allow of thy wits,* acknowledge your sanity. *woodcock,* (a proverbially stupid bird). *I am for all waters,* i.e., I can turn my hand to any trade.

---

delivered, released. *upshot,* conclusion. *Hey, Robin . . . lady does,* (the Clown sings an old ballad). *perdie,* certainly. *how fell you besides your five wits?,* i.e., how did you happen to become mad?. *notoriously,* outrageously. *propertied,* i.e., used me as a mere object, not a human being. *face me out of my wits,* i.e., impudently insist that I am mad. *Advise you,* consider carefully. *The minister is here,* (for the next few lines the Clown uses two voices, his own and that of Sir Topas). *God buy you,* God be with you, i.e., good-bye. *shent,* rebuked. *Well-a-day that you were,* alas, if only you were.

MALVOLIO: By this hand, I am. Good fool, some ink,
120   paper, and light; and convey what I will set down
   to my lady. It shall advantage thee more than ever
   the bearing of letter did.
CLOWN: I will help you to't. But tell me true, are you
   not mad indeed, or do you but counterfeit?°
MALVOLIO: Believe me, I am not. I tell thee true.
CLOWN: Nay, I'll ne'er believe a madman till I see his
   brains. I will fetch you light and paper and ink.
MALVOLIO: Fool, I'll requite it in the highest degree. I
   prithee be gone.
130 CLOWN: (Sings)

        I am gone, sir,
        And anon, sir,
      I'll be with you again,
        In a trice,
      Like to the old Vice,°
      Your need to sustain.°
      Who with dagger of lath,
      In his rage and his wrath,
      Cries "Ah ha" to the devil.
140   *Like a mad lad,*
      "Pare thy nails, dad."
      Adieu, goodman devil.°

   (Exit.)

ACT 4 / SCENE 3   OLIVIA's *garden.*

(Enter SEBASTIAN.*)*

SEBASTIAN: This is the air; that is the glorious sun;
   This pearl she gave me, I do feel't and see't;
   And though 'tis wonder that enwraps me thus,
   Yet 'tis not madness. Where's Antonio then?
   I could not find him at the Elephant;
   Yet there he was,° and there I found this credit,°
   That he did range the town to seek me out.
   His counsel now might do me golden service;
   For though my soul disputes well with my sense°
10   That this may be some error, but no madness,
   Yet doth this accident and flood of fortune
   So far exceed all instance,° all discourse,°
   That I am ready to distrust mine eyes
   And wrangle with my reason that persuades me
   To any other trust° but that I am mad,

Or else the lady's mad. Yet, if 'twere so,
She could not sway° her house, command her
   followers,
Take and give back affairs and their dispatch°
With such a smooth, discreet, and stable bearing
As I perceive she does. There's something in't   20
That is deceivable.° But here the lady comes.

(Enter OLIVIA *and* PRIEST.*)*

OLIVIA: Blame not this haste of mine. If you mean
   well,
Now go with me and with this holy man
Into the chantry by.° There, before him,
And underneath that consecrated roof,
Plight me the full assurance of your faith,
That my most jealious° and too doubtful soul
May live at peace. He shall conceal it
Whiles° you are willing it shall come to note,°
What time we will our celebration keep°   30
According to my birth. What do you say?
SEBASTIAN: I'll follow this good man and go with you
And having sworn truth, ever will be true.
OLIVIA: Then lead the way, good father, and heavens
   so shine
That they may fairly note° this act of mine.

(Exeunt.)

ACT 5 / SCENE 1   *Before* OLIVIA's *house.*

(Enter CLOWN *and* FABIAN.*)*

FABIAN: Now as thou lov'st me, let me see his° letter.
CLOWN: Good Master Fabian, grant me another re-
   quest.
FABIAN: Anything.
CLOWN: Do not desire to see this letter.
FABIAN: This is to give a dog, and in recompense desire
   my dog again.

(Enter DUKE, VIOLA, CURIO, *and* LORDS.*)*

DUKE: Belong you to the Lady Olivia, friends?
CLOWN: Ay, sir, we are some of her trappings.
DUKE: I know thee well. How dost thou, my good fel-   10
   low?
CLOWN: Truly, sir, the better for my foes, and the worse
   for my friends.
DUKE: Just the contrary: the better for thy friends.
CLOWN: No, sir, the worse.
DUKE: How can that be?

---

counterfeit, pretend. **Vice,** (in the morality plays, a
stock mischievous character who usually carried a wooden
dagger). **Your need to sustain,** i.e., in order to help you
resist the Devil. **Adieu, goodman devil,** (a much emended
line; "goodman" [Folio "good man"], a title for a yeoman
or any man of substance not of gentle birth, roughly cor-
responds to our "mister"). **was,** had been. **credit,** belief.
my soul disputes well with my sense, my reason agrees with
the evidence of my senses. **instance,** precedent. **discourse,** reason. **trust,** belief.

---

sway, rule. **Take and give . . . their dispatch,** i.e., assume and discharge the management of affairs. **deceivable,** deceptive. **chantry by,** nearby chapel. **jealious,** jealous, anxious. **Whiles,** until. **come to note,** be made public.
our celebration keep, celebrate our marriage ceremony (as
distinguished from the formal compact of betrothal).
fairly note, look with favor on. **his,** i.e., Malvolio's.

CLOWN: Marry, sir, they praise me and make an ass of
me. Now my foes tell me plainly I am an ass; so that
by my foes, sir, I profit in the knowledge of myself,
20   and by my friends I am abused;° so that, conclusions
to be as kisses,° if your four negatives° make your
two affirmatives,° why then, the worse for my
friends, and the better for my foes.

DUKE: Why, this is excellent.

CLOWN: By my troth, sir, no, though it please you to be
one of my friends.

DUKE: Thou shalt not be the worse for me. There's gold.

CLOWN: But that it would be double-dealing,° sir, I
would you could make it another.

30 DUKE: O, you give me ill counsel.

CLOWN: Put your grace° in your pocket, sir, for this
once, and let your flesh and blood obey it.

DUKE: Well, I will be so much a sinner to be a double-
dealer. There's another.°

CLOWN: *Primo, secundo, tertio*° is a good play;° and the
old saying is "The third pays for all." The triplex,°
sir, is a good tripping measure; or the bells of Saint
Bennet,° sir, may put you in mind—one, two, three.

DUKE: You can fool no more money out of me at this
40   throw.° If you will let your lady know I am here to
speak with her, and bring her along with you, it
may awake my bounty further.

CLOWN: Marry, sir, lullaby to your bounty till I come
again. I go, sir; but I would not have you to think
that my desire of having is the sin of covetousness.
But, as you say, sir, let your bounty take a nap; I
will awake it anon. (*Exit.*)

(*Enter* ANTONIO *and* OFFICERS.)

VIOLA: Here comes the man, sir, that did rescue me.

DUKE: That face of his I do remember well;
50   Yet when I saw it last, it was besmeared
As black as Vulcan° in the smoke of war.
A baubling° vessel was he captain of,
For shallow draught and bulk unprizable,°
With which such scathful° grapple did he make
With the most noble bottom° of our fleet
That very envy and the tongue of loss°

Cried fame and honor on him. What's the matter?

FIRST OFFICER: Orsino, this is that Antonio
That took the *Phoenix* and her fraught° from
Candy;°   60
And this is he that did the *Tiger* board
When your young nephew Titus lost his leg.
Here in the streets, desperate of shame and state,°
In private brabble° did we apprehend him.

VIOLA: He did me kindness, sir; drew on my side;°
But in conclusion put strange speech upon me.°
I know not what 'twas but distraction.°

DUKE: Notable° pirate, thou salt-water thief,
What foolish boldness brought thee to their mercies
Whom thou in terms so bloody and so dear°   70
Hast made thine enemies?

ANTONIO: Orsino, noble sir,
Be pleased that I shake off these names you give
me.
Antonio never yet was thief or pirate,
Though I confess, on base and ground enough,
Orsino's enemy. A witchcraft drew me hither.
That most ingrateful boy there by your side
From the rude sea's enraged and foamy mouth
Did I redeem. A wrack° past hope he was.
His life I gave him, and did thereto add   80
My love without retention or restraint,
All his in dedication. For his sake
Did I expose myself (pure° for his love)
Into the danger of this adverse° town;
Drew to defend him when he was beset;
Where being apprehended, his false cunning
(Not meaning to partake with me in danger)
Taught him to face me out of his acquaintance,°
And grew a twenty years removèd thing
While one would wink; denied me mine own purse,   90
Which I had recommended° to his use
Not half an hour before.

VIOLA: How can this be?

DUKE: When came he to this town?

ANTONIO: Today, my lord; and for three months
before,
No int'rim, not a minute's vacancy,
Both day and night did we keep company.

(*Enter* OLIVIA *and* ATTENDANTS.)

DUKE: Here comes the Countess; now heaven walks
on earth.

---

abused, deceived. *conclusions to be as kisses,* i.e., if
conclusions may be compared to kisses (when a coy girl's
repeated denials really mean assent). *negatives,* i.e., lips
(?). *affirmatives,* i.e., mouths (?). *double-dealing,* (1) giving twice (2) duplicity. *grace,* (1) title of nobility (2) generosity. *another,* i.e., coin. *Primo, secundo, tertio,* one,
two, three. *play,* child's game (?). *triplex,* triple time in
dancing. *Saint Bennet,* St. Benedict (a church). *throw,*
throw of the dice. *Vulcan,* Roman god of fire and patron
of blacksmiths. *baubling,* insignificant. *For shallow
draught and bulk unprizable,* i.e., virtually worthless on account of its small size. *scathful,* destructive. *bottom,* ship.
very envy and the tongue of loss, even enmity and the voice
of the losers.

---

fraught, freight, cargo. *Candy,* Candia, Crete. *desperate of shame and state,* i.e., recklessly disregarding his
shameful past behavior and the requirements of public
order. *brabble,* brawl. *drew on my side,* i.e., drew his
sword in my defense. *put strange speech upon me,* spoke
to me so oddly. *distraction,* madness. *Notable,* notorious.
dear, grievous. *wrack,* wreck. *pure,* purely. *adverse,*
unfriendly. *to face me out of his acquaintance,* i.e., brazenly
to deny any knowledge of me. *recommended,* given.

But for° thee, fellow: fellow, thy words are madness.
100 Three months this youth hath tended upon me;
But more of that anon. Take him aside.
OLIVIA: What would my lord, but that° he may not
    have,
Wherein Olivia may seem serviceable?
Cesario, you do not keep promise with me.
VIOLA: Madam?
DUKE: Gracious Olivia—
OLIVIA: What do you say, Cesario?—Good my lord°—
VIOLA: My lord would speak; my duty hushes me.
OLIVIA: If it be aught to the old tune, my lord,
110 It is as fat and fulsome° to mine ear
As howling after music.
DUKE: Still so cruel?
OLIVIA: Still so constant, lord.
DUKE: What, to perverseness? You uncivil lady,
To whose ingrate and unauspicious° altars
My soul the faithfull'st off'rings have breathed out
That e'er devotion tendered. What shall I do?
OLIVIA: Even what it please my lord, that shall become
    him.
DUKE: Why should I not, had I the heart to do it,
120 Like to th' Egyptian thief° at point of death,
Kill what I love?—a savage jealousy
That sometime savors nobly. But hear me this:
Since you to non-regardance° cast my faith,
And that° I partly know the instrument
That screws° me from my true place in your favor,
Live you the marble-breasted tyrant still.
But this your minion, whom I know you love,
And whom, by heaven I swear, I tender° dearly,
Him will I tear out of that cruel eye
130 Where he sits crownèd in his master's spite.
Come, boy, with me. My thoughts are ripe in
    mischief.
I'll sacrifice the lamb that I do love
To spite a raven's heart with a dove. *(Going.)*
VIOLA: And I, most jocund, apt,° and willingly,
To do you rest° a thousand deaths would die.

(Following.)

OLIVIA: Where goes Cesario?
VIOLA: After him I love
More than I love these eyes, more than my life,
More, by all mores,° than e'er I shall love wife.

But for, as for. **but that,** except that which (i.e., my love). **Good my lord,** i.e., please be silent (so Cesario may speak). **fat and fulsome,** gross and repulsive. **ingrate and unauspicious,** ungrateful and unpropitious. **th' Egyptian thief,** (in Heliodorus' *Ethiopica,* a Greek romance translated by Thomas Underdown about 1569, the bandit Thyamis, besieged in a cave, plans to kill the captive princess Clariclea, the object of his hopeless love; but in the darkness he kills another woman instead). **non-regardance,** neglect. **that,** since. **screws,** forces. **tender,** hold. **apt,** readily. **do you rest,** give you peace. **mores,** i.e., possible comparisons.

If I do feign, you witnesses above 140
Punish my life for tainting of my love!
OLIVIA: Ay me detested, how am I beguiled!
VIOLA: Who does beguile you? Who does do you
    wrong?
OLIVIA: Hast thou forgot thyself? Is it so long?
Call forth the holy father.

(Exit an ATTENDANT.)

DUKE: *(To* VIOLA*)* Come, away!
OLIVIA: Whither, my lord? Cesario, husband, stay.
DUKE: Husband?
OLIVIA: Ay, husband. Can he that deny?
DUKE: Her husband, sirrah?° 150
VIOLA: No, my lord, not I.
OLIVIA: Alas, it is the baseness of thy fear
That makes thee strangle thy propriety.°
Fear not, Cesario; take thy fortunes up;
Be that thou know'st thou art, and then thou art
As great as that° thou fear'st.

(Enter PRIEST.*)*

                 O, welcome, father!
Father, I charge thee by thy reverence
Here to unfold—though lately we intended
To keep in darkness what occasion now 160
Reveals before 'tis ripe—what thou dost know
Hath newly passed between this youth and me.
PRIEST: A contract° of eternal bond of love,
Confirmed by mutual joinder of your hands,
Attested by the holy close of lips,
Strength'nèd by interchangement of your rings;
And all the ceremony of this compact°
Sealed in my function,° by my testimony;
Since when, my watch hath told me, toward my
    grave
I have traveled but two hours. 170
DUKE: O thou dissembling cub, what wilt thou be
When time hath sowed a grizzle on thy case?°
Or will not else thy craft° so quickly grow
That thine own trip° shall be thine overthrow?
Farewell, and take her; but direct thy feet
Where thou and I, henceforth, may never meet.
VIOLA: My lord, I do protest.
OLIVIA: O, do not swear.
Hold little° faith, though thou hast too much fear.

(Enter SIR ANDREW.*)*

---

sirrah, (customary form of address to a menial). **strangle thy propriety,** deny your identity. **that,** him who (i.e., the Duke). **contract,** betrothal. **compact,** (accent on second syllable). **Sealed in my function,** i.e., ratified by me in my priestly office. **a grizzle on thy case,** gray hairs on your skin. **craft,** duplicity. **trip,** craftiness. **little,** i.e., at least a little.

180 ANDREW: For the love of God, a surgeon! Send one
presently° to Sir Toby.
OLIVIA: What's the matter?
ANDREW: H'as° broke my head across, and has given Sir
Toby a bloody coxcomb° too. For the love of God,
your help! I had rather than forty pound I were at
home.
OLIVIA: Who has done this, Sir Andrew?
ANDREW: The Count's gentleman, one Cesario. We took
him for a coward, but he's the very devil incardi-
190 nate.°
DUKE: My gentleman Cesario?
ANDREW: Od's lifelings,° here he is! You broke my head
for nothing; and that that I did, I was set on to do't
by Sir Toby.
VIOLA: Why do you speak to me? I never hurt you.
You drew your sword upon me without cause,
But I bespake you fair° and hurt you not.

(Enter [SIR] TOBY and CLOWN.)

ANDREW: If a bloody coxcomb be a hurt, you have hurt
me. I think you set nothing by a bloody coxcomb.
200 Here comes Sir Toby halting;° you shall hear more.
But if he had not been in drink, he would have
tickled you othergates° than he did.
DUKE: How now, gentleman! How is't with you?
TOBY: That's all one! Has hurt me, and there's th' end
on't. Sot,° didst see Dick Surgeon, sot?
CLOWN: O, he's drunk, Sir Toby, an hour agone. His
eyes were set° at eight i' th' morning.
TOBY: Then he's a rogue and a passy measures pavin.°
I hate a drunken rogue.
210 OLIVIA: Away with him! Who hath made this havoc with
them?
ANDREW: I'll help you, Sir Toby, because we'll be
dressed° together.
TOBY: Will you help—an ass-head and a coxcomb and
a knave, a thin-faced knave, a gull?
OLIVIA: Get him to bed, and let his hurt be looked to.

(Exeunt CLOWN, FABIAN, SIR TOBY, and SIR ANDREW.)

(Enter SEBASTIAN.)

SEBASTIAN: I am sorry, madam, I have hurt your
kinsman;
But had it been the brother of my blood,
220 I must have done no less with wit and safety.°
You throw a strange regard° upon me, and by that

I do perceive it hath offended you.
Pardon me, sweet one, even for the vows
We made each other but so late ago.
DUKE: One face, one voice, one habit,° and two
persons—
A natural perspective° that is and is not.
SEBASTIAN: Antonio, O my dear Antonio,
How have the hours racked and tortured me
Since I have lost thee!
ANTONIO: Sebastian are you?   230
SEBASTIAN: Fear'st thou° that,
Antonio?
ANTONIO: How have you made division of yourself?
An apple cleft in two is not more twin
Than these two creatures. Which is Sebastian?
OLIVIA: Most wonderful.
SEBASTIAN: Do I stand there? I never had a brother;
Nor can there be that deity in my nature
Of here and everywhere.° I had a sister,
Whom the blind waves and surges have devoured.   240
Of charity,° what kin are you to me?
What countryman? What name? What parentage?
VIOLA: Of Messaline; Sebastian was my father;
Such a Sebastian was my brother too;
So went he suited° to his watery tomb.
If spirits can assume both form and suit,°
You come to fright us.
SEBASTIAN: A spirit I am indeed,
But am in that dimension grossly clad
Which from the womb I did participate.°   250
Were you a woman, as the rest goes even,°
I should my tears let fall upon your cheek
And say, "Thrice welcome, drownèd Viola!"
VIOLA: My father had a mole upon his brow.
SEBASTIAN: And so had mine.
VIOLA: And died that day when Viola from her birth
Had numb'red thirteen years.
SEBASTIAN: O, that record° is lively in my soul!
He finishèd indeed his mortal act
That day that made my sister thirteen years.   260
VIOLA: If nothing lets° to make us happy both
But this my masculine usurped attire,
Do not embrace me till each circumstance
Of place, time, fortune do cohere and jump°
That I am Viola; which to confirm,

---

presently, immediately. **H'as,** he has. **coxcomb,** pate. **incardinate,** incarnate. **Od's lifelings,** by God's life. **bespake you fair,** addressed you courteously. **halting,** limping. **othergates,** otherwise. **Sot,** fool. **set,** closed. **passy measures pavin,** i.e., *passamezzo* pavan, a slow and stately dance of eight bars (hence its relevance to the surgeon whose eyes had "set at eight"). **be dressed,** have our wounds dressed. **with wit and safety,** i.e., with a sensible regard for my safety. **strange regard,** unfriendly look.

habit, costume. **A natural perspective,** i.e., a natural optical illusion (like that produced by a stereoscope, which converts two images into one). **Fear'st thou,** do you doubt. **Nor can there be . . . everywhere,** i.e., nor can I, like God, be everywhere at once. **Of charity,** out of simple kindness. **suited,** clothed. **form and suit,** body and clothing. **am in that dimension . . . participate,** i.e., clothed in the bodily form that, like other mortals, I acquired at birth. **as the rest goes even,** i.e., as other circumstances seem to indicate. **record,** history (accent on second syllable). **lets,** interferes. **cohere and jump,** i.e., fall together and agree.

I'll bring you to a captain in this town,
Where lie my maiden weeds;° by whose gentle help
I was preserved to serve this noble Count.
All the occurrence of my fortune since
270   Hath been between this lady and this lord.
SEBASTIAN: (*To* OLIVIA) So comes it, lady, you have
      been mistook.
But nature to her bias drew° in that.
You would have been contracted to a maid;
Nor are you therein, by my life, deceived:
You are betrothed both to a maid and man.
DUKE: Be not amazed; right noble is his blood.
If this be so, as yet the glass° seems true,
I shall have share in this most happy wrack.
      (*To* VIOLA) Boy, thou hast said to me a thousand
      times
280   Thou never shouldst love woman like to me.
VIOLA: And all those sayings will I over° swear,
And all those swearings keep as true in soul
As doth that orbèd continent° the fire
That severs day from night.
DUKE: Give me thy hand,
And let me see thee in thy woman's weeds.
VIOLA: The captain that did bring me first on shore
Hath my maid's garments. He upon some action
Is now in durance, at Malvolio's suit,°
290   A gentleman, and follower of my lady's.
OLIVIA: He shall enlarge° him. Fetch Malvolio hither.
And yet alas, now I remember me,
They say, poor gentleman, he's much distract.

(Enter CLOWN *with a letter, and* FABIAN.*)*

A most extracting° frenzy of mine own
From my remembrance clearly banished his.
How does he, sirrah?
CLOWN: Truly, madam, he holds Belzebub at the stave's
      end° as well as a man in his case° may do. H'as here
      writ a letter to you; I should have given't you today
300   morning. But as a madman's epistles are no gospels,
      so it skills° not much when they are delivered.
OLIVIA: Open't and read it.
CLOWN: Look then to be well edified, when the fool
      delivers the madman. (*Reads in a loud voice*) "By the
      Lord, madam"—
OLIVIA: How now? Art thou mad?

CLOWN: No, madam, I do but read madness. And your
      ladyship will have it as it ought to be, you must allow
      vox.°
OLIVIA: Prithee read i' thy right wits.   310
CLOWN: So I do, madonna; but to read his right wits is
      to read thus. Therefore perpend,° my princess, and
      give ear.
OLIVIA: (*To* FABIAN) Read it you, sirrah.
FABIAN: (*Reads*) "By the Lord, madam, you wrong me,
      and the world shall know it. Though you have put
      me into darkness, and given your drunken cousin
      rule over me, yet have I the benefit of my senses as
      well as your ladyship. I have your own letter that
      induced me to the semblance I put on; with the   320
      which I doubt not but to do myself much right, or
      you much shame. Think of me as you please. I leave
      my duty a little unthought of, and speak out of my
      injury.   THE MADLY USED MALVOLIO."
OLIVIA: Did he write this?
CLOWN: Ay, madam.
DUKE: This savors not much of distraction.
OLIVIA: See him delivered, Fabian; bring him hither.

(Exit FABIAN.*)*

My lord, so please you, these things further thought
      on,
To think me as well a sister as a wife,   330
One day shall crown th' alliance on't, so please you,
Here at my house and at my proper° cost.
DUKE: Madam, I am most apt° t' embrace your offer.
      (*To* VIOLA) Your master quits° you; and for your
      service done him,
So much against the mettle of your sex,
So far beneath your soft and tender breeding,
And since you called me master for so long,
Here is my hand; you shall from this time be
Your master's mistress.
OLIVIA: A sister; you are she.

(Enter [FABIAN, *with*] MALVOLIO.*)*

DUKE: Is this the madman?
OLIVIA: Ay, my lord, this same.
How now, Malvolio?
MALVOLIO: Madam, you have done me
      wrong,
Notorious° wrong.
OLIVIA: Have I, Malvolio? No.
MALVOLIO: Lady, you have. Pray you peruse that
      letter.
You must not now deny it is your hand.
Write from it° if you can, in hand or phrase,
Or say 'tis not your seal, not your invention.°   350

---

weeds, clothes. **nature to her bias drew,** i.e., nature followed her normal inclination. **glass,** i.e., the "natural perspective" of line 226. **over,** repeatedly. **orbèd continent,** in Ptolemaic astronomy, the sphere of the sun. **He upon some action . . . Malvolio's suit,** i.e., at Malvolio's instigation he is now imprisoned upon some legal charge. **enlarge,** release. **extracting,** i.e., obliterating (in that it draws me from all thoughts of Malvolio's "frenzy"). **he holds Belzebub at the stave's end,** i.e., he keeps the fiend at a distance. **case,** condition. **skills,** matters.

---

vox, i.e., an appropriately loud voice. **perpend,** pay attention. **proper,** own. **apt,** ready. **quits,** releases. **Notorious,** notable. **from it,** differently. **invention,** composition.

You can say none of this. Well, grant it then,
And tell me, in the modesty of honor,°
Why you have given me such clear lights of favor,
Bade me come smiling and cross-gartered to you,
To put on yellow stockings, and to frown
Upon Sir Toby and the lighter° people;
And, acting this in an obedient hope,
Why have you suffered me to be imprisoned,
Kept in a dark house, visited by the priest,
360 And made the most notorious geck and gull°
That e'er invention played on? Tell me why.
OLIVIA: Alas, Malvolio, this is not my writing,
Though I confess much like the character;
But, out of° question, 'tis Maria's hand.
And now I do bethink me, it was she
First told me thou wast mad; then cam'st in smiling,
And in such forms which here were presupposed°
Upon thee in the letter. Prithee be content.
This practice hath most shrewdly passed° upon
   thee;
370 But when we know the grounds and authors of it,
Thou shalt be both the plaintiff and the judge
Of thine own cause.
FABIAN: Good madam, hear me speak,
And let no quarrel, nor no brawl to come,
Taint the condition of this present hour,
Which I have wond'red at. In hope it shall not,
Most freely I confess myself and Toby
Set this device against Malvolio here,
Upon some stubborn and uncourteous parts°
380 We had conceived against him. Maria writ
The letter, at Sir Toby's great importance,°
In recompense whereof he hath married her.
How with a sportful malice it was followed
May rather pluck on° laughter than revenge,
If that° the injuries be justly weighed
That have on both sides passed.
OLIVIA: Alas, poor fool,° how have they baffled° thee!
CLOWN: Why, "some are born great, some achieve
   greatness, and some have greatness thrown upon
390   them." I was one, sir, in this interlude,° one Sir
   Topas, sir; but that's all one. "By the Lord, fool, I
   am not mad!" But do you remember, "Madam, why
   laugh you at such a barren rascal? And you smile
   not, he's gagged"? And thus the whirligig of time
   brings in his revenges.

MALVOLIO: I'll be revenged on the whole pack of you!

(Exit.)

OLIVIA: He hath been most notoriously abused.
DUKE: Pursue him and entreat him to a peace.
He hath not told us of the captain yet.
When that is known, and golden time convents,°   400
A solemn combination shall be made
Of our dear souls. Meantime, sweet sister,
We will not part from hence. Cesario, come—
For so you shall be while you are a man,
But when in other habits you are seen,
Orsino's mistress and his fancy's° queen.

(Exeunt [all but the CLOWN*].)*

*(*CLOWN *sings.°)*

   When that I was and a° little tiny boy,
      With hey, ho, the wind and the rain,
   A foolish thing was but a toy,°
      For the rain it raineth every day.   410

   But when I came to man's estate,
      With hey, ho, the wind and the rain,
   'Gainst knaves and thieves men shut their gate,
      For the rain it raineth every day.

   But when I came, alas, to wive,
      With hey, ho, the wind and the rain,
   By swaggering could I never thrive,
      For the rain it raineth every day.

   But when I came unto my beds,
      With hey, ho, the wind and the rain,   420
   With tosspots° still had drunken heads,
      For the rain it raineth every day.

   A great while ago the world begun,
      Hey, ho, the wind and the rain;
   But that's all one, our play is done,
      And we'll strive to please you every day.

(Exit.)

FINIS

---

in the modesty of honor, i.e., with a proper regard to
your own honor. *lighter,* lesser. *geck and gull,* fool and
dupe. *out of,* beyond. *presupposed,* imposed. *This practice hath most shrewdly passed,* i.e., this trick has most mischievously worked. *Upon some stubborn and uncourteous
parts,* i.e., because of some unyielding and discourteous
traits of character. *importance,* importunity. *pluck on,*
prompt. *If that,* if. *fool,* (here, a term of affection and
compassion). *baffled,* publicly humiliated. *interlude,* little
play.

---

convents, is suitable (?). *fancy's,* love's. *Clown sings,*
(since no source has been found for the Clown's song—
which certain editors have inexplicably denounced as dog-
gerel—we may assume that it is Shakespeare's). *and a,* a.
toy, trifle. *tosspots,* sots.

Figure 1. Malvolio (Donald Sinden) scrutinizes the fake letter, while behind the stylized "box tree," Fabian (Peter Geddis), Sir Toby (Bill Fraser) and Sir Andrew (Barrie Ingham) watch with amusement and indignant surprise, in the Royal Shakespeare Company production of *Twelfth Night*, directed by John Barton, 1969. (Photograph: Shakespeare Centre Library, Joe Cocks Studio Collection.)

Figure 2. The disguised Viola (Judi Dench) looks longingly at Orsino (Charles Thomas), while he, unaware of her feelings for him, listens to Feste's wistful song in the Royal Shakespeare Company production of *Twelfth Night,* directed by John Barton, 1969. (Photograph: Morris Newcombe.)

Figure 3. The disguised Viola (Judi Dench) listens with restrained anger to the clever repartee of the mourning Olivia (Lisa Harrow) in the Royal Shakespeare Company production of *Twelfth Night,* directed by John Barton, 1969. (Photograph: Shakespeare Centre Library, Joe Cocks Studio Collection.)

Figure 4. Sir Toby (Bill Fraser) and Sir Andrew (Jeffrey Dench, replacing Barrie Ingham) listen to Feste (Emrys James) remind them that "Youth's a stuff 'twill not endure" in the Royal Shakespeare Company production of *Twelfth Night*, directed by John Barton, 1969. (Photograph: Shakespeare Centre Library, Joe Cocks Studio Collection.)

Staging of *Twelfth Night*

REVIEW OF THE ROYAL SHAKESPEARE
COMPANY PRODUCTION, 1969, BY J. W.
LAMBERT

First, an unequivocal statement: the Royal Shakespeare Company's new production of *Twelfth Night* is superb, should not be missed, and *must* be shared with London in due time.

A schoolboy, back in 1932, I floated in a daze out of some London theater after seeing that famous "black and white" production. I can hardly remember anything about it, except Jean Forbes-Robertson's Viola and John Laurie's Feste; but it rapidly became in my innocent mind an idealized dream, mortal enemy of all its successors. Not quite mortal: in fact, many later productions have given intense pleasure, and many performances too. But not until last Thursday night did I feel again, from this play, that singular irradiation by a tranquil joy which is one true mark of aesthetic unity, or shiver so often with those mysterious frissons, like mild, beneficent electric shocks, which for me, as they were for Housman, are an infallible test of poetry, whether verbal or dramatic.

The great cold box in which *Pericles* and *The Winter's Tale* are played is here put away. Christopher Morley has set this play in a long receding wattle tunnel decorated by four stately, flickering candlesticks, but lit from the outside, sometimes a somber twilight umber, sometimes soaring into sunburst brilliance. No bright colors are allowed in Stephanie Howard's costumes, though a pleasing muslin flutter invades Lisa Harrow's fresh young Olivia as she emerges from the comfortable certainties of mourning into the perilous playground of desire. But the essential furniture is all a silvery white, including the shrubbery: a touch of affectation here, perhaps.

As the audience settles in, and the lights go down, there already sits Charles Thomas's slim and powerful Orsino, glowering luxuriously to the appropriate strains of Dowland's "Woeful heart with grief oppressed," most gently cadenced, first welcome sign that music—arranged with gratefully unobtrusive skill by Michael Tubbs—was to play its proper part in this most musical of comedies; Illyria, like Prospero's isle, is full of sweet sounds that give delight and hurt not. Full too of evocative echoes, notably of seabirds and the sea itself which threw Viola and Sebastian upon this magic shore, and sounds again, in their ears and in ours, as they stand in amazed recognition.

Viola comes stumbling out of the mist, held up by her sea-captain, sinks to the ground; and within a few minutes, long before her more famous moments, it is blessedly clear that Judi Dench has the measure of the part—clear from her seamless modulation out of exhaustion and despair into a brisk insistence upon throwing herself further into the arms of fate and under the mercy of time. This is a Viola who for all her tenderness is resilient and adaptable, just the wife for Orsino, that self-indulgent man of power. In her scenes with Mr. Thomas, she generates a splendid heat of passion, but I cannot say how, for there are no vulgarly obvious demonstrations of thwarted affection, any more than there are of her dismay at Olivia's advances. Miss Dench manages to be sturdy, steadfast and—if the word doesn't sound absurd—spiritual at the same time; not least in her tiny scene with the Fool and his tabor, where bickering upon a bench they seem to discover in each other the same bewildered hard-pressed love of life.

It is not really fanciful to say that Shakespeare himself speaks through Feste, as he skips from household to household, never at home. It is easy to play him as altogether too pathetic a creature; but Emrys James preserves a toughness behind the frailty of this barefoot, meal-white zany. He has too the invaluable gift of singing beautifully without sounding like a trained performer. The reduction of Sir Toby and Sir Andrew to melancholy silence with "O mistress mine" was enchantingly done, so was their awakening with "Peg o' Ramsay" and "The Twelve Days of Christmas"; an awesome silence gripped the theater as "Come away, Death" floated through Orsino's echoing hall. And when Feste came to Malvolio in his cellar Mr. James achieved a note of noncommittal shame which gave the scene a cruel power.

The Fool, the two knights and the Steward are perhaps the crux of the play, certainly the most difficult to get right. Shakespeare so often took stock comic characters, or indeed caricatures, and then effortlessly gave them so much depth that it is difficult to know where to stop in expanding their inherent richness. Here all, or almost all, is severity and naturalism. There is little buffoonery. Barrie Ingham's Sir Andrew is indeed given (on the strength of his first name?) a Scottish accent and bagpipes. But this particularization makes the poor aimless ass more real as he beadily scrabbles for the smallest coin in his sporran, or lumpishly proffers unwanted posies to Olivia. Bill Fraser's Sir Toby is unmistakably Falstaff far gone. He was, I think, tougher than Mr. Fraser can make him within this framework; defeated, yes, but not quite so desperately depressed. And for that matter I am positive that her lines do not call for the tired, pinched and anxious Maria that Brenda Bruce draws with affecting skill—affecting but regrettable, since Miss Bruce can transmit infectious glee better than any other actress I know.

And then Malvolio. Sick of self-love, Olivia acutely calls him; and so always playing a carefully maintained part. Thus Donald Sinden presents him, an almost Ibsenesque figure, a lightless torch of puritan ambition, appalled when others fail to play the role he allots them, all too easily gulled into thinking that they will. It is a true portrait, in a sense—and in any sense finely projected; but despite some neat comic moments, almost too grim.

I sense a stirring of protest—can this lugubrious catalogue be an account of the production hailed so rapturously in my opening paragraphs? Well, yes. The explanation lies in the clarity and force of the director's vision. Ever since Peter Hall brought him to Stratford from Cambridge ten years ago, even in the first stormy days when all might have come to naught, John Barton, once thought of as an academic among theater men, a theater man among academics, has clearly had much to contribute.

He has always, and rightly, been concerned that we should see and understand what he used to call the "under-text," or sub-text. And I have a suspicion that this passion is in some danger of running away with him. It is one thing to open our eyes to the deeper themes of a play, quite another to make the implicit explicit, the latent blatant. A delicate balance is called for here, too; but I have no doubt that, after what seem to me the excesses of *Troilus and Cressida,* and the possibly questionable emphasis in this *Twelfth Night,* Mr. Barton will find it. Besides, he soon developed a dazzling theatrical flair which is a joy in itself.

Questionable emphasis? As I recall again the innumerable enchantments of last Thursday night I find I hardly care, my words of warning fade like the last wisps of cloud on a ripening summer day, I beam gratitude to all the players and look forward to more from, I am convinced, a director standing upon the threshold of mature greatness.

THE TRAGEDY OF OTHELLO
The Moor of Venice

BY WILLIAM SHAKESPEARE

CHARACTERS

DUKE OF VENICE
BRABANTIO, *a senator, father to* DESDEMONA
SENATORS OF VENICE
GRATIANO, *brother to* BRABANTIO, *a noble Venetian*
LODOVICO, *kinsman to* BRABANTIO, *a noble Venetian*
OTHELLO, *the Moor, in the military service of Venice*
CASSIO, *an honorable lieutenant to* OTHELLO
IAGO, OTHELLO'S *ensign, a villain*
RODERIGO, *a gulled gentleman*
MONTANO, *governor of Cyprus*

CLOWN, *servant to* OTHELLO
DESDEMONA, *daughter to* BRABANTIO *and wife to* OTHELLO
EMILIA, *wife to* IAGO
BIANCA, *a courtesan*
GENTLEMEN, SAILORS, OFFICERS, MESSENGERS, HERALD, MUSICIANS, ATTENDANTS

SCENE

Venice and Cyprus.

ACT 1 / SCENE 1

(Enter RODERIGO *and* IAGO.*)*

RODERIGO: Tush, never tell me! I take it much
    unkindly
  That thou, Iago, who hast had my purse
  As if the strings were thine, shouldst know of this.°

IAGO: 'Sblood, but you will not hear me!
  If ever I did dream of such a matter,
  Abhor me.

RODERIGO: Thou told'st me thou didst hold him° in
  thy hate.

10 IAGO: Despise me if I do not. Three great ones of
  the city,
  In personal suit to make me his lieutenant,
  Off-capped to him; and by the faith of man,
  I know my price; I am worth no worse a place.
  But he, as loving his own pride and purposes,
  Evades them with a bombast circumstance.
  Horribly stuffed with epithets of war;
  And, in conclusion,
  Nonsuits° my mediators; for, "Certes," says he,
20 "I have already chose my officer."
  And what was he?
  Forsooth, a great arithmetician,°
  One Michael Cassio, a Florentine

(A fellow almost damned in a fair wife)°
That never set a squadron in the field,
Nor the division of a battle knows
More than a spinster,° unless the bookish theoric,
Wherein the togèd consuls° can propose
As masterly as he. Mere prattle without practice
Is all his soldiership. But he, sir, had th' election;   30
And I (of whom his eyes had seen the proof
At Rhodes, at Cyprus, and on other grounds
Christian and heathen) must be belee'd and
  calmed°
By debitor and creditor; this counter-caster,°
He, in good time, must his lieutenant be,
And I—God bless the mark!—his Moorship's
  ancient.°

RODERIGO: By heaven, I rather would have been his
  hangman.   40

IAGO: Why, there's no remedy; 'tis the curse of
  service.
  Preferment° goes by letter and affection,°

---

almost . . . wife, unexplainable phrase. Cassio is not married, nor is he about to be married. In the Italian novella that was the source for Shakespeare's play, Cassio is married, and perhaps Shakespeare intended to follow the novella when he began writing the play. *spinster,* spinner of thread; i.e., housewife, homemaker. *togèd consuls,* Senators dressed in togas; i.e., clothed for the council chamber, not the battlefield. *calmed,* have the wind taken out of my sails and left becalmed. *counter-caster,* accountant. *ancient,* ensign, standard-bearer. *Preferment,* advancement. *affection,* personal favoritism.

---

this, Desdemona's elopement with Othello. *him,* Othello. *Nonsuits,* rejects. *arithmetician,* person skilled in military calculations but not in actual warfare.

And not by old gradation,° where each second
Stood heir to th' first. Now, sir, be judge yourself,
Whether I in any just term am affined°
To love the Moor.

RODERIGO: I would not follow him then.

IAGO: O, sir, content you;
50 I follow him to serve my turn upon him.
We cannot all be masters, nor all masters
Cannot be truly followed. You shall mark
Many a duteous and knee-crooking knave
That, doting on his own obsequious bondage,
Wears out his time, much like his master's ass,
For naught but provender; and when he's old,
  cashiered.°
Whip me such honest knaves! Others there are
Who, trimmed in forms and visages of duty,
60 Keep yet their hearts attending on themselves;
And, throwing but shows of service on their lords,
'Do well thrive by them, and when they have lined
  their coats,
Do themselves homage. These fellows have some
  soul;
And such a one do I profess myself. For, sir,
It is as sure as you are Roderigo,
Were I the Moor, I would not be Iago.
In following him, I follow but myself;
70 Heaven is my judge, not I for love and duty,
But seeming so, for my own peculiar° end;
For when my outward action doth demonstrate
The native act and figure of my heart
In compliment extern,° 'tis not long after
But I will wear my heart upon my sleeve
For daws to peck at; I am not what I am.

RODERIGO: What a fortune does the thick-lips owe°
If he can carry't thus!

IAGO: Call up her father,
80 Rouse him. Make after him, poison his delight,
Proclaim him in the streets. Incense her kinsmen,
And though he in a fertile climate dwell,
Plague him with flies; though that his joy be joy,
Yet throw such changes of vexation on't
As it may lose some color.

RODERIGO: Here is her father's house. I'll call aloud.

IAGO: Do, with like timorous° accent and dire yell
As when, by night and negligence, the fire
Is spied in populous cities.

90 RODERIGO: What, ho, Brabantio! Signior Brabantio,
  ho!

IAGO: Awake! What, ho, Brabantio! Thieves! thieves!
  thieves!
Look to your house, your daughter, and your bags!
Thieves! thieves!

(BRABANTIO *at a window.*)

BRABANTIO (*above*): What is the reason of this terrible
  summons?
What is the matter there?

RODERIGO: Signior, is all your family within?

IAGO: Are your doors locked?   100

BRABANTIO: Why, wherefore ask you this?

IAGO: Zounds, sir, y'are robbed! For shame, put on
  your gown!
Your heart is burst; you have lost half your soul.
Even now, now, very now, an old black ram
Is tupping your white ewe. Arise, arise!
Awake the snorting° citizens with the bell,
Or else the devil will make a grandsire of you.
Arise, I say!

BRABANTIO: What, have you lost your wits?   110

RODERIGO: Most reverend signior, do you know my
  voice?

BRABANTIO: Not I. What are you?

RODERIGO: My name is Roderigo.

BRABANTIO: The worser welcome!
I have charged thee not to haunt about my doors.
In honest plainness thou hast heard me say
My daughter is not for thee; and now, in madness,
Being full of supper and distempr'ing° draughts,
Upon malicious bravery° dost thou come   120
To start° my quiet.

RODERIGO: Sir, sir, sir—

BRABANTIO: But thou must needs be sure
My spirit and my place have in them power
To make this bitter to thee.

RODERIGO: Patience, good sir.

BRABANTIO: What tell'st thou me of robbing? This is
  Venice;
My house is not a grange.°

RODERIGO: Most grave Brabantio,   130
In simple and pure soul I come to you.

IAGO: Zounds, sir, you are one of those that will not
serve God if the devil bid you. Because we come
to do you service, and you think we are ruffians,
you'll have your daughter covered with a **Barbary** horse; you'll have your nephews° neigh to
you; you'll have coursers for cousins,° and gennets for germans.°

BRABANTIO: What profane wretch art thou?

IAGO: I am one, sir, that comes to tell you your   140
daughter and the Moor are now making the
beast with two backs.

BRABANTIO: Thou art a villain.

IAGO: You are—a senator.

BRABANTIO: This thou shalt answer. I know thee,
  Roderigo.

---

gradation, seniority. affined, bound. cashiered,
dismissed. peculiar, personal. extern, external show.
owe, own. timorous, terrifying.

---

snorting, snoring. distemp'ring, intoxicating. bravery, bravado. start, upset. grange, isolated farmhouse.
nephews, grandsons. coursers for cousins, horses for
kinsmen. gennets for germans, Spanish horses for close
relatives.

RODERIGO: Sir, I will answer anything. But I beseech you,
If't be your pleasure and most wise consent,
150 As partly I find it is, that your fair daughter,
At this odd-even° and dull watch o' th' night,
Transported, with no worse nor better guard
But with a knave of common hire, a gondolier,
To the gross clasps of a lascivious Moor—
If this be known to you, and your allowance,
We then have done you bold and saucy° wrongs;
But if you know not this, my manners tell me
We have your wrong rebuke. Do not believe
That, from the sense of° all civility,
160 I thus would play and trifle with your reverence.
Your daughter, if you have not given her leave,
I say again, hath made a gross revolt,
Tying her duty, beauty, wit, and fortunes
In an extravagant and wheeling° stranger
Of here and everywhere. Straight satisfy yourself.
If she be in her chamber, or your house,
Let loose on me the justice of the state
For thus deluding you.
BRABANTIO: Strike on the tinder, ho!
170 Give me a taper! Call up all my people!
This accident° is not unlike my dream.
Belief of it oppresses me already.
Light, I say! Light! (Exit above.)
IAGO: Farewell, for I must leave you.
It seems not meet, nor wholesome to my place,
To be produced—as, if I stay, I shall—
Against the Moor. For I do know the state,
However this may gall him with some check,°
Cannot with safety cast° him; for he's embarked
180 With such loud reason to the Cyprus wars,
Which even now stand in act,° that for their souls
Another of his fathom° they have none
To lead their business; in which regard,
Though I do hate him as I do hell-pains,
Yet, for necessity of present life,
I must show out a flag and sign of love,
Which is indeed but sign. That you shall surely find him,
Lead to the Sagittary° the raisèd search;
190 And there will I be with him. So farewell. (Exit.)

(Enter, below, BRABANTIO, and SERVANTS with torches.)

BRABANTIO: It is too true an evil. Gone she is;
And what's to come of my despisèd time
Is naught but bitterness. Now, Roderigo,
Where didst thou see her?—O unhappy girl!—
With the Moor, say'st thou?—Who would be a father?—
How didst thou know 'twas she?—O, she deceives me
Past thought!—What said she to you?—Get more tapers!
200 Raise all my kindred!—Are they married, think you?
RODERIGO: Truly I think they are.
BRABANTIO: O heaven! How got she out? O treason of the blood!
Fathers, from hence trust not your daughters' minds
By what you see them act. Is there not charms
By which the property° of youth and maidhood
210 May be abused? Have you not read, Roderigo,
Of some such thing?
RODERIGO: Yes, sir, I have indeed.
BRABANTIO: Call up my brother.—O, would you had had her!—
Some one way, some another.—Do you know
Where we may apprehend her and the Moor?
RODERIGO: I think I can discover him, if you please
To get good guard and go along with me.
BRABANTIO: Pray you lead on. At every house I'll call;
I may command at most.—Get weapons, ho!
220 And raise some special officers of night.—
On, good Roderigo; I'll deserve° your pains.
(Exeunt.)

ACT 1 / SCENE 2

(Enter OTHELLO, IAGO, and ATTENDANTS with torches.)

IAGO: Though in the trade of war I have slain men,
Yet do I hold it very stuff o' th' conscience
To do no contrived murther. I lack iniquity
Sometimes to do me service. Nine or ten times
I had thought t' have yerked° him here under the ribs.
OTHELLO: 'Tis better as it is.
IAGO: Nay, but he prated,
And spoke such scurvy and provoking terms
Against your honor
10 That with the little godliness I have
I did full hard forbear him.° But I pray you, sir,
Are you fast married? Be assured of this,
That the magnifico° is much beloved,
And hath in his effect a voice potential
As double as the duke's.° He will divorce you,
Or put upon you what restraint and grievance

---

odd-even, around midnight, when the end of one day is indistinguishable from the beginning of the next. **saucy,** insolent. **the sense of,** contrary to. **extravagant and wheeling,** wandering and roving. **accident,** occurrence. **check,** reprimand. **cast,** dismiss. **stand in act,** are underway. **fathom,** ability. **Sagittary,** an inn.

---

property, nature. **deserve,** reward. **yerked,** stabbed. **did ... him,** had great difficulty restraining myself from attacking him. **magnifico,** Venetian nobleman (BARBANTIO). **voice ... duke's,** influence so strong it is like having two votes, as does the Duke of Venice.

The law, with all his might to enforce it on,
Will give him cable.°
20   OTHELLO: Let him do his spite.
My services which I have done the signiory°
Shall out-tongue his complaints. 'Tis yet to know°—
Which, when I know that boasting is an honor,
I shall promulgate—I fetch my life and being
From men of royal siege;° and my demerits°
May speak unbonneted° to as proud a fortune
As this that I have reached. For know, Iago,
But that I love the gentle Desdemona,
I would not my unhoused° free condition
30   Put into circumscription and confine
For the sea's worth.

(Enter CASSIO, OFFICERS, *with torches.)*

But look, what lights come yond?
IAGO: Those are the raisèd father and his friends.
You were best go in.
OTHELLO: Not I; I must be found.
My parts,° my title, and my perfect soul°
Shall manifest me rightly. Is it they?
IAGO: By Janus, I think no.
OTHELLO: The servants of the duke, and my
40   lieutenant.
The goodness of the night upon you, friends!
What is the news?
CASSIO: The duke does greet you, general;
And he requires your haste-post-haste appearance
Even on the instant.
OTHELLO: What's the matter, think you?
CASSIO: Something from Cyprus, as I may divine.
It is a business of some heat. The galleys
Have sent a dozen sequent° messengers
50   This very night at one another's heels,
And many of the consuls, raised and met,
Are at the duke's already. You have been hotly
called for;
When, being not at your lodging to be found,
The Senate hath sent about three several quests
To search you out.
OTHELLO: 'Tis well I am found by you.
I will but spend a word here in the house,
And go with you. *(Exit.)*
60   CASSIO: Ancient, what makes he here?
IAGO: Faith, he to-night hath boarded a land carack.°
If it prove lawful prize, he's made for ever.
CASSIO: I do not understand.
IAGO: He's married.
CASSIO: To who?

(Enter OTHELLO.)

IAGO: Marry, to—Come, captain, will you go?
OTHELLO: Have with you.
CASSIO: Here comes another troop to seek for you.

(Enter BRABANTIO, RODERIGO, *and others with lights
and weapons.)*

IAGO: It is Brabantio. General, be advised.
He comes to bad intent.   70
OTHELLO: Holla! Stand there!
RODERIGO: Signior, it is the Moor.
BRABANTIO: Down with him, thief!

(They draw on both sides.)

IAGO: You, Roderigo! Come, sir I am for you.
OTHELLO: Keep up your bright swords, for the dew
will rust them.
Good signior, you shall more command with years
Than with your weapons.
BRABANTIO: O thou foul thief, where has thou stowed
my daughter?   80
Damned as thou art, thou hast enchanted her!
For I'll refer me to all things of sense,°
If she in chains of magic were not bound,
Whether a maid so tender, fair, and happy,
So opposite to marriage that she shunned
The wealthy curlèd darlings of our nation,
Would ever have, t' incur a general mock,
Run from her guardage to the sooty bosom
Of such a thing as thou—to fear, not to delight.
Judge me the world if 'tis not gross in sense°   90
That thou hast practiced on her with foul charms,
Abused her delicate youth with drugs or minerals
That weaken motion.° I'll have't disputed on;°
'Tis probable, and palpable to thinking.
I therefore apprehend and do attach° thee
For an abuser of the world, a practicer
Of arts inhibited and out of warrant.°
Lay hold upon him. If he do resist,
Subdue him at his peril.
OTHELLO: Hold your hands,   100
Both you of my inclining and the rest.
Were it my cue to fight, I should have known it
Without a prompter. Where will you that I go
To answer this your charge?
BRABANTIO: To prison, till fit time
Of law and course of direct session
Call thee to answer.
OTHELLO: What if I do obey?
How may the duke be therewith satisfied,
Whose messengers are here about my side   110

---

cable, scope. *signiory,* Venetian government. *yet to
know,* still not known. *siege,* rank. *demerits,* merits.
speak unbonneted, without taking my hat off; i.e., on equal
terms. *unhoused,* unconfined. *parts,* personal qualities.
perfect soul, clear conscience. *sequent,* consecutive. *land
carack,* trading ship.

---

refer . . . sense, appeal to common sense. *gross in
sense,* obvious. *motion,* senses and mental powers. *disputed on,* tried in court. *attach,* arrest. *inhibited . . .
warrant,* prohibited and illegal.

Upon some present business of the state
To bring me to him?
OFFICER: 'Tis true, most worthy signior.
The duke's in council, and your noble self
I am sure is sent for.
BRABANTIO: How? The duke in council?
In this time of the night? Bring him away.
Mine's not an idle° cause. The duke himself,
Or any of my brothers of the state,
120   Cannot but feel this wrong as 'twere their own;
For if such actions may have passage free,
Bondslaves and pagans shall our statesmen be.
        (Exeunt.)

ACT 1 / SCENE 3

(Enter DUKE and SENATORS, set at a table, with lights
and ATTENDANTS.)

DUKE: There is no composition° in these news
That gives them credit.
1. SENATOR: Indeed they are disproportioned.
My letters say a hundred and seven galleys.
DUKE: And mine a hundred forty.
2. SENATOR: And mine two hundred.
But though they jump° not on a just account—
As in these cases where the aim° reports
'Tis oft with difference—yet do they all confirm
10   A Turkish fleet, and bearing up to Cyprus.
DUKE: Nay, it is possible enough to judgment.
I do not so secure me in the error°
But the main article I do approve°
In fearful sense.
SAILOR (within): What, ho! what, ho! what, ho!
OFFICER: A messenger from the galleys.

(Enter SAILOR.)

DUKE: Now, what's the business?
SAILOR: The Turkish preparation makes for Rhodes.
So was I bid report here to the state
20   By Signior Angelo.
DUKE: How say you by this change?
1. SENATOR: This cannot be
By no assay° of reason. 'Tis a pageant
To keep us in false gaze.° When we consider
Th' importancy of Cyprus to the Turk,
And let ourselves again but understand
That, as it more concerns the Turk than Rhodes,
So may he with more facile question bear it,°
For that it stands not in such warlike brace,°
30   But altogether lacks th' abilities
That Rhodes is dressed in—if we make thought of
this,

---

idle, trivial. composition, consistency. jump, agree.
aim, conjecture. secure . . . error, rely on inconsistencies.
approve, accept. assay, test. false gaze, looking the wrong
way. with . . . it, more easily capture. brace, prepared-
ness.

We must not think the Turk is so unskillful
To leave that latest which concerns him first,
Neglecting an attempt of ease and gain
To wake and wage° a danger profitless.
DUKE: Nay, in all confidence he's not for Rhodes.
OFFICER: Here is more news.

(Enter a MESSENGER.)

MESSENGER: The Ottomites, reverend and gracious,
Steering with due course toward the isle of Rhodes,   40
Have there injointed them with an after fleet.
1. SENATOR: Ay, so I thought. How many, as you
guess?
MESSENGER: Of thirty sail; and now they do restem
Their backward course, bearing with frank
appearance
Their purposes toward Cyprus. Signior Montano,
Your trusty and most valiant servitor,
With his free duty° recommends° you thus,
And prays you to believe him.   50
DUKE: 'Tis certain then for Cyprus.
Marcus Luccicos, is not he in town?
1. SENATOR: He's now in Florence.
DUKE: Write from us to him; post, post-haste
dispatch.

(Enter BRABANTIO, OTHELLO, CASSIO, IAGO,
RODERIGO, and OFFICERS.)

1. SENATOR: Here comes Brabantio and the valiant
Moor.
DUKE: Valiant Othello, we must straight employ you
Against the general enemy Ottoman.
(to BRABANTIO) I did not see you. Welcome, gentle   60
signior.
We lacked your counsel and your help to-night.
BRABANTIO: So did I yours. Good your grace, pardon
me.
Neither my place, nor aught I heard of business,
Hath raised me from my bed; nor doth the general
care
Take hold on me; for my particular grief
Is of so floodgate° and o'erbearing nature
That it engluts and swallows other sorrows,   70
And it is still itself.
DUKE: Why, what's the matter?
BRABANTIO: My daughter! O my daughter!
ALL: Dead?
BRABANTIO: Ay, to me.
She is abused, stol'n from me, and corrupted
By spells and medicines bought of mountebanks;
For nature so prepost'rously to err,
Being not deficient, blind, or lame of sense,
Sans° witchcraft could not.   80

---

wage, risk. free duty, freely given expression of
loyalty. recommends, informs. floodgate, overflowing.
sans, without.

DUKE: Whoe'er he be that in this foul proceeding
  Hath thus beguiled your daughter of herself,
  And you of her, the bloody book of law
  You shall yourself read in the bitter letter
  After your own sense; yea, though our proper° son
  Stood in your action.°
BRABANTIO: Humbly I thank your grace.
  Here is the man—this Moor, whom now, it seems,
  Your special mandate for the state affairs
90 Hath hither brought.
ALL: We are very sorry for't.
DUKE (to OTHELLO): What, in your own part, can you
  say to this?
BRABANTIO: Nothing, but this is so.
OTHELLO: Most potent, grave, and reverend signiors,
  My very noble, and approved good masters,
  That I have ta'en away this old man's daughter,
  It is most true; true I have married her.
  The very head and front° of my offending
100 Hath this extent, no more. Rude am I in my
    speech,
  And little blessed with the soft phrase of peace;
  For since these arms of mine had seven years' pith°
  Till now some nine moons wasted, they have used
  Their dearest action in the tented field;
  And little of this great world can I speak
  More than pertains to feats of broil and battle;
  And therefore little shall I grace my cause
  In speaking for myself. Yet, by your gracious
110   patience,
  I will a round° unvarnished tale deliver
  Of my whole course of love—what drugs, what
    charms,
  What conjuration, and what mighty magic
  (For such proceeding am I charged withal)
  I won his daughter.
BRABANTIO: A maiden never bold;
  Of spirit so still and quiet that her motion
  Blushed at herself;° and she—in spite of nature,
120 Of years, of country, credit, everything—
  To fall in love with what she feared to look on!
  It is a judgment maimed and most imperfect
  That will confess perfection so could err
  Against all rules of nature, and must be driven
  To find out practices of cunning hell
  Why this should be. I therefore vouch again
  That with some mixtures pow'rful o'er the blood,
  Or with some dram, conjured to this effect,
  He wrought upon her.
130 DUKE: To vouch this is no proof,
  Without more certain and more overt test
  Than these thin habits° and poor likelihoods

Of modern seeming° do prefer against him.
1. SENATOR: But, Othello, speak.
  Did you by indirect and forcèd courses
  Subdue and poison this young maid's affections?
  Or came it by request, and such fair question
  As soul to soul affordeth?
OTHELLO: I do beseech you,
  Send for the lady to the Sagittary   130
  And let her speak of me before her father.
  If you do find me foul in her report,
  The trust, the office, I do hold of you
  Not only take away, but let your sentence
  Even fall upon my life.
DUKE: Fetch Desdemona hither.
OTHELLO: Ancient, conduct them; you best know the
    place.

(Exit IAGO, with two or three ATTENDANTS.)

  And till she come, as truly as to heaven
  I do confess the vices of my blood,   140
  So justly to your grave ears I'll present
  How I did thrive in this fair lady's love,
  And she in mine.
DUKE: Say it, Othello.
OTHELLO: Her father loved me, oft invited me;
  Still questioned me the story of my life
  From year to year—the battles, sieges, fortunes
  That I have passed.
  I ran it through, even from my boyish days
  To th' very moment that he bade me tell it.   150
  Wherein I spake of most disastrous chances,
  Of moving accidents by flood and field;
  Of hairbreadth scapes i' th' imminent deadly
    breach;
  Of being taken by the insolent foe
  And sold to slavery; of my redemption thence
  And portance° in my travel's history;
  Wherein of anters° vast and deserts idle,°
  Rough quarries, rocks, and hills whose heads touch
    heaven,   160
  It was my hint to speak—such was the process;
  And of the Cannibals that each other eat,
  The Anthropophagi,° and men whose heads
  Do grow beneath their shoulders. This to hear
  Would Desdemona seriously incline;
  But still the house affairs would draw her thence;
  Which ever as she could with haste dispatch,
  She'd come again, and with a greedy ear
  Devour up my discourse. Which I observing,
  Took once a pliant° hour, and found good means 170
  To draw from her a prayer of earnest heart
  That I would all my pilgrimage dilate,°

---

our proper, my own. *stood . . . action*, were accused by you. *head and front*, the utmost. *pith*, strength. *round*, plain. *her motion . . . herself*, her own emotions made her blush. *thin habits*, slight appearing.

modern seeming, commonplace suppositions. *portance*, behavior. *anters*, caves. *idle*, barren. *Anthropophagi*, man-eaters. *pliant*, convenient. *dilate*, relate.

Whereof by parcels° she had something heard,
But not intentively.° I did consent,
And often did beguile her of her tears
When I did speak of some distressful stroke
That my youth suffered. My story being done,
She gave me for my pains a world of sighs.
She swore, i' faith, 'twas strange, 'twas passing
    strange;
180
'Twas pitiful, 'twas wondrous pitiful.
She wished she had not heard it; yet she wished
That heaven had made her such a man. She
    thanked me;
And bade me, if I had a friend that loved her,
I should but teach him how to tell my story,
And that would woo her. Upon this hint° I spake.
She loved me for the dangers I had passed,
And I loved her that she did pity them.
190
This only is the witchcraft I have used.
Here comes the lady. Let her witness it.

(*Enter* DESDEMONA, IAGO, ATTENDANTS.)

DUKE: I think this tale would win my daughter too.
    Good Brabantio,
Take up this mangled matter at the best.
Men do their broken weapons rather use
Than their bare hands.
BRABANTIO: I pray you hear her speak.
If she confess that she was half the wooer,
Destruction on my head if my bad blame
200
Light on the man! Come hither, gentle mistress.
Do you perceive in all this noble company
Where most you owe obedience?
DESDEMONA: My noble father,
I do perceive here a divided duty.
To you I am bound for life and education;
My life and education° both do learn me
How to respect you: you are the lord of duty;
I am hitherto your daughter. But here's my
    husband;
210
And so much duty as my mother showed
To you, preferring you before her father,
So much I challenge° that I may profess
Due to the Moor my lord.
BRABANTIO: God b' wi' ye! I have done.
Please it your grace, on to the state affairs.
I had rather to adopt a child than get° it.
Come hither, Moor.
I here do give thee that with all my heart
Which, but thou hast already, with all my heart
220
I would keep from thee. For your sake,° jewel,
I am glad at soul I have no other child;
For thy escape would teach me tyranny,

To hang clogs on them. I have done, my lord.
DUKE: Let me speak like yourself° and lay a sentence°
Which, as a grise° or step, may help these lovers
Into your favor.
When remedies are past, the griefs are ended
By seeing the worst, which late on hopes depended.
To mourn a mischief that is past and gone
Is the next way to draw new mischief on.
230
What cannot be preserved when fortune takes,
Patience her injury a mock'ry makes.
The robbed that smiles steals something from the
    thief;
He robs himself that spends a bootless° grief.
BRABANTIO: So let the Turk of Cyprus us beguile:
We lose it not so long as we can smile.
He bears the sentence well that nothing bears
But the free comfort which from thence he hears;
But he bears both the sentence and the sorrow
240
That to pay grief must of poor patience borrow.
These sentences, to sugar, or to gall,
Being strong on both sides, are equivocal.
But words are words. I never yet did hear
That the bruised heart was piecèd° through the
    ear.
Beseech you, now to the affairs of state.
DUKE: The Turk with a most mighty preparation
makes for Cyprus. Othello, the fortitude of the
place is best known to you; and though we have
250
there a substitute of most allowed° sufficiency,
yet opinion, a sovereign mistress of effects,°
throws a more safer voice on you. You must
therefore be content to slubber° the gloss of your
new fortunes with this more stubborn and bois-
terous expedition.
OTHELLO: The tyrant custom, most grave senators,
Hath made the flinty and steel couch of war
My thrice-driven° bed of down. I do agnize°
260
A natural and prompt alacrity
I find in hardness;° and do undertake
These present wars against the Ottomites.
Most humbly, therefore, bending to your state,
I crave fit disposition° for my wife,
Due reference of place, and exhibition,°
With such accommodation and besort°
As levels with her breeding.
DUKE: If you please,
Be't at her father's.
270
BRABANTIO: I'll not have it so.

---

by parcels, in bits and pieces. *intentively,* with full attention. *hint,* opportunity. *education,* upbringing, *challenge,* claim. *get,* beget. *for your sake,* because of what you have done.

Let . . . yourself, as you should. *sentence,* maxim. *grise,* degree. *bootless,* unavailing. *piecèd,* relieved. *allowed,* acknowledged. *effects,* of what should be done. *slubber,* sully. *thrice-driven,* thrice-winnowed; i.e., softest. *agnize,* recognize. *alacrity . . . hardness,* readiness to endure hardship. *disposition,* suitable provision. *reference . . . exhibition,* assignment of residence and allowance of money. *besort,* suitable company.

OTHELLO: Nor I.
DESDEMONA: Nor I. I would not there reside,
  To put my father in impatient thoughts
  By being in his eye. Most gracious duke,
  To my unfolding lend your prosperous° ear,
  And let me find a charter in your voice,
  To assist my simpleness.
DUKE: What would you, Desdemona?
DESDEMONA: That I did love the Moor to live with
280 him,
  My downright violence, and storm of fortunes,
  May trumpet to the world. My heart's subdued
  Even to the very quality of my lord.
  I saw Othello's visage in my mind,
  And to his honors and his valiant parts
  Did I my soul and fortunes consecrate.
  So that, dear lords, if I be left behind,
  A moth of peace, and he go to war,
  The rites for which I love him are bereft me,
290 And I a heavy interim shall support
  By his dear absence. Let me go with him.
OTHELLO: Let her have your voices.
  Vouch with me, heaven, I therefore beg it not
  To please the palate of my appetite,
  Nor to comply with heat°—the young affects°
  In me defunct—and proper° satisfaction;
  But to be free and bounteous to her mind;
  And heaven defend° your good souls that you
    think
300 I will your serious and great business scant
  For° she is with me. No, when light-winged toys
  Of feathered Cupid seel° with wanton dullness
  My speculative and officed instruments,°
  That° my disports corrupt and taint my business,
  Let housewives make a skillet of my helm,
  And all indign° and base adversities
  Make head against my estimation!°
DUKE: Be it as you shall privately determine,
  Either for her stay or going. Th' affair cries haste,
310 And speed must answer it. You must hence
    to-night.
DESDEMONA: To-night, my lord?
DUKE: This night.
OTHELLO: With all my heart.
DUKE: At nine i' th' morning here we'll meet again.
  Othello, leave some officer behind,
  And he shall our commission bring to you,
  With such things else of quality and respect
  As doth import° you.
320 OTHELLO: So please your grace, my ancient;
  A man he is of honesty and trust.

To his conveyance I assign my wife,
With what else needful your good grace shall think
To be sent after me.
DUKE: Let it be so.
  Good night to every one. (to BRABANTIO) And,
    noble signior,
  If virtue no delighted° beauty lack,
  Your son-in-law is far more fair than black.
1. SENATOR: Adieu, brave Moor. Use Desdemona   330
  well.
BRABANTIO: Look to her, Moor, if thou hast eyes to
  see:
  She has deceived her father, and may thee.
OTHELLO: My life upon her faith!

(Exeunt DUKE, SENATORS, OFFICERS, etc.)

  Honest Iago,
  My Desdemona must I leave to thee.
  I prithee let thy wife attend on her,
  And bring them after in the best advantage.°
  Come, Desdemona. I have but an hour   340
  Of love, of worldly matters and direction,
  To spend with thee. We must obey the time.

(Exit MOOR and DESDEMONA.)

RODERIGO: Iago,—
IAGO: What say'st thou, noble heart?
RODERIGO: What will I do, think'st thou?
IAGO: Why, go to bed and sleep.
RODERIGO: I will incontinently° drown myself.
IAGO: If thou dost, I shall never love thee after. Why,
  thou silly gentleman?
RODERIGO: It is silliness to live when to live is tor-   350
  ment; and then have we a prescription to die
  when death is our physician.
IAGO: O villainous! I have looked upon the world for
  four times seven years; and since I could distinguish betwixt a benefit and an injury, I never
  found man that knew how to love himself. Ere I
  would say I would drown myself for the love of a
  guinea hen, I would change my humanity with a
  baboon.
RODERIGO: What should I do? I confess it is my   360
  shame to be so fond, but it is not in my virtue to
  amend it.
IAGO: Virtue? a fig! 'Tis in ourselves that we are thus
  or thus. Our bodies are our gardens, to the
  which our wills are gardeners; so that if we will
  plant nettles or sow lettuce, set hyssop and weed
  up thyme, supply it with one gender° of herbs or
  distract it with many—either to have it sterile
  with idleness or manured with industry—why,
  the power and corrigible° authority of this lies in   370

---

prosperous, favorable. heat, sexual desire. young affects, excesses of youthful passion. proper, personal. defend, forbid. For, because. seel, blind. My . . . instruments, perceptual and mental powers. That, so that. indign, shameful. estimation, reputation. import, concern.

---

delighted, delightful. in . . . advantage, at the most opportune time. incontinently, immediately. gender, species. corrigible, corrective.

our wills. If the balance of our lives had not one scale of reason to poise another of sensuality, the blood and baseness of our natures would conduct us to most preposterous conclusions. But we have reason to cool our raging motions, our carnal stings, our unbitted° lusts; whereof I take this that you call love to be a sect or scion.°

RODERIGO: It cannot be.

IAGO: It is merely a lust of the blood and a permission
380 of the will. Come, be a man! Drown thyself? Drown cats and blind puppies! I have professed me thy friend, and I confess me knit to thy deserving with cables of perdurable° toughness. I could never better stead° thee than now. Put money in thy purse. Follow these wars; defeat thy favor° with an usurped beard. I say, put money in thy purse. It cannot be that Desdemona should long continue her love to the Moor—put money in thy purse—nor he his to
390 her. It was a violent commencement, and thou shalt see an answerable sequestration°—put but money in thy purse. These Moors are changeable in their wills—fill thy purse with money. The food that to him now is as luscious as locusts° shall be to him shortly as bitter as coloquintida.° She must change for youth: when she is sated with his body, she will find the error of her choice. She must have change, she must. Therefore put money in thy purse. If thou wilt
400 needs damn thyself, do it a more delicate way than drowning. Make° all the money thou canst. If sanctimony° and a frail vow betwixt an erring° barbarian and a supersubtle° Venetian be not too hard for my wits and all the tribe of hell, thou shalt enjoy her. Therefore make money. A pox of drowning! 'Tis clean out of the way. Seek thou rather to be hanged in compassing thy joy than to be drowned and go without her.

RODERIGO: Wilt thou be fast° to my hopes, if I depend
410 on the issue?

IAGO: Thou art sure of me. Go, make money. I have told thee often, and I retell thee again and again, I hate the Moor. My cause is hearted;° thine hath no less reason. Let us be conjunctive in our revenge against him. If thou canst cuckold him, thou dost thyself a pleasure, me a sport. There are many events in the womb of time, which will

be delivered. Traverse,° go, provide thy money! We have more of this to-morrow. Adieu.

RODERIGO: Where shall we meet i' th' morning? 420

IAGO: At my lodging.

RODERIGO: I'll be there with thee betimes.

IAGO: Go to, farewell.—Do you hear, Roderigo?

RODERIGO: What say you?

IAGO: No more of drowning, do you hear?

RODERIGO: I am changed.

IAGO: Go to, farewell. Put money enough in your purse.

RODERIGO: I'll sell my land. (Exit.)

IAGO: Thus do I ever make my fool my purse; 430
For I mine own gained knowledge should profane
If I would time expend with such a snipe°
But for my sport and profit. I hate the Moor;
And it is thought abroad that 'twixt my sheets
H'as done my office. I know not if't be true;
Yet I, for mere suspicion in that kind,
Will do as if for surety.° He holds me well;°
The better shall my purpose work on him.
Cassio's a proper° man. Let me see now;
To get his place, and to plume up my will° 440
In double knavery—How, how? Let's see:—
After some time, to abuse Othello's ear
That he is too familiar with his wife.
He hath a person and a smooth dispose°
To be suspected—framed to make women false.
The Moor is of a free and open nature
That thinks men honest that but seem to be so;
And will as tenderly be led by th' nose
As asses are.
I have't! It is engendered! Hell and night 450
Must bring this monstrous birth to the world's
light. (Exit.)

ACT 2 / SCENE 1

(Enter MONTANO and two GENTLEMEN.)

MONTANO: What from the cape can you discern at sea?

1. GENTLEMAN: Nothing at all: it is a high-wrought flood.
I cannot 'twixt the heaven and the main
Descry a sail.

MONTANO: Methinks the wind hath spoke aloud at land;
A fuller blast ne'er shook our battlements.
If it hath ruffianed so upon the sea, 10
What ribs of oak, when mountains melt on them,
Can hold the mortise?° What shall we hear of this?

---

unbitted, uncontrolled. *sect or scion,* cutting or offshoot. *perdurable,* everlasting. *stead,* help. *defeat . . . favor,* disguise yourself. *sequestration,* equally abrupt ending. *locusts,* sweet Mediterranean fruit. *coloquintida,* bitter apple, used as a purgative. *Make,* raise, or get together. *sanctimony,* religious ceremony. *erring,* vagabond. *supersubtle,* highly refined. *fast,* true. *cause . . . hearted,* rooted in my heart; i.e., deeply felt.

Traverse, march forward. *snipe,* woodcock; silly bird, i.e., fool. *will . . . surety,* as if it were a proven fact. *well,* in high regard. *proper,* handsome. *plume . . . will,* dress up my intentions. *dispose,* manner. *hold . . . mortise,* hold the joints together.

2. GENTLEMAN: A segregation° of the Turkish fleet.
For do but stand upon the foaming shore,
The chidden billow seems to pelt the clouds;
The wind-shaked surge, with high and monstrous mane,
Seems to cast water on the burning Bear
And quench the guards° of th' ever-fixèd pole.
20 I never did like molestation° view
On the enchafèd flood.
MONTANO: If that the Turkish fleet
Be not ensheltered and embayed, they are drowned;
It is impossible they bear it out.

(Enter a third GENTLEMAN.)

3. GENTLEMAN: News, lads! Our wars are done.
The desperate tempest hath so banged the Turks
That their designment halts.° A noble ship of Venice
30 Hath seen a grievous wrack and sufferance°
On most part of their fleet.
MONTANO: How? Is this true?
3. GENTLEMAN: The ship is here put in,
A Veronesa;° Michael Cassio,
Lieutenant to the warlike Moor Othello,
Is come on shore; the Moor himself at sea,
And is in full commission here for Cyprus.
MONTANO: I am glad on't. 'Tis a worthy governor.
3. GENTLEMAN: But this same Cassio, though he speak
40 of comfort
Touching the Turkish loss, yet he looks sadly
And prays the Moor be safe, for they were parted
With foul and violent tempest.
MONTANO: Pray heaven he be;
For I have served him, and the man commands
Like a full soldier. Let's to the seaside, ho!
As well to see the vessel that's come in
As to throw out our eyes for brave Othello,
Even till we make the main° and th' aerial blue
50 An indistinct regard.°
3. GENTLEMAN: Come, let's do so;
For every minute is expectancy
Of more arrivance.

(Enter CASSIO.)

CASSIO: Thanks, you the valiant of this warlike isle,
That so approve the Moor! O, let the heavens
Give him defense against the elements,
For I have lost him on a dangerous sea!
MONTANO: Is he well shipped?
CASSIO: His bark is stoutly timbered, and his pilot

Of very expert and approved allowance;° 60
Therefore my hopes, not surfeited to death,
Stand in bold cure.° *(Within)* A sail, a sail, a sail!

(Enter a MESSENGER.)

CASSIO: What noise?
MESSENGER: The town is empty; on the brow o' th' sea
Stand ranks of people, and they cry 'A sail!'
CASSIO: My hopes do shape him for the governor. *(A shot.)*
2. GENTLEMAN: They do discharge their shot of courtesy:
Our friends at least. 70
CASSIO: I pray you, sir, go forth
And give us truth who 'tis that is arrived.
2. GENTLEMAN: I shall. *(Exit.)*
MONTANO: But, good lieutenant, is your general wived?
CASSIO: Most fortunately. He hath achieved a maid
That paragons° description and wild fame;
One that excels the quirks of blazoning pens,°
And in th' essential vesture of creation
Does tire the ingener.° 80

(Enter SECOND GENTLEMAN.)

How now? Who has put in?
2. GENTLEMAN: 'Tis one Iago, ancient to the general.
CASSIO: H'as had most favorable and happy speed:
Tempests themselves, high seas, and howling winds,
The guttered° rocks and congregated sands,
Traitors ensteeped° to clog the guiltless keel,
As having sense of beauty, do omit
Their mortal° natures, letting go safely by
The divine Desdemona. 90
MONTANO: What is she?
CASSIO: She that I spake of, our great captain's captain,
Left in the conduct of the bold Iago,
Whose footing° here anticipates our thoughts
A se'nnight's° speed. Great Jove, Othello guard,
And swell his sail with thine own pow'rful breath,
That he may bless this bay with his tall ship,
Make love's quick pants in Desdemona's arms,
Give renewed fire to our extincted spirits, 100
And bring all Cyprus comfort!

(Enter DESDEMONA, IAGO, RODERIGO, and EMILIA with ATTENDANTS.)

---

segregation, scattering. **guards,** stars near the North Star. **molestation,** disturbance. **halts,** plan is crippled. **sufferance,** damage. **Veronesa,** ship furnished by Verona. **main,** sea. **indistinct regard,** indistinguishable.

expert . . . allowance, skill. **not surfeited . . . cure,** not having been overindulged stand a good chance of being fulfilled. **paragons,** surpasses. **quirk . . . pens,** ingenious descriptions of writers who seek to list all her beauties. **in . . . ingener,** her essential nature as it was created by God overwhelms the imagination of anyone who seeks to praise it. **guttered,** jagged. **ensteeped,** submerged. **mortal,** deadly. **footing,** landing. **se'nnight's,** week's.

O, behold!
The riches of the ship is come on shore!
Ye men of Cyprus, let her have your knees.
Hail to thee, lady! and the grace of heaven,
Before, behind thee, and on every hand,
Enwheel thee round!

DESDEMONA: I thank you, valiant Cassio.
What tidings can you tell me of my lord?

110 CASSIO: He is not yet arrived; nor know I aught
But that he's well and will be shortly here.

DESDEMONA: O but I fear! How lost you company?

CASSIO: The great contention of the sea and skies
Parted our fellowship. (Within) A sail, a sail! (A shot.)
But hark, A sail!

2. GENTLEMAN: They give their greeting to the
citadel;
This likewise is a friend.

CASSIO: See for the news.

(Exit GENTLEMAN.)

120 Good ancient, you are welcome. (to EMILIA)
Welcome, mistress.—
Let it not gall your patience, good Iago,
That I extend° my manners. 'Tis my breeding
That gives me this bold show of courtesy. (Kisses
EMILIA.)

IAGO: Sir, would she give you so much of her lips
As of her tongue she oft bestows on me,
You would have enough.

DESDEMONA: Alas, she has no speech!

130 IAGO: In faith, too much.
I find it still when I have list° to sleep.
Marry, before your ladyship, I grant,
She puts her tongue a little in her heart
And chides with thinking.

EMILIA: You have little cause to say so.

IAGO: Come on, come on! You are pictures out of
doors,
Bells in your parlors, wildcats in your kitchens,
Saints in your injuries, devils being offended,
140 Players° in your housewifery, and housewives° in
your beds.

DESDEMONA: O, fie upon thee, slanderer!

IAGO: Nay, it is true, or else I am a Turk:
You rise to play, and go to bed to work.

EMILIA: You shall not write my praise.

IAGO: No, let me not.

DESDEMONA: What wouldst thou write of me, if thou
shouldst praise me?

IAGO: O gentle lady, do not put me to't,
150 For I am nothing if not critical.

DESDEMONA: Come on, assay.°—There's one gone to
the harbor?

IAGO: Ay, madam.

DESDEMONA: I am not merry; but I do beguile
The thing I am by seeming otherwise.—
Come, how wouldst thou praise me?

IAGO: I am about it; but indeed my invention
Comes from my pate as birdlime° does from
frieze°—
It plucks out brains and all. But my Muse labors, 160
And thus she is delivered:
If she be fair° and wise, fairness and wit—
The one's for use, the other useth it.

DESDEMONA: Well praised! How if she be black° and
witty?

IAGO: If she be black, and thereto have a wit,
She'll find a white that shall her blackness fit.

DESDEMONA: Worse and worse!

EMILIA: How if fair and foolish?

IAGO: She never yet was foolish that was fair, 170
For even her folly° helped her to an heir.

DESDEMONA: These are old fond° paradoxes to make
fools laugh i' th' alehouse. What miserable praise
has thou for her that's foul° and foolish?

IAGO: There's none so foul, and foolish thereunto,
But does foul pranks which fair and wise ones do.

DESDEMONA: O heavy ignorance! Thou praisest the
worst best. But what praise couldst thou bestow
on a deserving woman indeed—one that in the
authority of her merit did justly put on the 180
vouch° of very malice itself?

IAGO: She that was ever fair, and never proud;
Had tongue at will, and yet was never loud;
Never lacked gold, and yet went never gay;°
Fled from her wish, and yet said 'Now I may';
She that, being angered, her revenge being nigh,
Bade her wrong stay,° and her displeasure fly;
She that in wisdom never was so frail
To change the cod's head for the salmon's tail;°
She that could think, and ne'er disclose her mind; 190
See suitors following, and not look behind:
She was a wight° (if ever such wight were)—

DESDEMONA: To do what?

IAGO: To suckle fools° and chronicle small beer.°

DESDEMONA: O most lame and impotent conclusion!
Do not learn of him, Emilia, though he be thy
husband. How say you, Cassio? Is he not a most
profane and liberal° counsellor?

CASSIO: He speaks home,° madam. You may relish
him more in the° soldier than in the scholar. 200

---

extend, show. list, desire. Players, actors. housewives, hussies. assay, try.

birdlime, sticky paste used to catch birds. frieze, coarse
cloth. fair, blonde. black, brunette. folly, wantonness.
fond, foolish. foul, ugly. put . . . vouch, compel the praise.
gay, extravagantly dressed. stay, sense of injury cease. To
. . . tail, to exchange something common but valuable for
something rare but useless. wight, person. fools, babies.
chronicle . . . beer, keep petty household accounts in order.
liberal, free-speaking; i.e., lewd. home, bluntly. in the, in
the character of.

IAGO (aside): He takes her by the palm. Ay well said, whisper! With as little a web as this will I ensnare as great a fly as Cassio. Ay, smile upon her, do! I will gyve° thee in thine own courtship,°—You say true; 'tis so, indeed!—If such tricks as these strip you out of your lieutenantry, it had been better you had not kissed your three fingers so oft— which now again you are most apt to play the sir° in. Very good! well kissed! an excellent curtsy!
210 'Tis so, indeed. Yet again your fingers to your lips? Would they were clyster pipes° for your sake! (Trumpet within.) The Moor! I know his trumpet.

CASSIO: 'Tis truly so.

DESDEMONA: Let's meet him and receive him.

CASSIO: Lo, where he comes.

(Enter OTHELLO and ATTENDANTS.)

OTHELLO: O my fair warrior!

DESDEMONA: My dear Othello!

OTHELLO: It gives me wonder great as my content
220 To see you here before me. O my soul's joy!
If after every tempest come such calms,
May the winds blow till they have wakened death!
And let the laboring bark climb hills of seas
Olympus-high, and duck again as low
As hell's from heaven! If it were now to die,
'Twere now to be most happy; for I fear
My soul hath her content so absolute
That not another comfort like to this
Succeeds in unknown fate.
230 DESDEMONA: The heavens forbid
But that our loves and comforts should increase
Even as our days do grow.

OTHELLO: Amen to that, sweet powers!
I cannot speak enough of this content;
It stops me here; it is too much of joy.
And this, and this, the greatest discords be (They kiss.)
That e'er our hearts shall make!

IAGO (aside): O, you are well tuned now!
240 But I'll set down° the pegs that make this music,
As honest as I am.

OTHELLO: Come, let us to the castle.
News, friends! Our wars are done; the Turks are drowned.
How does my old acquaintance of this isle?—
Honey, you shall be well desired° in Cyprus;
I have found great love amongst them. O my sweet,
I prattle out of fashion, and I dote
In mine own comforts. I prithee, good Iago,
250 Go to the bay and disembark my coffers.

Bring thou the master to the citadel;
He is a good one, and his worthiness
Does challenge much respect.—Come, Desdemona,
Once more well met at Cyprus.

(Exit OTHELLO with all but IAGO and RODERIGO.)

IAGO (to an ATTENDANT, who goes out): Do thou meet me presently at the harbor. (to RODERIGO) Come hither. If thou be'st valiant (as they say base men being in love have then a nobility in their natures more than is native to them), list me. The 260 lieutenant to-night watches on the court of guard.° First, I must tell thee this: Desdemona is directly in love with him.

RODERIGO: With him? Why, 'tis not possible.

IAGO: Lay thy finger thus,° and let thy soul be instructed. Mark me with what violence she first loved the Moor, but for bragging and telling her fantastical lies; and will she love him still for prating? Let not thy discreet heart think it. Her eye must be fed; and what delight shall she have to 270 look on the devil? When the blood is made dull with the act of sport, there should be, again to inflame it and to give satiety a fresh appetite, loveliness in favor, sympathy in years, manners, and beauties; all which the Moor is defective in. Now for want of these required conveniences,° her delicate tenderness will find itself abused, begin to heave the gorge,° disrelish and abhor the Moor. Very nature will instruct her in it and compel her to some second choice. Now, sir, that 280 is granted—as it is a most pregnant and unforced position—who stands so eminent in the degree of this fortune as Cassio does? A knave very voluble; no further conscionable than in putting on the mere form of civil and humane° seeming for the better compassing of his salt° and most hidden loose affection? Why, none! why, none! A slipper° and subtle knave; a finder-out of occasions; that has an eye can stamp and counterfeit advantages, though true 290 advantage never present itself; a devilish knave! Besides, the knave is handsome, young, and hath all those requisites in him that folly and green° minds look after. A pestilent complete knave! and the woman hath found him already.

RODERIGO: I cannot believe that in her; she's full of most blessed condition.

IAGO: Blessed fig's-end! The wine she drinks is made of grapes. If she had been blessed, she would

---

gyve, trap. courtship, courtly manners. sir, courtly gentleman. clyster pipes, syringes for an enema. set down, loosen. well desired, warmly welcomed.

watches . . . guard, has charge of the watch. thus, on your lips. conveniences, compatibilities. heave . . . gorge, be nauseated. humane, courteous. salt, lecherous. slipper, slippery. green, wanton and youthful.

300   never have loved the Moor. Blessed pudding!
Didst thou not see her paddle with the palm of
his hand? Didst not mark that?

RODERIGO: Yes, that I did; but that was but courtesy.

IAGO: Lechery, by this hand! an index and obscure
prologue to the history of lust and foul thoughts.
They met so near with their lips that their
breaths embraced together. Villainous thoughts,
Roderigo! When these mutualities so marshal
the way, hard at hand comes the master and

310   main exercise, th' incorporate° conclusion. Pish!
But, sir, be you ruled by me: I have brought you
from Venice. Watch you to-night; for the command, I'll lay't upon you. Cassio knows you not.
I'll not be far from you: do you find some occasion to anger Cassio, either by speaking too loud,
or tainting° his discipline, or from what other
course you please which the time shall more
favorably minister.

RODERIGO: Well.

320 IAGO: Sir, he is rash and very sudden in choler,° and
haply with his truncheon may strike at you. Provoke him that he may; for even out of that will I
cause these of Cyprus to mutiny; whose qual-
ification° shall come into no true taste again but
by the displanting of Cassio. So shall you have a
shorter journey to your desires by the means I
shall then have to prefer° them; and the imped-
iment most profitably removed without the
which there were no expectation of our prosper-

330   ity.

RODERIGO: I will do this if you can bring it to any
opportunity.

IAGO: I warrant thee. Meet me by and by at the
citadel; I must fetch his necessaries ashore.
Farewell.

RODERIGO: Adieu (Exit.)

IAGO: That Cassio loves her, I do well believe it;
That she loves him, 'tis apt and of great credit.°
The Moor, howbeit that I endure him not,

340 Is of a constant, loving, noble nature,
And I dare think he'll prove to Desdemona
A most dear husband. Now I do love her too;
Not out of absolute lust, though peradventure
I stand accountant for as great a sin,
But partly led to diet my revenge,
For that I do suspect the lusty Moor
Hath leaped into my seat; the thought whereof
Doth, like a poisonous mineral, gnaw my inwards;
And nothing can or shall content my soul

350 Till I am evened with him, wife for wife;
Or failing so, yet that I put the Moor
At least into a jealousy so strong

That judgment cannot cure. Which thing to do,
If this poor trash of Venice, whom I trash°
For his quick hunting, stand the putting on,°
I'll have our Michael Cassio on the hip,°
Abuse him to the Moor in the rank garb°
(For I fear Cassio with my nightcap too),
Make the Moor thank me, love me, and reward me
For making him egregiously an ass   360
And practicing upon° his peace and quiet
Even to madness. 'Tis here, but yet confused:
Knavery's plain face is never seen till used. (Exit.)

ACT 2 / SCENE 2

(Enter OTHELLO'S HERALD, with a proclamation.)

HERALD: It is Othello's pleasure, our noble and valiant general, that, upon certain tidings now arrived, importing the mere perdition° of the Turkish fleet, every man put himself into triumph;
some to dance, some to make bonfires, each man
to what sport and revels his addiction leads him.
For, besides these beneficial news, it is the celebration of his nuptial. So much was his pleasure
should be proclaimed. All offices° are open, and
there is full liberty of feasting from this present   10
hour of five till the bell have told eleven. Heaven
bless the isle of Cyprus and our noble general
Othello! (Exit.)

ACT 2 / SCENE 3

(Enter OTHELLO, DESDEMONA, CASSIO, and ATTEN-
DANTS.)

OTHELLO: Good Michael, look you to the guard
    to-night.
Let's teach ourselves that honorable stop,
Not to outsport discretion.

CASSIO: Iago hath direction what to do;
But not withstanding, with my personal eye
Will I look to't.

OTHELLO: Iago is most honest.
Michael, good night. To-morrow with your earliest
Let me have speech with you. (to DESDEMONA)   10
    Come, my dear love.
The purchase made, the fruits are to ensue;
That profit's yet to come 'tween me and you.—
Good night.

(Exit OTHELLO with DESDEMONA and ATTENDANTS.)
(Enter IAGO.)

---

incorporate, sexual. *tainting*, discrediting. *sudden in choler*, quick to anger. *qualification*, satisfaction. *prefer*, advance. *apt . . . credit*, probable and believable.

trash, hang weights on, as was done to hounds to restrain them from hunting too fast. *stand the putting on*, performs properly in response to my command. *on the hip*, in a vulnerable position (a term from wrestling). *rank garb*, coarse manner. *practicing upon*, plotting against. *perdition*, complete destruction. *offices*, kitchens and storerooms.

CASSIO: Welcome, Iago. We must to the watch.

IAGO: Not this hour, lieutenant; 'tis not yet ten o' th' clock. Our general cast° us thus early for the love of his Desdemona; who let us not therefore blame. He hath not yet made wanton the night with her, and she is sport for Jove.

20

CASSIO: She's a most exquisite lady.

IAGO: And, I'll warrant her, full of game.

CASSIO: Indeed, she's a most fresh and delicate creature.

IAGO: What an eye she has! Methinks it sounds a parley to provocation.

CASSIO: An inviting eye; and yet methinks right modest.

IAGO: And when she speaks, is it not an alarum° to love?

30

CASSIO: She is indeed perfection.

IAGO: Well, happiness to their sheets! Come, lieutenant, I have a stoup° of wine, and here without are a brace of Cyprus gallants that would fain have a measure to the health of black Othello.

CASSIO: Not to-night, good Iago. I have very poor and unhappy brains for drinking; I could well wish courtesy would invent some other custom of entertainment.

40

IAGO: O, they are our friends. But one cup! I'll drink for you.

CASSIO: I have drunk but one cup to-night, and that was craftily qualified° too; and behold what innovation° it makes here. I am unfortunate in the infirmity and dare not task my weakness with any more.

IAGO: What, man! 'Tis a night of revels: the gallants desire it.

CASSIO: Where are they?

50

IAGO: Here at the door; I pray you call them in.

CASSIO: I'll do't, but it dislikes me.° (Exit.)

IAGO: If I can fasten but one cup upon him
With that which he hath drunk to-night already,
He'll be as full of quarrel and offense
As my young mistress' dog. Now my sick fool
   Roderigo,
Whom love hath turned almost the wrong side out,
To Desdemona hath to-night caroused
Potations pottle-deep;° and he's to watch.

60

Three lads of Cyprus—noble swelling spirits,
That hold their honors in a wary distance,°
The very elements of this warlike isle—
Have I to-night flustered with flowing cups,
And they watch too. Now, 'mongst this flock of
   drunkards

---

    cast, dismissed.   **alarum**, trumpet signal.   **stoup**, two-quart tankard.   **craftily qualified**, carefully diluted. **innovation**, disturbing change.   **it dislikes me**, I don't want to.   **pottle-deep**, to the bottom of the tankard.   **hold ... distance**, are very touchy about their honor.

Am I to put our Cassio in some action
That may offend the isle.

(Enter CASSIO, MONTANO, and GENTLEMEN; SERVANTS following with wine.)

But here they come.
If consequence do but approve my dream,°
My boat sails freely, both with wind and stream.

70

CASSIO: 'Fore God, they have given me a rouse° already.

MONTANO: Good faith, a little one; not past a pint, as I am a soldier.

IAGO: Some wine, ho!

(Sings)

   And let me the canakin clink, clink;
   And let me the canakin clink.
      A soldier's a man;
      A life's but a span,
   Why then, let a soldier drink.

80

Some wine, boys!

CASSIO: 'Fore God, an excellent song!

IAGO: I learned it in England, where indeed they are most potent in potting. Your Dane, your German, and your swag-bellied Hollander—Drink, ho!—are nothing to your English.

CASSIO: Is your Englishman so expert in his drinking?

IAGO: Why, he drinks you with facility your Dane dead drunk; he sweats not to overthrow your Almain;° he gives your Hollander a vomit ere the next pottle can be filled.

90

CASSIO: To the health of our general!

MONTANO: I am for it, lieutenant, and I'll do you justice.

IAGO: O sweet England!

(Sings)

   King Stephen was a worthy peer;
      His breeches cost him but a crown;
   He held 'em sixpence all to dear,
      With that he called the tailor lown.°
   He was a wight of high renown,
      And thou art but of low degree.
   'Tis pride that pulls the country down;
      Then take thine auld cloak about thee.

100

Some wine, ho!

CASSIO: 'Fore God, this is a more exquisite song than the other.

IAGO: Will you hear't again?

    If ... dream, if events work out as I hope.   **rouse**, drink.   **Almain**, German.   **lown**, rascal.

CASSIO: No, for I hold him to be unworthy of his
110 place that does those things. Well, God's above
  all; and there be souls must be saved, and there
  be souls must not be saved.
IAGO: It's true, good lieutenant.
CASSIO: For mine own part—no offense to the general, nor any man of quality—I hope to be saved.
IAGO: And so do I too, lieutenant.
CASSIO: Ay, but by your leave, not before me. The
  lieutenant is to be saved before the ancient. Let's
  have no more of this; let's to our affairs.—God
120 forgive us our sins!—Gentlemen, let's look to our
  business. Do not think, gentlemen, I am drunk.
  This is my ancient; this is my right hand, and this
  is my left. I am not drunk now. I can stand well
  enough, and speak well enough.
ALL: Excellent well!
CASSIO: Why, very well then. You must not think
  then that I am drunk. *(Exit.)*
MONTANO: To th' platform, masters. Come, let's set
  the watch.
130 IAGO: You see this fellow that is gone before.
  He is a soldier fit to stand by Caesar
  And give direction; and do but see his vice.
  'Tis to his virtue a just equinox,°
  The one as long as th' other. 'Tis pity of him.
  I fear the trust Othello puts him in,
  On some odd time of his infirmity,
  Will shake this island.
MONTANO: But is he often thus?
IAGO: 'Tis evermore the prologue to his sleep:
140 He'll watch the horologe a double set°
  If drink rock not his cradle.
MONTANO: It were well
  The general were put in mind of it.
  Perhaps he sees it not, or his good nature
  Prizes the virtue that appears in Cassio
  And looks not on his evils. Is not this true?

(Enter RODERIGO.)

IAGO *(aside to him)*: How now, Roderigo?
  I pray you after the lieutenant, go!

(Exit RODERIGO.)

MONTANO: And 'tis great pity that the noble Moor
150 Should hazard such a place as his own second
  With one of an ingraft° infirmity.
  It were an honest action to say
  So to the Moor.
IAGO: Not I, for this fair island!
  I do love Cassio well and would do much
  To cure him of this evil. *(Within)* Help! help!
  But hark! What noise?

(Enter CASSIO, *driving in* RODERIGO.)

CASSIO: Zounds, you rogue! you rascal!
MONTANO: What's the matter, lieutenant?
CASSIO: A knave teach me my duty?   160
  I'll beat the knave into a twiggen° bottle.
RODERIGO: Beat me?
CASSIO: Dost thou prate, rogue? *(Strikes him.)*
MONTANO: Nay, good lieutenant! *(Stays him.)*
  Pray, sir, hold your hand.
CASSIO: Let me go, sir.
  Or I'll knock you o'er the mazzard.°
MONTANO: Come, come, you're drunk!
CASSIO: Drunk? *(They fight.)*
IAGO *(aside to* RODERIGO): Away, I say! Go out and cry 170
  a mutiny!

(Exit RODERIGO.)

  Nay, good lieutenant. God's will gentlemen!
  Help, ho!—lieutenant—sir—Montano—sir—
  Help, masters!—Here'a a goodly watch indeed!

(A bell rung.)

  Who's that which rings the bell? Diablo, ho!
  The town will rise. God's will, lieutenant, hold!
  You will be shamed for ever.

(Enter OTHELLO *and* GENTLEMEN *with weapons.)*

OTHELLO: What is the matter here?
MONTANO: Zounds, I bleed still. I am hurt to death.
  He dies!   180
OTHELLO: Hold for your lives!
IAGO: Hold, hold! Lieutenant—
  sir—Montano—gentlemen!
  Have you forgot all sense of place and duty?
  Hold! The general speaks to you. Hold, hold, for
  shame!
OTHELLO: Why, how now, ho? From whence ariseth
  this?
  Are we turned Turks, and to ourselves do that
  Which heaven hath forbid the Ottomites?   190
  For Christian shame put by this barbarous brawl!
  He that stirs next to carve for° his own rage
  Holds his soul light; he dies upon his motion.
  Silence that dreadful bell! It frights the isle
  From her propriety.° What's the matter, masters?
  Honest Iago, that looks dead with grieving,
  Speak. Who began this? On thy love, I charge thee.
IAGO: I do not know. Friends all but now, even now,
  In quarter, and in terms like bride and groom
  Devesting them for bed; and then, but now— 200
  As if some planet had unwitted men—
  Swords out, and tilting one at other's breast
  In opposition bloody. I cannot speak

---

  just equinox, exact equivalent. *watch ... set*, stay
awake two times around the clock. *ingraft*, ingrained.

  twiggen, wicker covered. *mazzard*, head. *carve for*,
indulge. *propriety*, natural condition.

Any beginning to this peevish odds.°
And would in action glorious I had lost
Those legs that brought me to a part of it!
OTHELLO: How comes it, Michael, you are thus
forgot?
CASSIO: I pray you pardon me; I cannot speak.
210 OTHELLO: Worthy Montano, you were wont be civil;
The gravity and stillness of your youth
The world hath noted, and your name is great
In mouths of wisest censure.° What's the matter
That you unlace your reputation thus
And spend your rich opinion° for the name
Of a night-brawler? Give me answer to't.
MONTANO: Worthy Othello, I am hurt to danger.
Your officer, Iago, can inform you,
While I spare speech, which something now
220 offends° me,
Of all that I do know; nor know I aught
By me that's said or done amiss this night,
Unless self-charity be sometimes a vice,
And to defend ourselves it be a sin
When violence assails us.
OTHELLO: Now, by heaven,
My blood begins my safer guides to rule,
And passion, having my best judgment collied,°
Assays to lead the way. If I once stir
230 Or do but lift this arm, the best of you
Shall sink in my rebuke. Give me to know
How this foul rout began, who set it on;
And he that is approved in° this offense,
Though he had twinned with me, both at a birth,
Shall lose me. What! in a town of war,
Yet wild, the people's hearts brimful of fear,
To manage° private and domestic quarrel?
In night, and on the court and guard of safety?
'Tis monstrous. Iago, who began't?
240 MONTANO: If partially affined, or leagued in office,°
Thou dost deliver more or less than truth,
Thou art no soldier.
IAGO: Touch me not so near.
I had rather have this tongue cut from my mouth
Than it should do offense to Michael Cassio;
Yet I persuade myself, to speak the truth
Shall nothing wrong him. Thus it is, general.
Montano and myself being in speech,
There comes a fellow crying out for help,
250 And Cassio following him with determined sword
To execute° upon him. Sir, this gentleman
Steps in to Cassio and entreats his pause.
Myself the crying fellow did pursue,
Lest by his clamor—as it so fell out—

The town might fall in fright. He, swift of foot,
Outran my purpose; and I returned the rather
For that I heard the clink and fall of swords,
And Cassio high in oath; which till to-night
I ne'er might say before. When I came back—
For this was brief—I found them close together   260
At blow and thrust, even as again they were
When you yourself did part them.
More of this matter cannot I report;
But men are men; the best sometimes forget.
Though Cassio did some little wrong to him,
As men in rage strike those that wish them best,
Yet surely Cassio I believe received
From him that fled some strange indignity,
Which patience could not pass.°
OTHELLO: I know, Iago,   270
Thy honesty and love doth mince this matter,
Making it light to Cassio. Cassio, I love thee;
But never more be officer of mine.

(Enter DESDEMONA, attended.)

Look if my gentle love be not raised up!
I'll make thee an example.
DESDEMONA: What's the matter?
OTHELLO: All's well now, sweeting; come away to bed.
(to Montano) Sir, for your hurts, myself will be your
surgeon.
Lead him off. (MONTANO is led off.)   280
Iago, look with care about the town
And silence those whom this vile brawl distracted.
Come, Desdemona: 'tis the soldiers' life
To have their balmy slumbers waked with strife.

(Exit with all but IAGO and CASSIO.)

IAGO: What, are you hurt, lieutenant?
CASSIO: Ay, past all surgery.
IAGO: Marry, God forbid!
CASSIO: Reputation, reputation, reputation! O, I
have lost my reputation! I have lost the immortal
part of myself, and what remains is bestial. My   290
reputation, Iago, my reputation!
IAGO: As I am an honest man, I thought you had
received some bodily wound. There is more
sense in that than in reputation. Reputation is an
idle and most false imposition; oft got without
merit and lost without deserving. You have lost
no reputation at all unless you repute yourself
such a loser. What, man! there are ways to recover the general again. You are but now cast in
his mood°—a punishment more in policy than in 300
malice, even so as one would beat his offenseless
dog to affright an imperious lion. Sue to him
again, and he's yours.
CASSIO: I will rather sue to be despised than to de-

---

peevish odds, childish quarrel. censure, judgment.
opinion, high reputation. offends, pains. collied, darkened. approved in, proved guilty of. manage, carry on.
partially . . . office, biased because of personal or official ties.
execute, work his will.

pass, ignore. cast . . . mood, dismissed because of his
anger.

ceive so good a commander with so slight, so
drunken, and so indiscreet an officer. Drunk!
and speak parrot!° and squabble! swagger!
swear! and discourse fustian° with one's own
shadow! O thou invisible spirit of wine, if thou
310   hast no name to be known by, let us call thee
devil!

IAGO: What was he that you followed with your
sword? What had he done to you?

CASSIO: I know not.

IAGO: Is't possible?

CASSIO: I remember a mass of things, but nothing
distinctly; a quarrel, but nothing wherefore. O
God, that men should put an enemy in their
mouths to steal away their brains! that we should
320   with joy, pleasance, revel, and applause transform outselves into beasts!

IAGO: Why, but you are now well enough. How come
you thus recovered?

CASSIO: It hath pleased the devil drunkenness to give
place to the devil wrath. One unperfectness
shows me another, to make me frankly despise
myself.

IAGO: Come, you are too severe a moraler. As the
time, the place, and the condition of this country
330   stands, I could heartily wish this had not so befall'n; but since it is as it is, mend it for your own
good.

CASSIO: I will ask him for my place again: he shall tell
me I am a drunkard! Had I as many mouths as
Hydra,° such an answer would stop them all. To
be now a sensible man, by and by a fool, and
presently a beast! O strange! Every inordinate
cup is unblest, and the ingredient is a devil.

IAGO: Come, come, good wine is a good familiar crea-
340   ture if it be well used. Exclaim no more against it.
And, good lieutenant, I think you think I love
you.

CASSIO: I have well approved° it, sir. I drunk!

IAGO: You or any man living may be drunk at some
time, man. I'll tell you what you shall do. Our
general's wife is now the general. I may say so in
this respect, for he hath devoted and given up
himself to the contemplation, mark, and de-
notement of her parts and graces. Confess your-
350   self freely to her; importune her help to put you
in your place again. She is of so free,° so kind, so
apt, so blessed a disposition she holds it a vice in
her goodness not to do more than she is re-
quested. This broken joint between you and her
husband entreat her to splinter;° and my fortunes against any lay° worth naming, this crack

of your love shall grow stronger than 'twas before.

CASSIO: You advise me well.

IAGO: I protest, in the sincerity of love and honest   360
kindness.

CASSIO: I think it freely; and betimes in the morning
will I beseech the virtuous Desdemona to undertake for me. I am desperate of my fortunes if
they check me here.

IAGO: You are in the right. Good night, lieutenant; I
must to the watch.

CASSIO: Good night, honest Iago.

(*Exit* CASSIO.)

IAGO: And what's he then that says I play the villain,
When this advice is free I give and honest,   370
Probal° to thinking, and indeed the course
To win the Moor again? For 'tis most easy
Th' inclining Desdemona to subdue°
In any honest suit; she's framed as fruitful°
As the free elements. And then for her
To win the Moor—were't to renounce his baptism,
All seals and symbols of redeemèd sin—
His soul is so enfettered to her love
That she may make, unmake, do what she list,°
Even as her appetite shall play the god   380
With his weak function. How am I then a villain
To counsel Cassio to this parallel course,
Directly to his good? Divinity° of hell!
When devils will the blackest sins put on,
They do suggest at first with heavenly shows,
As I do now. For whiles this honest fool
Plies Desdemona to repair his fortunes,
And she for him pleads strongly to the Moor,
I'll pour this pestilence into his ear,
That she repeals° him for her body's lust;   390
And by how much she strives to do him good,
She shall undo her credit with the Moor.
So will I turn her virtue into pitch,
And out of her own goodness make the net
That shall enmesh them all.

(*Enter* RODERIGO.)

How, now, Roderigo?

RODERIGO: I do follow here in the chase, not like a
hound that hunts, but one that fills up the cry.°
My money is almost spent; I have been to-night
exceedingly well cudgelled; and I think the issue   400
will be—I shall have so much experience for my
pains; and so, with no money at all, and a little
more wit, return again to Venice.

IAGO: How poor are they that have not patience!
What wound did ever heal but by degrees?

---

speak parrot, talk nonsense. **fustian,** bombastic gibberish. **Hydra,** many-headed monster of classical mythology. **approved,** proved. **free,** generous. **splinter,** bind
up with splints. **lay,** wager.

Probal, probable. **subdue,** persuade. **fruitful,** generous. **list,** pleases. **Divinity,** theology. **repeals,** pleads for
his reinstatement. **cry,** pack.

Thou know'st we work by wit, and not by
   witchcraft;
And wit depends on dilatory time.
Does't not go well? Cassio hath beaten thee,
410 And thou by that small hurt hast cashiered° Cassio.
Though other things grow fair against the sun,
Yet fruits that blossom first will first be ripe.
Content thyself awhile. By the mass, 'tis morning!
Pleasure and action make the hours seem short.
Retire thee; go where thou art billeted.
Away, I say! Thou shalt know more hereafter.
Nay, get thee gone!

(Exit RODERIGO.)

Two things are to be done;
My wife must move for Cassio to her mistress;
420 I'll set her on;
Myself the while to draw the Moor apart
And bring him jump° when he may Cassio find
Soliciting his wife. Ay, that's the way!
Dull not device by coldness and delay. *(Exit.)*

ACT 3 / SCENE 1

(Enter CASSIO, *with* MUSICIANS.)

CASSIO: Masters, play here, I will content° your pains:
   Something that's brief; and bid 'Good morrow,
   general.'

(They play.)
(Enter the CLOWN.)

CLOWN: Why, masters, ha' your instruments been at
   Naples, that they speak i' th' nose° thus?
MUSICIAN: How, sir, how?
CLOWN: Are these, I pray, called wind instruments?
MUSICIAN: Ay, marry, are they, sir.
CLOWN: O, thereby hangs a tail.
10 MUSICIAN: Whereby hangs a tale, sir?
CLOWN: Marry, sir, by many a wind instrument that I
   know. But, masters, here's money for you; and
   the general so likes your music that he desires
   you, for love's sake, to make no more noise with
   it.
MUSICIAN: Well, sir, we will not.
CLOWN: If you have any music that may not be heard,
   to't again: but, as they say, to hear music the
   general does not greatly care.
20 MUSICIAN: We have none such, sir.
CLOWN: Then put up your pipes in your bag, for I'll
   away. Go, vanish into air, away!

---

cashiered, brought about Cassio's discharge.   *jump,* at
the exact moment.   *content,* reward you for.   *Naples . . .*
nose, Naples was reputed to be a center of venereal disease,
and venereal diseases were thought to damage the structure
of the nose, resulting in a peculiar nasal sound.

(Exit MUSICIAN *with his fellows.)*

CASSIO: Dost thou hear, my honest friend?
CLOWN: No I hear not your honest friend. I hear you.
CASSIO: Prithee keep up thy quillets.° There's a poor
   piece of gold for thee. If the gentlewoman that
   attends the general's wife be stirring, tell her
   there's one Cassio entreats her a little favor of
   speech. Wilt thou do this?
CLOWN: She is stirring, sir. If she will stir hither, I 30
   shall seem to notify unto her.
CASSIO: Do, good my friend.

(Exit CLOWN.)
(Enter IAGO.)

In happy time, Iago.
IAGO: You have not been abed then!
CASSIO: Why, no; the day had broke
   Before we parted. I have made bold, Iago,
   To send in to your wife; my suit to her
   Is that she will to virtuous Desdemona
   Procure me some access.
IAGO: I'll send her to you presently;   40
   And I'll devise a mean to draw the Moor
   Out of the way, that your converse and business
   May be more free.
CASSIO: I humbly thank you, for't.

(Exit IAGO.)

I never knew
A Florentine more kind and honest.

(Enter EMILIA.)

EMILIA: Good morrow, good lieutenant. I am sorry
   For your displeasure; but all will sure be well.
   The general and his wife are talking of it,
   And she speaks for you stoutly. The Moor replies 50
   That he you hurt is of great fame in Cyprus
   And great affinity,° and that in wholesome wisdom
   He might not but refuse you; but he protests he
     loves you,
   And needs no other suitor but his likings
   To take the safest occasion by the front°
   To bring you in again.
CASSIO: Yet I beseech you,
   If you think fit, or that it may be done,
   Give me advantage of some brief discourse   60
   With Desdemona alone.
EMILIA: Pray you come in.
   I will bestow you where you shall have time
   To speak your bosom° freely.
CASSIO: I am much bound to you. *(Exeunt.)*

---

quillets, puns.   affinity, family connections.   *front,*
forelock.   *speak . . . bosom,* most private thoughts.

ACT 3 / SCENE 2

(Enter OTHELLO, IAGO, *and* GENTLEMEN.*)*

OTHELLO: These letters give, Iago, to the pilot
  And by him do my duties° to the Senate.
  That done, I will be walking on the works;°
  Repair there to me.
IAGO: Well, my good lord, I'll do't.
OTHELLO: This fortification, gentlemen, shall we
    see't?
GENTLEMEN: We'll wait upon your lordship. *(Exeunt.)*

ACT 3 / SCENE 3

(Enter DESDEMONA, CASSIO, *and* EMILIA.*)*

DESDEMONA: Be thou assured, good Cassio, I will do
  All my abilities in thy behalf.
EMILIA: Good madam, do. I warrant it grieves my
      husband
  As if the cause were his.
DESDEMONA: O, that's an honest fellow. Do not doubt,
    Cassio,
  But I will have my lord and you again
  As friendly as you were.
10 CASSIO: Bounteous madam,
  Whatever shall become of Michael Cassio,
  He's never anything but your true servant.
DESDEMONA: I know't; I thank you. You do love my
    lord;
  You have known him long; and be you well assured
  He shall in strangeness° stand no farther off
  Than in a politic distance.
CASSIO: Ay, but, lady,
  That policy may either last so long,
20 Or feed upon such nice° and waterish diet,
  Or breed itself so out of circumstance,
  That, I being absent, and my place supplied,
  My general will forget my love and service.
DESDEMONA: Do not doubt° that; before Emilia here
  I give thee warrant of thy place. Assure thee,
  If I do vow a friendship, I'll perform it
  To the last article. My lord shall never rest;
  I'll watch him tame° and talk him out of patience;
  His bed shall seem a school, his board a shrift;°
30 I'll intermingle everything he does
  With Cassio's suit. Therefore be merry, Cassio,
  For thy solicitor shall rather die
  Than give thy cause away.

(Enter OTHELLO *and* IAGO *at a distance.)*

EMILIA: Madam, here comes my lord.
CASSIO: Madam, I'll take my leave.

---

  duties, pay my respects. **works,** fortifications.
strangeness, aloofness. **nice,** trivial. **doubt,** fear. **tame,**
keep him awake (hawks were tamed by being kept awake).
shrift, confessional.

DESDEMONA: Why, stay, and hear me speak.
CASSIO: Madam, not now; I am very ill at ease,
  Unfit for my own purposes.
DESDEMONA: Well, do your discretion.

(Exit CASSIO.*)*

IAGO: Ha! I like not that.   40
OTHELLO: What dost thou say?
IAGO: Nothing, my lord; or if—I know not what.
OTHELLO: Was not that Cassio parted from my wife?
IAGO: Cassio, my lord? No, sure, I cannot think it,
  That he would steal away so guilty-like,
  Seeing you coming.
OTHELLO: I do believe 'twas he.
DESDEMONA: How now, my lord?
  I have been talking with a suitor here,
  A man that languishes in your displeasure.   50
OTHELLO: Who is't you mean?
DESDEMONA: Why, your lieutenant, Cassio. Good my
    lord,
  If I have any grace or power to move you,
  His present reconciliation° take;
  For if he be not one that truly loves you,
  That errs in ignorance, and not in cunning,
  I have no judgment in an honest face.
  I prithee call him back.
OTHELLO: Went he hence now?   60
DESDEMONA: Yes, faith; so humbled
  That he hath left part of his grief with me
  To suffer with him. Good love, call him back.
OTHELLO: Not now, sweet Desdemon; some other
    time.
DESDEMONA: But shall't be shortly?
OTHELLO: The sooner, sweet, for you.
DESDEMONA: Shall't be to-night at supper?
OTHELLO: No, not to-night.
DESDEMONA: To-morrow dinner then?   70
OTHELLO: I shall not dine at home;
  I meet the captains at the citadel.
DESDEMONA: Why then, to-morrow night, or Tuesday
    morn,
  On Tuesday noon or night, or Wednesday morn.
  I prithee name the time, but let it not
  Exceed three days. I' faith, he's penitent;
  And yet his trespass, in our common reason
  (Save that, they say, the wars must make examples
  Out of their best), is not almost° a fault   80
  T' incur a private check.° When shall he come?
  Tell me, Othello. I wonder in my soul
  What you could ask me that I should deny
  Or stand so mamm'ring on.° What? Michael Cassio,
  That came a-wooing with you, and so many a time,
  When I have spoke of you dispraisingly,

---

  reconciliation, accept his repentance. **almost,** hardly.
private check, even a private reprimand. **stand . . . on,** be so
hesitant to do.

Hath ta'en your part—to have so much to do
To bring him in? By'r Lady, I could do much—

OTHELLO: Prithee no more. Let him come when he
90   will!
I will deny thee nothing.

DESDEMONA: Why, this is not a boon;
'Tis as I should entreat you wear your gloves,
Or feed on nourishing dishes, or keep you warm,
Or sue to you to do a peculiar profit
To your own person. Nay, when I have a suit
Wherein I mean to touch your love indeed,
It shall be full of poise and difficult weight,
And fearful to be granted.

100   OTHELLO: I will deny thee nothing!
Whereon I do beseech thee grant me this,
To leave me but a little to myself.

DESDEMONA: Shall I deny you? No. Farewell, my lord.

OTHELLO: Farewell, my Desdemon: I'll come to thee
straight.

DESDEMONA: Emilia, come.—Be as your fancies teach
you;
Whate'er you be, I am obedient. (*Exit with* EMILIA.)

OTHELLO: Excellent wretch! Perdition catch my soul
110   But I do love thee! and when I love thee not,
Chaos is come again.

IAGO: My noble lord—

OTHELLO: What dost thou say, Iago?

IAGO: Did Michael Cassio, when you wooed my lady,
Know of your love?

OTHELLO: He did, from first to last. Why dost thou
ask?

IAGO: But for a satisfaction of my thought;
No further harm.

120   OTHELLO: Why of thy thought, Iago?

IAGO: I did not think he had been acquainted with
her.

OTHELLO: O, yes, and went between us very oft.

IAGO: Indeed?

OTHELLO: Indeed? Ay, indeed! Discern'st thou aught
in that?
Is he not honest?

IAGO: Honest, my lord?

OTHELLO: Honest. Ay, honest.

130   IAGO: My lord, for aught I know.

OTHELLO: What dost thou think?

IAGO: Think, my lord?

OTHELLO: Think, my lord?
By heaven, he echoes me,
As if there were some monster in his thought
Too hideous to be shown. Thou dost mean
something:
I heard thee say but now, thou lik'st not that,
When Cassio left my wife. What didst not like?

140   And when I told thee he was of my counsel
In my whole course of wooing, thou cried'st
'Indeed?'
And didst contract and purse thy brow together,

As if thou then hadst shut up in thy brain
Some horrible conceit.° If thou dost love me,
Show me thy thought.

IAGO: My lord, you know I love you.

OTHELLO: I think thou dost;
And, for° I know thou'rt full of love and honesty
And weigh'st thy words before thou giv'st them   150
breath,
Therefore these stops of thine fright me the more;
For such things in a false disloyal knave
Are tricks of custom; but in a man that's just
They are close dilations,° working from the heart
That passion cannot rule.

IAGO: For Michael Cassio,
I dare be sworn I think that he is honest.

OTHELLO: I think so too.

IAGO: Men should be what they seem;   160
Or those that be not, would they might seem none!

OTHELLO: Certain, men should be what they seem.

IAGO: Why then, I think Cassio's an honest man.

OTHELLO: Nay, yet there's more in this.
I prithee speak to me as to thy thinkings,
As thou dost ruminate, and give thy worst of
thoughts
The worst of words.

IAGO: Good my lord, pardon me:
Though I am bound to every act of duty,   170
I am not bound to that all slaves are free to.
Utter my thoughts? Why, say they are vile and
false,
As where's the palace whereinto foul things
Sometimes intrude not? Who has a breast so pure
But some uncleanly apprehensions
Keep leets° and law days, and in session sit
With meditations lawful?

OTHELLO: Thou dost conspire against thy friend,
Iago,   180
If thou but think'st him wronged, and mak'st his
ear
A stranger to thy thoughts.

IAGO: I do beseech you—
Though I perchance am vicious in my guess
(As I confess it is my nature's plague
To spy into abuses, and oft my jealousy°
Shapes faults that are not), that your wisdom yet
From one that so imperfectly conjects°
Would take no notice, nor build yourself a trouble 190
Out of his scattering and unsure observance.
It were not for your quiet nor your good,
Nor for my manhood, honesty, or wisdom,
To let you know my thoughts.

OTHELLO: What dost thou mean?

---

conceit, idea. ***for,*** because. ***close dilations,*** secret
feelings. ***leets,*** sessions of local courts. ***jealousy,*** suspicion.
conjects, conjectures.

IAGO: Good name in man and woman, dear my lord,
　　Is the immediate jewel of their souls.
　　Who steals my purse steals trash; 'tis something, nothing;
200　'Twas mine, 'tis his, and has been slave to thousands;
　　But he that filches from me my good name
　　Robs me of that which not enriches him
　　And makes me poor indeed.
OTHELLO: By heaven, I'll know thy thoughts!
IAGO: You cannot, if my heart were in your hand;
　　Nor shall not whilst 'tis in my custody.
OTHELLO: Ha!
IAGO: O, beware, my lord, of jealousy!
210　It is the green-eyed monster, which doth mock°
　　The meat it feeds on. That cuckold lives in bliss
　　Who, certain of his fate, loves not his wronger;
　　But O, what damnèd minutes tells he o'er
　　Who dotes, yet doubts—suspects, yet strongly loves!
OTHELLO: O misery!
IAGO: Poor and content is rich, and rich enough;
　　But riches fineless° is as poor as winter
　　To him that ever fears he shall be poor.
220　Good God, the souls of all my tribe defend
　　From jealousy!
OTHELLO: Why, why is this?
　　Think'st thou I'ld make a life of jealousy,
　　To follow still the changes of the moon
　　With fresh suspicions? No! To be once in doubt
　　Is once to be resolved. Exchange me for a goat
　　When I shall turn the business of my soul
　　To such exsufflicate and blown° surmises,
　　Matching thy inference. 'Tis not to make me
230　jealous
　　To say my wife is fair, feeds well, loves company,
　　Is free of speech, sings, plays, and dances well;
　　Where virtue is, these are more virtuous.
　　Nor from mine own weak merits will I draw
　　The smallest fear or doubt of her revolt,
　　For she had eyes, and chose me. No, Iago;
　　I'll see before I doubt; when I doubt, prove;
　　And on the proof there is no more but this—
　　Away at once with love or jealousy!
240　IAGO: I am glad of this; for now I shall have reason
　　To show the love and duty that I bear you
　　With franker spirit. Therefore, as I am bound,
　　Receive it from me. I speak not yet of proof.
　　Look to your wife; observe her well with Cassio;
　　Wear your eye thus, not jealous nor secure:
　　I would not have your free and noble nature,
　　Out of self-bounty,° be abused. Look to't.
　　I know our country disposition well:

In Venice they do let God see the pranks
　　They dare not show their husbands; their best　　250
　　conscience
　　Is not to leave't undone, but keep't unknown.
OTHELLO: Dost thou say so?
IAGO: She did deceive her father, marrying you;
　　And when she seemed to shake and fear your looks,
　　She loved them most.
OTHELLO: And so she did.
IAGO: Why, go to then!
　　She that, so young, could give out such a seeming　　260
　　To seel° her father's eyes up close as oak°—
　　He thought 'twas witchcraft—but I am much to blame.
　　I humbly do beseech you of your pardon
　　For too much loving you.
OTHELLO: I am bound to thee for ever.
IAGO: I see this hath a little dashed your spirits.
OTHELLO: Not a jot, not a jot.
IAGO: I' faith, I fear it has.
　　I hope you will consider what is spoke　　270
　　Comes from my love. But I do see y' are moved.
　　I am to pray you not to strain my speech
　　To grosser issues° nor to larger reach
　　Than to suspicion.
OTHELLO: I will not.
IAGO: Should you do so, my lord,
　　My speech should fall into such vile success°
　　As my thoughts aim not at. Cassio's my worthy friend—
　　My lord, I see y' are moved.　　280
OTHELLO: No, not much moved:
　　I do not think but Desdemona's honest.°
IAGO: Long live she so! and long live you to think so!
OTHELLO: And yet, how nature erring from itself—
IAGO: Ay, there's the point! as (to be bold with you)
　　Not to affect° many proposèd matches
　　Of her own clime, complexion, and degree,
　　Whereto we see in all things nature tends—
　　Foh! one may smell in such a will° most rank,
　　Foul disproportion, thoughts unnatural—　　290
　　But pardon me—I do not in position°
　　Distinctly speak of her; though I may fear
　　Her will, recoiling° to her better judgment,
　　May fall to match° you with her country forms,°
　　And happily° repent.
OTHELLO: Farewell, farewell!
　　If more thou dost perceive, let me know more.
　　Set on thy wife to observe. Leave me, Iago.

---

mock, play with; i.e., torture. **fineless,** boundless. **exsufflicate and blown,** inflated and flyblown. **self-bounty,** natural goodness.

seel, close; i.e., deceive. **oak,** close grained wood. **issues,** consequences. **vile success,** evil outcome. **honest,** chaste. **affect,** desire. **will,** desire. **in position,** in these assertions. **recoiling,** reverting. **fall to match,** happen to compare. **country forms,** appearance of her countrymen. **happily,** perchance.

IAGO: My lord, I take my leave. *(Going.)*

OTHELLO: Why did I marry? This honest creature doubtless

    Sees and knows more, much more, than he unfolds.

IAGO *(returns)*: My lord, I would I might entreat your honor

    To scan this thing no further: leave it to time.

    Although 'tis fit that Cassio have his place,

    For sure he fills it up with great ability,

    Yet, if you please to hold him off awhile,

300   You shall by that perceive him and his means.

    Note if your lady strain his entertainment°

    With any strong or vehement importunity;

    Much will be seen in that. In the mean time

    Let me be thought too busy in my fears

    (As worthy cause I have to fear I am)

    And hold her free.° I do beseech your honor.

OTHELLO: Fear not my government.°

IAGO: I once more take my leave. *(Exit.)*

OTHELLO: This fellow's of exceeding honesty,

310   And knows all qualities, with a learnèd spirit

    Of human dealings. If I do prove her haggard,°

    Though that her jesses° were my dear heartstrings,

    I'd whistle her off and let her down the wind°

    To prey at fortune. Haply, for I am black

    And have not those soft parts of conversation°

    That chamberers° have, or for I am declined

    Into the vale of years—yet that's not much—

    She's gone. I am abused, and my relief

    Must be to loathe her. O curse of marriage,

320   That we can call these delicate creatures ours,

    And not their appetites! I had rather be a toad

    And live upon the vapor of a dungeon

    Than keep a corner in the thing I love

    For others' uses. Yet 'tis the plague of great ones;

    Prerogatived° are they less than the base.

    'Tis destiny unshunnable, like death.

    Even then this forkèd plague° is fated to us

    When we do quicken.° Look where she comes.

(Enter DESDEMONA *and* EMILIA.*)*

    If she be false, O, then heaven mocks itself!

330   I'll not believe't.

DESDEMONA: How now, my dear Othello?

    Your dinner, and the generous° islanders

    By you invited, do attend your presence.

---

strain . . . entertainment, urge his reinstatement. **hold
her free,** consider her guiltless. **government,** self-control.
haggard, wild hawk. **jesses,** straps connected to the legs of a
hawk for keeping it under control. **whistle . . . wind,** turn
her loose and let her fly wherever her will might take her
(presumably to her self destruction). **soft . . . conversation,**
polished manners. **chamberers,** courtiers. **Prerogatived,**
privileged. **forkèd plague,** horns of a cuckold. **quicken,**
are born. **generous,** noble.

OTHELLO: I am to blame.

DESDEMONA: Why do you speak so faintly?

    Are you not well?

OTHELLO: I have a pain upon my forehead, here.

DESDEMONA: Faith, that's with watching;° 'twill away again.

    Let me but bind it hard, within this hour   340

    It will be well.

OTHELLO: Your napkin is too little

*(He pushes the handkerchief from him, and it falls
unnoticed.)*

    Let it alone. Come, I'll go in with you.

DESDEMONA: I am very sorry that you are not well.

(Exit with OTHELLO.*)*

EMILIA: I am glad I have found this napkin;

    This was her first remembrance from the Moor.

    My wayward husband hath a hundred times

    Wooed me to steal it; but she so loves the token

    (For he conjured her she should ever keep it)

    That she reserves it evermore about her   350

    To kiss and talk to. I'll have the work ta'en out°

    And give't Iago.

    What he will do with it heaven knows, not I;

    I nothing but° to please his fantasy.°

(Enter IAGO.*)*

IAGO: How now? What do you here alone?

EMILIA: Do not you chide; I have a thing for you.

IAGO: A thing for me? It is a common thing—

EMILIA: Ha?

IAGO: To have a foolish wife.

EMILIA: O, is that all? What will you give me now   360

    For that same handkerchief?

IAGO: What handkerchief?

EMILIA: What handkerchief!

    Why, that the Moor first gave to Desdemona;

    That which so often you did bid me steal.

IAGO: Hast stol'n it from her?

EMILIA: No, faith; she let it drop by negligence,

    And to th' advantage, I being here, took't up.

    Look, here it is.

IAGO: A good wench! Give it me.   370

EMILIA: What will you do with't, that you have been so earnest

    To have me filch it?

IAGO: Why, what's that to you?

EMILIA: If it be not for some purpose of import,

    Give't me again. Poor lady, she'll run mad

    When she shall lack it.

IAGO: Be not acknown on't;° I have use for it.

    Go, leave me.

---

watching, from lack of sleep. **taken out,** pattern
copied. **I nothing but,** my only desire is. **fantasy,** whim.
Be . . . it, pretend that you know nothing about it.

(*Exit* EMILIA.)

380 I will in Cassio's lodging lose this napkin
And let him find it. Trifles light as air
Are to the jealous confirmations strong
As proofs of holy writ. This may do something.
The Moor already changes with my poison:
Dangerous conceits are in their natures poisons,
Which at the first are scarce found to distaste,
But with a little act upon the blood
Burn like the mines of sulphur.

(*Enter* OTHELLO.)

I did say so.
390 Look where he comes! Not poppy nor
      mandragora,°
Nor all the drowsy syrups of the world,
Shall ever med'cine thee to that sweet sleep
Which thou owedst yesterday.
OTHELLO: Ha! ha! false to me?
IAGO: Why, how now, general? No more of that!
OTHELLO: Avaunt! be gone! Thou hast set me on the
      rack.
I swear 'tis better to be much abused
400 Than but to know't a little.
IAGO: How now, my lord?
OTHELLO: What sense had I of her stol'n hours of
      lust?
I saw't not, thought it not, it harmed not me;
I slept the next night well, fed well, was free° and
      merry;
I found not Cassio's kisses on her lips.
He that is robbed, not wanting what is stol'n,
Let him not know't, and he's not robbed at all.
410 IAGO: I am sorry to hear this.
OTHELLO: I had been happy if the general camp,
Pioneers° and all, had tasted her sweet body,
So I had nothing known. O, now for ever
Farewell the tranquil mind! farewell content!
Farewell the plumèd troop, and the big wars
That make ambition virtue! O, farewell!
Farewell the neighing steed and the shrill trump,
The spirit-stirring drum, th' ear-piercing fife,
The royal banner, and all quality,
420 Pride, pomp, and circumstance° of glorious war!
And O you mortal engines° whose rude throats
Th' immortal Jove's dread clamors counterfeit,°
Farewell! Othello's occupation's gone!
IAGO: Is't possible, my lord?
OTHELLO: Villain, be sure thou prove my love a
      whore!
Be sure of it; give me ocular proof;
Or, by the worth of man's eternal soul,

Thou hadst been better have been born a dog
Than answer my waked wrath! 430
IAGO: Is't come to this?
OTHELLO: Make me to see't; or at least so prove it
That the probation° bear no hinge nor loop
To hang a doubt on—or woe upon thy life!
IAGO: My noble lord—
OTHELLO: If thou dost slander her and torture me,
Never pray more; abandon all remorse;
On horror's head horrors accumulate;
Do deeds to make heaven weep, all earth amazed;
For nothing canst thou to damnation add 440
Greater than that.
IAGO: O grace! O heaven forgive me!
Are you a man? Have you a soul or sense?—
God b' wi' you! take mine office. O wretched fool,
That liv'st to make thine honesty a vice!
O monstrous world! Take note, take note, O world,
To be direct and honest is not safe.
I thank you for this profit;° and from hence
I'll love no friend, sith love breed such offense.
OTHELLO: Nay, Stay. Thou shouldst be honest. 450
IAGO: I should be wise; for honesty's a fool
And loses that it works for.
OTHELLO: By the world,
I think my wife be honest, and think she is not;
I think that thou art just, and think thou are not.
I'll have some proof. Her name, that was as fresh
As Dian's visage, is now begrimed and black
As mine own face. If there be cords, or knives,
Poison, or fire, or suffocating streams,
I'll not endure it. Would I were satisfied! 460
IAGO: I see, sir, you are eaten up with passion:
I do repent me that I put it to you.
You would be satisfied?
OTHELLO: Would? Nay, I will.
IAGO: And may; but how? how satisfied, my lord?
Would you, the supervisor, grossly gape on?
Behold her topped?
OTHELLO: Death and damnation! O!
IAGO: It were a tedious difficulty, I think,
To bring them to that prospect. Damn them then, 470
If ever mortal eyes do see them bolster°
More° than their own! What then? How then?
What shall I say? Where's satisfaction?
It is impossible you should see this,
Were they as prime° as goats, as hot as monkeys,
As salt° as wolves in pride,° and fools as gross
As ignorance made drunk. But yet, I say,
If imputation and strong circumstances
Which lead directly to the door of truth
Will give you satisfaction, you may have't. 480
OTHELLO: Give me a living reason she's disloyal.

---

mandragora, a narcotic. *free,* carefree. **Pioneers,**
lowest rank of soldier. *circumstance,* pageantry. **mortal
engines,** deadly artillery. *counterfeit,* imitate.

---

probation, proof. *profit,* lesson. *bolster,* lie together.
more, other. *prime,* lustful. *salt,* lecherous. *pride,* heat.

IAGO: I do not like the office.
But sith I am entered in this cause so far,
Pricked to't by foolish honesty and love,
I will go on. I lay with Cassio lately,
And being troubled with a raging tooth,
I could not sleep.
There are a kind of men so loose of soul
That in their sleeps will mutter their affairs.
490 One of this kind is Cassio.
In sleep, I heard him say, 'Sweet Desdemona,
Let us be wary, let us hide our loves!'
And then, sir, would he gripe° and wring my hand,
Cry, 'O sweet creature!' and then kiss me hard,
As if he plucked up kisses by the roots
That grew upon my lips; then laid his leg
Over my thigh, and sighed, and kissed, and then
Cried 'Cursèd fate that gave thee to the Moor!'
OTHELLO: O monstrous! monstrous!
500 IAGO: Nay, this was but his dream.
OTHELLO: But this denoted a foregone conclusion:
'Tis a shrewd doubt,° though it be but a dream.
IAGO: And this may help to thicken other proofs
That do demonstrate thinly.
OTHELLO: I'll tear her all to pieces!
IAGO: Nay, but be wise. Yet we see nothing done;
She may be honest yet. Tell me but this—
Have you not sometimes seen a handkerchief
Spotted with strawberries in your wife's hand?
510 OTHELLO: I gave her such a one; 'twas my first gift.
IAGO: I know not that; but such a handkerchief—
I am sure it was your wife's—did I to-day
See Cassio wipe his beard with.
OTHELLO: If't be that—
IAGO: If it be that, or any that was hers,
It speaks against her with the other proofs.
OTHELLO: O, that the slave had forty thousand lives!
One is too poor, too weak for my revenge.
Now do I see 'tis true. Look here, Iago:
520 All my fond love thus do I blow to heaven.
'Tis gone.
Arise, black vengeance, from the hollow hell!
Yield up, O love, thy crown and hearted throne
To tyrannous hate! Swell, bosom, with thy
fraught,°
For 'tis of aspics'° tongues!
IAGO: Yet be content.
OTHELLO: O, blood, blood, blood!
IAGO: Patience, I say. Your mind perhaps may
530 change.
OTHELLO: Never, Iago. Like to the Pontic sea,°
Whose icy current and compulsive course
Ne'er feels retiring ebb, but keeps due on
To the Propontic and the Hellespont,

Even so my bloody thoughts, with violent pace,
Shall ne'er look back, ne'er ebb to humble love,
Till that a capable° and wide revenge
Swallow them up. (He kneels.) Now, by yond marble
heaven,
In the due reverence of a sacred vow   540
I here engage my words.
IAGO: Do not rise yet. (IAGO kneels.)
Witness, you ever-burning lights above,
You elements that clip° us round about,
Witness that here Iago doth give up
The execution° of his wit, hands, heart
To wronged Othello's service! Let him command,
And to obey shall be in me remorse,°
What bloody business ever.

(They rise.)

OTHELLO: I greet thy love,   550
Not with vain thanks but with acceptance
bounteous,
And will upon the instant put thee to't.
Within these three days let me hear thee say
That Cassio's not alive.
IAGO: My friend is dead; 'tis done at your request.
But let her live.
OTHELLO: Damn her, lewd minx! O, damn her!
Come, go with me apart. I will withdraw
To furnish me with some swift means of death   560
For the fair devil. Now art thou my lieutenant.
IAGO: I am your own for ever. (Exeunt.)

ACT 3 / SCENE 4

(Enter DESDEMONA, EMILIA, and CLOWN.)

DESDEMONA: Do you know, sirrah, where Lieutenant
Cassio lies?°
CLOWN: I dare not say he lies anywhere.
DESDEMONA: Why, man?
CLOWN: He's a soldier, and for me to say a soldier lies
is stabbing.
DESDEMONA: Go to. Where lodges he?
CLOWN: To tell you where he lodges is to tell you
where I lie.
DESDEMONA: Can anything be made of this?   10
CLOWN: I know not where he lodges; and for me to
devise a lodging, and say he lies here or lies
there, were to lie in mine own throat.°
DESDEMONA: Can you enquire him out, and be
edified by report?
CLOWN: I will catechize the world for him; that is,
make questions and by them answer.
DESDEMONA: Seek him, bid him come hither. Tell him

---

gripe, grip. doubt, strong reason for suspicion.
fraught, burden. aspics', asps' (deadly poisonous snakes).
Pontic sea, Black Sea.

capable, comprehensive. clip, encompass. execution,
action. remorse, expression of pity (for Othello). lies,
lodges. lie...throat, tell an obvious lie.

20   I have moved my lord on his behalf and hope all
      will be well.
CLOWN: To do this is within the compass of man's wit,
    and therefore I'll attempt the doing of it. (Exit.)
DESDEMONA: Where should I lose that handkerchief,
    Emilia?
EMILIA: I know not, madam.
DESDEMONA: Believe me, I had rather have lost my
    purse
    Full of crusadoes;° and but my noble Moor
    Is true of mind, and made of no such baseness
30   As jealous creatures are, it were enough
    To put him to ill thinking.
EMILIA: Is he not jealous?
DESDEMONA: Who? he? I think the sun where he was
    born
    Drew all such humors° from him.

    (Enter OTHELLO.)

EMILIA: Look where he comes.
DESDEMONA: I will not leave him now till Cassio
    Be called to him.—How is't with you, my lord?
OTHELLO: Well, my good lady. (Aside) O, hardness to
40   dissemble!—
    How do you, Desdemona?
DESDEMONA: Well, my good lord.
OTHELLO: Give me your hand. This hand is moist, my
    lady.
DESDEMONA: It yet hath felt no age nor known no
    sorrow.
OTHELLO: This argues fruitfulness and liberal heart.
    Hot, hot, and moist. This hand of yours requires
    A sequester° from liberty, fasting and prayer,
50   Much castigation, exercise devout;
    For here's a young and sweating devil here
    That commonly rebels. 'Tis a good hand,
    A frank one.
DESDEMONA: You may, indeed, say so;
    For 'twas that hand that gave away my heart.
OTHELLO: A liberal hand! The hearts of old gave
    hands;
    But our new heraldry is hands, not hearts.
DESDEMONA: I cannot speak of this. Come now, your
60   promise!
OTHELLO: What promise, chuck?
DESDEMONA: I have sent to bid Cassio come speak
    with you.
OTHELLO: I have a salt and sorry rheum° offends me.
    Lend me thy handkerchief.
DESDEMONA: Here, my lord.
OTHELLO: That which I gave you.
DESDEMONA: I have it not about me.
OTHELLO: Not?

DESDEMONA: No, faith, my lord.
OTHELLO: That is a fault.
    That handkerchief
    Did an Egyptian° to my mother give.
    She was a charmer,° and could almost read
    The thoughts of people. She told her, while she
      kept it,
    'Twould make her amiable° and subdue my father
    Entirely to her love; but if she lost it
    Or made a gift of it, my father's eye
    Should hold her loathly, and his spirits should hunt   70
    After new fancies. She, dying, gave it me,
    And bid me, when my fate would have me wive,
    To give it her. I did so; and take heed on't;
    Make it a darling like your precious eye.
    To lose't or give't away were such perdition
    As nothing else could match.
DESDEMONA: Is't possible?
OTHELLO: 'Tis true. There's magic in the web of it.
    A sibyl° that had numbered in the world
    The sun to course two hundred compasses,   80
    In her prophetic fury sewed the work;
    The worms were hallowed that did breed the silk;
    And it was dyed in mummy° which the skillful
    Conserved° of maidens' hearts.
DESDEMONA: I' faith? Is't true?
OTHELLO: Most veritable. Therefore look to't well.
DESDEMONA: Then would to God that I had never
    seen't!
OTHELLO: Ha! Wherefore?
DESDEMONA: Why do you speak so startingly and   90
    rash?
OTHELLO: Is't lost? Is't gone? Speak, is it out o' th'
    way?
DESDEMONA: Heaven bless us!
OTHELLO: Say you?
DESDEMONA: It is not lost. But what an if it were?
OTHELLO: How?
DESDEMONA: I say it is not lost.
OTHELLO: Fetch't, let me see't!
DESDEMONA: Why, so I can, sir; but I will not now.   100
    This is a trick to put me from my suit:
    Pray you let Cassio be received again.
OTHELLO: Fetch me the handkerchief! My mind
    misgives.
DESDEMONA: Come, come!
    You'll never meet a more sufficient man.
OTHELLO: The handkerchief!
DESDEMONA: I pray talk me of Cassio.
OTHELLO: The handkerchief!
DESDEMONA: A man that all his time   110
    Hath founded his good fortunes on your love,
    Shared dangers with you—

---

crusadoes, Portuguese gold coins. *humors*, temperamental inclinations. *sequester*, removal. *rheum*, head cold.

Egyptian, Gypsy. *charmer*, magician. *amiable*, desirable. *sibyl*, prophetess. *mummy*, fluid derived from embalmed bodies. *conserved*, preserved.

OTHELLO: The handkerchief!

DESDEMONA: I'faith, you are to blame.

OTHELLO: Zounds! *(Exit.)*

EMILIA: Is not this man jealous?

DESDEMONA: I ne'er saw this before.
Sure there's some wonder in this handkerchief;
I am most unhappy in the loss of it.

120 EMILIA: 'Tis not a year or two shows us a man.
They are all but stomachs, and we all but food;
They eat us hungerly, and when they are full,
They belch us.

(Enter IAGO *and* CASSIO.)

Look you—Cassio and my husband!

IAGO: There is no other way; 'tis she must do't.
And lo the happiness!.° Go and importune her.

DESDEMONA: How now, good Cassio? What's the news
with you?

CASSIO: Madam, my former suit. I do beseech you

130 That by your virtuous means I may again
Exist, and be a member of his love
Whom I with all the office of my heart
Entirely honor. I would not be delayed.
If my offense be of such mortal kind
That neither service past, nor present sorrows,
Nor purposed merit in futurity,
Can ransom me into his love again,
But to know so must be my benefit.
So shall I clothe me in a forced content,

140 And shut myself up in some other course,
To fortune's alms.

DESDEMONA: Alas, thrice-gentle Cassio!
My advocation° is not now in tune.
My lord is not my lord; nor should I know him,
Were he in favor° as in humor altered.
So help me every spirit sanctified
As I have spoken for you all my best
And stood within the blank° of his displeasure
For my free speech! You must awhile be patient.

150 What I can do I will; and more I will
Than for myself I dare. Let that suffice you.

IAGO: Is my lord angry?

EMILIA: He went hence but now,
And certainly in strange unquietness.

IAGO: Can he be angry? I have seen the cannon
When it hath blown his ranks into the air
And, like the devil, from his very arm
Puffed his own brother—and can he be angry?
Something of moment then. I will go meet him.

160 There's matter in't indeed if he be angry.

DESDEMONA: I prithee do so.

(Exit IAGO.)

Something sure of state,
Either from Venice or some unhatched practice°
Made demonstrable here in Cyprus to him,
Hath puddled° his clear spirit; and in such cases
Men's natures wrangle with inferior things,
Though great ones are their object. 'Tis even so;
For let our finger ache, and it endues°
Our other, healthful members even to that sense
Of pain. Nay, we must think men are not gods, 170
Nor of them look for such observancy°
As fits the bridal. Beshrew me much, Emilia,
I was, unhandsome warrior as I am,
Arraigning his unkindness with my soul;
But now I find I had suborned the witness,
And he's indicted falsely.

EMILIA: Pray heaven it be state matters, as you think,
And no conception nor no jealous toy°
Concerning you.

DESDEMONA: Alas the day! I never gave him cause. 180

EMILIA: But jealous souls will not be answered so;
They are not ever jealous for the cause,
But jealous for they are jealous. 'Tis a monster
Begot upon itself, born on itself.

DESDEMONA: Heaven keep that monster from
Othello's mind!

EMILIA: Lady, amen.

DESDEMONA: I will go seek him. Cassio, walk here
about:
If I do find him fit, I'll move your suit 190
And seek to effect it to my uttermost.

CASSIO: I humbly thank your ladyship.

(Exeunt DESDEMONA *and* EMILIA.)
(Enter BIANCA.)

BIANCA: Save you, friend Cassio!

CASSIO: What make you from home?
How is it with you, my most fair Bianca?
I' faith, sweet love, I was coming to your house.

BIANCA: And I was going to your lodging, Cassio.
What, keep a week away? seven days and nights?
Eightscore eight hours? and lovers' absent hours,
More tedious than the dial° eightscore times? 200
O weary reck'ning!

CASSIO: Pardon me, Bianca:
I have this while with leaden thoughts been
pressed;
But I shall in a more continuate° time
Strike off this score of absence. Sweet Bianca,

(Gives her DESDEMONA's *handkerchief.)*

Take me this work out.

BIANCA: O Cassio, whence came this?
This is some token from a newer friend.

---

happiness, good luck. **advocation,** advocacy. **favor,** appearance. **blank,** center of a target.

unhatched practice, plot in the making. **puddled,** muddied. **endues,** brings. **observancy,** devoted attention. **toy,** fancy. **dial,** clock. **continuate,** uninterrupted.

210 To the felt absence now I feel a cause.
Is't come to this? Well, well.
CASSIO: Go to, woman!
Throw your vile guesses in the devil's teeth,
From whence you have them. You are jealous now
That this is from some mistress, some
remembrance.
No, by my faith, Bianca.
BIANCA: Why, whose is it?
CASSIO: I know not, sweet; I found it in my chamber.
220 I like the work well; ere it be demanded,
As like enough it will, I'd have it copied.
Take it and do't, and leave me for this time.
BIANCA: Leave you? Wherefore?
CASSIO: I do attend here on the general
And think it no addition, nor my wish,
To have him see me womaned.
BIANCA: Why, I pray you?
CASSIO: Not that I love you not.
BIANCA: But that you do not love me!
230 I pray you bring me on the way a little,
And say if I shall see you soon at night.
CASSIO: 'Tis but a little way that I can bring you,
For I attend here; but I'll see you soon.
BIANCA: 'Tis very good. I must be circumstanced.°

(Exeunt.)

ACT 4 / SCENE 1

(Enter OTHELLO and IAGO.)

IAGO: Will you think so?
OTHELLO: Think so, Iago?
IAGO: What,
To kiss in private?
OTHELLO: An unauthorized kiss.
IAGO: Or to be naked with her friend in bed
An hour or more, not meaning any harm?
OTHELLO: Naked in bed, Iago, and not mean harm?
It is hypocrisy against the devil.
10 They that mean virtuously, and yet do so,
The devil their virtue tempts, and they tempt
heaven.
IAGO: So they do nothing, 'tis a venial slip.
But if I give my wife a handkerchief—
OTHELLO: What then?
IAGO: Why, then 'tis hers, my lord; and being hers,
She may, I think, bestow't on any man.
OTHELLO: She is protectress of her honor too;
May she give that?
20 IAGO: Her honor is an essence that's not seen;
They have it very oft° that have it not.
But for the handkerchief—
OTHELLO: By heaven, I would most gladly have
forgot it!

Thou said'st—O, it comes o'er my memory
As doth the raven o'er the infected house,
Boding to all!—he had my handkerchief.
IAGO: Ay, what of that?
OTHELLO: That's not so good now.
IAGO: What 30
If I had said I had seen him do you wrong?
Or heard him say—as knaves be such abroad
Who having, by their own importunate suit,
Or voluntary dotage of some mistress,
Convincèd or supplied° them, cannot choose
But they must blab—
OTHELLO: Hath he said anything?
IAGO: He hath, my lord; but be you well assured,
No more than he'll unswear.
OTHELLO: What hath he said? 40
IAGO: Faith, that he did—I know not what he did.
OTHELLO: What? what?
IAGO: Lie—
OTHELLO: With her?
IAGO: With her, on her; what you will.
OTHELLO: Lie with her? lie on her?—We say lie on
her when they belie her.—Lie with her! Zounds,
that's fulsome.—Handkerchief—confessions—
handkerchief—To confess, and be hanged for
his labor—first to be hanged, and then to con- 50
fess! I tremble at it. Nature would not invest her-
self in such shadowing° passion without some in-
struction.° It is not words that shakes me
thus.—Pish! Noses, ears, and lips? Is't
possible?—Confess?—Handkerchief?—O devil!
(Falls in a trance.)
IAGO: Work on,
My med'cine work! Thus credulous fools are
caught,
And many worthy and chaste dames even thus,
All guiltless, meet reproach.—What, ho! my lord! 60
My lord, I say! Othello!

(Enter CASSIO.)

How now, Cassio?
CASSIO: What's the matter?
IAGO: My lord is fall'n into an epilepsy.
This is his second fit; he had one yesterday.
CASSIO: Rub him about the temples.
IAGO: No, forbear.
The lethargy must have his quiet course.
If not, he foams at mouth, and by and by
Breaks out to savage madness. Look, he stirs. 70
Do you withdraw yourself a little while.
He will recover straight. When he is gone,
I would on great occasion speak with you.

(Exit CASSIO.)

---

circumstanced, governed by circumstances.
They . . . oft, they often have the appearance of it.

Convincèd or supplied, overcome or gratified. **shadowing,** overwhelming. **instruction,** prompting, or cause.

How is it, general? Have you not hurt your head?
OTHELLO: Dost thou mock me?
IAGO: I mock you? No, by heaven.
    Would you would bear your fortune like a man!
OTHELLO: A hornèd man's° a monster and a beast.
IAGO: There's many a beast then in a populous city,
80   And many a civil monster.
OTHELLO: Did he confess it?
IAGO: Good, sir, be a man.
    Think every bearded fellow that's but yoked°
    May draw with you. There's millions now alive
    That nightly lie in those unproper° beds
    Which they dare swear peculiar:° your case is
      better.
    O, 'tis the spite of hell, the fiend's arch-mock,
    To lip a wanton in a secure° couch,
90   And to suppose her chaste! No, let me know;
    And knowing what I am, I know what she shall be.
OTHELLO: O, thou are wise! 'Tis certain.
IAGO: Stand you awhile apart;
    Confine yourself but in a patient list.°
    Whilst you were here, o'erwhelmèd with your
      grief—
    A passion most unsuiting such a man—
    Cassio came hither. I shifted him away
    And laid good 'scuse upon your ecstasy;°
100   Bade him anon return, and here speak with me;
    The which he promised. Do but encave° yourself
    And mark the fleers,° the gibes, and notable scorns
    That dwell in every region of his face;
    For I will make him tell the tale anew—
    Where, how, how oft, how long ago, and when
    He hath, and is again to cope° your wife.
    I say, but mark his gesture. Marry, patience!
    Or I shall say you are all in all in spleen,°
    And nothing of a man.
110 OTHELLO: Dost thou hear, Iago?
    I will be found most cunning in my patience;
    But—dost thou hear?—most bloody.
IAGO: That's not amiss;
    But yet keep time in all. Will you withdraw?

(OTHELLO retires.)

    Now will I question Cassio of Bianca,
    A huswife° that by selling her desires
    Buys herself bread and clothes. It is a creature
    That dotes on Cassio, as 'tis the strumpet's plague
    To beguile many and be beguiled by one.
120   He, when he hears of her, cannot refrain
    From the excess of laughter. Here he comes.

---

hornèd man, cuckold. **yoked,** married. **unproper,** not
exclusively their own. **peculiar,** exclusively their own.
secure, free from suspicion. **patient list,** within the
bounds of patience. **ecstasy,** trance. **encave,** conceal.
fleers, sneers. **cope,** meet. **all . . . spleen,** completely
overcome by emotion. **huswife,** hussy.

As he shall smile, Othello shall go mad;
    And his unbookish° jealousy must conster°
    Poor Cassio's smiles, gestures, and light behavior
    Quite in the wrong. How do you now, lieutenant?
CASSIO: The worser that you give me the addition°
    Whose want even kills me.
IAGO: Ply Desdemona well, and you are sure on't.
    Now, if this suit lay in Bianca's power,
    How quickly should you speed!   130
CASSIO: Alas, poor caitiff!°
OTHELLO: Look how he laughs already!
IAGO: I never knew a woman love man so.
CASSIO: Alas, poor rogue! I think, i' faith, she loves
    me.
OTHELLO: Now he denies it faintly, and laughs it out.
IAGO: Do you hear, Cassio?
OTHELLO: Now he importunes him
    To tell it o'er. Go to! Well said, well said!
IAGO: She gives it out that you shall marry her.   140
    Do you intend it?
CASSIO: Ha, ha, ha!
OTHELLO: Do you triumph, Roman? Do you
    triumph?
CASSIO: I marry her? What, a customer?° Prithee bear
    some charity to my wit; do not think it so un-
    wholesome. Ha, ha, ha!
OTHELLO: So, so, so, so! They laugh that win!
IAGO: Faith, the cry goes that you shall marry her.
CASSIO: Prithee say true.   150
IAGO: I am a very villain else.
OTHELLO: Have you scored° me? Well.
CASSIO: This is the monkey's own giving out. She is
    persuaded I will marry her out of her own love
    and flattery, not out of my promise.
OTHELLO: Iago beckons me; now he begins the story.
CASSIO: She was here even now; she haunts me in
    every place. I was t' other day talking on the sea
    bank with certain Venetians, and thither comes
    the bauble,° and by this hand, she falls me thus   160
    about my neck—
OTHELLO: Crying 'O dear Cassio!' as it were. His ges-
    ture imports it.
CASSIO: So hangs, and lolls, and weeps upon me; so
    hales and pulls me! Ha, ha, ha!
OTHELLO: Now he tells how she plucked him to my
    chamber.
    O, I see that nose of yours, but not that dog I shall
    throw't to.
CASSIO: Well, I must leave her company.   170

(Enter BIANCA.)

IAGO: Before me! Look where she comes.

---

unbookish, uninstructed. **conster,** construe. **addition,** title (of lieutenant). **caitiff,** wretch. **customer,** prostitute. **scored,** beaten. **bauble,** plaything.

CASSIO: 'Tis such another fitchew!° marry, a perfumed one. What do you mean by this haunting
of me?

BIANCA: Let the devil and his dam haunt you! What
did you mean by that same handkerchief you
gave me even now? I was a fine fool to take it. I
must take out the whole work? A likely piece of
work that you should find it in your chamber
180 and know not who left it there! This is some
minx's token, and I must take out the work?
There! Give it your hobby-horse.° Wheresoever
you had it, I'll take out no work on't.

CASSIO: How now, my sweet Bianca? How now? how
now?

OTHELLO: By heaven, that should be my handkerchief!

BIANCA: An you'll come to supper to-night, you may;
an you will not, come when you are next pre-
190 pared for. (Exit.)

IAGO: After her, after her!

CASSIO: Faith, I must; she'll rail i' th' street else.

IAGO: Will you sup there?

CASSIO: Yes, I intend so.

IAGO: Well, I may chance to see you; for I would very
fain speak with you.

CASSIO: Prithee come. Will you?

IAGO: Go to! say no more.

(Exit CASSIO.)

OTHELLO *(comes forward)*: How shall I murder him,
200 Iago?

IAGO: Did you perceive how he laughed at his vice?

OTHELLO: O Iago!

IAGO: And did you see the handkerchief?

OTHELLO: Was that mine?

IAGO: Yours, by this hand! And to see how he prizes
the foolish woman your wife! She gave it him,
and he hath giv'n it his whore.

OTHELLO: I would have him nine years a-killing!—A
fine woman! a fair woman! a sweet woman!

210 IAGO: Nay, you must forget that.

OTHELLO: Ay, let her rot, and perish, and be damned
to-night; for she shall not live. No, my heart is
turned to stone; I strike it, and it hurts my hand.
O, the world hath not a sweeter creature! She
might lie by an emperor's side and command
him tasks.

IAGO: Nay, that's not your way.

OTHELLO: Hang her! I do but say what she is. So delicate with her needle! an admirable musician! O
220 she will sing the savageness out of a bear! Of so
high and plenteous wit and invention—

IAGO: She's the worse for all this.

OTHELLO: O, a thousand thousand times! And then,
of so gentle° a condition!

IAGO: Ay, too gentle.°

OTHELLO: Nay, that's certain. But yet the pity of it,
Iago! O Iago, the pity of it, Iago!

IAGO: If you are so fond over her iniquity, give her
patent° to offend; for if it touch not you, it comes
near nobody. 230

OTHELLO: I will chop her into messes! Cuckold me!

IAGO: O, 'tis foul in her.

OTHELLO: With mine officer!

IAGO: That's fouler.

OTHELLO: Get me some poison, Iago, this night. I'll
not expostulate with her, lest her body and
beauty unprovide ° my mind again. This night,
Iago!

IAGO: Do it not with poison. Strangle her in her bed,
even the bed she hath contaminated. 240

OTHELLO: Good, good! The justice of it pleases. Very
good!

IAGO: And for Cassio, let me be his undertaker: you
shall hear more by midnight.

OTHELLO: Excellent good! *(A trumpet.)*
What trumpet is that same?

IAGO: Something from Venice, sure.

(Enter LODOVICO, DESDEMONA, and ATTENDANTS.)

'Tis Lodovico,
Come from the duke; and see, your wife is with
him. 250

LODOVICO: God save you, worthy general!

OTHELLO: With all my heart, sir.

LODOVICO: The duke and senators of Venice greet
you *(Gives him a letter.)*

OTHELLO: I kiss the instrument of their pleasures.

(Opens the letter and reads.)

DESDEMONA: And what's the news, good cousin
Lodovico?

IAGO: I am very glad to see you, signior.
Welcome to Cyprus.

LODOVICO: I thank you. How does Lieutenant Cassio? 260

IAGO: Lives, sir.

DESDEMONA: Cousin, there's fall'n between him and
my lord
An unkind breach; but you shall make all well.

OTHELLO: Are you sure of that?

DESDEMONA: My lord?

OTHELLO *(reads)*: 'This fail you not to do, as you
will—'

LODOVICO: He did not call; he's busy in the paper.
Is there division 'twixt thy lord and Cassio? 270

DESDEMONA: A most unhappy one. I would do much
T' atone° them, for the love I bear to Cassio.

OTHELLO: Fire and brimstone!

DESDEMONA: My lord?

OTHELLO: Are you wise?

---

fitchew, polecat; slang term for a whore. ***hobbyhorse,***
harlot. ***gentle,*** nobly born and bred.

gentle, generous. ***patent,*** license. ***unprovide,*** unsettle. ***T' atone,*** to reconcile.

DESDEMONA: What, is he angry?
LODOVICO: May be the letter moved him;
  For, as I think, they do command him home,
  Deputing Cassio in his government.
280 DESDEMONA: By my troth, I am glad on't.
OTHELLO: Indeed?
DESDEMONA: My lord?
OTHELLO: I am glad to see you mad.
DESDEMONA: Why, sweet Othello—
OTHELLO: Devil! *(Strikes her.)*
DESDEMONA: I have not deserved this.
LODOVICO: My lord, this would not be believed in
    Venice,
  Though I should swear I saw't. 'Tis very much.
290   Make her amends; she weeps.
OTHELLO: O devil, devil!
  If that the earth could teem with° woman's tears,
  Each drop she falls would prove a crocodile.
  Out of my sight!
DESDEMONA: I will not stay to offend you. *(Going.)*
LODOVICO: Truly, an obedient lady.
  I do beseech your lordship call her back.
OTHELLO: Mistress!
DESDEMONA: My lord?
300 OTHELLO: What would you with her, sir?
LODOVICO: Who? I, my lord?
OTHELLO: Ay! You did wish that I would make her
    turn.
  Sir, she can turn, and turn, and yet go on
  And turn again; and she can weep, sir, weep;
  And she's obedient; as you say, obedient,
  Very obedient.—Proceed you in your tears.—
  Concerning this, sir—O well-painted passion!—
  I am commanded home.—Get you away;
310   I'll send for you anon.—Sir, I obey the mandate
  And will return to Venice.—Hence, avaunt!

(Exit DESDEMONA.*)*

  Cassio shall have my place. And, sir, to-night
  I do entreat that we may sup together.
  You are welcome, sir, to Cyprus—Goats and
    monkeys! *(Exit.)*
LODOVICO: Is this the noble Moor whom our full
    Senate
  Call all in all sufficient? Is this the nature
  Whom passion could not shake? whose solid virtue
320   The shot of accident nor dart of chance
  Could neither graze nor pierce?
IAGO: He is much changed.
LODOVICO: Are his wits safe? Is he not light of brain?
IAGO: He's that he is; I may not breathe my censure.
  What he might be (if what he might, he is not)
  I would to heaven he were!
LODOVICO: What, strike his wife?
IAGO: Faith, that was not so well; yet would I knew
  That stroke would prove the worst!

LODOVICO: Is it his use?°   330
  Or did the letter work upon his blood
  And new-create this fault?
IAGO: Alas, alas!
  It is not honesty in me to speak
  What I have seen and known. You shall observe
    him,
  And his own courses will denote him so
  That I may save my speech. Do but go after
  And mark how he continues.
LODOVICO: I am sorry that I am deceived in him.   340
  (Exeunt.)

ACT 4 / SCENE 2

(Enter OTHELLO *and* EMILIA.*)*

OTHELLO: You have seen nothing then?
EMILIA: Nor ever heard, nor ever did suspect.
OTHELLO: Yes, you have seen Cassio and she
    together.
EMILIA: But then I saw no harm, and then I heard
  Each syllable that breath made up between them.
OTHELLO: What, did they never whisper?
EMILIA: Never, my lord.
OTHELLO: Nor send you out o' th' way?
EMILIA: Never.   10
OTHELLO: To fetch her fan, her gloves, her mask, nor
    nothing?
EMILIA: Never, my lord.
OTHELLO: That's strange.
EMILIA: I durst, my lord, to wager she is honest,
  Lay down my soul at stake. If you think other,
  Remove your thought; it doth abuse your bosom.
  If any wretch have put this in your head,
  Let heaven requite it with the serpent's curse!
  For if she be not honest, chaste, and true,   20
  There's no man happy; the purest of their wives
  Is foul as slander.
OTHELLO: Bid her come hither. Go.

(Exit EMILIA.*)*

  She says enough; yet she's a simple bawd
  That cannot say as much. This is a subtle whore,
  A closet lock and key of villainous secrets;
  And yet she'll kneel and pray; I have seen her do't.

(Enter DESDEMONA *and* EMILIA.*)*

DESDEMONA: My lord, what is your will?
OTHELLO: Pray, chuck, come hither.
DESDEMONA: What is your pleasure?   30
OTHELLO: Let me see your eyes.
  Look in my face.
DESDEMONA: What horrible fancy's this?
OTHELLO *(to* EMILIA*)*: Some of your function,°
  mistress.

---

teem with, be made pregnant by.

use, habit. **function,** go about your business; i.e.,
perform your function as the madam of a brothel.

Leave procreants alone and shut the door;
Cough or cry hem if anybody come.
Your mystery,° your mystery! Nay, dispatch!

(Exit EMILIA.)

DESDEMONA: Upon my knees, what doth your speech
40   import?
I understand a fury in your words,
But not the words.
OTHELLO: Why, what art thou?
DESDEMONA: Your wife, my lord; your true
And loyal wife.
OTHELLO: Come, swear it, damn thyself;
Lest, being like one of heaven, the devils
   themselves
Should fear to seize thee. Therefore be
50   double-damned—
Swear thou art honest.
DESDEMONA: Heaven doth truly know it.
OTHELLO: Heaven truly knows that thou art false as
   hell.
DESDEMONA: To whom, my lord? With whom? How
   am I false?
OTHELLO: Ah, Desdemon! away! away! away!
DESDEMONA: Alas the heavy day! Why do you weep?
Am I the motive° of these tears, my lord?
60 If haply you my father do suspect
An instrument of this your calling back,
Lay not your blame on me. If you have lost him,
Why, I have lost him too.
OTHELLO: Had it pleased heaven
To try me with affliction, had they rained
All kinds of sores and shames on my bare head,
Steeped me in poverty to the very lips,
Given to captivity me and my utmost hopes,
I should have found in some place of my soul
70 A drop of patience. But, alas, to make me
A fixèd figure for the time of scorn°
To point his slow unmoving finger at!
Yet could I bear that too; well, very well.
But there where I have garnered up my heart,
Where either I must live or bear no life,
The fountain from the which my current runs
Or else dries up—to be discarded thence,
Or keep it as a cistern for foul toads
To knot and gender in—turn thy complexion
80   there,°
Patience, thou young and rose-lipped cherubin!
Ay, there look grim as hell!
DESDEMONA: I hope my noble lord esteems me
   honest.
OTHELLO: O, ay; as summer flies are in the shambles,°
That quicken even with blowing.° O thou weed,

Who art so lovely fair, and smell'st so sweet,
That the sense aches at thee, would thou hadst
   ne'er been born!
DESDEMONA: Alas, what ignorant sin have I   90
   committed?
OTHELLO: Was this fair paper, this most goodly book,
Made to write 'whore' upon? What committed?
Committed? O thou public commoner!°
I should make very forges of my cheeks
That would to cinders burn up modesty,
Did I but speak thy deeds. What committed?
Heaven stops the nose at it, and the moon winks;°
The bawdy wind, that kisses all it meets,
Is hushed within the hollow mine of earth   100
And will not hear it. What committed?
Impudent strumpet!
DESDEMONA: By heaven, you do me wrong!
OTHELLO: Are not you a strumpet?
DESDEMONA: No, as I am a Christian!
If to preserve this vessel for my lord
From any other foul unlawful touch
Be not to be a strumpet, I am none.
OTHELLO: What, not a whore?
DESDEMONA: No, as I shall be saved!   110
OTHELLO: Is't possible?
DESDEMONA: O, heaven forgive us!
OTHELLO: I cry you mercy° then.
I took you for that cunning whore of Venice
That married with Othello.—*(Calling.)* You,
   mistress,
That have the office opposite to Saint Peter
And keep the gate of hell!

(Enter EMILIA.)

You, you, ay, you!
We have done our course; there's money for your   120
   pains:
I pray you turn the key, and keep our counsel.
   (Exit.)
EMILIA: Alas, what does this gentleman conceive?
How do you, madam? How do you, my good lady?
DESDEMONA: Faith, half asleep.
EMILIA: Good madam, what's the matter with my
   lord?
DESDEMONA: With who?
EMILIA: Why, with my lord, madam.
DESDEMONA: Who is thy lord?   130
EMILIA: He that is yours, sweet lady.
DESDEMONA: I have none. Do not talk to me, Emilia
I cannot weep; nor answer have I none
But what should go by water.° Prithee to-night
Lay on my bed my wedding sheets, remember;
And call thy husband hither.
EMILIA: Here's a change indeed! *(Exit.)*
DESDEMONA: 'Tis meet I should be used so, very meet.

---

mystery, trade. motive, cause. scorn, scornful world.
turn . . . there, change your color at that point. shambles,
slaughterhouses. quicken . . . blowing, come to life as soon
as their eggs are deposited.

public commoner, whore. winks, closes her eyes. cry
you mercy, beg your pardon. water, tears.

How have I been behaved, that he might stick
The small'st opinion° on my least misuse?°   140

(Enter IAGO and EMILIA.)

IAGO: What is your pleasure, madam? How is't with
    you?
DESDEMONA: I cannot tell. Those that do teach young
    babes
    Do it with gentle means and easy tasks:
    He might have chid me so; for, in good faith,
    I am a child to chiding.
IAGO: What is the matter, lady?
EMILIA: Alas, Iago, my lord hath so bewhored her,   150
    Thrown such despite and heavy terms upon her
    As true hearts cannot bear.
DESDEMONA: Am I that name, Iago?
IAGO: What name, fair lady?
DESDEMONA: Such as she says my lord did say I was.
EMILIA: He called her whore. A beggar in his drink
    Could not have laid such terms upon his callet.°
IAGO: Why did he so?
DESDEMONA: I do not know; I am sure I am none
    such.
IAGO: Do not weep, do not weep. Alas the day!   160
EMILIA: Hath she forsook so many noble matches,
    Her father and her country, all her friends,
    To be called whore? Would it not make one weep?
DESDEMONA: It is my wretched fortune.
IAGO: Beshrew him for't!
    How comes this trick° upon him?
DESDEMONA: Nay, heaven doth know.
EMILIA: I will be hanged if some eternal villain,
    Some busy and insinuating rogue,
    Some cogging,° cozening slave, to get some office,   170
    Have not devised this slander. I'll be hanged else.
IAGO: Fie, there is no such man! It is impossible.
DESDEMONA: If any such there be, heaven pardon
    him!
EMILIA: A halter pardon him! and hell gnaw his
    bones!
    Why should he call her whore? Who keeps her
    company?
    What place? what time? what form? what
    likelihood?   180
    The Moor's abused by some most villainous knave,
    Some base notorious knave, some scurvy fellow.
    O heaven, that such companions thou'dst unfold,°
    And put in every honest hand a whip
    To lash the rascals naked through the world
    Even from the east to th' west!
IAGO: Speak within door.°
EMILIA: O fie upon them! Some such squire he was
    That turned your wit the seamy side without
    And made you to suspect me with the Moor.   190

IAGO: You are a fool. Go to.
DESDEMONA: O good Iago,
    What shall I do to win my lord again?
    Good friend, go to him; for, by this light of heaven,
    I know not how I lost him. Here I kneel:
    If e'er my will did trespass 'gainst his love
    Either in discourse of thought or actual deed,
    Or that mine eyes, mine ears, or any sense
    Delighted them in any other form,
    Or that I do not yet, and ever did,   200
    And ever will (though he do shake me off
    To beggarly divorcement) love him dearly,
    Comfort forswear° me! Unkindness may do much;
    And his unkindness may defeat my life,
    But never taint my love. I cannot say "whore."
    It doth abhor me now I speak the word;
    To do the act that might th' addition earn
    Not the world's mass of vanity could make me.
IAGO: I pray you be content. 'Tis but his humor.
    The business of the state does him offense,   210
    And he does chide with you.
DESDEMONA: If 'twere no other—
IAGO: 'Tis but so, I warrant.

(Trumpets within.)

    Hark how these instruments summon you to
    supper.
    The messengers of Venice stay the meal.°
    Go in, and weep not. All things shall be well.

(Exeunt DESDEMONA and EMILIA.)
(Enter RODERIGO.)

    How now, Roderigo?
RODERIGO: I do not find that thou deal'st justly with
    me.   220
IAGO: What in the contrary?
RODERIGO: Every day thou daff'st me° with some de-
    vice, Iago, and rather, as it seems to me now,
    keep'st from me all conveniency° than suppliest
    me with the least advantage of hope. I will in-
    deed no longer endure it; nor am I yet per-
    suaded to put up in peace what already I have
    foolishly suffered.
IAGO: Will you hear me, Roderigo?
RODERIGO: Faith, I have heard too much; for your   230
    words and performance are no kin together.
IAGO: You charge me most unjustly.
RODERIGO: With naught but truth. I have wasted my-
    self out of means. The jewels you have had from
    me to deliver to Desdemona would half have
    corrupted a votarist.° You have told me she hath
    received them, and returned me expectations
    and comforts of sudden respect and acquaint-
    ance; but I find none.

---

opinion, suspicion. ***misuse,*** slightest misconduct. ***callet,*** whore. ***trick,*** strange behavior. ***cogging,*** cheating.
unfold, expose. ***within door,*** quietly.

Comfort forswear, happiness forsake. ***stay the meal,***
wait to eat. ***daff'st me,*** put me off. ***conveniency,*** opportunities (to meet with Desdemona). ***votarist,*** nun.

240 IAGO: Well, go to; very well.
RODERIGO: Very well! go to! I cannot go to, man; nor
'tis not very well. By this hand, I say 'tis very
scurvy, and begin to find myself fopped° in it.
IAGO: Very well.
RODERIGO: I tell you 'tis not very well. I will make
myself known to Desdemona. If she will return
me my jewels, I will give over my suit and repent
my unlawful solicitation; if not, assure yourself I
will seek satisfaction of you.
250 IAGO: You have said now.
RODERIGO: Ay, and said nothing but what I protest
intendment of doing.
IAGO: Why, now I see there's mettle in thee; and even
from this instant do build on thee a better opinion than ever before. Give me thy hand,
Roderigo. Thou hast taken against me a most
just exception; but yet I protest I have dealt most
directly in thy affair.
RODERIGO: It hath not appeared.
260 IAGO: I grant indeed it hath not appeared, and your
suspicion is not without wit and judgment. But,
Roderigo, if thou hast that in thee indeed which
I have greater reason to believe now than ever, I
mean purpose, courage, and valor, this night
show it. If thou the next night following enjoy
not Desdemona, take me from this world with
treachery and devise engines for° my life.
RODERIGO: Well, what is it? Is it within reason and
compass?
270 IAGO: Sir, there is especial commission come from
Venice to depute Cassio in Othello's place.
RODERIGO: Is that true? Why, then Othello and
Desdemona return again to Venice.
IAGO: O, no; he goes into Mauritania and takes away
with him the fair Desdemona, unless his abode
be lingered here by some accident; wherein none
can be so determinate° as the removing of Cassio.
RODERIGO: How do you mean removing of him?
280 IAGO: Why, by making him uncapable of Othello's
place—knocking out his brains.
RODERIGO: And that you would have me to do?
IAGO: Ay, if you dare do yourself a profit and a right.
He sups to-night with a harlotry, and thither will
I go to him. He knows not yet of his honorable
fortune. If you will watch his going thence,
which I will fashion to fall out between twelve
and one, you may take him at your pleasure. I
will be near to second your attempt, and he shall
290 fall between us. Come, stand not amazed at it,
but go along with me. I will show you such a
necessity in his death that you shall think yourself bound to put it on him. It is now high sup-

pertime, and the night grows to waste. About it!
RODERIGO: I will hear further reason for this.
IAGO: And you shall be satisfied. (Exeunt.)

ACT 4 / SCENE 3

(Enter OTHELLO, LODOVICO, DESDEMONA, EMILIA, and
ATTENDANTS.)

LODOVICO: I do beseech you, sir, trouble yourself no
further.
OTHELLO: O, pardon me; 'twill do me good to walk.
LODOVICO: Madam, good night. I humbly thank your
ladyship.
DESDEMONA: Your honor is most welcome.
OTHELLO: Will you walk, sir?
O, Desdemona—
DESDEMONA: My lord?
OTHELLO: Get you to bed on th' instant; I will be re-   10
turned forthwith. Dismiss your attendant there.
Look't be done.
DESDEMONA: I will, my lord.

(Exit OTHELLO, with LODOVICO and ATTENDANTS.)

EMILIA: How goes it now? He looks gentler than he
did.
DESDEMONA: He says he will return incontinent.°
He hath commanded me to go to bed,
And bade me to dismiss you.
EMILIA: Dismiss me?
DESDEMONA: It was his bidding; therefore, good   20
Emilia,
Give me my nightly wearing, and adieu.
We must not now displease him.
EMILIA: I would you had never seen him!
DESDEMONA: So would not I. My love doth so approve
him
That even his stubbornness,° his checks,° his
frowns—
Prithee unpin me—have grace and favor in them.
EMILIA: I have laid those sheets you bade me on the   30
bed.
DESDEMONA: All's one. Good faith, how foolish are
our minds!
If I do die before thee, prithee shroud me
In one of those same sheets.
EMILIA: Come, come! You talk.
DESDEMONA: My mother had a maid called Barbary.
She was in love; and he she loved proved mad°
And did forsake her. She had a song of 'Willow';
An old thing 'twas; but it expressed her fortune,   40
And she died singing it. That song to-night
Will not go from my mind; I have much to do
But to go hang my head all at one side
And sing it like poor Barbary. Prithee dispatch.

---

fopped, fooled. devise engines for, plots against. de-
terminate, effective.

incontinent, immediately. stubbornness, roughness.
checks, rebukes. mad, untrue.

EMILIA: Shall I go fetch your nightgown?
DESDEMONA: No, unpin me here.
 This Lodovico is a proper man.
EMILIA: A very handsome man.
DESDEMONA: He speaks well.
50 EMILIA: I know a lady in Venice would have walked
   barefoot to Palestine for a touch of his nether lip.
DESDEMONA (sings):

 The poor soul sat sighing by a sycamore tree,
   Sing all a green willow;
 Her hand on her bosom, her head on her knee,
   Sing willow, willow, willow.
 The fresh streams ran by her and murmured her
   moans;
   Sing willow, willow, willow;
60 *Her salt tears fell from her, and soft'ned the stones—*
Lay by these.

   Sing willow, willow, willow—

Prithee hie thee; he'll come anon.

 Sing all a green willow must be my garland.
 Let nobody blame him; his scorn I approve—

Nay, that's not next. Hark! who is't that knocks?
EMILIA: It is the wind.
DESDEMONA (sings):

 I called my love false love; but what said he then?
70   *Sing willow, willow, willow:*
 If I court moe women, you'll couch with moe men.

So, get thee gone; good night. Mine eyes do itch.
 Doth that bode weeping?
EMILIA: 'Tis neither here nor there.
DESDEMONA: I have heard it said so. O, these men,
   these men!
 Dost thou in conscience think—tell me, Emilia—
 That there be women do abuse their husbands
 In such gross kind?
80 EMILIA: There be some such, no question.
DESDEMONA: Wouldst thou do such a deed for all the
   world?
EMILIA: Why, would not you?
DESDEMONA: No, by this heavenly light!
EMILIA: Nor I neither by this heavenly light.
 I might do't as well i' th' dark.
DESDEMONA: Wouldst thou do such a deed for all the
   world?
EMILIA: The world's a huge thing; it is a great price
90   for a small vice.
DESDEMONA: Good troth, I think thou wouldst not.
EMILIA: By my troth, I think I should; and undo't
   when I had done it. Marry, I would not do such a
   thing for a joint-ring,° nor for measures of lawn,°

nor for gowns, petticoats, nor caps, nor any petty
 exhibition;° but, for all the whole world—'Ud's
 pity! who would not make her husband a cuckold to make him a monarch? I should venture
 purgatory for't.
DESDEMONA: Beshrew me if I would do such a wrong 100
 For the whole world.
EMILIA: Why, the wrong is but a wrong i' th' world;
 and having the world for your labor, 'tis a wrong
 in your own world, and you might quickly make
 it right.
DESDEMONA: I do not think there is any such woman.
EMILIA: Yes, a dozen; and as many to the vantage° as
 would store° the world they played for.
 But I do think it is their husbands' faults
 If wives do fall. Say that they slack their duties 110
 And pour our treasures into foreign laps;
 Or else break out in peevish jealousies,
 Throwing restraint upon us; or say they strike us,
 Or scant our former having° in despite°—
 Why, we have galls;° and though we have some
   grace,
 Yet have we some revenge. Let husbands know
 Their wives have sense like them. They see, and
   smell,
 And have their palates both for sweet and sour, 120
 As husbands have. What is it that they do
 When they change us for others? Is it sport?
 I think it is. And doth affection breed it?
 I think it doth. Is't frailty that thus errs?
 It is so too. And have not we affections,
 Desires for sport, and frailty, as men have?
 Then let them use us well; else let them know,
 The ills we do, their ills instruct us so.
DESDEMONA: Good night, good night. God me such
   usage° send, 130
 Not to pick bad from bad, but by bad mend!
 (Exeunt.)

ACT 5 / SCENE 1

(Enter IAGO and RODERIGO.)

IAGO: Here, stand behind this bulk;° straight will he
   come.
 Wear thy good rapier bare, and put it home.
 Quick, quick! Fear nothing; I'll be at thy elbow.
 It makes us, or it mars us—think on that,
 And fix most firm thy resolution.
RODERIGO: Be near at hand; I may miscarry in't.
IAGO: Here, at thy hand. Be bold, and take thy stand.
 (Stands aside.)
RODERIGO: I have no great devotion to the deed, 10

---

joint-ring, cheap ring.   **lawn,** fine linen.

petty exhibition, gift.   **vantage,** in addition.   **store,** populate.   **having,** allowance.   **despite,** spite.   **galls,** capacity to feel resentment.   **usage,** habits.   **bulk,** projecting store front.

10   And yet he hath given me satisfying reasons.
    'Tis but a man gone. Forth my sword! He dies!
  IAGO: I have rubbed this young quat° almost to the
    sense,°
    And he grows angry. Now whether he kill Cassio,
    Or Cassio him, or each do kill the other,
    Every way makes my gain. Live Roderigo,
    He calls me to a restitution large
    Of gold and jewels that I bobbed° from him
    As gifts to Desdemona.
20   It must not be. If Cassio do remain,
    He hath a daily beauty in his life
    That makes me ugly; and besides, the Moor
    May unfold me to him; there stand I in much peril.
    No, he must die. Be't so! I hear him coming.

(Enter CASSIO.)

  RODERIGO: I know his gait. 'Tis he. Villain, thou diest!
    (Makes a pass at CASSIO.)
  CASSIO: That thrust had been mine enemy indeed
    But that my coat is better than thou know'st.
    I will make proof of thine. *(Draws, and wounds*
    RODERIGO.)*
30   RODERIGO: O, I am slain!

    (IAGO darts from concealment behind CASSIO, wounds
    him in the leg, and exit.)

  CASSIO: I am maimed for ever. Help, ho! Murder!
    murder! *(Falls.)*

(Enter OTHELLO.)

  OTHELLO: The voice of Cassio. Iago keeps his word.
  RODERIGO: O, villain that I am!
  OTHELLO: It is even so.
  CASSIO: O, help, ho! light! a surgeon!
  OTHELLO: 'Tis he. O brave Iago, honest and just,
    That hast such noble sense of thy friend's wrong!
    Thou teachest me. Minion,° your dear lies dead,
40   And your unblest fate hies.° Strumpet, I come.
    Forth of my heart those charms, thine eyes, are
    blotted.
    Thy bed, lust-stained, shall with lust's blood be
    spotted. *(Exit.)*

(Enter LODOVICO and GRATIANO.)

  CASSIO: What, ho? No watch? No passage?° Murder!
    murder!
  GRATIANO: 'Tis some mischance. The cry is very
    direful.
  CASSIO: O, help!
50   LODOVICO: Hark!
  RODERIGO: O wretched villain!
  LODOVICO: Two or three groan. It is a heavy° night.

---

    quat, pimple. **to the sense,** raw. **bobbed,** swindled.
Minion, mistress. **hies,** hurries on. **passage,** passerby.
heavy, dark.

These may be counterfeits. Let's think't unsafe
    To come in to the cry without more help.
  RODERIGO: Nobody come? Then shall I bleed to
    death.
  LUDOVICO: Hark!

(Enter IAGO, with a light.)

  GRATIANO: Here's one comes in his shirt, with light
    and weapons.
  IAGO: Who's there? Whose noise is this that cries on   60
    murder?
  LODOVICO: We do not know.
  IAGO: Did not you hear a cry?
  CASSIO: Here, here! For heaven's sake, help me!
  IAGO: What's the matter?
  GRATIANO: This is Othello's ancient, as I take it.
  LODOVICO: The same indeed, a very valiant fellow.
  IAGO: What are you here that cry so grievously?
  CASSIO: Iago? O, I am spoiled, undone by villains!
    Give me some help.   70
  IAGO: O me, lieutenant! What villains have done this?
  CASSIO: I think that one of them is hereabout
    And I cannot make away.
  IAGO: O treacherous villains!
    (to LODOVICO and GRATIANO) What are you there?
    Come in, and give some help.
  RODERIGO: O, help me here!
  CASSIO: That's one of them.
  IAGO: O murd'rous slave! O villain! *(Stabs RODERIGO.)*
  RODERIGO: O damned Iago! O inhuman dog!   80
  IAGO: Kill men i' th' dark?—Where be these bloody
    thieves?—
    How silent is this town!—Ho! murder! murder!—
    What may you be? Are you of good or evil?
  LODOVICO: As you shall prove us, praise us.
  IAGO: Signior Lodovico?
  LODIVICO: He, sir.
  IAGO: I cry you mercy. Here's Cassio hurt by villains.
  GRATIANO: Cassio?
  IAGO: How is it, brother?   90
  CASSIO: My leg is cut in two.
  IAGO: Marry, heaven forbid!
    Light, gentlemen. I'll bind it with my shirt.

(Enter BIANCA.)

  BIANCA: What is the matter, ho? Who is't that cried?
  IAGO: Who is't that cried?
  BIANCA: O my dear Cassio! my sweet Cassio!
    O Cassio, Cassio, Cassio!
  IAGO: O notable strumpet!—Cassio, may you suspect
    Who they should be that thus have mangled you?
  CASSIO: No.   100
  GRATIANO: I am sorry to find you thus. I have been to
    seek you.
  IAGO: Lend me a garter. So. O for a chair
    To bear him easily hence!
  BIANCA: Alas, he faints! O Cassio, Cassio, Cassio!

IAGO: Gentlemen all, I do suspect this trash
　　To be a party in this injury.—
　　Patience awhile, good Cassio.—Come, come!
　　Lend me a light. Know we this face or no?
110　Alas, my friend and my dear countryman
　　Roderigo? No.—Yes, sure.—O heaven, Roderigo!
GRATIANO: What, of Venice?
IAGO: Even he, sir. Did you know him?
GRATIANO: Know him? Ay.
IAGO: Signior Gratiano? I cry you gentle pardon.
　　These bloody accidents must excuse my manners
　　That so neglected you.
GRATIANO: I am glad to see you.
IAGO: How do you, Cassio?—O, a chair, a chair!
GRATIANO: Roderigo?
120　IAGO: He, he, 'tis he! *(A chair brought in.)* O, that's well
　　　said;° the chair.
　　Some good man bear him carefully from hence.
　　I'll fetch the general's surgeon. *(to Bianca)* For you,
　　　mistress,
　　Save you your labor.—He that lies slain here,
　　　Cassio,
　　Was my dear friend. What malice was between
　　　you?
130　CASSIO: None in the world; nor do I know the man.
IAGO *(to BIANCA):* What, look you pale?—O, bear him
　　　out o' th' air.

　　(CASSIO and RODERIGO are borne off.)

　　Stay you, good gentlemen.—Look you pale,
　　　mistress?—
　　Do you perceive the gastness° of her eye?—
　　Nay, if you stare, we shall hear more anon.
　　Behold her well; I pray you look upon her.
　　Do you see, gentlemen? Nay, guiltiness will speak,
　　Though tongues were out of use.

　　(Enter EMILIA.)

140　EMILIA: 'Las, what's the matter? What's the matter,
　　　husband?
IAGO: Cassio hath here been set on in the dark
　　By Roderigo, and fellows that are scaped.
　　He's almost slain, and Roderigo dead.
EMILIA: Alas, good gentleman! alas, good Cassio!
IAGO: This is the fruit of whoring. Prithee, Emilia,
　　Go know of Cassio where he supped to-night.
　　(to BIANCA) What, do you shake at that?
BIANCA: He supped at my house; but I therefore
150　　shake not.
IAGO: O, did he so? I charge you go with me.
EMILIA: Fie, fie upon thee, strumpet!
BIANCA: I am no strumpet, but of life as honest
　　As you that thus abuse me.
EMILIA: As I? Foh! fie upon thee!

IAGO: Kind gentlemen, let's go see poor Cassio
　　dressed.
　　(to BIANCA) Come, mistress, you must tell's another
　　　tale.
　　Emilia, run you to the citadel　　　　　　　　　160
　　And tell my lord and lady what hath happed.

(Exit EMILIA.)

Will you go on afore?

(Exeunt all but IAGO.)

This is the night
That either makes me or fordoes° me quite. *(Exit.)*

ACT 5 / SCENE 2

*(DESDEMONA asleep in her bed. Enter OTHELLO with a
light.)*

OTHELLO: It is the cause,° it is the cause, my soul.
　　Let me not name it to you, you chaste stars!
　　It is the cause. Yet I'll not shed her blood,
　　Nor scar that whiter skin of hers than snow,
　　And smooth as monumental alabaster.
　　Yet she must die, else she'll betray more men.
　　Put out the light, and then put out the light.
　　If I quench thee, thou flaming minister,
　　I can again thy former light restore,
　　Should I repent me; but once put out thy light,　　10
　　Thou cunning'st pattern of excelling nature,
　　I know not where is that Promethean heat°
　　That can thy light relume.° When I have plucked
　　　the rose,
　　I cannot give it vital growth again;
　　It needs must wither. I'll smell thee on the tree. *(He
　　　kisses her.)*
　　O balmy breath, that dost almost persuade
　　Justice to break her sword! One more, one more!
　　Be thus when thou art dead, and I will kill thee,　　20
　　And love thee after. One more, and this the last!
　　So sweet was ne'er so fatal. I must weep,
　　But they are cruel tears. This sorrow's heavenly;
　　It strikes where it doth love. She wakes.
DESDEMONA: Who's there? Othello?
OTHELLO: Ay, Desdemona.
DESDEMONA: Will you come to bed, my lord?
OTHELLO: Have you prayed to-night, Desdemona?
DESDEMONA: Ay, my lord.
OTHELLO: If you bethink yourself of any crime　　　30
　　Unreconciled as yet to heaven and grace,
　　Solicit for it straight.
DESDEMONA: Alack, my lord, what may you mean by
　　that?
OTHELLO: Well, do it, and be brief; I will walk by.
　　I would not kill thy unprepared spirit.

---

well said, well done.　*gastness,* terror.

fordoes, destroys.　*cause,* cause of justice.　**Promethean heat,** divine fire.　*relume,* rekindle.

No, heaven forfend!° I would not kill thy soul.
DESDEMONA: Talk you of killing?
OTHELLO: Ay, I do.
40 DESDEMONA: Then heaven
Have mercy on me!
OTHELLO: Amen, with all my heart!
DESDEMONA: If you say so, I hope you will not kill me.
OTHELLO: Hum!
DESDEMONA: And yet I fear you; for you are fatal
then
When your eyes roll so. Why I should fear I know
not,
Since guiltiness I know not; but yet I feel I fear.
50 OTHELLO: Think on thy sins.
DESDEMONA: They are loves I bear to you.
OTHELLO: Ay, and for that thou diest.
DESDEMONA: That death's unnatural that kills for
loving.
Alas, why gnaw you so your nether lip?
Some bloody passion shakes your very frame.
These are portents; but yet I hope, I hope,
They do not point on me.
OTHELLO: Peace and be still!
60 DESDEMONA: I will so. What's the matter?
OTHELLO: That handkerchief which I so loved and
gave thee
Thou gav'st to Cassio.
DESDEMONA: No, by my life and soul!
Send for the man and ask him.
OTHELLO: Sweet soul, take heed,
Take heed of perjury; thou art on thy deathbed.
DESDEMONA: Ay, but not yet to die.
OTHELLO: Yes, presently.
70 Therefore confess thee freely of thy sin;
For to deny each article with oath
Cannot remove nor choke the strong conception°
That I do groan withal. Thou art to die.
DESDEMONA: Then Lord have mercy on me!
OTHELLO: I say amen.
DESDEMONA: And have you mercy too! I never did
Offend° you in my life; never loved Cassio
But with such general warranty of heaven
As I might love. I never gave him token.
80 OTHELLO: By heaven, I saw my handkerchief in's
hand!
O perjured woman! thou dost stone° my heart,
And mak'st me call what I intend to do
A murder, which I thought a sacrifice.
I saw the handkerchief.
DESDEMONA: He found it then.
I never gave it him. Send for him hither.
Let him confess a truth.
OTHELLO: He hath confessed.
90 DESDEMONA: What, my lord?

OTHELLO: That he hath used thee.
DESDEMONA: How? unlawfully?
OTHELLO: Ay.
DESDEMONA: He will not say so.
OTHELLO: No, his mouth is stopped.
Honest Iago hath ta'en order for't.°
DESDEMONA: O, my fear interprets. What, is he dead?
OTHELLO: Had all his hairs been lives, my great
revenge
Had stomach for them all. 100
DESDEMONA: Alas, he is betrayed, and I undone!
OTHELLO: Out, strumpet! Weep'st thou for him to my
face?
DESDEMONA: O, banish me, my lord, but kill me not!
OTHELLO: Down, strumpet!
DESDEMONA: Kill me to-morrow; let me live to-night!
OTHELLO: Nay, an you strive°—
DESDEMONA: But half an hour!
OTHELLO: Being done, there is no pause.
DESDEMONA: But while I say one prayer! 110
OTHELLO: It is too late. (Smothers her.)
DESDEMONA: O Lord, Lord, Lord!

(EMILIA at the door.)

EMILIA (calls within): My lord, my lord! What, ho, my
lord, my lord!
OTHELLO: What noise is this? Not dead? Not yet quite
dead?
I that am cruel am yet merciful;
I would not have thee linger in thy pain.
So, so.
EMILIA (within): What, ho! my lord, my lord! 120
OTHELLO: Who's there?
EMILIA (within): O, good my lord, I would speak a
word with you!
OTHELLO: Yes, 'tis Emilia.—By and by.—She's
dead.—
'Tis like she comes to speak of Cassio's death.
The noise was here. Ha! no more moving?
Still as the grave.—Shall she come in? Were't
good?—
I think she stirs again. No.—What's best to do? 130
If she come in, she'll sure speak to my wife.
My wife! my wife! what wife? I have no wife.
O, insupportable! O heavy hour!
Methinks it should be now a huge eclipse
Of sun and moon, and that th' affrighted globe
Should yawn° at alteration.
EMILIA (within): I do beseech you
That I may speak with you, O good my lord!
OTHELLO: I had forgot thee. O, come in, Emilia.
Soft, by and by.—Let me the curtains draw.— 140

(Closes the bed-curtains.)

---

forfend, forbid. conception, belief (of her being
guilty). offend, wrong. stone, turn to stone.

ta'en . . . for't, take measures to bring it about. strive,
struggle. yawn, open, as in an earthquake.

Where art thou?

(Opens the door.)

(Enter EMILIA.*)*

What's the matter with thee now?

EMILIA: O my good lord, yonder's foul murder done!

OTHELLO: What? Now?

EMILIA: But now, my lord.

OTHELLO: It is the very error° of the moon.
    She comes more nearer earth than she was wont
    And makes men mad.

EMILIA: Cassio, my lord, hath killed a young Venetian
150   Called Roderigo.

OTHELLO: Roderigo killed?
    And Cassio killed?

EMILIA: No, Cassio is not killed.

OTHELLO: Not Cassio killed? Then murder's out of
    tune,
    And sweet revenge grows harsh.

DESDEMONA: O, falsely, falsely murdered!

EMILIA: O Lord! what cry is that?

OTHELLO: That? What?

160 EMILIA: Out and alas! that was my lady's voice.
    Help! help, ho! help! O lady, speak again!
    Sweet Desdemona! O sweet mistress, speak!

DESDEMONA: A guiltless death I die.

EMILIA: O, who hath done this deed?

DESDEMONA: Nobody—I myself. Farewell.
    Commend me to my kind lord. O, farewell! *(She
    dies.)*

OTHELLO: Why, how should she be murd'red?

EMILIA: Alas, who knows?

OTHELLO: You heard her say herself, it was not I.

170 EMILIA: She said so. I must needs report the truth.

OTHELLO: She's like a liar gone to burning hell!
    'Twas I that killed her.

EMILIA: O, the more angel she,
    And you the blacker devil!

OTHELLO: She turned to folly, and she was a whore.

EMILIA: Thou dost belie her, and thou art a devil.

OTHELLO: She was false as water.

EMILIA: Thou art rash as fire to say
    That she was false. O, she was heavenly true!

180 OTHELLO: Cassio did top her. Ask thy husband else.
    O, I were damned beneath all depth in hell
    But that I did proceed upon just grounds
    To this extremity. Thy husband knew it all.

EMILIA: My husband?

OTHELLO: Thy husband.

EMILIA: That she was false to wedlock?

OTHELLO: Ay, with Cassio. Nay, had she been true,
    If heaven would make me such another world
    Of one entire and perfect chrysolite,
190   I'ld not have sold her for it.

---

error, straying from its natural course.

EMILIA: My husband?

OTHELLO: Ay, 'twas he that told me first.
    An honest man he is, and hates the slime
    That sticks on filthy deeds.

EMILIA: My husband?

OTHELLO: What needs this iterance?° Woman, I say
    thy husband.

EMILIA: O mistress, villainy hath made mocks with
    love!
    My husband say that she was false?   200

OTHELLO: He, woman.
    I say, thy husband. Dost understand the word?
    My friend, thy husband; honest, honest, Iago.

EMILIA: If he say so, may his pernicious soul
    Rot half a grain a day! he lies to th' heart.
    She was too fond of her most filthy bargain.

OTHELLO: Ha!

EMILIA: Do thy worst.
    This deed of thine is no more worthy heaven
    Than thou wast worthy her.   210

OTHELLO: Peace, you were best.

EMILIA: Thou hast not half the power to do me harm
    As I have to be hurt.° O gull! O dolt!
    As ignorant as dirt! thou hast done a deed—
    I care not for thy sword; I'll make thee known,
    Though I lost twenty lives. Help! help! O, help!
    The Moor hath killed my mistress! Murder!
    murder!

(Enter MONTANO, GRATIANO, IAGO, *and* OTHERS.*)*

MONTANO: What is the matter? How now, general?

EMILIA: O, are you come, Iago? You have done well,   220
    That men must lay their murders on your neck.

GRATIANO: What is the matter?

EMILIA: Disprove this villain, if thou be'st a man.
    He says thou told'st him that his wife was false.
    I know thou didst not; thou'rt not such a villain.
    Speak, for my heart is full.

IAGO: I told him what I thought, and told no more
    Than what he found himself was apt and true.

EMILIA: But did you ever tell him she was false?

IAGO: I did.   230

EMILIA: You told a lie, an odious damnèd lie!
    Upon my soul, a lie! a wicked lie!
    She false with Cassio? Did you say with Cassio?

IAGO: With Cassio, mistress. Go to, charm° your
    tongue.

EMILIA: I will not charm my tongue; I am bound to
    speak:
    My mistress here lies murdered in her bed—

ALL: O heavens forfend!

EMILIA: And your reports have set the murder on.   240

OTHELLO: Nay, stare not, masters. It is true indeed.

GRATIANO: 'Tis a strange truth.

---

iterance, repetition. **hurt,** to endure pain. **charm,**
cast a spell on; i.e., silence.

MONTANO: O monstrous act!

EMILIA: Villainy, villainy, villainy!
I think upon't—I think I smell't!—O villainy!
I thought so then.—I'll kill myself for grief.—
O villainy, villainy!

IAGO: What, are you mad? I charge you get you
home.

250 EMILIA: Good gentlemen, let me have leave to speak.
'Tis proper I obey him, but not now.
Perchance, Iago, I will ne'er go home.

OTHELLO: O! O! O! (Falls on the bed.)

EMILIA: Nay, lay thee down and roar!
For thou hast killed the sweetest innocent
That e'er did lift up eye.

OTHELLO: O, she was foul! (Rises.)
I scarce did know you, uncle. There lies your niece,
Whose breath, indeed, these hands have newly
260 stopped.
I know this act shows horrible and grim.

GRATIANO: Poor Desdemon! I am glad thy father's
dead.
Thy match was mortal to him, and pure grief
Shore° his old thread in twain. Did he live now,
This sight would make him do a desperate turn;°
Yea, curse his better angel from his side,
And fall to reprobation.°

OTHELLO: 'Tis pitiful; but yet Iago knows
270 That she with Cassio hath the act of shame
A thousand times committed. Cassio confessed it;
And she did gratify his amorous works
With the recognizance and pledge of love
Which I first gave her. I saw it in his hand.
It was a handkerchief, an antique token
My father gave my mother.

EMILIA: O God! O heavenly God!

IAGO: Zounds, hold your peace!

EMILIA: 'Twill out, 'twill out! I peace?
280 No, I will speak as liberal° as the north.°
Let heaven and men and devils, let them all,
All, all, cry shame against me, yet I'll speak.

IAGO: Be wise, and get you home.

EMILIA: I will not.

(IAGO draws and threatens EMILIA.)

GRATIANO: Fie!
Your sword upon a woman?

EMILIA: O thou dull Moor, that handkerchief thou
speak'st of
I found by fortune, and did give my husband;
290 For often with a solemn earnestness—
More than indeed belonged to such a trifle—
He begged of me to steal't.

IAGO: Villainous whore!

EMILIA: She give it Cassio? No, alas, I found it,
And I did give't my husband.

IAGO: Filth, thou liest!

EMILIA: By heaven, I do not, I do not, gentlemen.
O murd'rous coxcomb! what should such a fool
Do with so good a wife?

OTHELLO: Are there no stones° in heaven   300
But what serves for the thunder? Precious villain!

(The MOOR runs at IAGO, but is disarmed by MONTANO.
IAGO kills his wife.)

GRATIANO: The woman falls. Sure he hath killed his
wife.

(Exit IAGO.)

EMILIA: Ay, ay. O, lay me by my mistress' side.

GRATIANO: He's gone, but his wife's killed.

MONTANO: 'Tis a notorious villain. Take you this
weapon,
Which I have here recovered from the Moor.
Come, guard the door without, Let him not pass,
But kill him rather. I'll after the same villain,   310
For 'tis a damnèd slave.

(Exit MONTANO, with all but OTHELLO and EMILIA.)

OTHELLO: I am not valiant neither;
But every puny whipster° gets my sword.
But why should honor outlive honesty?
Let it go all.

EMILIA: What did thy song bode, lady?
Hark, canst thou hear me? I will play the swan,
And die in music (sings) 'Willow, willow, willow.'
Moor, she was chaste. She loved thee, cruel Moor:
So come my soul to bliss as I speak true.   320
So speaking as I think, I die, I die. (She dies.)

OTHELLO: I have another weapon in this chamber;
It is a sword of Spain, the Isebrook's° temper.
O, here it is.—Uncle, I must come forth.

GRATIANO (within): If thou attempt it, it will cost thee
dear.
Thou hast no weapon, and perforce must suffer.

OTHELLO: Look in upon me then and speak with me,
Or, naked° as I am, I will assault thee.

(Enter GRATIANO.)

GRATIANO: What is the matter?   330

OTHELLO: Behold, I have a weapon;
A better never did itself sustain
Upon a soldier's thigh. I have seen the day
That with this little arm and this good sword
I have made my way through more impediments
Than twenty times your stop.° But O vain boast!
Who can control his fate? 'Tis not so now.

Shore, cut. **turn,** deed. **reprobation,** be rejected by
God. **liberal,** unrestrainedly. **north,** blowing of the north
wind.

stones, thunderbolts. **whipster,** top-whipping boy.
Isebrook, Innsbruck, where the finest steel blades of the time
were forged. **naked,** unarmed. **stop,** power to stop.

Be not afraid, though you do see me weaponed.
Here is my journey's end, here is my butt,°
340 And very seamark° of my utmost sail.
Do you go back dismayed? 'Tis a lost° fear.
Man but a rush° against Othello's breast,
And he retires. Where should Othello go?
Now, how dost thou look now? O ill-starred wench!
Pale as thy smock! When we shall meet at compt,°
This look of thine will hurl my soul from heaven,
And fiends will snatch at it. Cold, cold, my girl?
Even like thy chastity.
O cursèd, cursèd slave! Whip me, ye devils,
350 From the possession of this heavenly sight!
Blow me about in the winds! roast me in sulphur!
Wash me in steep-down gulfs of liquid fire!
O Desdemona, Desdemona! dead!
O! O! O!

(Enter LODOVICO, MONTANO, IAGO *as prisoner, and* OF-
FICERS; CASSIO *in a chair.)*

LODOVICO: Where is this rash and most unfortunate
    man?
OTHELLO: That's he that was Othello. Here I am.
LODOVICO: Where is that viper? Bring the villain
    forth.
360 OTHELLO: I look down towards his feet°—but that's a
    fable.
If that thou be'st a devil, I cannot kill thee.

(Wounds IAGO.)

LODOVICO: Wrench his sword from him.

*(*OTHELLO *is disarmed.)*

IAGO: I bleed, sir, but not killed.
OTHELLO: I am not sorry neither. I'd have thee live;
    For in my sense, 'tis happiness to die.
LODOVICO: O thou Othello that wert once so good,
    Fall'n in the practice° of a damnèd slave,
    What shall be said to thee?
370 OTHELLO: Why, anything:
    An honorable murderer, if you will;
    For naught did I in hate, but all in honor.
LODOVICO: This wretch hath part confessed his
    villainy.
    Did you and he consent in Cassio's death?
OTHELLO: Ay.
CASSIO: Dear general, I never gave you cause.
OTHELLO: I do believe it, and I ask your pardon.
    Will you, I pray, demand that demi-devil
380 Why he hath thus ensnared my soul and body?
IAGO: Demand me nothing. What you know, you
    know.

---

butt, limit. seamark, beacon. lost, wasted. man ...
rush, wield a mere reed. compt, final accounting; i.e., Day
of Judgment. I ... feet, to see if they are cloven, as the
Devil's feet were believed to be. practice, plot.

From this time forth I never will speak word.
LODOVICO: What, not to pray?
GRATIANO: Torments will ope your lips.
OTHELLO: Well, thou dost best.
LODOVICO: Sir, you shall understand what hath
    befall'n,
    Which, as I think, you know not. Here is a letter
    Found in the pocket of the slain Roderigo;   390
    And here another. The one of them imports
    The death of Cassio to be undertook
    By Roderigo.
OTHELLO: O villain!
CASSIO: Most heathenish and most gross!
LODOVICO: Now here's another discontented paper
    Found in his pocket too; and this, it seems,
    Roderigo meant t' have sent this damnèd villain;
    But that, belike, Iago in the nick°
    Came in and satisfied him.   400
OTHELLO: O thou pernicious caitiff!—
    How came you, Cassio, by that handkerchief
    That was my wife's?
CASSIO: I found it in my chamber;
    And he himself confessed but even now
    That there he dropped it for a special purpose
    Which wrought to his desire.
OTHELLO: O fool! fool! fool!
CASSIO: There is besides in Roderigo's letter,
    How he upbraids Iago that he made him   410
    Brave° me upon the watch; whereon it came
    That I was cast;° and even but now he spake,
    After long seeming dead—Iago hurt him,
    Iago set him on.
LODOVICO: You must forsake this room and go with
    us.
    Your power and your command is taken off,
    And Cassio rules in Cyprus. For this slave,
    If there be any cunning cruelty
    That can torment him much and hold him long,   420
    It shall be his. You shall close prisoner rest
    Till the nature of your fault be known
    To the Venetian state. Come, bring away.
OTHELLO: Soft you! a word or two before you go.
    I have done the state some service, and they know't.
    No more of that. I pray you, in your letters,
    When you shall these unlucky deeds relate,
    Speak of me as I am. Nothing extenuate,
    Nor set down aught in malice. Then must you
        speak   430
    Of one that loved not wisely, but too well;
    Of one not easily jealous, but being, wrought,
    Perplexed° in the extreme; of one whose hand,
    Like the base Indian, threw a pearl away
    Richer than all his tribe; of one whose subdued
        eyes.

---

nick, nick of time.   Brave, defy.   cast, dismissed.
Perplexed, distraught.

Albeit unusèd to the melting mood,
Drop tears as fast as the Arabian trees
Their med'cinable gum. Set you down this.
440 And say besides that in Aleppo once,
Where a malignant and a turbaned Turk
Beat a Venetian and traduced the state,
I took by th' throat the circumcisèd dog
And smote him—thus. *(He stabs himself.)*
LODOVICO: O bloody period!°
GRATIANO: All that's spoke is marred.
OTHELLO: I kissed thee ere I killed thee. No way but
this,
Killing myself, to die upon a kiss. *(He falls upon the
bed and dies.)*
450 CASSIO: This did I fear, but thought he had no
weapon;

---

period, ending.

For he was great of heart.
LODOVICO *(to IAGO):* O Spartan dog,°
More fell° than anguish, hunger, or the sea!
Look on the tragic loading of this bed.
This is thy work. The object° poisons sight;
Let it be hid. Gratiano, keep the house,
And seize upon° the fortunes of the Moor,
For they succeed on you. To you, lord governor,
Remains the censure° of this hellish villain,   460
The time, the place, the torture. O enforce it!
Myself will straight abroad, and to the state
This heavy act with heavy heart relate. *(Exeunt.)*

Spartan dog, type of bloodhound, noted for its silence
and relentlessness. *fell,* cruel. *object,* spectacle. *seize
upon,* take possession. *censure,* legal sentencing.

Figure 1. The single set for the National Theatre production of *Othello,* directed by John Dexter, London, 1964. The three-part design of the set echoes the structural design at the back of the Renaissance English stage, illustrated in Figure 1 on page 160. (Photograph: Angus McBean, Harvard Theatre Collection.)

Figure 2. Othello (Laurence Olivier) and Iago (Frank Finlay) in the National Theatre production of *Othello,* directed by John Dexter, London, 1964. (Photograph: Angus McBean, Harvard Theatre Collection.)

Figure 3. Othello (Laurence Olivier) and Desdemona (Maggie Smith) in the National Theatre production of *Othello*, directed by John Dexter, London, 1964. (Photograph: Angus McBean, Harvard Theatre Collection.)

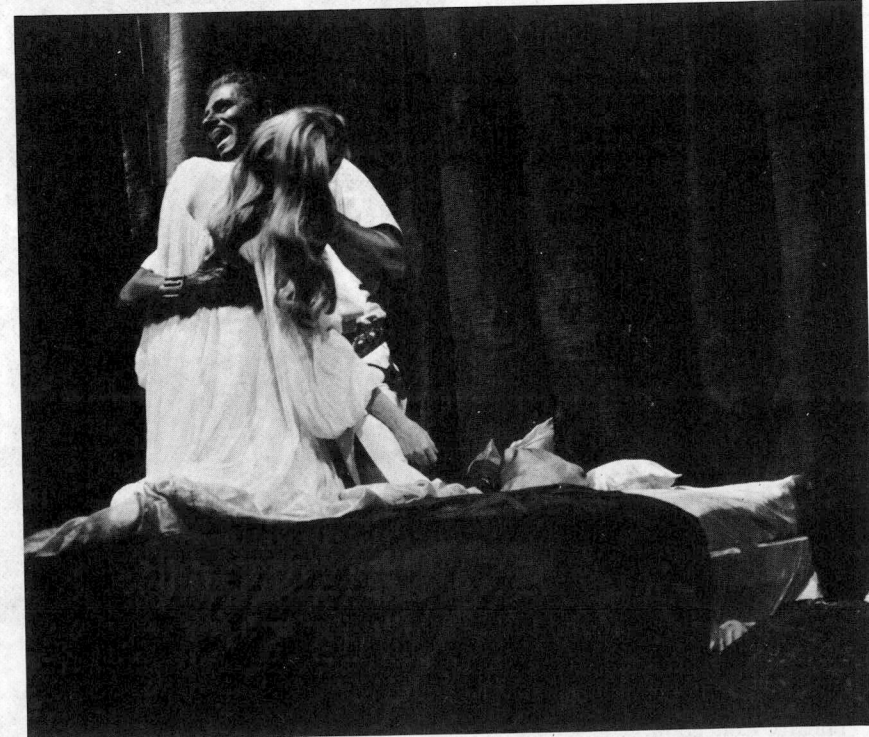

Figure 4. Othello (Laurence Olivier) hugs the dead body of Desdemona (Maggie Smith) as he gives his final speech in the National Theatre production of *Othello*, directed by John Dexter, London, 1964. (Photograph: Angus McBean, Harvard Theatre Collection.)

Staging of *Othello*

**REVIEW OF THE NATIONAL THEATRE
PRODUCTION, 1964, BY RONALD BRYDEN**

All posterity will want to know is how he played. John Dexter's National Theatre *Othello* is efficient and clear, if slow, and contains some intelligent minor novelties. But in the long run all that matters is that it left the stage as bare as possible for its athlete. What requires record is how he, tackling Burbage's role for the first time at 57, created the Moor.

He came on smelling a rose, laughing softly with a private delight; barefooted, ankleted, black. He had chosen to play a Negro. The story fits a true Moor better: one of those striding hawks, fierce in a narrow range of medieval passions, whose women still veil themselves like Henry Moore sleepers against the blowing sands of Nouakchott's surrealistically modern streets. But Shakespeare muddled, giving him the excuse to turn himself into a coastal African from below the Senegal: dark, thick-lipped, open, laughing.

He sauntered downstage, with a loose, bare-heeled roll of the buttocks; came to rest feet splayed apart, hip lounging outward. For him, the great Richard III of his day, the part was too simple. He had made it difficult and interesting for himself by studying, as scrupulously as he studied the flat vowels, dead grin and hunched time-steps of Archie Rice, how an African looks, moves, sounds. The make-up, exact in pigment, covered his body almost wholly: an hour's job at least. The hands hung big and graceful. The whole voice was characterised, the o's and the a's deepened, the consonants thickened with faint, guttural deliberation. 'Put up your bright swords, or de dew will rus' dem': not quite so crude, but in that direction.

It could have been caricature, an embarrassment. Instead, after the second performance, a well-known Negro actor rose in the stalls bravoing. For obviously it was done with love; with the main purpose of substituting for the dead grandeur of the Moorish empire one modern audiences could respond to: the grandeur of Africa. He was the continent, like a figure of Rubens allegory. In Cyprus, he strode ashore in a cloak and spiked helmet which brought to mind the medieval emirates of Ethiopia and Niger. Facing Doge and senators, he hooded his eyes in a pouting ebony mask: an old chief listening watchfully in tribal conclave. When he named them 'my masters' it was proudly edged: he had been a slave, their inquisition recalled his slavery, he reminded them in turn of his service and generalship.

He described Desdemona's encouragement smiling down at them, easy with sexual confidence. This was the other key to the choice of a Negro: Finlay's Iago, bony, crop-haired, staring with the fanatic mule-grin of a Mississippi redneck, was to be goaded by a small white man's sexual jealousy of the black, a jealousy sliding into ambiguous fascination. Like Yeats's crowd staring, sweating, at Don Juan's mighty thigh, this Iago gazed, licking dry lips, on a black one. All he need do is teach his own disease.

Mannerisms established, they were lifted into the older, broader imagery of the part. Leading Desdemona to bed, he pretended to snap at her with playful teeth. At Iago's first hints, he made a chuckling mock of twisting truth out of him by the ear. Then, during the temptation, he began to pace, turning his head sharply like a lion listening. The climax was his farewell to his occupation: bellowing the words as pure, wounded outcry, he hurled back his head until the ululating tongue showed pink against the roof of his mouth like a trumpeting elephant's. As he grew into a great beast, Finlay shrunk beside him, clinging to his shoulder like an ape, hugging his heels like a jackal.

He used every clue in the part, its most strenuous difficulties. Reassured by Desdemona's innocence, he bent to kiss her—and paused looking, sickened, at her lips. Long before his raging return, you knew he had found Cassio's kisses there. Faced with the lung-torturing hurdle of 'Like to the Pontic sea', he found a brilliant device for breaking the period: at 'Shall ne'er look back', he let the memories he was forswearing rush in and stop him, gasping with pain, until he caught breath. Then, at 'By yond marble heaven', he tore the crucifix from his neck (Iago, you recall, says casually Othello'd renounce his baptism for Desdemona) and, crouching forehead to ground, made his 'sacred vow' in the religion which caked Benin's altars with blood.

Possibly it was too early a climax, built to make a curtain of Iago's 'I am your own for ever.' In Act Four he could only repeat himself with increased volume, adding a humming animal moan as he fell into his fit, a strangler's look to the dangling hands, a sharper danger to the turns of his head as he questioned Emilia. But it gave him time to wind down to a superb returned dignity and tenderness for the murder. This became an act of love—at 'I would not have thee linger in thy pain' he threw aside the pillow and, stopping her lips with a kiss, strangled her. The last speech was spoken kneeling on the bed, her body

287

clutched upright to him as a shield for the dagger he turns on himself.

As he slumped beside her in the sheets, the current stopped. A couple of wigged actors stood awkwardly about. You could only pity them: we had seen history, and it was over. Perhaps it's as well to have seen the performance while still unripe, constructed in fragments, still knitting itself. Now you can see how it's done; later, it will be a torrent. But before it exhausts him, a film should be made. It couldn't save the whole truth, but it might save something the unborn should know.

REVIEW OF THE NATIONAL THEATRE PRODUCTION, 1964, BY THE LONDON *TIMES* DRAMATIC CRITIC

There have been few great Othellos in recent stage history. The late Frederick Walk was one contender for the title: and those who followed his work through the Irish hinterland claim the same for Anew McMaster. But in general postwar productions of the tragedy have centered on Iago and relegated the Moor to second position as a massively vulnerable dupe.

John Dexter's production emphatically reverses this relationship—as it could scarcely fail to do with Sir Laurence Olivier, for the first time in his career, playing the name part. But beyond the unalterable presence of an actor whose magnitude is unrivalled on the British stage, the production shows a determination to build up the role of the Moor at the expense of his malignant confidant.

A clue to the interpretation is given in the programme, which quotes F. R. Leavis's assessment of Iago as "not much more than a necessary piece of dramatic mechanism": less a character in himself than the embodiment of a concealed element in Othello's own nature. This role is certainly contained in the part; but to erect it into the whole truth amounts almost to mutilation. Iago is not merely on the level of a tempter in a miracle play: the part plainly exists in its own right, enigmatic perhaps, but freed with a personal vitality which keeps the riddle of his villany a permanently open question.

The penalties of translating the Leavis theory into action are graphically displayed in Frank Finlay's performance. Instead of the alert ensign, the resourceful actor who is all things to all men and who shapes his plot with the delight of an artist, we are confronted by a lumpish figure. The approach has some advantages. When all Othello's resistance has gone Iago clings about his neck almost with the embrace of a succubus—pouring poison into his ear in tones of satanic lullaby.

The physical attachment between him and the Moor—present from their first scene together with Othello playfully brushing his ancient's face with a bunch of flowers—often yields powerful effects. (Olivier is always at his best when he is in close tactile contact with an opponent.) But when Iago is left to play on lesser victims or to commune with himself, the part loses its coherence. Speed, changeable resourcefulness, nimble invention—all the qualities one expects are replaced by a plodding sameness, occasionally varied by arbitrary grotesqueness, and an unhappy attempt to humanize the character by introducing a whimpering note into the soliloquies.

The lack of a fully realized Iago seriously impoverishes the production—even in the Othello scenes, where Mr. Finlay's reading makes most sense. Othello needs an adversary, not an accomplice. As it is, Olivier's Othello stands as a heroic solo performance which is more remarkable for its technical mastery than for its power to move. Physically he departs from the image of the old soldier descended "into the vale of years." He presents a graceful, sensual figure to whom the duties of a bridegroom seem as familiar as those of the battlefield. His voice (a factor that has held him back from the part in the past) has acquired a measured deliberation and a new lower resonance: and—perhaps most striking of all—he has evolved a range of movement organically related to the part: a stance with feet apart and trunk thrown forward, and a use of oblique arm gestures and flattened palms of the hand.

Beautifully controlled at the beginning, where his modest playing suggests Salvini's "sleeping volcano", its underlying savagery becomes increasingly pronounced until—in the oath scene—he tears the cross from his neck and bows to the floor in atavistic obeisance to a barbaric god.

Of the other performances the best is Derek Jacobi's Cassio, who makes full use of his brief spell as lieutenant (for some reason uniformly pronounced "lootenant") to pull his rank over Iago and thus invite enmity. Maggie Smith's Desdemona is on very distant terms with the part. Obviously a mettlesome girl who would not for an instant have endured domestic tyranny, she introduces facetious modern inflexions (for instance her giggling reference to "These Men" in the bedchamber scene) which clash destructively with the character.

Jocelyn Herbert's set—a towering archway standing behind a slender draped wooden frame—partly solves the problem of the play's vagueness of locality and even manages to explain how Bianca comes to be wandering about in Othello's private quarters.

BEN JONSON

1572-1637

"He was better versed and knew more in Greek and Latin than all the poets in England. . . ." This heady appraisal of Jonson was made by Jonson himself during a boisterous conversation with the Scottish poet William Drummond. Yet the statement should not be taken simply as a sign of Jonson's bravado or as the overflow of Drummond's plentiful liquor supply, for Jonson was a profoundly learned man, even though he never received any formal education after he finished Westminster School in 1589. At Westminster, he studied under William Camden, a scholar and historian of international reputation, from whom he received a thorough training in the classics and a reverence for them that left its mark on everything he wrote. Jonson was not only the most learned, but also the most independent-minded dramatist of his age. After finishing school, he was forced by his stepfather to apprentice himself as a bricklayer, but after a year at this trade he fled the country and hired himself out as a soldier to fight on the side of Holland in its war against Spain. From 1597 on, we hear of him as a playwright, an actor, and, intermittently, a jailbird. In 1597, for example, he was arrested and imprisoned for his part as an actor and collaborator in *The Isle of Dogs,* a lost satiric comedy that was apparently so offensive in its topical references that it prompted the authorities to close the theaters temporarily. In 1598, his killing of a fellow actor in a duel would have taken him to the gallows had he not pled "benefit of clergy" (the ability to read and write). Combat came naturally to Jonson. Indeed, two of his plays, *Cynthia's Revels* (1600) and *Poetaster* (1601), contained such fierce attacks on several of his dramatic contemporaries that they fomented a satiric war in the theaters of the time.

The spirit of attack that so marks Jonson's life found theatrical form in satire, which he explained in the prologue to his first play, *Every Man in His Humour* (1598). There Jonson defined his dramatic art as being realistic in its method and satiric in its purpose, consisting of "deeds, and language, such as men do use:/ And persons, such as comedy would choose,/ When she would show an image of the times,/ And sport with human follies, not with crimes." In this dramatic manifesto, he was deliberately opposing himself to the romantic comedies, revenge tragedies, and English history plays that dominated the theater of his day. And in the play itself, he offers deftly drawn portraits of various Elizabethan character types—a solemn city gentleman, a plain-speaking country squire, a country bumpkin with city pretensions, a city simpleton with literary pretensions, a cowardly man with military pretensions, an ignorant water-bearer and his credulous wife, a witty young man and his ingenious servant, and a jealous husband. That gallery of portraits, which Jonson had drawn from Roman comedy and London life, was an immediate success, so much so that he quickly followed it with a companion piece, *Every Man Out of His Humour* (1599). The prologue for this play was not just a single speech, but an induction of almost three hundred lines in which three characters discuss the proper bases for dramatic satire. Their conversation distinguishes between true and false behavior, between behavior resulting from a psychological and physiological condition that the Elizabethans called a person's "humour," and behavior guided by social pretensions that Jonson called "affected humour." By exposing all the "affected humours" of his time, Jonson aimed to drive men and women out of their false social behavior, and he did so by producing such caricatures as the vainglorious traveller, the railing courtier, the fastidious dresser, and the officious lady.

The gallery of fools he portrayed in these early comedies clearly displayed his temperament and talent for the satiric art of social comedy. And during the years from 1606 to 1614, he deliberately followed his bent, turning out a series of comedies—*Volpone* (1606), *Epicoene* (1609), *The Alchemist* (1610), and *Bartholomew Fair* (1614)—that have established his reputation as one of the major social satirists of the English dramatic tradition. Jonson's comedies, in fact, established the tradition of social comedy on the English stage. His comedies of London life directly influenced his contemporaries, Middleton, Beaumont, and Fletcher, and led in turn to the Restoration comedies of sophisticated city life by Etherege, Wycherley, and Congreve, all of whom borrowed from Jonson and regarded him as their model. And they admired him not only for his satiric portraiture, but also for the perfection of his comic plots, which all depend on elaborate outwitting intrigues that are at once theatrically compelling and satirically significant. In *The Alchemist,* for example, Jonson constructs an elaborate con game in which three schemers—an Elizabethan underworld man with a smattering of alchemical jargon, a whore, and a servant with a knack for disguises—dupe a law clerk, a tobacco merchant, a gamester, a sensualist, a preacher, a deacon, and a young country gentleman. The brilliance of the play lies in the speed with which the crooks change styles and tricks to fit the next gull who enters—and in the dizzying buildup of comic situations as more and more of the characters try to claim their promised treasure at once.

Volpone also involves an elaborate con game in which a pack of scoundrels attempt to exploit a group of money-hungry fools, but it is a far grimmer work, for though Jonson claimed that his comedy sported "with human follies, not with crimes," the specimens shown to us in *Volpone* are not merely fools, but in several instances are morally despicable knaves. The names of the principal characters immediately suggest their depravity, for they are identified with the world of beasts. Thus, the lawyer Voltore is named for the vulture, the deaf old gentleman Corbaccio for the raven, the violent Corvino is a crow, while the chief schemers are Volpone, the fox, and his parasite Mosca, the fly. Even the more purely comic characters of the subplot share in the beast imagery: Sir Politic Would-Be, the gullible knight who imagines messages from spies in cabbages, reduces to Sir Pol, the parrot; his wife, Lady Politic Would-Be, chatters endlessly, like another parrot; and Peregrine, the young traveller, is named for a hunting falcon. The fools of the subplot, though in one sense apparently harmless, are also unwitting echoes of the knaves, and in fact they are also unwitting accomplices of the knaves, for the social pretensions of the Would-Bes play directly into the hands of Volpone's schemes at several points in the plot. Only Celia and Bonario escape the animal imagery, but they, too, are morally typed by their names, for Celia literally means heavenly, while Bonario signifies good-natured.

Although the central comic trick of *Volpone*—that of a man pretending to be sick—is a fairly common comic ploy and the plot ultimately turns into the tricking of the trickster, Jonson uses a variety of means to emphasize the darker implications of the trickery that pervades *Volpone*. Volpone's pretended sickness is mortal; the gulls are clustered around him, waiting for his death and the chance to inherit his great wealth; and the extremes to which they are willing to go, such as disinheriting a son and prostituting a wife, are cruel and unnatural. The language of the play also emphasizes its darker tones. Gold is not merely the object for which all strive, but becomes in Volpone's opening speech a substitute for God. The play's emphasis on disease and physical degeneration is, of course, part of the comic plot, but it is also a metaphor for the moral illness of this gold-dominated world. At the end of the play, the false sickness of Volpone is converted to real pain and all of his money given to the incurables, of which, spiritually, he is one.

Yet the play is also a comedy, and while we find the characters morally convulsive and thus disturbing, their deceptions and self-deceptions are also theatrically entertaining. The two chief tricksters, Volpone and Mosca, offer magnificent opportunities for actors: Volpone gets to play the invalid (complete with makeup and costume), as well as a mountebank seller of patent medicines, as well as the seducer, the invalid again, and finally an officer, while Mosca must continually play the triple role of the concerned servant of his "sick" master, the willing helper of each of the greedy gulls, and the schemer enjoying the success of his plot. Indeed, so attractive are these schemers in their ability to improvise and maneuver that we are repeatedly led to side with them against our better judgment, to give the fox the applause he asks for at the play's end. But that applause is only given, of course, if the actors and actresses are themselves virtuosos, as they appear to have been in the Guthrie Theater production of 1964. Reviews of that production, reprinted following the play, celebrated not only the exuberance of the actors and the orchestration of the director, but also the spectacle created by the designer. And photographs of the Guthrie production (see Figures 1, 2, and 3) display that spectacle in all of its comic and satiric aspects, from the wit of Volpone's disguises, to the folly of Sir Politic's poses, to the knavery of Corvino's greed.

VOLPONE, OR THE FOXE

BY BEN JONSON / TEXT AND NOTES BY PHILIP BROCKBANK

CHARACTERS

VOLPONE,° *a Magnifico*°
MOSCA,° *his Parasite*
VOLTORE,° *an Advocate*
CORBACCIO,° *an old Gentleman*
CORVINO,° *a Merchant*
AVOCATORI,° *four Magistrates*
NOTARIO, *the Register*°
NANO,° *a Dwarf*
CASTRONE, *an Eunuch*
GREGE (*a crowd*)
SIR POLITIC WOULD-BE, *a Knight*

PEREGRINE,° *a Gentleman-traveller*
BONARIO, *a young Gentleman*
FINE MADAME WOULD-BE, *the Knight's wife*
CELIA, *the Merchant's wife*
COMMANDADORI, *Officers*
MERCATORI, *three Merchants*
ANDROGYNO,° *a Hermaphrodite*
SERVITORE, *a Servant*
WOMEN

SCENE

Venice

THE ARGUMENT°

V OLPONE, childless, rich, feigns sick, despairs,
O ffers his state° to hopes of several heirs,
L ies languishing; his Parasite receives
P resents of all, assures, deludes: then weaves
O ther cross-plots, which ope themselves, are told.
N ew tricks for safety are sought; they thrive; when, bold,
E ach tempts th'other again, and all are sold.

PROLOGUE

Now, luck yet send us, and a little wit
  Will serve, to make our play hit;
According to the palates of the season,
  Here is rime, not empty of reason:
This we were bid to credit from our Poet,
  Whose true scope, if you would know it,
In all his poems, still, hath been this measure,
  To mix profit with your pleasure;
And not as some° (whose throats their envy failing)
10 Cry hoarsely, 'All he writes, is railing.'
And when his plays come forth, think they can flout them,
  With saying, 'He was a year° about them,'
To these there needs no lie, but this his creature,
  Which was, two months since, no feature;
And though he dares give them five lives to mend it,
  'Tis known, five weeks fully penned it;
From his own hand, without a coadjutor,°
  Novice, journeyman,° or tutor.
Yet, thus much I can give you, as a token   20
  Of his play's worth: no eggs are broken,
Nor quaking custards° with fierce teeth affrighted,
  Wherewith your rout are so delighted;
Nor hales he in a gull,° old ends° reciting,
  To stop gaps in his loose writing,
With such a deal of monstrous, and forced action;
  As might make Bet'lem a faction;°
Nor made he his play, for jests, stol'n from each table,
  But makes jests, to fit his fable.°
And, so presents quick° comedy, refined,   30
  As best critics have designed;
The laws of time, place, persons he observeth,
  From no needful rule he swerveth.
All gall, and copperas,° from his ink, he draineth,

Volpone, "an old fox, an old reinard, an old craftie, slie, subtle companion, sneaking lurking wily deceiver" (Florio, *A Worlde of Wordes* 1598). *Magnifico,* magnate of Venice. *Mosca,* "any kind of flye" (Florio); Beelzebub, the "Prince of Devils," is in Hebrew "the Lord of the flies." *Voltore,* "a ravenous bird called a vultur, a geyre or grap. Also a greedie cormorant" (Florio). *Corbaccio,* "a filthie great raven" (Florio). *Corvino,* crow; "of a ravens nature or colour" (Florio 1611). *Avocatori,* state prosecutors. *Register,* clerk of the court. *Nano,* Latin *nanus,* a dwarf. *Peregrine,* a hawk; a traveller. *Androgyno,* from Greek *andros* (man) and *gyne* (woman). *Argument,* the acrostic form is imitated from Plautus; *The Alchemist* also has one. *state,* estate. *as some,* specifically Marston in *The Dutch Curtezan* (prologue).

a year, "you nasty tortoise, you and your itchy poetry break out like Christmas, but once a year" (*Satiromastix* V. ii, 217). *coadjutor,* Jonson worked with collaborators on *Eastward Ho. journeyman,* qualified craftsman, more than novice but less than master. *quaking custards,* cowards; also perhaps custard-pie comedy, based on sport with huge custard at the Lord mayor's feast. *gull,* dupe, one who swallows anything (from gull-gorge). *ends,* tags. *make Bet'lem a faction,* either "make a party for the madhouse" or "enlist the support of the madhouse"; Bet'lem or Bedlam, was the asylum of St. Mary of Bethlehem. *fable,* plot. *quick,* lively. *gall, and copperas,* oak galls and iron sulphate, used to make ink; rancour was attributed to the gall-bladder and copperas is bitter.

Only, a little salt° remaineth,
Wherewith, he'll rub your cheeks, till, red with
    laughter,
They shall look fresh, a week after.

ACT I / SCENE 1

(VOLPONE's *house*)
(*Enter* VOLPONE, MOSCA.)

VOLPONE: Good morning to the day; and, next, my
    gold!
  Open the shrine°, that I may see my saint.

(MOSCA *reveals the treasure.*)

Hail the world's soul,° and mine! More glad than is
The teeming earth to see the longed-for sun
Peep through the horns of the celestial Ram,°
Am I, to view thy splendour, darkening his;
That, lying here, amongst my other hoards,
Show'st like a flame, by night; or like the day
Struck out of Chaos,° when all darkness fled
Unto the centre. O, thou sun of Sol,°
But brighter than thy father, let me kiss,
With adoration, thee, and every relic°
Of sacred treasure, in this blessed room.
Well did wise Poets, by thy glorious name
Title that age,° which they would have the best;
Thou being the best of things; and far
    transcending
All style of joy in children, parents, friends,
Or any other waking dream on earth.
Thy looks when they to Venus did ascribe,°
They should have given her twenty thousand
    Cupids;
Such are thy beauties, and our loves! Dear *saint*,
Riches, the dumb god,° that giv'st all men tongues;
That canst do nought, and yet mak'st men do all
    things;
The price of souls; even hell, with thee to boot,
Is made worth heaven! Thou art virtue, fame,
Honour, and all things else! Who can get thee,
He shall be noble, valiant, honest, wise°—

40

50

60

MOSCA: And what he will, sir. Riches are in fortune
  A greater good, than wisdom is in nature.°
VOLPONE: True, my beloved Mosca. Yet, I glory
  More in the cunning purchase° of my wealth,
  Than in the glad possession; since I gain
  No common way: I use no trade, no venture;
  I wound no earth with ploughshares; fat no beasts
  To feed the shambles°; have no mills for iron,
  Oil, corn, or men, to grind 'em° into poulder;   70
  I blow no subtle° glass; expose no ships
  To threat'nings of the furrow-faced sea;
  I turn° no moneys, in the public bank;
  Nor usure° private°—
MOSCA: No, sir, nor devour
  Soft prodigals. You shall ha' some will swallow
  A melting heir, as glibly as your Dutch
  Will pills of butter°, and ne'er purge for't
  Tear forth the fathers of poor families
  Out of their beds, and coffin them alive   80
  In some kind, clasping prison, where their bones
  May be forth-coming, when the flesh is rotten:
  But your sweet nature doth abhor these courses;
  You loathe, the widow's, or the orphan's tears
  Should wash your pavements; or their piteous cries
  Ring in your roofs; and beat the air, for
    vengeance—
VOLPONE: Right, Mosca, I do loathe it.
MOSCA: And besides, sir,
  You are not like the thresher,° that doth stand   90
  With a huge flail, watching a heap of corn,
  And, hungry, dares not taste the smallest grain,
  But feeds on mallows, and such bitter herbs;
  Not like the merchant, who hath filled his vaults
  With Romagnia,° and rich Candian wines,°
  Yet drinks the lees of Lombard's vinegar;
  You will not lie in straw, whilst moths, and worms
  Feed on your sumptuous hangings, and soft beds.
  You know the use of riches, and dare give, now,
  From that bright heap, to me, your poor observer,   100
  Or to your dwarf, or your hermaphrodite,
  Your eunuch, or what other household trifle
  Your pleasure allows maintenance—
VOLPONE: Hold thee,° Mosca,

(*Gives him money.*)

Take, of my hand; thou strik'st on truth, in all:
And they are envious term thee parasite.

---

salt is not used in ink, but iron sulphate was called "salt of iron" and Jonson needs it to introduce the following joke out of Horace (*Satires* I. x, 3). *shrine*, Volpone is at his devotions and the treasure has the aspect of a holy reliquary. *world's soul* with a pun on "sol," the sun; also perhaps the coin. *celestial Ram*, the sun enters Aries at the spring equinox. *day . . . Chaos*, the first day of creation (*Genesis* 1.2–4). *sun of Sol*, alchemy held gold to be the offspring of the sun. *relic*, i.e., the kind found in a shrine. *that age*, the Golden Age (described by Ovid, *Met.* 1.89–112). *Venus . . . ascribe*, following Homeric tradition the Latin poets often called Venus "golden" (*aurea*). *the dumb god*, "silence is golden." *Thou art . . . wise*, compare Horace, *Satires* II. iii, 94.

Riches . . . nature, "Better to be endowed by chance with riches than by nature with wisdom." *purchase*, procurance. *shambles*, slaughterhouse. *grind 'em*, i.e., exploit the men. *subtle*, tenous, delicate: Venice was famed for its glass. *turn*, exchange. *usure*, exchange at high interest. *Dutch . . . butter* a notorious Dutch weakness. *the thresher*, from Horace, *Satires* II. iii, 111. *Romagnia*, Rumney, a sweet Greek wine. *Candian wines*, Malmsey from Candy (Crete). *Hold thee*, keep yourself.

Call forth my dwarf, my eunuch, and my fool,
And let 'em make me sport. What should I do,
But cocker up my *genius,* and live free
110   To all delights, my fortune calls me to?
I have no wife, no parent, child, ally,
To give my substance to; but whom I make
Must be my heir: and this makes men observe° me.
This draws new clients,° daily, to my house,
Women, and men, of every sex and age,
That bring me presents, send me plate, coin,
    jewels,
With hope, that when I die (which they expect
Each greedy minute) it shall then return,
120   Tenfold, upon them; whilst some, covetous
Above the rest, seek to engross me, whole,
And counter-work, the one, unto the other,
Contend in gifts, as they would seem, in love:
All which I suffer, playing with their hopes,
And am content to coin 'em into profit,
And look upon their kindness, and take more,
And look on that; still bearing them in hand,°
Letting the cherry° knock against their lips,
And, draw it, by their mouths, and back again.
130   How now!

ACT 1 / SCENE 2

(Enter MOSCA, *with* NANO, ANDROGYNO, *and* CAS-
TRONE.)
(An entertainment follows.)

NANO: Now, room for fresh gamesters, who do will
    you to know,
      They do bring you neither play, nor University
      show;
And therefore do intreat you, that whatsoever they
    rehearse,°
      May not fare a whit the worse, for the false pace°
      of the verse.
If you wonder at this, you will wonder more, ere we
10   pass,
      For know *(pointing to* ANDROGYNO), here is
      enclosed the Soul of Pythagoras,
That juggler divine, as hereafter shall follow;
      Which soul, fast and loose,° sir, came first from
      Apollo,

And was breathed into Aethalides,° Mercurius his
    son,
      Where it had the gift to remember all that ever
      was done.
From thence it fled forth, and made quick   20
    transmigration
      To goldy-locked Euphorbus,° who was killed, in
      good fashion,
At the siege of old Troy, by the cuckold of Sparta.°
      Hermotimus was next (I find it in my charta)°
To whom it did pass, where no sooner it was
    missing,
      But with one Pyrrhus, of Delos,° it learned to go
      a-fishing:
And thence did it enter the Sophist of Greece.°   30
      From Pythagore, she went into a beautiful piece,
Hight° Aspasia, the meretrix°; and the next toss of
    her
      Was, again, of a whore, she became a
      philosopher,
Crates° the Cynic: as itself° does relate it.
      Since, kings, knights, and beggars, knaves, lords
      and fools gat it,
Besides, ox, and ass, camel, mule, goat, and brock,
      In all which it hath spoke, as in the cobbler's   40
      cock.°
But I come not here, to discourse of that matter,
      Or his one, two, or three, or his great oath, 'By
      Quater!'°
His musics,° his trigon, his golden thigh,°
      Or his telling how elements shift; but I
Would ask, how of late, thou has suffered
    translation,
      And shifted thy coat, in these days of
      reformation?°   50
ANDROGYNO: Like one of the reformèd,° a fool, as
    you see,
    Counting all old doctrine heresy.

---

cocker up, pamper, indulge (Latin, *indulgere genio*).
observe, "treat with ceremonious respect or reverence"
(OED). *clients,* followers who wait upon the patronage of
Volpone the Magnifico (ironic). *still,* continually. *bearing
. . . hand,* leading them on. *cherry,* in the game of chop-
cherry the player tried to bite a dangling cherry. *rehearse,*
recite. *false pace,* exemplified by Nano as he speaks; the
old-fashioned loose four-stress rhythm, with forced rhymes,
falsifies the natural sense. *fast and loose,* "slippery, hard to
catch," from a betting game in which one player guessed
whether or not a dagger was held fast in a belt intricately
folded by the other.

Aethalides, herald to the Argonauts and heir to an
omniscient memory. *Euphorbus,* the Trojan who first
wounded Patroclus *(Iliad* 17). *cuckold of Sparta,* Menelaus.
Hermotimus, a Greek philosopher. *charta,* paper, perhaps
Lucian's dialogue. *Pyrrhus, of Delos,* a philosopher; the
name and the allusion to fishing are supplied by Diogenes
Laertius without explanation. *Sophist of Greece,*
Pythagoras is so styled by Lucian. *Hight* (Old English),
named, called *Aspasia* mistress of Pericles. *meretrix,* courtesan. *Crates,* a pupil of Diogenes. *itself,* either the cock in
Lucian, or Androgyno. *cobbler's cock,* the cock tells the
story in Lucian. *Quater,* the Pythagorean trigon or triangle
of four, symbol of cosmic and moral harmony. *musics,*
Pythagorean theory related the spacing of the cosmic
spheres to the laws of harmony. *golden thigh,* attributed to
Pythagoras by his followers. *reformation,* the Protestant
reformation; Jonson was still a Catholic in 1606. *reformed,*
evidently the Puritans.

NANO: But not on thine own forbid meats° hast thou
    ventured?
ANDROGYNO: On fish, when first, a Carthusian° I
    entered.
NANO: Why, then thy dogmatical silence° hath left
    thee?
60 ANDROGYNO: Of that an obstreperous° lawyer bereft
    me.
NANO: O wonderful change! when Sir Lawyer
    forsook thee,
    For Pythagore's sake, what body then took thee?
ANDROGYNO: A good dull moyle.°
NANO: And how! by that means,
    Thou wert brought to allow of the eating of beans?
ANDROGYNO: Yes.
NANO: But, from the moyle, into whom did'st thou
70   pass?
ANDROGYNO: Into a very strange beast, by some
    writers called an ass;
    By others, a precise,° pure, illuminate° brother,
      Of those devour flesh, and sometimes one
        another;
    And will drop forth a libel, or a sanctified lie,
      Betwixt every spoonful of a nativity-pie.°
NANO: Now quit thee, for heaven, of that profane
    nation;
80   And gently, report thy next transmigration.
ANDROGYNO: To the same that I am.
NANO: A creature of delight?
    And, what is more than a fool, an
      hermaphrodite?
    Now pray thee, sweet soul, in all thy variation,
      Which body would'st thou choose, to take up thy
        station?
ANDROGYNO: Troth, this I am in, even here would I
    tarry.
90 NANO: 'Cause here, the delight of each sex thou canst
    vary?
ANDROGYNO: Alas, those pleasures be stale, and
    forsaken;
    No, 'tis your fool, wherewith I am so taken;
    The only one creature, that I can call blessed,
      For all other forms I have proved most
        distressed.
NANO: Spoke true, as thou wert in Pythagoras still.
    This learned opinion we celebrate will,
100   Fellow eunuch, as behoves us, with all our wit and
      art,

---

forbid meats, forbidden foods; Pythagoreans were forbidden fish and beans. **Carthusian,** an order strict in its
diet but allowing fish. **dogmatical silence,** Pythagoreans
were enjoined to a five-year silence, which might have been
maintained among the Carthusians. **obstreperous,** vociferous. **moyle,** mule. **precise,** "strict in religious observance,
puritanical" (*OED*). **illuminate,** visionary. **nativity-pie,**
Christmas pie, evading the word "mass." see *The Alchemist*
III. ii, 43.

To dignify that° whereof our selves are so great,
    and special a part.
VOLPONE: Now very, very pretty! Mosca, this
    Was thy invention?
MOSCA: If it please my patron,
    Not else.
VOLPONE: It doth, good Mosca.
MOSCA: Then it was, sir.

SONG°

Fools, they are the only nation°   110
Worth men's envy, or admiration;
Free from care, or sorrow-taking,
Selves, and others merry making:
All they speak, or do, is sterling.°
Your Fool, he is your great man's dearling,
And your ladies' sport, and pleasure;
Tongue, and bable° are his treasure.
E'en his face begetteth laughter,
And he speaks truth, free from slaughter;°
He's the grace of every feast,   120
And, sometimes, the chiefest guest;
Hath his trencher, and his stool,
When wit waits upon the fool.°
    O, who would not be
    He, he, he?

(One knocks without.)

VOLPONE: Who's that? Away!

(Exeunt NANO, CASTRONE.)

Look Mosca!
MOSCA: Fool, begone!

(Exit ANDROGYNO.)

    'Tis Signior Voltore, the advocate;
    I know him, by his knock.   130
VOLPONE: Fetch me my gown,
    My furs,° and night caps; say, my couch is
      changing:
    And let him entertain himself, awhile,
    Without i' th' gallery. Now, now, my clients
    Begin their visitation! vulture, kite,
    Raven, and gor-crow,° all my birds of prey,
    That think me turning carcass, now they come.
    I am not for 'em yet. How now? the news?

(Enter MOSCA.)

MOSCA: A piece of plate, sir.   140

---

that, i.e., folly. **Song,** it might be sung by the gro-
tesques, by Mosca alone, or by all. **nation,** sect. **sterling,**
capable of standing every test. **bable,** the fool's bauble or
sceptre; slang for phallus. **free from slaughter,** without
being called to account. **wit . . . fool,** the fool dines off his
host; wit waits upon the fool's words. **furs,** worn by the sick
for warmth. **gor-crow,** carrion crow.

VOLPONE: Of what bigness?

MOSCA: Huge,
Massy, and antique, with your name inscribed,
And arms engraven.

VOLPONE: Good! and not a fox
Stretched on the earth, with fine delusive sleights,
Mocking a gaping crow?° ha, Mosca?

MOSCA: Sharp, sir.

VOLPONE: Give me my furs. Why dost thou laugh so,
150   man?

MOSCA: I cannot choose, sir, when I apprehend
What thoughts he has, without, now, as he walks:
That this might be the last gift he should give;
That this would fetch you; if you died today,
And gave him all, what he should be tomorrow;
What large return would come of all his ventures;°
How he should worshipped be, and reverenced;
Ride, with his furs, and foot-cloths;° waited on
By herds of fools, and clients; have clear way
160   Made for his moyle, as lettered as himself;
Be called the great, and learned advocate:
And then concludes, there's nought impossible.

VOLPONE: Yes, to be learned, Mosca.

MOSCA: O, no: rich
Implies it. Hood an ass with reverend purple,°
So you can hide his two ambitious ears,
And he shall pass for a cathedral doctor.°

VOLPONE: My caps, my caps,° good Mosca. Fetch him
     in.

170 MOSCA: Stay, sir, your ointment° for your eyes.

VOLPONE: That's true;
Dispatch, dispatch; I long to have possession
Of my new present.

MOSCA: That, and thousands more,
I hope to see you lord of.

VOLPONE: Thanks, kind Mosca.

MOSCA: And that, when I am lost in blended dust,
And hundred such as I am, in succession—

VOLPONE: Nay, that were too much, Mosca.

180 MOSCA: You shall live,
Still, to delude these harpies.

VOLPONE: Loving Mosca!

     (Looking into a glass.)

'Tis well! My pillow now, and let him enter

     (Exit MOSCA.)

Now, my feigned cough, my phthisic,° and my
     gout,
My apoplexy, palsie, and catarrhs,
Help, with your forced functions, this my posture,°
Wherein, this three year, I have milked their
     hopes.
He comes, I hear him—uh! uh! uh! uh! O—   190

ACT 1 / SCENE 3

(Enter MOSCA, *with* VOLTORE *bearing plate.* VOLPONE
in bed.)

MOSCA: You still are what you were, sir. Only you,
Of all the rest, are he, commands his love:
And you do wisely, to preserve it, thus,
With early visitation, and kind notes°
Of your good meaning° to him, which, I know,
Cannot but come most grateful. Patron, sir!
Here's Signior Voltore is come—

VOLPONE: What say you?

MOSCA: Sir, Signior Voltore is come, this morning,
To visit you.   10

VOLPONE: I thank him.

MOSCA: And hath brought
A piece of antique plate, bought of St. Mark,°
With which he here presents you.

VOLPONE: He is welcome.
Pray him, to come more often.

MOSCA: Yes.

VOLTORE: What says he?

MOSCA: He thanks you, and desires you to see him
     often.   20

VOLPONE: Mosca!

MOSCA: My patron?

VOLPONE: Bring him near, where is he?
I long to feel his hand.

MOSCA *(guiding* VOLPONE's *hand)*: The plate is here,
     sir.

VOLTORE: How fare you, sir?

VOLPONE: I thank you, Signior Voltore.
Where is the plate? Mine eyes are bad.

VOLTORE *(putting it into his hand)*: I'm sorry   30
To see you still thus weak.

MOSCA *(aside)*: That he is not weaker.

VOLPONE: You are too munificent.

VOLTORE: No, sir, would to heaven,
I could as well give health to you, as that plate.

VOLPONE: You gave, sir, what you can. I thank you.
     Your love
Hath taste° in this, and shall not be unanswered.

---

fox . . . crow, for a similar application of the fable of the
crow, dropping its cheese as it sings for the adulatory fox,
see Horace, *Satires* II. v, 55.   *ventures,* enterprising invest-
ments.   *foot-cloths,* pageant drapery for a horse.   *reverend
purple,* crimson robes of a Doctor of Divinity.   *caps,* probably ear-caps, prompted by line 132; at this point, perhaps,
Volpone gets into bed.   *ointment,* to make his eyes sticky
and rheumy.   *Now . . . posture,* a sacrilegious invocation in
the epic manner to the powers of feigned disease.

---

phthisic, consumption or asthma.   *posture,* pose, imposture. "This and the following scenes are really a Roman
salutio i.e. the morning visit of clients to their patron so often
referred to and described by the satirists." (Rea).   *notes,*
signs.   *good meaning,* well-wishing.   *of St. Mark,* in St.
Mark's Square, celebrated for its goldsmiths' shops.   *Hath
taste in,* can be felt in.

I pray you see me often.
40 VOLTORE: Yes, I shall, sir.
VOLPONE: Be not far from me.
MOSCA (to VOLTORE): Do you observe that, sir?
VOLPONE: Hearken unto me, still: it will concern you.
MOSCA: You are a happy man, sir, know your good.
VOLPONE: I cannot now last long—
MOSCA: You are his heir, sir.
VOLTORE: Am I?
VOLPONE: I feel me going, uh! uh! uh! uh!
       I am sailing to my port, uh! uh! uh! uh!
50   And I am glad, I am so near my haven.
MOSCA: Alas, kind gentleman; well, we must all go—
VOLTORE: But, Mosca—
MOSCA: Age will conquer.
VOLTORE: Pray thee hear me.
       Am I inscribed his heir, for certain?
MOSCA: Are you?
       I do beseech you, sir, you will vouchsafe
       To write me, i' your family.° All my hopes
       Depend upon your worship. I am lost,
60   Except the rising sun do shine on me.
VOLTORE: It shall both shine, and warm thee, Mosca.
MOSCA: Sir,
       I am a man that have not done your love
       All the worst offices: here I wear your keys,°
       See all your coffers and your caskets locked,
       Keep the poor inventory of your jewels,
       Your plate, and monies; am your steward, sir,
       Husband your goods here.
VOLTORE: But am I sole heir?
70 MOSCA: Without a partner, sir, confirmed this
             morning;
       The wax is warm yet, and the ink scarce dry
       Upon the parchment.
VOLTORE: Happy, happy, me!
       By what good chance, sweet Mosca?
MOSCA: Your desert, sir;
       I know no second cause.
VOLTORE: Thy modesty
       Is loath to know it;° well, we shall requite it.
80 MOSCA: He ever liked your course,° sir, that first
             took° him.
       I, oft, have heard him say, how he admired
       Men of your large profession, that could speak
       To every cause, and things mere contraries,
       Till they were hoarse again, yet all be law;
       That, with most quick agility, could turn,
       And re-turn; make knots, and undo them;
       Give forkèd° counsel; take provoking gold°

---

write . . . family, names of servants were entered in a
"Household Book." **your keys,** i.e., Voltore's because Volpone's. **know it,** acknowledge it. **course,** way of doing
things. **took,** captivated. **large,** liberal, expansive and
eloquent. **forked,** equivocal. **provoking gold,** court fees
(provoke, "to call to a judge or court to take up one's cause"
(OED).

On either hand,° and put it up°: these men,
He knew, would thrive, with their humility.   90
And, for his part, he thought, he should be bless'd
To have his heir of such a suffering spirit,
So wise, so grave, of so perplexed° a tongue,
And loud withall, that would not wag, nor scarce
Lie still, without a fee; when every word
Your worship but lets fall, is a chequeen!°

(Another knocks.)

Who's that? one knocks; I would not have you seen,
       sir.
And yet—pretend you came, and went in haste;
I'll fashion an excuse. And gentle sir,   100
When you do come to swim, in golden lard,
Up to the arms, in honey, that your chin
Is born up stiff, with fatness of the flood,
Think on your vassal; but remember me:
I ha' not been your worst of clients.
VOLTORE: Mosca—
MOSCA: When will you have your inventory brought,
       sir?
Or see a copy of the will? *(Knocking again.)* Anon!
I'll bring 'em to you, sir. Away, be gone   110
Put business in your face.

       (Exit VOLTORE.)

VOLPONE: Excellent, Mosca!
       Come hither, let me kiss thee.
MOSCA: Keep you still, sir.
       Here is Corbaccio.
VOLPONE: Set the plate away.
       The vulture's gone, and the old raven's come.

ACT 1 / SCENE 4

MOSCA: Betake you to your silence, and your sleep.
       (Sets plate aside.) Stand there, and multiply. Now we
             shall see
       A wretch who is indeed more impotent
       Than this can feign to be; yet hopes to hop
       Over his grave. *(Enter CORBACCIO.)* Signior
             Corbaccio!
       You're very welcome, sir.
CORBACCIO: How does your patron?
MOSCA: Troth, as he did, sir, no amends.   10
CORBACCIO: What? mends he?
MOSCA: No, sir: he is rather worse.
CORBACCIO: That's well. Where is he?
MOSCA: Upon his couch, sir, newly fall'n asleep.
CORBACCIO: Does he sleep well?
MOSCA: No wink, sir, all this night,

---

either hand, for either party. **put it up,** either "deposit
it" or (Mosca's real meaning) "pocket it." **perplexed,** involved, puzzling. **chequeen** (F cecchine), Venetian gold
coin, sequin.

Nor yesterday, but slumbers.°
CORBACCIO: Good! He should take
Some counsel of physicians; I have brought him
20   An opiate here, from mine own doctor—
MOSCA: He will not hear of drugs.
CORBACCIO: Why? I myself
Stood by, while 't was made; saw all th' ingredients;
And know, it cannot but most gently work.
My life for his, 'tis but to make him sleep.
VOLPONE (aside): Ay, his last sleep, if he would take it.
MOSCA: Sir,
He has no faith in physic.
CORBACCIO: Say you, say you?
30 MOSCA: He has no faith in physic: he does think
Most of your° doctors are the greater danger,
And worse disease t'escape. I often have
Heard him protest, that your physician
Should never be his heir.
CORBACCIO: Not I his heir?
MOSCA: Not your physician, sir.
CORBACCIO: O, no, no, no,
I do not mean it.
MOSCA: No, sir, nor their fees
40   He cannot brook: he says, they flay° a man
Before they kill him.
CORBACCIO: Right, I do conceive° you.
MOSCA: And then, they do it by experiment;°
For which the law not only doth absolve 'em,
But gives them great reward: and he is loath
To hire his death, so.
CORBACCIO: It is true, they kill,
With as much licence, as a judge.
MOSCA: Nay, more;
50   For he but kills, sir, where the law condemns,
And these can kill him, too.
CORBACCIO: Ay, or me:
Or any man. How does his apoplex?°
Is that strong on him still?
MOSCA: Most violent.
His speech is broken, and his eyes are set,
His face drawn longer than 't was wont—
CORBACCIO: How? How?
Stronger than he was wont?
60 MOSCA: No, sir: his face
Drawn longer, than 't was wont.
CORBACCIO: O, good.
MOSCA: His mouth
Is ever gaping, and his eyelids hang.
CORBACCIO: Good.
MOSCA: A freezing numbness stiffens all his joints,
And makes the colour of his flesh like lead.
CORBACCIO: 'Tis good.

MOSCA: His pulse beats slow, and dull.
CORBACCIO: Good symptoms, still.   70
MOSCA: And, from his brain°—
CORBACCIO: Ha? how? Not from his brain?
MOSCA: Yes, sir, and from his brain—
CORBACCIO: I conceive you, good.
MOSCA: Flows a cold sweat, with a continual rheum,
Forth the resolvèd° corners of his eyes.
CORBACCIO: Is't possible? Yet I am better, ha!
How does he, with the swimming of his head?
MOSCA: O, sir, 'tis past the scotomy°; he, now,
Hath lost his feeling, and hath left° to snort,   80
You hardly can perceive him, that he breathes.
CORBACCIO: Excellent, excellent, sure I shall outlast
him:
This makes me young again, a score of years.
MOSCA: I was a-coming for you, sir.
CORBACCIO: Has he made his will?
What has he given me?
MOSCA: No, sir.
CORBACCIO: Nothing? ha?
MOSCA: He has not made his will, sir.   90
CORBACCIO: Oh, oh, oh.
What then did° Voltore, the lawyer, here?
MOSCA: He smelt a carcass, sir, when he but heard
My master was about his testament;
As I did urge him to it, for your good—
CORBACCIO: He came unto him, did he? I thought so.
MOSCA: Yes, and presented him this piece of plate.
CORBACCIO: To be his heir?
MOSCA: I do not know, sir.
CORBACCIO: True,   100
I know it too.
MOSCA: By your own scale,° sir.
CORBACCIO: Well,
I shall prevent° him, yet. See, Mosca, look,
Here, I have brought a bag of bright chequeens,
Will quite weigh down his plate.
MOSCA: Yea, marry, sir!
This is true physic, this your sacred medicine,
No talk of opiates, to this great elixir.°
CORBACCIO: 'Tis aurum palpabile,° if not potabile.°   110
MOSCA: It shall be ministered to him in his bowl?
CORBACCIO: Ay, do, do, do.

---

slumbers, dozes. **your,** i.e., doctors and physicians in general. **flay,** strip off skin. **conceive,** understand. **experiment,** trial upon the patient. **apoplex,** apoplexy; Hippocrates held the "strong apoplex" incurable.

from his brain, drainage of brain fluid was believed the last stage of strong apoplexy, and Corbaccio eagerly recognizes its significance. **resolved** slackened. **scotomy,** "dizziness accompanied by dimness of sight" (OED). **left,** ceased. **What then did,** F (Q But what did). **By . . . scale,** either "by your own estimation, without my help" or "judging by your own case." **prevent,** keep in front of. **weigh down,** outweigh; perhaps suggested by Mosca's "scale." **elixir,** alchemical essence fabled to make life eternal; analogous to the "stone" thought to eternalize base metal into gold. **arum . . . potabile,** "palpable, if not drinkable, gold." **aurum potabile,** was held a sovereign remedy for all diseases.

MOSCA: Most blessed cordial!°
　This will recover him.
CORBACCIO: Yes, do, do, do.
MOSCA: I think, it were not best, sir.
CORBACCIO: What?
MOSCA: To recover him.
CORBACCIO: O, no, no, no; by no means.
120　MOSCA: Why, sir, this
　Will work some strange effect, if he but feel it.
CORBACCIO: 'Tis true, therefore forbear, I'll take my
　venture:°
　Give me 't again.
MOSCA: At no hand, pardon me;
　You shall not do yourself that wrong, sir. I
　Will so advise you, you shall have it all.
CORBACCIO: How?
MOSCA: All, sir, 'tis your right, your own; no man
130　Can claim a part: 'tis yours, without a rival,
　Decreed by destiny.
CORBACCIO: How? how, good Mosca?
MOSCA: I'll tell you, sir. This fit he shall recover—
CORBACCIO: I do conceive you.
MOSCA: And, on first advantage°
　Of his gained° sense, will I re-importune him
　Unto the making of his testament;
　And show him this.
CORBACCIO: Good, good.
140　MOSCA: 'Tis better yet,
　If you will hear, sir.
CORBACCIO: Yes, with all my heart.
MOSCA: Now, would I counsel you, make home with
　speed;
　There, frame° a will: whereto° you shall inscribe
　My master your sole heir.
CORBACCIO: And disinherit
　My son?
MOSCA: O, sir, the better: for that colour°
150　Shall make it much more taking.°
CORBACCIO: O, but colour?
MOSCA: This will, sir, you shall send it unto me.
　Now, when I come to enforce,° as I will do,
　Your cares, your watchings, and your many
　prayers,
　Your more than many gifts, your this day's present,
　And, last, produce your will; where, without
　thought,
　Or least regard, unto your proper issue,°
160　A son so brave, and highly meriting,
　The stream of your diverted love hath thrown you
　Upon my master, and made him your heir:
　He cannot be so stupid, or stone dead,

But, out of conscience, and mere gratitude—
CORBACCIO: He must pronounce me, his?
MOSCA: 'Tis true.
CORBACCIO: This plot
　Did I think on before.
MOSCA: I do believe it.
CORBACCIO: Do you not believe it?　　　　　　　　170
MOSCA: Yes, sir.
CORBACCIO: Mine own project.
MOSCA: Which when he hath done, sir—
CORBACCIO: Published me his heir?
MOSCA: And you so certain to survive him—
CORBACCIO: Ay.
MOSCA: Being so lusty a man—
CORBACCIO: 'Tis true.
MOSCA: Yes, sir.
CORBACCIO: I thought on that too. See, how he　　180
　should be°
　The very organ,° to express my thoughts!
MOSCA: You have not only done yourself a good—
CORBACCIO: But multiplied it on my son?
MOSCA: 'Tis right, sir.
CORBACCIO: Still, my invention.
MOSCA: 'Las,° sir, heaven knows,
　It hath been all my study, all my care,
　(I e'en grow grey withal) how to work things—
CORBACCIO: I do conceive, sweet Mosca.　　　　190
MOSCA: You are he,
　For whom I labour, here.
CORBACCIO: Ay, do, do, do:
　I'll straight° about it. (Begins to go.)
MOSCA (aside): Rook go with you,° raven.
CORBACCIO: I know thee honest.
MOSCA: You do lie, sir.
CORBACCIO: And—
MOSCA: Your knowledge is no better than your ears,°
　sir.　　　　　　　　　　　　　　　　　　　200
CORBACCIO: I do not doubt, to be a father to thee.
MOSCA: Nor I, to gull my brother° of his blessing.
CORBACCIO: I may ha' my youth restored to me, why
　not?
MOSCA: Your worship is a precious ass—
CORBACCIO: What say'st thou?
MOSCA: I do desire your worship, to make haste, sir.
CORBACCIO: 'Tis done, 'tis done, I go.

(Exit CORBACCIO.)

VOLPONE (leaping up): O I shall burst;
　Let out my sides, let out my sides—
MOSCA: Contain

---

cordial, a medicine to invigorate the heart, e.g., potable gold. venture, i.e., the bag of gold. advantage, opportunity. gained regained. frame, devise. whereto, to the end that. colour, semblance. taking, attractive. enforce, urge. proper issue, own true offspring.

See . . . be, "See, if he isn't . . ." organ, medium instrument. 'Las, Alas. straight, immediately. Rook go with you, "may you be rooked." Your . . . ears, both a taunt and a strict truth. my brother, i.e., Corbaccio's son, with a glance at Jacob's cheating of Esau (Genesis 27).

Your flux° of laughter, sir. You know this hope
Is such a bait, it covers any hook.
VOLPONE: O, but thy working, and thy placing it!
I cannot hold; good rascal, let me kiss thee:
I never knew thee, in so rare a humour.°
MOSCA: Alas, sir, I but do, as I am taught;
Follow your grave instructions; give 'em words;°
Pour oil into their ears;° and send them hence.
220 VOLPONE: 'Tis true, 'tis true. What a rare punishment
Is avarice, to itself!
MOSCA: Ay, with our help, sir.
VOLPONE: So many cares, so many maladies,
So many fears attending old age,
Yea, death so often called on, as no wish
Can be more frequent with 'em, their limbs faint,
Their senses dull, their seeing, hearing, going,°
All dead before them; yea, their very teeth,
Their instruments of eating, failing them:
230 Yet this is reckoned life! Nay, here was 'one,
Is now gone home, that wishes to live longer!
Feels not his gout, nor palsy, feigns himself
Younger by scores of years, flatters his age,
With confident belying it, hopes he may
With charms, like Aeson,° have his youth restored:
And with these thoughts so battens,° as if fate
Would be as easily cheated on, as he,
And all turns air! (Another knocks.) Who's that,
    there, now? a third?
240 MOSCA: Close, to your couch again; I hear his voice.
It is Corvino, our spruce merchant.
VOLPONE (lying down): Dead.
MOSCA: Another bout,° sir, with your eyes. Who's
    there?

ACT 1 / SCENE 5

(Enter CORVINO.)

MOSCA: Signior Corvino! come most wished for! O,
    How happy were you, if you knew it, now!
CORVINO: Why? what? wherein?
MOSCA: The tardy hour is come, sir.
CORVINO: He is not dead?
MOSCA: Not dead, sir, but as good;
    He knows no man.
CORVINO: How shall I do, then?
MOSCA: Why, sir?
10 CORVINO: I have brought him, here, a pearl.
MOSCA: Perhaps he has
    So much remembrance left, as to know you, sir;
    He still calls on you, nothing but your name

Is in his mouth; is your pearl orient,° sir?
CORVINO: Venice was never owner of the like.
VOLPONE (faintly): Signior Corvino.
MOSCA: Hark.
VOLPONE: Signior Corvino.
MOSCA: He calls you, step and give it him. He's here,
    sir.   20
    And he has brought you a rich pearl.
CORVINO: How do you, sir?
    Tell him it doubles the twelfth carat.°
MOSCA: Sir,
    He cannot understand, his hearing's gone;
    And yet it comforts him, to see you—
CORVINO: Say,
    I have a diamant° for him, too.
MOSCA: Best show't, sir,
    Put it into his hand; 'tis only there   30
    He apprehends: he has his feeling, yet.

(VOLPONE seizes the pearl.)

See, how he grasps it!
CORVINO: 'Las, good gentleman!
    How pitiful the sight is!
MOSCA: Tut, forget, sir.
    The weeping of an heir should still be laughter,
    Under a visor.°
CORVINO: Why? am I his heir?
MOSCA: Sir, I am sworn, I may not show the will,
    Till he be dead; but, here has been Corbaccio,   40
    Here has been Voltore, here were others too,
    I cannot number 'em, they were so many,
    All gaping here for legacies, but I,
    Taking the vantage of his naming you,
    'Signior Corvino, Signior Corvino',° took
    Paper, and pen, and ink, and there I asked him,
    Whom he would have his heir? 'Corvino'. Who
    Should be executor? 'Corvino'. And
    To any question he was silent to,
    I still interpreted the nods he made,   50
    Through weakness, for consent; and sent home th'
        others,
    Nothing bequeathed them, but to cry, and curse.

(They embrace.)

CORVINO: O, my dear Mosca. Does he not perceive
    us?
MOSCA: No more than a blind harper.° He knows no
    man,
    No face of friend, nor name of any servant,
    Who 'twas that fed him last, or gave him drink:

---

flux, flow, morbid discharge. rare a humour, fine and inventive mood. give 'em words, deceive (proverbial). Pour ... ears, deceive with fulsome words (proverbial). going, ability to walk. Aeson, Jason's father, whose youth was restored by Medea's magic. battens, grows fat. Another bout, Mosca applies more ointment.

orient, eastern pearls were of superior value and brilliancy. carat, measure of weight of precious stones (then 3½ grains). diamant, Jonson anachronistically preferred this Middle English form. visor, a mask. Signior Corvino, Mosca mimics Volpone's feeble cry. blind harper, proverbial term for anonymous figure in a crowd.

60   Not those, he hath begotten, or brought up
      Can he remember.
      CORVINO: Has he children?
      MOSCA: Bastards,
      Some dozen, or more, that he begot on beggars,
      Gipsies, and Jews, and black-moors, when he was
        drunk.
      Knew you not that, sir? 'Tis the common fable,°
      The Dwarf, the Fool, the Eunuch are all his;
      He's the true father of his family,°
70   In all, save me: but he has given 'em nothing.
      CORVINO: That's well, that's well. Art sure he does not
        hear us?
      MOSCA: Sure, sir? Why, look you, credit your own
        sense. (Shouts in VOLPONE's ear.)
      The pox° approach, and add to your diseases,
      If it would send you hence the sooner, sir,
      For, your incontinence, it hath deserved it°
      Throughly and throughly, and the plague to boot.
      (to CORVINO.) You may come near, sir.
80   Would you once close
      Those filthy eyes of yours, that flow with slime,
      Like two frog-pits; and those same hanging cheeks,
      Covered with hide instead of skin—Nay, help, sir—
      That look like frozen dish-clouts, set on end.
      CORVINO: Or, like an old smoked wall, on which the
        rain
      Ran down in streaks.
      MOSCA: Excellent, sir, speak out;
      You may be louder yet; a culverin°
90   Dischargèd in his ear, would hardly bore it.
      CORVINO: His nose is like a common sewer, still
        running.
      MOSCA: 'Tis good! And what his mouth?
      CORVINO: A very draught.°
      MOSCA: O, stop it up— (Starts to smother him.)
      CORVINO: By no means.
      MOSCA: Pray you, let me.
      Faith, I could stifle him, rarely,° with a pillow,
      As well as any woman that should keep° him.
100   CORVINO: Do as you will, but I'll be gone.
      MOSCA: Be so;
      It is your presence makes him last so long.
      CORVINO: I pray you, use no violence.
      MOSCA: No, sir? why?
      Why should you be thus scrupulous, pray you, sir?
      CORVINO: Nay, at your discretion.
      MOSCA: Well, good sir, be gone.
      CORVINO: I will not trouble him now, to take my
        pearl?°

---

fable, story, report (not "fiction"). family, household,
pox, the great pox, syphilis. it . . . it, "your incontinence
hath deserved the pox." culverin, hand-gun. draught,
sink, cesspool. rarely, excellent. keep, keep house for,
look after. pearl, this, with the diamond, is still in Volpone's fist.

MOSCA: Puh! nor your diamant, What a needless care   110
  Is this afflicts you! (Takes the jewels.) Is not all, here,
    yours?
  Am not I here? whom you have made? your
    creature?
  That owe my being to you?
CORVINO: Grateful Mosca!
  Thou art my friend, my fellow, my companion,
  My partner, and shalt share in all my fortunes.
MOSCA: Excepting one.
CORVINO: What's that?   120
MOSCA: Your gallant° wife, sir.

(Exit CORVINO.)

  Now, is he gone; we had no other means
  To shoot him hence, but this.
VOLPONE: My divine Mosca!
  Thou hast today outgone thyself. (Another knocks.)
  Who's there?
  I will be troubled with no more. Prepare
  Me music, dances, banquets, all delights;
  The Turk is not more sensual in his pleasures
  Than will Volpone. (Exit MOSCA.) Let me see, a   130
    pearl!
  A diamant! plate! chequeens! Good morning's
    purchase;°
  Why, this is better than rob churches, yet;
  Or fat, by eating, once a month, a man. (Enter
    MOSCA.)
  Who is't?
MOSCA: The beauteous Lady Would-be, sir,
  Wife, to the English knight, Sir Politic Would-be,
  (This is the style, sir, is directed me)
  Hath sent to know, how you have slept tonight,   140
  And if you would be visited.
VOLPONE: Not now.
  Some three hours hence—
MOSCA: I told the squire so much.
VOLPONE: When I am high with mirth, and wine:
    then, then.
  'Fore heaven, I wonder at the desperate valour°
  Of the bold English, that they dare let loose
  Their wives, to all encounters!
MOSCA: Sir, this knight   150
  Had not his name for nothing, he is politic,
  And knows, how e'er his wife affect strange airs,
  She hath not yet the face, to be dishonest.°
  But, had she Signior Corvino's wife's face—
VOLPONE: Has she so rare a face?
MOSCA: O, Sir, the wonder,
  The blazing star of Italy! a wench

---

gallant, fine, beautiful. purchase, haul (thieves' cant).
desperate valour, the English were much wondered at in
Italy for the freedom they allowed their wives; the Italians
were reputed to incarcerate them. dishonest, unchaste.

O' the first year,° a beauty, ripe, as harvest!
Whose skin is whiter than a swan, all over!
160 Than silver, snow, or lillies! a soft lip,
Would tempt you to eternity of kissing!
And flesh that melteth, in the touch, to blood!
Bright as your gold! and lovely as your gold!
VOLPONE: Why had I not known this before?
MOSCA: Alas, sir,
Myself, but yesterday, discovered it.
VOLPONE: How might I see her?
MOSCA: O, not possible;
She's kept as warily as is your gold;
170 Never does come abroad,° never takes air
But at a window. All her looks are sweet,
As the first grapes, or cherries, and are watched
As near° as they are.
VOLPONE: I must see her—
MOSCA: Sir,
There is a guard, of ten spies thick, upon her;
All his whole household: each of which is set
Upon his fellow, and have all their charge,
When he goes out, when he comes in, examined.°
180 VOLPONE: I will go see her, though but at her window.
MOSCA: In some disguise, then.
VOLPONE: That is true. I must
Maintain mine own shape,° still, the same; we'll
think.

(*Exeunt* VOLPONE, MOSCA.)

ACT 2 / SCENE 1

(*The Square, before* CORVINO'S *house.*)
(*Enter* POLITIC WOULD-BE, PEREGRINE.)

SIR POLITIC: Sir, to a wise man, all the world's his soil.
It is not Italy, nor France, nor Europe,
That must bound me, if my fates call me forth.
Yet, I protest, it is no salt° desire
Of seeing countries, shifting a religion,
Nor any disaffection to the state
Where I was bred (and unto which I owe
My dearest plots°) hath brought me out; much less
That idle, antique, stale, grey-headed project
10 Of knowing° men's minds, and manners, with
Ulysses;
But a peculiar humour° of my wife's,
Laid for this height° of Venice, to observe,

To quote,° to learn the language, and so forth—
I hope you travel, sir, with licence?°
PEREGRINE: Yes.
SIR POLITIC: I dare the safelier converse—How long,
sir,
Since you left England?
PEREGRINE: Seven weeks.   20
SIR POLITIC: So lately!
You ha' not been with my lord ambassador?°
PEREGRINE: Not yet, sir.
SIR POLITIC: Pray you, what news, sir, vents° our
climate?
I heard, last night, a most strange thing reported
By some of my lord's followers, and I long
To hear, how 'twill be seconded.
PEREGRINE: What was't, sir?
SIR POLITIC: Marry, sir, of a raven, that should° build   30
In a ship royal of the King's.
PEREGRINE (*aside*): —This fellow
Does he gull° me, trow? or is gulled?—Your name,
sir?
SIR POLITIC: My name is Politic Would-be.
PEREGRINE (*aside*): O, that speaks him°—
A knight, sir?
SIR POLITIC: A poor knight, sir.
PEREGRINE: Your lady
Lies° here, in Venice, for intelligence   40
Of tires,° and fashions, and behaviour
Among the courtesans? The fine Lady Would-be?
SIR POLITIC: Yes, sir, the spider, and the bee,
oft-times,
Suck from one flower.
PEREGRINE: Good Sir Politic!
I cry your mercy;° I have heard much of you:
'Tis true, sir, of your raven.
SIR POLITIC: On your knowledge?°
PEREGRINE: Yes, and your lions whelping, in the   50
Tower.
SIR POLITIC: Another whelp!°
PEREGRINE: Another, sir.
SIR POLITIC: Now, heaven!
What prodigies be these? The fires at Berwick!°

O'the first year, perhaps "without blemish." *abroad,* out of the house. *near,* closely. *charge . . . examined,* i.e., each is questioned about the servant under his charge. *mine own shape,* i.e., his own apparent shape. *salt,* wanton (used of bitches on heat). *plots,* projects. *knowing . . . Ulysses,* alluding to the first lines of the *Odyssey.* *humour,* whim, obsession. *Laid for this height,* setting course for this latitude.

quote, make notes. *license,* warrant from the Lords of Council. *my lord ambassador,* Sir Henry Wotton was ambassador to Venice from 1604 to 1612; Sir Politic has been thought to caricature him. *vents,* "comes out of" or "publishes"; the rhetoric strains either usage. *should,* "it is said," from an Old English usage. *gull,* take in, fool. *speaks him,* expresses what he is. *Lies,* stays. *tires,* attires, head-dresses. *I cry your mercy,* I beg your pardon. *On your knowledge,* "your" may be impersonal, "This is known to be true?" *Another whelp!* Stow's *Annals* reports the whelping of King James's lions in the Tower on 5 August 1604 and 26 February 1605. *fires at Berwick,* ghostly battles on Halidon Hill near Berwick caused border alarms in 1604; aurora borealis has been suggested as contributory to this and other marvels of the time.

And the new star!° These things concurring,
  strange!
And full of omen! Saw you those meteors?°
PEREGRINE: I did, sir.
60 SIR POLITIC: Fearful! Pray you sir, confirm me,
Were there three porcpisces° seen, above the
  bridge,
As they give out?
PEREGRINE: Six, and a sturgeon, sir.
SIR POLITIC: I am astonished!
PEREGRINE: Nay, sir, be not so;
I'll tell you a greater prodigy, than these—
SIR POLITIC: What should these things portend!
PEREGRINE: The very day
70 (Let me be sure) that I put forth from London,
There was a whale discovered, in the river,
As high as Woolwich, that had waited there,
Few know how many months, for the subversion
Of the Stode fleet.°
SIR POLITIC: Is't possible? Believe it,
'Twas either sent from Spain, or the Archdukes!°
Spinola's° whale, upon my life, my credit!
Will they not leave these projects? Worthy sir,
Some other news.
80 PEREGRINE: Faith, Stone° the fool is dead,
And they do lack a tavern fool, extremely.
SIR POLITIC: Is Mas'° Stone dead?
PEREGRINE: He's dead, sir; why? I hope
You thought him not immortal? *(aside)*—O, this
  knight,
Were he well known, would be a precious thing
To fit our English stage: he that should write
But such a fellow, should be thought to feign
Extremely, if not maliciously.
90 SIR POLITIC: Stone dead!
PEREGRINE: Dead. Lord! how deeply, sir, you
  apprehend° it!

He was no kinsman to you?
SIR POLITIC: That I know of.°
Well! that same fellow was an unknown° fool.
PEREGRINE: And yet you knew him, it seems?
SIR POLITIC: I did so. Sir,
I knew him one of the most dangerous heads
Living within the state, and so I held him.
PEREGRINE: Indeed, sir? 100
SIR POLITIC: While he lived, in action.
He has received weekly intelligence,
Upon my knowledge, out of the Low Countries,
For all parts of the world, in cabbages;°
And those dispensed, again, t'ambassadors,
In oranges, musk-melons,° apricots,
Lemons, pome-citrons,° and such-like: sometimes
In Colchester oysters, and your Selsey cockles.°
PEREGRINE: You make me wonder!
SIR POLITIC: Sir, upon my knowledge. 110
Nay, I have observed him, at your public ordinary,°
Take his advertisement,° from a traveller
(A concealed statesman°) in a trencher of meat;
And, instantly, before the meal was done,
Convey an answer in a toothpick.
PEREGRINE: Strange!
How could this be, sir?
SIR POLITIC: Why, the meat was cut
So like his character,° and so laid, as he
Must easily read the cipher. 120
PEREGRINE: I have heard,
He could not read, sir.
SIR POLITIC: So 'twas given out,
In polity, by those that did employ him:
But he could read, and had your languages,
And to't, as sound a noddle°—
PEREGRINE: I have heard, sir,
That your baboons were spies; and that they were
A kind of subtle nation, near to China.
SIR POLITIC: Ay, ay, your *Mamuluchi.*° Faith, they had 130
Their hand in a French plot, or two; but they
Were so extremely given to women, as
They made discovery° of all: yet I
Had my advices° here, on Wednesday last,

---

the new star, Kepler discovered a nova in constellation Serpens in 1604; it was brighter than Jupiter and disappeared after two years. *meteors,* taken as ill omens, because an apparent disturbance of the cosmos. *porcpisces,* Jonson's spelling is retained with its correct etymology; Stow tells of "a great Porpus" taken from the Thames, and of "a very great whale" up river a few days later. *Stode fleet,* the English Merchant Adventurers were displaced from Hamburg and settled at Stade (Stode) at the mouth of the Elbe. *Archdukes* F (Q Arch-duke); the F reading may be the possessive (Archduke's) or it may be the correct style for Isabella and Albert, joint rulers of the Spanish Netherlands. *Spinola,* commander of the Spanish army in the Netherlands, often credited by the gullible with monstrous ingenuity; he was said to have hired a whale to drown London "by snuffing up the Thames and spouting it upon the City." *Stone,* in the spring of 1605 "Stone the fool" was whipped in Bridewell for "a blasphemous speech" in which he called the Lord Admiral a fool. *Mas'* master. *apprehend,* both "feel" and "understand."

That I know of, "not" understood before "that." *unknown,* i.e., not known for what he really was. *cabbages,* regularly imported from Holland at this time. *muskmelons,* common melons. *pome-citrons,* citrons, or limes. *Colchester oysters . . . Selsey cockles,* both delicacies in court circles. *ordinary,* tavern offering fixed prices. *advertisement,* instruction or information. *concealed statesman,* disguised agent of state. *character,* cipher, code. *noddle,* the back of the head and seat of the mind; perhaps less playful here than in its common use. *Mamuluchi,* a macaronic version of *mamalik,* Circassian slaves who came to rule Egypt in the thirteenth century; nothing to do with baboons or China. *discovery,* disclosure. *advices,* news, dispatches.

From one of their own coat,° they were returned,
Made their relations,° as the fashion is,
And now stand fair,° for fresh employment.

PEREGRINE (aside): —'Heart!°
This Sir Pol would be ignorant of nothing—
140   It seems, sir, you know all?

SIR POLITIC: Not all, sir. But,
I have some general notions; I do love
To note, and to observe: though I live out,
Free from the active torrent, yet I'd mark
The currents, and the passages of things,
For mine own private use; and know the ebbs,
And flows of state.

PEREGRINE: Believe it, sir, I hold
Myself, in no small tie,° unto my fortunes
150   For casting me thus luckily, upon you;
Whose knowledge, if your bounty equal it,
May do me great assistance, in instruction
For my behaviour, and my bearing, which
Is yet so rude, and raw.

SIR POLITIC: Why? came you forth
Empty of rules for travel?

PEREGRINE: Faith, I had
Some common ones, from out that vulgar
grammar,°
160   Which he that cried° Italian to me, taught me.

SIR POLITIC: Why, this it is, that spoils all our brave
bloods;
Trusting our hopeful gentry unto pedants:
Fellows of outside, and mere bark.° You seem
To be a gentleman, of ingenuous° race—
I not profess it, but my fate hath been
To be, where I have been consulted with,
In this high kind,° touching some great men's sons.
Persons of blood, and honour—
170   PEREGRINE (seeing people approach): Who be these, sir?

ACT 2 / SCENE 2

(Enter MOSCA and NANO, disguised, with materials for a
scaffold stage. A crowd follows.)

MOSCA: Under that window, there't must be. The
same.

SIR POLITIC: Fellows, to mount a bank°! Did your
instructor
In the dear° tongues, never discourse to you

Of the Italian mountebanks?

PEREGRINE: Yes, sir.

SIR POLITIC: Why,
Here shall you see one.

PEREGRINE: They are quacksalvers,°   10
Fellows, that live by venting° oils and drugs?

SIR POLITIC: Was that the character he gave you of
them?

PEREGRINE: As I remember.

SIR POLITIC: Pity his ignorance.
They are the only knowing men of Europe!
Great general scholars, excellent physicians,
Most admired statesmen, professed favourites,
And cabinet counsellors, to the greatest princes!
The only languaged men, of all the world!   20

PEREGRINE: And, I have heard, they are most lewd°
impostors;
Made all of terms, and shreds;° no less beliers°
Of great men's favours, than their own vile
medicines;
Which they will utter,° upon monstrous oaths:
Selling that drug, for twopence, ere they part,
Which they have valued at twelve crowns, before.

SIR POLITIC: Sir, calumnies are answered best with
silence: 30
Yourself shall judge. Who is it mounts, my friends?

MOSCA: Scoto of Mantua,° sir.

SIR POLITIC: Is't he? Nay, then
I'll proudly promise, sir, you shall behold
Another man, than has been phant'sied to you.
I wonder, yet, that he should mount his bank
Here, in this nook, that has been wont t'appear
In face of° the Piazza! Here, he comes.

(Enter VOLPONE, as a mountebank; with a crowd.)

VOLPONE (to NANO): Mount, zany.°

CROWD: Follow, follow, follow, follow, follow.   40

SIR POLITIC: See how the people follow him! He's a
man
May write ten thousand crowns, in bank, here.
Note,
Mark but his gesture: I do use to observe
The state he keeps, in getting up! (VOLPONE mounts
stage.)

PEREGRINE: 'Tis worth it, sir.

VOLPONE: Most noble gentlemen, and my worthy pat-
rons, it may seem strange, that I, your Scoto
Mantuano, who was ever wont to fix my bank in   50
face of the public Piazza, near the shelter of the

---

coat, side. relations, reports. stand fair, are well set.
'Heart, i.e., God's Heart! tie, obligation. vulgar grammar,
ordinary grammar book, apt to contain phrases and precepts; Florio's grammar may be intended. cried, called out,
intoned. bark, shell, outward appearance; may include
pun suggested by "cried." ingenuous, noble; Sir Politic
pauses to weigh Peregrine's potential. high hand, important capacity. mount a bank, from Italian monta in banco;
bank bench. dear, esteemed.

quacksalvers, a Dutch word for quackers about ointment; hence modern "quack." venting, vending. lewd,
ignorant. terms, and shreds, jargon, snatches and tags.
beliers, misreporters. utter, sell. Scoto of Mantua, renowned Italian juggler who visited Elizabeth's court in 1576.
In face of, facing on to. zany, clown and servant, comic
assistant.

Portico to the Procuratia,° should, now, after eight months' absence, from this illustrious city of Venice humbly retire myself, into an obscure nook of the Piazza.

SIR POLITIC: Did not I, now, object° the same?

PEREGRINE: Peace, sir.

VOLPONE: Let me tell you: I am not, as your Lombard proverb saith, cold on my feet,° or content to part with my commodities at a cheaper rate, than I accustomed: look not for it. Nor, that the calumnious reports of that impudent detractor, and shame to our profession—Alessandro Buttone,° I mean—who gave out, in public, I was condemned a sforzato° to the galleys, for poisoning the Cardinal Bembo's—cook,° hath at all attached,° much less dejected me. No, no, worthy gentlemen, to tell you true, I cannot endure, to see the rabble of these ground ciarlitani,° that spread their cloaks on the pavement, as if they meant to do feats of activity, and then come in, lamely, with their mouldy tales out of Boccaccio, like stale Tabarine,° the fabulist: some of them discoursing their travels, and of their tedious captivity in the Turk's galleys, when indeed, were the truth known, they were the Christian's galleys, where very temperately, they ate bread, and drunk water, as a wholesome penance, enjoined them by their confessors, for base pilferies.

SIR POLITIC: Note but his bearing, and contempt of these.

VOLPONE: These turdy-facy-nasty-paty-lousy-fartical° rogues, with one poor groat's-worth of unprepared antimony, finely wrapped up in several° scartoccios,° are able, very well, to kill their twenty a week, and play; yet, these meagre starved spirits, who have half stopped the organs of their minds with earthy oppilations,° want not their favourers among your shrivelled, salad°-eating artisans: who are overjoyed, that they may have

their half-pe'rth° of physic, though it purge 'em into another world, 't makes no matter.

SIR POLITIC: Excellent! Ha' you heard better language, sir?

VOLPONE: Well, let 'em go. And gentlemen, honourable gentlemen, know that for this time, our bank, being thus removed from the clamours of the canaglia,° shall be the scene of pleasure, and delight; for, I have nothing to sell, little, or nothing to sell.

SIR POLITIC: I told you, sir, his end.

PEREGRINE: You did so, sir.

VOLPONE: I protest, I, and my six servants, are not able to make of this precious liquor, so fast, as it is fetched away from my lodgings by gentlemen of your city; strangers of the Terra Firma°; worshipful merchants; ay, and senators too: who, ever since my arrival, have detained me to their uses, by their splendidous° liberalities. And worthily. For, what avails your rich man to have his magazines stuffed with moscadelli,° or of the purest grape, when his physicians prescribe him, on pain of death, to drink nothing but water, cocted° with aniseeds? O, health! health! the blessing of the rich! the riches of the poor! who can buy thee at too dear a rate, since there is no enjoying this world without thee? Be not then so sparing of your purses, honourable gentlemen, as to abridge the natural course of life—

PEREGRINE: You see his end?

SIR POLITIC: Ay, is't not good?

VOLPONE: For, when a humid flux, or catarrh, by the mutability of air, falls from your head, into an arm, or shoulder, or any other part; take you a ducat, or your chequeen of gold, and apply to the place affected: see, what good effect it can work. No, no, 'tis this blessed unguento,° this rare extraction, that hath only power to disperse all malignant humours,° that proceed, either of hot, cold, moist, or windy causes—

PEREGRINE: I would he had put in dry too.

SIR POLITIC: Pray you, observe.

Portico to the Procuratia, the arcaded residence of the Procurators on the north side of St. Mark's. **object,** possibly in archaic sense "put before the mind." **cold on my feet,** Italian, aver freddo a 'piedi, i.e., to be forced by poverty to sell cheaply. **Buttone,** the name of this rival owes nothing to fact. **sforzato,** "Sfortzati, gallie-slaves, prisoners perforce" (Florio 1598). **Bembo's—cook,** the pause insinuates "mistress"; Pietro Bembo (1470–1547), the great humanist, was born in Venice. **attached** arrested, constrained. **ground ciarlitani,** charlatans working on the ground, without a bank. **Tarbarine,** a famous zany in a touring Italian troop of the 1570s. **turdy . . . fartical,** an Aristophanic phrase, compounded of abusive improvisations. **several,** separate. **scartoccios,** "a coffin of paper for spice" (Florio 1598). **earthly oppilations,** gross obstructions, i.e., mundane concerns. **salad,** probably meaning "raw vegetables."

half-pe'rth, ha'p'orth. **canaglia,** "raskallie people onelie fit for dogs companie" (Florio 1598). **Terra Firma,** name for the mainland part of Venice. **splendidous,** common variant of "splendid." **magazines,** storehouses. **moscadelli,** "the wine Muscadine" (Florio 1598), muscatel. **cocted,** boiled. **unguento,** ointment. **malignant humours,** According to classical and medieval medical theory the four cardinal humours of the body were blood, phlegm, choler and melancholy, and they corresponded with the four elements—air (hot and moist), water (cold and moist), fire (hot and dry) and earth (cold and dry). Both pathological and temperamental traits were attributed to the dominance of one humour over the others, or to 'fluxes'—flowings of humours from one part of the body to another.

VOLPONE: To fortify the most indigest, and crude°
stomach, ay, were it of one that, through extreme weakness, vomited blood, applying only a
warm napkin to the place, after the unction, and
fricace°; for the *vertigine*°, in the head, putting
but a drop into your nostrils, likewise, behind the
ears; a most sovereign, and approved remedy:
140 the *mal caduco*°, cramps, convulsions, paralyses,
epilepsies, *tremor-cordia*,° retired nerves,° ill vap-
ours of the spleen, stoppings of the liver, the
stone, the strangury,° *hernia ventosa*,° *iliaca passio*°; stops a *disenteria* immediately; easeth the tor-
tion of the small guts; and cures *melancholia
hypocondriaca*,° being taken and applied, according to my printed receipt.° (*Pointing to his bill and
his glass.*) For, this is the physician, this the
150 medicine; this counsels, this cures; this gives the
direction, this works the effect: and, in sum, both
together may be termed an abstract of the
theoric, and practic in the Aesculapian° art.
'Twill cost you eight crowns. And, Zan Fritada,°
pray thee sing a verse, extempore, in honour of
it.

SIR POLITIC: How do you like him, sir?
PEREGRINE: Most strangely, I!
SIR POLITIC: Is not his language rare?
160 PEREGRINE: But° alchemy,
I never heard the like: or Broughton's° books.

(NANO *sings.*)

SONG

Had old Hippocrates, or Galen,°
That to their books put medicines all in,
But known this secret, they had never
(Of which they will be guilty ever)
Been murderers of so much paper,
Or wasted many a hurtless° taper:

No Indian drug had ere been fam'd,
Tobacco, sassafras° not named,
Ne yet of guacum one small stick, sir,   170
Nor Raymond Lully's° great elixir.
Ne had been known the Danish Gonswart,°
Or Paracelsus, with his long sword.°

PEREGRINE: All this, yet, will not do; eight crowns is
high.
VOLPONE: No more; gentlemen, if I had but time to
discourse to you the miraculous effects of this
my oil, surnamed *oglio del Scoto*; with the countless catalogue of those I have cured of th'afor-
said, and many more diseases; the patents and   180
privileges of all the princes and commonwealths
of Christendom; or but the depositions of those
that appeared on my part, before the signiory of
the *Sanita*,° and most learned college of physicians; where I was authorized, upon notice taken
of the admirable virtues of my medicaments, and
mine own excellency, in matter of rare, and unknown secrets, not only to dispense them publicly in this famous city, but in all the territories,
that happily joy under the government of the   190
most pious and magnificent states of Italy. But
may some other gallant fellow say, 'O, there be
divers that make profession to have as good, and
as experimented receipts as yours.' Indeed, very
many have assayed, like apes in imitation of that,
which is really and essentially in me, to make of
this oil; bestowed great cost in furnaces, stills,
alembics,° continual fires and preparation of the
ingredients (as indeed there goes to it six
hundred several° simples,° besides some quantity 200
of human fat, for the conglutination, which we
buy of the anatomists) but, when these prac-
titioners come to the last decoction,° blow, blow,°
puff, puff, and all flies *in fumo*: ha, ha, ha! Poor
wretches! I rather pity their folly, and indiscretion, than their loss of time, and money; for

---

crude, sour. *fricace,* massage. *vertigine,* dizziness.
mal caduco, falling sickness (epilepsy). *tremor-cordia,* heart
palpitations. *retired nerves,* shrunken sinews. *strangury,*
painful urination. *hernia ventosa,* gaseous protrusion (possibly strangulated hernia). *iliaca passio,* "pain and wring-
ing of the small guts" (Holland's *Pliny* II. 39). *melancholia
hypocondriaca,* melancholy was supposed to be seated in the
hypochondria—the soft parts of the body below the rib
cartilages. *receipt,* recipe. *Aesculapian,* after Aes-
culapius, Greek and Roman god of medicine. *Zan Fritada,*
Volpone calls Nano by the name of a celebrated zany (*fritada*
= pancake). *But,* "except for" or "pure." *Broughton,*
Hugh Broughton (1549–1612), rabbinical scholar and Puritan. *Hippocrates, or Galen,* Hippocrates (born *ca.* 460 B.C.)
invented the theory of humours and Galen (born *ca.* A.D.
130) expounded it; their authority in all medical matters was
still recognized in Jonson's time. *hurtless,* harmless.

Tobacco, sassafras, both used medicinally and newly
introduced from America. *guacum,* drug extracted from
resin of guaiacum tree. *Raymond Lully* (1235–1315), sage,
evangelist, and astrologer from Majorca; apocryphal alchemical works were ascribed to him posthumously, hence
the tradition that he discovered the elixir of life. *Danish
Gonswart,* unidentified: suggestions include a Dutch theologian (Wessel Gansfort) and a Danish Chemist (Berthold
Schwarz). *Paracelsus . . . sword,* Paracelsus was supposed
to have kept his quintessences in the pommel of his sword.
signiory of the Sanita, the "health masters" of Venice who
licensed physicians, drug-vendors and mountebanks.
alembics, alchemical stills. *several,* separate. *simples,*
remedies made from one herb only. *decoction,* boiling
down to extract essences. *blow, blow,* imitates the alchemist
at his furnace.

those may be covered by industry: but to be a
fool born, is a disease incurable. For my self, I
always from my youth have endeavoured to get
the rarest secrets, and book them; either in exchange, or for money: I spared not cost, nor
labour, where anything was worthy to be
learned. And gentlemen, honourable gentlemen, I will undertake, by virtue of chemical
art, out of the honourable hat, that covers your
head, to extract the four elements; that is to say,
the fire, air, water, and earth, and return you
your felt without burn, or stain. For, whilst
others have been at the balloo,° I have been at
my book; and am now past the craggy paths of
study, and come to the flowery plains of honour,
and reputation.

SIR POLITIC: I do assure you, sir, that is his aim.

VOLPONE: But, to our price—

PEREGRINE: And that withall, Sir Pol.

VOLPONE: You all know, honourable gentlemen, I
never valued this *ampulla*,° or vial, at less than
eight crowns, but for this time, I am content to
be deprived of it for six; six crowns is the price;
and less in courtesy, I know you cannot offer me:
take it, or leave it, howsoever, both it, and I, am
at your service. I ask you not, as the value of the
thing, for then I should demand of you a
thousand crowns, so the Cardinals Montalto,
Fernese,° the great Duke of Tuscany,° my gossip,° with divers other princes have given me; but
I despise money: only to show my affection to
you, honourable gentlemen, and your illustrious
state here, I have neglected the messages of
these princes, mine own offices,° framed my
journey hither, only to present you with the
fruits of my travels. *(to* NANO *and* MOSCA*)* Tune
your voices once more to the touch of your instruments, and give the honourable assembly
some delightful recreation.

PEREGRINE: What monstrous,° and most painful
circumstance
Is here, to get some three or four *gazets*!°
Some threepence, i' th' whole, for that 'twill come
to.

SONG

You that would last long, list to my song,
Make no more coil,° but buy of this oil.
Would you be ever fair? and young?
Stout of teeth? and strong of tongue?
Tart° of palate? quick of ear?
Sharp of sight? of nostril clear?
Moist of hand?° and light of foot?
Or, I will come nearer to it,
Would you live free from all diseases?
Do the act, your mistress pleases;   260
Yet fright all aches from your bones?°
Here's a medicine, for the nones.°

VOLPONE: Well, I am in a humour, at this time, to
make a present of the small quantity my coffer
contains: to the rich, in courtesy, and to the
poor, for God's sake. Wherefore, now mark; I
asked you six crowns; and six crowns, at other
times, you have paid me; you shall not give me
six crowns, or five, nor four, nor three, nor two,
nor one; nor half a ducat; no, nor a *moccenigo*°:   270
six—pence it will cost you, or six hundred
pound—expect no lower price, for by the banner
of my front,° I will not bate a *bagatine*°, that I will
have, only, a pledge of your loves, to carry something from amongst you, to show, I am not con-
temned by you. Therefore, now, toss your handkerchiefs,° cheerfully, cheerfully; and be advertised, that the first heroic spirit, that deigns to
grace me, with a handkerchief, I will give it a
little remembrance of something, beside, shall   280
please it better, than if I had presented it with a
double pistolet.°

PEREGRINE: Will you be that heroic spark,° Sir Pol?
O, see! the window has prevented you.

*(*CELIA *at the window° throws down her handkerchief.)*

VOLPONE: Lady, I kiss your bounty: and for this
timely grace, you have done your poor Scotto of
Mantua, I will return you, over and above my oil,
a secret of that high, and inestimable nature,

---

balloo (balloon), Venetian game. *ampulla*, "a thin
viole-glasse" (Florio 1598). *Cardinals Montalto, Fernese*,
Montalto became Pope Sixtus V in 1585; *Fernese* probably an
allusion to the notorious Alessandro Farnese who became
Pope Paul III in 1534 but there was also a later Cardinal
Alessandro Farnese (1520–1589). *Duke of Tuscany*, office
held by Cosimo de' Medici after 1569. *gossip*, godsib,
godfather; also "familiar acquaintance." *offices*, duties.
What monstrous . . . , Peregrine's speech is probably aside to
the audience. *gazets*, Venetian pennies, as Peregrine's
explanation indicates.

coil, pother, fuss. *Tart*, sharp, keen. *Moist of hand*,
the sign of "pith and livelihood" in *Venus & Adonis* 25–26.
aches . . . bones, probably alluding to venereal disease.
nones, nonce, occasion. *moccenigo*, "a kind of coine in
Venice" (Florio 1598) perhaps worth nine *gazets*. *banner of
my front*, displayed upon the scaffold, listing maladies and
cures. *bate*, abate. *bagatine*, "a little coine in Italie"
(Florio 1598) about a third of a farthing. *handkerchiefs*,
i.e., with the money knotted into a corner; the usual practice.
give it, i.e. the heroic spirit. *pistolet*, Spanish gold coin,
then worth about eighteen shillings. *spark*, gallant, brave
fellow. *Celia at the window*, presumably on the tarras or in
the window-stage; the text does not say when she first
appears.

shall make you for ever enamoured on that minute, wherein your eye first descended on so
mean, yet not altogether to be despised, an object. Here is a poulder°, concealed in this paper,
of which, if I should speak to the worth, nine
thousand volumes were but as one page, that
page as a line, that line as a word; so short is this
pilgrimage of man (which some call life) to the
expressing of it. Would I reflect on the price?
Why, the whole world were but as an empire,
that empire as a province, that province as a
290   bank, that bank as a private purse, to the purchase of it. I will, only, tell you; it is the poulder
that made Venus a goddess, given her by Apollo,
that kept her perpetually young, cleared her
wrinkles, firmed her gums, filled her skin, coloured her hair; from her, derived to Helen, and
at the sack of Troy, unfortunately, lost: till now,
in this our age, it was as happily recovered, by a
studious antiquary, out of some ruins of Asia,
who sent a moiety° of it, to the court of France
300   (but much sophisticated), wherewith the ladies
there, now, colour their hair. The rest, at this
present, remains with me; extracted to a quintessence: so that, wherever it but touches, in youth
it perpetually preserves, in age restores the complexion; seats your teeth, did they dance like virginal jacks,° firm as a wall; makes them white, as
ivory, that were black, as—

ACT 2 / SCENE 3

(Enter CORVINO.)

CORVINO: Spite o' the devil, and my shame! come
down here;
Come down! No house but mine to make your
scene?

(He beats away the mountebank.)

Signior Flaminio,° will you down, sir? down!
What, is my wife your Franciscina,° sir?
No windows on the whole Piazza, here,
To make your properties, but mine? but mine?
Heart! ere tomorrow, I shall be new christened,
10   And called the Pantalone di Besogniosi,°

---

poulder, powder; Jonson preferred this spelling (Latin
pulvis). moiety, a half, or a part. sophisticated, adulter-
ated. virginal jacks, strictly the pieces of wood bearing the
quills of the virginals, but sometimes erroneously used for
keys (the image derives from Rabelais). Flaminio, Flaminio
Scala, leading figure in the commedia, associated with Venice.
Franciscina, stock character of maid in the commedia. Pantalone di Besogniosi, stock Venetian character in the commedia; a lean old man in loose slippers, black cap and gown,
and red dress, his name derives him from a line of paupers,
and it was often his role to be cuckolded.

About the town. (Exit.)
PEREGRINE: What should this mean, Sir Pol?
SIR POLITIC: Some trick of state, believe it. I will
home.
PEREGRINE: It may be some design, on you.
SIR POLITIC: I know not.
I'll stand upon my guard.
PEREGRINE: It is your best, sir.
SIR POLITIC: This three weeks, all my advices, all my
letters,   20
They have been intercepted.
PEREGRINE: Indeed, sir?
Best have a care.
SIR POLITIC: Nay, so I will.
PEREGRINE: This knight,
I may not lose him, for my mirth, till night.

ACT 2 / SCENE 4

(VOLPONE's house.)
(Enter VOLPONE, MOSCA.)

VOLPONE: O, I am wounded,
MOSCA: Where, sir?
VOLPONE: Not without;
Those blows were nothing: I could bear them ever.
But angry Cupid, bolting° from her eyes,
Hath shot himself into me, like a flame;
Where, now, he flings about his burning heat,
As in a furnace, an ambitious fire°
Whose vent is stopped. The fight is all within me.
I cannot live, except thou help me, Mosca;   10
My liver° melts, and I, without the hope
Of some soft air, from her refreshing breath,
Am but a heap of cinders.
MOSCA: 'Las, good sir!
Would you had never seen her.
VOLPONE: Nay, would thou
Hadst never told me of her.
MOSCA: Sir, 'tis true;
I do confess, I was unfortunate,
And you unhappy: but I am bound in conscience,   20
No less than duty, to effect my best
To your release of torment, and I will, sir.
VOLPONE: Dear Mosca, shall I hope?
MOSCA: Sir, more than dear,
I will not bid you to despair of ought,
Within a human compass.
VOLPONE: O, there spoke
My better Angel. Mosca, take my keys,
Gold, plate and jewels, all's at thy devotion;°
Employ them, how thou wilt; nay, coin me,° too: 30

---

bolting, darting arrows (bolts). ambitious fire, rising,
swelling flames, recoiling to find other outlets. liver,
believed the seat of intense passions. devotion, disposal,
with pun on religious sense. coin me, render me into coin.

So thou, in this, but crown my longings.—Mosca?°
MOSCA: Use but your patience.
VOLPONE: So I have.
MOSCA: I doubt not
    To bring success to your desires.
VOLPONE: Nay, then,
    I not repent me of my late disguise.
MOSCA: If you can horn him,° sir, you need not.
40 VOLPONE: True:
    Besides, I never meant him for my heir.
    Is not the colour° o' my beard, and eyebrows,
    To make me known?
MOSCA: No jot.
VOLPONE: I did it well.
MOSCA: So well, would I could follow you in mine,°
    With half the happiness°; and, yet, I would
    Escape your *epilogue*.°
VOLPONE: But, were they gulled
    With a belief, that I was Scoto?
50 MOSCA: Sir,
    Scoto himself could hardly have distinguished!
    I have not time to flatter you, now, we'll part:
    And, as I prosper, so applaud my art. (*Exeunt.*)

ACT 2 / SCENE 5

(CORVINO'S *house*.)
(*Enter* CORVINO, CELIA.)

CORVINO: Death of mine honour, with the city's fool?
    A juggling, tooth-drawing,° prating mountebank?
    And at a public window? where, whilst he,
    With his strained action,° and his dole of faces,°
    To his drug lectures draws your itching ears,
    A crew of old, unmarried, noted lechers
    Stood leering up, like satyrs: and you smile
    Most graciously! and fan your favours forth,
    To give your hot spectators satisfaction!
10 What, was your mountebank their call? their
        whistle?°
    Or were you enamoured on his copper rings,
    His saffron jewel, with the toad-stone in't?
    Or his embroidered suit, with the cope-stitch°,
    Made of a hearse-cloth?° or his old tilt-feather?°

Or his starched beard?° Well! you shall have him,
    yes.
He shall come home, and minister unto you
The fricace, for the mother.° Or, let me see,
I think, you'd rather mount?° Would you not   20
    mount?
Why, if you'll mount, you may; yes truly, you may:
And so, you may be seen, down to th' foot.
Get you a cittern, Lady Vanity,°
And be a dealer,° with the virtuous man°;
Make one°: I'll but protest myself a cuckold,
And save your dowry.° I am a Dutchman,° I!
For, if you thought me an Italian,
You would be damned, ere you did this, you
    whore: 30
Thou'dst tremble, to imagine, that the murder
Of father, mother, brother, all thy race,
Should follow, as the subject of my justice.
CELIA: Good sir, have patience!
CORVINO: What couldst thou purpose
    Less to thyself, than, in this heat of wrath,
    And stung with my dishonour, I should strike

(*Takes his sword.*)

    This steel into thee, with as many stabs,
    As thou wert gazed upon with goatish eyes?
CELIA: Alas sir, be appeased! I could not think   40
    My being at the window should more, now,
    Move your impatience, than at other times.
CORVINO: No? not to seek, and entertain a parley,°
    With a known knave? before a multitude?
    You were an actor, with your handkerchief!
    Which he, most sweetly, kissed in the receipt,
    And might, no doubt, return it, with a letter,
    And point the place, where you might meet: your
        sister's,
    Your mother's, or your aunt's might serve the turn.   50
CELIA: Why, dear sir, when do I make these excuses?
    Or ever stir, abroad, but to the church?
    And that, so seldom—
CORVINO: Well, it shall be less;

---

crown, perfect, with pun on coin. —*Mosca?* expressing impatience at Mosca's thoughtful silence. *horn him,* cuckold him. *colour,* i.e., the fox's colour, red. *mine,* i.e., 'my art' (of disguise and mimicry). *happiness,* felicitous aptitude. *your epilogue,* i.e., the beating, but may hint at the end of Mosca's plot. *tooth-drawing,* the responsibility of mountebanks and barbers. *strained action,* extravagant gesture. *dole of faces,* mean repertory of expressions. *call . . . whistle,* alluding to the enticement of game-fowl. *toad-stone,* believed to lie between the toad's eyes and to have magical and restorative properties. *cope-stitch,* used to decorate a cope border. *hearse-cloth,* coffin drapery, here either cheap or stolen. *tilt-feather,* plume worn in tilting helmet; here perhaps found with the hearse-cloth.

starched beard, gummed and waxed beards were high fashion. *fricace, for the mother,* massage for hysteria, believed to be seated in the womb; Corvino puns on suggestions of seduction and birth. *mount.* i.e., the mountebank's platform, or the mountebank himself; another indecent pun affecting the meaning of "down to the foot." *cittern,* kind of zither or guitar, often carried by a mountebank's wench. *Lady Vanity,* a character in some morality plays, including that acted in *Sir Thomas More* IV. i. *be a dealer,* do a deal, trade with (hinting at prostitution). *virtuous man,* with sneering pun on "virtuoso." *Make one,* make a deal; mate. *protest,* declare. *save your dowry,* an adulteress was deprived of all her inheritance. *Dutchman,* believed to be long-suffering and phlegmatic. *parley,* conversation.

And thy restraint, before, was liberty
To what I now decree: and therefore, mark me.
First, I will have this bawdy light° dammed up;
And, till't be done, some two, or three yards off,
I'll chalk a line; o'er which, if thou but chance
60 To set thy desp'rate foot; more hell, more horror,
More wild, remorseless rage shall seize on thee,
Than on a conjurer that had heedless left
His circle's° safety, ere his devil was laid.
Then, here's a lock,° which I will hang upon thee;
And, now I think on't, I will keep thee backwards;
Thy lodging shall be backwards°; thy walks
    backwards;
Thy prospect—all be backwards; and no pleasure
That thou shalt know, but backwards. Nay, since
70   you force
My honest nature, know it is your own
Being too open, makes me use you thus.
Since you will not contain your subtle° nostrils
In a sweet room, but they must snuff the air
Of rank, and sweaty passengers°—(*Knock within.*)
One knocks.
Away, and be not seen, pain° of thy life;
Not look toward the window, if thou dost—
Nay, stay, hear this; let me not prosper, whore,
80 But I will make thee an anatomy,°
Dissect thee mine own self, and read a lecture
Upon thee, to the city, and in public.
Away! (*Exit* CELIA.) Who's there? (*Enter* SERVANT.)
SERVANT: 'Tis Signior Mosca, sir.

ACT 2 / SCENE 6

CORVINO: Let him come in, his master's dead. There's
    yet
    Some good, to help the bad. (*Enter* MOSCA.) My
        Mosca, welcome!
    I guess your news.
MOSCA: I fear you cannot, sir.
CORVINO: Is't not his death?
MOSCA: Rather the contrary.
CORVINO: Not his recovery?
10 MOSCA: Yes, sir.
CORVINO: I am cursed,
    I am bewitched, my crosses° meet to vex me.
    How? how? how? how?
MOSCA: Why, sir, with Scoto's oil!
    Corbaccio, and Voltore brought of it,
    Whilst I was busy in an inner room—

CORVINO: Death! that damned mountebank! But for
    the law,
    Now I could kill the rascal: 't cannot be,
    His oil should have that virtue. Ha' not I   20
    Known him a common rogue, come fiddling in
    To th' *osteria,*° with a tumbling whore,°
    And when he has done all his forced tricks, been
        glad
    Of a poor spoonful of dead wine, with flies in 't?
    It cannot be. All his ingredients
    Are a sheep's gall, a roasted bitch's marrow,
    Some few sod° earwigs, pounded caterpillars,
    A little capon's grease, and fasting spittle:°
    I know 'em, to a dram.   30
MOSCA: I know not, sir,
    But some on't, there, they poured into his ears,
    Some in his nostrils, and recovered him;
    Applying but the fricace.
COVINO: Pox o' that fricace.
MOSCA: And since, to seem the more officious,°
    And flattering of his health, there, they have had,
    At extreme fees,° the college of physicians
    Consulting on him, how they might restore him;
    Where one would have a cataplasm° of spices,   40
    Another, a flayed ape clapped to his breast,
    A third would ha' it a dog, a fourth an oil
    With wild cats' skins: at last, they all resolved
    That, to preserve him, was no other means,
    But some young woman must be straight sought
        out,
    Lusty, and full of juice, to sleep by him;
    And, to this service, most unhappily
    And most unwillingly, am I now employed,
    Which, here, I thought to pre-acquaint you with,   50
    For your advice, since it concerns you most,
    Because, I would not do that thing might cross
    Your ends,° on whom I have my whole
        dependence, sir:
    Yet, if I do it not, they may delate°
    My slackness to my patron, work me out
    Of his opinion; and there, all your hopes,
    Ventures, or whatsoever, are all frustrate.
    I do but tell you, sir. Besides, they are all
    Now striving, who shall first present him.°   60
        Therefore—°
    I could entreat you, briefly, conclude somewhat:°
    Prevent 'em if you can.
CORVINO: Death to my hopes!
    This is my villainous fortune! Best to hire

---

light, window. *circle,* the magician was supposed safe in his circle until the devil was "laid" to hell. *lock,* chastity belt. *backwards,* i.e., at the back of the house. *subtle,* insidiously acute. *passengers,* passers-by. *pain,* on pain. *Not look,* do not look. *anatomy,* body for anatomical demonstration; also moral analysis. *crosses,* afflictions; with a touch of ironic blasphemy.

osteria, inn. *tumbling whore,* disreputable acrobat (with indecent pun). *sod,* boiled. *fasting spittle,* here the saliva of the starving Scoto. *officious,* dutiful, zealous. *extreme fees,* the greatest cost. *cataplasm,* poultice. *cross Your ends,* obstruct your aims. *delate,* report. *present him,* i.e., with the young woman. *Therefore—,* the dash expresses an emphatic pause. *briefly, conclude somewhat,* quickly decide something.

Some common courtesan?

MOSCA: Ay, I thought of that, sir.
But they are all so subtle, full of art,
And age again° doting, and flexible,
70   So as—I cannot tell—we may perchance
Light on a quean,° may cheat us all.

CORVINO: 'Tis true.

MOSCA: No, no: it must be one, that has no tricks, sir,
Some simple thing, a creature, made unto it;°
Some wench you may command. Ha' you no
kinswoman?
God's so°—Think, think, think, think, think, think,
think, sir.
One o' the doctors offered, there, his daughter.

80   CORVINO: How?

MOSCA: Yes, Signior Lupo,° the physician.

CORVINO: His daughter!

MOSCA: And a virgin, sir. Why, alas
He knows the state of 's body, what it is;
That nought can warm his blood, sir, but a fever;
Nor any incantation raise his spirit;
A long forgetfulness hath seized that part.
Besides, sir, who shall know it? some one, or two—

CORVINO: I pray thee give me leave. *(Walks aside.)* If
90   any man
But I had had this luck—The thing, in't self,
I know, is nothing—Wherefore should not I
As well command my blood, and my affections,
As this dull doctor? In the point of honour,
The cases are all one, of wife, and daughter.

MOSCA *(aside)*: I hear him coming.

CORVINO: She shall do't: 'tis done.
'Slight,° if this doctor, who is not engaged,°
Unless 't be for his counsel, which is nothing,
100   Offer his daughter, what should I, that am
So deeply in? I will prevent him: wretch!
Covetous wretch! Mosca, I have determined.

MOSCA: How, sir?

CORVINO: We'll make all sure. The party, you wot of,
Shall be mine own wife, Mosca.

MOSCA: Sir, the thing,
But that I would not seem to counsel you,
I should have motioned° to you, at the first:
And, make your count,° you have cut all their
110   throats.
Why! 'tis directly taking a possession!°

Prevent 'em, beat 'em to it. *again*, on the other hand,
quean, strumpet. *made unto it*, made for the part; or
possibly "made to do it" by command. *God's so*, God's soul;
also corruption of *cazzo*, Italian for male organ. *Signior
Lupo*, Mr. Wolf; Mosca's invention parodies Jonson's own.
'Slight, God's light. *engaged*, involved. *motioned*, proposed. *make your count*, count on it; or possibly "count
your gains." *taking a possession*, Mosca uses the legal
phrase in a grotesque context.

And, in this next fit, we may let him go.
'Tis but to pull the pillow, from his head,
And he is throttled: 't had been done before,
But for your scrupulous doubts.

CORVINO: Ay, a plague on't,
My conscience fools my wit.° Well, I'll be brief,°
And so be thou, lest they should be before us;
Go home, prepare him, tell him, with what zeal
And willingness, I do it: swear it was,   120
On the first hearing, as thou mayst do, truly,
Mine own free motion.

MOSCA: Sir, I warrant you,
I'll so possess him with it, that the rest
Of his starved clients shall be banished, all;
And only you received. But come not, sir,
Until I send, for I have something else
To ripen,° for your good; you must not know it.

CORVINO: But do not you forget to send, now.

MOSCA: Fear not. *(Exit MOSCA.)*   130

ACT 2 / SCENE 7

CORVINO: Where are you, wife? my Celia? wife!

(Enter CELIA weeping.)

What, blubbering?
Come, dry those tears, I think, thou thought'st me
in earnest?
Ha? by this light, I talked so but to try thee.
Methinks, the lightness of the occasion
Should ha'confirmed° thee. Come, I am not
jealous.

CELIA: No?

CORVINO: Faith, I am not, I, nor never was: 10
It is a poor, unprofitable humour.
Do not I know, if women have a will,°
They'll do 'gainst all the watches° o' the world?
And that the fiercest spies, are tamed with gold?
Tut, I am confident in thee, thou shalt see't:
And see, I'll give thee cause too, to believe it.
Come, kiss me. Go, and make thee ready straight,
In all thy best attire, thy choicest jewels,
Put 'em all on, and with 'em, thy best looks:
We are invited to a solemn° feast,   20
At old Volpone's, where it shall appear
How far I am free, from jealousy, or fear.

ACT 3 / SCENE 1

(A Street.)
(Enter MOSCA.)

MOSCA: I fear, I shall begin to grow in love
With my dear self, and my most prosperous parts,°

---

wit, intelligence. *brief*, quick. *something ... ripen*,
i.e., the plot to disinherit Corbaccio's son. *confirmed*,
assured. *will*, sexual appetite. *watches*, watchmen, or
vigilances in general. *solemn*, formal, sumptuous. *parts*,
abilities.

They do so spring, and burgeon; I can feel
A whimsy° i' my blood: I know not how,
Success hath made me wanton. I could skip
Out of my skin, now, like a subtle° snake,
I am so limber. O! your parasite
Is a most precious thing, dropped from above,
Not bred 'mongst clods, and clotpoles, here on
    earth.
10   I muse the mystery° was not made a science,°
It is so liberally° professed! Almost
All the wise world is little else, in nature,
But parasites, or sub-parasites. And yet,
I mean not those, that have your bare town-art,°
To know, who's fit to feed 'em; have no house,
No family, no care, and therefore mould
Tales° for men's ears, to bait that sense; or get
Kitchen-invention,° and some stale receipts
20   To please the belly, and the groin°; not those,
With their court-dog-tricks, that can fawn, and
    fleer,°
Make their revènue out of legs and faces,°
Echo my lord, and lick away a moth:°
But your fine, elegant rascal, that can rise,
And stoop, almost together, like an arrow;
Shoot through the air, as nimbly as a star;
Turn short, as doth a swallow; and be here,
And there, and here, and yonder, all at once;
30   Present to any humour, all occasion;
And change a visor,° swifter, than a thought!
This is the creature, had the art born with him;
Toils not to learn it, but doth practise it
Out of most excellent nature: and such sparks,
Are the true parasites, others but their zanies.°

ACT 3 / SCENE 2

(Enter BONARIO.)

MOSCA: Who's this? Bonario? old Corbaccio's son?
    The person I was bound to seek. Fair sir,
    You are happ'ly met.
BONARIO: That cannot be, by thee.

---

    whimsy, vertigo, whirling.   *subtle,* applied to the snake
to signify its elusive movement, its texture and its traditional
cunning. *limber,* pliant, supple. *mystery,* professional
craft. *science,* branch of formal knowledge. *liberally,*
"widely practiced by gentlemen"; Mosca puns on the sense
describing the sciences "worthy of a free man" (see *OED*).
bare town-art, the minimal skills of a street parasite. *mould
Tales,* concoct scandal, with suggestion of shaping traps for
the ear. *Kitchen-invention,* perhaps new ways of preparing
old dishes ("stale receipts"); or possibly "kitchen gossip";
invention need not imply novelty (see *OED*). *groin,*
suggests that the receipts (recipes) include aphrodisiacs.
fleer, smile obsequiously. *legs and faces,* bows and smirks.
lick . . . moth, servile grooming; "moth" signified vermin in
general. *visor,* mask, hence "expression" or "role."
zanies, attendant clowns.

MOSCA: Why, sir?
BONARIO: Nay, 'pray thee know thy way, and leave
    me:
    I would be loath to interchange discourse,
    With such a mate, as thou art.
MOSCA: Courteous sir,   10
    Scorn not my poverty.
BONARIO: Not I, by heaven:
    But thou shalt give me leave to hate thy baseness.
MOSCA: Baseness?
BONARIO: Ay, answer me, is not thy sloth
    Sufficient argument? thy flattery?
    Thy means of feeding?
MOSCA: Heaven, be good to me,
    These imputations are too common, sir,
    And eas'ly stuck on virtue, when she's poor;   20
    You are unequal° to me, and howe'er
    Your sentence may be righteous, yet you are not,
    That ere you know me, thus, proceed in censure:
    St. Mark bear witness 'gainst you, 'tis inhuman.
    (weeps.)
BONARIO: What? does he weep? the sign is soft, and
    good!
    I do repent me, that I was so harsh.
MOSCA: 'Tis true, that, swayed by strong necessity,
    I am enforced to eat my careful° bread
    With too much obsequy; 'tis true, beside,   30
    That I am fain° to spin mine own poor raiment,
    Out of my mere observance,° being not born
    To a free fortune: but that I have done
    Base offices, in rending friends asunder,
    Dividing families, betraying counsels,
    Whispering false lies, or mining° men with praises,
    Trained° their credulity with perjuries,
    Corrupted chastity, or am in love
    With mine own tender ease, but would not rather
    Prove° the most rugged, and laborious course,   40
    That might redeem my present estimation;
    Let me here perish, in all hope of goodness.
BONARIO: This cannot be a personated passion!
    I was to blame, so to mistake thy nature;
    'Pray thee forgive me: and speak out thy business.
MOSCA: Sir, it concerns you; and though I may seem,
    At first, to make a main° offence, in manners,
    And in my gratitude, unto my master,
    Yet, for the pure love, which I bear all right,
    And hatred of the wrong, I must reveal it.   50
    This very hour, your father is in purpose
    To disinherit you—
BONARIO: How!
MOSCA: And thrust you forth,

---

    bound, on my way. *unequal,* unjust, but with allusion
to the difference of station. *careful,* hard-won. *fain,*
obliged. *observance,* dutiful service. *mining,* undermin-
ing. *Trained,* taken in, led on (see *OED*). *Prove,* undergo.
main, major.

As a mere stranger to his blood; 'tis true, sir:
The work no way engageth me, but, as
I claim an interest in the general state
Of goodness, and true virtue, which I hear
T'abound in you: and, for which mere respect,°
60   Without a second aim, sir, I have done it.
BONARIO: This tale hath lost thee much of the late
         trust,
    Thou hadst with me; it is impossible:
    I know not how to lend it any thought,
    My father should be so unnatural.
MOSCA: It is a confidence, that well becomes
    Your piety;° and formed, no doubt, it is,
    From your own simple innocence: which makes
    Your wrong more monstrous, and abhorred. But,
70   sir,
    I now, will tell you more. This very minute,
    It is, or will be doing; and, if you
    Shall be but pleased to go with me, I'll bring you,
    I dare not say where you shall see, but where
    Your ear shall be a witness of the deed;
    Hear yourself written bastard: and professed°
    The common issue of the earth.°
BONARIO: I'm mazed!
MOSCA: Sir, if I do it not, draw your just sword,
80   And score° your vengeance, on my front, and face;
    Make me your villain; you have too much wrong,
    And I do suffer for you, sir. My heart
    Weeps blood, in anguish—
BONARIO: Lead, I follow thee.

ACT 3 / SCENE 3

(VOLPONE's house.)
(Enter VOLPONE, followed by NANO, ANDROGYNO and CASTRONE.)

VOLPONE: Mosca stays long, methinks. Bring forth
         your sports
    And help to make the wretched time more sweet.
NANO: Dwarf, Fool, and Eunuch, well met here we
       be.
    A question it were now, whether° of us three,
    Being all, the known delicates° of a rich man.
    In pleasing him, claim the precedency can?
CASTRONE: I claim for myself.
10   ANDROGYNO: And, so doth the fool.
NANO: 'Tis foolish indeed: let me set you both to
       school.
    First, for your dwarf, he's little, and witty,
       And every thing, as it is little, is pretty;
    Else, why do men say to a creature of my shape,

So soon as they see him, 'It's a pretty little ape?'
And, why a pretty ape? but for pleasing imitation
    Of greater men's action, in a ridiculous fashion.
Beside, this feat° body of mind doth not crave
    Half the meat, drink, and cloth, one of your   20
       bulks wil have.
Admit, your fool's face be the mother of laughter,
    Yet, for his brain, it must always come after:
And, though that do feed him, it's a pitiful case.
    His body is beholding to such a bad face.

(One knocks.)

VOLPONE: Who's there? my couch; away, look Nano,
         see:
    Give me my caps, first—go, enquire!

(Exeunt NANO, ANDROGYNO, CASTRONE; VOLPONE to his bed.)

    Now, Cupid
    Send it be Mosca, and with fair return.°   30
NANO *(at the door)*: It is the beauteous madam—
VOLPONE: Would-be—is it?
NANO: The same.
VOLPONE: Now, torment on me; squire her in:
    For she will enter, or dwell here for ever.
    Nay, quickly, that my fit were past. I fear
    A second hell too, that my loathing this
    Will quite expel my appetite to the other:
    Would she were taking, now, her tedious leave.
    Lord, how it threats me, what I am to suffer!   40

ACT 3 / SCENE 4

(Enter NANO with LADY WOULD-BE.)

LADY WOULD-BE: I thank you, good sir. Pray you
         signify
    Unto your patron, I am here. This band°
    Shows not my neck enough—I trouble you, sir,
    Let me request you, bid one of my women
    Come hither to me—in good faith, I am dressed
    Most favourably ° today, it is no matter.

(Enter 1st WOMAN.)

    'Tis well enough. Look, see these petulant things!
    How they have done this!
VOLPONE: I do feel the fever   10
    Ent'ring, in at mine ears; O for a charm,
    To fright it hence.
LADY WOULD-BE: Come nearer: is this curl
    In his right place? or this? why is this higher
    Than all the rest? you ha'not washed your eyes,
       yet?
    Or do they not stand even i' your head?

---

for . . . respect, for which reason alone. *piety,* filial love (Latin *pietas*). *professed,* proclaimed. *common . . . earth,* of obscure or unknown parentage (Latin *terrae filius*). *score,* mark up. *front,* forehead or face. *whether,* which. *known delicates,* acknowledged indulgences.

feat, dainty. *fair return,* i.e., from a profitable venture. *band,* ruff or collar. *favourably,* pleasingly (but ironic).

Where's your fellow? call her. *(Exit* 1st WOMAN.*)*

NANO: Now, St. Mark
20   Deliver us: anon,° she'll beat her women,
        Because her nose is red.

(Enter 1st WOMAN *with* 2nd WOMAN.*)*

LADY WOULD-BE: I pray you, view
        This tire,° forsooth: are all things apt, or no?
1st WOMAN: One hair a little, here, sticks out,
        forsooth.
LADY WOULD-BE: Does't so forsooth? and where was
        your dear sight
        When it did so, forsooth? what now? bird-eyed?°
        And you, too? pray you both approach, and mend
30   it.
        Now, by that light, I muse, you're not ashamed!
        I, that have preached these things, so oft, unto you,
        Read you the principles, argued all the grounds,
        Disputed every fitness, every grace,°
        Called you to counsel of so frequent dressings—
NANO *(aside)*: More carefully, than of your fame,° or
        honour.
LADY WOULD-BE: Made you acquainted, what an
        ample dowry
40   The knowledge of these things would be unto you,
        Able, alone, to get you noble husbands
        At your return: and you, thus, to neglect it?
        Besides, you seeing what a curious° nation
        Th' Italians are, what will they say of me?
        'The English lady cannot dress herself.'—
        Here's a fine imputation, to our country!
        Well, go your ways, and stay, i'the next room.
        This fucus° was too coarse too, it's no matter.
        Good sir, you'll give 'em entertainment?

(Exeunt NANO, 1st *and* 2nd WOMEN.*)*

50   VOLPONE: The storm comes toward me.
LADY WOULD-BE: How does my Volp?
VOLPONE: Troubled with noise, I cannot sleep; I
        dreamt
        That a strange fury entered, now, my house,
        And, with the dreadful tempest of her breath,
        Did cleave my roof asunder.
LADY WOULD-BE: Believe me, and I
        Had the most fearful dream, could I remember 't—
VOLPONE: Out on my fate; I ha' given her the occasion
60   How to torment me: she will tell me hers.
LADY WOULD-BE: Methought, the golden mediocrity°
        Polite, and delicate—
VOLPONE: O, if you do love me,

No more; I sweat, and suffer, at the mention
        Of any dream: feel, how I tremble yet.
LADY WOULD-BE: Alas, good soul! the passion of the
        heart.°
        Seed-pearl° were good now, boiled with syrup of
        apples,
        Tincture of gold, and coral,° citron-pills,   70
        Your elecampane° root, myrobalanes°—
VOLPONE *(aside)*: Ay me, I have ta'en a grass-hopper
        by the wing.
LADY WOULD-BE: Burnt silk,° and amber,° you have
        muscadel
        Good i' the house—
VOLPONE: You will not drink, and part?
LADY WOULD-BE: No, fear not that. I doubt, we shall
        not get
        Some English saffron°—half a dram would serve—   80
        Your sixteen cloves, a little musk, dried mints,
        Bugloss,° and barley-meal—
VOLPONE: She's in again,
        Before I feigned diseases, now I have one.
LADY WOULD-BE: And these applied, with a right
        scarlet cloth°—
VOLPONE: Another flood of words! a very torrent!
LADY WOULD-BE: Shall I, sir, make you a poultice?
VOLPONE: No, no, no;
        I'm very well: you need prescribe no more.   90
LADY WOULD-BE: I have, a little, studied physic; but
        now,
        I'm all for music: save, i'the forenoons,°
        An hour, or two, for painting. I would have
        A lady, indeed, to have all, letters, and arts,
        Be able to discourse, to write, to paint,
        But principal, as Plato holds, your music,
        And so does wise Pythagoras, I take it,
        Is your true rapture; when there is concent°
        In face, in voice, and clothes: and is, indeed,   100
        Our sex's chiefest ornament.
VOLPONE: The poet,°
        As old in time, as Plato, and as knowing,
        Says that your highest female grace is silence.
LADY WOULD-BE: Which o' your poets? Petrarch? or
        Tasso? or Dante?

---

anon, shortly. **tire,** head-dress. **bird-eyed,** probably "pop-eyed," startled; possibly "short-sighted" or "timid." **preached . . . grace,** Lady Would-be deploys the terminology of formal rhetoric. **fame,** reputation. **curious,** particular about details. **fucus,** cosmetic paste. **golden mediocrity,** a travesty of the "golden mean."

passion of the heart, heartburn. **Seed-pearl,** said by Burton to "avail to the exhilaration of the heart" (*Anatomy of Melancholy* (1632), p. 376). **coral,** hung around the neck, supposed to drive away fears, devils and bad dreams. **elecampane,** plant with bitter aromatic leaves and root, used as stimulant. **myrobalanes,** astringent plum-like fruit prescribed for melancholy and agues. **Burnt silk,** taken in water for the small-pox. **amber,** used to perfume the air. **saffron,** then grown in England (e.g., at Saffron Walden) for medical and confectory use. **Bugloss,** recommended by Burton as a heart stimulant (*Anatomy* (1632), p. 373). **scarlet cloth,** another treatment for small-pox; the patient was wrapped in it. **forenoons,** mornings. **concent,** harmony, concord. **The poet,** i.e., Sophocles.

Guarini? Ariosto? Aretine?
Cieco di Hadria?° I have read them all.
VOLPONE: Is everything a cause, to my destruction?
110 LADY WOULD-BE: I think, I ha' two or three of 'em,
 about me.
VOLPONE: The sun, the sea will sooner, both, stand
 still,
Then her eternal tongue! nothing can scape it.
LADY WOULD-BE: Here's *Pastor Fido*°—
VOLPONE: Profess obstinate silence,
 That's now, my safest.
LADY WOULD-BE: All our English writers,
 I mean such, as are happy in th'Italian,
120 Will deign to steal out of this author, mainly;
Almost as much, as from Montagnié:
He has so modern, and facile a vein,
Fitting the time, and catching the court-ear.
Your Petrarch is more passionate, yet he,
In days of sonneting, trusted 'em, with much:°
Dante is hard, and few can understand him.
But, for a desperate wit,° there's Aretine!
Only, his pictures are a little obscene—
You mark me not?
140 VOLPONE: Alas, my mind's perturb'd.
LADY WOULD-BE: Why, in such cases, we must cure
 ourselves,
Make use of our philosophy—
VOLPONE: O'y me!
LADY WOULD-BE: And, as we find our passions do
 rebel,
Encounter 'em with reason; or divert 'em,
By giving scope unto some other humour
Of lesser danger: as, in politic bodies,°
150 There's nothing, more, doth overwhelm° the
 judgement,
And clouds the understanding, than too much
Settling, and fixing, and (as't were) subsiding
Upon one object. For the incorporating
Of these same outward things, into that part,
Which we call mental, leaves some certain faeces
That stop the organs, and, as Plato says,
Assassinates our knowledge.
VOLPONE: Now, the spirit
160 Of patience help me.

Cieco di Hadria, "the blind man of Adria," Luigi Groto
(1541–1585), a prolific, but minor, poet in comparison with
the five first named. *Pastor Fido,* Guarini's pastoral (1590),
translated into English as *The Faithful Shepherd* in 1602.
trusted ... much, left much in their keeping; Petrarch was
imitated as a sonneteer by Wyatt, Surrey, Sidney and
Spenser, among others. *desperate wit,* outrageous poet;
Aretino wrote a number of pornographic poems including
the sixteen *Sonneti lussoriosi* which were published to designs
by Giulio Romano in 1523. *politic bodies,* kingdom, states.
overwhelm ... knowledge, Lady Would-be's theories of obsession and perception are a travesty of Platonic thinking.

LADY WOULD-BE: Come, in faith, I must
Visit you more a days;° and make you well:
Laugh, and be lusty.
VOLPONE: My good angel save me!
LADY WOULD-BE: There was but one sole man, in all
 the world,
With whom I ere could sympathize; and he
Would lie you often, three, four hours together,
To hear me speak: and be, sometime, so rapt,
As he would answer me, quite from the purpose,   170
Like you, and you are like him, just. I'll discourse,
And't be but only, sir, to bring you asleep,
How we did spend our time, and loves, together,
For some six years.
VOLPONE: Oh, oh, oh, oh, oh, oh.
LADY WOULD-BE: For we were *coaetanei,*° and brought
 up—
VOLPONE (*aside*): Some power, some fate, some
 fortune rescue me!

ACT 3 / SCENE 5

(*Enter* MOSCA.)

MOSCA: God save you, madam!
LADY WOULD-BE: Good sir.
VOLPONE: Mosca! welcome,
 Welcome to my redemption!
MOSCA: Why, sir?
VOLPONE: Oh,
Rid me of this my torture, quickly, there;
My Madam, with the everlasting voice:
The bells, in time of pestilence,° ne'er made
Like noise, or were in that perpetual motion;   10
The cock-pit° comes not near it. All my house,
But now, steamed like a bath, with her thick breath.
A lawyer could not have been heard; nor scarce
Another woman, such a hail of words
She has let fall. For hell's sake, rid her hence.
MOSCA: Has she presented?
VOLPONE: O, I do not care,
I'll take her absence, upon any price,
With any loss.
MOSCA: Madam—   20
LADY WOULD-BE: I ha'brought your patron
A toy, a cap here, of mine own work—
MOSCA: 'Tis well,
I had forgot to tell you, I saw your knight,
Where you'd little think it—
LADY WOULD-BE: Where?
MOSCA: Marry,
Where yet, if you make haste, you may apprehend
 him,

---

more a days, on more days, more often (compare
"nowadays"). *coaetanei,* of the same age (*co-aetaneus*).
bells ... pestilence, death knells. *cock-pit,* to be found in
Venice or London; the Drury lane cock-pit was enclosed and
later became a theater.

30 Rowing upon the water in a gondola,
    With the most cunning courtesan of Venice.
LADY WOULD-BE: Is't true?
MOSCA: Pursue 'em, and believe your eyes:
    Leave me, to make your gift. *(Exit* LADY WOULD-BE.)
    I knew 'twould take.
    For lightly,° they that use themselves most licence,
    Are still° most jealous.
VOLPONE: Mosca, hearty thanks,
    For thy quick fiction, and delivery of me.
40 Now, to my hopes, what say'st thou?

    (Enter LADY WOULD-BE.)

LADY WOULD-BE: But do you hear, sir?—
VOLPONE: Again; I fear a paroxysm.
LADY WOULD-BE: Which way
    Rowed they together?
MOSCA: Toward the Rialto.
LADY WOULD-BE: I pray you lend me your dwarf.
MOSCA: I pray you, take him.

    (Exit LADY WOULD-BE.)

    Your hopes, sir, are like happy blossoms, fair,
    And promise timely fruit, if you will stay
50 But the maturing; keep you, at your couch,
    Corbaccio will arrive straight, with the will:
    When he is gone, I'll tell you more.
VOLPONE: My blood,
    My spirits are returned, I am alive:
    And like your wanton gamester, at *primero,*°
    Whose thought had whispered to him, not go less,
    Methinks I lie, and draw—for an encounter.

    *(*VOLPONE *draws the curtains across his bed.)*

ACT 3 / SCENE 6

*(*MOSCA *leads* BONARIO *in and hides him.)*

MOSCA: Sir, here concealed, you may hear all. But
    pray you
    Have patience, sir; *(One knocks)* the same's your
    father, knocks:
    I am compelled to leave you.
BONARIO: Do so. Yet,
    Cannot my thought imagine this a truth.

ACT 3 / SCENE 7

*(*MOSCA *admits* CORVINO *and* CELIA.)*

MOSCA: Death on me! you are come too soon, what
    meant you?
    Did not I say, I would send?
CORVINO: Yes, but I feared

    You might forget it, and then they prevent us.
MOSCA: Prevent? *(aside)*—Did e'er man haste so, for
    his horns?
    A courtier would not ply it so, for a place.—
    Well, now there's no helping it, stay here;
    I'll presently return. *(Moves toward* BONARIO.) 10
CORVINO: Where are you, Celia?
    You know not wherefore I have brought you
    hither?
CELIA: Not well, except° you told me.
CORVINO: Now, I will:
    Hark hither. *(They converse apart.)*
MOSCA *(to* BONARIO): Sir, your father hath sent word,
    It will be half an hour, ere he come;
    And therefore, if you please to walk, the while,
    Into that gallery—at the upper end, 20
    There are some books to entertain the time:
    And I'll take care, no man shall come unto you, sir.
BONARIO: Yes, I will stay there. *(aside)* I do doubt this
    fellow.

    (Exit BONARIO *to the gallery.)*

MOSCA: There, he is far enough; he can hear
    nothing:
    And, for his father, I can keep him off. *(Moves to*
    VOLPONE.)
CORVINO: Nay, now, there is no starting back; and
    therefore,
    Resolve upon it: I have so decreed. 30
    It must be done. Nor, would I move't° afore,
    Because I would avoid all shifts and tricks,
    That might deny me.
CELIA: Sir, let me beseech you,
    Affect° not these strange° trials; if you doubt
    My chastity, why lock me up, for ever:
    Make me the heir of darkness. Let me live,
    Where I may please your fears, if not your trust.
CORVINO: Believe it, I have no such humour, I.
    All that I speak, I mean; yet I am not mad: 40
    Not horn-mad,° see you? Go to, show yourself
    Obedient, and a wife.
CELIA: O heaven!
CORVINO: I say it,
    Do so.
CELIA: Was this the train?°
CORVINO: I've told you reasons;
    What the physicians have set down; how much,
    It may concern me; what my engagements are;
    My means°; and the necessity of those means, 50
    For my recovery: wherefore, if you be
    Loyal, and mine, be won, respect my venture.°

---

lightly, often, usually. *still,* always. *primero,* a gambling card-game resembling poker; Volpone puns on its technical terms "go less," "lie," "draw" and "encounter."

except, except what. *move,* urge. *Affect,* seek (not necessarily implying pretense). *strange,* exceptional, extreme. *horn-mad,* mad at being cuckholded, mad at the prospect, or mad to be so. *train,* trick, trap. *means,* financial resources. *venture,* enterprise.

CELIA: Before your honour?

CORVINO: Honour? tut, a breath;
There's no such thing, in nature: a mere term
Invented to awe fools. What is my gold
The worse, for touching? clothes for being looked
on?
Why, this's no more. An old, decrepit wretch,
60   That has no sense,° no sinew; takes his meat
With others' fingers; only knows to gape,
When you do scald his gums; a voice; a shadow;
And what can this man hurt you?

CELIA: Lord! what spirit
Is this hath entered him?

CORVINO: And for your fame,
That's such a jig°; as if I would go tell it,
Cry it, on the Piazza! who shall know it?
But he, that cannot speak it; and this fellow,
70   Whose lips are i' my pocket: save yourself,
If you'll proclaim't, you may. I know no other,
Should come to know it.

CELIA: Are heaven, and saints then nothing?
Will they be blind, or stupid?

CORVINO: How?

CELIA: Good sir,
Be jealous still, emulate them; and think
What hate they burn with, toward every sin.

CORVINO: I grant you: if I thought it were a sin,
80   I would not urge you. Should I offer this
To some young Frenchman, or hot Tuscan blood,
That had read Aretine, conned all his prints,
Knew every quirk° within lust's labyrinth,
And were professed critic,° in lechery:
And° I would look upon him, and applaud him,
This were a sin: but here, 'tis contrary,
A pious work, mere charity, for physic,
And honest polity, to assure mine own.°

CELIA: O heaven! canst thou suffer such a change?

90   VOLPONE: Thou art mine honour, Mosca, and my
pride,
My joy, my tickling, my delight! go, bring 'em.

MOSCA: Please you draw near, sir.

CORVINO: Come on, what—
You will not be rebellious? by that light—

(Drags her to the bed.)

MOSCA: Sir, Signior Corvino, here, is come to see
you—

VOLPONE: Oh!

MOSCA: And hearing of the consultation had,
100   So lately, for your health, is come to offer,
Or rather, sir, to prostitute—

CORVINO: Thanks, sweet Mosca.

MOSCA: Freely, unasked, or unentreated—

CORVINO: Well.

MOSCA: As the true, fervent instance of his love,
His own most fair and proper wife; the beauty,
Only of price,° in Venice—

CORVINO: 'Tis well urged.

MOSCA: To be your comfortress, and to preserve you.

VOLPONE: Alas, I'm past already! pray you, thank   110
him,
For his good care, and promptness, but for that,
'Tis a vain labour, e'en to fight 'gainst heaven;
Applying fire to a stone: —uh, uh, uh, uh.—
Making a dead leaf grow again. I take
His wishes gently, though; and, you may tell him,
What I've done for him: marry, my state is
hopeless!
Will him, to pray for me; and t'use his fortune,
With reverence, when he comes to't.   120

MOSCA: Do you hear, sir?
Go to him, with your wife.

CORVINO: Heart of my father!
Wilt thou persist thus? come, I pray thee, come.
Thou seest 'tis nothing: Celia! by this hand
I shall grow violent. Come, do't, I say.

CELIA: Sir, kill me, rather: I will take down poison,
Eat burning coals,° do anything—

CORVINO: Be damned!
Heart, I will drag thee hence, home, by the hair;   130
Cry thee a strumpet, through the streets; rip up
Thy mouth, unto thine ears; and slit thy nose,
Like a raw rotchet°—Do not tempt me, come.
Yield, I am loath—Death, I will buy some slave,°
Whom I will kill, and bind thee to him, alive;
And at my window, hang you forth: devising
Some monstrous crime, which I, in capital letters,
Will eat into thy flesh, with aquafortis,°
And burning corsives,° on this stubborn breast.
Now, by the blood, thou hast incensed, I'll do't.   140

CELIA: Sir, what you please, you may; I am your
martyr.

CORVINO: Be not thus obstinate, I ha' not deserved it:
Think, who it is, entreats you. Pray thee, sweet;
Good faith, thou shalt have jewels, gowns, attires,
What thou wilt think, and ask—Do, but, go kiss
him.
Or touch him, but. For my sake. At my suit.
This once. No? not? I shall remember this.
Will you disgrace me, thus? do you thirst my   150
undoing?

MOSCA: Nay, gentle lady, be advised.

CORVINO: No, no.
She has watched her time. God's precious,° this is
scurvy;

Only of price, of unique excellence. **Eat ... coals,**
Brutus's wife, Portia, died in this way. **rotchet,** the red
gurnet. **some slave,** this was Tarquin's threat to Lucrece.
aquafortis, nitric acid, used for etching. **corsives,** corro-
sives. **God's precious,** i.e., precious blood.

---

sense, sensory awareness. **jig,** trifle. **quirk,** sudden
twist. **professed critic,** qualified expert. **And,** if. **mine
own,** i.e., the inheritance.

'Tis very scurvy: and you are—
MOSCA: Nay, good sir.
CORVINO: An errant locust, by heaven, a locust.
    Whore,
    Crocodile,° that has thy tears prepared,
160 Expecting,° how thou'lt bid 'em flow.
MOSCA: Nay, pray you, sir,
    She will consider.
CELIA: Would my life would serve
    To satisfy—
CORVINO: 'Sdeath, if she would but speak to him,
    And save my reputation, 'twere somewhat;
    But, spitefully to affect my utter ruin°—
MOSCA: Ay, now you've put your fortune in her
    hands.
170 Why i'faith, it is her modesty, I must quit° her;
    If you were absent, she would be more coming;°
    I know it: and dare undertake for her.
    What woman can, before her husband? Pray you,
    Let us depart, and leave her, here.
CORVINO: Sweet Celia,
    Thou mayst redeem all, yet; I'll say no more:
    If not, esteem yourself as lost. (CELIA *starts to leave.*)
    Nay, stay there.

(*Exeunt* CORVINO, MOSCA.)

CELIA: O, God, and his good angels! whither, whither
180 Is shame fled human breasts? that with such ease,
    Men dare put off your honours, and their own?
    Is that, which ever was a cause of life,
    Now placed beneath the basest circumstance?
    And modesty an exile made, for money?
VOLPONE: Ay, in Corvino, and such earth-fed minds,

(*He leaps off from his couch.*)

    That never tasted the true heaven of love.
    Assure thee, Celia, he that would sell thee,
    Only for hope of gain, and that uncertain,
    He would have sold his part of paradise
190 For ready money, had he met a cope-man.°
    Why art thou mazed,° to see me thus revived?
    Rather applaud thy beauty's miracle;
    'Tis thy great work: that hath, not now alone,
    But sundry times, raised me, in several shapes,
    And, but this morning, like a mountebank,
    To see thee at thy window. Ay, before
    I would have left my practice,° for thy love,
    In varying figures, I would have contended

With the blue Proteus,° or the hornèd flood.°
    Now, art thou welcome.   200
CELIA: Sir!
VOLPONE: Nay, fly me not.
    Nor, let thy false imagination
    That I was bedrid, make thee think, I am so:
    Thou shalt not find it. I am, now, as fresh,
    As hot, as high, as in as jovial° plight,°
    As when, in that so celebrated scene,
    At recitation of our comedy,
    For entertainment of the great Valois,°
    I acted young Antinous°; and attracted   210
    The eyes, and ears of all the ladies present,
    T'admire each graceful gesture, note, and footing.

          SONG°

Come, my Celia, let us prove,°
While we can, the sports of love;
Time will not be ours, for ever,
He, at length, our good will sever;
Spend not then his gifts, in vain.
Suns, that set, may rise again:
But if, once, we lose this light,
'Tis with us perpetual night.   220
Why should we defer our joys?
Fame, and rumour are but toys.°
Cannot we delude the eyes
Of a few poor household spies?
Or his easier ears beguile,
Thus removèd, by our wile?
'Tis no sin, love's fruits to steal;
But the sweet thefts to reveal:
To be taken, to be seen,
These have crimes accounted been.   230

CELIA: Some *serene* blast me, or dire lightning strike
    This my offending face.
VOLPONE: Why droops my Celia?
    Thou hast in place of a base husband, found
    A worthy lover: use thy fortune well,
    With secrecy, and pleasure. See, behold,
    What thou art queen of; not in expectation,
    As I feed others; but possessed, and crowned.
    See, here, a rope of pearl; and each, more orient°

---

    errant, either "wandering" or "arrant, downright"; the senses are related and both applicable—"arrant, promiscuous parasite." **Crocodile,** believed to entice its victims with artful tears. **Expecting,** anticipating. **ruin**— (F ruin, Q ruin:), Q indicates that the thought is incomplete, or that Mosca interrupts it; some editors read "ruin!" **quit,** clear, acquit. **coming,** forthcoming, responsive. **cope-man,** chapman, dealer. **mazed,** bewildered. **practice,** scheming, intriguing. **figures,** appearances, shapes.

    blue Proteus, marine blue (Latin *caeruleus*); Menelaus contends with the many shapes of Proteus (*Odyssey* IV. 456–458). **hornèd flood,** the river-God Achelous who fought Hercules in the forms of bull, serpent, and man-bull; the shape may symbolize the river's branchings and its roar. **jovial,** born under Jupiter, and therefore apt to share Jove's convivial temperament and amorous propensities. **plight,** state, trim. **Valois,** Henry of Valois was entertained at Venice in 1574. **Antinous,** beautiful youth, minion of the Emperor Hadrian. **Song,** imitated largely from Catullus's fifth ode, *Vivamus, mea Lesbia*. **prove,** try. **toys,** trifles. **serene,** (French *serein*), twilight mist in hot countries; once thought noxious. **orient,** rare and fine.

240 Than that the brave Egyptian queen° caroused:
Dissolve, and drink 'em. See, a carbuncle,
May put out both the eyes of our St. Mark;°
A diamant, would have bought Lollia Paulina,°
When she came in, like star-light, hid with jewels,
That were the spoils of provinces; take these,
And wear, and lose 'em: yet remains an ear-ring
To purchase them again, and this whole state.
A gem, but worth a private patrimony,
Is nothing: we will eat such at a meal.
250 The heads of parrots, tongues of nightingales,
The brains of peacocks, and of ostriches
Shall be our food: and, could we get the phoenix,°
Though nature lost her kind, she were our dish.
CELIA: Good sir, these things might move a mind
    affected
With such delights; but I, whose innocence
Is all I can think wealthy, or worth th'enjoying,
And which once lost, I have nought to lose beyond
    it,
260 Cannot be taken with these sensual baits:
If you have conscience—
VOLPONE: 'Tis the beggar's virtue,
If thou hast wisdom, hear me, Celia.
Thy baths shall be the juice of July-flowers,°
Spirit of roses, and of violets,
The milk of unicorns,° and panthers' breath°
Gathered in bags, and mixed with Cretan wines.°
Our drink shall be preparèd gold, and amber;
Which we will take, until my roof whirl round
270 With the vertigo: and my dwarf shall dance,
My eunuch sing, my fool make up the antic.°
Whilst we, in changed shapes, act Ovid's tales,°
Thou, like Europa now, and I like Jove,°
Then I like Mars, and thou like Erycine,°

So, of the rest, till we have quite run through
And wearied all the fables of the gods.
Then will I have thee in more modern forms,
Attired like some sprightly dame of France,
Brave Tuscan lady, or proud Spanish beauty;
Sometimes, unto the Persian Sophy's° wife;   280
Or the Grand Signor's° mistress; and, for change,
To one of our most artful courtesans,
Or some quick° Negro, or cold Russian;
And I will meet thee, in as many shapes:
Where we may, so, transfuse° our wand'ring souls,
Out at our lips, and score up sums of pleasures,
    (Sings.)

That the curious shall not know,
How to tell them, as they flow;
And the envious, when they find
What their number is, be pined.°   290

CELIA: If you have ears that will be pierced; or eyes,
That can be opened; a heart, may be touched;
Or any part, that yet sounds man,° about you:
If you have touch of holy saints, or heaven,
Do me the grace, to let me scape. If not,
Be bountiful, and kill me. You do know,
I am a creature, hither ill betrayed,
By one, whose shame I would forget it were.
If you will deign me neither of these graces,
Yet feed your wrath, sir, rather than your lust;   300
(It is a vice, comes nearer manliness)
And punish that unhappy crime of nature,
Which you miscall my beauty: flay my face,
Or poison it, with ointments, for seducing
Your blood to this rebellion. Rub these hands,
With what may cause an eating leprosy,
E'en to my bones, and marrow: anything,
That may disfavour° me, save in my honour.
And I will kneel to you, pray for you, pay down
A thousand hourly vows, sir, for your health,   310
Report, and think you virtuous—
VOLPONE: Think me cold,
Frozen, and impotent, and so report me?
That I had Nestor's hernia,° thou wouldst think.
I do degenerate,° and abuse my nation,
To play with opportunity, thus long:
I should have done the act, and then parleyed.
Yield, or I'll force thee.

Egyptian queen, Pliny (*Naturalis Historia* IX.120) tells
how Cleopatra met Antony's challenge to spend a hundred
hundred thousand sesterces at a meal by drinking a priceless
pearl dissolved in vinegar. *both ... St. Mark,* perhaps an
image of St. Mark with gems for eyes, but none is recorded;
possibly two famous carbuncles in Venice, one in St. Mark's
treasury; possibly an extravagant sacrilegious metaphor.
Lollia Paulina, wife of the Emperor Caligula; an heiress
whose wealth was extorted from the provinces by her father;
Pliny describes her clad in jewels and glittering like the sun
at a bethrothal party. *phoenix,* the mythical Arabian bird,
supposed to renew itself from its own ashes every five
hundred years. *July-flowers,* gillyflowers (clove-scented
pinks). *milk of unicorns,* a delicacy found only here; but
powdered unicorn horn (from the rhinoceros) was used as
medicine. *panthers' breath,* panthers were said to attract
their prey by the sweetness of their scent. *Cretan wines,*
rather rich and sweet for bathing; there is evidence that
Mary Queen of Scots habitually bathed in wine. *antic,*
grotesque dance. *Ovid's tales,* i.e., *Metamorphoses. Europa
...Jove,* Zeus won Europa by playing with her in the form of
a bull before bearing her to Crete on his back. *Erycine,*
Venus, after her temple at Eryx in Sicily.

Sophy, the Shah, supreme ruler. *Grand Signor,* Sultan
of Turkey. *quick,* lively. *transfuse,* "to cause to flow from
one to another" (*OED*); the image is from Petronius, *Satyri-
con* 79. *pined,* tormented. *sounds man,* proclaims you a
man. *disfavour,* disfigure. *Nestor's hernia,* Nestor embodies the strengths as well as the weaknesses of age in
Homer's *Iliad;* this glance at his impotence is from Juvenal,
Satires VI, 326. *degenerate,* possibly used transitively
"cause my nation (Italy) to lose its ancestral virtue," but the
intransitive use is more probable.

CELIA: O! just God.

320 VOLPONE: In vain—

(BONARIO *leaps out from where Mosca had placed him.*)

BONARIO: Forbear, foul ravisher, libidinous swine,
Free the forced lady, or thou diest, impostor.
But that I am loath to snatch thy punishment
Out of the hand of justice, thou shouldst, yet,
Be made the timely sacrifice of vengeance,
Before this altar, and this dross,° thy idol.
Lady, let's quit the place, it is the den
Of villainy; fear nought, you have a guard:
And he, ere long, shall meet his just reward.

330 VOLPONE: Fall on me, roof, and bury me in ruin,
Become my grave, that wert my shelter. O!
I am unmasked, unspirited, undone,
Betrayed to beggary, to infamy—

ACT 3 / SCENE 8

(*Enter* MOSCA, *bleeding.*)

MOSCA: Where shall I run, most wretched shame of
men,
To beat out my unlucky brains?

VOLPONE: Here, here.
What! dost thou bleed?

MOSCA: O, that his well-driven sword
Had been so courteous to have cleft me down,
Unto the navel; ere I lived to see
My life, my hopes, my spirits, my patron, all

10 Thus desperately engaged,° by my error.

VOLPONE: Woe, on thy fortune.

MOSCA: And my follies, sir.

VOLPONE: Th'hast made me miserable.

MOSCA: And myself, sir.
Who would have thought, he would have
hearkened, so?

VOLPONE: What shall we do?

MOSCA: I know not, if my heart
Could expiate the mischance, I'd pluck it out.

20 Will you be pleased to hang me? or cut my throat?
And I'll requite you, sir. Let's die like Romans,°
Since we have lived, like Grecians.° (*They knock
without.*)

VOLPONE: Hark, who's there?
I hear some footing,° officers, the Saffi°
Come to apprehend us! I do feel the brand°
Hissing already, at my forehead: now,
Mine ears are boring.°

---

dross, "the scum thrown off from metals in smelting" (*OED*); a perverse dismissal of Volpone's gold. *engaged,* entangled. *like Romans,* stoically, by suicide. *like Grecians,* dissolutely and histrionically. *footing,* footsteps. *Saffi,* "Saffo, a catchpole, or sergeant" (Florio 1598); bailiffs. *brand,* Jonson himself was branded on the thumb for killing Gabriel Spencer. *boring,* this suggests ear-rings or ear-brandings for criminals, but no other evidence has been brought to bear.

MOSCA: To your couch, sir, you
Make that place good, however.° Guilty men
Suspect, what they deserve still. Signior Corbaccio! 30

ACT 3 / SCENE 9

(*Enter* CORBACCIO.)

CORBACCIO: Why! how now? Mosca!

(*Enter* VOLTORE *unseen.*)

MOSCA: O, undone, amazed,° sir.
Your son, I know not by what accident,
Acquainted with your purpose to my patron,
Touching your will, and making him your heir;
Entered our house with violence, his sword drawn,
Sought for you, called you wretch, unnatural,
Vowed he would kill you.

CORBACCIO: Me?

MOSCA: Yes, and my patron. 10

CORBACCIO: This act, shall disinherit him indeed:°
Here is the will.

MOSCA: 'Tis well, sir.

CORBACCIO: Right and well.
Be you as careful° now, for me.

MOSCA: My life, sir,
Is not more tendered,° I am only yours.

CORBACCIO: How does he? will he die shortly, thinkst
thou?

MOSCA: I fear 20
He'll outlast May.

CORBACCIO: Today?

MOSCA: No, last out May, sir.

CORBACCIO: Couldst thou not gi'him a dram?°

MOSCA: O, by no means, sir.

CORBACCIO: Nay, I'll not bid you.

VOLTORE (*aside*): This is a knave, I see.

MOSCA (*aside*): How! Signior Voltore! did he hear me?

VOLTORE: Parasite!

MOSCA: Who's that? O, sir, most timely welcome— 30

VOLTORE: Scarce,
To the discovery of your tricks, I fear.
You are his, only? and mine, also? are you not?

MOSCA: Who? I, sir!

VOLTORE: You sir, what device° is this
About a will?

MOSCA: A plot for you, sir.

VOLTORE: Come,
Put not your foists° upon me, I shall scent 'em.

MOSCA: Did you not hear it? 40

VOLTORE: Yes, I hear, Corbaccio
Hath made your patron, there, his heir.

MOSCA: 'Tis true,

Make . . . however, "keep up that role whatever you do." *amazed,* confused. *disinherit . . . indeed,* i.e., permanently. *careful,* solicitous. *tendered,* tenderly cared for. *dram,* dose. *device,* contrivance. *foists,* rogueries; also foist, "to smell or grow musty" (*OED*).

By my device, drawn to it by my plot,
With hope—
VOLTORE: Your patron should reciprocate?
And, you have promised?
MOSCA: For your good, I did, sir.
50 Nay more, I told his son, brought, hid him here,
Where he might hear his father pass the deed;
Being persuaded to it, by this thought, sir,
That the unnaturalness, first, of the act,
And then, his father's oft disclaiming° in him,
Which I did mean t'help on, would sure enrage
him
To do some violence upon his parent.
On which the law should take sufficient hold,
And you be stated° in a double hope:
Truth be my comfort, and my conscience,
60 My only aim was, to dig you a fortune
Out of these two, old rotten sepulchres—
VOLTORE: I cry thee mercy, Mosca.
MOSCA: Worth your patience,
And your great merit, sir. And, see the change!
VOLTORE: Why? what success?°
MOSCA: Most hapless!° you must help, sir.
Whilst we expected th'old raven, in comes
Corvino's wife, sent hither, by her husband—
VOLTORE: What, with a present?
70 MOSCA: No, sir, on visitation:
(I'll tell you how, anon) and, staying long,
The youth, he grows impatient, rushes forth,
Seizeth the lady, wounds me, makes me swear
(Or he would murder her, that was his vow)
T'affirm my patron to have° done her rape:
Which how unlike it is, you see! and, hence,
With that pretext, he's gone, t'accuse his father;
Defame my patron; defeat you—
VOLTORE: Where's her husband?
80 Let him be sent for, straight.
MOSCA: Sir, I'll go fetch him.
VOLTORE: Bring him, to the Scrutineo.°
MOSCA: Sir, I will.
VOLTORE: This must be stopped.
MOSCA: O, you do nobly, sir.
Alas, 'twas laboured all, sir, for your good;
Nor, was there any want of counsel, in the plot:
But fortune can, at any time, o'erthrow
The projects of a hundred learned clerks,° sir.
90 CORBACCIO: What's that?
VOLTORE: Wilt please you sir, to go along?

(*Exeunt* CORBACCIO, VOLTORE.)

MOSCA: Patron, go in, and pray for our success.
VOLPONE: Need makes devotion: heaven your labour
bless.

ACT 4 / SCENE 1

(*A street.*)
(*Enter* SIR POLITIC WOULD-BE, PEREGRINE.)

SIR POLITIC: I told you, sir, it was a plot°: you see
What observation is. You mentioned me,°
For some instructions: I will tell you, sir,
Since we are met, here, in this height° of Venice,
Some few particulars, I have set down,
Only for this meridian; fit to be known
Of your crude traveller, and they are these.
I will not touch, sir, at your° phrase,° or clothes,
For they are old.
PEREGRINE: Sir, I have better.   10
SIR POLITIC: Pardon,
I meant, as they are themes.°
PEREGRINE: O, sir, proceed:
I'll slander you no more of wit,° good sir.
SIR POLITIC: First, for your garb,° it must be grave,
and serious;
Very reserved, and locked; not tell a secret,
On any terms, not to your father; scarce
A fable,° but with caution; make sure choice
Both of your company, and discourse; beware,   20
You never speak a truth—
PEREGRINE: How!
SIR POLITIC: Not to strangers,
For those be they you must converse with, most;
Others I would not know,° sir, but at distance,
So as I still might be a saver, in 'em:°
You shall have tricks, else, passed upon you hourly.
And then, for your religion, profess none;
But wonder, at the diversity of all;
And, for your part, protest, were there no other 30
But simply the laws o'the land, you could content
you:
Nick Machiavel, and Monsieur Bodin,° both,
Were of this mind. Then, must you learn the use,
And handling of your silver fork,° at meals;
The metal° of your glass—these are main° matters,
With your Italian—and to know the hour,
When you must eat your melons, and your figs.

---

disclaiming in him, disowning; renouncing legal claim.
stated, instated. **success,** outcome. **hapless,** unfortunate.
to have, F (Q would have). **Scrutineo,** law court in Senate
House. **clerks,** scholars.

---

it was a plot, i.e., the mountebank scene. **mentioned
me,** asked me in passing (?) **height,** latitude. **your,** the
impersonal, familiar use which Peregrine affects to misinterpret. **phrase,** manner of speaking. **themes,** topics.
slander . . . wit, either "I'll no more misrepresent you for the
sake of being witty," or "I'll no more accuse you of being
quick-witted." **garb,** demeanour. **fable,** fiction. **know,**
acknowledge. **be . . . 'em,** "keep myself safe in respect to
them" (either from danger or from inconvenience).
Machiavel . . . Bodin, the sentiments are falsely attributed,
but Machiavelli did tend to subordinate religion to the state,
and Jean Bodin elaborated a theory of toleration. **fork,**
forks were not much used in England at this time. **metal,**
"the material used for making glass, in a molten state"
(*OED*); Sir Politic is exhibiting his technical knowledge.
main, of primary importance.

PEREGRINE: Is that a point of state, too?
50 SIR POLITIC: Here it is.
        For your Venetian, if he see a man
        Preposterous,° in the least, he has him straight;°
        He has: he strips him. I'll acquaint you, sir,
        I now have lived here, 'tis some fourteen months,
        Within the first week of my landing here,
        All took me for a citizen of Venice:
        I knew the forms so well—
    PEREGRINE (aside): And nothing else.
    SIR POLITIC: I had read Contarene,° took me a house,
60   Dealt with my Jews, to furnish it with moveables°—
        Well, if I could but find one man—one man.
        To mine own heart—whom I durst trust, I would—
    PEREGRINE: What? what, sir?
    SIR POLITIC: Make him rich, make him a fortune:
        He should not think, again. I would command it.
    PEREGRINE: As how?
    SIR POLITIC: With certain projects, that I have,
        Which, I may not discover.°
    PEREGRINE (aside): If I had
70   But one to wager with, I would lay odds, now,
        He tells me, instantly.
    SIR POLITIC: One is (and that
        I care not greatly, who knows) to serve the state
        Of Venice, with red herrings, for three years,
        And at a certain rate, from Rotterdam,
        Where I have correspondence.° There's a letter,
        Sent me from one o' the States,° and to that
            purpose;
        He cannot write his name, but that's his mark.
80 PEREGRINE: He is a chandler?°
    SIR POLITIC: No, a cheesemonger.
        There are some other too, with whom I treat,
        About the same negotiation;
        And, I will not undertake it: for, 'tis thus,
        I'll do 't with ease, I've cast° it all. Your hoy°
        Carries but three men in her, and a boy;
        And she shall make me three returns, a year:
        So, if there come but one of three, I save,
        If two, I can defalk.° But, this is now,
90   If my main project fail.
    PEREGRINE: Then, you have others?
    SIR POLITIC: I should be loath to draw the subtle air°

Preposterous, back-to-front, in the wrong order. **has him straight**, sums him up instantly. *Contarene*, Cardinal Gasparo Contarini published a book on Venice, *De Magistratibus et Republica Venetorum* (1589), translated into English in 1599. *moveables*, at this time commonly distinguished from fixed furnishings. *discover*, reveal. *correspondence*, connections. *one o'the States*, a member of the Dutch assembly, the States-General. *chandler?* Peregrine speculates from the greasy state of the letter. *cast*, reckoned. *hoy*, Dutch coastal vessel, meant for short hauls. *defalk*, allow a deduction, perhaps on the price of the herrings, but the financial strategy is obscure. *subtle air*, atmosphere of intrigue.

Of such a place, without my thousand aims.
        I'll not dissemble sir, where'er I come
        I love to be considerative°; and, 'tis true,
        I have, at my free hours, thought upon
        Some certain goods, unto the state of Venice,
        Which I do call my cautions°: and, sir, which
        I mean, in hope of pension, to propound
        To the Great Council, then unto the Forty,   100
        So to the Ten.° My means° are made already—
    PEREGRINE: By whom?
    SIR POLITIC: Sir, one, that though his place be
            obscure,
        Yet, he can sway, and they will hear him. He's
        A *commendatore*.
    PEREGRINE: What, a common sergeant?°
    SIR POLITIC: Sir, such as they are, put it in their
            mouths,°
        What they should say, sometimes: as well as   110
            greater.
        I think I have my notes, to show you—
    PEREGRINE: Good, sir.
    SIR POLITIC: But, you shall swear unto me, on your
            gentry,
        Not to anticipate—
    PEREGRINE: I, sir?
    SIR POLITIC: Nor reveal
        A circumstance—My paper is not with me.
    PEREGRINE: O, but, you can remember, sir.   120
    SIR POLITIC: My first is,
        Concerning tinder-boxes. You must know,
        No family is, here, without its box.
        Now sir, it being so portable a thing,
        Put case,° that you, or I were ill affected
        Unto the state; sir, with it in our pockets,
        Might not I go into the *arsenale*?°
        Or you? come out again? and none the wiser?
    PEREGRINE: Except yourself, sir.
    SIR POLITIC: Go to, then. I, therefore,   130
        Advertise° to the state, how fit it were,
        That none, but such as were known patriots,
        Sound lovers of their country, should be suffered
        T'enjoy them in their houses: and, even those,
        Sealed,° at some office, and, at such a bigness,
        As might not lurk in pockets.
    PEREGRINE: Admirable!
    SIR POLITIC: My next is, how t'enquire, and be
            resolved,

---

considerative, prudently deliberate. *cautions*, can mean "precautions," but taken here "in hope of pension." *Great ... Ten*, the administrative hierarchy of Venice. *means*, means of access, contacts. *sergeant*, officer charged with the arrest or summoning of offenders. *their mouths*, i.e., the mouths of the great. *Put case*, "say for example." *arsenale*, Sir Politic may use the Italian pronunciation; the Arsenal of Venice housed all its ships and weapons. *Advertise*, make known. *Sealed*, registered under seal.

140   By present demonstration,° whether a ship,
    Newly arrived from Soria,° or from
    Any suspected part of all the Levant,
    Be guilty of the plague: and, where they use,
    To lie out forty, fifty days, sometimes,
    About the Lazaretto,° for their trial;
    I'll save that charge, and loss unto the merchant,
    And, in an hour, clear the doubt.
PEREGRINE: Indeed, sir?
SIR POLITIC: Or—I will lose my labour.
150 PEREGRINE: My faith, that's much.
SIR POLITIC: Nay, sir, conceive me. 'Twill cost me, in
    onions,°
    Some thirty *livres*°—
PEREGRINE: Which is one pound sterling.
SIR POLITIC: Beside my water-works: for this I do, sir.
    First, I bring in your ship, 'twixt two brick walls;
    (But those the state shall venture°) on the one
    I strain° me a fair tarpaulin; and, in that,
    I stick my onions, cut in halves: the other
160   Is full of loop-holes, out at which, I thrust
    The noses of my bellows; and, those bellows
    I keep, with water-works, in perpetual motion,
    (Which is the easiest matter of a hundred).
    Now, sir, your onion, which doth naturally
    Attract th'infection, and your bellows, blowing
    The air upon him, will show (instantly)
    By his changed colour, if there be contagion,
    Or else, remain as fair, as at the first.
    Now 'tis known, 'tis nothing.
170 PEREGRINE: You are right, sir.
SIR POLITIC: I would I had my note.°
PEREGRINE: Faith, so would I:
    But, you ha' done well, for once, sir.
SIR POLITIC: Were I false,°
    Or would be made so, I could show you reasons,
    How I could sell this state, now, to the Turk;
    Spite of their gallies, or their—°
PEREGRINE: Pray you, Sir Pol.
SIR POLITIC: I have 'em not, about me.
180 PEREGRINE: That I feared.
    They're there, sir?
SIR POLITIC: No, this is my diary.
    Wherein I note my actions of the day.
PEREGRINE: Pray you, let's see, sir. What is here?
    '*Notandum,*
    A rat had gnawn my spur-leathers;
    notwithstanding,

    I put on new, and did go forth: but, first,
    I threw three beans over the threshold.° *Item,*
    I went, and bought two tooth-picks,° whereof one   190
    I burst, immediately, in a discourse
    With a Dutch merchant, 'bout *ragion del stato.*°
    From him I went, and paid a *moccenigo,*
    For piecing my silk stockings; by the way,
    I cheapened sprats°: and at St. Mark's I urined,'
    Faith, these are politic notes!
SIR POLITIC: Sir, I do slip
    No action of my life, thus, but I quote° it.
PEREGRINE: Believe me it is wise!
SIR POLITIC: Nay, sir, read forth.   200

ACT 4 / SCENE 2

(*Enter* LADY WOULD-BE, NANO *and two* WOMEN)

LADY WOULD-BE: Where should this loose° knight be,
    trow? sure, he's housed.
NANO: Why, then he's fast.
LADY WOULD-BE: Ay, he plays both, with me:
    I pray you, stay. This heat will do more harm
    To my complexion, than his heart is worth.
    (I do not care° to hinder, but to take him)
    How it comes off! (*Rubbing her face*)
1ST WOMAN: My master's yonder.
LADY WOULD-BE: Where?   10
2nd WOMAN: With a young gentleman.
LADY WOULD-BE: That same's the party!
    In man's apparel. Pray you, sir, jog my knight:
    I will be tender to his reputation,
    However he demerit.°
SIR POLITIC: My lady?
PEREGRINE: Where?
SIR POLITIC: 'Tis she indeed, sir, you shall know her.
    She is,
    Were she not mine, a lady of that merit,   20
    For fashion, and behaviour; and, for beauty
    I durst compare—
PEREGRINE: It seems, you are not jealous,
    That dare commend her.
SIR POLITIC: Nay, and for discourse—
PEREGRINE: Being your wife, she cannot miss° that.
SIR POLITIC (*the parties meet*): Madam,
    Here is a gentleman, pray you, use him, fairly,
    He seems a youth, but he is—

---

present demonstration, on-the-spot proof. **Soria,** Syria. **Lazaretto,** pest-house; two were established in islands of the Gulf of Venice after the plagues of 1423 and 1576. **onions,** supposed to protect against the plague by gathering the infection. **livre,** French coin. **venture,** invest in. **strain,** stretch. **note,** possibly note of patent. **false,** traitorous. **or their—** Sir Politic breaks off as he searches for his papers.

A rat ... threshold, some details here are owed to Theophrastus's Character of a Superstitious Man. **tooth-picks,** for the fashion of using toothpicks expressively see *King John* I. i., 190–193. **ragion del stato,** reasons and affairs of state. **cheapened sprats,** by haggling; Coryat tells how Venetian gentlemen did their own shopping in the market. **quote,** note. **loose,** the game of fast-and-loose. **I do not care to,** I am not anxious to. **demerit,** merits blame. **miss,** lack.

30 LADY WOULD-BE: None?

SIR POLITIC: Yes, one

Has put his face, as soon,° into the world—

LADY WOULD-BE: You mean, as early? but today?

SIR POLITIC: How's this!

LADY WOULD-BE: Why in this habit, sir, you
apprehend me.

Well, Master Would-be, this doth not become you;

I had thought, the odour, sir, of your good name,

Had been more precious to you; that you would

40 not

Have done this dire massacre,° on your honour;

One of your gravity, and rank, besides!

But, knights, I see, care little for the oath

They make to ladies: chiefly, their own ladies.

SIR POLITIC: Now, by my spurs, the symbol of my
knight-hood—

PEREGRINE (aside): Lord! how his brain is humbled,°
for an oath.

SIR POLITIC: I reach° you not.

50 LADY WOULD-BE: Right, sir, your polity°

May bear it through,° thus. (to PEREGRINE) Sir, a
word with you.

I would be loath, to contest publicly,

With any gentlewoman; or to seem

Froward,° or violent (as The Courtier says)

It comes too near rusticity, in a lady,

Which I would shun, by all means: and, however

I may deserve from Master Would-be, yet,

T'have one fair gentlewoman, thus, be made

60 Th'unkind instrument, to wrong another,

And one she knows not; ay, and to persever:

In my poor judgment, is not warranted

From being a solecism° in our sex,

If not in manners.

PEREGRINE: How is this!

SIR POLITIC: Sweet madam,

Come nearer to your aim.

LADY WOULD-BE: Marry, and will, sir.

Since you provoke me, with your impudence,

70 And laughter of your light land-siren, here,

Your Sporus,° your hermaphrodite—

PEREGRINE: What's here?

Poetic fury, and historic° storms!

SIR POLITIC: The gentleman, believe it, is of worth,

And of our nation.

LADY WOULD-BE: Ay, your Whitefriars nation°!

Come, I blush for you, Master Would-be, I;

And am ashamed, you should ha' no more
forehead,°

Than, thus, to be the patron, or St. George   80

To a lewd harlot, a base fricatrice,°

A female devil, in a male outside.

SIR POLITIC (to PEREGRINE): Nay,

And you be° such a one, I must bid adieu

To your delights! The case° appears too liquid.°

(Exit SIR POLITIC.)

LADY WOULD-BE: Ay, you may carry't clear, with your
state-face!°

But, for your carnival° concupiscence,°

Who here is fled for liberty of conscience,°

From furious persecution of the marshal,   90

Her will I disple.°

PEREGRINE: This is fine, i'faith!

And do you use this,° often? is this part

Of your wit's exercise, 'gainst you have occasion?

Madam—

LADY WOULD-BE: Go to, sir.

PEREGRINE: Do you hear me, lady?

Why, if your knight have set you to beg shirts,°

Or to invite me home, you might have done it

A nearer° way, by far.   100

LADY WOULD-BE: This cannot work you,

Out of my snare.

PEREGRINE: Why? am I in it, then?

Indeed, your husband told me, you were fair,

And so you are; only your nose inclines,

That side, that's next the sun, to the queen-apple.°

LADY WOULD-BE: This cannot be endured, by any
patience.

---

as soon, at so early an age; but the phrase is open to Lady Would-be's wilful misinterpretation. **massacre,** accented on second syllable here. **humbled,** brought low—down to his spurs; editors have here found a sneer at King James's readiness to create new knights. **reach,** understand. **polity,** policy, cunning bluff. **bear it through,** carry it off. **Froward,** refractory. **solecism,** a grammatical, not a sexual, impropriety; the word is itself a solecism here. **Sporus,** minion castrated and "married" by Nero. **historic,** perhaps "epoch-making."

Whitefriars nation, Whitefriars was a "liberty" under the old priory charter, inside the City of London but outside its jurisdiction; it became almost a miniature state for outcasts. **forehead,** "capacity for blushing, modesty" (OED). **fricatrice,** whore (Latin, fricare, to rub). **you be,** addressed either to Lady Would-be or to Peregrine. **case,** possibly "mask" or "disguise." **liquid,** "transparent, easily seen through" or "amorphous, hard to grasp"; and Lady Would-be may be sobbing. **state-face,** politic countenance. **carnival,** probably for "carnal." **concupiscence,** for "concupiscent (woman)." **liberty of conscience,** freedom from religious persecution; the prison marshal is conceived as the persecutor and concupiscence as the religion. **disple,** ed. (FQ disc'ple) "to subject to discipline; especially as a religious practice" (OED). **use this,** act like this. **beg shirts,** Lady Would-be is evidently tugging at Peregrine's shirt. **nearer,** more direct. **queen-apple,** perhaps a quince, or early variety of apple; Lady Would-be's nose is red on one side.

ACT 4 / SCENE 3

(Enter MOSCA.)

MOSCA: What's the matter, madam?

LADY WOULD-BE: If the Senate
Right not my quest,° in this; I will protest° 'em,
To all the world, no aristocracy.

MOSCA: What is the injury, lady?

LADY WOULD-BE: Why, the callet,
You told me of, here I have ta'en disguised.

MOSCA: Who? this? what means your ladyship? the
creature

10 I mentioned to you, is apprehended, now,
Before the Senate, you shall see her—

LADY WOULD-BE: Where?

MOSCA: I'll bring you to her. This young gentleman
I saw him land, this morning, at the port.

LADY WOULD-BE: Is't possible! how has my judgement
wandered!
Sir, I must, blushing, say to you, I have erred:
And plead you pardon.

PEREGRINE: What! more changes, yet?

20 LADY WOULD-BE: I hope, you ha'not the malice to
remember
A gentlewoman's passion. If you stay,
In Venice, here, please you to use me,° sir—

MOSCA: Will you go, madam?

LADY WOULD-BE: Pray you, sir, use me. In faith,
The more you see me, the more I shall conceive,°
You have forgot our quarrel.

PEREGRINE: This is rare!
Sir Politic Would-be? no, Sir Politic Bawd!

30 To bring me, thus, acquainted with his wife!
Well, wise Sir Pol: since you have practised,° thus,
Upon my freshmanship, I'll try your salt-head,°
What proof it is against a counter-plot.

ACT 4 / SCENE 4

(The Scrutineo.)

(Enter VOLTORE, CORBACCIO, CORVINO, MOSCA.)

VOLTORE: Well, now you see the carriage° of the
business,
Your constancy is all, that is required
Unto the safety of it.

MOSCA: Is the lie
Safely conveyed amongst us? is that sure?
Knows every man his burden?°

CORVINO: Yes.

MOSCA: Then, shrink not.

CORVINO *(aside to* MOSCA): But, knows the advocate   10
the truth?

MOSCA: O, sir,
By no means. I devised a formal° tale,
That salved° your reputation. But, be valiant, sir.

CORVINO: I fear no one, but him; that, this his
pleading
Should make him stand for a co-heir—

MOSCA: Co-halter.
Hang him: we will but use his tongue, his noise,
As we do Croaker's here. *(Pointing to* CORBACCIO.)   20

CORVINO: Ay, what shall he do?

MOSCA: When we ha' done, you mean?

CORVINO: Yes.

MOSCA: Why, we'll think:
Sell him for mummia,° he's half dust already.
(to VOLTORE) Do not you smile, to see this buffalo,°
(Pointing to CORVINO.)
How he doth sport it with his head?—*(aside)* I
should
If all were well, and past. *(to* CORBACCIO) Sir, only
you
Are he, that shall enjoy the crop of all,   30
And these not know for whom they toil.

CORBACCIO: Ay, peace.

MOSCA *(to* CORVINO): But you shall eat it.° *(Then to*
VOLTORE *again.)* Much! Worshipful sir,
Mercury° sit upon your thund'ring tongue,
Or the French Hercules,° and make your language
As conquering as his club, to beat along,
As with a tempest, flat, our adversaries:
But, much more, yours, sir.

VOLTORE: Here they come, ha' done.   40

MOSCA: I have another witness, if you need, sir,
I can produce.

VOLTORE: Who is it?

MOSCA: Sir, I have her.

ACT 4 / SCENE 5

(Enter four AVOCATORI, BONARIO, CELIA, NOTARIO,
COMMENDATORI *and* OTHERS.)

---

quest, petition. **protest,** proclaim. **use me,** Lady
Would-be intends to be socially useful but her rhetoric
insinuates her readiness to be Peregrine's mistress. **conceive,** understand; become pregnant. **practised,** plotted;
Peregrine thinks he has been gulled. **salt-head,** seasoned,
experienced; salacious, bawdy. **carriage,** management.
burden, refrain of a song; hence "part in the performance."

formal, "elaborately constructed, circumstantial" *(OED)*.
salved, healed, made good. **mummia,** a medicinal preparation from the substance of mummies; fake mummy was
made from baked corpses. **buffalo,** alluding to the cuckold's horns that the "formal tale" sets upon Corvino. **eat
it,** i.e., the crop, the legacy; Corvino may overhear the words
to Corbaccio. **Mercury,** god of eloquence and of trade; also
associated with trickery and theft. **French Hercules,** Hercules was fabled to have fathered the Celts in Gaul while
returning from the far west with the oxen of Geryon; as the
Celtic Hercules he was the symbol of eloquence.

1st AVOCATORE: The like of this the Senate never
    heard of.
2nd AVOCATORE: 'Twill come most strange to them,
    when we report it.
4th AVOCATORE: The gentlewoman has been ever
    held
    Of unreprovèd name.
3rd AVOCATORE: So, the young man.
4th AVOCATORE: The more unnatural part that of his
10   father.
2nd AVOCATORE: More of the husband.
1st AVOCATORE: I not know to give
    His act a name, it is so monstrous!
4th AVOCATORE: But the impostor, he is a thing
    created
    T'exceed example!°
1st AVOCATORE: And all after times!°
2nd AVOCATORE: I never heard a true voluptuary
    Described, but him.
20 3rd AVOCATORE: Appear yet those were cited?°
NOTARIO: All, but the old magnifico, Volpone.
1st AVOCATORE: Why is not he here?
MOSCA: Please your fatherhoods,
    Here is his advocate. Himself's, so weak,
    So feeble—
4th AVOCATORE: What are you?
BONARIO: His parasite,
    His knave, his pandar: I beseech the court,
    He may be forced to come, that your grave eyes
30   May bear strong witness of his strange impostures.
VOLTORE: Upon my faith, and credit, with your
    virtues,
    He is not able to endure the air.
2nd AVOCATORE: Bring him, however.
3rd AVOCATORE: We will see him.
4th AVOCATORE: Fetch him.
VOLTORE: Your fatherhoods' fit pleasures be obeyed,
    Be sure, the sight will rather move your pities,
    Than indignation; may it please the court,
40   In the meantime, he may be heard in me:
    I know this place most void of prejudice,
    And therefore crave it, since we have no reason
    To fear our truth should hurt our cause.
3rd AVOCATORE: Speak free.
VOLTORE: Then know, most honoured fathers, I
    must now
    Discover, to your strangely abused ears,
    The most prodigious, and most frontless° piece
    Of solid impudence, and treachery,
50   That ever vicious nature yet brought forth
    To shame the state of Venice. This lewd woman
    (That wants° no artificial looks, or tears,
    To help the visor,° she has now put on)

Hath long been known a close° adulteress,
To that lascivious youth there; not suspected,
I say, but known; and taken, in the act,
With him; and by this man, the easy husband,
Pardoned: whose timeless° bounty makes him,
    now,
Stand here, the most unhappy, innocent person, 60
That ever man's own goodness made accused.
For these, not knowing how to owe° a gift
Of that dear grace,° but with their shame; being
    placed
So above all powers of their gratitude,°
Began to hate the benefit; and, in place
Of thanks, devise t'extirp° the memory
Of such an act. Wherein, I pray your fatherhoods,
To observe the malice, yea, the rage of creatures
Discovered in their evils; and what heart° 70
Such take, even from their crimes. But that, anon,
Will more appear. This gentleman, the father,
Hearing of this foul fact, with many others,
Which daily struck at his too-tender ears,
And, grieved in nothing more, than that he could
    not
Preserve himself a parent (his son's ills°
Growing to that strange flood) at last decreed
To disinherit him.
1st AVOCATORE: These be strange turns!° 80
2nd AVOCATORE: The young man's fame was ever
    fair, and honest.
VOLTORE: So much more full of danger is his vice,
    That can beguile so, under shade of virtue.
    But as I said, my honoured sires, his father
    Having this settled purpose, (by what means
    To him betrayed, we know not) and this day
    Appointed for the deed; that parricide,
    (I cannot style him better) by confederacy°
    Preparing this his paramour to be there, 90
    Entered Volpone's house (who was the man
    Your fatherhoods must understand, designed°
    For the inheritance) there sought his father:
    But, with what purpose sought he him, my lords?
    (I tremble to pronounce it, that a son
    Unto a father, and to such a father
    Should have so foul, felonious intent)
    It was, to murder him. When, being prevented
    By his more happy absence, what then did he?
    Not check his wicked thoughts; no, now new deeds: 100
    (Mischief doth ever° end, where it begins)

---

example, precedent. after times, i.e., future possibilities. cited, summoned, called as witnesses. frontless,
shameless. wants, lacks. visor, mask.

---

close, secret. timeless, untimely. owe, acknowledge
(= own), or "properly possess." gift . . . grace, "so precious
and unmerited a gift (of pardon)." So . . . gratitude, i.e., in
a position of indebtedness beyond the reach of their powers
of gratitude. extirp, extirpate, eradicate. heart, hardness
of heart; impudent courage. ills, evils. turns, turns of
event. confederacy, conspiracy. designed, designated.
ever, the reading "never" has been proposed and followed
by some editors, but "ever" means "what begins badly ends
badly."

An act of horror, fathers! he dragged forth
The agèd gentleman, that had there lain, bed-rid,
Three years, and more, out of his innocent couch,
Naked, upon the floor, there left him; wounded
His servant in the face; and, with this strumpet,
The stale° to his forged practice,° who was glad
To be so active, (I shall here desire
Your fatherhoods to note but my collections,°

110 As most remarkable) thought, at once, to stop
His father's ends;° discredit his free choice,
In the old gentleman;° redeem themselves,
By laying infamy upon this man,
To whom, with blushing, they should owe° their
   lives.

1st AVOCATORE: What proofs have you of this?

BONARIO: Most honoured fathers,
I humbly crave, there be no credit given
To this man's mercenary tongue.

120 2nd AVOCATORE: Forbear.

BONARIO: His soul moves in his fee.

3rd AVOCATORE: O, sir.

BONARIO: This fellow,
For six sols° more, would plead against his maker.

1st AVOCATORE: You do forget yourself.

VOLTORE: Nay, nay, grave fathers,
Let him have scope: can any man imagine
That he will spare his accuser, that would not
Have spared his parent?

130 1st AVOCATORE: Well, produce your proofs.

CELIA: I would I could forget, I were a creature.

VOLTORE: Signior Corbaccio.

4th AVOCATORE: What is he?

VOLTORE: The father.

2nd AVOCATORE: Has he had an oath?

NOTARIO: Yes.

CORBACCIO: What must I do now?

NOTARIO: Your testimony's craved.

CORBACCIO: Speak to the knave?

140 I'll ha' my mouth, first, stopped with earth; my
   heart
Abhors his knowledge°: I disclaim° in him.

1st AVOCATORE: But, for what cause?

CORBACCIO: The mere portent° of nature.
He is an utter stranger, to my loins.

BONARIO: Have they made° you to this!

CORBACCIO: I will not hear thee,
Monster of men, swine, goat, wolf, parricide,
Speak not, thou viper.

BONARIO: Sir, I will sit down,   150
And rather wish my innocence should suffer,
Than I resist the authority of a father.

VOLTORE: Signior Corvino.

2nd AVOCATORE: This is strange!

1st AVOCATORE: Who's this?

NOTARIO: The husband.

4th AVOCATORE: Is he sworn?

NOTARIO: He is.

3rd AVOCATORE: Speak then.

CORVINO: This woman, please your fatherhoods, is a   160
   whore,
Of most hot exercise, more than a partridge,°
Upon record—

1st AVOCATORE: No more.

CORVINO: Neighs, like a jennet.°

NOTARIO: Preserve the honour of the court.

CORVINO: I shall,
And modesty of your most reverend ears.
And yet, I hope that I may say, these eyes
Have seen her glued unto that piece of cedar;   170
That fine well-timbered° gallant: and that, here,°
The letters may be read, thorough the horn,°
That makes the story perfect.°

MOSCA: Excellent! sir.

CORVINO: There is no shame in this, now, is there?

MOSCA: None.

CORVINO: Or if I said, I hoped that she were onward°
To her damnation, if there be a hell
Greater than whore, and woman; a good Catholic
May make the doubt.   180

3rd AVOCATORE: His grief hath made him frantic.

1st AVOCATORE: Remove him, hence.

2nd AVOCATORE: Look to the woman. *(She swoons.)*

CORVINO: Rare!
Prettily feigned! again!

4th AVOCATORE: Stand from about her.

1st AVOCATORE: Give her the air.

3rd AVOCATORE *(to MOSCA)*: What can you say?

MOSCA: My wound,
May't please your wisdoms, speaks for me, received   190
In aid of my good patron, when he missed
His sought-for father, when that well-taught dame
Had her cue given her, to cry out a rape.

BONARIO: O, most laid° impudence! Fathers—

3rd AVOCATORE: Sir, be silent,
You had your hearing free,° so must they theirs.

2nd AVOCATORE: I do begin to doubt th'imposture
   here.

---

stale, lure; "a prostitute of the lowest class employed as a decoy by thieves" *(OED).* *forged practice,* contrived plot. *collections,* conclusions. *ends,* purposes, aims. *gentleman,* i.e., Volpone. *owe,* acknowledge as due. *sols,* French coins worth one twentieth of a livre. *his knowledge,* knowledge of him. *disclaim,* deny kinship. *portent,* ominous freak; suggesting unnatural birth and leading to the denial of paternity. *made,* forced, or possibly "shaped."

partridge, described by Pliny as the most concupiscent of creatures *(Nat. Hist.* X. 102). *jennet,* small Spanish horse. *well-timbered,* well-built. *here,* Corvino holds his forked fingers to his forehead to give himself cuckold's horns. *letters . . . horn,* punning on "horn-book," a primer (so-called because protected by translucent horn). *perfect,* complete. *onward,* well on the way. *laid,* plotted. *free,* i.e., from interruption

4th AVOCATORE: This woman, has too many moods.

200 VOLTORE: Grave fathers,
　　She is a creature, of a most professed,
　　And prostituted lewdness.

CORVINO: Most impetuous!
　　Unsatisfied, grave fathers!

VOLTORE: May her feignings
　　Not take your wisdoms; but this day, she baited°
　　A stranger, a grave knight, with her loose eyes,
　　And more lascivious kisses. This man saw 'em
　　Together, on the water, in a gondola.

210 MOSCA: Here is the lady herself, that saw 'em too,
　　Without°; who, then, had in the open streets
　　Pursued them, but for saving her knight's honour.

1st AVOCATORE: Produce that lady.

2nd AVOCATORE: Let her come. (*Exit* MOSCA.)

4th AVOCATORE: These things
　　They strike, with wonder!

3rd AVOCATORE: I am turned a stone!

ACT 4 / SCENE 6

(*Enter* MOSCA *with* LADY WOULD-BE.)

MOSCA: Be resolute, madam.

LADY WOULD-BE: Ay, this same is she.
　　Out, thou chameleon° harlot: now, thine eyes
　　Vie tears with the hyaena°: dar'st thou look
　　Upon my wrongèd face? I cry your pardons.
　　I fear, I have, forgettingly, transgressed
　　Against the dignity of the court—

2nd AVOCATORE: No, madam.

LADY WOULD-BE: And been exorbitant°—

10 4th AVOCATORE: You have not, lady.
　　These proofs are strong.

LADY WOULD-BE: Surely, I had no purpose,
　　To scandalize your honours, or my sex's.

3rd AVOCATORE: We do believe it.

LADY WOULD-BE: Surely, you may believe it.

2nd AVOCATORE: Madam, we do.

LADY WOULD-BE: Indeed, you may; my breeding
　　Is not so coarse—

4th AVOCATORE: We know it.

20 LADY WOULD-BE: To offend
　　With pertinacy—

3rd AVOCATORE: Lady.

LADY WOULD-BE: Such a presence:
　　No, surely.

1st AVOCATORE: We well think it.

LADY WOULD-BE: You may think it.

1st AVOCATORE: Let her o'ercome.° (*to* BONARIO) What
　　witnesses have you,
　　To make good your report?

BONARIO: Our consciences— 30

CELIA: And heaven, that never fails the innocent.

4th AVOCATORE: These are no testimonies.

BONARIO: Not in your courts,
　　Where multitude,° and clamour, overcomes.

1st AVOCATORE: Nay, then you do wax insolent.

VOLTORE: Here, here,

(VOLPONE *is brought in, as impotent.°*)

　　The testimony comes, that will convince,
　　And put to utter dumbness their bold tongues.
　　See here, grave fathers, here's the ravisher,
　　The rider on men's wives, the great impostor, 40
　　The grand voluptuary! do you not think,
　　These limbs should affect venery?° or these eyes
　　Covet a concubine? pray you, mark these hands.
　　Are they not fit to stroke a lady's breasts?
　　Perhaps, he doth dissemble?

BONARIO: So he does.

VOLTORE: Would you ha'him tortured?

BONARIO: I would have him proved.°

VOLTORE: Best try him, then, with goads, or burning
　　irons; 50
　　Put him to the strappado:° I have heard,
　　The rack° had cured the gout, faith, give it him,
　　And help° him of a malady, be courteous.
　　I'll undertake, before these honoured fathers,
　　He shall have, yet, as many left diseases,
　　As she has known adulterers, or thou strumpets.
　　O, my most equal° hearers, if these deeds,
　　Acts, of this bold, and most exorbitant° strain,
　　May pass with sufferance, what one citizen,
　　But owes the forfeit of his life, yea fame, 60
　　To him that dares traduce him°? which of you
　　Are safe, my honoured fathers? I would ask,
　　With leave of your grave fatherhoods, if their plot
　　Have any face, or colour like to truth?
　　Or if, unto the dullest nostril, here,
　　It smell not rank, and most abhorred slander?
　　I crave your care of this good gentleman,
　　Whose life is much endangered, by their fable°;

---

　　baited, enticed. *Without*, outside. *chameleon*, its colour changes made it a symbol of fraud and treachery; Lady Would-be alludes to the inconstant appearance of her quarry. *hyaena*, another symbol of treachery because it attracted its victims by its quasi-human cry (but not by its tears). *exorbitant*, beyond bounds, outrageous.

o'ercome, prevail, have the last word. *multitude*, numbers (not necessarily a crowd). *impotent*, totally disabled; Lady Would-be may kiss Volpone at this point, or when he is borne out. *affect venery*, enjoy sexual pleasure; or "affect" may = "effect." *proved*, put to the proof, tested. *strappado*, a form of torture; the victim is hoisted by a rope binding his wrists behind his back, then dropped with a jerk. *rack ... gout*, a common sentiment. *help*, relieve. *equal*, just. *exorbitant strain*, outrageous nature. *what ... traduce him*, "what single citizen would there be whose life, and indeed reputation, would not be forfeitable to any who had the impudence to slander him?" *fable*, falsehood, or plot.

And, as for them, I will conclude with this,

70   That vicious persons when they are hot, and
     fleshed°
     In impious acts, their constancy° abounds:
     Damned deeds are done with greatest confidence.

1st AVOCATORE: Take 'em to custody, and sever
     them.°

(CELIA and BONARIO taken out.)

2nd AVOCATORE: 'Tis pity, two such prodigies° should
     live.

1st AVOCATORE: Let the old gentleman be returned,
     with care:

80   I'm sorry, our credulity wronged him. *(VOLPONE
     borne off)*

4th AVOCATORE: These are two creatures!

3rd AVOCATORE: I have an earthquake in me!

2nd AVOCATORE: Their shame, even in their cradles,
     fled their faces.

4th AVOCATORE: You've done a worthy service to the
     state, sir,
     In their discovery.

1st AVOCATORE: You shall hear, ere night,
     What punishment the court decrees upon 'em.

90   VOLTORE: We thank your fatherhoods.

(Exeunt AVOCATORI, NOTARIO, OFFICERS.)

     How did you like it?

MOSCA: Rare.
     I'd ha'your tongue, sir, tipped with gold, for this;
     I'd ha'you be the heir to the whole city;
     The earth I'd have want men, ere you want living:°
     They're bound to erect your statue, in St. Mark's.
     Signior Corvino, I would have you go,
     And show yourself, that you have conquered.

CORVINO: Yes.

100 MOSCA: It was much better, that you should profess
     Yourself a cuckold, thus; than that the other°
     Should have been proved.

CORVINO: Nay, I considered that:
     Now, it is her fault—

MOSCA: Then, it had been yours.

CORVINO: True, I do doubt this advocate, still.

MOSCA: I'faith,
     You need not, I dare ease you of that care.

CORVINO: I trust thee, Mosca.

110 MOSCA: As your own soul, sir.

CORBACCIO: Mosca!

MOSCA: Now for your business, sir.

CORBACCIO: How? ha'you business?

MOSCA: Yes, yours, sir.

CORBACCIO: O, none else?

MOSCA: None else, not I.

CORBACCIO: Be careful then.

MOSCA: Rest you, with both your eyes,° sir.

CORBACCIO: Dispatch it—

MOSCA: Instantly.   120

CORBACCIO: And look, that all,
     Whatever, be put in,° jewels, plate, monies,
     Household stuff, bedding, curtains.

MOSCA: Curtain-rings, sir,
     Only, the advocate's fee must be deducted.

CORBACCIO: I'll pay him now: you'll be too prodigal.

MOSCA: Sir, I must tender it.°

CORBACCIO: Two chequeens is well?

MOSCA: No, six, sir.

CORBACCIO: 'Tis too much.   130

MOSCA: He talked a great while.
     You must consider that, sir.

CORBACCIO: Well, there's three—

MOSCA: I'll give it him.

CORBACCIO: Do so, and there's for thee. *(Exit
     CORBACCIO.)*

MOSCA: Bountiful bones°! What horrid strange
     offence
     Did he commit 'gainst nature, in his youth,
     Worthy his age°? you see, sir, how I work
     Unto your ends; take you no notice.°   140

VOLTORE: No,
     I'll leave you.

MOSCA: All is yours; *(Exit VOLTORE.)* the devil, and all:
     Good advocate.—Madame, I'll bring you home.

LADY WOULD-BE: No, I'll go see your patron.

MOSCA: That you shall not:
     I'll tell you, why. My purpose is to urge
     My patron to reform° his will; and, for
     The zeal you've shown today, whereas before
     You were but third, or fourth, you shall be now   150
     Put in the first: which would appear as begged,
     If you were present. Therefore—

LADY WOULD-BE: You shall sway° me. *(Exeunt MOSCA,
     LADY WOULD-BE.)*

ACT 5 / SCENE 1

(VOLPONE's house.)
(Enter VOLPONE°.)

VOLPONE: Well, I am here; and all this brunt° is past:
     I ne'er was in dislike with my disguise,
     Till this fled° moment; here, 'twas good, in private,

---

fleshed, inured. *constancy,* resolution. *sever them,*
keep them apart. *prodigies,* monsters, unnatural creatures.
want living, lack a livelihood. *the other,* i.e., the procura-
tion of his wife for Volpone.

Rest . . . eyes, "relax completely." *put in,* i.e., in the
inventory of the inheritance. *tender it,* give it him. *Bountiful bones!* apt to the meanness and leanness of Corbaccio.
Worthy . . . age, "deserving an old age like this." *take . . .
notice,* "ignore me"; perhaps Lady Would-be is watching.
reform, recast. *sway,* rule. *Enter Volpone,* Volpone may
be carried in, discovered on his litter, or be back in his bed.
brunt, shock, crisis. *fled,* past.

But, in your public—*Cavè*°, whilst I breathe. *(Gets up.)*
'Fore God, my left leg 'gan to have the cramp;
And I apprehended,° straight,° some power had struck me
With a dead palsy: well, I must be merry,
And shake it off. A many° of these fears
10   Would put me into some villainous disease,
Should they come thick upon me: I'll prevent 'em.
Give me a bowl of lusty wine, to fright
This humour from my heart. *(He drinks.)* Hum, hum, hum!
'Tis almost gone, already: I shall conquer.
Any device, now, of rare, ingenious knavery,
That would possess me with a violent laughter,
Would make me up, again! *(Drinks again.)* So, so, so, so.
20   This heat is life°; 'tis blood, by this time: Mosca!

ACT 5 / SCENE 2

(Enter MOSCA.*)*

MOSCA: How now, sir? does the day look clear again?
Are we recovered? and wrought° out of error,
Into our way? to see our path, before us?
Is our trade free, once more?
VOLPONE: Exquisite Mosca!
MOSCA: Was it not carried learnedly?
VOLPONE: And stoutly.
Good wits are greatest in extremities.
MOSCA: It were a folly, beyond thought, to trust
10   Any grand act unto a cowardly spirit:
You are not taken with it, enough,° methinks?
VOLPONE: O, more, than if I had enjoyed the wench:
The pleasure of all woman-kind's not like it.
MOSCA: Why, now you speak, sir. We must, here, be fixed;
Here, we must rest; this is our masterpiece:
We cannot think, to go beyond this.
VOLPONE: True.
Thou'st played thy prize, my precious Mosca.
20   MOSCA: Nay, sir,
To gull the court—
VOLPONE: And, quite divert the torrent
Upon the innocent.
MOSCA: Yes, and to make

So rare a music out of discords—
VOLPONE: Right,
That, yet, to me's the strangest°! how thou'st borne it!
That these, being so divided 'mongst themselves,
Should not scent somewhat, or in me, or° thee,   30
Or doubt their own side.
MOSCA: True, they will not see't.
Too much lights blinds 'em, I think. Each of 'em
Is so possessed,° and stuffed with his own hopes,
That anything, unto the contrary,
Never so true, or never so apparent,
Never so palpable, they will resist it—
VOLPONE: Like a temptation of the devil.
MOSCA: Right, sir.
Merchants may talk of trade, and your great   40
signiors
Of land, that yields well; but if Italy
Have any glebe,° more fruitful, than these fellows,
I am deceived. Did not your advocate rare?°
VOLPONE: O—'My most honoured fathers, my grave fathers,
Under correction of your fatherhoods.
What face of truth, is here? If these strange deeds
May pass, most honoured fathers'—I had much ado   50
To forbear laughing.
MOSCA: 'T seemed to me, you sweat,° sir.
VOLPONE: In troth, I did a little.
MOSCA: But confess, sir,
Were you not daunted?°
VOLPONE: In good faith, I was
A little in a mist; but not dejected:
Never, but still myself.
MOSCA: I think° it, sir.
Now, so truth help me, I must needs say this, sir,   60
And, out of conscience, for your advocate:
He's taken pains, in faith, sir, and deserved,
(In my poor judgement, I speak it, under favour,°
Not to contrary you, sir) very richly—
Well—to be cozened.°
VOLPONE: 'Troth, and I think so too,
By that I heard him, in the latter end.
MOSCA: O, but before, sir; had you heard him, first,
Draw it to certain heads,° then aggravate,°

Cavè (Latin), beware; Volpone may ask the audience to keep a look-out while he relaxes, or he may address the warning to himself. *apprehended*, felt. *straight*, immediately. *many*, used as a noun (compare "a great many"). *This heat is life*, Volpone identifies the response of his blood to wine with the processes by which the body's vital heat is generated. *wrought . . . way*, Mosca talks with mock piety. *You . . . enough*, Mosca may sense that Volpone is already thinking of the next device, towards which the dialogue now subtly moves.

strangest, most wonderful and ingenious; the word 'strange' is important in this act. *or . . . or*, either . . . or. *possessed*, the sense hovers between "possessing" and "possessed by"; another key word. *glebe*, earth, soil. *rare*, rarely. *sweat*, sweated; Mosca insists that Volpone was afraid. *daunted*, "dazed" or "abashed"; Volpone's reply meets both senses, he was a little confused (*in a mist*) but not downcast (*dejected*). *think*, believe. *under favour*, "with your permission"; Mosca now parodies Voltore. *cozened*, cheated. *heads*, chief points of a discourse (*OED*). *aggravate*, put weight upon, solemnly emphasize with *gravitas*.

70   Then use his vehement figures°—I looked still,
     When he would shift a shirt°; and, doing this
     Out of pure love, no hope of gain—
VOLPONE: 'Tis right.
     I cannot answer° him, Mosca, as I would,
     Not yet; but, for thy sake, at thy entreaty,
     I will begin, even now, to vex 'em all:
     This very instant.
MOSCA: Good, sir.
VOLPONE: Call the dwarf,
80   And eunuch, forth.
MOSCA: Castrone, Nano!

(Enter CASTRONE *and* NANO.*)*

NANO: Here.
VOLPONE: Shall we have a jig,° now?
MOSCA: What you please, sir.
VOLPONE: Go,
     Straight, give out, about the streets, you two,
     That I am dead; do it with constancy,°
     Sadly,° do you hear? impute it to the grief
     Of this late slander.

(Exeunt CASTRONE *and* NANO.*)*

90   MOSCA: What do you mean,° sir?
VOLPONE: O,
     I shall have, instantly, my vulture, crow,
     Raven, come flying hither, on the news,
     To peck for carrion, my she-wolf, and all,
     Greedy, and full of expectation—
MOSCA: And then to have it ravished from their
       mouths?
VOLPONE: 'Tis true, I will ha' thee put on a gown,
     And take upon thee,° as thou wert mine heir;
100   Show 'em a will: open that chest, and reach
     Forth one of those, that has° the blanks.° I'll
       straight
     Put in thy name.
MOSCA: It will be rare, sir.
VOLPONE: Ay,
     When they e'en° gape, and find themselves
       deluded—
MOSCA: Yes.
VOLPONE: And thou use them scurvily. Dispatch,
110   Get on thy gown.
MOSCA: But, what, sir, if they ask
     After the body?
VOLPONE: Say, it was corrupted.

MOSCA: I'll say it stunk, sir; and was fain° t'have it
     Coffined up instantly, and sent away.
VOLPONE: Anything, what thou wilt. Hold, here's my
     will.
     Get thee a cap, a count-book,° pen and ink,
     Papers afore thee; sit, as thou wert taking
     An inventory of parcels:° I'll get up,   120
     Behind the curtain, on a stool, and hearken;
     Sometime, peep over; see, how they do look;
     With what degrees, their blood doth leave their
       faces!
     O, 'twill afford me a rare meal of laughter.
MOSCA: Your advocate will turn stark dull,° upon it.
VOLPONE: It will take off his oratory's edge.
MOSCA: But your *clarissimo,*° old round-back, he
     Will crump you, like a hog-louse,° with the touch.
VOLPONE: And what Corvino?   130
MOSCA: O, sir, look for him,
     Tomorrow morning, with a rope, and a dagger,°
     To visit all the streets; he must run mad.
     My lady too, that came into the court,
     To bear false witness, for your worship—
VOLPONE: Yes,
     And kissed me 'fore the fathers; when my face
     Flowed all with oils—
MOSCA: And sweat, sir. Why, your gold
     Is such another medicine, it dries up   140
     All those offensive savours! It transforms
     The most deformed, and restores 'em lovely,
     As 'twere the strange poetical girdle.° Jove
     Could not invent, t' himself, a shroud more subtle,
     To pass Acrisius'° guards. It is the thing
     Makes all the world her grace, her youth, her
       beauty.
VOLPONE: I think, she loves me.
MOSCA: Who? the lady,° sir?
     She's jealous of you.   150
VOLPONE: Do'st thou say so? *(Knocking without.)*
MOSCA: Hark,
     There's some already.
VOLPONE: Look.
MOSCA: It is the vulture:
     He has the quickest scent.

---

vehement figures, may refer to figures of both speech and gesture. **shift a shirt,** change a shirt; a figure for Voltore's gesticulations. **answer,** repay. **a jig,** a jest, "some sport"; a burlesque "jig" sometimes followed serious drama in the Elizabethan theater, which may be the point here. **with constancy,** firmly, or perhaps "with straight faces." **Sadly,** gravely. **mean,** intend. **take upon thee,** assume the part. **has,** i.e., have. **blanks,** spaces for the legatee's names. **e'en,** just, doing nothing else but.

fain, i.e., "I was fain (obliged)." **count-book,** account book. **parcels,** lots, items. **dull,** insensible; but Volpone replies to the sense "blunt." **clarissimo,** a Venetian grandee. **crump . . . louse,** "curl up like a wood-louse." **rope . . . dagger,** stock properties of suicidal or homicidal madness induced by despair; compare Hieronimo's madness (once played by Jonson) in *The Spanish Tragedy* IV.iv. **poetical girdle,** the Folio adds the explanation 'Cestus' after 'Jove'; it was possibly meant as a correction to replace 'girdle'; Cestus, the girdle of Venus described by Homer, could transfigure ugliness and awaken passion even in old age. **Acrisius,** the father of Danae; he shut her in a tower of brass but Jove reached her in a shower of gold. **the lady,** presumably Lady Would-be, but some have supposed Celia.

VOLPONE: I'll to my place, *(conceals himself.)*
Thou, to thy posture.°
MOSCA: I am set.
160 VOLPONE: But, Mosca,
Play the artificer° now, torture 'em, rarely.

ACT 5 / SCENE 3

(Enter VOLTORE.*)*

VOLTORE: How now, my Mosca?
MOSCA: Turkey carpets,° nine—
VOLTORE: Taking an inventory? that is well.
MOSCA: Two suits of bedding, tissue°—
VOLTORE: Where's the will?
Let me read that, the while.

(Enter CORBACCIO *carried in a chair.)*

CORBACCIO: So, set me down:
And get you home. *(Exeunt* PORTERS.*)*
VOLTORE: Is he come, now, to trouble us?
10 MOSCA: Of cloth of gold, two more—
CORBACCIO: Is it done, Mosca?
MOSCA: Of several velvets,° eight—
VOLTORE: I like his care.
CORBACCIO: Dost thou not hear?

(Enter CORVINO.*)*

CORVINO: Ha! is the hour come, Mosca?

*(*VOLPONE *peeps from behind a traverse.)*

VOLPONE *(aside)*: Ay, now they muster.
CORVINO: What does the advocate here?
Or this Corbaccio?
CORBACCIO: What do these here?

(Enter LADY WOULD-BE.*)*

20 LADY WOULD-BE: Mosca!
Is his thread° spun?
MOSCA: Eight chests of linen—
VOLPONE *(aside)*: My fine dame Would-be, too!
CORVINO: Mosca, the will,
That I may show it these, and rid 'em hence.
MOSCA: Six chests of diaper,° four of damask—There.
(Gives them the will.)
CORBACCIO: Is that the will?
MOSCA: Down-beds, and bolsters—
VOLPONE *(aside)*: Rare!
30 Be busy still. Now, they begin to flutter:

---

posture, pose, act. *Play the artificer,* "do a craftsman's job," with pun on the sense "trickster." *Turkey carpets,* then used as table and wall drapery. *tissue,* cloth woven with gold or silver. *velvets,* velvet hangings (several = separate). *thread,* of the Three Fates: Clothos spun the thread of life, Lachesis measured it, and Atropos cut it; but the phrase was a popular pomposity. *diaper,* fabric with diamond-like pattern.

They never think of me. Look, see, see, see!
How their swift eyes run over the long deed,
Unto the name, and to the legacies,
What is bequeathed them, there—
MOSCA: Ten suits of hangings°—
VOLPONE *(aside)*: Ay, i'their garters,° Mosca. Now,
their hopes
Are at the gasp.°
VOLTORE: Mosca the heir!
CORBACCIO: What's that? 40
VOLPONE *(aside)*: My advocate is dumb, look to my
merchant,
He has heard of some strange storm, a ship is lost,
He faints: my lady will swoon. Old glazen-eyes,°
He hath not reached his despair, yet.
CORBACCIO: All these
Are out of hope, I am sure the man.
CORVINO: But, Mosca—
MOSCA: Two cabinets—
CORVINO: Is this in earnest? 50
MOSCA: One
Of ebony—
CORVINO: Or, do you but delude me?
MOSCA: The other, mother of pearl—I am very busy.
Good faith, it is a fortune thrown upon me—
Item, one salt° of agate—not my seeking.
LADY WOULD-BE: Do you hear, sir?
MOSCA: A perfumed box—'pray you forbear,
You see I am troubled°—made of an onyx—
LADY WOULD-BE: How! 60
MOSCA: Tomorrow, or next day, I shall be at leisure,
To talk with you all.
CORVINO: Is this my large hope's issue?
LADY WOULD-BE: Sir, I must have a fairer answer.
MOSCA: Madam!
Marry, and shall: pray you, fairly° quit my house.
Nay, raise no tempest with your looks; but, hark
you:
Remember, what your ladyship offered me,
To put you in, an heir; go to, think on't. 70
And what you said, e'en your best madams did
For maintenance, and why not you? enough.
Go home, and use the poor Sir Pol, your knight,
well;
For fear I tell some riddles°: go, be melancholic.
(Exit LADY WOULD-BE.*)*
VOLPONE *(aside)*: O, my fine devil!
CORVINO: Mosca, pray you a word.
MOSCA: Lord! will not you take your dispatch hence,
yet?

---

suits of hangings, sets for four-poster bed. *garters,* Volpone puns on the popular jibe "Hang yourself in your own garters." *gasp,* last gasp. *glazen-eyes,* Corbaccio wears spectacles. *salt,* salt-cellar. *troubled,* busy, being put to some trouble; or perhaps "vexed." *fairly,* probably "well and truly," completely. *riddles,* mysteries, secrets.

80   Methinks, of all, you should have been th'example.°
Why should you stay, here? with what thought?
   what promise?
Hear you, do not you know, I know you an ass?
And that you would, most fain, have been a wittol,°
If fortune would have let you? that you are
A declared cuckold, on good terms?° this pearl,
You'll say, was yours? right: this diamant?
I'll not deny't, but thank you. Much here, else?
It may be so. Why, think that these good works
90   May help to hide your bad: I'll not betray you,
Although you be but extraordinary,°
And have it only in title, if sufficeth.
Go home, be melancholic too, or mad. (*Exit*
   CORVINO.)
VOLPONE (*aside*): Rare, Mosca! how this villainy
   becomes him!
VOLTORE: Certain, he doth delude all these, for me.
CORBACCIO: Mosca, the heir?
VOLPONE (*aside*): O, his four eyes have found it!
CORBACCIO: I'm cozened, cheated, by a parasite slave;
100   Harlot° thou'st gulled me.
MOSCA: Yes, sir. Stop your mouth,
Or I shall draw the only tooth, is left.
Are not you he, that filty covetous wretch,
With the three legs,° that here, in hope of prey,
Have, any time this three year, snuffed about,
With your most grov'ling nose; and would have
   hired
Me to the poisoning of my patron? sir?
Are not you he, that have, today, in court,
110   Professed the disinheriting of your son?
Perjured yourself? Go home, and die, and stink;
If you but croak a syllable, all comes out:
Away and call your porters, go, go, stink. (*Exit*
   CORBACCIO.)
VOLPONE (*aside*): Excellent varlet!
VOLTORE: Now, my faithful Mosca,
I find thy constancy—
MOSCA: Sir?
VOLTORE: Sincere.
120   MOSCA: A table
Of porphyry—I mar'l,° you'll be thus troublesome.
VOLTORE: Nay, leave off now, they are gone.
MOSCA: Why, who are you?
What, who did send for you? O, cry your mercy,
Reverend sir! good faith, I am grieved for you,

That any chance° of mine should thus defeat
Your, I must needs say, most deserving travails:
But, I protest, sir, it was cast upon me,
And I could, almost, wish to be without it,
But that the will o'the dead, must be observed.   130
Marry, my joy is, that you need it not,
You have a gift, sir, thank your education,
Will never let you want,° while there are men,
And malice, to breed causes.° Would I had
But half the like, for all my fortune, sir.
If I have any suits (as I do hope,
Things being so easy, and direct, I shall not)
I will make bold with your obstreperous° aid,
Conceive me, for your fee,° sir. In meantime,
You, that have so much law, I know ha' the   140
   conscience,
Not to be covetous of what is mine.
Good sir, I thank you for my plate°: 'twill help
To set up a young man. Good faith, you look
As you were costive; best go home, and purge, sir.
   (*Exit* VOLTORE.)
VOLPONE (*coming out*): Bid him, eat lettuce° well: my
   witty mischief,
Let me embrace thee. O, that I could now
Transform thee to a Venus—Mosca, go,
Straight, take my habit of *clarissimo*;   150
And walk the streets; be seen, torment 'em more:
We must pursue, as well as plot. Who would
Have lost this feast?
MOSCA: I doubt it will lose them.°
VOLPONE: O, my recovery shall recover all.
That I could now but think on some disguise,
To meet 'em in: and ask 'em questions.
How I would vex 'em still, at every turn!
MOSCA: Sir, I can fit you.
VOLPONE: Canst thou?   160
MOSCA: Yes, I know
One of the *commendatori*,° sir, so like you,
Him will I straight make drunk, can bring you his
   habit.
VOLPONE: A rare disguise, and answering thy brain!
O, I will be a sharp disease unto 'em.
MOSCA: Sir, you must look for curses—
VOLPONE: Till they burst;
The Fox fares ever best, when he is cursed.°

---

example, i.e., in leading the way when "dispatched."
wittol, conniving cuckold. **on good terms,** i.e., outspokenly
so, fair and square. **extraordinary,** in title only (as Mosca
explains); used of offices held extra to the establishment.
Harlot, base-born fellow. **three legs,** i.e., with his stick; in
the riddle of the Sphinx, the child goes upon four legs, the
man on two, and the old man on three. **mar'l,** marvel.

chance, good fortune. **want,** be in need. **causes,**
law-suits. **obstreperous,** vociferous. **Conceive ... fee,** "I
shall expect to pay the usual fee, you understand." **plate,**
i.e., that presented by Voltore. **lettuce,** a recognized treatment for constipation, and for frenzy. **doubt ... them,**
possibly "I doubt if it will get rid of them," but Volpone's
reply interprets "I fear it will lose them to us as a source of
income." **commendatori,** a term for the court officers,
sergeants at law. **Fox ... cursed,** a proverb; the fox is only
cursed by the hunter when he gets away.

ACT 5 / SCENE 4

(SIR POLITIC WOULD-BE's *house*.)
(*Enter* PEREGRINE *disguised, and three* MERCHANTS.)

PEREGRINE: Am I enough disguised?
1st MERCHANT: I warrant° you.
PEREGRINE: All my ambition is to fright him, only.
2nd MERCHANT: If you could ship him away, 'twere
    excellent.
3rd MERCHANT: To Zant,° or to Aleppo?
PEREGRINE: Yes, and ha'his
    Adventures put i'the *Book of Voyages*,°
    And his gulled° story registered, for truth?
10 Well, gentlemen, when I am in, a while,
    And that you think us warm in our discourse,
    Know your approaches.°
1st MERCHANT: Trust it to our care. (*Exeunt*
    MERCHANTS.)

(*Enter* WAITING WOMAN.)

PEREGRINE: Save you, fair lady. Is Sir Pol within?
WOMAN: I do not know, sir.
PEREGRINE: Pray you, say unto him,
    Here is a merchant, upon earnest° business,
    Desires to speak with him.
WOMAN: I will see, sir.
20 PEREGRINE: Pray you. (*Exit* WOMAN.)
    I see, the family is all female, here.

(*Enter* WAITING WOMAN.)

WOMAN: He says, sir, he has weighty affairs of state,
    That now require him whole°—some other time
    You may possess him.°
PEREGRINE: Pray you, may again,
    If those require him whole, these will exact him,°
    Whereof I bring him tidings. (*Exit* WOMAN.) What
    might be
    His grave affair of state, now? how to make
30 Bolognian sausages, here, in Venice, sparing°
    One o' th'ingredients.

(*Enter* WAITING WOMAN.)

WOMAN: Sir, he says, he knows
    By your word, tidings,° that you are no statesman,
    And therefore, wills you stay.
PEREGRINE: Sweet, pray you return him,°

I have not read so many proclamations,
    And studied them, for words, as he has done;
    But—Here he deigns to come. (*Exit* WOMAN.)

(*Enter* SIR POLITIC WOULD-BE.)

SIR POLITIC: Sir, I must crave
    Your courteous pardon. There hath chanced,   40
    today,
    Unkind disaster, 'twixt my lady, and me:
    And I was penning my apology
    To give her satisfaction, as you came, now.
PEREGRINE: Sir, I am grieved, I bring you worse
    disaster;
    The gentleman, you met at the port, today,
    That told you, he was newly arrived—
SIR POLITIC: Ay, was
    A fugitive-punk?°   50
PEREGRINE: No, sir, a spy, set on you:
    And, he has made relation° to the Senate,
    That you professed to him, to have a plot,
    To sell the state of Venice, to the Turk.
SIR POLITIC: O me!
PEREGRINE: For which, warrants are signed by this
    time,
    To apprehend you, and to search your study,
    For papers—
SIR POLITIC: Alas, sir. I have none, but notes,   60
    Drawn out of play-books—
PEREGRINE: All the better, sir.
SIR POLITIC: And some essays.° What shall I do?
PEREGRINE: Sir, best
    Convey yourself into a sugar-chest,
    Or, if you could lie round,° a frail° were rare:
    And I could send you, aboard.
SIR POLITIC: Sir, I but talked so,
    For discourse sake, merely. (*They knock without.*)
PEREGRINE: Hark, they are there.   70
SIR POLITIC: I am a wretch, a wretch.
PEREGRINE: What will you do, sir?
    H'you ne'er a currant-butt to leap into?
    They'll put you to the rack, you must be sudden.°
SIR POLITIC: Sir, I have an engine°—
3rd MERCHANT (*off-stage*): Sir Politic Would-be?
2nd MERCHANT (*off-stage*): Where is he?
SIR POLITIC: That I have thought upon, before time.
PEREGRINE: What is it?
SIR POLITIC: —I shall ne'er endure the torture.—   80
    Marry, it is, sir, of a tortoise-shell,°
    Fitted,° for these extremities: 'pray you sir, help
    me.

---

warrant, assure. ***Zant***, Zante, one of the Ionian
islands, and a Venetian possession at the time. ***Book of
Voyages***, Hakluyt's *Principal Navigations* was published in its
enlarged form in 1598–1600, but there were other books of
voyages too. ***gulled story***, "the story of his gulling." ***Know
. . . approaches***, get ready to enter (perhaps nautical jargon).
earnest, weighty. ***require . . . whole***, require his whole
attention. ***possess him***, have his company. ***exact him***,
probably "force him out," extract him from his study (see
OED). ***sparing***, leaving out. ***tidings***, Sir Politic's word is
"intelligence." ***return him***, answer him.

---

punk, prostitute. ***made relation***, Peregrine now uses
state language. ***essays***, a literary form that Jonson despised. ***lie round***, curl up. ***frail***, rush basket for figs.
sudden, quick. ***engine***, device, contrivance. ***tortoise-shell***,
a feature of the Venetian market; the tortoise was a symbol
of polity. ***Fitted***, suited.

Here, I've a place, sir, to put back my legs,—
Please you to lay it on, sir—with this cap,
And my black gloves, I'll lie, sir, like a tortoise,
Till they are gone.
PEREGRINE: And, call you this an engine?
SIR POLITIC: Mine own device°—good sir, bid my
90   wife's women
To burn my papers.°

(MERCHANTS rush in.)

1st MERCHANT: Where's he hid?
3rd MERCHANT: We must,
And will, sure, find him.
2nd MERCHANT: Which is his study?
1st MERCHANT: What
Are you, sir?
PEREGRINE: I'm a merchant, that came here
To look upon this tortoise.
100 3rd MERCHANT: How?
1st MERCHANT: St. Mark!
What beast is this?
PEREGRINE: It is a fish.
2nd MERCHANT: Come out, here.
PEREGRINE: Nay, you may strike him, sir, and tread
upon him:
He'll bear a cart.
1st MERCHANT: What, to run over him?
PEREGRINE: Yes.
110 3rd MERCHANT: Let's jump upon him.
2nd MERCHANT: Can he not go?
PEREGRINE: He creeps, sir.
1st MERCHANT: Let's see him creep. *(Prods him.)*
PEREGRINE: No, good sir, you will hurt him.
2nd MERCHANT: Heart, I'll see him creep; or prick his
guts.
3rd MERCHANT: Come out, here.
PEREGRINE: Pray you sir. *(to SIR POLITIC)* Creep a
little!
120 1st MERCHANT: Forth!
2nd MERCHANT: Yet further.
PEREGRINE: Good sir! *(to SIR POLITIC)* Creep!
2nd MERCHANT: We'll see his legs.

(They pull off the shell and discover him.)

3rd MERCHANT: God's so—, he has garters!
1st MERCHANT: Ay, and gloves!
2nd MERCHANT: Is this
Your fearful tortoise?
PEREGRINE *(throwing off his disguise)*: Now, Sir Pol, we
are even;
130 For your next project, I shall be prepared:
I am sorry for the funeral of your notes, sir.

1st MERCHANT: 'Twere a rare motion,° to be seen in
Fleet Street!
2nd MERCHANT: Ay, i'the term.°
1st MERCHANT: Or Smithfield,° in the fair.
3rd MERCHANT: Methinks, 'tis but a melancholic
sight!
PEREGRINE: Farewell, most politic tortoise. *(Exeunt
PEREGRINE, MERCHANTS.)*

(Enter WAITING WOMAN.)

SIR POLITIC: Where's my lady?   140
Knows she of this?
WOMAN: I know not, sir.
SIR POLITIC: Enquire. *(Exit WOMAN.)*
O, I shall be the fable of all feasts;
The freight of the *gazetti*;° ship-boys' tale;
And, which is more, even talk for ordinaries.°

(Enter WAITING WOMAN.)

WOMAN: My lady's come most melancholic, home,
She says, sir, she will straight to sea, for physic.°
SIR POLITIC: And I, to shun, this place, and clime for
ever;   150
Creeping, with house, on back: and think it well,
To shrink my poor head, in my politic shell.

ACT 5 / SCENE 5

(VOLPONE's house.)
*(Enter VOLPONE, MOSCA; the first, in the habit° of a
Commendatore: the other, of a Clarissimo.)*

VOLPONE: Am I then like him?
MOSCA: O, sir, you are he:
No man can sever° you.
VOLPONE: Good.
MOSCA: But, what am I?
VOLPONE: 'Fore heaven, a brave *clarissimo*, thou
becom'st it!
Pity, thou wert not born one.
MOSCA: If I hold°
My made one, 'twill be well.   10
VOLPONE: I'll go, and see
What news, first, at the court. *(Exit VOLPONE.)*
MOSCA: Do so. My Fox

---

device, invention (of own devising). **burn my papers,** Peregrine must tell the woman to do this as the merchants rush in and look around.

motion, puppet-show. **term,** the law term, when the lawyers of the Inns of Court were in residence and their clients in town. **Smithfield,** site of Bartholomew Fair; Jonson's *Bartholomew Fair* features a puppet-show. **freight ... gazetti,** i.e., carried by the news-sheets. **ordinary,** tavern. **physic,** medical treatment, recuperation. **habit,** Gifford describes the dress as "a black stuff gown and a red cap with two gilt buttons in front." **sever,** separate, distinguish. **hold,** either "keep up" or "remain in" the assumed role; Mosca equivocates between modesty and guile.

Is out on his hole,° and, ere he shall re-enter,
I'll make him languish in his borrowed case,°
Except° he come to composition,° with me:
Androgyno, Castrone, Nano!

(Enter ANDROGYNO, CASTRONE, NANO.*)*

ALL: Here.
MOSCA: Go recreate° yourselves, abroad;° go, sport.
    (Exeunt the three.)
20 So, now I have the keys, and am possessed.°
    Since he will, needs, be dead, afore his time,
    I'll bury him, or gain by him. I'm his heir:
    And so will keep me,° till he share at least.
    To cozen him of all, were but a cheat
    Well placed; no man would construe it a sin:
    Let his sport pay for't,° this is called the Fox-trap.

(Exit MOSCA.*)*

ACT 5 / SCENE 6

(A Street.)
(Enter CORBACCIO *and* CORVINO.*)*

CORBACCIO: They say, the court is set.
CORVINO: We must maintain
    Our first tale good, for both our reputations.
CORBACCIO: Why? mine's no tale: my son would,
    there, have killed me.
CORVINO: That's true, I had forgot: mine is, I am
    sure.
    But, for your will, sir.
CORBACCIO: Ay, I'll come upon° him,
10   For that, hereafter, now his patron's dead.

(Enter VOLPONE *disguised.)*

VOLPONE: Signior Corvino! and Corbaccio! sir,
    Much joy unto you.
CORVINO: Of what?
VOLPONE: The sudden good,
    Dropped down upon you—
CORBACCIO: Where?
VOLPONE: And none knows how—
    From old Volpone, sir.
CORBACCIO: Out, errant° knave.
20 VOLPONE: Let not your too much wealth, sir, make
    you furious.
CORBACCIO: Away, thou varlet.
VOLPONE: Why sir?

CORBACCIO: Dost thou mock me?
VOLPONE: You mock the world,° sir, did you not
    change° wills?
CORBACCIO: Out, harlot.
VOLPONE: O! belike you are the man,
    Signior Corvino? Faith, you carry it well;
    You grow not mad withal: I love your spirit.   30
    You are not over-leavened,° with your fortune.
    You should ha'some would swell,° now, like a
    wine-fat,°
    With such an autumn°—Did he gi' you all, sir?
CORVINO: Avoid,° you rascal.
VOLPONE: Troth, your wife has shown
    Herself a very woman°: but, you are well,
    You need not care, you have a good estate,
    To bear it out,° sir: better by this chance.
    Except Corbaccio have a share?   40
CORBACCIO: Hence, varlet.
VOLPONE: You will not be aknown,° sir: why, 'tis wise.
    Thus do all gamesters, at all games, dissemble.
    No man will seem to win. *(Exeunt* CORBACCIO,
    CORVINO*)*
    Here, comes my vulture,
    Heaving his beak up i'the air, and snuffing.

ACT 5 / SCENE 7

(Enter VOLTORE *to* VOLPONE.*)*

VOLTORE: Outstripped thus, by a parasite? a slave?
    Would run on errands? and make legs,° for
    crumbs?
    Well, what I'll do—
VOLPONE: The court stays° for your worship.
    I e'en rejoice, sir, at your worship's happiness,
    And that it fell into so learned hands,
    That understand the fingering.—
VOLTORE: What do you mean?
VOLPONE: I mean to be a suitor to your worship,   10
    For the small tenement,° out of reparations°;
    That, at the end of your long row of houses,
    By the Piscaria°: it was, in Volpone's time,
    Your predecessor, ere he grew diseased,
    A handsome, pretty, customed,° bawdy-house,
    As any was in Venice (none dispraised)
    But fell with him; his body, and that house
    Decayed, together.
VOLTORE: Come, sir, leave your prating.

Fox . . . hole, alluding to the boys' game, Fox-in-the-Hole; players hop, and strike each other with gloves and light thongs. *case,* disguise. *Except,* unless. *composition,* agreement, compromise. *recreate,* refresh, amuse. *abroad,* outside. *possessed,* in possession (but the word has its other potentials). *keep me,* remain. *let . . . for't,* "Let his amusement compensate his loss," but "sport" is also apt for the hunting and hunted fox. *come upon,* "make a demand or claim upon" (*OED*). *errant* = arrant.

mock the world, "are laughing at everyone." *change,* exchange. *over-leavened,* puffed up (as with too much yeast). *You . . . swell,* "You'd have some swelling . . ." *wine-fat,* wine-vat. *autumn,* i.e., harvest. *avoid,* be gone! *a very woman,* a woman indeed. *bear it out,* carry it off. *aknown,* acknowledged (to be the heir). *make legs,* bow and scrape. *stays,* waits. *tenement,* house. *reparations,* repair(s). *Piscaria,* fish-market. *customed,* well patronized.

20 VOLPONE: Why, if your worship gave me but your
      hand,
   That I may ha'the refusal;° I have done.
   'Tis a mere toy to you, sir; candle-rents:°
   As your learn'd worship knows—
VOLTORE: What do I know?
VOLPONE: Marry, no end of your wealth, sir, God
      decrease° it!
VOLTORE: Mistaking knave! what, mock'st thou my
      misfortune?
30 VOLPONE: His blessing on your heart, sir, would
      'twere more.

(Exit VOLTORE.*)*

—Now, to my first, again; at the next corner.
(Watches, apart.)

ACT 5 / SCENE 8

(Enter CORBACCIO, CORVINO, [MOSCA *passant°].)*

CORBACCIO: See, in our habit! see the impudent
      varlet!
CORVINO: That I could shoot mine eyes at him, like
      gun-stones°!
VOLPONE: But, is this true, sir, of the parasite?
CORBACCIO: Again, t'afflict us? monster!
VOLPONE: In good faith, sir,
   I'm heartily grieved, a beard of your grave length°
   Should be so over-reached, I never brooked
20   That parasite's hair, methought his nose should
      cozen:
   There still was somewhat, in his look, did promise
   The bane° of a *clarissimo.*
CORBACCIO: Knave—
VOLPONE: Methinks,
   Yet you, that are so traded° i'the world,
   A witty merchant, the fine bird, Corvino,
   That have such moral emblems° on your name,
   Should not have sung your shame; and dropped
30   your cheese:
   To let the Fox laugh at your emptiness.°
CORVINO: Sirrah, you think, the privilege of the
      place,°
   And your red saucy cap, that seems, to me,

Nailed to your jolt-head,° with those two
      chequeens,°
Can warrant° your abuses; come you, hither:
You shall perceive, sir, I dare beat you. Approach.
VOLPONE: No haste, sir, I do know your valour, well:
   Since you durst publish what you are, sir.   40
CORVINO: Tarry,
   I'd speak, with you.
VOLPONE: Sir, sir, another time—
CORVINO: Nay, now.
VOLPONE: O God, sir! I were a wise man,
   Would stand° the fury of a distracted cuckold.

*(*MOSCA *walks by 'em.)*

CORBACCIO: What! come again?
VOLPONE: Upon 'em, Mosca; save me!
CORBACCIO: The air's infected, where he breathes.
CORVINO: Let's fly him.   50
VOLPONE: Excellent basilisk!° turn upon the vulture.

ACT 5 / SCENE 9

(Enter VOLTORE.*)*

VOLTORE: Well, flesh-fly,° it is summer with you, now;
   Your winter will come on.
MOSCA: Good advocate,
   Pray thee, not rail, nor threaten out of place, thus;
   Thou'lt make a solecism, as madam says.
   Get you a biggin° more: your brain breaks loose.
VOLTORE: Well, sir.
VOLPONE: Would you ha' me beat the insolent slave?
   Throw dirt, upon his first good clothes?
VOLTORE: This same
   Is, doubtless, some familiar!°   10
VOLPONE: Sir, the court
   In troth, stays for you. I am mad,° a mule,°

---

    refusal, i.e., "first refusal."   **candle-rents,** rents from deteriorating property (self-consuming, like candles). **decrease,** a calculated Dogberryism for 'increase'; hence the double force of Voltore's response "Mistaking knave." *MOSCA passant,* i.e., crosses the stage in his role of *clarissimo.* **gun-stones,** stone cannon-shot. **beard . . . length,** "one so old and wise," but probably literal too. **bane,** ruin, destruction. **traded,** experienced. **moral emblems,** Corvino's name recalls the crow that dropped its cheese to sing to the fox. **emptiness,** i.e., of belly and of head. **place,** station, rank (as a commendatore).

    jolt-head, block-head.   **chequeens,** i.e., the coin-like buttons of his hat. **warrant,** sanction, protect by official authority. **stand,** withstand. **basilisk,** or cockatrice, a fabulous reptile hatched by a serpent from a cock's egg and capable of killing by its glance. **flesh-fly,** a blow-fly, the meaning of "Mosca." **biggin,** lawyer's cap or coif. **familiar,** i.e., "some fellow of the same household." **mad,** furiotones, stone cannon-shot. **beard . . . length,** "one so old and wise," but probably literal too. **bane,** ruin, destruction. **traded,** experienced. **moral emblems,** Corvino's name recalls the crow that dropped its cheese to sing to the fox. **emptiness,** i.e., of belly and of head. **place,** station, rank (as a commendatore). **jolthead,** block-head. **chequeens,** i.e., the coin-like buttons of his hat. **warrant,** sanction, protect by official authority. **stand,** withstand. **basilisk,** or cockatrice, a fabulous reptile hatched by a serpent from a cock's egg and capable of killing by its glance. **flesh-fly,** a blow-fly, the meaning of "Mosca." **biggin,** lawyer's cap or coif. **familiar,** i.e., "some fellow of the same household." **mad,** furious (that). **mule,** mules were customarily ridden by lawyers.

That never read Justinian,° should get up,
And ride an advocate. Had you no quirk,°
To avoid gullage,° sir, by such a creature?
I hope you do but jest; he has not done't:
This's but confederacy,° to blind the rest.
You are the heir?
20 VOLTORE: A strange, officious,
    Troublesome knave! thou dost torment me.
VOLPONE: I know—
    It cannot be, sir, that you should be cozened;
    'Tis not within the wit of man, to do it:
    You are so wise, so prudent—and, 'tis fit,
    That wealth, and wisdom still, should go together.

ACT 5 / SCENE 10

(The Scrutineo.)
(Enter Four AVOCATORI, NOTARIO, COMMENDATORI,
BONARIO, CELIA, CORBACCIO, CORVINO.)

1st AVOCATORE: Are all the parties, here?
NOTARIO: All, but the advocate.
2nd AVOCATORE: And, here he comes.

(Enter VOLTORE, with VOLPONE disguised.)

1st AVOCATORE: Then bring 'em forth to sentence.
VOLTORE: O, my most honoured fathers, let your
        mercy
    Once win upon° your justice, to forgive—
    I am distracted—
VOLPONE *(aside)*: What will he do, now?
10 VOLTORE: O,
    I know not which t'address myself to, first,
    Whether your fatherhoods, or these innocents—
CORVINO *(aside)*: Will he betray himself?
VOLTORE: Whom, equally,
    I have abused, out of most covetous ends°—
CORVINO *(to CORBACCIO)*: The man is mad!
CORBACCIO: What's that?
CORVINO: He is possessed.°
VOLTORE: For which, now struck in conscience, here I
20   prostrate
    Myself, at your offended feet, for pardon.
1st and 2nd AVOCATORI: Arise!
CELIA: O heaven, how just thou art?
VOLPONE *(aside)*: I'm caught
    I'mine own noose—
CORVINO *(to CORBACCIO)*: Be constant,° sir, nought
        now
    Can help, but impudence.°

1st AVOCATORE: Speak forward.
COMMENDATORE: Silence!   30
VOLTORE: It is not passion° in me, reverend fathers,
    But only conscience, my good sires,
    That makes me, now, tell truth. That parasite,
    That knave hath been the instrument of all.
2nd AVOCATORE: Where is that knave? fetch him!
VOLPONE: I go. *(Exit VOLPONE.)*
CORVINO: Grave fathers,
    This man's distracted; he confessed it, now:°
    For, hoping to be old Volpone's heir,
    Who now is dead—   40
3rd AVOCATORE: How?
2nd AVOCATORE: Is Volpone dead?
CORVINO: Dead since, grave fathers—
BONARIO: O, sure vengeance!
1st AVOCATORE: Stay,
    Then, he was no deceiver?
VOLTORE: O no, none:
    The parasite, grave fathers—
CORVINO: He does speak,
    Out of mere envy, 'cause the servant's made°   50
    The thing, he gaped for°; please your fatherhoods,
    This is the truth: though, I'll not justify
    The other, but he may° be some-deal° faulty.
VOLTORE: Ay, to your hopes, as well as mine,
        Corvino:
    But I'll use modesty.° Pleaseth your wisdoms
    To view these certain notes, and but confer° them;

(Gives them papers.)

    As I hope favour, they shall speak clear truth.
CORVINO: The devil has entered him!
BONARIO: Or bides in you.   60
4th AVOCATORE: We have done ill, by a public officer°
    To send for him, if he be heir.
2nd AVOCATORE: For whom?
4th AVOCATORE: Him, that they call the parasite.
3rd AVOCATURE: 'Tis true;
    He is a man, of great estate, now left.
4th AVOCATORE: Go you, and learn his name, and say,
        the court
    Entreats his presence, here; but, to the clearing
    Of some few doubts. *(Exit NOTARIO.)*   70
2nd AVOCATORE: This same's a labyrinth!
1st AVOCATORE: Stand you unto your first report?
CORVINO: My state,°
    My life, my fame—
BONARIO *(aside)*: Where is it?

Justinian, i.e., the *Corpus Jurus Civilis*, the Roman code of law compiled under the direction of Justinian I. *quirk*, trick. *gullage*, being gulled. *confederacy*, i.e., between Mosca and Voltore. *win upon*, overcome. *ends*, purposes, motives. *possessed*, i.e., of a devil. *constant*, firm, consistent. *impudence*, unblushing effrontery.

passion, frenzy. *now*, just now. *made*, achieved, grabbed. *gaped for*, hungered after. *but he may*, "he may yet." *some-deal*, somewhere. *modesty*, moderation. *certain*, "particular" or perhaps "reliable." *confer*, either "compare" or "consult together about." *public officer*, describing the status of Volpone as commendatore. *state*, estate.

CORVINO: Are at the stake.°
1st AVOCATORE: Is yours so too?
CORBACCIO: The advocate's a knave:
    And has a forked tongue—
80 2nd AVOCATORE: Speak to the point.
CORBACCIO: So is the parasite, too.
1st AVOCATORE: This is confusion.
VOLTORE: I do beseech your fatherhoods, read but
    those.
CORVINO: And credit nothing, the false spirit hath
    writ:
    It cannot be, but he is possessed, grave fathers.

ACT 5 / SCENE 11

(A Street.)
(Enter VOLPONE.)

VOLPONE: To make a snare, for mine own neck! and
    run
    My head into it, wilfully! with laughter!
    When I had newly scaped, was free, and clear!
    Out of mere wantonness! O, the dull devil°
    Was in this brain of mine, when I devised it;
    And Mosca gave it second;° he must now
    Help to sear° up this vein, or we bleed dead.

(Enter NANO, ANDROGYNO, CASTRONE.)

    How now! who let you loose? whither go you, now?
10   What? to buy ginger-bread? or to drown kitlings?°
NANO: Sir, master Mosca called us out of doors.
    And bid us all go play, and took the keys.
ANDROGYNO: Yes.
VOLPONE: Did master Mosca take the keys? why, so!
    I am farther in. These are my fine conceits!°
    I must be merry, with a mischief to me!°
    What a vile wretch was I, that could not bear
    My fortune° soberly? I must ha' my crotchets!°
    And my conundrums!° well, go you, and seek him:
20   His meaning may be truer, than my fear.
    Bid him, he straight come to me, to the court;
    Thither will I, and, if't be possible,
    Unscrew° my advocate, upon° new hopes:
    When I provoked him, then I lost myself.

Are . . . stake, "are all staked on the truth of what I have
said." *dull devil,* "devil of stupidity." *gave it second,*
seconded it. *sear,* cauterise, stem blood with hot iron. *buy
. . . kitlings,* presumably the pastimes of self-indulgent and
malicious children. *conceits,* notions, schemes. *with . . .
to me,* either reflective, "with this mischievous result," or
imprecatory, "a mischief take me!" *fortune,* i.e., good
fortune in surviving the court action, or perhaps "wealth."
crotchets, whimsical fancies, perverse conceits (*OED*). *conundrums,* whims, crochets. *Unscrew,* i.e., "dislodge him
from his present course"; or perhaps "unwind him" as if he
were a loaded cross-bow. *upon,* used to indicate manner—
"in" or "by."

ACT 5 / SCENE 12

(The Scrutineo.)
*(Four AVOCATORI, NOTARIO, VOLTORE, BONARIO,
CELIA, CORBACCIO, CORVINO, COMMENDATORI.)*

1st AVOCATORE *(with VOLTORE's notes)*: These things
    can ne'er be reconciled. He, here,
    Professeth, that the gentleman was wronged;
    And that the gentlewoman was brought thither,
    Forced by her husband: and there left.
VOLTORE: Most true.
CELIA: How ready is heaven to those, that pray!
1st AVOCATORE: But, that
    Volpone would have ravished her, he holds
    Utterly false; knowing his impotence.   10
CORVINO: Grave fathers, he is possessed; again, I say,
    Possessed: nay, if there be possession,
    And obsession,° he has both.
3rd AVOCATORE: Here comes our officer.

(Enter VOLPONE, disguised.)

VOLPONE: The parasite will straight be here, grave
    fathers.
4th AVOCATORE: You might invent° some other name,
    sir varlet.°
3rd AVOCATORE: Did not the notary meet him?
VOLPONE: Not that I know.   20
4th AVOCATORE: His coming will clear all.
2nd AVOCATORE: Yet it is misty.
VOLTORE: May't please your fatherhoods—

(VOLPONE whispers to the Advocate.)

VOLPONE: Sir, the parasite
    Willed me to tell you, that his master lives;
    That you are still the man; your hopes, the same;
    And this was, only a jest—
VOLTORE: How?
VOLPONE: Sir, to try
    If you were firm, and how you stood affected.°   30
VOLTORE: Art sure he lives?
VOLPONE: Do I live, sir?°
VOLTORE: O me!
    I was too violent.
VOLPONE: Sir, you may redeem it—
    They said, you were possessed; fall down, and seem
    so:
    I'll help to make it good. *(VOLTORE falls.)*
    God bless the man!

---

obsession, "actuation by the devil or an evil spirit from
without" (*OED*). *invent,* find. *varlet,* menial or knave
(here used to slight the commendatore). *how . . . affected,*
"which way you were inclined," "how you would feel and
act." *Do . . . sir?* Volpone evidently discloses his identity to
Voltore, perhaps by showing his red hair, or a signet ring.

40   (aside) Stop your wind hard,° and swell—See, see,
          see, see!
      He vomits crooked pins! his eyes are set,
      Like a dead hare's, hung in a poulter's° shop!
      His mouth's running away!° do you see, signior?
      Now, 'tis in his belly.
CORVINO: Ay, the devil!
VOLPONE: Now, in his throat.
CORVINO: Ay, I perceive it plain.
VOLPONE: 'Twill out, 'twill out; stand clear. See,
50   where it flies!
      In shape of a blue toad, with a bat's wings!
      Do not you see it, sir?
CORBACCIO: What? I think I do.
CORVINO: 'Tis too manifest.
VOLPONE: Look! he comes t'himself!
VOLTORE: Where am I?
VOLPONE: Take good heart, the worst is past, sir.
      You are dispossessed.
1st AVOCATORE: What accident is this?
60 2nd AVOCATORE: Sudden, and full of wonder!
3rd AVOCATORE: If he were
      Possessed, as it appears, all this is nothing.
CORVINO: He has been, often, subject to these fits.
1st AVOCATORE: Show him that writing, do you know
      it, sir?
VOLPONE (aside to VOLTORE): Deny it, sir, forswear it,
      know it not.
VOLTORE: Yes, I do know it well, it is my hand:°
      But all, that it contains, is false.
70 BONARIO: O practice!
2nd AVOCATORE: What maze is this!
1st AVOCATORE: Is he not guilty, then,
      Whom you, there, name the parasite?
VOLTORE: Grave fathers,
      No more than, his good patron, old Volpone.
4th AVOCATORE: Why, he is dead?
VOLTORE: O no, my honoured fathers.
      He lives—
1st AVOCATORE: How! lives?
80 VOLTORE: Lives.
2nd AVOCATORE: This is subtler° yet!
3rd AVOCATORE: You said he was dead!
VOLTORE: Never.
3rd AVOCATORE (to CORVINO): You said so!
CORVINO: I heard so.
4th AVOCATORE: Here comes the gentleman, make
      him way.

      (Enter MOSCA as clarissimo.)

3rd AVOCATORE: A stool!

4th AVOCATORE (aside): A proper° man! and were
      Volpone dead,   90
      A fit match for my daughter.
3rd AVOCATORE: Give him way.
VOLPONE (aside to MOSCA): Mosca, I was almost lost,
      the advocate
      Had betrayed all; but, now, it is recovered:°
      All's o'the hinge° again—say, I am living.
MOSCA: What busy° knave is this! most reverend
      fathers,
      I sooner, had attended your grave pleasures,
      But that my order, for the funeral   100
      Of my dear patron did require me—
VOLPONE (aside): Mosca!
MOSCA: Whom I intend to bury, like a gentleman.
VOLPONE (aside): Aye, quick,° and cozen me of all.
2nd AVOCATORE: Still stranger!
      More intricate!
1st AVOCATORE: And come about° again!
4th AVOCATORE (aside): It is a match, my daughter is
      bestowed.
MOSCA (aside to VOLPONE): Will you give me half?   110
VOLPONE (aside to MOSCA): First, I'll be hanged.
MOSCA (aside to VOLPONE): I know,
      Your voice is good, cry° not so loud.
1st AVOCATORE: Demand°
      The advocate. Sir, did you not affirm,
      Volpone was alive?
VOLPONE: Yes, and he is;
      This gent'man told me so. (aside to MOSCA) Thou
      shalt have half.
MOSCA: Whose drunkard is this same? speak some   120
      that know him:
      I never saw his face. (aside to VOLPONE) I cannot now
      Afford it you so cheap.
VOLPONE (aside to MOSCA): No?
1st AVOCATORE: What say you?
VOLTORE: The officer told me.
VOLPONE: I did, grave fathers,
      And will maintain, he lives, with mine own life.
      And, that this creature told me. (Aside) I was born
      With all good° stars my enemies.   130
MOSCA: Most grave fathers,
      If such an insolence, as this, must pass°
      Upon me, I am silent; 'twas not this,
      For which you sent, I hope.
2nd AVOCATORE: Take him away.
VOLPONE (aside): Mosca!
3rd AVOCATORE: Let him be whipped,—

Stop your wind, hold your breath. **poulter's,** poulter-
ers. **running away,** twisting from one side to the other.
hand, handwriting. **subtler,** more elusive and bewildering.

proper, handsome. **recovered,** got back again; covered
up again. **o' the hinge,** running smoothly, no longer
unhinged (o' = on). **busy,** officious. **quick,** alive. **come
about,** turned round, reversed. **cry,** shout. **Demand,** ask.
good, propitious. **pass,** be allowed.

VOLPONE (*aside*): Wilt thou betray me?
    Cozen me?
140 3rd AVOCATORE: And taught to bear himself
    Toward a person of his rank.
4th AVOCATORE: Away. (VOLPONE *is seized.*)
MOSCA: I humbly thank your fatherhoods.
VOLPONE (*aside*): Soft, soft: whipped?
    And lose all that I have? if I confess.
    It cannot be much more.
4th AVOCATORE (*to* MOSCA): Sir, are you married?
VOLPONE: They'll be allied,° anon;° I must be
    resolute:

(*He puts off his disguise.*)

150   The Fox shall, here, uncase.°
MOSCA: Patron!
VOLPONE: Nay, now,
    My ruins shall not come alone; your match
    I'll hinder sure: my substance shall not glue° you,
    Nor screw° you, into a family.
MOSCA: Why, patron!
VOLPONE: I am Volpone, and this is my knave;°
    This, his own knave; this, avarice's fool;°
    This, a chimera° of wittol,° fool, and knave;
160   And, reverend fathers, since we all can hope
    Nought, but a sentence, let's not now despair it.°
    You hear me brief.
CORVINO: May it please your fatherhoods—
COMMENDATORE: Silence!
1st AVOCATORE: The knot is now undone, by miracle!
2nd AVOCATORE: Nothing can be more clear.
3rd AVOCATORE: Or can more prove
    These innocent.
1st AVOCATORE: Give 'em their liberty.
170 BONARIO: Heaven could not, long, let such gross
    crimes be hid.
2nd AVOCATORE: If this be held the highway to get
    riches,
    May I be poor.
3rd AVOCATORE: This's° not the gain, but torment.
1st AVOCATORE: These possess wealth, as sick men
    possess fevers,
    Which, trulier, may be said to possess them.
2nd AVOCATORE: Disrobe that parasite.
180 CORVINO, MOSCA: Most honoured fathers—
1st AVOCATORE: Can you plead ought to stay the
    course of justice?

    If you can, speak.
CORVINO, VOLTORE: We beg favour.
CELIA: And mercy.
1st AVOCATORE: You hurt your innocence, suing for
    the guilty.
    Stand forth; and first, the parasite. You appear
    T'have been the chiefest minister,° if not plotter,
    In all these lewd° impostures; and now, lastly,   190
    Have, with your impudence, abused the court,
    And habit of a gentleman of Venice,
    Being a fellow of no birth, or blood:
    For which, our sentence is, first thou be whipped;
    Then live perpetual prisoner in our gallies.
VOLPONE: I thank you, for him.
MOSCA: Bane° to thy woolvish nature.
1st AVOCATORE: Deliver him to the Saffi.° (MOSCA *is
    led off.*) Thou, Volpone,
    By blood, and rank a gentleman, canst not fall   200
    Under like censure; but our judgement on thee
    Is, that thy substance all be straight confiscate
    To the hospital, of the *Incurabili*:°
    And, since the most was gotten by imposture,
    By feigning lame, gout, palsy, and such diseases,
    Thou art to lie in prison, cramped with irons,
    Till thou be'st sick, and lame indeed. Remove him.
VOLPONE: This is called mortifying° of a fox.
    (VOLPONE *is led off.*)
1st AVOCATORE: Thou, Voltore, to take away the
    scandal   210
    Thou hast given all worthy men, of thy profession,
    Art banished from their fellowship, and our state.
    Corbaccio!—bring him near. We here possess
    Thy son, of all thy state; and confine thee
    To the monastery of *San Spirito*:°
    Where, since thou knew'st not how to live well here,
    Thou shalt be learn'd to die well.
CORBACCIO: Ha! what said he?
COMMENDATORE: You shall know anon, sir.
1st AVOCATORE: Thou, Corvino, shalt   220
    Be straight embarked from thine own house, and
    rowed
    Round about Venice, through the Grand Canal,
    Wearing a cap, with fair, long ass's ears,
    Instead of horns: and, so to mount, a paper
    Pinned on thy breast, to the berlino°—
CORVINO: Yes,

---

allied, i.e., by a marriage bargain. *anon*, in a moment.
uncase, remove disguise, perhaps with a suggestion of the
fox breaking cover. *Patron!* Mosca is apparently startled
back into his servile role. *glue*, suggests a parasitic attachment. *screw*, suggests a tortuous one. *knave*, menial;
rogue. *fool*, dupe. *chimera*, mythical beast with a lion-
head, goat-body and serpent-tail; hence a triple monster.
wittol, conniving cuckold. *let's . . . it*, "let us not despair for
want of a sentence." *This's*, i.e., riches.

minister, agent, instrument. *lewd*, wicked, base.
Bane, death. *Saffi*, bailiffs. *Incurabili*, the Hospital of
Incurables was founded in Venice in 1522 for the treatment
of venereal disease; the punishment is therefore particularly
appropriate. *mortifying*, several senses are relevant:
humiliating; rendering dead to the world and the flesh by
spiritual discipline; hanging game to make it tender. *San
Spirito*, the monastery of the Holy Spirit stood on the
Giudecca canal. *berlino*, pillory.

And, have mine eyes beat out with stinking fish,
Bruised fruit, and rotten eggs—'Tis well. I'm glad,
230 I shall not see my shame, yet.

1st AVOCATORE: And to expiate
Thy wrongs done to thy wife, thou art to send her
Home, to her father, with her dowry trebled:
And these are all your judgements—

ALL: Honoured fathers.

1st AVOCATORE: Which may not be revoked. Now,
    you begin,
When crimes are done, and past, and to be
    punished,
240 To think what your crimes are: away with them!
Let all, that see these vices thus rewarded,
Take heart, and love to study 'em. Mischiefs feed

Like beasts, till they be fat, and then they bleed.
    (Exeunt.)

(To speak the Epilogue.)

VOLPONE: The seasoning of a play is the applause.
Now, though the Fox be punished by the laws,
He, yet, doth hope there is no suffering due,
For any fact,° which he hath done 'gainst you;
If there be, censure him: here he, doubtful, stands.
If not, fare jovially, and clap your hands.

THE END

---

fact, crime (as in the legal phrase "after the fact").

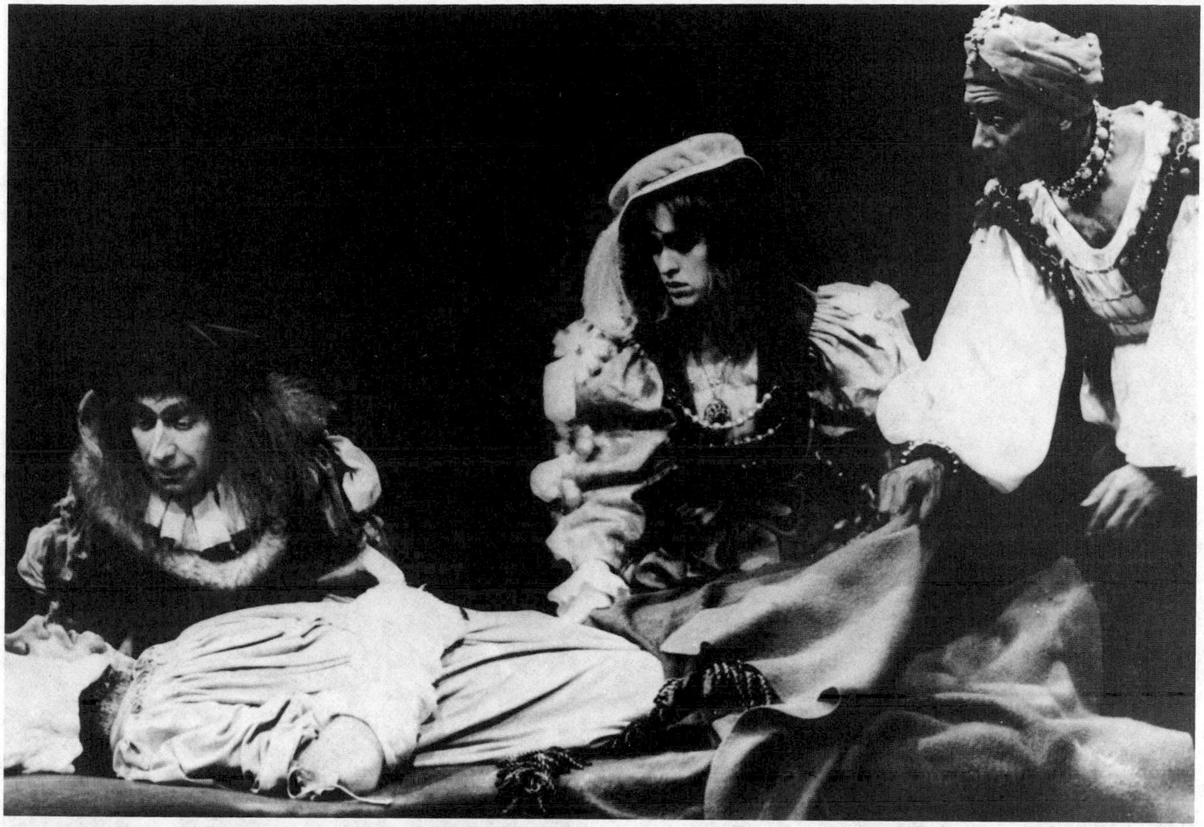

Figure 1. Voltore (Ken Ruta, *left*) stares at the body of Volpone (Douglas Campbell), disguised as a sick and dying man, while Androgyno (Katherine Emery, *center*) and Castrone (Graham Browne, *right*) look on with feigned concern in the Guthrie Theater Company production of *Volpone,* directed by Tyrone Guthrie and designed by Tanya Moiseiwitsch, Minneapolis, 1964. (Photograph: Courtesy of the Guthrie Theater.)

Figure 2. Corvino (Claude Woolman) entreats his wife Celia (Kristina Callahan) to make herself ready for a visit to Volpone in the Guthrie Theater Company production of *Volpone,* directed by Tyrone Guthrie and designed by Tanya Moiseiwitsch, Minneapolis, 1964. (Photograph: Courtesy of the Guthrie Theater.)

Figure 3. Volpone (Douglas Campbell, *left*), disguised as the mountebank Scoto of Mantua, extols his quack remedies to the crowd, while Sir Politic Would-Be (Lee Richardson, *right*) listens attentively in the Guthrie Theater Company production of *Volpone,* directed by Tyrone Guthrie and designed by Tanya Moiseiwitsch, Minneapolis, 1964. (Photograph: Courtesy of the Guthrie Theater.)

Staging of *Volpone*

**REVIEW OF THE GUTHRIE THEATER
PRODUCTION, 1964, BY JOHN K. SHERMAN**

My guess is that Tyrone Guthrie's production of Ben Jonson's "Volpone," fourth play of the Minnesota Theater Company's current season, will tote up as his most brilliant achievement to date in Minneapolis, when the votes are in.

It is mad, it is breath-taking in its energy and beautiful to look at, it is farce raised to the nth degree. It is a potent mixture of scalding satire and leaping fantasy. It is a 17th century three-ring circus. Above all, it is exuberantly and quintessentially theatrical—something the like of which could not be found or as fully enjoyed in any other medium than that of the living stage.

Least of all, I should add, on the printed page. Reading the play last week, I wondered how in the world its jagged and gnarled verse, its antiquated language, its far-fetched and dated figures of speech could be brought alive on a mid-20th century stage. Guthrie, I thought to myself, makes things too hard for himself and his company.

The current production proves, among other things, that the play-on-stage is the thing, and that some play scripts (O'Neill's, for example, in modern drama) are unprepossessing anywhere but on the stage. Paradoxically, however, this is the one play you should read before attending a performance. Why? Because it will give you some needed bearings as to what is going on.

"Volpone" is as thick with obscure allusions and literary double-talk as T. S. Eliot's "Waste Land." Jonson was a learned man who, unfortunately, liked to show off his learning. The play's dialogue is so crowded with references to events of the time, to classical literature and other matters known only to a well-educated man, that it took a very knowing spectator, even in the year of 1606 to catch all of them. In the play's reading version, there are almost more footnotes than text.

My point is that by reading the play—and a real chore it is—and by following up some of the footnote material, you perceive the drift and point of scenes which on stage come out in fountains and torrents of English that are often unintelligible on a word-to-word basis. And you'll discover, too, that you don't have to understand every consecutive word any more than you do in Italian opera.

I shouldn't over-emphasize this obscurity. As a matter of fact, "Volpone" at the Guthrie Theater triumphantly emerges, both in meaning and treatment, as a grotesque masquerade on the theme of human deterioration resulting from greed and self-seeking in general. Materialism as a deadly and dehumanizing force has never been attacked with more savage satire, or with more hilarious low comedy.

Volpone (the Fox) as you recall, receives valuable presents from his avaricious friends who hope, by such gifts, to become heirs to the wealth of a man they believe to be dying. Mosca (the Fly) abets his perfectly healthy master in acquiring riches by such deception, in luring a luscious and reluctant matron to his den, and in framing a court trial where injustice penalizes the innocent and rewards the corrupt.

In the end, of course, the gold-obsessed Volpone and his sly Mosca overreach themselves and get their deserts along with the other predators.

The joy to be found in this production is that of seeing members of the company stepping forth in bizarre caricatures which are a marvel of makeup, costuming, and flamboyant action. The play is actually a series of plays-within-a-play, following each other with knockabout speed and the precision of a ballet.

Douglas Campbell's Volpone is marvelously protean in his disguises of sick man, mountebank, ravenous seducer and derisive man-about-town.

This is a magnificent performance by any definition, vocally a prodigious feat from its mighty roars to its senile quaverings, and in action a veritable catalogue of comic-heroic capers . . . a portrayal unfailingly resourceful in every twist of the plot.

The slippery schemer and "stage manager" Mosca is personified in a snickering, light-stepping, cynical arabesque of action by George Grizzard, whose versatility seems to increase every time we see him.

The three buzzards who prey on the "dying" Volpone are masterpieces of extravagant impersonation—Ken Ruta as the clawing Voltore, the Vulture; Robert Pastene as the loathsome Corbaccio, the Raven, deaf and nearly blind; and Claude Woolman as the violent and despicable wife-seller, Corvino, the Crow.

The stage is full of such fantastic and over-drawn types: Lee Richardson as the fatuous and harebrained Sir Politick Would-Be; Ruth Nelson as his loose-tongued lady, Michael Levin as his baffled confidant, plus the peculiar trio of servants in Volpone's household—Sandy McCallum as the dwarf, Graham Brown as the eunuch and Katherine Emery as the hermaphrodite. "Straight" roles of the two much-abused innocents are a hysterical Celia by Kristina

347

Callahan and a manly boob, Bonnario, by Thomas Slater.

The singing from time to time (to music by Dominick Argento), the slapstick of the street scene where Volpone sets up his medicine show, the rough-house courtroom scenes, in fact the whole swarming action from start to finish combines high elegance with outright burlesque. Tanya Moiseiwitsch's stage design and costuming are most fetching and elaborate, a spectacle in themselves.

REVIEW OF THE GUTHRIE THEATER PRODUCTION, 1964, BY THOMAS WILLIS

In the service of this dark, outrageous, even merciless dissection of our vicious nature, the Guthrie has focused all its resources. In keeping with the renaissance Venetian setting, Tanya Moiseiwitsch has backed the action with a balcony the full width of the stage supported by serpentine gold columns. The chests of treasure are themselves treasures, being painted with oval-framed scenes of town, water, and sky.

Taking her cue from Volpone's description of his predators, "vulture, raven, kite, and gorcrow," she costumes the trio in black, with beaks for noses, great feather collars to preen and puff, clawed gloves, and a hawk's crest. Mosca, the fly, is in blue-bottle black, glinting indigo and green. And Volpone is all fox red, from bed to collar, except when disguised—then he changes to silver fox.

The Tyrone Guthrie directing conceit, like so many of his best, is operatic. Volpone is part Don Juan with a different object of desire, part Dulcamara, part John Wellington Wells, but all cruel renaissance sensualist.

He hires as familiars a hemaphrodite, a eunuch, and a dwarf, but as much for their musical skill as their freakish pleasantry. Disguised as mountebank in search of his Celia, he mounts a stirring potion sale, ending with a virtuoso trip up a ladder, across the top of the cart, and onto his lady's balcony for a "Deh, vieni alla finestra" spoken to a humming accompaniment from the trio below. When the jealous husband storms out, Volpone takes the short way down, launching himself straight out into space to be caught—Bolshoi Ballet style—by the men below.

Having once seen and heard—for this Volpone, like all good renaissance gentlemen, is singer and speaker—Douglas Campbell's way with the role, you are not likely to forget it. A voluptuary from the start, he manages to be funny and diabolically cruel at the same time. The scene in the locked chamber, where he pursues the innocent wife sent as sacrificial lamb by her husband, partially disrobes her, and throws her on the bed, all the while singing "To Ce-e-e-elia" in best period style and with a surprisingly good baritone, will do for a start.

George Grizzard's buzzing Mosca—he really does go "bzzz, bzzz" when he's thinking—is a wonderfully intelligent foil, clever, sinuous, and with more style than we would have believed possible on the basis of his other roles. The buzzard trio—Claude Woolman, Ken Ruta, and Robert Pastene—have aped the aviary with obvious relish and skill. Kristina Callahan's bewildered Celia maintains thruout her calamitous role a most appealing puzzlement. Neither of the Politick Would-Be's—Lee Richardson and Ruth Nelson—are up to the others, and it is a severe letdown when a dash of real buffoonery is indicated.

At the end of the retributory trial, conducted in frozen motion style to avoid the short scene changes, vice is suitably punished with imprisonment, banishment, and fines. Afterward, everyone breaks character for a contrapuntal madrigal in a "Don Giovanni" ending, accompanied by an unseen instrumental ensemble. Mr. Campbell and Mr. Jonson have the last word—everyone else stops in midsyllable—urging the audience to "fare jovially and clap your hands." That everyone does is no surprise.

JOHN WEBSTER

ca. 1580–1630

John Webster wrote two of the grimmest tragedies ever to appear on the English stage, or on any other. These two plays, *The White Devil* (1612) and *The Duchess of Malfi* (1614), embody a vision of human depravity that is altogether as dark as the convulsive spectacles of Euripides, and they express that vision in a style that is as dazzling as the poetry of Shakespeare. The vision and the style of these two plays alone have earned Webster a permanent place in the dramatic tradition. Most of his other works were joint efforts—two lively comedies of London life, *Westward Ho* (1604) and *Northward Ho* (1605), and a rambling history play, *Sir Thomas Wyatt* (1607), done in collaboration with Thomas Dekker; a classically unified tragedy, *Appius and Virginia* (1608), and a tragicomedy, *A Cure for a Cuckold* (1625), done in collaboration with Thomas Heywood. Aside from these collaborative works, Webster turned out at least two other plays on his own, a tragedy that has not survived about the Machiavellian Duke of Guise, and a tragicomedy, *The Devil's Law Case* (1623), featuring another Machiavellian villain, in this case a wealthy Neapolitan merchant. Other plays of the time have been attributed to Webster, but the attributions are too doubtful to provide any reliable insight into his career as a playwright.

Webster's theatrical career is, in fact, remarkably obscure, as uncertain as the dates of his birth and death. Exactly how he was occupied during his lifetime can be inferred only from the circumstances connected with the writing, production, and publication of his few surviving plays, for records of the period contain virtually no information of his whereabouts or his doings. No doubt, he was highly active in the London theaters of his day, writing as he did for a number of different companies, in collaboration with at least two different dramatists. He evidently kept up with the work of his contemporaries, for in his preface to *The White Devil*, he went out of his way to comment on "the full and heightened style" of Chapman, "the laboured and understanding works" of Jonson, "the no less worthy composures" of Beaumont and Fletcher, and "the right happy and copious industry" of Shakespeare, Dekker, and Heywood. Apparently, most dramatists of the period were also familiar with Webster, for when *The Duchess of Malfi* was published in 1623, three of his contemporaries prepared prefatory poems in honor of Webster and his play. One of them, John Ford, went so far as to "Crown him a poet, whom nor Rome nor Greece/Transcend in all theirs for a masterpiece." Ford was obviously carried away by the occasion, yet his lavish praise clearly indicates that Webster was well known and admired in the theatrical world of renaissance London.

Webster's popularity was at least in part the product of the theatrical fads he exploited in his two most famous plays, for both *The White Devil* and *The Duchess of Malfi* combine elements from several types of English drama that were in vogue at the end of the sixteenth and the beginning of the seventeenth centuries. Both plays draw heavily on the lurid conventions of Senecan revenge tragedy that Kyd had popularized in *The Spanish Tragedy*. Indeed, they are filled with ghastly and grisly events of one spectacular kind or another—with ghosts, mad scenes, macabre dumb shows, and sensational murders, ranging from poisonings, to stabbings, to broken necks. These nightmarish events are masterminded by diabolically ingenious and fiendishly cruel villains—Machiavellian antagonists whose cruelty and guile harken back to the power-crazed types that Marlowe had popularized twenty years earlier in *Tamburlaine, The Jew of Malta,* and *Edward II.* To top it all off, these sinister characters are let loose to work their havoc in the world of renaissance Italy, a world that was popularly imagined by many Englishmen to be the epitome of corruption and decadence. That sensational image of Italian life had already been dramatized in numerous plays of the period—for example, in Marston's *The Malcontent,* in Jonson's *Volpone,* and in Tourneur's *The Revenger's Tragedy.* Webster was thus capitalizing on proven theatrical commodities in both *The White Devil* and *The Duchess of Malfi.*

He was also capitalizing on proven historical and literary commodities, for both plays are based on popular stories of actual events that took place in sixteenth century Italy. *The Duchess of Malfi,* for example, dramatizes a tragic love story that Webster had found in a widely read collection of tales, *The Palace of Pleasure* (1567), by William Painter. Painter's story of the duchess was itself a translation of a tale he had discovered in another collection, *Histoires Tragiques* (1565), by the French writer Belleforest. Belleforest's story was in turn a translation and extensive embellishment of a tale he had found in yet another collection, *Novelle* (1554), by the Italian writer Matteo Bandello. And Bandello's story was drawn from events that had actually occurred over a period of time ranging from 1500 to 1513. In *The Duchess of Malfi,* Webster was working with a sensational love story that had proven its tragic appeal over the course of a century, capturing the imagination of readers and writers in Italy, France, and England.

Although Webster had a surefire story and surefire dramatic techniques for bringing it to life on stage, he was by no means aiming simply to create a melodramatic thriller in *The Duchess of Malfi.* If that had been his purpose, he need only have dramatized the star-crossed love story he found in Painter's collection—a story drawn out at great length by narrative commentary yet identical in its plot and characters to Bandello's much shorter account. Webster, however, did not interpret the story as it had been by all of its previous tellers. He did not regard it simply as the pitiful spectacle of a calamitous marriage between persons of different social rank. Consequently, he made large-scale revisions in his source, revisions that can readily be seen by comparing Bandello's tale to the play itself. In Bandello's story, for example, attention is focussed almost exclusively on the Duchess and Antonio—first on their unsuccessful efforts to conceal their marriage, then on their futile attempts to elude the reprisal of her brothers who oppose the marriage. As a result, the two brothers remain shadowy figures, known simply by the bare fact of their opposition. Actually, they are so vague and indistinct as characters that Bandello refers to them simply as "the Cardinal and the other brother," or as "the Argonese brothers." But in Webster's play, they are clearly distinguished from one another, each moved by profoundly different motives to oppose the marriage— the Cardinal by family pride, Ferdinand by incestuous desire. Indeed, in

Webster's play the two brothers become major characters in their own right, with their decadent and malign impulses as compelling as the defiant love of the Duchess and Antonio.

Even more striking than the expanded role of the brothers is the transformation of Bosola, who appears only once in Bandello's story when he is mentioned at the end as the murderer of Antonio. But in the play, Bosola is in the limelight from the very first scene to the very last, not merely as the hired agent of the two brothers, but also as the malcontent critic of their corrupting influence, and finally as the avenger of the injustice they have inflicted on the Duchess and Antonio. In his paradoxical role as culprit, critic, and avenger, Bosola epitomizes the ambiguous view of human nature that emerges from the behavior of all the characters in the play, for the Cardinal and Ferdinand are not shown as being completely unregenerate, nor for that matter are Antonio and the Duchess presented as being completely guileless. In Webster's hands the story of the duchess turns into a searching study of a morally chaotic world, a world in which private impulse, public sanction, and moral law are hopelessly entangled, so much so that all the characters who populate the world are victims of its moral chaos, even those who are ostensibly the victimizers.

Because Webster offers a highly complex, rather than a melodramatically simple, view of good and evil, *The Duchess of Malfi* is an extremely difficult play to realize accurately on the stage. Directors, for example, are faced with the problem of how to stage a decadent world without being carried away by sensationalism alone. They are also faced with the problem of how to establish moral distinctions between the Duchess, Antonio, Bosola, Ferdinand, and the Cardinal, without overlooking their psychological relationships and affinities to one another. These and other staging problems are discussed in the interview with Jean Gascon, who directed the Stratford Festival production in 1971. Gascon's solutions are reflected in the photographs from his production that show two dramatically parallel scenes from Act 1—Ferdinand procuring the services of Bosola (see Figure 1) and the Duchess wooing Antonio (Figure 2)— as well as the banishment scene from Act 3, when the Duchess and Antonio are banished by the Cardinal and the state of Ancona (Figure 3). These photographs and the review by Clive Barnes clearly show that Gascon succeeded in communicating what he—and Webster—intended to reveal in the play: "the difficulty of virtue in a sea of corruption."

THE DUCHESS OF MALFI

BY JOHN WEBSTER / NOTES BY J. DENNIS HUSTON AND ALVAN B. KERNAN

CHARACTERS

BOSOLA, *gentleman of the Duchess' horse*
FERDINAND, *Duke of Calabria*
CARDINAL, *his brother*
ANTONIO, *steward of the Duchess' household*
DELIO, *his friend*
FOROBOSCO
MALATESTE, *a count*
The Marquis of PESCARA
SILVIO, *a lord*
CASTRUCHIO, *an old lord*
RODERIGO, *lord*

GRISOLAN, *lord*
THE DUCHESS, *sister of Ferdinand and the Cardinal*
CARIOLA, *her woman*
JULIA, *wife to Castruchio and mistress to the Cardinal*
The DOCTOR
COURT OFFICERS
The several madmen, including: ASTROLOGER, TAILOR, PRIEST, DOCTOR
OLD LADY
THREE YOUNG CHILDREN
TWO PILGRIMS
ATTENDANTS, LADIES, EXECUTIONERS

ACT 1 / SCENE 1

(The DUCHESS' palace in Amalfi)
(Enter ANTONIO and DELIO.)

DELIO: You are welcome to your country, dear
    Antonio,
You have been long in France, and you return
A very formal Frenchman, in your habit.°
How do you like the French court?
ANTONIO: I admire it;
In seeking to reduce both State and people
To a fixed order, their judicious king
Begins at home. Quits° first his royal palace
10 Of flatt'ring sycophants, of dissolute,
And infamous persons, which° he sweetly terms
His Master's masterpiece, the work of Heaven,
Consid'ring duly, that a prince's court
Is like a common fountain, whence should flow
Pure silver-drops in general. But if't chance
Some cursed example poison't near the head,°
Death and diseases through the whole land spread.
And what is't makes this blessèd government,
But a most provident council, who dare freely
20 Inform him° the corruption of the times?
Though some o' th' court hold it presumption
To instruct princes what they ought to do,
It is a noble duty to inform them
What they ought to foresee. Here comes Bosola,
The only court-gall:° yet I observe his railing
Is not for simple love of piety:

Indeed he rails at those things which he wants,
Would be as lecherous, covetous, or proud,
Bloody, or envious, as any man,
If he had means to be so.—Here's the Cardinal.   30

(Enter BOSOLA and the CARDINAL)

BOSOLA: I do haunt you still.
CARDINAL: So.
BOSOLA: I have done you better service than to be
    slighted thus. Miserable age, where only the°
    reward of doing well, is the doing of it!
CARDINAL: You enforce° your merit too much.
BOSOLA: I fell into the galleys in your service, where,
    for two years together, I wore two towels instead
    of a shirt, with a knot on the shoulder, after the   40
    fashion of a Roman mantle. Slighted thus, I will
    thrive some way: blackbirds fatten best in hard
    weather,° why not I, in these dog days?°
CARDINAL: Would you could become honest,—
BOSOLA: With all your divinity, do but direct me the
    way to it. I have known many travel far for it,
    and yet return as arrant knaves, as they went
    forth; because they carried themselves always
    along with them.° *(Exit CARDINAL)* Are you
    gone? Some fellows, they say, are possessed with
    the devil, but this great fellow were able to   50
    possess the greatest devil, and make him worse.
ANTONIO: He hath denied thee some suit?
BOSOLA: He and his brother are like plum trees, that
    grow crooked over standing° pools, they are rich,

---

habit, dress.   **Quits,** empties.   **which,** modifies either the "royal palace" or the process of ridding.   **head,** both the source of the fountain and the chief of state.   **Inform him,** inform him about.   **court-gall,** both a sore spot in the court and a bitter railer against the court.

only the, the only.   **enforce,** emphasize.   **blackbirds . . . weather,** It was commonly thought that blackbirds grew fat in cold weather—perhaps because their ruffled feathers made them seem heavier then.   **dog days,** corrupt times.   **because . . . them,** because they could not get away from the evil within themselves.   **standing,** stagnant.

and o'erladen with fruit, but none but crows, pies,° and caterpillars feed on them. Could I be one of their flatt'ring panders, I would hang on their ears like a horseleech, till I were full, and then drop off. I pray, leave me. Who would rely
60   upon these miserable dependences,° in expectation to be advanced tomorrow? What creature ever fed worse, than hoping Tantalus;° nor ever died any man more fearfully, than he that hoped for a pardon? There are rewards for hawks, and dogs, when they have done us service; but for a soldier, that hazards his limbs in a battle, nothing but a kind of geometry° is his last supportation.

DELIO: Geometry?

BOSOLA: Ay, to hang in a fair pair of slings, take his
70   latter swing in the world, upon an honorable pair of crutches, from hospital to hospital. Fare ye well sir, and yet do not you scorn us; for places in the court are but like beds in the hospital, where this man's head lies at that man's foot, and so lower and lower. *(Exit* BOSOLA*.)*

DELIO: I knew this fellow seven years in the galleys,° For a notorious murther, and 'twas thought The Cardinal suborned° it: he was released By the French general, Gaston de Foix°
80   When he recovered Naples.

ANTONIO: 'Tis great pity He should be thus neglected: I have heard He's very valiant. This foul melancholy Will poison all his goodness; for, I'll tell you, If too immoderate sleep be truly said To be an inward rust unto the soul, It then doth follow want of action Breeds all black malcontents, and their close rearing,°
80   Like moths in cloth, do hurt for want of wearing.°

---

pies, magpies.   *dependences,* social inferiority that makes one dependent upon the favors of another.   *Tantalus,* a wrongdoer who was punished in Hades by being set, thirsty and hungry, in a pool of water that receded whenever he tried to drink from it and under a tree whose fruit he could never reach.   *kind of geometry,* hanging in a stiff, angular position.   *seven . . . galleys,* This statement only appears to contradict Bosola's previous complaint. His claim there that for two years—an arbitrary identification of an indefinite period of time—he has gone without a change of clothes is presented as an illustration of the wretched conditions imposed upon galley slaves.   *suborned it,* secretly induced him to do it.   *Gaston de Foix,* Webster is confused here, for although Gaston de Foix was a French general who won an important victory over the Spanish and papal armies at Ravenna in 1512, he had nothing to do with the conquest of Naples in 1501: at that time he was only thirteen years old.   *their . . . rearing,* their self-centered invidious brooding.   *do hurt,* hurts (the verb governs "close rearing," but it is given a plural form because of its proximity to "moths in cloth").   *wearing,* exposure to the air (of action).

ACT 1 / SCENE 2

*(*DELIO *and* ANTONIO *pass into the inner stage, where* CASTRUCHIO,° SILVIO, RODERIGO, *and* GRISOLAN *are entering.)*

DELIO: The presence° 'gins to fill. You promised me To make me the partaker of the natures Of° some of your great courtiers.

ANTONIO: The Lord Cardinal's And other strangers', that are now in court? I shall. Here comes the great Calabrian duke.

(Enter FERDINAND *and* ATTENDANTS.*)*

FERDINAND: Who took the ring° oft'nest?

SILVIO: Antonio Bologna, my lord.

FERDINAND: Our sister Duchess' great master° of her
10   household? Give him the jewel.—When shall we leave this sportive action, and fall to action indeed?

CASTRUCHIO: Methinks, my lord, you should not desire to go to war in person.

FERDINAND *(aside):* Now for some gravity:—why, my lord?

CASTRUCHIO: It is fitting a soldier arise to be a prince, but not necessary a prince descend to be a captain!

FERDINAND: No?
20

CASTRUCHIO: No my lord, he were far better do it by a deputy.

FERDINAND: Why should he not as well sleep, or eat, by a deputy? This might take idle, offensive, and base office from him, whereas the other deprives him of honor.

CASTRUCHIO: Believe my experience: that realm is never long in quiet where the ruler is a soldier.

FERDINAND: Thou toldst me thy wife could not endure fighting.
30

CASTRUCHIO: True, my lord.

FERDINAND: And of a jest she broke of° a captain she met full of wounds: I have forgot it.

CASTRUCHIO: She told him, my lord, he was a pitiful fellow, to lie, like the children of Ismael,° all in tents.°

FERDINAND: Why, there's a wit were able to undo all the chirurgeons° o' the city, for although gallants should quarrel, and had drawn their weapons,
40   and were ready to go to it; yet her persuasions

Castruchio The name is meant to suggest impotence. *presence,* presence chamber, where nobility received official visitors.   *To . . . Of,* to tell me about the characters of.   *took the ring,* won at jousting (by carrying off a ring with one's lance).   *great master,* steward.   *broke of,* told about.   *children of Ismael,* Arabs.   *tents,* a pun, meaning both "tents" in the modern sense and also rolls of lint used for dressing wounds.   *chirurgeons,* surgeons.

would make them put up.°
CASTRUCHIO: That she would, my lord.
  How do you like my Spanish jennet?°
RODERIGO: He is all fire.
FERDINAND: I am of Pliny's opinion.° I think he was
  begot by the wind; he runs as if he were ballas-
  sed° with quicksilver.°
SILVIO: True, my lord, he reels from the tilt° often.
50 RODERIGO and GRISOLAN: Ha, ha, ha!
FERDINAND: Why do you laugh? Methinks you that
  are courtiers should be my touchwood:° take fire
  when I give fire; that is, laugh when I laugh,
  were the subject never so witty—
CASTRUCHIO: True, my lord, I myself have heard a
  very good jest, and have scorned to seem to have
  so silly° a wit, as to understand it.
FERDINAND: But I can laugh at your fool, my lord.
CASTRUCHIO: He cannot speak, you know, but he
60 makes faces; my lady cannot abide him.
FERDINAND: No?
CASTRUCHIO: Not endure to be in merry company:
  for she says too much laughing, and too much
  company, fills her too full of the wrinkle.°
FERDINAND: I would then have a mathematical in-
  strument° made for her face, that she might not
  laugh out of compass.° I shall shortly visit you at
  Milan, Lord Silvio.
SILVIO: Your grace shall arrive most welcome.
70 FERDINAND: You are a good horseman, Antonio; you
  have excellent riders in France, what do you
  think of good horsemanship?
ANTONIO: Nobly, my lord: as out of the Grecian
  horse° issued many famous princes: so out of
  brave horsemanship, arise the first sparks of
  growing resolution, that raise the mind to noble
  action.
FERDINAND: You have bespoke it worthily.

(Enter DUCHESS, CARDINAL, CARIOLA,° JULIA, *and*
ATTENDANTS.)

SILVIO: Your brother, the Lord Cardinal, and sister
  Duchess.   80
CARDINAL: Are the galleys come about?°
GRISOLAN: They are, my lord.
FERDINAND: Here's the Lord Silvio, is come to take his
  leave.
DELIO *(aside to* ANTONIO): Now sir, your promise:
  what's that Cardinal? I mean his temper? They
  say he's a brave fellow, will play his five thousand
  crowns at tennis, dance, court ladies, and one
  that hath fought single combats.
ANTONIO: Some such flashes° superficially hang on   90
  him, for form; but observe his inward character:
  he is a melancholy churchman. The spring in his
  face is nothing but the engend'ring of toads:°
  where he is jealous of any man, he lays worse
  plots for them, than ever was imposed on Hercules,° for he strews in his way flatterers, panders, intelligencers, atheists, and a thousand
  such political° monsters. He should have been
  Pope, but instead of coming to it by the primitive
  decency° of the Church, he did bestow bribes, so   100
  largely and so impudently as if he would have
  carried it away without Heaven's knowledge.
  Some good he hath done—
DELIO: You have given too much of him. What's his
  brother?
ANTONIO: The Duke there? a most perverse and
  turbulent nature:
  What appears in him mirth, is merely outside;
  If he laugh heartily, it is to laugh
  All honesty out of fashion.   110
DELIO: Twins?°
ANTONIO: In quality:
  He° speaks with others' tongues, and hears men's
  suits
  With others' ears, will seem to sleep o' th' bench
  Only to entrap offenders in their answers;
  Dooms men to death by information,°
  Rewards, by hearsay.°

there's . . . up, The sexual innuendoes in this speech—
obvious in "drawn their weapons," "go to it," and "put up"
and probable in "undo" and "persuasions"—suggest both
Julia's promiscuity and Ferdinand's licentiousness. The
lewdness prevalent in Ferdinand's idiom suggests powerful
incestuous desires, not fully suppressed. *jennet,* a small
Spanish horse. *Pliny's opinion,* In his *Natural History,* Pliny
wrote that some Portuguese mares were impregnated by the
West Wind. *ballassed,* ballasted. *quicksilver,* the element
mercury, noted for its mobility. *reels . . . tilt,* shies away
from the ring that is the target in tilting. *touchwood,*
tinder. *silly,* simple. *fills . . . wrinkle,* There is in this
speech a sexual pun, which Castruchio, who is stupidly
innocent of his wife's unfaithfulness, does not recognize. *wrinkle,* both a physical and a moral blemish and,
here, pudendum as well. *mathematical instrument,* some
compasslike device for confining movement. *out of compass,* to excess. *Grecian horse.* The huge wooden horse
which the Greeks secretly filled with their best and noblest
soldiers and which the Trojans foolishly transported within
the walls of their city.

Cariola, Cariola's name, like Castruchio's, is themati-
cally appropriate. A "carriolo" was, among other things, a
trundle bed, which servants like Cariola used to sleep in so
that they might remain accessible to their mistresses. *come
about,* returned to port. *flashes,* examples of showy behavior. *spring . . . toads,* countenance of nobility hides a
vicious, scheming temperament. *Hercules,* a mythical hero,
considered the strongest mortal, who performed twelve
superhuman "labors." *political,* plotting. *primitive decency,* simple and straightforward honesty. *Twins,* Are
these two brothers twins, then? *He,* Ferdinand. *information,* the testimony of informers. *Dooms . . . hearsay,* Antonio implies that Ferdinand's judgments are arbitrary and
cruel, for the testimony of informers, who are paid for what
they say, is hardly more reliable evidence than hearsay.
When Ferdinand is their judge, men are doomed to death or
rewarded indiscriminately as he chooses.

DELIO: Then the law to him
120 Is like a foul black cobweb to a spider:
He makes it his dwelling, and a prison
To entangle those shall feed him.°
ANTONIO: Most true:
He ne'er pays debts, unless they be shrewd turns,°
And those he will confess that he doth owe.
Last, for his brother there, the Cardinal:
They that do flatter him most say oracles°
Hang at his lips, and verily I believe them:
For the devil speaks in them.
130 But for their sister, the right noble Duchess,
You never fixed your eye on three fair medals,
Cast in one figure, of so different temper.°
For her discourse, it is so full of rapture,
You only will begin, then to be sorry
When she doth end her speech; and wish, in
      wonder,
She held it less vainglory to talk much
Than your penance, to hear her.° Whilst she
      speaks,
140 She throws upon a man so sweet a look,
That it were able to raise one to a galliard°
That lay in a dead palsy; and to° dote
On that sweet countenance. But in that look
There speaketh so divine a continence,
As cuts off all lascivious and vain hope.
Her days are practiced° in such noble virtue,
That sure her nights, nay more, her very sleeps,
Are more in heaven, than other ladies' shrifts.°
Let all sweet ladies break their flatt'ring glasses,°
150 And dress themselves in her.°
DELIO: Fie, Antonio,
You play the wire-drawer° with her
      commendations.
ANTONIO: I'll case the picture up.° Only thus much°—
All her particular worth grows to this sum:
She stains° the time past, lights the time to come.

---

those . . . him, those that he feeds upon. *shrewd turns,* evil doings. *oracles,* words of great wisdom. *You . . . temper,* You have never seen three medals depicting the same figure which are made of such different kinds of metal as these three people. *You . . . her,* a deceptively difficult statement, which may be paraphrased: Just when you have begun (to feel this rapture), you will become sorry that she had ended her speech. And then, under the wonder of her spell, you will wish that she thought it more noble ("less vainglory") to talk a great deal than she thought it discomforting to you ("your penance") to hear her talk. *galliard,* a lively dance. *and to,* and (it is also able to make one). *practiced,* habitually spent. *shrifts,* confessions to a priest. *glasses,* mirrors. *And . . . her,* and follow her example. *wire-drawer,* one who draws out a wire from metal and, metaphorically, one who overextends the limits of truth. *I'll . . . up,* I'll put this picture of her (that I have presented) away. *Only . . . much,* Only this will I say in summary. *stains,* deprives of luster.

CARIOLA: You must attend my lady, in the gallery,
Some half an hour hence.
ANTONIO: I shall. *(Exeunt ANTONIO and DELIO.)*
FERDINAND: Sister, I have a suit to you.°   160
DUCHESS: To me, sir?
FERDINAND: A gentleman here: Daniel de Bosola,
One that was in the galleys.
DUCHESS: Yes, I know him.
FERDINAND: A worthy fellow h'is. Pray let me entreat
      for
The provisorship of your horse.°
DUCHESS: Your knowledge of him
Commends him, and prefers him.
FERDINAND: Call him hither.   170

(Exit ATTENDANT.)

We are now upon parting.° Good Lord Silvio
Do us commend to all our noble friends
At the leaguer.°
SILVIO: Sir, I shall.
DUCHESS: You are for Milan?
SILVIO: I am.
DUCHESS: Bring the caroches.° We'll bring you down
      to the haven.

(Exeunt DUCHESS, CARIOLA, SILVIO, CASTRUCHIO, RODERIGO, GRISOLAN, JULIA, and ATTENDANTS.)

CARDINAL: Be sure you entertain that Bosola
For your intelligence.° I would not be seen in't.   180
And therefore many times I have slighted him
When he did court our furtherance, as this
      morning.
FERDINAND: Antonio, the great master of her
      household
Had been far fitter.
CARDINAL: You are deceived in him,
His nature is too honest for such business.—
He comes: I'll leave you.

(Enter BOSOLA.)

BOSOLA: I was lured° to you. *(Exit CARDINAL.)*   190
FERDINAND: My brother here, the Cardinal, could
      never
Abide you.
BOSOLA: Never since he was in my debt.
FERDINAND: May be some oblique character in your
      face
Made him suspect you?
BOSOLA: Doth he study physiognomy?
There's no more credit to be given to th' face,

---

a . . . you, one who has a request to make of you. *let . . . horse,* Let me entreat you to let him serve as your groom. *upon parting,* preparing to leave. *leaguer,* camp. *caroches,* coaches. *entertain . . . intelligence,* use Bosola to gather information secretly. *lured,* called, with the implicit idea of "enticed into a trap."

200   Than to a sick man's urine, which some call
      The physician's whore, because she cozens him.°
      He did suspect me wrongfully.
    FERDINAND: For that
      You must give great men leave to take their times:
      Distrust doth cause us seldom be° deceived;
      You see, the oft shaking of the cedar tree
      Fastens it more at root.
    BOSOLA: Yet take heed:
      For to suspect a friend unworthily,
210   Instructs him the next way° to suspect you,
      And prompts him to deceive you.
    FERDINAND: There's gold.
    BOSOLA: So:
      What follows? Never rained such showers as these
      Without thunderbolts i' th' tail of them.°
      Whose throat must I cut?
    FERDINAND: Your inclination to shed blood rides
      post°
      Before my occasion to use you. I give you that°
220   To live i' th' court, here, and observe the Duchess,
      To note all the particulars of her havior:
      What suitors do solicit her for marriage
      And whom she best affects. She's a young widow:
      I would not have her marry again.
    BOSOLA: No, sir?
    FERDINAND: Do not you ask the reason, but be
      satisfied
      I say I would not.
    BOSOLA: It seems you would create me
230   One of your familiars.
    FERDINAND: Familiar? what's that?
    BOSOLA: Why, a very quaint invisible devil in flesh,
      An intelligencer.
    FERDINAND: Such a kind of thriving thing
      I would wish thee; and ere long, thou mayst arrive
      At a higher place° by't.
    BOSOLA (trying to give the money back): Take your
      devils,
      Which hell calls angels°: these cursed gifts would
240   make
      You a corrupter, me an impudent traitor,

There's . . . him, Most kinds of sickness would not be recognizable in a urinary analysis. *seldom be,* to be seldom. *the . . . way,* in the quickest way. *Never . . . them,* Bosola here refers to the mythical story in which Zeus transforms himself into a shower of gold in order to possess Danae, who is imprisoned in a brass tower. The obscene use of the word "tail" in this speech provides almost as good an example of Bosola's cynicism as his bold conclusion: "Whose throat must I cut?" *rides post,* rides swiftly, upon horseback, changing mounts often. *I . . . that,* I command you. *higher place,* the kind of ambiguous statement that is characteristic of villains in Renaissance drama. Ferdinand may mean either a better social position or a scaffold (from which to be hanged). *angels,* gold coins, which derived their name from the image of the archangel Michael on them.

      And should I take these they'd take me to hell.
    FERDINAND: Sir, I'll take nothing from you that I have
      given.
      There is a place that I procured for you
      This morning, the provisorship o' th' horse,
      Have you heard on't?
    BOSOLA: No.
    FERDINAND: 'Tis yours; is't not worth thanks?
    BOSOLA: I would have you curse yourself now, that   250
      your bounty,
      Which makes men truly noble,° e'er should make
      Me a villain: oh, that to avoid ingratitude
      For the good deed you have done me, I must do
      All the ill man can invent. Thus the devil
      Candies all sins o'er,° and what Heaven terms vild,°
      That names he complimental.°
    FERDINAND: Be yourself.
      Keep your old garb of melancholy: 'twill express
      You envy those that stand above your reach,   260
      Yet strive not to come near 'em. This will gain
      Access to private lodgings, where yourself
      May, like a politic dormouse,—
    BOSOLA: As I have seen some,
      Feed in a lord's dish, half asleep, not seeming
      To listen to any talk, and yet these rogues
      Have cut his throat in a dream.° What's my place?
      The provisorship o' th' horse? say then my
      corruption
      Grew out of horse dung. I am your creature.   270
    FERDINAND: Away!
    BOSOLA: Let good men, for good deeds, covet good
      fame,
      Since place and riches oft are bribes of shame;
      Sometimes the devil doth preach. (*Exit* BOSOLA.)

    (*Enter* CARDINAL, DUCHESS, *and* CARIOLA.)

    CARDINAL: We are to part from you: and your own
      discretion
      Must now be your director.
    FERDINAND: You are a widow:
      You know already what man is; and therefore   280
      Let not youth, high promotion, eloquence,—
    CARDINAL: No, nor any thing without the addition,
      honor,
      Sway your high blood.
    FERDINAND: Marry? they are most luxurious,°
      Will° wed twice.
    CARDINAL: O fie!
    FERDINAND: Their livers° are more spotted

Which . . . noble, because money gives man a position of nobility in society. *Candies . . . o'er,* makes sins seem tempting. *vild,* vile. *complimental,* worthy of compliment, good. *in a dream,* while he slept. *luxurious,* incontinent. *Will,* who will. *livers,* The liver was believed to be the source of passion.

Than Laban's sheep.°

290 DUCHESS: Diamonds are of most value,
They say, that have passed through most jewelers'
hands.
FERDINAND: Whores, by that rule, are precious.
DUCHESS: Will you hear me?
I'll never marry—
CARDINAL: So most widows say,
But commonly that motion° lasts no longer
Than the turning of an hourglass; the funeral
sermon
300 And it, end both together.
FERDINAND: Now hear me:
You live in a rank pasture; here, i' th' court,
There is a kind of honeydew° that's deadly:
'Twill poison your fame;° look to't; be not cunning,
For they whose faces do belie their hearts
Are witches, ere they arrive at twenty years,
Ay, and give the devil suck.
DUCHESS: This is terrible good counsel.
FERDINAND: Hypocrisy is woven of a fine small
310 thread,
Subtler than Vulcan's engine:° yet, believe't,
Your darkest actions, nay, your privat'st thoughts,
Will come to light.
CARDINAL: You may flatter yourself,
And take your own choice, privately be married
Under the eaves of night—
FERDINAND: Think't the best voyage
That e'er you made; like the irregular crab,
Which, though't goes backward, thinks that it goes
320 right,
Because it goes its own way; but observe,
Such weddings may more properly be said
To be executed, than celebrated.
CARDINAL: The marriage night
Is the entrance into some prison.
FERDINAND: And those joys,
Those lustful pleasures, are like heavy sleeps
Which do forerun man's mischief.°
CARDINAL: Fare you well.
330 Wisdom begins at the end:° remember it. (Exit
CARDINAL.)
DUCHESS: I think this speech between you both was
studied,
It came so roundly off.
FERDINAND: You are my sister,
This was my father's poniard:° do you see,

I'd be loath to see't look rusty,° 'cause 'twas his.
I would have you to give o'er these chargeable°
revels;
A visor and a mask° are whispering-rooms°   340
That were ne'er built for goodness: fare ye well.
And women like that part, which, like the lamprey,°
Hath ne'er a bone in't.
DUCHESS: Fie sir!
FERDINAND: Nay,
I mean the tongue—variety of courtship°—
What cannot a neat knave with a smooth tale
Make a woman believe? Farewell, lusty widow.
(Exit FERDINAND.)
DUCHESS: Shall this move me? If all my royal kindred
Lay in my way unto this marriage,   350
I'd make them my low footsteps.° And even now,
Even in this hate, as men in some great battles,
By apprehending danger, have achiev'd
Almost impossible actions (I have heard soldiers
say so),
So I, through frights and threat'nings, will assay
This dangerous venture. Let old wives report
I winked, and chose a husband. Cariola,
To thy known secrecy I have given up
More than my life, my fame.°   360
CARIOLA: Both shall be safe:
For I'll conceal this secret from the world
As warily as those that trade in poison
Keep poison from their children.
DUCHESS: Thy protestation
Is ingenious° and hearty: I believe it.
Is Antonio come?
CARIOLA: He attends you.
DUCHESS: Good, dear soul,
Leave me; but place thyself behind the arras,   370
Where thou mayst overhear us. Wish me good
speed,
For I am going into a wilderness,
Where I shall find nor path, nor friendly clew°
To be my guide.

(CARIOLA goes behind the curtain, and the DUCHESS
draws the traverse to reveal ANTONIO.)

I sent for you. Sit down:
Take pen and ink, and write. Are you ready?
ANTONIO: Yes.

Laban's sheep, In Laban's flock were many spotted sheep (Genesis 30:29–43). *motion,* resolution. *honeydew,* a sweet, sticky substance secreted by some plants. *fame,* reputation. *Vulcan's engine,* the net that Vulcan used to catch his wife, Venus, and her paramour, Mars. *mischief,* misfortune. *Wisdom . . . end,* considers the end before beginning an action. *poniard,* dagger.

I'd . . . rusty, I would not like to see it covered with your blood ("rusty"). *chargeable,* expensive. *visor . . . mask,* part of the costume used by lords and ladies participating in the revelry of a masque. *whispering-rooms,* small rooms where secret, often amorous, interviews were held. *lamprey,* eel-like fish. *variety of courtship,* (the source of) variety in courtship (because it can express love in so many different ways). *footsteps,* steppingstones. *fame,* reputation. *ingenious,* straightforward. *clew,* something that helps one out of a labyrinth.

DUCHESS: What did I say?

380 ANTONIO: That I should write somewhat.

DUCHESS: Oh, I remember:
After these triumphs and this large expense
It's fit, like thrifty husbands,° we inquire
What's laid up for tomorrow.

ANTONIO: So please your beauteous excellence.

DUCHESS: Beauteous?
Indeed I thank you. I look young for your sake:
You have ta'en my cares upon you.

ANTONIO: I'll fetch your grace

390 The particulars of your revenue and expense.

DUCHESS: Oh, you are an upright treasurer, but you mistook,°
For when I said I meant to make inquiry
What's laid up for tomorrow, I did mean
What's laid up yonder for me.

ANTONIO: Where?

DUCHESS: In heaven.
I am making my will, as 'tis fit princes should,
In perfect memory, and I pray, sir, tell me

400 Were not one better make it smiling, thus,
Than in deep groans and terrible ghastly looks,
As if the gifts we parted with procured
That violent distraction?

ANTONIO: Oh, much better.

DUCHESS: If I had a husband now, this care were quit;
But I intend to make you overseer.
What good deed shall we first remember? Say.

ANTONIO: Begin with that first good deed, began i' th' world,

410 After man's creation, the sacrament of marriage.
I'd have you first provide for a good husband;
Give him all.

DUCHESS: All?

ANTONIO: Yes, your excellent self.

DUCHESS: In a winding sheet?

ANTONIO: In a couple.

DUCHESS: St. Winifred!° that were a strange will.

ANTONIO: 'Twere strange
If there were no will in you to marry again.

420 DUCHESS: What do you think of marriage?

ANTONIO: I take't, as those that deny purgatory:
It locally° contains or heaven, or hell;
There's no third place in't.

DUCHESS: How do you affect° it?

ANTONIO: My banishment, feeding my melancholy,
Would often reason thus:—

DUCHESS: Pray, let's hear it.

ANTONIO: Say a man never marry, nor have children,

What takes that from him? only the bare name
Of being a father, or the weak delight   430
To see the little wanton° ride a-cock-horse
Upon a painted stick, or hear him chatter
Like a taught starling.

DUCHESS: Fie, fie, what's all this?
One of your eyes is bloodshot, use my ring to't.
They say 'tis very sovereign:° 'twas my wedding ring,
And I did vow never to part with it,
But to my second husband.

ANTONIO: You have parted with it now.   440

DUCHESS: Yes, to help your eyesight.

ANTONIO: You have made me stark blind.

DUCHESS: How?

ANTONIO: There is a saucy and ambitious devil
Is dancing in this circle.°

DUCHESS: Remove him.

ANTONIO: How?

DUCHESS: There needs small conjuration,° when your finger
May do it: thus, is it fit?°   450

(She puts the ring on his finger and he kneels.)

ANTONIO: What said you?

DUCHESS: Sir,
This goodly roof of yours is too low built;°
I cannot stand upright in't, nor discourse
Without° I raise it higher: raise yourself,
Or if you please, my hand° to help you: so.
(Raises him.)

ANTONIO: Ambition, madam, is a great man's madness
That is not kept in chains and close-pent rooms,
But in fair lightsome lodgings, and is girt   460
With the wild noise of prattling visitants,°
Which makes it lunatic, beyond all cure.
Conceive not I am so stupid,° but I aim
Whereto your favors tend. But he's a fool
That, being a-cold, would thrust his hand i' th' fire
To warm them.

DUCHESS: So, now the ground's broke,
You may discover what a wealthy mine
I make you lord of.

ANTONIO: O my unworthiness!   470

DUCHESS: You were ill° to sell yourself.
This dark'ning of your worth is not like that
Which tradesmen use° i' th' city; their false lights

---

husbands, a pun, meaning both "stewards" and "married men." **mistook,** misunderstood (me). **St. Winifred,** a Welsh saint of the seventh century who was beheaded by Caradoc ap Alauc when she rejected his amorous advances. **locally,** in itself. **affect,** feel about.

wanton, fellow. **sovereign,** effective. **circle,** the ring. **small conjuration,** little magic. **it is fit,** Does it fit? **This . . . built,** Your humble attitude makes me uncomfortable. **Without,** unless. **my hand,** (here is) my hand. **visitants,** visitors. **so stupid,** so lunatic (as to be ambitious). **ill,** ill-advised. **tradesmen use,** Food shops were kept dark so that buyers could not closely examine a tradesman's wares.

Are to rid° bad wares off. And I must tell you
If you will know where breathes a complete man,
(I speak it without flattery), turn your eyes
And progress through° yourself.
ANTONIO: Were there nor heaven, nor hell,
 I should be honest: I have long served virtue,
480 And ne'er ta'en wages of her.
DUCHESS: Now she pays it.
 The misery of us that are born great:
 We are forced to woo, because none dare woo us.
 And as a tyrant doubles with his words,°
 And fearfully° equivocates, so we
 Are forced to express our violent passions
 In riddles and in dreams, and leave the path
 Of simple virtue, which was never made
 To seem the thing it is not. Go, go brag
490 You have left me heartless; mine is in your bosom:
 I hope 'twill multiply love there. You do tremble:
 Make not your heart so dead a piece of flesh
 To fear more than to love me. Sir, be confident,
 What is't distracts you? This is flesh and blood, sir,
 'Tis not the figure cut in alabaster
 Kneels at my husband's tomb.° Awake, awake,
   man!
 I do here put off all vain ceremony,
 And only do appear to you, a young widow
500 That claims you for her husband, and like a widow,
 I use but half a blush in't.°
ANTONIO: Truth speak for me,
 I will remain the constant sanctuary
 Of your good name.
DUCHESS: I thank you, gentle love,
 And 'cause° you shall not come to me in debt,
 Being now my steward, here upon your lips
 I sign your *Quietus est.*° This you should have
   begged now:
510 I have seen children oft eat sweetmeats thus,
 As fearful to devour them too soon.
ANTONIO: But for your brothers?
DUCHESS: Do not think of them:
 All discord without° this circumference
 Is only to be pitied, and not feared.
 Yet, should they know it, time will easily
 Scatter the tempest.
ANTONIO: These words should be mine,
 And all the parts you have spoke, if some part of it

Would not have savored° flattery.   520
DUCHESS: Kneel.

(Enter CARIOLA.*)*

ANTONIO: Ha?
DUCHESS: Be not amazed; this woman's of my
   counsel.
 I have heard lawyers say, a contract in a chamber,
 Per verba [de] presenti,° is absolute marriage.
 Bless, Heaven, this sacred gordian,° which let
   violence
 Never untwine.
ANTONIO: And may our sweet affections, like the   530
   spheres,
 Be still° in motion.°
DUCHESS: Quick'ning,° and make
 The like soft music.°
ANTONIO: That we may imitate the loving palms,
 Best emblem of a peaceful marriage,
 That ne'er bore fruit divided.°
DUCHESS: What can the Church force more?
ANTONIO: That Fortune may not know an accident
 Either of joy or sorrow, to divide   540
 Our fixèd wishes.
DUCHESS: How can the Church build faster?
 We now are man and wife, and 'tis the Church
 That must but echo this. Maid,° stand apart,
 I now am blind.°
ANTONIO: What's your conceit° in this?
DUCHESS: I would have you lead your fortune by the
   hand,
 Unto your marriage bed:
 (You speak in me this, for we now are one)   550
 We'll only lie, and talk together, and plot
 T'appease my humorous° kindred; and if you
   please,
 Like the old tale, in *Alexander and Lodowick,*°
 Lay a naked sword between us, keep us chaste.
 Oh, let me shroud° my blushes in your bosom,

---

rid, pass. **progress through**, look carefully at. **doubles ... words**, employs phrases with ambiguous, double meanings. **fearfully**, causing fear (in others). **'Tis ... tomb**, The whiteness of alabaster made it, like marble, suitable for use in funeral monuments. The Duchess' reference here is, no doubt, to a statue that marks her first husband's tomb. **I ... in't**, I have been made bold by my experience. **'cause**, so that. **Quietus est**, This phrase, which was often used in account books, literally means "It is finished," and in this instance the reference is to Antonio's obligations as steward. **without**, outside.

savored, resembled. **Per ... presenti**, "through words of the present (tense)": the lovers henceforth accept each other as husband and wife, in a contract that is legally valid. **gordian**, a knot that cannot be untied. **still**, always. **like ... motion**, Planets were thought to revolve around the earth in concentric, transparent, spherical shells. **Quick'ning**, stirring to life. **music**, The harmonious motion of the planets in the spheres was supposed to make sweet music. **That ... divided**, Fruit-bearing palm trees were thought to depend for their productivity upon a male palm tree. **Maid**, Cariola. **I ... blind**, I have been made blind by love (because I have eyes only for Antonio). **conceit**, meaning. **humorous**, volatile, subject to many humors. **Alexander and Lodowick**, two legendary friends so alike no one could tell them apart; so true was Lodowick to their friendship that he married the Princess of Hungaria in Alexander's name and then every night placed a naked sword in the bed between himself and the Princess in order to keep from wronging Alexander. **shroud**, bury.

Since 'tis the treasury of all my secrets.

(ANTONIO *and the* DUCHESS *begin to exit slowly.*)

CARIOLA: Whether the spirit of greatness, or of
woman
560   Reign most in her, I know not, but it shows
A fearful madness: I owe her much of pity.
(*Exeunt.*)

ACT 2 / SCENE 1

(*The* DUCHESS' *palace about a year later*)
(*Enter* BOSOLA *and* CASTRUCHIO.)

BOSOLA: You say you would fain be taken for an
eminent courtier?

CASTRUCHIO: 'Tis the very main° of my ambition.

BOSOLA: Let me see, you have a reasonable good face
for't already, and your nightcap° expresses your
ears sufficient largely.° I would have you learn to
twirl the strings of your band° with a good grace;
and in a set speech, at th'end of every sentence,
to hum three or four times, or blow your nose till
it smart again, to recover your memory. When
10   you come to be a president° in criminal causes, if
you smile upon a prisoner, hang him, but if you
frown upon him and threaten him, let him be
sure to scape the gallows.

CASTRYCGUI: I would be a very merry president,—

BOSOLA: Do not sup a-nights; 'twill beget you an
admirable wit.

CASTRUCHIO: Rather it would make me have a good
stomach° to quarrel, for they say your roaring
20   boys° eat meat seldom, and that makes them so
valiant. But how shall I know whether the people
take me for an eminent fellow?

BOSOLA: I will teach a trick to know it: give out you lie
a-dying, and if you hear the common people
curse you, be sure you are taken for one of the
prime nightcaps.°

(*Enter* OLD LADY.)

You come from painting now?

OLD LADY: From what?

BOSOLA: Why, from your scurvy face-physic.° To
30   behold thee not painted inclines somewhat near
a miracle. These, in thy face here, were deep ruts
and foul sloughs° the last progress.° There was a
lady in France that, having had the smallpox,
flayed the skin off her face, to make it more

level; and whereas before she looked like a
nutmeg grater,° after she resembled an abortive
hedgehog.°

OLD LADY: Do you call this painting?

BOSOLA: No, no, but you call it careening° of an old
morphewed° lady, to make her disembogue° 40
again. There's rough-cast° phrase to your plastic.°

OLD LADY: It seems you are well acquainted with my
closet?°

BOSOLA: One would suspect it for a shop of witchcraft, to find in it the fat of serpents, spawn of
snakes, Jews' spittle, and their young children's
ordure, and all these for the face. I would sooner
eat a dead pigeon,° taken from the soles of the
feet of one sick of the plague, than kiss one of 50
you fasting.° Here are two of you, whose sin of
your youth is the very patrimony of the physician,° makes him renew his footcloth° with the
spring, and change his high-prized° courtesan
with the fall of the leaf: I do wonder you do not
loathe yourselves. Observe my meditation now:
    What thing is in this outward form of man
    To be beloved? We account it ominous,
    If nature do produce a colt, or lamb,
    A fawn, or goat, in any limb resembling 60
    A man; and fly from't as a prodigy.°
    Man stands amazed to see his deformity,
    In any other creature but himself.
    But in our own flesh, though we bear
      diseases
    Which have their true names only ta'en from
      beasts,
    As the most ulcerous wolf,° and swinish
      measle;°
    Though we are eaten up of lice and worms, 70
    And though continually we bear about us
    A rotten and dead body, we delight
    To hide it in rich tissue:° all our fear,
    Nay, all our terror, is lest our physician

---

main, goal. *nightcap,* the coif, a white cap worn by lawyers. *expresses . . . largely,* makes your ears stick out far enough. *band,* white tabs that were also part of the lawyer's official costume. *president,* presiding judge. *good stomach,* predisposition. *roaring boys,* bullies, quarrelsome young men. *nightcaps,* lawyers. *face-physic,* a preparation that purges the face of unwanted layers of skin. *sloughs,* both "ditches" and "layers of dead skin." *the . . . progress,* the last time a journey was made by our ruler (and by the coach of time across your face).

nutmeg grater, because her face was so pock-marked. *hedgehog,* In flaying, the skin would be removed in strips that would roll up and stick out like spines on a hedgehog. *careening,* scraping. *morphewed,* covered with scaly skin. *disembogue,* set out on a journey. *rough-cast,* cast in a kind of rough plaster. *There's . . . plastic,* There's language as ugly as your appearance. *plastic,* molding. *closet,* most private room. *dead pigeon,* Pigeons were sometimes pressed against plague sores in the hope that the poison would be drawn to the birds and out of the sores. *fasting,* when your stomach is empty (and your breath foul). *whose . . . physician,* whose sins of lust in your youth have infected you with syphilis, and have thus guaranteed the physician an income for life. *footcloth,* decorative accouterments for a horse, which advertised the eminence of the owner. *high-prized,* both highly prized and high-priced. *prodigy,* unnatural monster. *wolf,* ulcer. *swinish measle,* leprosy. *rich tissue,* elaborate clothing.

Should put us in the ground, to be made
  sweet.
Your wife's gone to Rome. You two couple,°
  and get you
To the wells at Lucca,° to recover° your aches.

(*Exeunt* CASTRUCHIO *and* OLD LADY.)

80   I have other work on foot: I observe our
        Duchess
      Is sick a-days, she pukes, her stomach seethes,°
      The fins° of her eyelids look most teeming
        blue,°
      She wanes i' th' cheek, and waxes fat i' th'
        flank;
      And, contrary to our Italian fashion,
      Wears a loose-bodied gown. There's somewhat
        in't.
90   I have a trick may chance discover it,
      A pretty one; I have brought some apricocks,°
      The first our spring yields.°

(*Enter* ANTONIO *and* DELIO.)

DELIO (*aside*): And so long since married?
      You amaze me.
ANTONIO (*aside*): Let me seal your lips for ever,
      For did I think that anything but th' air
      Could carry these words from you, I should wish
      You had no breath at all. (*to* BOSOLA) Now sir, in
        your contemplation?°
100   You are studying to become a great wise fellow?
BOSOLA: Oh sir, the opinion° of wisdom is a foul
      tetter,° that runs all over a man's body: if simplic-
      ity direct us to have no° evil, it directs us to a
      happy being. For the subtlest folly proceeds
      from the subtlest wisdom. Let me be simply
      honest.
ANTONIO: I do understand your inside.°
BOSOLA: Do you so?
ANTONIO: Because you would not seem to appear to
110   th' world
      Puffed up with your preferment, you continue
      This out-of-fashion melancholy; leave it, leave it.
BOSOLA: Give me leave to be honest in any phrase, in
      any compliment whatsoever. Shall I confess my-
      self to you? I look no higher than I can reach:
      they are the gods, that must ride on winged
      horses; a lawyer's mule of a slow pace will both

suit my disposition and business. For, mark me,
  when a man's mind rides faster than his horse
  can gallop they quickly both tire.   120
ANTONIO: You would look up to heaven, but I think
      The devil, that rules i' th' air, stands in your lights.
BOSOLA: Oh, sir, you are lord of the ascendant,° chief
      man with the Duchess: a duke was your cousin-
      german,° removed. Say you were lineally de-
      scended from King Pippin,° or he himself, what
      of this? Search the heads of the greatest rivers in
      the world, you shall find them but bubbles of
      water. Some would think the souls of princes
      were brought forth by some more weighty cause   130
      than those of meaner persons; they are de-
      ceived; there's the same hand to them: the like
      passions sway them; the same reason that makes
      a vicar go to law for a tithe pig° and undo his
      neighbors, makes them° spoil a whole province,
      and batter down goodly cities with the cannon.

(*Enter* DUCHESS *and* LADIES.)

DUCHESS: Your arm, Antonio; do I not grow fat?
      I am exceeding short-winded. Bosola,
      I would have you, sir, provide for me a litter,
      Such a one, as the Duchess of Florence rode in.   140
BOSOLA: The Duchess used one, when she was great
      with child.
DUCHESS: I think she did. (*to one of her* LADIES) Come
      hither, mend my ruff,°
      Here. When?° Thou art such a tedious lady; and
      Thy breath smells of lemon peels;° would thou
      hadst done;°
      Shall I sound° under thy fingers? I am
      So troubled with the mother.°
BOSOLA (*aside*): I fear too much.   150
DUCHESS (*to* ANTONIO): I have heard you say that the
      French courtiers
      Wear their hats on 'fore the King.
ANTONIO: I have seen it.
DUCHESS: In the presence?°
ANTONIO: Yes.
DUCHESS: Why should not we bring up that fashion?
      'Tis ceremony more than duty that consists

---

couple, join, both as traveling and as sleeping companions. *wells at Lucca,* warm springs near Pisa. *recover,*
heal. *seethes,* is violently agitated. *fins,* edges. *teeming
blue,* the blue color characteristic of the eyelids of pregnant
women. *apricocks,* apricots. *I . . . yields,* Bosola intends
to find out if the Duchess is pregnant by offering her
apricots and thus appealing to the strong craving for fruit
that is often demonstrated by pregnant women. *in your
contemplation,* (Have we interrupted you while you were
rapt) in contemplation? *opinion,* teachings. *tetter,* skin
disease, eczema. *have no,* have nothing to do with. *inside,*
the true nature that you are covering up.

lord . . . ascendant, ruling power. *cousin-german,* first
("germane") cousin. *King Pippin,* father of Charlemagne.
tithe pig, a pig owed to the vicar as a tithe. *them,* princes.
ruff, a lace collar. *When,* an expression of impatience.
peels, In the first three editions of the play, the word is
spelled "pils" and "pills," which could mean either pills or
peels. Though the spelling becomes "peels" in the fourth
edition, we cannot know for certain whether this waiting-
woman sweetened her breath with lemon peels or with little
lemon pills. *would . . . done,* I wish you were finished.
sound, swoon. *mother,* the name Elizabethans gave to a
kind of hysteria that was accompanied by swelling in the
throat and choking. The pun on the obvious meaning of
"mother" is also intended, and it is this meaning of the word
that Bosola refers to in his subsequent aside. *presence,*
presence chamber.

In the removing of a piece of felt:
160 Be you the example to the rest o' th' court;
Put on your hat first.
ANTONIO: You must pardon me:
I have seen, in colder countries than in France,°
Nobles stand bare° to th' prince; and the distinction
Methought showed reverently.
BOSOLA: I have a present for your grace.
DUCHESS: For me, sir?
BOSOLA: Apricocks, madam.
DUCHESS: O sir, where are they?
170 I have heard of none to-year.°
BOSOLA (aside): Good, her color rises.
DUCHESS: Indeed, I thank you: they are wondrous
fair ones.
What an unskillful fellow is our gardener!
We shall have none this month.
BOSOLA: Will not your grace pare them?
DUCHESS: No, they taste of musk,° methinks; indeed
they do.
BOSOLA: I know not: yet I wish your grace had pared
180 'em.
DUCHESS: Why?
BOSOLA: I forgot to tell you the knave gard'ner,
Only to raise his profit by them the sooner,
Did ripen them in horse dung.
DUCHESS: Oh, you jest.°
(to ANTONIO) You shall judge: pray taste one.
ANTONIO: Indeed, madam,
I do not love the fruit.
DUCHESS: Sir, you are loath
190 To rob us of our dainties: 'tis a delicate fruit,
They say they are restorative?°
BOSOLA: 'Tis a pretty art,
This grafting.°
DUCHESS: 'Tis so: a bett'ring of nature.
BOSOLA: To make a pippin grow upon a crab,°
A damson on a blackthorn.° (aside) How greedily
she eats them!
A whirlwind strike off these bawd farthingales,°
For, but for that, and the loose-bodied gown,
200 I should have discovered apparently°
The young springal° cutting a caper in her belly.
DUCHESS: I thank you, Bosola: they were right good
ones,
If they do not make me sick.

ANTONIO: How now, madam?
DUCHESS: This green fruit and my stomach are not
friends.
How they swell me!
BOSOLA (aside): Nay, you are too much swelled
already.   210
DUCHESS: Oh, I am in an extreme cold sweat,
BOSOLA: I am very sorry. (Exit.)
DUCHESS: Lights to my chamber! O, good Antonio,
I fear I am undone. (Exit DUCHESS.)
DELIO: Lights there, lights!
ANTONIO: O my most trusty Delio, we are lost:
I fear she's fall'n in labor, and there's left
No time for her remove.
DELIO: Have you prepared
Those ladies to attend her? and procured   220
That politic° safe conveyance for the midwife
Your Duchess plotted?°
ANTONIO: I have.
DELIO: Make use then of this forced occasion:°
Give out that Bosola hath poisoned her,
With these apricocks. That will give some color°
For her keeping close.°
ANTONIO: Fie, fie, the physicians
Will then flock to her.
DELIO: For that you may pretend   240
She'll use some prepared antidote of her own,
Lest the physicians should repoison her.
ANTONIO: I am lost in amazement. I know not what to
think on't. (Exeunt.)

ACT 2 / SCENE 2

(A hall in the DUCHESS' palace)
(Enter BOSOLA and OLD LADY.)

BOSOLA: So, so: there's no question but her tetch-
iness° and most vulturous eating of the apricocks
are apparent signs of breeding— (to the OLD
LADY) Now?
OLD LADY: I am in haste, sir.
BOSOLA: There was a young waiting-woman, had a
monstrous desire to see the glasshouse°—
OLD LADY: Nay, pray let me go!
BOSOLA: And it was only to know what strange in-   10
strument° it was, should swell up a glass to the
fashion of a woman's belly.
OLD LADY: I will hear no more of the glasshouse; you
are still abusing women!
BOSOLA: Who, I? no, only by the way now and then,
mention your frailties. The orange tree bears
ripe and green fruit and blossoms altogether.
And some of you give entertainment for pure

---

in ... France, i.e., in England. **bare,** bare-headed.
to-year, this year. **musk,** an animal secretion used in
making perfume. **Oh, you jest,** The Duchess' unruffled
reaction to Bosola's vile suggestion attests to the intensity of
her desire for fruit. **restorative,** healthful. **grafting,** a
double-entendre, referring to propagation both in fruit
trees and in human beings (because the physical union in
sexual intercourse can be considered another form of grafting). **pippin, crab,** different kinds of apples. **damson,
blackthorn,** different kinds of plums. **farthingales,** hooped
petticoats. **apparently,** openly manifesting itself. **sprin-
gal,** youth.

---

politic, secret. **plotted,** planned. **forced occasion,**
circumstances forced upon us. **color,** reason. **close,** privately shut away. **tetchiness,** touchiness. **apparent,** obvious. **glasshouse,** glass factory. **instrument,** a double-
entendre.

love, but more, for more precious reward. The
lusty spring smells well,° but drooping autumn
20 tastes well. If we have the same golden showers
that rained in the time of Jupiter the Thunderer,
you have the same Danaes still, to hold up their
laps to receive them.° Didst thou never study the
mathematics?
OLD LADY: What's that, sir?
BOSOLA: Why, to know the trick how to make a many
lines meet in one center.° Go, go; give your
foster daughters° good counsel: tell them, that
the devil takes delight to hang at a woman's
30 girdle, like a false rusty watch, that she cannot
discern how the time passes.° (Exit OLD LADY.)

(Enter ANTONIO, DELIO, RODERIGO, GRISOLAN.)

ANTONIO: Shut up the court gates.
RODERIGO: Why sir? What's the danger?
ANTONIO: Shut up the posterns° presently,° and call
All the officers o' th' court.
GRISOLAN: I shall instantly. (Exit.)
ANTONIO: Who keeps the key o' th' park gate?
RODERIGO: Forobosco.
ANTONIO: Let him bring't presently. (Exit RODERIGO.)

(Enter SERVANTS, GRISOLAN, RODERIGO.)

40 FIRST SERVANT: Oh, gentlemen o' th' court, the
foulest treason!
BOSOLA (aside): If that these apricocks should be
poisoned now,
Without my knowledge!
FIRST SERVANT: There was taken even now
A Switzer in the Duchess' bedchamber.
SECOND SERVANT: A Switzer?°
FIRST SERVANT: With a pistol in his great codpiece.°
BOSOLA: Ha, ha, ha.
50 FIRST SERVANT: The codpiece was the case for't.
SECOND SERVANT: There was a cunning traitor.

Who would have searched his codpiece?
FIRST SERVANT: True, if he kept out of the ladies'
chambers.
And all the moulds of his buttons were leaden
bullets.
SECOND SERVANT: Oh wicked cannibal: a firelock in's
codpiece?
FIRST SERVANT: 'Twas a French plot, upon my life.
SECOND SERVANT: To see what the devil can do.   60
ANTONIO: All the officers here?
SERVANTS: We are.
ANTONIO: Gentlemen,
We have lost much plate° you know; and but this
evening
Jewels, to the value of four thousand ducats
Are missing in the Duchess' cabinet.°
Are the gates shut?
FIRST SERVANT: Yes.
ANTONIO: 'Tis the Duchess' pleasure   70
Each officer be locked into his chamber
Till the sun-rising; and to send the keys
Of all their chests, and of their outward doors
Into her bedchamber. She is very sick.
RODERIGO: At her pleasure.°
ANTONIO: She entreats you take't not ill. The
innocent
Shall be the more approved° by it.
BOSOLA: Gentlemen o' th' wood yard,° where's your
Switzer now?   80
FIRST SERVANT: By this hand, 'twas credibly reported
by one o' th' black guard.° (Exeunt BOSOLA,
RODERIGO, and SERVANTS.)
DELIO: How fares it with the Duchess?
ANTONIO: She's exposed
Unto the worst of torture, pain, and fear.
DELIO: Speak to her all happy comfort.
ANTONIO: How I do play the fool with mine own
danger!°
You are this night, dear friend, to post to Rome;°   90
My life lies in your service.
DELIO: Do not doubt me.
ANTONIO: Oh, 'tis far from me: and yet fear presents
me
Somewhat° that looks like danger.
DELIO: Believe it,
'Tis but the shadow of your fear, no more:
How superstitiously we mind° our evils!
The throwing down salt, or crossing of a hare;
Bleeding at nose, the stumbling of a horse: 100

The . . . well, The lusty young woman and the aging
whore both find something rewarding in love—one, the act
itself; the other, the money she receives for it. ***If . . . them,***
Bosola's argument here is simply that where there are men
who are willing to pay for love, there are women to sell it.
Why . . . center, another obscene reference to the lap of a
whore. ***foster daughters,*** women for whom she serves as a
midwife. ***the . . . passes,*** Because the devil impassions men
with desires even for women who are old, women are
deluded into thinking that they have not lost the beauty of
their youth (and have, consequently, not grown old). ***post-
erns,*** back gates. ***presently,*** now, at this present moment.
Switzer, a Swiss mercenary. ***With . . . codpiece,*** The codpiece was a baglike flap formerly worn in the front of men's
breeches and since replaced by the fly. Bosola's laughter
upon hearing that the pistol has been hidden in the Switzer's
codpiece results from his recognition of the obvious
double-entendre in "pistol"—a double-entendre that is developed by the servants in the succeeding speeches.

plate, money. ***in . . . cabinet,*** from the Duchess'
chamber. ***At . . . pleasure,*** perhaps an unintentional pun.
approved, proven good. ***wood yard,*** place where firewood
was cut. ***black guard,*** kitchen servants. ***How . . . danger,***
What a fool I am to increase the possibility of revealing our
secret marriage (by having a child). ***Rome,*** where the
Duchess' brothers are. ***Somewhat,*** something. ***mind,***
notice.

Or singing of a cricket, are of power
To daunt whole man in us.° Sir, fare you well:
I wish you all the joys of a blessèd father;
And, for my faith, lay this° unto your breast,
Old friends, like old swords, still are trusted best.

(Exit DELIO.)

(Enter CARIOLA *with a child.)*

CARIOLA: Sir, you are the happy father of a son:
  Your wife commends him to you.
ANTONIO: Blessèd comfort!
  For heaven's sake tend her well: I'll presently
110 Go set a figure° for's nativity. *(Exeunt.)*

ACT 2 / SCENE 3

(A hall in the DUCHESS' *palace)*
(Enter BOSOLA *with a dark lanthorn.°)*

BOSOLA: Sure I did hear a woman shriek: list, ha?
  And the sound came, if I received it right,
  From the Duchess' lodgings; there's some
    stratagem
  In the confining all our courtiers
  To their several wards. I must have part of° it,
  My intelligence° will freeze else. List again,
  It may be 'twas the melancholy bird,
  Best friend of silence, and of solitariness,
10 The owl, that screamed so—ha!—Antonio?

(Enter ANTONIO *with a candle, his sword drawn.)*

ANTONIO: I heard some noise: who's there? What art
    thou? Speak.
BOSOLA: Antonio! Put not your face nor body
  To such a forced expression of fear—
  I am Bosola, your friend.
ANTONIO: Bosola!
  (aside) This mole does undermine me—heard you
    not
  A noise even now?
20 BOSOLA: From whence?
ANTONIO: From the Duchess' lodging.
BOSOLA: Not I. Did you?
ANTONIO: I did, or else I dreamed.
BOSOLA: Let's walk towards it.
ANTONIO: No. It may be 'twas
  But the rising of the wind.
BOSOLA: Very likely
  Methinks 'tis very cold, and yet you sweat.
  You look wildly.
30 ANTONIO: I have been setting a figure

To . . . us, to rob us of all our bravery. *this,* my faith.
set a figure, check the horoscope for. *dark lanthorn,* a
lantern with only one opening, which could be closed to shut
off the light (often used by someone who wanted to move
stealthily at night.) *have . . . of,* find out about. *intelligence,* information gathered as a spy.

For the Duchess' jewels.°
BOSOLA: Ah, and how falls your question?
  Do you find it radical?°
ANTONIO: What's that to you?
  'Tis rather to be questioned what design,
  When all men were commanded to their lodgings,
  Makes you a nightwalker.
BOSOLA: In sooth I'll tell you:
  Now all the court's asleep, I thought the devil
  Had least to do here; I came to say my prayers, 40
  And if it do offend you I° do so,
  You are a fine courtier.
ANTONIO *(aside):* This fellow will undo me.
  You gave the Duchess apricocks today;
  Pray heaven they were not poisoned.
BOSOLA: Poisoned! a Spanish fig°
  For the imputation!
ANTONIO: Traitors are ever confident,
  Till they are discovered. There were jewels stol'n
    too, 50
  In my conceit,° none are to be suspected
  More than yourself.
BOSOLA: You are a false steward.
ANTONIO: Saucy slave! I'll pull thee up by the roots.
BOSOLA: May be the ruin will crush you to pieces.
ANTONIO: You are an impudent snake indeed, sir,
  Are you scarce warm, and do you show your sting?°
[BOSOLA: . . .°
ANTONIO]: You libel well, sir.
BOSOLA: No sir, copy it out, 60
  And I will set my hand to't.°
ANTONIO: My nose bleeds.
  One that were superstitious would count
  This ominous—when it merely comes° by chance.
  Two letters, that are wrought here for my name
  Are drowned in blood!°

I . . . jewels, I have been checking a horoscope (to see if
I can trace) the Duchess' jewels. *radical,* resolvable by
astrology. *I,* that I. *Spanish fig,* an expression of contempt, accompanied by the obscene gesture of thrusting the
thumb between the forefinger and the middle finger. *conceit,* opinion. *Are . . . sting,* The reference is to the fiftieth
fable of Aesop. "The Countryman and the Snake." A
villager finds a snake almost frozen and takes it home to
warm it by the fire, but as soon as it is revived by the heat, the
serpent tries to attack the countryman's wife and children.
The reference to Bosola as "scarce warm" here is motivated
by the fact that he has only recently been appointed to the
provisorship of the Duchess' horses. *Bosola,* A speech
seems to be missing here. *copy . . . to't,* Make your charges
formally, and I will set my hand to the task of answering
them. (Otherwise, be quiet). *merely comes,* in actuality
comes merely. *Two . . . blood,* Exactly what Antonio is
referring to here is a mystery. He may be holding two
handkerchiefs, embroidered with his initials, that he has
used to absorb the blood from his nosebleed; or he may hold
two official letters that required his signature as steward and
have become spotted with blood.

Mere accident. For you, sir, I'll take order:°
I' th' morn you shall be safe.° *(aside)* 'Tis that must
70   color
Her lying-in. *(to* BOSOLA) Sir, this door you pass not.
I do not hold it fit that you come near
The Duchess' lodgings till you have quit° yourself;
(aside) The great are like the base; nay, they are the
    same,
When they seek shameful ways to avoid shame.
(Exit.)
BOSOLA: Antonio hereabout did drop a paper,
Some of your help, false friend:° oh, here it is.
What's here?—a child's nativity calculated?
80 *(Reads.)* The Duchess was delivered of a son, 'tween
the hours twelve and one, in the night: Anno
Dom: 1504.—That's this year—*decimo nono
Decembris,*—That's this night—taken according
to the Meridian of Malfi—That's our Duchess:
happy discovery!—The Lord of the first house,°
being combust° in the ascendant, signifies short
life, and Mars being in a human sign, joined to
the tail of the Dragon, in the eighth house, doth
threaten a violent death; *Caetera non scrutantur.*°
90 Why now 'tis most apparent. This precise° fellow
Is the Duchess' bawd:° I have it to my wish.°
This is a parcel of intelligency°
Our courtiers were cased up° for! It needs must
    follow,
That I must be committed, on pretense
Of poisoning her, which I'll endure and laugh at.
If one could find the father now—but that
Time will discover. Old Castruchio
I' th' morning posts to Rome; by him I'll send
100 A letter, that shall make her brothers' galls
O'erflow their livers. This was a thrifty way.°
Though lust do mask in ne'er so strange disguise
She's oft found witty, but is never wise. *(Exit.)*

ACT 2 / SCENE 4

(The CARDINAL'*s palace in Rome)*
(Enter CARDINAL *and* JULIA.)

CARDINAL: Sit: thou art my best of wishes. Prithee tell
    me

What trick didst thou invent to come to Rome
Without thy husband?
JULIA: Why, my lord, I told him
I came to visit an old anchorite°
Here, for devotion.
CARDINAL: Thou art a witty° false one:
I mean to him.
JULIA: You have prevailèd with me   10
Beyond my strongest thoughts: I would not° now
Find you inconstant.
CARDINAL: Do not put thyself
To such a voluntary torture, which proceeds
Out of your own guilt.
JULIA: How, my lord?
CARDINAL: You fear
My constancy, because you have approved°
Those giddy and wild turnings in yourself.
JULIA: Did you e'er find them?   20
CARDINAL: Sooth, generally for women:
A man might strive to make glass malleable,
Ere he should make them fixed.
JULIA: So, my lord!—
CARDINAL: We had need go borrow that fantastic
    glass°
Invented by Galileo the Florentine,
To view another spacious world i' th' moon,
And look to find a constant woman there.
JULIA: This is very well, my lord.   30
CARDINAL: Why do you weep?
Are tears your justification? The selfsame tears
Will fall into your husband's bosom, lady,
With a loud protestation that you love him
Above the world. Come, I'll love you wisely,
That's jealously, since I am very certain
You cannot make me cuckold.°
JULIA: I'll go home
To my husband.
CARDINAL: You may thank me, lady,   40
I have taken you off your melancholy perch,
Bore you upon my fist, and showed you game,
And let you fly at it. I pray thee, kiss me.°
When thou wast with thy husband, thou wast
    watched
Like a tame elephant:° (still you are to thank me)

I'll . . . order, I'll issue an order for your arrest. *safe,* in custody. *quit,* acquitted yourself (of any blame for her sickness). *false friend,* the dark lantern (associated with secret, underhanded dealings proceeding under the cover of night). *Lord . . . house,* the planet that controls the boy's nativity. *combust,* burned up by being too near the sun (and, therefore, having lost its power). *Caetera non scrutantur,* The rest (of the horoscope) remains unexamined. *precise,* (seemingly) strait-laced. *bawd,* pander. *I . . . wish,* I have succeeded in getting what I wanted (i.e. important secret information). *parcel of intelligency,* a piece of really significant information. *cased up,* ordered to keep to their quarters. *thrifty way,* shrewd scheme.

---

anchorite hermit. *witty,* an ironic echo of the same word from the closing line of the preceding scene. *I . . . not,* I could not bear to. *approved,* given vent to. *fantastic glass,* telescope. *I . . . cuckold,* You cannot make me a cuckold (because I am not married to you). *I . . . me,* The Cardinal's imagery here is derived from the sport of falconry, but there are double-entendres in what he says—a habit of speech that links him psychologically with his brother. *tame elephant,* Elephants were tamed by being kept awake for so long that they would do anything in order to sleep.

Thou hadst only kisses from him, and high
   feeding,°
But what delight was that? 'Twas just like one
50   That hath a little fing'ring on the lute,
Yet cannot tune it:° (still you are to thank me)
JULIA: You told me of a piteous wound i' th' heart,
And a sick liver, when you wooed me first,
And spake like one in physic.°
CARDINAL: Who's that?

(Enter SERVANT.*)*

Rest firm, for my affection to thee,
Lightning moves slow to't.
SERVANT: Madam, a gentleman
That's come post from Malfi desires to see you.
60   CARDINAL: Let him enter; I'll withdraw. *(Exit.)*
SERVANT: He says
Your husband, old Castruchio, is come to Rome,
Most pitifully tired with riding post. *(Exit* SERVANT.*)*

(Enter DELIO.*)*

JULIA: Signior Delio! *(aside)* 'Tis one of my old suitors.
DELIO: I was bold to come and see you.
JULIA: Sir, you are welcome.
DELIO: Do you lie° here?
JULIA: Sure° your own experience
Will satisfy you no; our Roman prelates
70   Do not keep lodging for ladies.
DELIO: Very well.
I have brought you no commendations from your
   husband,
For I know none by him.
JULIA: I hear he's come to Rome?
DELIO: I never knew man and beast, of a horse and a
   knight,
So weary of each other. If he had had a good back,
He would have undertook to have borne his horse,
80   His breach° was so pitifully sore.
JULIA: Your laughter
Is my pity.°
DELIO: Lady, I know not whether
You want money, but I have brought you some.
JULIA: From my husband?
DELIO: No, from mine own allowance.°
JULIA: I must hear the condition, ere I be bound to
take it.
DELIO: Look on't, 'tis gold. Hath it not a fine color?
90   JULIA: I have a bird more beautiful.

DELIO: Try the sound on't.°
JULIA: A lute string far exceeds it;
It hath no smell, like cassia° or civet;°
Nor is it physical,° though some fond° doctors
Persuade us, seethe't in cullises.° I'll tell you,
This is a creature bred by— *(Enter* SERVANT.*)*
SERVANT: Your husband's come,
Hath delivered a letter to the Duke of Calabria,
That, to my thinking, hath put him out of his wits.
(Exit SERVANT.*)*
JULIA: Sir, you hear.   100
Pray let me know your business and your suit,
As briefly as can be.
DELIO: With good speed. I would wish you,
At such time, as you are nonresident
With your husband, my mistress.
JULIA: Sir, I'll go ask my husband if I shall,
And straight return your answer. *(Exit.)*
DELIO: Very fine,
Is this her wit or honesty° that speaks thus?   110
I heard one say the Duke was highly moved
With a letter sent from Malfi. I do fear
Antonio is betrayed. How fearfully
Shows his ambition now; unfortunate Fortune!
They pass through whirlpools, and deep woes do
   shun,
Who the event weigh, ere the action's done. *(Exit.)*

ACT 2 / SCENE 5

(Enter CARDINAL, *and* FERDINAND, *furious, with a
letter.)*

FERDINAND: I have this night digged up a mandrake.°
CARDINAL: Say you?
FERDINAND: And I am grown mad with't.   10
CARDINAL: What's the prodigy?°
FERDINAND: Read there, a sister damned; she's loose,
   i' th' hilts:°
Grown a notorious strumpet.
CARDINAL: Speak lower.
FERDINAND: Lower?
Rogues do not whisper't now, but seek to
   publish't—
As servants do the bounty of their lords—
Aloud; and with a covetous, searching eye,   20

---

high feeding, Obscene jokes are directed at Castruchio's
impotence, which makes him capable only of kissing Julia.
tune it, make it play a tune. **in physic,** under the care of a
physician. **lie,** stay. **Sure,** surely. **breach,** behind. **Your
. . . pity,** Julia's answer here is purposely ambiguous. She
may be saying either "What you laugh at, I pity," or "What
you laugh at makes my position (as Castruchio's wife)
pitiful." **allowance,** income.

Look . . . it, As Delio proposes a liaison with her, Julia
thinks about the Cardinal, her present lover, and she unconsciously replies to Delio's proposition by employing the same
kind of imagery (from falconry and lute-playing) that the
Cardinal has just finished using. **cassia,** cinnamon. **civet,**
an animal secretion used in making perfume. **physical,**
health-restoring. **fond,** foolish. **Nor . . . cullises,** Nor is it
health-restoring—though some foolish doctors argue to the
contrary—when it is boiled in a broth. **cullises,** broths.
honesty, chastity. **mandrake,** a root that was thought to
induce madness if plucked. **prodigy,** unnatural event.
loose . . .hilts, unchaste.

To mark who note them. Oh, confusion seize her:
She hath had most cunning bawds to serve her
   turn,
And more secure conveyances° for lust,
Than towns of° garrison, for service.

CARDINAL: Is't possible?
Can this be certain?

FERDINAND: Rhubarb,° oh for rhubarb
To purge this choler; here's the cursèd day°
To prompt my memory, and here't shall stick°
Till of her bleeding heart I make a sponge
To wipe it out.

CARDINAL: Why do you make yourself
So wild a tempest?

FERDINAND: Would I could be one,
That I might toss her palace 'bout her ears,
30 Root up her goodly forests, blast her meads,°
And lay her general territory as waste,
As she hath done her honor's.

CARDINAL: Shall our blood,
The royal blood of Aragon and Castile,
Be thus attainted?

FERDINAND: Apply desperate physic,
We must not now use balsamum,° but fire,
The smarting cupping-glass,° for that's the mean
To purge infected blood, such blood as hers.
40 There is a kind of pity in mine eye;
I'll give it to my handkercher, and now 'tis here:
I'll bequeath this° to her bastard.

CARDINAL: What to do?

FERDINAND: Why, to make soft lint for his mother's
   wounds,
When I have hewèd her to pieces.

CARDINAL: Cursed creature!
Unequal nature, to place women's hearts
So far upon the left side.°

50 FERDINAND: Foolish men,
That e'er will trust their honor in a bark,
Made of so slight, weak bulrush as a woman,
Apt every minute to sink it!

CARDINAL: Thus ignorance, when it hath purchased
   honor
It cannot wield it.

FERDINAND: Methinks I see her laughing,
Excellent hyena!° Talk to me somewhat, quickly,
Or my imagination will carry me

To see her in the shameful act of sin.   60

CARDINAL: With whom?

FERDINAND: Happily,° with some strong-thighed
   bargeman;
Or one o' th' wood yard, that can quoit the sledge°
Or toss the bar, or else some lovely squire
That carries coals up to her privy lodgings.

CARDINAL: You fly beyond your reason.

FERDINAND: Go to, mistress!°
'Tis not your whore's milk, that shall quench my
   wildfire,   70
But your whore's blood.

CARDINAL: How idly shows this rage! which carries
   you,
As men conveyed by witches, through the air
On violent whirlwinds. This intemperate noise
Fitly resembles deaf men's shrill discourse,
Who talk aloud, thinking all other men
To have their imperfection.

FERDINAND: Have not you
My palsy?   80

CARDINAL: Yes, I can be angry
Without this rupture;° there is not in nature
A thing, that makes man so deformed, so beastly,
As doth intemperate anger. Chide yourself.
You have diverse men, who never yet expressed
Their strong desire of rest but by unrest,
By vexing of themselves. Come, put yourself
In tune.

FERDINAND: So, I will only study° to seem
The thing I am not. I could kill her now,   90
In you, or in myself,° for I do think
It is some sin in us, heaven doth revenge
By her.

CARDINAL: Are you stark mad?

FERDINAND: I would have their bodies
Burnt in a coal-pit, with the ventage° stopped
That their cursed smoke might not ascend to
   heaven;
Or dip the sheets they lie in, in pitch or sulphur,
Wrap them in't, and then light them like a match;   100
Or else to boil their bastard to a cullis,
And give't his lecherous father, to renew
The sin of his back.°

CARDINAL: I'll leave you.

FERDINAND: Nay, I have done;
I am confident, had I been damned in hell,
And should have heard of this, it would have put
   me

---

secure conveyances, secret arrangements. *towns of,* towns (have) of. *Rhubarb,* thought to cure men of excessive anger by purging them of it. *here's . . . day,* Ferdinand refers here to the horoscope that Bosola has enclosed. *To prompt,* to keep in. *meads,* meadows. *balsamum,* healing ointment. *cupping-glass,* a small vacuum glass used for drawing blood. *this,* the handkerchief. *to . . . side,* It was thought that only the hearts of deceitful persons were located on the left ("sinister") side. *hyena,* Its lechery, as well as its laughter, makes it an appropriate image for Ferdinand to use here.

Happily, probably, by hap. *quoit the sledge,* throw the hammer. *mistress,* Ferdinand jealously rails agains the Duchess—as if she were a mistress who had deserted him for another lover. *rupture,* complete lack of control. *study,* work. *I could . . . myself,* I could kill you, and even myself, now. *ventage,* chimney. *to . . . back,* to make him, literally, take his son back.

Into a cold sweat. In, in, I'll go sleep:
110　Till I know who leaps my sister, I'll not stir.
That known, I'll find scorpions to string my whips,
And fix her in a general eclipse.° (*Exeunt.*)

ACT 3 / SCENE 1

(*The* DUCHESS' *palace at Amalfi, a few years later*)
(*Enter* ANTONIO *and* DELIO.)

ANTONIO:　Our noble friend, my most beloved Delio,
Oh, you have been a stranger long at court,
Came you along with the Lord Ferdinand?

DELIO:　I did, sir, and how fares your noble Duchess?

ANTONIO:　Right fortunately well. She's an excellent
Feeder of pedigrees: since you last saw her,
She hath had two children more, a son and
　daughter.

DELIO:　Methinks 'twas yesterday. Let me but wink,
10　And not behold your face,° which to mine eye
Is somewhat leaner: verily I should dream
It were within this half hour.

ANTONIO:　You have not been in law,° friend Delio,
Nor in prison, nor a suitor at the court,
Nor begged the reversion° of some great man's
　place,
Nor troubled with an old wife, which° doth make
Your time so insensibly° hasten.

DELIO:　Pray sir tell me,
20　Hath not this news arrived yet to the ear
Of the Lord Cardinal?

ANTONIO:　I fear it hath;
The Lord Ferdinand, that's newly come to court,
Doth bear himself right dangerously.

DELIO:　Pray why?

ANTONIO:　He is so quiet, that he seems to sleep
The tempest out, as dormice do in winter;
Those houses that are haunted are most still,
Till the devil be up.

30　DELIO:　What say the common people?

ANTONIO:　The common rabble do directly say
She is a strumpet.

DELIO:　And your graver heads,
Which would be politic,° what censure they?

ANTONIO:　They do observe I grow to infinite
　purchase°
The left-hand° way, and all suppose the Duchess
Would amend it, if she could. For, say they,
Great princes, though they grudge their officers
40　Should have such large and unconfinèd means

To get wealth under them, will not complain
Lest thereby they should make them odious
Unto the people. For other obligation
Of love, or marriage, between her and me,
They never dream of.

(*Enter* FERDINAND, DUCHESS, *and* BOSOLA.)

DELIO:　The Lord Ferdinand
Is going to bed.

FERDINAND:　I'll instantly to bed,
For I am weary: I am to bespeak
A husband for you.°　　　　　　　　　　　50

DUCHESS:　For me, sir! pray who is't?

FERDINAND:　The great Count Malateste.°

DUCHESS:　Fie upon him,
A count? He's a mere stick of sugar candy,°
You may look quite thorough° him: when I choose
A husband, I will marry for your honor.

FERDINAND:　You shall do well in't. How is't,° worthy
　Antonio?

DUCHESS:　But, sir, I am to have private conference
　with you,　　　　　　　　　　　　　　60
About a scandalous report is spread
Touching mine honor.

FERDINAND:　Let me be ever deaf to't:
One of Pasquil's paper bullets,° court calumny,
A pestilent air, which princes' palaces
Are seldom purged of. Yet, say that it were true,
I pour it in your bosom,° my fixed love
Would strongly excuse, extenuate, nay, deny
Faults were they apparent in you. Go, be safe
In your own innocency.　　　　　　　　70

DUCHESS:　Oh blessed comfort:
This deadly air is purged. (*Exeunt* DUCHESS,
　ANTONIO, DELIO.)

FERDINAND:　Her guilt treads on
Hot burning cultures.° Now, Bosola,
How thrives our intelligence?°

BOSOLA:　Sir, uncertainly:
'Tis rumored she hath had three bastards, but
By whom we may go read i' th' stars.°

FERDINAND:　Why some
Hold opinion all things are written there.　　80

BOSOLA:　Yes, if we could find spectacles to read
　them;

I am . . . you, I am to speak in favor of a prospective husband for you. ***Count Malateste,*** a name Webster chose probably for the effect of the obscene pun. ***He's . . . candy,*** He is of little worth. ***thorough,*** through. ***How is't,*** How is business? ***Pasquil's . . . bullets,*** satirical attacks. (Pasquil, or Pasquin, was the name given a statue to which Italian writers commonly affixed satires.) ***pour . . . bosom,*** I confess to you that. ***cultures,*** the iron blade in the front of a plow. In medieval England, people could demonstrate their innocence of a crime if they could walk unharmed on red-hot cultures. ***intelligence,*** system for spying. ***we . . . stars,*** we cannot determine by any factual evidence.

And . . . eclipse, and cast her forever into darkness.
Let . . . face, It seems hardly more than a wink's time since I last saw your face. ***in law,*** involved in a legal case. ***reversion,*** right of succession to. ***which,*** because you are not involved in any of these tedious undertakings. ***insensibly,*** exceeding the powers of the senses to record. ***politic,*** more prudent. ***purchase,*** wealth. ***left-hand,*** underhanded.

I do suspect, there hath been some sorcery
Used on the Duchess.
FERDINAND: Sorcery? To what purpose?
BOSOLA: To make her dote on some desertless fellow,
  She shames to acknowledge.
FERDINAND: Can your faith give way
  To think there's power in potions or in charms
90 To make us love, whether we will or no?
BOSOLA: Most certainly.
FERDINAND: Away, these are mere gulleries,° horrid
    things
  Invented by some cheating mountebanks°
  To abuse us. Do you think that herbs or charms
  Can force the will? Some trials have been made
  In the foolish practice. But the ingredients
  Were lenative poisons,° such as are of force
  To make the patient mad; and straight the witch
100 Swears, by equivocation,° they are in love.
  The witchcraft lies in her° rank blood: this night
  I will force confession from her. You told me
  You had got, within these two days, a false key°
  Into her bedchamber.
BOSOLA: I have.
FERDINAND: As I would wish.°
BOSOLA: What do you intend to do?
FERDINAND: Can you guess?
BOSOLA: No.
110 FERDINAND: Do not ask then.
  He that can compass° me, and know my drifts,°
  May say he hath put a girdle 'bout the world,°
  And sounded all her quicksands.
BOSOLA: I do not
  Think so.
FERDINAND: What do you think then, pray?
BOSOLA: That you
  Are your own chronicle too much,° and grossly
  Flatter yourself.
120 FERDINAND: Give me thy hand; I thank thee.
  I never gave pension° but to flatterers
  Till I entertained thee: farewell,
  That friend a great man's ruin strongly checks,
  Who rails into his belief° all his defects. (Exeunt.)

ACT 3 / SCENE 2

(The DUCHESS' bedchamber)
(Enter DUCHESS, ANTONIO, and CARIOLA.)

DUCHESS: Bring me the casket hither, and the glass;°
  You get no lodging here tonight, my lord.
ANTONIO: Indeed, I must persuade one.
DUCHESS: Very good:
  I hope in time 'twill grow into a custom,
  That noblemen shall come with cap and knee,°
  To purchase a night's lodging of their wives.
ANTONIO: I must lie here.
DUCHESS: Must? you are a lord of misrule.°
ANTONIO: Indeed, my rule is only in the night. 10
DUCHESS: To what use will you put me?
ANTONIO: We'll sleep together.
DUCHESS: Alas, what pleasure can two lovers find in
  sleep?
CARIOLA: My lord, I lie with her often, and I know
  She'll much disquiet you.
ANTONIO: See, you are complained of.
CARIOLA: For she's the sprawling'st bedfellow.
ANTONIO: I shall like her the better for that.
CARIOLA: Sir, shall I ask you a question? 20
ANTONIO: I pray thee Cariola.
CARIOLA: Wherefore still, when you lie with my lady
  Do you rise° so early?
ANTONIO: Laboring men,
  Count the clock oft'nest, Cariola,
  Are glad when their task's ended.
DUCHESS: I'll stop your mouth.

(Kisses him.)

ANTONIO: Nay, that's but one. Venus had two soft
    doves
  To draw her chariot: I must have another. 30

(Kisses her.)

  When wilt thou marry, Cariola?
CARIOLA: Never, my lord.
ANTONIO: O fie upon this single life: forego it.
  We read how Daphne,° for her peevish slight°
  Became a fruitless bay tree; Syrinx° turned
  To the pale empty reed; Anaxarete°
  Was frozen into marble: whereas those
  Which married, or proved kind unto their friends°
  Were, by a gracious influence, transhaped
  Into the olive, pomegranate, mulberry; 40
  Became flowers, precious stones, or eminent stars.
CARIOLA: This is vain poetry; but I pray you tell me,

---

gulleries, tricks. *mountebanks*, charlatans, pitchmen who mounted benches and peddled their wares, which were usually elixirs and cure-alls. *lenative poisons*, powerful drugs. *by equivocation*, by equating love with madness. *her*, the Duchess'. *false key*, pass key. *As ... wish*, I want it. *compass*, comprehend. *drifts*, secret schemes. *put ... world*, traveled around the world (i.e. has done everything). *Are ... much*, talk too much about the enormity of your deeds. *pension*, reward for service. *belief*, awareness.

glass, mirror. *with ... knee*, on bended knee, with cap in hand. *lord of misrule*, master of the court revels (which were held at night). *rise*, a double-entendre. *Daphne*, a nymph who, pursued by Pan, was transformed into a bay tree at her own entreaty. *peevish slight*, foolish rejection of Pan. *Syrinx*, a nymph who was changed into a reed in order to escape Pan's pursuit. *Anaxarete*, a mythical Grecian queen who scorned the advances of Iphis and stood unmoved as he hanged himself, for which she was punished by being turned into marble. *friends*, lovers.

If there were proposed me wisdom, riches, and
   beauty,
In three several young men, which should I
   choose?
ANTONIO: 'Tis a hard question. This was Paris' case,°
   And he was blind in't, and there was great cause:
   For how was't possible he could judge right,
50 Having three amorous goddesses in view,
   And they stark naked? 'Twas a motion°
   Were able to benight the apprehension°
   Of the severest counselor of Europe.
   Now I look on both your faces, so well formed,
   It puts me in mind of a question I would ask.
CARIOLA: What is't?
ANTONIO: I do wonder why hard-favored° ladies,
   For the most part, keep worse-favored
     waiting-women
60 To attend them, and cannot endure fair ones.
DUCHESS: Oh, that's soon answered.
   Did you ever in your life know an ill painter
   Desire to have his dwelling next door to the shop
   Of an excellent picture maker? 'Twould disgrace
   His face-making,° and undo him. I prithee
   When were we so merry? My hair tangles.
ANTONIO (aside to CARIOLA): Pray thee, Cariola, let's
   steal forth° the room,
   And let her talk to herself: I have diverse times
70 Served her the like when she hath chafed
     extremely.
   I love to see her angry—softly Cariola. (Exeunt
   ANTONIO and CARIOLA.)
DUCHESS: Doth not the color of my hair 'gin to
   change?
   When I wax grey, I shall have all the court
   Powder their hair with arras,° to be like me:
   You have cause to love me, I entered you into° my
   heart

(Enter FERDINAND, unseen.)

80 Before you would vouchsafe to call for the keys.
   We shall one day have my brothers take° you
   napping.

Methinks his presence, being now in court,
Should make you keep your own bed, but you'll say
Love mixed with fear is sweetest. I'll assure you
You shall get no more children till my brothers
Consent to be your gossips.° Have you lost your
   tongue?

(In the mirror she sees FERDINAND holding a poniard.)

'Tis welcome:
For know, whether I am doomed to live, or die, 90
I can do both like a prince.

(FERDINAND gives her a poniard.)

FERDINAND: Die then, quickly.
   Virtue, where art thou hid? What hideous thing
   Is it, that doth eclipse thee?
DUCHESS: Pray, sir, hear me—
FERDINAND: Or is it true, thou art but a bare name,
   And no essential thing?
DUCHESS: Sir—
FERDINAND: Do not speak.
DUCHESS: No sir: 100
   I will plant my soul in mine ears, to hear you.°
FERDINAND: Oh most imperfect light of human
   reason,
   That mak'st us so unhappy, to foresee
   What we can least prevent. Pursue thy wishes
   And glory in them: there's in shame no comfort,
   But to be past all bounds and sense of shame.
DUCHESS: I pray sir, hear me: I am married—
FERDINAND: So!
DUCHESS: Happily,° not to your liking, but for that 110
   Alas, your shears do come untimely now
   To clip the bird's wings, that's already flown.
   Will you see my husband?
FERDINAND: Yes, if I could change
   Eyes with a basilisk.°
DUCHESS: Sure, you came hither
   By his confederacy.°
FERDINAND: The howling of a wolf
   Is music to thee, screech owl; prithee, peace.
   Whate'er thou art that hast enjoyed my sister, 120
   (For I am sure thou hear'st me), for thine own sake
   Let me not know thee. I came hither prepared
   To work thy discovery, yet am now persuaded

Paris' case, Paris, the handsomest of men, was asked to judge who among the goddesses was the fairest—Hera, Athena, or Aphrodite. Because all three of the goddesses, who stood naked before him, were beautiful, he could not choose a winner; so each offered him a reward as a bribe. Hera promised greatness. Athena offered success in war, and Aphrodite told him that she would give him the most beautiful woman in the world for his wife. Finally, he judged Aphrodite the winner, and she subsequently helped him to carry off Helen, with disastrous consequences for himself and his city. *motion,* spectacle. *benight the apprehension,* obscure the judgment. *hard-favored,* unattractive. *face-making,* a pun, meaning both portrait-painting and make-up work. *forth,* forth from. *arras,* a white powder. *entered . . . into,* offered you. *take,* discover.

gossips, sponsors at a baptism. *I will . . . you,* I will listen to you with the utmost attention. *Happily,* probably. *basilisk,* a legendary reptile that could kill with a look. *By his confederacy,* The Duchess remains hopeful, thinking that Ferdinand's appearance has been arranged with Antonio. But she is, of course, mistaken, and the indefiniteness of her reference in the phrase "By his confederacy" emphasizes the magnitude of her error. It is not a "confederacy" with Antonio that has prompted Ferdinand's appearance; instead it is his emotional and psychological commitment to the forces of evil and destruction represented by the basilisk.

It would beget such violent effects
As would damn° us both. I would not for ten
  millions
I had beheld thee; therefore, use all means
I never may have knowledge of thy name;
Enjoy thy lust still, and a wretched life,
130 On that condition. And for thee, vild° woman,
If thou do wish thy lecher may grow old
In thy embracements, I would have thee build
Such a room for him, as our anchorites°
To holier use inhabit. Let not the sun
Shine on him, till he's dead. Let dogs and monkeys
Only converse with him, and such dumb things
To whom nature denies use° to sound his name.
Do not keep a paraquito, lest she learn it;
If thou do love him, cut out thine own tongue,
140 Lest it bewray him.
DUCHESS: Why might not I marry?
I have not gone about, in this, to create
Any new world, or custom.
FERDINAND: Thou art undone:
And thou hast ta'en that massy sheet of lead
That hid thy husband's bones, and folded it
About my heart.
DUCHESS: Mine bleeds for't.
FERDINAND: Thine? thy heart?
150 What should I name't, unless a hollow bullet°
Filled with unquenchable wildfire?
DUCHESS: You are in this
Too strict,° and were you not my princely brother
I would say too willful. My reputation
Is safe.
FERDINAND: Dost thou know what reputation is?
I'll tell thee, to small purpose, since th'instruction
Comes now too late:
Upon a time° Reputation, Love and Death
160 Would° travel o'er the world: and it was concluded
That they should part, and take three several ways.
Death told them they should find him in great
  battles,
Or cities plagued with plagues. Love gives them
  counsel
To inquire for him 'mongst unambitious
  shepherds,
Where dow'ries were not talked of, and sometimes
'Mongst quiet kindred, that had nothing left
170 By their dead parents. "Stay," quoth Reputation,
"Do not forsake me: for it is my nature,
If once I part from any man I meet,
I am never found again." And so, for you:
You have shook hands with° Reputation,
And made him invisible. So fare you well.

I will never see you more.
DUCHESS: Why should only I,
Of all the other princes of the world
Be cased up, like a holy relic? I have youth,
And a little beauty.   180
FERDINAND: So you have some virgins°
That are witches. I will never see thee more. (Exit.)

(Enter CARIOLA and ANTONIO with a pistol.)

DUCHESS: You saw this apparition?°
ANTONIO: Yes: we are
Betrayed. How came he hither? I should turn
This, to thee, for that. (Points the pistol at CARIOLA.)
CARIOLA: Pray, sir, do; and when
That you have cleft my heart, you shall read there
Mine innocence.
DUCHESS: That gallery° gave him entrance.   190
ANTONIO: I would this terrible thing would come
  again,
That, standing on my guard, I might relate°
My warrantable love. Ha! what means this?
DUCHESS: He left this with me. (She shows the poniard.)
ANTONIO: And, it seems, did wish
You would use it on yourself?
DUCHESS: His action seemed
To intend so much.°
ANTONIO: This hath a handle to't   200
As well as a point: turn it towards him, and
So fasten the keen edge in his rank gall.

(Knocking.)

How now? Who knocks? More earthquakes?°
DUCHESS: I stand
As if a mine, beneath my feet, were ready
To be blown up.
CARIOLA: 'Tis Bosola.
DUCHESS: Away!
Oh misery, methinks unjust actions
Should wear these masks and curtains, and not we. 210
You must instantly part hence: I have fashioned it°
already. (Exit ANTONIO.)

(Enter BOSOLA.)

BOSOLA: The Duke your brother is ta'en up in a
  whirlwind;
Hath took horse, and's rid post to Rome.
DUCHESS: So late?
BOSOLA: He told me, as he mounted into th' saddle,
You were undone.
DUCHESS: Indeed, I am very near it.

---

damn, The first quarto edition reads "dampe." vild,
vile. anchorites, hermits. use, skill. hollow bullet, cannon ball. strict, unyielding. Upon a time, once. would,
wished to. shook...with, parted from.

So ... virgins, So, you know, have some virgins.
apparition, the sudden and unexpected appearance of Ferdinand. gallery, upstairs corridor (in this case, the upper
stage). relate, demonstrate. intend so much, imply as
much. earthquakes, serious problems. fashioned it, contrived a plan.

220 BOSOLA: What's the matter?
DUCHESS: Antonio, the master of our household,
  Hath dealt so falsely with me in's accounts:
  My brother stood engaged° with me for money
  Ta'en up of° certain Neapolitan Jews,
  And Antonio lets the bonds be forfeit.
BOSOLA: Strange. *(aside)* This is cunning.
DUCHESS: And hereupon
  My brother's bills at Naples are protested
  Against.° Call up our officers.
230 BOSOLA: I shall. *(Exit.)*

  (Enter ANTONIO.*)*

DUCHESS: The place that you must fly to, is Ancona.
  Hire a house there. I'll send after you
  My treasure, and my jewels. Our weak safety
  Runs upon enginous wheels:° short syllables
  Must stand for periods.° I must now accuse you
  Of such a feignèd crime, as Tasso calls
  Magnanima mensogna: a noble lie,
  'Cause it must shield our honors—Hark, they are
    coming.

  (Enter BOSOLA *and* OFFICERS. *The* DUCHESS *and* AN-
  TONIO *begin their feigned dispute.)*

240 ANTONIO: Will your grace hear me?
DUCHESS: I have got well by° you: you have yielded
    me
  A million of loss; I am like to inherit
  The people's curses for your stewardship.
  You had the trick, in audit time, to be sick
  Till I had signed your *Quietus;* and that cured you
  Without help of a doctor. Gentlemen,
  I would have this man be an example to you all:
  So shall you hold my favor. I pray let him;°
250 For h'as done that, alas, you would not think of;
  And, because I intend to be rid of him,
  I mean not to publish.° Use your fortune
    elsewhere.
ANTONIO: I am strongly armed to brook my
    overthrow,
  As commonly men bear with a hard year:
  I will not blame the cause on't; but do think
  The necessity of my malevolent star
  Procures this, not her humor.° O, the inconstant
260 And rotten ground of service, you may see;
  'Tis ev'n like him that, in a winter night,
  Takes a long slumber o'er a dying fire,

As loth to part from't, yet parts thence as cold
As when he first sat down.
DUCHESS: We do confiscate,
  Towards the satisfying of your accounts,
  All that you have.
ANTONIO: I am all yours; and 'tis very fit
  All mine should be so.
DUCHESS: So, sir, you have your pass.°   270
ANTONIO: You may see, gentlemen, what 'tis to serve
  A prince with body and soul. *(Exit.)*
BOSOLA: Here's an example for extortion: what mois-
  ture is drawn out of the sea, when foul weather
  comes, pours down, and runs into the sea again.
DUCHESS: I would know what are your opinions
  Of this Antonio.
SECOND OFFICER: He could not abide to see a pig's
  head gaping.° I thought your grace would find
  him a Jew.°   280
THIRD OFFICER: I would you had been his officer, for
  your own sake.
FOURTH OFFICER: You would have had more money.
FIRST OFFICER: He stopped his ears with black wool,
  and to those came to him for money said he was
  thick of hearing.
SECOND OFFICER: Some said he was an hermaphro-
  dite,° for he could not abide a woman.
FOURTH OFFICER: How scurvy proud he would look,
  when the treasury was full. Well, let him go.   290
FIRST OFFICER: Yes, and the chippings of the butt'ry°
  fly after him, to scour his gold chain.°
DUCHESS: Leave us. What do you think of these?°
  (Exeunt OFFICERS.*)*
BOSOLA: That these are rogues, that in's prosperity,
  But to have waited on his fortune, could have
    wished
  His dirty stirrup riveted through their noses:
  And followed after's° mule, like a bear in a ring.°
  Would have prostituted their daughters to his lust;
  Made their first-born intelligencers;° thought none 300
    happy
  But such as were born under his blessed planet;
  And wore his livery. And do these lice drop off
    now?
  Well, never look to have the like° again;
  He hath left a sort of flatt'ring rogues behind him;
  Their doom must follow. Princes pay flatterers,

---

engaged, committed.   *Ta'en up of,* borrowed from.
protested Against, called in for payment.   *Runs . . . wheels,*
depends upon speed and ingenuity.   *periods,* well-
proportioned sentences.   *got . . . by,* had enough of.   *let
hm,* let him go.   *publish,* publicly announce (what he has
done).   *but . . . humor,* This overthrow has been brought
about by evil Fortune's unalterable decree, not by the
capriciousness of the Duchess.

pass, leave to go.   *gaping,* He could not stand to see
people feasting on pork (because he hated feasting in
general and the eating of pork in particular).   *Jew,* an
unusually clever miser.   *hermaphrodite,* an individual having both male and female sexual characteristics.   *chippings
. . . butt'ry,* bread crumbs, used for polishing gold.   *gold
chain,* steward's badge of office.   *these,* these officers.
after's, after Antonio's.   *like . . . ring,* Rings were thrust
through the noses of bears so that they could be marched in
procession before bearbaiting events.   *intelligencers,* spies.
the like, one as good as Antonio.

In their own money. Flatterers dissemble their
   vices,
310 And they dissemble their lies:° that's justice.
Alas, poor gentleman,—
DUCHESS: Poor! he hath amply filled his coffers.
BOSOLA: Sure he was too honest. Pluto° the god of
   riches,
When he's sent by Jupiter° to any man,
He goes limping, to signify that wealth
That comes on God's name, comes slowly; but
   when he's sent
On the devil's errand, he rides post and comes in by
320   scuttles.°
Let me show you what a most unvalued° jewel
You have, in a wanton humor, thrown away
To bless the man shall° find him. He was an
   excellent
Courtier, and most faithful; a soldier that thought
   it
As beastly to know his own value too little,
As devilish to acknowledge it too much:
Both his virtues and form deserved a far better
330   fortune.
His discourse rather delighted to judge itself, than
   show itself.°
His breast was filled with all perfection,
And yet it seemed a private whisp'ring room:
It made so little noise of't.
DUCHESS: But he was basely descended.
BOSOLA: Will you make yourself a mercenary herald,
Rather to examine men's pedigrees, than virtues?
You shall want° him:
340 For know an honest statesman to a prince,
Is like a cedar, planted by a spring:
The spring bathes the tree's root; the grateful tree
Rewards it with his shadow. You have not done so;
I would sooner swim to the Bermoothas° on
Two politicians'° rotten bladders, tied
Together with an intelligencer's heartstring,
Than depend on so changeable a prince's favor.
Fare thee well, Antonio, since the malice of the
   world
350 Would needs down with thee, it cannot be said yet
That any ill happened unto thee,
Considering thy fall was accompanied with virtue.
DUCHESS: Oh, you render me excellent music.

BOSOLA: Say you?
DUCHESS: This good one that you speak of—is my
   husband.
BOSOLA: Do I not dream? Can this ambitious age
Have so much goodness in't as to prefer
A man merely for worth, without these shadows
Of wealth, and painted honors? possible?°   360
DUCHESS: I have had three children by him.
BOSOLA: Fortunate lady,
For you have made your private nuptial bed
The humble and fair seminary° of peace.
No question but many an unbeneficed° scholar
Shall pray for you for this deed, and rejoice
That some preferment in the world can yet
Arise from merit. The virgins of your land
That have no dowries shall hope your example
Will raise them to rich husbands. Should you want 370
Soldiers, 'twould make the very Turks and Moors
Turn Christians, and serve you for this act.
Last, the neglected poets of your time,
In honor of this trophy° of a man,
Raised by that curious engine,° your white hand,
Shall thank you in your grave for't; and make that
More reverend than all the cabinets°
Of living princes. For Antonio,
His fame shall likewise flow from many a pen,
When heralds shall want coats, to sell to men.°   380
DUCHESS: As I taste comfort, in this friendly speech,
So would I find concealment°—
BOSOLA: Oh the secret of my prince,
Which I will wear on th' inside of my heart.
DUCHESS: You shall take charge of all my coin and
   jewels
And follow him, for he retires himself
To Ancona.
BOSOLA: So.
DUCHESS: Whither, within few days,   390
I mean to follow thee.
BOSOLA: Let me think:
I would wish your grace to feign a pilgrimage
To Our Lady of Loretto, scarce seven leagues
From fair Ancona, so may you depart
Your country with more honor and your flight
Will seem a princely progress,° retaining
Your usual train about you.
DUCHESS: Sir, your direction
Shall lead me, by the hand.   400
CARIOLA: In my opinion,
She were better progress to the baths at Lucca,°

Flatterers . . . lies, Flatterers pretend that princes do not
have vices, and princes pretend that flatterers do not lie.
Pluto, actually King of the Underworld; the god of riches
was Plutus. Webster's error in this case may, however, be
intentional, for he may want to emphasize the extent to
which Bosola's thinking is dominated by the power of
blackness. *Jupiter,* king of the gods. *by scuttles,* runs
quickly. *unvalued,* invaluable. *man shall,* man who shall.
to . . . itself, to be sound, rather than showy. *want,* miss.
Bermoothas, Bermuda, which was thought of as a distant and
primitive island. *politicians,* self-interested schemers.

possible, (Is it) possible? *seminary,* seed bed. *unbe-
neficed,* not supported by a lord. *trophy,* prize. *engine,*
source of power. *cabinets,* advisors. *When . . . men,* when
heralds no longer shall deal in the corrupt practice of selling
coats of arms to men (i.e., when men are rewarded for virtue
rather than for bribery). *concealment,* secrecy. *progress,*
official journey. *Lucca,* a resort near Pisa.

Or go visit the Spa°
In Germany: for, if you will believe me,
I do not like this jesting with religion,
This feigned pilgrimage.
DUCHESS: Thou art a superstitious fool!
  Prepare us instantly for our departure.
  Past sorrows, let us moderately lament them;
410 For those to come, seek wisely to prevent them.

  (Exit DUCHESS with CARIOLA.)

BOSOLA: A politician is the devil's quilted° anvil:
  He fashions all sins on him, and the blows
  Are never heard; he may work in a lady's chamber,
  As here for proof. What rests,° but I reveal
  All to my lord? Oh, this base quality
  Of intelligencer! Why, every quality i' th' world
  Prefers but gain, or commendation.°
  Now for this act, I am certain to be raised:
  And men that paint weeds to the life° are praised.
  (Exit.)

ACT 3 / SCENE 3

(The CARDINAL's palace in Rome)
(Enter CARDINAL, FERDINAND, MALATESTE, PESCARA, SILVIO, DELIO.)

CARDINAL: Must we turn soldier then?
MALATESTE: The Emperor,°
  Hearing your worth that way, ere you attained
  This reverend garment, joins you in commission
  With the right fortunate soldier, the Marquis of
    Pescara°
  And the famous Lannoy.°
CARDINAL: He that had the honor
  Of taking the French king° prisoner?
10 MALATESTE: The same.
  Here's a plot° drawn for a new fortification
  At Naples.
FERDINAND: This great Count Malateste,° I perceive
  Hath got employment.
DELIO: No employment my lord,
  A marginal note in the muster book,° that he is

A voluntary lord.°
FERDINAND: He's no soldier?
DELIO: He has worn gunpowder, in's hollow tooth,
  For the toothache.   20
SILVIO: He comes to the leaguer° with a full intent
  To eat fresh beef, and garlic; means to stay
  Till the scent be gone,° and straight return to court.
DELIO: He hath read all the late service,°
  As the city chronicle° relates it,
  And keeps two pewterers going, only to express
  Battles in model.°
SILVIO: Then he'll fight by the book.°
DELIO: By the almanac, I think,
  To choose good days and shun the critical.°   30
  That's his mistress' scarf.
SILVIO: Yes, he protests
  He would do much for that taffeta,—
DELIO: I think he would run away from a battle
  To save it from taking° prisoner.
SILVIO: He is horribly afraid
  Gunpowder will spoil the perfume on't,—
DELIO: I saw a Dutchman break his pate° once
  For calling him pot-gun;° he made his head
  Have a bore in't, like a musket.   40
SILVIO: I would he had made a touchhole° to't.°
  He is indeed a guarded sumpter-cloth°
  Only for the remove° of the court

  (Enter BOSOLA.)

PESCARA: Bosola arrived? What should be the
    business?
  Some falling out amongst the cardinals?
  These factions amongst great men, they are like
  Foxes when their heads are divided:°
  They carry fire in their tails, and all the country
  About them goes to wrack for't.   50
SILVIO: What's that Bosola?
DELIO: I knew him in Padua—a fantastical° scholar,
  like such who study to know how many knots was
  in Hercules' club; of what color Achilles'° beard
  was, or whether Hector° were not troubled with

Spa, a town in Belgium famous for its mineral waters. r its mineral waters. *quilted*, covered with a sound-absorbing material. *rests*, remains. *Why . . . commendation*, Every quality of character leads to some reward: (if the quality is evil), the reward is gain; (if it is good), the prize is only commendation. *to the life*, so that they seem lifelike. *Emperor*, Charles V, the greatest of all Hapsburg emperors, who ruled from 1519 to 1558. *Marquis of Pescara*, the soldier who commanded the Italian army in its victory over Francis I of France at Pavia in 1525. *Lannoy*, Viceroy of Naples, one of the Italian commanders at Pavia and a favorite of Charles V. *French king*, Francis I, who would surrender his sword at Pavia only to Lannoy. *plot*, diagram. *Malateste*, the ruling family in Rimini, Italy, during the sixteenth century. *muster book*, a register of the officers and men in a military unit.

voluntary lord, a lord who volunteers for military service. *leaguer*, alliance. *Till . . . gone*, until the good food is eaten. *all . . . service*, all about the recent military maneuvers. *city chronicle*, official reports about the affairs of a city. *model*, miniature reproductions (with pewter soldiers). *by the book*, according to some generally accepted treatise on military strategy. *critical*, days of crisis. *taking*, being taken. *break his pate*, strike him across the head. *pot-gun*, popgun, a braggart. *touchhole*, the vent in firearms through which the charge was ignited. *I . . . to't*, I wish he had burst his false pride completely. *guarded sumpter-cloth*, ornamental blanket. *remove*, location. *heads are divided*, when they are tied tail to tail (cf. Judges 15:4). *fantastical*, pursuing foolish fantasies. *Achilles*, the greatest Greek warrior in the Trojan War. *Hector*, the greatest Trojan warrior.

the toothache. He hath studied himself half
blear-eyed to know the true symmetry of
Caesar's nose by a shoeing horn.° And this he did
to gain the name of a speculative man.

60   PESCARA: Mark Prince Ferdinand,
A very salamander° lives in's eye,
To mock the eager violence of fire.

SILVIO: That cardinal hath made more bad faces with
his oppression than ever Michael Angelo made
good ones: he lifts up's nose,° like a foul por-
poise° before a storm,—

PESCARA: The Lord Ferdinand laughs.

DELIO: Like a deadly cannon, that lightens° ere it
smokes.

70   PESCARA: These are your true pangs of death,
The pangs of life, that struggle with great
statesmen,°—

DELIO: In such a deformèd silence,° witches whisper
their charms.

CARDINAL (on the other side of the stage): Doth she make
religion her riding hood
To keep her from the sun and tempest?°

FERDINAND: That!°
That damns her. Methinks her fault and beauty

80   Blended together show like leprosy:
The whiter, the fouler. I make it a question
Whether her beggarly brats were ever christened.

CARDINAL: I will instantly solicit the state of Ancona
To have them banished.

FERDINAND (to the CARDINAL): You are for° Loretto?
I shall not be at your ceremony;° fare you well.

(to BOSOLA) Write to the Duke of Malfi, my young
nephew
She had by her first husband, and acquaint him

90   With's mother's honesty.

BOSOLA: I will.

FERDINAND: Antonio!
A slave, that only smelled of ink and counters°
And ne'er in's life looked like a gentleman

---

to . . . horn, to learn that Caesar's nose was as symmetri-
cal and well-tapered as a shoehorn. *salamander,* thought
capable of living in fire. *lifts up's nose,* He sniffs around
for trouble. *foul porpoise,* The appearance of porpoises
around a ship was believed to be a warning of foul weather
to come. *lightens,* gives off light (of fire). *These . . .
statesmen,* This passage is confusing enough to be textually
corrupt: it is difficult to see how "The pangs of life, that
struggle with great statesmen" can be an accurate description of "true pangs of death." But whether there is a textual
corruption in this passage or not, its implication is that the
whispered secrets between the Cardinal and Ferdinand are
directed toward evil ends. *In . . . silence,* in such unnatural
whispers. *sun . . . tempest,* the Cardinal, who theoretically
represents the light of God, and Ferdinand, whose anger is
violent, like a tempest. *That,* That is correct! *for,* headed
for. *ceremony,* his official installation as a soldier. *counters,* pieces of wood or bone used in keeping accounts.

But in the audit time.° Go, go presently;
Draw me out an hundred and fifty of our horse,
And meet me at the fort bridge.° (Exeunt.)

ACT 3 / SCENE 4

(Loretto)
(Enter TWO PILGRIMS to the Shrine of Our Lady of
Loretto.)

FIRST PILGRIM: I have not seen a goodlier shrine than
this;
Yet I have visited many.

SECOND PILGRIM: The Cardinal of Aragon
Is this day to resign his cardinal's hat;°
His sister Duchess likewise is arrived
To pay her vow of pilgrimage. I expect
A noble ceremony.

FIRST PILGRIM: No question.—They come.

(Here the ceremony of the Cardinal's installment in the
habit of a soldier: performed in delivering up his cross,
hat, robes, and ring at the shrine, and investing him with
sword, helmet, shield, and spurs. Then ANTONIO, and the
DUCHESS, and their children, having presented themselves at the shrine, are (by a form of banishment in dumb
show expressed towards them by the CARDINAL and the
state of ANCONA) banished. During all which ceremony
this ditty is sung to very solemn music, by diverse churchmen; and then exeunt.)

The author disclaims this ditty to be his.

Arms and honors deck thy story   10
To thy fame's eternal glory.
Adverse fortune ever fly thee;
No disastrous fate come nigh thee.

I alone will sing thy praises,
Whom to honor virtue raises;
And thy study that divine is,
Bent to martial discipline is.
Lay aside all those robes lie by thee,
Crown thy arts with arms; they'll beautify thee.

O worthy of worthiest name, adorned in this   20
manner,
Lead bravely thy forces on, under war's warlike
banner.
O mayst thou prove fortunate in all martial
courses,
Guide thou still by skill, in arts and forces:
Victory attend thee nigh, whilst fame sings loud thy
powers;

But . . . time, In audit time, the Duke implies Antonio
made enough money to qualify as a gentleman. *fort bridge,*
draw-bridge. *to . . . hat,* resigning his church position (to
become a soldier).

Triumphant conquest crown thy head, and
30   blessings pour down showers.

FIRST PILGRIM: Here's a strange turn of state: who
        would have thought
    So great a lady would have matched herself
    Unto so mean° a person? Yet the Cardinal
    Bears himself much too cruel.
SECOND PILGRIM: They are banished.
FIRST PILGRIM: But I would ask what power hath this
        state
    Of Ancona, to determine of° a free prince?
40 SECOND PILGRIM: They are a free state, sir, and her
        brother showed
    How that the Pope, forehearing of her looseness,
    Hath seized into th' protection of the Church
    The dukedom which she held as dowager.°
FIRST PILGRIM: But by what justice?
SECOND PILGRIM: Sure I think by none,
    Only her brother's instigation.
FIRST PILGRIM: What was it, with such violence he
        took
50   Off from her finger?
SECOND PILGRIM: 'Twas her wedding ring,
    Which he vowed shortly he would sacrifice
    To his revenge.
FIRST PILGRIM: Alas Antonio!
    If that a man be thrust into a well,
    No matter who sets hand to't,° his own weight
    Will bring him sooner to th' bottom. Come, let's
        hence.
    Fortune makes this conclusion general:
60   All things do help th' unhappy man to fall. (*Exeunt.*)

ACT 3 / SCENE 5

(*Somewhere near Loretto*)
(*Enter* ANTONIO, DUCHESS, CHILDREN, CARIOLA, SER-
VANTS.)

DUCHESS: Banished Ancona?
ANTONIO: Yes, you see what power
    Lightens° in great men's breath.
DUCHESS: Is all our train
    Shrunk to this poor remainder?
ANTONIO: These poor men,
    Which have got little in your service, vow
    To take your fortune.° But your wiser buntings,°
    Now they are fledged,° are gone.
10 DUCHESS: They have done wisely.

This puts me in mind of death: physicians thus,
    With their hands full of money, use to give o'er°
    Their patients.
ANTONIO: Right° the fashion of the world:
    From decayed fortunes every flatterer shrinks;
    Men cease to build where the foundation sinks.
DUCHESS: I had a very strange dream tonight.
ANTONIO: What was't?
DUCHESS: Methought I wore my coronet of state,
    And on a sudden all the diamonds   20
    Were changed to pearls.
ANTONIO: My interpretation
    Is, you'll weep shortly; for to me, the pearls
    Do signify your tears.
DUCHESS: The birds that live i' th' field
    On the wild benefit of nature live
    Happier than we; for they may choose their mates,
    And carol their sweet pleasures to the spring.

(*Enter* BOSOLA *with a letter, which he gives to the*
DUCHESS.)

BOSOLA: You are happily o'erta'en.
DUCHESS: From my brother?   30
BOSOLA: Yes, from the Lord Ferdinand, your
        brother,
    All love, and safety—
DUCHESS: Thou dost blanch mischief;
    Wouldst make it white.° See, see, like to calm
        weather
    At sea before a tempest, false hearts speak fair
    To those they intend most mischief. (*She reads a
    letter.*)
    "Send Antonio to me; I want his head in a
        business."   40
    A politic equivocation—
    He doth not want your counsel, but your head:
    That is, he cannot sleep till you be dead.
    And here's another pitfall, that's strewed o'er
    With roses. Mark it, 'tis a cunning one:
        "I stand engaged for your husband for several
        debts at Naples. Let not that trouble him: I had
        rather have his heart than his money."
    And I believe so too.
BOSOLA: What do you believe?   50
DUCHESS: That he so much distrusts my husband's
        love,
    He will by no means believe his heart is with him
    Until he see it. The devil is not cunning enough
    To circumvent us in riddles.
BOSOLA: Will you reject that noble and free league
    Of amity and love which I present you?
DUCHESS: Their league is like that of some politic°
        kings

---

mean, of a low social class. *determine of,* pass judgment against. *dowager,* property received by a widow upon
the death of her husband. *sets . . . to't,* gives him the initial
push. *Lightens,* explodes. *take . . . fortune,* endure your
misfortune with you. *buntings,* little birds. *are fledged,*
have acquired enough feathers to fly.

---

o'er, up. *Right,* such is. *Thou . . . white,* You try to
cover the blackness of your evil intentions with the whiteness
(of feigned friendliness). *politic,* conniving.

60 Only to make themselves of strength and power
To be our after-ruin. Tell them so.
BOSOLA: And what from you?
ANTONIO: Thus tell him: I will not come.
BOSOLA: And what of this?
ANTONIO: My brothers° have dispersed
Bloodhounds abroad, which till I hear are muzzled
No truce—though hatched with ne'er such politic
skill—
Is safe that hangs upon our enemies' will.°
70 I'll not come at them.
BOSOLA: This proclaims your breeding.
Every small thing draws a base mind to fear,
As the adamant° draws iron. Fare you well, sir;
You shall shortly hear from's. (Exit.)
DUCHESS: I suspect some ambush:
Therefore, by all my love, I do conjure you
To take your eldest son and fly towards Milan.
Let us not venture all this poor remainder
In one unlucky bottom.°
80 ANTONIO: You counsel safely.
Best of my life, farewell. Since we must part,
Heaven hath a hand in't: but no otherwise
Than as some curious artist takes in sunder
A clock or watch, when it is out of frame,°
To bring't in better order.
DUCHESS: I know not which is best,
To see you dead, or part with you. Farewell, boy,
Thou art happy, that thou hast not understanding
To know thy misery. For all our wit
90 And reading brings us to a truer sense
Of sorrow. In the eternal Church, sir,
I do hope we shall not part thus.
ANTONIO: O be of comfort,
Make patience a noble fortitude:
And think not how unkindly° we are used.
Man, like to cassia,° is proved best being bruised.
DUCHESS: Must I, like to a slave-born Russian,
Account it praise to suffer tyranny?
And yet, O Heaven, thy heavy hand is in't.
100 I have seen my little boy oft scourge his top,°
And compared myself to't: nought made me e'er
go right,
But Heaven's scourge stick.
ANTONIO: Do not weep:
Heaven fashioned us of nothing; and we strive
To bring ourselves to nothing. Farewell, Cariola,
And thy sweet armful°. (to the DUCHESS) If I do never

see thee more,
Be a good mother to your little ones,
And save them from the tiger: fare you well.   110
DUCHESS: Let me look upon you once more, for that
speech
Came from a dying father: your kiss is colder
Than I have seen an holy anchorite
Give to a dead man's skull.
ANTONIO: My heart is turned to a heavy lump of
lead,°
With which I sound my danger: fare you well. (Exit
with elder SON.)
DUCHESS: My laurel is all witherèd.
CARIOLA: Look, madam, what a troop of armèd men   120
Make° toward us.

(Enter BOSOLA with a guard, all wearing armored
masks.)

DUCHESS: O, they are very welcome:
When Fortune's wheel is overcharged with°
princes,
The weight makes it move swift. I would have my
ruin
Be sudden. I am your adventure,° am I not?
BOSOLA: You are. You must see your husband no
more,—
DUCHESS: What devil art thou, that counterfeits   130
Heaven's thunder?
BOSOLA: Is that terrible? I would have you tell me
whether
Is that note worse that° frights the silly birds
Out of the corn, or that which doth allure them
To the nets? You have harkened to the last too
much.
DUCHESS: O misery! like to a rusty o'erchargèd
cannon,
Shall I never fly in pieces? Come: to what prison?   140
BOSOLA: To none.
DUCHESS: Whither then?
BOSOLA: To your palace.
DUCHESS: I have heard that Charon's° boat serves to
convey
All o'er the dismal lake, but brings none back again.
BOSOLA: Your brothers mean you safety and pity.
DUCHESS: Pity!
With such a pity men preserve alive
Pheasants and quails, when they are not fat enough   150
To be eaten.
BOSOLA: These are your children?

---

brothers, brothers-in-law. **which ... will,** Until those
bloodhounds are tied up, no truce that depends on our
enemies' good will is safe for us—no matter how skillfully
couched in ambiguous language it may be. **adamant,**
magnet. **bottom,** the hold of a ship (i.e., in one precarious
place). **frame,** order. **unkindly,** both evilly and unnaturally. **cassia,** bark that, when pounded, is a source of
cinnamon. **scourge his top,** spin his toy top. **sweet armful,**
the babies she holds.

lump of lead, Sailors took depth readings by dropping
heavy lumps of lead overboard. **Make,** the verb is plural
because of its proximity to "men." **overcharged with,**
turned over by (the weight of the princes tied to it).
adventure, what you venture after. **whether ... worse that,**
which note is worse, that which. **Charon,** the old boatman
who ferried the souls of the dead across the river Styx to
Hades.

DUCHESS: Yes.

BOSOLA: Can they prattle?°

DUCHESS: No.
But I intend, since they were born accursed,
Curses shall be their first language.

BOSOLA: Fie, madam!
Forget this base, low fellow.

160 DUCHESS: Were I a man,
I'd beat that counterfeit face° into thy other—

BOSOLA: One of no birth.

DUCHESS: Say that he was born mean:
Man is most happy, when's own actions
Be arguments and examples of his virtue.

BOSOLA: A barren, beggarly virtue.

DUCHESS: I prithee, who is greatest? Can you tell?
Sad tales befit my woe: I'll tell you one.
A salmon, as she swam unto the sea,
170 Met with a dogfish, who encounters her
With this rough language: "Why are thou so bold
To mix thyself with our high state of floods°
Being no eminent courtier, but one
That for the calmest and fresh time o' th' year
Dost live in shallow rivers, rankst thyself
With silly smelts and shrimps? And darest thou
Pass by our° dogship° without reverence?"
"O," quoth the salmon, "sister, be at peace:
Thank Jupiter, we both have passed the net.
180 Our value never can be truly known,
Till in the fisher's basket we be shown;
I' th' market then my price may be the higher,
Even when I am nearest to the cook, and fire."
So, to great men, the moral may be stretched:
Men oft are valued high,° when th'are most
wretched.
But, come, whither you please. I am armed 'gainst
misery,
Bent to all sways of the oppressor's will.
190 There's no deep valley, but near some great hill.°
(*Exeunt.*)

ACT 4 / SCENE 1

(*In a prison somewhere near Loretto*)
(*Enter* FERDINAND *and* BOSOLA.)

FERDINAND: How doth our sister Duchess bear
herself
In her imprisonment?

BOSOLA: Nobly. I'll describe her:
She's sad, as one long used to't, and she seems

Rather to welcome the end of misery
Than shun it—a behavior so noble,
As gives a majesty to adversity.
You may discern the shape of loveliness
More perfect in her tears, than in her smiles. 10
She will muse four hours together, and her silence,
Methinks, expresseth more than if she spake.

FERDINAND: Her melancholy seems to be fortified
With a strange disdain.

BOSOLA: 'Tis so, and this restraint
(Like English mastives, that grow fierce with tying)
Makes her too passionately apprehend
Those pleasures she's kept from.

FERDINAND: Curse upon her!
I will no longer study in the book 20
Of another's heart:° inform her what I told you.
(*Exit.*)

(BOSOLA *enters the* DUCHESS' *inner-stage prison.*)

BOSOLA: All comfort to, your grace;—

DUCHESS: I will have none.
'Pray thee, why dost thou wrap thy poisoned pills
In gold and sugar?°

BOSOLA: Your elder brother, the Lord Ferdinand,
Is come to visit you, and sends you word,
'Cause once he rashly made a solemn vow
Never to see you more. He comes i' th' night,
And prays you, gently, neither torch nor taper 30
Shine in your chamber. He will kiss your hand;
And reconcile himself, but, for his vow,
He dares not see you.

DUCHESS: At his pleasure.
Take hence the lights: he's come. (*Exeunt* SERVANTS
with lights.)

(*Enter* FERDINAND.)

FERDINAND: Where are you?

DUCHESS: Here sir.

FERDINAND: This darkness suits you well.

DUCHESS: I would ask your pardon.

FERDINAND: You have it; 40
For I account it the honorabl'st revenge
Where I may kill, to pardon.° Where are your cubs?

DUCHESS: Whom?

FERDINAND: Call them your children;
For though our national law distinguish bastards
From true legitimate issue, compassionate nature
Makes them all equal.

DUCHESS: Do you visit me for this?
You violate a sacrament o' th' Church°

---

prattle, talk. *counterfeit face,* the armored visor.
high . . . floods, the deep sea (of the court's high intrigue).
our, The plural was used in any address to royal persons.
dogship, a term of abuse, satirizing such types of formal
address as "your lordship." *valued high,* judged worthy (by
God). *There's . . . hill,* Even in despair man finds cause for
hope—in the power of God.

I . . . heart, I will no longer waste my time trying to
figure out what is in her heart. *why . . . sugar,* Why do you
cover up your hatred and evil designs with feigned courtesy?
For . . . pardon, For I consider it most honorable to pardon,
when I could kill. *sacrament . . . Church,* her marriage to
Antonio, which she believes is recognized by the eternal
Church.

50 Shall make you howl in hell for't.
    FERDINAND: It had been well,
      Could you have lived thus° always, for indeed
      You were too much i' th' light.° But no more;
      I come to seal my peace with you: here's a hand,

    (Gives her a dead man's hand.)

      To which you have vowed much love; the ring°
        upon't
      You gave.
    DUCHESS: I affectionately kiss it.
    FERDINAND: Pray do, and bury the print of it in your
60   heart.
      I will leave this ring with you, for a love-token,
      And the hand, as sure as the ring. And do not
        doubt
      But you shall have the heart too. When you need a
        friend
      Send it to him that owed° it: you shall see
      Whether he can aid you.
    DUCHESS: You are very cold.
      I fear you are not well after your travel.
70   Ha lights!—Oh, horrible!
    FERDINAND: Let her have lights enough. (Exit.)

    (Enter SERVANTS with lights.)

    DUCHESS: What witchcraft doth he practice,° that he
      hath left
      A dead man's hand here?—

    (Here is discovered, behind a traverse, the artificial fig-
    ures of ANTONIO and his children, appearing as if they
    were dead.)

    BOSOLA: Look you, here's the piece from which 'twas
      ta'en.
      He doth present you this sad spectacle
      That, now you know directly they are dead,
      Hereafter you may wisely cease to grieve
80   For that which cannot be recovered.
    DUCHESS: There is not between heaven and earth one
      wish
      I stay for after this. It wastes me more,
      Than were't my picture, fashioned out of wax,
      Stuck with a magical needle, and then buried
      In some foul dunghill.° And yond's an excellent
        property

    For a tyrant, which I would account mercy,—
    BOSOLA: What's that?
    DUCHESS: If they would bind me to that lifeless   90
      trunk,°
      And let me freeze to death.
    BOSOLA: Come, you must live.
    DUCHESS: That's the greatest torture souls feel in
      hell:
      In hell that they must live, and cannot die.
      Portia,° I'll new kindle thy coals again,
      And revive the rare and almost dead example
      Of a loving wife.
    BOSOLA: O, fie! despair? remember   100
      You are a Christian.°
    DUCHESS: The Church enjoins fasting:
      I'll starve myself to death.
    BOSOLA: Leave this vain sorrow;
      Things, being at the worst, begin to mend:
      The bee when he hath shot his sting into your hand
      May then play with your eyelid.°
    DUCHESS: Good comfortable° fellow,
      Persuade a wretch that's broke upon the wheel°
      To have all his bones new set: entreat him live,   110
      To be executed again. Who must dispatch me?
      I account this world a tedious theater,
      For I do play a part in't 'gainst my will.
    BOSOLA: Come, be of comfort, I will save your life.
    DUCHESS: Indeed, I have not leisure to tend so small a
      business.
    BOSOLA: Now, by my life, I pity you.
    DUCHESS: Thou art a fool then,
      To waste thy pity on a thing so wretched
      As cannot pity itself. I am full of daggers.   120
      Puff! let me blow these vipers from me.

    (She turns to a SERVANT.)

      What are you?
    SERVANT: One that wishes you long life.
    DUCHESS: I would thou wert hanged for the horrible
      curse
      Thou hast given me: I shall shortly grow° one
      Of the miracles of pity. I'll go pray. No,
      I'll go curse.
    BOSOLA: Oh fie!
    DUCHESS: I could curse the stars.   130
    BOSOLA: Oh, fearful!

---

thus, in darkness. *too . . . light,* too conspicuous. *ring,* her wedding ring, which was earlier seized by the Cardinal. *owed,* owned. *What . . . practice,* A dead man's hand was one of the charms used in attempts to cure madness by witchcraft. *my . . . dunghill,* The reference here is to the black-magic practice of putting an evil spell on someone by sticking pins into a doll that looks like him. By then burying the doll in a dunghill, the magician calls upon supernatural spirits to curse even the corpse of the intended victim by denying it proper burial.

lifeless trunk, (the statue of) dead Antonio. *Portia,* Brutus' wife, who committed suicide by swallowing red-hot coals after she heard of her husband's death. *You . . . Christian,* Suicide is forbidden by Christianity. *The . . . eyelid,* After it has used its stinger on your hand, the bee may sit even on your eyelid without being able to do any harm. *comfortable,* free from pain. *broke . . . wheel,* In Webster's time, men were tortured by being bound to a wheel and then stretched until their bones broke under the strain. *grow,* become.

DUCHESS: And those three smiling seasons of the year
Into a Russian winter—nay, the world
To its first chaos.°
BOSOLA: Look you, the stars shine still.
DUCHESS: Oh, but you must
Remember, my curse hath a great way to go:
Plagues, that make lanes through largest families,
Consume them.
140 BOSOLA: Fie lady!
DUCHESS: Let them° like tyrants
Never be remembered, but for the ill they have
done:
Let all the zealous prayers of mortifièd
Churchmen forget them,—
BOSOLA: O uncharitable!
DUCHESS: Let heaven, a little while, cease crowning
martyrs
To punish them.
150 Go, howl them this, and say I long to bleed.
It is some mercy when men kill with speed. (Exit
with SERVANTS.)

(Enter FERDINAND.)

FERDINAND: Excellent, as I would wish: she's plagued
in art.°
These presentations are but framed in wax
By the curious° master in that quality,
Vincentio Lauriola,° and she takes them
For true, substantial bodies.
BOSOLA: Why do you do this?
FERDINAND: To bring her to despair.
160 BOSOLA: 'Faith,° end here,
And go no farther in your cruelty.
Send her a penitential garment, to put on
Next to her delicate skin, and furnish her
With beads° and prayerbooks.
FERDINAND: Damn her! that body of hers,
While that my blood ran pure in't, was more worth
Than that which thou wouldst comfort, called a
soul.°
I will send her masques° of common courtesans,
170 Have her meat served up by bawds and ruffians,
And 'cause she'll needs be° mad, I am resolved
To remove forth° the common hospital

And . . . chaos, And (I could curse) spring, summer, and fall so that they became one long winter; in fact I could wish the world restored to its original state of chaos. *them,* her brothers. *she . . . art,* She was tormented by these wax figures. *curious,* ingenious. *Vincentio Lauriola,* historically unidentifiable, but here he is clearly meant to be a skillful wax-worker. *'Faith,* an interjection, contracted from "in faith." *beads,* rosary beads. *that . . . soul,* There is in this declaration—because the Duchess' body is its focus—another unconscious suggestion of Ferdinand's sexual desires for his sister. *masques,* courtly entertainments. *needs be,* willfully continues to be. *forth,* from.

All the mad folk, and place them near her lodging.
There let them practice° together, sing, and dance,
And act their gambols to the full o' th' moon:°
If she can sleep the better for it, let her.
Your work is almost ended.
BOSOLA: Must I see her again?
FERDINAND: Yes.
BOSOLA: Never.   180
FERDINAND: You must.
BOSOLA: Never in mine own shape;°
That's forfeited by my intelligence°
And this last cruel lie. When you send me next,
The business shall be comfort.
FERDINAND: Very likely.°
Thy pity is nothing of kin to thee. Antonio
Lurks about Milan; thou shalt shortly thither,
To feed a fire as great as my revenge,
Which ne'er will slack till it have spent his fuel; 190
Intemperate agues make physicians cruel. (Exeunt.)

ACT 4 / SCENE 2

(The same place)
(Enter DUCHESS and CARIOLA.)

DUCHESS: What hideous noise was that?
CARIOLA: 'Tis the wild consort
Of madmen, lady, which your tyrant brother
Hath placed about your lodging. This tyranny,
I think, was never practiced till this hour.
DUCHESS: Indeed, I thank him: nothing but noise
and folly
Can keep me in my right wits, whereas reason
And silence make me stark mad. Sit down.
Discourse to me some dismal tragedy.   10
CARIOLA: O 'twill increase your melancholy.
DUCHESS: Thou art deceived;
To hear of greater grief would lessen mine.
This is a prison?
CARIOLA: Yes, but you shall live
To shake this durance° off.
DUCHESS: Thou art a fool:
The robin red-breast and the nightingale
Never live long in cages.
CARIOLA: Pray dry your eyes.   20
What think you of, madam?
DUCHESS: Of nothing:
When I muse thus, I sleep.
CARIOLA: Like a madman, with your eyes open?
DUCHESS: Dost thou think we shall know one another
In th' other world?
CARIOLA: Yes, out of question.

---

practice, carry on their activities. *full . . . moon,* the time when madmen were thought to be most mad. *in . . . shape,* without being disguised. *intelligence,* work as a spy. *Very likely,* a cynical rejoinder, because Bosola will then offer her the "comfort" of death. *durance,* hardship.

DUCHESS: O, that it were possible we might
But hold some two days' conference with the dead:
40   From them I should learn somewhat I am sure
I never shall know here. I'll tell thee a miracle;
I am not mad yet, to my cause of sorrow.°
Th' heaven o'er my head seems made of molten
   brass,
The earth of flaming sulphur, yet I am not mad.
I am acquainted with sad misery,
As the tanned galley slave is with his oar.
Necessity makes me suffer constantly,
And custom makes it easy. Who do I look like now?
50   CARIOLA: Like to your picture in the gallery,
A deal of life in show,° but none in practice:°
Or rather like some reverend monument
Whose ruins are even pitied.
DUCHESS: Very proper:
And Fortune seems only to have her eyesight,°
To behold my tragedy.
How now! What noise is that? (Enter SERVANT.)
SERVANT: I am come to tell you,
Your brother hath intended you some sport.°
60   A great physician when the Pope was sick
Of a deep melancholy, presented him
With several sorts of madmen, which wild object,
Being full of change and sport, forced him to
   laugh,
And so th'imposthume° broke: the selfsame cure
The Duke intends on you.
DUCHESS: Let them come in.
SERVANT: There's a mad lawyer, and a secular priest,
A doctor that hath forfeited his wits
70   By jealousy; an astrologian
That in his works said such a day o' th' month
Should be the day of doom, and, failing of't,
Ran mad; an English tailor, crazed i' th' brain
With the study of new fashion; a gentleman usher°
Quite beside himself with care to keep in mind
The number of his lady's salutations
Or "How do you?" she employed him in each
   morning;°
A farmer too, an excellent knave in grain,°
80   Mad, 'cause he was hindered transportation;°

And let° one broker,° that's mad, loose to these,
You'd think the devil were among them.
DUCHESS: Sit Cariola. Let them loose when you
   please,
For I am chained to endure all your tyranny.

(Enter MADMEN. Here, by a MADMAN, this song is sung
to a dismal kind of music.)

   O let us howl, some heavy note,
      Some deadly-dogg'd howl,
   Sounding, as from the threat'ning throat,
      Of beasts and fatal fowl.
   As ravens, screech owls, bulls, and bears,   90
      We'll bell,° and bawl our parts,
   Till irksome noise have cloyed your ears,
      And corrosived° your hearts.
   At last when as our choir wants breath,
      Our bodies being blest,
   We'll sing like swans, to welcome death,
      And die in love and rest.

MAD ASTROLOGER: Doomsday not come yet? I'll draw
   it nearer by a perspective,° or make a glass that
   shall set all the world on fire upon an instant. I   100
   cannot sleep; my pillow is stuffed with a litter of
   porcupines.
MAD LAWYER: Hell is a mere glasshouse,° where the
   devils are continually blowing up women's souls
   on hollow irons,° and the fire never goes out.
MAD PRIEST: I will lie with every woman in my parish
   the tenth night: I will tithe them over like
   haycocks.°
MAD DOCTOR: Shall my pothecary° outgo° me, because I am a cuckold? I have found out his   110
   roguery: he makes alum° of his wife's urine and
   sells it to Puritans, that have sore throats with
   over-straining.°
MAD ASTROLOGER: I have skill in heraldry.
MAD LAWYER: Hast?
MAD ASTROLOGER: You do give for your crest a woodcock's° head, with the brains picked out on't. You
   are a very ancient gentleman.
MAD PRIEST: Greek is turned Turk;° we are only to be

---

to ... sorrow, which is why I feel sorrow. show,
appearance. practice, action, Fortune ... eyesight, Traditionally, the goddess Fortune was pictured as blindfolded
because she distributed her rewards so arbitrarily. Here the
Duchess implies that momentarily Fortune's blindfold has
been removed so that she can see the sad results of her
handiwork. sport, entertainment. imposthume, ulcer
(which caused the melancholy). usher, an attendant who
walks before a person of rank, greeting guests and introducing strangers. How ... morning, a double-entendre, meaning the usher was made to serve her sexually as well as
socially. in grain, both "in the grain trade" and "in essence
(a knave)." hindered transportation, denied export.

let, turn. broker, pawnbroker. bell, bellow. corro-
sived, corroded. perspective, telescope. glasshouse, a factory where glass is made. blowing ... irons, A sexual
meaning is implicit in this statement, and in most of the
lunatic raving that follows; these madmen, like Lear on the
heath, are acutely conscious of the intensity of man's sexual
desires. haycocks, stacks of hay, but an obscene pun is
intended as well. pothecary, druggist. outgo, get the best
of. alum, an astringent formerly used to treat inflamed
tissue. over-straining, singing too loudly and, also, straining too much of the life out of religion. woodcock, thought
to be a stupid bird. Greek ... Turk, The Greek text of the
Bible has been made to serve nonbelievers (all non-
Puritans).

120 saved by the Helvetian translation.°

MAD ASTROLOGER (*to* LAWYER): Come on sir, I will lay the law to you.°

MAD LAWYER: Oh, rather lay° a corrosive: the law will eat to the bone.

MAD PRIEST: He that drinks but to satisfy nature is damned.

MAD DOCTOR: If I had my glass° here, I would show a sight should make all the women here call me mad doctor.

130 MAD ASTROLOGER (*pointing to* PRIEST): What's he, a ropemaker?°

MAD LAWYER: No, no, no, a snuffling° knave that, while he shows the tombs, will have his hand in a wench's placket.°

MAD PRIEST: Woe to the caroche° that brought home my wife from the masque at three o'clock in the morning; it had a large featherbed in it.

MAD DOCTOR: I have pared the devil's nails° forty times, roasted them in raven's eggs, and cured agues with them.

140 MAD PRIEST: Get me three hundred milch° bats, to make possets° to procure sleep.

MAD DOCTOR: All the college may throw their caps° at me; I have made a soap-boiler costive:° it was my masterpiece—

(*Here the dance consisting of eight* MADMEN, *with music answerable thereunto, after which* BOSOLA, *like an old man, enters.*)

DUCHESS: Is he mad too?

SERVANT: Pray question him; I'll leave you. (*Exeunt* SERVANT *and* MADMEN.)

BOSOLA: I am come to make thy tomb.

150 DUCHESS: Ha, my tomb?
    Thou speakst as if I lay upon my deathbed,
    Gasping for breath. Dost thou perceive me sick?

BOSOLA: Yes, and the more dangerously, since thy sickness is insensible.°

DUCHESS: Thou art not mad, sure; dost know me?

BOSOLA: Yes.

DUCHESS: Who am I?

BOSOLA: Thou art a box of worm seed,° at best but° a salvatory of green mummy.° What's this flesh? a little cruded° milk, fantastical puff paste:° our 160 bodies are weaker than those paper prisons boys use to keep flies in, more contemptible—since ours is to preserve earthworms. Didst thou ever see a lark in a cage? such is the soul in the body: this world is like her little turf of grass° and the heaven o'er our heads, like her looking glass,° only gives us a miserable knowledge of the small compass of our prison.

DUCHESS: Am not I thy Duchess?

BOSOLA: Thou art some great woman, sure; for riot° 170 begins to sit on thy forehead (clad in grey hairs) twenty years sooner than on a merry milkmaid's. Thou sleepst worse, than if a mouse should be forced to take up her lodging in a cat's ear. A little infant, that breeds its teeth, should it lie with thee, would cry out, as if thou wert the more unquiet bedfellow.°

DUCHESS: I am Duchess of Malfi still.

BOSOLA: That makes thy sleeps so broken:
    Glories, like glowworms, afar off shine bright, 180
    But looked to near, have neither heat nor light.

DUCHESS: Thou art very plain.°

BOSOLA: My trade is to flatter the dead, not the living: I am a tombmaker.

DUCHESS: And thou comst to make my tomb?

BOSOLA: Yes.

DUCHESS: Let me be a little merry;
    Of what stuff wilt thou make it?

BOSOLA: Nay, resolve me° first. Of what fashion?

DUCHESS: Why, do we grow fantastical° in our 190 deathbed?
    Do we affect fashion in the grave?

BOSOLA: Most ambitiously. Princes' images on their tombs
    Do not lie as they were wont, seeming to pray
    Up to heaven, but with their hands under their cheeks,°
    As if they died of the toothache. They are not carved
    With their eyes fixed upon the stars; but, as 200
    Their minds were wholly bent upon the world,
    The selfsame way they seem to turn their faces.

DUCHESS: Let me know fully therefore the effect
    Of this thy dismal preparation,

Helvetian translation, the translation of the Bible officially approved by the Puritans. *I . . . you,* I will explain the church law to you. *Oh . . . lay,* You might just as well apply. *glass,* some sort of magnifying glass. *ropemaker,* i.e. one who is in league with the hangman. *snuffling,* sanctimonious. *placket,* both "pocket" and "pudendum." *caroche,* a luxurious carriage. *I . . . nails,* I have brought the devil under my control. *milch,* milk-bearing. *possets,* a hot drink made of sweetened, spiced milk curdled with ale or wine. *throw . . . caps,* vainly seek to surpass me in skill. *I . . . costive,* I have made one who boils soap constipated (an unusual accomplishment because soap was an essential element used in manufacturing suppositories). *insensible,* not apparent to the senses. *box . . . seed,* a box of food for worms. *but,* only.

---

salvatory . . . mummy, either a container for an unripened mummy (because you are still alive) or an ointment box for fresh mummia, a drug derived from embalmed bodies. *cruded,* curdled. *puff-paste,* a light pastry. *turf of grass, looking glass,* articles that were put into bird cages in an attempt to keep the captured birds happy. *riot,* lines of sorrow that disturb the previous order of beauty. *A . . . bedfellow,* You sleep more restlessly than a baby cutting teeth. *plain,* plain-spoken. *resolve me,* Answer my question. *fantastical,* obsessed by fantasies. *with . . . cheeks,* in a semirecumbent position.

This talk, fit for a charnel.°
BOSOLA: Now I shall;

(Enter EXECUTIONERS with a coffin, cords, and a bell.)

Here is a present from your princely brothers,
And may it arrive welcome, for it brings
Last benefit, last sorrow.
210 DUCHESS: Let me see it.
I have so much obedience in my blood
I wish it in their veins, to do them good.
BOSOLA: This is your last presence chamber.
CARIOLA: O my sweet lady!
DUCHESS: Peace! it affrights not me.
BOSOLA: I am the common bellman,°
That usually is sent to condemned persons,
The night before they suffer.
DUCHESS: Even now thou saidst
220 Thou wast a tomb-maker?
BOSOLA: 'Twas to bring you
By degrees to mortification.° Listen:

(Rings the bell.)

Hark, now every thing is still,
The screech owl and the whistler shrill°
Call upon our dame,° aloud,
And bid her quickly don her shroud.
Much you had of land and rent,
Your length in clay's now competent.
A long war disturbed your mind;
230 Here your perfect peace is signed.
Of what is't fools make such vain keeping?
Sin° their conception, their birth, weeping:
Their life, a general mist of error,
Their death, a hideous storm of terror.
Strew your hair with powders sweet:
Don clean linen, bathe your feet,
And the foul fiend° more to check,
A crucifix let bless your neck.
'Tis now full tide 'tween night and day,
240 End your groan, and come away.

(EXECUTIONERS approach.)

CARIOLA: Hence, villains, tyrants, murderers. Alas!
What will you do with my lady? Call for help.
DUCHESS: To whom? To our next neighbors? They
are mad-folks.
BOSOLA: Remove that noise.

(EXECUTIONERS seize CARIOLA, who struggles.)

DUCHESS: Farewell, Cariola,

In my last will I have not much to give:
A many hundred guests have fed upon me;
Thine will be a poor reversion.°
CARIOLA: I will die with her.   250
DUCHESS: I pray thee, look thou givst my little boy
Some syrup for his cold, and let the girl
Say her prayers, ere she sleep. (CARIOLA is forced
off.)
Now, what you please.
What death?
BOSOLA: Strangling. Here are your executioners.
DUCHESS: I forgive them:
The apoplexy, catarrh,° or cough o' th' lungs
Would do as much as they do.
BOSOLA: Doth not death fright you?   260
DUCHESS: Who would be afraid on't?
Knowing to meet such excellent company
In th' other world.
BOSOLA: Yet, methinks,
The manner of your death should much afflict
you;
This cord should terrify you?
DUCHESS: Not a whit:
What would it pleasure me, to have my throat cut
With diamonds? or to be smotherèd   270
With cassia? or to be shot to death with pearls?
I know death hath ten thousand several doors
For men to take their exits; and 'tis found
They go on such strange geometrical hinges,
You may open them both ways.° Any way, for
heaven sake,
So I were out of your whispering. Tell my brothers
That I perceive death, now I am well awake,
Best gift is they can give, or I can take.
I would fain put off my last woman's fault: 280
I'll not be tedious to you.
EXECUTIONERS: We are ready.
DUCHESS: Dispose my breath how please you, but my
body
Bestow upon my women, will you?
EXECUTIONERS: Yes.
DUCHESS: Pull, and pull strongly, for your able
strength
Must pull down heaven upon me—
Yet stay, heaven-gates are not so highly archèd   290
As princes' palaces: they that enter there
Must go upon their knees. (She kneels.) Come
violent death,
Serve for mandragora° to make me sleep.
Go tell my brothers, when I am laid out,
They then may feed in quiet. (They strangle her.)
BOSOLA: Where's the waiting woman?
Fetch her. Some other strangle the children.

---

charnel, cemetery. bellman, one who was supposed to
drive evil spirits away from the soul. 'Twas . . . mortification, It was to get you accustomed to the idea of dying.
whistler shrill, a bird whose song was supposed to be a
foreboding of evil. our dame, the Duchess. Sin, The
word here assumes the meanings of both "since" and "sin"
(which attends man's conception). foul fiend, the devil.

reversion, estate passed on to her. catarrh, hemor-
rhage. You . . . ways, Death may come and get you, or you
may go to it (by committing suicide). mandragora, a plant
formerly used as a narcotic.

(Exeunt EXECUTIONERS.*)*
(Enter one with CARIOLA.*)*

Look you, there sleeps your mistress.

300 CARIOLA: O you are damned
Perpetually for this. My turn is next,
Is't not so ordered?

BOSOLA: Yes, and I am glad
You are so well prepared for't.

CARIOLA: You are deceived sir,
I am not prepared for't. I will not die;
I will first come to my answer, and know
How I have offended.

BOSOLA: Come, dispatch her.
310 You kept her° counsel; now you shall keep ours.

CARIOLA: I will not die—I must not—I am contracted
To a young gentleman.

EXECUTIONER *(showing the noose)*: Here's your
wedding ring.

CARIOLA: Let me but speak with the Duke. I'll
discover
Treason to his person.

BOSOLA: Delays: throttle her.

EXECUTIONER: She bites and scratches.

320 CARIOLA: If you kill me now,
I am damned. I have not been at confession
This two years.

BOSOLA: When!°

CARIOLA: I am quick with child.°

BOSOLA: Why then,
Your credit's saved.° Bear her into th' next room
Let this lie still.

*(*EXECUTIONERS *strangle* CARIOLA *and exeunt with her
body.)*
(Enter FERDINAND.*)*

FERDINAND: Is she dead?

BOSOLA: She is what
330 You'd have her. But here begin your pity.

*(*BOSOLA *draws the traverse and shows the children
strangled.)*

Alas, how have these offended?

FERDINAND: The death
Of young wolves is never to be pitied.

BOSOLA: Fix your eye here.

FERDINAND: Constantly.

BOSOLA: Do you not weep?
Other sins only speak; murther shrieks out:
The element of water moistens the earth,
But blood flies upwards and bedews the heavens.

FERDINAND: Cover her face. Mine eyes dazzle:° she   340
died young.

BOSOLA: I think not so: her infelicity
Seemed to have years too many.

FERDINAND: She and I were twins:
And should I die this instant I had lived
Her time to a minute.

BOSOLA: It seems she was born first:
You have bloodily approved° the ancient truth,
That kindred commonly do worse agree°
Than remote strangers.   350

FERDINAND: Let me see her face again—
Why didst not thou pity her? What an excellent
Honest man mightst thou have been
If thou'hadst borne her to some sanctuary!
Or, bold in a good cause, opposed thyself
With thy advancèd sword above thy head,
Between her innocence and my revenge!
I bade thee, when I was distracted of my wits,
Go kill my dearest friend, and thou hast done't.
For let me examine well the cause.   360
What was the meanness of her match to me?
Only, I must confess, I had a hope,
Had she continued widow, to have gained
An infinite mass of treasure by her death;°
And that was the main cause—her marriage,
That drew a stream of gall quite through my heart.
For thee (as we observe in tragedies
That a good actor many times is cursed
For playing a villain's part), I hate thee for't.
And, for my sake, say thou hast done much ill, well. 370

BOSOLA: Let me quicken your memory, for I perceive
You are falling into ingratitude. I challenge
The reward due to my service.

FERDINAND: I'll tell thee,
What I'll give thee—

BOSOLA: Do.

FERDINAND: I'll give thee a pardon
For this murther.

BOSOLA: Ha?

FERDINAND: Yes: and 'tis   380
The largest bounty I can study° to do thee.
By what authority didst thou execute
This bloody sentence?

BOSOLA: By yours.

FERDINAND: Mine? Was I her judge?
Did any ceremonial form of law

---

her, the Duchess'. **When,** an exclamation of impatience. **quick . . . child,** pregnant. (Criminals who were pregnant were sometimes granted a stay of execution until the birth of the child.) **Your . . . saved,** Your reputation is saved—because your death will prevent you from bearing a bastard child.

dazzle, are dazzled. **approved,** proven. **do . . . agree,** differ more. **Only . . . death,** The Duke, desperately searching for the reason why he found his sister's marriage to Antonio so hateful, here presents an obvious rationalization: even if the Duchess had died without remarrying, her estate would have gone to her first son, the young Duke of Malfi. The real explanation for Ferdinand's intense jealousy of Antonio is, of course, too frightening for him to admit, or even to recognize consciously. **study,** consciously bring myself.

Doom her to not-being? Did a complete jury
Deliver her conviction up i' th' court?
Where shalt thou find this judgment registered
390 Unless in hell? See, like a bloody fool
Th' hast forfeited thy life, and thou shalt die for't.
BOSOLA: The office of justice is perverted quite
When one thief hangs another. Who shall dare
To reveal this?
FERDINAND: Oh, I'll tell thee:
The wolf shall find her grave and scrape it up,
Not to devour the corpse, but to discover
The horrid murther.
BOSOLA: You, not I, shall quake for't.
400 FERDINAND: Leave me.
BOSOLA: I will first receive my pension.°
FERDINAND: You are a villain.
BOSOLA: When your ingratitude
Is judge, I am so—
FERDINAND: O horror!
That not the fear of Him which binds the devils
Can prescribe man obedience.
Never look upon me more.
BOSOLA: Why fare thee well.
410 Your brother and yourself are worthy men;
You have a pair of hearts are hollow graves—
Rotten, and rotting others. And your vengeance,
Like two chained bullets,° still goes arm in arm.
You may be brothers, for treason, like the plague,
Doth take much in a blood.° I stand like one
That long hath ta'en a sweet and golden dream:
I am angry with myself, now that I wake.
FERDINAND: Get thee into some unknown part o' th'
world,
420 That I may never see thee.
BOSOLA: Let me know
Wherefore I should be thus neglected? Sir,
I served your tyranny, and rather strove
To satisfy yourself, than all the world;
And though I loathed the evil, yet I loved
You that did counsel it, and rather sought
To appear a true servant than an honest man.
FERDINAND: I'll go hunt the badger° by owl-light:°
'Tis a deed of darkness. (Exit.)
430 BOSOLA: He's much distracted. Off my painted
honor!°
While with vain hopes our faculties we tire,
We seem to sweat in ice and freeze in fire.°
What would I do, were this to do again?
I would not change my peace of conscience

---

pension, reward for services. **chained bullets,** Cannon balls were sometimes chained together to increase the extent of their destructive force. **take . . . blood,** runs in the blood of particular families. **badger,** an animal that avoided daylight. **owl-light,** night. **I'll . . . owl-light,** I shall henceforth carry out my activities in darkness. **painted honor,** false sense of importance, as a spy for Ferdinand. **We . . . fire,** We are always uncomfortably restless and unsatisfied.

For all the wealth of Europe. She stirs; here's life.
Return, fair soul, from darkness, and lead mine
Out of this sensible° hell. She's warm; she breathes:
Upon thy pale lips I will melt my heart
To store them with fresh color. Who's there?   440
Some cordial drink!° Alas! I dare not call:
So pity would destroy pity.° Her eye opes,
And heaven in it seems to ope, that late was shut,
To take me up to mercy.
DUCHESS: Antonio!
BOSOLA: Yes, madam, he is living,
The dead bodies you saw were but feigned statues;
He's reconciled to your brothers: the Pope hath
wrought
The atonement.   450
DUCHESS: Mercy. (She dies.)
BOSOLA: Oh, she's gone again: there the cords of life
broke.
Oh sacred innocence, that sweetly sleeps
On turtles'° feathers, whilst a guilty conscience
Is a black register, wherein is writ
All our good deeds and bad, a perspective
That shows us hell. That we cannot be suffered
To do good when we have a mind to it!
This is manly sorrow: 460
These tears, I am very certain, never grew
In my mother's milk. My estate° is sunk
Below the degree of fear: where were
These penitent fountains while she was living?
Oh, they were frozen up! Here is a sight
As direful to my soul as is the sword
Unto a wretch hath slain his father. Come,
I'll bear thee hence,
And execute thy last will—that's deliver
Thy body to the reverend dispose   470
Of some good women: that the cruel tyrant
Shall not deny me. Then I'll post to Milan,
Where somewhat I will speedily enact
Worth my dejection.° (Exit carrying the body.)

ACT 5 / SCENE 1

(A public place in Milan)
(Enter ANTONIO and DELIO.)

ANTONIO: What think you of my hope of
reconcilement
To the Aragonian brethren?
DELIO: I misdoubt it,
For though they have sent their letters of safe
conduct

---

sensible, apparent to the senses. **cordial drink,** medicine to induce revival. **So . . . pity,** By pitying her and calling out for help, I would only destroy her whom I pity because Ferdinand would return and kill her. **turtles,** turtledoves (traditionally a symbol of love and peace). **estate,** condition. **Worth my dejection,** keeping with my abasement.

For your repair° to Milan, they appear
But nets to entrap you. The Marquis of Pescara,
Under whom you hold certain land in cheat,°
10 Much 'gainst his noble nature, hath been moved
To seize those lands, and some of his dependants
Are at this instant making it their suit
To be invested in your revenues.
I cannot think they mean well to your life
That do deprive you of your means of life,
Your living.
ANTONIO: You are still an heretic.°
To any safety I can shape myself.
DELIO: Here comes the Marquis. I will make myself
20 Petitioner for some part of your land,
To know whether° it is flying.°
ANTONIO: I pray do.

(Enter PESCARA.)

DELIO: Sir, I have a suit to you.
PESCARA: To me?
DELIO: An easy one:
There is the citadel of St. Bennet,°
With some demesnes,° of late in the possession
Of Antonio Bologna; please you bestow them on
me?
30 PESCARA: You are my friend. But this is such a suit
Nor fit for me to give, nor you to take.
DELIO: No sir?
PESCARA: I will give you ample reason for't
Soon, in private. Here's the Cardinal's mistress.

(Enter JULIA.)

JULIA: My lord, I am grown your poor petitioner,
And should be an ill beggar had I not
A great man's letter here, the Cardinal's,
To court you in my favor.

(She gives him a letter.)

PESCARA: He entreats for you
40 The citadel of St. Bennet, that belonged
To the banished Bologna.
JULIA: Yes.
PESCARA: I could not have thought of a friend I could
Rather pleasure with it: 'tis yours.
JULIA: Sir, I thank you.
And he shall know how doubly I am engaged,
Both in your gift and speediness of giving,
Which makes your grant the greater. (Exit.)
ANTONIO (aside): How they fortify
50 Themselves with my ruin!

DELIO: Sir, I am
Little bound to you.
PESCARA: Why?
DELIO: Because you denied this suit to me, and gave't
To such a creature.
PESCARA: Do you know what it was?
It was Antonio's land—not forfeited
By course of law, but ravished from his throat
By the Cardinal's entreaty. It were not fit
I should bestow so main a piece of wrong 60
Upon my friend: 'tis a gratification
Only due to a strumpet; for it is injustice.
Shall I sprinkle the pure blood of innocents
To make these followers I call my friends
Look ruddier° upon me? I am glad
This land, ta'en from the owner by such wrong,
Returns again unto so foul an use,
As salary for his lust. Learn, good Delio,
To ask noble things of me, and you shall find
I'll be a noble giver. 70
DELIO: You instruct me well.
ANTONIO (aside): Why, here's a man, now, would
fright° impudence
From sauciest beggars.
PESCARA: Prince Ferdinand's come to Milan
Sick, as they give out, of an apoplexy;
But some say 'tis a frenzy. I am going
To visit him. (Exit.)
ANTONIO: 'Tis a noble old fellow.°
DELIO: What course do you mean to take, Antonio? 80
ANTONIO: This night I mean to venture all my
fortune,
Which is no more than a poor ling'ring life,
To the Cardinal's worst of malice.° I have got
Private access to his chamber, and intend
To visit him, about the mid of night,
As once his brother did our noble Duchess.°
It may be that the sudden apprehension
Of danger—for I'll go in mine own shape—,
When he shall see it fraight° with love and duty, 90
May draw the poison out of him, and work
A friendly reconcilement. If it fail,
Yet it shall rid me of this infamous calling,°
For better fall once, than be ever falling.

repair, return. in cheat, subject to return to the lord only if the tenant dies without an heir or if he commits a felony. heretic, skeptic. whether, The second and third quarto editions read "whither," it . . . flying, it is wantonly being given away. St. Bennet, St. Benedict. demesnes, land attached to the citadel.

ruddier, more glowingly. fright, drive away. old fellow, The Marquis of Pescara never actually lived to be an "old fellow"; he died when he was thirty-six. There is, however, a good reason why Webster makes him old: that way he commands respect as one who has lived long enough to become wise. To . . . malice, against the worst malice of the Cardinal. As . . . Duchess, The reference is to the time that Ferdinand came unexpectedly into the Duchess' bedchamber while she was combing her hair and readying herself for bed. Antonio does not yet know about the murderous visit that Ferdinand made while the Duchess was in prison. fraight, abounding with. infamous calling, life of disgrace.

DELIO: I'll second you in all danger; and, howe'er,
    My life keeps rank with yours.
ANTONIO: You are still my loved and best friend.
    (Exeunt.)

ACT 5 / SCENE 2

(The palace of the Aragonian brothers in Milan)
(Enter PESCARA and DOCTOR.)

PESCARA: Now, doctor, may I visit your patient?
DOCTOR: If't please your lordship, but he's instantly
    To take the air here in the gallery,
    By my direction.
PESCARA: Pray thee, what's his disease?
DOCTOR: A very pestilent disease, my lord,
    They call lycanthropia.°
PESCARA: What's that?
    I need a dictionary to't.
10 DOCTOR: I'll tell you:
    In those that are possessed with't there o'erflows
    Such melancholy humor, they imagine
    Themselves to be transformèd into wolves,
    Steal forth to churchyards in the dead of night,
    And dig dead bodies up: as two nights since
    One met the Duke, 'bout midnight in a lane
    Behind St. Mark's church, with the leg of a man
    Upon his shoulder; and he howled fearfully—
    Said he was a wolf; only the difference
20   Was a wolf's skin was hairy on the outside,
    His on the inside. Bade them take their swords,
    Rip up his flesh, and try. Straight I was sent for,
    And having ministered to him, found his grace
    Very well recoverèd.
PESCARA: I am glad on't.
DOCTOR: Yet not without some fear
    Of a relapse. If he grow to his fit again,
    I'll go a nearer way to work with him
    Than ever Paracelsus° dreamed of. If
30   They'll give me leave, I'll buffet his madness out of
      him.
    Stand aside: he comes.

    (Enter CARDINAL, FERDINAND, MALATESTE, and
    BOSOLA, *who remains behind.)*

FERDINAND: Leave me.
MALATESTE: Why doth your lordship love this solitar-
    iness?
FERDINAND: Eagles commonly fly alone. They are
    crows, daws,° and starlings that flock together.
    Look, what's that follows me?
MALATESTE: Nothing, my lord.
40 FERDINAND: Yes.

MALATESTE: 'Tis your shadow.
FERDINAND: Stay it; let it not haunt me.
MALATESTE: Impossible, if you move, and the sun
    shine.
FERDINAND: I will throttle it.

    (He attacks his shadow.)

MALATESTE: Oh, my lord, you are angry with noth-
    ing.
FERDINAND: You are a fool. How is't possible I should
    catch my shadow unless I fall upon't? When I go
    to hell, I mean to carry a bribe: for, look you,   50
    good gifts evermore make way for the worst per-
    sons.
PESCARA: Rise, good my lord.
FERDINAND: I am studying the art of patience.
PESCARA: 'Tis a noble virtue—
FERDINAND: To drive six snails before me, from this
    town to Moscow; neither use goad nor whip to
    them, but let them take their own time—the pa-
    tient'st man i' th' world match me for an experi-
    ment! And I'll crawl after like a sheep-biter.°   60
CARDINAL: Force him up.

    (They make FERDINAND stand up.)

FERDINAND: Use me well, you were best.°
    What I have done, I have done. I'll confess
    nothing.
DOCTOR: Now let me come to him. Are you mad, my
    lord?
    Are you out of your princely wits?
FERDINAND: What's he?
PESCARA: Your doctor.
FERDINAND: Let me have his beard sawed off, and his   70
    eyebrows
    Filed more civil.°
DOCTOR: I must do mad tricks with him,
    For that's the only way on't. I have brought
    Your grace a salamander's° skin, to keep you
    From sun-burning.
FERDINAND: I have cruel sore eyes.
DOCTOR: The white of a cockatrice° egg is present
    remedy.
FERDINAND: Let it be a new-laid one, you were best.   80
    Hide me from him: physicians are like kings:
    They brook no contradiction.
DOCTOR: Now he begins

---

    sheep-biter, a sheep-stealing dog.   *you ... best,* an
interjectory phrase meaning "you would be well-advised to."
Let ... civil, I wish his appearance were not so hostile.
salamander, thought capable of living in fire.   *cockatrice,* a
legendary monster with the head, wings, and legs of a cock
and the tail of a serpent. Because most of its power was
thought to be vested in its eyes—its look was deadly—and
because egg whites were often used in treating sore eyes, the
white of a cockatrice's egg would theoretically be an ideal
remedy for the affliction the Duke complains of.

lycanthropia, a mania in which the victim imagines
himself a wolf.   *Paracelsus,* a German physician and alchemist noted for his radical way of treating diseases.
daws, crowlike birds.

To fear me; now let me alone with him.

(FERDINAND *tries to take off his gown;* CARDINAL *seizes him.*)

CARDINAL: How now, put off your gown?
DOCTOR: Let me have some forty urinals filled with
  rose-water: he and I'll go pelt one another with
  them: now he begins to fear me. Can you fetch a
  frisk,° sir? (*aside to* CARDINAL) Let him go; let him
90 go upon my peril. I find by his eye, he stands in
  awe of me: I'll make him as tame as a dormouse.

(CARDINAL *releases* FERDINAND.)

FERDINAND: Can you fetch your frisks, sir! I will
  stamp him into a cullis;° flay off his skin to cover
  one of the anatomies.° This rogue hath set i' th'
  cold yonder, in Barber-Chirurgeons' Hall.°
  Hence, hence! you are all of you like beasts for
  sacrifice: (*throws the* DOCTOR *down and beats him*)
  there's nothing left of you, but tongue and belly,°
  flattery and lechery. (*Exit.*)
100 PESCARA: Doctor, he did not fear you throughly.°
DOCTOR: True, I was somewhat too forward.
BOSOLA (*aside*): Mercy upon me! What a fatal
  judgment
  Hath fall'n upon this Ferdinand!
PESCARA: Knows your grace
  What accident hath brought unto the Prince
  This strange distraction?
CARDINAL (*aside*): I must feign somewhat.° Thus they
  say it grew:
110 You have heard it rumored for these many years,
  None of our family dies but there is seen
  The shape of an old woman, which is given
  By tradition to us to have been murdered
  By her nephews, for her riches. Such a figure
  One night, as the Prince sat up late at's book,
  Appeared to him; when crying out for help,
  The gentlemen of's chamber found his grace
  All on a cold sweat, altered much in face
  And language. Since which apparition
120 He hath grown worse and worse, and I much fear
  He cannot live.
BOSOLA: Sir, I would speak with you.

---

fetch a frisk, dance a caper. cullis, broth, made partly
by pounding fowl. anatomies, skeletons. Barber-
Chirurgeons' Hall, the place where barber-surgeons went to
pick up corpses of executed felons, which they used for
anatomical experiments. tongue and belly, In ancient religious ceremonies, the tongues and entrails of sacrificial
animals were left for the gods. But Ferdinand intends
another meaning as well: in his despair he sees man as
essentially a deceiver and a creature of appetite; he is not a
complex, integrated human being, but only a tongue and a
belly. throughly, completely. feign somewhat, make up
something.

PESCARA: We'll leave your grace,
  Wishing to the sick Prince, our noble lord,
  All health of mind and body.
CARDINAL: You are most welcome.

(*Exeunt* PESCARA, MALATESTE, *and* DOCTOR.)

Are you come? (*aside*) So—this fellow must not
  know
By any means I had intelligence
In° our Duchess' death. For, though I counseled it, 130
The full of all th' engagement° seemed to grow
From Ferdinand. Now sir, how fares our sister?
I do not think but sorrow makes her look
Like to an oft-dyed garment. She shall now
Taste comfort from me—Why do you look so
  wildly?
Oh, the fortune of your master here, the Prince,
Dejects you, but be you of happy comfort:
If you'll do one thing for me I'll entreat,
Though he had a cold tombstone o'er his bones, 140
I'll make you what you would be.
BOSOLA: Anything?
  Give it me in a breath,° and let me fly to't:
  They that think long, small expedition win,°
  For musing much o' th' end, cannot begin.

(*Enter* JULIA.)

JULIA: Sir, will you come in to supper?
CARDINAL: I am busy! Leave me!
JULIA (*aside*): What an excellent shape hath that
  fellow! (*Exit.*)
CARDINAL: 'Tis thus: Antonio lurks here in Milan; 150
  Inquire him out, and kill him. While he lives,
  Our sister cannot marry, and I have thought
  Of an excellent match for her. Do this, and style
  me°
  Thy advancement.
BOSOLA: But by what means shall I find him out?
CARDINAL: There is a gentleman called Delio
  Here in the camp, that hath been long approved°
  His loyal friend. Set eye upon that fellow,
  Follow him to mass; may be Antonio, 160
  Although he do account religion
  But a school-name,° for fashion of the world
  May accompany him. Or else go inquire out
  Delio's confessor, and see if you can bribe
  Him to reveal it. There are a thousand ways
  A man might find to trace him—as, to know°
  What fellows haunt the Jews for taking up°
  Great sums of money, for sure he's in want;

---

had . . . In, had a part in the planning of. full . . .
engagement, everything to do with the deed. in a breath,
quickly. small . . . win, accomplish little. style me, call me
the means to. hath . . . approved, has long proved to be.
school-name, mere word. know, find out. for taking up, to
borrow.

  Or else go to th' picture makers, and learn
170 Who brought her picture lately.° Some of these
  Happily may take—
BOSOLA: Well, I'll not freeze i' th' business,
  I would see that wretched° thing, Antonio,
  Above all sights i' th' world.
CARDINAL: Do, and be happy.° *(Exit.)*
BOSOLA: This fellow doth breed basilisks° in's eyes,
  He's nothing else but murder: yet he seems
  Not to have notice of the Duchess' death.
  'Tis his cunning. I must follow his example:
180 There cannot be a surer way to trace,
  Than that of an old fox.

   (Enter JULIA, *pointing a pistol at him.)*

JULIA: So, sir, you are well met.
BOSOLA: How now?
JULIA: Nay, the doors are fast enough.
  Now sir, I will make you confess your treachery.
BOSOLA: Treachery?
JULIA: Yes, confess to me
  Which of my women 'twas hired to put
  Love-powder into my drink?
190 BOSOLA: Love-powder?
JULIA: Yes, when I was at Malfi—
  Why should I fall in love with such a face else?
  I have already suffered for thee so much pain,
  The only remedy to do me good
  Is to kill my longing.
BOSOLA: Sure, your pistol holds
  Nothing but perfumes or kissing comfits.°
   Excellent lady,
  You have a pretty way on't to discover°
200 Your longing. Come, come, I'll disarm you
  And arm you thus— *(embraces her)* yet this is
   wondrous strange.
JULIA: Compare thy form and my eyes together,
  You'll find my love no such great miracle.
  (Kisses him.) Now you'll say

  I am a wanton. This nice° modesty in ladies
  Is but a troublesome familiar°
  That haunts them.
BOSOLA: Know you me, I am a blunt soldier.°
JULIA: The better: 210
  Sure, there wants fire where there are no lively
   sparks
  Of roughness.
BOSOLA: And I want compliment.°
JULIA: Why, ignorance
  In courtship cannot make you do amiss,
  If you have a heart to do well.
BOSOLA: You are very fair.
JULIA: Nay, if you lay beauty to my charge,
  I must plead unguilty.   220
BOSOLA: Your bright eyes
  Carry a quiver of darts in them,° sharper
  Than sunbeams.
JULIA: You will mar me with commendation.
  Put yourself to the charge of courting me,
  Whereas now I woo you.
BOSOLA *(aside)*: I have it, I will work upon this
   creature.
  Let us grow more amorously familiar.
  If the great Cardinal now should see me thus, 230
  Would he not count me a villain?
JULIA: No, he might count me a wanton,
  Not lay a scruple of offense on you:
  For if I see and steal a diamond,
  The fault is not i' th' stone, but in me, the thief
  That purloins it. I am sudden with you:
  We that are great women of pleasure, use to cut
   off°
  These uncertain wishes and unquiet longings,
  And in an instant join the sweet delight 240
  And the pretty excuse together; had you been i' th'
   street
  Under my chamber window, even there
  I should have courted you.
BOSOLA: Oh, you are an excellent lady.
JULIA: Bid me do somewhat for you presently
  To express I love you.
BOSOLA: I will, and if you love me,
  Fail not to effect it.
  The Cardinal is grown wondrous melancholy; 250
  Demand the cause, let him not put you off
  With feigned excuse; discover the main ground
  on't.
JULIA: Why would you know this?

Or . . . lately, The exact meaning of this passage is difficult to determine: "brought" may be a printer's misreading of "bought." If the verb is "brought," the passage is an obvious development of the Cardinal's idea that Antonio is "in want": needing cash, he has sold a miniature of the Duchess to a dealer. If, however, the verb is "bought," the "Who" governing it is ambiguous. It may refer either to "picture makers" or to Antonio, depending on whether he has sold his wife's picture to get money or bought it as a keepsake. Most modern editions emend to "bought," but because the first quarto reading seems to develop logically out of the Cardinal's thought, "brought" is here retained. *wretched,* an equivocation, meaning either despicable or pitiable. *be happy,* Be happy (in the advancement that will follow as a result of your seeing him). *basilisk,* a mythical monster that could kill with a look. *kissing comfits,* breath sweeteners. *discover,* make known.

---

nice, foolish. *familiar,* family spirit. *blunt soldiers,* a double-entendre, like most of the language in this interview. *compliment,* The homonym, "complement," is also implied. *Your . . . them,* Cupid was supposed to afflict people with love by shooting them with enchanted darts, and it was through the eyes that love was most commonly thought to enter the body. *use . . . off,* are in the habit of dispensing with.

BOSOLA: I have depended on him,
And I hear that he is fallen in some disgrace
With the Emperor. If he be, like the mice
That forsake falling houses,° I would shift
To other dependence.

260 JULIA: You shall not need follow the wars:°
I'll be your maintenance.

BOSOLA: And I your loyal servant;
But I cannot leave my calling.

JULIA: Not leave an
Ungrateful general for the love of a sweet lady?
You are like some, cannot sleep in featherbeds,
But must have blocks for their pillows.

BOSOLA: Will you do this?

JULIA: Cunningly.

270 BOSOLA: Tomorrow I'll expect th'intelligence.

JULIA: Tomorrow!° Get you into my cabinet;°
You shall have it with you:° do not delay me—
No more than I do you. I am like one
That is condemned: I have my pardon promised,
But I would see it sealed. Go, get you in;
You shall see me wind my tongue about his heart
Like a skein of silk. (BOSOLA *withdraws behind the
traverse.*)

(*Enter* CARDINAL.)

CARDINAL: Where are you? (*Enter* SERVANTS.)

SERVANTS: Here.

280 CARDINAL: Let none, upon your lives,
Have conference with the Prince Ferdinand,
Unless I know it. (*aside*) In this distraction
He may reveal the murther. (*Exeunt* SERVANTS.)
Yond's my ling'ring consumption:
I am weary of her; and by any means
Would be quit of—

JULIA: How now, my lord?
What ails you?

CARDINAL: Nothing.

290 JULIA: Oh, you are much altered:
Come, I must be your secretary,° and remove
This lead from off your bosom—What's the
matter?

CARDINAL: I may not tell you.

JULIA: Are you so far in love with sorrow,
You cannot part with part of it? or think you
I cannot love your grace when you are sad,
As well as merry? or do you suspect
I, that have been a secret to your heart
300 These many winters, cannot be the same
Unto your tongue?

---

like . . . houses, Mice were thought to desert old houses just before they fell down. *follow the wars,* follow after the Cardinal when he goes to war. *Tomorrow,* Not tomorrow, but now! *cabinet,* closet. *with you,* at your appearance. *secretary,* one entrusted with secrets.

CARDINAL: Satisfy thy longing.
The only way to make thee keep my counsel
Is not to tell thee.

JULIA: Tell your echo this—
Or flatterers, that, like echoes, still report
What they hear, though most imperfect—and not
me;
For, if that you be true unto yourself,
I'll know.°   310

CARDINAL: Will you rack me?°

JULIA: No, judgment shall
Draw it from you. It is an equal fault
To tell one's secrets unto all, or none.

CARDINAL: The first argues folly.

JULIA: But the last, tyranny.

CARDINAL: Very well. Why, imagine I have
committed
Some secret deed which I desire the world
May never hear of!   320

JULIA: Therefore may not I know it?
You have concealed for me as great a sin
As adultery. Sir, never was occasion
For perfect trial of my constancy
Til now. Sir, I beseech you.

CARDINAL: You'll repent it.

JULIA: Never.

CARDINAL: It hurries thee to ruin: I'll not tell thee.
Be well advised, and think what danger 'tis
To receive a prince's secrets. They that do,   330
Had need have their breasts hooped with adamant°
To contain them. I pray thee yet be satisfied.
Examine thine own frailty; 'tis more easy
To tie knots, than unloose them. 'Tis a secret
That, like a ling'ring poison, may chance lie
Spread in thy veins, and kill thee seven year hence.

JULIA: Now you dally with° me.

CARDINAL: No more. Thou shalt know it.
By my appointment,° the great Duchess of Malfi
And two of her young children, four nights since,   340
Were strangled.

JULIA: Oh heaven! Sir, what have you done?

CARDINAL: How now? How settles this? Think you
your bosom
Will be a grave dark and obscure enough
For such a secret?

JULIA: You have undone yourself, sir.

CARDINAL: Why?

JULIA: It lies not in me to conceal it.

CARDINAL: No?   350
Come, I will swear you to't upon this book.

JULIA: Most religiously.

CARDINAL: Kiss it.

For . . . know, for you can be true to yourself only by telling me. *rack me,* put me upon the rack. *adamant,* unyielding steel. *dally with,* make a fool of. *appointment,* order.

(She kisses a Bible.)

Now you shall never utter it. Thy curiosity
Hath undone thee: thou'rt poisoned with that
    book.
Because I knew thou couldst not keep my counsel.
I have bound thee to't by death.

(Enter BOSOLA.*)*

BOSOLA: For pity sake, hold.
360 CARDINAL: Ha, Bosola!
JULIA *(to the* CARDINAL*)*: I forgive you
This equal piece of justice you have done,
For I betrayed your counsel to that fellow:
He overheard it. That was the cause I said
It lay not in me to conceal it.
BOSOLA: Oh foolish woman,
Couldst not thou have poisoned him?
JULIA: 'Tis weakness,
Too much to think what should have been done. I
370   go,
I know not whither. *(Dies.)*
CARDINAL: Wherefore comst thou hither?
BOSOLA: That I might find a great man, like yourself,
Not out of his wits, as the Lord Ferdinand,
To remember my service.
CARDINAL: I'll have thee hewed in pieces.
BOSOLA: Make not yourself such a promise of that life
Which is not yours to dispose of.
CARDINAL: Who placed thee here?
380 BOSOLA: Her lust, as she intended.
CARDINAL: Very well,
Now you know me for your fellow murderer.
BOSOLA: And wherefore should you lay fair marble
    colors°
Upon your rotten purposes to° me?
Unless you imitate some that do plot great treasons,
And when they have done, go hide themselves i' th'
    graves
Of those were actors in't.
390 CARDINAL: No more: there is a fortune attends thee.
BOSOLA: Shall I go sue to Fortune any longer?
'Tis the fool's pilgrimage.
CARDINAL: I have honors in store for thee.
BOSOLA: There are a many ways that conduct to
    seeming
Honor, and some of them very dirty ones.
CARDINAL: Throw to the devil
Thy melancholy. The fire burns well,
What need we keep a stirring of't, and make
400   A greater smother?° Thou wilt kill Antonio?
BOSOLA: Yes.
CARDINAL: Take up that body.
BOSOLA: I think I shall
Shortly grow the common bier for churchyards!

---

fair . . . colors, paint to make wood look like marble.
to, toward.   *smother,* smoke.

CARDINAL: I will allow thee some dozen of attendants,
To aid thee in the murther.
BOSOLA: Oh, by no means: physicians that apply
    horseleeches to any rank swelling use to cut off
    their tails, that the blood may run through them
    the faster. Let me have no train° when I go to   410
    shed blood, lest it make me have a greater—
    when I ride to the gallows.
CARDINAL: Come to me after midnight, to help to
    remove that body to her own lodging. I'll give
    out she died o' th' plague; 'twill breed the less
    inquiry after her death.
BOSOLA: Where's Castruchio her husband?
CARDINAL: He's rode to Naples to take possession of
    Antonio's citadel.
BOSOLA: Believe me, you have done a very happy   420
    turn.
CARDINAL: Fail not to come. There is the master key
Of our lodgings, and by that you may conceive
What trust I plant in you. *(Exit.)*
BOSOLA: You shall find me ready.
Oh poor Antonio, though nothing be so needful
To thy estate, as pity, yet I find
Nothing so dangerous. I must look to my footing;
In such slippery ice-pavements men had need
To be frost-nailed° well: they may break their necks   430
    else.
The precedent's here afore me: how this man
Bears up in blood!° seems fearless! Why, 'tis well:
Security° some men call the suburbs of hell,
Only a dead wall between. Well, good Antonio,
I'll seek thee out; and all my care shall be
To put thee into safety from the reach
Of these most cruel biters, that have got
Some of thy blood already. It may be
I'll join with thee in a most just revenge.   440
The weakest arm is strong enough, that strikes
With the sword of justice. Still methinks the
    Duchess
Haunts me—there, there!—'tis nothing but my
    melancholy.
O penitence, let me truly taste thy cup,
That throws men down, only to raise them up.
    (Exit.)

ACT 5 / SCENE 3

(Somewhere near the DUCHESS' *grave)*
(Enter ANTONIO *and* DELIO. ECHO *from the* DUCHESS'
grave.)

DELIO: Yond's the Cardinal's window. This
    fortification

---

no train, no procession at my back (waiting to betray
me).   *frost-nailed,* equipped with hobnailed boots for gripping the ice.   *Bears . . . blood,* shows his courage.   *Security,*
lack of danger.

Grew from the ruins of an ancient abbey.
And to yond side o' th' river lies a wall,
Piece of a cloister, which in my opinion
Gives the best echo that you ever heard;
So hollow, and so dismal, and withal
So plain in the distinction° of our words,
That may have supposed it is a spirit
410   That answers.
ANTONIO: I do love these ancient ruins:
We never tread upon them, but we set
Our foot upon some reverend history,
And, questionless,° here in this open court,
Which now lies naked to the injuries
Of stormy weather, some men lie interred
Loved the Church so well and gave so largely to't
They thought it should have canopied their bones
Till doomsday. But all things have their end:
420   Churches and cities, which have diseases like to
     men,
Must have like death that we have.
ECHO: *Like death that we have.*
DELIO: Now the echo hath caught you.
ANTONIO: It groaned, methought, and gave
A very deadly accent!
ECHO: *Deadly accent.*
DELIO: I told you 'twas a pretty one. You may make it
A huntsman or a falconer, a musician,
430   Or a thing of sorrow.
ECHO: *A thing of sorrow.*
ANTONIO: Ay, sure, that suits it best.
ECHO: *That suits it best.*
ANTONIO: 'Tis very like my wife's voice.
ECHO: *Ay, wife's voice.*
DELIO: Come, let's walk farther from't.
I would not have you go to th' Cardinal's tonight.
Do not.
ECHO: *Do not.*
440   DELIO: Wisdom doth not more moderate wasting
     sorrow
Than time.° Take time for't: be mindful of thy
     safety.
ECHO: *Be mindful of thy safety.*
ANTONIO: Necessity compels me:
Make scrutiny throughout the passages°
Of your own life; you'll find it impossible
To fly your fate.
ECHO: *O fly your fate.*
450   DELIO: Hark, the dead stones seem to have pity on
     you
And give you good counsel.
ANTONIO: Echo, I will not talk with thee,
For thou art a dead thing.

ECHO: *Thou art a dead thing.*
ANTONIO: My Duchess is asleep now,
And her little ones—I hope sweetly. Oh, heaven
Shall I never see her more?
ECHO: *Never see her more.*
ANTONIO: I marked not one° repetition of the Echo   460
But that: and, on the sudden, a clear light
Presented me a face folded in sorrow.
DELIO: Your fancy, merely.
ANTONIO: Come, I'll be out of this ague;°
For to live thus, is not indeed to live:
It is a mockery, and abuse of life.
I will not henceforth save myself by halves.
Lose all, or nothing.
DELIO: Your own virtue save you!
I'll fetch your eldest son, and second you.   470
It may be that the sight of his° own blood,
Spread in so sweet a figure, may beget
The more compassion.
ANTONIO: However, fare you well.
Though in our miseries Fortune hath a part
Yet in our noble sufferings she hath none.
Contempt of pain—that we may call our own.
    (*Exeunt.*)

ACT 5 / SCENE 4

(*The palace of the Aragonian brothers in Milan*)
(*Enter* CARDINAL, PESCARA, MALATESTE, RODERIGO,
GRISOLAN.)

CARDINAL: You shall not watch tonight by the sick
     Prince;
His grace is very well recovered.
MALATESTE: Good my lord, suffer us.°
CARDINAL: Oh, by no means:
The noise and change of object in his eye
Doth more distract him. I pray, all to bed;
And though you hear him in his violent fit,
Do not rise, I entreat you.
PESCARA: So sir, we shall not—   10
CARDINAL: Nay, I must have you promise
Upon your honors, for I was enjoined to't
By himself; and he seemed to urge it sensibly.°
PESCARA: Let our honors bind this trifle.
CARDINAL: Nor any of your followers.
PESCARA: Neither.
CARDINAL: It may be, to make trial of your promise,
When he's asleep, myself will rise, and feign
Some of his mad tricks, and cry out for help,
And feign myself in danger.   20
MALATESTE: If your throat were cutting,

I . . . one, I did not notice the significance of one.
ague, a sickness characterized by intermittent chills and
fever.   *his,* the Cardinal's family's.   *suffer us,* Allow us then
to watch over him.   *sensibly,* when he was in full possession
of his senses.

---

distinction, articulation.   *questionless,* unquestionably.
Wisdom . . . time, Wisdom does not alleviate the pain of
consuming sorrow any better than time(?).   *passages,*
events.

I'd not come at you, now I have protested against it.
CARDINAL: Why, I thank you. (*Withdraws.*)
GRISOLAN: 'Twas a foul storm tonight.
RODERIGO: The Lord Ferdinand's chamber shook
    like an osier.°
MALATESTE: 'Twas nothing but pure kindness in the
    devil,
    To rock his own child.

(*Exeunt* RODERIGO, MALATESTE, PESCARA, GRISOLAN.)

30 CARDINAL: The reason why I would not suffer these
    About my brother is because at midnight
    I may with better privacy convey
    Julia's body to her own lodging. O, my conscience!
    I would pray now, but the devil takes away my
      heart
    For having any confidence in prayer.
    About this hour I appointed Bosola
    To fetch the body: when he hath served my turn,
    He dies. (*Exit.*)

(*Enter* BOSOLA.)

40 BOSOLA: Ha! 'twas the Cardinal's voice. I heard him
      name
    Bosola, and my death—listen, I hear one's footing.

(*Enter* FERDINAND.)

FERDINAND: Strangling is a very quiet death.
BOSOLA: Nay, then, I see I must stand upon my
    guard.
FERDINAND: What say' to that? Whisper, softly: do
    you agree to't?
    So it must be done i' th' dark: the Cardinal
    Would not for a thousand pounds the doctor
50   should see it. (*Exit.*)
BOSOLA: My death is plotted; here's° the consequence
    of murther.°
    We value not desert, nor Christian breath,
    When we know black deeds must be cured with
    death. (*Withdraws.*)

(*Enter* ANTONIO *and a* SERVANT.)

SERVANT: Here stay, sir, and be confident, I pray:
    I'll fetch a dark lanthorn. (*Exit.*)
ANTONIO: Could I take him
    At his prayers, there were hope of pardon.
60 BOSOLA: Fall right my sword:

(*Half-crazed by fears that he will be murdered,* BOSOLA
mistakes ANTONIO *for the Cardinal or one of the hen-
chmen and runs him through, from behind.*)

    I'll not give thee so much leisure as to pray.
ANTONIO: Oh, I am gone. Thou hast ended a long
    suit.

---

osier, willow tree. **here's,** the plotting of my death.
murther, (my doing) murder.

In a minute.
BOSOLA: What art thou?
ANTONIO: A most wretched thing,
    That only have thy benefit in death.
    To appear myself.° (*Enter* SERVANT *with a dark
    lanthorn.*)
SERVANT: Where are you sir?
ANTONIO: Very near my home.° Bosola?   70
SERVANT: Oh misfortune!
BOSOLA (*to* SERVANT): Smother thy pity, thou art dead
    else—Antonio!
    The man I would have saved 'bove mine own life!
    We are merely the stars' tennis balls, struck and
    banded°
    Which way please them. Oh, good Antonio,
    I'll whisper one thing in thy dying ear,
    Shall make thy heart break quickly. Thy fair
    Duchess   80
    And two sweet children—
ANTONIO: Their very names
    Kindle a little life in me.
BOSOLA: Are murdered!
ANTONIO: Some men have wished to die
    At the hearing of sad tidings: I am glad
    That I shall do't in sadness. I would not now
    Wish my wounds balmed, nor healed: for I have no
    use
    To put my life to. In all our quest of greatness,   90
    Like wanton boys whose pastime is their care,
    We follow after bubbles, blown in th'air.
    Pleasure of life, what is't? only the good hours
    Of an ague; merely a preparative to rest,
    To endure vexation. I do not ask
    The process of my death. Only commend me
    To Delio.
BOSOLA: Break, heart!
ANTONIO: And let my son fly the courts of princes.
    (*Dies.*)
BOSOLA: Thou seemst to have loved Antonio?   100
SERVANT: I brought him hither,
    To have reconciled him to the Cardinal.
BOSOLA: I do not ask thee that.
    Take him up, if thou tender thine own life,
    And bear him where the Lady Julia
    Was wont to lodge. Oh, my fate moves swift.
    I have this Cardinal in the forge already;
    Now I'll bring him to th' hammer (O direful
    misprision!°)
    I will not imitate things glorious,   110
    No more than base:° I'll be mine own example.
    (*to the* SERVANT) On, on! And look thou represent,°

That . . . myself, The only benefit that I get from you in
death is to be again myself (and no longer have to run and
hide). **home,** final resting place. **banded,** bandied. **misprision,** mistake. **No . . . base,** any more than I will seek to
copy what is base. **represent,** imitate.

for silence,
The thing thou bearst. *(Exeunt.)*

ACT 5 / SCENE 5

(Enter CARDINAL, *with a book.)*

CARDINAL: I am puzzled in a question about hell:
He° says in hell there's one material fire,
And yet it shall not burn all men alike.
Lay him by. How tedious is a guilty conscience!
When I look into the fishponds in my garden,
Methinks I see a thing armed with a rake°
That seems to strike at me. Now? Art thou come?

(Enter BOSOLA *and* SERVANT, *with* ANTONIO's *body.)*

Thou lookst ghastly:
There sits in thy face some great determination,
10 Mixed with some fear.
BOSOLA: Thus it lightens into° action:
I am come to kill thee.
CARDINAL: Ha? Help! our guard!
BOSOLA: Thou art deceived:
They are out of thy howling.
CARDINAL: Hold, and I will faithfully divide
Revenues with thee.
BOSOLA: Thy prayers and proffers
Are both unseasonable.
20 CARDINAL: Raise the watch:
We° are betrayed!
BOSOLA: I have confined your flight:
I'll suffer you to retreat to Julia's chamber,
But no further.
CARDINAL: Help! We are betrayed!

(Enter PESCARA, MALATESTE, RODERIGO, *and* GRISO-
LAN, *above.)*

MALATESTE: Listen.
CARDINAL: My dukedom for rescue!
RODERIGO: Fie upon his counterfeiting.
MALATESTE: Why, 'tis not the Cardinal.
30 RODERIGO: Yes, yes, 'tis he:
But I'll see him hanged ere I'll go down to him.
CARDINAL: Here's a plot upon me! I am assaulted! I
am lost,
Unless some rescue!
GRISOLAN: He doth this pretty well,
But it will not serve to laugh me° out of mine
honor.°
CARDINAL: The sword's at my throat!

He, the author of the book.   *armed . . . rake,* The devil
was traditionally thought to carry a fork of some sort.
lightens into, shows itself as it rises to.   *We,* The Cardinal
uses the royal "we" here, perhaps in an unconscious attempt
to establish his authority over Bosola, and certainly in an
effort to summon others to his help.   *laugh me,* trick me.
mine honor, my vow to him not to interfere.

RODERIGO: You would not bawl so loud then.
MALATESTE: Come, come. Let's go to bed: he told us   40
thus much aforehand.
PESCARA: He wished you should not come at him, but
believ't,
The accent of the voice sounds not in jest.
I'll down to him, howsoever, and with engines°
Force ope the doors. *(Exit.)*
RODERIGO: Let's follow him aloof,
And note how the Cardinal will laugh at him.
(Exeunt above.)
BOSOLA: There's for you first:
'Cause you shall not unbarricade the door   50
To let in rescue.

(He kills the SERVANT.)*

CARDINAL: What cause hast thou to pursue my life?
BOSOLA: Look there.
CARDINAL: Antonio!
BOSOLA: Slain by my hand unwittingly.
Pray, and be sudden:° when thou killedst thy sister,
Thou tookst from Justice her most equal balance,
And left her naught but her sword.
CARDINAL: O mercy!

(He falls to his knees.)

BOSOLA: Now it seems thy greatness was only   60
outward:
For thou fallst faster of thyself than calamity
Can drive thee. I'll not waste longer time. There.

(Stabs the CARDINAL.)*

CARDINAL: Thou hast hurt me.
BOSOLA: Again. *(Stabs him again.)*
CARDINAL: Shall I die like a leveret,°
Without any resistance? Help! help! help!
I am slain.

(Enter FERDINAND.)*

FERDINAND: Th'alarum?° give me a fresh horse.
Rally the vaunt-guard,° or the day is lost.   70
Yield, yield! I give you the honor of arms,
Shake my sword over you. Will you yield?
CARDINAL: Help me! I am your brother.
FERDINAND: The devil!
My brother fight upon the adverse party!

(He wounds the CARDINAL, *and, in the scuffle, gives*
BOSOLA *his death wound.)*

There flies your ransom.°
CARDINAL: Oh, justice,
I suffer now for what hath former been:

---

engines, tools.   *'Cause,* so that.   *sudden,* quick.
leveret, small hare.   *alarum,* the trumpet call to arms.
vaunt-guard, the foremost ranks of the army.   *ransom,*
(chance for) being ransomed.

Sorrow is held the eldest child of sin.
80 FERDINAND: Now you're brave fellows. Caesar's fortune was harder than Pompey's; Caesar died in
the arms of prosperity, Pompey at the feet of
disgrace. You both died in the field; the pain's
nothing. Pain many times is taken away with the
apprehension of greater—as the toothache with
the sight of a barber° that comes to pull it out:
there's philosophy for you.
BOSOLA: Now my revenge is perfect.° Sink, thou main
cause
90 Of my undoing!—The last part of my life
Hath done me best service.

(He kills FERDINAND.)

FERDINAND: Give me some wet hay:° I am broken
winded.
I do account this world but a dog kennel:
I will vault credit, and affect high pleasures
Beyond death.°
BOSOLA: He seems to come to himself,
Now he's so near the bottom.
FERDINAND: My sister! oh, my sister! there's the cause
100 on't.
Whether we fall by ambition, blood, or lust,
Like diamonds, we are cut with our own dust. (Dies)
CARDINAL: Thou hast thy payment too.
BOSOLA: Yes, I hold my weary soul in my teeth:
'Tis ready to part from me. I do glory
That thou, which stoodst like a huge pyramid
Begun upon a large and ample base,
Shalt end in a little point, a kind of nothing.

(Enter PESCARA, MALATESTE, RODERIGO, and GRISO-
LAN.)

PESCARA: How now, my lord?
110 MALATESTE: O sad disaster!
RODERIGO: How comes this?
BOSOLA: Revenge!—for the Duchess of Malfi,
murderèd
By th'Aragonian brethren; for Antonio,
Slain by this hand; for lustful Julia,
Poisoned by this man; and lastly, for myself,
That was an actor in the main of all,
Much 'gainst mine own good nature, yet i' th' end
Neglected.°

PESCARA: How now, my lord?   120
CARDINAL: Look to my brother:
He° gave us these large wounds as we were
struggling
Here i' th' rushes.° And now, I pray, let me
Be laid by, and never thought of. (Dies.)
PESCARA: How fatally, it seems, he did withstand°
His own rescue!
MALATESTE: Thou wretched thing of blood,
How came Antonio by his death?
BOSOLA: In a mist—I know not how—   130
Such a mistake as I have often seen
In a play. Oh, I am gone—
We are only like dead walls or vaulted graves
That, ruined, yield no echo. Fare you well.
It may be pain, but no harm, to me to die
In so good a quarrel. Oh this gloomy world,
In what a shadow or deep pit of darkness
Doth, womanish° and fearful,° mankind live?
Let worthy minds ne'er stagger in distrust
To suffer death or shame for what is just: 140
Mine is another voyage. (Dies.)
PESCARA: The noble Delio, as I came to th' palace,
Told me of Antonio's being here, and showed me
A pretty gentleman, his son and heir.

(Enter DELIO with ANTONIO's son.)

MALATESTE: O, sir, you come too late.
DELIO: I heard so, and
Was armed° for't ere I came. Let us make noble use
Of this great ruin, and join all our force
To establish this young hopeful gentleman
In's mother's right. These wretched, eminent°   150
things
Leave no more fame behind 'em, than should one
Fall in a frost and leave his print in snow:
As soon as the sun shines, it ever melts
Both form and matter. I have ever thought
Nature doth nothing so great for great men,
As when she's pleased to make them lords of truth:
Integrity of life is fame's best friend,
Which nobly, beyond death, shall crown the end.
(Exeunt.)

---

barber, Barbers served also as surgeons at this time.
perfect, complete. wet hay, thought to be the best food for
a broken-winded horse. I . . . death, I will leap over things
credited to be of worth in this world, and I will strive after
the true pleasures that lie beyond death. yet . . . Neglected,
"Which, ultimately, I neglected."

He, Bosola. rushes, Greens and reeds were sometimes
used to cover cold castle floors. withstand, offer opposition
to (by counseling us against). womanish, timorous. fearful, both frightened and frightening. armed, prepared.
eminent, conspicuous.

Figure 1. Ferdinand (Roland Hewgill, *right*) bribes Bosola (Powys Thomas) to spy on the Duchess in the Stratford Festival production of *The Duchess of Malfi*, directed by Jean Gascon and designed by Desmond Heeley, Stratford, Ontario, 1971. (Photograph: Douglas Spillane. Courtesy of the Stratford Festival.)

Figure 2. The Duchess (Pat Galloway) woos Antonio (Barry MacGregor) in the Stratford Festival production of *The Duchess of Malfi*, directed by Jean Gascon and designed by Desmond Heeley, Stratford, Ontario, 1971. (Photograph: Douglas Spillane. Courtesy of the Stratford Festival.)

Figure 3. Antonio (Barry MacGregor), the Duchess (Pat Galloway), and various church figures form a tableau depicting the banishment scene at Loretto in the Stratford Festival production of *The Duchess of Malfi*, directed by Jean Gascon and designed by Desmond Heeley, Stratford, Ontario, 1971. (Photograph: Douglas Spillane. Courtesy of the Stratford Festival.)

Staging of *The Duchess of Malfi*

INTERVIEW WITH JEAN GASCON, DIRECTOR
OF THE 1971 STRATFORD FESTIVAL
PRODUCTION OF *THE DUCHESS OF MALFI,* BY
BRADFORD S. FIELD, JR.

FIELD: I was looking at some of the photographs of *The Duchess of Malfi* on its tour and of the play as it opened here. I noticed that on the tour the Cardinal was in one costume, but that you recostumed the character entirely for the production here. What kind of discovery did you make that led to that change?

GASCON: We were after a kind of monolithic idea of the Cardinal, and the costume that first turned out was much too light and didn't give that kind of pyramidal shape that I was looking for. As happens very often in the theatre, we didn't have a chance to re-do it before the tour. This happened with a lot of the costumes in *Malfi*. We took a lot of risks in the original designs. Some worked and some didn't, and after the tour, when we had a chance to make changes, we did so. We had originally decided on a kind of no-period costume, one that would reflect a degraded court, a sick court. We expanded that design idea much further after the tour in Minneapolis and Ottawa, because we were going much further in the whole production with this idea of a decadent, corrupted, sick court.

FIELD: Does this decadence strike a chord in a modern audience's heart?

GASCON: Well, it's not the same kind of decadence . . . decadence can become a kind of cliché too. There's Roman decadence, and there are other kinds, Italian Renaissance decadence, that can be just a tableau of beautiful costumes, and we wanted to go against that . . .

FIELD: Aside from the costumes, did you have to make any other adjustments as you went along? Were there any other problems, say, in interpretation that were difficult?

GASCON: The two really difficult problems that we had were, first, to establish in the *Duchess of Malfi* the relationships within the family. It's not spelled out in the dialogue, but there's obviously an incestuous love felt by Ferdinand for his sister. To show that, and to show the relationship of the Cardinal to the other two, is very intricate work. Ferdinand is a deranged man. They are like twins, really, Ferdinand and the sister. They come from the same cell, I think, in Webster's mind, except that one went rotten and the other went beautiful. There's a lot of Ferdinand in the Duchess and a lot of the Duchess in Ferdinand, and that is very tricky to establish. The second problem was the difficulty of defining the character of

Bosola. A marvelous character, a disenchanted, bitter man, but what is disturbing is that within him you can feel that he never became "somebody" in that society because the society wouldn't allow it.

FIELD: Even though he had all the talent to be so?

GASCON: He had everything! The whole equipment was there—the intelligence, the dedication, the courage. And he lost it all . . . it reminded me at one point of some Brechtian characters. Brecht establishes that people—whether they be Peachums or Schweiks—will do anything, when it's a question of survival, and that it's not their fault if they do wrong. It's the society that is rotten, when the only way to survive in it is to be anti-social, when they cannot fulfill their own lives.

FIELD: So that Bosola is a good example, or rather a horrible example, of wasted capacity.

GASCON: Absolutely! In the view of Brecht, and of Webster, the man that has everything should succeed in a well-organized society; in a well-organized society a man like Bosola would have a chance to be a great man.

FIELD: In these two general problems can you put your finger on a specific speech or piece of stage action that exemplifies the problem, like establishing the relationship between the brother and the sister?

GASCON: As I said, it's really not in the dialogue . . . a question we ask about Ferdinand is, why is he so concerned about that Duchess, why does he punish her so much? The reason, we see finally, is incestuous love, and in the production itself you have to make that clear to the audience at the beginning of the play, so they know what you're talking about. We started with a tableau—and that is really a very difficult thing to make succeed—where Antonio is talking about the corruption of the court from the upper balcony, and down below all the courtiers are doing their business, trying to get some job or another, people moving around in a kind of dream-like light. In that scene, we tried to establish some close physical contact between the brother and the sister, contacts that were sexual for Ferdinand, but not for the Duchess. We had to be careful. These things may mean too much, more than you want them to mean. You have to make sure that your point of view toward the play is registered in the house.

FIELD: The house . . . when you know what kind of audience you are going to get all summer long, how much does that affect the way you interpret the play?

GASCON: Doesn't affect me at all. And I don't think it should. I always hope for success, but when you tackle a difficult play like *Duchess of Malfi* you cannot worry about things like this so-called relevance. You must go for clarity, clarity of thinking, of emotion, of all the physical elements. Then people can really understand what you are talking about.

FIELD: You spoke earlier of the danger of having something mean more that you had expected it to. Did any scenes in *Duchess of Malfi* surprise you? Any of them give more or different things than you expected?

GASCON: One thing turned out better than we expected. In Webster there is a scene in pantomime, the banishment of the Duchess at Loretto in the cathedral. That point in the Jacobean tragedy is a very important moment—but there's no text.

FIELD: These peasants try to explain it, don't they?

GASCON: The peasants come in before it, talking about the scene, and then after that commenting on the scene, but there's no scene written. About three weeks before we opened the play I suddenly had serious doubts about that scene, and I went to the designer, Desmond Heeley, and I said, maybe, you know, the play wouldn't lose anything if we don't do that scene. And I could see him nearly bursting into tears; we had both worked so hard on that concept. For us it was a very important moment in the play. At the beginning when we were doing our homework on it, I had thought it was a very important moment, but suddenly in the rehearsals of it, because there was no text—and no costumes—and no light—and no sounds . . .

FIELD: And no audience . . .

GASCON: And no audience, then suddenly it looked ludicrous. We said, "What are we doing here?" Even the actors were saying, "What is this thing about?" And finally, fortunately, we convinced each other that our first idea was a good one, and that we had to go on with it, still not sure that we would keep it. I remember the first time that we produced it in front of a few people here in Stratford, the first technical dress rehearsal, with the sounds, and the lights, and the costumes and all that—people thought it was a marvelous theatrical moment, a kind of summing up of the whole style of the production, a style that was very bold, very gutsy and menacing and cruel— and that moment seemed to be the pinnacle of the production.

FIELD: So it wasn't a surprise but more a fulfillment of your hopes.

GASCON: The surprise was because we had had our doubts about it. We had stopped believing in it. It teaches you a lesson, to trust your instinct. It's half analytic and half emotional.

FIELD: Half analytical . . . it should not be something that you know that you can impose upon the text.

GASCON: No, it has to come from the play that influences you, and suddenly inside yourself, in some strange way, your guts are affected and your imagination is affected, and suddenly you see what is the best way to illuminate "what I think the play is about," to do it that way. But if you do it from the outside, then you go for gimmicks; and when you go for gimmicks, there's a great chance of it not working at all.

REVIEW OF THE STRATFORD FESTIVAL PRODUCTION, 1971, BY CLIVE BARNES

Not for the first time—and probably not for the last, because institutions breed traditions—the second night of the Stratford Festival offset the slight disappointment of the first. Last night's production of John Webster's "The Duchess of Malfi" was a most cogent performance of a thrillingly evil play.

Why are Webster and the other Jacobean playwrights so deplorably neglected, and then—when produced—maltreated by directors, actors, critics and audiences alike? "The Duchess of Malfi," like "The White Devil," should have a place in any classic repertory, yet it is an unjustifiable rarity. I have only seen it

a couple of times before—notably with John Gielgud as Ferdinand.

The play itself is full of black blood and diamond poetry. It seems to represent two genres, the revenge play—although who is revenging whom is never quite clear—and the malcontent play. Both kinds would have been very familiar to their original audiences, and Webster's virtuosity would be better appreciated in its historical context.

The play is in a way illogical, but it has its own dark consistency. The Duchess of Malfi is a young widow with two brothers, Ferdinand, the Duke of Calabria, and the Cardinal. They do not wish the Duchess to marry—we never quite know why, although this production persuasively suggests that Ferdinand had incestuous desires for her.

The Duchess determines to marry, or at least take a lover, and her choice falls upon Antonio, her steward. Antonio loves her dearly and they have three children. Ferdinand has placed in the Duchess's court a spy, Bosola, who is nominally Master of the Horse to the Duchess, but in reality is a creature of the Duke. Bosola is one of the most interesting villains in literature—for his villainy is philosophic and honest. He is the complete rational madman and a monster of undirected purpose.

At last—and it must be admitted that Bosola is a very unperceptive spy—the Duchess's deceptions are discovered, and Ferdinand resolves to punish her. He parts her from her husband, and after torturing her in an attempt to send her mad, he and his brother have her murdered.

What follows is carnage incarnate. Such principal characters that have not been already murdered are now dispatched, and the final scene is positively infested with bodies. Not to be murdered in a Webster play would be the death of any actor of ambition—indeed the equivalent of a walk-on part.

Yet it is a great play. Even the story itself has been stabbed to tatters by unlikelihood, and yet this terrible galliard of death has its own momentum and dignity. Webster had a strange melancholy, and a mind of macabre power. Imagine the scene where the Duke is trying to send the Duchess of Malfi mad.

He arranges to see her in the pitch of night—all is dark. He gives her his hand, and leaves her—holding the hand, which he says is the severed hand of her lover, Antonio. It isn't, but that is hardly the point. Then again Webster's poetry appeals to the heart, whereas Shakespeare so often appeals more to the mind. Some of Webster's lines, such as "I am the Duchess of Malfi still," have no intellectual pretensions to poetic diction, but in their place they strike home like a poignard.

The play has been directed by Jean Gascon, Strat-

ford's artistic director, and he has done a very fine job. He has deliberately concentrated on simplicity and pace. There is no scenery—apart from Tanya Moiseiwitsch's permanent setting, and a few sparse properties. The costumes by Desmond Heeley are both gorgeous and fantastic. They have a wayward decadence to them that is just right. But spectacle Mr. Gascon uses sparingly. The famous scene of the Duchess and Antonio being excommunicated is handled with grandeur but tact, and even the madness scenes and the terrible murder of the Duchess is kept as cool as cold steel.

Mr. Gascon seems to have plucked an unusual theme from the play—the difficulty of virtue in a sea of corruption—which adds to the ambivalence of Bosola, that crazy mixed-up villain, but also serves to give the play a new depth and direction. This is a rotten world, both playwright and director are saying, so why expect anything of morality. And yet morality must be served—even to the final mound of fresh bleeding corpses.

Pat Galloway is splendid as the Duchess. She has the quick sensuality and the loyal constancy, the aristocratic mien and the quite unsentimental poignancy of a great woman dispatched before her time. The rest of the cast moved well in her sphere.

The actor cannot be blamed, but Mr. Gascon's decision to make Bosola a mistaken villain and a bluff man of honor does detract from the character and the play—the role should have a random malevolence, a serpent hypocrisy, and a fine Italian hand. This, for the rest of his reading, Mr. Gascon sacrificed, leaving Powys Thomas, playing the part, to pick up the pieces, which of course he couldn't. This was the one unconvincing character.

The diabolical brothers were excellently done, with Roland Hewgill villainously mad as the Duke and William Needles deadly, lizardlike and voluntary as the Cardinal. I admired also the honesty and dignity of Barry MacGregor's Antonio.

This is the kind of production and acting that has made the Canadian Stratford company among the most admired in the English-speaking world.

NEOCLASSICAL
THEATER

In the middle of the seventeenth century, drama moved indoors and stayed there. It moved from daylight to candlelight, from large open-air theaters, some capable of seating as many as 2000, to relatively small auditoriums, usually accommodating no more than 700. And this radical shift in the environment of drama produced not only a radically different theatrical experience, but also called forth radically different changes in the conception of drama itself. This change in the theatrical environment had already been anticipated by developments dating back to the early sixteenth century, when indoor theaters began to be built in the banqueting halls of Italy and in remodelled tennis courts in France. English private theaters, located in former monasteries such as Blackfriars and Whitefriars, began in the late 1500s. In all these spaces, the stage usually occupied one end of a long hall, and the audience watched from side galleries and from the floor in front of the stage. By the last third of the seventeenth century, theaters reflecting this design had become standard throughout the major dramatic centers in Europe, and these theaters were conventionally equipped with a proscenium arch framing the stage, a design derived from Italian stage architecture of the sixteenth century. In English theaters of the later seventeenth century, a sizable forestage, recalling the platform of the Elizabethan public theater, extended beyond the proscenium, and double doors, also in front of the proscenium, gave actors ready access to this favored acting area (see Figure 1). French theaters of the same period have a much shallower forestage, no doors, and, in some cases, benches to seat members of the audience on stage behind the proscenium (see Figure 2). In both theaters, the pit, or floor area directly in front of the stage, is shared by standing and seated spectators. Earlier, this space had been entirely given to standing room or left vacant so that the royal party could have an uninterrupted view of the stage.

Just as the English and French had borrowed from the Italians in their use of a proscenium arch, so they turned to Italy for the sets they were to display behind the picture frame of the arch. Italian set design had been pioneered by Sebastian Serlio, who created in his lengthy treatise, *Architettura* (1545), a set of detailed drawings for three typical sets, which he based on his reading of a classical Roman treatise. His dependence on a classical source is only one of the many instances that account for the term neoclassicism. Later designers simplified his three-dimensional details into painted ones and substituted flat wings for the angle wings Serlio had used. At first, the elaborate Italianate sets were used primarily for court entertainments—masques in early seventeenth century England, and court ballets in mid-seventeenth century France. But the very possibility of being able to represent different locales by changing a painted backdrop and wings (instead of saying "So this is the Forest of Arden" and expecting the audience to imagine the new locale) led to a new and crucial feature in theater architecture. Because flats that are to be shifted require

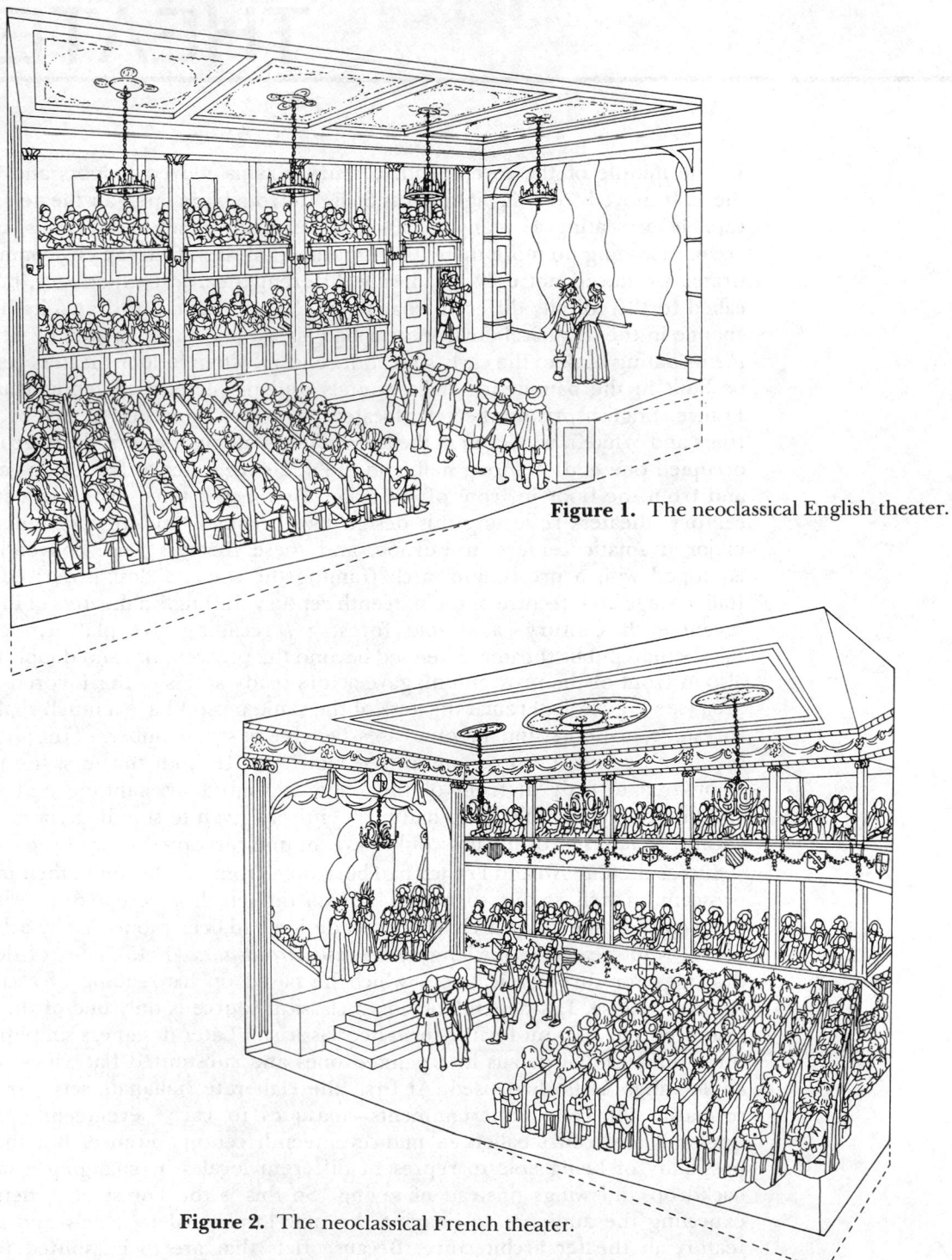

Figure 1. The neoclassical English theater.

Figure 2. The neoclassical French theater.

machinery, or stagehands, or both, to move them, it became necessary to conceal such backstage efforts. Designers began by using plain flats for concealing the activity, but gradually looked for a permanent frame for the stage: the proscenium arch. While the proscenium masked backstage maneuverings, it also detached the space on stage from the space in the remainder of the theater, and thus separated the actors from the audience. Lighting changes also reinforced this separation. In the drawings reproduced here, we see chandeliers with candles lighting both the audience and the stage. But in the late seventeenth century, footlights were added, and more attention was given to lighting the stage alone. And in the eighteenth century, dimming devices (such as lowering the candle footlights) were invented, lamps began to replace candles, and lamps with reflectors were placed *behind* the proscenium arch, focusing light more sharply on the acting area.

Still, the theaters of this period are nothing like the darkened auditoriums of today, and audiences then would not have wished them so, since they came to the theater to be seen as much as to see. For English audiences after 1660 (the date of the restoration of the monarchy and the restoration of theatrical activity), the playhouse was the place to meet friends, to talk, to flirt, to eat and drink. Prologues to Restoration plays frequently comment on the audience's behavior and especially on the attention of those in the pit (still the cheapest seats) to orange-women, prostitutes, and young men trying to be witty. The performance, it might almost be said, ran simultaneously onstage and offstage. Well-known liaisons between actresses and nobles brought performers and audience together even more closely. In a famous painting by the satiric artist, William Hogarth, of the final scene from Gay's *The Beggar's Opera* (1728), an actress can be seen gazing not only at the actor who should command her exclusive attention, but also at the Duke of Bolton, her real-life lover, who sits in an onstage box. The costuming of most plays in contemporary dress added to the mirror effect, since people onstage looked very much like those offstage. Paintings of the famous actor, David Garrick, for example, show him wearing the standard wig and dress of the mid-eighteenth century—for Macbeth! Actors owned their own wardrobes, and, like the audience members, spent lavish amounts on a single costume. The stage picture was thus likely to be highly gorgeous, but not necessarily consistent, and certainly not historically accurate.

The similarities between onstage and offstage behavior can be found in the plays as well as in performance practices. Indeed, the two are closely related, particularly in the social comedies of Etherege, Wycherley, Congreve, Molière, Goldsmith, and Sheridan. In these plays the audience could easily see itself. *The Man of Mode,* for example, reflects the fashionable activities of London society, for its characters, like members of the audience themselves, are seen promenading in St. James Park and planning illicit assignations at the theater. In France, Molière also finds a wide range of satiric targets that mirror the life of his audience—from the bourgeois who try to be upper class to the fashionable salon society obsessed with trivial affairs. But even when he comes close to satirizing his own audience directly, he is careful to leave an escape route, for his onstage characters are always highly exaggerated versions of actual experience, and their exaggeration is usually the source of his mockery.

The relation of drama to actual experience was, in fact, a central issue in critical theories of the period, most of which were derived from Italian commentaries on classical criticism. The treatises of Minturno, Scaliger, and Castelvetro, which sought to define literary art or to comment on Aristotle and Horace, argued for "verisimilitude," likeness to truth, and formulated a number of elaborate rules to bring drama closer to reality. But for them, reality was to be achieved not through having the stage life exactly like real life, but through abiding by certain normative conditions. Tragedy, for example, was to follow the norms of elevated speech, characters of high rank, and plots with unhappy endings, while comedy was to use a more colloquial style befitting its middle- or lower-class characters, and was to end happily. Verisimilitude also demanded that certain events, especially violent ones, be kept offstage, since they were thought unlikely to be convincing onstage. Finally, a play was to deal only with a single series of incidents, occurring in a single locale, within a period of twenty-four hours or less. These famous, even notorious, "unities" of action, place, and time were thought to support verisimilitude, since an audience in a theater presumably knew that it had been in the same place for several hours only, and in that limited time it could not believe a multitude of actions taking place.

Such theories, called neoclassical because they are based on reinterpretations of classical texts, could not, of course, last forever. And by the end of the eighteenth century, one of England's great literary critics, Samuel Johnson, a man thoroughly steeped in neoclassical theory, offered a common sense repudiation of the rules in his *Preface to Shakespeare:*

> The truth is, that the spectators are always in their senses, and know, from the first act to the last, that the stage is only a stage, and that the players are only players. They come to hear a certain number of lines recited with just gesture and elegant modulation. The lines relate to some action, and an action must be in some place; but the different actions that complete a story may be in places very remote from each other; and where is the absurdity of allowing that space to represent first Athens, and then Sicily, which was always known to be neither Sicily nor Athens, but a modern theater?

But by the end of the eighteenth century, staging techniques were being designed to make spectators forget they were in a theater. The development of machinery for changing sets, the elaboration of scenery painting, and the increased use of sophisticated lighting that would focus primarily on the stage were clear indications of a growing interest in making the stage picture look "real," in creating a detailed theatrical illusion. Acting styles, too, edged slightly closer to "realistic" portrayal of characters. In these ways, the theater's move indoors led eventually to drama that focussed almost totally on the individual character, showing how external environment and inner emotional life together shape the destiny of the individual.

MOLIÈRE

1622–1673

Molière, the preeminent comic dramatist in the history of French theater, was also known in his own time as the director and the leading actor of the major theatrical company in Paris. He was, in fact, so thoroughly a man of the stage that once he became involved in it, after a brief period of studying law, he abandoned his given name, Jean-Baptiste Poquelin, and replaced it with the singular one by which he has since been known. His theatrical career began in 1643, when he formed a small company, known as the Illustre Théâtre, with a family of talented actors, the Béjarts. But their enterprise failed so badly that Molière was temporarily imprisoned for debts, and the company was forced to leave Paris. They regrouped themselves in the provinces and toured the countryside from 1645 to 1658, a period when Molière evidently trained himself in every aspect of the theater from set-building to playwriting. During this time, for example, he witnessed the touring Italian companies and steeped himself in their extensive repertoire of comic techniques—techniques of the *commedia dell'arte,* such as stock characters, slapstick routines (known as *lazzi*), intrigue plots, and conventional "surprise" endings. By the end of this period, Molière had also become director of the troupe, which he had enlarged and improved by attracting some of the most accomplished actors and actresses of his day. When he took his troupe back to Paris in 1658, having arranged a special performance for the youthful Louis XIV and his court, Molière won the king's favor and was granted permission to remain in Paris and perform at the Théâtre du Petit-Bourbon, one of the few existing theaters in the city. He had won over the king, it should be noted, not by his troupe's production of a tragedy of Corneille, but by his comic performance in *The Amorous Doctor,* a farcical afterpiece he had written himself.

Molière's genius was clearly attuned to the world of comedy, and it led his troupe ultimately to be commissioned as chief entertainers to the court of Louis XIV. In 1661 he gained control of the theater in the Palais Royal, and in 1665 his group was formally designated "The King's Company." Throughout his career in Paris, Molière wrote approximately thirty theatrical pieces, some known as *comédies-ballets,* which were plays interspersed with music and dancing for presentation to the court at Versailles, and others that were purely dramatic for staging in his own theater at the Palais Royal. The *comédies-ballets* were notable not only for their music, dancing, and spectacular scenic effects, but also because the ballet sections were often performed by members of the court, including the King himself. Yet these works were conceived by Molière to be fully worked out plays as well. In fact, one of Molière's most famous comedies, *The Would-Be-Gentleman* (1670), was a *comédie-ballet,* designed at the King's command to include a musical section with a Turkish theme. This material could easily be omitted from the work, as indeed it was by Molière when he produced it as an entirely dramatic work in 1671 at the Palais Royal.

Whether writing entertainments for the court or plays for the public,

Molière's comic purpose was always the same: to expose through laughter the follies of society. Even so, his satiric treatment of various social types often aroused the displeasure of some members in the fashionable world who felt he was engaging in personal assaults on their reputation. In his own defense, he wrote a play about the theater itself, *The Versailles Impromptu* (1663), in which one of the characters offers a very revealing conversation he has had with Molière about the purpose of his comedies:

> His aim, he said, is to portray types and not individuals, and all the people who appear in his plays are imaginary, phantoms if you like; he invents them as he goes along, in such a way as to entertain the audience; and he would be embarrassed if they resembled actual people . . . and I agree with him. Why bother to pin such and such a trait on so-and-so when his characters have traits that could fit a hundred different people? The business of comedy is to present the flaws common to all men, and especially the men of our time.

In revealing human flaws, Molière typically designed his plays to focus on the comically absurd behavior of a single character who is controlled by a singular obsession. Arnolphe, for example, in *The School for Wives* (1662) is a forty-two-year-old man so desirous of being married yet so fearful of being cuckolded that he has contrived to raise a young girl of six in almost monastic seclusion for thirteen years, assuming that her total ignorance of other men and her rigorous instruction in the duties of a wife will make her completely obedient to him. But shortly after the play opens, the young girl Agnès is discovered by a young man, and the delicious progress of their courtship comically exposes the major weakness in Arnolphe's fanatically designed plan—he has failed to realize that a marriage can truly be secured only by love. Harpagon, on the other hand, the title character of *The Miser* (1668), is so avaricious that he is even willing to marry off his young daughter to a much older man, simply because the man is willing to marry her, as Harpagon gleefully reports, "without a dowry." And Orgon, the main character in *Tartuffe* (1669), is so fanatically devoted to the sham holy man Tartuffe that he worries more about the welfare of Tartuffe than about anyone else in his own family. When he is told that his wife is suffering from a fever, his reply is comically inappropriate: "Ah. And Tartuffe?" Indeed, Orgon is so blindly devoted to Tartuffe that he persistently refuses to see the hypocrisy of Tartuffe until he is nearly undone by it.

The obsessions of these characters are usually called to their attention—and to ours—by the presence of reasonable and sensible persons in their world. Sometimes these *raisonneurs* (rational commentators) are servants, sometimes friends, sometimes close relatives of the obsessed characters, but whatever their status, they repeatedly fail to bring them to their senses through rational appeals. Only the power of extremely painful experience seems capable of curing these characters, and thus Molière displays the extremity of their fixations. Although their obsessions are huge—and hugely funny—these characters are not only magnificent in their delusions, but they are also intensely human in their attachments to them. And thus Molière conceives his obsessed characters so that we will not only laugh at them but will also comprehend their pain. How else can an audience respond when Arnolphe finally recognizes that Agnès loves someone else and turns to the audience expressing his hurt and frustration? Moments such as these, as well as the sustained allegiance of the *raisonneurs* in their world, suggest that Molière intended us to see these misguided characters—whose roles he so often performed himself—as deserving both our judgment and our sympathy.

In *The Misanthrope* (1666), we are once again faced with an obsessed figure, Alceste, who produces conflicting reactions, but for far more complicated reasons than Molière's comedies usually contain. Unlike his counterparts, Alceste is obsessed with an admirable idea—namely, a belief that honesty and integrity are the most important bases of all human relationships. Consequently, he is moved to condemn his society as being filled with shallow flirts and sycophants, with hypocrites who praise people to their faces and mock them as soon as they are gone. And surely Alceste is right in condemning these characters in his world. But surely Philinte, the *raisonneur* friend of Alceste, is also correct in recognizing that a brutally frank honesty such as Alceste recommends would be the undoing of society itself. Beyond the questions raised by Philinte, we are also forced to see that Alceste is so obsessed with his vision that he sees himself as the only sincere person in his world, and thus he appears to be a supremely self-regarding egotist. And to top off these contradictions, Alceste is in love with the most beautiful—and the most insincere—woman in his society, so that he is trapped between what he believes and what he feels.

The doubts raised by Alceste's demands for sincerity coupled with his love for Célimène find their structural analogue in the to-and-fro motion of the play. The setting, appropriately, is Célimène's house, the center of social activity, and Alceste is constantly being taken away either by his legal affairs or by his anger with Célimène, yet he repeatedly returns, always attempting to get Célimène to understand his true feelings and admit to her own. In the gathering action that brings more and more people on stage, we come to expect the comic recognition and resolution customary in the finales of Molière's other works. But in the final act, Molière reverses this pattern and our expectations. The movement instead is one of gradual dispersal. Célimène's sarcastic condemnation of her own circle alienates her admirers and they slowly leave; Alceste, in turn, asks her to flee society with him, but she refuses, so he angrily rejects her; and the play ends with only a slight note of hope as Philinte and Éliante, the two *raisonneurs* go after Alceste, hoping to change his bitter mood. The play ends very much as it began—in a stalemate.

Still, the serious issues raised by *The Misanthrope* and the ambiguous tone of its ending are counterpointed, both on the page and on the stage, by deliciously witty speeches and comic characters. Richard Wilbur's translation has caught the epigrammatic quality of the original; in fact, Wilbur's translation of this and other plays (*The School for Wives* and *Tartuffe*) have rekindled interest in Molière on stages across the country. Wilbur's translation is discussed in the review following the text of a 1968 production by the APA-Phoenix Repertory Company, and photographs of this production clearly show the detailed period costumes and set devices the APA used to evoke the self-conscious style of the society that so offended Alceste. The elaborate surfaces of that style are blatantly conveyed in the costumes of Acaste and Clitandre (see Figure 1), much as Alceste's opposition to it is displayed in his unstylish lankness, his plain clothes, and his uncoiffured hair (see Figure 2). And in his bewildered look we see the play's paradox: society's honest man must necessarily be an outsider; he will ridicule society's pretensions without changing them one wit.

THE MISANTHROPE

BY MOLIÈRE / TRANSLATED BY RICHARD WILBUR

CHARACTERS

ALCESTE, *in love with Célimène*
PHILINTE, *Alceste's friend*
ORONTE, *in love with Célimène*
CÉLIMÈNE, *Alceste's beloved*
ELIANTE, *Célimène's cousin*
ARSINOÉ, *a friend of Célimène's*
ACASTE, *marquess*

CLITANDRE, *marquess*
BASQUE, *Célimène's servant*
A GUARD *of the Marshalsea*
DUBOIS, *Alceste's valet*

SCENE

The scene throughout is in Célimène's house at Paris.

ACT 1

(The scene opens on PHILINTE *and* ALCESTE.*)*

PHILINTE: Now, what's got into you?

ALCESTE *(seated)*: Kindly leave me alone.

PHILINTE: Come, come, what is it? This lugubrious
    tone . . .

ALCESTE: Leave me, I said; you spoil my solitude.

PHILINTE: Oh, listen to me, now, and don't be rude.

ALCESTE: I choose to be rude, Sir, and to be hard of
    hearing.

PHILINTE: These ugly moods of yours are not
    endearing;
    Friends though we are, I really must insist . . .

ALCESTE *(abruptly rising)*: Friends? Friends, you say?
    Well, cross me off your list.
    I've been your friend till now, as you well know;
    But after what I saw a moment ago
    I tell you flatly that our ways must part.
    I wish no place in a dishonest heart.

PHILINTE: Why, what have I done, Alceste? Is this
    quite just?

ALCESTE: My God, you ought to die of self-disgust.
    I call your conduct inexcusable, Sir,
    And every man of honor will concur.
    I see you almost hug a man to death,
    Exclaim for joy until you're out of breath,
    And supplement these loving demonstrations
    With endless offers, vows, and protestations;
    Then when I ask you "Who was that?", I find
    That you can barely bring his name to mind!
    Once the man's back is turned, you cease to love
      him,
    And speak with absolute indifference of him!
    By God, I say it's base and scandalous
    To falsify the heart's affections thus;
    If I caught myself behaving in such a way,
    I'd hang myself for shame, without delay.

PHILINTE: It hardly seems a hanging matter to me;
    I hope that you will take it graciously
    If I extend myself a slight reprieve,
    And live a little longer, by your leave.

ALCESTE: How dare you joke about a crime so grave? 40

PHILINTE: What crime? How else are people to
    behave?

ALCESTE: I'd have them be sincere, and never part
    With any word that isn't from the heart.

PHILINTE: When someone greets us with a show of
    pleasure,
    It's but polite to give him equal measure,
    Return his love the best that we know how,
    And trade him offer for offer, vow for vow.

ALCESTE: No, no, this formula you'd have me follow, 50
    However fashionable, is false and hollow,
    And I despise the frenzied operations
    Of all these barterers of protestations,
    These lavishers of meaningless embraces,
    These utterers of obliging commonplaces,
    Who court and flatter everyone on earth
    And praise the fool no less than the man of worth.
    Should you rejoice that someone fondles you,
    Offers his love and service, swears to be true,
    And fills your ears with praises of your name, 60
    When to the first damned fop he'll say the same?
    No, no: no self-respecting heart would dream
    Of prizing so promiscuous an esteem;
    However high the praise, there's nothing worse
    Than sharing honors with the universe.
    Esteem is founded on comparison:
    To honor all men is to honor none.
    Since you embrace this indiscriminate vice,
    Your friendship comes at far too cheap a price;
    I spurn the easy tribute of a heart 70
    Which will not set the worthy man apart:
    I choose, Sir, to be chosen; and in fine,
    The friend of mankind is no friend of mine.

PHILINTE: But in polite society, custom decrees
    That we show certain outward courtesies. . . .

ALCESTE: Ah, no! We should condemn with all our
    force
    Such false and artificial intercourse.
    Let men behave like men; let them display
    Their inmost hearts in everything they say;
    Let the heart speak, and let our sentiments

Not mask themselves in silly compliments.
PHILINTE: In certain cases it would be uncouth
And most absurd to speak the naked truth;
With all respect for your exalted notions,
It's often best to veil one's true emotions.
Wouldn't the social fabric come undone
If we were wholly frank with everyone?
Suppose you met with someone you couldn't bear;
80 Would you inform him of it then and there?
ALCESTE: Yes.
PHILINTE: Then you'd tell old Emilie it's pathetic
The way she daubs her features with cosmetic
And plays the gay coquette at sixty-four?
ALCESTE: I would.
PHILINTE: And you'd call Dorilas a bore,
And tell him every ear at court is lame
From hearing him brag about his noble name?
ALCESTE: Precisely.
90 PHILINTE: Ah, you're joking.
ALCESTE: *Au contraire*°:
In this regard there's none I'd choose to spare.
All are corrupt; there's nothing to be seen
In court or town but aggravates my spleen.°
I fall into deep gloom and melancholy
When I survey the scene of human folly,
Finding on every hand base flattery,
Injustice, fraud, self-interest, treachery. . . .
Ah, it's too much; mankind has grown so base,
100 I mean to break with the whole human race.
PHILINTE: This philosophic rage is a bit extreme;
You've no idea how comical you seem;
Indeed, we're like those brothers in the play
Called *School for Husbands*,° one of whom was
prey . . .
ALCESTE: Enough, now! None of your stupid similes.
PHILINTE: Then let's have no more tirades, if you
please.
The world won't change, whatever you say or do;
110 And since plain speaking means so much to you,
I'll tell you plainly that by being frank
You've earned the reputation of a crank,
And that you're thought ridiculous when you rage
And rant against the manners of the age.
ALCESTE: So much the better; just what I wish to hear.
No news could be more grateful to my ear.
All men are so detestable in my eyes,
I should be sorry if they thought me wise.
PHILINTE: Your hatred's very sweeping, is it not?
120 ALCESTE: Quite right: I hate the whole degraded lot.

PHILINTE: Must all poor human creatures be
embraced,
Without distinction, by your vast distaste?
Even in these bad times, there are surely a few . . .
ALCESTE: No, I include all men in one dim view:
Some men I hate for being rogues; the others
I hate because they treat the rogues like brothers,
And, lacking a virtuous scorn for what is vile,
Receive the villain with a complaisant smile.
Notice how tolerant people choose to be   130
Toward that bold rascal who's at law with me.°
His social polish can't conceal his nature;
One sees at once that he's a treacherous creature;
No one could possibly be taken in
By those soft speeches and that sugary grin.
The whole world knows the shady means by which
The low-brow's grown so powerful and rich,
And risen to a rank so bright and high
That virtue can but blush, and merit sigh.
Whenever his name comes up in conversation,   140
None will defend his wretched reputation;
Call him knave, liar, scoundrel, and all the rest,
Each head will nod, and no one will protest.
And yet his smirk is seen in every house,
He's greeted everywhere with smiles and bows,
And when there's any honor that can be got
By pulling strings, he'll get it, like as not.
My God! It chills my heart to see the ways
Men come to terms with evil nowadays;
Sometimes, I swear, I'm moved to flee and find   150
Some desert land unfouled by humankind.
PHILINTE: Come, let's forget the follies of the times
And pardon mankind for its petty crimes;
Let's have an end of rantings and of railings,
And show some leniency toward human failings.
This world requires a pliant rectitude;
Too stern a virtue makes one stiff and rude;
Good sense views all extremes with detestation,
And bids us to be noble in moderation.
The rigid virtues of the ancient days   160
Are not for us; they jar with all our ways
And ask of us too lofty a perfection.
Wise men accept their times without objection,
And there's no greater folly, if you ask me
Than trying to reform society.
Like you, I see each day a hundred and one
Unhandsome deeds that might be better done,
But still, for all the faults that meet my view,
I'm never known to storm and rave like you.
I take men as they are, or let them be,   170
And teach my soul to bear their frailty;
And whether in court or town, whatever the scene,

Au contraire, "On the contrary." **spleen**, The traditional seat of anger. **School for Husbands**, In Molière's
School For Husbands (1661) Sganarelle and Ariste also view
human nature in contrasting ways, one critically, the other
with philosophical indulgence.

---

at law, that is, who has a lawsuit against me.

My phlegm's° as philosophic as your spleen.
ALCESTE: This phlegm which you so eloquently
      commend,
   Does nothing ever rile it up, my friend?
   Suppose some man you trust should treacherously
   Conspire to rob you of your property,
   And do his best to wreck your reputation?
   Wouldn't you feel a certain indignation?
PHILINTE: Why, no. These faults of which you so
180   complain
   Are part of human nature, I maintain,
   And it's no more a matter for disgust
   That men are knavish, selfish and unjust,
   Than that the vulture dines upon the dead,
   And wolves are furious, and apes ill-bred.
ALCESTE: Shall I see myself betrayed, robbed, torn to
      bits,
   And not . . . Oh, let's be still and rest our wits.
   Enough of reasoning, now. I've had my fill.
190 PHILINTE: Indeed, you would do well, Sir, to be still.
   Rage less at your opponent, and give some thought
   To how you'll win this lawsuit that he's brought.
ALCESTE: I assure you I'll do nothing of the sort.
PHILINTE: Then who will plead your case before the
      court?
ALCESTE: Reason and right and justice will plead for
      me.
PHILINTE: Oh, Lord! What judges do you plan to
      see?°
200 ALCESTE: Why, none. The justice of my cause is clear.
PHILINTE: Of course, man; but there's politics to
      fear. . . .
ALCESTE: No, I refuse to lift a hand. That's flat.
   I'm either right, or wrong.
PHILINTE: Don't count on that.
ALCESTE: No, I'll do nothing.
PHILINTE: Your enemy's influence
   Is great, you know . . .
ALCESTE: That makes no difference.
210 PHILINTE: It will; you'll see.
ALCESTE: Must honor bow to guile?
   If so, I shall be proud to lose the trial.
PHILINTE: Oh, really . . .
ALCESTE: I'll discover by this case
   Whether or not men are sufficiently base
   And impudent and villainous and perverse
   To do me wrong before the universe.
PHILINTE: What a man!
ALCESTE: Oh, I could wish, whatever the cost,
220   Just for the beauty of it, that my trial were lost.
PHILINTE: If people heard you talking so, Alceste,

---

   phlegm's, one of the four humours, or basic fluids,
thought to determine temperament. An excess of phlegm
made one slow, lazy, and complacent. *judges . . . see,* the
common practice of the time was to solicit the favor of
judges and make them gifts.

   They'd split their sides. Your name would be a jest.
ALCESTE: So much the worse for jesters.
PHILINTE: May I enquire
   Whether this rectitude you so admire,
   And these hard virtues you're enamored of
   Are qualities of the lady whom you love?
   It much surprises me that you, who seem
   To view mankind with furious disesteem,
   Have yet found something to enchant your eyes   230
   Amidst a species which you so despise.
   And what is more amazing, I'm afraid,
   Is the most curious choice your heart has made.
   The honest Eliante is fond of you,
   Arsinoé, the prude, admires you too;
   And yet your spirit's been perversely led
   To choose the flighty Célimène instead,
   Whose brittle malice and coquettish ways
   So typify the manners of our days.
   How is it that the traits you most abhor   240
   Are bearable in this lady you adore?
   Are you so blind with love that you can't find them?
   Or do you contrive, in her case, not to mind them?
ALCESTE: My love for that young widow's not the kind
   That can't perceive defects; no, I'm not blind.
   I see her faults, despite my ardent love,
   And all I see I fervently reprove.
   And yet I'm weak; for all her falsity,
   That woman knows the art of pleasing me,
   And though I never cease complaining of her,   250
   I swear I cannot manage not to love her.
   Her charm outweighs her faults; I can but aim
   To cleanse her spirit in my love's pure flame.
PHILINTE: That's no small task; I wish you all success.
   You think then that she loves you?
ALCESTE: Heavens, yes!
   I wouldn't love her did she not love me.
PHILINTE: Well, if her taste for you is plain to see,
   Why do these rivals cause you such despair?
ALCESTE: True love, Sir, is possessive, and cannot   260
      bear
   To share with all the world. I'm here today
   To tell her she must send that mob away.
PHILINTE: If I were you, and had your choice to
      make,
   Eliante, her cousin, would be the one I'd take;
   That honest heart, which cares for you alone,
   Would harmonize far better with your own.
ALCESTE: True, true: each day my reason tells me so;
   But reason doesn't rule in love, you know.   270
PHILINTE: I fear some bitter sorrow is in store;
   This love . . .

   (Enter ORONTE.)

ORONTE *(to ALCESTE)*: The servants told me at the
      door
   That Eliante and Célimène were out,
   But when I heard, dear Sir, that you were about,
   I came to say, without exaggeration,

That I hold you in the vastest admiration,
And that it's always been my dearest desire
280 To be the friend of one I so admire.
I hope to see my love of merit requited,
And you and I in friendship's bond united.
I'm sure you won't refuse—if I may be frank—
A friend of my devotedness—and rank. (*During this
    speech of Oronte's,* ALCESTE *is abstracted, and seems
    unaware that he is being spoken to. He only breaks off
    his reverie when* ORONTE *says:*)
It was for you, if you please, that my words were
    intended
ALCESTE: For me, Sir?
ORONTE: Yes, for you. You're not offended?
ALCESTE: By no means. But this much surprises
290   me. . . .
The honor comes most unexpectedly. . . .
ORONTE: My high regard should not astonish you;
    The whole world feels the same. It is your due.
ALCESTE: Sir . . .
ORONTE: Why, in all the State there isn't one
    Can match your merits; they shine, Sir, like the
    sun.
ALCESTE: Sir . . .
ORONTE: You are higher in my estimation
300   Than all that's most illustrious in the nation.
ALCESTE: Sir . . .
ORONTE: If I lie, may heaven strike me dead!
    To show you that I mean what I have said,
    Permit me, Sir, to embrace you most sincerely,
    And swear that I will prize our friendship dearly.
    Give me your hand. And now, Sir, if you choose,
    We'll make our vows,
ALCESTE: Sir . . .
ORONTE: What! You refuse?
310 ALCESTE: Sir, it's a very great honor you extend:
    But friendship is a sacred thing, my friend;
    It would be profanation to bestow
    The name of friend on one you hardly know.
    All parts are better played when well-rehearsed;
    Let's put off friendship, and get acquainted first.
    We may discover it would be unwise
    To try to make our natures harmonize.
ORONTE: By heaven! You're sagacious to the core;
    This speech has made me admire you even more.
320 Let time, then, bring us closer day by day;
    Meanwhile, I shall be yours in every way.
    If, for example, there should be anything
    You wish at court, I'll mention it to the King.
    I have his ear, of course; it's quite well known
    That I am much in favor with the throne.
    In short, I am your servant. And now, dear friend,
    Since you have such fine judgment, I intend
    To please you, if I can, with a small sonnet°
    I wrote not long ago. Please comment on it,

---

sonnet, during this period the term "sonnet" applied to
any lyric poem.

And tell me whether I ought to publish it.   330
ALCESTE: You must excuse me, Sir; I'm hardly fit
    To judge such matters.
ORONTE: Why not?
ALCESTE: I am, I fear,
    Inclined to be unfashionably sincere.
ORONTE: Just what I ask; I'd take no satisfaction
    In anything but your sincere reaction.
    I beg you not to dream of being kind.
ALCESTE: Since you desire it, Sir, I'll speak my mind.
ORONTE: *Sonnet.* It's a sonnet. . . . "Hope" . . . The   340
    poem's addressed
    To a lady who wakened hopes within my breast.
    "Hope" . . . this is not the pompous sort of thing,
    Just modest little verses, with a tender ring.
ALCESTE: Well, we shall see.
ORONTE: "Hope" . . . I'm anxious to hear
    Whether the style seems properly smooth and
    clear,
    And whether the choice of words is good or bad.
ALCESTE: We'll see, we'll see.   350
ORONTE: Perhaps I ought to add
    That it took me only a quarter-hour to write it.
ALCESTE: The time's irrelevant, Sir; kindly recite it.
ORONTE (*reading*): "Hope comforts us awhile, t'is true,
    Lulling our cares with careless laughter,
    And yet such joy is full of rue,
    My Phyllis, if nothing follows after."
PHILINTE: I'm charmed by this already; the style's
    delightful.
ALCESTE (*sotto voce, to* PHILINTE): How can you say   360
    that? Why, the thing is frightful.
ORONTE: "Your fair face smiled on me awhile,
    But was it kindness so to enchant me?
    'Twould have been fairer not to smile,
    If hope was all you meant to grant me."
PHILINTE: What a clever thought! How handsomely
    you phrase it!
ALCESTE (*sotto voce to* PHILINTE): You know the thing is
    trash. How dare you praise it?
ORONTE: "If it's to be my passion's fate   370
    Thus everlastingly to wait,
    Then death will come to set me free:
    For death is fairer than the fair;
    Phyllis, to hope is to despair
    When one must hope eternally."
PHILINTE: The close is exquisite—full of feeling and
    grace.
ALCESTE (*sotto voce, aside*): Oh, blast the close; you'd
    better close your face
    Before you send your lying soul to hell.   380
PHILINTE: I can't remember a poem I've liked so well.
ALCESTE (*sotto voce, aside*): Good Lord!
ORONTE (*to* PHILINTE): I fear you're flattering me a
    bit.
PHILINTE: Oh, no!
ALCESTE (*sotto voce, aside*): What else d'you call it, you
    hypocrite?

ORONTE (*to* ALCESTE): But you, Sir, keep your promise
    now: don't shrink
390   From telling me sincerely what you think.
ALCESTE: Sir, these are delicate matters; we all desire
    To be told that we've the true poetic fire.
    But once, to one whose name I shall not mention,
    I said, regarding some verse of his invention,
    That gentlemen should rigorously control
    That itch to write which often afflicts the soul;
    That one should curb the heady inclination
    To publicize one's little avocation;
    And that in showing off one's works of art
400   One often plays a very clownish part.
ORONTE: Are you suggesting in a devious way
    That I ought not . . .
ALCESTE: Oh, that I do not say.
    Further, I told him that no fault is worse
    Than that of writing frigid, lifeless verse,
    And that the merest whisper of such a shame
    Suffices to destroy a man's good name.
ORONTE: D'you mean to say my sonnet's dull and
    trite?
410   ALCESTE: I don't say that. But I went on to cite
    Numerous cases of once-respected men
    Who came to grief by taking up the pen.
ORONTE: And am I like them? Do I write so poorly?
ALCESTE: I don't say that. But I told this person, "Surely
    You're under no necessity to compose;
    Why you should wish to publish, heaven knows.
    There's no excuse for printing tedious rot
    Unless one writes for bread, as you do not.
420   Resist temptation, then, I beg of you;
    Conceal your pastimes from the public view;
    And don't give up, on any provocation,
    Your present high and courtly reputation,
    To purchase at a greedy printer's shop
    The name of silly author and scribbling fop."
    These were the points I tried to make him see.
ORONTE: I sense that they are also aimed at me;
    But now—about my sonnet—I'd like to be told . . .
ALCESTE: Frankly, that sonnet should be
430   pigeonholed.
    You've chosen the worst models to imitate.
    The style's unnatural. Let me illustrate:

    For example, "Your fair face smiled on me awhile,"
    Followed by, " 'Twould have been fairer not to
        smile!"
    Or this: "such joy is full of rue;"
    Or this: "For death is fairer than the fair;"
    Or, "Phyllis, to hope is to despair
        When one must hope eternally!"

440   This artificial style, that's all the fashion,
    Has neither taste, nor honesty, nor passion;
    It's nothing but a sort of wordy play,

And nature never spoke in such a way.
What, in this shallow age, is not debased?
Our fathers, though less refined, had better taste;
I'd barter all that men admire today
For one old love-song I shall try to say:

"If the King had given me for my own
Paris, his citadel,
And I for that must leave alone   450
Her whom I love so well,
I'd say the to the Crown,
Take back your glittering town;
My darling is more fair, I swear,
My darling is more fair."

The rhyme's not rich, the style is rough and old,
But don't you see that it's the purest gold
Beside the tinsel nonsense now preferred,
And that there's passion in its every word?

"If the King had given me for my own   460
Paris, his citadel,
And I for that must leave alone
Her whom I love so well,
I'd say then to the Crown,
Take back your glittering town;
My darling is more fair, I swear,
My darling is more fair."

There speaks a loving heart. (*to* PHILINTE) You're
    laughing, eh?
Laugh on, my precious wit. Whatever you say,   470
I hold that song's worth all the bibelots°
That people hail today with "ah's" and "oh's."
ORONTE: And I maintain my sonnet's very good.
ALCESTE: It's not at all surprising that you should.
    You have your reasons; permit me to have mine
    For thinking that you cannot write a line.
ORONTE: Others have praised my sonnet to the skies.
ALCESTE: I lack their art of telling pleasant lies.
ORONTE: You seem to think you've got no end of wit.
ALCESTE: To praise your verse, I'd need still more of   480
    it.
ORONTE: I'm not in need of your approval, Sir.
ALCESTE: That's good; you couldn't have it if you
    were.
ORONTE: Come now, I'll lend you the subject of my
    sonnet;
    I'd like to see you try to improve upon it.
ALCESTE: I might, by chance, write something just as
    shoddy;
    But then I wouldn't show it to everybody.   490
ORONTE: You're most opinionated and conceited.

---

bibelots, trinkets.

ALCESTE: Go find your flatterers, and be better
    treated.
ORONTE: Look here, my little fellow, pray watch your
    tone.
ALCESTE: My great big fellow, you'd better watch
    your own.
PHILINTE (*stepping between them*): Oh, please, please,
    gentlemen! This will never do.
500 ORONTE: The fault is mine, and I leave the field to
    you.
    I am your servant, Sir, in every way.
ALCESTE: And I, Sir, am your most abject valet. (*Exit*
    ORONTE.)
PHILINTE: Well, as you see, sincerity in excess
    Can get you into a very pretty mess;
    Oronte was hungry for appreciation. . . .
ALCESTE: Don't speak to me.
PHILINTE: What?
ALCESTE: No more conversation.
510 PHILINTE: Really, now . . .
ALCESTE: Leave me alone.
PHILINTE: If I . . .
ALCESTE: Out of my sight!
PHILINTE: But what . . .
ALCESTE: I won't listen.
PHILINTE: But . . .
ALCESTE: Silence!
PHILINTE: Now, is it polite . . .
ALCESTE: By heaven, I've had enough. Don't follow
520   me.
PHILINTE: Ah, you're just joking. I'll keep you
    company (*They go out.*)

ACT 2

(*Enter* ALCESTE *and* CÉLIMÈNE.)

ALCESTE: Shall I speak plainly, Madam? I confess
    Your conduct gives me infinite distress,
    And my resentment's grown too hot to smother.
    Soon, I foresee, we'll break with one another.
    If I said otherwise, I should deceive you;
    Sooner or later, I shall be forced to leave you,
    And if I swore that we shall never part,
    I should misread the omens of my heart.
CÉLIMÈNE: You kindly saw me home, it would appear,
10   So as to pour invectives in my ear.
ALCESTE: I've no desire to quarrel. But I deplore
    Your inability to shut the door
    On all these suitors who beset you so.
    There's what annoys me, if you care to know.
CÉLIMÈNE: Is it my fault that all these men pursue
    me?
    Am I to blame if they're attracted to me?
    And when they gently beg an audience,
    Ought I to take a stick and drive them hence?
20 ALCESTE: Madam, there's no necessity for a stick;
    A less responsive heart would do the trick.

    Of your attractiveness I don't complain;
    But those your charms attract, you then detain
    By a most melting and receptive manner,
    And so enlist their hearts beneath your banner.
    It's the agreeable hopes which you excite
    That keep these lovers round you day and night;
    Were they less liberally smiled upon,
    That sighing troop would very soon be gone.
    But tell me, Madam, why it is that lately   30
    This man Clitandre interests you so greatly?
    Because of what high merits do you deem
    Him worthy of the honor of your esteem?
    Is it that your admitting glances linger
    On the splendidly long nail of his little finger?
    Or do you share the general deep respect
    For the blond wig he chooses to affect?
    Are you in love with his embroidered hose?
    Do you adore his ribbons and his bows?
    Or is it that this paragon bewitches   40
    Your tasteful eye with his vast German breeches?°
    Perhaps his giggle, or his falsetto voice,
    Makes him the latest gallant of your choice?
CÉLIMÈNE: You're much mistaken to resent him so.
    Why I put up with him you surely know:
    My lawsuit's very shortly to be tried,
    And I must have his influence on my side.
ALCESTE: Then lose your lawsuit, Madam, or let it
    drop.
    Don't torture me by humoring such a fop.   50
CÉLIMÈNE: You're jealous of the whole world, Sir.
ALCESTE: That's true,
    Since the whole world is well-received by you.
CÉLIMÈNE: That my good nature is so unconfined
    Should serve to pacify your jealous mind;
    Were I to smile on one, and scorn the rest,
    Then you might have some cause to be distressed.
ALCESTE: Well, if I mustn't be jealous, tell me, then,
    Just how I'm better treated than other men.
CÉLIMÈNE: You know you have my love. Will that not   60
    do?
ALCESTE: What proof have I that what you say is true?
CÉLIMÈNE: I would expect, Sir, that my having said it
    Might give the statement a sufficient credit.
ALCESTE: But how can I be sure that you don't tell
    The selfsame thing to other men as well?
CÉLIMÈNE: What a gallant speech! How flattering to
    me!
    What a sweet creature you make me out to be!
    Well then, to save you from the pangs of doubt,   70
    All that I've said I hereby cancel out;
    Now, none but yourself shall make a monkey of
    you:
    Are you content?

---

breeches, fashionable wide breeches called *rhingraves,* after
the Rhingrave Frederick, Governor of Maestricht.

ALCESTE: Why, why am I doomed to love you?
I swear that I shall bless the blissful hour
When this poor heart's no longer in your power!
I make no secret of it: I've done my best
To exorcise this passion from my breast;
80 But thus far all in vain; it will not go;
It's for my sins that I must love you so.
CELIMENE: Your love for me is matchless, Sir; that's
clear.
ALCESTE: Indeed, in all the world it has no peer;
Words can't describe the nature of my passion,
And no man ever loved in such a fashion.
CELIMENE: Yes, it's a brand-new fashion, I agree:
You show your love by castigating me,
And all your speeches are enraged and rude.
90 I've never been so furiously wooed.
ALCESTE: Yet you could calm that fury, if you chose.
Come, shall we bring our quarrels to a close?
Let's speak with open hearts, then, and begin . . .

(Enter BASQUE.)

CELIMENE: What is it?
BASQUE: Acaste is here.
CELIMENE: Well, send him in. *(Exit BASQUE.)*
ALCESTE: What! Shall we never be alone at all?
You're always ready to receive a call,
And you can't bear, for ten ticks of the clock,
100 Not to keep open house for all who knock.
CELIMENE: I couldn't refuse him: he'd be most put
out.
ALCESTE: Surely that's not worth worrying about.
CELIMENE: Acaste would never forgive me if he
guessed
That I consider him a dreadful pest.
ALCESTE: If he's a pest, why bother with him then?
CELIMENE: Heavens! One can't antagonize such men;
Why, they're the chartered gossips of the court,
110 And have a say in things of every sort.
One must receive them, and be full of charm;
They're no great help, but they can do you harm,
And though your influence be ever so great,
They're hardly the best people to alienate.
ALCESTE: I see, dear lady, that you could make a case
For putting up with the whole human race;
These friendships that you calculate so nicely . . .

(BASQUE re-enters.)

BASQUE: Madam, Clitandre is here as well.
ALCESTE: Precisely.
120 CELIMENE: Where are you going?
ALCESTE: Elsewhere.
CELIMENE: Stay.
ALCESTE: No, no.
CELIMENE: Stay, Sir.
ALCESTE: I can't.
CELIMENE: I wish it.
ALCESTE: No, I must go.

I beg you, Madam, not to press the matter;
You know I have no taste for idle chatter.
CELIMENE: Stay: I command you.   130
ALCESTE: No, I cannot stay.
CELIMENE: Very well; you have my leave to go away.

(Enter ELIANTE, PHILINTE, ACASTE, and CLITANDRE.)

ELIANTE *(to CÉLIMÈNE)*: The Marquesses have kindly
come to call.
Were they announced?
CELIMENE: Yes. Basque, bring chairs for all.

(BASQUE provides the chairs and exits.)

(to ALCESTE): You haven't gone?
ALCESTE: No; and I shan't depart
Till you decide who's foremost in your heart.
CELIMENE: Oh, hush.   140
ALCESTE: It's time to choose; take them, or me.
CELIMENE: You're mad.
ALCESTE: I'm not, as you shall shortly see.
CELIMENE: Oh?
ALCESTE: You'll decide.
CELIMENE: You're joking now, dear friend.
ALCESTE: No, no; you'll choose; my patience is at an
end.
CLITANDRE: Madam, I come from court, where poor
Cléonte   150
Behaved like a perfect fool, as is his wont.
Has he no friend to counsel him, I wonder,
And teach him less unerringly to blunder?
CELIMENE: It's true, the man's a most accomplished
dunce;
His gauche behavior charms the eye at once;
And every time one sees him, on my word,
His manner's grown a trifle more absurd.
ACASTE: Speaking of dunces, I've just now conversed
With old Damon, who's one of the very worst;   160
I stood a lifetime in the broiling sun
Before his dreary monologue was done.
CELIMENE: Oh, he's a wondrous talker, and has the
power
To tell you nothing hour after hour:
If, by mistake, he ever came to the point,
The shock would put his jawbone out of joint.
ELIANTE *(to PHILINTE)*: The conversation takes its
usual turn,
And all our dear friends' ears will shortly burn.   170
CLITANDRE: Timante's a character, Madam.
CELIMENE: Isn't he, though?
A man of mystery from top to toe,
Who moves about in a romantic mist
On secret missions which do not exist.
His talk is full of eyebrows and grimaces;
How tired one gets of his momentous faces;
He's always whispering something confidential
Which turns out to be quite inconsequential;
Nothing's too slight for him to mystify;

He even whispers when he says "good-by."
ACASTE: Tell us about Géralde.
CELIMENE: That tiresome ass.
He mixes only with the titled class,
And fawns on dukes and princes, and is bored
With anyone who's not at least a lord.
The man's obsessed with rank, and his discourses
Are all of hounds and carriages and horses;
He uses Christian names with all the great,
180 And the word "Milord," with him, is out of date.
CLITANDRE: He's very taken with Bélise, I hear.
CELIMENE: She is the dreariest company, poor dear.
Whenever she comes to call, I grope about
To find some topic which will draw her out,
But, owing to her dry and faint replies,
The conversation wilts, and droops, and dies.
In vain one hopes to animate her face
By mentioning the ultimate commonplace;
But sun or shower, even hail or frost
190 Are matters she can instantly exhaust.
Meanwhile her visit, painful though it is,
Drags on and on through mute eternities,
And though you ask the time, and yawn, and yawn,
She sits there like a stone and won't be gone.
ACASTE: Now for Adraste.
CELIMENE: Oh, that conceited elf
Has a gigantic passion for himself;
He rails against the court, and cannot bear it
That none will recognize his hidden merit;
200 All honors given to others give offense
To his imaginary excellence.
CLITANDRE: What about young Cléon? His house,
they say,
Is full of the best society, night and day.
CELIMENE: His cook has made him popular, not he:
It's Cléon's table that people come to see.
ELIANTE: He gives a splendid dinner, you must
admit.
CELIMENE: But must he serve himself along with it?
210 For my taste, he's a most insipid dish
Whose presence sours the wine and spoils the fish.
PHILINTE: Damis, his uncle, is admired no end.
What's your opinion, Madam?
CELIMENE: Why, he's my friend.
PHILINTE: He seems a decent fellow, and rather
clever.
CELIMENE: He works too hard at cleverness, however.
I hate to see him sweat and struggle so
To fill his conversation with bons mots.°
220 Since he's decided to become a wit
His taste's so pure that nothing pleases it;
He scolds at all the latest books and plays,
Thinking that wit must never stoop to praise,
That finding fault's a sign of intellect,

That all appreciation is abject,
And that by damning everything in sight
One shows oneself in a distinguished light.
He's scornful even of our conversations:
Their trivial nature sorely tries his patience;
He folds his arms, and stands above the battle,   230
And listens sadly to our childish prattle.
ACASTE: Wonderful, Madam! You've hit him off
precisely.
CLITANDRE: No one can sketch a character so nicely.
ALCESTE: How bravely, Sirs, you cut and thrust at all
These absent fools, till one by one they fall:
But let one come in sight, and you'll at once
Embrace the man you lately called a dunce,
Telling him in a tone sincere and fervent
How proud you are to be his humble servant.   240
CLITANDRE: Why pick on us? Madame's been
speaking, Sir,
And you should quarrel, if you must, with her.
ALCESTE: No, no, by God, the fault is yours, because
You lead her on with laughter and applause,
And make her think that she's the more delightful
The more her talk is scandalous and spiteful.
Oh, she would stoop to malice far, far less
If no such claque° approved her cleverness.
It's flatterers like you whose foolish praise   250
Nourishes all the vices of these days.
PHILINTE: But why protest when someone ridicules
Those you'd condemn, yourself, as knaves or fools?
CÉLIMENE: Why, Sir? Because he loves to make a fuss.
You don't expect him to agree with us,
When there's an opportunity to express
His heaven-sent spirit of contrariness?
What other people think, he can't abide;
Whatever they say, he's on the other side;
He lives in deadly terror of agreeing;   260
Twould make him seem an ordinary being.
Indeed, he's so in love with contradiction,
He'll turn against his most profound conviction
And with a furious eloquence deplore it,
If only someone else is speaking for it.
ALCESTE: Go on, dear lady, mock me as you please;
You have your audience in ecstasies.
PHILINTE: But what she says is true: you have a way
Of bridling at whatever people say;
Whether they praise or blame, your angry spirit   270
Is equally unsatisfied to hear it.
ALCESTE: Men, Sir, are always wrong, and that's the
reason
That righteous anger's never out of season;
All that I hear in all their conversation
Is flattering praise or reckless condemnation.
CELIMENE: But . . .
ALCESTE: No, no, Madam, I am forced to state

---

bons mots, witty sayings.

claque, band of followers.

That you have pleasures which I deprecate,
280 And that these others, here, are much to blame
For nourishing the faults which are your shame.
CLITANDRE: I shan't defend myself, Sir; but I vow
I'd thought this lady faultless until now.
ACASTE: I see her charms and graces, which are
many;
But as for faults, I've never noticed any.
ALCESTE: I see them, Sir; and rather than ignore
them,
I strenuously criticize her for them.
290 The more one loves, the more one should object
To every blemish, every least defect.
Were I this lady, I would soon get rid
Of lovers who approved of all I did,
And by their slack indulgence and applause
Endorsed my follies and excused my flaws.
CELIMENE: If all hearts beat according to your
measure,
The dawn of love would be the end of pleasure;
And love would find its perfect consummation
300 In ecstasies of rage and reprobation.
ELIANTE: Love, as a rule, affects men otherwise,
And lovers rarely love to criticize.
They see their lady as a charming blur,
And find all things commendable in her.
If she has any blemish, fault, or shame,
They will redeem it by a pleasing name.
The pale-faced lady's lily-white, perforce;
The swarthy one's a sweet brunette, of course;
The spindly lady has a slender grace;
310 The fat one has a most majestic pace;
The plain one, with her dress in disarray,
They classify as *beauté négligée*,°
The hulking one's a goddess in their eyes,
The dwarf, a concentrate of Paradise;
The haughty lady has a noble mind;
The mean one's witty, and the dull one's kind;
The chatterbox has liveliness and verve,
The mute one has a virtuous reserve.
So lovers manage, in their passion's cause,
320 To love their ladies even for their flaws.
ALCESTE: But I still say . . .
CELIMENE: I think it would be nice
To stroll around the gallery once or twice.
What! You're not going, Sirs?
CLITANDRE and ACASTE: No, Madam, no.
ALCESTE: You seem to be in terror lest they go.
Do what you will, Sirs; leave, or linger on,
But I shan't go till after you are gone.
ACASTE: I'm free to linger, unless I should perceive
330 Madame is tired, and wishes me to leave.
CLITANDRE: And as for me, I needn't go today
Until the hour of the King's *coucher*.°

CELIMENE (*to* ALCESTE): You're joking, surely?
ALCESTE: Not in the least; we'll see
Whether you'd rather part with them, or me.

(*Enter* BASQUE.)

BASQUE (*to* ALCESTE): Sir, there's a fellow here who
bids me state
That he must see you, and that it can't wait.
ALCESTE: Tell him that I have no such pressing
affairs. 340
BASQUE: It's a long tailcoat that this fellow wears,
With gold all over.
CELIMENE (*to* ALCESTE): You'd best go down and see.
Or—have him enter.

(ALCESTE *indicates to* BASQUE *to show the visitor in. Exit*
BASQUE.)
(*Enter a* GUARD *of the Marshalsea.*°)

ALCESTE (*confronting the* GUARD): Well, what do you
want with me?
Come in, Sir.
GUARD: I've a word, Sir, for your ear.
ALCESTE: Speak it aloud, Sir; I shall strive to hear.
GUARD: The Marshals have instructed me to say 350
You must report to them without delay.
ALCESTE: Who? Me, Sir?
GUARD: Yes, Sir; you.
ALCESTE: But what do they want?
PHILINTE (*to* ALCESTE): To scotch your silly quarrel
with Oronte.
CELIMENE (*to* PHILINTE): What quarrel?
PHILINTE: Oronte and he have fallen out
Over some verse he spoke his mind about;
The Marshals wish to arbitrate the matter. 360
ALCESTE: Never shall I equivocate or flatter!
PHILINTE: You'd best obey their summons; come, let's
go.
ALCESTE: How can they mend our quarrel, I'd like to
know?
Am I to make a cowardly retraction,
And praise those jingles to his satisfaction?
I'll not recant; I've judged that sonnet rightly.
It's bad.
PHILINTE: But you might say so more politely. . . . 370
ALCESTE: I'll not back down; his verses make me sick.
PHILINTE: If only you could be more politic!
But come, let's go.
ALCESTE: I'll go, but I won't unsay
A single word.
PHILINTE: Well, let's be on our way.
ALCESTE: Till I am ordered by my lord the King
To praise that poem, I shall say the thing
Is scandalous, by God, and that the poet

---

beauté négligée, "careless beauty." *coucher*, an evening
reception held in the King's bedchamber.

Marshalsea, The Marshalsea Tribunal handled quarrels among members of the nobility.

380   Ought to be hanged for having the nerve to show
      it. *(to* CLITANDRE *and* ACASTE, *who are laughing)*
    By heaven, Sirs, I really didn't know
    That I was being humorous.
CELIMENE: Go, Sir, go;
    Settle your business.
ALCESTE: I shall, and when I'm through,
    I shall return to settle things with you.

(Exit ALCESTE *with the* GUARD. *The others withdraw.)*

ACT 3

(Enter CLITANDRE *and* ACASTE.)

CLITANDRE: Dear Marquess, how contented you
    appear;
    All things delight you, nothing mars your cheer.
    Can you, in perfect honesty, declare
    That you've a right to be so debonair?
ACASTE: By Jove, when I survey myself, I find
    No cause whatever for distress of mind.
    I'm young and rich; I can in modesty
    Lay claim to an exalted pedigree;
10   And owing to my name and my condition
    I shall not want for honors and position.
    Then as to courage, that most precious trait,
    I seem to have it, as was proved of late
    Upon the field of honor, where my bearing,
    They say, was very cool and rather daring.
    I've wit, of course; and taste in such perfection
    That I can judge without the least reflection,
    And at the theater, which is my delight,
    Can make or break a play on opening night,
20   And lead the crowd in hisses or bravos,
    And generally be known as one who knows.
    I'm clever, handsome, gracefully polite;
    My waist is small, my teeth are strong and white;
    As for my dress, the world's astonished eyes
    Assure me that I bear away the prize.
    I find myself in favor everywhere,
    Honored by men, and worshipped by the fair;
    And since these things are so, it seems to me
    I'm justified in my complacency.
30 CLITANDRE: Well, if so many ladies hold you dear,
    Why do you press a hopeless courtship here?
ACASTE: Hopeless, you say? I'm not the sort of fool
    That likes his ladies difficult and cool.
    Men who are awkward, shy, and peasantish
    May pine for heartless beauties, if they wish,
    Grovel before them, bear their cruelties,
    Woo them with tears and sighs and bended knees,
    And hope by dogged faithfulness to gain
    What their poor merits never could obtain.
40   For men like me, however, it makes no sense
    To love on trust, and foot the whole expense.
    Whatever any lady's merits be,
    I think, thank God, that I'm as choice as she;
    That if my heart is kind enough to burn

    For her, she owes me something in return;
    And that in any proper love affair
    The partners must invest an equal share.
CLITANDRE: You think, then, that our hostess favors
    you?
ACASTE: I've reason to believe that that is true.   50
CLITANDRE: How did you come to such a mad
    conclusion?
    You're blind, dear fellow. This is sheer delusion.
ACASTE: All right, then: I'm deluded and I'm blind.
CLITANDRE: Whatever put the notion in your mind?
ACASTE: Delusion.
CLITANDRE: What persuades you that you're right?
ACASTE: I'm blind.
CLITANDRE: But have you any proofs to cite?
ACASTE: I tell you I'm deluded.   60
CLITANDRE: Have you, then,
    Received some secret pledge from Célimène?
ACASTE: Oh, no; she scorns me.
CLITANDRE: Tell me the truth, I beg.
ACASTE: She just can't bear me.
CLITANDRE: Ah, don't pull my leg.
    Tell me what hope she's given you, I pray.
ACASTE: I'm hopeless, and it's you who win the day.
    She hates me thoroughly, and I'm so vexed
    I mean to hang myself on Tuesday next.   70
CLITANDRE: Dear Marquess, let us have an armistice
    And make a treaty. What do you say to this?
    If ever one of us can plainly prove
    That Célimène encourages his love,
    The other must abandon hope, and yield,
    And leave him in possession of the field.
ACASTE: Now, there's a bargain that appeals to me;
    With all my heart, dear Marquess, I agree.
    But hush.

(Enter CÉLIMÈNE.)

CELIMENE: Still here?   80
CLITANDRE: T'was love that stayed our feet.
CELIMENE: I think I heard a carriage in the street.
    Whose is it? D'you know?

(Enter BASQUE.)

BASQUE: Madame. Arsinoé is here.
CELIMENTE: Arsinoé, you say? Oh, dear.
BASQUE: Eliante is entertaining her below. *(Exit.)*
CELIMENE: What brings the creature here, I'd like to
    know?
ACASTE: They say she's dreadfully prudish, but in
    fact   90
    I think her piety . . .
CELIMENE: It's all an act.
    At heart she's worldly, and her poor success
    In snaring men explains her prudishness.
    It breaks her heart to see the beaux and gallants
    Engrossed by other women's charms and talents,
    And so she's always in a jealous rage

Against the faulty standards of the age.
She lets the world believe that she's a prude
100   To justify her loveless solitude,
And strives to put a band of moral shame
On all the graces that she cannot claim.
But still she'd love a lover; and Alceste
Appears to be the one she'd love the best.
His visits here are poison to her pride;
She seems to think I've lured him from her side;
And everywhere, at court or in the town,
The spiteful, envious woman runs me down.
In short, she's just as stupid as can be,
110   Vicious and arrogant in the last degree,
And . . .

(Enter ARSINOÉ.*)*

Ah! What happy chance has brought you here?
I've thought about you ever so much, my dear.

ARSINOE: I've come to tell you something you should
        know.
CELIMENE: How good of you to think of doing so!

*(*CLITANDRE *and* ACASTE *go out, laughing.)*

ARSINOE: It's just as well those gentlemen didn't tarry.
CELIMENE: Shall we sit down?
ARSINOE: That won't be necessary.
120   Madam, the flame of friendship ought to burn
Brightest in matters of the most concern,
And as there's nothing which concerns us more
Than honor, I have hastened to your door
To bring you, as your friend, some information
About the status of your reputation.
I visited, last night, some virtuous folk,
And, quite by chance, it was of you they spoke;
There was I fear no tendency to praise
Your light behavior and your dashing ways.
130   The quantity of gentlemen you see
And your by now notorious coquetry
Were both so vehemently criticized
By everyone, that I was much surprised.
Of course, I needn't tell you where I stood;
I came to your defense as best I could,
Assured them you were harmless, and declared
Your soul was absolutely unimpaired.
But there are some things, you must realize,
One can't excuse, however hard one tries,
140   And I was forced at least into conceding
That your behavior, Madam, is misleading,
That it makes a bad impression, giving rise
To ugly gossip and obscene surmise,
And that if you were more *overtly* good,
You wouldn't be so much misunderstood.
Not that I think you've been unchaste.—No! No!
The saints preserve me from a thought so low!
But mere good conscience never did suffice;
One must avoid the outward show of vice.
150   Madam, you're too intelligent, I'm sure,
To think my motives anything but pure

In offering you this counsel—which I do
Out of a zealous interest in you.
CELIMENE: Madam, I haven't taken you amiss;
I'm very much obliged to you for this;
And I'll at once discharge the obligation
By telling you about *your* reputation.
You've been so friendly as to let me know
What certain people say of me, and so
I mean to follow your benign example   160
By offering you a somewhat similar sample.
The other day, I went to an affair
And found some most distinguished people there
Discussing piety, both false and true.
The conversation soon came round to you.
Alas! Your prudery and bustling zeal
Appeared to have a very slight appeal.
Your affectation of a grave demeanor,
Your endless talk of virtue and of honor,
The aptitude of your suspicious mind   170
For finding sin where there is none to find,
Your towering self-esteem, that pitying face
With which you contemplate the human race,
Your sermonizings and your sharp aspersions
On people's pure and innocent diversions—
All these were mentioned, Madam, and, in fact,
Were roundly and concertedly attacked.
"What good," they said, "are all those outward
        shows,
When everything belies her pious pose?   180
She prays incessantly; but then, they say,
She beats her maids and cheats them of their pay;
She shows her zeal in every holy place,
But still she's vain enough to paint her face;
She holds that naked statues are immoral,
But with a naked *man* she'd have no quarrel."
Of course, I said to everybody there
That they were being viciously unfair;
But still they were disposed to criticize you,
And all agreed that someone should advise you   190
To leave the morals of the world alone,
And worry rather more about your own.
They felt that one's self-knowledge should be great
Before one thinks of setting others straight;
That one should learn the art of living well
Before one threatens other men with hell.
And that the Church is best equipped, no doubt,
To guide our souls and root our vices out.
Madam, you're too intelligent, I'm sure,
To think my motives anything but pure   200
In offering you this counsel—which I do
Out of a zealous interest in you.
ARSINOE: I dared not hope for gratitude, but I
Did not expect so acid a reply;
I judge, since you've been so extremely tart,
That my good counsel pierced you to the heart.
CELIMENE: Far from it, Madam. Indeed, it seems to
        me
We ought to trade advice more frequently.

210   One's vision of oneself is so defective
       That it would be an excellent corrective.
       If you are willing, Madam, let's arrange
       Shortly to have another frank exchange
       In which we'll teach each other, *entre nous*,°
       What you've heard tell of me, and I of you.
    ARSINOE: Oh, people never censure you, my dear;
       It's me they criticize. Or so I hear.
    CELIMENE: Madam, I think we either blame or praise
       According to our taste and length of days.
220   There is a time of life for coquetry,
       And there's a season, too, for prudery.
       When all one's charms are gone, it is, I'm sure,
       Good strategy to be devout and pure:
       It makes one seem a little less forsaken.
       Some day, perhaps, I'll take the road you've taken:
       Time brings all things. But I have time aplenty,
       And see no cause to be a prude at twenty.
    ARSINOE: You give your age in such a gloating tone
       That one would think I was an ancient crone;
230   We're not so far apart, in sober truth,
       That you can mock me with a boast of youth!
       Madam, you baffle me. I wish I knew
       What moves you to provoke me as you do.
    CELIMENE: For my part, Madam, I should like to
         know
       Why you abuse me everywhere you go.
       Is it my fault, dear lady, that your hand
       Is not, alas, in very great demand?
       If men admire me, if they pay me court
240   And daily make me offers of the sort
       You'd dearly love to have them make to you,
       How can I help it? What would you have me do?
       If what you want is lovers, please feel free
       To take as many as you can from me.
    ARSINOE: Oh, come. D'you think the world is losing
         sleep
       Over that flock of lovers which you keep,
       Or that we find it difficult to guess
       What price you pay for their devotedness?
250   Surely you don't expect us to suppose
       Mere merit could attract so many beaux?
       It's not your virtue that they're dazzled by;
       Nor is it virtuous love for which they sigh.
       You're fooling no one, Madam; the world's not
         blind;
       There's many a lady heaven has designed
       To call men's noblest, tenderest feelings out,
       Who has no lovers dogging her about;
       From which it's plain that lovers nowadays
260   Must be acquired in bold and shameless ways,
       And only pay one court for such reward
       As modesty and virtue can't afford.

       Then don't be quite so puffed up, if you please,
       About your tawdry little victories;
       Try, if you can, to be a shade less vain,
       And treat the world with somewhat less disdain.
       If one were envious of your amours,
       One soon could have a following like yours;
       Lovers are no great trouble to collect
       If one prefers them to one's self-respect.   270
    CELIMENE: Collect them then, my dear; I'd love to see
       You demonstrate that charming theory;
       Who knows, you might . . .
    ARSINOE: Now, Madam, that will do;
       It's time to end this trying interview.
       My coach is late in coming to your door,
       Or I'd have taken leave of you before.
    CELIMENE: Oh, please don't feel that you must rush
         away;
       I'd be delighted, Madam, if you'd stay.   280
       However, lest my conversation bore you,
       Let me provide some better company for you;
       This gentleman, who comes most apropos,
       Will please you more than I could do, I know.

    (Enter ALCESTE.*)*

       Alceste, I have a little note to write
       Which simply must go out before tonight;
       Please entertain Madame; I'm sure that she
       Will overlook my incivility. *(Exit.)*
    ARSINOE: Well, Sir, our hostess graciously contrives
       For us to chat until my coach arrives;   290
       And I shall be forever in her debt
       For granting me this little tête-à-tête.°
       We women very rightly give our hearts
       To men of noble character and parts,
       And your especial merits, dear Alceste,
       Have roused the deepest sympathy in my breast.
       Oh, how I wish they had sufficient sense
       At court, to recognize your excellence!
       They wrong you greatly, Sir. How it must hurt you
       Never to be rewarded for your virtue!   300
    ALCESTE: Why, Madam, what cause have I to feel
         aggrieved?
       What great and brilliant thing have I achieved?
       What service have I rendered to the King
       That I should look to him for anything?
    ARSINOE: Not everyone who's honored by the State
       Has done great services. A man must wait
       Till time and fortune offer him the chance.
       Your merit, Sir, is obvious at a glance,
       And . . .   310
    ALCESTE: Ah, forget my merit; I'm not neglected.
       The court, I think, can hardly be expected
       To mine men's souls for merit, and unearth

---

entre nous, "between us."

tête-à-tête, literally head-to-head; i.e., private conversation.

Our hidden virtues and our secret worth.

ARSINOE: *Some* virtues, though, are far too bright to
   hide;
   Yours are acknowledged, Sir, on every side.
   Indeed, I've heard you warmly praised of late
   By persons of considerable weight.

320 ALCESTE: This fawning age has praise for everyone,
   And all distinctions, Madam, are undone.
   All things have equal honor nowadays,
   And no one should be gratified by praise.
   To be admired, one only need exist,
   And every lackey's on the honors list.

ARSINOE: I only wish, Sir, that you had your eye
   On some position at court, however high;
   You'd only have to hint at such a notion
   For me to set the proper wheels in motion;
330 I've certain friendships I'd be glad to use
   To get you any office you might choose.

ALCESTE: Madam, I fear that any such ambition
   Is wholly foreign to my disposition.
   The soul God gave me isn't of the sort
   That prospers in the weather of a court.
   It's all too obvious that I don't possess
   The virtues necessary for success.
   My one great talent is for speaking plain;
   I've never learned to flatter or to feign;
340 And anyone so stupidly sincere
   Had best not seek a courtier's career.
   Outside the court, I know, one must dispense
   With honors, privilege, and influence;
   But still one gains the right, foregoing these,
   Not to be tortured by the wish to please.
   One needn't live in dread of snubs and slights,
   Nor praise the verse that every idiot writes,
   Nor humor silly Marquesses, nor bestow
   Politic sighs on Madam So-and-So.

ARSINOE: Forget the court, then; let the matter rest.
   But I've another cause to be distressed
   About your present situation, Sir.
   It's to your love affair that I refer.
   She whom you love, and who pretends to love you,
   Is, I regret to say, unworthy of you.

ALCESTE: Why, Madam! Can you seriously intend
   To make so grave a charge against your friend?

ARSINOE: Alas, I must. I've stood aside too long
   And let that lady do you grievous wrong;
360 But now my debt to conscience shall be paid:
   I tell you that your love has been betrayed.

ALCESTE: I thank you, Madam; you're extremely
   kind.
   Such words are soothing to a lover's mind.

ARSINOE: Yes, though she *is* my friend, I say again
   You're very much too good for Célimène.
   She's wantonly misled you from the start.

ALCESTE: You may be right; who knows another's
   heart?
370 But ask yourself if it's the part of charity

To shake my soul with doubts of her sincerity.

ARSINOE: Well, if you'd rather be a dupe than doubt
   her,
   That's your affair. I'll say no more about her.

ALCESTE: Madam, you know that doubt and vague
   suspicion
   Are painful to a man in my position;
   It's most unkind to worry me this way
   Unless you've some real proof of what you say.

ARSINOE: Sir, say no more: all doubt shall be   380
   removed,
   And all that I've been saying shall be proved.
   You've only to escort me home, and there
   We'll look into the heart of this affair.
   I've ocular° evidence which will persuade you
   Beyond a doubt, that Célimène's betrayed you.
   Then, if you're saddened by that revelation,
   Perhaps I can provide some consolation. *(They go
   out.)*

ACT 4

(Enter ELIANTE *and* PHILINTE.)

PHILINTE: Madam, he acted like a stubborn child;
   I thought they never would be reconciled;
   In vain we reasoned, threatened, and appealed;
   He stood his ground and simply would not yield.
   The Marshals, I feel sure, have never heard
   An argument so splendidly absurd.
   "No, gentlemen," said he, "I'll not retract.
   His verse is bad: extremely bad, in fact.
   Surely it does the man no harm to know it.
   Does it disgrace him, not to be a poet?   20
   A gentleman may be respected still,
   Whether he writes a sonnet well or ill.
   That I dislike his verse should not offend him;
   In all that touches honor, I commend him;
   He's noble, brave, and virtuous—but I fear
   He can't in truth be called a sonneteer.
   I'll gladly praise his wardrobe; I'll endorse
   His dancing, or the way he sits a horse;
   But, gentlemen, I cannot praise his rhyme.
   In fact, it ought to be a capital crime   30
   For anyone so sadly unendowed
   To write a sonnet, and read the thing aloud."
   At length he fell into a gentler mood
   And, striking a concessive attitude,
   He paid Oronte the following courtesies:
   "Sir, I regret that I'm so hard to please,
   And I'm profoundly sorry that your lyric
   Failed to provoke me to a panegyric."
   After these curious words, the two embraced,
   And then the hearing was adjourned—in haste.   40

---

ocular, visible.

ELIANTE: His conduct has been very singular lately;
    Still, I confess that I respect him greatly.
    The honesty in which he takes such pride
    Has—to my mind—its, noble, heroic side.
    In this false age, such candor seem outrageous;
    But I could wish that it were more contagious.
PHILINTE: What most intrigues me in our friend
    Alceste
    Is the grand passion that rages in his breast.
50   The sullen humors he's compounded of
    Should not, I think, dispose his heart to love;
    But since they do, it puzzles me still more
    That he should choose your cousin to adore.
ELIANTE: It does, indeed, belie the theory
    That love is born of gentle sympathy,
    And that the tender passion must be based
    On sweet accords of temper and of taste.
PHILINTE: Does she return his love, do you suppose?
ELIANTE: Ah, that's a difficult question, Sir. Who
60   knows?
    How can we judge the truth of her devotion?
    Her heart's a stranger to its own emotion.
    Sometimes it thinks it loves, when no love's there;
    At other times it loves quite unaware.
PHILINTE: I rather think Alceste is in for more
    Distress and sorrow than he's bargained for;
    Were he of my mind, Madam, his affection
    Would turn in quite a different direction,
    And we would see him more responsive to
70   The kind regard which he receives from you.
ELIANTE: Sir, I believe in frankness, and I'm inclined,
    In matters of the heart, to speak my mind.
    I don't oppose his love for her; indeed,
    I hope with all my heart that he'll succeed,
    And were it in my power, I'd rejoice
    In giving him the lady of his choice.
    But if, as happens frequently enough
    In love affairs, he meets with a rebuff—
    If Célimène should grant some rival's suit—
80   I'd gladly play the role of substitute;
    Nor would his tender speeches please me less
    Because they'd once been made without success.
PHILINTE: Well, Madam, as for me, I don't oppose
    Your hopes in this affair; and heaven knows
    That in my conversations with the man
    I plead your cause as often as I can.
    But if those two should marry, and so remove
    All chance that he will offer you his love,
    Then I'll declare my own, and hope to see
90   Your gracious favor pass from him to me.
    In short, should you be cheated of Alceste,
    I'd be most happy to be second best.
ELIANTE: Philinte, you're teasing.
PHILINTE: Ah, Madam, never fear;
    No words of mine were ever so sincere,
    And I shall live in fretful expectation
    Till I can make a fuller declaration.

(*Enter* ALCESTE.)

ALCESTE: Avenge me, Madam! I must have
    satisfaction,
    Or this great wrong will drive me to distraction! 100
ELIANTE: Why, what's the matter? What's upset you
    so?
ALCESTE: Madam, I've had a mortal, mortal blow
    If Chaos repossessed the universe,
    I swear I'd not be shaken any worse.
    I'm ruined. . . . I can say no more. . . . My soul . . .
ELIANTE: Do, try, Sir, to regain your self-control.
ALCESTE: Just heaven! Why were so much beauty and
    grace
    Bestowed on one so vicious and so base? 110
ELIANTE: Once more, Sir, tell us. . . .
ALCESTE: My world has gone to wrack;
    I'm—I'm betrayed; she's stabbed me in the back:
    Yes, Célimène (who would have thought it of her?)
    Is false to me, and has another lover.
ELIANTE: Are you quite certain? Can you prove these
    things?
PHILINTE: Lovers are prey to wild imaginings
    And jealous fancies. No doubt there's some
    mistake. . . . 120
ALCESTE: Mind your own business, Sir, for heaven's
    sake.
    (*to* ELIANTE) Madam, I have the proof that you
    demand
    Here in my pocket, penned by her own hand.
    Yes, all the shameful evidence one could want
    Lies in this letter written to Oronte—
    Oronte! Whom I felt sure she couldn't love,
    And hardly bothered to be jealous of.
PHILINTE: Still, in a letter, appearances may deceive; 130
    This may not be so bad as you belive.
ALCESTE: Once more I beg you, Sir, to let me be;
    Tend to your own affairs; leave mine to me.
ELIANTE: Compose yourself; this anguish that you
    feel . . .
ALCESTE: Is something, Madam, you alone can heal.
    My outraged heart, beside itself with grief,
    Appeals to you for comfort and relief.
    Avenge me on your cousin, whose unjust
    And faithless nature has deceived my trust; 140
    Avenge a crime your pure soul must detest.
ELIANTE: But how, Sir?
ALCESTE: Madam, this heart within my breast
    Is yours; pray take it; redeem my heart from her,
    And so avenge me on my torturer.
    Let her be punished by the fond emotion,
    The ardent love, the bottomless devotion,
    The faithful worship which this heart of mine
    Will offer up to yours as to a shrine.
ELIANTE: You have my sympathy, Sir, in all you 150
    suffer;
    Nor do I scorn the noble heart you offer;

But I suspect you'll soon be mollified,
And this desire for vengeance will subside.
When some beloved hand has done us wrong
We thirst for retribution—but not for long;
However dark the deed that she's committed,
A lovely culprit's very soon acquitted.
Nothing's so stormy as an injured lover,
160 And yet no storm so quickly passes over.
ALCESTE: No, Madam, no—this is no lovers' spat;
I'll not forgive her; it's gone too far for that;
My mind's made up; I'll kill myself before
I waste my hopes upon her any more.
Ah, here she is. My wrath intensifies.
I shall confront her with her tricks and lies,
And crush her utterly, and bring you then
A heart no longer slave to Célimène. *(Exit ELIANTE
and PHILINTE.)*

(Enter CÉLIMÈNE.)

ALCESTE *(aside)*: Sweet heaven, help me to control my
170 passion.
CELIMENE *(to ALCESTE)*: Oh, Lord. Why stand there
staring in that fashion?
And what d'you mean by those dramatic sighs,
And that malignant glitter in your eyes?
ALCESTE: I mean that sins which cause the blood to
freeze
Look innocent beside your treacheries;
That nothing Hell's or Heaven's wrath could do
Ever produced so bad a thing as you.
180 CELIMENE: Your compliments were always sweet and
pretty.
ALCESTE: Madam, it's not the moment to be witty.
No, blush and hang your head; you've ample
reason,
Since I've the fullest evidence of your treason.
Ah, this is what my sad heart prophesied;
Now all my anxious fears are verified;
My dark suspicion and my gloomy doubt
Divined the truth, and now the truth is out.
190 For all your trickery, I was not deceived;
It was my bitter stars that I believed.
But don't imagine that you'll go scot-free;
You shan't misuse me with impunity.
I know that love's irrational and blind;
I know the heart's not subject to the mind,
And can't be reasoned into beating faster;
I know each soul is free to choose its master;
Therefore had you but spoken from the heart,
Rejecting my attentions from the start,
200 I'd have no grievance, or at any rate
I could complain of nothing but my fate.
Ah, but so falsely to encourage me—
That was a treason and a treachery
For which you cannot suffer too severely,
And you shall pay for that behavior dearly.
Yes, now I have no pity, not a shred;

My temper's out of hand; I've lost my head;
Shocked by the knowledge of your
double-dealings,
My reason can't restrain my savage feelings; 210
A righteous wrath deprives me of my senses,
And I won't answer for the consequences.
CELIMENE: What does this outburst mean? Will you
please explain?
Have you, by any chance, gone quite insane?
ALCESTE: Yes, yes, I went insane the day I fell
A victim to your black and fatal spell,
Thinking to meet with some sincerity
Among the treacherous charms that beckoned me.
CELIMENE: Pooh. Of what treachery can you 220
complain?
ALCESTE: How sly you are, how cleverly you feign!
But you'll not victimize me any more.
Look: here's a document you've seen before.
This evidence, which I acquired today,
Leaves you, I think, without a thing to say.
CELIMENE: Is this what sent you into such a fit?
ALCESTE: You should be blushing at the sight of it.
CELIMENE: Ought I to blush? I truly don't see why.
ALCESTE: Ah, now you're being bold as well as sly; 230
Since there's no signature, perhaps you'll claim . . .
CELIMENE: I wrote it, whether or not it bears my
name.
ALCESTE: And you can view with equanimity
This proof of your disloyalty to me!
CELIMENE: Oh, don't be so outrageous and extreme.
ALCESTE: You take this matter lightly, it would seem.
Was it no wrong to me, no shame to you,
That you should send Oronte this billet-doux?°
CELIMENE: Oronte! Who said it was for him? 240
ALCESTE: Why, those
Who brought me this example of your prose.
But what's the difference? If you wrote the letter
To someone else, it pleases me no better.
My grievance and your guilt remain the same.
CELIMENE: But need you rage, and need I blush for
shame,
If this was written to a *woman* friend?
ALCESTE: Ah! Most ingenious. I'm impressed no end;
And after that incredible evasion 250
Your guilt is clear. I need no more persuasion.
How dare you try so clumsy a deception?
D'you think I'm wholly wanting in perception?
Come, come, let's see how brazenly you'll try
To bolster up so palpable a lie:
Kindly construe this ardent closing section
As nothing more than sisterly affection!
Here, let me read it. Tell me, if you dare to,
That this is for a woman . . .
CELIMENE: I don't care to. 260

---

billet-doux, love letter.

What right have you to badger and berate me,
And so highhandedly interrogate me?
ALCESTE: Now, don't be angry; all I ask of you
Is that you justify a phrase or two . . .
CELIMENE: No, I shall not. I utterly refuse,
And you may take those phrases as you choose.
ALCESTE: Just show me how this letter could be meant
For a woman's eyes, and I shall be content.
CELIMENE: No, no, it's for Oronte; you're perfectly
270   right.
I welcome his attentions with delight,
I prize his character and his intellect,
And everything is just as you suspect.
Come, do your worst now; give your rage free rein;
But kindly cease to bicker and complain.
ALCESTE (aside): Good God! Could anything be more
inhuman?
Was ever a heart so mangled by a woman?
When I complain of how she has betrayed me,
280   She bridles, and commences to upbraid me!
She tries my tortured patience to the limit;
She won't deny her guilt; she glories in it!
And yet my heart's too faint and cowardly
To break these chains of passion, and be free,
To scorn her as it should, and rise above
This unrewarded, mad, and bitter love.
(to CÉLIMÈNE): Ah, traitress, in how confident a
fashion
You take advantage of my helpless passion,
290   And use my weakness for your faithless charms
To make me once again throw down my arms!
But do at least deny this black transgression;
Take back that mocking and perverse confession;
Defend this letter and your innocence,
And I, poor fool, will aid in your defense.
Pretend, pretend, that you are just and true,
And I shall make myself believe in you.
CELIMENE: Oh, stop it. Don't be such a jealous dunce,
Or I shall leave off loving you at once.
300   Just why should I pretend? What could impel me.
To stoop so low as that? And kindly tell me
Why, if I loved another, I shouldn't merely
Inform you of it, simply and sincerely!
I've told you where you stand, and that admission
Should altogether clear me of suspicion;
After so generous a guarantee,
What right have you to harbor doubts of me?
Since women are (from natural reticence)
Reluctant to declare their sentiments,
310   And since the honor of our sex requires
That we conceal our amorous desires,
Ought any man for whom such laws are broken
To question what the oracle has spoken?
Should he not rather feel an obligation
To trust that most obliging declaration?
Enough, now. Your suspicions quite disgust me;
Why should I love a man who doesn't trust me?

I cannot understand why I continue,
Fool that I am, to take an interest in you.
I ought to choose a man less prone to doubt,   320
And give you something to be vexed about.
ALCESTE: Ah, what a poor enchanted fool I am;
These gentle words, no doubt, were all a sham;
But destiny requires me to entrust
My happiness to you, and so I must.
I'll love you to the bitter end, and see
How false and treacherous you dare to be.
CELIMENE: No, you don't really love me as you ought.
ALCESTE: I love you more than can be said or
thought;   330
Indeed, I wish you were in such distress
That I might show my deep devotedness.
Yes, I could wish that you were wretchedly poor,
Unloved, uncherished, utterly obscure;
That fate had set you down upon the earth
Without possessions, rank, or gentle birth;
Then, by the offer of my heart, I might
Repair the great injustice of your plight;
I'd raise you from the dust, and proudly prove
The purity and vastness of my love.   340
CELIMENE: This is a strange benevolence indeed!
God grant that I may never be in need. . . .
Ah, here's Monsieur Dubois, in quaint disguise.

(Enter MONSIEUR DUBOIS.)

ALCESTE: Well, why this costume? Why those
frightened eyes?
What ails you?
DUBOIS: Well, sir, things are most mysterious.
ALCESTE: What do you mean?
DUBOIS: I fear they're very serious.
ALCESTE: What?   350
DUBOIS: Shall I speak more loudly?
ALCESTE: Yes; speak out.
DUBOIS: Isn't there someone here, Sir?
ALCESTE: Speak, you lout!
Stop wasting time.
DUBOIS: Sir, we must slip away.
ALCESTE: How's that?
DUBOIS: We must decamp without delay.
ALCESTE: Explain yourself.
DUBOIS: I tell you we must fly.   360
ALCESTE: What for?
DUBOIS: We mustn't pause to say good-by.
ALCESTE: Now what d'you mean by all of this, you
clown?
DUBOIS: I mean, Sir, that we've got to leave this town.
ALCESTE: I'll tear you limb from limb and joint from
joint
If you don't come more quickly to the point.
DUBOIS: Well, Sir, today a man in a black suit,
Who wore a black and ugly scowl to boot,   370
Left us a document scrawled in such a hand
As even Satan couldn't understand.

424 / THE MISANTHROPE

It bears upon your lawsuit, I don't doubt;
But all hell's devils couldn't make it out.
ALCESTE: Well, well, go on. What then? I fail to see
How this event obliges us to flee.
DUBOIS: Well, Sir: an hour later, hardly more,
A gentleman who's often called before
Came looking for you in an anxious way.
380   Not finding you, he asked me to convey
(Knowing I could be trusted with the same)
The following message.... Now, what *was* his
name?
ALCESTE: Forget his name, you idiot. What did he
say?
DUBOIS: Well, it was one of your friends, Sir, anyway.
He warned you to begone, and he suggested
That if you stay, you may well be arrested.
ALCESTE: What? Nothing more specific? Think, man,
390   think!
DUBOIS: No, Sir. He had me bring him pen and ink,
And dashed you off a letter which, I'm sure,
Will render things distinctly less obscure.
ALCESTE: Well—let me have it!
CELIMENE: What *is* this all about?
ALCESTE: God knows; but I have hopes of finding
out.
How long am I to wait, you blitherer?
DUBOIS (*after a protracted search for the letter*): I must
400   have left it on your table, Sir.
ALCESTE: I ought to ...
CELIMENE: No, no, keep your self-control;
Go find out what's behind his rigmarole.
ALCESTE: It seems that fate, no matter what I do,
Has sworn that I may not converse with you;
But, Madam, pray permit your faithful lover
To try once more before the day is over.

(DUBOIS *and* ALCESTE *leave, then* CÉLIMÈNE *with-draws.*)

ACT 5

(*Enter* ALCESTE *and* PHILINTE.)

ALCESTE: No, it's too much. My mind's made up, I tell
you.
PHILINTE: Why should this blow, however hard,
compel you ...
ALCESTE: No, no, don't waste your breath in
argument;
Nothing you say will alter my intent;
This age is vile, and I've made up my mind
To have no further commerce with mankind.
10   Did not truth, honor, decency, and the laws
Oppose my enemy and approve my cause?
My claims were justified in all men's sight;
I put my trust in equity and right;
Yet, to my horror and the world's disgrace,
Justice is mocked, and I have lost my case!

A scoundrel whose dishonesty is notorious
Emerges from another lie victorious!
Honor and right condone his brazen fraud,
While rectitude and decency applaud!
Before his smirking face, the truth stands charmed,   20
And virtue conquered, and the law disarmed!
His crime is sanctioned by a court decree!
And not content with what he's done to me,
The dog now seeks to ruin me by stating
That I composed a book now circulating,
A book so wholly criminal and vicious
That even to speak its title is seditious!
Meanwhile Oronte, my rival, lends his credit
To the same libelous tale, and helps to spread it!
Oronte! A man of honor and of rank,   30
With whom I've been entirely fair and frank;
Who sought me out and forced me, willy-nilly,
To judge some verse I found extremely silly;
And who, because I properly refused
To flatter him, or see the truth abused,
Abets my enemy in a rotten slander!
There's the reward of honesty and candor!
The man will hate me to the end of time
For failing to commend his wretched rhyme!
And not this man alone, but all humanity   40
Do what they do from interest and vanity;
They prate of honor, truth, and righteousness,
But lie, betray, and swindle nonetheless.
Come then: man's villainy is too much to bear;
Let's leave this jungle and this jackal's lair.
Yes! Treacherous and savage race of men,
You shall not look upon my face again.
PHILINTE: Oh, don't rush into exile prematurely;
Things aren't as dreadful as you make them,
surely.   50
It's rather obvious, since you're still at large,
That people don't believe your enemy's charge.
Indeed, his tale's so patently untrue
That it may do more harm to him than you.
ALCESTE: Nothing could do that scoundrel any harm:
His frank corruption is his greatest charm,
And, far from hurting him, a further shame
Would only serve to magnify his name.
PHILINTE: In any case, his bald prevarication
Has done no injury to your reputation,   60
And you may feel secure in that regard.
As for your lawsuit, it should not be hard
To have the case reopened, and contest
This judgment ...
ALCESTE: No, no, let the verdict rest.
Whatever cruel penalty it may bring,
I wouldn't have it changed for anything.
It shows the times' injustice with such clarity
That I shall pass it down to our posterity
As a great proof and signal demonstration   70
Of the black wickedness of this generation.
It may cost twenty thousand francs; but I

Shall pay their twenty thousand, and gain thereby
The right to storm and rage at human evil,
And send the race of mankind to the devil.
PHILINTE: Listen to me. . . .
ALCESTE: Why? What can you possibly say?
Don't argue, Sir; your labor's thrown away.
Do you propose to offer lame excuses
80   For men's behavior and the times' abuses?
PHILINTE: No, all you say I'll readily concede:
This is a low, conniving age indeed;
Nothing but trickery prospers nowadays,
And people ought to mend their shabby ways.
Yes, man's a beastly creature; but must we then
Abandon the society of men?
Here in the world, each human frailty
Provides occasion for philosophy,
And that is virtue's noblest exercise;
90   If honesty shone forth from all men's eyes,
If every heart were frank and kind and just,
What could our virtues do but gather dust
(Since their employment is to help us bear
The villainies of men without despair)?
A heart well-armed with virtue can endure. . . .
ALCESTE: Sir, you're a matchless reasoner, to be sure;
Your words are fine and full of cogency;
But don't waste time and eloquence on me.
My reason bids me go, for my own good.
100   My tongue won't lie and flatter as it should;
God knows what frankness it might next commit,
And what I'd suffer on account of it.
Pray let me wait for Célimène's return
In peace and quiet. I shall shortly learn,
By her response to what I have in view,
Whether her love for me is feigned or true.
PHILINTE: Till then, let's visit Eliante upstairs.
ALCESTE: No, I am too weighed down with somber
   cares.
110   Go to her, do; and leave me with my gloom
Here in the darkened corner of this room.
PHILINTE: Why, that's no sort of company, my friend;
I'll see if Eliante will not descend.

(Exit PHILINTE, ALCESTE *withdraws to a corner.)*
(Enter CÉLIMÈNE *and* ORONTE.)

ORONTE: Yes, Madam, if you wish me to remain
Your true and ardent lover, you must deign
To give me some more positive assurance.
All this suspense is quite beyond endurance.
If your heart shares the sweet desires of mine,
Show me as much by some convincing sign;
120   And here's the sign I urgently suggest:
That you no longer tolerate Alceste,
But sacrifice him to my love, and sever
All your relations with the man forever.
CELIMENE: Why do you suddenly dislike him so?
You praised him to the skies not long ago.

ORONTE: Madam, that's not the point. I'm here to find
Which way your tender feelings are inclined.
Choose, if you please, between Alceste and me,
And I shall stay or go accordingly.   130
ALCESTE (*emerging from the corner*): Yes, Madam,
   choose; this gentleman's demand
Is wholly just, and I support his stand.
I too am true and ardent; I too am here
To ask you that you make your feelings clear.
No more delays, now; no equivocation;
The time has come to make your declaration.
ORONTE: Sir, I've no wish in any way to be
An obstacle to your felicity.
ALCESTE: Sir, I've no wish to share her heart with   140
   you;
That may sound jealous, but at least it's true.
ORONTE: If, weighing us, she leans in your direction
   . . .
ALCESTE: If she regard you with the least affection
   . . .
ORONTE: I swear I'll yield her to you there and then.
ALCESTE: I swear I'll never see her face again.
ORONTE: Now, Madam, tell us what we've come to
   hear.
ALCESTE: Madam, speak openly and have no fear.
ORONTE: Just say which one is to remain your lover.   150
ALCESTE: Just name one name, and it will all be over.
ORONTE: What! Is it possible that you're undecided?
ALCESTE: What! Can your feelings possibly be
   divided?
CELIMENE: Enough: this inquisition's gone too far:
How utterly unreasonable you are!
Not that I couldn't make the choice with ease;
My heart has no conflicting sympathies;
I know full well which one of you I favor,
And you'd not see me hesitate or waver.   160
But how can you expect me to reveal
So cruelly and bluntly what I feel?
I think it altogether too unpleasant
To choose between two men when both are
   present;
One's heart has means more subtle and more kind
Of letting its affections be divined,
Nor need one be uncharitably plain
To let a lover know he loves in vain.
ORONTE: No, no, speak plainly; I for one can stand it.   170
I beg you to be frank.
ALCESTE: And I demand it.
The simple truth is what I wish to know,
And there's no need for softening the blow.
You've made an art of pleasing everyone,
But now your days of coquetry are done:
You have no choice now, Madam, but to choose,
For I'll know what to think if you refuse;
I'll take your silence for a clear admission
That I'm entitled to my worst suspicion.   180
ORONTE: I thank you for this ultimatum, Sir,

And I may say I heartily concur.

CELIMENE: Really, this foolishness is very wearing:
Must you be so unjust and overbearing?
Haven't I told you why I must demur?
Ah, here's Eliante; I'll put the case to her.

(*Enter* ELIANTE *and* PHILINTE.)

Cousin, I'm being persecuted here
By these two persons, who, it would appear,
Will not be satisfied till I confess
190 Which one I love the more, and which the less,
And tell the latter to his face that he
Is henceforth banished from my company.
Tell me, has ever such a thing been done?

ELIANTE: You'd best not turn to me, I'm not the one
To back you in a matter of this kind:
I'm all for those who frankly speak their mind.

ORONTE: Madam, you'll search in vain for a defender.

ALCESTE: You're beaten, Madam, and may as well
surrender.

200 ORONTE: Speak, speak, you must; and end this awful
strain.

ALCESTE: Or don't, and your position will be plain.

ORONTE: A single word will close this painful scene.

ALCESTE: But if you're silent, I'll know what you
mean.

(*Enter* ARSINOÉ, ACASTE, *and* CLITANDRE.)

ACASTE (*to* CÉLIMÈNE): Madam, with all due
deference, we two
Have come to pick a little bone with you.

CLITANDRE (*to* ORONTE *and* ALCESTE): I'm glad you're
210   present, Sirs; as you'll soon learn,
Our business here is also your concern.

ARSINOÉ (*to* CÉLIMÈNE): Madam, I visit you so soon
again
Only because of these two gentlemen,
Who came to me indignant and aggrieved
About a crime too base to be believed.
Knowing your virtue, having such confidence in it,
I couldn't think you guilty for a minute,
In spite of all their telling evidence;
220 And, rising above our little difference,
I've hastened here in friendship's name to see
You clear yourself of this great calumny.

ACASTE: Yes, Madam, let us see with what composure
You'll manage to respond to this disclosure.
You lately sent Clitandre this tender note.

CLITANDRE: And this one, for Acaste, you also wrote.

ACASTE (*to* ORONTE *and* ALCESTE): You'll recognize this
writing, Sirs, I think;
The lady is so free with pen and ink
230 That you must know it all too well, I fear.
But listen: this is something you should hear.

"How absurd you are to condemn my lighthear-
tedness in society, and to accuse me of being

happiest in the company of others. Nothing could
be more unjust; and if you do not come to me
instantly and beg pardon for saying such a thing, I
shall never forgive you as long as I live. Our big
bumbling friend the Viscount . . ."

What a shame that he's not here.

"Our big bumbling friend the Viscount, whose 240
name stands first in your complaint, is hardly a
man to my taste; and ever since the day I watched
him spending three-quarters of an hour spitting
into a well, so as to make circles in the water, I have
been unable to think highly of him. As for the little
Marquess . . ."

In all modesty, gentlemen, that is I.

"As for the little Marquess, who sat squeezing my
hand for such a long while yesterday, I find him in
all respects the most trifling creature alive; and the 250
only things of value about him are his cape and his
sword. As for the man with the green ribbons . . ."

(*to* ALCESTE): It's your turn now, Sir.

"As for the man with the green ribbons, he
amuses me now and then with his bluntness and his
bearish ill-humor; but there are many times indeed
when I think him the greatest bore in the world.
And as for the sonneteer . . ."

(*to* ORONTE): Here's your helping.

"And as for the sonneteer, who has taken it into 260
his head to be witty, and insists on being an author
in the teeth of opinion, I simply cannot be bothered
to listen to him, and his prose wearies me quite as
much as his poetry. Be assured that I am not always
so well-entertained as you suppose; that I long for
your company, more than I dare to say, at all these
entertainments to which people drag me; and that
the presence of those one loves is the true and
perfect seasoning to all one's pleasures."

CLITANDRE: And now for me. 270

"Clitandre, whom you mention, and who so
pesters me with his saccharine speeches, is the last
man on earth for whom I could feel any affection.
He is quite mad to suppose that I love him, and so
are you, to doubt that you are loved. Do come to
your senses; exchange your suppositions for his;
and visit me as often as possible, to help me bear
the annoyance of his unwelcome attentions."

It's a sweet character that these letters show,
And what to call it, Madam, you well know. 280

290 Enough. We're off to make the world acquainted
     With this sublime self-portrait that you've painted.
ACASTE: Madam, I'll make you no farewell oration;
     No, you're not worthy of my indignation.
     Far choicer hearts than yours, as you'll discover,
     Would like this little Marquess for a lover.

     (Exit ACASTE *and* CLITANDRE.*)*

ORONTE: So! After all those loving letters you wrote,
     You turn on me like this, and cut my throat!
     And your dissembling, faithless heart, I find,
300 Has pledged itself by turns to all mankind!
     How blind I've been! But now I clearly see;
     I thank you, Madam, for enlightening me.
     My heart is mine once more, and I'm content;
     The loss of it shall be your punishment
     (to ALCESTE*)* Sir, she is yours; I'll seek no more to stand
     Between your wishes and this lady's hand. *(Exit.)*
ARSINOE *(to* CÉLIMÈNE*)*: Madam, I'm forced to speak.
     I'm far too stirred
310 To keep my counsel, after what I've heard.
     I'm shocked and staggered by your want of morals.
     It's not my way to mix in others' quarrels;
     But really, when this fine and noble spirit,
     This man of honor and surpassing merit,
     Laid down the offering of his heart before you,
     How *could* you . . .
ALCESTE: Madam, permit me, I implore you,
     To represent myself in this debate.
     Don't bother, please, to be my advocate.
320 My heart, in any case, could not afford
     To give your services their due reward;
     And if I chose, for consolation's sake,
     Some other lady, t'would not be you I'd take.
ARSINOE: What makes you think you could, Sir? And
     how dare you
     Imply that I've been trying to ensnare you?
     If you can for a moment entertain
     Such flattering fancies, you're extremely vain.
     I'm not so interested as you suppose
330 In Célimène's discarded gigolos.
     Get rid of that absurd illusion, do.
     Women like me are not for such as you.
     Stay with this creature, to whom you're so attached;
     I've never seen two people better matched.

     (Exit ARSINOÉ.*)*

ALCESTE *(to* CÉLIMÈNE*)*: Well, I've been still
     throughout this exposé,
     Till everyone but me has said his say.
     Come, have I shown sufficient self-restraint?
     And may I now . . .
340 CELIMENE: Yes, make your just complaint.
     Reproach me freely, call me what you will;
     You've every right to say I've used you ill.
     I've wronged you, I confess it; and in my shame

I'll make no effort to escape the blame.
The anger of those others I could despise;
My guilt toward you I sadly recognize.
Your wrath is wholly justified, I fear;
I know how culpable I must appear,
I know all things bespeak my treachery,
And that, in short, you've grounds for hating me.   350
Do so; I give you leave.
ALCESTE: Ah, traitress—how,
     How should I cease to love you, even now?
     Though mind and will were passionately bent
     On hating you, my heart would not consent.
     (to ELIANTE *and* PHILINTE*)* Be witness to my
     madness, both of you;
     See what infatuation drives one to;
     But wait; my folly's only just begun,
     And I shall prove to you before I'm done   360
     How strange the human heart is, and how far
     From rational we sorry creatures are.
     (to CÉLIMÈNE*)* Woman, I'm willing to forget your
     shame,
     And clothe your treacheries in a sweeter name;
     I'll call them youthful errors, instead of crimes,
     And lay the blame on these corrupting times.
     My one condition is that you agree
     To share my chosen fate, and fly with me
     To that wild, trackless, solitary place   370
     In which I shall forget the human race.
     Only by such a course can you atone
     For those atrocious letters; by that alone
     Can you remove my present horror of you,
     And make it possible for me to love you.
CELIMENTE: What! *I* renounce the world at my young
     age,
     And die of boredom in some hermitage?
ALCESTE: Ah, if you really loved me as you ought,
     You wouldn't give the world a moment's thought; 380
     Must you have me, and all the world beside?
CELIMENE: Alas, at twenty one is terrified
     Of solitude. I fear I lack the force
     And depth of soul to take so stern a course.
     But if my hand in marriage will content you,
     Why, there's a plan which I might well consent to,
     And . . .
ALCESTE: No, I detest you now. I could excuse
     Everything else, but since you thus refuse
     To love me wholly, as a wife should do,   390
     And see the world in me, as I in you,
     Go! I reject your hand, and disenthrall
     My heart from your enchantments, once for all.
     (Exit CÉLIMÈNE.*)*
ALCESTE *(to* ELIANTE*)*: Madam, your virtuous beauty
     has no peer;
     Of all this world, you only are sincere;
     I've long esteemed you highly, as you know;
     Permit me ever to esteem you so,
     And if I do not now request your hand,

Forgive me, Madam, and try to understand.
I feel unworthy of it; I sense that fate
Does not intend me for the married state,
That I should do you wrong by offering you
My shattered heart's unhappy residue,
And that in short . . .

ELIANTE: Your argument's well taken:
Nor need you fear that I shall feel forsaken.
Were I to offer him this hand of mine,

410 Your friend Philinte, I think, would not decline.

PHILINTE: Ah, Madam, that's my heart's most
    cherished goal,

For which I'd gladly give my life and soul.

ALCESTE (*to* ELIANTE *and* PHILINTE): May you be true
    to all you now profess,
And so deserve unending happiness.
Meanwhile, betrayed and wronged in everything,
I'll flee this bitter world where vice is king,
And seek some spot unpeopled and apart
Where I'll be free to have an honest heart. (*Exit*   420
ALCESTE.)

PHILINTE: Come, Madam, let's do everything we can
To change the mind of this unhappy man. (*They
    follow him.*)

Figure 1. Acaste (Brian Bedford, *left*) Eliante (Patricia Conolly, *standing*), Célimène (Christine Pickles), and Clitandre (Joseph Bird) in the A.P.A. Repertory Company production of *The Misanthrope*, directed by Stephen Porter, designed by James Tilton, and presented by the Professional Theater Program of the University of Michigan, Ann Arbor, 1968. (Photograph: University Productions of the University of Michigan.)

Figure 2. Alceste (Richard Easton, *center*) expresses his dismay upon learning from the Guard of the Marshalsea (Michael Durrell) that he must appear in court to settle his quarrel with Oronte; Philinte (Sydney Walker, *left*) and Eliante (Patricia Conolly, *left*) show their concern for Alceste's predicament, Célimène (Christine Pickles) expresses her surprise, while Acaste (Brian Bedford, *right*) and Clitandre (Joseph Bird, *far right*) look on with an air of pretended concern in the A.P.A. Repertory Company production of *The Misanthrope*, directed by Stephen Porter and designed by James Tilton, New York, 1968. (Photograph: Van Williams.)

Staging of *The Misanthrope*

REVIEW OF THE A.P.A.-PHOENIX THEATER
PRODUCTION, 1968, BY CLIVE BARNES

Of course, Molière's "The Misanthrope" is, as of last night, the best play in town, and gratifyingly the A.P.A. Repertory Company comes close enough to doing it justice. I only hope Broadway audiences, so thinly nurtured on what often passes for wit on our stages, will have the sense to flock to it.

The play is timely. It might be said that it is always the function of a masterpiece to be timely, but in the case of "The Misanthrope" its social attitudes find a mockingly telling echo in our society. Molière was writing of a Paris dominated by the French court of the mid-17th century. A society as mannered as a ruffle and as hypocritical as a duelist's courtesy.

Bad verse gushed out of society's faucet; manners were a comedy; comedies were manners, and all manner of bows, scrapes, bobs, bows and falsities eased the daily traffic of human intercourse and quite obviated the need for honesty. Into this society comes Alceste, who, sadness of sadness, not only has the bad taste to speak his mind but, alas and alas, also is head over rapier in love with Celimene, who is all coquetry, all wiles, all deceit and all entrancements. In short, a witch of the first water.

Celimene, who is as surrounded with lovers as a lap dog might be with cushions, is the very epitome of the age. She is a gossip who cannot bear to hear a good word about anyone, and she relates the bad word with such a pretty display of dazzling malice that her barbs go out to her victims as sharp as Cupid's arrows.

Against such a woman the bluff and honest Alceste has no defenses. He rampages through polite society telling people to their face things that should be said only behind their backs, and as a result he has become a misanthrope, determined to abandon a society he finds false and the company of men he finds abhorrent. But then, there is always Celimene to lead him back to the straight and narrow primrose path.

It is a play that mixes humor and humanity so skillfully that anyone wanting to know what a comedy really is could well study it. The characters of the play—with the ill-contrasted lovers set against a background of tittlers and tattlers—are sweetly balanced, and progress of the play is exquisite right up to the masterly conclusion, which is wittily inconclusive.

Molière provides one great scene after another as the characters pirouette round, flicking one another like fencers. Yet beyond the wit and the dazzle, the insults and the ripostes, lies a serious play of a man disgusted by the false values he finds around him. Molière is too humane to be a satirist. He never loads the battle; he never really takes sides. Alceste is not only the one completely honest man in the play, he is also the one prig, and is not a little pompous.

His very aggressiveness is comic, and he sometimes protests so much that he seems to take as much pleasure out of his protestation as out of his virtue. No, perhaps, Molière's ideal is conveyed better in the characters of his friend Philante and Eliante, Celimene's cousin, who, in the words of Philante, hold that "in polite society, custom decrees that we show certain outward courtesies." Celimene, faithless yet vivacious, has a lesson to learn, but then so has Alceste.

What often stands in the way of Molière in English is the incredible difficulty of translating the poet's rhymed couplets while preserving rhyme, sense, rhythm, wit and sensibility. Richard Wilbur's marvelous translation does this. It is supple and subtle, it trips affectionately off the tongue with the rise and fall of natural speech to it, and the wit shimmers at its heart like a priceless diamond on a bed of velvet.

The A.P.A. rose manfully to the challenge, helped manfully by the swiftly naturalistic staging of Stephen Porter, who let the language speak for itself and the play make its own points. Although the company is dangerously shallow in depth, Richard Easton made an excellent Alceste, bluff, comically—but never too comically—wronged and surprisingly warm, as if at times he was not only the dupe of Celimene but also of his own unbending rectitude.

The other outstanding performance came from Brian Bedford—who in only his second performance with the company is shaping up as the right kind of repertory star—as the foppish Acaste. Mr. Bedford uses both his eyes and teeth with such exceptional virtuosity that one might easily overlook his perfect period manners, in which only Mr. Easton could rival him, and his deftly accurate comic timing. Keene Curtis, yet another of Celimene's suitors, also gave a very well-judged portrayal, with one gorgeous scene in which he reads a sonnet to Mr. Easton, asks for an honest opinion and disconcertingly receives it.

The women (Rosemary Harris come home wherever you are!) do not come off so well. Christine Pickles, however, makes a very brave attempt at Celimene, and has the right looks, the right voice and even the right spirit. But at this performance they somehow failed to come together at the right time; it was a portrayal almost right, and on another night might well prove more memorable than on this.

431

GEORGE ETHEREGE

1635–1691

Sir George Etherege—diplomat, dramatist, man-about-town—perfectly exemplifies the spirit of sophisticated Restoration society. Pleasure was his goal, and he hungered after it ceaselessly, even during his appointment as Minister to Ratisbon (1685–1688), when he scandalized the German aristocrats with his losses at gambling and his triumphs in love. Carousing, gambling, talking, whoring, writing—these were the forms of his pleasure, just as they were the delights of other men in the giddy world of London's high society for at least thirty years after the Restoration of monarchy to England in 1660. Like Charles II, the king who restored monarchy and who was the model for the sophisticated men of the age, Etherege conducted his life with the unaffected grace and polish of a true wit. He came to be known by his friends as "easie" Etherege, and he numbered among his companions the most brilliant and rakish young men of the age—the "court wits"—Henry Savile, Sir Charles Sedley, and John Wilmot, the "wicked" Earl of Rochester. They admired him for his wit, his skeptical attitudes, his libertine values, and he prided himself on his "noble laziness of mind." Had he been less of a gentleman, he might have been more of a dramatist, but his "noble laziness" made it impossible for him to take the stage seriously. For Etherege, as for many dramatists of his day, writing was a fashionable pastime but not a serious profession.

He wrote only three plays: *The Comical Revenge; or, Love in a Tub* (1664); *She Wou'd if She Cou'd* (1668); and *The Man of Mode, or, Sir Fopling Flutter* (1676). But these plays, particularly the last two, are preeminent examples of Restoration social comedy. *She Wou'd if She Cou'd* was, in fact, the first play of the period to give itself over entirely to the fashionable spots, the witty capers, the smart talk, the lively people, and the hangers-on of sophisticated London society. Its main action focuses on the lively courtship of two witty young women from the country, Ariana and Gatty, by two rakish young men of the town, Courtall and Freeman. As their tag names suggest, the women are gadabouts seeking the idle and harmless pleasures of the town, while the men are hedonists pursuing sexual satisfaction without the restraints of marriage. And the comic wit of their courtship derives from this basic tension. Set off against these lively young people are the would-be wits, such as the Cockwoods and other country types, who aspire to the ways of the city without the intelligence or verve to achieve sophistication. *She Wou'd if She Cou'd* is a sustained contrast between true and false wit according to the standards of Restoration society, and thus it charmed the critics, as well as the court, and three years after its premiere was still being talked of as "the best comedy that has been written since the Restoration of the stage."

The Man of Mode, according to chroniclers of the period, also "met with extraordinary success" and "got a great deal of money" from its opening run in the theater. Its initial success was at least in part the result of striking similarities that the audience seemed to find between the chief male characters in the play and well-known members of the Restoration smart set. Some people thought that

433

Etherege was portraying himself in the sexual escapades of Dorimant; others believed that "that base man Mr. Dorimant" was a replica of the "wicked" Earl of Rochester. Medley was associated with Sir Charles Sedley, and Sir Fopling with Beau Hewitt, an eminent fop of the day. But Dryden was closer to the truth when he reminded the audience in his epilogue to the play that "every man is safe from what he feared,/ For no one fool is hunted from the herd." As its ambiguous title suggests, the play is not about one fool in particular, but about modish life-styles in general—about the nature of existence in a highly sophisticated society and the consequences of a commitment to its unique social values. In this respect it bears comparison with Molière's *The Misanthrope*.

But while the protagonist of Molière's play is a critic of his society, the hero of Etherege's play, namely Dorimant, is the supreme embodiment of his society's values. His status as rake-hero is epitomized in such outlandish activities as cheerfully breaking off with one mistress in the presence of the woman he will next seduce, casually sending a guinea to a whore for a box at the opera, kissing his latest mistress while his valet ties up the bed-linen and his friends wait outside, all the while quoting lines from poetry that perfectly suit his situation. In these and similar activities, Dorimant epitomizes the wit, the grace, the libertinism, and the cynicism that also reappear in other rake-heroes, such as Horner in Wycherley's *The Country Wife* (1675), Valentine in Congreve's *Love for Love* (1695), and both Mirabell and Fainall (the hero and villain) in Congreve's *The Way of the World* (1700).

In contrast to Dorimant who is the true "man of mode," Etherege gives us a dazzling comic portrait in the titular "man of mode," Sir Fopling Flutter. Young Bellair and Dorimant sum him up neatly:

He thinks himself the pattern of modern gallantry.
He is indeed the pattern of modern foppery.

Sir Fopling is the English counterpart of Acaste, Clitandre, and Oronte in *The Misanthrope*. Happily lost in his French clothes, French phrases, and consuming self-esteem (Figure 1), he cannot see the discrepancy between what he wants to be and what he really is. In his excesses and self-delusions he is a model for other Restoration fools, such as Witwoud and Petulant of Congreve's *The Way of the World* (1700), Lord Foppington of Vanbrugh's *The Relapse* (1697), and even survives into the eighteenth century with Bob Acres of Sheridan's *The Rivals* (1775) and Crabtree as well as Sir Benjamin Backbite of Sheridan's *The School for Scandal* (1777).

The ambivalence created by the presence of two "men of mode" is further echoed in Dorimant's relationships with women. While the play exposes his cynicism in callously manipulating Loveit (see Figure 2), it also presents the moments when genuine feelings form the basis of lasting personal relationships.

But even as *The Man of Mode* shows us a world that values Dorimant for his wit and social intelligence, it also exposes the cynicism of that world as it is manifest in Dorimant's callous manipulation of Loveit (see Figure 2). More importantly, it marks the beginning of the move in English comic drama toward recognizing genuine feeling as the basis of lasting personal relationships. Thus, while Dorimant and Harriet flirt with each other in public (see Figure 3), they then turn to the audience to confess their vulnerability. For example, when Harriet hears Dorimant speak of the change in her facial expression, she tells us, "I feel as great a change within, but he shall never know it." So, too, after Dorimant finds that Harriet won't easily give in to him, he reveals to us, "I love her and dare not let her know it. I fear sh'as an ascendant o'er me and may revenge the wrongs I have done her sex." In moments such as these, their mutual emotional repression comically reveals the painful price that comes from a commitment to the elegant style of their society. *The Way of the World* displays the problem of emotional vulnerability even more clearly in Mirabell who directly confesses his love for Millamant to his friends. When she teases him by saying "What would you give that you could help loving me?" she then forces him to the witty and painfully honest confession, "I would give something that you did not know I could not help it." Such moments of sincerity look forward to the surprising climax of Farquhar's *The Beaux' Stratagem* (1707) in which a married couple who are unsuited to each other cheerfully agree to divorce rather than continuing the facade and farce of their marriage.

The valuing of truth in human relationships, a truth that may lie hidden, consciously or unconsciously, under the wit of the characters, has led modern directors to look to Restoration comedy not just for a source of elegant period pieces, but also for characters and situations that seem contemporary in their implications. When *The Man of Mode* was produced in 1971 by the Royal Shakespeare Company, the director (Terry Hands) deliberately broke away from a detailed period setting, as he explains in the interview following the text. The set for his production featured a magnified version of Newton's cradle (see Figure 4), a piece contemporary with the play (as a Restoration scientific model), but also familiar to its modern audience (as a popular game-object). This device, together with the modern costumes, provoked differing reactions from audiences and critics, as can be seen in the two reviews reprinted following the text. But the modern style of the production evidently did give the actors the freedom to discover the reality of the play's emotions.

THE MAN OF MODE
Or, Sir Fopling Flutter

BY GEORGE ETHEREGE / TEXT AND NOTES BY GEORGE NETTLETON AND ARTHUR CASE

CHARACTERS

MR. DORIMANT
MR. MEDLEY
OLD BELLAIR
YOUNG BELLAIR
SIR FOPLING FLUTTER
LADY TOWNLEY
EMILIA
MRS. LOVEIT
BELLINDA
LADY WOODVILL

HARRIET, *her daughter*
PERT, *a waiting woman*
BUSY, *a waiting woman*
A SHOEMAKER
AN ORANGE WOMAN
THREE SLOVENLY BULLIES
TWO CHAIRMEN
MR. SMIRK, *a Parson*
HANDY, *a Valet-de-chambre*
PAGES, FOOTMEN, *etc.*

PROLOGUE

By Sir Car Scroope, Baronet°

Like dancers on the ropes poor poets fare,
Most perish young, the rest in danger are;
This, one would think, should make our authors
    wary,
But, gamester-like, the giddy fools miscarry.
A lucky hand or two so tempts 'em on,
They cannot leave off play till they're undone.
With modest fears a muse does first begin,
Like a young wench newly enticed to sin;
But tickled once with praise, by her good will,
The wanton fool would never more lie still.
'Tis an old mistress you'll meet here tonight,
Whose charms you once have looked on with delight.
But now of late such dirty drabs have known ye,
A muse o'th' better sort's ashamed to own ye.
Nature well drawn, and wit, must now give place
To gaudy nonsense and to dull grimace;
Nor is it strange that you should like so much
That kind of wit, for most of yours is such.
But I'm afraid that while to France we go,
To bring you home fine dresses, dance, and show,
The stage, like you, will but more foppish grow.
Of foreign wares, why should we fetch the scum,
When we can be so richly served at home?
For heav'n be thanked, 'tis not so wise an age
But your own follies may supply the stage.
Though often plowed, there's no great fear the soil
Should barren grow by the too frequent toil;

While at your doors are to be daily found
Such loads of dunghill to manure the ground.
'Tis by your follies that we players thrive,
As the physicians by diseases live;
And as each year some new distemper reigns,
Whose friendly poison helps to increase their gains,
So among you there starts up every day
Some new, unheard-of fool for us to play.
Then, for your own sakes be not too severe,
Nor what you all admire at home, damn here;
Since each is fond of his own ugly face,
Why should you, when we hold it, break the glass?

ACT 1 / SCENE 1

(A dressing room. A table covered with a toilet; clothes laid ready.)

(Enter DORIMANT *in his gown and slippers, with a note in his hand, made up, repeating verses.)*

DORIMANT: Now for some ages had the pride of Spain
Made the sun shine on half the world in vain.°

(Then looking on the note.)

'For Mrs. Loveit.'—What a dull, insipid thing is a billet-doux written in cold blood, after the heat of the business is over! It is a tax upon good nature which I have here been laboring to pay, and have done it, but with as much regret as ever fanatic paid the Royal Aid or church duties.°

Sir Car Scroope, one of the most popular of "the mob of gentlemen who wrote with ease."

Here as elsewhere in the play, Dorimant recites lines from the seventeenth century poet, Edmund Waller. *church duties,* taxes levied in support of the civil and ecclesiastical government.

'Twill have the same fate, I know, that all my notes to her have had of late; 'twill not be thought kind enough. 'Faith, women are i'the right when they jealously examine our letters, for in them we always first discover our decay of passion.—Hey! Who waits?

(Enter HANDY.*)*

HANDY: Sir—

DORIMANT: Call a footman.

HANDY: None of 'em are come yet.

DORIMANT: Dogs! Will they ever lie snoring abed till noon?

HANDY: 'Tis all one, sir; if they're up, you indulge 'em so they're ever poaching after whores all the morning.

DORIMANT: Take notice henceforward who's wanting in his duty; the next clap he gets, he shall rot for an example. What vermin are those chattering without?

HANDY: Foggy° Nan, the orange-woman, and Swearing Tom, the shoemaker.

DORIMANT: Go, call in that over-grown jade with the flasket° of guts before her; fruit is refreshing in a morning.

(Exit HANDY.*)*

   It is not that I love you less
   Than when before your feet I lay—

(Enter ORANGE-WOMAN *and* HANDY.*)*

How now, double tripe, what news do you bring?

ORANGE WOMAN: News! Here's the best fruit has come to town t'year; gad, I was up before four o'clock this morning and bought all the choice i'the market.

DORIMANT: The nasty refuse of your shop.

ORANGE WOMAN: You need not make mouths at it; I assure you, 'tis all culled ware.

DORIMANT: The citizens buy better on a holiday in their walk to Totnam.°

ORANGE WOMAN: Good or bad, 'tis all one; I never knew you commend anything. Lord! would the ladies had heard you talk of 'em as I have done! *(Sets down the fruit.)* Here, bid your man give me an angel.°

DORIMANT *(to* HANDY*)*: Give the bawd her fruit again.

ORANGE WOMAN: Well, on my conscience, there never was the like of you!—God's my life, I had almost forgot to tell you there is a young gentlewoman lately come to town with her mother, that is so taken with you.

DORIMANT: Is she handsome?

ORANGE WOMAN: Nay,° gad, there are few finer women, I tell you but so, and a hugeous fortune, they say. Here, eat this peach. It comes from the stone;° 'tis better than any Newington° y'have tasted.

DORIMANT *(taking the peach)*: This fine woman, I'll lay my life, is some awkward, ill-fashioned country toad who, not having above four dozen of black hairs on her head, has adorned her baldness with a large, white fruz,° that she may look sparkishly in the forefront of the King's box at an old play.

ORANGE WOMAN: Gad, you'd change your note quickly if you did but see her.

DORIMANT: How came she to know me?

ORANGE WOMAN: She saw you yesterday at the Change;° she told me you came and fooled with the woman at the next shop.

DORIMANT: I remember there was a mask observed me, indeed. Fooled, did she say?

ORANGE WOMAN: Ay; I vow she told me twenty things you said, too, and acted with her head and with her body so like you—

(Enter MEDLEY.*)*

MEDLEY: Dorimant, my life, my joy, my darling sin! How dost thou? *(Embraces* DORIMANT.*)*

ORANGE WOMAN: Lord, what a filthy trick these men have got of kissing one another! *(she spits.)*

MEDLEY: Why do you suffer this cartload of scandal to come near you and make your neighbors think you so improvident to need a bawd?

ORANGE WOMAN *(to* DORIMANT*)*: Good, now! we shall have it you did but want° him to help you! Come, pay me for my fruit.

MEDLEY: Make us thankful for it,° huswife, bawds are as much out of fashion as gentlemen-ushers;° none but old formal ladies use the one, and none but foppish old stagers° employ the other. Go! You are an insignificant brandy bottle.

DORIMANT: Nay, there you wrong her; three quarts of Canary is her business.

ORANGE WOMAN: What you please, gentlemen.

DORIMANT: To him! give him as good as he brings.

ORANGE WOMAN: Hang him, there is not such another

Foggy, bloated.   *flasket,* a long shallow basket or tub. *Totnam,* Tottenham, a northern suburb of London.   *angel,* a gold coin worth ten shillings.

Nay, a meaningless interjection equivalent to "why!" *stone,* the meaning of this phrase is not clear: it may be either that the fruit was sun-ripened upon a tree trained against a stone wall, or that it was a freestone peach. *Newington,* the center of a fruit-growing district in Kent. *fruz,* a frizzy arrangement of artificial hair. *Change,* The New Exchange in the Strand. *want,* need. *Make . . . it,* i.e., God make us thankful for it. *gentlemen-ushers,* male attendants upon a lady. *old stagers,* old hands.

heathen in the town again, except it be the shoemaker without.

MEDLEY: I shall see you hold up your hand at the bar next sessions for murder, huswife; that shoemaker can take his oath you are in fee with the doctors to sell green fruit to the gentry, that the crudities may breed diseases.

ORANGE WOMAN (to DORIMANT): Pray, give me my money.

DORIMANT: Not a penny! When you bring the gentlewoman hither you spoke of, you shall be paid.

ORANGE WOMAN: The gentlewoman! the gentlewoman may be as honest° as your sisters for aught I know. Pray, pay me, Mr. Dorimant, and do not abuse me so; I have an honester way of living—you know it.

MEDLEY: Was there ever such a resty° bawd!

DORIMANT: Some jade's tricks she has, but she makes amends when she's in good humor.—Come, tell me the lady's name and Handy shall pay you.

ORANGE WOMAN: I must not; she forbid me.

DORIMANT: That's a sure sign she would have you.°

MEDLEY: Where does she live?

ORANGE WOMAN: They lodge at my house.

MEDLEY: Nay, then she's in a hopeful way.

ORANGE WOMAN: Good Mr. Medley, say your pleasure of me, but take heed how you affront my house! God's my life!—'in a hopeful way!'

DORIMANT: Prithee, peace! What kind of woman's the mother?

ORANGE WOMAN: A goodly, grave gentlewoman. Lord, how she talks against the wild young men o' the town! As for your part, she thinks you an arrant devil; should she see you, on my conscience she would look if you had not a cloven foot.

DORIMANT: Does she know me?

ORANGE WOMAN: Only by hearsay; a thousand horrid stories have been told her of you, and she believes 'em all.

MEDLEY: By the character this should be the famous Lady Woodvill and her daughter Harriet.

ORANGE WOMAN: The devil's in him for guessing, I think.

DORIMANT: Do you know 'em?

MEDLEY: Both very well; the mother's a great admirer of the forms and civility of the last age.

DORIMANT: An antiquated beauty may be allowed to be out of humor at the freedoms of the present. This is a good account of the mother; pray, what is the daughter?

MEDLEY: Why, first, she's an heiress—vastly rich.

DORIMANT: And handsome?

MEDLEY: What alteration a twelvemonth may have bred in her I know not, but a year ago she was the beautifullest creature I ever saw: a fine, easy, clean shape; light brown hair in abundance; her features regular; her complexion clear and lively; large, wanton eyes; but above all, a mouth that has made me kiss it a thousand times in imagination; teeth white and even, and pretty, pouting lips, with a little moisture ever hanging on them, that look like the Provins° rose fresh on the bush, ere the morning sun has quite drawn up the dew.

DORIMANT: Rapture! mere° rapture!

ORANGE WOMAN: Nay, gad, he tells you true; she's a delicate creature.

DORIMANT: Has she wit?

MEDLEY: More than is usual in her sex, and as much malice. Then, she's as wild as you would wish her, and has a demureness in her looks that makes it so surprising.

DORIMANT: Flesh and blood cannot hear this and not long to know her.

MEDLEY: I wonder what makes her mother bring her up to town; an old doting keeper cannot be more jealous of his mistress.

ORANGE WOMAN: She made me laugh yesterday; there was a judge came to visit 'em, and the old man, she told me, did so stare upon her, and when he saluted her smacked so heartily. Who would think it of 'em?

MEDLEY: God-a-mercy, judge!°

DORIMANT: Do 'em right; the gentlemen of the long robe° have not been wanting by their good examples to countenance the crying sin o' the nation.

MEDLEY: Come, on with your trappings; 'tis later than you imagine.

DORIMANT: Call in the shoemaker, Handy.

ORANGE WOMAN: Good Mr. Dorimant, pay me. Gad, I had rather give you my fruit than stay to be abused by that foul-mouthed rogue; what you gentlemen say, it matters not much, but such a dirty fellow does one more disgrace.

DORIMANT (to HANDY): Give her ten shillings—(to ORANGE-WOMAN) and be sure you tell the young gentlewoman I must be acquainted with her.

ORANGE WOMAN: Now do you long to be tempting this pretty creature. Well, heavens mend you!

MEDLEY: Farewell, bog!°

(Exit ORANGE-WOMAN and HANDY.)

---

honest, chaste. resty, restive. have you, i.e., have you tell me.

Provins, the town of Provins, some 50 miles E.S.E. of Paris, is still noted for its trade in roses. mere, pure. God-a-mercy, judge, an ironical exclamation of applause, equivalent to "Well done, judge!" gentlemen ... robe, lawyers. bog, fat person.

—Dorimant, when did you see your *pisaller,*° as you call her, Mrs. Loveit?

DORIMANT: Not these two days.

MEDLEY: And how stand affairs between you?

DORIMANT: There has been great patching of late, much ado; we make a shift to hang together.

MEDLEY: I wonder how her mighty spirit bears it.

DORIMANT: Ill enough, on all conscience; I never knew so violent a creature.

MEDLEY: She's the most passionate in her love and the most extravagant in her jealousy of any woman I ever heard of. What note is that?

DORIMANT: An excuse I am going to send her for the neglect I am guilty of.

MEDLEY: Prithee, read it.

DORIMANT: No; but if you will take the pains, you may.

MEDLEY *(reads):*

I never was a lover of business, but now I have a just reason to hate it, since it has kept me these two days from seeing you. I intend to wait upon you in the afternoon, and in the pleasure of your conversation forget all I have suffered during this tedious absence.

This business of yours, Dorimant, has been with a vizard° at the playhouse; I have had an eye on you. If some malicious body should betray you, this kind note would hardly make your peace with her.

DORIMANT: I desire no better.

MEDLEY: Why, would her knowledge of it oblige you?

DORIMANT: Most infinitely; next to the coming to a good understanding with a new mistress, I love a quarrel with an old one. But the devil's in't! there has been such a calm in my affairs of late, I have not had the pleasure of making a woman so much as break her fan, to be sullen, or forswear herself, these three days.

MEDLEY: A very great misfortune. Let me see; I love mischief well enough to forward this business myself. I'll about it presently, and though I know the truth of what y'ave done will set her a-raving, I'll heighten it a little with invention, leave her in a fit o' the mother,° and be here again before y'are ready.

DORIMANT: Pray, stay; you may spare yourself the labor. The business is undertaken already by one who will manage it with as much address, and I think with a little more malice than you can.

MEDLEY: Who i'the devil's name can this be!

DORIMANT: Why, the vizard—that very vizard you saw me with.

MEDLEY: Does she love mischief so well as to betray herself to spite another?

DORIMANT: Not so neither, Medley. I will make you comprehend the mystery: this mask, for a farther confirmation of what I have been these two days swearing to her, made me yesterday at the playhouse make her a promise before her face utterly to break off with Loveit, and, because she tenders° my reputation and would not have me do a barbarous thing, has contrived a way to give me a handsome occasion.

MEDLEY: Very good.

DORIMANT: She intends about an hour before me, this afternoon, to make Loveit a visit, and, having the privilege, by reason of a professed friendship between them, to talk of her concerns—

MEDLEY: Is she a friend?

DORIMANT: Oh, an intimate friend!

MEDLEY: Better and better; pray, proceed.

DORIMANT: She means insensibly to insinuate a discourse of me and artificially raise her jealousy to such a height that, transported with the first motions of her passion, she shall fly upon me with all the fury imaginable as soon as ever I enter; the quarrel being thus happily begun, I am to play my part, confess and justify all my roguery, swear her impertinence and ill-humor makes her intolerable, tax her with the next fop that comes into my head, and in a huff march away, slight her, and leave her to be taken by whosoever thinks it worth his time to lie down before her.

MEDLEY: This vizard is a spark and has a genius that makes her worthy of yourself, Dorimant.

(Enter HANDY, SHOEMAKER, *and* FOOTMAN.)

DORIMANT: You rogue there, who sneak like a dog that has flung down a dish! if you do not mend your waiting, I'll uncase you° and turn you loose to the wheel of fortune. *(Giving* HANDY *the letter.)* Handy, seal this and let him run with it presently. *(Exit* FOOTMAN.)

MEDLEY: Since y'are resolved on a quarrel, why do you send her this kind note?

DORIMANT: To keep her at home in order to the business—*(to the* SHOEMAKER*)* How now, you drunken sot?

SHOEMAKER: 'Zbud, you have no reason to talk; I have not had a bottle of sack of yours in my belly this fortnight.

MEDLEY: The orange woman says your neighbors take notice what a heathen you are, and design to inform the bishop and have you burned for an atheist.

---

pisaller, makeshift.   *vizard,* mask; by metonymy, a masked person.   *fit . . . mother,* hysteria.

tenders, cherishes.   *uncase you,* strip you (of your livery).

SHOEMAKER: Damn her, dunghill, if her husband does not remove her, she stinks so, the parish intend to indict him for a nuisance.

MEDLEY: I advise you like a friend; reform your life. You have brought the envy of the world upon you by living above yourself. Whoring and swearing are vices too genteel for a shoemaker.

SHOEMAKER: 'Zbud, I think you men of quality will grow as unreasonable as the women. You would ingross° the sins of the nation; poor folks can no sooner be wicked but th'are railed at by their betters.

DORIMANT: Sirrah, I'll have you stand i'the pillory for this libel!

SHOEMAKER: Some of you deserve it, I'm sure; there are so many of 'em, that our journeymen nowadays, instead of harmless ballads, sing nothing but your damned lampoons.

DORIMANT: Our lampoons, you rogue!

SHOEMAKER: Nay, good master, why should not you write your own commentaries as well as Cæsar?

MEDLEY: The rascal's read, I perceive.

SHOEMAKER: You know the old proverb—ale and history.°

DORIMANT: Draw on my shoes, sirrah.

SHOEMAKER: Here's a shoe—!

DORIMANT: —Sits with more wrinkles than there are in an angry bully's forehead!

SHOEMAKER: 'Zbud, as smooth as your mistress's skin does upon her! So; strike your foot in home. 'Zbud, if e'er a monsieur of 'em all make more fashionable ware, I'll be content to have my ears whipped off with my own paring knife.

MEDLEY: And served up in a ragout instead of coxcombs to a company of French shoemakers for a collation.

SHOEMAKER: Hold, hold! Damn 'em, caterpillars! let 'em feed upon cabbage.—Come master, your health this morning next my heart now!

DORIMANT: Go, get you home and govern your family better! Do not let your wife follow you to the alehouse, beat your whore, and lead you home in triumph.

SHOEMAKER: 'Zbud, there's never a man i'the town lives more like a gentleman with his wife than I do. I never mind her motions,° she never inquires into mine; we speak to one another civilly, hate one another heartily, and because 'tis vulgar to lie and soak° together, we have each of us our several° settle-bed.

DORIMANT (to HANDY): Give him half a crown.

MEDLEY: Not without he will promise to be bloody drunk.

SHOEMAKER: 'Tope' 's the word i'the eye of the world. (HANDY gives him money; he invites HANDY, in dumbshow, to join him in a drink.) For my master's honor, Robin!

DORIMANT: Do not debauch my servants, sirrah.

SHOEMAKER: I only tip him the wink; he knows an alehouse from a hovel. (Exit SHOEMAKER.)

DORIMANT (to HANDY): My clothes, quickly.

MEDLEY: Where shall we dine today?

(Enter YOUNG BELLAIR.)

DORIMANT: Where you will; here comes a good third man.

YOUNG BELLAIR: Your servant, gentlemen.

MEDLEY: Gentle sir, how will you answer this visit to your honorable mistress? 'Tis not her interest you should keep company with men of sense who will be talking reason.

YOUNG BELLAIR: I do not fear her pardon; do you but grant me yours for my neglect of late.

MEDLEY: Though y'ave made us miserable by the want of your good company, to show you I am free from all resentment, may the beautiful cause of our misfortune give you all the joys happy lovers have shared ever since the world began.

YOUNG BELLAIR: You wish me in heaven, but you believe me on my journey to hell.

MEDLEY: You have a good strong faith, and that may contribute much towards your salvation. I confess I am but of an untoward constitution, apt to have doubts and scruples—and in love they are no less distracting than in religion. Were I so near marriage, I should cry out by fits as I ride in my coach, 'Cuckold, cuckold!' with no less fury than the mad fanatic does 'glory!' in Bethlem.°

YOUNG BELLAIR: Because religion makes some run mad must I live an atheist?

MEDLEY: Is it not great indiscretion for a man of credit, who may have money enough on his word, to go and deal with Jews, who for little sums make men enter into bonds and give judgments?

YOUNG BELLAIR: Preach no more on this text. I am determined, and there is no hope of my conversion.

DORIMANT (to HANDY, who is fiddling about him): Leave your unnecessary fiddling; a wasp that's buzzing

---

ingross, monopolize. ale and history, the proverb has not been identified: it may have been a vernacular equivalent of the Latin in vino veritas, referring to the frankness of an intoxicated person. motions, actions. soak, get drunk. several, individual.

Bethlem, Bethlehem Hospital, more commonly known as Bedlam, an asylum for the insane, in Moorfields. The fanatic referred to may have been Oliver Cromwell's mad porter.

about a man's nose at dinner is not more trouble-some than thou art.

HANDY: You love to have your clothes hang just, sir.

DORIMANT: I love to be well dressed, sir, and think it no scandal to my understanding.

HANDY: Will you use the essence or orange flower water?

DORIMANT: I will smell as I do today, no offence to the ladies' noses.

HANDY: Your pleasure, sir. (*Exit* HANDY.)

DORIMANT: That a man's excellency should lie in neatly tying of a ribband or a cravat! How care-ful's nature in furnishing the world with neces-sary coxcombs!

YOUNG BELLAIR: That's a mighty pretty suit of yours, Dorimant.

DORIMANT: I am glad't has your approbation.

YOUNG BELLAIR: No man in town has a better fancy in his clothes than you have.

DORIMANT: You will make me have an opinion of my genius.

MEDLEY: There is a great critic, I hear, in these mat-ters lately arrived piping hot from Paris.

YOUNG BELLAIR: Sir Fopling Flutter, you mean.

MEDLEY: The same.

YOUNG BELLAIR: He thinks himself the pattern of modern gallantry.

DORIMANT: He is indeed the pattern of modern fop-pery.

MEDLEY: He was yesterday at the play, with a pair of gloves up to his elbows, and a periwig more exactly curled than a lady's head newly dressed for a ball.

YOUNG BELLAIR: What a pretty lisp he has!

DORIMANT: Ho! that he affects in imitation of the people of quality of France.

MEDLEY: His head stands, for the most part, on one side, and his looks are more languishing than a lady's when she lolls at stretch in her coach or leans her head carelessly against the side of a box i'the playhouse.

DORIMANT: He is a person indeed of great acquired follies.

MEDLEY: He is like many others, beholding to his education for making him so eminent a cox-comb; many a fool had been lost to the world had their indulgent parents wisely bestowed neither learning nor good breeding on 'em.

YOUNG BELLAIR: He has been, as the sparkish word is, 'brisk upon the ladies' already. He was yesterday at my Aunt Townley's and gave Mrs. Loveit a catalogue of his good qualities under the charac-ter of a complete gentleman, who, according to Sir Fopling, ought to dress well, dance well, fence well, have a genius for love letters, an agreeable voice for a chamber, be very amorous, something discreet, but not overconstant.

MEDLEY: Pretty ingredients to make an accomplished person!

DORIMANT: I am glad he pitched upon Loveit.

YOUNG BELLAIR: How so?

DORIMANT: I wanted a fop to lay to her charge, and this is as pat as may be.

YOUNG BELLAIR: I am confident she loves no man but you.

DORIMANT: The good fortune were enough to make me vain, but that I am in my nature modest.

YOUNG BELLAIR: Hark you, Dorimant.—With your leave, Mr. Medley; 'tis only a secret concerning a fair lady.

MEDLEY: Your good breeding, sir, gives you too much trouble, you might have whispered without all this ceremony.

YOUNG BELLAIR (*to* DORIMANT): How stand your af-fairs with Bellinda of late?

DORIMANT: She's a little jilting baggage.

YOUNG BELLAIR: Nay, I believe her false enough, but she's ne'er the worse for your purpose; she was with you yesterday in a disguise at the play.

DORIMANT: There we fell out and resolved never to speak to one another more.

YOUNG BELLAIR: The occasion?

DORIMANT: Want of courage to meet me at the place appointed. These young women apprehend lov-ing as much as the young men do fighting, at first; but once entered, like them too, they all turn bullies straight.

(*Enter* HANDY.)

HANDY (*to* YOUNG BELLAIR): Sir, your man without de-sires to speak with you.

YOUNG BELLAIR: Gentlemen, I'll return immediately. (*Exit* YOUNG BELLAIR.)

MEDLEY: A very pretty fellow this.

DORIMANT: He's handsome, well bred, and by much the most tolerable of all the young men that do not abound in wit.

MEDLEY: Ever well dressed, always complaisant, and seldom impertinent. You and he are grown very intimate, I see.

DORIMANT: It is our mutual interest to be so: it makes the women think the better of his understand-ing, and judge more favorably of my reputation; it makes him pass upon some for a man of very good sense, and I upon others for a very civil person.

MEDLEY: What was that whisper?

DORIMANT: A thing which he would fain have known, but I did not think it fit to tell him; it might have frighted him from his honorable intentions of marrying.

MEDLEY: Emilia—give her her due—has the best reputation of any young woman about the town who has beauty enough to provoke detraction;

her carriage is unaffected, her discourse modest—not at all censorious nor pretending, like the counterfeits of the age.

DORIMANT: She's a discreet maid, and I believe nothing can corrupt her but a husband.

MEDLEY: A husband?

DORIMANT: Yes, a husband. I have known many women make a difficulty of losing a maidenhead, who have afterwards made none of making a cuckold.

MEDLEY: This prudent consideration, I am apt to think, has made you confirm poor Bellair in the desperate resolution he has taken.

DORIMANT: Indeed, the little hope I found there was of her, in the state she was in, has made me by my advice contribute something towards the changing of her condition.

(Enter YOUNG BELLAIR.)

—Dear Bellair, by heavens, I thought we had lost thee! men in love are never to be reckoned on when we would form a company.

YOUNG BELLAIR: Dorimant, I am undone. My man has brought the most surprising news i'the world.

DORIMANT: Some strange misfortune is befallen your love.

YOUNG BELLAIR: My father came to town last night and lodges i'the very house where Emilia lies.

MEDLEY: Does he know it is with her you are in love?

YOUNG BELLAIR: He knows I love, but knows not whom, without some officious sot has betrayed me.

DORIMANT: Your Aunt Townley is your confidant and favors the business.

YOUNG BELLAIR: I do not apprehend any ill office from her. I have received a letter, in which I am commanded by my father to meet him at my aunt's this afternoon. He tells me farther he has made a match for me and bids me resolve to be obedient to his will or expect to be disinherited.

MEDLEY: Now's your time, Bellair; never had lover such an opportunity of giving a generous proof of his passion.

YOUNG BELLAIR: As how, I pray?

MEDLEY: Why, hang an estate, marry Emilia out of hand, and provoke your father to do what he threatens; 'tis but despising a coach, humbling yourself to a pair of goloshes,° being out of countenance when you meet your friends, pointed at and pitied wherever you go by all the amorous fops that know you, and your fame will be immortal.

YOUNG BELLAIR: I could find in my heart to resolve not to marry at all.

goloshes, pattens or clogs.

DORIMANT: Fie, fie! That would spoil a good jest and disappoint the well-natured town of an occasion of laughing at you.

YOUNG BELLAIR: The storm I have so long expected hangs o'er my head and begins to pour down upon me; I am on the rack and can have no rest till I'm satisfied in what I fear. Where do you dine?

DORIMANT: At Long's or Locket's.°

MEDLEY: At Long's let it be.

YOUNG BELLAIR: I'll run and see Emilia and inform myself how matters stand. If my misfortunes are not so great as to make me unfit for company, I'll be with you. (Exit YOUNG BELLAIR.)

(Enter a FOOTMAN with a letter.)

FOOTMAN (to DORIMANT): Here's a letter, sir.

DORIMANT: The superscription's right: 'For Mr. Dorimant.'

MEDLEY: Let's see; the very scrawl and spelling of a true-bred whore.

DORIMANT: I know the hand, the style is admirable, I assure you.

MEDLEY: Prithee, read it.

DORIMANT (reads):

I told a you you dud not love me, if you dud, you wou'd have seen me again ere now. I have no money and am very mallicolly; pray send me a guynie to see the operies.

Your servant to command,
Molly.

MEDLEY: Pray, let the whore have a favorable answer, that she may spark it in a box and do honor to her profession.

DORIMANT: She shall, and perk up i'the face of quality. (to HANDY) Is the coach at the door?

HANDY: You did not bid me send for it.

DORIMANT: Eternal blockhead! (HANDY offers to go out.) Hey, sot—

HANDY: Did you call me, sir?

DORIMANT: I hope you have no just exception to the name, sir?

HANDY: I have sense, sir.

DORIMANT: Not so much as a fly in winter.—How did you come, Medley?

MEDLEY: In a chair.

FOOTMAN (to DORIMANT): You may have a hackney coach if you please, sir.

DORIMANT: I may ride the elephant if I please, sir. Call another chair and let my coach follow to Long's.

Long's, Locket's, fashionable taverns, one in the Haymarket, the other in Charing Cross.

Be calm, ye great parents, etc.

(*Exeunt, singing.*)

ACT 2 / SCENE 1

(LADY TOWNLEY's *house*)
(*Enter my* LADY TOWNLEY *and* EMILIA.)

LADY TOWNLEY: I was afraid, Emilia, all had been discovered.

EMILIA: I tremble with the apprehension still.

LADY TOWNLEY: That my brother should take lodgings i'the very house where you lie!

EMILIA: 'Twas lucky we had timely notice to warn the people to be secret. He seems to be a mighty good-humored old man.

LADY TOWNLEY: He ever had a notable smirking way with him.

EMILIA: He calls me rogue, tells me he can't abide me, and does so bepat me.

LADY TOWNLEY: On my word, you are much in his favor then.

EMILIA: He has been very inquisitive, I am told, about my family, my reputation, and my fortune.

LADY TOWNLEY: I am confident he does not i'the least suspect you are the woman his son's in love with.

EMILIA: What should make him, then, inform himself so particularly of me?

LADY TOWNLEY: He was always of a very loving temper himself; it may be he has a doting fit upon him—who knows?

EMILIA: It cannot be.

(*Enter* YOUNG BELLAIR.)

LADY TOWNLEY: Here comes my nephew.—Where did you leave your father?

YOUNG BELLAIR: Writing a note within. Emilia, this early visit looks as if some kind jealousy would not let you rest at home.

EMILIA: The knowledge I have of my rival gives me a little cause to fear your constancy.

YOUNG BELLAIR: My constancy! I vow—

EMILIA: Do not vow. Our love is frail as is our life and full as little in our power; and are you sure you shall outlive this day?

YOUNG BELLAIR: I am not; but when we are in perfect health, 'twere an idle thing to fright ourselves with the thoughts of sudden death.

LADY TOWNLEY: Pray, what has passed between you and your father i'the garden?

YOUNG BELLAIR: He's firm in his resolution, tells me I must marry Mrs. Harriet, or swears he'll marry himself and disinherit me. When I saw I could not prevail with him to be more indulgent, I dissembled an obedience to his will, which has composed his passion and will give us time—and, I hope, opportunity—to deceive him.

(*Enter* OLD BELLAIR *with a note in his hand.*)

LADY TOWNLEY: Peace, here he comes!

OLD BELLAIR: Harry, take this and let your man carry it for me to Mr. Fourbe's° chamber, my lawyer i'the Temple.° (*Exit* YOUNG BELLAIR.) (*to* EMILIA) Neighbor, a dod! I am glad to see thee here.— Make much of her, sister; she's one of the best of your acquaintance. I like her countenance and her behavior well; she has a modesty that is not common i'this age, a dod, she has!

LADY TOWNLEY: I know her value, brother, and esteem her accordingly.

OLD BELLAIR: Advise her to wear a little more mirth in her face; a dod, she's too serious.

LADY TOWNLEY: The fault is very excusable in a young woman.

OLD BELLAIR: Nay, a dod, I like her ne'er the worse. A melancholy beauty has her charms. I love a pretty sadness in a face, which varies now and then, like changeable colors, into a smile.

LADY TOWNLEY: Methinks you speak very feelingly, brother.

OLD BELLAIR: I am but five and fifty, sister, you know—an age not altogether unsensible.—(*to* EMILIA) Cheer up, sweetheart! I have a secret to tell thee may chance to make thee merry. We three will make collation together anon; i'the meantime, mum, I can't abide you! go, I can't abide you!

(*Enter* YOUNG BELLAIR.)

—Harry, come! you must along with me to my Lady Woodvill's.—I am going to slip the boy at° a mistress.

YOUNG BELLAIR: At a wife, sir, you would say.

OLD BELLAIR: You need not look so glum, sir; a wife is no curse when she brings the blessing of a good estate with her; but an idle town flirt, with a painted face, a rotten reputation, and a crazy fortune, a dod! is the devil and all, and such a one I hear you are in league with.

YOUNG BELLAIR: I cannot help detraction, sir.

OLD BELLAIR: Out! 'A pize° o' their breeches, there are keeping fools° enough for such flaunting baggages, and they are e'en too good for 'em.— (*to* EMILIA) Remember 'night. Go, y'are a rogue, y'are a rogue! Fare you well, fare you well!—(*to* YOUNG BELLAIR) Come, come, come along, sir!

(*Exeunt* OLD *and* YOUNG BELLAIR.)

Fourbe's, "Fourbe" is a "label" name, meaning a cheat. **Temple,** the center of the life in the legal profession in London, lying between Fleet Street and the Thames. **slip . . . at,** release the boy in pursuit of (a hunting term). **pize,** a meaningless imprecation of uncertain origin. **keeping fools,** i.e., keepers of mistresses.

LADY TOWNLEY: On my word, the old man comes on apace; I'll lay my life he's smitten.

EMILIA: This is nothing but the pleasantness of his humor.

LADY TOWNLEY: I know him better than you. Let it work; it may prove lucky.

(*Enter a* PAGE.)

PAGE: Madam, Mr. Medley has sent to know whether a visit will not be troublesome this afternoon.

LADY TOWNLEY: Send him word his visits never are so.

(*Exit* PAGE.)

EMILIA: He's a very pleasant man.

LADY TOWNLEY: He's a very necessary man among us women; he's not scandalous i'the least, perpetually contriving to bring good company together, and always ready to stop up a gap at ombre; then, he knows all the little news o'the town.

EMILIA: I love to hear him talk o'the intrigues; let 'em be never so dull in themselves, he'll make 'em pleasant i'the relation.

LADY TOWNLEY: But he improves things so much one can take no measure of the truth from him. Mr. Dorimant swears a flea or a maggot is not made more monstrous by a magnifying glass than a story is by his telling it.

(*Enter* MEDLEY.)

EMILIA: Hold, here he comes.

LADY TOWNLEY: Mr. Medley.

MEDLEY: Your servant, madam.

LADY TOWNLEY: You have made yourself a stranger of late.

EMILIA: I believe you took a surfeit of ombre last time you were here.

MEDLEY: Indeed, I had my belly full of that termagant, Lady Dealer. There never was so unsatiable a carder;° an old gleeker° never loved to sit to't like her. I have played with her now at least a dozen times till she 'as worn out all her fine complexion and her tour° would keep in curl no longer.

LADY TOWNLEY: Blame her not, poor woman; she loves nothing so well as a black ace.°

MEDLEY: The pleasure I have seen her in when she has had hope in drawing for a matadore!

EMILIA: 'Tis as pretty sport to her as persuading masks off is to you, to make discoveries.

LADY TOWNLEY: Pray, where's your friend Mr. Dorimant?

MEDLEY: Soliciting his affairs; he's a man of great employment—has more mistresses now depending than the most eminent lawyer in England has causes.°

EMILIA: Here has been Mrs. Loveit so uneasy and out of humor these two days.

LADY TOWNLEY: How strangely love and jealousy rage in that poor woman!

MEDLEY: She could not have picked out a devil upon earth so proper to torment her; h'as made her break a dozen or two of fans already, tear half a score points° in pieces, and destroy hoods and knots° without number.

LADY TOWNLEY: We heard of a pleasant serenade he gave her t'other night.

MEDLEY: A Danish serenade with kettle-drums and trumpets.

EMILIA: Oh, barbarous!

MEDLEY: What! You are of the number of the ladies whose ears are grown so delicate since our operas you can be charmed with nothing but *flûtes douces*° and French hautboys?°

EMILIA: Leave your raillery, and tell us, is there any new wit come forth—songs or novels?

MEDLEY: A very pretty piece of gallantry, by an eminent author, called *The Diversions of Bruxelles,*° very necessary to be read by all old ladies who are desirous to improve themselves at questions and commands, blindman's buff, and the like fashionable recreations.

EMILIA: Oh, ridiculous!

MEDLEY: Then there is *The Art of Affectation,* written by a late beauty of quality, teaching you how to draw up your breasts, stretch up your neck, to thrust out your breech, to play with your head, to toss up your nose, to bite your lips, to turn up your eyes, to speak in a silly, soft tone of a voice, and use all the foolish French words that will infallibly make your person and conversation charming; with a short apology at the latter end in the behalf of young ladies who notoriously wash° and paint though they have naturally good complexions.

EMILIA: What a deal of stuff you tell us!

MEDLEY: Such as the town affords, madam. The Russians, hearing the great respect we have for foreign dancing, have lately sent over some of their best balladines,° who are now practising a famous ballet which will be suddenly° danced at

---

carder, card-player.   *gleeker,* player of gleek (an old card game).   *tour,* a crescent-shaped front of false hair. *black ace,* in the game of ombre the black aces were two of the three highest trumps, which were known as "matadores."

causes, cases.   *score points,* lace kerchiefs.   *knots,* bows of ribbon.   *flûtes douces,* high-pitched flutes.   *hautboys,* oboes.   *The Diversions of Bruxelles,* this book, and that named by Medley in his next speech, appear to be the creations of his imagination.   *who ... wash,* use cosmetic washes.   *balladines,* ballet dancers.   *suddenly,* shortly.

the Bear Garden.°

LADY TOWNLEY: Pray, forbear your idle stories, and give us an account of the state of love as it now stands.

MEDLEY: Truly, there has been some revolutions in those affairs—great chopping and changing among the old, and some new lovers whom malice, indiscretion, and misfortune have luckily brought into play.

LADY TOWNLEY: What think you of walking into the next room and sitting down before you engage in this business?

MEDLEY: I wait upon you, and I hope (though women are commonly unreasonable) by the plenty of scandal I shall discover, to give you very good content, ladies. (Exeunt.)

ACT 2 / SCENE 2

(MRS. LOVEIT's lodgings)

(Enter MRS. LOVEIT and PERT. MRS. LOVEIT putting up a letter, then pulling out her pocket-glass and looking in it.)

MRS. LOVEIT: Pert.

PERT: Madam?

MRS. LOVEIT: I hate myself, I look so ill today.

PERT: Hate the wicked cause on't, that base man Mr. Dorimant, who makes you torment and vex yourself continually.

MRS. LOVEIT: He is to blame, indeed.

PERT: To blame to be two days without sending, writing, or coming near you, contrary to his oath and covenant! 'Twas to much purpose to make him swear! I'll lay my life there's not an article but he has broken—talked to the vizards i'the pit, waited upon the ladies from the boxes to their coaches, gone behind the scenes, and fawned upon those little insignificant creatures, the players. 'Tis impossible for a man of his inconstant temper to forbear, I'm sure.

MRS. LOVEIT: I know he is a devil, but he has something of the angel yet undefaced in him, which makes him so charming and agreeable that I must love him, be he never so wicked.

PERT: I little thought, madam, to see your spirit tamed to this degree, who banished poor Mr. Lackwit but for taking up another lady's fan in your presence.

MRS. LOVEIT: My knowing of such odious fools contributes to the making of me love Dorimant the better.

PERT: Your knowing of Mr. Dorimant, in my mind, should rather make you hate all mankind.

MRS. LOVEIT: So it does, besides himself.

PERT: Pray, what excuse does he make in this letter?

MRS. LOVEIT: He has had business.

PERT: Business in general terms would not have been a current excuse for another. A modish man is always very busy when he is in pursuit of a new mistress.

MRS. LOVEIT: Some fop has bribed you to rail at him. He had business; I will believe it, and will forgive him.

PERT: You may forgive him anything, but I shall never forgive him his turning me into ridicule, as I hear he does.

MRS. LOVEIT: I perceive you are of the number of those fools his wit has made his enemies.

PERT: I am of the number of those he's pleased to rally, madam, and if we may believe Mr. Wagfan and Mr. Caperwell, he sometimes makes merry with yourself too, among his laughing companions.

MRS. LOVEIT: Blockheads are as malicious to witty men as ugly women are to the handsome; 'tis their interest, and they make it their business to defame 'em.

PERT: I wish Mr. Dorimant would not make it his business to defame you.

MRS. LOVEIT: Should he, I had rather be made infamous by him than owe my reputation to the dull discretion of those fops you talk of.

(Enter BELLINDA.)

—Bellinda! (Running to her.)

BELLINDA: My dear!

MRS. LOVEIT: You have been unkind of late.

BELLINDA: Do not say unkind—say unhappy.

MRS. LOVEIT: I could chide you. Where have you been these two days?

BELLINDA: Pity me rather, my dear; where I have been so tired with two or three country gentlewomen, whose conversation has been more unsufferable than a country fiddle.

MRS. LOVEIT: Are they relations?

BELLINDA: No; Welsh acquaintance I made when I was last year at St. Winifred's.° They have asked me a thousand questions of the modes and intrigues of the town, and I have told 'em almost as many things for news that hardly were so when their gowns were in fashion.

MRS. LOVEIT: Provoking creatures! How could you endure 'em?

BELLINDA (aside): Now to carry on my plot. Nothing but love could make me capable of so much falsehood. 'Tis time to begin, lest Dorimant

---

Bear Garden, there were several bear-gardens, used not only for bear-baiting, but for other entertainments. It is not clear which one is referred to here.

St. Winifred's, St. Winifred's Well, a famed miraculous spring in Flintshire, Wales, near the modern Holywell.

should come before her jealousy has stung her.—(*Laughs, and then speaks on.*) I was yesterday at a play with 'em, where I was fain to show 'em the living as the man at Westminster does the dead: 'That is Mrs. Such-a-one, admired for her beauty; that is Mr. Such-a-one, cried up for a wit; that is sparkish Mr. Such-a-one, who keeps reverend Mrs. Such-a-one; and there sits fine Mrs. Such-a-one who was lately cast off by my Lord Such-a-one.'

MRS. LOVEIT: Did you see Dorimant there?

BELLINDA: I did, and imagine you were there with him and have no mind to own it.

MRS. LOVEIT: What should make you think so?

BELLINDA: A lady masked in a pretty *déshabillé*, whom Dorimant entertained with more respect than the gallants do a common vizard.

MRS. LOVEIT (*aside*): Dorimant at the play entertaining a mask! Oh, heavens!

BELLINDA (*aside*): Good!

MRS. LOVEIT: Did he stay all the while?

BELLINDA: Till the play was done, and then led her out, which confirms me it was you.

MRS. LOVEIT: Traitor!

PERT: Now you may believe he had business, and you may forgive him too.

MRS. LOVEIT: Ingrateful, perjured man!

BELLINDA: You seem so much concerned, my dear, I fear I have told you unawares what I had better have concealed for your quiet.

MRS. LOVEIT: What manner of shape had she?

BELLINDA: Tall and slender. Her motions were very genteel; certainly she must be some person of condition.

MRS. LOVEIT: Shame and confusion be ever in her face when she shows it!

BELLINDA: I should blame your discretion for loving that wild man, my dear, but they say he has a way so bewitching that few can defend their hearts who know him.

MRS. LOVEIT: I will tear him from mine or die i'the attempt.

BELLINDA: Be more moderate.

MRS. LOVEIT: Would I had daggers, darts, or poisoned arrows in my breast, so I could but remove the thoughts of him from thence!

BELLINDA: Fie, fie! your transports are too violent, my dear; this may be but an accidental gallantry, and 'tis likely ended at her coach.

PERT: Should it proceed farther, let your comfort be, the conduct Mr. Dorimant affects will quickly make you know your rival, ten to one let you see her ruined, her reputation exposed to the town—a happiness none will envy her but yourself, madam.

MRS. LOVEIT: Whoe'er she be, all the harm I wish her is, may she love him as well as I do and may he give her as much cause to hate him.

PERT: Never doubt the latter end of your curse, madam.

MRS. LOVEIT: May all the passions that are raised by neglected love—jealousy, indignation, spite, and thirst of revenge—eternally rage in her soul, as they do now in mine. (*Walks up and down with a distracted air.*)

(*Enter a* PAGE.)

PAGE: Madam, Master Dorimant—

MRS. LOVEIT: I will not see him.

PAGE: I told him you were within, madam.

MRS. LOVEIT: Say you lied—say I'm busy—shut the door—say anything!

PAGE: He's here, madam.

(*Enter* DORIMANT.)

DORIMANT: They taste of death who do at heaven arrive;
But we this paradise approach alive.

(*to* MISTRESS LOVEIT) What, dancing *The Galloping Nag*° without a fiddle? (*Offers to catch her by the hand; she flings away and walks on. He, pursuing her.*) I fear this restlessness of the body, madam, proceeds from an unquietness of the mind. What unlucky accident puts you out of humor? A point ill washed, knots spoiled i'the making up, hair shaded awry, or some other little mistake in setting you in order?

PERT: A trifle, in my opinion, sir, more inconsiderable than any you mention.

DORIMANT: O Mrs. Pert! I never knew you sullen enough to be silent; come, let me know the business.

PERT: The business, sir, is the business that has taken you up these two days. How have I seen you laugh at men of business, and now to become a man of business yourself!

DORIMANT: We are not masters of our affections; our inclinations daily alter: now we love pleasure, and anon we shall dote on business. Human frailty will have it so, and who can help it?

MRS. LOVEIT: Faithless, inhuman, barbarous man—

DORIMANT (*aside*): Good! Now the alarm strikes.

MRS. LOVEIT: Without sense of love, of honor, or of gratitude, tell me, for I will know, what devil masked she was you were with at the play yesterday?

DORIMANT: Faith, I resolved as much as you, but the devil was obstinate and would not tell me.

MRS. LOVEIT: False in this as in your vows to me!—you do know.

DORIMANT: The truth is, I did all I could to know.

The Galloping Nag, a country dance.

MRS. LOVEIT: And dare you own it to my face? Hell and furies! *(Tears her fan in pieces.)*

DORIMANT: Spare your fan, madam; you are growing hot and will want it to cool you.

MRS. LOVEIT: Horror and distraction seize you! Sorrow and remorse gnaw your soul, and punish all your perjuries to me! *(Weeps.)*

DORIMANT *(turning to BELLINDA):*

So thunder breaks the cloud in twain
And makes a passage for the rain.

(to BELLINDA) Bellinda, you are the devil that have raised this storm; you were at the play yesterday and have been making discoveries to your dear.

BELLINDA: Y'are the most mistaken man i'the world.

DORIMANT: It must be so, and here I vow revenge—resolve to pursue and persecute you more impertinently than ever any loving fop did his mistress, hunt you i'the Park,° trace you i'the Mail,° dog you in every visit you make, haunt you at the plays and i'the drawing-room, hang my nose in your neck and talk to you whether you will or no, and ever look upon you with such dying eyes till your friends grow jealous of me, send you out of town, and the world suspect your reputation.—*(in a lower voice.)* At my Lady Townley's when we go from hence. *(He looks kindly on BELLINDA.)*

BELLINDA: I'll meet you there.

DORIMANT: Enough.

MRS. LOVEIT *(pushing DORIMANT away):* Stand off! You sha' not stare upon her so.

DORIMANT: Good; there's one made jealous already.

MRS. LOVEIT: Is this the constancy you vowed?

DORIMANT: Constancy at my years! 'Tis not a virtue in season; you might as well expect the fruit the autumn ripens i'the spring.

MRS. LOVEIT: Monstrous principle!

DORIMANT: Youth has a long journey to go, madam; should I have set up my rest° at the first inn I lodged at, I should never have arrived at the happiness I now enjoy.

MRS. LOVEIT: Dissembler, damned dissembler!

DORIMANT: I am so, I confess: good nature and good manners corrupt me. I am honest in my inclinations, and would not, wer't not to avoid offence,

make a lady a little in years believe I think her young, willfully mistake art for nature, and seem as fond of a thing I am weary of as when I doted on't in earnest.

MRS. LOVEIT: False man!

DORIMANT: True woman!

MRS. LOVEIT: Now you begin to show yourself.

DORIMANT: Love gilds us over and makes us show fine things to one another for a time, but soon the gold wears off and then again the native brass appears.

MRS. LOVEIT: Think on your oaths, your vows, and protestations, perjured man!

DORIMANT: I made 'em when I was in love.

MRS. LOVEIT: And therefore ought they not to bind? Oh, impious!

DORIMANT: What we swear at such a time may be a certain proof of a present passion, but to say truth, in love there is no security to be given for the future.

MRS. LOVEIT: Horrid and ingrateful, begone, and never see me more!

DORIMANT: I am not one of those troublesome coxcombs, who, because they were once well received, take the privilege to plague a woman with their love ever after. I shall obey you, madam, though I do myself some violence.

(He offers to go and MRS. LOVEIT pulls him back.)

MRS. LOVEIT: Come back! You sha' not go! Could you have the ill-nature to offer it?

DORIMANT: When love grows diseased, the best thing we can do is to put it to a violent death. I cannot endure the torture of a ling'ring and consumptive passion.

MRS. LOVEIT: Can you think mine sickly?

DORIMANT: Oh, 'tis desperately ill. What worse symptoms are there than your being always uneasy when I visit you, your picking quarrels with me on slight occasions, and in my absence kindly list'ning to the impertinences of every fashionable fool that talks to you?

MRS. LOVEIT: What fashionable fool can you lay to my charge?

DORIMANT: Why, the very cock-fool of all those fools—Sir Fopling Flutter.

MRS. LOVEIT: I never saw him in my life but once.

DORIMANT: The worse woman you, at first sight to put on all your charms, to entertain him with that softness in your voice, and all that wanton kindness in your eyes you so notoriously affect when you design a conquest.

MRS. LOVEIT: So damned a lie did never malice yet invent. Who told you this?

DORIMANT: No matter. That ever I should love a woman that can dote on a senseless caper, a tawdry French ribband, and a formal cravat!

Park, probably referring to Hyde Park, which was more fashionable than St. James's Park at this time. **Mail,** the Mall (to use the more common spelling) was a long tract in St. James's Park originally laid out for playing the game of paille-maille (pall-mall): at this time, and for many years, thereafter, a place of fashionable resort. Not to be confused with Pall Mall, some four hundred yards to the north, where the game was played earlier in the century. **set . . . rest,** taken up my permanent abode.

MRS. LOVEIT: You make me mad.

DORIMANT: A guilty conscience may do much. Go on—be the game-mistress o' the town, and enter° all our young fops as fast as they come from travel.

MRS. LOVEIT: Base and scurrilous!

DORIMANT: A fine mortifying reputation 'twill be for a woman of your pride, wit, and quality!

MRS. LOVEIT: This jealousy's a mere pretence, a cursed trick of your own devising. I know you.

DORIMANT: Believe it and all the ill of me you can: I would not have a woman have the least good thought of me, that can think well of Fopling. Farewell! Fall to, and much good may do you with your coxcomb.

MRS. LOVEIT: Stay, oh stay! and I will tell you all.

DORIMANT: I have been told too much already. (*Exit* DORIMANT.)

MRS. LOVEIT: Call him again!

PERT: E'en let him go—a fair riddance.

MRS. LOVEIT: Run, I say, call him again! I will have him called!

PERT: The devil should carry him away first were it my concern. (*Exit* PERT.)

BELLINDA: H'as frighted me from the very thoughts of loving men. For heaven's sake, my dear, do not discover° what I told you! I dread his tongue as much as you ought to have done his friendship.

(*Enter* PERT.)

PERT: He's gone, madam.

MRS. LOVEIT: Lightning blast him!

PERT: When I told him you desired him to come back, he smiled, made a mouth at me, flung into his coach, and said—

MRS. LOVEIT: What did he say?

PERT: 'Drive away!' and then repeated verses.

MRS. LOVEIT: Would I had made a contract to be a witch when first I entertained this greater devil, monster, barbarian! I could tear myself in pieces. Revenge—nothing but revenge can ease me. Plague, war, famine, fire—all that can bring universal ruin and misery on mankind—with joy I'd perish to have you in my power but this moment. (*Exit* MRS. LOVEIT.)

PERT: Follow, madam; leave her not in this outrageous passion! (PERT *gathers up the things.*)

BELLINDA (*aside*): H'as given me the proof which I desired of his love,
But 'tis a proof of his ill-nature too.
I wish I had not seen him use her so.
I sigh to think that Dorimant may be
One day as faithless and unkind to me. (*Exeunt.*)

ACT 3 / SCENE 1

(LADY WOODVILL's *lodgings*)
(*Enter* HARRIET *and* BUSY, *her woman.*)

BUSY: Dear madam, let me set that curl in order.

HARRIET: Let me alone; I will shake 'em all out of order.

BUSY: Will you never leave this wildness?

HARRIET: Torment me not.

BUSY: Look! There's a knot falling off.

HARRIET: Let it drop.

BUSY: But one pin, dear madam.

HARRIET: How do I daily suffer under thy officious fingers!

BUSY: Ah, the difference that is between you and my Lady Dapper! how uneasy she is if the least thing be amiss about her!

HARRIET: She is indeed most exact; nothing is ever wanting to make her ugliness remarkable.

BUSY: Jeering people say so.

HARRIET: Her powdering, painting, and her patching never fail in public to draw the tongues and eyes of all the men upon her.

BUSY: She is, indeed, a little too pretending.

HARRIET: That woman should set up for beauty as much in spite of nature as some men have done for wit!

BUSY: I hope without offence one may endeavor to make one's self agreeable.

HARRIET: Not when 'tis impossible. Women then ought to be no more fond of dressing than fools should be of talking; hoods and modesty, masks and silence, things that shadow and conceal— they should think of nothing else.

BUSY: Jesu! Madam, what will your mother think is become of you? For heaven's sake go in again!

HARRIET: I won't.

BUSY: This is the extravagant'st thing that ever you did in your life, to leave her and a gentleman who is to be your husband.

HARRIET: My husband! Hast thou so little wit to think I spoke what I meant when I overjoyed her in the country with a low curtsey and 'What you please, madam; I shall ever be obedient'?

BUSY: Nay, I know not, you have so many fetches.°

HARRIET: And this was one, to get her up to London. Nothing else, I assure thee.

BUSY: Well, the man, in my mind, is a fine man.

HARRIET: The man indeed wears his clothes fashionably and has a pretty, negligent way with him, very courtly and much affected; he bows, and talks, and smiles so agreeably, as he thinks.

BUSY: I never saw anything so genteel.

HARRIET: Varnished over with good breeding, many

---

enter, initiate.   *discover*, disclose.

fetches, tricks.

a blockhead makes a tolerable show.

BUSY: I wonder you do not like him.

HARRIET: I think I might be brought to endure him, and that is all a reasonable woman should expect in a husband; but there is duty i'the case, and like the haughty Merab, I

Find much aversion in my stubborn mind,

Which

Is bred by being promised and designed.

BUSY: I wish you do not design your own ruin. I partly guess your inclinations, madam—that Mr. Dorimant—

HARRIET: Leave your prating and sing some foolish song or other.

BUSY: I will—the song you love so well ever since you saw Mr. Dorimant. (Sings.)

SONG

When first Amintas charmed my heart,
My heedless sheep began to stray;
The wolves soon stole the greatest part,
And all will now be made a prey.

Ah, let not love your thoughts possess,
'Tis fatal to a shepherdess;
The dang'rous passion you must shun,
Or else like me be quite undone.

HARRIET: Shall I be paid down by a covetous parent for a purchase? I need no land; no, I'll lay myself out all in love. It is decreed—

(*Enter* YOUNG BELLAIR.)

YOUNG BELLAIR: What generous resolution are you making, madam?

HARRIET: Only to be disobedient, sir.

YOUNG BELLAIR: Let me join hands with you in that—

HARRIET: With all my heart; I never thought I should have given you mine so willingly. Here I, Harriet—

YOUNG BELLAIR: And I, Harry—

HARRIET: Do solemnly protest—

YOUNG BELLAIR: And vow—

HARRIET: That I with you—

YOUNG BELLAIR: And I with you—

BOTH: Will never marry.

HARRIET: A match!

YOUNG BELLAIR: And no match! How do you like this indifference now?

HARRIET: You expect I should take it ill, I see.

YOUNG BELLAIR: 'Tis not unnatural for you women to be a little angry: you miss a conquest, though you

would slight the poor man were he in your power.

HARRIET: There are some, it may be, have an eye like Bart'lomew°—big enough for the whole fair; but I am not of the number, and you may keep your gingerbread. 'Twill be more acceptable to the lady whose dear image it wears, sir.

YOUNG BELLAIR: I must confess, madam, you came a day after the fair.

HARRIET: You own then you are in love?

YOUNG BELLAIR: I do.

HARRIET: The confidence is generous, and in return I could almost find in my heart to let you know my inclinations.

YOUNG BELLAIR: Are you in love?

HARRIET: Yes, with this dear town, to that degree I can scarce endure the country in landscapes and in hangings.

YOUNG BELLAIR: What a dreadful thing 'twould be to be hurried back to Hampshire!

HARRIET: Ah, name it not!

YOUNG BELLAIR: As for us, I find we shall agree well enough. Would we could do something to deceive the grave people!

HARRIET: Could we delay their quick proceeding, 'twere well. A reprieve is a good step towards the getting of a pardon.

YOUNG BELLAIR: If we give over the game, we are undone. What think you of playing it on booty?°

HARRIET: What do you mean?

YOUNG BELLAIR: Pretend to be in love with one another; 'twill make some dilatory excuses we may feign pass the better.

HARRIET: Let us do't, if it be but for the dear pleasure of dissembling.

YOUNG BELLAIR: Can you play your part?

HARRIET: I know not what it is to love, but I have made pretty remarks° by being now and then where lovers meet. Where did you leave their gravities?

YOUNG BELLAIR: I'th' next room. Your mother was censuring our modern gallant.

(*Enter* OLD BELLAIR *and* LADY WOODVILL.)

HARRIET: Peace! here they come. I will lean against this wall and look bashfully down upon my fan, while you, like an amorous spark, modishly entertain me.

LADY WOODVILL (*to* OLD BELLAIR): Never go about to

Bart'lomew, Bartholomew Fair, held annually in Smithfield, in the eastern quarter of London, for several days about St. Bartholomew's Day (Aug. 24), was extensive and popular. **playing on booty,** gamesters who joined together secretly to swindle a third player and divide the gains. **remarks,** observations.

excuse 'em; come, come, it was not so when I was a young woman.

OLD BELLAIR: A dod, they're something disrespectful—

LADY WOODVILL: Quality was then considered, and not rallied by every fleering° fellow.

OLD BELLAIR: Youth will have its jest—a dod, it will.

LADY WOODVILL: 'Tis good breeding now to be civil to none but players and Exchange women;° they are treated by 'em as much above their condition as others are below theirs.

OLD BELLAIR: Out! a pize on 'em! talk no more. The rogues ha' got an ill habit of preferring beauty no matter where they find it.

LADY WOODVILL: See your son and my daughter; they have improved their acquaintance since they were within.

OLD BELLAIR: A dod, methinks they have! let's keep back and observe.

YOUNG BELLAIR (to HARRIET): Now for a look and gestures that may persuade 'em I am saying all the passionate things imaginable—

HARRIET: Your head a little more on one side. Ease yourself on your left leg and play with your right hand.

YOUNG BELLAIR: Thus, is it not?

HARRIET: Now set your right leg firm on the ground, adjust your belt, then look about you.

YOUNG BELLAIR: A little exercising will make me perfect.

HARRIET: Smile, and turn to me again very sparkish.

YOUNG BELLAIR: Will you take your turn and be instructed?

HARRIET: With all my heart!

YOUNG BELLAIR: At one motion play your fan, roll your eyes, and then settle a kind look upon me.

HARRIET: So!

YOUNG BELLAIR: Now spread your fan, look down upon it, and tell° the sticks with a finger.

HARRIET: Very modish!

YOUNG BELLAIR: Clap your hand up to your bosom, hold down your gown. Shrug a little, draw up your breasts, and let 'em fall again gently, with a sigh or two, etc.

HARRIET: By the good instructions you give, I suspect you for one of those malicious observers who watch people's eyes, and from innocent looks make scandalous conclusions.

YOUNG BELLAIR: I know some, indeed, who out of mere love to mischief are as vigilant as jealousy itself, and will give you an account of every glance that passes at a play and i'th' Circle.°

HARRIET: 'Twill not be amiss now to seem a little pleasant.

YOUNG BELLAIR: Clap your fan, then, in both your hands, snatch it to your mouth, smile, and with a lively motion fling your body a little forwards. So! Now spread it, fall back on the sudden, cover your face with it and break out into a loud laughter—take up, look grave, and fall a-fanning of yourself—Admirably well acted!

HARRIET: I think I am pretty apt at these matters.

OLD BELLAIR (to LADY WOODVILL): A dod, I like this well!

LADY WOODVILL: This promises something.

OLD BELLAIR: Come! there is love i'th'case, a dod there is, or will be. What say you, young lady?

HARRIET: All in good time, sir; you expect we should fall to and love as game-cocks fight, as soon as we are set together. A dod, y'are unreasonable!

OLD BELLAIR: A dod, sirrah, I like thy wit well.

(Enter a SERVANT.)

SERVANT: The coach is at the door, madam.

OLD BELLAIR: Go, get you and take the air together.

LADY WOODVILL: Will not you go with us?

OLD BELLAIR: Out! a pize! A dod, I ha' business and cannot. We shall meet at night at my sister Townley's.

YOUNG BELLAIR (aside): He's going to Emilia. I overheard him talk of a collation. (Exeunt.)

ACT 3 / SCENE 2

(LADY TOWNLEY's drawing-room.)
(Enter LADY TOWNLEY, EMILIA, and MR. MEDLEY.)

LADY TOWNLEY: I pity the young lovers we last talked of, though to say truth their conduct has been so indiscreet they deserve to be unfortunate.

MEDLEY: Y'have had an exact account, from the great lady i'th' box down to the little orange wench.

EMILIA: Y'are a living libel, a breathing lampoon. I wonder you are not torn in pieces.

MEDLEY: What think you of setting up an office of intelligence for these matters? The project may get money.

LADY TOWNLEY: You would have great dealings with country ladies.

MEDLEY: More than Muddiman° has with their husbands.

(Enter BELLINDA.)

---

fleering, grimacing. *Exchange women,* shop-women in the New Exchange. *tell,* count. *Circle,* perhaps the reference here is to the inner circle at Court.

Muddiman, Henry Muddiman (1629–1692), editor of the *London Gazette,* and also for some thirty years the author of handwritten news-letters which circulated widely among country gentlemen.

LADY TOWNLEY: Bellinda, what has been become of you? We have not seen you here of late with your friend Mrs. Loveit.

BELLINDA: Dear creature, I left her but now so sadly afflicted!

LADY TOWNLEY: With her old distemper, jealousy!

MEDLEY: Dorimant has played her some new prank.

BELLINDA: Well, that Dorimant is certainly the worst man breathing.

EMILIA: I once thought so.

BELLINDA: And do you not think so still?

EMILIA: No, indeed!

BELLINDA: Oh, Jesu!

EMILIA: The town does him a great deal of injury, and I will never believe what it says of a man I do not know, again, for his sake.

BELLINDA: You make me wonder.

LADY TOWNLEY: He's a very well-bred man.

BELLINDA: But strangely ill-natured.

EMILIA: Then he's a very witty man.

BELLINDA: But a man of no principles.

MEDLEY: Your man of principles is a very fine thing, indeed.

BELLINDA: To be preferred to men of parts by women who have regard to their reputation and quiet. Well, were I minded to play the fool, he should be the last man I'd think of.

MEDLEY: He has been the first in many ladies' favors, though you are so severe, madam.

LADY TOWNLEY: What he may be for a lover, I know not; but he's a very pleasant acquaintance, I am sure.

BELLINDA: Had you seen him use Mrs. Loveit as I have done, you would never endure him more.

EMILIA: What, he has quarreled with her again!

BELLINDA: Upon the slightest occasion; he's jealous of Sir Fopling.

LADY TOWNLEY: She never saw him in her life but yesterday, and that was here.

EMILIA: On my conscience, he's the only man in town that's her aversion! How horribly out of humor she was all the while he talked to her!

BELLINDA: And somebody has wickedly told him—

EMILIA: Here he comes.

(Enter DORIMANT.)

MEDLEY: Dorimant! you are luckily come to justify yourself: here's a lady—

BELLINDA: —Has a word or two to say to you from a disconsolate person.

DORIMANT: You tender your reputation too much, I know, madam, to whisper with me before this good company.

BELLINDA: To serve Mrs. Loveit I'll make a bold venture.

DORIMANT: Here's Medley, the very spirit of scandal.

BELLINDA: No matter!

EMILIA: 'Tis something you are unwilling to hear, Mr. Dorimant.

LADY TOWNLEY: Tell him, Bellinda, whether he will or no.

BELLINDA: Mrs. Loveit—

DORIMANT: Softly! these are laughers; you do not know 'em.

BELLINDA *(to* DORIMANT *apart)*: In a word, y'ave made me hate you, which I thought you never could have done.

DORIMANT: In obeying your commands.

BELLINDA: 'Twas a cruel part you played. How could you act it?

DORIMANT: Nothing is cruel to a man who could kill himself to please you. Remember five o'clock tomorrow morning!

BELLINDA: I tremble when you name it.

DORIMANT: Be sure you come!

BELLINDA: I sha'not.

DORIMANT: Swear you will!

BELLINDA: I dare not.

DORIMANT: Swear, I say!

BELLINDA: By my life—by all the happiness I hope for—

DORIMANT: You will.

BELLINDA: I will!

DORIMANT: Kind!

BELLINDA: I am glad I've sworn. I vow I think I should ha' failed you else!

DORIMANT: Surprisingly kind! In what temper did you leave Loveit?

BELLINDA: Her raving was prettily over, and she began to be in a brave way of defying you and all your works. Where have you been since you went from thence?

DORIMANT: I looked in at the play.

BELLINDA: I have promised, and must return to her again.

DORIMANT: Persuade her to walk in the Mail this evening.

BELLINDA: She hates the place and will not come.

DORIMANT: Do all you can to prevail with her.

BELLINDA: For what purpose?

DORIMANT: Sir Fopling will be here anon; I'll prepare him to set upon her there before me.

BELLINDA: You persecute her too much, but I'll do all you'll ha' me.

DORIMANT *(aloud)*: Tell her plainly 'tis grown so dull a business I can drudge on no longer.

EMILIA: There are afflictions in love, Mr. Dorimant.

DORIMANT: You women make 'em, who are commonly as unreasonable in that as you are at play—without the advantage be on your side, a man can never quietly give over when he's weary.

MEDLEY: If you would play without being obliged to complaisance, Dorimant, you should play in public places.

DORIMANT: Ordinaries° were a very good thing for that, but gentlemen do not of late frequent 'em. The deep play is now in private houses.

(BELLINDA *offering to steal away*.)

LADY TOWNLEY: Bellinda, are you leaving us so soon?

BELLINDA: I am to go to the park with Mrs. Loveit, madam. (*Exit* BELLINDA.)

LADY TOWNLEY: This confidence° will go nigh to spoil this young creature.

MEDLEY: 'Twill do her good, madam. Young men who are brought up under practicing lawyers prove the abler counsel when they come to be called to the bar themselves.

DORIMANT: The town has been very favorable to you this afternoon, my Lady Townley; you use to have an *embarras*° of chair and coaches at your door, an uproar of footmen in your hall, and a noise of fools above here.

LADY TOWNLEY: Indeed, my house is the general rendezvous, and next to the playhouse is the common refuge of all the young idle people.

EMILIA: Company is a very good thing, madam, but I wonder you do not love it a little more chosen.

LADY TOWNLEY: 'Tis good to have an universal taste; we should love wit, but for variety be able to divert ourselves with the extravagancies of those who want it.

MEDLEY: Fools will make you laugh.

EMILIA: For once or twice, but the repetition of their folly after a visit or two grows tedious and unsufferable.

LADY TOWNLEY: You are a little too delicate, Emilia.

(*Enter a* PAGE.)

PAGE: Sir Fopling Flutter, madam, desires to know if you are to be seen.

LADY TOWNLEY: Here's the freshest fool in town, and one who has not cloyed you yet.—Page!

PAGE: Madam!

LADY TOWNLEY: Desire him to walk up. (*Exit* PAGE.)

DORIMANT: Do not you fall on him, Medley, and snub him. Soothe him up in his extravagance; he will show the better.

MEDLEY: You know I have a natural indulgence for fools and need not this caution, sir.

(*Enter* SIR FOPLING FLUTTER *with his Page after him*.)

SIR FOPLING FLUTTER: Page, wait without. (*to* LADY TOWNLEY) Madam, I kiss your hands. I see yesterday was nothing of chance; the *belles assemblées*° form themselves here every day. (*to*

EMILIA) Lady, your servant.—Dorimant, let me embrace thee! Without lying, I have not met with any of my acquaintance who retain so much of Paris as thou dost—the very air thou hadst when the marquise mistook thee i'th' Tuileries and cried, 'Hey, Chevalier!' and then begged thy pardon.

DORIMANT: I would fain wear in fashion as long as I can, sir; 'tis a thing to be valued in men as well as baubles.

SIR FOPLING FLUTTER: Thou art a man of wit and understands the town. Prithee, let thee and I be intimate; there is no living without making some good man the confidant of our pleasures.

DORIMANT: 'Tis true! but there is no man so improper for such a business as I am.

SIR FOPLING FLUTTER: Prithee, why hast thou so modest an opinion of thyself?

DORIMANT: Why, first, I could never keep a secret in my life; and then, there is no charm so infallibly makes me fall in love with a woman as my knowing a friend loves her. I deal honestly with you.

SIR FOPLING FLUTTER: Thy humor's very gallant, or let me perish! I knew a French count so like thee!

LADY TOWNLEY: Wit, I perceive, has more power over you than beauty, Sir Fopling, else you would not have let this lady stand so long neglected.

SIR FOPLING FLUTTER (*to* EMILIA): A thousand pardons, madam; some civility's due of course upon the meeting of a long absent friend. The *éclat*° of so much beauty, I confess, ought to have charmed me sooner.

EMILIA: The *brillant*° of so much good language, sir, has much more power than the little beauty I can boast.

SIR FOPLING FLUTTER: I never saw anything prettier than this high work on your *point d'Espagne*.°

EMILIA: 'Tis not so rich as *point de Venise*.

SIR FOPLING FLUTTER: Not altogether, but looks cooler and is more proper for the season.— Dorimant, is not that Medley?

DORIMANT: The same, sir.

SIR FOPLING FLUTTER: Forgive me, sir; in this *embarras*° of civilities I could not come to have you in my arms sooner. You understand an equipage° the best of any man in town, I hear.

MEDLEY: By my own you would not guess it.

SIR FOPLING FLUTTER: There are critics who do not write, sir.

MEDLEY: Our peevish poets will scarce allow it.

SIR FOPLING FLUTTER: Damn 'em, they'll allow no man

___

Ordinaries, taverns. *confidence*, intimacy. *embarras*, blockade. *belles assemblées*, gatherings of fashionable people.

éclat, splendor. *brillant*, brilliance. *point d'Espagne*, point lace. *embarras*, crush. *equipage*, retinue of personal attendants.

wit who does not play the fool like themselves and show it! Have you taken notice of the galleshº I brought over?

MEDLEY: Oh, yes! 't has quite another air than th' English makes.

SIR FOPLING FLUTTER: 'Tis as easily known from an English tumbrilº as an Inns of courtº man is from one of us.

DORIMANT: True; there is a bel airº in galleshes as well as men.

MEDLEY: But there are few so delicate to observe it.

SIR FOPLING FLUTTER: The world is generally very grossierº here, indeed.

LADY TOWNLEY (to EMILIA): He's very fine.

EMILIA: Extreme proper.º

SIR FOPLING FLUTTER (overhearing): A slight suit I made to appear in at my first arrival—not worthy your consideration, ladies.

DORIMANT: The pantaloon is very well mounted.

SIR FOPLING FLUTTER: The tassels are new and pretty.

MEDLEY: I never saw a coat better cut.

SIR FOPLING FLUTTER: It makes me show long waisted, and, I think, slender.

DORIMANT: That's the shape our ladies dote on.

MEDLEY: Your breech, though, is a handful too high, in my eye, Sir Fopling.

SIR FOPLING FLUTTER: Peace, Medley! I have wished it lower a thousand times, but a pox on't! 'twill not be.

LADY TOWNSEND: His gloves are well fringed, large, and graceful.

SIR FOPLING FLUTTER: I was always eminent for being bien ganté.º

EMILIA: He wears nothing but what are originals of the most famous hands in Paris.

SIR FOPLING FLUTTER: You are in the right, madam.

LADY TOWNLEY: The suit!

SIR FOPLING FLUTTER: Barroy.º

EMILIA: The garniture!º

SIR FOPLING FLUTTER: Le Gras.

MEDLEY: The shoes!

SIR FOPLING FLUTTER: Piccar.

DORMINANT: The periwig!

SIR FOPLING FLUTTER: Chedreux.

LADY TOWNLEY: } The gloves!
EMILIA:

SIR FOPLING FLUTTER: Orangerie—you know the smell, ladies.—Dorimant, I could find in my heart for an amusement to have a gallantry with some of our English ladies.

DORIMANT: 'Tis a thing no less necessary to confirm the reputation of your wit than a duel will be to satisfy the town of your courage.

SIR FOPLING FLUTTER: Here was a woman yesterday—

DORIMANT: Mistress Loveit.

SIR FOPLING FLUTTER: You have named her.

DORIMANT: You cannot pitch on a better for your purpose.

SIR FOPLING FLUTTER: Prithee, what is she?

DORIMANT: A person of quality, and one who has a restº of reputation enough to make the conquest considerable; besides, I hear she likes you too.

SIR FOPLING FLUTTER: Methoughts she seemed, though, very reserved and uneasy all the time I entertained her.

DORIMANT: Grimace and affectation! You will see her i' th' Mail tonight.

SIR FOPLING FLUTTER: Prithee, let thee and I take the air together.

DORIMANT: I am engaged to Medley, but I'll meet you at Saint James's and give you some information upon the which you may regulate your proceedings.

SIR FOPLING FLUTTER: All the world will be in the Park tonight. Ladies, 'twere pity to keep so much beauty longer within doors and rob the Ringº of all those charms that should adorn it.—Hey, page!

(Enter PAGE.)

See that all my people be ready.

(PAGE goes out again.)

—Dorimant, au revoir. (Exit.)

MEDLEY: A fine, mettled coxcomb.

DORIMANT: Brisk and insipid.

MEDLEY: Pert and dull.

EMILIA: However you despise him, gentlemen, I'll lay my life he passes for a wit with many.

DORIMANT: That may very well be; Nature has her cheats, stumsº a brain, and puts sophisticate dulness often on the tasteless multitude for true wit and good humor. Medley, come!

MEDLEY: I must go a little way; I will meet you i'the Mail.

DORIMANT: I'll walk through the garden thither.—(to the women) We shall meet anon and bow.

LADY TOWNLEY: Not to-night. We are engaged about a business the knowledge of which may make you laugh hereafter.

---

gallesh, caleche, an open carriage. tumbril, a heavy cart. Inns of Court man, lawyer, or other professional man, resident in one of the "Temples." bel air, fashionable mode. grossier, coarse. proper, handsome, elegant. bien ganté, well-gloved. Barroy, this name and those which follow are those of fashionable Parisian tradesmen. garniture, trimmings.

---

rest, remnant. Ring, a circular course in Hyde Park, used for riding and driving. stums, revives (a term usually employed in connection with the reclamation of wine or ale).

MEDLEY: Your servant, ladies.
DORIMANT: 'Au revoir,' as Sir Fopling says.

(*Exeunt* MEDLEY *and* DORIMANT.)

LADY TOWNLEY: The old man will be here immediately.
EMILIA: Let's expect° him i'th' garden.
LADY TOWNLEY: 'Go! you are a rogue.'
EMILIA: 'I can't abide you.' (*Exeunt.*)

ACT 3 / SCENE 3

(*The Mail*)
(*Enter* HARRIET *and* YOUNG BELLAIR, *she pulling him.*)

HARRIET: Come along.
YOUNG BELLAIR: And leave your mother!
HARRIET: Busy will be sent with a hue and cry after us, but that's no matter.
YOUNG BELLAIR: 'Twill look strangely in me.
HARRIET: She'll believe it a freak of mine and never blame your manners.
YOUNG BELLAIR: What reverend acquaintance is that she has met?
HARRIET: A fellow-beauty of the last king's time,° though by the ruins you would hardly guess it. (*Exeunt.*)

(*Enter* DORIMANT *and crosses the stage.*) (*Enter* YOUNG BELLAIR *and* HARRIET.)

YOUNG BELLAIR: By this time your mother is in a fine taking.
HARRIET: If your friend Mr. Dorimant were but here now, that she might find me talking with him!
YOUNG BELLAIR: She does not know him, but dreads him, I hear, of all mankind.
HARRIET: She concludes if he does but speak to a woman, she's undone—is on her knees every day to pray heaven defend me from him.
YOUNG BELLAIR: You do not apprehend him so much as she does?
HARRIET: I never saw anything in him that was frightful.
YOUNG BELLAIR: On the contrary, have you not observed something extreme delightful in his wit and person?
HARRIET: He's agreeable and pleasant, I must own, but he does so much affect being so, he displeases me.
YOUNG BELLAIR: Lord, madam! all he does and says is so easy and so natural.
HARRIET: Some men's verses seem so to the unskillful, but labor i'the one and affectation in the other to the judicious plainly appear.

YOUNG BELLAIR: I never heard him accused of affectation before.

(*Enter* DORIMANT *and stares upon her.*)

HARRIET: It passes on the easy town, who are favorably pleased in him to call it humor.

(*Exeunt* YOUNG BELLAIR *and* HARRIET.)

DORIMANT: 'Tis she! it must be she—that lovely hair, that easy shape, those wanton eyes, and all those melting charms about her mouth which Medley spoke of! I'll follow the lottery and put in for a prize with my friend Bellair. (*Exit* DORIMANT *repeating:*)

In love the victors from the vanquished fly;
They fly that wound, and they pursue that die.

(*Enter* YOUNG BELLAIR *and* HARRIET *and after them* DORIMANT *standing at a distance.*)

YOUNG BELLAIR: Most people prefer High Park° to this place.
HARRIET: It has the better reputation, I confess; but I abominate the dull diversions there—the formal bows, the affected smiles, the silly by-words and amorous tweers° in passing. Here one meets with a little conversation now and then.
YOUNG BELLAIR: These conversations have been fatal to some of your sex, madam.
HARRIET: It may be so; because some who want temper° have been undone by gaming, must others who have it wholly deny themselves the pleasure of play?
DORIMANT (*coming up gently and bowing to her*): Trust me, it were unreasonable, madam.
HARRIET (*she starts and looks grave*): Lord, who's this?
YOUNG BELLAIR: Dorimant!
DORIMANT: Is this the woman your father would have you marry?
YOUNG BELLAIR: It is.
DORIMANT: Her name?
YOUNG BELLAIR: Harriet.
DORIMANT: I am not mistaken; she's handsome.
YOUNG BELLAIR: Talk to her; her wit is better than her face. We were wishing for you but now.
DORIMANT (*to* HARRIET): Overcast with seriousness o'the sudden! A thousand smiles were shining in that face but now; I never saw so quick a change of weather.
HARRIET (*aside*): I feel as great a change within, but he shall never know it.
DORIMANT: You were talking of play, madam. Pray, what may be your stint?°

---

expect, await.   *last king's time*, of the reign of Charles I, which had ended more than a quarter of a century earlier.

High Park, an alternative name for Hyde Park. *tweers*, leers.   *temper*, self-control.   *stint*, pre-determined amount, after the loss of which the gamester intends to cease playing.

HARRIET: A little harmless discourse in public walks, or at most an appointment in a box, barefaced, at the playhouse; you are for masks and private meetings, where women engage for all they are worth, I hear.

DORIMANT: I have been used to deep play, but I can make one at small game when I like my gamester well.

HARRIET: And be so unconcerned you'll ha' no pleasure in't.

DORIMANT: Where there is a considerable sum to be won, the hope of drawing people in makes every trifle considerable.

HARRIET: The sordidness of men's natures, I know, makes 'em willing to flatter and comply with the rich, though they are sure never to be the better for 'em.

DORIMANT: 'Tis in their power to do us good, and we despair not but at some time or other they may be willing.

HARRIET: To men who have fared in this town like you, 'twould be a great mortification to live on hope. Could you keep a Lent for a mistress?

DORIMANT: In expectation of a happy Easter and, though time be very precious, think forty days well lost to gain your favor.

HARRIET: Mr. Bellair, let us walk; 'tis time to leave him. Men grow dull when they begin to be particular.

DORIMANT: Y'are mistaken; flattery will not ensue, though I know y' are greedy of the praises of the whole Mail.

HARRIET: You do me wrong.

DORIMANT: I do not. As I followed you, I observed how you were pleased when the fops cried, 'She's handsome, very handsome! by God she is!' and whispered aloud your name; the thousand several forms you put your face into; then, to make yourself more agreeable, how wantonly you played with your head, flung back your locks, and looked smilingly over your shoulder at 'em!

HARRIET: I do not go begging the men's, as you do the ladies', good liking, with a sly softness in your looks and a gentle slowness in your bows as you pass by 'em—as thus, sir. (Acts him.) Is not this like you?

(Enter LADY WOODVILL and BUSY.)

YOUNG BELLAIR: Your mother, madam.

(Pulls HARRIET; she composes herself.)

LADY WOODVILL: Ah, my dear child Harriet!

BUSY (aside): Now is she so pleased with finding her again she cannot chide her.

LADY WOODVILL: Come away!

DORIMANT: 'Tis now but high Mail,° madam—the

---

high Mail, the busiest hour of the Mall's social activities.

---

most entertaining time of all the evening.

HARRIET: I would fain see that Dorimant, mother, you so cry out of for a monster, he's in the Mail, I hear.

LADY WOODVILL: Come away then! The plague is here and you should dread the infection.

YOUNG BELLAIR: You may be misinformed of the gentleman.

LADY WOODVILL: Oh, no! I hope you do not know him. He is the prince of all the devils in the town—delights in nothing but in rapes and riots!

DORIMANT: If you did but hear him speak, madam!

LADY WOODVILL: Oh, he has a tongue, they say, would tempt the angels to a second fall.

(Enter SIR FOPLING with his equipage, six FOOTMEN and a PAGE.)

SIR FOPLING FLUTTER: Hey! Champagne, Norman, La Rose, La Fleur, La Tour, La Verdure!— Dorimant—

LADY WOODVILL: Here, here he is among this rout! He names him! Come away, Harriet; come away!

(Exeunt LADY WOODVILL, HARRIET, BUSY, and YOUNG BELLAIR.)

DORIMANT: This fool's coming has spoiled all. She's gone, but she has left a pleasing image of herself behind that wanders in my soul—it must not settle there.

SIR FOPLING FLUTTER: What reverie is this? Speak, man!

DORIMANT: Snatcht from myself, how far behind
Already I behold the shore!

(Enter MEDLEY.)

MEDLEY: Dorimant, a discovery! I met with Bellair.

DORIMANT: You can tell me no news, sir; I know all.

MEDLEY: How do you like the daughter?

DORIMANT: You never came so near truth in your life as you did in her description.

MEDLEY: What think you of the mother?

DORIMANT: Whatever I think of her, she thinks very well of me, I find.

MEDLEY: Did she know you?

DORIMANT: She did not; whether she does now or no, I know not. Here was a pleasant scene towards, when in came Sir Fopling, mustering up his equipage, and at the latter end named me and frighted her away.

MEDLEY: Loveit and Bellinda are not far off; I saw 'em alight at St. James's.

DORIMANT: Sir Fopling! hark you, a word or two. (Whispers.) Look you do not want assurance.

SIR FOPLING FLUTTER: I never do on these occasions.

DORIMANT: Walk on; we must not be seen together. Make your advantage of what I have told you. The next turn you will meet the lady.

SIR FOPLING FLUTTER: Hey! Follow me all!

(Exeunt SIR FOPLING *and his equipage.)*

DORIMANT: Medley, you shall see good sport anon between Loveit and this Fopling.

MEDLEY: I thought there was something toward, by that whisper.

DORIMANT: You know a worthy principle of hers?

MEDLEY: Not to be so much as civil to a man who speaks to her in the presence of him she professes to love.

DORIMANT: I have encouraged Fopling to talk to her tonight.

MEDLEY: Now you are here, she will go nigh to beat him.

DORIMANT: In the humor she's in, her love will make her do some very extravagant thing doubtless.

MEDLEY: What was Bellinda's business with you at my Lady Townley's?

DORIMANT: To get me to meet Loveit here in order to an *éclaircissement.*° I made some difficulty of it and have prepared this rencounter to make good my jealousy.

MEDLEY: Here they come.

(Enter MRS. LOVEIT, BELLINDA, *and* PERT.*)*

DORIMANT: I'll meet her and provoke her with a deal of dumb civility in passing by, then turn short and be behind her when Sir Fopling sets upon her—

See how unregarded now
That piece of beauty passes.

(Exeunt DORIMANT *and* MEDLEY.*)*

BELLINDA: How wonderful respectfully he bowed!

PERT: He's always over-mannerly when he has done a mischief.

BELLINDA: Methoughts, indeed, at the same time he had a strange, despising countenance.

PERT: The unlucky look he thinks becomes him.

BELLINDA: I was afraid you would have spoke to him, my dear.

MRS. LOVEIT: I would have died first; he shall no more find me the loving fool he has done.

BELLINDA: You love him still?

MRS. LOVEIT: No!

PERT: I wish you did not.

MRS. LOVEIT: I do not, and I will have you think so.—What made you hale me to this odious place, Bellinda?

BELLINDA: I hate to be hulched up° in a coach; walking is much better.

MRS. LOVEIT: Would we could meet Sir Fopling now!

BELLINDA: Lord, would you not avoid him?

MRS. LOVEIT: I would make him all the advances that may be.

BELLINDA: That would confirm Dorimant's suspicion, my dear.

MRS. LOVEIT: He is not jealous; but I will make him so, and be revenged a way he little thinks on.

BELLINDA *(aside)*: If she should make him jealous, that may make him fond of her again. I must dissuade her from it.—Lord, my dear, this will certainly make him hate you.

MRS. LOVEIT: 'Twill make him uneasy, though he does not care for me. I know the effects of jealousy on men of his proud temper.

BELLINDA: 'Tis a fantastic remedy; its operations are dangerous and uncertain.

MRS. LOVEIT: 'Tis the strongest cordial we can give to dying love: it often brings it back when there's no sign of life remaining. But I design not so much the reviving of his, as my revenge.

(Enter SIR FOPLING *and his equipage.)*

SIR FOPLING FLUTTER: Hey! Bid the coachman send home four of his horses and bring the coach to Whitehall;° I'll walk over the Park.—(*to* MRS. LOVEIT) Madam, the honor of kissing your fair hands is a happiness I missed this afternoon at my Lady Townley's.

MRS. LOVEIT: You were very obliging, Sir Fopling, the last time I saw you there.

SIR FOPLING FLUTTER: The preference was due to your wit and beauty. (*to* BELLINDA) Madam, your servant; there never was so sweet an evening.

BELLINDA: 'T has drawn all the rabble of the town hither.

SIR FOPLING FLUTTER: 'Tis pity there's not an order made that none but the *beau monde* should walk here.

MRS. LOVEIT: 'Twould add much to the beauty of the place. See what a sort° of nasty fellows are coming!

(Enter four ill-fashioned fellows singing:)

'Tis not for kisses alone
So long I have made my address,—

MRS. LOVEIT: Fo! Their periwigs are scented with tobacco so strong—

SIR FOPLING FLUTTER: It overcomes our pulvilio.° Methinks I smell the coffee-house they come from.

1 MAN: Dorimant's convenient,° Madam Loveit.

éclaircissement, understanding. *hulched up,* huddled up like a hunchback.

Whitehall, the palace on the east side of St. James's Park; at this time (and until its destruction by fire in 1698) the royal residence. *sort,* group. *pulvilio,* scented cosmetic powder. *convenient,* mistress.

2 MAN: I like the oily buttock° with her.
3 MAN: What spruce prig° is that?
1 MAN: A caravan° lately come from Paris.
2 MAN: Peace! they smoke.°

(All of them coughing; exeunt singing:)

    There's something else to be done,
    Which you cannot choose but guess.

(Enter DORIMANT and MEDLEY.)

DORIMANT: They're engaged.
MEDLEY: She entertains him as if she liked him!
DORIMANT: Let us go forward—seem earnest in discourse and show ourselves; then you shall see how she'll use him.
BELLINDA: Yonder's Dorimant, my dear.
MRS. LOVEIT *(aside to BELLINDA)*: I see him. He comes insulting, but I will disappoint him in his expectation. *(to SIR FOPLING)* I like this pretty, nice humor of yours, Sir Fopling.—*(to BELLINDA)* With what a loathing eye he looked upon those fellows!
SIR FOPLING FLUTTER: I sat near one of 'em at a play today and was almost poisoned with a pair of cordovan gloves he wears.
MRS. LOVEIT: Oh, filthy cordovan! How I hate the smell! *(Laughs in a loud, affected way.)*
SIR FOPLING FLUTTER: Did you observe, madam, how their cravats hung loose an inch from their neck and what a frightful air it gave 'em?
MRS. LOVEIT: Oh, I took particular notice of one that is always spruced up with a deal of dirty skycolored ribband.
BELLINDA: That's one of the walking flageolets° who haunt the Mail o'nights.
MRS. LOVEIT: Oh, I remember him, h'has a hollow tooth enough to spoil the sweetness of an evening.
SIR FOPLING FLUTTER: I have seen the tallest walk the streets with a dainty pair of boxes° neatly buckled on.
MRS. LOVEIT: And a little foot-boy at his heels, pocket-high, with a flat cap, a dirty face—
SIR FOPLING FLUTTER: And a snotty nose.
MRS. LOVEIT: Oh, odious!—There's many of my own sex with that Holborn equipage° trig° to Gray's Inn° Walks and now and then travel hither on a Sunday.

---

oily buttock, smooth-appearing prostitute. **prig,** top. **caravan,** gull, "easy mark." **smoke,** observe (us). **flageolets,** tall, thin men. **boxes,** presumably pattens or clogs. **Holborn equipage,** middle-class sort of attendance. **trig,** walk briskly. **Gray's Inn,** the gardens of this, one of the Inns of Court, were apparently the middle-class equivalent of the Mall.

MEDLEY *(to DORIMANT)*: She takes no notice of you.
DORIMANT: Damn her! I am jealous of a counterplot.
MRS. LOVEIT: Your liveries are the finest, Sir Fopling—oh, that page! that page is the prettily'st dressed—they are all Frenchmen.
SIR FOPLING FLUTTER: There's one damned English blockhead among 'em; you may know him by his mien.
MRS. LOVEIT: Oh, that's he—that's he! What do you call him?
SIR FOPLING FLUTTER: Hey—I know not what to call him—
MRS. LOVEIT: What's your name?
FOOTMAN: John Trott, madam.
SIR FOPLING FLUTTER: Oh, unsufferable! Trott, Trott, Trott! There's nothing so barbarous as the names of our English servants.—What countryman are you, sirrah?
FOOTMAN: Hampshire, sir.
SIR FOPLING FLUTTER: Then Hampshire be your name. Hey, Hampshire!
MRS. LOVEIT: Oh, that sound—that sound becomes the mouth of a man of quality!
MEDLEY: Dorimant, you look a little bashful on the matter.
DORIMANT: She dissembles better than I thought she could have done.
MEDLEY: You have tempted her with too luscious a bait. She bites at the coxcomb.
DORIMANT: She cannot fall from loving me to that.
MEDLEY: You begin to be jealous in earnest.
DORIMANT: Of one I do not love—
MEDLEY: You did love her.
DORIMANT: The fit has long been over.
MEDLEY: But I have known men fall into dangerous relapses when they have found a woman inclining to another.
DORIMANT *(to himself)*: He guesses the secret of my heart. I am concerned, but dare not show it, lest Bellinda should mistrust all I have done to gain her.
BELLINDA *(aside)*: I have watched his look and find no alteration there. Did he love her, some signs of jealousy would have appeared.
DORIMANT *(to MRS. LOVEIT)*: I hope this happy evening, madam, has reconciled you to the scandalous Mail. We shall have you now hankering° here again—
MRS. LOVEIT: Sir Fopling, will you walk?
SIR FOPLING FLUTTER: I am all obedience, madam.
MRS. LOVEIT: Come along then, and let's agree to be malicious on all the ill-fashioned things we meet.
SIR FOPLING FLUTTER: We'll make a critique on the whole Mail, madam.

---

hankering, loitering about.

MRS. LOVEIT: Bellinda, you shall engage°—

BELLINDA: To the reserve of our friends,° my dear.

MRS. LOVEIT: No! no exceptions!

SIR FOPLING FLUTTER: We'll sacrifice all to our diversion.

MRS. LOVEIT: All—all.

SIR FOPLING FLUTTER: All.

BELLINDA: All? Then let it be.

(*Exeunt* SIR FOPLING, MRS. LOVEIT, BELINDA, *and* PERT, *laughing.*)

MEDLEY: Would you had brought some more of your friends, Dorimant, to have been witnesses of Sir Fopling's disgrace and your triumph.

DORIMANT: 'Twere unreasonable to desire you not to laugh at me; but pray do not expose me to the town this day or two.

MEDLEY: By that time you hope to have regained your credit.

DORIMANT: I know she hates Fopling and only makes use of him in hope to work me on again; had it not been for some powerful considerations which will be removed tomorrow morning, I had made her pluck off this mask and show the passsion that lies panting under.

(*Enter a* FOOTMAN.)

MEDLEY: Here comes a man from Bellair with news of your last adventure.

DORIMANT: I am glad he sent him; I long to know the consequence of our parting.

FOOTMAN: Sir, my master desires you to come to my Lady Townley's presently° and bring Mr. Medley with you. My Lady Woodvill and her daughter are there.

MEDLEY: Then all's well, Dorimant.

FOOTMAN: They have sent for the fiddles and mean to dance. He bid me tell you, sir, the old lady does not know you, and would have you own yourself to be Mr. Courtage. They are all prepared to receive you by that name.

DORIMANT: That foppish admirer of quality, who flatters the very meat at honorable tables and never offers love to a woman below a lady-grandmother.

MEDLEY: You know the character you are to act, I see.

DORIMANT: This is Harriet's contrivance—wild, witty, lovesome, beautiful, and young!—Come along, Medley.

MEDLEY: This new woman would well supply the loss of Loveit.

DORIMANT: That business must not end so; before tomorrow sun is set. I will revenge and clear it.

And you and Loveit, to her cost, shall find,
I fathom all the depths of womankind. (*Exeunt.*)

ACT 4 / SCENE 1

(LADY TOWNLEY'S *drawing-room*)
(*The scene opens with the fiddles playing a country dance. Enter* DORIMANT *and* LADY WOODVILL, YOUNG BELLAIR *and* MRS. HARRIET, OLD BELLAIR *and* EMILIA, MR. MEDLEY *and* LADY TOWNLEY, *as having just ended the dance.*)

OLD BELLAIR: So, so, so!—a smart bout, a very smart bout, a dod!

LADY TOWNLEY: How do you like Emilia's dancing, brother?

OLD BELLAIR: Not at all—not at all!

LADY TOWNLEY: You speak not what you think, I am sure.

OLD BELLAIR: No matter for that; go, bid her dance no more. It don't become her—it don't become her. Tell her I say so. (*aside*) A dod, I love her!

DORIMANT (*to* LADY WOODVILL): All people mingle nowadays, madam. And in public places women of quality have the least respect showed 'em.

LADY WOODVILL: I protest you say the truth, Mr. Courtage.

DORIMANT: Forms and ceremonies, the only things that uphold quality and greatness, are now shamefully laid aside and neglected.

LADY WOODVILL: Well, this is not the women's age, let 'em think what they will. Lewdness is the business now; love was the business in my time.

DORIMANT: The women, indeed, are little beholding to the young men of this age; they're generally only dull admirers of themselves, and make their court to nothing but their periwigs and their cravats, and would be more concerned for the disordering of 'em, though on a good occasion, than a young maid would be for the tumbling of her head or handkercher.

LADY WOODVILL: I protest you hit 'em.

DORIMANT: They are very assiduous to show themselves at court, well dressed, to the women of quality, but their business is with the stale mistresses of the town, who are prepared to receive their lazy addresses by industrious old lovers who have cast 'em off and made 'em easy.

HARRIET (*to* MEDLEY): He fits my mother's humor so well, a little more and she'll dance a kissing dance with him anon.

MEDLEY: Dutifully observed, madam.

DORIMANT (*to* LADY WOODVILL): They pretend to be great critics in beauty. By their talk you would think they liked no face, and yet they can dote on an ill one if it belong to a laundress or a tailor's daughter. They cry, 'A woman's past her prime at twenty, decayed at four-and-twenty, old and unsufferable at thirty.'

LADY WOODVILL: Unsufferable at thirty! That they are in the wrong, Mr. Courtage, at five-and-thirty, there are living proofs enough to convince 'em.

DORIMANT: Ay, madam. There's Mrs. Setlooks, Mrs. Droplip, and my Lady Lowd; show me among all our opening buds a face that promises so much beauty as the remains of theirs.

LADY WOODVILL: The depraved appetite of this vicious age tastes nothing but green fruit, and loathes it when 'tis kindly° ripened.

DORIMANT: Else so many deserving women, madam, would not be so untimely neglected.

LADY WOODVILL: I protest, Mr. Courtage, a dozen such good men as you would be enough to atone for that wicked Dorimant and all the under° debauchees of the town. (HARRIET, EMILIA, YOUNG BELLAIR, MEDLEY, and LADY TOWNLEY *break out into a laughter.*)—What's the matter there?

MEDLEY: A pleasant mistake, madam, that a lady has made, occasions a little laughter.

OLD BELLAIR: Come, come, you keep 'em idle! They are impatient till the fiddles play again.

DORIMANT: You are not weary, madam?

LADY WOODVILL: One dance more, I cannot refuse you, Mr. Courtage.

(They dance. After the dance OLD BELLAIR, *singing and dancing up to* EMILIA.)

EMILIA: You are very active, sir.

OLD BELLAIR: A dod, sirrah! when I was a young fellow I could ha' capered up to my woman's gorget.°

DORIMANT *(to* LADY WOODVILL*)*: You are willing to rest yourself, madam—

LADY TOWNLEY *(to* LADY WOODVILL*)*: We'll walk into my chamber and sit down.

MEDLEY: Leave us Mr. Courtage; he's a dancer, and the young ladies are not weary yet.

LADY WOODVILL: We'll send him out again.

HARRIET: If you do not quickly, I know where to send for Mr. Dorimant.

LADY WOODVILL: This girl's head, Mr. Courtage, is ever running on that wild fellow.

DORIMANT: 'Tis well you have got her a good husband, madam; that will settle it.

(Exeunt LADY TOWNLEY, LADY WOODVILL, *and* DORIMANT.*)*

OLD BELLAIR *(to* EMILIA*)*: A dod, sweetheart, be advised and do not throw thyself away on a young, idle fellow.

---

kindly, naturally.   **under,** lesser.   **capered . . . gorget,** kicked as high as my partner's neck-piece.

EMILIA: I have no such intention, sir.

OLD BELLAIR: Have a little patience! Thou shalt have the man I spake of. A dod, he loves thee and will make a good husband—but no words!

EMILIA: But, sir—

OLD BELLAIR: No answer—out a pize! peace! and think on't.

(Enter DORIMANT.*)*

DORIMANT: Your company is desired within, sir.

OLD BELLAIR: I go, I go! Good Mr. Courtage, fare you well!—*(to* EMILIA*)* Go, I'll see you no more!

EMILIA: What have I done, sir?

OLD BELLAIR: You are ugly, you are ugly!—Is she not, Mr. Courtage?

EMILIA: Better words or I shan't abide you.

OLD BELLAIR: Out a pize; a dod, what does she say? Hit her a pat for me there. *(Exit* OLD BELLAIR.*)*

MEDLEY: You have charms for the whole family.

DORIMANT: You'll spoil all with some unseasonable jest, Medley.

MEDLEY: You see I confine my tongue and am content to be a bare spectator, much contrary to my nature.

EMILIA: Methinks, Mr. Dorimant, my Lady Woodvill is a little fond of you.

DORIMANT: Would her daughter were!

MEDLEY: It may be you find her so. Try her—you have an opportunity.

DORIMANT: And I will not lose it.—Bellair, here's a lady has something to say to you.

YOUNG BELLAIR: I wait upon her.—Mr. Medley, we have both business with you.

DORIMANT: Get you all together then. *(to* HARRIET*)* That demure curtsey is not amiss in jest, but do not think in earnest it becomes you.

HARRIET: Affectation is catching, I find; from your grave bow I got it.

DORIMANT: Where had you all that scorn and coldness in your look?

HARRIET: From nature, sir; pardon my want of art. I have not learnt those softnesses and languishings which now in faces are so much in fashion.

DORIMANT: You need 'em not; you have a sweetness of your own, if you would but calm your frowns and let it settle.

HARRIET: My eyes are wild and wand'ring like my passions, and cannot yet be tied to rules of charming.

DORMINANT: Women indeed, have a method of managing those messengers of love. Now they will look as if they would kill, and anon they will look as if they were dying. They point and rebate° their glances, the better to invite us.

---

point and rebate, sharpen and blunt.

HARRIET: I like this variety well enough, but hate the set face that always looks as if it would say, 'Come love me!'—a woman who at plays makes the *doux yeux*° to a whole audience and at home cannot forbear 'em to her monkey.

DORIMANT: Put on a gentle smile and let me see how well it will become you.

HARRIET: I am sorry my face does not please you as it is, but I shall not be complaisant and change it.

DORIMANT: Though you are obstinate, I know 'tis capable of improvement, and shall do you justice, madam, if I chance to be at Court when the critics of the Circle pass their judgment; for thither you must come.

HARRIET: And expect to be taken in pieces, have all my features examined, every motion censured, and on the whole be condemned to be but pretty, or a beauty of the lowest rate. What think you?

DORIMANT: The women—nay, the very lovers who belong to the drawing-room—will maliciously allow you more than that: they always grant what is apparent, that they may the better be believed when they name concealed faults they cannot easily be disproved in.

HARRIET: Beauty runs as great a risk exposed at Court as wit does on the stage, where the ugly and the foolish all are free to censure.

DORIMANT (*aside*): I love her and dare not let her know it; I fear sh'as an ascendant o'er me and may revenge the wrongs I have done her sex. (*to her*) Think of making a party, madam; love will engage.

HARRIET: You make me start! I did not think to have heard of love from you.

DORIMANT: I never knew what 'twas to have a settled ague yet, but now and then have had irregular fits.

HARRIET: Take heed! Sickness after long health is commonly more violent and dangerous.

DORIMANT (*aside*): I have took the infection from her, and feel the disease now spreading in me. (*to her*) Is the name of love so frightful that you dare not stand it?

HARRIET: 'Twill do little execution out of your mouth on me, I am sure.

DORIMANT: It has been fatal—

HARRIET: To some easy women, but we are not all born to one destiny. I was informed you use to laugh at love and not make it.

DORIMANT: The time has been, but now I must speak—

HARRIET: If it be on that idle subject, I will put on my serious look, turn my head carelessly from you, drop my lip, let my eyelids fall and hang half o'er my eyes—thus, while you buzz a speech of an hour long in my ear, and I answer never a word. Why do you not begin?

DORIMANT: That the company may take notice how passionately I make advances of love, and how disdainfully you receive 'em!

HARRIET: When your love's grown strong enough to make you bear being laughed at, I'll give you leave to trouble me with it. Till when pray forbear, sir.

(*Enter* SIR FOPLING *and others in masks.*)

DORIMANT: What's here—masquerades?

HARRIET: I thought that foppery had been left off, and people might have been in private with a fiddle.

DORIMANT: 'Tis endeavored to be kept on foot still by some who find themselves the more acceptable the less they are known.

YOUNG BELLAIR: This must be Sir Fopling.

MEDLEY: That extraordinary habit shows it.

YOUNG BELLAIR: What are the rest?

MEDLEY: A company of French rascals whom he picked up in Paris and has brought over to be his dancing equipage on these occasions. Make him own himself; a fool is very troublesome when he presumes he is incognito.

SIR FOPLING FLUTTER (*to* HARRIET): Do you know me?

HARRIET: Ten to one but I guess at you.

SIR FOPLING FLUTTER: Are you women as fond of a vizard as we men are?

HARRIET: I am very fond of a vizard that covers a face I do not like, sir.

YOUNG BELLAIR: Here are no masks, you see, sir, but those which came with you. This was intended a private meeting; but because you look like a gentleman, if you will discover yourself and we know you to be such, you shall be welcome.

SIR FOPLING FLUTTER (*pulling off his mask*): Dear Bellair!

MEDLEY: Sir Fopling! How came you hither?

SIR FOPLING FLUTTER: Faith, as I was coming late from Whitehall, after the King's *couchée*,° one of my people told me he had heard fiddles at my Lady Townley's, and—

DORIMANT: You need not say any more, sir.

SIR FOPLING FLUTTER: Dorimant, let me kiss thee.

DORIMANT: Hark you, Sir Fopling—(*whispers.*)

SIR FOPLING FLUTTER: Enough, enough, Courtage.— A pretty kind of young woman that, Medley. I observed her in the Mail—more *éveillée*° than our English women commonly are. Prithee, what is she?

MEDLEY: The most noted coquette in town. Beware of her.

SIR FOPLING FLUTTER: Let her be what she will, I know how to take my measures. In Paris the mode is to flatter the prude, laugh at the *faux-prude*, make serious love to the *demi-prude*, and only rally with the *coquette*. Medley, what think you?

MEDLEY: That for all this smattering of the mathematics, you may be out in your judgment at tennis.

SIR FOPLING FLUTTER: What a *coq-à-l'âne*° is this? I talk of women and thou answer'st tennis.

MEDLEY: Mistakes will be for want of apprehension.

SIR FOPLING FLUTTER: I am very glad of the acquaintance I have with this family.

MEDLEY: My lady truly is a good woman.

SIR FOPLING FLUTTER: Ah, Dorimant—Courtage, I would say—would thou hadst spent the last winter in Paris with me! When thou wert there, La Corneus and Sallyes were the only habitudes we had: a comedian would have been a *bonne fortune*.° No stranger ever passed his time so well as I did some months before I came over. I was well received in a dozen families where all the women of quality used to visit; I have intrigues to tell thee more pleasant than ever thou read'st in a novel.

HARRIET: Write 'em, sir, and oblige us women. Our language wants such little stories.

SIR FOPLING FLUTTER: Writing, madam, 's a mechanic part of wit. A gentleman should never go beyond a song or a billet.

HARRIET: Bussy° was a gentleman.

SIR FOPLING FLUTTER: Who, d'Ambois?°

MEDLEY: Was there ever such a brisk blockhead?

HARRIET: Not d'Ambois, sir, but Rabutin—he who writ the loves of France.

SIR FOPLING FLUTTER: That may be, madam; many gentlemen do things that are below 'em. Damn your authors, Courtage; women are the prettiest things we can fool away our time with.

HARRIET: I hope ye have wearied yourself to-night at Court, sir, and will not think of fooling with anybody here.

SIR FOPLING FLUTTER: I cannot complain of my fortune there, madam.—Dorimant—

DORIMANT: Again!

SIR FOPLING FLUTTER: Courtage—a pox on't!—I have something to tell thee. When I had made my court within, I came out and flung myself upon the mat under the state° i'th' outward room, i'th' midst of half a dozen beauties who were withdrawn to jeer among themselves, as they called it.

DORIMANT: Did you know 'em?

SIR FOPLING FLUTTER: Not one of 'em, by heavens!—not I. But they were all your friends.

DORIMANT: How are you sure of that?

SIR FOPLING FLUTTER: Why, we laughed at all the town—spared nobody but yourself. They found me a man for their purpose.

DORIMANT: I know you are malicious, to your power.°

SIR FOPLING FLUTTER: And faith, I had occasion to show it, for I never saw more gaping fools at a ball or on a birthday.°

DORIMANT: You learned who the women were?

SIR FOPLING FLUTTER: No matter; they frequent the drawing-room.

DORIMANT: —And entertain themselves pleasantly at the expense of all the fops who come there.

SIR FOPLING FLUTTER: That's their bus'ness. Faith, I sifted 'em,° and find they have a sort of wit among them.—Ah, filthy! *(Pinches a tallow candle.)*

DORIMANT: Look, he has been pinching the tallow candle.

SIR FOPLING FLUTTER: How can you breathe in a room where there's grease frying?—Dorimant, thou art intimate with my lady; advise her, for her own sake and the good company that comes hither, to burn wax lights.

HARRIET: What are these masquerades who stand so obsequiously at a distance?

SIR FOPLING FLUTTER: A set of balladines whom I picked out of the best in France and brought over with a *flute-douce* or two—my servants. They shall entertain you.

HARRIET: I had rather see you dance yourself, Sir Fopling.

SIR FOPLING FLUTTER: And I had rather do it—all the company knows it—but, madam—

MEDLEY: Come, come, no excuses, Sir Fopling!

SIR FOPLING FLUTTER: By heavens, Medley—

MEDLEY: Like a woman I find you must be struggled with before one brings you to what you desire. *(They converse in dumb-show.)*

HARRIET *(aside)*: Can he dance?

EMILIA: And fence and sing too, if you'll believe him.

DORIMANT: He has no more excellence in his heels than in his head. He went to Paris a plain,

---

coq-à-l'âne, nonsense. *bonne fortune*, piece of good luck. *Bussy*, Roger de Rabutin, Comte de Bussy, author of the *Histoire amoureuse des Gaules:* still living at this time, despite the implication of Harriet's "was." *d'Ambois*, Sir Fopling displays his actual ignorance of the fashionable world of Paris by supposing Harriet refers to the sixteenth-century French adventurer, who was well-known to the English as the hero of Chapman's play of the same name.

state, canopy. *to . . . power*, to the extent of your power. *birthday*, at a celebration of the king's birthday. *sifted 'em*, examined.

bashful English blockhead, and is returned a fine undertaking° French fop.

MEDLEY (*to* HARRIET): I cannot prevail.

SIR FOPLING FLUTTER: Do not think it want of complaisance, madam.

HARRIET: You are too well bred to want that, Sir Fopling. I believe it want of power.

SIR FOPLING FLUTTER: By heavens, and so it is! I have sat up so damned late and drunk so cursed hard since I came to this lewd town, that I am fit for nothing but low dancing now—a *courante,* a *bourrée,* or a *menuet.*° But St. André° tells me, if I will but be regular, in one month I shall rise again. Pox on this debauchery! (*Endeavors at a caper.*)

EMILIA: I have heard your dancing much commended.

SIR FOPLING FLUTTER: It had the good fortune to please in Paris. I was judged to rise within an inch as high as the Basque° in an entry° I danced there.

HARRIET (*to* EMILIA): I am mightily taken with this fool; let us sit.—Here's a seat, Sir Fopling.

SIR FOPLING FLUTTER: At your feet, madam; I can be nowhere so much at ease.—By your leave, gown. (*Sits at* HARRIET'*s feet.*)

HARRIET:
EMILIA: } Ah, you'll spoil it!

SIR FOPLING FLUTTER: No matter; my clothes are my creatures. I make 'em to make my court to you ladies. (*to his servants*) Hey! *Qu'on commence!*° (*Dance.*) —To an English dancer, English motions. I was forced to entertain° this fellow (*pointing to* JOHN TROTT), one of my set miscarrying.—Oh, horrid! Leave your damned manner of dancing and put on the French air: have you not a pattern before you?—Pretty well! imitation in time may bring him to something.

(*After the dance, enter* OLD BELLAIR, LADY WOODVILL, *and* LADY TOWNLEY.)

OLD BELLAIR: Hey, a dod, what have we here— a mumming?

LADY WOODVILL: Where's my daughter? Harriet!

DORIMANT: Here, here, madam! I know not but under these disguises there may be dangerous sparks; I gave the young lady warning.

LADY WOODVILL: Lord! I am so obliged to you, Mr. Courtage.

HARRIET: Lord, how you admire this man!

LADY WOODVILL: What have you to except against him?

HARRIET: He's a fop.

LADY WOODVILL: He's not a Dorimant, a wild extravagant fellow of the times.

HARRIET: He's a man made up of forms and commonplaces sucked out of the remaining lees of the last age.

LADY WOODVILL: He's so good a man that, were you not engaged—

LADY TOWNLEY: You'll have but little night to sleep in.

LADY WOODVILL: Lord, 'tis perfect day.°

DORIMANT (*aside*): The hour is almost come I appointed Bellinda, and I am not so foppishly in love here to forget. I am flesh and blood yet.

LADY TOWNLEY: I am very sensible,° madam. (*Bowing.*)

LADY WOODVILL: Lord, madam! (*Bowing.*)

HARRIET: Look! in what a struggle is my poor mother yonder!

YOUNG BELLAIR: She has much ado to bring out the compliment.

DORIMANT: She strains hard for it.

HARRIET: See, see! her head tottering, her eyes staring, and her under lip trembling—

DORIMANT: Now—now she's in the very convulsions of her civility. (*aside*) 'Sdeath, I shall lose Bellinda! I must fright her hence; she'll be an hour in this fit of good manners else. (*to* LADY WOODVILL) Do you not know Sir Fopling, madam?

LADY WOODVILL: I have seen that face—oh, heaven! 'tis the same we met in the Mail. How came he here?

DORIMANT: A fiddle, in this town, is a kind of fop-call; no sooner it strikes up but the house is besieged with an army of masquerades straight.

LADY WOODVILL: Lord! I tremble, Mr. Courtage. For certain, Dorimant is in the company.

DORIMANT: I cannot confidently say he is not. You had best be gone. I will wait upon you; your daughter is in the hands of Mr. Bellair.

LADY WOODVILL: I'll see her before me.—Harriet, come away.

YOUNG BELLAIR: Lights! lights!

LADY TOWNLEY: Light, down there!

OLD BELLAIR: A dod, it needs not—

DORIMANT (*calling to the Servants without*): Call my Lady Woodvill's coach to the door quickly.

(*Exeunt* YOUNG BELLAIR, HARRIET, LADY TOWNLEY, DORIMANT, *and* LADY WOODVILL.)

---

undertaking, enterprising, bold. *courante . . . menuet,* dances that did not require "capers" (high kicks). *St. André,* a famous French dancing-master. *Basque,* usually explained as the skirt of a coat—but this would scarcely be a leap to boast of. Perhaps the reference is to a contemporary Basque professional dancer. *entry,* a dance performed as an interlude in an entertainment. *Qu'on commence!,* begin *entertain,* engage, hire.

perfect day, broad daylight. *sensible,* aware (of your courtesy to me).

OLD BELLAIR: Stay, Mr. Medley: let the young fellows do that duty; we will drink a glass of wine together. 'Tis good after dancing. (*indicating* SIR FOPLING.) What mumming° spark is that?

MEDLEY: He is not to be comprehended in few words.

SIR FOPLING FLUTTER: Hey, La Tour!

MEDLEY: Whither away, Sir Fopling?

SIR FOPLING FLUTTER: I have business with Courtage.

MEDLEY: He'll but put the ladies into their coach and come up again.

OLD BELLAIR: In the meantime I'll call for a bottle.

(*Exit* OLD BELLAIR.)

(*Enter* YOUNG BELLAIR.)

MEDLEY: Where's Dorimant?

YOUNG BELLAIR: Stol'n home. He has had business waiting for him there all this night, I believe, by an impatience I observed in him.

MEDLEY: Very likely; 'tis but dissembling drunkenness, railing at his friends, and the kind soul will embrace the blessing and forget the tedious expectation.

SIR FOPLING FLUTTER: I must speak with him before I sleep.

YOUNG BELLAIR (*to* MEDLEY): Emilia and I are resolved on that business.

MEDLEY: Peace! here's your father.

(*Enter* OLD BELLAIR *and a* BUTLER *with a bottle of wine.*)

OLD BELLAIR: The women are all gone to bed.—Fill, boy!—Mr. Medley, begin a health.

MEDLEY (*whispers*): To Emilia!

OLD BELLAIR: Out a pize! she's a rogue, and I'll not pledge you.

MEDLEY: I know you will.

OLD BELLAIR: A dod, drink it, then!

SIR FOPLING FLUTTER: Let us have the new bacchic.

OLD BELLAIR: A dod, that is a hard word. What does it mean, sir?

MEDLEY: A catch or drinking-song.

OLD BELLAIR: Let us have it then.

SIR FOPLING FLUTTER: Fill the glasses round and draw up in a body.—Hey, music! (*They sing.*)

The pleasures of love and the joys of good wine
To perfect our happiness wisely we join.
We to beauty all day
Give the sovereign sway
And her favorite nymphs devoutly obey.
At the plays we are constantly making our court,
And when they are ended we follow the sport
To the Mall and the Park,
Where we love till 'tis dark.

Then sparkling champagne
Puts an end to their reign;
It quickly recovers
Poor languishing lovers;
Makes us frolic and gay, and drowns all our sorrow.
But alas! we relapse again on the morrow.
    Let every man stand
    With his glass in his hand,
And briskly discharge at the word of command:
    Here's a health to all those
    Whom to-night we depose!
Wine and beauty by turns great souls should inspire;
Present all together! and now, boys, give fire!

(*They drink.*)

OLD BELLAIR: A dod, a pretty business and very merry!

SIR FOPLING FLUTTER: Hark you; Medley, let you and I take the fiddles and go waken Dorimant.

MEDLEY: We shall do him a courtesy, if it be as I guess. For after the fatigue of this night he'll quickly have his belly full and be glad of an occasion to cry, 'Take away, Handy!'

YOUNG BELLAIR: I'll go with you, and there we'll consult about affairs, Medley.

OLD BELLAIR (*looks on his watch*): A dod, 'tis six o'clock!

SIR FOPLING FLUTTER: Let's away, then.

OLD BELLAIR: Mr. Medley, my sister tells me you are an honest man—and a dod, I love you. Few words and hearty—that's the way with old Harry, old Harry.

SIR FOPLING FLUTTER (*to his Servants*): Light your flambeaux. Hey!

OLD BELLAIR: What does the man mean?

MEDLEY: 'Tis day, Sir Fopling.

SIR FOPLING FLUTTER: No matter, our serenade will look the greater. (*Exeunt omnes.*)

ACT 4 / SCENE 2

(DORIMANT'S *lodging. A table, a candle, a toilet, etc.* HANDY, *tying up linen.*)
(*Enter* DORIMANT *in his gown, and* BELLINDA.)

DORIMANT: Why will you be gone so soon?

BELLINDA: Why did you stay out so late?

DORIMANT: Call a chair, Handy.—What makes you tremble so?

BELLINDA: I have a thousand fears about me. Have I not been seen, think you?

DORIMANT: By nobody but myself and trusty Handy.

BELLINDA: Where are all your people?

DORIMANT: I have dispersed 'em on sleeveless° errands. What does that sigh mean?

BELLINDA: Can you be so unkind to ask me? Well—

---

mumming, masquerading.

sleeveless, useless.

(sighs)—were it to do again—

DORIMANT: We should do it, should we not?

BELLINDA: I think we should—the wickeder man you to make me love so well. Will you be discreet now?

DORIMANT: I will.

BELLINDA: You cannot.

DORIMANT: Never doubt it.

BELLINDA: I will not expect it.

DORIMANT: You do me wrong.

BELLINDA: You have no more power to keep the secret than I had not to trust you with it.

DORIMANT: By all the joys I have had and those you keep in store—

BELLINDA: You'll do for my sake what you never did before.

DORIMANT: By that truth thou hast spoken, a wife shall sooner betray herself to her husband.

BELLINDA: Yet I had rather you should be false in this than in another thing you promised me.

DORIMANT: What's that?

BELLINDA: That you would never see Loveit more but in public places—in the Park, at Court and plays.

DORIMANT: 'Tis not likely a man should be fond of seeing a damned old play when there is a new one acted.

BELLINDA: I dare not trust your promise.

DORIMANT: You may—

BELLINDA: This does not satisfy me. You shall swear you never will see her more.

DORIMANT: I will, a thousand oaths. By all—

BELLINDA: Hold! You shall not, now I think on't better.

DORIMANT: I will swear!

BELLINDA: I shall grow jealous of the oath and think I owe your truth to that, not to your love.

DORIMANT: Then, by my love; no other oath I'll swear.

(Enter HANDY.*)*

HANDY: Here's a chair.

BELLINDA: Let me go.

DORIMANT: I cannot.

BELLINDA: Too willingly, I fear.

DORIMANT: Too unkindly feared. When will you promise me again?

BELLINDA: Not this fortnight.

DORIMANT: You will be better than your word.

BELLINDA: I think I shall. Will it not make you love me less? *(Starting.)* Hark! What fiddles are these? *(Fiddles without.)*

DORIMANT: Look out, Handy. *(Exit* HANDY *and returns.)*

HANDY: Mr. Medley, Mr. Bellair, and Sir Fopling; they are coming up.

DORIMANT: How got they in?

HANDY: The door was open for the chair.

BELLINDA: Lord, let me fly!

DORIMANT: Here, here, down the back stairs! I'll see you into your chair.

BELLINDA: No, no! Stay and receive 'em. And be sure you keep your word and never see Loveit more. Let it be a proof of your kindness.

DORIMANT: It shall.—Handy, direct her.—*(Kissing her hand.)* Everlasting love go along with thee. *(Exeunt* BELLINDA *and* HANDY.*)*

(Enter YOUNG BELLAIR, MEDLEY, *and* SIR FOPLING.*)*

YOUNG BELLAIR: Not abed yet?

MEDLEY: You have had an 'irregular fit,' Dorimant.

DORIMANT: I have.

YOUNG BELLAIR: And is it off already?

DORIMANT: Nature has done her part, gentlemen; when she falls kindly to work, great cures are effected in little time, you know.

SIR FOPLING FLUTTER: We thought there was a wench in the case, by the chair that waited. Prithee, make us a *confidence*.

DORIMANT: Excuse me.

SIR FOPLING FLUTTER: *Le sage* Dorimant! Was she pretty?

DORIMANT: So pretty she may come to keep her coach and pay parish duties if the good humor of the age continue.

MEDLEY: And be of the number of the ladies kept by public-spirited men for the good of the whole town.

SIR FOPLING FLUTTER *(dancing by himself)*: Well said, Medley.

YOUNG BELLAIR: See Sir Fopling dancing!

DORIMANT: You are practising and have a mind to recover, I see.

SIR FOPLING FLUTTER: Prithee, Dorimant, why hast not thou a glass hung up here? A room is the dullest thing without one.

YOUNG BELLAIR: Here is company to entertain you.

SIR FOPLING FLUTTER: But I mean in case of being alone. In a glass a man may entertain himself—

DORIMANT: The shadow of himself, indeed.

SIR FOPLING FLUTTER: —Correct the errors of his motions and his dress.

MEDLEY: I find, Sir Fopling, in your solitude you remember the saying of the wise man, and study yourself.°

SIR FOPLING FLUTTER: 'Tis the best diversion in our retirements. Dorimant, thou art a pretty fellow and wear'st thy clothes well, but I never saw thee have a handsome cravat. Were they made up like mine, they'd give another air to thy face. Prithee, let me send my man to dress thee but one day; by

---

study yourself, this saying is attributed to several of the Seven Wise Men of Greece, most frequently to Thales.

heavens, an Englishman cannot tie a ribbon.

DORIMANT: They are something clumsy fisted—

SIR FOPLING FLUTTER: I have brought over the prettiest fellow that ever spread a toilet. He served some time under Merille,° the greatest *genie* in the world for a *valet-de-chambre*.

DORIMANT: What! he who formerly belonged to the Duke of Candale?

SIR FOPLING FLUTTER: The same, and got him his immortal reputation.

DORIMANT: Y'have a very fine brandenburgh° on, Sir Fopling.

SIR FOPLING FLUTTER: It serves to wrap me up after the fatigue of a ball.

MEDLEY: I see you often in it, with your periwig tied up.

SIR FLOPLING FLUTTER: We should not always be in a set dress; 'tis more *en cavalier*° to appear now and then in a *deshabillé*.

MEDLEY: Pray, how goes your business with Loveit?

SIR FOPLING FLUTTER: You might have answered yourself in the Mail last night. Dorimant, did you not see the advances she made me? I have been endeavoring at a song.

DORIMANT: Already!

SIR FOPLING FLUTTER: 'Tis my *coup d'essai*° in English: I would fain have thy opinion of it.

DORIMANT: Let's see it.

SIR FOPLING FLUTTER: Hey, page, give me my song.—Bellair, here; thou hast a pretty voice—sing it.

YOUNG BELLAIR: Sing it yourself, Sir Fopling.

SIR FOPLING: Excuse me.

YOUNG BELLAIR: You learnt to sing in Paris.

SIR FOPLING: I did—of Lambert,° the greatest master in the world. But I have his own fault, a weak voice, and care not to sing out of a *ruelle*.°

DORIMANT (*aside*): A *ruelle* is a pretty cage for a singing fop, indeed.

YOUNG BELLAIR (*reads the song*):

How charming Phillis is, how fair!
    Ah, that she were as willing
To ease my wounded heart of care,
    And make her eyes less killing.
I sigh, I sigh, I languish now,
    And love will not let me rest;
I drive about the Park and bow,
    Still as I meet my dearest.

Merille, subsequently valet to the Duke of Orleans, brother of Louis XIV and an even more eminent figure in French society than the Duke of Candale, whom Dorimant mentions in his next speech. *brandenburgh*, morning gown. *en cavalier*, fashionable. *coup d'essai*, first attempt. *Lambert*, Michel Lambert, master of chamber music to Louis XIV. *ruelle*, except in a lady's bedchamber (sc. at a levee).

SIR FOPLING FLUTTER: Sing it! sing it, man; it goes to a pretty new tune which I am confident was made by Baptiste.°

MEDLEY: Sing it yourself, Sir Fopling, he does not know the tune.

SIR FOPLING: I'll venture. (SIR FOPLING *sings*.)

DORIMANT: Ay, marry! now 'tis something. I shall not flatter you, Sir Fopling; there is not much thought in't, but 'tis passionate and well turned.

MEDLEY: After the French way.

SIR FOPLING: That I aimed at. Does it not give you a lively image of the thing? Slap! down goes the glass,° and thus we are at it. (*He bows and grimaces.*)

DORIMANT: It does, indeed, I perceive, Sir Fopling. You'll be the very head of the sparks who are lucky in compositions of this nature.

(*Enter* SIR FOPLING'S FOOTMAN.)

SIR FOPLING FLUTTER: La Tour, is the bath ready?

FOOTMAN: Yes, sir.

SIR FOPLING FLUTTER: *Adieu donc, mes chers.* (*Exit* SIR FOPLING.)

MEDLEY: When have you your revenge on Loveit, Dorimant?

DORIMANT: I will but change my linen and about it.

MEDLEY: The powerful considerations which hindered have been removed then?

DORIMANT: Most luckily this morning. You must along with me; my reputation lies at stake there.

MEDLEY: I am engaged to Bellair.

DORIMANT: What's your business?

MEDLEY: Ma-tri-mony, an't like you.

DORIMANT: It does not, sir.

YOUNG BELLAIR: It may in time, Dorimant: What think you of Mrs. Harriet?

DORIMANT: What does she think of me?

YOUNG BELLAIR: I am confident she loves you.

DORIMANT: How does it appear?

YOUNG BELLAIR: Why, she's never well but when she's talking of you—but then, she finds all the faults in you she can. She laughs at all who commend you—but then, she speaks ill of all who do not.

DORIMANT: Women of her temper betray themselves by their over-cunning. I had once a growing love with a lady who would always quarrel with me when I came to see her, and yet was never quiet if I stayed a day from her.

YOUNG BELLAIR: My father is in love with Emilia.

DORIMANT: That is a good warrant for your proceedings. Go on and prosper; I must to Loveit. Medley, I am sorry you cannot be a witness.

MEDLEY: Make her meet Sir Fopling again in the

Baptiste, Jean Baptiste Lully, composer, and director of opera for Louis XIV. *glass*, the glass window of the coach.

same place and use him ill before me.

DORIMANT: That may be brought about, I think. I'll be at your aunt's anon and give you joy, Mr. Bellair.

YOUNG BELLAIR: You had not best think of Mrs. Harriet too much; without church security there's no taking up° there.

DORIMANT: I may fall into the snare too. But—
The wise will find a difference in our fate;
You wed a woman, I a good estate. (*Exeunt.*)

ACT 4 / SCENE 3

(*The street before* MRS. LOVEIT's *lodgings*)
(*Enter the chair with* BELLINDA; *the men set it down and open it.* BELLINDA *starting.*)

BELLINDA (*surprised*): Lord, where am I?—in the Mail! Whither have you brought me?

1 CHAIRMAN: You gave us no directions, madam.

BELLINDA (*aside*): The fright I was in made me forget it.

1 CHAIRMAN: We use to carry a lady from the Squire's hither.

BELLINDA (*aside*): This is Loveit: I am undone if she sees me.—Quickly, carry me away!

1 CHAIRMAN: Whither, an't like your honor?

BELLINDA: Ask no questions—

(*Enter* MRS. LOVEIT's FOOTMAN.)

FOOTMAN: Have you seen my lady, madam?

BELLINDA: I am just come to wait upon her.

FOOTMAN: She will be glad to see you, madam. She sent me to you this morning to desire your company, and I was told you went out by five o'clock.

BELLINDA (*aside*): More and more unlucky!

FOOTMAN: Will you walk in, madam?

BELLINDA: I'll discharge my chair and follow. Tell your mistress I am here. (*Exit* FOOTMAN. BELLINDA *gives the* CHAIRMEN *money.*) Take this, and if ever you should be examined, be sure you say you took me up in the Strand over against the Exchange, as you will answer it to Mr. Dorimant.

CHAIRMEN: We will, an't like your honor. (*Exeunt* CHAIRMEN.)

BELLINDA: Now to come off, I must on—
In confidence and lies some hope is left;
'Twere hard to be found out in the first theft.
(*Exit.*)

ACT 5 / SCENE 1

(MRS. LOVEIT's *lodgings*)
(*Enter* MRS. LOVEIT *and* PERT, *her woman.*)

PERT: Well! in my eyes Sir Fopling is no such despicable person.

MRS. LOVEIT: You are an excellent judge!

PERT: He's as handsome a man as Mr. Dorimant, and as great a gallant.

MRS. LOVEIT: Intolerable! Is't not enough I submit to his impertinences, but must I be plagued with yours too?

PERT: Indeed, madam—

MRS. LOVEIT: 'Tis false, mercenary malice—

(*Enter her* FOOTMAN.)

FOOTMAN: Mrs. Bellinda, madam.

MRS. LOVEIT: What of her?

FOOTMAN: She's below.

MRS. LOVEIT: How came she?

FOOTMAN: In a chair; Ambling Harry brought her.

MRS. LOVEIT (*aside*): He bring her! His chair stands near Dorimant's door and always brings me from thence. (*to* FOOTMAN) Run and ask him where he took her up. (*Exit* FOOTMAN.) Go! there is no truth in friendship neither. Women, as well as men, all are false—or all are so to me, at least.

PERT: You are jealous of her too?

MRS. LOVEIT: You had best tell her I am. 'Twill become the liberty you take of late. This fellow's bringing of her, her going out by five o'clock—I know not what to think.

(*Enter* BELLINDA.)

—Bellinda, you are grown an early riser, I hear.

BELLINDA: Do you not wonder, my dear, what made me abroad so soon?

MRS. LOVEIT: You do not use to be so.

BELLINDA: The country gentlewomen I told you of (Lord, they have the oddest diversions!) would never let me rest till I promised to go with them to the markets this morning to eat fruit and buy nosegays.

MRS. LOVEIT: Are they so fond of a filthy nosegay?

BELLINDA: They complain of the stinks of the town, and are never well but when they have their noses in one.

MRS. LOVEIT: There are essences and sweet waters.

BELLINDA: Oh, they cry out upon perfumes, they are unwholesome; one of 'em was falling into a fit with the smell of these *nerolii.*°

MRS. LOVEIT: Methinks in complaisance you should have had a nosegay too.

BELLINDA: Do you think, my dear, I could be so loathsome, to trick myself up with carnations and stock-gillyflowers? I begged their pardon and told them I never wore anything but orange flowers and tuberose. That which made me

---

taking up, taking up quarters.

nerolii, essences of orange.

willing to go, was a strange desire I had to eat some fresh nectarines.

MRS. LOVEIT: And had you any?

BELLINDA: The best I ever tasted.

MRS. LOVEIT: Whence came you now?

BELLINDA: From their lodgings, where I crowded out of a coach and took a chair to come and see you, my dear.

MRS. LOVEIT: Whither did you send for that chair?

BELLINDA: 'T was going by empty.

MRS. LOVEIT: Where do these country gentlewomen lodge, I pray?

BELLINDA: In the Strand over against the Exchange.

PERT: That place is never without a nest of 'em. They are always, as one goes by, fleering in balconies or staring out of windows.

(Enter FOOTMAN.)

MRS. LOVEIT (to the FOOTMAN): Come hither! (Whispers.)

BELLINDA (aside): This fellow by her order has been questioning the chairman. I threatened 'em with the name of Dorimant; if they should have told truth, I am lost forever.

MRS. LOVEIT: In the Strand, said you?

FOOTMAN: Yes, madam; over against the Exchange.
(Exit FOOTMAN.)

MRS. LOVEIT (aside): She's innocent, and I am much to blame.

BELLINDA (aside): I am so frightened, my countenance will betray me.

MRS. LOVEIT: Bellinda, what makes you look so pale?

BELLINDA: Want of my usual rest and jolting up and down so long in an odious hackney.

(FOOTMAN returns.)

FOOTMAN: Madam, Mr. Dorimant.

MRS. LOVEIT: What makes him here?

BELLINDA (aside): Then I am betrayed, indeed. H'has broke his word, and I love a man that does not care for me!

MRS. LOVEIT: Lord, you faint, Bellinda!

BELLINDA: I think I shall—such an oppression here on the sudden.

PERT: She has eaten too much fruit, I warrant you.

MRS. LOVEIT: Not unlikely.

PERT: 'Tis that lies heavy on her stomach.

MRS. LOVEIT: Have her into my chamber, give her some surfeit water,° and let her lie down a little.

PERT: Come, madam! I was a strange° devourer of fruit when I was young—so ravenous—

(Exeunt BELLINDA, and PERT, leading her off.)

MRS. LOVEIT: Oh, that my love would be but calm

awhile, that I might receive this man with all the scorn and indignation he deserves!

(Enter DORIMANT.)

DORIMANT: Now for a touch of Sir Fopling to begin with.—'Hey, page, give positive order that none of my people stir. Let the canaille wait as they should do.' Since noise and nonsense have such powerful charms.

I, that I may successful prove,
Transform myself to what you love.

MRS. LOVEIT: If that would do, you need not change from what you are: you can be vain and loud enough.

DORIMANT: But not with so good a grace as Sir Fopling.—'Hey, Hampshire!'—'Oh, that sound, that sound becomes the mouth of a man of quality!'

MRS. LOVEIT: Is there a thing so hateful as a senseless mimic?

DORIMANT: He's a great grievance indeed to all who, like yourself, madam, love to play the fool in quiet.

MRS. LOVEIT: A ridiculous animal, who has more of the ape than the ape has of the man in him!

DORIMANT: I have as mean an opinion of a sheer° mimic as yourself; yet were he all ape, I should prefer him to the gay, the giddy, brisk, insipid, noisy fool you dote on.

MRS. LOVEIT: Those noisy fools, however you despise 'em, have good qualities which weigh more (or ought at least) with us women than all the pernicious wit you have to boast of.

DORIMANT: That I may hereafter have a just value for their merit, pray do me the favor to name 'em.

MRS. LOVEIT: You'll despise 'em as the dull effects of ignorance and vanity; yet I care not if I mention some. First, they really admire us, while you at best but flatter us well.

DORIMANT: Take heed! Fools can dissemble too.

MRS. LOVEIT: They may, but not so artificially° as you. There is no fear they should deceive us. Then, they are assiduous, sir; they are ever offering us their service, and always waiting on our will.

DORIMANT: You owe that to their excessive idleness. They know not how to entertain themselves at home, and find so little welcome abroad they are fain to fly to you who countenance 'em, as a refuge against the solitude they would be otherwise condemned to.

MRS. LOVEIT: Their conversation, too, diverts us better.

---

surfeit water, a medicine to counteract excessive eating.
strange, notable, extraordinary.

sheer, pure, mere.　artificially, artfully.

DORIMANT: Playing with your fan, smelling to your gloves, commending your hair, and taking notice how 'tis cut and shaded after the new way—

MRS. LOVEIT: Were it sillier than you can make it, you must allow 'tis pleasanter to laugh at others than to be laughed at ourselves, though never so wittily. Then, though they want skill to flatter us, they flatter themselves so well they save us the labor. We need not take that care and pains to satisfy 'em of our love, which we so often lose on you.

DORIMANT: They commonly, indeed, believe too well of themselves, and always better of you than you deserve.

MRS. LOVEIT: You are in the right. They have an implicit faith in us which keeps 'em from prying narrowly into our secrets and saves us the vexatious trouble of clearing doubts which your subtle and causeless jealousies every moment raise.

DORIMANT: There is an inbred falsehood in women which inclines 'em still to them whom they may most easily deceive.

MRS. LOVEIT: The man who loves above his quality does not suffer more from the insolent impertinence of his mistress than the woman who loves above her understanding does from the arrogant presumptions of her friend.

DORIMANT: You mistake the use of fools; they are designed for properties, and not for friends. You have an indifferent stock of reputation left yet. Lose it all like a frank gamester on the square; 'twill then be time enough to turn rook° and cheat it up again on a good, substantial bubble.°

MRS. LOVEIT: The old and the ill-favored are only fit for properties, indeed, but young and handsome fools have met with kinder fortunes.

DORIMANT: They have, to the shame of your sex be it spoken! 'Twas this, the thought of this, made me by a timely jealousy endeavor to prevent the good fortune you are providing for Sir Fopling. But against a woman's frailty all our care is vain.

MRS. LOVEIT: Had I not with a dear experience bought the knowledge of your falsehood, you might have fooled me yet. This is not the first jealousy you have feigned, to make a quarrel with me and get a week to throw away on some such unknown, inconsiderable slut as you have been lately lurking with at plays.

DORIMANT: Women, when they would break off with a man, never want th' address to turn the fault on him.

MRS. LOVEIT: You take a pride of late in using of me

ill, that the town may know the power you have over me, which now (as unreasonably as yourself) expects that I (do me all the injuries you can) must love you still.

DORIMANT: I am so far from expecting that you should, I begin to think you never did love me.

MRS. LOVEIT: Would the memory of it were so wholly worn out in me, that I did doubt it too! What made you come to disturb my growing quiet?

DORIMANT: To give you joy of your growing infamy.

MRS. LOVEIT: Insupportable! Insulting devil!—this from you, the only author of my shame! This from another had been but justice, but from you 'tis a hellish and inhumane outrage. What have I done?

DORIMANT: A thing that puts you below my scorn, and makes my anger as ridiculous as you have made my love.

MRS. LOVEIT: I walked last night with Sir Fopling.

DORIMANT: You did, madam, and you talked and laughed aloud, 'Ha, ha, ha!'—Oh, that laugh! that laugh becomes the confidence of a woman of quality.

MRS. LOVEIT: You who have more pleasure in the ruin of a woman's reputation than in the endearments of her love, reproach me not with yourself—and I defy you to name the man can lay a blemish on my fame.

DORIMANT: To be seen publicly so transported with the vain follies of that notorious fop, to me is an infamy below the sin of prostitution with another man.

MRS. LOVEIT: Rail on! I am satisfied in the justice of what I did; you have provoked me to't.

DORIMANT: What I did was the effect of a passion whose extravagancies you have been willing to forgive.

MRS. LOVEIT: And what I did was the effect of a passion you may forgive if you think it.

DORIMANT: Are you so indifferent grown?

MRS. LOVEIT: I am.

DORIMANT: Nay, then 'tis time to part. I'll send you back your letters you have so often asked for. I have two or three of 'em about me.

MRS. LOVEIT: Give 'em me.

DORIMANT: You snatch as if you thought I would not. There! (giving her the letters) and may the perjuries in 'em be mine if e'er I see you more! (Offers to go; she catches him.)

MRS. LOVEIT: Stay!

DORIMANT: I will not.

MRS. LOVEIT: You shall.

DORIMANT: What have you to say?

MRS. LOVEIT: I cannot speak it yet.

DORIMANT: Something more in commendation of the fool.—Death, I want patience; let me go!

MRS. LOVEIT: I cannot. (aside) I can sooner part with

_____

rook, sharper, swindler.   bubble, dupe.

the limbs that hold him.—I hate that nauseous fool; you know I do.

DORIMANT: Was it the scandal you were fond of then?

MRS. LOVEIT: Y'had raised my anger equal to my love—a thing you ne'er could do before, and in revenge I did—I know not what I did. Would you would not think on't any more!

DORIMANT: Should I be willing to forget it, I shall be daily minded of it; 'twill be a commonplace for all the town to laugh at me, and Medley, when he is rhetorically drunk, will ever be declaiming on it in my ears.

MRS. LOVEIT: 'Twill be believed a jealous spite. Come, forget it.

DORIMANT: Let me consult my reputation; you are too careless of it. (Pauses.) You shall meet Sir Fopling in the Mail again tonight.

MRS. LOVEIT: What mean you?

DORIMANT: I have thought on it, and you must. 'Tis necessary to justify my love to the world. You can handle a coxcomb as he deserves when you are not out of humor, madam.

MRS. LOVEIT: Public satisfaction for the wrong I have done you! This is some new device to make me more ridiculous.

DORIMANT: Hear me!

MRS. LOVEIT: I will not.

DORIMANT: You will be persuaded.

MRS. LOVEIT: Never!

DORIMANT: Are you so obstinate?

MRS. LOVEIT: Are you so base?

DORIMANT: You will not satisfy my love?

MRS. LOVEIT: I would die to satisfy that; but I will not, to save you from a thousand racks, do a shameless thing to please your vanity.

DORIMANT: Farewell, false woman!

MRS. LOVEIT: Do—go!

DORIMANT: You will call me back again.

MRS. LOVEIT: Exquisite fiend, I knew you came but to torment me!

(Enter BELLINDA and PERT.)

DORIMANT (surprised): Bellinda here!

BELLINDA (aside): He starts and looks pale! The sight of me has touched his guilty soul.

PERT: 'Twas but a qualm, as I said—a little indigestion; the surfeit water did it, madam, mixed with a little mirabilis.°

DORIMANT (aside): I am confounded, and cannot guess how she came hither!

MRS. LOVEIT: 'Tis your fortune, Bellinda, ever to be here when I am abused by this prodigy of ill-nature.

BELLINDA: I am amazed to find him here. How has he the face to come near you?

DORIMANT (aside): Here is fine work towards! I never was at such a loss before.

BELLINDA: One who makes a public profession of breach of faith and ingratitude—I loathe the sight of him.

DORIMANT (aside): There is no remedy; I must submit to their tongues now, and some other time bring myself off as well as I can.

BELLINDA: Other men are wicked; but then, they have some sense of shame. He is never well but when he triumphs—nay, glories to a woman's face in his villainies.

MRS. LOVEIT: You are in the right, Bellinda, but methinks your kindness for me makes you concern yourself too much with him.

BELLINDA: It does indeed, my dear. His barbarous carriage° to you yesterday made me hope you ne'er would see him more, and the very next day to find him here again, provokes me strangely. But because I know you love him, I have done.

DORIMANT: You have reproached me handsomely, and I deserve it for coming hither; but—

PERT: You must expect it, sir. All women will hate you for my lady's sake.

DORIMANT (aside to BELLINDA): Nay, if she begins too, 'tis time to fly; I shall be scolded to death else. (Aloud) I am to blame in some circumstances, I confess; but as to the main, I am not so guilty as you imagine. I shall seek a more convenient time to clear myself.

MRS. LOVEIT: Do it now. What impediments are here?

DORIMANT: I want time, and you want temper.

MRS. LOVEIT: These are weak pretenses.

DORIMANT: You were never more mistaken in your life; and so farewell. (DORIMANT flings off.)

MRS. LOVEIT: Call a footman, Pert, quickly; I will have him dogged.

PERT: I wish you would not, for my quiet and your own.

MRS. LOVEIT: I'll find out the infamous cause of all our quarrels, pluck her mask off, and expose her barefaced to the world! (Exit PERT.)

BELLINDA (aside): Let me but escape this time, I'll never venture more.

MRS. LOVEIT: Bellinda, you shall go with me.

BELLINDA: I have such a heaviness hangs on me with what I did this morning, I would fain go home and sleep, my dear.

MRS. LOVEIT: Death and eternal darkness! I shall never sleep again. Raging fevers seize the world and make mankind as restless all as I am! (Exit MRS. LOVEIT.)

---

mirabilis, aqua mirabilis, an old-fashioned restorative, made of spirits of wine and a variety of spices.

carriage, demeanor.

BELLINDA: I knew him false and helped to make him so. Was not her ruin enough to fright me from the danger? It should have been, but love can take no warning. (*Exit* BELLINDA.)

ACT 5 / SCENE 2

(LADY TOWNLEY's *house*)
(*Enter* MEDLEY, YOUNG BELLAIR, LADY TOWNLEY, EMILIA, *and* SMIRK, *a Chaplain.*)

MEDLEY: Bear up, Bellair, and do not let us see that repentance in thine we daily do in married faces.

LADY TOWNLEY: This wedding will strangely surprise my brother when he knows it.

MEDLEY: Your nephew ought to conceal it for a time, madam; since marriage has lost its good name, prudent men seldom expose their own reputations till 'tis convenient to justify their wives.

OLD BELLAIR (*without*): Where are you all there? Out, a dod! will nobody hear?

LADY TOWNLEY: My brother! Quickly, Mr. Smirk, into this closet! you must not be seen yet.

(SMIRK *goes into the closet.*)

(*Enter* OLD BELLAIR *and* LADY TOWNLEY'S PAGE.)

OLD BELLAIR: Desire Mr. Fourbe to walk into the lower parlor; I will be with him presently. (*to* YOUNG BELLAIR) Where have you been sir, you could not wait on me to-day?

YOUNG BELLAIR: About a business.

OLD BELLAIR: Are you so good at business? A dod, I have a business too, you shall dispatch out of hand, sir.—Send for a parson, sister; my Lady Woodvill and her daughter are coming.

LADY TOWNLEY: What need you huddle up things thus?

OLD BELLAIR: Out a pize! youth is apt to play the fool, and 'tis not good it should be in their power.

LADY TOWNLEY: You need not fear your son.

OLD BELLAIR: H' has been idling this morning, and a dod, I do not like him. (*to* EMILIA) How dost thou do, sweetheart?

EMILIA: You are very severe, sir—married in such haste.

OLD BELLAIR: Go to, thou'rt a rogue, and I will talk with thee anon. Here's my Lady Woodvill come.

(*Enter* LADY WOODVILL, HARRIET, *and* BUSY.)

—Welcome, madam; Mr. Fourbe's below with the writings.

LADY WOODVILL: Let us down and make an end then.

OLD BELLAIR: Sister, show the way. (*to* YOUNG BELLAIR, *who is talking to* HARRIET) Harry, your business lies not there yet.—Excuse him till we have done, lady, and then, a dod, he shall be for thee. Mr. Medley, we must trouble you to be a witness.

MEDLEY: I luckily came for that purpose, sir.

(*Exeunt* OLD BELLAIR, YOUNG BELLAIR, LADY TOWNLEY, *and* LADY WOODVILL.)

BUSY: What will you do, madam?

HARRIET: Be carried back and mewed up in the country again—run away here—anything rather than be married to a man I do not care for! Dear Emilia, do thou advise me.

EMILIA: Mr. Bellair is engaged, you know.

HARRIET: I do, but know not what the fear of losing an estate may fright him to.

EMILIA: In the desperate condition you are in, you should consult with some judicious man. What think you of Mr. Dorimant?

HARRIET: I do not think of him at all.

BUSY (*aside*): She thinks of nothing else, I am sure.

EMILIA: How fond your mother was of Mr. Courtage!

HARRIET: Because I contrived the mistake to make a little mirth you believe I like the man.

EMILIA: Mr. Bellair believes you love him.

HARRIET: Men are seldom in the right when they guess at a woman's mind. Would she whom he loves loved him no better!

BUSY (*aside*): That's e'en well enough, on all conscience.

EMILIA: Mr. Dorimant has a great deal of wit.

HARRIET: And takes a great deal of pains to show it.

EMILIA: He's extremely well fashioned.

HARRIET: Affectedly grave, or ridiculously wild and apish.

BUSY: You defend him still against your mother!

HARRIET: I would not were he justly rallied, but I cannot hear anyone undeservedly railed at.

EMILIA: Has your woman learnt the song you were so taken with?

HARRIET: I was fond of a new thing; 'tis dull at a second hearing.

EMILIA: Mr. Dorimant made it.

BUSY: She knows it, madam, and has made me sing it at least a dozen times this morning.

HARRIET: Thy tongue is as impertinent as thy fingers.

EMILIA: You have provoked her.

BUSY: 'Tis but singing the song and I shall appease her.

EMILIA: Prithee, do.

HARRIET: She has a voice will grate your ears worse than a cat-call, and dresses so ill she's scarce fit to trick up a yeoman's daughter on a holiday.

(BUSY *sings.*)

SONG
BY SIR C. S.°

As Amoret with Phyllis sat,
  One evening on the plain,
And saw the charming Strephon wait
  To tell the nymph his pain;

The threat'ning danger to remove,
  She whispered in her ear,
'Ah, Phyllis, if you would not love,
  This shepherd do not hear!

'None ever had so strange an art,
  His passion to convey
Into a list'ning virgin's heart,
  And steal her soul away.

'Fly, fly betimes, for fear you give
  Occasion for your fate.'
'In vain,' said she; 'in vain I strive!
  Alas, 'tis now too late.'

(*Enter* DORIMANT.)

DORIMANT: Music so softens and disarms the mind—

HARRIET: That not one arrow does resistance find.

DORIMANT: Let us make use of the lucky minute, then.

HARRIET (*aside, turning from* DORIMANT): My love springs with my blood into my face; I dare not look upon him yet.

DORIMANT: What have we here? the picture of celebrated beauty giving audience in public to a declared lover?

HARRIET: Play the dying fop and make the piece complete, sir.

DORIMANT: What think you if the hint were well improved—the whole mystery° of making love pleasantly designed and wrought in a suit of hangings?°

HARRIET: 'Twere needless to execute fools in effigy who suffer daily in their own persons.

DORIMANT (*to* EMILIA, *aside*): Mrs. Bride, for such I know this happy day has made you—

EMILIA (*aside*): Defer the formal joy you are to give me, and mind your business with her. (*Aloud.*) Here are dreadful preparations, Mr. Dorimant—writings sealing, and a parson sent for.

DORIMANT: To marry this lady—

BUSY: Condemned she is, and what will become of her I know not, without you generously engage in a rescue.

C.S., almost certainly Sir Car Scroope, who wrote the prologue. **mystery,** art. **designed . . . hangings,** drawn and embroidered in a set of draperies.

DORIMANT: In this sad condition, madam, I can do no less than offer you my service.

HARRIET: The obligation is not great; you are the common sanctuary for all young women who run from their relations.

DORIMANT: I have always my arms open to receive the distressed. But I will open my heart and receive you, where none yet did ever enter. You have filled it with a secret, might I but let you know it—

HARRIET: Do not speak it if you would have me believe it; your tongue is so famed for falsehood, 'twill do the truth an injury. (*Turns away her head.*)

DORIMANT: Turn not away, then, but look on me and guess it.

HARRIET: Did you not tell me there was no credit to be given to faces?—that women nowadays have their passions as much at will as they have their complexions, and put on joy and sadness, scorn and kindness, with the same ease they do their paint and patches? Are they the only counterfeits?

DORIMANT: You wrong your own while you suspect my eyes. By all the hope I have in you, the inimitable color in your cheeks is not more free from art than are the sighs I offer.

HARRIET: In men who have been long hardened in sin we have reason to mistrust the first signs of repentance.

DORIMANT: The prospect of such a heaven will make me persevere and give you marks that are infallible.

HARRIET: What are those?

DORIMANT: I will renounce all the joys I have in friendship and in wine, sacrifice to you all the interest I have in other women—

HARRIET: Hold! Though I wish you devout, I would not have you turn fanatic. Could you neglect these a while and make a journey into the country?

DORIMANT: To be with you, I could live there and never send one thought to London.

HARRIET: Whate'er you say, I know all beyond High Park's a desert to you, and that no gallantry can draw you farther.

DORIMANT: That has been the utmost limit of my love; but now my passion knows no bounds, and there's no measure to be taken of what I'll do for you from anything I ever did before.

HARRIET: When I hear you talk thus in Hampshire I shall begin to think there may be some little truth enlarged upon.

DORIMANT: Is this all? Will you not promise me—?

HARRIET: I hate to promise; what we do then is expected from us and wants much of the welcome it finds when it surprises.

DORIMANT: May I not hope?

HARRIET: That depends on you and not on me, and 'tis to no purpose to forbid it. *(Turns to* BUSY.*)*

BUSY: Faith, madam, now I perceive the gentleman loves you too, e'en let him know your mind, and torment yourselves no longer.

HARRIET: Dost think I have no sense of modesty?

BUSY: Think, if you lose this you may never have another opportunity.

HARRIET: May he hate me (a curse that frights me when I speak it), if ever I do a thing against the rules of decency and honor.

DORIMANT *(to* EMILIA*):* I am beholding to you for your good intentions, madam.

EMILIA: I thought the concealing of our marriage from her might have done you better service.

DORIMANT: Try her again.

EMILIA: What have you resolved, madam? The time draws near.

HARRIET: To be obstinate and protest against this marriage.

(Enter LADY TOWNLEY *in haste.)*

LADY TOWNLEY *(to* EMILIA*):* Quickly, quickly! let Mr. Smirk out of the closet.

*(*SMIRK *comes out of the closet.)*

HARRIET: A parson! *(to* DORIMANT*)* Had you laid him in here?

DORIMANT: I knew nothing of him.

HARRIET: Should it appear you did, your opinion of my easiness may cost you dear.

(Enter OLD BELLAIR, YOUNG BELLAIR, MEDLEY, *and* LADY WOODVILL.*)*

OLD BELLAIR: Out a pize! the canonical hour° is almost past. Sister, is the man of God come?

LADY TOWNLEY: He waits your leisure.

OLD BELLAIR *(to* SMIRK*):* By your favor, sir.—A dod, a pretty spruce fellow. What may we call him?

LADY TOWNLEY: Mr. Smirk—my Lady Biggot's chaplain.

OLD BELLAIR: A wise woman! a dod, she is. The man will serve for the flesh as well as the spirit. *(to* SMIRK*)* Please you, sir, to commission a young couple to go to bed together a God's name?—Harry!

YOUNG BELLAIR: Here, sir.

OLD BELLAIR: Out a pize! Without your mistress in your hand!

SMIRK: Is this the gentleman?

OLD BELLAIR: Yes, sir.

___

canonical hour, the time (at this period from eight to twelve o'clock in the morning) during which a marriage could be legally performed.

SMIRK: Are you not mistaken, sir?

OLD BELLAIR: A dod, I think not, sir.

SMIRK: Sure, you are, sir!

OLD BELLAIR: You look as if you would forbid the banns, Mr. Smirk. I hope you have no pretension to the lady.

SMIRK: Wish him joy, sir; I have done him the good office to-day already.

OLD BELLAIR: Out a pize! What do I hear?

LADY TOWNLEY: Never storm, brother; the truth is out.

OLD BELLAIR: How say you, sir? Is this your wedding day?

YOUNG BELLAIR: It is, sir.

OLD BELLAIR: And a dod, it shall be mine, too. *(to* EMILIA*)* Give me thy hand, sweetheart. What dost thou mean? Give me thy hand, I say.

*(*EMILIA *kneels and* YOUNG BELLAIR.*)*

LADY TOWNLEY: Come, come! give her your blessing; this is the woman your son loved and is married to.

OLD BELLAIR: Ha! cheated! cozened! and by your contrivance, sister!

LADY TOWNLEY: What would you do with her? She's a rogue and you can't abide her.

MEDLEY: Shall I hit her a pat for you, sir?

OLD BELLAIR *(flinging away):* A dod, you are all rogues, and I never will forgive you.

LADY TOWNLEY: Whither? Whither away?

MEDLEY: Let him go and cool awhile.

LADY WOODVILL *(to* DORIMANT*):* Here's a business broke out now, Mr. Courtage; I am made a fine fool of.

DORIMANT: You see the old gentleman knew nothing of it.

LADY WOODVILL: I find he did not. I shall have some trick put upon me if I stay in this wicked town any longer.—Harriet, dear child, where art thou? I'll into the country straight.

OLD BELLAIR: A dod, madam, you shall hear me first.

(Enter MRS. LOVEIT *and* BELLINDA*)*

MRS. LOVEIT: Hither my man dogged him.

BELLINDA: Yonder he stands, my dear.

MRS. LOVEIT: I see him *(aside)* and with him the face that has undone me. Oh, that I were but where I might throw out the anguish of my heart! Here it must rage within and break it.

LADY TOWNLEY: Mrs. Loveit! Are you afraid to come forward?

MRS. LOVEIT: I was amazed to see so much company here in a morning. The occasion sure is extraordinary.

DORIMANT *(aside):* Loveit and Bellinda! The devil owes me a shame to-day and I think never will have done paying it.

MRS. LOVEIT: Married! dear Emilia! How am I transported with the news!

HARRIET (to DORIMANT): I little thought Emilia was the woman Mr. Bellair was in love with. I'll chide her for not trusting me with the secret.

DORIMANT: How do you like Mrs. Loveit?

HARRIET: She's a famed mistress of yours, I hear.

DORIMANT: She has been, on occasion.

OLD BELLAIR (to LADY WOODVILL): A dod, madam, I cannot help it.

LADY WOODVILL: You need make no more apologies, sir.

EMILIA (to MRS. LOVEIT): The old gentleman's excusing himself to my Lady Woodvill.

MRS. LOVEIT: Ha, ha, ha! I never heard of anything so pleasant!

HARRIET (to DORIMANT): She's extremely overjoyed at something.

DORIMANT: At nothing. She is one of those hoyting° ladies who gaily fling themselves about and force a laugh when their aching hearts are full of discontent and malice.

MRS. LOVEIT: O heaven! I was never so near killing myself with laughing.—Mr. Dorimant, are you a brideman?

LADY WOODVILL: Mr. Dorimant!—Is this Mr. Dorimant, madam?

MRS. LOVEIT: If you doubt it, your daughter can resolve you, I suppose.

LADY WOODVILL: I am cheated too—basely cheated!

OLD BELLAIR: Out a pize! what's here? More knavery yet?

LADY WOODVILL: Harriet, on my blessing come away, I charge you!

HARRIET: Dear mother, do but stay and hear me.

LADY WOODVILL: I am betrayed and thou art undone, I fear.

HARRIET: Do not fear it; I have not, nor never will, do anything against my duty—believe me, dear mother, do!

DORIMANT (to MRS. LOVEIT): I had trusted you with this secret but that I knew the violence of your nature would ruin my fortune, as now unluckily it has. I thank you, madam.

MRS. LOVEIT: She's an heiress, I know, and very rich.

DORIMANT: To satisfy you, I must give up my interest wholly to my love. Had you been a reasonable woman, I might have secured 'em both and been happy.

MRS. LOVEIT: You might have trusted me with anything of this kind—you know you might. Why did you go under a wrong name?

DORIMANT: The story is too long to tell you now. Be

satisfied, this is the business; this is the mask has kept me from you.

BELLINDA (aside): He's tender of my honor though he's cruel to my love.

MRS. LOVEIT: Was it no idle mistress, then?

DORIMANT: Believe me, a wife to repair the ruins of my estate, that needs it.

MRS. LOVEIT: The knowledge of this makes my grief hang lighter on my soul, but I shall never be more happy.

DORIMANT: Bellinda!

BELLINDA: Do not think of clearing yourself with me; it is impossible. Do all men break their words thus?

DORIMANT: Th'extravagant words they speak in love. 'Tis as unreasonable to expect we should perform all we promise then, as do all we threaten when we are angry. When I see you next—

BELLINDA: Take no notice of me, and I shall not hate you.

DORIMANT: How came you to Mrs. Loveit?

BELLINDA: By a mistake the chairmen made for want of my giving them directions.

DORIMANT: 'Twas a pleasant one. We must meet again.

BELLINDA: Never.

DORIMANT: Never!

BELLINDA: When we do, may I be as infamous as you are false.

LADY TOWNLEY (to LADY WOODVILL): Men of Mr. Dorimant's character always suffer in the general opinion of the world.

MEDLEY: You can make no judgment of a witty man from common fame, considering the prevailing faction, madam.

OLD BELLAIR: A dod, he's in the right.

MEDLEY: Besides, 'tis a common error among women to believe too well of them they know, and too ill of them they don't.

OLD BELLAIR: A dod, he observes well.

LADY TOWNLEY: Believe me, madam, you will find Mr. Dorimant as civil a gentleman as you thought Mr. Courtage.

HARRIET: If you would but know him better—

LADY WOODVILL: You have a mind to know him better! Come away! You shall never see him more.

HARRIET: Dear mother, stay!

LADY WOODVILL: I wo'not be consenting to your ruin.

HARRIET: Were my fortune in your power—

LADY WOODVILL: Your person is.

HARRIET: Could I be disobedient, I might take it out of yours and put it into his.

LADY WOODVILL: 'Tis that you would be at; you would marry this Dorimant.

HARRIET: I cannot deny it; I would, and never will marry any other man.

LADY WOODVILL: Is this the duty that you promised?

---

hoyting, hoydenish, romping.

HARRIET: But I will never marry him against your will.

LADY WOODVILL (aside): She knows the way to melt my heart.—(to HARRIET) Upon yourself light your undoing!

MEDLEY (to OLD BELLAIR): Come, sir, you have not the heart any longer to refuse your blessing.

OLD BELLAIR: A dod, I ha'not.—Rise, and God bless you both! Make much of her, Harry; she deserves thy kindness. (to EMILIA) A dod, sirrah, I did not think it had been in thee.

(*Enter* SIR FOPLING *and* PAGE.)

SIR FOPLING FLUTTER: 'Tis a damned windy day.— Hey, page, is my periwig right?

PAGE: A little out of order, sir.

SIR FOPLING FLUTTER: Pox o' this apartment! It wants an antechamber to adjust oneself in. (to MRS. LOVEIT) Madam, I came from your house, and your servants directed me hither.

MRS. LOVEIT: I will give order hereafter they shall direct you better.

SIR FOPLING FLUTTER: The great satisfaction I had in the Mail last night has given me much disquiet since.

MRS. LOVEIT: 'Tis likely to give me more than I desire.

SIR FOPLING FLUTTER (aside): What the devil makes her so reserved?—Am I guilty of an indiscretion, madam?

MRS. LOVEIT: You will be of a great one if you continue your mistake, sir.

SIR FOPLING FLUTTER: Something puts you out of humor.

MRS. LOVEIT: The most foolish, inconsiderable thing that ever did.

SIR FOPLING FLUTTER: Is it in my power?

MRS. LOVEIT: To hang or drown it. Do one of 'em and trouble me no more.

SIR FOPLING FLUTTER: So *fière*? *Serviteur,* madam!°— Medley, where's Dorimant?

MEDLEY: Methinks the lady has not made you those advances today she did last night, Sir Fopling.

SIR FOPLING FLUTTER: Prithee, do not talk of her!

MEDLEY: She would be a *bonne fortune*.

SIR FOPLING FLUTTER: Not to me at present.

MEDLEY: Not so?

SIR FOPLING FLUTTER: An intrigue now would be but a temptation to me to throw away that vigor on one which I mean shall shortly make my court to the whole sex in a ballet.

MEDLEY: Wisely considered, Sir Fopling.

SIR FOPLING FLUTTER: No one woman is worth the loss of a cut° in a caper.

MEDLEY: Not when 'tis so universally designed.

LADY WOODVILL: Mr. Dorimant, everyone has spoke so much in your behalf that I can no longer doubt but I was in the wrong.

MRS. LOVEIT (to BELLINDA): There's nothing but falsehood and impertinence in this world; all men are villains or fools. Take example from my misfortunes. Bellinda, if thou wouldst be happy, give thyself wholly up to goodness.

HARRIET (to MRS. LOVEIT): Mr. Dorimant has been your God Almighty long enough; 'tis time to think of another.

MRS. LOVEIT: Jeered by her! I will lock myself up in my house and never see the world again.

HARRIET: A nunnery is the more fashionable place for such a retreat, and has been the fatal consequence of many a *belle passion*.

MRS. LOVEIT (aside): Hold, heart, till I get home! Should I answer, 'twould make her triumph greater. (*Is going out.*)

DORIMANT: Your hand, Sir Fopling—

SIR FOPLING FLUTTER: Shall I wait upon you, madam?

MRS. LOVEIT: Legion of fools, as many devils take thee! (*Exit* MRS. LOVEIT.)

MEDLEY: Dorimant, I pronounce thy reputation clear; and henceforward when I would know anything of woman, I will consult no other oracle.

SIR FOPLING FLUTTER (gazing after MRS. LOVEIT): Stark mad, by all that's handsome!—Dorimant, thou hast engaged me in a pretty business.

DORIMANT: I have not leisure now to talk about it.

OLD BELLAIR (indicating SIR FOPLING): Out a pize! what does this man of mode do here again?

LADY TOWNLEY: He'll be an excellent entertainment within, brother, and is luckily come to raise the mirth of the company.

LADY WOODVILL: Madam, I take my leave of you.

LADY TOWNLEY: What do you mean, madam?

LADY WOODVILL: To go this afternoon part of my way to Hartly.°

OLD BELLAIR: A dod, you shall stay and dine first! Come, we will all be good friends, and you shall give Mr. Dorimant leave to wait upon you and your daughter in the country.

LADY WOODVILL: If his occasions bring him that way, I have now so good an opinion of him, he shall be welcome.

HARRIET: —To a great rambling, lone house that looks as it were not inhabited, the family's so small. There you'll find my mother, an old lame aunt, and myself, sir, perched up on chairs at a distance in a large parlor, sitting moping like

---

so fière? Serviteur, madam, so fierce? Your servant, madam! *cut,* a rapid "twiddling" of the feet by a dancer who has sprung in the air.

Hartly, Hartley Row, Hampshire, about half-way between London and Salisbury.

three or four melancholy birds in a spacious volary.° Does not this stagger your resolution?

DORIMANT: Not at all, madam. The first time I saw you you left me with the pangs of love upon me, and this day my soul has quite given up her liberty.

HARRIET: This is more dismal than the country! Emilia, pity me, who am going to that sad place. Methinks I hear the hateful noise of rooks already—kaw, kaw, kaw! There's music in the worst cry° in London—'My dill and cowcumbers to pickle!'

OLD BELLAIR: Sister, knowing of this matter, I hope you have provided us some good cheer.

LADY TOWNLEY: I have, brother, and the fiddles too.

OLD BELLAIR: Let 'em strike up, then; the young lady shall have a dance before she departs. *(Dance.)*

(After the dance.)—So! now we'll in and make this an arrant wedding-day. *(To the pit.)*

And if these honest gentlemen rejoice,
A dod, the boy has made a happy choice.

(Exeunt omnes.)

EPILOGUE

By Mr. Dryden

Most modern wits such monstrous fools have shown,
They seemed not of heav'n's making, but their own.
Those nauseous harlequins in farce may pass,
But there goes more to a substantial ass.
Something of man must be exposed to view
That, gallants, they may more resemble you.

Sir Fopling is a fool so nicely writ,
The ladies would mistake him for a wit;
And when he sings, talks loud, and cocks,° would cry,
'I vow, methinks he's pretty company!
So brisk, so gay, so travelled, so refined,
As he took pains to graff upon his kind.'°
True fops help nature's work and go to school,
To file and finish God A'mighty's fool.
Yet none Sir Fopling him, or him, can call;
He's knight o'th' shire,° and represents ye all.
From each he meets, he culls whate'er he can;
Legion's his name, a people in a man.
His bulky folly gathers as it goes
And, rolling o'er you, like a snowball grows.
His various modes from various fathers follow;
One taught the toss,° and one the new French
        wallow.°
His sword-knot, this; his cravat, this designed;
And this, the yard-long snake° he twirls behind.
From one the sacred periwig he gained,
Which wind ne'er blew, nor touch of hat profaned.
Another's diving bow he did adore,
Which with a shog° casts all the hair before
Till he with full decorum brings it back,
And rises with a water spaniel shake.
As for his songs (the ladies' dear delight),
Those sure he took from most of you who write.
Yet every man is safe from what he feared,
For no one fool is hunted from the herd.

---

volary, aviary. *cry,* street-vendor's cry.

cocks, cocks his hat. *graff . . . kind,* as if he had taken pains to improve his natural talents. *shire,* a representative (properly, in parliament). *toss,* an upward jerk of the head. *wallow,* a rolling gait. *snake,* a long curl or tail attached to a wig. *shog,* a shake.

Figure 1. Sir Fopling Flutter (John Wood), dressed in a striking costume and wig, effusively greets Harriet (Helen Mirren) at Lady Townley's ball, while a sardonic Dorimant (Alan Howard) looks on in the Royal Shakespeare Company production of *The Man of Mode*, directed by Terry Hands, 1971. (Photograph: Donald Cooper, Photostage Limited.)

Figure 2. Dorimant (Alan Howard) taunts his current (and soon-to-be former) mistress Mrs. Loveit (Vivien Merchant) in the Royal Shakespeare Company production of *The Man of Mode*, directed by Terry Hands, 1971. (Photograph: Donald Cooper, Photostage Limited.)

Figure 3. Harriet (Helen Mirren) flirts with Dorimant (Alan Howard) while Emilia (Isla Blair) watches in the background during the Royal Shakespeare Company production of *The Man of Mode*, directed by Terry Hands, 1971. (Photograph: Donald Cooper, Photostage Limited.)

Figure 4. Dorimant (Alan Howard) contemplates the giant Newton's cradle that was the main feature of Timothy O'Brien's set for the Royal Shakespeare Company production of *The Man of Mode,* directed by Terry Hands, 1971. (Photograph: Donald Cooper, Photostage Limited.)

Staging of *The Man of Mode*

INTERVIEW WITH DIRECTOR TERRY HANDS
AND DESIGNER TIMOTHY O'BRIEN OF
THE ROYAL SHAKESPEARE COMPANY
PRODUCTION, 1971, BY ROBERT WATERHOUSE

THE MAN OF MODE by Sir George Etherege, a new arrival in the Royal Shakespeare Company's repertoire at the Aldwych, is the seventh RSC production directed by Terry Hands and designed by Timothy O'Brien. Their partnership, begun in 1968 with the notable reconstitution of *The Merry Wives of Windsor*, and continued with *The Latent Heterosexual, Pericles, Women Beware Women, Bartholomew Fair*, and—earlier this year—*The Merchant of Venice*. The current production of *Man of Mode*, only the second time it has been seen professionally acted in some 200 years, is an interesting attempt to put a Restoration comedy into a roughly contemporary setting, and is consistent with the RSC's policy of exploring the less well known texts. For the first in *P&P*'s new series investigating notable director-designer partnerships, Robert Waterhouse went to the Aldwych to discuss with Terry Hands and Timothy O'Brien their approach to the play and to working with each other.

WATERHOUSE: Why *Man of Mode*?

HANDS: First of all the text. We thought it was good prose of a kind which hadn't been heard for a long time. The reason why it hadn't been done for about 200 years was that its moral philosophy was abhorrent to the eighteenth and nineteenth centuries. The behaviour of its characters upset nineteenth century morality. This absence from the stage gave us the opportunity to present a Restoration play as though it was new, written yesterday. People could come and see it without any preconceptions.

WATERHOUSE: But it remains a Restoration comedy, doesn't it? Isn't it very stylised in the way that it's written?

HANDS: Some of it is. Half the text is straight naturalistic prose of a kind John Osborne would be proud of; the other half is written in the artificial terms of those who delight in speaking to impress others. But people do that as well today. This play was written in 1676, some 16 years after the Restoration itself; it has the label of a Restoration comedy but our understanding of Restoration drama derives from a tradition of playing it, not from a knowledge of the period. The little that we do know about the Restoration style suggests that it was a sort of cabaret: they put in Pop numbers, the latest fashions and anything that was exciting on the scene. Restoration drama doesn't appear to have been the kind of finger twirling mannered performance we've become used to.

WATERHOUSE: Did your approach open up many design possibilities?

HANDS: Well, only about 40 lines of text actually relate to the period. This left us free to concentrate on trying to create the effect on the audience of today that the play might have had upon the audience in its own time rather than presenting an erroneous museum facsimile. We wanted a design concept that would delight the audience, enable them to see themselves in the play like the 1676 audience might have seen themselves, but be sufficiently removed for them to get the satirical points and be amused by the goings on.

O'BRIEN: Also, we found to our pleasure when we examined the play that it was not a late example of Restoration comedy, where the form is very set, but that it had affinities with Jacobean theatre; we found we were dealing with a comedy where we could sympathise with the characters and see their problems in terms of ours. I recently met a girl in Hampshire who had been to see *Man of Mode*—she was a totally normal member, if that can be imagined, of the theatre going public. She told me that the play had excited her and that afterwards she went through St. James's Park and thought "What a pity the park isn't expressed in terms of the silver balls used in the set; it's much more fun that way."

WATERHOUSE: The night I saw the play the audience responded much more in the second act than the first.

HANDS: But what did you think?

WATERHOUSE: I thought the text might have been taken more by the scruff of its neck. How much editing did you do?

HANDS: Very little.

WATERHOUSE: The first act in particular was overlong and slow in getting the carnival atmosphere you say you wanted.

HANDS: Editing the first act wouldn't solve very much because one of the things Etherege does is spend one and a quarter hours in getting his characters on stage. The last character isn't introduced until the fifth scene; by then he's ready to start his play so the reason why the second half is more interesting is that the play only begins with the last scene of the first

479

half. The danger is to regard it as a farce, which it isn't.

WATERHOUSE: Isn't there a problem, then, of not knowing on what levels to read the characters?

O'BRIEN: The play divides up into artificial and natural characters.

HANDS: The two main artificial characters, Mrs. Loveit and Sir Fopling Flutter, have to be rejected at the end from a hierarchical society which is graded from the most natural up to the most artificial.

O'BRIEN: In one instance, however, something contradictory to the point we're making happens. In Scene 8 Sir Fopling comes to Dorimant's house to examine the bed for traces of Belinda's ruin and is astonished at the urbanity of Dorimant at being able to conceal it. In a passage after that Sir Fopling becomes tremendously alive inside his artificial limits. Someone says 'Look, Sir Fopling's dancing' and he's up on a cloud at the end of a wonderfully successful party where he has felt himself the real comet in the sky, and he's celebrating this so nakedly in his Brandenberg with its soft colours and weaving about the stage like some marvellous happy moth. Then he explains that he has written a song, which is teased out of him. It's read over and he's persuaded to sing it. He stands on the bed, starts to sing, and suddenly realises it's a much better song then he remembered. Almost with tears of pride he sings. Then he sits down and his friends say: 'Of its kind it couldn't be bettered and it's particularly remarkable for being in the French manner.' 'That's what I aimed at,' he says, bursts into tears, and then makes a marvelous gesture: he cries 'Slap, down goes the glass and we're at it.' That's not artificial, it's someone so enthusiastic, so capable of enjoying himself, that the artificiality has vanished. At that point the play is really consummate.

HANDS: If one is watching this scene without the benefit, or hindrance, of twenty or thirty years theatre experience, it all becomes as clear as a bell. I'm sure most younger audiences would allow Sir Fopling to develop as he goes along, not stereotype him. It's very much a doing of your own thing play. The reason why we tried a more contemporary approach is that the play has so many points of contact with real life; behaving naturally is the crux of the Dorimant-Harriet relationship. In order to point up this the play shows every other layer of behaviour; most Restoration plays do the same. I'd like to see other directors and designers go through all the Restoration plays and put them into some recognisable form. Look how badly we do Molière in this country. Really appallingly badly. Molière was a great showman; if there happened to be a team of jugglers around he would put them into the play. There was none of this reverential rubbish about manners and the way people behave. I would passionately like to see

Molière with new songs. Surely there is a way to get him back into common currency.

O'BRIEN: One should emphasise in parallel the much quieter virtues of an approach with which the audience can associate easily, so that it is understood that people, not puppets, are on stage. There should be no translation into the superficial fads of the moment. We have made the odd mistake in the past when searching for a contemporary point of contact in introducing flip things which have nothing to do with fundamentals.

WATERHOUSE: So when you got down to thinking about stage design and costumes what were your fundamentals?

O'BRIEN: We started thinking in terms of the Restoration—wouldn't you? But one of the problems in doing a play in period is that you have truthfully to involve your cast in a whole study of how to handle the Restoration idiom—an obstacle to be surmounted before the text can be served.

WATERHOUSE: And that wasn't worthwhile?

HANDS: It wasn't possible. Nobody knows exactly what they did. Also, nobody really knows how people behaved in the streets.

O'BRIEN: If you give people Restoration clothes you impose on them a style of movement and behaviour which has everything to do with the problems they're facing but nothing very much to do with the emotions and situations they're trying to express.

HANDS: Costume of any period is designed more to reveal than to conceal certain parts of the body. The parts revealed are those of particular sexual or, more often than not, aesthetic interest to the period, and at the time of the Restoration much men's clothing was designed to reveal the calf. Taste is catholic today about which parts of the body you reveal, but the calf isn't one of them. So what's the point in a play where men are chasing women and women chasing men because they both fancy each other, all dressed in a sexual aesthetic which has no relevance to the audience?

WATERHOUSE: Was this a major consideration?

HANDS: Absolutely. The complexity of the play is who is chasing whom, so surely you need to put it into a context which the audience can understand. It seemed crucial to begin with trousers. We looked at modern clothes, deciding what they did and why they did it, then Tim started to develop a costume from his idea of what our men would want to show: chests and arms, if you like biceps. So the sleeves became fuller than modern clothes, the chest area was more distinct—but not so much that the audience wouldn't understand what was going on. It was a very rich world, too; we wanted to convey wealth, colour, flamboyance. If the play were done in Restoration costume, only the sophisticated half of the audience would respond; there's an enormous new audience which wants to see plays it can relate to. Everything I do is angled towards people who may be walking into that theatre for the very first time.

O'BRIEN: It's interesting how one's faith is confirmed. We were painting the set in a South London workshop with the help of young people who had been either to art schools or to a university, and one of them took a look at the model and asked me to explain what the play was about, which I did in terms of Dorimant as the libertine forced by Harriet to see her not as another conquest but as someone for whom it might be worth changing himself. The boy then said the set struck him as something like a 'new restoration.' His words were an absolute echo of something Terry and I tried to formulate very early on.

HANDS: I was once in a school with Theatregoround when we asked a boy why he didn't go to the theatre. He replied that he had no interest in seeing "Some bloke poncing around in a crown." He's right. Who does want to see someone poncing around in a crown? There's a big audience who do, of course, and who scream if they can't see people poncing about in crowns, but there are large numbers who would just as soon see people in tracksuits. The theatre is no more than animated story telling, after all. Every other period except our own—and they were all more successful than ours in getting audiences into the theatre—used a form of heightened modern dress. But don't get the idea that we knew from the start where we were going to get: much of this production developed during rehearsals.

O'BRIEN: This often happens when a designer and director are planning a show. In bald terms you can guess at your destination; But you cannot be confident that this destination is well-chosen. So you begin to work but are constantly haunted by alternatives. Sometimes you long to have it revealed to you that the traditional mode is correct because that can solve so much—it means you'll be working in a language understood within the profession and one that you hope still has validity and carrying power to the public. However, on this occasion, we were constantly disappointed in any such hope; we kept having to try to find a heightened modern version, and that's when the gradient gets steep because you must be frightfully careful of wrong associations and you have to invent extremely accurately. A lot of the designer's and director's work is preventing a wrong audience reaction on the way to provoking an intensified right reaction. You work slowly forward, discarding things to the point where, you hope, every component in the production points to the same end.

WATERHOUSE: You're talking about after you made the model?

O'BRIEN: In the event, and it need not have been so, we found our way in through the set.

WATERHOUSE: How long did you actually have to prepare this production?

O'BRIEN: Not as long as usual because *Man of Mode* was a replacement for another play rather late in the day; I was working on *Enemies* with David Jones, and we had about a fortnight from that opening night to the start of the new rehearsals. Normally we have design thought out when we begin rehearsals, though it is often modified. This time we had only the first version of the set available when we talked to the actors. It wasn't, in fact, as terrifying as it first seemed because the actors contributed enormously to our ideas. I was anxious enough, though, since whatever you need physically has to be made after it is designed. People ask me whether I would like to come to decisions earlier or later: the answer is that one wants to take decisions as late as possible, in the light of as much information as possible, but with enough time remaining for these decisions to become concrete objects.

WATERHOUSE: A pretty tall order.

O'BRIEN: Of course. But the designer who is responsible for the provision of designs as well as the designing process is both the procrastinator and the expeditor. If he takes regrets away from a production they are not only that the wrong decisions were made but that they were poorly carried out for lack of time, because there's a process of digestion necessary for manufacture as well as thought.

WATERHOUSE: Does this need for time lead to clashes with directors?

HANDS: Clashes waste time.

O'BRIEN: That's right.

HANDS: You cannot afford to waste time, and when you have only a short preparation period you're really dependent on one another. This was our seventh play together, so even though we had little time we knew each other's shorthands. Normally we have a couple of months to formulate our ideas and then up to ten weeks' rehearsal at Stratford. But even then, why quarrel? Theatre is such a collaborative process—in English theatre you can't really rule where one man's job starts and another ends. The art is to get all the strands knotted for the first night.

WATERHOUSE: But do you work better under pressure?

HANDS: There's never any shortage of pressure in the RSC and I don't think it helps matters to close up the time allowed as well.

O'BRIEN: There are two distinct ways of working—which may not really be as distinct as they at first seem. There's the sifting and harvesting process when you have a lot of time. The other way, when you have little time, the sifting process suffers. You need instant sifting, followed by instant decisions.

WATERHOUSE: By instant you mean two or three days?

O'BRIEN: Yes. Sometimes crucial matters have to be decided over a weekend that you would perhaps have liked a fortnight to discuss. This should lead us into certain forms of caution. We never say we're unhappy in public, but obviously we are more uncomfortable at some times than others. One of the nightmares is the temptation to think that you have time to do the sifting when you patently haven't, because that leads to real neurosis. One of the things which Terry and I are beginning to consider is how much damage is done by the wrong sort of delay. We belong to a theatre where every liberty can be taken to come to the right conclusion. That's the form. I think sometimes it would be wise to come to the conclusion a little

more sharply because other processes need their elbow room—amongst them is the process of rehearsing the actors. If you're still in a conceptual turmoil when rehearsing actors everybody suffers from the irresolution that is apparent.

HANDS: This is terribly important. The actors must be the prime consideration because they are the ones who finally have to go out and play out that gigantic bluff in front of the audience. To work under pressure, or not under pressure, is unimportant; what is worrying is when the processes get in the way of the actors' development within the play. On *Man of Mode*, where we were working under tremendous pressure of time, three actors had their entire costumes changed because we had made a hasty decision which was inaccurate.

REVIEW OF THE ROYAL SHAKESPEARE COMPANY PRODUCTION, 1971, BY IRVING WARDLE

Like Amsterdam's specialist brothels, Restoration comedy was formerly tolerated as a libertine entertainment on the understanding that it made no contact with the flow of normal life. One of the main achievements in the past decade of classical production is its release from this ghetto by the elimination of that *cordon sanitaire* once known as "Restoration style." Plenty of productions exemplify this process, but none more completely than Terry Hands's version of *The Man of Mode* which admits not only the human content of the play but allows it a sense of continuity stretching back to Shakespeare and forward into our own time. Rarely has the RSC's classical-contemporary policy been more fully vindicated.

This is claimed as the first London revival of the comedy since 1766: but Prospect Productions mounted it in Yorkshire a few years ago, and the memory of that show, with its standard parade of bloodless gallants and simpering mistresses, heightens the sense of what has been gained at the Aldwych. Comparatively decorous though its text is, *The Man of Mode* is hard to take as an artificial comedy as its fun is unusually cruel. The intrigue turns at least as much on the tactics of dropping women as picking them up; and Dorimant, the principal lover, acts as much from sadism and ruthless vanity as from desire.

Timothy O'Brien's beautiful set derives from a familiar modern living toy, a framework of suspended steel balls, here magnified into a constellation of silver orbs hanging over the stage and gliding into new positions for changes of scene. The costume, long dresses for the girls, and velvet suits (worn with broad brimmed hats) for the men, further locates the piece in a cool playground for the modern peacock generation whose dances and pastoral lyrics go to a John Dankworth score. Here Dorimant (Alan Howard) voluptuously starts the day, relishing the prospect of rejecting a mistress and stripping off to drop into his morning bath to await news of the latest virgins in town. Howard plays Dorimant with a crooked auburn-bearded grin and a body twisted by his own intrigues; you never question his capacities to get things moving, but there is no appeal whatever to sympathy and you relish his humiliations as much as his successes.

This is important, because the full gesture of the production is one of benevolence. In this sense it joins hands, say, with Mr. Hands's production of *The Merry Wives*; an action in which many mean things happen, but which finally develops into a celebration of fecundity from which no one is excluded; not even David Waller's Old Bellair, who goes through the show pinching the bottom of his son's beloved, or

Vivien Merchant, who camps up the discarded Mrs. Loveit into the purple-gowned likeness of a Sunset Boulevard has-been.

The clue to the interpretation may well have been the character for which the play is best remembered: Sir Fopling Flutter, the first of the Restoration's line of Francophile clowns. The point about Sir Fopling is that everyone wants him to do his thing: he is a cause of entertainment, not irritation, to the other characters. And from the first moment of John Wood's performance, torpedoing his white walking stick into the wings, it is clear that he is to be the source of much more than malicious mockery.

Francophile snobbery is one of the basic comic clichés; but by the end Wood has earned sympathy even for that (as in his delight at finding the one English follower in his retinue starting to speak French). It is a lovely, highly vulnerable performance which reestablishes Mr. Wood as a major asset to the company. Helen Mirren's Harriet, tousled amid her immaculate companions, hurtles through the action as an embodiment of rebellious natural life: never more so than when she and Terence Taplin mime a tender courtship scene for the benefit of two matchmaking elders.

REVIEW OF THE ROYAL SHAKESPEARE COMPANY PRODUCTION, 1971, BY STANLEY PRICE

THE RSC have clearly disinterred the dramatic remains of Sir George Etherege for some theatrical purpose. For a start the play stands at a fascinating point in dramatic evolution, a post-Jacobean melodrama conceived in terms of early Restoration comedy. In Etherege the Restoration style takes its earliest shape in substituting the pursuit of sex and the acquisition of dowry for the murkier Jacobean motivations of murder, incest and revenge. Dorimant, the play's principal, emerges as a positively Jacobean villain who uses sex as a weapon in a private war against fashionable society, womankind in general, and himself in particular. The character of the hell-bent rake, Dorimant, supposedly modelled on the Earl of Rochester, was presumably so familiar to contemporary audiences that Etherege thought it unnecessary to delve into any psychological motivations. Dorimant goes about his sexual intrigues and revenges without so much as a motivational by-your-leave. I don't know when the word 'weapon' first came into use in the vernacular for the male member, but in Etherege it achieves something of an exact apotheosis. Dorimant, whether conceived as hero or anti-hero, has his cake and eats it frequently. At the play's end he bags his beautiful, spirited heiress and foreswears fashionable London for married life in the country. He accepts his fate with the resigned self-sacrifice of the contemporary rake who knew full well the wogs really began North of Hyde Park.

Terry Hands' production of The Man of Mode seeks, as is currently modish with 17th Century drama, to put all this sexual plot and counter-plot into a more modern setting. While I know and can frequently sympathise with the arguments in favour of this treatment for over-worked classics, I am more dubious about their validity when applied to lesser-known works. There is the inescapable implication that the director knows the play won't stand firmly on its own two feet, but is important chiefly because of its appositeness to our own time. The snag here is that one spends a great deal of time at such productions pursuing private mental red herrings and not listening to the play. In this form of director's theatre what is at issue is not what the playwright's attitude was to his own time, but what the director's attitude is to our own.

Despite some fascinating programme notes and quotes on Sir George Etherege that show him as wit, gambler, courtier, diplomat and lecher, a veritable prototype for a Restoration comedy, I'm not sure that I took away from this production any strong idea of Etherege's own attitude to his society. Nor do I see at all clearly what Terry Hands' attitude is to that society, or what exact historical or sociological parallels he finds with our own. It is too easy and glib to claim that surfeit of sex and materialism link us to the Restoration admass. After all in what societies hasn't the urge for as much bed and board as possible played a dominant role? Possibly Terry Hands wished to express such universality, but to do so he has fallen for a hodge-podge of styles that confuse rather than elucidate the issues.

His designer, Timothy O'Brien, has used the device of Newton's Cradle to stunning effect. Rescued from scientific obscurity by the Heal's-Habitat nexus as a conversation-piece for the trendy front-parlour, O'Brien has created a gigantic version of the Cradle that encompasses the stage. The six suspended silver spheres are used at different levels and angles to signify scene changes, and help give the production pace as well as an air of fashionable abstract interior décor. The costumes and music, however, veer alarmingly in several directions and periods. The men's fashions seem to strive after King's Road modern but are more in line with the pastel, poetic suits of Gilbert and Sullivan's *Patience*. The women are dressed-up all diaphanous, but Vivien Merchant's Mrs. Loveit is dressed and made-up as though for a '30s Hollywood movie. John Dankworth's music produces one tuneful melody fetchingly sung by Lila Kaye, that would grace any modern musical, but for the rest he appears to be striving for a style that will marry rock and gavotte.

This uneasiness of style carries over into the acting of the play's two stars, Alan Howard and Vivien Merchant, who give performances very much at odds with the straight Restoration comedy style of the rest of the cast. Howard comes down heavily on the interpretation of Dorimant as Jacobean villain. He is a morose, self-tormented lecher who rasps his lines in a series of extended cadences that lure the ear away from an understanding of the complicated plot that Dorimant is at great pains to explain in the first scenes. As Mrs. Loveit, Dorimant's much-abused mistress, Vivien Merchant invests the character with such high-strung histrionics that she seems about to undertake the assassination of Duncan rather than a mere assignation in the Mall. At the serious level at which Miss Merchant takes the part the play's comedy becomes insupportable and the whole production goes out of the window.

For the rest the casting is more fortunate and stylistically in period. The whole production is lifted by the arrival of John Wood. He gives a totally captivating and outrageous display of High French camp as Sir Fopling Flutter, the character that is clearly the blueprint from which Vanburgh created his Lord Foppington. His high moment comes in a splendidly ludicrous but accurate replica of the famous Versailles masque with Sir Fopling as the Sun King. Helen Mirren makes a delightful Harriet, the county heiress of independent mind, and has a hilariously-mimed scene of phoney courtship with Terence Taplin as Bellair. Julian Glover is a smoothly voyeuristic Medley, and Brenda Bruce spreads ineffable good cheer as a permissive dowager. As the laid and discarded Bellinda, Frances de la Tour again shows, after her Miss Hoyden and her Helena in *A Midsummer Night's Dream*, that she is the RSC's most natural comedienne.

In my view *Man of Mode* is good entertainment, stylistically at sea. Its parts are better than its whole, which is perhaps fitting for Sir George Etherege was a gentleman much interested in parts, as an extract from one of his ambassadorial letters from the Diet of Ratisbon, 1687, shows " . . . The best fortune I have had here has been a player something handsomer, and as much as a jilt as Mrs. Barry. Nevertheless this is a Country to satisfy Sir Robert Parker's vanity, for few foul their fingers with touching of a C*** that does not belong to a Countess." Clearly diplomatic bags ain't what they used to be!

RICHARD BRINSLEY SHERIDAN

1751—1816

By the age of twenty-six, Richard Brinsley Sheridan had achieved remarkable successes both in his personal and his professional life. He had married the beautiful Miss Linley with whom he had eloped to France to save her from an unwelcome suitor; he had survived two duels with her frustrated suitor; his first play, *The Rivals,* had been successfully presented at Covent Garden and later in the same year, 1775, his comic opera, *The Duenna,* began a run that would stretch to an amazing 75 performances; he had bought the well-known Drury Lane theater; and *The School for Scandal,* his most famous play, opened there with great success on May 7, 1777. Sheridan's remaining years in the theater were much less noteworthy. He was constantly plagued by debts—running a theater is an expensive business—and he wrote only two more plays: *The Critic* (1779), a witty burlesque of the theatrical process itself; and *Pizarro,* a melodrama adapted from a German source. His interest subsequently turned to politics, and when he died he was given a large public funeral and buried in Westminster Abbey.

The Rivals and *The School for Scandal,* Sheridan's two masterpieces, are not only brilliant theatrical works in themselves, but mark an important moment in English comedy—the return of wit and humor to the stage. For most of the eighteenth century, reactions against the so-called "Immorality and Profaneness of the English Stage" (the words are from the title of Jeremy Collier's famous attack of 1698 on Restoration comedy) had turned comedy away from laughter into melodrama filled with moral and emotional appeals. Such drama is usually referred to as "sentimental comedy," and its characteristics were succinctly described by Oliver Goldsmith, the author of the other great comedy of the late eighteenth century, *She Stoops to Conquer* (1773), in his "Essay on the Theater; or, A Comparison between Laughing and Sentimental Comedy" (1773):

> In these plays almost all the characters are good and exceedingly generous; they are lavish enough of their *tin* money on the stage: and though they want humor, have abundance of sentiment and feeling. If they happen to have faults or foibles, the spectator is taught not only to pardon but to applaud them, in consideration of the goodness of their hearts; so that folly, instead of being ridiculed, is commended, and the comedy aims at touching our passions without the power of being truly pathetic.

As Goldsmith implies here and makes explicit elsewhere in his essay, the spirit of sentimental comedy runs counter to the great tradition of corrective laughter that begins in Greek comedy, finds compelling force in the comedies of Ben Jonson, and dominates the later seventeenth century both in the plays of Molière and those of the English Restoration playwrights.

Sheridan also responded to such "weeping comedy" with his own "laughing comedy," *The Rivals,* which quickly reveals his intentions in the second scene, where he introduces a young woman of markedly sentimental tendencies—so marked, indeed, that they are clearly meant to be a comic caricature. Her name, Lydia Languish, clearly denotes her sentimental excesses, as do the mawkish titles of the books in her library: *The Reward of Constancy, The Fatal Connection, The Mistakes of the Heart,* and *The Delicate Mistress.* Although Lydia is the comedy's romantic heroine, she is nonetheless an extremely silly girl, overwhelmed with romantic notions that Sheridan constantly undercuts. The play's genuine humor, however, derives not from the problems of Lydia, but from the schemes of her lover, Captain Absolute, who disguises himself to woo her and then experiences the comic complications that result from his double identity. Even more memorable to most audiences are two characters whose language is a perpetual source of comic delight: Bob Acres and Mrs. Malaprop. Acres, a country gentleman, figures in the plot as a rival to Absolute for Lydia's hand, but his real stage function is to amuse the audience with his attempts at fashionable dress and speech. Again Sheridan pokes fun at the excesses of sentiment, for Acres is intent on swearing so that "the oath should be an echo to the sense; and this we call the *oath referential* or *sentimental swearing.*" Even more extreme as a figure of affectation and humor is Mrs. Malaprop, whose name has given the word "malapropism" to our language. Her expressed concern for the correct use of language makes the repeatedly garbled language of her speeches even more ludicrous: "but above all, Sir Anthony, she should be mistress of orthodoxy, that she might not mis-spell and mis-pronounce words so shamefully as girls usually do; and likewise that she might reprehend the true meaning of what she is saying."

The School for Scandal at first seems an extension of Sheridan's attack on sentimental comedy, especially considering the satiric portrayal of Joseph Surface, who is praised as a "man of sentiment," when, as his last name implies, he is actually a man of deception. But it should be noted that the moral and emotional sentiments Joseph expresses are themselves neither offensive nor necessarily false. Instead, Sheridan attacks Joseph's *pose* as a man who makes moral statements—"to smile at the jest which plants a thorn in another's breast is to become a principal in the slander"—while actually scheming to slander his brother Charles and steal his beloved. And though Joseph Surface is the subtlest, the most cunning, of the scandal-mongers because he wears the mask of moral concern, he is by no means the only one in the play. With such tag names as Lady Sneerwell, Mrs. Candour, Crabtree, Snake, and Sir Benjamin Backbite, Sheridan, like Molière in *The Misanthrope,* creates an entire gallery of malicious gossips to populate his school for scandal.

Although Sheridan attacks malice masquerading as sentiment, he also presents the value of true sentiment, of genuine feelings that prompt generous actions. In Act IV, scene i, when the seemingly rakish Charles refuses to sell the portrait of his uncle, Sir Oliver, because "The old fellow has been very good to me and, egad, I'll keep his picture while I've a room to put it in," the improvident generosity of his impulse wins him the affection of the disguised Oliver. Similarly, the play's climactic and most intricately structured scene, the "screen scene," is a masterful blend of witty double-entendre, farcical maneuverings, and at the end honest feelings. The scene's tension builds slowly as Lady Teazle, then her husband Sir Peter, and finally Charles Surface enter Joseph's library, creating a situation that we hope will finally lead to the revelation of Joseph's duplicity. And when the revelation comes, with the toppling of the screen and the discovery of Lady Teazle's hiding place, we get not only the punch line to the long joke, but something more. While Lady Teazle has been hiding behind the screen she has had a chance to hear Sir Peter's open confession of his love for her, his young, headstrong wife. And when she is discovered, she responds not with the expected evasion, but with a frank acknowledgment of her faults and a promise to be a better wife.

Because the play encompasses so many moods, it can be performed in a variety of ways, as it has been on the contemporary stage. The customary choice has been to aim for a high style reminiscent of fashionable eighteenth century society. But the actors in the Stratford, Ontario production of 1970 were praised by Clive Barnes for avoiding "any preconceptions they may have about English high comedy style." And Michael Langham, that production's director, makes clear in an interview following the text that he tried to emphasize the "soiled" quality of the scandalmongers (see Figure 1), much as he tried to portray the realistic side of the relationship between Sir Peter Teazle and Lady Teazle (see Figure 2). As both the painful action of the portrait scene (see Figure 3) and the vigorous action in the screen scene suggest (see Figure 4), Langham deliberately moved away from the "icy artifice of most modern stagings" so as to convey the complex world of the play. But no matter how it is staged, *The School for Scandal* remains a masterful blend of wit and true sentiment.

THE SCHOOL FOR SCANDAL

BY RICHARD BRINSLEY SHERIDAN / TEXT AND NOTES BY GEORGE NETTLETON AND ARTHUR CASE

CHARACTERS

SIR PETER TEAZLE
SIR OLIVER SURFACE
JOSEPH SURFACE
CHARLES SURFACE
CRABTREE
SIR BENJAMIN BACKBITE
ROWLEY
TRIP
MOSES

SNAKE
CARELESS *and other Companions to* CHARLES SURFACE
SERVANTS, *etc.*
LADY TEAZLE
MARIA
LADY SNEERWELL
MRS. CANDOUR

SCENE
London

PROLOGUE

By David Garrick, Esq.

A School for Scandal! tell me, I beseech you,
Needs there a school this modish art to teach you?
No need of lessons now, the knowing think—
We might as well be taught to eat and drink.
Caused by a dearth of scandal, should the vapors
Distress our fair ones—let 'em read the papers;
Their own pow'rful mixtures such disorders hit;
Crave what they will, there's *quantum sufficit.*°
  'Lord!' cries my Lady Wormwood (who loves tattle,
And puts much salt and pepper in her prattle),
Just ris'n at noon, all night at cards when threshing
Strong tea and scandal—'Bless me, how refreshing!
Give me the papers, Lisp—how bold and free! (*Sips.*)
Last night Lord L—(*sips*) *was caught with Lady D*—
For aching heads what charming sal volatile! (*Sips.*)
If Mrs. B—*will still continue flirting,*
We hope she'll DRAW, *or we'll* UNDRAW *the curtain.*
Fine satire, poz°—in public all abuse it,
But by ourselves (*sips*), our praise we can't refuse it.
Now, Lisp, read *you*—there, at that dash and star.'°
'Yes, ma'am.—*A certain Lord had best beware,*
Who lives not twenty miles from Grosv'nor Square;
For should he Lady W—*find willing,*
WORMWOOD *is bitter*'—'Oh! that's me! the villain!
Throw it behind the fire, and never more
Let that vile paper come within my door.'—

---

quantum sufficit, plenty. *poz*, positively. *dash and star.* a frequent method of veiled reference to the names of those involved in fashionable intrigues.

Thus at our friends we laugh, who feel the dart;
To reach our feelings, we ourselves must smart.
Is our young bard so young, to think that he
Can stop the full spring-tide of calumny?
Knows he the world so little, and its trade?
Alas! the devil is sooner raised than laid.
So strong, so swift, the monster there's no gagging:
Cut Scandal's head off—still the tongue is wagging.
Proud of your smiles once lavishly bestow'd,
Again your young Don Quixote takes the road:
To show his gratitude, he draws his pen,
And seeks this hydra, Scandal, in his den.
For your applause all perils he would through—
He'll fight—that's *write*—a cavalliero true,
Till every drop of blood—that's *ink*—is spilt for you.

ACT 1 / SCENE 1

(LADY SNEERWELL'S *house*)
(LADY SNEERWELL *at the dressing-table*–SNAKE *drinking chocolate.*)

LADY SNEERWELL: The paragraphs, you say, Mr. Snake, were all inserted?

SNAKE: They were madam, and as I copied them myself in a feigned hand, there can be no suspicion whence they came.

LADY SNEERWELL: Did you circulate the reports of Lady Brittle's intrigue with Captain Boastall?

SNAKE: That is in as fine a train as your ladyship could wish,—in the common course of things, I think it must reach Mrs. Clackit's ears within four-and-twenty hours; and then, you know, the business is as good as done.

LADY SNEERWELL: Why, truly, Mrs. Clackit has a very pretty talent, and a great deal of industry.

SNAKE: True, madam, and has been tolerably successful in her day:—to my knowledge, she has been the cause of six matches being broken off, and three sons being disinherited, of four forced elopements, as many close confinements, nine separate maintenances, and two divorces;—nay, I have more than once traced her causing a *Tête-à-Tête* in the *Town and Country Magazine,°* when the parties perhaps had never seen each other's faces before in the course of their lives.

LADY SNEERWELL: She certainly has talents, but her manner is gross.

SNAKE: 'Tis very true,—she generally designs well, has a free tongue, and a bold invention; but her coloring is too dark, and her outline often extravagant. She wants that *delicacy of hint,* and *mellowness of sneer,* which distinguish your ladyship's scandal.

LADY SNEERWELL: Ah! you are partial, Snake.

SNAKE: Not in the least; everybody allows that Lady Sneerwell can do more with *a word* or *a look* than many can with the most labored detail, even when they happen to have a little truth on their side to support it.

LADY SNEERWELL: Yes, my dear Snake; and I am no hypocrite to deny the satisfaction I reap from the success of my efforts. Wounded myself, in the early part of my life, by the envenomed tongue of slander, I confess I have since known no pleasure equal to the reducing others to the level of my own injured reputation.

SNAKE: Nothing can be more natural. But Lady Sneerwell, there is one affair in which you have lately employed me, wherein, I confess, I am at a loss to guess your motives.

LADY SNEERWELL: I conceive you mean with respect to my neighbor, Sir Peter Teazle, and his family?

SNAKE: I do; here are two young men, to whom Sir Peter has acted as a kind of guardian since their father's death; the elder possessing the most amiable character, and universally well spoken of; the youngest, the most dissipated and extravagant young fellow in the kingdom, without friends or character,—the former an avowed admirer of your ladyship, and apparently your favorite; the latter attached to Maria, Sir Peter's ward, and confessedly beloved by her. Now, on the face of these circumstances, it is utterly unaccountable to me, why you, the widow of a city knight, with a good jointure, should not close with the passion of a man of such character and expectations as Mr. Surface; and more so why you should be so uncommonly earnest to destroy the mutual attachment subsisting between his brother Charles and Maria.

LADY SNEERWELL: Then, at once to unravel this mystery, I must inform you that love has no share whatever in the intercourse between Mr. Surface and me.

SNAKE: No!

LADY SNEERWELL: His real attachment is to Maria, or her fortune; but finding in his brother a favored rival, he has been obliged to mask his pretensions, and profit by my assistance.

SNAKE: Yet still I am more puzzled why you should interest yourself in his success.

LADY SNEERWELL: Heav'ns! how dull you are! Cannot you surmise the weakness which I hitherto, through shame, have concealed even from *you?* Must I confess that Charles—that libertine, that extravagant, that bankrupt in fortune and reputation—that he it is for whom I am thus anxious and malicious, and to gain whom I would sacrifice everything?

SNAKE: Now, indeed, your conduct appears consistent; but how came you and Mr. Surface so confidential?

LADY SNEERWELL: For our mutual interest. I have found him out a long time since—I know him to be artful, selfish, and malicious—in short, a sentimental knave.

SNAKE: Yet, Sir Peter vows he has not his equal in England—and, above all, he praises him as a man of sentiment.

LADY SNEERWELL: True; and with the assistance of his sentiment and hypocrisy he has brought Sir Peter entirely into his interest with regard to Maria.

(Enter SERVANT.*)*

SERVANT: Mr. Surface.

LADY SNEERWELL: Show him up. *(Exit* SERVANT.*)* He generally calls about this time. I don't wonder at people's giving him to me for a lover.

(Enter JOSEPH SURFACE.*)*

JOSEPH SURFACE: My dear Lady Sneerwell, how do you do to-day? Mr. Snake, your most obedient.

LADY SNEERWELL: Snake has just been arraigning me on our mutual attachment, but I have informed him of our real views; you know how useful he has been to us; and, believe me, the confidence is not ill placed.

JOSEPH SURFACE: Madam, it is impossible for me to suspect a man of Mr. Snake's sensibility and discernment.

LADY SNEERWELL: Well, well, no compliments now;—but tell me when you saw your mistress, Maria—or, what is more material to me, your brother.

Town and Country Magazine, Since 1769, this magazine had published monthly sketches of fashionable intrigues.

JOSEPH SURFACE: I have not seen either since I left you; but I can inform you that they never meet. Some of your stories have taken a good effect on Maria.

LADY SNEERWELL: Oh, my dear Snake! the merit of this belongs to you. But do your brother's distresses increase?

JOSEPH SURFACE: Every hour;—I am told he has had another execution in the house yesterday; in short, his dissipation and extravagance exceed any thing I ever heard of.

LADY SNEERWELL: Poor Charles!

JOSEPH SURFACE: True, madam;—notwithstanding his vices, one can't help feeling for him.—Aye, poor Charles! I'm sure I wish it was in *my* power to be of any essential service to him.—For the man who does not share in the distresses of a brother, even though merited by his own misconduct, deserves—

LADY SNEERWELL: O lud! you are going to be moral, and forget that you are among friends.

JOSEPH SURFACE: Egad, that's true!—I'll keep that sentiment till I see Sir Peter. However, it is certainly a charity to rescue Maria from such a libertine, who, if he is to be reclaimed, can be so only by a person of your ladyship's superior accomplishments and understanding.

SNAKE: I believe, Lady Sneerwell, here's company coming,—I'll go and copy the letter I mentioned to you.—Mr. Surface, your most obedient. (*Exit* SNAKE.)

JOSEPH SURFACE: Sir, your very devoted.—Lady Sneerwell, I am very sorry you have put any further confidence in that fellow.

LADY SNEERWELL: Why so?

JOSEPH SURFACE: I have lately detected him in frequent conference with old Rowley, who was formerly my father's steward, and has never, you know, been a friend of mine.

LADY SNEERWELL: And do you think he would betray us?

JOSEPH SURFACE: Nothing more likely: take my word for't, Lady Sneerwell, that fellow hasn't virtue enough to be faithful even to his own villainy.—Hah! Maria!

(*Enter* MARIA.)

LADY SNEERWELL: Maria, my dear, how do you do?—What's the matter?

MARIA: Oh! there is that disagreeable lover of mine, Sir Benjamin Backbite, has just called at my guardian's, with his odious uncle, Crabtree; so I slipped out, and run hither to avoid them.

LADY SNEERWELL: Is that all?

JOSEPH SURFACE: If my brother Charles had been of the party, ma'am, perhaps you would not have been so much alarmed.

LADY SNEERWELL: Nay, now you are severe; for I dare swear the truth of the matter is, Maria heard *you* were here;—but, my dear, what has Sir Benjamin done, that you should avoid him so?

MARIA: Oh, he has done nothing—but 'tis for what he has said,—his conversation is a perpetual libel on all his acquaintance.

JOSEPH SURFACE: Aye, and the worst of it is, there is no advantage in not knowing him; for he'll abuse a stranger just as soon as his best friend—and his uncle's as bad.

LADY SNEERWELL: Nay, but we should make allowance; Sir Benjamin is a wit and a poet.

MARIA: For my part, I own, madam, wit loses its respect with me, when I see it in company with malice.—What do you think, Mr. Surface?

JOSEPH SURFACE: Certainly, madam; to smile at the jest which plants a thorn in another's breast is to become a principal in the mischief.

LADY SNEERWELL: Pshaw! there's no possibility of being witty without a little ill nature: the malice of a good thing is the barb that makes it stick.—What's your opinion, Mr. Surface?

JOSEPH SURFACE: To be sure, madam, that conversation, where the spirit of raillery is suppressed, will ever appear tedious and insipid.

MARIA: Well I'll not debate how far scandal may be allowable; but in a man, I am sure, it is always contemptible.—We have pride, envy, rivalship, and a thousand motives to depreciate each other; but the male slanderer must have the cowardice of a woman before he can traduce one.

(*Enter* SERVANT.)

SERVANT: Madam, Mrs. Candour is below, and, if your ladyship's at leisure, will leave her carriage.

LADY SNEERWELL: Beg her to walk in. (*Exit* SERVANT.) Now Maria, however here is a character to your taste; for, though Mrs. Candour is a little talkative, everybody allows her to be the best-natured and best sort of woman.

MARIA: Yes, with a very gross affectation of good nature and benevolence, she does more mischief than the direct malice of old Crabtree.

JOSEPH SURFACE: I'faith 'tis very true, Lady Sneerwell; whenever I hear the current running against the characters of my friends, I never think them in such danger as when Candour undertakes their defence.

LADY SNEERWELL: Hush!—here she is!

(*Enter* MRS. CANDOUR.)

MRS. CANDOUR: My dear Lady Sneerwell, how have you been this century?—Mr. Surface, what news do you hear?—though indeed it is no matter, for I think one hears nothing else but scandal.

JOSEPH SURFACE: Just so, indeed, madam.

MRS. CANDOUR: Ah, Maria! child,—what, is the whole affair off between you and Charles? His extravagance, I presume—the town talks of nothing else.

MARIA: I am very sorry, ma'am, the town has so little to do.

MRS. CANDOUR: True, true, child: but there is no stopping people's tongues.—I own I was hurt to hear it, as indeed I was to learn, from the same quarter, that your guardian, Sir Peter, and Lady Teazle have not agreed lately so well as could be wished.

MARIA: 'Tis strangely impertinent for people to busy themselves so.

MRS. CANDOUR: Very true, child, but what's to be done? People will talk—there's no preventing it.—Why, it was but yesterday I was told that Miss Gadabout had eloped with Sir Filigree Flirt.—But, Lord! there's no minding what one hears—though, to be sure, I had this from very good authority.

MARIA: Such reports are highly scandalous.

MRS. CANDOUR: So they are, child—shameful, shameful! But the world is so censorious, no character escapes.—Lord, now who would have suspected your friend, Miss Prim, of an indiscretion? Yet such is the ill-nature of people, that they say her uncle stopped her last week, just as she was stepping into the York Diligence with her dancing-master.

MARIA: I'll answer for't there are no grounds for the report.

MRS. CANDOUR: Oh, no foundation in the world, I dare swear; no more, probably, than for the story circulated last month of Mrs. Festino's affair with Colonel Cassino;—though, to be sure, that matter was never rightly cleared up.

JOSEPH SURFACE: The license of invention some people take is monstrous indeed.

MARIA: 'Tis so.—But, in my opinion, those who report such things are equally culpable.

MRS. CANDOUR: To be sure, they are; tale-bearers are as bad as the tale-makers—'tis an old observation, and a very true one—but what's to be done, as I said before? how will you prevent people from talking?—To-day, Mrs. Clackit assured me Mr. and Mrs. Honeymoon were at last become mere man and wife, like the rest of their acquaintances.—She likewise hinted that a certain widow, in the next street, had got rid of her dropsy and recovered her shape in a most surprising manner. And at the same time Miss Tattle, who was by, affirmed that Lord Buffalo had discovered his lady at a house of no extraordinary fame—and that Sir Harry Bouquet and Tom Saunter were to measure swords on a similar provocation. But, Lord, do you think I would report these things! No, no! tale-bearers, as I said before, are just as bad as tale-makers.

JOSEPH SURFACE: Ah! Mrs. Candour, if everybody had your forbearance and good nature!

MRS. CANDOUR: I confess, Mr. Surface, I cannot bear to hear people attacked behind their backs, and when ugly circumstances come out against one's acquaintance I own I always love to think the best.—By the bye, I hope it is not true that your brother is absolutely ruined?

JOSEPH SURFACE: I am afraid his circumstances are very bad indeed, ma'am.

MRS. CANDOUR: Ah!—I heard so—but you must tell him to keep up his spirits—everybody almost is in the same way! Lord Spindle, Sir Thomas Splint, Captain Quinze, and Mr. Nickit—all up, I hear, within this week; so, if Charles is undone, he'll find half his acquaintances ruined too—and that, you know, is a consolation.

JOSEPH SURFACE: Doubtless, ma'am—a very great one.

(Enter SERVANT.)

SERVANT: Mr. Crabtree and Sir Benjamin Backbite.
(Exit SERVANT.)

LADY SNEERWELL: So, Maria, you see your lover pursues you; positively you shan't escape.

(Enter CRABTREE and SIR BENJAMIN BACKBITE.)

CRABTREE: Lady Sneerwell, I kiss your hands. Mrs. Candour, I don't believe you are acquainted with my nephew, Sir Benjamin Backbite? Egad, ma'am, he has a pretty wit, and is a pretty poet too; isn't he, Lady Sneerwell?

SIR BENJAMIN: O fie, uncle!

CRABTREE: Nay, egad it's true—I'll back him at a rebus or a charade against the best rhymer in the kingdom. Has your ladyship heard the epigram he wrote last week on Lady Frizzle's feather catching fire?—Do, Benjamin, repeat it—or the charade you made last night extempore at Mrs. Drowzie's conversazione.—Come now; your *first* is the name of a fish, your *second* a great naval commander, and—

SIR BENJAMIN: Uncle, now—prithee—

CRABTREE: I'faith, ma'am, 'twould surprise you to hear how ready he is at these things.

LADY SNEERWELL: I wonder, Sir Benjamin, you never publish anything.

SIR BENJAMIN: To say truth, ma'am, 'tis very vulgar to print; and, as my little productions are mostly satires and lampoons on particular people, I find they circulate more by giving copies in confidence to the friends of the parties—however, I have some love elegies, which, when favored with this lady's smiles, I mean to give to the public.

CRABTREE: 'Fore heav'n, ma'am, they'll immortalize you!—you'll be handed down to posterity like Petrarch's Laura, or Waller's Sacharissa.°

SIR BENJAMIN: Yes, madam, I think you will like them, when you shall see them on a beautiful quarto page, where a neat rivulet of text shall murmur through a meadow of margin. 'Fore gad, they will be the most elegant things of their kind!

CRABTREE: But, ladies, that's true—have you heard the news?

MRS. CANDOUR: What, sir, do you mean the report of—

CRABTREE: No, ma'am, that's not it.—Miss Nicely is going to be married to her own footman.

MRS. CANDOUR: Impossible!

CRABTREE: Ask Sir Benjamin.

SIR BENJAMIN: 'Tis very true, ma'am—everything is fixed, and the wedding liveries bespoke.

CRABTREE: Yes—and they *do* say there were pressing reasons for it.

LADY SNEERWELL: Why, I *have* heard something of this before.

MRS. CANDOUR: It can't be—and I wonder any one should believe such a story of so prudent a lady as Miss Nicely.

SIR BENJAMIN: O lud! ma'am, that's the very reason 'twas believed at once. She has always been so *cautious* and so *reserved,* that everybody was sure there was some reason for it at bottom.

MRS. CANDOUR: Why, to be sure, a tale of scandal is as fatal to the credit of a prudent lady of her stamp as a fever is generally to those of the strongest constitutions; but there is a sort of puny, sickly reputation that is always ailing, yet will outlive the robuster characters of a hundred prudes.

SIR BENJAMIN: True, madam, there are valetudinarians in reputation as well as constitution, who, being conscious of their weak part, avoid the least breath of air, and supply their want of stamina by care and circumspection.

MRS. CANDOUR: Well, but this may be all a mistake. You know, Sir Benjamin, very trifling circumstances often give rise to the most injurious tales.

CRABTREE: That they do, I'll be sworn, ma'am. Did you ever hear how Miss Piper came to lose her lover and her character last summer at Tunbridge?—Sir Benjamin, you remember it?

SIR BENJAMIN: Oh, to be sure!—the most whimsical circumstance—

LADY SNEERWELL: How was it, pray?

CRABTREE: Why, one evening, at Mrs. Ponto's assembly, the conversation happened to turn on the difficulty of breeding Nova Scotia sheep in this country. Says a young lady in company, 'I have known instances of it; for Miss Letitia Piper, a first cousin of mine, had a Nova Scotia sheep that produced her twins.' 'What!' cries the old Dowager Lady Dundizzy (who you know is as deaf as a post), 'has Miss Piper had twins?' This mistake, as you may imagine, threw the whole company into a fit of laughing. However, 'twas the next morning everywhere reported, and in a few days believed by the whole town, that Miss Letitia Piper had actually been brought to bed of a fine boy and a girl—and in less than a week there were people who could name the father, and the farm-house where the babies were put out to nurse!

LADY SNEERWELL: Strange, indeed!

CRABTREE: Matter of fact, I assure you.—O lud! Mr. Surface, pray is it true that your uncle, Sir Oliver, is coming home?

JOSEPH SURFACE: Not that I know of, indeed, sir.

CRABTREE: He has been in the East Indias a long time. You can scarcely remember him, I believe.—Sad comfort, whenever he returns, to hear how your brother has gone on!

JOSEPH SURFACE: Charles has been imprudent, sir, to be sure; but I hope no busy people have already prejudiced Sir Oliver against him,—he may reform.

SIR BENJAMIN: To be sure he may—for my part I never believed him to be so utterly void of principle as people say—and though he has lost all his friends, I am told nobody is better spoken of by the Jews.

CRABTREE: That's true, egad, nephew. If the old Jewry were a ward, I believe Charles would be an alderman; no man more popular there, 'fore gad! I hear he pays as many annuities as the Irish tontine; and that, whenever he's sick, they have prayers for the recovery of his health in the Synagogue.

SIR BENJAMIN: Yet no man lives in greater splendor.—They tell me, when he entertains his friends, he can sit down to dinner with a dozen of his own securities; have a score of tradesmen waiting in the antechamber, and an officer behind every guest's chair.

JOSEPH SURFACE: This may be entertainment to you, gentlemen, but you pay very little regard to the feelings of a brother.

MARIA: Their malice is intolerable!—Lady Sneerwell,

Sacharissa, Edmund Waller's poetical name for Lady Dorothy Sidney.

I must wish you a good morning—I'm not very well. (*Exit* MARIA.)

MRS. CANDOUR: O dear! she changes color very much!

LADY SNEERWELL: Do, Mrs. Candour, follow her—she may want assistance.

MRS. CANDOUR: That I will, with all my soul, ma'am.—Poor dear girl! who knows what her situation may be! (*Exit* MRS. CANDOUR.)

LADY SNEERWELL: 'Twas nothing but that she could not bear to hear Charles reflected on, notwithstanding their difference.

SIR BENJAMIN: The young lady's *penchant* is obvious.

CRABTREE: But, Benjamin, you mustn't give up the pursuit for that; follow her, and put her into good humor. Repeat her some of your own verses.—Come, I'll assist you.

SIR BENJAMIN: Mr. Surface, I did not mean to hurt you; but depend upon't your brother is utterly undone. (*Going.*)

CRABTREE: O lud, aye! undone as ever man was— can't raise a guinea. (*Going.*)

SIR BENJAMIN: And everything sold, I'm told, that was movable. (*Going.*)

CRABTREE: I have seen one that was at his house—not a thing left but some empty bottles that were overlooked, and the family pictures, which I believe are framed in the wainscot. (*Going.*)

SIR BENJAMIN: And I am very sorry to hear also some bad stories against him. (*Going.*)

CRABTREE: Oh, he has done many mean things, that's certain. (*Going.*)

SIR BENJAMIN: But, however, as he's your brother— (*Going.*)

CRABTREE: We'll tell you all, another opportunity.

(*Exeunt* CRABTREE *and* SIR BENJAMIN.)

LADY SNEERWELL: Ha, ha, ha! 'tis very hard for them to leave a subject they have not quite run down.

JOSEPH SURFACE: And I believe the abuse was no more acceptable to your ladyship than to Maria.

LADY SNEERWELL: I doubt° her affections are farther engaged than we imagined; but the family are to be here this evening, so you may as well dine where you are, and we shall have an opportunity of observing farther;—in the meantime, I'll go and plot mischief, and you shall study sentiments. (*Exeunt.*)

ACT 1 / SCENE 2

(SIR PETER TEAZLE'S *house.*)
(*Enter* SIR PETER.)

SIR PETER: When an old bachelor takes a young wife, what is he to expect?—'Tis now six months since

---

doubt, suspect.

Lady Teazle made me the happiest of men—and I have been the miserablest dog ever since that ever committed wedlock! We tift a little going to church, and came to a quarrel before the bells were done ringing. I was more than once nearly choked with gall during the honeymoon, and had lost all comfort in life before my friends had done wishing me joy! Yet I chose with caution—a girl bred wholly in the country, who never knew luxury beyond one silk gown, nor dissipation above the annual gala of a race ball. Yet now she plays her part in all the extravagant fopperies of the fashion and the town, with as ready a grace as if she had never seen a bush nor a grass-plat out of Grosvenor Square! I am sneered at by my old acquaintance—paragraphed in the newspapers. She dissipates my fortune, and contradicts all my humors; yet the worst of it is, I doubt I love her, or I should never bear all this. However, I'll never be weak enough to own it.

(*Enter* ROWLEY.)

ROWLEY: Oh! Sir Peter, your servant,—how is it with you, sir?

SIR PETER: Very bad, Master Rowley, very bad;—I meet with nothing but crosses and vexations.

ROWLEY: What can have happened to trouble you since yesterday?

SIR PETER: A good question to a married man!

ROWLEY: Nay, I'm sure your lady, Sir Peter, can't be the cause of your uneasiness.

SIR PETER: Why, has anyone told you she was dead?

ROWLEY: Come, come, Sir Peter, you love her, notwithstanding your tempers don't exactly agree.

SIR PETER: But the fault is entirely hers, Master Rowley. I am, myself, the sweetest-tempered man alive, and hate a teasing temper—and so I tell her a hundred times a day.

ROWLEY: Indeed!

SIR PETER: Aye; and what is very extraordinary, in all our disputes she is always in the wrong! But Lady Sneerwell, and the set she meets at her house, encourage the perverseness of her disposition. Then, to complete my vexations, Maria, my ward, whom I ought to have the power of a father over, is determined to turn rebel too, and absolutely refuses the man whom I have long resolved on for her husband;—meaning, I suppose, to bestow herself on his profligate brother.

ROWLEY: You know, Sir Peter, I have always taken the liberty to differ with you on the subject of these two young gentlemen. I only wish you may not be deceived in your opinion of the elder. For Charles, my life on't! he will retrieve his errors yet. Their worthy father, once my honored master, was, at his years, nearly as wild a spark; yet, when he died, he did not leave a more benevolent heart to lament his loss.

SIR PETER: You are wrong, Master Rowley. On their father's death, you know, I acted as a kind of guardian to them both, till their uncle Sir Oliver's Eastern liberality gave them an early independence; of course, no person could have more opportunities of judging of their hearts, and I was never mistaken in my life. Joseph is indeed a model for the young men of the age. He is a man of sentiment, and acts up to the sentiments he professes; but, for the other, take my word for't, if he had any grains of virtue by descent, he has dissipated them with the rest of his inheritance. Ah! my old friend, Sir Oliver, will be deeply mortified when he finds how part of his bounty has been misapplied.

ROWLEY: I am sorry to find you so violent against the young man, because this may be the most critical period of his fortune. I came hither with news that will surprise you.

SIR PETER: What! let me hear.

ROWLEY: Sir Oliver *is* arrived, and at this moment in town.

SIR PETER: How! you astonish me! I thought you did not expect him this month.

ROWLEY: I did not; but his passage has been remarkably quick.

SIR PETER: Egad, I shall rejoice to see my old friend,—'tis sixteen years since we met—we have had many a day together; but does he still enjoin us not to inform his nephews of his arrival?

ROWLEY: Most strictly. He means, before it is known, to make some trial of their dispositions.

SIR PETER: Ah! There needs no art to discover their merits—however, he shall have his way; but, pray, does he know I am married?

ROWLEY: Yes, and will soon wish you joy.

SIR PETER: What, as we drink health to a friend in a consumption! Ah, Oliver will laugh at me—we used to rail at matrimony together—but he has been steady to his text. Well, he must be at my house, though—I'll instantly give orders for his reception. But, Master Rowley, don't drop a word that Lady Teazle and I ever disagree.

ROWLEY: By no means.

SIR PETER: For I should never be able to stand Noll's jokes; so I'd have him think, Lord forgive me! that we are a very happy couple.

ROWLEY: I understand you—but then you must be very careful not to differ while he's in the house with you.

SIR PETER: Egad, and so we must—and that's impossible. Ah! Master Rowley, when an old bachelor marries a young wife, he deserves—no—the crime carries the punishment along with it. (*Exeunt.*)

ACT 2 / SCENE 1

(SIR PETER TEAZLE'S *house*)
(*Enter* SIR PETER *and* LADY TEAZLE.)

SIR PETER: Lady Teazle, Lady Teazle, I'll not bear it!

LADY TEAZLE: Sir Peter, Sir Peter, you may bear it or not, as you please; but I ought to have my own way in everything, and what's more, I *will* too.—What! though I was educated in the country, I know very well that women of fashion in London are accountable to nobody after they are married.

SIR PETER: Very well, ma'am, very well,—so a husband is to have no influence, no authority?

LADY TEAZLE: Authority! No, to be sure—if you wanted authority over me, you should have adopted me, and not married me; I am sure you were old enough.

SIR PETER: Old enough!—aye, there it is!—Well, well, Lady Teazle, though my life may be made unhappy by your temper, I'll not be ruined by your extravagance.

LADY TEAZLE: My extravagance! I'm sure I'm not more extravagant than a woman of fashion ought to be.

SIR PETER: No, no, madam, you shall throw away no more sums on such unmeaning luxury. 'Slife! to spend as much to furnish your dressing room with flowers in winter as would suffice to turn the Pantheon° into a greenhouse, and give a *fête champêtre*° at Christmas!

LADY TEAZLE: Lord, Sir Peter, am I to blame because flowers are dear in cold weather? You should find fault with the climate, and not with me. For my part, I am sure I wish it was spring all the year round, and that roses grew under one's feet!

SIR PETER: Oons! madam—if you had been born to this, I shouldn't wonder at your talking thus.—But you forget what your situation was when I married you.

LADY TEAZLE: No, no, I don't; 'twas a very disagreeable one, or I should never have married *you*.

SIR PETER: Yes, yes, madam, you were then in somewhat an humbler style—the daughter of a plain country squire. Recollect, Lady Teazle, when I saw you first, sitting at your tambour,° in a pretty figured linen gown, with a bunch of keys by your side, your hair combed smooth over a roll, and

---

Pantheon, a fashionable concert-hall in Oxford Street. *fête champêtre,* an open-air festival. *tambour,* embroidery frame.

your apartment hung round with fruits in worsted, of your own working.

LADY TEAZLE: O, yes! I remember it very well, and a curious life I led—my daily occupation to inspect the dairy, superintend the poultry, and make extracts from the family receipt-book, and comb my aunt Deborah's lap-dog.

SIR PETER: Yes, yes, ma'am, 'twas so indeed.

LADY TEAZLE: And then, you know, my evening amusements! To draw patterns for ruffles, which I had not the materials to make; to play Pope Joan° with the curate; to read a novel to my aunt; or to be stuck down to an old spinet to strum my father to sleep after a fox-chase.

SIR PETER: I am glad you have so good a memory. Yes, madam, these were the recreations I took you from; but now you must have your own coach—*vis-á-vis*—and three powdered footmen before your chair and, in summer, a pair of white cats° to draw you to Kensington Gardens.—No recollection, I suppose, when you were content to ride double, behind the butler, on a docked coach-horse?

LADY TEAZLE: No—I swear I never did that—I deny the butler and the coach-horse.

SIR PETER: This, madam, was your situation—and what have I not done for you? I have made you a woman of fashion, of fortune, of rank—in short, I have made you my wife.

LADY TEAZLE: Well, then, and there is but one thing more you can make me to add to the obligation—and that is—

SIR PETER: My widow, I suppose?

LADY TEAZLE: Hem! hem!

SIR PETER: Thank you, madam—but don't flatter yourself; for though your ill-conduct may disturb my peace, it shall never break my heart, I promise you: however, I am equally obliged to you for the hint.

LADY TEAZLE: Then why will you endeavor to make yourself so disagreeable to me, and thwart me in every little elegant expense?

SIR PETER: 'Slife, madam, I say, had you any of these elegant expenses when you married me?

LADY TEAZLE: Lud, Sir Peter! would you have me be out of fashion?

SIR PETER: The fashion, indeed! what had you to do with the fashion before you married me?

LADY TEAZLE: For my part, I should think you would like to have your wife thought a woman of taste.

SIR PETER: Aye—there's another precious circumstance!—a charming set of acquaintance you have made there!

LADY TEAZLE: That's very true, indeed, Sir Peter! and, *after* having married you, I am sure I should never pretend to taste again! But now, Sir Peter, if we have finished our daily jangle, I presume I may go to my engagement at Lady Sneerwell's?

SIR PETER: Aye—there's another precious circumstance!—a charming set of acquaintance you have made there!

LADY TEAZLE: Nay, Sir Peter, they are people of rank and fortune, and remarkably tenacious of reputation.

SIR PETER: Yes, egad, they are tenacious of reputation with a vengeance; for they don't choose anybody should have a character but themselves! Such a crew! Ah! many a wretch has rid on a hurdle° who has done less mischief than those utterers of forged tales, coiners of scandal,—and clippers of reputation.

LADY TEAZLE: What! would you restrain the freedom of speech?

SIR PETER: Oh! they have made you just as bad as any one of the society.

LADY TEAZLE: Why, I believe I do bear a part with a tolerable grace. But I vow I have no malice against the people I abuse; when I say an ill-natured thing, 'tis out of pure good humor—and I take it for granted they deal exactly in the same manner with me. But, Sir Peter, you know you promised to come to Lady Sneerwell's too.

SIR PETER: Well, well, I'll call in just to look after my own character.

LADY TEAZLE: Then, indeed, you must make haste after me or you'll be too late.—So good-bye to ye. (*Exit* LADY TEAZLE.)

SIR PETER: So—I have gained much by my intended expostulations! Yet with what a charming air she contradicts everything I say, and how pleasingly she shows her contempt of my authority! Well, though I can't make her love me, there is a great satisfaction in quarreling with her; and I think she never appears to such advantage as when she's doing everything in her power to plague me. (*Exit.*)

ACT 2 / SCENE 2

(LADY SNEERWELL'S)

(LADY SNEERWELL, MRS. CANDOUR, CRABTREE, SIR BENJAMIN BACKBITE, *and* JOSEPH SURFACE.)

LADY SNEERWELL: Nay, positively, we will hear it.

JOSEPH SURFACE: Yes, yes, the epigram, by all means.

Pope Joan, an old-fashioned game of cards. *cats,* ponies.

hurdle, rough cart on which criminals were taken to the place of execution.

SIR BENJAMIN: Plague on't, uncle! 'tis mere nonsense.

CRABTREE: No, no; 'fore gad, very clever for an extempore!

SIR BENJAMIN: But, ladies, you should be acquainted with the circumstance,—you must know that one day last week, as Lady Betty Curricle was taking the dust in Hyde Park, in a sort of duodecimo° phaëton, she desired me to write some verses on her ponies; upon which, I took out my pocket-book, and in one moment produced the following:

'Sure never were seen two such beautiful ponies! Other horses are clowns, and these macaronies! Nay, to give 'em this title I'm sure isn't wrong— Their legs are so slim and their tails are so long.'

CRABTREE: There, ladies—done in the smack of a whip, and on horseback too!

JOSEPH SURFACE: A very Phœbus, mounted—indeed, Sir Benjamin.

SIR BENJAMIN: O dear sir—trifles—trifles.

(Enter LADY TEAZLE and MARIA.)

MRS. CANDOUR: I must have a copy.

LADY SNEERWELL: Lady Teazle, I hope we shall see Sir Peter.

LADY TEAZLE: I believe he'll wait on your ladyship presently.

LADY SNEERWELL: Maria, my love, you look grave. Come, you shall sit down to cards with Mr. Surface.

MARIA: I take very little pleasure in cards—however, I'll do as your ladyship pleases.

LADY TEAZLE (aside): I am surprised Mr. Surface should sit down with her.—I thought he would have embraced this opportunity of speaking to me before Sir Peter came.

MRS. CANDOUR: Now, I'll die but you are so scandalous, I'll forswear your society.

LADY TEAZLE: What's the matter, Mrs. Candour?

MRS. CANDOUR: They'll not allow our friend Miss Vermilion to be handsome.

LADY SNEERWELL: Oh, surely, she's a pretty woman.

CRABTREE: I am very glad you think so, ma'am.

MRS. CANDOUR: She has a charming fresh color.

LADY TEAZLE: Yes, when it is fresh put on.

MRS. CANDOUR: O fie! I'll swear her color is natural—I have seen it come and go.

LADY TEAZLE: I dare swear you have, ma'am—it goes of a night, and comes again in the morning.

MRS. CANDOUR: Ha! ha! ha! how I hate to hear you talk so! But surely, now, her sister is, or was, very handsome.

CRABTREE: Who? Mrs. Evergreen?—O Lord! she's six-and-fifty if she's an hour!

MRS. CANDOUR: Now positively you wrong her; fifty-two or fifty-three is the utmost—and I don't think she looks more.

SIR BENJAMIN: Ah! there is no judging by her looks, unless one could see her face.

LADY SNEERWELL: Well, well, if Mrs. Evergreen does take some pains to repair the ravages of time, you must allow she effects it with great ingenuity; and surely that's better than the careless manner in which the widow Ochre caulks her wrinkles.

SIR BENJAMIN: Nay, now, Lady Sneerwell, you are severe upon the widow. Come, come, it is not that she paints so ill—but, when she has finished her face, she joins it on so badly to her neck, that she looks like a mended statue, in which the connoisseur may see at once that the head's modern, though the trunk's antique!

CRABTREE: Ha! ha! ha! well said, nephew!

MRS. CANDOUR: Ha! ha! ha! Well, you make me laugh, but I vow I hate you for't.— What do you think of Miss Simper?

SIR BENJAMIN: Why, she has very pretty teeth.

LADY TEAZLE: Yes; and on that account, when she is neither speaking nor laughing (which very seldom happens), she never absolutely shuts her mouth, but leaves it always on a jar, as it were.

MRS. CANDOUR: How can you be so ill-natured?

LADY TEAZLE: Nay, I allow even that's better than the pains Mrs. Prim takes to conceal her losses in front. She draws her mouth till it positively resembles the aperture of a poor's-box,° and all her words appear to slide out edgeways.

LADY SNEERWELL: Very well, Lady Teazle; I see you can be a little severe.

LADY TEAZLE: In defence of a friend it is but justice;—but here comes Sir Peter to spoil our pleasantry.

(Enter SIR PETER TEAZLE.)

SIR PETER: Ladies, your most obedient—Mercy on me, here is the whole set! a character dead at every word, I suppose. (aside)

MRS. CANDOUR: I am rejoiced you are come. Sir Peter. They have been so censorious. They will allow good qualities to nobody—not even good nature to our friend Mrs. Pursy.

LADY TEAZLE: What, the fat dowager who was at Mrs. Codille's last night?

MRS. CANDOUR: Nay, her bulk is her misfortune; and, when she takes such pains to get rid of it, you ought not to reflect on her.

---

duodecimo, diminutive.

poor's box, Referring to the narrow slit in the top of the church contribution-box for the poor of the parish.

LADY SNEERWELL: That's very true, indeed.

LADY TEAZLE: Yes, I know she almost lives on acids and small whey; laces herself by pulleys; and often, in the hottest noon of summer, you may see her on a little squat pony, with her hair platted up behind like a drummer's, and puffing round the Ring° on a full trot.

MRS. CANDOUR: I thank you, Lady Teazle, for defending her.

SIR PETER: Yes, a good defence, truly.

MRS. CANDOUR: But Sir Benjamin is as censorious as Miss Sallow.

CRABTREE: Yes, and she is a curious being to pretend to be censorious!—an awkward gawky, without any one good point under heaven.

MRS CANDOUR: Positively you shall not be so very severe. Miss Sallow is a relation of mine by marriage, and, as for her person, great allowance is to be made; for, let me tell you, a woman labors under many disadvantages who tries to pass for a girl at six-and-thirty.

LADY SNEERWELL: Though, surely, she is handsome still—and for the weakness in her eyes, considering how much she reads by candle-light, it is not to be wondered at.

MRS. CANDOUR: True; and then as to her manner, upon my word I think it is particularly graceful, considering she never had the least education; for you know her mother was a Welch milliner, and her father a sugar-baker at Bristol.

SIR BENJAMIN: Ah! you are both of you too good-natured!

SIR PETER: Yes, damned good-natured! This their own relation! mercy on me! (aside)

SIR BENJAMIN: And Mrs. Candour is of so moral a turn she can sit for an hour to hear Lady Stucco talk sentiment.

LADY TEAZLE: Nay, I vow Lady Stucco is very well with the dessert after dinner; for she's just like the French fruit one cracks for mottoes—made up of paint and proverb.

MRS. CANDOUR: Well, I never will join in ridiculing a friend; and so I constantly tell my cousin Ogle, and you all know what pretensions she has to be critical in beauty.

CRABTREE: Oh, to be sure! she has herself the oddest countenance that ever was seen; 'tis a collection of features from all the different countries of the globe.

SIR BENJAMIN: So she has, indeed—an Irish front!

CRABTREE: Caledonian locks!

SIR BENJAMIN: Dutch nose!

CRABTREE: Austrian lip!

SIR BENJAMIN: Complexion of a Spaniard!

CRABTREE: And teeth à la Chinoise!

SIR BENJAMIN: In short, her face resembles a table d'hôte at Spa—where no two guests are of a nation—

CRABTREE: Or a congress at the close of a general war—wherein all the members, even to her eyes, appear to have a different interest, and her nose and chin are the only parties likely to join issue.

MRS. CANDOUR: Ha! ha! ha!

SIR PETER: Mercy on my life!—a person they dine with twice a week! (aside)

LADY SNEERWELL: Go—go—you are a couple of provoking toads.

MRS. CANDOUR: Nay, but I vow you shall not carry the laugh off so—for give me leave to say, that Mrs. Ogle—

SIR PETER: Madam, madam, I beg your pardon—there's no stopping these good gentlemen's tongues. But when I tell you, Mrs. Candour, that the lady they are abusing is a particular friend of mine—I hope you'll not take her part.

LADY SNEERWELL: Well said, Sir Peter! but you are a cruel creature—too phlegmatic yourself for a jest, and too peevish to allow wit on others.

SIR PETER: Ah, madam, true wit is more nearly allied to good nature than your ladyship is aware of.

LADY TEAZLE: True, Sir Peter; I believe they are so near akin that they can never be united.

SIR BENJAMIN: Or rather, madam, suppose them man and wife, because one so seldom sees them together.

LADY TEAZLE: But Sir Peter is such an enemy to scandal, I believe he would have it put down by parliament.

SIR PETER: 'Fore heaven, madam, if they were to consider the sporting with reputation of as much importance as poaching on manors, and pass An Act for the Preservation of Fame, I believe many would thank them for the bill.

LADY SNEERWELL: O lud! Sir Peter; would you deprive us of our privileges?

SIR PETER: Aye, madam; and then no person should be permitted to kill characters or run down reputations, but qualified old maids and disappointed widows.

LADY SNEERWELL: Go, you monster!

MRS. CANDOUR: But sure you would not be quite so severe on those who report what they hear.

SIR PETER: Yes, madam, I would have law merchant° for them too; and in all cases of slander currency, whenever the drawer of the lie was not to be found, the injured parties should have a right to come on any of the indorsers.

Ring, the fashionable drive originally laid out in Hyde Park by Charles II.

law merchant, mercantile law.

CRABTREE: Well, for my part, I believe there never was a scandalous tale without some foundation.

LADY SNEERWELL: Come, ladies, shall we sit down to cards in the next room?

(Enter SERVANT *and whispers* SIR PETER.*)*

SIR PETER: I'll be with them directly.— *(Exit* SERVANT.*)* I'll get away unperceived. *(aside)*

LADY SNEERWELL: Sir Peter, you are not leaving us?

SIR PETER: Your ladyship must excuse me; I'm called away by particular business—but I leave my character behind me. *(Exit* SIR PETER.*)*

SIR BENJAMIN: Well certainly, Lady Teazle, that lord of yours is a strange being; I could tell you some stories of him would make you laugh heartily, if he wasn't your husband.

LADY TEAZLE: O pray don't mind that—come, do let's hear them.

(They join the rest of the company, all talking as they are going into the next room.)

JOSEPH SURFACE *(rising with* MARIA*)*: Maria, I see you have no satisfaction in this society.

MARIA: How is it possible I should? If to raise malicious smiles at the infirmities and misfortunes of those who have never injured us be the province of wit or humor, heaven grant me a double portion of dulness!

JOSEPH SURFACE: Yet they appear more ill-natured than they are; they have no malice at heart.

MARIA: Then is their conduct still more contemptible; for, in my opinion, nothing could excuse the intemperance of their tongues but a natural and ungovernable bitterness of mind.

JOSEPH SURFACE: But can you, Maria, feel thus for others, and be unkind to me alone? Is hope to be denied the tenderest passion?

MARIA: Why will you distress me by renewing this subject?

JOSEPH SURFACE: Ah, Maria! you would not treat me thus, and oppose your guardian, Sir Peter's will, but that I see that profligate Charles is still a favored rival.

MARIA: Ungenerously urged! But, whatever my sentiments of that unfortunate young man are, be assured I shall not feel more bound to give him up, because his distresses have lost him the regard even of a brother.

*(*LADY TEAZLE *returns.)*

JOSEPH SURFACE: Nay, but, Maria, do not leave me with a frown—by all that's honest, I swear—Gad's life, here's Lady Teazle. *(aside)* You must not—no, you shall not—for, though I have the greatest regard for Lady Teazle—

MARIA: Lady Teazle!

JOSEPH SURFACE: Yet were Sir Peter to suspect—

LADY TEAZLE *(coming forward)*: What's this, pray? Do you take her for me?—Child, you are wanted in the next room.— *(Exit* MARIA.*)* What is all this, pray?

JOSEPH SURFACE: Oh, the most unlucky circumstance in nature! Maria has somehow suspected the tender concern I have for your happiness, and threatened to acquaint Sir Peter with her suspicions, and I was just endeavoring to reason with her when you came.

LADY TEAZLE: Indeed! but you seemed to adopt a very tender mode of reasoning—do you *usually* argue on your knees?

JOSEPH SURFACE: Oh, she's a child—and I thought a little bombast—but, Lady Teazle, when are you to give me your judgment on my library, as you promised?

LADY TEAZLE: No, no—I begin to think it would be imprudent, and you know I admit you as a lover no further than *fashion* requires.

JOSEPH SURFACE: True—a mere Platonic cicisbeo,° what every London wife is *entitled* to.

LADY TEAZLE: Certainly, one must not be out of the fashion; however, I have so many of my country prejudices left, that, though Sir Peter's ill humor may vex me ever so, it never shall provoke me to—

JOSEPH SURFACE: The only revenge in your power. Well, I applaud your moderation.

LADY TEAZLE: Go—you are an insinuating wretch! But we shall be missed—let us join the company.

JOSEPH SURFACE: But we had best not return together.

LADY TEAZLE: Well, don't stay—for Maria shan't come to hear any more of your *reasoning*, I promise you. *(Exit* LADY TEAZLE.*)*

JOSEPH SURFACE: A curious dilemma, truly, my politics have run me into! I wanted, at first, only to ingratiate myself with Lady Teazle, that she might not be my enemy with Maria; and I have, I don't know how, become her serious lover. Sincerely I begin to wish I had never made such a point of gaining so *very good* a character, for it has led me into so many cursed rogueries that I doubt I shall be exposed at last. *(Exit.)*

ACT 2 / SCENE 3

*(*SIR PETER'S*)*
(Enter SIR OLIVER SURFACE *and* ROWLEY.*)*

SIR OLIVER: Ha! ha! ha! and so my old friend is married, hey?—a young wife out of the country.—Ha! ha! ha!—that he should have

---

cicisbeo, gallant to a married woman.

stood bluff° to old bachelor so long, and sink into a husband at last!

ROWLEY: But you must not rally him on the subject, Sir Oliver; 'tis a tender point, I assure you, though he has been married only seven months.

SIR OLIVER: Then he has been just half a year on the stool of repentance!—Poor Peter! But you say he has entirely given up Charles—never sees him, hey?

ROWLEY: His prejudice against him is astonishing, and I am sure greatly increased by a jealousy of him with Lady Teazle, which he has been industriously led into by a scandalous society in the neighborhood, who have contributed not a little to Charles's ill name; whereas the truth is, I believe, if the lady is partial to either of them, his brother is the favorite.

SIR OLIVER: Aye,—I know there are a set of malicious, prating, prudent gossips, both male and female, who murder characters to kill time, and will rob a young fellow of his good name before he has years to know the value of it,—but I am not to be prejudiced against my nephew by such, I promise you! No, no;—if Charles has done nothing false or mean, I shall compound for his extravagance.—

ROWLEY: Then, my life on't, you will reclaim him.— Ah, sir, it gives me new life to find that *your* heart is not turned against him, and that the son of my good old master has one friend, however, left.

SIR OLIVER: What! shall I forget, Master Rowley, when I was at his years myself? Egad, my brother and I were neither of us very *prudent* youths— and yet, I believe, you have not seen many better men than your old master was?

ROWLEY: Sir, 'tis this reflection gives me assurance that Charles may yet be a credit to his family.— But here comes Sir Peter.

SIR OLIVER: Egad so he does!—Mercy on me, he's greatly altered, and seems to have a settled married look! One may read husband in his face at this distance!

(*Enter* SIR PETER TEAZLE.)

SIR PETER: Hah! Sir Oliver—my old friend! Welcome to England a thousand times!

SIR OLIVER: Thank you, thank you, Sir Peter! and i'faith I am glad to find you well, believe me!

SIR PETER: Ah! 'tis a long time since we met—sixteen years, I doubt, Sir Oliver, and many a cross accident in the time.

SIR OLIVER: Aye, I have had my share—but, what! I find you are married, hey, my old boy?—Well, well, it can't be helped—and so I wish you joy with all my heart!

---

stood bluff, steadfast.

SIR PETER: Thank you, thank you, Sir Oliver—Yes, I have entered into the happy state—but we'll not talk of that now.

SIR OLIVER: True, true, Sir Peter; old friends should not begin on grievances at first meeting. No, no, no.

ROWLEY (*to* SIR OLIVER): Take care, pray, sir.

SIR OLIVER: Well, so one of my nephews is a wild rogue, hey?

SIR PETER: Wild! Ah! my old friend, I grieve for your disappointment there—he's a lost young man, indeed; however, his brother will make you amends; Joseph is, indeed, what a youth should be—everybody in the world speaks well of him.

SIR OLIVER: I am sorry to hear it—he has too good a character to be an honest fellow.—Everybody speaks well of him! Psha! then he has bowed as low to knaves and fools as to the honest dignity of genius or virtue.

SIR PETER: What, Sir Oliver! do you blame him for not making enemies?

SIR OLIVER: Yes, if he has merit enough to deserve them.

SIR PETER: Well, well—you'll be convinced when you know him. 'Tis edification to hear him converse—he professes the noblest sentiments.

SIR OLIVER: Ah, plague of his sentiments! If he salutes me with a scrap of morality in his mouth, I shall be sick directly. But, however, don't mistake me, Sir Peter; I don't mean to defend Charles's errors—but, before I form my judgment of either of them, I intend to make a trial of their hearts—and my friend Rowley and I have planned something for the purpose.

ROWLEY: And Sir Peter shall own for once he has been mistaken.

SIR PETER: Oh, my life on Joseph's honor!

SIR OLIVER: Well, come, give us a bottle of good wine, and we'll drink the lad's health, and tell you our scheme.

SIR PETER: *Allons,* then!

SIR OLIVER: And don't, Sir Peter, be so severe against your old friend's son. Odds my life! I am not sorry that he has run out of the course a little; for my part, I hate to see prudence clining to the green succors of my youth; 'tis like ivy round a sapling, and spoils the growth of the tree. (*Exeunt.*)

ACT 3 / SCENE 1

(SIR PETER'S)

(SIR PETER TEAZLE, SIR OLIVER SURFACE, *and* ROWLEY.)

SIR PETER: Well, then—we will see this fellow first, and have our wine afterwards. But how is this,

Master Rowley? I don't see the jet° of your scheme.

ROWLEY: Why, sir, this Mr. Stanley, whom I was speaking of, is nearly related to them, by their mother; he was once a merchant in Dublin, but has been ruined by a series of undeserved misfortunes. He has applied, by letter, since his confinement, both to Mr. Surface and Charles—from the former he has received nothing but evasive promises of future service, while Charles has done all that his extravagance has left him power to do; and he is, at this time, endeavoring to raise a sum of money, part of which, in the midst of his own distresses, I know he intends for the service of poor Stanley.

SIR OLIVER: Ah! he is my brother's son.

SIR PETER: Well, but how is Sir Oliver personally to—

ROWLEY: Why, sir, I will inform Charles and his brother that Stanley has obtained permission to apply in person to his friends, and, as they have neither of them ever seen him, let Sir Oliver assume his character, and he will have a fair opportunity of judging at least of the benevolence of their dispositions; and believe me, sir, you will find in the youngest brother one who, in the midst of folly and dissipation, has still, as our immortal bard expresses it,—

> 'a tear for pity, and a hand
> Open as day, for melting charity.'°

SIR PETER: Psha! What signifies his having an open hand or purse either, when he has nothing left to give? Well, well, make the trial, if you please; but where is the fellow whom you brought for Sir Oliver to examine, relative to Charles's affairs?

ROWLEY: Below, waiting his commands, and no one can give him better intelligence.—This, Sir Oliver, is a friendly Jew, who, to do him justice, had done everything in his power to bring your nephew to a proper sense of his extravagance.

SIR PETER: Pray let us have him in.

ROWLEY: Desire Mr. Moses to walk upstairs.

SIR PETER: But why should you suppose he will speak the truth?

ROWLEY: Oh, I have convinced him that he has no chance of recovering certain sums advanced to Charles but through the bounty of Sir Oliver, who he knows is arrived; so that you may depend on his fidelity to his own interest. I have also another evidence in my power, one Snake, whom I have detected in a matter little short of forgery, and shall shortly produce to remove

some of *your* prejudices, Sir Peter, relative to Charles and Lady Teazle.

SIR PETER: I have heard too much on that subject.

ROWLEY: Here comes the honest Israelite.

(Enter MOSES.)

—This is Sir Oliver.

SIR OLIVER: Sir, I understand you have lately had great dealings with my nephew Charles.

MOSES: Yes, Sir Oliver—I have done all I could for him, but he was ruined before he came to me for assistance.

SIR OLIVER: That was unlucky, truly—for you have had no opportunity of showing your talents.

MOSES: None at all—I hadn't the pleasure of knowing his distresses—till he was some thousands worse than nothing.

SIR OLIVER: Unfortunate, indeed! But I suppose you have done all in your power for him, honest Moses?

MOSES: Yes, he knows that. This very evening I was to have brought him a gentleman from the city, who doesn't know him, and will, I believe, advance him some money.

SIR PETER: What, one Charles has never had money from before?

MOSES: Yes; Mr. Premium, of Crutched Friars°—formerly a broker.

SIR PETER: Egad, Sir Oliver, a thought strikes me!—Charles, you say, doesn't know Mr. Premium?

MOSES: Not at all.

SIR PETER: Now then, Sir Oliver, you may have a better opportunity of satisfying yourself than by an old romancing tale of a poor relation;—go with my friend Moses, and represent Mr. Premium, and then I'll answer for't, you will see your nephew in all his glory.

SIR OLIVER: Egad, I like this idea better than the other and I may visit Joseph afterwards, as old Stanley.

SIR PETER: True—so you may.

ROWLEY: Well, this is taking Charles rather at a disadvantage, to be sure. However, Moses—you understand Sir Peter, and will be faithful?

MOSES: You may depend upon me,—this is near the time I was to have gone.

SIR OLIVER: I'll accompany you as soon as you please, Moses; but hold! I have forgot one thing—how the plague shall I be able to pass for a Jew?

MOSES: There's no need—the principal is Christian.

SIR OLIVER: Is he?—I'm sorry to hear it—but, then again, an't I rather too smartly dressed to look like a money-lender?

---

jet, point, gist. *a tear . . . charity,* from *Henry IV, Part II,* IV. iv. 31–32.

Crutched Friars, a street, not far from the Tower of London, named from an old Convent of Crossed or Crouched Friars.

SIR PETER: Not at all; 'twould not be out of character, if you went in your own carriage—would it, Moses?

MOSES: Not in the least.

SIR OLIVER: Well, but how must I talk? there's certainly some cant of usury, and mode of treating, that I ought to know.

SIR PETER: Oh, there's not much to learn—the great point, as I take it, is to be exorbitant enough in your demands—hey, Moses?

MOSES: Yes, that's a very great point.

SIR OLIVER: I'll answer for't I'll not be wanting in that. I'll ask him eight or ten per cent on the loan, at least.

MOSES: If you ask him no more than that, you'll be discovered immediately.

SIR OLIVER: Hey! What the plague! how much then?

MOSES: That depends upon the circumstances. If he appears not very anxious for the supply, you should require only forty or fifty per cent; but if you find him in great distress, and want the moneys very bad—you may ask double.

SIR PETER: A good honest trade you're learning, Sir Oliver!

SIR OLIVER: Truly I think so—and not unprofitable.

MOSES: Then, you know, you haven't the moneys yourself, but are forced to borrow them for him of a friend.

SIR OLIVER: Oh! I borrow it of a friend, do I?

MOSES: Yes, and your friend is an unconscionable dog, but you can't help it.

SIR OLIVER: My friend is an unconscionable dog, is he?

MOSES: Yes, and he himself has not the moneys by him—but is forced to sell stock at a great loss.

SIR OLIVER: He is forced to sell stock, is he, at a great loss, is he? Well, that's very kind of him.

SIR PETER: I'faith, Sir Oliver—Mr. Premium, I mean—you'll soon be master of the trade. But, Moses! wouldn't you have him run out a little against the Annuity Bill?° That would be in character, I should think.

MOSES: Very much.

ROWLEY: And lament that a young man now must be at years of discretion before he is suffered to ruin himself?

MOSES: Aye, great pity!

SIR PETER: And abuse the public for allowing merit to an act whose only object is to snatch misfortune and imprudence from the rapacious relief of usury, and give the minor a chance of inheriting

Annuity Bill, the Annuity Bill, presented in the House of Commons April 29, 1777, and passed in May (after the first performance of *The S. for S.*) was aimed to safeguard minors against grantors of life annuities.

his estate without being undone by coming into possession.

SIR OLIVER: So, so—Moses shall give me further instructions as we go together.

SIR PETER: You will not have much time, for your nephew lives hard by.

SIR OLIVER: Oh, never fear! my tutor appears so able, that though Charles lived in the next street, it must be my own fault if I am not a complete rogue before I turn the corner. (*Exeunt* SIR OLIVER *and* MOSES.)

SIR PETER: So now I think Sir Oliver will be convinced;—you are partial, Rowley, and would have prepared Charles for the other plot.

ROWLEY: No, upon my word, Sir Peter.

SIR PETER: Well, go bring me this Snake, and I'll hear what he has to say presently.—I see Maria, and want to speak with her.—(*Exit* ROWLEY.) I should be glad to be convinced my suspicions of Lady Teazle and Charles were unjust. I have never yet opened my mind on this subject to my friend Joseph—I'm determined I will do it—*he* will give me his opinion sincerely.

(*Enter* MARIA.)

So, child, has Mr. Surface returned with you?

MARIA: No, sir—he was engaged.

SIR PETER: Well, Maria, do you not reflect, the more you converse with that amiable young man, what return his partiality for you deserves?

MARIA: Indeed, Sir Peter, your frequent importunity on this subject distresses me extremely—you compel me to declare, that I know no man who has ever paid me a particular attention whom I would not prefer to Mr. Surface.

SIR PETER: So,—here's perverseness! No, no, Maria, 'tis Charles only whom you would prefer—'tis evident his vices and follies have won your heart.

MARIA: This is unkind, sir—you know I have obeyed you in neither seeing nor corresponding with him; I have heard enough to convince me that he is unworthy my regard. Yet I cannot think it culpable, if, while my understanding severely condemns his vices, my heart suggests some pity for his distresses.

SIR PETER: Well, well, pity him as much as you please, but give your heart and hand to a worthier object.

MARIA: Never to his brother!

SIR PETER: Go, perverse and obstinate! But take care, madam; you have never yet known what the authority of a guardian is—don't compel me to inform you of it.

MARIA: I can only say, you shall not have *just* reason. 'Tis true, by my father's will, I am for a short period bound to regard you as his substitute, but must cease to think you so, when you would compel me to be miserable. (*Exit* MARIA.)

SIR PETER: Was ever man so crossed as I am! everything conspiring to fret me!—I had not been involved in matrimony a fortnight, before her father, a hale and hearty man, died—on purpose, I believe, for the pleasure of plaguing me with the care of his daughter. But here comes my helpmate! She appears in great good humor. How happy I should be if I could tease her into loving me, though but a little!

(*Enter* LADY TEAZLE.)

LADY TEAZLE: Lud! Sir Peter, I hope you haven't been quarreling with Maria—it isn't using me well to be ill humored when I am not by.

SIR PETER: Ah, Lady Teazle, you might have the power to make me good humored at all times.

LADY TEAZLE: I am sure I wish I had—for I want you to be in charming sweet temper at this moment. Do be good humored now, and let me have two hundred pounds, will you?

SIR PETER: Two hundred pounds! what, an't I to be in a good humor without paying for it! But speak to me thus, and i'faith there's nothing I could refuse you. You shall have it; but seal me a bond for the repayment.

LADY TEAZLE: O no—there—my note of hand will do as well.

SIR PETER (*kissing her hand*): And you shall no longer reproach me with not giving you an independent settlement,—I mean shortly to surprise you; but shall we always live thus, hey?

LADY TEAZLE: If you please. I'm sure I don't care how soon we leave off quarreling, provided you'll own *you* were tired first.

SIR PETER: Well—then let our future contest be, who shall be most obliging.

LADY TEAZLE: I assure you, Sir Peter, good nature becomes you. You look now as you did before we were married!—when you used to walk with me under the elms, and tell me stories of what a gallant you were in your youth, and chuck me under the chin, you would, and ask me if I thought I could love an old fellow, who would deny me nothing—didn't you?

SIR PETER: Yes, yes, and you were as kind and attentive.

LADY TEAZLE: Aye, so I was, and would always take your part, when my acquaintance used to abuse you, and turn you into ridicule.

SIR PETER: Indeed!

LADY TEAZLE: Aye, and when my cousin Sophy has called you a stiff, peevish old bachelor, and laughed at me for thinking of marrying one who might be my father, I have always defended you—and said I didn't think you so ugly by any

means, and that I dared say you'd make a very good sort of a husband.

SIR PETER: And you prophesied right—and we shall certainly now be the happiest couple—

LADY TEAZLE: And never differ again!

SIR PETER: No, never!—though at the same time, indeed, my dear Lady Teazle, you must watch your temper very narrowly; for all in all our little quarrels, my dear, if you recollect, my love, you always began first.

LADY TEAZLE: I beg your pardon, my dear Sir Peter: indeed, you always gave the provocation.

SIR PETER: Now, see, my angel! take care—*contradicting* isn't the way to keep friends.

LADY TEAZLE: Then don't *you* begin it, my love!

SIR PETER: There, now! you—you are going on—you don't perceive, my life, that you are just doing the very thing which you know always makes me angry.

LADY TEAZLE: Nay, you know if you will be angry without any reason—

SIR PETER: There now! you want to quarrel again.

LADY TEAZLE: No, I am sure I don't—but, if you will be so peevish—

SIR PETER: There now! who begins first?

LADY TEAZLE: Why, you, to be sure. I said nothing—but there's no bearing your temper.

SIR PETER: No, no, madam, the fault's in your own temper.

LADY TEAZLE: Aye, you are just what my cousin Sophy said you would be.

SIR PETER: Your cousin Sophy is a forward, impertinent gipsy.

LADY TEAZLE: You are a great bear, I'm sure, to abuse my relations.

SIR PETER: Now may all the plagues of marriage be doubled on me, if ever I try to be friends with you any more!

LADY TEAZLE: So much the better.

SIR PETER: No, no, madam; 'tis evident you never cared a pin for me, and I was a madman to marry you—a pert, rural coquette, that had refused half the honest squires in the neighborhood!

LADY TEAZLE: And I am sure I was a fool to marry you—an old dangling bachelor, who was single at fifty, only because he never could meet with any one who would have him.

SIR PETER: Aye, aye, madam; but you were pleased enough to listen to me—*you* never had such an offer before.

LADY TEAZLE: No! didn't I refuse Sir Twivy Tarrier, who everybody said would have been a better match—for his estate is just as good as yours—and he has broke his neck since we have been married.

SIR PETER: I have done with you, madam! You are an unfeeling, ungrateful—but there's an end of everything. I believe you capable of anything that's bad. Yes, madam, I now believe the reports relative to you and Charles, madam—yes, madam, you and Charles—are not without grounds—

LADY TEAZLE: Take care, Sir Peter! you had better not insinuate any such thing! I'll not be suspected with*out cause,* I promise you.

SIR PETER: Very well, madam! very well! a separate maintenance as soon as you please. Yes, madam, or a divorce! I'll make an example of myself for the benefit of all old bachelors. Let us separate, madam.

LADY TEAZLE: Agreed! agreed! And now, my dear Sir Peter, we are of a mind once more, we may be the *happiest couple,* and *never differ again,* you know: ha! ha! Well, you are going to be in a passion, I see, and I shall only interrupt you.—so bye! bye! *(Exit.)*

SIR PETER: Plagues and tortures! can't I make her angry neither? Oh, I am the miserablest fellow! But I'll not bear her presuming to keep her temper—no! she may break my heart, but she shan't keep her temper. *(Exit.)*

ACT 3 / SCENE 2

*(*CHARLES'S *house)*
(Enter TRIP, MOSES, *and* SIR OLIVER SURFACE.*)*

TRIP: Here, Master Moses! if you'll stay a moment, I'll try whether—what's the gentleman's name?

SIR OLIVER: Mr. Moses, what *is* my name? *(aside)*

MOSES: Mr. Premium.

TRIP: Premium—very well. *(Exit* TRIP, *taking snuff.)*

SIR OLIVER: To judge by the servants, one wouldn't believe the master was ruined. But what!—sure, this was my brother's house?

MOSES: Yes, sir; Mr. Charles bought it of Mr. Joseph, with the furniture, pictures, &c., just as the old gentleman left it—Sir Peter thought it a great piece of extravagance in him.

SIR OLIVER: In my mind, the other's economy in *selling* it to him was more reprehensible by half.

(Re-enter TRIP.*)*

TRIP: My master says you must wait, gentlemen; he has company, and he can't speak with you yet.

SIR OLIVER: If he knew *who* it was wanted to see him, perhaps he wouldn't have sent such a message.

TRIP: Yes, yes, sir; he knows *you* are here—I didn't forget little Premium—no, no, no.

SIR OLIVER: Very well—and I pray, sir, what may be your name?

TRIP: Trip, sir—my name is Trip, at your service.

SIR OLIVER: Well, then, Mr. Trip, you have a pleasant sort of a place here, I guess.

TRIP: Why, yes—here are three or four of us pass our time agreeably enough; but then our wages are sometimes a little in arrear—and not very great either—but fifty pounds a year, and find our own bags and bouquets.°

SIR OLIVER *(aside)*: Bags and bouquets! halters and bastinadoes!

TRIP: But *à propos,* Moses, have you been able to get me that little bill discounted?

SIR OLIVER *(aside)*: Wants to raise money, too!—mercy on me. Has his distresses, I warrant, like a lord,—and affects creditors and duns.

MOSES: 'Twas not to be done, indeed, Mr. Trip. *(Gives the note.)*

TRIP: Good lack, you surprise me! My friend Brush has indorsed it, and I thought when he put his mark on the back of a bill 'twas as good as cash.

MOSES: No, 'twouldn't do.

TRIP: A small sum—but twenty pounds. Hark'ee, Moses, do you think you couldn't get it me by way of annuity?

SIR OLIVER *(aside)*: An annuity! ha! ha! ha! a footman raise money by way of annuity! Well done, luxury, egad!

MOSES: But you must insure your place.

TRIP: Oh, with all my heart! I'll insure my place, and my life too, if you please.

SIR OLIVER *(aside)*: It's more than I would your neck.

TRIP: But then, Moses, it must be done before this d—d register° takes place—one wouldn't like to have one's name made public, you know.

MOSES: No, certainly. But is there nothing you could deposit?

TRIP: Why, nothing capital of my master's wardrobe has dropped lately; but I could give you a morgage on some of his winter clothes, with equity of redemption before November—or you shall have the reversion of the French velvet, or a post-obit° on the blue and silver;—these, I should think, Moses, with a few pair of point ruffles, as a collateral security—hey, my little fellow?

MOSES: Well, well. *(Bell rings.)*

TRIP: Gad, I heard the bell! I believe, gentlemen, I can now introduce you. Don't forget the annuity, little Moses! This way, gentlemen, insure my place, you know.

---

bags and bouquets, footman's trappings. The back-hair of the bag-wig was enclosed in an ornamental bag. *register,* another reference to the Annuity Bill of 1777, proposed on April 29, and passed in May. It provided "for registering the Grants of Life Annuities." *post-obit,* future claim.

SIR OLIVER (aside): If the man be a shadow of his master, this is the temple of dissipation indeed! (Exeunt.)

ACT 3 / SCENE 3

(CHARLES SURFACE, CARELESS, and others at a table with wine, etc.)

CHARLES SURFACE: 'Fore heaven, 'tis true!—there's the great degeneracy of the age. Many of our acquaintance have taste, spirit, and politeness; but plague on't, they won't drink.

CARELESS: It is so, indeed, Charles! they give in to all the substantial luxuries of the table, and abstain from nothing but wine and wit.

CHARLES SURFACE: Oh, certainly society suffers by it intolerably! for now, instead of the social spirit of raillery that used to mantle over a glass of bright Burgundy, their conversation is become just like the Spa-water they drink, which has all the pertness and flatulence of champagne, without its spirit or flavor.

1 GENTLEMAN: But what are they to do who love play better than wine?

CARELESS: True! there's Harry diets himself for gaming, and is now under a hazard regimen.°

CHARLES SURFACE: Then he'll have the worst of it. What! you wouldn't train a horse for the course by keeping him from corn! For my part, egad, I am now never so successful as when I am a little merry—let me throw on a bottle of champagne, and I never lose—at least I never feel my losses, which is exactly the same thing.

2 GENTLEMAN: Aye, that I believe.

CHARLES SURFACE: And, then, what man can pretend to be a believer in love, who is an abjurer of wine? 'Tis the test by which the lover knows his own heart. Fill a dozen bumpers to a dozen beauties, and she that floats at top is the maid that has bewitched you.

CARELESS: Now then, Charles, be honest, and give us your real favorite.

CHARLES SURFACE: Why, I have withheld her only in compassion to you. If I toast her, you must give a round of her peers—which is impossible—on earth.

CARELESS: Oh, then we'll find some canonised vestals or heathen goddesses that will do, I warrant!

CHARLES SURFACE: Here then, bumpers, you rogues! bumpers! Maria! Maria!—(Drink.)

1 GENTLEMAN: Maria who?

CHARLES: O, damn the surname!—'tis too formal to be registered in Love's calendar—but now, Sir Toby Bumper, beware—we must have beauty superlative.

CARELESS: Nay, never study, Sir Toby: we'll stand to the toast, though your mistress should want an eye—and you know you have a song will excuse you.

SIR TOBY: Egad, so I have! and I'll give him the song instead of the lady. (Sings.)

SONG AND CHORUS

Here's to the maiden of bashful fifteen;
  Here's to the widow of fifty;
Here's to the flaunting extravagannt quean,
  And here's to the housewife that's thrifty.
Chorus. *Let the toast pass—*
  Drink to the lass—
I'll warrant she'll prove an excuse for the glass.
Here's to the charmer whose dimples we prize:
  Now to the maid who has none, sir;
Here's to the girl with a pair of blue eyes,
  And here's to the nymph with but one, sir.
Chorus. *Let the toast pass, &c.*

Here's to the maid with a bosom of snow:
  Now to her that's as brown as a berry:
Here's to the wife with a face full of woe,
  And now for the damsel that's merry.
Chorus. *Let the toast pass, &c.*

For let 'em be clumsy, or let 'em be slim,
  Young or ancient, I care not a feather:
So fill a pint bumper quite up to the brim,
  —And let us e'en toast 'em together.
Chorus. *Let the toast pass, &c.*

ALL: Bravo! Bravo!

(Enter TRIP, and whispers CHARLES SURFACE.)

CHARLES SURFACE: Gentlemen, you must excuse me a little.—Careless, take the chair, will you?

CARELESS: Nay, prithee, Charles, what now? This is one of your peerless beauties, I suppose, has dropped in by chance?

CHARLES SURFACE: No, faith! To tell you the truth, 'tis a Jew and a broker, who are come by appointment.

CARELESS: Oh, damn it! let's have the Jew in—

1 GENTLEMAN: Aye, and the broker too, by all means.

2 GENTLEMAN: Yes, yes, the Jew and the broker.

CHARLES SURFACE: Egad, with all my heart!—Trip, bid the gentlemen walk in.—(Exit TRIP.) Though there's one of them a stranger, I can tell you.

CARELESS: Charles, let us give them some generous Burgundy, and perhaps they'll grow conscientious.

CHARLES SURFACE: Oh, hang 'em, no! wine does but

---

hazard regimen, "keeps in strict training for gambling."

draw forth a man's *natural* qualities; and to make *them* drink would only be to whet their knavery.

(Enter TRIP, SIR OLIVER SURFACE, *and* MOSES.)

CHARLES SURFACE: So, honest Moses; walk in, pray, Mr. Premium—that's the gentleman's name, isn't it, Moses?

MOSES: Yes, sir.

CHARLES SURFACE: Set chairs, Trip.—Sit down, Mr. Premium.—Glasses, Trip —Sit down, Moses.—Come, Mr. Premium, I'll give you a sentiment; here's 'Success to usury!'—Moses, fill the gentleman a bumper.

MOSES: Success to usury!

CARELESS: Right, Moses—usury is prudence and industry, and deserves to succeed.

SIR OLIVER: Then here's—All the success it deserves!

CARELESS: No, no, that won't do! Mr. Premium, you have demurred to the toast, and must drink it in a pint bumper.

1 GENTLEMAN: A pint bumper, at least.

MOSES: Oh, pray, sir, consider—Mr. Premium's a gentleman.

CARELESS: And therefore loves good wine.

2 GENTLEMAN: Give Moses a quart glass—this is mutiny, and a high contempt of the chair.

CARELESS: Here, now for't! I'll see justice done, to the last drop of my bottle.

SIR OLIVER: Nay, pray, gentlemen—I did not expect this usage.

CHARLES SURFACE: No, hang it, Careless, you shan't; Mr. Premium's a stranger.

SIR OLIVER *(aside)*: Odd! I wish I was well out of this company.

CARELESS: Plague on 'em then! if they won't drink, we'll not sit down with 'em. Come, Harry, the dice are in the next room.—Charles, you'll join us—when you have finished your business with these gentlemen?

CHARLES SURFACE: I will! I will!—*(Exeunt Gentlemen.)* Careless!

CARELESS *(returning)*: Well!

CHARLES SURFACE: Perhaps I may want *you.*

CARELESS: Oh, you know I am always ready—word, note, or bond, 'tis all the same to me. *(Exit.)*

MOSES: Sir, this is Mr. Premium, a gentleman of the strictest honor and secrecy; and always performs what he undertakes. Mr. Premium, this is—

CHARLES SURFACE: Pshaw! have done! Sir, my friend Moses is a very honest fellow, but a little slow at expression; he'll be an hour giving us our titles. Mr. Premium, the plain state of the matter is this—I am an extravagant young fellow who wants money to borrow; you I take to be a prudent old fellow, who has got money to lend. I am blockhead enough to give fifty per cent sooner than not have it; and you, I presume, are rogue

enough to take a hundred if you could get it. Now, sir, you see we are acquainted at once, and may proceed to business without farther ceremony.

SIR OLIVER: Exceeding frank, upon my word. I see, sir, you are not a man of many compliments.

CHARLES SURFACE: Oh, no, sir! plain dealing in business I always think best.

SIR OLIVER: Sir, I like you the better for't. However, you are mistaken in one thing—I have no money to lend, but I believe I could procure some of a friend; but then he's an unconscionable dog—isn't he, Moses? And must sell stock to accommodate you—mustn't he, Moses?

MOSES: Yes, indeed! You know I always speak the truth, and scorn to tell a lie!

CHARLES SURFACE: Right! People that expect truth generally do. But these are trifles, Mr. Premium. What! I know money isn't to be bought without paying for't!

SIR OLIVER: Well, but what security could you give? You have no land, I suppose?

CHARLES SURFACE: Not a mole-hill, nor a twig, but what's in beau-pots° out at the window!

SIR OLIVER: Nor any stock, I presume?

CHARLES SURFACE: Nothing but live stock—and that's only a few pointers and ponies. But pray, Mr. Premium, are you acquainted at all with any of my connections?

SIR OLIVER: Why, to say truth, I am.

CHARLES SURFACE: Then you must know that I have a devilish rich uncle in the East Indies, Sir Oliver Surface, from whom I have the greatest expectations.

SIR OLIVER: That you have a wealthy uncle, I have heard—but how your expectations will turn out is more, I believe, than you can tell.

CHARLES SURFACE: Oh, no!—there can be no doubt—they tell me I'm a prodigious favorite—and that he talks of leaving me everything.

SIR OLIVER: Indeed! this is the first I've heard on't.

CHARLES SURFACE: Yes, yes, 'tis just so.—Moses knows 'tis true; don't you, Moses?

MOSES: Oh, yes! I'll swear to't.

SIR OLIVER *(aside)*: Egad, they'll persuade me presently I'm at Bengal.

CHARLES SURFACE: Now I propose, Mr. Premium, if it's agreeable to you, a post-obit on Sir Oliver's life; though at the same time the old fellow has been so liberal to me that I give you my word I should be very sorry to hear anything had happened to him.

SIR OLIVER: Not more than *I* should, I assure you. But the bond you mention happens to be just the

---

beau-pots, large ornamental flower-pots.

worst security you could offer me—for I might live to a hundred and never recover the principal.

CHARLES SURFACE: Oh, yes, you would!—the moment Sir Oliver dies, you know, you'd come on me for the money.

SIR OLIVER: Then I believe I should be the most unwelcome dun you ever had in your life.

CHARLES SURFACE: What! I suppose you are afraid now that Sir Oliver is too good a life?

SIR OLIVER: No, indeed I am not—though I have heard he is as hale and healthy as any man of his years in Christendom.

CHARLES SURFACE: There again you are misinformed. No, no, the climate has hurt him considerably, poor uncle Oliver. Yes, he breaks apace, I'm told—and so much altered lately that his nearest relations don't know him.

SIR OLIVER: No! Ha! ha! ha! so much altered lately that his relations don't know him! Ha! ha! ha! that's droll, egad—ha! ha! ha!

CHARLES SURFACE: Ha! ha!—you're glad to hear that, little Premium.

SIR OLIVER: No, no, I'm not.

CHARLES SURFACE: Yes, yes, you are—ha! ha! ha!—you know that mends your chance.

SIR OLIVER: But I'm told Sir Oliver is coming over—nay, some say he is actually arrived.

CHARLES SURFACE: Pshaw! sure I must know better than you whether he's come or not. No, no, rely on't, he is at this moment at Calcutta, isn't he, Moses?

MOSES: Oh yes, certainly.

SIR OLIVER: Very true, as you say, you must know better than I, though I have it from pretty good authority—haven't I, Moses?

MOSES: Yes, most undoubted!

SIR OLIVER: But, sir, as I understand you want a few hundreds immediately, is there nothing you would dispose of?

CHARLES SURFACE: How do you mean?

SIR OLIVER: For instance, now—I have heard—that your father left behind him a great quantity of massy old plate.

CHARLES SURFACE: O lud! that's gone long ago—Moses can tell you how better than I can.

SIR OLIVER: Good lack! all the family race-cups and corporation bowls! (aside) —Then it was also supposed that his library was one of the most valuable and complete.

CHARLES SURFACE: Yes, yes, so it was—vastly too much so for a private gentleman—for my part, I was always of a communicative disposition, so I thought it a shame to keep so much knowledge to myself.

SIR OLIVER (aside): Mercy on me! learning that had run in the family like an heirloom!—(Aloud) Pray, what are become of the books?

CHARLES SURFACE: You must inquire of the auctioneer, Master Premium, for I don't believe even Moses can direct you there.

MOSES: I never meddle with books.

SIR OLIVER: So, so, nothing of the family property left, I suppose?

CHARLES SURFACE: Not much, indeed; unless you have a mind to the family pictures. I have got a room full of ancestors above—and if you have a taste for old paintings, egad, you shall have 'em a bargain!

SIR OLIVER: Hey! and the devil! sure, you wouldn't sell your forefathers, would you?

CHARLES SURFACE: Every man of 'em, to the best bidder.

SIR OLIVER: What! your great-uncles and aunts?

CHARLES SURFACE: Aye, and my great-grandfathers and grandmothers too.

SIR OLIVER: Now I give him up!—(aside) What the plague, have you no vowels for your own kindred? Odd's life! do you take me for Shylock in the play, that you would raise money of me on your own flesh and blood?

CHARLES SURFACE: Nay, my little broker, don't be angry: what need you care, if you have your money's worth?

SIR OLIVER: Well, I'll be the purchaser—I think I can dispose of the family.—(aside) Oh, I'll never forgive him this! never!

(Enter CARELESS.)

CARELESS: Come, Charles, what keeps you?

CHARLES SURFACE: I can't come yet. I'faith! we are going to have a sale above—here's little Premium will buy all my ancestors!

CARELESS: Oh, burn your ancestors!

CHARLES SURFACE: No, he may do that afterwards, if he pleases. Stay, Careless, we want you; egad, you shall be auctioneer—so come along with us.

CARELESS: Oh, have with you, if that's the case.—I can handle a hammer as well as a dice box!

SIR OLIVER: Oh, the profligates!

CHARLES SURFACE: Come, Moses, you shall be appraiser, if we want one.—Gad's life, little Premium, you don't seem to like the business.

SIR OLIVER: Oh, yes, I do, vastly! Ha! ha! yes, yes, I think it a rare joke to sell one's family by auction—ha! ha!—(aside) Oh, the prodigal!

CHARLES SURFACE: To be sure! when a man wants money, where the plague should he get assistance, if he can't make free with his own relations? (Exeunt.)

ACT 4 / SCENE 1

(Picture-room at CHARLES'S.*)*
(Enter CHARLES SURFACE, SIR OLIVER SURFACE, MOSES, *and* CARELESS.*)*

CHARLES SURFACE: Walk in, gentlemen, pray walk in!— here they are, the family of the Surfaces, up to the Conquest.

SIR OLIVER: And, in my opinion, a goodly collection.

CHARLES SURFACE: Aye, aye, these are done in true spirit of portrait-painting—no volunteer grace or expression—not like the works of your modern Raphael, who gives you the strongest resemblance, yet contrives to make your own portrait independent of you; so that you may sink the original and not hurt the picture. No, no; the merit of these is the inveterate likeness—all stiff and awkward as the originals, and like nothing in human nature beside!

SIR OLIVER: Ah! we shall never see such figures of men again.

CHARLES SURFACE: I hope not. Well, you see, Master Premium, what a domestic character I am—here I sit of an evening surrounded by my family. But come, get to your pulpit, Mr. Auctioneer—here's an old gouty chair of my grandfather's will answer the purpose.

CARELESS: Aye, aye, this will do. But, Charles, I have ne'er a hammer; and what's an auctioneer without his hammer?

CHARLES SURFACE: Egad, that's true. What parchment have we here? *(Takes down a roll.)* 'Richard, heir to Thomas'—our genealogy in full. Here, Careless, you shall have no common bit of mahogany—here's the family tree for you, you rogue—this shall be your hammer, and now you may knock down my ancestors with their own pedigree.

SIR OLIVER *(aside)*: What an unnatural rogue!—an *ex post facto* parricide!

CARELESS: Yes, yes, here's a list of your generation indeed;—faith, Charles, this is the most convenient thing you could have found for the business, for 'twill serve not only as a hammer, but a catalogue into the bargain.—But come, begin—A-going, a-going, a-going!

CHARLES SURFACE: Bravo, Careless! Well, here's my great uncle, Sir Richard Raviline, a marvellous good general in his day, I assure you. He served in all the Duke of Marlborough's wars, and got that

cut over his eye at the battle of Malplaquet.° What say you, Mr. Premium? look at him—there's a hero for you! not cut out of his feathers, as your modern clipped captains are, but enveloped in wig and regimentals, as a general should be. What do you bid?

MOSES: Mr. Premium would have you speak.

CHARLES SURFACE: Why, then, he shall have him for ten pounds, and I am sure that's not dear for a staff-officer.

SIR OLIVER: Heaven deliver me! his famous uncle Richard for ten pounds!—Very well, sir, I take him at that.

CHARLES SURFACE: Careless, knock down my uncle Richard.—Here, now, is a maiden sister of his, my great-aunt Deborah, done by Kneller,° thought to be in his best manner, and a very formidable likeness. There she is, you see, a shepherdess feeding her flock. You shall have her for five pounds ten— the sheep are worth the money.

SIR OLIVER: Ah! poor Deborah! a woman who set such a value on herself!—Five pound ten—she's mine.

CHARLES SURFACE: Knock down my aunt Deborah! Here, now, are two that were a sort of cousins of theirs.—You see, Moses, these pictures were done some time ago, when beaux wore wigs, and the ladies wore their own hair.

SIR OLIVER: Yes, truly, head-dresses appear to have been a little lower in those days.

CHARLES SURFACE: Well, take that couple for the same.

MOSES: 'Tis a good bargain.

CHARLES SURFACE: Careless!—This, now, is a grandfather of my mother's, a learned judge, well known on the western circuit.—What do you rate him at, Moses?

MOSES: Four guineas.

CHARLES SURFACE: Four guineas! Gad's life, you don't bid me the price of his wig.—Mr. Premium, *you* have more respect for the woolsack;° do let us knock his lordship down at fifteen.

SIR OLIVER: By all means.

CARELESS: Gone!

CHARLES SURFACE: And there are two brothers of his, William and Walter Blunt, Esquires, both mem-

---

battle of Malplaquet, on September 11, 1709.

Kneller, Sir Godfrey Kneller (1648–1723), who painted many portraits of English sovereigns and nobles. **woolsack,** "for lawyers." The reference to the Lord Chancellor's seat on the Woolsack in the House of Lords is here meant as the symbol of the profession of law.

bers of Parliament, and noted speakers; and, what's very extraordinary, I believe this is the first time they were ever bought and sold.

SIR OLIVER: That's very extraordinary, indeed! I'll take them at your own price, for the honor of Parliament.

CARELESS: Well said, little Premium! I'll knock 'em down at forty.

CHARLES SURFACE: Here's a jolly fellow—I don't know what relation, but he was mayor of Manchester; take him at eight pounds.

SIR OLIVER: No, no—six will do for the mayor.

CHARLES SURFACE: Come, make it guineas, and I'll throw you the two aldermen there into the bargain.

SIR OLIVER: They're mine.

CHARLES SURFACE: Careless, knock down the mayor and aldermen. But, plague on't! we shall be all day retailing in this manner; do let us deal wholesale—what say you, little Premium? Give me three hundred pounds for the rest of the family in the lump.

CARELESS: Aye, aye, that will be the best way.

SIR OLIVER: Well, well, anything to accommodate you; they are mine. But there is one portrait which you have always passed over.

CARELESS: What, that ill-looking little fellow over the settee?

SIR OLIVER: Yes, sir, I mean that; though I don't think him so ill-looking a little fellow, by any means.

CHARLES SURFACE: What, that? Oh, that's my uncle Oliver! 'Twas done before he went to India.

CARELESS: Your uncle Oliver! Gad, then you'll never be friends, Charles. That, now, to me, is as stern a looking rogue as ever I saw—an unforgiving eye, and a damned disinheriting countenance! an inveterate knave, depend on't. Don't you think so, little Premium?

SIR OLIVER: Upon my soul, sir, I do not; I think it is as honest a looking face as any in the room, dead or alive. But I suppose your uncle Oliver goes with the rest of the lumber?

CHARLES SURFACE: No, hang it! I'll not part with poor Noll. The old fellow has been very good to me, and, egad, I'll keep his picture while I've a room to put it in.

SIR OLIVER: The rogue's my nephew after all! (aside)—But, sir, I have somehow taken a fancy to that picture.

CHARLES SURFACE: I'm sorry for't, for you certainly will not have it. Oons! haven't you got enough of 'em?

SIR OLIVER: I forgive him everything! (aside) But, sir, when I take a whim in my head, I don't value money. I'll give you as much for that as for all the rest.

CHARLES SURFACE: Don't tease me, master broker; I tell you I'll not part with it, and there's an end on't.

SIR OLIVER: How like his father the dog is!— (Aloud) Well, well, I have done.—I did not perceive it before, but I think I never saw such a resemblance.—Well, sir—here's a draught for your sum.

CHARLES SURFACE: Why, 'tis for eight hundred pounds!

SIR OLIVER: You will not let Sir Oliver go?

CHARLES SURFACE: Zounds! no! I tell you, once more.

SIR OLIVER: Then never mind the difference; we'll balance another time. But give me your hand on the bargain; you are an honest fellow, Charles—I beg pardon, sir, for being so free.— Come, Moses.

CHARLES SURFACE: Egad, this is a whimsical old fellow!—but hark'ee, Premium, you'll prepare lodgings for these gentlemen.

SIR OLIVER: Yes, yes, I'll send for them in a day or two.

CHARLES SURFACE: But hold—do now—send a genteel conveyance for them, for, I assure you, they were most of them used to ride in their own carriages.

SIR OLIVER: I will, I will, for all but—Oliver.

CHARLES SURFACE: Aye, all but the little honest nabob.

SIR OLIVER: You're fixed on that?

CHARLES SURFACE: Peremptorily.

SIR OLIVER: A dear extravagant rogue!—Good day!—Come, Moses,—Let me hear now who dares call him profligate! (Exeunt SIR OLIVER and MOSES.)

CARELESS: Why, this is the oddest genius of the sort I ever saw!

CHARLES SURFACE: Egad, he's the prince of brokers, I think. I wonder how the devil Moses got acquainted with so honest a fellow.—Ha! here's Rowley.—Do, Careless, say I'll join the company in a moment.

CARELESS: I will—but don't let that old blockhead persuade you to squander any of that money on old musty debts, or any such nonsense; for tradesmen, Charles, are the most exorbitant fellows!

CHARLES SURFACE: Very true, and paying them is only encouraging them.

CARELESS: Nothing else.

CHARLES SURFACE: Aye, aye, never fear.—(Exit CARELESS.) So! this was an odd old fellow, indeed! Let me see, two-thirds of this is mine by right—five hundred and thirty pounds. 'Fore heaven! I find one's ancestors are more valuable relations than I took 'em for!—Ladies and gentlemen, your most obedient and very grateful humble servant.

(Enter ROWLEY.)

Ha! old Rowley! egad, you are just come in time to take leave of your old acquaintance.

ROWLEY: Yes, I heard they were going. But I wonder you can have such spirits under so many distresses.

CHARLES SURFACE: Why, there's the point—my distresses are so many, that I can't afford to part with my spirits; but I shall be rich and splenetic, all in good time. However, I suppose you are surprised that I am not more sorrowful at parting with so many near relations; to be sure, 'tis very affecting; but rot 'em, you see they never move a muscle, so why should I?

ROWLEY: There's no making you serious a moment.

CHARLES SURFACE: Yes, faith: I am so now. Here, my honest Rowley, here, get me this changed, and take a hundred pounds of it immediately to old Stanley.

ROWLEY: A hundred pounds! Consider only—

CHARLES SURFACE: Gad's life, don't talk about it! poor Stanley's wants are pressing, and, if you don't make haste, we shall have some one call that has a better right to the money.

ROWLEY: Ah! there's the point! I never will cease dunning you with the old proverb—

CHARLES SURFACE: 'Be *just* before you're *generous,* hey!—Why, so I would if I could; but Justice is an old lame hobbling beldame, and I can't get her to keep pace with Generosity, for the soul of me.

ROWLEY: Yet, Charles, believe me, one hour's reflection—

CHARLES SURFACE: Aye, aye, it's all very true; but, hark'ee, Rowley, while I have, by heaven I'll give—so, damn your economy! and now for hazard. (*Exit.*)

ACT 4 / SCENE 2

(*The parlor*)
(*Enter* SIR OLIVER SURFACE *and* MOSES.)

MOSES: Well, sir, I think, as Sir Peter said, you have seen Mr. Charles in high glory: 'tis great pity he's so extravagant.

SIR OLIVER: True, but he wouldn't sell my picture.

MOSES: And loves wine and women so much.

SIR OLIVER: But he wouldn't sell my picture!

MOSES: And games so deep.

SIR OLIVER: But he wouldn't sell my picture. Oh, here's Rowley.

(*Enter* ROWLEY.)

ROWLEY: So, Sir Oliver, I find you have made a purchase—

SIR OLIVER: Yes, yes, our young rake has parted with his ancestors like old tapestry.

ROWLEY: And here has he commissioned me to re-deliver your part of the purchase-money—I mean, though, in your necessitous character of old Stanley.

MOSES: Ah! there is the pity of all: he is so damned charitable.

ROWLEY: And I left a hosier and two tailors in the hall, who, I'm sure, won't be paid, and this hundred would satisfy 'em.

SIR OLIVER: Well, well, I'll pay his debts—and his benevolence too; but now I am no more a broker, and you shall introduce me to the elder brother as old Stanley.

ROWLEY: Not yet awhile; Sir Peter, I know, means to call there about this time.

(*Enter* Trip.)

TRIP: O gentlemen, I beg pardon for not showing you out; this way—Moses, a word. (*Exeunt* TRIP *and* MOSES.)

SIR OLIVER: There's a fellow for you! Would you believe it, that puppy intercepted the Jew on our coming, and wanted to raise money before he got to his master!

ROWLEY: Indeed!

SIR OLIVER: Yes, they are now planning an annuity business. Ah, Master Rowley, in my days, servants were content with the follies of their masters, when they were worn a little threadbare—but now they have their vices, like their birthday clothes,° with the gloss on. (*Exeunt.*)

ACT 4 / SCENE 3

(*A library in* JOSEPH SURFACE'S *house*)
(JOSEPH SURFACE *and* SERVANT.)

JOSEPH SURFACE: No letter from Lady Teazle?

SERVANT: No, sir.

JOSEPH SURFACE (*aside*): I am surprised she hasn't sent, if she's prevented from coming. Sir Peter certainly does not suspect me. Yet I wish I may not lose the heiress, through the scrape I have drawn myself in with the wife; however, Charles's imprudence and bad character are great points in my favor. (*Knocking.*)

SERVANT: Sir, I believe that must be Lady Teazle.

JOSEPH SURFACE: Hold! See whether it is or not, before you go to the door—I have a particular message for you, if it should be my brother.

SERVANT: 'Tis her ladyship, sir; she always leaves her chair at the milliner's in the next street.

JOSEPH SURFACE: Stay, stay—draw that screen before the window—that will do;—my opposite neighbor is a maiden lady of so curious a tem-

---

birthday clothes, ceremonial dress for the King's Birthday celebrations per.—(SERVANT *draws the screen and exits.*) I have a difficult hand to play in this affair. Lady Teazle has lately suspected my views on Maria; but she must by no means be let into that secret,—at least, not till I have her more in my power.

(*Enter* LADY TEAZLE.)

LADY TEAZLE: What, sentiment in soliloquy! Have you been very impatient now? O lud! don't pretend to look grave. I vow I couldn't come before.

JOSEPH SURFACE: O madam, punctuality is a species of constancy, a very unfashionable quality in a lady.

LADY TEAZLE: Upon my word, you ought to pity me. Do you know that Sir Peter is grown so ill-tempered to me of late, and so jealous of Charles too—that's the best of the story, isn't it?

JOSEPH SURFACE (*aside*): I am glad my scandalous friends keep that up.

LADY TEAZLE: I am sure I wish he would let Maria marry him, and then perhaps he would be confinced; don't you, Mr. Surface?

JOSEPH SURFACE (*aside*): Indeed I do not.—Oh, certainly I do! for then my dear Lady Teazle would also be convinced how wrong her suspicions were of my having any design on the silly girl.

LADY TEAZLE: Well, well, I'm inclined to believe you. But isn't it provoking, to have the most ill-natured things said to one? And there's my friend Lady Sneerwell has circulated I don't know how many scandalous tales of me! and all without any foundation, too—that's what vexes me.

JOSEPH SURFACE: Aye, madam, to be sure, that *is* the provoking circumstance—without foundation! yes, yes, there's the mortification, indeed; for when a scandalous story is believed against one, there certainly is no comfort like the consciousness of having deserved it.

LADY TEAZLE: No, to be sure—then I'd forgive their malice; but to attack me, who am really so innocent, and who never say an ill-natured thing of anybody—that is, of any friend—and then Sir Peter, too, to have him so peevish, and so suspicious, when I know the integrity of my own heart—indeed 'tis monstrous!

JOSEPH SURFACE: But, my dear Lady Teazle, 'tis your own fault if you suffer it. When a husband entertains a groundless suspicion of his wife, and withdraws his confidence from her, the original compact is broke, and she owes it to the honor of her sex to endeavor to outwit him.

LADY TEAZLE: Indeed! So that, if he suspects me without cause, it follows that the best way of curing his jealousy is to give him reason for't?

JOSEPH SURFACE: Undoubtedly—for your husband should never be deceived in you: and in that case it becomes *you* to be frail in compliment to *his* discernment.

LADY TEAZLE: To be sure, what you say is very reasonable, and when the consciousness of my own innocence—

JOSEPH SURFACE: Ah, my dear madam, there is the great mistake; 'tis this very conscious innocence that is of the greatest prejudice to you. What is it makes you negligent of forms, and careless of the world's opinion? why, the *consciousness* of your innocence. What makes you thoughtless in your conduct, and apt to run into a thousand little imprudences? why, the *consciousness* of your innocence. What makes you impatient of Sir Peter's temper and outrageous at his suspicions? why, the *consciousness* of your own innocence!

LADY TEAZLE: 'Tis very true!

JOSEPH SURFACE: Now, my dear Lady Teazle, if you would but once make a trifling *faux pas*, you can't conceive how cautious you would grow—and how ready to humor and agree with your husband.

LADY TEAZLE: Do you think so?

JOSEPH SURFACE: Oh, I'm sure on't; and then you would find all scandal would cease at once, for—in short, your character at present is like a person in a plethora, absolutely dying of too much health.

LADY TEAZLE: So, so; then I perceive your prescription is, that I must sin in my own defence, and part with my virtue to preserve my reputation?

JOSEPH SURFACE: Exactly so, upon my credit, ma'am.

LADY TEAZLE: Well, certainly this is the oddest doctrine, and the newest receipt for avoiding calumny?

JOSEPH SURFACE: An infallible one, believe me. *Prudence,* like *experience,* must be paid for.

LADY TEAZLE: Why, if my understanding were once convinced—

JOSEPH SURFACE: Oh, certainly, madam, your understanding *should* be convinced. Yes, yes—heaven forbid I should persuade you to do anything you *thought* wrong. No, no, I have too much honor to desire it.

LADY TEAZLE: Don't you think we may as well leave honor out of the argument?

JOSEPH SURFACE: Ah, the ill effects of your country education, I see, still remain with you.

LADY TEAZLE: I doubt they do, indeed; and I will fairly own to you, that if I could be persuaded to do wrong, it would be by Sir Peter's ill-usage sooner than your honorable logic, after all.

JOSEPH SURFACE: Then, by this hand, which he is unworthy of— (*Taking her hand.*)

(*Re-enter* SERVANT.)

'Sdeath, you blockhead—what do you want?

SERVANT: I beg pardon, sir, but I thought you wouldn't choose Sir Peter to come up without announcing him.

JOSEPH SURFACE: Sir Peter!—Oons—the devil!

LADY TEAZLE: Sir Peter! O lud! I'm ruined! I'm ruined!

SERVANT: Sir, 'twasn't I let him in.

LADY TEAZLE: Oh! I'm undone! What will become of me, now, Mr. Logic?—Oh! mercy, he's on the stairs—I'll get behind here—and if ever I'm so imprudent again— (*Goes behind the screen.*)

JOSEPH SURFACE: Give me that book. (*Sits down. SERVANT pretends to adjust his hair.*)

(*Enter SIR PETER TEAZLE.*)

SIR PETER: Aye, ever improving himself!—Mr. Surface, Mr. Surface—

JOSEPH SURFACE: Oh, my dear Sir Peter, I beg your pardon. (*Gaping, and throws away the book.*) I have been dozing over a stupid book. Well, I am much obliged to you for this call. You haven't been here, I believe, since I fitted up this room. Books, you know, are the only things I am a coxcomb in.

SIR PETER: 'Tis very neat indeed. Well, well, that's proper; and you make even your screen a source of knowledge—hung, I perceive, with maps.

JOSEPH SURFACE: Oh, yes, I find great use in that screen.

SIR PETER: I dare say you must—certainly—when you want to find anything in a hurry.

JOSEPH SURFACE (*aside*): Aye, or to hide anything in a hurry either.

SIR PETER: Well, I have a little private business—

JOSEPH SURFACE: You needn't stay. (*to SERVANT*)

SERVANT: No, sir. (*Exit.*)

JOSEPH SURFACE: Here's a chair, Sir Peter—I beg—

SIR PETER: Well, now we are alone, there is a subject, my dear friend, on which I wish to unburden my mind to you—a point of the greatest moment to my peace: in short, my good friend, Lady Teazle's conduct of late has made me extremely unhappy.

JOSEPH SURFACE: Indeed! I am very sorry to hear it.

SIR PETER: Yes, 'tis but too plain she has not the least regard for me; but what's worse, I have pretty good authority to suspect she must have formed an attachment to another.

JOSEPH SURFACE: You astonish me!

SIR PETER: Yes! and, between ourselves, I think I have discovered the person.

JOSEPH SURFACE: How! you alarm me exceedingly.

SIR PETER: Aye, my dear friend, I knew you would sympathize with me!

JOSEPH SURFACE: Yes, believe me, Sir Peter, such a discovery would hurt me just as much as it would you.

SIR PETER: I am convinced of it.—Ah! it is a happiness to have a friend whom one can trust even with one's family secrets. But have you no guess who I mean?

JOSEPH SURFACE: I haven't the most distant idea. It can't be Sir Benjamin Backbite!

SIR PETER: O, no! What say you to Charles?

JOSEPH SURFACE: My brother! impossible!

SIR PETER: Ah, my dear friend, the goodness of your own heart misleads you—you judge of others by yourself.

JOSEPH SURFACE: Certainly, Sir Peter, the heart that is conscious of its own integrity is ever slow to credit another's treachery.

SIR PETER: True; but your brother has no sentiment—you never hear him talk so.

JOSEPH SURFACE: Yet I can't but think Lady Teazle herself has too much principle—

SIR PETER: Aye; but what's her principle against the flattery of a handsome, lively young fellow?

JOSEPH SURFACE: That's very true.

SIR PETER: And then, you know, the difference of our ages makes it very improbable that she should have any great affection for me; and if she were to be frail, and I were to make it public, why the town would only laugh at me, the foolish old bachelor who had married a girl.

JOSEPH SURFACE: That's true, to be sure—they *would* laugh.

SIR PETER: Laugh! aye, and make ballads, and paragraphs, and the devil knows what of me.

JOSEPH SURFACE: No, you must never make it public.

SIR PETER: But then again—that the nephew of my old friend, Sir Oliver, should be the person to attempt such a wrong, hurts me more nearly.

JOSEPH SURFACE: Aye, there's the point. When ingratitude barbs the dart of injury, the wound has double danger in it.

SIR PETER: Aye—I, that was, in a manner, left his guardian—in whose house he had been so often entertained—who never in my life denied him—my advice!

JOSEPH SURFACE: Oh, 'tis not to be credited! There *may* be a man capable of such baseness, to be sure; but, for my part, till you can give me positive proofs, I cannot but doubt it. However, if it should be proved on him, he is no longer a brother of mine! I disclaim kindred with him—for the man who can break through the laws of hospitality, and attempt the wife of his friend, deserves to be branded as the pest of society.

SIR PETER: What a difference there is between you! What noble sentiments!

JOSEPH SURFACE: Yet I cannot suspect Lady Teazle's honor.

SIR PETER: I am sure I wish to think well of her, and to remove all ground of quarrel between us. She has lately reproached me more than once with having made no settlement on her; and, in our last quarrel, she almost hinted that she should not break her heart if I was dead. Now, as we seem to differ in our ideas of expense, I have resolved she shall be her own mistress in that respect for the future; and, if I *were* to die, she shall find that I have not been inattentive to her interest while living. Here, my friend, are the drafts of two deeds, which I wish to have your opinion on. By one, she will enjoy eight hundred a year independent while I live; and, by the other, the bulk of my fortune after my death.

JOSEPH SURFACE: This conduct, Sir Peter, is indeed truly generous.— *(aside)* I wish it may not corrupt my pupil.

SIR PETER: Yes, I am determined she shall have no cause to complain, though I would not have her acquainted with the latter instance of my affection yet awhile.

JOSEPH SURFACE: Nor I, if I could help it. *(aside)*

SIR PETER: And now, my dear friend, if you please, we will talk over the situation of your hopes with Maria.

JOSEPH SURFACE *(softly)*: No, no, Sir Peter; another time, if you please.

SIR PETER: I am sensibly chagrined at the little progress you seem to make in her affection.

JOSEPH SURFACE: I beg you will not mention it. What are my disappointments when your happiness is in debate! *(Softly.)*—'Sdeath, I shall be ruined every way! *(aside)*

SIR PETER: And though you are so averse to my acquainting Lady Teazle with your passion, I am sure she's not your enemy in the affair.

JOSEPH SURFACE: Pray, Sir Peter, now oblige me. I am really too much affected by the subject we have been speaking on to bestow a thought on my own concerns. The man who is entrusted with his friend's distresses can never—

(Enter SERVANT.)

Well, sir?

SERVANT: Your brother, sir, is speaking to a gentleman in the street, and says he knows you are within.

JOSEPH SURFACE: 'Sdeath, blockhead—I'm not within—I'm out for the day.

SIR PETER: Stay—hold—a thought has struck me—you shall be at home.

JOSEPH SURFACE: Well, well, let him up.—*(Exit SERVANT.)* He'll interrupt Sir Peter—however—

SIR PETER: Now, my good friend, oblige me, I entreat you. Before Charles comes, let me conceal myself somewhere; then do you tax him on the point we have been talking on, and his answers may satisfy me at once.

JOSEPH SURFACE: O, fie, Sir Peter! would you have me join in so mean a trick?—to trepan my brother so?

SIR PETER: Nay, you tell me you are *sure* he is innocent; if so, you do him the greatest service by giving him an opportunity to clear himself, and you will set my heart at rest. Come, you shall not refuse me; here, behind the screen will be *(Goes to the screen.)*—Hey! what the devil! there seems to be *one* listener here already—I'll swear I saw a petticoat!

JOSEPH SURFACE: Ha! ha! ha! Well, this is ridiculous enough. I'll tell you, Sir Peter, though I hold a man of intrigue to be a most despicable character, yet you know, it doesn't follow that one is to be an absolute Joseph either! Hark'ee! 'tis a little French milliner, a silly rogue that plagues me—and having some character—on your coming, she ran behind the screen.

SIR PETER: Ah, you rogue!—But, egad, she has overheard all I have been saying of my wife.

JOSEPH SURFACE: Oh, 'twill never go any further, you may depend on't!

SIR PETER: No! then, i'faith, let her hear it out.—Here's a closet will do as well.

JOSEPH SURFACE: Well, go in then.

SIR PETER: Sly rogue! sly rogue! *(Goes into the closet.)*

JOSEPH SURFACE: A very narrow escape, indeed! and a curious situation I'm in, to part man and wife in this manner.

LADY TEAZLE *(peeping from the screen)*: Couldn't I steal off?

JOSEPH SURFACE: Keep close, my angel!

SIR PETER *(peeping out)*: Joseph, tax him home.

JOSEPH SURFACE: Back, my dear friend!

LADY TEAZLE *(peeping)*: Couldn't you lock Sir Peter in?

JOSEPH SURFACE: Be still, my life!

SIR PETER *(peeping)*: You're sure the little milliner won't blab?

JOSEPH SURFACE: In, in, my dear Sir Peter!—'Fore gad, I wish I had a key to the door.

(Enter CHARLES SURFACE.)

CHARLES SURFACE: Hollo! brother, what has been the matter? Your fellow would not let me up at first. What! have you had a Jew or a wench with you?

JOSEPH SURFACE: Neither, brother, I assure you.

CHARLES SURFACE: But what has made Sir Peter steal off? I thought he had been with you.

JOSEPH SURFACE: He was, brother; but, hearing *you* were coming, he did not choose to stay.

CHARLES SURFACE: What! was the old gentleman afraid I wanted to borrow money of him!

JOSEPH SURFACE: No, sir: but I am sorry to find, Charles, that you have lately given that worthy man grounds for great uneasiness.

CHARLES SURFACE: Yes, they tell me I do that to a great many worthy men. But how so, pray?

JOSEPH SURFACE: To be plain with you, brother, he thinks you are endeavoring to gain Lady Teazle's affections from him.

CHARLES SURFACE: Who, I? O lud! not I, upon my word.—Ha! ha! ha! so the old fellow has found out that he has got a young wife, has he?—or, what's worse, has her ladyship discovered that she has an old husband?

JOSEPH: This is no subject to jest on, brother.—He who can laugh—

CHARLES SURFACE: True, true, as you were going to say—then, seriously, I never had the least idea of what you charge me with, upon my honor.

JOSEPH SURFACE: Well, it will give Sir Peter great satisfaction to hear this. (Aloud.)

CHARLES SURFACE: To be sure, I once thought the lady seemed to have taken a great fancy to me; but, upon my soul, I never gave her the least encouragement. Besides, you know my attachment to Maria.

JOSEPH SURFACE: But sure, brother, even if Lady Teazle had betrayed the fondest partiality for you—

CHARLES SURFACE: Why, look'ee, Joseph, I hope I shall never deliberately do a dishonorable action—but if a pretty woman were purposely to throw herself in my way—and that pretty woman married to a man old enought to be her father—

JOSEPH SURFACE: Well!

CHARLES SURFACE: Why, I believe I should be obliged to borrow a little of your morality, that's all.—But brother, do you know now that you surprise me exceedingly, by naming me with Lady Teazle; for, faith, I always understood you were her favorite.

JOSEPH SURFACE: Oh, for shame, Charles! This retort is foolish.

CHARLES SURFACE: Nay, I swear I have seen you exchange such significant glances—

JOSEPH SURFACE: Nay, nay, sir, this is no jest—

CHARLES SURFACE: Egad, I'm serious! Don't you remember—one day, when I called here—

JOSEPH SURFACE: Nay, prithee, Charles—

CHARLES SURFACE: And found you together—

JOSEPH SURFACE: Zounds, sir, I insist—

CHARLES SURFACE: And another time, when your servant—

JOSEPH SURFACE: Brother, brother, a word with you!—(aside) Gad, I must stop him.

CHARLES SURFACE: Informed me, I say, that—

JOSEPH SURFACE: Hush! I beg your pardon, but Sir Peter has overheard all we have been saying—I knew you would clear yourself, or I should not have consented.

CHARLES SURFACE: How Sir Peter! Where is he?

JOSEPH SURFACE: Softly, there! (Points to the closet.)

CHARLES SURFACE: Oh, 'fore heaven, I'll have him out.—Sir Peter, come forth!

JOSEPH SURFACE: No, no—

CHARLES SURFACE: I say, Sir Peter, come into court.—(Pulls in SIR PETER.) What! my old guardian!—What—turn inquisitor, and take evidence, incog.?

SIR PETER: Give me your hand, Charles—I believe I have suspected you wrongfully—but you mustn't be angry with Joseph—'twas my plan!

CHARLES SURFACE: Indeeed!

SIR PETER: But I acquit you. I promise you I don't think near so ill of you as I did. What I have heard has given me great satisfaction.

CHARLES SURFACE: Egad, then, 'twas lucky you didn't hear any more. Wasn't it, Joseph? (Half aside)

SIR PETER: Well, well, I believe you.

JOSEPH SURFACE: Would they were both out of the room!

SIR PETER: And in future, perhaps, we may not be such strangers.

(Enter SERVANT who whispers JOSEPH SURFACE.)

JOSEPH SURFACE: Lady Sneerwell!—stop her by all means— (Exit SERVANT.) Gentlemen— I beg pardon—I must wait on you downstairs—here's a person come on particular business.

CHARLES SURFACE: Well, you can see him in another room. Sir Peter and I haven't met a long time, and I have something to say to him.

JOSEPH SURFACE: They must not be left together.—I'll send Lady Sneerwell away, and return directly.—(aside) Sir Peter, not a word on the French milliner. (Exit JOSEPH SURFACE.)

SIR PETER: Oh! not for the world!—Ah, Charles, if you associated more with your brother, one might indeed hope for your reformation. He is a man of sentiment.—Well, there is nothing in the world so noble as a man of sentiment!

CHARLES SURFACE: Pshaw! he is too moral by half, and so apprehensive of his good name, as he calls it, that I suppose he would as soon let a priest into his house as a girl.

SIR PETER: No, no.—come, come,—you wrong him. No, no, Joseph is no rake, but he is not such a saint in that respect either,—I have a great mind to tell him—we should have a laugh! (aside)

CHARLES SURFACE: Oh, hang him! he's a very anchorite, a young hermit!

SIR PETER: Hark'ee—you must not abuse him; he may chance to hear of it again, I promise you.

CHARLES SURFACE: Why, you won't tell him?

SIR PETER: No—but—this way.—(aside) Egad, I'll tell

him.—Hark'ee, have you a mind to have a good laugh at Joseph?

CHARLES SURFACE: I should like it of all things.

SIR PETER: Then, i'faith, we will!—I'll be quit with him for discovering me. *(aside)*—He had a girl with him when I called.

CHARLES SURFACE: What! Joseph? you jest.

SIR PETER: Hush!—a little—French milliner—and the best of the jest is—she's in the room now.

CHARLES SURFACE: The devil she is!

SIR PETER: Hush! I tell you. *(Points to the screen.)*

CHARLES SURFACE: Behind the screen! 'Slife, let's unveil her!

SIR PETER: No, no, he's coming:—you shan't, indeed!

CHARLES SURFACE: Oh, egad, we'll have a peep at the little milliner!

SIR PETER: Not for the world!—Joseph will never forgive me.

CHARLES SURFACE: I'll stand by you—

SIR PETER *(struggling with* CHARLES*)*: Odds, here he is!

*(*JOSEPH SURFACE *enters just as* CHARLES *throws down the screen.)*

CHARLES SURFACE: Lady Teazle, by all that's wonderful!

SIR PETER: Lady Teazle, by all that's horrible!

CHARLES SURFACE: Sir Peter, this is one of the smartest French milliners I ever saw. Egad, you seem all to have been diverting yourselves here at hide and seek—and I don't see who is out of the secret. Shall I beg your ladyship to inform me?—Not a word!—Brother, will you please to explain this matter? What! Morality dumb too!—Sir Peter, though I *found* you in the dark, perhaps you are not so now! All mute! Well—though *I* can make nothing of the affair, I suppose you perfectly understand one another; so I'll leave you to yourselves.—*(Going.)* Brother, I'm sorry to find you *have given that worthy man so much uneasiness.*—Sir Peter! there's nothing *in the world so noble as a man of sentiment!* (*Exit* CHARLES.)

(They stand for some time looking at each other.)

JOSEPH SURFACE: Sir Peter—notwithstanding I confess that appearances are against me—if you will afford me your patience—I make no doubt but I shall explain everything to your satisfaction.

SIR PETER: If you please—

JOSEPH SURFACE: The fact is, sir, that Lady Teazle, knowing my pretensions to your ward Maria—I say, sir, Lady Teazle, being apprehensive of the jealousy of your temper—and knowing my friendship to the family—she, sir, I say—called here—in order that—I might explain those pretensions—but on your coming—being apprehensive—as I said—of your jealousy—she withdrew—and this, you may depend on't is the whole truth of the matter.

SIR PETER: A very clear account, upon my word; and I dare swear the lady will vouch for every article of it.

LADY TEAZLE *(coming forward)*: For not one word of it, Sir Peter!

SIR PETER: How! don't you think it worth while to agree in the lie?

LADY TEAZLE: There is not one syllable of truth in what that gentleman has told you.

SIR PETER: I believe you, upon my soul, ma'am!

JOSEPH SURFACE *(aside)*: 'Sdeath, madam, will you betray me?

LADY TEAZLE: Good Mr. Hypocrite, by your leave, I will speak for myself.

SIR PETER: Aye, let her alone, sir; you'll find she'll make out a better story than *you*, without prompting.

LADY TEAZLE: Hear me, Sir Peter!—I came here on no matter relating to your ward, and even ignorant of this gentleman's pretensions to her—but I came, seduced by his insidious arguments, at least to listen to his pretended passion, if not to sacrifice *your* honor to his baseness.

SIR PETER: Now, I believe, the truth *is* coming, indeed!

JOSEPH SURFACE: The woman's mad!

LADY TEAZLE: No, sir; she's recovered her senses, and your own arts have furnished her with the means.—Sir Peter, I do not expect you to credit me—but the tenderness you expressed for me, when I am sure you could not think I was a witness to it, has penetrated to my heart, and had I left the place without the shame of this discovery, my future life should have spoken the sincerity of my gratitude. As for that smooth-tongue hypocrite, who would have seduced the wife of his too credulous friend, while he affected honorable addresses to his ward—I behold him now in a light so truly despicable, that I shall never again respect myself for having listened to him. *(Exit.)*

JOSEPH SURFACE: Notwithstanding all this, Sir Peter, heaven knows—

SIR PETER: That you are a villain!—and so I leave you to your conscience.

JOSEPH SURFACE: You are too rash, Sir Peter; you shall hear me. The man who shuts out conviction by refusing to—

SIR PETER: Oh!—

(Exeunt, JOSEPH SURFACE *following and speaking.)*

ACT 5 / SCENE 1

(The library in JOSEPH SURFACE'S *house.)*
(Enter JOSEPH SURFACE *and* SERVANT.)*

JOSEPH SURFACE: Mr. Stanley! why should you think I would see him? you *must* know he comes to ask something.

SERVANT: Sir, I should not have let him in, but that Mr. Rowley came to the door with him.

JOSEPH SURFACE: Pshaw! blockhead! to suppose that I should *now* be in a temper to receive visits from poor relations!—Well, shy don't you show the fellow up?

SERVANT: I will, sir—Why sir, it was not my fault that Sir Peter discovered my lady—

JOSEPH SURFACE: Go, fool! (*Exit* SERVANT.) Sure, Fortune never played a man of my policy such a trick before! My character with Sir Peter, my hopes with Maria, destroyed in a moment! I'm in a rare humor to listen to other people's distresses! I shan't be able to bestow even a benevolent sentiment on Stanley.—So! here he comes, and Rowley with him. I must try to recover myself—and put a little charity into my face, however. (*Exit.*)

(*Enter* SIR OLIVER SURFACE *and* ROWLEY.)

SIR OLIVER: What! does he avoid us? That was he, was it not?

ROWLEY: It was, sir—but I doubt you are come a little too abruptly—his nerves are so weak, that the sight of a poor relation may be too much for him.—I should have gone first to break you to him.

SIR OLIVER: A plague of his nerves!—Yet this is he whom Sir Peter extols as a man of the most benevolent way of thinking!

ROWLEY: As to his way of thinking, I cannot pretend to decide; for, to do him justice, he appears to have as much speculative benevolence as any private gentleman in the kingdom, though he is seldom so sensual as to indulge himself in the exercise of it.

SIR OLIVER: Yet has a string of charitable sentiments, I suppose, at his fingers' ends!

ROWLEY: Or, rather, at his tongue's end, Sir Oliver; for I believe there is no sentiment he has more faith in than that 'Charity begins at home.'

SIR OLIVER: And his, I presume, is of that domestic sort which never stirs abroad at all.

ROWLEY: I doubt you'll find it so;—but he's coming—I mustn't seem to interrupt you; and you know, immediately as you leave him, I come in to announce your arrival in your real character.

SIR OLIVER: True; and afterwards you'll meet me at Sir Peter's.

ROWLEY: Without losing a moment. (*Exit* ROWLEY.)

SIR OLIVER: So! I don't like the complaisance of his features.

(*Re-enter* JOSEPH SURFACE.)

JOSEPH SURFACE: Sir, I beg you ten thousand pardons for keeping you a moment waiting—Mr. Stanley, I presume.

SIR OLIVER: At your service.

JOSEPH SURFACE: Sir, I beg you will do me the honor to sit down—I entreat you, sir.

SIR OLIVER: Dear sir—there's no occasion.—Too civil by half! (*aside*)

JOSEPH SURFACE: I have not the pleasure of knowing you, Mr. Stanley; but I am extremely happy to see you look so well. You were nearly related to my mother, I think, Mr. Stanley?

SIR OLIVER: I was sir—so nearly that my present poverty, I fear, may do discredit to her wealthy children—else I should not have presumed to trouble you.

JOSEPH SURFACE: Dear sir, there needs no apology: he that is in distress, though a stranger, has a right to claim kindred with the wealthy;—I am sure I wish *I* was one of that class, and had it in my power to offer you even a small relief.

SIR OLIVER: If your uncle, Sir Oliver, were here, I should have a friend.

JOSEPH SURFACE: I wish he were, sir, with all my heart: you should not want an advocate with him, believe me, sir.

SIR OLIVER: I should not *need* one—my distresses would recommend me; but I imagined his bounty had enabled *you* to become the agent of his charity.

JOSEPH SURFACE: My dear sir, you were strangely misinformed. Sir Oliver is a worthy man, a very worthy sort of man; but—avarice, Mr. Stanley, is the vice of age. I will tell you, my good sir, in confidence, what he has done for me has been a mere nothing; though people, I know, have thought otherwise, and for my part, I never chose to contradict the report.

SIR OLIVER: What! has he never transmitted you bullion! rupees!° pagodas!°

JOSEPH SURFACE: O dear sir, nothing of the kind! No, no; a few presents now and then—china—shawls—Congo tea—avadavats,° and Indian crackers°—little more, believe me.

SIR OLIVER (*aside*): Here's gratitude for twelve thousand pounds!—Avadavats and Indian crackers!

JOSEPH SURFACE: Then, my dear sir, you have heard, I doubt not, of the extravagance of my brother;

---

rupees, silver coins of India, then valued at two shillings. *pagodas,* gold coins of India, then valued at eight shillings. *avadavats,* small singing-birds of India, having red and black plumage. *Indian crackers,* fire-crackers with colored wrappers.

516 / THE SCHOOL FOR SCANDAL   ACT 5 / SCENE 2

there are very few would credit what I have done for that unfortunate young man.

SIR OLIVER: Not I, for one! *(aside)*

JOSEPH SURFACE: The sums I have lent him! Indeed I have been exceedingly to blame—it was an amiable weakness: however, I don't pretend to defend it—and now I feel it doubly culpable, since it has deprived me of the pleasure of serving *you*, Mr. Stanley, as my heart dictates.

SIR OLIVER *(aside)*: Dissembler!—Then, sir, you cannot assist me?

JOSEPH SURFACE: At present, it grieves me to say, I cannot; but, whenever I have the ability, you may depend upon hearing from me.

SIR OLIVER: I am extremely sorry—

JOSEPH SURFACE: Not more than I am, believe me; to pity, without the power to relieve, is still more painful than to ask and be denied.

SIR OLIVER: Kind sir, your most obedient humble servant.

JOSEPH SURFACE: You leave me deeply affected, Mr. Stanley.—William, be ready to open the door.

SIR OLIVER: O dear sir, no ceremony.

JOSEPH SURFACE: Your very obedient.

SIR OLIVER: Sir, your most obsequious.

JOSEPH SURFACE: You may depend upon hearing from me, whenever I can be of service.

SIR OLIVER: Sweet sir, you are too good.

JOSEPH SURFACE: In the meantime I wish you health and spirits.

SIR OLIVER: Your ever grateful and perpetual humble servant.

JOSEPH SURFACE: Sir, yours as sincerely.

SIR OLIVER: Now I am satisfied! *(Exit.)*

JOSEPH SURFACE *(solus)*: This is one bad effect of a good character; it invites applications from the unfortunate, and there needs no small degree of address to gain the reputation of benevolence without incurring the expense. The silver ore of pure charity is an expensive article in the catalogue of a man's good qualities; whereas the sentimental French plate I use instead of it makes just as good a show, and pays no tax.

(Enter ROWLEY.)

ROWLEY: Mr. Surface, your servant—I was apprehensive of interrupting you—though my business demands immediate attention—as this note will inform you.

JOSEPH SURFACE: Always happy to see Mr. Rowley.— *(Reads.)* How! 'Oliver—Surface!'—My uncle arrived!

ROWLEY: He is, indeed—we have just parted—quite well, after a speedy voyage, and impatient to embrace his worthy nephew.

JOSEPH SURFACE: I am astonished!—William! stop Mr. Stanley, if he's not gone.

ROWLEY: Oh! he's out of reach, I believe.

JOSEPH SURFACE: Why didn't you let me know this when you came in together?

ROWLEY: I thought you had particular business. But I must be gone to inform your brother, and appoint him here to meet his uncle. He will be with you in a quarter of an hour.

JOSEPH SURFACE: So he says. Well I am strangely overjoyed at his coming.—*(aside)* Never, to be sure, was anything so damned unlucky!

ROWLEY: You will be delighted to see how well he looks.

JOSEPH SURFACE: Oh! I'm rejoiced to hear it.—*(aside)* Just at this time!

ROWLEY: I'll tell him how impatiently you expect him.

JOSEPH SURFACE: Do, do; pray give my best duty and affection. Indeed, I cannot express the sensations I feel at the thought of seeing him.—*(Exit ROWLEY.)* Certainly his coming just at this time is the cruellest piece of ill fortune. *(Exit.)*

ACT 5 / SCENE 2

(At SIR PETER'S*)*
(Enter MRS. CANDOUR *and* MAID.*)*

MAID: Indeed, ma'am, my lady will see nobody at present.

MRS. CANDOUR: Did you tell her it was her friend Mrs. Candour?

MAID: Yes, madam; but she begs you will excuse her.

MRS. CANDOUR: Do go again; I shall be glad to see her, if it be only for a moment, for I am sure she must be in great distress. *(Exit* MAID.*)* Dear heart, how provoking! I'm not mistress of half the circumstances! We shall have the whole affair in the newspapers, with the names of the parties at length, before I have dropped the story at a dozen houses.

(Enter SIR BENJAMIN BACKBITE.*)*

O dear Sir Benjamin! you have heard, I suppose—

SIR BENJAMIN: Of Lady Teazle and Mr. Surface—

MRS. CANDOUR: And Sir Peter's discovery—

SIR BENJAMIN: Oh, the strangest piece of business, to be sure!

MRS. CANDOUR: Well, I never was so surprised in my life. I am so sorry for all parties, indeed I am.

SIR BENJAMIN: Now, I don't pity Sir Peter at all—he was so extravagantly partial to Mr. Surface.

MRS. CANDOUR: Mr. Surface! Why, 'twas with Charles Lady Teazle was detected.

SIR BENJAMIN: No such thing—Mr. Surface is the gallant.

MRS. CANDOUR: No, no—Charles is the man. 'Twas Mr. Surface brought Sir Peter on purpose to discover them.

SIR BENJAMIN: I tell you I have it from one—

MRS. CANDOUR: And I have it from one—

SIR BENJAMIN: Who had it from one, who had it—

MRS. CANDOUR: From one immediately—But here's Lady Sneerwell; perhaps she knows the whole affair.

(Enter LADY SNEERWELL.*)*

LADY SNEERWELL: So, my dear Mrs. Candour, here's a sad affair of our friend Lady Teazle!

MRS. CANDOUR: Aye, my dear friend, who could have thought it—

LADY SNEERWELL: Well, there's no trusting appearances; though, indeed, she was always too lively for me.

MRS. CANDOUR: To be sure, her manners were a little too free—but she was very young!

LADY SNEERWELL: And had, indeed, some good qualities.

MRS. CANDOUR: So she had, indeed. But have you heard the particulars?

LADY SNEERWELL: No; but everybody says that Mr. Surface—

SIR BENJAMIN: Aye, there, I told you—Mr. Surface was the man.

MRS. CANDOUR: No, no, indeed—the assignation was with Charles.

LADY SNEERWELL: With Charles! You alarm me, Mrs. Candour.

MRS. CANDOUR: Yes, yes, he was the lover. Mr. Surface—do him justice—was only the informer.

SIR BENJAMIN: Well, I'll not dispute with yout, Mrs. Candour; but, be it which it may, I hope that Sir Peter's wound will not—

MRS. CANDOUR: Sir Peter's wound! Oh, mercy! I didn't hear a word of their fighting.

LADY SNEERWELL: Nor I, a syllable.

SIR BENJAMIN: No! what, no mention of the duel?

MRS. CANDOUR: Not a word.

SIR BENJAMIN: O Lord—yes, yes, they fought before they left the room.

LADY SNEERWELL: Pray let us hear.

MRS. CANDOUR: Aye, do oblige us with the duel.

SIR BENJAMIN: 'Sir,' says Sir Peter—immediately after the discovery—'you are a most ungrateful fellow.'

MRS, CANDOUR: Aye, to Charles—

SIR BENJAMIN: No, no—to Mr. Surface—'a most ungrateful fellow; and old as I am, sir,' says he, 'I insist on immediate satisfaction.'

MRS. CANDOUR: Aye, that must have been to Charles; for 'tis very unlikely Mr. Surface should go to fight in his house.

SIR BENJAMIN: 'Gad's life, ma'am, not at all—'giving me immediate satisfaction.'—On this, madam, Lady Teazle, seeing Sir Peter in such danger, ran out of the room in strong hysterics, and Charles after her, calling out for hartshorn and water! Then, madam, they began to fight with swords—

(Enter CRABTREE.*)*

CRABTREE: With pistols, nephew—I have it from undoubted authority.

MRS. CANDOUR: O Mr. Crabtree, then it is all true!

CRABTREE: Too true, indeed, ma'am, and Sir Peter's dangerously wounded—

SIR BENJAMIN: By a thrust of in *seconde*° quite through his left side—

CRABTREE: By a bullet lodged in the thorax.

MRS. CANDOUR: Mercy on me! Poor Sir Peter!

CRABTREE: Yes, ma'am—though Charles would have avoided the matter, if he could.

MRS. CANDOUR: I knew Charles was the person.

SIR BENJAMIN: Oh, my uncle, I see, knows nothing of the matter.

CRABTREE: But Sir Peter taxed him with the basest ingratitude—

SIR BENJAMIN: That I told you, you know.

CRABTREE: Do, nephew, let me speak!—and insisted on an immediate—

SIR BENJAMIN: Just as I said.

CRABTREE: Odds life, nephew, allow others to know something too! A pair of pistols lay on the bureau (for Mr. Surface, it seems, had come the night before late from Salt-Hill, where he had been to see the Montem° with a friend, who has a son at Eton), so, unluckily, the pistols were left charged.

SIR BENJAMIN: I heard nothing of this.

CRABTREE: Sir Peter forced Charles to take one, and they fired, it seems, pretty nearly together. Charles's shot took place, as I told you, and Sir Peter's missed; but, what is very extraordinary, the ball struck against a little bronze Pliny that stood over the chimney-piece, grazed out of the window at a right angle, and wounded the postman, who was just coming to the door with a double letter from Northamptonshire.

SIR BENJAMIN: My uncle's account is more circumstantial, I must confess; but I believe mine is the true one, for all that.

LADY SNEERWELL *(aside)*: I am more interested in this affair than they imagine, and must have better information. *(Exit* LADY SNEERWELL.*)*

SIR BENJAMIN *(after a pause looking at each other)*: Ah! Lady Sneerwell's alarm is very easily accounted for.

CRABTREE: Yes, yes, they certainly *do* say—but that's neither here nor there.

---

seconde, a term in fencing. *Montem,* It was formerly the custom of Eton school boys to go to Salt-Hill *(processus ad montem)* every third year on Whit-Tuesday, and levy *salt-money* from the onlookers at the ceremony.

MRS. CANDOUR: But, pray, where is Sir Peter at present?

CRABTREE: Oh! they brought him home, and he is now in the house, though the servants are ordered to deny it.

MRS. CANDOUR: I believe so, and Lady Teazle, I suppose, attending him.

CRABTREE: Yes, yes; I saw one of the faculty enter just before me.

SIR BENJAMIN: Hey! who comes here?

CRABTREE: Oh, this is he—the physician, depend on't.

MRS. CANDOUR: Oh, certainly! it must be the physician; and now we shall know.

(Enter SIR OLIVER SURFACE.)

CRABTREE: Well, doctor, what hopes?

MRS. CANDOUR: Aye, doctor, how's your patient?

SIR BENJAMIN: Now, doctor, isn't it a wound with a small-sword?

CRABTREE: A bullet lodged in the thorax, for a hundred!

SIR OLIVER: Doctor! a wound with a small-sword! and a bullet in the thorax?—Oons! are you mad, good people?

SIR BENJAMIN: Perhaps, sir, you are not a doctor?

SIR OLIVER: Truly, I am to thank you for my degree, if I am.

CRABTREE: Only a friend of Sir Peter's then, I presume. But, sir, you must have heard of this accident?

SIR OLIVER: Not a word!

CRABTREE: Not of his being dangerously wounded?

SIR OLIVER: The devil he is!

SIR BENJAMIN: Run through the body—

CRABTREE: Shot in the breast—

SIR BENJAMIN: By one Mr. Surface—

CRABTREE: Aye, the younger.

SIR OLIVER: Hey! what the plague! you seem to differ strangely in your accounts—however, you agree that Sir Peter is dangerously wounded.

SIR BENJAMIN: Oh, yes, we agree there.

CRABTREE: Yes, yes, I believe there can be no doubt of that.

SIR OLIVER: Then, upon my word, for a person in that situation, he is the most imprudent man alive—for here he comes, walking as if nothing at all were the matter.

(Enter SIR PETER TEAZLE.)

Odds heart, Sir Peter! you are come in good time, I promise you; for we had just given you over.

SIR BENJAMIN: Egad, uncle, this is the most sudden recovery!

SIR OLIVER: Why, man! what do you do out of bed with a small-sword through your body, and a bullet lodged in your thorax?

SIR PETER: A small-sword and a bullet?

SIR OLIVER: Aye; these gentlemen would have killed you without law or physic, and wanted to dub me a doctor—to make me an accomplice.

SIR PETER: Why, what is all this?

SIR BENJAMIN: We rejoice, Sir Peter, that the story of the duel is not true, and are sincerely sorry for your other misfortunes.

SIR PETER: So, so; all over the town already. (aside)

CRABTREE: Though, Sir Peter, you were certainly vastly to blame to marry at all, at your years.

SIR PETER: Sir, what business is that of yours?

MRS. CANDOUR: Though, indeed, as Sir Peter made so good a husband, he's very much to be pitied.

SIR PETER: Plague on your pity, ma'am! I desire none of it.

SIR BENJAMIN: However, Sir Peter, you must not mind the laughing and jests you will meet with on this occasion.

SIR PETER: Sir, I desire to be master in my own house.

CRABTREE: 'Tis no uncommon case, that's one comfort.

SIR PETER: I insist on being left to myself: without ceremony, I insist on your leaving my house directly!

MRS. CANDOUR: Well, well, we are going; and depend on't, we'll make the best report of you we can.

SIR PETER: Leave my house!

CRABTREE: And tell how hardly you have been treated.

SIR PETER: Leave my house!

SIR BENJAMIN: And how patiently you bear it.

SIR PETER: Fiends! vipers! furies! Oh! that their own venom would choke them!

(Exeunt MRS. CANDOUR, SIR BENJAMIN BACKBITE, CRABTREE, etc.)

SIR OLIVER: They are very provoking indeed, Sir Peter.

(Enter ROWLEY.)

ROWLEY: I heard high words—what has ruffled you, Sir Peter?

SIR PETER: Pshaw! what signifies asking? Do I ever pass a day without my vexations?

SIR OLIVER: Well, I'm not inquisitive—I come only to tell you that I have seen both my nephews in the manner we proposed.

SIR PETER: A precious couple they are!

ROWLEY: Yes, and Sir Oliver is convinced that your judgment was right, Sir Peter.

SIR OLIVER: Yes, I find Joseph is indeed the man, after all.

ROWLEY: Yes, as Sir Peter says, he's a man of sentiment.

SIR OLIVER: And acts up to the sentiments he professes.

ROWLEY: It certainly is edification to hear him talk.

SIR OLIVER: Oh, he's a model for the young men of the age! But how's this, Sir Peter? you don't join in your friend Joseph's praise, as I expected.

SIR PETER: Sir Oliver, we live in a damned wicked world, and the fewer we praise the better.

ROWLEY: What! do *you* say so, Sir Peter, who were never mistaken in your life?

SIR PETER: Pshaw! plague on you both! I see by your sneering you have heard the whole affair. I shall go mad among you!

ROWLEY: Then, to fret you no longer, Sir Peter, we are indeed acquainted with it all. I met Lady Teazle coming from Mr. Surface's, so humbled that she deigned to request me to be her advocate with you.

SIR PETER: And does Sir Oliver know all too?

SIR OLIVER: Every circumstance.

SIR PETER: What, of the closet—and the screen, hey?

SIR OLIVER: Yes, yes, and the little French milliner. Oh, I have been vastly diverted with the story! ha! ha!

SIR PETER: 'Twas very pleasant.

SIR OLIVER: I never laughed more in my life, I assure you: ha! ha!

SIR PETER: O, vastly diverting! ha! ha!

ROWLEY: To be sure, Joseph with his sentiments! ha! ha!

SIR PETER: Yes, yes, his sentiments! ha! ha! A hypocritical villain!

SIR OLIVER: Aye, and that rogue Charles to pull Sir Peter out of the closet: ha! ha!

SIR PETER: Ha! ha! 'twas devilish entertaining, to be sure!

SIR OLIVER: Ha! ha! Egad, Sir Peter, I should like to have seen your face when the screen was thrown down: ha! ha!

SIR PETER: Yes, yes, my face when the screen was thrown down: ha! ha! Oh, I must never show my head again!

SIR OLIVER: But come, come, it isn't fair to laugh at you neither, my old friend—though, upon my soul, I can't help it.

SIR PETER: Oh, pray don't restrain your mirth on my account—it does not hurt me at all! I laugh at the whole affair myself. Yes, yes, I think being a standing jest for all one's acquaintances a very happy situation. O yes, and then of a morning to read the paragraphs about Mr. S—, Lady T—, and Sir P—, will be so entertaining!

ROWLEY: Without affectation, Sir Peter, you may despise the ridicule of fools. But I see Lady Teazle going towards the next room; I am sure you must desire a reconciliation as earnestly as she does.

SIR OLIVER: Perhaps my being here prevents her coming to you. Well, I'll leave honest Rowley to mediate between you; but he must bring you all presently to Mr. Surface's, where I am not returning, if not to reclaim a libertine, at least to expose hypocrisy.

SIR PETER: Ah! I'll be present at your discovering yourself there with all my heart—though 'tis a vile unlucky place for discoveries!

ROWLEY: We'll follow. (*Exit* SIR OLIVER SURFACE.)

SIR PETER: She is not coming here, you see, Rowley.

ROWLEY: No, but she has left the door of that room open, you perceive. See, she is in tears!

SIR PETER: Certainly a little mortification appears very becoming in a wife! Don't you think it will do her good to let her pine a little?

ROWLEY: Oh, this is ungenerous in you!

SIR PETER: Well, I know not what to think. You remember, Rowley, the letter I found of hers, evidently intended for Charles!

ROWLEY: A mere forgery, Sir Peter! laid in your way on purpose. This is one of the points which I intend *Snake* shall give you conviction on.

SIR PETER: I wish I were once satisfied of that. She looks this way. What a remarkably elegant turn of the head she has! Rowley, I'll go to her.

ROWLEY: Certainly.

SIR PETER: Though, when it is known that we are reconciled, people will laugh at me ten times more!

ROWLEY: Let them laugh, and retort their malice only by showing them you are happy in spite of it.

SIR PETER: I'faith, so I will! and, if I'm not mistaken, we may yet be the happiest couple in the country.

ROWLEY: Nay, Sir Peter—he who once lays aside suspicion—

SIR PETER: Hold, my dear Rowley! if you have any regard for me, never let me hear you utter anything like a sentiment—I have had enough of them to serve me the rest of my life. (*Exeunt.*)

ACT 5 / SCENE 3

(*The library in* JOSEPH SURFACE'S *house*)
(JOSEPH SURFACE *and* LADY SNEERWELL.)

LADY SNEERWELL: Impossible! Will not Sir Peter immediately be reconciled to Charles, and of consequence no longer oppose his union with Maria? The thought is distraction to me!

JOSEPH SURFACE: Can passion furnish a remedy?

LADY SNEERWELL: No, nor cunning either. Oh, I was a fool, an idiot, to league with such a blunderer!

JOSEPH SURFACE: Sure, Lady Sneerwell, *I* am the greatest sufferer; yet you see I bear the accident with calmness.

LADY SNEERWELL: Because the disappointment doesn't reach your *heart*; your *interest* only attached you to Maria. Had you felt for *her* what *I* have for that ungrateful libertine, neither your temper nor hypocrisy could prevent your showing the sharpness of your vexation.

JOSEPH SURFACE: But why should your reproaches fall on *me* for this disappointment?

LADY SNEERWELL: Are you not the cause of it? What had you to do to bate in your pursuit of Maria to pervert Lady Teazle by the way? Had you not a sufficient field for your roguery in blinding Sir Peter, and supplanting your brother? I hate such an avarice of crimes; 'tis an unfair monopoly, and never prospers.

JOSEPH SURFACE: Well, I admit I have been to blame. I confess I deviated from the direct road of wrong, but I don't think we're so totally defeated neither.

LADY SNEERWELL: No!

JOSEPH SURFACE: You tell me you have made a trial of Snake since we met, and that you still believe him faithful to us—

LADY SNEERWELL: I do believe so.

JOSEPH SURFACE: And that he has undertaken, should it be necessary, to swear and prove that Charles is at this time contracted by vows and honor to your ladyship—which some of his former letters to you will serve to support?

LADY SNEERWELL: This, indeed, might have assisted.

JOSEPH SURFACE: Come, come; it is not too late yet.— *(Knocking at the door.)* But hark! this is probably my uncle, Sir Oliver: retire to that room; we'll consult farther when he's gone.

LADY SNEERWELL: Well! but if *he* should find you out too—

JOSEPH SURFACE: Oh, I have no fear of that. Sir Peter will hold his tongue for his own credit's sake— and you may depend on't I shall soon discover Sir Oliver's weak side!

LADY SNEERWELL: I have no diffidence of your abilities—only be constant to one roguery at a time. *(Exit.)*

JOSEPH SURFACE: I will, I will! So! 'tis confounded hard, after such bad fortune, to be baited by one's confederate in evil. Well, at all events, my character is so much better than Charles's, that I certainly—hey!—what!—this is not Sir Oliver, but old Stanley again! Plague on't! that he should return to leave me just now! We shall have Sir Oliver come and find him here—and—

(Enter SIR OLIVER SURFACE.)

Gad's life, Mr. Stanley, why have you come back to plague me just at this time? You must not stay now, upon my word.

SIR OLIVER: Sir, I hear your uncle Oliver is expected here, and though he has been so penurious to *you*, I'll try what he'll do for *me.*

JOSEPH SURFACE: Sir, 'tis impossible for you to stay now, so I must beg—Come any other time, and I promise you, you shall be assisted.

SIR OLIVER: No: Sir Oliver and I must be acquainted.

JOSEPH SURFACE: Zounds, sir! then I insist on your quitting the room directly.

SIR OLIVER: Nay, sir!

JOSEPH SURFACE: Sir, I insist on't!—Here, William! show this gentleman out. Since you compel me, sir—not one moment—this is such insolence! *(Going to push him out.)*

(Enter CHARLES SURFACE.)

CHARLES SURFACE: Heyday! what's the matter now? What the devil, have you got hold of my little broker here? Zounds, brother, don't hurt little Premium. What's the matter, my little fellow?

JOSEPH SURFACE: So! he has been with you, too, has he?

CHARLES SURFACE: To be sure he has! Why, 'tis as honest a little— but sure, Joseph, you have not been borrowing money too, have you?

JOSEPH SURFACE: Borrowing! no! But, brother, you know here we expect Sir Oliver every—

CHARLES SURFACE: O gad, that's true! Noll mustn't find the little broker here, to be sure.

JOSEPH SURFACE: Yet, Mr. Stanley insists—

CHARLES SURFACE: Stanley! why his name is Premium.

JOSEPH SURFACE: No, no, Stanley.

CHARLES SURFACE: No, no, Premium.

JOSEPH SURFACE: Well, no matter which—but—

CHARLES SURFACE: Aye, aye, Stanley or Premium, 'tis the same thing, as you say; for I suppose he goes by half a hundred names, besides A.B.'s° at the coffee houses.

JOSEPH SURFACE: Death! here's Sir Oliver at the door. *(Knocking again.)* Now I beg, Mr. Stanley—

CHARLES SURFACE: Aye, and I beg, Mr. Premium—

SIR OLIVER: Gentlemen—

JOSEPH SURFACE: Sir, by heaven you shall go!

CHARLES SURFACE: Aye, out with him, certainly.

SIR OLIVER: This violence—

JOSEPH SURFACE: 'Tis your own fault.

CHARLES SURFACE: Out with him, to be sure. *(Both forcing SIR OLIVER out.)*

(Enter SIR PETER and LADY TEAZLE, MARIA, and ROW-LEY.)

SIR PETER: My old friend, Sir Oliver—hey! What in the name of wonder!—Here are dutiful nephews!—assault their uncle at the first visit!

LADY TEAZLE: Indeed, Sir Oliver, 'twas well we came in to rescue you.

A.B.'s, a reference to appointments at the coffee-houses made under concealed names.

ROWLEY: Truly it was; for I perceive, Sir Oliver, the character of old Stanley was no protection to you.

SIR OLIVER: Nor of Premium either: the necessities of the *former* could not extort a shilling from *that* benevolent gentleman; and now, egad, I stood a chance of faring worse than my ancestors, and being knocked down without being bid for.

(After a pause, JOSEPH *and* CHARLES *turning to each other.)*

JOSEPH SURFACE: Charles!

CHARLES SURFACE: Joseph!

JOSEPH SURFACE: 'Tis now complete!

CHARLES SURFACE: Very!

SIR OLIVER: Sir Peter, my friend, and Rowley too—look on that elder nephew of mine. You know what he has already received from my bounty; and you know also how gladly I would have regarded half my fortune as held in trust for him—judge, then, my disappointment in discovering him to be destitute of truth—charity—and gratitude!

SIR PETER: Sir Oliver, I should be more surprised at this declaration, if I had not myself found him selfish, treacherous, and hypocritical!

LADY TEAZLE: And if the gentleman pleads not guilty to these, pray let him call *me* to his character.

SIR PETER: Then, I believe, we need add no more.—If he knows himself, he will consider it as the most perfect punishment that he is known to the world.

CHARLES SURFACE *(aside)*: If they talk this way to *Honesty,* what will they say to *me,* by and by?

*(*SIR PETER, LADY TEAZLE, *and* MARIA *retire.)*

SIR OLIVER: As for that prodigal, his brother, there—

CHARLES SURFACE *(aside)*: Aye, now comes my turn: the damned family pictures will ruin me!

JOSEPH SURFACE: Sir Oliver!—uncle!—will you honor me with a hearing?

CHARLES SURFACE *(aside)*: Now if Joseph would make one of his long speeches, I might recollect myself a little.

SIR OLIVER *(to* JOSEPH SURFACE*)*: I suppose you would undertake to justify yourself entirely?

JOSEPH SURFACE: I trust I could.

SIR OLIVER: Pshaw!—Well, sir! and *you* (to CHARLES) could justify yourself too, I suppose?

CHARLES SURFACE: Not that I know of, Sir Oliver.

SIR OLIVER: What!—Little Premium has been let too much into the secret, I presume?

CHARLES SURFACE: True, sir; but they were family secrets, and should never be mentioned again, you know.

ROWLEY: Come, Sir Oliver, I know you cannot speak of Charles's follies with anger.

SIR OLIVER: Odd's heart, no more I can—nor with gravity either. Sir Peter, do you know the rogue bargained with me for all his ancestors—sold me judges and generals by the foot—and maiden aunts as cheap as broken china.

CHARLES SURFACE: To be sure, Sir Oliver, I did make a little free with the family canvas, that's the truth on't. My ancestors may certainly rise in evidence against me, there's no denying it; but believe me sincere when I tell you—and upon my soul I would not say it if I was not—that if I do not appear mortified at the exposure of my follies, it is because I feel at this moment the warmest satisfaction in seeing you, my liberal benefactor.

SIR OLIVER: Charles, I believe you. Give me your hand again; the ill-looking little fellow over the settee has made your peace.

CHARLES SURFACE: Then, sir, my gratitude to the original is still increased.

LADY TEAZLE *(pointing to* MARIA*)*: Yet, I believe, Sir Oliver, here is one whom Charles is still more anxious to be reconciled to.

SIR OLIVER: Oh, I have heard of his attachment there; and, with the young lady's pardon, if I construe right—that blush—

SIR PETER: Well, child, speak your sentiments.

MARIA: Sir, I have little to say, but that I shall rejoice to hear that he is happy; for me, whatever claim I had to his affection, I willingly resign it to one who has a better title.

CHARLES SURFACE: How, Maria!

SIR PETER: Heyday! what's the mystery now? While he appeared an incorrigible rake, you would give your hand to no one else; and now that he is likely to reform, I warrant you won't have him.

MARIA: His own heart—and Lady Sneerwell know the cause.

CHARLES SURFACE: Lady Sneerwell!

JOSEPH SURFACE: Brother, it is with great concern I am obliged to speak on this point, but my regard to justice compels me, and Lady Sneerwell's injuries can no longer be concealed. *(Goes to the door.)*

(Enter LADY SNEERWELL.*)*

SIR PETER: So! another French milliner!—Egad, he has one in every room in the house, I suppose!

LADY SNEERWELL: Ungrateful Charles! Well may you be surprised, and feel for the indelicate situation which your perfidy has forced me into.

CHARLES SURFACE: Pray, uncle, is this another plot of yours? For, as I have life, I don't understand it.

JOSEPH SURFACE: I believe, sir, there is but the evidence of one person more necessary to make it extremely clear.

SIR PETER: And that person, I imagine, is Mr. Snake.—Rowley, you were perfectly right to bring him with us, and pray let him appear.

ROWLEY: Walk in, Mr. Snake.

(Enter SNAKE.*)*

I thought his testimony might be wanted; however, it happens unluckily, that he comes to confront Lady Sneerwell, and not to support her.

LADY SNEERWELL: Villain! Treacherous to me at last! *(aside)* —Speak, fellow, have *you* too conspired against me?

SNAKE: I beg your ladyship ten thousand pardons: you paid me extremely liberally for the lie in question; but I have unfortunately been offered double to speak the truth.

SIR PETER: Plot and counterplot, egad—I wish your ladyship joy of the success of your negotiation.

LADY SNEERWELL: The torments of shame and disappointment on you all!

LADY TEAZLE: Hold, Lady Sneerwell—before you go, let me thank you for the trouble you and that gentleman have taken, in writing letters to me from Charles, and answering them yourself; and let me also request you to make my respects to the Scandalous College, of which you are president, and inform them, that Lady Teazle, licentiate, begs leave to return the diploma they granted her, as she leaves off practice, and kills characters no longer.

LADY SNEERWELL: You too, madam!—provoking—insolent! May your husband live these fifty years! *(Exit.)*

SIR PETER: Oons! what a fury!

LADY TEAZLE: A malicious creature, indeed!

SIR PETER: Hey! not for her last wish?

LADY TEAZLE: Oh, no!

SIR OLIVER: Well, sir, and what have you to say now?

JOSEPH SURFACE: Sir, I am so confounded, to find that Lady Sneerwell could be guilty of suborning Mr. Snake in this manner, to impose on us all, that I know not what to say; however, lest her revengeful spirit should prompt her to injure my brother, I had certainly better follow her directly. *(Exit.)*

SIR PETER: Moral to the last drop!

SIR OLIVER: Aye, and marry her, Joseph, if you can.—Oil and vinegar, egad! you'll do very well together.

ROWLEY: I believe we have no more occasion for Mr. Snake at present.

SNAKE: Before I go, I beg pardon once for all, for whatever uneasiness I have been the humble instrument of causing to the parties present.

SIR PETER: Well, well, you have made atonement by a good deed at last.

SNAKE: But I must request of the company, that it shall never be known.

SIR PETER: Hey! what the plague! are you ashamed of having done a right thing once in your life?

SNAKE: Ah, sir—consider I live by the badness of my character—I have nothing but my infamy to depend on! and, if it were once known that I had been betrayed into an honest action, I should lose every friend I have in the world.

SIR OLIVER: Well, well—we'll not traduce you by saying anything in your praise, never fear. *(Exit* SNAKE.*)*

SIR PETER: There's a precious rogue! yet that fellow is a writer and a critic!

LADY TEAZLE: See, Sir Oliver, there needs no persuasion now to reconcile your nephew and Maria. *(*CHARLES *and* MARIA *apart.)*

SIR OLIVER: Aye, aye, that's as it should be, and, egad, we'll have the wedding to-morrow morning.

CHARLES SURFACE: Thank you, my dear uncle.

SIR PETER: What, you rogue! don't you ask the girl's consent first?

CHARLES SURFACE: Oh, I have done that a long time—above a minute ago—and she has looked yes.

MARIA: For shame, Charles!—I protest, Sir Peter, there has not been a word—

SIR OLIVER: Well, then, the fewer the better—may your love for each other never know abatement.

SIR PETER: And may you live as happily together as Lady Teazle and I—intend to do!

CHARLES SURFACE: Rowley, my old friend, I am sure you congratulate me; and I suspect that I owe you much.

SIR OLIVER: You do, indeed, Charles.

ROWLEY: If my efforts to serve you had not succeeded you would have been in my debt for the attempt—but deserve to be happy—and you overpay me.

SIR PETER: Aye, honest Rowley always said you would reform.

CHARLES SURFACE: Why as to reforming, Sir Peter, I'll make no promises, and that I take to be a proof that I intend to set about it.—But here shall be my monitor—my gentle guide.—Ah! can I leave the virtuous path those eyes illumine?

Though thou, dear maid, shouldst waive thy
　　beauty's sway,
Thou still must rule, because I *will* obey:
An humbled fugitive from Folly view,
No sanctuary near but *Love* and—You;

(To the audience.)

> *You* can, indeed, each anxious fear remove.
> For even *Scandal* dies, if *you* approve.

FINIS

EPILOGUE
By George Colman°

(Spoken by LADY TEAZLE.*)*

I, who was late so volatile and gay,
Like a trade-wind must now blow all one way,
Bend all my cares, my studies, and my vows,
To one old rusty weathercock—my spouse!
So wills our virtuous bard—the motley Bayes°
Of crying epilogues and laughing plays!
    Old bachelors, who marry smart young wives,
Learn from our play to regulate your lives:
Each bring his dear to town, all faults upon her—
London will prove the very source of honor.
Plunged fairly in, like a cold bath it serves,
When principles relax, to brace the nerves.
    Such is my case;—and yet I might deplore
That the gay dream of dissipation's o'er;
And say, ye fair, was ever lively wife,
Born with a genius for the highest life,
Like me untimely blasted in her bloom,
Like me condemned to such a dismal doom?
Save money—when I just knew how to waste it!
Leave London—just as I began to taste it!
Must I then watch the early crowing cock,
The melancholy ticking of a clock;
In the lone rustic hall for ever pounded,
With dogs, cats, rats, and squalling brats surrounded?
With humble curates can I now retire,

(While good Sir Peter boozes with the squire,)
And at backgammon mortify my soul,
That pants for loo,° or flutters at a vole?°
Seven's the main!° Dear sound!—that must expire,
Lost at hot cockles,° round a Christmas fire!
The transient hour of fashion too soon spent,
Farewell the tranquil mind, farewell content!°
Farewell the plumèd head, the cushioned tête,
That takes the cushion from its proper seat!
That spirit-stirring drum!°—card drums I mean,
Spadille°—odd trick—pam°—basto°—king and
    queen!
And you, ye knockers, that, with brazen throat,
The welcome visitors' approach denote;
Farewell! all quality of high renown,
Pride, pomp, and circumstance of glorious town!
Farewell! your revels I partake no more,
And Lady Teazle's occupation's o'er!
All this I told our bard—he smiled, and said 'twas
    clear,
I ought to play deep tragedy next year.
Meanwhile he drew wise morals from his play,
And in these solemn periods stalked away:—
'Blest were the fair like you; her faults who stopped,
And closed her follies when the curtain dropped!
No more in vice or error to engage,
Or play the fool at large on life's great stage.

George Colman, author of *The Jealous Wife.* **Bayes,**
poet, dramatist (from Bayes in *The Rehearsal*).

---

    loo, a favorite eighteenth-century game of cards. **flut-
ters . . . vole,** winning all the tricks. **main,** in hazard, the
caster of the dice "called his *main*" by naming a number from
five to nine. **hot cockles,** "A play in which one kneels, and
covering his eyes lays his head in another's lap and guesses
who struck him." **Farewell . . . content,** These lines parody
Othello's soliloquy, III, iii, 347–357. **drum,** Fashionable
card-party. **Spadille,** the ace of spades. **pam,** the knave of
clubs. **basto,** the ace of clubs.

Figure 1. Sir Benjamin Backbite (Eric Donkin, *center foreground*) recites
one of his malicious epigrams to entertain Mrs. Candour (Jane Casson,
left), Joseph Surface (Robin Gammell, *center background*), and Lady
Sneerwell (Pat Galloway, *right*) in the Stratford Festival production of
The School for Scandal, directed by Michael Langham and designed by
Leslie Hurry, Stratford, Ontario, 1970. (Photograph: Douglas Spillane.
Courtesy of the Stratford Festival.)

Figure 2. Sir Peter Teazle (Stephen Murray) berates Lady Teazle (Helen
Carey) for the extravagance of her fashionable inclinations in the Stratford Festival production of *The School for Scandal,* directed by Michael
Langham and designed by Leslie Hurry, Stratford, Ontario, 1970. (Photograph: Douglas Spillane. Courtesy of the Stratford Festival.)

Figure 3. Charles Surface (Barry MacGregor, *left*) offers to sell the portrait of his great-aunt Deborah to Sir Oliver Surface (Mervyn Blake), here posing as the broker Mr. Premium, in the Stratford Festival production of *The School for Scandal*, directed by Michael Langham and designed by Leslie Hurry, Stratford, Ontario, 1970. (Photograph: Douglas Spillane. Courtesy of the Stratford Festival.)

Figure 4. Sir Peter Teazle (Stephen Murray, *left*) tries to prevent Charles (Barry MacGregor) from pulling away the screen that purportedly conceals Joseph's mistress in the Stratford Festival production of *The School for Scandal*, directed by Michael Langham and designed by Leslie Hurry, Stratford, Ontario, 1970. (Photograph: Douglas Spillane. Courtesy of the Stratford Festival.)

Staging of *The School for Scandal*

INTERVIEW WITH MICHAEL LANGHAM,
DIRECTOR OF THE 1970 STRATFORD
PRODUCTION, BY BRADFORD S. FIELD, JR.

FIELD: I hear that *The School for Scandal* at Stratford was very successful.

LANGHAM: It was very well received, but, like all plays written for an eighteenth century theatre, rather difficult to arrange for a thrust stage like the one at Stratford.

FIELD: From the reviews you got you seem to have had no real trouble.

LANGHAM: Only technical problems, but it was a very confident production. We had a tone pitched at about the right level. We tried to avoid the usual icy artifice of most modern staging. It is clear to anyone who reads the play that the idiom of the language is not modern, but rather a special one.

FIELD: Wit, polish, repartee . . .

LANGHAM: Like that. It was written for an audience which had not yet lost the art of conversation. And the idiom affects everything else, the way one walks, for instance, was more a matter of displaying oneself than of getting from A to B in a straight line.

FIELD: Then you strove for some type of artifice, such as that in Restoration comedy.

LANGHAM: Yes and no. In the manner of speech and movement yes. The play itself imitates that earlier dramatic style. But by Sheridan's day that style was a century old. His play is in content not nearly so, ah, bumptious.

FIELD: How do you avoid a Restoration style when you do a play that imitates a Restoration style?

LANGHAM: It wasn't a Restoration style we sought to avoid, but modern versions of it. It's become a theatrical convention, you know, to suppose that since the language is so neat and precise in plays like these, that the society is, also.

FIELD: Then your production presented a society that was dirty?

LANGHAM: Not smutty, but soiled. Characters walked about with chickenshit on their boots. Their toilet facilities were primitive. For example, we began the play with only Snake on stage. Lady Sneerwell was off stage, shouting her lines. When she came in she was carrying an armful of gossip sheets, obviously having been sitting on the john. And that was only a beginning. She entered bald. We had a bald wig on her. And in her shift. During the rest of the scene we saw her gradual transformation as she dressed, and built up this fantastic facade. It was a good visual image, heavily impressed on the audience, to show how much *The School for Scandal* is about facades.

FIELD: You especially emphasized that point?

LANGHAM: Well, that's only one theme. Did you ever notice how much reference there is in the play to the loss of the American colonies?

FIELD: None, that I can remember.

LANGHAM: None at all. It was occurring right at that time, yet the play ignores it, as, I think, the Englishman of that time tended to do. Most interest was centered in the progress of the East India Company. That is where Sir Oliver returns from, India.

FIELD: Still, there has to be something in a play to interest a modern audience.

LANGHAM: Yes, well, the play is very funny, that's timeless enough.

FIELD: But lots of plays are funny. Why choose *The School for Scandal?*

LANGHAM: In the production we did at Stratford we saw the play revealing a changeover in the leadership of the country from the old aristocrats to the new merchant classes. Sir Oliver is a representative of that old class and tries to exemplify its virtues. And in the portrait scene, where all those old ancestors are being sold off without pity, we can see that changeover in a way just as striking as Lady Sneerwell's facades. The scene, as we played it, had almost a heartbreaking quality.

FIELD: Then your appeal to the modern audience is to show them the realistic basis of the action.

LANGHAM: Yes, the Teazle-plot fits that approach quite well. Lady Teazle was revealed as really from the country, but on the make, you know . . . oh, not just a bumpkin, more of a hoyden. Sir Peter we made not ludicrous but poignant, pointing out the dangers and difficulties of that kind of marriage.

FIELD: What was the most serious problem which you had to work out in staging this play?

LANGHAM: Well, I suppose I would have to say our greatest problem was a kind of North American infelicity with language!

FIELD: Surely not actors!

LANGHAM: Yes. In England the problem is not so serious. People in fact still do enjoy a tradition of facility of words and complicated phrasing; but over here, while the language, the tone, is much more open and direct, that's not much help in projecting the delicate facades that are offered by Sheridan's language. So we had some hard work to overcome that.

FIELD: Which scenes or characters in the play gave you more trouble than others?

LANGHAM: Sneerwell's role gave us problems because she reappears after such a long absence that we had to worry about re-establishing her character. Oh, there were some little things, too. In the last scene when it seems clear that Maria has won Charles—and Lady Sneerwell had had a secret lust for him—she goes for Maria's eyes with her nails. Charles holds her back and her wig falls off, revealing the hideous bald dome again. Well, in a theatre an audience often thinks that a wig's falling off must be a mistake. So we had to add some *further* business with everyone on stage re-acting with elaborate revulsion at the sight of her—to underscore the point that it was an intended part of the play.

FIELD: Were there parts that worked out better than you expected?

LANGHAM: Yes . . . the music, and the final moments . . . we finished the play with a tableau. We had a marvelous musical score by Stanley Silverman. In tone and style it ranged from 1776 then worked its way up to 1969 in the middle, and then back again, so at the end of the play the music—and the tone of the whole production—had returned to the tone of the eighteenth century. We sang a period song among the central characters as the scandal-mongers all leaned out from the wings to discover what they might overhear, and so we brought the cast on together for a final tableau.

REVIEW OF THE STRATFORD PRODUCTION, 1970, BY CLIVE BARNES

Gossip, malice and hypocrisy, like the poor, will always be with us, and therefore every production of Sheridan's exquisite comedy, "The School for Scandal," can hardly fail to be timely. Michael Langham's new production of the play seen for the first time at the Stratford Festival last night is more than timely, it is well-timed.

The rough vigor and dramatic ambiguity of the opening night's "Merchant of Venice" could be completely forgotten in the volatile brilliance of this "School for Scandal," which showed the company off to its best advantage.

This is such a good play, with all its plots and counterplots intermeshing like the parts of a watch, with Sheridan's timeless jokes as funny as ever, and with Sheridan's insight into his fellow beings as sharp as a surgeon's scalpel.

Two brothers—one the perfect hypocrite, the other a hellbent rake—are vying for both the good will of their rich uncle and the hand of an equally rich heiress. It is 18th-century fashionable London, a world dominated by tattle, appearances, costumes and money.

The conniving hypocrite, Joseph Surface, is exposed; the good-natured rake, Charles Surface, gets fortune, bride and reformation, and Sir Peter Teazle, guardian of the young heiress, obtains reconciliation with his young, and hitherto flighty, country wife, Lady Teazle. It all works merrily and morally enough, with wit and truth enough to spare for everyone.

Mr. Langham, who was director of the Stratford Festival from 1955 until 1967, has returned for the first time, and here gives Sheridan his due. In the past I have not always numbered myself among Mr. Langham's greatest admirers. He seemed too arch a disciple of that bad old Tyrone Guthrie school of directing, where every story had to tell a picture, while gimmickeries ran riot and devil take the playwright.

This "School for Scandal," however, seems to find Mr. Langham in a most un-Guthrie-like mood of clarity and simplicity. To be sure, he feels impelled to end the piece with a tableau of piercing irrelevance. Also for some reason, the jollifications of Charles and his friends are accompanied by a kind of thinly baroque version of rock music, which might perhaps be termed "Mr. Bach Goes to Rock," and is a little vulgar and obvious. Yet, for the rest I have nothing but praise.

What it seems that Mr. Langham has achieved is to persuade his cast to forget any preconceptions they may have about English high comedy style. As a result, not only is there a much more interesting, much more alive feel to the playing, but you also get actors actually playing roles such as Joseph Surface and Sir Peter, rather than actors playing Sir John Gielgud and Sir Ralph Richardson playing Joseph Surface and Sir Peter. It is an enormous difference.

And Mr. Langham himself, if I can say this without offering offense, appears a new man. Gone are those circular dances for his actors that he once seemed to find integral to staging on a thrust stage, gone are those exaggerations of character actors blinking knowingly through inches of make-up, and gone are most of the tricks and the foibles. This was a beautiful production.

The actors have responded. Robin Gammell's unctuous yet oddly not unattractive Joseph Surface is perfect in every glance and every inflection. He plays the role as if it were farce rather than comedy—it is a very pushing, physical performance—and the result is fresh and appealing. As the honest, if wayward, brother, Barry MacGregor shows just the right hazy generosity of spirit. More than in most productions, these two contrasting brothers (rather like Hogarth's "Idle and Industrious Apprentices" seen through Sheridan's more worldly eyes) become the focal point of the play as, I suspect, the playwright intended.

As a result of this focus, the fighting Teazles quite rightly step back a little into the play's mechanism. However, Stephen Murray's natural friendly and avuncular Sir Peter is a portrayal of great quality, and is matched by the girlish flightiness of Helen Carey as Lady Teazle.

Of the rest, there are many good performances, including those of the scandalous scholastics, Jane Casson, Bernard Behrens, Eric Donkin, Pat Galloway and Robin Marshall, and I liked also the bluffness of Mervyn Blake as Sir Oliver Surface and James Blendick as the faithful Rowley.

A fine evening, then, much aided by the handsome and stylish scenery and costumes by Leslie Hurry. Incidentally, and apropos of almost nothing, in the director's note given in the program, Mr. Langham reminds us all that the phrase "the silent majority" originated with Homer. The dear old Greek used it to describe the dead. It is amazing how many gaps in an education can be filled in by assiduous theatergoing.

MODERN THEATER

Modern drama, like modern painting and other forms of modern art, developed not in the twentieth century, as might be casually assumed, but during the nineteenth century. It was born out of a widespread reaction against the subject matters, forms, and methods of staging that had prevailed in many eighteenth- and early nineteenth-century plays—against aristocratic or exotic heroes and heroines, against the rigorous unities of a neoclassical tragedy or the flamboyant events of a romantic melodrama, against declamatory styles of acting or spectacular forms of setting, against theatrical conventions that were regarded as being too far from the truth of ordinary existence. "Reality," in turn, became a watchword among early modern dramatists, actors, directors, and set designers. Indeed, the realistic impulse in one form or another so heavily influenced theater through the first half of the twentieth century that the history of modern drama may well be understood in terms of the movements that grew out of realism, either as a refinement of it or as a reaction against it.

Realism in its most literal sense developed out of a desire to bring the stage into greater conformity with the surface details of ordinary human experience. This impulse first manifested itself in the efforts of set designers to create a full-scale visual illusion in the theater, to make the stage setting look like an interior place where ordinary people actually lived and worked—or, as one recent director has put it, to show "a real chair in a real setting." This concept of staging clearly required a set more visually plausible than the sliding wings and canvas backdrops of the neoclassical stage, which usually depicted doors and windows, sometimes even chairs, by means of perspective painting on the backdrop, instead of incorporating movable doors, windows, and furniture.

To create the illusion of a three-dimensional interior, nineteenth-century set designers devised a set composed of flats arranged to form connected walls enclosing three sides of the stage, with the fourth wall removed so that the audience could look into a stage room that spatially seemed just like a real one. The realistic illusion of this stage design, known as the box set, was enhanced by movable windows and doors built into the walls of the back or side flats, as well as by false thickness pieces built into the window and door openings, which gave them an air of solidity. When the interior walls of the set were decorated and hung with fixtures, and when the floor space enclosed by the walls was equipped with rugs, furniture, and other props, the stage resembled a real room in every respect (see Figure 1). By the middle of the nineteenth century, the box set had been used in theaters throughout Europe, and its subsequent importance to the history of drama may be seen in the fact that detailed interiors figure prominently in almost all the plays written in the modern realistic tradition, such as Ibsen's *A Doll's House,* Strindberg's *Miss Julie,* Chekhov's *The Cherry Orchard,* Shaw's *Pygmalion,* O'Casey's *Juno and the Paycock,* and Williams' *Cat on a Hot Tin Roof.*

The development of the box set took place during the same period as major technological advances in lighting. Gaslights, as well as lime or calcium light, superseded oil lamps during the first half of the nineteenth century, making

Figure 1. The box set decorated with wall and window hangings, as well as with furniture and props, to create the illusion of an actual room.

possible not only a greater degree of power and control in stage lighting, but also a variety of realistic effects, such as the illusion of sunlight, moonlight, or lamplight coming through doors and windows. During the second half of the nineteenth century, the invention of the carbon arc lamp and finally the incandescent lamp not only freed theaters from the terrible fire hazards of gaslights, but also encouraged directors and designers to invent elaborately realistic lighting effects.

Acting styles were slower to approximate the natural gestures, movements, and tones of voices appropriate to realistic staging, in part because the declamatory style of romantic acting was highly popular with audiences, but also because anything less pronounced would have been inadequate to make a clearly audible and visual impression in the cavernous theaters common during the late eighteenth century and much of the nineteenth. The auditoriums in these theaters were typically based on a design that was calculated to accommodate as large an audience as possible—sometimes as many as four thousand—with little concern for the needs of the actors or of the spectators. That design can readily be understood by first imagining a large cylinder at whose base is seated the majority of the audience, looking at a large opening that has been pierced in the cylinder to form the proscenium arch of the stage (see Figure 2). Then imagine that the builders or remodelers of such theaters, in order to fit in more paying spectators, hung balconies at four or five levels around the inside walls of the cylinder above the base (see Figure 3). Clearly, an actor or actress performing in these theaters had to develop an exaggerated style of movement, gesture, and intonation to make an impact on the audience sitting in those balconies.

But during the late nineteenth and early twentieth centuries, theater architecture began to undergo significant modifications, which were intended to create better acoustical, visual, and spatial arrangements for actors and spectators. Cylindrical designs were gradually abandoned in favor of fan-shaped auditoriums with rising tiers of seats, all facing the stage (see Figure 4). In auditoriums based on this design—a design that now prevails in many commercial, community, and college theaters—the clear sightlines and favorable acoustics made it possible for performers to develop and use a more natural style of acting. And where theaters of this design were not available, directors

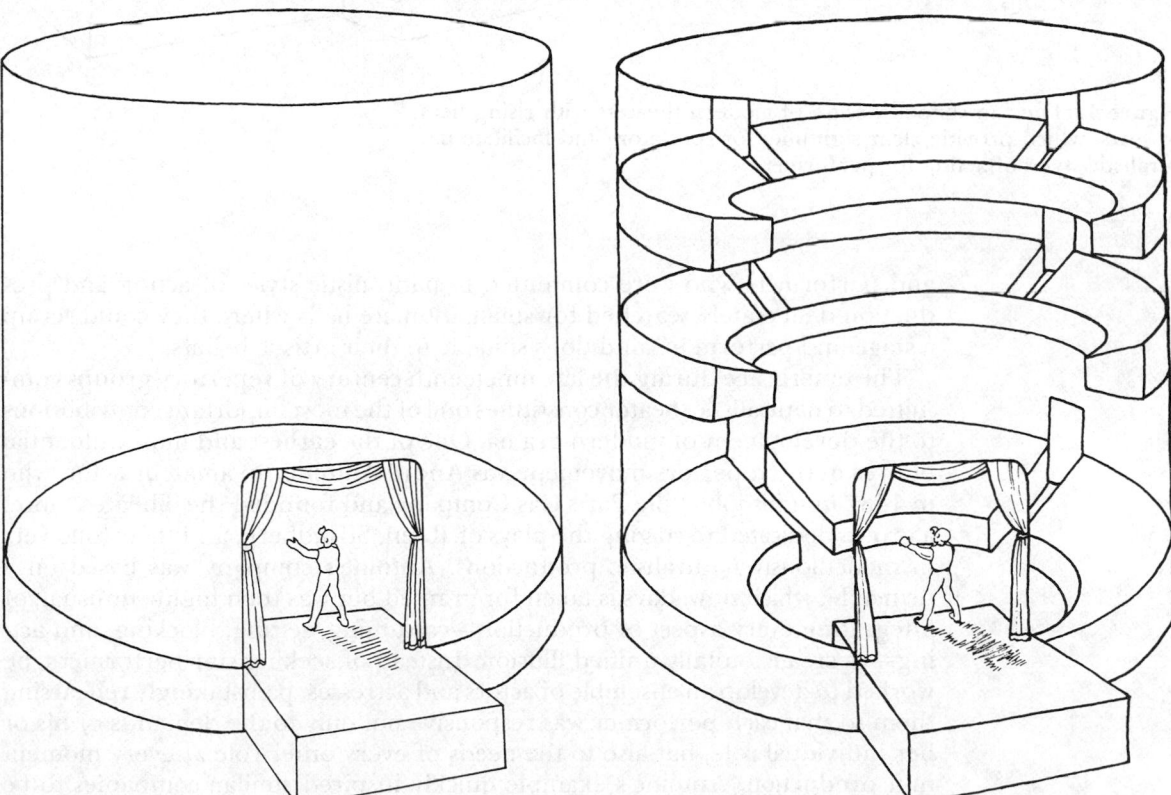

Figure 2. The cylindrical design of late eighteenth- and early nineteenth-century theaters.

Figure 3. The cylindrically designed theater, showing multiple balconies remote from the actor on stage.

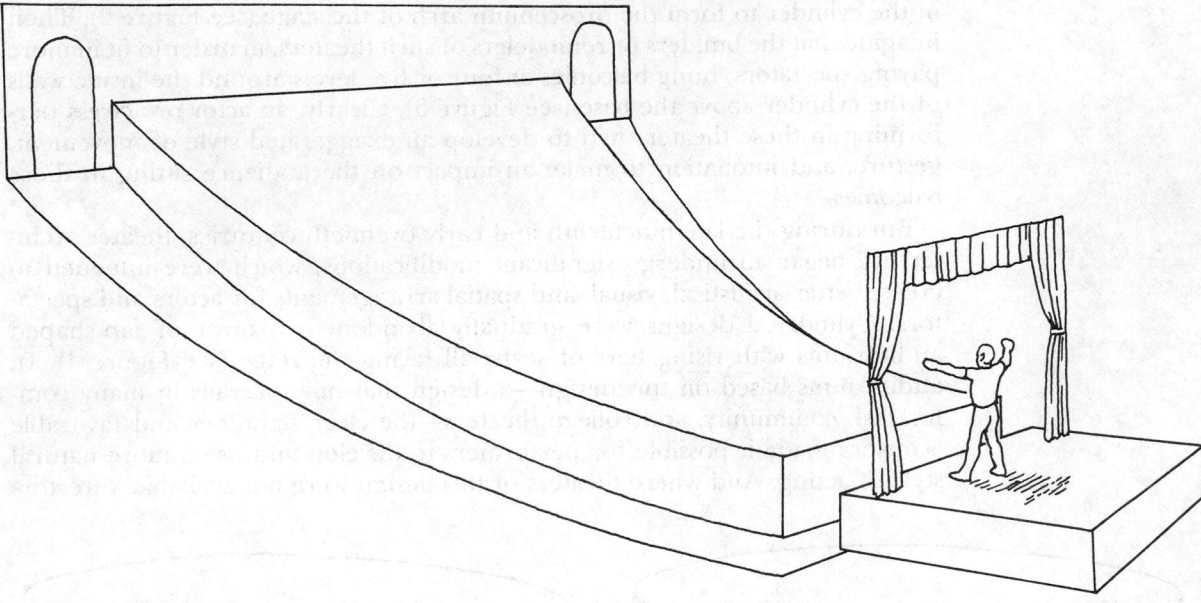

Figure 4. The fan-shaped design of modern theaters with rising tiers of seats, which provide clear sightlines for spectators and facilitate naturalistic styles of acting for performers.

and performers who were committed to naturalistic styles of acting and production deliberately searched for small, intimate halls where they could set up a stage and perform in conditions suitable to their artistic beliefs.

The emergence during the late nineteenth century of repertory groups committed to naturalistic theater constitutes one of the most important contributions to the development of modern drama. One of the earliest and most influential figures in this repertory movement was André Antoine, an amateur actor, who in 1887 quit his job at the Paris Gas Company and founded the Théâtre Libre, a group dedicated to staging the plays of Ibsen, Strindberg, and their followers in meticulously naturalistic productions. Antoine's company was based on a principle, which nowadays is taken for granted but was then highly unusual, of integrating every aspect of production—costuming, setting, blocking, and acting—to create a totally unified illusion. Instead of seeking star performers, he worked to develop an ensemble of actors and actresses, painstakingly rehearsing them so that each performer was responsive not only to the demands of his or her individual role, but also to the needs of every other role at every moment in a production. Antoine's example quickly inspired similar companies to be formed throughout Europe and America.

The most well-known and influential organization to develop during the early repertory movement was the Moscow Art Theater, founded in 1898 by Konstantin Stanislavsky, an amateur actor and director, and by Vladimir Nemirovich-Danchenko, a successful playwright. The Moscow Art Theater achieved its early fame by producing the plays of Chekhov in a style that accentuated their emotional and psychological subtlety. This style entailed not only a detailed attention to elements of staging—including even the use of music to underline important emotional moments—but also a carefully defined method of acting, propounded by Stanislavsky, whose fundamental purpose was to create "the inner life of a human spirit." Stanislavsky's method, which he subsequently expounded in several highly influential books—among them *My Life in Art* (1924) and *An Actor Prepares* (1926)—required actors to think "about the inner side of a role, and how to create its spiritual life through the help of the internal process of living the part. You must live it by actually experiencing feelings that are analogous to it, each and every time you repeat the process of creating it." The illusion of reality, as Stanislavsky defined it, depended on using the theater to dramatize not simply the external but, more important, the internal condition of human experience.

Stanislavsky's emphasis on the "inner side of a role," on "living the part," would have been impossible without dramatic roles that called for such an approach, without plays that offer probing studies of psychologically complex characters in complex social, domestic, and personal situations. In this profound sense, realistic and naturalistic drama originated not from an interest in representing the surface details, the literal image, of human activity, but out of a concern with reflecting the environmental and psychological conditions that account for the problematic quality of ordinary human experience. In this sense Ibsen is often considered the "father" of modern drama. Beginning in 1877, for example, Ibsen wrote a series of realistic "problem" plays, in which he systematically shattered popular illusions about such then sacred institutions as marriage and religion—plays in which he showed the inner life of his characters as they come to recognize the painful realities of their personal situations. Chekhov dramatized a similar kind of experience in his turn-of-the-century plays, though he presented his characters as being at once comic, pitiable, and admirably human in their futile efforts to overcome both the romantic illusions and the banal necessities of their existence. Strindberg exposed even harsher realities in his naturalistic dramatizations of the sexual antagonism between men and women.

In portraying characters, the early modern dramatists relied not only on the psychological nuances of dialogue and action, but also on the emblematic significances of the box set itself, for its detailed interiors may be seen as tangibly revealing not only a particular place in which the characters exist, but also exposing the quality of their existence. In *A Doll's House*, for example, the setting called for in Ibsen's stage directions—a room cluttered with bric-a-brac and overstuffed chairs—is as stifling and deceiving as the marriage of Nora and Helmer. In Chekhov's *The Cherry Orchard*, the cozy nursery where the play begins and ends is an emblem of the childish and irrepressibly romantic illusions that govern the thoughts of Ranevskaya and Gayev and that make them incapable of coming to terms with the changing society around them. And in *Miss Julie*, the kitchen, which constitutes the setting for the entire play, is a continual reminder of the cultural and psychological servitude that Jean, the valet, is bent on overthrowing.

Though the realism of box sets and the naturalism of psychologically motivated characters was dramatically compelling, modern drama also developed along nonrealistic and even anti-realistic lines. As early as 1835, a young medical researcher named Georg Büchner began writing plays that challenged the romantic historical dramas of Germany's Friedrich Schiller, plays whose protagonists (Mary Stuart, William Tell, Joan of Arc) are clearly heroic figures. Though Büchner's first play, *Danton's Death,* dealt with the major political event of the eighteenth century, the French Revolution, his treatment of it was decidedly nonromantic, both in characterization and in style. Instead of blank verse and classical dramatic structure, Büchner turned to prose and an almost cinematic juxtaposition of scenes. Büchner, in fact, was so far ahead of his time that editions of his work did not even appear until the second half of the century. Indeed, the first performance of *Woyzeck,* Büchner's major work, did not take place until 1913, one hundred years after his birth.

By the late nineteenth century, various anti-realistic tendencies—known as symbolism, expressionism, and surrealism—had already taken form in the critical statements and plays of *avant-garde* dramatists. Proponents of these counter-realistic movements argued that dramatic truth was not to be found in the tangible surfaces of a box set nor even in the intangible life of a psychologically complex character, but in symbols, images, legends, myths, fantasies, dreams, and other mysterious manifestations of spirituality, subjectivity, or the unconscious. Symbolists, for example, claimed the existence of a higher truth than was evident in external reality, and they aimed to create in the theater a mysterious and quasi-religious experience. Expressionists believed that truth existed not in the external appearance of reality but in the subjective perception of reality, no matter how psychologically distorted that perception might be, and they often sought to dramatize how the world appears to a disturbed and convulsive mind. Surrealists claimed that truth was to be found not in the logic of everyday events but in the irrational processes of the unconscious mind, and they tried to re-create the strange combinations of the familiar and the mysterious that often take place in dreams.

From a late twentieth-century perspective, these various anti-realistic tendencies now seem commonplace, but in their own day they were revolutionary, and they attracted not only experimental writers, but major dramatists who had already established themselves as masters of realistic and naturalistic drama. Ibsen's late plays, especially *The Lady from the Sea* (1888) and *When We Dead Awaken* (1899) are manifestly symbolic not only in their titles but also in their settings and in their action. Although Strindberg began by writing such naturalistic plays as *The Father* (1887) and *Miss Julie* (1888), he later turned to the fantasy world of *A Dream Play* (1901) and the haunting, personal symbolism of *The Ghost Sonata* (1907). Even Shaw, so thoroughly committed to a theater of intellectual and social realism, wrote a five-play parable set in the Garden of Eden, Mesopotamia, as well as England both in his own time and the future in *Back to Methusaleh* (1920). For the American playwright O'Neill, symbolic and expressionistic drama came early in his career rather than at the end, in the psychologically distorted perceptions of *The Emperor Jones* (1920), the symbolic events of *The Hairy Ape* (1922), and the expressionistic symbols of *The Great God Brown* (1926). In Italy, Luigi Pirandello dramatized the enduring struggle between appearance and reality by bringing on stage both "actors" and "characters," the latter group dizzying in their simultaneous reality and nonreality. And though the Spanish playwright Garcia Lorca called his last play, *The House of Bernarda Alba* (1936), "a photographic document," the text begins with symbolic insistence on the "very white room" in Bernarda's house, and ends with Bernarda insisting on the spiritual whiteness of her youngest daughter: "My daughter died a virgin."

Symbolic drama of the early modern period was mirrored in a variety of staging techniques that were often intentionally designed to obliterate any hint of a realistic environment. In France, the main exponent of symbolist staging was Aurelien-Marie Lugné-Poe, who established an avant-garde repertory group, known as the Théâtre de l'Oeuvre, which was dedicated to the production of symbolist plays. In Lugné-Poe's productions, scenery was often reduced to painted, abstract backdrops; props and furniture were often minimal or nonexistent; lighting was often minimal and dispersed instead of focussed; and actors strived to evoke a mood rather than to reveal psychological motivation. Expressionistic stagings, which were largely developed in German theater during the 1920s, replaced representational settings with expressively stylized backdrops, showing exterior or interior locations that had been distorted and exaggerated in color and shape; lighting was often harshly focussed or nervously scattered; and actors strived through disjointed movements and telegraphic speech patterns to evoke human behavior as it might be perceived by a psychologically convulsive personality. Surrealistic stagings, which were launched by Antonin Artaud and André Breton in Parisian theaters of the 1920s, pushed productions even further toward expressive abstraction in backdrops, costumes, lighting, and acting styles.

By the end of the twenties, these counterrealistic movements, though polemically extreme in their practices, had worked substantial changes in the style of drama and of theatrical production—changes that resulted in a synthesis of realistic and naturalistic methods with symbolic, expressionistic, or surrealistic techniques. The power of such a synthesis was convincingly displayed in the work of Bertolt Brecht, the major German playwright and director of the twentieth century. From the 1920s through the early 1950s, Brecht wrote an extensive series of plays that were simultaneously realistic in their depiction of human motives and values, expressionistic in their episodic structure, and politically explicit in their ideology. And he created stagings for his plays with the Berliner Ensemble that used realistic costumes and set pieces combined with an abstract backdrop, visible lighting instruments, visible scene changing, and scene titles or other messages projected onto the backdrop. By means of this synthesis, Brecht aimed both to engage an audience in the situation of his characters and to distance them sufficiently so that they would be provoked to think about its social and political implications. Once Brecht had established the theatrical power of such a synthesis, it gradually came to be a dominant approach in serious theater of the twentieth century. Tennessee Williams, for example, blended realism and expressionism in all of his plays, beginning with his notes on music, lighting, and pantomime for *The Glass Menagerie* (1944) and continuing with his emphasis on the bedroom and the bed in *Cat on a Hot Tin Roof* (1955). So, when Arthur Miller's *Death of a Salesman* (1949) opened on Broadway with a striking combination of naturalistic and expressionistic effects, both in the physical set and in the play's structure, his mixture of styles evoked almost no surprise at all.

GEORG BÜCHNER

1813–1837

Though he died quite young, Georg Büchner led three distinctly different lives. His first and most successful was as a medical researcher and lecturer, a profession that came naturally to the son of a doctor. Büchner was educated at Darmstadt in his native Germany, and then in 1831 went to Strasbourg to study medicine but after two years returned to Germany, conforming to a state law that required students from Hesse (the region in which Büchner lived) to study at the state university. Here he began his second life as a student revolutionary, involved in an underground society aimed at attacking the regime of Ludwig II, grand duke of Hesse. As coauthor of *The Hessian Courier* (1834), a manifesto against the extortionist tactics of the grand duke, Büchner attempted to arouse his readers by reminding them of the French Revolution and its disappointing political aftermath: France, only temporarily a republic, became again a monarchy, and Germany, frightened by the violence in France, gave its people constitutions that served to quiet revolt rather than establish true freedom. To escape possible arrest, Büchner left Germany for Strasbourg in 1835, finished his medical studies, wrote a treatise on the nervous system of the barbel (a large fish), and then on the strength of that treatise moved to Zurich in late 1836, where he was offered a lectureship. A promising career as a teacher and researcher, if not as a revolutionary, seemed to open before him, only to close on February 19, 1837, when he died of typhoid fever.

In the last few years before his death, Büchner had also begun to lead a third life, that of a dramatist. At first, playwriting may have seemed merely a way to make money, since he composed his first work, *Danton's Death*, in 1835 and sent it to a well-known editor, together with a letter indicating that he was financially strapped. But after his return to Strasbourg, Büchner translated two plays by Victor Hugo and wrote a second play, *Leonce and Lena* (1836), in response to a competition for the best German comedy; his manuscript arrived after the deadline and so was not eligible. His third play, *Woyzeck*, must also date from 1836, but it remained in manuscript form, in several incomplete drafts. A fourth play, *Pietro Aretino*, survives only in its title.

Büchner's choice to write about the French Revolution at a time when he was desperate for money and planning to leave Germany to avoid arrest may have contributed to his distinctly unheroic portrayal of major figures from the Revolution. Set in 1794, near the end of the Reign of Terror, *Danton's Death* focuses on internal power struggles rather than the larger social context. In this play, Robespierre and Saint-Just are portrayed as coldly calculating individuals who use abstractions such as "freedom" and "humanity" to hide their manipulative search for power. But Georges Danton, rather than heroically opposing these men, seems strangely passive, refusing to leave Paris even though his friends warn him, preferring to spend his time not only with his wife, Julie, but with numerous prostitutes. Though he rouses himself during his trial to remind his accusers of his actions in the early days of the Revolution, he sinks at the play's end to a fatalistic aphorism: "The world is chaos. Nothingness is the world-god yet to be born." Büchner's historical play never glorifies the Revolution. In keeping with this unglorified view of the Revolution, *Danton's Death* is written in prose rather than blank verse, and it presents the voices not only of Danton and Robespierre but of nameless citizens and of powerless women. "What are we but puppets, manipulated on wires by unknown powers?" asks Danton as he muses to Julie about the rightness of his actions, a metaphor used as stage setting in Jonathan Miller's 1971 production, which featured side boxes with headless mannequins, as well as projections of Roman statues.

Büchner's vision of human beings as puppets emerges again in *Leonce and Lena*, a play that superficially seems completely different from *Danton's Death* and its specific historical context. Büchner sets up a fairy-tale world in which Prince Leonce, unwilling to accept an arranged marriage, and Princess Lena, equally unwilling to sacrifice herself, both disguise themselves and run away. Of course, they meet and fall in love, but the names of their countries, Popo and Pipi, with their echoes of excrement and urination, should alert us to the darker side of the fairy-tale world. In the final scene, disguised as "two world-famous automatons," Leonce and Lena are married. When they remove their masks, they find that instead of "escaping into Paradise" they "have been deceived." Though the tone of the play is light, the storyline clearly argues the inability of human beings to control their destinies.

Though *Danton's Death* and *Leonce and Lena* are strikingly different in setting and tone, though one play deals with actual figures of the French Revolution and the other with imaginary and comic royal personages, both plays are "costume dramas," requiring the creation of a world noticeably unlike the one in which Büchner actually lived. In contrast, *Woyzeck* is based on a real murder that took place in Leipzig in 1821, when Johann Christian Woyzeck stabbed his ex-mistress seven times. Woyzeck's execution did not take place until three years after the murder because of several appeals; but two investigations by a court-appointed physician, Johann Clarus, concluded that Woyzeck was legally responsible for his actions. While these reports, available to Büchner through his father, aimed at justifying Woyzeck's execution, they also included many of the details that might well have been used to argue for extenuating circumstances, particularly Woyzeck's claims that he had visions and heard voices.

Yet *Woyzeck*'s peculiar force comes not from its basis in real life but from Büchner's extraordinarily stripped-down style. Gone are the long speeches of argument that punctuate *Danton's Death*; gone are the long pseudo-meditations of *Leonce and Lena*. Instead, the characters in *Woyzeck* speak in short, choppy phrases, in allusions rather than explanations, in snatches of songs or of biblical quotations. Such a style fits the central character who finds it difficult to express his feelings, and who finally seeks refuge in violent action rather than in language. Significantly, the characters in this play who *can* speak freely are the ones we most mistrust: the Captain who preaches a meaningless morality while driving Woyzeck mad with his insinuations about Marie, Woyzeck's common-law wife, and the Doctor, who preaches human freedom to the man he is using for his bizarre scientific experiments. Gone too is any attempt at linear development or an intrigue plot. In its place is a series of short scenes, some involving just four or six speeches. The language, the action, the motivation, the scene structure—all are fragmentary.

Fragmentary is more than a metaphor for the form and content of *Woyzeck*; it is an accurate description of the playtext itself. For unlike any other work in this volume, *Woyzeck* is incomplete. It exists only in a manuscript that contains four different versions or groupings of scenes: one contains twenty-one scenes, a second has nine scenes, a third has two scenes, and the fourth has seventeen scenes. Some scenes seem to be revisions of others, while others appear only once. These different versions raise a host of questions about Büchner's unresolved intentions. Does the play begin with Woyzeck and Andres in the field (as in two sequences of the manuscript) or with the fair (Scene 3 in our text), thereby immediately introducing Woyzeck, Marie, and the Sergeant who will become her new lover? How many times does Woyzeck tell Andres he hears a voice telling him to stab only to be met with the prosaic remedy of "brandy with a painkiller in it" (Scene 13)? The scene appears in two different forms, and one might reasonably argue that Büchner meant it to appear just once, or that he wanted the scene in twice, to emphasize Woyzeck's "voices" and Andres's lack of sympathy. Scenes 18 and 27 appear on a separate page of the manuscript and nowhere else, with no indication of where Büchner meant to put them. The choice to use Scene 27 as the final scene is also an interpretation of one of the play's unresolved questions. Does Woyzeck drown himself after throwing away the knife he used to kill Marie, perhaps because of guilt (the last lines of Scene 24 echo Lady Macbeth's famous lines), or does he merely wash himself off and return to town where his child seems to reject him (Scene 27)?

Thus, every reader of the play is, to some extent, acting as its editor, just as Henry J. Schmidt has titled his translation in this volume a "reconstruction of the text." Schmidt has worked from the most complete modern edition of the play available and has considered all the variant scenes, as well as the order that the manuscript does suggest for certain scenes. But, as Mel Gussow suggests in his review of the New York Shakespeare Festival production, "the play is open to free-handed interpretation" and to various production styles. In this production, JoAnne Akalaitis draws on images from the twentieth century, such as the antiseptically white mechanic chair in which the Captain sits while Woyzeck shaves him (see Figure 1). The townspeople who surround Woyzeck after the murder wear clothes evoking the 1930s and 1940s (see Figure 2). Images of the concentration camps dominate the production: Gussow explicitly links Woyzeck to a prisoner at Dachau, while the murder of Marie (see Figure 3) takes place in what seems to be an empty shower room, evoking memories of the "shower rooms" that were really gas chambers in which thousands of prisoners died. These visual reminders of the prejudice and hatred of the twentieth century testify to the play's enduring power. Though the fragmentary nature of the play on the page may at times frustrate editors and readers, the play onstage shows us pieces of a life that coalesce into an emblem of contemporary pain and despair.

WOYZECK

BY GEORG BÜCHNER / A RECONSTRUCTION OF THE ORIGINAL TEXT TRANSLATED BY HENRY J. SCHMIDT

CHARACTERS

FRANZ WOYZECK
MARIE
CAPTAIN
DOCTOR
DRUM MAJOR
SERGEANT
ANDRES
MARGRET
BARKER ⎫
ANNOUNCER ⎬ *can be played by one actor*
OLD MAN ⎭
CHILD
JEW
INNKEEPER

FIRST APPRENTICE
SECOND APPRENTICE
KARL, *an idiot*
KATEY
GRANDMOTHER
FIRST CHILD
SECOND CHILD
THIRD CHILD
FIRST PERSON
SECOND PERSON
COURT CLERK
JUDGE
SOLDIERS, STUDENTS, YOUNG MEN, GIRLS,
   CHILDREN

1

(Open field. The town in the distance.)

(WOYZECK and ANDRES are cutting branches in the bushes.)

WOYZECK: Hey, Andres! That streak across the grass— that's where heads roll at night. Once somebody picked one up, thought it was a hedgehog. Three days and three nights, and he was lying in a coffin. *(Softly.)* Andres, it was the Freemasons.° That's it— the Freemasons! Shh!

ANDRES: *(Sings.)*

   I saw two big rabbits
   Chewing up the green, green grass . . .

WOYZECK: Shh! Something's moving!

ANDRES:

   Chewing up the green, green grass
   Till it all was gone.

WOYZECK: Something's moving behind me—under me. *(Stamps on the ground.)* Hollow! You hear that? It's all hollow down there. The Freemasons!

ANDRES: I'm scared.

WOYZECK: It's so quiet—that's strange. You feel like holding your breath. Andres!

ANDRES: What?

WOYZECK: Say something! *(Stares off into the distance.)* Andres! Look how bright it is! There's fire raging around the sky, and a noise is coming down like trumpets. It's coming closer! Let's go! Don't look back! *(Drags him into the bushes.)*

ANDRES: *(After a pause.)* Woyzeck! Do you still hear it?

WOYZECK: Quiet, everything's quiet, like the world was dead.

ANDRES: Listen! They're drumming. We've got to get back.

2

(The town.)

(MARIE with her CHILD at the window. MARGRET. A parade goes by, the DRUM MAJOR leading.)

MARIE: *(Rocking the CHILD in her arms.)* Hey, boy! Ta-ra-ra-ra! You hear it? They're coming.

MARGRET: What a man, like a tree!

MARIE: He stands on his feet like a lion. *(The DRUM MAJOR greets them.)*

MARGRET: Say, what a friendly look you gave him, neighbor. We're not used to that from you.

MARIE: *(Sings.)*

   A soldier is a handsome fellow . . .

MARGRET: Your eyes are still shining.

MARIE: So what? Why don't you take *your* eyes to the Jew and have them polished—maybe they'll shine enough to sell as two buttons.

Freemasons, an international secret society.

540

MARGRET: What? Why, Mrs. Virgin! I'm a decent woman, but you—you can stare through seven pairs of leather pants!

MARIE: Bitch! (*Slams the window shut.*) Come on, boy. What do they want from us, anyway? You're only the son of a whore, and you make your mother happy with your bastard face. Ta-ta! (*Sings.*)

> *Maiden, how sorrow can sting,*
> *You've got a son but no ring!*
> *Oh, who cares what is right,*
> *I'll sing to you all night:*
> *Rockabye baby, my baby are you,*
> *Nobody cares what we do.*
>
> *Johnny, hitch up your six horses fleet,*
> *Go bring them something to eat.*
> *From oats they will turn,*
> *From water they'll turn,*
> *Only cool wine will be fine, hooray!*
> *Only cool wine will be fine.*

(*A knock at the window.*)

MARIE: Who's that? Is that you, Franz? Come on in!

WOYZECK: I can't. Have to go to roll call.

MARIE: What's the matter with you, Franz?

WOYZECK: (*Mysteriously.*) Marie, there was something out there again—a lot. Isn't it written: "And lo, the smoke of the country went up as the smoke of a furnace"?°

MARIE: Franz . . .

WOYZECK: It followed me until I reached town. What's going to happen?

MARIE: Franz!

WOYZECK: I've got to go. (*He leaves.*)

MARIE: That man! He's seeing things. He didn't even look at his own child. He'll go crazy with those thoughts of his. Why are you so quiet, son? Are you scared? It's getting so dark, you'd think you were blind. Usually there's a light shining in. I can't stand it. It frightens me. (*Goes off.*)

3

(*Fair booths. Lights. People.*)

(*An* OLD MAN *sings to a barrel organ, a* CHILD *dances.*)

OLD MAN:

> *How long we live, just time will tell,*
> *We all have got to die,*
> *We know that very well!*

MARIE: Hey! Wow!

WOYZECK: Poor man, old man! Poor child! Little child! Cares and fairs! Hey, Marie, should I . . . ?

MARIE: Even a fool must have some sense to be able to say: Foolish world! Beautiful world!

BARKER: (*In front of a booth, with a* WOMAN *wearing pants. He presents a costumed monkey. The* BARKER *speaks with a French accent.*) Gentlemen! Gentlemen! Look at this creature, as God made it—he's nothing, nothing at all. Now see the effect of art: he walks upright, wears coat and pants, carries a sword! Ho! Take a bow! Presto—you're a baron. Give me a kiss! (*The monkey trumpets.*) The little fellow is musical. Ladies and gentlemen, here is to be seen the astronomical horse and the little cannery-birds°—they're favorites of all potentates of Europe—they're members of all learned societies. They'll tell you everything: how old you are, how many children you have, what kind of illnesses. (*Points to the monkey.*) He shoots a pistol, stands on one leg. It's all education; he has merely a beastly reason, or rather a very reasonable beastliness—he's no dumb individual like a lot of people, present company excepted. Observe the progress of civilization. Everything progresses—a horse, a monkey, a cannery-bird! The monkey is already a soldier. That's not much—it's the lowest level of the human race. Enter! The presentation will begin. The commencement of the beginning will start immediately.

WOYZECK: Want to?

MARIE: All right. It ought to be good. Look at his tassels—and the woman's got pants on!

(SERGEANT. DRUM MAJOR.)

SERGEANT: Hold it! Over there. Look at her! What a piece!

DRUM MAJOR: Goddamn! Good enough for the propagation of cavalry regiments and the breeding of drum majors!

SERGEANT: Look how she holds her head—you'd think that black hair would pull her down like a weight. And those eyes, black . . .

DRUM MAJOR: It's like looking down a well or a chimney. Come on, after her!

MARIE: (*Entering the booth.*) Those lights! My eyes!

WOYZECK: Yeah, like a barrel of black cats with fiery eyes. Hey, what a night!

(*Inside the booth.*)

ANNOUNCER: (*Presenting a horse.*) Show your talent! Show your beastly wisdom. Put human society to shame. Gentlemen, this animal that you see here, with a tail on his body, with his four hoofs, is a

---

"And lo, . . . furnace," Gen. 19:28, the destruction of Sodom and Gomorrah.

cannery-birds, the Barker says *Canaillevogel* instead of *Kanarienvogel,* meaning "canaries."

member of all learned societies, is a professor at
our university with whom the students learn to ride
and fight. That was simple comprehension. Now
think with double *raison.*° What do you do when
you think with double *raison?* Is there in the learned
société° an ass? (*The horse shakes its head.*) Now you
understand double *raison?* That is beastiognomy.°
Yes, that is no dumb animal, that's a person! A
human being, a beastly human being, but still an
animal, *une bête.* (*The horse behaves improperly.*) That's
right, put *société* to shame. You see, the beast is still
nature, unideal nature. Take a lesson from him.
Go ask the doctor, it's very unhealthy.° All this
means: Man, be natural. You were created from
dust, sand, dirt. Do you want to be more than dust,
sand, dirt? Observe his reason: he can add, but he
can't count on his fingers. How come? He simply
can't express himself, explain himself. He's a transformed person! Tell the gentlemen what time it is.
Does anyone have a watch—a watch?

SERGEANT: A watch! (*Slowly and grandly he pulls a watch
out of his pocket.*) There you are.

MARIE: This I've got to see. (*She climbs into the first row.
The* SERGEANT *helps her.*)

4

(*Room.*)

(MARIE *sits with her* CHILD *on her lap, a piece of mirror
in her hand.*)

MARIE: (*Looks at herself in the mirror.*) These stones really
sparkle! What kind are they? What did he call
them? Go to sleep, son! Shut your eyes tight. (*The*
CHILD *covers his eyes with his hands.*) Tighter—stay
quiet or he'll come get you. (*Sings.*)

Close up your shop, fair maid,
A gypsy boy's in the glade.
He'll lead you by the hand
Off into gypsyland.

(*Looks in the mirror again.*) It must be gold. The likes of
us only have a little corner in the world and a little piece
of mirror, but my mouth is just as red as the great ladies
with their mirrors from top to toe, and handsome lords
who kiss their hands. I'm just a poor woman. (*The* CHILD
sits up.) Shh, son, eyes shut! Look, the sandman! He's
running along the wall. (*She flashes with the mirror.*) Eyes
shut, or he'll look into them, and you'll go blind.

(WOYZECK *enters behind her. She jumps up with her
hands over her ears.*)

---

raison, reason. *société,* company. **beastiognomy,** *vieh-
sionomik:* a pun on "beast" and "physiognomy." **unhealthy,**
meaning "to hold it in."

WOYZECK: What's that you got there?
MARIE: Nothing.
WOYZECK: Something's shining under your fingers.
MARIE: An earring. I found it.
WOYZECK: I've never found anything like that. Two at
once.
MARIE: What am I—a whore?
WOYZECK: It's all right, Marie. Look, the boy's asleep.
Lift him up under his arms, the chair's hurting him.
Those shiny drops on his forehead; everything un-
der the sun is work. Sweat, even in our sleep. Us
poor people! Here's some more money, Marie, my
pay and some from my captain.
MARIE: Bless you, Franz.
WOYZECK: I have to go. See you tonight, Marie. Bye.
MARIE: (*Alone, after a pause.*) What a bitch I am. I could
stab myself. Oh, what a world! Everything goes to
hell anyhow, man and woman alike.

5

(*The* CAPTAIN. WOYZECK.)

(*The* CAPTAIN *in a chair,* WOYZECK *shaves him.*)

CAPTAIN: Take it easy, Woyzeck, take it easy. One thing
at a time. You're making me dizzy. You're going to
finish early today—what am I supposed to do with
the extra ten minutes? Woyzeck, just think, you've
still got a good thirty years to live, thirty years!
That's 360 months, and days, hours, minutes! What
are you going to do with that ungodly amount of
time? Get organized, Woyzeck.
WOYZECK: Yes, Cap'n.
CAPTAIN: I fear for the world when I think about eternity. Activity, Woyzeck, activity! Eternal—that's
eternal—that is—eternal—you realize that, of
course. But then again it's not eternal, it's only a
moment, yes, a moment. Woyzeck, it frightens me
to think that the earth rotates in one day. What a
waste of time! What will come of that? Woyzeck, I
can't look at a mill wheel anymore or I get melancholy.
WOYZECK: Yes, Cap'n.
CAPTAIN: Woyzeck, you always look so upset. A good
man doesn't act like that, a good man with a good
conscience. Say something, Woyzeck. What's the
weather like?
WOYZECK: It's bad, Cap'n, bad—wind.
CAPTAIN: I can feel it, there's something rapid out
there. A wind like that reminds me of a mouse.
(*Cunningly.*) I believe it's coming from the south-
north.
WOYZECK: Yes, Cap'n.
CAPTAIN: Ha-ha-ha! South-north! Ha-ha-ha! Oh, are
you stupid, terribly stupid! (*Sentimentally.*) Woyzeck,
you're a good man, a good man—(*With dignity.*) but
Woyzeck, you've got no morality. Morality—that's

when you are moral, you understand. It's a good word. You have a child without the blessing of the church, as our Reverend Chaplain says, without the blessing of the church. *I* didn't make that up.

WOYZECK: Cap'n, the good Lord isn't going to look at a poor worm only because amen was said over it before it was created. The Lord said: "Suffer little children to come unto me."

CAPTAIN: What's that you're saying? What kind of a crazy answer is that? You're getting me all confused. When I say *you*, I mean you—you!

WOYZECK: Us poor people. You see, Cap'n—money, money. If you don't have money . . . Just try to raise your own kind on morality in this world. After all, we're flesh and blood. The likes of us are unhappy in this world and in the next. I guess if we ever got to Heaven, we'd have to help with the thunder.

CAPTAIN: Woyzeck, you have no virtue. You're not a virtuous person. Flesh and blood? When I'm lying at the window after it has rained, and I watch the white stockings as they go tripping down the street—damn it, Woyzeck, then love comes all over me. I've got flesh and blood, too. But Woyzeck, virtue, virtue! How else could I make time go by? I always say to myself: you're a virtuous man, *(Sentimentally.)* a good man, a good man.

WOYZECK: Yes, Cap'n, virtue! I haven't figured it out yet. You see, us common people, we don't have virtue. We act like nature tells us. But if I was a gentleman, and had a hat and a watch and a topcoat and could talk refined, then I'd be virtuous, too. Virtue must be nice, Cap'n. But I'm just a poor guy.

CAPTAIN: That's fine, Woyzeck. You're a good man, a good man. But you think too much, that's unhealthy. You always look so upset. This discussion has really worn me out. You can go now—and don't run like that! Slowly, nice and slow down the street.

6

(MARIE. DRUM MAJOR.)

DRUM MAJOR: Marie!

MARIE: *(Looking at him expressively.)* Go march up and down for me. A chest like a bull and a beard like a lion. Nobody else is like that. No woman is prouder than me.

DRUM MAJOR: Sundays when I have my plumed helmet and my white gloves—goddamn, Marie! The prince always says: man, you're quite a guy!

MARIE: *(Mockingly.)* Aw, go on! *(Goes up to him.)* What a man!

DRUM MAJOR: What a woman! Hell, let's breed a race of drum majors, hey? *(He embraces her.)*

MARIE: *(Moody.)* Leave me alone!

DRUM MAJOR: You wildcat!

MARIE: *(Violently.)* Just try to touch me!

DRUM MAJOR: You've got the devil in your eyes.

MARIE: For all I care. What does it matter?

7

(On the street.)

(MARIE. WOYZECK.)

WOYZECK: *(Stares at her, shakes his head.)* Hm! I don't see anything, I don't see anything. Oh, I should be able to see it; I should be able to grab it with my fists.

MARIE: *(Intimidated.)* What's the matter, Franz? You're out of your mind, Franz.

WOYZECK: A sin so fat and so wide—it stinks enough to smoke the angels out of Heaven. You've got a red mouth, Marie. No blister on it? Good-bye, Marie. You're as beautiful as sin. Can mortal sin be so beautiful?

MARIE: Franz, you're delirious.

WOYZECK: Damn it! Was he standing here like this, like this?

MARIE: As the day is long and the world is old, lots of people can stand on one spot, one after another.

WOYZECK: I saw him.

MARIE: You can see all sorts of things if you've got two eyes and aren't blind, and the sun is shining.

WOYZECK: With my own eyes!

MARIE: *(Fresh.)* So what!

8

(At the DOCTOR's.*)*

(WOYZECK. *The* DOCTOR.)

DOCTOR: What is this I hear, Woyzeck? A man of honor!

WOYZECK: What is it, Doctor?

DOCTOR: I saw it, Woyzeck. You pissed on the street, you pissed on the wall like a dog. And you get two cents a day. Woyzeck, that's bad. The world's getting bad, very bad.

WOYZECK: But Doctor, the call of nature . . .

DOCTOR: The call of nature, the call of nature! Nature! Haven't I proved that the *musculus constrictor vesicae°* is subject to the will? Nature! Woyzeck, man is free. In man alone is individuality exalted to freedom. Couldn't hold it in! *(Shakes his head, puts his hands behind his back, and paces back and forth.)* Did you eat your peas already, Woyzeck? I'm revolutionizing science, I'll blow it sky-high. Urea ten per cent, ammonium chloride, hyperoxidic. Woyzeck, try pissing again. Go in there and try.

WOYZECK: I can't, Doctor.

---

musculus constrictor vesicae, muscle controlling the bladder.

DOCTOR: (*With emotion.*) But pissing on the wall! I have it in writing. Here's the contract. I saw it all—saw it with my own eyes. I was just holding my nose out the window, letting the sun's rays hit it, so as to examine the process of sneezing. (*Goes up to him.*) No, Woyzeck, I'm not getting angry. Anger is unhealthy, unscientific. I am calm, perfectly calm. My pulse is beating at its usual sixty, and I tell you this in all cold-bloodedness. Now, who would get excited about a human being, a human being? If it were a Proteus that were dying—! But you shouldn't have pissed on the wall . . .

WOYZECK: You see, Doctor, sometimes you've got a certain character, a certain structure. But with nature, that's something else, you see, with nature. (*He cracks his knuckles.*) That's like—how should I put it—for example . . .

DOCTOR: Woyzeck, you're philosophizing again.

WOYZECK: (*Confidingly.*) Doctor, have you ever seen anything of double nature? When the sun's standing high at noon and the world seems to be going up in flames, I've heard a terrible voice talking to me!

DOCTOR: Woyzeck, you've got an *aberratio!*°

WOYZECK: (*Puts his finger to his nose.*) The toadstools, Doctor. There—that's where it is. Have you seen how they grow in patterns? If only someone could read that.

DOCTOR: Woyzeck, you've got a marvelous *aberratio mentalis partialis,*° second species, beautifully developed. Woyzeck, you're getting a raise. Second species: fixed idea with a generally rational condition. You're doing everything as usual? Shaving your captain?

WOYZECK: Yes, sir.

DOCTOR: Eating your peas?

WOYZECK: Same as ever, Doctor. My wife gets the money for the household.

DOCTOR: Going on duty?

WOYZECK: Yes, sir.

DOCTOR: You're an interesting case. Subject Woyzeck, you're getting a raise. Now behave yourself. Show me your pulse! Yes.

9

(*Street.*)

(CAPTAIN. DOCTOR. *The* CAPTAIN *comes panting down the street, stops, pants, looks around.*)

CAPTAIN: Doctor, I feel sorry for horses when I think that the poor beasts have to go everywhere on foot. Don't run like that! Don't wave your cane around in the air like that! You'll run yourself to death that way. A good man with a good conscience doesn't go so fast. A good man . . . (*He catches the* DOCTOR *by the coat.*) Doctor, allow me to save a human life. You're racing . . . Doctor, I'm so melancholy. I get so emotional. I always start crying when I see my coat hanging on the wall—there it is.

DOCTOR: Hm! Bloated, fat, thick neck, apoplectic constitution. Yes, Captain, you might be stricken by an *apoplexia cerebralis.*° But you might get it just on one side and be half paralyzed, or—best of all—you might become mentally affected and just vegetate from then on. Those are approximately your prospects for the next four weeks. Moreover, I can assure you that you will be a most interesting case, and if, God willing, your tongue is partially paralyzed, we'll make immortal experiments.

CAPTAIN: Doctor, don't frighten me! People have been known to die of fright, of pure, sheer fright. I can see them now, with flowers in their hands—but they'll say, he was a good man, a good man. You damn coffin nail!

DOCTOR: (*Holds out his hat.*) What's this, Captain? That's brain-less!

CAPTAIN: (*Makes a crease.*) What's this, Doctor? That's increase!

DOCTOR: I take my leave, most honorable Mr. Drill-prick.

CAPTAIN: Likewise, dearest Mr. Coffin Nail.

(WOYZECK *comes running down the street.*)

CAPTAIN: Hey, Woyzeck, why are you running past us like that? Stay here, Woyzeck. You're running around like an open razor blade. You might cut someone! You're running like you had to shave a regiment of castrates and would be hanged while the last hair was disappearing. But about those long beards—what was I going to say? Woyzeck—those long beards . . .

DOCTOR: A long beard on the chin. Pliny° speaks of it. Soldiers should be made to give them up.

CAPTAIN: (*Continues.*) Hey? What about those long beards? Say, Woyzeck, haven't you found a hair from a beard in your soup bowl yet? Hey? You understand, of course, a human hair, from the beard of an engineer, a sergeant, a—drum major? Hey, Woyzeck? But you've got a decent wife. Not like others.

WOYZECK: Yes, sir! What are you trying to say, Cap'n?

CAPTAIN: Look at the face he's making! Now, it doesn't necessarily have to be in the soup, but if you hurry around the corner, you might find one on a pair of

---

aberratio, aberration. *aberratio mentalis partialis,* partial aberration.

apoplexia cerebralis, brain tumor. *Pliny,* Roman scholar (A.D. 23–79), although the story that Alexander the Great ordered his soldiers to shave their beards to prevent the enemy from grabbing them actually derives from the Greek historian Plutarch (A.D. 46–119).

lips—a pair of lips, Woyzeck. I know what love is, too, Woyzeck. Say! You're as white as chalk!

WOYZECK: Cap'n, I'm just a poor devil—and that's all I have in the world. Cap'n, if you're joking . . .

CAPTAIN: Joking? Me? Who do you think you are?

DOCTOR: Your pulse, Woyzeck, your pulse—short, hard, skipping, irregular.

WOYZECK: Cap'n, the earth is hot as hell—for me it's ice cold! Ice cold—hell is cold, I'll bet. It can't be! God! God! It can't be!

CAPTAIN: Listen, fellow, how'd you like to be shot, how'd you like to have a couple of bullets in your head? You're looking daggers at me; but I only mean well, because you're a good man, Woyzeck, a good man.

DOCTOR: Facial muscles rigid, tense, occasionally twitching. Posture erect, tense.

WOYZECK: I'm going. A lot is possible. A man! A lot is possible. The weather's nice, Cap'n. Look: such a beautiful, hard, rough sky—you'd almost feel like pounding a block of wood into it and hanging yourself on it, only because of the hyphen between yes, and yes again—and no. Cap'n, yes and no? Is no to blame for yes, or yes for no? I'll have to think about that. (*Goes off with long strides, first slowly, then ever faster.*)

DOCTOR: (*Races after him.*) A phenomenon! Woyzeck! Another raise!

CAPTAIN: These people make me dizzy. Look at them go—that tall rascal takes off like the shadow before a spider, and the short one—he's trotting along. The tall one is lightning and the short one is thunder. Ha-ha! After them. Grotesque! Grotesque!

10

(*The guardroom.*)

(WOYZECK. ANDRES.)

ANDRES: (*Sings.*)

> Our hostess has a pretty maid,
> She's in her garden night and day,
> She sits inside her garden . . .

WOYZECK: Andres!

ANDRES: Huh?

WOYZECK: Nice weather.

ANDRES: Sunday weather. There's music outside town. All the broads are out there already, everybody's sweating—it's really moving along.

WOYZECK: (*Restlessly.*) A dance, Andres. They're dancing.

ANDRES: Yeah, at the Horse and at the Star.

WOYZECK: Dancing, dancing.

ANDRES: Big deal. (*Sings.*)

> She sits inside her garden,
> Until the bells have all struck twelve,
> And stares at all the soldiers.

WOYZECK: Andres, I can't keep still.

ANDRES: Stupid!

WOYZECK: I've got to get out of here. I can't see straight. Dancing. Dancing. With their hot hands. Damn it, Andres!

ANDRES: What do you want?

WOYZECK: I've got to go.

ANDRES: With that broad?

WOYZECK: I've got to get out. It's so hot in here.

11

(*Inn.*)

(*The windows are open, a dance. Benches in front of the house.* APPRENTICES.)

FIRST APPRENTICE:

> This shirt I've got, I don't know whose,
> My soul it stinks like booze . . .

SECOND APPRENTICE: Brother, shall I in friendship bore a hole in your nature? Onward! I want to bore a hole in your nature. I'm quite a guy, too, you know. I'm going to kill all the fleas on his body.

FIRST APPRENTICE: My soul, my soul it stinks like booze. Even money must eventually decay. Forget-me-not! Oh, is this world beautiful! Brother, I could cry a rain barrel full of tears. I wish our noses were two bottles and we could pour them down each other's throats.

OTHERS: (*In chorus.*)

> A hunter from the west
> Once went riding through the woods.
> Hip-hip, hooray! A hunter's life is always gay,
> O'er meadow and o'er stream,
> Oh, hunting is my dream!

(WOYZECK *stands at the window.* MARIE *and the* DRUM MAJOR *dance past without seeing him.*)

MARIE: (*Dancing by.*) On! and on, on and on!

WOYZECK: (*Chokes.*) On and on! On and on! (*Jumps up violently and sinks back on the bench.*) On and on, on and on. (*Beats his hands together.*) Spin around, roll around. Why doesn't God blow out the sun so that everything can roll around in lust, man and woman, man and beast. They'll do it in broad daylight, they'll do it on our hands, like flies. Woman! That woman is hot, hot! On and on, on and on. (*Jumps up.*) The bastard! Look how he's grabbing her, grabbing her body! He—he's got her now, like I used to have her!

FIRST APPRENTICE: *(Preaches on the table.)* Yet when a wanderer stands leaning against the stream of time and/or gives answer in the wisdom of God, asking himself: Why does Man exist? Why does Man exist? But verily I say unto you: how could the farmer, the cooper, the shoemaker, the doctor exist if God hadn't created man? How could the tailor exist if God hadn't given man a feeling of shame? How could the soldier exist, if men didn't feel the necessity of killing one another? Therefore, do not ye despair, yes, yes, life is lovely and fine, yet all that is earthly is passing, even money must eventually decay. In conclusion, my dear friends, let us piss crosswise so that a Jew will die.

12

(Open field.)

WOYZECK: On and on! On and on! Shh! Music! *(Stretches out on the ground.)* Ha—what—what are you saying? Louder, louder . . . stab—stab the bitch to death? Stab—stab the bitch to death. Should I? Must I? Do I hear it over there, is the wind saying it too? It goes on and on—stab her to death . . . to death.

13

(Night.)

(ANDRES *and* WOYZECK *in a bed.*)

WOYZECK: *(Shakes* ANDRES.*)* Andres! Andres! I can't sleep. When I close my eyes, everything starts turning, and I hear the fiddles, on and on, on and on, and then there's a voice from the wall. Don't you hear anything?

ANDRES: Oh, yeah. Let them dance! God bless us, amen. *(Falls asleep again.)*

WOYZECK: It keeps saying: stab, stab! And it floats between my eyes like a knife.

ANDRES: Drink some brandy with a painkiller in it. That'll cut your fever.

14

(Inn.)

(DRUM MAJOR. WOYZECK. ONLOOKERS.)

DRUM MAJOR: I'm a man! *(Pounds his chest.)* A man, you hear? Who wants to start something? If you're not drunk as a lord, stay away from me. I'll shove your nose up your ass. I'll . . . *(To* WOYZECK.*)* Man, have a drink. A man gotta drink. I wish the world was booze, booze.

WOYZECK: *(Whistles.)*

DRUM MAJOR: You bastard, you want me to pull your tongue out of your throat and wrap it around you?

(They wrestle, WOYZECK *loses.)* You want me to leave you enough breath to fart with?

(WOYZECK *sits on the bench, exhausted and trembling.*)

DRUM MAJOR: He thinks he's so great. Ha!

Oh, brandy, that's my life,
Oh, brandy gives me courage!

AN ONLOOKER: He sure got his.
ANOTHER: He's bleeding.
WOYZECK: One thing after another.

15

(Shop.)

(WOYZECK. *The* JEW.)

WOYZECK: The pistol costs too much.
JEW: Well, do you want it or don't you?
WOYZECK: How much is the knife?
JEW: It's good and straight. You want to cut your throat with it? Well, how about it? I'll give it to you as cheap as anybody else. Your death'll be cheap—but not for nothing. How about it? You'll have an economical death.
WOYZECK: That can cut more than just bread.
JEW: Two cents.
WOYZECK: There! *(Goes off.)*
JEW: There! Like it was nothing. But it's money! The dog.

16

(Room.)

(MARIE. KARL, *the idiot.* CHILD.)

MARIE: *(Leafs through the Bible.)* "And no guile is found in his mouth"° . . . My God! my God! Don't look at me. *(Pages further.)* "And the scribes and Pharisees brought unto him a woman taken in adultery, and set her in the midst . . . And Jesus said unto her, 'Neither do I condemn thee: go, and sin no more'"° *(Clasps her hands together.)* My God! My God, I can't. God, just give me enough strength to pray. *(The* CHILD *snuggles up to her.)* The boy is like a knife in my heart. Karl! He's sunning himself.
KARL: *(Lies on the ground and tells himself fairy tales on his fingers.)* This one has a golden crown—he's a king. Tomorrow I'll go get the queen's child. Blood sausage says, come on, liver sausage! *(He takes the* CHILD *and is quiet.)*
MARIE: Franz hasn't come, not yesterday, not today. It's getting hot in here. *(She opens the window.)* "And

---

"*And no guile . . . mouth,*" 1 Peter 2:22.   "***And the scribes . . . more,***" John 8:3–11.

stood at his feet weeping, and began to wash his feet with tears, and did wipe them with the hairs of her head, and kissed his feet, and anointed them with ointment."° (*Beats her breast.*) It's all dead! Savior, Savior, I wish I could anoint your feet!

17

(*Barracks.*)

(ANDRES. WOYZECK *rummages through his things.*)

WOYZECK: This jacket isn't part of the uniform, Andres. You can use it, Andres. The crucifix is my sister's—so's the little ring. I've got an icon, too—two hearts in beautiful gold. It was in my mother's Bible, and it says:

May pain be my reward,
Through pain I love my Lord.

Lord, like Thy body, red and sore,
So be my heart forevermore.

My mother can only feel the sun shining on her hands now. That doesn't matter.
ANDRES: (*Blankly, answers to everything.*) Yeah.
WOYZECK: (*Pulls out a piece of paper.*) Friedrich Johann Franz Woyzeck, soldier, rifleman in the second regiment, second battalion, fourth company, born on the Feast of the Annunciation. Today I'm thirty years, seven months, and twelve days old.
ANDRES: Franz, you better go to the hospital. You poor guy—drink brandy with a painkiller in it. That'll kill the fever.
WOYZECK: You know, Andres, when the carpenter nails those boards together, nobody knows who's going to be lying between them.

18

(*The* DOCTOR'S *courtyard.*)

(STUDENTS *below, the* DOCTOR *at the attic window.*)

DOCTOR: Gentlemen, I am on the roof like David when he saw Bathsheba,° but all I see are panties hanging in the garden of the girls' boarding house. Gentlemen, we are dealing with the important question of the relationship of subject to object. If we take only one of the things in which the organic self-affirmation of the Divine manifests itself to such a high degree, and examine its relationship to space,

to the earth, to the planetary system . . . gentlemen, if I throw this cat out of the window, how will it relate to the *centrum gravitationis*° and to its own instinct? Hey, Woyzeck. (*Shouts.*) Woyzeck! (DOCTOR *comes down.*)
WOYZECK: Doctor, it bites!
DOCTOR: The fellow holds the beast so tenderly, like it was his own grandmother!
WOYZECK: Doctor, I've got the shivers.
DOCTOR: (*Elated.*) Say, that's wonderful, Woyzeck! (*Rubs his hands. He takes the cat.*) What's this, gentlemen—a new species of rabbit louse, a beautiful species. (*He pulls out a magnifying glass.*) Gentlemen—(*The cat runs off.*) gentlemen, that animal has no scientific instinct. Gentlemen, instead of that you can see something else. Take note of this man—for a quarter of a year he hasn't eaten anything but peas. Notice the result. Feel how uneven his pulse is. There—and the eyes.
WOYZECK: Doctor, everything's getting black. (*He sits down.*)
DOCTOR: Courage! Just a few more days, Woyzeck, and then it'll be all over. Feel him, gentlemen, feel him. (STUDENTS *feel his temples, pulse, and chest.*) Apropos, Woyzeck *wiggle your ears for the gentlemen. I meant to show it to you before. He uses two muscles. Come on, hop to it!
WOYZECK: Oh, Doctor!
DOCTOR: You dog, do I have to wiggle them for you? Are you going to act like the cat? This, gentlemen, represents a transition to the donkey, frequently resulting from being brought up by women and from the use of the mother tongue. How much hair has your mother pulled out for a tender memory? It's gotten very thin in the last few days. Yes, the peas, gentlemen.

19

(*Street.*)

(MARIE *with little girls in front of the house door.* GRANDMOTHER. *Then* WOYZECK.)

GIRLS:

How bright the sun on Candlemas Day,
On fields of golden grain.
As two by two they marched along
Down the country lane.
The pipers up in front,
The fiddlers in a chain.
Their red socks . . .

"*And stood at his feet . . . ointment,*" Luke 7:37–38.
David when he saw Bathsheba, cf. 2 Sam. 11:2ff.

---

centrum gravitationis, center of gravity.

FIRST CHILD: I don't like it!
SECOND CHILD: What do you want, anyway?
THIRD CHILD: Why'd you start it?
SECOND CHILD: Yeah, why?
FIRST CHILD: Because!
SECOND CHILD: Why because?
THIRD CHILD: Who's going to sing—? *(Looks questioningly around the circle and points to the* FIRST CHILD.*)*
FIRST CHILD: I can't.
ALL THE CHILDREN: Marie, you sing to us.
MARIE: Come, you little crabs.

(Children's games: "Ring-around-a-rosy" and "King Herod."°)

Grandmother, tell a story.
GRANDMOTHER: Once upon a time, there was a poor little child with no father and no mother. Everything was dead, and no one was left in the whole world. Everything was dead, and the child went and cried day and night. And since nobody was left on the earth, he wanted to go up to the heavens, 'cause the moon was looking at him so friendly, and when he finally got to the moon, the moon was a piece of rotten wood, and then he went to the sun, and when he got there, the sun was a wilted sunflower, and when he got to the stars, they were little golden flies stuck up there like the shrike° sticks them on the blackthorn; and when he wanted to go back down to the earth, the earth was an upset pot, and the child was all alone, and he sat down and cried, and there he sits to this day, all alone.
WOYZECK: Marie!
MARIE: *(Startled.)* What is it?
WOYZECK: Marie, we have to go. It's time.
MARIE: Where to?
WOYZECK: How do I know?

20

(Evening. The town in the distance.)

*(*MARIE. WOYZECK.*)*

MARIE: That must be the town back there. It's dark.
WOYZECK: Stay here. Come on, sit down.
MARIE: But I have to get back.
WOYZECK: You won't get sore feet.
MARIE: What's gotten into you!
WOYZECK: Do you know how long it's been, Marie?
MARIE: Two years since Pentecost.°

"King Herod," the name of the children's game or rhyme derives from the biblical figure who ordered the massacre of children (Matt. 2). *shrike,* also known as the "butcher bird" because it impales its prey on thorns. *Pentecost,* Christian festival commemorating the revelation of the Holy Spirit to the apostles.

WOYZECK: Do you know how long it's going to be?
MARIE: I've got to go make supper.
WOYZECK: Are you freezing, Marie? But you're warm. How hot your lips are! Hot—the hot breath of a whore—but I'd give heaven and earth to kiss them once more. Once you're cold, you don't freeze anymore. The morning dew won't make you freeze.
MARIE: What are you talking about?
WOYZECK: Nothing. *(Silence.)*
MARIE: Look how red the moon is.
WOYZECK: Like a bloody blade.
MARIE: What are you up to? Franz, you're so pale. *(He pulls out the knife.)* Franz—wait! For God's sake—help!
WOYZECK: Take that and that! Can't you die? There! There! Ah—she's still twitching. Not yet? Not yet? Still alive? *(Keeps on stabbing.)* Are you dead? Dead! Dead! *(People approach, he runs off.)*

21

(Two people.)

FIRST PERSON: Wait!
SECOND PERSON: You hear it? Shh! Over there!
FIRST PERSON: Ooh! There! What a sound!
SECOND PERSON: That's the water, it's calling. Nobody has drowned for a long time. Let's go. It's bad to hear things like that.
FIRST PERSON: Ooh! There it is again. Like someone dying.
SECOND PERSON: It's weird. It's so foggy—gray mist everywhere and the beetles humming like broken bells. Let's get out of here!
FIRST PERSON: No—it's too clear, too loud. Up this way. Come on.

22

(Inn.)

*(*WOYZECK. KATEY. KARL. INNKEEPER. *People.)*

WOYZECK: Dance, all of you, on and on. Sweat and stink. He'll get you all in the end. *(Sings.)*

Our hostess has a pretty maid,
She's in her garden night and day,
She sits inside her garden,
Until the bells have all struck twelve,
And stares at all the soldiers.

(He dances.) Come on, Katey! Sit down! I'm hot, hot. *(He takes off his jacket.)* That's the way it is: the devil takes one and lets the other go. Katey, you're hot! Why? Katey, you'll be cold someday, too. Be reasonable. Can't you sing something?
KATEY: *(Sings.)*

For Swabian hills I do not yearn,
And flowing gowns I always spurn,
For flowing gowns and pointed shoes
A servant girl should never choose.

WOYZECK: No, no shoes. You can go to hell without
shoes, too.
KATEY: *(Dances.)*

For shame, my love, I'm not your own,
Just keep your money and sleep alone.

WOYZECK: Yes, you're right! I don't want to make my-
self bloody.
KATEY: But what's that on your hand?
WOYZECK: Who? Me?
KATEY: Red . . . blood! *(People gather around.)*
WOYZECK: Blood? Blood.
INNKEEPER: Ooh. Blood.
WOYZECK: I guess I must have cut myself on my right
hand.
INNKEEPER: But how'd it get on your elbow?
WOYZECK: I wiped it off.
INNKEEPER: What! With your right hand on your right
elbow? You're talented.
KARL: And then the giant said: I smell, I smell, I smell
human flesh. Phew! That stinks already.
WOYZECK: Damn it, what do you want? What do you
care? Get away, or the first one who . . . God damn
it! You think I killed someone? Am I a murderer?
What are you staring at? Look at yourselves! Out
of my way! *(He runs out.)*

23

(Night. The town in the distance.)

(WOYZECK alone.)

WOYZECK: The knife? Where's the knife? Here's where
I left it. It'll give me away! Closer, still closer! What
kind of a place is this? What's that I hear? Something's moving. Shh! Over there. Marie? Ah—
Marie! Quiet. Everything's quiet! You're so pale,
Marie. Why is that red thread around your neck?
Who helped you earn that for your sins? They
made you black, black! Now I've made you white.
Your black hair looks so wild. Didn't you do your
braids today? Something's lying over there! Cold,
wet, still. Got to get away from here. The knife, the
knife—is that it? There! People—over there. *(He
runs off.)*

24

(WOYZECK at a pond.)

WOYZECK: Down it goes! *(He throws the knife in.)* It sinks
like a stone in the dark water. The moon is like a

bloody blade. Is the whole world going to give me
away? No—it's too far in front—when people go
swimming—*(He goes into the pond and throws it far
out.)* All right, now—but in the summer, when they
go diving for shells . . . Oh, it'll rust. Who'll recognize it? I wish I'd smashed it! Am I still bloody? I
better wash myself. There's a spot—and there's another.°

25

(Street.)

(Children.)

FIRST CHILD: Come on! Marie!
SECOND CHILD: What's wrong?
FIRST CHILD: Don't you know? Everybody's gone out
there already. Someone's lying there!
SECOND CHILD: Where?
FIRST CHILD: To the left through the forest, near that
red cross.
SECOND CHILD: Let's go, so we can still see something.
Otherwise they'll carry her away.

26

(COURT CLERK, DOCTOR, JUDGE.)

CLERK: A good murder, a real murder, a beautiful murder. As good a murder as you'd ever want to see.
We haven't had one like this for a long time.

27

(KARL. The CHILD. WOYZECK.)

KARL: *(Holds the CHILD on his lap.)* He fell in the water,
he fell in the water, he fell in the water.
WOYZECK: Son—Christian!
KARL: *(Stares at him.)* He fell in the water.
WOYZECK: *(Wants to caress the CHILD, who turns away and
screams.)* My God!
KARL: He fell in the water.
WOYZECK: Christian, you'll get a horsey. Da-da! *(The
CHILD resists. To KARL.)* Here, go buy the boy a hor-
sey.
KARL: *(Stares at him.)*
WOYZECK: Hop-hop! Horsey!
KARL: *(Cheers.)* Hop-hop! Horsey! Horsey! *(Runs off with
the CHILD.)*

(WOYZECK remains, alone.)

There's a spot . . . another, cf. *Macbeth* 5.1.

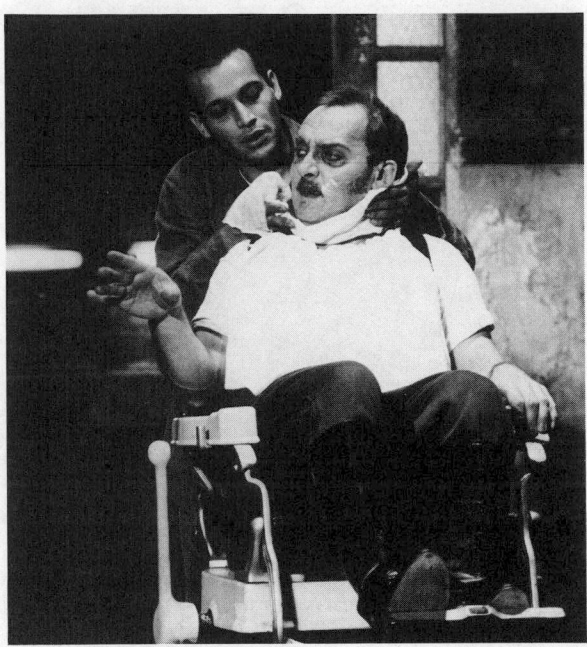

Figure 1. Woyzeck (Jesse Borrego) shaves the Captain (Zach Grenier) in the 1992 New York Shakespeare Festival production, directed by JoAnne Akalaitis. (Photograph: Martha Swope.)

Figure 2. The townspeople stare at Woyzeck (Jesse Borrego) after the murder of Marie in the 1992 New York Shakespeare Festival production, directed by JoAnne Akalaitis. (Photograph: Martha Swope.)

Figure 3. The murder of Marie (Sheila Tousey) takes place in slow motion, focusing attention on Woyzeck's (Jesse Borrego) upraised hand and Marie's attempt to stop the knife's descent in the 1992 New York Shakespeare Festival production, directed by JoAnne Akalaitis. (Photograph: Martha Swope).

Staging of *Woyzeck*

REVIEW OF THE NEW YORK SHAKESPEARE
FESTIVAL PRODUCTION, 1992, BY MEL
GUSSOW

The title character in "Woyzeck" is, we are told, "running around like an open razor blade." The image, in common with the play itself, is as precise as it is terrifying. Woyzeck, a military barber and the most ordinary of common men, is overcome by dementia. He hears strange sounds, sees visions and is driven to a desperate act of murder. Along with "Danton's Death," the play certified Georg Büchner's reputation as the first modern playwright. Written in the 1830's and discovered as fragments after the author's death, the work foreshadowed explorations by Kafka, Brecht and Beckett. The modernism of Büchner is basic to JoAnne Akalaitis's compelling production of the Joseph Papp Public Theater in New York.

Because of the nonlinear style and the focus on an irrational antihero, the play is open to free-handed interpretation. In search of "Woyzeck," Ms. Akalaitis uses alternate scenes and extracts from early drafts of the play, filtering Henry J. Schmidt's translation through her fervid theatrical imagination. The difficulty this director has had in dealing with Shakespeare is not in evidence in her treatment of Büchner.

In the reordering of scenes the play gains in momentum, accruing intensity and psychological awareness as Woyzeck moves through the last stages of his calamitous life. The director has given greater centricity to the role of Marie, Woyzeck's common-law wife and the object of his homicidal impulse. But of course this is still Woyzeck's tragedy, as he is crushed by people and events beyond his control.

Ms. Akalaitis has accentuated the folk elements within the play, crucial to Büchner, for whom this was a ballad-like dramatization of an actual occurrence. Philip Glass's sizzling music is often paired with folk-style lyrics by Paul Schmidt, and martial clog dancing adds to the ritualistic background.

In contrast to the stark simplicity of Richard Foreman's version of the play several seasons ago at Hartford Stage, Ms. Akalaitis's approach has a visual richness. The productions are equally valid but they are so dissimilar in concept that they could be staged together in repertory. Naturally they share the same themes, characters and impact.

Ms. Akalaitis takes a cue from her own early work as a director and playwright with Mabou Mines, in terms of using imagery to enhance a text, as she did in "Dressed Like an Egg," her lush collage of the life of Colette. With "Woyzeck," she seems to be influenced by German Expressionist art. In scene after scene there are striking stage pictures of people caught in a frenzy or in a moment of aggrieved anticipation.

The military barracks that is the central environment of the play would need no conversion to become a concentration camp. As designed by Marina Draghici, who did the impressive settings for Caryl Churchill's "Mad Forest," the scenery simulates all the coldness and malevolence of a life in confinement. The bare plastered walls and streaked windows, evocatively lighted by Mimi Jordan Sherin, are like conjurations of the paintings of Anselm Kiefer.

Woyzeck (Jesse Borrego) tears across the stage in a fever. In his rag uniform and with a haunted look in his deep-set eyes, Mr. Borrego resembles a prisoner of Dachau suddenly released and brought into a blinding light. Repeatedly he is transfixed like an apparition in a nightmare.

Shaving his captain (Zach Grenier), Woyzeck strops his razor for so long that it seems as if he is sharpening his blade for slaughter. The autocratic officer flinches as the barber approaches his chair; still he never stops badgering his subordinate. Wherever Woyzeck turns, he is besieged, even, as it turns out, in his home, up to then his single sanctuary. In response, he tries to outrun his demons.

In those moments when things stand still, velocity is replaced by what could be called frieze frames. Townspeople sit in a line as in a pew and a grandmother tells the bleakest and most Büchnerian of fairy tales: "Once upon a time there was a poor child with no father and no mother; everything was dead, and no one was left in the whole world."

Ms. Akalaitis uses her painterly eye to illuminate motifs, but along the way there are a few questionable directorial choices. The production begins awkwardly with a film clip of Mr. Borrego climbing rocks. This is apparently a scene from Ms. Akalaitis's adaptation of other Büchner works, which she entitled "Leon and Lena (Lenz)," and presented at the Guthrie Theater. The film has no direct bearing on the play we are seeing. The carnival sequence is surprisingly mundane and a scene of soldiers showering detracts from a later, symbolic moment when Woyzeck tries to wash away his bloody deed.

Furthermore, some of the acting lacks resilience, even allowing for the fact that those characters who have no names, like the drum major, are intended to be emblematic. But the production is anchored by the actors in the three most important roles: the commandingly imperious Mr. Grenier as the captain, Sheila Tousey as Marie and Mr. Borrego, who grasps the tortured essence of Woyzeck.

When he turns against Marie, who has been his only source of stability, he attacks her as if she were the incarnation of everything that had been bedeviling him. The scene is staged with ferocity: the victim is helpless, the murderer uncontrollable. Around the time he was creating "Woyzeck," Büchner wrote a letter to his parents in which he commented on German militarism and what he considered to be the brute force of the law. He asked, "Aren't we in an eternal state of violence?" That question and its accompanying cry for help are searingly captured by the playwright and by Ms. Akalaitis as his contemporary interpreter.

HENRIK IBSEN

When Ibsen was born, his father was a prosperous merchant in Skien, a small town in the southeastern part of Norway, but by the time Ibsen was eight his father had gone bankrupt and the family was compelled to leave its spacious home for quarters in an attic apartment filled with the abandoned possessions of a previous tenant. Ibsen never forgot that painful reversal of fortune. In fact, he recorded its details in an unfinished autobiography that he began in 1881. That early exposure to human suffering was to leave its mark on many of his plays, not in any specific autobiographical sense, but in a general concern with the economic, social, and psychological conditions that afflict the lives of ordinary men and women.

During his early dramatic career, from 1851 to 1867, when he was still influenced by the style and subject matter of romantic theater, Ibsen wrote a series of plays in blank verse, most of them based on Norwegian myth and history. Yet even in these works, particularly *Brand* (1866) and *Peer Gynt* (1867), Ibsen revealed a concern with moral and social issues that was to characterize his later plays. In Brand he created a protagonist so single-mindedly committed to his religious ministry that he sacrifices first his child, then his wife, and ultimately himself to the fulfillment of his mission; then in the character of Peer Gynt, the demonic antithesis of Brand, he created a protagonist so committed to his own selfish desires that he devotes his life to a series of fanatically deceitful adventures with which he deceives even himself, until at the moment of his death he discovers his irredeemable hollowness. Although *Brand* and *Peer Gynt* made Ibsen famous and financially secure, they were the last works he was to write in the tradition of romantic drama.

Beginning with *The League of Youth* (1869), a play that attacked the hypocrisy of provincial politics and politicians, Ibsen turned from history, myth, and folklore to contemporary social problems, from romantic idealism to realistic drama, from verse to prose. In *The Pillars of Society* (1877), he continued his iconoclastic aims by exposing the disreputable behavior of a socially respectable businessman and by reforming him through the agency of a socially liberated woman. Having attacked business and politics, he then went after the most sacred of all social institutions—marriage—by making the heroine of this next play, *A Doll's House* (1879), a young wife who gradually becomes aware that she has been turned into a helpless child by her husband, whom she abandons after discovering that he is an emotional hypocrite. Ibsen's audience was shocked by the ending of *A Doll's House,* but he was unrelenting in his attack and answered their outrage with *Ghosts* (1881), whose heroine heeds the advice of her minister to remain with her husband and, therefore, must spend the rest of her life concealing her own feelings and the truth about her husband's dissolute behavior. Ibsen's frank treatment of syphilis in *Ghosts,* and his implicit attack on Norwegian social and religious values, roused even stronger criticism than *A Doll's House.* It is not surprising that Ibsen's next play, *An Enemy of the People*

(1882), dealt with the difficulty of being the outsider who brings unpleasant truths to the attention of the community. Then, in a startling reversal, Ibsen made the truth bringer in *The Wild Duck* (1884) a morally ambiguous figure, so intent on forcing long-hid secrets into the open that he destroys an entire family. In his late, symbolic plays, particularly *Rosmersholm* (1886), *Hedda Gabler* (1890), and *The Master Builder* (1892), Ibsen moved away from his concern with social problems into a psychological exploration of emotionally and sexually driven individuals who become entangled in self-destructive personal relationships.

This body of plays quickly earned Ibsen the reputation of a fighting social realist—a description applied to him by his Anglo-Irish contemporary, George Bernard Shaw, in *The Quintessence of Ibsenism* (1891). And from his own time to this day, many of Ibsen's prose plays have been interpreted primarily as pieces of social criticism. *A Doll's House,* for example, is frequently celebrated nowadays as an attack on male chauvinism and an affirmation of womens' rights. And there is much about the relationship of Torvald and Nora that supports this interpretation, not the least of which is his nearly total subjugation and humiliation of her—his conception of her as his "little songbird" and "doll"—as well as her final rejection of his belief that "First and foremost, you're a wife and a mother," and her consequent decision "to think things out for myself and try to find my own answer." Yet it is also important to recognize that *A Doll's House,* like Ibsen's other prose plays, is first and foremost a psychologically realistic work about a human being in an ordinary world who slowly and painfully comes to an extraordinary understanding about the importance of personal integrity in human affairs. That special understanding leads Nora to assert that "I am first and foremost a human being." And that belief leads her at last to leave Torvald not because he has subjugated her, but because he has profoundly disappointed her by valuing his material welfare and social status more highly than her human love. So it is that she is moved to tell Torvald "you neither think nor talk like the man I could share my life with." The implication of these remarks seems to be that she could have forgiven him everything had he finally been true to her hopeful vision of him. Her departure, then, might well be seen as the logical consequence of her shattered illusions about Torvald, rather than an assertion of her woman's rights.

Ibsen himself may well have meant to show both Nora and Torvald as being imprisoned in their relationship, even though for years the play has been read as his plea for female emancipation. Ibsen explicitly disclaimed a feminist interpretation of the play several years after its production, when speaking to a meeting of the Norwegian Association for Women's Rights: "I must decline the honor of being said to have worked for the Women's Rights movement. I am not even very sure what Women's Rights are. To me it has been a question of human rights." Given Ibsen's disclaimer, the play might well be interpreted as a skillfully constructed piece that begins as a suspense story (Will Nora be able to keep Torvald from learning her guilty secret?), but develops into a painfully probing exposure of a human relationship based on misunderstanding and lack of communication, a relationship that denies both individuals their human rights. As Nora accurately observes near the end, "In eight whole years—longer even—ever since we first met, we've never exchanged a serious word on any serious thing." The problem of the play, in this sense, appears to be less an issue of Nora's rights than the issue of what a marriage must be if it is to achieve the "miracle of miracles"—a true and lasting relationship that allows both partners their human rights.

Just the same, readers and spectators may find themselves troubled by the plausibility of Nora's transformation from a naive young wife into a resolutely independent human being—from someone who at the beginning of the play is given over to relishing her macaroons, begging money from Torvald, and flirting with Dr. Rank into someone who at the end is able to abandon all of these comfortable pleasures, as well as her children, without having any "idea what will happen to me." This transformation provides a major problem for any actress who plays the role of Nora, as Walter Kerr noted in his review of the 1971 production starring Claire Bloom: "How does one turn an enchanting child into a dominating adult, especially when the transition is missing?" To do so, as Kerr makes clear in his review, evidently requires an actress to convey more than mere childishness in the beginning, even as it requires her to convey something other than mere domination at the end. And photographs of Claire Bloom performing the role of Nora show that in the beginning of the play she did suggest a degree of thoughtful reservation far exceeding that of a child (see Figure 1), much as at the end of the play she expressed a sense of painful awareness and resoluteness not to be expected of a merely dominating adult (see Figures 2 and 3). In her facial expression, as in the austere clothing she wears during the final scene, Claire Bloom portrays Nora as someone who is clearly aware that in slamming the door on Torvald she has relinquished a set of emotional ties that still tug at her without any clear sense of what will become of her.

A DOLL'S HOUSE

BY HENRIK IBSEN / TRANSLATED BY MICHAEL MEYER

CHARACTERS

TORVALD HELMER, *a lawyer*
NORA, *his wife*
DR. RANK
MRS. LINDE
NILS KROGSTAD, *also a lawyer*
The HELMERS' *three small children*

ANNE-MARIE, *their nurse*
HELEN, *the maid*
A PORTER

SCENE

The action takes place in the Helmers' apartment.

ACT 1

(A comfortably and tastefully, but not expensively furnished room. Backstage right a door leads out to the hall; backstage left, another door to HELMER's study. Between these two doors stands a piano. In the middle of the left-hand wall is a door, with a window downstage of it. Near the window, a round table with armchairs and a small sofa. In the right-hand wall, slightly upstage, is a door; downstage of this, against the same wall, a stove lined with porcelain tiles, with a couple of armchairs and a rocking-chair in front of it. Between the stove and the side door is a small table. Engravings on the wall. A what-not with china and other bric-a-brac; a small bookcase with leather-bound books. A carpet on the floor; a fire in the stove. A winter day.

A bell rings in the hall outside. After a moment, we hear the front door being opened. NORA enters the room, humming contentedly to herself. She is wearing outdoor clothes and carrying a lot of parcels, which she puts down on the table right. She leaves the door to the hall open; through it, we can see a PORTER carrying a Christmas tree and a basket. He gives these to the MAID, who has opened the door for them.)

NORA: Hide that Christmas tree away, Helen. The children mustn't see it before I've decorated it this evening. *(to the PORTER, taking out her purse)* How much—?

PORTER: A shilling.

NORA: Here's half a crown. No, keep it.

(The PORTER touches his cap and goes. NORA closes the door. She continues to laugh happily to herself as she removes her coat, etc. She takes from her pocket a bag containing macaroons and eats a couple. Then she tiptoes across and listens at her husband's door.)

NORA: Yes, he's here. *(Starts humming again as she goes over to the table, right.)*

HELMER *(from his room)*: Is that my skylark twittering out there?

NORA *(opening some of the parcels)*: It is!

HELMER: Is that my squirrel rustling?

NORA: Yes!

HELMER: When did my squirrel come home?

NORA: Just now. *(Pops the bag of macaroons in her pocket and wipes her mouth.)* Come out here, Torvald, and see what I've bought.

HELMER: You mustn't disturb me! *(Short pause, then he opens the door and looks in, his pen in his hand.)* Bought, did you say? All that? Has my little squanderbird been overspending again?

NORA: Oh, Torvald, surely we can let ourselves go a little this year! It's the first Christmas we don't have to scrape.

HELMER: Well, you know, we can't afford to be extravagant.

NORA: Oh yes, Torvald, we can be a little extravagant now. Can't we? Just a tiny bit? You've got a big salary now, and you're going to make lots and lots of money.

HELMER: Next year, yes. But my new salary doesn't start till April.

NORA: Pooh; we can borrow till then.

HELMER: Nora! *(Goes over to her and takes her playfully by the ear.)* What a little spendthrift you are! Suppose I were to borrow fifty pounds today, and you spent it all over Christmas, and then on New Year's Eve a tile fell off a roof on to my head—

NORA *(puts her hand over his mouth)*: Oh, Torvald! Don't say such dreadful things!

HELMER: Yes, but suppose something like that did happen? What then?

NORA: If anything as frightful as that happened, it wouldn't make much difference whether I was in debt or not.

HELMER: But what about the people I'd borrowed from?

NORA: Them? Who cares about them? They're strangers.

HELMER: Oh, Nora, Nora, how like a woman! No, but seriously, Nora, you know how I feel about this. No debts! Never borrow! A home that is founded on debts can never be a place of freedom and beauty. We two have stuck it out bravely up to now; and we shall continue to do so for the short time we still have to.

NORA *(goes over toward the stove)*: Very well, Torvald. As you say.

HELMER *(follows her)*: Now, now! My little songbird mustn't droop her wings. What's this? Is little squirrel sulking? *(Takes out his purse.)* Nora; guess what I've got here!

NORA *(turns quickly)*: Money!

HELMER: Look. *(Hands her some banknotes.)* I know how these small expenses crop up at Christmas.

NORA *(counts them)*: One—two—three—four. Oh, thank you, Torvald, thank you! I should be able to manage with this.

HELMER: You'll have to.

NORA: Yes, yes, of course I will. But come over here, I want to show you everything I've bought. And so cheaply! Look, here are new clothes for Ivar— and a sword. And a horse and a trumpet for Bob. And a doll and a cradle for Emmy—they're nothing much, but she'll pull them apart in a few days. And some bits of material and handkerchiefs for the maids. Old Anne-Marie ought to have had something better, really.

HELMER: And what's in that parcel?

NORA *(cries)*: No, Torvald, you mustn't see that before this evening!

HELMER: Very well. But now, tell me, you little spendthrift, what do you want for Christmas?

NORA: Me? Oh, pooh, I don't want anything.

HELMER: Oh, yes, you do. Now tell me, what, within reason, would you most like?

NORA: No, I really don't know. Oh, yes—Torvald—!

HELMER: Well?

NORA *(plays with his coat-buttons, not looking at him)*: If you really want to give me something, you could—you could—

HELMER: Come on, out with it.

NORA *(quickly)*: You could give me money, Torvald. Only as much as you feel you can afford; then later I'll buy something with it.

HELMER: But, Nora—

NORA: Oh yes, Torvald dear, please! Please! Then I'll wrap up the notes in pretty gold paper and hang them on the Christmas tree. Wouldn't that be fun?

HELMER: What's the name of that little bird that can never keep any money?

NORA: Yes, yes, squanderbird; I know. But let's do as I say, Torvald; then I'll have time to think about what I need most. Isn't that the best way? Mm?

HELMER *(smiles)*: To be sure it would be, if you could keep what I gave you and really buy yourself something with it. But you'll spend it on all sorts of useless things for the house, and then I'll have to put my hand in my pocket again.

NORA: Oh, but Torvald—

HELMER: You can't deny it, Nora dear. *(Puts his arm round her waist.)* The squanderbird's a pretty little creature, but she gets through an awful lot of money. It's incredible what an expensive pet she is for a man to keep.

NORA: For shame! How can you say such a thing? I save every penny I can.

HELMER *(laughs)*: That's quite true. Every penny you can. But you can't.

NORA *(hums and smiles, quietly gleeful)*: Hm. If you only knew how many expenses we larks and squirrels have, Torvald.

HELMER: You're a funny little creature. Just like your father used to be. Always on the look-out for some way to get money, but as soon as you have any it just runs through your fingers, and you never know where it's gone. Well, I suppose I must take you as you are. It's in your blood. Yes, yes, yes, these things are hereditary, Nora.

NORA: Oh, I wish I'd inherited more of Papa's qualities.

HELMER: And I wouldn't wish my darling little songbird to be any different from what she is. By the way, that reminds me. You look awfully— how shall I put it?—awfully guilty today.

NORA: Do I—

HELMER: Yes, you do. Look me in the eyes.

NORA *(looks at him)*: Well?

HELMER *(wags his finger)*: Has my little sweet-tooth been indulging herself in town today, by any chance?

NORA: No, how can you think of such a thing?

HELMER: Not a tiny little digression into a pastry shop?

NORA: No, Torvald, I promise—

HELMER: Not just a wee jam tart?

NORA: Certainly not.

HELMER: Not a little nibble at a macaroon?

NORA: No, Torvald—I promise you, honestly—

HELMER: There, there. I was only joking.

NORA *(goes over to the table, right)*: You know I could never act against your wishes.

HELMER: Of course not. And you've given me your word—*(Goes over to her.)* Well, my beloved Nora, you keep your little Christmas secrets to yourself. They'll be revealed this evening, I've no doubt, once the Christmas tree has been lit.

NORA: Have you remembered to invite Dr. Rank?

HELMER: No. But there's no need; he knows he'll be dining with us. Anyway, I'll ask him when he comes this morning. I've ordered some good wine. Oh, Nora, you can't imagine how I'm looking forward to this evening.

NORA: So am I. And, Torvald, how the children will love it!

HELMER: Yes, it's a wonderful thing to know that one's position is assured and that one has an ample income. Don't you agree? It's good to know that, isn't it?

NORA: Yes, it's almost like a miracle.

HELMER: Do you remember last Christmas? For three whole weeks you shut yourself away every evening to make flowers for the Christmas tree, and all those other things you were going to surprise us with. Ugh, it was the most boring time I've ever had in my life.

NORA: I didn't find it boring.

HELMER (smiles): But it all came to nothing in the end, didn't it?

NORA: Oh, are you going to bring that up again? How could I help the cat getting in and tearing everything to bits?

HELMER: No, my poor little Nora, of course you couldn't. You simply wanted to make us happy, and that's all that matters. But it's good that those hard times are past.

NORA: Yes, it's wonderful.

HELMER: I don't have to sit by myself and be bored. And you don't have to tire your pretty eyes and your delicate little hands—

NORA (claps her hands): No, Torvald, that's true, isn't it—I don't have to any longer? Oh, it's really all just like a miracle. (Takes his arm.) Now, I'm going to tell you what I thought we might do, Torvald. As soon as Christmas is over—(A bell rings in the hall.) Oh, there's the doorbell. (Tidies up one or two things in the room.) Someone's coming. What a bore.

HELMER: I'm not at home to any visitors. Remember!

MAID (in the doorway): A lady's called, madam. A stranger.

NORA: Well, ask her to come in.

MAID: And the doctor's here too, sir.

HELMER: Has he gone to my room?

MAID: Yes, sir.

(HELMER goes into his room. The MAID shows in MRS. LINDE, who is dressed in travelling clothes, and closes the door.)

MRS. LINDE (shyly and a little hesitantly): Good evening, Nora.

NORA (uncertainly): Good evening—

MRS. LINDE: I don't suppose you recognize me.

NORA: No, I'm afraid I— Yes, wait a minute— surely—(Exclaims.) Why, Christine! Is it really you?

MRS. LINDE: Yes, it's me.

NORA: Christine! And I didn't recognize you! But how could I—? (More quietly.) How you've changed, Christine!

MRS. LINDE: Yes, I know. It's been nine years—nearly ten—

NORA: Is it so long? Yes, it must be. Oh, these last eight years have been such a happy time for me!

So you've come to town? All that way in winter! How brave of you!

MRS. LINDE: I arrived by the steamer this morning.

NORA: Yes, of course—to enjoy yourself over Christmas. Oh, how splendid! We'll have to celebrate! But take off your coat. You're not cold, are you? (Helps her off with it.) There! Now let's sit down here by the stove and be comfortable. No, you take the armchair. I'll sit here in the rocking-chair. (Clasps MRS. LINDE's hands.) Yes, now you look like your old self. It was just at first that— you've got a little paler, though, Christine. And perhaps a bit thinner.

MRS. LINDE: And older, Nora. Much, much older.

NORA: Yes, perhaps a little older. Just a tiny bit. Not much. (Checks herself suddenly and says earnestly.) Oh, but how thoughtless of me to sit here and chatter away like this! Dear, sweet Christine, can you forgive me?

MRS. LINDE: What do you mean, Nora?

NORA (quietly): Poor Christine, you've become a widow.

MRS. LINDE: Yes. Three years ago.

NORA: I know, I know—I read it in the papers. Oh, Christine, I meant to write to you so often, honestly. But I always put it off, and something else always cropped up.

MRS. LINDE: I understand, Nora dear.

NORA: No, Christine, it was beastly of me. Oh, my poor darling, what you've gone through! And he didn't leave you anything?

MRS. LINDE: No.

NORA: No children, either?

MRS. LINDE: No.

NORA: Nothing at all, then?

MRS. LINDE: Not even a feeling of loss or sorrow.

NORA (looks incredulously at her): But, Christine, how is that possible?

MRS. LINDE (smiles sadly and strokes NORA's hair): Oh, these things happen, Nora.

NORA: All alone. How dreadful that must be for you. I've three lovely children. I'm afraid you can't see them now, because they're out with nanny. But you must tell me everything—

MRS. LINDE: No, no, no. I want to hear about you.

NORA: No, you start. I'm not going to be selfish today. I'm just going to think about you. Oh, but there's one thing I must tell you. Have you heard of the wonderful luck we've just had?

MRS. LINDE: No. What?

NORA: Would you believe it—my husband's just been made manager of the bank!

MRS. LINDE: Your husband? Oh, how lucky—!

NORA: Yes, isn't it? Being a lawyer is so uncertain, you know, especially if one isn't prepared to touch any case that isn't—well—quite nice. And of course Torvald's been very firm about that—and

I'm absolutely with him. Oh, you can imagine how happy we are! He's joining the bank in the New Year, and he'll be getting a big salary, and lots of percentages too. From now on we'll be able to live quite differently—we'll be able to do whatever we want. Oh, Christine, it's such a relief! I feel so happy! Well, I mean, it's lovely to have heaps of money and not to have to worry about anything. Don't you think?

MRS. LINDE: It must be lovely to have enough to cover one's needs, anyway.

NORA: Not just our needs! We're going to have heaps and heaps of money!

MRS. LINDE (smiles): Nora, Nora, haven't you grown up yet? When we were at school you were a terrible little spendthrift.

NORA (laughs quietly): Yes, Torvald still says that. (Wags her finger.) But "Nora, Nora" isn't as silly as you think. Oh, we've been in no position for me to waste money. We've both had to work.

MRS. LINDE: You too?

NORA: Yes, little things—fancy work, crocheting, embroidery and so forth. (Casually.) And other things too. I suppose you know Torvald left the Ministry when we got married? There were no prospects for promotion in his department, and of course he needed more money. But the first year he overworked himself quite dreadfully. He had to take on all sorts of extra jobs, and worked day and night. But it was too much for him, and he became frightfully ill. The doctors said he'd have to go to a warmer climate.

MRS. LINDE: Yes, you spent a whole year in Italy, didn't you?

NORA: Yes. It wasn't easy for me to get away, you know. I'd just had Ivar. But of course we had to do it. Oh, it was a marvelous trip! And it saved Torvald's life. But it cost an awful lot of money, Christine.

MRS. LINDE: I can imagine.

NORA: Two hundred and fifty pounds. That's a lot of money, you know.

MRS. LINDE: How lucky you had it.

NORA: Well, actually, we got it from my father.

MRS. LINDE: Oh, I see. Didn't he die just about that time?

NORA: Yes, Christine, just about then. Wasn't it dreadful, I couldn't go and look after him. I was expecting little Ivar any day. And then I had my poor Torvald to care for—we really didn't think he'd live. Dear, kind Papa! I never saw him again, Christine. Oh, it's the saddest thing that's happened to me since I got married.

MRS. LINDE: I know you were very fond of him. But you went to Italy—?

NORA: Yes. Well, we had the money, you see, and the doctors said we mustn't delay. So we went the month after Papa died.

MRS. LINDE: And your husband came back completely cured?

NORA: Fit as a fiddle!

MRS. LINDE: But—the doctor?

NORA: How do you mean?

MRS. LINDE: I thought the maid said that the gentleman who arrived with me was the doctor.

NORA: Oh yes, that's Doctor Rank, but he doesn't come because anyone's ill. He's our best friend, and he looks us up at least once every day. No, Torvald hasn't had a moment's illness since we went away. And the children are fit and healthy and so am I. (Jumps up and claps her hands.) Oh God, oh God, Christine, isn't it a wonderful thing to be alive and happy! Oh, but how beastly of me! I'm only talking about myself. (Sits on a footstool and rests her arms on MRS. LINDE's knee.) Oh, please don't be angry with me! Tell me, is it really true you didn't love your husband? Why did you marry him, then?

MRS. LINDE: Well, my mother was still alive; and she was helpless and bedridden. And I had my two little brothers to take care of. I didn't feel I could say no.

NORA: Yes, well, perhaps you're right. He was rich then, was he?

MRS. LINDE: Quite comfortably off, I believe. But his business was unsound, you see, Nora. When he died it went bankrupt, and there was nothing left.

NORA: What did you do?

MRS. LINDE: Well, I had to try to make ends meet somehow, so I started a little shop, and a little school, and anything else I could turn my hand to. These last three years have been just one endless slog for me, without a moment's rest. But now it's over, Nora. My poor dear mother doesn't need me any more; she's passed away. And the boys don't need me either; they've got jobs now and can look after themselves.

NORA: How relieved you must feel—

MRS. LINDE: No, Nora. Just unspeakably empty. No one to live for any more. (Gets up restlessly.) That's why I couldn't bear to stay out there any longer, cut off from the world. I thought it'd be easier to find some work here that will exercise and occupy my mind. If only I could get a regular job—office work of some kind—

NORA: Oh but, Christine, that's dreadfully exhausting; and you look practically finished already. It'd be much better for you if you could go away somewhere.

MRS. LINDE (goes over to the window): I have no Papa to pay for my holidays, Nora.

NORA (gets up): Oh, please don't be angry with me.

MRS. LINDE: My dear Nora, it's I who should ask you

not to be angry. That's the worst thing about this kind of situation—it makes one so bitter. One has no one to work for; and yet one has to be continually sponging for jobs. One has to live; and so one becomes completely egocentric. When you told me about this luck you've just had with Torvald's new job—can you imagine?—I was happy not so much on your account, as on my own.

NORA: How do you mean? Oh, I understand. You mean Torvald might be able to do something for you?

MRS. LINDE: Yes, I was thinking that.

NORA: He will too, Christine. Just you leave it to me. I'll lead up to it so delicately, so delicately; I'll get him in the right mood. Oh, Christine, I do so want to help you.

MRS. LINDE: It's sweet of you to bother so much about me, Nora. Especially since you know so little of the worries and hardships of life.

NORA: You say *I* know little of—?

MRS. LINDE (*smiles*): Well, good heavens—those bits of fancy work of yours—well, really—! You're a child, Nora.

NORA (*tosses her head and walks across the room*): You shouldn't say that so patronizingly.

MRS. LINDE: Oh?

NORA: You're like the rest. You all think I'm incapable of getting down to anything serious—

MRS. LINDE: My dear—

NORA: You think I've never had any worries like the rest of you.

MRS. LINDE: Nora dear, you've just told me about all your difficulties—

NORA: Pooh—that! (*Quietly.*) I haven't told you about the big thing.

MRS. LINDE: What big thing? What do you mean?

NORA: You patronize me, Christine; but you shouldn't. You're proud that you've worked so long and so hard for your mother.

MRS. LINDE: I don't patronize anyone, Nora. But you're right—I am both proud and happy that I was able to make my mother's last months on earth comparatively easy.

NORA: And you're also proud at what you've done for your brothers.

MRS. LINDE: I think I have a right to be.

NORA: I think so too. But let me tell you something, Christine. I too have done something to be proud and happy about.

MRS. LINDE: I don't doubt it. But—how do you mean?

NORA: Speak quietly! Suppose Torvald should hear! He mustn't, at any price—no one must know, Christine—no one but you.

MRS. LINDE: But what is this?

NORA: Come over here. (*Pulls her down on to the sofa beside her.*) Yes, Christine—I too have done some-thing to be happy and proud about. It was I who saved Torvald's life.

MRS. LINDE: Saved his—? How did you save it?

NORA: I told you about our trip to Italy. Torvald couldn't have lived if he hadn't managed to get down there—

MRS. LINDE: Yes, well—your father provided the money—

NORA (*smiles*): So Torvald and everyone else thinks. But—

MRS. LINDE: Yes?

NORA: Papa didn't give us a penny. It was I who found the money.

MRS. LINDE: You? All of it?

NORA: Two hundred and fifty pounds. What do you say to that?

MRS. LINDE: But Nora, how could you? Did you win a lottery or something?

NORA (*scornfully*): Lottery? (*Sniffs.*) What would there be to be proud of in that?

MRS. LINDE: But where did you get it from, then?

NORA (*hums and smiles secretively*): Hm; tra-la-la-la!

MRS. LINDE: You couldn't have borrowed it.

NORA: Oh? Why not?

MRS. LINDE: Well, a wife can't borrow money without her husband's consent.

NORA (*tosses her head*): Ah, but when a wife has a little business sense, and knows how to be clever—

MRS. LINDE: But Nora, I simply don't understand—

NORA: You don't have to. No one has said I borrowed the money. I could have got it in some other way. (*Throws herself back on the sofa.*) I could have got it from an admirer. When a girl's as pretty as I am—

MRS. LINDE: Nora, you're crazy!

NORA: You're dying of curiosity now, aren't you, Christine?

MRS. LINDE: Nora, dear, you haven't done anything foolish?

NORA (*sits up again*): Is it foolish to save one's husband's life?

MRS. LINDE: I think it's foolish if without his knowledge you—

NORA: But the whole point was that he mustn't know! Great heavens, don't you see? He hadn't to know how dangerously ill he was. I was the one they told that his life was in danger and that only going to a warm climate could save him. Do you suppose I didn't try to think of other ways of getting him down there? I told him how wonderful it would be for me to go abroad like other young wives: I cried and prayed; I asked him to remember my condition, and said he ought to be nice and tender to me; and then I suggested he might quite easily borrow the money. But then he got almost angry with me, Christine. He said I was frivolous, and that it was his duty as a husband not to pander to my moods and caprices—I think that's what he called them. Well, well, I thought, you've got to be saved somehow. And then I thought of a way—

MRS. LINDE: But didn't your husband find out from your father that the money hadn't come from him?

NORA: No, never. Papa died just then. I'd thought of letting him into the plot and asking him not to tell. But since he was so ill—! And as things turned out, it didn't become necessary.

MRS. LINDE: And you've never told your husband about this?

NORA: For heaven's sake, no! What an idea! He's frightfully strict about such matters. And besides—he's so proud of being a *man*—it'd be so painful and humiliating for him to know that he owed anything to me. It'd completely wreck our relationship. This life we have built together would no longer exist.

MRS. LINDE: Will you never tell him?

NORA (thoughtfully, half-smiling): Yes—some time, perhaps. Years from now, when I'm no longer pretty. You mustn't laugh! I mean of course, when Torvald no longer loves me as he does now; when it no longer amuses him to see me dance and dress up and play the fool for him. Then it might be useful to have something up my sleeve. (Breaks off.) Stupid, stupid, stupid! That time will never come. Well, what do you think of my big secret, Christine? I'm not completely useless, am I? Mind you, all this has caused me a frightful lot of worry. It hasn't been easy for me to meet my obligations punctually. In case you don't know, in the world of business there are things called quarterly instalments and interest, and they're a terrible problem to cope with. So I've had to scrape a little here and save a little there as best I can. I haven't been able to save much on the housekeeping money, because Torvald likes to live well, and I couldn't let the children go short of clothes—I couldn't take anything out of what he gives me for them. The poor little angels!

MRS. LINDE: So you've had to stint yourself, my poor Nora?

NORA: Of course. Well, after all, it was my problem. Whenever Torvald gave me money to buy myself new clothes, I never used more than half of it; and I always bought what was cheapest and plainest. Thank heaven anything suits me, so that Torvald's never noticed. But it made me a bit sad sometimes, because it's lovely to wear pretty clothes. Don't you think?

MRS. LINDE: Indeed it is.

NORA: And then I've found one or two other sources of income. Last winter I managed to get a lot of copying to do. So I shut myself away and wrote every evening, late into the night. Oh, I often got so tired. But it was great fun, though, sitting there working and earning money. It was almost like being a man.

MRS. LINDE: But how much have you managed to pay off like this?

NORA: Well, I can't say exactly. It's awfully difficult to keep an exact check on these kind of transactions. I only know I've paid everything I've managed to scrape together. Sometimes I really didn't know where to turn. (Smiles.) Then I'd sit here and imagine some rich old gentleman had fallen in love with me—

MRS. LINDE: What! What gentleman?

NORA: Silly! And that now he'd died and when they opened his will it said in big letters: "Everything I possess is to be paid forthwith to my beloved Mrs. Nora Helmer in cash."

MRS. LINDE: But, Nora dear, who was this gentleman?

NORA: Great heavens, don't you understand? There wasn't any old gentleman; he was just something I used to dream up as I sat here evening after evening wondering how on earth I could raise the money. But what does it matter? The old bore can stay imaginary as far as I'm concerned, because now I don't have to worry any longer! (Jumps up.) Oh, Christine, isn't it wonderful! I don't have to worry any more! No more troubles! I can play all day with the children, I can fill the house with pretty things, just the way Torvald likes. And, Christine, it'll soon be spring, and the air'll be fresh and the skies blue,—and then perhaps we'll be able to take a little trip somewhere. I shall be able to see the sun again. Oh, yes, yes, it's a wonderful thing to be alive and happy!

(The bell rings in the hall.)

MRS. LINDE (gets up): You've a visitor. Perhaps I'd better go.

NORA: No, stay. It won't be for me. It's someone for Torvald—

MAID (in the doorway): Excuse me, madam, a gentleman's called who says he wants to speak to the master. But I didn't know—seeing as the doctor's with him—

NORA: Who is this gentleman?

KROGSTAD (in the doorway): It's me, Mrs. Helmer.

(MRS. LINDE starts, composes herself and turns away to the window.)

NORA (takes a step towards him and whispers tensely): You? What is it? What do you want to talk to my husband about?

KROGSTAD: Business—you might call it. I hold a minor post in the bank, and I hear your husband is to become our new chief—

NORA: Oh—then it isn't—?

KROGSTAD: Pure business, Mrs. Helmer. Nothing more.

NORA: Well, you'll find him in his study.

(*Nods indifferently as she closes the hall door behind him. Then she walks across the room and sees to the stove.*)

MRS. LINDE: Nora, who was that man?

NORA: A lawyer called Krogstad.

MRS. LINDE: It was him, then.

NORA: Do you know that man?

MRS. LINDE: I used to know him—some years ago. He was a solicitor's clerk in our town, for a while.

NORA: Yes, of course, so he was.

MRS. LINDE: How he's changed!

NORA: He was very unhappily married, I believe.

MRS. LINDE: Is he a widower now?

NORA: Yes, with a lot of children. Ah, now it's alight.

(*She closes the door of the stove and moves the rocking-chair a little to one side.*)

MRS. LINDE: He does—various things now, I hear?

NORA: Does he? It's quite possible—I really don't know. But don't let's talk about business. It's so boring.

(DR. RANK *enters from* HELMER'S *study.*)

RANK (*still in the doorway*): No, no, my dear chap, don't see me out. I'll go and have a word with your wife. (*Closes the door and notices* MRS. LINDE.) Oh, I beg your pardon. I seem to be *de trop* here too.

NORA: Not in the least. (*Introduces them.*) Dr. Rank. Mrs. Linde.

RANK: Ah! A name I have often heard in this house. I believe I passed you on the stairs as I came up.

MRS. LINDE: Yes. Stairs tire me; I have to take them slowly.

RANK: Oh, have you hurt yourself?

MRS. LINDE: No, I'm just a little run down.

RANK: Ah, is that all? Then I take it you've come to town to cure yourself by a round of parties?

MRS. LINDE: I have come here to find work.

RANK: Is that an approved remedy for being run down?

MRS. LINDE: One has to live, Doctor.

RANK: Yes, people do seem to regard it as a necessity.

NORA: Oh, really, Dr. Rank. I bet you want to stay alive.

RANK: You bet I do. However miserable I sometimes feel, I still want to go on being tortured for as long as possible. It's the same with all my patients; and with people who are morally sick, too. There's a moral cripple in with Helmer at this very moment—

MRS. LINDE (*softly*): Oh!

NORA: Whom do you mean?

RANK: Oh, a lawyer fellow called Krogstad—you wouldn't know him. He's crippled all right; morally twisted. But even he started off by announcing, as though it were a matter of enormous importance, that he had to live.

NORA: Oh? What did he want to talk to Torvald about?

RANK: I haven't the faintest idea. All I heard was something about the bank.

NORA: I didn't know that Krog—that this man Krogstad had any connection with the bank.

RANK: Yes, he's got some kind of job down there. (*to* MRS. LINDE) I wonder if in your part of the world you too have a species of human being that spends its time fussing around trying to smell out moral corruption? And when they find a case they give him some nice, comfortable position so that they can keep a good watch on him. The healthy ones just have to lump it.

MRS. LINDE: But surely it's the sick who need care most?

RANK (*shrugs his shoulders*): Well, there we have it. It's that attitude that's turning human society into a hospital.

(NORA, *lost in her own thoughts, laughs half to herself and claps her hands.*)

RANK: Why are you laughing? Do you really know what society is?

NORA: What do I care about society? I think it's a bore. I was laughing at something else—something frightfully funny. Tell me, Dr. Rank—will everyone who works at the bank come under Torvald now?

RANK: Do you find that particularly funny?

NORA (*smiles and hums*): Never mind! Never you mind! (*Walks around the room.*) Yes, I find it very amusing to think that we—I mean, Torvald—has obtained so much influence over so many people. (*Takes the paper bag from her pocket.*) Dr. Rank, would you like a small macaroon?

RANK: Macaroons! I say! I thought they were forbidden here.

NORA: Yes, well, these are some Christine gave me.

MRS. LINDE: What? I—?

NORA: All right, all right, don't get frightened. You weren't to know Torvald had forbidden them. He's afraid they'll ruin my teeth. But, dash it—for once—! Don't you agree, Dr. Rank? Here! (*Pops a macaroon into his mouth.*) You too, Christine. And I'll have one too. Just a little one. Two at the most. (*Begins to walk round again.*) Yes, now I feel really, really happy. Now there's just one thing in the world I'd really love to do.

RANK: Oh? And what is that?

NORA: Just something I'd love to say to Torvald.

RANK: Well, why don't you say it?

NORA: No, I daren't. It's too dreadful.

MRS. LINDE: Dreadful?

RANK: Well, then, you'd better not. But you can say it to us. What is it you'd so love to say to Torvald?

NORA: I've the most extraordinary longing to say: "Bloody hell!"

RANK: Are you mad?

MRS. LINDE: My dear Nora—!

RANK: Say it. Here he is.

NORA (hiding the bag of macaroons): Ssh! Ssh!

(HELMER, with his overcoat on his arm and his hat in his hand, enters from his study.)

NORA (goes to meet him): Well, Torvald dear, did you get rid of him?

HELMER: Yes, he's just gone.

NORA: May I introduce you—? This is Christine. She's just arrived in town.

HELMER: Christine—? Forgive me, but I don't think—

NORA: Mrs. Linde, Torvald dear. Christine Linde.

HELMER: Ah. A childhood friend of my wife's, I presume?

MRS. LINDE: Yes, we knew each other in earlier days.

NORA: And imagine, now she's traveled all this way to talk to you.

HELMER: Oh?

MRS. LINDE: Well, I didn't really—

NORA: You see, Christine's frightfully good at office work, and she's mad to come under some really clever man who can teach her even more than she knows already—

HELMER: Very sensible, madam.

NORA: So when she heard you'd become head of the bank—it was in her local paper—she came here as quickly as she could and—Torvald, you will, won't you? Do a little something to help Christine? For my sake?

HELMER: Well, that shouldn't be impossible. You are a widow, I take it, Mrs. Linde?

MRS. LINDE: Yes.

HELMER: And you have experience of office work?

MRS. LINDE: Yes, quite a bit.

HELMER: Well then, it's quite likely I may be able to find some job for you—

NORA (claps her hands): You see, you see!

HELMER: You've come at a lucky moment, Mrs. Linde.

MRS. LINDE: Oh, how can I ever thank you—?

HELMER: There's absolutely no need. (Puts on his overcoat.) But now I'm afraid I must ask you to excuse me—

RANK: Wait. I'll come with you.

(He gets his fur coat from the hall and warms it at the stove.)

NORA: Don't be long, Torvald dear.

HELMER: I'll only be an hour.

NORA: Are you going too, Christine?

MRS. LINDE (puts on her outdoor clothes): Yes, I must start to look round for a room.

HELMER: Then perhaps we can walk part of the way together.

NORA (helps her): It's such a nuisance we're so cramped here—I'm afraid we can't offer to—

MRS. LINDE: Oh, I wouldn't dream of it. Goodbye, Nora dear, and thanks for everything.

NORA: Au revoir. You'll be coming back this evening, of course. And you too, Dr. Rank. What? If you're well enough? Of course you'll be well enough. Wrap up warmly, though.

(They go out, talking, into the hall. Children's voices are heard from the stairs.)

NORA: Here they are! Here they are!

(She runs out and opens the door. ANNE-MARIE, the nurse, enters with the children.)

NORA: Come in, come in! (Stoops down and kisses them.) Oh, my sweet darlings—! Look at them, Christine! Aren't they beautiful?

RANK: Don't stand here chattering in this draught!

HELMER: Come, Mrs. Linde. This is for mothers only.

(DR. RANK, HELMER, and MRS. LINDE go down the stairs. The NURSE brings the children into the room. NORA follows, and closes the door to the hall.)

NORA: How well you look! What red cheeks you've got! Like apples and roses! (The children answer her inaudibly as she talks to them.) Have you had fun? That's splendid. You gave Emmy and Bob a ride on the sledge? What, both together? I say! What a clever boy you are, Ivar! Oh, let me hold her for a moment, Anne-Marie! My sweet little baby doll! (Takes the smallest child from the NURSE and dances with her.) Yes, yes, Mummy will dance with Bob too. What? Have you been throwing snowballs? Oh, I wish I'd been there! No, don't—I'll undress them myself, Anne-Marie. No, please let me; it's such fun. Go inside and warm yourself; you look frozen. There's some hot coffee on the stove. (The NURSE goes into the room on the left. NORA takes off the children's outdoor clothes and throws them anywhere while they all chatter simultaneously.) What? A big dog ran after you? But he didn't bite you? No, dogs don't bite lovely little baby dolls. Leave those parcels alone, Ivar. What's in them? Ah, wouldn't you like to know! No, no; it's nothing nice. Come on, let's play a game. What shall we play? Hide and seek. Yes, let's play hide and seek. Bob shall hide first. You want me to? All right, let me hide first.

(NORA and the children play around the room, and in the adjacent room to the left, laughing and shouting. At *length* NORA *hides under the table. The children rush in, look, but cannot find her. Then they hear her half-stifled laughter, run to the table, lift up the cloth and see her. Great excitement. She crawls out as though to frighten them. Further excitement. Meanwhile, there has been a knock on the door leading from the hall, but no one has noticed it. Now the door is half-opened and* KROGSTAD *enters. He waits for a moment; the game continues.)*

KROGSTAD: Excuse me, Mrs. Helmer—

NORA *(turns with a stifled cry and half jumps up)*: Oh! What do you want?

KROGSTAD: I beg your pardon; the front door was ajar. Someone must have forgotten to close it.

NORA *(gets up)*: My husband is not at home, Mr. Krogstad.

KROGSTAD: I know.

NORA: Well, what do you want here, then?

KROGSTAD: A word with you.

NORA: With—? *(to the children, quietly)* Go inside to Anne-Marie. What? No, the strange gentleman won't do anything to hurt Mummy. When he's gone we'll start playing again.

(She takes the children into the room on the left and closes the door behind them.)

NORA *(uneasy, tense)*: You want to speak to me?

KROGSTAD: Yes.

NORA: Today? But it's not the first of the month yet.

KROGSTAD: No, it is Christmas Eve. Whether or not you have a merry Christmas depends on you.

NORA: What do you want? I can't give you anything today—

KROGSTAD: We won't talk about that for the present. There's something else. You have a moment to spare?

NORA: Oh, yes. Yes, I suppose so; though—

KROGSTAD: Good. I was sitting in the café down below and I saw your husband cross the street—

NORA: Yes.

KROGSTAD: With a lady.

NORA: Well?

KROGSTAD: Might I be so bold as to ask: was not that lady a Mrs. Linde?

NORA: Yes.

KROGSTAD: Recently arrived in town?

NORA: Yes, today.

KROGSTAD: She is a good friend of yours, is she not?

NORA: Yes, she is. But I don't see—

KROGSTAD: I used to know her too once.

NORA: I know.

KROGSTAD: Oh? You've discovered that. Yes, I thought you would. Well then, may I ask you a straight question: is Mrs. Linde to be employed at the bank?

NORA: How dare you presume to cross-examine me, Mr. Krogstad? You, one of my husband's em-ployees? But since you ask, you shall have an answer. Yes, Mrs. Linde is to be employed by the bank. And I arranged it, Mr. Krogstad. Now you know.

KROGSTAD: I guessed right, then.

NORA *(walks up and down the room)*: Oh, one has a little influence, you know. Just because one's a woman it doesn't necessarily mean that—When one is in a humble position, Mr. Krogstad, one should think twice before offending someone who—hm—

KROGSTAD: —who has influence?

NORA: Precisely.

KROGSTAD *(changes his tone)*: Mrs. Helmer, will you have the kindness to use your influence on my behalf?

NORA: What? What do you mean?

KROGSTAD: Will you be so good as to see that I keep my humble position at the bank?

NORA: What do you mean? Who is thinking of removing you from your position?

KROGSTAD: Oh, you don't need to play the innocent with me. I realize it can't be very pleasant for your friend to risk bumping into me; and now I also realize whom I have to thank for being hounded out like this.

NORA: But I assure you—

KROGSTAD: Look, let's not beat about the bush. There's still time, and I'd advise you to use your influence to stop it.

NORA: But, Mr. Krogstad, I have no influence!

KROGSTAD: Oh? I thought you just said—

NORA: But I didn't mean it like that! I? How on earth could you imagine that I would have any influence over my husband?

KROGSTAD: Oh, I've known your husband since we were students together. I imagine he has his weaknesses like other married men.

NORA: If you speak impertinently of my husband, I shall show you the door.

KROGSTAD: You're a bold woman, Mrs. Helmer.

NORA: I'm not afraid of you any longer. Once the New Year is in, I'll soon be rid of you.

KROGSTAD *(more controlled)*: Now listen to me, Mrs. Helmer. If I'm forced to, I shall fight for my little job at the bank as I would fight for my life.

NORA: So it sounds.

KROGSTAD: It isn't just the money; that's the last thing I care about. There's something else—well, you might as well know. It's like this, you see. You know of course, as everyone else does, that some years ago I committed an indiscretion.

NORA: I think I did hear something—

KROGSTAD: It never came into court; but from that day, every opening was barred to me. So I turned my hand to the kind of business you know about. I had to do something; and I don't think I was one of the worst. But now I want to give up all that. My sons are growing up; for their sake, I must try to regain what respectability I can. This job in the bank was the first step on the ladder. And now your husband wants to kick me off that ladder back into the dirt.

NORA: But my dear Mr. Krogstad, it simply isn't in my power to help you.

KROGSTAD: You say that because you don't want to help me. But I have the means to make you.

NORA: You don't mean you'd tell my husband that I owe you money?

KROGSTAD: And if I did?

NORA: That'd be a filthy trick! (*Almost in tears.*) This secret that is my pride and my joy—that he should hear about it in such a filthy, beastly way—hear about it from you! It'd involve me in the most dreadful unpleasantness—

KROGSTAD: Only—unpleasantness?

NORA (*vehemently*): All right, do it! You'll be the one who'll suffer. It'll show my husband the kind of man you are, and then you'll never keep your job.

KROGSTAD: I asked you whether it was merely domestic unpleasantness you were afraid of.

NORA: If my husband hears about it, he will of course immediately pay you whatever is owing. And then we shall have nothing more to do with you.

KROGSTAD (*Takes a step closer*): Listen, Mrs. Helmer. Either you've a bad memory or else you know very little about financial transactions. I had better enlighten you.

NORA: What do you mean?

KROGSTAD: When your husband was ill, you came to me to borrow two hundred and fifty pounds.

NORA: I didn't know anyone else.

KROGSTAD: I promised to find that sum for you—

NORA: And you did find it.

KROGSTAD: I promised to find that sum for you on certain conditions. You were so worried about your husband's illness and so keen to get the money to take him abroad that I don't think you bothered much about the details. So it won't be out of place if I refresh your memory. Well—I promised to get you the money in exchange for an I.O.U., which I drew up.

NORA: Yes, and which I signed.

KROGSTAD: Exactly. But then I added a few lines naming your father as security for the debt. This paragraph was to be signed by your father.

NORA: Was to be? He did sign it.

KROGSTAD: I left the date blank for your father to fill in when he signed this paper. You remember, Mrs. Helmer?

NORA: Yes, I think so—

KROGSTAD: Then I gave you back this I.O.U. for you to post to your father. Is that not correct?

NORA: Yes.

KROGSTAD: And of course you posted it at once; for within five or six days you brought it along to me with your father's signature on it. Whereupon I handed you the money.

NORA: Yes, well. Haven't I repaid the instalments as agreed?

KROGSTAD: Mm—yes, more or less. But to return to what we were speaking about—that was a difficult time for you just then, wasn't it, Mrs. Helmer?

NORA: Yes, it was.

KROGSTAD: Your father was very ill, if I am not mistaken.

NORA: He was dying.

KROGSTAD: He did in fact die shortly afterwards?

NORA: Yes.

KROGSTAD: Tell me, Mrs. Helmer, do you by any chance remember the date of your father's death? The day of the month, I mean.

NORA: Papa died on the twenty-ninth of September.

KROGSTAD: Quite correct; I took the trouble to confirm it. And that leaves me with a curious little problem—(*Takes out a paper.*)—which I simply cannot solve.

NORA: Problem? I don't see—

KROGSTAD: The problem, Mrs. Helmer, is that your father signed this paper three days after his death.

NORA: What? I don't understand—

KROGSTAD: Your father died on the twenty-ninth of September. But look at this. Here your father has dated his signature the second of October. Isn't that a curious little problem, Mrs. Helmer? (*Nora is silent.*) Can you suggest any explanation? (*She remains silent.*) And there's another curious thing. The words "second of October" and the year are written in a hand which is not your father's, but which I seem to know. Well, there's a simple explanation to that. Your father could have forgotten to write in the date when he signed, and someone else could have added it before the news came of his death. There's nothing criminal about that. It's the signature itself I'm wondering about. It *is* genuine, I suppose, Mrs. Helmer? It was your father who wrote his name here?

NORA (*after a short silence, throws back her head and looks defiantly at him*): No, it was not. It was I who wrote Papa's name there.

KROGSTAD: Look, Mrs. Helmer, do you realize this is a dangerous admission?

NORA: Why? You'll get your money.

KROGSTAD: May I ask you a question? Why didn't you send this paper to your father?

NORA: I couldn't. Papa was very ill. If I'd asked him to sign this, I'd have had to tell him what the money was for. But I couldn't have told him in his condition that my husband's life was in danger. I couldn't have done that!

KROGSTAD: Then you would have been wiser to have given up your idea of a holiday.

NORA: But I couldn't! It was to save my husband's life. I couldn't put it off.

KROGSTAD: But didn't it occur to you that you were being dishonest towards me?

NORA: I couldn't bother about that. I didn't care about you. I hated you because of all the beastly difficulties you'd put in my way when you knew how dangerously ill my husband was.

KROGSTAD: Mrs. Helmer, you evidently don't appreciate exactly what you have done. But I can assure you that it is no bigger nor worse a crime then the one I once committed, and thereby ruined my whole social position.

NORA: You? Do you expect me to believe that you would have taken a risk like that to save your wife's life?

KROGSTAD: The law does not concern itself with motives.

NORA: Then the law must be very stupid.

KROGSTAD: Stupid or not, if I show this paper to the police, you will be judged according to it.

NORA: I don't believe that. Hasn't a daughter the right to shield her father from worry and anxiety when he's old and dying? Hasn't a wife the right to save her husband's life? I don't know much about the law, but there must be something somewhere that says that such things are allowed. You ought to know about that, you're meant to be a lawyer, aren't you? You can't be a very good lawyer, Mr. Krogstad.

KROGSTAD: Possibly not. But business, the kind of business we two have been transacting—I think you'll admit I understand something about that? Good. Do as you please. But I tell you this. If I get thrown into the gutter for a second time, I shall take you with me.

(He bows and goes out through the hall.)

NORA (stands for a moment in thought, then tosses her head): What nonsense! He's trying to frighten me! I'm not that stupid. (Busies herself gathering together the children's clothes; then she suddenly stops.) But—? No, it's impossible. I did it for love, didn't I?

THE CHILDREN (in the doorway, left): Mummy, the strange gentleman's gone out into the street.

NORA: Yes, yes, I know. But don't talk to anyone about the strange gentleman. You hear? Not even to Daddy.

CHILDREN: No, Mummy, Will you play with us again now?

NORA: No, no. Not now.

CHILDREN: Oh but, Mummy, you promised!

NORA: I know, but I can't just now. Go back to the nursery. I've got a lot to do. Go away, my darlings, go away. (She pushes them gently into the other room, and closes the door behind them. She sits on the sofa, takes up her embroidery, stitches for a few moments, but soon stops.) No! (Throws the embroidery aside, gets up, goes to the door leading to the hall and calls.) Helen! Bring in the Christmas tree! (She goes to the table on the left and opens the drawer in it; then pauses again.) No, but it's utterly impossible!

MAID (enters with the tree): Where shall I put it, madam?

NORA: There, in the middle of the room.

MAID: Will you be wanting anything else?

NORA: No, thank you. I have everything I need.

(The MAID puts down the tree and goes out.)

NORA (busy decorating the tree): Now—candles here—and flowers here. That loathsome man! Nonsense, nonsense, there's nothing to be frightened about. The Christmas tree must be beautiful. I'll do everything that you like, Torvald. I'll sing for you, dance for you—

(HELMER, with a bundle of papers under his arm, enters.)

NORA: Oh—are you back already?

HELMER: Yes. Has anyone been here?

NORA: Here? No.

HELMER: That's strange. I saw Krogstad come out of the front door.

NORA: Did you? Oh yes, that's quite right—Krogstad was here for a few minutes.

HELMER: Nora, I can tell from your face, he's been here and asked you to put in a good word for him.

NORA: Yes.

HELMER: And you were to pretend you were doing it of your own accord? You weren't going to tell me he'd been here? He asked you to do that too, didn't he?

NORA: Yes, Torvald. But—

HELMER: Nora, Nora! And you were ready to enter into such a conspiracy? Talking to a man like that, and making him promises—and then, on top of it all, to tell me an untruth!

NORA: An untruth?

HELMER: Didn't you say no one had been here? (Wags his finger.) My little songbird must never do that again. A songbird must have a clean beak to sing with; otherwise she'll starting twittering out of tune. (Puts his arm around her waist.) Isn't that the way we want things? Yes, of course it is. (Lets go of her.) So let's hear no more about that. (Sits down in front of the stove.) Ah, how cosy and peaceful it is here. (Glances for a few moments at his papers.)

NORA (busy with the tree, after a short silence): Torvald.

HELMER: Yes.

NORA: I'm terribly looking forward to that fancy

dress ball at the Stenborgs on Boxing Day.

HELMER: And I'm terribly curious to see what you're going to surprise me with.

NORA: Oh, it's so maddening.

HELMER: What is?

NORA: I can't think of anything to wear. It all seems so stupid and meaningless.

HELMER: So my little Nora's come to that conclusion, has she?

NORA (behind his chair, resting her arms on its back): Are you very busy, Torvald?

HELMER: Oh—

NORA: What are those papers?

HELMER: Just something to do with the bank.

NORA: Already?

HELMER: I persuaded the trustees to give me authority to make certain immediate changes in the staff and organization. I want to have everything straight by the New Year.

NORA: Then that's why this poor man Krogstad—

HELMER: Hm.

NORA (still leaning over his chair, slowly strokes the back of his head): If you hadn't been so busy, I was going to ask you an enormous favour, Torvald.

HELMER: Well, tell me. What was it to be?

NORA: You know I trust your taste more than anyone's. I'm so anxious to look really beautiful at the fancy dress ball. Torvald, couldn't you help me to decide what I shall go as, and what kind of costume I ought to wear?

HELMER: Aha! So little Miss Independent's in trouble and needs a man to rescue her, does she?

NORA: Yes, Torvald. I can't get anywhere without your help.

HELMER: Well, well, I'll give the matter thought. We'll find something.

NORA: Oh, how kind of you! (Goes back to the tree. Pause.) How pretty these red flowers look! But, tell me is it so dreadful, this thing that Krogstad's done?

HELMER: He forged someone else's name. Have you any idea what that means?

NORA: Mightn't he have been forced to do it by some emergency?

HELMER: He probably just didn't think—that's what usually happens. I'm not so heartless as to condemn a man for an isolated action.

NORA: No, Torvald, of course not!

HELMER: Men often succeed in re-establishing themselves if they admit their crime and take their punishment.

NORA: Punishment?

HELMER: But Krogstad didn't do that. He chose to try and trick his way out of it; and that's what has morally destroyed him.

NORA: You think that would—?

HELMER: Just think how a man with that load on his conscience must always be lying and cheating and dissembling; how he must wear a mask even in the presence of those who are dearest to him, even his own wife and children! Yes, the children. That's the worst danger, Nora.

NORA: Why?

HELMER: Because an atmosphere of lies contaminates and poisons every corner of the home. Every breath that the children draw in such a house contains the germs of evil.

NORA (comes closer behind him): Do you really believe that?

HELMER: Oh, my dear, I've come across it so often in my work at the bar. Nearly all young criminals are the children of mothers who are constitutional liars.

NORA: Why do you say mothers?

HELMER: It's usually the mother; though of course the father can have the same influence. Every lawyer knows that only too well. And yet this fellow Krogstad has been sitting at home all these years poisoning his children with his lies and pretences. That's why I say that, morally speaking, he is dead. (Stretches out his hands toward her.) So my pretty little Nora must promise me not to plead his case. Your hand on it. Come, come, what's this? Give me your hand. There. That's settled, now. I assure you it'd be quite impossible for me to work in the same building as him. I literally feel physically ill in the presence of a man like that.

NORA (draws her hand from his and goes over to the other side of the Christmas tree) How hot it is in here! And I've so much to do.

HELMER (gets up and gathers his papers): Yes, and I must try to get some of this read before dinner. I'll think about your costume too. And I may even have something up my sleeve to hang in gold paper on the Christmas tree. (Lays his hand on her head.) My precious little songbird!

(He goes into his study and closes the door.)

NORA (softly, after a pause): It's nonsense. It must be. It's impossible. It must be impossible!

NURSE (in the doorway, left): The children are asking if they can come in to Mummy.

NORA: No, no, no; don't let them in! You stay with them, Anne-Marie.

NURSE: Very good, madam. (Closes the door.)

NORA (pale with fear): Corrupt my little children—! Poison my home! (Short pause. She throws back her head.) It isn't true! It couldn't be true!

ACT 2

(The same room. In the corner by the piano the Christmas tree stands, stripped and disheveled, its candles burned to their sockets. NORA's outdoor clothes lie on the sofa. She is *alone in the room, walking restlessly to and fro. At length she stops by the sofa and picks up her coat.)*

NORA *(drops the coat again)*: There's someone coming! *(Goes to the door and listens.)* No, it's no one. Of course—no one'll come today, it's Christmas Day. Nor tomorrow. But perhaps—! *(Opens the door and looks out.)* No. Nothing in the letter-box. Quite empty. *(Walks across the room.)* Silly, silly. Of course he won't do anything. It couldn't happen. It isn't possible. Why, I've three small children.

(The NURSE, *carrying a large cardboard box, enters from the room on the left.)*

NURSE: I found those fancy dress clothes at last, madam.

NORA: Thank you. Put them on the table.

NURSE *(does so)*: They're all rumpled up.

NORA: Oh, I wish I could tear them into a million pieces!

NURSE: Why, madam! They'll be all right. Just a little patience.

NORA: Yes, of course. I'll go and get Mrs. Linde to help me.

NURSE: What, out again? In this dreadful weather? You'll catch a chill, madam.

NORA: Well, that wouldn't be the worst. How are the children?

NURSE: Playing with their Christmas presents, poor little dears. But—

NORA: Are they still asking to see me?

NURSE: They're so used to having their Mummy with them.

NORA: Yes, but, Anne-Marie, from now on I shan't be able to spend so much time with them.

NURSE: Well, children get used to anything in time.

NORA: Do you think so? Do you think they'd forget their mother if she went away from them—for ever?

NURSE: Mercy's sake, madam! For ever!

NORA: Tell me, Anne-Marie—I've so often wondered. How could you bear to give your child away—to strangers?

NURSE: But I had to when I came to nurse my little Miss Nora.

NORA: Do you mean you wanted to?

NURSE: When I had the chance of such a good job? A poor girl what's got into trouble can't afford to pick and choose. That good-for-nothing didn't lift a finger.

NORA: But your daughter must have completely forgotten you.

NURSE: Oh no, indeed she hasn't. She's written to me twice, once when she got confirmed and then again when she got married.

NORA *(hugs her)*: Dear old Anne-Marie, you were a good mother to me.

NURSE: Poor little Miss Nora, you never had any mother but me.

NORA: And if my little ones had no one else, I know you would—no, silly, silly, silly! *(Opens the cardboard box.)* Go back to them, Anne-Marie. Now I must—Tomorrow you'll see how pretty I shall look.

NURSE: Why, there'll be no one at the ball as beautiful as my Miss Nora.

(She goes into the room, left.)

NORA *(begins to unpack the clothes from the box, but soon throws them down again)* Oh, if only I dared go out! If I could be sure no one would come and nothing would happen while I was away! Stupid, stupid! No one will come. I just musn't think about it. Brush this muff. Pretty gloves, pretty gloves! Don't think about it, don't think about it! One, two, three, four, five, six—*(Cries.)* Ah—they're coming—!

(She begins to run towards the door, but stops uncertainly. MRS. LINDE *enters from the hall, where she has been taking off her outdoor clothes.)*

NORA: Oh, it's you, Christine. There's no one else out there, is there? Oh, I'm so glad you've come.

MRS. LINDE: I hear you were at my room asking for me.

NORA: Yes, I just happened to be passing. I want to ask you to help me with something. Let's sit down here on the sofa. Look at this. There's going to be a fancy dress ball tomorrow night upstairs at Consul Stenborg's, and Torvald wants me to go as a Neapolitan fisher-girl and dance the tarantella. I learned it on Capri.

MRS. LINDE: I say, are you going to give a performance?

NORA: Yes, Torvald says I should. Look, here's the dress. Torvald had it made for me in Italy; but now it's all so torn, I don't know—

MRS. LINDE: Oh, we'll soon put that right; the stitching's just come away. Needle and thread? Ah, here we are.

NORA: You're being awfully sweet.

MRS. LINDE *(sews)*: So you're going to dress up tomorrow, Nora? I must pop over for a moment to see how you look. Oh, but I've completely forgotten to thank you for that nice evening yesterday.

NORA *(gets up and walks across the room)*: Oh, I didn't think it was as nice as usual. You ought to have come to town a little earlier, Christine. . . . Yes, Torvald understands how to make a home look attractive.

MRS. LINDE: I'm sure you do, too. You're not your father's daughter for nothing. But tell me. Is Dr. Rank always in such low spirits as he was yesterday?

NORA: No, last night it was very noticeable. But he's got a terrible disease; he's got spinal tuberculosis, poor man. His father was a frightful creature who kept mistresses and so on. As a result Dr. Rank has been sickly ever since he was a child—you understand—

MRS. LINDE (puts down her sewing): But, my dear Nora, how on earth did you get to know about such things?

NORA (walks about the room): Oh, don't be silly, Christine—when one has three children, one comes into contact with women who—well, who know about medical matters, and they tell one a thing or two.

MRS. LINDE (sews again; a short silence): Does Dr. Rank visit you every day?

NORA: Yes, every day. He's Torvald's oldest friend, and a good friend to me too. Dr. Rank's almost one of the family.

MRS. LINDE: But, tell me—is he quite sincere? I mean, doesn't he rather say the sort of thing he thinks people want to hear?

NORA: No, quite the contrary. What gave you that idea?

MRS. LINDE: When you introduced me to him yesterday, he said he'd often heard my name mentioned here. But later I noticed your husband had no idea who I was. So how could Dr. Rank—?

NORA: Yes, that's quite right, Christine. You see, Torvald's so hopelessly in love with me that he wants to have me all to himself—those were his very words. When we were first married, he got quite jealous if I as much as mentioned any of my old friends back home. So naturally, I stopped talking about them. But I often chat with Dr. Rank about that kind of thing. He enjoys it, you see.

MRS. LINDE: Now listen, Nora. In many ways you're still a child; I'm a bit older than you and have a little more experience of the world. There's something I want to say to you. You ought to give up this business with Dr. Rank.

NORA: What business?

MRS. LINDE: Well, everything. Last night you were speaking about this rich admirer of yours who was going to give you money—

NORA: Yes, and who doesn't exist—unfortunately. But what's that got to do with—?

MRS. LINDE: Is Dr. Rank rich?

NORA: Yes.

MRS. LINDE: And he has no dependents?

NORA: No, no one. But—

MRS. LINDE: And he comes here to see you every day?

NORA: Yes, I've told you.

MRS. LINDE: But how dare a man of his education be so forward?

NORA: What on earth are you talking about?

MRS. LINDE: Oh, stop pretending, Nora. Do you think I haven't guessed who it was who lent you that two hundred pounds?

NORA: Are you out of your mind? How could you imagine such a thing? A friend, someone who comes here every day! Why, that'd be an impossible situation!

MRS. LINDE: Then it really wasn't him?

NORA: No, of course not. I've never for a moment dreamed of—anyway, he hadn't any money to lend then. He didn't come into that till later.

MRS. LINDE: Well, I think that was a lucky thing for you, Nora dear.

NORA: No, I could never have dreamed of asking Dr. Rank—though I'm sure that if I ever did ask him—

MRS. LINDE: But of course you won't.

NORA: Of course not. I can't imagine that it should ever become necessary. But I'm perfectly sure that if I did speak to Dr. Rank—

MRS. LINDE: Behind your husband's back?

NORA: I've got to get out of this other business; and that's been going on behind his back. I've got to get out of it.

MRS. LINDE: Yes, well, that's what I told you yesterday. But—

NORA (walking up and down): It's much easier for a man to arrange these things than a woman—

MRS. LINDE: One's own husband, yes.

NORA: Oh, bosh. (Stops walking.) When you've completely repaid a debt, you get your I.O.U. back, don't you?

MRS. LINDE: Yes, of course.

NORA: And you can tear it into a thousand pieces and burn the filthy, beastly thing!

MRS. LINDE (looks hard at her, puts down her sewing and gets up slowly): Nora, you're hiding something from me.

NORA: Can you see that?

MRS. LINDE: Something has happened since yesterday morning. Nora, what is it?

NORA (goes toward her): Christine! (Listens.) Ssh! There's Torvald. Would you mind going into the nursery for a few minutes? Torvald can't bear to see sewing around. Anne-Marie'll help you.

MRS. LINDE (gathers some of her things together): Very well. But I shan't leave this house until we've talked this matter out.

(She goes into the nursery, left. As she does so, HELMER enters from the hall.)

NORA (runs to meet him): Oh, Torvald dear, I've been so longing for you to come back!

HELMER: Was that the dressmaker?

NORA: No, it was Christine. She's helping me mend

my costume. I'm going to look rather splendid in that.

HELMER: Yes, that was quite a bright idea of mine, wasn't it?

NORA: Wonderful! But wasn't it nice of me to give in to you?

HELMER (takes her chin in his hand): Nice—to give in to your husband? All right, little silly, I know you didn't mean it like that. But I won't disturb you. I expect you'll be wanting to try it on.

NORA: Are you going to work now?

HELMER: Yes. (Shows her a bundle of papers.) Look at these. I've been down to the bank—(Turns to go into his study.)

NOVA: Torvald.

HELMER (stops): Yes.

NORA: If little squirrel asked you really prettily to grant her a wish—

HELMER: Well?

NORA: Would you grant it to her?

HELMER: First I should naturally have to know what it was.

NORA: Squirrel would do lots of pretty tricks for you if you granted her wish.

HELMER: Out with it, then.

NORA: Your little skylark would sing in every room—

HELMER: My little skylark does that already.

NORA: I'd turn myself into a little fairy and dance for you in the moonlight, Torvald.

HELMER: Nora, it isn't that business you were talking about this morning?

NORA (comes closer): Yes, Torvald—oh, please! I beg of you!

HELMER: Have you really the nerve to bring that up again?

NORA: Yes, Torvald, yes, you must do as I ask! You must let Krogstad keep his place at the bank!

HELMER: My dear Nora, his is the job I'm giving to Mrs. Linde.

NORA: Yes, that's terribly sweet of you. But you can get rid of one of the other clerks instead of Krogstad.

HELMER: Really, you're being incredibly obstinate. Just because you thoughtlessly promised to put in a word for him, you expect me to—

NORA: No, it isn't that, Helmer. It's for your own sake. That man writes for the most beastly newspapers—you said so yourself. He could do you tremendous harm. I'm so dreadfully frightened of him—

HELMER: Oh, I understand. Memories of the past. That's what's frightening you.

NORA: What do you mean?

HELMER: You're thinking of your father, aren't you?

NORA: Yes, yes. Of course. Just think what those dreadful men wrote in the papers about Papa! The most frightful slanders. I really believe it

would have lost him his job if the Ministry hadn't sent you down to investigate, and you hadn't been so kind and helpful to him.

HELMER: But my dear little Nora, there's a considerable difference between your father and me. Your father was not a man of unassailable reputation. But I am; and I hope to remain so all my life.

NORA: But no one knows what spiteful people may not dig up. We could be so peaceful and happy now, Torvald—we could be free from every worry—you and I and the children. Oh, please Torvald, please—!

HELMER: The very fact of your pleading his cause makes it impossible for me to keep him. Everyone at the bank already knows that I intend to dismiss Krogstad. If the rumor got about that the new manager had allowed his wife to persuade him to change his mind—

NORA: Well, what then?

HELMER: Oh, nothing, nothing. As long as my little Miss Obstinate gets her way—! Do you expect me to make a laughing-stock of myself before my entire staff—give people the idea that I am open to outside influence? Believe me, I'd soon feel the consequences! Besides—there's something else that makes it impossible for Krogstad to remain in the bank while I am its manager.

NORA: What is that?

HELMER: I might conceivably have allowed myself to ignore his moral obloquies—

NORA: Yes, Torvald, surely?

HELMER: And I hear he's quite efficient at his job. But we—well, we were schoolfriends. It was one of those friendships that one enters into over-hastily and so often comes to regret later in life. I might as well confess the truth. We—well, we're on Christian name terms. And the tactless idiot makes no attempt to conceal it when other people are present. On the contrary, he thinks it gives him the right to be familiar with me. He shows off the whole time, with "Torvald this," and "Torvald that." I can tell you, I find it damned annoying. If he stayed, he'd make my position intolerable.

NORA: Torvald, you can't mean this seriously.

HELMER: Oh? And why not?

NORA: But it's so petty.

HELMER: What did you say? Petty? You think I am petty?

NORA: No, Torvald dear, of course you're not. That's just why—

HELMER: Don't quibble! You call my motives petty. Then I must be petty too. Petty! I see. Well, I've had enough of this. (Goes to the door and calls into the hall.) Helen!

NORA: What are you going to do?

HELMER (*searching among his papers*): I'm going to settle this matter once and for all. (*The* MAID *enters.*) Take this letter downstairs at once. Find a messenger and see that he delivers it. Immediately! The address is on the envelope. Here's the money.

MAID: Very good, sir. (*Goes out with the letter.*)

HELMER (*putting his papers in order*): There now, little Miss Obstinate.

NORA (*tensely*): Torvald—what was in that letter?

HELMER: Krogstad's dismissal.

NORA: Call her back, Torvald! There's still time. Oh, Torvald, call her back! Do it for my sake—for your own sake—for the children! Do you hear me, Torvald? Please do it! You don't realize what this may do to us all!

HELMER: Too late.

NORA: Yes. Too late.

HELMER: My dear Nora, I forgive you this anxiety. Though it is a bit of an insult to me. Oh, but it is! Isn't it an insult to imply that I should be frightened by the vindictiveness of a depraved hack journalist? But I forgive you, because it so charmingly testifies to the love you bear me. (*Takes her in his arms.*) Which is as it should be, my own dearest Nora. Let what will happen, happen. When the real crisis comes, you will not find me lacking in strength or courage. I am man enough to bear the burden for us both.

NORA (*fearfully*): What do you mean?

HELMER: The whole burden, I say—

NORA (*calmly*): I shall never let you do that.

HELMER: Very well. We shall share it, Nora—as man and wife. And that is as it should be. (*Caresses her.*) Are you happy now? There, there, there; don't look at me with those frightened little eyes. You're simply imagining things. You go ahead now and do your tarantella, and get some practice on that tambourine. I'll sit in my study and close the door. Then I won't hear anything, and you can make all the noise you want. (*Turns in the doorway.*) When Dr. Rank comes, tell him where to find me. (*He nods to her, goes into his room with his papers and closes the door.*)

NORA (*desperate with anxiety, stands as though transfixed, and whispers*): He said he'd do it. He will do it. He will do it, and nothing'll stop him. No, never that. I'd rather anything. There must be some escape—! Some way out—! (*The bell rings in the hall.*) Dr. Rank—! Anything but that! Anything, I don't care—!

(*She passes her hand across her face, composes herself, walks across and opens the door to the hall.* DR. RANK *is standing there, hanging up his fur coat. During the following scene it begins to grow dark.*)

NORA: Good evening, Dr. Rank. I recognized your ring. But you mustn't go in to Torvald yet. I think he's busy.

RANK: And—you?

NORA (*as he enters the room and she closes the door behind him*): Oh, you know very well I've always time to talk to you.

RANK: Thank you. I shall avail myself of that privilege as long as I can.

NORA: What do you mean by that? As long as you *can*?

RANK: Yes. Does that frighten you?

NORA: Well, it's rather a curious expression. Is something going to happen?

RANK: Something I've been expecting to happen for a long time. But I didn't think it would happen quite so soon.

NORA (*seizes his arm*): What is it? Dr. Rank, you must tell me!

RANK (*sits down by the stove*): I'm on the way out. And there's nothing to be done about it.

NORA (*sighs with relief*): Oh, it's you—?

RANK: Who else? No, it's no good lying to oneself. I am the most wretched of all my patients, Mrs. Helmer. These last few days I've been going through the books of this poor body of mine, and I find I am bankrupt. Within a month I may be rotting up there in the churchyard.

NORA: Ugh, what a nasty way to talk!

RANK: The facts aren't exactly nice. But the worst is that there's so much else that's nasty to come first. I've only one more test to make. When that's done I'll have a pretty accurate idea of when the final disintegration is likely to begin. I want to ask you a favor. Helmer's a sensitive chap, and I know how he hates anything ugly. I don't want him to visit me when I'm in hospital—

NORA: Oh but, Dr. Rank—

RANK: I don't want him there. On any pretext. I shan't have him allowed in. As soon as I know the worst, I'll send you my visiting card with a black cross on it, and then you'll know that the final filthy process has begun.

NORA: Really, you're being quite impossible this evening. And I did hope you'd be in a good mood.

RANK: With death on my hands? And all this to atone for someone else's sin? Is there justice in that? And in every single family, in one way or another, the same merciless law of retribution is at work—

NORA (*holds her hands to her ears*): Nonsense! Cheer up! Laugh!

RANK: Yes, you're right. Laughter's all the damned thing's fit for. My poor innocent spine must pay for the fun my father had as a gay young lieutenant.

NORA (*at the table, left*): You mean he was too fond of asparagus and *foie gras*?

RANK: Yes; and truffles too.

NORA: Yes, of course, truffles, yes. And oysters too, I suppose?

RANK: Yes, oysters, oysters. Of course.

NORA: And all that port and champagne to wash them down. It's too sad that all those lovely things should affect one's spine.

RANK: Especially a poor spine that never got any pleasure out of them.

NORA: Oh yes, that's the saddest thing of all.

RANK (looks searchingly at her): Hm—

NORA (after a moment): Why did you smile?

RANK: No, it was you who laughed.

NORA: No, it was you who smiled, Dr. Rank!

RANK (gets up): You're a worse little rogue than I thought.

NORA: Oh, I'm full of stupid tricks today.

RANK: So it seems.

NORA (puts both her hands on his shoulders): Dear, dear Dr. Rank, you mustn't die and leave Torvald and me.

RANK: Oh, you'll soon get over it. Once one is gone, one is soon forgotten.

NORA (looks at him anxiously): Do you believe that?

RANK: One finds replacements, and then—

NORA: Who will find a replacement?

RANK: You and Helmer both will, when I am gone. You seem to have made a start already, haven't you? What was this Mrs. Linde doing here yesterday evening?

NORA: Aha! But surely you can't be jealous of poor Christine?

RANK: Indeed I am. She will be my successor in this house. When I have moved on, this lady will—

NORA: Ssh—don't speak so loud! She's in there!

RANK: Today again? You see!

NORA: She's only come to mend my dress. Good heavens, how unreasonable you are! (Sits on the sofa.) Be nice now, Dr. Rank. Tomorrow you'll see how beautifully I shall dance; and you must imagine that I'm doing it just for you. And for Torvald, of course; obviously. (Takes some things out of the box.) Dr. Rank, sit down here and I'll show you something.

RANK (sits): What's this?

NORA: Look here! Look!

RANK: Silk stockings!

NORA: Flesh-coloured. Aren't they beautiful? It's very dark in here now, of course, but tomorrow—! No, no, no; only the soles. Oh well, I suppose you can look a bit higher if you want to.

RANK: Hm—

NORA: Why are you looking so critical? Don't you think they'll fit me?

RANK: I can't really give you a qualified opinion on that.

NORA (looks at him for a moment): Shame on you! (Flicks him on the ear with the stockings.) Take that. (Puts them back in the box.)

RANK: What other wonders are to be revealed to me?

NORA: I shan't show you anything else. You're being naughty.

(She hums a little and looks among the things in the box.)

RANK (after a short silence): When I sit here like this being so intimate with you, I can't think—I cannot imagine what would have become of me if I had never entered this house.

NORA (smiles): Yes, I think you enjoy being with us, don't you?

RANK (more quietly, looking into the middle distance): And now to have to leave it all—

NORA: Nonsense. You're not leaving us.

RANK (as before): And not to be able to leave even the most wretched token of gratitude behind; hardly even a passing sense of loss; only an empty place, to be filled by the next comer.

NORA: Suppose I were to ask you to—? No—

RANK: To do what?

NORA: To give me proof of your friendship—

RANK: Yes, yes?

NORA: No, I mean—to do me a very great service—

RANK: Would you really for once grant me that happiness?

NORA: But you've no idea what it is.

RANK: Very well, tell me, then.

NORA: No, but, Dr. Rank, I can't. It's far too much—I want your help and advice, and I want you to do something for me.

RANK: The more the better. I've no idea what it can be. But tell me. You do trust me, don't you?

NORA: Oh, yes, more than anyone. You're my best and truest friend. Otherwise I couldn't tell you. Well then, Dr. Rank—there's something you must help me to prevent. You know how much Torvald loves me—he'd never hesitate for an instant to lay down his life for me—

RANK (leans over toward her): Nora—do you think he is the only one—?

NORA (with a slight start): What do you mean?

RANK: Who would gladly lay down his life for you?

NORA (sadly): Oh, I see.

RANK: I swore to myself I would let you know that before I go. I shall never have a better opportunity. . . . Well, Nora, now you know that. And now you also know that you can trust me as you can trust nobody else.

NORA (rises; calmly and quietly): Let me pass, please.

RANK (makes room for her but remains seated): Nora—

NORA (in the doorway to the hall): Helen, bring the lamp. (Goes over to the stove.) Oh, dear Dr. Rank, this was really horrid of you.

RANK (gets up): That I have loved you as deeply as anyone else has? Was that horrid of me?

NORA: No—but that you should go and tell me. That was quite unnecessary—

RANK: What do you mean? Did you know, then—?

(The MAID *enters with the lamp, puts it on the table and goes out.)*

RANK: Nora—Mrs. Helmer—I am asking you, did you know this?

NORA: Oh, what do I know, what did I know, what didn't I know—I really can't say. How could you be so stupid, Dr. Rank? Everything was so nice.

RANK: Well, at any rate now you know that I am ready to serve you, body and soul. So—please continue.

NORA *(looks at him)*: After this?

RANK: Please tell me what it is.

NORA: I can't possibly tell you now.

RANK: Yes, yes! You mustn't punish me like this. Let me be allowed to do what I can for you.

NORA: You can't do anything for me now. Anyway, I don't need any help. It was only my imagination—you'll see. Yes, really. Honestly. *(Sits in the rocking chair, looks at him and smiles.)* Well, upon my word you *are* a fine gentleman, Dr. Rank. Aren't you ashamed of yourself, now that the lamp's been lit?

RANK: Frankly, no. But perhaps I ought to say— *adieu?*

NORA: Of course not. You will naturally continue to visit us as before. You know quite well how Torvald depends on your company.

RANK: Yes, but you?

NORA: Oh, I always think it's enormous fun having you here.

RANK: That was what misled me. You're a riddle to me, you know. I'd often felt you'd just as soon be with me as with Helmer.

NORA: Well, you see, there are some people whom one loves, and others whom it's almost more fun to be with.

RANK: Oh yes, there's some truth in that.

NORA: When I was at home, of course I loved Papa best. But I always used to think it was terribly amusing to go down and talk to the servants; because they never told me what I ought to do; and they were such fun to listen to.

RANK: I see. So I've taken their place?

NORA *(jumps up and runs over to him)*: Oh, dear sweet Dr. Rank, I didn't mean that at all. But I'm sure you understand—I feel the same about Torvald as I did about Papa.

MAID *(enters from the hall)*: Excuse me, madam. *(Whispers to her and hands her a visiting card.)*

NORA *(glances at the card)*: Oh! *(Puts it quickly in her pocket.)*

RANK: Anything wrong?

NORA: No, no, nothing at all. It's just something

that—it's my new dress.

RANK: What? But your costume is lying over there.

NORA: Oh—that, yes—but there's another—I ordered it specially—Torvald mustn't know—

RANK: Ah, so that's your big secret?

NORA: Yes, yes. Go in and talk to him—he's in his study—keep him talking for a bit—

RANK: Don't worry. He won't get away from me. *(Goes into* HELMER's *study.)*

NORA *(to the* MAID*)*: Is he waiting in the kitchen?

MAID: Yes, madam, he came up the back way—

NORA: But didn't you tell him I had a visitor?

MAID: Yes, but he wouldn't go.

NORA: Wouldn't go?

MAID: No, madam, not until he'd spoken with you.

NORA: Very well, show him in; but quietly. Helen, you mustn't tell anyone about this. It's a surprise for my husband.

MAID: Very good, madam. I understand. *(Goes.)*

NORA: It's happening. It's happening after all. No, no, no, it can't happen, it mustn't happen.

(She walks across and bolts the door of HELMER's *study. The* MAID *opens the door from the hall to admit* KROGSTAD, *and closes it behind him. He is wearing an overcoat, heavy boots and a fur cap.)*

NORA *(goes toward him.)*: Speak quietly. My husband's at home.

KROGSTAD: Let him hear.

NORA: What do you want from me?

KROGSTAD: Information.

NORA: Hurry up, then. What is it?

KROGSTAD: I suppose you know I've been given the sack.

NORA: I couldn't stop it, Mr. Krogstad. I did my best for you, but it didn't help.

KROGSTAD: Does your husband love you so little? He knows what I can do to you, and yet he dares to—

NORA: Surely you don't imagine I told him?

KROGSTAD: No, I didn't really think you had. It wouldn't have been like my old friend Torvald Helmer to show that much courage—

NORA: Mr. Krogstad, I'll trouble you to speak respectfully of my husband.

KROGSTAD: Don't worry, I'll show him all the respect he deserves. But since you're so anxious to keep this matter hushed up, I presume you're better informed than you were yesterday of the gravity of what you've done?

NORA: I've learned more than you could ever teach me.

KROGSTAD: Yes, a bad lawyer like me—

NORA: What do you want from me?

KROGSTAD: I just wanted to see how things were with you, Mrs. Helmer. I've been thinking about you all day. Even duns and hack journalists have hearts, you know.

NORA: Show some heart, then. Think of my little children.

KROGSTAD: Have you and your husband thought of mine? Well, let's forget that. I just wanted to tell you, you don't need to take this business too seriously. I'm not going to take any action for the present.

NORA: Oh, no—you won't, will you? I knew it.

KROGSTAD: It can all be settled quite amicably. There's no need for it to become public. We'll keep it among the three of us.

NORA: My husband must never know about this.

KROGSTAD: How can you stop him? Can you pay the balance of what you owe me?

NORA: Not immediately.

KROGSTAD: Have you any means of raising the money during the next few days?

NORA: None that I would care to use.

KROGSTAD: Well, it wouldn't have helped anyway. However much money you offered me now I wouldn't give you back that paper.

NORA: What are you going to do with it?

KROGSTAD: Just keep it. No one else need ever hear about it. So in case you were thinking of doing anything desperate—

NORA: I am.

KROGSTAD: Such as running away—

NORA: I am.

KORGSTAD: Or anything more desperate—

NORA: How did you know?

KROGSTAD: —just give up the idea.

NORA: How did you know?

ᴋʀᴏɢsᴛᴀᴅ: Most of us think of that at first. I did. But I hadn't the courage—

NORA (dully): Neither have I.

KROGSTAD (relieved): It's true, isn't it? You haven't the courage either?

NORA: No. I haven't. I haven't.

KROGSTAD: It'd be a stupid thing to do anyway. Once the first little domestic explosion is over. . . . I've got a letter in my pocket here addressed to your husband—

NORA: Telling him everything?

KROGSTAD: As delicately as possibly.

NORA (quickly): He must never see that letter. Tear it up. I'll find the money somehow—

KROGSTAD: I'm sorry, Mrs. Helmer, I thought I'd explained—

NORA: Oh, I don't mean the money I owe you. Let me know how much you want from my husband, and I'll find it for you.

KROGSTAD: I'm not asking your husband for money.

NORA: What do you want, then?

KROGSTAD: I'll tell you. I want to get on my feet again, Mrs. Helmer. I want to get to the top. And your husband's going to help me. For eighteen months now my record's been clean. I've been in hard straits all that time; I was content to fight my way back inch by inch. Now I've been chucked back into the mud, and I'm not going to be satisfied with just getting back my job. I'm going to get to the top, I tell you. I'm going to get back into the bank, and it's going to be higher up. Your husband's going to create a new job for me—

NORA: He'll never do that!

KROGSTAD: Oh, yes he will. I know him. He won't dare to risk a scandal. And once I'm in there with him, you'll see! Within a year I'll be his right-hand man. It'll be Nils Krogstad who'll be running that bank, not Torvald Helmer!

NORA: That will never happen.

KROGSTAD: Are you thinking of—?

NORA: Now I *have* the courage.

KROGSTAD: Oh, you can't frighten me. A pampered little pretty like you—

NORA: You'll see! You'll see!

KROGSTAD: Under the ice? Down in the cold, black water? And then, in the spring to float up again, ugly, unrecognizable, hairless—?

NORA: You can't frighten me.

KROGSTAD: And you can't frighten me. People don't do such things, Mrs. Helmer. And anyway, what'd be the use? I've got him in my pocket.

NORA: But afterwards? When I'm no longer—?

KROGSTAD: Have you forgotten that then your reputation will be in my hands? (She looks at him speechlessly.) Well, I've warned you. Don't do anything silly. When Helmer's read my letter, he'll get in touch with me. And remember, it's your husband who's forced me to act like this. And for that I'll never forgive him. Goodbye, Mrs. Helmer. (He goes out through the hall.)

NORA (runs to the hall door, opens it a few inches and listens): He's going. He's not going to give him the letter. Oh, no, no, it couldn't possibly happen. (Opens the door a little wider). What's he doing? Standing outside the front door. He's not going downstairs. Is he changing his mind? Yes, he—!

(A letter falls into the letter-box. KROGSTAD's footsteps die away down the stairs.)

NORA (with a stifled cry, runs across the room toward the table by the sofa. A pause): In the letter-box. (Steals timidly over toward the hall door.) There it is! Oh, Torvald, Torvald! Now we're lost!

MRS. LINDE (enters from the nursery with NORA's costume): Well, I've done the best I can. Shall we see how it looks—?

NORA (whispers hoarsely): Christine, come here.

MRS. LINDE (throws the dress on the sofa): What's wrong

with you? You look as though you'd seen a ghost!

NORA: Come here. Do you see that letter? There—look—through the glass of the letter-box.

MRS. LINDE: Yes, yes, I see it.

NORA: That letter's from Krogstad—

MRS. LINDE: Nora! It was Krogstad who lent you the money!

NORA: Yes. And now Torvald's going to discover everything.

MRS. LINDE: Oh, believe me, Nora, it'll be best for you both.

NORA: You don't know what's happened. I've committed a forgery—

MRS. LINDE: But, for heaven's sake—!

NORA: Christine, all I want is for you to be my witness.

MRS. LINDE: What do you mean? Witness what?

NORA: If I should go out of my mind—and it might easily happen—

MRS. LINDE: Nora!

NORA: Or if anything else should happen to me—so that I wasn't here any longer—

MRS. LINDE: Nora, Nora, you don't know what you're saying!

NORA: If anyone should try to take the blame, and say it was all his fault—you understand—?

MRS. LINDE: Yes, yes—but how can you think—?

NORA: Then you must testify that it isn't true, Christine. I'm not mad—I know exactly what I'm saying—and I'm telling you, no one else knows anything about this. I did it entirely on my own. Remember that.

MRS. LINDE: All right. But I simply don't understand—

NORA: Oh, how could you understand? A miracle—is—about to happen.

MRS. LINDE: Miracle?

NORA: Yes. A miracle. But it's so frightening, Christine. It *mustn't* happen, not for anything in the world.

MRS. LINDE: I'll go over and talk to Krogstad.

NORA: Don't go near him. He'll only do something to hurt you.

MRS. LINDE: Once upon a time he'd have done anything for my sake.

NORA: He?

MRS. LINDE: Where does he live?

NORA: Oh, how should I know—? Oh yes, wait a moment—! (*Feels in her pocket.*) Here's his card. But the letter, the letter—!

HELMER (*from his study, knocks on the door*): Nora!

NORA (*cries in alarm*): What is it?

HELMER: Now, now, don't get alarmed. We're not coming in, you've closed the door. Are you trying on your costume?

NORA: Yes, yes—I'm trying on my costume. I'm going to look so pretty for you, Torvald.

MRS. LINDE (*who has been reading the card*): Why, he lives just round the corner.

NORA: Yes; but it's no use. There's nothing to be done now. The letter's lying there in the box.

MRS. LINDE: And your husband has the key?

NORA: Yes, he always keeps it.

MRS. LINDE: Krogstad must ask him to send the letter back unread. He must find some excuse—

NORA: But Torvald always opens the box at just about this time—

MRS. LINDE: You must stop him. Go in and keep him talking. I'll be back as quickly as I can.

(*She hurries out through the hall.*)

NORA (*goes over to* HELMER's *door, opens it and peeps in*): Torvald!

HELMER (*offstage*): Well, may a man enter his own drawing room again? Come on, Rank, now we'll see what—(*In the doorway.*) But what's this?

NORA: What, Torvald dear?

HELMER: Rank's been preparing me for some great transformation scene.

RANK (*in the doorway*): So I understood. But I seem to have been mistaken.

NORA: Yes, no one's to be allowed to see me before tomorrow night.

HELMER: But, my dear Nora, you look quite worn out. Have you been practising too hard?

NORA: No, I haven't practised at all yet.

HELMER: Well, you must.

NORA: Yes, Torvald, I must, I know. But I can't get anywhere without your help. I've completely forgotten everything.

HELMER: Oh, we'll soon put that to rights.

NORA: Yes, help me, Torvald. Promise me you will? Oh, I'm so nervous. All those people—! You must forget everything except me this evening. You mustn't think of business—I won't even let you touch a pen. Promise me, Torvald?

HELMER: I promise. This evening I shall think of nothing but you—my poor, helpless little darling. Oh, there's just one thing I must see to—(*Goes toward the hall door.*)

NORA: What do you want out there?

HELMER: I'm only going to see if any letters have come.

NORA: No, Torvald, no!

HELMER: Why, what's the matter?

NORA: Torvald, I beg you. There's nothing there.

HELMER: Well, I'll just make sure.

(*He moves toward the door.* NORA *runs to the piano and plays the first bars of the tarantella.*)

HELMER (*at the door, turns*): Aha!

NORA: I can't dance tomorrow if I don't practise with you now.

HELMER (goes over to her): Are you really so frightened, Nora dear?

NORA: Yes, terribly frightened. Let me start practising now, at once—we've still time before dinner. Oh, do sit down and play for me, Torvald dear. Correct me, lead me, the way you always do.

HELMER: Very well, my dear, if you wish it.

(He sits down at the piano. NORA seizes the tambourine and a long multi-coloured shawl from the cardboard box, wraps the latter hastily around her, then takes a quick leap into the center of the room.)

NORA: Play for me! I want to dance!

(HELMER plays and NORA dances. DR. RANK stands behind HELMER at the piano and watches her.)

HELMER (as he plays): Slower, slower!

NORA: I can't!

HELMER: Not so violently, Nora.

NORA: I must!

HELMER (stops playing): No, no, this won't do at all.

NORA (laughs and swings her tambourine): Isn't that what I told you?

RANK: Let me play for her.

HELMER (gets up): Yes, would you? Then it'll be easier for me to show her.

(RANK sits down at the piano and plays. NORA dances more and more wildly. HELMER has stationed himself by the stove and tries repeatedly to correct her, but she seems not to hear him. Her hair works loose and falls over her shoulders; she ignores it and continues to dance. MRS. LINDE enters.)

MRS. LINDE (stands in the doorway as though tongue-tied): Ah—!

NORA (as she dances): Christine, we're having such fun!

HELMER: But, Nora darling, you're dancing as if your life depended on it.

NORA: It does.

HELMER: Rank, stop it! This is sheer lunacy. Stop it, I say!

(RANK ceases playing. NORA suddenly stops dancing.)

HELMER (goes over to her): I'd never have believed it. You've forgotten everything I taught you.

NORA (throws away the tambourine): You see!

HELMER: I'll have to show you every step.

NORA: You see how much I need you! You must show me every step of the way. Right to the end of the dance. Promise me you will, Torvald?

HELMER: Never fear. I will.

NORA: You mustn't think about anything but me—today or tomorrow. Don't open any letters—don't even open the letter-box—

HELMER: Aha, you're still worried about that fellow—

NORA: Oh, yes, yes, him too.

HELMER: Nora, I can tell from the way you're behaving, there's a letter from him already there.

NORA: I don't know. I think so. But you mustn't read it now. I don't want anything ugly to come between us till it's all over.

RANK (quietly, to HELMER): Better give her her way.

HELMER (puts his arm around her): My child shall have her way. But tomorrow night, when your dance is over—

NORA: Then you will be free.

MAID (appears in the doorway, right): Dinner is served, madam.

NORA: Put out some champagne, Helen.

MAID: Very good, madam. (Goes.)

HELMER: I say! What's this, a banquet?

NORA: We'll drink champagne until dawn! (Calls.) And, Helen! Put out some macaroons! Lots of macaroons—for once!

HELMER (takes her hands in his): Now, now, now. Don't get so excited. Where's my little songbird, the one I know?

NORA: All right. Go and sit down—and you too, Dr. Rank. I'll be with you in a minute. Christine, you must help me put my hair up.

RANK (quietly, as they go): There's nothing wrong, is there? I mean, she isn't—er—expecting—?

HELMER: Good heavens no, my dear chap. She just gets scared like a child sometimes—I told you before—

(They go out right.)

NORA: Well?

MRS. LINDE: He's left town.

NORA: I saw it from your face.

MRS. LINDE: He'll be back tomorrow evening. I left a note for him.

NORA: You needn't have bothered. You can't stop anything now. Anyway, it's wonderful really, in a way—sitting here and waiting for the miracle to happen.

MRS. LINDE: Waiting for what?

NORA: Oh, you wouldn't understand. Go in and join them. I'll be with you in a moment.

(MRS. LINDE goes into the dining-room.)

NORA (stands for a moment as though collecting herself. Then she looks at her watch): Five o'clock. Seven hours till midnight. Then another twenty-four hours till midnight tomorrow. And then the tarantella will be finished. Twenty-four and seven? Thirty-one hours to live.

HELMER (appears in the doorway, right): What's happened to my little songbird?

NORA (runs to him with here arms wide): Your songbird is here!

ACT 3

(The same room. The table which was formerly by the sofa has been moved into the centre of the room; the chairs *surround it as before. The door to the hall stands open. Dance music can be heard from the floor above.* MRS. LINDE *is seated at the table, absent-mindedly glancing through a book. She is trying to read, but seems unable to keep her mind on it. More than once she turns and listens anxiously toward the front door.)*

MRS. LINDE *(looks at her watch)*: Not here yet. There's not much time left. Please God he hasn't—! *(Listens again.)* Ah, here he is. *(Goes out into the hall and cautiously opens the front door. Footsteps can be heard softly ascending the stairs. She whispers.)* Come in. There's no one here.

KROGSTAD *(in the doorway)*: I found a note from you at my lodgings. What does this mean?

MRS. LINDE: I must speak with you.

KROGSTAD: Oh? And must our conversation take place in this house?

MRS. LINDE: We couldn't meet at my place; my room has no separate entrance. Come in. We're quite alone. The maid's asleep, and the Helmers are at the dance upstairs.

KROGSTAD *(comes into the room)*: Well, well! So the Helmers are dancing this evening? Are they indeed?

MRS. LINDE: Yes, why not?

KROGSTAD: True enough. Why not?

MRS. LINDE: Well, Krogstad. You and I must have a talk together.

KROGSTAD: Have we two anything further to discuss?

MRS. LINDE: We have a great deal to discuss.

KROGSTAD: I wasn't aware of it.

MRS. LINDE: That's because you've never really understood me.

KROGSTAD: Was there anything to understand? It's the old story, isn't it—a woman chucking a man because something better turns up?

MRS. LINDE: Do you really think I'm so utterly heartless? You think it was easy for me to give you up?

KROGSTAD: Wasn't it?

MRS. LINDE: Oh, Nils, did you really believe that?

KROGSTAD: Then why did you write to me the way you did?

MRS. LINDE: I had to. Since I had to break with you, I thought it my duty to destroy all the feelings you had for me.

KROGSTAD *(clenches his fists)*: So that was it. And you did this for money!

MRS. LINDE: You mustn't forget I had a helpless mother to take care of, and two little brothers. We couldn't wait for you, Nils. It would have been so long before you'd had enough to support us.

KROGSTAD: Maybe. But you had no right to cast me off for someone else.

MRS. LINDE: Perhaps not. I've often asked myself that.

KROGSTAD *(more quietly)*: When I lost you, it was just as though all solid ground had been swept from under my feet. Look at me. Now I am a shipwrecked man, clinging to a spar.

MRS. LINDE: Help may be near at hand.

KROGSTAD: It was near. But then you came, and stood between it and me.

MRS. LINDE: I didn't know, Nils. No one told me till today that this job I'd found was yours.

KROGSTAD: I believe you, since you say so. But now you know, won't you give it up?

MRS. LINDE: No—because it wouldn't help you even if I did.

KROGSTAD: Wouldn't it? I'd do it all the same.

MRS. LINDE: I've learned to look at things practically. Life and poverty have taught me that.

KROGSTAD: And life has taught me to distrust fine words.

MRS. LINDE: Then it's taught you a useful lesson. But surely you still believe in actions?

KROGSTAD: What do you mean?

MRS. LINDE: You said you were like a shipwrecked man clinging to a spar.

KROGSTAD: I have good reason to say it.

MRS. LINDE: I'm in the same position as you. No one to care about, no one to care for.

KROGSTAD: You made your own choice.

MRS. LINDE: I had no choice—then.

KROGSTAD: Well?

MRS. LINDE: Nils, suppose we two shipwrecked souls could join hands?

KROGSTAD: What are you saying?

MRS. LINDE: Castaways have a better chance of survival together than on their own.

KROGSTAD: Christine!

MRS. LINDE: Why do you suppose I came to this town?

KROGSTAD: You mean—you came because of me?

MRS. LINDE: I must work if I'm to find life worth living. I've always worked, for as long as I can remember; it's been the greatest joy of my life—my only joy. But now I'm alone in the world, and I feel so dreadfully lost and empty. There's no joy in working just for oneself. Oh, Nils, give me something—someone—to work for.

KROGSTAD: I don't believe all that. You're just being hysterical and romantic. You want to find an excuse for self-sacrifice.

MRS. LINDE: Have you ever known me to be hysterical?

KROGSTAD: You mean you really—? Is it possible? Tell me—you know all about my past?

MRS. LINDE: Yes.

KROGSTAD: And you know what people think of me here?

MRS. LINDE: You said just now that with me you might have become a different person.

KROGSTAD: I know I could have.

MRS. LINDE: Could it still happen?

KROGSTAD: Christine—do you really mean this?

Yes—you do—I see it in your face. Have you really the courage—?

MRS. LINDE: I need someone to be a mother to; and your children need a mother. And you and I need each other. I believe in you, Nils. I am afraid of nothing—with you.

KROGSTAD (clasps her hands): Thank you, Christine—thank you! Now I shall make the world believe in me as you do! Oh—but I'd forgotten—

MRS. LINDE (listens): Ssh! The tarantella! Go quickly, go!

KROGSTAD: Why? What is it?

MRS. LINDE: You hear that dance? As soon as it's finished, they'll be coming down.

KROGSTAD: All right, I'll go. It's no good, Christine. I'd forgotten—you don't know what I've just done to the Helmers.

MRS. LINDE: Yes, Nils. I know.

KROGSTAD: And yet you'd still have the courage to—?

MRS. LINDE: I know what despair can drive a man like you to.

KROGSTAD: Oh, if only I could undo this!

MRS. LINDE: You can. Your letter is still lying in the box.

KROGSTAD: Are you sure?

MRS. LINDE: Quite sure. But—

KROGSTAD (looks searchingly): Is that why you're doing this? You want to save your friend at any price? Tell me the truth. Is that the reason?

MRS. LINDE: Nils, a woman who has sold herself once for the sake of others doesn't make the same mistake again.

KROGSTAD: I shall demand my letter back.

MRS. LINDE: No, no.

KROGSTAD: Of course I shall. I shall stay here till Helmer comes down. I'll tell him he must give me back my letter—I'll say it was only to do with my dismissal, and that I don't want him to read it—

MRS. LINDE: No, Nils, you mustn't ask for that letter back.

KROGSTAD: But—tell me—wasn't that the real reason you asked me to come here?

MRS. LINDE: Yes—at first, when I was frightened. But a day has passed since then, and in that time I've seen incredible things happen in this house. Helmer must know the truth. This unhappy secret of Nora's must be revealed. They must come to a full understanding; there must be an end of all these shiftings and evasions.

KROGSTAD: Very well. If you're prepared to risk it. But one thing I can do—and at once—

MRS. LINDE (listens): Hurry! Go, go! The dance is over. We aren't safe here another moment.

KROGSTAD: I'll wait for you downstairs.

MRS. LINDE: Yes, do. You can see me home.

KROGSTAD: I've never been so happy in my life before!

(He goes through the front door. The door leading from the room into the hall remains open.)

MRS. LINDE (tidies the room a little and gets her hat and coat): What a change! Oh, what a change! Someone to work for—to live for! A home to bring joy into! I won't let this chance of happiness slip through my fingers. Oh, why don't they come? (Listens.) Ah, here they are. I must get my coat on.

(She takes her hat and coat. HELMER's and NORA's voices become audible outside. A key is turned in the lock and HELMER leads NORA almost forcibly into the hall. She is dressed in an Italian costume with a large black shawl. He is in evening dress, with a black cloak.)

NORA (still in the doorway, resisting him): No, no, no—not in here! I want to go back upstairs. I don't want to leave so early.

HELMER: But my dearest Nora—

NORA: Oh, please, Torvald, please! Just another hour!

HELMER: Not another minute, Nora, my sweet. You know what we agreed. Come along, now. Into the drawing-room. You'll catch cold if you stay out here.

(He leads her, despite her efforts to resist him, gently into the room.)

MRS. LINDE: Good evening.

NORA: Christine!

HELMER: Oh, hullo, Mrs. Linde. You still here?

MRS. LINDE: Please forgive me. I did so want to see Nora in her costume.

NORA: Have you been sitting here waiting for me?

MRS. LINDE: Yes, I got here too late, I'm afraid. You'd already gone up. And I felt I really couldn't go back home without seeing you.

HELMER (takes off NORA's shawl): Well, take a good look at her. She's worth looking at, don't you think? Isn't she beautiful, Mrs. Linde?

MRS. LINDE: Oh, yes, indeed—

HELMER: Isn't she unbelievably beautiful? Everyone at the party said so. But dreadfully stubborn she is, bless her pretty little heart. What's to be done about that? Would you believe it, I practically had to use force to get her away!

NORA: Oh, Torvald, you're going to regret not letting me stay—just half an hour longer.

HELMER: Hear that, Mrs. Linde? She dances her tarantella—makes a roaring success—and very well deserved—though possibly a trifle too realistic—more so than was aesthetically necessary, strictly speaking. But never mind that. Main thing is—she had a success—roaring success. Was I going to let her stay on after that and spoil the impression? No, thank you. I took my beautiful little Capri signorina—my capricious little Capricienne, what?—under my arm—a swift round of the ballroom, a curtsey to the company, and, as they say in novels, the beautiful apparition disappeared! An exit should always be dramatic, Mrs. Linde. But unfortunately that's just what I can't get Nora to realize. I say, it's hot in here. *(Throws his cloak on a chair and opens the door to his study.)* What's this? It's dark in here. Ah, yes, of course—excuse me. *(Goes in and lights a couple of candles.)*

NORA *(whispers swiftly, breathlessly)*: Well?

MRS. LINDE *(quietly)*: I've spoken to him.

NORA: Yes?

MRS. LINDE: Nora—you must tell your husband everything.

NORA *(dully)*: I knew it.

MRS. LINDE: You've nothing to fear from Krogstad. But you must tell him.

NORA: I shan't tell him anything.

MRS. LINDE: Then the letter will.

NORA: Thank you, Christine. Now I know what I must do. Ssh!

HELMER *(returns)*: Well, Mrs. Linde, finished admiring her?

MRS. LINDE: Yes. Now I must say good night.

HELMER: Oh, already? Does this knitting belong to you?

MRS. LINDE *(takes it)*: Thank you, yes. I nearly forgot it.

HELMER: You knit, then?

MRS. LINDE: Why, yes.

HELMER: Know what? You ought to take up embroidery.

MRS. LINDE: Oh? Why?

HELMER: It's much prettier. Watch me, now. You hold the embroidery in your left hand, like this, and then you take the needle in your right hand and go in and out in a slow, easy movement—like this. I am right, aren't I?

MRS. LINDE: Yes, I'm sure—

HELMER: But knitting, now—that's an ugly business—can't help it. Look—arms all huddled up—great clumsy needles going up and down—makes you look like a damned Chinaman. I say, that really was a magnificent champagne they served us.

MRS. LINDE: Well, good night, Nora. And stop being stubborn. Remember!

HELMER: Quite right, Mrs. Linde!

MRS. LINDE: Good night, Mr. Helmer.

HELMER *(accompanies her to the door)*: Good night, good night! I hope you'll manage to get home all right? I'd gladly—but you haven't far to go, have you? Good night, good night. *(She goes. He closes the door behind her and returns.)* Well, we've got rid of her at last. Dreadful bore that woman is!

NORA: Aren't you very tired, Torvald?

HELMER: No, not in the least.

NORA: Aren't you sleepy?

HELMER: Not a bit. On the contrary, I feel extraordinarily exhilarated. But what about you? Yes, you look very sleepy and tired.

NORA: Yes, I am very tired. Soon I shall sleep.

HELMER: You see, you see! How right I was not to let you stay longer!

NORA: Oh, you're always right, whatever you do.

HELMER *(kisses her on the forehead)*: Now my little songbird's talking just like a real big human being. I say, did you notice how cheerful Rank was this evening?

NORA: Oh? Was he? I didn't have a chance to speak with him.

HELMER: I hardly did. But I haven't seen him in such a jolly mood for ages. *(Look at her for a moment, then comes closer.)* I say, it's nice to get back to one's home again, and be all alone with you. Upon my word, you're a distractingly beautiful young woman.

NORA: Don't look at me like that, Torvald!

HELMER: What, not look at my most treasured possession? At all this wonderful beauty that's mine, mine alone, all mine.

NORA *(goes round to the other side of the table)*: You mustn't talk to me like that tonight.

HELMER *(follows her)*: You've still the tarantella in your blood, I see. And that makes you even more desirable. Listen! Now the other guests are beginning to go. *(More quietly.)* Nora—soon the whole house will be absolutely quiet.

NORA: Yes, I hope so.

HELMER: Yes, my beloved Nora, of course you do! Do you know—when I'm out with you among other people like we were tonight, do you know why I say so little to you, why I keep so aloof from you, and just throw you an occasional glance? Do you know why I do that? It's because I pretend to myself that you're my secret mistress, my clandestine little sweetheart, and that nobody knows there's anything at all between us.

NORA: Oh, yes, yes, yes—I know you never think of anything but me.

HELMER: And then when we're about to go, and I wrap the shawl round your lovely young shoulders, over this wonderful curve of your neck— Then I pretend to myself that you are my young bride, that we've just come from the wedding, that I'm taking you to my house for the first time—that, for the first time, I am alone with you—quite alone with you, as you stand there young and trembling and beautiful. All evening I've had no eyes for anyone but you. When I saw you dance the tarantella, like a huntress, a temptress, my blood grew hot, I couldn't stand it any longer! That was why I seized you and dragged you down here with me—

NORA: Leave me, Torvald! Get away from me! I don't want all this.

HELMER: What? Now, Nora, you're joking with me. Don't want, don't want—? Aren't I your husband—?

(There is a knock on the front door.)

NORA *(starts)*: What was that?

HELMER *(goes toward the hall)*: Who is it?

RANK *(outside)*: It's me. May I come in for a moment?

HELMER *(quietly, annoyed)*: Oh, what does he want now? *(Calls.)* Wait a moment. *(Walks over and opens the door.)* Well! Nice of you not to go by without looking in.

RANK: I thought I heard your voice, so I felt I had to say goodbye. *(His eyes travel swiftly around the room.)* Ah, yes—these dear rooms, how well I know them. What a happy, peaceful home you two have.

HELMER: You seemed to be having a pretty happy time yourself upstairs.

RANK: Indeed I did. Why not? Why shouldn't one make the most of this world? As much as one can, and for as long as one can. The wine was excellent—

HELMER: Especially the champagne.

RANK: You noticed that too? It's almost incredible how much I managed to get down.

NORA: Torvald drank a lot of champagne too, this evening.

RANK: Oh?

NORA: Yes. It always makes him merry afterwards.

RANK: Well, why shouldn't a man have a merry evening after a well-spent day?

HELMER: Well-spent? Oh, I don't know that I can claim that.

RANK *(slaps him across the back)*: I can, though, my dear fellow!

NORA: Yes, of course, Dr. Rank—you've been carrying out a scientific experiment today, haven't you?

RANK: Exactly.

HELMER: Scientific experiment! Those are big words for my little Nora to use!

NORA: And may I congratulate you on the finding?

RANK: You may indeed.

NORA: It was good, then?

RANK: The best possible finding—both for the doctor and the patient. Certainty.

NORA *(quickly)*: Certainty?

RANK: Absolute certainty. So aren't I entitled to have a merry evening after that?

NORA: Yes, Dr. Rank. You were quite right to.

HELMER: I agree. Provided you don't have to regret it tomorrow.

RANK: Well, you never get anything in this life without paying for it.

NORA: Dr. Rank—you like masquerades, don't you?

RANK: Yes, if the disguises are sufficiently amusing.

NORA: Tell me. What shall we two wear at the next masquerade?

HELMER: You little gadabout! Are you thinking about the next one already?

RANK: We two? Yes, I'll tell you. You must go as the Spirit of Happiness—

HELMER: You try to think of a costume that'll convey that.

RANK: Your wife need only appear as her normal, everyday self—

HELMER: Quite right! Well said! But what are you going to be? Have you decided that?

RANK: Yes, my dear friend. I have decided that.

HELMER: Well?

RANK: At the next masquerade, I shall be invisible.

HELMER: Well, that's a funny idea.

RANK: There's a big, black hat—haven't you heard of the invisible hat? Once it's over your head, no one can see you any more.

HELMER *(represses a smile)*: Ah yes, of course.

RANK: But I'm forgetting what I came for. Helmer, give me a cigar. One of your black Havanas.

HELMER: With the greatest pleasure. *(Offers him the box.)*

RANK *(takes one and cuts off the tip)*: Thank you.

NORA *(strikes a match)*: Let me give you a light.

RANK: Thank you. *(She holds out the match for him. He lights his cigar.)* And now—goodbye.

HELMER: Goodbye, my dear chap, goodbye.

NORA: Sleep well, Dr. Rank.

RANK: Thank you for that kind wish.

NORA: Wish me the same.

RANK: You? Very well—since you ask. Sleep well. And thank you for the light. *(He nods to them both and goes.)*

HELMER *(quietly)*: He's been drinking too much.

NORA *(abstractedly)*: Perhaps.

(HELMER takes his bunch of keys from his pocket and goes out into the hall.)

NORA: Torvald, what do you want out there?

HELMER: I must empty the letter-box. It's absolutely full. There'll be no room for the newspapers in the morning.

NORA: Are you going to work tonight?

HELMER: You know very well I'm not. Hullo, what's this? Someone's been at the lock.

NORA: At the lock—?

HELMER: Yes, I'm sure of it. Who on earth—? Surely not one of the maids? Here's a broken hairpin. Nora, it's yours—

NORA *(quickly)*: Then it must have been the children.

HELMER: Well, you'll have to break them of that habit. Hm, hm. Ah, that's done it. *(Takes out the contents of the box and calls into the kitchen.)* Helen! Helen!

Put out the light on the staircase. *(Comes back into the drawing room with the letters in his hand and closes the door to the hall.)* Look at this! You see how they've piled up? *(Glances through them.)* What on earth's this?

NORA *(at the window)*: The letter! Oh, no, Torvald, no!

HELMER: Two visiting cards—from Rank.

NORA: From Dr. Rank?

HELMER *(looks at them)*: Peter Rank, M.D. They were on top. He must have dropped them in as he left.

NORA: Has he written anything on them?

HELMER: There's a black cross above his name. Look. Rather gruesome, isn't it? It looks just as though he was announcing his death.

NORA: He is.

HELMER: What? Do you know something? Has he told you anything?

NORA: Yes. When these cards come, it means he's said goodbye to us. He wants to shut himself up in his house and die.

HELMER: Ah, poor fellow. I knew I wouldn't be seeing him for much longer. But so soon—! And now he's going to slink away and hide like a wounded beast.

NORA: When the time comes, it's best to go silently. Don't you think so, Torvald?

HELMER *(walks up and down)*: He was so much a part of our life. I can't realize that he's gone. His suffering and loneliness seemed to provide a kind of dark background to the happy sunlight of our marriage. Well, perhaps it's best this way. For him, anyway. *(Stops walking.)* And perhaps for us too, Nora. Now we have only each other. *(Embraces her.)* Oh, my beloved wife—I feel as though I could never hold you close enough. Do you know, Nora, often I wish some terrible danger might threaten you, so that I could offer my life and my blood, everything, for your sake.

NORA *(tears herself loose and says in a clear, firm voice)*: Read your letters now, Torvald.

HELMER: No, no. Not tonight. Tonight I want to be with you, my darling wife—

NORA: When your friend is about to die—?

HELMER: You're right. This news has upset us both. An ugliness has come between us; thoughts of death and dissolution. We must try to forget them. Until then—you go to your room; I shall go to mine.

NORA *(throws her arms round his neck)*: Good night, Torvald! Good night!

HELMER *(kisses her on the forehead)*: Good night, my darling little songbird. Sleep well, Nora. I'll go and read my letters.

(He goes into the study with the letters in his hand, and closes the door.)

NORA *(wild-eyed, fumbles around, seizes HELMER's cloak, throws it round herself and whispers quickly, hoarsely)*: Never see him again. Never. Never. Never. *(Throws the shawl over her head.)* Never see the children again. Them too. Never. Never. Oh—the icy black water! Oh—that bottomless—that—! Oh, if only it were all over! Now he's got it—he's reading it. Oh, no, no! Goodbye, Torvald! Goodbye, my darlings!

(She turns to run into the hall. As she does so, HELMER throws open his door and stands there with an open letter in his hand.)

HELMER: Nora!

NORA *(shrieks)*: Ah—!

HELMER: What is this? Do you know what is in this letter?

NORA: Yes, I know. Let me go! Let me go!

HELMER *(holds her back)*: Go? Where?

NORA *(tries to tear herself loose)*: You mustn't try to save me, Torvald!

HELMER *(staggers back)*: Is it true? Is it true, what he writes? Oh, my God! No, no—it's impossible, it can't be true!

NORA: It *is* true. I've loved you more than anything else in the world.

HELMER: Oh, don't try to make silly excuses.

NORA *(takes a step toward him)*: Torvald—

HELMER: Wretched woman! What have you done?

NORA: Let me go! You're not going to suffer for my sake. I won't let you!

HELMER: Stop being theatrical. *(Locks the front door.)* You're going to stay here and explain yourself. Do you understand what you've done? Answer me! Do you understand?

NORA *(looks unflinchingly at him and, her expression growing colder, says)*: Yes. Now I am beginning to understand.

HELMER *(walking round the room)*: Oh, what a dreadful awakening! For eight whole years—she who was my joy and my pride—a hypocrite, a liar—worse, worse—a criminal! Oh, the hideousness of it! Shame on you, shame!

(NORA is silent and stares unblinkingly at him.)

HELMER *(stops in front of her)*: I ought to have guessed that something of this sort would happen. I should have foreseen it. All your father's recklessness and instability—be quiet!—I repeat, all your father's recklessness and instability he has handed on to you. No religion, no morals, no sense of duty! Oh, how I have been punished for closing my eyes to his faults! I did it for your sake. And now you reward me like this.

NORA: Yes. Like this.

HELMER: Now you have destroyed all my happiness. You have ruined my whole future. Oh, it's too dreadful to contemplate! I am in the power of a man who is completely without scruples. He can do what he likes with me, demand what he pleases, order me to do anything—I dare not disobey him. I am condemned to humiliation and ruin simply for the weakness of a woman.

NORA: When I am gone from this world, you will be free.

HELMER: Oh, don't be melodramatic. Your father was always ready with that kind of remark. How would it help me if you were "gone from this world," as you put it? It wouldn't assist me in the slightest. He can still make all the facts public; and if he does, I may quite easily be suspected of having been an accomplice in your crime. People may think that I was behind it—that it was I who encouraged you! And for all this I have to thank you, you whom I have carried on my hands through all the years of our marriage! Now do you realize what you've done to me?

NORA (coldly calm): Yes.

HELMER: It's so unbelievable I can hardly credit it. But we must try to find some way out. Take off that shawl. Take it off, I say! I must try to buy him off somehow. This thing must be hushed up at any price. As regards our relationship—we must appear to be living together just as before. Only appear, of course. You will therefore continue to reside here. That is understood. But the children shall be taken out of your hands. I dare no longer entrust them to you. Oh, to have to say this to the woman I once loved so dearly—and whom I still—! Well, all that must be finished. Henceforth there can be no question of happiness; we must merely strive to save what shreds and tatters—(The front door bell rings. HELMER starts.) What can that be? At this hour? Surely not—? He wouldn't—? Hide yourself, Nora. Say you're ill.

(NORA does not move. HELMER goes to the door of the room and opens it. The MAID is standing half-dressed in the hall.)

MAID: A letter for madam.

HELMER: Give it me. (Seizes the letter and shuts the door.) Yes, it's from him. You're not having it. I'll read this myself.

NORA: Read it.

HELMER (by the lamp): I hardly dare to. This may mean the end for us both. No. I must know. (Tears open the letter hastily; reads a few lines; looks at a piece of paper which is enclosed with it; utters a cry of joy.) Nora! (She looks at him questioningly.) Nora! No—I must read it once more. Yes, yes, it's true! I am saved! Nora, I am saved!

NORA: What about me?

HELMER: You too, of course. We're both saved, you and I. Look! He's returning your I.O.U. He writes that he is sorry for what has happened—a happy accident has changed his life—oh, what does it matter what he writes? We are saved, Nora! No one can harm you now. Oh, Nora, Nora—no, first let me destroy this filthy thing. Let me see—! (Glances at the I.O.U.) No, I don't want to look at it. I shall merely regard the whole business as a dream. (He tears the I.O.U. and both letters into pieces, throws them into the stove and watches them burn.) There. Now they're destroyed. He wrote that ever since Christmas Eve you've been—oh, these must have been three dreadful days for you, Nora.

NORA: Yes. It's been a hard fight.

HELMER: It must have been terrible—seeing no way out except—no, we'll forget the whole sordid business. We'll just be happy and go on telling ourselves over and over again: "It's over! It's over!" Listen to me, Nora. You don't seem to realize. It's over! Why are you looking so pale? Ah, my poor little Nora, I understand. You can't believe that I have forgiven you. But I have, Nora. I swear it to you. I have forgiven you everything. I know that what you did you did for your love of me.

NORA: That is true.

HELMER: You have loved me as a wife should love her husband. It was simply that in your inexperience you chose the wrong means. But do you think I love you any the less because you don't know how to act on your own initiative? No, no. Just lean on me. I shall counsel you. I shall guide you. I would not be a true man if your feminine helplessness did not make you doubly attractive in my eyes. You mustn't mind the hard words I said to you in those first dreadful moments when my whole world seemed to be tumbling about my ears. I have forgiven you, Nora. I swear it to you; I have forgiven you.

NORA: Thank you for your forgiveness.

(She goes out through the door, right.)

HELMER: No, don't go—(Looks in.) What are you doing there?

NORA (offstage): Taking off my fancy dress.

HELMER (by the open door): Yes, do that. Try to calm yourself and get your balance again, my frightened little songbird. Don't be afraid. I have broad wings to shield you. (Begins to walk around near the door.) How lovely and peaceful this little home of ours is, Nora. You are safe here; I shall watch over you like a hunted dove which I have snatched unharmed from the claws of the falcon. Your wildly beating little heart shall find peace with me. It will happen, Nora; it will take time, but it will happen, believe me. Tomorrow all this will seem quite different. Soon everything will be as it was before. I shall no longer need to remind you that I have forgiven you; your own heart will tell you that it is true. Do you really think I could ever bring myself to disown you, or even to reproach you? Ah, Nora, you don't understand what goes on in a husband's heart. There is something indescribably wonderful and satisfying for a husband in knowing that he has forgiven his wife—forgiven her unreservedly, from the bottom of his heart. It means that she has become his property in a double sense; he has, as it were, brought her into the world anew; she is now not only his wife but also his child. From now on that is what you shall be to me, my poor, helpless, bewildered little creature. Never be frightened of anything again, Nora. Just open your heart to me. I shall be both your will and your conscience. What's this? Not in bed? Have you changed?

NORA *(in her everyday dress)*: Yes, Torvald. I've changed.

HELMER: But why now—so late—?

NORA: I shall not sleep tonight.

HELMER: But, my dear Nora—

NORA *(looks at her watch)*: It isn't that late. Sit down here, Torvald. You and I have a lot to talk about.

(She sits down on one side of the table.)

HELMER: Nora, what does this mean? You look quite drawn—

NORA: Sit down. It's going to take a long time. I've a lot to say to you.

HELMER *(sits down on the other side of the table)*: You alarm me, Nora. I don't understand you.

NORA: No, that's just it. You don't understand me. And I've never understood you—until this evening. No, don't interrupt me. Just listen to what I have to say. You and I have got to face facts, Torvald.

HELMER: What do you mean by that?

NORA *(after a short silence)*: Doesn't anything strike you about the way we're sitting here?

HELMER: What?

NORA: We've been married for eight years. Does it occur to you that this is the first time that we two, you and I, man and wife, have ever had a serious talk together?

HELMER: Serious? What do you mean, serious?

NORA: In eight whole years—no, longer—ever since we first met—we have never exchanged a serious word on a serious subject.

HELMER: Did you expect me to drag you into all my worries—worries you couldn't possibly have helped me with?

NORA: I'm not talking about worries. I'm simply saying that we have never sat down seriously to try to get to the bottom of anything.

HELMER: But, my dear Nora, what on earth has that got to do with you?

NORA: That's just the point. You have never understood me. A great wrong has been done to me, Torvald. First by Papa, and then by you.

HELMER: What? But we two have loved you more than anyone in the world!

NORA *(shakes her head)*: You have never loved me. You just thought it was fun to be in love with me.

HELMER: Nora, what kind of a way is this to talk?

NORA: It's the truth, Torvald. When I lived with Papa, he used to tell me what he thought about everything, so that I never had any opinions but his. And if I did have any of my own, I kept them quiet, because he wouldn't have liked them. He called me his little doll, and he played with me just the way I played with my dolls. Then I came here to live in your house—

HELMER: What kind of a way is that to describe our marriage?

NORA *(undisturbed)*: I mean, then I passed from Papa's hands into yours. You arranged everything the way you wanted it, so that I simply took over your taste in everything—or pretended I did—I don't really know—I think it was a little of both—first one and then the other. Now I look back on it, it's as if I've been living here like a pauper, from hand to mouth. I performed tricks for you, and you gave me food and drink. But that was how you wanted it. You and Papa have done me a great wrong. It's your fault that I have done nothing with my life.

HELMER: Nora, how can you be so unreasonable and ungrateful? Haven't you been happy here?

NORA: No; never. I used to think I was; but I haven't ever been happy.

HELMER: Not—not happy?

NORA: No. I've just had fun. You've always been very kind to me. But our home has never been anything but a playroom. I've been your doll-wife, just as I used to be Papa's doll-child. And the children have been my dolls. I used to think it was fun when you came in and played with me, just as they think it's fun when I go in and play games with them. That's all our marriage has been, Torvald.

HELMER: There may be a little truth in what you say, though you exaggerate and romanticize. But from now on it'll be different. Playtime is over. Now the time has come for education.

NORA: Whose education? Mine or the children's?

HELMER: Both yours and the children's, my dearest Nora.

NORA: Oh, Torvald, you're not the man to educate me into being the right wife for you.

HELMER: How can you say that?

NORA: And what about me? Am I fit to educate the children?

HELMER: Nora!

NORA: Didn't you say yourself a few minutes ago that you dare not leave them in my charge?

HELMER: In a moment of excitement. Surely you don't think I meant it seriously?

NORA: Yes. You were perfectly right. I'm not fitted to educate them. There's something else I must do first. I must educate myself. And you can't help me with that. It's something I must do by myself. That's why I'm leaving you.

HELMER (*jumps up*): What did you say?

NORA: I must stand on my own feet if I am to find out the truth about myself and about life. So I can't go on living here with you any longer.

HELMER: Nora, Nora!

NORA: I'm leaving you now, at once. Christine will put me up for tonight—

HELMER: You're out of your mind! You can't do this! I forbid you!

NORA: It's no use your trying to forbid me any more. I shall take with me nothing but what is mine. I don't want anything from you, now or ever.

HELMER: What kind of madness is this?

NORA: Tomorrow I shall go home—I mean, to where I was born. It'll be easiest for me to find some kind of a job there.

HELMER: But you're blind! You've no experience of the world—

NORA: I must try to get some, Torvald.

HELMER: But to leave your home, your husband, your children! Have you thought what people will say?

NORA: I can't help that. I only know that I must do this.

HELMER: But this is monstrous! Can you neglect your most sacred duties?

NORA: What do you call my most sacred duties?

HELMER: Do I have to tell you? Your duties towards your husband, and your children.

NORA: I have another duty which is equally sacred.

HELMER: You have not. What on earth could that be?

NORA: My duty towards myself.

HELMER: First and foremost you are a wife and a mother.

NORA: I don't believe that any longer. I believe that I am first and foremost a human being, like you—or anyway, that I must try to become one. I know most people think as you do, Torvald, and I know there's something of the sort to be found in books. But I'm no longer prepared to accept what people say and what's written in books. I must think things out for myself, and try to find my own answer.

HELMER: Do you need to ask where your duty lies in your own home? Haven't you an infallible guide in such matters—your religion?

NORA: Oh, Torvald, I don't really know what religion means.

HELMER: What are you saying?

NORA: I only know what Pastor Hansen told me when I went to confirmation. He explained that religion meant this and that. When I get away from all this and can think things out on my own, that's one of the questions I want to look into. I want to find out whether what Pastor Hansen said was right—or anyway, whether it is right for me.

HELMER: But it's unheard of for so young a woman to behave like this! If religion cannot guide you, let me at least appeal to your conscience. I presume you have some moral feelings left? Or—perhaps you haven't? Well, answer me.

NORA: Oh, Torvald, that isn't an easy question to answer. I simply don't know. I don't know where I am in these matters. I only know that these things mean something quite different to me from what they do to you. I've learned now that certain laws are different from what I'd imagined them to be; but I can't accept that such laws can be right. Has a woman really not the right to spare her dying father pain, or save her husband's life? I can't believe that.

HELMER: You're talking like a child. You don't understand how society works.

NORA: No, I don't. But now I intend to learn. I must try to satisfy myself which is right, society or I.

HELMER: Nora, you're ill; you're feverish. I almost believe you're out of your mind.

NORA: I've never felt so sane and sure in my life.

HELMER: You feel sure that it is right to leave your husband and your children?

NORA: Yes. I do.

HELMER: Then there is only one possible explanation.

NORA: What?

HELMER: That you don't love me any longer.

NORA: No, that's exactly it.

HELMER: Nora! How can you say this to me?

NORA: Oh, Torvald, it hurts me terribly to have to say it, because you've always been so kind to me. But I can't help it. I don't love you any longer.

HELMER (*controlling his emotions with difficulty*): And you feel quite sure about this too?

NORA: Yes, absolutely sure. That's why I can't go on living here any longer.

HELMER: Can you also explain why I have lost your love?

NORA: Yes, I can. It happened this evening, when the

miracle failed to happen. It was then that I realized you weren't the man I'd thought you to be.

HELMER: Explain more clearly. I don't understand you.

NORA: I've waited so patiently, for eight whole years—well, good heavens, I'm not such a fool as to suppose that miracles occur every day. Then this dreadful thing happened to me, and then I *knew:* "Now the miracle will take place!" When Krogstad's letter was lying out there, it never occurred to me for a moment that you would let that man trample over you. I *knew* that you would say to him: "Publish the facts to the world." And when he had done this—

HELMER: Yes, what then? When I'd exposed my wife's name to shame and scandal—

NORA: Then I was certain that you would step forward and take all the blame on yourself, and say: "I am the one who is guilty!"

HELMER: Nora!

NORA: You're thinking I wouldn't have accepted such a sacrifice from you? No, of course I wouldn't! But what would my word have counted for against yours? That was the miracle I was hoping for, and dreading. And it was to prevent it happening that I wanted to end my life.

HELMER: Nora, I would gladly work for you night and day, and endure sorrow and hardship for your sake. But no man can be expected to sacrifice his honor, even for the person he loves.

NORA: Millions of women have done it.

HELMER: Oh, you think and talk like a stupid child.

NORA: That may be. But you neither think nor talk like the man I could share my life with. Once you'd got over your fright—and you weren't frightened of what might threaten me, but only of what threatened you—once the danger was past, then as far as you were concerned it was exactly as though nothing had happened. I was your little songbird just as before—your doll whom henceforth you would take particular care to protect from the world because she was so weak and fragile. *(Gets up.)* Torvald, in that moment I realized that for eight years I had been living here with a complete stranger, and had borne him three children—! Oh, I can't bear to think of it! I could tear myself to pieces!

HELMER *(sadly):* I see it, I see it. A gulf has indeed opened between us. Oh, but Nora—couldn't it be bridged?

NORA: As I am now, I am no wife for you.

HELMER: I have the strength to change.

NORA: Perhaps—if your doll is taken from you.

HELMER: But to be parted—to be parted from you! No, no, Nora, I can't conceive of it happening!

NORA *(goes into the room, right):* All the more necessary that it should happen.

(She comes back with her outdoor things and a small traveling-bag, which she puts down on a chair by the table.)

HELMER: Nora, Nora, not now! Wait till tomorrow!

NORA *(puts on her coat):* I can't spend the night in a strange man's house.

HELMER: But can't we live here as brother and sister, then—?

NORA *(fastens her hat):* You know quite well it wouldn't last. *(Puts on her shawl.)* Goodbye, Torvald. I don't want to see the children. I know they're in better hands than mine. As I am now, I can be nothing to them.

HELMER: But some time, Nora—some time—?

NORA: How can I tell? I've no idea what will happen to me.

HELMER: But you are my wife, both as you are and as you will be.

NORA: Listen, Torvald. When a wife leaves her husband's house, as I'm doing now, I'm told that according to the law he is freed of any obligations towards her. In any case, I release you from any such obligations. You mustn't feel bound to me in any way, however small, just as I shall not feel bound to you. We must both be quite free. Here is your ring back. Give me mine.

HELMER: That too?

NORA: That too.

HELMER: Here it is.

NORA: Good. Well, now it's over. I'll leave the keys here. The servants know about everything to do with the house—much better than I do. Tomorrow, when I have left town, Christine will come to pack the things I brought here from home. I'll have them sent on after me.

HELMER: This is the end then! Nora, will you never think of me any more?

NORA: Yes, of course. I shall often think of you and the children and this house.

HELMER: May I write to you, Nora?

NORA: No. Never. You mustn't do that.

HELMER: But at least you must let me send you—

NORA: Nothing. Nothing.

HELMER: But if you should need help—?

NORA: I tell you, no. I don't accept things from strangers.

HELMER: Nora—can I never be anything but a stranger to you?

NORA *(picks up her bag):* Oh, Torvald! Then the miracle of miracles would have to happen.

HELMER: The miracle of miracles?

NORA: You and I would both have to change so much

that—oh, Torvald, I don't believe in miracles any longer.

HELMER: But I want to believe in them. Tell me. We should have to change so much that—?

NORA: That life together between us two could become a marriage. Goodbye.

(She goes out through the hall.)

HELMER *(sinks down on a chair by the door and buries his face in his hands)*: Nora! Nora! *(Looks round and gets up.)* Empty! She's gone! *(A hope strikes him.)* The miracle of miracles—?

(The street door is slammed shut downstairs.)

Figure 1. Nora (Claire Bloom) shows Torvald (Donald Madden) a doll that she has bought as a Christmas present for one of their children in the Playhouse production of *A Doll's House*, directed by Patrick Garland, New York, 1971. (Photograph: Henry Grossman.)

Figure 2. Torvald (Donald Madden) berates Nora (Claire Bloom) after reading the blackmail letter from Krogstad in the Playhouse production of *A Doll's House*, directed by Patrick Garland, New York, 1971. (Photograph: Henry Grossman.)

Figure 3. Nora (Claire Bloom) prepares to leave Torvald (Donald Madden) in the final scene of the Playhouse production of *A Doll's House*, directed by Patrick Garland, New York, 1971. The transformation of Nora that Claire Bloom sought to project through her performance of the role may be seen by comparing her facial expression and costume in this photograph with those shown in Figures 1 and 2. (Photograph: Henry Grossman.)

Staging of *A Doll's House*

REVIEW OF THE PLAYHOUSE PRODUCTION, NEW
YORK, 1971, BY WALTER KERR

The difficulty with Ibsen today is that we must try to take two separate things seriously, the playwright's ideas and the playwright's playwriting. The ideas, of course, present no particular problem. One has only to listen to Claire Bloom's last long speech in the current—and very sleek—revival of "A Doll's House," which will soon be alternating with "Hedda Gabler" at the Playhouse, or to glance at the brief excerpts from Ibsen's "Notes for a Modern Tragedy" that have been included in the program to know that the ideas were sound, advanced, on target. "A woman cannot be herself in modern society," the notes read, "It is an exclusively male society, with laws made by men and with prosecutors and judges who assess female conduct from a male standpoint." Kate Millett sounds old-fashioned beside that.

But how, how, how do you take the playwriting seriously? From what vantage point, what perch or roost or perspective in time, can you attend, without doubling up, to the spectacle of a woman so determined to keep a secret from her husband that she promptly spills it, virtually within his hearing, to the very first acquaintance who walks in the door? Add to that the fact that she hasn't seen the acquaintance in years, and doesn't even recognize her when they do meet, and you've got a rather peculiar secret-keeper on your hands.

Peculiar things are going to keep happening, peculiar and predictable. Ibsen did work by notebook, which means that he jotted down most logically all the little twists and turns of motivation he was going to need and then clipped them together to make a scene whether they precisely flowed or not. If they didn't flow, he forced them ("Tell me, is it true you didn't love your husband?").

The terrible danger in this shuffled-note method is that you are going to hear the papers rustling, the clips slipping on. You can't *help* hearing them. And so you know, infallibly, that the moment the child-wife Nora exclaims "Oh, God, it's good to be alive and happy!," a doorbell will ring and a furtive fellow will slip in who's going to bring down her doll's house in ruins. Just as you know, with a certainty close to hilarity, that when Nora's fatuous lord and master, Torvald, exclaims "I often wish you were threatened with some impending disaster so that I could risk everything!," disaster is not only impending but here. Torvald has only to go to the mailbox ("I'm going to see if there's any mail"), slit open the first letter to hand, and the fat is in the fire. (In the current production, the fat is not only in the fire, Nora is on the floor, having been hurled there by a vigorous spouse who, it turns out, is willing to risk nothing.)

The underpinnings are all transparent, line by line and blow by blow, and we must struggle to induce in ourselves a state of mind that holds humor at bay in honor of the social proposition being so implausibly stated. It's a real battle, one that is often lost; Ibsen believed in his mechanics as well as in his creed, and we cannot. The effort isn't exacerbating, especially; we needn't come away exhausted from it. It is possible to look at the foolishness and feel fond, if not doting, as we wait for the message that is going to come of it all. But it's nip and tuck the whole way, and the thin ice of the situation poses extremely thorny problems for actors.

It's not only a matter of how the good lady doing Nora is going to try to stitch together the two parts of the role, the giddy, fawning creature who is willing to leap up and down like a puppy dog snatching at proffered bones for two acts and the serene, stern woman who lays down the new law in Act 3, having matured wonderfully during intermission. It's a matter of how everyone onstage, pompous husband, long-lost confidante, sniveling blackmailer, dying Dr. Rank who is willing to offer Nora his love with his next-to-last breath, is going to get us past the preposterous and into the ringing preachment. Do they try to steal home, eliding all that is awkward as quietly as possible? Do they rush it, pouncing upon line two before we have quite noticed line one? Do they stylize it, lifting themselves into daguerreotype postures that plainly have little to do with reality?

The present company, under Patrick Garland's direction, has tried taking it by storm, with a bit of the daguerreotype thrown in. Donald Madden, a Torvald who might well see Dr. Rank about hypertension, glides across the highly lacquered floor (this Nora has such difficulty getting money out of her husband that you feel he won't even allow the lady carpeting) to exchange his wife's swift kisses for quickly palmed coins as though the two were Harlequins giving a summer-park performance in a high wind. Robert Gerringer, the forger who has come to accuse Nora of forgery (motives do get piggy-backed in this odd way), keeps his mouth open and working so that no matter who is talking his teeth will show.

All work at a high pitch and in some fever, as though a Racinian *tirade* might spin off into space at any moment. (If you have never seen "A Doll's

House," and I was stunned to discover how many first-nighters never had, this is a crystal-clear reading of it, laid out like silverware.) And there are some genuine successes within the near-stylization. Roy Shuman's Dr. Rank, for instance, is highly mannered: head thrown back, hands always on the point of clapping, eyes darting this way and that as he bluntly, briskly mocks himself and his approaching death. The effect is perfect, that of a man already halfway to the horizon waving farewell with his thumb to his nose. I have never seen the part more robustly or more persuasively played. Patricia Elliott's Kristine, so quickly privy to Nora's secrets, speaks vast amounts of exposition exquisitely, then zeroes in fiercely upon the play's point as she grips her shawl severely and remembers that her only happiness has lain in work.

But what of Nora? Claire Bloom has made, I think, an admirable choice, though a choice with a canker to it. Most Noras won't sacrifice the opportunity to charm, to be bird-like and winsome and if possible adorable, during the first two acts. And you can't entirely blame *them*. Nora is, as written in these acts, a ninny underneath, a girl who really can't feel any sympathy for creditors because, after all, they're "strangers," a girl who, though her secret debt is much on her mind, hasn't the faintest notion of how much of it she's paid off. She subsists, it would seem, on macaroons. But actresses who go for charm and a pretty mindlessness are stuck with the last act. How does one turn an enchanting child into a dominating adult, especially when the transition is missing?

Miss Bloom tries to create the transition from the beginning, which is surely an intelligent thing to do. Even as her Nora is nestling her pretty head against her husband's waistcoat while she seduces him with quick flattery into giving her old friend a job, there is a strain about the eyes, an indication of an intelligence withheld, that adds initial dimension to the role. Where most Noras seem to have an instinct for being playful, fluttering as to the cocoon born, Miss Bloom's playfulness is plainly put on, a trick she has learned, a device that does not wholly engage her.

She is constantly listening to herself make the sounds a pompous husband expects, aware of their insincerity and worried about the gulf between what she is doing and what she might be feeling. Faintly alienated from the outset, she has given us a base for the play's ending. The reserve that we felt in her was the conscience that might have been awakened at any time but is not in fact awakened until it is time to make that speech and slam that door.

The catch to doing it this way, because the part is split in the writing, is a curious sense of heartlessness that overtakes Nora en route. Being to a degree disengaged, she seems not only indifferent to her children and extremely obtuse about her friend Kristine's personal problems but horrendously cold-blooded about the devoted Dr. Rank. He announces his impending death and she scarcely looks up from her sewing. He makes a gesture of love toward her, a gesture that has to be disinterested because he will never see her again, and she recoils as though he had proposed, perhaps, another forgery. Clipping the butterfly's wings leaves us with something of a dragonfly. Or are we merely being given a bit of "Hedda" ahead of time?

Miss Bloom works honorably, looks well, arrives at her last scene logically, and doesn't seem anyone you'd care to trust your heart with (I'm not thinking of Torvald, who is an oaf, but, say, of Dr. Rank, who is not). Miss Bloom has cooled Nora to make the way for the ultimate avalanche; the move does take away anything that was ever very appealing about her.

Good try. The problem, which persists, lies in the play. Ibsen simply could not, or did not, get his meaning and his method to match up. When he speaks of "laws made by men" and "judges who assess female conduct from a male standpoint," we know exactly what he is talking about. We also know that he is right. But the technical illustration in the play proper runs like this. Nora has forged her father's signature to get money to help her ailing husband, who must not know he is being helped. Why didn't she have her father sign the document? Because he, too, was ailing; she didn't want to trouble him. Thus there are two kinds of law: male law (don't forge) and female law (don't bother father). Serious as the point is, the illustration can only make us smile.

The actors must try to make us contain the smile, which, in this revival, they occasionally do.

AUGUST STRINDBERG

1849—1912

Throughout his life Strindberg suffered from a variety of psychological anxieties and compulsions, and throughout his career he exploited his personal and psychic life in his novels, short stories, poetry, essays, and plays. He was raised in Stockholm, Sweden, the fourth of twelve children and the first born in wedlock. His mother died when he was thirteen, and his father immediately married the housekeeper. Strindberg himself was married three times and divorced three times, and each of his marriages was a tormenting experience both for him and the woman, particularly his first marriage to Siri von Essen, an aspiring actress of little talent who divorced her husband, a baron, in order to marry Strindberg. Before the marriage, Strindberg had worked briefly in various jobs, as a tutor, a telegraph clerk, an actor, and a librarian, but once he became involved with Siri he devoted himself almost exclusively to his writing. They remained married from 1877 to 1891, but long before they were divorced their affection for one another had given way to sexual quarrels, mutual jealousies, and bitter recriminations. During the disintegration of the marriage, Strindberg turned out a series of autobiographical novels, among them *A Fool's Defence* (1886), based on his involvement with Siri and her former husband, as well as a series of powerful naturalistic plays, all dealing with forms of psychological and sexual strife between men and women, including *The Father* (1887), *Miss Julie* (1888), *The Creditors* (1889), and *The Stronger* (1890).

Strindberg was married once again in 1893, this time to a young Austrian journalist, but their relationship quickly disintegrated into many of the same patterns that had characterized his first marriage. And by 1894 Strindberg himself was beginning to experience a psychological disintegration that was to extend over the next two years, a period during which he suffered from a profound sense of guilt and spiritual torment, as well as from a variety of paranoic hallucinations, focussing both on supernatural powers and on the doctor to whom he eventually committed himself for treatment. During this period he immersed himself in the mystical works of Emanuel Swedenborg and other religious writers, as well as turning his hand to painting and experiments in alchemy. By 1897, he had already chronicled his psychological and spiritual crisis in a thinly veiled novel, *Inferno*, and by 1898 he had begun another immensely productive period of writing that was to continue until the end of his life. Overall, he produced more than seventy plays and dramatic fragments.

During the period following his psychological inferno, Strindberg turned out a series of twenty-one chronicle plays, many of them in the manner of Shakespeare's, dealing with figures and periods in Swedish history from the thirteenth to the eighteenth century. But the most important plays of his later period reflect the preoccupations that flowed from his spiritual crisis, and they are concerned with the exposure of evil, as in *The Dance of Death* (1901), *A Dream Play* (1902), and *The Ghost Sonata* (1907), or with guilt and expiation, as in *Crime and Crime* (1899) and *Easter* (1901), or with spiritual pilgrimage, as in *To Damascus*

(1898–1904) and *The Great Highway* (1909). In these plays, Strindberg turned away from the purely naturalistic methods of his earlier plays, using expressionistic and symbolic techniques to dramatize his troubled vision of human experience. In *A Dream Play,* for example, the world is seen entirely through the experience and perception of the Daughter of Indra, the child of a deity, whose descent to earth and subsequent encounters with various human beings reflect and reproduce, as Strindberg explained in his note on the play, "the disconnected but apparently logical form of a dream." Because it is a dream, "Anything can happen; everything is possible and probable . . . The characters are split, double and multiply; they evaporate, crystallise, scatter and converge. But a single consciousness holds sway over them all—that of the dreamer." The dreamer, of course, was Strindberg himself, and the disconnected events of the play vividly project his melancholy vision of the human landscape. *The Ghost Sonata* is another expressionistic and symbolic fantasy, this time displaying the macabre spectacle of a demonic household as it is progressively unveiled to the eyes of a young student—clearly Strindberg's alter ego—who ends the play by proclaiming the world to be "this madhouse, this prison, this charnelhouse." In their expressionistic techniques, these later plays prefigure a major aspect of modern and contemporary drama. In their preoccupation with dreams and the disconnected logic of psychic experience, they are arresting parallels to the work of Freud, whose first important study of the unconscious, *The Interpretation of Dreams,* did not appear until 1900.

But even in his naturalistic plays of the eighties, such as *Miss Julie*, Strindberg was advanced for his time, both in his dramatic techniques and in his psychological insight. He took great pains to identify his innovations in a lengthy "Foreword" to *Miss Julie* that he wrote after the play was accepted for publication. He called attention, for example, to the improvisational miming of Kristin early in the play, to the improvisational miming and dancing of the peasants, and to the improvisational monologue of Kristin mumbling in her sleep. He was aware of the classical precedents for mime, dancing, and monologue in drama, much as he was aware of the Italian Renaissance precedents for improvisational performance, but he also recognized that realistic conventions of his time had excluded these dramatic possibilities from the stage, whereas he considered them not only consistent with, but essential to a naturalistic illusion. In the same context, he also called attention to the fact that the play is designed to be staged without intermission, and that the set is to be diagonally arranged, "so that the actors may play full-face and in half-profile when they are sitting opposite one another at the table." He might also have pointed out that the action is set in a kitchen that really functions, for the play begins with Kristin frying a piece of kidney on the stove, and it reaches a climax with Jean beheading Julie's greenfinch on the kitchen chopping block. In all these respects, Strindberg carried naturalistic theater further than any of his contemporaries—extending it to its logical and psychological limits.

In the psychological conception of Jean and Julie, as well as in the unfolding of their relationship, Strindberg also challenged his contemporaries, particularly Emile Zola, the first major proponent of naturalistic drama, who in 1874 had written a manifesto proclaiming that heredity and environment are the sole determinants of human nature and behavior, and that dramatists are, therefore, obliged to reflect these circumstances in their plays. Strindberg, however, was clearly not content to limit himself to so narrow a conception of human behavior as he makes clear in the "Foreword" to *Miss Julie:*

> I see Miss Julie's tragic fate to be the result of many circumstances: the mother's character, the father's mistaken upbringing of the girl, her own weak nature, and the influence of her fiancé on a weak, degenerate mind. Also, more directly, the festive mood of Midsummer Eve, her father's absence, her monthly indisposition, her pre-occupation with animals, the excitement of dancing, the magic of dusk, the strongly aphrodisiac influence of flowers, and finally the chance that drives the couple into a room alone—to which must be added the urgency of the excited man.
>
> My treatment of the theme, morever, is neither exclusively physiological nor psychological. I have not put the blame wholly on the inheritance from her mother, nor on her physical condition at the time, nor on immorality. I have not even preached a moral sermon; in the absence of a priest I leave this to the cook.
>
> I congratulate myself on this multiplicity of motives as being up-to-date, and if others have done the same thing before me, then I congratulate myself on not being alone in my "paradoxes," as all innovations are called.

Strindberg's comments here and elsewhere in the "Foreword" may well serve as a warning against trying to interpret the play within any kind of simplistic framework. It is an enactment of a class struggle, as Strindberg notes, and as is repeatedly evident in the play from the dialogue and action of Julie, Jean, and Kristin. It is also, in part, an enactment of sexual warfare, as Strindberg and the play make painfully clear. But these two aspects of the conflict are inextricably woven together and complicated further by the subtle aspects of personality that mark both Jean and Julie as individuals rather than social or sexual types. The unfolding of their conflict is thus continually surprising and revealing, and until the very end of the play when Julie walks out of the kitchen with the razor in her hand the resolution of their conflict is never predictable, though it is thoroughly plausible.

Because of the complexity and the intensity of their struggle, *Miss Julie* is an extremely difficult play to produce, as noted in one of the reviews of the National Theatre production reprinted following the text. Photographs of that production show Albert Finney as Jean and Maggie Smith as Julie at various moments during their conflict—from their initial confrontation in the kitchen (see Figure 1) to their long conversation following the departure of the peasants (see Figure 2), to the final moments of the play (see Figure 3). Although their facial expressions clearly betray a lack of ferocity that one of the reviewers criticized in the production, they do show Jean's unnerving callousness, and they also suggest the subtle unfolding of Julie's tragic demise.

MISS JULIE
A Naturalistic Tragedy

BY AUGUST STRINDBERG / TRANSLATED BY ELIZABETH SPRIGGE

CHARACTERS

MISS JULIE, *aged 25*
JEAN, *the valet, aged 30*
KRISTIN, *the cook, aged 35*

SCENE:

The large kitchen of a Swedish manor house in a country district in the 1880s.

(Midsummer Eve.
The kitchen has three doors, two small ones into JEAN'S *and* KRISTIN'S *bedrooms, and a large, glass-fronted double one, opening on to a courtyard. This is the only way to the rest of the house.*
Through these glass doors can be seen part of a fountain with a cupid, lilac bushes in flower and the tops of some Lombardy poplars. On one wall are shelves edged with scalloped paper on which are kitchen utensils of copper, iron and tin.
To the left is the corner of a large tiled range and part of its chimney-hood, to the right the end of the servants' dinner table with chairs beside it.
The stove is decorated with birch boughs, the floor strewn with twigs of juniper. On the end of the table is a large Japanese spice jar full of lilac.
There are also an ice-box, a scullery table and a sink.
Above the double door hangs a big old-fashioned bell; near it is a speaking-tube.
A fiddle can be heard from the dance in the barn near-by.
KRISTIN *is standing at the stove, frying something in a pan. She wears a light-colored cotton dress and a big apron.*
JEAN *enters, wearing livery and carrying a pair of large riding-boots with spurs, which he puts in a conspicuous place.)*

JEAN: Miss Julie's crazy again to-night, absolutely crazy.

KRISTIN: Oh, so you're back, are you?

JEAN: When I'd taken the Count to the station, I came back and dropped in at the Barn for a dance. And who did I see there but our young lady leading off with the gamekeeper. But the moment she sets eyes on me, up she rushes and invites me to waltz with her. And how she waltzed—I've never seen anything like it! She's crazy.

KRISTIN: Always has been, but never so bad as this last fortnight since the engagement was broken off.

JEAN: Yes, that was a pretty business, to be sure. He's a decent enough chap, too, even if he isn't rich.

Oh, but they're choosy! *(Sits down at the end of the table.)* In any case, it's a bit odd that our young—er—lady would rather stay at home with yokels than go with her father to visit her relations.

KRISTIN: Perhaps she feels a bit awkward, after that bust-up with her fiancé.

JEAN: Maybe. That chap had some guts, though. Do you know the sort of thing that was going on, Kristin? I saw it with my own eyes, though I didn't let on I had.

KRISTIN: You saw them . . . ?

JEAN: Didn't I just! Came across the pair of them one evening in the stable-yard. Miss Julie was doing what she called "training" him. Know what that was? Making him jump over her riding-whip— the way you teach a dog. He did it twice and got a cut each time for his pains, but when it came to the third go, he snatched the whip out of her hand and broke it into smithereens. And then he cleared off.

KRISTIN: What goings on! I never did!

JEAN: Well, that's how it was with that little affair . . . Now, what have you got for me, Kristin? Something tasty?

KRISTIN *(serving from the pan to his plate)*: Well, it's just a little bit of kidney I cut off their joint.

JEAN *(smelling it)*: Fine! That's my special delice. *(Feels the plate.)* But you might have warmed the plate.

KRISTIN: When you choose to be finicky you're worse than the Count himself. *(Pulls his hair affectionately.)*

JEAN *(crossly)*: Stop pulling my hair. You know how sensitive I am.

KRISTIN: There, there! It's only love, you know.

(JEAN eats. KRISTIN brings a bottle of beer.)

JEAN: Beer on Midsummer Eve? No thanks! I've got something better than that. *(From a drawer in the table brings out a bottle of red wine with a yellow seal.)*

Yellow seal, see! Now get me a glass. You use a glass with a stem of course when you're drinking it straight.

KRISTIN (*giving him a wine-glass*): Lord help the woman who gets you for a husband, you old fusser! (*She puts the beer in the ice-box and sets a small saucepan on the stove.*)

JEAN: Nonsense! You'll be glad enough to get a fellow as smart as me. And I don't think it's done you any harm, people calling me your fiancé. (*Tastes the wine.*) Good, Very good indeed. But not quite warmed enough. (*Warms the glass in his hand.*) We bought this in Dijon. Four francs the liter without the bottle, and duty on top of that. What are you cooking now? It stinks.

KRISTIN: Some bloody muck Miss Julie wants for Diana.

JEAN: You should be more refined in your speech, Kristin. But why should you spend a holiday cooking for that bitch? Is she sick or what?

KRISTIN: Yes, she's sick. She sneaked out with the pug at the lodge and got in the usual mess. And that, you know, Miss Julie won't have.

JEAN: Miss Julie's too high-and-mighty in some respects, and not enough in others, just like her mother before her. The Countess was more at home in the kitchen and cowsheds than anywhere else, but would she ever go driving with only one horse? She went round with her cuffs filthy, but she had to have the coronet on the cuff-links. Our young lady—to come back to her—hasn't any proper respect for herself or her position. I mean she isn't refined. In the Barn just now she dragged the gamekeeper away from Anna and made him dance with her—no waiting to be asked. We wouldn't do a think like that. But that's what happens when the gentry try to behave like the common people—they become common ... Still she's a fine girl. Smashing! What shoulders! And what—er—etcetera!

KRISTIN: Oh come off it! I know what Clara says, and she dresses her.

JEAN: Clara? Pooh, you're all jealous! But I've been out riding with her ... and as for her dancing!

KRISTIN: Listen, Jean. You will dance with me, won't you, as soon as I'm through.

JEAN: Of course I will.

KRISTIN: Promise?

JEAN: Promise? When I say I'll do a thing I do it. Well thanks for the supper. It was a real treat. (*Corks the bottle.*)

(JULIE *appears in the doorway, speaking to someone outside.*)

JULIE: I'll be back in a moment. Don't wait.

(JEAN *slips the bottle into the drawer and rises respectfully.*

JULIE *enters and joins* KRISTIN *at the stove.*)

Well, have you made it? (KRISTIN *signs that* JEAN *is near them.*)

JEAN (*gallantly*): Have you ladies got some secret?

JULIE (*flipping his face with her handkerchief*): You're very inquisitive.

JEAN: What a delicious smell! Violets.

JULIE (*coquettishly*): Impertinence! Are you an expert of scent too? I must say you know how to dance. Now don't look. Go away. (*The music of a schottische begins.*)

JEAN (*with impudent politeness*): Is it some witches' brew you're cooking on Midsummer Eve? Something to tell your stars by, so you can see your future?

JULIE (*sharply*): If you could see that you'd have good eyes. (*to* KRISTIN) Put it in a bottle and cork it tight. Come and dance this schottische with me, Jean.

JEAN (*hesitating*): I don't want to be rude, but I've promised to dance this one with Kristin.

JULIE: Well, she can have another, can't you, Kristin? You'll lend me Jean, won't you?

KRISTIN (*bottling*): It's nothing to do with me. When you're so condescending, Miss, it's not his place to say no. Go on, Jean, and thank Miss Julie for the honor.

JEAN: Frankly speaking, Miss, and no offense meant, I wonder if it's wise for you to dance twice running with the same partner, specially as those people are so ready to jump to conclusions.

JULIE (*flaring up*): What did you say? What sort of conclusions? What do you mean?

JEAN (*meekly*): As you choose not to understand, Miss Julie, I'll have to speak more plainly. It looks bad to show a preference for one of your retainers when they're all hoping for the same unusual favor.

JULIE: Show a preference! The very idea! I'm surprised at you. I'm doing the people an honor by attending their ball when I'm mistress of the house, but if I'm really going to dance, I mean to have a partner who can lead and doesn't make me look ridiculous.

JEAN: If those are your orders, Miss, I'm at your service.

JULIE (*gently*): Don't take it as an order. Tonight we're all just people enjoying a party. There's no question of class. So now give me your arm. Don't worry, Kristin, I shan't steal your sweetheart.

(JEAN *gives* JULIE *his arm and leads her out. Left alone,* KRISTIN *plays her scene in an unhurried, natural way, humming to the tune of the schottische, played on a distant violin. She clears* JEAN's *place, washes up and puts things away, then takes off her apron, brings out a small mirror from a drawer, props it against the jar of lilac, lights a candle, warms a small pair of tongs and curls her fringe. She goes to the door and listens, then turning back to the table finds* MISS JULIE's *handkerchief. She smells it, then meditatively smooths it out and folds it. Enter* JEAN.)

JEAN: She really *is* crazy. What a way to dance! With people standing grinning at her too from behind the doors. What's got into her, Kristin?

KRISTIN: Oh, it's just her time coming on. She's always queer then. Are you going to dance with me now?

JEAN: Then you're not wild with me for cutting that one.

KRISTIN: You know I'm not—for a little thing like that. Besides, I know my place.

JEAN (*putting his arm round her waist*): You're a sensible girl, Kristin, and you'll make a very good wife . . .

(*Enter* JULIE, *unpleasantly surprised.*)

JULIE (*with forced gaiety*): You're a fine beau—running away from your partner.

JEAN: Not away, Miss Julie, but as you see back to the one I deserted.

JULIE (*changing her tone*): You really can dance, you know. But why are you wearing your livery on a holiday. Take it off at once.

JEAN: Then I must ask you to go away for a moment, Miss. My black coat's here. (*Indicates it hanging on the door to his room.*)

JULIE: Are you so shy of me—just over changing a coat? Go into your room then—or stay here and I'll turn my back.

JEAN: Excuse me then, Miss. (*He goes to his room and is partly visible as he changes his coat.*)

JULIE: Tell me, Kristin, is Jean your fiancé? You seem very intimate.

KRISTIN: My fiancé? Yes, if you like. We call it that.

JULIE: Call it?

KRISTIN: Well, you've had a fiancé yourself, Miss, and . . .

JULIE: But we really were engaged.

KRISTIN: All the same it didn't come to anything.

(JEAN *returns in his black coat.*)

JULIE: *Très gentil, Monsieur Jean. Très gentil.*

JEAN: *Vous voulez plaisanter, Madame.*

JULIE: *Et vous voulez parler français.*° Where did you learn it?

JEAN: In Switzerland, when I was steward at one of the biggest hotels in Lucerne.

JULIE: You look quite the gentleman in that get-up. Charming. (*Sits at the table.*)

Très . . . gentil, Very nice, Monsieur Jean, very nice. *Vous . . . Madame,* You like to joke, Madame. *Et . . . français,* And you want to speak French.

JEAN: Oh, you're just flattering me!

JULIE (*annoyed*): Flattering you?

JEAN: I'm too modest to believe you would pay real compliments to a man like me, so I must take it you are exaggerating—that this is what's known as flattery.

JULIE: Where on earth did you learn to make speeches like that? Perhaps you've been to the theater a lot.

JEAN: That's right. And traveled a lot too.

JULIE: But you come from this neighborhood, don't you?

JEAN: Yes, my father was a laborer on the next estate—the District Attorney's place. I often used to see you, Miss Julie, when you were little, though you never noticed me.

JULIE: Did you really?

JEAN: Yes. One time specially I remember . . . but I can't tell you about that.

JULIE: Oh do! Why not? This is just the time.

JEAN: No, I really can't now. Another time perhaps.

JULIE: Another time means never. What harm in now?

JEAN: No harm, but I'd rather not. (*Points to* KRISTIN, *now fast asleep.*) Look at her.

JULIE: She'll make a charming wife, won't she? I wonder if she snores.

JEAN: No, she doesn't, but she talks in her sleep.

JULIE (*cynically*): How do you know she talks in her sleep?

JEAN (*brazenly*): I've heard her. (*Pause. They look at one another.*)

JULIE: Why don't you sit down?

JEAN: I can't take such a liberty in your presence.

JULIE: Supposing I order you to.

JEAN: I'll obey.

JULIE: Then sit down. No, wait a minute. Will you get me a drink first?

JEAN: I don't know what's in the ice-box. Only beer, I expect.

JULIE: There's no only about it. My taste is so simple I prefer it to wine.

(JEAN *takes a bottle from the ice-box, fetches a glass and plate and serves the beer.*)

JEAN: At your service.

JULIE: Thank you. Won't you have some yourself?

JEAN: I'm not really a beer-drinker, but if it's an order. . . .

JULIE: Order? I should have thought it was ordinary manners to keep your partner company.

JEAN: That's a good way of putting it. (*He opens another bottle and fetches a glass.*)

JULIE: Now drink my health. (*He hesitates.*) I believe the man really is shy.

(JEAN *kneels and raises his glass with mock ceremony.*)

JEAN: To the health of my lady!

JULIE: Bravo! Now kiss my shoe and everything will be perfect. (*He hesitates, then boldly takes hold of her foot and lightly kisses it.*) Splendid. You ought to have been an actor.

JEAN (*rising*): We can't go on like this, Miss Julie. Someone might come in and see us.

JULIE: Why would that matter?

JEAN: For the simple reason that they'd talk. And if you knew the way their tongues were wagging out there just now, you . . .

JULIE: What were they saying? Tell me. Sit down.

JEAN (*sitting*): No offense meant, Miss, but . . . well, their language wasn't nice, and they were hinting . . . oh, you know quite well what. You're not a child, and if a lady's seen drinking alone at night with a man—and a servant at that—then . . .

JULIE: Then what? Besides, we're not alone. Kristin's here.

JEAN: Yes, asleep.

JULIE: I'll wake her up. (*Rises.*) Kristin, are you asleep? (KRISTIN *mumbles in her sleep.*) Kristin! Goodness, how she sleeps!

KRISTIN (*in her sleep*): The Count's boots are cleaned—put the coffee on—yes, yes, at once . . . (*Mumbles incoherently.*)

JULIE (*tweaking her nose*): Wake up, can't you!

JEAN (*sharply*): Let her sleep.

JULIE: What?

JEAN: When you've been standing at the stove all day you're likely to be tired at night. And sleep should be respected.

JULIE (*changing her tone*): What a nice idea. It does you credit. Thank you for it. (*Holds out her hand to him.*) Now come out and pick some lilac for me. (*During the following* KRISTIN *goes sleepily in to her bedroom.*)

JEAN: Out with you, Miss Julie?

JULIE: Yes.

JEAN: It wouldn't do. It really wouldn't.

JULIE: I don't know what you mean. You can't possibly imagine that . . .

JEAN: I don't, but others do.

JULIE: What? That I'm in love with the valet?

JEAN: I'm not a conceited man, but such a thing's been known to happen, and to these rustics nothing's sacred.

JULIE: You, I take it, are an aristocrat.

JEAN: Yes, I am.

JULIE: And I am coming down in the world.

JEAN: Don't come down, Miss Julie. Take my advice. No one will believe you came down of your own accord. They'll all say you fell.

JULIE: I have a higher opinion of our people than you. Come and put it to the test. Come on. (*Gazes into his eyes.*)

JEAN: You're very strange, you know.

JULIE: Perhaps I am, but so are you. For that matter everything is strange. Life, human beings, everything, just scum drifting about on the water until it sinks—down and down. That reminds me of a dream I sometimes have, in which I'm on top of a pillar and can't see any way of getting down. When I look down I'm dizzy; I have to get down but I haven't the courage to jump. I can't stay there and I long to fall, but I don't fall. There's no respite. There can't be any peace at all for me until I'm down, right down on the ground. And if I did get to the ground I'd want to be under the ground . . . Have you ever felt like that?

JEAN: No. In my dream I'm lying under a great tree in a dark wood. I want to get up, up to the top of it, and look out over the bright landscape where the sun is shining and rob that high nest of its golden eggs. And I climb and climb, but the trunk is so thick and smooth and it's so far to the first branch. But I know if I can once reach that first branch I'll go to the top just as if I'm on a ladder. I haven't reached it yet, but I shall get there, even if only in my dreams.

JULIE: Here I am chattering about dreams with you. Come on. Only into the park. (*She takes his arm and they go toward the door.*)

JEAN: We must sleep on nine midsummer flowers tonight; then our dreams will come true, Miss Julie. (*They turn at the door. He has a hand to his eye.*)

JULIE: Have you got something in your eye? Let me see.

JEAN: Oh, it's nothing. Just a speck of dust. It'll be gone in a minute.

JULIE: My sleeve must have rubbed against you. Sit down and let me see to it. (*Takes him by the arm and makes him sit down, bends his head back and tries to get the speck out with the corner of her handkerchief.*) Keep still now, quite still. (*Slaps his hand.*) Do as I tell you. Why, I believe you're trembling, big, strong man though you are! (*Feels his biceps.*) What muscles!

JEAN (*warning*): Miss Julie!

JULIE: Yes, Monsieur Jean?

JEAN: *Attention. Je ne suis qu'un homme.*°

JULIE: Will you stay still! There now. It's out. Kiss my hand and say thank you.

JEAN (*rising*): Miss Julie, listen, Kristin's gone to bed now. Will you listen?

JULIE: Kiss my hand first.

JEAN: Very well, but you'll have only yourself to blame.

JULIE: For what?

JEAN: For what! Are you still a child at twenty-five? Don't you know it's dangerous to play with fire?

Attention . . . homme, Careful, I'm only a man.

JULIE: Not for me. I'm insured.

JEAN (*bluntly*): No, you're not. And even if you are, there's still stuff here to kindle a flame.

JULIE: Meaning yourself?

JEAN: Yes. Not because I'm me, but because I'm a man and young and . . .

JULIE: And good looking? What incredible conceit! A Don Juan perhaps? Or a Joseph? Good Lord, I do believe you are a Joseph!

JEAN: Do you?

JULIE: I'm rather afraid so.

(JEAN *goes boldly up and tries to put his arms round her and kiss her. She boxes his ears.*)

How dare you!

JEAN: Was that in earnest or a joke?

JULIE: In earnest.

JEAN: Then what went before was in earnest too. You take your games too seriously and that's dangerous. Anyhow I'm tired of playing now and beg leave to return to my work. The Count will want his boots first thing and it's past midnight now.

JULIE: Put those boots down.

JEAN: No. This is my work, which it's my duty to do. But I never undertook to be your playfellow and I never will be. I consider myself too good for that.

JULIE: You're proud.

JEAN: In some ways—not all.

JULIE: Have you ever been in love?

JEAN: We don't put it that way, but I've been gone on quite a few girls. And once I went sick because I couldn't have the one I wanted. Sick, I mean, like those princes in the Arabian Nights who couldn't eat or drink for love.

JULIE: Who was she? (*No answer.*) Who was she?

JEAN: You can't force me to tell you that.

JULIE: If I ask as an equal, ask as a—friend? Who was she?

JEAN: You.

JULIE (*sitting*): How absurd!

JEAN: Yes, ludicrous if you like. That's the story I wouldn't tell you before, see, but now I will . . . Do you know what the world looks like from below? No, you don't. No more than the hawks and falcons do whose backs one hardly ever sees because they're always soaring up aloft. I lived in a laborer's hovel with seven other children and a pig, out in the gray fields where there isn't a single tree. But from the window I could see the wall round the Count's park with apple-trees above it. That was the Garden of Eden, guarded by many terrible angels with flaming swords. All the same I and the other boys managed to get to the tree of life. Does all this make you despise me?

JULIE: Goodness, all boys steal apples!

JEAN: You say that now, but all the same you do despise me. However, one time I went into the Garden of Eden with my mother to weed the onion beds. Close to the kitchen garden there was a Turkish pavilion hung all over with jasmine and honeysuckle. I hadn't any idea what it was used for, but I'd never seen such a beautiful building. People used to go in and then come out again, and one day the door was left open. I crept up and saw the walls covered with pictures of kings and emperors, and the windows had red curtains with fringes—you know now what the place was, don't you? I . . . (*Breaks off a piece of lilac and holds it for* JULIE *to smell. As he talks, she takes it from him.*) I had never been inside the manor, never seen anything but the church, and this was more beautiful. No matter where my thoughts went, they always came back—to that place. The longing went on growing in me to enjoy it fully, just once. *Enfin,*° I sneaked in, gazed and admired. Then I heard someone coming. There was only one way out for the gentry, but for me there was another and I had no choice but to take it. (JULIE *drops the lilac on the table.*) Then I took to my heels, plunged through the raspberry canes, dashed across the strawberry beds and found myself on the rose terrace. There I saw a pink dress and a pair of white stockings—it was you. I crawled into a weed pile and lay there right under it among prickly thistles and damp rank earth. I watched you walking among the roses and said to myself: "If it's true that a thief can get to heaven and be with the angels, it's pretty strange that a laborer's child here on God's earth mayn't come in the park and play with the Count's daughter."

JULIE (*sentimentally*): Do you think all poor children feel the way you did?

JEAN (*taken aback, then rallying*): *All* poor children? . . . Yes, of course they do. Of course.

JULIE: It must be terrible to be poor.

JEAN (*with exaggerated distress*): Oh yes, Miss Julie, yes. A dog may lie on the Countess's sofa, a horse may have his nose stroked by a young lady, but a servant . . . (*Change of tone.*) well, yes, now and then you meet one with guts enough to rise in the world, but how often? Anyhow, do you know what I did? Jumped into the millstream with my clothes on, was pulled out and got a hiding. But the next Sunday, when Father and all the rest went to Granny's, I managed to get left behind. Then I washed with soap and hot water, put my

---

Enfin, Well.

best clothes on and went to church so as to see you. I did see you and went home determined to die. But I wanted to die beautifully and peacefully, without any pain. Then I remembered it was dangerous to sleep under an elder bush. We had a big one in full bloom, so I stripped it and climbed into the oats-bin with the flowers. Have you ever noticed how smooth oats are? Soft to touch as human skin . . . Well, I closed the lid and shut my eyes, fell asleep, and when they woke me I was very ill. But I didn't die, as you see. What I meant by all that I don't know. There was no hope of winning you—you were simply a symbol of the hopelessness of ever getting out of the class I was born in.

JULIE: You put things very well, you know. Did you go to school?

JEAN: For a while. But I've read a lot of novels and been to the theater. Besides, I've heard educated folk talking—that's what's taught me most.

JULIE: Do you stand round listening to what we're saying?

JEAN: Yes, of course. And I've heard quite a bit too! On the carriage box or rowing the boat. Once I heard you, Miss Julie, and one of your young lady friends . . .

JULIE: Oh! Whatever did you hear?

JEAN: Well, it wouldn't be nice to repeat it. And I must say I was pretty startled. I couldn't think where you had learnt such words. Perhaps, at bottom, there isn't as much difference between people as one's led to believe.

JULIE: How dare you! We don't behave as you do when we're engaged.

JEAN (looking hard at her): Are you sure? It's no use making out so innocent to me.

JULIE: The man I gave my love to was a scoundrel.

JEAN: That's what you always say—afterward.

JULIE: Always?

JEAN: I think it must be always. I've heard the expression several times in similar circumstances.

JULIE: What circumstances?

JEAN: Like those in question. The last time . . .

JULIE (rising): Stop. I don't want to hear any more.

JEAN: Nor did she—curiously enough. May I go to bed now please?

JULIE (gently): Go to bed on Midsummer Eve?

JEAN: Yes. Dancing with that crowd doesn't really amuse me.

JULIE: Get the key of the boathouse and row me out on the lake. I want to see the sun rise.

JEAN: Would that be wise?

JULIE: You sound as though you're frightened for your reputation.

JEAN: Why not? I don't want to be made a fool of, nor to be sent packing without references when I'm trying to better myself. Besides, I have Kristin to consider.

JULIE: So now it's Kristin.

JEAN: Yes, but it's you I'm thinking about too. Take my advice and go to bed.

JULIE: Am I to take orders from you?

JEAN: Just this once, for your own sake. Please. It's very late and sleepiness goes to one's head and makes one rash. Go to bed. What's more, if my ears don't deceive me, I hear people coming this way. They'll be looking for me, and if they find us here, you're done for.

(The CHORUS approaches, singing. During the following dialogue the song is heard in snatches, and in full when the peasants enter.)

Out of the wood two women came,
Tridiri-ralla, tridiri-ra.
The feet of one were bare and cold,
Tridiri-ralla-la.

The other talked of bags of gold,
Tridiri-ralla, tridiri-ra.
But neither had a sou to her name,
Tridiri-ralla-la.

The bridal wreath I give to you,
Tridiri-ralla, tridiri-ra.
But to another I'll be true,
Tridiri-ralla-la.

JULIE: I know our people and I love them, just as they do me. Let them come. You'll see.

JEAN: No, Miss Julie, they don't love you. They take your food, then spit at it. You must believe me. Listen to them, just listen to what they're singing . . . No, don't listen.

JULIE (listening): What are they singing?

JEAN: They're mocking—you and me.

JULIE: Oh no! How horrible! What cowards!

JEAN: A pack like that's always cowardly. But against such odds there's nothing we can do but run away.

JULIE: Run away? Where to? We can't get out and we can't go into Kristin's room.

JEAN: Into mine then. Necessity knows no rules. And you can trust me. I really am your true and devoted friend.

JULIE: But supposing . . . supposing they were to look for you in there?

JEAN: I'll bolt the door, and if they try to break in I'll shoot. Come on. (Pleading.) Please come.

JULIE (tensely): Do you promise . . . ?

JEAN: I swear!

(JULIE goes quickly into his room and he excitedly follows her. Led by the fiddler, the peasants enter in festive attire *with flowers in their hats. They put a barrel of beer and a keg of spirits, garlanded with leaves, on the table, fetch glasses and begin to carouse. The scene becomes a ballet. They form a ring and dance and sing and mime. "Out of the wood two women came." Finally they go out, still singing.* JULIE *comes in alone. She looks at the havoc in the kitchen, wrings her hands, then takes out her powder puff and powders her face.* JEAN *enters in high spirits.)*

JEAN: Now you see! And you heard, didn't you? Do you still think it's possible for us to stay here?

JULIE: No, I don't. But what can we do?

JEAN: Run away. Far away. Take a journey.

JULIE: Journey? But where to?

JEAN: Switzerland. The Italian lakes. Ever been there?

JULIE: No. Is it nice?

JEAN: Ah! Eternal summer, oranges, evergreens . . . ah!

JULIE: But what would we do there?

JEAN: I'll start a hotel. First-class accommodation and first-class customers.

JULIE: Hotel?

JEAN: There's life for you. New faces all the time, new languages—no time for nerves or worries, no need to look for something to do—work rolling up of its own accord. Bells ringing night and day, trains whistling, buses coming and going, and all the time gold pieces rolling on to the counter. There's life for you!

JULIE: For *you*. And I?

JEAN: Mistress of the house, ornament of the firm. With your looks, and your style . . . oh, it's bound to be a success! Terrific! You'll sit like a queen in the office and set your slaves in motion by pressing an electric button. The guests will file past your throne and nervously lay their treasure on your table. You've no idea the way people tremble when they get their bills. I'll salt the bills and you'll sugar them with your sweetest smiles. Ah, let's get away from here! *(Produces a time-table.)* At once, by the next train. We shall be at Malmö at six-thirty, Hamburg eight-forty next morning, Frankfort-Basle the following day, and Como by the St. Gotthard Pass in—let's see— three days. Three days!

JULIE: That's all very well. But Jean, you must give me courage. Tell me you love me. Come and take me in your arms.

JEAN *(reluctantly)*: I'd like to, but I daren't. Not again in this house. I love you—that goes without saying. You can't doubt that, Miss Julie, can you?

JULIE *(shyly, very feminine)*: Miss? Call me Julie. There aren't any barriers between us now. Call me Julie.

JEAN *(uneasily)*: I can't. As long as we're in this house, there *are* barriers between us. There's the past

and there's the Count. I've never been so servile to anyone as I am to him. I've only to hear his bell and I shy like a horse. Even now, when I look at his boots, standing there so proud and stiff, I feel my back beginning to bend. *(Kicks the boots.)* It's those old, narrow-minded notions drummed into us as children . . . but they can soon be forgotten. You've only got to get to another country, a republic, and people will bend themselves double before my porter's livery. Yes, double they'll bend themselves, but I shan't. I wasn't born to bend. I've got guts. I've got character, and once I reach that first branch, you'll watch me climb. Today I'm valet, next year I'll be proprietor, in ten years I'll have made a fortune, and then I'll go to Rumania, get myself decorated and I may, I only say *may*, mind you, end up as a Count.

JULIE *(sadly)*: That would be very nice.

JEAN: You see in Rumania one can buy a title, and then you'll be a Countess after all. My Countess.

JULIE: What do I care about all that? I'm putting those things behind me. Tell me you love me, because if you don't . . . if you don't, what am I?

JEAN: I'll tell you a thousand times over—later. But not here. No sentimentality now or everything will be lost. We must consider this thing calmly like reasonable people. *(Takes a cigar, cuts and lights it.)* You sit down there and I'll sit here and we'll talk as if nothing happened.

JULIE: My God, have you no feelings at all?

JEAN: Nobody has more. But I know how to control them.

JULIE: A short time ago you were kissing my shoe. And now . . .

JEAN *(harshly)*: Yes, that was then. Now we have something else to think about.

JULIE: Don't speak to me so brutally.

JEAN: I'm not. Just sensibly. One folly's been committed, don't let's have more. The Count will be back at any moment and we've got to settle our future before that. Now, what do you think of my plans? Do you approve?

JULIE: It seems a very good idea—but just one thing. Such a big undertaking would need a lot of capital. Have you got any?

JEAN *(chewing his cigar)*: I certainly have. I've got my professional skill, my wide experience, and my knowledge of foreign languages. That's capital worth having, it seems to me.

JULIE: But it won't buy even one railway ticket.

JEAN: Quite true. That's why I need a backer to advance some ready cash.

JULIE: How could you get that at a moment's notice?

JEAN: You must get it, if you want to be my partner.

JULIE: I can't. I haven't any money of my own. *(Pause.)*

JEAN: Then the whole thing's off.

JULIE: And . . . ?

JEAN: We go on as we are.

JULIE: Do you think I'm going to stay under this roof as your mistress? With everyone pointing at me. Do you think I can face my father after this? No. Take me away from here, away from this shame, this humiliation. Oh my God, what have I done? My God, my God! *(Weeps.)*

JEAN: So that's the tune now, is it? What have you done? Same as many before you.

JULIE *(hysterically)*: And now you despise me. I'm falling, I'm falling.

JEAN: Fall as far as me and I'll lift you up again.

JULIE: Why was I so terribly attracted to you? The weak to the strong, the falling to the rising? Or was it love? Is that love? Do you know what love is?

JEAN: Do I? You bet I do. Do you think I never had a girl before?

JULIE: The things you say, the things you think!

JEAN: That's what life's taught me, and that's what I am. It's no good getting hysterical or giving yourself airs. We're both in the same boat now. Here, my dear girl, let me give you a glass of something special. *(Opens the drawer, takes out the bottle of wine and fills two used glasses.)*

JULIE: Where did you get that wine?

JEAN: From the cellar.

JULIE: My father's burgundy.

JEAN: Why not, for his son-in-law?

JULIE: And I drink beer.

JEAN: That only shows your taste's not so good as mine.

JULIE: Thief!

JEAN: Are you going to tell on me?

JULIE: Oh God! The accomplice of a petty thief! Was I blind drunk? Have I dreamt this whole night? Midsummer Eve, the night for innocent merrymaking.

JEAN: Innocent, eh?

JULIE: Is anyone on earth as wretched as I am now?

JEAN: Why should *you* be? After such a conquest. What about Kristin in there? Don't you think she has any feelings?

JULIE: I did think so, but I don't any longer. No. A menial is a menial . . .

JEAN: And a whore is a whore.

JULIE *(falling to her knees, her hands clasped)*: O God in heaven, put an end to my miserable life! Lift me out of this filth in which I'm sinking. Save me! Save me!

JEAN: I must admit I'm sorry for you. When I was in the onion bed and saw you up there among the roses, I . . . yes, I'll tell you now . . . I had the same dirty thoughts as all boys.

JULIE: You, who wanted to die because of me?

JEAN: In the oats-bin? That was just talk.

JULIE: Lies, you mean.

JEAN *(getting sleepy)*: More or less. I think I read a story in some paper about a chimney-sweep who shut himself up in a chest full of lilac because he'd been summonsed for not supporting some brat . . .

JULIE: So this is what you're like.

JEAN: I had to think up something. It's always the fancy stuff that catches the women.

JULIE: Beast!

JEAN: *Merde!*

JULIE: Now you have seen the falcon's back.

JEAN: Not exactly its *back*.

JULIE: I was to be the first branch.

JEAN: But the branch was rotten.

JULIE: I was to be a hotel sign.

JEAN: And I the hotel.

JULIE: Sit at your counter, attract your clients and cook their accounts.

JEAN: I'd have done that myself.

JULIE: That any human being can be so steeped in filth!

JEAN: Clean it up then.

JULIE: Menial! Lackey! Stand up when I speak to you.

JEAN: Menial's whore, lackey's harlot, shut your mouth and get out of here! Are you the one to lecture me for being coarse? Nobody of my kind would ever be as coarse as you were tonight. Do you think any servant girl would throw herself at a man that way? Have you ever seen a girl of my class asking for it like that? I haven't. Only animals and prostitutes.

JULIE *(broken)*: Go on. Hit me, trample on me—it's all I deserve. I'm rotten. But help me! If there's any way out at all, help me.

JEAN *(more gently)*: I'm not denying myself a share in the honor of seducing you, but do you think anybody in my place would have dared look in your direction if you yourself hadn't asked for it? I'm still amazed . . .

JULIE: And proud.

JEAN: Why not? Though I must admit the victory was too easy to make me lose my head.

JULIE: Go on hitting me.

JEAN *(rising)*: No. On the contrary I apologize for what I've said. I don't hit a person who's down—least of all a woman. I can't deny there's a certain satisfaction in finding that what dazzled one below was just moonshine, that the falcon's back is gray after all, that there's powder on the lovely cheek, that polished nails can have black tips, that the handkerchief is dirty although it smells of scent. On the other hand it hurts to find that what I was struggling to reach wasn't high and isn't real. It hurts to see you fallen so low you're far lower than your own cook. Hurts like when you see the last flowers of summer lashed to pieces by rain and turned to mud.

JULIE: You're talking as if you're already my superior.

JEAN: I am. I might make you a Countess, but you could never make me a Count, you know.

JULIE: But I am the child of a Count, and you could never be that.

JEAN: True, but I might be the father of Counts if . . .

JULIE: You're a thief. I'm not.

JEAN: There are worse things than being a thief—much lower. Besides, when I'm in a place I regard myself as a member of the family to some extent, as one of the children. You don't call it stealing when children pinch a berry from over-laden bushes. (*His passion is roused again.*) Miss Julie, you're a glorious woman, far too good for a man like me. You were carried away by some kind of madness, and now you're trying to cover up your mistake by persuading yourself you're in love with me. You're not, although you may find me physically attractive, which means your love's no better than mine. But I wouldn't be satisfied with being nothing but an animal for you, and I could never make you love me.

JULIE: Are you sure?

JEAN: You think there's a chance? Of my loving you, yes, of course. You're beautiful, refined (*Takes her hand.*) educated, and you can be nice when you want to be. The fire you kindle in a man isn't likely to go out. (*Puts his arm round her.*) You're like mulled wine, full of spices, and your kisses . . . (*He tries to pull her to him, but she breaks away.*)

JULIE: Let go of me! You won't win me that way.

JEAN: Not that way, how then? Not by kisses and fine speeches, not by planning the future and saving you from shame? How then?

JULIE: How? How? I don't know. There isn't any way. I loathe you—loathe you as I loathe rats, but I can't escape from you.

JEAN: Escape with me.

JULIE (*pulling herself together*): Escape? Yes, we must escape. But I'm so tired. Give me a glass of wine. (*He pours it out. She looks at her watch.*) First we must talk. We still have a little time. (*Empties the glass and holds it out for more.*)

JEAN: Don't drink like that. You'll get tipsy.

JULIE: What's that matter?

JEAN: What's it matter? It's vulgar to get drunk. Well, what have you got to say?

JULIE: We've got to run away, but we must talk first—or rather, I must, for so far you've done all the talking. You've told me about your life, now I want to tell you about mine, so that we really know each other before we begin this journey together.

JEAN: Wait. Excuse my saying so, but don't you think you may be sorry afterward if you give away your secrets to me?

JULIE: Aren't you my friend?

JEAN: On the whole. But don't rely on me.

JULIE: You can't mean that. But anyway everyone knows my secrets. Listen. My mother wasn't well-born; she came of quite humble people, and was brought up with all those new ideas of sex-equality and women's rights and so on. She thought marriage was quite wrong. So when my father proposed to her, she said she would never become his *wife* . . . but in the end she did. I came into the world, as far as I can make out, against my mother's will, and I was left to run wild, but I had to do all the things a boy does—to prove women are as good as men. I had to wear boys' clothes; I was taught to handle horses—and I wasn't allowed in the dairy. She made me groom and harness and go out hunting; I even had to try to plough. All the men on the estate were given the women's jobs, and the women the men's, until the whole place went to rack and ruin and we were the laughing-stock of the neighborhood. At last my father seemed to have come to his senses and rebelled. He changed everything and ran the place his own way. My mother got ill—I don't know what was the matter with her, but she used to have strange attacks and hide herself in the attic or the garden. Sometimes she stayed out all night. Then came the great fire which you have heard people talking about. The house and the stables and the barns—the whole place burnt to the ground. In very suspicious circumstances. Because the accident happened the very day the insurance had to be renewed, and my father had sent the new premium, but through some carelessness of the messenger it arrived too late. (*Refills her glass and drinks.*)

JEAN: Don't drink any more.

JULIE: Oh, what does it matter? We were destitute and had to sleep in the carriages. My father didn't know how to get money to rebuild, and then my mother suggested he should borrow from an old friend of hers, a local brick manufacturer. My father got the loan and, to his surprise, without having to pay interest. So the place was rebuilt. (*Drinks.*) Do you know who set fire to it?

JEAN: Your lady mother.

JULIE: Do you know who the brick manufacturer was?

JEAN: Your mother's lover?

JULIE: Do you know whose the money was?

JEAN: Wait . . . no, I don't know that.

JULIE: It was my mother's.

JEAN: In other words the Count's, unless there was a

settlement.

JULIE: There wasn't any settlement. My mother had a little money of her own which she didn't want my father to control, so she invested it with her— friend.

JEAN: Who grabbed it.

JULIE: Exactly. He appropriated it. My father came to know all this. He couldn't bring an action, couldn't pay his wife's lover, nor prove it was his wife's money. That was my mother's revenge because he made himself master in his own house. He nearly shot himself then—at least there's a rumor he tried and didn't bring it off. So he went on living, and my mother had to pay dearly for what she'd done. Imagine what those five years were like for me. My natural sympathies were with my father, yet I took my mother's side, because I didn't know the facts. I'd learnt from her to hate and distrust men— you know how she loathed the whole male sex. And I swore to her I'd never become the slave of any man.

JEAN: And so you got engaged to that attorney.

JULIE: So that he should be my slave.

JEAN: But he wouldn't be.

JULIE: Oh yes, he wanted to be, but he didn't have the chance. I got bored with him.

JEAN: Is that what I saw—in the stable-yard?

JULIE: What did you see?

JEAN: What I saw was him breaking off the engagement.

JULIE: That's a lie. It was I who broke it off. Did he say it was him? The cad.

JEAN: He's not a cad. Do you hate men, Miss Julie?

JULIE: Yes . . . most of the time. But when that weakness comes, oh . . . the shame!

JEAN: Then do you hate me?

JULIE: Beyond words. I'd gladly have you killed like an animal.

JEAN: Quick as you'd shoot a mad dog, eh?

JULIE: Yes.

JEAN: But there's nothing here to shoot with—and there isn't a dog. So what do we do now?

JULIE: Go abroad.

JEAN: To make each other miserable for the rest of our lives?

JULIE: No, to enjoy ourselves for a day or two, for a week, for as long as enjoyment lasts, and then— to die . . .

JEAN: Die? How silly! I think it would be far better to start a hotel.

JULIE (without listening): . . . die on the shores of Lake Como, where the sun always shines and at Christmas time there are green trees and glowing oranges.

JEAN: Lake Como's a rainy hole and I didn't see any oranges outside the shops. But it's a good place for tourists. Plenty of villas to be rented by— er—honeymoon couples. Profitable business that. Know why? Because they all sign a lease for six months and all leave after three weeks.

JULIE (naïvely): After three weeks? Why?

JEAN: They quarrel, of course. But the rent has to be paid just the same. And then it's let again. So it goes on and on, for there's plenty of love although it doesn't last long.

JULIE: You don't want to die with me?

JEAN: I don't want to die at all. For one thing I like living and for another I consider suicide's a sin against the Creator who gave us life.

JULIE: You believe in God—you?

JEAN: Yes, of course. And I go to church every Sunday. Look here. I'm tired of all this. I'm going to bed.

JULIE: Indeed! And do you think I'm going to leave things like this? Don't you know what you owe the woman you've ruined?

JEAN (taking out his purse and throwing a silver coin on the table): There you are. I don't want to be in anybody's debt.

JULIE (pretending not to notice the insult): Don't you know what the law is?

JEAN: There's no law unfortunately that punishes a woman for seducing a man.

JULIE: But can you see anything for it but to go abroad, get married and then divorce?

JEAN: What if I refuse this mésalliance?

JULIE: Mésalliance?

JEAN: Yes for me. I'm better bred than you, see! Nobody in my family committed arson.

JULIE: How do you know?

JEAN: Well, you can't prove otherwise, because we haven't any family records outside the Registrar's office. But I've seen your family tree in that book on the drawing-room table. Do you know who the founder of your family was? A miller who let his wife sleep with the King one night during the Danish war. I haven't any ancestors like that. I haven't any ancestors at all, but I might become one.

JULIE: This is what I get for confiding in someone so low, for sacrificing my family honor . . .

JEAN: Dishonor! Well, I told you so. One shouldn't drink because then one talks. And one shouldn't talk.

JULIE: Oh, how ashamed I am, how bitterly ashamed! If at least you loved me!

JEAN: Look here—for the last time—what do you want? Am I to burst into tears? Am I to jump over your riding whip? Shall I kiss you and carry you off to Lake Como for three weeks, after which . . . What am I to do? What do you want? This is getting unbearable, but that's what comes of playing around with women. Miss Julie, I can see how miserable you are; I know you're going through hell, but I don't understand you. We don't have scenes like this; we don't go in for hating each other. We make love for fun in our spare time, but we haven't all day and all night for it like you. I think you must be ill. I'm sure you're ill.

JULIE: Then you must be kind to me. You sound almost human now.

JEAN: Well, be human yourself. You spit at me, then won't let me wipe it off—on you.

JULIE: Help me, help me! Tell me what to do, where to go.

JEAN: Jesus, as if I knew!

JULIE: I've been mad, raving mad, but there must be a way out.

JEAN: Stay here and keep quiet. Nobody knows anything.

JULIE: I can't. People do know. Kristin knows.

JEAN: They don't know and they wouldn't believe such a thing.

JULIE (hesitating): But—it might happen again.

JEAN: That's true.

JULIE: And there might be—consequences.

JEAN (in panic): Consequences! Fool that I am I never thought of that. Yes, there's nothing for it but to go. At once. I can't come with you. That would be a complete give-away. You must go alone—abroad—anywhere.

JULIE: Alone! Where to? I can't.

JEAN: You must. And before the Count gets back. If you stay, we know what will happen. Once you've sinned you feel you might as well go on, as the harm's done. Then you get more and more reckless and in the end you're found out. No. You must go abroad. Then write to the Count and tell him everything, except that it was me. He'll never guess that—and I don't think he'll want to.

JULIE: I'll go if you come with me.

JEAN: Are you crazy, woman? "Miss Julie elopes with valet." Next day it would be in the headlines, and the Count would never live it down.

JULIE: I can't go. I can't stay. I'm so tired, so completely worn out. Give me orders. Set me going. I can't think any more, can't act . . .

JEAN: You see what weaklings you are. Why do you give yourselves airs and turn up your noses as if you're the lords of creation? Very well, I'll give you your orders. Go upstairs and dress. Get money for the journey and come down here again.

JULIE (softly): Come up with me.

JEAN: To your room? Now you've gone crazy again. (Hesitates a moment.) No! Go along at once. (Takes her hand and pulls her to the door.)

JULIE (as she goes): Speak kindly to me, Jean.

JEAN: Orders always sound unkind. Now you know. Now you know.

(Left alone, JEAN sighs with relief, sits down at the table, takes out a note-book and pencil and adds up figures, now and then aloud. Dawn begins to break. KRISTIN enters dressed for church, carrying his white dickey and tie.)

KRISTIN: Lord Jesus, look at the state the place is in! What have you been up to? (Turns out the lamp.)

JEAN: Oh, Miss Julie invited the crowd in. Did you sleep through it? Didn't you hear anything?

KRISTIN: I slept like a log.

JEAN: And dressed for church already.

KRISTIN: Yes, you promised to come to Communion with me today.

JEAN: Why, so I did. And you've got my bib and tucker. I see. Come on then. (Sits. KRISTIN begins to put his things on. Pause. Sleepily.) What's the lesson today?

KRISTIN: It's about the beheading of John the Baptist, I think.

JEAN: That's sure to be horribly long. Hi, you're choking me! Oh Lord, I'm so sleepy, so sleepy!

KRISTIN: Yes, what have you been doing up all night? You look absolutely green.

JEAN: Just sitting here talking with Miss Julie.

KRISTIN: She doesn't know what's proper, that one. (Pause.)

JEAN: I say, Kristin.

KRISTIN: What?

JEAN: It's queer really, isn't it, when you come to think of it? Her.

KRISTIN: What's queer?

JEAN: The whole thing. (Pause.)

KRISTIN (looking at the half-filled glasses on the table): Have you been drinking together too?

JEAN: Yes.

KRISTIN: More shame you. Look me straight in the face.

JEAN: Yes.

KRISTIN: Is it possible? Is it possible?

JEAN (after a moment): Yes, it is.

KRISTIN: Oh! This I would never have believed. How low!

JEAN: You're not jealous of her, surely?

KRISTIN: No, I'm not. If it had been Clara or Sophie I'd have scratched your eyes out. But not of her. I don't know why; that's how it is though. But it's disgusting.

JEAN: You're angry with her then.

KRISTIN: No. With you. It was wicked of you, very very wicked. Poor girl. And, mark my words, I won't stay here any longer now—in a place where one can't respect one's employers.

JEAN: Why should one respect them?

KRISTIN: You should know since you're so smart. But you don't want to stay in the service of people who aren't respectable, do you? I wouldn't demean myself.

JEAN: But it's rather a comfort to find out they're no better than us.

KRISTIN: I don't think so. If they're no better there's nothing for us to live up to. Oh and think of the Count! Think of him. He's been through so much already. No I won't stay in the place any longer. A fellow like you too! If it had been that attorney now or somebody of her own class . . .

JEAN: Why, what's wrong with . . .

KRISTIN: Oh, you're all right in your own way, but when all's said and done there is a difference between one class and another. No, this is something I'll never be able to stomach. That our young lady who was so proud and so down on men you'd never believe she'd let one come near her should go and give herself to one like you. She who wanted to have poor Diana shot for running after the lodge-keeper's pug. No. I must say . . . ! Well, I won't stay here any longer. On the twenty-fourth of October, I quit.

JEAN: And then?

KRISTIN: Well, since you mention it, it's about time you began to look around, if we're ever going to get married.

JEAN: But what am I to look for? I shan't get a place like this when I'm married.

KRISTIN: I know you won't. But you might get a job as porter or caretaker in some public institution. Government rations are small but sure, and there's a pension for the widow and children.

JEAN: That's all very fine, but it's not in my line to start thinking at once about dying for my wife and children. I must say I had rather bigger ideas.

KRISTIN: You and your ideas! You've got obligations too, and you'd better start thinking about them.

JEAN: Don't *you* start pestering me about obligations. I've had enough of that. (*Listens to a sound upstairs.*) Anyway we've got plenty of time to work things out. Go and get ready now and we'll be off to church.

KRISTIN: Who's that walking about upstairs?

JEAN: Don't know—unless it's Clara.

KRISTIN (*going*): You don't think the Count could have come back without our hearing him?

JEAN (*scared*): The Count? No, he can't have. He'd have rung for me.

KRISTIN: God help us! I've never known such goings on. (*Exit.*)

(*The sun has now risen and is shining on the treetops. The light gradually changes until it slants in through the windows.* JEAN *goes to the door and beckons.* JULIE *enters in traveling clothes, carrying a small bird-cage covered with a cloth which she puts on a chair.*)

JULIE: I'm ready.

JEAN: Hush! Kristin's up.

JULIE (*in a very nervous state*): Does she suspect anything?

JEAN: Not a thing. But, my God, what a sight you are!

JULIE: Sight! What do you mean?

JEAN: You're white as a corpse and—pardon me—your face is dirty.

JULIE: Let me wash then. (*Goes to the sink and washes her face and hands.*) There. Give me a towel. Oh! The sun is rising!

JEAN: And that breaks the spell.

JULIE: Yes. The spell of Midsummer Eve . . . But listen, Jean. Come with me. I've got the money.

JEAN (*skeptically*): Enough?

JULIE: Enough to start with. Come with me. I can't travel alone today. It's Midsummer Day, remember. I'd be packed into a suffocating train among crowds of people who'd all stare at me. And it would stop at every station while I yearned for wings. No, I can't do that. I simply can't. There will be memories too; memories of Midsummer Days when I was little. The leafy church—birch and lilac—the gaily spread dinner table, relatives, friends—everything in the park—dancing and music and flowers and fun. Oh, however far you run away—there'll always be memories in the baggage car—and remorse and guilt.

JEAN: I will come with you, but quickly now then, before it's too late. At once.

JULIE: Put on your things. (*Picks up the cage.*)

JEAN: No luggage, mind. That would give us away.

JULIE: No, only what we can take with us in the carriage.

JEAN (*fetching his hat*): What on earth have you got there? What is it?

JULIE: Only my greenfinch. I don't want to leave it behind.

JEAN: Well, I'll be damned! We're to take a bird-cage along, are we? You're crazy. Put that cage down.

JULIE: It's the only thing I'm taking from my home. The only living creature who cares for me since Diana went off like that. Don't be cruel. Let me take it.

JEAN: Put that cage down, I tell you—and don't talk so loud. Kristin will hear.

JULIE: No, I won't leave it in strange hands. I'd rather you killed it.

JEAN: Give the little beast here then and I'll wring its neck.

JULIE: But don't hurt it, don't . . . no, I can't.

JEAN: Give it here, I *can*.

JULIE (*taking the bird out of the cage and kissing it*): Dear little Serena, must you die and leave your mistress?

JEAN: Please don't make a scene. It's *your* life and

future we're worrying about. Come on, quick now!

(He snatches the bird from her, puts it on a board and picks up a chopper. JULIE *turns away.)*

You should have learnt how to kill chickens instead of target-shooting. Then you wouldn't faint at a drop of blood.

JULIE *(screaming)*: Kill me too! Kill me! You who can butcher an innocent creature without a quiver. Oh, how I hate you, how I loathe you! There is blood between us now. I curse the hour I first saw you. I curse the hour I was conceived in my mother's womb.

JEAN: What's the use of cursing. Let's go.

JULIE *(going to the chopping-block as if drawn against her will)*: No, I won't go yet. I can't ... I must look. Listen! There's a carriage. *(Listens without taking her eyes off the board and chopper.)* You don't think I can bear the sight of blood. You think I'm so weak. Oh, how I should like to see your blood and your brains on a chopping-block! I'd like to see the whole of your sex swimming like that in a sea of blood. I think I could drink out of your skull, bathe my feet in your broken breast and eat your heart roasted whole. You think I'm weak. You think I love you, that my womb yearned for your seed and I want to carry your offspring under my heart and nourish it with my blood. You think I want to bear your child and take your name. By the way, what is your name? I've never heard your surname. I don't suppose you've got one. I should be "Mrs. Hovel" or "Madam Dunghill." You dog wearing my collar, you lackey with my crest on your buttons! I share you with my cook; I'm my own servant's rival! Oh! Oh! Oh! ... You think I'm a coward and will run away. No, now I'm going to stay—and let the storm break. My father will come back ... find his desk broken open ... his money gone. Then he'll ring the bell—twice for the valet—and then he'll send for the police ... and I shall tell everything. Everything. Oh how wonderful to make an end of it all—a real end! He has a stroke and dies and that's the end of all of us. Just peace and quietness ... eternal rest. The coat of arms broken on the coffin and the Count's line extinct ... But the valet's line goes on in an orphanage, wins laurels in the gutter and ends in jail.

JEAN: There speaks the noble blood! Bravo, Miss Julie. But now, don't let the cat out of the bag.

*(*KRISTIN *enters dressed for church, carrying a prayer-book.* JULIE *rushes to her and flings herself into her arms for protection.)*

JULIE: Help me, Kristin! Protect me from this man!

KRISTIN *(unmoved and cold)*: What goings-on for a feast day morning! *(Sees the board.)* And what a filthy mess. What's it all about? Why are you screaming and carrying on so?

JULIE: Kristin, you're a woman and my friend. Beware of that scoundrel!

JEAN *(embarrassed)*: While you ladies are talking things over, I'll go and shave. *(Slips into his room.)*

JULIE: You must understand. You must listen to me.

KRISTIN: I certainly don't understand such loose ways. Where are you off to in those traveling clothes? And he had his hat on, didn't he, eh?

JULIE: Listen, Kristin. Listen, I'll tell you everything.

KRISTIN: I don't want to know anything.

JULIE: You must listen.

KRISTIN: What to? Your nonsense with Jean? I don't care a rap about that; it's nothing to do with me. But if you're thinking of getting him to run off with you, we'll soon put a stop to that.

JULIE *(very nervously)*: Please try to be calm, Kristin, and listen. I can't stay here, nor can Jean—so we must go abroad.

KRISTIN: Hm, hm!

JULIE *(brightening)*: But you see, I've had an idea. Supposing we all three go—abroad—to Switzerland and start a hotel together ... I've got some money, you see ... and Jean and I could run the whole thing—and I thought you would take charge of the kitchen. Wouldn't that be splendid? Say yes, do. If you come with us everything will be fine. Oh do say yes! *(Puts her arms round* KRISTIN.)*

KRISTIN *(coolly thinking)*: Hm, hm.

JULIE *(presto tempo)*: You've never traveled, Kristin. You should go abroad and see the world. You've no idea how nice it is traveling by train—new faces all the time and new countries. On our way through Hamburg we'll go to the zoo—you'll love that—and we'll go to the theater and the opera too ... and when we get to Munich there'll be the museums, dear, and pictures by Rubens and Raphael—the great painters, you know ... You've heard of Munich, haven't you? Where King Ludwig lived—you know, the king who went mad, ... We'll see his castles—some of his castles are still just like in fairy-tales ... and from there it's not far to Switzerland—and the Alps. Think of the Alps, Kristin dear, covered with snow in the middle of summer ... and there are oranges there and trees that are green the whole year round ...

*(*JEAN *is seen in the door of his room, sharpening his razor on a strop which he holds with his teeth and his left hand. He listens to the talk with satisfaction and now and then nods approval.* JULIE *continues, tempo prestissimo.)*

And then we'll get a hotel ... and I'll sit at the desk, while Jean receives the guests and goes out

marketing and writes letters . . . There's life for
you! Trains whistling, buses driving up, bells
ringing upstairs and downstairs . . . and I shall
make out the bills—and I shall cook them too . . .
you've no idea how nervous travelers are when it
comes to paying their bills. And you—you'll sit
like a queen in the kitchen . . . of course there
won't be any standing at the stove for you. You'll
always have to be nicely dressed and ready to be
seen, and with your looks—no, I'm not flattering
you—one fine day you'll catch yourself a husband . . . some rich Englishman, I shouldn't
wonder—they're the ones who are easy *(Slowing
down.)* to catch . . . and then we'll get rich and
build ourselves a villa on Lake Como . . . of
course it rains there a little now and then—but
(Dully.) the sun must shine there too
sometimes—even though it seems gloomy—and
if not—then we can come home again—come
back—*(Pause.)*—here—or somewhere else . . .

KRISTIN: Look here, Miss Julie, do you believe all that
yourself?

JULIE *(exhausted)*: Do I believe it?

KRISTIN: Yes.

JULIE *(wearily)*: I don't know. I don't believe anything
any more. *(Sinks down on the bench; her head in her
arms on the table.)* Nothing. Nothing at all.

KRISTIN *(turning to JEAN)*: So you meant to beat it, did
you?

JEAN *(disconcerted, putting the razor on the table)*: Beat it?
What are you talking about? You've heard Miss
Julie's plan, and though she's tired now with
being up all night, it's a perfectly sound plan.

KRISTIN: Oh, is it? If you thought I'd work for
that . . .

JEAN *(interrupting)*: Kindly use decent language in
front of your mistress. Do you hear?

KRISTIN: Mistress?

JEAN: Yes.

KRISTIN: Well, well, just listen to that!

JEAN: Yes, it would be a good thing if you did listen
and talked less. Miss Julie is your mistress and
what's made you lose your respect for her now
ought to make you feel the same about yourself.

KRISTIN: I've always had enough self-respect—

JEAN: To despise other people.

KRISTIN: —not to go below my own station. Has the
Count's cook ever gone with the groom or the
swineherd? Tell me that.

JEAN: No, you were lucky enough to have a high-class
chap for your beau.

KRISTIN: High-class all right—selling the oats out of
the Count's stable.

JEAN: You're a fine one to talk—taking a commission
on the groceries and bribes from the butcher.

KRISTIN: What the devil . . . ?

JEAN: And now you can't feel any respect for your
employers. You, you!

KRISTIN: Are you coming to church with me? I
should think you need a good sermon after your
fine deeds.

JEAN: No, I'm not going to church today. You can go
alone and confess your own sins.

KRISTIN: Yes, I'll do that and bring back enough
forgiveness to cover yours too. The Saviour
suffered and died on the cross for all our sins,
and if we go to Him with faith and a penitent
heart, He takes all our sins upon Himself.

JEAN: Even grocery thefts?

JULIE: Do you believe that, Kristin?

KRISTIN: That is my living faith, as sure as I stand
here. The faith I learnt as a child and have kept
ever since, Miss Julie. "But where sin abounded,
grace did much more abound."

JULIE: Oh, if I had your faith! Oh, if . . .

KRISTIN: But you see you can't have it without God's
special grace, and it's not given to all to have that.

JULIE: Who is it given to then?

KRISTIN: That's the great secret of the workings of
grace, Miss Julie. God is no respecter of persons,
and with Him the last shall be first . . .

JULIE: Then I suppose He does respect the last.

KRISTIN *(continuing)*: . . . and it is easier for a camel to
go through the eye of a needle than for a rich
man to enter into the kingdom of God. That's
how it is, Miss Julie. Now I'm going—alone, and
on my way I shall tell the groom not to let any of
the horses out, in case anyone should want to
leave before the Count gets back. Good-by.
(Exit.)

JEAN: What a devil! And all on account of a greenfinch.

JULIE *(wearily)*: Never mind the greenfinch. Do you
see any way out of this, any end to it?

JEAN *(pondering)*: No.

JULIE: If you were in my place, what would you do?

JEAN: In your place? Wait a bit. If I was a woman—a
lady of rank who had—fallen. I don't know. Yes,
I do know now.

JULIE *(picking up the razor and making a gesture)*: This?

JEAN: Yes. But *I* wouldn't do it, you know. There's a
difference between us.

JULIE: Because you're a man and I'm a woman? What
is the difference?

JEAN: The usual difference—between man and
woman.

JULIE *(holding the razor)*: I'd like to. But I can't. My
father couldn't either, that time he wanted to.

JEAN: No, he didn't want to. He had to be revenged
first.

JULIE: And now my mother is revenged again,
through me.

JEAN: Didn't you ever love your father, Miss Julie?

JULIE: Deeply, but I must have hated him too—
unconsciously. And he let me be brought up to
despise my own sex, to be half woman, half man.

Whose fault is what's happened? My father's, my mother's, or my own? My own? I haven't anything that's my own. I haven't one single thought that I didn't get from my father, one emotion that didn't come from my mother, and as for this last idea—about all people being equal—I got that from him, my fiancé—that's why I call him a cad. How can it be my fault? Push the responsibility on to Jesus, like Kristin does? No, I'm too proud and—thanks to my father's teaching—too intelligent. As for all that about a rich person not being able to get into heaven, it's just a lie, but Kristin, who has money in the savings-bank, will certainly not get in. Whose fault is it? What does it matter whose fault it is? In any case I must take the blame and bear the consequences.

JEAN: Yes, but . . . (*There are two sharp rings on the bell.* JULIE *jumps to her feet.* JEAN *changes into his livery.*) The Count is back. Supposing Kristin . . . (*Goes to the speaking-tube, presses it and listens.*)

JULIE: Has he been to his desk yet?

JEAN: This is Jean, sir. (*Listens.*) Yes, sir. (*Listens.*) Yes, sir, very good, sir. (*Listens.*) At once, sir? (*Listens.*) Very good, sir. In half an hour.

JULIE (*in panic*): What did he say? My God, what did he say?

JEAN: He ordered his boots and his coffee in half an hour.

JULIE: Then there's half an hour . . . Oh, I'm so tired! I can't do anything. Can't be sorry, can't run away, can't stay, can't live—can't die. Help me. Order me, and I'll obey like a dog. Do me this last service—save my honor, save his name. You know what I ought do to, but haven't the strength to do. Use your strength and order me to do it.

JEAN: I don't know why—I can't now—I don't understand . . . It's just as if this coat made me—I can't give you orders—and now that the Count has spoken to me—I can't quite explain, but . . . well, that devil of a lackey is bending my back again. I believe if the Count came down now and ordered me to cut my throat, I'd do it on the spot.

JULIE: Then pretend you're him and I'm you. You did some fine acting before, when you knelt to

me and played the aristocrat. Or . . . Have you ever seen a hypnotist at the theater? (*He nods.*) He says to the person "Take the broom," and he takes it. He says "Sweep," and he sweeps . . .

JEAN: But the person has to be asleep.

JULIE (*as if in a trance*): I am asleep already . . . the whole room has turned to smoke—and you look like a stove—a stove like a man in black with a tall hat—your eyes are glowing like coals when the fire is low—and your face is a white patch like ashes. (*The sunlight has now reached the floor and lights up* JEAN.) How nice and warm it is! (*She holds out her hands as though warming them at a fire.*) And so light—and so peaceful.

JEAN (*putting the razor in her hand*): Here is the broom. Go now while it's light—out to the barn—and . . . (*Whispers in her ear.*)

JULIE (*waking*): Thank you. I am going now—to rest. But just tell me that even the first can receive the gift of grace.

JEAN: The first? No, I can't tell you that. But wait . . . Miss Julie, I've got it! You aren't one of the first any longer. You're one of the last.

JULIE: That's true, I'm one of the very last. I *am* the last. Oh! . . . But now I can't go. Tell me again to go.

JEAN: No, I can't now either. I can't.

JULIE: And the first shall be last.

JEAN: Don't think, don't think. You're taking my strength away too and making me a coward. What's that? I thought I saw the bell move . . . To be so frightened of a bell! Yes, but it's not just a bell. There's somebody behind it—a hand moving it—and something else moving the hand—and if you stop your ears—if you stop your ears—yes, then it rings louder than ever. Rings and rings until you answer—and then it's too late. Then the police come and . . . and . . . (*The bell rings twice loudly.* JEAN *flinches, then straightens himself up.*) It's horrible. But there's no other way to end it . . . Go!

(JULIE *walks firmly out through the door.*)

CURTAIN

Figure 1. Julie (Maggie Smith) waves her scented handkerchief at Jean (Albert Finney) in the National Theatre production of *Miss Julie*, directed by Michael Elliott, London, 1966. (Photograph: Angus McBean, Harvard Theatre Collection.)

Figure 2. Jean (Albert Finney) and Julie (Maggie Smith) during a pause in their long conversation, after the peasants have departed, in the National Theatre production of *Miss Julie*, directed by Michael Elliott, London, 1966. (Photograph: Zoë Dominic, London.)

Figure 3. Julie (Maggie Smith) holds her greenfinch in her hands while Jean (Albert Finney) waits ready to behead it on the chopping board in the National Theatre production of *Miss Julie,* directed by Michael Elliott, London, 1966. (Photograph: Angus McBean, Harvard Theatre Collection.)

Staging of *Miss Julie*

**REVIEW OF THE NATIONAL THEATRE
PRODUCTION, 1966, BY THE LONDON *TIMES*
DRAMA CRITIC**

Miss Julie brings Mr. Finney and Miss Smith together in Strindberg's sexual dual between servant and mistress. The duel itself comes over with less than its usual ferocity as the production gives as much emphasis to the private fantasies of the antagonists as to their actual encounter. Jean's dream of social advancement and Julie's dream of falling to destruction are the real things: each to the other is only the accidental means of embodying them. Not that Michael Elliott's production is lacking in aggressiveness: Miss Smith's erotic arrogance in the first scene is matched by the casual brutality with which Mr. Finney at the end chops off the tame bird's head.

But it is rather that the partners (Julie in particular) are acting under a somnambulistic spell. The production does not stretch Miss Smith far enough away from comedy; and her voice is still obstinately without pathos. But Mr. Finney's Jean is a subtle compound of materialism and social pretension; and there is a fine icy Christine by Jeanne Watts, who gives the claustrophobic drama a link with the outer world. The pantomine interlude, alas, has defeated Mr. Elliott like other directors before him.

**REVIEW OF THE NATIONAL THEATRE
PRODUCTION, 1966, BY HUGH LEONARD**

Second nights can be dangerous. Actors loosen their collars, tuck in their frayed nerve-ends and uncross their fingers. A happy tiredness descends on the company like fall-out; and the first casualty is timing. Then a drawer sticks, a line is fluffed and a laugh comes at the wrong place. Panic sets in, and last night's champagne goes incurably flat. Perhaps this was what happened to *Miss Julie* at the National Theatre, but Michael Elliott's direction wasn't quite up to the task to begin with. This is a veritable bitch of a play, in which a miss is as bad as a mile. Big guns are needed; and although Mr. Elliott had them, they were trained in the wrong direction. For great stretches of time we were obliged to look at the back of Albert Finney's head and at Maggie Smith in half-profile. Savagely emotional scenes were played at a murmur in dingy lighting and a set which reduced Strindberg's 'large kitchen' to a pokey room with swaying roofbeams. The callous beheading of the chaffinch generated hardly an 'ugh!', and the play's ending was so indeterminately staged that the audience sat in puzzled silence waiting for more.

Not that the production was a disaster. But it wasn't Strindberg either. Mr. Finney's valet was good, but muted; and, as Miss Julie, Miss Smith wasn't nearly patrician enough. To fall spectacularly, one needs height first and foremost; and it is Julie's pretensions which dictate her suicide. With no discernible social gap existing between Julie and her father's valet, half the play's values were lost. Miss Smith is always delightful to watch and listen to; but this isn't her part any more than Strindberg is suited to Mr. Elliott.

ANTON CHEKHOV

1860-1904

Anton Chekhov was born in Taganrog, a Crimean resort not far from Yalta, where he wrote his last play, *The Cherry Orchard,* when he was dying of tuberculosis. Although his grandfather had been a serf who amassed enough money not only to buy his freedom but also an estate, his father, plagued by the debts of an unsuccessful grocery, was forced to leave Taganrog and move the family to Moscow. Chekhov himself remained in Taganrog to finish his schooling, but his years there could hardly have been pleasant ones, for his poverty compelled him to earn money by doing homework for his fellow students, and Taganrog itself, like most seaside resorts of that era, was filled with the sick and aged. So it is not surprising that the resorts that appear repeatedly in Chekhov's works, such as the "villas" that Lopahin proposes to build along the river bank, are always associated with tedium and futility. By 1880, Chekhov, too, had left Taganrog and moved to Moscow, where he entered medical school and started to write short stories to help support himself and his family. He became a physician and practiced medicine for a time, yet he gradually came to spend more and more effort on his writing, less and less on medicine. By 1888, he was practicing only during epidemics, when there was a shortage of doctors, whereas he was writing so much that he had already published 300 stories. During the 1880s, Chekhov had also started writing for the stage—first one-act plays, which he began doing in 1884, the year of his graduation from medical school, then full-length works, the earliest of which appeared in 1887. Most of his one-act plays are farcical studies of middle-class aspirations to sophisticated society, such as *The Boor* and *The Marriage Proposal,* which were well received and still continue to be performed. His early full-length works, such as *Ivanov* (1887), and *The Wood Demon* (1889), an early version of *Uncle Vanya,* were bitter failures, so much so that he did not write another serious full-length play until *The Seagull* (1896), which was first produced in St. Petersburg.

The Seagull, a psychologically realistic play, which bears witness to the drama of human loneliness and frustration, failed dismally in its opening production, for it was a radical departure from Russian theatrical tastes of the time. Chekhov's audience was unaccustomed to his low-key realism, to his subtle revelations of character, to his apparently plotless drama of Russian life, for this kind of drama was completely at odds with the melodramatic thrillers then being imported from Paris. The Russian actors were also unprepared for it, since they had never tried, nor seen, any style of performance other than the bombastic acting of the period that had been popularized by the English actor Edmund Kean. And the management of the theater where it was produced did not give the actors much of a chance to develop an appropriately low-key style, allowing them only nine days for rehearsals. *The Seagull* was literally laughed off the stage in St. Petersburg. Although Chekhov vowed never to write another play, he did permit *The Seagull* to be printed in a literary magazine, where it caught the interest of two wealthy young men, Constantin Stanislavski and Vladimir Nemirovich-

Danchenko, whose theatrical ambitions brought them together in 1898 to form the Moscow Art Theater. This group was based on the new principles of ensemble acting then being attempted throughout Europe, where acting companies were following the model established by the German troupe of the Duke of Saxe-Meinegen. But Stanislavski and Nemirovich-Danchenko were not content simply to develop an ensemble. They aimed to develop an acting company with a distinctively new style of performance, a style that was understated rather than overstated, realistic instead of melodramatic. That style was perfectly attuned to the psychological nuances of *The Seagull,* and thus they chose to conclude their first season with a revival of the play. That revival turned out to be the making of both Chekhov and the Moscow Art Theater, for though the rest of their season had been a series of failures, *The Seagull* was met with thunderous applause by the audience.

Chekhov's plays do not actually try to elicit dynamic roars of approval. Indeed, they are all wry, sometimes wearied, sometimes satirical displays of futility in human behavior—of the inability to act decisively, even when such action would seem to be easily within the range of human capacity. In *Uncle Vanya* (1899), for example, the central character learns that the professor for whom he has slaved without reward is not the personification of wisdom, as he had thought, but is instead a mediocre academic windbag. Consequently, he is moved to shoot the professor at point-blank range, but misses him. And he is seen at the end of the play repressing the knowledge he has of his own wasted life, unlearning what he has learned by a titanic effort in futility. Chekhov's next play, *The Three Sisters* (1901), is a study of shared futility, enacted by the title characters, who though left with an ample inheritance never fulfill any of their personal hopes, professional ambitions, or mundane desires, not even the simple desire that moves them throughout the play: to go to Moscow. *The Three Sisters* was followed three years later by the production of *The Cherry Orchard* in January 1904, six months before Chekhov died of tuberculosis.

The Cherry Orchard may be seen as a full-scale version of cultural futility—of the inability of an old aristocratic social order to preserve itself, of the inability of a new bourgeois order to find meaning in anything beyond the acquisition of money and land. Everyone in the play owns, wants to own, or wants to maintain ownership of someone or something, and the play witnesses everyone gaining or losing the things they wish to own. Whether the audience is to laugh at this spectacle, or to weep, or simply to be bemused, is a difficult question. Chekhov called the play a comedy, and he apparently intended it to be comic, judging from correspondence with Stanislavski and Nemirovich-Danchenko. Yet Stanislavski's letters just as clearly show that he did not consider it a comedy at all—that he viewed it as a tragic expression of Russian life:

> It is not a comedy, not a farce, as you wrote—it is a tragedy no matter if you do indicate a way out into a better world in the last act . . . when I read it for the second time . . . I wept like a woman, I tried to control myself, but could not. I can hear you say: "But please, this is a farce . . ." No, for the ordinary person this is a tragedy.

Stanislavski's decision to produce the play as a tragedy moved Chekhov to complain that he was turning it into a piece of sniveling sentimentality, and Stanislavski did modify his interpretation somewhat during the next thirty years that he produced it, but he never came around to seeing the characters as laughable.

The conflict between Chekhov and Stanislavski is, of course, irreconcilable, because the play repeatedly hovers between the comic and the tragic. Yet Peter Brook's production, first staged in Paris in 1981, then performed in New York in 1988, seems to have achieved the delicate combination of moods which the play evokes. One has only to look at the contrasting shots of Mrs. Ranevsky, Lopakhin, and Gayev (see Figures 1 and 2) to see what Brook and his actors achieved. As seen in Figure 1, Mrs. Ranevsky dances with delight to be back in her old home, while Gayev looks on and Lopakhin, still the outsider, the peasant, sits on the floor; later (see Figure 2), Lopakhin tells Mrs. Ranevsky that she must sell the cherry orchard, and the set look on her face reveals both sadness and defiance. Again Gayev looks on, as he does throughout the play, never really accomplishing anything in spite of his many speeches, but this time his expression reflects his sister's melancholy. The characters and their feelings stand out with particular force because, as Frank Rich notes in his review following the text, Brook has avoided any kind of elaborate scenery, restricting himself just to Oriental rugs and a few other suggestive furnishings. This choice, seemingly a strange one for a play set in an ample country house in nineteenth-century Russia, nonetheless reflects the play's constant evocation of places, people, and ways of life which are out of sight, and often out of reach, such as Paris, or Mrs. Ranevsky's lover, or Pishchik's daughter Dashenka, or the cherry orchard, though each has an almost-palpable reality. Without detailed sets and furnishings, the actors must conjure up both the onstage and the offstage realities—and in so doing, demonstrate that all of those realities are equally unstable and, at last, equally unreachable.

THE CHERRY ORCHARD

BY ANTON CHEKHOV / TRANSLATED BY DAVID MAGARSHACK

CHARACTERS

LYUBOV (LYUBA) ANDREYEVNA RANEVSKY, *a landowner*
ANYA, *her daughter, aged seventeen*
VARYA, *her adopted daughter, aged twenty-four*
LEONID ANDREYEVICH GAYEV, *Mrs. Ranevsky's brother*
YERMOLAY ALEXEYEVICH LOPAKHIN, *a businessman*
PETER (PYOTR) SERGEYEVICH TROFIMOV, *a student*
BORIS BORISOVICH SIMEONOV-PISHCHIK, *a landowner*
CHARLOTTE IVANOVNA, *a governess*
SIMON PANTELEYEVICH YEPIKHODOV, *a clerk*

DUNYASHA, *a maid*
FIRS, *a manservant, aged eighty-seven*
YASHA, *a young manservant*
A HIKER
A STATIONMASTER
A POST OFFICE CLERK
GUESTS *and* SERVANTS

SCENE

The action takes place on MRS. RANEVSKY'S *estate.*

ACT 1

(A room which is still known as the nursery. One of the doors leads to ANYA'S *room. Daybreak; the sun will be rising soon. It is May. The cherry trees are in blossom, but it is cold in the orchard. Morning frost. The windows of the room are shut. Enter* DUNYASHA, *carrying a candle, and* LOPAKHIN *with a book in his hand.)*

LOPAKHIN: The train's arrived, thank goodness. What's the time?

DUNYASHA: Nearly two o'clock, sir. *(Blows out the candle.)* It's light already.

LOPAKHIN: How late was the train? Two hours at least. *(Yawns and stretches.)* What a damn fool I am! Came here specially to meet them at the station and fell asleep. . . . Sat down in a chair and dropped off. What a nuisance! Why didn't you wake me?

DUNYASHA: I thought you'd gone, sir. *(Listens.)* I think they're coming.

LOPAKHIN *(listening):* No. . . . I should have been there to help them with the luggage and so on. *(Pause.)* Mrs. Ranevsky's been abroad for five years. I wonder what she's like now. . . . She's such a nice person. Simple, easy-going. I remember when I was a lad of fifteen, my late father—he used to keep a shop in the village—punched me in the face and made my nose bleed. We'd gone into the yard to fetch something, and he was drunk. Mrs. Ranevsky—I remember it as if it happened yesterday, she was such a young girl then and so slim—took me to the washstand in this very room, the nursery. "Don't cry, little peasant," she said, "it won't matter by the time you're wed." *(Pause.)* Little peasant . . . It's quite true my father was a peasant, but here I am wearing a white waistcoat and brown shoes. A dirty peasant in a fashionable shop. . . . Except, of course, that I'm a rich man now, rolling in money. But, come to think of it, I'm a plain peasant still. . . . *(Turns the pages of his book.)* Been

reading this book and haven't understood a word. Fell asleep reading it.

(Pause.)

DUNYASHA: The dogs have been awake all night; they know their masters are coming.

LOPAKHIN: What's the matter, Dunyasha? Why are you in such a state?

DUNYASHA: My hands are shaking. I think I'm going to faint.

LOPAKHIN: A little too refined, aren't you, Dunyasha? Quite the young lady. Dress, hair. It won't do, you know. Remember your place!

(Enter YEPIKHODOV *with a bunch of flowers; he wears a jacket and brightly polished high-boots which squeak loudly; on coming in, he drops the flowers.)*

YEPIKHODOV *(picking up the flowers):* The gardener sent these. Said to put them in the dining room. *(Hands the flowers to* DUNYASHA.)

LOPAKHIN: Bring me some kvass while you're about it.

DUNYASHA: Yes, sir. *(Goes out.)*

YEPIKHODOV: Thirty degrees, morning frost, and the cherry trees in full bloom. Can't say I think much of our climate, sir. *(Sighs.)* Our climate isn't particularly accommodating, is it, sir? Not when you want it to be, anyway. And another thing. The other day I bought myself this pair of boots, and believe me, sir, they squeak so terribly that it's more than a man can endure. Do you happen to know of something I could grease them with?

LOPAKHIN: Go away. You make me tired.

YEPIKHODOV: Every day, sir, I'm overtaken by some calamity. Not that I mind. I'm used to it. I just smile. *(*DUNYASHA *comes in and hands* LOPAKHIN *the kvass.)* I'll be off. *(Bumps into a chair and knocks it over.)* There you are, sir. *(Triumphantly.)* You see, sir, pardon the expression, this sort of circumstance . . . I mean to say . . . Remarkable! Quite remarkable! *(Goes out.)*

DUNYASHA: I simply must tell you, sir: Yepikhodov has proposed to me.

LOPAKHIN: Oh?

DUNYASHA: I really don't know what to do, sir. He's ever such a quiet fellow, except that sometimes he starts talking and you can't understand a word he says. It sounds all right and it's ever so moving, only you can't make head or tail of it. I like him a little, I think. I'm not sure though. He's madly in love with me. He's such an unlucky fellow, sir. Every day something happens to him. Everyone teases him about it. They've nicknamed him Twenty-two Calamities.

LOPAKHIN *(listens)*: I think I can hear them coming.

DUNYASHA: They're coming! Goodness, I don't know what's the matter with me. I've gone cold all over.

LOPAKHIN: Yes, they are coming all right. Let's go and meet them. Will she recognize me? We haven't seen each other for five years.

DUNYASHA *(agitated)*: I'm going to faint. Oh dear, I'm going to faint!

(Two carriages can be heard driving up to the house. LOPAKHIN and DUNYASHA go out quickly. The stage is empty. People can be heard making a noise in the adjoining rooms. FIRS, who has been to meet MRS. RANEVSKY at the station, walks across the stage hurriedly, leaning on a stick. He wears an old-fashioned livery coat and a top hat; he keeps muttering to himself, but it is impossible to make out a single word. The noise offstage becomes louder. A voice is heard: "Let's go through here." MRS. RANEVSKY, ANYA, and CHARLOTTE, with a lap dog on a little chain, all wearing traveling clothes, VARYA, wearing an overcoat and a head scarf, GAYEV, SIMEONOV-PISHCHIK, LOPAKHIN, DUNYASHA, carrying a bundle and an umbrella, and other SERVANTS with luggage walk across the stage.)

ANYA: Let's go through here. Remember this room, Mother?

MRS. RANEVSKY *(joyfully, through tears)*: The nursery!

VARYA: It's so cold. My hands are quite numb. *(to MRS. RANEVSKY)* Your rooms, the white one and the mauve one, are just as you left them, Mother dear.

MRS. RANEVSKY: The nursery! My dear, my beautiful room! I used to sleep here when I was a little girl. *(Cries.)* I feel like a little girl again now. *(Kisses her brother and VARYA, and then her brother again.)* Varya is the same as ever. Looks like a nun. And I also recognized Dunyasha. *(Kisses DUNYASHA.)*

GAYEV: The train was two hours late. How do you like that? What a way to run a railway!

CHARLOTTE *(to PISHCHIK)*: My dog also eats nuts.

PISHCHIK *(surprised)*: Good Lord!

(All, except ANYA and DUNYASHA, go out.)

DUNYASHA: We thought you'd never come. *(Helps ANYA off with her coat and hat.)*

ANYA: I haven't slept for four nights on our journey. Now I'm chilled right through.

DUNYASHA: You left before Easter. It was snowing and freezing then. It's different now, isn't it? Darling Anya! *(Laughs and kisses her.)* I've missed you so much, my darling, my precious! Oh, I must tell you at once! I can't keep it to myself a minute longer. . . .

ANYA *(apathetically)*: What is it this time?

DUNYASHA: Our clerk, Yepikhodov, proposed to me after Easter.

ANYA: Always the same. *(Tidying her hair.)* I've lost all my hairpins. *(She is so tired, she can hardly stand.)*

DUNYASHA: I don't know what to think. He loves me so much, so much!

ANYA *(tenderly, looking through the door into her room)*: My own room, my own windows, just as if I'd never been away! I'm home again! As soon as I get up in the morning, I'll run out into the orchard. . . . Oh, if only I could sleep. I didn't sleep all the way back, I was so worried.

DUNYASHA: Mr. Trofimov arrived the day before yesterday.

ANYA *(joyfully)*: Peter!

DUNYASHA: He's asleep in the bathhouse. He's been living there. Afraid of being a nuisance, he says. *(Glancing at her watch.)* I really ought to wake him, except that Miss Varya told me not to. "Don't you dare wake him!" she said.

(VARYA comes in with a bunch of keys at her waist.)

VARYA: Dunyasha, coffee quick! Mother's asking for some.

DUNYASHA: I won't be a minute! *(Goes out.)*

VARYA: Well, thank goodness you're all back. You're home again, my darling. *(Caressing her.)* My darling is home again! My sweet child is home again.

ANYA: I've had such an awful time!

VARYA: I can imagine it.

ANYA: I left before Easter. It was terribly cold then. All the way Charlotte kept talking and doing her conjuring tricks. Why did you force Charlotte on me?

VARYA: But you couldn't have gone alone, darling, could you? You're only seventeen!

ANYA: In Paris it was also cold and snowing. My French is awful. I found Mother living on the fourth floor. When I got there, she had some French visitors, a few ladies and an old Catholic priest with a book. The place was full of tobacco smoke and terribly uncomfortable. Suddenly I felt sorry for Mother, so sorry that I took her head in my arms, held it tightly, and couldn't let go. Afterwards Mother was very sweet to me. She was crying all the time.

VARYA *(through tears)*: Don't go on, Anya. Please don't.

ANYA: She'd already sold her villa near Mentone. She had nothing left. Nothing! I hadn't any money, either. There was hardly enough for the journey. Mother just won't understand! We had dinner at the station and she would order the most expensive things and tip the waiters a ruble each. Charlotte was just the same. Yasha, too, demanded to be given the same kind of food. It was simply awful! You see, Yasha is Mother's manservant. We've brought him back with us.

VARYA: Yes, I've seen the scoundrel.

ANYA: Well, what's been happening? Have you paid the interest on the mortgage?

VARYA: Heavens, no!

ANYA: Dear, oh dear . . .

VARYA: The estate will be up for sale in August.

ANYA: Oh dear!

LOPAKHIN *(puts his head through the door and bleats)*: Bah-h-h! *(Goes out.)*

VARYA *(through tears)*: Oh, I'd like to hit him! *(Shakes her fist.)*

ANYA *(gently embracing* VARYA*)*: Varya, has he proposed to you? *(*VARYA *shakes her head.)* But he loves you. Why don't you two come to an understanding? What are you waiting for?

VARYA: I don't think anything will come of it. He's so busy. He can't be bothered with me. Why, he doesn't even notice me. I wish I'd never known him. I can't stand the sight of him. Everyone's talking about our wedding, everyone's congratulating me, while there's really nothing in it. It's all so unreal. Like a dream. *(In a different tone of voice.)* You've got a new brooch. Like a bee, isn't it?

ANYA *(sadly)*: Yes, Mother bought it. *(Goes to her room, talking quite happily, like a child.)* You know, I went up in a balloon in Paris!

VARYA: My darling's home again! My dearest one's home again! *(*DUNYASHA *has come back with a coffeepot and is making coffee;* VARYA *is standing at the door of* ANYA's *room.)* All day long, darling, I'm busy about the house, and all the time I'm dreaming, dreaming. If only we could find a rich husband for you! My mind would be at rest then. I'd go into a convent and later on a pilgrimage to Kiev . . . to Moscow. Just keep going from one holy place to another. On and on. . . . Wonderful!

ANYA: The birds are singing in the orchard. What's the time?

VARYA: It's past two. It's time you were asleep, darling. *(Goes into* ANYA's *room.)* Wonderful!

(Enter YASHA *with a traveling rug and a small bag.)*

YASHA *(crossing the stage, in an affected genteel voice)*: May I be permitted to go through here?

DUNYASHA: I can hardly recognize you, Yasha. You've changed so much abroad.

YASHA: Hmmm . . . And who are you, may I ask?

DUNYASHA: When you left, I was no bigger than this. *(Shows her height from the floor with her hand.)* I'm Dunyasha, Fyodor Kozoedov's daughter. Don't you remember me?

YASHA: Mmmm . . . Juicy little cucumber! *(Looks round, then puts his arms around her; she utters a little scream and drops a saucer.* YASHA *goes out hurriedly.)*

VARYA *(in the doorway, crossly)*: What's going on there?

DUNYASHA *(in tears)*: I've broken a saucer.

VARYA: That's lucky.

ANYA *(coming out of her room)*: Mother must be told Peter's here.

VARYA: I gave orders not to wake him.

ANYA *(pensively)*: Father died six years ago. A month after our brother, Grisha, was drowned in the river. Such a pretty little boy. He was only seven. Mother took it badly. She went away, went away never to come back. *(Shudders.)* Peter Trofimov was Grisha's tutor. He might remind her . . .

*(*FIRS *comes in, wearing a jacket and a white waistcoat.)*

FIRS *(walks up to the coffeepot anxiously)*: Madam will have her coffee here. *(Puts on white gloves.)* Is the coffee ready? *(Sternly, to* DUNYASHA.*)* You there! Where's the cream?

DUNYASHA: Oh dear! *(Goes out quickly.)*

FIRS *(fussing round the coffeepot)*: The nincompoop! *(Muttering to himself.)* She's come from Paris. . . . Master used to go to Paris. . . . Aye, by coach. . . . *(Laughs.)*

VARYA: What are you talking about, Firs?

FIRS: Sorry, what did you say? *(Joyfully.)* Madam is home again! Home at last! I can die happy now. *(Weeps with joy.)*

(Enter MRS. RANEVSKY, GAYEV, [LOPAKHIN], *and* SIMEONOV-PISHCHIK, *the last one wearing a Russian long-waisted coat of expensive cloth and wide trousers. As he enters,* GAYEV *moves his arms and body as if he were playing billiards.)*

MRS. RANEVSKY: How does it go now? Let me think. Pot the red in the corner. Double into the middle pocket.

GAYEV: And straight into the corner! A long time ago, Lyuba, you and I slept in this room. Now I'm fifty-one. . . . Funny, isn't it!

LOPAKHIN: Aye, time flies.

GAYEV: I beg your pardon?

LOPAKHIN: "Time flies," I said.

GAYEV: The place reeks of patchouli.

ANYA: I'm off to bed. Good night, Mother. *(Kisses her mother.)*

MRS. RANEVSKY: My sweet little darling! *(Kisses her hands.)* You're glad to be home, aren't you? I still can't believe it.

ANYA: Good night, Uncle.

GAYEV *(kissing her face and hands)*: God bless you. You're so like your mother! *(to his sister)* You were just like her at that age, Lyuba.

(ANYA shakes hands with LOPAKHIN and PISHCHIK. Goes out and shuts the door behind her.)

MRS. RANEVSKY: She's terribly tired.

PISHCHIK: It was a long journey.

VARYA *(to LOPAKHIN and PISHCHIK)*: Well, gentlemen, it's past two o'clock. You mustn't outstay your welcome, must you?

MRS. RANEVSKY *(laughs)*: You're just the same, Varya. *(Draws VARYA to her and kisses her.)* Let me have my coffee first and then we'll all go. *(FIRS puts a little cushion under her feet.)* Thank you, Firs dear. I've got used to having coffee. I drink it day and night. Thank you, Firs, thank you, my dear old man. *(Kisses FIRS.)*

VARYA: I'd better make sure they've brought all the things in. *(Goes out.)*

MRS. RANEVSKY: Is it really me sitting here? *(Laughs.)* I feel like jumping about, waving my arms. *(Covers her face with her hands.)* And what if it's all a dream? God knows, I love my country. I love it dearly. I couldn't look out of the train for crying. *(Through tears.)* But, I suppose I'd better have my coffee. Thank you, Firs, thank you, dear old man. I'm so glad you're still alive.

FIRS: The day before yesterday . . .

GAYEV: He's a little deaf.

LOPAKHIN: At five o'clock I've got to leave for Kharkov. What a nuisance! I wish I could have had a good look at you, a good talk with you. You're still as magnificent as ever.

PISHCHIK *(breathing heavily)*: Lovelier, I'd say. Dressed in the latest Paris fashion. If only I were twenty years younger—ho-ho-ho!

LOPAKHIN: This brother of yours says that I'm an ignorant oaf, a tightfisted peasant, but I don't mind. Let him talk. All I want is that you should believe in me as you used to, that you should look at me as you used to with those wonderful eyes of yours. Merciful heavens! My father was a serf of your father and your grandfather, but you, you alone, did so much for me in the past that I forgot everything, and I love you just as if you were my own flesh and blood, more than my own flesh and blood.

MRS. RANEVSKY: I can't sit still, I can't. . . . *(Jumps up and walks about the room in great agitation.)* This happiness is more than I can bear. Laugh at me if you like. I'm making such a fool of myself. Oh, my darling little bookcase . . . *(Kisses the bookcase.)* My sweet little table . . .

GAYEV: You know, of course, that Nanny died here while you were away.

MRS. RANEVSKY *(sits down and drinks her coffee)*: Yes, God rest her soul. They wrote to tell me about it.

GAYEV: Anastasy, too, is dead. Boss-eyed Peter left me for another job. He's with the Police Superintendent in town now. *(Takes a box of fruit drops out of his pocket and sucks one.)*

PISHCHIK: My daughter Dashenka—er—wishes to be remembered to you.

LOPAKHIN: I'd like to say something very nice and cheerful to you. *(Glances at his watch.)* I shall have to be going in a moment and there isn't much time to talk. As you know, your cherry orchard's being sold to pay your debts. The auction is on the twenty-second of August. But there's no need to worry, my dear. You can sleep soundly. There's a way out. Here's my plan. Listen carefully, please. Your estate is only about twelve miles from town, and the railway is not very far away. Now, all you have to do is break up your cherry orchard and the land along the river into building plots and lease them out for country cottages. You'll then have an income of at least twenty-five thousand a year.

GAYEV: I'm sorry, but what utter nonsense!

MRS. RANEVSKY: I don't quite follow you, Lopakhin.

LOPAKHIN: You'll be able to charge your tenants at least twenty-five rubles a year for a plot of about three acres. I bet you anything that if you advertise now, there won't be a single plot left by the autumn. They will all be snapped up. In fact, I congratulate you. You are saved. The site is magnificent and the river is deep enough for bathing. Of course, the place will have to be cleared, tidied up. . . . I mean, all the old buildings will have to be pulled down, including, I'm sorry to say, this house, but it isn't any use to anybody any more, is it? The old cherry orchard will have to be cut down.

MRS. RANEVSKY: Cut down? My dear man, I'm very sorry but I don't think you know what you're talking about. If there's anything of interest, anything quite remarkable, in fact, in the whole county, it's our cherry orchard.

LOPAKHIN: The only remarkable thing about this orchard is that it's very large. It only produces a crop every other year, and even then you don't know what to do with the cherries. Nobody wants to buy them.

GAYEV: Why, you'll find our orchard mentioned in the encyclopedia.

LOPAKHIN *(glancing at his watch)*: If we can't think of anything and if we can't come to any decision, it won't be only your cherry orchard but your whole estate that will be sold at auction on the twenty-second of August. Make up your mind. I tell you, there is no other way. Take my word for it. There isn't.

FIRS: In the old days, forty or fifty years ago, the cherries used to be dried, preserved, made into jam, and sometimes—

GAYEV: Do shut up, Firs.

FIRS: —and sometimes cartloads of dried cherries were sent to Moscow and Kharkov. Fetched a lot of money, they did. Soft and juicy, those cherries were. Sweet and such a lovely smell . . . They knew the recipe then. . . .

MRS. RANEVSKY: And where's the recipe now?

FIRS: Forgotten. No one remembers it.

PISHCHIK (to MRS. RANEVSKY): What was it like in Paris? Eh? Eat any frogs?

MRS. RANEVSKY: I ate crocodiles.

PISHCHIK: Good Lord!

LOPAKHIN: Till recently there were only the gentry and the peasants in the country. Now we have holiday-makers. All our towns, even the smallest, are surrounded by country cottages. I shouldn't be surprised if in twenty years the holiday-maker multiplies enormously. All your holiday-maker does now is drink tea on the veranda, but it's quite in the cards that if he becomes the owner of three acres of land, he'll do a bit of farming on the side, and then your cherry orchard will become a happy, prosperous, thriving place.

GAYEV (indignantly): What nonsense!

(Enter VARYA and YASHA.)

VARYA: I've got two telegrams in here for you, Mother dear. (Picks out a key and unlocks the old-fashioned bookcase with a jingling noise.) Here they are.

MRS. RANEVSKY: They're from Paris. (Tears the telegrams up without reading them.) I've finished with Paris.

GAYEV: Do you know how old this bookcase is, Lyuba? Last week I pulled out the bottom drawer and saw some figures burned into it. This bookcase was made exactly a hundred years ago. What do you think of that? Eh? We ought really to celebrate its centenary. An inanimate object, but say what you like, it's a bookcase after all.

PISHCHIK (amazed): A hundred years! Good Lord!

GAYEV: Yes, indeed. It's quite something. (Feeling round the bookcase with his hands.) Dear, highly esteemed bookcase, I salute you. For over a hundred years you have devoted yourself to the glorious ideals of goodness and justice. Throughout the hundred years your silent appeal to fruitful work has never faltered. It sus-tained (through tears) in several generations of our family, their courage and faith in a better future and fostered in us the ideals of goodness and social consciousness.

(Pause.)

LOPAKHIN: Aye. . . .

MRS. RANEVSKY: You haven't changed a bit, have you, darling Leonid?

GAYEV (slightly embarrassed): Off the right into a corner! Pot into the middle pocket!

LOPAKHIN (glancing at his watch): Well, afraid it's time I was off.

YASHA (handing MRS. RANEVSKY her medicine): Your pills, ma'am.

PISHCHIK: Never take any medicines, dear lady. I don't suppose they'll do you much harm. but they won't do you any good either. Here, let me have 'em, my dear lady. (Takes the box of pills from her, pours the pills into the palm of his hand, blows on them, puts them all into his mouth, and washes them down with kvass.) There!

MRS. RANEVSKY (alarmed): You're mad!

PISHCHIK: Swallowed the lot.

LOPAKHIN: The glutton!

(All laugh.)

FIRS: He was here at Easter, the gentleman was. Ate half a bucketful of pickled cucumbers, he did. . . .(Mutters.)

MRS. RANEVSKY: What is he saying?

VARYA: He's been muttering like that for the last three years. We've got used to it.

YASHA: Old age!

(CHARLOTTE, in a white dress, very thin and tightly laced, a lorgnette dangling from her belt, crosses the stage.)

LOPAKHIN: I'm sorry, Miss Charlotte, I haven't had the chance of saying how-do-you-do to you. (Tries to kiss her hand.)

CHARLOTTE (snatching her hand away): If I let you kiss my hand, you'll want to kiss my elbow, then my shoulder . . .

LOPAKHIN: It's not my lucky day. (They all laugh.) My dear Charlotte, show us a trick, please.

MRS. RANEVSKY: Yes, do show us a trick, Charlotte.

CHARLOTTE: I won't. I'm off to bed. (Goes out.)

LOPAKHIN: We'll meet again in three weeks. (Kisses MRS. RANEVSKY's hand.) Good-bye for now. I must go. (to GAYEV) So long. (Embraces PISHCHIK.) So long. (Shakes hands with VARYA and then with FIRS and YASHA.) I wish I didn't have to go. (to MRS. RANEVSKY) Let me know if you make up your mind about the country cottages. If you decide to go ahead, I'll get you a loan of fifty thousand or more. Think it over seriously.

VARYA (angrily): For goodness' sake, go!

LOPAKHIN: I'm going, I'm going. . . .(Goes out.)

GAYEV: The oaf! However, I'm sorry. Varya's going to marry him, isn't she? He's Varya's intended.

VARYA: Don't say things you'll be sorry for, Uncle.

MRS. RANEVSKY: But why not, Varya? I should be only too glad. He's a good man.

PISHCHIK: A most admirable fellow, to tell the truth. My Dashenka—er—also says that—er—says all sorts of things. (Drops off and snores, but wakes up immediately.) By the way, my dear lady, you will lend me two hundred and forty rubles, won't you? Must pay the interest on the mortgage tomorrow.

VARYA (terrified): We have no money; we haven't!

MRS. RANEVSKY: We really haven't any, you know.

PISHCHIK: Have a good look around—you're sure to find it. (Laughs.) I never lose hope. Sometimes I think it's all over with me, I'm done for, then—hey presto—they build a railway over my land and pay me for it. Something's bound to turn up, if not today, then tomorrow. I'm certain of it. Dashenka might win two hundred thousand. She's got a ticket in the lottery, you know.

MRS. RANEVSKY: Well, I've finished my coffee. Now to bed.

FIRS (brushing GAYEV's clothes admonishingly): Put the wrong trousers on again, sir. What am I to do with you?

VARYA (in a low voice): Anya's asleep. (Opens a window quietly.) The sun has risen. It's no longer cold. Look, Mother dear. What lovely trees! Heavens, what wonderful air! The starlings are singing.

GAYEV (opens another window.): The orchard's all white. Lyuba, you haven't forgotten, have you? The long avenue there—it runs on and on, straight as an arrow. It gleams on moonlit nights. Remember? You haven't forgotten, have you?

MRS. RANEVSKY (looking through the window at the orchard): Oh, my childhood, oh, my innocence! I slept in this nursery. I used to look out at the orchard from here. Every morning happiness used to wake with me. The orchard was just the same in those days. Nothing has changed. (Laughs happily.) White, all white! Oh, my orchard! After the dark, rainy autumn and the cold winter, you're young again, full of happiness; the heavenly angels haven't forsaken you. If only this heavy load could be lifted from my heart; if only I could forget my past!

GAYEV: Well, and now they're going to sell the orchard to pay our debts. Funny, isn't it?

MRS. RANEVSKY: Look! Mother's walking in the orchard in . . . a white dress! (Laughs happily.) It is Mother!

GAYEV: Where?

VARYA: Really, Mother dear, what are you saying?

MRS. RANEVSKY: There's no one there. I just imagined it. Over there, on the right, near the turning to the summer house, a little white tree's leaning over. It looks like a woman. (Enter TROFIMOV. He is dressed in a shabby student's uniform and wears glasses.) What an amazing orchard! Masses of white blossom. A blue sky . . .

TROFIMOV: I say, Mrs. Ranevsky . . .(She looks round at him.) I've just come to say hello. I'll go at once. (Kisses her hand warmly.) I was told to wait till morning, but I—I couldn't, I couldn't.

(MRS. RANEVSKY gazes at him in bewilderment.)

VARYA (through tears): This is Peter Trofimov.

TROFIMOV: Peter Trofimov. Your son Grisha's old tutor. I haven't changed so much, have I?

(MRS. RANEVSKY embraces him and weeps quietly.)

GAYEV (embarrassed): There, there, Lyuba.

VARYA (cries): I did tell you to wait till tomorrow, didn't I, Peter?

MRS. RANEVSKY: Grisha, my . . . little boy. Grisha . . . my son.

VARYA: It can't be helped, Mother. It was God's will.

TROFIMOV (gently, through tears): Now, now . . .

MRS. RANEVSKY (weeping quietly): My little boy died, drowned. Why? Why, my friend? (More quietly.) Anya's asleep in there and here I am shouting, making a noise. . . . Well, Peter? You're not as good-looking as you were, are you? Why not? Why have you aged so much?

TROFIMOV: A peasant woman in a railway carriage called me "a moth-eaten gentleman."

MRS. RANEVSKY: You were only a boy then. A charming young student. Now you're growing thin on top, you wear glasses. . . . You're not still a student, are you? (Walks toward the door.)

TROFIMOV: I expect I shall be an eternal student.

MRS. RANEVSKY (kisses her brother and then VARYA): Well, go to bed now. You, Leonid, have aged too.

PISHCHIK (following her): So, we're off to bed now, are we? Oh dear, my gout! I think I'd better stay the night here. Now, what about letting me have the—er—two hundred and forty rubles tomorrow morning, dear lady? Early tomorrow morning. . . .

GAYEV: He does keep on, doesn't he?

PISHCHIK: Two hundred and forty rubles—to pay the interest on the mortgage.

MRS. RANEVSKY: But I haven't any money, my dear man.

PISHCHIK: I'll pay you back, dear lady. Such a trifling sum.

MRS. RANEVSKY: Oh, all right. Leonid will let you have it. Let him have it, Leonid.

GAYEV: Let him have it? The hell I will.

MRS. RANEVSKY: What else can we do? Let him have it,

please. He needs it. He'll pay it back.

(MRS. RANEVSKY, TROFIMOV, PISHCHIK, *and* FIRS *go out.* GAYEV, VARYA, *and* YASHA *remain.*)

GAYEV: My sister hasn't got out of the habit of throwing money about. (*to* YASHA) Out of my way, fellow. You reek of the hen house.

YASHA (*grins*): And you, sir, are the same as ever.

GAYEV: I beg your pardon? (*to* VARYA) What did he say?

VARYA (*to* YASHA): Your mother's come from the village. She's been sitting in the servants' quarters since yesterday. She wants to see you.

YASHA: Oh, bother her!

VARYA: You shameless bounder!

YASHA: I don't care. She could have come tomorrow, couldn't she? (*Goes out.*)

VARYA: Dear Mother is just the same as ever. Hasn't changed a bit. If you let her, she'd give away everything.

GAYEV: I suppose so. (*Pause.*) When a lot of remedies are suggested for an illness, it means that the illness is incurable. I've been thinking, racking my brains; I've got all sorts of remedies, lots of them, which, of course, means that I haven't got one. It would be marvelous if somebody left us some money. It would be marvelous if we found a very rich husband for Anya. It would be marvelous if one of us went to Yaroslavl to try our luck with our great-aunt, the Countess. She's very rich, you know. Very rich.

VARYA (*crying*): If only God would help us.

GAYEV: Don't howl! Our aunt is very rich, but she doesn't like us. First, because my sister married a lawyer and not a nobleman. . . . (ANYA *appears in the doorway.*) She did not marry a nobleman, and she has not been leading an exactly blameless life, has she? She's a good, kind, nice person. I love her very much. But, however much you try to make allowances for her, you have to admit that she is an immoral woman. You can sense it in every movement she makes.

VARYA (*in a whisper*): Anya's standing in the doorway.

GAYEV: I beg your pardon? (*Pause.*) Funny thing, there's something in my right eye. Can't see properly. On Thursday, too, in the district court . . .

(ANYA *comes in.*)

VARYA: Why aren't you asleep, Anya?

ANYA: I can't sleep, I can't.

GAYEV: My little darling! (*Kisses* ANYA's *face and hands.*) My dear child! (*Through tears.*) You're not my niece, you're my angel. You're everything to me. Believe me. Do believe me.

ANYA: I believe you, Uncle. Everyone loves you, everyone respects you, but, dear Uncle, you shouldn't talk so much. What were you saying just now about Mother, about your own sister? What did you say it for?

GAYEV: Well, yes, yes. (*He takes her hand and covers his face with it.*) You're quite right. It was dreadful. Dear God, dear God, help me! That speech I made to the bookcase today—it was so silly. The moment I finished it, I realized how silly it was.

VARYA: It's quite true, Uncle dear. You oughtn't to talk so much. Just don't talk, that's all.

ANYA: If you stopped talking, you'd feel much happier yourself.

GAYEV: Not another word. (*Kisses* ANYA's *and* VARYA's *hands.*) Not another word. Now to business. Last Thursday I was at the county court, and, well—er—I met a lot of people there, and we started talking about this and that, and—er—it would seem that we might manage to raise some money on a promissory note and pay the interest to the bank.

VARYA: Oh, if only God would help us!

GAYEV: I shall be there again on Tuesday, and I'll have another talk. (*to* VARYA) For goodness' sake, don't howl! (*to* ANYA) Your mother will have a talk with Lopakhin. I'm sure he won't refuse her. After you've had your rest, you'll go to Yaroslavl to see your great-aunt, the Countess. That's how we shall tackle the problem from three different sides, and I'm sure we'll get it settled. The interest we shall pay. Of that I'm quite sure. (*Puts a fruit drop in his mouth.*) I give you my word of honor, I swear by anything you like, the estate will not be sold! (*Excitedly.*) Why, I'll stake my life on it! Here's my hand; call me a rotten scoundrel if I allow the auction to take place. I stake my life on it!

ANYA (*has regained her composure; she looks happy*): You're so good, Uncle dear! So clever! (*Embraces him.*) I'm no longer worried now. Not a bit worried. I'm happy.

(*Enter* FIRS.)

FIRS (*reproachfully*): Have you no fear of God, sir? When are you going to bed?

GAYEV: Presently, presently. Go away, Firs. Never mind, I'll undress this time. Well, children, bye-bye now. More about it tomorrow. Now you must go to bed. (*Kisses* ANYA *and* VARYA.) I'm a man of the eighties. People don't think much of that time, but let me tell you, I've suffered a great deal for my convictions during my life. It's not for nothing that the peasants love me. You have to know your peasant, you have to know how to—

ANYA: There you go again, Uncle.

VARYA: Please, Uncle dear, don't talk so much.

FIRS (*angrily*): Sir!

GAYEV: I'm coming, I'm coming. You two go to bed. Off two cushions into the middle. Pot the white!

(GAYEV *goes out,* FIRS *shuffling off after him.*)

ANYA: I'm not worried any longer now. I don't feel like going to Yaroslavl. I don't like my great-aunt, but I'm no longer worried. I ought to thank Uncle for that. (*Sits down.*)

VARYA: I ought to go to bed, and I shall be going in a moment, I must tell you first that something unpleasant happened here while you were away. You know, of course, that only a few old servants live in the old servants' quarters: Yefimushka, Polia, Evstigney, and, well, also Karp. They had been letting some tramps sleep there, but I didn't say anything about it. Then I heard that they were telling everybody that I'd given orders for them to be fed on nothing but dried peas. I'm supposed to be a miser, you see. It was all that Evstigney's doing. Well, I said to myself, if that's how it is, you just wait! So I sent for Evstigney. (*Yawns.*) He comes. "What do you mean," I said, "Evstigney, you silly old fool?" (*Looks at* ANYA) Darling! (*Pause.*) Asleep . . . (*Takes* ANYA *by the arm.*) Come to bed, dear. . . . Come on! (*Leads her by the arm.*) My darling's fallen asleep. Come along. (*They go out. A shepherd's pipe is heard playing from far away on the other side of the orchard.* TROFIMOV *walks across the stage and, catching sight of* VARYA *and* ANYA, *stops.*) Shh! She's asleep, asleep. Come along, my sweet.

ANYA (*softly, half asleep*): I'm so tired. . . . I keep hearing harness bells. Uncle . . . dear . . . Mother and Uncle . . .

VARYA: Come on, my sweet, come on. . . .

(*They go into* ANYA's *room.*)

TROFIMOV (*deeply moved*): My sun! My spring!

CURTAIN

ACT 2

(*Open country. A small tumbledown wayside chapel. Near it, a well, some large stones, which look like old gravestones, and an old bench. A road can be seen leading to* GAYEV's *estate. On one side, a row of tall dark poplars; it is there that the cherry orchard begins. In the distance, some telegraph poles, and far, far away on the horizon, the outlines of a large town that is visible only in very fine, clear weather. The sun is about to set.* CHARLOTTE, YASHA, *and* DUNYASHA *are sitting on the bench;* YEPIKHODOV *is standing nearby and is playing a guitar; they all sit sunk in thought.* CHARLOTTE *wears a man's old peaked hat; she has taken a shotgun from her shoulder and is adjusting the buckle on the strap.*)

CHARLOTTE (*pensively*): I haven't a proper passport, I don't know how old I am, and I can't help thinking that I'm still a young girl. When I was a little girl, my father and mother used to travel the fairs and give performances—very good ones. I used to do the *salto mortale* and all sorts of other tricks. When Father and Mother died, a German lady adopted me and began educating me. Very well. I grew up and became a governess, but where I came from and who I am, I do not know. Who my parents were, I do not know either. They may not even have been married. I don't know. (*Takes a cucumber out of her pocket and starts eating it.*) I don't know anything. (*Pause.*) I'm longing to talk to someone, but there is no one to talk to. I haven't anyone. . . .

YEPIKHODOV (*plays his guitar and sings*): "What care I for the world and its bustle? What care I for my friends and my foes?" . . . Nice to play a mandolin.

DUNYASHA: It's a guitar, not a mandolin. (*She looks at herself in a hand mirror and powders her face.*)

YEPIKHODOV: To a madman in love, it's a mandolin. (*Sings softly.*) "If only my heart was warmed by the fire of love requited."

(YASHA *joins in.*)

CHARLOTTE: How terribly these people sing! Ugh! Like hyenas.

DUNYASHA (*to* YASHA): All the same, you're ever so lucky to have been abroad.

YASHA: Why, of course. Can't help agreeing with you there. (*Yawns, then lights a cigar.*)

YEPIKHODOV: Stands to reason. Abroad, everything's in excellent complexion. Been like that for ages.

YASHA: Naturally.

YEPIKHODOV: I'm a man of some education, I read all sorts of remarkable books, but what I simply can't understand is where it's all leading to. I mean, what do I really want—to live or to shoot myself? In any case, I always carry a revolver. Here it is. (*Shows them his revolver.*)

CHARLOTTE: That's done. Now I can go. (*Puts the shotgun over her shoulder.*) You're a very clever man, Yepikhodov. You frighten me to death. Women must be madly in love with you. Brrr! (*Walking away.*) These clever people are all so stupid. I've no one to talk to. Always alone, alone, I've no one, and who I am and what I am for is a mystery. (*Walks off slowly.*)

YEPIKHODOV: Strictly speaking, and apart from all other considerations, what I ought to say about myself, among other things, is that Fate treats me without mercy, like a storm a small boat. Even supposing I'm mistaken, why in that case should I wake up this morning and suddenly find a spider of quite enormous dimensions on my chest? As big as that. *(Uses both hands to show the spider's size.)* Or again, I pick up a jug of kvass and there's something quite outrageously indecent in it, like a cockroach. *(Pause.)* Have you ever read Buckle's *History of Civilization*? *(Pause.)* May I have a word or two with you, Dunyasha?

DUNYASHA: Oh, all right. What is it?

YEPIKHODOV: I'd be very much obliged if you'd let me speak to you in private. *(Sighs.)*

DUNYASHA *(embarrassed)*: All right, only first bring me my cape, please. It's hanging near the wardrobe. It's so damp here.

YEPIKHODOV: Very well, I'll fetch it. . . . Now I know what to do with my revolver. *(Picks up his guitar and goes out strumming it.)*

YASHA: Twenty-two Calamities! A stupid fellow, between you and me. *(Yawns.)*

DUNYASHA: I hope to goodness he won't shoot himself. *(Pause.)* I'm ever so nervous. I can't help being worried all the time. I was taken into service when I was a little girl, and now I can't live like a peasant any more. See my hands? They're ever so white, as white as a young lady's. I've become so nervous, so sensitive, so like a lady. I'm afraid of everything. I'm simply terrified. So if you deceived me, Yasha, I don't know what would happen to my nerves.

YASHA *(kisses her)*: Little cucumber! Mind you, I expect every girl to be respectable. What I dislike most is for a girl to misbehave herself.

DUNYASHA: I've fallen passionately in love with you, Yasha. You're so educated. You can talk about anything.

(Pause.)

YASHA *(yawning)*: You see, in my opinion, if a girl is in love with somebody, it means she's immoral. *(Pause.)* It is so pleasant to smoke a cigar in the open air. *(Listens.)* Someone's coming. It's them. . . . *(*DUNYASHA *embraces him impulsively.)* Please go home and look as if you've been down to the river for a swim. Take that path or they'll think I had arranged to meet you here. Can't stand that sort of thing.

DUNYASHA *(coughing quietly)*: Your cigar has given me an awful headache. *(Goes out.)*

*(*YASHA *remains sitting near the chapel. Enter* MRS. RANEVSKY, GAYEV, *and* LOPAKHIN.*)*

LOPAKHIN: You must make up your minds once and for all. There's not much time left. After all, it's quite a simple matter. Do you agree to lease your land for country cottages or don't you? Answer me in one word: yes or no. Just one word.

MRS. RANEVSKY: Who's been smoking such horrible cigars here? *(Sits down.)*

GAYEV: Now that they've built the railway, things are

much more convenient. *(Sits down)*. We've been to town for lunch—pot the red in the middle! I really should have gone in to have a game first.

MRS. RANEVSKY: There's plenty of time.

LOPAKHIN: Just one word. *(Imploringly.)* Please give me your answer!

GAYEV *(yawns)*: I beg your pardon?

MRS. RANEVSKY *(looking in her purse)*: Yesterday I had a lot of money, but I've hardly any left today. My poor Varya! Tries to economize by feeding everybody on milk soup and the old servants in the kitchen on peas, and I'm just throwing money about stupidly. *(Drops her purse, scattering some gold coins.)* Goodness gracious, all over the place! *(She looks annoyed.)*

YASHA: Allow me to pick 'em up, madam. It won't take a minute. *(Starts picking up the coins.)*

MRS. RANEVSKY: Thank you, Yasha. Why on earth did I go out to lunch? That disgusting restaurant of yours with its stupid band, and those tablecloths smelling of soap. Why did you have to drink so much, Leonid? Or eat so much? Or talk so much? You did talk a lot again in the restaurant today and all to no purpose. About the seventies and the decadents . . . And who to? Talking about the decadents to waiters!

LOPAKHIN: Aye. . . .

GAYEV *(waving his arm)*: I'm incorrigible, that's clear. *(Irritably to* YASHA.*)* What are you hanging around here for?

YASHA *(laughs)*: I can't hear your voice without laughing, sir.

GAYEV *(to his sister)*: Either he or I.

MRS. RANEVSKY: Go away, Yasha. Run along.

YASHA *(returning the purse to* MRS. RANEVSKY*)*: At once, madam. *(Is hardly able to suppress his laughter.)* This very minute. *(Goes out.)*

LOPAKHIN: The rich merchant Deriganov is thinking of buying your estate. I'm told he's coming to the auction himself.

MRS. RANEVSKY: Where did you hear that?

LOPAKHIN: That's what they're saying in town.

GAYEV: Our Yaroslavl great-aunt has promised to send us money, but when and how much we do not know.

LOPAKHIN: How much will she send? A hundred thousand? Two hundred?

MRS. RANEVSKY: Well, I hardly think so. Ten or fifteen thousand at most. We must be thankful for that.

LOPAKHIN: I'm sorry, but such improvident people as you, such peculiar, unbusinesslike people, I've never met in my life! You're told in plain language that your estate's going to be sold, and you don't seem to understand.

MRS. RANEVSKY: But what are we to do? Tell us, please.

LOPAKHIN: I tell you every day. Every day I go on repeating the same thing over and over again. You must let out the cherry orchard and the land for country cottages, and you must do it now, as quickly as possible. The auction is on top of you! Try to understand! The moment you decide to let your land, you'll be able to raise as much money as you like, and you'll be saved.

MRS. RANEVSKY: Country cottages, holiday-makers— I'm sorry, but it's so vulgar.

GAYEV: I'm of your opinion entirely.

LOPAKHIN: I shall burst into tears or scream or have a fit. I can't stand it. You've worn me out! *(to* GAYEV*)* You're a silly old woman!

GAYEV: I beg your pardon?

LOPAKHIN: A silly old woman! *(He gets up to go.)*

MRS. RANEVSKY *(in dismay)*: No, don't go. Please stay. I beg you. Perhaps we'll think of something.

LOPAKHIN: What is there to think of?

MRS. RANEVSKY: Please don't go. I beg you. Somehow I feel so much more cheerful with you here. *(Pause.)* I keep expecting something to happen, as though the house was going to collapse on top of us.

GAYEV *(deep in thought)*: Cannon off the cushion. Pot into the middle pocket. . . .

MRS. RANEVSKY: I'm afraid we've sinned too much—

LOPAKHIN: You sinned!

GAYEV *(putting a fruit drop into his mouth)*: They say I squandered my entire fortune on fruit drops. *(Laughs.)*

MRS. RANEVSKY: Oh, my sins! . . . I've always thrown money about aimlessly, like a madwoman. Why, I even married a man who did nothing but pile up debts. My husband died of champagne. He drank like a fish. Then, worse luck, I fell in love with someone, had an affair with him, and it was just at that time—it was my first punishment, a blow that nearly killed me—that my boy was drowned in the river here. I went abroad, never to come back, never to see that river again. I shut my eyes and ran, beside myself, and *he* followed me—pitilessly, brutally. I bought a villa near Mentone because *he* had fallen ill. For the next three years I knew no rest, nursing him day and night. He wore me out. Everything inside me went dead. Then, last year, I had to sell the villa to pay my debts. I left for Paris, where he robbed me, deserted me, and went to live with another woman. I tried to poison myself. Oh, it was all so stupid, so shaming. . . . It was then that I suddenly felt an urge to go back to Russia, to my homeland, to my daughter. *(Dries her eyes.)* Lord, O Lord, be merciful! Forgive me my sins! Don't punish me any more! *(Takes a telegram from her pocket.)* I received this telegram from Paris today. He asks me to forgive him. He implores me to go back. *(Tears up the telegram.)* What's that? Music? *(Listens intently.)*

GAYEV: That's our famous Jewish band. Remember? Four fiddles, a flute, and a double bass.

MRS. RANEVSKY: Does it still exist? We ought to arrange a party and have them over to the house.

LOPAKHIN *(listening)*: I don't hear anything. *(Sings quietly.)* "And the Germans, if you pay 'em, will turn a Russian into a Frenchman." *(Laughs.)* I saw an excellent play at the theatre last night. It was very amusing.

MRS. RANEVSKY: I don't suppose it was amusing at all. You shouldn't be watching plays, but should be watching yourselves more often. What dull lives you live. What nonsense you talk.

LOPAKHIN: Perfectly true. Let's admit quite frankly that the life we lead is utterly stupid. *(Pause.)* My father was a peasant, an idiot. He understood nothing. He taught me nothing. He just beat me when he was drunk and always with a stick. As a matter of fact, I'm just as big a blockhead and an idiot myself. I never learnt anything, and my handwriting is so abominable that I'm ashamed to let people see it.

MRS. RANEVSKY: You ought to get married, my friend.

LOPAKHIN: Yes. That's true.

MRS. RANEVSKY: Married to our Varya. She's a nice girl.

LOPAKHIN: Aye. . . .

MRS. RANEVSKY: Her father was a peasant too. She's a hard-working girl, and she loves you. That's the important thing. Why, you've been fond of her for a long time yourself.

LOPAKHIN: Very well. I've no objection. She's a good girl.

(Pause.)

GAYEV: I've been offered a job in a bank. Six thousand a year. Have you heard, Lyuba?

MRS. RANEVSKY: You in a bank! You'd better stay where you are.

(FIRS comes in carrying an overcoat.)

FIRS *(to GAYEV)*: Please put it on, sir. It's damp out here.

GAYEV *(putting on the overcoat)*: You're a damned nuisance, my dear fellow.

FIRS: Come along, sir. Don't be difficult. . . . This morning, too, you went off without saying a word. *(Looks him over.)*

MRS. RANEVSKY: How you've aged, Firs!

FIRS: What's that, ma'am?

LOPAKHIN: Your mistress says you've aged a lot.

FIRS: I've been alive a long time. They were trying to marry me off before your dad was born. . . . *(Laughs.)* When freedom came, I was already chief valet. I refused to accept freedom and

628 / THE CHERRY ORCHARD

stayed on with my master. (*Pause.*) I well remember how glad everyone was, but what they
were glad about, they did not know themselves.

LOPAKHIN: It wasn't such a bad life before, was it? At
least, they flogged you.

FIRS (*not hearing him*): I should say so. The peasants
stuck to their masters and the masters to their
peasants. Now everybody does what he likes.
You can't understand nothing.

GAYEV: Shut up, Firs. I have to go to town tomorrow.
I've been promised an introduction to a general
who might lend us some money on a promissory
note.

LOPAKHIN: Nothing will come of it. You won't pay the
interest, either. You may be sure of that.

MRS. RANEVSKY: Oh, he's just imagining things. There
aren't any generals.

(*Enter* TROFIMOV, ANYA, *and* VARYA.)

GAYEV: Here they are at last.

ANYA: There's Mother.

MRS. RANEVSKY (*affectionately*): Come here, come here,
my dears. (*Embracing* ANYA *and* VARYA.) If you
only knew how much I love you both. Sit down
beside me. That's right.

(*All sit down.*)

LOPAKHIN: Our eternal student is always walking
about with the young ladies.

TROFIMOV: Mind your own business.

LOPAKHIN: He's nearly fifty and he's still a student.

TROFIMOV: Do drop your idiotic jokes.

LOPAKHIN: Why are you so angry, you funny fellow?

TROFIMOV: Well, stop pestering me.

LOPAKHIN (*laughs*): Tell me, what do you think of me?

TROFIMOV: Simply this: You're a rich man and you'll
soon be a millionaire. Now, just as a beast of prey
devours everything in its path and so helps to
preserve the balance of nature, so you, too,
perform a similar function.

(*They all laugh.*)

VARYA: You'd better tell us about the planets, Peter.

MRS. RANEVSKY: No, let's carry on with what we were
talking about yesterday.

TROFIMOV: What was that?

GAYEV: Pride.

TROFIMOV: We talked a lot yesterday, but we didn't
arrive at any conclusion. As you see it, there's
something mystical about the proud man. You
may be right for all I know. But try to look at it
simply, without being too clever. What sort of
pride is it, is there any sense in it. if, physiologi-
cally, man is far from perfect? If, in fact, he is, in
the vast majority of cases, coarse, stupid, and

profoundly unhappy? It's time we stopped admiring ourselves. All we must do is—work!

GAYEV: We're going to die all the same.

TROFIMOV: Who knows? And what do you mean by
"we're going to die"? A man may possess a
hundred senses. When he dies, he loses only the
five we know. The other ninety-five live on.

MRS. RANEVSKY: How clever you are, Peter!

LOPAKHIN (*ironically*): Oh, frightfully!

TROFIMOV: Mankind marches on, perfecting its powers. Everything that is incomprehensible to us
now, will one day become familiar and comprehensible. All we have to do is to work and do
our best to assist those who are looking for truth.
Here in Russia only a few people are working so
far. The vast majority of the educated people I
know, do nothing. They aren't looking for anything. They are quite incapable of doing any
work. They call themselves intellectuals, but
speak to their servants as inferiors and treat the
peasants like animals. They're not particularly
keen on their studies, they don't do any serious
reading, they are bone idle, they merely talk
about science, and they understand very little
about art. They are all so solemn, they look so
very grave, they talk only of important matters,
they philosophize. Yet anyone can see that our
workers are abominably fed, sleep on bare
boards, thirty and forty to a room—bedbugs
everywhere, stench, damp, moral turpitude. It's
therefore obvious that all our fine phrases are
merely a way of deluding ourselves and others.
Tell me, where are all those children's crèches
people are talking so much about? Where are the
reading rooms? You find them only in novels.
Actually, we haven't any. All we have is dirt,
vulgarity, brutality. I dislike and I'm frightened
of all these solemn countenances, just as I'm
frightened of all serious conversations. Why not
shut up for once?

LOPAKHIN: Well, I get up at five o'clock in the morning. I work from morning till night, and I've
always lots of money on me—mine and other
people's—and I can see what the people around
me are like. One has only to start doing something to realize how few honest, decent people
there are about. Sometimes when I lie awake, I
keep thinking; Lord, you've given us vast forests,
boundless plains, immense horizons, and living
here, we ourselves ought really to be giants—

MRS. RANEVSKY: You want giants, do you? They're all
right only in fairy tales. Elsewhere they frighten
me. (YEPIKHODOV *crosses the stage in the background,
playing his guitar. Pensively.*) There goes
Yepikhodov.

ANYA (*pensively*): There goes Yepikhodov.

GAYEV: The sun's set, ladies and gentlemen.

TROFIMOV: Yes.

GAYEV (*softly, as though declaiming*): Oh, nature, glorious nature! Glowing with eternal radiance, beautiful and indifferent, you, whom we call Mother, uniting in yourself both life and death, you—life-giver and destroyer . . .

VARYA (*imploringly*): Darling Uncle!

ANYA: Uncle, again!

TROFIMOV: You'd far better pot the red in the middle.

GAYEV: Not another word! Not another word!

(*They all sit deep in thought. Everything is still. The silence is broken only by the subdued muttering of* FIRS. *Suddenly a distant sound is heard. It seems to come from the sky, the sound of a breaking string, slowly dying away, melancholy.*)

MRS. RANEVSKY: What's that?

LOPAKHIN: I don't know. I expect a bucket must have broken somewhere far away in a coal mine, but somewhere a very long distance away.

GAYEV: Perhaps it was a bird, a heron or something.

TROFIMOV: Or an eagle-owl.

MRS. RANEVSKY (*shudders*): It makes me feel dreadful for some reason.

(*Pause.*)

FIRS: Same thing happened before the misfortune: the owl hooted and the samovar kept hissing.

GAYEV: Before what misfortune?

FIRS: Before they gave us our freedom.

(*Pause.*)

MRS. RANEVSKY: Come, let's go in, my friends. It's getting dark. (*to* ANYA) There are tears in your eyes. What's the matter, darling. (*Embraces her.*)

ANYA: It's nothing, Mother. Nothing.

TROFIMOV: Someone's coming.

(*A* HIKER *appears. He wears a shabby white peaked cap and an overcoat; he is slightly drunk.*)

HIKER: Excuse me, is this the way to the station?

GAYEV: Yes, follow that road.

HIKER: I'm greatly obliged to you sir. (*Coughs.*) Glorious weather . . . (*Declaiming.*) Brother, my suffering brother, come to the Volga, you whose groans . . . (*to* VARYA) Mademoiselle, won't you give thirty kopecks to a starving Russian citizen?

(VARYA, *frightened, utters a little scream.*)

LOPAKHIN (*angrily*): There's a limit to the most disgraceful behavior.

MRS. RANEVSKY (*at a loss*): Here, take this. (*Looks for some money in her purse.*) No silver. Never mind, have this gold one.

HIKER: Profoundly grateful to you, ma'am. (*Goes out.*)

(*Laughter.*)

VARYA (*frightened*): I'm going away. I'm going away. Good heavens, Mother dear, there's no food for the servants in the house, and you gave him a gold sovereign!

MRS. RANEVSKY: What's to be done with a fool like me? I'll give you all I have when we get home. You'll lend me some more money, Lopakhin, won't you?

LOPAKHIN: With pleasure.

MRS. RANEVSKY: Let's go in. It's time. By the way, Varya, we've found you a husband here. Congratulations.

VARYA (*through tears*): This isn't a joking matter, Mother.

LOPAKHIN: Okhmelia, go to a nunnery!

GAYEV: Look at my hands. They're shaking. It's a long time since I had a game of billiards.

LOPAKHIN: Okhmelia, O nymph, remember me in your prayers!

MRS. RANEVSKY: Come along, come along, it's almost supper time.

VARYA: That man frightened me. My heart's still pounding.

LOPAKHIN: Let me remind you, ladies and gentlemen: The cherry orchard is up for sale on the twenty-second of August. Think about it! Think!

(*They all go out except* TROFIMOV *and* ANYA.)

ANYA (*laughing*): I'm so glad the hiker frightened Varya. Now we are alone.

TROFIMOV: Varya's afraid we might fall in love. That's why she follows us around for days on end. With her narrow mind she cannot grasp that we are above love. The whole aim and meaning of our life is to bypass everything that is petty and illusory, that prevents us from being free and happy. Forward! Let us march on irresistibly toward the bright star shining there in the distance! Forward! Don't lag behind, friends!

ANYA (*clapping her hands excitedly*): You talk so splendidly! (*Pause.*) It's so heavenly here today!

TROFIMOV: Yes, the weather is wonderful.

ANYA: What have you done to me, Peter? Why am I no longer as fond of the cherry orchard as before? I loved it so dearly. I used to think there was no lovelier place on earth than our orchard.

TROFIMOV: The whole of Russia is our orchard. The earth is great and beautiful. There are lots of lovely places on it. (*Pause.*) Think, Anya: your grandfather, your great-grandfather, and all your ancestors owned serfs. They owned living souls. Can't you see human beings looking at you from every cherry tree in your orchard, from every leaf and every tree trunk? Don't you hear their voices? To own living souls—that's what has changed you all so much, you who are living now and those who lived before you. That's why your mother, you yourself, and your uncle no longer realize that you are living on borrowed capital, at other people's expense, at the expense of those whom you don't admit farther than your entrance hall. We are at least two hundred years behind the times. We haven't got anything at all. We have no definite attitude toward our past. We just philosophize, complain of depression, or drink vodka. Isn't it abundantly clear that before we start living in the present, we must atone for our past, make an end of it? And atone for it we can only by suffering, by extraordinary, unceasing labor. Understand that, Anya.

ANYA: The house we live in hasn't really been ours for a long time. I'm going to leave it. I give you my word.

TROFIMOV: If you have the keys of the house, throw them into the well and go away. Be free as the wind.

ANYA (rapturously): How well you said it!

TROFIMOV: Believe me, Anya, believe me! I'm not yet thirty, I'm young, I'm still a student, but I've been through hell more than once. I'm driven from pillar to post. In winter I'm half-starved, I'm ill, worried, poor as a beggar. You can't imagine the terrible places I've been to! And yet, always, every moment of the day and night, my heart was full of ineffable visions of the future. I feel, I'm quite sure, that happiness is coming, Anya. I can see it coming already.

ANYA (pensively): The moon is rising.

(YEPIKHODOV can be heard playing the same sad tune as before on his guitar. The moon rises. Somewhere near the poplars VARYA is looking for ANYA and calling, "Anya, where are you?")

TROFIMOV: Yes, the moon is rising. (Pause.) There it is—happiness! It's coming nearer and nearer. Already I can hear its footsteps, and if we never see it, if we never know it, what does that matter? Others will see it.

VARYA (offstage): Anya, where are you?

TROFIMOV: That Varya again! (Angrily.) Disgusting!

ANYA: Never mind, let's go to the river. It's lovely there.

TROFIMOV: Yes, let's.

(They go out.)

VARYA (offstage): Anya! Anya!

CURTAIN

ACT 3

(The drawing room, separated by an archway from the ballroom. A candelabra is alight. The Jewish band can be heard playing in the entrance hall. It is the same band that is mentioned in Act Two. Evening. In the ballroom people are dancing the Grande Ronde. SIMEONOV-PISHCHIK's voice can be heard crying out, "Promenade à une paire!" They all come out into the drawing room: PISHCHIK and CHARLOTTE the first couple, TROFIMOV and MRS. RANEVSKY the second, ANYA and a POST OFFICE CLERK the third, VARYA and the STATIONMASTER the fourth, and so on. VARYA is quietly crying and dries her eyes as she dances. The last couple consists of DUNYASHA and a partner. They walk across the drawing room. PISHCHIK shouts, "Grande Ronde balancez!" and "Les cavaliers à genoux et remerciez vos dames!")

(FIRS, wearing a tailcoat, brings in soda water on a tray. PISHCHIK and TROFIMOV come into the drawing room.)

PISHCHIK: I've got high blood-pressure. I've had two strokes already, and I find dancing hard work. But, as the saying goes, if you're one of a pack, wag your tail, whether you bark or not. As a matter of fact, I'm as strong as a horse. My father, may he rest in peace, liked his little joke, and speaking about our family pedigree, he used to say that the ancient Simeonov-Pishchiks came from the horse that Caligula had made a senator. (Sits down.) But you see, the trouble is that I have no money. A hungry dog believes only in meat. (Snores, but wakes up again at once.) I'm just the same. All I can think of is money.

TROFIMOV: There really is something horsy about you.

PISHCHIK: Well, a horse is a good beast. You can sell a horse.

(From an adjoining room comes the sound of people playing billiards. VARYA appears in the ballroom under the archway.)

TROFIMOV (teasing her): Mrs. Lopakhin! Mrs. Lopakhin!

VARYA (angrily): Moth-eaten gentleman!

TROFIMOV: Well, I am a moth-eaten gentleman and proud of it.

VARYA (brooding bitterly): We've hired a band, but how we are going to pay for it, I don't know. (Goes out.)

TROFIMOV (to PISHCHIK): If the energy you have wasted throughout your life looking for money to pay the interest on your debts had been spent on something else, you'd most probably have succeeded in turning the world upside down.

PISHCHIK: Nietzsche, the famous philosopher—a great man, a man of great intellect—says in his works that there's nothing wrong about forging bank notes.

TROFIMOV: Have you read Nietzsche?

PISHCHIK: Well, actually, Dashenka told me about it. I don't mind telling you, though, that in my present position I might even forge bank notes. The day after tomorrow I've got to pay three hundred and ten rubles. I've already got one hundred and thirty. (*Feels his pockets in alarm.*) My money's gone, I've lost my money! (*Through tears.*) Where is it? (*Happily.*) Ah, here it is, in the lining. Lord the shock brought me out in a cold sweat!

(*Enter* MRS. RANEVSKY *and* CHARLOTTE.)

MRS. RANEVSKY (*hums a popular Georgian dance tune*): Why is Leonid so late? What's he doing in town? (*to* DUNYASHA) Offer the band tea, please.

TROFIMOV: I don't suppose the auction has taken place.

MRS. RANEVSKY: What a time to have a band! What a time to give a party! Oh, well, never mind. (*Sits down and hums quietly.*)

CHARLOTTE (*hands* PISHCHIK *a pack of cards*): Here's a pack of cards. Think of a card.

PISHCHIK: All right.

CHARLOTTE: Now shuffle the pack. That's right. Now give it to me. Now, then, my dear Mr. Pishchik, *eins, zwei, drei!* Look in your breast pocket. Is it there?

PISHCHIK (*takes the card out of his breast pocket*): The eight of spades! Absolutely right! (*Surprised.*) Good Lord!

CHARLOTTE (*holding a pack of cards on the palm of her hand, to* TROFIMOV): Tell me, quick, what's the top card?

TROFIMOV: Well, let's say the queen of spades.

CHARLOTTE: Here it is. (*to* PISCHIK): What's the top card now?

PISHCHIK: The ace of hearts.

CHARLOTTE: Here you are! (*Claps her hands and the pack of cards disappears.*) What lovely weather we're having today. (*A mysterious female voice, which seems to come from under the floor, answers: "Oh yes, glorious weather, madam!"*) You're my ideal, you're so nice! (*The voice: "I like you very much too, madam."*)

STATIONMASTER (*clapping his hands*): Bravo, Madam Ventriloquist!

PISHCHIK (*looking surprised*): Good Lord! Enchanting, Miss Charlotte, I'm simply in love with you.

CHARLOTTE: In love! Are you sure you can love? *Guter Mensch, aber schlecter Musikant.* [A good man, but a poor musician.]

TROFIMOV (*claps* PISHCHIK *on the shoulder*): Good old horse!

CHARLOTTE: Attention, please. One more trick. (*She takes a rug from a chair.*) Here's a very good rug. I'd like to sell it. (*Shaking it.*) Who wants to buy it?

PISHCHIK (*surprised*): Good Lord!

CHARLOTTE: *Eins, zwei, drei!* (*Quickly snatching up the rug, which she had let fall, she reveals* ANYA *standing behind it.* ANYA *curtseys, runs to her mother, embraces her, and runs back to the ballroom, amid general enthusiasm.*)

MRS. RANEVSKY (*applauding*): Bravo, bravo!

CHARLOTTE: Now, once more. *Eins, zwei, drei!* (*Lifts the rug; behind it stands* VARYA, *who bows.*)

PISHCHIK (*surprised*): Good Lord!

CHARLOTTE: The end! (*Throws the rug over* PISHCHIK, *curtseys, and runs off to the ballroom.*)

PISHCHIK (*running after her*): The hussy! What a woman, eh? What a woman! (*Goes out.*)

MRS. RANEVSKY: Still no Leonid. I can't understand what he can be doing in town all this time. It must be over now. Either the estate has been sold or the auction didn't take place. Why keep us in suspense so long?

VARYA (*trying to comfort her*): I'm certain Uncle must have bought it.

TROFIMOV (*sarcastically*): Oh, to be sure!

VARYA: Our great-aunt sent him power of attorney to buy the estate in her name and transfer the mortgage to her. She's done it for Anya's sake. God will help us and Uncle will buy it. I'm sure of it.

MRS. RANEVSKY: Your great-aunt sent fifteen thousand to buy the estate in her name. She doesn't trust us—but the money wouldn't even pay the interest. (*She covers her face with her hands.*) My whole future is being decided today, my future. . . .

TROFIMOV (*teasing* VARYA): Mrs. Lopakhin!

VARYA (*crossly*): Eternal student! Expelled twice from the university, weren't you?

MRS. RANEVSKY: Why are you so cross, Varya? He's teasing you about Lopakhin. Well, what of it? Marry Lopakhin if you want to. He is a nice, interesting man. If you don't want to, don't marry him. Nobody's forcing you, darling.

VARYA: I regard such a step seriously, Mother dear. I don't mind being frank about it: He is a nice man, and I like him.

MRS. RANEVSKY: Well, marry him. What are you waiting for? That's what I can't understand.

VARYA: But, Mother dear, I can't very well propose to him myself, can I? Everyone's been talking to me about him for the last two years. Everyone! But he either says nothing or makes jokes. I quite understand. He's making money. He has his business to think of, and he hasn't time for me. If I had any money, just a little, a hundred rubles, I'd give up everything and go right away as far as possible. I'd have gone into a convent.

TROFIMOV: Wonderful!

VARYA (*to* TROFIMOV): A student ought to be intelligent! (*In a gentle voice, through tears.*) How plain you've grown, Peter! How you've aged! *(to* MRS. RANEVSKY, *no longer crying)* I can't live without having something to do, Mother! I must be doing something all the time.

(Enter YASHA.*)*

YASHA *(hardly able to restrain his laughter)*: Yepikhodov's broken a billiard cue! *(Goes out.)*

VARYA: What's Yepikhodov doing here? Who gave him permission to play billiards? Can't understand these people! *(Goes out.)*

MRS. RANEVSKY: Don't tease her, Peter. Don't you see she is unhappy enough already?

TROFIMOV: She's a bit too conscientious. Pokes her nose into other people's affairs. Wouldn't leave me and Anya alone all summer. Afraid we might have an affair. What business is it of hers? Besides, the idea never entered my head. Such vulgarity is beneath me. We are above love.

MRS. RANEVSKY: So, I suppose I must be beneath love. *(In great agitation.)* Why isn't Leonid back? All I want to know is: Has the estate been sold or not? Such a calamity seems so incredible to me that I don't know what to think. I'm completely at a loss. I feel like screaming, like doing something silly. Help me, Peter. Say something. For God's sake, say something!

TROFIMOV: What does it matter whether the estate's been sold today or not? The estate's been finished and done with long ago. There's no turning back. The road to it is closed. Stop worrying, my dear. You mustn't deceive yourself. Look the truth straight in the face for once in your life.

MRS. RANEVSKY: What truth? You can see where truth is and where it isn't, but I seem to have gone blind. I see nothing. You boldly solve all important problems, but tell me, dear boy, isn't it because you're young, isn't it because you haven't had the time to live through the consequences of any of your problems? You look ahead boldly, but isn't it because you neither see nor expect anything terrible to happen to you, because life is still hidden from your young eyes? You're bolder, more honest, you see much deeper than any of us, but think carefully, try to understand our position, be generous even a little, spare me. I was born here, you know. My father and mother lived here, and my grandfather also. I love this house. Life has no meaning for me without the cherry orchard, and if it has to be sold, then let me be sold with it. *(Embraces* TROFIMOV *and kisses him on the forehead.)* Don't you see, my son was drowned here. *(Weeps.)* Have pity on me, my good, kind friend.

TROFIMOV: You know I sympathize with you with all my heart.

MRS. RANEVSKY: You should have put it differently. *(Takes out her handkerchief. A telegram falls on the floor.)* My heart is so heavy today. You can't imagine how heavy. I can't bear this noise. The slightest sound makes me shudder. I'm trembling all over. I'm afraid to go to my room. I'm terrified to be alone. . . . Don't condemn me, Peter. I love you as my own son. I'd gladly let Anya marry you, I swear I would. Only, my dear boy, you must study, you must finish your course at the university. You never do anything. You just drift from one place to another. That's what's so strange. Isn't that so? Isn't it? And you should do something about your beard. Make it grow, somehow. *(Laughs.)* You are funny!

TROFIMOV *(picking up the telegram)*: I have no wish to be handsome.

MRS. RANEVSKY: That telegram's from Paris. I get one every day. Yesterday and today. That wild man is ill again, in trouble again. He asks me to forgive him. He begs me to come back to him, and I really think I ought to be going back to Paris to be near him for a bit. You're looking very stern, Peter. But what's to be done, my dear boy? What am I to do? He's ill. He's lonely. He's unhappy. Who'll look after him there? Who'll stop him from doing something silly? Who'll give him his medicine at the right time? And, why hide it? Why be silent about it? I love him. That's obvious. I love him. I love him. He's a millstone round my neck and he's dragging me down to the bottom with him, but I love the millstone, and I can't live without it. *(Presses* TROFIMOV's *hand.)* Don't think badly of me, Peter. Don't say anything. Don't speak.

TROFIMOV *(through tears)*: For God's sake—forgive my being so frank, but he left you penniless!

MRS. RANEVSKY: No, no, no! You mustn't say that. *(Puts her hands over her ears.)*

TROFIMOV: Why, he's a scoundrel, and you're the only one who doesn't seem to know it. He's a petty scoundrel, a nonentity.

MRS. RANEVSKY *(angry but restraining herself)*: You're twenty-six or twenty-seven, but you're still a schoolboy—a sixth-grade schoolboy!

TROFIMOV: What does that matter?

MRS. RANEVSKY: You ought to be a man. A person of your age ought to understand people who are in love. You ought to be in love yourself. You ought to fall in love. *(Angrily.)* Yes! Yes! And you're not so pure either. You're just a prude, a ridiculous crank, a freak!

TROFIMOV *(horrified)*: What is she saying?

MRS. RANEVSKY: "I'm above love!" You're not above

love, you're simply what Firs calls a nincompoop. Not have a mistress at your age!

TROFIMOV (*horrified*): This is terrible! What is she saying? (*Walks quickly into the ballroom, clutching his head.*) It's dreadful! I can't! I'll go away! (*Goes out but immediately comes back.*) All is at an end between us! (*Goes out into the hall.*)

MRS. RANEVSKY (*shouting after him*): Peter, wait! You funny boy, I was only joking. Peter!

(*Someone can be heard running rapidly up the stairs and then suddenly falling downstairs with a crash.* ANYA *and* VARYA *scream, followed immediately by laughter.*)

MRS. RANEVSKY: What's happened?

ANYA (*laughing, runs in*): Peter's fallen down the stairs! (*Runs out.*)

MRS. RANEVSKY: What an eccentric! (*The* STATIONMASTER *stands in the middle of the ballroom and recites "The Fallen Woman" by Alexey Tolstoy. The others listen. But he has hardly time to recite a few lines when the sound of a waltz comes from the entrance hall, and the recitation breaks off. Everyone dances.* TROFIMOV, ANYA, VARYA, *and* MRS. RANEVSKY *enter from the hall.*) Well, Peter dear, you pure soul, I'm sorry. . . . Come, let's dance. (*Dances with* TROFIMOV.)

(ANYA *and* VARYA *dance together.* FIRS *comes in and stands his walking stick near the side door.* YASHA *has also come in from the drawing room and is watching the dancing.*)

YASHA: Well, Grandpa!

FIRS: I'm not feeling too well. We used to have generals, barons, and admirals at our dances before, but now we send for the post office clerk and the stationmaster. Even they are not too keen to come. Afraid I'm getting weak. The old master, the mistress's grandfather that is, used to give us powdered sealing wax for medicine. It was his prescription for all illnesses. I've been taking sealing wax every day for the last twenty years or more. That's perhaps why I'm still alive.

YASHA: You make me sick, Grandpa. (*Yawns*). I wish you was dead.

FIRS: Ugh, you nincompoop! (*Mutters.*)

(TROFIMOV *and* MRS. RANEVSKY *dance in the ballroom and then in the drawing room.*)

MRS. RANEVSKY: *Merci.* I think I'll sit down a bit. (*Sits down.*) I'm tired.

(*Enter* ANYA.)

ANYA (*agitated*): A man in the kitchen said just now that the cherry orchard has been sold today.

MRS. RANEVSKY: Sold? Who to?

ANYA: He didn't say. He's gone away now.

(ANYA *dances with* TROFIMOV; *both go off to the ballroom.*)

YASHA: Some old man gossiping, madam. A stranger.

FIRS: Master Leonid isn't here yet. Hasn't returned. Wearing his light autumn overcoat. He might catch cold. Oh, these youngsters!

MRS. RANEVSKY: I shall die! Yasha, go and find out who bought it.

YASHA: But he's gone, the old man has. (*Laughs.*)

MRS. RANEVSKY (*a little annoyed*): Well, what are you laughing at? What are you so pleased about?

YASHA: Yepikhodov's a real scream. Such a fool. Twenty-two Calamities!

MRS. RANEVSKY: Firs, where will you go if the estate's sold?

FIRS: I'll go wherever you tell me, ma'am.

MRS. RANEVSKY: You look awful! Are you ill? You'd better go to bed.

FIRS: Me to bed, ma'am? (*Ironically.*) If I goes to bed, who's going to do the waiting? Who's going to look after everything? I'm the only one in the whole house.

YASHA (*to* MRS. RANEVSKY): I'd like to ask you a favor, madam. If you go back to Paris, will you take me with you? It's quite impossible for me to stay here. (*Looking round, in an undertone.*) You know perfectly well yourself what an uncivilized country this is—the common people are so immoral—and besides, it's so boring here, the food in the kitchen is disgusting, and on top of it, there's that old Firs wandering about, muttering all sorts of inappropriate words. Take me with you, madam, please!

(*Enter* PISHCHIK.)

PISHCHIK: May I have the pleasure of a little dance, fair lady? (MRS. RANEVSKY *goes with him.*) I'll have one hundred and eighty rubles off you all the same, my dear, charming lady. . . . I will, indeed. (*They dance.*) One hundred and eighty rubles. . . .

(*They go into the ballroom.*)

YASHA (*singing softly*): "Could you but feel the agitated beating of my heart."

(*In the ballroom a woman in a gray top hat and check trousers can be seen jumping about and waving her arms. Shouts of "Bravo, Charlotte! Bravo!"*)

DUNYASHA (*stops to powder her face*): Miss Anya told me to join the dancers because there are lots of gentlemen and very few ladies. But dancing makes me dizzy and my heart begins beating so fast. I say, Firs, the post office clerk said something to me just now that quite took my breath away.

(*The music becomes quieter.*)

FIRS: What did he say to you?

DUNYASHA: "You're like a flower," he said.

YASHA (*yawning*): What ignorance! (*Goes out.*)

DUNYASHA: Like a flower! I'm ever so delicate, and I love people saying nice things to me!

FIRS: You'll come to a bad end, my girl. Mark my words.

(*Enter* YEPIKHODOV.)

YEPIKHODOV: You seem to avoid me, Dunyasha. Just as if I was some insect. (*Sighs.*) Oh, life!

DUNYASHA: What do you want?

YEPIKHODOV: No doubt you may be right. (*Sighs.*) But, of course, if one looks at things from a certain point of view, then, if I may say so and if you'll forgive my frankness, you have reduced me absolutely to a state of mind. I know what Fate has in store for me. Every day some calamity overtakes me, but I got used to it so long ago that I just look at my Fate and smile. You gave me your word, and though I—

DUNYASHA: Let's talk about it some other time. Leave me alone now. Now, I am dreaming. (*Plays with her fan.*)

YEPIKHODOV: Every day some calamity overtakes me, and I—let me say it quite frankly—why, I just smile, laugh even.

(*Enter* VARYA *from the ballroom.*)

VARYA: Are you still here, Simon! What an ill-mannered fellow you are, to be sure! (*to* DUNYASHA) Be off with you, Dunyasha. (*to* YEPIKHODOV) First you go and play billiards and break a cue, and now you wander about the drawing room as if you were a guest.

YEPIKHODOV: It's not your place to reprimand me, if you don't mind my saying so.

VARYA: I'm not reprimanding you. I'm telling you. All you do is drift about from one place to another without ever doing a stroke of work. We're employing an office clerk, but goodness knows why.

YEPIKHODOV (*offended*): Whether I work or drift about, whether I eat or play billards, is something which only people older than you, people who know what they're talking about, should decide.

VARYA: How dare you talk to me like that? (*Flaring up.*) How dare you? I don't know what I'm talking about, don't I? Get out of here! This instant!

YEPIKHODOV (*cowed*): Express yourself with more delicacy, please.

VARYA (*beside herself*): Get out of here this minute! Out! (*He goes toward the door, and she follows him.*) Twenty-two Calamities! Don't let me see you here again! Never set foot here again! (*YEPIKHODOV goes out. He can be heard saying behind the door: "I'll lodge a complaint."*) Oh, so you're coming back, are you? (*Picks up the stick which* FIRS *has left near the door.*) Come on, come on, I'll show you! Coming are you? Well, take that! (*Swings the stick as* LOPAKHIN *comes in.*)

LOPAKHIN: Thank you very much!

VARYA (*angrily and derisively*): I'm so sorry!

LOPAKHIN: It's quite all right. Greatly obliged to you for the kind reception.

VARYA: Don't mention it. (*Walks away, then looks round and inquires gently.*) I didn't hurt you, did I?

LOPAKHIN: Oh no, not at all. There's going to be an enormous bump on my head for all that.

(*Voices in the ballroom: "Lopakhin's arrived. Lopakhin!"*)

PISHCHIK: Haven't heard from you or seen you for ages, my dear fellow! (*Embraces* LOPAKHIN.) Do I detect a smell of brandy, dear boy? We're doing very well here, too.

(*Enter* MRS. RANEVSKY.)

MRS. RANEVSKY: Is it you, Lopakhin? Why have you been so long? Where's Leonid?

LOPAKHIN: He came back with me. He'll be here in a moment.

MRS. RANEVSKY (*agitated*): Well, what happened? Did the auction take place? Speak, for heaven's sake!

LOPAKHIN (*embarrassed, fearing to betray his joy*): The auction was over by four o'clock. We missed our train and had to wait till half past nine. (*With a deep sigh.*) Oh dear, I'm afraid I feel a little dizzy.

(*Enter* GAYEV. *He carries some parcels in his right hand and wipes away his tears with his left.*)

MRS. RANEVSKY: What's the matter, Leonid? Well! (*Impatiently, with tears.*) Quick, tell me for heaven's sake!

GAYEV (*doesn't answer, only waves his hands resignedly; to* FIRS, *weeping*): Here, take these—anchovies, Kerch herrings . . . I've had nothing to eat all day. I've had a terrible time. (*The door of the billiard room is open; the click of billiard balls can be heard and* YASHA's *voice: "Seven and eighteen!"* GAYEV's *expression changes. He is no longer crying.*) I'm awfully tired. Come and help me change, Firs.

(*GAYEV goes off through the ballroom to his own room, followed by* FIRS.)

PISHCHIK: Well, what happened at the auction? Come, tell us!

MRS. RANEVSKY: Has the cherry orchard been sold?

LOPAKHIN: It has.

MRS. RANEVSKY: Who bought it?

LOPAKHIN: I bought it. (*Pause.* MRS. RANEVSKY *is crushed; she would have collapsed on the floor if she had not been standing near an armchair.* VARYA *takes the keys from her belt, throws them on the floor in the center of the drawing room, and goes out.)* I bought it! One moment, please, ladies and gentlemen. I feel dazed. I can't talk. . . . *(Laughs.)* Deriganov was already there when we got to the auction. Gayev had only fifteen thousand, and Deriganov began his bidding at once with thirty thousand over and above the mortgage. I realized the position at once and took up his challenge. I bid forty. He bid forty-five. He kept raising his bid by five thousand and I by adding another ten thousand. Well, it was soon over. I bid ninety thousand on top of the arrears, and the cherry orchard was knocked down to me. Now the cherry orchard is mine! Mine! *(Laughs loudly.)* Merciful heavens, the cherry orchard's mine! Come on, tell me, tell me I'm drunk. Tell me I'm out of my mind. Tell me I'm imagining it all. *(Stamps his feet.)* Don't laugh at me! If my father and my grandfather were to rise from their graves and see what's happened, see how their Yermolay, their beaten and half-literate Yermolay, Yermolay who used to run around barefoot in winter, see how that same Yermolay bought this estate, the most beautiful estate in the world! I've bought the estate where my father and grandfather were slaves, where they weren't even allowed inside the kitchen. I must be dreaming. I must be imagining it all. It can't be true. It's all a figment of your imagination, shrouded in mystery. *(Picks up the keys, smiling affectionately.)* She's thrown down the keys. Wants to show she's no longer the mistress here. *(Jingles the keys.)* Oh well, never mind. *(The band is heard tuning up.)* Hey you, musicians, play something! I want to hear you. Come, all of you! Come and watch Yermolay Lopakhin take an axe to the cherry orchard. Watch the trees come crashing down. We'll cover the place with country cottages, and our grandchildren and great-grandchildren will see a new life springing up here. Strike up the music! *(The band plays.* MRS. RANEVSKY *has sunk into a chair and is weeping bitterly. Reproachfully.)* Why did you not listen to me? You poor dear, you will never get it back now. *(With tears.)* Oh, if only all this could be over soon, if only our unhappy, disjointed life could somehow be changed soon.

PISHCHIK *(takes his arm, in an undertone)*: She's crying. Let's go into the ballroom. Let's leave her alone. Come on. *(Takes his arm and leads him away to the ballroom.)*

LOPAKHIN: What's the matter? You there in the band, play up, play up! Let's hear you properly. Let's have everything as I want it now. *(Ironically.)* Here comes the new landowner, the owner of the cherry orchard! *(Knocks against a small table*

accidentally and nearly knocks over the candelabra.) I can pay for everything!

*(*LOPAKHIN *goes out with* PISHCHIK. *There is no one left in the ballroom except* MRS. RANEVSKY, *who remains sitting in a chair, hunched up and crying bitterly. The band plays quietly.* ANYA *and* TROFIMOV *come in quickly.* ANYA *goes up to her mother and kneels in front of her.* TROFIMOV *remains standing by the entrance to the ballroom.)*

ANYA: Mother, Mother, why are you crying? My dear, good, kind Mother, my darling Mother, I love you; God bless you, Mother. The cherry orchard is sold. It's gone. That's true, quite true, but don't cry, Mother. You still have your life ahead of you, and you've still got your kind and pure heart. . . . Come with me, darling. Come. Let's go away from here. We shall plant a new orchard, an orchard more splendid than this one. You will see it, you will understand, and joy, deep, serene joy, will steal into your heart, sink into it like the sun in the evening, and you will smile, Mother! Come, darling! Come!

CURTAIN

ACT 4

(The scene is the same as in the first act. There are no curtains at the windows or pictures on the walls. Only a few pieces of furniture are left. They have been stacked in one corner as if for sale. There is a feeling of emptiness. Near the front door and at the back of the stage, suitcases, traveling bags, etc., are piled up. The door on the left is open and the voices of VARYA *and* ANYA *can be heard.* LOPAKHIN *stands waiting.* YASHA *is holding a tray with glasses of champagne. In the entrance hall* YEPIKHODOV *is tying up a box. There is a constant murmur of voices offstage, the voices of peasants who have come to say good-bye.* GAYEV's *voice is heard: "Thank you, my dear people, thank you.")*

YASHA: The peasants have come to say good-bye. In my opinion, sir, the peasants are decent enough fellows, but they don't understand a lot.

(The murmur of voices dies away. MRS. RANEVSKY *and* GAYEV *come in through the entrance hall; she is not crying, but she is pale. Her face is quivering. She cannot speak.)*

GAYEV: You gave them your purse, Lyuba. You shouldn't. You really shouldn't!

MRS. RANEVSKY: I—I couldn't help it. I just couldn't help it.

(Both go out.)

LOPAKHIN *(calling through the door after them)*: Please take a glass of champagne. I beg you. One glass each before we leave. I forgot to bring any from town, and I could find only one bottle at the station. Please! *(Pause.)* Why, don't you want any? *(Walks away from the door.)* If I'd known, I wouldn't have bought it. Oh well, I don't think I'll have any, either. *(YASHA puts the tray down carefully on a chair.)* You'd better have some, Yasha.

YASHA: Thank you, sir. To those who're going away! And here's to you, sir, who're staying behind! *(Drinks.)* This isn't real champagne. Take it from me, sir.

LOPAKHIN: Paid eight rubles a bottle. *(Pause.)* Damn cold here.

YASHA: The stoves haven't been lit today. We're leaving, anyway. *(Laughs.)*

LOPAKHIN: What's so funny?

YASHA: Oh, nothing. Just feeling happy.

LOPAKHIN: It's October, but it might just as well be summer: it's so sunny and calm. Good building weather. *(Glances at his watch and calls through the door.)* I say, don't forget the train leaves in forty-seven minutes. In twenty minutes we must start for the station. Hurry up!

(TROFIMOV comes in from outside, wearing an overcoat.)

TROFIMOV: I think it's about time we were leaving. The carriages are at the door. Where the blazes could my galoshes have got to? Disappeared without a trace. *(Through the door.)* Anya, I can't find my galoshes! Can't find them!

LOPAKHIN: I've got to go to Kharkov. I'll leave with you on the same train. I'm spending the winter in Kharkov. I've been hanging about here too long. I'm worn out with having nothing to do. I can't live without work. Don't know what to do with my hands. They just flop about as if they belonged to someone else.

TROFIMOV: Well, we'll soon be gone and then you can resume your useful labors.

LOPAKHIN: Come on, have a glass of champagne.

TROFIMOV: No, thank you.

LOPAKHIN: So you're off to Moscow, are you?

TROFIMOV: Yes. I'll see them off to town, and I'm off to Moscow tomorrow.

LOPAKHIN: I see. I suppose the professors have stopped lecturing while you've been away. They're all waiting for you to come back.

TROFIMOV: Mind your own business.

LOPAKHIN: How many years have you been studying at the university?

TROFIMOV: Why don't you think of something new for a change? This is rather old, don't you think?—and stale. *(Looking for his galoshes.)* I don't suppose we shall ever meet again, so let me give you a word of advice as a farewell gift: Don't wave your arms about. Get rid of the habit of throwing your arms about. And another thing: To build country cottages in the hope that in the fullness of time vacationers will become landowners is the same as waving your arms about. Still, I like you in spite of everything. You've got fine sensitive fingers, like an artist's, and you have a fine sensitive soul.

LOPAKHIN *(embraces him)*: My dear fellow, thanks for everything. Won't you let me lend you some money for your journey? You may need it.

TROFIMOV: Need it? Whatever for?

LOPAKHIN: But you haven't any, have you?

TROFIMOV: Oh, but I have. I've just got some money for a translation. Got it here in my pocket. *(Anxiously.)* Where could those galoshes of mine have got to?

VARYA *(from another room)*: Oh, take your filthy things! *(Throws a pair of galoshes onto the stage.)*

TROFIMOV: Why are you so cross, Varya? Good heavens, these are not my galoshes!

LOPAKHIN: I had about three thousand acres of poppy sown last spring. Made a clear profit of forty thousand. When my poppies were in bloom, what a beautiful sight they were! Well, so you see, I made forty thousand and I'd be glad to lend you some of it because I can afford to. So why be so high and mighty? I'm a peasant. . . . I'm offering it to you without ceremony.

TROFIMOV: Your father was a peasant, my father was a pharmacist, all of which proves exactly nothing. *(LOPAKHIN takes out his wallet.)* Put it back! Put it back! If you offered me two hundred thousand, I wouldn't accept it. I'm a free man. Everything you prize so highly, everything that means so much to all of you, rich or poor, has no more power over me than a bit of fluff blown about in the air. I can manage without you. I can pass you by. I'm strong and proud. Mankind is marching toward a higher truth, toward the greatest happiness possible on earth, and I'm in the front ranks!

LOPAKHIN: Will you get there?

TROFIMOV: I will. *(Pause.)* I will get there or show others the way to get there.

(The sound of an axe striking a tree can be heard in the distance.)

LOPAKHIN: Well, good-bye, my dear fellow. Time to go. You and I are trying to impress one another, but life goes on regardless. When I work hard for hours on end, I can think more clearly, and then I can't help feeling that I, too, know what I live for. Have you any idea how many people in Russia exist goodness only knows why? However, no matter. It isn't they who make the world go round. I'm told Gayev has taken a job at the bank at six thousand a year. He'll never stick to it. Too damn lazy.

ANYA *(in the doorway)*: Mother asks you not to begin

cutting the orchard down till she's gone.

TROFIMOV: Really, haven't you any tact at all? (*Goes out through the hall.*)

LOPAKHIN: Sorry, I'll see to it at once, at once! The damned idiots! (*Goes out after* TROFIMOV.)

ANYA: Has Firs been taken to the hospital?

YASHA: I told them to this morning. They must have taken him, I should think.

ANYA (*to* YEPIKHODOV, *who is crossing the ballroom*): Please find out if Firs has been taken to the hospital.

YASHA (*offended*): I told Yegor this morning. I haven't got to tell him a dozen times, have I?

YEPIKHODOV: Old man Firs, if you want my final opinion, is beyond repair, and it's high time he was gathered to his fathers. So far as I'm concerned, I can only envy him. (*Puts a suitcase on a hatbox and squashes it.*) There, you see! I knew it. (*Goes out.*)

YASHA (*sneeringly*): Twenty-two Calamities!

VARYA (*from behind the door*): Has Firs been taken to the hospital?

ANYA: He has.

VARYA: Why didn't they take the letter for the doctor?

ANYA: We'd better send it on after him. (*Goes out.*)

VARYA (*from the next room*): Where's Yasha? Tell him his mother's here. She wants to say good-bye to him.

YASHA (*waves his hand impatiently*): Oh, that's too much!

(*All this time* DUNYASHA *has been busy with the luggage. Now that* YASHA *is alone, she goes up to him.*)

DUNYASHA: You haven't even looked at me once, Yasha. You're going away, leaving me behind. (*Bursts out crying and throws her arms around his neck.*)

YASHA: Must you cry? (*Drinks champagne.*) I'll be back in Paris in a week. Tomorrow we catch the express and off we go! That's the last you'll see of us. I can hardly believe it, somehow. *Vive la France!* I hate it here. It doesn't suit me at all. It's not the kind of life I like. I'm afraid it can't be helped. I've had enough of all this ignorance. More than enough. (*Drinks champagne.*) So what's the use of crying? Behave yourself and you won't end up crying.

DUNYASHA (*powdering her face, looking in a hand mirror*): Write to me from Paris, please. I did love you, Yasha, after all. I loved you so much. I'm such an affectionate creature, Yasha.

YASHA: They're coming here. (*Busies himself around the suitcases, humming quietly.*)

(*Enter* MRS. RANEVSKY, GAYEV, ANYA, *and* CHARLOTTE.)

GAYEV: We ought to be going. There isn't much time left. (*Looking at* YASHA.) Who's smelling of pickled herrings here?

MRS. RANEVSKY: In another ten minutes we ought to be getting into the carriages. (*Looks round the room.*) Good-bye, dear house, good-bye, old grandfather house! Winter will pass, spring will come, and you won't be here any more. They'll have pulled you down. The things these walls have seen! (*Kisses her daughter affectionately.*) My precious one, you look radiant. Your eyes are sparkling like diamonds. Happy? Very happy?

ANYA: Oh yes, very! A new life is beginning, Mother!

GAYEV (*gaily*): It is, indeed. Everything's all right now. We were all so worried and upset before the cherry orchard was sold, but now, when everything has been finally and irrevocably settled, we have all calmed down and even cheered up. I'm a bank official now, a financier. Pot the red in the middle. As for you, Lyuba, say what you like, but you too are looking a lot better. There's no doubt about it.

MRS. RANEVSKY: Yes, my nerves are better, that's true. (*Someone helps her on with her hat and coat.*) I sleep well. Take my things out, Yasha. It's time. (*to* ANYA) We'll soon be seeing each other again, darling. I'm going to Paris. I'll live there on the money your great-aunt sent from Yaroslavl to buy the estate—three cheers for Auntie!—but the money won't last long, I'm afraid.

ANYA: You'll come home soon, Mother, very soon. I'm going to study, pass my school exams, and then I'll work and help you. We shall read all sorts of books together, won't we, Mother? (*Kisses her mother's hands.*) We shall read during the autumn evenings. We'll read lots and lots of books, and a new, wonderful world will open up to us. (*Dreamily.*) Oh, do come back, Mother!

MRS. RANEVSKY: I'll come back, my precious. (*Embraces her daughter.*)

(*Enter* LOPAKHIN. CHARLOTTE *quietly hums a tune.*)

GAYEV: Happy Charlotte! She's singing!

CHARLOTTE (*picks up a bundle that looks like a baby in swaddling clothes*): My darling baby, go to sleep, my baby. (*A sound of a baby crying is heard.*) Hush, my sweet, my darling boy. (*The cry is heard again.*) Poor little darling, I'm so sorry for you! (*Throws the bundle down.*) So you will find me another job, won't you? I can't go on like this.

LOPAKHIN: We'll find you one, don't you worry.

GAYEV: Everybody's leaving us. Varya's going away. All of a sudden, we're no longer wanted.

CHARLOTTE: I haven't anywhere to live in town. I must go away. (*Sings quietly.*) It's all the same to me. . . .

(*Enter* PISHCHIK.)

LOPAKHIN: The nine days' wonder!

PISHCHIK (*out of breath*): Oh dear, let me get my breath back! I'm all in. Dear friends . . . a drink of water, please.

GAYEV: Came to borrow some money, I'll be bound. Not from me this time. Better make myself scarce. (*Goes out.*)

PISHCHIK: Haven't seen you for ages, dearest lady. (*to* LOPAKHIN) You here too? Glad to see you . . . man of immense intellect. . . . Here, that's for you, take it. (*Gives* LOPAKHIN *money.*) Four hundred rubles. That leaves eight hundred and forty I still owe you.

LOPAKHIN (*puzzled, shrugging his shoulders*): I must be dreaming. Where did you get it?

PISHCHIK: One moment . . . Terribly hot . . . Most extraordinary thing happened. Some Englishmen came to see me. They found some kind of white clay on my land. (*to* MRS. RANEVSKY) Here's four hundred for you too, beautiful ravishing lady. (*Gives her the money.*) The rest later. (*Drinks some water.*) Young fellow in the train just now was telling me that some—er—great philosopher advises people to jump off roofs. "Jump!" he says, and that'll solve all your problems. (*With surprise.*) Good Lord! More water, please.

LOPAKHIN: Who were these Englishmen?

PISHCHIK: I let them a plot of land with the clay on a twenty-four years' lease. And now you must excuse me, my friends. I'm in a hurry. Must be rushing off somewhere else. To Znoykov's, to Kardamonov's . . . Owe them all money. (*Drinks.*) Good-bye. I'll look in on Thursday.

MRS. RANEVSKY: We're just leaving for town. I'm going abroad tomorrow.

PISHCHIK: What? (*In a worried voice.*) Why are you going to town? Oh! I see! The furniture, the suitcases . . . Well, no matter. (*Through tears.*) No matter. Men of immense intellect, these Englishmen. . . . No matter. . . . No matter. I wish you all the best. May God help you. . . . No matter. Everything in this world comes to an end. (*Kisses* MRS. RANEVSKY'*s hand.*) When you hear that my end has come, remember the—er—old horse and say: Once there lived a man called Simeonov-Pishchik; may he rest in peace. Remarkable weather we've been having. . . . Yes. (*Goes out in great embarrassment, but immediately comes back and says, standing in the doorway.*) My Dashenka sends her regards. (*Goes out.*)

MRS. RANEVSKY: Well, we can go now. I'm leaving with two worries on my mind. One concerns Firs. He's ill. (*With a glance at her watch.*) We still have about five minutes.

ANYA: Firs has been taken to the hospital, Mother. Yasha sent him off this morning.

MRS. RANEVSKY: My other worry concerns Varya. She's used to getting up early and working. Now that she has nothing to do, she's like a fish out of water. She's grown thin and pale, and she's always crying, poor thing. (*Pause.*) You must have noticed it, Lopakhin. As you very well know, I'd always hoped to see her married to you. Indeed, everything seemed to indicate that you two would get married. (*She whispers to* ANYA, *who nods to* CHARLOTTE, *and they both go out.*) She loves you, you like her, and I simply don't know why you two always seem to avoid each other. I don't understand it.

LOPAKHIN: To tell you the truth, neither do I. The whole thing's odd somehow. If there's still time, I'm ready even now. . . . Let's settle it at once and get it over. I don't feel I'll ever propose to her without you here.

MRS. RANEVSKY: Excellent! Why, it shouldn't take more than a minute. I'll call her at once.

LOPAKHIN: And there's champagne here too. Appropriate to the occasion. (*Looks at the glasses.*) They're empty. Someone must have drunk it. (YASHA *coughs.*) Lapped it up, I call it.

MRS. RANEVSKY (*excitedly*): Fine! We'll go out. Yasha, *allez!* I'll call her. (*Through the door.*) Varya, leave what you're doing and come here for a moment. Come on.

(MRS. RANEVSKY *goes out with* YASHA.)

LOPAKHIN (*glancing at his watch*): Aye. . . .

(*Pause. Behind the door suppressed laughter and whispering can be heard. Enter* VARYA.)

VARYA (*spends a long time examining the luggage*): Funny, can't find it.

LOPAKHIN: What are you looking for?

VARYA: Packed it myself, and can't remember.

(*Pause.*)

LOPAKHIN: Where are you going now, Varya?

VARYA: Me? To the Ragulins'. I've agreed to look after their house—to be their housekeeper, I suppose.

LOPAKHIN: In Yashnevo, isn't it? About fifty miles from here. (*Pause.*) Aye. . . . So life's come to an end in this house.

VARYA (*examining the luggage*): Where can it be? Must have put it in the trunk. Yes, life's come to an end in this house. It will never come back.

LOPAKHIN: I'm off to Kharkov by the same train. Lots to see to there. I'm leaving Yepikhodov here to keep an eye on things. I've given him the job.

VARYA: Have you?

LOPAKHIN: This time last year it was already snowing, you remember. Now it's calm and sunny. A bit cold, though. Three degrees of frost.

VARYA: I haven't looked. *(Pause.)* Anyway, our thermometer's broken.

(Pause. A voice from outside, through the door: "Mr. Lopakhin!")

LOPAKHIN *(as though he had long been expecting this call)*: Coming! *(Goes out quickly.)*

(VARYA sits down on the floor, lays her head on a bundle of clothes, and sobs quietly. The door opens and MRS. RANEVSKY comes in cautiously.)

MRS. RANEVSKY: Well? *(Pause.)* We must go.

VARYA *(no longer crying, dries her eyes)*: Yes, it's time, Mother dear. I'd like to get to the Ragulins' today, I only hope we don't miss the train.

MRS. RANEVSKY *(calling through the door.)*: Anya, put your things on.

(Enter ANYA, followed by GAYEV and CHARLOTTE. GAYEV wears a warm overcoat with a hood. SERVANTS and COACHMEN come in. YEPIKHODOV is busy with the luggage.)

MRS. RANEVSKY: Now we can be on our way.

ANYA *(joyfully)*: On our way. Oh, yes!

GAYEV: My friends, my dear, dear friends, leaving this house for good, how can I remain silent, how can I, before parting from you, refrain from expressing the feelings which now pervade my whole being—

ANYA *(imploringly)*: Uncle!

VARYA: Uncle dear, please don't.

GAYEV *(dejectedly)*: Double the red into the middle. . . . Not another word!

(Enter TROFIMOV, followed by LOPAKHIN.)

TROFIMOV: Well, ladies and gentlemen, it's time to go.

LOPAKHIN: Yepikhodov, my coat!

MRS. RANEVSKY: Let me sit down a minute. I feel as though I've never seen the walls and ceilings of this house before. I look at them now with such eagerness, with such tender emotion. . . .

GAYEV: I remember when I was six years old sitting on this window sill on Trinity Sunday and watching Father going to church.

MRS. RANEVSKY: Have all the things been taken out?

LOPAKHIN: I think so. *(To YEPIKHODOV as he puts on his coat.)* Mind, everything's all right here, Yepikhodov.

YEPIKHODOV *(in a hoarse voice)*: Don't you worry, sir.

LOPAKHIN: What's the matter with your voice?

YEPIKHODOV: I've just had a drink of water and I must have swallowed something.

YASHA *(contemptuously)*: What ignorance!

MRS. RANEVSKY: There won't be a soul left in this place when we've gone.

LOPAKHIN: Not till next spring.

(VARYA pulls an umbrella out of a bundle of clothes with such force that it looks as if she were going to hit someone with it; LOPAKHIN pretends to be frightened.)

VARYA: Good heavens, you didn't really think that—

TROFIMOV: Come on, let's get into the carriages! It's time. The train will be in soon.

VARYA: There are your galoshes, Peter. By that suitcase. *(Tearfully.)* Oh, how dirty they are, how old. . . .

TROFIMOV *(putting on his galoshes)*: Come along, ladies and gentlemen.

(Pause.)

GAYEV *(greatly put out, afraid of bursting into tears)*: Train . . . station . . . in off into the middle pocket . . . double the white into the corner.

MRS. RANEVSKY: Come along!

LOPAKHIN: Is everyone here? No one left behind? *(Locks the side door on the left.)* There are some things in there. I'd better keep it locked. Come on!

ANYA: Good-bye, old house! Good-bye, old life!

TROFIMOV: Welcome new life!

(TROFIMOV goes out with ANYA. VARYA casts a last look round the room and goes out unhurriedly. YASHA and CHARLOTTE, carrying her lap dog, go out.)

LOPAKHIN: So, it's till next spring. Come along, ladies and gentlemen. Till we meet again. *(Goes out.)*

(MRS. RANEVSKY and GAYEV are left alone. They seem to have been waiting for this moment. They fling their arms around each other, sobbing quietly, restraining themselves, as though afraid of being overheard.)

GAYEV *(in despair)*: My sister! My sister!

MRS. RANEVSKY: Oh, my dear, my sweet, my beautiful orchard! My life, my youth, my happiness, good-bye! . . .

ANYA *(offstage, happily, appealingly)*: Mo-ther!

TROFIMOV *(offstage, happily, excited)*: Where are you?

MRS. RANEVSKY: One last look at the walls and the windows. Mother loved to walk in this room.

GAYEV: My sister, my sister!

ANYA *(offstage)*: Mo-ther!

TROFIMOV *(offstage)*: Where are you?

MRS. RANEVSKY: We're coming.

(They go out. The stage is empty. The sound of all the doors being locked is heard, then of carriages driving off. It grows quiet. The silence is broken by the muffled noise of an axe striking a tree, sounding forlorn and sad. Footsteps can be heard. FIRS appears from the door on the right. He is dressed, as always, in a jacket and white waistcoat. He is wearing slippers. He looks ill.)

FIRS *(walks up to the door and tries the handle)*: Locked! They've gone. *(Sits down on the sofa.)* Forgot all about me. Never mind. Let me sit down here for a bit. Forgotten to put on his fur coat, the young master has. Sure of it. Gone off in his light overcoat. *(Sighs anxiously.)* I should have seen to it. . . . Oh, these youngsters! *(Mutters something which cannot be understood.)* My life's gone just as if I'd never lived. . . . *(Lies down.)* I'll lie down a bit. No strength left, Nothing's left. Nothing. Ugh, you—nincompoop! *(Lies motionless.)*

(A distant sound is heard, which seems to come from the sky, the sound of a breaking string, slowly dying away, melancholy. It is followed by silence, broken only by the sound of an axe striking a tree far away in the orchard.)

CURTAIN

Figure 1. Mrs. Ranevsky (Natasha Parry) dances with delight to be back in her old home, while Gayev (Erland Josephson) looks on and Lopakhin (Brian Dennehy) sits on the floor in the Peter Brook production of *The Cherry Orchard,* directed by Peter Brook, 1988. (Photograph: Martha Swope.)

Figure 2. Lopakhin (Brian Dennehy) tells Mrs. Ranevsky (Natasha Parry) that she must sell the cherry orchard, while Gayev (Erland Josephson) looks on, the melancholy expression on his face echoing that of his sister, in the Peter Brook production of *The Cherry Orchard,* directed by Peter Brook, 1988. (Photograph: Martha Swope.)

Staging of *The Cherry Orchard*

REVIEW OF THE PETER BROOK PRODUCTION, 1988, BY FRANK RICH

It is not until the final act of *The Cherry Orchard* that the malevolent thud of an ax signals the destruction of a family's ancestral estate and, with it, the traumatic uprooting of a dozen late-nineteenth-century Russian lives. But in Peter Brook's production of Chekhov's play, the landscape seems to have been cleared before Act I begins. Mr. Brook has stripped *The Cherry Orchard* of its scenery, its front curtain, its intermissions. Even the house in which the play unfolds—the Brooklyn Academy of Music's semirestored Majestic Theater—looks half-demolished, a once-genteel palace of gilt and plush now a naked, faded shell of crumbling brick, chipped paint and forgotten hopes.

What little decorative elegance remains can be found on the vast stage floor, which Mr. Brook has covered, as is his wont, with dark Oriental rugs. And that—plus an extraordinary international cast, using a crystalline new translation by Elisaveta Lavrova—proves to be all that's needed. On this director's magic carpets, *The Cherry Orchard* flies. By banishing all forms of theatrical realism except the only one that really matters—emotional truth—Mr. Brook has found the pulse of a play that its author called "not a drama but a comedy, in places almost a farce." That pulse isn't to be confused with the somber metronomic beat of the Act IV ax—the Stanislavskian gloom that Chekhov so despised—and it isn't the kinetic, too frequently farcical gait of Andrei Serban's fascinating 1977 production at Lincoln Center. The real tone of *The Cherry Orchard* is that of a breaking string—that mysterious unidentifiable offstage sound that twice interrupts the action, unnerving the characters and audience alike with the sensation that unfathomable life is inexorably rushing by.

We feel that strange tingle, an exquisite pang of joy and suffering, again and again. When the beautiful Natasha Parry, as the bankrupt landowner Lyubov, returns to her estate from Paris, her brimming eyes take in the vast reaches of the auditorium in a single sweeping glance of nostalgic longing. But when she says, "I feel like a little girl again," the husky darkness of her voice fills in the scarred decades since childhood, relinquishing the girlishness even as it is reclaimed. Later, Miss Parry will simply sit in a chair, quietly crying, as Brian Dennehy, in the role of the merchant Lopakhin, announces that he has purchased her estate at auction. Lopakhin, whose ancestors were serfs on the land he now owns, can't help celebrating his purchase, but his half-jig of victory is slowly tempered by the realization that he has forfeited any chance of affection from the aristocratic woman he has just bought out. A bear of a man, Mr. Dennehy ends up prostrate on the floor behind Miss Parry's chair, tugging ineffectually at her hem. We're left with an indelible portrait of not one but two well-meaning souls who have lost what they most loved by recognizing their own desires too late.

That Lopakhin is as sympathetic and complex a figure as Lyubov, rather than a malicious arriviste, is a tribute not just to Mr. Dennehy's performance but also to Mr. Brook's entire approach to the play. When Trofimov (Zeljko Ivanek), the eternal student, angrily tells Miss Parry to "face the truth" for once in her life, she responds rhetorically, "What truth?" The director, like Chekhov, recognizes that there is no one truth. Each character must be allowed his own truth—a mixture of attributes and convictions that can't easily be typed or judged. Mr. Dennehy gives us both sides (and more) of the man whom Trofimov variously calls a "beast of prey" and "a fine, sensitive soul." Mr. Ivanek does the same with Trofimov, providing a rounded view of the sometimes foolish but fundamentally idealistic young man whose opinions swing so wildly. Though the student may look immature telling off Lyubov or Lopakhin, his vision of a happier future is so stirring that Mr. Ivanek quite rightly prompts the moon to rise while proclaiming it ("I can feel my happiness coming—I can see it!") at the end of Act II.

Miss Parry, Mr. Dennehy and Mr. Ivanek are all brilliant under Mr. Brook's guidance, and they're not alone. As Lyubov's brother, Gaev—a forlorn representative of Czarist Russia's obsolete, decaying nobility—the Swedish actor Erland Josephson embodies the fossilized remains of a civilization. Elegant of bearing yet fuzzy of expression, his voice mellifluous yet childlike, he snaps into focus only when drifting into imaginary billiard games. One of the evening's comic high points is his absurdly gratuitous tribute to a century-old family bookcase, but the hilarity of his futility is matched by the poignance of his Act III entrance, in which his exhausted posture and sad, dangling bundle of anchovy and herring tins announce the estate's sale to his sister well before Lopakhin does.

As Firs, the octogenarian family retainer, Roberts Blossom is a tall, impish, bearded figure in formal black, stooping over his cane—a spindly, timeless ghost from the past, as rooted to the soil as the trees we never see. Stephanie Roth is a revelation as Varya, whose fruitless religious piety is balanced by a bravery that saves her from despair when her last prayer for happiness, a marriage proposal from Lopakhin, flickers and then dies in Mr. Dennehy's eyes. Linda Hunt (Charlotta), Jan Triska (Yepikhodov) and Mike Nussbaum (Pishchik) find the melancholy humor of true Old World clowns in their subsidiary, more broadly conceived roles. If the play's younger generation—Rebecca Miller (Anya), Kate Mailer (Dunyasha) and David Pierce (Yasha)—is not of the same class, holding one's own with a company of this stature is no small achievement in itself.

In keeping with his work with the actors, Mr. Brook's staging has a supple, airy flow that avoids cheap laughs or sentimentality yet is always strikingly theatrical. In Act III, the reveling dancers twirl around velvet screens in choreographic emulation of the ricocheting rumors of the estate's sale. Throughout the evening, the transitions of mood are lightning fast. In an instant, Miss Parry's reminiscence of her son's drowning can be dispelled by the jaunty strains of a nearby band. Neither Lyubov nor anyone else is allowed the self-pity that would plunge *The Cherry Orchard* from the flickering tearfulness of regret into the maudlin sobs of phony high drama.

The mood that is achieved instead, though not tragic, recalls Mr. Brook's *Endgame*-inspired *King Lear* of the 1960s. Beckett is definitely on the director's mind, as is evident not just from the void in which he sets the play but also by his explicit evocation of the Beckett humor in several scenes. When Miss Hunt's governess gives her monologue describing her utter lack of identity—she doesn't know who she is or where she came from—it's a cheeky, center-stage effusion of existential verbal slapstick, with a vegetable for a prop, right out of *Waiting for Godot* or *Happy Days*. When, at evening's end, old Firs

is locked by accident in the mansion, we're keenly aware of the repetition of the word "nothing" in his final speech. As Mr. Blossom falls asleep in his easy chair, illuminated by a bare shaft of light and accompanied by the far-off sound of the ax, one can't be blamed for thinking of Krapp reviewing his last tape.

But the delicate connections Mr. Brook draws between Beckett and Chekhov are inevitable and to the point, not arch and pretentious, and they help explain why this *Cherry Orchard* is so right. Though Chekhov was dying when he wrote this play, he didn't lose his perspective on existence and the people who endure it. Horrible, inexplicable things happen to the characters in *The Cherry Orchard*—the shadow of death is always cloaking their shoulders, as it does Beckett's lost souls—but, as Mr. Brook writes in the program, "they have not given up." They simply trudge on, sometimes with their senses of humor intact, sometimes with a dogged faith in the prospects for happiness.

That's the human comedy, and, if it isn't riotously funny, one feels less alone in the solitary plight, indeed exhilarated, watching it unfold on stage as honestly and buoyantly and poetically as a dream. This is a *Cherry Orchard* that pauses for breath only when life does, for people to recoup after dying a little. I think Mr. Brook has given us the Chekhov production that every theatergoer fantasizes about but, in my experience, almost never finds.

BERNARD SHAW

1856–1950

Shaw did not write his first play until he was thirty-six, but by the time of his death he had written forty-seven full-length plays as well as a number of playlets and thus had become one of the most prolific dramatists in the history of the English theater. He was born and raised in Dublin in the midst of an unhappy marriage, his father an unsuccessful merchant who turned to drink, his mother a talented singer who scorned the domestic chores of tending a household. By the time he was fifteen, he had dropped out of school, where according to his own account he learned only that schools are a form of imprisonment; by the time he was twenty he had abandoned an office job in Dublin and gone to live in London with his mother, who was a professional teacher of music. Shaw had vowed never to do another "honest day's work" but to make his way in the world as a writer, and from 1876 to 1885 he leaned on his mother for financial support while he turned out five novels, none of which he was able to get published.

Although the early 1880s were a period of literary frustration for Shaw, they proved to be a time in which he made intellectual discoveries that were to influence most of his thinking and writing. In 1882 he first heard about Karl Marx and subsequently became a lifelong convert to socialism, confessing later that "the importance of the economic basis of society dawned on me" and that "Marx made a man of me." Then in 1884, having studied *Das Kapital* in a Marxist reading circle, he joined the Fabians, a socialist group that, though influenced by Marx, regarded the state not as a class structure to be overthrown but as a social mechanism to be gradually altered and used for the promotion of public welfare. To achieve this goal, Shaw and his Fabian colleagues publicized their positions on every economic, political, and social issue of the day—from local government reform to reform of the poor laws, from trade unionism to women's rights—making their views known in leaflets, newspapers, pamphlets, and books, in lecture halls and on street corners. By the late 1880s Shaw was also writing art criticism, book reviews, and music criticism for several London newspapers. And in 1891, he also made his views known on the state of drama by publishing *The Quintessence of Ibsenism,* a fiery little book in which he sought to awaken English theatergoers to the social consciousness embodied in Ibsen's plays.

Having sharpened his prose on so wide a variety of cultural and social issues, Shaw himself was uniquely prepared to become the English counterpart of Ibsen, and in 1892 he launched his theatrical career with *Widowers' Houses,* a dramatic attack on the evils of slum landlordism, which he showed to be an emblem of the capitalist system. But even in this first play, as in nearly all of the others he was to write, Shaw's dramatic technique was vastly different from that of Ibsen. Whereas Ibsen had probed the inner lives and problems of his characters in plays suffused with a Scandinavian air of gloom, Shaw turned his characters into witty spokespersons for his social and political views. Shaw's experience in politics and critical reviewing had clearly taught him that comic wit is often the most powerful means of awakening an audience and winning its support.

In the years that followed his first play, Shaw used his comic techniques to expose and satirize an astonishing array of follies or evils in economics, politics, society, theology, morality, and science. In *Mrs. Warren's Profession* (1893), a play about prostitution, he showed that "rich men without conviction are more dangerous in modern society than poor women without chastity." In *Arms and the Man* (1894), he mocked romantic notions about love and war by making his hero a blunt realist who throws away his cartridges and replaces them with chocolates because he knows enough to realize that cartridges will be useless during a cavalry charge but chocolates will be invaluable after the charge is over. In *Candida* (1895), he challenged conventional ideas of marriage by creating as his heroine a very superior woman whose strength is revealed to lie in the way she conceals her strength. In *Caesar and Cleopatra* (1899), he mocked Shakespeare's view of Roman history, as it had been presented in *Julius Caesar* and *Antony and Cleopatra,* by turning Cleopatra into a naive and fearful sixteen-year-old, who is schooled in political wisdom by the hero of the play, Caesar. For Shaw, Caesar was a "naturally great" man precisely because he was free from conventional moral beliefs as well as charmingly self-aware of his limitations.

Though Shaw saw clearly how human beings are often imprisoned by conventional morality, he could imagine the possibility of human beings and social institutions liberating themselves as well. In *Major Barbara* (1905), he created one of his most compelling embodiments of the "life force," Andrew Undershaft, who overturns sentimental moralizing about poverty by providing well-paying jobs rather than Salvation Army handouts; the munitions maker is thus both the merchant of destruction and the creator of meaningful labor. And yet when the weapons of Undershaft came to dominate Europe during World War I, Shaw was quick to dramatize the destructive social and political bankruptcy of his generation. For example, in *Heartbreak House* (1919, though he began writing it in 1913), Shaw portrayed his withering vision of "cultured, leisured Europe before the war," by showing it to be incapable of shaking off its laziness and shallowness. Later, *Saint Joan* (1923) dramatized the tragic conflict between political institutions and genius, ending with a scene in which the martyred Joan returns as a dream-vision twenty-five years after she has been burnt. But when she offers to return as a living woman, everyone shrinks from the prospect in dismay.

Shaw expounded his views not only in his plays but also in prefaces and notes that he wrote for the published versions of the plays. By means of these commentaries, which were often as long as the plays themselves, Shaw used his incisive prose style to explicate his characters, plots, and themes as well as to gain a wider audience for his ideas than was possible in the theater. *Man and Superman* (1903), for example, which brilliantly dramatizes Shaw's ideas of the "life force" and "creative evolution," was published with a lengthy essay on modern society and the need for the superman and with a tract called "The Revolutionists Handbook and Pocket Companion," which had been mentioned in the first act of the play.

For *Pygmalion* (1913), Shaw provided not only a preface but, more strikingly, an afterword, reprinted here following the play, in which he went on to explain what happened to his characters after the play. Shaw's insistence in the afterword that Henry Higgins, the phonetics teacher, and Eliza Doolittle, the Cockney flower girl, whose speech—and life—he transforms, *would not* get married constitutes an extraordinary attempt to control the audience's experience and understanding of the play as fully as possible. That Shaw ever attempted to exert such total control over his audience seems particularly ironic given the fact that both the play itself and the myth on which it is based are concerned with the problems that arise when one human being tries to exert such control over another. Within the play, Shaw explores the theme of control by turning the story of the mythical Greek sculptor, Pygmalion, who created a beautiful statue and then saw it come to life, into the story of Higgins, who transforms a "draggletailed guttersnipe" into "a duchess." He corrects her accent, teaches her proper grammar, dresses her in beautiful clothes, and then watches with pride as the once dirty-faced flower girl moves successfully into "polite society."

But Shaw shows us that the reshaping of Eliza raises serious questions about any attempt to control or shape the lives of other people, especially those over whom one has some power, whether the power comes from class status or money or gender. Even before Higgins starts to teach Eliza, his housekeeper Mrs. Pearce asks, "And what is to become of her when youve finished your teaching?" Higgins's reply is flippant: "Whats to become of her if I leave her in the gutter?" Though Colonel Pickering, Higgins's friend, addresses Eliza politely as "Miss Doolittle," he is astonished to find out that Eliza has run away after her success at the ball and asks naively, "What did we do to her?" From Eliza's point of view, what they have done, rather than make a princess out of Cinderella, is destroy her life as a flower girl without offering her any new possibilities. Yet in the process of railing against her predicament, Eliza discovers that she has become independent, that she can teach others what Higgins has taught her. The real transformation, as Higgins realizes, is not in her speech but in her soul: "I said I'd make a women of you; and I have."

Having made a woman of Eliza, Higgins comes tantalizingly close to finding himself in the situation of his mythic counterpart Pygmalion, who fell in love with the statue he had created. Thus Shaw examines the theme of control by dramatizing its effect not only on Eliza but also on Higgins—on the controller as well as on the one controlled. In flirting constantly with the possibility of a romantic relationship between Higgins and Eliza, Shaw ultimately invites his audience to ponder the fascinating—and disturbing—question of whether a seemingly amoral and heartless creator can be redeemed or transformed by his creation. Though Shaw left the question open in the play itself and answered it negatively in the afterword, the film of *Pygmalion*, for which Shaw wrote the screenplay and received an Academy Award, ends with a scene which implies a distinctly different answer from his afterword. Specifically, as Higgins is shown sitting alone in his study, listening to the recording he made when Eliza first appeared there, Eliza herself returns, her own voice replacing the mechanical one. Shaw probably did not write this scene, though he seems to have given it tacit approval, but it is the very same scene which also comes at the end of *My Fair Lady* (1956), the highly successful musical based on *Pygmalion*.

Yet, as Ronald Bryden's review of the 1974 London production of *Pygmalion* makes clear, Shaw's insistence that Eliza does not marry Higgins is also stage-worthy and even more relevant to contemporary audiences. Though Higgins may have power because of his education and because he is a man, he is finally unwilling to change and to grow or, in Alec McCowen's portrayal, to grow up. By contrast, Diana Rigg's Eliza, beginning as a messy figure with tattered gloves and wildly feathered hat (see Figure 1) can change, as she is transformed first into an elegantly gowned woman who fascinates polite society (see Figure 3). But the real transformation is internal. Rigg's Eliza ends as a poised figure even with Higgins's hand on her throat (see Figure 2). Indeed, the look on her face makes clear that, while she may be attracted to Higgins, she can also resist both the visible threat and the implied caress. Yet the fact that Shaw had to argue so long for that resistance indicates the enduring power of the desire for romance, a desire *Pygmalion* continues to evoke and to question.

PYGMALION

BY BERNARD SHAW

PRINCIPAL CHARACTERS IN THE ORDER OF THEIR APPEARANCE

CLARA EYNSFORD HILL *daughter of*

MRS EYNSFORD HILL *a lady*

FREDDY EYNSFORD HILL *the lady's son*

ELIZA DOOLITTLE *a flower girl*

COLONEL PICKERING *British officer, amateur phonetician*

PROFESSOR HENRY HIGGINS *a phonetician*

MRS. PEARCE *Professor Higgins's housekeeper*

ALFRED DOOLITTLE *Eliza's father, a dust (garbage) man*

MRS HIGGINS *Professor Higgins's mother*

PERIOD

The present

PREFACE TO PYGMALION
A PROFESSOR OF PHONETICS

As will be seen later on, Pygmalion needs, not a preface, but a sequel, which I have supplied in its due place.

The English have no respect for their language, and will not teach their children to speak it. They spell it so abominably that no man can teach himself what it sounds like. It is impossible for an Englishman to open his mouth without making some other Englishman hate or despise him. German and Spanish are accessible to foreigners: English is not accessible even to Englishmen. The reformer England needs today is an energetic phonetic enthusiast: that is why I have made such a one the hero of a popular play. There have been heroes of that kind crying in the wilderness for many years past. When I became interested in the subject towards the end of the eighteen-seventies, the illustrious Alexander Melville Bell, the inventor of Visible Speech, had emigrated to Canada, where his son invented the telephone; but Alexander J. Ellis was still a London patriarch, with an impressive head always covered by a velvet skull cap, for which he would apologize to public meetings in a very courtly manner. He and Tito Pagliardini, another phonetic veteran, were men whom it was impossible to dislike. Henry Sweet, then a young man, lacked their sweetness of character: he was about as conciliatory to conventional mortals as Ibsen or Samuel Butler. His great ability as a phonetician (he was, I think, the best of them all at his job) would have entitled him to high official recognition, and perhaps enabled him to popularize his subject, but for his Satanic contempt for all academic dignitaries and persons in general who thought more of Greek than of phonetics. Once, in the days when the Imperial Institute rose in South Kensington, and Joseph Chamberlain was booming the Empire, I induced the editor of a leading monthly review to commission an article from Sweet on the imperial importance of his subject. When it arrived, it contained nothing but a savagely derisive attack on a professor of language and literature whose chair Sweet regarded as proper to a phonetic expert only. The article, being libellous, had to be returned as impossible; and I had to renounce my dream of dragging its author into the limelight. When I met him afterwards, for the first time for many years, I found to my astonishment that he, who had been a quite tolerably presentable young man, had actually managed by sheer scorn to alter his personal appearance until he had become a sort of walking repudiation of Oxford and all its traditions. It must have been largely in his own despite that he was squeezed into something called a Readership of phonetics there. The future of phonetics rests probably with his pupils, who all swore by him; but nothing could bring the man himself into any sort of compliance with the university to which he nevertheless clung by divine right in an intensely Oxonian way. I daresay his papers, if he has left any, include some satires that may be published without too destructive results fifty years hence. He was, I believe, not in the least an illnatured man: very much the opposite, I should say; but he would not suffer fools gladly.

Those who knew him will recognize in my third act the allusion to the patent shorthand in which he used to write postcards, and which may be acquired from a four and sixpenny manual published by the Clarendon Press. The postcards which Mrs Higgins describes are such as I have received from Sweet. I would decipher a sound which a cockney would represent by *zerr*, and a Frenchman by *seu*, and then write demanding with some heat what on earth it meant. Sweet, with boundless contempt for my stupidity, would reply that it not only meant but obviously was the word Result, as no other word containing that sound, and capable of making sense with the context, existed in any language spoken on earth. That less expert mortals should require fuller indications was beyond Sweet's patience. Therefore, though the whole point of his Current Shorthand is that it can express every sound in the language perfectly, vowels as well as consonants, and that your hand has to make no stroke except the easy and current ones with which you write m, n, and u, l, p, and q, scribbling them at whatever angle comes easiest to you, his unfortunate determination to make this remarkable and quite legible script serve also as a shorthand reduced it in his own practice to the most inscrutable of cryptograms. His true objective was the provision of a full, accurate, legible script for our noble but ill-dressed language; but he was led past that by his contempt for the popular Pitman system of shorthand, which he called the Pitfall system. The triumph of Pitman was a triumph of business organization: there was a weekly paper to persuade you to learn Pitman: there were cheap textbooks and exercise books and transcripts of speeches for you to copy, and schools where experienced teachers coached you up to the necessary proficiency. Sweet could not organize his market in that fashion. He might as well have been the Sybil who tore up the leaves of prophecy that nobody would attend to. The four and sixpenny manual, mostly in his lithographed handwriting, that was never vulgarly advertized, may perhaps some day be taken up by a syndicate and pushed upon the public as The Times pushed the Encyclopædia Britannica; but until then it will certainly not prevail against Pitman. I have bought three copies of it during my lifetime; and I am informed by the publishers that its cloistered existence is still a steady and healthy one. I actually learned the system two several times; and yet the shorthand in which I am writing these lines is Pitman's. And the reason is, that my secretary cannot transcribe Sweet, having been perforce taught in the schools of Pitman. Therefore, Sweet railed at Pitman as vainly as Thersites railed at Ajax: his raillery, however it may have eased his soul, gave no popular vogue to Current Shorthand.

Pygmalion Higgins is not a portrait of Sweet, to whom the adventure of Eliza Doolittle would have been impossible; still, as will be seen, there are touches of Sweet in the play. With Higgins's physique and temperament Sweet might have set the Thames on fire. As it was, he impressed himself professionally on Europe to an extent that made his comparative personal obscurity, and the failure of Oxford to do justice to his eminence, a puzzle to foreign specialists in his subject. I do not blame Oxford, because I think Oxford is quite right in demanding a certain social amenity from its nurslings (heaven knows it is not exorbitant in its requirements!); for although I well know how hard it is for a man of genius with a seriously underrated subject to maintain serene and kindly relations with the men who underrate it, and who keep all the best places for less important subjects which they profess without originality and sometimes without much capacity for them, still, if he overwhelms them with wrath and disdain, he cannot expect them to heap honors on him.

Of the later generations of phoneticians I know little. Among them towers the Poet Laureate, to whom perhaps Higgins may owe his Miltonic sympathies, though here again I must disclaim all portraiture. But if the play makes the public aware that there are such people as phoneticians, and that they are among the most important people in England at present, it will serve its turn.

I wish to boast that Pygmalion has been an extremely successful play all over Europe and North America as well as at home. It is so intensely and deliberately didactic, and its subject is esteemed so dry, that I delight in throwing it at the heads of the wiseacres who repeat the parrot cry that art should never be didactic. It goes to prove my contention that art should never be anything else.

Finally, and for the encouragement of people troubled with accents that cut them off from all high employment, I may add that the change wrought by Professor Higgins in the flower-girl is neither impossible nor uncommon. The modern concierge's daughter who fulfils her ambition by playing the Queen of Spain in Ruy Blas at the Théâtre Français is only one of many thousands of men and women who have sloughed off their native dialects and acquired a new tongue. But the thing has to be done scientifically, or the last state of the aspirant may be worse than the first. An honest and natural slum dialect is more tolerable than the attempt of a phonetically untaught person to imitate the vulgar dialect of the golf club; and I am sorry to say that in spite of the efforts of our Royal Academy of Dramatic Art, there is still too much sham golfing English on our stage, and too little of the noble English of Forbes Robertson.

ACT 1

(*Covent Garden at 11.15 p.m. Torrents of heavy summer rain. Cab whistles blowing frantically in all directions. Pedestrians running for shelter into the market and under the portico of St Paul's Church, where there are already several people, among them a lady and her daughter in evening dress. They are all peering out gloomily at the rain, except one man with his back turned to the rest, who seems wholly preoccupied with a notebook in which he is writing busily.*
The church clock strikes the first quarter.)

THE DAUGHTER (*in the space between the central pillars, close to the one on her left*): I'm getting chilled to the bone. What can Freddy be doing all this time? He's been gone twenty minutes.

THE MOTHER (*on her daughter's right*): Not so long. But he ought to have got us a cab by this.

A BYSTANDER (*on the lady's right*): He wont get no cab not until half-past eleven, missus, when they come back after dropping their theatre fares.

THE MOTHER: But we must have a cab. We cant stand here until half-past eleven. It's too bad.

THE BYSTANDER: Well, it aint my fault, missus.

THE DAUGHTER: If Freddy had a bit of gumption, he would have got one at the theatre door.

THE MOTHER: What could he have done, poor boy?

THE DAUGHTER: Other people got cabs. Why couldnt he?

(FREDDY *rushes in out of the rain from the Southampton Street side, and comes between them closing a dripping umbrella. He is a young man of twenty, in evening dress, very wet round the ankles.*)

THE DAUGHTER: Well, havnt you got a cab?

FREDDY: Theres not one to be had for love or money.

THE MOTHER: Oh, Freddy, there must be one. You cant have tried.

THE DAUGHTER: It's too tiresome. Do you expect us to go and get one ourselves?

FREDDY: I tell you theyre all engaged. The rain was so sudden: nobody was prepared; and everybody had to take a cab. Ive been to Charing Cross one way and nearly to Ludgate Circus the other; and they were all engaged.

THE MOTHER: Did you try Trafalgar Square?

FREDDY: There wasnt one at Trafalgar Square.

THE DAUGHTER: Did you try?

FREDDY: I tried as far as Charing Cross station. Did you expect me to walk to Hammersmith?

THE DAUGHTER: You havnt tried at all.

THE MOTHER: You really are very helpless, Freddy. Go again; and dont come back until you have found a cab.

FREDDY: I shall simply get soaked for nothing.

THE DAUGHTER: And what about us? Are we to stay here all night in this draught, with next to nothing on? You selfish pig—

FREDDY: Oh, very well: I'll go, I'll go. (*He opens his umbrella and dashes off Strandwards, but comes into collision with a flower girl, who is hurrying in for shelter, knocking her basket out of her hands. A blinding flash of lightning, followed instantly by a rattling peal of thunder, orchestrates the incident.*)

THE FLOWER GIRL: Nah then, Freddy: look wh' y' gowin, deah.

FREDDY: Sorry (*he rushes off*).

THE FLOWER GIRL (*picking up her scattered flowers and replacing them in the basket*): Theres menners f' yer! Te-oo banches o voylets trod into the mad. (*She sits down on the plinth of the column, sorting her flowers, on the lady's right. She is not at all an attractive person. She is perhaps eighteen, perhaps twenty, hardly older. She wears a little sailor hat of black straw that has long been exposed to the dust and soot of London and has seldom if ever been brushed. Her hair needs washing rather badly: its mousy color can hardly be natural. She wears a shoddy black coat that reaches nearly to her knees and is shaped*

to her waist. She has a brown skirt with a coarse apron. Her boots are much the worse for wear. She is no doubt as clean as she can afford to be; but compared to the ladies she is very dirty. Her features are no worse than theirs; but their condition leaves something to be desired; and she needs the services of a dentist.*)

THE MOTHER: How do you know that my son's name is Freddy, pray?

THE FLOWER GIRL: Ow, eez ye-ooa san, is e? Wal, fewd dan y' de-ooty bawmz a mather should, eed now betten to spawl a pore gel's flahrzn than ran awy athaht pyin. Will ye-oo py me f'them? (*Here, with apologies, this desperate attempt to present her dialect without a phonetic alphabet must be abandoned as unintelligible outside London.*)

THE DAUGHTER: Do nothing of the sort, mother. The idea!

THE MOTHER: Please allow me, Clara. Have you any pennies?

THE DAUGHTER: No. I've nothing smaller than sixpence.

THE FLOWER GIRL (*hopefully*): I can give you change for a tanner, kind lady.

THE MOTHER (*to* CLARA): Give it to me. (CLARA *parts reluctantly.*) Now (*to the girl*) this is for your flowers.

THE FLOWER GIRL: Thank you kindly, lady.

THE DAUGHTER: Make her give you the change. These things are only a penny a bunch.

THE MOTHER: Do hold your tongue, Clara. (*To the girl*) You can keep the change.

THE FLOWER GIRL: Oh, thank you, lady.

THE MOTHER: Now tell me how you know that young gentleman's name.

THE FLOWER GIRL: I didnt.

THE MOTHER: I heard you call him by it. Dont try to deceive me.

THE FLOWER GIRL (*protesting*): Who's trying to deceive you? I called him Freddy or Charlie same as you might yourself if you was talking to a stranger and wished to be pleasant. (*She sits down beside her basket.*)

THE DAUGHTER: Sixpence thrown away! Really, mamma, you might have spared Freddy that. (*She retreats in disgust behind the pillar.*)

(*An elderly gentleman of the amiable military type rushes into the shelter, and closes a dripping umbrella. He is in the same plight as* FREDDY, *very wet about the ankles. He is in evening dress, with a light overcoat. He takes the place left vacant by the daughter's retirement.*)

THE GENTLEMAN: Phew!

THE MOTHER (*to the gentleman*): Oh, sir, is there any sign of its stopping?

THE GENTLEMAN: I'm afraid not. It started worse than ever about two minutes ago (*he goes to the plinth beside the flower girl; puts up his foot on it; and stoops to turn down his trouser ends.*)

THE MOTHER: Oh dear! (*She retires sadly and joins her daughter.*)

THE FLOWER GIRL (*taking advantage of the military gentleman's proximity to establish friendly relations with him*): If it's worse, it's a sign it's nearly over. So cheer up, Captain; and buy a flower off a poor girl.

THE GENTLEMAN: I'm sorry. I havnt any change.

THE FLOWER GIRL: I can give you change, Captain.

THE GENTLEMAN: For a sovereign? Ive nothing less.

THE FLOWER GIRL: Garn! Oh do buy a flower off me, Captain. I can change half-a-crown. Take this for tuppence.

THE GENTLEMAN: Now dont be troublesome: theres a good girl. (*Trying his pockets*) I really havnt any change—Stop: heres three hapence, if thats any use to you (*he retreats to the other pillar*).

THE FLOWER GIRL (*disappointed, but thinking three halfpence better than nothing*): Thank you, sir.

THE BYSTANDER (*to the girl*): You be careful: give him a flower for it. Theres a bloke here behind taking down every blessed word youre saying. (*All turn to the man who is taking notes.*)

THE FLOWER GIRL (*springing up terrified*): I aint done nothing wrong by speaking to the gentleman. Ive a right to sell flowers if I keep off the kerb. (*Hysterically*) I'm a respectable girl: so help me, I never spoke to him except to ask him to buy a flower off me. (*General hubbub, mostly sympathetic to the flower girl, but deprecating her excessive sensibility. Cries of* Dont start hollerin. Who's hurting you? Nobody's going to touch you. Whats the good of fussing? Steady on. Easy easy, *etc., come from the elderly staid spectators, who pat her comfortingly. Less patient ones bid her shut her head, or ask her roughly what is wrong with her. A remoter group, not knowing what the matter is, crowd in and increase the noise with question and answer:* Whats the row? Whatshe do? Where is he? A tec taking her down. What! him? Yes: him over there: Took money off the gentleman, *etc. The flower girl, distraught and mobbed, breaks through them to the gentleman, crying wildly*) Oh, sir, dont let him charge me. You dunno what it means to me. Theyll take away my character and drive me on the streets for speaking to gentlemen. They—

THE NOTE TAKER (*coming forward on her right, the rest crowding after him*): There, there, there, there! who's hurting you, you silly girl? What do you take me for?

THE BYSTANDER: It's all right: he's a gentleman: look at his boots. (*Explaining to the note taker*) She thought you was a copper's nark, sir.

THE NOTE TAKER (*with quick interest*): Whats a copper's nark?

THE BYSTANDER (*inapt at definition*): It's a—well, it's a copper's nark, as you might say. What else would you call it? A sort of informer.

THE FLOWER GIRL (*still hysterical*): I take my Bible oath I never said a word—

THE NOTE TAKER (*overbearing but good-humored*): Oh, shut up, shut up. Do I look like a policeman?

THE FLOWER GIRL (*far from reassured*): Then what did you take down my words for? How do I know whether you took me down right? You just shew me what youve wrote about me. (*The note taker opens his book and holds it steadily under her nose, though the pressure of the mob trying to read it over his shoulders would upset a weaker man.*) Whats that? That aint proper writing. I cant read that.

THE NOTE TAKER: I can. (*Reads, reproducing her pronunciation exactly*) "Cheer ap, Keptin; n' baw ya flahr orf a pore gel."

THE FLOWER GIRL (*much distressed*): It's because I called him Captain. I meant no harm. (*To the gentleman*) Oh, sir, dont let him lay a charge agen me for a word like that. You—

THE GENTLEMAN: Charge! I make no charge. (*To the note taker*) Really, sir, if you are a detective, you need not begin protecting me against molestation by young women until I ask you. Anybody could see that the girl meant no harm.

THE BYSTANDERS GENERALLY (*demonstrating against police espionage*): Course they could. What business is it of yours? You mind your own affairs. He wants promotion, he does. Taking down people's words! Girl never said a word to him. What harm if she did? Nice thing a girl cant shelter from the rain without being insulted, etc., etc., etc. (*She is conducted by the more sympathetic demonstrators back to her plinth, where she resumes her seat and struggles with her emotion.*)

THE BYSTANDER: He aint a tec. He's a blooming busybody: thats what he is. I tell you, look at his boots.

THE NOTE TAKER (*turning on him genially*): And how are all your people down at Selsey?

THE BYSTANDER (*suspiciously*): Who told you my people come from Selsey?

THE NOTE TAKER: Never you mind. They did. (*To the girl*) How do you come to be up so far east? You were born in Lisson Grove.

THE FLOWER GIRL (*appalled*): Oh, what harm is there in my leaving Lisson Grove? It wasnt fit for a pig to live in; and I had to pay four-and-six a week. (*In tears*) Oh, boo—hoo—oo—

THE NOTE TAKER: Live where you like; but stop that noise.

THE GENTLEMAN (*to the girl*): Come, come! he cant touch you: you have a right to live where you please.

A SARCASTIC BYSTANDER (*thrusting himself between the note taker and the gentleman*): Park Lane, for instance. I'd like to go into the Housing Question with you, I would.

THE FLOWER GIRL (*subsiding into a brooding melancholy over her basket, and talking very low-spiritedly to herself*): I'm a good girl, I am.

THE SARCASTIC BYSTANDER (*not attending to her*): Do you know where I come from?

THE NOTE TAKER (*promptly*): Hoxton.

(*Titterings. Popular interest in the note taker's performance increases.*)

THE SARCASTIC ONE (*amazed*): Well, who said I didnt? Bly me! You know everything, you do.

THE FLOWER GIRL (*still nursing her sense of injury*): Aint no call to meddle with me, he aint.

THE BYSTANDER (*to her*): Of course he aint. Dont you stand it from him. (*To the note taker*) See here: what call have you to know about people what never offered to meddle with you? Wheres your warrant?

SEVERAL BYSTANDERS (*encouraged by this seeming point of law*): Yes: wheres your warrant?

THE FLOWER GIRL: Let him say what he likes. I dont want to have no truck with him.

THE BYSTANDER: You take us for dirt under your feet, dont you? Catch you taking liberties with a gentleman!

THE SARCASTIC BYSTANDER: Yes: tell him where he come from if you want to go fortune-telling.

THE NOTE TAKER: Cheltenham, Harrow, Cambridge, and India.

THE GENTLEMAN: Quite right. (*Great laughter. Reaction in the note taker's favor. Exclamations of* He knows all about it. Told him proper. Hear him tell the toff where he come from? *etc.*) May I ask, sir, do you do this for your living at a music hall?

THE NOTE TAKER: Ive thought of that. Perhaps I shall some day.

(*The rain has stopped; and the persons on the outside of the crowd begin to drop off.*)

THE FLOWER GIRL (*resenting the reaction*): He's no gentleman, he aint, to interfere with a poor girl.

THE DAUGHTER (*out of patience, pushing her way rudely to the front and displacing the gentleman, who politely retires to the other side of the pillar*): What on earth is Freddy doing? I shall get pneumonia if I stay in this draught any longer.

THE NOTE TAKER (*to himself, hastily making a note of her pronunciation of "monia"*): Earlscourt.

THE DAUGHTER (*violently*): Will you please keep your impertinent remarks to yourself.

THE NOTE TAKER: Did I say that out loud? I didnt mean to. I beg your pardon. Your mother's Epsom, unmistakably.

THE MOTHER (*advancing between her daughter and the note taker*): How very curious! I was brought up in Largelady Park, near Epsom.

THE NOTE TAKER (*uproariously amused*): Ha! ha! What a devil of a name! Excuse me. (*To the daughter*) You want a cab, do you?

THE DAUGHTER: Dont dare speak to me.

THE MOTHER: Oh please, please, Clara. (*Her daughter repudiates her with an angry shrug and retires haughtily.*) We should be so grateful to you, sir, if you found us a cab. (*The note taker produces a whistle.*) Oh, thank you. (*She joins her daughter.*)

(*The note taker blows a piercing blast.*)

THE SARCASTIC BYSTANDER: There! I knowed he was a plain-clothes copper.

THE BYSTANDER: That aint a police whistle: thats a sporting whistle.

THE FLOWER GIRL (*still preoccupied with her wounded feelings*): He's no right to take away my character. My character is the same as any lady's.

THE NOTE TAKER: I dont know whether youve noticed it; but the rain stopped about two minutes ago.

THE BYSTANDER: So it has. Why didnt you say so before? and us losing our time listening to your silliness! (*He walks off towards the Strand.*)

THE SARCASTIC BYSTANDER: I can tell where you come from. You come from Anwell. Go back there.

THE NOTE TAKER (*helpfully*): Hanwell.

THE SARCASTIC BYSTANDER (*affecting great distinction of speech*): Thenk you, teacher. Haw haw! So long (*he touches his hat with mock respect and strolls off*).

THE FLOWER GIRL: Frightening people like that! How would he like it himself?

THE MOTHER: It's quite fine now, Clara. We can walk to a motor bus. Come. (*She gathers her skirts above her ankles and hurries off towards the Strand.*)

THE DAUGHTER: But the cab—(*her mother is out of hearing*). Oh, how tiresome! (*She follows angrily.*)

(*All the rest have gone except the note taker, the gentleman, and the flower girl, who sits arranging her basket and still pitying herself in murmurs.*)

THE FLOWER GIRL: Poor girl! Hard enough for her to live without being worrited and chivied.

THE GENTLEMAN (*returning to his former place on the note taker's left*): How do you do it, if I may ask?

THE NOTE TAKER: Simply phonetics. The science of speech. Thats my profession: also my hobby. Happy is the man who can make a living by his hobby! You can spot an Irishman or a Yorkshireman by his brogue. *I* can place any man within six miles. I can place him within two miles in London. Sometimes within two streets.

THE FLOWER GIRL: Ought to be ashamed of himself, unmanly coward!

THE GENTLEMAN: But is there a living in that?

THE NOTE TAKER: Oh yes. Quite a fat one. This is an age of upstarts. Men begin in Kentish Town with £80 a year, and end in Park Lane with a hundred thousand. They want to drop Kentish Town; but they give themselves away every time they open their mouths. Now I can teach them—

THE FLOWER GIRL: Let him mind his own business and leave a poor girl—

THE NOTE TAKER (*explosively*): Woman: cease this detestable boohooing instantly; or else seek the shelter of some other place of worship.

THE FLOWER GIRL (*with feeble defiance*): Ive a right to be here if I like, same as you.

THE NOTE TAKER: A woman who utters such depressing and disgusting sounds has no right to be anywhere—no right to live. Remember that you are a human being with a soul and the divine gift of articulate speech: that your native language is the language of Shakespeare and Milton and The Bible: and dont sit there crooning like a bilious pigeon.

THE FLOWER GIRL (*quite overwhelmed, looking up at him in mingled wonder and deprecation without daring to raise her head*): Ah-ah-ah-ow-ow-ow-oo!

THE NOTE TAKER (*whipping out his book*): Heavens! what a sound! (*He writes; then holds out the book and reads, reproducing her vowels exactly*) Ah-ah-ah-ow-ow-ow-oo!

THE FLOWER GIRL (*tickled by the performance, and laughing in spite of herself*): Garn!

THE NOTE TAKER: You see this creature with her kerb-stone English: the English that will keep her in the gutter to the end of her days. Well, sir, in three months I could pass that girl off as a duchess at an ambassador's garden party. I could even get her a place as lady's maid or shop assistant, which requires better English. Thats the sort of thing I do for commercial millionaires. And on the profits of it I do genuine scientific work in phonetics, and a little as a poet on Miltonic lines.

THE GENTLEMAN: I am myself a student of Indian dialects; and—

THE NOTE TAKER (*eagerly*): Are you? Do you know Colonel Pickering, the author of Spoken Sanscrit?

THE GENTLEMAN: I am Colonel Pickering. Who are you?

THE NOTE TAKER: Henry Higgins, author of Higgins's Universal Alphabet.

PICKERING (*with enthusiasm*): I came from India to meet you.

HIGGINS: I was going to India to meet you.

PICKERING: Where do you live?

HIGGINS: 27A Wimpole Street. Come and see me tomorrow.

PICKERING: I'm at the Carlton. Come with me now and lets have a jaw over some supper.

HIGGINS: Right you are.

THE FLOWER GIRL (*to* PICKERING, *as he passes her*): Buy a flower, kind gentleman. I'm short for my lodging.

PICKERING: I really havnt any change. I'm sorry (*he goes away*).

HIGGINS (*shocked at the girl's mendacity*): Liar. You said you could change half-a-crown.

THE FLOWER GIRL (*rising in desperation*): You ought to be stuffed with nails, you ought. (*Flinging the basket at his feet*) Take the whole blooming basket for sixpence.

(*The church clock strikes the second quarter.*)

HIGGINS (*hearing in it the voice of God, rebuking him for his Pharisaic want of charity to the poor girl*): A reminder. (*He raises his hat solemnly; then throws a handful of money into the basket and follows* PICKERING.)

THE FLOWER GIRL (*picking up a half-crown*): Ah-ow-ooh! (*Picking up a couple of florins*) Aaah-ow-ooh! (*Picking up several coins*) Aaaaaah-ow-ooh! (*Picking up a half-sovereign*) Aaaaaaaaaaah-ow-ooh!!!

FREDDY (*springing out of a taxicab*): Got one at last. Hallo! (*To the girl*) Where are the two ladies that were here?

THE FLOWER GIRL: They walked to the bus when the rain stopped.

FREDDY: And left me with a cab on my hands! Damnation!

THE FLOWER GIRL (*with grandeur*): Never mind, young man. I'm going home in a taxi. (*She sails off to the cab. The driver puts his hand behind him and holds the door firmly shut against her. Quite understanding his mistrust, she shews him her handful of money.*) Eightpence aint no object to me, Charlie. (*He grins and opens the door.*) Angel Court, Drury Lane, round the corner of Micklejohn's oil shop. Lets see how fast you can make her hop it. (*She gets in and pulls the door to with a slam as the taxicab starts.*)

FREDDY: Well, I'm dashed!

ACT 2

(*Next day at 11 a.m.* HIGGINS's *laboratory in Wimpole Street. It is a room on the first floor, looking on the street, and was meant for the drawing room. The double doors are in the middle of the back wall; and persons entering find in the corner to their right two tall file cabinets at right angles to one another against the walls. In this corner stands a flat writing-table, on which are a phonograph, a laryngoscope, a row of tiny organ pipes with bellows, a set of lamp chimneys for singing flames with burners attached to a gas plug in the wall by an india-rubber tube, several tuning-forks of different sizes, a life-size image of half a human head, shewing in section the vocal organs, and a box containing a supply of wax cylinders for the phonograph.*

Further down the room, on the same side, is a fireplace, with a comfortable leather-covered easy-chair at the side of the hearth nearest the door, and a coal-scuttle. There is a clock on the mantelpiece. Between the fireplace and the phonograph table is a stand for newspapers.

On the other side of the central door, to the left of the visitor, is a cabinet of shallow drawers. On it is a telephone and the telephone directory. The corner beyond, and most of the side wall, is occupied by a grand piano, with the keyboard at the end furthest from the door, and a bench for the player extending the full length of the keyboard. On the piano is a dessert dish heaped with fruit and sweets, mostly chocolates.

The middle of the room is clear. Besides the easy-chair, the piano bench, and two chairs at the phonograph table, there is one stray chair. It stands near the fireplace. On the walls, engravings: mostly Piranesis and mezzotint portraits. No paintings.

PICKERING *is seated at the table, putting down some cards and a tuning-fork which he has been using.* HIGGINS *is standing up near him, closing two or three file drawers which are hanging out. He appears in the morning light as a robust, vital, appetizing sort of man of forty or thereabouts, dressed in a professional-looking black frock-coat with a white linen collar and black silk tie. He is of the energetic, scientific type, heartily, even violently interested in everything that can be studied as a scientific subject, and careless about himself and other people, including their feelings. He is, in fact, but for his years and size, rather like a very impetuous baby "taking notice" eagerly and loudly, and requiring almost as much watching to keep him out of unintended mischief. His manner varies from genial bullying when he is in a good humor to stormy petulance when anything goes wrong; but he is so entirely frank and void of malice that he remains likeable even in his least reasonable moments.)*

HIGGINS *(as he shuts the last drawer)*: Well, I think thats the whole show.

PICKERING: It's really amazing. I havnt taken half of it in, you know.

HIGGINS: Would you like to go over any of it again?

PICKERING *(rising and coming to the fireplace, where he plants himself with his back to the fire)*: No, thank you; not now. I'm quite done up for this morning.

HIGGINS *(following him, and standing beside him on his left)*: Tired of listening to sounds?

PICKERING: Yes. It's a fearful strain. I rather fancied myself because I can pronounce twenty-four distinct vowel sounds; but your hundred and thirty beat me. I cant hear a bit of difference between most of them.

HIGGINS *(chuckling, and going over to the piano to eat sweets)*: Oh, that comes with practice. You hear no difference at first; but you keep on listening, and presently you find theyre all as different as A from B. *(MRS PEARCE looks in: she is HIGGINS's housekeeper.)* Whats the matter?

MRS PEARCE *(hesitating, evidently perplexed)*: A young woman wants to see you sir.

HIGGINS: A young woman! What does she want?

MRS PEARCE: Well, sir, she says youll be glad to see her when you know what she's come about. She's quite a common girl, sir. Very common indeed. I should have sent her away, only I thought perhaps you wanted her to talk into your machines. I hope Ive not done wrong; but really you see such queer people sometimes—youll excuse me, I'm sure, sir—

HIGGINS: Oh, thats all right, Mrs Pearce. Has she an interesting accent?

MRS PEARCE: Oh, something dreadful, sir, really. I dont know how you can take an interest in it.

HIGGINS *(to PICKERING)*: Lets have her up. Shew her up, Mrs Pearce *(he rushes across to his working table and picks out a cylinder to use on the phonograph)*.

MRS PEARCE *(only half resigned to it)*: Very well, sir. It's for you to say. *(She goes downstairs.)*

HIGGINS: This is rather a bit of luck. I'll shew you how I make records. We'll set her talking; and I'll take it down first in Bell's visible Speech; then in broad Romic; and then we'll get her on the phonograph so that you can turn her on as often as you like with the written transcript before you.

MRS PEARCE *(returning)*: This is the young woman, sir.

(The flower girl enters in state. She has a hat with three ostrich feathers, orange, sky-blue, and red. She has a nearly clean apron, and the shoddy coat has been tidied a little. The pathos of this deplorable figure, with its innocent vanity and consequential air, touches PICKERING, who has already straightened himself in the presence of MRS PEARCE . But as to HIGGINS, the only distinction he makes between men and women is that when he is neither bullying nor exclaiming to the heavens against some feather-weight cross, he coaxes women as a child coaxes its nurse when it wants to get anything out of her.)

HIGGINS *(brusquely, recognizing her with unconcealed disappointment, and at once, babylike, making an intolerable grievance of it)*: Why, this is the girl I jotted down last night. She's no use: Ive got all the records I want of the Lisson Grove lingo; and I'm not going to waste another cylinder on it. *(To the girl)* Be off with you: I dont want you.

THE FLOWER GIRL: Dont you be so saucy. You aint heard what I come for yet. *(To MRS PEARCE, who is waiting at the door for further instructions)* Did you tell him I come in a taxi?

MRS PEARCE: Nonsense, girl! what do you think a gentleman like Mr Higgins cares what you came in?

THE FLOWER GIRL: Oh, we are proud! He aint above giving lessons, not him: I heard him say so. Well, I aint come here to ask for any compliment; and if my money's not good enough I can go elsewhere.

HIGGINS: Good enough for what?

THE FLOWER GIRL: Good enough for ye-oo. Now you know, dont you? I'm come to have lessons, I am. And to pay for em too: make no mistake.

HIGGINS *(stupent)*: Well!!! *(Recovering his breath with a gasp)* What do you expect me to say to you?

THE FLOWER GIRL: Well, if you was a gentleman, you might ask me to sit down, I think. Dont I tell you I'm bringing you business?

HIGGINS: Pickering: shall we ask this baggage to sit down, or shall we throw her out of the window?

THE FLOWER GIRL *(running away in terror to the piano, where she turns at bay)*: Ah-ah-oh-ow-ow-ow-oo! *(Wounded and whimpering)* I wont be called a baggage when Ive offered to pay like any lady.

(Motionless, the two men stare at her from the other side of the room, amazed.)

PICKERING *(gently)*: What is it you want, my girl?

THE FLOWER GIRL: I want to be a lady in a flower shop stead of selling at the corner of Tottenham Court Road. But they wont take me unless I can talk more genteel. He said he could teach me. Well, here I am ready to pay him—not asking any favor—and he treats me as if I was dirt.

MRS PEARCE: How can you be such a foolish ignorant

girl as to think you could afford to pay Mr Higgins?

THE FLOWER GIRL: Why shouldnt I? I know what lessons cost as well as you do; and I'm ready to pay.

HIGGINS: How much?

THE FLOWER GIRL (coming back to him, triumphant): Now youre talking! I thought youd come off it when you saw a chance of getting back a bit of what you chucked at me last night. (Confidently) Youd had a drop in, hadnt you?

HIGGINS (peremptorily): Sit down.

THE FLOWER GIRL: Oh, if youre going to make a compliment of it—

HIGGINS (thundering at her): Sit down.

MRS PEARCE (severely): Sit down, girl. Do as youre told.

(She places the stray chair near the hearthrug between HIGGINS and PICKERING, and stands behind it waiting for the girl to sit down.)

THE FLOWER GIRL: Ah-ah-ah-ow-ow-oo! (She stands, half rebellious, half bewildered.)

PICKERING (very courteous): Wont you sit down?

LIZA (coyly): Dont mind if I do. (She sits down. PICKERING returns to the hearthrug.)

HIGGINS: Whats your name?

THE FLOWER GIRL: Liza Doolittle.

HIGGINS (declaiming gravely):

Eliza, Elizabeth, Betsy, and Bess,
They went to the woods to get a bird's nes':

PICKERING: They found a nest with four eggs in it:

HIGGINS: They took one apiece, and left three in it.

(They laugh heartily at their own wit.)

LIZA: Oh, dont be silly.

MRS PEARCE: You mustnt speak to the gentleman like that.

LIZA: Well, why wont he speak sensible to me?

HIGGINS: Come back to business. How much do you propose to pay me for the lessons?

LIZA: Oh, I know whats right. A lady friend of mine gets French lessons for eighteenpence an hour from a real French gentleman. Well, you wouldnt have the face to ask me the same for teaching me my own language as you would for French; so I wont give more than a shilling. Take it or leave it.

HIGGINS (walking up and down the room, rattling his keys and his cash in his pockets): You know, Pickering, if you consider a shilling, not as a simple shilling, but as a percentage of this girl's income, it works out as fully equivalent to sixty or seventy guineas from a millionaire.

PICKERING: How so?

HIGGINS: Figure it out. A millionaire has about £150 a day. She earns about half-a-crown.

LIZA (haughtily): Who told you I only—

HIGGINS (continuing): She offers me two-fifths of her day's income for a lesson. Two-fifths of a millionaire's income for a day would be somewhere about £60. It's handsome. By George, it's enormous! it's the biggest offer I ever had.

LIZA (rising, terrified): Sixty pounds! What are you talking about? I never offered you sixty pounds. Where would I get—

HIGGINS: Hold your tongue.

LIZA (weeping): But I aint got sixty pounds. Oh—

MRS PEARCE: Dont cry, you silly girl. Sit down. Nobody is going to touch your money.

HIGGINS: Somebody is going to touch you, with a broomstick, if you dont stop snivelling. Sit down.

LIZA (obeying slowly): Ah-ah-ah-ow-oo-o! One would think you was my father.

HIGGINS: If I decide to teach you, I'll be worse than two fathers to you. Here (he offers her his silk handkerchief)!

LIZA: Whats this for?

HIGGINS: To wipe your eyes. To wipe any part of your face that feels moist. Remember: thats your handkerchief; and thats your sleeve. Dont mistake the one for the other if you wish to become a lady in a shop.

(LIZA, utterly bewildered, stares helplessly at him.)

MRS PEARCE: It's no use talking to her like that, Mr Higgins: she doesnt understand you. Besides, youre quite wrong: she doesnt do it that way at all (she takes the handkerchief).

LIZA (snatching it): Here! You give me that handkerchief. He give it to me, not to you.

PICKERING (laughing): He did. I think it must be regarded as her property, Mrs Pearce.

MRS PEARCE (resigning herself): Serve you right, Mr Higgins.

PICKERING: Higgins: I'm interested. What about the ambassador's garden party? I'll say youre the greatest teacher alive if you make that good. I'll bet you all the expenses of the experiment you cant do it. And I'll pay for the lessons.

LIZA: Oh, you are real good. Thank you, Captain.

HIGGINS (tempted, looking at her): It's almost irresistible. She's so deliciously low—so horribly dirty—

LIZA (protesting extremely): Ah-ah-ah-ah-ow-ow-oo-oo!!! I aint dirty: I washed my face and hands afore I come, I did.

PICKERING: Youre certainly not going to turn her head with flattery, Higgins.

MRS PEARCE (uneasy): Oh, dont say that, sir: theres more ways than one of turning a girl's head; and nobody can do it better than Mr Higgins, though he may not always mean it. I do hope, sir, you wont encourage him to do anything foolish.

HIGGINS (becoming excited as the idea grows on him): What is life but a series of inspired follies? The difficulty is to find them to do. Never lose a chance: it doesnt come every day. I shall make a duchess of this draggletailed guttersnipe.

LIZA (*strongly deprecating this view of her*): Ah-ah-ah-ow-ow-oo!

HIGGINS (*carried away*): Yes: in six months—in three if she has a good ear and a quick tongue—I'll take her anywhere and pass her off as anything. We'll start today: now! this moment! Take her away and clean her, Mrs Pearce. Monkey Brand, if it wont come off any other way. Is there a good fire in the kitchen?

MRS PEARCE (*protesting*): Yes; but—

HIGGINS (*storming on*): Take all her clothes off and burn them. Ring up Whiteley or somebody for new ones. Wrap her up in brown paper til they come.

LIZA: Youre no gentleman, youre not, to talk of such things. I'm a good girl, I am; and I know what the like of you are, I do.

HIGGINS: We want none of your Lisson Grove prudery here, young woman. Youve got to learn to behave like a duchess. Take her away, Mrs Pearce. If she gives you any trouble, wallop her.

LIZA (*springing up and running between* PICKERING *and* MRS PEARCE *for protection*): No! I'll call the police, I will.

MRS PEARCE: But Ive no place to put her.

HIGGINS: Put her in the dustbin.

LIZA: Ah-ah-ah-ow-ow-oo!

PICKERING: Oh come, Higgins! be reasonable.

MRS PEARCE (*resolutely*): You must be reasonable, Mr Higgins: really you must. You cant walk over everybody like this.

(HIGGINS, *thus scolded, subsides. The hurricane is succeeded by a zephyr of amiable surprise.*)

HIGGINS (*with professional exquisiteness of modulation*): I walk over everybody! My dear Mrs Pearce, my dear Pickering, I never had the slightest intention of walking over anyone. All I propose is that we should be kind to this poor girl. We must help her to prepare and fit herself for her new station in life. If I did not express myself clearly it was because I did not wish to hurt her delicacy, or yours.

(LIZA, *reassured, steals back to her chair.*)

MRS PEARCE (*to* PICKERING): Well, did you ever hear anything like that, sir?

PICKERING (*laughing heartily*): Never, Mrs Pearce: never.

HIGGINS (*patiently*): Whats the matter?

MRS PEARCE: Well, the matter is, sir, that you cant take a girl up like that as if you were picking up a pebble on the beach.

HIGGINS: Why not?

MRS PEARCE: Why not! But you dont know anything about her. What about her parents? She may be married.

LIZA: Garn!

HIGGINS: There! As the girl very properly says, Garn! Married indeed! Dont you know that a woman of that class looks a worn out drudge of fifty a year after she's married?

LIZA: Whood marry me?

HIGGINS (*suddenly resorting to the most thrillingly beautiful low tones in his best elocutionary style*): By George, Eliza, the streets will be strewn with the bodies of men shooting themselves for your sake before Ive done with you.

MRS PEARCE: Nonsense sir. You mustnt talk like that to her.

LIZA (*rising and squaring herself determinedly*): I'm going away. He's off his chump, he is. I dont want no balmies teaching me.

HIGGINS (*wounded in his tenderest point by her insensibility to his elocution*): Oh, indeed! I'm mad, am I? Very well, Mrs Pearce: you neednt order the new clothes for her. Throw her out.

LIZA (*whimpering*): Nah-ow. You got no right to touch me.

MRS PEARCE: You see now what comes of being saucy. (*Indicating the door*) This way, please.

LIZA (*almost in tears*): I didnt want no clothes. I wouldnt have taken them (*she throws away the handkerchief*). I can buy my own clothes.

HIGGINS (*deftly retrieving the handkerchief and intercepting her on her reluctant way to the door*): Youre an ungrateful wicked girl. This is my return for offering to take you out of the gutter and dress you beautifully and make a lady of you.

MRS PEARCE: Stop, Mr Higgins. I wont allow it. It's you that are wicked. Go home to your parents, girl; and tell them to take better care of you.

LIZA: I aint got no parents. They told me I was big enough to earn my own living and turned me out.

MRS PEARCE: Wheres your mother?

LIZA: I aint got no mother. Her that turned me out was my sixth stepmother. But I done without them. And I'm a good girl, I am.

HIGGINS: Very well, then, what on earth is all this fuss about? The girl doesnt belong to anybody—is no use to anybody but me. (*He goes to* MRS PEARCE *and begins coaxing.*) You can adopt her, Mrs Pearce: I'm sure a daughter would be a great amusement to you. Now dont make any more fuss. Take her downstairs; and—

MRS PEARCE: But whats to become of her? Is she to be paid anything? Do be sensible, sir.

HIGGINS: Oh, pay her whatever is necessary: put it down in the housekeeping book. (*Impatiently*) What on earth will she want with money? She'll have her food and her clothes. She'll only drink if you give her money.

LIZA (*turning on him*): Oh you are a brute. It's a lie: nobody ever saw the sign of liquor on me. (*She goes back to her chair and plants herself there defiantly.*)

PICKERING (*in good-humored remonstrance*): Does it occur to you, Higgins, that the girl has some feelings?

HIGGINS (*looking critically at her*): Oh no, I dont think so. Not any feelings that we need bother about. (*Cheerily*) Have you, Eliza?

LIZA: I got my feelings same as anyone else.

HIGGINS (*to* PICKERING, *reflectively*): You see the difficulty?

PICKERING: Eh? What difficulty?

HIGGINS: To get her to talk grammar. The mere pronunciation is easy enough.

LIZA: I dont want to talk grammar. I want to talk like a lady.

MRS PEARCE: Will you please keep to the point, Mr Higgins? I want to know on what terms the girl is to be here. Is she to have any wages? And what is to become of her when youve finished your teaching? You must look ahead a little.

HIGGINS (*impatiently*): Whats to become of her if I leave her in the gutter? Tell me that, Mrs Pearce.

MRS PEARCE: Thats her own business, not yours, Mr Higgins.

HIGGINS: Well, when Ive done with her, we can throw her back into the gutter; and then it will be her own business again; so thats all right.

LIZA: Oh, youve no feeling heart in you: you dont care for nothing but yourself (*she rises and takes the floor resolutely*). Here! Ive had enough of this. I'm going (*making for the door*). You ought to be ashamed of yourself, you ought.

HIGGINS (*snatching a chocolate cream from the piano, his eyes suddenly beginning to twinkle with mischief*): Have some chocolates, Eliza.

LIZA (*halting, tempted*): How do I know what might be in them? Ive heard of girls being drugged by the like of you.

(HIGGINS *whips out his penknife; cuts a chocolate in two; puts one half into his mouth and bolts it; and offers her the other half.*)

HIGGINS: Pledge of good faith, Eliza. I eat one half: you eat the other. (LIZA *opens her mouth to retort: he pops the half chocolate into it.*) You shall have boxes of them, barrels of them, every day. You shall live on them. Eh?

LIZA (*who has disposed of the chocolate after being nearly choked by it*): I wouldnt have ate it, only I'm too ladylike to take it out of my mouth.

HIGGINS: Listen, Eliza. I think you said you came in a taxi.

LIZA: Well, what if I did? Ive as good a right to take a taxi as anyone else.

HIGGINS: You have, Eliza; and in future you shall have as many taxis as you want. You shall go up and down and round the town in a taxi every day. Think of that, Eliza.

MRS PEARCE: Mr Higgins: youre tempting the girl. It's not right. She should think of the future.

HIGGINS: At her age! Nonsense! Time enough to think of the future when you havnt any future to think of. No, Eliza: do as this lady does: think of other people's futures; but never think of your own. Think of chocolates, and taxis, and gold, and diamonds.

LIZA: No: I dont want no gold and no diamonds. I'm a good girl, I am. (*She sits down again, with an attempt at dignity.*)

HIGGINS: You shall remain so, Eliza, under the care of Mrs Pearce. And you shall marry an officer in the Guards, with a beautiful moustache: the son of a marquis, who will disinherit him for marrying you, but will relent when he sees your beauty and goodness—

PICKERING: Excuse me, Higgins; but I really must interfere. Mrs Pearce is quite right. If this girl is to put herself in your hands for six months for an experiment in teaching, she must understand thoroughly what she's doing.

HIGGINS: How can she? She's incapable of understanding anything. Besides, do any of us understand what we are doing? If we did, would we ever do it?

PICKERING: Very clever, Higgins; but not sound sense. (*To* ELIZA) Miss Doolittle—

LIZA (*overwhelmed*): Ah-ah-ow-oo!

HIGGINS: There! Thats all youll get out of Eliza. Ah-ah-ow-oo! No use explaining. As a military man you ought to know that. Give her her orders: thats what she wants. Eliza: you are to live here for the next six months, learning how to speak beautifully, like a lady in a florist's shop. If youre good and do whatever youre told, you shall sleep in a proper bedroom, and have lots to eat, and money to buy chocolates and take rides in taxis. If youre naughty and idle you will sleep in the back kitchen among the black beetles, and be walloped by Mrs Pearce with a broomstick. At the end of six months you shall go to Buckingham Palace in a carriage, beautifully dressed. If the King finds out youre not a lady, you will be taken by the police to the Tower of London, where your head will be cut off as a warning to other presumptuous flower girls. If you are not found out, you shall have a present of seven-and-sixpence to start life with as a lady in a shop. If you refuse this offer you will be a most ungrateful and wicked girl; and the angels will weep for you. (*To* PICKERING) Now are you satisfied, Pickering? (*To* MRS PEARCE) Can I put it more plainly and fairly, Mrs Pearce?

MRS PEARCE (*patiently*): I think youd better let me speak to the girl properly in private. I dont know that I can take charge of her or consent to the arrangement at all. Of course I know you dont mean her any harm; but when you get what you call interested in people's accents, you never think or care what may happen to them or you. Come with me, Eliza.

HIGGINS: Thats all right. Thank you, Mrs Pearce. Bundle her off to the bath-room.

LIZA (*rising reluctantly and suspiciously*): Youre a great bully, you are. I wont stay here if I dont like. I wont let nobody wallop me. I never asked to go to Bucknam Palace, I didnt. I was never in trouble with the police, not me. I'm a good girl—

MRS PEARCE: Dont answer back, girl. You dont understand the gentleman. Come with me. (*She leads the way to the door, and holds it open for* ELIZA.)

LIZA (*as she goes out*): Well, what I say is right. I wont go near the King, not if I'm going to have my head cut off. If I'd known what I was letting myself in for, I wouldnt have come here. I always been a good girl; and I never offered to say a word to him; and I dont owe him nothing; and I dont care; and I wont be put upon; and I have my feelings the same as anyone else—

(MRS PEARCE *shuts the door; and* ELIZA'S *plaints are no longer audible.* PICKERING *comes from the hearth to the chair and sits astride it with his arms on the back.*)

PICKERING: Excuse the straight question, Higgins. Are you a man of good character where women are concerned?

HIGGINS (*moodily*): Have you ever met a man of good character where women are concerned?

PICKERING: Yes: very frequently.

HIGGINS (*dogmatically, lifting himself on his hands to the level of the piano, and sitting on it with a bounce*): Well, I havnt. I find that the moment I let a woman make friends with me, she becomes jealous, exacting, suspicious, and a damned nuisance. I find that the moment I let myself make friends with a woman, I become selfish and tyrannical. Women upset everything. When you let them into your life, you find that the woman is driving at one thing and youre driving at another.

PICKERING: At what, for example?

HIGGINS (*coming off the piano restlessly*): Oh, Lord knows! I suppose the woman wants to live her own life; and the man wants to live his; and each tries to drag the other on to the wrong track. One wants to go north and the other south; and the result is that both have to go east, though they both hate the east wind. (*He sits down on the bench at the keyboard.*) So here I am, a confirmed old bachelor, and likely to remain so.

PICKERING (*rising and standing over him gravely*): Come, Higgins! You know what I mean. If I'm to be in this business I shall feel responsible for that girl. I hope it's understood that no advantage is to be taken of her position.

HIGGINS: What! That thing! Sacred, I assure you. (*Rising to explain*) You see, she'll be a pupil; and teaching would be impossible unless pupils were sacred. Ive taught scores of American millionairesses how to speak English: the best looking women in the world.

I'm seasoned. They might as well be blocks of wood. *I* might as well be a block of wood. It's—

(MRS PEARCE *opens the door. She has* ELIZA'S *hat in her hand.* PICKERING *retires to the easy-chair at the hearth and sits down.*)

HIGGINS (*eagerly*): Well, Mrs Pearce: is it all right?

MRS PEARCE (*at the door*): I just wish to trouble you with a word, if I may, Mr Higgins.

HIGGINS: Yes, certainly. Come in. (*She comes forward.*) Dont burn that, Mrs Pearce. I'll keep it as a curiosity. (*He takes the hat.*)

MRS PEARCE: Handle it carefully, sir, please. I had to promise her not to burn it; but I had better put it in the oven for a while.

HIGGINS (*putting it down hastily on the piano*): Oh! thank you. Well, what have you to say to me?

PICKERING: Am I in the way?

MRS PEARCE: Not at all, sir. Mr Higgins: will you please be very particular what you say before the girl?

HIGGINS (*sternly*): Of course. I'm always particular about what I say. Why do you say this to me?

MRS PEARCE (*unmoved*): No, sir: youre not at all particular when youve mislaid anything or when you get a little impatient. Now it doesnt matter before me: I'm used to it. But you really must not swear before the girl.

HIGGINS (*indignantly*): *I* swear! (*Most emphatically*) I never swear. I detest the habit. What the devil do you mean?

MRS PEARCE (*stolidly*): Thats what I mean, sir. You swear a great deal too much. I dont mind your damning and blasting, and what the devil and where the devil and who the devil—

HIGGINS: Mrs Pearce: this language from your lips! Really!

MRS PEARCE (*not to be put off*): —but there is a certain word I must ask you not to use. The girl has just used it herself because the bath was too hot. It begins with the same letter as bath. She knows no better: she learnt it at her mother's knee. But she must not hear it from your lips.

HIGGINS (*loftily*): I cannot charge myself with having ever uttered it, Mrs Pearce. (*She looks at him steadfastly. He adds, hiding an uneasy conscience with a judicial air*) Except perhaps in a moment of extreme and justifiable excitement.

MRS PEARCE: Only this morning, sir, you applied it to your boots, to the butter, and to the brown bread.

HIGGINS: Oh, that! Mere alliteration, Mrs Pearce, natural to a poet.

MRS PEARCE: Well, sir, whatever you choose to call it, I beg you not to let the girl hear you repeat it.

HIGGINS: Oh, very well, very well. Is that all?

MRS PEARCE: No, sir. We shall have to be very particular with this girl as to personal cleanliness.

HIGGINS: Certainly. Quite right. Most important.

MRS PEARCE: I mean not to be slovenly about her dress or untidy in leaving things about.

HIGGINS (going to her solemnly): Just so. I intended to call your attention to that. (He passes on to PICKERING, who is enjoying the conversation immensely.) It is these little things that matter, Pickering. Take care of the pence and the pounds will take care of themselves is as true of personal habits as of money. (He comes to anchor on the hearthrug, with the air of a man in an unassailable position.)

MRS PEARCE: Yes, sir. Then might I ask you not to come down to breakfast in your dressing-gown, or at any rate not to use it as a napkin to the extent you do, sir. And if you would be so good as not to eat everything off the same plate, and to remember not to put the porridge saucepan out of your hand on the clean tablecloth, it would be a better example to the girl. You know you nearly choked yourself with a fishbone in the jam only last week.

HIGGINS (routed from the hearthrug and drifting back to the piano): I may do these things sometimes in absence of mind; but surely I dont do them habitually. (Angrily) By the way: my dressing-gown smells most damnably of benzine.

MRS PEARCE: No doubt it does, Mr Higgins. But if you will wipe your fingers—

HIGGINS (yelling): Oh very well, very well: I'll wipe them in my hair in future.

MRS PEARCE: I hope youre not offended, Mr Higgins.

HIGGINS (shocked at finding himself thought capable of an unamiable sentiment): Not at all, not at all. Youre quite right, Mrs Pearce: I shall be particularly careful before the girl. Is that all?

MRS PEARCE: No, sir. Might she use some of those Japanese dresses you brought from abroad? I really cant put her back into her old things.

HIGGINS: Certainly. Anything you like. Is that all?

MRS PEARCE: Thank you, sir. Thats all. (She goes out.)

HIGGINS: You know, Pickering, that woman has the most extraordinary ideas about me. Here I am, a shy, diffident sort of man. Ive never been able to feel really grown-up and tremendous, like other chaps. And yet she's firmly persuaded that I'm an arbitrary overbearing bossing kind of person. I cant account for it.

(MRS PEARCE returns.)

MRS PEARCE: If you please, sir, the trouble's beginning already. Theres a dustman downstairs, Alfred Doolittle, wants to see you. He says you have his daughter here.

PICKERING (rising): Phew! I say! (He retreats to the hearthrug.)

HIGGINS (promptly): Send the blackguard up.

MRS PEARCE: Oh, very well, sir. (She goes out.)

PICKERING: He may not be a blackguard, Higgins.

HIGGINS: Nonsense. Of course he's a blackguard.

PICKERING: Whether he is or not, I'm afraid we shall have some trouble with him.

HIGGINS (confidently): Oh no: I think not. If theres any trouble he shall have it with me, not I with him. And we are sure to get something interesting out of him.

PICKERING: About the girl?

HIGGINS: No. I mean his dialect.

PICKERING: Oh!

MRS PEARCE (at the door): Doolittle, sir. (She admits DOOLITTLE and retires.)

(ALFRED DOOLITTLE is an elderly but vigorous dustman, clad in the costume of his profession, including a hat with a back brim covering his neck and shoulders. He has well marked and rather interesting features, and seems equally free from fear and conscience. He has a remarkably expressive voice, the result of a habit of giving vent to his feelings without reserve. His present pose is that of wounded honor and stern resolution.)

DOOLITTLE (at the door, uncertain which of the two gentlemen is his man): Professor Higgins?

HIGGINS: Here. Good morning. Sit down.

DOOLITTLE: Morning, Governor. (He sits down magisterially) I come about a very serious matter, Governor.

HIGGINS (to PICKERING): Brought up in Hounslow. Mother Welsh, I should think. (DOOLITTLE opens his mouth, amazed. HIGGINS continues) What do you want, Doolittle?

DOOLITTLE (menacingly): I want my daughter: thats what I want. See?

HIGGINS: Of course you do. Youre her father, arnt you? You dont suppose anyone else wants her, do you? I'm glad to see you have some spark of family feeling left. She's upstairs. Take her away at once.

DOOLITTLE (rising, fearfully taken aback): What!

HIGGINS: Take her away. Do you suppose I'm going to keep your daughter for you?

DOOLITTLE (remonstrating): Now, now, look here, Governor. Is this reasonable? Is it fairity to take advantage of a man like this? The girl belongs to me. You got her. Where do I come in? (He sits down again.)

HIGGINS: Your daughter had the audacity to come to my house and ask me to teach her how to speak properly so that she could get a place in a flowershop. This gentleman and my housekeeper have been here all the time. (Bullying him) How dare you come here and attempt to blackmail me? You sent her here on purpose.

DOOLITTLE (protesting): No, Governor.

HIGGINS: You must have. How else could you possibly know that she is here?

DOOLITTLE: Dont take a man up like that, Governor.

HIGGINS: The police shall take you up. This is a plant— a plot to extort money by threats. I shall telephone for the police. (He goes resolutely to the telephone and opens the directory.)

DOOLITTLE: Have I asked you for a brass farthing? I leave it to the gentleman here: have I said a word about money?

HIGGINS (*throwing the book aside and marching down on* DOOLITTLE *with a poser*): What else did you come for?

DOOLITTLE (*sweetly*): Well, what would a man come for? Be human, Governor.

HIGGINS (*disarmed*): Alfred: did you put her up to it?

DOOLITTLE: So help me, Governor, I never did. I take my Bible oath I aint seen the girl these two months past.

HIGGINS: Then how did you know she was here?

DOOLITTLE ("*most musical, most melancholy*"): I'll tell you, Governor, if youll only let me get a word in. I'm willing to tell you. I'm wanting to tell you. I'm waiting to tell you.

HIGGINS: Pickering: this chap has a certain natural gift of rhetoric. Observe the rhythm of his native wood-notes wild. "I'm willing to tell you: I'm wanting to tell you: I'm waiting to tell you." Sentimental rhetoric! thats the Welsh strain in him. It also accounts for his mendacity and dishonesty.

PICKERING: Oh, please, Higgins: I'm west country myself. (*To* DOOLITTLE) How did you know the girl was here if you didnt send her?

DOOLITTLE: It was like this, Governor. The girl took a boy in the taxi to give him a jaunt. Son of her landlady, he is. He hung about on the chance of her giving him another ride home. Well, she sent him back for her luggage when she heard you was willing for her to stop here. I met the boy at the corner of Long Acre and Endell Street.

HIGGINS: Public house. Yes?

DOOLITTLE: The poor man's club, Governor: why shouldnt I?

PICKERING: Do let him tell his story, Higgins.

DOOLITTLE: He told me what was up. And I ask you, what was my feelings and my duty as a father? I says to the boy, "You bring me the luggage," I says—

PICKERING: Why didnt you go for it yourself?

DOOLITTLE: Landlady wouldnt have trusted me with it, Governor. She's that kind of woman: you know. I had to give the boy a penny afore he trusted me with it, the little swine. I brought it to her just to oblige you like, and make myself agreeable. Thats all.

HIGGINS: How much luggage?

DOOLITTLE: Musical instrument, Governor. A few pictures, a trifle of jewelry, and a bird-cage. She said she didnt want no clothes. What was I to think from that, Governor? I ask you as a parent what was I to think?

HIGGINS: So you came to rescue her from worse than death, eh?

DOOLITTLE (*appreciatively: relieved at being so well understood*): Just so, Governor. Thats right.

PICKERING: But why did you bring her luggage if you intended to take her away?

DOOLITTLE: Have I said a word about taking her away? Have I now?

HIGGINS (*determinedly*): Youre going to take her away, double quick. (*He crosses to the hearth and rings the bell.*)

DOOLITTLE (*rising*): No, Governor. Dont say that. I'm not the man to stand in my girl's light. Heres a career opening for her, as you might say; and—

(MRS PEARCE *opens the door and awaits orders.*)

HIGGINS: Mrs Pearce: this is Eliza's father. He has come to take her away. Give her to him. (*He goes back to the piano, with an air of washing his hands of the whole affair.*)

DOOLITTLE: No. This is a misunderstanding. Listen here—

MRS PEARCE: He cant take her away, Mr Higgins: how can he? You told me to burn her clothes.

DOOLITTLE: Thats right. I cant carry the girl through the streets like a blooming monkey, can I? I put it to you.

HIGGINS: You have put it to me that you want your daughter. Take your daughter. If she has no clothes go out and buy her some.

DOOLITTLE (*desperate*): Wheres the clothes she come in? Did I burn them or did your missus here?

MRS PEARCE: I am the housekeeper, if you please. I have sent for some clothes for your girl. When they come you can take her away. You can wait in the kitchen. This way, please.

(DOOLITTLE, *much troubled, accompanies her to the door; then hesitates; finally turns confidentially to* HIGGINS.)

DOOLITTLE: Listen here, Governor. You and me is men of the world, aint we?

HIGGINS: Oh! Men of the world, are we? Youd better go, Mrs Pearce.

MRS PEARCE: I think so, indeed, sir. (*She goes, with dignity.*)

PICKERING: The floor is yours, Mr Doolittle.

DOOLITTLE (*to* PICKERING): I thank you, Governor. (*To* HIGGINS, *who takes refuge on the piano bench, a little overwhelmed by the proximity of his visitor; for* DOOLITTLE *has a professional flavor of dust about him.*) Well, the truth is, Ive taken a sort of fancy to you, Governor; and if you want the girl, I'm not so set on having her back home again but what I might be open to an arrangement. Regarded in the light of a young woman, she's a fine handsome girl. As a daughter she's not worth her keep; and so I tell you straight. All I ask is my rights as a father; and youre the last man alive to expect me to let her go for nothing; for I can see youre one of the straight sort, Governor. Well, whats a five-pound note to you?

And whats Eliza to me? (*He returns to his chair and sits down judicially.*)

PICKERING: I think you ought to know, Doolittle, that Mr Higgins's intentions are entirely honorable.

DOOLITTLE: Course they are, Governor. If I thought they wasnt, I'd ask fifty.

HIGGINS (*revolted*): Do you mean to say, you callous rascal, that you would sell your daughter for £50?

DOOLITTLE: Not in a general way I wouldnt; but to oblige a gentleman like you I'd do a good deal, I do assure you.

PICKERING: Have you no morals, man?

DOOLITTLE (*unabashed*): Cant afford them, Governor. Neither could you if you was as poor as me. Not that I mean any harm, you know. But if Liza is going to have a bit out of this, why not me too?

HIGGINS (*troubled*): I dont know what to do, Pickering. There can be no question that as a matter of morals it's a positive crime to give this chap a farthing. And yet I feel a sort of rough justice in his claim.

DOOLITTLE: Thats it, Governor. Thats all I say. A father's heart, as it were.

PICKERING: Well, I know the feeling; but really it seems hardly right—

DOOLITTLE: Dont say that, Governor. Dont look at it that way. What am I, Governors both? I ask you, what am I? I'm one of the undeserving poor: thats what I am. Think of what that means to a man. It means that he's up agen middle class morality all the time. If theres anything going, and I put in for a bit of it, it's always the same story: "Youre undeserving; so you cant have it." But my needs is as great as the most deserving widow's that ever got money out of six different charities in one week for the death of the same husband. I dont need less than a deserving man: I need more. I dont eat less hearty than him; and I drink a lot more. I want a bit of amusement, cause I'm a thinking man. I want cheerfulness and a song and a band when I feel low. Well, they charge me just the same for everything as they charge the deserving. What is middle class morality? Just an excuse for never giving me anything. Therefore, I ask you, as two gentlemen, not to play that game on me. I'm playing straight with you. I aint pretending to be deserving. I'm undeserving; and I mean to go on being undeserving. I like it; and thats the truth. Will you take advantage of a man's nature to do him out of the price of his own daughter what he's brought up and fed and clothed by the sweat of his brow until she's growed big enough to be interesting to you two gentlemen? Is five pounds reasonable? I put it to you; and I leave it to you.

HIGGINS (*rising, and going over to* PICKERING): Pickering: if we were to take this man in hand for three months, he could choose between a seat in the Cabinet and a popular pulpit in Wales.

PICKERING: What do you say to that, Doolittle?

DOOLITTLE: Not me, Governor, thank you kindly. Ive heard all the preachers and all the prime ministers—for I'm a thinking man and game for politics or religion or social reform same as all the other amusements—and I tell you it's a dog's life any way you look at it. Undeserving poverty is my line. Taking one station in society with another, it's—it's—well, it's the only one that has any ginger in it, to my taste.

HIGGINS: I suppose we must give him a fiver.

PICKERING: He'll make a bad use of it, I'm afraid.

DOOLITTLE: Not me, Governor, so help me I wont. Dont you be afraid that I'll save it and spare it and live idle on it. There wont be a penny of it left by Monday: I'll have to go to work same as if I'd never had it. It wont pauperize me, you bet. Just one good spree for myself and the missus, giving pleasure to ourselves and employment to others, and satisfaction to you to think it's not been throwed away. You couldnt spend it better.

HIGGINS (*taking out his pocket book and coming between* DOOLITTLE *and the piano*): This is irresistible. Lets give him ten. (*He offers two notes to the dustman.*)

DOOLITTLE: No, Governor. She wouldnt have the heart to spend ten; and perhaps I shouldnt neither. Ten pounds is a lot of money: it makes a man feel prudent like; and then goodbye to happiness. You give me what I ask you, Governor: not a penny more, and not a penny less.

PICKERING: Why dont you marry that missus of yours? I rather draw the line at encouraging that sort of immorality.

DOOLITTLE: Tell her so, Governor: tell her so. *I'm* willing. It's me that suffers by it. Ive no hold on her. I got to be agreeable to her. I got to give her presents. I got to buy her clothes something sinful. I'm a slave to that woman, Governor, just because I'm not her lawful husband. And she knows it too. Catch her marrying me! Take my advice, Governor: marry Eliza while she's young and dont know no better. If you dont youll be sorry for it after. If you do, she'll be sorry for it after; but better her than you, because youre a man, and she's only a woman and dont know how to be happy anyhow.

HIGGINS: Pickering: if we listen to this man another minute, we shall have no convictions left. (*To* DOOLITTLE) Five pounds I think you said.

DOOLITTLE: Thank you kindly, Governor.

HIGGINS: Youre sure you wont take ten?

DOOLITTLE: Not now. Another time, Governor.

HIGGINS (*handing him a five-pound note*): Here you are.

DOOLITTLE: Thank you, Governor. Good morning. (*He hurries to the door, anxious to get away with his booty. When he opens it he is confronted with a dainty and exquisitely clean young Japanese lady in a simple blue cotton kimono printed cunningly with small white jasmine blossoms.* MRS PEARCE *is with her. He gets out of her way deferentially and apologizes.)* Beg pardon, miss.

THE JAPANESE LADY: Garn! Dont you know your own daughter?

DOOLITTLE: ⎱ *(exclaiming* ⎰ Bly me! it's Eliza!
HIGGINS: ⎰ *simultaneously)* ⎱ Whats that! This!
PICKERING: ⎰   ⎱ By Jove!

LIZA: Dont I look silly?

HIGGINS: Silly?

MRS PEARCE *(at the door)*: Now, Mr Higgins, please dont say anything to make the girl conceited about herself.

HIGGINS *(conscientiously)*: Oh! Quite right, Mrs Pearce. *(To* ELIZA*)* Yes: damned silly.

MRS PEARCE: Please, sir.

HIGGINS *(correcting himself)*: I mean extremely silly.

LIZA: I should look all right with my hat on. *(She takes up her hat; puts it on; and walks across the room to the fireplace with a fashionable air.)*

HIGGINS: A new fashion, by George! And it ought to look horrible!

DOOLITTLE *(with fatherly pride)*: Well, I never thought she'd clean up as good looking as that, Governor. She's a credit to me, aint she?

LIZA: I tell you, it's easy to clean up here. Hot and cold water on tap, just as much as you like, there is. Woolly towels, there is; and a towel horse so hot, it burns your fingers. Soft brushes to scrub yourself, and a wooden bowl of soap smelling like primroses. Now I know why ladies is so clean. Washing's a treat for them. Wish they saw what it is for the like of me!

HIGGINS: I'm glad the bathroom met with your approval.

LIZA: It didnt: not all of it; and I dont care who hears me say it. Mrs Pearce knows.

HIGGINS: What was wrong, Mrs Pearce?

MRS PEARCE *(blandly)*: Oh, nothing sir. It doesnt matter.

LIZA: I had a good mind to break it. I didnt know which way to look. But I hung a towel over it, I did.

HIGGINS: Over what?

MRS. PEARCE: Over the looking-glass, sir.

HIGGINS: Doolittle: you have brought your daughter up too strictly.

DOOLITTLE: Me! I never brought her up at all, except to give her a lick of a strap now and again. Dont put it on me, Governor. She aint accustomed to it, you see: thats all. But she'll soon pick up your free-and-easy ways.

LIZA: I'm a good girl, I am; and I won't pick up no free-and-easy ways.

HIGGINS: Eliza: if you say again that youre a good girl, your father shall take you home.

LIZA: Not him. You dont know my father. All he come here for was to touch you for some money to get drunk on.

DOOLITTLE: Well, what else would I want money for?

To put into the plate in church, I suppose. *(She puts out her tongue at him. He is so incensed by this that* PICKERING *presently finds it necessary to step between them.)* Dont you give me none of your lip; and dont let me hear you giving this gentleman any of it neither, or youll hear from me about it. See?

HIGGINS: Have you any further advice to give her before you go, Doolittle? Your blessing, for instance.

DOOLITTLE: No, Governor: I aint such a mug as to put up my children to all I know myself. Hard enough to hold them in without that. If you want Eliza's mind improved, Governor, you do it yourself with a strap. So long, gentlemen. *(He turns to go.)*

HIGGINS *(impressively)*: Stop. Youll come regularly to see your daughter. It's your duty, you know. My brother is a clergyman; and he could help you in your talks with her.

DOOLITTLE *(evasively)*: Certainly. I'll come, Governor. Not just this week, because I have a job at a distance. But later on you may depend on me. Afternoon, Gentlemen. Afternoon, maam. *(He takes off his hat to* MRS PEARCE, *who disdains the salutation and goes out. He winks at* HIGGINS, *thinking him probably a fellow-sufferer from* MRS PEARCE's *difficult disposition, and follows her.)*

LIZA: Dont you believe the old liar. He'd as soon you set a bull-dog on him as a clergyman. You wont see him again in a hurry.

HIGGINS: I dont want to, Eliza. Do you?

LIZA: Not me. I dont want never to see him again, I dont. He's a disgrace to me, he is, collecting dust, instead of working at his trade.

PICKERING: What is his trade, Eliza?

LIZA: Taking money out of other people's pockets into his own. His proper trade's a navvy; and he works at it sometimes too—for exercise—and earns good money at it. Aint you going to call me Miss Doolittle any more?

PICKERING: I beg your pardon, Miss Doolittle. It was a slip of the tongue.

LIZA: Oh, I dont mind; only it sounded so genteel. I should just like to take a taxi to the corner of Tottenham Court Road and get out there and tell it to wait for me, just to put the girls in their place a bit. I wouldnt speak to them, you know.

PICKERING: Better wait til we get you something really fashionable.

HIGGINS: Besides, you shouldnt cut your old friends now that you have risen in the world. Thats what we call snobbery.

LIZA: You dont call the like of them my friends now, I should hope. Theyve took it out of me often enough with their ridicule when they had the chance; and now I mean to get a bit of my own back. But if I'm to have fashionable clothes, I'll wait. I should like to have some. Mrs Pearce says youre going to give me some to wear in bed at night different to what I wear in the daytime; but it do seem a waste of money when you could get something to shew. Besides, I never could fancy changing into cold things on a winter night.

MRS PEARCE (*coming back*): Now, Eliza. The new things have come for you to try on.

LIZA: Ah-ow-oo-ooh! (*She rushes out.*)

MRS PEARCE (*following her*): Oh, dont rush about like that, girl. (*She shuts the door behind her.*)

HIGGINS: Pickering: we have taken on a stiff job.

PICKERING (*with conviction*): Higgins: we have.

ACT 3

(*It is* MRS HIGGINS's *at-home day. Nobody has yet arrived. Her drawing room, in a flat on Chelsea Embankment, has three windows looking on the river; and the ceiling is not so lofty as it would be in an older house of the same pretension. The windows are open, giving access to a balcony with flowers in pots. If you stand with your face to the windows, you have the fireplace on your left and the door in the right-hand wall close to the corner nearest the windows.*

MRS HIGGINS was brought up on Morris and Burne Jones; and her room, which is very unlike her son's room in Wimpole Street, is not crowded with furniture and little tables and nicknacks. In the middle of the room there is a big ottoman; and this, with the carpet, the Morris wall-papers, and the Morris chintz window curtains and brocade covers of the ottoman and its cushions, supply all the ornament, and are much too handsome to be hidden by odds and ends of useless things. A few good oil-paintings from the exhibitions in the Grosvenor Gallery thirty years ago (the Burne Jones, not the Whistler side of them) are on the walls. The only landscape is a Cecil Lawson on the scale of a Rubens. There is a portrait of MRS HIGGINS *as she was when she defied fashion in her youth in one of the beautiful Rossettian costumes which, when caricatured by people who did not understand, led to the absurdities of popular estheticism in the eighteen-seventies.*

In the corner diagonally opposite the door MRS HIGGINS, *now over sixty and long past taking the trouble to dress out of the fashion, sits writing at an elegantly simple writing-table with a bell button within reach of her hand. There is a Chippendale chair further back in the room between her and the window nearest her side. At the other side of the room, further forward, is an Elizabethan chair roughly carved in the taste of Inigo Jones. On the same side a piano in a decorated case. The corner between the fireplace and the window is occupied by a divan cushioned in Morris chintz.*

It is between four and five in the afternoon.

The door is opened violently; and HIGGINS *enters with his hat on.*)

MRS HIGGINS (*dismayed*): Henry (*scolding him*)! What are

you doing here to-day? It is my at-home day: you promised not to come. (*As he bends to kiss her, she takes his hat off, and presents it to him.*)

HIGGINS: Oh bother! (*He throws the hat down on the table.*)

MRS HIGGINS: Go home at once.

HIGGINS (*kissing her*): I know, mother. I came on purpose.

MRS HIGGINS: But you mustnt. I'm serious, Henry. You offend all my friends: they stop coming whenever they meet you.

HIGGINS: Nonsense! I know I have no small talk; but people dont mind. (*He sits on the settee.*)

MRS HIGGINS: Oh! dont they? Small talk indeed! What about your large talk? Really, dear, you mustnt stay.

HIGGINS: I must. Ive a job for you. A phonetic job.

MRS HIGGINS: No use, dear. I'm sorry; but I cant get round your vowels; and though I like to get pretty postcards in your patent shorthand, I always have to read the copies in ordinary writing you so thoughtfully send me.

HIGGINS: Well, this isnt a phonetic job.

MRS HIGGINS: You said it was.

HIGGINS: Not your part of it. Ive picked up a girl.

MRS HIGGINS: Does that mean that some girl has picked you up?

HIGGINS: Not at all. I dont mean a love affair.

MRS HIGGINS: What a pity!

HIGGINS: Why?

MRS HIGGINS: Well, you never fall in love with anyone under forty-five. When will you discover that there are some rather nice-looking young women about?

HIGGINS: Oh, I cant be bothered with young women. My idea of a lovable woman is something as like you as possible. I shall never get into the way of seriously liking young women: some habits lie too deep to be changed. (*Rising abruptly and walking about, jingling his money and his keys in his trouser pockets*) Besides, theyre all idiots.

MRS HIGGINS: Do you know what you would do if you really loved me, Henry?

HIGGINS: Oh bother! What? Marry, I suppose?

MRS HIGGINS: No. Stop fidgeting and take your hands out of your pockets. (*With a gesture of despair, he obeys and sits down again.*) Thats a good boy. Now tell me about the girl.

HIGGINS: She's coming to see you.

MRS HIGGINS: I dont remember asking her.

HIGGINS: You didnt. *I* asked her. If youd known her you wouldnt have asked her.

MRS HIGGINS: Indeed! Why?

HIGGINS: Well, it's like this. She's a common flower girl. I picked her off the kerbstone.

MRS HIGGINS: And invited her to my at-home!

HIGGINS (*rising and coming to her to coax her*): Oh, thatll be all right. Ive taught her to speak properly; and she has strict orders as to her behavior. She's to keep to two subjects: the weather and everybody's

health—Fine day and How do you do, you know—
and not to let herself go on things in general. That
will be safe.

MRS HIGGINS: Safe! To talk about our health! about our
insides! perhaps about our outsides! How could you
be so silly, Henry?

HIGGINS (*impatiently*): Well, she must talk about something. (*He controls himself and sits down again.*) Oh,
she'll be all right: dont you fuss. Pickering is in it
with me. Ive a sort of bet on that I'll pass her off as
a duchess in six months. I started on her some
months ago; and she's getting on like a house on
fire. I shall win my bet. She has a quick ear; and
she's been easier to teach than my middle-class pupils because she's had to learn a complete new language. She talks English almost as you talk French.

MRS HIGGINS: Thats satisfactory, at all events.

HIGGINS: Well, it is and it isnt.

MRS HIGGINS: What does that mean?

HIGGINS: You see, Ive got her pronunciation all right;
but you have to consider not only how a girl pronounces, but what she pronounces; and thats
where—

(*They are interrupted by the parlor-maid, announcing
guests.*)

THE PARLOR-MAID: Mrs and Miss Eynsford Hill. (*She
withdraws.*)

HIGGINS: Oh Lord! (*He rises; snatches his hat from the table;
and makes for the door; but before he reaches it his mother
introduces him.*)

(MRS and MISS EYNSFORD HILL *are the mother and
daughter who sheltered from the rain in Covent Garden.
The mother is well bred, quiet, and has the habitual
anxiety of straitened means. The daughter has acquired
a gay air of being very much at home in society: the
bravado of genteel poverty.*)

MRS EYNSFORD HILL (*to* MRS HIGGINS): How do you do?
(*They shake hands.*)

MISS EYNSFORD HILL: How d'you do? (*She shakes.*)

MRS HIGGINS (*introducing*): My son Henry.

MRS EYNSFORD HILL: Your celebrated son! I have so
longed to meet you, Professor Higgins.

HIGGINS (*glumly, making no movement in her direction*): Delighted. (*He backs against the piano and bows
brusquely.*)

MISS EYNSFORD HILL (*going to him with confident familiarity*): How do you do?

HIGGINS (*staring at her*): Ive seen you before somewhere.
I havnt the ghost of a notion where; but Ive heard
your voice. (*Drearily*) It doesnt matter. Youd better
sit down.

MRS HIGGINS: I'm sorry to say that my celebrated son
has no manners. You mustnt mind him.

MISS EYNSFORD HILL (*gaily*): I dont. (*She sits in the Elizabethan chair.*)

MRS EYNSFORD HILL (*a little bewildered*): Not at all. (*She
sits on the ottoman between her daughter and* MRS HIG-
GINS, *who has turned her chair away from the writing
table.*)

HIGGINS: Oh, have I been rude? I didnt mean to be.

(*He goes to the central window, through which, with his
back to the company, he contemplates the river and the
flowers in Battersea Park on the opposite bank as if they
were a frozen desert.
The parlor-maid returns, ushering in* PICKERING.)

THE PARLOR-MAID: Colonel Pickering. (*She withdraws.*)

PICKERING: How do you do, Mrs Higgins?

MRS HIGGINS: So glad youve come. Do you know Mrs
Eynsford Hill—Miss Eynsford Hill? (*Exchange of
bows. The* COLONEL *brings the Chippendale chair a little
forward between* MRS HILL *and* MRS HIGGINS, *and sits
down.*)

PICKERING: Has Henry told you what weve come for?

HIGGINS (*over his shoulder*): We were interrupted: damn
it!

MRS HIGGINS: Oh Henry, Henry, really!

MRS EYNSFORD HILL (*half rising*): Are we in the way?

MRS HIGGINS (*rising and making her sit down again*): No,
no. You couldnt have come more fortunately: we
want you to meet a friend of ours.

HIGGINS (*turning hopefully*): Yes, by George! We want
two or three people. Youll do as well as anybody
else.

(*The parlor-maid returns, ushering* FREDDY.)

THE PARLOR-MAID: Mr Eynsford Hill.

HIGGINS (*almost audibly, past endurance*): God of Heaven!
another of them.

FREDDY (*shaking hands with* MRS HIGGINS): Ahdedo?

MRS HIGGINS: Very good of you to come. (*Introducing*)
Colonel Pickering.

FREDDY (*bowing*): Ahdedo?

MRS HIGGINS: I dont think you know my son, Professor
Higgins.

FREDDY (*going to* HIGGINS): Ahdedo?

HIGGINS (*looking at him much as if he were a pickpocket*): I'll
take my oath Ive met you before somewhere.
Where was it?

FREDDY: I dont think so.

HIGGINS (*resignedly*): It dont matter, anyhow. Sit down.

(*He shakes* FREDDY's *hand, and almost slings him on to
the ottoman with his face to the windows; then comes
round to the other side of it.*)

HIGGINS: Well, here we are, anyhow! (*He sits down on the
ottoman next* MRS EYNSFORD HILL, *on her left.*) And
now, what the devil are we going to talk about until
Eliza comes?

MRS HIGGINS: Henry: you are the life and soul of the
Royal Society's soirées; but really youre rather
trying on more commonplace occasions.

HIGGINS: Am I? Very sorry. (*Beaming suddenly*) I suppose I am, you know. (*Uproariously*) Ha, ha!

MISS EYNSFORD HILL (*who considers* HIGGINS *quite eligible matrimonially*): I sympathize. *I* havnt any small talk. If people would only be frank and say what they really think!

HIGGINS (*relapsing into gloom*): Lord forbid!

MRS EYNSFORD HILL (*taking up her daughter's cue*): But why?

HIGGINS: What they think they ought to think is bad enough, Lord knows; but what they really think would break up the whole show. Do you suppose it would be really agreeable if I were to come out now with what *I* really think?

MISS EYNSFORD HILL (*gaily*): Is it so very cynical?

HIGGINS: Cynical! Who the dickens said it was cynical? I mean it wouldnt be decent.

MRS EYNSFORD HILL (*seriously*): Oh! I'm sure you dont mean that, Mr Higgins.

HIGGINS: You see, we're all savages, more or less. We're supposed to be civilized and cultured—to know all about poetry and philosophy and art and science, and so on; but how many of us know even the meanings of these names? (*To* MISS HILL) What do you know of poetry? (*To* MRS HILL) What do you know of science? (*Indicating* FREDDY) What does he know of art or science or anything else? What the devil do you imagine I know of philosophy?

MRS HIGGINS (*warningly*): Or of manners, Henry?

THE PARLOR-MAID (*opening the door*): Miss Doolittle. (*She withdraws.*)

HIGGINS (*rising hastily and running to* MRS HIGGINS): Here she is, mother. (*He stands on tiptoe and makes signs over his mother's head to* ELIZA *to indicate to her which lady is her hostess*).

(ELIZA, *who is exquisitely dressed, produces an impression of such remarkable distinction and beauty as she enters that they all rise, quite fluttered. Guided by* HIGGINS's *signals, she comes to* MRS HIGGINS *with studied grace.*)

LIZA (*speaking with pedantic correctness of pronunciation and great beauty of tone*): How do you do, Mrs Higgins? (*She gasps slightly in making sure of the H in* HIGGINS, *but is quite successful.*) Mr Higgins told me I might come.

MRS HIGGINS (*cordially*): Quite right: I'm very glad indeed to see you.

PICKERING: How do you do, Miss Doolittle?

LIZA (*shaking hands with him*): Colonel Pickering, is it not?

MRS EYNSFORD HILL: I feel sure we have met before, Miss Doolittle. I remember your eyes.

LIZA: How do you do? (*She sits down on the ottoman gracefully in the place just left vacant by* HIGGINS.)

MRS EYNSFORD HILL (*introducing*): My daughter Clara.

LIZA: How do you do?

CLARA (*impulsively*): How do you do? (*She sits down on the ottoman beside* ELIZA, *devouring her with her eyes.*)

FREDDY (*coming to their side of the ottoman*): Ive certainly had the pleasure.

MRS EYNSFORD HILL (*introducing*): My son Freddy.

LIZA: How do you do?

(FREDDY *bows and sits down in the Elizabethan chair, infatuated.*)

HIGGINS (*suddenly*): By George, yes: it all comes back to me! (*They stare at him.*) Covent Garden! (*Lamentably*) What a damned thing!

MRS HIGGINS: Henry, please! (*He is about to sit on the edge of the table*) Dont sit on my writing-table: youll break it.

HIGGINS (*sulkily*): Sorry.

(*He goes to the divan, stumbling into the fender and over the fire-irons on his way; extricating himself with muttered imprecations; and finishing his disastrous journey by throwing himself so impatiently on the divan that he almost breaks it.* MRS HIGGINS *looks at him, but controls herself and says nothing.*
A long and painful pause ensues.)

MRS HIGGINS (*at last, conversationally*): Will it rain, do you think?

LIZA: The shallow depression in the west of these islands is likely to move slowly in an easterly direction. There are no indications of any great change in the barometrical situation.

FREDDY: Ha! ha! how awfully funny!

LIZA: What is wrong with that, young man? I bet I got it right.

FREDDY: Killing!

MRS EYNSFORD HILL: I'm sure I hope it wont turn cold. Theres so much influenza about. It runs right through our whole family regularly every spring.

LIZA (*darkly*): My aunt died of influenza: so they said.

MRS EYNSFORD HILL (*clicks her tongue sympathetically*): !!!

LIZA (*in the same tragic tone*): But it's my belief they done the old woman in.

MRS HIGGINS (*puzzled*): Done her in?

LIZA: Y-e-e-e-es, Lord love you! Why should she die of influenza? She come through diphtheria right enough the year before. I saw her with my own eyes. Fairly blue with it, she was. They all thought she was dead; but my father he kept ladling gin down her throat til she came to so sudden that she bit the bowl off the spoon.

MRS EYNSFORD HILL (*startled*): Dear me!

LIZA (*piling up the indictment*): What call would a woman with that strength in her have to die of influenza? What become of her new straw hat that should have come to me? Somebody pinched it; and what I say is, them as pinched it done her in.

MRS EYNSFORD HILL: What does doing her in mean?

HIGGINS (*hastily*): Oh, thats the new small talk. To do a person in means to kill them.

MRS EYNSFORD HILL (*to* ELIZA, *horrified*): You surely dont believe that your aunt was killed?

LIZA: Do I not! Them she lived with would have killed her for a hat-pin, let alone a hat.

MRS EYNSFORD HILL: But it cant have been right for your father to pour spirits down her throat like that. It might have killed her.

LIZA: Not her. Gin was mother's milk to her. Besides, he'd poured so much down his own throat that he knew the good of it.

MRS EYNSFORD HILL: Do you mean that he drank?

LIZA: Drank! My word! Something chronic.

MRS EYNSFORD HILL: How dreadful for you!

LIZA: Not a bit. It never did him no harm what I could see. But then he did not keep it up regular. (*Cheerfully*) On the burst, as you might say, from time to time. And always more agreeable when he had a drop in. When he was out of work, my mother used to give him fourpence and tell him to go out and not come back until he'd drunk himself cheerful and loving-like. Theres lots of women has to make their husbands drunk to make them fit to live with. (*Now quite at her ease*) You see, it's like this. If a man has a bit of a conscience, it always takes him when he's sober; and then it makes him low-spirited. A drop of booze just takes that off and makes him happy. (*To* FREDDY, *who is in convulsions of suppressed laughter*) Here! what are you sniggering at?

FREDDY: The new small talk. You do it so awfully well.

LIZA: If I was doing it proper, what was you laughing at? (*To* HIGGINS) Have I said anything I oughtnt?

MRS HIGGINS (*interposing*): Not at all, Miss Doolittle.

LIZA: Well, thats a mercy, anyhow. (*Expansively*) What I always say is—

HIGGINS (*rising and looking at his watch*): Ahem!

LIZA (*looking round at him; taking the hint; and rising*): Well: I must go. (*They all rise.* FREDDY *goes to the door.*) So pleased to have met you. Goodbye. (*She shakes hands with* MRS HIGGINS.)

MRS HIGGINS: Goodbye.

LIZA: Goodbye, Colonel Pickering.

PICKERING: Goodbye, Miss Doolittle. (*They shake hands.*)

LIZA (*nodding to the others*): Goodbye, all.

FREDDY (*opening the door for her*): Are you walking across the Park, Miss Doolittle? If so—

LIZA: Walk! Not bloody likely. (*Sensation.*) I am going in a taxi. (*She goes out.*)

(PICKERING *gasps and sits down.* FREDDY *goes out on the balcony to catch another glimpse of* ELIZA.)

MRS EYNSFORD HILL (*suffering from shock*): Well, I really cant get used to the new ways.

CLARA (*throwing herself discontentedly into the Elizabethan chair*): Oh, it's all right, mamma, quite right. People will think we never go anywhere or see anybody if you are so old-fashioned.

MRS EYNSFORD HILL: I daresay I am very old-fashioned; but I do hope you wont begin using that expression, Clara. I have got accustomed to hear you talking about men as rotters, and calling everything filthy and beastly; though I do think it horrible and unladylike. But this last is really too much. Dont you think so, Colonel Pickering?

PICKERING: Dont ask me. Ive been away in India for several years; and manners have changed so much that I sometimes dont know whether I'm at a respectable dinner-table or in a ship's forecastle.

CLARA: It's all a matter of habit. Theres no right or wrong in it. Nobody means anything by it. And it's so quaint, and gives such a smart emphasis to things that are not in themselves very witty. I find the new small talk delightful and quite innocent.

MRS EYNSFORD HILL (*rising*): Well, after that, I think it's time for us to go.

(PICKERING *and* HIGGINS *rise.*)

CLARA (*rising*): Oh yes: we have three at-homes to go to still. Goodbye, Mrs Higgins. Goodbye, Colonel Pickering. Goodbye, Professor Higgins.

HIGGINS (*coming grimly at her from the divan, and accompanying her to the door*): Goodbye. Be sure you try on that small talk at the three at-homes. Dont be nervous about it. Pitch it in strong.

CLARA (*all smiles*): I will. Goodbye. Such nonsense, all this early Victorian prudery!

HIGGINS (*tempting her*): Such damned nonsense!

CLARA: Such bloody nonsense!

MRS EYNSFORD HILL (*convulsively*): Clara!

CLARA: Ha! ha! (*She goes out radiant, conscious of being thoroughly up to date, and is heard descending the stairs in a stream of silvery laughter.*)

FREDDY (*to the heavens at large*): Well, I ask you— (*He gives it up, and comes to* MRS HIGGINS.) Goodbye.

MRS HIGGINS (*shaking hands*): Goodbye. Would you like to meet Miss Doolittle again?

FREDDY (*eagerly*): Yes, I should, most awfully.

MRS HIGGINS: Well, you know my days.

FREDDY: Yes. Thanks awfully. Goodbye. (*He goes out.*)

MRS EYNSFORD HILL: Goodbye, Mr Higgins.

HIGGINS: Goodbye. Goodbye.

MRS EYNSFORD HILL (*to* PICKERING): It's no use. I shall never be able to bring myself to use that word.

PICKERING: Dont. It's not compulsory, you know. Youll get on quite well without it.

MRS EYNSFORD HILL: Only, Clara is so down on me if I am not positively reeking with the latest slang. Goodbye.

PICKERING: Goodbye. (*They shake hands.*)

MRS EYNSFORD HILL (*to* MRS HIGGINS): You mustnt mind Clara. (PICKERING, *catching from her lowered tone that this is not meant for him to hear, discreetly joins* HIGGINS *at the window.*) We're so poor! and she gets so few parties, poor child! She doesnt quite know. (MRS HIGGINS, *seeing that her eyes are moist, takes her hand sympathetically and goes with her to the door.*) But the boy is nice. Dont you think so?

MRS HIGGINS: Oh, quite nice. I shall always be delighted to see him.

MRS EYNSFORD HILL: Thank you, dear. Goodbye. (*She goes out.*)

HIGGINS (*eagerly*): Well? Is Eliza presentable? (*He swoops on his mother and drags her to the ottoman, where she sits down in* ELIZA's *place with her son on her left.*)

(PICKERING *returns to his chair on her right.*)

MRS HIGGINS: You silly boy, of course she's not presentable. She's a triumph of your art and of her dressmaker's; but if you suppose for a moment that she doesnt give herself away in every sentence she utters, you must be perfectly cracked about her.

PICKERING: But dont you think something might be done? I mean something to eliminate the sanguinary element from her conversation.

MRS HIGGINS: Not as long as she is in Henry's hands.

HIGGINS (*aggrieved*): Do you mean that my language is improper?

MRS HIGGINS: No, dearest: it would be quite proper—say on a canal barge; but it would not be proper for her at a garden party.

HIGGINS (*deeply injured*): Well I must say—

PICKERING (*interrupting him*): Come, Higgins: you must learn to know yourself. I havnt heard such language as yours since we used to review the volunteers in Hyde Park twenty years ago.

HIGGINS (*sulkily*): Oh, well, if you say so, I suppose I dont always talk like a bishop.

MRS HIGGINS (*quieting* HENRY *with a touch*): Colonel Pickering: will you tell me what is the exact state of things in Wimpole Street?

PICKERING (*cheerfully: as if this completely changed the subject*): Well, I have come to live there with Henry. We work together at my Indian Dialects; and we think it more convenient—

MRS HIGGINS: Quite so. I know all about that: it's an excellent arrangement. But where does this girl live?

HIGGINS: With us, of course. Where should she live?

MRS HIGGINS: But on what terms? Is she a servant? If not, what is she?

PICKERING (*slowly*): I think I know what you mean, Mrs Higgins.

HIGGINS: Well, dash me if *I* do! Ive had to work at the girl every day for months to get her to her present pitch. Besides, she's useful. She knows where my things are, and remembers my appointments and so forth.

MRS HIGGINS: How does your housekeeper get on with her?

HIGGINS: Mrs Pearce? Oh, she's jolly glad to get so much taken off her hands; for before Eliza came, she used to have to find things and remind me of my appointments. But she's got some silly bee in her bonnet about Eliza. She keeps saying "You dont think sir": doesnt she, Pick?

PICKERING: Yes: thats the formula. "You dont think, sir." Thats the end of every conversation about Eliza.

HIGGINS: As if I ever stop thinking about the girl and her confounded vowels and consonants. I'm worn out, thinking about her, and watching her lips and her teeth and her tongue, not to mention her soul, which is the quaintest of the lot.

MRS HIGGINS: You certainly are a pretty pair of babies, playing with your live doll.

HIGGINS: Playing! The hardest job I ever tackled: make no mistake about that, mother. But you have no idea how frightfully interesting it is to take a human being and change her into a quite different human being by creating a new speech for her. It's filling up the deepest gulf that separates class from class and soul from soul.

PICKERING (*drawing his chair closer to* MRS HIGGINS *and bending over to her eagerly*): Yes: it's enormously interesting. I assure you, Mrs Higgins, we take Eliza very seriously. Every week—every day almost—there is some new change. (*Closer again*) We keep records of every stage—dozens of gramophone disks and photographs—

HIGGINS (*assailing her at the other ear*): Yes, by George: it's the most absorbing experiment I ever tackled. She regularly fills our lives up: doesnt she, Pick?

PICKERING: We're always talking Eliza.

HIGGINS: Teaching Eliza.

PICKERING: Dressing Eliza.

MRS HIGGINS: What!

HIGGINS: Inventing new Elizas.

HIGGINS:		You know, she has the most extraordinary quickness of ear:
PICKERING:	(*speaking together*)	I assure you, my dear Mrs Higgins, that girl
HIGGINS:		just like a parrot. Ive tried her with every
PICKERING:		is a genius. She can play the piano quite beautifully.
HIGGINS:		possible sort of sound that a human being can make—
PICKERING:		We have taken her to classical concerts and to music
HIGGINS:		Continental dialects, African dialects, Hottentot
PICKERING:		halls; and it's all the same to her: she plays everything
HIGGINS:		clicks, things it took me years to get hold of; and
PICKERING:		she hears right off when she comes home, whether it's
HIGGINS:		she picks them up like a shot, right away, as if she had
PICKERING:		Beethoven and Brahms or Lehar and Lionel Monckton;
HIGGINS:		been at it all her life.
PICKERING:		though six months ago, she'd never as much as touched a piano—

MRS HIGGINS (*putting her fingers in her ears, as they are by this time shouting one another down with an intolerable noise*): Sh-sh-sh—sh! (*They stop.*)

PICKERING: I beg your pardon. (*He draws his chair back apologetically.*)

HIGGINS: Sorry. When Pickering starts shouting nobody can get a word in edgeways.

MRS HIGGINS: Be quiet, Henry. Colonel Pickering: dont you realize that when Eliza walked into Wimpole Street, something walked in with her?

PICKERING: Her father did. But Henry soon got rid of him.

MRS HIGGINS: It would have been more to the point if her mother had. But as her mother didnt something else did.

PICKERING: But what?

MRS HIGGINS (*unconsciously dating herself by the word*): A problem.

PICKERING: Oh, I see. The problem of how to pass her off as a lady.

HIGGINS: I'll solve that problem. Ive half solved it already.

MRS HIGGINS: No, you two infinitely stupid male creatures: the problem of what is to be done with her afterwards.

HIGGINS: I dont see anything in that. She can go her own way, with all the advantages I have given her.

MRS HIGGINS: The advantages of that poor woman who was here just now! The manners and habits that disqualify a fine lady from earning her own living without giving her a fine lady's income! Is that what you mean?

PICKERING (*indulgently, being rather bored*): Oh, that will be all right, Mrs Higgins. (*He rises to go.*)

HIGGINS (*rising also*): We'll find her some light employment.

PICKERING: She's happy enough. Dont you worry about her. Goodbye. (*He shakes hands as if he were consoling a frightened child, and makes for the door.*)

HIGGINS: Anyhow, theres no good bothering now. The thing's done. Goodbye, mother. (*He kisses her, and follows* PICKERING.)

PICKERING (*turning for a final consolation*): There are plenty of openings. We'll do whats right. Goodbye.

HIGGINS (*to* PICKERING *as they go out together*): Let's take her to the Shakespear exhibition at Earls Court.

PICKERING: Yes: lets. Her remarks will be delicious.

HIGGINS: She'll mimic all the people for us when we get home.

PICKERING: Ripping. (*Both are heard laughing as they go downstairs.*)

MRS HIGGINS (*rises with an impatient bounce, and returns to her work at the writing-table. She sweeps a litter of disarranged papers out of her way; snatches a sheet of paper from her stationery case; and tries resolutely to write. At the third line she gives it up; flings down her pen; grips the table angrily and exclaims*): Oh, men! men!! men!!!

ACT 4

(*The Wimpole Street laboratory. Midnight. Nobody in the room. The clock on the mantelpiece strikes twelve. The fire is not alight: it is a summer night.*

Presently HIGGINS *and* PICKERING *are heard on the stairs.*)

HIGGINS (*calling down to* PICKERING): I say, Pick: lock up, will you? I shant be going out again.

PICKERING: Right. Can Mrs Pearce go to bed? We dont want anything more, do we?

HIGGINS: Lord, no!

(ELIZA *opens the door and is seen on the lighted landing in opera cloak, brilliant evening dress, and diamonds, with fan, flowers, and all accessories. She comes to the hearth, and switches on the electric lights there. She is tired: her pallor contrasts strongly with her dark eyes and hair; and her expression is almost tragic. She takes off her cloak; puts her fan and flowers on the piano; and sits down on the bench, brooding and silent.* HIGGINS, *in evening dress, with overcoat and hat, comes in, carrying a smoking jacket which he has picked up downstairs. He takes off the hat and overcoat; throws them carelessly on the newspaper stand; disposes of his coat in the same way; puts on the smoking jacket; and throws himself wearily into the easy-chair at the hearth.* PICKERING, *similarly attired, comes in. He also takes off his hat and overcoat, and is about to throw them on* HIGGINS's *when he hesitates.*)

PICKERING: I say: Mrs Pearce will row if we leave these things lying about in the drawing room.

HIGGINS: Oh, chuck them over the bannisters into the hall. She'll find them there in the morning and put them away all right. She'll think we were drunk.

PICKERING: We are, slightly. Are there any letters?

HIGGINS: I didnt look. (PICKERING *takes the overcoats and hats and goes downstairs.* HIGGINS *begins half singing half yawning an air from La Fanciulla del Golden West. Suddenly he stops and exclaims*) I wonder where the devil my slippers are!

(ELIZA *looks at him darkly; then rises suddenly and leaves the room.*

HIGGINS *yawns again, and resumes his song.*

PICKERING *returns, with the contents of the letter-box in his hand.*)

PICKERING: Only circulars, and this coroneted billet-doux for you. (*He throws the circulars into the fender, and posts himself on the hearthrug, with his back to the grate.*)

HIGGINS (*glancing at the billet-doux*): Money-lender. (*He throws the letter after the circulars.*)

(ELIZA *returns with a pair of large down-at-heel slippers. She places them on the carpet before* HIGGINS, *and sits as before without a word.*)

HIGGINS (*yawning again*): Oh Lord! What an evening!

What a crew! What a silly tomfoolery! (*He raises his shoe to unlace it, and catches sight of the slippers. He stops unlacing and looks at them as if they had appeared there of their own accord.*) Oh! theyre there, are they?

PICKERING (*stretching himself*): Well, I feel a bit tired. It's been a long day. The garden party, a dinner party, and the opera! Rather too much of a good thing. But youve won your bet, Higgins. Eliza did the trick, and something to spare, eh?

HIGGINS (*fervently*): Thank God it's over!

(ELIZA *flinches violently; but they take no notice of her; and she recovers herself and sits stonily as before.*)

PICKERING: Were you nervous at the garden party? *I* was. Eliza didnt seem a bit nervous.

HIGGINS: Oh, she wasnt nervous. I knew she'd be all right. No: it's the strain of putting the job through all these months that has told on me. It was interesting enough at first, while we were at the phonetics; but after that I got deadly sick of it. If I hadnt backed myself to do it I should have chucked the whole thing up two months ago. It was a silly notion: the whole thing has been a bore.

PICKERING: Oh come! the garden party was frightfully exciting. My heart began beating like anything.

HIGGINS: Yes, for the first three minutes. But when I saw we were going to win hands down, I felt like a bear in a cage, hanging about doing nothing. The dinner was worse: sitting gorging there for over an hour, with nobody but a damned fool of a fashionable woman to talk to! I tell you, Pickering, never again for me. No more artificial duchesses. The whole thing has been simple purgatory.

PICKERING: Youve never been broken in properly to the social routine. (*Strolling over to the piano*) I rather enjoy dipping into it occasionally myself: it makes me feel young again. Anyhow, it was a great success: an immense success. I was quite frightened once or twice because Eliza was doing it so well. You see, lots of the real people cant do it at all: theyre such fools that they think style comes by nature to people in their position; and so they never learn. Theres always something professional about doing a thing superlatively well.

HIGGINS: Yes: thats what drives me mad: the silly people dont know their own silly business. (*Rising*) However, it's over and done with; and now I can go to bed at last without dreading tomorrow.

(ELIZA's *beauty becomes murderous.*)

PICKERING: I think I shall turn in too. Still, it's been a great occasion: a triumph for you. Goodnight. (*He goes.*)

HIGGINS (*following him*): Goodnight. (*Over his shoulder, at the door*) Put out the lights, Eliza; and tell Mrs Pearce not to make coffee for me in the morning: I'll take tea. (*He goes out.*)

(ELIZA *tries to control herself and feel indifferent as she rises and walks across to the hearth to switch off the lights. By the time she gets there she is on the point of screaming. She sits down in* HIGGINS's *chair and holds on hard to the arms. Finally she gives way and flings herself furiously on the floor, raging.*)

HIGGINS (*in despairing wrath outside*): What the devil have I done with my slippers? (*He appears at the door.*)

LIZA (*snatching up the slippers, and hurling them at him one after the other with all her force*): There are your slippers. And there. Take your slippers; and may you never have a day's luck with them!

HIGGINS (*astounded*): What on earth—! (*He comes to her.*) Whats the matter? Get up. (*He pulls her up.*) Anything wrong?

LIZA (*breathless*): Nothing wrong—with you. Ive won your bet for you, havnt I? Thats enough for you. *I* dont matter, I suppose.

HIGGINS: You won my bet! You! Presumptuous insect! *I* won it. What did you throw those slippers at me for?

LIZA: Because I wanted to smash your face. I'd like to kill you, you selfish brute. Why didnt you leave me where you picked me out of—in the gutter? You thank God it's all over, and that now you can throw me back again there, do you? (*She crisps her fingers frantically.*)

HIGGINS (*looking at her in cool wonder*): The creature is nervous, after all.

LIZA (*gives a suffocated scream of fury, and instinctively darts her nails at his face*): !!

HIGGINS (*catching her wrists*): Ah! would you? Claws in, you cat. How dare you shew your temper to me? Sit down and be quiet. (*He throws her roughly into the easy-chair.*)

LIZA (*crushed by superior strength and weight*): Whats to become of me? Whats to become of me?

HIGGINS: How the devil do I know whats to become of you? What does it matter what becomes of you?

LIZA: You dont care. I know you dont care. You wouldnt care if I was dead. I'm nothing to you—not so much as them slippers.

HIGGINS (*thundering*): Those slippers.

LIZA (*with bitter submission*): Those slippers. I didnt think it made any difference now.

(*A pause.* ELIZA *hopeless and crushed.* HIGGINS *a little uneasy.*)

HIGGINS (*in his loftiest manner*): Why have you begun going on like this? May I ask whether you complain of your treatment here?

LIZA: No.

HIGGINS: Has anybody behaved badly to you? Colonel Pickering? Mrs Pearce? Any of the servants?

LIZA: No.

HIGGINS: I presume you dont pretend that *I* have treated you badly?

LIZA: No.

HIGGINS: I am glad to hear it. *(He moderates his tone.)* Perhaps youre tired after the strain of the day. Will you have a glass of champagne? *(He moves towards the door.)*

LIZA: No. *(Recollecting her manners)* Thank you.

HIGGINS *(good-humored again)*: This has been coming on you for some days. I suppose it was natural for you to be anxious about the garden party. But thats all over now. *(He pats her kindly on the shoulder. She writhes.)* Theres nothing more to worry about.

LIZA: No. Nothing more for you to worry about. *(She suddenly rises and gets away from him by going to the piano bench, where she sits and hides her face.)* Oh God! I wish I was dead.

HIGGINS *(staring after her in sincere surprise)*: Why? In heaven's name, why? *(Reasonably, going to her)* Listen to me, Eliza. All this irritation is purely subjective.

LIZA: I dont understand. I'm too ignorant.

HIGGINS: It's only imagination. Low spirits and nothing else. Nobody's hurting you. Nothing's wrong. You go to bed like a good girl and sleep it off. Have a little cry and say your prayers: that will make you comfortable.

LIZA: I heard your prayers. "Thank God it's all over!"

HIGGINS *(impatiently)*: Well, dont you thank God it's all over? Now you are free and can do what you like.

LIZA *(pulling herself together in desperation)*: What am I fit for? What have you left me fit for? Where am I to go? What am I to do? Whats to become of me?

HIGGINS *(enlightened, but not at all impressed)*: Oh thats whats worrying you, is it? *(He thrusts his hands into his pockets, and walks about in his usual manner, rattling the contents of his pockets, as if condescending to a trivial subject out of pure kindness.)* I shouldnt bother about it if I were you. I should imagine you wont have much difficulty in settling yourself somewhere or other, though I hadnt quite realized that you were going away. *(She looks quickly at him: he does not look at her, but examines the dessert stand on the piano and decides that he will eat an apple.)* You might marry, you know. *(He bites a large piece out of the apple and munches it noisily.)* You see, Eliza, all men are not confirmed old bachelors like me and the Colonel. Most men are the marrying sort (poor devils!); and youre not bad-looking: it's quite a pleasure to look at you sometimes—not now, of course, because youre crying and looking as ugly as the very devil; but when youre all right and quite yourself, youre what I should call attractive. That is, to the people in the marrying line, you understand. You go to bed and have a good nice rest; and then get up and look at yourself in the glass; and you wont feel so cheap.

(ELIZA again looks at him, speechless, and does not stir. The look is quite lost on him: he eats his apple with a dreamy expression of happiness, as it is quite a good one.)

HIGGINS *(a genial afterthought occurring to him)*: I daresay my mother could find some chap or other who would do very well.

LIZA: We were above that at the corner of Tottenham Court Road.

HIGGINS *(waking up)*: What do you mean?

LIZA: I sold flowers. I didnt sell myself. Now youve made a lady of me I'm not fit to sell anything else. I wish youd left me where you found me.

HIGGINS *(slinging the core of the apple decisively into the grate)*: Tosh, Eliza. Dont you insult human relations by dragging all this cant about buying and selling into it. You neednt marry the fellow if you dont like him.

LIZA: What else am I to do?

HIGGINS: Oh, lots of things. What about your old idea of a florist's shop? Pickering could set you up in one: he's lots of money. *(Chuckling)* He'll have to pay for all those togs you have been wearing today; and that, with the hire of the jewellery, will make a big hole in two hundred pounds. Why, six months ago you would have thought it the millennium to have a flower shop of your own. Come! youll be all right. I must clear off to bed: I'm devilish sleepy. By the way, I came down for something: I forget what it was.

LIZA: Your slippers.

HIGGINS: Oh yes, of course. You shied them at me. *(He picks them up, and is going out when she rises and speaks to him.)*

LIZA: Before you go, sir—

HIGGINS *(dropping the slippers in his surprise at her calling him Sir)*: Eh?

LIZA: Do my clothes belong to me or to Colonel Pickering?

HIGGINS *(coming back into the room as if her question were the very climax of unreason)*: What the devil use would they be to Pickering?

LIZA: He might want them for the next girl you pick up to experiment on.

HIGGINS *(shocked and hurt)*: Is that the way you feel towards us?

LIZA: I dont want to hear anything more about that. All I want to know is whether anything belongs to me. My own clothes were burnt.

HIGGINS: But what does it matter? Why need you start bothering about that in the middle of the night?

LIZA: I want to know what I may take away with me. I dont want to be accused of stealing.

HIGGINS *(now deeply wounded)*: Stealing! You shouldnt have said that, Eliza. That shews a want of feeling.

LIZA: I'm sorry. I'm only a common ignorant girl; and in my station I have to be careful. There cant be any feelings between the like of you and the like of me. Please will you tell me what belongs to me and what doesnt?

HIGGINS *(very sulky)*: You may take the whole damned

houseful if you like. Except the jewels. Theyre hired. Will that satisfy you? *(He turns on his heel and is about to go in extreme dudgeon.)*

LIZA *(drinking in his emotion like nectar, and nagging him to provoke a further supply)*: Stop, please. *(She takes off her jewels.)* Will you take these to your room and keep them safe? I dont want to run the risk of their being missing.

HIGGINS *(furious)*: Hand them over. *(She puts them into his hands.)* If these belonged to me instead of to the jeweller, I'd ram them down your ungrateful throat. *(He perfunctorily thrusts them into his pockets, unconsciously decorating himself with the protruding ends of the chains.)*

LIZA *(taking a ring off)*: This ring isnt the jeweller's: it's the one you bought me in Brighton. I dont want it now. *(HIGGINS dashes the ring violently into the fireplace, and turns on her so threateningly that she crouches over the piano with her hands over her face, and exclaims)* Dont you hit me.

HIGGINS: Hit you! You infamous creature, how dare you accuse me of such a thing? It is you who have hit me. You have wounded me to the heart.

LIZA *(thrilling with hidden joy)*: I'm glad. Ive got a little of my own back, anyhow.

HIGGINS *(with dignity, in his finest professional style)*: You have caused me to lose my temper: a thing that has hardly ever happened to me before. I prefer to say nothing more tonight. I am going to bed.

LIZA *(pertly)*: Youd better leave a note for Mrs Pearce about the coffee; for she wont be told by me.

HIGGINS *(formally)*: Damn Mrs Pearce; and damn the coffee; and damn you; and damn my own folly in having lavished hard-earned knowledge and the treasure of my regard and intimacy on a heartless guttersnipe. *(He goes out with impressive decorum, and spoils it by slamming the door savagely.)*

(ELIZA smiles for the first time; expresses her feelings by a wild pantomime in which an imitation of HIGGINS's exit is confused with her own triumph; and finally goes down on her knees on the hearthrug to look for the ring.)

ACT 5

(MRS HIGGINS's drawing room. She is at her writing-table as before. The parlor-maid comes in.)

THE PARLOR-MAID *(at the door)*: Mr Henry, maam, is downstairs with Colonel Pickering.

MRS HIGGINS: Well, shew them up.

THE PARLOR-MAID: Theyre using the telephone, maam. Telephoning to the police, I think.

MRS HIGGINS: What!

THE PARLOR-MAID *(coming further in and lowering her voice)*: Mr Henry is in a state, maam. I thought I'd better tell you.

MRS HIGGINS: If you had told me that Mr Henry was not in a state it would have been more surprising. Tell them to come up when theyve finished with the police. I suppose he's lost something.

THE PARLOR-MAID: Yes, maam *(going)*.

MRS HIGGINS: Go upstairs and tell Miss Doolittle that Mr Henry and the Colonel are here. Ask her not to come down til I send for her.

THE PARLOR-MAID: Yes, maam.

(HIGGINS bursts in. He is, as the parlor-maid has said, in a state.)

HIGGINS: Look here, mother: heres a confounded thing!

MRS HIGGINS: Yes, dear. Good morning. *(He checks his impatience and kisses her, whilst the parlor-maid goes out.)* What is it?

HIGGINS: Eliza's bolted.

MRS HIGGINS *(calmly continuing her writing)*: You must have frightened her.

HIGGINS: Frightened her! nonsense! She was left last night, as usual, to turn out the lights and all that; and instead of going to bed she changed her clothes and went right off: her bed wasnt slept in. She came in a cab for her things before seven this morning; and that fool Mrs Pearce let her have them without telling me a word about it. What am I to do?

MRS HIGGINS: Do without, I'm afraid, Henry. The girl has a perfect right to leave if she chooses.

HIGGINS *(wandering distractedly across the room)*: But I cant find anything. I dont know what appointments Ive got. I'm—*(PICKERING comes in. MRS HIGGINS puts down her pen and turns away from the writing-table.)*

PICKERING *(shaking hands)*: Good morning, Mrs Higgins. Has Henry told you? *(He sits down on the ottoman.)*

HIGGINS: What does that ass of an inspector say? Have you offered a reward?

MRS HIGGINS *(rising in indignant amazement)*: You dont mean to say you have set the police after Eliza.

HIGGINS: Of course. What are the police for? What else could we do? *(He sits in the Elizabethan chair.)*

PICKERING: The inspector made a lot of difficulties. I really think he suspected us of some improper purpose.

MRS HIGGINS: Well, of course he did. What right have you to go to the police and give the girl's name as if she were a thief, or a lost umbrella, or something? Really! *(She sits down again, deeply vexed.)*

HIGGINS: But we want to find her.

PICKERING: We cant let her go like this, you know, Mrs Higgins. What were we to do?

MRS HIGGINS: You have no more sense, either of you, than two children. Why—

(The parlor-maid comes in and breaks off the conversation.)

THE PARLOR-MAID: Mr Henry: a gentleman wants to see you very particular. He's been sent on from Wimpole Street.

HIGGINS: Oh, bother! I cant see anyone now. Who is it?

THE PARLOR-MAID: A Mr Doolittle, sir.

PICKERING: Doolittle! Do you mean the dustman?

THE PARLOR-MAID: Dustman! Oh no, sir: a gentleman.

HIGGINS (*springing up excitedly*): By George, Pick, it's some relative of hers that she's gone to. Somebody we know nothing about. (*To the parlor-maid*) Send him up, quick.

THE PARLOR-MAID: Yes, sir. (*She goes.*)

HIGGINS (*eagerly, going to his mother*): Genteel relatives! now we shall hear something. (*He sits down in the Chippendale chair.*)

MRS HIGGINS: Do you know any of her people?

PICKERING: Only her father: the fellow we told you about.

THE PARLOR-MAID (*announcing*): Mr Doolittle. (*She withdraws.*)

(DOOLITTLE *enters. He is brilliantly dressed in a new fashionable frock-coat, with white waistcoat and grey trousers. A flower in his buttonhole, a dazzling silk hat, and patent leather shoes complete the effect. He is too concerned with the business he has come on to notice* MRS HIGGINS. *He walks straight to* HIGGINS, *and accosts him with vehement reproach.*)

DOOLITTLE (*indicating his own person*): See here! Do you see this? You done this.

HIGGINS: Done what, man?

DOOLITTLE: This, I tell you. Look at it. Look at this hat. Look at this coat.

PICKERING: Has Eliza been buying you clothes?

DOOLITTLE: Eliza! not she. Not half. Why would she buy me clothes?

MRS HIGGINS: Good morning, Mr Doolittle. Wont you sit down?

DOOLITTLE (*taken aback as he becomes conscious that he has forgotten his hostess*): Asking your pardon, maam. (*He approaches her and shakes her proffered hand.*) Thank you. (*He sits down on the ottoman, on* PICKERING'S *right.*) I am that full of what has happened to me that I cant think of anything else.

HIGGINS: What the dickens has happened to you?

DOOLITTLE: I shouldnt mind if it had only happened to me: anything might happen to anybody and nobody to blame but Providence, as you might say. But this is something that you done to me: yes, you, Henry Higgins.

HIGGINS: Have you found Eliza? Thats the point.

DOOLITTLE: Have you lost her?

HIGGINS: Yes.

DOOLITTLE: You have all the luck, you have. I aint found her; but she'll find me quick enough now after what you done to me.

MRS HIGGINS: But what has my son done to you, Mr Doolittle?

DOOLITTLE: Done to me! Ruined me. Destroyed my happiness. Tied me up and delivered me into the hands of middle class morality.

HIGGINS (*rising intolerantly and standing over* DOOLITTLE): Youre raving. Youre drunk. Youre mad. I gave you five pounds. After that I had two conversations with you, at half-a-crown an hour. Ive never seen you since.

DOOLITTLE: Oh! Drunk! am I? Mad! am I? Tell me this. Did you or did you not write a letter to an old blighter in America that was giving five millions to found Moral Reform Societies all over the world, and that wanted you to invent a universal language for him?

HIGGINS: What! Ezra D. Wannafeller! He's dead. (*He sits down again carelessly.*)

DOOLITTLE: Yes: he's dead; and I'm done for. Now did you or did you not write a letter to him to say that the most original moralist at present in England, to the best of your knowledge, was Alfred Doolittle, a common dustman.

HIGGINS: Oh, after your last visit I remember making some silly joke of the kind.

DOOLITTLE: Ah! you may well call it a silly joke. It put the lid on me right enough. Just give him the chance he wanted to shew that Americans is not like us: that they recognize and respect merit in every class of life, however humble. Them words is in his blooming will, in which, Henry Higgins, thanks to your silly joking, he leaves me a share in his Predigested Cheese Trust worth three thousand a year on condition that I lecture for his Wannafeller Moral Reform World League as often as they ask me up to six times a year.

HIGGINS: The devil he does! Whew! (*Brightening suddenly*) What a lark!

PICKERING: A safe thing for you, Doolittle. They wont ask you twice.

DOOLITTLE: It aint the lecturing I mind. I'll lecture them blue in the face, I will, and not turn a hair. It's making a gentleman of me that I object to. Who asked him to make a gentleman of me? I was happy. I was free. I touched pretty nigh everybody for money when I wanted it, same as I touched you, Henry Higgins. Now I am worrited; tied neck and heels; and everybody touches me for money. It's a fine thing for you, says my solicitor. Is it? says I. You mean it's a good thing for you, I says. When I was a poor man and had a solicitor once when they found a pram in the dust cart, he got me off, and got shut of me and got me shut of him as quick as he could. Same with the doctors: used to shove me out of the hospital before I could hardly stand on my legs, and nothing to pay. Now they finds out that I'm not a healthy man and cant live unless they looks after me twice a day. In the house I'm not let do a hand's turn for myself: somebody else must do it and touch me for it. A year ago I hadnt a relative in the world except two or three that wouldnt speak to me. Now Ive fifty, and not a decent week's wages among the lot of them. I have to live for others and not for myself: thats middle class morality. You talk of losing Eliza. Dont you be anxious: I bet she's on my doorstep by this: she that could support herself easy by selling flowers if I wasnt respectable. And the next one to touch me will be you, Henry Higgins. I'll have to learn to speak middle class language from you, instead of speaking proper English. Thats where youll come in; and I daresay thats what you done it for.

MRS HIGGINS: But, my dear Mr Doolittle, you need not suffer all this if you are really in earnest. Nobody can force you to accept this bequest. You can repudiate it. Isnt that so, Colonel Pickering?

PICKERING: I believe so.

DOOLITTLE (*softening his manner in deference to her sex*): Thats the tragedy of it, maam. It's easy to say chuck it; but I havnt the nerve. Which of us has? We're all intimidated. Intimidated, maam: thats what we are. What is there for me if I chuck it but the workhouse in my old age? I have to dye my hair already to keep my job as a dustman. If I was one of the deserving poor, and had put by a bit, I could chuck it; but then why should I, acause the deserving poor might as well be millionaires for all the happiness they ever has. They dont know what happiness is. But I, as one of the undeserving poor, have nothing between me and the pauper's uniform but this here blasted three thousand a year that shoves me into the middle class. (Excuse the expression, maam: youd use it yourself if you had my provocation.) Theyve got you every way you turn: it's a choice between the Skilly of the workhouse and the Char Bydis of the middle class; and I havnt the nerve for the workhouse. Intimidated: thats what I am. Broke. Bought up. Happier men than me will call for my dust, and touch me for their tip; and I'll look on helpless, and envy them. And thats what your son has brought me to. (*He is overcome by emotion.*)

MRS HIGGINS: Well, I'm very glad youre not going to do anything foolish, Mr Doolittle. For this solves the problem of Eliza's future. You can provide for her now.

DOOLITTLE (*with melancholy resignation*): Yes, maam: I'm expected to provide for everyone now, out of three thousand a year.

HIGGINS (*jumping up*): Nonsense! he cant provide for her. He shant provide for her. She doesnt belong to him. I paid him five pounds for her. Doolittle: either youre an honest man or a rogue.

DOOLITTLE (*tolerantly*): A little of both, Henry, like the rest of us: a little of both.

HIGGINS: Well, you took that money for the girl; and you have no right to take her as well.

MRS HIGGINS: Henry: dont be absurd. If you want to know where Eliza is, she is upstairs.

HIGGINS (*amazed*): Upstairs!!! Then I shall jolly soon fetch her downstairs. (*He makes resolutely for the door.*)

MRS HIGGINS (*rising and following him*): Be quiet, Henry. Sit down.

HIGGINS: I—

MRS HIGGINS: Sit down, dear; and listen to me.

HIGGINS: Oh very well, very well, very well. (*He throws himself ungraciously on the ottoman, with his face towards the windows.*) But I think you might have told us this half an hour ago.

MRS HIGGINS: Eliza came to me this morning. She passed the night partly walking about in a rage, partly trying to throw herself into the river and being afraid to, and partly in the Carlton Hotel. She told me of the brutal way you two treated her.

HIGGINS (*bounding up again*): What!

PICKERING (*rising also*): My dear Mrs Higgins, she's been telling you stories. We didnt treat her brutally. We hardly said a word to her; and we parted on particularly good terms. (*Turning on* HIGGINS.) Higgins: did you bully her after I went to bed?

HIGGINS: Just the other way about. She threw my slippers in my face. She behaved in the most outrageous way. I never gave her the slightest provocation. The slippers came bang into my face the moment I entered the room—before I had uttered a word. And used perfectly awful language.

PICKERING (*astonished*): But why? What did we do to her?

MRS HIGGINS: I think I know pretty well what you did. The girl is naturally rather affectionate, I think. Isnt she, Mr Doolittle?

DOOLITTLE: Very tender-hearted, maam. Takes after me.

MRS HIGGINS: Just so. She had become attached to you both. She worked very hard for you, Henry! I dont think you quite realize what anything in the nature of brain work means to a girl like that. Well, it seems that when the great day of trial came, and she did this wonderful thing for you without making a single mistake, you two sat there and never said a word to her, but talked together of how glad you were that it was all over and how you had been bored with the whole thing. And then you were surprised because she threw your slippers at you! *I* should have thrown the fire-irons at you.

HIGGINS: We said nothing except that we were tired and wanted to go to bed. Did we, Pick?

PICKERING (*shrugging his shoulders*): That was all.

MRS HIGGINS (*ironically*): Quite sure?

PICKERING: Absolutely. Really, that was all.

MRS HIGGINS: You didnt thank her, or pet her, or admire her, or tell her how splendid she'd been.

HIGGINS (*impatiently*): But she knew all about that. We didnt make speeches to her, if thats what you mean.

PICKERING (*conscience stricken*): Perhaps we were a little inconsiderate. Is she very angry?

MRS HIGGINS (*returning to her place at the writing-table*): Well, I'm afraid she wont go back to Wimpole Street, especially now that Mr Doolittle is able to keep up the position you have thrust on her; but she says she is quite willing to meet you on friendly terms and to let bygones be bygones.

HIGGINS (*furious*): Is she, by George? Ho!

MRS HIGGINS: If you promise to behave yourself, Henry, I'll ask her to come down. If not, go home; for you have taken up quite enough of my time.

HIGGINS: Oh, all right. Very well. Pick: you behave yourself. Let us put on our best Sunday manners for this creature that we picked out of the mud. (*He flings himself sulkily into the Elizabethan chair.*)

DOOLITTLE (*remonstrating*): Now, now, Henry Higgins! have some consideration for my feelings as a middle class man.

MRS HIGGINS: Remember your promise, Henry. (*She presses the bell-button on the writing-table.*) Mr Doolittle: will you be so good as to step out on the balcony for a moment. I dont want Eliza to have the shock of your news until she has made it up with these two gentlemen. Would you mind?

DOOLITTLE: As you wish, lady. Anything to help Henry to keep her off my hands. (*He disappears through the window.*)

(*The parlor-maid answers the bell.* PICKERING *sits down in* DOOLITTLE's *place.*)

MRS HIGGINS: Ask Miss Doolittle to come down, please.

THE PARLOR-MAID: Yes, maam. (*She goes out.*)

MRS HIGGINS: Now, Henry: be good.

HIGGINS: I am behaving myself perfectly.

PICKERING: He is doing his best, Mrs Higgins.

(*A pause.* HIGGINS *throws back his head; stretches out his legs; and begins to whistle.*)

MRS HIGGINS: Henry, dearest, you dont look at all nice in that attitude.

HIGGINS (*pulling himself together*): I was not trying to look nice, mother.

MRS HIGGINS: It doesnt matter, dear. I only wanted to make you speak.

HIGGINS: Why?

MRS HIGGINS: Because you cant speak and whistle at the same time.

(HIGGINS *groans. Another very trying pause.*)

HIGGINS (*springing up, out of patience*): Where the devil is that girl? Are we to wait here all day?

(ELIZA *enters, sunny, self-possessed, and giving a staggeringly convincing exhibition of ease of manner. She carries a little work-basket, and is very much at home.* PICKERING *is too much taken aback to rise.*)

LIZA: How do you do, Professor Higgins? Are you quite well?

HIGGINS (*choking*): Am I—(*He can say no more.*)

LIZA: But of course you are: you are never ill. So glad to see you again, Colonel Pickering. (*He rises hastily; and they shake hands.*) Quite chilly this morning, isnt it? (*She sits down on his left. He sits beside her.*)

HIGGINS: Dont you dare try this game on me. I taught it to you; and it doesnt take me in. Get up and come home; and dont be a fool.

(ELIZA *takes a piece of needlework from her basket, and begins to stitch at it, without taking the least notice of this outburst.*)

MRS HIGGINS: V⬛⬛icely put, indeed, Henry. No woman could⬛⬛st such an invitation.

HIGGINS: You let her alone, mother. Let her speak for herself. You will jolly soon see whether she has an idea that I havnt put into her head or a word that I havnt put into her mouth. I tell you I have created this thing out of the squashed cabbage leaves of Covent Garden; and now she pretends to play the fine lady with me.

MRS HIGGINS (*placidly*): Yes, dear; but youll sit down, wont you?

(HIGGINS *sits down again, savagely.*)

LIZA (*to* PICKERING, *taking no apparent notice of* HIGGINS, *and working away deftly*): Will you drop me altogether now that the experiment is over, Colonel Pickering?

PICKERING: Oh dont. You mustnt think of it as an experiment. It shocks me, somehow.

LIZA: Oh, I'm only a squashed cabbage leaf—

PICKERING (*impulsively*): No.

LIZA (*continuing quietly*): —but I owe so much to you that I should be very unhappy if you forgot me.

PICKERING: It's very kind of you to say so, Miss Doolittle.

LIZA: It's not because you paid for my dresses. I know you are generous to everybody with money. But it was from you that I learnt really nice manners; and that is what makes one a lady, isnt it? You see it was so very difficult for me with the example of Professor Higgins always before me. I was brought up to be just like him, unable to control myself, and using bad language on the slightest provocation. And I should never have known that ladies and gentlemen didnt behave like that if you hadnt been there.

HIGGINS: Well!!

PICKERING: Oh, thats only his way, you know. He doesnt mean it.

LIZA: Oh, *I* didnt mean it either, when I was a flower girl. It was only my way. But you see I did it; and thats what makes the difference after all.

PICKERING: No doubt. Still, he taught you to speak; and I couldnt have done that, you know.

LIZA (*trivially*): Of course: that is his profession.

HIGGINS: Damnation!

LIZA (*continuing*): It was just like learning to dance in the fashionable way: there was nothing more than that in it. But do you know what began my real education?

PICKERING: What?

LIZA (*stopping her work for a moment*): Your calling me Miss Doolittle that day when I first came to Wimpole Street. That was the beginning of self-respect for me. (*She resumes her stitching.*) And there were a hundred little things you never noticed, because they came naturally to you. Things about standing up and taking off your hat and opening doors—

PICKERING: Oh, that was nothing.

LIZA: Yes: things that shewed you thought and felt about me as if I were something better than a scullery-maid; though of course I know you would have been just the same to a scullery-maid if she had been let into the drawing room. You never took off your boots in the dining room when I was there.

PICKERING: You mustnt mind that. Higgins takes off his boots all over the place.

LIZA: I know. I am not blaming him. It is his way, isnt it? But it made such a difference to me that you didnt do it. You see, really and truly, apart from the things anyone can pick up (the dressing and the proper way of speaking, and so on), the difference between a lady and a flower girl is not how she behaves, but how she's treated. I shall always be a flower girl to Professor Higgins, because he always treats me as a flower girl, and always will; but I know I can be a lady to you, because you always treat me as a lady, and always will.

MRS HIGGINS: Please dont grind your teeth, Henry.

PICKERING: Well, this is really very nice of you, Miss Doolittle.

LIZA: I should like you to call me Eliza, now, if you would.

PICKERING: Thank you. Eliza, of course.

LIZA: And I should like Professor Higgins to call me Miss Doolittle.

HIGGINS: I'll see you damned first.

MRS HIGGINS: Henry! Henry!

PICKERING (*laughing*): Why dont you slang back at him? Dont stand it. It would do him a lot of good.

LIZA: I cant. I could have done it once; but now I cant go back to it. Last night, when I was wandering about, a girl spoke to me; and I tried to get back into the old way with her; but it was no use. You told me, you know, that when a child is brought to a foreign country, it picks up the language in a few weeks, and forgets its own. Well, I am a child in your country. I have forgotten my own language, and can speak nothing but yours. Thats the real break-off with the corner of Tottenham Court Road. Leaving Wimpole Street finishes it.

PICKERING (*much alarmed*): Oh! but youre coming back to Wimpole Street, arnt you? Youll forgive Higgins?

HIGGINS (*rising*): Forgive! Will she, by George! Let her go. Let her find out how she can get on without us. She will relapse into the gutter in three weeks without me at her elbow.

(DOOLITTLE *appears at the center window. With a look of dignified reproach at* HIGGINS, *he comes slowly and silently to his daughter, who, with her back to the window, is unconscious of his approach.*)

PICKERING: He's incorrigible, Eliza. You wont relapse, will you?

LIZA: No: not now. Never again. I have learnt my lesson. I dont believe I could utter one of the old sounds if I tried. (DOOLITTLE *touches her on her left shoulder. She drops her work, losing her self-possession utterly at the spectacle of her father's splendor*) A-a-a-a-a-ah-ow-ooh!

HIGGINS (*with a crow of triumph*): Aha! Just so. A-a-a-a-ahowooh! A-a-a-a-ahowooh! A-a-a-a-ahowooh! Victory! Victory! (*He throws himself on the divan, folding his arms, and spraddling arrogantly.*)

DOOLITTLE: Can you blame the girl? Dont look at me like that, Eliza. It aint my fault. Ive come into some money.

LIZA: You must have touched a millionaire this time, dad.

DOOLITTLE: I have. But I'm dressed something special today. I'm going to St George's, Hanover Square. Your stepmother is going to marry me.

LIZA (*angrily*): Youre going to let yourself down to marry that low common woman!

PICKERING (*quietly*): He ought to, Eliza. (*To* DOOLITTLE) Why has she changed her mind?

DOOLITTLE (*sadly*): Intimidated, Governor. Intimidated. Middle class morality claims its victim. Wont you put on your hat, Liza, and come and see me turned off?

LIZA: If the Colonel says I must, I—I'll (*almost sobbing*) I'll demean myself. And get insulted for my pains, like enough.

DOOLITTLE: Dont be afraid: she never comes to words with anyone now, poor woman! respectability has broke all the spirit out of her.

PICKERING (*squeezing* ELIZA's *elbow gently*): Be kind to them, Eliza. Make the best of it.

LIZA (*forcing a little smile for him through her vexation*): Oh well, just to shew theres no ill feeling. I'll be back in a moment. (*She goes out.*)

DOOLITTLE (*sitting down beside* PICKERING): I feel uncommon nervous about the ceremony, Colonel. I wish youd come and see me through it.

PICKERING: But youve been through it before, man. You were married to Eliza's mother.

DOOLITTLE: Who told you that, Colonel?

PICKERING: Well, nobody told me. But I concluded—naturally—

DOOLITTLE: No: that aint the natural way, Colonel: it's only the middle class way. My way was always the undeserving way. But dont say nothing to Eliza. She dont know: I always had a delicacy about telling her.

PICKERING: Quite right. We'll leave it so, if you dont mind.

DOOLITTLE: And youll come to the church, Colonel, and put me through straight?

PICKERING: With pleasure. As far as a bachelor can.

MRS HIGGINS: May I come, Mr Doolittle? I should be very sorry to miss your wedding.

DOOLITTLE: I should indeed be honored by your condescension, maam; and my poor old woman would take it as a tremenjous compliment. She's been very low, thinking of the happy days that are no more.

MRS HIGGINS (rising): I'll order the carriage and get ready. (The men rise, except HIGGINS.) I shant be more than fifteen minutes. (As she goes to the door ELIZA comes in, hatted and buttoning her gloves.) I'm going to the church to see your father married, Eliza. You had better come in the brougham with me. Colonel Pickering can go on with the bridegroom.

(MRS HIGGINS goes out. ELIZA comes to the middle of the room between the center window and the ottoman. PICKERING joins her.)

DOOLITTLE: Bridegroom! What a word! It makes a man realize his position, somehow. (He takes up his hat and goes towards the door.)

PICKERING: Before I go, Eliza, do forgive him and come back to us.

LIZA: I dont think papa would allow me. Would you, dad?

DOOLITTLE (sad but magnanimous): They played you off very cunning, Eliza, them two sportsmen. If it had been only one of them, you could have nailed him. But you see, there was two; and one of them chaperoned the other, as you might say. (To PICKERING) It was artful of you, Colonel; but I bear no malice: I should have done the same myself. I been the victim of one woman after another all my life; and I dont grudge you two getting the better of Eliza. I shant interfere. It's time for us to go, Colonel. So long, Henry. See you in St George's, Eliza. (He goes out.)

PICKERING (coaxing): Do stay with us, Eliza. (He follows Doolittle.)

(ELIZA goes out on the balcony to avoid being alone with HIGGINS. He rises and joins her there. She immediately comes back into the room and makes for the door; but he goes along the balcony quickly and gets his back to the door before she reaches it.)

HIGGINS: Well, Eliza, youve had a bit of your own back, as you call it. Have you had enough? and are you going to be reasonable? Or do you want any more?

LIZA: You want me back only to pick up your slippers and put up with your tempers and fetch and carry for you.

HIGGINS: I havnt said I wanted you back at all.

LIZA: Oh, indeed. Then what are we talking about?

HIGGINS: About you, not about me. If you come back I shall treat you just as I have always treated you. I cant change my nature; and I dont intend to change my manners. My manners are exactly the same as Colonel Pickering's.

LIZA: Thats not true. He treats a flower girl as if she was a duchess.

HIGGINS: And I treat a duchess as if she was a flower girl.

LIZA: I see. (She turns away composedly, and sits on the ottoman, facing the window.) The same to everybody.

HIGGINS: Just so.

LIZA: Like father.

HIGGINS (grinning, a little taken down): Without accepting the comparison at all points, Eliza, it's quite true that your father is not a snob, and that he will be quite at home in any station of life to which his eccentric destiny may call him. (Seriously) The great secret, Eliza, is not having bad manners or good manners or any other particular sort of manners, but having the same manner for all human souls: in short, behaving as if you were in Heaven, where there are no third-class carriages, and one soul is as good as another.

LIZA: Amen. You are a born preacher.

HIGGINS (irritated): The question is not whether I treat you rudely, but whether you ever heard me treat anyone else better.

LIZA (with sudden sincerity): I dont care how you treat me. I dont mind your swearing at me. I dont mind a black eye: Ive had one before this. But (standing up and facing him) I wont be passed over.

HIGGINS: Then get out of my way; for I wont stop for you. You talk about me as if I were a motor bus.

LIZA: So you are a motor bus: all bounce and go, and no consideration for anyone. But I can do without you: dont think I cant.

HIGGINS: I know you can. I told you you could.

LIZA (wounded, getting away from him to the other side of the ottoman with her face to the hearth): I know you did, you brute. You wanted to get rid of me.

HIGGINS: Liar.

LIZA: Thank you. (She sits down with dignity.)

HIGGINS: You never asked yourself, I suppose, whether I could do without you.

LIZA (earnestly): Dont you try to get round me. Youll have to do without me.

HIGGINS (arrogant): I can do without anybody. I have my own soul: my own spark of divine fire. But (with sudden humility) I shall miss you, Eliza. (He sits down near her on the ottoman.) I have learnt something from your idiotic notions: I confess that humbly and gratefully. And I have grown accustomed to your voice and appearance. I like them, rather.

LIZA: Well, you have both of them on your gramophone and in your book of photographs. When you feel lonely without me, you can turn the machine on. It's got no feelings to hurt.

HIGGINS: I cant turn your soul on. Leave me those feelings; and you can take away the voice and the face. They are not you.

LIZA: Oh, you are a devil. You can twist the heart in a girl as easy as some could twist her arms to hurt her. Mrs Pearce warned me. Time and again she has wanted to leave you; and you always got round her at the last minute. And you dont care a bit for her. And you dont care a bit for me.

HIGGINS: I care for life, for humanity; and you are a part of it that has come my way and been built into my house. What more can you or anyone ask?

LIZA: I wont care for anybody that doesnt care for me.

HIGGINS: Commercial principles, Eliza. Like (reproducing her Covent Garden pronunciation with professional exactness) s'yollin voylets (selling violets), isnt it?

LIZA: Dont sneer at me. It's mean to sneer at me.

HIGGINS: I have never sneered in my life. Sneering doesnt become either the human face or the human soul. I am expressing my righteous contempt for Commercialism. I dont and wont trade in affection. You call me a brute because you couldnt buy a claim on me by fetching my slippers and finding my spectacles. You were a fool: I think a woman fetching a man's slippers is a disgusting sight: did I ever fetch your slippers? I think a good deal more of you for throwing them in my face. No use slaving for me and then saying you want to be cared for: who cares for a slave? If you come back, come back for the sake of good fellowship; for youll get nothing else. Youve had a thousand times as much out of me as I have out of you; and if you dare to set up your little dog's tricks of fetching and carrying slippers against my creation of a Duchess Eliza, I'll slam the door in your silly face.

LIZA: What did you do it for if you didnt care for me?

HIGGINS (heartily): Why, because it was my job.

LIZA: You never thought of the trouble it would make for me.

HIGGINS: Would the world ever have been made if its maker had been afraid of making trouble? Making life means making trouble. Theres only one way of escaping trouble; and thats killing things. Cowards, you notice, are always shrieking to have troublesome people killed.

LIZA: I'm no preacher: I dont notice things like that. I notice that you dont notice me.

HIGGINS (jumping up and walking about intolerantly): Eliza: youre an idiot. I waste the treasures of my Miltonic mind by spreading them before you. Once for all, understand that I go my way and do my work without caring twopence what happens to either of us. I am not intimidated, like your father and your stepmother. So you can come back or go to the devil: which you please.

LIZA: What am I to come back for?

HIGGINS (bounding up on his knees on the ottoman and leaning over it to her): For the fun of it. Thats why I took you on.

LIZA (with averted face): And you may throw me out tomorrow if I dont do everything you want me to?

HIGGINS: Yes; and you may walk out tomorrow if I dont do everything you want me to.

LIZA: And live with my stepmother?

HIGGINS: Yes, or sell flowers.

LIZA: Oh! if I only could go back to my flower basket! I should be independent of both you and father and all the world! Why did you take my independence from me? Why did I give it up? I'm a slave now, for all my fine clothes.

HIGGINS: Not a bit. I'll adopt you as my daughter and settle money on you if you like. Or would you rather marry Pickering?

LIZA (looking fiercely round at him): I wouldnt marry you if you asked me; and youre nearer my age than what he is.

HIGGINS (gently): Than he is: not "than what he is."

LIZA (losing her temper and rising): I'll talk as I like. Youre not my teacher now.

HIGGINS (reflectively): I dont suppose Pickering would, though. He's as confirmed an old bachelor as I am.

LIZA: Thats not what I want; and dont you think it. Ive always had chaps enough wanting me that way. Freddy Hill writes to me twice and three times a day, sheets and sheets.

HIGGINS (disagreeably surprised): Damn his impudence! (He recoils and finds himself sitting on his heels.)

LIZA: He has a right to if he likes, poor lad. And he does love me.

HIGGINS (getting off the ottoman): You have no right to encourage him.

LIZA: Every girl has a right to be loved.

HIGGINS: What! By fools like that?

LIZA: Freddy's not a fool. And if he's weak and poor and wants me, may be he'd make me happier than my betters that bully me and dont want me.

HIGGINS: Can he make anything of you? Thats the point.

LIZA: Perhaps I could make something of him. But I never thought of us making anything of one another; and you never think of anything else. I only want to be natural.

HIGGINS: In short, you want me to be as infatuated about you as Freddy? Is that it?

LIZA: No I dont. Thats not the sort of feeling I want from you. And dont you be too sure of yourself or of me. I could have been a bad girl if I'd liked. Ive seen more of some things than you, for all your learning. Girls like me can drag gentlemen down to make love to them easy enough. And they wish each other dead the next minute.

HIGGINS: Of course they do. Then what in thunder are we quarrelling about?

LIZA (much troubled): I want a little kindness. I know I'm

a common ignorant girl, and you a book-learned gentleman; but I'm not dirt under your feet. What I done (*correcting herself*) what I did was not for the dresses and the taxis: I did it because we were pleasant together and I come—came—to care for you; not to want you to make love to me, and not forgetting the difference between us, but more friendly like.

HIGGINS: Well, of course. Thats just how I feel. And how Pickering feels. Eliza: youre a fool.

LIZA: Thats not a proper answer to give me (*she sinks on the chair at the writing-table in tears*).

HIGGINS: It's all youll get until you stop being a common idiot. If youre going to be a lady, youll have to give up feeling neglected if the men you know dont spend half their time snivelling over you and the other half giving you black eyes. If you cant stand the coldness of my sort of life, and the strain of it, go back to the gutter. Work til you are more a brute than a human being; and then cuddle and squabble and drink til you fall asleep. Oh, it's a fine life, the life of the gutter. It's real: it's warm: it's violent: you can feel it through the thickest skin: you can taste it and smell it without any training or any work. Not like Science and Literature and Classical Music and Philosophy and Art. You find me cold, unfeeling, selfish, dont you? Very well: be off with you to the sort of people you like. Marry some sentimental hog or other with lots of money, and a thick pair of lips to kiss you with and a thick pair of boots to kick you with. If you cant appreciate what youve got, youd better get what you can appreciate.

LIZA (*desperate*): Oh, you are a cruel tyrant. I cant talk to you: you turn everything against me: I'm always in the wrong. But you know very well all the time that youre nothing but a bully. You know I cant go back to the gutter, as you call it, and that I have no real friends in the world but you and the Colonel. You know well I couldnt bear to live with a low common man after you two; and it's wicked and cruel of you to insult me by pretending I could. You think I must go back to Wimpole Street because I have nowhere else to go but father's. But dont you be too sure that you have me under your feet to be trampled on and talked down. I'll marry Freddy, I will, as soon as he's able to support me.

HIGGINS (*sitting down beside her*): Rubbish! you shall marry an ambassador. You shall marry the Governor-General of India or the Lord-Lieutenant of Ireland, or somebody who wants a deputy-queen. I'm not going to have my masterpiece thrown away on Freddy.

LIZA: You think I like you to say that. But I havnt forgot what you said a minute ago; and I wont be coaxed round as if I was a baby or a puppy. If I cant have kindness, I'll have independence.

HIGGINS: Independence? Thats middle class blasphemy. We are all dependent on one another, every

soul of us on earth.

LIZA (*rising determinedly*): I'll let you see whether I'm dependent on you. If you can preach, I can teach. I'll go and be a teacher.

HIGGINS: Whatll you teach, in heaven's name?

LIZA: What you taught me. I'll teach phonetics.

HIGGINS: Ha! ha! ha!

LIZA: I'll offer myself as an assistant to Professor Nepean.

HIGGINS (*rising in a fury*): What! That impostor! that humbug! that toadying ignoramus! Teach him my methods! my discoveries! You take one step in his direction and I'll wring your neck. (*He lays hands on her.*) Do you hear?

LIZA (*defiantly non-resistant*): Wring away. What do I care? I knew youd strike me some day. (*He lets her go, stamping with rage at having forgotten himself, and recoils so hastily that he stumbles back into his seat on the ottoman.*) Aha! Now I know how to deal with you. What a fool I was not to think of it before! You cant take away the knowledge you gave me. You said I had a finer ear than you. And I can be civil and kind to people, which is more than you can. Aha! Thats done you, Henry Higgins, it has. Now I dont care that (*snapping her fingers*) for your bullying and your big talk. I'll advertize it in the papers that your duchess is only a flower girl that you taught, and that she'll teach anybody to be a duchess just the same in six months for a thousand guineas. Oh, when I think of myself crawling under your feet and being trampled on and called names, when all the time I had only to lift up my finger to be as good as you, I could just kick myself.

HIGGINS (*wondering at her*): You damned impudent slut, you! But it's better than snivelling; better than fetching slippers and finding spectacles, isnt it? (*Rising*) By George, Eliza, I said I'd make a woman of you; and I have. I like you like this.

LIZA: Yes: you turn round and make up to me now that I'm not afraid of you, and can do without you.

HIGGINS: Of course I do, you little fool. Five minutes ago you were like a millstone round my neck. Now youre a tower of strength: a consort battleship. You and I and Pickering will be three old bachelors together instead of only two men and a silly girl.

(MRS HIGGINS *returns, dressed for the wedding.* ELIZA *instantly becomes cool and elegant.*)

MRS HIGGINS: The carriage is waiting, Eliza. Are you ready?

LIZA: Quite. Is the Professor coming?

MRS HIGGINS: Certainly not. He cant behave himself in church. He makes remarks out loud all the time on the clergyman's pronunciation.

LIZA: Then I shall not see you again, Professor. Goodbye. (*She goes to the door.*)

MRS HIGGINS (*coming to* HIGGINS): Goodbye, dear.

HIGGINS: Goodbye, mother. (*He is about to kiss her, when*

he recollects something.) Oh, by the way, Eliza, order a ham and a Stilton cheese, will you? And buy me a pair of reindeer gloves, number eights, and a tie to match that new suit of mine, at Eale & Binman's. You can choose the color. *(His cheerful, careless, vigorous voice shows that he is incorrigible.)*

LIZA *(disdainfully)*: Buy them yourself. *(She sweeps out.)*

MRS HIGGINS: I'm afraid youve spoiled that girl, Henry. But never mind, dear: I'll buy you the tie and gloves.

HIGGINS *(sunnily)*: Oh, dont bother. She'll buy em all right enough. Goodbye.

(They kiss. MRS HIGGINS *runs out.* HIGGINS *left alone, rattles his cash in his pocket; chuckles; and disports himself in a highly self-satisfied manner.)*

*   *   *

The rest of the story need not be shewn in action, and indeed, would hardly need telling if our imaginations were not so enfeebled by their lazy dependence on the ready-mades and reach-me-downs of the ragshop in which Romance keeps its stock of "happy endings" to misfit all stories. Now, the history of Eliza Doolittle, though called a romance because the transfiguration it records seems exceedingly improbable, is common enough. Such transfigurations have been achieved by hundreds of resolutely ambitious young women since Nell Gwynne set them the example by playing queens and fascinating kings in the theatre in which she began by selling oranges. Nevertheless, people in all directions have assumed, for no other reason than that she became the heroine of a romance, that she must have married the hero of it. This is unbearable, not only because her little drama, if acted on such a thoughtless assumption, must be spoiled, but because the true sequel is patent to anyone with a sense of human nature in general, and of feminist instinct in particular.

Eliza, in telling Higgins she would not marry him if he asked her, was not coquetting: she was announcing a well-considered decision. When a bachelor interests, and dominates, and teaches, and becomes important to a spinster, as Higgins with Eliza, she always, if she has character enough to be capable of it, considers very seriously indeed whether she will play for becoming that bachelor's wife, especially if he is so little interested in marriage that a determined and devoted woman might capture him if she set herself resolutely to do it. Her decision will depend a good deal on whether she is really free to choose; and that, again, will depend on her age and income. If she is at the end of her youth, and has no security for her livelihood, she will marry him because she must marry anybody who will provide for her. But at Eliza's age a good-looking girl does not feel that pressure: she feels free to pick and choose. She is therefore guided by her instinct in the matter. Eliza's instinct tells her not to marry Higgins. It does not tell her to give him up. It is not in the slightest doubt as to his remaining one of the strongest personal interests in her

life. It would be very sorely strained if there was another woman likely to supplant her with him. But as she feels sure of him on that last point, she has no doubt at all as to her course, and would not have any, even if the difference of twenty years in age, which seems so great to youth, did not exist between them.

As our own instincts are not appealed to by her conclusion, let us see whether we cannot discover some reason in it. When Higgins excused his indifference to young women on the ground that they had an irresistible rival in his mother, he gave the clue to his inveterate old-bachelordom. The case is uncommon only to the extent that remarkable mothers are uncommon. If an imaginative boy has a sufficiently rich mother who has intelligence, personal grace, dignity of character without harshness, and a cultivated sense of the best art of her time to enable her to make her house beautiful, she sets a standard for him against which very few women can struggle, besides effecting for him a disengagement of his affections, his sense of beauty, and his idealism from his specifically sexual impulses. This makes him a standing puzzle to the huge number of uncultivated people who have been brought up in tasteless homes by commonplace or disagreeable parents, and to whom, consequently, literature, painting, sculpture, music, and affectionate personal relations come as modes of sex if they come at all. The word passion means nothing else to them; and that Higgins could have a passion for phonetics and idealize his mother instead of Eliza, would seem to them absurd and unnatural. Nevertheless, when we look round and see that hardly anyone is too ugly or disagreeable to find a wife or a husband if he or she wants one, whilst many old maids and bachelors are above the average in quality and culture, we cannot help suspecting that the disentanglement of sex from the associations with which it is so commonly confused, a disentanglement which persons of genius achieve by sheer intellectual analysis, is sometimes produced or aided by parental fascination.

Now, though Eliza was incapable of thus explaining to herself Higgins's formidable powers of resistance to the charm that prostrated Freddy at the first glance, she was instinctively aware that she could never obtain a complete grip of him, or come between him and his mother (the first necessity of the married woman). To put it shortly, she knew that for some mysterious reason he had not the makings of a married man in him, according to her conception of a husband as one to whom she would be his nearest and fondest and warmest interest. Even had there been no mother-rival, she would still have refused to accept an interest in herself that was secondary to philosophic interests. Had Mrs Higgins died, there would still have been Milton and the Universal Alphabet. Landor's remark that to those who have the greatest power of loving, love is a secondary affair, would not have recommended Landor to Eliza. Put that along with her resentment of Higgins's domineering superiority, and her mistrust of his coaxing cleverness in getting round her and evading her wrath when he had gone too far with his impetuous bullying, and you will see that Eliza's instinct had good grounds for warning her not to marry her Pygmalion.

And now, whom did Eliza marry? For if Higgins was a predestinate old bachelor, she was most certainly not a predestinate old maid. Well, that can be told very shortly to those who have not guessed it from the indications she has herself given them.

Almost immediately after Eliza is stung into proclaiming her considered determination not to marry Higgins, she mentions the fact that young Mr Frederick Eynsford Hill is pouring out his love for her daily through the post. Now Freddy is young, practically twenty years younger than Higgins: he is a gentleman (or, as Eliza would qualify him, a toff), and speaks like one; he is nicely dressed, is treated by the Colonel as an equal, loves her unaffectedly, and is not her master, nor ever likely to dominate her in spite of his advantage of social standing. Eliza has no use for the foolish romantic tradition that all women love to be mastered, if not actually bullied and beaten. "When you go to women," says Nietzsche, "take your whip with you." Sensible despots have never confined that precaution to women: they have taken their whips with them when they have dealt with men, and been slavishly idealized by the men over whom they have flourished the whip much more than by women. No doubt there are slavish women as well as slavish men: and women, like men, admire those that are stronger than themselves. But to admire a strong person and to live under that strong person's thumb are two different things. The weak may not be admired and hero-worshipped; but they are by no means disliked or shunned; and they never seem to have the least difficulty in marrying people who are too good for them. They may fail in emergencies; but life is not one long emergency: it is mostly a string of situations for which no exceptional strength is needed, and with which even rather weak people can cope if they have a stronger partner to help them out. Accordingly, it is a truth everywhere in evidence that strong people, masculine or feminine, not only do not marry stronger people, but do not shew any preference for them in selecting their friends. When a lion meets another with a louder roar "the first lion thinks the last a bore." The man or woman who feels strong enough for two, seeks for every other quality in a partner than strength.

The converse is also true. Weak people want to marry strong people who do not frighten them too much; and this often leads them to make the mistake we describe metaphorically as "biting off more than they can chew." They want too much for too little; and when the bargain is unreasonable beyond all bearing, the union becomes impossible: it ends in the weaker party being either discarded or borne as a cross, which is worse. People who are not only weak, but silly or obtuse as well, are often in these difficulties.

This being the state of human affairs, what is Eliza fairly sure to do when she is placed between Freddy and Higgins? Will she look forward to a lifetime of fetching Higgins's slippers or to a lifetime of Freddy fetching hers? There can be no doubt about the answer. Unless Freddy is biologically repulsive to her, and Higgins biologically attractive to a degree that overwhelms all her other instincts, she will, if she marries either of them, marry Freddy.

And that is just what Eliza did.

Complications ensued; but they were economic, not romantic. Freddy had no money and no occupation. His mother's jointure, a last relic of the opulence of Largelady Park, had enabled her to struggle along in Earlscourt with an air of gentility, but not to procure any serious secondary education for her children, much less give the boy a profession. A clerkship at thirty shillings a week was beneath Freddy's dignity, and extremely distasteful to him besides. His prospects consisted of a hope that if he kept up appearances somebody would do something for him. The something appeared vaguely to his imagination as a private secretaryship or a sinecure of some sort. To his mother it perhaps appeared as a marriage to some lady of means who could not resist her boy's niceness. Fancy her feelings when he married a flower girl who had become déclassée under extraordinary circumstances which were now notorious!

It is true that Eliza's situation did not seem wholly ineligible. Her father, though formerly a dustman, and now fantastically disclassed, had become extremely popular in the smartest society by a social talent which triumphed over every prejudice and every disadvantage. Rejected by the middle class, which he loathed, he had shot up at once into the highest circles by his wit, his dustmanship (which he carried like a banner), and his Nietzschean transcendence of good and evil. At intimate ducal dinners he sat on the right hand of the Duchess; and in country houses he smoked in the pantry and was made much of by the butler when he was not feeding in the dining room and being consulted by cabinet ministers. But he found it almost as hard to do all this on four thousand a year as Mrs Eynsford Hill to live in Earlscourt on an income so pitiably smaller that I have not the heart to disclose its exact figure. He absolutely refused to add the last straw to his burden by contributing to Eliza's support.

Thus Freddy and Eliza, now Mr and Mrs Eynsford Hill, would have spent a penniless honeymoon but for a wedding present of £500 from the Colonel to Eliza. It lasted a long time because Freddy did not know how to spend money, never having had any to spend, and Eliza, socially trained by a pair of old bachelors, wore her clothes as long as they held together and looked pretty, without the least regard to their being many months out of fashion. Still, £500 will not last two young people for ever; and they both knew, and Eliza felt as well, that they must shift for themselves in the end. She could quarter herself on Wimpole Street because it had come to be her home; but she was quite aware that she ought not to quarter Freddy there, and that it would not be good for his character if she did.

Not that the Wimpole Street bachelors objected. When she consulted them, Higgins declined to be bothered about her housing problem when that solution was so simple. Eliza's desire to have Freddy in the house with her seemed of no more importance than if she had wanted an extra piece of bedroom furniture. Pleas as to Freddy's character, and the moral obligation on him to earn his own living, were lost on Higgins. He denied that Freddy had any character, and declared that if he tried to do any useful work some competent person would have the trouble of undoing it: a procedure involving a net loss to the community, and great unhappiness to Freddy himself, who was obviously intended by Nature for such light work as amusing Eliza, which, Higgins declared, was a much more useful and honorable occupation than working in the city. When Eliza referred again to her project of teaching phonetics, Higgins abated not a jot of his violent opposition to it. He said she was not within ten years of being qualified to meddle with his pet subject; and as it was evident that the Colonel agreed with him, she felt she could not go against them in this grave matter, and that she had no right, without Higgins's consent, to exploit the knowledge he had given her; for his knowledge seemed to her as much his private property as his watch: Eliza was no communist. Besides, she was superstitiously devoted to them both, more entirely and frankly after her marriage than before it.

It was the Colonel who finally solved the problem, which had cost him much perplexed cogitation. He one day asked Eliza, rather shyly, whether she had quite given up her notion of keeping a flower shop. She replied that she had thought of it, but had put it out of her head, because the Colonel had said, that day at Mrs Higgins's, that it would never do. The Colonel confessed that when he said that, he had not quite recovered from the dazzling impression of the day before. They broke the matter to Higgins that evening. The sole comment vouchsafed by him very nearly led to a quarrel with Eliza. It was to the effect that she would have in Freddy an ideal errand boy.

Freddy himself was next sounded on the subject. He said he had been thinking of a shop himself; though it had presented itself to his pennilessness as a small place in which Eliza should sell tobacco at one counter whilst he sold newspapers at the opposite one. But he agreed that it would be extraordinarily jolly to go early every morning with Eliza to Covent Garden and buy flowers on the scene of their first meeting: a sentiment which earned him many kisses from his wife. He added that he had always been afraid to propose anything of the sort, because Clara would make an awful row about a step that must damage her matrimonial chances, and his mother could not be expected to like it after clinging for so many years to that step of the social ladder on which retail trade is impossible.

This difficulty was removed by an event highly unexpected by Freddy's mother. Clara, in the course of her incursions into those artistic circles which were the highest within her reach, discovered that her conversational qualifications were expected to include a grounding in the novels of Mr H. G. Wells. She borrowed them in various directions so energetically that she swallowed them all within two months. The result was a conversion of a kind quite common today. A modern Acts of the Apostles would fill fifty whole Bibles if anyone were capable of writing it.

Poor Clara, who appeared to Higgins and his mother as a disagreeable and ridiculous person, and to her own mother as in some inexplicable way a social failure, had never seen herself in either light; for though to some extent ridiculed and mimicked in West Kensington like everybody else there, she was accepted as a rational and normal—or shall we say inevitable?—sort of human being. At worst they called her The Pusher; but to them no more than to herself had it ever occurred that she was pushing the air, and pushing it in a wrong direction. Still, she was not happy. She was growing desperate. Her one asset, the fact that her mother was what the Epsom greengrocer called a carriage lady, had no exchange value, apparently. It had prevented her from getting educated, because the only education she could have afforded was education with the Earlscourt greengrocer's daughter. It had led her to seek the society of her mother's class; and that class simply would not have her, because she was much poorer than the greengrocer, and, far from being able to afford a maid, could not afford even a housemaid, and had to scrape along at home with an illiberally treated general servant. Under such circumstances nothing could give her an air of being a genuine product of Largelady Park. And yet its tradition made her regard a marriage with anyone within her reach as an unbearable humiliation. Commercial people and professional people in a small way were odious to her. She ran after painters and novelists; but she did not charm them; and her bold attempts to pick up and practice artistic and literary talk irritated them. She was, in short, an utter failure, an ignorant, incompetent, pretentious, unwelcome, penniless, useless little snob; and though she did not admit these disqualifications (for nobody ever faces unpleasant truths of this kind until the possibility of a way out dawns on them) she felt their effects too keenly to be satisfied with her position.

Clara had a startling eyeopener when, on being suddenly wakened to enthusiasm by a girl of her own age who dazzled her and produced in her a gushing desire to take her for a model, and gain her friendship, she discovered that this exquisite apparition had graduated from the gutter in a few months time. It shook her so violently, that when Mr H. G. Wells lifted her on the point of his puissant pen, and placed her at the angle of view from which the life she was leading and the society to which she clung appeared in its true relation to real human needs and worthy social structure, he effected a conversion and a conviction of sin comparable to the most sensational feats of General Booth or Gypsy Smith. Clara's snobbery went bang. Life suddenly began to move with her. Without knowing how or why, she began to make friends and enemies. Some of the acquaintances to whom she had been a tedious or indifferent or ridiculous affliction, dropped her: others became cordial. To her amazement she found that some "quite nice" people were saturated with Wells, and that this accessibility to ideas was the secret of their niceness. People she had thought deeply religious, and had tried to conciliate on that track with disastrous results, suddenly took an interest in her, and revealed a hostility to conventional religion which she had never conceived possible except among the most desperate characters. They made her read Galsworthy; and Galsworthy exposed the vanity of Largelady Park and finished her. It exasperated her to think that the dungeon in which she had languished for so many unhappy years had been unlocked all the time, and that the impulses she had so carefully struggled with and stifled for the sake of keeping well with society, were precisely those by which alone she could have come into any sort of sincere human contact. In the radiance of these discoveries, and the tumult of their reaction, she made a fool of herself as freely and conspicuously as when she so rashly adopted Eliza's expletive in Mrs Higgins's drawing room; for the new-born Wellsian had to find her bearings almost as ridiculously as a baby; but nobody hates a baby for its ineptitudes, or thinks the worse of it for trying to eat the matches; and Clara lost no friends by her follies. They laughed at her to her face this time; and she had to defend herself and fight it out as best she could.

When Freddy paid a visit to Earlscourt (which he never did when he could possibly help it) to make the desolating announcement that he and his Eliza were thinking of blackening the Largelady scutcheon by opening a shop, he found the little household already convulsed by a prior announcement from Clara that she also was going to work in an old furniture shop in Dover Street, which had been started by a fellow Wellsian. This appointment Clara owed, after all, to her old social accomplishment of Push. She had made up her mind that, cost what it might, she would see Mr Wells in the flesh; and she had achieved her end at a garden party. She had better luck than so rash an enterprise deserved. Mr Wells came up to her expectations. Age had not withered him, nor could custom stale his infinite variety in half an hour. His pleasant neatness and compactness, his small hands and feet, his teeming ready brain, his unaffected accessibility, and a certain fine apprehensiveness which stamped him as susceptible from his topmost hair to his tipmost toe, proved irresistible. Clara talked of nothing else for weeks and weeks afterwards. And as she happened to talk to the lady of the furniture shop, and that lady also desired above all things to know Mr Wells and sell pretty things to him, she offered Clara a job on the chance of achieving that end through her.

And so it came about that Eliza's luck held, and the expected opposition to the flower shop melted away. The shop is in the arcade of a railway station not very far from the Victoria and Albert Museum; and if you live in that neighborhood you may go there any day and buy a buttonhole from Eliza.

Now here is a last opportunity for romance. Would you not like to be assured that the shop was an immense success, thanks to Eliza's charms and her early business experience in Covent Garden? Alas! the truth is the truth: the shop did not pay for a long time, simply because Eliza and her Freddy did not know how to keep it. True, Eliza had not to begin at the very beginning: she knew the names and prices of the cheaper flowers; and her elation was unbounded when she found that Freddy, like all youths educated at cheap, pretentious, and thoroughly inefficient schools, knew a little Latin. It was very little, but enough to make him appear to her a Porson or Bentley, and to put him at his ease with botanical nomenclature. Unfortunately he knew nothing else; and Eliza, though she could count money up to eighteen shillings or so, and had acquired a certain familiarity with the language of Milton from her struggles to qualify herself for winning Higgins's bet, could not write out a bill without utterly disgracing the establishment. Freddy's power of stating in Latin that Balbus built a wall and that Gaul was divided into three parts did not carry with it the slightest knowledge of accounts or business: Colonel Pickering had to explain to him what a cheque book and a bank account meant. And the pair were by no means easily teachable. Freddy backed up Eliza in her obstinate refusal to believe that they could save money by engaging a bookkeeper with some knowledge of the business. How, they argued, could you possibly save money by going to extra expense when you already could not make both ends meet? But the Colonel, after making the ends meet over and over again, at last gently insisted; and Eliza, humbled to the dust by having to beg from him so often, and stung by the uproarious derision of Higgins, to whom the notion of Freddy succeeding at anything was a joke that never palled, grasped the fact that business, like phonetics, has to be learned.

On the piteous spectacle of the pair spending their evenings in shorthand schools and polytechnic classes, learning bookkeeping and typewriting with incipient junior clerks, male and female, from the elementary schools, let me not dwell. There were even classes at the London School of Economics, and a humble personal appeal to the director of that institution to recommend a course bearing on the flower business. He, being a humorist, explained to them the method of the celebrated Dickensian essay on Chinese Metaphysics by the gentleman who read an article on China and an article on Metaphysics and combined the information. He suggested that they should combine the London School with Kew Gardens. Eliza, to whom the procedure of the Dickensian gentleman seemed perfectly correct (as in fact it was) and not in the least funny (which was her only ignorance), took his advice with entire gravity. But the effort that cost her the deepest humiliation was a request to Higgins, whose pet artistic fancy, next to Milton's verse, was caligraphy, and who himself wrote a most beautiful Italian hand, that he would teach her to write. He declared that she was congenitally incapable of forming a single letter worthy of the least of Milton's words; but she persisted; and again he suddenly threw himself into the task of teaching her with a combination of stormy intensity, concentrated patience, and occasional bursts of interesting disquisition on the beauty and nobility, the august mission and destiny, of human handwriting. Eliza ended by acquiring an extremely uncommercial script which was a positive extension of her personal beauty, and spending three times as much on stationery as anyone else because certain qualities and shapes of paper became indispensible to her. She could not even address an envelope in the usual way because it made the margins all wrong.

Their commercial schooldays were a period of disgrace and despair for the young couple. They seemed to be learning nothing about flower shops. At last they gave it up as hopeless, and shook the dust of the shorthand schools, and the polytechnics, and the London School of Economics from their feet for ever. Besides, the business was in some mysterious way beginning to take care of itself. They had somehow forgotten their objections to employing other people. They came to the conclusion that their own way was the best, and that they had really a remarkable talent for business. The Colonel, who had been compelled for some years to keep a sufficient sum on current account at his bankers to make up their deficits, found that the provision was unnecessary: the young people were prospering. It is true that there was not quite fair play between them and their competitors in trade. Their week-ends in the country cost them nothing, and saved them the price of their Sunday dinners; for the motor car was the Colonel's; and he and Higgins paid the hotel bills. Mr F. Hill, florist and greengrocer (they soon discovered that there was money in asparagus; and asparagus led to other vegetables), had an air which stamped the business as classy; and in private life he was still Frederick Eynsford Hill, Esquire. Not that there was any swank about him: nobody but Eliza knew that he had been christened Frederick Challoner. Eliza herself swanked like anything.

That is all. That is how it has turned out. It is astonishing how much Eliza still manages to meddle in the housekeeping at Wimpole Street in spite of the shop and her own family. And it is notable that though she never nags her husband, and frankly loves the Colonel as if she were his favorite daughter, she has never got out of the habit of nagging Higgins that was established on the fatal night when she won his bet for him. She snaps his head off on the faintest provocation, or on none. He no longer dares to tease her by assuming an abysmal inferiority of Freddy's mind to his own. He storms and bullies and derides: but she stands up to him so ruthlessly that the Colonel has to ask her from time to time to be kinder to Higgins; and it is the only request of his that brings a mulish expression into her face. Nothing but some emergency or calamity great enough to break down all likes and dislikes, and throw them both back on their common humanity—and may they be spared any such trial!—will ever alter this. She knows that Higgins does not need her, just as her father did not need her. The very scrupulousness with which he told her that day that he had become used to having her there, and dependent on her for all sorts of little services, and that he should miss her if she went away (it would never have occurred to Freddy or the Colonel to say anything of the sort) deepens her inner certainty that she is "no more to him than them slippers"; yet she has a sense, too, that his indifference is deeper than the infatuation of commoner souls. She is immensely interested in him. She has even secret mischievous moments in which she wishes she could get him alone, on a desert island, away from all ties and with nobody else in the world to consider, and just drag him off his pedestal and see him making love like any common man. We all have private imaginations of that sort. But when it comes to business, to the life that she really leads as distinguished from the life of dreams and fancies, she likes Freddy and she likes the Colonel; and she does not like Higgins and Mr Doolittle. Galatea never does quite like Pygmalion: his relation to her is too godlike to be altogether agreeable.

Figure 1. A shabbily dressed and hesitant Eliza (Diana Rigg) listens to Higgins (Alec McCowen) explaining his plan to teach her how to speak properly. The 1974 London production was directed by John Dexter. (Photograph: Zoë Dominic, London.)

Figure 2. After insisting that she can teach phonetics herself, a poised and elegant Eliza (Diana Rigg) looks up at Higgins (Alec McCowen) with mingled fascination and resistance as he threatens to wring her neck. The 1974 London production was directed by John Dexter. (Photograph: Zoë Dominic. London.)

Figure 3. Beautifully outfitted, Eliza (Diana Rigg, *center*) tries out her new pronunciation and vocabulary at Mrs. Higgins's tea party. Listening to her are, *left to right*, Mrs. Higgins (Ellen Pollock), Colonel Pickering (Jack May), Mrs. Eynsford Hill (Margaret Ward), Clara Eynsford Hill (Sarah Atkinson), Higgins (Alec McCowen) and Freddy Eynsford Hill (Anthony Naylor). The richly detailed set and costumes were designed by Jocelyn Herbert and Andrew Sanders for the 1974 London production, directed by John Dexter. (Photograph: Zoë Dominic, London.)

Staging of *Pygmalion*

**REVIEW OF THE LONDON PRODUCTION, 1974,
BY RONALD BRYDEN**

As a rule, Norfolk has no flatness to match the second night of a show acclaimed to be a hit by the morning papers singing together. The nervous chemistry which triggered ovations is spent. The exhausted cast, carousing all night, have already passed from excitement to boredom at the certainty of a long run. The audience, serious playgoers in real clothes as opposed to the first night's fancy dress rout of backers' friends, sit baffled, wondering what the shouting was about. The revival of *Pygmalion* at the Old New, as I shall always think of the Albery Theatre, was the exception. Clearly the cast found it impossible to believe a success, in these days, wholly earned and deserved. Even at the second performance [they] were still beavering away earning it all over again.

Presumably they needed reassurance that one could market *My Fair Lady* without the songs and sentiment. Joy to the world, they were wrong. The man deserving their success most is Eddie Kulukundis, first impresario to recognise that beneath the mountain of royalties from Lerner and Loewe's extravaganza lay the 20th century classic ripest for rediscovery. Alongside the familiar pleasure of the real Eliza Doolittle's revelation within the bedraggled Covent Garden guttersnipe runs, in this production, the pleasure of the revelation of the play Shaw really wrote, crisp and twice as pertinent as the day he wrote it.

Did you think the day gone by when a comedy about a Cockney learning to talk Knightsbridge posh had anything to say to our cultural revolution, with its thousand local accents blooming together in the halls of Reith? You were thinking of the wrong play: not Shaw's but Alan Lerner's. Shaw's Professor Higgins is a modern phoneticist, with no preference between the accents by which England's classes proclaim themselves—'good English' to him is simply clear English, attainable only by foreigners, and he's as scathing about Mayfair's drawl as about Eliza's tortured vowels. The high point of the Shaw version isn't Cinderella going to the ball, but Cinderella shying the slipper in the prince's face and asking what made him think any girl in her right mind could want a life as useless as a princess's?

For, of course, there never was a ball scene in Shaw's *Pygmalion*. He pretended he left it out because it would cost too much even for Beerbohm Tree's Edwardian palace of spectacle, Her Majesty's. In fact, he knew perfectly well it could only obscure his real story line, as it has so fatally for the two generations brought up on Anthony Asquith's pre-war film and Lerner and Loewe's coster fantasia. One of the keenest pleasures of John Dexter's production is the beautifully ruthless cut

from Mrs. Higgins' third-act question, 'What's to become of her afterwards?', to afterwards itself—Eliza slumped despairingly in her diamonds on the same stool where she timidly perched on her arrival in Higgins' laboratory, fit for nothing but evenings as pointless and boring as the one she's just spent.

Indeed, the play has so many modern resonances you wonder whether Shaw wasn't in fact the last of the prophets. Acquired in a fit of absent-mindedness, Eliza in her helpless gentrification could stand for any former British colony left to its own devices with the crippling legacy of a one-crop economy, an education system geared to Oxbridge entry and class structure based on shades of Nordic pallor. Until Soyinka, one of the Naipauls or their equal replaces it, *Pygmalion* is the best play on post-imperialism we have. It's also the best answer yet to Germaine Greer and sisters. When Eliza sniffles about what she's been 'made into' by her masters in speech, Higgins roars at her to forget how men treat her and stand on her own feet—she won't be independent until she stops whining for men to recognise her independence, and takes it.

So that, for the first time since Beerbohm Tree bowdlerised the final curtain by tossing flowers to the departing Mrs. Patrick Campbell, the happy ending is the one Shaw wrote. Eliza takes her independence and goes out slamming the door, to turn Freddie Eynsford Hill into the same sort of full-grown human being Higgins has goaded her to become. Any other conclusion would be as bathetic as Mrs. Gandhi pleading for India's reannexation by the United Kingdom or Mrs. Pankhurst telling Lloyd George she didn't really want votes for women, thank you, she'd only done it because she secretly enjoyed forcible feeding.

The impossibility of Higgins and Eliza finally falling into each other's arms is underlined here by the presence of Alec McCowen and Diana Rigg in the roles. They make the characters fundamentally incompatible by being the same kind of actors. The strongest weapon of both is precision, verging on over-calculatedness. One can imagine their two minds meeting in the phonetic lessons, revelling in precise discrimination of sounds and precise imitation of them. Once their precision turns to any larger relationship between the pedant and his Galatea, it's clear the negotiations can never succeed. Precisely as Millamant and Mirabell hammer out the terms of their marriage contract in *The Way of the World,* this Eliza and Higgins haggle over the fine print of a possible merger and recognise that it will not work.

Neither is perfectly cast. The second level of Shaw's

joke was that his 'companion dreadnoughts' should be played by two sacred monsters of theatrical egotism like Tree and Mrs. Pat. He was fortunate that George Alexander's refusal of the play gave Higgins to Tree, the ultimate actor-manager. Higgins could become a parody of Tree's Svengali, a power-mad scientist into whose clutches the flower-girl falls, only to destroy him with the greater monstrosity of her Cockney sanity. (The nearest modern approach to Tree's Higgins would surely be Donald Sinden's; may it be soon.) McCowen can't play that. Instead he mines the role for the nuggets of psychology with which Shaw underpinned Tree's flamboyance: Higgins' admission that he never feels completely grown-up among other men; his dependence on his mother; his defensive barricading of himself behind the minutiae of a science concerned with self-presentation.

McCowen's precision can flower here—watch the marvellous, three-second movement with which he drops Eliza's hat when his housekeeper warns him of lice, shakes his fingers fastidiously, tells himself not to be ridiculous and hides the gesture by plunging his hands under his arms in a habitual Napoleonic stance of self-sufficiency. Instead of virtuoso floods of actor-managerish charm and temperament, he gives the subtext: the insecurity which makes Higgins all bark, botanical and canine. It's a colder reading than usual, but not without emotion. Implicit in his teaching of Eliza is his recognition of a being in the same need to learn self-presentation as himself. When she walks out at the end, his shoulders sag in recognition that he has created in her a strength beyond his own.

Against the odds, he earns success in the role. So in another way does Diana Rigg. The germ of Shaw's comedy was his detection beneath Mrs. Pat's *grande dame* languors of a coarse, quarrelsome strain of Cockney vulgarity. That layer of the part is beyond Miss Rigg, so she cleverly builds her performance from its other pole.

Her Cockney is not raucous but muffled: she makes its uncertainty Eliza's. The girl who walks into Higgins' parlour is only a fraction of herself. She mumbles, talks to herself, uses her limbs awkwardly. In the tea-party scene, she is a doll coming to life, Coppélia spinning out of control as selfhood floods into her wooden gestures.

Her brand of preciseness comes into its own here: I've never seen it played better. In the final acts, intelligence can take over. Eliza is herself, contained, exact and beautiful. The self-pity is played as a duty to herself, part of her negotiations with Higgins, but it's clear she would rather know where she stands than risk ambiguity staying with him. The incompleteness of characterisation is turned into the character: the full Eliza is only there at the end of the play. You can fault individual early bits, but you can't fault the whole conception, its acuteness or skill.

The leads justify casting against the grain by evolving during their performances. Bob Hoskins' Doolittle is all there from the moment he takes the stage, a philosophical walrus who puts a curve on his rhetoric rather as sealions curve their torsos to catch a fish. Ellen Pollock's Mrs. Higgins shapes itself beautifully against the two leads: you can see her demonstrating to Eliza the meaning of graceful movement, while relishing with a private vanity her son's admiration of it. So does Hilda Fenemore's Mrs. Pearce: it's clear that the housekeeper has found Higgins' weakness and exploits it, whereas once she finds Eliza's strength she stands back and washes her hands of her. The dove-tailing of these performances I suppose is John Dexter's special triumph: it's the tightest-woven stage household we've seen since his *Woman Killed With Kindness*. Jocelyn Herbert's and Andrew Sanders' sets are probably the best summary of the production: a shade diagrammatic, drawn rather than embodied, they earn success by sheer accuracy of line. It's a better kind of success, I'd say, than many more full-blown.

LUIGI PIRANDELLO

1867–1936

Pirandello's life was in many respects as problematic as the existence of the characters in his plays, and he playfully acknowledged its confusion by declaring himself to be "the son of Chaos." His father was actually the owner of a lucrative sulfur mine, and Pirandello was born on his father's country estate in a southern Sicilian locale, whose name was derived from the Greek word, chaos. Although his father had intended him to have a career in business, Pirandello was already writing poetry by the time he was sixteen, and when he was eighteen, having failed in a brief business venture, his father sent him off to the University of Rome. He subsequently attended the University of Bonn, where in 1891 he earned a doctorate in philology, but instead of pursuing a career in teaching and research he returned to Rome and immersed himself in writing poetry and fiction. By 1894, he had already published two volumes of poetry and a collection of short stories. Also in 1894, he was married off in an arrangement negotiated by his father and another sulfur-mine owner who wanted to unite their business interests. For its first ten years, the marriage was evidently a happy one, supported by the substantial wealth of both sets of parents, but in 1904 both sulfur mines were destroyed by a flood. The news of this disaster was so shocking to Pirandello's wife that she fainted on hearing it, was subsequently completely paralyzed for six months, and then gradually went insane. Pirandello was forced to take a position teaching literature at a girl's school, an arrangement that provoked his wife to have hysterical fits of jealousy. Her derangement repeatedly caused her to become physically violent, yet Pirandello persisted in taking care of her himself for fifteen years, until in 1919 his friends finally convinced him to have her committed to a mental institution.

Pirandello continued to write during all the years of living through his wife's insanity and through the insanity of World War I, which divided his allegiances between Germany, a country he admired for its learning and scholarship, and Italy, his own country, which entered the conflict in 1916 on the side of the English and French. By 1916, he had published several volumes of short stories, several novels, several collections of poetry, and three one-act plays, and in virtually all these works he expressed a relativistic view of existence that he appears to have been driven to by the chaotic nature of his own personal experience. In his most well-known novel, *The Late Mattia Pascal* (1905), for example, he told the story of a man who discovers that because he left some belongings on a bridge everyone thinks he has committed suicide. Having made this discovery, the man decides to capitalize on the misunderstanding by trying to start a new life, free of the deceptions and role-playing that had characterized his old one. But he at once realizes that he must take a new role, in order to prevent his earlier identity from being discovered, and thus gradually recognizes that his personality is not his own creation, but an appearance forced on him by what is expected in his own society.

The predicament of Mattia Pascal epitomizes Pirandello's persistent concerns: the inescapable compulsion of human beings to play roles, to assume so many guises, in fact, that they can never be certain even of their own personal character, much less that of anyone else they encounter in the world. Pirandello explicitly defined his concern with these problems in 1920, shortly before the appearance of *Six Characters in Search of an Author* (1922):

> I think that life is a very sad piece of buffoonery: because we have in ourselves, without being able to know why, wherefore or whence, the need to deceive ourselves constantly by creating a reality (one for each and never the same for all), which from time to time is discovered to be vain and illusory.

The vanity and the illusoriness of this "buffoonery" provided Pirandello with the grounds for all of his writing:

> My art is full of bitter compassion for all those who deceive themselves; but this compassion cannot fail to be followed by the ferocious derision of destiny which condemns man to deception.

His "bitter compassion," fed by the irrationality of the war, evidently moved him to turn to playwriting, for between 1916 and 1921 in a fury of productivity he produced a total of fifteen plays.

Pirandello dramatized his relativistic vision most explicitly in a play appropriately titled *Right You Are, If You Think You Are* (1917), which depicts the futile attempts of an Italian community to unravel the truth about a husband, his wife, and his mother-in-law who have come to live in their city. The mother-in-law, for example, tells one story about their situation, which is subsequently contradicted by that of the husband, who appears to demonstrate that his mother-in-law is insane, but his version of their situation is, in turn, discredited by another story from his mother-in-law that appears to prove that he is a madman, and the action of the play repeatedly complicates the problem of determining the truth about the family without ever resolving it. As the wife (who appears only at the end of the play) says, "I am the one that each of you thinks I am." Truth is thus presented to be as unstable, as variable, as the differing perceptions of every member in the community. The maddening implications of this vision were dramatized by Pirandello in *Enrico IV* (1922), a play that portrays the schizophrenic experience of a man who recovers from a long psychotic delusion about himself only to perpetuate his madness as a deliberate pose. But at the end of the play, his deliberate choice turns into an eternal necessity, when he kills a man who has accused him of being sane and finds that in order to escape a charge of murder he must retreat forever into the role of being a madman.

By the end of his life, Pirandello had dramatized his haunting view of existence in nearly forty plays, but none of them achieved the enduring fame of *Six Characters in Search of an Author* (1922). Its unique dramatic power is in large part the result of Pirandello's reclaiming of a traditional dramatic form—the play within the play—and a traditional dramatic metaphor for the vanity of existence—"Life's but . . . a poor player that struts and frets his hour upon the stage and then is heard no more." Pirandello has used these traditional elements to present his relativistic vision in its most disturbingly complicated form. From the moment the six characters appear on stage seeking an author to tell their story and a producer to dramatize their experience, Pirandello gradually unfolds the dizzying ramifications of his relativistic view: in the Father's repeated explanations of it that the Producer repeatedly denies even in the face of the hopeless confusion unfolding before him, in the repeated attempts of the Stepdaughter to have the story played from her perspective that the Father repeatedly claims to be a distortion of his true character, in the almost inarticulate desire of the Mother to have her older son express the affection and forgiveness that she feels is warranted from her point of view, in the Son's attempt to proclaim his lack of complicity in the gruesome tragedy despite being one of the villains of the piece, and, of course, in the inability of any of the characters or actors to understand each other at all. The play moves inexorably to its final frenzy of yelling, one side shouting "Reality!" the other "Make-believe!" And Pirandello's symbolic comment on this confusion is to plunge the theater into darkness, so that even the Producer, so staunchly sure of the truth, cannot see where he is going. Although the play is clearly an enactment of Pirandello's relativistic philosophy, it may also be seen as dramatizing the problematic relationship between art and life, between performance and existence. The characters' search for an author may also be viewed as a compelling psychological study of the anxiety—even the schizophrenia—that results from the felt absence of a stable authority figure. Even the Father, the traditional image of authority, is seeking a reliable source of authority, but the only authority figure in the play, the Producer, is equally unreliable.

When *Six Characters* was first produced in Rome, the audience turned into a madhouse of excitement at the end of the play. When it was produced in Paris in 1923, it stunned the French theatrical world and led to a torrent of dramatic imitations. Wherever and whenever it is produced, in fact, it provokes the excitement of audiences and critics, as evidenced by the review of the American Conservatory Theater production, reprinted following the text. Photographs of that production clearly show the haunting expressions and gestures the performers displayed in acting the roles of the six characters (see Figures 1 and 2) as well as the outrage of the Stepdaughter at the moment the Father is attempting to seduce her (Figure 3), a moment epitomizing Pirandello's disturbing view of experience.

SIX CHARACTERS IN SEARCH OF AN AUTHOR

BY LUIGI PIRANDELLO / TRANSLATED BY FREDERICK MAY

CHARACTERS OF THE PLAY IN THE MAKING

THE FATHER
THE MOTHER
THE STEPDAUGHTER
THE SON
THE BOY (*nonspeaking*)
THE LITTLE GIRL (*nonspeaking*)
MADAME PACE (*who is called into being*)

THE STAGE MANAGER
THE PROMPTER
THE PROPERTY MAN
THE FOREMAN OF THE STAGE CREW
THE PRODUCER'S SECRETARY
THE COMMISSIONAIRE
STAGE HANDS AND OTHER THEATRE PERSONNEL

THE ACTORS IN THE COMPANY

THE PRODUCER (*Director*)
THE LEADING LADY
THE LEADING MAN
THE SECOND FEMALE LEAD (*referred to as* THE SECOND
ACTRESS *in the text.*)
THE INGENUE
THE JUVENILE LEAD
OTHER ACTORS AND ACTRESSES

SCENE

Daytime: The Stage of a Theatre

N.B. The play has neither acts nor scenes. Its performance will be interrupted twice: once—though the curtain will not be lowered—when the PRODUCER *and the principal* CHARACTERS *go away to write the script and the* ACTORS *leave the stage, and a second time when the Man on the Curtain lets it fall by mistake.*

ACT 1

(*When the audience enters the auditorium the curtain is up and the stage is just as it would be during the daytime. There is no set and there are no wings; it is empty and in almost total darkness. This is in order that right from the very beginning the audience shall receive the impression of being present, not at a performance of a carefully rehearsed play, but at a performance of a play that suddenly happens.*

Two small flights of steps, one right and one left, give access to the stage from the auditorium.

On the stage itself, the prompter's dome has been removed, and is standing just to one side of the prompt box.

Downstage, on the other side, a small table and an armchair with its back turned to the audience have been set for the Producer.

Two more small tables, one rather larger than the other, together with several chairs, have been set downstage so that they are ready if needed for the rehearsal. There are other chairs scattered about to the left and to the right for the actors, and, in the background, to one side and almost hidden, there is a pianoforte.

When the house lights go down the FOREMAN *comes on to the stage through the back door. He is dressed in blue dungarees and carries his tools in a bag slung at his belt. From a corner at the back of the stage he takes one or two*

slats of wood, brings them down front, kneels down and starts nailing them together. At the sound of his hammer the STAGE MANAGER rushes in from the direction of the dressing-rooms.)

STAGE MANAGER: Hey! What are you doing?

FOREMAN: What am I doing? Hammering . . . nails.

STAGE MANAGER: At this time of day? (*He looks at his watch.*) It's gone half-past ten! The Producer'll be here any minute now and he'll want to get on with his rehearsal.

FOREMAN: And let me tell *you* something . . . I've got to have time to do *my* work, too.

STAGE MANAGER: You'll get it, you'll get it. . . . But you can't do that *now*.

FOREMAN: When can I do it then?

STAGE MANAGER: After the rehearsal. Now, come on. . . . Clear up all this mess, and let me get on with setting the second act of *The Game As He Played It*.

(*The* FOREMAN *gathers his pieces of wood together, muttering and grumbling all the while, and goes off. Meanwhile, the* ACTORS OF THE COMPANY *have begun to come on to the stage through the door back. First one comes in, then another, then two together . . . just as they please. There are nine or ten of them in all–as many as you would suppose you would need for the rehearsal of Pirandello's play,* The Game As He Played It, *which*

692

has been called for today. As they come in they greet one another and the STAGE MANAGER with a cheery 'Good morning'. Some of them go off to their dressing-rooms; others, and among them the PROMPTER, who is carrying the prompt copy rolled up under his arm, remain on the stage, waiting for the PRODUCER to come and start the rehearsal. While they are waiting—some of them standing, some seated about in small groups—they exchange a few words among themselves. One lights a cigarette, another complains about the part that he's been given and a third reads out an item of news from a theatrical journal for the benefit of the other actors. It would be best if all the ACTORS and ACTRESSES could be dressed in rather bright and gay clothes. This first improvised scene should be played very naturally and with great vivacity. After a while, one of the comedy men can sit down at the piano and start playing a dance-tune. The younger ACTORS and ACTRESSES start dancing.)

STAGE MANAGER (clapping his hands to restore order): Come on, now, come on! That's enough of that! Here's the producer!

(The music and dancing come to a sudden stop. The ACTORS turn and look out into the auditorium and see the PRODUCER, who is coming in through the door. He comes up the gangway between the stalls, bowler hat on head, stick under arm, and a large cigar in his mouth, to the accompaniment of a chorus of 'Good-mornings' from the ACTORS and climbs up one of the flights of steps on to the stage. His SECRETARY offers him his post—a newspaper or so, a script.)

PRODUCER: Any letters?

SECRETARY: None at all. This is all the post there is.

PRODUCER (handing him back the script): Put it in my office. (Then, looking around and turning to the STAGE MANAGER.) Oh, you can't see a thing here! Ask them to give us a spot of light, please.

STAGE MANAGER: Right you are!

(He goes off to give the order and a short while after the whole of the right side of the stage, where the ACTORS are standing, is lit up by a bright white light. In the meantime the PROMPTER has taken his place in his box, switched on his light and spread his script out in front of him.)

PRODUCER (clapping his hands): Come on, let's get started! (to the STAGE MANAGER) Anyone missing?

STAGE MANAGER: The Leading Lady.

PRODUCER: As usual! (Looks at his watch.) We're ten minutes late already. Make a note, will you, please, to remind me to give her a good talking-to about being so late! It might teach her to get to rehearsals on time in the future.

(He has scarcely finished his rebuke when the voice of the LEADING LADY is heard at the back of the auditorium.)

LEADING LADY: No, please don't! Here I am! Here I am! (She is dressed completely in white, with a large and rather dashing and provocative hat, and is carrying a dainty little lap-dog. She runs down the aisle and hastily climbs up the steps on to the stage.)

PRODUCER: You've set your heart on always keeping us waiting, haven't you?

LEADING LADY: Forgive me! I hunted everywhere for a taxi so that I should get here on time! But you haven't started yet, anyway. And I don't come on immediately. (Then, calling the STAGE MANAGER by name, she gives him the lap-dog.) Please put him in my dressing-room . . . and mind you shut the door!

PRODUCER (grumblingly): And she has to bring a dog along too! As if there weren't enough dogs around here! (He claps his hands again and turns to the PROMPTER.) Come on now, let's get on with Act II of The Game As He Played It. (He sits down in the armchair.) Now, ladies and gentlemen, who's on?

(The ACTORS and ACTRESSES clear away from the front of the stage and go and sit to one side, except for the three who start the scene, and the LEADING LADY. She has paid no attention to the PRODUCER's question and has seated herself at one of the little tables.)

PRODUCER (to the LEADING LADY): Ah! So you're in this scene, are you?

LEADING LADY: Me? Oh, no!

PRODUCER (annoyed): Then for God's sake get off!

(And the LEADING LADY gets up and goes and sits with the others.)

PRODUCER (to the PROMPTER): Now, let's get started!

PROMPTER (reading from his script): "The house of Leone Gala. A strange room, half dining-room, half study."

PRODUCER (turning to the STAGE MANAGER): We'll use the red set.

STAGE MANAGER (making a note on a sheet of paper): The red set. Right!

PROMPTER (continuing to read from his script): "A table laid for a meal and a desk with books and papers. Bookshelves with books on them. Glass-fronted cupboards containing valuable china. A door back leading into Leone's bedroom. A side door left, leading into the kitchen. The main entrance is right."

PRODUCER (getting up and pointing): Right! Now listen carefully—over there, the main entrance. And over here, the kitchen. (Turning to the ACTOR who is to play the part of Socrates.) You'll make your entrances and exits this side. (to the STAGE MANAGER) We'll have that green-baize door at the back there . . . and some curtains. (He goes and sits down again.)

STAGE MANAGER (making a note): Right you are!

PROMPTER (*reading*): "Scene I. Leone Gala, Guido Venanzi, Filippo, who is called Socrates." (*to the* PRODUCER) Do I have to read the stage directions as well?

PRODUCER: Yes, yes, of course! I've told you that a hundred times!

PROMPTER (*reading*): "When the curtain rises. Leone Gala, wearing a cook's hat and apron, is busy beating an egg in a basin, with a wooden spoon. Filippo, also dressed as a cook, is beating another egg. Guido Venanzi is sitting listening to them."

LEADING MAN (*to the* PRODUCER): Excuse me, but do I really have to wear a cook's hat?

PRODUCER (*irritated by this observation*): So it seems! That's certainly what's written there! (*He points to the script.*)

LEADING MAN: Forgive me for saying so, but it's ridiculous.

PRODUCER (*bounding to feet in fury*): Ridiculous! Ridiculous! What do you expect me to do if the French haven't got any more good comedies to send us, and we're reduced to putting on plays by Pirandello? And if you can understand *his* plays . . . you're a better man than I am! He deliberately goes out of his way to annoy people, so that by the time the play's through everybody's fed up . . . actors, critics, audience, everybody! (*The* ACTORS *laugh. Then getting up and going over to the* LEADING MAN, *the* PRODUCER *cries.*) Yes, my dear fellow, a cook's hat! And you beat eggs! And do you think that, having these eggs to beat, you then have nothing more on your hands? Oh, no, not a bit of it. . . . You have to represent the shell of the eggs that you're beating! (*The* ACTORS *start laughing again and begin to make ironical comments among themselves.*) Shut up! And listen when I'm explaining things! (*Turning again to the* LEADING MAN.) Yes, my dear fellow, the shell . . . or, as you might say, the empty form of reason, without that content of instinct which is blind! You are reason and your wife is instinct, in a game where you play the parts which have been given you. And all the time you're playing your part, you are the self-willed puppet of yourself. Understand?

LEADING MAN (*spreading out his hands*): Me? No!

PRODUCER (*returning to his seat*): Neither do I! However, let's get on with it! It's going to be a wonderful flop, anyway! (*In a confidential tone.*) I suggest you turn to the audience a bit more . . . about three-quarters face. Otherwise, what with the abstruseness of the dialogue, and the audience's not being able to hear you, the whole thing'll go to hell. (*Clapping his hands again.*) Now, come along! *Come along!* Let's get started!

PROMPTER: Excuse me, sir, do you mind if I put the top back on my box? There's a bit of a draught.

PRODUCER: Of course! Go ahead! Go ahead!

(*Meanwhile the* COMMISSIONAIRE *has entered the auditorium. He is wearing a braided cap and, having covered the length of the aisle, he comes up to the edge of the stage to announce the arrival of the* SIX CHARACTERS *to the* PRODUCER. *They have followed the* COMMISSIONAIRE *into the auditorium and have walked behind him as he has come up to the stage. They look about them, a little perplexed and a little dismayed.*

In any production of this play it is imperative that the producer should use every means possible to avoid any confusion between the SIX CHARACTERS *and the* ACTORS. *The placing of the two groups, as they will be indicated in the stage-directions once the* CHARACTERS *are on the stage, will no doubt help. So, too, will their being lit in different colors. But the most effective and most suitable method of distinguishing them that suggests itself, is the use of special masks for the* CHARACTERS, *masks specially made from some material which will not grow limp with perspiration and will at the same time be light enough to be worn by the actors playing these parts. They should be cut so as to leave the eyes, the nose and the mouth free. In this way the deep significance of the play can be brought out. The* CHARACTERS *should not, in fact, appear as phantasms, but as created realities, unchangeable creations of the imagination and, therefore, more real and more consistent than the ever-changing naturalness of the* ACTORS.

The masks will assist in giving the impression of figures constructed by art, each one fixed immutably in the expression of that sentiment which is fundamental to it. That is to say in REMORSE *for the* FATHER, REVENGE *for the* STEPDAUGHTER, CONTEMPT *for the* SON *and* SORROW *for the* MOTHER. *Her mask should have wax tears fixed in the corners of the eyes and coursing down the cheeks, just like those which are carved and painted in the representations of the Mater Dolorosa that are to be seen in churches.*

Her dress, too, should be of a special material and cut. It should be severely plain, its folds stiff, giving in fact the appearance of having been carved, and not of being made of any material that you can just go out and buy or have cut-out and made up into a dress by any ordinary dressmaker.

The FATHER *is a man of about fifty. He is not bald but his reddish hair is thin at the temples. His moustache is thick and coils over his still rather youthful-looking mouth, which all too often falls open in a purposeless, uncertain smile. His complexion is pale and this is especially noticeable when one has occasion to look at his forehead, which is particularly broad. His blue, oval-shaped eyes are very clear and piercing. He is wearing a dark jacket and light-coloured trousers. At times his manner is all sweetness and light, at others it is hard and harsh.*

The MOTHER *appears as a woman crushed and ter-*

rified by an intolerable weight of shame and abasement. She is dressed in a modest black and wears a thick crepe widow's veil. When she lifts her veil she reveals a wax-like face; it is not, however at all sickly looking. She keeps her eyes downcast all the time. The STEPDAUGHTER, *who is eighteen, is defiant, bold, arrogant—almost shamelessly so. She is very beautiful. She, too, is dressed in mourning but carries it with a decided air of showy elegance. She shows contempt for the very timid, dejected, half-frightened manner of her younger brother, a rather grubby and unprepossessing* BOY *of fourteen, who is also dressed in black. On the other hand she displays a very lively tenderness for her small sister, a* LITTLE GIRL *of about four, who is wearing a white frock with a black silk sash round her waist.*

The SON *is a tall young man of twenty-two. He is wearing a mauve-coloured overcoat and has a long green scarf twisted round his neck. He appears as if he has stiffened into an attitude of contempt for the* FATHER *and of supercilious indifference toward the* MOTHER.*)*

COMMISSIONAIRE *(cap in hand):* Excuse me, sir.

PRODUCER *(snapping at him rudely):* Now what's the matter?

COMMISSIONAIRE: There are some people here, sir, asking for you.

(The PRODUCER *and the* ACTORS *turn in astonishment and look out into the auditorium.)*

PRODUCER *(furiously):* But I've got a rehearsal on at the moment! And you know quite well that no one's allowed in here while a rehearsal's going on. *(Then addressing the* CHARACTERS.) Who are you? What do you want?

FATHER *(he steps forward, followed by the others, and comes to the foot of one of the flights of steps):* We are here in search of an author.

PRODUCER *(caught between anger and utter astonishment):* In search of an author? Which author?

FATHER: Any author, sir.

PRODUCER: But there's no author here. . . . We're rehearsing a new play.

STEPDAUGHTER *(vivaciously, as she rushes up the steps):* So much the better! Then so much the better, sir! We can be your new play.

ONE OF THE ACTORS *(amidst the lively comments and laughter of the others):* Oh, just listen to her! *Listen* to her!

FATHER *(following the* STEPDAUGHTER *on to the stage):* Yes, but if there isn't any author. . . . *(to the* PRODUCER) Unless you'd like to be the author. . . .

(Holding the LITTLE GIRL *by the hand, the* MOTHER, *followed by the* BOY, *climbs up the first steps leading to the stage and stands there expectantly. The* SON *remains morosely below.)*

PRODUCER: Are you people trying to be funny?

FATHER: No. . . . How can you suggest such a thing? On the contrary, we are bringing you a terrible and grievous drama.

STEPDAUGHTER: And we might make your fortune for you.

PRODUCER: Perhaps you'll do me the kindness of getting out of this theatre! We've got no time to waste on lunatics!

FATHER *(he is wounded by this, but replies in a gentle tone):* Oh . . . But you know very well, don't you, that life is full of things that are infinitely absurd, things that, for all their impudent absurdity, have no need to masquerade as truth, because they are true.

PRODUCER: What the devil are you talking about?

FATHER: What I'm saying is that reversing the usual order of things, forcing oneself to a contrary way of action, may well be construed as madness. As, for instance, when we create things which have all the appearance of reality in order that they shall look like the realities themselves. But allow me to observe that if this indeed be madness, it is, nonetheless, the sole *raison d'etre* of your profession.

(The ACTORS *stir indignantly at this.)*

PRODUCER *(getting up and looking him up and down):* Oh, yes? do you think ours is a profession of lunatics, do you?

FATHER: Yes, making what isn't true *seem* true . . . without having to . . . for fun. . . . Isn't it your function to give life on the stage to imaginary characters?

PRODUCER *(immediately, making himself spokesman for the growing anger of his actors):* I should like you to know, my dear sir, that the actor's profession is a most noble one. and although nowadays, with things in the state they are, our playwrights give us stupid comedies to act, and puppets to represent instead of men, I'd have you know that it is our boast that we have given life, here on these very boards, to immortal works!

(The ACTORS *satisfiedly murmur their approval and applaud the* PRODUCER.)*

FATHER *(breaking in and following hard on his argument):* There you are! Oh, that's it exactly! To living beings . . . to beings who are more alive than those who breathe and wear clothes! Less real, perhaps, but truer! We're in complete agreement!

(The ACTORS *look at each other in utter astonishment.)*

PRODUCER: But . . . What on earth! . . . But you said just now . . .

FATHER: No, I said that because of your . . . because

you shouted at us that you had no time to waste on lunatics . . . while nobody can know better than you that nature makes use of the instrument of human fantasy to pursue her work of creation on a higher level.

PRODUCER: True enough! True enough! But where does all this get us?

FATHER: Nowhere. I only wish to show you that one is born into life in so many ways, in so many forms. . . . As a tree, or as a stone; as water or as a butterfly. . . . Or as a woman. And that one can be born a character.

PRODUCER (ironically, feigning amazement): And you together with these other people, were born a character?

FATHER: Exactly. And alive, as you see. (The PRODUCER and the ACTORS burst out laughing as if at some huge joke.) (Hurt.) I'm sorry that you laugh like that because, I repeat, we carry within ourselves a terrible and grievous drama, as you can deduce for yourselves from this woman veiled in black.

(And so saying, he holds out his hand to the MOTHER and helps her up the last few steps and, continuing to hold her hand, leads her with a certain tragic solemnity to the other side of the stage, which immediately lights up with a fantastic kind of light. The LITTLE GIRL and the BOY follow their MOTHER. Next the SON comes up and goes and stands to one side, in the background. Then the STEPDAUGHTER follows him on to the stage; she stands downstage, leaning against the proscenium arch. The ACTORS are at first completely taken-aback and then, caught in admiration at this development, they burst into applause—just as if they had had a show put on for their benefit.)

PRODUCER (at first utterly astonished and then indignant): Shut up! what the . . . ! (Then turning to the CHARACTERS.) And you get out of here! Clear out of here! (to the STAGE MANAGER) For God's sake, clear them out!

STAGE MANAGER (coming forward, but then stopping as if held back by some strange dismay): Go away! Go away!

FATHER (to the PRODUCER): No, no! Listen. . . . We. . . .

PRODUCER (shouting): I tell you, we've got work to do!

LEADING MAN: You can't go about playing practical jokes like this. . . .

FATHER (resolutely coming forward): I wonder at your incredulity. Is it perhaps that you're not accustomed to seeing the characters created by an author leaping to life up here on the stage, when they come face to face with each other? Or is it, perhaps, that there's no script there (He points to the prompt box.) that contains us?

STEPDAUGHTER (smiling, she steps toward the PRODUCER; then, in a wheedling voice): Believe me, sir, we really are six characters . . . and very, very interesting! But we've been cut adrift.

FATHER (brushing her aside): Yes, that's it, we've been cut adrift. (And then immediately to the PRODUCER.) In the sense, you understand, that the author who created us as living beings, either couldn't or wouldn't put us materially into the world of art. And it was truly a crime . . . because he who has the good fortune to be born a living character may snap his fingers at Death even. He will never die! Man . . . The writer . . . The instrument of creation . . . Will die. . . . But what is created by him will never die. And in order to live eternally he has not the slightest need of extraordinary gifts or of accomplishing prodigies. Who was Sancho Panza? Who was Don Abbondio? And yet they live eternally because—living seeds—they had the good fortune to find a fruitful womb—a fantasy which knew how to raise and nourish them, and to make them live through all eternity.

PRODUCER: All this is very, very fine indeed. . . . But what do you want here?

FATHER: We wish to live, sir!

PRODUCER (ironically): Through all eternity?

FATHER: No sir; just a moment . . . in you.

AN ACTOR: Listen to him! . . . listen to him!

LEADING LADY: They want to live in us!

JUVENILE LEAD (pointing to the STEPDAUGHTER): I've no objection . . . so long as I get her.

FATHER: Listen! Listen! The play is in the making. (to the PRODUCER) But if you and your actors are willing, we can settle it all between us without further delay.

PRODUCER (annoyed): But what do you want to settle? We don't go in for that sort of concoction here! We put on comedies and dramas here.

FATHER: Exactly! That's the very reason why we came to you.

PRODUCER: And where's the script?

FATHER: It is in us, sir. (The ACTORS laugh.) The drama is in us. We are the drama and we are impatient to act it—so fiercely does our inner passion urge us on.

STEPDAUGHTER (scornful, treacherous, alluring, with deliberate shamelessness): My passion. . . . If you only knew! My passion . . . for him! (She points to the FATHER and makes as if to embrace him, but then bursts into strident laughter.)

FATHER (at once, angrily): You keep out of this for the moment! And please don't laugh like that!

STEPDAUGHTER: Oh . . . mayn't I? Then perhaps you'll allow me, ladies and gentlemen. . . . Although it's scarcely two months since my father died . . . just you watch how I can dance and sing! (Mischievously she starts to sing Dave Stamper's

"Prends garde à Tchou-Tchin-Tchou" in the fox-trot or slow one-step version by François Salabert. She sings the first verse, accompanying it with a dance.)

Les chinois sont un peuple malin,
De Shangai à Pékin,
Ils ont mis des écriteaux partout:
Prenez garde à Tchou-Tchin-Tchou!

(While she is singing and dancing, the ACTORS, *and especially the younger ones, as if attracted by some strange fascination, move toward her and half raise their hands as though to catch hold of her. She runs away, and when the* ACTORS *burst into applause, and the* PRODUCER *rebukes her, she stands where she is, quietly, abstractedly, and as if her thoughts were far away.)*

ACTORS and ACTRESSES *(laughing and clapping)*: Well done! Jolly good!

PRODUCER *(irately)*: Shut up! What do you think this is . . . a cabaret? *(Then taking the* FATHER *a little to one side, he says with a certain amount of consternation.)* Tell me something. . . . Is she mad?

FATHER: What do you mean, mad? It's worse than that!

STEPDAUGHTER *(immediately rushing up to the* PRODUCER*)*: Worse! Worse! Oh it's something very much worse than that! Listen! Let's put this drama on at once . . . Please! Then you'll see that at a certain moment I . . . when this little darling here. . . . *(Takes the* LITTLE GIRL *by the hand and brings her over to the* PRODUCER.*)* . . . Isn't she a dear? *(Takes her in her arms and kisses her.)* You little darling! . . . You dear little darling! *(Puts her down again, adding in a moved tone, almost without wishing to.)* Well, when God suddenly takes this child away from her poor mother, and that little imbecile there *(Roughly grabbing hold of the* BOY *by the sleeve and thrusting him forward.)* does the stupidest of all stupid things, like the idiot he is *(Pushing him back toward the* MOTHER.*)* . . . Then you will see me run away. Yes, I shall run away! And, oh, how I'm longing for that moment to come! Because after all the very intimate things that have happened between him and me *(With a horrible wink in the direction of the* FATHER.*)* I can't remain any longer with these people . . . having to witness my mother's anguish because of that queer fish there *(Pointing to the* SON.*)* Look at him! Look at him! See how indifferent, how frigid he is . . . because he's the legitimate son . . . *he* is! He despises me, he despises him *(Pointing to the* BOY.*)*, he despises that dear little creature. . . . Because we're bastards! Do you understand? . . . Because we're *bastards! (She goes up to the* MOTHER *and embraces her.)* And he doesn't want to recog-

nize this poor woman as his mother. . . . This poor woman . . . who is the mother of us all! He looks down at her as if she were only the mother of us three bastards! The wretch! *(She says all this very quickly and very excitedly. She raises her voice at the word 'bastards' and the final "wretch" is delivered in a low voice and almost spat out.)*

MOTHER *(to the* PRODUCER, *an infinity of anguish in her voice)*: Please, in the name of these two little children . . . I beg you. . . . *(She grows faint and sways on her feet.)* Oh, my God! *(Consternation and bewilderment among the* ACTORS.*)*

FATHER *(rushing over to support her, accompanied by most of the* ACTORS*)*: Quick . . . a chair. . . . A chair for this poor widow!

ACTORS *(rushing over)*: Has she fainted? Has she fainted?

PRODUCER: Quick, get a chair . . . get a chair!

(One of the ACTORS *brings a chair, the others stand around, anxious to help in any way they can. The* MOTHER *sits on the chair; she attempts to prevent the* FATHER *from lifting the veil which hides her face.)*

FATHER: Look at her. . . . Look at her. . . .

MOTHER: No, no! My God! Stop it, please!

FATHER: Let them see you. *(He lifts her veil.)*

MOTHER *(rising and covering her face with her hands in desperation)*: I beg you, sir, . . . Don't let this man carry out his plan! You must prevent him. . . . It's horrible!

PRODUCER *(utterly dumbfounded)*: I don't get this at all. . . . I haven't got the slightest idea what you're talking about. *(to the* FATHER*)* Is this lady your wife?

FATHER *(immediately)*: Yes, sir, my wife.

PRODUCER: Then how does it come about that she's a widow if you're still alive?

(The ACTORS *find relief for their bewilderment and astonishment in a noisy burst of laughter.)*

FATHER *(wounded, speaking with sharp resentment)*: Don't laugh! Don't laugh like that, for pity's sake! It is in this fact that her drama lies. She had another man. Another man who ought to be here.

MOTHER *(with a cry)*: No! No!

STEPDAUGHTER: He's got the good luck to be dead. . . . He died two months ago, as I just told you. We're still wearing mourning for him, as you can see.

FATHER: But it's not because he's dead that he's not here. No, he's not here because . . . Look at her! Look at her, please, and you'll understand immediately! Her drama does not lie in the love of two men for whom she, being incapable of love, could feel nothing. . . . Unless, perhaps, it be a little gratitude . . . to him, not to me. She is not a woman. . . . She is a mother. And her drama. . . . And how powerful it is! How powerful it is! . . . Her drama lies entirely, in fact, in these four children. . . . The children of the two men that she had.

MOTHER: Did you say that I had them? Do you dare to say that I *had* these two men . . . to suggest that I wanted them? *(to the* PRODUCER*)* It was his doing. He gave him to me! He forced him on me! He forced me. . . . He forced me to go away with that other man!

STEPDAUGHTER *(at once, indignantly)*: It's not true!

MOTHER *(startled)*: Not true?

STEPDAUGHTER: It's not true! It's not true, I say.

MOTHER: And what can you possibly know about it?

STEPDAUGHTER: It's not true! *(to the* PRODUCER*)* Don't believe her! Do you know why she said that? Because of him. *(Pointing to the* SON.*)* That's why she said it! Because she tortures herself, wears herself out with anguish, because of the indifference of that son of hers. She wants him to believe that if she abandoned him when he was two years old it was because he *(Pointing to the* FATHER.*)* forced her to do it.

MOTHER *(forcefully)*: He forced me to do it! He forced me, as God is my witness! *(to the* PRODUCER*)* Ask him *(Pointing to her* HUSBAND.*)* if it's not true! Make him tell my son! She *(Pointing to her* DAUGHTER.*)* knows nothing at all about the matter.

STEPDAUGHTER: I know that while my father lived you were always happy. . . . You had a peaceful and contented life together. Deny it if you can!

MOTHER: I don't deny it! No. . . .

STEPDAUGHTER: He was always most loving, always kindness itself towards you. *(to the* BOY, *angrily)* Isn't it true? Go on. . . . Say it's true! Why don't you speak, you stupid little idiot?

MOTHER: Leave the poor boy alone! Why do you want to make me appear an ungrateful woman? I don't want to say anything against your father. . . . I only said that it wasn't my fault, and that it wasn't just to satisfy my own desires that I left his house and abandoned my son.

FATHER: What she says is true. It was my doing.

(There is a pause.)

LEADING MAN *(to the other* ACTORS*)*: My God! What a show!

LEADING LADY: And we're the audience this time!

JUVENILE LEAD: For once in a while.

PRODUCER *(who is beginning to show a lively interest)*: Let's listen to this! Let's hear what they've got to say! *(And saying this he goes down the steps into the auditorium and stands in front of the stage, as if to get an impression of the scene from the audience's point of view.)*

SON *(without moving from where he is, speaking coldly, softly, ironically)*: Yes! Listen to the chunk of philosophy you're going to get now. He will tell you all about the Demon of Experiment.

FATHER: You're a cynical idiot, as I've told you a hundred times. *(Down to the* PRODUCER.*)* He mocks me because of this expression that I've discovered in my own defence.

SON *(contemptuously)*: Words! Words!

FATHER: Yes! Words! Words! They can always bring consolation to us. . . . To everyone of us. . . . When we're confronted by something for which there's no explanation. . . . When we're face to face with an evil that consumes us. . . . The consolation of finding a word that tells us nothing, but that brings us peace.

STEPDAUGHTER: And dulls our sense of remorse, too. Yes! That above all!

FATHER: Dulls our sense of remorse? No, that's not true. It wasn't with words alone that I quietened remorse within me.

STEPDAUGHTER: No, you did it with a little money as well. Yes! Oh, yes! with a little money as well! With the hundred lire that he was going to offer me . . . as payment, ladies and gentlemen!

(A movement of horror on the part of the ACTORS.*)*

SON *(contemptuously to his* STEPSISTER*)*: That was vile!

STEPDAUGHTER: Vile? There they were, in a pale blue envelope, on the little mahogany table in the room behind Madame Pace's shop. Madame Pace. . . . One of those *Madames* who pretend to sell *Robes et Manteaux* so that they can attract us poor girls from decent families into their workrooms.

SON: And she's bought the right to tyrannise over the whole lot of us with those hundred lire that he was going to pay her. . . . But by good fortune. . . . And let me emphasise this. . . . He had no reason to pay her anything.

STEPDAUGHTER: Yes, but it was a very near thing! Oh, yes, it was, you know! *(She bursts out laughing.)*

MOTHER *(rising to protest)*: For shame! For shame!

STEPDAUGHTER *(immediately)*: Shame? No! This is my revenge! I'm trembling with desire. . . . Simply trembling with desire to live that scene! That room. . . . Over there the divan, the long mirror and a screen. . . . And in front of the window that little mahogany table. . . . And the pale blue envelope with the hundred lire inside. Yes, I can see it quite clearly! I'd only have to stretch out my hand and I could pick it up! But you gentlemen really ought to turn your backs now, because I'm almost naked. I no longer blush, because he's the one who does the blushing now.

(Pointing to FATHER.*)* But, let me tell you, he was very pale then. . . . Very pale indeed! *(to the* PRODUCER*)* You can believe *me!*

PRODUCER: I haven't the vaguest idea what you're talking about!

FATHER: I can well believe it! When you get things hurled at you like that. Put your foot down. . . . And let me speak before you believe all these horrible slanders she's so viciously heaping upon me. . . . Without letting me get a word of explanation in.

STEPDAUGHTER: Ah, but this isn't the place for your long-winded fairy-stories, you know!

FATHER: But I'm not going to. . . . I want to explain things to him!

STEPDAUGHTER: Oh yes . . . I bet you do! You'll explain everything so that it suits you, won't you?

(At this point the PRODUCER *comes back on stage to restore order.)*

FATHER: But can't you see that here we have the cause of all the trouble! In the use of words! Each one of us has a whole world of things inside him. . . . And each one of us has his own particular world. How can we understand each other if into the words which I speak I put the sense and the value of things as I understand them within myself. . . . While at the same time whoever is listening to them inevitably assumes them to have the sense and value that they have for him. . . . The sense and value that they have in the world that he has within him? We think we understand one another. . . . But we never really do understand! Look at this situation, for example! All my pity, all the pity that I feel for this woman *(Pointing to the* MOTHER*)* she sees as the most ferocious cruelty.

MOTHER: But you turned me out of the house!

FATHER: There! Do you hear? I turned her out! She really believed that I was turning her out!

MOTHER: You know how to talk . . . I don't. . . . But believe me *(Turning to the* PRODUCER.*)* after he had married me. . . . Goodness knows why! For I was a poor, humble woman. . . .

FATHER: But it was just because of that. . . . It was your humility that I loved in you. I married you for your humility, believing . . . *(He breaks off, for she is making gestures of contradiction. Then, seeing how utterly impossible it is to make her understand him, he opens his arms wide in a gesture of despair and turns to the* PRODUCER.*)* No! . . . You see? She says no! It's terrifying, believe me! It's really terrifying, this deafness *(He taps his forehead.).* . . . This mental deafness of hers! Affection. . . . Yes! . . . For her children! But deaf . . . Mentally deaf. . . . Deaf to the point of desperation.

STEPDAUGHTER: True enough! But now you make

him tell us what good all his cleverness has ever done us.

FATHER: If we could only foresee all the ill that can result from the good that we believe we are doing.

(Meanwhile the LEADING LADY, *with ever-increasing fury, has been watching the* LEADING MAN, *who is busy carrying on a flirtation with the* STEPDAUGHTER. *Unable to stand it any longer she now steps forward and says to the* PRODUCER.*)*

LEADING LADY: Excuse me, but are you going on with the rehearsal?

PRODUCER: Why, of course! Of course! But just at the moment I want to hear what these people have to say!

JUVENILE LEAD: This is really something quite new!

INGENUE: It's most interesting!

LEADING LADY: For those that are interested! *(And she looks meaningly in the direction of the* LEADING MAN.*)*

PRODUCER *(to the* FATHER*)*: But you'll have to explain everything clearly. *(He goes and sits down.)*

FATHER: Yes. . . . Well. . . . You see . . . I had a poor man working under me. . . . He was my secretary, and devoted to me. . . . Who understood her in every way . . . In everything *(Pointing to the* MOTHER.*)* Oh, there wasn't the slightest suspicion of anything wrong. He was a good man. A humble man. . . . Just like her. . . . They were incapable . . . both of them . . . not only of doing evil . . . but even of thinking it!

STEPDAUGHTER: So, instead, he thought about it for them! And then got on with it.

FATHER: It's not true! I thought that what I should be doing would be for their good. . . . And for mine, too . . . I confess it! Yes, things had come to such a pass that I couldn't say a single word to either of them without their immediately exchanging an understanding look. . . . Without the one's immediately trying to catch the other's eye. . . . For advice as to how to take what I had said. . . . So that I shouldn't get into a bad temper. As you'll readily appreciate it was enough to keep me in a state of continual fury. . . . Of intolerable exasperation!

PRODUCER: But. . . . Forgive my asking. . . . Why didn't you give this secretary of yours the sack?

FATHER: That's exactly what I did do, as a matter of fact. But then I had to watch that poor woman wandering forlornly about the house like some poor lost creature . . . Like one of those stray animals you take in out of charity.

MOTHER: But . . .

FATHER *(immediately turning on her, as if to forestall what she is about to say)*: Your son! You were going to tell him about your son, weren't you?

MOTHER: But first of all he tore my son away from me!

FATHER: Not out of any desire to be cruel though! I took him away so that, by living in the country, in contact with Nature, he might grow up strong and healthy.

STEPDAUGHTER (pointing to him, ironically): And just look at him!

FATHER (immediately): And is it my fault, too, that he's grown up the way he has? I sent him to a wet-nurse in the country . . . a peasant's wife . . . because my wife didn't seem strong enough to me. . . . Although she came of a humble family, and it was for that reason that I'd married her! Just a whim maybe. . . . But then . . . what was I to do? I've always had this cursed longing for a certain solid moral healthiness.

(At this the STEPDAUGHTER breaks out afresh into noisy laughter.)

Make her stop that noise! I can't stand it!

PRODUCER: Be quiet! Let me hear what he has to say, for God's sake!

(At the PRODUCER'S rebuke she immediately returns to her former attitude. . . . Absorbed and distant, a half-smile on her lips. The PRODUCER comes down off the stage again to see how it looks from the auditorium.)

FATHER: I could no longer stand the sight of that woman near me (Pointing to the MOTHER.) Not so much because of the irritation she caused me . . . the nausea . . . the very real nausea with which she inspired me. . . . But rather because of the pain . . . the pain and the anguish that I was suffering on her account.

MOTHER: And he sent me away!

FATHER: Well provided with everything. . . . To that other man. . . . So that she might be free of me.

MOTHER: And so that he might be free as well!

FATHER: Yes, I admit it. And a great deal of harm came as a result of it. . . . But I meant well. . . . And I did it more for her sake than for my own. I swear it! (He folds his arms. Then immediately turning to the MOTHER.) Did I ever lose sight of you? Tell me, did I ever lose sight of you until that fellow took you away suddenly to some other town . . . all unknown to me. . . . Just because he'd got some queer notion into his head about the interest I was showing in you. . . . An interest which was pure, I assure you, sir. . . . Without the slightest suspicion of any ulterior motive about it! I watched the new little family that grew up around her with incredible tenderness. She can testify to that. (He points to the STEPDAUGHTER.)

STEPDAUGHTER: Oh, I most certainly can! I was such a sweet little girl. . . . Such a sweet little girl, you see. . . . With plaits down to my shoulders . . . and my knickers a little bit longer than my frock. I used to see him standing there by the door of the school as I came out. He came to see how I was growing up. . . .

FATHER: Oh, this is vile! Treacherous! Infamous!

STEPDAUGHTER: Oh, no! What makes you say it's infamous?

FATHER: It's infamous! Infamous! (Then turning excitedly to the PRODUCER he goes on in an explanatory tone.) After she'd gone away (Pointing to the MOTHER.), my house suddenly seemed empty. She had been a burden on my spirit, but she had filled my house with her presence! Left alone I wandered through the rooms like some lost soul. This boy here (Pointing to the SON), having been brought up away from home. . . . I don't know . . . But . . . but when he returned home he no longer seemed to be my son. With no mother to link him to me, he grew up entirely on his own. . . . A creature apart . . . absorbed in himself . . . with no tie of intellect or affection to bind him to me. And then. . . . And, strange as it may seem, it's the simple truth . . . I became curious about her little family. . . . Gradually I was attracted to this family which had come into being as a result of what I had done. And the thought of it began to fill the emptiness that I felt all around me. I felt a real need . . . a very real need . . . to believe that she was happy, at peace, absorbed in the simple everyday duties of life. I wanted to look on her as being fortunate because she was far removed from the complicated torments of my spirit. And so, to have some proof of this, I used to go and watch that little girl come out of school.

STEPDAUGHTER: I should just say he did! He used to follow me along the street. He would smile at me and when I reached home he'd wave to me . . . like this. I would look at him rather provocatively, opening my eyes wide. I didn't know who he might be. I told my mother about him and she knew at once who it must be. (The MOTHER nods agreement.) At first she didn't want to let me go to school again. . . . And she kept me away for several days. And when I did go back, I saw him waiting for me at the door again . . . looking ridiculous . . . with a brown paper bag in his hand. He came up to me and patted me. . . . And then he took a lovely large straw hat out of the bag . . . with lots of lovely roses on it . . . And all for me.

PRODUCER: This is a bit off the point, you know.

SON (contemptuously): Yes. . . . Literature! Literature!

FATHER: Literature indeed! This is life! Passion!

PRODUCER: It may be. But you certainly can't act this sort of stuff!

FATHER: I agree with you. Because all this is only

leading up to the main action. I'm not suggesting that this part should be acted. And as a matter of fact, as you can quite well see, she (Pointing to the STEPDAUGHTER.) is no longer that little girl with plaits down to her shoulders. . . .

STEPDAUGHTER: . . . and her knickers a little bit longer than her frock!

FATHER: It is now that the drama comes! Something new, something complex. . . .

STEPDAUGHTER (coming forward, her voice gloomy, fierce): As soon as my father died. . . .

FATHER (at once, not giving her a chance to continue): . . . they fell into the most wretched poverty! They came back here. . . . And because of her stupidity (Pointing to the MOTHER.) I didn't know a thing about it. It's true enough that she can hardly write her own name. . . . But she might have got her daughter or that boy to write and tell me that they were in need!

MOTHER: Now tell me, sir, how was I to know that this was how he'd feel?

FATHER: That's exactly where you went wrong, in never having got to know how I felt about something.

MOTHER: After so many years away from him. . . . And after all that had happened. . . .

FATHER: And is it my fault that that fellow took you away from here as he did? (Turning to the PRODUCER.) I tell you, they disappeared overnight. . . . He'd found some sort of a job away from here . . . I couldn't trace them at all. . . . So, of necessity, my interest in them dwindled. And this was how it was for quite a number of years. The drama broke out, unforeseen, and violent in its intensity, when they returned. . . . When I was impelled by the demands of my miserable flesh, which is still alive with desire. . . . Oh, the wretchedness, the unutterable wretchedness of the man who's alone and who detests the vileness of casual affairs! When he's not old enough to do without a woman, and not really young enough to be able to go and look for one without feeling a sense of shame. Wretchedness, did I say? It's horrible! It's horrible! Because no woman is any longer capable of giving him love. And when he realises this, he ought to do without. . . . Yes, yes, I know! . . . Each one of us, when he appears before his fellow men, is clothed with a certain dignity. But deep down inside himself he knows what unconfessable things go on in the secrecy of his own heart. We give way . . . we give way to temptation. . . . Only to rise up again immediately, filled with a great eagerness to reestablish our dignity in all its solid entirety. . . . Just as if it were a tombstone on some grave in which we had buried, in which we had hidden from our eyes, every sign, and the very memory itself of our shame. And everyone is just like that! Only there are some of us who lack the courage to talk about certain things.

STEPDAUGHTER: They've got the courage to do them, though. . . . All of them!

FATHER: Yes, all of them! But only in secret! And that's why it needs so much more courage to talk about them! A man's only got to mention these things, and the words have hardly left his lips before he's been labelled a cynic. And all the time it's not true. He's just like everybody else. . . . In fact he's better than they are, because he's not afraid to reveal with the light of his intelligence that red blush of shame which is inherent in human bestiality. . . . That shame to which bestial man closes his eyes, in order not to see it. And woman. . . . Yes, woman. . . . What kind of a being is she? She looks at you, tantalisingly, invitingly. You take her in your arms. And no sooner is she clasped firmly in your arms than she shuts her eyes. It is the sign of her mission, the sign by which she says to man. "Blind yourself, for I am blind."

STEPDAUGHTER: And what about when she no longer shuts her eyes? When she no longer feels the need to hide her blushing shame from herself by closing her eyes? When she sees instead . . . dry-eyed and dispassionate . . . the blushing shame of man, who has blinded himself without love? Oh, what disgust, what unutterable disgust, does she feel then for all these intellectual complications, for all this philosophy which reveals the beast in man and then tries to save him, tries to excuse him . . . I just can't stand here and listen to him! Because when a man is obliged to 'simplify' life bestially like that—when he throws overboard every vestige of 'humanity', every chaste desire, every pure feeling. . . . All sense of idealism, of duty, or modesty and of shame. . . . Then nothing is more contemptible, infuriating and revoltingly nauseating than their maudlin remorse. . . . Those crocodile tears!

PRODUCER: Now let's get back to the point! Let's get to the point! This is just a lot of beating about the bush!

FATHER: Very well. But a fact is like a sack. . . . When it's empty it won't stand up. And in order to make it stand up you must first of all pour into it all the reasons and all the feelings which have caused it to exist. I couldn't possibly be expected to know that when that man died and they returned here in such utter poverty, she (Pointing to the MOTHER.) would go out to work as a dress-maker in order to support the children. . . . Nor that, of all people, she'd gone to work for that . . . for Madame Pace.

STEPDAUGHTER: Who's a high-class dress-maker, if

you ladies and gentlemen would really like to know. On the surface she does work for only the best sort of people. But she arranges things so that these fine ladies act as a screen ... without prejudice to the others ... who are only so-so.

MOTHER: Believe me, it never entered my head for one moment that that old hag gave me work because she had her eye on my daughter. ...

STEPDAUGHTER: Poor Mummy! Do you know what that woman used to do when I took her back the work that my mother had done? She would point out to me how the material had been ruined by giving it to my mother to sew. ... Oh, she'd grumble about this! And she'd grumble about that! And so, you understand, I had to pay for it. ... And all the time this poor creature thought she was sacrificing herself for me and for those two children, as she sat up all night sewing away at work for Madame Pace. (*Gestures and exclamations of indignation from the* ACTORS.)

PRODUCER (*immediately*): And it was there, one day, that you met ...

STEPDAUGHTER (*pointing to the* FATHER): ... him! Yes, him! An old client! Now there's a scene for you to put on! Absolutely superb!

FATHER: With her ... the Mother ... arriving. ...

STEPDAUGHTER (*immediately, treacherously*): ... almost in time!

FATHER (*a cry*): No! In time! In time! Fortunately I recognized her in time! And I took them all back home with me! Now you can imagine what the situation is like for both of us. She, just as you see her. ... And I no longer able to look her in the face.

STEPDAUGHTER: It's utterly ridiculous! How can I possibly be expected, after all that, to be a modest young miss ... well-bred and virtuous ... in accordance with his confounded aspirations for a "solid moral healthiness"?

FATHER: My drama lies entirely in this one thing. ... In my being conscious that each one of us believes himself to be a single person. But it's not true. ... Each one of us is many persons. ... Many persons ... according to all the possibilities of being that there are within us. ... With some people we are one person. ... With others we are somebody quite different. ... And all the time we are under the illusion of always being one and the same person for everybody. ... We believe that we are always this one person in whatever it is we may be doing. But it's not true! It's not true! And we see this very clearly when by some tragic chance we are, as it were, caught up whilst in the middle of doing something and find ourselves suspended in midair. And then we perceive that all of us was not in what we were doing, and that it would, there-

fore, be an atrocious injustice to us to judge us by that action alone ... to keep us suspended like that. ... To keep us in a pillory ... throughout all existence ... as if our whole life were completely summed up in that one deed. Now do you understand the treachery of this girl? She surprised me somewhere where I shouldn't have been ... and doing something that I shouldn't have been doing with her. ... She surprised an aspect of me that should never have existed for her. And now she is trying to attach to me a reality such as I could never have expected I should have to assume for her. ... The reality that lies in one fleeting, shameful moment of my life. And this, this above all, is what I feel most strongly about. And as you can see, the drama acquires a tremendous value from this concept. Then there's the position of the others. ... His ...(*Pointing to the* SON.)

SON (*shrugging his shoulders scornfully*): Leave me alone! I've got nothing to do with all this!

FATHER: What do you mean ... you've got nothing to do with all this?

SON: I've got nothing to do with it. ... And I don't want to have anything to do with it, because, as you quite well know, I wasn't meant to be mixed up in all this with the rest of you!

STEPDAUGHTER: Common, that's what we are! And he's a fine gentleman! But, as you may have noticed, every now and again I fix him with a contemptuous look, and he lowers his eyes. ... Because he knows the harm he's done me!

SON (*scarcely looking at her*): I?

STEPDAUGHTER: Yes, you! You! It's all your fault that I became a prostitute! (*A movement of horror from the* ACTORS.) Did you or did you not deny us, by the attitude you adopted—I won't say the intimacy of your home—but even that mere hospitality which makes guests feel at their ease? We were invaders who had come to disturb the kingdom of your legitimacy. I should just like you (*This to the* PRODUCER.) to be present at certain little scenes that took place between him and me. He says that I tyrannised over everybody. ... But it was just because of the way that he behaved that I took advantage of the thing that he calls 'vile.' ... Why I exploited the reason for my coming into his house with my mother ... Who is his mother as well! And I went into that house as mistress of it!

SON (*slowly coming forward*): It's all very easy for them. ... It's fine sport. ... All of them ganging up against me. But just imagine the position of a son whose fate it is one fine day, while he's sitting quietly at home, to see arriving an impudent and brazen young woman who asks for his father— and heaven knows what her business is with him!

Later he sees her come back, as brazen as ever, bringing that little girl with her. And finally he sees her treating her father—without knowing in the least why—in a very equivocal and very much to-the-point manner . . . asking him for money, in a tone of voice which leads you to suppose that he must give it to her. . . . Must give it to her, because he has every obligation to do so. . . .

FATHER: As indeed I have! It's an obligation I owe your mother!

SON: How should I know that? When had I never seen or even heard of her? Then one day I see her arrive with *her* (Pointing to the STEPDAUGHTER.) together with that boy and the little girl. And they say to me, "This is *your* mother, too, you know." Little by little I begin to understand. . . . Largely as a result of the way she goes on (*Pointing to the* STEPDAUGHTER *again.*). . . . Why is it that they've come to live with us. . . . So suddenly . . . So unexpectedly. . . . What I feel, what I experience, I neither wish, nor am able, to express. I wouldn't even wish to confess it to myself. No action, therefore, can be hoped for from me in this affair. Believe me, I am a dramatically unrealised character . . . and I do not feel the least bit at ease in their company. So please leave me out of it!

FATHER: What! But it's just because you're like that . . .

SON (*in violent exasperation*): And what do you know about it? How do you know what I'm like? When have you ever bothered yourself about me?

FATHER: I admit it! I admit it! But isn't that a dramatic situation in itself? This aloofness of yours, which is so cruel to me and to your mother. . . . Your mother who returns home and sees you almost for the first time . . . You're so grown up that she doesn't recognise you, but she knows that you're her son. (*Pointing to the* MOTHER *and addressing the* PRODUCER.) There, look! She's crying!

STEPDAUGHTER (*angrily, stamping her foot*): Like the fool she is!

FATHER (*pointing to the* STEPDAUGHTER): She can't stand him! (*Then returning to the subject of the* SON.) He says he's got nothing to do with all this, when, as a matter of fact, almost the whole action hinges on him. Look at that little boy. . . . See how he clings to his mother all the time, frightened and humiliated. . . . And it's *his* fault that he's like that! Perhaps his position is the most painful of all. . . . More than any of them he feels himself to be an outsider. And so the poor little chap feels mortified, humiliated at being taken into my home . . . out of charity, as it were. (*Confidentially.*) He's just like his father. Humble. . . . Doesn't say a word. . . .

PRODUCER: I don't think it's a good idea to have him in. You've no idea what a nuisance boys are on the stage.

FATHER: Oh, . . . but he won't be a nuisance for long . . . He disappears almost immediately. And the little girl, too. . . . In fact, she's the first to go.

PRODUCER: This is excellent! I assure you I find this all very interesting. . . . Very interesting indeed! I can see we've got the makings of a pretty good play here.

STEPDAUGHTER (*trying to butt in*): When you've got a character like me!

FATHER (*pushing her to one side in his anxiety to hear what decision the* PRODUCER *has come to*): You be quiet!

PRODUCER (*continuing, heedless of the interruption*): And it's certainly something new. . . . Ye-es! . . .

FATHER: Absolutely brand new!

PRODUCER: You had a nerve, though. I must say. . . . Coming here and chucking the idea at me like that. . . .

FATHER: Well, you understand, born as we are for the stage. . . .

PRODUCER: Are you amateur actors?

FATHER: No . . . I say that we're born for the stage because . . .

PRODUCER: Oh, don't try and con me with that one! You're an old hand at this game.

FATHER: No. I only act as much as anyone acts the part that he sets himself to perform, or the part that he is given in life. And in me it is passion itself, as you can see, that always becomes a little theatrical of its own accord . . . as it does in everyone . . . once it becomes exalted.

PRODUCER: Oh well, that as may be! That as may be! . . . But you do understand, without an author . . . I could give you the address of somebody who'd . . .

FATHER: No! . . . Look here. . . . You be the author!

PRODUCER: Me? What the devil are you talking about?

FATHER: Yes, you! You! Why not?

PRODUCER: Because I've never written anything in my life! That's why not!

FATHER: Then why not try your hand at it now? There's nothing to it. Everybody's doing it! And your job's made all the easier for you because we are here, all of us, alive before you. . . .

PRODUCER: That's not enough!

FATHER: Not enough? When you see us live our drama . . .

PRODUCER: Yes! Yes! But we'll still need somebody to write the play.

FATHER: No. . . . Someone to take it down possibly, while we act it out, scene by scene. It'll be quite sufficient if we make a rough sketch of it first and then have a run through.

PRODUCER (*climbing back on to the stage, tempted by*

this): H'm! . . . You almost succeed in tempting me. . . . H'm! It would be rather fun! We could certainly have a shot at it.

FATHER: Of course! Oh, you'll see what wonderful scenes'll emerge! I can tell you what they are here and now.

PRODUCER: You tempt me. . . . You tempt me. . . . Let's have a go at it! . . . Come with me into my office. (*Turning to the* ACTORS.) You can have a few minutes' break. . . . But don't go too far away. I want you all back again in about a quarter of an hour or twenty minutes. (*To the* FATHER.) Well, let's see what we can make of it! We might get something really extraordinary out of it. . . .

FATHER: There's no *might* about it! They'd better come along too, don't you think? (*Pointing to the other* CHARACTERS.)

PRODUCER: Yes, bring 'em along! Bring 'em along! (*Starts going off and then turns back to the* ACTORS.) Now remember, don't be late back! You've got a quarter of an hour!

(*The* PRODUCER *and the* SIX CHARACTERS *cross the stage and disappear. The* ACTORS *remain looking at one another in astonishment.*)

LEADING MAN: Is he serious? What's he going to do?

JUVENILE LEAD: This is utter madness!

A THIRD ACTOR: Does he expect us to knock up a play in five minutes?

JUVENILE LEAD: Yes . . . like the actors in the old Comedia dell'Arte.

LEADING LADY: Well, if he thinks that I'm going to have anything to do with fun and games of that sort. . . .

INGENUE: And you certainly don't catch me joining in!

A FOURTH ACTOR: I should like to know who those people are. (*He is alluding to the* CHARACTERS.)

THIRD ACTOR: Who do you think they're likely to be? They're probably escaped lunatics. . . . Or crooks!

JUVENILE LEAD: And does he really take what they say seriously?

INGENUE: Vanity! That's what it is. . . . The vanity of appearing as an author!

LEADING MAN: It's absolutely unheard of! If the stage has come to this. . . .

A FIFTH ACTOR: I'm rather enjoying it!

THIRD ACTOR: Oh, well! After all, we shall have the pleasure of seeing what comes of it all!

(*And talking among themselves in this way the* ACTORS *leave the stage. Some go out through the door back, some go in the direction of the dressing-rooms. The curtain remains up.*)
(*The performance is suspended for twenty minutes.*)

ACT 2

(*The call-bells ring, warning the audience that the performance is about to be resumed. The* ACTORS, *the* STAGE MANAGER, *the* FOREMAN *of the stage crew, the* PROMPTER *and the* PROPERTY MAN *reassemble on stage. Some come from the dressing-rooms, some through the door back, some even from the auditorium. The* PRODUCER *enters from his office accompanied by the* SIX CHARACTERS. *The houselights are extinguished and the stage lighting is as before.*)

PRODUCER: Now come on, ladies and gentlemen! Are we all here? Let me have your attention please! Now let's make a start! (*Then calls the* FOREMAN.)

FOREMAN: Yes, sir?

PRODUCER: Set the stage for the parlour scene. A couple of flats and a door will do. As quickly as you can!

(*The* FOREMAN *runs off at once to carry out this order and is setting the stage as directed whilst the* PRODUCER *is making his arrangements with the* STAGE MANAGER, *the* PROPERTY MAN, *the* PROMPTER *and the* ACTORS. *The flats he has set up are painted in pink and gold stripes.*)

PRODUCER (*to* PROPERTY MAN): Just have a look, please, and see if we've got some sort of sofa or divan in the props room.

PROPERTY MAN: There's the green one, sir.

STEPDAUGHTER: No, no, green won't do! It was yellow . . . yellow flowered plush. . . . A huge thing . . . and most comfortable.

PROPERTY MAN: Well, we haven't got anything like that.

PRODUCER: It doesn't matter! Give me what there is!

STEPDAUGHTER: What do you mean, it doesn't matter? Madame Pace's famous sofa!

PRODUCER: We only want it for this run-through. Please don't interfere. (*to the* STAGE MANAGER) Oh, and see if we've got a shop-window . . . something rather long and narrowish is what we want.

STEPDAUGHTER: And a little table . . . the little mahogany table for the pale blue envelope.!

STAGE MANAGER (*to* PRODUCER): There's that little one. . . . You know, the gold-painted one.

PRODUCER: That'll do fine! Shove it on!

FATHER: You need a long mirror.

STEPDAUGHTER: And the screen! I must have a screen, please. . . . Else how can I manage?

STAGE MANAGER: Don't you worry, Miss! We've got masses of them!

PRODUCER (*to the* STEPDAUGHTER): And some clotheshangers and so on, h'm?

STEPDAUGHTERS: Oh, yes, lots!

PRODUCER (*to the* STAGE MANAGER): See how many we've got and get somebody to bring them up.

STAGE MANAGER: Right you are, sir, I'll see to it!

(The STAGE MANAGER *goes off about his business and while the* PRODUCER *is talking to the* PROMPTER *and later to the* CHARACTERS *and* ACTORS, *he gets the stage hands to bring up the furniture and properties and proceeds to arrange them in what he thinks is the best sort of order.)*

PRODUCER *(to the* PROMPTER*)*: Now if you'll get into position while they're setting the stage. . . . Look, here's an outline of the thing. . . . Act I . . . Act II . . . *(he holds out some sheets of paper to him)*. But you'll really have to excel yourself this time.

PROMPTER: You mean, take it down in shorthand?

PRODUCER *(pleasantly surprised)*: Oh, good man! Can you do shorthand?

PROMPTER: I mayn't know much about prompting, but shorthand. . . .

PRODUCER: Better and better. *(Turning to a* STAGE-HAND.*)* Go and get some paper out of my room. . . . A large wadge. . . . As much as you can find!

(The STAGE-HAND *hurries off and returns shortly with a thick wad of paper which he gives to the* PROMPTER.*)*

PRODUCER *(to the* PROMPTER*)*: Follow the scenes closely as we play them and try to fix the lines . . . or at least the most important ones. *(Then, turning to the* ACTORS.*)* Right, ladies and gentlemen, clear the stage, please! No, come over this side *(He waves them over to his left.)* . . . and pay careful attention to what goes on.

LEADING LADY: Excuse me, but we . . .

PRODUCER *(forestalling what she is going to say)*: There won't be any improvising to do, don't you worry!

LEADING MAN: What do we have to do, then?

PRODUCER: Nothing. For the moment all you've got to do is to stay over there and watch what happens. You'll get your parts later. Just now we're going to have a rehearsal . . . or as much of one as we can in the circumstances! And they'll be doing the rehearsing. *(He points to the* CHARACTERS.*)*

FATHER *(in consternation, as if he had tumbled from the clouds into the midst of all the confusion on stage)*. We are? But, excuse me, in what way will it be a rehearsal?

PRODUCER: Well . . . a rehearsal . . . a rehearsal for their benefit. *(He points to the* ACTORS.*)*

FATHER: But if we're the characters . . .

PRODUCER: Just so, "the characters." But it's not characters that act here. It's actors who do the acting here. The characters remain there, in the script. *(He points to the prompt-box.)* . . . When there is a script!

FATHER: Precisely! And since there is no script and you have the good fortune to have the characters here alive before your very eyes. . . .

PRODUCER: Oh, this is wonderful! Do you want to do everything on your own? Act . . . present yourselves to the public!

FATHER: Yes, just as we are.

PRODUCER: And let me tell you you'd make a wonderful sight!

LEADING MAN: And what use should we be then?

PRODUCER: You're not going to pretend that you can act, are you? Why, it's enough to make a cat laugh. . . . *(And as a matter of fact, the* ACTORS *burst out laughing.)* There you are, you see, they're laughing at the idea! *(Then, remembering.)* But, to the point! I must tell you what your parts are. That's not so very difficult. They pretty well cast themselves. *(to the* SECOND ACTRESS*)* You, the MOTHER. *(to the* FATHER*)* We'll have to find a name for her.

FATHER: Amalia.

PRODUCER: But that's your wife's name. We can hardly call her by her real name.

FATHER: And why not, when that's her name? But, perhaps, it is has to be that lady . . . *(A slight gesture to indicate the* SECOND ACTRESS.*)* I see *her* *(Pointing to the* MOTHER.*)* as Amalia. But do as you like. . . . *(His confusion grows.)* I don't know what to say to you. . . . I'm already beginning. . . . I don't know how to express it . . . to hear my own words ringing false . . . as if they had another sound from the one I had meant to give them. . . .

PRODUCER: Now don't you worry about that! Don't you worry about it at all! We'll think about how to get the right tone of voice. And as for the name. . . . If you want it to be Amalia, Amalia it shall be. Or we'll find some other name. Just for the present we'll refer to the characters in this way. *(to the* JUVENILE LEAD*)* You, the Son . . . *(to the* LEADING LADY*)* And you'll play the Stepdaughter, of course. . . .

STEPDAUGHTER *(excitedly)*: What! What did you say? That woman there. . . . Me! *(She bursts out laughing.)*

PRODUCER *(angrily)*: And what's making you laugh?

LEADING LADY *(indignantly)*: Nobody has ever dared to laugh at me before! Either you treat me with respect or I'm walking out!

STEPDAUGHTER: Oh, no, forgive me! I wasn't laughing at you.

PRODUCER *(to* STEPDAUGHTER*)*: You should feel yourself honoured to be played by . . .

LEADING LADY *(immediately, disdainfully)*: . . . "that woman there."

STEPDAUGHTER: But my remark wasn't meant as a criticism of you . . . I was thinking about myself. . . . Because I can't see myself in you at all. I don't know how to . . . you're not a bit like me!

FATHER: Yes, that's the point I wanted to make! Look . . . all that we express. . . .

PRODUCER: What do you mean . . . *all that you express?* Do you think that this whatever-it-is that you express is something you've got inside you? Not a bit of it.

FATHER: Why . . . aren't even the things we express our own?

PRODUCER: Of course they aren't! The things that you express become material here for the actors, who give it body and form, voice and gesture. And, let me tell you, my actors have given expression to much loftier material than this. This stuff of yours is so trivial that, believe me, if it comes off on the stage, the credit will all be due to my actors.

FATHER: I don't dare to contradict you! But please believe me when I tell you that we . . . who have these bodies . . . these features. . . . Who are as you see us now . . . We are suffering horribly. . . .

PRODUCER (*cutting in impatiently*): . . . But the make-up will remedy all that. . . . At least as far as your faces are concerned!

FATHER: Perhaps. . . . But what about our voices? . . . What about our gestures? . . .

PRODUCER: Now, look here! You, as yourself, just cannot exist here! Here there's an actor who'll play you. And let that be an end to all this argument!

FATHER: I understand. . . . And now I think I see why our author didn't wish to put us on the stage after all. . . . He saw us as we are. . . . Alive. . . . He saw us as living beings. . . . I don't want to offend your actors. . . . Heaven forbid that I should! . . . But I think that seeing myself acted now . . . by I don't know whom . . .

LEADING MAN (*rising with some dignity and coming over, followed by a laughing group of young actresses*): By me, if you have no objection.

FATHER (*humbly, mellifluously*): I am deeply honoured, sir. (*He bows.*) But. . . . Well. . . . I think that however much of his art this gentleman puts into absorbing me into himself. . . . However much he wills it. . . . (*He becomes confused.*)

LEADING MAN: Go on! Go on! (*The actresses laugh.*)

FATHER: Well, I should say that the performance he'll give. . . . Even if he makes himself up to look as much like me as he can. . . . I should say that with his figure . . . (*All the* ACTORS *laugh.*) . . . it will be difficult for it to be a performance of me . . . of me as I really am. It will rather be . . . leaving aside the question of his appearance. . . . It will be how he interprets what I am . . . how he sees me. . . . If he sees me as anything at all. . . . And not as I, deep down within myself, feel myself to be. And it certainly seems to me that whoever is called upon to criticise us will have to take this into account.

PRODUCER: So you're already thinking about what the critics will say, are you? And here I am, still trying to get the play straight! The critics can say what they like. We'd be much better occupied in thinking about getting the play on. . . . If we can. (*Stepping out of the group and looking around him.*) Now, come on, let's make a start! Is everything ready? (to the ACTORS and CHARACTERS) Come on, don't clutter up the place! Let me see how it looks! (*He comes down from the stage.*) And now, don't let's lose any more time! (to the STEP-DAUGHTER) Do you think the set looks all right?

STEPDAUGHTER: To be perfectly honest, I just don't recognise it at all!

PRODUCER: Good Lord, you surely didn't hope that we were going to reconstruct that room behind Madame Pace's shop here on the stage, did you? (to the FATHER) You did tell me it had flowered wallpaper, didn't you?

FATHER: Yes, white.

PRODUCER: Well, it's not white—and it's got stripes on it—but it'll have to do! As for the furniture, I think we've more or less got everything we need. Bring that little table down here a bit! (*The* STAGE-HANDS *do so. Then he says to the* PROPERTY MAN.) Now, will you go and get an envelope. . . . A pale blue one if you can. . . . And give it to that gentleman. (*He points to the* FATHER.)

PROPERTY MAN: The kind you put letters in?

PRODUCER *and* FATHER: Yes, the kind you put letters in!

PROPERTY MAN: Yes, sir! At once, sir! (*Exit.*)

PRODUCER: Now, come on! First scene—the young lady. (*The* LEADING LADY *comes forward.*) No! No! Wait a moment! I said the young lady! (*Pointing to the* STEPDAUGHTER.) You stay there and watch. . . .

STEPDAUGHTER (*immediately adding*): . . . how I make it live!

LEADING LADY (*resentfully*): I'll know how to make it live, don't you worry, once I get started!

PRODUCER (*with his hands to his head*): Ladies and gentlemen, don't let's have any arguing! Please! Right! Now . . . The first scene is between the young lady and Madame Pace. Oh! (*He looks around rather helplessly and then comes back on stage.*) What about this Madame Pace?

FATHER: She's not with us, sir.

PRODUCER: And what do we do about her?

FATHER: But she's alive! She's alive too!

PRODUCER: Yes, yes! But where is she?

FATHER: If you'll just allow me to have a word with your people. . . . (*Turning to the* ACTRESSES.) I wonder if you ladies would do me the kindness of lending me your hats for a moment.

THE ACTRESSES (*a chorus . . . half-laughing, half-surprised*): What? Our hats?

What did he say?
Why?
Listen to the man!

PRODUCER: What are you going to do with the women's hats?

(The ACTORS *laugh*.)

FATHER: Oh, nothing . . . I just want to put them on these pegs for a moment. And perhaps one of you ladies would be so kind as to take off your coat, too.

THE ACTORS (*laughter and surprise in their voices*): Their coats as well? And after that? The man must be mad!

ONE OR TWO OF THE ACTRESSES (*surprise and laughter in their voices*): But why?
Only our coats?

FATHER: So that I can hang them here. . . . Just for a moment or so. . . . Please do me this favour. Will you?

THE ACTRESSES (*they take off their hats. One or two take off their coats as well, all laughing the while. They go over and hang the coats here and there on the pegs and hangers*):
And why not?
Here you are!
This really is funny!
Do we have to put them on show?

FATHER: Precisely. . . . You have to put them on show . . . Like this!

PRODUCER: Is one allowed to know what you're up to?

FATHER: Why yes. If we set the stage better, who knows whether she may not be attracted by the objects of her trade and perhaps appear among us. . . . (*He invites them to look toward the door at the back of the stage*.) Look! Look!

(*The door opens and* MADAME PACE *comes in and takes a few steps forward. She is an enormously fat old harridan of a woman, wearing a pompous carrot-coloured tow wig with a red rose stuck into one side of it, in the Spanish manner. She is heavily made up and dressed with clumsy elegance in a stylish red silk dress. In one hand she carries an ostrich feather fan; the other hand is raised and a lighted cigarette is poised between two fingers. Immediately they see this apparition, the* ACTORS *and the* PRODUCER *bound off the stage with howls of fear, hurling themselves down the steps into the auditorium and making as if to dash up the aisle. The* STEPDAUGHTER, *however, rushes humbly up to* MADAME PACE, *as if greeting her mistress*.)

STEPDAUGHTER (*rushing up to her*): Here she is! Here she is!

FATHER (*beaming*): It's Madame Pace! What did I tell you? Here she is!

PRODUCER (*his first surprise overcome, he is now indignant*): What sort of a game do you call this?

LEADING MAN:⎫ *almost at the* ⎫ Hang it all, what's
JUVENILE LEAD:⎬ *same moment* ⎬ going on?
INGENUE: ⎪ *and all* ⎪ Where did *she* spring
LEADING LADY:⎭ *speaking at* ⎭ from?
            once. They were keeping
                       her in reserve!
                       So it's back to the
                       music hall and
                       conjuring tricks, is it?

FATHER (*dominating the protesting voices*): One moment, please! Why should you wish to destroy this prodigy of reality, which was born, which was evoked, attracted and formed by this scene itself? . . . A reality which has more right to live here than you have. . . . Because it is so very much more alive than you are. . . . Why do you want to spoil it all, just because of some niggling, vulgar convention of truth? . . . Which of you actresses will be playing the part of Madame Pace? Well, *that* woman *is* Madame Pace! Grant me at least that the actress who plays her will be less true than she is. . . . For *she* is Madame Pace in person! Look! My daughter recognised her and went up to her at once. Now, watch the scene! Just watch it! (*Hesitantly the* PRODUCER *and the* ACTORS *climb back on to the stage. But while the* ACTORS *have been protesting and the* FATHER *has been replying to them, the scene between the* STEPDAUGHTER *and* MADAME PACE *has begun. It is carried on in an undertone, very quietly—naturally in fact—in a manner that would be quite impossible on the stage. When the* ACTORS *obey the* FATHER'S *demand that they shall watch what is happening, they see that* MADAME PACE *has already put her hand under the* STEPDAUGHTER'S *chin to raise her head and is talking to her. Hearing her speak in a completely unintelligible manner they are held for a moment. But almost immediately their attention flags*.)

PRODUCER: Well?

LEADING MAN: But what's she saying?

LEADING LADY: We can't hear a thing!

JUVENILE LEAD: Speak up! Louder!

STEPDAUGHTER (*she leaves* MADAME PACE *and comes down to the group of* ACTORS. MADAME PACE *smiles—a priceless smile*): Did you say, 'Louder?' What do you mean, 'Louder?' What we're talking about is scarcely the sort of thing to be shouted from the roof-tops. I was able to yell it out just now so that I could shame *him* (*Pointing to the* FATHER.) . . . so that I could have my revenge! But it's quite another matter for Madame Pace. . . . It would mean prison for her.

PRODUCER: Indeed? So that's how it is, is it? But let me tell you something, my dear young lady. . . . Here in the theatre you've got to make yourself heard! The way you're doing this bit at the moment even those of us who're on stage can't hear you! Just imagine what it'll be like with an audience out front. This scene's got to be got over. And anyway there's nothing to prevent you from speaking up when you're on together. . . . We shan't be here to listen to you. . . . We're only here now because it's a rehearsal. Pretend you're alone in the room behind the shop, where nobody can hear you.

(The STEPDAUGHTER *elegantly, charmingly—and with a mischievous smile—wags her finger two or three times in disagreement.*)

PRODUCER: What do you mean, 'No?'

STEPDAUGHTER (*in a mysterious whisper*): There's someone who'll hear us if she (*Pointing to* MADAME PACE.) speaks up.

PRODUCER (*in utter consternation*): Do you mean to say that there's somebody else who's going to burst in on us? (*The* ACTORS *make as if to dive off the stage again.*)

FATHER: No! No! They're alluding to me. I have to be there, waiting behind the door. . . . And Madame Pace knows it. So, if you'll excuse me, I'll go. . . . So that I'm all ready to make my entrance. (*He starts off toward the back of the stage.*)

PRODUCER (*stopping him*): No! No! Wait a moment! When you're here you have to respect the conventions of the theatre! Before you get ready to go on to that bit. . . .

STEPDAUGHTER: No! Let's get on with it at once! At once! I'm dying with desire, I tell you . . . to live this scene. . . . To live it! If he wants to get on with it right away, I'm more than ready!

PRODUCER (*shouting*): But first of all, the scene between you and her (*Pointing to* MADAME PACE.) has got to be over! Do you understand?

STEPDAUGHTER: Oh, my God! She's just been telling me what you already know. . . . That once again my mother's work has been badly done. . . . That the dress is spoilt . . . And that I must be patient if she is to go on helping us in our misfortune.

MADAME PACE (*stepping forward, a grand air of importance about her*): But, yes, señor, porque I not want to make profit . . . to take advantage. . . .

PRODUCER (*more than a touch of terror in his voice*): What? Does she speak like that?

(*The* ACTORS *burst into noisy laughter.*)

STEPDAUGHTER (*laughing too*): Yes, she speaks like that, half in English, half in Spanish. . . . It's most comical.

MADAME PACE: Ah, no, it does not to me seem good manners that you laugh of me when I . . . force myself to . . . hablar, as I can, English, señor!

PRODUCER: Indeed, no! It's very wrong of us! You speak like that! Yes, speak like that, Madame!

It'll bring the house down! We couldn't ask for anything better. It'll bring a little comic relief into the crudity of the situation. Yes, you talk like that! It's absolutely wonderful!

STEPDAUGHTER: Wonderful! And why not? When you hear a certain sort of suggestion made to you in a lingo like that. . . . There's not much doubt about what your answer's going to be. . . . Because it almost seems like a joke. You feel inclined to laugh when you hear there's an 'old señor', who wants to 'amuse himself with me'. An 'old señor', eh, Madame?

MADAME PACE: Not so very old. . . . Not quite so young, yes? And if he does not please to you. . . . Well, he has . . . prudencia.

MOTHER (*absorbed as they are in the scene, the* ACTORS *have been paying no attention to her. Now, to their amazement and consternation, she leaps up and attacks* MADAME PACE. *At her cry they jump, then hasten smilingly to restrain her, for she, meanwhile, has snatched off* MADAME PACE'S *wig and has thrown it to the ground*): You old devil! You old witch! You murderess! Oh, my daughter!

STEPDAUGHTER (*rushing over to restrain her* MOTHER): No, Mummy, no! Please!

FATHER (*rushing over at the same time*): Calm yourself, my dear! Just be calm! Now . . . come and sit down again!

MOTHER: Take that woman out of my sight, then!

(*In the general excitement the* PRODUCER, *too, has rushed over and the* STEPDAUGHTER *now turns to him.*)

STEPDAUGHTER: It's impossible for my mother to remain here!

FATHER (*to the* PRODUCER): They can't be here together. That's why, when we first came, that woman wasn't with us. If they're on at the same time the whole thing is inevitably given away in advance.

PRODUCER: It doesn't matter! It doesn't matter a bit! This is only a first run-through. . . . Just to give us a rough idea how it goes. Everything'll come in useful . . . I can sort out the bits and pieces later. . . . I'll make something out of it, even if it is all jumbled up. (*Turning to the* MOTHER *and leading her back to her chair.*) Now, please be calm, and sit down here, nice and quietly.

(*Meanwhile the* STEPDAUGHTER *has gone down centre stage again. She turns to* MADAME PACE.)

STEPDAUGHTER: Go on, Madame, go on!

MADAME PACE (*offended*): Ah, no thank you! Here I do not do nothing more with your mother present!

STEPDAUGHTER: Now, come on! Show in the 'old señor' who wants to 'amuse himself with me'. (*Turning imperiously on the rest.*) Yes, this scene has got to be played. So let's get on with it! (*to*

MADAME PACE) You can go!

MADAME PACE: Ah, I am going . . . I am going. . . . Most assuredly I am going! (*Exit furiously, ramming her wig back on and glowering at the* ACTORS, *who mockingly applaud her.*)

STEPDAUGHTER (*to the* FATHER): And now you make your entrance! There's no need for you to go out and come in again! Come over here! Pretend that you've already entered! Now, I'm standing here modestly, my eyes on the ground. Come on! Speak up! Say, 'Good afternoon, Miss,' in that special tone of voice . . . you know. . . . Like somebody who's just come in from the street.

PRODUCER (*by this time he is down off the stage*): Listen to her! Are you running this rehearsal, or am I? (*To the* FATHER, *who is looking perplexed and undecided*) Go on, do as she tells you! Go to the back of the stage. . . . Don't exit! . . . And then come forward again.

(*The* FATHER *does as he is told. He is troubled and very pale. But as he approaches from the back of the stage he smiles, already absorbed in the reality of his created life. He smiles as if the drama which is about to break upon him is as yet unknown to him. The* ACTORS *become intent on the scene which is beginning.*)

PRODUCER (*whispering quickly to the* PROMPTER, *who has taken up his position*): Get ready to write now!

THE SCENE

FATHER (*coming forward, a new note in his voice*): Good afternoon, Miss.

STEPDAUGHTER (*her head bowed, speaking with restrained disgust*): Good afternoon!

FATHER (*studying her a little, looking up into her face from under the brim of her hat [which almost hides it], and perceiving that she is very young, exclaims, almost to himself, a little out of complacency, a little, too, from the fear of compromising himself in a risky adventure*): H'm! But. . . . M'm. . . . This won't be the first time, will it? The first time that you've been here?

STEPDAUGHTER (*as before*): No, sir.

FATHER: You've been in here before? (*And since the* STEPDAUGHTER *nods in affirmation.*) More than once? (*He waits a little while for her reply, resumes his study of her, again looking up into her face from under the brim of her hat, smiles and then says.*) Then . . . well . . . it shouldn't any longer be so. . . . May I take off your hat?

STEPDAUGHTER (*immediately forestalling him, unable to restrain her disgust*): No, sir, I'll take it off myself! (*Convulsed, she hurriedly takes it off.*)

(*The* MOTHER *is on tenterhooks throughout. The* TWO CHILDREN *cling to their* MOTHER *and they, she and the* SON *form a group on the side opposite the* ACTORS, *watching the scene. The* MOTHER *follows the words and the actions of the* STEPDAUGHTER *and the* FATHER *with varying expressions of sorrow, of indignation, of anxiety and of horror; from time to time she hides her face in her hands and sobs.*)

MOTHER: Oh, my God! My God!

FATHER (*he remains for a moment as if turned to stone by this sob. Then he resumes in the same tone of voice as before*): Here, let me take it. I'll hang it up for you. (*He takes the hat from her hands.*) But such a charming, such a dear little head really ought to have a much smarter hat than this! Would you like to come and help me choose one from among these hats of Madame's? Will you?

INGENUE (*breaking in*): Oh, I say! Those are *our* hats!

PRODUCER (*at once, furiously*): For God's sake, shut up! Don't try to be funny! We're doing our best to rehearse this scene, in case you weren't aware of the fact! (*Turning to* STEPDAUGHTER.) Go on from where you left off, please.

STEPDAUGHTER (*continuing*): No thank you, sir.

FATHER: Come now, don't say no. Do say you'll accept it. . . . Just to please me. I shall be most upset if you won't. . . . Look, here are some rather nice ones. And then it would please Madame. She puts them out on show on purpose, you know.

STEPDAUGHTER: No . . . listen! I couldn't wear it.

FATHER: You're thinking perhaps about what they'll say when you come home wearing a new hat? Well now, shall I tell you what to do? Shall I tell you what to say when you get home?

STEPDAUGHTER (*quickly—she is at the end of her tether*): No, it's not that! I couldn't wear it because I'm . . . As you see. . . . You should have noticed already . . . (*indicating her black dress.*)

FATHER: That you're in mourning! Of course. . . . Oh, forgive me! Of course! Oh, I beg your pardon! Believe me. . . . I'm most profoundly sorry. . . .

STEPDAUGHTER (*summoning all her strength and forcing herself to conquer her contempt, her indignation and her nausea*): Stop! Please don't say any more! I really ought to be thanking you. There's no need for you to feel so very sorry or upset! Please don't give another thought to what I said! I, too, you understand. . . . (*Tries hard to smile and adds.*) I really must forget that I'm dressed like this!

PRODUCER (*interrupting them; he climbs back on the stage and turns to the* PROMPTER): Hold it! Stop a minute! Don't write that down. Leave out that last bit. (*Turning to the* FATHER *and the* STEPDAUGHTER.) It's going very well! Very well indeed! (*Then to the* FATHER.) And then you go on as we arranged. (*to the* ACTORS) Rather delightful, that bit where he offers her the hat, don't you think?

STEPDAUGHTER: Ah, but the best bit's coming now! Why aren't we going on?

PRODUCER: Now be patient, please! Just for a little while! *(Turning to the* ACTORS.*)* Of course it'll have to be treated rather lightly. . . .

LEADING MAN: . . . M'm . . . and put over slickly. . . .

LEADING LADY: Of course! There's nothing difficult about it at all. *(to the* LEADING MAN*)* Shall we try it now?

LEADING MAN: As far as I'm . . . I'll go and get ready for my entrance. *(Exits to take up his position outside the door back.)*

PRODUCER *(to the* LEADING LADY*)*: Now, look. . . . The scene between you and Madame Pace is finished. I'll get down to writing it up properly afterwards. You're standing. . . . Where are you going?

LEADING LADY: Just a moment! I want to put my hat back on. . . . *(Goes over, takes her hat down and puts it on.)*

PRODUCER: Good! Now you stand here. With your head bowed down a bit.

STEPDAUGHTER *(amused)*: But she's not dressed in black!

LEADING LADY: I *shall* be dressed in black. . . . And much more becomingly than you are!

PRODUCER *(to the* STEPDAUGHTER*)*: Shut up . . . please! And watch! You'll learn something. *(Claps his hands.)* Now come on! Let's get going! Entrance! *(He goes down from the stage again to see how it looks from out front. The door back opens and the* LEADING MAN *steps forward. He has the lively, raffish, self-possessed air of an elderly gallant. The playing of this scene by the* ACTORS *will appear from the very first words as something completely different from what was played before, without its having, even in the slightest degree, the air of a parody. It should appear rather as if the scene has been touched up. Quite naturally the* FATHER *and the* STEPDAUGHTER, *not being able to recognise themselves at all in the* LEADING LADY *and* LEADING MAN, *yet hearing them deliver the very words they used, react in a variety of ways, now with a gesture, now with a smile, with open protest even, to the impression they receive. They are surprised, lost in wonder, in suffering . . . as we shall see. The* PROMPTER'S *voice is clearly heard throughout the scene.)*

LEADING MAN: Good afternoon, Miss!

FATHER *(immediately, unable to restrain himself)*: No! No! *(And the* STEPDAUGHTER, *seeing the* LEADING MAN *enter in this way, bursts out laughing.)*

PRODUCER *(infuriated)*: Shut up! And once and for all . . . Stop that laughing! We shan't get anywhere if we go on like this!

STEPDAUGHTER *(moving away from the proscenium)*: Forgive me . . . but I couldn't help laughing! This lady *(Pointing to the* LEADING LADY.*)* stands just where you put her, without budging an inch . . . But if she's meant to be me.

. . . I can assure you that if I heard anybody saying 'Good afternoon' to me in that way and in that tone of voice I'd burst out laughing. . . . So I had to, you see.

FATHER *(coming forward a little, too)*: Yes, that's it exactly. . . . His manner. . . . The tone of voice. . . .

PRODUCER: To hell with your manner and your tone of voice! Just stand to one side, if you don't mind, and let me get a look at this rehearsal.

LEADING MAN *(coming forward)*: Now if I've got to play an old fellow who's coming into a house of rather doubtful character. . . .

PRODUCER: Oh, don't take any notice of him! Now, *please!* Start again, please! It was going very nicely. *(There is a pause—he is clearly waiting for the* LEADING MAN *to begin again.)* Well?

LEADING MAN: Good afternoon, Miss.

LEADING LADY: Good afternoon!

LEADING MAN *(repeating the* FATHER'S *move—that is, looking up into the* LEADING LADY'S *face from under the brim of her hat; but then expressing very clearly first his satisfaction and then his fear)*: M'm . . . this won't be the first time, I hope. . . .

FATHER *(unable to resist the temptation to correct him)*: Not 'hope'—'will it?', 'will it?'

PRODUCER: You say 'will it?' . . . It's a question.

LEADING MAN *(pointing to the* PROMPTER*)*: I'm sure he said, 'hope.'

PRODUCER: Well, it's all one! 'Hope' or whatever it was! Go on, please! Go on. . . . Oh, there was one thing . . . I think perhaps it ought not to be quite so heavy. . . . Hold on, I'll show you what I mean. Watch me. . . . *(Comes back on to the stage. Then, making his entrance, he proceeds to play the part.)* Good afternoon, Miss.

LEADING LADY: Good afternoon. . . .

PRODUCER: M'm. . . . *(Turning to the* LEADING MAN *to impress on him the way he has looked up at the* LEADING LADY *from under the brim of her hat.)* Surprise, fear and satisfaction. *(Then turning back to the* LEADING LADY.*)* It won't be the first time, will it, that you've been here? *(Turning again to the* LEADING MAN *enquiringly.)* Is that clear? *(to the* LEADING LADY*)* And then you say, 'No, sir.' *(to the* LEADING MAN*)* There you are. . . . It wants to be a little more . . . what shall I say? . . . A little more *flexible.* A little more *souple!* *(He goes down from the stage again.)*

LEADING LADY: No, sir. . . .

LEADING MAN: You've been here before? More than once?

PRODUCER: Wait a minute! You must let her *(pointing to the* LEADING LADY.*)* get her nod in first. You've been here before? *(The* LEADING LADY *lifts her head a little, closing her eyes painfully as if in disgust and then when the* PRODUCER *says* DOWN, *nods twice.)*

STEPDAUGHTER (*unable to restrain herself*): Oh, my God! (*And immediately she puts her hand over her mouth to stifle her laughter.*)

PRODUCER (*turning*): What's the matter?

STEPDAUGHTER (*immediately*): Nothing! Nothing!

PRODUCER (*to the* LEADING MAN): It's your cue. . . . Carry straight on.

LEADING MAN: More than once? Well then . . . Come along . . . May I take off your hat? (*The* LEADING MAN *says this last line in such a tone of voice and accompanies it with such a gesture that the* STEPDAUGHTER, *who has remained with her hands over her mouth, can no longer restrain herself. She tries desperately to prevent herself from laughing but a noisy burst of laughter comes irresistibly through her fingers.*)

LEADING LADY (*turning indignantly*): I'm not going to stand here and be made a fool of by that woman!

LEADING MAN: And neither am I. Let's pack the whole thing in.

PRODUCER (*shouting at the* STEPDAUGHTER): Once and for all, will you shut up!

STEPDAUGHTER: Yes. . . . Forgive me, please! . . . Forgive me!

PRODUCER: The trouble with you is that you've got no manners! You go too far!

FATHER (*trying to intervene*): Yes, sir, you're quite right! Quite right! But you must forgive her. . . .

PRODUCER (*climbing back on to the stage*): What do you want me to forgive? It's absolutely disgusting the way she's behaving!

FATHER: Yes. . . . But . . . Oh, believe me . . . Believe me, it has such a strange effect. . . .

PRODUCER: Strange! How do you mean, 'Strange'? What's so strange about it?

FATHER: You see, sir, I admire . . . I admire your ac-.tors . . . That gentleman there (*Pointing to the* LEADING MAN.) and that lady (*Pointing to the* LEADING LADY.) . . . But . . . Well . . . The truth is . . . They're certainly not us!

PRODUCER: I should hope not! How do you expect them to be you if they're actors?

FATHER: Just so, actors. And they play our parts well, both of them. But when they act . . . To us they seem to be doing something quite different. They want to be the same . . . And all the time they just aren't.

PRODUCER: But how aren't they the same? What are they then?

FATHER: Something that becomes theirs . . . And no longer ours.

PRODUCER: But that's inevitable! I've told you that already.

FATHER: Yes. I understand . . . I understand that. . . .

PRODUCER: Well then, let's hear no more on the subject! (*Turning to the* ACTORS.) We'll run through it later by ourselves in the usual way. I've always had a strong aversion to holding rehearsals with the author present. He's never satisfied! (*Turning to the* FATHER *and the* STEPDAUGHTER.) Now, come on, Let's get on with it! And let's see if we can have no more laughing! (*to the* STEPDAUGHTER.)

STEPDAUGHTER: Oh, I shan't laugh any more! I promise you! My big bit's coming now. . . . Just you wait and see!

PRODUCER: Well, then. . . . When you say, 'Please don't give another thought to what I said! I, too, you understand. . . .' (*Turning to the* FATHER.) You come in at once with, 'I understand! I understand!' and immediately ask . . .

STEPDAUGHTER (*interrupting him*): What? What does he ask?

PRODUCER: . . . why you're in mourning.

STEPDAUGHTER: Oh, no! That's not it at all! Listen! When I told him that I mustn't think about my being in mourning, do you know what his answer was? 'Well, then, let's take this little frock off at once, shall we!'

PRODUCER: That would be wonderful! Wonderful! That *would* bring the house down!

STEPDAUGHTER: But it's the truth!

PRODUCER: But what's the truth got to do with it? Acting's what we're here for! Truth's all very fine. . . . But only up to a point.

STEPDAUGHTER: And what do you want then?

PRODUCER: You'll see! You'll see. Leave everything to me.

STEPDAUGHTER: No, I won't! What you'd like to do, no doubt, is to concoct a romantic, sentimental little affair out of my disgust, out of all the reasons, each more cruel, each viler than the other, why I am this sort of woman, why I am what I am! An affair with him! He asks me why I'm in mourning and I reply with tears in my eyes that my father died only two months ago. No! No! He must say what he said then, 'Well, then, let's take this little frock off at once, shall we? And I . . . my heart still grieving for my father's death. . . . I went behind there. . . . Do you understand? . . . There, behind that screen! And then, my fingers trembling with shame and disgust, I took off my frock, undid my brassiere. . . .

PRODUCER (*running his hands through his hair*): For God's sake! What on earth are you saying, girl?

STEPDAUGHTER (*crying out excitedly*): The truth! The truth!

PRODUCER: Yes, it probably is the truth! I'm not denying it! And I understand . . . I fully appreciate all your horror: But you must realise that we simply can't put this kind of thing on the stage.

STEPDAUGHTER: Oh, you can't, can't you? If that's how things are, thanks very much! I'm going!

PRODUCER: No! No! Look here! . . .

STEPDAUGHTER: I'm going! I'm not stopping here! You worked it all out together, didn't you? . . . The pair of you. . . . You and him. . . . When you were in there. . . . You worked out what was going to be possible on the stage. Oh, thanks very much! I understand! He wants to jump to the bit where he presents his spiritual torments! *(This is said harshly.)* But I want to present my own drama! *Mine! Mine!*

PRODUCER *(his shoulders shaking with annoyance)*: Ah! There we have it! *Your* drama! Look here . . . you'll have to forgive me for telling you this . . . but there isn't only your part to be considered! Each of the others has his drama, too. *(He points to the* FATHER.*)* He has his and your Mother has hers. You can't have one character coming along like this, becoming too prominent, invading the stage in and out of season and overshadowing all the rest. All the characters must be contained within one harmonious picture, and presenting only what it is proper to present. I'm very well aware that everyone carries a complete life within himself and that he wants to put it before the whole world. But it's here that we run into difficulties: how are we to bring out only just so much as is absolutely necessary? . . . And at the same time, of course, to take into account all the other characters. . . . And yet in that small fragment we have to be able to hint at all the rest of the secret life of that character. Ah, it would be all very pleasant if each character could have a nice little monologue. . . . Or without making any bones about it, give a lecture, in which he could tell his audience what's bubbling and boiling away inside him. *(His tone is good-humoured, conciliatory.)* You must restrain yourself. And believe me, it's in your own interest, too. Because all this fury . . . this exasperation and this disgust . . . They make a bad impression. Especially when . . . And pardon me for mentioning this. . . . You yourself have confessed that you'd had other men there at Madame Pace's before him. . . . And more than once!

STEPDAUGHTER *(bowing her head. She pauses a moment in recollection and then, a deeper note in her voice)*: That is true! But you must remember that those other men mean *him* for me, just as much as he himself does!

PRODUCER *(uncomprehending)*: What? The other men mean *him*? What do you mean?

STEPDAUGHTER: Isn't it true that in the case of someone who's gone wrong, the person who was responsible for the first fault is responsible for all the faults which follow? And in my case, he is responsible. . . . Has been ever since before I was born. Look at him, and see if it isn't true!

PRODUCER: Very well, then! And does this terrible weight of remorse that is resting on his spirit seem so slight a thing to you? Give him the chance of acting it!

STEPDAUGHTER: How? How can he act all his 'noble' remorse, all his 'moral' torments, if you want to spare him all the horror of one day finding in his arms. . . . After he had asked her to take off her frock . . . her grief still undulled by time. . . . The horror of finding in his arms that child. . . . A woman now, and a fallen woman already. . . . That child whom he used to go and watch as she came out of school? *(She says these last words in a voice trembling with emotion. The* MOTHER, *hearing her talk like this, is overcome by distress which expresses itself at first in stifled sobs. Finally she breaks out into a fit of bitter crying. Everyone is deeply moved. There is a long pause.)*

STEPDAUGHTER *(gravely and resolutely, as soon as the* MOTHER *shows signs of becoming a little quieter)*: At the moment we are here, unknown as yet by the public. Tomorrow you will present us as you wish. . . . Making up your play in your own way. But would you really like to see our drama? To see it flash into life as it did in reality?

PRODUCER: Why, of course! I couldn't ask for anything better, so that from now on I can use as much as possible of it.

STEPDAUGHTER: Well, then, ask my Mother to leave us.

MOTHER *(rising, her quiet weeping changed to a sharp cry)*: No! No! Don't you allow them to do it! Don't allow them to do it!

PRODUCER: But it's only so that I can see how it goes.

MOTHER: I can't bear it! I can't bear it!

PRODUCER: But since it's already happened, I don't understand!

MOTHER: No, it's happening now! It happens all the time! My torment is no pretence, sir. I am alive and I am present always. . . . At every moment of my torment . . . A torment which is for ever renewing itself. Always alive and always present. But those two children there . . . Have you heard them say a single word? They can no longer speak! They cling to me still. . . . In order to keep my torment living and present! But for themselves they no longer exist! They no longer exist! And she *(Pointing to the* STEPDAUGHTER.*)* . . . She has run away. . . . Run away from me and is lost. . . . Lost! . . . And if I see her here before me it is for this reason and for this reason alone. . . . To renew at all times. . . . Forever. . . . To bring before me again, present and living, the anguish that I have suffered on her account too.

FATHER *(solemnly)*: The eternal moment, as I told you, sir. She *(He points to the* STEPDAUGHTER.*)* . . . She is here in order to fix me. . . . To hold me suspended throughout all eternity. . . . In the pillory of that one fleeting shameful moment in my life. She cannot renounce her role . . . And you, sir, cannot really spare me my agony.

PRODUCER: Quite so, but I didn't say that I wouldn't present it. As a matter of fact it'll form the basis of the first act. . . . Up to the point where she surprises you (*Pointing to the* MOTHER.)

FATHER: That is right. Because it is my sentence. All our passion. . . . All our suffering. . . . Which must culminate in *her* cry. (*Pointing to the* MOTHER.)

STEPDAUGHTER: I can still hear it ringing in my ears! That cry sent me mad! You can play me just as you like . . . It doesn't matter. Dressed, if you like, provided that I can have my arms bare at least. . . . Just my arms bare. . . . Because, you see, standing there. . . . (*She goes up to the* FATHER *and rests her head on his chest.*) With my head resting on his chest like this . . . and with my arms round his neck . . . I could see a vein throbbing away in my arm. And then . . . Just as if that pulsing vein alone gave me a sense of horror . . . I shut my eyes tight and buried my head in his chest. (*Turning towards the* MOTHER.) Scream, Mummy! Scream! (*She buries her head in the* FATHER's *chest and, raising her shoulders as if in order not to hear the cry, adds in a voice stifled with torment.*) Scream, as you screamed then!

MOTHER (*rushing upon them to separate them*): No! No! She's my daughter! (*And having torn her daughter away.*) You brute! You brute! She's my daughter! Can't you see that she's my daughter?

PRODUCER (*retreating at the cry right up to the footlights, amid the general dismay of the* ACTORS): Excellent! Excellent! And then . . . Curtain! Curtain!

FATHER (*rushing over to him convulsively*): Yes, because that's how it really happened!

PRODUCER (*quite convinced, admiration in his voice*): Oh, yes, we must have the curtain there. . . . That cry and then . . . Curtain! Curtain!

(*At the repeated shouts of the* PRODUCER *the* STAGE-HAND *on the curtain lets it down, leaving the* PRODUCER *and the* FATHER *between it and the footlights.*)

PRODUCER (*looking up, his arms raised*): Oh, the damned fool! I say, 'Curtain' . . . Meaning that I want the act to end there. . . . And he really does go and bring the curtain down. (*to the* FATHER, *lifting up a corner of the curtain.*) Oh, yes! That's absolutely wonderful! Very good indeed! That'll get them! There's no *if* or *but* about it. . . . That line and then . . . *Curtain!* We've got something in that first act . . . or I'm a Dutchman! (*Disappears through the curtain with the* FATHER.)

ACT 3

(*When the curtain goes up again the audience sees that the* STAGE-HANDS *have dismantled the previous set and put on in its place a small garden fountain. On one side of the stage the* ACTORS *are sitting in a row, and on the other side, the* CHARACTERS. *The* PRODUCER *is standing in a meditative attitude in the middle of the stage with his hand clenched over his mouth. There is a brief pause.*)

PRODUCER (*with a shrug of his shoulders*): Oh, well! . . . Let's get on with Act II! Now if you'll only leave it all to me, as we agreed, everything'll sort itself out.

STEPDAUGHTER: This is where we make our entry into his house . . . (*Pointing to the* FATHER.) In spite of him! (*Pointing to the* SON.)

PRODUCER (*out of patience*): Yes, yes! But leave it to me, I tell you!

STEPDAUGHTER: Well. . . . So long as it's made quite clear that it was against his wishes.

MOTHER (*from the corner, shaking her head*): For all the good that's come of it. . . .

STEPDAUGHTER (*turning to her quickly*): That doesn't matter! The more harm that it's done us, the more remorse for him!

PRODUCER (*impatiently*): I understand all that! I'll take it all into account! don't you worry about it!

MOTHER (*a supplicant note in her voice*): But I do beg you, sir . . . To set my conscience at rest. . . . To make it quite plain that I tried in every way I could to . . .

STEPDAUGHTER (*interrupting contemptuously and continuing her* MOTHER's *speech*): . . . to pacify me, to persuade me not to get my own back. . . . (*to the* PRODUCER) Go on . . . do what she asks you! Give her that satisfaction. . . . Because she's quite right, you know! I'm enjoying myself no end, because . . . Well, just look . . . The meeker she is, the more she tries to wriggle her way into his heart, the more he holds himself aloof, the more distant he becomes. I can't think why she bothers!

PRODUCER: Are we going to get started on the second act or are we not?

STEPDAUGHTER: I won't say another word! But, you know, it won't be possible to play it all in the garden, as you suggested.

PRODUCER: Why not?

STEPDAUGHTER: Because he (*Pointing to the* SON *again.*) shuts himself up in his room all the time. . . . Holding himself aloof. . . . And, what's more, there's all the boy's part. . . . Poor bewildered little devil. . . . As I told you, all that takes place indoors.

PRODUCER: I know all about that! On the other hand you do understand that we can hardly stick up notices telling the audience what the scene is. . . . Or change the set three or four times in one act.

LEADING MAN: They used to in the good old days.

PRODUCER: Oh, yes. . . . When the intelligence of the audience was about up to the level of that little girl's there. . . .

LEADING LADY: And it does make it easier to get the sense of illusion.

FATHER (*immediately, rising*): Illusion, did you say? For Heaven's sake, please don't use the word illusion! Please don't use that word. . . . It's a particularly cruel one for us!

PRODUCER (*astounded*): And why's that?

FATHER: It's cruel! Cruel! You should have known that!

PRODUCER: What ought we to say then? We were referring to the illusion that we have to create on this stage . . . for the audience. . . .

LEADING MAN: . . . with our acting. . . .

PRODUCER: . . . the illusion of a reality!

FATHER: I understand, sir. But you . . . Perhaps you can't understand us. Forgive me! Because . . . you see . . . for you and for your actors, all this is only . . . and quite rightly so. . . . All this is only a game.

LEADING LADY (*indignantly interrupting him*): What do you mean, a game? We're not children! We're serious actors!

FATHER: I don't deny it! And in fact, in using the term, I was referring to your art which must, as this gentleman has said, create a perfect illusion of reality.

PRODUCER: Precisely!

FATHER: Now just consider the fact that we (*Pointing quickly to himself and to the other* FIVE CHARACTERS.) as ourselves, have no other reality outside this illusion!

PRODUCER (*in utter astonishment, looking round at his actors who show the same bewildered amazement*): And what does all that mean?

FATHER (*the ghost of a smile on his face. There is a brief pause while he looks at them all*): As I said. . . . What other reality should we have? What for you is an illusion that you have to create, for us, on the other hand, is our sole reality. The only reality we know. (*There he takes a step or two toward the* PRODUCER *and adds.*) But it's not only true in our case, you know. Just think it over. (*He looks into his eyes.*) Can you tell me who you are? (*And he stands there pointing his index finger at him.*)

PRODUCER (*disturbed, a half-smile on his lips*): What? Who am I? I'm myself!

FATHER: And suppose I were to tell you that that wasn't true? Suppose I told you that you were me? . . .

PRODUCER: I should say that you were mad! (*The* ACTORS *laugh.*)

FATHER: You're quite right to laugh, because here everything's a game. (*to the* PRODUCER) And you can object, therefore, that it's only in fun that that gentleman (*Pointing to the* LEADING MAN.) who is *himself* must be *me* who, on the contrary, am myself. . . . That is, *the person you see here.* There, you see. I've caught you in a trap! (*The* ACTORS *laugh again.*)

PRODUCER (*annoyed*): But you said all this not ten minutes ago! Do we have to go over all that again?

FATHER: No. As a matter of fact that wasn't what I intended. I should like to invite you to abandon this game . . . (*Looking at the* LEADING LADY *as if to forestall what she will say.*) Your art! Your art! . . . The game that it is customary for you and your actors to play here in this theatre. And once again I ask you in all seriousness. . . . Who are you?

PRODUCER (*turning to the* ACTORS *in utter amazement, an amazement not unmixed with irritation*): What a cheek the fellow has! A man who calls himself a character comes here and asks me who I am!

FATHER (*with dignity, but in no way haughtily*): A character, sir, may always ask a man who he is. Because a character has a life which is truly his, marked with his own special characteristics. . . . And as a result he is always somebody! Whilst a man. . . . And I'm not speaking of you personally at the moment. . . . Man in general . . . Can quite well be nobody.

PRODUCER: That as may be! But you're asking *me* these questions. Me, do you understand? The Producer! The boss!

FATHER (*softly, with gentle humility*): But only in order to know if you, you as you really are now, are seeing yourself as, for instance, after all the time that has gone by, you see yourself as you were at some point in the past. . . . With all the illusions that you had then . . . with everything . . . all the things you had deep down inside you . . . everything that made up your external world . . . everything as it appeared to you then . . . and as it *was,* as it was in reality for you then! Well . . . thinking back on those illusions which you no longer have . . . on all those things that no longer *seem* to be what they *were* once upon a time . . . don't you feel that . . . I won't say these boards. . . . No! . . . That the very earth itself is slipping away from under your feet, when you reflect that in the same way this *you* that you now feel yourself to be . . . all your reality as it is today . . . is destined to seem an illusion tomorrow?

PRODUCER (*not having understood much of all this, and somewhat taken aback by this argument*): Well? And where does all this get us, anyway?

FATHER: Nowhere. I only want to make you see that if

we *(Again pointing to himself and to the other* CHARACTERS.*)* have no reality outside the world of illusion, it would be as well if you mistrusted your own reality. . . . The reality that you breathe and touch today . . . Because like the reality of yesterday, it is fated to reveal itself as a mere illusion tomorrow.

PRODUCER *(deciding to make fun of him)*: Oh, excellent! And so you'd say that you and this play of yours that you've been putting on for my benefit are more real than I am?

FATHER *(with the utmost seriousness)*: Oh, without a doubt.

PRODUCER: Really?

FATHER: I thought that you'd understood that right from the very beginning.

PRODUCER: More real than I am?

FATHER: If your reality can change from one day to the next. . . .

PRODUCER: But everybody knows that it can change like that! It's always changing. . . . Just like everybody else's.

FATHER *(with a cry)*: No, ours doesn't change! You see. . . . That's the difference between us! Our reality doesn't change. . . . It can't change. . . . It can never be in any way different from what it is. . . . Because it is already fixed. . . . Just as it is. . . . For ever! For ever it is *this* reality. . . . It's terrible! . . . This immutable reality. . . . It should make you shudder to come near us!

PRODUCER *(quickly, suddenly struck by an idea. He moves over and stands squarely in front of him)*: I should like to know, however, when anyone ever saw a character step out of his part and begin a long dissertation on it like the one you've just been making. . . . Expounding it. . . . Explaining it. . . . Can you tell me? . . . I've never seen it happen before!

FATHER: You have never seen it happen before because authors usually hide the details of their work of creation. Once the characters are alive. . . . Once they are standing truly alive before their author. . . . He does nothing but follow the words and gestures that they suggest to him. . . . And he must want them to be what they themselves want to be. For woe betide him if he doesn't do what they wish him to do! When a character is born he immediately acquires such an independence . . . Even of his own author. . . . That everyone can imagine him in a whole host of situations in which his author never thought of placing him. . . . They can even imagine his acquiring, sometimes, a significance that the author never dreamt of giving him.

PRODUCER: Yes. . . . I know all that!

FATHER: Well, then, why are you so astonished at seeing us? Just imagine what a misfortune it is for a character to be born alive. . . . Created by the imagination of an author who afterwards sought to deny him life. . . . Now tell me whether a character who has been left unrealised in this way. . . . Living, yet without a life. . . . Whether this character hasn't the right to do what we are doing now. . . . Here and now. . . . For your benefit? . . . After we had spent . . . Oh, such ages, believe me! . . . Doing it for his benefit . . . Trying to persuade him, trying to urge him to realise us. . . . First of all I would present myself to him. . . . Then she would . . . *(Pointing to the* STEPDAUGHTER.*)* . . . And then her poor Mother. . . .

STEPDAUGHTER *(coming forward as if in a trance)*: Yes, what he says is true. . . . I would go and tempt him. . . . There, in his gloomy study. . . . Just at twilight. . . . He would be sitting there, sunk in an armchair. . . . Not bothering to stir himself and switch on the light. . . . Content to let the room get darker and darker. . . . Until the whole room was filled with a darkness that was alive with our presence. . . . We were there to tempt him. . . . *(And then, as if she saw herself as still in that study and irritated by the presence of all those actors.)* Oh, go away. . . . All of you! Leave us alone! Mummy . . . and her son. . . . I and the little girl. . . . The boy by himself. . . . Always by himself. . . . Then he and I together. *(A faint gesture in the direction of the* FATHER*)* And then. . . . By myself. . . . By myself . . . alone in that darkness. *(A sudden turn round as if she wished to seize and fix the vision that she has of herself, the living vision of herself that she sees shining in the darkness.)* Yes, my life! Ah, what scenes, what wonderful scenes we suggested to him! And I . . . I tempted him more than any of them. . . .

FATHER: Indeed you did! And it may well be that it's all your fault that he wouldn't give us the life we asked for. . . . You were too persistent. . . . Too impudent. . . . You exaggerated too much. . . .

STEPDAUGHTER: What? When it was he who wanted me to be what I am? *(She goes up to the* PRODUCER *and says confidentially.)* I think it's much more likely that he refused because he felt depressed . . . or because of his contempt for the theatre. . . . Or at least, for the present-day theatre with all its pandering to the box-office. . . .

PRODUCER: Let's get on! Let's get on, for God's sake! Let's have some action!

STEPDAUGHTER: It looks to me as if we've got too much action for you already. . . . Just staging our entry into his house. *(Pointing to the* FATHER.*)* You yourself said that you couldn't stick up notices or be changing the set every five minutes.

PRODUCER: And neither can we! Of course we can't! What we've got to do is to combine and group all the action into one continuous well-knit scene. . . . Not the sort of thing that you want. . . . With, first of all, your younger brother coming home from school and wandering about the house like some lost soul. . . . Hiding behind doors and brooding on a plan that . . . What did you say it does to him?

STEPDAUGHTER: Dries him up. . . . Shrivels him up completely.

PRODUCER: M'm! Well, as you said. . . . And all the time you can see it more and more clearly in his eyes. . . . Wasn't that what you said?

STEPDAUGHTER: Yes. . . . just look at him! (*Pointing to where he is standing by his* MOTHER.)

PRODUCER: And then, at the same time, you want the child to be playing in the garden, blissfully unaware of everything. The boy in the house, the little girl in the garden. . . . I ask you!

STEPDAUGHTER: Yes . . . happily playing in the sun! That is the only pleasure that I have. . . . Her happiness. . . . All the joy that she gets from playing in the garden. . . . After the wretchedness and the squalor of that horrible room where we all four slept together. . . . And she had to sleep with me. . . . Just think of it. . . . My vile contaminated body next to hers! . . . With her holding me tight in her loving, innocent, little arms! She only had to get a glimpse of me in the garden and she'd run up to me and take me by the hand. She wasn't interested in the big flowers . . . she'd run about looking for the . . . 'weeny' ones. . . . So that she could point them out to me. . . . And she'd be so happy. . . . So excited. . . . (*As she says this she is torn by the memory of it all and gives a long, despairing cry, dropping her head on to her hands which are lying loosely on the little table in front of her. At the sight of her emotion everyone is deeply moved. The* PRODUCER *goes up to her almost paternally and says comfortingly.*)

PRODUCER: We'll have the garden in . . . don't you worry. . . . We'll have the garden scene in. . . . Just you wait and see. . . . You'll be quite satisfied with how I arrange it. . . . We'll play everything in the garden. (*Calling a* STAGE-HAND.) Hey (*his name*)! Let me have something in the shape of a tree or two. . . . A couple of not-too-large cypresses in front of this fountain! (*Two small cypresses descend from the flies. The* FOREMAN *dashes up and fixes them with struts and nails.*)

PRODUCER (*to the* STEPDAUGHTER): That'll do. . . . For the moment anyway. . . . It'll give us a rough idea. (*Calls to the* STAGE-HAND *again.*) Oh (*his name*), let me have something for a sky, will you?

STAGE HAND (*up aloft*): Eh?

PRODUCER: Something for a sky! A flat to go behind the fountain! (*And a white backcloth descends from the flies.*)

PRODUCER: Not white! I said I wanted a sky! Oh, well, it doesn't matter. . . . Leave it! Leave it! . . . I'll fix it myself. . . . (*Calls.*) Hey! . . . You there on the lights! . . . Everything off. . . . And let me have the moonlight blues on! . . . Blues in the batten! . . . A couple of blue spots on the backcloth! . . . Yes, that's it! That's just right!

(*There is now a mysterious moonlit effect about the scene, and the* ACTORS *are prompted to move about and to speak as they would if they were indeed walking in a moonlit garden.*)

PRODUCER (*to the* STEPDAUGHTER): There, do you see? Now the Boy, instead of hiding behind doors inside the house, can move about the garden and hide behind these trees. But, you know, it'll be rather difficult to find a little girl to play that scene with you. . . . The one where she shows you the flowers. (*Turning to the* BOY.) Now come down here a bit! Let's see how it works out! (*Then, since the* BOY *doesn't move.*) Come on! Come on! (*He drags him forward and tries to make him hold his head up. But after every attempt down it falls again.*) Good God, here's a fine how d'ye do. . . . There's something queer about this boy. . . . What's the matter with him? . . . My God, he'll have to say *something*. . . . (*He goes up to him, puts a hand on his shoulder and places him behind one of the trees.*) Now. . . . Forward a little! . . . Let me see you! . . . M'm! . . . Now hide yourself. . . . That's it! Now try popping your head out a bit. . . . Take a look round. . . . (*He goes to one side to study the effect and the* BOY *does what he has been told to do. The* ACTORS *look on, deeply affected and quite dismayed.*) That's excellent! . . . Yes, excellent! (*Turning again to the* STEPDAUGHTER.) Suppose the little girl were to catch sight of him there as he was looking out, and run over to him. . . . Wouldn't that drag a word or two out of him?

STEPDAUGHTER (*rising*): It's no use your hoping that he'll speak. . . . At least not so long as *he's* here. (*Pointing to the* SON.) If you want him to speak, you'll have to send *him* away first.

SON (*going resolutely toward the steps down into the auditorium*): Willingly! I'm only too happy to oblige. Nothing could possibly suit me better!

PRODUCER (*immediately catching hold of him*): Hey! Oh no you don't! Where are you going? You hang on a minute!

(*The* MOTHER *rises in dismay, filled with anguish at the thought that he really is going away. She instinctively raises her arms to prevent him from going, without, however, moving from where she is standing.*)

SON (*he has reached the footlights*): I tell you . . . There's absolutely nothing for me to do here! Let me go, please! Let me go! (*This to the* PRODUCER.)

PRODUCER: What do you mean . . . There's nothing for you to do?

STEPDAUGHTER (*placidly, ironically*): Don't bother to hold him back! He won't go away!

FATHER: He has to play that terrible scene with his Mother in the garden.

SON (*immediately, fiercely, resolutely*): I'm not playing anything! I've said that all along! (*To the PRODUCER*) Let me go!

STEPDAUGHTER (*running over, then addressing the PRODUCER*) Do you mind? (*She gets him to lower the hand with which he has been restraining the SON.*) Let him go! (*Then turning to the SON, as soon as the PRODUCER has dropped his arm.*) Well, go on. . . . Leave us!

(*The SON stands where he is, still straining in the direction of the steps, but, as if held back by some mysterious force, he cannot go down them. Then, amidst the utter dismay and anxious bewilderment of the ACTORS, he wanders slowly along the length of the footlights in the direction of the other flight of steps. Once there, he again finds himself unable to descend, much as he would wish to. The STEPDAUGHTER has watched his progress intently, her eyes challenging, defiant. Now she bursts out laughing.*)

STEPDAUGHTER: He can't, you see! He can't leave us! He must remain here. . . . He has no choice but to remain with us! He's chained to us. . . . Irrevocably! But if I . . . Who really do run away when what is inevitable happens. . . . And I run away because of my hatred for him. . . . I run away just because I can no longer bear the sight of him. . . . Well, if I can still stay here. . . . If I can still put up with his company and with having to have him here before my eyes. . . . Do you think it's likely that he can run away? Why, he was to stay here with that precious father of his. . . . With his mother. . . . Because now she has no other children but him. . . . (*Turning to her MOTHER.*) Come on, Mummy! Come on. . . . (*Turning to the PRODUCER and pointing to the MOTHER.*) There. . . . you see. . . . She'd got up to prevent him from going. . . . (*to her MOTHER, as if willing her actions by some magic power*) Come on! Come on! (*Then to the PRODUCER.*) You can imagine just how reluctant she is to give this proof of her affection in front of your actors. But so great is her desire to be with him that . . . There! . . . You see? . . . She's willing to live out again her scene with him! (*And as a matter of fact the MOTHER has gone up to her SON, and scarcely has the STEPDAUGHTER finished speaking before she makes a gesture to indicate her agreement.*)

SON (*immediately*): No! No! You're not going to drag me into this! If I can't get away, I shall stay here!

But I repeat that I'm not going to do any acting at all!

FATHER (*trembling with excitement, to the PRODUCER*): You can force him to act!

SON: Nobody can force me!

FATHER: I can and I will!

STEPDAUGHTER: Wait! Wait! First of all the little girl has to go to the fountain. . . . (*Goes over to the LITTLE GIRL. She drops on to her knees in front of her and takes her face in her hands.*) Poor little darling. . . . You're looking so bewildered. . . . With those beautiful eyes. . . . You must be wondering just where you are. We're on a stage, dear! What's a stage? Well . . . It's a place where you play at being serious. They put on plays here. And now we're putting a play on. Really and truly! Even you. . . . (*Embracing her, clasping her to her breast and rocking her for a moment or so*) Oh, you little darling. . . . My dear little darling, what a terrible play for you. . . . What a horrible end they've thought out for you! The garden, the fountain. . . . Yes, it's a make-believe fountain . . . The pity is, darling, that everything's make-believe here . . . But perhaps you like a make-believe fountain better than a real one. . . . So that you can play in it. . . . M'm? No. . . . It'll be a game for the others. . . . Not for you unfortunately . . . Because you're real. . . . And you really play by a real fountain. . . . A lovely big green one, with masses of bamboo palms casting shadows. . . . Looking at your reflection in the water. . . . And lots and lots of little baby ducklings swimming about in it, breaking the shadow into a thousand little ripples. You try to take hold of one of the ducklings. . . . (*With a shriek which fills everybody with dismay.*) No, Rosetta, no! Your Mummy's not looking after you. . . . And all because of that swine there. . . . Her son! I feel as if all the devils in hell were loose inside me. . . . And he . . . (*Leaves the LITTLE GIRL and turns with her usual scorn to the BOY.*) What are you doing . . . drooping there like that? . . . Always the little beggar-boy! It'll be your fault too if that baby drowns. . . . Because of the way you go on. . . . As if I didn't pay for everybody when I got you into this house. (*Seizing his arm to make him take his hand out of his pocket.*) What have you got there? What are you trying to hide? Out with it! Take that hand out of your pocket! (*She snatches his hand out of his pocket and to everybody's horror reveals that it is clenched round a revolver. She looks at him for a little while, as if satisfied. Then she says somberly.*) M'm! Where did you get that gun from? . . . And how did you manage to lay your hands on it? (*And since the BOY, in his utter dismay—his eyes are staring and vacant—does not reply.*) You idiot! If I'd been you I shouldn't have killed myself. . . . I'd have killed one of *them*. . . . Or the pair of them! Father and son together! (*She hides them behind the cypress tree where he was lurking before. Then she takes the* LITTLE GIRL *by the hand and leads her towards the fountain. She puts her into the basin of the fountain, and makes her lie down so that she is completely hidden. Finally she goes down on her knees and buries her head in her hands on the rim of the basin of the fountain.*)

PRODUCER: That's it! Good! (*Turning to the* SON.) And at the same time. . . .

SON (*angrily*): What do you mean . . . 'And at the same time'? Oh, no! . . . Nothing of the sort! There never was any scene between her and me! (*Pointing to the* MOTHER.) You make her tell you what really happened! (*Meanwhile the* SECOND ACTRESS *and the* JUVENILE LEAD *have detached themselves from the group of* ACTORS *and are standing gazing intently at the* MOTHER *and the* SON *so that later thay can act these parts.*)

MOTHER: Yes, it's true, sir! I'd gone to his room at the time.

SON: There! Did you hear? To my room! Not into the garden!

PRODUCER: That doesn't matter at all! As I said we'll have to run all the action together into one composite scene!

SON (*becoming aware that the* JUVENILE LEAD *is studying him*): What do you want?

JUVENILE LEAD: Nothing! I was just looking at you.

SON (*turning to the* SECOND ACTRESS): Oh! . . . And *you're* here too, are you? All ready to play *her* part, I suppose? (*Pointing to the* MOTHER.)

PRODUCER: That's the idea! And if you want my opinion you ought to be damned grateful for all the attention they're paying you.

SON: Indeed? Thank you! But hasn't it dawned on you yet that you aren't going to be able to stage this play? Not even the tiniest vestige of us is to be found in you. . . . And all the time your actors are studying us from the outside. Do you think it's possible for us to live confronted by a mirror which, not merely content with freezing us in that particular picture which is the fixing of our expression, has to throw an image back at us which we can no longer recognise? . . . Our own features, yes. . . . But twisted into a horrible grimace.

FATHER: He's quite right! He's quite right, you know!

PRODUCER (*to the* JUVENILE LEAD *and* SECOND ACTRESS): Right you are! Get back with the others!

SON: It's no use your bothering! I'm not having anything to do with this!

PRODUCER: You be quiet for the moment, and let me listen to what your mother has to say. (*to the* MOTHER) You were saying? . . . You'd gone to his room? . . .

MOTHER: Yes, I'd gone to his room. . . . I couldn't bear the strain any longer! I wanted to pour out my heart to him. . . . I wanted to tell him of all the anguish that was tormenting me. . . . But as soon as he saw me come in . . .

SON: There was no scene between us! I rushed out of the room. . . . I didn't want to get involved in any scenes! Because I never have been involved in any! Do you understand?

MOTHER: Yes! That *is* what happened! That is what happened.

PRODUCER: But for the purposes of this play we've simply *got* to have a scene between you and him! Why . . . it's absolutely *essential!*

MOTHER: I'm quite ready to take part in one! Oh, if you could only find some way to give me an opportunity of speaking to him . . . if only for a moment. . . . So that I can pour out my heart to him!

FATHER (*going up to the* SON, *in a great rage*): You'll do what she asks, do you understand? You'll do what your Mother asks!

SON (*more stubbornly than ever*): I'm doing nothing!

FATHER (*taking hold of him by the lapels of his coat and shaking him*): My God, you'll do what I tell you! Or else . . . Can't you hear how she's pleading with you? Haven't you a spark of feeling in you for your Mother?

SON (*grappling with the* FATHER): No, I haven't! For God's sake, let's have done with all this. . . . Once and for all, let's have done with it!

(*General agitation. The* MOTHER *is terrified and tries to get between them in order to separate them.*)

MOTHER: Please! Please!

FATHER (*without relinquishing his hold*): You must obey me! You *must!*

SON (*struggling with him and finally hurling him to the ground. He falls near the steps amidst general horror*): What's come over you? Why are you in this terrible state of frenzy? Haven't you any sense of decency? . . . Going about parading your shame. . . . And ours, too. I'm having nothing to do with this affair! Nothing, do you hear? And by making this stand I am interpreting the wishes of our author, who didn't wish to put us on the stage!

PRODUCER: Oh, God! You come along here and . . .

SON (*pointing to the* FATHER): *He* did! I didn't.

PRODUCER: Aren't you here now?

SON: It was he who wanted to come. . . . And he dragged us all along with him. Then the pair of them went in there with you and agreed on what was to go into the play. But he didn't only stick to what really did occur. . . . No, as if that wasn't enough for any man, he had to put in things that never even happened.

PRODUCER: Well, then, you tell me what really happened! You can at least do that! You rushed out of your room without saying a word?

SON (*he hesitates for a moment*): Without saying a word!

I didn't want to get involved in a scene!

PRODUCER (*pressing him*): And then? What did you do then?

SON (*everybody's attention is on him; amidst the anguished silence he takes a step or two across the front of the stage*): Nothing. . . . As I was crossing the garden . . . (*He breaks off and becomes gloomy and absorbed.*)

PRODUCER (*urging him to speak, very much moved by this extraordinary reserve*): Well? As you were crossing the garden?

SON (*in exasperation, shielding his face with his arm*): Why do you want to force me to tell you? It's horrible!

(*The* MOTHER *is trembling all over and stifled sobs come from her as she looks toward the fountain.*)

PRODUCER (*slowly, quietly . . . he has seen where the* MOTHER *is looking and he now turns to the* SON *with growing apprehension*): The little girl?

SON (*staring straight in front of him, out into the auditorium*): There . . . In the fountain. . . .

FATHER (*from where he is on the floor, pointing with tender pity to the* MOTHER): She was following him. . . .

PRODUCER (*anxiously to the* SON): And what did you do?

SON (*slowly, continuing to stare in front of him*): I rushed up to the fountain. . . . I was about to dive in and fish her out. . . . Then all of a sudden I pulled up short. . . . Behind that tree I saw something that made my blood run cold. . . . The boy. . . . The boy was standing there. . . . Stock still. . . . With madness in his eyes. . . . Staring like some insane creature at his little sister, who was lying drowned in the fountain! (*The* STEPDAUGHTER, *who has all this while been bent over the fountain in order to hide the* LITTLE GIRL, *is sobbing desperately—her sobs coming like an echo from the background. There is a pause.*) I moved towards him. . . . And then . . . (*And from behind the trees where the* BOY *is hidden a revolver shot rings out.*)

MOTHER (*with a heartrending cry she rushes behind the trees accompanied by the* SON *and all the* ACTORS. *There is general confusion*): Oh, my son! My son! (*And then amidst the general hubbub and shouting.*) Help! Oh, help!

PRODUCER (*amidst all the shouting, he tries to clear a space while the* BOY *is carried off behind the skycloth*): Is he wounded? Is he badly hurt?

(*By now everybody, except for the* PRODUCER *and the* FATHER, *who is still on the ground by the steps, has disappeared behind the skycloth. They can be heard muttering and exclaiming in great consternation. Then first from one side, then from the other, the* ACTORS *re-enter.*)

LEADING LADY (*re-entering right, very much moved*): He's dead, poor boy! He's dead! Oh what a terrible thing to happen!

LEADING MAN (*re-entering left, laughing*): What do you mean, dead? It's all make-believe! It's all just a pretence! Don't get taken in by it!

OTHER ACTORS (*entering from the right*): Make-believe? Pretence? Reality! Reality! He's dead!

OTHERS (*from the left*): No! Make-believe! It's all a pretence!

FATHER (*rising and crying out to them*): What do you mean, pretence? Reality, ladies and gentlemen, reality! Reality! (*And desperation in his face, he too disappears behind the backcloth.*)

PRODUCER (*at the end of his tether*): Pretence! Reality! Go to hell, the whole lot of you! Lights! Lights! Lights!

(*The stage and the auditorium are suddenly flooded with very bright light. The* PRODUCER *breathes again as if freed from a tremendous burden. They all stand there looking into one another's eyes, in an agony of suspense and dismay.*)

PRODUCER: My God! Nothing like this has ever happened to me before! I've lost a whole day on their account! (*He looks at his watch.*) You can go home now. . . . All of you! There's nothing we can do now! It's too late to start rehearsing again! I'll see you all this evening. (*And as soon as the* ACTORS *have said 'Goodbye!' and gone he calls out to the* ELECTRICIAN.) Hey (*his name*) Everything off! (*He has hardly got the words out before the theatre is plunged for a moment into utter darkness.*) Hell! You might at least leave me one light on, so that I can see where I'm going!

(*And immediately behind the backcloth, a green flood lights up. It projects the silhouettes of the* CHARACTERS [*minus the* BOY *and the* LITTLE GIRL], *clear-cut and huge, on to the backcloth. The* PRODUCER *is terrified and leaps off the stage. As he does so the green flood is switched off—rather as if its having come on in the first instance had been due to the* ELECTRICIAN'S *having pulled the wrong switch—and the stage is again lit in blue. Slowly the* CHARACTERS *come in and advance to the front of the stage. The* SON *comes in first, from the right, followed by the* MOTHER, *who has her arms outstretched toward him. Then the* FATHER *comes in from the left. They stop halfway down the stage and stand there like people in a trance. Last of all the* STEPDAUGHTER *comes in from the left and runs toward the steps which lead down into the auditorium. With her foot on the top step she stops for a moment to look at the other three and bursts into strident laughter. Then she hurls herself down the steps and runs up the aisle. She stops at the back of the auditorium and turns to look at the three figures standing on the stage. She bursts out laughing again. And when she has disappeared from the auditorium you can still hear her terrible laughter coming from the foyer beyond. A short pause and then,* CURTAIN.)

Figure 1. The Little Girl, the Boy, the Stepdaughter (Barbara Colby), the Son (Paul Shenar), the Mother (Josephine Nichols), and the Father (Richard Dysart) in the American Conservatory Theater production of *Six Characters in Search of an Author,* directed by William Ball and Byron Ringland, San Francisco, 1967. (Photograph: Hank Kranzler.)

Figure 2. The six characters *(standing right)* explain their situation to the producer and actors *(seated left)* in the American Conservatory Theater production of *Six Characters in Search of an Author,* directed by William Ball and Byron Ringland, San Francisco, 1967. (Photograph: Hank Kranzler.)

SIX CHARACTERS IN SEARCH OF AN AUTHOR / 721

Figure 3. The Father as played by The Leading Man (William Patterson) attempts to seduce the Stepdaughter as played by The Leading Lady (Michael Learned) in the American Conservatory Theater production of *Six Characters in Search of an Author,* directed by William Ball and Byron Ringland, San Francisco, 1967. (Photograph: Hank Kranzler.)

Staging of *Six Characters in Search of an Author*

REVIEW OF THE AMERICAN CONSERVATORY
THEATER PRODUCTION, 1967, BY JEANNE
MILLER

The American Conservatory Theater's production of Luigi Pirandello's "Six Characters in Search of an Author" combines all the elements of a suspense melodrama, a philosophical riddle and a black comedy.

It opened last night at Marines' Theater, directed by William Ball and Byron Ringland who have freed the play of many of its enigmas. The tragi-comedy begins quite hilariously with a theatrical company in rehearsal—ACT itself, as a matter of fact, preparing a scene from Brandon Thomas' "Charley's Aunt."

The performers are bouncy and energetic, dressed in brightly colored hippie clothing. Therefore, the appearance of the six characters, starkly garbed in black and undulating in a silent and choreographed lament, strikes an instant and eerie note of fascinating menace.

This same level of paradox is admirably sustained throughout the evening, as the drama veers from the tortured self-analysis of the characters to the shallow interpretation of their passionate history by the actors.

The characters who break into the rehearsal have been abandoned by the author who created them and doomed to wander endlessly unless someone records their story.

The director of the acting company, after futilely attempting to evict them from the theater, finally agrees to have their grim tale portrayed by his troupe. Pandemonium ensues when the actors make a superficial travesty out of the characters' tragic plight.

Richard A. Dysart, who plays the father, is the principal spokesman for Pirandello's cerebrations about reality and illusion. In the hands of a less talented actor, this exposition could easily descend to the level of a windy intellectual exercise. But Dysart infuses his role with such tormented and guilt-ridden emotion that he is enormously moving, especially when he lucidly projects the playwright's thesis about the permanence and value of art in contrast to the absurdity and transiency of life.

Josephine Nichols, too, is excellent as the hapless mother whose frozen, hollow-eyed despair is especially poignant. As the step-daughter, Barbara Colby approaches her role with a steely erotic abandon that is exceedingly effective.

Paul Shenar is properly arrogant and disdainful as the embittered son. And Scott Hylands is engaging as the befuddled director who becomes fascinated and finally distraught by the behavior of the characters. Dion Chesse is also outstanding as the actor who portrays the father.

A note of mordant humor as well as high camp is introduced by the appearance of an actor, Jay Doyle, who plays the role of Madame Pace, the brothel-keeper.

Ball and Ringland have wittily and intelligently kept the production rippling and singing with tremendous theatrical vitality.

SEAN O'CASEY

1880–1964

Although the Abbey Theatre of Dublin did not produce any of his plays until he was forty-three, and though he permanently left Ireland three years later—angered by the tempestuous reception of his work and saddened by the political self-destructiveness of his countrymen—Sean O'Casey remains the most distinguished dramatist of Irish experience to have emerged in the twentieth century or in any other period. The youngest of thirteen children, of whom only five survived, O'Casey (christened John Casey by his Protestant parents) was born and raised amid the poverty and squalor of Dublin's overpopulated tenements, in a painful world that he evocatively detailed in his monumental six-volume autobiography. As a child, he suffered not only from a miserable diet consisting all too often of nothing more than bread and tea, but also from an eye disease that left him nearly blind as an adult. After his father's death when O'Casey was only six, he was raised by his mother, whose heroic struggle to support her surviving children clearly inspired his conception of the brave and devoted women who figure prominently in his best-known dramas of Irish experience, *The Shadow of a Gunman* (1923), *Juno and the Paycock* (1924), and *The Plough and the Stars* (1926).

Young O'Casey also suffered from the tyranny of incompetent schoolmasters, whose brutality moved him to quit school before he was thirteen and to take on a series of unskilled jobs as a candlemaker, dockhand, hod carrier, and road-worker—jobs that brought him into touch with the life and language of the common laborers and the down-and-outers, who also figure in his early dramas of urban Irish experience. Having quit school, he taught himself, with the help of his older sister, to read and write. And, with the encouragement of an older brother, he took part in amateur theatrical performances that exposed him to the works of Shakespeare and of Dion Boucicault, an Irish melodramatic play-wright who dominated the popular Irish, English, and American stages throughout much of the late nineteenth century. Thus, by the age of eighteen, he had already tried his hand at playwriting, though he was never able to get these early plays published or produced.

By his early twenties, O'Casey had also become involved with various nationalistic groups that aimed at gaining Irish independence from Britain. Inspired by the nationalistic movement, he not only learned to play the bagpipes and founded a pipers band, but he also learned the Irish language, taught it to fellow workers in the Gaelic League, and even went so far as to Gaelicize his name to Sean O'Cathasaigh. By his late-thirties, however, O'Casey had become disillusioned with the impractical and often self-serving behavior of the Irish nationalistic leaders as well as with the factionalism that developed among such competing groups as the "Free Staters," who were willing to accept partial independence for Ireland within the British Empire, and the "Diehards," who believed only in complete independence for Ireland. Such factionalism gave rise to the bitterly divisive civil war of 1922. Thus, during his early-forties, he Anglicized his surname to O'Casey.

O'Casey's impatience with the impractical idealism of his countrymen is reflected, in *Juno and the Paycock,* by Johnny Boyle's assertion that "a principle's a principle," which his mother counters with her assertion that "you lost your best principle, me boy, when you lost your arm; them's the only sort o' principles that's any good to a workin' man." In speaking for the principles of "a workin' man," Juno Boyle voices O'Casey's enduring interest in the plight of the impoverished Irish laborer, reflected in his affiliation with the Irish labor unions during the bitter general strike of 1913 and in the Socialist thinking he clearly espouses in such proletarian "morality" plays as *Within the Gates* (1934) and *The Star Turns Red* (1940). Ultimately, in his later visionary plays, such as *Red Roses for Me* (1942) and *Cock-a-doodle Dandy* (1949), O'Casey moves beyond any kind of doctrinaire thinking to an affirmation of the life force itself.

Though the visionary fantasies of his later plays are often seen as diverging radically from the naturalistic mode of his earlier work, O'Casey's writing is almost always characterized by a complex and quite daring mixture of theatrical elements and situations, which finally make it difficult, if not misleading, to attempt a clear-cut categorization of any of his plays. In *The Shadow of a Gunman,* for example, the first of his plays to be staged by the Abbey Theatre, O'Casey sets the action in a Dublin tenement house during the 1920 guerilla warfare between the Irish Republican Army and the British Black and Tans. But within this harshly naturalistic setting, he portrays both the comic and the tragic consequences of his characters' various masquerades, illusions, and self-delusions, by contrasting the vanity of a self-styled poet, with the cowardice of a mock-heroic clown, with the courage of an impressionable young working girl. So, too, in one of his best-known later plays, *Red Roses for Me,* O'Casey sets the action in the impoverished world of working-class Dublin during the general strike of 1913. Yet, over the course of the play, he depicts not only the comic squabbles and the pathetic sufferings of his characters, but also the miraculous, though temporary, transformation of their world through the dream vision of an idealized Ireland.

The technique of juxtaposing the heroic and the mock-heroic is central to both *Juno and the Paycock* and *The Plough and the Stars.* The plot of *Juno,* for example, blends melodrama (the ambiguously-stated will, as well as the pregnant and abandoned girl) with real tragedy (the betrayal of Robbie Tancred, the abduction of Johnny Boyle, and the self-destruction of Ireland). Similarly, *The Plough and the Stars* dramatizes the events of a major moment in Irish history— the Easter Rising of 1916—from the viewpoint of the ordinary people who are both part of history and trapped by it. Even more controversially, O'Casey repeatedly questions the validity of the bloody struggle for Irish independence by associating it with braggart and cowardly characters, as well as by emphasizing its toll upon the women, who are shown losing their families or their lives as a result of events related to the Irish struggle.

O'Casey's exploration of his culture is nowhere more complexly dramatized than in *Juno and the Paycock,* which swirls around a number of strikingly different characters and moods: the comic posturings of Jack Boyle and the slapstick pratfalls of his companion Joxer (see Figure 1); the increasingly pathetic situation of Johnny Boyle and Mary Boyle, brother and sister each trapped by their own misguided choices; the effusive jollity of Maisie Madigan; the visionary prayer of the bereaved Mrs. Tancred (see Figure 2); and always the compassionate yet practical generosity of Juno. This rich tapestry of characters is further complicated by O'Casey's ambiguous depiction of them. Mary Boyle, for example, is both the victimized girl and the slogan-spouting young woman who frets about the color of her hair ribbon; Juno is the only practical and stabilizing element in her family, yet she never really tries to restrain Boyle from spending the inheritance they have not yet received; and Boyle, though selfish and pompous, is also an enduringly comic figure derived from both the braggadocio of Roman comedy and the vainly blustering stage Irishman, whose language and posture are laughably far above his station in life. Johnny Boyle epitomizes O'Casey's ambiguous conception of his characters, and a powerful actor in the role can easily make us share his torment (see Figure 3) even while we recognize his political treachery.

The difficulty of balancing these widely varying characters, moods, and situations is reflected in the two reviews of the 1980 Royal Shakespeare Company production that are reprinted following the text of the play. Though responding to the same production, these reviewers perceive it and judge it quite differently. Derek Mahon, for example, laments its lack of "star turns," its failure to display "the vividness of personality" that animates the strikingly different characters, whereas John Elsom applauds the carefully orchestrated "naturalism" that unifies all the scenes and thus overcomes "the combination of tragedy and farce" that has often troubled audiences and critics. The disagreement of these reviewers reflects the quarrel about the play's serio-comic ending, which juxtaposes the poignant spectacle of Juno, echoing Mrs. Tancred's prayer to "Take away this murdherin' hate, an' give us Thine own eternal love!" with the return of Joxer and Boyle, both drunk. Their concluding slapstick appearance has so often troubled readers, directors, and spectators that it was cut from a professional recording made in the 1950s, which led O'Casey to defend it as "the comic highlight (and the tragic highlight too) of the play."

JUNO AND THE PAYCOCK

BY SEAN O'CASEY

CHARACTERS IN THE PLAY

'CAPTAIN' JACK BOYLE
JUNO BOYLE, *his wife*
JOHNNY BOYLE } *their children*
MARY BOYLE
'JOXER' DALY
MRS. MAISIE MADIGAN
'NEEDLE' NUGENT, *a tailor*
MRS. TANCRED
JERRY DEVINE
CHARLES BENTHAM, *a school teacher*
AN IRREGULAR MOBILIZER
TWO IRREGULARS
A COAL-BLOCK VENDOR

} *Residents in the Tenement*

A SEWING MACHINE MAN
TWO FURNITURE REMOVAL MEN
TWO NEIGHBOURS

SCENE

ACT 1—*The living apartment of a two-roomed tenancy of the Boyle family, in a tenement house in Dublin.*
ACT 2—*The same.*
ACT 3—*The same.*
A few days elapse between Acts 1 and 2, and two months between Acts 2 and 3.
During Act 3 the curtain is lowered for a few minutes to denote the lapse of one hour.
Period of the play, 1922.

ACT 1

The living-room of a two-room tenancy occupied by the Boyle family in a tenement house in Dublin. Left, a door leading to another part of the house; left of door a window looking into the street; at back a dresser; farther to right at back, a window looking into the back of the house. Between the window and the dresser is a picture of the Virgin; below the picture, on a bracket, is a crimson bowl in which a floating votive light is burning. Farther to the right is a small bed partly concealed by cretonne hangings strung on a twine. To the right is the fireplace; near the fireplace is a door leading to the other room. Beside the fireplace is a box containing coal. On the mantelshelf is an alarm clock lying on its face. In a corner near the window looking into the back is a galvanized bath. A table and some chairs. On the table are breakfast things for one. A teapot is on the hob and a frying-pan stands inside the fender. There are a few books on the dresser and one on the table. Leaning against the dresser is a long-handled shovel—the kind invariably used by labourers when turning concrete or mixing mortar. Johnny Boyle is sitting crouched beside the fire. Mary with her jumper off—it is lying on the back of a chair—is arranging her hair before a tiny mirror perched on the table. Beside the mirror is stretched out the morning paper, which she looks at when she isn't gazing into the mirror. She is a well-made and good-looking girl of twenty-two. Two forces are working in her mind—one, through the circumstances of her life, pulling her back; the other, through the influence of books she has read, pushing her forward. The opposing forces are apparent in her speech and her manners, both of which are degraded by her environment, and improved by her acquaintance—slight though it be—with literature. The time is early forenoon.

MARY: (*Looking at the paper*) On a little by-road, out be-yant Finglas, he was found.

(MRS. BOYLE *enters by door on right; she has been shopping and carries a small parcel in her hand. She is forty-five years of age, and twenty years ago she must have been a pretty woman; but her face has now assumed that look which ultimately settles down upon the faces of the women of the working-class; a look of listless monotony and harassed anxiety, blending with an expression of mechanical resistance. Were circumstances favourable, she would probably be a handsome, active and clever woman.*)

MRS. BOYLE: Isn't he come in yet?

MARY: No, mother.

MRS. BOYLE: Oh, he'll come in when he likes; struttin' about the town like a paycock with Joxer, I suppose. I hear all about Mrs. Tancred's son is in this mornin's paper.

MARY: The full details are in it this mornin'; seven wounds he had—one entherin' the neck, with an exit wound beneath the left shoulder-blade; another in the left breast penethratin' the heart, an' . . .

JOHNNY: (*Springing up from the fire*) Oh, quit that readin' for God's sake! Are yous losin' all your feelin's? It'll soon be that none of you'll read anythin' that's not about butcherin'!

(*He goes quickly into the room on left.*)

MARY: He's gettin' very sensitive, all of a sudden!

MRS. BOYLE: I'll read it myself, Mary, by an' by, when I come home. Everybody's sayin' that he was a Die-hard—thanks be to God that Johnny had nothin' to do with him this long time. . . . (*Opening the parcel and taking out some sausages, which she places on a plate*) Ah, then, if that father o' yours doesn't come in soon for his breakfast, he may go without any; I'll not wait much longer for him.

MARY: Can't you let him get it himself when he comes in?

MRS. BOYLE: Yes, an' let him bring in Joxer Daly along with him? Ay, that's what he'd like an' that's what he's waitin' for—till he thinks I'm gone to work, an' then sail in with the boul' Joxer, to burn all the coal an' dhrink all the tea in the place, to show them what a good Samaritan he is! But I'll stop here till he comes in, if I have to wait till to-morrow mornin'.

Voice of JOHNNY *inside*: Mother!

MRS. BOYLE: Yis?

Voice of JOHNNY: Bring us in a dhrink o' wather.

MRS. BOYLE: Bring in that fella a dhrink o' wather, for God's sake, Mary.

MARY: Isn't he big an' able enough to come out an' get it himself?

MRS. BOYLE: If you weren't well yourself you'd like somebody to bring you in a dhrink o' wather.

(She brings in drink and returns.)

MRS. BOYLE: Isn't it terrible to have to be waitin' this way! You'd think he was bringin' twenty poun's a week into the house the way he's going on. He wore out the Health Insurance long ago, he's afther wearin' out the unemployment dole, an', now, he's thryin' to wear out me! An' constantly singin', no less, when he ought always to be on his knees offerin' up a Novena for a job!

MARY: (*Trying a ribbon fillet-wise around her head*) I don't like this ribbon, ma; I think I'll wear the green—it looks betther than the blue.

MRS. BOYLE: Ah, wear whatever ribbon you like, girl, only don't be botherin' me. I don't know what a girl on strike wants to be wearin' a ribbon round her head for, or silk stockin's on her legs either; it's wearin' them things that make the employers think they're givin' yous too much money.

MARY: The hour is past now when we'll ask the employers' permission to wear what we like.

MRS. BOYLE: I don't know why you wanted to walk out for Jennie Claffey; up to this you never had a good word for her.

MARY: What's the use of belongin' to a Trades Union if you won't stand up for your principles? Why did they sack her? It was a clear case of victimization. We couldn't let her walk the streets, could we?

MRS. BOYLE: No, of course yous couldn't—yous wanted to keep her company. Wan victim wasn't enough. When the employers sacrifice wan victim, the Trades Unions go wan betther be sacrificin' a hundred.

MARY: It doesn't matther what you say, ma—a principle's a principle.

MRS. BOYLE: Yis; an' when I go into oul' Murphy's to-morrow, an' he gets to know that, instead o' payin' all, I'm goin' to borry more, what'll he say when I tell him a principle's a principle? What'll we do if he refuses to give us any more on tick?

MARY: He daren't refuse—if he does, can't you tell him he's paid?

MRS. BOYLE: It's lookin' as if he was paid, whether he refuses or no.

*(*JOHNNY *appears at the door on left. He can be plainly seen now; he is a thin, delicate fellow, something younger than* MARY. *He has evidently gone through a rough time. His face is pale and drawn; there is a tremulous look of indefinite fear in his eyes. The left sleeve of his coat is empty, and he walks with a slight halt.)*

JOHNNY: I was lyin' down; I thought yous were gone. Oul' Simon Mackay is thrampin' about like a horse over me head, an' I can't sleep with him—they're like thunder-claps in me brain! The curse o'—God forgive me for goin' to curse!

MRS. BOYLE: There, now; go back an' lie down again an' I'll bring you in a nice cup o' tay.

JOHNNY: Tay, tay, tay! You're always thinkin' o' tay. If a man was dyin', you'd thry to make him swally a cup o' tay!

(He goes back.)

MRS. BOYLE: I don't know what's goin' to be done with him. The bullet he got in the hip in Easter Week was bad enough; but the bomb that shatthered his arm in the fight in O'Connell Street put the finishin' touch on him. I knew he was makin' a fool of himself. God knows I went down on me bended knees to him not to go agen the Free State.

MARY: He stuck to his principles, an', no matther how you may argue, ma, a principle's a principle.

Voice of JOHNNY: Is Mary goin' to stay here?

MARY: No, I'm not goin' to stay here; you can't expect me to be always at your beck an' call, can you?

Voice of JOHNNY: I won't stop here be meself!

MRS. BOYLE: Amn't I nicely handicapped with the whole o' yous! I don't know what any o' yous ud do without your ma. (*To* JOHNNY) Your father'll be here in a minute, an' if you want anythin', he'll get it for you.

JOHNNY: I hate assin' him for anythin'. . . . He hates to be assed to stir. . . . Is the light lightin' before the picture o' the Virgin?

MRS. BOYLE: Yis, yis! The wan inside to St. Anthony isn't enough, but he must have another wan to the Virgin here!

*(*JERRY DEVINE *enters hastily. He is about twenty-five, well set, active and earnest. He is a type, becoming very common now in the Labour Movement, of a mind knowing enough to make the mass of his associates, who know*

less, a power, and too little to broaden that power for the benefit of all. MARY *seizes her jumper and runs hastily into room left.*)

JERRY: (*Breathless*) Where's the Captain, Mrs. Boyle, where's the Captain?

MRS. BOYLE: You may well ass a body that: he's wherever Joxer Daly is—dhrinkin' in some snug or another.

JERRY: Father Farrell is just afther stoppin' to tell me to run up an' get him to go to the new job that's goin' on in Rathmines; his cousin is foreman o' the job, an' Father Farrell was speakin' to him about poor Johnny an' his father bein' idle so long, an' the foreman told Father Farrell to send the Captain up an' he'd give him a start—I wondher where I'd find him?

MRS. BOYLE: You'll find he's ayther in Ryan's or Foley's.

JERRY: I'll run round to Ryan's—I know it's a great house o' Joxer's.

(*He rushes out.*)

MRS. BOYLE: (*Piteously*) There now, he'll miss that job, or I know for what! If he gets win' o' the word, he'll not come back till evenin', so that it'll be too late. There'll never be any good got out o' him so long as he goes with that shouldher-shruggin' Joxer. I killin' meself workin', an' he shtruttin' about from mornin' till night like a paycock!

(*The steps of two persons are heard coming up a flight of stairs. They are the footsteps of* CAPTAIN BOYLE *and* JOXER. CAPTAIN BOYLE *is singing in a deep, sonorous, self-honoring voice.*)

THE CAPTAIN: Sweet Spirit, hear me prayer! Hear . . . oh . . . hear . . . me prayer . . . hear, oh, hear . . . Oh, he . . . ar . . . oh, he . . . ar . . . me . . . pray . . . er!

JOXER: (*Outside*) Ah, that's a darlin' song, a daaarlin' song!

MRS. BOYLE: (*Viciously*) Sweet spirit hear his prayer! Ah, then, I'll take me solemn affeydavey, it's not for a job he's prayin'!

(*She sits down on the bed so that the cretonne hangings hide her from the view of those entering.*
      THE CAPTAIN *comes in. He is a man of about sixty; stout, grey-haired and stocky. His neck is short, and his head looks like a stone ball that one sometimes sees on top of a gate-post. His cheeks, reddish-purple, are puffed out, as if he were always repressing an almost irrepressible ejaculation. On his upper lip is a crisp, tightly cropped moustache; he carries himself with the upper part of his body slightly thrown back, and his stomach slightly thrust forward. His walk is a slow, consequential strut. His clothes are dingy, and he wears a faded seaman's-cap with a glazed peak.*)

BOYLE: (*To* JOXER, *who is still outside*) Come on, come in, Joxer; she's gone out long ago, man. If there's nothing else to be got, we'll furrage out a cup o' tay, anyway. It's the only bit I get in comfort when she's away. 'Tisn't Juno should be her pet name at all, but Deirdre of the Sorras, for she's always grousin'.

(JOXER *steps cautiously into the room. He may be younger than the* CAPTAIN *but he looks a lot older. His face is like a bundle of crinkled paper; his eyes have a cunning twinkle; he is spare and loosely built; he has a habit of constantly shrugging his shoulders with a peculiar twitching movement, meant to be ingratiating. His face is invariably ornamented with a grin.*)

JOXER: It's a terrible thing to be tied to a woman that's always grousin'. I don't know how you stick it—it ud put years on me. It's a good job she has to be so ofen away, for (*with a shrug*) when the cat's away, the mice can play!

BOYLE: (*With a commanding and complacent gesture*) Pull over to the fire, Joxer, an' we'll have a cup o' tay in a minute.

JOXER: Ah, a cup o' tay's a darlin' thing, a daaarlin' thing—the cup that cheers but doesn't . . .

(JOXER's *rhapsody is cut short by the sight of* JUNO *coming forward and confronting the two cronies. Both are stupefied.*)

MRS. BOYLE: (*With sweet irony—poking the fire, and turning her head to glare at* JOXER) Pull over to the fire, Joxer Daly, an' we'll have a cup o' tay in a minute! Are you sure, now, you wouldn't like an egg?

JOXER: I can't stop, Mrs. Boyle; I'm in a desperate hurry, a desperate hurry.

MRS. BOYLE: Pull over to the fire, Joxer Daly; people is always far more comfortabler here than they are in their own place.

(JOXER *makes hastily for the door.* BOYLE *stirs to follow him; thinks of something to relieve the situation—stops, and says suddenly:*)

Joxer!

JOXER: (*At door ready to bolt*) Yis?

BOYLE: You know the foreman o' that job that's goin' on down in Killesther, don't you, Joxer?

JOXER: (*Puzzled*) Foreman—Killesther?

BOYLE: (*With a meaning look*) He's a butty o' yours, isn't he?

JOXER: (*The truth dawning on him*) The foreman at Killesther—oh yis, yis. He's an oul' butty o' mine—oh, he's a darlin' man, a daaarlin' man.

BOYLE: Oh, then, it's a sure thing. It's a pity we didn't go down at breakfast first thing this mornin'—we might ha' been working now; but you didn't know it then.

JOXER: (*With a shrug*) It's betther late than never.

BOYLE: It's nearly time we got a start, anyhow; I'm fed up knockin' round, doin' nothin'. He promised you—gave you the straight tip?

JOXER: Yis. 'Come down on the blow o' dinner,' says he, 'an' I'll start you, an' any friend you like to brin' with you.' 'Ah,' says I, 'you're a darlin' man, a daaarlin' man.'

BOYLE: Well, it couldn't come at a bether time—we're a long time waitin' for it.

JOXER: Indeed we were; but it's a long lane that has no turnin'.

BOYLE: The blow up for dinner is at one—wait till I see what time it 'tis.

(He goes over to the mantelpiece, and gingerly lifts the clock.)

MRS. BOYLE: Min' now, how you go on fiddlin' with that clock—you know the least little thing sets it asthray.

BOYLE: The job couldn't come at a bether time; I'm feelin' in great fettle, Joxer. I'd hardly believe I ever had a pain in me legs, an' last week I was nearly crippled with them.

JOXER: That's bether an' bether; ah, God never shut wan door but He opened another!

BOYLE: It's only eleven o'clock; we've lashin's o' time. I'll slip on me oul' moleskins afther breakfast, an' we can saunther down at our ayse. *(Putting his hand on the shovel)* I think, Joxer, we'd bether bring our shovels?

JOXER: Yis, Captain, yis; it's bether to go fully prepared an' ready for all eventualities. You bring your long-tailed shovel, an' I'll bring me navvy. We mighten' want them, an', then agen, we might: for want of a nail the shoe was lost, for want of a shoe the horse was lost, an' for want of a horse the man was lost—aw, that's a darlin' proverb, a daarlin' . . .

(As JOXER is finishing his sentence, MRS. BOYLE approaches the door and JOXER retreats hurriedly. She shuts the door with a bang.)

BOYLE: *(Suggestively)* We won't be long pullin' ourselves together agen when I'm working for a few weeks.

(MRS. BOYLE takes no notice.)

BOYLE: The foreman on the job is an oul' butty o' Joxer's; I have an idea that I know him meself. *(Silence)* . . . There's a button off the back o' me moleskin trousers. . . . If you leave out a needle an' thread I'll sew it on meself. . . . Thanks be to God, the pains in me legs is gone, anyhow!

MRS. BOYLE: *(With a burst)* Look here, Mr. Jacky Boyle, them yarns won't go down with Juno. I know you an' Joxer Daly of an oul' date, an' if you think you're able to come it over me with them fairy tales, you're in the wrong shop.

BOYLE: *(Coughing subduedly to relieve the tenseness of the situation)* U-u-u-ugh!

MRS. BOYLE: Butty o' Joxer's! Oh, you'll do a lot o' good as long as you continue to be a butty o' Joxer's!

BOYLE: U-u-u-ugh!

MRS. BOYLE: Shovel! Ah, then, me boyo, you'd do far more work with a knife an' fork than ever you'll do with a shovel! If there was e'er a genuine job goin' you'd be dh'other way about—not able to lift your arms with the pains in your legs! Your poor wife slavin' to keep the bit in your mouth, an' you gallivantin' about all the day like a paycock!

BOYLE: It ud be bether for a man to be dead, bether for a man to be dead.

MRS. BOYLE: *(Ignoring the interruption)* Everybody callin' you 'Captain', an' you only wanst on the wather, in an oul' collier from here to Liverpool, when anybody, to listen or look at you, ud take you for a second Christo For Columbus!

BOYLE: Are you never goin' to give us a rest?

MRS. BOYLE: Oh, you're never tired o' lookin' for a rest.

BOYLE: D'ye want to dhrive me out o' the house?

MRS. BOYLE: It ud be easier to dhrive you out o' the house than to dhrive you into a job. Here, sit down an' take your breakfast—it may be the last you'll get, for I don't know where the next is goin' to come from.

BOYLE: If I get this job we'll be all right.

MRS. BOYLE: Did ye see Jerry Devine?

BOYLE: *(Testily)* No, I didn't see him.

MRS. BOYLE: No, but you seen Joxer. Well, he was here lookin' for you.

BOYLE: Well, let him look!

MRS. BOYLE: Oh, indeed, he may well look, for it ud be hard for him to see you, an' you stuck in Ryan's snug.

BOYLE: I wasn't in Ryan's snug—I don't go into Ryan's.

MRS. BOYLE: Oh, is there a mad dog there? Well, if you weren't in Ryan's you were in Foley's.

BOYLE: I'm telling you for the last three weeks I haven't tasted a dhrop of intoxicatin' liquor. I wasn't in ayther wan snug or dh'other—I could swear that on a prayer-book—I'm as innocent as the child unborn!

MRS. BOYLE: Well, if you'd been in for your breakfast you'd ha' seen him.

BOYLE: *(Suspiciously)* What does he want me for?

MRS. BOYLE: He'll be back any minute an' then you'll soon know.

BOYLE: I'll dhrop out an' see if I can meet him.

MRS. BOYLE: You'll sit down an' take your breakfast, an' let me go to me work, for I'm an hour late already waitin' for you.

BOYLE: You needn't ha' waited, for I'll take no breakfast—I've a little spirit left in me still!

MRS. BOYLE: Are you goin' to have your breakfast—yes or no?

BOYLE: *(Too proud to yield)* I'll have no breakfast—yous can keep your breakfast. *(Plaintively)* I'll knock out a bit somewhere, never fear.

MRS. BOYLE: Nobody's goin' to coax you—don't think that.

(She vigorously replaces the pan and the sausages in the press.)

BOYLE: I've a little spirit left in me still.

(JERRY DEVINE enters hastily.)

JERRY: Oh, here you are at last! I've been searchin' for you everywhere. The foreman in Foley's told me you hadn't left the snug with Joxer ten minutes before I went in.

MRS. BOYLE: An' he swearin' on the holy prayer-book that he wasn't in no snug!

BOYLE: *(To JERRY)* What business is it o' yours whether I was in a snug or no? What do you want to be gallopin' about afther me for? Is a man not to be allowed to leave his house for a minute without havin' a pack o' spies, pimps an' informers cantherin' at his heels?

JERRY: Oh, you're takin' a wrong view of it, Mr. Boyle; I simply was anxious to do you a good turn. I have a message for you from Father Farrell: He says that if you go to the job that's on in Rathmines, an' ask for Foreman Managan, you'll get a start.

BOYLE: That's all right, but I don't want the motions of me body to be watched the way an asthronomer ud watch a star. If you're folleyin' Mary aself, you've no pereeogative to be folleyin' me. *(Suddenly catching his thigh)* U-ugh, I'm afther gettin' a terrible twinge in me right leg!

MRS. BOYLE: Oh, it won't be very long now till it travels into your left wan. It's miraculous that whenever he scents a job in front of him, his legs begin to fail him! Then, me bucko, if you lose this chance, you may go an' furrage for yourself!

JERRY: This job'll last for some time too, Captain, an' as soon as the foundations are in, it'll be cushy enough.

BOYLE: Won't it be a climbin' job? How d'ye expect me to be able to go up a ladder with these legs? An', if I get up aself, how am I goin' to get down agen?

MRS. BOYLE: *(Viciously)* Get wan o' the labourers to carry you down in a hod! You can't climb a laddher, but you can skip like a goat into a snug!

JERRY: I wouldn't let myself be let down that easy, Mr. Boyle; a little exercise, now, might do you all the good in the world.

BOYLE: It's a docthor you should have been, Devine—maybe you know more about the pains in me legs than meself that has them?

JERRY: *(Irritated)* Oh, I know nothin' about the pains in your legs; I've brought the message that Father Farrell gave me, an' that's all I can do.

MRS. BOYLE: Here, sit down an' take your breakfast, an' go an' get ready; an' don't be actin' as if you couldn't pull a wing out of a dead bee.

BOYLE: I want no breakfast, I tell you; it ud choke me afther all that's been said. I've a little spirit left in me still.

MRS. BOYLE: Well, let's see your spirit, then, an' go in at wanst an' put on your moleskin trousers!

BOYLE: *(Moving towards the door on left)* It ud be bether for a man to be dead! U-ugh! There's another twinge in me other leg! Nobody but meself knows the sufferin' I'm goin' through with the pains in these legs o' mine!

(He goes into the room on left as MARY comes out with her hat in her hand.)

MRS. BOYLE: I'll have to push off now, for I'm terrible late already, but I was determined to stay an' hunt that Joxer this time.

(She goes off.)

JERRY: Are you going out, Mary?

MARY: It looks like it when I'm putting on my hat, doesn't it?

JERRY: The bitther word agen, Mary.

MARY: You won't allow me to be friendly with you; if I thry, you deliberately misundherstand it.

JERRY: I didn't always misundherstand it; you were often delighted to have the arms of Jerry around you.

MARY: If you go on talkin' like this, Jerry Devine, you'll make me hate you!

JERRY: Well, let it be either a weddin' or a wake! Listen, Mary, I'm standin' for the Secretaryship of our Union. There's only one opposin' me; I'm popular with all the men, an' a good speaker—all are sayin' that I'll get elected.

MARY: Well?

JERRY: The job's worth three hundred an' fifty pounds a year, Mary. You an' I could live nice an' cosily on that; it would lift you out o' this place an' . . .

MARY: I haven't time to listen to you now—I have to go.

(She is going out, when JERRY bars the way.)

JERRY: *(Appealingly)* Mary, what's come over you with me for the last few weeks? You hardly speak to me, an' then only a word with a face o' bitterness on it. Have you forgotten, Mary, all the happy evenin's that were as sweet as the scented hawthorn that sheltered the sides o' the road as we saunthered through the country?

MARY: That's all over now. When you get your new job, Jerry, you won't be long findin' a girl far better than I am for your sweetheart.

JERRY: Never, never, Mary! No matther what happens, you'll always be the same to me.

MARY: I must be off; please let me go, Jerry.

JERRY: I'll go a bit o' the way with you.

MARY: You needn't, thanks; I want to be by meself.

JERRY: *(Catching her arm)* You're goin' to meet another fella; you've clicked with someone else, me lady!

MARY: That's no concern o' yours, Jerry Devine; let me go!

JERRY: I saw yous comin' out o' the Cornflower Dance Class, an' you hangin' on his arm—a thin, lanky strip of a Micky Dazzler, with a walkin'-stick an' gloves!

Voice of JOHNNY: (*Loudly*) What are you doin' there—pullin' about everything!

Voice of BOYLE: (*Loudly and viciously*) I'm puttin' on me moleskin trousers!

MARY: You're hurtin' me arm! Let me go, or I'll scream, an' then you'll have the oul' fella out on top of us!

JERRY: Don't be so hard on a fella, Mary, don't be so hard.

BOYLE: (*Appearing at the door*) What's the meanin' of all this hillabaloo?

MARY: Let me go, let me go!

BOYLE: D'ye hear me—what's all this hillabaloo about?

JERRY: (*Plaintively*) Will you not give us one kind word, one kind word, Mary?

BOYLE: D'ye hear me talkin' to yous? What's all this hillabaloo for?

JERRY: Let me kiss your hand, your little, tiny, white hand!

BOYLE: Your little, tiny, white hand—are you takin' leave o' your senses, man?

(MARY *breaks away and rushes out.*)

BOYLE: This is nice goin's on in front of her father!

JERRY: Ah, dhry up, for God's sake!

(*He follows* MARY.)

BOYLE: Chiselurs don't care a damn now about their parents, they're bringin' their fathers' grey hairs down with sorra to the grave, an' laughin' at it, laughin' at it. Ah, I suppose it's just the same everywhere—the whole worl's in a state o' chassis! (*He sits by the fire*) Breakfast! Well, they can keep their breakfast for me. Not if they went down on their bended knees would I take it—I'll show them I've a little spirit left in me still! (*He goes over to the press, takes out a plate and looks at it*) Sassige! Well, let her keep her sassige. (*He returns to the fire, takes up the teapot and gives it a gentle shake*) The tea's wet right enough.

(*A pause; he rises, goes to the press, takes out the sausage, puts it on the pan, and puts both on the fire. He attends the sausage with a fork.*)

BOYLE: (*Singing*)

When the robins nest agen,
And the flowers are in bloom,
When the Springtime's sunny smile seems to banish all
   sorrow an' gloom;
Then me bonny blue-ey'd lad, if me heart be true till
   then—
He's promised he'll come back to me,
When the robins nest agen!

(*He lifts his head at the high note, and then drops his eyes to the pan.*)

BOYLE: (*Singing*)

When the . . .

(*Steps are heard approaching; he whips the pan off the fire and puts it under the bed, then sits down at the fire. The door opens and a bearded man looking in says:*)

You don't happen to want a sewin' machine?

BOYLE: (*Furiously*) No, I don't want e'er a sewin' machine!

(*He returns the pan to the fire, and commences to sing again.*)

BOYLE: (*Singing*)

When the robins nest agen,
And the flowers they are in bloom,
He's . . .

(*A thundering knock is heard at the street door.*)

BOYLE: There's a terrible tatheraraa—that's a stranger—that's nobody belongin' to the house.

(*Another loud knock.*)

JOXER: (*Sticking his head in at the door*) Did ye hear them tatherarahs?

BOYLE: Well, Joxer, I'm not deaf.

JOHNNY: (*Appearing in his shirt and trousers at the door on left; his face is anxious and his voice is tremulous*) Who's that at the door; who's that at the door? Who gave that knock—d'ye yous hear me—are yous deaf or dhrunk or what?

BOYLE: (*To* JOHNNY) How the hell do I know who 'tis? Joxer, stick your head out o' the window an' see.

JOXER: An' mebbe get a bullet in the kisser? Ah, none o' them thricks for Joxer! It's betther to be a coward than a corpse!

BOYLE: (*Looking cautiously out of the window*) It's a fella in a thrench coat.

JOHNNY: Holy Mary, Mother o' God, I . . .

BOYLE: He's goin' away—he must ha' got tired knockin'.

(JOHNNY *returns to the room on left.*)

BOYLE: Sit down an' have a cup o' tay, Joxer.

JOXER: I'm afraid the missus ud pop in on us agen before we'd know where we are. Somethin's tellin' me to go at wanst.

BOYLE: Don't be superstitious, man; we're Dublin men, an' not boyos that's only afther comin' up from the bog o' Allen—though if she did come in, right enough, we'd be caught like rats in a thrap.

JOXER: An' you know the sort she is—she wouldn't listen to reason—an' wanse bitten twice shy.

BOYLE: (*Going over to the window at back*) If the worst

came to the worst, you could dart out here, Joxer; it's only a dhrop of a few feet to the roof of the return room, an' the first minute she goes into dh'other room I'll give you the bend, an' you can slip in an' away.

JOXER: (*Yielding to the temptation*) Ah, I won't stop very long anyhow. (*Picking up a book from the table*) Whose is the buk?

BOYLE: Aw, one o' Mary's; she's always readin' lately—nothin' but thrash, too. There's one I was lookin' at dh'other day: three stories, *The Doll's House, Ghosts,* an' *The Wild Duck*—buks only fit for chiselurs!

JOXER: Didja ever rade *Elizabeth, or Th' Exile o' Sibayria?* . . . Ah, it's a darlin' story, a daarlin' story!

BOYLE: You eat your sassige, an' never min' *Th' Exile o' Sibayria.*

(*Both sit down;* BOYLE *fills out tea, pours gravy on* JOXER's *plate, and keeps the sausage for himself.*)

JOXER: What are you wearin' your moleskin trousers for?

BOYLE: I have to go to a job, Joxer. Just afther you'd gone, Devine kem runnin' in to tell us that Father Farrell said if I went down to the job that's goin' on in Rathmines I'd get a start.

JOXER: Be the holy, that's good news!

BOYLE: How is it good news? I wondher if you were in my condition, would you call it good news?

JOXER: I thought . . .

BOYLE: You thought! You think too sudden sometimes, Joxer. D'ye know, I'm hardly able to crawl with the pains in me legs!

JOXER: Yis, yis; I forgot the pains in your legs. I know you can do nothin' while they're at you.

BOYLE: You forgot; I don't think any of yous realize the state I'm in with the pains in my legs. What ud happen if I had to carry a bag o' cement?

JOXER: Ah, any man havin' the like of them pains id be down an' out, down an' out.

BOYLE: I wouldn't mind if he had said it to meself; but, no, oh no, he rushes in an' shouts it out in front o' Juno, an' you know what Juno is, Joxer. We all know Devine knows a little more than the rest of us, but he doesn't act as if he did; he's a good boy, sober, able to talk an' all that, but still . . .

JOXER: Oh ay; able to argufy, but still . . .

BOYLE: If he's runnin' afther Mary, aself, he's not goin' to be runnin' afther me. Captain Boyle's able to take care of himself. Afther all, I'm not gettin' brought up on Virol. I never heard him usin' a curse; I don't believe he was ever dhrunk in his life—sure he's not like a Christian at all!

JOXER: You're afther takin' the word out o' me mouth—afther all, a Christian's natural, but he's unnatural.

BOYLE: His oul' fella was just the same—a Wicklow man.

JOXER: A Wicklow man! That explains the whole thing.

I've met many a Wicklow man in me time, but I never met wan that was any good.

BOYLE: 'Father Farrell,' says he, 'sent me down to tell you.' Father Farrell! . . . D'ye know, Joxer, I never like to be beholden to any o' the clergy.

JOXER: It's dangerous, right enough.

BOYLE: If they do anything for you, they'd want you to be livin' in the Chapel. . . . I'm goin' to tell you somethin', Joxer, that I wouldn't tell to anybody else—the clergy always had too much power over the people in this unfortunate country.

JOXER: You could sing that if you had an air to it!

BOYLE: (*Becoming enthusiastic*) Didn't they prevent the people in '47 from seizin' the corn, an' they starvin'; didn't they down Parnell; didn't they say that hell wasn't hot enough nor eternity long enough to punish the Fenians? We don't forget, we don't forget them things, Joxer. If they've taken everything else from us, Joxer, they've left us our memory.

JOXER: (*Emotionally*) For mem'ry's the only friend that grief can call its own, that grief . . . can . . . call . . . its own!

BOYLE: Father Farrell's beginnin' to take a great intherest in Captain Boyle; because of what Johnny did for his country, says he to me wan day. It's a curious way to reward Johnny be makin' his poor oul' father work. But that's what the clergy want, Joxer—work, work, work for me an' you; havin' us mulin' from mornin' till night, so that they may be in bether fettle when they come hoppin' round for their dues! Job! Well, let him give his job to wan of his hymn-singin', prayer-spoutin', craw-thumpin' Confraternity men!

(*The voice of a coal-block vendor is heard chanting in the street.*)

Voice of COAL VENDOR: Blocks . . . coal-blocks! Blocks . . . coal-blocks!

JOXER: God be with the young days when you were steppin' the deck of a manly ship, with the win' blowin' a hurricane through the masts, an' the only sound you'd hear was, 'Port your helm!' an' the only answer, 'Port it is, sir!'

BOYLE: Them was days, Joxer, them was days. Nothin' was too hot or too heavy for me then. Sailin' from the Gulf o' Mexico to the Antanartic Ocean. I seen things, I seen things, Joxer, that no mortal man should speak about that knows his Catechism. Ofen, an' ofen, when I was fixed to the wheel with a marlin-spike, an' the win's blowin' fierce an' the waves lashin' an' lashin', till you'd think every minute was goin' to be your last, an' it blowed, an' blowed—blew is the right word, Joxer, but blowed is what the sailors use. . . .

JOXER: Aw, it's a darlin' word, a daarlin' word.

BOYLE: An', as it blowed an' blowed, I ofen looked up

at the sky an' assed meself the question—what is the stars, what is the stars?

Voice of COAL VENDOR: Any blocks, coal-blocks; blocks, coal-blocks!

JOXER: Ah, that's the question, that's the question—what is the stars?

BOYLE: An' then, I'd have another look, an' I'd ass meself—what is the moon?

JOXER: Ah, that's the question—what is the moon, what is the moon?

(Rapid steps are heard coming towards the door. BOYLE *makes desperate efforts to hide everything;* JOXER *rushes to the window in a frantic effort to get out;* BOYLE *begins to innocently lilt 'Oh, me darlin' Jennie, I will be thrue to thee', when the door is opened, and the black face of the* COAL VENDOR *appears.)*

COAL VENDOR: D'yez want any blocks?

BOYLE: *(With a roar)* No, we don't want any blocks!

JOXER: *(Coming back with a sigh of relief)* That's afther puttin' the heart across me—I could ha' sworn it was Juno. I'd betther be goin', Captain; you couldn't tell the minute Juno'd hop in on us.

BOYLE: Let her hop in; we may as well have it out first as at last. I've made up me mind—I'm not goin' to do only what she damn well likes.

JOXER: Them sentiments does you credit, Captain; I don't like to say anything as between man an' wife, but I say as a butty, as a butty, Captain, that you've stuck it too long, an' that it's about time you showed a little spunk.

How can a man die betther than facin' fearful odds,
For th' ashes of his fathers an' the temples of his gods?

BOYLE: She has her rights—there's no one denyin' it, but haven't I me rights too?

JOXER: Of course you have—the sacred rights o' man!

BOYLE: Today, Joxer, there's goin' to be issued a proclamation be me, establishin' an independent Republic, an' Juno'll have to take an oath of allegiance.

JOXER: Be firm, be firm, Captain; the first few minutes'll be the worst: if you gently touch a nettle it'll sting you for your pains; grasp it like a lad of mettle, an' as soft as silk remains!

Voice of JUNO *outside*: Can't stop, Mrs. Madigan—I haven't a minute!

JOXER: *(Flying out of the window)* Holy God, here she is!

BOYLE: *(Packing the things away with a rush in the press)* I knew that fella ud stop till she was in on top of us!

(He sits down by the fire.)
JUNO *enters hastily; she is flurried and excited.)*

JUNO: Oh, you're in—you must have been only afther comin' in?

BOYLE: No, I never went out.

JUNO: It's curious, then, you never heard the knockin'.

(She puts her coat and hat on bed.)

BOYLE: Knockin'? Of course I heard the knockin'.

JUNO: An' why didn't you open the door, then? I suppose you were so busy with Joxer that you hadn't time.

BOYLE: I haven't seen Joxer since I seen him before. Joxer! What ud bring Joxer here?

JUNO: D'ye mean to tell me that the pair of yous wasn't collogin' together here when me back was turned?

BOYLE: What ud we be collogin' together about? I have somethin' else to think of besides collogin' with Joxer. I can swear on all the holy prayer-books . . .

MRS. BOYLE: That you weren't in no snug! Go on in at wanst now, an' take off that moleskin trousers o' yours, an' put on a collar an' tie to smarten yourself up a bit. There's a visitor comin' with Mary in a minute, an' he has great news for you.

BOYLE: A job, I suppose; let us get wan first before we start lookin' for another.

MRS. BOYLE: That's the thing that's able to put the win' up you. Well, it's no job, but news that'll give you the chance o' your life.

BOYLE: What's all the mystery about?

MRS. BOYLE: G'win an' take off the moleskin trousers when you're told!

*(*BOYLE *goes into room on left.*
MRS. BOYLE *tidies up the room, puts the shovel under the bed, and goes to the press.)*

MRS. BOYLE: Oh, God bless us, looka the way everything's thrun about! Oh, Joxer was here, Joxer was here!

*(*MARY *enters with* CHARLIE BENTHAM; *he is a young man of twenty-five, tall, good-looking, with a very high opinion of himself generally. He is dressed in a brown coat, brown knee-breeches, grey stockings, a brown sweater, with a deep blue tie; he carries gloves and a walking-stick.)*

MRS. BOYLE: *(Fussing round)* Come in, Mr. Bentham; sit down, Mr. Bentham, in this chair; it's more comfortabler than that, Mr. Bentham. Himself'll be here in a minute; he's just takin' off his trousers.

MARY: Mother!

BENTHAM: Please don't put yourself to any trouble, Mrs. Boyle—I'm quite all right here, thank you.

MRS. BOYLE: An' to think of you knowin' Mary, an' she knowin' the news you had for us, an' wouldn't let on; but it's all the more welcomer now, for we were on our last lap!

Voice of JOHNNY *inside*: What are you kickin' up all the racket for?

BOYLE: *(Roughly)* I'm takin' off me moleskin trousers!

JOHNNY: Can't you do it, then, without lettin' th' whole house know you're takin' off your trousers? What d'ye want puttin' them on an' takin' them off again?

BOYLE: Will you let me alone, will you let me alone? Am

I never goin' to be done thryin' to please th' whole o' yous?

MRS. BOYLE: (*To* BENTHAM) You must excuse th' state o' th' place, Mr. Bentham; th' minute I turn me back that man o' mine always makes a litther o' th' place, a litther o' th' place.

BENTHAM: Don't worry, Mrs. Boyle; it's all right, I assure . . .

BOYLE: (*Inside*) Where's me braces; where in th' name o' God did I leave me braces? . . . Ay, did you see where I put me braces?

JOHNNY: (*Inside, calling out*) Ma, will you come in here an' take da away ou' o' this or he'll dhrive me mad.

MRS. BOYLE: (*Going towards the door*) Dear, dear, dear, that man'll be lookin' for somethin' on th' day o' Judgement. (*Looking into room and calling to* BOYLE) Look at your braces, man, hangin' round your neck!

BOYLE: (*Inside*) Aw, Holy God!

MRS. BOYLE: (*Calling*) Johnny, Johnny, come out here for a minute.

JOHNNY: Ah, leave Johnny alone, an' don't be annoyin' him!

MRS. BOYLE: Come on, Johnny, till I inthroduce you to Mr. Bentham. (*To* BENTHAM) My son, Mr. Bentham; he's afther goin' through the mill. He was only a chiselur of a Boy Scout in Easter Week, when he got hit in the hip; and his arm was blew off in the fight in O'Connell Street. (JOHNNY *comes in.*) Here he is, Mr. Bentham; Mr. Bentham, Johnny. None can deny he done his bit for Irelan', if that's goin' to do him any good.

JOHNNY: (*Boastfully*) I'd do it agen, ma, I'd do it agen; for a principle's a principle.

MRS. BOYLE: Ah, you lost your best principle, me boy, when you lost your arm; them's the only sort o' principles that's any good to a workin' man.

JOHNNY: Ireland only half free'll never be at peace while she has a son left to pull a trigger.

MRS. BOYLE: To be sure, to be sure—no bread's a lot betther than half a loaf. (*Calling loudly in to* BOYLE) Will you hurry up there?

(BOYLE *enters in his best trousers, which aren't too good, and looks very uncomfortable in his collar and tie.*)

MRS. BOYLE: This is my husband; Mr. Boyle, Mr. Bentham.

BENTHAM: Ah, very glad to know you, Mr. Boyle. How are you?

BOYLE: Ah, I'm not too well at all; I suffer terrible with pains in me legs. Juno can tell you there what . . .

MRS. BOYLE: You won't have many pains in your legs when you hear what Mr. Bentham has to tell you.

BENTHAM: Juno! What an interesting name! It reminds one of Homer's glorious story of ancient gods and heroes.

BOYLE: Yis, doesn't it? You see, Juno was born an' chris-

tened in June; I met her in June; we were married in June, an' Johnny was born in June, so wan day I says to her, 'You should ha' been called Juno,' an' the name stuck to her ever since.

MRS. BOYLE: Here, we can talk o' them things agen; let Mr. Bentham say what he has to say now.

BENTHAM: Well, Mr. Boyle, I suppose you'll remember a Mr. Ellison of Santry—he's a relative of yours, I think.

BOYLE: (*Viciously*) Is it that prognosticator an' procrastinator! Of course I remember him.

BENTHAM: Well, he's dead, Mr. Boyle . . .

BOYLE: Sorra many'll go into mournin' for him.

MRS. BOYLE: Wait till you hear what Mr. Bentham has to say, an' then, maybe, you'll change your opinion.

BENTHAM: A week before he died he sent for me to write his will for him. He told me that there were two only that he wished to leave his property to: his second cousin, Michael Finnegan of Santry, and John Boyle, his first cousin, of Dublin.

BOYLE: (*Excitedly*) Me, is it me, me?

BENTHAM: You, Mr. Boyle; I'll read a copy of the will that I have here with me, which has been duly filed in the Court of Probate.

(*He takes a paper from his pocket and reads:*)

6th February 1922

This is the last Will and Testament of William Ellison, of Santry, in the County of Dublin. I hereby order and wish my property to be sold and divided as follows:—

£20 to the St. Vincent de Paul Society.

£60 for Masses for the repose of my soul (5s. for each Mass).

The rest of my property to be divided between my first and second cousins.

I hereby appoint Timothy Buckly, of Santry, and Hugh Brierly, of Coolock, to be my Executors.

(*Signed*) WILLIAM ELLISON.
HUGH BRIERLY.
TIMOTHY BUCKLY.
CHARLES BENTHAM, N.T.

BOYLE: (*Eagerly*) An' how much'll be comin' out of it, Mr. Bentham?

BENTHAM: The Executors told me that half of the property would be anything between £1500 and £2000.

MARY: A fortune, father, a fortune!

JOHNNY: We'll be able to get out o' this place now, an' go somewhere we're not known.

MRS. BOYLE: You won't have to trouble about a job for awhile, Jack.

BOYLE: (*Fervently*) I'll never doubt the goodness o' God agen.

BENTHAM: I congratulate you, Mr. Boyle.

(*They shake hands.*)

BOYLE: An' now, Mr. Bentham, you'll have to have a wet.

BENTHAM: A wet?

BOYLE: A wet—a jar—a boul!

MRS. BOYLE: Jack, you're speakin' to Mr. Bentham, an' not to Joxer.

BOYLE: (*Solemnly*) Juno . . . Mary . . . Johnny . . . we'll have to go into mournin' at wanst. . . . I never expected that poor Bill ud die so sudden. . . . Well, we all have to die some day . . . you, Juno, to-day . . . an' me, maybe, to-morrow. . . . It's sad, but it can't be helped. . . . Requiescat in pace . . . or, usin' our oul' tongue like St. Patrick or St. Bridget, Guh sayeree jeea ayera!

MARY: Oh, father, that's not Rest in Peace; that's God save Ireland.

BOYLE: U-u-ugh, it's all the same—isn't it a prayer? . . . Juno, I'm done with Joxer; he's nothin' but a prognosticator an' a . . .

JOXER: (*Climbing angrily through the window and bounding into the room*) You're done with Joxer, are you? Maybe you thought I'd stop on the roof all the night for you! Joxer out on the roof with the win' blowin' through him was nothin' to you an' your friend with the collar an' tie!

MRS. BOYLE: What in the name o' God brought you out on the roof; what were you doin' there?

JOXER: (*Ironically*) I was dhreamin' I was standin' on the bridge of a ship, an' she sailin' the Antartic Ocean, an' it blowed, an' blowed, an' I lookin' up at the sky an' sayin', what is the stars, what is the stars?

MRS. BOYLE: (*Opening the door and standing at it*) Here, get ou' o' this, Joxer Daly; I was always thinkin' you had a slate off.

JOXER: (*Moving to the door*) I have to laugh every time I look at the deep-sea sailor; an' a row on a river ud make him seasick!

BOYLE: Get ou' o' this before I take the law into me own hands!

JOXER: (*Going out*) Say aw rewaeawr, but not good-bye. Lookin' for work, an' prayin' to God he won't get it!

(*He goes.*)

MRS. BOYLE: I'm tired tellin' you what Joxer was; maybe now you see yourself the kind he is.

BOYLE: He'll never blow the froth off a pint o' mine agen, that's a sure thing. Johnny . . . Mary . . . you're to keep yourselves to yourselves for the future. Juno, I'm done with Joxer. . . . I'm a new man from this out. . . .

(*Clasping* JUNO's *hand, and singing emotionally:*)

O, me darlin' Juno, I will be thrue to thee;
Me own, me darlin' Juno, you're all the world to me.

CURTAIN

ACT 2

The same, but the furniture is more plentiful, and of a vulgar nature. A glaringly upholstered armchair and lounge; cheap pictures and photos everywhere. Every available spot is ornamented with huge vases filled with artificial flowers. Crossed festoons of colored paper chains stretch from end to end of ceiling. On the table is an old attaché case. It is about six in the evening, and two days after the First Act. BOYLE, *in his shirt-sleeves, is voluptuously stretched on the sofa; he is smoking a clay pipe. He is half asleep. A lamp is lighting on the table. After a few moments' pause the voice of* JOXER *is heard singing softly outside at the door—'Me pipe I'll smoke, as I dhrive me moke—are you there, Mor . . . ee . . . ar . . . i . . . teee!'*

BOYLE: (*Leaping up, takes a pen in his hand and busies himself with papers*) Come along, Joxer, me son, come along.

JOXER: (*Putting his head in*) Are you be yourself?

BOYLE: Come on, come on; that doesn't matther; I'm masther now, an' I'm goin' to remain masther.

(JOXER *comes in.*)

JOXER: How d'ye feel now, as a man o' money?

BOYLE: (*Solemnly*) It's a responsibility, Joxer, a great responsibility.

JOXER: I suppose 'tis now, though you wouldn't think it.

BOYLE: Joxer, han' me over that attackey case on the table there. (JOXER *hands the case.*) Ever since the Will was passed I've run hundreds o' dockyments through me han's—I tell you, you have to keep your wits about you.

(*He busies himself with papers.*)

JOXER: Well, I won't disturb you; I'll dhrop in when . . .

BOYLE: (*Hastily*) It's all right, Joxer, this is the last one to be signed to-day.

(*He signs a paper, puts in into the case, which he shuts with a snap, and sits back pompously in the chair.*)

Now, Joxer, you want to see me; I'm at your service— what can I do for you, me man?

JOXER: I've just dhropped in with the £3:5s. that Mrs. Madigan riz on the blankets an' table for you, an' she says you're to be in no hurry payin' it back.

BOYLE: She won't be long without it; I expect the first cheque for a couple o' hundhred any day. There's the five bob for yourself—go on, take it, man; it'll not be the last you'll get from the Captain. Now an' agen we have our differ, but we're there together all the time.

JOXER: Me for you, an' you for me, like the two Musketeers.

BOYLE: Father Farrell stopped me to-day an' tole me how glad he was I fell in for the money.

JOXER: He'll be stoppin' you ofen enough now; I suppose it was 'Mr.' Boyle with him?

BOYLE: He shuk me be the han' . . .

JOXER: (*Ironically*) I met with Napper Tandy, an' he shuk me be the han'!

BOYLE: You're seldom asthray, Joxer, but you're wrong shipped this time. What you're sayin' of Father Farrell is very near to blasfeemey. I don't like any one to talk disrespectful of Father Farrell.

JOXER: You're takin' me up wrong, Captain; I wouldn't let a word be said agen Father Farrell—the heart o' the rowl, that's what he is; I always said he was a darlin' man, a daarlin' man.

BOYLE: Comin' up the stairs who did I meet but that bummer, Nugent. 'I seen you talkin' to Father Farrell,' says he, with a grin on him. 'He'll be folleyin' you,' says he, 'like a Guardian Angel from this out'—all the time the oul' grin on him, Joxer.

JOXER: I never seen him yet but he had that oul' grin on him!

BOYLE: 'Mr. Nugent,' says I, 'Father Farrell is a man o' the people, an', as far as I know the History o' me country, the priests was always in the van of the fight for Irelan's freedom.'

JOXER: (*Fervently*)

Who was it led the van, Soggart Aroon?
Since the fight first began, Soggart Aroon?

BOYLE: 'Who are you tellin'?' says he. 'Didn't they let down the Fenians, an' didn't they do in Parnell? An' now . . .' 'You ought to be ashamed o' yourself,' says I, interruptin' him, 'not to know the History o' your country.' An' I left him gawkin' where he was.

JOXER: Where ignorance 's bliss 'tis folly to be wise; I wondher did he ever read the Story o' Irelan'.

BOYLE: Be J. L. Sullivan? Don't you know he didn't.

JOXER: Ah, it's a darlin' buk, a daarlin' buk!

BOYLE: You'd betther be goin', now, Joxer; his Majesty, Bentham, 'll be here any minute, now.

JOXER: Be the way things is lookin', it'll be a match between him an' Mary. She's thrun over Jerry altogether. Well, I hope it will, for he's a darlin' man.

BOYLE: I'm glad you think so—I don't. (*Irritably*) What's darlin' about him?

JOXER: (*Nonplussed*) I only seen him twiced; if you want to know me, come an' live with me.

BOYLE: He's too dignified for me—to hear him talk you'd think he knew as much as a Boney's Oraculum. He's given up his job as teacher, an' is goin' to become a solicitor in Dublin—he's been studyin' law. I suppose he thinks I'll set him up, but he's wrong shipped. An' th' other fella—Jerry's as bad. The two o' them ud give you a pain in your face, listenin' to them; Jerry believin' in nothin', an' Bentham believin' in everythin'. One that says all is God an' no man; an' th' other that says all is man an' no God!

JOXER: Well, I'll be off now.

BOYLE: Don't forget to dhrop down afther awhile; we'll have a quiet jar, an' a song or two.

JOXER: Never fear.

BOYLE: An' tell Mrs. Madigan that I hope we'll have the pleasure of her organization at our little enthertainment.

JOXER: Righto; we'll come down together.

(*He goes out.*
JOHNNY *comes from room on left, and sits down moodily at the fire.* BOYLE *looks at him for a few moments, and shakes his head. He fills his pipe.*)

Voice of JUNO *at the door*: Open the door, Jack; this thing has me nearly kilt with the weight.

(BOYLE *opens the door.* JUNO *enters carrying the box of a gramophone, followed by* MARY *carrying the horn and some parcels.* JUNO *leaves the box on the table and flops into a chair.*)

JUNO: Carryin' that from Henry Street was no joke.

BOYLE: U-u-ugh, that's a grand-lookin' insthrument—how much was it?

JUNO: Pound down, an' five to be paid at two shillin's a week.

BOYLE: That's reasonable enough.

JUNO: I'm afraid we're runnin' into too much debt; first the furniture, an' now this.

BOYLE: The whole lot won't be much out of £2000.

MARY: I don't know what you wanted a gramophone for—I know Charlie hates them; he says they're destructive of real music.

BOYLE: Desthructive of music—that fella ud give you a pain in your face. All a gramophone wants is to be properly played; its thrue wondher is only felt when everythin's quiet—what a gramophone wants is dead silence!

MARY: But, father, Jerry says the same; afther all, you can only appreciate music when your ear is properly trained.

BOYLE: That's another fella ud give you a pain in your face. Properly thrained! I suppose you couldn't appreciate football unless your fut was properly thrained.

MRS. BOYLE: (*To* MARY) Go on in ower that an' dress, or Charlie'll be in on you, an' tea nor nothin'll be ready.

(MARY *goes into room left.*)

MRS. BOYLE: (*Arranging table for tea*) You didn't look at our new gramophone, Johnny?

JOHNNY: 'Tisn't gramophones I'm thinking of.

MRS. BOYLE: An' what is it you're thinkin' of, allanna?

JOHNNY: Nothin', nothin', nothin'.

MRS. BOYLE: Sure, you must be thinkin' of somethin'; it's yourself that has yourself the way y'are; sleepin'

wan night in me sisther's, an' the nex' in your father's brother's—you'll get no rest goin' on that way.

JOHNNY: I can rest nowhere, nowhere, nowhere.

MRS. BOYLE: Sure, you're not thryin' to rest anywhere.

JOHNNY: Let me alone, let me alone, let me alone, for
God's sake.

(A knock at street door.)

MRS. BOYLE: (*In a flutter*) Here he is; here's Mr. Bentham!

BOYLE: Well, there's room for him; it's a pity there's not
a brass band to play him in.

MRS. BOYLE: We'll han' the tea round, an' not be clus-
thered round the table, as if we never seen nothin'.

(Steps are heard approaching, and JUNO *opening the
door, allows* BENTHAM *to enter.)*

JUNO: Give your hat an' stick to Jack, there . . . sit down,
Mr. Bentham . . . no, not there . . . in th' easy chair
be the fire . . . there, that's bether. Mary'll be out
to you in a minute.

BOYLE: (*Solemnly*) I seen be the paper this mornin' that
Consols was down half per cent. That's serious, min'
you, an' shows the whole counthry's in a state o'
chassis.

MRS. BOYLE: What's Consols, Jack?

BOYLE: Consols? Oh, Consols is—oh, there's no use
tellin' women what Consols is—th' wouldn't un-
dherstand.

BENTHAM: It's just as you were saying, Mr. Boyle . . .

(MARY enters, charmingly dressed.)

BENTHAM: Oh, good evening, Mary; how pretty you're
looking!

MARY: (*Archly*) Am I?

BOYLE: We were just talkin' when you kem in, Mary; I
was tellin' Mr. Bentham that the whole counthry's
in a state o' chassis.

MARY: (*To* BENTHAM) Would you prefer the green or
the blue ribbon round me hair, Charlie?

MRS. BOYLE: Mary, your father's speakin'.

BOYLE: (*Rapidly*) I was jus' tellin' Mr. Bentham that the
whole counthry's in a state o' chassis.

MARY: I'm sure you're frettin', da, whether it is or no.

MRS. BOYLE: With all our churches an' religions, the
worl's not a bit the better.

BOYLE: (*With a commanding gesture*) Tay!

(MARY and MRS. BOYLE dispense the tea.)

MRS. BOYLE: An' Irelan's takin' a leaf out o' the worl's
buk; when we got the makin' of our own laws I
thought we'd never stop to look behind us, but
instead of that we never stopped to look before us!
If the people ud folley up their religion bether
there'd be a bether chance for us—what do you
think, Mr. Bentham?

BENTHAM: I'm afraid I can't venture to express an opinion on that point, Mrs. Boyle; dogma has no attraction for me.

MRS. BOYLE: I forgot you didn't hold with us: what's
this you said you were?

BENTHAM: A Theosophist, Mrs. Boyle.

MRS. BOYLE: An' what in the name o' God's a Theosophist?

BOYLE: A Theosophist, Juno, 's a—tell her, Mr. Bentham, tell her.

BENTHAM: It's hard to explain in a few words: The-
osophy's founded on The Vedas, the religious
books of the East. Its central theme is the existence
of an all-pervading Spirit—the Life-Breath. Nothing really exists but this one Universal Life-Breath.
And whatever even seems to exist separately from
this Life-Breath, doesn't really exist at all. It is all
vital force in man, in all animals, and in all vegeta-
tion. This Life-Breath is called the Prawna.

MRS. BOYLE: The Prawna! What a comical name!

BOYLE: Prawna; yis, the Prawna. (*Blowing gently through
his lips*) That's the Prawna!

MRS. BOYLE: Whisht, whisht, Jack.

BENTHAM: The happiness of man depends upon his
sympathy with this Spirit. Men who have reached
a high state of excellence are called Yogi. Some men
become Yogi in a short time, it may take others
millions of years.

BOYLE: Yogi! I seen hundreds of them in the streets
o' San Francisco.

BENTHAM: It is said by these Yogi that if we practise
certain mental exercises we would have powers denied to others—for instance, the faculty of seeing
things that happen miles and miles away.

MRS. BOYLE: I wouldn't care to meddle with that sort o'
belief; it's a very curious religion, altogether.

BOYLE: What's curious about it? Isn't all religions curious?—if they weren't, you wouldn't get any one to
believe them. But religions is passin' away—they've
had their day like everything else. Take the real
Dublin people, f'rinstance: they know more about
Charlie Chaplin an' Tommy Mix than they do about
SS. Peter an' Paul!

MRS. BOYLE: You don't believe in ghosts, Mr. Bentham?

MARY: Don't you know he doesn't, mother?

BENTHAM: I don't know that, Mary. Scientists are beginning to think that what we call ghosts are sometimes
seen by persons of a certain nature. They say that
sensational actions, such as the killing of a person,
demand great energy, and that energy lingers in
the place where the action occurred. People may
live in the place and see nothing, when someone
may come along whose personality has some peculiar connection with the energy of the place, and,
in a flash, the person sees the whole affair.

JOHNNY: (*Rising swiftly, pale and affected*) What sort o'
talk is this to be goin' on with? Is there nothin'
bether to be talkin' about but the killin' o' people?

My God, isn't it bad enough for these things to happen without talkin' about them!

(*He hurriedly goes into the room on left.*)

BENTHAM: Oh, I'm very sorry, Mrs. Boyle; I never thought . . .

MRS. BOYLE: (*Apologetically*) Never mind, Mr. Bentham, he's very touchy.

(*A frightened scream is heard from* JOHNNY *inside.*)

MRS. BOYLE: Mother of God, what's that?

(*He rushes out again, his face pale, his lips twitching, his limbs trembling.*)

JOHNNY: Shut the door, shut the door, quick, for God's sake! Great God, have mercy on me! Blessed Mother o' God, shelter me, shelther your son!

MRS. BOYLE: (*Catching him in her arms*) What's wrong with you? What ails you? Sit down, sit down, here, on the bed . . . there now . . . there now.

MARY: Johnny, Johnny, what ails you?

JOHNNY: I seen him, I seen him . . . kneelin' in front o' the statue . . . merciful Jesus, have pity on me!

MRS. BOYLE: (*To* BOYLE) Get him a glass o' whisky . . . quick, man, an' don't stand gawkin'.

(BOYLE *gets the whisky.*)

JOHNNY: Sit here, sit here, mother . . . between me an' the door.

MRS. BOYLE: I'll sit beside you as long as you like, only tell me what was it came across you at all?

JOHNNY: (*After taking some drink*) I seen him. . . . I seen Robbie Tancred kneelin' down before the statue . . . an' the red light shinin' on him . . . an' when I went in . . . he turned an' looked at me . . . an' I seen the woun's bleedin' in his breast. . . . Oh, why did he look at me like that? . . . it wasn't my fault that he was done in. . . . Mother o' God, keep him away from me!

MRS. BOYLE: There, there, child, you've imagined it all. There was nothin' there at all—it was the red light you seen, an' the talk we had put all the rest into your head. Here, dhrink more o' this—it'll do you good. . . . An', now, stretch yourself down on the bed for a little. (*To* BOYLE) Go in, Jack, an' show him it was only in his own head it was.

BOYLE: (*Making no move*) E-e-e-e-eh; it's all nonsense; it was only a shadda he saw.

MARY: Mother o' God, he made me heart lep!

BENTHAM: It was simply due to an overwrought imagination—we all get that way at times.

MRS. BOYLE: There, dear, lie down in the bed, an' I'll put the quilt across you . . . e-e-e-eh, that's it . . . you'll be as right as the mail in a few minutes.

JOHNNY: Mother, go into the room an' see if the light's lightin' before the statue.

MRS. BOYLE: (*To* BOYLE) Jack, run in an' see if the light's lightin' before the statue.

BOYLE: (*To* MARY) Mary, slip in an' see if the light's lightin' before the statue.

(MARY *hesitates to go in.*)

BENTHAM: It's all right; Mary, I'll go.

(*He goes into the room; remains for a few moments, and returns.*)

BENTHAM: Everything's just as it was—the light burning bravely before the statue.

BOYLE: Of course; I knew it was all nonsense.

(*A knock at the door.*)

BOYLE: (*Going to open the door*) E-e-e-e-eh.

(*He opens it, and* JOXER, *followed by* MRS. MADIGAN, *enters.* MRS. MADIGAN *is a strong, dapper little woman of about forty-five; her face is almost always a widespread smile of complacency. She is a woman who, in manner at least, can mourn with them that mourn, and rejoice with them that do rejoice. When she is feeling comfortable, she is inclined to be reminiscent; when others say anything, or following a statement made by herself, she has a habit of putting her head a little to one side, and nodding it rapidly several times in succession, like a bird pecking at a hard berry. Indeed, she has a good deal of the bird in her, but the bird instinct is by no means a melodious one. She is ignorant, vulgar and forward, but her heart is generous withal. For instance, she would help a neighbor's sick child; she would probably kill the child, but her intention would be to cure it; she would be more at home helping a drayman to lift a fallen horse. She is dressed in a rather soiled grey dress and a vivid purple blouse; in her hair is a huge comb, ornamented with huge colored beads. She enters with a gliding step, beaming smile and nodding head.* BOYLE *receives them effusively.*)

BOYLE: Come on in, Mrs. Madigan; come on in; I was afraid you weren't comin'. . . . (*Slyly*) There's some people able to dhress, ay, Joxer?

JOXER: Fair as the blossoms that bloom in the May, an' sweet as the scent of the new-mown hay. . . . Ah, well she may wear them.

MRS. MADIGAN: (*Looking at* MARY) I know some as are as sweet as the blossoms that bloom in the May—oh, no names, no pack dhrill!

BOYLE: An' now I'll inthroduce the pair o' yous to Mary's intended: Mr. Bentham, this is Mrs. Madigan, an oul' back-parlour neighbour, that, if she could help it at all, ud never see a body shuk!

BENTHAM: (*Rising, and tentatively shaking the hand of* MRS. MADIGAN) I'm sure, it's a great pleasure to know you, Mrs. Madigan.

MRS. MADIGAN: An' I'm goin' to tell you, Mr. Bentham, you're goin' to get as nice a bit o' skirt in Mary, there, as ever you seen in your puff. Not like some of the dhressed-up dolls that's knockin' about lookin' for men when it's a skelpin' they want. I remember, as well as I remember yesterday, the day she was born—of a Tuesday, the 25th o' June, in the year 1901, at thirty-three minutes past wan in the day be Foley's clock, the pub at the corner o' the street. A cowld day it was too, for the season o' the year, an' I remember sayin' to Joxer, there, who I met comin' up th' stairs, that the new arrival in Boyle's ud grow up a hardy chiselur if it lived, an' that she'd be somethin' one o' these days that nobody suspected, an' so signs on it, here she is today, goin' to be married to a young man lookin' as if he'd be fit to commensurate in any position in life it ud please God to call him!

BOYLE: (*Effusively*) Sit down, Mrs. Madigan, sit down, me oul' sport. (*To* BENTHAM) This is Joxer Daly, Past Chief Ranger of the Dear Little Shamrock Branch of the Irish National Foresters, an oul' front-top neighbour, that never despaired, even in the darkest days of Ireland's sorra.

JOXER: Nil desperandum, Captain, nil desperandum.

BOYLE: Sit down, Joxer, sit down. The two of us was ofen in a tight corner.

MRS. BOYLE: Ay, in Foley's snug!

JOXER: An' we kem out of it flyin', we kem out of it flyin', Captain.

BOYLE: An' now for a dhrink—I know yous won't refuse an oul' friend.

MRS. MADIGAN: (*To* JUNO) Is Johnny not well, Mrs. . . .

MRS. BOYLE: (*Warningly*) S-s-s-sh.

MRS. MADIGAN: Oh, the poor darlin'.

BOYLE: Well, Mrs. Madigan, is it tea or what?

MRS. MADIGAN: Well, speakin' for meself, I jus' had me tea a minute ago, an' I'm afraid to dhrink any more—I'm never the same when I dhrink too much tay. Thanks, all the same, Mr. Boyle.

BOYLE: Well, what about a bottle o' stout or a dhrop o' whisky?

MRS. MADIGAN: A bottle o' stout ud be a little too heavy for me stummock afther me tay. . . . A-a-ah, I'll thry the ball o' malt.

(BOYLE *prepares the whisky.*)

MRS. MADIGAN: There's nothin' like a ball o' malt occasional like—too much of it isn't good. (*To* BOYLE, *who is adding water*) Ah, God, Johnny, don't put too much wather on it! (*She drinks.*) I suppose yous'll be lavin' this place.

BOYLE: I'm looking for a place near the sea; I'd like the place that you might say was me cradle, to be me grave as well. The sea is always callin' me.

JOXER: She is callin', callin', callin', in the win' an' on the sea.

BOYLE: Another dhrop o' whisky, Mrs. Madigan?

MRS. MADIGAN: Well, now, it ud be hard to refuse seein' the suspicious times that's in it.

BOYLE: (*With a commanding gesture*) Song! . . . Juno . . . Mary . . . 'Home to Our Mountains'!

MRS. MADIGAN: (*Enthusiastically*) Hear, hear!

JOXER: Oh, tha's a darlin' song, a daarlin' song!

MARY: (*Bashfully*) Ah no, da; I'm not in a singin' humour.

MRS. MADIGAN: Gawn with you, child, an' you only goin' to be marrid; I remember as well as I remember yesterday,—it was on a lovely August evenin', exactly, accordin' to date, fifteen years ago, come the Tuesday folleyin' the nex' that's comin' on, when me own man—*the Lord be good to him*—an' me was sittin' shy together in a doty little nook on a counthry road, adjacent to The Stiles. 'That'll scratch your lovely, little white neck,' says he, ketchin' hould of a danglin' bramble branch, holdin' clusters of the loveliest flowers you ever seen, an' breakin' it off, so that his arm fell, accidental like, roun' me waist, an' as I felt it tightenin', an' tightenin', an' tightenin', I thought me buzzom was every minute goin' to burst out into a roystherin' song about

'The little green leaves that were shakin' on the threes,
The gallivantin' buttherflies, an' buzzin' o' the bees!'

BOYLE: Ordher for the song!

JUNO: Come on, Mary—we'll do our best.

(JUNO *and* MARY *stand up, and choosing a suitable position, sing simply* 'Home to Our Mountains'. *They bow to the company, and return to their places.*)

BOYLE: (*Emotionally, at the end of song*) Lull . . . me . . . to . . . rest!

JOXER: (*Clapping his hands*) Bravo, bravo! Darlin' girulls, darlin' girulls!

MRS. MADIGAN: Juno, I never seen you in bether form.

BENTHAM: Very nicely rendered indeed.

MRS. MADIGAN: A noble call, a noble call!

MRS. BOYLE: What about yourself, Mrs. Madigan?

(*After some coaxing,* MRS. MADIGAN *rises, and in a quavering voice sings the following verse:*)

If I were a blackbird I'd whistle and sing;
I'd follow the ship that my thrue love was in;
An' on the top riggin', I'd there build me nest,
An' at night I would sleep on me Willie's white breast!

(*Becoming husky, amid applause, she sits down.*)

MRS. MADIGAN: Ah, me voice is too husky now, Juno; though I remember the time when Maisie Madigan could sing like a nightingale at matin' time. I remember as well as I remember yesterday, at a party given to celebrate the comin' of the first chiselur to Annie an' Benny Jimeson—who was the barber, yous may remember, in Henrietta Street, that, after Easter Week, hung out a green, white an' orange pole, an' then, when the Tans started their Jazz dancin', whipped it in agen, an' stuck out a red, white an' blue wan instead, givin' as an excuse that a barber's pole was strictly non-political—singin' 'An' You'll Remember Me' with the top notes quiverin' in a dead hush of pethrified attention, folleyed be a clappin' o' han's that shuk the tumblers on the table, an' capped by Jimeson, the barber, sayin' that it was the best rendherin' of 'You'll Remember Me' he ever heard in his natural!

BOYLE: (*Peremptorily*) Ordher for Joxer's song!

JOXER: Ah no, I couldn't; don't ass me, Captain.

BOYLE: Joxer's song, Joxer's song—give us wan of your shut-eyed wans.

(JOXER *settles himself in his chair; takes a drink; clears his throat; solemnly closes his eyes, and begins to sing in a very querulous voice:*)

She is far from the lan' where her young hero sleeps,
An' lovers around her are sighing   (*He hesitates.*)
An' lovers around her are sighin' . . . sighin' . . .
    sighin' . . .   (*A pause*)

BOYLE: (*Imitating* JOXER)

And lovers around her are sighing!

What's the use of you thryin' to sing the song if you don't know it?

MARY: Thry another one, Mr. Daly—maybe you'd be more fortunate.

MRS. MADIGAN: Gawn, Joxer; thry another wan.

JOXER: (*Starting again*)

I have heard the mavis singin' his love song to the
    morn;
I have seen the dew-dhrop clingin' to the rose jus' newly
    born; but . . . but . . . (*frantically*) To the rose jus'
    newly born . . . newly born . . . born.

JOHNNY: Mother, put on the gramophone, for God's sake, an' stop Joxer's bawlin'.

BOYLE: (*Commandingly*) Gramophone! . . . I hate to see fellas thryin' to do what they're not able to do.

(BOYLE *arranges the gramophone, and is about to start it, when voices are heard of persons descending the stairs.*)

MRS. BOYLE: (*Warningly*) Whisht, Jack, don't put it on, don't put it on yet; this must be poor Mrs. Tancred comin' down to go to the hospital—I forgot all about them bringin' the body to the church tonight. Open the door, Mary, an' give them a bit o' light.

(MARY *opens the door, and* MRS. TANCRED—*a very old women, obviously shaken by the death of her son—appears, accompanied by several neighbors. The first few phrases are spoken before they appear.*)

FIRST NEIGHBOUR: It's a sad journey we're goin' on, but God's good, an' the Republicans won't be always down.

MRS. TANCRED: Ah, what good is that to me now? Whether they're up or down—it won't bring me darlin' boy from the grave.

MRS. BOYLE: Come in an' have a hot cup o' tay, Mrs. Tancred, before you go.

MRS. TANCRED: Ah, I can take nothin' now, Mrs. Boyle—I won't be long afther him.

FIRST NEIGHBOUR: Still an' all, he died a noble death, an' we'll bury him like a king.

MRS. TANCRED: An' I'll go on livin' like a pauper. Ah, what's the pains I suffered bringin' him into the world to carry him to his cradle, to the pains I'm sufferin' now, carryin' him out o' the world to bring him to his grave!

MARY: It would be better for you not to go at all, Mrs. Tancred, but to stay at home beside the fire with some o' the neighbours.

MRS. TANCRED: I seen the first of him, an' I'll see the last of him.

MRS. BOYLE: You'd want a shawl, Mrs. Tancred; it's a cowld night, an' the win's blowin' sharp.

MRS. MADIGAN: (*Rushing out*) I've a shawl above.

MRS. TANCRED: Me home is gone now; he was me only child, an' to think that he was lyin' for a whole night stretched out on the side of a lonely country lane, with his head, his darlin' head, that I ofen kissed an' fondled, half hidden in the wather of a runnin' brook. An' I'm told he was the leadher of the ambush where me nex' door neighbour, Mrs. Mannin', lost her Free State soldier son. An' now here's the two of us oul' women, standin' one on each side of a scales o' sorra, balanced be the bodies of our two dead darlin' sons. (MRS. MADIGAN *returns, and wraps a shawl around her.*) God bless you, Mrs. Madigan. . . . (*She moves slowly towards the door*) Mother o' God, Mother o' God, have pity on the pair of us! . . . O Blessed Virgin, where were you when me darlin' son was riddled with bullets, when me darlin' son was riddled with bullets! . . . Sacred Heart of the Crucified Jesus, take away our hearts o' stone . . . an' give us hearts o' flesh! . . . Take away this murdherin' hate . . . an' give us Thine own eternal love!

(*They pass out of the room.*)

MRS. BOYLE: (*Explanatorily to* BENTHAM) That was Mrs. Tancred of the two-pair back; her son was found, e'er yestherday, lyin' out beyant Finglas riddled with bullets. A Die-hard he was, be all accounts. He was a nice quiet boy, but lattherly he went to hell, with his Republic first, an' Republic last an' Republic over all. He often took tea with us here, in the oul' days, an' Johnny, there, an' him used to be always together.

JOHNNY: Am I always to be havin' to tell you that he was no friend o' mine? I never cared for him, an' he

could never stick me. It's not because he was Commandant of the Battalion that I was Quarther-
Masther of, that we were friends.

MRS. BOYLE: He's gone now—the Lord be good to him!
God help his poor oul' creature of a mother, for no
matther whose friend or enemy he was, he was her
poor son.

BENTHAM: The whole thing is terrible, Mrs. Boyle; but
the only way to deal with a mad dog is to destroy
him.

MRS. BOYLE: An' to think of me forgettin' about him
bein' brought to the church to-night, an' we singin'
an' all, but it was well we hadn't the gramophone
goin', anyhow.

BOYLE: Even if we had aself. We've nothin' to do with
these things, one way or t'other. That's the Government's business, an' let them do what we're payin'
them for doin'.

MRS. BOYLE: I'd like to know how a body's not to mind
these things; look at the way they're afther leavin'
the people in this very house. Hasn't the whole
house, nearly, been massacreed? There's young
Dougherty's husband with his leg off; Mrs. Travers
that had her son blew up be a mine in Inchegeela,
in Co. Cork; Mrs. Mannin' that lost wan of her sons
in an ambush a few weeks ago, an' now, poor Mrs.
Tancred's only child gone west with his body made
a collandher of. Sure, if it's not our business, I don't
know whose business it is.

BOYLE: Here, there, that's enough about them things;
they don't affect us, an' we needn't give a damn. If
they want a wake, well, let them have a wake. When
I was a sailor, I was always resigned to meet with a
wathery grave; an' if they want to be soldiers, well,
there's no use o' them squealin' when they meet a
soldier's fate.

JOXER: Let me like a soldier fall—me breast expandin'
to th' ball!

MRS. BOYLE: In wan way, she deserves all she got; for
lately, she let th' Die-hards make an open house of
th' place; an' for th' last couple of months, either
when th' sun was risin' or when th' sun was settin',
you had C.I.D. men burstin' into your room, assin'
you where were you born, where were you christened, where were you married, an' where would
you be buried!

JOHNNY: For God's sake, let us have no more o' this talk.

MRS. MADIGAN: What about Mr. Boyle's song before we
start th' gramophone?

MARY: (Getting her hat, and putting it on) Mother, Charlie
and I are goin' out for a little sthroll.

MRS. BOYLE: All right, darlin'.

BENTHAM: (Going out with MARY) We won't be long away,
Mrs. Boyle.

MRS. MADIGAN: Gwan, Captain, gwan.

BOYLE: E-e-e-eh, I'd want to have a few more jars in
me, before I'd be in fettle for singin'.

JOXER: Give us that poem you writ t'other day. (To the

rest) Aw, it's a darlin' poem, a daarlin' poem.

MRS. BOYLE: God bless us, is he startin' to write poetry!

BOYLE: (Rising to his feet) E-e-e-e-eh.

(He recites in an emotional, consequential manner the
following verses:)

> Shawn an' I were friends, sir, to me he was all in all.
> His work was very heavy and his wages were very
> small.
> None betther on th' beach as Docker, I'll go bail,
> 'Tis now I'm feelin' lonely, for to-day he lies in jail.
> He was not what some call pious—seldom at church
> or prayer;
> For the greatest scoundrels I know, sir, goes every
> Sunday there.
> Fond of his pint—well, rather, but hated the Boss by
> creed
> But never refused a copper to comfort a pal in need.

E-e-e-e-eh.

(He sits down.)

MRS. MADIGAN: Grand, grand; you should folly that up,
you should folly that up.

JOXER: It's a daarlin' poem!

BOYLE: (Delightedly) E-e-e-e-eh.

JOHNNY: Are yous goin' to put on th' gramophone tonight, or are yous not?

MRS. BOYLE: Gwan, Jack, put on a record.

MRS. MADIGAN: Gwan, Captain, gwan.

BOYLE: Well, yous'll want to keep a dead silence.

(He sets a record, starts the machine, and it begins to
play 'If you're Irish, come into the Parlour'. As the tune
is in full blare, the door is suddenly opened by a brisk,
little bald-headed man, dressed circumspectly in a black
suit; he glares fiercely at all in the room; he is 'NEEDLE'
NUGENT, a tailor. He carries his hat in his hand.)

NUGENT: (Loudly, above the noise of the gramophone) Are
yous goin' to have that thing bawlin' an' the funeral
of Mrs. Tancred's son passin' the house? Have none
of yous any respect for the Irish people's National
regard for the dead?

(BOYLE stops the gramophone.)

MRS. BOYLE: Maybe, Needle Nugent, it's nearly time we
had a little less respect for the dead, an' a little more
regard for the livin'.

MRS. MADIGAN: We don't want you, Mr. Nugent, to
teach us what we learned at our mother's knee. You
don't look yourself as if you were dyin' of grief; if
y'ass Maisie Madigan anything, I'd call you a real
thrue Die-hard an' live-soft Republican, attendin'
Republican funerals in the day, an' stoppin' up half
the night makin' suits for the Civic Guards!

(Persons are heard running down to the street, some saying, 'Here it is, here it is.' NUGENT *withdraws, and the rest, except* JOHNNY, *go to the window looking into the street, and look out. Sounds of a crowd coming nearer are heard; portion are singing:)*

> To Jesus' Heart all burning
> With fervent love for men,
> My heart with fondest yearning
> Shall raise its joyful strain.
> While ages course along,
> Blest be with loudest song
> The Sacred Heart of Jesus
> By every heart and tongue.

MRS. BOYLE: Here's the hearse, here's the hearse!

BOYLE: There's t'oul' mother walkin' behin' the coffin.

MRS. MADIGAN: You can hardly see the coffin with the wreaths.

JOXER: Oh, it's a darlin' funeral, a daarlin' funeral!

MRS. MADIGAN: W'd have a betther view from the street.

BOYLE: Yes—this place ud give you a crick in your neck.

(They leave the room, and go down. JOHNNY *sits moodily by the fire.*
A young man enters; he looks at JOHNNY *for a moment.)*

THE YOUNG MAN: Quarther-Masther Boyle.

JOHNNY: *(With a start)* The Mobilizer!

THE YOUNG MAN: You're not at the funeral?

JOHNNY: I'm not well.

THE YOUNG MAN: I'm glad I've found you; you were stoppin' at your aunt's; I called there but you'd gone. I've to give you an ordher to attend a Battalion Staff meetin' the night afther to-morrow.

JOHNNY: Where?

THE YOUNG MAN: I don't know; you're to meet me at the Pillar at eight o'clock; then we're to go to a place I'll be told of to-night; there we'll meet a mothor that'll bring us to the meeting. They think you might be able to know somethin' about them that gave the bend where Commandant Tancred was shelterin'.

JOHNNY: I'm not goin', then. I know nothing about Tancred.

THE YOUNG MAN: *(At the door)* You'd betther come for your own sake—remember your oath.

JOHNNY: *(Passionately)* I won't go! Haven't I done enough for Ireland! I've lost me arm, an' me hip's desthroyed so that I'll never be able to walk right agen! Good God, haven't I done enough for Ireland?

THE YOUNG MAN: Boyle, no man can do enough for Ireland!

(He goes.)

(Faintly in the distance the crowd is heard saying:)

> Hail, Mary, full of grace, the Lord is with Thee;
> Blessed art Thou amongst women, and blessed, etc.

CURTAIN

ACT 3

The same as Act 2. It is about half-past six on a November evening; a bright fire burns in the grate; MARY, *dressed to go out, is sitting on a chair by the fire, leaning forward, her hands under her chin, her elbows on her knees. A look of dejection, mingled with uncertain anxiety, is on her face. A lamp, turned low, is lighting on the table. The votive light under the picture of the Virgin gleams more redly than ever.* MRS. BOYLE *is putting on her hat and coat. It is two months later.*

MRS. BOYLE: An' has Bentham never even written to you since—not one line for the past month?

MARY: *(Tonelessly)* Not even a line, mother.

MRS. BOYLE: That's very curious. . . . What came between the two of yous at all? To leave you so sudden, an' yous so great together. . . . To go away t' England, an' not to even leave you his address. . . . The way he was always bringin' you to dances, I thought he was mad afther you. Are you sure you said nothin' to him?

MARY: No, mother—at least nothing that could possibly explain his givin' me up.

MRS. BOYLE: You know you're a bit hasty at times, Mary, an' say things you shouldn't say.

MARY: I never said to him what I shouldn't say, I'm sure of that.

MRS. BOYLE: How are you sure of it?

MARY: Because I love him with all my heart and soul, mother. Why, I don't know; I often thought to myself that he wasn't the man poor Jerry was, but I couldn't help loving him, all the same.

MRS. BOYLE: But you shouldn't be frettin' the way you are; when a woman loses a man, she never knows what she's afther losin', to be sure, but, then, she never knows what she's afther gainin', either. You're not the one girl of a month ago—you look like one pinin' away. It's long ago I had a right to bring you to the doctor, instead of waitin' till to-night.

MARY: There's no necessity, really, mother, to go to the doctor; nothing serious is wrong with me—I'm run down and disappointed, that's all.

MRS. BOYLE: I'll not wait another minute; I don't like the look of you at all. . . . I'm afraid we made a mistake in throwin' over poor Jerry. . . . He'd have been betther for you than that Bentham.

MARY: Mother, the best man for a woman is the one for whom she has the most love, and Charlie had it all.

MRS. BOYLE: Well, there's one thing to be said for him—he couldn't have been thinkin' of the money, or he wouldn't ha' left you . . . it must ha' been somethin' else.

MARY: (*Wearily*) I don't know . . . I don't know, mother . . . only I think . . .

MRS. BOYLE: What d'ye think?

MARY: I imagine . . . he thought . . . we weren't . . . good enough for him.

MRS. BOYLE: An' what was he himself, only a school teacher? Though I don't blame him for fightin' shy of people like that Joxer fella an' that oul' Madigan wan—nice sort o' people for your father to introduce to a man like Mr. Bentham. You might have told me all about this before now, Mary; I don't know why you like to hide everything from your mother; you knew Bentham, an' I'd ha' known nothin' about it if it hadn't bin for the Will; an' it was only to-day, afther long coaxin', that you let out that he's left you.

MARY: It would have been useless to tell you—you wouldn't understand.

MRS. BOYLE: (*Hurt*) Maybe not. . . . Maybe I wouldn't understand. . . . Well, we'll be off now.

(*She goes over to door left, and speaks to* BOYLE *inside.*)

MRS. BOYLE: We're goin' now to the doctor's. Are you goin' to get up this evenin'?

BOYLE: (*From inside*) The pains in me legs is terrible! It's me should be poppin' off to the doctor instead o' Mary, the way I feel.

MRS. BOYLE: Sorra mend you! A nice way you were in last night—carried in in a frog's march, dead to the world. If that's the way you'll go on when you get the money it'll be the grave for you, an asylum for me and the Poorhouse for Johnny.

BOYLE: I thought you were goin'?

MRS. BOYLE: That's what has you as you are—you can't bear to be spoken to. Knowin' the way we are, up to our ears in debt, it's a wondher you wouldn't ha' got up to go to th' solicitor's an' see if we could ha' gotten a little o' the money even.

BOYLE: (*Shouting*) I can't be goin' up there night, noon an' mornin', can I? He can't give the money till he gets it, can he? I can't get blood out of a turnip, can I?

MRS. BOYLE: It's nearly two months since we heard of the Will, an' the money seems as far off as ever. . . . I suppose you know we owe twenty pouns to oul' Murphy?

BOYLE: I've a faint recollection of you tellin' me that before.

MRS. BOYLE: Well, you'll go over to the shop yourself for the things in future—I'll face him no more.

BOYLE: I thought you said you were goin'?

MRS. BOYLE: I'm goin' now; come on, Mary.

BOYLE: Ey, Juno, ey!

MRS. BOYLE: Well, what d'ye want now?

BOYLE: Is there e'er a bottle o' stout left?

MRS. BOYLE: There's two o' them here still.

BOYLE: Show us in one o' them an' leave t'other there till I get up. An' throw us in the paper that's on the table, an' the bottle o' Sloan's Liniment that's in th' drawer.

MRS. BOYLE: (*Getting the liniment and the stout*) What paper is it you want—the *Messenger*?

BOYLE: *Messenger*! The *News o' the World*!

(MRS. BOYLE *brings in the things asked for, and comes out again.*)

MRS. BOYLE: (*At door*) Mind the candle, now, an' don't burn the house over our heads. I left t'other bottle o' stout on the table.

(*She puts bottle of stout on table. She goes out with* MARY. *A cork is heard popping inside.*
A pause; then outside the door is heard the voice of JOXER *lilting softly: 'Me pipe I'll smoke, as I dhrive me moke . . . are you . . . there . . . Mor . . . ee . . . ar . . . i . . . teee!' A gentle knock is heard, and after a pause the door opens, and* JOXER, *followed by* NUGENT, *enters.*)

JOXER: Be God, they must be all out; I was thinkin' there was somethin' up when he didn't answer the signal. We seen Juno an' Mary goin', but I didn't see him, an' it's very seldom he escapes me.

NUGENT: He's not goin' to escape me—he's not goin' to be let go to the fair altogether.

JOXER: Sure, the house couldn't hould them lately; an' he goin' about like a mastherpiece of the Free State counthry; forgettin' their friends; forgettin' God— wouldn't even lift his hat passin' a chapel! Sure they were bound to get a dhrop! An' you really think there's no money comin' to him afther all?

NUGENT: Not as much as a red rex, man; I've been a bit anxious this long time over me money, an' I went up to the solicitor's to find out all I could—ah, man, they were goin' to throw me down the stairs. They toul' me that the oul' cock himself had the stairs worn away comin' up afther it, an' they black in the face tellin' him he'd get nothin'. Some way or another that the Will is writ he won't be entitled to get as much as a make!

JOXER: Ah, I thought there was somethin' curious about the whole thing; I've bin havin' sthrange dhreams for the last couple o' weeks. An' I notice that that Bentham fella doesn't be comin' here now—there must be somethin' on the mat there too. Anyhow, who, in the name o' God, ud leave anythin' to that oul' bummer? Sure it ud be unnatural. An' the way Juno an' him's been throwin' their weight about for the last few months! Ah, him that goes a borrowin' goes a sorrowin'!

NUGENT: Well, he's not goin' to throw his weight about in the suit I made for him much longer. I'm tellin' you seven pouns aren't to be found growin' on the bushes these days.

JOXER: An' there isn't hardly a neighbour in the whole street that hasn't lent him money on the strength of what he was goin' to get, but they're after backing the wrong horse. Wasn't it a mercy o' God that I'd nothin' to give him! The softy I am, you know, I'd ha' lent him me last juice! I must have had somebody's good prayers. Ah, afther all, an honest man's the noblest work o' God!

(BOYLE *coughs inside.*)

JOXER: Whisht, damn it, he must be inside in bed.
NUGENT: Inside o' bed or outside of it, he's goin' to pay me for that suit, or give it back—he'll not climb up my back as easily as he thinks.
JOXER: Gwan in at wanst, man, an' get it off him, an' don't be a fool.
NUGENT: (*Going to door left, opening it and looking in*) Ah, don't disturb yourself, Mr. Boyle; I hope you're not sick?
BOYLE: Th' oul' legs, Mr. Nugent, the oul' legs.
NUGENT: I just called over to see if you could let me have anything off the suit.
BOYLE: E-e-e-eh, how much is this it is?
NUGENT: It's the same as it was at the start—seven pouns.
BOYLE: I'm glad you kem, Mr. Nugent; I want a good heavy top-coat—Irish frieze, if you have it. How much would a top-coat like that be, now?
NUGENT: About six pouns.
BOYLE: Six pouns—six an' seven, six an' seven is thirteen—that'll be thirteen pouns I'll owe you.

(JOXER *slips the bottle of stout that is on the table into his pocket.* NUGENT *rushes into the room, and returns with suit on his arm; he pauses at the door.*)

NUGENT: You'll owe me no thirteen pouns. Maybe you think you're bether able to owe it than pay it!
BOYLE: (*Frantically*) Here, come back to hell ower that— where're you goin' with them clothes o' mine?
NUGENT: Where am I goin' with them clothes o' yours? Well, I like your damn cheek!
BOYLE: Here, what am I goin' to dhress meself in when I'm goin' out?
NUGENT: What do I care what you dhress yourself in! You can put yourself in a bolsther cover, if you like.

(*He goes towards the other door, followed by* JOXER.)

JOXER: What'll he dhress himself in! Gentleman Jack an' his frieze coat!

(*They go out.*)

BOYLE: (*Inside*) Ey, Nugent; ey, Mr. Nugent, Mr. Nugent!

(*After a pause* BOYLE *enters hastily, buttoning the braces of his moleskin trousers; his coat and vest are on his arm;*

he throws these on a chair and hurries to the door on right.)

BOYLE: Ey, Mr. Nugent, Mr. Nugent!
JOXER: (*Meeting him at the door*) What's up, what's wrong, Captain?
BOYLE: Nugent's been here an' took away me suit—the only things I had to go out in!
JOXER: Tuk your suit—for God's sake! An' what were you doin' while he was takin' them?
BOYLE: I was in bed when he stole in like a thief in the night, an' before I knew even what he was thinkin' of, he whipped them from the chair an' was off like a redshank!
JOXER: An' what, in the name o' God, did he do that for?
BOYLE: What did he do it for? How the hell do I know what he done it for?—jealousy an' spite, I suppose.
JOXER: Did he not say what he done it for?
BOYLE: Amn't I afther tellin' you that he had them whipped up an' was gone before I could open me mouth?
JOXER: That was a very sudden thing to do; there mus' be somethin' behin' it. Did he hear anythin', I wondher?
BOYLE: Did he hear anythin'?—you talk very queer, Joxer—what could he hear?
JOXER: About you not gettin' the money, in some way or t'other?
BOYLE: An' what ud prevent me from gettin' th' money?
JOXER: That's jus' what I was thinkin'—what ud prevent you from gettin' the money—nothin', as far as I can see.
BOYLE: (*Looking round for bottle of stout, with an exclamation*) Aw, holy God!
JOXER: What's up, Jack?
BOYLE: He must have afther lifted the bottle o' stout that Juno left on the table!
JOXER: (*Horrified*) Ah no, ah no; he wouldn't be afther doin' that now.
BOYLE: An' who done it then? Juno left a bottle o' stout here, an' it's gone—it didn't walk, did it?
JOXER: Oh, that's shockin'; ah, man's inhumanity to man makes countless thousands mourn!
MRS. MADIGAN: (*Appearing at the door*) I hope I'm not disturbin' you in any discussion on your forthcomin' legacy—if I may use the word—an' that you'll let me have a barny for a minute or two with you, Mr. Boyle.
BOYLE: (*Uneasily*) To be sure, Mrs. Madigan—an oul' friend's always welcome.
JOXER: Come in the evenin', come in th' mornin'; come when you're assed, or come without warnin', Mrs. Madigan.
BOYLE: Sit down, Mrs. Madigan.
MRS. MADIGAN: (*Ominously*) Th' few words I have to say can be said standin'. Puttin' aside all formularies, I

suppose you remember me lendin' you some time ago three pouns that I raised on blankets an' furniture in me uncle's?

BOYLE: I remember it well. I have it recorded in me book—three pouns five shillings from Maisie Madigan, raised on articles pawned; an', item: fourpence, given to make up the price of a pint, on th' principle that no bird ever flew on wan wing; all to be repaid at par, when the ship comes home.

MRS. MADIGAN: Well, ever since I shoved in the blankets I've been perishing with th' cowld, an' I've decided, if I'll be too hot in th' next' world aself, I'm not goin' to be too cowld in this wan; an' consequently, I want me three pouns, if you please.

BOYLE: This is a very sudden demand, Mrs. Madigan, an' can't be met; but I'm willin' to give you a receipt in full, in full.

MRS. MADIGAN: Come on, out with th' money, an' don't be jack-actin'.

BOYLE: You can't get blood out of a turnip, can you?

MRS. MADIGAN: (*Rushing over and shaking him*) Gimme me money, y'oul' reprobate, or I'll shake the worth of it out of you!

BOYLE: Ey, houl' on, there; houl' on, there! You'll wait for your money now, me lassie!

MRS. MADIGAN: (*Looking around the room and seeing the gramophone*) I'll wait for it, will I? Well, I'll not wait long; if I can't get th' cash, I'll get th' worth of it.

(*She catches up the gramophone.*)

BOYLE: Ey, ey, there, wher'r you goin' with that?

MRS. MADIGAN: I'm goin' to th' pawn to get me three quid five shillins; I'll brin' you th' ticket, an' then you can do what you like, me bucko.

BOYLE: You can't touch that, you can't touch that! It's not my property, an' it's not ped for yet!

MRS. MADIGAN: So much th' better. It'll be an ayse to me conscience, for I'm takin' what doesn't belong to you. You're not goin' to be swankin' it like a paycock with Maisie Madigan's money—I'll pull some o' th' gorgeous feathers out o' your tail!

(*She goes off with the gramophone.*)

BOYLE: What's th' world comin' to at all? I ass you, Joxer Daly, is there any morality left anywhere?

JOXER: I wouldn't ha' believed it, only I seen it with me own two eyes. I didn't think Maisie Madigan was that sort o' woman; she has either a sup taken, or she's heard somethin'.

BOYLE: Heard somethin'—about what, if it's not any harm to ass you?

JOXER: She must ha' heard some rumour or other that you weren't goin' to get th' money.

BOYLE: Who says I'm not goin' to get th' money?

JOXER: Sure, I don't know—I was only sayin'.

BOYLE: Only sayin' what?

JOXER: Nothin'.

BOYLE: You were goin' to say somethin'—don't be a twisther.

JOXER: (*Angrily*) Who's a twisther?

BOYLE: Why don't you speak your mind, then?

JOXER: You never twisted yourself—no, you wouldn't know how!

BOYLE: Did you ever know me to twist; did you ever know me to twist?

JOXER: (*Fiercely*) Did you ever do anythin' else! Sure, you can't believe a word that comes out o' your mouth.

BOYLE· Here, get out, ower o' this; I always knew you were a prognosticator an' a procrastinator!

JOXER: (*Going out as* JOHNNY *comes in*) The anchor's weighed, farewell, ree . . . mem . . . ber . . . me. Jacky Boyle, Esquire, infernal rogue an' damned liar.

JOHNNY: Joxer an' you at it agen?—when are you goin' to have a little respect for yourself, an' not be always makin' a show of us all?

BOYLE: Are you goin' to lecture me now?

JOHNNY: Is mother back from the doctor yet, with Mary?

(MRS. BOYLE *enters; it is apparent from the serious look on her face that something has happened. She takes off her hat and coat without a word and puts them by. She then sits down near the fire, and there is a few moments' pause.*)

BOYLE: Well, what did the doctor say about Mary?

MRS. BOYLE: (*In an earnest manner and with suppressed agitation*) Sit down here, Jack; I've something to say to you . . . about Mary.

BOYLE: (*Awed by her manner*) About . . . Mary?

MRS. BOYLE: Close that door there and sit down here.

BOYLE: (*Closing the door*) More throuble in our native land, is it? (*He sits down.*) Well, what is it?

MRS. BOYLE: It's about Mary.

BOYLE: Well, what about Mary—there's nothin' wrong with her, is there?

MRS. BOYLE: I'm sorry to say there's a gradle wrong with her.

BOYLE: A gradle wrong with her! (*Peevishly*) First Johnny an' now Mary; is the whole house goin' to become an hospital! It's not consumption, is it?

MRS. BOYLE: No . . . it's not consumption . . . it's worse.

JOHNNY: Worse! Well, we'll have to get her into some place ower this, there's no one here to mind her.

MRS. BOYLE: We'll all have to mind her now. You might as well know now, Johnny, as another time. (*To* BOYLE) D'ye know what the doctor said to me about her, Jack?

BOYLE: How ud I know—I wasn't there, was I?

MRS. BOYLE: He told me to get her married at wanst.

BOYLE: Married at wanst! An' why did he say the like o' that?

MRS. BOYLE: Because Mary's goin' to have a baby in a short time.

BOYLE: Goin' to have a baby!—my God, what'll Bentham say when he hears that?

MRS. BOYLE: Are you blind, man, that you can't see that it was Bentham that has done this wrong to her?

BOYLE: (*Passionately*) Then he'll marry her, he'll have to marry her!

MRS. BOYLE: You know he's gone to England, an' God knows where he is now.

BOYLE: I'll folly him, I'll folly him, an' bring him back, an' make him do her justice. The scoundrel, I might ha' known what he was, with his yogees an' his prawna!

MRS. BOYLE: We'll have to keep it quiet till we see what we can do.

BOYLE: Oh, isn't this a nice thing to come on top o' me, an' the state I'm in! A pretty show I'll be to Joxer an' to that oul' wan, Madigan! Amn't I afther goin' through enough without havin' to go through this!

MRS. BOYLE: What you an' I'll have to go through'll be nothin' to what poor Mary'll have to go through; for you an' me is middlin' old, an' most of our years is spent; but Mary'll have maybe forty years to face an' handle, an' every wan of them'll be tainted with a bitther memory.

BOYLE: Where is she? Where is she till I tell her off? I'm tellin' you when I'm done with her she'll be a sorry girl!

MRS. BOYLE: I left her in me sister's till I came to speak to you. You'll say nothin' to her, Jack; ever since she left school she's earned her livin', an' your fatherly care never throubled the poor girl.

BOYLE: Gwan, take her part agen her father! But I'll let you see whether I'll say nothin' to her or no! Her an' her readin'! That's more o' th' blasted nonsense that has the house fallin' down on top of us! What did th' likes of her, born in a tenement house, want with readin'? Her readin's afther bringin' her to a nice pass—oh, it's madnin', madnin', madnin'!

MRS. BOYLE: When she comes back say nothin' to her, Jack, or she'll leave this place.

BOYLE: Leave this place! Ay, she'll leave this place, an' quick too!

MRS. BOYLE: If Mary goes, I'll go with her.

BOYLE: Well, go with her! Well, go, th' pair o' yous! I lived before I seen yous, an' I can live when yous are gone. Isn't this a nice thing to come rollin' in on top o' me afther all your prayin' to St. Anthony an' The Little Flower! An' she's a Child o' Mary, too—I wonder what'll the nuns think of her now? An' it'll be bellows'd all over th' disthrict before you could say Jack Robinson; an' whenever I'm seen they'll whisper, 'That's th' father of Mary Boyle that had th' kid be th' swank she used to go with; d'ye know, d'ye know?' To be sure they'll know—more about it than I will meself!

JOHNNY: She should be dhriven out o' th' house she's brought disgrace on!

MRS. BOYLE: Hush, you, Johnny. We needn't let it be bellows'd all over the place; all we've got to do is to leave this place quietly an' go somewhere where we're not known an' nobody'll be th' wiser.

BOYLE: You're talkin' like a two-year-oul', woman. Where'll we get a place ou' o' this—places aren't that easily got.

MRS. BOYLE: But, Jack, when we get the money . . .

BOYLE: Money—what money?

MRS. BOYLE: Why, oul' Ellison's money, of course.

BOYLE: There's no money comin' from oul' Ellison, or any one else. Since you've heard of wan throuble, you might as well hear of another. There's no money comin' to us at all—the Will's a wash-out!

MRS. BOYLE: What are you sayin', man—no money?

JOHNNY: How could it be a wash-out?

BOYLE: The boyo that's afther doin' it to Mary done it to me as well. The thick made out the Will wrong; he said in th' Will, only first cousin an' second cousin, instead of mentionin' our names, an' now any one that thinks he's a first cousin or second cousin t'oul' Ellison can claim the money as well as me, an' they're springin' up in hundreds, an' comin' from America an' Australia, thinkin' to get their whack out of it, while all the time the lawyers is gobblin' it up, till there's not as much as ud buy a stockin' for your lovely daughter's baby!

MRS. BOYLE: I don't believe it, I don't believe it, I don't believe it!

JOHNNY: Why did you say nothin' about this before?

MRS. BOYLE: You're not serious, Jack; you're not serious!

BOYLE: I'm tellin' you the scholar, Bentham, made a banjax o' th' Will; instead o' sayin', 'th' rest o' me property to be divided between me first cousin, Jack Boyle, an' me second cousin, Mick Finnegan, o' Santhry', he writ down only, 'me first an' second cousins', an' the world an' his wife are afther th' property now.

MRS. BOYLE: Now I know why Bentham left poor Mary in th' lurch; I can see it all now—oh, is there not even a middlin' honest man left in th' world?

JOHNNY: (*To* BOYLE) An' you let us run into debt, an' you borreyed money from everybody to fill yourself with beer! An' now you tell us the whole thing's a washout! Oh, if it's thrue, I'm done with you, for you're worse than me sisther Mary!

BOYLE: You hole your tongue, d'ye hear? I'll not take any lip from you. Go an' get Bentham if you want satisfaction for all that's afther happenin' us.

JOHNNY: I won't hole me tongue, I won't hole me tongue! I'll tell you what I think of you, father an' all you are . . . you . . .

MRS. BOYLE: Johnny, Johnny, Johnny, for God's sake, be quiet!

JOHNNY: I'll not be quiet, I'll not be quiet; he's a nice father, isn't he? Is it any wondher Mary went asthray, when . . .

MRS. BOYLE: Johnny, Johnny, for my sake be quiet—for your mother's sake!

BOYLE: I'm goin' out now to have a few dhrinks with th' last few makes I have, an' tell that lassie o' yours not to be here when I come back; for if I lay me eyes on her, I'll lay me hans on her, an' if I lay me hans on her, I won't be accountable for me actions!

JOHNNY: Take care somebody doesn't lay his hans on you—y'oul' . . .

MRS. BOYLE: Johnny, Johnny!

BOYLE: (At door, about to go out) Oh, a nice son, an' a nicer daughter, I have. (Calling loudly upstairs) Joxer, Joxer, are you there?

JOXER: (From a distance) I'm here, More . . . ee . . . aar . . . i . . . tee!

BOYLE: I'm goin' down to Foley's—are you comin'?

JOXER: Come with you? With that sweet call me heart is stirred; I'm only waiting for the word, an' I'll be with you, like a bird!

(BOYLE and JOXER pass the door going out.)

JOHNNY: (Throwing himself on the bed) I've a nice sisther, an' a nice father, there's no bettin' on it. I wish to God a bullet or a bomb had whipped me ou' o' this long ago! Not one o' yous, not one o' yous, have any thought for me!

MRS. BOYLE: (With passionate remonstrance) If you don't whisht, Johnny, you'll drive me mad. Who has kep' th' home together for the past few years—only me? An' who'll have to bear th' biggest part o' this throuble but me?—but whinin' an' whingin' isn't goin' to do any good.

JOHNNY: You're to blame yourself for a gradle of it—givin' him his own way in everything, an' never assin' to check him, no mather what he done. Why didn't you look afther th' money? why . . .

(There is a knock at the door; MRS. BOYLE opens it; JOHNNY rises on his elbow to look and listen; two men enter.)

FIRST MAN: We've been sent up be th' Manager of the Hibernian Furnishings Co., Mrs. Boyle, to take back the furniture that was got a while ago.

MRS. BOYLE: Yous'll touch nothin' here—how do I know who yous are?

FIRST MAN: (Showing a paper) There's the ordher, ma'am. (Reading) A chest o' drawers, a table, wan easy an' two ordinary chairs; wan mirror; wan chestherfield divan, an' a wardrobe an' two vases (To his comrade) Come on, Bill, it's afther knockin'-off time already.

JOHNNY: For God's sake, mother, run down to Foley's an' bring father back, or we'll be left without a stick.

(The men carry out the table.)

MRS. BOYLE: What good would it be?—you heard what he said before he went out.

JOHNNY: Can't you thry? He ought to be here, an' the like of this goin' on.

(MRS. BOYLE puts a shawl around her, as MARY enters.)

MARY: What's up, mother? I met men carryin' away the table, an' everybody's talking about us not gettin' the money after all.

MRS. BOYLE: Everythin's gone wrong, Mary, everythin'. We're not gettin' a penny out o' the Will, not a penny—I'll tell you all when I come back; I'm goin' for your father.

(She runs out.)

JOHNNY: (To MARY, who has sat down by the fire) It's a wondher you're not ashamed to show your face here, afther what has happened.

(JERRY enters slowly; there is a look of earnest hope on his face. He looks at MARY for a few moments.)

JERRY: (Softly) Mary!

(MARY does not answer.)

JERRY: Mary, I want to speak to you for a few moments, may I?

(MARY remains silent; JOHNNY goes slowly into room on left.)

JERRY: Your mother has told me everything, Mary, and I have come to you. . . . I have come to tell you, Mary, that my love for you is greater and deeper than ever. . . .

MARY: (With a sob) Oh, Jerry, Jerry, say no more; all that is over now; anything like that is impossible now!

JERRY: Impossible? Why do you talk like that, Mary?

MARY: After all that has happened.

JERRY: What does it matter what has happened? We are young enough to be able to forget all those things. (He catches her hand) Mary, Mary, I am pleading for your love. With Labour, Mary, humanity is above everything; we are the Leaders in the fight for a new life. I want to forget Bentham, I want to forget that you left me—even for a while.

MARY: Oh, Jerry, Jerry, you haven't the bitter word of scorn for me after all.

JERRY: (Passionately) Scorn! I love you, love you, Mary!

MARY: (Rising, and looking him in the eyes) Even though . . .

JERRY: Even though you threw me over for another man; even though you gave me many a bitter word!

MARY: Yes, yes, I know; but you love me, even though . . . even though . . . I'm . . . goin' . . . goin' . . . (He looks at her questioningly, and fear gathers in his eyes) Ah, I was thinkin' so. . . . You don't know everything!

JERRY: (*Poignantly*) Surely to God, Mary, you don't mean that . . . that . . . that . . .

MARY: Now you know all, Jerry; now you know all!

JERRY: My God, Mary, have you fallen as low as that?

MARY: Yes, Jerry, as you say, I have fallen as low as that.

JERRY: I didn't mean it that way, Mary . . . it came on me so sudden, that I didn't mind what I was sayin'. . . . I never expected this—your mother never told me. . . . I'm sorry . . . God knows, I'm sorry for you, Mary.

MARY: Let us say no more, Jerry; I don't blame you for thinkin' it's terrible. . . . I suppose it is. . . . Everybody'll think the same . . . it's only as I expected—your humanity is just as narrow as the humanity of the others.

JERRY: I'm sorry, all the same. . . . I shouldn't have troubled you. . . . I wouldn't if I'd known. . . . If I can do anything for you . . . Mary . . . I will.

(*He turns to go, and halts at the door.*)

MARY: Do you remember, Jerry, the verses you read when you gave the lecture in the Socialist Rooms some time ago, on Humanity's Strife with Nature?

JERRY: The verses—no; I don't remember them.

MARY: I do. They're runnin' in me head now—

> An' we felt the power that fashion'd
> All the lovely things we saw,
> That created all the murmur
> Of an everlasting law,
> Was a hand of force an' beauty,
> With an eagle's tearin' claw.
>
> Then we saw our globe of beauty
> Was an ugly thing as well,
> A hymn divine whose chorus
> Was an agonizin' yell;
> Like the story of a demon,
> That an angel had to tell;
>
> Like a glowin' picture by a
> Hand unsteady, brought to ruin;
> Like her craters, if their deadness
> Could give life unto the moon;
> Like the agonizing horror
> Of a violin out of tune.

(*There is a pause, and* DEVINE *goes slowly out.*)

JOHNNY: (*Returning*) Is he gone?

MARY: Yes.

(*The two men re-enter.*)

FIRST MAN: We can't wait any longer for t'oul' fella—sorry, Miss, but we have to live as well as th' nex' man.

(*They carry out some things.*)

JOHNNY: Oh, isn't this terrible! . . . I suppose you told him everything . . . couldn't you have waited for a few days? . . . he'd have stopped th' takin' of the things, if you'd kep' your mouth shut. Are you burnin' to tell every one of the shame you've brought on us?

MARY: (*Snatching up her hat and coat*) Oh, this is unbearable!

(*She rushes out.*)

FIRST MAN: (*Re-entering*) We'll take the chest o' drawers next—it's the heaviest.

(*The votive light flickers for a moment, and goes out.*)

JOHNNY: (*In a cry of fear*) Mother o' God, the light's afther goin' out!

FIRST MAN: You put the win' up me the way you bawled that time. The oil's all gone, that's all.

JOHNNY: (*With an agonizing cry*) Mother o' God, there's a shot I'm afther gettin'!

FIRST MAN: What's wrong with you, man? Is it a fit you're takin'?

JOHNNY: I'm afther feelin' a pain in me breast, like the tearin' by of a bullet!

FIRST MAN: He's goin' mad—it's a wondher they'd leave a chap like that here by himself.

(TWO IRREGULARS *enter swiftly; they carry revolvers; one goes over to* JOHNNY; *the other covers the two furniture men.*)

FIRST IRREGULAR: (*To the men, quietly and incisively*) Who are you?—what are yous doin' here?—quick!

FIRST MAN: Removin' furniture that's not paid for.

IRREGULAR: Get over to the other end of the room an' turn your faces to the wall—quick!

(*The two men turn their faces to the wall, with their hands up.*)

SECOND IRREGULAR: (*To* JOHNNY) Come on, Sean Boyle, you're wanted; some of us have a word to say to you.

JOHNNY: I'm sick, I can't—what do you want with me?

SECOND IRREGULAR: Come on, come on; we've a distance to go, an' haven't much time—come on.

JOHNNY: I'm an oul' comrade—yous wouldn't shoot an oul' comrade.

SECOND IRREGULAR: Poor Tancred was an oul' comrade o' yours, but you didn't think o' that when you gave him away to the gang that sent him to his grave. But we've no time to waste; come on—here, Dermot, ketch his arm. (*To* JOHNNY) Have you your beads?

JOHNNY: Me beads! Why do you ass me that, why do you ass me that?

SECOND IRREGULAR: Go on, go on, march!

JOHNNY: Are yous goin' to do in a comrade?—look at me arm, I lost it for Ireland.

SECOND IRREGULAR: Commandant Tancred lost his life for Ireland.

JOHNNY: Sacred Heart of Jesus, have mercy on me! Mother o' God, pray for me—be with me now in the agonies o' death! . . . Hail, Mary, full o' grace . . . the Lord is . . . with Thee.

(They drag out JOHNNY BOYLE, *and the curtain falls. When it rises again the most of the furniture is gone.* MARY *and* MRS. BOYLE, *one on each side, are sitting in a darkened room, by the fire; it is an hour later.)*

MRS. BOYLE: I'll not wait much longer . . . what did they bring him away in the mothor for? Nugent says he thinks they had guns . . . is me throubles never goin' to be over? . . . If anything ud happen to poor Johnny, I think I'd lose me mind. . . . I'll go to the Police Station, surely they ought to be able to do somethin'.

(Below is heard the sound of voices.)

MRS. BOYLE: Whisht, is that something? Maybe, it's your father, though when I left him in Foley's he was hardly able to lift his head. Whisht!

(A knock at the door, and the voice of MRS. MADIGAN, *speaking very softly):* Mrs. Boyle, Mrs. Boyle.

*(*MRS. BOYLE *opens the door.)*

MRS. MADIGAN: Oh, Mrs. Boyle, God an' His Blessed Mother be with you this night!

MRS. BOYLE: *(Calmly)* What is it, Mrs. Madigan? It's Johnny—something about Johnny.

MRS. MADIGAN: God send it's not, God send it's not Johnny!

MRS. BOYLE: Don't keep me waitin', Mrs. Madigan; I've gone through so much lately that I feel able for anything.

MRS. MADIGAN: Two polismen below wantin' you.

MRS. BOYLE: Wantin' me; an' why do they want me?

MRS. MADIGAN: Some poor fella's been found, an' they think it's, it's . . .

MRS. BOYLE: Johnny, Johnny!

MARY: *(With her arms round her mother)* Oh, mother, mother, me poor, darlin' mother.

MRS. BOYLE: Hush, hush, darlin'; you'll shortly have your own throuble to bear. *(To* MRS. MADIGAN*)* An' why do the polis think it's Johnny, Mrs. Madigan?

MRS. MADIGAN: Because one o' the doctors knew him when he was attendin' with his poor arm.

MRS. BOYLE: Oh, it's thrue, then; it's Johnny, it's me son, me own son!

MARY: Oh, it's thrue, it's thrue what Jerry Devine says—there isn't a God, there isn't a God; if there was He wouldn't let these things happen!

MRS. BOYLE: Mary, you mustn't say them things. We'll want all the help we can get from God an' His Blessed Mother now! These things have nothin' to do with the Will o' God. Ah, what can God do agen the stupidity o' men!

MRS. MADIGAN: The polis want you to go with them to the hospital to see the poor body—they're waitin' below.

MRS. BOYLE: We'll go. Come, Mary, an' we'll never come back here agen. Let your father furrage for himself now; I've done all I could an' it was all no use—he'll be hopeless till the end of his days. I've got a little room in me sisther's where we'll stop till your throuble is over, an' then we'll work together for the sake of the baby.

MARY: My poor little child that'll have no father!

MRS. BOYLE: It'll have what's far betther—it'll have two mothers.

A ROUGH VOICE *shouting from below:* Are yous goin' to keep us waitin' for yous all night?

MRS. MADIGAN: *(Going to the door, and shouting down)* Take your hour, there, take your hour! If yous are in such a hurry, skip off, then, for nobody wants you here—if they did yous wouldn't be found. For you're the same as yous were undher the British Government—never where yous are wanted! As far as I can see, the Polis as Polis, in this city, is Null an' Void!

MRS. BOYLE: We'll go, Mary, we'll go; you to see your poor dead brother, an' me to see me poor dead son!

MARY: I dhread it, mother, I dhread it!

MRS. BOYLE: I forgot, Mary, I forgot; your poor oul' selfish mother was only thinkin' of herself. No, no, you mustn't come—it wouldn't be good for you. You go on to me sisther's an' I'll face th' ordeal meself. Maybe I didn't feel sorry enough for Mrs. Tancred when her poor son was found as Johnny's been found now—because he was a Die-hard! Ah, why didn't I remember that then he wasn't a Die-hard or a Stater, but only a poor dead son! It's well I remember all that she said—an' it's my turn to say it now: What was the pain I suffered, Johnny, bringin' you into the world to carry you to your cradle, to the pains I'll suffer carryin' you out o' the world to bring you to your grave! Mother o' God, Mother o' God, have pity on us all! Blessed Virgin, where were you when me darlin' son was riddled with bullets, when me darlin' son was riddled with bullets? Sacred Heart o' Jesus, take away our hearts o' stone, and give us hearts o' flesh! Take away this murdherin' hate, an' give us Thine own eternal love!

(They all go slowly out. There is a pause; then a sound of shuffling steps on the stairs outside. The door opens and BOYLE *and* JOXER, *both of them very drunk, enter.)*

BOYLE: I'm able to go no farther. . . . Two polis, ey . . . what were they doin' here, I wondher? . . . Up to no good, anyhow . . . an' Juno an' that lovely daughter o' mine with them. (*Taking a sixpence from his pocket and looking at it*) Wan single, solitary tanner left out of all I borreyed . . . (*He lets it fall*) The last o' the Mohicans. . . . The blinds is down, Joxer, the blinds is down!

JOXER: (*Walking unsteadily across the room, and anchoring at the bed*) Put all . . . your throubles . . . in your oul' kit-bag . . . an' smile . . . smile . . . smile!

BOYLE: The counthry'll have to steady itself . . . it's goin' . . . to hell. . . . Where'r all . . . the chairs . . . gone to . . . steady itself, Joxer. . . . Chairs'll . . . have to . . . steady themselves. . . . No matther . . . what any one may . . . say. . . . Irelan's sober . . . is Irelan' . . . free.

JOXER: (*Stretching himself on the bed*) Chains . . . an' . . . slaveree . . . that's a darlin' motto . . . a daaarlin' . . . motto!

BOYLE: If th' worst comes . . . to th' worse . . . I can join

a . . . flyin' . . . column. . . . I done . . . me bit . . . in Easther Week . . . had no business . . . to . . . be . . . there . . . but Captain Boyle's Captain Boyle!

JOXER: Breathes there a man with soul . . . so . . . de . . . ad . . . this . . . me . . . o . . . wn, me nat . . . ive l . . . an'!

BOYLE: (*Subsiding into a sitting posture on the floor*) Commandant Kelly died . . . in them . . . arms . . . Joxer. . . . Tell me Volunteer Butties . . . says he . . . that . . . I died for . . . Irelan'!

JOXER: D'jever rade Willie . . . Reilly . . . an' his own . . . Colleen . . . Bawn? It's a darlin' story, a daarlin' story!

BOYLE: I'm telling you . . . Joxer . . . th' whole worl's . . . in a terr . . . ible state o' . . . chassis!

CURTAIN

Figure 1. Joxer (John Rogan) and "Captain" Boyle (Norman Rodway) enjoy a surreptitious breakfast in the shabby Dublin tenement in the Royal Shakespeare Company production of *Juno and the Paycock,* directed by Trevor Nunn, 1980. (Photograph: Donald Cooper, Photostage Limited.)

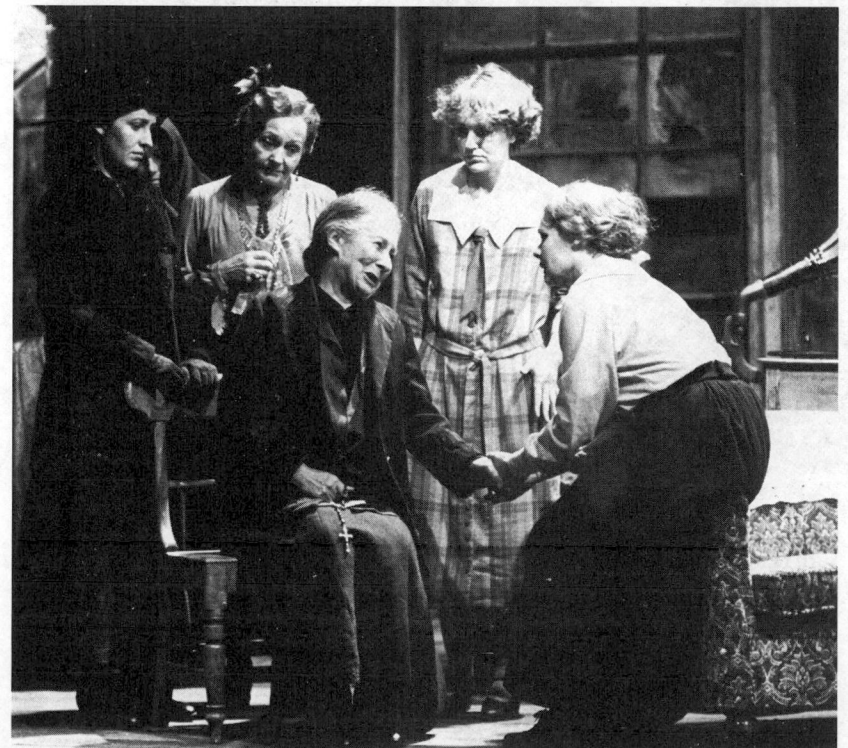

Figure 2. Juno (Judi Dench) tries to comfort Mrs. Tancred (Marie Kean), while neighbors (Frankie Cosgrave, Denyse Alexander, *partially hidden,* and Doreen Keogh) and Juno's daughter Mary (Dearbhla Molloy) look sympathetically at the grieving old woman in the Royal Shakespeare Company production of *Juno and the Paycock,* directed by Trevor Nunn, 1980. (Photograph: Donald Cooper, Photostage Limited.)

Figure 3. Johnny Boyle (Gerard Murphy), frightened and angered after hearing of the betrayal of Mary and the loss of his family's financial hopes, clings to his mother, Juno (Judi Dench), in the Royal Shakespeare Company production of *Juno and the Paycock*, directed by Trevor Nunn, 1980. (Photograph: Donald Cooper/Photostage.)

Staging of *Juno and the Paycock*

REVIEW OF THE ROYAL SHAKESPEARE
COMPANY PRODUCTION, 1980,
BY DEREK MAHON

There was a group of American undergraduates at the Aldwych on the night I saw the RSC revival of *Juno and the Paycock,* and I wondered if they could have guessed, without being told, that this was one of the great plays of the twentieth century. Amazed by the listlessness of the first act, I took some time to realize that it was intentional, not the result of a virus among the cast. Trevor Nunn's production adopts a radically different approach to O'Casey's masterpiece from the one to which we have long been accustomed. Subduing the star turns in the interest of the whole, he has come up with a slow-moving, low-keyed version which is more insidiously depressing than any I have yet seen, if adequate on its own terms. An interesting line of inquiry perhaps, but not a recipe for artistic success.

Nunn's strategy is mistaken because the play is composed of star turns. It is a play about character, even "characters," as well as circumstances, and to eschew vividness of personality, a vividness the playwright certainly intended, is to lose a vital dimension of the play, and the one that makes it great. The Boyles and their neighbours are victims of circumstance, granted; but they must be allowed to be more than that, or we make of a complex and exhilarating work a piece of doleful social realism. Not even that. The reality of the long-demolished Dublin tenements is not here, or only partly so; as any reader of O'Casey's autobiographies will know, the irrepressible high spirits were, in those surroundings, as much a fact of life as the squalor.

Norman Rodway as Boyle and John Rogan as Joxer are, therefore, not so much disappointing as infuriating. Deflected by the rationale of the production from playing their marvelous parts to the full, they give us, respectively, a dejected and irritable codger apparently endowed with sober self-knowledge, and a whining creep devoid of even superficial charm. When Boyle announces defiantly to Juno, "I've a little spirit left in me still," he is boasting, but it should not be an empty boast, as the liveliness of his fancy and the trenchancy of his self-dramatizing balderdash make clear. Self-dramatizing in a literal sense; for he and Joxer conduct their own little play within the play, oddly prefiguring Estragon and Vladimir, though much of the fun of that goes by the board here.

On the plus side, Gerard Murphy brings more presence to the part of the maimed and frightened Johnny than is usually the case. O'Casey himself, during rehearsals for the original Abbey production, habitually referred to *Juno* as "the play about Johnny Boyle"— meaning, perhaps, that Johnny represented in his own person all the desperation of a people living, like the Boyles, on impossible dreams. Nobody in the play pays him much heed, and the part is too often treated as a nuisance, like Johnny himself; but that isn't the case here. And Judi Dench is a memorable Juno; her bitterness qualified by an essential sweetness, she alone of the cast shines through the doctrinaire opacity.

I described Boyle as "self-dramatizing," and the theme of the play is the price of his self-dramatization— even, it might be said, the price of drama. In terms of the Boyles' family life, that price is disintegration and chaos. So too in the political sphere, where theatrical postures and heightened language have led to civil war. "Give us one of your shut-eyed ones," says Boyle to Joxer during a sing-song; and Joxer forgets the words. "Shut-eyed ones," for O'Casey as for Dr. Cruise O'Brien in our own day, are the source of half the misery of Ireland; yet they are a seemingly indispensable part of the drama: even the RSC permits itself the liberty of introducing and concluding each act with a snatch of the kind of demotic Dublin melody of which O'Casey evidently took a dim view. This is unfortunate; the effect is to cheapen and trivialize the play itself.

It is Juno's distinction that she resists the blandishments of drama and song, and her misfortune that she (and her daughter Mary, despite her half-baked socialism) sees the only alternative in a mirage of middle-class gentility. The power of the play resides in its intellectual battle with its own emotional appeal. Clear-sighted though it may be, *Juno and the Paycock* is also O'Casey's great "shut-eyed one." The struggle within the artefact itself is of central importance, and to tilt the balance so completely in Juno's favour, by denying Boyle his measure of magnetism, however specious, is to forfeit a crucial tension.

I have never seen a better production of *Juno and the Paycock* than Trevor Nunn's, and I do not expect to see one. It had the characteristics of Nunn's work at its best, a sensitivity to detail, rhythm, clarity and self-confidence; but it also lifted Sean O'Casey's play out of that slightly condescending slot of the mind to which many critics, including me, have assigned it. Nobody doubts the power of certain scenes, particularly the accumulation of disasters which leads to Mrs. Boyle's courageous speech in the last act—"Take away this murdherin' hate," and few question either the humor of the Joxer Daly/Captain Boyle scenes, which too easily confirm the British impression of the Irish as a charming, feckless race.

But the combination of tragedy and farce has been queried, as if O'Casey, self-taught, from a poor family, had not acquired the sophistication to distinguish between the two. Some scenes, too, have been held to betray a literary self-consciousness, as if O'Casey wanted to remind his audience that he, like Mary Boyle, has been reading Ibsen. Mrs. Madigan's flattery of Mary— "I remember, as well as I remember yesterday, the day she was born"—recalls the Nurse's speech in *Romeo and Juliet*; while the sing-song at the end of Act Two, where the Boyle family, supposedly enriched by an inheritance, gather with their friends around the new gramophone on the new three-piece suite, can seem like padding, as if O'Casey, uncertain how to complete the scene without anticipating the revelations to come, had resorted to music-hall nostalgia.

For these and other reasons, *Juno and the Paycock* has been regarded as a rich and powerful play, but far from a masterpiece. Nunn's production, however, faultlessly cast, turns the supposed weaknesses into strengths. The contrast between Judi Dench's determination as Juno and Norman Rodway's fecklessness as the Captain are shown as two sides to the Irish despair, one carrying on against the odds while the other gives up too soon. Nunn brings out the family likenesses in the next generation: Dearbhla Molloy's Mary actually looks like a younger Juno, particularly when the two sing together sweetly and shyly, and there is the same impetuousness in love which landed poor Juno with the Captain. If we need a justification for the family sing-song, here it is—the perpetuation of follies, because, on a darker note, Gerard Murphy's Johnny Boyle skulks in fear on the party fringes and the funeral of a neighbor's son interrupts the proceedings. "If you're Irish," runs the record, "Come into the parlour"—and a mourning mother in widow's black does.

The RSC production is rooted in naturalism—the broken bike by the grimy window—but it never slumps into an accumulation of irrelevant details. Nunn has managed to bring the play together so that each moment of each scene fits into the whole, and we are not left just with another sad anecdote from Dublin in the troublesome Twenties, but with an orchestrated hymn against all poverty, despair and hate. It is deeply moving, without being sentimental or sententious, and establishes Nunn as the best British director of our time.

FEDERICO GARCIA LORCA

1898–1936

Before he was executed by the Fascists at the beginning of the Spanish civil war, Lorca had written twelve plays. But his last three works—tragedies of rural life—are such powerful evocations of an archetypal conflict between passionate human instincts and traditional codes of conduct that they alone have been sufficient to establish his reputation as the most culturally conscious and theatrically intense dramatist to emerge in Spain during the twentieth century. He was born near the city of Granada, in southern Spain, a region deeply influenced by the Andalusian and gypsy folk traditions of balladry and dance—traditions that left their mark on both his poetry and plays. He was also influenced by his wealthy father and his cultivated mother who evidently encouraged him to develop his widely varied artistic talents, for he was not only a poet and playwright, but also an accomplished pianist and painter. By the time he was eight, he was already improvising plays in the courtyard of his parents' home, and before he entered the University of Granada at the age of sixteen he was writing ballads, poems, and prose descriptions of the Spanish landscape that he subsequently included in published collections of his works. When he entered the University, he planned to study for a career in the law, but he quickly changed his mind and moved on to studies in philosophy and literature, which he continued at the University of Madrid. When he moved to Madrid in 1919, he had already published *Impressions and Landscapes* (1918), an evocative series of impressions based on his travels throughout Spain, and he had in hand a manuscript of poems that he shared with his fellow students in public readings. Lorca, in fact, was an inveterate performer, and throughout his life he evidently took much greater pleasure in reading his works or seeing them produced than in rushing them into print. He usually published his work well after it had been written, and much of it remained unpublished even at the time of his death.

Lorca's playwriting career began in earnest during the 1920s, a period when he experimented in a variety of forms and turned out a number of works, including a parable play about a cockroach who becomes entranced by the enchanting world of a butterfly, a comedy based on the traditional Spanish puppet character Don Cristobal, a series of farces based on the films of Buster Keaton, a surrealist work involving a young man, his fiancée, a mannequin, a dead child, and a cat, a verse play about Mariana Pineda, a nineteenth-century figure who died in the liberation of Madrid, and a tragic farce about an old bachelor who falls in love with a naive and sensual young girl. These works, together with his numerous public readings, as well as the publication of two collections of poems and a collection of ballads, had turned Lorca into a widely celebrated Spanish writer by the end of the 1920s. In 1929, he left Spain temporarily to visit Paris and London, before traveling to America, where he spent a year at Columbia University, but he evidently did not find New York a congenial place, and by 1930 he had left to visit Cuba, Argentina, and other Latin American countries before returning permanently to Spain.

His travel abroad had also apparently turned him away from all the cosmopolitan movements in drama that were then astir in the major theatrical centers, for when he returned to Spain in 1931, he organized a government-sponsored theatrical troupe and began touring the provinces, producing the Spanish classics of the seventeenth century, wherever he could find an audience in small Spanish towns and villages. His sustained immersion in the folk life of the Spanish provinces also must have led him to develop the subjects that resulted in the major works of his career—his three tragedies of rural experience—which he wrote during his last five years. In each of these, he focused on the predicament of characters who are torn between their allegiance to traditional Spanish codes of honor and religious belief, on the one hand, and their passionate human desires, on the other. And, in each case, he dramatized the tragic frustration of natural human impulses that he evidently perceived as the inescapable outcome of being forced to submit to rigid and anachronistic codes of behavior. Lorca's emphasis on such frustration may also reflect a covert attack on a variety of repressive forces in his own life: the dogmatic power of the Catholic church, the political conservatism of the governing Fascists who would execute Lorca in 1936, and the hostility of a predominantly heterosexual society that degraded and ostracized homosexuals like himself.

In the earliest of the tragedies, *Blood Wedding* (1933), a work heavily interspersed with lyric scenes, Lorca dramatized the primal power of the blood in the person of a young woman "burning with desire," who finds herself betrothed and married to a man whom she regards as "a little bit of water." Immediately after the marriage ceremony she runs off with another man, the husband of her cousin, a man whose family had killed the father and brother of her own husband in a blood feud, but a man whom she had always loved because he was for her "a dark river, choked with brush, that brought near me the undertone of its rushes and its whispered song." The two lovers thus violate all the codes of belief and honor in their community and escape into the forest, where they are pursued by the newly married groom, which results in a doubly fatal encounter between the groom and his rival. The bride is thus left "without a single man ever having seen himself in the whiteness of my breasts," a condition that is at once the measure of her conventional purity and her intense frustration. And the mother of the groom, in a final chorus, is seen lamenting the death of her last son at the hands of the same family that had previously killed her husband and her other son. The conflict between traditional codes and human desires is, therefore, presented as bringing profound suffering to all the central characters, old and young, conventional and rebellious alike. In his second tragedy of rural experience, *Yerma* (1934), Lorca examined the plight of a married woman, whose frustrated maternal desire ultimately drives her to the act of killing her impotent and unsympathetic husband—an act that in turn moves her to cry out "I'm going to rest without ever waking to see whether my blood has announced the coming of new blood. My body barren forever."

Like his other mature plays, *The House of Bernarda Alba*, finished in 1936 a few months before Lorca's death but not produced until 1945, is dramatically preoccupied with the frustration of natural human desire. And like these other plays, it dramatizes this problem by focusing on the experience of women, exploring the sentiment voiced by Amelia, "To be born a woman's the worst possible punishment." Indeed, in this play there are no men on stage at all, though every speech resounds either with the memory of Bernarda's recently dead husband or with the yearning of all her daughters for the virile figure of Pepe el Romano. The world of the play, as indicated by its title, is dominated by Bernarda, whose tyrannical honor and pride and piety and repressiveness are epitomized by the starkly white color of her house, by the black colors of mourning she enforces upon her daughters, and by her big stick that thumps over and over again on the stage. The play repeatedly emphasizes repression: Bernarda's announcement of eight years of mourning, Maria Josefa gagged so that she won't shout, the stallion locked in the stall. Even when La Poncia, the earthy maid who is willing to confront Bernarda directly, imagines revenge, she invokes the prevailing sense of a household that is really a prison: "Then I'll lock myself up in a room with her and spit in her face—for a whole year."

Staging a play whose characters almost always seem at emotional breaking points is not easy, but Nuria Espert, a well-known Spanish actress and director, succeeded in her 1986 production (first staged at the Lyric, Hammersmith, then transferred to the West End). As Michael Billington points out in his review, and as a number of other critics noted, the set itself was crucial, its white stone walls and barred windows harshly looming over the black-clad actresses (see Figure 1). Espert's three older actresses, differing noticeably in physical stature, emphasize the conflict between contrasting views of womanhood. Patricia Hayes as Maria Josefa appears always in white (see Figure 3), symbolizing both the bride she wishes to become and the innocence of the lamb she carries in the last act, an innocence her daughter Bernarda has imprisoned and thus distorted into madness. Glenda Jackson's thin angular features and her ramrod-straight posture (see Figure 3) aptly reflect Bernarda's condemnation of everyone beneath her in social standing or in moral outlook. Joan Plowright's rounder features and full curls (see Figure 2) suggest that La Poncia is a woman able to remember her husband with delight, a woman able to understand the sexual longings of Martirio and Adela, longings that Bernarda can only try to repress. Given the irrepressibility of such desires, it's not surprising that Bernarda at the end turns into a screaming banshee, driving off Pepe el Romano (see Figure 4) and thus driving Adela to suicide. She may command her house, but it is a house dominated by death.

THE HOUSE OF BERNARDA ALBA
A Drama about Women in the Villages of Spain

BY FEDERICO GARCIA LORCA / TRANSLATED BY JAMES GRAHAM-LUJÁN AND RICHARD L. O'CONNELL

CHARACTERS

BERNARDA *(age 60)*
MARIA JOSEFA, *Bernarda's Mother (age 80)*
ANGUSTIAS, *Bernarda's Daughter (age 39)*
MAGDALENA, *Bernarda's Daughter (age 30)*
AMELIA, *Bernarda's Daughter (age 27)*
MARTIRIO, *Bernarda's Daughter (age 24)*
ADELA, *Bernarda's Daughter (age 20)*

A MAID *(age 50)*
LA PONCIA, *A Maid (age 60)*
PRUDENCIA *(age 50)*
Women in Mourning

The writer states that these Three Acts are intended as a photographic document.

ACT 1

(A very white room in BERNARDA ALBA'S *house. The walls are white. There are arched doorways with jute curtains tied back with tassels and ruffles. Wicker chairs. On the walls, pictures of unlikely landscapes full of nymphs or legendary kings.*

It is summer. A great brooding silence fills the stage. It is empty when the curtain rises. Bells can be heard tolling outside.)

FIRST SERVANT *(entering)*: The tolling of those bells hits me right between the eyes.

PONCIA *(she enters, eating bread and sausage)*: More than two hours of mumbo jumbo. Priests are here from all the towns. The church looks beautiful. At the first responsory for the dead, Magdalena fainted.

FIRST SERVANT: She's the one who's left most alone.

PONCIA: She's the only one who loved her father. Ay! Thank God we're alone for a little. I came over to eat.

FIRST SERVANT: If Bernarda sees you . . . !

PONCIA: She's not eating today so she'd just as soon we'd all die of hunger! Domineering old tyrant! But she'll be fooled! I opened the sausage crock.

FIRST SERVANT *(with an anxious sadness)*: Couldn't you give me some for my little girl, Poncia?

PONCIA: Go ahead! And take a fistful of peas too. She won't know the difference today.

VOICE *(within)*: Bernarda!

PONCIA: There's the grandmother! Isn't she locked up tight?

FIRST SERVANT: Two turns of the key.

PONCIA: You'd better put the cross-bar up too. She's got the fingers of a lock-picker!

VOICE *(within)*: Bernarda!

PONCIA *(shouting)*: She's coming! *(to the* SERVANT*)* Clean everything up good. If Bernarda doesn't find things shining, she'll pull out the few hairs I have left.

SERVANT: What a woman!

PONCIA: Tyrant over everyone around her. She's perfectly capable of sitting on your heart and watching you die for a whole year without turning off that cold little smile she wears on her wicked face. Scrub, scrub those dishes!

SERVANT: I've got blood on my hands from so much polishing of everything.

PONCIA: She's the cleanest, she's the decentest, she's the highest everything! A good rest her poor husband's earned!

(The bells stop.)

SERVANT: Did all the relatives come?

PONCIA: Just hers. His people hate her. They came to see him dead and make the sign of the cross over him; that's all.

SERVANT: Are there enough chairs?

PONCIA: More than enough. Let them sit on the floor. When Bernarda's father died people stopped coming under this roof. She doesn't want them to see her in her "domain." Curse her!

SERVANT: She's been good to you.

PONCIA: Thirty years washing her sheets. Thirty years eating her leftovers. Nights of watching when she had a cough. Whole days peeking through a crack in the shutters to spy on the neighbors and carry her the tale. Life without secrets one from the other. But in spite of that—curse her! May the "pain of the piercing nail" strike her in the eyes.

SERVANT: Poncia!

PONCIA: But I'm a good watchdog! I bark when I'm told and bite beggars' heels when she sics me on 'em. My sons work in her fields—both of them already married, but one of these days I'll have enough.

SERVANT: And then . . . ?

PONCIA: Then I'll lock myself up in a room with her and spit in her face—a whole year. "Bernarda, here's for this, that and the other!" Till I leave her—just like a lizard the boys have squashed. For that's what she is—she and her whole family! Not that I envy her her life. Five girls are left her, five ugly daughters—not counting Angustias the eldest, by her first husband, who has money—the rest of them, plenty of eyelets to embroider, plenty of linen petticoats, but bread and grapes when it comes to inheritance.

SERVANT: Well, I'd like to have what they've got!

PONCIA: All we have is our hands and a hole in God's earth.

SERVANT: And that's the only earth they'll ever leave to us—to us who have nothing!

PONCIA (at the cupboard): This glass has some specks.

SERVANT: Neither soap nor rag will take them off.

(The bells toll.)

PONCIA: The last prayer! I'm going over and listen. I certainly like the way our priest sings. In the Pater Noster his voice went up, and up—like a pitcher filling with water little by little. Of course, at the end his voice cracked, but it's glorious to hear it. No, there never was anybody like the old Sacristan—Tronchapinos. At my mother's Mass, may she rest in peace, he sang. The walls shook—and when he said "Amen," it was as if a wolf had come into the church.

(Imitating him.)

A-a-a-a-men!

(She starts coughing.)

SERVANT: Watch out—you'll strain your windpipe!

PONCIA: I'd rather strain something else!

(Goes out laughing.)

(The SERVANT scrubs. The bells toll.)

SERVANT (imitating the bells): Dong, dong, dong. Dong, dong, dong. May God forgive him!

BEGGAR WOMAN (at the door, with a little girl): Blesséd be God!

SERVANT: Dong, dong, dong. I hope he waits many years for us! Dong, dong, dong.

BEGGAR (loudly, a little annoyed): Blesséd be God!

SERVANT (annoyed): Forever and ever!

BEGGAR: I came for the scraps.

(The bells stop tolling.)

SERVANT: You can go right out the way you came in. Today's scraps are for me.

BEGGAR: But you have somebody to take care of you—and my little girl and I are all alone!

SERVANT: Dogs are alone too, and they live.

BEGGAR: They always give them to me.

SERVANT: Get out of here! Who let you in anyway? You've already tracked up the place.

(The BEGGAR WOMAN and LITTLE GIRL leave. The SERVANT goes on scrubbing.)

Floors finished with oil, cupboards, pedestals, iron beds—but us servants, we can suffer in silence—and live in mud huts with a plate and a spoon. I hope someday not a one will be left to tell it.

(The bells sound again.)

Yes, yes—ring away. Let them put you in a coffin with gold inlay and brocade to carry it on— you're no less dead than I'll be, so take what's coming to you, Antonio María Benavides—stiff in your broadcloth suit and your high boots— take what's coming to you! You'll never again lift my skirts behind the corral door!

(From the rear door, two by two, women in mourning with large shawls and black skirts and fans, begin to enter. They come in slowly until the stage is full.)

SERVANT (breaking into a wail): Oh, Antonio María Benavides, now you'll never see these walls, nor break bread in this house again! I'm the one who loved you most of all your servants.

(Pulling her hair.)

Must I live on after you've gone? Must I go on living?

(The two hundred women finish coming in, and BERNARDA and her five daughters enter. BERNARDA leans on a cane.)

BERNARDA (to the SERVANT): Silence!

SERVANT (weeping): Bernarda!

BERNARDA: Less shrieking and more work. You should have had all this cleaner for the wake. Get out. This isn't your place.

(The SERVANT goes off crying.)

The poor are like animals—they seem to be made of different stuff.

FIRST WOMAN: The poor feel their sorrows too.

BERNARDA: But they forget them in front of a plateful of peas.

FIRST GIRL (timidly): Eating is necessary for living.

BERNARDA: At your age one doesn't talk in front of older people.

WOMAN: Be quiet, child.

BERNARDA: I've never taken lessons from anyone. Sit down.

(They sit down. Pause. Loudly.)

Magdalena, don't cry. If you want to cry, get under your bed. Do you hear me?

SECOND WOMAN *(to BERNARDA)*: Have you started to work the fields?

BERNARDA: Yesterday.

THIRD WOMAN: The sun comes down like lead.

FIRST WOMAN: I haven't known heat like this for years.

(Pause. They all fan themselves.)

BERNARDA: Is the lemonade ready?

PONCIA: Yes, Bernarda.

(She brings in a large tray full of little white jars which she distributes.)

BERNARDA: Give the men some.

PONCIA: They're already drinking in the patio.

BERNARDA: Let them get out the way they came in. I don't want them walking through here.

A GIRL *(to ANGUSTIAS)*: Pepe el Romano was with the men during the service.

ANGUSTIAS: There he was.

BERNARDA: His mother was there. She saw his mother. Neither she nor I saw Pepe . . .

GIRL: I thought . . .

BERNARDA: The one who *was* there was Darajalí, the widower. Very close to your Aunt. We all of us saw him.

SECOND WOMAN *(aside, in a low voice)*: Wicked, worse than wicked woman!

THIRD WOMAN: A tongue like a knife!

BERNARDA: Women in church shouldn't look at any man but the priest—and him only because he wears skirts. To turn your head is to be looking for the warmth of corduroy.

FIRST WOMAN: Sanctimonious old snake!

PONCIA *(between her teeth)*: Itching for a man's warmth.

BERNARDA *(beating with her cane on the floor)*: Bless éd be God!

ALL *(crossing themselves)*: Forever blesséd and praised.

BERNARDA: Rest in peace with holy company at your head.

ALL: Rest in peace!

BERNARDA: With the Angel Saint Michael, and his sword of justice.

ALL: Rest in peace!

BERNARDA: With the key that opens, and the hand that locks.

ALL: Rest in peace!

BERNARDA: With the most blesséd, and the little lights of the field.

ALL: Rest in peace!

BERNARDA: With our holy charity, and all souls on land and sea.

ALL: Rest in peace!

BERNARDA: Grant rest to your servant, Antonio María Benavides, and give him the crown of your blesséd glory.

ALL: Amen.

BERNARDA *(she rises and chants)*: *Requiem aeternam donat eis domine.*

ALL *(standing and chanting in the Gregorian fashion)*: *Et lux perpetua luce ab eis.*

(They cross themselves.)

FIRST WOMAN: May you have health to pray for his soul. *(They start filing out.)*

THIRD WOMAN: You won't lack loaves of hot bread.

SECOND WOMAN: Nor a roof for your daughters.

(They are all filing in front of BERNARDA and going out. ANGUSTIAS leaves by the door to the patio.)

FOURTH WOMAN: May you go on enjoying your wedding wheat.

PONCIA *(she enters, carrying a money bag)*: From the men—this bag of money for Masses.

BERNARDA: Thank them—and let them have a glass of brandy.

GIRL *(to MAGDALENA)*: Magdalena . . .

BERNARDA *(to MAGDALENA, who is starting to cry)*: Sh-h-h-h!

(She beats with her cane on the floor.)
(All the women have gone out.)

BERNARDA *(to the women who have just left)*: Go back to your houses and criticize everything you've seen! I hope it'll be many years before you pass under the archway of my door again.

PONCIA: You've nothing to complain about. The whole town came.

BERNARDA: Yes, to fill my house with the sweat from their wraps and the poison of their tongues.

AMELIA: Mother, don't talk like that.

BERNARDA: What other way is there to talk about this cursed village with no river—this village full of wells where you drink water always fearful it's been poisoned?

PONCIA: Look what they've done to the floor!

BERNARDA: As though a herd of goats had passed through.

(PONCIA cleans the floor.)

Adela, give me a fan.

ADELA: Take this one.

(She gives her a round fan with green and red flowers.)

BERNARDA (*throwing the fan on the floor*): Is that the fan to give to a widow? Give me a black one and learn to respect your father's memory.

MARTIRIO: Take mine.

BERNARDA: And you?

MARTIRIO: I'm not hot.

BERNARDA: Well, look for another, because you'll need it. For the eight years of mourning, not a breath of air will get in this house from the street. We'll act as if we'd sealed up doors and windows with bricks. That's what happened in my father's house—and in my grandfather's house. Meantime, you can all start embroidering your hope-chest linens. I have twenty bolts of linen in the chest from which to cut sheets and coverlets. Magdalena can embroider them.

MAGDALENA: It's all the same to me.

ADELA (*sourly*): If you don't want to embroider them—they can go without. That way yours will look better.

MAGDALENA: Neither mine nor yours. I know I'm not going to marry. I'd rather carry sacks to the mill. Anything except sit here day after day in this dark room.

BERNARDA: That's what a woman is for.

MAGDALENA: Cursed be all women.

BERNARDA: In this house you'll do what I order. You can't run with the story to your father any more. Needle and thread for women. Whiplash and mules for men. That's the way it has to be for people who have certain obligations.

(ADELA *goes out.*)

VOICE: Bernarda! Let me out!

BERNARDA (*calling*): Let her out now!

(The FIRST SERVANT *enters.*)

FIRST SERVANT: I had a hard time holding her. In spite of her eighty years, your mother's strong as an oak.

BERNARDA: It runs in the family. My grandfather was the same way.

SERVANT: Several times during the wake I had to cover her mouth with an empty sack because she wanted to shout out to you to give her dishwater to drink at least, and some dogmeat, which is what she says you feed her.

MARTIRIO: She's mean!

BERNARDA (*to* SERVANT): Let her get some fresh air in the patio.

SERVANT: She took her rings and the amethyst earrings out of the box, put them on, and told me she wants to get married.

(The daughters laugh.)

BERNARDA: Go with her and be careful she doesn't get near the well.

SERVANT: You don't need to be afraid she'll jump in.

BERNARDA: It's not that— but the neighbors can see her there from their windows.

(The SERVANT *leaves.*)

MARTIRIO: We'll go change our clothes.

BERNARDA: Yes, but don't take the kerchiefs from your heads.

(ADELA *enters.*)

And Angustias?

ADELA (*meaningfully*): I saw her looking out through the cracks of the back door. The men had just gone.

BERNARDA: And you, what were *you* doing at the door?

ADELA: I went there to see if the hens had laid.

BERNARDA: But the men had already gone!

ADELA (*meaningfully*): A group of them were still standing outside.

BERNARDA (*furiously*): Angustias! Angustias!

ANGUSTIAS (*entering*): Did you want something?

BERNARDA: For what—and at whom—were you looking?

ANGUSTIAS: Nobody.

BERNARDA: Is it decent for a woman of your class to be running after a man the day of her father's funeral? Answer me! Whom were you looking at?

(*Pause.*)

ANGUSTIAS: I . . .

BERNARDA: Yes, you!

ANGUSTIAS: Nobody.

BERNARDA: Soft! Honeytongue!

(She strikes her.)

PONCIA (*running to her*): Bernarda, calm down!

(She holds her. ANGUSTIAS *weeps.*)

BERNARDA: Get out of here, all of you!

(They all go out.)

PONCIA: She did it not realizing what she was doing—although it's bad, of course. It really disgusted me to see her sneak along to the patio. Then she stood at the window listening to the men's talk, which, as usual, was not the sort one should listen to.

BERNARDA: That's what they come to funerals for. (*With curiosity.*) What were they talking about?

PONCIA: They were talking about Paca la Roseta. Last night they tied her husband up in a stall, stuck her on a horse behind the saddle, and carried her away to the depths of the olive grove.

BERNARDA: And what did she do?

PONCIA: She? She was just as happy—they say her

breasts were exposed and Maximiliano held on to her as if he were playing a guitar. Terrible!

BERNARDA: And what happened?

PONCIA: What had to happen. They came back almost at daybreak. Paca la Roseta with her hair loose and a wreath of flowers on her head.

BERNARDA: She's the only bad woman we have in the village.

PONCIA: Because she's not from here. She's from far away. And those who went with her are the sons of outsiders too. The men from here aren't up to a thing like that.

BERNARDA: No, but they like to see it, and talk about it, and suck their fingers over it.

PONCIA: They were saying a lot more things.

BERNARDA (looking from side to side with a certain fear): What things?

PONCIA: I'm ashamed to talk about them.

BERNARDA: And my daughter heard them?

PONCIA: Of course!

BERNARDA: That one takes after her Aunts: white and mealy-mouthed and casting sheep's eyes at any little barber's compliment. Oh, what one has to go through and put up with so people will be decent and not too wild!

PONCIA: It's just that your daughters are of an age when they ought to have husbands. Mighty little trouble they give you. Angustias must be much more than thirty now.

BERNARDA: Exactly thirty-nine.

PONCIA: Imagine. And she's never had a beau . . .

BERNARDA (furiously): None of them has ever had a beau and they've never needed one! They get along very well.

PONCIA: I didn't mean to offend you.

BERNARDA: For a hundred miles around there's no one good enough to come near them. The men in this town are not of their class. Do you want me to turn them over to the first shepherd?

PONCIA: You should have moved to another town.

BERNARDA: That's it. To sell them!

PONCIA: No, Bernarda, to change. . . . Of course, any place else, they'd be the poor ones.

BERNARDA: Hold your tormenting tongue!

PONCIA: One can't even talk to you. Do we, or do we not share secrets?

BERNARDA: We do not. You're a servant and I pay you. Nothing more.

PONCIA: But . . .

FIRST SERVANT (entering): Don Arturo's here. He's come to see about dividing the inheritance.

BERNARDA: Let's go. (to the SERVANT) You start whitewashing the patio. (to LA PONCIA) And you start putting all the dead man's clothes away in the chest.

PONCIA: We could give away some of the things.

BERNARDA: Nothing—not a button even! Not even the cloth we covered his face with.

(She goes out slowly, leaning on her cane. At the door she turns to look at the two servants. They go out. She leaves.) (AMELIA and MARTIRIO enter.)

AMELIA: Did you take the medicine?

MARTIRIO: For all the good it'll do me.

AMELIA: But you took it?

MARTIRIO: I do things without any faith, but like clockwork.

AMELIA: Since the new doctor came you look livelier.

MARTIRIO: I feel the same.

AMELIA: Did you notice? Adelaida wasn't at the funeral.

MARTIRIO: I know. Her sweetheart doesn't let her go out even to the front doorstep. Before, she was gay. Now, not even powder on her face.

AMELIA: These days a girl doesn't know whether to have a beau or not.

MARTIRIO: It's all the same.

AMELIA: The whole trouble is all these wagging tongues that won't let us live. Adelaida has probably had a bad time.

MARTIRIO: She's afraid of our mother. Mother is the only one who knows the story of Adelaida's father and where he got his lands. Everytime she comes here, Mother twists the knife in the wound. Her father killed his first wife's husband in Cuba so he could marry her himself. Then he left her there and went off with another woman who already had one daughter, and then he took up with this other girl, Adelaida's mother, and married her after his second wife died insane.

AMELIA: But why isn't a man like that put in jail?

MARTIRIO: Because men help each other cover up things like that and no one's able to tell on them.

AMELIA: But Adelaida's not to blame for any of that.

MARTIRIO: No. But history repeats itself. I can see that everything is a terrible repetition. And she'll have the same fate as her mother and grandmother—both of them wife to the man who fathered her.

AMELIA: What an awful thing!

MARTIRIO: It's better never to look at a man. I've been afraid of them since I was a little girl. I'd see them in the yard, yoking the oxen and lifting grain sacks, shouting and stamping, and I was always afraid to grow up for fear one of them would suddenly take me in his arms. God has made me weak and ugly and has definitely put such things away from me.

AMELIA: Don't say that! Enrique Humanas was after you and he liked you.

MARTIRIO: That was just people's ideas! One time I stood in my nightgown at the window until daybreak because he let me know through his shepherd's little girl that he was going to come, and he didn't. It was all just talk. Then he married someone else who had more money than I.

AMELIA: And ugly as the devil.

MARTIRIO: What do men care about ugliness? All they care about is lands, yokes of oxen, and a submissive bitch who'll feed them.

AMELIA: Ay!

(MAGDALENA enters.)

MAGDALENA: What are you doing?

MARTIRIO: Just here.

AMELIA: And you?

MAGDALENA: I've been going through all the rooms. Just to walk a little, and look at Grandmother's needlepoint pictures—the little woolen dog, and the black man wrestling with the lion—which we liked so much when we were children. Those were happier times. A wedding lasted ten days and evil tongues weren't in style. Today people are more refined. Brides wear white veils, just as in the cities, and we drink bottled wine, but we rot inside because of what people might say.

MARTIRIO: Lord knows what went on then!

AMELIA (to MAGDALENA): One of your shoelaces has come untied.

MAGDALENA: What of it?

AMELIA: You'll step on it and fall.

MAGDALENA: One less!

MARTIRIO: And Adela?

MAGDALENA: Ah! She put on the green dress she made to wear for her birthday, went out to the yard, and began shouting: "Chickens! Chickens, look at me!" I had to laugh.

AMELIA: If Mother had only seen her!

MAGDALENA: Poor little thing! She's the youngest one of us and still has her illusions. I'd give something to see her happy.

(Pause. ANGUSTIAS crosses the stage, carrying some towels.)

ANGUSTIAS: What time is it?

MAGDALENA: It must be twelve.

ANGUSTIAS: So late?

AMELIA: It's about to strike.

(ANGUSTIAS goes out.)

MAGDALENA (meaningfully): Do you know what?

(Pointing after ANGUSTIAS.)

AMELIA: No.

MAGDALENA: Come on!

MARTIRIO: I don't know what you're talking about!

MAGDALENA: Both of you know it better than I do, always with your heads together, like two little sheep, but not letting anybody else in on it. I mean about Pepe el Romano!

MARTIRIO: Ah!

MAGDALENA (mocking her): Ah! The whole town's talking about it. Pepe el Romano is coming to marry Angustias. Last night he was walking around the house and I think he's going to send a declaration soon.

MARTIRIO: I'm glad. He's a good man.

AMELIA: Me too. Angustias is well off.

MAGDALENA: Neither one of you is glad.

MARTIRIO: Magdalena! What do you mean?

MAGDALENA: If he were coming because of Angustias' looks, for Angustias as a woman, I'd be glad too, but he's coming for her money. Even though Angustias is our sister, we're her family here and we know she's old and sickly, and always has been the least attractive one of us! Because if she looked like a dressed-up stick at twenty, what can she look like now, now that she's forty?

MARTIRIO: Don't talk like that. Luck comes to the one who least expects it.

AMELIA: But Magdalena's right after all! Angustias has all her father's money; she's the only rich one in the house and that's why, now that Father's dead and the money will be divided, they're coming for her.

MAGDALENA: Pepe el Romano is twenty-five years old and the best looking man around here. The natural thing would be for him to be after you, Amelia, or our Adela, who's twenty—not looking for the least likely one in this house, a woman who, like her father, talks through her nose.

MARTIRIO: Maybe he likes that!

MAGDALENA: I've never been able to bear your hypocrisy.

MARTIRIO: Heavens!

(ADELA enters.)

MAGDALENA: Did the chickens see you?

ADELA: What did you want me to do?

AMELIA: If Mother sees you, she'll drag you by your hair!

ADELA: I had a lot of illusions about this dress. I'd planned to put it on the day we were going to eat watermelons at the well. There wouldn't have been another like it.

MARTIRIO: It's a lovely dress.

ADELA: And one that looks very good on me. It's the best thing Magdalena's ever cut.

MAGDALENA: And the chickens, what did they say to you?

ADELA: They presented me with a few fleas that riddled my legs.

(They laugh.)

MARTIRIO: What you can do is dye it black.

MAGDALENA: The best thing you can do is give it to Angustias for her wedding with Pepe el Romano.

ADELA (*with hidden emotion*): But Pepe el Romano . . .

AMELIA: Haven't you heard about it?

ADELA: No.

MAGDALENA: Well, now you know!

ADELA: But it can't be!

MAGDALENA: Money can do anything.

ADELA: Is that why she went out after the funeral and stood looking through the door?

(*Pause.*)

And that man would . . .

MAGDALENA: Would do anything.

(*Pause.*)

MARTIRIO: What are you thinking, Adela?

ADELA: I'm thinking that this mourning has caught me at the worst moment of my life for me to bear it.

MAGDALENA: You'll get used to it.

ADELA (*bursting out, crying with rage*): I will not get used to it! I can't be locked up. I don't want my skin to look like yours. I don't want my skin's whiteness lost in these rooms. Tomorrow I'm going to put on my green dress and go walking in the streets. I want to go out!

(*The* FIRST SERVANT *enters.*)

MAGDALENA (*in a tone of authority*): Adela!

SERVANT: The poor thing! How she misses her father. . . .

(*She goes out.*)

MARTIRIO: Hush!

AMELIA: What happens to one will happen to all of us.

(ADELA *grows calm.*)

MAGDALENA: The servant almost heard you.

SERVANT (*entering*): Pepe el Romano is coming along at the end of the street.

(AMELIA, MARTIRIO *and* MAGDALENA *run hurriedly.*)

MAGDALENA: Let's go see him!

(*They leave rapidly.*)

SERVANT (*to* ADELA): Aren't you going?

ADELA: It's nothing to me.

SERVANT: Since he has to turn the corner, you'll see him better from the window of your room.

(*The* SERVANT *goes out.* ADELA *is left on the stage, standing doubtfully; after a moment, she also leaves rapidly, going toward her room.* BERNARDA *and* LA PONCIA *come in.*)

BERNARDA: Damned portions and shares.

PONCIA: What a lot of money is left to Angustias!

BERNARDA: Yes.

PONCIA: And for the others, considerably less.

BERNARDA: You've told me that three times now, when you know I don't want it mentioned! Considerably less; a lot less! Don't remind me any more.

(ANGUSTIAS *comes in, her face heavily made up.*)

Angustias!

ANGUSTIAS: Mother.

BERNARDA: Have you dared to powder your face? Have you dared to wash your face on the day of your father's death?

ANGUSTIAS: He wasn't my father. Mine died a long time ago. Have you forgotten that already?

BERNARDA: You owe more to this man, father of your sisters, than to your own. Thanks to him, your fortune is intact.

ANGUSTIAS: We'll have to see about that first!

BERNARDA: Even out of decency! Out of respect!

ANGUSTIAS: Let me go out, mother!

BERNARDA: Let you go out? After I've taken that powder off your face, I will. Spineless! Painted hussy! Just like your aunts!

(*She removes the powder violently with her handkerchief.*)

Now get out!

PONCIA: Bernarda, don't be so hateful!

BERNARDA: Even though my mother is crazy, I still have my five senses and I know what I'm doing.

(*They all enter.*)

MAGDALENA: What's going on here?

BERNARDA: Nothing's "going on here"!

MAGDALENA (*to* ANGUSTIAS): If you're fighting over the inheritance, you're the richest one and can hang on to it all.

ANGUSTIAS: Keep your tongue in your pocketbook!

BERNARDA (*beating on the floor*): Don't fool yourselves into thinking you'll sway me. Until I go out of this house feet first I'll give the orders for myself and for you!

(*Voices are heard and* MARIA JOSEFA, BERNARDA'S *mother, enters. She is very old and has decked out her head and breast with flowers.*)

MARIA JOSEFA: Bernarda, where is my mantilla? Nothing, nothing of what I own will be for any of you. Not my rings nor my black moiré dress. Because not a one of you is going to marry—not a one. Bernarda, give me my necklace of pearls.

BERNARDA (*to the* SERVANT): Why did you let her get in here?

SERVANT (*trembling*): She got away from me!

MARIA JOSEFA: I ran away because I want to marry—I

want to get married to a beautiful manly man from the shore of the sea. Because here the men run from women.

BERNARDA: Hush, hush, Mother!

MARIA JOSEFA: No, no—I won't hush. I don't want to see these single women, longing for marriage, turning their hearts to dust; and I want to go to my home town. Bernarda, I want a man to get married to and be happy with!

BERNARDA: Lock her up!

MARIA JOSEFA: Let me go out, Bernarda!

(*The* SERVANT *seizes* MARIA JOSEFA.)

BERNARDA: Help her, all of you!

(*They all grab the old woman.*)

MARIA JOSEFA: I want to get away from here! Bernarda! To get married by the shore of the sea—by the shore of the sea!

(*Quick, curtain.*)

ACT 2

(*A white room in* BERNARDA'*s house. The doors on the left lead to the bedrooms.* BERNARDA'*s* DAUGHTERS *are seated on low chairs, sewing.* MAGDALENA *is embroidering.* LA PONCIA *is with them.*)

ANGUSTIAS: I've cut the third sheet.

MARTIRIO: That one goes to Amelia.

MAGDALENA: Angustias, shall I put Pepe's initials here too?

ANGUSTIAS (*dryly*): No.

MAGDALENA (*calling, from off stage to* ADELA): Adela, aren't you coming?

AMELIA: She's probably stretched out on the bed.

PONCIA: Something's wrong with that one. I find her restless, trembling, frightened—as if a lizard were between her breasts.

MARTIRIO: There's nothing, more or less, wrong with her than there is with all of us.

MAGDALENA: All of us except Angustias.

ANGUSTIAS: I feel fine, and anybody who doesn't like it can pop.

MAGDALENA: We all have to admit the nicest things about you are your figure and your tact.

ANGUSTIAS: Fortunately, I'll soon be out of this hell.

MAGDALENA: Maybe you won't get out!

MARTIRIO: Stop this talk!

ANGUSTIAS: Besides, a good dowry is better than dark eyes in one's face!

MAGDALENA: All you say just goes in one ear and out the other.

AMELIA (*to* LA PONCIA): Open the patio door and see if we can get a bit of a breeze.

(LA PONCIA *opens the door.*)

MARTIRIO: Last night I couldn't sleep because of the heat.

AMELIA: Neither could I.

MAGDALENA: I got up for a bit of air. There was a black storm cloud and a few drops even fell.

PONCIA: It was one in the morning and the earth seemed to give off fire. I got up too. Angustias was still at the window with Pepe.

MAGDALENA (*with irony*): That late? What time did he leave?

ANGUSTIAS: Why do you ask, if you saw him?

AMELIA: He must have left about one-thirty.

ANGUSTIAS: Yes. How did you know?

AMELIA: I heard him cough and heard his mare's hoofbeats.

PONCIA: But I heard him leave around four.

ANGUSTIAS: It must have been someone else!

PONCIA: No, I'm sure of it!

AMELIA: That's what it seemed to me, too.

MAGDALENA: That's very strange!

(*Pause.*)

PONCIA: Listen, Angustias, what did he say to you the first time he came by your window?

ANGUSTIAS: Nothing. What should he say? Just talked.

MARTIRIO: It's certainly strange that two people who never knew each other should suddenly meet at a window and be engaged.

ANGUSTIAS: Well, I didn't mind.

AMELIA: I'd have felt very strange about it.

ANGUSTIAS: No, because when a man comes to a window he knows, from all the busybodies who come and go and fetch and carry, that he's going to be told "yes."

MARTIRIO: All right, but he'd have to ask you.

ANGUSTIAS: Of course!

AMELIA (*inquisitively*): And how did he ask you?

ANGUSTIAS: Why, no way:—"You know I'm after you. I need a good, well brought up woman, and that's you—if it's agreeable."

AMELIA: These things embarrass me!

ANGUSTIAS: They embarrass me too, but one has to go through it!

PONCIA: And did he say anything more?

ANGUSTIAS: Yes, he did all the talking.

MARTIRIO: And you?

ANGUSTIAS: I couldn't have said a word. My heart was almost coming out of my mouth. It was the first time I'd ever been alone at night with a man.

MAGDALENA: And such a handsome man.

ANGUSTIAS: He's not bad looking!

PONCIA: Those things happen among people who have an idea how to do things, who talk and say and move their hand. The first time my husband, Evaristo the Short-tailed, came to my window . . . Ha! Ha! Ha!

AMELIA: What happened?

PONCIA: It was very dark. I saw him coming along

and as he went by he said, "Good evening." "Good evening," I said. Then we were both silent for more than half an hour. The sweat poured down my body. Then Evaristo got nearer and nearer as if he wanted to squeeze in through the bars and said in a very low voice—"Come here and let me feel you!"

(*They all laugh.* AMELIA *gets up, runs, and looks through the door.*)

AMELIA: Ay, I thought mother was coming!

MAGDALENA: What she'd have done to us!

(*They go on laughing.*)

AMELIA: Sh-h-h! She'll hear us.

PONCIA: Then he acted very decently. Instead of getting some other idea, he went to raising birds, until he died. You aren't married but it's good for you to know, anyway, that two weeks after the wedding a man gives up the bed for the table, then the table for the tavern, and the woman who doesn't like it can just rot, weeping in a corner.

AMELIA: You liked it.

PONCIA: I learned how to handle him!

MARTIRIO: Is it true that you sometimes hit him?

PONCIA: Yes, and once I almost poked out one of his eyes!

MAGDALENA: All women ought to be like that!

PONCIA: I'm one of your mother's school. One time I don't know what he said to me, and then I killed all his birds—with the pestle!

(*They laugh.*)

MAGDALENA: Adela, child! Don't miss this.

AMELIA: Adela!

(*Pause.*)

MAGDALENA: I'll go see!

(*She goes out.*)

PONCIA: That child is sick!

MARTIRIO: Of course. She hardly sleeps!

PONCIA: What *does* she do, then?

MARTIRIO: How do I know what she does?

PONCIA: You probably know better than we do, since you sleep with just a wall between you.

ANGUSTIAS: Envy gnaws on people.

AMELIA: Don't exaggerate.

AUGUSTIAS: I can tell it in her eyes. She's getting the look of a crazy woman.

MARTIRIO: Don't talk about crazy women. This is one place you're not allowed to say that word.

(MAGDALENA *and* ADELA *enter.*)

MAGDALENA: Didn't you say she was asleep?

ADELA: My body aches.

MARTIRIO (*with a hidden meaning*): Didn't you sleep well last night?

ADELA: Yes.

MARTIRIO: Then?

ADELA (*loudly*): Leave me alone. Awake or asleep, it's no affair of yours. I'll do whatever I want to with my body.

MARTIRIO: I was just concerned about you!

ADELA: Concerned?—curious! Weren't you sewing? Well, continue! I wish I were invisible so I could pass through a room without being asked where I was going!

SERVANT (*entering*): Bernarda is calling you. The man with the laces is here.

(*All but* ADELA *and* LA PONCIA *go out, and as* MARTIRIO *leaves, she looks fixedly at* ADELA.)

ADELA: Don't look at me like that! If you want, I'll give you my eyes, for they're younger, and my back to improve that hump you have, but look the other way when I go by.

PONCIA: Adela, she's your sister, and the one who most loves you besides!

ADELA: She follows me everywhere. Sometimes she looks in my room to see if I'm sleeping. She won't let me breathe, and always, "Too bad about that face!" "Too bad about that body! It's going to waste!" But I won't let that happen. My body will be for whomever I choose.

PONCIA (*insinuatingly, in a low voice*): For Pepe el Romano, no?

ADELA (*frightened*): What do you mean?

PONCIA: What I said, Adela!

ADELA: Shut up!

PONCIA (*loudly*): Don't you think I've noticed?

ADELA: Lower your voice!

PONCIA: Then forget what you're thinking about!

ADELA: What do you know?

PONCIA: We old ones can see through walls. Where do you go when you get up at night?

ADELA: I wish you were blind!

PONCIA: But my head and hands are full of eyes, where something like this is concerned. I couldn't possibly guess your intentions. Why did you sit almost naked at your window, and with the light on and the window open, when Pepe passed by the second night he came to talk with your sister?

ADELA: That's not true!

PONCIA: Don't be a child! Leave your sister alone. And if you like Pepe el Romano, keep it to yourself.

(ADELA *weeps.*)

Besides, who says you can't marry him? Your sister Angustias is sickly. She'll die with her first child. Narrow waisted, old—and out of my experience I can tell you she'll die. Then Pepe will do what all widowers do in these parts: he'll marry the youngest and most beautiful, and that's you. Live on that hope, forget him, anything; but don't go against God's law.

ADELA: Hush!

PONCIA: I won't hush!

ADELA: Mind your own business. Snooper, traitor!

PONCIA: I'm going to stick to you like a shadow!

ADELA: Instead of cleaning the house and then going to bed and praying for the dead, you root around like an old sow about goings on between men and women—so you can drool over them.

PONCIA: I keep watch; so people won't spit when they pass our door.

ADELA: What a tremendous affection you've suddenly conceived for my sister.

PONCIA: I don't have any affection for any of you. I want to live in a decent house. I don't want to be dirtied in my old age!

ADELA: Save your advice. It's already too late. For I'd leap not over you, just a servant, but over my mother to put out this fire I feel in my legs and my mouth. What can you possibly say about me? That I lock myself in my room and will not open the door? That I don't sleep? I'm smarter than you! See if you can catch the hare with your hands.

PONCIA: Don't defy me, Adela, don't defy me! Because I can shout, light lamps, and make bells ring.

ADELA: Bring four thousand yellow flares and set them about the walls of the yard. No one can stop what has to happen.

PONCIA: You like him that much?

ADELA: That much! Looking in his eyes I seem to drink his blood in slowly.

PONCIA: I won't listen to you.

ADELA: Well, you'll have to. I've been afraid of you. But now I'm stronger than you!

(ANGUSTIAS enters.)

ANGUSTIAS: Always arguing!

PONCIA: Certainly. She insists that in all this heat I have to go bring her I don't know what from the store.

ANGUSTIAS: Did you buy me the bottle of perfume?

PONCIA: The most expensive one. And the face powder. I put them on the table in your room.

(ANGUSTIAS goes out.)

ADELA: And be quiet!

PONCIA: We'll see!

(MARTIRIO and AMELIA enter.)

MARTIRIO (to ADELA): Did you see the laces?

AMELIA: Angustias', for her wedding sheets, are beautiful.

ADELA (to MARTIRIO, who is carrying some lace): And these?

MARTIRIO: They're for me. For a nightgown.

ADELA (with sarcasm): One needs a sense of humor around here!

MARTIRIO (meaningfully): But only for me to look at. I don't have to exhibit myself before anybody.

PONCIA: No one ever sees us in our nightgowns.

MARTIRIO (meaningfully, looking at ADELA): Sometimes they don't! But I love nice underwear. If I were rich, I'd have it made of Holland Cloth. It's one of the few tastes I've left.

PONCIA: These laces are beautiful for babies' caps and christening gowns. I could never afford them for my own. Now let's see if Augustias will use them for hers. Once she starts having children, they'll keep her running night and day.

MAGDALENA: I don't intend to sew a stitch on them.

AMELIA: And much less bring up some stranger's children. Look how our neighbors across the road are—making sacrifices for four brats.

PONCIA: They're better off than you. There at least they laugh and you can hear them fight.

MARTIRIO: Well, you go work for them, then.

PONCIA: No, fate has sent me to this nunnery!

(Tiny bells are heard distantly as though through several thicknesses of wall.)

MAGDALENA: It's the men going back to work.

PONCIA: It was three o'clock a minute ago.

MARTIRIO: With this sun!

ADELA (sitting down): Ay! If only we could go out in the fields too!

MAGDALENA (sitting down): Each class does what it has to!

MARTIRIO (sitting down): That's it!

AMELIA (sitting down): Ay!

PONCIA: There's no happiness like that in the fields right at this time of year. Yesterday morning the reapers arrived. Forty or fifty handsome young men.

MAGDALENA: Where are they from this year?

PONCIA: From far, far away. They came from the mountains! Happy! Like weathered trees! Shouting and throwing stones! Last night a woman who dresses in sequins and dances, with an accordion, arrived, and fifteen of them made a deal with her to take her to the olive grove. I saw them from far away. The one who talked with her was a boy with green eyes—tight knit as a sheaf of wheat.

AMELIA: Really?

ADELA: Are you sure?

PONCIA: Years ago another one of those women came here, and I myself gave my eldest son some money so he could go. Men need things like that.

ADELA: Everything's forgiven *them*.

AMELIA: To be born a woman's the worst possible punishment.

MAGDALENA: Even our eyes aren't our own.

(A distant song is heard, coming nearer.)

PONCIA: There they are. They have a beautiful song.

AMELIA: They're going out to reap now.

CHORUS:

The reapers have set out
Looking for ripe wheat;
They'll carry off the hearts
Of any girls they meet.

(Tambourines and carrañacas are heard. Pause. They all listen in the silence cut by the sun.)

AMELIA: And they don't mind the sun!

MARTIRIO: They reap through flames.

ADELA: How I'd like to be a reaper so I could come and go as I pleased. Then we could forget what's eating us all.

MARTIRIO: What do you have to forget?

ADELA: Each one of us has something.

MARTIRIO *(intensely)*: Each one!

PONCIA: Quiet! Quiet!

CHORUS *(very distantly)*:

Throw wide your doors and windows,
You girls who live in the town
The reaper asks you for roses
With which to deck his crown.

PONCIA: What a song!

MARTIRIO *(with nostalgia)*:

Throw wide your doors and windows,
You girls who live in the town.

ADELA *(passionately)*:

The reaper asks you for roses
With which to deck his crown.

(The song grows more distant.)

PONCIA: Now they're turning the corner.

ADELA: Let's watch them from the window of my room.

PONCIA: Be careful not to open the shutters too much because they're likely to give them a push to see who's looking.

(The three leave. MARTIRIO is left sitting on the low chair with her head between her hands.)

AMELIA *(drawing near her)*: What's wrong with you?

MARTIRIO: The heat makes me feel ill.

AMELIA: And it's no more than that?

MARTIRIO: I was wishing it were November, the rainy days, the frost—anything except this unending summertime.

AMELIA: It'll pass and come again.

MARTIRIO: Naturally.

(Pause.)

What time did you go to sleep last night?

AMELIA: I don't know. I sleep like a log. Why?

MARTIRIO: Nothing. Only I thought I heard someone in the yard.

AMELIA: Yes?

MARTIRIO: Very late.

AMELIA: And weren't you afraid?

MARTIRIO: No. I've heard it other nights.

AMELIA: We'd better watch out! Couldn't it have been the shepherds?

MARTIRIO: The shepherds come at six.

AMELIA: Maybe a young, unbroken mule?

MARTIRIO *(to herself, with double meaning)*: That's it! That's it. An unbroken little mule.

AMELIA: We'll have to set a watch.

MARTIRIO: No. No. Don't say anything. It may be I've just imagined it.

AMELIA: Maybe.

(Pause. AMELIA starts to go.)

MARTIRIO: Amelia!

AMELIA *(at the door)*: What?

(Pause.)

MARTIRIO: Nothing.

(Pause.)

AMELIA: Why did you call me?

(Pause.)

MARTIRIO: It just came out. I didn't mean to.

(Pause.)

AMELIA: Lie down for a little.

ANGUSTIAS *(she bursts in furiously, in a manner that makes a great contrast with previous silence)*: Where's that picture of Pepe I had under my pillow? Which one of you has it?

MARTIRIO: No one.

AMELIA: You'd think he was a silver St. Bartholomew.

ANGUSTIAS: Where's the picture?

(PONCIA, MAGDALENA and ADELA enter.)

ADELA: What picture?

ANGUSTIAS: One of you has hidden it from me.

MAGDALENA: Do you have the effrontery to say that?

ANGUSTIAS: I had it in my room, and now it isn't there.

MARTIRIO: But couldn't it have jumped out into the yard at midnight? Pepe likes to walk around in the moonlight.

ANGUSTIAS: Don't joke with me! When he comes I'll tell him.

PONCIA: Don't do that! Because it'll turn up.

(*Looking at* ADELA.)

ANGUSTIAS: I'd like to know which one of you has it.

ADELA (*looking at* MARTIRIO): Somebody has it! But not me!

MARTIRIO (*with meaning*): Of course not you!

BERNARDA (*entering with her cane*): What scandal is this in my house in the heat's heavy silence? The neighbors must have their ears glued to the walls.

ANGUSTIAS: They've stolen my sweetheart's picture!

BERNARDA (*fiercely*): Who? Who?

ANGUSTIAS: They have!

BERNARDA: Which one of you?

(*Silence.*)

Answer me!

(*Silence.*) (*To* LA PONCIA.)

Search their rooms! Look in their beds. This comes of not tying you up with shorter leashes. But I'll teach you now! (*to* ANGUSTIAS) Are you sure?

ANGUSTIAS: Yes.

BERNARDA: Did you look everywhere?

ANGUSTIAS: Yes, Mother.

(*They all stand in an embarrassed silence.*)

BERNARDA: At the end of my life—to make me drink the bitterest poison a mother knows. (*to* PONCIA) Did you find it?

PONCIA: Here it is.

BERNARDA: Where did you find it?

PONCIA: It was . . .

BERNARDA: Say it! Don't be afraid.

PONCIA (*wonderingly*): Between the sheets in Martirio's bed.

BERNARDA (*to* MARTIRIO): Is that true?

MARTIRIO: It's true.

BERNARDA (*advancing on her, beating her with her cane*): You'll come to a bad end yet, you hypocrite! Trouble maker!

MARTIRIO (*fiercely*): Don't hit me, Mother!

BERNARDA: All I want to!

MARTIRIO: If I let you! You hear me? Get back!

PONCIA: Don't be disrespectful to your mother!

ANGUSTIAS (*holding* BERNARDA): Let her go, please!

BERNARDA: Not even tears in your eyes.

MARTIRIO: I'm not going to cry just to please you.

BERNARDA: Why did you take the picture?

MARTIRIO: Can't I play a joke on my sister? What else would I want it for?

ADELA (*leaping forward, full of jealousy*): It wasn't a joke! You never liked to play jokes. It was something else bursting in her breast—trying to come out. Admit it openly now.

MARTIRIO: Hush, and don't make me speak; for if I should speak the walls would close together one against the other with shame.

ADELA: An evil tongue never stops inventing lies.

BERNARDA: Adela!

MAGDALENA: You're crazy.

AMELIA: And you stone us all with your evil suspicions.

MARTIRIO: But some others do things more wicked!

ADELA: Until all at once they stand forth stark naked and the river carries them along.

BERNARDA: Spiteful!

ANGUSTIAS: It's not my fault Pepe el Romano chose me!

ADELA: For your money.

ANGUSTIAS: Mother!

BERNARDA: Silence!

MARTIRIO: For your fields and your orchards.

MAGDALENA: That's only fair.

BERNARDA: Silence, I say! I saw the storm coming but I didn't think it'd burst so soon. Oh, what an avalanche of hate you've thrown on my heart! But I'm not old yet—I have five chains for you, and this house my father built, so not even the weeds will know of my desolation. Out of here!

(*They go out.* BERNARDA *sits down desolately.* LA PONCIA *is standing close to the wall.* BERNARDA *recovers herself, and beats on the floor.*)

I'll have to let them feel the weight of my hand! Bernarda, remember your duty!

PONCIA: May I speak?

BERNARDA: Speak. I'm sorry you heard. A stranger is always out of place in a family.

PONCIA: What I've seen, I've seen.

BERNARDA: Angustias must get married right away.

PONCIA: Certainly. We'll have to get her away from here.

BERNARDA: Not her, him!

PONCIA: Of course. He's the one to get away from here. You've thought it all out.

BERNARDA: I'm not thinking. These are things that shouldn't and can't be thought out. I give orders.

PONCIA: And you think he'll be satisfied to go away?

BERNARDA (*rising*): What are you imagining now?

PONCIA: He will, of course, marry Angustias.

BERNARDA: Speak up! I know you well enough to see that your knife's out for me.

PONCIA: I never knew a warning could be called murder.

BERNARDA: Have you some "warning" for me?

PONCIA: I'm not making any accusations, Bernarda. I'm only telling you to open your eyes and you'll see.

BERNARDA: See what?

PONCIA: You've always been smart, Bernarda. You've

seen other people's sins a hundred miles away. Many times I've thought you could read minds. But, your children are your children, and now you're blind.

BERNARDA: Are you talking about Martirio?

PONCIA: Well, yes—about Martirio . . .

(With curiosity.)

I wonder why she hid the picture?

BERNARDA *(shielding her daughter)*: After all, she says it was a joke. What else could it be?

PONCIA *(scornfully)*: Do you believe that?

BERNARDA *(sternly)*: I don't merely believe it. It's so!

PONCIA: Enough of this. We're talking about your family. But if we were taking about your neighbor across the way, what would it be?

BERNARDA: Now you're beginning to pull the point of the knife out.

PONCIA *(always cruelly)*: No, Bernarda. Something very grave is happening here. I don't want to put the blame on your shoulders, but you've never given your daughters any freedom. Martirio is lovesick. I don't care what you say. Why didn't you let her marry Enrique Humanas? Why, on the very day he was coming to her window did you send him a message not to come?

BERNARDA *(loudly)*: I'd do it a thousand times over! My blood won't mingle with the Humanas' while I live! His father was a shepherd.

PONCIA: And you see now what's happening to you with these airs!

BERNARDA: I have them because I can afford to. And you don't have them because you know where you came from!

PONCIA *(with hate)*: Don't remind me! I'm old now. I've always been grateful for your protection.

BERNARDA *(emboldened)*: You don't seem so!

PONCIA *(with hate, behind softness)*: Martirio will forget this.

BERNARDA: And if she doesn't—the worse for her. I don't believe this is that "very grave thing" that's happening here. Nothing's happening here. It's just that you wish it would! And if it should happen one day, you can be sure it won't go beyond these walls.

PONCIA: I'm not so sure of that! There are people in town who can also read hidden thoughts, from afar.

BERNARDA: How you'd like to see me and my daughters on our way to a whorehouse!

PONCIA: No one knows her own destiny!

BERNARDA: I know my destiny! And my daughters'! The whorehouse was for a certain woman, already dead. . . .

PONCIA *(fiercely)*: Bernarda, respect the memory of my mother!

BERNARDA: Then don't plague me with your evil thoughts!

(Pause.)

PONCIA: I'd better stay out of everything.

BERNARDA: That's what you ought to do. Work and keep your mouth shut. The duty of all who work for a living.

PONCIA: But we can't do that. Don't you think it'd be better for Pepe to marry Martirio or . . . yes! . . . Adela?

BERNARDA: No, I *don't* think so.

PONCIA *(with meaning)*: Adela! She's Romano's real sweetheart!

BERNARDA: Things are never the way we want them!

PONCIA: But it's hard work to turn them from their destined course. For Pepe to be with Angustias seems wrong to me—and to other people—and even to the wind. Who knows if they'll get what they want?

BERNARDA: There you go again! Sneaking up on me—giving me bad dreams. But I won't listen to you, because if all you say should come to pass—I'd scratch your face.

PONCIA: Frighten someone else with that.

BERNARDA: Fortunately, my daughters respect me and have never gone against my will!

PONCIA: That's right! But, as soon as they break loose they'll fly to the rooftops!

BERNARDA: And I'll bring them down with stones!

PONCIA: Oh, yes! You were always the bravest one!

BERNARDA: I've always enjoyed a good fight!

PONCIA: But aren't people strange. You should see Angustias' enthusiasm for her lover, at her age! And he seems very smitten too. Yesterday my oldest son told me that when he passed by with the oxen at four-thirty in the morning they were still talking.

BERNARDA: At four-thirty?

ANGUSTIAS *(entering)*: That's a lie!

PONCIA: That's what he told me.

BERNARDA *(to ANGUSTIAS)*: Speak up!

ANGUSTIA: For more than a week Pepe has been leaving at one. May God strike me dead if I'm lying.

MARTIRIO *(entering)*: I heard him leave at four too.

BERNARDA: But did you see him with your eyes?

MARTIRIO: I didn't want to look out. Don't you talk now through the side window?

ANGUSTIAS: We talk through my bedroom window.

(ADELA appears at the door.)

MARTIRIO: Then . . .

BERNARDA: What's going on here?

PONCIA: If you're not careful, you'll find out! At least Pepe was at *one* of your windows—and at four in the morning too!

BERNARDA: Are you sure of that?

PONCIA: You can't be sure of anything in this life!

ADELA: Mother, don't listen to someone who wants us to lose everything we have.

BERNARDA: I know how to take care of myself! If the townspeople want to come bearing false witness against me, they'll run into a stone wall! Don't any of you talk about this! Sometimes other people try to stir up a wave of filth to drown us.

MARTIRIO: I don't like to lie.

PONCIA: So there must be something.

BERNARDA: There won't be anything. I was born to have my eyes always open. Now I'll watch without closing them 'til I die.

ANGUSTIAS: I have the right to know.

BERNARDA: You don't have any right except to obey. No one's going to fetch and carry for me. (*to* LA PONCIA) And don't meddle in our affairs. No one will take a step without my knowing it.

SERVANT (*entering*): There's a big crowd at the top of the street, and all the neighbors are at their doors!

BERNARDA (*to* PONCIA): Run see what's happening!

(*The* GIRLS *are about to run out.*)

Where are you going? I always knew you for window-watching women and breakers of your mourning. All of you, to the patio!

(*They go out.* BERNARDA *leaves. Distant shouts are heard.*)

(MARTIRIO *and* ADELA *enter and listen, not daring to step farther than the front door.*)

MARTIRIO: You can be thankful I didn't happen to open my mouth.

ADELA: I would have spoken too.

MARTIRIO: And what were you going to say? Wanting isn't doing!

ADELA: I do what I can and what happens to suit me. You've wanted to, but haven't been able.

MARTIRIO: You won't go on very long.

ADELA: I'll have everything!

MARTIRIO: I'll tear you out of his arms!

ADELA (*pleadingly*): Martirio, let me be!

MARTIRIO: None of us will have him!

ADELA: He wants me for his house!

MARTIRIO: I saw how he embraced you!

ADELA: I didn't want him to. It's as if I were dragged by a rope.

MARTIRIO: I'll see you dead first!

(MAGDALENA *and* ANGUSTIAS *look in. The tumult is increasing. A* SERVANT *enters with* BERNARDA. PONCIA *also enters from another door.*)

PONCIA: Bernarda!

BERNARDA: What's happening?

PONCIA: Librada's daughter, the unmarried one, had a child and no one knows whose it is!

ADELA: A child?

PONCIA: And to hide her shame she killed it and hid it under the rocks, but the dogs, with more heart than most Christians, dug it out and, as though directed by the hand of God, left it at her door. Now they want to kill her. They're dragging her through the streets—and down the paths and across the olive groves the men are coming, shouting so the fields shake.

BERNARDA: Yes, let them all come with olive whips and hoe handles—let them all come and kill her!

ADELA: No, not to kill her!

MARTIRIO: Yes—and let us go out too!

BERNARDA: And let whoever loses her decency pay for it!

(*Outside a woman's shriek and a great clamor is heard.*)

ADELA: Let her escape! Don't you go out!

MARTIRIO (*looking at* ADELA): Let her pay what she owes!

BERNARDA (*at the archway*): Finish her before the guards come! Hot coals in the place where she sinned!

ADELA (*holding her belly*): No! No!

BERNARDA: Kill her! Kill her!

(*Curtain.*)

ACT 3

(*Four white walls, lightly washed in blue, of the interior patio of* BERNARDA ALBA's *house. The doorways, illumined by the lights inside the rooms, give a tenuous glow to the stage. At the center there is a table with a shaded oil lamp about which* BERNARDA *and her* DAUGHTERS *are eating.* LA PONCIA *serves them.* PRUDENCIA *sits apart. When the curtain rises, there is a great silence interrupted only by the noise of plates and silverware.*)

PRUDENCIA: I'm going. I've made you a long visit.

(*She rises.*)

BERNARDA: But wait, Prudencia. We never see one another.

PRUDENCIA: Have they sounded the last call to rosary?

PONCIA: Not yet.

(PRUDENCIA *sits down again.*)

BERNARDA: And your husband, how's he getting on?

PRUDENCIA: The same.

BERNARDA: We never see him either.

PRUDENCIA: You know how he is. Since he quarrelled with his brothers over the inheritance, he hasn't used the front door. He takes a ladder and climbs over the back wall.

BERNARDA: He's a real man! And your daughter?

PRUDENCIA: He's never forgiven her.

BERNARDA: He's right.

PRUDENCIA: I don't know what he told you. I suffer because of it.

BERNARDA: A daughter who's disobedient stops being a daughter and becomes an enemy.

PRUDENCIA: I let water run. The only consolation I've left is to take refuge in the church, but, since I'm losing my sight, I'll have to stop coming so the children won't make fun of me.

(A heavy blow is heard against the walls.)

What's that?

BERNARDA: The stallion. He's locked in the stall and he kicks against the wall of the house.

(Shouting.)

Tether him and take him out in the yard!

(In a lower voice.)

He must be too hot.

PRUDENCIA: Are you going to put the new mares to him?

BERNARDA: At daybreak.

PRUDENCIA: You've known how to increase your stock.

BERNARDA: By dint of money and struggling.

PONCIA *(interrupting)*: And she has the best herd in these parts. It's a shame that prices are low.

BERNARDA: Do you want a little cheese and honey?

PRUDENCIA: I have no appetite.

(The blow is heard again.)

PONCIA: My God!

PRUDENCIA: It quivered in my chest.

BERNARDA *(rising, furiously)*: Do I have to say things twice? Let him out to roll on the straw.

(Pause. Then, as though speaking to the STABLEMAN.)

Well then, lock the mares in the corral, but let him run free or he may kick down the walls.

(She returns to the table and sits again.)

Ay, what a life!

PRUDENCIA: You have to fight like a man.

BERNARDA: That's it.

(ADELA gets up from the table.)

Where are you going?

ADELA: For a drink of water.

BERNARDA *(raising her voice)*: Bring a pitcher of cool water. *(to ADELA)* You can sit down. *(ADELA sits down.)*

PRUDENCIA: And Angustias, when will she get married?

BERNARDA: They're coming to ask for her within three days.

PRUDENCIA: You must be happy.

ANGUSTIAS: Naturally!

AMELIA *(to MAGDALENA)*: You've spilled the salt!

MAGDALENA: You can't possibly have worse luck than you're having.

AMELIA: It always brings bad luck.

BERNARDA: That's enough!

PRUDENCIA *(to ANGUSTIAS)*: Has he given you the ring yet?

ANGUSTIAS: Look at it.

(She holds it out.)

PRUDENCIA: It's beautiful. Three pearls. In my day, pearls signified tears.

ANGUSTIAS: But things have changed now.

ADELA: I don't think so. Things go on meaning the same. Engagement rings should be diamonds.

PONCIA: The most appropriate.

BERNARDA: With pearls or without them, things are as one proposes.

MARTIRIO: Or as God disposes.

PRUDENCIA: I've been told your furniture is beautiful.

BERNARDA: It cost sixteen thousand *reales*.

PONCIA *(interrupting)*: The best is the wardrobe with the mirror.

PRUDENCIA: I never saw a piece like that.

BERNARDA: We had chests.

PRUDENCIA: The important thing is that everything be for the best.

ADELA: And that you never know.

BERNARDA: There's no reason why it shouldn't be.

(Bells are heard very distantly.)

PRUDENCIA: The last call. *(to ANGUSTIAS)* I'll be coming back to have you show me your clothes.

ANGUSTIAS: Whenever you like.

PRUDENCIA: Good evening—God bless you!

BERNARDA: Good-bye, Prudencia.

ALL FIVE DAUGHTERS *(at the same time)*: God go with you!

(Pause. PRUDENCIA goes out.)

BERNARDA: Well, we've eaten.

(They rise.)

ADELA: I'm going to walk as far as the gate to stretch my legs and get a bit of fresh air.

(MAGDALENA sits down in a low chair and leans against the wall.)

AMELIA: I'll go with you.

MARTIRIO: I too.

ADELA *(with contained hate)*: I'm not going to get lost!

AMELIA: One needs company at night.

(They go out. BERNARDA sits down. ANGUSTIAS is clearing the table.)

BERNARDA: I've told you once already! I want you to talk to your sister Martirio. What happened about the picture was a joke and you must forget it.

ANGUSTIAS: You know she doesn't like me.

BERNARDA: Each one knows what she thinks inside. I don't pry into anyone's heart, but I want to put up a good front and have family harmony. You understand?

ANGUSTIAS: Yes.

BERNARDA: Then that's settled.

MAGDALENA (she is almost asleep): Besides, you'll be gone in no time.

(She falls asleep.)

ANGUSTIAS: Not soon enough for me.

BERNARDA: What time did you stop talking last night?

ANGUSTIAS: Twelve-thirty.

BERNARDA: What does Pepe talk about?

ANGUSTIAS: I find him absent-minded. He always talks to me as though he were thinking of something else. If I ask him what's the matter, he answers—"We men have our worries."

BERNARDA: You shouldn't ask him. And when you're married, even less. Speak if he speaks, and look at him when he looks at you. That way you'll get along.

ANGUSTIAS: But, Mother, I think he's hiding things from me.

BERNARDA: Don't try to find out. Don't ask him, and above all, never let him see you cry.

ANGUSTIAS: I should be happy, but I'm not.

BERNARDA: It's all the same.

ANGUSTIAS: Many nights I watch Pepe very closely through the window bars and he seems to fade away—as though he were hidden in a cloud of dust like those raised by the flocks.

BERNARDA: That's just because you're not strong.

ANGUSTIAS: I hope so!

BERNARDA: Is he coming tonight?

ANGUSTIAS: No, he went into town with his mother.

BERNARDA: Good, we'll get to bed early. Magdalena!

ANGUSTIAS: She's asleep.

(ADELA, MARTIRIO and AMELIA enter.)

AMELIA: What a dark night!

ADELA: You can't see two steps in front of you.

MARTIRIO: A good night for robbers, for anyone who needs to hide.

ADELA: The stallion was in the middle of the corral. White. Twice as large. Filling all the darkness.

AMELIA: It's true. It was frightening. Like a ghost.

ADELA: The sky has stars as big as fists.

MARTIRIO: This one stared at them till she almost cracked her neck.

ADELA: Don't you like them up there?

MARTIRIO: What goes on over the roof doesn't mean a thing to me. I have my hands full with what happens under it.

ADELA: Well, that's the way it goes with you!

BERNARDA: And it goes the same for you as for her.

ANGUSTIAS: Good night.

ADELA: Are you going to bed now?

ANGUSTIAS: Yes, Pepe isn't coming tonight.

(She goes out.)

ADELA: Mother, why, when a stars falls or lightning flashes, does one say:
  Holy Barbara, blessed on high
  May your name be in the sky
  With holy water written high?

BERNARDA: The old people know many things we've forgotten.

AMELIA: I close my eyes so I won't see them.

ADELA: Not I. I like to see what's quiet and been quiet for years on end, running with fire.

MARTIRIO: But all that has nothing to do with us.

BERNARDA: And it's better not to think about it.

ADELA: What a beautiful night! I'd like to stay up till very late and enjoy the breeze from the fields.

BERNARDA: But we have to go to bed. Magdalena!

AMELIA: She's just dropped off.

BERNARDA: Magdalena!

MAGDALENA (annoyed): Leave me alone!

BERNARDA: To bed!

MAGDALENA (rising, in a bad humor): You don't give anyone a moment's peace!

(She goes off grumbling.)

AMELIA: Good night!

(She goes out.)

BERNARDA: You two get along, too.

MARTIRIO: How is it Angustias' sweetheart isn't coming tonight?

BERNARDA: He went on a trip.

MARTIRIO (looking at ADELA): Ah!

ADELA: I'll see you in the morning!

(She goes out. MARTIRIO drinks some water and goes out slowly, looking at the door to the yard. LA PONCIA enters.)

PONCIA: Are you still here?

BERNARDA: Enjoying this quiet and not seeing anywhere the "very grave thing" that's happening here—according to you.

PONCIA: Bernarda, let's not go any further with this.

BERNARDA: In this house there's no question of a yes or a no. My watchfulness can take care of anything.

PONCIA: Nothing's happening outside. That's true, all right. Your daughters act and are as though stuck in a cupboard. But neither you nor anyone else can keep watch inside a person's heart.

BERNARDA: My daughters breathe calmly enough.

PONCIA: That's your business, since you're their mother. I have enough to do just with serving you.

BERNARDA: Yes, you've turned quiet now.

PONCIA: I keep my place—that's all.

BERNARDA: The trouble is you've nothing to talk about. If there were grass in this house, you'd make it your business to put the neighbors' sheep to pasture here.

PONCIA: I hide more than you think.

BERNARDA: Do your sons still see Pepe at four in the morning? Are they still repeating this house's evil litany?

PONCIA: They say nothing.

BERNARDA: Because they can't. Because there's nothing for them to sink their teeth in. And all because my eyes keep constant watch!

PONCIA: Bernarda, I don't want to talk about this because I'm afraid of what you'll do. But don't you feel so safe.

BERNARDA: Very safe!

PONCIA: Who knows, lightning might strike suddenly. Who knows but what all of a sudden, in a rush of blood, your heart might stop.

BERNARDA: Nothing will happen here. I'm on guard now against all your suspicions.

PONCIA: All the better for you.

BERNARDA: Certainly, all the better!

SERVANT (entering): I've just finished with the dishes. Is there anything else, Bernarda?

BERNARDA (rising): Nothing. I'm going to get some rest.

PONCIA: What time do you want me to call you?

BERNARDA: No time. Tonight I intend to sleep well.

(She goes out.)

PONCIA: When you're powerless against the sea, it's easier to turn your back on it and not look at it.

SERVANT: She's so proud! She herself pulls the blindfold over her eyes.

PONCIA: I can do nothing. I tried to head things off, but now they frighten me too much. You feel this silence?—in each room there's a thunderstorm—and the day it breaks, it'll sweep all of us along with it. But I've said what I had to say.

SERVANT: Bernarda thinks nothing can stand against her, yet she doesn't know the strength a man has among women alone.

PONCIA: It's not all the fault of Pepe el Romano. It's true last year he was running after Adela; and she was crazy about him—but she ought to keep her place and not lead him on. A man's a man.

SERVANT: And some there are who believe he didn't have to talk many times with Adela.

PONCIA: That's true.

(In a low voice.)

And some other things.

SERVANT: I don't know what's going to happen here.

PONCIA: How I'd like to sail across the sea and leave this house, this battleground, behind!

SERVANT: Bernarda's hurrying the wedding and it's possible nothing will happen.

PONCIA: Things have gone much too far already. Adela is set no matter what comes, and the rest of them watch without rest.

SERVANT: Martirio too . . . ?

PONCIA: That one's the worst. She's a pool of poison. She sees El Romano is not for her, and she'd sink the world if it were in her hand to do so

SERVANT: How bad they all are!

PONCIA: They're women without men, that's all. And in such matters even blood is forgotten. Sh-h-h-h!

(She listens.)

SERVANT: What's the matter?

PONCIA (she rises): The dogs are barking.

SERVANT: Someone must have passed by the back door.

(ADELA enters wearing a white petticoat and corselet.)

PONCIA: Aren't you in bed yet?

ADELA: I want a drink of water.

(She drinks from a glass on the table.)

PONCIA: I imagined you were asleep.

ADELA: I got thirsty and woke up. Aren't you two going to get some rest?

SERVANT: Soon now.

(ADELA goes out.)

PONCIA: Let's go.

SERVANT: We've certainly earned some sleep. Bernarda doesn't let me rest the whole day.

PONCIA: Take the light.

SERVANT: The dogs are going mad.

PONCIA: They're not going to let us sleep.

(They go out. The stage is left almost dark. MARIA JOSEFA enters with a lamb in her arms.)

MARIA JOSEFA (singing):
Little lamb, child of mine,
Let's go to the shore of the sea,
The tiny ant will be at his doorway,
I'll nurse you and give you your bread.
Bernarda, old leopard-face,
And Magdalena, hyena-face,
Little lamb . . .
Rock, rock-a-bye,
Let's go to the palms at Bethlehem's gate.

(She laughs.)

> Neither you nor I would want to sleep
> The door will open by itself
> And on the beach we'll go and hide
> In a little coral cabin.
> Bernarda, old leopard-face,
> And Magdalena, hyena-face,
> Little lamb . . .
> Rock, rock-a-bye,
> Let's go to the palms at Bethlehem's gate.

(She goes off singing.)

(ADELA enters. She looks about cautiously and disappears out the door leading to the corral. MARTIRIO enters by another door and stands in anguished watchfulness near the center of the stage. She also is in petticoats. She covers herself with a small black scarf. MARIA JOSEFA crosses before her.)

MARTIRIO: Grandmother, where are you going?

MARIA JOSEFA: You are going to open the door for me? Who are you?

MARTIRIO: How did you get out here?

MARIA JOSEFA: I escaped. You, who are you?

MARTIRIO: Go back to bed.

MARIA JOSEFA: You're Martirio. Now I see you. Martirio, face of a martyr. And when are you going to have a baby? I've had this one.

MARTIRIO: Where did you get that lamb?

MARIA JOSEFA: I know it's a lamb. But can't a lamb be a baby? It's better to have a lamb than not to have anything. Old Bernarda, leopard-face, and Magdalena, hyena-face!

MARTIRIO: Don't shout.

MARIA JOSEFA: It's true. Everything's very dark. Just because I have white hair you think I can't have babies, but I can—babies and babies and babies. This baby will have white hair, and I'd have *this* baby, and another, and this *one* other; and with all of us with snow white hair we'll be like the waves—one, then another, and another. Then we'll all sit down and all of us will have white heads, and we'll be seafoam. Why isn't there any seafoam here? Nothing but mourning shrouds here.

MARTIRIO: Hush, hush.

MARIA JOSEFA: When my neighbor had a baby, I'd carry her some chocolate and later she'd bring me some, and so on—always and always and always. You'll have white hair, but your neighbors won't come. Now I have to go away, but I'm afraid the dogs will bite me. Won't you come with me as far as the fields? I don't like fields. I like houses, but open houses, and the neighbor women asleep in their beds with their little tiny tots, and the men outside sitting in their chairs. Pepe el Romano is a giant. All of you love him. But he's going to devour you because you're

grains of wheat. No, not grains of wheat. Frogs with no tongues!

MARTIRIO *(angrily)*: Come, off to bed with you.

(She pushes her.)

MARIA JOSEFA: Yes, but then you'll open the door for me, won't you?

MARTIRIO: Of course.

MARIA JOSEFA *(weeping)*:
> Little lamb, child of mine,
> Let's go to the shore of the sea,
> The tiny ant will be at his doorway,
> I'll nurse you and give you your bread.

(MARTIRIO locks the door through which MARIA JOSEFA came out and goes to the yard door. There she hesitates, but goes two steps farther.)

MARTIRIO *(in a low voice)*: Adela! *(Pause. She advances to the door. Then, calling.)* Adela!

(ADELA enters. Her hair is disarranged.)

ADELA: And what are you looking for me for?

MARTIRIO: Keep away from him.

ADELA: Who are you to tell me that?

MARTIRIO: That's no place for a decent woman.

ADELA: How you wish *you'd* been there!

MARTIRIO *(shouting)*: This is the moment for me to speak. This can't go on.

ADELA: This is just the beginning. I've had strength enough to push myself forward—the spirit and looks you lack. I've seen death under this roof, and gone out to look for what was mine, what belonged to me.

MARTIRIO: That soulless man came for another woman. You pushed yourself in front of him.

ADELA: He came for the money, but his eyes were always on me.

MARTIRIO: I won't allow you to snatch him away. He'll marry Angustias.

ADELA: You know better than I he doesn't love her.

MARTIRIO: I know.

ADELA: You know because you've seen—he loves me, me!

MARTIRIO *(desperately)*: Yes.

ADELA *(close before her)*: He loves me, *me!* He loves me, *me!*

MARTIRIO: Stick me with a knife if you like, but don't tell me that again.

ADELA: That's why you're trying to fix it so I won't go away with him. It makes no difference to you if he puts his arms around a woman he doesn't love. Nor does it to me. He could be a hundred years with Angustias, but for him to have his arms around me seems terrible to you—because you too love him! You love him!

MARTIRIO (*dramatically*): Yes! Let me say it without hiding my head. Yes! my breast's bitter, bursting like a pomegranate. I love him!

ADELA (*impulsively, hugging her*): Martirio, Martirio, I'm not to blame!

MARTIRIO: Don't put your arms around me! Don't try to smooth it over. My blood's no longer yours, and even though I try to think of you as a sister, I see you as just another woman.

(*She pushes her away.*)

ADELA: There's no way out here. Whoever has to drown—let her drown. Pepe is mine. He'll carry me to the rushes along the river bank. . . .

MARTIRIO: He won't!

ADELA: I can't stand this horrible house after the taste of his mouth. I'll be what he wants me to be. Everybody in the village against me, burning me with their fiery fingers; pursued by those who claim they're decent, and I'll wear, before them all, the crown of thorns that belongs to the mistress of a married man.

MARTIRIO: Hush!

ADELA: Yes, yes. (*In a low voice.*) Let's go to bed. Let's let him marry Angustias. I don't care any more, but I'll go off alone to a little house where he'll come to see me whenever he wants, whenever he feels like it.

MARTIRIO: That'll never happen! Not while I have a drop of blood left in my body.

ADELA: Not just weak you, but a wild horse I could force to his knees with just the strength of my little finger.

MARTIRIO: Don't raise that voice of yours to me. It irritates me. I have a heart full of a force so evil that, without my wanting to be, I'm drowned by it.

ADELA: You show us the way to love our sisters. God must have meant to leave me alone in the midst of darkness because I can see you as I've never seen you before.

(*A whistle is heard and* ADELA *runs toward the door, but* MARTIRIO *gets in front of her.*)

MARTIRIO: Where are you going?

ADELA: Get away from that door!

MARTIRIO: Get by me if you can!

ADELA: Get away!

(*They struggle.*)

MARTIRIO (*shouts*): Mother! Mother!

ADELA: Let me go!

(BERNARDA *enters. She wears petticoats and a black shawl.*)

BERNARDA: Quiet! Quiet! How poor I am without even a man to help me!

MARTIRIO (*pointing to* ADELA): She was with him. Look at those skirts covered with straw!

BERNARDA (*going furiously toward Adela*): That's the bed of a bad woman!

ADELA (*facing her*): There'll be an end to prison voices here! (ADELA *snatches away her mother's cane and breaks it in two.*) This is what I do with the tyrant's cane. Not another step. No one but Pepe commands me!

(MAGDALENA *enters.*)

MAGDALENA: Adela!

(LA PONCIA *and* ANGUSTIAS *enter.*)

ADELA: I'm his. (*to* ANGUSTIAS) Know that—and go out in the yard and tell him. He'll be master in this house.

ANGUSTIAS: My God!

BERNARDA: The gun! Where's the gun?

(*She rushes out.* LA PONCIA *runs ahead of her.* AMELIA *enters and looks on frightened, leaning her head against the wall. Behind her comes* MARTIRIO.)

ADELA: No one can hold me back!

(*She tries to go out.*)

ANGUSTIAS (*holding her*): You're not getting out of here with your body's triumph! Thief! Disgrace of this house!

MAGDALENA: Let her go where we'll never see her again!

(*A shot is heard.*)

BERNARDA (*entering*): Just try looking for him now!

MARTIRIO (*entering*): That does away with Pepe el Romano.

ADELA: Pepe! My God! Pepe!

(*She runs out.*)

PONCIA: Did you kill him?

MARTIRIO: No. He raced away on his mare!

BERNARDA: It was my fault. A woman can't aim.

MAGDALENA: Then, why did you say . . . ?

MARTIRIO: For her! I'd like to pour a river of blood over her head!

PONCIA: Curse you!

MAGDALENA: Devil!

BERNARDA: Although it's better this way!

(*A thud is heard.*)

Adela! Adela!

PONCIA (*at her door*): Open this door!

BERNARDA: Open! Don't think the walls will hide your shame!

SERVANT (*entering*): All the neighbors are up!

BERNARDA (*in a low voice, but like a roar*): Open! Or I'll knock the door down!

(Pause. Everything is silent.)

Adela!

(She walks away from the door.)

A hammer!

(LA PONCIA throws herself against the door. It opens and she goes in. As she enters, she screams and backs out.)

What is it?

PONCIA (*she puts her hands to her throat*): May we never die like that!

(The SISTERS fall back. The SERVANT crosses herself. BERNARDA screams and goes forward.)

Don't go in!

BERNARDA: No, not I! Pepe, you're running now, alive in the darkness, under the trees, but another day you'll fall. Cut her down! My daughter died a virgin. Take her to another room and dress her as though she were a virgin. No one will say anything about this! She died a virgin. Tell them, so that at dawn, the bells will ring twice.

MARTIRIO: A thousand times happy she, who had him.

BERNARDA: And I want no weeping. Death must be looked at face to face. Silence!

(To one daughter.)

Be still, I said!

(To another daughter.)

Tears when you're alone! We'll drown ourselves in a sea of mourning. She, the youngest daughter of Bernarda Alba, died a virgin. Did you hear me? Silence, silence, I said. Silence!

CURTAIN

Figure 1. The entire household of Bernarda Alba and the neighbor women join in mourning for Bernarda's late husband in Nuria Espert's 1986 production at the Lyric, Hammersmith. (Photograph: Donald Cooper, Photostage Limited.)

Figure 2. Poncia (Joan Plowright, *arms outstretched*) tells Angustias (Julie Legrand, *left*), Magdalena (Christine Edmonds), Amelia (Chloe Salaman), and Martirio (Deborah Findlay) about her courtship in Nuria Espert's 1986 production at the Lyric, Hammersmith. (Photograph: Donald Cooper, Photostage Limited.)

Figure 3. Maria Josefa (Patricia Hayes, *center*) insists that she wants to marry; Bernarda (Glenda Jackson) stares at her in anger, and Poncia (Joan Plowright) tries to restrain her in Nuria Espert's 1986 production at the Lyric, Hammersmith. (Photograph: Donald Cooper, Photostage Limited.)

Figure 4. "Just try looking for him now!" screams Bernarda Alba (Glenda Jackson, *center,* with rifle) after firing at Pepe el Romano; Adela (Amanda Root, *standing right*) is about to rush out, distraught, to her death in Nuria Espert's 1986 production (as seen at the Globe Theatre in 1987). (Photograph: Donald Cooper, Photostage Limited.)

Staging of *The House of Bernarda Alba*

**REVIEW OF THE LYRIC, HAMMERSMITH,
PRODUCTION, 1988, BY MICHAEL BILLINGTON**

The British theatre suddenly seems to be shedding its insularity. Peter James's internationalist policy at the Lyric, Hammersmith, brings us a moving, austerely impressive production of Lorca's 50-year-old *The House of Bernarda Alba,* directed by Nuria Espert, that proves several things: that British actresses can play Spanish tragedy, that Lorca is translatable (at least by Robert David Macdonald), and that a suburban theatre can yield a production that would not disgrace—indeed would enhance—the stages of our national companies.

The set has a lot to do with it. Ezio Frigerio (Strehler's designer) has taken the title literally and made the house one of the stars of the evening. Lorca's play is about the passion and frustration of the five, immured daughters of the widowed, tyrannical Bernarda Alba: and Frigerio has surrounded them by towering, white, age-pocked Granada walls inset with tiny, barred windows and culminating in a grating, flagstone floor.

The impression, simultaneously, is of a prison courtyard, a nunnery and an asylum: and, even if the sense of Andalusian heat is not very strong, the claustrophobia is heightened by the lowering space and by Franca Squarciatino's black costumes giving the women the look of bottled insects.

The difficulty lies in creating, for an English audience, a world dominated by honour, tradition, toil and sexual restraint from which there is only one escape: an arranged marriage has been fixed between the eldest daughter, Angustias, and the unseen Pepe El Romano who, it tragically transpires, is the lover of her youngest sister, Adela.

The power of Lorca's play lies in its portrait of a specific family but even in the canopied courtyard while outside the men go off to harvest. They are enclosed by the house, history, sexual custom and an overpowering sense of fate. "I should be happy but I'm not," says Angustias. "It's all the same either way," her mother replies, sealing their collective doom.

Nuria Espert breaks through Anglo-Saxon optimism to create this sense of entrapment and she does this by assembling a crack company in which no one is allowed to give a selfish-star-performance. Gillian Hanna's Maid, dutifully scrubbing stone floors and driven mad by the noise of the funeral bells, is as vital to the atmosphere as Glenda Jackson's tyrannical matriarch who rules over her brood like a female leopard (she even brandishes a claw at a recalcitrant daughter) and who howls with sadistic relish as an errant village woman is dragged through the streets.

At first hard to distinguish, her five daughters gradually take on individual life: Deborah Findlay's Martirio, caressing a black-stockinged ankle as she talks of the men yoking bullocks in the yard, implies a sensuality balefully repressed, while Amanda Root's Adela in her green dress embodies a dream of freedom.

But the vital tonal contrast is supplied by Joan Plowright in a marvellous performance as the servant Poncia: she is earthy, robust, sensual but the way she smooths the nap of the folded linen evokes a lifetime of drudgery and suggests she is as much part of a doomed, mechanistic universe as the sisters. Patricia Hayes, stark-naked in a white shift, also gives a highly courageous performance as the mad, locked-in grandmother symbolising the fate awaiting Bernarda's daughters.

A needless interval dissipates the tension. But otherwise this is a vivid realisation of Lorca's play that conveys much of its meaning through a series of resonant images: of the sisters breaking into dreamy, private dances as the men go off to reap and of the family dining in a corner of the courtyard in a state of imprisoned festivity. Nuria Espert has put before us an enclosed world: at the same time, she has opened up the possibility of Lorca on the British stage.

BERTOLT BRECHT

The social and political upheavals of the twentieth century profoundly influenced Brecht's life and his plays. World War I put an end to his medical studies in Munich and marked the beginning of his intense political consciousness, which he expressed in "The Legend of the Dead Soldier" (1918), a poem the Nazis were later to cite as evidence for denying him German citizenship. Shortly after the war, in 1919, he took part in an unsuccessful revolution in his native Bavaria, a bitter experience that provided the basis for his first successful play, *Drums in the Night* (1922). By 1922, Brecht had also become "dramaturg" (a resident playwright and adapter) at the Munich Kammerspiele, a theater for which he wrote *In the Jungle of the Cities* (1923). There, too, he directed *Edward II* (1924), his revision of Marlowe's history play, in a striking production that featured a battle scene with the faces of the soldiers painted starkly white.

But it was in Berlin, where Brecht moved in 1924, that he was to become widely known—and where he was to develop his revolutionary concept of "epic theater": a form of drama and dramatic production intended to provoke spectators into a heightened social and political awareness, rather than involve them emotionally in a realistic or naturalistic situation. To prevent spectators from empathizing with his characters, Brecht advocated an "alienation effect" both in acting and playwriting. Brecht's approach to acting directly countered the method of Stanislavsky. Brecht asked actors to distance themselves from the inner life of a role and not immerse themselves in it, to deliver lines in a mocking or dispassionate tone instead of an emotionally convincing voice, and in general to act a part in a manner that conveyed the awareness of being a performer rather than the involvement of being a character. To jerk spectators into a heightened social and political consciousness, Brecht abandoned the carefully elaborated plots of realistic drama in favor of an episodic structure he learned from reading and viewing of the expressionistic political plays of his German contemporaries. Brecht created this jerky, episodic effect by using short scenes in rapidly changing locales, with frequent shifts from prose to verse to song. And to further awaken the audience to his political message, Brecht incorporated a variety of nonrealistic staging devices used by the radical German producer Erwin Piscator—posters, slide projections, motion pictures, stylized sets, and garish lighting effects.

Brecht synthesized all these elements for the first time in *Man Is Man* (1926), a fiercely anti-colonial, anti-war play, which is set in India during the British imperial rule and depicts the transformation of a poor dock worker into a soldier and military hero—a transformation that also changes him from a human being into a monster of nature. Two years later, Brecht produced his most popular and successful piece of epic theater, *The Threepenny Opera* (1928), a biting attack on capitalistic society, a society in which "money rules the world," and in which "Mankind can keep alive thanks to its brilliance in keeping its humanity repressed." To this political satire, Brecht joins romantic satire, mocking Polly Peachum's naive attachment to the lusty Macheath. The fame and money Brecht gained from this work, the popularity of which derived not just from Brecht's clever reworking of John Gay's *The Beggar's Opera* (1728) but from Kurt Weill's pungent score, gave Brecht the freedom to create a wide variety of theatrical works: his dogmatically Marxist plays, which he called "lehrstücke" (literally, learning pieces), including *The Measures Taken* (1930) and *The Exception and the Rule* (1930); his less dogmatic but still socialist plays, such as *The Mother* (1932) and *St. Joan of the Stockyards* (1932); and his other musical collaborations with Weill, *Happy End* (1929), *The Rise and Fall of the City of Mahagonny* (1929), and *The Seven Deadly Sins* (1933). The overtly didactic message in all these plays was, in essence, a challenge to the audience to change an existing social order that Brecht perceived as enslaving human beings through bureaucracy, war, and capitalism.

In 1933, political upheaval once again altered the course of Brecht's life, for when Hitler came to power Brecht was compelled to flee Nazi Germany—the communist politics of his plays had led to the danger of his being tried for high treason. He stayed briefly in Switzerland, then made his home in Denmark until 1939, when an impending Nazi invasion of that country forced him to move his family and his acting company to Sweden. But in 1940, the fear that Sweden would be invaded drove Brecht and his entourage to Finland. In 1941, he obtained a visa to the United States and settled in Santa Monica, California, where he lived until 1947, when his communist allegiances brought him under investigation by the House Committee on Un-American Activities, and he was forced to return to Germany. He spent his remaining years in East Berlin, where he devoted himself primarily to producing his already written plays and to turning his acting company, the Berliner Ensemble, into one of the most distinguished theatrical groups in the world.

During his exile from Germany, Brecht composed his most powerful plays—among them *Mother Courage and Her Children* (1939), *The Good Woman of Setzuan* (1943), *The Caucasian Chalk Circle* (1945), and *Galileo*, which he wrote and rewrote between 1938 and 1954. In all of these plays, the overt, even strident didacticism of his earlier Marxist plays gives way to a broader socialist message. Oppression is still the enemy, but in these plays it is seen as residing not only in social institutions, but in the acts of individual human beings. And it is in these plays, too, that the split between Brecht's theories of epic theater and his actual practice become most noticeable, for the plays seem to invite an audience to become passionately involved in the problems of their central characters. Although Brecht's notes on Mother Courage repeatedly emphasize the distasteful qualities he had hoped to reveal in her—her pettiness, her moral deformity, her incurable political ignorance—audiences invariably become engaged by her tenacity and idomitability. The female protagonist of *The Good Woman of Setzuan* must adopt male disguise and ruthless behavior in order to enjoy the good fortune which suddenly befalls her, but although Brecht offers no solution to her dilemma (how can one be good and still survive in a grasping, materialistic world?), the strength of Shen Te's idealism still engages the audience's sympathies. And although Brecht's notes to *Galileo* indicate that he meant to portray the famous scientist as having betrayed his calling, the play itself invites a more spacious and sympathetic view of the man.

Brecht's three versions of the play show his continuing fascination with the character of Galileo as well as his perception that Galileo's recantation of his scientific discoveries could be interpreted in a variety of ways. In the first version, written in 1938 and titled *The Earth Moves*, Galileo's revolutionary experiments and discoveries are depicted as profoundly disturbing to the religious authorities because they replace a geocentric view of planetary relationships with a heliocentric one and thereby remove human beings from the center of God's universe—a decentering that challenges the centrality of the Catholic church itself. But after 1945, when American war planes dropped atom bombs on Hiroshima and Nagasaki, Brecht, aided by Charles Laughton, rewrote the play in English to mock not only the institutions of the church but also Galileo himself as a kind of self-serving intellectual who would do anything, even recant his own scientific work, to save his skin. In this version, the play turns into a condemnation of the scientist as a man who might have changed human understanding but who failed to do so and in that failure indirectly contributed to something as horrific as the dropping of the bomb. The play's final version, in German again, is the longest, containing Brecht's bitterest attack on Galileo's failure to resist the Inquisition.

The balance and clarity of the "Laughton version" reflect the unusual working conditions that created the text. Meeting every morning in Laughton's large house overlooking the Pacific Ocean, the famous actor who spoke no German and the famous playwright whose English was limited, communicated through their common language—theatrical gesture. Brecht reports that he would act out a piece of dialogue in "bad English or even in German," Laughton would act it back in "proper English," and finally Brecht would consent to a line which Laughton would then write down.

Photographs from the 1947 New York production show Laughton's ability to convey different facets of Galileo's personality: his wary suspicion of the Inquisitor (Figure 1), his comfortably relaxed enjoyment of his friends (Figure 2), and his intense concentration (Figure 3). In that final photograph, one sees too the pain of the "stony and scientifically accurate self-knowledge" that Irwin Shaw found so memorable. Galileo's chilling view of himself as a man who betrayed his profession seemed for Irwin Shaw "the very core of truth." Yet the play follows Galileo's long speech of self-recrimination with Andrea's view that Galileo's recantation was strategic, something that enabled him to live and continue his writing. Who, then, has the last word? In the play's final scene, Andrea smuggles Galileo's manuscript out of Italy, trying to explain the truth to a young boy just as Galileo had explained it to him. And though the almost-blind Galileo can no longer see the sky, it is nonetheless bright.

GALILEO

BY BERTOLT BRECHT / TRANSLATED BY CHARLES LAUGHTON

It is my opinion that the earth is very noble and admirable by reason of so many and so different alterations and generations which are incessantly made therein.

—GALILEO GALILEI

CHARACTERS

GALILEO GALILEI
ANDREA SARTI, *two actors: boy and man*
MRS. SARTI
LUDOVICO MARSILI
PRIULI, *the curator*
SAGREDO, GALILEO's *friend*
VIRGINIA GALILEI
TWO SENATORS
MATTI, *an iron founder*
PHILOSOPHER, *later*, RECTOR OF THE UNIVERSITY
ELDERLY LADY
YOUNG LADY
FEDERZONI, *assistant to* GALILEO
MATHEMATICIAN
LORD CHAMBERLAIN
FAT PRELATE
TWO SCHOLARS
TWO MONKS
INFURIATED MONK
OLD CARDINAL
ATTENDANT MONK

CHRISTOPHER CLAVIUS
LITTLE MONK
TWO SECRETARIES
CARDINAL BELLARMIN
CARDINAL BARBERINI
CARDINAL INQUISITOR
YOUNG GIRL
HER FRIEND
GIUSEPPE
STREET SINGER
HIS WIFE
REVELLER
A LOUD VOICE
INFORMER
TOWN CRIER
OFFICIAL
PEASANT
CUSTOMS OFFICER
BOY
SENATORS, OFFICIALS, PROFESSORS, LADIES, GUESTS, CHILDREN

There are two wordless roles: The Doge in scene 2 and Prince Cosmo de Medici in scene 4. The ballad of scene 9 is filled out by a pantomime: among the individuals in the pantomimic crowd are three extras (including the "King of Hungary"), Cobbler's Boy, Three Children, Peasant Woman, Monk, Rich Couple, Dwarf, Beggar, and Girl.

SCENE 1

In the year sixteen hundred and nine
Science' light began to shine.
At Padua City, in a modest house
Galileo Galilei set out to prove
The sun is still, the earth is on the move.

(GALILEO's *scantily furnished study. Morning.* GALILEO *is washing himself. A barefooted boy,* ANDREA, *son of his housekeeper,* MRS. SARTI, *enters with a big astronomical model.*)

GALILEO: Where did you get that thing?
ANDREA: The coachman brought it.
GALILEO: Who sent it?
ANDREA: It said "From the Court of Naples" on the box.
GALILEO: I don't want their stupid presents. Illuminated manuscripts, a statue of Hercules the size of an elephant—they never send money.
ANDREA: But isn't this an astronomical instrument, Mr. Galilei?
GALILEO: This is an antique too. An expensive toy.
ANDREA: What's it for?

GALILEO: It's a map of the sky according to the wise men of ancient Greece. Bosh! We'll try and sell it to the university. They still teach it there.
ANDREA: How does it work, Mr. Galilei?
GALILEO: It's complicated.
ANDREA: I think I could understand it.
GALILEO (*interested*): Maybe. Let's begin at the beginning. Description!
ANDREA: There are metal rings, a lot of them.
GALILEO: How many?
ANDREA: Eight.
GALILEO: Correct. And?
ANDREA: There are words painted on the bands.
GALILEO: What words?
ANDREA: The names of stars.
GALILEO: Such as?
ANDREA: Here is a band with the sun on it and on the inside band is the moon.
GALILEO: Those metal bands represent crystal globes, eight of them.
ANDREA: Crystal?
GALILEO: Like huge soap bubbles one inside the other and the stars are supposed to be tacked on to them.

Spin the band with the sun on it. (ANDREA *does*.) You see the fixed ball in the middle?

ANDREA: Yes.

GALILEO: That's the earth. For two thousand years man has chosen to believe that the sun and all the host of stars revolve about him. Well. The Pope, the Cardinals, the princes, the scholars, captains, merchants, housewives, have pictured themselves squatting in the middle of an affair like that.

ANDREA: Locked up inside?

GALILEO (*triumphant*): Ah!

ANDREA: It's like a cage.

GALILEO: So you sensed that. (*Against the model*.) I like to think the ships began it.

ANDREA: Why?

GALILEO: They used to hug the coasts and then all of a sudden they left the coasts and spread over the oceans. A new age was coming. I was on to it years ago. I was a young man, in Siena. There was a group of masons arguing. They had to raise a block of granite. It was hot. To help matters, one of them wanted to try a new arrangement of ropes. After five minutes' discussion, out went a method which had been employed for a thousand years. The millennium of faith is ended, said I, this is the millennium of doubt. And we are pulling out of that contraption. The sayings of the wise men won't wash anymore. Everybody, at last, is getting nosy. I predict that in our time astronomy will become the gossip of the marketplace and the sons of fishwives will pack the schools.

ANDREA: You're off again, Mr. Galilei. Give me the towel. (*He wipes some soap from* GALILEO's *back*.)

GALILEO: By that time, with any luck, they will be learning that the earth rolls around the sun, and that their mothers, the captains, the scholars, the princes, and the Pope are rolling with it.

ANDREA: That turning-round-business is no good. I can see with my own eyes that the sun comes up in one place in the morning and goes down in a different place in the evening. It doesn't stand still, I can see it move.

GALILEO: You see nothing, all you do is gawk. Gawking is not seeing. (*He puts the iron washstand in the middle of the room*.) Now: that's the sun. Sit down. (ANDREA *sits on a chair*. GALILEO *stands behind him*.) Where is the sun, on your right or on your left?

ANDREA: Left.

GALILEO: And how will it get to the right?

ANDREA: By your putting it there, of course.

GALILEO: Of course? (*He picks* ANDREA *up, chair and all, and carries him round to the other side of the washstand*.) Now where is the sun?

ANDREA: On the right.

GALILEO: And did it move?

ANDREA: I did.

GALILEO: Wrong. Stupid! The chair moved.

ANDREA: But I was on it.

GALILEO: Of course. The chair is the earth, and you're sitting on it.

(MRS. SARTI, *who has come in with a glass of milk and a roll, has been watching*.)

MRS. SARTI: What are you doing with my son, Mr. Galilei?

ANDREA: Now, mother, you don't understand.

MRS. SARTI: You understand, don't you? Last night he tried to tell me that the earth goes round the sun. You'll soon have him saying that two times two is five.

GALILEO (*eating his breakfast*): Apparently we are on the threshold of a new era, Mrs. Sarti.

MRS. SARTI: Well, I hope we can pay the milkman in this new era. A young gentleman is here to take private lessons and he is well-dressed and don't you frighten him away like you did the others. Wasting your time with Andrea! (*To* ANDREA.) How many times have I told you not to wheedle free lessons out of Mr. Galilei? (MRS. SARTI *goes*.)

GALILEO: So you thought enough of the turning-round-business to tell your mother about it.

ANDREA: Just to surprise her.

GALILEO: Andrea, I wouldn't talk about our ideas outside.

ANDREA: Why not?

GALILEO: Certain of the authorities won't like it.

ANDREA: Why not, if it's the truth?

GALILEO (*laughs*): Because we are like the worms who are little and have dim eyes and can hardly see the stars at all, and the new astronomy is a framework of guesses or very little more—yet.

(MRS. SARTI *shows in* LUDOVICO MARSILI, *a presentable young man*.)

GALILEO: This house is like a marketplace. (*Pointing to the model*.) Move that out of the way! Put it down there!

(LUDOVICO *does*.)

LUDOVICO: Good morning, sir. My name is Ludovico Marsili.

GALILEO (*reading a letter of recommendation he has brought*): You came by way of Holland and your family lives in the Campagna? Private lessons, thirty scudi a month.

LUDOVICO: That's all right, of course, sir.

GALILEO: What is your subject?

LUDOVICO: Horses.

GALILEO: Aha.

LUDOVICO: I don't understand science, sir.

GALILEO: Aha.

LUDOVICO: They showed me an instrument like that in Amsterdam. You'll pardon me, sir, but it didn't make sense to me at all.

GALILEO: It's out of date now.

(ANDREA *goes.*)

LUDOVICO: You'll have to be patient with me, sir. Nothing in science makes sense to me.

GALILEO: Aha.

LUDOVICO: I saw a brand new instrument° in Amsterdam. A tube affair. "See things five times as large as life!" It had two lenses, one at each end, one lens bulged and the other was like that. (*Gesture.*) Any normal person would think that different lenses cancel each other out. They didn't! I just stood and looked a fool.

GALILEO: I don't quite follow you. What does one see enlarged?

LUDOVICO: Church steeples, pigeons, boats. Anything at a distance.

GALILEO: Did you yourself—see things enlarged?

LUDOVICO: Yes, sir.

GALILEO: And the tube had two lenses? Was it like this? (*He has been making a sketch.*)

(LUDOVICO *nods.*)

GALILEO: A recent invention?

LUDOVICO: It must be. They only started peddling it on the streets a few days before I left Holland.

GALILEO (*starts to scribble calculations on the sketch; almost friendly*): Why do you bother your head with science? Why don't you just breed horses?

(*Enter* MRS. SARTI. GALILEO *doesn't see her. She listens to the following.*)

LUDOVICO: My mother is set on the idea that science is necessary nowadays for conversation.

GALILEO: Aha. You'll find Latin or philosophy easier. (MRS. SARTI *catches his eye.*) I'll see you on Tuesday afternoon.

LUDOVICO: I shall look forward to it, sir.

GALILEO: Good morning. (*He goes to the window and shouts into the street.*) Andrea! Hey, Redhead, Redhead!

MRS. SARTI: The curator of the museum is here to see you.

---

brand new instrument, The telescope was thought erroneously to have been invented by Hans Lippershey, who made and sold telescopes in Middelburg, Netherlands, in 1608. When he applied for a patent, he was refused on the grounds that the idea was widespread. Telescopes were available for sale in Paris in 1609, then Germany, Italy, and London in the same year. Galileo reinvented the instrument by calculating the mathematical relationship of the focal lengths of lenses. His versions were on the order of ten times more powerful than those available, and they also permitted the viewer to see things right side up, which Lippershey's did not.

GALILEO: Don't look at me like that. I took him, didn't I?

MRS. SARTI: I caught your eye in time.

GALILEO: Show the curator in.

(*She goes. He scribbles something on a new sheet of paper. The* CURATOR *comes in.*)

CURATOR: Good morning, Mr. Galilei.

GALILEO: Lend me a scudo. (*He takes it and goes to the window, wrapping the coin in the paper on which he has been scribbling.*) Redhead, run to the spectacle-maker and bring me two lenses; here are the measurements. (*He throws the paper out of the window. During the following scene* GALILEO *studies his sketch of the lenses.*)

CURATOR: Mr. Galilei, I have come to return your petition for an honorarium. Unfortunately I am unable to recommend your request.

GALILEO: My good sir, how can I make ends meet on five hundred scudi?

CURATOR: What about your private students?

GALILEO: If I spend all my time with students, when am I to study? My particular science is on the threshold of important discoveries. (*He throws a manuscript on the table.*) Here are my findings on the laws of falling bodies. That should be worth two hundred scudi.

CURATOR: I am sure that any paper of yours is of infinite worth, Mr. Galilei. . . .

GALILEO: I was limiting it to two hundred scudi.

CURATOR (*cool*): Mr. Galilei, if you want money and leisure, go to Florence. I have no doubt Prince Cosmo de Medici will be glad to subsidize you, but eventually you will be forbidden to think—in the name of the Inquisition. (GALILEO *says nothing.*) Now let us not make a mountain out of a molehill. You are happy here in the Republic of Venice but you need money. Well, that's human, Mr. Galilei, may I suggest a simple solution? You remember that chart you made for the army to extract cube roots without any knowledge of mathematics? Now that was practical!

GALILEO: Bosh!

CURATOR: Don't say bosh about something that astounded the Chamber of Commerce. Our city elders are businessmen. Why don't you invent something useful that will bring them a little profit?

GALILEO (*playing with the sketch of the lenses; suddenly*): I see. Mr. Priuli, I may have something for you.

CURATOR: You don't say so.

GALILEO: It's not quite there yet, but . . .

CURATOR: You've never let me down yet, Galilei.

GALILEO: You are always an inspiration to me, Priuli.

CURATOR: You are a great man: a discontented man, but I've always said you are a great man.

GALILEO (*tartly*): My discontent, Priuli, is for the most part with myself. I am forty-six years of age and have achieved nothing which satisfies me.

CURATOR: I won't disturb you any further.

GALILEO: Thank you. Good morning.

CURATOR: Good morning. And thank you.

(*He goes.* GALILEO *sighs.* ANDREA *returns, bringing lenses.*)

ANDREA: One scudo was not enough. I had to leave my cap with him before he'd let me take them away.

GALILEO: We'll get it back someday. Give them to me.
(*He takes the lenses over to the window, holding them in the relation they would have in a telescope.*)

ANDREA: What are those for?

GALILEO: Something for the senate. With any luck, they will rake in two hundred scudi. Take a look!

ANDREA: My, things look close! I can read the copper letters on the bell in the Campanile. And the washerwomen by the river, I can see their washboards!

GALILEO: Get out of the way. (*Looking through the lenses himself.*) Aha!

SCENE 2

No one's virtue is complete:
Great Galileo liked to eat.
You will not resent, we hope,
The truth about his telescope.

(*The great arsenal of Venice, overlooking the harbor full of ships.* SENATORS *and* OFFICIALS *on one side,* GALILEO, *his daughter* VIRGINIA, *and his friend* SAGREDO *on the other side. They are dressed in formal, festive clothes.* VIRGINIA *is fourteen and charming. She carries a velvet cushion on which lies a brand new telescope. Behind* GALILEO *are some* ARTISANS *from the arsenal. There are onlookers,* LUDOVICO *amongst them.*)

CURATOR (*announcing*): Senators, Artisans of the Great Arsenal of Venice; Mr. Galileo Galilei, professor of mathematics at your University of Padua.

(GALILEO *steps forward and starts to speak.*)

GALILEO: Members of the High Senate! Gentlemen: I have great pleasure, as director of this institute, in presenting for your approval and acceptance an entirely new instrument originating from this our great arsenal of the Republic of Venice. As professor of mathematics at your University of Padua, your obedient servant has always counted it his privilege to offer you such discoveries and inventions as might prove lucrative to the manufacturers and merchants of our Venetian Republic. Thus, in all humility, I tender you this, my optical tube, or telescope, constructed, I assure you, on the most scientific and Christian principles, the product of seventeen years patient research at your University of Padua.

(GALILEO *steps back. The* SENATORS *applaud.*)

SAGREDO (*aside to* GALILEO): Now you will be able to pay your bills.

GALILEO: Yes. It will make money for them. But you realize that it is more than a money-making gadget?—I turned it on the moon last night . . .

CURATOR (*in his best chamber-of-commerce manner*): Gentlemen: Our Republic is to be congratulated not only because this new acquisition will be one more feather in the cap of Venetian culture . . . (*polite applause*) . . . not only because our own Mr. Galilei has generously handed this fresh product of his teeming brain entirely over to you, allowing you to manufacture as many of these highly salable articles as you please. . . . (*Considerable applause.*) But Gentlemen of the Senate, has it occurred to you that—with the help of this remarkable new instrument—the battle fleet of the enemy will be visible to us a full two hours before we are visible to him? (*Tremendous applause.*)

GALILEO (*aside to* SAGREDO): We have been held up three generations for lack of a thing like this. I want to go home.

SAGREDO: What about the moon?

GALILEO: Well, for one thing, it doesn't give off its own light.

CURATOR (*continuing his oration*): And now, Your Excellency, and Members of the Senate, Mr. Galilei entreats you to accept the instrument from the hands of his charming daughter Virginia.

(*Polite applause. He beckons to* VIRGINIA *who steps forward and presents the telescope to the* DOGE.)

CURATOR (*during this*): Mr. Galilei gives his invention entirely into your hands, Gentlemen, enjoining you to construct as many of these instruments as you may please.

(*More applause. The* SENATORS *gather round the telescope, examining it, and looking through it.*)

GALILEO (*aside to* SAGREDO): Do you know what the Milky Way is made of?

SAGREDO: No.

GALILEO: I do.

CURATOR (*interrupting*): Congratulations, Mr. Galilei. Your extra five hundred scudi a year are safe.

GALILEO: Pardon? What? Of course, the five hundred scudi! Yes!

(*A prosperous man is standing beside the* CURATOR.)

CURATOR: Mr. Galilei, Mr. Matti of Florence.

MATTI: You're opening new fields, Mr. Galilei. We could do with you at Florence.

CURATOR: Now, Mr. Matti, leave something to us poor Venetians.

MATTI: It is a pity that a great republic has to seek an excuse to pay its great men their right and proper dues.

CURATOR: Even a great man has to have an incentive. (*He joins the* SENATORS *at the telescope.*)

MATTI: I am an iron founder.

GALILEO: Iron founder!

MATTI: With factories at Pisa and Florence. I wanted to talk to you about a machine you designed for a friend of mine in Padua.

GALILEO: I'll put you on to someone to copy it for you, I am not going to have the time.—How are things in Florence?

(*They wander away.*)

FIRST SENATOR (*peering*): Extraordinary! They're having their lunch on that frigate. Lobsters! I'm hungry!

(*Laughter.*)

SECOND SENATOR: Oh, good heavens, look at her! I must tell my wife to stop bathing on the roof. When can I buy one of these things?

(*Laughter.* VIRGINA *has spotted* LUDOVICO *among the onlookers and drags him to* GALILEO.)

VIRGINIA (*to* LUDOVICO): Did I do it nicely?

LUDOVICO: I thought so.

VIRGINIA: Here's Ludovico to congratulate you, father.

LUDOVICO (*embarrassed*): Congratulations, sir.

GALILEO: I improved it.

LUDOVICO: Yes, sir. I am beginning to understand science.

(GALILEO *is surrounded.*)

VIRGINIA: Isn't father a great man?

LUDOVICO: Yes.

VIRGINIA: Isn't that new thing father made pretty?

LUDOVICO: Yes, a pretty red. Where I saw it first it was covered in green.

VIRGINIA: What was?

LUDOVICO: Never mind. (*A short pause.*) Have you ever been to Holland?

(*They go. All Venice is congratulating* GALILEO, *who wants to go home.*)

SCENE 3

January ten, sixteen ten;
Galileo Galilei abolishes heaven.

(GALILEO's *study at Padua. It is night.* GALILEO *and* SAGREDO *at a telescope.*)

SAGREDO (*softly*): The edge of the crescent is jagged. All along the dark part, near the shiny crescent, bright particles of light keep coming up, one after the other and growing larger and merging with the bright crescent.

GALILEO: How do you explain those spots of light?

SAGREDO: It can't be true . . .

GALILEO: It *is* true: they are high mountains.

SAGREDO: On a star?

GALILEO: Yes. The shining particles are mountain peaks catching the first rays of the rising sun while the slopes of the mountains are still dark, and what you see is the sunlight moving down from the peaks into the valleys.

SAGREDO: But this gives the lie to all the astronomy that's been taught for the last two thousand years.

GALILEO: Yes. What you are seeing now has been seen by no other man beside myself.

SAGREDO: But the moon can't be an earth with mountains and valleys like our own any more than the earth can be a star.

GALILEO: The moon *is* an earth with mountains and valleys—and the earth *is* a star. As the moon appears to us, so we appear to the moon. From the moon, the earth looks something like a crescent, sometimes like a half-globe, sometimes a full globe, and sometimes it is not visible at all.

SAGREDO: Galileo, this is frightening.

(*An urgent knocking on the door.*)

GALILEO: I've discovered something else, something even more astonishing.

(*More knocking.* GALILEO *opens the door and the* CURATOR *comes in.*)

CURATOR: There it is—your "miraculous optical tube." Do you know that this invention he so picturesquely termed "the fruit of seventeen years research" will be on sale tomorrow for two scudi apiece at every street corner in Venice? A shipload of them has just arrived from Holland.

SAGREDO: Oh, dear!

(GALILEO *turns his back and adjusts the telescope.*)

CURATOR: When I think of the poor gentlemen of the senate who believed they were getting an invention they could monopolize for their own profit. . . . Why, when they took their first look through the glass, it was only by the merest chance that they didn't see a peddler, seven times enlarged, selling tubes exactly like it at the corner of the street.

SAGREDO: Mr. Priuli, with the help of this instrument, Mr. Galilei has made discoveries that will revolutionize our concept of the universe.

CURATOR: Mr. Galilei provided the city with a first rate water pump and the irrigation works he designed function splendidly. How was I to expect this?

GALILEO (*still at the telescope*): Not so fast, Priuli. I may be on the track of a very large gadget. Certain of the stars appear to have regular movements. If there were a clock in the sky, it could be seen from anywhere. That might be useful for your shipowners.

CURATOR: I won't listen to you. I listened to you before, and as a reward for my friendship you have made me the laughingstock of the town. You can laugh— you got your money. But let me tell you this: you've destroyed my faith in a lot of things, Mr. Galilei. I'm disgusted with the world. That's all I have to say. (*He storms out.*)

GALILEO (*embarrassed*): Businessmen bore me, they suffer so. Did you see the frightened look in his eyes when he caught sight of a world not created solely for the purpose of doing business?

SAGREDO: Did you know that telescopes had been made in Holland?

GALILEO: I'd heard about it. But the one I made for the Senators was twice as good as any Dutchman's. Besides, I needed the money. How can I work, with the tax collector on the doorstep? And my poor daughter will never acquire a husband unless she has a dowry, she's not too bright. And I like to buy books—all kinds of books. Why not? And what about my appetite? I don't think well unless I eat well. Can I help it if I get my best ideas over a good meal and a bottle of wine? They don't pay me as much as they pay the butcher's boy. If only I could have five years to do nothing but research! Come on. I am going to show you something else.

SAGREDO: I don't know that I want to look again.

GALILEO: This is one of the brighter nebulae of the Milky Way. What do you see?

SAGREDO: But it's made up of stars—countless stars.

GALILEO: Countless worlds.

SAGREDO (*hesitating*): What about the theory that the earth revolves round the sun? Have you run across anything about that?

GALILEO: No. But I noticed something on Tuesday that might prove a step towards even that. Where's Jupiter? There are four lesser stars near Jupiter. I happened on them on Monday but didn't take any particular note of their position. On Tuesday I looked again. I could have sworn they had moved. They have changed again. Tell me what you see.

SAGREDO: I only see three.

GALILEO: Where's the fourth? Let's get the charts and settle down to work.

(*They work and the lights dim. The lights go up again. It is near dawn.*)

GALILEO: The only place the fourth can be is round at the back of the larger star where we cannot see it. This means there are small stars revolving around a big star. Where are the crystal shells now that the stars are supposed to be fixed to?

SAGREDO: Jupiter can't be attached to anything: there are other stars revolving round it.

GALILEO: There is no support in the heavens. (SAGREDO *laughs awkwardly.*) Don't stand there looking at me as if it weren't true.

SAGREDO: I suppose it is true. I'm afraid.

GALILEO: Why?

SAGREDO: What do you think is going to happen to you for saying that there is another sun around which other earths revolve? And that there are only stars and no difference between earth and heaven? Where is God then?

GALILEO: What do you mean?

SAGREDO: God? Where is God?

GALILEO (*angrily*): Not there! Any more than he'd be here—if creatures from the moon came down to look for him!

SAGREDO: Then where is He?

GALILEO: I'm not a theologian: I'm a mathematician.

SAGREDO: You are a human being! (*Almost shouting.*) Where is God in your system of the universe?

GALILEO: Within ourselves. Or—nowhere.

SAGREDO: Ten years ago a man was burned at the stake for saying that.

GALILEO: Giordano Bruno° was an idiot: he spoke too soon. He would never have been condemned if he could have backed up what he said with proof.

SAGREDO (*incredulously*): Do you really believe proof will make any difference?

GALILEO: I believe in the human race. The only people that can't be reasoned with are the dead. Human beings are intelligent.

SAGREDO: Intelligent—or merely shrewd?

GALILEO: I know they call a donkey a horse when they want to sell it, and a horse a donkey when they want to buy it. But is that the whole story? Aren't they susceptible to truth as well? (*He fishes a small pebble out of his pocket.*) If anybody were to drop a stone . . . (*drops the pebble*) . . . and tell them that it didn't fall, do you think they would keep quiet? The evidence of your own eyes is a very seductive thing. Sooner or later everybody must succumb to it.

SAGREDO: Galileo, I am helpless when you talk.

(*A church bell has been ringing for some time, calling people to Mass. Enter* VIRGINIA, *muffled up for Mass, carrying a candle, protected from the wind by a globe.*)

VIRGINIA: Oh, father, you promised to go to bed tonight, and it's five o'clock again.

GALILEO: Why are you up at this hour?

VIRGINIA: I'm going to Mass with Mrs. Sarti. Ludovico is going too. How was the night, father?

Giordano Bruno, Bruno (1548–1600), one of the most distinguished Italian Renaissance thinkers, lectured in England, France, Germany, and other countries in Europe before being imprisoned for heresy by the Inquisition. After a period of confinement and a lengthy trial, he was burned at the stake. He believed, like Galileo, in the Copernican view of astronomy, which asserted that the earth rotated around the sun.

GALILEO: Bright.

VIRGINIA: What did you find through the tube?

GALILEO: Only some little specks by the side of a star. I must draw attention to them somehow. I think I'll name them after the Prince of Florence. Why not call them the Medicean planets? By the way, we may move to Florence. I've written to His Highness, asking if he can use me as Court Mathematician.

VIRGINIA: Oh, father, we'll be at the court!

SAGREDO (amazed): Galileo!

GALILEO: My dear Sagredo, I must have leisure. My only worry is that His Highness after all may not take me. I'm not accustomed to writing formal letters to great personages. Here, do you think this is the right sort of thing?

SAGREDO (reads and quotes): "Whose sole desire is to reside in Your Highness' presence—the rising sun of our great age." Cosmo de Medici is a boy of nine.

GALILEO: The only way a man like me can land a good job is by crawling on his stomach. Your father, my dear, is going to take his share of the pleasures of life in exchange for all his hard work, and about time too. I have no patience, Sagredo, with a man who doesn't use his brains to fill his belly. Run along to Mass now.

(VIRGINIA goes.)

SAGREDO: Galileo, do not go to Florence.

GALILEO: Why not?

SAGREDO: The monks are in power there.

GALILEO: Going to Mass is a small price to pay for a full belly. And there are many famous scholars at the court of Florence.

SAGREDO: Court monkeys.

GALILEO: I shall enjoy taking them by the scruff of the neck and making them look through the telescope.

SAGREDO: Galileo, you are traveling the road to disaster. You are suspicious and skeptical in science, but in politics you are as naive as your daughter! How can people in power leave a man at large who tells the truth, even if it be the truth about the distant stars? Can you see the Pope scribbling a note in his diary: "10th of January, 1610, Heaven abolished"? A moment ago, when you were at the telescope, I saw you tied to the stake, and when you said you believed in proof, I smelt burning flesh!

GALILEO: I am going to Florence.

(Before the next scene a curtain with the following legend on it is lowered:

By setting the name of Medici in the sky, I am bestowing immortality upon the stars. I commend myself to you as your most faithful and devoted servant, whose sole desire is to reside in Your Highness' presence, the rising sun of our great age.

—GALILEO GALILEI)

SCENE 4

(GALILEO's house at Florence. Well-appointed. GALILEO is demonstrating his telescope to PRINCE COSMO DE MEDICI, a boy of nine, accompanied by his LORD CHAMBERLAIN, LADIES AND GENTLEMEN OF THE COURT, and an assortment of university PROFESSORS. With GALILEO are ANDREA and FEDERZONI, the new assistant (an old man). MRS. SARTI stands by. Before the scene opens the voice of the PHILOSOPHER can be heard.)

VOICE OF THE PHILOSOPHER: Quaedam miracula universi. Orbes mystice canorae, arcus crystallini, circulatio corporum coelestium. Cyclorum epicyclorumque intoxicatio, integritas tabulae chordarum et architectura elata globorum coelestium.

GALILEO: Shall we speak in everyday language? My colleague Mr. Federzoni does not understand Latin.

PHILOSOPHER: Is it necessary that he should?

GALILEO: Yes.

PHILOSOPHER: Forgive me. I thought he was your mechanic.

ANDREA: Mr. Federzoni is a mechanic and a scholar.

PHILOSOPHER: Thank you, young man. If Mr. Federzoni insists . . .

GALILEO: I insist.

PHILOSOPHER: It will not be as clear, but it's your house. Your Highness . . . (The PRINCE is ineffectually trying to establish contact with ANDREA.) I was about to recall to Mr. Galilei some of the wonders of the universe as they are set down for us in the Divine Classics. (The LADIES "ah.") Remind him of the "mystically musical spheres, the crystal arches, the circulation of the heavenly bodies—"

ELDERLY LADY: Perfect poise!

PHILOSOPHER: "—the intoxication of the cycles and epicycles, the integrity of the tables of chords and the enraptured architecture of the celestial globes."

ELDERLY LADY: What diction!

PHILOSOPHER: May I pose the question: Why should we go out of our way to look for things that can only strike a discord in this ineffable harmony?

(The LADIES applaud.)

FEDERZONI: Take a look through here—you'll be interested.

ANDREA: Sit down here, please.

(The PROFESSORS laugh.)

MATHEMATICIAN: Mr. Galilei, nobody doubts that your brain child—or is it your adopted brain child?—is brilliantly contrived.

GALILEO: Your Highness, one can see the four stars as large as life, you know.

(The PRINCE looks to the ELDERLY LADY for guidance.)

MATHEMATICIAN: Ah. But has it occurred to you that an eyeglass through which one sees such phenomena might not be a too reliable eyeglass?

GALILEO: How is that?

MATHEMATICIAN: If one could be sure you would keep your temper, Mr. Galilei, I could suggest that what one sees in the eyeglass and what is in the heavens are two entirely different things.

GALILEO (*quietly*): You are suggesting fraud?

MATHEMATICIAN: No! How could I, in the presence of His Highness?

ELDERLY LADY: The gentlemen are just wondering if Your Highness' stars are really, really there!

(Pause.)

YOUNG LADY (*trying to be helpful*): Can one see the claws on the Great Bear?

GALILEO: And everything on Taurus the Bull.

FEDERZONI: Are you going to look through it or not?

MATHEMATICIAN: With the greatest of pleasure.

(Pause. Nobody goes near the telescope. All of a sudden the boy ANDREA *turns and marches pale and erect past them through the whole length of the room. The* GUESTS *follow with their eyes.)*

MRS. SARTI (*as he passes her*): What is the matter with you?

ANDREA (*shocked*): They are wicked.

PHILOSOPHER: Your Highness, it is a delicate matter and I had no intention of bringing it up, but Mr. Galilei was about to demonstrate the impossible. His new stars would have broken the outer crystal sphere—which we know of on the authority of Aristotle. I am sorry.

MATHEMATICIAN: The last word.

FEDERZONI: He had no telescope.

MATHEMATICIAN: Quite.

GALILEO (*keeping his temper*): "Truth is the daughter of Time, not of Authority." Gentlemen, the sum of our knowledge is pitiful. It has been my singular good fortune to find a new instrument which brings a small patch of the universe a little bit closer. It is at your disposal.

PHILOSOPHER: Where is all this leading?

GALILEO: Are we, as scholars, concerned with where the truth might lead us?

PHILOSOPHER: Mr. Galilei, the truth might lead us anywhere!

GALILEO: I can only beg you to look through my eyeglass.

MATHEMATICIAN (*wild*): If I understand Mr. Galilei correctly, he is asking us to discard the teachings of two thousand years.

GALILEO: For two thousand years we have been looking at the sky and didn't see the four moons of Jupiter, and there they were all the time. Why defend shaken teachings? You should be doing the shaking. (*The* PRINCE *is sleepy.*) Your Highness! My work in the Great Arsenal of Venice brought me in daily contact with sailors, carpenters, and so on. These men are unread. They depend on the evidence of their senses. But they taught me many new ways of doing things. The question is whether these gentlemen here want to be found out as fools by men who might not have had the advantages of a classical education but who are not afraid to use their eyes. I tell you that our dockyards are stirring with that same high curiosity which was the true glory of Ancient Greece.

(Pause.)

PHILOSOPHER: I have no doubt Mr. Galilei's theories will arouse the enthusiasm of the dockyards.

CHAMBERLAIN: Your Highness, I find to my amazement that this highly informative discussion has exceeded the time we had allowed for it. May I remind Your Highness that the State Ball begins in three-quarters of an hour?

(The COURT *bows low.)*

ELDERLY LADY: We would really have liked to look through your eyeglass, Mr. Galilei, wouldn't we, Your Highness?

(The PRINCE *bows politely and is led to the door.* GALILEO *follows the* PRINCE, CHAMBERLAIN, *and* LADIES *towards the exit. The* PROFESSORS *remain at the telescope.)*

GALILEO (*almost servile*): All anybody has to do is look through the telescope, Your Highness.

*(*MRS. SARTI *takes a plate with candies to the* PRINCE *as he is walking out.)*

MRS. SARTI: A piece of homemade candy, Your Highness?

ELDERLY LADY: Not now. Thank you. It is too soon before His Highness' supper.

PHILOSOPHER: Wouldn't I like to take that thing to pieces.

MATHEMATICIAN: Ingenious contraption. It must be quite difficult to keep clean. (*He rubs the lens with his handkerchief and looks at the handkerchief.*)

FEDERZONI: We did not paint the Medicean stars on the lens.

ELDERLY LADY (*to the* PRINCE, *who has whispered something to her*): No, no, no, there is nothing the matter with your stars!

CHAMBERLAIN (*across the stage to* GALILEO): His Highness will of course seek the opinion of the greatest living authority: Christopher Clavius, Chief Astronomer to the Papal College in Rome.

SCENE 5

Things take indeed a wondrous turn
When learned men do stoop to learn.

Clavius, we are pleased to say,
Upheld Galileo Galilei.

(A burst of laughter is heard and the curtains reveal a
hall in the Collegium Romanum. HIGH CHURCHMEN,
MONKS, and SCHOLARS standing about talking and
laughing. GALILEO by himself in a corner.)

FAT PRELATE (shaking with laughter): Hopeless! Hopeless!
Hopeless! Will you tell me something people won't
believe?

A SCHOLAR: Yes, that you don't love your stomach!

FAT PRELATE: They'd believe that. They only do not
believe what's good for them. They doubt the devil,
but fill them up with some fiddle-de-dee about the
earth rolling like a marble in the gutter and they
swallow it hook, line, and sinker. Sancta simplicitas!

(He laughs until the tears run down his cheeks. The others
laugh with him. A group has formed whose members
boisterously begin to pretend they are standing on a rolling globe.)

A MONK: It's rolling fast, I'm dizzy. May I hold on to
you, Professor? (He sways dizzily and clings to one of
the SCHOLARS for support.)

THE SCHOLAR: Old Mother Earth's been at the bottle
again. Whoa!

MONK: Hey! Hey! We're slipping off! Help!

SECOND SCHOLAR: Look! There's Venus! Hold me, lads.
Whee!

SECOND MONK: Don't, don't hurl us off on to the moon.
There are nasty sharp mountain peaks on the
moon, brethren!

VARIOUSLY: Hold tight! Hold tight! Don't look down!
Hold tight! It'll make you giddy!

FAT PRELATE: And we cannot have giddy people in Holy
Rome.

(They rock with laughter. An INFURIATED MONK comes
out from a large door at the rear holding a Bible in his
hand and pointing out a page with his finger.)

INFURIATED MONK: What does the Bible say—"Sun,
stand thou still on Gideon and thou, moon, in the
valley of Ajalon." Can the sun come to a standstill
if it doesn't ever move? Does the Bible lie?

FAT PRELATE: How did Christopher Clavius, the greatest astronomer we have, get mixed up in an investigation of this kind?

INFURIATED MONK: He's in there with his eye glued to
that diabolical instrument.

FAT PRELATE (to GALILEO, who has been playing with his
pebble and has dropped it): Mr. Galilei, something
dropped down.

GALILEO: Monsignor, are you sure it didn't drop up?

INFURIATED MONK: As astronomers we are aware that
there are phenomena which are beyond us, but
man can't expect to understand everything!

(Enter a very OLD CARDINAL leaning on a MONK for
support. Others move aside.)

OLD CARDINAL: Aren't they out yet? Can't they reach a
decision on that paltry matter? Christopher Clavius
ought to know his astronomy after all these years.
I am informed that Mr. Galilei transfers mankind
from the center of the universe to somewhere on
the outskirts. Mr. Galilei is therefore an enemy of
mankind and must be dealt with as such. Is it conceivable that God would trust this most precious
fruit of His labor to a minor frolicking star? Would
He have sent His Son to such a place? How can
there be people with such twisted minds that they
believe what they're told by the slave of a multiplication table?

FAT PRELATE (quietly to CARDINAL): The gentleman is
over there.

OLD CARDINAL: So you are the man. You know my eyes
are not what they were, but I can see you bear a
striking resemblance to the man we burned. What
was his name?

MONK: Your Eminence must avoid excitement the doctor said . . .

OLD CARDINAL (disregarding him): So you have degraded
the earth despite the fact that you live by her and
receive everything from her. I won't have it! I won't
have it! I won't be a nobody on an inconsequential
star briefly twirling hither and thither. I tread the
earth, and the earth is firm beneath my feet, and
there is no motion to the earth, and the earth is the
center of all things, and I am the center of the earth,
and the eye of the Creator is upon me. About me
revolve, affixed to their crystal shells, the lesser
lights of the stars and the great light of the sun,
created to give light upon me that God might see
me—Man, God's greatest effort, the center of creation. "In the image of God created He him." Immortal . . . (His strength fails him and he catches for the
MONK for support.)

MONK: You mustn't overtax your strength, Your Eminence.

(At this moment the door at the rear opens and CHRIS-
TOPHER CLAVIUS enters followed by his ASTRONOMERS.
He strides hastily across the hall, looking neither to right
nor left. As he goes by we hear him say—)

CLAVIUS: He is right.

(Deadly silence. All turn to GALILEO.)

OLD CARDINAL: What is it? Have they reached a decision?

(No one speaks.)

MONK: It is time that Your Eminence went home.

(The hall is emptying fast. One LITTLE MONK who had
entered with CLAVIUS speaks to GALILEO.)

LITTLE MONK: Mr. Galilei, I heard Father Clavius say: "Now it's for the theologians to set the heavens right again." You have won.

(Before the next scene a curtain with the following legend on it is lowered:

. . . As these new astronomical charts enable us to determine longitudes at sea and so make it possible to reach the new continents by the shortest routes, we would beseech Your Excellency to aid us in reaching Mr. Galilei, mathematician to the Court of Florence, who is now in Rome . . .
—From a letter written by a member of the Genoa Chamber of Commerce and Navigation to the Papal Legation)

SCENE 6

When Galileo was in Rome
A Cardinal asked him to his home
He wined and dined him as his guest
And only made one small request.

(CARDINAL BELLARMIN's house in Rome. Music is heard and the chatter of many guests. Two SECRETARIES are at the rear of the stage at a desk. GALILEO, his daughter VIRGINIA, now twenty-one and LUDOVICO MARSILI, who has become her fiancé, are just arriving. A few GUESTS, standing near the entrance with masks in their hands, nudge each other and are suddenly silent. GALILEO looks at them. They applaud him politely and bow.)

VIRGINIA: O father! I'm so happy. I won't dance with anyone but you, Ludovico.

GALILEO (*to a SECRETARY*): I was to wait here for His Eminence.

FIRST SECRETARY: His Eminence will be with you in a few minutes.

VIRGINIA: Do I look proper?

LUDOVICO: You are showing some lace.

(GALILEO puts his arms around their shoulders.)

GALILEO (*quoting mischievously*): Fret not, daughter, if perchance
You attract a wanton glance.
The eyes that catch a trembling lace
Will guess the heartbeat's quickened pace.
Lovely woman still may be
Careless with felicity.

VIRGINIA (*to GALILEO*): Feel my heart.

GALILEO (*to LUDOVICO*): It's thumping.

VIRGINIA: I hope I always say the right thing.

LUDOVICO: She's afraid she's going to let us down.

VIRGINIA: Oh, I want to look beautiful.

GALILEO: You'd better. If you don't they'll start saying all over again that the earth doesn't turn.

LUDOVICO (*laughing*): It *doesn't* turn, sir.

(GALILEO laughs.)

GALILEO: Go and enjoy yourselves. (*He speaks to one of the SECRETARIES.*) A large fête?

FIRST SECRETARY: Two hundred and fifty guests, Mr. Galilei. We have represented here this evening most of the great families of Italy, the Orsinis, the Villanis, the Nuccolis, the Soldanieris, the Canes, the Lecchis, the Estensis, the Colombinis, the . . .

(VIRGINIA comes running back.)

VIRGINIA: Oh father, I didn't tell you: you're famous.

GALILEO: Why?

VIRGINIA: The hairdresser in the Via Vittorio kept four other ladies waiting and took me first. (*Exit.*)

GALILEO (*at the stairway, leaning over the well*): Rome!

(Enter CARDINAL BELLARMIN, wearing the mask of a lamb, and CARDINAL BARBERINI, wearing the mask of a dove.)

SECRETARIES: Their Eminences, Cardinals Bellarmin and Barberini.

(The CARDINALS lower their masks.)

GALILEO (*to BELLARMIN*): Your Eminence.

BELLARMIN: Mr. Galilei, Cardinal Barberini.

GALILEO: Your Eminence.

BARBERINI: So you are the father of that lovely child!

BELLARMIN: Who is inordinately proud of being her father's daughter.

(They laugh.)

BARBERINI (*points his finger at GALILEO*): "The sun riseth and setteth and returneth to its place," saith the Bible. What saith Galilei?

GALILEO: Appearances are notoriously deceptive, Your Eminence. Once when I was so high, I was standing on a ship that was pulling away from the shore and I shouted, "The shore is moving!" I know now that it was the ship which was moving.

BARBERINI (*laughs*): You can't catch that man. I tell you, Bellarmin, his moons around Jupiter are hard nuts to crack. Unfortunately for me I happened to glance at a few papers on astronomy once. It is harder to get rid of than the itch.

BELLARMIN: Let's move with the times. If it makes navigation easier for sailors to use new charts based on a new hypothesis let them have them. We only have to scotch doctrines that contradict Holy Writ.

(He leans over the balustrade of the well and acknowledges various GUESTS.)

BARBERINI: But Bellarmin, you haven't caught on to this fellow. The scriptures don't satisfy him. Copernicus does.

GALILEO: Copernicus? "He that withholdeth corn the people shall curse him." Book of Proverbs.

BARBERINI: "A prudent man concealeth knowledge." Also Book of Proverbs.

GALILEO: "Where no oxen are, the stable is clean, but much increase is by the strength of the ox."

BARBERINI: "He that ruleth his spirit is better than he that taketh a city."

GALILEO: "But a broken spirit drieth up the bones." (*Pause.*) "Doth not wisdom cry?"

BARBERINI: "Can one walk on hot coals and his feet not be scorched?"—Welcome to Rome, Friend Galileo. You recall the legend of our city's origin? Two small boys found sustenance and refuge with a she-wolf and from that day we have paid the price for the she-wolf's milk. But the place is not bad. We have everything for your pleasure—from a scholarly dispute with Bellarmin to ladies of high degree. Look at that woman flaunting herself. No? He wants a weighty discussion! All right! (*To* GALILEO.) You people speak in terms of circles and ellipses and regular velocities—simple movements that the human mind can grasp—very convenient—but suppose Almighty God had taken it into his head to make the stars move like that . . . (*he describes an irregular motion with his fingers through the air*) . . . then where would you be?

GALILEO: My good man—the Almighty would have endowed us with brains like that . . . (*repeats the movement*) . . . so that we could grasp the movements . . . (*repeats the movement*) . . . like that. I believe in the brain.

BARBERINI: I consider the brain inadequate. He doesn't answer. He is too polite to tell me he considers *my* brain inadequate. What is one to do with him? Butter wouldn't melt in his mouth. All he wants to do is to prove that God made a few boners in astronomy. God didn't study his astronomy hard enough before he composed Holy Writ. (*To the* SECRETARIES.) Don't take anything down. This is a scientific discussion among friends.

BELLARMIN (*to* GALILEO): Does it not appear more probable—even to you—that the Creator knows more about his work than the created?

GALILEO: In his blindness man is liable to misread not only the sky but also the Bible.

BELLARMIN: The interpretation of the Bible is a matter for the ministers of God. (GALILEO *remains silent.*) At last you are quiet. (*He gestures to the* SECRETARIES. *They start writing.*) Tonight the Holy Office has decided that the theory according to which the earth goes around the sun is foolish, absurd, and a heresy. I am charged, Mr. Galilei, with cautioning you to abandon these teachings. (*To the* FIRST SECRETARY.) Would you repeat that?

FIRST SECRETARY (*reading*): "His Eminence, Cardinal Bellarmin, to the aforesaid Galilei: The Holy Office has resolved that the theory according to which the earth goes around the sun is foolish, absurd, and a heresy. I am charged, Mr. Galilei, with cautioning you to abandon these teachings."

GALILEO (*rocking on his base*): But the facts!

BARBERINI (*consoling*): Your findings have been ratified by the Papal Observatory, Galilei. That should be most flattering to you . . .

BELLARMIN (*cutting in*): The Holy Office formulated the decree without going into details.

GALILEO (*to* BARBERINI): Do you realize, the future of all scientific research is . . .

BELLARMIN (*cutting in*): Completely assured, Mr. Galilei. It is not given to man to know the truth: it is granted to him to seek after the truth. Science is the legitimate and beloved daughter of the Church. She must have confidence in the Church.

GALILEO (*infuriated*): I would not try confidence by whistling her too often.

BARBERINI (*quickly*): Be careful what you're doing—you'll be throwing out the baby with the bath water, friend Galilei. (*Serious.*) We need you more than you need us.

BELLARMIN: Well, it is time we introduced our distinguished friend to our guests. The whole country talks of him!

BARBERINI: Let us replace our masks, Bellarmin. Poor Galilei hasn't got one.

(*He laughs. They take* GALILEO *out.*)

FIRST SECRETARY: Did you get his last sentence?

SECOND SECRETARY: Yes. Do you have what he said about believing in the brain?

(*Another cardinal—the* INQUISITOR—*enters.*)

INQUISITOR: Did the conference take place?

(*The* FIRST SECRETARY *hands him the papers and the* INQUISITOR *dismisses the* SECRETARIES. *They go. The* INQUISITOR *sits down and starts to read the transcription. Two or three* YOUNG LADIES *skitter across the stage; they see the* INQUISITOR *and curtsy as they go.*)

YOUNG GIRL: Who was that?

HER FRIEND: The Cardinal Inquisitor.

(*They giggle and go. Enter* VIRGINIA. *She curtsies as she goes. The* INQUISITOR *stops her.*)

INQUISITOR: Good evening, my child. Beautiful night. May I congratulate you on your betrothal? Your young man comes from a fine family. Are you staying with us here in Rome?

VIRGINIA: Not now, Your Eminence. I must go home to prepare for the wedding.

INQUISITOR: Ah. You are accompanying your father to Florence. That should please him. Science must be cold comfort in a home. Your youth and warmth will keep him down to earth. It is easy to get lost up there. (*He gestures to the sky.*)

VIRGINIA: He doesn't talk to me about the stars, Your Eminence.

INQUISITOR: No. (*He laughs.*) They don't eat fish in the fisherman's house. I can tell you something about astronomy. My child, it seems that God has blessed our modern astronomers with imaginations. It is quite alarming! Do you know that the earth—which we old fogies supposed to be so large—has shrunk to something no bigger than a walnut, and the new universe has grown so vast that prelates—and even cardinals—look like ants. Why, God Almighty might lose sight of a Pope! I wonder if I know your Father Confessor.

VIRGINIA: Father Christopherus, from Saint Ursula's at Florence, Your Eminence.

INQUISITOR: My dear child, your father will need you. Not so much now perhaps, but one of these days. You are pure, and there is strength in purity. Greatness is sometimes, indeed often, too heavy a burden for those to whom God has granted it. What man is so great that he has no place in a prayer? But I am keeping you, my dear. Your fiancé will be jealous of me, and I am afraid your father will never forgive me for holding forth on astronomy. Go to your dancing and remember me to Father Christopherus.

(VIRGINIA *kisses his ring and runs off. The* INQUISITOR *resumes his reading.*)

SCENE 7

Galileo, feeling grim,
A young monk came to visit him.
The monk was born of common folk.
It was of science that they spoke.

(*Garden of Florentine Ambassador in Rome. Distant hum of a great city.* GALILEO *and the* LITTLE MONK *of scene 5 are talking.*)

GALILEO: Let's hear it. That robe you're wearing gives you the right to say whatever you want to say. Let's hear it.

LITTLE MONK: I have studied physics, Mr. Galilei.

GALILEO: That might help us if it enabled you to admit that two and two are four.

LITTLE MONK: Mr. Galilei, I have spent four sleepless nights trying to reconcile the decree that I have read with the moons of Jupiter that I have seen. This morning I decided to come to see you after I had said Mass.

GALILEO: To tell me that Jupiter has no moons?

LITTLE MONK: No, I found out that I think the decree a wise decree. It has shocked me into realizing that free research has its dangers. I have had to decide to give up astronomy. However, I felt the impulse to confide in you some of the motives which have impelled even a passionate physicist to abandon his work.

GALILEO: Your motives are familiar to me.

LITTLE MONK: You mean, of course, the special powers invested in certain commissions of the Holy Office? But there is something else. I would like to talk to you about my family. I do not come from the great city. My parents are peasants in the Campagna, who know about the cultivation of the olive tree, and not much about anything else. Too often these days when I am trying to concentrate on tracking down the moons of Jupiter, I see my parents. I see them sitting by the fire with my sister, eating their curded cheese. I see the beams of the ceiling above them, which the smoke of centuries has blackened, and I can see the veins stand out on their toil-worn hands, and the little spoons in their hands. They scrape a living, and underlying their poverty there is a sort of order. There are routines. The routine of scrubbing the floors, the routine of the seasons in the olive orchard, the routine of paying taxes. The troubles that come to them are recurrent troubles. My father did not get his poor bent back all at once, but little by little, year by year, in the olive orchard; just as year after year, with unfailing regularity, childbirth has made my mother more and more sexless. They draw the strength they need to sweat with their loaded baskets up the stony paths, to bear children, even to eat, from the sight of the trees greening each year anew, from the reproachful face of the soil, which is never satisfied, and from the little church and Bible texts they hear there on Sunday. They have been told that God relies upon them and that the pageant of the world has been written around them that they may be tested in the important or unimportant parts handed out to them. How could they take it, were I to tell them that they are on a lump of stone ceaselessly spinning in empty space, circling around a second-rate star? What, then, would be the use of their patience, their acceptance of misery? What comfort, then, the Holy Scriptures, which have mercifully explained their crucifixion? The Holy Scriptures would then be proved full of mistakes. No, I see them begin to look frightened. I see them slowly put their spoons down on the table. They would feel cheated. "There is no eye watching over us, after all," they would say. "We have to start out on our own, at our time of life. Nobody has planned a part for us beyond this wretched one on a worthless star. There is no meaning in our misery. Hunger is just not having eaten. It is no test of strength. Effort is just stooping and carrying. It is not a virtue." Can you understand that I read into the decree of the Holy Office a noble motherly pity and a great goodness of the soul?

GALILEO (*embarrasssed*): Hm, well at least you have found out that it is not a question of the satellites of Jupiter, but of the peasants of the Campagna! And don't try to break me down by the halo of beauty that radiates from old age. How does a pearl develop in an oyster? A jagged grain of sand makes its way into the oyster's shell and makes its life unbearable. The oyster exudes slime to cover the grain of sand and the slime eventually hardens into a pearl. The oyster nearly dies in the process. To hell with the pearl, give me the healthy oyster! And virtues are not exclusive to misery. If your parents were prosperous and happy, they might develop the virtues of happiness and prosperity. Today the virtues of exhaustion are caused by the exhausted land. For that my new water pumps could work more wonders than their ridiculous superhuman efforts. Be fruitful and multiply: for war will cut down the population, and our fields are barren! (*A pause.*) Shall I lie to your people?

LITTLE MONK: We must be silent from the highest of motives: the inward peace of less fortunate souls.

GALILEO: My dear man, as a bonus for not meddling with your parents' peace, the authorities are tendering me, on a silver platter, persecution-free, my share of the fat sweated from your parents, who, as you know, were made in God's image. Should I condone this decree, my motives might not be disinterested: easy life, no persecution, and so on.

LITTLE MONK: Mr. Galilei, I am a priest.

GALILEO: You are also a physicist. How can new machinery be evolved to domesticate the river water if we physicists are forbidden to study, discuss, and pool our findings about the greatest machinery of all, the machinery of the heavenly bodies? Can I reconcile my findings on the paths of falling bodies with the current belief in the tracks of witches on broom sticks? (*A pause.*) I am sorry—I shouldn't have said that.

LITTLE MONK: You don't think that the truth, if it is the truth, would make its way without us?

GALILEO: No! No! No! As much of the truth gets through as we push through. You talk about the Campagna peasants as if they were the moss on their huts. Naturally, if they don't get a move on and learn to think for themselves, the most efficient of irrigation systems cannot help them. I can see their divine patience, but where is their divine fury?

LITTLE MONK (*helpless*): They are old!

(GALILEO *stands for a moment, beaten; he cannot meet the* LITTLE MONK's *eyes. He takes a manuscript from the table and throws it violently on the ground.*)

LITTLE MONK: What is that?

GALILEO: Here is writ what draws the ocean when it ebbs and flows. Let it lie there. Thou shalt not read. (LITTLE MONK *has picked up the manuscript.*) Already!

An apple of the tree of knowledge, he can't wait, he wolfs it down. He will rot in hell for all eternity. Look at him, where are his manners?—Sometimes I think I would let them imprison me in a place a thousand feet beneath the earth where no light could reach me, if in exchange I could find out what stuff that is: "Light." The bad thing is that, when I find something, I have to boast about it like a lover or a drunkard or a traitor. That is a hopeless vice and leads to the abyss. I wonder how long I shall be content to discuss it with my dog!

LITTLE MONK (*immersed in the manuscript*): I don't understand this sentence.

GALILEO: I'll explain it to you, I'll explain it to you.

(*They are sitting on the floor.*)

SCENE 8

Eight long years with tongue in cheek
Of what he knew he did not speak.
Then temptation grew too great
And Galileo challenged fate.

(GALILEO's *house in Florence again.* GALILEO *is supervising his* ASSISTANTS—ANDREA, FEDERZONI, *and the* LITTLE MONK—*who are about to prepare an experiment.* MRS. SARTI *and* VIRGINIA *are at a long table sewing bridal linen. There is a new telescope, larger than the old one. At the moment it is covered with a cloth.*)

ANDREA (*looking up a schedule*): Thursday. Afternoon. Floating bodies again. Ice, bowl of water, scales, and it says here an iron needle. Aristotle.

VIRGINIA: Ludovico likes to entertain. We must take care to be neat. His mother notices every stitch. She doesn't approve of father's books.

MRS. SARTI: That's all a thing of the past. He hasn't published a book for years.

VIRGINIA: That's true. Oh Sarti, it's fun sewing a trousseau.

MRS. SARTI: Virginia, I want to talk to you. You are very young, and you have no mother, and your father is putting those pieces of ice in water, and marriage is too serious a business to go into blind. Now you should go to see a real astronomer from the university and have him cast your horoscope so you know where you stand. (VIRGINIA *giggles.*) What's the matter?

VIRGINIA: I've been already.

MRS. SARTI: Tell Sarti.

VIRGINIA: I have to be careful for three months now because the sun is in Capricorn, but after that I get a favorable ascendant, and I can undertake a journey if I am careful of Uranus, as I'm a Scorpion.

MRS. SARTI: What about Ludovico?

VIRGINIA: He's a Leo, the astronomer said. Leos are sensual. (*Giggles.*)

(*There is a knock at the door, it opens. Enter the* RECTOR OF THE UNIVERSITY, *the philosopher of scene 4, bringing a book.*)

RECTOR (*to* VIRGINIA): This is about the burning issue of the moment. He may want to glance over it. My faculty would appreciate his comments. No, don't disturb him now, my dear. Every minute one takes of your father's time is stolen from Italy. (*He goes.*)

VIRGINIA: Federzoni! The rector of the university brought this.

(FEDERZONI *takes it.*)

GALILEO: What's it about?

FEDERZONI (*spelling*): DE MACULIS IN SOLE.

ANDREA: Oh, it's on the sun spots!

(ANDREA *comes to one side, and the* LITTLE MONK *the other, to look at the book.*)

ANDREA: A new one!

(FEDERZONI *resentfully puts the book into their hands and continues with the preparation of the experiment.*)

ANDREA: Listen to this dedication. (*Quotes.*) "To the greatest living authority on physics, Galileo Galilei."—I read Fabricius' paper the other day. Fabricius says the spots are clusters of planets between us and the sun.

LITTLE MONK: Doubtful.

GALILEO (*noncommittal*): Yes?

ANDREA: Paris and Prague hold that they are vapors from the sun. Federzoni doubts that.

FEDERZONI: Me? You leave me out. I said "hm," that was all. And don't discuss new things before me. I can't read the material, it's in Latin. (*He drops the scales and stands trembling with fury.*) Tell me, can I doubt anything?

(GALILEO *walks over and picks up the scales silently. Pause.*)

LITTLE MONK: There is happiness in doubting, I wonder why.

ANDREA: Aren't we going to take this up?

GALILEO: At the moment we are investigating floating bodies.

ANDREA: Mother has baskets full of letters from all over Europe asking his opinion.

FEDERZONI: The question is whether you can afford to remain silent.

GALILEO: I cannot afford to be smoked on a wood fire like a ham.

ANDREA (*surprised*): Ah. You think the sun spots may have something to do with that again? (GALILEO *does not answer.*)

ANDREA: Well, we stick to fiddling about with bits of ice in water. That can't hurt you.

GALILEO: Correct.—Our thesis!

ANDREA: All things that are lighter than water float, and all things that are heavier sink.

GALILEO: Aristotle says—

LITTLE MONK (*reading out of a book, translating*): "A broad and flat disk of ice, although heavier than water, still floats, because it is unable to divide the water."

GALILEO: Well. Now I push the ice below the surface. I take away the pressure of my hands. What happens?

(*Pause.*)

LITTLE MONK: It rises to the surface.

GALILEO: Correct. It seems to be able to divide the water as it's coming up, doesn't it?

LITTLE MONK: Could it be lighter than water after all?

GALILEO: Aha!

ANDREA: Then all things that are lighter than water float, and all things that are heavier sink. Q.e.d.°

GALILEO: Not at all. Hand me that iron needle. Heavier than water? (*They all nod.*) A piece of paper. (*He places the needle on a piece of paper and floats it on the surface of the water. Pause.*) Do not be hasty with your conclusion. (*Pause.*) What happens?

FEDERZONI: The paper has sunk, the needle is floating.

VIRGINIA: What's the matter?

MRS. SARTI: Every time I hear them laugh it sends shivers down my spine.

(*There is a knocking at the outer door.*)

MRS. SARTI: Who's that at the door?

(*Enter* LUDOVICO. VIRGINIA *runs to him. They embrace.* LUDOVICO *is followed by a* SERVANT *with baggage.*)

MRS. SARTI: Well!

VIRGINIA: Oh! Why didn't you write that you were coming?

LUDOVICO: I decided on the spur of the moment. I was over inspecting our vineyards at Bucciole. I couldn't keep away.

GALILEO: Who's that?

LITTLE MONK: Miss Virginia's intended. What's the matter with your eyes?

GALILEO (*blinking*): Oh yes, it's Ludovico, so it is. Well! Sarti, get a jug of that Sicilian wine, the old kind. We celebrate.

Q.e.d., In Latin, *quod erat demonstrandum,* "which was to be demonstrated," the usual ending on a logical examination using Aristotelian logic. The point is that it is not demonstrated; the experiment with the needle and the paper demonstrates the power of surface tension, which contradicts Andrea's earlier statement. Experimentation, in other words, is the final arbiter of what is true, not rules such as Andrea establishes.

(*Everybody sits down.* MRS. SARTI *has left, followed by* LUDOVICO'S SERVANT.)

GALILEO: Well, Ludovico, old man. How are the horses?

LUDOVICO: The horses are fine.

GALILEO: Fine.

LUDOVICO: But those vineyards need a firm hand. (*To* VIRGINIA.) You look pale. Country life will suit you. Mother's planning on September.

VIRGINIA: I suppose I oughtn't, but stay here, I've got something to show you.

LUDOVICO: What?

VIRGINIA: Never mind. I won't be ten minutes. (*She runs out.*)

LUDOVICO: How's life these days, sir?

GALILEO: Dull.—How was the journey?

LUDOVICO: Dull.—Before I forget, mother sends her congratulations on your admirable tact over the latest rumblings of science.

GALILEO: Thank her from me.

LUDOVICO: Christopher Clavius had all Rome on its ears. He said he was afraid that the turning-around-business might crop up again on account of these spots on the sun.

ANDREA: Clavius is on the same track! (*To* LUDOVICO.) My mother's baskets are full of letters from all over Europe asking Mr. Galilei's opinion.

GALILEO: I am engaged in investigating the habits of floating bodies. Any harm in that?

(MRS. SARTI *reenters, followed by the* SERVANT. *They bring wine and glasses on a tray.*)

GALILEO (*hands out the wine*): What news from the Holy City, apart from the prospect of my sins?

LUDOVICO: The Holy Father is on his death bed. Hadn't you heard?

LITTLE MONK: My goodness! What about the succession?

LUDOVICO: All the talk is of Barberini.

GALILEO: Barberini?

ANDREA: Mr. Galilei knows Barberini.

LITTLE MONK: Cardinal Barberini is a mathematician.

FEDERZONI: A scientist in the chair of Peter!

(*Pause.*)

GALILEO (*cheering up enormously*): This means change. We might live to see the day, Federzoni, when we don't have to whisper that two and two are four. (*To* LUDOVICO.) I like this wine. Don't you, Ludovico?

LUDOVICO: I like it.

GALILEO: I know the hill where it is grown. The slope is steep and stony, the grape almost blue. I am fond of this wine.

LUDOVICO: Yes, sir.

GALILEO: There are shadows in this wine. It is almost sweet but just stops short.—Andrea, clear that stuff away, ice, bowl and needle.—I cherish the conso-

lations of the flesh. I have no patience with cowards who call them weaknesses. I say there is a certain achievement in enjoying things.

(*The* PUPILS *get up and go to the experiment table.*)

LITTLE MONK: What are we to do?

FEDERZONI: He is starting on the sun.

(*They begin with clearing up.*)

ANDREA (*singing in a low voice*): The Bible proves the earth stands still,
The Pope, he swears with tears:
The earth stands still. To prove it so
He takes it by the ears.

LUDOVICO: What's the excitement?

MRS. SARTI: You're not going to start those hellish goings-on again, Mr. Galilei?

ANDREA: And gentlefolk, they say so too.
Each learned doctor proves,
(If you grease his palm): The earth stands still.
And yet—and yet it moves.

GALILEO: Barberini is in the ascendant, so your mother is uneasy, and you're sent to investigate me. Correct me if I am wrong, Ludovico. Clavius is right: These spots on the sun interest me.

ANDREA: We might find out that the sun also revolves. How would you like that, Ludovico?

GALILEO: Do you like my wine, Ludovico?

LUDOVICO: I told you I did, sir.

GALILEO: You really like it?

LUDOVICO: I like it.

GALILEO: Tell me, Ludovico, would you consider going so far as to accept a man's wine or his daughter without insisting that he drop his profession? I have no wish to intrude, but have the moons of Jupiter affected Virginia's bottom?

MRS. SARTI: That isn't funny, it's just vulgar. I am going for Virginia.

LUDOVICO (*keeps her back*): Marriages in families such as mine are not arranged on a basis of sexual attraction alone.

GALILEO: Did they keep you back from marrying my daughter for eight years because I was on probation?

LUDOVICO: My future wife must take her place in the family pew.

GALILEO: You mean, if the daughter of a bad man sat in your family pew, your peasants might stop paying the rent?

LUDOVICO: In a sort of way.

GALILEO: When I was your age, the only person I allowed to rap me on the knuckles was my girl.

LUDOVICO: My mother was assured that you had undertaken not to get mixed up in this turning-around-business again, sir.

GALILEO: We had a conservative Pope then.

MRS. SARTI: Had! His Holiness is not dead yet!

GALILEO (*with relish*): Pretty nearly.

MRS. SARTI: That man will weigh a chip of ice fifty times, but when it comes to something that's convenient, he believes it blindly. "Is His Holiness dead?"—"Pretty nearly!"

LUDOVICO: You will find, sir, if His Holiness pàsses away, the new Pope, whoever he turns out to be, will respect the convictions held by the solid families of the country.

GALILEO (*to* ANDREA): That remains to be seen.—Andrea, get out the screen. We'll throw the image of the sun on our screen to save our eyes.

LITTLE MONK: I thought you'd been working at it. Do you know when I guessed it? When you didn't recognize Mr. Marsili.

MRS. SARTI: If my son has to go to hell for sticking to you, that's my affair, but you have no right to trample on your daughter's happiness.

LUDOVICO (*to his* SERVANT): Giuseppe, take my baggage back to the coach, will you?

MRS. SARTI: This will kill her. (*She runs out, still clutching the jug.*)

LUDOVICO (*politely*): Mr. Galilei, if we Marsilis were to countenance teachings frowned on by the church, it would unsettle our peasants. Bear in mind: these poor people in their brute state get everything upside down. They are nothing but animals. They will never comprehend the finer points of astronomy. Why, two months ago a rumor went around, an apple had been found on a pear tree, and they left their work in the fields to discuss it.

GALILEO (*interested*): Did they?

LUDOVICO: I have seen the day when my poor mother has had to have a dog whipped before their eyes to remind them to keep their place. Oh, you may have seen the waving corn from the window of your comfortable coach. You have, no doubt, nibbled our olives, and absentmindedly eaten our cheese, but you can have no idea how much responsibility that sort of thing entails.

GALILEO: Young man, I do not eat my cheese absentmindedly. (*To* ANDREA.) Are we ready?

ANDREA: Yes, sir.

GALILEO (*leaves* LUDOVICO *and adjusts the mirror*): You would not confine your whippings to dogs to remind your peasants to keep their places, would you, Marsili?

LUDOVICO (*after a pause*): Mr. Galilei, you have a wonderful brain, it's a pity.

LITTLE MONK (*astonished*): He threatened you.

GALILEO: Yes. And he threatened you too. We might unsettle his peasants. Your sister, Fulganzio, who works the lever of the olive press, might laugh out loud if she heard the sun is not a gilded coat of arms but a lever too. The earth turns because the sun turns it.

ANDREA: That could interest his steward too and even his money lender—and the seaport towns . . .

FEDERZONI: None of them speak Latin.

GALILEO: I might write in plain language. The work we do is exacting. Who would go through the strain for less than the population at large!

LUDOVICO: I see you have made your decision. It was inevitable. You will always be a slave of your passions. Excuse me to Virginia, I think it's as well I don't see her now.

GALILEO: The dowry is at your disposal at any time.

LUDOVICO: Good afternoon. (*He goes, followed by the* SERVANT.)

ANDREA: Exit Ludovico. To hell with all Marsilis, Villanis, Orsinis, Canes, Nuccolis, Soldanieris . . .

FEDERZONI: . . . who ordered the earth stand still because their castles might be shaken loose if it revolves . . .

LITTLE MONK: . . . and who only kiss the Pope's feet as long as he uses them to trample on the people. God made the physical world, God made the human brain. God will allow physics.

ANDREA: They will try to stop us.

GALILEO: Thus we enter the observation of these spots on the sun in which we are interested, at our own risk, not counting on protection from a problematical new Pope . . .

ANDREA: . . . but with great likelihood of dispelling Fabricius' vapors, and the shadows of Paris and Prague, and of establishing the rotation of the sun . . .

GALILEO: . . . and with *some* likelihood of establishing the rotation of the sun. My intention is not to prove that I was right but to find out *whether* I was right. "Abandon hope all ye who enter—an observation." Before assuming these phenomena are spots, which would suit us, let us first set about proving that they are not—fried fish. We crawl by inches. What we find today we will wipe from the blackboard tomorrow and reject it—unless it shows up again the day after tomorrow. And if we find anything which would suit us, that thing we will eye with particular distrust. In fact, we will approach this observing of the sun with the implacable determination to prove that the earth stands still and only if hopelessly defeated in this pious undertaking can we allow ourselves to wonder if we may not have been right all the time: the earth revolves. Take the cloth off the telescope and turn it on the sun.

(*Quietly they start work. When the corruscating image of the sun is focused on the screen,* VIRGINIA *enters hurriedly, her wedding dress on, her hair disheveled,* MRS. SARTI *with her, carrying her wedding veil. The two women realize what has happened.* VIRGINIA *faints.* ANDREA, LITTLE MONK, *and* GALILEO *rush to her.* FEDERZONI *continues working.*)

SCENE 9

On April Fool's Day, thirty two,
Of science there was much ado.
People had learned from Galilei:
They used his teaching in their way.

(*Around the corner from the marketplace a* STREET SINGER *and his* WIFE, *who is costumed to represent the earth in a skeleton globe made of thin bands of brass, are holding the attention of a sprinkling of representative citizens, some in masquerade who were on their way to see the carnival procession. From the marketplace the noise of an impatient crowd.*)

BALLAD SINGER (*accompanied by his* WIFE *on the guitar*): When the Almighty made the universe
He made the earth and then he made the sun.
Then round the earth he bade the sun to turn—
That's in the Bible, Genesis, Chapter One.
And from that time all beings here below
Were in obedient circles meant to go:

Around the Pope the cardinals
Around the cardinals the bishops
Around the bishops the secretaries
Around the secretaries the aldermen
Around the aldermen the craftsmen
Around the craftsmen the servants
Around the servants the dogs, the chickens, and
the beggars.

(*A conspicuous* REVELLER—*henceforth called the* SPINNER—*has slowly caught on and is exhibiting his idea of spinning around. He does not lose dignity, he faints with mock grace.*)

BALLAD SINGER: Up stood the learned Galileo
Glanced briefly at the sun
And said: "Almighty God was wrong
In Genesis, Chapter One!"

Now that was rash, my friends, it is no matter small
For heresy will spread today like foul diseases.
Change Holy Writ, forsooth? What will be left at
all?
Why: each of us would say and do just what he
pleases!

(*Three wretched* EXTRAS, *employed by the chamber of commerce, enter. Two of them, in ragged costumes, moodily bear a litter with a mock throne. The third sits on the throne. He wears sacking, a false beard, a prop crown, he carries a prop orb and sceptre, and around his chest the inscription* "THE KING OF HUNGARY." *The litter has a card with* "No. 4" *written on it. The litter bearers dump him down and listen to the* BALLAD SINGER.)

BALLAD SINGER: Good people, what will come to pass
If Galileo's teachings spread?
No altar boy will serve the Mass
No servant girl will make the bed.

Now that is grave, my friends, it is no matter small:
For independent spirit spreads like foul diseases!
(Yet life is sweet and man is weak and after all—
How nice it is, for a little change, to do just as one
pleases!)

(*The* BALLAD SINGER *takes over the guitar. His* WIFE *dances around him, illustrating the motion of the earth. A* COBBLER'S BOY *with a pair of resplendent lacquered boots hung over his shoulder has been jumping up and down in mock excitement. There are three more* CHILDREN, *dressed as grownups among the* SPECTATORS, *two together and a single one with mother. The* COBBLER'S BOY *takes the three* CHILDREN *in hand, forms a chain, and leads it, moving to the music, in and out among the* SPECTATORS, *"whipping" the chain so that the last child bumps into people. On the way past a* PEASANT WOMAN, *he steals an egg from her basket. She gestures to him to return it. As he passes her again he quietly breaks the egg over her head. The* KING OF HUNGARY *ceremoniously hands his orb to one of his bearers, marches down with mock dignity, and chastises the* COBBLER'S BOY. *The parents remove the three* CHILDREN. *The unseemliness subsides.*)

BALLAD SINGER: The carpenters take wood and build
Their houses—not the church's pews.
And members of the cobblers' guild
Now boldly walk the streets—in shoes.
The tenant kicks the noble lord
Quite off the land he owned—like that!
The milk his wife once gave the priest
Now makes (at last!) her children fat.

Ts, ts, ts, ts, my friends, this is no matter small
For independent spirit spreads like foul diseases
People must keep their place, some down and some
on top!
(Though it is nice, for a little change, to do just as
one pleases!)

(*The* COBBLER'S BOY *has put on the lacquered boots he was carrying. He struts off. The* BALLAD SINGER *takes over the guitar again. His* WIFE *dances around him in increased tempo. A* MONK *has been standing near a* RICH COUPLE, *who are in subdued costly clothes, without masks: shocked at the song, he now leaves. A* DWARF *in the costume of an astronomer turns his telescope on the departing* MONK, *thus drawing attention to the* RICH COUPLE. *In imitation of the* COBBLER'S BOY, *the* SPINNER *forms a chain of grownups. They move to the music, in and out, and between the* RICH COUPLE. *The* SPINNER *changes the* GENTLEMAN's *bonnet for the ragged hat of a* BEGGAR. *The* GENTLEMAN *decides to take this in good part, and a* GIRL *is emboldened to take his dagger. The* GENTLEMAN *is miffed, throws the* BEGGAR's *hat back. The* BEGGAR *discards the* GENTLEMAN's *bonnet and drops it on the ground. The* KING OF HUNGARY *has walked from his throne, taken an egg from the* PEASANT WOMAN, *and paid for it. He now ceremoniously breaks it over the* GENTLEMAN's *head as he is bending down to pick up his bonnet. The* GENTLEMAN *conducts the* LADY *away from the scene. The* KING OF HUNGARY, *about to resume his throne, finds one of the* CHILDREN *sitting on it. The* GENTLEMAN *returns to retrieve his dagger. Merriment. The* BALLAD SINGER *wanders off. This is part of his routine. His* WIFE *sings to the* SPINNER.)

WIFE: Now speaking for myself I feel
That I could also do with a change.
You know, for me . . . (*Turning to a reveller*)
. . . *you have appeal*
Maybe tonight we could arrange . . .

(*The* DWARF-ASTRONOMER *has been amusing the people by focusing his telescope on her legs. The* BALLAD SINGER *has returned.*)

BALLAD SINGER: No, no, no, no, no, stop, Galileo, stop!
For independent spirit spreads like foul diseases
People must keep their place, some down and
some on top!
(Though it is nice, for a little change, to do just as
one pleases!)

(*The* SPECTATORS *stand embarrassed. A* GIRL *laughs loudly.*)

BALLAD SINGER AND HIS WIFE: Good people who have
trouble here below
In serving cruel lords and gentle Jesus
Who bids you turn the other cheek just so . . .
(*With mimicry.*)
While they prepare to strike the second blow:
Obedience will never cure your woe
So each of you wake up and do just as he pleases!

(*The* BALLAD SINGER *and his* WIFE *hurriedly start to try to sell pamphlets to the* SPECTATORS.)

BALLAD SINGER: Read all about the earth going round
the sun, two centesimi only. As proved by the great
Galileo. Two centesimi only. Written by a local
scholar. Understandable to one and all. Buy one
for your friends, your children and your aunty
Rosa, two centesimi only. Abbreviated but complete. Fully illustrated with pictures of the planets,
including Venus, two centesimi only.

(*During the speech of the* BALLAD SINGER *we hear the carnival procession approaching followed by laughter. A* REVELLER *rushes in.*)

REVELLER: The procession!

(*The litter bearers speedily joggle out the* KING OF HUNGARY. *The* SPECTATORS *turn and look at the first float of the procession, which now makes its appearance. It bears a gigantic figure of* GALILEO, *holding in one hand an open Bible with the pages crossed out. The other hand points to the Bible, and the head mechanically turns from side to side as if to say "No! No!")*

A LOUD VOICE: Galileo, the Bible killer!

(*The laughter from the marketplace becomes uproarious. The* MONK *comes flying from the marketplace followed by delighted* CHILDREN.)

SCENE 10

The depths are hot, the heights are chill
The streets are loud, the court is still.

(*Antechamber and staircase in the Medicean palace in Florence.* GALILEO, *with a book under his arm, waits with his* DAUGHTER *to be admitted to the presence of the* PRINCE.)

VIRGINIA: They are a long time.

GALILEO: Yes.

VIRGINIA: Who is that funny-looking man? (*She indicates the* INFORMER *who has entered casually and seated himself in the background, taking no apparent notice of* GALILEO.)

GALILEO: I don't know.

VIRGINIA: It's not the first time I have seen him around.
He gives me the creeps.

GALILEO: Nonsense. We're in Florence, not among robbers in the mountains of Corsica.

VIRGINIA: Here comes the Rector.

(*The* RECTOR *comes down the stairs.*)

GALILEO: Gaffone is a bore. He attaches himself to you.

(*The* RECTOR *passes, scarcely nodding.*)

GALILEO: My eyes are bad today. Did he acknowledge
us?

VIRGINIA: Barely. (*Pause.*) What's in your book? Will
they say it's heretical?

GALILEO: You hang around church too much. And getting up at dawn and scurrying to Mass is ruining
your skin. You pray for me, don't you?

(*A* MAN *comes down the stairs.*)

VIRGINIA: Here's Mr. Matti. You designed a machine
for his iron foundries.

MATTI: How were the squabs, Mr. Galilei? (*Low.*) My
brother and I had a good laugh the other day. He
picked up a racy pamphlet against the Bible somewhere. It quoted you.

GALILEO: The squabs, Matti, were wonderful, thank
you again. Pamphlets I know nothing about. The
Bible and Homer are my favorite reading.

MATTI: No necessity to be cautious with me, Mr. Galilei.
I am on your side. I am not a man who knows about
the motions of the stars, but you have championed
the freedom to teach new things. Take that mechanical cultivator they have in Germany which you
described to me. I can tell you, it will never be used
in this country. The same circles that are hampering
you now will forbid the physicians at Bologna to cut

up corpses for research. Do you know, they have such things as money markets in Amsterdam and in London? Schools for business, too. Regular papers with news. Here we are not even free to make money. I have a stake in your career. They are against iron foundries because they say the gathering of so many workers in one place fosters immorality! If they ever try anything, Mr. Galilei, remember you have friends in all walks of life including an iron founder. Good luck to you. (*He goes.*)

GALILEO: Good man, but need he be so affectionate in public? His voice carries. They will always claim him as their spiritual leader particularly in places where it doesn't help me at all. I have written a book about the mechanics of the firmament, that is all. What they do or don't do with it is not my concern.

VIRGINIA (*loud*): If people only knew how you disagreed with those goings-on all over the country last All Fools' day.

GALILEO: Yes. Offer honey to a bear, and lose your arm if the beast is hungry.

VIRGINIA (*low*): Did the Prince ask you to come here today?

GALILEO: I sent word I was coming. He will want the book, he has paid for it. My health hasn't been any too good lately. I may accept Sagredo's invitation to stay with him in Padua for a few weeks.

VIRGINIA: You couldn't manage without your books.

GALILEO: Sagredo has an excellent library.

VIRGINIA: We haven't had this month's salary yet—

GALILEO: Yes. (*The* CARDINAL INQUISITOR *passes down the staircase. He bows deeply in answer to* GALILEO'*s bow.*) What is he doing in Florence? If they try to do anything to me, the new Pope will meet them with an iron NO. And the Prince is my pupil, he would never have me extradited.

VIRGINIA: Psst. The Lord Chamberlain.

(*The* LORD CHAMBERLAIN *comes down the stairs.*)

LORD CHAMBERLAIN: His Highness had hoped to find time for you, Mr. Galilei. Unfortunately, he has to leave immediately to judge the parade at the Riding Academy. On what business did you wish to see His Highness?

GALILEO: I wanted to present my book to His Highness.

LORD CHAMBERLAIN: How are your eyes today?

GALILEO: So, so. With His Highness' permission, I am dedicating the book . . .

LORD CHAMBERLAIN: Your eyes are a matter of great concern to His Highness. Could it be that you have been looking too long and too often through your marvelous tube? (*He leaves without accepting the book.*)

VIRGINIA (*greatly agitated*): Father, I am afraid.

GALILEO: He didn't take the book, did he? (*Low and resolute.*) Keep a straight face. We are not going home, but to the house of the lens-grinder. There is a coach and horses in his backyard. Keep your eyes to the front, don't look back at that man.

(*They start. The* LORD CHAMBERLAIN *comes back.*)

LORD CHAMBERLAIN: Oh, Mr. Galilei! His Highness has just charged me to inform you that the Florentine Court is no longer in a position to oppose the request of the Holy Inquisition to interrogate you in Rome.

SCENE 11

The Pope

(*A chamber in the Vatican. The* POPE, URBAN VIII—*formerly* CARDINAL BARBERINI—*is giving audience to the* CARDINAL INQUISITOR. *The trampling and shuffling of many feet is heard throughout the scene from the adjoining corridors. During the scene the* POPE *is being robed for the conclave he is about to attend: at the beginning of the scene he is plainly* BARBERINI, *but as the scene proceeds he is more and more obscured by grandiose vestments.*)

POPE: No! No! No!

INQUISITOR (*referring to the owners of the shuffling feet*): Doctors of all chairs from the universities, representatives of the special orders of the church, representatives of the clergy as a whole who have come believing with childlike faith in the word of God as set forth in the Scriptures, who have come to hear Your Holiness confirm their faith: and Your Holiness is really going to tell them that the Bible can no longer be regarded as the alphabet of truth?

POPE: I will not set myself up against the multiplication table. No!

INQUISITOR: Ah, that is what these people say, that it is the multiplication table. Their cry is, "The figures compel us," but where do these figures come from? Plainly they come from doubt. These men doubt everything. Can society stand on doubt and not on faith? "Thou are my master, but I doubt whether it is for the best." "This is my neighbor's house and my neighbor's wife, but why shouldn't they belong to me?" After the plague, after the new war, after the unparalleled disaster of the Reformation, your dwindling flock look to their shepherd, and now the mathematicians turn their tubes on the sky and announce to the world that you have not the best advice about the heavens either—up to now your only uncontested sphere of influence. This Galilei started meddling in machines at an early age. Now that men in ships are venturing on the great oceans—I am not against that of course—they are putting their faith in a brass bowl they call a compass and not in Almighty God.

POPE: This man is the greatest physicist of our time. He is the light of Italy, and not just any muddlehead.

INQUISITOR: Would we have had to arrest him otherwise? This bad man knows what he is doing, not writing his books in Latin, but in the jargon of the marketplace.

POPE (occupied with the shuffling feet): That was not in the best of taste. (A pause.) These shuffling feet are making me nervous.

INQUISITOR: May they be more telling than my words, Your Holiness. Shall all these go from you with doubt in their hearts?

POPE: This man has friends. What about Versailles?° What about the Viennese court? They will call Holy Church a cesspool for defunct ideas. Keep your hands off him.

INQUISITOR: In practice it will never get far. He is a man of the flesh. He would soften at once.

POPE: He has more enjoyment in him than any man I ever saw. He loves eating and drinking and thinking. To excess. He indulges in thinking bouts! He cannot say no to an old wine or a new thought. (Furious.) I do not want a condemnation of physical facts. I do not want to hear battle cries: Church, church, church! Reason, reason, reason! (Pause.) These shuffling feet are intolerable. Has the whole world come to my door?

INQUISITOR: Not the whole world, Your Holiness. A select gathering of the faithful.

(Pause.)

POPE (exhausted): It is clearly understood: he is not to be tortured. (Pause.) At the very most, he may be shown the instruments.

INQUISITOR: That will be adequate, Your Holiness. Mr. Galilei understands machinery.

(The eyes of BARBERINI look helplessly at the CARDINAL INQUISITOR from under the completely assembled panoply of POPE URBAN VIII.)

SCENE 12

June twenty-second, sixteen thirty-three,
A momentous date for you and me.
Of all the days that was the one
An age of reason could have begun.

(Again the garden of the Florentine Ambassador at Rome, where GALILEO's assistants wait the news of the trial. The LITTLE MONK and FEDERZONI are attempting to concentrate on a game of chess. VIRGINIA kneels in a corner, praying and counting her beads.)

Versailles, The Pope refers to Versailles as the center of the French court, even though Louis XIV's massive palace would not be built until the 1660s.

LITTLE MONK: The Pope didn't even grant him an audience.

FEDERZONI: No more scientific discussions.

ANDREA: The "Discorsi" will never be finished. The sum of his findings. They will kill him.

FEDERZONI (stealing a glance at him): Do you really think so?

ANDREA: He will never recant.

(Silence.)

LITTLE MONK: You know when you lie awake at night how your mind fastens on to something irrelevant. Last night I kept thinking: if only they would let him take his little stone in with him, the appeal-to-reason-pebble that he always carries in his pocket.

FEDERZONI: In the room *they'll* take him to, he won't have a pocket.

ANDREA: But he will not recant.

LITTLE MONK: How can they beat the truth out of a man who gave his sight in order to see?

FEDERZONI: Maybe they can't.

(Silence.)

ANDREA (speaking about VIRGINIA): She is praying that he will recant.

FEDERZONI: Leave her alone. She doesn't know whether she's on her head or on her heels since they got hold of her. They brought her Father Confessor from Florence.

(The INFORMER of scene 10 enters.)

INFORMER: Mr. Galilei will be here soon. He may need a bed.

FEDERZONI: Have they let him out?

INFORMER: Mr. Galilei is expected to recant at five o'clock. The big bell of Saint Marcus will be rung and the complete text of his recantation publicly announced.

ANDREA: I don't believe it.

INFORMER: Mr. Galilei will be brought to the garden gate at the back of the house, to avoid the crowds collecting in the streets. (He goes.)

(Silence.)

ANDREA: The moon is an earth because the light of the moon is not her own. Jupiter is a fixed star, and four moons turn around Jupiter, therefore we are not shut in by crystal shells. The sun is the pivot of our world, therefore the earth is not the center. The earth moves, spinning about the sun. And he showed us. You can't make a man unsee what he has seen.

(Silence.)

FEDERZONI: Five o'clock is one minute.

(VIRGINIA prays louder.)

ANDREA: Listen all of you, they are murdering the truth.

(He stops up his ears with his fingers. The two other pupils do the same. FEDERZONI *goes over to the* LITTLE MONK, *and all of them stand absolutely still in cramped positions. Nothing happens. No bell sounds. After a silence, filled with the murmur of* VIRGINIA's *prayers,* FEDERZONI *runs to the wall to look at the clock. He turns around, his expression changed. He shakes his head. They drop their hands.)*

FEDERZONI: No. No bell. It is three minutes after.
LITTLE MONK: He hasn't.
ANDREA: He held true. It is all right, it is all right.
LITTLE MONK: He did not recant.
FEDERZONI: No.

(They embrace each other, they are delirious with joy.)

ANDREA: So force cannot accomplish everything. What has been seen can't be unseen. Man is constant in the face of death.
FEDERZONI: June 22, 1633: dawn of the age of reason. I wouldn't have wanted to go on living if he had recanted.
LITTLE MONK: I didn't say anything, but I was in agony. Oh, ye of little faith!
ANDREA: I was sure.
FEDERZONI: It would have turned our morning to night.
ANDREA: It would have been as if the mountain had turned to water.
LITTLE MONK *(kneeling down, crying)*: Oh God, I thank Thee.
ANDREA: Beaten humanity can lift its head. A man has stood up and said "no."

(At this moment the bell of Saint Marcus begins to toll. They stand like statues. VIRGINIA *stands up.)*

VIRGINIA: The bell of Saint Marcus. He is not damned.

(From the street one hears the TOWN CRIER *reading* GALILEO's *recantation.)*

TOWN CRIER: I, Galileo Galilei, Teacher of Mathematics and Physics, do hereby publicly renounce my teaching that the earth moves. I foreswear this teaching with a sincere heart and unfeigned faith and detest and curse this and all other errors and heresies repugnant to the Holy Scriptures.

(The lights dim; when they come up again the bell of Saint Marcus is petering out. VIRGINIA *has gone but the* SCHOLARS *are still there waiting.)*

ANDREA *(loud)*: The mountain did turn to water.

*(*GALILEO *has entered quietly and unnoticed. He is changed, almost unrecognizable. He has heard* ANDREA. *He waits some seconds by the door for somebody to greet him. Nobody does. They retreat from him. He goes slowly and, because of his bad sight, uncertainly, to the front of the stage where he finds a chair, and sits down.)*

ANDREA: I can't look at him. Tell him to go away.

FEDERZONI: Steady.
ANDREA *(hysterically)*: He saved his big gut.
FEDERZONI: Get him a glass of water.

(The LITTLE MONK *fetches a glass of water for* ANDREA. *Nobody acknowledges the presence of* GALILEO, *who sits silently on his chair listening to the voice of the* TOWN CRIER, *now in another street.)*

ANDREA: I can walk. Just help me a bit.

(They help him to the door.)

ANDREA *(in the door)*: "Unhappy is the land that breeds no hero."
GALILEO: No, Andrea: "Unhappy is the land that needs a hero."

(Before the next scene a curtain with the following legend on it is lowered:

You can plainly see that if a horse were to fall from a height of three or four feet, it could break its bones, whereas a dog would not suffer injury. The same applies to a cat from a height of as much as eight or ten feet, to a grasshopper from the top of a tower, and to an ant falling down from the moon. Nature could not allow a horse to become as big as twenty horses nor a giant as big as ten men, unless she were to change the proportions of all its members, particularly the bones. Thus the common assumption that great and small structures are equally tough is obviously wrong.
—From the *Discorsi)*

SCENE 13

1633–1642.
Galileo Galilei remains a prisoner
of the Inquisition until his death.

(A country house near Florence. A large room simply furnished. There is a huge table, a leather chair, a globe of the world on a stand, and a narrow bed. A portion of the adjoining anteroom is visible, and the front door which opens into it.)
(An OFFICIAL OF THE INQUISITION *sits on guard in the anteroom.)*
(In the large room, GALILEO *is quietly experimenting with a bent wooden rail and a small ball of wood. He is still vigorous but almost blind.)*
(After a while there is a knocking at the outside door. The OFFICIAL *opens it to a* PEASANT *who brings a plucked goose.* VIRGINIA *comes from the kitchen. She is past forty.)*

PEASANT *(handing the goose to* VIRGINIA*)*: I was told to deliver this here.
VIRGINIA: I didn't order a goose.
PEASANT: I was told to say it's from someone who was passing through.

(VIRGINIA *takes the goose, surprised. The* OFFICIAL *takes it from her and examines it suspiciously. Then, reassured, he hands it back to her. The* PEASANT *goes.* VIRGINIA *brings the goose in to* GALILEO.)

VIRGINIA: Somebody who was passing through sent you something.

GALILEO: What is it?

VIRGINIA: Can't you see it?

GALILEO: No. (*He walks over.*) A goose. Any name?

VIRGINIA: No.

GALILEO (*weighing the goose*): Solid.

VIRGINIA (*cautiously*): Will you eat the liver, if I have it cooked with a little apple?

GALILEO: I had my dinner. Are you under orders to finish me off with food?

VIRGINIA: It's not rich. And what is wrong with your eyes again? You should be able to see it.

GALILEO: You were standing in the light.

VIRGINIA: I was not.—You haven't been writing again?

GALILEO (*sneering*): What do you think?

(VIRGINIA *takes the goose out into the anteroom and speaks to the* OFFICIAL.)

VIRGINIA: You had better ask Monsignor Carpula to send the doctor. Father couldn't see this goose across the room.—Don't look at me like that. He has not been writing. He dictates everything to me, as you know.

OFFICIAL: Yes?

VIRGINIA: He abides by the rules. My father's repentance is sincere. I keep an eye on him (*She hands him the goose.*) Tell the cook to fry the liver with an apple and an onion. (*She goes back into the large room.*) And you have no business to be doing that with those eyes of yours, father.

GALILEO: You may read me some Horace.

VIRGINIA: We should go on with your weekly letter to the Archbishop. Monsignor Carpula to whom we owe so much was all smiles the other day because the Archbishop had expressed his pleasure at your collaboration.

GALILEO: Where were we?

VIRGINIA (*sits down to take his dictation*): Paragraph four.

GALILEO: Read what you have.

VIRGINIA: "The position of the church in the matter of the unrest at Genoa. I agree with Cardinal Spoletti in the matter of the unrest among the Venetian ropemakers . . ."

GALILEO: Yes. (*Dictates.*) I agree with Cardinal Spoletti in the matter of the unrest among the Venetian ropemakers: it is better to distribute good nourishing food in the name of charity than to pay them more for their bellropes. It being surely better to strengthen their faith than to encourage their acquisitiveness. St. Paul says: Charity never faileth.— How is that?

VIRGINIA: It's beautiful, father.

GALILEO: It couldn't be taken as irony?

VIRGINIA: No. The Archbishop will like it. It's so practical.

GALILEO: I trust your judgment. Read it over slowly.

VIRGINIA: "The position of the Church in the matter of the unrest . . ."

(*There is a knocking at the outside door.* VIRGINIA *goes into the anteroom. The* OFFICIAL *opens the door. It is* ANDREA.)

ANDREA: Good evening. I am sorry to call so late, I'm on my way to Holland. I was asked to look him up. Can I go in?

VIRGINIA: I don't know whether he will see you. You never came.

ANDREA: Ask him.

(GALILEO *recognizes the voice. He sits motionless.* VIRGINIA *comes in to* GALILEO.)

GALILEO: Is that Andrea?

VIRGINIA: Yes. (*Pause.*) I will send him away.

GALILEO: Show him in.

(VIRGINIA *shows* ANDREA *in.* VIRGINIA *sits,* ANDREA *remains standing.*)

ANDREA (*cool*): Have you been keeping well, Mr. Galilei?

GALILEO: Sit down. What are you doing these days? What are you working on? I heard it was something about hydraulics in Milan.

ANDREA: As he knew I was passing through, Fabricius of Amsterdam asked me to visit you and inquire about your health.

(*Pause.*)

GALILEO: I am very well.

ANDREA (*formally*): I am glad I can report you are in good health.

GALILEO: Fabricius will be glad to hear it. And you might inform him that, on account of the depth of my repentance, I live in comparative comfort.

ANDREA: Yes, we understand that the church is more than pleased with you. Your complete acceptance has had its effect. Not one paper expounding a new thesis has made its appearance in Italy since your submission.

(*Pause.*)

GALILEO: Unfortunately there are countries not under the wing of the church. Would you not say the erroneous condemned theories are still taught— there?

ANDREA (*relentless*): Things are almost at a standstill.

GALILEO: Are they? (*Pause.*) Nothing from Descartes in Paris?

ANDREA: Yes. On receiving the news of your recantation, he shelved his treatise on the nature of light.

GALILEO: I sometimes worry about my assistants whom I led into error. Have they benefited by my example?

ANDREA: In order to work I have to go to Holland.

GALILEO: Yes.

ANDREA: Federzoni is grinding lenses again, back in some shop.

GALILEO: He can't read the books.

ANDREA: Fulganzio, our little monk, has abandoned research and is resting in peace in the church.

GALILEO: So. (*Pause.*) My superiors are looking forward to my spiritual recovery. I am progressing as well as can be expected.

VIRGINIA: You are doing well, father.

GALILEO: Virginia, leave the room.

(VIRGINIA *rises uncertainly and goes out.*)

VIRGINIA (*to the* OFFICIAL): He was his pupil, so now he is his enemy.—Help me in the kitchen.

(*She leaves the anteroom with the* OFFICIAL.)

ANDREA: May I go now, sir?

GALILEO: I do not know why you came, Sarti. To unsettle me? I have to be prudent.

ANDREA: I'll be on my way.

GALILEO: As it is, I have relapses. I completed the "Discorsi."

ANDREA: You completed what?

GALILEO: My "Discorsi."

ANDREA: How?

GALILEO: I am allowed pen and paper. My superiors are intelligent men. They know the habits of a lifetime cannot be broken abruptly. But they protect me from any unpleasant consequences: they lock my pages away as I dictate them. And I should know better than to risk my comfort. I wrote the "Discorsi" out again during the night. The manuscript is in the globe. My vanity has up to now prevented me from destroying it. If you consider taking it, you will shoulder the entire risk. You will say it was pirated from the original in the hands of the Holy Office.

(ANDREA, *as in a trance, has gone to the globe. He lifts the upper half and gets the book. He turns the pages as if wanting to devour them. In the background the opening sentences of the* Discorsi *appear:*

MY PURPOSE IS TO SET FORTH A VERY NEW
SCIENCE DEALING WITH A VERY ANCIENT
SUBJECT—MOTION. . . . AND I HAVE
DISCOVERED BY EXPERIMENT SOME PROPERTIES
OF IT WHICH ARE WORTH KNOWING. . . .)

GALILEO: I had to employ my time somehow.

(*The text disappears.*)

ANDREA: Two new sciences! This will be the foundation stone of a new physics.

GALILEO: Yes. Put it under your coat.

ANDREA: And we thought you had deserted. (*In a low voice.*) Mr. Galilei, how can I begin to express my shame. Mine has been the loudest voice against you.

GALILEO: That would seem to have been proper. I taught you science and I decried the truth.

ANDREA: Did you? I think not. Everything is changed!

GALILEO: What is changed?

ANDREA: You shielded the truth from the oppressor. Now I see! In your dealings with the Inquisition you used the same superb common sense you brought to physics.

GALILEO: Oh!

ANDREA: We lost our heads. With the crowd at the street corners we said: "He will die, he will never surrender!" You came back: "I surrendered but I am alive." We cried: "Your hands are stained!" You say: "Better stained than empty."

GALILEO: "Better stained than empty."—It sounds realistic. Sounds like me.

ANDREA: And I of all people should have known. I was twelve when you sold another man's telescope to the Venetian Senate, and saw you put it to immortal use. Your friends were baffled when you bowed to the Prince of Florence: Science gained a wider audience. You always laughed at heroics. "People who suffer bore me," you said. "Misfortunes are due mainly to miscalculations." And: "If there are obstacles, the shortest line between two points may be the crooked line."

GALILEO: It makes a picture.

ANDREA: And when you stooped to recant in 1633, I should have understood that you were again about your business.

GALILEO: My business being?

ANDREA: Science. The study of the properties of motion, mother of the machines which will themselves change the ugly face of the earth.

GALILEO: Aha!

ANDREA: You gained time to write a book that only you could write. Had you burned at the stake in a blaze of glory they would have won.

GALILEO: They have won. And there is no such thing as a scientific work that only one man can write.

ANDREA: Then why did you recant, tell me that!

GALILEO: I recanted because I was afraid of physical pain.

ANDREA: No!

GALILEO: They showed me the instruments.

ANDREA: It was not a plan?

GALILEO: It was not.

(*Pause.*)

ANDREA: But you have contributed. Science has only

one commandment: contribution. And you have contributed more than any man for a hundred years.

GALILEO: Have I? Then welcome to my gutter, dear colleague in science and brother in treason: I sold out, you are a buyer. The first sight of the book! His mouth watered and his scoldings were drowned. Blessed be our bargaining, whitewashing, death-fearing community!

ANDREA: The fear of death is human.

GALILEO: Even the church will teach you that to be weak is not human. It is just evil.

ANDREA: The church, yes! But science is not concerned with our weaknesses.

GALILEO: No? My dear Sarti, in spite of my present convictions, I may be able to give you a few pointers as to the concerns of your chosen profession.

(*Enter* VIRGINIA *with a platter.*)

In my spare time, I happen to have gone over this case. I have spare time.—Even a man who sells wool, however good he is at buying wool cheap and selling it dear, must be concerned with the standing of the wool trade. The practice of science would seem to call for valor. She trades in knowledge, which is the product of doubt. And this new art of doubt has enchanted the public. The plight of the multitude is old as the rocks, and is believed to be basic as the rocks. But now they have learned to doubt. They snatched the telescopes out of our hands and had them trained on their tormentors: prince, official, public moralist. The mechanism of the heavens was clearer, the mechanism of their courts was still murky. The battle to measure the heavens is won by doubt; by credulity the Roman housewife's battle for milk will always be lost. Word is passed down that this is of no concern to the scientist who is told he will only release such of his findings as do not disturb the peace, that is, the peace of mind of the well-to-do. Threats and bribes fill the air. Can the scientist hold out on the numbers?—For what reason do you labor? I take it the intent of science is to ease human existence. If you give way to coercion, science can be crippled, and your new machines may simply suggest new drudgeries. Should you then, in time, discover all there is to be discovered, your progress must then become a progress away from the bulk of humanity. The gulf might even grow so wide that the sound of your cheering at some new achievement would be echoed by a universal howl of horror.—As a scientist I had an almost unique opportunity. In my day astronomy emerged into the marketplace. At that particular time, had one man put up a fight, it could have had wide repercussions. I have come to believe that I was never in real danger; for some years I was as strong as the authorities, and I sur-

rendered my knowledge to the powers that be, to use it, no, not *use* it, *abuse* it, as it suits their ends. I have betrayed my profession. Any man who does what I have done must not be tolerated in the ranks of science.

(VIRGINIA, *who has stood motionless, puts the platter on the table.*)

VIRGINIA: You are accepted in the ranks of the faithful, father.

GALILEO (*sees her*): Correct. (*He goes over to the table.*) I have to eat now.

VIRGINIA: We lock up at eight.

ANDREA: I am glad I came. (*He extends his hand.* GALILEO *ignores it and goes over to his meal.*)

GALILEO (*examining the plate; to* ANDREA): Somebody who knows me sent me a goose. I still enjoy eating.

ANDREA: And your opinion is now that the "new age" was an illusion?

GALILEO: Well.—This age of ours turned out to be a whore, spattered with blood. Maybe, new ages look like blood-spattered whores. Take care of yourself.

ANDREA: Yes. (*Unable to go.*) With reference to your evaluation of the author in question—I do not know the answer. But I cannot think that your savage analysis is the last word.

GALILEO: Thank you, sir.

(OFFICIAL *knocks at the door.*)

VIRGINIA (*showing* ANDREA *out*): I don't like visitors from the past, they excite him.

(*She lets him out. The* OFFICIAL *closes the iron door.* VIRGINIA *returns.*)

GALILEO (*eating*): Did you try and think who sent the goose?

VIRGINIA: Not Andrea.

GALILEO: Maybe not. I gave Redhead his first lesson; when he held out his hand, I had to remind myself he is teaching now.—How is the sky tonight?

VIRGINIA (*at the window*): Bright.

(GALILEO *continues eating.*)

SCENE 14

*The great book o'er the border went
And, good folk, that was the end.
But we hope you'll keep in mind
You and I were left behind.*

(*Before a little Italian customs house early in the morning.* ANDREA *sits upon one of his traveling trunks at the barrier and reads* GALILEO's *book. The window of a small house is still lit, and a big grotesque shadow, like an old witch and her cauldron, falls upon the house wall beyond.*)

Barefoot CHILDREN *in rags see it and point to the little house.)*

CHILDREN (*singing*): One, two, three, four, five, six,
Old Marina is a witch.
At night, on a broomstick she sits
And on the church steeple she spits.

CUSTOMS OFFICER (*to* ANDREA): Why are you making this journey?

ANDREA: I am a scholar.

CUSTOMS OFFICER (*to his* CLERK): Put down under "reason for leaving the country": Scholar. (*He points to the baggage.*) Books! Anything dangerous in these books?

ANDREA: What is dangerous?

CUSTOMS OFFICER: Religion. Politics.

ANDREA: These are nothing but mathematical formulas.

CUSTOMS OFFICER: What's that?

ANDREA: Figures.

CUSTOMS OFFICER: Oh, figures. No harm in figures. Just wait a minute, sir, we will soon have your papers stamped. (*He exits with* CLERK.)

(*Meanwhile, a little council of war among the* CHILDREN *has taken place.* ANDREA *quietly watches. One of the* BOYS, *pushed forward by the others, creeps up to the little house from which the shadow comes and takes the jug of milk on the doorstep.*)

ANDREA (*quietly*): What are you doing with that milk?

BOY (*stopping in mid-movement*): She is a witch.

(*The other* CHILDREN *run away behind the customs house. One of them shouts, "Run, Paolo!"*)

ANDREA: Hmm!—And because she is a witch she mustn't have milk. Is that the idea?

BOY: Yes.

ANDREA: And how do you know she is a witch?

BOY (*points to shadow on house wall*): Look!

ANDREA: Oh! I see.

BOY: And she rides on a broomstick at night—and she bewitches the coachman's horses. My cousin Luigi looked through the hole in the stable roof, that the snowstorm made, and heard the horses coughing something terrible.

ANDREA: Oh!—How big was the hole in the stable roof?

BOY: Luigi didn't tell. Why?

ANDREA: I was asking because maybe the horses got sick because it was cold in the stable. You had better ask Luigi how big that hole is.

BOY: You are not going to say Old Marina isn't a witch, because you can't.

ANDREA: No, I can't say she isn't a witch. I haven't looked into it. A man can't know about a thing he hasn't looked into, or can he?

BOY: No!—But THAT! (*He points to the shadow.*) She is stirring hell-broth.

ANDREA: Let's see. Do you want to take a look? I can lift you up.

BOY: You lift me to the window, mister! (*He takes a sling shot out of his pocket.*) I can really bash her from there.

ANDREA: Hadn't we better make sure she is a witch before we shoot? I'll hold that.

(*The* BOY *puts the milk jug down and follows him reluctantly to the window.* ANDREA *lifts the boy up so that he can look in.*)

ANDREA: What do you see?

BOY (*slowly*): Just an old girl cooking porridge.

ANDREA: Oh! Nothing to it then. Now look at her shadow, Paolo.

(*The* BOY *looks over his shoulder and back and compares the reality and the shadow.*)

BOY: The big thing is a soup ladle.

ANDREA: Ah! A ladle! You see, I would have taken it for a broomstick, but I haven't looked into the matter as you have, Paolo. Here is your sling.

CUSTOMS OFFICER (*returning with the* CLERK *and handing* ANDREA *his papers*): All present and correct. Good luck, sir.

(ANDREA *goes, reading* GALILEO's *book. The* CLERK *starts to bring his baggage after him. The barrier rises.* ANDREA *passes through, still reading the book. The* BOY *kicks over the milk jug.*)

BOY (*shouting after* ANDREA): She *is* a witch! She *is* a witch!

ANDREA: You saw with your own eyes: think it over!

(*The* BOY *joins the others. They sing.*)

One, two, three, four, five, six,
Old Marina is a witch.
At night, on a broomstick she sits
And on the church steeple she spits.

(*The* CUSTOMS OFFICERS *laugh.* ANDREA *goes.*)

Figure 1. Galileo (Charles Laughton) glances warily at the Inquisitor (John Carradine) while Virginia (Joan McCracken) curtsies demurely in the 1947 New York production directed by Joseph Losey. (Photograph: Billy Rose Theatre Collection. The New York Public Library for the Performing Arts. Astor, Lenox, and Tilden Foundations.)

Figure 2. A relaxed Galileo (Charles Laughton) chats with his co-workers and Ludovico while Mrs. Sarti (Hester Sondergard) looks on disapprovingly. Around the table are Ludovico (Philip Swander), Andrea (Nehemiah Persoff), and the Little Monk (Donald Symington), while Federzoni (Dwight Marfield) stands in the background. The 1947 New York production was directed by Joseph Losey. (Photograph: Billy Rose Theatre Collection. The New York Public Library for the Performing Arts. Astor, Lenox, and Tilden Foundations.)

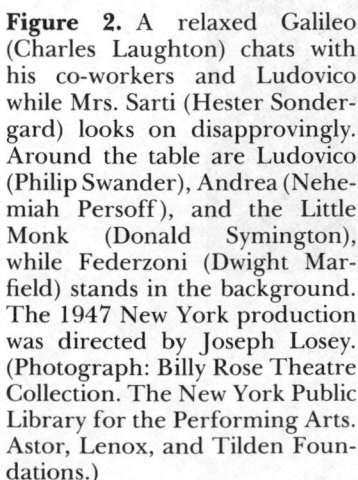

Figure 3. Almost blind, the imprisoned Galileo (Charles Laughton) "is experimenting with a bent wooden rail and a small ball of wood" in the final scene of the 1947 New York production directed by Joseph Losey. (Photograph: Billy Rose Theatre Collection. The New York Public Library for the Performing Arts. Astor, Lenox, and Tilden Foundations.)

Staging of *Galileo*

REVIEW OF THE NEW YORK PRODUCTION, 1947, BY IRWIN SHAW

There has been considerable discussion, some of it quite acrimonious, about the propriety of having an institution called the Experimental Theatre put on a work in which an actor of Charles Laughton's standing plays the leading part. The argument has leaked over to include the Experimental Theatre's next production, "Skipper Next to God," with John Garfield. According to the critics of the enterprise, it would seem that nothing a well-known actor can do on a stage can properly be considered an experiment. This, of course, is nonsense, and the sponsors of the project are to be congratulated for fulfilling handsomely, in Bertolt Brecht's "Galileo," the promise of the organization's title.

The play is noble in theme, relentlessly unconventional in execution, and it permits Laughton to escape, if only for six performances, the absurd, minor warblings which have recently been his lot in Hollywood. Equipped with an abstract set, a fluttering gauze curtain that is drawn at the end of each scene by a small boy with a pole, projections of Renaissance drawings and paintings, and intermittent choruses with music by Hanns Eisler, sung by three choirboys, it could hardly be called a standard Broadway performance.

Aside from its technical innovations, the story of Galileo's martyrdom by Authority is bitterly apposite for today's audiences. The heresy hunters are almost as busy today in Washington as they ever were in Florence, and recantations fill the air in a medieval blizzard of fear. *Time, Life* and Hearst have replaced the rack, and the Representative from New Jersey has donned the Inquisitor's dark satin. The sobbing "I was wrong" of the matinee idol is now to be heard, instead of the "I have sinned" of the old astronomer, but the pattern, as Brecht bleakly points out, is the same. Truth dies with conformity, this year or last.

Cool demands. Brecht's method of saying these things, in accordance with his theories of the "Epic" theater, is abstract, cold and didactic. He assumes the air of the passionless teacher lecturing to students who are not so bright as they should be. He disdains all emotionalism; scornfully, he refuses to amuse us with the usual dramatist's tricks. His characters are symbols, not people; his action the functioning of huge forces, not the clash of human beings. The final effect is interesting, but aggravating. We get the unpleasant feeling that Brecht regards the human race, or at least that part of it which goes to the theater, as animals equipped with only the most rudimentary ability to reason. His Olympian condescension is bound to annoy us, even when we agree with him most heartily.

Joseph Losey's staging meets, I suppose, with Brecht's cool demands, but it is only in three magnificently searching and eloquent scenes in the second half that the play comes really alive. One is in a garden, in which a young monk tells Galileo the reasons of conscience for which he is giving up the study of physics; another is in the Pope's robing room, in which the humanitarian prelate is forced by the logic of his position to agree to the limited torture of the scientist; and the third is the last scene of the play, in which Galileo explores the most profound and complex depths of compromise, cowardice and treachery.

It is in this scene, seated quietly on the almost empty stage, that Laughton gives us one of the most memorable moments of the recent theater. With a stony and scientifically accurate self-knowledge, he appraises himself and the world. Tragically clear, half-victor half-victim, the old giant delivers himself of a monumental monologue, and for a time, on the stage of the Maxine Elliot, we seem to be at the very core of truth.

It is devoutly to be hoped that the commercial theater will rise to the challenge of "Galileo" and put it on the boards where all may see it.

EUGENE O'NEILL

1888–1953

Before his death of a rare degenerative disease that made it almost impossible for him to write during the last several years of his life, O'Neill produced more than fifty plays whose theatrical range and vision have firmly established him as the greatest playwright in the history of American drama. From the very beginning of his life the theater was an inextricable part of his experience, for he was the son of one of America's most famous matinee idols, the romantic actor James O'Neill, who achieved theatrical fame as the star of *The Count of Monte Cristo* and continued to tour in the play until he was well into his sixties. O'Neill himself was born in a hotel in the theater district of New York, and during his early childhood he travelled with his father on theatrical tours that took him throughout the United States. The chaotic life of his father's career and the morphine addiction that his mother developed after taking the drug to alleviate the pain of O'Neill's birth were also an indelible part of his experience, which he reflected in a number of late autobiographical plays that constitute the greatest achievement of his career, among them *Long Day's Journey into Night* (1940) and *A Moon for the Misbegotten* (1943). In these and other late plays, O'Neill confronted the most painful aspects of his family's and his own personal experience—his father's extramarital affairs, his mother's morphine addiction, his brother's inability to hold a job, his father's alcoholism, his brother's alcoholism, his own alcoholism that drove him to attempt suicide at a Bowery bar in 1912, and the endless cycle of bitter accusation and shamefaced apology that consumed the family throughout his life, leaving him obsessively torn between love and hatred for all its members. But the writing of these plays was more than a psychological milestone of honestly confronting his own past, for they also represent the artistic climax to his many years of searching for an appropriate dramatic form in which to convey his vision of modern experience.

O'Neill turned to playwriting in 1912, after a hectic period of several years, during which he got secretly married to a young woman whom he promptly left to go prospecting for gold in Honduras, then returned after a year to join his father as an actor and assistant stage manager on tour, went to sea again for a brief period, returned and took a job as a reporter on a small town newspaper in Connecticut, and then came down with tuberculosis, brought on no doubt by his dissolute life, which forced him to be hospitalized for an extended period of time. During 1912, he became an avid reader of drama and decided to make his career as a dramatist. He began writing plays in 1913, enrolled in a playwriting course at Harvard during 1914, moved to Greenwich Village in 1915, and there joined up with a group of *avant-garde* writers who had formed a repertory company, called the Provincetown Players, which became one of the most influential groups in American theater, largely because of the plays that O'Neill produced for them during his early career.

O'Neill began by writing a series of one-act plays based on his earlier experiences at sea, strictly realistic plays in which he dramatized the illusions and preoccupations of men adrift in the world. By the early 1920s, he had begun writing full-length plays, still drawing on his fascination with the sea, but conveying a complex vision of tragic fate and frustration, as in the Pulitzer Prize-winning *Beyond the Horizon* (1920) and *Anna Christie* (1921). He then began to experiment with expressionistic techniques in *The Emperor Jones* (1920), a one-act psychodrama about a Negro "emperor" who flees a palace revolution and succumbs to his own fantasies and "the Little Formless Fears." The most striking innovation in this play was O'Neill's use of a drumbeat that began at pulse rate and gradually accelerated as Jones came closer and closer to death, ceasing only when he died. In *The Hairy Ape* (1922), O'Neill went even further with expressionist techniques by using contrastive symbolic settings (a furnace room versus fashionable Fifth Avenue), as well as choral speeches, and socially emblematic characters to dramatize the destruction of a young stoker, named Yank, who is unable to move outside of his class.

By the mid-1920s, his fascination with Freudian psychology had already become manifest in *Desire Under the Elms* (1924), a play dramatizing the tragic sexual attraction between a young man and his young stepmother. Then in *The Great God Brown* (1926), he used expressionistic techniques to dramatize what he was later to call the "profound hidden conflicts of the mind," by having the actors wear masks, as in Greek drama, to reflect their assumed personalities. By the late 1920s, his absorption with Freudian psychology had carried him so far into experimental theater that he tried to reveal the inner thoughts of his characters by having them interrupt their dialogue and express their hidden feelings in monologue to the audience, a strategy he used in his nine-act play *Strange Interlude* (1928). In *Days without End* (1934), he carried his expressionistic rendering of Freudian themes to the logical extreme by having two actors play the conflicting sides of the main character. Yet even during this period when he was exploring the psychopathology of the human mind, he was also working in more realistic and naturalistic modes that anticipated the style of his late plays. In *Mourning Becomes Electra* (1931), a trilogy based on the *Oresteia* of Aeschylus, O'Neill dramatized the tragic fate of a family across several generations—a fate determined not by pride, as in the Greek drama, but by sexual instincts, psychic guilt, suicide, and remorse. During the early 1930s, he also wrote his only comedy, *Ah, Wilderness* (1933), a nostalgic work in the realistic style that depicts a family very much like his own, but which offers an idyllic family picture that was to be strikingly reversed in the years to follow.

Finally, in the late 1930s, he began to face up to his own past, first with *The Iceman Cometh* (1939), which was set in a saloon very much like the one where he had lived and had tried to kill himself, and which dramatized at length O'Neill's painful awareness of human frailty and self-deception. In *Long Day's Journey into Night* (1940), he was able "to face my dead at last," and he did so by turning the four members of his family—his father, mother, brother Jamie, and himself—into the "four haunted Tyrones," whose love-hate conflicts he completely exposed, but exposed with compassion, understanding, and forgiveness. Finally, in 1943, he completed his last autobiographical play, *A Moon for the Misbegotten*, a work based on the life of his alcoholic brother Jamie. It was the last of O'Neill's plays to be produced during his lifetime, and it almost never got staged at all.

The first production, in 1947, floundered in Columbus, was attacked by the Chamber of Commerce in Pittsburgh, censored by the police in Detroit, and never made it to New York until ten years later in 1957. And when it finally did get to New York, four years after O'Neill had died, the critics treated it as roughly as the businessmen and police had ten years earlier. Only in 1968, in a production at Circle in the Square, did it finally find a receptive audience, though when it was revived again in the mid-1970s critics were ready to recognize it as one of O'Neill's finest plays, possibly even his greatest.

Like his other late autobiographical plays, *A Moon for the Misbegotten* is written in the style of what O'Neill himself called "faithful realism." Yet it is by no means an easy play to witness or produce. It calls for two exceptional performers, one of them a huge woman, "so oversize for a woman that she is almost a freak," and the other an actor capable of sustaining a third act monologue that goes on for several pages. Josie, the oversized virgin, whom everyone thinks of as a whore, gets a bottle of real bourbon, hoping to seduce Jim Tyrone, the cynical New York drunk, and so get him to marry her. But the planned seduction turns into a long confession by Jim, and the embrace that is meant to produce a shotgun marriage produces instead "a strangely tragic picture"—"this big sorrowful woman hugging a haggard-faced, middle-aged drunkard against her breast as if he were a sick child." A theatrically parallel tableau of hopelessness also appears in *A Long Day's Journey into Night*, at the end of the play, when the three drunken Tyrone men sit silently listening to the drugged Mary Tyrone. But *A Moon for the Misbegotten* moves beyond the momentary stasis to the waking-up, both literally and spiritually, when Jim awakens and tries to pretend that his confession did not happen, but then finally admits that he does remember and is glad to remember. Josie's final line is thus full of compassion, when she says gently to an empty stage, "May you have your wish and die in your sleep soon, Jim, darling. May you rest forever in forgiveness and peace."

The most memorable production of the play took place in 1973, when Colleen Dewhurst and Jason Robards, Jr., joined forces with the director José Quintero. Quintero had already directed *Long Day's Journey into Night*, in 1955, and Robards had played the role of Jamie Tyrone in that same production. In Colleen Dewhurst, they found an actress who could encompass Josie, both physically and emotionally. She was capable of the raucous, even coarse behavior that characterizes Josie for much of the first two acts (see Figure 2), and yet she could also show the understanding and compassion necessary as she listens to Jim throughout much of Act 3 (see Figure 3). Miss Dewhurst received rave notices from the critics, as reflected in the review reprinted following the text. The set for that production was an evocative rather than detailed re-creation of the farmhouse where the action of the play is located (see Figure 1), with its base in real objects, in the wooden floor, the rocks, and the chairs, just as the play has its roots in the reality of O'Neill's tormented past. Yet the set was also free of those objects, implying the world beyond, just as the play itself hints at a future free of guilt.

A MOON FOR THE MISBEGOTTEN

BY EUGENE O'NEILL

CHARACTERS

JOSIE HOGAN
PHIL HOGAN, *her father*
MIKE HOGAN, *her brother*
JAMES TYRONE, JR.
T. STEDMAN HARDER

SCENE

ACT 1: *The farmhouse. Around noon. Early September, 1923.* ACT 2: *The same, but with the interior of sitting room revealed—11 o'clock that night;* ACT 3: *The same as Act 1. No time elapses between Acts 2 and 3;* ACT 4: *The same—Dawn of the following morning.*

The play takes place in Connecticut at the home of tenant farmer, Phil Hogan, between the hours of noon on a day in early September, 1923, and the sunrise of the following day.

The house is not, to speak mildly, a fine example of New England architecture, placed so perfectly in its setting that it appears a harmonious part of the landscape, rooted in the earth. It has been moved to its present site, and looks it. An old box-like, clapboarded affair, with a shingled roof and brick chimney, it is propped up about two feet above ground by layers of timber blocks. There are two windows on the lower floor of this side of the house which faces front, and one window on the floor above. These windows have no shutters, curtains or shades. Each has at least one pane missing, a square of cardboard taking its place. The house had once been painted a repulsive yellow with brown trim, but the walls now are a blackened and weathered gray, flaked with streaks and splotches of dim lemon. Just around the left corner of the house, a flight of steps leads to the front door.

To make matters worse, a one-story, one-room addition has been tacked on at right. About twelve feet long by six high, this room which is JOSIE HOGAN'S bedroom, is evidently homemade. Its walls and sloping roof are covered with tar paper, faded to dark gray. Close to where it joins the house, there is a door with a flight of three unpainted steps leading to the ground. At right of door is a small window.

From these steps there is a footpath going around an old pear tree, at right-rear, through a field of hay stubble to a patch of woods. The same path also extends left to join a dirt road which leads up from the county highway (about a hundred yards off left) to the front door of the house, and thence back through a scraggly orchard of apple trees to the barn. Close to the house, under the window next to JOSIE'S bedroom, there is a big boulder with a flat-top.

ACT 1

(It is just before noon. The day is clear and hot.

The door of JOSIE'S bedroom opens and she comes out on the steps, bending to avoid bumping her head.

JOSIE is twenty-eight. She is so oversize for a woman that she is almost a freak—five feet eleven in her stockings and weighs around one hundred and eighty. Her sloping shoulders are broad, her chest deep with large, firm breasts, her waist wide but slender by contrast with her hips and thighs. She has long smooth arms, immensely strong, although no muscles show. The same is true of her legs.

She is more powerful than any but an exceptionally strong man, able to do the manual labor of two ordinary men. But there is no mannish quality about her. She is all woman.

The map of Ireland is stamped on her face, with its long upper lip and small nose, thick black eyebrows, black hair as coarse as a horse's mane, freckled, sunburned fair skin, high cheekbones and heavy jaw. It is not a pretty face, but her large dark-blue eyes give it a note of beauty, and her smile, revealing even white teeth, gives it charm.

She wears a cheap, sleeveless, blue cotton dress. Her feet are bare, the soles earth-stained and tough as leather.

She comes down the steps and goes left to the corner of the house and peers around it toward the barn. Then she moves swiftly to the right of the house and looks back.)

JOSIE: Ah, thank God. *(She goes back toward the steps as her brother, MIKE, appears hurrying up from right-rear.)*

(MIKE HOGAN is twenty, about four inches shorter than his sister. He is sturdily built, but seems almost puny compared to her. He has a common Irish face, its expression sullen, or slyly cunning, or primly self-righteous. He never forgets that he is a good Catholic, faithful to all the observances, and so is one of the élite of Almighty God in a world of damned sinners composed of Protestants and bad Catholics. In brief, MIKE is a New England Irish Catholic Puritan, Grade B, and an extremely irritating youth to have around.)

(MIKE wears dirty overalls, a sweat-stained brown shirt. He carries a pitchfork.)

JOSIE: Bad luck to you for a slowpoke. Didn't I tell you half-past eleven?

MIKE: How could I sneak here sooner with him peeking round the corner of the barn to catch me if I took a minute's rest, the way he always does? I had to wait till he went to the pig pen. (*He adds viciously.*) Where he belongs, the old hog! (JOSIE's *right arm strikes with surprising swiftness and her big hand lands on the side of his jaw. She means it to be only a slap, but his head jerks back and he stumbles, dropping the pitchfork, and pleads cringingly.*) Don't hit me, Josie! Don't, now!

JOSIE (*quietly*): Then keep your tongue off him. He's my father, too, and I like him, if you don't.

MIKE (*out of her reach—sullenly*): You're two of a kind, and a bad kind.

JOSIE (*good naturedly*): I'm proud of it. And I didn't hit you, or you'd be flat on the ground. It was only a love tap to waken your wits, so you'll use them. If he catches you running away, he'll beat you half to death. Get your bag now. I've packed it. It's inside the door of my room with your coat laid over it. Hurry now, while I see what he's doing. (*She moves quickly to peer around the corner of the house at left. He goes up the steps into her room and returns carrying an old coat and a cheap bulging satchel. She comes back.*) There's no sight of him. (MIKE *drops the satchel on the ground while he puts on the coat.*) I put everything in the bag. You can change to your Sunday suit in the can at the station or in the train, and don't forget to wash your face. I know you want to look your best when our brother, Thomas, sees you on his doorstep. (*Her tone becomes derisively amused.*) And him way up in the world, a noble sergeant of the Bridgeport police. Maybe he'll get you on the force. It'd suit you. I can see you leading drunks to the lockup while you give them a lecture on temperance. Or if Thomas can't get you a job, he'll pass you along to our brother, John, the noble barkeep in Meriden. He'll teach you the trade. You'll make a nice one, who'll never steal from the till, or drink, and who'll tell customers they've had enough and better go home just when they're beginning to feel happy. (*She sighs regretfully.*) Ah, well, Mike, you was born a priest's pet, and there's no help for it.

MIKE: That's right! Make fun of me again, because I want to be decent.

JOSIE: You're worse than decent. You're virtuous.

MIKE: Well that's a thing nobody can say about—(*He stops, a bit ashamed, but mostly afraid to finish.*)

JOSIE (*amused*): About me? No, and what's more, they don't. (*She smiles mockingly.*) I know what a trial it's been to you, Mike, having a sister who's the scandal of the neighborhood.

MIKE: It's you that's saying it, not me. I don't want to part with hard feelings. And I'll keep on praying for you.

JOSIE (*roughly*): Och! To hell with your prayers!

MIKE (*stiffly*): I'm going. (*He picks up his bag.*)

JOSIE (*her manner softening*): Wait. (*She comes to him.*) Don't mind my rough tongue, Mike. I'm sorry to see you go, but it's the best thing for you. That's why I'm helping you, the same as I helped Thomas and John. You can't stand up to the Old Man any more than Thomas or John could, and the old divil would always keep you a slave. I wish you all the luck in the world, Mike. I know you'll get on—and God bless you. (*Her voice has softened, and she blinks back tears. She kisses him—then fumbling in the pocket of her dress, pulls out a little roll of one-dollar bills and presses it in his hand.*) Here's a little present over your fare. I took it from his little green bag, and won't he be wild when he finds out! But I can handle him.

MIKE (*enviously*): You can. You're the only one. (*Gratefully moved for a second.*) Thank you, Josie. You've a kind heart. (*Then virtuously.*) But I don't like taking stolen money.

JOSIE: Don't be a bigger jackass than you are already. Tell your conscience it's a bit of the wages he's never given you.

MIKE: That's true, Josie. It's rightfully mine. (*He shoves the money into his pocket.*)

JOSIE: Get along now, so you won't miss the trolley. And don't forget to get off the train at Bridgeport. Give my love to Thomas and John. No, never mind. They've not written me in years. Give them a boot in the tail for me.

MIKE: That's nice talk for a woman. You've a tongue as dirty as the Old Man's.

JOSIE (*impatiently*): Don't start preaching, like you love to, or you'll never go.

MIKE: You're as bad as he is, almost. It's his influence made you what you are, and him always scheming how he'll cheat people, selling them a broken-down nag or a sick cow or pig that he's doctored up to look good for a day or two. It's no better than stealing, and you help him.

JOSIE: I do. Sure, it's grand fun.

MIKE: You ought to marry and have a home of your own away from this shanty and stop your shameless ways with men. (*He adds, not without moral satisfaction.*) Though it'd be hard to find a decent man who'd have you now.

JOSIE: I don't want a decent man, thank you. They're no fun. They're all sticks like you. And I wouldn't marry the best man on earth and be tied down to him alone.

MIKE (*with a cunning leer*): Not even Jim Tyrone, I suppose? (*She stares at him.*) You'd like being tied to money, I know that, and he'll be rich when his mother's estate is settled. (*Sarcastically.*) I suppose you've never thought of that? Don't tell me! I've watched you making sheep's eyes at him.

JOSIE (contemptuously): So I'm leading Jim on to propose, am I?

MIKE: I know it's crazy, but maybe you're hoping if you got hold of him alone when he's mad drunk— Anyway, talk all you please to put me off, I'll bet my last penny you've cooked up some scheme to hook him, and the Old Man put you up to it. Maybe he thinks if he caught you with Jim and had witnesses to prove it, and his shotgun to scare him—

JOSIE (controlling her anger): You're full of bright thoughts. I wouldn't strain my brains any more, if I was you.

MIKE: Well, I wouldn't put it past the Old Man to try any trick. And I wouldn't put it past you, God forgive you. You've never cared about your virtue, or what man you went out with. You've always been brazen as brass and proud of your disgrace. You can't deny that, Josie.

JOSIE: I don't. (Then ominously.) You'd better shut up now. I've been holding my temper, because we're saying good-bye. (She stands up.) But I'm losing patience.

MIKE (hastily): Wait till I finish and you won't be mad at me. I was going to say I wish you luck with your scheming, for once. I hate Jim Tyrone's guts, with his quotin' Latin and his high-toned Jesuit College education, putting on airs as if he was too good to wipe his shoes on me, when he's nothing but a drunken bum who never done a tap of work in his life, except acting on the stage while his father was alive to get him the jobs. (Vindictively.) I'll pray you'll find a way to nab him, Josie, and skin him out of his last nickel!

JOSIE (makes a threatening move toward him): One more word out of you— (Then contemptuously.) You're a dirty tick and it'd serve you right if I let you stay gabbing until Father came and beat you to a jelly, but I won't. I'm too anxious to be rid of you. (Roughly.) Get out of here, now! Do you think he'll stay all day with the pigs, you gabbing fool? (She goes left to peer around the corner of the house— with real alarm.) There he is coming up to the barn. (MIKE grabs the satchel, terrified. He slinks swiftly around the corner and disappears along the path to the woods, right-rear. She keeps watching her father and does not notice MIKE's departure.) He's looking toward the meadow. He sees you're not working. He's running down there. He'll come here next. You'd better run for your life! (She peeks around the corner again—with amused admiration.) Look at my poor old father pelt. He's as spry on his stumpy legs as a yearling—and as full of rage as a nest of wasps! (She laughs and comes back to look along the path to the woods.) Well, that's

the last of you, Mike, and good riddance. It was the little boy you used to be that I had to mother, and not you, I stole the money for. (This dismisses him. She sighs.) Well, himself will be here in a minute. I'd better be ready. (She reaches in her bedroom corner by the door and takes out a sawed-off broom handle.) Not that I need it, but it saves his pride. (She sits on the steps with the broom handle propped against the steps near her right hand. A moment later, her father, PHIL HOGAN, comes running up from left-rear and charges around the corner of the house, his arms pumping up and down, his fists clenched, his face full of fighting fury.)

(HOGAN is fifty-five, about five feet six. He has a thick neck, lumpy, sloping shoulders, a barrel-like trunk, stumpy legs, and big feet. His arms are short and muscular, with large hairy hands. His head is round with thinning sandy hair. His face is fat with a snub nose, long upper lip, big mouth, and little blue eyes with bleached lashes and eyebrows that remind one of a white pig's. He wears heavy brogans, filthy overalls, and a dirty short-sleeved undershirt. Arms and face are sunburned and freckled. On his head is an old wide-brimmed hat of coarse straw that would look more becoming on a horse. His voice is high-pitched with a pronounced brogue.)

HOGAN (stops as he turns the corner and sees her— furiously): Where is he? Is he hiding in the house? I'll wipe the floors with him, the lazy bastard! (Turning his anger against her.) Haven't you a tongue in your head, you great slut you?

JOSIE (with provoking calm): Don't be calling me names, you bad-tempered old hornet, or maybe I'll lose my temper, too.

HOGAN: To hell with your temper, you overgrown cow!

JOSIE: I'd rather be a cow than an ugly little buck goat. You'd better sit down and cool off. Old men shouldn't run around raging in the noon sun. You'll get sunstroke.

JOGAN: To hell with sunstroke! Have you seen him?

JOSIE: Have I seen who?

HOGAN: Mike! Who else would I be after, the Pope? He was in the meadow, but the minute I turned my back he sneaked off. (He sees the pitchfork.) There's his pitchfork! Will you stop your lying!

JOSIE: I haven't said I didn't see him.

HOGAN: Then don't try to help him hide from me, or— Where is he?

JOSIE: Where you'll never find him.

HOGAN: We'll soon see! I'll bet he's in your room under the bed, the cowardly lump! (He moves toward the steps.)

JOSIE: He's not. He's gone like Thomas and John before him to escape your slave-driving.

HOGAN (stares at her incredulously): You mean he's run off to make his own way in the world?

JOSIE: He has. So make up your mind to it, and sit down.

HOGAN (*baffled, sits on the boulder and takes off his hat to scratch his head–with a faint trace of grudging respect*): I'd never dream he had that much spunk. (*His temper rising again.*) And I know damned well he hadn't, not without you to give him the guts and help him, like the great soft fool you are!

JOSIE: Now don't start raging again, Father.

HOGAN (*seething*): You've stolen my satchel to give him, I suppose, like you did before for Thomas and John?

JOSIE: It was my satchel, too. Didn't I help you in the trade for the horse, when you got the Crowleys to throw in the satchel for good measure? I was up all night fixing that nag's forelegs so his knees wouldn't buckle together till after the Crowleys had him a day or two.

HOGAN (*forgets his anger to grin reminiscently*): You've a wonderful way with animals, God bless you. And do you remember the two Crowleys came back to give me a beating, and I licked them both?

JOSIE (*with calculating flattery*): You did. You're a wonderful fighter. Sure, you could give Jack Dempsey himself a run for his money.

HOGAN (*with sharp suspicion*): I could, but don't try to change the subject and fill me with blarney.

JOSIE: All right. I'll tell the truth then. They were getting the best of you till I ran out and knocked one of them tail over tin cup against the pigpen.

HOGAN (*outraged*): You're a liar! They was begging for mercy before you came. (*Furiously.*) You thief, you! You stole my fine satchel for that lump! And I'll bet that's not all. I'll bet, like when Thomas and John sneaked off, you— (*He rises from the boulder threateningly.*) Listen, Josie, if you found where I had my little green bag, and stole money to give to that lousy altar boy, I'll—

JOSIE (*rises from the steps with the broom handle in her right hand*): Well, I did. So now what'll you do? Don't be threatening me. You know I'll beat better sense in your skull if you lay a finger on me.

HOGAN: I never yet laid hands on a woman—not when I was sober—but if it wasn't for that club— (*Bitterly.*) A fine curse God put on me when he gave me a daughter as big and strong as a bull, and as vicious and disrespectful. (*Suddenly his eyes twinkle and he grins admiringly.*) Be God, look at you standing there with the club! If you ain't the damnedest daughter in Connecticut, who is? (*He chuckles and sits on the boulder again.*)

JOSIE (*laughs and sits on the steps putting the club away*): And if you ain't the damnedest father in Connecticut, who is?

HOGAN (*takes a clay pipe and plug of tobacco and knife from his pocket. He cuts the plug and stuffs his pipe–without rancor*): How much did you steal, Josie?

JOSIE: Six dollars only.

HOGAN: *Only!* Well, God grant someone with wits will see that dopey gander at the depot and sell him the railroad for the six. (*Grumbling.*) It isn't the money I mind, Josie—

JOSIE: I know. Sure, what do you care for money? You'd give your last penny to the first beggar you met—if he had a shotgun pointed at your heart!

HOGAN: Don't be teasing. You know what I mean. It's the thought of that pious lump having my money that maddens me. I wouldn't put it past him to drop it in the collection plate next Sunday, he's that big a jackass.

JOSIE: I knew when you'd calmed down you'd think it worth six dollars to see the last of him.

HOGAN (*finishes filling his pipe*): Well, maybe I do. To tell the truth, I never liked him. (*He strikes a match on the seat of his overalls and lights his pipe.*) And I never liked Thomas and John, either.

JOSIE (*amused*): You've the same bad luck in sons I have in brothers.

HOGAN (*puffs ruminatively*): They all take after your mother's family. She was the only one in it had spirit, God rest her soul. The rest of them was a pious lousy lot. They wouldn't dare put food in their mouths before they said grace for it. They was too busy preaching temperance to have time for a drink. They spent so much time confessing their sins, they had no chance to do any sinning. (*He spits disgustedly.*) The scum of the earth! Thank God, you're like me and your mother.

JOSIE: I don't know if I should thank God for being like you. Sure, everyone says you're a wicked old tick, as crooked as a corkscrew.

HOGAN: I know. They're an envious lot, God forgive them. (*They both chuckle. He pulls on his pipe reflectively.*) You didn't get much thanks from Mike, I'll wager, for your help.

JOSIE: Oh, he thanked me kindly. And then he started to preach about my sins—and yours.

HOGAN: Oho, did he? (*Exploding.*) For the love of God, why didn't you hold him till I could give him one good kick for a parting blessing!

JOSIE: I near gave him one myself.

HOGAN: When I think your poor mother was killed bringing that crummy calf into life! (*Vindictively.*) I've never set foot in a church since, and never will. (*A pause. He speaks with a surprising sad gentleness.*) A sweet woman. Do you remember her, Josie? You were only a little thing when she died.

JOSIE: I remember her well. (*With a teasing smile which is half sad.*) She was the one could put you in your place when you'd come home drunk and want to tear down the house for the fun of it.

HOGAN (*with admiring appreciation*): Yes, she could do

it, God bless her. I only raised my hand to her once—just a slap because she told me to stop singing, it was after daylight. The next moment I was on the floor thinking a mule had kicked me. *(He chuckles.)* Since you've grown up, I've had the same trouble. There's no liberty in my own home.

JOSIE: That's lucky—or there wouldn't be any home.

HOGAN *(after a pause of puffing on his pipe)*: What did that donkey, Mike, preach to you about?

JOSIE: Oh, the same as ever—that I'm the scandal of the countryside, carrying on with men without a marriage license.

HOGAN *(gives her a strange, embarrassed glance and then looks away. He does not look at her during the following dialogue. His manner is casual)*: Hell roast his soul for saying it. But it's true enough.

JOSIE *(defiantly)*: It is, and what of it? I don't care a damn for the scandal.

HOGAN: No. You do as you please and to hell with everyone.

JOSIE: Yes, and that goes for you, too, if you are my father. So don't you start preaching too.

HOGAN: Me, preach? Sure, the divil would die laughing. Don't bring me into it. I learned long since to let you go your own way because there's no controlling you.

JOSIE: I do my work and I earn my keep and I've a right to be free.

HOGAN: You have. I've never denied it.

JOSIE: No. You've never. I've often wondered why a man that likes fights as much as you didn't grab at the excuse of my disgrace to beat the lights out of the men.

HOGAN: Wouldn't I look a great fool, when everyone knows any man who tried to make free with you, and you not willing, would be carried off to the hospital? Anyway, I wouldn't want to fight an army. You've had too many sweethearts.

JOSIE *(with a proud toss of her head—boastfully)*: That's because I soon get tired of any man and give him his walking papers.

HOGAN: I'm afraid you were born to be a terrible wanton woman. But to tell the truth, I'm well satisfied you're what you are, though I shouldn't say it, because if you was the decent kind, you'd have married some fool long ago, and I'd have lost your company and your help on the farm.

JOSIE *(with a trace of bitterness)*: Leave it to you to think of your own interest.

HOGAN *(puffs on his pipe)*: What else did my beautiful son, Mike, say to you?

JOSIE: Oh, he was full of stupid gab, as usual. He gave me good advice—

HOGAN *(grimly)*: That was kind of him. It must have been good—

JOSIE: I ought to marry and settle down—if I could

find a decent man who'd have me, which he was sure I couldn't.

HOGAN *(beginning to boil)*: I tell you, Josie, it's going to be the saddest memory of my life I didn't get one last swipe at him!

JOSIE: So the only hope, he thought, was for me to catch some indecent man, who'd have money coming to him I could steal.

HOGAN *(gives her a quick, probing side glance—casually)*: He meant Jim Tyrone?

JOSIE: He did. And the dirty tick accused you and me of making up a foxy scheme to trap Jim. I'm to get him alone when he's crazy drunk and lead him on to marry me. *(She adds in a hard, scornful tone.)* As if that would ever work. Sure, all the pretty little tarts on Broadway, New York, must have had a try at that, and much good it did them.

HOGAN *(again with a quick side glance—casually)*: They must have, surely. But that's in the city where he's suspicious. You never can tell what he mightn't do here in the country, where he's innocent, with a moon in the sky to fill him with poetry and a quart of bad hootch inside of him.

JOSIE *(turns on him angrily)*: Are you taking Mike's scheme seriously, you old goat?

HOGAN: I'm not. I only thought you wanted my opinion. *(She regards him suspiciously, but his face is blank, as if he hadn't a thought beyond enjoying his pipe.)*

JOSIE *(turning away)*: And if that didn't work, Mike said maybe we had a scheme that I'd get Jim in bed with me and you'd come with witnesses and a shotgun, and catch him there.

HOGAN: Faith, me darlin' son never learnt that from his prayer book! He must have improved his mind on the sly.

JOSIE: The dirty tick!

HOGAN: Don't call him a tick. I don't like ticks but I'll say this for them, I never picked one off me yet was a hypocrite.

JOSIE: Him daring to accuse us of planning a rotten trick like that on Jim!

HOGAN *(as if he misunderstood her meaning)*: Yes, it's as old as the hills. Everyone's heard of it. But it still works now and again, I'm told, and sometimes an old trick is best because it's so ancient no one would suspect you'd try it.

JOSIE *(staring at him resentfully)*: That's enough out of you, Father. I never can tell to this day, when you put that dead mug on you, whether you're joking or not, but I don't want to hear any more—

HOGAN *(mildly)*: I thought you wanted my honest opinion on the merits of Mike's suggestion.

JOSIE: Och, shut up, will you? I know you're only trying to make game of me. You like Jim and you'd never play a dirty trick on him, not even if I was willing.

HOGAN: No—not unless I found he was playing one on me.

JOSIE: Which he'd never.

HOGAN: No, I wouldn't think of it, but my motto in life is never trust anyone too far, not even myself.

JOSIE: You've reason for the last. I've often suspected you sneak out of bed in the night to pick your own pockets.

HOGAN: I wouldn't call it a dirty trick on him to get you for a wife.

JOSIE (exasperatedly): God save us, are you off on that again?

HOGAN: Well, you've put marriage in my head and I can't help considering the merits of the case, as they say. Sure, you're two of a kind, both great disgraces. That would help make a happy marriage because neither of you could look down on the other.

JOSIE: Jim mightn't think so.

HOGAN: You mean he'd think he was marrying beneath his station? He'd be a damned fool if he had that notion, for his Old Man who'd worked up from nothing to be rich and famous didn't give a damn about station. Didn't I often see him working on his grounds in clothes I wouldn't put on a scarecrow, not caring who saw him? (With admiring affection.) God rest him, he was a true Irish gentleman.

JOSIE: He was, and didn't you swindle him, and make me help you at it? I remember when I was a slip of a girl, and you'd get a letter saying his agent told him you were a year behind in the rent, and he'd be damned if he'd stand for it, and he was coming here to settle the matter. You'd make me dress up, with my hair brushed and a ribbon in it, and leave me to soften his heart before he saw you. So I'd skip down the path to meet him, and make a courtesy, and hold on to his hand, and bat my eyes at him and lead him in the house, and offer him a drink of the good whiskey you didn't keep for company, and gape at him and tell him he was the handsomest man in the world, and the fierce expression he'd put on for you would go away.

HOGAN (chuckles): You did it wonderful. You should have gone on the stage.

JOSIE (dryly): Yes, that's what he'd tell me, and he'd reach in his pocket and take out a half dollar, and ask me if you hadn't put me up to it. So I'd say yes, you had.

HOGAN (sadly): I never knew you were such a black traitor, and you only a child.

JOSIE: And then you'd come and before he could get a word out of him, you'd tell him you'd vacate the premises unless he lowered the rent and painted the house.

HOGAN: Be God, that used to stop him in his tracks.

JOSIE: It didn't stop him from saying you were the damnedest crook ever came out of Ireland.

HOGAN: He said it with admiration. And we'd start drinking and telling stories, and singing songs, and by the time he left we were both too busy cursing England to worry over the rent. (He grins affectionately.) Oh, he was a great man entirely.

JOSIE: He was. He always saw through your tricks.

HOGAN: Didn't I know he would? Sure, all I wanted was to give him the fun of seeing through them so he couldn't be hard-hearted. That was the real trick.

JOSIE (stares at him): You old devil, you've always a trick hidden behind your tricks, so no one can tell at times what you're after.

HOGAN: Don't be suspicious. Sure, I'd never try to fool you. You know me too well. But we've gone off the track. It's Jim we're discussing, not his father. I was telling you I could see the merit in your marrying him.

JOSIE (exasperatedly): Och, a cow must have kicked you in the head this morning.

HOGAN: I'd never give it a thought if I didn't know you had a soft spot in your heart for him.

JOSIE (resentfully): Well, I haven't! I like him, if that's what you mean, but it's only to talk to, because he's educated and quiet-spoken and has politeness even when he's drunkest, and doesn't roar around cursing and singing, like some I could name.

HOGAN: If you could see the light in your eyes when he blarneys you—

JOSIE (roughly): The light in me foot! (Scornfully.) I'm in love with him, you'll be saying next!

HOGAN (ignores this): And another merit of the case is, he likes you.

JOSIE: Because he keeps dropping in here lately? Sure, it's only when he gets sick of the drunks at the Inn, and it's more to joke with you than see me.

HOGAN: It's your happiness I'm considering when I recommend your using your wits to catch him, if you can.

JOSIE (jeeringly): If!

HOGAN: Who knows? With all the sweethearts you've had, you must have a catching way with men.

JOSIE (boastfully): Maybe I have. But that doesn't mean—

HOGAN: If you got him alone tonight—there'll be a beautiful moon to fill him with poetry and loneliness, and—

JOSIE: That's one of Mike's dirty schemes.

HOGAN: Mike be damned! Sure, that's every woman's scheme since the world was created. Without it there'd be no population. (*Persuasively.*) There'd be no harm trying it, anyway.

JOSIE: And no use, either. (*Bitterly.*) Och, Father, don't play the jackass with me. You know, and I know, I'm an ugly overgrown lump of a woman, and the men that want me are no better than stupid bulls. Jim can have all the pretty, painted little Broadway girls he wants—and dancers on the stage, too—when he comes into his estate. That's the kind he likes.

HOGAN: I notice he's never married one. Maybe he'd like a fine strong handsome figure of a woman for a change, with beautiful eyes and hair and teeth and a smile.

JOSIE (*pleased, but jeering*): Thank you kindly for your compliments. Now I know a cow kicked you in the head.

HOGAN: If you think Jim hasn't been taking in your fine points, you're a fool.

JOSIE: You mean you've noticed him? (*Suddenly furious.*) Stop your lying!

HOGAN: Don't fly in a temper. All I'm saying is, there may be a chance in it to better yourself.

JOSIE (*scornfully*): Better myself by being tied down to a man who's drunk every night of his life? No thank you!

HOGAN: Sure, you're strong enough to reform him. A taste of that club you've got, when he came home to you paralyzed, and in a few weeks you'd have him a dirty prohibitionist.

JOSIE (*seriously*): It's true, if I was his wife, I'd cure him of drinking himself to death, if I had to kill him. (*Then angrily.*) Och, I'm sick of your crazy gab, Father! Leave me alone!

HOGAN: Well, let's put it another way. Don't tell me you couldn't learn to love the estate he'll come into.

JOSIE (*resentfully*): Ah, I've been waiting for that. That's what Mike said again. Now we've come to the truth behind all your blather of my liking him or him liking me. (*Her manner changing—defiantly.*) All right then. Of course I'd love the money. Who wouldn't? And why shouldn't I get my hands on it, if I could? He's bound to be swindled out of it, anyway. He'll go back to the Broadway he thinks is heaven, and by the time the pretty little tarts, and the barroom sponges and racetrack touts and gamblers are through with him he'll be picked clean. I'm no saint, God knows, but I'm decent and deserving compared to those scum.

HOGAN (*eagerly*): Be God, now you're using your wits. And where there's a will there's a way. You and me have never been beat when we put our brains together. I'll keep thinking it over, and you do the same.

JOSIE (*with illogical anger*): Well, I won't! And you keep your mad scheming to yourself. I won't listen to it.

HOGAN (*as if he were angry, too*): All right. The divil take you. It's all you'll hear from me. (*He pauses—then with great seriousness, turning to her.*) Except one thing— (*As she starts to shut him up—sharply.*) I'm serious, and you'd better listen, because it's about this farm. which is home to us.

JOSIE (*surprised, stares at him*): What about the farm?

HOGAN: Don't forget, if we have lived on it twenty years, we're only tenants and we could be thrown out on our necks any time. (*Quickly.*) Mind you, I don't say Jim would ever do it, rent or no rent, or let the executors do it, even if they wanted, which they don't, knowing they'd never find another tenant.

JOSIE: What's worrying you, then?

HOGAN: This. I've been afraid lately the minute the estate is out of probate, Jim will sell the farm.

JOSIE (*exasperatedly*): Of course he will! Hasn't he told us and promised you can buy it on easy time payments at the small price you offered?

HOGAN: Jim promises whatever you like when he's full of whiskey. He might forget a promise as easy when he's drunk enough.

JOSIE (*indignantly*): He'd never! And who'd want it except us? No one ever has in all the years—

HOGAN: Someone has lately. The agent got an offer last month, Jim told me, bigger than mine.

JOSIE: Och, Jim loves to try and get your goat. He was kidding you.

HOGAN: He wasn't. I can tell. He said he told the agent to tell whoever it was the place wasn't for sale.

JOSIE: Of course he did. Did he say who'd made the offer?

HOGAN: He didn't know. It came through a real-estate man who wouldn't tell who his client was. I've been trying to guess, but I can't think of anyone crazy enough unless it'd be some damn fool of a millionaire buying up land to make a great estate for himself, like our beautiful neighbor, Harder, the Standard Oil thief, did years ago. (*He adds with bitter fervency.*) May he roast in hell and his Limey superintendent with him!

JOSIE: Amen to that. (*Then, scornfully.*) This land for an estate? And if there was an offer, Jim's refused it, and that ends it. He wouldn't listen to any offer, after he's given his word to us.

HOGAN: Did I say he would—when he's in his right mind? What I'm afraid of is, he might be led into it sometime when he has one of his sneering bitter drunks on and talks like a Broadway crook himself, saying money is the only thing in the world, and everything and anyone can be bought if the price is big enough. You've heard him.

JOSIE: I have. But he doesn't fool me at all. He only acts like he's hard and shameless to get back at life when it's tormenting him—and who doesn't? *(He gives her a quick, curious side glance which she doesn't notice.)*

HOGAN: Or take the other kind of queer drunk he gets on sometimes when, without any reason you can see, he'll suddenly turn strange, and look sad, and stare at nothing as if he was mourning over some ghost inside him, and—

JOSIE: I think I know what comes over him when he's like that. It's the memory of his mother comes back and his grief for her death. *(Pityingly.)* Poor Jim.

HOGAN *(ignoring this)*: And whiskey seems to have no effect on him, like water off a duck's back. He'll keep acting natural enough, and you'd swear he wasn't bad at all, but the next day you find his brain was so paralyzed he don't remember a thing until you remind him? He's done a lot of mad things, when he was that way, he was sorry for after.

JOSIE *(scornfully)*: What drunk hasn't? But he'd never— *(Resentfully.)* I won't have you suspecting Jim without any cause, d'you hear me!

HOGAN: I don't suspect him. All I've said is, when a man gets as queer drunk as Jim, he doesn't know himself what he mightn't do, and we'd be damned fools if we didn't fear the possibility, however small it is, and do all we can to guard against it.

JOSIE: There's no possibility! And how could we guard against it, if there was?

HOGAN: Well, you can put yourself out to be extra nice to him, for one thing.

JOSIE: How nice is extra nice?

HOGAN: You ought to know. But here's one tip. I've noticed when you talk rough and brazen like you do to other men, he may grin like they do, as if he enjoyed it, but he don't. So watch your tongue.

JOSIE *(with a defiant toss of her head)*: I'll talk as I please, and if he don't like it he can lump it! *(Scornfully.)* I'm to pretend I'm a pure virgin, I suppose? That would fool him, wouldn't it, and him hearing all about me from the men at the Inn? *(She gets to her feet, abruptly changing the subject.)* We're wasting the day, blathering. *(Then her face hardening.)* If he ever went back on his word, no matter how drunk he was, I'd be with you in any scheme you made against him, no matter how dirty. *(Hastily.)* But it's all your nonsense. I'd never believe it. *(She comes and picks up the pitchfork.)* I'll go to the meadow and finish Mike's work. You needn't fear you'll miss his help on the farm.

HOGAN: A hell of a help! A weak lazy back and the appetitie of a drove of starving pigs! *(As she turns to go—suddenly bellicose.)* Leaving me, are you? When it's dinner time? Where's my dinner, you lazy cow?

JOSIE: There's stew on the stove, you bad-tempered runt. Go in and help yourself. I'm not hungry. Your gab has bothered my mind. I need hard work in the sun to clear it. *(She starts to go off toward rear-right.)*

HOGAN *(glancing down the road, off left-front)*: You'd better wait. There's a caller coming to the gate—and if I'm not mistaken, it's the light of your eyes himself.

JOSIE *(angrily)*: Shut up! *(She stares off—her face softens and grows pitying.)* Look at him when he thinks no one is watching, with his eyes on the ground. Like a dead man walking slow behind his own coffin. *(Then roughly.)* Faith, he must have a hangover. He sees us now. Look at the bluff he puts up, straightening himself and grinning. *(Resentfully.)* I don't want to meet him. Let him make jokes with you and play the old game about a drink you both think is such fun. That's all he comes for, anyway. *(She starts off again.)*

HOGAN: Are you running away from him? Sure, you must be afraid you're in love. *(JOSIE halts instantly and turns back defiantly. He goes on.)* Go in the house now, and wash your face, and tidy your dress, and give a touch to your hair. You want to look decent for him.

JOSIE *(angrily)*: I'll go in the house, but only to see the stew ain't burned, for I supposed you'll have the foxiness to ask him to have a bit to eat to keep in his good graces.

HOGAN: Why shouldn't I ask him? I know damned well he has no appetite this early in the day, but only a thirst.

JOSIE: Och, you make me sick, you sly miser! *(She goes through her bedroom, slamming the door behind her. HOGAN refills his pipe, pretending he doesn't notice TYRONE approaching, his eyes bright with droll expectation. JIM TYRONE enters along the road from the highway, left.)*

(TYRONE is in his early forties, around five feet nine, broad-shouldered and deep-chested. His naturally fine physique has become soft and soggy from dissipation, but his face is still good-looking despite its unhealthy puffiness and the bags under the eyes. He has thinning dark hair, parted and brushed back to cover a bald spot. His eyes are brown, the whites congested and yellowish. His nose, big and aquiline, gives his face a certain Mephistophelian quality which is accentuated by his habitually cynical expression. But when he smiles without sneering, he still has the ghost of a former youthful irresponsible Irish charm—that of the beguiling ne'er-do-well, sentimental and romantic. It is his humor and charm which have kept him attractive to women, and popular with men as a drinking

companion. He is dressed in an expensive dark-brown suit, tight-fitting and drawn in at the waist, dark-brown made-to-order shoes and silk socks, a white silk shirt, silk handkerchief in breast pocket, a dark tie. This get-up suggests that he follows a style set by well-groomed Broadway gamblers who would like to be mistaken for Wall Street brokers.)

(He has had enough pick-me-ups to recover from morning-after nausea and steady his nerves. During the following dialogue, he and HOGAN *are like players at an old familiar game where each knows the other's moves, but which still amuses them.)*

TYRONE *(approaches and stands regarding* HOGAN *with a sardonic relish.* HOGAN *scratches a match on the seat of his overalls and lights his pipe, pretending not to see him.* TYRONE *recites with feeling)*:
"*Fortunate senex, ergo tua rura manebunt,
et tibi magna satis, quamvis lapis omnia nudus.*"

HOGAN *(mutters)*: It's the landlord again, and my shotgun not handy. *(He looks up at* TYRONE.*)* Is it Mass you're saying, Jim? That was Latin. I know it by ear. What the hell—insult does it mean?

TYRONE: Translated very freely into Irish English, something like this. *(He imitates* HOGAN'S *brogue.)* "Ain't you the lucky old bastard to have this beautiful farm, if it is full of nude rocks."

HOGAN: I like that part about the rocks. If cows could eat them this place would make a grand dairy farm. *(He spits.)* It's easy to see you've a fine college education. It must be a big help to you conversing with whores and barkeeps.

TYRONE: Yes, a very valuable worldly asset. I was once offered a job as office boy—until they discovered I wasn't qualified because I had no Bachelor of Arts diploma. There had been a slight misunderstanding just before I was to graduate.

HOGAN: Between you and the Fathers? I'll wager!

TYRONE: I made a bet with another Senior I could get a tart from the Haymarket to visit me, introduce her to the Jebs as my sister—and get away with it.

HOGAN: But you didn't?

TYRONE: Almost. It was a memorable day in the halls of learning. All the students were wise and I had them rolling in the aisles as I showed Sister around the grounds, accompanied by one of the Jebs. He was a bit suspicious at first, but Dutch Maisie—her professional name—had no make-up on, and was dressed in black, and had eaten a pound of Sen-Sen to kill the gin on her breath, and seemed such a devout girl that he forgot his suspicions. *(He pauses.)* Yes, all would have been well, but she was a mischievous minx, and had her own ideas of improving on my joke. When she was saying good-bye to Father Fuller, she added innocently: "Christ, Father, it's nice and quiet out here away from the damned Sixth

Avenue El. I wish to hell I could stay here!" *(Dryly.)* But she didn't, and neither did I.

HOGAN *(chuckles delightedly)*: I'll bet you didn't. God bless Dutch Maisie! I'd like to have known her.

TYRONE *(sits down on the steps—with a change of manner)*: Well, how's the Duke of Donegal this fine day?

HOGAN: Never better.

TYRONE: Slaving and toiling as usual, I see.

HOGAN: Hasn't a poor man a right to his noon rest without being sneered at by his rich landlord?

TYRONE: "Rich" is good. I would be, if you'd pay up your back rent.

HOGAN: You ought to pay me, instead, for occupying this rockpile, miscalled a farm. *(His eyes twinkling.)* But I have fine reports to give you of a promising harvest. The milkweed and the thistles is in thriving condition, and I never saw the poison ivy so bounteous and beautiful. *(*TYRONE *laughs. Without their noticing,* JOSIE *appears in the doorway behind* TYRONE. *She has tidied up and arranged her hair. She smiles down at* JIM, *her face softening, pleased to hear him laugh.)*

TYRONE: You win. Where did Josie go, Phil? I saw her here—

HOGAN: She ran in the house to make herself beautiful for you.

JOSIE *(breaks in roughly)*: You're a liar. *(To* TYRONE, *her manner one of bold, free-and-easy familiarity.)* Hello, Jim.

TYRONE *(starts to stand up)*: Hello, Josie.

JOSIE *(puts a hand on his shoulder and pushes him down)*: Don't get up. Sure, you know I'm no lady. *(She sits on the top step—banteringly.)* How's my fine Jim this beautiful day? You don't look so bad. You must have stopped at the Inn for an eye-opener—or ten of them.

TYRONE: I've felt worse. *(He looks up at her sardonically.)* And how's my Virgin Queen of Ireland?

JOSIE: Yours, is it? Since when? And don't be miscalling me a virgin. You'll ruin my reputation, if you spread that lie about me. *(She laughs.* TYRONE *is staring at her. She goes on quickly.)* How is it you're around so early? I though you never got up till afternoon.

TYRONE: Couldn't sleep. One of those heebie-jeebie nights when the booze keeps you awake instead of— *(He catches her giving him a pitying look—irritably.)* But what of it!

JOSIE: Maybe you had no woman in bed with you, for a change. It's a terrible thing to break the habit of years.

TYRONE *(shrugs his shoulders)*: Maybe.

JOSIE: What's the matter with the tarts in town, they let you do it? I'll bet the ones you know on Broadway, New York, wouldn't neglect their business.

TYRONE (*pretends to yawn boredly*): Maybe not. (*Then irritably.*) Cut out the kidding, Josie. It's too early.

HOGAN (*who has been taking everything in without seeming to*): I told you not to annoy the gentleman with your rough tongue.

JOSIE: Sure I thought I was doing my duty as hostess making him feel at home.

TYRONE (*stares at her again*): Why all the interest lately in the ladies of the profession, Josie?

JOSIE: Oh, I've been considering joining their union. It's easier living than farming, I'm sure. (*Then resentfully.*) You think I'd starve at it, don't you because your fancy is for dainty dolls of women! But other men like—

TYRONE (*with sudden revulsion*): For God's sake, cut out that kind of talk, Josie! It sounds like hell.

JOSIE (*stares at him startledly—then resentfully*): Oh, it does, does it? (*Forcing a scornful smile.*) I'm shocking you, I suppose? (HOGAN *is watching them both, not missing anything in their faces, while he seems intent on his pipe.*)

TYRONE (*looking a bit sheepish and annoyed at himself for his interest—shrugs his shoulders*): No. Hardly. Forget it. (*He smiles kiddingly.*) Anyway, who told you I fall for the dainty dolls? That's all a thing of the past. I like them tall and strong and voluptuous, now, with beautiful big breasts. (*She blushes and looks confused and is furious with herself for doing so.*)

HOGAN: There you are, Josie, darlin'. Sure he couldn't speak fairer than that.

JOSIE (*recovers herself*): He couldn't, indeed. (*She pats* TYRONE's *head—playfully.*) You're a terrible blarneying liar, Jim, but thank you just the same. (TYRONE *turns his attention to* HOGAN. *He winks at* JOSIE *and begins in an exaggeratedly casual manner.*)

TYRONE: I don't blame you, Mr. Hogan, for taking it easy on such a blazing hot day.

HOGAN (*doesn't look at him. His eyes twinkle*): Hot, did you say? I find it cool, meself. Take off your coat if you're hot, Mister Tyrone.

TYRONE: One of the most stifling days I've ever known. Isn't it, Josie?

JOSIE (*smiling*): Terrible. I know you must be perishing.

HOGAN: I wouldn't call it a damned bit stifling.

TYRONE: It parches the membranes in your throat.

HOGAN: The what? Never mind. I can't have them, for my throat isn't parched at all. If yours is, Mister Tyrone, there's a well full of water at the back.

TYRONE: Water? That's something people wash with, isn't it? I mean, some people.

HOGAN: So I've heard. But, like you, I find it hard to believe. It's a dirty habit. They must be foreigners.

TYRONE: As I was saying, my throat is parched after the long dusty walk I took just for the pleasure of being your guest.

HOGAN: I don't remember inviting you, and the road is hard macadam with divil a speck of dust, and it's less than a quarter mile from the Inn here.

TYRONE: I didn't have a drink at the Inn. I was waiting until I arrived here, knowing that you—

HOGAN: Knowing I'd what?

TYRONE: Your reputation as a generous host—

HOGAN: The world must be full of liars. So you didn't have a drink at the Inn? Then it must be the air itself smells of whiskey today, although I didn't notice it before you came. You've gone on the water-wagon, I suppose? Well, that's fine, and I ask pardon for misjudging you.

TYRONE: I've wanted to go on the wagon for the past twenty-five years, but the doctors have strictly forbidden it. It would be fatal—with my weak heart.

HOGAN: So you've a weak heart? Well, well, and me thinking all along it was your head. I'm glad you told me. I was just going to offer you a drink, but whiskey is the worst thing—

TYRONE: The Docs say it's a matter of life and death. I must have a stimulant—one big drink, at least, whenever I strain my heart walking in the hot sun.

HOGAN: Walk back to the Inn, then, and give it a good strain, so you can buy yourself two big drinks.

JOSIE (*laughing*): Ain't you the fools, playing that old game between you, and both of you pleased as punch!

TYRONE (*gives up with a laugh*): Hasn't he ever been known to loosen up, Josie?

JOSIE: You ought to know. If you need a drink you'll have to buy it from him or die of thirst.

TYRONE: Well, I'll bet this is one time he's going to treat.

HOGAN: Be God, I'll take that bet!

TYRONE: After you've heard the news I've got for you, you'll be so delighted you won't be able to drag out the old bottle quick enough.

HOGAN: I'll have to be insanely delighted.

JOSIE (*full of curiosity*): Shut up, Father. What news, Jim?

TYRONE: I have it off the grapevine that a certain exalted personage will drop in on you before long.

HOGAN: It's the sheriff again. I know by the pleased look on your mug.

TYRONE: Not this time. (*He pauses tantalizingly.*)

JOSIE: Bad luck to you, can't you tell us who?

TYRONE: A more eminent grafter than the sheriff— (*Sneeringly.*) A leading aristocrat in our Land of the Free and Get-Rich-Quick, whose boots are licked by one and all—and one of the Kings of our Republic by Divine Right of Inherited Swag. In short, I refer to your good neighbor, T. Stedman Harder, Standard Oil's sappiest child, whom I know you both love so dearly. (*There is a pause after this announcement.* HOGAN *and* JOSIE *stiffen, and their eyes begin to glitter. But they can't believe their luck at first.*)

HOGAN (*in an ominous whisper*): Did you say Harder is coming to call on us, Jim?

JOSIE: It's too good to be true.

TYRONE (*watching them with amusement*): No kidding. The great Mr. Harder intends to stop here on his way back to lunch from a horseback ride.

JOSIE: How do you know?

TYRONE: Simpson told me. I ran into him at the Inn.

HOGAN: That English scum of a superintendent!

TYRONE: He was laughing himself sick. He said he suggested the idea to Harder—told him you'd be overwhelmed with awe if he deigned to interview you in person.

HOGAN: Overwhelmed isn't the word. Is it, Josie?

JOSIE: It isn't indeed, Father.

TYRONE: For once in his life, Simpson is cheering for you. He doesn't like his boss. In fact, he asked me to tell you he hopes you kill him.

HOGAN (*disdainfully*): To hell with the Limey's good wishes. I'd like both of them to call together.

JOSIE: Ah, well, we can't have everything. (*to* TYRONE) What's the reason Mr. Harder decided to notice poor, humble scum the like of us?

TYRONE (*grinning*): That's right, Josie. Be humble. He'll expect you to know your place.

HOGAN: Will he now? Well, well. (*With a great happy sigh.*) This is going to be a beautiful day entirely.

JOSIE: But what's Harder's reason, Jim?

TYRONE: Well, it seems he has an ice pond on his estate.

HOGAN: Oho! So that's it!

TYRONE: Yes. That's it. Harder likes to keep up the good old manorial customs. He clings to his ice pond. And your pigpen isn't far from his ice pond.

HOGAN: A nice little stroll for the pigs, that's all.

TYRONE: And somehow Harder's fence in that vicinity has a habit of breaking down.

HOGAN: Fences are queer things. You can't depend on them.

TYRONE: Simpson says he's had it repaired a dozen times, but each time on the following night it gets broken down again.

JOSIE: What a strange thing! It must be the bad fairies. I can't imagine who else could have done it. Can you, Father?

HOGAN: I can't, surely.

TYRONE: Well, Simpson can. He knows you did it and he told his master so.

HOGAN (*disdainfully*): Master is the word. Sure, the

English can't live unless they have a lord's backside to kiss, the dirty slaves.

TYRONE: The result of those breaks in the fence is that your pigs stroll—as you so gracefully put it—stroll through to wallow happily along the shores of the ice pond.

HOGAN: Well, why not? Sure, they're fine ambitious American-born pigs and they don't miss any opportunities. They're like Harders' father who made the money for him.

TYRONE: I agree, but for some strange reason Harder doesn't look forward to the taste of pig in next summer's ice water.

HOGAN: He must be delicate. Remember he's delicate, Josie, and leave your club in the house. (*He bursts into joyful menacing laughter.*) Oh, be God and be Christ in the mountains! I've pined to have a quiet word with Mr. Harder for years, watching him ride past in his big shiny automobile with his snoot in the air, and being tormented always by the complaints of his Limey superintendent. Oh, won't I welcome him!

JOSIE: Won't *we*, you mean. Sure, I love him as much as you.

HOGAN: I'd kiss you, Jim, for this beautiful news, if you wasn't so damned ugly. Maybe Josie'll do it for me. She has a stronger stomach.

JOSIE: I will! He's earned it. (*She pulls* TYRONE's *head back and laughingly kisses him on the lips. Her expression changes. She looks startled and confused, stirred and at the same time frightened. She forces a scornful laugh.*) Och, there's no spirit in you! It's like kissing a corpse.

TYRONE (*gives her a strange surprised look—mockingly*): Yes? (*Turning to* HOGAN.) Well, how about that drink, Phil? I'll leave it to Josie if drinks aren't on the house.

HOGAN: *I* won't leave it to Josie. She's prejudiced, being in love.

JOSIE (*angrily*): Shut up, you old liar! (*Then guiltily, forcing a laugh.*) Don't talk nonsense to sneak out of treating Jim.

HOGAN (*sighing*): All right, Josie. Go get the bottle and one small glass, or he'll never stop nagging me. I can turn my back, so the sight of him drinking free won't break my heart. (JOSIE *gets up, laughing, and goes in the house.* HOGAN *peers at the road off left.*) On his way back to lunch you said? Then it's time— (*Fervently.*) O Holy Joseph, don't let the bastard change his mind!

TYRONE (*beginning to have qualms*): Listen, Phil. Don't get too enthusiastic. He has a big drag around here, and he'll have you pinched, sure as hell, if you beat him up.

HOGAN: Och, I'm no fool. (JOSIE *comes out with a bottle and a tumbler.*) Will you listen to this, Josie. He's warning me not to give Harder a beating—as if

I'd dirty my hands on the scum.

JOSIE: As if we'd need to. Sure, all we want is a quiet chat with him.

HOGAN: That's all. As neighbor to neighbor.

JOSIE *(hands* TYRONE *the bottle and tumbler)*: Here you are, Jim. Don't stint yourself.

HOGAN *(mournfully)*: A fine daughter! I tell you a small glass and you give him a bucket! *(As* TYRONE *pours a big drink, grinning at him, he turns away with a comic shudder.)* That's a fifty-dollar drink, at least.

TYRONE: Here's luck, Phil.

HOGAN: I hope you drown. *(*TYRONE *drinks and makes a wry face.)*

TYRONE: The best chicken medicine I've ever tasted.

HOGAN: That's gratitude for you! Here, pass me the bottle. A drink will warm up my welcome for His Majesty. *(He takes an enormous swig from the bottle.)*

JOSIE *(looking off left)*: There's two horseback riders on the county road now.

HOGAN: Praise be to God! It's him and a groom. *(He sets the bottle on top of the boulder.)*

JOSIE: That's McCabe. An old sweetheart of mine. *(She glances at* TYRONE *provokingly—then suddenly worried and protective.)* You get in the house, Jim. If Harder sees you here, he'll lay the whole blame on you.

TYRONE: Nix, Josie. You don't think I'm going to miss this, do you?

JOSIE: You can sit inside by my window and take in everything. Come on, now, don't be stubborn with me. *(She puts her hands under his arms and lifts him to his feet as easily as if he was a child—banteringly.)* Go into my beautiful bedroom. It's a nice place for you.

TYRONE *(kiddingly)*: Just what I've been thinking for some time, Josie.

JOSIE *(boldly)*: Sure, you've never given me a sign of it. Come up tonight and we'll spoon in the moonlight and you can tell me your thoughts.

TYRONE: That's a date. Remember, now.

JOSIE: It's you who'll forget. Go inside now, before it's too late. *(She gives him a shove inside and closes the door.)*

HOGAN *(has been watching the visitor approach)*: He's dismounting—as graceful as a scarecrow, and his poor horse longing to give him a kick. Look at Mac grinning at us. Sit down, Josie. *(She sits on the steps, he on the boulder.)* Pretend you don't notice him. *(T. STEDMAN HARDER appears at left. They act as if they didn't see him.* HOGAN *knocks out his pipe on the palm of his hand.)*

*(*HARDER *is in his late thirties but looks younger because his face is unmarked by worry, ambition, or any of the common hazards of life. No matter how long he lives, his four undergraduate years will always be for him the most significant in his life, and the moment of his highest achievement the time he was tapped for an exclusive Senior Society at the Ivy university to which his father had given millions. Since that day he has felt no need for further aspiring, no urge to do anything except settle down on his estate and live the life of a country gentleman, mildly interested in saddle horses and sport models of foreign automobiles. He is not the blatantly silly, playboy heir to millions whose antics make newspaper headlines. He doesn't drink much except when he attends his class reunion every spring—the most exciting episode of each year for him. He doesn't give wild parties, doesn't chase after musical-comedy cuties, is a mildly contented husband and father of three children. A not unpleasant man, affable, good-looking in an ordinary way, sunburnt and healthy, beginning to take on fat, he is simply immature, naturally lethargic, a bit stupid. Coddled from birth, everything arranged and made easy for him, deferred to because of his wealth, he usually has the self-confident attitude of acknowledged superiority, but assumes a supercilious insecure air when dealing with people beyond his ken. He is dressed in a beautifully tailored English tweed coat and whipcord riding breeches, immaculately polished English riding boots with spurs, and carries a riding crop in his hand.)*

(It would be hard to find anyone more ill-equipped for combat with the HOGANS. *He has never come in contact with anyone like them. To make matters easier for them he is deliberate in his speech, slow on the uptake, and has no sense of humor. The experienced strategy of the* HOGANS *in verbal battle is to take the offensive at once and never let an opponent get set to hit back. Also, they use a beautifully co-ordinated, bewildering change of pace, switching suddenly from jarring shouts to low, confidential vituperation. And they exaggerate their Irish brogues to confuse an enemy still further.)*

HARDER *(walks toward* HOGAN—*stiffly)*.: Good morning. I want to see the man who runs this farm.

HOGAN *(surveys him deliberately, his little pig eyes gleaming with malice)*: You do, do you? Well, you've seen him. So run along now and play with your horse, and don't bother me. *(He turns to* JOSIE, *who is staring at* HARDER, *much to his discomfiture, as if she had discovered a cockroach in her soup.)* D'you see what I see, Josie? Be God, you'll have to give that damned cat of yours a spanking for bringing it to our doorstep.

HARDER *(determined to be authoritative and command respect—curtly)*: Are you Hogan?

HOGAN *(insultingly)*: I am *Mister* Philip Hogan—to a gentleman.

JOSIE *(glares at* HARDER*)*: Where's your manners, you spindle-shanked jockey? Were you brought up in a stable?

HARDER *(does not fight with ladies, and especially not with this lady—ignoring her)*: My name is Harder. *(He obviously expects them to be immediately impressed and apologetic.)*

HOGAN *(contemptuously)*: Who asked you your name, me little man?

JOSIE: Sure, who in the world cares who the hell you are?

HOGAN: But if you want to play politeness, we'll play with you. Let me introduce you to my daughter, Harder—Miss Josephine Hogan.

JOSIE *(petulantly)*: I don't want to meet him, Father. I don't like his silly sheep's face, and I've no use for jockeys, anyway. I'll wager he's no damned good to a woman. *(From inside her bedroom comes a burst of laughter. This revelation of an unseen audience startles* HARDER. *He begins to look extremely unsure of himself.)*

HOGAN: I don't think he's a jockey. It's only the funny pants he's wearing. I'll bet if you asked his horse, you'd find he's no cowboy either. *(to* HARDER, *jeeringly)* Come, tell us the truth, me honey. Don't you kiss your horse each time you mount and beg him, please don't throw me today, darlin', and I'll give you an extra bucket of oats. *(He bursts into an extravagant roar of laughter, slapping his thigh, and* JOSIE *guffaws with him, while they watch the disconcerting effect of this theatrical mirth on* HARDER.*)*

HARDER *(beginning to lose his temper)*: Listen to me, Hogan! I didn't come here— *(He is going to add "to listen to your damned jokes" or something like that, but* HOGAN *silences him.)*

HOGAN *(shouts)*: What? What's that you said? *(He stares at the dumbfounded* HARDER *with droll amazement, as if he couldn't believe his ears.)* You didn't come here? *(He turns to* JOSIE–*in a whisper.)* Did you hear that, Josie? *(He takes off his hat and scratches his head in comic bewilderment.)* Well, that's a puzzle, surely. How d'you suppose he got here?

JOSIE: Maybe the stork brought him, bad luck to it for a dirty bird. *(Again* TYRONE'S *laughter is heard from the bedroom.)*

HARDER *(so off balance now he can only repeat angrily)*: I said I didn't come here—

HOGAN *(shouts)*: Wait! Wait, now! *(Threateningly.)* We've had enough of that. Say it a third time and I'll send my daughter to telephone the asylum.

HARDER *(forgetting he's a gentleman)*: Damn you, I'm the one who's had enough—!

JOSIE *(shouts)*: Hold your dirty tongue! I'll have no foul language in my presence.

HOGAN: Och, don't mind him, Josie. He's said he isn't here, anyway, so we won't talk to him behind his back. *(He regards* HARDER *with pitying contempt.)* Sure, ain't you the poor crazy creature? Do you want us to believe you're a ghost?

HARDER *(notices the bottle on the boulder for the first time—tries to be contemptuously tolerant and even to smile*

with condescending disdain): Ah! I understand now. You're drunk. I'll come back sometime when you're sober—or send Simpson— *(He turns away, glad of an excuse to escape.)*

JOSIE *(jumps up and advances on him menacingly)*: No, you don't! You'll apologize first for insulting a lady—insinuating I'm drunk this early in the day—or I'll knock some good breeding in you!

HARDER *(actually frightened now)*: I—I said nothing about you—

HOGAN *(gets up to come between them)*: Aisy now, Josie. He didn't mean it. He don't know what he means, the poor loon. *(to* HARDER–*pityingly)* Run home, that's a good lad, before your keeper misses you.

HARDER *(hastily)*: Good day. *(He turns eagerly toward left but suddenly* HOGAN *grabs his shoulder and spins him around–then shifts his grip to the lapel of* HARDER'S *coat.)*

HOGAN *(grimly)*: Wait now, me Honey Boy. I'll have a word with you, if you plaze. I'm beginning to read some sense into this. You mentioned that English bastard, Simpson. I know who you are now.

HARDER *(outraged)*: Take your hands off me, you drunken fool. *(He raises his riding crop.)*

JOSIE *(grabs it and tears it from his hand with one powerful twist–fiercely)*: Would you strike my poor infirm old father, you coward, you!

HARDER *(calling for help)*: McCabe!

HOGAN: Don't think McCabe will hear you, if you blew Gabriel's horn. He knows I or Josie can lick him with one hand. *(Sharply)* Josie! Stand between us and the gate. *(*JOSIE *takes her stand where the path meets the road. She turns her back for a moment, shaking with suppressed laughter, and waves her hand at* MC CABE *and turns back.* HOGAN *releases his hold on* HARDER'S *coat.)* There now. Don't try running away or my daughter will knock you senseless. *(He goes on grimly before* HARDER *can speak.)* You're the blackguard of a millionaire that owns the estate next to ours, ain't you? I've been meaning to call on you, for I've a bone to pick with you, you bloody tyrant! But I couldn't bring myself to set foot on land bought with Standard Oil money that was stolen from the poor it ground in the dust beneath its dirty heel—land that's watered with the tears of starving widows and orphans—*(He abruptly switches from this eloquence to a matter-of-fact tone.)* But never mind that, now. I won't waste words trying to reform a born crook. *(Fiercely, shoving his dirty unshaven face almost into* HARDER'S.*)* What I want to know is, what the hell d'you mean by your contemptible trick of breaking down your fence to entice my poor pigs to take their death in your ice pond? *(There is a shout of laughter from* JOSIE'S *bedroom, and* JOSIE *doubles up and holds her sides.* HARDER *is so flabbergasted by this mad accusation he cannot even sputter. But* HOGAN *acts as if he'd denied it–savagely.)* Don't lie, now! None of your damned Standard Oil excuses, or be Jaysus, I'll break you in half! Haven't I mended that fence morning after morning, and seen the footprints where you had sneaked up in the night to pull it down again. How many times have I mended that fence, Josie?

JOSIE: If it's once, it's a hundred, Father.

HOGAN: Listen, me little millionaire! I'm a peaceful, mild man that believes in live and let live, and as long as the neighboring scum leaves me alone, I'll let them alone, but when it comes to standing by and seeing my poor pigs murthered one by one—! Josie! How many pigs is it caught their death of cold in his damned ice pond and died of pneumonia?

JOSIE: Ten of them, Father. And ten more died of cholera after drinking the dirty water in it.

HOGAN: All prize pigs, too! I was offered two hundred dollars apiece for them. Twenty pigs at two hundred, that's four thousand. And a thousand to cure the sick and cover funeral expenses for the dead. Call it four thousand you owe me. *(Furiously.)* And you'll pay it, or I'll sue you, so help me Christ! I'll drag you in every court in the land! I'll paste your ugly mug on the front page of every newspaper as a pig-murdering tyrant! Before I'm through with you, you'll think you're the King of England at an Irish wake! *(With a quick change of pace to a wheedling confidential tone.)* Tell me now, if it isn't a secret, whatever made you take such a savage grudge against pigs? Sure, it isn't reasonable for a Standard Oil man to hate hogs.

HARDER *(manages to get in three sputtering words)*: I've had enough—!

HOGAN *(with a grin)*: Be God, I believe you! *(Switching to fierceness and grabbing his lapel again.)* Look out, now! Keep your place and be soft-spoken to your betters! You're not in your shiny automobile now with your funny nose cocked so you won't smell the poor people. *(He gives him a shake.)* And let me warn you! I have to put up with a lot of pests on this heap of boulders some joker once called a farm. There's a cruel skinflint of a landlord who swindles me out of my last drop of whiskey, and there's poison ivy, and ticks, and potato bugs, and there's snakes and skunks! But, be God, I draw the line somewhere, and I'll be damned if I'll stand for a Standard Oil man trespassing! So will you kindly get the hell out of here before I plant a kick on your backside that'll land you in the Atlantic Ocean! *(He gives* HARDER *a shove.)* Beat it now! *(*HARDER *tries to make some sort of dis-*

dainfully dignified exit. But he has to get by JOSIE.*)*

JOSIE *(leers at him idiotically)*: Sure, you wouldn't go without a word of good-bye to me, would you, darlin'? Don't scorn me just because you have on your jockey's pants. *(In a hoarse whisper.)* Meet me tonight, as usual, down by the pigpen. *(*HARDER'S *retreat becomes a rout. He disappears on left, but a second later his voice, trembling with anger, is heard calling back threateningly.)*

HARDER: If you dare touch that fence again, I'll put this matter in the hands of the police!

HOGAN *(shouts derisively)*: And I'll put it in my lawyer's hands and in the newspapers! *(He doubles up with glee.)* Look at him fling himself on his nag and spur the poor beast! And look at McCabe behind him! He can hardly stay in the saddle for laughing! *(He slaps his thigh.)* O Jaysus, this is a great day for the poor and oppressed! I'll do no more work! I'll go down to the Inn and spend money and get drunk as Moses!

JOSIE: Small blame to you. You deserve it. But you'll have your dinner first, to give you a foundation. Come on, now. *(They turn back toward the house. From inside another burst of laughter from* TYRONE *is heard.* JOSIE *smiles.)* Listen to Jim still in stitches. It's good to hear him laugh as if he meant it. *(*TYRONE *appears in the doorway of her bedroom.)*

TYRONE: O God, my sides are sore. *(They all laugh together. He joins them at the left corner of the house.)*

JOSIE: It's dinner time. Will you have a bite to eat with us, Jim? I'll boil you some eggs.

HOGAN: Och, why do you have to mention eggs? Don't you know it's the one thing he might eat? Well, no matter. Anything goes today. *(He gets the bottle of whiskey.)* Come in, Jim. We'll have a drink while Josie's fixing the grub. *(They start to go in the front door,* HOGAN *in the lead.)*

TYRONE *(suddenly–with sardonic amusement)*: Wait a minute. Let us pause to take a look at this very valuable property. Don't you notice the change, Phil? Every boulder on the place has turned to solid gold.

HOGAN: What the hell—? You didn't get the D.T.'s from my whiskey, I know that.

TYRONE: No D.T.'s about it. This farm has suddenly become a gold mine. You know that offer I told you about? Well, the agent did a little detective work and he discovered it came from Harder. He doesn't want the damned place but he dislikes you as a neighbor and he thinks the best way to get rid of you would be to become your landlord.

HOGAN: The sneaking skunk! I'm sorry I didn't give him that kick.

TYRONE: Yes. So am I. That would have made the place even more valuable. But as it is, you did nobly. I expect him to double or triple his first offer. In fact, I'll bet the sky is the limit now.

HOGAN (*gives* JOSIE *a meaningful look*): I see your point! But we're not worrying you'd ever forget your promise to us for any price.

TYRONE: Promise? What promise? You know what Kipling wrote: (*Paraphrasing the "Rhyme of the Three Sealers."*) There's never a promise of God or man goes north of ten thousand bucks.

HOGAN: D'you hear him, Josie? We can't trust him.

JOSIE: Och, you know he's kidding.

HOGAN: I don't! I'm becoming suspicious.

TYRONE (*a trace of bitterness beneath his amused tone*): That's wise dope, Phil. Trust and be a sucker. If I were you, I'd be seriously worried. I've always wanted to own a gold mine—so I could sell it.

JOSIE (*bursts out*): Will you shut up your rotten Broadway blather!

TYRONE (*stares at her in surprise*): Why so serious and indignant, Josie? You just told your unworthy Old Man I was kidding. (*to* HOGAN) At last, I've got you by the ears, Phil. We must have a serious chat about when you're going to pay that back rent.

HOGAN (*groans*): A landlord who's a blackmailer! Holy God, what next! (JOSIE *is smiling with relief now.*)

TYRONE: And you, Josie, please remember when I keep that moonlight date tonight I expect you to be very sweet to me.

JOSIE (*with a bold air*): Sure, you don't have to blackmail me. I'd be that to you, anyway.

HOGAN: Are you laying plots in my presence to seduce my only daughter? (*Then philosophically.*) Well, what can I do? I'll be drunk at the Inn, so how could I prevent it? (*He goes up the steps.*) Let's eat, for the love of God. I'm starving. (*He disappears inside the house.*)

JOSIE (*with an awkward playful gesture, takes* TYRONE *by the hand*): Come along, Jim.

TYRONE (*smiles kiddingly*): Afraid you'll lose me? Swell chance! (*His eyes fix on her breasts—with genuine feeling*). You have the most beautiful breasts in the world, do you know it, Josie?

JOSIE (*pleased—shyly*): I don't—but I'm happy if you think— (*Then quickly.*) But I've no time now to listen to your kidding, with my mad old father waiting for his dinner. So come on. (*She tugs at his hand and he follows her up the steps. Her manner changes to worried solicitude.*) Promise me you'll eat something, Jim. You've got to eat. You can't go on the way you are, drinking and never eating, hardly. You're killing yourself.

TYRONE (*sardonically*): That's right. Mother me, Josie, I love it.

JOSIE (*bullyingly*): I will, then. You need one to take care of you. (*They disappear inside the house.*)

ACT 2

(*Scene: The same, with the wall of the living room removed. It is a clear warm moonlight night, around eleven o'clock.*

JOSIE *is sitting on the steps before the front door. She has changed to her Sunday best, a cheap dark-blue dress, black stockings and shoes. Her hair is carefully arranged, and by way of adornment a white flower is pinned on her bosom. She is hunched up, elbows on knees, her chin in her hands. There is an expression on her face we have not seen before, a look of sadness and loneliness and humiliation.*

She sighs and gets slowly to her feet, her body stiff from sitting long in the same position. She goes into the living room, fumbles around for a box of matches, and lights a kerosene lamp on the table.

The living room is small, low-ceilinged, with faded, fly-specked wallpaper, a floor of bare boards. It is cluttered up with furniture that looks as if it had been picked up at a fire sale. There is a table at center, a disreputable old Morris chair beside it; two ugly sideboards, one at left, the other at right-rear; a porch rocking-chair, painted green, with a hole in its cane bottom; a bureau against the rear wall, with two chairs on either side of a door to the kitchen. On the bureau is an alarm clock which shows the time to be five past eleven. At right-front is the door to JOSIE'S *bedroom.*)

JOSIE (*looks at the clock—dully*): Five past eleven, and he said he'd be here around nine. (*Suddenly in a burst of humiliated anger, she tears off the flower pinned to her bosom and throws it in the corner.*) To hell with you, Jim Tyrone! (*From down the road, the quiet of the night is shattered by a burst of melancholy song. It is unmistakably* HOGAN'S *voice wailing an old Irish lament at the top of his lungs.* JOSIE *starts—then frowns irritably.*) What's bringing him home an hour before the Inn closes? He must be more paralyzed than ever I've known him. (*She listens to the singing—grimly.*) Ah, here you come, do you, as full as a tick! I'll give you a welcome, if you start cutting up! I'm in no mood to put up with you. (*She goes into her bedroom and returns with her broomstick club. Outside the singing grows louder as* HOGAN *approaches the house. He only remembers one verse of the song and he has been repeating it.*)

HOGAN:

Oh the praties they grow small
Over here, over here,
Oh, the praties they grow small
Over here.
Oh the praties they grow small
And we dig them in the fall
And we eat them skins and all
Over here, over here.

(*He enters left-front, weaving and lurching a bit. But*

he is not as drunk as he appears. Or rather, he is one of those people who can drink an enormous amount and be absolutely plastered when they want to be for their own pleasure, but at the same time are able to pull themselves together when they wish and be cunningly clear-headed. Just now, he is letting himself go and getting great satisfaction from it. He pauses and bellows belligerently at the house) Hurroo! Down with all tyrants, male and female! To hell with England, and God damn Standard Oil!

JOSIE *(shouts back)*: Shut up your noise, you crazy old billy goat!

HOGAN *(hurt and mournful)*: A sweet daughter and a sweet welcome home in the dead of night. *(Beginning to boil.)* Old goat! There's respect for you! *(Angrily–starting for the front door.)* Crazy billy goat, is it? Be God, I'll learn you manners! *(He pounds on the door with his fist.)* Open the door! Open this door, I'm saying, before I drive a fist through it, or kick it into flinders! *(He gives it a kick.)*

JOSIE: It's not locked, you drunken old loon! Open it yourself!

HOGAN *(turns the knob and stamps in)*: Drunken old loon, am I? Is that the way to address your father?

JOSIE: No. It's too damned good for him.

HOGAN: It's time I taught you a lesson. Be Jaysus, I'll take you over my knee and spank your tail, if you are as big as a cow! *(He makes a lunge to grab her.)*

JOSIE: Would you, though! Take that, then! *(She raps him smartly, but lightly, on his bald spot with the end of her broom handle.)*

HOGAN *(with an exaggerated howl of pain)*: Ow! *(His anger evaporates and he rubs the top of his head ruefully–with bitter complaint.)* God forgive you, it's a great shame to me I've raised a daughter so cowardly she has to use a club.

JOSIE *(puts her club on the table–grimly)*: Now I've no club.

HOGAN *(evades the challenge)*: I never thought I'd see the day when a daughter of mine would be such a coward as to threaten her old father when he's helpless drunk and can't hit back. *(He slumps down on the Morris chair.)*

JOSIE: Ah, that's better. Now that little game is over. *(Then angrily.)* Listen to me, Father. I have no patience left, so get up from that chair, and go in your room, and go to bed, or I'll take you by the scruff of your neck and the seat of your pants and throw you in and lock the door on you! I mean it now! *(On the verge of angry tears.)* I've had all I can bear this night, and I want some peace and sleep, and not to listen to an old lush!

HOGAN *(appears drunker, his head wagging, his voice thick, his talk rambling)*: That's right. Fight with me. My own daughter has no feelings or sympathy. As if

I hadn't enough after what's happened tonight.

JOSIE *(with angry disgust)*: Och, don't try— *(Then curiously.)* What's happened? I thought something must be queer, you coming home before the Inn closed, but then I thought maybe for once you'd drunk all you could hold. *(Scathingly.)* And, God pity you, if you ain't that full, you're damned close to it.

HOGAN: Go on. Make fun of me. Old lush! You wouldn't feel so comical, if— *(He stops, mumbling to himself.)*

JOSIE: If what?

HOGAN: Never mind. Never mind. I didn't come home to fight, but seek comfort in your company. And if I was singing coming along the road, it was only because there's times you have to sing to keep from crying.

JOSIE: I can see you crying!

HOGAN: You will. And you'll see yourself crying, too, when— *(He stops again and mumbles to himself.)*

JOSIE: When what! *(Exasperatedly.)* Will you stop your whiskey drooling and talk plain?

HOGAN *(thickly)*: No matter. No matter. Leave me alone.

JOSIE *(angrily)*: That's good advice. To hell with you! I know your game. Nothing at all has happened. All you want is to keep me up listening to your guff. Go to your room, I'm saying, before—

HOGAN: I won't. I couldn't sleep with my thoughts tormented the way they are. I'll stay here in this chair, and you go to your room and let me be.

JOSIE *(snorts)*: And have you singing again in a minute and smashing the furniture—

HOGAN: Sing, is it? Are you making fun again? I'd give a keen of sorrow or howl at the moon like an old mangy hound in his sadness if I knew how, but I don't. So rest aisy. You won't hear a sound from me. Go on and snore like a pig to your heart's content. *(He mourns drunkenly.)* A fine daughter! I'd get more comfort from strangers.

JOSIE: Och, for God's sake, dry up! You'll sit in the dark then. I won't leave the lamp lit for you to tip over and burn down the house. *(She reaches out to turn down the lamp.)*

HOGAN *(thickly)*: Let it burn to the ground. A hell of a lot I care if it burns.

JOSIE *(in the act of turning down the lamp, stops and stares at him, puzzled and uneasy)*: I never heard you talk that way before, no matter how drunk you were. *(He mumbles. Her tone becomes persuasive.)* What's happened to you, Father?

HOGAN *(bitterly)*: Ah it's "Father" now, is it, not old billy goat? Well, thank God for small favors. *(With heavy sarcasm.)* Oh, nothing's happened to me at all, at all. A trifle, only. I wouldn't waste your time mentioning it, or keep you up when you want sleep so bad.

JOSIE (angrily): Och, you old loon, I'm sick of you. Sleep it off till you get some sense. (She reaches for the lamp again.)

HOGAN: Sleep it off? We'll see if you'll sleep it off when you know— (He lapses into drunken mumbling.)

JOSIE (again stares at him): Know what, Father?

HOGAN (mumbles): The son of a bitch!

JOSIE (trying a light tone): Sure, there's a lot of those in the neighborhood. Which one do you mean? Is Harder on your mind again?

HOGAN (thickly): He's one and a prize one, but I don't mean him. I'll say this for Harder, you know what to expect from him. He's no wolf in sheep's clothing, nor a treacherous snake in the grass who stabs you in the back with a knife—

JOSIE (apprehensive now—forces a joke): Sure, if you've found a snake who can stab you with a knife, you'd better join the circus with him and make a pile of money.

HOGAN (bitterly): Make jokes, God forgive you! You'll soon laugh from the wrong end of your mouth! (He mumbles.) Pretending he's our friend! The lying bastard!

JOSIE (bristles resentfully): Is it Jim Tyrone you're calling hard names?

HOGAN: That's right. Defend him, you big soft fool! Faith, you're a prize dunce! You've had a good taste of believing his word, waiting hours for him dressed up in your best like a poor sheep without pride or spirit—

JOSIE (stung): Shut up! I was calling him a lying bastard myself before you came, and saying I'd never speak to him again. And I knew all along he'd never remember to keep his date after he got drunk.

HOGAN: He's not so drunk he forgot to attend to business.

JOSIE (as if she hadn't heard—defiantly): I'd have stayed up anyway a beautiful night like this to enjoy the moonlight, if there wasn't a Jim Tyrone in the world.

HOGAN (with heavy sarcasm): In your best shoes and stockings? Well, well. Sure, the moon must feel flattered by your attentions.

JOSIE (furiously): You won't feel flattered if I knock you tail over tincup out of that chair! And stop your whiskey gabble about Jim. I see what you're driving at with your dark hints and curses, and if you think I'll believe— (With forced assurance.) Sure, I know what's happened as well as if I'd been there. Jim saw you'd got drunker than usual and you were an easy mark for a joke, and he made a goat of you!

HOGAN (bitterly): Goat again! (He struggles from his chair and stands swaying unsteadily—with offended dignity.) All right, I won't say another word. There's no use telling the truth to a bad-tempered woman in love.

JOSIE: Love be damned! I hate him now!

HOGAN: Be Christ, you have me stumped. A great proud slut who's played games with half the men around here, and now you act like a numbskull virgin that can't believe a man would tell her a lie!

JOSIE (threateningly): If you're going to your room, you'd better go quick!

HOGAN (fixes his eyes on the door at rear—with dignity): That's where I'm going, yes—to talk to myself so I'll know someone with brains is listening. Good night to you, Miss Hogan. (He starts—swerves left—tries to correct this and lurches right and bumps against her, clutching the supporting arm she stretches out.)

JOSIE: God help you, if you try to go upstairs now, you'll end up in the cellar.

HOGAN (hanging on to her arm and shoulder—maudlinly affectionate now): You're right. Don't listen to me. I'm wrong to bother you. You've had sorrow enought this night. Have a good sleep, while you can, Josie, darlin'—and good night and God bless you. (He tries to kiss her, but she wards him off and steers him back to the chair.)

JOSIE: Sit down before you split in pieces on the floor and I have to get a wheelbarrow to collect you. (She dumps him in the chair where he sprawls limply, his chin on his chest.)

HOGAN (mumbles dully): It's too late. It's all settled. We're helpless, entirely.

JOSIE (really worried now): How is it all settled? If you're helpless, I'm not. (Then as he doesn't reply—scornfully.) It's the first time I ever heard you admit you were licked. And it's the first time I ever saw you so paralyzed you couldn't shake the whiskey from your brains and get your head clear when you wanted. Sure, that's always been your pride—and now look at you, the stupid object you are, mumbling and drooling!

HOGAN (struggles up in his chair—angrily): Shut up your insults! Be God, I can get my head clear if I like! (He shakes his head violently.) There! It's clear. I can tell you each thing that happened tonight as clear as if I'd not taken a drop, if you'll listen and not keep calling me a liar.

JOSIE: I'll listen, now I see you have hold of your wits.

HOGAN: All right, then. I'll begin at the beginning when him and me left here, and you gave him a sweet smile, and rolled your big beautiful cow's eyes at him, and wiggled your backside, and stuck out your beautiful breasts you know he admires, and said in a sick sheep's voice. "Don't forget our moonlight date, Jim."

JOSIE (with suppressed fury): You're a—! I never—! You old—!

HOGAN: And he said: "You bet I won't forget, Josie."

JOSIE: The lying crook!

HOGAN (*his voice begins to sink into a dejected monotone*): We went to the Inn and started drinking whiskey. And I got drunk.

JOSIE (*exasperatedly*): I guessed that! And Jim got drunk, too. And then what?

HOGAN (*dully*): Who knows how drunk he got? He had one of his queer fits when you can't tell. He's the way I told you about this morning, when he talks like a Broadway crook, who'd sell his soul for a price, and there's a sneering divil in him, and he loves to pick out the weakness in people and say cruel, funny things that flay the hide off them, or play cruel jokes on them. (*With sudden rage.*) God's curse on him, I'll wager he's laughing to himself this minute, thinking it's the cutest joke in the world, the fools he made of us. You in particular. Be God, I had my suspicions, at least, but your head was stuffed with mush and love, and you wouldn't—

JOSIE (*furiously*): You'll tell that lie about my love once too often! And I'll play a joke on him yet that'll make him sorry he—

HOGAN (*sunk in drunken defeatism again*): It's too late. You shouldn't have let him get away from you to the Inn. You should have kept him here. Then maybe, if you'd got him drunk enough you could have— (*His head nodding, his eyes blinking—thickly.*) But it's no good talking now—no good at all—no good—

JOSIE (*gives him a shake*): Keep hold of your wits or I'll give you a cuff on both ears! Will you stop blathering like an old woman and tell me plainly what he's done!

HOGAN: He's agreed to sell the farm, that's what! Simpson came to the Inn to see him with a new offer from Harder. Ten thousand, cash.

JOSIE (*overwhelmed*): Ten thousand! Sure, three is all it's worth at most. And two was what you offered that Jim promised—

HOGAN: What's money to Harder? After what we did to him, all he wants is revenge. And here's where he's foxy. Simpson must have put him up to it knowing how Jim hates it here living on a small allowance, and he longs to go back to Broadway and his whores. Jim won't have to wait for his half of the cash till the estate's settled. Harder offers to give him five thousand cash as a loan against the estate the second the sale is made. Jim can take the next train to New York.

JOSIE (*tensely, on the verge of tears*): And Jim accepted? I don't believe it!

HOGAN: Don't then. Be God, you'll believe it tomorrow. Harder proposed that he meet with Jim and the executors in the morning and settle it, and Jim promised Simpson he would.

JOSIE (*desperately*): Maybe he'll get so drunk he'll never remember—

HOGAN: He won't. Harder's coming in his automobile to pick him up and make sure of him. Anyway don't think because he forgot you were waiting—in the moonlight, eating your heart out, that he'd ever miss a date with five thousand dollars, and all the pretty whores of Broadway he can buy with it.

JOSIE (*distractedly*): Will you shut up! (*Angrily.*) And where were you when all this happened? Couldn't you do anything to stop it, you old loon?

HOGAN: I couldn't. Simpson came and sat at the table with us—

JOSIE: And you let him!

HOGAN: Jim invited him. Anyway, I wanted to find out what trick he had up his sleeve, and what Jim would do. When it was all over, I got up and took a swipe at Simpson, but I missed him. (*With drunken sadness.*) I was too drunk—too drunk—too drunk— I missed him, God forgive me! (*His chin sinks on his chest and his eyes shut.*)

JOSIE (*shakes him*): If you don't keep awake, be God, I won't miss you!

HOGAN: I was going to take a swipe at Jim, too, but I couldn't do it. My heart was too broken with sorrow. I'd come to love him like a son—a real son of my heart!—to take the place of that jackass, Mike, and me two other jackasses.

JOSIE (*her face hard and bitter*): I think now Mike was the only one in this house with sense.

HOGAN: I was too drowned in sorrow by his betraying me—and you he'd pretended to like so much. So I only called him a dirty lying skunk of a treacherous bastard, and I turned my back on him and left the Inn, and I made myself sing on the road so he'd hear, and they'd all hear in the Inn, to show them I didn't care a damn.

JOSIE (*scathingly*): Sure, wasn't you the hero! A hell of a lot of good—

HOGAN: Ah, well, I suppose the temptation was too great. He's weak, with one foot in the grave from whiskey. Maybe we shouldn't blame him.

JOSIE (*her eyes flashing*): Not blame him? Well, I blame him, God damn him! Are you making excuses for him, you old fool!

HOGAN: I'm not. He's a dirty snake! But I was thinking how do I know what I wouldn't do for five thousand cash, and how do you know what you wouldn't do?

JOSIE: Nothing could make me betray him! (*Her face grows hard and bitter.*) Or it couldn't before. There's nothing I wouldn't do now. (HOGAN *suddenly begins to chuckle.*) Do you think I'm lying? Just give me a chance—

HOGAN: I remembered something. (*He laughs drunk-*

enly.) Be Christ, Josie, for all his Broadway wisdom about women, you've made a prized damned fool of him and that's some satisfaction!

JOSIE (*bewildered*): How'd you mean?

HOGAN: You'll never believe it. Neither did I, But he kept on until, be God, I saw he really meant it.

JOSIE: Meant what?

HOGAN: It was after he'd turned queer—early in the night before Simpson came. He started talking about you, as if you was on his mind, worrying him—and before he finished I take my oath I began to hope you could really work Mike's first scheme on him, if you got him alone in the moonlight, because all his gab was about his great admiration for you.

JOSIE: Och! The liar!

HOGAN: He said you had great beauty in you that no one appreciated but him.

JOSIE (*shakenly*): You're lying.

HOGAN: Great strength, you had, and great pride, he said—and great goodness, no less! But here's where you've made a prize jackass of him, like I said. (*With a drunken leer.*) Listen now, darlin', and don't drop dead with amazement. (*He leans toward her and whispers.*) He believes you're a virgin! (JOSIE *stiffens as if she'd been insulted.* HOGAN *goes on.*) He does, so help me! He means it, the poor dunce! He thinks you're a poor innocent virgin! He thinks it's all boasting and pretending you've done about being a slut. (*He chuckles.*) A virgin, no less! You!

JOSIE (*furiously*): Stop saying it! Boasting and pretending, am I? The dirty liar!

HOGAN: Faith, you don't have to tell me. (*Then he looks at her in drunken surprise–thickly.*) Are you taking it as an insult? Why the hell don't you laugh? Be God, you ought to see what a stupid sheep that makes him.

JOSIE (*forces a laugh*): I do see it.

HOGAN (*chuckling drunkenly*): Oh, be God, I've just remembered another thing, Josie. I know why he didn't keep his date with you. It wasn't that he'd forgot. He remembered well enough, for he talked about it—

JOSIE: You mean he deliberately, knowing I'd be waiting— (*Fiercely.*) God damn him!

HOGAN: He as much as told me his reason, though he wouldn't come out with it plain, me being your father. His conscience was tormenting him. He's going to leave you alone and not see you again—for your sake, because he loves you! (*He chuckles.*)

JOSIE (*looks stricken and bewildered–her voice trembling*): Loves me? You're making it up.

HOGAN: I'm not. I know it sounds crazy but—

JOSIE: What did he mean, for my sake?

HOGAN: Can't you see? You're a pure virgin to him,

but all the same there's things besides your beautiful soul he feels drawn to, like your beautiful hair and eyes, and—

JOSIE (*strickenly*): Och, don't Father! You know I'm only a big—

HOGAN (*as if she hadn't spoken*): So he'll keep away from temptation because he can't trust himself, and it'd be a sin on his conscience if he was to seduce you. (*He laughs drunkenly.*) Oh, be God! If that ain't rich!

JOSIE (*her voice trembles*): So that was his reason— (*Then angrily.*) So he thinks all he has to do is crook a finger and I'll fall for him, does he, the vain Broadway crook!

HOGAN (*chuckling*): Be Jaysus, it was the maddest thing in the world, him gabbing like a soft loon about you—and there at the bar in plain sight was two of the men you've been out with, the gardener at Smith's, and Regan, the chauffeur for Driggs, having a drink together!

JOSIE (*with a twitching smile*): It must have been mad, surely. I wish I'd been there to laugh up my sleeve. (*Angry.*) But what's all his crazy lying blather got to do with him betraying us and selling the place?

HOGAN (*at once, hopelessly dejected again*): Nothing at all. I only thought you'd like to know you'd had that much revenge.

JOSIE: A hell of a revenge! I'll have a better one than that on him— or I'll try to! I'm not like you, owning up I'm beaten and crying wurra-wurra like a coward and getting hopeless drunk! (*She gives him a shake.*) Get your wits about you and answer me this: Did Simpson get him to sign a paper?

HOGAN: No, but what good is that? In the morning he'll sign all they shove in front of him.

JOSIE: It's this good. It means we still have a chance. Or I have.

HOGAN: What chance? Are you going to beg him to take pity on us?

JOSIE: I'll see him in hell first! There's another chance, and a good one. But I'll need your help— (*Angrily.*) And look at you, your brains drowned in whiskey, so I can't depend on you!

HOGAN (*rousing himself*): You can, if there's any chance. Be God, I'll make myself as sober as a judge for you in the wink of an eye! (*Then dejectedly.*) But what can you do now, darlin'? You haven't even got him here. He's down at the Inn sitting alone, drinking and dreaming of the little whores he'll be with tomorrow night on Broadway.

JOSIE: I'll get him here! I'll humble my pride and go down to the Inn for him! And if he doesn't want to come I've a way to make him. I'll raise a scene and pretend I'm in a rage because he forgot his date. I'll disgrace him till he'll be glad to come with me to shut me up. I know his weakness, and it's his vanity about his women. If I was a dainty, pretty tart he'd be proud I'd raise a rumpus about him. But when it's a big, ugly hulk like me— (*She falters and forces herself to go on.*) If he ever was tempted to want me, he'd be ashamed of it. That's the truth behind the lies he told you of his conscience and his fear he might ruin me, God damn him!

HOGAN: No, he meant it, Josie. But never mind that now. Let's say you've got him here. Then what will you do?

JOSIE: I told you this morning if he ever broke his promise to us I'd do anything and not mind how crooked it was. And I will! Your part in it is to come at sunrise with witnesses and catch us in— (*She falters.*)

HOGAN: In bed, is it? Then it's Mike's second scheme you're thinking about?

JOSIE: I told you I didn't care how dirty a trick— (*With a hard bitter laugh.*) The dirtier the better now!

HOGAN: But how'll you get him in bed, with all his honorable scruples, thinking you're a virgin? But I'm forgetting he stayed away because he was afraid he'd be tempted. So maybe—

JOSIE (*tensely*): For the love of God, don't harp on his lies. He won't be tempted at all. But I'll get him so drunk he'll fall asleep and I'll carry him in and put him in bed—

HOGAN: Be God, that's the way! But you'll have to get a pile of whiskey down him. You'll never do it unless you're more sociable and stop looking at him the way you do, whenever he takes a drink, as if you was praying Almighty God to forgive a poor drunkard. You've got to encourage him. The best way would be for you to drink with him. It would put him at his ease and unsuspecting, and it'd give you courage, too, so you'd act bold for a change instead of giving him brazen talk he's tired of hearing, while you act shy as a mouse.

JOSIE (*gives her father a bitter, resentful look*): You're full of sly advice all of a sudden, ain't you? You dirty little tick!

HOGAN (*angrily*): Didn't you tell me to get hold of my wits? Be God if you want me drunk, I've only to let go. That'd suit me. I want to forget my sorrow, and I've no faith in your scheme because you'll be too full of scruples. Like the drinking. You're such a virtuous teetotaller—

JOSIE: I've told you I'd do anything now! (*Then confusedly.*) All I meant was, it's not right, a father to tell his daughter how to— (*Then angrily.*) I don't need your advice. Haven't I had every man I want around here?

HOGAN: Ah, thank God, that sounds natural! Be God, I thought you'd started playing virgin with me just because the Broadway sucker thinks you're one.

JOSIE (*furiously*): Shut up! I'm not playing anything. And don't worry I can't do my part of the trick.

HOGAN: That's the talk! But let me get it all clear. I come at sunrise with my witnesses, and you've forgot to lock your door, and we walk in, and there's the two of you in bed, and I raise the roof and threaten him if he don't marry you—

JOSIE: Marry him? After what he's done to us? I wouldn't marry him now if he was the last man on earth! All we want is a paper signed by him with witnesses that he'll sell the farm to you for the price you offered, and not to Harder.

HOGAN: Well, that's justice, but that's all it is. I thought you wanted to make him pay for his black treachery against us, the dirty bastard!

JOSIE: I do want! (*She again gives him a bitter resentful glance.*) It's the estate money you're thinking of, isn't it? Leave it to you! (*Hastily.*) Well, so am I! I'd like to get my hooks on it! (*With a hard, brazen air.*) Be God, if I'm to play whore, I deserve my pay! We'll make him sign a paper he owes me ten thousand dollars the minute the estate is settled. (*She laughs.*) How's that? I'll bet none of his tarts on Broadway ever got a thousandth part of that out of him, no matter how dainty and pretty! (*Laughing again.*) And here's what'll be the greatest joke to teach him a lesson. He'll pay for it for nothing! I'll get him in bed but I'll never let him—

HOGAN (*with delighted admiration*): Och, by Jaysus, Josie, that's the best yet! (*He slaps his thigh enthusiastically.*) Oh, that'll teach him to doublecross his friends! That'll show him two can play at tricks! And him believing you so innocent! Be God, you'll make him the prize sucker of the world! Won't I roar inside me when I see his face in the morning! (*He bursts into coarse laughter.*)

JOSIE (*again with illogical resentment*): Stop laughing! You're letting yourself be drunk again. (*Then with a hard, business-like air.*) We've done enough talking. Let's start—

HOGAN: Wait, now. There's another thing. Just what do you want me to threaten him with when I catch you? That we'll sue him for outraging your virtue? Sure, his lawyer would have all your old flames in the witness box, till the jury would think you'd been faithful to the male inhabitants of America. So what threat—I can't think of any he wouldn't laugh at.

JOSIE (*tensely*): Well I can! Do I have to tell you his weakness again? It's his vanity about women, and his Broadway pride he's so wise no woman could fool him. It's the disgrace to his vanity—being caught with the likes of me— (*Falteringly, but forcing herself to go on.*) My mug beside his in all the newspapers—the New York papers, too—he'll see the whole of Broadway splitting their sides laughing at him—and he'll give anything to keep us quiet, I tell you. He will! I know him! So don't worry— (*She ends up on the verge of bitter humiliated tears.*)

HOGAN (*without looking at her–enthusiastic again*): Be God, you're right!

JOSIE (*gives him a bitter glance–fiercely*): Then get the hell out of that chair and let's start it! (*He gets up. She surveys him resentfully.*) You're steady on your pins, ain't you, you scheming old thief, now there's the smell of money around! (*Quickly.*) Well, I'm glad. I know I can depend on you now. You'll walk down to the Inn with me and hide outside until you see me come out with him. Then you can sneak in the Inn yourself and pick the witnesses to stay up with you. But mind you don't get drunk again, and let them get too drunk.

HOGAN: I won't, I take my oath! (*He pats her on the shoulder approvingly.*) Be God, you've got the proud, fighting spirit in you that never says die, and you make me ashamed of my weakness. You're that eager now, be damned if I don't almost think you're glad of the excuse!

JOSIE (*stiffens*): Excuse for what, you old—

HOGAN: To show him no man can get the best of you—what else?—like you showed all the others.

JOSIE: I'll show him to his sorrow! (*Then abruptly, starting for the screen door at left.*) Come on. We've no time to waste. (*But when she gets to the door, she appears suddenly hesitant and timid–hurriedly.*) Wait. I'd better give a look at myself in the mirror. (*In a brazen tone.*) Sure, those in my trade have to look their best! (*She hurries back across the room into her bedroom and closes the door.* HOGAN *stares after her. Abruptly he ceases to look like a drunk who, by an effort, is keeping himself half-sober. He is a man who has been drinking a lot but is still clear-headed and has complete control of himself.*)

HOGAN (*watches the crack under* JOSIE'S *door and speaks half-aloud to himself, shaking his head pityingly*): A look in the mirror and she's forgot to light her lamp! (*Remorsefully.*) God forgive me, it's bitter medicine. But it's the only way I can see that has a chance now. (JOSIE'S *door opens. At once, he is as he was. She comes out, a fixed smile on her lips, her head high, her face set defiantly. But she has evidently been crying.*)

JOSIE (*brazenly*): There, now. Don't I look ten thousand dollars' worth to any drunk?

HOGAN: You look a million, darlin'!

JOSIE (*goes to the screen door and pushes it open with the manner of one who has burned all bridges*): Come

along, then. (*She goes out. He follows close on her heels. She stops abruptly on the first step–startledly.*) Look! There's someone on the road—

HOGAN (*pushes past her down the steps–peering off left-front–as if aloud to himself, in dismay*): Be God, it's him! I never thought—

JOSIE (*as if aloud to herself*): So he didn't forget—

HOGAN (*quickly*): Well, it proves he can't keep away from you, and that'll make it easier for you— (*Then furiously.*) Oh, the dirty, double-crossing bastard! The nerve of him! Coming to call on you, after making you wait for hours, thinking you don't know what he's done to us this night, and it'll be a fine cruel joke to blarney you in the moonlight, and you trusting him like a poor sheep, and never suspecting—

JOSIE (*stung*): Shut up! I'll teach him who's the joker! I'll let him go on as if you hadn't told me what he's done—

HOGAN: Yes, don't let him suspect it, or you wouldn't fool him. He'd know you were after revenge. But he can see me here now. I can't sneak away or he'd be suspicious. We've got to think of a new scheme quick to get me away—

JOSIE (*quickly*): I know how. Pretend you're as drunk as when you came. Make him believe you're so drunk you don't remember what he's done, so he can't suspect you told me.

HOGAN: I will. Be God, Josie, damned if I don't think he's so queer drunk himself he don't remember, or he'd never come here.

JOSIE: The drunker he is the better! (*Lowering her voice–quickly.*) He's turned in the gate where he can hear us. Pretend we're fighting and I'm driving you off till you're sober. Say you won't be back tonight. It'll make him sure he'll have the night alone with me. You start the fight.

HOGAN (*becomes at once very drunk. He shouts*): Put me out of my own home, will you, you undutiful slut!

JOSIE: Celebration or not, I'll have no drunks cursing and singing all night. Go back to the Inn.

HOGAN: I will! I'll get a room and two bottles and stay drunk as long as I please!

JOSIE: Don't come back till you've slept it off, or I'll wipe the floor with you! (TYRONE *enters, left-front. He does not appear to be drunk–that is, he shows none of the usual symptoms. He seems much the same as in Act 1. The only perceptible change is that his eyes have a peculiar fixed, glazed look, and there is a certain vague quality in his manner and speech, as if he were a bit hazy and absent-minded.*)

TYRONE (*dryly*): Just in time for the Big Bout. Or is this the final round?

HOGAN (*whirls on him unsteadily*): Who the hell— (*Peering at him.*) Oh, it's you, is it?

TYRONE: What was the big idea, Phil, leaving me flat?

HOGAN: Leave you flat? Be Jaysus, that reminds me I owe you a swipe on the jaw for something. What was it? Be God, I'm too drunk to remember. But here it is, anyway. (*He turns loose a round-house swing that misses* TYRONE *by a couple of feet, and reels away.* TYRONE *regards him with vague surprise.*)

JOSIE: Stop it, you damned old fool, and get out of here!

HOGAN: Taking his side against your poor old father, are you? A hell of a daughter! (*He draws himself up with drunken dignity.*) Don't expect me home tonight, Miss Hogan, or tomorrow either, maybe. You can take your bad temper out on your sweetheart here. (*He starts off down the road, left-front, with a last word over his shoulder.*) Bad luck to you both. (*He disappears. A moment later he begins to bawl his mournful Irish song.*) "Oh, the praties they grow small, Over here, over here," etc. (*During a part of the following scene the song continues to be heard at intervals, receding as he gets farther off on his way to the Inn.*)

JOSIE: Well, thank God. That's good riddance. (*She comes to* TYRONE, *who stands staring after* HOGAN *with a puzzled look.*)

TYRONE: I've never seen him that stinko before. Must have got him all of a sudden. He didn't seem so lit up at the Inn, but I guess I wasn't paying much attention.

JOSIE (*forcing a playful air*): I should think, if you were a real gentleman, you'd be apologizing to me, not thinking of him. Don't you know you're two hours and a half late? I oughtn't to speak to you, if I had any pride.

TYRONE (*stares at her curiously*): You've got too damn much pride, Josie. That's the trouble.

JOSIE: And just what do you mean by that, Jim?

TYRONE (*shrugs his shoulders*): Nothing. Forget it. I do apologize, Josie. I'm damned sorry. Haven't any excuse. Can't think up a lie. (*Staring at her curiously again.*) Or, now I think of it, I had a damned good honorable excuse, but— (*He shrugs.*) Nuts. Forget it.

JOSIE: Holy Joseph, you're full of riddles tonight. Well, I don't need excuses. I forgive you, anyway, now you're here. (*She takes his hand—playfully.*) Come on now and we'll sit on my bedroom steps and be romantic in the moonlight, like we planned to. (*She leads him there. He goes along in an automatic way, as if only half-conscious of what he is doing. She sits on the top step and pulls him down on the step beneath her. A pause. He stares vaguely at nothing. She bends to give him an uneasy appraising glance.*)

TYRONE (*suddenly, begins to talk mechanically*): Had to get out of the damned Inn. I was going batty alone there. The old heebie-jeebies. So I came to you. (*He pauses—then adds with strange, wondering*

sincerity.) I've really begun to love you a lot, Josie.

JOSIE (*blurts out bitterly*): Yes, you've proved that tonight, haven't you? (*Hurriedly regaining her playful tone.*) But never mind. I said I'd forgive you for being so late. So go on about love. I'm all ears.

TYRONE (*as if he hadn't listened*): I thought you'd have given me up and gone to bed. I remember I had some nutty idea I'd get in bed with you—just to lie with my head on your breast.

JOSIE (*moved in spite of herself—but keeps her bold, playful tone*): Well, maybe I'll let you— (*Hurriedly.*) Later on, I mean. The night's young yet, and we'll have it all to ourselves. (*Boldly again.*) But here's for a starter. (*She puts her arms around him and draws him back till his head is on her breast.*) There, now.

TYRONE (*relaxes—simply and gratefully*): Thanks, Josie. (*He closes his eyes. For a moment, she forgets everything and stares down at his face with a passionate, possessive tenderness. A pause. From far-off on the road to the Inn,* HOGAN'S *mournful song drifts back through the moonlight quiet: "Oh, the praties they grow small, Over here, over here."* TYRONE *rouses himself and straightens up. He acts embarrassed, as if he felt he'd been making a fool of himself—mockingly.*) Hark, Hark, the Donegal lark! "Thou wast not born for death, immortal bird." Can't Phil sing anything but that damned dirge, Josie? (*She doesn't reply. He goes on hazily.*) Still, it seems to belong tonight—in the moonlight—or in my mind—(*He quotes.*)

"Now more than ever seems it rich to die,
To cease upon the midnight with no pain.
In such an ecstasy!"

(*He has recited this with deep feeling. Now he sneers.*) Good God! Ode to Phil the Irish Nightingale! I must have the D.T.'s.

JOSIE (*her face grown bitter*): Maybe it's only your bad conscience.

TYRONE (*starts guiltily and turns to stare into her face—suspiciously*): What put that in your head? Conscience about what?

JOSIE (*quickly*): How would I know, if you don't? (*Forcing a playful tone.*) For the sin of wanting to be in bed with me. Maybe that's it.

TYRONE (*with strange relief*): Oh. (*A bit shamefacedly.*) Forget that stuff, Josie. I was half nutty.

JOSIE (*bitterly*): Och, for the love of God, don't apologize as if you was ashamed of— (*She catches herself.*)

TYRONE (*with a quick glance at her face*): All right. I certainly won't apologize—if you're not kicking. I was afraid I might have shocked your modesty.

JOSIE (*roughly*): *My* modesty? Be God, I didn't know I had any left.

TYRONE (*draws away from her–irritably*): Nix, Josie. Lay off that line, for tonight at least. (*He adds slowly.*) I'd like tonight to be different.

JOSIE: Different from what? (*He doesn't answer. She forces a light tone.*) All right. I'll be as different as you please.

TYRONE (*simply*): Thanks, Josie. Just be yourself. (*Again as if he were ashamed, or afraid he had revealed some weakness–off-handedly.*) This being out in the moonlight instead of the lousy Inn isn't a bad bet, at that. I don't know why I hang out in that dump, except I'm even more bored in the so-called good hotels in this hick town.

JOSIE (*trying to examine his face without his knowing*): Well, you'll be back on Broadway soon now, won't you?

TYRONE: I hope so.

JOSIE: Then you'll have all the pretty little tarts to comfort you when you get your sorrowful spell on.

TYRONE: Oh, to hell with the rough stuff, Josie! You promised you'd can it tonight.

JOSIE (*tensely*): You're a fine one to talk of promises!

TYRONE (*vaguely surprised by her tone*): What's the matter? Still sore at me for being late?

JOSIE (*quickly*): I'm not. I was teasing you. To prove there's no hard feelings, how would you like a drink? But I needn't ask. (*She gets up.*) I'll get a bottle of his best.

TYRONE (*mechanically*): Fine. Maybe that will have some kick. The booze at the Inn didn't work tonight.

JOSIE: Well, this'll work. (*She starts to go into her bedroom. He sits hunched up on the step, staring at nothing. She pauses in the doorway to glance back. The hard, calculating expression on her face softens. For a second she stares at him, bewildered by her conflicting feelings. Then she goes inside, leaving the door open. She opens the door from her room to the lighted living room, and is seen going to the kitchen on the way to the cellar. She has left the door from the living room to her bedroom open and the light reveals a section of the bedroom framed in the doorway behind TYRONE. The foot of the bed which occupies most of the room can be seen, and that is all except that the walls are unpainted pine boards. TYRONE continues to stare at nothing, but becomes restless. His hands and mouth twitch.*)

TYRONE (*suddenly, with intense hatred*): You rotten bastard! (*He springs to his feet–fumbles in his pockets for cigarettes–strikes a match which lights up his face, on which there is now an expression of miserable guilt. His hand is trembling so violently he cannot light the cigarette.*)

ACT 3

(*Scene: The living-room wall has been replaced and all we see now of its lighted interior is through the two win-dows. Otherwise, everything is the same, and this Act follows the preceding without any lapse of time. TYRONE is still trying with shaking hands to get his cigarette lighted. Finally he succeeds, and takes a deep inhale, and starts pacing back and forth a few steps, as if in a cell of his own thought. He swears defensively.*) God damn it. You'll be crying in your beer in a minute. (*He begins to sing sneeringly half under his breath a snatch from an old sob song, popular in the Nineties*)

"And baby's cries can't waken her
In the baggage coach ahead."

(*His sneer changes to a look of stricken guilt and grief*) Christ! (*He seems about to break down and sob but he fights this back*) Cut it out, you drunken fool! (*JOSIE can be seen through the windows, returning from the kitchen. He turns with a look of relief and escape*) Thank God! (*He sits on the boulder and waits. JOSIE stops by the table in the living room to turn down the lamp until only a dim light remains. She has a quart of whiskey under her arm, two tumblers, and a pitcher of water. She goes through her bedroom and appears in the outer doorway. TYRONE gets up*) Ah! At last the old booze! (*He relieves her of the pitcher and tumblers as she comes down the steps.*)

JOSIE (*with a fixed smile*): You'd think I'd been gone years. You didn't seem so perishing for a drink.

TYRONE (*in his usual, easy, kidding way*): It's you I was perishing for. I've been dying of loneliness—

JOSIE: You'll die of lying some day. But I'm glad you're alive again. I thought when I left you really were dying on me.

TYRONE: No such luck.

JOSIE: Och, don't talk like that. Come on have a drink. We'll use the boulder for a table and I'll be barkeep. (*He puts the pitcher and tumblers on the boulder and she uncorks the bottle. She takes a quick glance at his face–startledly.*) What's come over you, Jim? You look as if you've seen a ghost.

TYRONE (*looks away–dryly*): I have. My own. He's punk company.

JOSIE: Yes, it's the worst ghost of all, your own. Don't I know? But this will keep it in place. (*She pours a tumbler half full of whiskey and hands it to him.*) Here. But wait till I join you. (*She pours the other tumbler half full.*)

TYRONE (*surprised.*): Hello! I thought you never touched it.

JOSIE (*glibly*): I have on occasion. And this is one. I don't want to be left out altogether from celebrating our victory over Harder. (*She gives him a sharp bitter glance. Meeting his eyes, which are regarding her with puzzled wonder, she forces a laugh.*) Don't look at me as if I was up to some game. A drink or two will make me better company, and help me enjoy the moon and the night with you. Here's luck. (*She touches his glass with hers.*)

TYRONE (*shrugs his shoulders*): All right. Here's luck. (*They drink. She gags and sputters. He pours water in her glass. She drinks it. He puts his glass and the pitcher back on the boulder. He keeps staring at her with a puzzled frown.*)

JOSIE: Some of it went down the wrong way.

TYRONE: So I see. That'll teach you to pour out baths instead of drinks.

JOSIE: It's the first time I ever heard you complain a drink was too big.

TYRONE: Yours was too big.

JOSIE: I'm my father's daughter. I've a strong head. So don't worry I'll pass out and you'll have to put me to bed. (*She gives a little bold laugh.*) Sure, that's a beautiful notion. I'll have to pretend I'm—

TYRONE (*irritably*): Nix on the raw stuff, Josie. Remember you said—

JOSIE (*resentment in her kidding*): I'd be different? That's right. I'm forgetting it's your pleasure to have me pretend I'm an innocent virgin tonight.

TYRONE (*in a strange tone that is almost threatening*): If you don't look out, I'll call you on that bluff, Josie. (*He stares at her with a deliberate sensualist's look that undresses her.*) I'd like to. You know that, don't you?

JOSIE (*boldly*): I don't at all. You're the one who's bluffing.

TYRONE (*grabs her in his arms—with genuine passion*): Josie! (*Then as suddenly lets her go.*) Nix. Let's cut it out. (*He turns away. Her face betrays the confused conflict within her of fright, passion, happiness, and bitter resentment. He goes on with an abrupt change of tone.*) How about another drink? That's honest-to-God old bonded Bourbon. How the devil did Phil get hold of it?

JOSIE: Tom Lombardo, the bootlegger, gave him a case for letting him hide a truckload in our barn when the agents were after him. He stole it from a warehouse on faked permits. (*She pours out drinks as she speaks, a half tumblerful for him, a small one for herself.*) Here you are. (*She gives him his drink—smiles at him coquettishly, beginning to show the effect of her big drink by her increasingly bold manners.*) Let's sit down where the moon will be in our eyes and we'll see romance. (*She takes his arm and leads him to her bedroom steps. She sits on the top step, pulling him down beside her but on the one below. She raises her glass.*) Here's hoping before the night's out you'll have more courage and kiss me at least.

TYRONE (*frowns—then kiddingly*): That's a promise. Here's how. (*He drains his tumbler. She drinks half of hers. He puts his glass on the ground beside him. A pause. She tries to read his face without his noticing. He seems to be lapsing again into vague preoccupation.*)

JOSIE: Now don't sink back half-dead-and-alive in

dreams the way you were before.

TYRONE (*quickly*): I'm not. I had a good final dose of heebie-jeebies when you were in the house. That's all for tonight. (*He adds a bit maudlinly, his two big drinks beginning to affect him.*) Let the dead past bury its dead.

JOSIE: That's the talk. There's only tonight, and the moon, and us—and the bonded Bourbon. Have another drink, and don't wait for me.

TYRONE: Not now, thanks. They're coming too fast. (*He gives her a curious, cynically amused look.*) Trying to get me soused, Josie?

JOSIE (*starts—quickly*): I'm not. Only to get you feeling happy, so you'll forget all sadness.

TYRONE (*kiddingly*): I might forget all my honorable intentions, too. So look out.

JOSIE: I'll look forward to it—and I hope that's another promise, like the kiss you owe me. If you're suspicious I'm trying to get you soused—well, here goes. (*She drinks what is left in her glass.*) There, now. I must be scheming to get myself soused, too.

TYRONE: Maybe you are.

JOSIE (*resentfully*): If I was, it'd be to make you feel at home. Don't all the pretty little Broadway tarts get soused with you?

TYRONE (*irritably*): There you go again with that old line!

JOSIE: All right, I won't! (*Forcing a laugh.*) I must be eaten up with jealousy for them, that's it.

TYRONE: You needn't be. They don't belong.

JOSIE: And I do?

TYRONE: Yes. You do.

JOSIE: For tonight only, you mean?

TYRONE: We've agreed there is only tonight—and it's to be different from any past night—for both of us.

JOSIE (*in a forced, kidding tone*): I hope it will be. I'll try to control my envy for your Broadway flames. I suppose it's because I have a picture of them in my mind as small and dainty and pretty—

TYRONE: They're just gold-digging tramps.

JOSIE (*as if he hadn't spoken*): While I'm only a big, rough, ugly cow of a woman.

TYRONE: Shut up! You're beautiful.

JOSIE (*jeeringly, but her voice trembles*): God pity the blind!

TYRONE: You're beautiful to me.

JOSIE: It must be the Bourbon—

TYRONE: You're real and healthy and clean and fine and warm and strong and kind—

JOSIE: I have a beautiful soul, you mean?

TYRONE: Well, I don't know much about ladies' souls— (*He takes her hand.*) But I do know you're beautiful. (*He kisses her hand.*) And I love you a lot—in my fashion.

JOSIE (*stammers*): Jim— (*Hastily forcing her playful tone.*) Sure, you're full of fine compliments all of a sudden, and I ought to show you how pleased I am. *(She pulls his head back and kisses him on the lips–a quick, shy kiss.)* That's for my beautiful soul.

TYRONE *(The kiss arouses his physical desire. He pulls her head down and stares into her eyes)*: You have a beautiful strong body, too, Josie—and beautiful eyes and hair, and a beautiful smile and beautiful warm breasts. *(He kisses her on the lips. She pulls back frightenedly for a second–then returns his kiss. Suddenly he breaks away–in a tone of guilty irritation.)* Nix! Nix! Don't be a fool, Josie. Don't let me pull that stuff.

JOSIE *(triumphant for a second)*: You meant it! I know you meant it! *(Then with resentful bitterness– roughly.)* Be God, you're right I'm a damned fool to let you make me forget you're the greatest liar in the world! *(Quickly.)* I mean, the greatest kidder. And now, how about another drink?

TYRONE *(staring at nothing–vaguely)*: You don't get me, Josie. You don't know—and I hope you never will know—

JOSIE *(blurts out bitterly)*: Maybe I know more than you think.

TYRONE *(as if she hadn't spoken)*: There's always the aftermath that poisons you. I don't want you to be poisoned—

JOSIE: Maybe you know what you're talking about—

TYRONE: And I don't want to be poisoned myself— not again—not with you. *(He pauses–slowly.)* There have been too many nights—and dawns. This must be different. I want— *(His voice trails off into silence.)*

JOSIE *(trying to read his face–uneasily)*: Don't get in one of your queer spells, now. *(She gives his shoulder a shake–forcing a light tone.)* Sure, I don't think you know what you want. Except another drink. I'm sure you want that. And I want one, too.

TYRONE *(recovering himself)*: Fine! Grand idea. *(He gets up and brings the bottle from the boulder. He picks up his tumbler and pours a big drink. She is holding out her tumbler but he ignores it.)*

JOSIE: You're not polite, pouring your own first.

TYRONE: I said a drink was a grand idea—for me. Not for you. You skip this one.

JOSIE *(resentfully)*: Oh, I do, do I? Are you giving me orders?

TYRONE: Yes. Take a big drink of moonlight instead.

JOSIE *(angrily)*: You'll pour me a drink, if you please, Jim Tyrone, or—

TYRONE *(stares at her–then shrugs his shoulders)*: All right, if you want to take it that way, Josie. It's your funeral. *(He pours a drink into her tumbler.)*

JOSIE *(ashamed but defiant–stiffly)*: Thank you kindly. *(She raises her glass–mockingly.)* Here's to tonight. *(*TYRONE *is staring at her, a strange bitter disgust in his eyes. Suddenly he slaps at her hand. knocking the glass to the ground.)*

TYRONE *(his voice hard with repulsion)*: I've slept with drunken tramps on too many nights!

JOSIE *(stares at him, too startled and bewildered to be angry. Her voice trembles with surprising meekness)*: All right, Jim, if you don't want me to—

TYRONE *(now looks as bewildered by his action as she does)*: I'm sorry, Josie. Don't know what the drink got into me. *(He picks up her glass.)* Here. I'll pour you another.

JOSIE *(still meek)*: No, thank you. I'll skip this one. *(She puts the glass on the ground.)* But you drink up.

TYRONE: Thanks. *(He gulps down his drink. Mechanically, as if he didn't know what he was doing, he pours another. Suddenly he blurts out with guilty loathing.)* That fat blonde pig on the train—I got her drunk! That's why— *(He stops guiltily.)*

JOSIE *(uneasily)*: What are you talking about? What train?

TYRONE: No train. Don't mind me. *(He gulps down the drink and pours another with the same strange air of acting unconsciously.)* Maybe I'll tell you—later, when I'm— That'll cure you—for all time! *(Abruptly he realizes what he is saying. He gives the characteristic shrug of shoulders–cynically.)* Nuts! The Brooklyn boys are talking again. I guess I'm more stewed than I thought—in the center of the old bean, at least. *(Dully.)* I better beat it back to the Inn and go to bed and stop bothering you, Josie.

JOSIE *(bullyingly–and pityingly)*: Well, you won't, not if I have to hold you. Come on now, bring your drink and sit down like you were before. *(He does so. She pats his cheek–forcing a playful air.)* That's a good boy. And I won't take any more whiskey. I've all the effect from it I want already. Everything is far away and doesn't matter—except the moon and its dreams, and I'm part of the dreams—and you are, too. *(She adds with a rueful little laugh.)* I keep forgetting the thing I've got to remember. I keep hoping it's a lie, even though I know I'm a damned fool.

TYRONE *(hazily)*: Damned fool about what?

JOSIE: Never mind. *(Forcing a laugh.)* I've just had a thought. If my poor old father had seen you knocking his prize whiskey on the ground—Holy Joseph, he'd have had three paralytic strokes!

TYRONE *(grins)*: Yes, I can picture him, *(He pauses– with amused affection.)* But that's all a fake. He loves to play tightwad, but the people he likes know better. He'd give them his shirt. He's a grand old scout, Josie. *(A bit maudlin.)* The only real friend I've got left—except you. I love his guts.

JOSIE *(tensely–sickened by his hypocrisy)*: Och, for the love of God—!

TYRONE *(shrugs his shoulders)*: Yes, I suppose that does sound like moaning-at-the-bar stuff. But I mean it.

JOSIE: Do you? Well, I know my father's virtues without you telling me.

TYRONE: You ought to appreciate him because he worships the ground you walk on—and he knows you a lot better than you think. *(He turns to smile at her teasingly.)* As well as I do—almost.

JOSIE *(defensively)*: That's not saying much. Maybe I can guess what you think you know— *(Forcing a contemptuous laugh.)* If it's that, God pity you, you're a terrible fool.

TYRONE *(teasingly)*: If it's what? I haven't said anything.

JOSIE: You'd better not, or I'll die laughing at you. *(She changes the subject abruptly.)* Why don't you drink up? It makes me nervous watching you hold it as if you didn't know it was there.

TYRONE: I didn't, at that. *(He drinks.)*

JOSIE: And have another.

TYRONE *(a bit drunkenly)*: Will a whore go to a picnic? Real bonded Bourbon. That's my dish. *(He goes to the boulder for the bottle. He is as steady on his feet as if he were completely sober.)*

JOSIE *(in a light tone)*: Bring the bottle back so it'll be handy and you won't have to leave me. I miss you.

TYRONE *(comes back with the bottle. He smiles at her cynically)*: Still trying to get me soused, Josie?

JOSIE: I'm not such a fool—with your capacity.

TYRONE: You better watch your step. It might work—and then think of how disgusted you'd feel with me lying beside you, probably snoring, as you watched the dawn come. You don't know—

JOSIE *(defiantly)*: The hell I don't! Isn't that the way I've felt with every one of them, after?

TYRONE *(as if he hadn't heard—bitterly)*: But take it from me, I know. I've seen too God-damned many dawns creeping grayly over too many dirty windows.

JOSIE *(ignores this—boldly)*: But it might be different with you. Love could make it different. And I've been head over heels in love ever since you said you loved my beautiful soul. *(Again he doesn't seem to have heard—resentfully.)* Don't stand there like a loon, mourning over the past. Why don't you pour yourself a drink and sit down?

TYRONE *(looks at the bottle and tumbler in his hands, as if he'd forgotten them—mechanically)*: Sure thing. Real bonded Bourbon. I ought to know. If I had a dollar for every drink of it I had before Prohibition, I'd hire our dear bully, Harder, for a valet. *(JOSIE stiffens and her face hardens.* TYRONE *pours a drink and sets the bottle on the ground. He looks up suddenly into her eyes—warningly.)* You'd better remember I said you had beautiful eyes and hair—and breasts.

JOSIE: I remember you did. *(She tries to be calculatingly enticing.)* So sit down and I'll let you lay your head—

TYRONE: No. If you won't watch your step, I've got to. *(He sits down but doesn't lean back.)* And don't let me get away with pretending I'm so soused I don't know what I'm doing. I always know. Or part of me does. That's the trouble. *(He pauses—then bursts out in a strange threatening tone.)* You better look out, Josie. She was tickled to death to get me pie-eyed. Had an idea she could roll me, I guess. She wasn't so tickled about it—later on.

JOSIE: What she? *(He doesn't reply. She forces a light tone.)* I hope you don't think I'm scheming to roll you.

TYRONE *(vaguely)*: What? *(Coming to—indignantly.)* Of course not. What are you talking about? For God's sake, you're not a tart.

JOSIE *(roughly)*: No, I'm a fool. I'm always giving it away.

TYRONE *(angrily)*: That lousy bluff again, eh? You're a liar! For Christ sake, quit that smut stuff, can't you!

JOSIE *(stung)*: Listen to me, Jim! Drunk or not, don't you talk that way to me or—

TYRONE: How about your not talking the old smut stuff to me? You promised you'd be yourself. *(Pauses—vaguely.)* You don't get it, Josie. You see, she was one of the smuttiest talking pigs I've ever listened to.

JOSIE: What she? Do you mean the blonde on the train?

TYRONE *(starts—sharply)*: Train? Who told you—? *(Quickly.)* Oh—that's right—I did say— *(Vaguely.)* What blonde? What's the difference? Coming back from the Coast. It was long ago. But it seems like tonight. There is no present or future—only the past happening over and over again—now. You can't get away from it. *(Abruptly.)* Nuts! To hell with that crap.

JOSIE: You came back from the Coast about a year ago after—*(She checks herself.)*

TYRONE *(dully)*: Yes. After Mama's death. *(Quickly.)* But I've been to the Coast a lot of times during my career as a third-rate ham. I don't remember which time—or anything much—except I was pie-eyed in a drawing room for the whole four days. *(Abruptly.)* What were we talking about before? What a grand guy Phil is. You ought to be glad you've got him for a father. Mine was an old bastard.

JOSIE: He wasn't! He was one of the finest, kindest gentlemen ever lived.

TYRONE *(sneeringly)*: Outside the family, sure. Inside, he was a lousy tightwad bastard.

JOSIE *(repelled)*: You ought to be ashamed!

TYRONE: To speak ill of the dead? Nuts! He can't hear, and he knows I hated him, anyway—as much as he hated me. I'm glad he's dead. So is he. Or he ought to be. Everyone ought to be, if they have any sense. Out of a bum racket. At peace. *(He shrugs his shoulders.)* Nuts! What of it?

JOSIE *(tensely)*: Don't Jim. I hate you when you talk like that. *(Forcing a light tone.)* Do you want to spoil our beautiful moonlight night? And don't be telling me of your old flames, on trains or not. I'm too jealous.

TYRONE *(with a shudder of disgust)*: Of that pig? *(He drinks his whiskey as if to wash a bad taste from his mouth—then takes one of her hands in both of his—simply.)* You're a fool to be jealous of anyone. You're the only woman I care a damn about.

JOSIE *(deeply stirred, in spite of herself—trembling)*: Jim, don't— *(Forcing a tense little laugh.)* All right, I'll try and believe that—for tonight.

TYRONE *(simply)*: Thanks, Josie. *(A pause. He speaks in a tone of random curiosity.)* Why did you say a while ago I'd be leaving for New York soon?

JOSIE *(stiffens—her face hardening)*: Well, I was right, wasn't I? *(Unconsciously she tries to pull her hand away.)*

TYRONE: Why are you pulling your hand away?

JOSIE *(stops)*: Was I? *(Forcing a smile.)* I suppose because it seems crazy for you to hold my big ugly paw so tenderly. But you're welcome to it, if you like.

TYRONE: I do like. It's strong and kind and warm—like you. *(He kisses it.)*

JOSIE *(tensely)*: Och, for the love of God—! *(She jerks her hand away—then hastily forces a joking tone.)* Wasting kisses on my hand! Sure, even the moon is laughing at us.

TYRONE: Nuts for the moon! I'd rather have one light on Broadway than all the moons since Rameses was a pup. *(He takes cigarettes from his pocket and lights one.)*

JOSIE *(her eyes searching his face, lighted up by the match)*: You'll be taking a train back to your dear old Broadway tomorrow night, won't you?

TYRONE *(still holding the burning match, stares at her in surprise)*: Tomorrow night? Where did you get that?

JOSIE: A little bird told me.

TYRONE *(blows out the match in a cloud of smoke)*: You'd better give that bird the bird. By the end of the week, is the right dope. Phil got his dates mixed.

JOSIE *(quickly)*: He didn't tell me. He was too drunk to remember anything.

TYRONE: He was sober when I told him. I called up the executors when we reached the Inn after leaving here. They said the estate would be out of probate within a few days. I told Phil the glad tidings and bought drinks for all and sundry. There was quite a celebration. Funny, Phil wouldn't remember that.

JOSIE *(bewildered—not knowing what to believe)*: It is—funny.

TYRONE *(shrugs his shoulders)*: Well, he's stewed to the ears. That always explains anything. *(Then strangely.)* Only sometimes it doesn't.

JOSIE: No—sometimes it doesn't.

TYRONE *(goes on without real interest, talking to keep from thinking)*: Phil certainly has a prize bun on to-night. He never took a punch at me before. And that drivel he talked about owing me one—What got into his head, I wonder.

JOSIE *(tensely)*: How would I know, if you don't?

TYRONE: Well, I don't. Not unless—I remember I did try to get his goat. Simpson sat down with us. Harder sent him to see me. You remember after Harder left here I said the joke was on you, that you'd made this place a gold mine. I was kidding, but I had the right dope. What do you think he told Simpson to offer? Ten grand! On the level, Josie.

JOSIE *(tense)*: So you accepted?

TYRONE: I told Simpson to tell Harder I did. I de-cided the best way to fix him was to let him think he'd got away with it, and then when he comes tomorrow morning to drive me to the executor's office, I'll tell him what he can do with himself, his bankroll, and tin oil tanks.

JOSIE *(knows he is telling the truth—so relieved she can only stammer stupidly)*: So that's—the truth of it.

TYRONE *(smiles)*: Of course, I did it to kid Phil, too. He was right there, listening. But I know I didn't fool him.

JOSIE *(weakly)*: Maybe you did fool him, for once. But I don't know.

TYRONE: And that's why he took a swing at me? *(He laughs, but there is a forced note to it.)* Well, if so, it's one hell of a joke on him. *(His tone becomes hurt and bitter.)* All the same, I'll be good and sore, Josie. I promised this place wouldn't be sold ex-cept to him. What the hell does he think I am? He ought to know I wouldn't double-cross you and him for ten million!

JOSIE *(giving away at last to her relief and joy)*: Don't I know! Oh, Jim, darling! *(She hugs him passionately and kisses him on the lips.)* I knew you'd never—I told him— *(She kisses him again.)* Oh, Jim, I love you.

TYRONE *(again with a strange, simple gratitude)*: Thanks, Josie. I mean, for not believing I'm a rotten louse. Everyone else believes it—including myself—for a damned good reason. *(Abruptly changing the subject.)* I'm a fool to let this stuff about Phil get under my skin, but— Why, I re-member telling him tonight I'd even written my brother and got his okay on selling the farm to him. And Phil thanked me. He seemed touched and grateful. You wouldn't think he'd forget that.

JOSIE *(her face hard and bitter)*: I wouldn't, indeed. There's a lot of things he'll have to explain when he comes at sun— *(Hastily.)* When he comes back. *(She pauses—then bursts out.)* The damned old schemer, I'll teach him to— *(Again checking herself.)* to act like a fool.

TYRONE *(smiles)*: You'll get out the old club, eh? What a bluff you are, Josie. *(Teasingly.)* You and your loves, Messalina—when you've never—

JOSIE *(with a faint spark of her old defiance)*: You're a liar.

TYRONE: "Pride is the sin by which the angels fell." Are you going to keep that up—with me?

JOSIE *(feebly)*: You think I've never because no one would—because I'm a great ugly cow—

TYRONE *(gently)*: Nuts! You could have had any one of them. You kidded them till you were sure they wanted you. That was all you wanted. And then you slapped them groggy when they tried for more. But you had to keep convincing your-self—

JOSIE *(tormentedly)*: Don't, Jim.

TYRONE: You can take the truth, Josie—from me. Because you and I belong to the same club. We can kid the world but we can't fool ourselves, like most people, no matter what we do—nor escape ourselves no matter where we run away. Whether it's the bottom of a bottle, or a South Sea Island, we'd find our own ghosts there wait-ing to greet us— "sleepless with pale com-memorative eyes," as Rossetti wrote. *(He sneers to himself.)* The old poetic bull, eh? Crap! *(Reverting to a teasing tone.)* You don't ask how I saw through your bluff, Josie. You pretend too much. And so do the guys. I've listened to them at the Inn. They all lie to each other. No one wants to admit all he got was a slap in the puss, when he thinks a lot of other guys made it. You can't blame them. And they know you don't give a damn how they lie. So—

JOSIE: For the love of God, Jim! Don't!

TYRONE: Phil is wise to you, of course, but although he knew I knew, he would never admit it until tonight.

JOSIE *(startled—vindictively)*: So he admitted it, did he? Wait till I get hold of him!

TYRONE: He'll never admit it to you. He's afraid of hurting you.

JOSIE: He is, is he? Well— *(Almost hysterically.)* For the love of God, can't you shut up about him!

TYRONE *(glances up at her, surprised—then shrugs his shoul-ders)*: Oh, all right. I wanted to clear things up, that's all—for Phil's sake as well as yours. You have a hell of a license to be sore. He's the one who ought to be. Don't you realize what a lousy position you've put him in with your brazen-trollop act?

JOSIE *(tensely)*: No. He doesn't care, except to use me in his scheming. He—

TYRONE: Don't be a damned fool. Of course he cares. And so do I. *(He turns and pulls her head down and kisses her on the lips.)* I care, Josie. I love you.

JOSIE *(with pitiful longing)*: Do you, Jim? Do you? *(She forces a trembling smile—faintly.)* Then I'll confess the truth to you. I've been a crazy fool. I am a virgin. *(She begins to sob with a strange forlorn shame and humiliation.)* And now you'll never—and I want you to—now more than ever—because I love you more than ever, after what's happened—*(Suddenly she kisses him with fierce pas-sion.)* But you will! I'll make you! To hell with your honorable scruples! I know you want me! I couldn't believe that until tonight—but now I know. It's in your kisses! *(She kisses him again—with passionate tenderness.)* Oh, you great fool! As if I gave a damn what happened after! I'll have had tonight and your love to remember for the rest of my days! *(She kisses him again.)* Oh, Jim darling, haven't you said yourself there's only tonight? *(She whispers tenderly.)* Come. Come with me. *(She gets to her feet, pulling at his arm—with a little self-mocking laugh.)* But I'll have to make you leave before sunrise. I mustn't forget that.

TYRONE *(a strange change has come over his face. He looks her over now with a sneering cynical lust. He speaks thickly as if he was suddenly very drunk)*: Sure thing, Kiddo. What the hell else do you suppose I came for? I've been kidding myself. *(He steps up beside her and puts his arm around her and presses his body to hers.)* You're the goods, Kid. I've wanted you all along. Love, nuts! I'll show you what love is. I know what you want, Bright Eyes. *(She is staring at him now with a look of frightened horror. He kisses her roughly.)* Come on, Baby Doll, let's hit the hay. *(He pushes her back in the doorway.)*

JOSIE *(strickenly)*: Jim! Don't! *(She pulls his arms away so violently that he staggers back and would fall down the steps if she didn't grab his arm in time. As it is he goes down on one knee. She is on the verge of collapse herself—brokenly.)* Jim! I'm not a whore.

TYRONE *(remains on one knee—confusedly, as if he didn't know what had happened)*: What the hell? Was I trying to rape you, Josie? Forget it. I'm drunk—not responsible. *(He gets to his feet, stag-gering a bit, and steps down to the ground.)*

JOSIE *(covering her face with her hands)*: Oh, Jim! *(She sobs.)*

TYRONE *(with vague pity)*: Don't cry. No harm done. You stopped me, didn't you? *(She continues to sob. He mutters vaguely, as if talking to himself.)* Must have drawn a blank for a while. Nuts! Cut out the faking. I knew what I was doing. *(Slowly, star-ing before him.)* But it's funny. I *was* seeing things. That's the truth, Josie. For a moment I thought you were that blonde pig— *(Hastily.)* The old heebie-jeebies. Hair of the dog. *(He gropes around *for the bottle and his glass.*) I'll have another shot—

JOSIE (*takes her hands from her face–fiercely*): Pour the whole bottle down your throat, if you like! Only stop talking! (*She covers her face with her hands and sobs again.*)

TYRONE (*stares at her with a hurt and sad expression–dully*): Can't forgive me, eh? You ought to. You ought to thank me for letting you see— (*He pauses, as if waiting for her to say something, but she remains silent. He shrugs his shoulders, pours out a big drink mechanically.*) Well, here's how. (*He drinks and puts the bottle and glass on the ground–dully.*) That was a nightcap. Our moonlight romance seems to be a flop, Josie. I guess I'd better go.

JOSIE (*dully*): Yes. You'd better go. Good night.

TYRONE: Not good night. Good-bye.

JOSIE (*lifts her head*): Good-bye?

TYRONE: Yes. I won't see you again before I leave for New York. I was a damned fool to come tonight. I hoped—But you don't get it. How could you? So what's the good— (*He shrugs his shoulders hopelessly and turns toward the road.*)

JOSIE: Jim!

TYRONE (*turning back—bitter accusation in his tone now*): Whore? Who said you were a whore? But I warned you, didn't I, if you kept on— Why did you have to act like one, asking me to come to bed? That wasn't what I came here for. And you promised tonight would be different. Why the hell did you promise that, if all you wanted was what all the others want, if that's all love means to you? (*Then guiltily.*) Oh, Christ, I don't mean that, Josie. I know how you feel, and if I could give you happiness— But it wouldn't work. You don't know me. I'd poison it for myself and for you. I've poisoned it already, haven't I, but it would be a million times worse after— No matter how I tried not to. I'd make it like all the other nights—for you, too. You'd lie awake and watch the dawn come with disgust, with nausea retching your memory, and the wine of passion poets blab about, a sour aftertaste in your mouth of Dago red ink! (*He gives a sneering laugh.*)

JOSIE (*distractedly*): Oh, Jim, don't! Please don't!

TYRONE: You'd hate me and yourself—not for a day or two but for the rest of your life. (*With a perverse, jeering note of vindictive boastfulness in his tone.*) Believe me, Kid, when I poison them, they stay poisoned!

JOSIE (*with dull bitterness*): Good-bye, Jim.

TYRONE (*miserably hurt and sad for a second—appealingly*): Josie— (*Gives the characteristic shrug of his shoulders—simply.*) Good-bye. (*He turns toward the road—bitterly.*) I'll find it hard to forgive, too. I came here asking for love—just for this one night, because I thought you loved me. (*Dully.*) Nuts. To hell with it. (*He starts away.*)

JOSIE (*watches him for a second, fighting the love that, in* spite of her, responds to his appeal—then she springs up and runs to him—with fierce, possessive, maternal tenderness*): Come here to me, you great fool, and stop your silly blather. There's nothing to hate you for. There's nothing to forgive. Sure, I was only trying to give you happiness, because I love you. I'm sorry I was so stupid and didn't see— But I see now. and you'll find I have all the love you need. (*She gives him a hug and kisses him. There is passion in her kiss but it is a tender, protective maternal passion, which he responds to with an instant grateful yielding.*)

TYRONE (*simply*): Thanks, Josie. You're beautiful. I love you. I knew you'd understand.

JOSIE: Of course I do. Come, now. (*She leads him back, her arm around his waist.*)

TYRONE: I didn't want to leave you. You know that.

JOSIE: Indeed I know it. Come now. We'll sit down. (*She sits on the top step and pulls him down on the step below her.*) That's it—with my arm around you. Now lay your head on my breast—the way you said you wanted to do.— (*He lets his head fall back on her breast. She hugs him—gently.*) There, now. Forget all about my being a fool and forgive— (*Her voice trembles—but she goes on determinedly.*) Forgive my selfishness, thinking only of myself. Sure, if there's one thing I owe you tonight, after all my lying and scheming, it's to give you the love you need, and it'll be my pride and my joy— (*Forcing a trembling echo of her playful tone.*) It's easy enough, too, for I have all kinds of love for you—and maybe this is the greatest of all— because it costs so much. (*She pauses, looking down at his face. He has closed his eyes and his haggard, dissipated face looks like a pale mask in the moonlight—at peace as a death mask is at peace. She becomes frightened.*) Jim! Don't look like that!

TYRONE (*opens his eyes—vaguely*): Like what?

JOSIE (*quickly*): It's the moonlight. It makes you look so pale, and with your eyes closed—

TYRONE (*simply*): You mean I looked dead?

JOSIE: No! As if you'd fallen asleep.

TYRONE (*speaks in a tired, empty tone, as if he felt he ought to explain something to her—something which no longer interests him*): Listen, and I'll tell you a little story, Josie. All my life I had just one dream. From the time I was a kid, I loved race-horses. I thought they were the most beautiful things in the world. I liked to gamble, too. So the big dream was that some day I'd have enough dough to play a cagey system of betting on favorites, and follow the horses south in the winter, and come back north with them in the spring, and be at the track every day. It seemed that would be the ideal life—for me. (*He pauses.*)

JOSIE: Well, you'll be able to do it.

TYRONE: No. I won't be able to do it, Josie. That's the joke. I gave it a try-out before I came up here. I borrowed some money on my share of the estate, and started going to tracks. But it didn't work. I played my system, but I found I didn't care if I won or lost. The horses were beautiful, but I found myself saying to myself, what of it? Their beauty didn't mean anything. I found that every day I was glad when the last race was over, and I could go back to the hotel—and the bottle in my room. *(He pauses, staring into the moonlight with vacant eyes.)*

JOSIE *(uneasily)*: Why did you tell me this?

TYRONE *(in the same listless monotone)*: You said I looked dead. Well, I am.

JOSIE: You're not! *(She hugs him protectively.)* Don't talk like that!

TYRONE: Ever since Mama died.

JOSIE *(deeply moved—pityingly)*: I know. I've felt all along it was that sorrow was making you— *(She pauses—gently.)* Maybe if you talked about your grief for her, it would help you. I think it must be all choked up inside you, killing you.

TYRONE *(in a strange warning tone)*: You'd better look out, Josie.

JOSIE: Why?

TYRONE *(quickly, forcing his cynical smile)*: I might develop a crying jag, and sob on your beautiful breast.

JOSIE *(gently)*: You can sob all you like.

TYRONE: Don't encourage me. You'd be sorry. *(A deep conflict shows in his expression and tone. He is driven to go on in spite of himself.)* But if you're such a glutton for punishment— After all, I said I'd tell you later, didn't I?

JOSIE *(puzzled)*: You said you'd tell me about the blonde on the train.

TYRONE: She's part of it. I lied about that. *(He pauses—then blurts out sneeringly.)* You won't believe it could have happened. Or if you did believe, you couldn't understand or forgive— *(Quickly.)* But you might. You're the one person who might. Because you really love me. And because you're the only woman I've ever met who understands the lousy rotten things a man can do when he's crazy drunk, and draws a blank— especially when he's nutty with grief to start with.

JOSIE *(hugging him tenderly)*: Of course I'll understand, Jim, darling.

TYRONE *(stares into the moonlight—hauntedly)*: But I didn't draw a blank. I tried to. I drank enough to knock out ten men. But it didn't work. I knew what I was doing. *(He pauses—dully.)* No, I can't tell you, Josie. You'd loathe my guts, and I couldn't blame you.

JOSIE: No! I'll love you no matter what—

TYRONE *(with strange triumphant harshness)*: All right! Remember that's a promise! *(He pauses—starts to speak—pauses again.)*

JOSIE *(pityingly)*: Maybe you'd better not—if it will make you suffer.

TYRONE: Trying to welch now, eh? It's too late. You've got me started. Suffer? Christ, I ought to suffer! *(He pauses. Then he closes his eyes. It is as if he had to hide from sight before he can begin. He makes his face expressionless. His voice becomes impersonal and objective, as though what he told concerned some man he had known, but had nothing to do with him. This is the only way he can start telling the story.)* When Mama died, I'd been on the wagon for nearly two years. Not even a glass of beer. Honestly. And I know I would have stayed on. For her sake. She had no one but me. The Old Man was dead. My brother had married—had a kid—had his own life to live. She'd lost him. She had only me to attend to things for her and take care of her. She'd always hated my drinking. So I quit. It made me happy to do it. For her. Because she was all I had, all I cared about. Because I loved her. *(He pauses.)* No one would believe that now, who knew— But I did.

JOSIE *(gently)*: I know how much you loved her.

TYRONE: We went out to the Coast to see about selling a piece of property the Old Man had bought there years ago. And one day she suddenly became ill. Got rapidly worse. Went into a coma. Brain tumor. The docs said, no hope. Might never come out of coma. I went crazy. Couldn't face losing her. The old booze yen got me. I got drunk and stayed drunk. And I began hoping she'd never come out of the coma, and see I was drinking again. That was my excuse, too—that she'd never know. And she never did. *(He pauses—then sneeringly.)* Nix! Kidding myself again. I know damned well just before she died she recognized me. She saw I was drunk. Then she closed her eyes so she couldn't see, and was glad to die! *(He opens his eyes and stares into the moonlight as if he saw this deathbed scene before him.)*

JOSIE *(soothingly)*: Ssshh. You only imagine that because you feel guilty about drinking.

TYRONE *(as if he hadn't heard, closes his eyes again)*: After that, I kept so drunk I did draw a blank most of the time, but I went through the necessary motions and no one guessed how drunk— *(He pauses.)* But there are things I can never forget—the undertakers, and her body in a coffin with her face made up. I couldn't hardly recognize her. She looked young and pretty like someone I remembered meeting long ago. Practically a stranger. To who I was a stranger. Cold and indifferent. Not worried about me any more. Free at last. Free from worry. From pain. From me. I stood looking down at her, and something happened to me. I found I couldn't feel anything. I knew I ought to be heartbroken but I couldn't feel anything. I seemed dead, too. I knew I ought to cry. Even a crying jag would look better than just standing there. But I couldn't cry. I cursed to myself, "You dirty bastard, it's Mama. You loved her, and now she's dead. She's gone away from you forever. Never, never again—" But it had no effect. All I did was try to explain to myself, "She's dead. What does she care now if I cry or not, or what I do? It doesn't matter a damn to her. She's happy to be where I can't hurt her ever again. She's rid of me at last. For God's sake, can't you leave her alone even now? For God's sake, can't you let her rest in peace?" (*He pauses—then sneeringly.*) But there were several people around and I knew they expected me to show something. Once a ham, always a ham! So I put on an act. I flopped on my knees and hid my face in my hands and faked some sobs and cried, "Mama! Mama! My dear mother!" But all the time I kept saying to myself, "You lousy ham! You God-damned lousy ham! Christ, in a minute you'll start singing 'Mother Macree'!" (*He opens his eyes and gives a tortured, sneering laugh, staring into the moonlight.*)

JOSIE (*horrified, but still deeply pitying*): Jim! Don't! It's past. You've punished yourself. And you were drunk. You didn't mean—

TYRONE (*again closes his eyes*): I had to bring her body East to be buried beside the Old Man. I took a drawing room and hid in it with a case of booze. She was in her coffin in the baggage car. No matter how drunk I got, I couldn't forget that for a minute. I found I couldn't stay alone in the drawing room. It became haunted. I was going crazy. I had to go out and wander up and down the train looking for company. I made such a public nuisance of myself that the conductor threatened if I didn't quit, he'd keep me locked in the drawing room. But I'd spotted one passenger who was used to drunks and could pretend to like them, if there was enough dough in it. She had parlor house written all over her—a blonde pig who looked more like a whore than twenty-five whores, with a face like an overgrown doll's and a come-on smile as cold as a polar bear's feet. I bribed the porter to take a message to her and that night she sneaked into my drawing room. She was bound for New York, too. So every night—for fifty bucks a night— (*He opens his eyes and now he stares torturedly through the moonlight into the drawing room.*)

JOSIE (*her face full of revulsion—stammers*): Oh, how could you! (*Instinctively she draws away, taking her arms from around him.*)

TYRONE: How could I? I don't know. But I did. I suppose I had some mad idea she could make me forget—what was in the baggage car ahead.

JOSIE: Don't. (*She draws back again so he has to raise his head from her breast. He doesn't seem to notice this.*)

TYRONE: No, it couldn't have been that. Because I didn't seem to want to forget. It was like some plot I had to carry out. The blonde—she didn't matter. She was only something that belonged in the plot. It was as if I wanted revenge—because I'd been left alone—because I knew I was lost, without any hope left—that all I could do would be drink myself to death, because no one was left who could help me. (*His face hardens and a look of cruel vindictiveness comes into it—with a strange horrible satisfaction in his tone.*) No, I didn't forget even in that pig's arms! I remembered the last two lines of a lousy tear-jerker song I'd heard when I was a kid kept singing over and over in my brain.

"And baby's cries can't waken her
In the baggage coach ahead."

JOSIE (*distractedly*): Jim!

TYRONE: I couldn't stop it singing. I didn't want to stop it!

JOSIE: Jim! For the love of God. I don't want to hear!

TYRONE (*after a pause—dully*): Well, that's all—except I was too drunk to go to her funeral.

JOSIE: Oh! (*She has drawn away from him as far as she can without getting up. He becomes aware of this for the first time and turns slowly to stare at her.*)

TYRONE (*dully*): Don't want to touch me now, eh? (*He shrugs his shoulders mechanically.*) Sorry. I'm a damned fool. I shouldn't have told you.

JOSIE (*her horror ebbing as her love and protective compassion returns—moves nearer him—haltingly*): Don't, Jim. Don't say—I don't want to touch you. It's—a lie. (*She puts a hand on his shoulder.*)

TYRONE (*as if she hadn't spoken—with hopeless longing*): Wish I could believe in the spiritualists' bunk. If I could tell her it was because I missed her so much and couldn't forgive her for leaving me—

JOSIE: Jim! For the love of God—!

TYRONE (*unheeding*): She'd understand and forgive me, don't you think? She always did. She was simple and kind and pure of heart. She was beautiful. You're like her deep in your heart. That's why I told you. I thought— (*Abruptly his expression becomes sneering and cynical—harshly.*) My mistake. Nuts! Forget it. Time I got a move on. I don't like your damned moon, Josie. It's an ad for the past. (*He recites mockingly*)

"It is the very error of the moon:
She comes more nearer earth than she was wont,
And makes men mad."

(*He moves*) I'll grab the last trolley for town. There'll be a speak open, and some drunk laughing. I need a laugh. (*He starts to get up.*)

JOSIE (*throws her arms around him and pulls him back—*

tensely): No! You won't go! I won't let you! *(She hugs him close—gently.)* I understand now, Jim, darling, and I'm proud you came to me as the one in the world you know loves you enough to understand and forgive—and I do forgive!

TYRONE *(lets his head fall back on her breast—simply)*: Thanks, Josie, I knew you—

JOSIE: As *she* forgives, do you hear me! As *she* loves and understands and forgives!

TYRONE *(simply)*: Yes, I know she— *(His voice breaks.)*

JOSIE *(bends over him with a brooding maternal tenderness)*: That's right. Do what you came for, my darling. It isn't drunken laughter in a speakeasy you want to hear at all, but the sound of yourself crying your heart's repentance against her breast. *(His face is convulsed. He hides it on her breast and sobs rackingly. She hugs him more tightly and speaks softly, staring into the moonlight.)* She hears. I feel her in the moonlight, her soul wrapped in it like a silver mantle, and I know she understand and forgives me, too, and her blessing lies on me. *(A pause. His sobs begin to stop exhaustedly. She looks down at him again and speaks soothingly as she would to a child.)* There. There, now. *(He stops. She goes on in a gentle, bullying tone.)* You're a fine one, wanting to leave me when the night I promised I'd give you has just begun, our night that'll be different from all the others, with a dawn that won't creep over dirty windowpanes but will wake in the sky like a promise of God's peace in the soul's dark sadness. *(She smiles a little amused smile.)* Will you listen to me, Jim! I must be a poet. Who would have guessed it? Sure, love is a wonderful mad inspiration! *(A pause. She looks down. His eyes are closed. His face against her breast looks pale and haggard in the moonlight. Calm with the drained, exhausted peace of death. For a second she is frightened. Then she realizes and whispers softly.)* Asleep. *(In a tender crooning tone like a lullaby.)* That's right. Sleep in peace, my darling. *(Then with sudden anguished longing.)* Oh, Jim, Jim, maybe my love could still save you, if you could want it enough! *(She shakes her head.)* No. That can never be. *(Her eyes leave his face to stare up at the sky. She looks weary and stricken and sad. She forces a defensive, self-derisive smile.)* God forgive me, it's a fine end to all my scheming, to sit here with the dead hugged to my breast, and the silly mug of the moon grinning down, enjoying the joke!

ACT 4

(Scene: Same as Act Three. It is dawn. The first faint streaks of color, heralding the sunrise, appear in the eastern sky at left.

JOSIE sits in the same position on the steps, as if she had not moved, her arms around TYRONE. He is still asleep, his head on her breast. His face has the same exhausted, death-like repose. JOSIE's face is set in an expression of numbed, resigned sadness. Her body sags tiredly. In spite of her strength, holding herself like this for hours, for fear of waking him, is becoming too much for her.

The two make a strangely tragic picture in the wan dawn light—this big sorrowful woman hugging a haggard-faced, middle-aged drunkard against her breast, as if he were a sick child.

HOGAN appears at left-rear, coming from the barn. He approaches the corner of the house stealthily on tiptoe. Wisps of hay stick to his clothes and his face is swollen and sleepy, but his little pig's eyes are sharply wide awake and sober. He peeks around the corner, and takes in the two on the steps. His eyes fix on JOSIE's face in a long, probing stare.)

JOSIE *(speaks in a low grim tone)*: Stop hiding, Father. I heard you sneak up. *(He comes guiltily around the corner. She keeps her voice low, but her tone is commanding.)* Come here, and be quiet about it. *(He obeys meekly, coming as far as the boulder silently, his eyes searching her face, his expression becoming guilty and miserable at what he sees. She goes on in the same tone, without looking at him.)* Talk low, now. I don't want him wakened— *(She adds strangely.)* Not until the dawn has beauty in it.

HOGAN *(worriedly)*: What? *(He decides it's better for the present to ask no questions. His eyes fall on TYRONE's face. In spite of himself, he is startled—in an awed, almost frightened whisper.)* Be god, he looks dead!

JOSIE *(strangely)*: Why wouldn't he? He is.

HOGAN: Is?

JOSIE: Don't be a fool. Can't you see him breathing? Dead asleep, I mean. Don't stand there gawking. Sit down. *(He sits meekly on the boulder. His face betrays a guilty dread of what is coming. There is a pause in which she doesn't look at him but, he keeps glancing at her, growing visibly more uneasy. She speaks bitterly.)* Where's your witnesses?

HOGAN *(guiltily)*: Witnesses? *(Then forcing an amused grin.)* Oh, be God, if that ain't a joke on me! Sure I got so blind drunk at the Inn I forgot all about our scheme and came home and went to sleep in the hayloft.

JOSIE *(her expression harder and more bitter)*: You're a liar.

HOGAN: I'm not. I just woke up. Look at the hay sticking to me. That's proof.

JOSIE: I'm not thinking of that, and well you know it. *(With bitter voice.)* So you just woke up—did you?—and then came sneaking here to see if the scheme behind your scheme had worked!

HOGAN *(guiltily)*: I don't know what you mean.

JOSIE: Don't lie any more, Father. This time, you've told one too many. *(He starts to defend himself but the look on her face makes him think better of it and he remains uneasily silent. A pause.)*

HOGAN *(finally has to blurt out)*: Sure, if I'd brought the witnesses, there's nothing for them to witness that—

JOSIE: No. You're right there. There's nothing. Nothing at all. *(She smiles strangely.)* Except a great miracle they'd never believe, or you either.

HOGAN: What miracle?

JOSIE: A virgin who bears a dead child in the night, and the dawn finds her still a virgin. If that isn't a miracle, what is?

HOGAN *(uneasily)*: Stop talking so queer. You give me the shivers. *(He attempts a joking tone.)* Is it you who's the virgin? Faith, that *would* be a miracle, no less! *(He forces a chuckle.)*

JOSIE: I told you to stop lying, Father.

HOGAN: What lie? *(He stops and watches her face worriedly. She is silent, as if she were not aware of him now. Her eyes are fixed on the wanton sky.)*

JOSIE *(as if to herself)*: It'll be beautiful soon, and I can wake him.

HOGAN *(can't resist his anxiety any longer)*: Josie, darlin'! For the love of God, can't you tell me what happened to you?

JOSIE *(her face hard and bitter again)*: I've told you once. Nothing.

HOGAN: Nothing? If you could see the sadness in your face—

JOSIE: What woman doesn't sorrow for the man she loved who has died? But there's pride in my heart, too.

HOGAN *(tormentedly)*: Will you stop talking as if you'd gone mad in the night! *(Raising his voice—with revengeful anger.)* Listen to me! If Jim Tyrone has done anything to bring you sorrow— *(TYRONE stirs in his sleep and moans, pressing his face against her breast as if for protection. She looks down at him and hugs him close.)*

JOSIE *(croons softly)*: There, there, my darling. Rest in peace a while longer. *(Turns on her father angrily and whispers.)* Didn't I tell you to speak low and not wake him! *(She pauses—then quietly.)* He did nothing to bring me sorrow. It was my mistake. I thought there was still hope. I didn't know he'd died already—that it was a damned soul coming to me in the moonlight, to confess and be forgiven and find peace for a night—

HOGAN: Josie! Will you stop!

JOSIE *(after a pause—dully)*: He'd never do anything to hurt me. You know it. *(Self-mockingly.)* Sure, hasn't he told me I'm beautiful to him and he loves me—in his fashion. *(Then matter-of-factly.)* All that happened was that he got drunk and he had one of his crazy notions he wanted to sleep the way he is, and I let him sleep. *(With forced roughness.)* And, be God, the night's over. I'm half dead with tiredness and sleepiness. It's that you see in my face, not sorrow.

HOGAN: Don't try to fool me, Josie. I—

JOSIE *(her face hard and bitter—grimly)*: Fool you, is it? It's you who made a fool of me with your lies, thinking you'd use me to get your dirty greasy paws on the money he'll have!

HOGAN: No! I swear by all the saints—

JOSIE: You'd swear on a Bible while you were stealing it! *(Grimly.)* Listen to me, Father. I didn't call you here to answer questions about what's none of your business. I called you here to tell you I've seen through all the lies you told last night to get me to— *(As he starts to speak.)* Shut up! I'll do the talking now. You weren't drunk. You were only putting it on as part of your scheme—

HOGAN *(quietly)*: I wasn't drunk, no. I admit that, Josie. But I'd had slews of drinks and they were in my head or I'd never have the crazy dreams—

JOSIE *(with biting scorn)*: Dreams, is it? The only dream you've ever had, or will have, is of yourself counting a fistful of dirty money, and divil a care how you got it, or who you robbed or made suffer!

HOGAN *(winces—pleadingly)*: Josie!

JOSIE: Shut up! *(Scathingly.)* I'm sure you've made up a whole new set of lies and excuses. You're that cunning and clever, but you can save your breath. They wouldn't fool me now. I've been fooled once too often. *(He gives her a frightened look, as if something he had dreaded has happened. She goes on, grimly accusing.)* You lied about Jim selling the farm. You knew he was kidding. You knew the estate would be out of probate in a few days, and he'd go back to Broadway, and you had to do something quick or you'd lose the last chance of getting your greedy hooks on his money.

HOGAN *(miserably)*: No. It wasn't that, Josie.

JOSIE: You saw how hurt and angry I was because he'd kept me waiting here, and you used that. You knew I loved him and wanted him and you used that. You used all you knew about me— Oh, you did it clever! You ought to be proud! You worked it so it was me who did all the dirty scheming— You knew I'd find out from Jim you'd lied about the farm, but not before your lie had done its work—made me go after him, get him drunk, get drunk myself so I could be shameless—and when the truth did come out, wouldn't it make me love him all the more and be more shameless and willing? Don't tell me you didn't count on that, and you such a clever schemer! And if he once had me, knowing I was a virgin, didn't you count on his honor and remorse, and his loving me in his fashion, to make him offer to marry me? Sure, why wouldn't he, you thought. It wouldn't hold him. He'd go back to Broadway just the same and never see me again. But there'd be money in it, and when he'd finished killing himself, I'd be his legal widow and get what's left.

HOGAN (*miserably*): No! It wasn't that.

JOSIE: But what's the good of talking? It's all over. I've only one more word for you, Father, and it's this: I'm leaving you today, like my brothers left. You can live alone and work alone your cunning schemes on yourself.

HOGAN (*after a pause—slowly*): I knew you'd be bitter against me, Josie, but I took the chance you'd be so happy you wouldn't care how—.

JOSIE (*as if she hadn't heard, looking at the eastern sky which is now glowing with color*): Thank God, it's beautiful. It's time. (*to* HOGAN) Go in the house and stay there till he's gone. I don't want you around to start some new scheme. (*He looks miserable, starts to speak, thinks better of it, and meekly tiptoes past her up the steps and goes in, closing the door quietly after him. She looks down at* TYRONE. *Her face softens with a maternal tenderness—sadly.*) I hate to bring you back to life, Jim, darling. If you could have died in your sleep, that's what you would have liked, isn't it? (*She gives him a gentle shake.*) Wake up, Jim. (*He moans in his sleep and presses more closely against her. She stares at his face.*) Dear God, let him remember that one thing and forget the rest. That will be enough for me. (*She gives him a more vigorous shake.*) Jim! Wake up, do you hear? It's time.

TYRONE (*half wakens without opening his eyes—mutters*): What the hell? (*Dimly conscious of a woman's body—cynically.*) Again, eh? Same old stuff. Who the hell are you, sweetheart? (*Irritably.*) What's the big idea, waking me up? What time is it?

JOSIE: It's dawn.

TYRONE (*still without opening his eyes*): Dawn? (*He quotes drowsily.*)

"But I was desolate and sick of an old passion,
When I awoke and found the dawn was gray."

(*Then with a sneer*) They're all gray. Go to sleep, Kid—and let me sleep. (*He falls asleep again.*)

JOSIE (*tensely*): This one isn't gray, Jim. It's different from all the others—(*She sees he is asleep—bitterly.*) He'll have forgotten. He'll never notice. And I'm the whore on the train to him now, not— (*Suddenly she pushes him away from her and shakes him roughly.*) Will you wake up, for God's sake! I've had all I can bear—

TYRONE (*still half asleep*): Hey! Cut out the rough stuff, Kid. What? (*Awake now, blinking his eyes—with dazed surprise.*) Josie.

JOSIE (*still bitter*): That's who, and none of your damned tarts! (*She pushes him.*) Get up now, so you won't fall asleep again. (*He does so with difficulty, still in a sleepy daze, his body stiff and cramped. She conquers her bitter resentment and puts on her old* free-and-easy kidding tone with him, but all the time waiting to see how much he will remember.) You're stiff and cramped, and no wonder. I'm worse from holding you, if that's any comfort. (*She stretches and rubs her numbed arms, groaning comically.*) Holy Joseph, I'm a wreck entirely. I'll never be the same. (*Giving him a quick glance.*) You look as if you'd drawn a blank and were wondering how you got here. I'll bet you don't remember a thing.

TYRONE (*moving his arms and legs gingerly—sleepily*): I don't know. Wait till I'm sure I'm still alive.

JOSIE: You need an eye-opener. (*She picks up the bottle and glass and pours him a drink.*) Here you are.

TYRONE (*takes the glass mechanically*): Thanks, Josie. (*He goes and sits on the boulder, holding the drink as if he had no interest in it.*)

JOSIE (*watching him*): Drink up or you'll be asleep again.

TYRONE: No, I'm awake now, Josie. Funny. Don't seem to want a drink. Oh, I've got a head all right. But no heebie-jeebies—yet.

JOSIE: That's fine. It must be a pleasant change—

TYRONE: It is. I've got a nice, dreamy peaceful hangover for once—as if I'd had a sound sleep without nightmares.

JOSIE: So you did. Divil a nightmare. I ought to know. Wasn't I holding you and keeping them away?

TYRONE: You mean you— (*Suddenly.*) Wait a minute. I remember now I was sitting alone at a table in the Inn, and I suddenly had a crazy notion I'd come up here and sleep with my head on your— So that's why I woke up in your arms. (*Shamefacedly.*) And you let me get away with it. You're a nut, Josie.

JOSIE: Oh, I didn't mind.

TYRONE: You must have seen how blotto I was, didn't you?

JOSIE: I did. You were as full as a tick.

TYRONE: Then why didn't you give me the bum's rush?

JOSIE: Why would I? I was glad to humor you.

TYRONE: For God's sake, how long was I cramped on you like that?

JOSIE: Oh, a few hours, only.

TYRONE: God, I'm sorry, Josie, but it's your own fault for letting me—

JOSIE: Och, don't be apologizing. I was glad of the excuse to stay awake and enjoy the beauty of the moon.

TYRONE: Yes, I can remember what a beautiful night it was.

JOSIE: Can you? I'm glad of that, Jim. You seemed to enjoy it the while we were sitting here together before you fell asleep.

TYRONE: How long a while was that?

JOSIE: Not long. Less than an hour, anyway.

TYRONE: I suppose I bored the hell out of you with a

lot of drunken drivel.

JOSIE: Not a lot, no. But some. You were full of blarney, saying how beautiful I was to you.

TYRONE (earnestly): That wasn't drivel, Josie. You were. You are. You always will be.

JOSIE: You're a wonder, Jim. Nothing can stop you, can it? Even me in the light of dawn, looking like something you'd put in the field to scare the crows from the corn. You'll kid at the Day of Judgment.

TYRONE (impatiently): You know damned well it isn't kidding. You're not a fool. You can tell.

JOSIE (kiddingly): All right, then, I'm beautiful and you love me—in your fashion.

TYRONE: "In my fashion," eh? Was I reciting poetry to you? That must have been hard to take.

JOSIE: It wasn't. I liked it. It was all about beautiful nights and the romance of the moon.

TYRONE: Well, there was some excuse for that, anyway. It sure was a beautiful night. I'll never forget it.

JOSIE: I'm glad, Jim.

TYRONE: What other bunk did I pull on you—or I mean, did old John Barleycorn pull?

JOSIE: Not much. You were mostly quiet and sad—in a kind of daze, as if the moon was in your wits as well as whiskey.

TYRONE: I remember I was having a grand time at the Inn, celebrating with Phil, and then suddenly, for no reason, all the fun went out of it, and I was more melancholy than ten Hamlets. (He pauses.) Hope I didn't tell you the sad story of my life and weep on your bosom, Josie.

JOSIE: You didn't. The one thing you talked a lot about was that you wanted the night with me to be different from all the other nights you'd spent with women.

TYRONE (with revulsion): God, don't make me think of those tramps now! (Then with deep, grateful feeling.) It sure was different, Josie. I may not remember much, but I know how different it was from the way I feel now. None of my usual morning-after stuff—the damned sick remorse that makes you wish you'd died in your sleep so you wouldn't have to face the rotten things you're afraid you said and did the night before, when you were so drunk you didn't know what you were doing.

JOSIE: There's nothing you said or did last night for you to regret. You can take my word for it.

TYRONE (as if he hadn't heard—slowly): It's hard to describe how I feel. It's a new one on me. Sort of at peace with myself and this lousy life—as if all my sins had been forgiven— (He becomes self conscious—cynically.) Nuts with that sin bunk, but you know what I mean.

JOSIE (tensely): I do, and I'm happy you feel that way, Jim. (A pause. She goes on.) You talked about how you'd watched too many dawns come creeping grayly over dirty windowpanes, with some tart snoring beside you—

TYRONE (winces): Have a heart. Don't remind me of that now, Josie. Don't spoil this dawn! (A pause. She watches him tensely. He turns slowly to face the east, where the sky is now glowing with all the colors of an exceptionally beautiful sunrise. He stares, drawing a deep breath. He is profoundly moved but immediately becomes self-conscious and tries to sneer it off—cynically.) God seems to be putting on quite a display. I like Belasco better. Rise of curtain, Act-Four stuff. (Her face has fallen into lines of bitter hurt, but he adds quickly and angrily.) God damn it! Why do I have to pull that lousy stuff? (With genuine deep feeling.) God, it's beautiful, Josie! I—I'll never forget it—here with you.

JOSIE (her face clearing—simply): I'm glad, Jim. I was hoping you'd feel beauty in it—by way of a token.

TYRONE (watching the sunrise—mechanically): Token of what?

JOSIE: Oh, I don't know. Token to me that—never mind. I forget what I meant. (Abruptly changing the subject.) Don't think I woke you just to admire the sunrise. You're on a farm, not Broadway, and it's time for me to start work, not go to bed. (She gets to her feet and stretches. There is a growing strain behind her free-and-easy manner.) And that's a hint, Jim. I can't stay entertaining you. So go back to the Inn, that's a good boy. I know you'll understand the reason, and not think I'm tired of your company. (She forces a smile.)

TYRONE (gets up): Of course, I understand. (He pauses—then blurts out guiltily.) One more question. You're sure I didn't get out of order last night—and try to make you, or anything like that.

JOSIE: You didn't. You kidded back when I kidded you, the way we always do. That's all.

TYRONE: Thank God for that. I'd never forgive myself if—I wouldn't have asked you except I've pulled some pretty rotten stuff when I was drawing a blank. (He becomes conscious of the forgotten drink he has in his hand.) Well, I might as well drink this. The bar at the Inn won't be open for hours. (He drinks—then looks pleasantly surprised.) I'll be damned! That isn't Phil's rotgut. That's real, honest-to-God bonded Bourbon. Where— (This clicks in his mind and suddenly he remembers everything and JOSIE sees that he does. The look of guilt and shame and anguish settles over his face. Instinctively he throws the glass away, his first reaction one of loathing for the drink which brought back memory. He feels JOSIE staring at him and fights desperately to control his voice and expression.) Real Bourbon. I remember now you said a bootlegger gave it to Phil. Well, I'll run along and let you do your work. See you later, Josie. (*He turns toward the road.*)

JOSIE (*strickenly*): No! Don't, Jim! Don't go like that! You won't see me later. You'll never see me again now, and I know that's best for us both, but I can't bear to have you ashamed you wanted my love to comfort your sorrow—when I'm so proud I could give it. (*Pleadingly.*) I hoped, for your sake, you wouldn't remember, but now you do, I want you to remember my love for you gave you peace for a while.

TYRONE (*stares at her fighting with himself. He stammers defensively*): I don't know what you're talking about. I don't remember—

JOSIE (*sadly*): All right, Jim. Neither do I then. Good-bye, and God bless you. (*She turns as if to go up the steps into the house.*)

TYRONE (*stammers*): Wait, Josie! (*Coming to her.*) I'm a liar! I'm a louse! Forgive me, Josie. I do remember! I'm glad I remember! I'll never forget your love! (*He kisses her on the lips.*) Never! (*Kissing her again.*) Never, do you hear! I'll always love you, Josie. (*He kisses her again.*) Good-bye—and God bless you! (*He turns away and walks quickly down the road off left without looking back. She stands, watching him go, for a moment, then she puts her hands over her face, her head bent, and sobs.* HOGAN *comes out of her room and stands on top of the steps. He looks after* TYRONE *and his face is hard with bitter anger.*)

JOSIE (*sensing his presence, stops crying and lifts her head—dully*): I'll get your breakfast in a minute, Father.

HOGAN: To hell with my breakfast! I'm not a pig that has no other thought but eating! (*Then pleadingly.*) Listen, darlin'. All you said about my lying and scheming, and what I hoped would happen, is true. But it wasn't his money, Josie. I did see it was the last chance—the only one left to bring the two of you to stop your damned pretending, and face the truth that you loved each other. I wanted you to find happiness—by hook or crook, one way or another, what did I care how? I wanted to save him, and hoped he'd see that only your love could— It was his talk of the beauty he saw in you that made me hope— And I knew he'd never go to bed with you even if you'd let him unless he married you. And if I gave a thought to his money at all, that was the least of it, and why shouldn't I want to have you live in ease and comfort for a change, like you deserve, instead of in this shanty on a lousy farm, slaving for me? (*He pauses—miserably.*) Can't you believe that's the truth, Josie, and not feel so bitter against me?

JOSIE (*her eyes still following* TYRONE—*gently*): I know it's the truth, Father. I'm not bitter now. Don't be afraid I'm going to leave you. I only said it to punish you for a while.

HOGAN (*with humble gratitude*): Thank God for that, darlin'.

JOSIE (*forces a teasing smile and a little of her old manner*): A ginger-haired, crooked old goat like you to be playing Cupid!

HOGAN (*his face lights up joyfully. He is almost himself again—ruefully*): You had me punished, that's sure. I was thinking after you'd gone I'd drown myself in Harder's ice pond. There was this consolation in it, I knew that the bastard would never look at a piece of ice again without remembering me. (*She doesn't hear this. Her thoughts are on the receding figure of* TYRONE *again.* HOGAN *looks at her sad face worriedly—gently.*) Don't darlin'. Don't be hurting yourself. (*Then as she still doesn't hear, he puts on his old, fuming irascible tone.*) Are you going to moon at the sunrise forever, and me with the sides of my stomach knocking together?

JOSIE (*gently*): Don't worry about me, Father. It's over now. I'm not hurt. I'm only sad for him.

HOGAN: For him? (*He bursts out in a fit of smoldering rage.*) May the blackest curse from the pit of hell—

JOSIE (*with an anguished cry*): Don't, Father! I love him!

HOGAN (*subsides, but his face looks sorrowful and old—dully*): I didn't mean it. I know whatever happened he meant no harm to you. It was life I was cursing—(*With a trace of his natural manner.*) And, be God, that's a waste of breath, if it does deserve it. (*Then as she remains silent—miserably.*) Or maybe I was cursing myself for a damned old scheming fool, like I ought to.

JOSIE (*turns to him, forcing a teasing smile*): Look out. I might say Amen to that. (*Gently.*) Don't be sad, Father. I'm all right—and I'm well content here with you. (*Forcing her teasing manner again.*) Sure, living with you has spoilt me for any other man, anyway. There'd never be the same fun or excitement.

HOGAN (*plays up to this—in his fuming manner*): There'll be excitement if I don't get my breakfast soon, but it won't be fun, I'm warning you!

JOSIE (*forcing her usual reaction to his threats*): Och, don't be threatening me, you bad-tempered old tick. Let's go in the house and I'll get your damned breakfast.

HOGAN: Now you're talking. (*He goes in the house through her room. She follows him as far as the door—then turns for a last look down the road.*)

JOSIE (*her face sad, tender and pitying—gently*): May you have your wish and die in your sleep soon, Jim, darling. May you rest forever in forgiveness and peace. (*She turns slowly and goes into the house.*)

CURTAIN

Figure 1. Josie (Colleen Dewhurst) and Tyrone (Jason Robards) in front of the realistic/symbolic set for the José Quintero production of *A Moon for the Misbegotten*, New York, 1974. (Photograph: Martha Swope.)

Figure 2. Josie (Colleen Dewhurst) and Tyrone (Jason Robards) in the José Quintero production of *A Moon for the Misbegotten*, New York, 1974. (Photograph: Martha Swope.)

Figure 3. Hogan (Ed Flanders) reproves Josie (Colleen Dewhurst) as she cradles Tyrone (Jason Robards) in her arms in the José Quintero production of *A Moon for the Misbegotten,* New York, 1974. (Photograph: Martha Swope.)

Staging of *A Moon for the Misbegotten*

REVIEW OF THE NEW YORK PRODUCTION, 1974, BY WALTER KERR

Colleen Dewhurst is a beautiful woman giving a beautiful performance in the newest revival of Eugene O'Neill's "A Moon for the Misbegotten" (which also just happens to be a beautiful play, possibly O'Neill's best), and I find nothing more fetching about her performance than her witchlike way with an unfinished sentence.

Unfinished sentences can be hell for actors, often because the playwright has had no thought to complete and has simply handed the performer the task of implying one. They can hang there, limp as on a washline, ready to blow any which way a wind happens along. Not in Miss Dewhurst's firmly ruled kingdom, though. In "A Moon for the Misbegotten" she is, in her shanty-Irish father's words, "big and strong as a bull, and as vicious and disrespectful," and she is waiting, in the early kerosene-lit moonlight, for a visit from one of her betters. The visitor is to be Jason Robards, member of an acting family, handsomely educated, already half-broken by drink. He should be, in the opinion of a canny father, readily seduceable.

In fact, Father Ed Flanders (another stunning performance) has the night's course well planned into the dawn. He will slip off to a bar and get himself drunk enough to be utterly unable to prevent anything Mr. Robards may have in mind. It is Miss Dewhurst's business to see to it that Mr. Robards's mind takes a right turn. At this point in the conniving, the actress suddenly turns on the aged leprechaun who is whispering goat-songs in her ear.

Eyes blazing, her hair pulled taut from a clear forehead, arm ever-ready to take a stick to her mentor, she lets him know what she thinks of "a father telling his daughter how to—" and there lets the sentence die. The special splendor of the moment is that it doesn't die. The obvious finish to the line is "to seduce a man," and, if that were all, it wouldn't be much. By letting it break where O'Neill broke it, and by reaching out to join her playwright creatively, Miss Dewhurst fills the void with a heartful of contending emotions. What is left over, and unsaid, is that she wants the love of the man, that she wants it on her own terms, that she is terribly, terribly afraid she is not going to get it, and that seduction—if she knew anything at all about it—would waste the last ounce of goodness in two malformed lives. That's a lot, but it's all there.

It is difficult to take your eyes off Miss Dewhurst,

whether she is smiling or in fury. She has a smile that behaves strangely. Most smiles, when they are about to crack in dismay, crack downward. Hers shatters upward, sustaining the shape of happiness while a telltale quaver makes a lie of the crescent corners of her mouth. Her face seems actually to brighten under the hint of pain, a sense of unruly merriment tries hard to assert itself, a vixenish gaiety becomes permanent companion of disaster.

The effect is enormously touching, and it blends ever so easily with the roustabout humors of her donnybrooks with her father. The racy, fork-tongued, rattle-on chaffings between Miss Dewhurst and Mr. Flanders are exhilaratingly designed by director José Quintero, and they remind you, in case you've forgotten, that when O'Neill wanted to write comedy, he had only to pick up an alternate pen and let another kind of theater-ink flow, an apparently inexhaustible knowhow takeover.

But "A Moon for the Misbegotten" is not, in the end, comedy, which is where Miss Dewhurst's unfinished sentences and upsweep dismays, and Jason Robards come in. Mr. Robards begins brilliantly, self-conscious not only about his natty 1923 clothes but about his need for a drink, his need for a woman who will not turn out to be a whore, his need for nothing so much as an impossible forgiveness.

The shaking hand with which he lights a cigarette as their tryst together is to begin establishes its outcome; the succulent surrender to a first taste of a drink she brings him outlines precisely the one comfort this doomed man can know. The detail—an uneasy balance on a treacherous planet, fingers at his collar, palms scraping the nap of jacket and trousers as though something dirty could be wiped away—is graphic, conscientiously arrived at, intelligently used.

I have one important reservation about the production and feel something of an ingrate for bringing it up. But at the invitational preview I attended, the terrifying "almost" of the third act—the teasing possibility that against all odds two rattled, emotionally starved, yearning and yet distrustful misfits will somehow find a crooked way to an ultimate meeting—simply didn't happen. We know that it *can't* happen, that it was never in the cards; but that is for the fourth act to say. Here, with all of the anger and ugliness and awkward groping allowed for, there must be a rhythm that moves toward fusion, toward a coming-together of the far ends of the earth. Without it, without its momentary false promise, the play is too much of a piece, each movement reiterating the other.

Mr. Robards, possibly out of over-concern that each moment will be technically right, continually aborts that promised rhythm, lurching away in self-disgust and trying to spit from his mouth the venom of lost years so often that the design becomes fragmented, the contrast stalemated. I may have seen an unduly edgy performance; certainly it is a matter that continued performance can correct. But there were times when I wanted to collar the man and order him to stay with the scene, stay with the woman, until O'Neill's play could come as close as it dared to a psychic embrace. *Then* it might be shattered, letting us see the remorse-ridden figure as truly dead. It is the crest of the wave, before it collapses on the beach, that is missing, leaving me with slightly fonder memories of the 1968 production at the downtown Circle in the Square.

If I suggest that "Moon for the Misbegotten" just may be O'Neill's richest work for the theater, it is because the free creative impulse is allowed more play here than in the directly autobiographical "Long Day's Journey Into Night." The Robards role is, of course, rooted in O'Neill's older brother. The other figures, however, draw upon, and demand, vast imaginative resources; life is made on the wing rather than painstakingly remembered. It is an honest life, and for O'Neill, an unusually lyric one; the crafty, the damned, and the forgiving breathe.

ARTHUR MILLER

1915–

Although Miller has written only a dozen or so plays, he is viewed throughout the world as one of America's most eminent contemporary dramatists. His *Death of a Salesman* (1949) is probably the most famous American play of the twentieth century, for it has come to be seen by millions of people as a consummate dramatization of the most disturbing aspects in the modern American version of "success." Theatrical success came relatively early in Miller's own career, yet he worked arduously to achieve it. He was born in Harlem at a time when his father was still struggling to establish a successful clothing manufacturing business, and he was raised in a suburb of Brooklyn after his father's business had become well established. But the depression of 1929 nearly ruined his father, so that when Miller graduated from high school in 1932, he had to take a job in an automobile warehouse to save up enough money to be able to attend college at the University of Michigan. During his four years at Michigan, he studied playwriting and he won a number of playwriting contests that also helped him to work his way through college. After graduating from Michigan, he worked briefly for the playwriting project the federal government was then supporting to help sustain dramatists during the depression, and subsequently he found work writing radio plays for CBS and later for the Cavalcade of America. During the war, he was unable to serve in the military because of a football injury he had suffered in high school, so instead he began writing radio plays and other pieces to help support civilian morale at home. Before the end of the war, he had also completed his first full-length play to be produced on Broadway, *The Man Who Had All the Luck* (1944), and though it closed after only four performances, it clearly anticipated the concern with moral responsibility and guilt that has been central to virtually all of Miller's work for the theater.

Miller's next play, *All My Sons* (1947), won the New York Drama Critics Circle award for the best play of the season, and it quickly established him as a serious playwright in the socially conscious tradition of Ibsen. When the play was first produced, Miller went out of his way in a press interview to declare his concern with moral and social issues:

> In all my plays and books I try to take setting and dramatic situations from life which involve real questions of right and wrong. Then I set out, rather implacably and in the most realistic situations I can find, the moral dilemma and try to point a real, though hard, path out. I don't see how you can write anything decent without using the question of right and wrong as the basis.

And in *All My Sons* he clearly focussed on the issue of moral responsibility by portraying the crisis that is produced when a small armaments manufacturer is discovered by his son to have sold defective airplane parts to the army, making him responsible for the death of a number of wartime pilots. The father, Joe Keller, seeks to justify himself to his son by claiming that he had wanted to preserve the business and support his family, but the son, Chris, maintains that "There's a universe outside and you're responsible to it." When Keller discovers that his other son, an air corps pilot himself, has been driven to suicide by the discovery of his guilt, he finally is forced to acknowledge his moral responsibility for a world beyond the limits of his own family: "I think to him they were all my sons. And I guess they were." And that recognition drives him to commit suicide himself.

Joe Keller's morally blind commitment to "dollars and cents" clearly anticipated Willy Loman's commitment to "success" in *Death of a Salesman*, much as the shattering of Joe Keller's self-delusion anticipated the shattering of Willy's "dream." But in *Death of a Salesman*, Miller did not confine himself to exposing the ramifications of a fatally wrong moral decision, and in the case of Willy Loman he chose to explore the ramifications of a fatally wrong way of life—a way of life distinctively American in its commitment to a naive idea of success. To invest his play with such broad social implications, Miller chose for his protagonist an archetypal figure in American culture—the travelling salesman—and he endowed that figure with all the conventional American aspirations, including not only the desire to succeed by being "well liked," but also the desire to be respected by one's friends, to be loved and admired by one's family, to contribute to the success of one's children, to pay one's bills on time, and to own one's own home. Then, in order to explore the failure of such middle-class values, Miller made the strategic decision of focussing on the archetypal salesman at the most vulnerable moment in his life, when he is "tired to death" by his age and by the disappointment of all his hopes. That, in essence, is the formula for the play, but the play itself goes far beyond the formula, largely because Miller does not confine himself to making an indictment of American cultural values.

The play can, of course, be read as an exposure of the cruelty, the cynicism, the stupidity, and the immorality that result from a blind commitment to American materialistic values, for those qualities are repeatedly displayed in Willy's behavior toward his wife, his sons, his friends, and his boss, as well as in Happy's behavior toward Willy, the boss' behavior toward Willy, and above all in the symbolic spectacle of Willy's brother Ben preaching the law of the jungle to Biff: "Never fight fair with a stranger, boy. You'll never get out of the jungle that way." The play can also be read as a tragedy of the common man—a view of the work that Miller sought to define in an essay he published along with the play, called "Tragedy and the Common Man." In that essay, he sought to challenge the traditional notion of the tragic figure as being necessarily "well placed" or "exalted," arguing that "the very same mental processes" are to be found in the "lowly," in particular, "the underlying fear of being displaced, the disaster inherent in being torn away from our chosen image of what and who we are in the world." And certainly it can be said that Willy displays that archetypal fear throughout the play, much as he displays the indignation that Miller regards as the inevitable result of being displaced: "the fateful wound from which the inevitable events spiral is the wound of indignity, and its dominant force is indignation. Tragedy, then, is the consequence of a man's total compulsion to evaluate himself justly."

But the power of the play, at last, derives less from its socially conscious tragic vision than from the way that Miller dramatizes that vision by concentrating on Willy's mental and emotional experience during the moment of his tragic crisis. Willy would not, after all, be such a compelling figure if he were merely a common social type. He is, in fact, highly particularized through the detailed exposure of his tortured consciousness—through the expressionistic presentation of his mental processes as he repeatedly shifts back and forth between past and present experience, mingling memory with immediate reality with hallucination. When he is shown, for example, in the first act, on the verge of embracing his wife, Linda, only to find himself engulfed by the memory of his adulterous escapade with another woman, Willy is poignantly revealed as a particular human being overwhelmed by guilt and by the painful isolation that it creates between him and his family. His sense of isolation, of course, increases throughout the play as he is incessantly bombarded both by painful memories from the past and disappointments in the present. Yet he does not simply acquiesce to the relentless flow of events in his world and in his mind, but seeks to resist them, indeed to alter them with all the force of his being. And though he is finally driven to relinquish his being in the act of resistance, he does so not out of a will to succeed, or to be "well liked," but out of a wholly selfless love for his family. In doing so, he thus escapes from the enslavement of being a salesman and becomes a person bound by authentic human attachments, free at last "to do the right thing."

In the years immediately following its first appearance, *Death of a Salesman* was interpreted in the United States and throughout the world as being primarily a statement about American culture, but its persistent appeal to audiences suggests that it speaks to even larger concerns—to the dismay that all human beings experience when they find themselves unable to accept what they have done to others, what others have done to them, and what they have become as a consequence. These dimensions of the play have recently moved directors and producers to revive it and stage it so as to emphasize the deeply human struggle that Willy goes through in the process of facing up to his illusions. This approach, for example, was taken by the famous movie and stage actor, George C. Scott, in a production he directed and starred in during 1974. A review of Scott's production, reprinted following the text, explains how he staged the play in order to emphasize the emotional, mental, and psychological struggle that Willy experiences. Photographs of Scott in the role of Willy clearly reveal that he was able to convey the man's fatigue (see Figure 1), his guilt (see Figure 3), his love for his family (see Figure 2), and thus his ultimate dignity.

DEATH OF A SALESMAN

BY ARTHUR MILLER

CHARACTERS

WILLY LOMAN
LINDA
BIFF
HAPPY
BERNARD
THE WOMAN
CHARLEY
UNCLE BEN
HOWARD WAGNER

JENNY
STANLEY
MISS FORSYTHE
LETTA

SCENE

The action takes place in WILLY LOMAN's *house and yard and in various places he visits in the New York and Boston of today.*

ACT 1

(A melody is heard, played upon a flute. It is small and fine, telling of grass and trees and the horizon. The curtain rises.

Before us is the Salesman's house. We are aware of towering, angular shapes behind it, surrounding it on all sides. Only the blue light of the sky falls upon the house and forestage; the surrounding area shows an angry glow of orange. As more light appears, we see a solid vault of apartment houses around the small, fragile-seeming home. An air of the dream clings to the place, a dream rising out of reality. The kitchen at center seems actual enough, for there is a kitchen table with three chairs, and a refrigerator. But no other fixtures are seen. At the back of the kitchen there is a draped entrance, which leads to the living-room. To the right of the kitchen, on a level raised two feet, is a bedroom furnished only with a brass bedstead and a straight chair. On a shelf over the bed a silver athletic trophy stands. A window opens onto the apartment house at the side.

Behind the kitchen, on a level raised six and a half feet, is the boys' bedroom, at present barely visible. Two beds are dimly seen, and at the back of the room a dormer window. [This bedroom is above the unseen living-room.] At the left a stairway curves up to it from the kitchen.

The entire setting is wholly or, in some places, partially transparent. The roof-line of the house is one-dimensional; under and over it we see the apartment buildings. Before the house lies an apron, curving beyond the forestage into the orchestra. This forward area serves as the back yard as well as the locale of all WILLY's *imaginings and of his city scenes. Whenever the action is in the present the actors observe the imaginary wall-lines, entering the house only through its door at the left. But in the scenes of the past these boundaries are broken, and characters enter or leave a room by stepping "through" a wall onto the forestage.*

From the right, WILLY LOMAN, *the Salesman, enters, carrying two large sample cases. The flute plays on. He hears but is not aware of it. He is past sixty years of age, dressed quietly. Even as he crosses the stage to the doorway of the house, his exhaustion is apparent. He unlocks the door, comes into the kitchen, and thankfully lets his burden down, feeling the soreness of his palms. A word-sigh escapes his lips—it might be "Oh, boy, oh, boy." He closes the door, then carries his cases out into the living-room, through the draped kitchen doorway.*

LINDA, *his wife, has stirred in her bed at the right. She gets out and puts on a robe, listening. Most often jovial, she has developed an iron repression of her exceptions to* WILLY's *behavior—she more than loves him, she admires him, as though his mercurial nature, his temper, his massive dreams and little cruelties, served her only as sharp reminders of the turbulent longings within him, longings which she shares but lacks the temperament to utter and follow to their end.)*

LINDA *(hearing* WILLY *outside the bedroom, calls with some trepidation)*: Willy!

WILLY: It's all right. I came back.

LINDA: Why? What happened? *(Slight pause.)* Did something happen, Willy?

WILLY: No, nothing happened.

LINDA: You didn't smash the car, did you?

WILLY *(with casual irritation)*: I said nothing happened. Didn't you hear me?

LINDA: Don't you feel well?

WILLY: I'm tired to the death. *(The flute has faded away. He sits on the bed beside her, a little numb.)* I couldn't make it. I just couldn't make it, Linda.

LINDA *(very carefully, delicately)*: Where were you all day? You look terrible.

WILLY: I got as far as a little above Yonkers. I stopped for a cup of coffee. Maybe it was the coffee.

LINDA: What?

WILLY *(after a pause)*: I suddenly couldn't drive any

more. The car kept going off onto the shoulder, y'know?

LINDA *(helpfully)*: Oh. Maybe it was the steering again. I don't think Angelo knows the Studebaker.

WILLY: No, it's me, it's me. Suddenly I realize I'm goin' sixty miles an hour and I don't remember the last five minutes. I'm—I can't seem to—keep my mind to it.

LINDA: Maybe it's your glasses. You never went for your new glasses.

WILLY: No, I see everything. I came back ten miles an hour. It took me nearly four hours from Yonkers.

LINDA *(resigned)*: Well, you'll just have to take a rest, Willy, you can't continue this way.

WILLY: I just got back from Florida.

LINDA: But you didn't rest your mind. Your mind is overactive, and the mind is what counts, dear.

WILLY: I'll start out in the morning. Maybe I'll feel better in the morning. *(She is taking off his shoes.)* These goddam arch supports are killing me.

LINDA: Take an aspirin. Should I get you an aspirin? It'll soothe you.

WILLY *(with wonder)*: I was driving along, you understand? And I was fine. I was even observing the scenery. You can imagine, me looking at scenery, on the road every week of my life. But it's so beautiful up there, Linda, the trees are so thick, and the sun is warm. I opened the windshield and just let the warm air bathe over me. And then all of a sudden I'm goin' off the road! I'm tellin' ya, I absolutely forgot I was driving. If I'd've gone the other way, over the white line I might've killed somebody. So I went on again—and five minutes later I'm dreamin' again, and I nearly—*(He presses two fingers against his eyes.)* I have such thoughts, I have such strange thoughts.

LINDA: Willy, dear. Talk to them again. There's no reason why you can't work in New York.

WILLY: They don't need me in New York. I'm the New England man. I'm vital in New England.

LINDA: But you're sixty years old. They can't expect you to keep traveling every week.

WILLY: I'll have to send a wire to Portland. I'm supposed to see Brown and Morrison tomorrow morning at ten o'clock to show the line. Goddammit, I could sell them! *(He starts putting on his jacket.)*

LINDA *(taking the jacket from him)*: Why don't you go down to the place tomorrow and tell Howard you've simply got to work in New York? You're too accommodating, dear.

WILLY: If old man Wagner was alive I'd a been in charge of New York now! That man was a prince, he was a masterful man. But that boy of his, that Howard, he don't appreciate. When I

was north the first time, the Wagner Company didn't know where New England was!

LINDA: Why don't you tell those things to Howard, dear?

WILLY *(encouraged)*: I will, I definitely will. Is there any cheese?

LINDA: I'll make you a sandwich.

WILLY: No, go to sleep. I'll take some milk. I'll be up right away. The boys in?

LINDA: They're sleeping. Happy took Biff on a date tonight.

WILLY *(interested)*: That so?

LINDA: It was so nice to see them shaving together, one behind the other, in the bathroom. And going out together. You notice? The whole house smells of shaving lotion.

WILLY: Figure it out. Work a lifetime to pay off a house. You finally own it, and there's nobody to live in it.

LINDA: Well, dear, life is a casting off. It's always that way.

WILLY: No, no, some people—some people accomplish something. Did Biff say anything after I went this morning?

LINDA: You shouldn't have criticized him, Willy, especially after he just got off the train. You mustn't lose your temper with him.

WILLY: When the hell did I lose my temper? I simply asked him if he was making any money. Is that a criticism?

LINDA: But, dear, how could he make any money?

WILLY *(worried and angered)*: There's such an undercurrent in him. He became a moody man. Did he apologize when I left this morning?

LINDA: He was crestfallen, Willy. You know how he admires you. I think if he finds himself, then you'll both be happier and not fight any more.

WILLY: How can he find himself on a farm? Is that a life? A farmhand? In the beginning, when he was young, I thought, well, a young man, it's good for him to tramp around, take a lot of different jobs. But it's more than ten years now and he has yet to make thirty-five dollars a week!

LINDA: He's finding himself, Willy.

WILLY: Not finding yourself at the age of thirty-four is a disgrace!

LINDA: Shh!

WILLY: The trouble is he's lazy, goddammit!

LINDA: Willy, please!

WILLY: Biff is a lazy bum.

LINDA: They're sleeping. Get something to eat. Go on down.

WILLY: Why did he come home? I would like to know what brought him home.

LINDA: I don't know. I think he's still lost, Willy. I think he's very lost.

WILLY: Biff Loman is lost. In the greatest country in

the world a young man with such—personal attractiveness, gets lost. And such a hard worker. There's one thing about Biff—he's not lazy.

LINDA: Never.

WILLY (*with pity and resolve*): I'll see him in the morning; I'll have a nice talk with him. I'll get him a job selling. He could be big in no time. My God! Remember how they used to follow him around in high school? When he smiled at one of them their faces lit up. When he walked down the street . . . (*He loses himself in reminiscences.*)

LINDA (*trying to bring him out of it*): Willy, dear, I got a new kind of American-type cheese today. It's whipped.

WILLY: Why do you get American when I like Swiss?

LINDA: I just thought you'd like a change—

WILLY: I don't want a change! I want Swiss cheese. Why am I always being contradicted?

LINDA (*with a covering laugh*): I thought it would be a surprise.

WILLY: Why don't you open a window in here, for God's sake?

LINDA (*with infinite patience*): They're all open, dear.

WILLY: The way they boxed us in here. Bricks and windows, windows and bricks.

LINDA: We should've bought the land next door.

WILLY: The street is lined with cars. There's not a breath of fresh air in the neighborhood. The grass don't grow any more, you can't raise a carrot in the back yard. They should've had a law against apartment houses. Remember those two beautiful elm trees out there? When I and Biff hung the swing between them?

LINDA: Yeah, like being a million miles from the city.

WILLY: They should've arrested the builder for cutting those down. They massacred the neighborhood. (*Lost.*) More and more I think of those days, Linda. This time of year it was lilac and wisteria. And then the peonies would come out, and the daffodils. What fragrance in this room!

LINDA: Well, after all, people had to move somewhere.

WILLY: No, there's more people now.

LINDA: I don't think there's more people. I think—

WILLY: There's more people! That's what's ruining this country! Population is getting out of control. The competition is maddening! Smell the stink from that apartment house! And another one on the other side . . . How can they whip cheese?

(*On* WILLY's *last line,* BIFF *and* HAPPY *raise themselves up in their beds, listening.*)

LINDA: Go down, try it. And be quiet.

WILLY (*turning to* LINDA, *guiltily*): You're not worried about me, are you, sweetheart?

BIFF: What's the matter?

HAPPY: Listen!

LINDA: You've got too much on the ball to worry about.

WILLY: You're my foundation and my support, Linda.

LINDA: Just try to relax, dear. You make mountains out of molehills.

WILLY: I won't fight him any more. If he wants to go back to Texas, let him go.

LINDA: He'll find his way.

WILLY: Sure. Certain men just don't get started till later in life. Like Thomas Edison, I think. Or B. F. Goodrich. One of them was deaf. (*He starts for the bedroom doorway.*) I'll put my money on Biff.

LINDA: And Willy—if it's warm Sunday we'll drive in the country. And we'll open the windshield, and take lunch.

WILLY: No, the windshields don't open on the new cars.

LINDA: But you opened it today.

WILLY: Me? I didn't. (*He stops.*) Now isn't that peculiar! Isn't that a remarkable—(*He breaks off in amazement and fright as the flute is heard distantly.*)

LINDA: What, darling?

WILLY: That is the most remarkable thing.

LINDA: What, dear?

WILLY: I was thinking of the Chevvy. (*Slight pause.*) Nineteen twenty-eight . . . when I had that red Chevvy—(*Breaks off.*) That funny? I coulda sworn I was driving that Chevvy today.

LINDA: Well, that's nothing. Something must've reminded you.

WILLY: Remarkable. Ts. Remember those days? The way Biff used to simonize that car? The dealer refused to believe there was eighty thousand miles on it. (*He shakes his head.*) Heh! (*to* LINDA) Close your eyes, I'll be right up. (*He walks out of the bedroom.*)

HAPPY (*to* BIFF): Jesus, maybe he smashed up the car again!

LINDA (*calling after* WILLY): Be careful on the stairs, dear! The cheese is on the middle shelf! (*She turns, goes over to the bed, takes his jacket, and goes out of the bedroom.*)

(*Light has risen on the boys' room. Unseen,* WILLY *is heard talking to himself, "Eighty thousand miles," and a little laugh.* BIFF *gets out of bed, comes downstage a bit, and stands attentively.* BIFF *is two years older than his brother* HAPPY, *well built, but in these days bears a worn air and seems less self-assured. He has succeeded less, and his dreams are stronger and less acceptable than* HAPPY's. HAPPY *is tall, powerfully made. Sexuality is like a visible color on him, or a scent that many women have discovered. He, like his brother, is lost, but in a different way, for he has never allowed himself to turn his face toward defeat and is thus more confused and hard-skinned, although seemingly more content.*)

HAPPY *(getting out of bed)*: He's going to get his license taken away if he keeps that up. I'm getting nervous about him, y'know, Biff?

BIFF: His eyes are going.

HAPPY: No, I've driven with him. He sees all right. He just doesn't keep his mind on it. I drove into the city with him last week. He stops at a green light and then it turns red and he goes. *(He laughs.)*

BIFF: Maybe he's color-blind.

HAPPY: Pop? Why he's got the finest eye for color in the business. You know that.

BIFF *(sitting down on his bed)*: I'm going to sleep.

HAPPY: You're not still sour on Dad, are you, Biff?

BIFF: He's all right, I guess.

WILLY *(underneath them, in the living-room)*: Yes, sir, eighty thousand miles—eighty-two thousand!

BIFF: You smoking?

HAPPY *(holding out a pack of cigarettes)*: Want one?

BIFF *(taking a cigarette)*: I can never sleep when I smell it.

WILLY: What a simonizing job, heh!

HAPPY *(with deep sentiment)*: Funny, Biff, y'know? Us sleeping in here again? The old beds. *(He pats his bed affectionately.)* All the talk that went across those two beds, huh? Our whole lives.

BIFF: Yeah. Lotta dreams and plans.

HAPPY *(with a deep and masculine laugh)*: About five hundred women would like to know what was said in this room.

(They share a soft laugh.)

BIFF: Remember that big Betsy something—what the hell was her name—over on Bushwick Avenue?

HAPPY *(combing his hair)*: With the collie dog!

BIFF: That's the one. I got you in there, remember?

HAPPY: Yeah, that was my first time—I think. Boy, there was a pig! *(They laugh, almost crudely.)* You taught me everything I know about women. Don't forget that.

BIFF: I bet you forgot how bashful you used to be. Especially with girls.

HAPPY: Oh, I still am, Biff.

BIFF: Oh, go on.

HAPPY: I just control it, that's all. I think I got less bashful and you got more so. What happened, Biff? Where's the old humor, the old confidence? *(He shakes* BIFF's *knee.* BIFF *gets up and moves restlessly about the room.)* What's the matter?

BIFF: Why does Dad mock me all the time?

HAPPY: He's not mocking you, he—

BIFF: Everything I say there's a twist of mockery on his face. I can't get near him.

HAPPY: He just wants you to make good, that's all. I wanted to talk to you about Dad for a long time, Biff. Something's—happening to him. He—talks to himself.

BIFF: I noticed that this morning. But he always mumbled.

HAPPY: But not so noticeable. It got so embarrassing I sent him to Florida. And you know something? Most of the time he's talking to you.

BIFF: What's he say about me?

HAPPY: I can't make it out.

BIFF: What's he say about me?

HAPPY: I think the fact that you're not settled, that you're still kind of up in the air . . .

BIFF: There's one or two other things depressing him, Happy.

HAPPY: What do you mean?

BIFF: Never mind. Just don't lay it all to me.

HAPPY: But I think if you just got started—I mean—is there any future for you out there?

BIFF: I tell ya, Hap, I don't know what the future is. I don't know—what I'm supposed to want.

HAPPY: What do you mean?

BIFF: Well, I spent six or seven years after high school trying to work myself up. Shipping clerk, salesman, business of one kind or another. And it's a measly manner of existence. To get on that subway on the hot mornings in summer. To devote your whole life to keeping stock, or making phone calls, or selling or buying. To suffer fifty weeks of the year for the sake of a two-week vacation, when all you really desire is to be outdoors, with your shirt off. And always to have to get ahead of the next fella. And still—that's how you build a future.

HAPPY: Well, you really enjoy it on a farm? Are you content out there?

BIFF *(with rising agitation)*: Hap, I've had twenty or thirty different kinds of jobs since I left home before the war, and it always turns out the same. I just realized it lately. In Nebraska when I herded cattle, and the Dakotas, and Arizona, and now in Texas. It's why I came home now, I guess, because I realized it. This farm I work on, it's spring there now, see? And they've got about fifteen new colts. There's nothing more inspiring or—beautiful then the sight of a mare and a new colt. And it's cool there now, see? Texas is cool now, and it's spring. And whenever spring comes to where I am, I suddenly get the feeling, my God, I'm not gettin' anywhere! What the hell am I doing, playing around with horses, twenty-eight dollars a week! I'm thirty-four years old, I oughta be makin' my future. That's when I come running home. And now, I get here, and I don't know what to do with myself. *(After a pause.)* I've always made a point of not wasting my life, and everytime I come back here I know that all I've done is to waste my life.

HAPPY: You're a poet, you know that, Biff? You're a—you're an idealist!

BIFF: No, I'm mixed up very bad. Maybe I oughta get married. Maybe I oughta get stuck into something. Maybe that's my trouble. I'm like a boy. I'm not married, I'm not in business, I just—I'm like a boy. Are you content, Hap? You're a success, aren't you? Are you content?

HAPPY: Hell, no!

BIFF: Why? You're making money, aren't you?

HAPPY (moving about with energy, expressiveness): All I can do now is wait for the merchandise manager to die. And suppose I get to be merchandise manager? He's a good friend of mine, and he just built a terrific estate on Long Island. And he lived there about two months and sold it, and now he's building another one. He can't enjoy it once it's finished. And I know that's just what I would do. I don't know what the hell I'm workin' for. Sometimes I sit in my apartment—all alone. And I think of the rent I'm paying. And it's crazy. But then, it's what I always wanted. My own apartment, a car, and plenty of women. And still, goddammit, I'm lonely.

BIFF (with enthusiasm): Listen, why don't you come out West with me?

HAPPY: You and I, heh?

BIFF: Sure, maybe we could buy a ranch. Raise cattle, use our muscles. Men built like we are should be working out in the open.

HAPPY (avidly): The Loman Brothers, heh?

BIFF (with vast affection): Sure, we'd be known all over the counties!

HAPPY (enthralled): That's what I dream about, Biff. Sometimes I want to just rip my clothes off in the middle of the store and outbox that goddam merchandise manager. I mean I can outbox, outrun, and outlift anybody in that store, and I have to take orders from those common, petty sons-of-bitches till I can't stand it any more.

BIFF: I'm tellin' you, kid, if you were with me I'd be happy out there.

HAPPY (enthused): See, Biff, everybody around me is so false that I'm constantly lowering my ideals . . .

BIFF: Baby, together we'd stand up for one another, we'd have someone to trust.

HAPPY: If I were around you—

BIFF: Hap, the trouble is we weren't brought up to grub for money. I don't know how to do it.

HAPPY: Neither can I!

BIFF: Then let's go!

HAPPY: The only thing is—what can you make out there?

BIFF: But look at your friend. Builds an estate and then hasn't the peace of mind to live in it.

HAPPY: Yeah, but when he walks into the store the waves part in front of him. That's fifty-two thousand dollars a year coming through the revolving door, and I got more in my pinky finger than he's got in his head.

BIFF: Yeah, but you just said—

HAPPY: I gotta show some of those pompous, self-important executives over there that Hap Loman can make the grade. I want to walk into the store the way he walks in. Then I'll go with you, Biff. We'll be together yet, I swear. But take those two we had tonight. Now weren't they gorgeous creatures?

BIFF: Yeah, yeah, most gorgeous I've had in years.

HAPPY: I get that any time I want, Biff. Whenever I feel disgusted. The only trouble is, it gets like bowling or something. I just keep knockin' them over and it doesn't mean anything. You still run around a lot?

BIFF: Naa. I'd like to find a girl—steady, somebody with substance.

HAPPY: That's what I long for.

BIFF: Go on! You'd never come home.

HAPPY: I would! Somebody with character, with resistance! Like Mom, y'know? You're gonna call me a bastard when I tell you this. That girl Charlotte I was with tonight is engaged to be married in five weeks. (He tries on his new hat.)

BIFF: No kiddin'!

HAPPY: Sure, the guy's in line for the vice-presidency of the store. I don't know what gets into me, maybe I just have an overdeveloped sense of competition or something, but I went and ruined her, and furthermore I can't get rid of her. And he's the third executive I've done that to. Isn't that a crummy characteristic? And to top it all, I go to their weddings! (Indignantly, but laughing.) Like I'm not supposed to take bribes. Manufacturers offer me a hundred-dollar bill now and then to throw an order their way. You know how honest I am, but it's like this girl, see. I hate myself for it. Because I don't want the girl, and, still, I take it and—I love it!

BIFF: Let's go to sleep.

HAPPY: I guess we didn't settle anything, heh?

BIFF: I just got one idea that I think I'm going to try.

HAPPY: What's that?

BIFF: Remember Bill Oliver?

HAPPY: Sure, Oliver is very big now. You want to work for him again?

BIFF: No, but when I quit he said something to me. He put his arm on my shoulder, and he said, "Biff, if you ever need anything, come to me."

HAPPY: I remember that. That sounds good.

BIFF: I think I'll go to see him. If I could get ten thousand or even seven or eight thousand dollars I could buy a beautiful ranch.

HAPPY: I bet he'd back you. 'Cause he thought highly of you, Biff. I mean, they all do. You're well liked, Biff. That's why I say to come back here, and we both have the apartment. And I'm tellin' you, Biff, any babe you want . . .

BIFF: No, with a ranch I could do the work I like and still be something. I just wonder though. I wonder if Oliver still thinks I stole that carton of basketballs.

HAPPY: Oh, he probably forgot that long ago. It's almost ten years. You're too sensitive. Anyway, he didn't really fire you.

BIFF: Well, I think he was going to. I think that's why I quit. I was never sure whether he knew or not. I know he thought the world of me, though. I was the only one he'd let lock up the place.

WILLY (below): You gonna wash the engine, Biff?

HAPPY: Shh!

(BIFF looks at HAPPY, who is gazing down, listening. WILLY is mumbling in the parlor.)

HAPPY: You hear that?

(They listen. WILLY laughs warmly.)

BIFF (growing angry): Doesn't he know Mom can hear that?

WILLY: Don't get your sweater dirty, Biff!

(A look of pain crosses BIFF's face.)

HAPPY: Isn't that terrible? Don't leave again, will you? You'll find a job here. You gotta stick around. I don't know what to do about him, it's getting embarrassing.

WILLY: What a simonizing job!

BIFF: Mom's hearing that!

WILLY: No kiddin', Biff, you got a date? Wonderful!

HAPPY: Go on to sleep. But talk to him in the morning, will you?

BIFF (reluctantly getting into bed): With her in the house. Brother!

HAPPY (getting into bed): I wish you'd have a good talk with him.

(The light on their room begins to fade.)

BIFF (to himself in bed): That selfish, stupid . . .

HAPPY: Sh . . . Sleep, Biff.

(Their light is out. Well before they have finished speaking, WILLY's form is dimly seen below in the darkened kitchen. He opens the refrigerator, searches in there, and takes out a bottle of milk. The apartment houses are fading out, and the entire house and surroundings become covered with leaves. Music insinuates itself as the leaves appear.)

WILLY: Just wanna be careful with those girls, Biff, that's all. Don't make any promises. No promises of any kind. Because a girl, y'know, they always believe what you tell 'em, and you're very young, Biff, you're too young to be talking seriously to girls.

(Light rises on the kitchen. WILLY, talking, shuts the refrigerator door and comes downstage to the kitchen table. He pours milk into a glass. He is totally immersed in himself, smiling faintly.)

WILLY: Too young entirely, Biff. You want to watch your schooling first. Then when you're all set, there'll be plenty of girls for a boy like you. (He smiles broadly at a kitchen chair.) That so? The girls pay for you? (He laughs.) Boy, you must really be makin' a hit.

(WILLY is gradually addressing—physically—a point offstage, speaking through the wall of the kitchen, and his voice has been rising in volume to that of a normal conversation.)

WILLY: I been wondering why you polish the car so careful. Ha! Don't leave the hubcaps, boys. Get the chamois to the hubcaps. Happy, use newspaper on the windows, it's the easiest thing. Show him how to do it, Biff! You see, Happy? Pad it up, use it like a pad. That's it, that's it, good work. You're doin' all right, Hap. (He pauses, then nods in approbation for a few seconds, then looks upward.) Biff, first thing we gotta do when we get time is clip that big branch over the house. Afraid it's gonna fall in a storm and hit the roof. Tell you what. We get a rope and sling her around, and then we climb up there with a couple of saws and take her down. Soon as you finish the car, boys, I wanna see ya. I got a surprise for you, boys.

BIFF (offstage): Whatta ya got, Dad?

WILLY: No, you finish first. Never leave a job till you're finished—remember that. (Looking toward the "big trees.") Biff, up in Albany I saw a beautiful hammock. I think I'll buy it next trip, and we'll hang it right between those two elms. Wouldn't that be something? Just swingin' there under those branches. Boy, that would be . . .

(YOUNG BIFF and YOUNG HAPPY appear from the direction WILLY was addressing. HAPPY carries rags and a pail of water. BIFF, wearing a sweater with a block "S," carries a football.)

BIFF (pointing in the direction of the car offstage): How's that, Pop, professional?

WILLY: Terrific. Terrific job, boys. Good work, Biff.

HAPPY: Where's the surprise, Pop?

WILLY: In the back seat of the car.

HAPPY: Boy! (He runs off.)

BIFF: What is it, Dad? Tell me, what'd you buy?

WILLY (laughing, cuffs him): Never mind, something I want you to have.

BIFF (turns and starts off): What is it, Hap?

HAPPY (offstage): It's a punching bag!

BIFF: Oh, Pop!

WILLY: It's got Gene Tunney's signature on it!

(HAPPY *runs onstage with a punching bag.*)

BIFF: Gee, how'd you know we wanted a punching bag?

WILLY: Well, it's the finest thing for the timing.

HAPPY (*lies down on his back and pedals with his feet*): I'm losing weight, you notice, Pop?

WILLY (*to* HAPPY): Jumping rope is good too.

BIFF: Did you see the new football I got?

WILLY (*examining the ball*): Where'd you get a new ball?

BIFF: The coach told me to practice my passing.

WILLY: That so? And he gave you the ball, heh?

BIFF: Well, I borrowed it from the locker room. (*He laughs confidentially.*)

WILLY (*laughing with him at the theft*): I want you to return that.

HAPPY: I told you he wouldn't like it!

BIFF (*angrily*): Well, I'm bringing it back!

WILLY (*stopping the incipient argument, to* HAPPY): Sure, he's gotta practice with a regulation ball, doesn't he? (*to* BIFF) Coach'll probably congratulate you on your initiative!

BIFF: Oh, he keeps congratulating my initiative all the time, Pop.

WILLY: That's because he likes you. If somebody else took that ball there'd be an uproar. So what's the report, boys, what's the report?

BIFF: Where'd you go this time, Dad? Gee we were lonesome for you.

WILLY (*pleased, puts an arm around each boy and they come down to the apron*): Lonesome, heh?

BIFF: Missed you every minute.

WILLY: Don't say? Tell you a secret, boys. Don't breathe it to a soul. Someday I'll have my own business, and I'll never have to leave home any more.

HAPPY: Like Uncle Charley, heh?

WILLY: Bigger than Uncle Charley! Because Charley is not—liked. He's liked, but he's not—well liked.

BIFF: Where'd you go this time, Dad?

WILLY: Well, I got on the road, and I went north to Providence. Met the Mayor.

BIFF: The Mayor of Providence!

WILLY: He was sitting in the hotel lobby.

BIFF: What'd he say?

WILLY: He said, "Morning!" and I said, "You got a fine city here, Mayor." And then he had coffee with me. And then I went to Waterbury. Waterbury is a fine city. Big clock city, the famous Waterbury clock. Sold a nice bill there. And then Boston—Boston is the cradle of the Revolution. A fine city. And a couple of other towns in Mass., and on to Portland and Bangor and straight home!

BIFF: Gee, I'd love to go with you sometime, Dad.

WILLY: Soon as summer comes.

HAPPY: Promise?

WILLY: You and Hap and I, and I'll show you all the towns. America is full of beautiful towns and fine, upstanding people. And they know me, boys, they know me up and down New England. The finest people. And when I bring you fellas up, there'll be an open sesame for all of us, 'cause one thing, boys: I have friends. I can park my car in any street in New England, and the cops protect it like their own. This summer, heh?

BIFF *and* HAPPY (*together*): Yeah! You bet!

WILLY: We'll take our bathing suits.

HAPPY: We'll carry your bags, Pop!

WILLY: Oh, won't that be something! Me comin' into the Boston stores with you boys carryin' my bags. What a sensation!

(BIFF *is prancing around, practicing passing the ball.*)

WILLY: You nervous, Biff, about the game?

BIFF: Not if you're gonna be there.

WILLY: What do they say about you in school, now that they made you captain?

HAPPY: There's a crowd of girls behind him everytime the classes change.

BIFF (*taking* WILLY's *hand*): This Saturday, Pop, this Saturday—just for you, I'm going to break through for a touchdown.

HAPPY: You're supposed to pass.

BIFF: I'm takin' one play for Pop. You watch me, Pop, and when I take off my helmet, that means I'm breakin' out. Then you watch me crash through that line!

WILLY (*kisses* BIFF): Oh, wait'll I tell this in Boston!

(BERNARD *enters in knickers. He is younger than* BIFF, *earnest and loyal, a worried boy.*)

BERNARD: Biff, where are you? You're supposed to study with me today.

WILLY: Hey, looka Bernard. What're you lookin' so anemic about, Bernard?

BERNARD: He's gotta study, Uncle Willy. He's got Regents next week.

HAPPY (*tauntingly, spinning* BERNARD *around*): Let's box, Bernard!

BERNARD: Biff! (*He gets away from* HAPPY.) Listen, Biff, I heard Mr. Birnbaum say that if you don't start studyin' math he's gonna flunk you, and you won't graduate. I heard him!

WILLY: You better study with him, Biff. Go ahead now.

BERNARD: I heard him!

BIFF: Oh, Pop, you didn't see my sneakers! (*He holds up a foot for* WILLY *to look at.*)

WILLY: Hey, that's a beautiful job of printing!

BERNARD (*wiping his glasses*): Just because he printed University of Virginia on his sneakers doesn't mean they've got to graduate him, Uncle Willy!

WILLY (*angrily*): What're you talking about? With scholarships to three universities they're gonna flunk him?

BERNARD: But I heard Mr. Birnbaum say—

WILLY: Don't be a pest, Bernard! (*to his boys*) What an anemic!

BERNARD: Okay, I'm waiting for you in my house, Biff.

(BERNARD *goes off. The* LOMANS *laugh.*)

WILLY: Bernard is not well liked, is he?

BIFF: He's liked, but he's not well liked.

HAPPY: That's right, Pop.

WILLY: That's just what I mean. Bernard can get the best marks in school, y'understand, but when he gets out in the business world, y'understand, you are going to be five times ahead of him. That's why I thank Almighty God you're both built like Adonises. Because the man who makes an appearance in the business world, the man who creates personal interest, is the man who gets ahead. Be liked and you will never want. You take me, for instance. I never have to wait in line to see a buyer. "Willy Loman is here!" That's all they have to know, and I go right through.

BIFF: Did you knock them dead, Pop?

WILLY: Knocked 'em cold in Providence, slaughtered 'em in Boston.

HAPPY (*on his back, pedaling again*): I'm losing weight, you notice, Pop?

(LINDA *enters, as of old, a ribbon in her hair, carrying a basket of washing.*)

LINDA (*with youthful energy*): Hello, dear!

WILLY: Sweetheart!

LINDA: How'd the Chevvy run?

WILLY: Chevrolet, Linda, is the greatest car ever built. (*to the boys*) Since when do you let your mother carry wash up the stairs?

BIFF: Grab hold there, boy!

HAPPY: Where to, Mom?

LINDA: Hang them up on the line. And you better go down to your friends, Biff. The cellar is full of boys. They don't know what to do with themselves.

BIFF: Ah, when Pop comes home they can wait!

WILLY (*laughs appreciatively*): You better go down and tell them what to do, Biff.

BIFF: I think I'll have them sweep out the furnace room.

WILLY: Good work, Biff.

BIFF (*goes through wall-line of kitchen to doorway at back and calls down*): Fellas! Everybody sweep out the furnace room! I'll be right down!

VOICES: All right! Okay, Biff.

BIFF: George and Sam and Frank, come out back! We're hangin' up the wash! Come on, Hap, on the double! (*He and* HAPPY *carry out the basket.*)

LINDA: The way they obey him!

WILLY: Well, that's training, the training. I'm tellin' you, I was sellin' thousands and thousands, but I had to come home.

LINDA: Oh, the whole block'll be at that game. Did you sell anything?

WILLY: I did five hundred gross in Providence and seven hundred gross in Boston.

LINDA: No! Wait a minute, I've got a pencil. (*She pulls pencil and paper out of her apron pocket.*) That makes your commission . . . Two hundred—my God! Two hundred and twelve dollars!

WILLY: Well, I didn't figure it yet, but . . .

LINDA: How much did you do?

WILLY: Well, I—I did—about a hundred and eighty gross in Providence. Well, no—it came to—roughly two hundred gross on the whole trip.

LINDA (*without hesitation*): Two hundred gross. That's . . . (*She figures.*)

WILLY: The trouble was that three of the stores were half closed for inventory in Boston. Otherwise I woulda broke records.

LINDA: Well, it makes seventy dollars and some pennies. That's very good.

WILLY: What do we owe?

LINDA: Well, on the first there's sixteen dollars on the refrigerator—

WILLY: Why sixteen?

LINDA: Well, the fan belt broke, so it was a dollar eighty.

WILLY: But it's brand new.

LINDA: Well, the man said that's the way it is. Till they work themselves in, y'know.

(*They move through the wall-line into the kitchen.*)

WILLY: I hope we didn't get stuck on that machine.

LINDA: They got the biggest ads of any of them!

WILLY: I know, it's a fine machine. What else?

LINDA: Well, there's nine-sixty for the washing machine. And for the vacuum cleaner there's three and a half due on the fifteenth. Then the roof, you got twenty-one dollars remaining.

WILLY: It don't leak, does it?

LINDA: No, they did a wonderful job. Then you owe Frank for the carburetor.

WILLY: I'm not going to pay that man! That goddam Chevrolet, they ought to prohibit the manufacture of that car!

LINDA: Well, you owe him three and a half. And odds and ends, comes to around a hundred and twenty dollars by the fifteenth.

WILLY: A hundred and twenty dollars! My God, if business don't pick up I don't know what I'm gonna do!

LINDA: Well, next week you'll do better.

WILLY: Oh, I'll knock 'em dead next week. I'll go to

Hartford. I'm very well liked in Hartford. You know, the trouble is, Linda, people don't seem to take to me.

(They move onto the forestage.)

LINDA: Oh, don't be foolish.

WILLY: I know it when I walk in. They seem to laugh at me.

LINDA: Why? Why would they laugh at you? Don't talk that way, Willy.

(WILLY moves to the edge of the stage. LINDA goes into the kitchen and starts to darn stockings.)

WILLY: I don't know the reason for it, but they just pass me by. I'm not noticed.

LINDA: But you're doing wonderful, dear. You're making seventy to a hundred dollars a week.

WILLY: But I gotta be at it ten, twelve hours a day. Other men—I don't know—they do it easier. I don't know why—I can't stop myself—I talk too much. A man oughta come in with a few words. One thing about Charley. He's a man of few words, and they respect him.

LINDA: You don't talk too much, you're just lively.

WILLY *(smiling)*: Well, I figure, what the hell, life is short, a couple of jokes. *(to himself)* I joke too much! *(The smile goes.)*

LINDA: Why? You're—

WILLY: I'm fat. I'm very—foolish to look at, Linda. I didn't tell you, but Christmas time I happened to be calling on F.H. Stewarts, and a salesman I know, as I was going in to see the buyer I heard him say something about—walrus. And I—I cracked him right across the face. I won't take that. I simply will not take that. But they do laugh at me. I know that.

LINDA: Darling . . .

WILLY: I gotta overcome it. I know I gotta overcome it. I'm not dressing to advantage, maybe.

LINDA: Willy, darling, you're the handsomest man in the world—

WILLY: Oh, no, Linda.

LINDA: To me you are. *(Slight pause.)* The handsomest.

(From the darkness is heard the laughter of a woman. Willy doesn't turn to it, but it continues through LINDA's lines.)

LINDA: And the boys, Willy. Few men are idolized by their children the way you are.

(Music is heard as behind a scrim, to the left of the house, THE WOMAN, dimly seen, is dressing.)

WILLY *(with great feeling)*: You're the best there is, Linda, you're a pal, you know that? On the road—on the road I want to grab you sometimes and just kiss the life outa you.

(The laughter is loud now, and he moves into a brightening area at the left, where THE WOMAN has come from behind the scrim and is standing, putting on her hat, looking into a "mirror" and laughing.)

WILLY: 'Cause I get so lonely—especially when business is bad and there's nobody to talk to. I get the feeling that I'll never sell anything again, that I won't make a living for you, or a business, a business for the boys. *(He talks through THE WOMAN's subsiding laughter; THE WOMAN primps at the "mirror.")* There's so much I want to make for—

THE WOMAN: Me? You didn't make me, Willy. I picked you.

WILLY *(pleased)*: You picked me?

THE WOMAN *(who is quite proper-looking, WILLY's age)*: I did. I've been sitting at that desk watching all the salesmen go by, day in, day out. But you've got such a sense of humor, and we do have such a good time together, don't we?

WILLY: Sure, sure. *(He takes her in his arms.)* Why do you have to go now?

THE WOMAN: It's two o'clock . . .

WILLY: No, come on in! *(He pulls her.)*

THE WOMAN: . . . my sisters'll be scandalized. When'll you be back?

WILLY: Oh, two weeks about. Will you come up again?

THE WOMAN: Sure thing. You do make me laugh. It's good for me. *(She squeezes his arm, kisses him.)* And I think you're a wonderful man.

WILLY: You picked me, heh?

THE WOMAN: Sure. Because you're so sweet. And such a kidder.

WILLY: Well, I'll see you next time I'm in Boston.

THE WOMAN: I'll put you right through to the buyers.

WILLY *(slapping her bottom)*: Right, well, bottoms up!

THE WOMAN *(slaps him gently and laughs)*: You just kill me, Willy. *(He suddenly grabs her and kisses her roughly.)* You kill me. And thanks for the stockings. I love a lot of stockings. Well, good night.

WILLY: Good night. And keep your pores open!

THE WOMAN: Oh, Willy!

(THE WOMAN bursts out laughing, and LINDA's laughter blends in. THE WOMAN disappears into the dark. Now the area at the kitchen table brightens. LINDA is sitting where she was at the kitchen table, but now is mending a pair of her silk stockings.)

LINDA: You are, Willy. The handsomest man. You've got no reason to feel that—

WILLY *(coming out of THE WOMAN's dimming area and going over to LINDA)*: I'll make it all up to you, Linda, I'll—

LINDA: There's nothing to make up, dear. You're doing fine, better than—

WILLY *(noticing her mending)*: What's that?

LINDA: Just mending my stockings. They're so expensive—

WILLY (angrily, taking them from her): I won't have you mending stockings in this house! Now throw them out!

(LINDA puts the stockings in her pocket.)

BERNARD (entering on the run): Where is he? If he doesn't study!

WILLY (moving to the forestage, with great agitation): You'll give him the answers!

BERNARD: I do, but I can't on a Regents! That's a state exam! They're liable to arrest me!

WILLY: Where is he? I'll whip him, I'll whip him!

LINDA: And he'd better give back that football, Willy, it's not nice.

WILLY: Biff! Where is he? Why is he taking everything?

LINDA: He's too rough with the girls, Willy. All the mothers are afraid of him!

WILLY: I'll whip him!

BERNARD: He's driving the car without a license!

(THE WOMAN's laugh is heard.)

WILLY: Shut up!

LINDA: All the mothers—

WILLY: Shut up!

BERNARD (backing quietly away and out): Mr. Birnbaum says he's stuck up.

WILLY: Get outa here!

BERNARD: If he doesn't buckle down he'll flunk math!
(He goes off.)

LINDA: He's right, Willy, you've gotta—

WILLY (exploding at her): There's nothing the matter with him! You want him to be a worm like Bernard? He's got spirit, personality . . .

(As he speaks, LINDA, almost in tears, exits into the living-room. WILLY is alone in the kitchen, wilting and staring. The leaves are gone. It is night again, and the apartment houses look down from behind.)

WILLY: Loaded with it. Loaded! What is he stealing? He's giving it back, isn't he? Why is he stealing? What did I tell him? I never in my life told him anything but decent things.

(HAPPY in pajamas has come down the stairs; WILLY suddenly becomes aware of HAPPY's presence.)

HAPPY: Let's go now, come on.

WILLY (sitting down at the kitchen table): Huh! Why did she have to wax the floors herself? Everytime she waxes the floors she keels over. She knows that!

HAPPY: Shh! Take it easy. What brought you back tonight?

WILLY: I got an awful scare. Nearly hit a kid in Yonkers. God! Why didn't I go to Alaska with my brother Ben that time! Ben! That man was a genius, that man was success incarnate! What a mistake! He begged me to go.

HAPPY: Well, there's no use in—

WILLY: You guys! There was a man started with the clothes on his back and ended up with diamond mines!

HAPPY: Boy, someday I'd like to know how he did it.

WILLY: What's the mystery? The man knew what he wanted and went out and got it! Walked into a jungle, and comes out, the age of twenty-one, and he's rich! The world is an oyster, but you don't crack it open on a mattress!

HAPPY: Pop, I told you I'm gonna retire you for life.

WILLY: You'll retire me for life on seventy goddam dollars a week? And your women and your car and your apartment, and you'll retire me for life! Christ's sake, I couldn't get past Yonkers today! Where are you guys, where are you? The woods are burning! I can't drive a car!

(CHARLEY has appeared in the doorway. He is a large man, slow of speech, laconic, immovable. In all he says, despite what he says, there is pity, and, now, trepidation. He has a robe over pajamas, slippers on his feet. He enters the kitchen.)

CHARLEY: Everything all right?

HAPPY: Yeah, Charley, everything's . . .

WILLY: What's the matter?

CHARLEY: I heard some noise. I thought something happened. Can't we do something about the walls? You sneeze in here, and in my house hats blow off.

HAPPY: Let's go to bed, Dad, Come on.

(CHARLEY signals to HAPPY to go.)

WILLY: You go ahead, I'm not tired at the moment.

HAPPY (to WILLY): Take it easy, huh? (He exits.)

WILLY: What're you doin' up?

CHARLEY (sitting down at the kitchen table opposite WILLY): Couldn't sleep good. I had a heartburn.

WILLY: Well, you don't know how to eat.

CHARLEY: I eat with my mouth.

WILLY: No, you're ignorant. You gotta know about vitamins and things like that.

CHARLEY: Come on, let's shoot. Tire you out a little.

WILLY (hesitantly): All right. You got cards?

CHARLEY (taking a deck from his pocket): Yeah, I got them. Someplace. What is it with those vitamins?

WILLY (dealing): They build up your bones. Chemistry.

CHARLEY: Yeah, but there's no bones in a heartburn.

WILLY: What are you talkin' about? Do you know the first thing about it?

CHARLEY: Don't get insulted.

WILLY: Don't talk about something you don't know anything about.

(They are playing. Pause.)

CHARLEY: What're you doin' home?

WILLY: A little trouble with the car.

CHARLEY: Oh. *(Pause.)* I'd like to take a trip to California.

WILLY: Don't say.

CHARLEY: You want a job?

WILLY: I got a job, I told you that. *(After a slight pause.)* What the hell are you offering me a job for?

CHARLEY: Don't get insulted.

WILLY: Don't insult me.

CHARLEY: I don't see no sense in it. You don't have to go on this way.

WILLY: I got a good job. *(Slight pause.)* What do you keep comin' in here for?

CHARLEY: You want me to go?

WILLY *(after a pause, withering)*: I can't understand it. He's going back to Texas again. What the hell is that?

CHARLEY: Let him go.

WILLY: I got nothin' to give him, Charley, I'm clean, I'm clean.

CHARLEY: He won't starve. None a them starve. Forget about him.

WILLY: Then what have I got to remember?

CHARLEY: You take it too hard. To hell with it. When a deposit bottle is broken you don't get your nickel back.

WILLY: That's easy enough for you to say.

CHARLEY: That ain't easy for me to say.

WILLY: Did you see the ceiling I put up in the living-room?

CHARLEY: Yeah, that's a piece of work. To put up a ceiling is a mystery to me. How do you do it?

WILLY: What's the difference?

CHARLEY: Well, talk about it.

WILLY: You gonna put up a ceiling?

CHARLEY: How could I put up a ceiling?

WILLY: Then what the hell are you bothering me for?

CHARLEY: You're insulted again.

WILLY: A man who can't handle tools is not a man. You're disgusting.

CHARLEY: Don't call me disgusting, Willy.

(UNCLE BEN, carrying a valise and an umbrella, enters the forestage from around the right corner of the house. He is a stolid man, in his sixties, with a mustache and an authoritative air. He is utterly certain of his destiny, and there is an aura of far places about him. He enters exactly as WILLY speaks.)

WILLY: I'm getting awfully tired, Ben.

(BEN's music is heard. BEN looks around at everything.)

CHARLEY: Good, keep playing; you'll sleep better. Did you call me Ben?

(BEN looks at his watch.)

WILLY: That's funny. For a second there you reminded me of my brother Ben.

BEN: I only have a few minutes. *(He strolls, inspecting the place.* WILLY *and* CHARLEY *continue playing.)*

CHARLEY: You never heard from him again, heh? Since that time?

WILLY: Didn't Linda tell you? Couple of weeks ago we got a letter from his wife in Africa. He died.

CHARLEY: That so.

BEN *(chuckling)*: So this is Brooklyn, eh?

CHARLEY: Maybe you're in for some of his money.

WILLY: Naa, he had seven sons. There's just one opportunity I had with that man . . .

BEN: I must make a train, William. There are several properties I'm looking at in Alaska.

WILLY: Sure, sure! If I'd gone with him to Alaska that time, everything would've been totally different.

CHARLEY: Go on, you'd froze to death up there.

WILLY: What're you talking about?

BEN: Opportunity is tremendous in Alaska, William. Surprised you're not up there.

WILLY: Sure, tremendous.

CHARLEY: Heh?

WILLY: There was the only man I ever met who knew the answers.

CHARLEY: Who?

BEN: How are you all?

WILLY *(taking a pot, smiling)*: Fine, fine.

CHARLEY: Pretty sharp tonight.

BEN: Is Mother living with you?

WILLY: No, she died a long time ago.

CHARLEY: Who?

BEN: That's too bad. Fine specimen of a lady, Mother.

WILLY *(to CHARLEY)*: Heh?

BEN: I'd hoped to see the old girl.

CHARLEY: Who died?

BEN: Heard anything from Father, have you?

WILLY *(unnerved)*: What do you mean, who died?

CHARLEY *(taking a pot)*: What're you talkin' about?

BEN *(looking at his watch)*: William, it's half-past eight!

WILLY *(as though to dispel his confusion he angrily stops CHARLEY's hand)*: That's my build!

CHARLEY: I put the ace—

WILLY: If you don't know how to play the game I'm not gonna throw my money away on you!

CHARLEY *(rising)*: It was my ace, for God's sake!

WILLY: I'm through, I'm through!

BEN: When did Mother die?

WILLY: Long ago. Since the beginning you never knew how to play cards.

CHARLEY *(picks up the cards and goes to the door)*: All right! Next time I'll bring a deck with five aces.

WILLY: I don't play that kind of game!

CHARLEY *(turning to him)*: You ought to be ashamed of yourself!

WILLY: Yeah?

CHARLEY: Yeah! (*He goes out.*)

WILLY (*slamming the door after him*): Ignoramus!

BEN (*as* WILLY *comes toward him through the wall-line of the kitchen*): So you're William.

WILLY (*shaking* BEN'S *hand*): Ben! I've been waiting for you so long! What's the answer? How did you do it?

BEN: Oh, there's a story in that.

(LINDA *enters the forestage, as of old, carrying the wash basket.*)

LINDA: Is this Ben?

BEN (*gallantly*): How do you do, my dear.

LINDA: Where've you been all these years? Willy's always wondered why you—

WILLY (*pulling* BEN *away from her impatiently*): Where is Dad? Didn't you follow him? How did you get started?

BEN: Well, I don't know how much you remember.

WILLY: Well, I was just a baby, of course, only three or four years old—

BEN: Three years and eleven months.

WILLY: What a memory, Ben!

BEN: I have many enterprises, William, and I have never kept books.

WILLY: I remember I was sitting under the wagon in—was it Nebraska?

BEN: It was South Dakota, and I gave you a bunch of wild flowers.

WILLY: I remember you walking away down some open road.

BEN (*laughing*): I was going to find Father in Alaska.

WILLY: Where is he?

BEN: At that age I had a very faulty view of geography, William. I discovered after a few days that I was heading due south, so instead of Alaska, I ended up in Africa.

LINDA: Africa!

WILLY: The Gold Coast!

BEN: Principally diamond mines.

LINDA: Diamond mines!

BEN: Yes, my dear. But I've only a few minutes—

WILLY: No! Boys! Boys! (*YOUNG BIFF and HAPPY appear.*) Listen to this. This is your Uncle Ben, a great man! Tell my boys, Ben!

BEN: Why, boys, when I was seventeen I walked into the jungle, and when I was twenty-one I walked out. (*He laughs.*) And by God I was rich.

WILLY (*to the boys*): You see what I been talking about? The greatest things can happen!

BEN (*glancing at his watch*): I have an appointment in Ketchikan Tuesday week.

WILLY: No, Ben! Please tell about Dad. I want my boys to hear. I want them to know the kind of stock they spring from. All I remember is a man with a big beard, and I was in Mamma's lap, sitting around a fire, and some kind of high music.

BEN: His flute. He played the flute.

WILLY: Sure, the flute, that's right!

(*New music is heard, a high, rollicking tune.*)

BEN: Father was a very great and a very wild-hearted man. We would start in Boston, and he'd toss the whole family into the wagon, and then he'd drive the team right across the country; through Ohio, and Indiana, Michigan, Illinois, and all the Western states. And we'd stop in the towns and sell the flutes that he'd made on the way. Great inventor, Father. With one gadget he made more in a week than a man like you could make in a lifetime.

WILLY: That's just the way I'm bringing them up, Ben—rugged, well liked, all-around.

BEN: Yeah? (*to* BIFF) Hit that, boy—hard as you can. (*He pounds his stomach.*)

BIFF: Oh, no, sir!

BEN (*taking boxing stance*): Come on, get to me! (*He laughs.*)

WILLY: Go to it, Biff! Go ahead, show him!

BIFF: Okay! (*He cocks his fists and starts in.*)

LINDA (*to* WILLY): Why must he fight, dear?

BEN (*sparring with* BIFF): Good boy! Good boy!

WILLY: How's that, Ben, heh?

HAPPY: Give him the left, Biff!

LINDA: Why are you fighting?

BEN: Good boy! (*Suddenly comes in, trips* BIFF, *and stands over him, the point of his umbrella poised over* BIFF'S *eye.*)

LINDA: Look out, Biff!

BIFF: Gee!

BEN (*patting* BIFF'S *knee*): Never fight fair with a stranger, boy. You'll never get out of the jungle that way. (*Taking* LINDA'S *hand and bowing.*) It was an honor and a pleasure to meet you, Linda.

LINDA (*withdrawing her hand coldly, frightened*): Have a nice—trip.

BEN (*to* WILLY): And good luck with your—what do you do?

WILLY: Selling.

BEN: Yes. Well . . . (*He raises his hand in farewell to all.*)

WILLY: No, Ben, I don't want you to think . . . (*He takes* BEN'S *arm to show him.*) It's Brooklyn. I know, but we hunt too.

BEN: Really, now.

WILLY: Oh, sure, there's snakes and rabbits and—that's why I moved out here. Why, Biff can fell any one of these trees in no time! Boys! Go right over to where they're building the apartment house and get some sand. We're gonna rebuild the entire front stoop right now! Watch this, Ben!

BIFF: Yes, sir! On the double, Hap!

HAPPY (*as he and* BIFF *run off*): I lost weight, Pop, you notice?

(CHARLEY *enters in knickers, even before the boys are gone.*)

CHARLEY: Listen, if they steal any more from that building the watchman'll put the cops on them!

LINDA (*to* WILLY): Don't let Biff . . .

(BEN *laughs lustily.*)

WILLY: You shoulda seen the lumber they brought home last week. At least a dozen six-by-tens worth all kinds a money.

CHARLEY: Listen, if that watchman—

WILLY: I gave them hell, understand. But I got a couple of fearless characters there.

CHARLEY: Willy, the jails are full of fearless characters.

BEN (*clapping* WILLY *on the back, with a laugh at* CHARLEY): And the stock exchange, friend!

WILLY (*joining in* BEN's *laughter*): Where are the rest of your pants?

CHARLEY: My wife bought them.

WILLY: Now all you need is a golf club and you can go upstairs and go to sleep. (*to* BEN) Great athlete! Between him and his son Bernard they can't hammer a nail!

BERNARD (*rushing in*): The watchman's chasing Biff!

WILLY (*angrily*): Shut up! He's not stealing anything!

LINDA (*alarmed, hurrying off left*): Where is he? Biff, dear! (*She exits.*)

WILLY (*moving toward the left, away from* BEN): There's nothing wrong. What's the matter with you?

BEN: Nervy boy. Good!

WILLY (*laughing*): Oh, nerves of iron, that Biff!

CHARLEY: Don't know what it is. My New England man comes back and he's bleedin', they murdered him up there.

WILLY: It's contacts, Charley, I got important contacts!

CHARLEY (*sarcastically*): Glad to hear it, Willy. Come in later, we'll shoot a little casino. I'll take some of your Portland money. (*He laughs at* WILLY *and exits.*)

WILLY (*turning to* BEN): Business is bad, it's murderous. But not for me, of course.

BEN: I'll stop by on my way back to Africa.

WILLY (*longingly*): Can't you stay a few days? You're just what I need, Ben, because I—I have a fine position here, but I—well, Dad left when I was such a baby and I never had a chance to talk to him and I still feel—kind of temporary about myself.

BEN: I'll be late for my train.

(*They are at opposite ends of the stage.*)

WILLY: Ben, my boys—can't we talk? They'd go into the jaws of hell for me, see, but I—

BEN: William, you're being first-rate with your boys. Outstanding, manly chaps!

WILLY (*hanging on to his words*): Oh, Ben, that's good to hear! Because sometimes I'm afraid that I'm not teaching them the right kind of—Ben, how should I teach them?

BEN (*giving great weight to each word, and with a certain vicious audacity*): William, when I walked into the jungle, I was seventeen. When I walked out I was twenty-one. And, by God, I was rich! (*He goes off into darkness around the right corner of the house.*)

WILLY: . . . was rich! That's just the spirit I want to imbue them with! To walk into a jungle! I was right! I was right! I was right!

(BEN *is gone, but* WILLY *is still speaking to him as* LINDA, *in nightgown and robe, enters the kitchen, glances around for* WILLY, *then goes to the door of the house, looks out and sees him. Comes down to his left. He looks at her.*)

LINDA: Willy, dear? Willy?

WILLY: I was right!

LINDA: Did you have some cheese? (*He can't answer.*) It's very late, darling. Come to bed, heh?

WILLY (*looking straight up*): Gotta break your neck to see a star in this yard.

LINDA: You coming in?

WILLY: Whatever happened to that diamond watch fob? Remember? When Ben came from Africa that time? Didn't he give me a watch fob with a diamond in it?

LINDA: You pawned it, dear. Twelve, thirteen years ago. For Biff's radio correspondence course.

WILLY: Gee, that was a beautiful thing. I'll take a walk.

LINDA: But you're in your slippers.

WILLY (*starting to go around the house at the left*): I was right! I was! (*Half to* LINDA, *as he goes, shaking his head.*) What a man! There was a man worth talking to. I was right!

LINDA (*calling after* WILLY): But in your slippers, Willy!

(WILLY *is almost gone when* BIFF, *in his pajamas, comes down the stairs and enters the kitchen.*)

BIFF: What is he doing out there?

LINDA: Sh!

BIFF: God Almighty, Mom, how long has he been doing this?

LINDA: Don't, he'll hear you.

BIFF: What the hell is the matter with him?

LINDA: It'll pass by morning.

BIFF: Shouldn't we do anything?

LINDA: Oh, my dear, you should do a lot of things, but there's nothing to do, so go to sleep.

(HAPPY *comes down the stair and sits on the steps.*)

HAPPY: I never heard him so loud, Mom.

LINDA: Well, come around more often; you'll hear him. (*She sits down at the table and mends the lining of* WILLY's *jacket.*)

BIFF: Why didn't you ever write me about this, Mom?

LINDA: How would I write to you? For over three months you had no address.

BIFF: I was on the move. But you know I thought of you all the time. You know that, don't you, pal?

LINDA: I know, dear, I know. But he likes to have a letter. Just to know that there's still a possibility for better things.

BIFF: He's not like this all the time, is he?

LINDA: It's when you come home he's always the worst.

BIFF: When I come home?

LINDA: When you write you're coming, he's all smiles, and talks about the future, and—he's just wonderful. And then the closer you seem to come, the more shaky he gets, and then, by the time you get here, he's arguing, and he seems angry at you. I think it's just that maybe he can't bring himself to—to open up to you. Why are you so hateful to each other? Why is that?

BIFF (*evasively*): I'm not hateful, Mom.

LINDA: But you no sooner come in the door than you're fighting!

BIFF: I don't know why. I mean to change. I'm tryin', Mom, you understand?

LINDA: Are you home to stay now?

BIFF: I don't know. I want to look around, see what's doin'.

LINDA: Biff, you can't look around all your life, can you?

BIFF: I just can't take hold, Mom. I can't take hold of some kind of a life.

LINDA: Biff, a man is not a bird, to come and go with the springtime.

BIFF: Your hair . . . (*He touches her hair.*) Your hair got so gray.

LINDA: Oh, it's been gray since you were in high school. I just stopped dyeing it, that's all.

BIFF: Dye it again, will ya? I don't want my pal looking old. (*He smiles.*)

LINDA: You're such a boy! You think you can go away for a year and . . . You've got to get it into your head now that one day you'll knock on this door and there'll be strange people here—

BIFF: What are you talking about? You're not even sixty, Mom.

LINDA: But what about your father?

BIFF (*lamely*): Well, I meant him too.

HAPPY: He admires Pop.

LINDA: Biff, dear, if you don't have any feeling for him, then you can't have any feeling for me.

BIFF: Sure I can, Mom.

LINDA: No. You can't just come to see me, because I love him. (*With a threat, but only a threat, of tears.*) He's the dearest man in the world to me, and I won't have anyone making him feel unwanted and low and blue. You've got to make up your mind now, darling, there's no leeway any more. Either he's your father and you pay him that respect, or else you're not to come here. I know he's not easy to get along with—nobody knows that better than me—but . . .

WILLY (*from the left, with a laugh*): Hey, hey, Biffo!

BIFF (*starting to go out after* WILLY): What the hell is the matter with him? (HAPPY *stops him.*)

LINDA: Don't—don't go near him!

BIFF: Stop making excuses for him! He always, always wiped the floor with you. Never had an ounce of respect for you.

HAPPY: He's always had respect for—

BIFF: What the hell do you know about it?

HAPPY (*surlily*): Just don't call him crazy!

BIFF: He's got no character—Charley wouldn't do this. Not in his own house—spewing out that vomit from his mind.

HAPPY: Charley never had to cope with what he's got to.

BIFF: People are worse off than Willy Loman. Believe me, I've seen them!

LINDA: Then make Charley your father, Biff. You can't do that, can you? I don't say he's a great man. Willy Loman never made a lot of money. His name was never in the paper. He's not the finest character that ever lived. But he's a human being, and a terrible thing is happening to him. So attention must be paid. He's not to be allowed to fall into his grave like an old dog. Attention, attention must be finally paid to such a person. You called him crazy—

BIFF: I didn't mean—

LINDA: No, a lot of people think he's lost his—balance. But you don't have to be very smart to know what his trouble is. The man is exhausted.

HAPPY: Sure!

LINDA: A small man can be just as exhausted as a great man. He works for a company thirty-six years this March, opens up unheard-of territories to their trademark, and now in his old age they take his salary away.

HAPPY (*indignantly*): I didn't know that, Mom.

LINDA: You never asked, my dear! Now that you get your spending money someplace else you don't trouble your mind with him.

HAPPY: But I gave you money last—

LINDA: Christmas time, fifty dollars! To fix the hot water it cost ninety-seven fifty! For five weeks he's been on straight commission, like a beginner, an unknown!

876 / DEATH OF A SALESMAN

BIFF: Those ungrateful bastards!

LINDA: Are they any worse than his sons? When he brought them business, when he was young, they were glad to see him. But now his old friends, the old buyers that loved him so and always found some order to hand him in a pinch— they're all dead, retired. He used to be able to make six, seven calls a day in Boston. Now he takes his valises out of the car and puts them back and takes them out again and he's exhausted. Instead of walking he talks now. He drives seven hundred miles, and when he gets there no one knows him any more, no one welcomes him. And what goes through a man's mind, driving seven hundred miles home without having earned a cent? Why shouldn't he talk to himself? Why? When he has to go to Charley and borrow fifty dollars a week and pretend to me that it's his pay? How long can that go on? How long? You see what I'm sitting here and waiting for? And you tell me he has no character? The man who never worked a day but for your benefit? When does he get the medal for that? Is this his reward—to turn around at the age of sixty-three and find his sons, who he loved better than his life, one a philandering bum—

HAPPY: Mom!

LINDA: That's all you are, my baby! (to BIFF) And you! What happened to the love you had for him? You were such pals! How you used to talk to him on the phone every night! How lonely he was till he could come home to you!

BIFF: All right, Mom. I'll live here in my room, and I'll get a job. I'll keep away from him, that's all.

LINDA: No, Biff. You can't stay here and fight all the time.

BIFF: He threw me out of this house, remember that.

LINDA: Why did he do that? I never knew why.

BIFF: Because I know he's a fake and he doesn't like anybody around who knows!

LINDA: Why a fake? In what way? What do you mean?

BIFF: Just don't lay it all at my feet. It's between me and him—that's all I have to say. I'll chip in from now on. He'll settle for half my pay check. He'll be all right. I'm going to bed. (He starts for the stairs.)

LINDA: He won't be all right.

BIFF (turning on the stairs, furiously): I hate this city and I'll stay here. Now what do you want?

LINDA: He's dying, Biff.

(HAPPY turns quickly to her, shocked.)

BIFF (after a pause): Why is he dying?

LINDA: He's been trying to kill himself.

BIFF (with great horror): How?

LINDA: I live from day to day.

BIFF: What're you talking about?

LINDA: Remember I wrote you that he smashed up the car again? In February?

BIFF: Well?

LINDA: The insurance inspector came. He said that they have evidence. That all these accidents in the last year—weren't—weren't—accidents.

HAPPY: How can they tell that? That's a lie.

LINDA: It seems there's a woman . . . (She takes a breath as . . .)

BIFF (sharply but contained): What woman?

LINDA (simultaneously): . . . and this woman . . .

LINDA: What?

BIFF: Nothing. Go ahead.

LINDA: What did you say?

BIFF: Nothing. I just said what woman?

HAPPY: What about her?

LINDA: Well, it seems she was walking down the road and saw his car. She says that he wasn't driving fast at all, and that he didn't skid. She says he came to that little bridge, and then deliberately smashed into the railing, and it was only the shallowness of the water that saved him.

BIFF: Oh, no, he probably just fell asleep again.

LINDA: I don't think he fell asleep.

BIFF: Why not?

LINDA: Last month . . . (With great difficulty.) Oh, boys, it's so hard to say a thing like this! He's just a big stupid man to you, but I tell you there's more good in him than in many other people. (She chokes, wipes her eyes.) I was looking for a fuse. The lights blew out, and I went down the cellar. And behind the fuse box—it happened to fall out—was a length of rubber pipe—just short.

HAPPY: No kidding?

LINDA: There's a little attachment on the end of it. I knew right away. And sure enough, on the bottom of the water heater there's a new little nipple on the gas pipe.

HAPPY (angrily): That—jerk.

BIFF: Did you have it taken off?

LINDA: I'm—I'm ashamed to. How can I mention it to him? Every day I go down and take away that little rubber pipe. But, when he comes home, I put it back where it was. How can I insult him that way? I don't know what to do. I live from day to day, boys. I tell you, I know every thought in his mind. It sounds so old-fashioned and silly, but I tell you he put his whole life into you and you've turned your backs on him. (She is bent over in the chair, weeping, her face in her hands.) Biff, I swear to God! Biff, his life is in your hands!

HAPPY (to BIFF): How do you like that damned fool!

BIFF (kissing her): All right, pal, all right. It's all settled now. I've been remiss. I know that, Mom. But now I'll stay, and I swear to you, I'll apply myself. (Kneeling in front of her, in a fever of self-reproach)

It's just—you see, Mom, I don't fit in business. Not that I won't try. I'll try, and I'll make good.

HAPPY: Sure you will. The trouble with you in business was you never tried to please people.

BIFF: I know, I—

HAPPY: Like when you worked for Harrison's. Bob Harrison said you were tops, and then you go and do some damn fool thing like whistling whole songs in the elevator like a comedian.

BIFF (*against* HAPPY): So what? I like to whistle sometimes.

HAPPY: You don't raise a guy to a responsible job who whistles in the elevator!

LINDA: Well, don't argue about it now.

HAPPY: Like when you'd go off and swim in the middle of the day instead of taking the line around.

BIFF (*his resentment rising*): Well, don't you run off? You take off sometimes, don't you? On a nice summer day?

HAPPY: Yeah, but I cover myself!

LINDA: Boys!

HAPPY: If I'm going to take a fade the boss can call any number where I'm supposed to be and they'll swear to him that I just left. I'll tell you something that I hate to say, Biff, but in the business world some of them think you're crazy.

BIFF (*angered*): Screw the business world!

HAPPY: All right, screw it! Great, but cover yourself!

LINDA: Hap, Hap!

BIFF: I don't care what they think! They've laughed at Dad for years, and you know why? Because we don't belong in this nuthouse of a city! We should be mixing cement on some open plain, or—or carpenters. A carpenter is allowed to whistle!

(WILLY *walks in from the entrance of the house, at left.*)

WILLY: Even your grandfather was better than a carpenter. (*Pause. They watch him.*) You never grew up. Bernard does not whistle in the elevator, I assure you.

BIFF (*as though to laugh* WILLY *out of it*): Yeah, but you do, Pop.

WILLY: I never in my life whistled in an elevator! And who in the business world thinks I'm crazy!

BIFF: I didn't mean it like that, Pop. Now don't make a whole thing out of it, will ya?

WILLY: Go back to the West! Be a carpenter, a cowboy, enjoy yourself!

LINDA: Willy, he was just saying—

WILLY: I heard what he said!

HAPPY (*trying to quiet* WILLY): Hey, Pop, come on now . . .

WILLY (*continuing over* HAPPY'S *line*): They laugh at me, heh? Go to Filene's, go to the Hub, go to Slattery's, Boston. Call out the name Willy Loman and see what happens! Big shot!

BIFF: All right, Pop.

WILLY: Big!

BIFF: All right!

WILLY: Why do you always insult me?

BIFF: I didn't say a word. (*to* LINDA) Did I say a word?

LINDA: He didn't say anything, Willy.

WILLY (*going to the doorway of the living-room*): All right, good night, good night.

LINDA: Willy, dear, he just decided . . .

WILLY (*to* BIFF): If you get tired hanging around tomorrow, paint the ceiling I put up in the living-room.

BIFF: I'm leaving early tomorrow.

HAPPY: He's going to see Bill Oliver, Pop.

WILLY (*interestedly*): Oliver? For what?

BIFF (*with reserve, but trying, trying*): He always said he'd stake me. I'd like to go into business, so maybe I can take him up on it.

LINDA: Isn't that wonderful?

WILLY: Don't interrupt. What's wonderful about it? There's fifty men in the City of New York who'd stake him. (*to* BIFF) Sporting goods?

BIFF: I guess so. I know something about it and—

WILLY: He knows something about it! You know sporting goods better than Spalding, for God's sake! How much is he giving you?

BIFF: I don't know, I didn't even see him yet, but—

WILLY: Then what're you talkin' about?

BIFF (*getting angry*): Well, all I said was I'm gonna see him, that's all!

WILLY (*turning away*): Ah, you're counting your chickens again.

BIFF (*starting left for the stairs*): Oh, Jesus, I'm going to sleep!

WILLY (*calling after him*): Don't curse in this house!

BIFF (*turning*): Since when did you get so clean?

HAPPY (*trying to stop them*): What a . . .

WILLY: Don't use that language to me! I won't have it!

HAPPY (*grabbing* BIFF, *shouts*): Wait a minute! I got an idea. I got a feasible idea. Come here, Biff, let's talk this over now, let's talk some sense here. When I was down in Florida last time, I thought of a great idea to sell sporting goods. It just came back to me. You and I, Biff—we have a line, the Loman Line. We train a couple of weeks, and put on a couple of exhibitions, see?

WILLY: That's an idea!

HAPPY: Wait! We form two basketball teams, see? Two water-polo teams. We play each other. It's a million dollars' worth of publicity. Two brothers, see? The Loman Brothers. Displays in the Royal Palms—all the hotels. And banners over the ring and the basketball court; "Loman Brothers." Baby, we could sell sporting goods!

WILLY: This is a one-million-dollar idea!

LINDA: Marvelous!

BIFF: I'm in great shape as far as that's concerned.

HAPPY: And the beauty of it is, Biff, it wouldn't be like a business. We'd be out playin' ball again . . .

BIFF (*enthused*): Yeah, that's . . .

WILLY: Million-dollar . . .

HAPPY: And you wouldn't get fed up with it, Biff. It'd be the family again. There'd be the old honor, and comradeship, and if you wanted to go off for a swim or somethin'—well, you'd do it! Without some smart cooky gettin' up ahead of you!

WILLY: Lick the world! You guys together could absolutely lick the civilized world.

BIFF: I'll see Oliver tomorrow. Hap, if we could work that out . . .

LINDA: Maybe things are beginning to—

WILLY (*wildly enthused, to* LINDA): Stop interrupting! (*To* BIFF) But don't wear sport jacket and slacks when you see Oliver.

BIFF: No, I'll—

WILLY: A business suit, and talk as little as possible, and don't crack any jokes.

BIFF: He did like me. Always liked me.

LINDA: He loved you!

WILLY (*to* LINDA): Will you stop! (*to* BIFF) Walk in very serious. You are not applying for a boy's job. Money is to pass. Be quiet, fine, and serious. Everybody likes a kidder, but nobody lends him money.

HAPPY: I'll try to get some myself, Biff. I'm sure I can.

WILLY: I see great things for you kids. I think your troubles are over. But remember, start big and you'll end big. Ask for fifteen. How much you gonna ask for?

BIFF: Gee, I don't know—

WILLY: And don't say "Gee." "Gee" is a boy's word. A man walking in for fifteen thousand dollars does not say "Gee!"

BIFF: Ten, I think would be top though.

WILLY: Don't be so modest. You always started too low. Walk in with a big laugh. Don't look worried. Start off with a couple of your good stories to lighten things up. It's not what you say, it's how you say it—because personality always wins the day.

LINDA: Oliver always thought the highest of him—

WILLY: Will you let me talk?

BIFF: Don't yell at her, Pop, will ya?

WILLY (*angrily*): I was talking, wasn't I?

BIFF: I don't like you yelling at her all the time, and I'm tellin' you, that's all.

WILLY: What're you, takin' over this house?

LINDA: Willy—

WILLY (*turning on her*): Don't take his side all the time, goddammit!

BIFF (*furiously*): Stop yelling at her!

WILLY (*suddenly pulling on his cheek, beaten down, guilt ridden*): Give my best to Bill Oliver—he may remember me. (*He exits through the living-room doorway.*)

LINDA (*her voice subdued*): What'd you have to start that for? (BIFF *turns away.*) You see how sweet he was as soon as you talked hopefully? (*She goes over to* BIFF.) Come up and say good night to him. Don't let him go to bed that way.

HAPPY: Come on, Biff, let's buck him up.

LINDA: Please, dear. Just say good night. It takes so little to make him happy. Come. (*She goes through the living-room doorway, calling upstairs from within the living-room.*) Your pajamas are hanging in the bathroom, Willy!

HAPPY (*looking toward where* LINDA *went out*): What a woman! They broke the mold when they made her. You know that, Biff?

BIFF: He's off salary. My God, working on commission!

HAPPY: Well, let's face it: he's no hot-shot selling man. Except that sometimes, you have to admit, he's a sweet personality.

BIFF (*deciding*): Lend me ten bucks, will ya? I want to buy some new ties.

HAPPY: I'll take you to a place I know. Beautiful stuff. Wear one of my striped shirts tomorrow.

BIFF: She got gray. Mom got awful old. Gee, I'm gonna go in to Oliver tomorrow and knock him for a—

HAPPY: Come on up. Tell that to Dad. Let's give him a whirl. Come on.

BIFF (*steamed up*): You know, with ten thousand bucks, boy!

HAPPY (*as they go into the living-room*): That's the talk, Biff, that's the first time I've heard the old confidence out of you! (*From within the living-room, fading off.*) You're gonna live with me, kid, and any babe you want just say the word . . . (*The last lines are hardly heard. They are mounting the stairs to their parents' bedroom.*)

LINDA (*entering her bedroom and addressing* WILLY, *who is in the bathroom. She is straightening the bed for him*): Can you do anything about the shower? It drips.

WILLY (*from the bathroom*): All of a sudden everything falls to pieces! Goddam plumbing, oughta be sued, those people. I hardly finished putting it in and the thing . . . (*His words rumble off.*)

LINDA: I'm just wondering if Oliver will remember him. You think he might?

WILLY (*coming out of the bathroom in his pajamas*): Remember him? What's the matter with you, you crazy? If he'd've stayed with Oliver he'd be on top by now! Wait'll Oliver gets a look at him. You don't know the average caliber any more. The average young man today—(*He is getting into bed.*)—is got a caliber of zero. Greatest thing in the world for him was to bum around.

(BIFF *and* HAPPY *enter the bedroom. Slight pause.*)

WILLY (*stops short, looking at* BIFF): Glad to hear it, boy.

HAPPY: He wanted to say good night to you, sport.

WILLY *(to* BIFF): Yeah. Knock him dead, boy. What'd you want to tell me?

BIFF: Just take it easy, Pop. Good night. *(He turns to go.)*

WILLY *(unable to resist):* And if anything falls off the desk while you're talking to him—like a package or something—don't you pick it up. They have office boys for that.

LINDA: I'll make a big breakfast—

WILLY: Will you let me finish? *(to* BIFF) Tell him you were in the business in the West. Not farm work.

BIFF: All right, Dad.

LINDA: I think everything—

WILLY *(going right through her speech):* And don't undersell yourself. No less than fifteen thousand dollars.

BIFF *(unable to bear him):* Okay. Good night, Mom. *(He starts moving.)*

WILLY: Because you got a greatness in you, Biff, remember that. You got all kinds a greatness . . . *(He lies back, exhausted.* BIFF *walks out.)*

LINDA *(calling after* BIFF): Sleep well, darling!

HAPPY: I'm gonna get married, Mom. I wanted to tell you.

LINDA: Go to sleep, dear.

HAPPY *(going):* I just wanted to tell you.

WILLY: Keep up the good work. *(*HAPPY *exits.)* God . . . remember that Ebbets Field game? The championship of the city?

LINDA: Just rest. Should I sing to you?

WILLY: Yeah. Sing to me. *(*LINDA *hums a soft lullaby.)* When that team came out—he was the tallest, remember?

LINDA: Oh, yes. And in gold.

*(*BIFF *enters the darkened kitchen, takes a cigarette and leaves the house. He comes downstage into a golden pool of light. He smokes, staring at the night.)*

WILLY: Like a young god. Hercules—something like that. And the sun, the sun all around him. Remember how he waved to me? Right up from the field, with the representatives of three colleges standing by? And the buyers I brought, and the cheers when he came out—Loman, Loman, Loman! God Almighty, he'll be great yet. A star like that, magnificent, can never really fade away!

(The light on WILLY *is fading. The gas heater begins to glow through the kitchen wall, near the stairs, a blue flame beneath red coils.)*

LINDA *(timidly):* Willy dear, what has he got against you?

WILLY: I'm so tired. Don't talk any more.

*(*BIFF *slowly returns to the kitchen. He stops, stares toward the heater.)*

LINDA: Will you ask Howard to let you work in New York?

WILLY: First thing in the morning. Everything'll be all right.

*(*BIFF *reaches behind the heater and draws out a length of rubber tubing. He is horrified and turns his head toward* WILLY's *room, still dimly lit, from which the strains of* LINDA's *desperate but monotonous humming rise.)*

WILLY *(staring through the window into the moonlight):* Gee, look at the moon moving between the buildings!

*(*BIFF *wraps the tubing around his hand and quickly goes up the stairs.)*

ACT 2

(Music is heard, gay and bright. The curtain rises as the music fades away. WILLY, *in shirt sleeves, is sitting at the kitchen table, sipping coffee, his hat in his lap.* LINDA *is filling his cup when she can.)*

WILLY: Wonderful coffee. Meal in itself.

LINDA: Can I make you some eggs?

WILLY: No. Take a breath.

LINDA: You look so rested, dear.

WILLY: I slept like a dead one. First time in months. Imagine, sleeping till ten on a Tuesday morning. Boys left nice and early, heh?

LINDA: They were out of here by eight o'clock.

WILLY: Good work!

LINDA: It was so thrilling to see them leaving together. I can't get over the shaving lotion in this house!

WILLY *(smiling):* Mmm—

LINDA: Biff was very changed this morning. His whole attitude seemed to be hopeful. He couldn't wait to get downtown to see Oliver.

WILLY: He's heading for a change. There's no question, there simply are certain men that take longer to get—solidified. How did he dress?

LINDA: His blue suit. He's so handsome in that suit. He could be a—anything in that suit!

*(*WILLY *gets up from the table.* LINDA *holds his jacket for him.)*

WILLY: There's no question, no question at all. Gee, on the way home tonight I'd like to buy some seeds.

LINDA *(laughing):* That'd be wonderful. But not enough sun gets back there. Nothing'll grow any more.

WILLY: You wait, kid, before it's all over we're gonna get a little place out in the country, and I'll raise some vegetables, a couple of chickens . . .

LINDA: You'll do it yet, dear.

*(*WILLY *walks out of his jacket.* LINDA *follows him.)*

WILLY: And they'll get married, and come for a weekend. I'd built a little guest house. 'Cause I got so many fine tools, all I'd need would be a little lumber and some peace of mind.

LINDA (*joyfully*): I sewed the lining . . .

WILLY: I could build two guest houses, so they'd both come. Did he decide how much he's going to ask Oliver for?

LINDA (*getting him into the jacket*): He didn't mention it, but I imagine ten or fifteen thousand. You going to talk to Howard today?

WILLY: Yeah, I'll put it to him straight and simple. He'll just have to take me off the road.

LINDA: And Willy, don't forget to ask for a little advance, because we've got the insurance premium. It's the grace period now.

WILLY: That's a hundred . . . ?

LINDA: A hundred and eight, sixty-eight. Because we're a little short again.

WILLY: Why are we short?

LINDA: Well, you had the motor job on the car . . .

WILLY: That goddam Studebaker!

LINDA: And you got one more payment on the refrigerator . . .

WILLY: But it just broke again!

LINDA: Well, it's old, dear.

WILLY: I told you we should've bought a well-advertised machine. Charley bought a General Electric and its twenty years old and it's still good, that son-of-a-bitch.

LINDA: But, Willy—

WILLY: Whoever heard of a Hastings refrigerator? Once in my life I would like to own something outright before it's broken! I'm always in a race with the junkyard! I just finished paying for the car and it's on its last legs. The refrigerator consumes belts like a goddamn maniac. They time those things. They time them so when you finally paid for them, they're used up.

LINDA (*buttoning up his jacket as he unbuttons it*): All told, about two hundred dollars would carry us, dear. But that includes the last payment on the mortgage. After this payment, Willy, the house belongs to us.

WILLY: It's twenty-five years!

LINDA: Biff was nine years old when we bought it.

WILLY: Well, that's a great thing. To weather a twenty-five year mortgage is—

LINDA: It's an accomplishment.

WILLY: All the cement, the lumber, the reconstruction I put in this house! There ain't a crack to be found in it any more.

LINDA: Well, it served its purpose.

WILLY: What purpose? Some stranger'll come along, move in, and that's that. If only Biff would take this house, and raise a family . . . (*He starts to go.*) Good-by, I'm late.

LINDA (*suddenly remembering*): Oh, I forgot! You're supposed to meet them for dinner.

WILLY: Me?

LINDA: At Frank's Chop House on Forty-eighth near Sixth Avenue.

WILLY: Is that so! How about you?

LINDA: No, just the three of you. They're gonna blow you to a big meal!

WILLY: Don't say! Who thought of that?

LINDA: Biff came to me this morning, Willy, and he said, "Tell Dad, we want to blow him to a big meal." Be there six o'clock. You and your two boys are going to have dinner.

WILLY: Gee whiz! That's really somethin'. I'm gonna knock Howard for a loop, kid. I'll get an advance, and I'll come home with a New York job. Goddammit, now I'm gonna do it!

LINDA: Oh, that's the spirit, Willy!

WILLY: I will never get behind a wheel the rest of my life!

LINDA: It's changing, Willy, I can feel it changing!

WILLY: Beyond a question. G'by, I'm late. (*He starts to go again.*)

LINDA (*calling after him as she runs to the kitchen table for a handkerchief*): You got your glasses?

WILLY (*feels for them, then comes back in*): Yeah, yeah, got my glasses.

LINDA (*giving him the handkerchief*): And a handkerchief.

WILLY: Yeah, handkerchief.

LINDA: And your saccharine?

WILLY: Yeah, my saccharine.

LINDA: Be careful on the subway stairs.

(*She kisses him, and a silk stocking is seen hanging from her hand.* WILLY *notices it.*)

WILLY: Will you stop mending stockings? At least while I'm in the house. It gets me nervous. I can't tell you. Please.

(LINDA *hides the stocking in her hand as she follows* WILLY *across the forestage in front of the house.*)

LINDA: Remember, Frank's Chop House.

WILLY (*passing the apron*): Maybe beets would grow out there.

LINDA (*laughing*): But you tried so many times.

WILLY: Yeah. Well, don't work hard today. (*He disappears around the right corner of the house.*)

LINDA: Be careful!

(*As* WILLY *vanishes,* LINDA *waves to him. Suddenly the phone rings. She runs across the stage and into the kitchen and lifts it.*)

LINDA: Hello? Oh, Biff! I'm so glad you called, I just . . . Yes, sure, I just told him. Yes, he'll be there for dinner at six o'clock, I didn't forget. Listen, I was just dying to tell you. You know that little rubber pipe I told you about? That he connected to the gas heater? I finally decided to go down the cellar this morning and take it away and destroy it. But it's gone! Imagine? He took it away himself, it isn't there! (*She listens.*) When? Oh, then you took it. Oh—nothing, it's just that I'd hoped he'd taken it away himself. Oh, I'm not worried, darling, because this morning he left in such high spirits, it was like the old days! I'm not afraid any more. Did Mr. Oliver see you? . . . Well, you wait there then. And make a nice impression on him, darling. Just don't perspire too much before you see him. And have a nice time with Dad. He may have big news too! . . . That's right, a New York job. And be sweet to him tonight, dear. Be loving to him. Because he's only a little boat looking for a harbor. (*She is trembling with sorrow and joy.*) Oh, that's wonderful, Biff, you'll save his life. Thanks, darling. Just put your arm around him when he comes into the restaurant. Give him a smile. That's the boy . . . Goodby, dear. . . . You got your comb? . . . That's fine. Good-by, Biff dear.

(*In the middle of her speech,* HOWARD WAGNER, *thirty-six, wheels on a small typewriter table on which is a wire-recording machine and proceeds to plug it in. This is on the left forestage. Light slowly fades on* LINDA *as it rises on* HOWARD. HOWARD *is intent on threading the machine and only glances over his shoulder as* WILLY *appears.*)

WILLY: Pst! Pst!

HOWARD: Hello, Willy, come in.

WILLY: Like to have a little talk with you, Howard.

HOWARD: Sorry to keep you waiting. I'll be with you in a minute.

WILLY: What's that, Howard?

HOWARD: Didn't you ever see one of these? Wire recorder.

WILLY: Oh. Can we talk a minute?

HOWARD: Records things. Just got delivery yesterday. Been driving me crazy, the most terrific machine I ever saw in my life. I was up all night with it.

WILLY: What do you do with it?

HOWARD: I bought it for dictation, but you can do anything with it. Listen to this. I had it home last night. Listen to what I picked up. The first one is my daughter. Get this. (*He flicks the switch and "Roll out the Barrel" is heard being whistled.*) Listen to that kid whistle.

WILLY: That is lifelike, isn't it?

HOWARD: Seven years old. Get that tone.

WILLY: Ts, ts. Like to ask a little favor if you . . .

(*The whistling breaks off, and the voice of* HOWARD's *daughter is heard.*)

HIS DAUGHTER: "Now you, Daddy."

HOWARD: She's crazy for me! (*Again the same song is whistled.*) That's me! Ha! (*He winks.*)

WILLY: You're very good!

(*The whistling breaks off again. The machine runs silent for a moment.*)

HOWARD: Sh! Get this now, this is my son.

HIS SON: "The capital of Alabama is Montgomery; the capital of Arizona is Phoenix; the capital of Arkansas is Little Rock; the capital of California is Sacramento . . ." (*and on, and on.*)

HOWARD (*holding up five fingers*): Five years old, Willy!

WILLY: He'll make an announcer some day!

HIS SON (*continuing*): "The capital . . ."

HOWARD: Get that—alphabetical order! (*The machine breaks off suddenly.*) Wait a minute. The maid kicked the plug out.

WILLY: It certainly is a—

HOWARD: Sh, for God's sake!

HIS SON: "It's nine o'clock, Bulova watch time. So I have to go to sleep."

WILLY: That really is—

HOWARD: Wait a minute! The next is my wife.

(*They wait.*)

HOWARD'S VOICE: "Go on, say something." (*Pause.*) "Well, you gonna talk?"

HIS WIFE: "I can't think of anything."

HOWARD'S VOICE: "Well, talk—it's turning."

HIS WIFE (*shyly, beaten*): "Hello." (*Silence.*) "Oh, Howard, I can't talk into this . . ."

HOWARD (*snapping the machine off*): That was my wife.

WILLY: This is a wonderful machine. Can we—

HOWARD: I tell you, Willy, I'm gonna take my camera, and my bandsaw, and all my hobbies, and out they go. This is the most fascinating relaxation I ever found.

WILLY: I think I'll get one myself.

HOWARD: Sure, they're only a hundred and a half. You can't do without it. Supposing you wanna hear Jack Benny, see? But you can't be at home at that hour. So you tell the maid to turn the radio on when Jack Benny comes on, and this automatically goes on with the radio . . .

WILLY: And when you come home you . . .

HOWARD: You can come home twelve o'clock, one o'clock, any time you like, and you get yourself a Coke and sit yourself down, throw the switch, and there's Jack Benny's program in the middle of the night!

WILLY: I'm definitely going to get one. Because lots of time I'm on the road, and I think to myself, what I must be missing on the radio!

HOWARD: Don't you have a radio in the car?

WILLY: Well, yeah, but who ever thinks of turning it on?

HOWARD: Say, aren't you supposed to be in Boston?

WILLY: That's what I want to talk to you about, Howard. You got a minute? (*He draws a chair in from the wing.*)

HOWARD: What happened? What're you doing here?

WILLY: Well . . .

HOWARD: You didn't crack up again, did you?

WILLY: Oh, no. No . . .

HOWARD: Geez, you had me worried there for a minute. What's the trouble?

WILLY: Well, tell you the truth, Howard. I've come to the decision that I'd rather not travel any more.

HOWARD: Not travel! Well, what'll you do?

WILLY: Remember, Christmas time, when you had the party here? You said you'd try to think of some spot for me here in town.

HOWARD: With us?

WILLY: Well, sure.

HOWARD: Oh, yeah, yeah, I remember. Well, I couldn't think of anything for you, Willy.

WILLY: I tell ya, Howard. The kids are all grown up, y'know. I don't need much any more. If I could take home—well, sixty-five dollars a week, I could swing it.

HOWARD: Yeah, but Willy, see I—

WILLY: I tell ya why, Howard. Speaking frankly and between the two of us, y'know—I'm just a little tired.

HOWARD: Oh, I could understand that, Willy. But you're a road man, Willy, and we do a road business. We've only got a half-dozen salesmen on the floor here.

WILLY: God knows, Howard, I never asked a favor of any man. But I was with the firm when your father used to carry you in here in his arms.

HOWARD: I know that, Willy, but—

WILLY: Your father came to me the day you were born and asked me what I thought of the name of Howard, may he rest in peace.

HOWARD: I appreciate that, Willy, but there just is no spot here for you. If I had a spot I'd slam you right in, but I just don't have a single solitary spot.

(*He looks for his lighter.* WILLY *has picked it up and gives it to him. Pause.*)

WILLY (*with increasing anger*): Howard, all I need to set my table is fifty dollars a week.

HOWARD: But where am I going to put you, kid?

WILLY: Look, it isn't a question of whether I can sell merchandise, is it?

HOWARD: No, but it's a business, kid, and everybody's gotta pull his own weight.

WILLY (*desperately*): Just let me tell you a story, Howard—

HOWARD: 'Cause you gotta admit, business is business.

WILLY (*angrily*): Business is definitely business, but just listen for a minute. You don't understand this. When I was a boy—eighteen, nineteen—I was already on the road. and there was a question in my mind as to whether selling had a future for me. Because in those days I had a yearning to go to Alaska. See, there were three gold strikes in one month in Alaska, and I felt like going out. Just for the ride, you might say.

HOWARD (*barely interested*): Don't say.

WILLY: Oh, yeah, my father lived many years in Alaska. He was an adventurous man. We've got quite a little streak of self-reliance in our family. I thought I'd go out with my older brother and try to locate him, and maybe settle in the North with the old man. And I was almost decided to go, when I met a salesman in the Parker House. His name was Dave Singleman. And he was eighty-four years old, and he'd drummed merchandise in thirty-one states. And old Dave, he'd go up to his room, y'understand, put on his green velvet slippers—I'll never forget—and pick up his phone and call the buyers, and without ever leaving his room, at the age of eighty-four, he made his living. And when I saw that, I realized that selling was the greatest career a man could want. 'Cause what could be more satisfying than to be able to go, at the age of eighty-four, into twenty or thirty different cities, and pick up a phone, and be remembered and loved and helped by so many different people? Do you know? when he died—and by the way he died the death of a salesman, in his green velvet slippers in the smoker of the New York, New Haven and Hartford, going into Boston—when he died, hundreds of salesmen and buyers were at his funeral. Things were sad on a lotta trains for months after that. (*He stands up.* HOWARD *has not looked at him.*) In those days there was personality in it, Howard. There was respect, and comradeship, and gratitude in it. Today, it's all cut and dried, and there's no chance for bringing friendship to bear—or personality. You see what I mean? They don't know me any more.

HOWARD (*moving away, to the right*): That's just the thing, Willy.

WILLY: If I had forty dollars a week—that's all I'd need. Forty dollars, Howard.

HOWARD: Kid, I can't take blood from a stone, I—

WILLY (*desperation is on him now*): Howard, the year Al Smith was nominated, your father came to me and—

HOWARD (*starting to go off*): I've got to see some people, kid.

WILLY (*stopping him*): I'm talking about your father! There were promises made across this desk! You mustn't tell me you've got people to see—I put thirty-four years into this firm, Howard, and now I can't pay my insurance! You can't eat the orange and throw the peel away—a man is not a piece of fruit! *(After a pause.)* Now pay attention. Your father—in 1928 I had a big year. I averaged a hundred and seventy dollars a week in commissions.

HOWARD *(impatiently)*: Now, Willy, you never averaged—

WILLY *(banging his hand on the desk)*: I averaged a hundred and seventy dollars a week in the year of 1928! And your father came to me—or rather, I was in the office here—it was right over this desk—and he put his hand on my shoulder—

HOWARD *(getting up)*: You'll have to excuse me, Willy, I gotta see some people. Pull yourself together. *(Going out.)* I'll be back in a little while.

(On HOWARD's *exit, the light of his chair grows very bright and strange.)*

WILLY: Pull myself together! What the hell did I say to him? My God, I was yelling at him! How could I! *(*WILLY *breaks off, staring at the light, which occupies the chair, animating it. He approaches this chair, standing across the desk from it.)* Frank, Frank, don't you remember what you told me that time? How you put your hand on my shoulder, and Frank . . . *(He leans on the desk and as he speaks the dead man's name he accidentally switches on the recorder, and instantly)*

HOWARD'S SON: ". . . of New York is Albany. The capital of Ohio is Cincinnati, the capital of Rhode Island is . . ." *(The recitation continues.)*

WILLY *(leaping away with fright, shouting)*: Ha! Howard! Howard! Howard!

HOWARD *(rushing in)*: What happened?

WILLY *(pointing at the machine, which contines nasally, childishly, with the capital cities)*: Shut it off! Shut it off!

HOWARD *(pulling the plug out)*: Look, Willy . . .

WILLY *(pressing his hands to his eyes)*: I gotta get myself some coffee. I'll get some coffee . . .

*(*WILLY *starts to walk out.* HOWARD *stops him.)*

HOWARD *(rolling up the cord)*: Willy, Look . . .

WILLY: I'll go to Boston.

HOWARD: Willy, you can't go to Boston for us.

WILLY: Why can't I go?

HOWARD: I don't want you to represent us. I've been meaning to tell you for a long time now.

WILLY: Howard, are you firing me?

HOWARD: I think you need a good long rest, Willy.

WILLY: Howard—

HOWARD: And when you feel better, come back, and we'll see if we can work something out.

WILLY: But I gotta earn money, Howard. I'm in no position to—

HOWARD: Where are your sons? Why don't your sons

give you a hand?

WILLY: They're working on a very big deal.

HOWARD: This is no time for false pride, Willy. You go to your sons and you tell them that you're tired. You've got two great boys, haven't you?

WILLY: Oh, no question, no question, but in the meantime . . .

HOWARD: Then that's that, heh?

WILLY: All right, I'll go to Boston tomorrow.

HOWARD: No, no.

WILLY: I can't throw myself on my sons. I'm not a cripple!

HOWARD: Look, kid, I'm busy this morning.

WILLY *(grasping* HOWARD's *arm)*: Howard, you've got to let me go to Boston!

HOWARD *(hard, keeping himself under control)*: I've got a line of people to see this morning. Sit down, take five minutes, and pull yourself together, and then go home, will ya? I need the office, Willy. *(He starts to go; turns, remembering the recorder, starts to push off the table holding the recorder.)* Oh, yeah. Whenever you can this week, stop by and drop off the samples. You'll feel better, Willy, and then come back and we'll talk. Pull yourself together, kid, there's people outside.

*(*HOWARD *exits, pushing the table off left.* WILLY *stares into space, exhausted. Now the music is heard—*BEN's *music—first distantly, then closer, closer. As* WILLY *speaks,* BEN *enters from the right. He carries valise and umbrella.)*

WILLY: Oh, Ben, how did you do it? What is the answer? Did you wind up the Alaska deal already?

BEN: Doesn't take much time if you know what you're doing. Just a short business trip. Boarding ship in an hour. Wanted to say good-by.

WILLY: Ben, I've got to talk to you.

BEN *(glancing at his watch)*: Haven't the time, William.

WILLY *(crossing the apron to* BEN*)*: Ben, nothing's working out. I don't know what to do.

BEN: Now look here, William. I've bought timberland in Alaska and I need a man to look after things for me.

WILLY: God, timberland! Me and my boys in those grand outdoors!

BEN: You've a new continent at your doorstep, William. Get out of these cities, they're full of talk and time payments and courts of law. Screw on your fists and you can fight for a fortune up there.

WILLY: Yes, yes! Linda, Linda!

*(*LINDA *enters as of old, with the wash.)*

LINDA: Oh, you're back?

BEN: I haven't much time.

WILLY: No, wait! Linda, he's got a proposition for me in Alaska.

LINDA: But you've got—(to BEN) He's got a beautiful job here.

WILLY: But in Alaska, kid, I could—

LINDA: You're doing well enough, Willy!

BEN (to LINDA): Enough for what, my dear?

LINDA (frightened of BEN and angry at him): Don't say those things to him! Enough to be happy right here, right now. (to WILLY, while BEN laughs) Why must everybody conquer the world? You're well liked, and the boys love you, and someday—(to BEN)—why, old man Wagner told him just the other day that if he keeps it up he'll be a member of the firm, didn't he, Willy?

WILLY: Sure, sure. I am building something with this firm, Ben, and if a man is building something he must be on the right track, mustn't he?

BEN: What are you building? Lay your hand on it. Where is it?

WILLY (hesitantly): That's true, Linda, there's nothing.

LINDA: Why? (to BEN) There's a man eighty-four years old—

WILLY: That's right, Ben, that's right. When I look at that man I say, what is there to worry about?

BEN: Bah!

WILLY: It's true, Ben. All he has to do is go into any city, pick up the phone, and he's making his living and you know why?

BEN (picking up his valise): I've got to go.

WILLY (holding BEN back): Look at this boy!

(BIFF, in his high school sweater, enters carrying suitcase. HAPPY carries BIFF's shoulder guards, gold helmet, and football pants.)

WILLY: Without a penny to his name, three great universities are begging for him, and from there the sky's the limit, because it's not what you do, Ben. It's who you know and the smile on your face! It's contacts, Ben, contacts! The whole wealth of Alaska passes over the lunch table at the Commodore Hotel, and that's the wonder, the wonder of this century, that a man can end with diamonds here on the basis of being liked! (He turns to BIFF.) And that's why when you get out on that field today it's important. Because thousands of people will be rooting for you and loving you. (to BEN, who has again begun to leave) And Ben! when he walks into a business office his name will sound out like a bell and all the doors will open to him! I've seen it, Ben, I've seen it a thousand times! You can't feel it with your hand like timber, but it's there!

BEN: Good-by, William.

WILLY: Ben, am I right? Don't you think I'm right? I value your advice.

BEN: There's a new continent at your doorstep, William. You could walk out rich. Rich! (He is gone.)

WILLY: We'll do it here, Ben! You hear me? We're gonna do it here!

(YOUNG BERNARD rushes in. The gay music of the Boys is heard.)

BERNARD: Oh, gee, I was afraid you left already!

WILLY: Why? What time is it?

BERNARD: It's half-past one!

WILLY: Well, come on, everybody! Ebbets Field next stop! Where's the pennants? (He rushes through the wall-line of the kitchen and out into the living-room.)

LINDA (to BIFF): Did you pack fresh underwear?

BIFF (who has been limbering up): I want to go!

BERNARD: Biff, I'm carrying your helmet, ain't I?

HAPPY: No, I'm carrying the helmet.

BERNARD: Oh, Biff, you promised me.

HAPPY: I'm carrying the helmet.

BERNARD: How am I going to get in the locker room?

LINDA: Let him carry the shoulder guards. (She puts her coat and hat on in the kitchen.)

BERNARD: Can I, Biff? 'Cause I told everybody I'm going to be in the locker room.

HAPPY: In Ebbets Field it's the clubhouse.

BERNARD: I meant the clubhouse, Biff!

HAPPY: Biff!

BIFF (grandly, after a slight pause): Let him carry the shoulder guards.

HAPPY (as he gives BERNARD the shoulder guards): Stay close to us now.

(WILLY rushes in with the pennants.)

WILLY (handing them out): Everybody wave when Biff comes out on the field. (HAPPY and BERNARD run off.) You set now, boy?

(The music has died away.)

BIFF: Ready to go, Pop. Every muscle is ready.

WILLY (at the edge of the apron): You realize what this means?

BIFF: That's right, Pop.

WILLY (feeling BIFF's muscles): You're comin' home this afternoon captain of the All-Scholastic Championship Team of the City of New York.

BIFF: I got it, Pop. And remember, pal, when I take off my helmet, that touchdown is for you.

WILLY: Let's go! (He is starting out, with his arm around BIFF, when CHARLEY enters, as of old, in knickers.) I got no room for you, Charley.

CHARLEY: Room? For what?

WILLY: In the car.

CHARLEY: You goin' for a ride? I wanted to shoot some casino.

WILLY (furiously): Casino! (Incredulously.) Don't you realize what today is?

LINDA: Oh, he knows, Willy. He's just kidding you.

WILLY: That's nothing to kid about!

CHARLEY: No, Linda, what's goin' on?

LINDA: He's playing in Ebbets Field.

CHARLEY: Baseball in this weather?

WILLY: Don't talk to him. Come on, come on! *(He is pushing them out.)*

CHARLEY: Wait a minute, didn't you hear the news?

WILLY: What?

CHARLEY: Don't you listen to the radio? Ebbets Field just blew up.

WILLY: You go to hell! *(CHARLEY laughs. Pushing them out.)* Come on, come on! We're late.

CHARLEY *(as they go)*: Knock a homer, Biff, knock a homer!

WILLY *(the last to leave, turning to CHARLEY)*: I don't think that was funny, Charley. This is the greatest day of his life.

CHARLEY: Willy, when are you going to grow up?

WILLY: Yeah, heh? When this game is over, Charley, you'll be laughing out of the other side of your face. They'll be calling him another Red Grange. Twenty-five thousand a year.

CHARLEY *(kidding)*: Is that so?

WILLY: Yeah, that's so.

CHARLEY: Well, then, I'm sorry, Willy. But tell me something.

WILLY: What?

CHARLEY: Who is Red Grange?

WILLY: Put up your hands. Goddam you, put up your hands!

(CHARLEY, chuckling, shakes his head and walks away, around the left corner of the stage. WILLY follows him. The music rises to a mocking frenzy.)

WILLY: Who the hell do you think you are, better than everybody else? You don't know everything, you big, ignorant, stupid . . . Put up your hands!

(Light rises, on the right side of the forestage, on a small table in the reception room of CHARLEY's office. Traffic sounds are heard. BERNARD, now mature, sits whistling to himself. A pair of tennis rackets and an overnight bag are on the floor beside him.)

WILLY *(offstage)*: What are you walking away for? Don't walk away! If you're going to say something say it to my face! I know you laugh at me behind my back. You'll laugh out of the other side of your goddam face after this game. Touchdown! Touchdown! Eighty thousand people! Touchdown! Right between the goal posts.

(BERNARD is a quiet, earnest, but self-assured young man. WILLY's voice is coming from right upstage now. BERNARD lowers his feet off the table and listens. JENNY, his father's secretary, enters.)

JENNY *(distressed)*: Say, Bernard, will you go out in the hall?

BERNARD: What is that noise? Who is it?

JENNY: Mr. Loman. He just got off the elevator.

BERNARD *(getting up)*: Who's he arguing with?

JENNY: Nobody. There's nobody with him. I can't deal with him any more, and your father gets all upset everytime he comes. I've got a lot of typing to do, and your father's waiting to sign it. Will you see him?

WILLY *(entering)*: Touchdown! Touch—*(He sees JENNY.)* Jenny, Jenny, good to see you. How're ya? Workin'? Or still honest?

JENNY: Fine. How've you been feeling?

WILLY: Not much any more, Jenny. Ha, ha! *(He is surprised to see the rackets.)*

BERNARD: Hello, Uncle Willy.

WILLY *(almost shocked)*: Bernard! Well, look who's here! *(He comes quickly, guiltily, to BERNARD and warmly shakes his hand.)*

BERNARD: How are you? Good to see you.

WILLY: What are you doing here?

BERNARD: Oh, just stopped by to see Pop. Get off my feet till my train leaves. I'm going to Washington in a few minutes.

WILLY: Is he in?

BERNARD: Yes, he's in his office with the accountant. Sit down.

WILLY *(sitting down)*: What're you going to do in Washington?

BERNARD: Oh, just a case I've got there, Willy.

WILLY: That so? *(Indicating the rackets.)* You going to play tennis there?

BERNARD: I'm staying with a friend who's got a court.

WILLY: Don't say. His own tennis court. Must be fine people, I bet.

BERNARD: They are, very nice. Dad tells me Biff's in town.

WILLY *(with a big smile)*: Yeah, Biff's in. Working on a very big deal, Bernard.

BERNARD: What's Biff doing?

WILLY: Well, he's been doing very big things in the West. But he decided to establish himself here. Very big. We've having dinner. Did I hear your wife had a boy?

BERNARD: That's right. Our second.

WILLY: Two boys! What do you know!

BERNARD: What kind of a deal has Biff got?

WILLY: Well, Bill Oliver—very big sporting-goods man—he wants Biff very badly. Called him in from the West. Long distance, carte blanche, special deliveries. Your friends have their own private tennis court?

BERNARD: You still with the old firm, Willy?

WILLY *(after a pause)*: I'm—I'm overjoyed to see how you made the grade, Bernard, overjoyed. It's an encouraging thing to see a young man really—

really—Looks very good for Biff—very—*(He breaks off, then.)* Bernard—*(He is so full of emotion, he breaks off again.)*

BERNARD: What is it, Willy?

WILLY *(small and alone)*: What—what's the secret?

BERNARD: What secret?

WILLY: How—how did you? Why didn't he ever catch on?

BERNARD: I wouldn't know that, Willy.

WILLY *(confidentially, desperately)*: You were his friend, his boyhood friend. There's something I don't understand about it. His life ended after that Ebbets Field game. From the age of seventeen nothing good ever happened to him.

BERNARD: He never trained himself for anything.

WILLY: But he did, he did. After high school he took so many correspondence courses. Radio mechanics; television; God knows what, and never made the slightest mark.

BERNARD *(taking off his glasses)*: Willy, do you want to talk candidly?

WILLY *(rising, faces BERNARD)*: I regard you as a very brilliant man, Bernard. I value your advice.

BERNARD: Oh, the hell with the advice, Willy. I couldn't advise you. There's just one thing I've always wanted to ask you. When he was supposed to graduate, and the math teacher flunked him—

WILLY: Oh, that son-of-a-bitch ruined his life.

BERNARD: Yeah, but, Willy, all he had to do was go to summer school and make up that subject.

WILLY: That's right, that's right.

BERNARD: Did you tell him not to go to summer school?

WILLY: Me? I begged him to go. I ordered him to go!

BERNARD: Then why wouldn't he go?

WILLY: Why? Why! Bernard, that question has been trailing me like a ghost for the last fifteen years. He flunked the subject, and laid down and died like a hammer hit him!

BERNARD: Take it easy, kid.

WILLY: Let me talk to you—I got nobody to talk to. Bernard, Bernard, was it my fault? Y'see? It keeps going around in my mind, maybe I did something to him. I got nothing to give him.

BERNARD: Don't take it so hard.

WILLY: Why did he lay down? What is the story there? You were his friend!

BERNARD: Willy, I remember, it was June, and our grades came out. And he'd flunked math.

WILLY: That son-of-a-bitch!

BERNARD: No, it wasn't right then. Biff just got very angry, I remember, and he was ready to enroll in summer school.

WILLY *(surprised)*: He was?

BERNARD: He wasn't beaten by it at all. But then, Willy, he disappeared from the block for almost a month. And I got the idea that he'd gone up to New England to see you. Did he have a talk with you then?

(WILLY stares in silence.)

BERNARD: Willy?

WILLY *(with a strong edge of resentment in his voice)*: Yeah, he came to Boston. What about it?

BERNARD: Well, just that when he came back—I'll never forget this, it always mystifies me. Because I'd thought so well of Biff, even though he'd always taken advantage of me. I loved him, Willy, y'know? And he came back after that month and took his sneakers—remember those sneakers with "University of Virginia" printed on them? He was so proud of those, wore them every day. And he took them down in the cellar, and burned them up in the furnace. We had a fist fight. It lasted at least half an hour. Just the two of us, punching each other down the cellar, and crying right through it. I've often thought of how strange it was that I knew he'd given up his life. What happened in Boston, Willy?

(WILLY looks at him as at an intruder.)

BERNARD: I just bring it up because you asked me.

WILLY *(angrily)*: Nothing. What do you mean, "What happened?" What's that got to do with anything?

BERNARD: Well, don't get sore.

WILLY: What are you trying to do, blame it on me? If a boy lays down is that my fault?

BERNARD: Now, Willy, don't get—

WILLY: Well, don't—don't talk to me that way! What does that mean, "What happened?"

(CHARLEY enters. He is in his vest, and he carries a bottle of bourbon.)

CHARLEY: Hey, you're going to miss that train. *(He waves the bottle.)*

BERNARD: Yeah, I'm going. *(He takes the bottle.)* Thanks, Pop. *(He picks up his rackets and bag.)* Good-by, Willy, and don't worry about it. You know, "If at first you don't succeed . . ."

WILLY: Yes, I believe in that.

BERNARD: But sometimes, Willy, it's better for a man just to walk away.

WILLY: Walk away?

BERNARD: That's right.

WILLY: But if you can't walk away?

BERNARD *(after a slight pause)*: I guess that's when it's tough. *(Extending his hand.)* Good-by, Willy.

WILLY *(shaking BERNARD's hand)*: Good-by, boy.

CHARLEY *(an arm on BERNARD's shoulder)*: How do you like this kid? Gonna argue a case in front of the Supreme Court.

BERNARD *(protesting)*: Pop!

WILLY (*genuinely shocked, pained, and happy*): No! The Supreme Court!

BERNARD: I gotta run. 'By, Dad!

CHARLEY: Knock 'em dead, Bernard!

(BERNARD *goes off.*)

WILLY (*as* CHARLEY *takes out his wallet*): The Supreme Court! And he didn't even mention it!

CHARLEY (*counting out money on the desk*): He don't have to—he's gonna do it.

WILLY: And you never told him what to do, did you? You never took any interest in him.

CHARLEY: My salvation is that I never took any interest in anything. There's some money—fifty dollars. I got an accountant inside.

WILLY: Charley, look . . . (*With difficulty.*) I got my insurance to pay. If you can manage it—I need a hundred and ten dollars.

(CHARLEY *doesn't reply for a moment; merely stops moving.*)

WILLY: I'd draw it from my bank but Linda would know, and I . . .

CHARLEY: Sit down, Willy.

WILLY (*moving toward the chair*): I'm keeping an account of everything, remember. I'll pay every penny back. (*He sits.*)

CHARLEY: Now listen to me, Willy.

WILLY: I want you to know I appreciate . . .

CHARLEY (*sitting down on the table*): Willy, what're you doin'? What the hell is goin' on in your head?

WILLY: Why? I'm simply . . .

CHARLEY: I offered you a job. You can make fifty dollars a week. And I won't send you on the road.

WILLY: I've got a job.

CHARLEY: Without pay? What kind of a job is a job without pay? (*He rises.*) Now, look, kid, enough is enough. I'm no genius but I know when I'm being insulted.

WILLY: Insulted!

CHARLEY: Why don't you want to work for me?

WILLY: What's the matter with you? I've got a job.

CHARLEY: Then what're you walkin' in here every week for?

WILLY (*getting up*): Well, if you don't want me to walk in here—

CHARLEY: I am offering you a job.

WILLY: I don't want your goddam job!

CHARLEY: When the hell are you going to grow up?

WILLY (*furiously*): You big ignoramus, if you say that to me again I'll rap you one! I don't care how big you are! (*He's ready to fight.*)

(Pause.)

CHARLEY (*kindly, going to him*): How much do you need, Willy?

WILLY: Charley, I'm strapped, I'm strapped. I don't know what to do. I was just fired.

CHARLEY: Howard fired you?

WILLY: That snotnose. Imagine that? I named him. I named him Howard.

CHARLEY: Willy, when're you gonna realize that them things don't mean anything? You named him Howard, but you can't sell that. The only thing you got in this world is what you can sell. And the funny thing is that you're a salesman, and you don't know that.

WILLY: I've always tried to think otherwise, I guess. I always felt that if a man was impressive, and well liked, that nothing—

CHARLEY: Why must everybody like you? Who liked J. P. Morgan? Was he impressive? In a Turkish bath he'd look like a butcher. But with his pockets on he was very well liked. Now listen, Willy, I know you don't like me, and nobody can say I'm in love with you, but I'll give you a job because—just for the hell of it, put it that way. Now what do you say?

WILLY: I—I just can't work for you, Charley.

CHARLEY: What're you, jealous of me?

WILLY: I can't work for you, that's all, don't ask me why.

CHARLEY (*angered, takes out more bills*): You been jealous of me all your life, you damned fool! Here, pay your insurance. (*He puts the money in* WILLY's *hand.*)

WILLY: I'm keeping strict accounts.

CHARLEY: I've got some work to do. Take care of yourself. And pay your insurance.

WILLY (*moving to the right*): Funny, y'know? After all the highways, and the trains, and the appointments, and the years, you end up worth more dead than alive.

CHARLEY: Willy, nobody's worth nothin' dead. (*After a slight pause.*) Did you hear what I said?

(WILLY *stands still, dreaming.*)

CHARLEY: Willy!

WILLY: Apologize to Bernard for me when you see him. I didn't mean to argue with him. He's a fine boy. They're all fine boys, and they'll end up big—all of them. Someday they'll all play tennis together. Wish me luck, Charley. He saw Bill Oliver today.

CHARLEY: Good luck.

WILLY (*on the verge of tears*): Charley, you're the only friend I got. Isn't that a remarkable thing? (*He goes out.*)

CHARLEY: Jesus!

(CHARLEY *stares after him a moment and follows. All light blacks out. Suddenly raucous music is heard, and a red glow rises behind the screen at right.* STANLEY, *a young waiter, appears, carrying a table, followed by* HAPPY, *who is carrying two chairs.*)

STANLEY (*putting the table down*): That's all right, Mr. Loman, I can handle it myself. (*He turns and takes the chairs from* HAPPY *and places them at the table.*)

HAPPY (*glancing around*): Oh, this is better.

STANLEY: Sure, in the front there you're in the middle of all kinds a noise. Whenever you got a party, Mr. Loman, you just tell me and I'll put you back here. Y'know, there's a lotta people they don't like it private, because when they go out they like to see a lotta action around them because they're sick and tired to stay in the house by theirself. But I know you, you ain't from Hackensack. You know what I mean?

HAPPY (*sitting down*): So how's it coming, Stanley?

STANLEY: Ah, it's a dog's life. I only wish during the war they'd a took me in the Army. I coulda been dead by now.

HAPPY: My brother's back, Stanley.

STANLEY: Oh, he come back, heh? From the Far West.

HAPPY: Yeah, big cattle man, my brother, so treat him right. And my father's coming too.

STANLEY: Oh, your father too!

HAPPY: You got a couple of nice lobsters?

STANLEY: Hundred per cent, big.

HAPPY: I want them with the claws.

STANLEY: Don't worry, I don't give you no mice. (HAPPY *laughs.*) How about some wine? It'll put a head on the meal.

HAPPY: No. You remember, Stanley, that recipe I brought you from overseas? With the champagne in it?

STANLEY: Oh, yeah, sure. I still got it tacked up yet in the kitchen. But that'll have to cost a buck apiece anyways.

HAPPY: That's all right.

STANLEY: What'd you, hit a number or somethin'?

HAPPY: No, it's a little celebration. My brother is—I think he pulled off a big deal today. I think we're going into business together.

STANLEY: Great! That's the best for you. Because a family business, you know what I mean?—that's the best.

HAPPY: That's what I think.

STANLEY: 'Cause what's the difference? Somebody steals? It's in the family. Know what I mean? (*Sotto voce.*) Like this bartender here. The boss is goin' crazy what kinda leak he's got in the cash register. You put it in but it don't come out.

HAPPY (*raising his head*): Sh!

STANLEY: What?

HAPPY: You notice I wasn't lookin' right or left, was I?

STANLEY: No.

HAPPY: And my eyes are closed.

STANLEY: So what's the—?

HAPPY: Strudel's comin'.

STANLEY (*catching on, looks around*): Ah, no, there's no—

(*He breaks off as a furred, lavishly dressed girl enters and sits at the next table. Both follow her with their eyes.*)

STANLEY: Geez, how'd ya know?

HAPPY: I got radar or something. (*Staring directly at her profile.*) Oooooooo . . . Stanley.

STANLEY: I think that's for you, Mr. Loman.

HAPPY: Look at that mouth. Oh, God. And the binoculars.

STANLEY: Geez, you got a life, Mr. Loman.

HAPPY: Wait on her.

STANLEY (*going to the girl's table*): Would you like a menu, ma'am?

GIRL: I'm expecting someone, but I'd like a—

HAPPY: Why don't you bring her—excuse me, miss, do you mind? I sell champagne, and I'd like you to try my brand. Bring her a champagne, Stanley.

GIRL: That's awfully nice of you.

HAPPY: Don't mention it. It's all company money. (*He laughs.*)

GIRL: That's a charming product to be selling, isn't it?

HAPPY: Oh, gets to be like everything else. Selling is selling, y'know.

GIRL: I suppose.

HAPPY: You don't happen to sell, do you?

GIRL: No, I don't sell.

HAPPY: Would you object to a compliment from a stranger? You ought to be on a magazine cover.

GIRL (*looking at him a little archly*): I have been.

(STANLEY *comes in with a glass of champagne.*)

HAPPY: What'd I say before, Stanley? You see? She's a cover girl.

STANLEY: Oh, I could see, I could see.

HAPPY (*to the* GIRL): What magazine?

GIRL: Oh, a lot of them. (*She takes the drink.*) Thank you.

HAPPY: You know what they say in France, don't you? "Champagne is the drink of the complexion"—Hya, Biff!

(BIFF *has entered and sits with* HAPPY.)

BIFF: Hello, kid. Sorry I'm late.

HAPPY: I just got here. Uh, Miss—?

GIRL: Forsythe.

HAPPY: Miss Forsythe, this is my brother.

BIFF: Is Dad here?

HAPPY: His name is Biff. You might've heard of him. Great football player.

GIRL: Really? What team?

HAPPY: Are you familiar with football?

GIRL: No, I'm afraid I'm not.

HAPPY: Biff is quarterback with the New York Giants.

GIRL: Well, that is nice, isn't it? *(She drinks.)*

HAPPY: Good health.

GIRL: I'm happy to meet you.

HAPPY: That's my name. Hap. It's really Harold, but at West Point they called me Happy.

GIRL *(now really impressed)*: Oh, I see. How do you do? *(She turns her profile.)*

BIFF: Isn't Dad coming?

HAPPY: You want her?

BIFF: Oh, I could never make that.

HAPPY: I remember the time that idea would never come into your head. Where's the old confidence, Biff?

BIFF: I just saw Oliver—

HAPPY: Wait a minute. I've got to see that old confidence again. Do you want her? She's on call.

BIFF: Oh, no. *(He turns to look at the GIRL.)*

HAPPY: I'm telling you. Watch this. *(Turning to the GIRL.)* Honey? *(She turns to him.)* Are you busy?

GIRL: Well, I am . . . but I could make a phone call.

HAPPY: Do that, will you, honey? And see if you can get a friend. We'll be here for a while. Biff is one of the greatest football players in the country.

GIRL *(standing up)*: Well, I'm certainly happy to meet you.

HAPPY: Come back soon.

GIRL: I'll try.

HAPPY: Don't try, honey, try hard.

(The GIRL exits. STANLEY follows, shaking his head in bewildered admiration.)

HAPPY: Isn't that a shame now? A beautiful girl like that? That's why I can't get married. There's not a good woman in a thousand. New York is loaded with them, kid!

BIFF: Hap, look—

HAPPY: I told you she was on call!

BIFF *(strangely unnerved)*: Cut it out, will ya? I want to say something to you.

HAPPY: Did you see Oliver?

BIFF: I saw him all right. Now look, I want to tell Dad a couple of things and I want you to help me.

HAPPY: What? Is he going to back you?

BIFF: Are you crazy? You're out of your goddam head, you know that?

HAPPY: Why? What happened?

BIFF *(breathlessly)*: I did a terrible thing today, Hap. It's been the strangest day I ever went through. I'm all numb, I swear.

HAPPY: You mean he wouldn't see you?

BIFF: Well, I waited six hours for him, see? All day. Kept sending my name in. Even tried to date his secretary so she'd get me to him, but no soap.

HAPPY: Because you're not showin' the old confidence, Biff. He remembered you, didn't he?

BIFF *(stopping HAPPY with a gesture)*: Finally, about five

o'clock, he comes out. Didn't remember who I was or anything. I felt like such an idiot, Hap.

HAPPY: Did you tell him my Florida idea?

BIFF: He walked away. I saw him for one minute. I got so mad I could've torn the walls down! How the hell did I ever get the idea I was a salesman there? I even believed myself that I'd been a salesman for him! And then he gave me one look and—I realized what a ridiculous lie my whole life has been! We've been talking in a dream for fifteen years. I was a shipping clerk.

HAPPY: What'd you do?

BIFF *(with great tension and wonder)*: Well, he left, see. And the secretary went out. I was all alone in the waiting-room. I don't know what came over me, Hap. The next thing I know I'm in his office—paneled walls, everything. I can't explain it. I—Hap, I took his fountain pen.

HAPPY: Geez, did he catch you?

BIFF: I ran out. I ran down all eleven flights. I ran and ran and ran.

HAPPY: That was an awful dumb—what'd you do that for?

BIFF *(agonized)*: I don't know, I just—wanted to take something, I don't know. You gotta help me, Hap, I'm gonna tell Pop.

HAPPY: You crazy? What for?

BIFF: Hap, he's got to understand that I'm not the man somebody lends that kind of money to. He thinks I've been spiting him all these years and it's eating him up.

HAPPY: That's just it. You tell him something nice.

BIFF: I can't.

HAPPY: Say you got a lunch date with Oliver tomorrow.

BIFF: So what do I do tomorrow?

HAPPY: You leave the house tomorrow and come back at night and say Oliver is thinking it over. And he thinks it over for a couple of weeks, and gradually it fades away and nobody's the worse.

BIFF: But it'll go on forever!

HAPPY: Dad is never so happy as when he's looking forward to something!

(WILLY enters.)

HAPPY: Hello, scout!

WILLY: Gee, I haven't been here in years!

(STANLEY has followed WILLY in and sets a chair for him. STANLEY starts off but HAPPY stops him.)

HAPPY: Stanley!

(STANLEY stands by, waiting for an order.)

BIFF *(going to WILLY with guilt, as to an invalid)*: Sit down, Pop. You want a drink?

WILLY: Sure, I don't mind.

BIFF: Let's get a load on.

WILLY: You look worried.

BIFF: N-no. (*to* STANLEY) Scotch all around. Make it doubles.

STANLEY: Doubles, right. (*He goes.*)

WILLY: You had a couple already, didn't you?

BIFF: Just a couple, yeah.

WILLY: Well, what happened, boy? (*Nodding affirmatively, with a smile.*) Everything go all right?

BIFF (*takes a breath, then reaches out and grasps* WILLY's *hand*): Pal . . . (*He is smiling bravely, and* WILLY *is smiling too.*) I had an experience today.

HAPPY: Terrific, Pop.

WILLY: That so? What happened?

BIFF (*high, slightly alcoholic, above the earth*): I'm going to tell you everything from first to last. It's been a strange day. (*Silence. He looks around, composes himself as best he can, but his breath keeps breaking the rhythm of his voice.*) I had to wait quite a while for him, and—

WILLY: Oliver?

BIFF: Yeah, Oliver. All day, as a matter of cold fact. And a lot of—instances—facts, Pop, facts about my life came back to me. Who was it, Pop? Who ever said I was a salesman with Oliver?

WILLY: Well, you were.

BIFF: No, Dad, I was a shipping clerk.

WILLY: But you were practically—

BIFF (*with determination*): Dad, I don't know who said it first, but I was never a salesman for Bill Oliver.

WILLY: What're you talking about?

BIFF: Let's hold on to the facts tonight, Pop. We're not going to get anywhere bullin' around. I was a shipping clerk.

WILLY (*angrily*): All right, now listen to me—

BIFF: Why don't you let me finish?

WILLY: I'm not interested in stories about the past or any crap of that kind because the woods are burning, boys, you understand? There's a big blaze going on all around. I was fired today.

BIFF (*shocked*): How could you be?

WILLY: I was fired, and I'm looking for a little good news to tell your mother, because the woman has waited and the woman has suffered. The gist of it is that I haven't got a story left in my head, Biff. So don't give me a lecture about facts and aspects. I am not interested. Now what've you got to say to me?

(STANLEY *enters with three drinks. They wait until he leaves.*)

WILLY: Did you see Oliver?

BIFF: Jesus, Dad!

WILLY: You mean you didn't go up there?

HAPPY: Sure he went up there.

BIFF: I did. I—saw him. How could they fire you?

WILLY (*on the edge of his chair*): What kind of a welcome did he give you?

BIFF: He won't even let you work on commission?

WILLY: I'm out! (*Driving.*) So tell me, he gave you a warm welcome?

HAPPY: Sure, Pop, sure!

BIFF (*driven*): Well, it was kind of—

WILLY: I was wondering if he'd remember you. (*to* HAPPY.) Imagine, man doesn't see him for ten, twelve years, and gives him that kind of a welcome!

HAPPY: Damn right!

BIFF (*trying to return to the offensive*): Pop, look—

WILLY: You know why he remembered you, don't you? Because you impressed him in those days.

BIFF: Let's talk quietly and get this down to the facts, huh?

WILLY (*as though* BIFF *had been interrupting*): Well, what happened? It's great news, Biff. Did he take you into his office or'd you talk in the waiting-room?

BIFF: Well, he came in, see, and—

WILLY (*with a big smile*): What'd he say? Betcha he threw his arm around you.

BIFF: Well, he kinda—

WILLY: He's a fine man. (*to* HAPPY) Very hard man to see, y'know.

HAPPY (*agreeing*): Oh, I know.

WILLY (*to* BIFF): Is that where you had the drinks?

BIFF: Yeah, he gave me a couple of—no, no!

HAPPY (*cutting in*): He told him my Florida idea.

WILLY: Don't interrupt. (*to* BIFF) How'd he react to the Florida idea?

BIFF: Dad, will you give me a minute to explain?

WILLY: I've been waiting for you to explain since I sat down here! What happened? He took you into his office and what?

BIFF: Well—I talked. And—and he listened, see.

WILLY: Famous for the way he listens, y'know. What was his answer?

BIFF: His answer was—(*He breaks off, suddenly angry.*) Dad, you're not letting me tell you what I want to tell you!

WILLY (*accusing, angered*): You didn't see him, did you?

BIFF: I did see him!

WILLY: What'd you insult him or something? You insulted him, didn't you?

BIFF: Listen, will you let me out of it, will you just let me out of it!

HAPPY: What the hell!

WILLY: Tell me what happened!

BIFF (*to* HAPPY): I can't talk to him!

(*A single trumpet note jars the ear. The light of green leaves stains the house, which holds the air of night and a dream.* YOUNG BERNARD *enters and knocks on the door of the house.*)

YOUNG BERNARD (*frantically*): Mrs. Loman, Mrs. Loman!

HAPPY: Tell him what happened!

BIFF (to HAPPY): Shut up and leave me alone!

WILLY: No, no! You had to go and flunk math!

BIFF: What math? What're you talking about?

YOUNG BERNARD: Mrs. Loman, Mrs. Loman!

(LINDA appears in the house, as of old.)

WILLY (wildly): Math, math, math!

BIFF: Take it easy, Pop!

YOUNG BERNARD: Mrs. Loman!

WILLY (furiously): If you hadn't flunked you'd've been set by now!

BIFF: Now, look, I'm gonna tell you what happened, and you're going to listen to me.

YOUNG BERNARD: Mrs. Loman!

BIFF: I waited six hours—

HAPPY: What the hell are you saying?

BIFF: I kept sending in my name but he wouldn't see me. So finally he . . . (He continues unheard as light fades low on the restaurant.)

YOUNG BERNARD: Biff flunked math!

LINDA: No!

YOUNG BERNARD: Birnbaum flunked him! They won't graduate him!

LINDA: But they have to. He's gotta go to the university. Where is he? Biff! Biff!

YOUNG BERNARD: No, he left. He went to Grand Central.

LINDA: Grand— You mean he went to Boston!

YOUNG BERNARD: Is Uncle Willy in Boston?

LINDA: Oh, maybe Willy can talk to the teacher. Oh, the poor, poor boy!

(Light on house area snaps out.)

BIFF (at the table, now audible, holding up a gold fountain pen): . . . so I'm washed up with Oliver, you understand? Are you listening to me?

WILLY (at a loss): Yeah, sure. If you hadn't flunked—

BIFF: Flunked what? What're you talking about?

WILLY: Don't blame everything on me! I didn't flunk math—you did! What pen?

HAPPY: That was awful dumb, Biff, a pen like that is worth—

WILLY (seeing the pen for the first time): You took Oliver's pen?

BIFF (weakening): Dad, I just explained it to you.

WILLY: You stole Bill Oliver's fountain pen!

BIFF: I didn't exactly steal it! That's just what I've been explaining to you!

HAPPY: He had it in his hand and just then Oliver walked in, so he got nervous and stuck it in his pocket!

WILLY: My God, Biff!

BIFF: I never intended to do it, Dad!

OPERATOR'S VOICE: Standish Arms, good evening!

WILLY (shouting): I'm not in my room!

BIFF (frightened): Dad, what's the matter? (He and HAPPY stand up.)

OPERATOR: Ringing Mr. Loman for you!

WILLY: I'm not there, stop it!

BIFF (horrified, gets down on one knee before WILLY): Dad, I'll make good, I'll make good. (WILLY tries to get to his feet. BIFF holds him down.) Sit down now.

WILLY: No, you're no good, you're no good for anything.

BIFF: I am, Dad, I'll find something else, you understand? Now don't worry about anything. (He holds up WILLY's face.) Talk to me, Dad.

OPERATOR: Mr. Loman does not answer. Shall I page him?

WILLY (attempting to stand, as though to rush and silence the OPERATOR): No, no, no!

HAPPY: He'll strike something, Pop.

WILLY: No, no . . .

BIFF (desperately, standing over WILLY): Pop, listen! Listen to me! I'm telling you something good. Oliver talked to his partner about the Florida idea. You listening? He—he talked to his partner, and he came to me . . . I'm going to be all right, you hear? Dad, listen to me, he said it was just a question of the amount!

WILLY: Then you . . . got it?

HAPPY: He's gonna be terrific, Pop!

WILLY (trying to stand): Then you got it, haven't you? You got it! You got it!

BIFF (agonized, holds WILLY down): No, no. Look, Pop. I'm supposed to have lunch with them tomorrow. I'm just telling you this so you'll know that I can still make an impression, Pop. And I'll make good somewhere, but I can't go tomorrow, see?

WILLY: Why not? You simply—

BIFF: But the pen, Pop!

WILLY: You give it to him and tell him it was an oversight!

HAPPY: Sure, have lunch tomorrow!

BIFF: I can't say that—

WILLY: You were doing a crossword puzzle and accidentally used his pen!

BIFF: Listen, kid, I took those balls years ago, now I walk in with his fountain pen? That clinches it, don't you see? I can't face him like that! I'll try elsewhere.

PAGE'S VOICE: Paging Mr. Loman!

WILLY: Don't you want to be anything?

BIFF: Pop, how can I go back?

WILLY: You don't want to be anything, is that what's behind it?

BIFF (now angry at WILLY for not crediting his sympathy): Don't take it that way! You think it was easy walking into that office after what I'd done to him? A team of horses couldn't have dragged me back to Bill Oliver!

WILLY: Then why'd you go?

BIFF: Why did I go? Why did I go! Look at you! Look

at what's become of you!

(*Off left,* THE WOMAN *laughs.*)

WILLY: Biff, you're going to go to that lunch tomorrow, or—

BIFF: I can't go. I've got no appointment!

HAPPY: Biff, for . . . !

WILLY: Are you spiting me?

BIFF: Don't take it that way! Goddammit!

WILLY (*strikes* BIFF *and falters away from the table*): You rotten little louse! Are you spiting me?

THE WOMAN: Someone's at the door, Willy!

BIFF: I'm no good, can't you see what I am?

HAPPY (*separating them*): Hey, you're in a restaurant! Now cut it out, both of you! (*The* GIRLS *enter.*) Hello, girls, sit down.

(THE WOMAN *laughs, off left.*)

MISS FORSYTHE: I guess we might as well. This is Letta.

THE WOMAN: Willy, are you going to wake up?

BIFF (*ignoring* WILLY): How're ya, miss, sit down. What do you drink?

MISS FORSYTHE: Letta might not be able to stay long.

LETTA: I gotta get up very early tomorrow. I got jury duty. I'm so excited! Were you fellows ever on a jury?

BIFF: No, but I been in front of them! (*The* GIRLS *laugh.*) This is my father.

LETTA: Isn't he cute? Sit down with us, Pop.

HAPPY: Sit him down, Biff!

BIFF (*going to him*): Come on, slugger, drink us under the table. To hell with it! Come on, sit down, pal.

(*On* BIFF's *last insistence,* WILLY *is about to sit.*)

THE WOMAN (*now urgently*): Willy, are you going to answer the door!

(THE WOMAN's *call pulls* WILLY *back. He starts right, befuddled.*)

BIFF: Hey, where are you going?

WILLY: Open the door.

BIFF: The door?

WILLY: The washroom . . . the door . . . where's the door?

BIFF (*leading* WILLY *to the left*): Just go straight down.

(WILLY *moves left.*)

THE WOMAN: Willy, Willy, are you going to get up, get up, get up, get up?

(WILLY *exits left.*)

LETTA: I think it's sweet you bring your daddy along.

MISS FORSYTHE: Oh, he isn't really your father!

BIFF (*at left, turning to her resentfully*): Miss Forsythe, you've just seen a prince walk by. A fine, troubled prince. A hard-working, unappreciated

prince. A pal, you understand? A good companion. Always for his boys.

LETTA: That's so sweet.

HAPPY: Well, girls, what's the program? We're wasting time. Come on, Biff. Gather round. Where would you like to go?

BIFF: Why don't you do something for him?

HAPPY: Me!

BIFF: Don't you give a damn for him, Hap?

HAPPY: What're you talking about? I'm the one who—

BIFF: I sense it, you don't give a good goddam about him. (*He takes the rolled-up hose from his pocket and puts it on the table in front of* HAPPY.) Look what I found in the cellar, for Christ's sake. How can you bear to let it go on?

HAPPY: Me? Who goes away? Who runs off and—

BIFF: Yeah, but he doesn't mean anything to you. You could help him—I can't! Don't you understand what I'm talking about? He's going to kill himself, don't you know that?

HAPPY: Don't I know it! Me!

BIFF: Hap, help him! Jesus . . . help him . . . Help me, help me, I can't bear to look at his face! (*Ready to weep, he hurries out, up right.*)

HAPPY (*starting after him*): Where are you going?

MISS FORSYTHE: What's he so mad about?

HAPPY: Come on, girls, we'll catch up with him.

MISS FORSYTHE (*as* HAPPY *pushes her out*): Say, I don't like that temper of his!

HAPPY: He's just a little overstrung, he'll be all right!

WILLY (*off left, as* THE WOMAN *laughs*): Don't answer! Don't answer!

LETTA: Don't you want to tell your father—

HAPPY: No, that's not my father. He's just a guy. Come on, we'll catch Biff, and, honey, we're going to paint this town! Stanley, where's the check! Hey, Stanley!

(*They exit.* STANLEY *looks toward left.*)

STANLEY (*calling to* HAPPY *indignantly*): Mr. Loman! Mr. Loman!

(STANLEY *picks up a chair and follows them off. Knocking is heard off left.* THE WOMAN *enters, laughing.* WILLY *follows her. She is in a black slip, he is buttoning his shirt. Raw, sensuous music accompanies their speech.*)

WILLY: Will you stop laughing? Will you stop?

THE WOMAN: Aren't you going to answer the door? He'll wake the whole hotel.

WILLY: I'm not expecting anybody.

THE WOMAN: Whyn't you have another drink, honey, and stop being so damn self-centered?

WILLY: I'm so lonely.

THE WOMAN: You know you ruined me, Willy? From now on, whenever you come to the office, I'll see that you go right through to the buyers. No waiting at my desk any more, Willy. You ruined me.

WILLY: That's nice of you to say that.

THE WOMAN: Gee, you are self-centered! Why so sad? You are the saddest, self-centeredest soul I ever did see-saw. (*She laughs. He kisses her.*) Come on inside, drummer boy. It's silly to be dressing in the middle of the night. (*As knocking is heard.*) Aren't you going to answer the door?

WILLY: They're knocking on the wrong door.

THE WOMAN: But I felt the knocking. And he heard us talking in here. Maybe the hotel's on fire!

WILLY (*his terror rising*): It's a mistake.

THE WOMAN: Then tell him to go away!

WILLY: There's nobody there.

THE WOMAN: It's getting on my nerves, Willy. There's somebody standing out there and it's getting on my nerves!

WILLY (*pushing her away from him*): All right, stay in the bathroom here, and don't come out. I think there's a law in Massachusetts about it, so don't come out. It may be that new room clerk. He looked very mean. So don't come out. It's a mistake, there's no fire.

(*The knocking is heard again. He takes a few steps away from her, and she vanishes into the wing. The light follows him, and now he is facing* YOUNG BIFF, *who carries a suitcase.* BIFF *steps toward him. The music is gone.*)

BIFF: Why didn't you answer?

WILLY: Biff! What are you doing in Boston?

BIFF: Why didn't you answer? I've been knocking for five minutes, I called you on the phone—

WILLY: I just heard you. I was in the bathroom and had the door shut. Did anything happen home?

BIFF: Dad—I let you down.

WILLY: What do you mean?

BIFF: Dad . . .

WILLY: Biffo, what's this about? (*Putting his arm around* BIFF.) Come on, let's go downstairs and get you a malted.

BIFF: Dad, I flunked math.

WILLY: Not for the term?

BIFF: The term. I haven't got enough credits to graduate.

WILLY: You mean to say Bernard wouldn't give you the answers?

BIFF: He did, he tried, but I only got a sixty-one.

WILLY: And they wouldn't give you four points?

BIFF: Birnbaum refused absolutely. I begged him, Pop, but he won't give me those points. You gotta talk to him before they close the school. Because if he saw the kind of man you are, and you just talked to him in your way, I'm sure he'd come through for me. The class came right before practice, see, and I didn't go enough. Would you talk to him? He'd like you, Pop. You know the way you could talk.

WILLY: You're on. We'll drive right back.

BIFF: Oh, Dad, good work! I'm sure he'll change it for you!

WILLY: Go downstairs and tell the clerk I'm checkin' out. Go right down.

BIFF: Yes, sir! See, the reason he hates me, Pop—one day he was late for class so I got up at the blackboard and imitated him. I crossed my eyes and talked with a lithp.

WILLY (*laughing*): You did? The kids like it?

BIFF: They nearly died laughing!

WILLY: Yeah? What'd you do?

BIFF: The thquare root of thixthy twee is . . . (WILLY *bursts out laughing;* BIFF *joins him.*) And in the middle of it he walked in!

(WILLY *laughs and* THE WOMAN *joins in offstage.*)

WILLY (*without hesitation*): Hurry downstairs and—

BIFF: Somebody in there?

WILLY: No, that was next door.

(THE WOMAN *laughs offstage.*)

BIFF: Somebody got in your bathroom!

WILLY: No, it's the next room, there's a party—

THE WOMAN (*enters, laughing. She lisps this*): Can I come in? There's something in the bathtub, Willy, and it's moving!

(WILLY *looks at* BIFF, *who is staring open-mouthed and horrified at* THE WOMAN.)

WILLY: Ah—you better go back to your room. They must be finished painting by now. They're painting her room so I let her take a shower here. Go back, go back . . . (*He pushes her.*)

THE WOMAN (*resisting*): But I've got to get dressed Willy, I can't—

WILLY: Get out of here! Go back, go back . . . (*Suddenly striving for the ordinary.*) This is Miss Francis, Biff, she's a buyer. They're painting her room. Go back, Miss Francis, go back . . .

THE WOMAN: But my clothes, I can't go out naked in the hall!

WILLY (*pushing her offstage*): Get outa here! Go back, go back!

(BIFF *slowly sits down on his suitcase as the argument continues offstage.*)

THE WOMAN: Where's my stockings? You promised me stockings, Willy!

WILLY: I have no stockings here!

THE WOMAN: You had two boxes of size nine sheers for me, and I want them!

WILLY: Here, for God's sake, will you get outa here!

THE WOMAN (*enters holding a box of stockings*): I just hope there's nobody in the hall. That's all I hope. (*to* BIFF) Are you football or baseball?

BIFF: Football.

THE WOMAN (*angry, humiliated*): That's me too. G'night. (*She snatches her clothes from* WILLY, *and walks out.*)

WILLY (*after a pause*): Well, better get going. I want to get to the school first thing in the morning. Get my suits out of the closet. I'll get my valise. (BIFF *doesn't move.*) What's the matter? (BIFF *remains motionless, tears falling.*) She's a buyer. Buys for J. H. Simmons. She lives down the hall—they're painting. You don't imagine—(*He breaks off. After a pause.*) Now listen, pal, she's just a buyer. She sees merchandise in her room and they have to keep it looking just so . . . (*Pause. Assuming command.*) All right, get my suits. (BIFF *doesn't move.*) Now stop crying and do as I say. I gave you an order. Biff, I gave you an order! Is that what you do when I give you an order? How dare you cry! (*Putting his arm around* BIFF.) Now look, Biff, when you grow up you'll understand about these things. You mustn't—you mustn't overemphasize a thing like this. I'll see Birnbaum first thing in the morning.

BIFF: Never mind.

WILLY (*getting down beside* BIFF): Never mind! He's going to give you those points. I'll see to it.

BIFF: He wouldn't listen to you.

WILLY: He certainly will listen to me. You need those points for the U. of Virginia.

BIFF: I'm not going there.

WILLY: Heh? If I can't get him to change that mark you'll make it up in summer school. You've got all summer to—

BIFF (*his weeping breaking from him*): Dad . . .

WILLY (*infected by it*): Oh, my boy . . .

BIFF: Dad . . .

WILLY: She's nothing to me, Biff. I was lonely, I was terribly lonely.

BIFF: You—you gave her Mama's stockings! (*His tears break through and he rises to go.*)

WILLY (*grabbing for* BIFF): I gave you an order!

BIFF: Don't touch me, you—liar!

WILLY: Apologize for that!

BIFF: You fake! You phony little fake! You fake! (*Overcome, he turns quickly and weeping fully goes out with his suitcase.* WILLY *is left on the floor on his knees.*)

WILLY: I gave you an order! Biff, come back here or I'll beat you! Come back here! I'll whip you!

(STANLEY *comes quickly in from the right and stands in front of* WILLY.)

WILLY (*shouts at* STANLEY): I gave you an order . . .

STANLEY: Hey, let's pick it up, pick it up, Mr. Loman. (*He helps* WILLY *to his feet.*) Your boys left with the chippies. They said they'll see you home.

(*A second waiter watches some distance away.*)

WILLY: But we were supposed to have dinner together.

(*Music is heard,* WILLY'S *theme.*)

STANLEY: Can you make it?

WILLY: I'll—sure, I can make it. (*Suddenly concerned about his clothes.*) Do I—I look all right?

STANLEY: Sure, you look all right. (*He flicks a speck off* WILLY'S *lapel.*)

WILLY: Here—here's a dollar.

STANLEY: Oh, your son paid me. It's all right.

WILLY (*putting it in* STANLEY'S *hand*): No, take it. You're a good boy.

STANLEY: Oh, no, you don't have to . . .

WILLY: Here—here's some more, I don't need it any more. (*After a slight pause.*) Tell me—is there a seed store in the neighborhood?

STANLEY: Seeds? You mean like to plant?

(*As* WILLY *turns,* STANLEY *slips the money back into his jacket pocket.*)

WILLY: Yes. Carrots, peas . . .

STANLEY: Well, there's hardware stores on Sixth Avenue, but it may be too late now.

WILLY (*anxiously*): Oh, I'd better hurry. I've got to get some seeds. (*He starts off to the right.*) I've got to get some seeds, right away. Nothing's planted. I don't have a thing in the ground.

(WILLY *hurries out as the light goes down.* STANLEY *moves over to the right after him, watches him off. The other waiter has been staring at* WILLY.)

STANLEY (*to the waiter*): Well, whatta you looking at?

(*The waiter picks up the chairs and moves off right. Stanley takes the table and follows him. The light fades on this area. There is a long pause, the sound of the flute coming over. The light gradually rises on the kitchen, which is empty.* HAPPY *appears at the door of the house, followed by* BIFF. HAPPY *is carrying a large bunch of long-stemmed roses. He enters the kitchen, looks around for* LINDA. *Not seeing her, he turns to* BIFF, *who is just outside the house door, and makes a gesture with his hands, indicating "Not here, I guess." He looks into the living-room and freezes. Inside,* LINDA, *unseen, is seated,* WILLY'S *coat on her lap. She rises ominously and quietly and moves toward* HAPPY, *who backs up into the kitchen, afraid.*)

HAPPY: Hey, what're you doing up? (LINDA *says nothing but moves toward him implacably.*) Where's Pop? (*He keeps backing to the right, and now* LINDA *is in full view in the doorway to the living-room.*) Is he sleeping?

LINDA: Where were you?

HAPPY (*trying to laugh it off*): We met two girls, Mom, very fine types. Here, we brought you some flowers. (*Offering them to her.*) Put them in your room, Ma.

(She knocks them to the floor at BIFF's *feet. He has now come inside and closed the door behind him. She stares at* BIFF, *silent.)*

HAPPY: Now, what'd you do that for? Mom, I want you to have some flowers—

LINDA *(cutting* HAPPY *off, violently to* BIFF*)*: Don't you care whether he lives or dies?

HAPPY *(going to the stairs)*: Come upstairs, Biff.

BIFF *(with a flare of disgust, to* HAPPY*)*: Go away from me! *(to* LINDA*)* What do you mean, lives or dies? Nobody's dying around here, pal.

LINDA: Get out of my sight! Get out of here!

BIFF: I wanna see the boss.

LINDA: You're not going near him!

BIFF: Where is he? *(He moves into the living-room and* LINDA *follows.)*

LINDA *(shouting after* BIFF*)*: You invite him for dinner. He looks forward to it all day—*(*BIFF *appears in his parents' bedroom, looks around, and exits.)*—and then you desert him there. There's no stranger you'd do that to!

HAPPY: Why? He had a swell time with us. Listen, when I—*(*LINDA *comes back into the kitchen.)*—desert him I hope I don't outlive the day!

LINDA: Get out of here!

HAPPY: Now look, Mom . . .

LINDA: Did you have to go to women tonight? You and your lousy rotten whores!

*(*BIFF *re-enters the kitchen.)*

HAPPY: Mom, all we did was follow Biff around trying to cheer him up! *(To* BIFF*)* Boy, what a night you gave me!

LINDA: Get out of here, both of you, and don't come back! I don't want you tormenting him any more. Go on now, get your things together! *(to* BIFF*)* You can sleep in his apartment. *(She starts to pick up the flowers and stops herself.)* Pick up this stuff, I'm not your maid any more. Pick it up, you bum, you!

*(*HAPPY *turns his back to her in refusal.* BIFF *slowly moves over and gets down on his knees, picking up the flowers.)*

LINDA: You're a pair of animals! No one, not another living soul would have had 'the cruelty to walk out on that man in a restaurant!

BIFF *(not looking at her)*: Is that what he said?

LINDA: He didn't have to say anything. He was so humiliated he nearly limped when he came in.

HAPPY: But, Mom, he had a great time with us—

BIFF *(cutting him off violently)*: Shut up!

(Without another word, HAPPY *goes upstairs.)*

LINDA: You! You didn't even go in to see if he was all right!

BIFF *(still on the floor in front of* LINDA, *the flowers in his hand; with self-loathing)*: No. Didn't. Didn't do a damned thing. How do you like that, heh? Left him babbling in a toilet.

LINDA: You louse. You . . .

BIFF: Now you hit it on the nose! *(He gets up, throws the flowers in the wastebasket).* The scum of the earth, and you're looking at him!

LINDA: Get out of here!

BIFF: I gotta talk to the boss, Mom. Where is he?

LINDA: You're not going near him. Get out of this house!

BIFF *(with absolute assurance, determination)*: No. We're gonna have an abrupt conversation, him and me.

LINDA: You're not talking to him!

(Hammering is heard from outside the house, off right. BIFF *turns toward the noise.)*

LINDA *(suddenly pleading)*: Will you please leave him alone?

BIFF: What's he doing out there?

LINDA: He's planting the garden!

BIFF *(quietly)*: Now? Oh, my God!

*(*BIFF *moves outside,* LINDA *following. The light dies down on them and comes up on the center of the apron as* WILLY *walks into it. He is carrying a flashlight, a hoe, and a handful of seed packets. He raps the top of the hoe sharply to fix it firmly, and then moves to the left, measuring off the distance with his foot. He holds the flashlight to look at the seed packets, reading off the instructions. He is in the blue of night.)*

WILLY: Carrots . . . quarter-inch apart. Rows . . . one-foot rows. *(He measures it off.)* One foot. *(He puts down a package and measures off.)* Beets. *(He puts down another package and measures again.)* Lettuce. *(He reads the package, puts it down.)* One foot—*(He breaks off as* BEN *appears at the right and moves slowly down to him.)* What a proposition, ts, ts. Terrific, terrific. 'Cause she's suffered, Ben, the woman has suffered. You understand me? A man can't go out the way he came in, Ben, a man has got to add up to something. You can't, you can't— *(*BEN *moves toward him as though to interrupt.)* You gotta consider, now. Don't answer so quick. Remember, it's a guaranteed twenty-thousand-dollar proposition. Now look, Ben, I want you to go through the ins and outs of this thing with me. I've got nobody to talk to, Ben, and the woman has suffered, you hear me?

BEN *(standing still, considering)*: What's the proposition?

WILLY: It's twenty thousand dollars on the barrelhead. Guaranteed, gilt-edged, you understand?

BEN: You don't want to make a fool of yourself. They might not honor the policy.

WILLY: How can they dare refuse? Didn't I work like

a coolie to meet every premium on the nose? And now they don't pay off? Impossible!

BEN: It's called a cowardly thing, William.

WILLY: Why? Does it take more guts to stand here the rest of my life ringing up a zero?

BEN (*yielding*): That's a point, William. (*He moves, thinking, turns.*) And twenty thousand—that *is* something one can feel with the hand, it is there.

WILLY (*now assured, with rising power*): Oh, Ben, that's the whole beauty of it! I see it like a diamond, shining in the dark, hard and rough, that I can pick up and touch in my hand. Not like—like an appointment! This would not be another damned-fool appointment, Ben, and it changes all the aspects. Because he thinks I'm nothing, see, and so he spites me. But the funeral— (*Straightening up.*) Ben, that funeral will be massive! They'll come from Maine, Massachusetts, Vermont, New Hampshire! All the old-timers with the strange license plates—that boy will be thunder-struck, Ben, because he never realized—I am known! Rhode Island, New York, New Jersey—I am known, Ben, and he'll see it with his eyes once and for all. He'll see what I am, Ben! He's in for a shock, that boy!

BEN (*coming down to the edge of the garden*): He'll call you a coward.

WILLY (*suddenly fearful*): No, that would be terrible.

BEN: Yes. And a damned fool.

WILLY: No, no, he mustn't, I won't have that! (*He is broken and desperate.*)

BEN: He'll hate you, William.

(*The gay music of the* BOYS *is heard.*)

WILLY: Oh, Ben, how do we get back to all the great times? Used to be so full of light, and comradeship, the sleigh-riding in winter, and the ruddiness on his cheeks. And always some kind of good news coming up, always something nice coming up ahead. And never even let me carry the valises in the house, and simonizing, simonizing that little red car! Why, why can't I give him something and not have him hate me?

BEN: Let me think about it. (*He glances at his watch.*) I still have a little time. Remarkable proposition, but you've got to be sure you're not making a fool of yourself.

(BEN *drifts off upstage and goes out of sight.* BIFF *comes down from the left.*)

WILLY (*suddenly conscious of* BIFF, *turns and looks up at him, then begins picking up the packages of seeds in confusion*): Where the hell is that seed? (*Indignantly*) You can't see nothing out here! They boxed in the whole goddam neighborhood!

BIFF: There are people all around here. Don't you realize that?

WILLY: I'm busy. Don't bother me.

BIFF (*taking the hoe from* WILLY): I'm saying good-by to you, Pop. (WILLY *looks at him, silent, unable to move.*) I'm not coming back any more.

WILLY: You're not going to see Oliver tomorrow?

BIFF: I've got no appointment, Dad.

WILLY: He put his arm around you, and you've got no appointment?

BIFF: Pop, get this now, will you? Everytime I've left it's been a fight that sent me out of here. Today I realized something about myself and I tried to explain it to you and I—I think I'm just not smart enough to make any sense out of it for you. To hell with whose fault it is or anything like that. (*He takes* WILLY's *arm.*) Let's just wrap it up, heh? Come on in, we'll tell Mom. (*He gently tries to pull* WILLY *to left.*)

WILLY (*frozen, immobile, with guilt in his voice*): No, I don't want to see her.

BIFF: Come on! (*He pulls again, and* WILLY *tries to pull away.*)

WILLY (*highly nervous*): No, no, I don't want to face her.

BIFF (*tries to look into* WILLY's *face, as if to find the answer there*): Why don't you want to see her?

WILLY (*more harshly now*): Don't bother me, will you?

BIFF: What do you mean, you don't want to see her? You don't want them calling you yellow, do you? This isn't your fault; it's me, I'm a bum. Now come inside! (WILLY *strains to get away.*) Did you hear what I said to you?

(WILLY *pulls away and quickly goes by himself into the house.* BIFF *follows.*)

LINDA (*to* WILLY): Did you plant, dear?

BIFF (*at the door, to* LINDA): All right, we had it out. I'm going and I'm not writing any more.

LINDA (*going to* WILLY *in the kitchen*): I think that's the best way, dear. 'Cause there's no use drawing it out, you'll just never get along.

(WILLY *doesn't respond.*)

BIFF: People ask where I am and what I'm doing, you don't know, and you don't care. That way it'll be off your mind and you can start brightening up again. All right? That clears it, doesn't it? (WILLY *is silent, and* BIFF *goes to him.*) You gonna wish me luck, scout? (*He extends his hand.*) What do you say?

LINDA: Shake his hand, Willy.

WILLY (*turning to her, seething with hurt*): There's no necessity to mention the pen at all, y'know.

BIFF (*gently*): I've got no appointment, Dad.

WILLY (*erupting fiercely*): He put his arm around . . . ?

BIFF: Dad, you're never going to see what I am, so what's the use of arguing? If I strike oil I'll send you a check. Meantime forget I'm alive.

WILLY (to LINDA): Spite, see?

BIFF: Shake hands, Dad.

WILLY: Not my hand.

BIFF: I was hoping not to go this way.

WILLY: Well, this is the way you're going. Good-by.

(BIFF *looks at him a moment, then turns sharply and goes to the stairs.*)

WILLY (*stops him with*): May you rot in hell if you leave this house!

BIFF (*turning*): Exactly what is it that you want from me?

WILLY: I want you to know, on the train, in the mountains, in the valleys, wherever you go, that you cut down your life for spite!

BIFF: No, no.

WILLY: Spite, spite, is the word of your undoing! And when you're down and out, remember what did it. When you're rotting somewhere beside the railroad tracks, remember, and don't you dare blame it on me!

BIFF: I'm not blaming it on you!

WILLY: I won't take the rap for this, you hear?

(HAPPY *comes down the stairs and stands on the bottom step, watching.*)

BIFF: That's just what I'm telling you!

WILLY (*sinking into a chair at the table, with full accusation*): You're trying to put a knife in me—don't think I don't know what you're doing!

BIFF: All right, phony! Then let's lay it on the line. (*He whips the rubber tube out of his pocket and puts it on the table.*)

HAPPY: You crazy—

LINDA: Biff! (*She moves to grab the hose, but BIFF holds it down with his hand.*)

BIFF: Leave it there! Don't move it!

WILLY (*not looking at it*): What is that?

BIFF: You know goddam well what that is.

WILLY (*caged, wanting to escape*): I never saw that.

BIFF: You saw it. The mice didn't bring it into the cellar! What is this supposed to do, make a hero out of you? This supposed to make me sorry for you?

WILLY: Never heard of it.

BIFF: There'll be no pity for you, you hear it? No pity!

WILLY (*to LINDA*): You hear the spite!

BIFF: No, you're going to hear the truth—what you are and what I am!

LINDA: Stop it!

WILLY: Spite!

HAPPY (*coming down toward BIFF*): You cut it now!

BIFF (*to HAPPY*): The man don't know who we are! The man is gonna know! (*to WILLY*) We never told the truth for ten minutes in this house!

HAPPY: We always told the truth!

BIFF (*turning on him*): You big blow, are you the assis-

tant buyer? You're one of the two assistants to the assistant, aren't you?

HAPPY: Well, I'm practically—

BIFF: You're practically full of it! We all are! And I'm through with it. (*to WILLY*) Now hear this, Willy, this is me.

WILLY: I know you!

BIFF: You know why I had no address for three months? I stole a suit in Kansas City and I was in jail. (*to LINDA, who is sobbing*) Stop crying. I'm through with it.

(LINDA *turns away from them, her hands covering her face.*)

WILLY: I suppose that's my fault!

BIFF: I stole myself out of every good job since high school!

WILLY: And whose fault is that?

BIFF: And I never got anywhere because you blew me so full of hot air I could never stand taking orders from anybody! That's whose fault it is!

WILLY: I hear that!

LINDA: Don't, Biff!

BIFF: It's goddam time you heard that! I had to be boss big shot in two weeks, and I'm through with it!

WILLY: Then hang yourself! For spite, hang yourself!

BIFF: No! Nobody's hanging himself, Willy! I ran down eleven flights with a pen in my hand today. And suddenly I stopped, you hear me? And in the middle of that office building, do you hear this? I stopped in the middle of that building and I saw—the sky. I saw the things that I love in this world. The work and the food and time to sit and smoke. And I looked at the pen and said to myself, what the hell am I grabbing this for? Why am I trying to become what I don't want to be? What am I doing in an office, making a contemptuous, begging fool of myself, when all I want is out there, waiting for me the minute I say I know who I am! Why can't I say that, Willy? (*He tries to make WILLY face him, but WILLY pulls away and moves to the left.*)

WILLY (*with hatred, threateningly*): The door of your life is wide open!

BIFF: Pop! I'm a dime a dozen, and so are you!

WILLY (*turning on him now in an uncontrolled outburst*): I am not a dime a dozen! I am Willy Loman and you are Biff Loman!

(BIFF *starts for WILLY, but is blocked by HAPPY. In his fury, BIFF seems on the verge of attacking his father.*)

BIFF: I am not a leader of men, Willy, and neither are you. You were never anything but a hard-working drummer who landed in the ash can like all the rest of them! I'm one dollar an hour, Willy! I tried seven states and couldn't raise it. A buck an hour! Do you gather my meaning? I'm not bringing home any prizes any more, and you're going to stop waiting for me to bring them home!

WILLY (*directly to* BIFF): You vengeful, spiteful mut!

(BIFF *breaks from* HAPPY. WILLY, *in fright, starts up the stairs.* BIFF *grabs him.*)

BIFF (*at the peak of his fury*): Pop, I'm nothing! I'm nothing, Pop. Can't you understand that? There's no spite in it any more. I'm just what I am, that's all.

(BIFF'*s fury has spent itself, and he breaks down, sobbing, holding on to* WILLY, *who dumbly fumbles for* BIFF'*s face.*)

WILLY (*astonished*): What're you doing? What're you doing? (*to* LINDA) Why is he crying?

BIFF (*crying, broken*): Will you let me go, for Christ's sake? Will you take that phony dream and burn it before something happens? (*Struggling to contain himself, he pulls away and moves to the stairs.*) I'll go in the morning. Put him—put him to bed. (*Exhausted,* BIFF *moves up the stairs to his room.*)

WILLY (*after a long pause, astonished, elevated*): Isn't that—isn't that remarkable? Biff—he likes me!

LINDA: He loves you, Willy!

HAPPY (*deeply moved*): Always did, Pop.

WILLY: Oh, Biff! (*Staring wildly.*) He cried! Cried to me. (*He is choking with his love, and now cries out his promise.*) That boy—that boy is going to be magnificent!

(BEN *appears in the light just outside the kitchen.*)

BEN: Yes, outstanding, with twenty thousand behind him.

LINDA (*sensing the racing of his mind, fearfully, carefully*): Now come to bed, Willy. It's all settled now.

WILLY (*finding it difficult not to rush out of the house*): Yes, we'll sleep. Come on. Go to sleep, Hap.

BEN: And it does take a great kind of a man to crack the jungle.

(*In accents of dread,* BEN'*s idyllic music starts up.*)

HAPPY (*his arm around* LINDA): I'm getting married, Pop, don't forget it. I'm changing everything. I'm gonna run that department before the year is up. You'll see, Mom. (*He kisses her.*)

BEN: The jungle is dark but full of diamonds, Willy.

(WILLY *turns, moves, listening to* BEN.)

LINDA: Be good. You're both good boys, just act that way, that's all.

HAPPY: 'Night, Pop. (*He goes upstairs.*)

LINDA (*to* WILLY): Come, dear.

BEN (*with greater force*): One must go in to fetch a diamond out.

WILLY (*to* LINDA, *as he moves slowly along the edge of the kitchen, toward the door*): I just want to get settled down, Linda. Let me sit alone for a little.

LINDA (*almost uttering her fear*): I want you upstairs.

WILLY (*taking her in his arms*): In a few minutes, Linda. I couldn't sleep right now. Go on, you look awful tired. (*He kisses her.*)

BEN: Not like an appointment at all. A diamond is rough and hard to the touch.

WILLY: Go on now. I'll be right up.

LINDA: I think this is the only way, Willy.

WILLY: Sure, it's the best thing.

BEN: Best thing!

WILLY: The only way. Everything is gonna be—go on, kid, go to bed. You look so tired.

LINDA: Come right up.

WILLY: Two minutes.

(LINDA *goes into the living-room, then reappears in her bedroom.* WILLY *moves just outside the kitchen door.*)

WILLY: Loves me. (*Wonderingly.*) Always loved me. Isn't that a remarkable thing? Ben, he'll worship me for it!

BEN (*with promise*): It's dark there, but full of diamonds.

WILLY: Can you imagine that magnificence with twenty thousand dollars in his pocket?

LINDA (*calling from her room*): Willy! Come up!

WILLY (*calling into the kitchen*): Yes! Yes. Coming! It's very smart, you realize that, don't you sweetheart? Even Ben sees it. I gotta go, baby. 'By! 'By! (*Going over to* BEN, *almost dancing*) Imagine? When the mail comes he'll be ahead of Bernard again!

BEN: A perfect proposition all around.

WILLY: Did you see how he cried to me? Oh, if I could kiss him, Ben!

BEN: Time, William, time!

WILLY: Oh, Ben, I always knew one way or another we were gonna make it, Biff and I!

BEN (*looking at his watch*): The boat. We'll be late. (*He moves slowly off into the darkness.*)

WILLY (*elegiacally, turning to the house*): Now when you kick off, boy, I want a seventy-yard boot, and get right down the field under the ball, and when you hit, hit low and hit hard, because it's important, boy. (*He swings around and faces the audience.*) There's all kinds of important people in the stands, and the first thing you know . . . (*Suddenly realizing he is alone.*) Ben! Ben, where do I . . . ? (*He makes a sudden movement of search.*) Ben, how do I . . . ?

LINDA (*calling*): Willy, you coming up?

WILLY (*uttering a gasp of fear, whirling about as if to quiet her*): Sh! (*He turns around as if to find his way; sounds, faces, voices, seem to be swarming in upon him and he flicks at them, crying.*) Sh! Sh! (*Suddenly *music, faint and high, stops him. It rises in intensity, almost to an unbearable scream. He goes up and down on his toes, and rushes off around the house.)* Shhh!

LINDA: Willy?

(There is no answer. LINDA *waits.* BIFF *gets up off his bed. He is still in his clothes.* HAPPY *sits up.* BIFF *stands listening.)*

LINDA *(with real fear)*: Willy, answer me! Willy!

(There is the sound of a car starting and moving away at full speed.)

LINDA: No!

BIFF *(rushing down the stairs)*: Pop!

(As the car speeds off, the music crashes down in a frenzy of sound, which becomes the soft pulsation of a single cello string. BIFF *slowly returns to his bedroom. He and* HAPPY *gravely don their jackets.* LINDA *slowly walks out of her room. The music has developed into a dead march. The leaves of day are appearing over everything.* CHARLEY *and* BERNARD, *somberly dressed, appear and knock on the kitchen door.* BIFF *and* HAPPY *slowly descend the stairs to the kitchen as* CHARLEY *and* BERNARD *enter. All stop a moment when* LINDA, *in clothes of mourning, bearing a little bunch of roses, comes through the draped doorway into the kitchen. She goes to* CHARLEY *and takes his arm. Now all move toward the audience, through the wall-line of the kitchen. At the limit of the apron,* LINDA *lays down the flowers, kneels, and sits back on her heels. All stare down at the grave.)*

REQUIEM

CHARLEY: It's getting dark, Linda.

*(*LINDA *doesn't react. She stares at the grave.)*

BIFF: How about it, Mom? Better get some rest, heh? They'll be closing the gate soon.

*(*LINDA *makes no move. Pause.)*

HAPPY *(deeply angered)*: He had no right to do that. There was no necessity for it. We would've helped him.

CHARLEY *(grunting)*: Hmmm.

BIFF: Come along, Mom.

LINDA: Why didn't anybody come?

CHARLEY: It was a very nice funeral.

LINDA: But where are all the people he knew? Maybe they blame him.

CHARLEY: Naa. It's a rough world, Linda. They wouldn't blame him.

LINDA: I can't understand it. At this time especially. First time in thirty-five years we were just about free and clear. He only needed a little salary. He was even finished with the dentist.

CHARLEY: No man only needs a little salary.

LINDA: I can't understand it.

BIFF: There were a lot of nice days. When he'd come home from a trip; or on Sundays, making the stoop; finishing the cellar; putting on the new porch; when he built the extra bathroom; and put up the garage. You know something, Charley, there's more of him in that front stoop than in all the sales he ever made.

CHARLEY: Yeah. He was a happy man with a batch of cement.

LINDA: He was so wonderful with his hands.

BIFF: He had the wrong dreams. All, all, wrong.

HAPPY *(almost ready to fight* BIFF*)*: Don't say that!

BIFF: He never knew who he was.

CHARLEY *(stopping* HAPPY*'s movement and reply. To* BIFF*)*: Nobody dast blame this man. You don't understand: Willy was a salesman. And for a salesman, there is no rock bottom to the life. He don't put a bolt to a nut, he don't tell you the law or give you medicine. He's a man way out there in the blue, riding on a smile and a shoeshine. And when they start not smiling back—that's an earthquake. And then you get yourself a couple of spots on your hat, and you're finished. Nobody dast blame this man. A salesman is got to dream, boy. It comes with the territory.

BIFF: Charley, the man didn't know who he was.

HAPPY *(infuriated)*: Don't say that!

BIFF: Why don't you come with me, Happy?

HAPPY: I'm not licked that easily. I'm staying right in this city and I'm gonna beat this racket! *(He looks at* BIFF, *his chin set.)* The Loman Brothers!

BIFF: I know who I am, kid,

HAPPY: All right, boy. I'm gonna show you and everybody else that Willy Loman did not die in vain. He had a good dream. It's the only dream you can have—to come out number-one man. He fought it out here, and this is where I'm gonna win it for him.

BIFF *(with a hopeless glance at* HAPPY, *bends toward his mother)*: Let's go, Mom.

LINDA: I'll be with you in a minute. Go on, Charley. *(He hesitates.)* I want to, just for a minute. I never had a chance to say good-by.

*(*CHARLEY *moves away, followed by* HAPPY. BIFF *remains a slight distance up and left of* LINDA. *She sits there, summoning herself. The flute begins, not far away, playing behind her speech.)*

LINDA: Forgive me, dear, I can't cry. I don't know what it is, but I can't cry. I don't understand it. Why did you ever do that? Help me, Willy, I can't cry. It seems to me that you're just on another trip. I keep expecting you. Willy, dear, I can't cry. Why did you do it? I search and search and I search, and I can't understand it, Willy. I made the last payment on the house today. Today, dear. And there'll be nobody home. *(A sob rises in her throat.)* We're free and clear. *(Sobbing more fully, released.)* We're free. *(BIFF comes slowly toward her.)* We're free . . . We're free . . .

(BIFF lifts her to her feet and moves out up right with her in his arms. LINDA sobs quietly. BERNARD and CHARLEY come together and follow them, followed by HAPPY. *Only the music of the flute is left on the darkening stage as over the house the hard towers of the apartment buildings rise into sharp focus, and*

THE CURTAIN FALLS

Figure 1. Willy (George C. Scott) leans against the refrigerator shortly after returning home from his trip to Yonkers at the opening of the Circle in the Square production of *Death of a Salesman,* directed by George C. Scott, New York, 1975. (Photograph: Inge Morath, Magnum Photos, Inc.)

Figure 2. Willy (George C. Scott), during the enactment of a pleasant memory, tells Young Happy (Harvey Keitel, *left*) and Young Biff (James Farentino, *right*) to help their mother Linda (Teresa Wright) carry up the wash in the Circle in the Square production of *Death of a Salesman*, directed by George C. Scott, New York, 1975. (Photograph: Inge Morath, Magnum Photos, Inc.)

Figure 3. Willy (George C. Scott), during the enactment of a painful memory, tries to explain away the presence of The Woman (Patricia Quinn) with whom he has been discovered by Biff (James Farentino) in the Circle in the Square production of *Death of a Salesman*, directed by George C. Scott, New York, 1975. (Photograph: Inge Morath, Magnum Photos, Inc.)

Staging of *Death of a Salesman*

REVIEW OF THE CIRCLE IN THE SQUARE
PRODUCTION, 1975, BY WALTER KERR

Attention has been paid. In reviving Arthur Miller's "Death of a Salesman" at Circle in the Square, and in taking on the part of the self-doomed but perpetually incurable Willy Loman himself, director-star George C. Scott has first of all behaved not as director or as star but as servant of a play, a piece of work in the hand. Furthermore, he has not behaved as though he were serving an old play, a familiar play, a play whose ancient echoes were so overwhelming that a kind of fearful obeisance was the best that could be offered it. He has chosen not to remember it, or to remember other people's remembrances of it, but to pay attention to its undeniably powerful, still most affecting, but extraordinarily ambiguous voice. Not what Elia Kazan once heard in it, not what Lee J. Cobb once heard in it, perceptive and just as they may have been. But, with one sharp ear cocked, what is it saying *now*?

This is not simply a matter of muting the lines we recall all too well. Mr. Scott has a fascinating trick—it is more than a trick, it is a heart-rending trait of character—of burying a phrase like "He's liked, but he's not well liked" by making it part of a compulsive contradiction, hurling it so hot on the heels of the contrary line preceding it that you must take the two in balance and believe neither. Listen to him, without transition, pause, or apparent dishonesty, breathlessly bracketing "I'm very well liked, the only thing is people don't take to me" and making both sense and agony of it. Or, glorying in his talent for regaling his New England buyers. "I'm full of jokes, I tell too many jokes," with the savagery of the latter seeming to bite off his own braggart head.

There is much savagery in Mr. Scott's performance—he comes on like the last bald American eagle dead set for a final reckoning—but it is more than the quite normal savagery of his customary stage deportment, it is a savagery uncovered in the near-manic, electrifying shifts of mood, boast and bile back to back, of Arthur Miller's play. And it completely disrupts my *own* (perhaps faulty) memory of the original production, its original meaning. I remember assuming that Willy Loman had once been a successful salesman, had once done well by his wife and boys, had once made "a smile and a shoeshine" work for him. That the dream (the American dream of success by back-slapping and coming in Number One on all sales charts?) had eventually collapsed of its own essential vacuousness was the pathos of the moment, but the pathos of the moment was a somewhat recent discovery, a realization, not a permanence recognized from the beginning.

With Mr. Scott it is certainly otherwise. Quite apart from absorbing the catch-phrases by which we identify the play into a relentless, run-on "yes-no" that is Willy Loman's never-ending private torment, Mr. Scott makes us hear lines we seem never to have heard before. He is speaking to his outrageously successful brother, Ben, despoiler of the Gold Coast, reaper of fabulous Alaskan harvests. Ben is older than Willie, got started sooner than Willy. Ben even remembers their father, a man who played a flute as he carted the family from state to state across the American landscape.

But the father died before Willy could quite know him, or know himself in relation to any father. "I still feel a little *temporary* about myself," he says, reflectively, with unconscious grief, to the solid, if almost mythical, brother who never felt temporary about anything. Mr. Scott's Willy always had to compensate, to inflate his indeterminate place in the scheme of things, to substitute for his sickened hollowness an equally hollow image in which only others—only his adoring sons—could possibly believe. He has been a shell from the beginning, filling himself with borrowed life, life that could be borrowed from successful salesmen he admired, life that might be borrowed—on a kind of promissory note—from the coming success of his two boys.

This becomes stunningly clear in a scene almost impossible to contemplate, given Mr. Scott's intensely mesmerizing presence. Willy is to recall a day, early in his career, when he listened to a salesman, an 84-year-old master-drummer, in his room at the Parker House, making an ample, indestructible living by doing nothing more than reach for a phone and run up orders by the dozen. He must make us believe that this one eavesdropping image of success has given him his goal in life, a self-image strong enough to sustain him. And he must do it while the man he is talking to, an employer about to fire him now that he is an exhausted 62, is paying no heed at all, incapable of being moved by anything he says.

To begin with, it is unthinkable that anyone within Mr. Scott's feverish, concentrated range should not listen to him. And if we can bring ourselves to believe that the man is not listening, then why should we listen? The essence of the sequence is the deaf dismissal of Mr. Scott's dreams. And yet it happens both ways, creating stage magic of the highest order. Our own absorption in Mr. Scott's passionate recollection of things past is total: we see everything he sees, the room's furnishings, the drummer's posture, the waves of power reaching out to envelope Mr. Scott. At the same time the actor is able to distance himself from his indifferent employer, to isolate himself with *us*, to the point where we hear what no one else can hear, share what no one else can share. The doubleness is devastating; I still don't believe it.

And, at the same time Mr. Scott is alternately drawing his teeth across his lower lip and lifting the corners of his mouth in a mirthless but expansive smile, abruptly shifting from snarl to endearment, Teresa Wright, as his wife, is creating the perfect complement to his instability. Face severely in repose, voice rarely raised, she is both patient and rock-hard in her steadfast coping with home truths. She is not deceived, not even by love. But she does love. And her love has the toughness that will tolerate neither lies nor laments from her failed children.

Their father is an ordinary man; they are to find no blame in him for that. Ordinary men become exhausted as surely as great men do; the exhaustion is just as real, no guilt is to be lodged against it. She has heard her husband letting himself in by night beneath the naked bulb over the back door, sigh as he dropped his satchels, greet her encouragingly, explosively betray his own chagrin in sudden envy of men who have "accomplished something." She knows he has accomplished nothing, hadn't an identity to do it with. The boys are not to say so. "Attention must be paid" to ordinary men, exhausted or not. There is no rhetoric in Miss Wright as she speaks the words, no lumpy quasi-poetry. She is speaking a harsh truth, harshly. Let the boys be "bums," if that is what they are to be. And let them honor their father, who would have honored them if he had only known how. If we are to shed tears, and we do, they fall on granite.

Between Mr. Scott and the superb Miss Wright, "Death of a Salesman" becomes a play of persons, not of social prophecy or some archetypal proclamation of an already failed American myth. It is too richly contradictory, too intimately detailed, too ambiguously loving and desperate, for mere abstraction; its weaknesses and its toughnesses are tangible, not distantly theoretical. If the work now seems tantalizing in its implications, the implications are more nearly those that endlessly badgered O'Neill: it is illusions that destroy. "We never told the truth for one minute in this house" is a cry near the end in a house that cannot stand; to the last, Willy Loman is imagining that, somehow or other, the $20,000 in insurance money that will come with his death will guarantee the successful future of his elder, equally emptied-out son. Death goes right on dreaming.

Mr. Miller's play holds, contains its own complex meaning that is beyond facile ideological analysis, lives and moves and has its being in the mercury of its ravaged, hoping, falsely jovial, forgiving, unforgiving figures. At the preview I saw, the evening's momentum was interrupted at least once, possibly due to an errant light cue; and because the act-endings are insufficiently italicized, I think the production might profit from having a single intermission rather than two, though that may be demanding something too much of Mr. Scott's unhusbanded energies. But the whole is handsomely acted—James Farentino, Harvey Keitel, and Chuck Patterson are particularly fine— and Mr. Scott's staging is as restlessly right as his performance; he is endlessly on his feet though he knows that his feet will betray him before they can ever see him home.

TENNESSEE WILLIAMS

1911–1983

Despite his first name, a nickname he adopted during his college days, Williams was born in Mississippi and lived there until 1918, when his father, a travelling salesman, was promoted to an office in St. Louis. That move to the midwest, according to Williams, was a "tragic" experience. He was mocked for his southern accent, he was pained by the heightened awareness of being poor, and thus he never adjusted to life in St. Louis. Looking back on his childhood there, Williams once described it as "the beginning of the social consciousness which I think has marked most of my writing." Williams lived in St. Louis until his mid-twenties, and those years with his family—with his tyrannical father, his overprotective mother, and his mentally withdrawn sister—evidently gave rise to the acute psychological awareness that has also marked virtually all of his writing. Those years with his family in St. Louis certainly must have given rise to his abiding concern with the painful experience of the outsider: the artist, the dreamer, the physically crippled, the mentally disturbed, and the sexually driven. As a child, he had been afflicted by diptheria, which for many years left him with paralyzed legs and weakened kidneys. As a teenager, he suffered the taunts of his father who repeatedly called him "Miss Nancy" because of his literary inclinations. In his mid-twenties, he worked himself into a nervous and physical breakdown, selling shoes during the day at his father's insistence and writing plays late into the night to escape his miserable existence. During this time he also witnessed the permanent mental breakdown of his introverted sister, with whom he had been close throughout his years in Mississippi and St. Louis.

These painful experiences of his childhood and youth clearly provided Williams with material for his first major stage success, *The Glass Menagerie* (1944), "a memory play," whose protagonist-narrator, Tom Wingfield is clearly modelled on Williams himself, much as Laura Wingfield is modelled on Williams' sister Rose. Tom, for example, is portrayed as a poet and dreamer, yearning for escape from the suffocating world of business, while Laura is depicted as a pathologically shy young woman who lives in a private world of glass animals and old phonograph records. Indeed, it might well be said that Williams has reflected the personality and disposition of his father, or his mother, or his sister, or himself in virtually all his work. His father's personality is echoed in the cynically practical and coarsely domineering men who often figure prominently in his plays, such as Stanley Kowalski of *A Streetcar Named Desire* (1947) or Big Daddy in *Cat on a Hot Tin Roof* (1955). His mother is echoed in the long-suffering women who patiently endure the afflictions of being married to these domineering characters, such as Stella Kowalski or Big Mama. His sister is echoed in psychologically fragile women who have retreated from life, such as Blanche, a faded southern "gentlewoman," who clings desperately to the memory of her lost plantation in *A Streetcar Named Desire,* or Alma, the virginal spinster in *Summer and Smoke* (1948), or Hannah Jelkes, the "ethereal, almost ghostly" figure in *The Night of the Iguana* (1961). And Williams's homosexual self, a self he did not acknowledge publicly for many years, is echoed in the relationship between Brick and Skipper in *Cat on a Hot Tin Roof*. Indeed, Williams has echoed himself in all his artists, and poets, and dreamers—men and women characters alike—who suffer from the brutality of the coarsely practical worlds they inhabit.

But Williams by no means limited himself to characters modeled on his own family, as is evident simply from all the lusty and vigorous women who figure in his plays, such as Serafina in *The Rose Tattoo* (1950), or Maxine Faulk in *The Night of the Iguana,* or Maggie in *Cat on a Hot Tin Roof*. Indeed, it would be mistaken to regard Williams as a strictly autobiographical dramatist, for he repeatedly transformed his personal experience so that his characters, while echoing aspects of his family, are by no means exactly like them at all. And the aspects that Williams chose to echo are occasioned by his persistent concern with the experience of the outsider in modern society, and with the implications of that experience as it is manifest in human loneliness, in the inability of human beings to communicate with one another, and in the irrepressible need to create illusions through which they can escape from the loneliness and painfulness of their existence.

In dramatizing these aspects of experience, Williams was never content to settle for a strictly realistic method of presentation. In his "Production Notes" to *The Glass Menagerie,* for example, he attacked "the straight realistic play with its genuine frigidaire and authentic ice-cubes" by comparing it to a mere "photographic likeness," which he considered inadequate to convey the truth of human experience. To bring the audience closer to the truth, Williams argued in favor of "expressionism and all other unconventional techniques in drama." In *The Glass Menagerie* he relied heavily on suggestive music, lighting, and pantomime to evoke the memories of Tom Wingfield. His notes to the play reveal that he intended even to convey comments on Tom's staged memories through the device of projecting images or phrases on a screen—a device from the epic theater of Brecht. Although Williams agreed to omitting the screen device in the original production of the play, he has persisted in using other techniques of expressionistic theater to evoke the mood and quality of his characters' experience. In his "Notes for the Designer" at the beginning of *Cat on a Hot Tin Roof,* Williams clearly blends realistic and expressionistic approaches by describing the stage furniture in meticulous detail and then concluding with the direction that "the walls below the ceiling should dissolve mysteriously into air." He even turns the furniture into a form of symbolic statement by noting that Brick's "*huge* console combination of radio-phonograph (hi-fi with three speakers) TV set *and* liquor cabinet . . . is a very complete and compact little shrine to virtually all the comforts and illusions behind which we hide from such things as the characters in the play are faced with."

The entire set for *Cat on a Hot Tin Roof*—the bedroom of Brick and Maggie—is a richly symbolic location, for the "big double bed" that it contains tangibly reflects the frustrating relationship of Maggie and Brick, and the bedroom as a whole evokes the problematic relationship of Skipper and Brick through the memories it contains of its original owners, "a pair of old bachelors who shared this room all their lives together." In fact, the image of the bedroom and all that it begets—or fails to beget—is a central concern for everyone in the play, for Big

Daddy and Big Mama, for Gooper and Mae alike. It is thus highly appropriate that all the struggles within the family take place within this haunting room.

Despite its frankly suggestive set, when the play opened, the critic Walter Kerr called it "a beautifully written, perfectly directed, stunningly acted play of evasion: evasion on the part of its principal character, evasion perhaps on the part of its playwright." He was referring, of course, to the play's persistent concern with the relationship of Brick and Skipper, the exact nature of which is never clearly established. Williams knew that the relationship would raise questions as to whether or not it was homosexual, and thus he took the unusual step of inserting an interpretative comment into the middle of the play:

> The thing they're discussing, timidly and painfully on the side of BIG DADDY, fiercely, violently on BRICK's side, is the inadmissible thing that SKIPPER died to disavow between them. The fact that if it existed it had to be disavowed to "keep face" in the world they lived in, may be at the heart of the "mendacity" that BRICK drinks to kill his disgust with. It may be the root of his collapse. Or maybe it is only a single manifestation of it, not even the most important. The bird that I hope to catch in the net of this play is not the solution of one man's pyschological problem.

In making such remarks, Williams, still putting the matter into the conditional, raises the idea that the problem is not what kind of relationship Brick and Skipper had, but their need, created by "the world they lived in" to "keep face." The more important issue, both for Brick and for Williams, is "mendacity." Everyone in the play is guilty of mendacity—of lying, betrayal, and manipulation. And the lies persist only because Big Daddy and Big Mama want to believe them, a condition that suggests the root of public lying is the act of lying to oneself. Williams' concern with the wilful perpetuation of illusions is reflected also in the structure of the play, for the first act centers on Maggie trying to get Brick to look at her, while the second act reaches its climax with Big Daddy forcing Brick to look at himself, and the third act derives its power from Brick's final refusal to let Maggie sustain any illusions about him.

Because all the characters in the play are so determinedly bent on their ways, yet so undone by the ways they have chosen for themselves, they require very complex performances from actors and actresses—performances that convey both their wilfulness and their vulnerability. These qualities were evidently achieved by the American Shakespeare Theater when it revived the play in 1974, as can be seen from a review of that production reprinted following the text. Photographs from that production convey the sensuality and the helplessness Eizabeth Ashley brought to the role of Maggie (see Figure 1), much as they reveal the obstinacy and the air of defeat Keir Dullea gave to the role of Brick (see Figures 1 and 2). They also show the blustery power of Fred Gwynne in the role of Big Daddy (see Figures 3 and 4). Although weakened by disease, that power is still seen in the play as being great enough to hobble virtually everyone in his world.

CAT ON A HOT TIN ROOF

BY TENNESSEE WILLIAMS

CHARACTERS

MARGARET

BRICK

MAE, *sometimes called* SISTER WOMAN

BIG MAMA

DIXIE, *a little girl*

BIG DADDY

REVEREND TOOKER

GOOPER, *sometimes called* BROTHER MAN

DOCTOR BAUGH, *pronounced "Baw"*

LACEY, *a Negro servant*

SOOKEY, *another*

CHILDREN

NOTES FOR THE DESIGNER

The set is the bed-sitting room of a plantation home in the Mississippi Delta. It is along an upstairs gallery which probably runs around the entire house; it has two pairs of very wide doors opening onto the gallery, showing white balustrades against a fair summer sky that fades into dusk and night during the course of the play, which occupies precisely the time of its performance, excepting, of course, the fifteen minutes of intermission.

Perhaps the style of the room is not what you would expect in the home of the Delta's biggest cotton-planter. It is Victorian with a touch of the Far East. It hasn't changed much since it was occupied by the original owners of the place, Jack Straw and Peter Ochello, a pair of old bachelors who shared this room all their lives together. In other words, the room must evoke some ghosts; it is gently and poetically haunted by a relationship that must have involved a tenderness which was uncommon. This may be irrelevant or unnecessary, but I once saw a reproduction of a faded photograph of the verandah of Robert Louis Stevenson's home on that Samoan Island where he spent his last years, and there was a quality of tender light on weathered wood, such as porch furniture made of bamboo and wicker, exposed to tropical suns and tropical rains, which came to mind when I thought about the set for this play, bringing also to mind the grace and comfort of light, the reassurance it gives, on a late and fair afternoon in summer, the way that no matter what, even dread of death, is gently touched and soothed by it. For the set is the background for a play that deals with human extremities of emotion, and it needs that softness behind it.

The bathroom door, showing only pale-blue tile and silver towel racks, is in one side wall; the hall door in the opposite wall. Two articles of furniture need mention: a big double bed which staging should make a functional part of the set as often as suitable, the surface of which should be slightly raked to make figures on it seen more easily; and against the wall space between the two huge double doors upstage: a monumental monstrosity peculiar to our times, a huge console combination of radio-phonograph (hi-fi with three speakers) TV set and liquor cabinet, bearing and containing many glasses and bottles, all in one piece, which is a combination of muted silver tones, and the opalescent tones of reflecting glass, a chromatic link, this thing, between the sepia (tawny gold) tones of the interior and the cool (white and blue) tones of the gallery and sky. This piece of furniture (?!), this monument, is a very complete and compact little shrine to virtually all the comforts and illusions behind which we hide from such things as the characters in the play are faced with.

The set should be far less realistic than I have so far implied in this description of it. I think the walls below the ceiling should dissolve mysteriously into air; the set should be roofed by the sky; stars and moon suggested by traces of milky pallor, as if they were observed through a telescope lens out of focus.

Anything else I can think of? Oh, yes, fanlights (transoms shaped like an open glass fan) above all the doors in the set, with panes of blue and amber, and above all, the designer should take as many pains to give the actors room to move about freely (to show their restlessness, their passion for breaking out) as if it were a set for a ballet.

An evening in summer. The action is continuous, with two intermissions.

ACT 1

(At the rise of the curtain someone is taking a shower in the bathroom, the door of which is half open. A pretty young woman, with anxious lines in her face, enters the bedroom and crosses to the bathroom door.)

MARGARET *(shouting above roar of water)*: One of those no-neck monsters hit me with a hot buttered biscuit so I have t' change!

(MARGARET's voice is both rapid and drawling. In her long speeches she has the vocal tricks of a priest delivering a liturgical chant, the lines are almost sung, always continuing a little beyond her breath so she has to gasp for another. Sometimes she intersperses the lines with a little wordless singing, such as "da-da-daaa!")

(Water turns off and BRICK calls out to her, but is still unseen. A tone of politely feigned interest, masking indifference, or worse, is characteristic of his speech with MARGARET.)

BRICK: Wha'd you say, Maggie? Water was on s' loud I couldn't hearya. . . .

MARGARET: Well, I!—just remarked that!—one of th' no-neck monsters messed up m' lovely lace dress so I got t'—cha-a-ange. . . . (She opens and kicks shut drawers of the dresser.)

BRICK: Why d'ya call Gooper's kiddies no-neck monsters?

MARGARET: Because they've got no necks! Isn't that a good enough reason?

BRICK: Don't they have any necks?

MARGARET: None visible. Their fat little heads are set on their fat little bodies without a bit of connection.

BRICK: That's too bad.

MARGARET: Yes, it's too bad because you can't wring their necks if they've got no necks to wring! Isn't that right, honey? (She steps out of her dress, stands in a slip of ivory satin and lace.) Yep, they're no-neck monsters, all no-neck people are monsters . . .

(Children shriek downstairs.)

Hear them? Hear them screaming? I don't know where their voice boxes are located since they don't have necks. I tell you I got so nervous at that table tonight I thought I would throw back my head and utter a scream you could hear across the Arkansas border an' parts of Louisiana an' Tennessee. I said to your charming sister-in-law, Mae, honey, couldn't you feed those precious little things at a separate table with an oilcloth cover? They make such a mess an' the lace cloth looks so pretty! She made enormous eyes at me and said, "Ohhh, noooooo! On Big Daddy's birthday? Why, he would never forgive me!" Well, I want you to know, Big Daddy hadn't been at the table two minutes with those five no-neck monsters slobbering and drooling over their food before he threw down his fork an' shouted, "Fo' God's sake, Gooper, why don't you put them pigs at a trough in th' kitchen?"—Well, I swear, I simply could have di-ieed!

Think of it, Brick, they've got five of them and number six is coming. They've brought the whole bunch down here like animals to display at a county fair. Why, they have those children doin' tricks all the time! "Junior, show Big Daddy how you do this, show Big Daddy how you do that, say your little piece fo' Big Daddy, Sister. Show your dimples, Sugar. Brother, show Big Daddy how you stand on your head!"—It goes on all the time, along with constant little remarks and innuendos about the fact that you and I have not produced any children, are totally childless and therefore totally useless!—Of course it's comical but it's also disgusting since it's so obvious what they're up to!

BRICK (without interest): What are they up to, Maggie?

MARGARET: Why, you know what they're up to!

BRICK (appearing): No, I don't know what they're up to.

(He stands there in the bathroom doorway drying his hair with a towel and hanging onto the towel rack because one ankle is broken, plastered and bound. He is still slim and firm as a boy. His liquor hasn't started tearing him down outside. He has the additional charm of that cool air of detachment that people have who have given up the struggle. But now and then, when disturbed, something flashes behind it, like lightning in a fair sky, which shows that at some deeper level he is far from peaceful. Perhaps in a stronger light he would show some signs of deliquescence, but the fading, still warm, light from the gallery treats him gently.)

MARGARET: I'll tell you what they're up to, boy of mine!—They're up to cutting you out of your father's estate, and—

(She freezes momentarily before her next remark. Her voice drops as if it were somehow a personally embarrassing admission.)

—Now we know that Big Daddy's dyin' of—cancer. . . .

(There are voices on the lawn below: long-drawn calls across distance. MARGARET raises her lovely bare arms and powders her armpits with a light sigh.)

(She adjusts the angle of a magnifying mirror to straighten an eyelash, then rises fretfully saying.)

There's so much light in the room it—

BRICK (softly but sharply): Do we?

MARGARET: Do we what?

BRICK: Know Big Daddy's dyin' of cancer?

MARGARET: Got the report today.

BRICK: Oh . . .

MARGARET (letting down bamboo blinds which cast long, gold-fretted shadows over the room): Yep, got th' report just now . . . it didn't surprise me, Baby. . . .

(Her voice has range, and music; sometimes it drops low as a boy's and you have a sudden image of her playing boy's games as a child.)

I recognized the symptoms soon's we got here last spring, and I'm willin' to bet you that Brother Man and his wife were pretty sure of it, too. That more than likely explains why their usual summer migration to the coolness of the Great Smokies was passed up this summer in favor of—hustlin' down here ev'ry whipstitch with their whole screamin' tribe! And why so many allusions have been made to Rainbow Hill lately. You know what Rainbow Hill is? Place that's famous for treatin' alcoholics an' dope fiends in the movies!

BRICK: I'm not in the movies.

MARGARET: No, and you don't take dope. Otherwise you're a perfect candidate for Rainbow Hill, Baby, and that's where they aim to ship you—over my dead body! Yep, over my dead body they'll ship you there, but nothing would please them better. Then Brother Man could get a-hold of the purse strings and dole out remittances to us, maybe get power of attorney and sign checks for us and cut off our credit wherever, whenever he wanted! Son-of-a-bitch! How'd you like that, Baby?—Well, you've been doin' just about ev'rything in your power to bring it about, you've just been doin' ev'rything you can think of to aid and abet them in this scheme of theirs! Quittin' work, devoting yourself to the occupation of drinkin'!—Breakin' your ankle last night on the high school athletic field: doin' what? Jumpin' hurdles? At two or three in the morning? Just fantastic! Got in the paper. *Clarksdale Register* carried a nice little item about it, human interest story about a well-known former athlete stagin' a one-man track meet on the Glorious Hill High School athletic field last night, but was slightly out of condition and didn't clear the first hurdle! Brother Man Gooper claims he exercised his influence t' keep it from goin' out over AP or UP or every goddam "P."

But, Brick? You still have one big advantage!

(During the above swift flood of words, BRICK has reclined with contrapuntal leisure on the snowy surface of the bed and has rolled over carefully on his side or belly.)

BRICK *(wryly)*: Did you *say* something, Maggie?

MARGARET: Big Daddy dotes on you, honey. And he can't stand Brother Man and Brother Man's wife, that monster of fertility, Mae. Know how I know? By little expressions that flicker over his face when that woman is holding fo'th on one of her choice topics such as—how she refused twilight sleep!—when the twins were delivered! Because she feels motherhood's an experience that a woman ought to experience fully!—in order to fully appreciate the wonder and beauty of it! HAH!—and how she made Brother Man come in an' stand beside her in the delivery room so he would not miss out on the "wonder and beauty" of it either!—producin' those no-neck monsters. . . .

(A speech of this kind would be antipathetic from almost anybody but MARGARET; she makes it oddly funny, because her eyes constantly twinkle and her voice shakes with laughter which is basically indulgent.)

—Big Daddy shares my attitude toward those

two! As for me, well—I give him a laugh now and then and he tolerates me. In fact!—I sometimes suspect that Big Daddy harbors a little unconscious "lech" fo' me. . . .

BRICK: What makes you think that Big Daddy has a lech for you, Maggie?

MARGARET: Way he always drops his eyes down my body when I'm talkin' to him, drops his eyes to my boobs and licks his old chops! Ha ha!

BRICK: That kind of talk is disgusting.

MARGARET: Did anyone ever tell you that you're an ass-aching Puritan, Brick?

I think it's mighty fine that that ole fellow, on the doorstep of death, still takes in my shape with what I think is deserved appreciation!

And you wanta know something else? Big Daddy didn't know how many little Maes and Goopers had been produced! "How many kids have you got?" he asked at the table, just like Brother Man and his wife were new acquaintances to him! Big Mama said he was jokin', but that ole boy wasn't jokin', Lord, no!

And when they infawmed him that they had five already and were turning out number six!—the news seemed to come as a sort of unpleasant surprise . . .

(Children yell below.)

Scream, monsters!

(Turns to BRICK with a sudden, gay, charming smile which fades as she notices that he is not looking at her but into fading gold space with a troubled expression.)
(It is constant rejection that makes her humor "bitchy.")

Yes, you should of been at that supper-table, Baby.

(Whenever she calls him "baby" the word is a soft caress.)

Y'know, Big Daddy, bless his ole sweet soul, he's the dearest ole thing in the world, but he does hunch over his food as if he preferred not to notice anything else. Well, Mae an' Gooper were side by side at the table, direckly across from Big Daddy, watchin' his face like hawks while they jawed an' jabbered about the cuteness an' brilliance of th' no-neck monsters!

(She giggles with a hand fluttering at her throat and her breast and her long throat arched.)
(She comes downstage and recreates the scene with voice and gesture.)

And the no-neck monsters were ranged around the table, some in high chairs and some on th' *Books of Knowledge*, all in fancy little paper caps in honor of Big Daddy's birthday, and all through dinner, well, I want you to know that Brother Man an' his partner never once, for one moment, stopped exchanging pokes an' pinches an' kicks an' signs an' signals!—Why, they were like a couple of cardsharps fleecing a sucker.—Even Big Mama, bless her ole sweet soul, she isn't th' quickest an' brightest thing in the world, she finally noticed, at last, an' said to Gooper, "Gooper, what are you an' Mae makin' all these signs at each other about?"—I swear t' goodness, I nearly choked on my chicken!

(MARGARET, *back at the dressing table, still doesn't see* BRICK. *He is watching her with a look that is not quite definable—Amused? shocked? contemptuous?—part of those and part of something else.*)

Y'know—your brother Gooper still cherishes the illusion he took a giant step up the social ladder when he married Miss Mae Flynn of the Memphis Flynns.

But I have a piece of Spanish news for Gooper. The Flynns never had a thing in this world but money and they lost that, they were nothing at all but fairly successful climbers. Of course, Mae Flynn came out in Memphis eight years before I made my debut in Nashville, but I had friends at Ward-Belmont who came from Memphis and they used to come to see me and I used to go to see them for Christmas and spring vacations, and so I know who rates an' who doesn't rate in Memphis society. Why, y'know ole Papa Flynn, he barely escaped doing time in the Federal pen for shady manipulations on th' stock market when his chain stores crashed, and as for Mae having been a cotton carnival queen, as they remind us so often, lest we forget, well, that's one honor that I don't envy her for!—Sit on a brass throne on a tacky float an' ride down Main Street, smilin', bowin', and blowin' kisses to all the trash on the street—

(*She picks out a pair of jeweled sandals and rushes to the dressing table.*)

Why, year before last, when Susan McPheeters was singled out fo' that honor, y' know what happened to her? Y'know what happened to poor little Susie McPheeters?

BRICK (*absently*): No. What happened to little Susie McPheeters?

MARGARET: Somebody spit tobacco juice in her face.

BRICK (*dreamily*): Somebody spit tobacco juice in her face?

MARGARET: That's right, some old drunk leaned out of a window in the Hotel Gayoso and yelled, "Hey, Queen, hey, hey, there, Queenie!" Poor Susie looked up and flashed him a radiant smile and he shot out a squirt of tobacco juice right in poor Susie's face.

BRICK: Well, what d'you know about that.

MARGARET (*gaily*): What do I know about it? I was there, I saw it!

BRICK (*absently*): Must have been kind of funny.

MARGARET: Susie didn't think so. Had hysterics. Screamed like a banshee. They had to stop th' parade an' remove her from her throne an' go on with—

(*She catches sight of him in the mirror, gasps slightly, wheels about to face him. Count ten.*)

—Why are you looking at me like that?

BRICK (*whistling softly, now*): Like what, Maggie?

MARGARET (*intensely, fearfully*): The way y' were lookin' at me just now, befo' I caught your eye in the mirror and you started t' whistle! I don't know how t' describe it but it froze my blood!—I've caught you lookin' at me like that so often lately. What are you thinkin' of when you look at me like that?

BRICK: I wasn't conscious of lookin' at you, Maggie.

MARGARET: Well, I was conscious of it! What were you thinkin'?

BRICK: I don't remember thinking of anything, Maggie.

MARGARET: Don't you think I know that—? Don't you—?—Think I know that—?

BRICK (*cooly*): Know *what*, Maggie?

MARGARET (*struggling for expression*): That I've gone through this—*hideous!*—*transformation*, become—*hard!* Frantic! (*Then she adds, almost tenderly.*) —*cruel!!*

That's what you've been observing in me lately. How could y' help but observe it? That's all right. I'm not—thin-skinned any more, can't afford t' be thin-skinned any more. (*She is now recovering her power.*) —But Brick? Brick?

BRICK: Did you say something?

MARGARET: I was *goin'* t' say something; that I get—lonely. Very!

BRICK: Ev'rybody gets that . . .

MARGARET: Living with someone you love can be lonelier—than living entirely *alone!*—if the one that y' love doesn't love you. . . .

(*There is a pause.* BRICK *hobbles downstage and asks, without looking at her.*)

BRICK: Would you like to live alone, Maggie?

(*Another pause: then—after she has caught a quick, hurt breath.*)

MARGARET: *No!—God!—I wouldn't!*

(*Another gasping breath. She forcibly controls what must have been an impulse to cry out. We see her deliberately, very forcibly, going all the way back to the world in which you can talk about ordinary matters.*)

Did you have a nice shower?

BRICK: Uh-huh.

MARGARET: Was the water cool?

BRICK: No.

MARGARET: But it made y' feel fresh, huh?

BRICK: Fresher. . . .

MARGARET: I know something would make y' feel *much* fresher!

BRICK: What?

MARGARET: An alcohol rub. Or cologne, a rub with cologne!

BRICK: That's good after a workout but I haven't been workin' out, Maggie.

MARGARET: You've kept in good shape, though.

BRICK (*indifferently*): You think so, Maggie?

MARGARET: I always thought drinkin' men lost their looks, but I was plainly mistaken.

BRICK (*wryly*): Why, thanks, Maggie.

MARGARET: You're the only drinkin' man I know that it never seems t' put fat on.

BRICK: I'm gettin' softer, Maggie.

MARGARET: Well, sooner or later it's bound to soften you up. It was just beginning to soften up Skipper when— (*She stops short.*) I'm sorry. I never could keep my fingers off a sore—I wish you *would* lose your looks. If you did it would make the martyrdom of Saint Maggie a little more bearable. But no such goddam luck. I actually believe you've gotten better looking since you've gone on the bottle. Yeah, a person who didn't know you would think you'd never had a tense nerve in your body or a strained muscle.

(*There are sounds of croquet on the lawn below: the click of mallets, light voices, near and distant.*)

Of course, you always had that detached quality as if you were playing a game without much concern over whether you won or lost, and not that you've lost the game, not lost but just quit playing, you have that rare sort of charm that usually only happens in very old or hopelessly sick people, the charm of the defeated.—You look so cool, so cool, so enviably cool.

REVEREND TOOKER (*off stage right*): Now looka here, boy, lemme show you how to get outa that!

MARGARET: They're playing croquet. The moon has appeared and it's white, just beginning to turn a little bit yellow. . . .

You were a wonderful lover. . . .

Such a wonderful person to go to bed with, and I think mostly because you were really indifferent to it. Isn't that right? Never had any anxiety about it, did it naturally, easily, slowly, with absolute confidence and perfect calm, more like opening a door for a lady or seating her at a table than giving expression to any longing for her. Your indifference made you wonderful at lovemaking—*strange?*—but true. . . .

REVEREND TOOKER: Oh! That's a beauty.

DOCTOR BAUGH: Yeah. I got you boxed.

MARGARET: You know, if I thought you would never, never, *never* make love to me again—I would go downstairs to the kitchen and pick out the longest and sharpest knife I could find and stick it straight into my heart, I swear that I would!

REVEREND TOOKER: Watch out, you're gonna miss it.

DOCTOR BAUGH: You just don't know me, boy!

MARGARET: But one thing I don't have is the charm of the defeated, my hat is still in the ring, and I am determined to win!

(*There is the sound of croquet mallets hitting croquet balls.*)

REVEREND TOOKER: Mmm—You're too slippery for me.

MARGARET: —What is the victory of a cat on a hot tin roof?—I wish I knew. . . .

Just staying on it, I guess, as long as she can. . . .

DOCTOR BAUGH: Jus' like an eel, boy, jus' like an eel!

(*More croquet sounds.*)

MARGARET: Later tonight I'm going to tell you I love you an' maybe by that time you'll be drunk enough to believe me. Yes, they're playing croquet. . . .

Big Daddy is dying of cancer. . . .

What were you thinking of when I caught you looking at me like that? Were you thinking of Skipper?

(BRICK *takes up his crutch, rises.*)

Oh, excuse me, forgive me, but laws of silence don't work! No, laws of silence don't work. . . .

(BRICK *crosses to the bar, takes a quick drink, and rubs his head with a towel.*)

Laws of silence don't work. . . .

When something is festering in your memory or your imagination, laws of silence don't work, it's just like shutting a door and locking it on a house on fire in hope of forgetting that the house is burning. But not facing a fire doesn't put it out. Silence about a thing just magnifies it. It grows and festers in silence, becomes malignant. . . .

(*He drops his crutch.*)

BRICK: Give me my crutch.

(*He has stopped rubbing his hair dry but still stands hanging onto the towel rack in a white towel-cloth robe.*)

MARGARET: Lean on me.

BRICK: No, just give me my crutch.

MARGARET: Lean on my shoulder.

BRICK: *I don't want to lean on your shoulder, I want my crutch!*

(This is spoken like sudden lightning.)

Are you going to give me my crutch or do I have to get down on my knees on the floor and—

MARGARET: *Here, here, take it, take it! (She has thrust the crutch at him.)*

BRICK *(hobbling out)*: Thanks . . .

MARGARET: We mustn't scream at each other, the walls in this house have ears. . . .

(He hobbles directly to liquor cabinet to get a new drink.)

—but that's the first time I've heard you raise your voice in a long time, Brick. A crack in the wall?—Of composure?
—I think that's a good sign. . . .
A sign of nerves in a player on the defensive!

(BRICK turns and smiles at her cooly over his fresh drink.)

BRICK: It just hasn't happened yet, Maggie.

MARGARET: What?

BRICK: The click I get in my head when I've had enough of this stuff to make me peaceful. . . .
Will you do me a favor?

MARGARET: Maybe I will. What favor?

BRICK: Just, just keep your voice down!

MARGARET *(in a hoarse whisper)*: I'll do you that favor, I'll speak in a whisper, if not shut up completely, if *you* will do *me* a favor and make that drink your last one till after the party.

BRICK: What party?

MARGARET: Big Daddy's birthday party.

BRICK: Is this Big Daddy's birthday?

MARGARET: You know this is Big Daddy's birthday!

BRICK: No, I don't, I forgot it.

MARGARET: Well, I remembered it for you. . . .

(They are both speaking as breathlessly as a pair of kids after a fight, drawing deep exhausted breaths and looking at each other with faraway eyes, shaking and panting together as if they had broken apart from a violent struggle.)

BRICK: Good for you, Maggie.

MARGARET: You just have to scribble a few lines on this card.

BRICK: You scribble something, Maggie.

MARGARET: It's got to be your handwriting; it's your present, I've given him my present; it's got to be your handwriting!

(The tension between them is building again, the voices becoming shrill once more.)

BRICK: I didn't get him a present.

MARGARET: I got one for you.

BRICK: All right. You write the card, then.

MARGARET: And have him know you didn't remember his birthday?

BRICK: I didn't remember his birthday.

MARGARET: You don't have to prove you didn't!

BRICK: I don't want to fool him about it.

MARGARET: Just write "Love, Brick!" for God's—

BRICK: No.

MARGARET: You've *got* to!

BRICK: I don't have to do anything I don't want to do. You keep forgetting the conditions on which I agreed to stay on living with you.

MARGARET *(out before she knows it)*: I'm not living with you. We occupy the same cage.

BRICK: You've got to remember the conditions agreed on.

SONNY *(off stage)*: Mommy, give it to me. I had it first.

MAE: Hush.

MARGARET: They're impossible conditions!

BRICK: Then why don't you—?

SONNY: I want it, I want it!

MAE: Get away!

MARGARET: HUSH! Who is out there? Is somebody at the door?

(There are footsteps in hall.)

MAE *(outside)*: May I enter a moment?

MARGARET: OH, *you!* Sure. Come in, Mae.

(MAE enters bearing aloft the bow of a young lady's archery set.)

MAE: Brick, is this thing yours?

MARGARET: Why, Sister Woman—that's my Diana Trophy. Won it at the intercollegiate archery contest on the Ole Miss campus.

MAE: It's a mighty dangerous thing to leave exposed round a house full of nawmal rid-blooded children, attracted t'weapons.

MARGARET: "Nawmal rid-blooded children attracted t'weapons" ought t'be taught to keep their hands off things that don't belong to them.

MAE: Maggie, honey, if you had children of your own you'd know how funny that is. Will you please lock this up and put the key out of reach?

MARGARET: Sister Woman, nobody is plotting the destruction of your kiddies. —Brick and I still have our special archers' license. We're goin' deer-huntin' on Moon Lake as soon as the season starts. I love to run with dogs through chilly woods, run, run leap over obstructions— *(She goes into the closet carrying the bow.)*

MAE: How's the injured ankle, Brick?

BRICK: Doesn't hurt. Just itches.

MAE: Oh, my! Brick—Brick, you should've been downstairs after supper! Kiddies put on a show. Polly played the piano, Buster an' Sonny drums, an' then they turned out the lights an' Dixie an' Trixie puhfawmed a toe dance in fairy costume with *spahklus!* Big Daddy just beamed! He just beamed!

MARGARET *(from the closet with a sharp laugh):* Oh, I bet. It breaks my heart that we missed it! *(She reenters.)* But Mae? Why did y'give dawgs' names to all your kiddies?

MAE: *Dogs'* names?

MARGARET *(sweetly):* Dixie, Trixie, Buster, Sonny, Polly!—Sounds like four dogs and a parrot . . .

MAE: Maggie?

(MARGARET turns with a smile.)

Why are you so catty?

MARGARET: Cause I'm a cat! But why can't *you* take a joke, Sister Woman?

MAE: Nothin' pleases me more than a joke that's funny. You know the real names of our kiddies. Buster's real name is Robert. Sonny's real name is Saunders. Trixie's real name is Marlene and Dixie's—

(GOOPER downstairs calls for her. "Hey, Mae! Sister Woman, intermission is over!"—she rushes to door, saying.)

Intermission is over! See ya later!

MARGARET: I wonder what Dixie's real name is?

BRICK: Maggie, being catty doesn't help things any . . .

MARGARET: I know! *WHY!*—Am I so catty?—Cause I'm consumed with envy an' eaten up with longing?—Brick, I'm going to lay out your beautiful Shantung silk suit from Rome and one of your monogrammed silk shirts. I'll put your cuff links in it, those lovely star sapphires I get you to wear so rarely. . . .

BRICK: I can't get trousers on over this plaster cast.

MARGARET: Yes, you can, I'll help you.

BRICK: I'm not going to get dressed, Maggie.

MARGARET: Will you just put on a pair of white silk pajamas?

BRICK: Yes, I'll do that, Maggie.

MARGARET: *Thank* you, thank you so *much!*

BRICK: Don't mention it.

MARGARET: *Oh, Brick!* How long does it have t' go on? This punishment? Haven't I done time enough, haven't I served my term, can't I apply for a—pardon?

BRICK: Maggie, you're spoiling my liquor. Lately your voice always sounds like you'd been running upstairs to warn somebody that the house was on fire!

MARGARET: Well, no wonder, no wonder. Y'know what I feel like, Brick?
    I feel all the time like a cat on a hot tin roof!

BRICK: Then jump off the roof, jump off it, cats can jump off roofs and land on their four feet uninjured!

MARGARET: Oh, yes!

BRICK: Do it!—fo' God's sake, do it . . .

MARGARET: Do what?

BRICK: Take a lover!

MARGARET: I can't see a man but you! Even with my eyes closed, I just see you! Why don't you get ugly, Brick, why don't you please get fat or ugly or something so I could stand it? *(She rushes to hall door, opens it, listens.)* The concert is still going on! Bravo, no-necks, bravo! *(She slams and locks door fiercely.)*

BRICK: What did you lock the door for?

MARGARET: To give us a little privacy for a while.

BRICK: You know better, Maggie.

MARGARET: No, I don't know better. . . .

(She rushes to gallery doors, draws the rose-silk drapes across them.)

BRICK: Don't make a fool of yourself.

MARGARET: I don't mind makin' a fool of myself over you!

BRICK: I mind, Maggie. I feel embarrassed for you.

MARGARET: Feel embarrassed! But don't continue my torture. I can't live on and on under these circumstances.

BRICK: You agreed to—

MARGARET: I know but—

BRICK: —Accept that condition!

MARGARET: *I CAN'T! I CAN'T! I CAN'T! (She seizes his shoulder.)*

BRICK: Let go!

(He breaks away from her and seizes the small boudoir chair and raises it like a lion-tamer facing a big circus cat.)
(Count five. She stares at him with her fist pressed to her mouth, then bursts into shrill, almost hysterical laughter. He remains grave for a moment, then grins and puts the chair down.)
(BIG MAMA calls through closed door.)

BIG MAMA: Son? Son? Son?

BRICK: What is it, Big Mama?

BIG MAMA *(outside):* Oh, son! We got the most wonderful news about Big Daddy. I just had t' run up an' tell you right this— *(She rattles the knob.)* —What's this door doin', locked, faw? You all think there's robbers in the house?

MARGARET: Big Mama, Brick is dressin', he's not dressed yet.

BIG MAMA: That's all right, it won't be the first time I've seen Brick not dressed. Come on, open this door!

(MARGARET, with a grimace, goes to unlock and open the hall door, as BRICK hobbles rapidly to the bathroom and kicks the door shut. BIG MAMA has disappeared from the hall.)

MARGARET: Big Mama?

(BIG MAMA *appears through the opposite gallery doors behind* MARGARET, *huffing and puffing like an old bulldog. She is a short, stout woman; her sixty years and 170 pounds have left her somewhat breathless most of the time; she's always tensed like a boxer, or rather, a Japanese wrestler. Her "family" was maybe a little superior to* BIG DADDY's *but not much. She wears a black or silver lace dress and at least half a million in flashy gems. She is very sincere.*)

BIG MAMA (*loudly, startling* MARGARET): Here—I come through Gooper's and Mae's gall'ry door. Where's Brick? *Brick*—Hurry on out of there, son, I just have a second and want to give you the news about Big Daddy.—I hate locked doors in a house. . . .

MARGARET (*with affected lightness*): I've noticed you do, Big Mama, but people have got to have *some* moments of privacy, don't they?

BIG MAMA: No, ma'am, not in *my* house. (*Without pause.*) Whacha took off you' dress faw? I thought that little lace dress was so sweet on yuh, honey.

MARGARET: I thought it looked sweet on me, too, but one of m' cute little table-partners used it for a napkin so—!

BIG MAMA (*picking up stockings on floor*): What?

MARGARET: You know, Big Mama, Mae and Gooper's so touchy about those children—thanks, Big Mama . . .

(BIG MAMA *has thrust the picked-up stockings in* MARGARET's *hand with a grunt.*)

—that you just don't dare to suggest there's any room for improvement in their—

BIG MAMA: Brick, hurry out!—Shoot, Maggie, you just don't like children.

MARGARET: I do SO like children! Adore them!—well brought up!

BIG MAMA (*gentle—loving*): Well, why don't you have some and bring them up well, then, instead of all the time pickin' on Gooper's an' Mae's?

GOOPER (*shouting up the stairs*): Hey, hey, Big Mama, Betsy an' Hugh got to go, waitin' t' tell yuh g'by!

BIG MAMA: Tell 'em to hold their hawses, I'll be right down in a jiffy!

GOOPER: Yes ma'am!

(*She turns to the bathroom door and calls out.*)

BIG MAMA: Son? Can you hear me in there?

(*There is a muffled answer.*)

We just got the full report from the laboratory at the Ochsner Clinic, completely negative, son, ev'rything negative, right on down the line! Nothin' a-tall's wrong with him but some little functional thing called a spastic colon. Can you hear me, son?

MARGARET: He can hear you, Big Mama.

BIG MAMA: Then why don't he say something? God Almighty, a piece of news like that should make him shout. It made *me* shout, I can tell you. I shouted and sobbed and fell right down on my knees!—Look! (*She pulls up her skirt.*) See the bruises where I hit my kneecaps? Took both doctors to haul me back on my feet!

(*She laughs—she always laughs like hell at herself.*)

Big Daddy was furious with me! But ain't that wonderful news?

(*Facing bathroom again, she continues.*)

After all the anxiety we been through to git a report like that on Big Daddy's birthday? Big Daddy tried to hide how much of a load that news took off his mind, but didn't fool *me*. He was mighty close to crying about it *himself*!

(*Goodbyes are shouted downstairs, and she rushes to door.*)

GOOPER: Big Mama!

BIG MAMA: *Hold those people down there, don't let them go!*—Now, git dressed, we're comin' up to this room fo' Big Daddy's birthday party because of your ankle.—How's his ankle, Maggie?

MARGARET: Well, he broke it, Big Mama.

BIG MAMA: I know he broke it.

(*A phone is ringing in hall. A Negro voice answers: "Mistuh Polly's res'dence."*)

I mean does it hurt him much still.

MARGARET: I'm afraid I can't give you that information, Big Mama. You'll have to ask Brick if it hurts much still or not.

SOOKEY (*in the hall*): It's Memphis, Mizz Polly, it's Miss Sally in Memphis.

BIG MAMA: Awright, Sookey.

(BIG MAMA *rushes into the hall and is heard shouting on the phone.*)

Hello, Miss Sally. How are you, Miss Sally?—Yes, well, I was just gonna call you about it. *Shoot!*

MARGARET: Brick, don't!

(BIG MAMA *raises her voice to a bellow.*)

BIG MAMA: *Miss Sally? Don't ever call me from the Gayoso Lobby, too much talk goes on in that hotel lobby, no wonder you can't hear me!* Now listen, Miss Sally. They's nothin' serious wrong with Big Daddy. We got the report just now, they's nothin' wrong but a thing called a—spastic! SPASTIC!—colon . . . (*She appears at the hall door and calls to* MARGARET.) —Maggie, come out here and talk to that fool on the phone. I'm shouted breathless!

MARGARET (*goes out and is heard sweetly at phone*): Miss Sally? This is Brick's wife, Maggie. So nice to hear your voice. Can you hear *mine?* Well, *good!*—Big Mama just wanted you to know that they've got the report from the Ochsner Clinic and what Big Daddy has is a spastic colon. Yes. Spastic colon, Miss Sally. That's right, spastic colon. *G'bye, Miss Sally, hope I'll see you real soon!*

(*Hangs up a little before* MISS SALLY *was probably ready to terminate the talk. She returns through the hall door.*)

She heard me perfectly. I've discovered with deaf people the thing to do is not shout at them but just enunciate clearly. My rich old Aunt Cornelia was deaf as the dead but I could make her hear me just by sayin' each word slowly, distinctly, close to her ear. I read her the *Commercial Appeal* ev'ry night, read her the classified ads in it, even, she never missed a word of it. But was she a mean ole thing! Know what I got when she died? Her unexpired subscriptions to five magazines and the Book-of-the-Month Club and a LIBRARY full of ev'ry dull book ever written! All else went to her hellcat of a sister . . . meaner than she was, even!

(BIG MAMA *has been straightening things up in the room during this speech.*)

BIG MAMA (*closing closet door on discarded clothes*): Miss Sally sure is a case! Big Daddy says she's always got her hand out fo' something. He's not mistaken. That poor ole thing always has her hand out fo' somethin'. I don't think Big Daddy gives her as much as he should.

GOOPER: Big Mama! Come on now! Betsy and Hugh can't wait no longer!

BIG MAMA (*shouting*): I'm comin'!

(*She starts out. At the hall door, turns and jerks a forefinger, first toward the bathroom door, then toward the liquor cabinet, meaning:* "Has BRICK *been drinking?"* MARGARET *pretends not to understand, cocks her head and raises her brows as if the pantomimic performance was completely mystifying to her.*)

(BIG MAMA *rushes back to* MARGARET.)

Shoot! Stop playin' so dumb!—I mean has he been drinkin' that stuff much yet?

MARGARET (*with a little laugh*): Oh! I think he had a highball after supper.

BIG MAMA: Don't laugh about it!—some single men stop drinkin' when they git married and others start! Brick never touched liquor before he—!

MARGARET (*crying out*): *THAT'S NOT FAIR!*

BIG MAMA: Fair or not fair I want to ask you a question, one question: D'you make Brick happy in bed?

MARGARET: Why don't you ask if he makes *me* happy in bed?

BIG MAMA: Because I know that—

MARGARET: *It works both ways!*

BIG MAMA: Something's not right! You're childless and my son drinks!

GOOPER: Come on, Big Mama!

(GOOPER *has called her downstairs and she has rushed to the door on the line above. She turns at the door and points at the bed.*)

—When a marriage goes on the rocks, the rocks are *there*, right *there!*

MARGARET: *That's*—

(BIG MAMA *has swept out of the room and slammed the door.*)

—not—*fair* . . .

(MARGARET *is alone, completely alone, and she feels it. She draws in, hunches her shoulders, raises her arms with fists clenched, shuts her eyes tight as a child about to be stabbed with a vaccination needle. When she opens her eyes again, what she sees is the long oval mirror and she rushes straight to it, stares into it with a grimace and says:* "Who are you?"—*Then she crouches a little and answers herself in a different voice which is high, thin, mocking:* "I am Maggie the Cat!"—*Straightens quickly as bathroom door opens a little and* BRICK *calls out to her.*)

BRICK: Has Big Mama gone?

MARGARET: She's gone.

(*He opens the bathroom door and hobbles out, with his liquor glass now empty, straight to the liquor cabinet. He is whistling softly.* MARGARET's *head pivots on her long, slender throat to watch him.*)

(*She raises a hand uncertainly to the base of her throat, as if it was difficult for her to swallow, before she speaks.*)

You know, our sex life didn't just peter out in the usual way, it was cut off short, long before the natural time for it to, and it's going to revive again, just as sudden as that. I'm confident of it. That's what I'm keeping myself attractive for. For the time when you'll see me again like other men see me. Yes, like other men see me. They still see me, Brick, and they like what they see. Uh-huh. Some of them would give their—
  Look, Brick!

(*She stands before the long oval mirror, touches her breast and then her hips with her two hands.*)

How high my body stays on me!—Nothing has fallen on me—not a fraction. . . .

(*Her voice is soft and trembling: a pleading child's. At this moment as he turns to glance at her—a look which is like a player passing a ball to another player, third down and goal to go—she has to capture the audience in a grip so tight that she can hold it till the first intermission without any lapse of attention.)*

Other men still want me. My face looks strained, sometimes, but I've kept my figure as well as you've kept yours, and men admire it. I still turn heads on the street. Why, last week in Memphis everywhere that I went men's eyes burned holes in my clothes, at the country club and in restaurants and department stores, there wasn't a man I met or walked by that didn't just eat me up with his eyes and turn around when I passed him and look back at me. Why, at Alice's party for her New York cousins, the best-lookin' man in the crowd—followed me upstairs and tried to force his way in the powder room with me, followed me to the door and tried to force his way in!

BRICK: Why didn't you let him, Maggie?

MARGARET: Because I'm not that common, for one thing. Not that I wasn't almost tempted to. You like to know who it was? It was Sonny Boy Maxwell, that's who!

BRICK: Oh, yeah, Sonny Boy Maxwell, he was a good end-runner but had a little injury to his back and had to quit.

MARGARET: He has no injury now and has no wife and still has a lech for me!

BRICK: I see no reason to lock him out of a powder room in that case.

MARGARET: And have someone catch me at it? I'm not that stupid. Oh, I might sometime cheat on you with someone, since you're so insultingly eager to have me do it!—But if I do, you can be damned sure it will be in a place and a time where no one but me and the man could possibly know. Because I'm not going to give you any excuse to divorce me for being unfaithful or anything else. . . .

BRICK: Maggie, I wouldn't divorce you for being unfaithful or anything else. Don't you know that? Hell. I'd be relieved to know that you'd found yourself a lover.

MARGARET: Well, I'm taking no chances. No, I'd rather stay on this hot tin roof.

BRICK: A hot tin roof's 'n uncomfo'table place t' stay on. . . . *(He starts to whistle softly.)*

MARGARET *(through his whistle)*: Yeah, but I can stay on it just as long as I have to.

BRICK: You could leave me, Maggie.

(He resumes whistle. She wheels about to glare at him.)

MARGARET: *Don't want to and will not!* Besides if I did, you don't have a cent to pay for it but what you get from Big Daddy and he's dying of cancer!

(For the first time a realization of BIG DADDY's doom seems to penetrate to BRICK's consciousness, visibly, and he looks at MARGARET.)

BRICK: Big Mama just said he *wasn't*, that the report was okay.

MARGARET: That's what she thinks because she got the same story that they gave Big Daddy. And was just as taken in by it as he was, poor ole things. . . .

But tonight they're going to tell her the truth about it. When Big Daddy goes to bed, they're going to tell her that he is dying of cancer. *(She slams the dresser drawer.)*—It's malignant and it's terminal.

BRICK: Does Big Daddy know it?

MARGARET: Hell, do they *ever* know it? Nobody says, "You're dying." You have to fool them. They have to fool *themselves*.

BRICK: Why?

MARGARET: *Why?* Because human beings dream of life everlasting, that's the reason! But most of them want it on earth and not in heaven.

(He gives a short, hard laugh at her touch of humor.)

Well. . . . *(She touches up her mascara.)* That's how it is, anyhow. . . . *(She looks about.)* Where did I put down my cigarette? Don't want to burn up the home-place, at least not with Mae and Gooper and their five monsters in it!

(She has found it and sucks at it greedily. Blows out smoke and continues.)

So this is Big Daddy's last birthday. And Mae and Gooper, they know it, oh, *they* know it, all right. They got the first information from the Ochsner Clinic. That's why they rushed down here with their no-neck monsters. Because. Do you know something? Big Daddy's made no will? Big Daddy's never made out any will in his life, and so this campaign's afoot to impress him, forcibly as possible, with the fact that you drink and I've borne no children!

(He continues to stare at her a moment, then mutters something sharp but not audible and hobbles rather rapidly out onto the long gallery in the fading, much faded, gold light.)

MARGARET *(continuing her liturgical chant)*: Y'know, I'm *fond* of Big Daddy, I am genuinely fond of that old man, I really *am*, you know. . . .

BRICK *(faintly, vaguely)*: Yes, I know you are. . . .

MARGARET: I've always sort of admired him in spite of his coarseness, his four-letter words and so forth. Because Big Daddy *is* what he *is*, and he makes no bones about it. He hasn't turned gentleman farmer, he's still a Mississippi redneck, as much of a redneck as he must have been when he was just overseer here on the old Jack Straw and Peter Ochello place. But he got hold of it an' built it into th' biggest an' finest plantation in the Delta.—I've always *liked* Big Daddy. . . .

(She crosses to the proscenium.)

Well, this is Big Daddy's last birthday. I'm sorry about it. But I'm facing the facts. It takes money to take care of a drinker and that's the office that I've been elected to lately.

BRICK: You don't have to take care of me.

MARGARET: Yes, I do. Two people in the same boat have got to take care of each other. At least you want money to buy more Echo Spring when this supply is exhausted, or will you be satisfied with a ten-cent beer?

Mae an' Gooper are plannin' to freeze us out of Big Daddy's estate because you drink and I'm childless. But we can defeat that plan. We're *going* to defeat that plan!

Brick, y'know, I've been so God damn disgustingly poor all my life!—That's the *truth*, Brick!

BRICK: I'm not sayin' it isn't.

MARGARET: Always had to suck up to people I couldn't stand because they had money and I was poor as Job's turkey. You don't know what that's like. Well, I'll tell you, it's like you would feel a thousand miles away from Echo Spring!—And had to get back to it on that broken ankle . . . without a crutch!

That's how it feels to be as poor as Job's turkey and have to suck up to relatives that you hated because they had money and all you had was a bunch of hand-me-down clothes and a few old moldy three-per-cent government bonds. My daddy loved his liquor, he fell in love with his liquor the way you've fallen in love with Echo Spring!—And my poor Mama, having to maintain some semblance of social position, to keep appearances up, on an income of one hundred and fifty dollars a month on those old government bonds!

When I came out, the year that I made my debut, I had just two evening dresses! One Mother made me from a pattern in *Vogue*, the other a hand-me-down from a snotty rich cousin I hated!

—The dress that I married you in was my grandmother's weddin' gown. . . .

So that's why I'm like a cat on a hot tin roof!

(BRICK is still on the gallery. Someone below calls up to him in a warm Negro voice, "Hiya, Mistuh Brick, how yuh feelin'?" BRICK raises his liquor glass as if that answered the question.)

MARGARET: You can be young without money, but you can't be old without it. You've got to be old *with* money because to be old without it is just too awful, you've got to be one or the other, either young or *with money*, you can't be old and *without* it.—That's the *truth*, Brick. . . .

(BRICK whistles softly, vaguely.)

Well, now I'm dressed, I'm all dressed, there's nothing else for me to do. *(Forlornly, almost fearfully.)* I'm dressed, all dressed, nothing else for me to do. . . .

(She moves about restlessly, aimlessly, and speaks, as if to herself.)

What am I—? Oh!—my bracelets. . . .

(She starts working a collection of bracelets over her hands onto her wrists, about six on each, as she talks.)

I've thought a whole lot about it and now I know when I made my mistake. Yes, I made my mistake when I told you the truth about that thing with Skipper. Never should have confessed it, a fatal error, tellin' you about that thing with Skipper.

BRICK: Maggie, shut up about Skipper. I mean it, Maggie; you got to shut up about Skipper.

MARGARET: You ought to understand that Skipper and I—

BRICK: You don't think I'm serious, Maggie? You're fooled by the fact that I am saying this quiet? Look, Maggie. What you're doing is a dangerous thing to do. You're—you're—you're—foolin' with something that—nobody ought to fool with.

MARGARET: This time I'm going to finish what I have to say to you. Skipper and I made love, if love you could call it, because it made both of us feel a little bit closer to you. You see, you son of a bitch, you asked too much of people, of me, of him, of all the unlucky poor damned sons of bitches that happen to love you, and there was a whole pack of them, yes, there was a pack of them besides me and Skipper, you asked too goddam much of people that loved you, you—superior creature!—you godlike being!—And so we made love to each other to dream it was you, both of us! Yes, yes, yes! Truth, truth! What's so awful about it? I like it, I think the truth is—yeah! I shouldn't have told you. . . .

BRICK *(holding his head unnaturally still and uptilted a bit)*: It was Skipper that told me about it. Not you, Maggie.

MARGARET: I told you!

BRICK: After he told me!

MARGARET: What does it matter who—?

DIXIE: I got your mallet, I got your mallet.

TRIXIE: Give it to me, give it to me, IT's mine.

(BRICK turns suddenly out upon the gallery and calls.)

BRICK: Little girl! Hey, little girl!

LITTLE GIRL *(at a distance)*: What, Uncle Brick?

BRICK: Tell the folks to come up!—Bring everybody upstairs!

TRIXIE: It's mine, it's mine.

MARGARET: I can't stop myself! I'd go on telling you this in front of them all, if I had to!

BRICK: Little girl, Go on, go on, will you? Do what I told you, call them!

DIXIE: Okay.

MARGARET: Because it's got to be told and you, you!—you never let me!

(She sobs, then controls herself, and continues almost calmly.)

It was one of those beautiful, ideal things, they tell about in the Greek legends, it couldn't be anything else, you being you, and that's what made it so sad, and that's what made it so awful, because it was love that never could be carried through to anything satisfying or even talked about plainly.

BRICK: Maggie, you gotta stop this.

MARGARET: Brick, I tell you, you got to believe me, Brick, I *do* understand all about it! I—I think it was—*noble!* Can't you tell I'm sincere when I say I respect it? My only point, the only point that I'm making, is life has got to be allowed to continue even after the *dream* of life is —all— over. . . .

(BRICK *is without his crutch. Leaning on furniture, he crosses to pick it up as she continues as if possessed by a will outside herself.*)

Why I remember when we double-dated at college, Gladys Fitzgerald and I and you and Skipper, it was more like a date between you and Skipper. Gladys and I were just sort of tagging along as if it was necessary to chaperone you!—to make a good public impression—

BRICK (*turns to face her, half lifting his crutch*): Maggie, you want me to hit you with this crutch? Don't you know I could kill you with this crutch?

MARGARET: Good, Lord, man, d' you think I'd care if you did?

BRICK: One man has one great good true thing in his life. One great good thing which is true!—I had friendship with Skipper.—You are naming it dirty!

MARGARET: I'm not naming it dirty! I am naming it clean.

BRICK: Not love with you, Maggie, but friendship with Skipper was that one great true thing, and you are naming it dirty!

MARGARET: Then you haven't been listenin', not understood what I'm saying! I'm naming it so damn clean that it killed poor Skipper!—You two had something that had to be kept on ice, yes, incor-

ruptible, yes!—and death was the only icebox where you could keep it. . . .

BRICK: I married you, Maggie. Why would I marry you, Maggie, if I was—?

MARGARET: Brick, let me finish!—I know, believe me I know, that it was only Skipper that harbored even any *unconscious* desire for anything not perfectly pure between you two!—Now let me skip a little. You married me early that summer we graduated out of Ole Miss, and we were happy, weren't we, we were blissful, yes, hit heaven together ev'ry time that we loved! But that fall you an' Skipper turned down wonderful offers of jobs in order to keep on bein' football heroes— pro-football heroes. You organized the Dixie Stars that fall, so you could keep on bein' teammates forever! But somethin' was not right with it!—*Me included!*—between you. Skipper began hittin' the bottle . . . you got a spinal injury— couldn't play the Thanksgivin' game in Chicago, watched it on TV from a traction bed in Toledo. I joined Skipper. The Dixie Stars lost because poor Skipper was drunk. We drank together that night all night in the bar of the Blackstone and when cold day was comin' up over the Lake an' we were comin' out drunk to take a dizzy look at it, I said, "SKIPPER! STOP LOVIN' MY HUSBAND OR TELL HIM HE'S GOT TO LET YOU ADMIT IT TO HIM!"—one way or another!

HE SLAPPED ME HARD ON THE MOUTH!—then turned and ran without stopping once, I am sure, all the way back into his room at the Blackstone. . . .

—When I came to his room that night, with a little scratch like a shy little mouse at his door, he made that pitiful, ineffectual little attempt to prove that what I had said wasn't true. . . .

(BRICK *strikes at her with crutch, a blow that shatters the gemlike lamp on the table.*)

—In this way, I destroyed him, by telling him truth that he and his world which he was born and raised in, yours and his world, had told him could not be told?

From then on Skipper was nothing at all but a receptacle for liquor and drugs. . . .

—*Who shot cock robin? I with my*— (*She throws back her head with tight shut eyes.*) —*merciful arrow!*

(BRICK *strikes at her; misses.*)

Missed me!—Sorry,—I'm not tryin' to whitewash my behavior, Christ, no! Brick, I'm not good. I don't know why people have to pretend to be good, nobody's good. The rich or the well-to-do can afford to respect moral patterns, conventional moral patterns, but I could never afford to, yeah, but—I'm honest! Give me credit for just that, will you *please*?—Born poor, raised poor, expect to die poor unless I manage to get us something out of what Big Daddy leaves when he dies of cancer! But Brick?!—*Skipper is dead! I'm alive!* Maggie the cat is—

(BRICK *hops awkwardly forward and strikes at her again with his crutch.*)

—alive! I am alive, alive! I am . . .

(*He hurls the crutch at her, across the bed she took refuge behind, and pitches forward on the floor as she completes her speech.*)

—alive!

(*A little girl,* DIXIE, *bursts into the room, wearing an Indian war bonnet and firing a cap pistol at* MARGARET *and shouting:* "Bang, bang, bang!")
(*Laughter downstairs floats through the open hall door.* MARGARET *had crouched gasping to bed at child's entrance. She now rises and says with cool fury.*)

Little girl, your mother or someone should teach you—(*gasping*)—to knock at a door before you come into a room. Otherwise people might think that you—lack—good breeding. . . .
DIXIE: Yanh, yanh, yanh, what is Uncle Brick doin' on th' floor?
BRICK: I tried to kill your Aunt Maggie, but I failed—and I fell. Little girl, give me my crutch so I can get up off th' floor.
MARGARET: Yes, give your uncle his crutch, he's a cripple, honey, he broke his ankle last night jumping hurdles on the high school athletic field!
DIXIE: What were you jumping hurdles for, Uncle Brick?
BRICK: Because I used to jump them, and people like to do what they used to do, even after they've stopped being able to do it. . . .
MARGARET: That's right, that's your answer, now go away, little girl.

(DIXIE *fires cap pistol at* MARGARET *three times.*)

Stop, you stop that, monster! You little no-neck monster! (*She seizes the cap pistol and hurls it through gallery door.*)
DIXIE (*with a precocious instinct for the cruelest thing*): You're *jealous!*—You're just jealous because you can't have babies!

(*She sticks out her tongue at* MARGARET *as she sashays past her with her stomach stuck out, to the gallery.* MARGARET *slams the gallery doors and leans panting against them. There is a pause.* BRICK *has replaced his spilt drink and sits, faraway, on the great four-poster bed.*)

MARGARET: You see?—they gloat over us being child-less, even in front of their five little no-neck monsters!

(*Pause. Voices approach on the stairs.*)

Brick?—I've been to a doctor in Memphis, a—a gynecologist. . . .
I've been completely examined, and there is no reason why we can't have a child whenever we want one. And this is my time by the calendar to conceive. Are you listening to me? Are you? Are you LISTENING TO ME!
BRICK: Yes. I hear you, Maggie. (*His attention returns to her inflamed face.*) —But how in hell on earth do you imagine—that you're going to have a child by a man that can't stand you?
MARGARET: That's a problem that I will have to work out. (*She wheels about to face the hall door.*)
MAE (*off stage left*): Come on, Big Daddy. We're all goin' up to Brick's room.

(*From off stage left, voices:* REVEREND TOOKER, DOCTOR BAUGH, MAE.)

MARGARET: *Here they come!*

(*The lights dim.*)

ACT 2

(*There is no lapse of time.* MARGARET *and* BRICK *are in the same positions they held at the end of Act 1.*)

MARGARET (*at door*): *Here they come!*

(BIG DADDY *appears first, a tall man with a fierce, anxious look, moving carefully not to betray his weakness even, or especially, to himself.*)

GOOPER: I read in the *Register* that you're getting a new memorial window.

(*Some of the people are approaching through the hall, others along the gallery: voices from both directions.* GOOPER *and* REVEREND TOOKER *become visible outside gallery doors, and their voices come in clearly.*)
(*They pause outside as* GOOPER *lights a cigar.*)

REVEREND TOOKER (*vivaciously*): Oh, but St. Paul's in Grenada has three memorial windows, and the latest one is a Tiffany stained-glass window that cost twenty-five hundred dollars, a picture of Christ the Good Shepherd with a Lamb in His arms.
MARGARET: Big Daddy.
BIG DADDY: Well, Brick.
BRICK: Hello Big Daddy.—Congratulations!
BIG DADDY: —Crap. . . .
GOOPER: Who give that window, Preach?
REVEREND TOOKER: Clyde Fletcher's widow. Also presented St. Paul's with a baptismal font.

GOOPER: Y'know what somebody ought t' give your church is a *coolin'* system, Preach.

MAE (*almost religiously*): Let's see now, they've had their *tyyy*-phoid shots, and their tetanus shots, their diptheria shots and their hepatitis shots and their polio shots, they got *those* shots every month from May through September, and— Gooper? Hey! Gooper!—What all have the kiddies been shot faw?

REVEREND TOOKER: Yes, siree, Bob! And y'know what Gus Hamma's family gave in his memory to the church at Two Rivers? A complete new stone parish-house with a basketball court in the basement and a—

BIG DADDY (*uttering a loud barking laugh which is far from truly mirthful*): Hey, Preach! What's all this talk about memorials, Preach? Y' think somebody's about t' kick off around here? 'S that it?

(*Startled by this interjection,* REVEREND TOOKER *decides to laugh at the question almost as loud as he can.*)

(*How he would answer the question we'll never know, as he's spared that embarrassment by the voice of* GOOPER's *wife,* MAE, *rising high and clear as she appears with* "DOC" BAUGH, *the family doctor, through the hall door.*)

MARGARET (*overlapping a bit*): Turn on the hi-fi, Brick! Let's have some music t' start th' party with!

BRICK: You turn it on, Maggie.

(*The talk becomes so general that the room sounds like a great aviary of chattering birds. Only* BRICK *remains unengaged, leaning upon the liquor cabinet with his faraway smile, an ice cube in a paper napkin with which he now and then rubs his forehead. He doesn't respond to* MARGARET's *command. She bounds forward and stoops over the instrument panel of the console.*)

GOOPER: We gave 'em that thing for a third anniversay present, got three speakers in it.

(*The room is suddenly blasted by the climax of a Wagnerian opera or a Beethoven symphony.*)

BIG DADDY: *Turn that dam thing off!*

(*Almost instant silence, almost instantly broken by the shouting charge of* BIG MAMA, *entering through the hall door like a charging rhino.*)

BIG MAMA: *Wha's my Brick, wha's mah precious baby!!*

BIG DADDY: *Sorry! Turn it back on!*

(*Everyone laughs very loud.* BIG DADDY *is famous for his jokes at* BIG MAMA's *expense, and nobody laughs louder at these jokes than* BIG MAMA *herself, though sometimes they're pretty cruel and* BIG MAMA *has to pick up or fuss with something to cover the hurt that the loud laugh doesn't quite cover.*)

(*On this occasion, a happy occasion because the dread in her heart has also been lifted by the false report on* BIG

DADDY's *condition, she giggles, grotesquely, coyly, in* BIG DADDY's *direction and bears down upon* BRICK, *all very quick and alive.*)

BIG MAMA: Here he is, here's my precious baby! What's that you've got in your hand? You put that liquor down, son, your hand was made fo' holdin' somethin' better than that!

GOOPER: Look at Brick put it down!

(BRICK *has obeyed* BIG MAMA *by draining the glass and handing it to her. Again everyone laughs, some high, some low.*)

BIG MAMA: Oh, you bad boy, you, you're my bad little boy. Give Big Mama a kiss, you bad boy, you!— Look at him shy away, will you? Brick never liked bein' kissed or made a fuss over, I guess because he's always had too much of it!

Son, you turn that thing off!

(BRICK *has switched on the TV set.*)

I can't stand TV, radio was bad enough but TV has gone it one better, I mean—(*plops wheezing in chair*)—one worse, ha ha! Now what'm I sittin' down here faw? I want t' sit next to my sweetheart on the sofa, hold hands with him and love him up a little!

(BIG MAMA *has on a black and white figured chiffon. The large irregular patterns, like the markings of some massive animal, the luster of her great diamonds and many pearls, the brilliants set in the silver frames of her glasses, her riotous voice, booming laugh, have dominated the room since she entered.* BIG DADDY *has been regarding her with a steady grimace of chronic annoyance.*)

BIG MAMA (*still louder*): Preacher, Preacher, hey, Preach! Give me you' hand an' help me up from this chair!

REVEREND TOOKER: None of your tricks, Big Mama!

BIG MAMA: What tricks? You give me you' hand so I can get up an'—

(REVEREND TOOKER *extends her his hand. She grabs it and pulls him into her lap with a shrill laugh that spans an octave in two notes.*)

Ever seen a preacher in a fat lady's lap? Hey, hey, folks! Ever seen a preacher in a fat lady's lap?

(BIG MAMA *is notorious throughout the Delta for this sort of inelegant horseplay.* MARGARET *looks on with indulgent humor, sipping Dubonnet "on the rocks" and watching* BRICK, *but* MAE *and* GOOPER *exchange signs of humorless anxiety over these antics, the sort of behavior which* MAE *thinks may account for their failure to quite get in with the smartest young married set in Memphis, despite all. One of the Negroes,* LACY *or* SOOKEY, *peeks in, cackling. They are waiting for a sign to bring in the* cake and champagne. *But* BIG DADDY's *not amused. He doesn't understand why, in spite of the infinite mental relief he's received from the doctor's report, he still has these same old fox teeth in his guts. "This spastic condition is something else," he says to himself, but aloud he roars at* BIG MAMA.)

BIG DADDY: *BIG MAMA, WILL YOU QUIT HORSIN'?*—You're too old an' too fat fo' that sort of crazy kid stuff an' besides a woman with your blood pressure—she had two hundred last spring!—is riskin' a stroke when you mess around like that. . . .

(MAE *blows on a pitch pipe.*)

BIG MAMA: *Here comes Big Daddy's birthday!*

(*Negroes in white jackets enter with an enormous birthday cake ablaze with candles and carrying buckets of champagne with satin ribbons about the bottle necks.* MAE *and* GOOPER *strike up song, and everybody, including the* NEGROES *and* CHILDREN, *joins in. Only* BRICK *remains aloof.*)

EVERYONE:
Happy birthday to you.
Happy birthday to you.
Happy birthday, Big Daddy—

(*Some sing: "Dear, Big Daddy!"*)

Happy birthday to you.

(*Some sing: "How old are you?"*)
(MAE *has come down center and is organizing her children like a chorus. She gives them a barely audible: "One, two, three!" and they are off in the new tune.*)

CHILDREN:
Skinamarinka—dinka—dink
Skinamarinka—do
We love you.
Skinamarinka—dinka—dink
Skinamarinka—do.

(*All together, they turn to* BIG DADDY.)

Big Daddy, you!

(*They turn back front, like a musical comedy chorus.*)

We love you in the morning;
We love you in the night.
We love you when we're with you,
And we love you out of sight.
Skinamarinka—dinka—dink
Skinamarinka—do.

(MAE *turns to* BIG MAMA.)

Big Mama, too!

(BIG MAMA *bursts into tears. The* NEGROES *leave.*)

BIG DADDY: Now Ida, what the hell is the matter with you?

MAE: She's just so happy.

BIG MAMA: I'm just so happy, Big Daddy, I have to cry or something.

(*Sudden and loud in the hush.*)

Brick, do you know the wonderful news that Doc Baugh got from the clinic about Big Daddy? Big Daddy's one hundred per cent!

MARGARET: Isn't that wonderful?

BIG MAMA: He's just one hundred per cent. Passed the examination with flying colors. Now that we know there's nothing wrong with Big Daddy but a spastic colon, I can tell you something. I was worried sick, half out of my mind, for fear Big Daddy might have a thing like—

(MARGARET *cuts through this speech, jumping up and exclaiming shrilly.*)

MARGARET: Brick, honey, aren't you going to give Big Daddy his birthday present?

(*Passing by him, she snatches his liquor glass from him.*)
(*She picks up a fancily wrapped package.*)

Here it is, Big Daddy, this is from Brick!

BIG MAMA: This is the biggest birthday Big Daddy's ever had, a hundred presents and bushels of telegrams from—

MAE (*at same time*): What is it, Brick?

GOOPER: I bet 500 to 50 that Brick don't *know* what it is.

BIG MAMA: The fun of presents is not knowing what they are till you open the package. Open your present, Big Daddy.

BIG DADDY: Open it you'self. I want to ask Brick somethin'! Come here, Brick.

MARGARET: Big Daddy's callin' you, Brick. (*She is opening the package.*)

BRICK: Tell Big Daddy I'm crippled.

BIG DADDY: I see you're crippled. I want to know how you got crippled.

MARGARET (*making diversionary tactics*): *Oh, look, oh, look, why, it's a cashmere robe!* (*She holds the robe up for all to see.*)

MAE: You sound surprised, Maggie.

MARGARET: I never saw one before.

MAE: That's funny.—*Hah!*

MARGARET (*turning on her fiercely, with a brilliant smile*): *Why is it funny? All my family ever had was family—and luxuries such as cashmere robes still surprise me!*

BIG DADDY (*ominously*): Quiet!

MAE (*heedless in her fury*): I don't see how you could be so surprised when you bought it yourself at Loewenstein's in Memphis last Saturday. You know how I know?

BIG DADDY: I said, Quiet!

MAE: —I know because the salesgirl that sold it to you waited on me and said, Oh, Mrs. Pollitt, your sister-in-law just bought a cashmere robe for your husband's father!

MARGARET: Sister Woman! Your talents are wasted as a housewife and mother, you really ought to be with the FBI or—

BIG DADDY: QUIET!

(REVEREND TOOKER's *reflexes are slower than the others'. He finishes a sentence after the bellow.*)

REVEREND TOOKER (*to* DOC BAUGH): —the Stork and the Reaper are running neck and neck!

(*He starts to laugh gaily when he notices the silence and* BIG DADDY's *glare. His laugh dies falsely.*)

BIG DADDY: Preacher, I hope I'm not butting in on more talk about memorial stained-glass windows, am I, Preacher?

(REVEREND TOOKER *laughs feebly, then coughs dryly in the embarrassed silence.*)

Preacher?

BIG MAMA: Now, Big Daddy, don't you pick on Preacher!

BIG DADDY (*raising his voice*): You ever hear that expression all hawk and no spit? You bring that expression to mind with that little dry cough of yours, all hawk an' no spit. . . .

(*The pause is broken only by a short startled laugh from* MARGARET, *the only one there who is conscious of and amused by the grotesque.*)

MAE (*raising her arms and jangling her bracelets*): I wonder if the mosquitoes are active tonight?

BIG DADDY: What's that, Little Mama? Did you make some remark?

MAE: Yes, I said I wondered if the mosquitoes would eat us alive if we went out on the gallery for a while.

BIG DADDY: Well, if they do, I'll have your bones pulverized for fertilizer!

BIG MAMA (*quickly*): Last week we had an airplane spraying the place and I think it done some good, at least I haven't had a—

BIG DADDY (*cutting her speech*): Brick, they tell me, if what they tell me is true, that you done some jumping last night on the high school athletic field?

BIG MAMA: Brick, Big Daddy is talking to you, son.

BRICK (*smiling vaguely over his drink*): What was that, Big Daddy?

BIG DADDY: They said you done some jumping on the high school track field last night.

BRICK: That's what they told me, too.

BIG DADDY: Was it jumping or humping that you were doing out there? What were you doing out there at three A.M., layin' a woman on that cinder track?

BIG MAMA: Big Daddy, you are off the sick-list, now, and I'm not going to excuse you for talkin' so—

BIG DADDY: Quiet!

BIG MAMA: —*nasty* in front of Preacher and—

BIG DADDY: *QUIET!*—I ast you, Brick, if you was cuttin' you'self a piece o' poon-tang last night on that cinder track? I thought maybe you were chasin' poon-tang on that track an' tripped over something in the heat of the chase—'sthat it?

(GOOPER *laughs, loud and false, others nervously following suit.* BIG MAMA *stamps her foot, and purses her lips, crossing to* MAE *and whispering something to her as* BRICK *meets his father's hard, intent, grinning stare with a slow, vague smile that he offers all situations from behind the screen of his liquor.*)

BRICK: No, sir, I don't think so. . . .

MAE (*at the same time, sweetly*): Reverend Tooker, let's you and I take a stroll on the widow's walk.

(*She and the preacher go out on the gallery as* BIG DADDY *says.*)

BIG DADDY: Then what the hell were you doing out there at three o'clock in the morning?

BRICK: Jumping the hurdles, Big Daddy, runnin' and jumpin' the hurdles, but those high hurdles have gotten too high for me, now.

BIG DADDY: Cause you was drunk?

BRICK (*his vague smile fading a little*): Sober I wouldn't have tried to jump the *low* ones. . . .

BIG MAMA (*quickly*): Big Daddy, blow out the candles on your birthday cake!

MARGARET (*at the same time*): I want to propose a toast to Big Daddy Pollitt on his sixty-fifth birthday, the biggest cotton planter in—

BIG DADDY (*bellowing with fury and disgust*): *I told you to stop it, now stop it, quit this—!*

BIG MAMA (*coming in front of* BIG DADDY *with the cake*).: Big Daddy, I will not allow you to talk that way, not even on your birthday, I—

BIG DADDY: I'll talk like I want to on my birthday, Ida, or any other goddam day of the year and anybody here that don't like it knows what they can do!

BIG MAMA: You don't mean that!

BIG DADDY: What makes you think I don't mean it?

(*Meanwhile various discreet signals have been exchanged and* GOOPER *has also gone out on the gallery.*)

BIG MAMA: I just know you don't mean it.

BIG DADDY: You don't know a goddam thing and you never did!

BIG MAMA: Big Daddy, you don't mean that.

BIG DADDY: Oh, yes, I do, oh, yes, I do, I mean it! I

put up with a whole lot of crap around here because I thought I was dying. And you thought I was dying and you started taking over, well, you can stop taking over now, Ida, because I'm not gonna die, you can just stop now this business of taking over because you're not taking over because I'm not dying, I went through the laboratory and the goddam exploratory operation and there's nothing wrong with me but a spastic colon. And I'm not dying of cancer which you thought I was dying of. Ain't that so? Didn't you think that I was dying of cancer, Ida?

(*Almost everybody is out on the gallery but the two old people glaring at each other across the blazing cake.*)
(BIG MAMA'*s chest heaves and she presses a fat fist to her mouth.*)
(BIG DADDY *continues, hoarsely.*)

Ain't that so, Ida? Didn't you have an idea I was dying of cancer and now you could take control of this place and everything on it? I got that impression, I seemed to get that impression. Your loud voice everywhere, your fat old body butting in here and there!

BIG MAMA: Hush! The Preacher!
BIG DADDY: Fuck the goddam preacher!

(BIG MAMA *gasps loudly and sits down on the sofa which is almost too small for her.*)

Did you hear what I said? I said fuck the goddam preacher!

(*Somebody closes the gallery doors from outside just as there is a burst of fireworks and excited cries from the children.*)

BIG MAMA: I never seen you act like this before and I can't think what's got in you!
BIG DADDY: I went through all that laboratory and operation and all just so I would know if you or me was boss here! Well, now it turns out that I am and you ain't—and that's my birthday present—and my cake and champagne!—because for three years now you been gradually taking over. Bossing. Talking. Sashaying your fat old body around the place I made! I made this place! I was overseer on it! I was the overseer on the old Straw and Ochello plantation. I quit school at ten! I quit school at ten years old and went to work like a nigger in the fields. And I rose to be overseer of the Straw and Ochello plantation. And old Straw died and I was Ochello's partner and the place got bigger and bigger and bigger and bigger and bigger! I did all that myself with no goddam help from you, and now you think you're just about to take over. Well, I am just about to tell you that you are not just about to take over, you are not just about to take

over a God damn thing. Is that clear to you, Ida? Is that very plain to you, now? Is that understood completely? I been through the laboratory from A to Z. I've had the goddam exploratory operation, and nothing is wrong with me but a spastic colon—made spastic, I guess, by *disgust!* By all the goddam lies and liars that I have had to put up with, and all the goddam hypocrisy that I lived with all these forty years that we been livin' together!

Hey! Ida!! Blow out the candles on the birthday cake! Purse up your lips and draw a deep breath and blow out the goddam candles on the cake!

BIG MAMA: Oh, Big Daddy, oh, oh, oh, Big Daddy!
BIG DADDY: What's the matter with you?
BIG MAMA: *In all these years you never believed that I loved you??*
BIG DADDY: Huh?
BIG MAMA: *And I did. I did so much. I did love you!—I even loved your hate and your hardness, Big Daddy!* (*She sobs and rushes awkwardly out onto the gallery.*)
BIG DADDY (*to himself*): *Wouldn't it be funny if that was true....*

(*A pause is followed by a burst of light in the sky from the fireworks.*)

BRICK! HEY, BRICK!

(*He stands over his blazing birthday cake.*)
(*After some moments,* BRICK *hobbles in on his crutch, holding his glass.* MARGARET *follows him with a bright, anxious smile.*)

I didn't call you, Maggie. I called Brick.
MARGARET: I'm just delivering him to you.

(*She kisses* BRICK *on the mouth which he immediately wipes with the back of his hand. She flies girlishly back out.* BRICK *and his father are alone.*)

BIG DADDY: Why did you do that?
BRICK: Do what, Big Daddy?
BIG DADDY: Wipe her kiss off your mouth like she'd spit on you.
BRICK: I don't know. I wasn't conscious of it.
BIG DADDY: That woman of yours has a better shape on her than Gooper's but somehow or other they got the same look about them.
BRICK: What sort of look is that, Big Daddy?
BIG DADDY: I don't know how to describe it but it's the same look.
BRICK: They don't look peaceful, do they?
BIG DADDY: No, they sure in hell don't.
BRICK: They look nervous as cats?
BIG DADDY: That's right, they look nervous as cats.
BRICK: Nervous as a couple of cats on a hot tin roof?
BIG DADDY: That's right, boy, they look like a couple

of cats on a hot tin roof. It's funny that you and Gooper being so different would pick out the same type of woman.

BRICK: Both of us married into society, Big Daddy.

BIG DADDY: Crap . . . I wonder what gives them both that look?

BRICK: Well. They're sittin' in the middle of a big piece of land, Big Daddy, twenty-eight thousand acres is a pretty big piece of land and so they're squaring off on it, each determined to knock off a bigger piece of it than the other whenever you let it go.

BIG DADDY: I got a surprise for those women. I'm not gonna let it go for a long time yet if that's what they're waiting for.

BRICK: That's right, Big Daddy. You just sit tight and let them scratch each other's eyes out. . . .

BIG DADDY: You bet your life I'm going to sit tight on it and let those sons of bitches scratch their eyes out, ha ha ha. . . .

But Gooper's wife's a good breeder, you got to admit she's fertile. Hell, at supper tonight she had them all at the table and they had to put a couple of extra leafs in the table to make room for them, she's got five head of them, now, and another one's comin'.

BRICK: Yep, number six is comin'. . . .

BIG DADDY: Six hell, she'll probably drop a litter next time. Brick, you know, I swear to God, I don't know the way it happens?

BRICK: The way what happens, Big Daddy?

BIG DADDY: You git you a piece of land, by hook or crook, an' things start growin' on it, things accumulate on it, and the first thing you know it's completely out of hand, completely out of hand!

BRICK: Well, they say nature hates a vacuum, Big Daddy.

BIG DADDY: That's what they say, but sometimes I think that a vacuum is a hell of a lot better than some of the stuff that nature replaces it with.

Is someone out there by that door?

GOOPER: Hey Mae.

BRICK: Yep.

BIG DADDY: Who? (*He has lowered his voice.*)

BRICK: Someone int'rested in what we say to each other.

BIG DADDY: Gooper?—GOOPER!

(*After a discreet pause,* MAE *appears in the gallery door.*)

MAE: Did you call Gooper, Big Daddy?

BIG DADDY: Aw, it was you.

MAE: Do you want Gooper, Big Daddy?

BIG DADDY: No, and I don't want you. I want some privacy here, while I'm having a confidential talk with my son Brick. Now it's too hot in here to close them doors, but if I have to close those fuckin' doors in order to have a private talk with

my son Brick, just let me know and I'll close 'em. Because I hate eavesdroppers, I don't like any kind of sneakin' an' spyin'.

MAE: Why, Big Daddy—

BIG DADDY: You stood on the wrong side of the moon, it threw your shadow!

MAE: I was just—

BIG DADDY: You was just nothing but *spyin'* an' you *know* it!

MAE (*begins to sniff and sob*): Oh, Big Daddy, you're so unkind for some reason to those that really love you!

BIG DADDY: Shut up, shut up, shut up! I'm going to move you and Gooper out of that room next to this! It's none of your goddam business what goes on in here at night between Brick an' Maggie. You listen at night like a couple of rutten peekhole spies and go and give a report on what you hear to Big Mama an' she comes to me and says they say such and such and so and so about what they heard goin' on between Brick an' Maggie, and Jesus, it makes me sick. I'm goin' to move you an' Gooper out of that room, I can't stand sneakin' an' spyin', it makes me puke. . . .

(MAE *throws back her head and rolls her eyes heavenward and extends her arms as if invoking God's pity for this unjust martyrdom; then she presses a handkerchief to her nose and flies from the room with a loud swish of skirts.*)

BRICK (*now at the liquor cabinet*): They listen, do they?

BIG DADDY: Yeah. They listen and give reports to Big Mama on what goes on in here between you and Maggie. They say that— (*He stops as if embarrassed.*) —You won't sleep with her, that you sleep on the sofa. Is that true or not true? If you don't like Maggie, get rid of Maggie!—What are you doin' there now?

BRICK: Fresh'nin up my drink.

BIG DADDY: Son, you know you got a real liquor problem?

BRICK: Yes, sir, yes, I know.

BIG DADDY: Is that why you quit sports-announcing, because of this liquor problem?

BRICK: Yes, sir, yes, sir, I guess so.

(*He smiles vaguely and amiably at his father across his replenished drink.*)

BIG DADDY: Son, don't guess about it, it's too important.

BRICK (*vaguely*): Yes, sir.

BIG DADDY: And listen to me, don't look at the damn chandelier. . . .

(*Pause.* BIG DADDY's *voice is husky.*)

—Somethin' else we picked up at th' big fire sale in Europe.

(Another pause.)

Life is important. There's nothing else to hold onto. A man that drinks is throwing his life away. Don't do it, hold onto your life. There's nothing else to hold onto. . . .

Sit down over here so we don't have to raise our voices, the walls have ears in this place.

BRICK *(hobbling over to sit on the sofa beside him)*: All right, Big Daddy.

BIG DADDY: Quit!—how'd that come about? Some disappointment?

BRICK: I don't know. Do you?

BIG DADDY: I'm askin' you, God damn it! How in hell would I know if you don't?

BRICK: I just got out there and found that I had a mouth full of cotton. I was always two or three beats behind what was goin' on on the field and so I—

BIG DADDY: Quit!

BRICK *(amiably)*: Yes, quit.

BIG DADDY: Son?

BRICK: Huh?

BIG DADDY *(inhales loudly and deeply from his cigar; then bends suddenly a little forward, exhaling loudly and raising a hand to his forehead)*: Whew!—ha ha!—I took in too much smoke, it made me a little lightheaded. . . .

(The mantel clock chimes.)

Why is it so damn hard for people to talk?

BRICK: Yeah. . . .

(The clock goes on sweetly chiming till it has completed the stroke of ten.)

—Nice peaceful-soundin' clock, I like to hear it all night. . . .

(He slides low and comfortable on the sofa; BIG DADDY *sits straight and rigid with some unspoken anxiety. All his gestures are tense and jerky as he talks. He wheezes and pants and sniffs through his nervous speech, glancing quickly, shyly, from time to time, at his son.)*

BIG DADDY: We got that clock the summer we wint to Europe, me an' Big Mama on that damn Cook's Tour, never such an awful time in my life. I'm tellin' you, son, those gooks over there, they gouge your eyeballs out in their grand hotels. And Big Mama bought more stuff than you could haul in a couple of boxcars, that's no crap. Everywhere she wint on this whirlwind tour, she bought, bought, bought. Why, half that stuff she bought is still crated up in the cellar, under water last spring! *(He laughs.)*

That Europe is nothin' on earth but a great big auction, that's all it is, that bunch of old worn-out places, it's just a big firesale, the whole

fuckin' thing, an' Big Mama wint wild in it, why, you couldn't hold that woman with a mule's harness! Bought, bought, bought!—lucky I'm a rich man, yes siree, Bob, an' half that stuff is mildewin' in th' basement. It's lucky I'm a rich man, it sure is lucky, well, I'm a rich man, Brick, yep, I'm a mighty rich man. *(His eyes light up for a moment.)*

Y'know how much I'm worth? Guess, Brick! Guess how much I'm worth!

*(*BRICK *smiles vaguely over his drink.)*

Close on ten million in cash an' blue-chip stocks, outside, mind you, of twenty-eight thousand acres of the richest land this side of the valley Nile!

But a man can't buy his life with it, he can't buy back his life with it when his life has been spent, that's one thing not offered in the Europe fire-sale or in the American markets or any markets on earth, a man can't buy his life with it, he can't buy back his life when his life is finished.

That's a sobering thought, a very sobering thought, and that's a thought that I was turning over in my head, over and over and over—until today. . . .

I'm wiser and sadder, Brick, for this experience which I just gone through. They's one thing else that I remember in Europe.

BRICK: What is that, Big Daddy?

BIG DADDY: The hills around Barcelona in the country of Spain and the children running over those bare hills in their bare skins beggin' like starvin' dogs with howls and screeches, and how fat the priests are on the streets of Barcelona, so many of them and so fat and so pleasant, ha ha!—Y'know I could feed that country? I got money enough to feed that goddam country, but the human animal is a selfish beast and I don't reckon the money I passed out there to those howling children in the hills around Barcelona would more than upholster the chairs in this room, I mean pay to put a new cover on this chair!

Hell, I threw them money like you'd scatter feed corn for chickens, I threw money at them just to get rid of them long enought to climb back into th' car and—drive away. . . .

And then in Morocco, them Arabs, why, I remember one day in Marrakech, that old walled Arab city, I set on a broken-down wall to have a cigar, it was fearful hot there and this Arab woman stood in the road and looked at me till I was embarrassed, she stood stock still in the dusty hot road and looked at me till I was embarrassed. But listen to this. She had a naked child with her, a little naked girl with her, barely able to toddle, and after a while she set this child on the ground and give her a push and whispered something to her.

This child come toward me, barely able t' walk, come toddling up to me and—

Jesus, it makes you sick to' remember a thing like this!

It stuck out its hand and tried to unbutton my trousers!

That child was not yet five! Can you believe me? Or do you think that I am making this up? I wint back to the hotel and said to Big Mama, Git packed! We're clearing out of this country. . . .

BRICK: Big Daddy, you're on a talkin' jag tonight.

BIG DADDY *(ignoring this remark)*: Yes, sir, that's how it is, the human animal is a beast that dies but the fact that he's dying don't give him pity for others, no, sir, it—

—Did you say something?

BRICK: Yes.

BIG DADDY: What?

BRICK: Hand me over that crutch so I can get up.

BIG DADDY: Where you goin'?

BRICK: I'm takin' a little short trip to Echo Spring.

BIG DADDY: To where?

BRICK: Liquor cabinet. . . .

BIG DADDY: Yes, sir, boy— *(He hands BRICK the crutch)* —the human animal is a beast that dies and if he's got money he buys and buys and buys and I think the reason he buys everything he can buy is that in the back of his mind he has the crazy hope that one of his purchases will be life everlasting!—Which it never can be. . . . The human animal is a beast that—

BRICK *(at the liquor cabinet)*: Big Daddy, you sure are shootin' th' breeze here tonight.

(There is a pause and voices are heard outside.)

BIG DADDY: I been quiet here lately, spoke not a word, just sat and stared into space. I had something heavy weighing on my mind but tonight that load was took off me. That's why I'm talking.—The sky looks diff'rent to me. . . .

BRICK: You know what I like to hear most?

BIG DADDY: What?

BRICK: Solid quiet. Perfect unbroken quiet.

BIG DADDY: Why?

BRICK: Because it's more peaceful.

BIG DADDY: Man, you'll hear a lot of that in the grave. *(He chuckles agreeably.)*

BRICK: Are you through talkin' to me?

BIG DADDY: Why are you so anxious to shut me up?

BRICK: Well, sir, ever so often you say to me, Brick, I want to have a talk with you, but when we talk, it never materializes. Nothing is said. You sit in a chair and gas about this and that and I look like I listen. I try to look like I listen, but I don't listen, not much. Communication is—awful hard be-tween people an'—somehow between you and me, it just don't—happen.

BIG DADDY: Have you ever been scared? I mean have you ever felt downright terror of something? *(He gets up.)* Just one moment. *(He looks off as if he were going to tell an important secret.)*

Brick?

BRICK: What?

BIG DADDY: Son, I thought I had it!

BRICK: Had what? Had what, Big Daddy?

BIG DADDY: Cancer!

BRICK: Oh . . .

BIG DADDY: I thought the old man made out of bones had laid his cold and heavy hand on my shoulder!

BRICK: Well, Big Daddy, you kept a tight mouth about it.

BIG DADDY: A pig squeals. A man keeps a tight mouth about it, in spite of a man not having a pig's advantage.

BRICK: What advantage is that?

BIG DADDY: Ignorance—of mortality—is a comfort. A man don't have that comfort, he's the only living thing that conceives of death, that knows what it is. The others go without knowing which is the way that anything living should go, go without knowing, without any knowledge of it, and yet a pig squeals, but a man sometimes, he can keep a tight mouth about it. Sometimes he—

(There is a deep smoldering ferocity in the old man.)

—can keep a tight mouth about it. I wonder if—

BRICK: What, Big Daddy?

BIG DADDY: A whiskey highball would injure this spastic condition?

BRICK: No, sir, it might do it good.

BIG DADDY *(grins suddenly, wolfishly)*: Jesus, I can't tell you! The sky is open! Christ, it's open again! It's open boy, it's open!

(BRICK looks down at his drink.)

BRICK: You feel better, Big Daddy?

BIG DADDY: Better? Hell! I can breathe!—All of my life I been like a doubled up fist. . . . *(He pours a drink.)* —Poundin', smashin', drivin'!—now I'm going to loosen these doubled-up hands and touch things *easy* with them. . . .

(He spreads his hands as if caressing the air.)

You know what I'm contemplating?

BRICK *(vaguely)*: No, sir. What are you contemplating?

BIG DADDY: Ha ha!—*Pleasure!*—pleasure with *women!*

(BRICK's smile fades a little but lingers.)

—Yes, boy. I'll tell you something that you might

not guess. I still have desire for women and this is my sixty-fifth birthday.

BRICK: I think that's mighty remarkable, Big Daddy.

BIG DADDY: Remarkable?

BRICK: *Admirable*, Big Daddy.

BIG DADDY: You're damn right it is, remarkable and admirable both. I realize now that I never had me enough. I let many chances slip by because of scruples about it, scruples, convention—crap.... All that stuff is bull, bull, bull!—It took the shadow of death to make me see it. Now that shadow's lifted, I'm going to cut loose and have, what is it they call it, have me a—ball!

BRICK: A ball, huh?

BIG DADDY: That's right, a ball, a ball! Hell!—I slept with Big Mama till, let's see, five years ago, till I was sixty and she was fifty-eight, and never even liked her, never did!

(*The phone has been ringing down the hall.* BIG MAMA *enters, exclaiming.*)

BIG MAMA: Don't you men hear that phone ring? I heard it way out on the gall'ry.

BIG DADDY: There's five rooms off this front gall'ry that you could go through. Why do you go through this one?

(BIG MAMA *makes a playful face as she bustles out the hall door.*)

Hunh!—Why, when Big Mama goes out of a room, I can't remember what that woman looks like—

BIG MAMA: Hello.

BIG DADDY: But when Big Mama comes back into the room, boy, then I see what she looks like, and I wish I didn't.

(*Bends over laughing at this joke till it hurts his guts and he straightens with a grimace. The laugh subsides to a chuckle as he puts the liquor glass a little distrustfully down the table.*)

BIG MAMA: Hello, Miss Sally.

(BRICK *has risen and hobbled to the gallery doors.*)

BIG DADDY: Hey! Where you goin'?

BRICK: Out for a breather.

BIG DADDY: Not yet you ain't. Stay here till this talk is finished, young fellow.

BRICK: I thought it was finished, Big Daddy.

BIG DADDY: It ain't even begun.

BRICK: My mistake. Excuse me. I just wanted to feel that river breeze.

BIG DADDY: Set back in that chair.

(BIG MAMA's *voice rises, carrying down the hall.*)

BIG MAMA: Miss Sally, you're a case! You're a caution, Miss Sally.

BIG DADDY: Jesus, she's talking to my old maid sister again.

BIG MAMA: Why didn't you give me a chance to explain it to you?

BIG DADDY: Brick, this stuff burns me.

BIG MAMA: Well, goodbye, now, Miss Sally. You come down real soon. Big Daddy's dying to see you.

BIG DADDY: Crap!

BIG MAMA: Yaiss, goodbye, Miss Sally....

(*She hangs up and bellows with mirth.* BIG DADDY *groans and covers his ears as she approaches.*)

(*Bursting in*)

Big Daddy, that was Miss Sally callin' from Memphis again! You know what she done, Big Daddy? She called her doctor in Memphis to git him to tell her what that spastic thing is! Ha-HAAAA!—And called back to tell me how relieved she was that—Hey! Let me in!

(BIG DADDY *has been holding the door half closed against her.*)

BIG DADDY: Naw I ain't. I told you not to come and go through this room. You just back out and go through those five other rooms.

BIG MAMA: Big Daddy? Big Daddy? Oh, Big Daddy!—You didn't mean those things you said to me, did you?

(*He shuts door firmly against her but she still calls.*)

Sweetheart? Sweetheart? Big Daddy? You didn't mean those awful things you said to me?—I know you didn't. I know you didn't mean those things in your heart....

(*The childlike voice fades with a sob and her heavy footsteps retreat down the hall.* BRICK *has risen once more on his crutches and starts for the gallery again.*)

BIG DADDY: All I ask of that woman is that she leave me alone. But she can't admit to herself that she makes me sick. That comes of having slept with her too many years. Should of quit much sooner but that old woman she never got enough of it—and I was good in bed ... I never should of wasted so much of it on her.... They say you got just so many and each one is numbered. Well, I got a few left in me, a few, and I'm going to pick me a good one to spend 'em on! I'm going to pick me a choice one, I don't care how much she costs, I'll smother her in—minks! Ha ha! I'll strip her naked and smother her in minks and choke her with diamonds! Ha ha! I'll strip her naked and choke her with diamonds and smother her with minks and hump her from hell to breakfast. *Ha aha ha ha ha!*

MAE (*gaily at door*): Who's that laughin' in there?

GOOPER: Is Big Daddy laughin' in there?

BIG DADDY: Crap!—them two—*drips.* . . .

(He goes over and touches BRICK's *shoulder.)*

Yes, son. Brick, boy.—I'm *happy!* I'm happy, son, I'm happy!

(He chokes a little and bites his under lip, pressing his head quickly, shyly against his son's head and then, coughing with embarrassment, goes uncertainly back to the table where he set down the glass. He drinks and makes a grimace as it burns his guts. BRICK *sighs and rises with effort.)*

What makes you so restless? Have you got ants in your britches?

BRICK: Yes, sir . . .

BIG DADDY: Why?

BRICK: —Something—hasn't happened. . . .

BIG DADDY: Yeah? What is that!

BRICK *(sadly)*: —the click. . . .

BIG DADDY: Did you say click?

BRICK: Yes, click.

BIG DADDY: What click?

BRICK: A click that I get in my head that makes me peaceful.

BIG DADDY: I sure in hell don't know what you're talking about, but it disturbs me.

BRICK: It's just a mechanical thing.

BIG DADDY: What is a mechanical thing?

BRICK: This click that I get in my head that makes me peaceful. I got to drink till I get it. It's just a mechanical thing, something like a—like a—like a—

BIG DADDY: Like a—

BRICK: Switch clicking off in my head, turning the hot light off and the cool night on and— *(He looks up, smiling sadly.)* —all of a sudden there's —peace!

BIG DADDY *(whistles long and soft with astonishment; he goes back to* BRICK *and clasps his son's two shoulders)* Jesus! I didn't know it had gotten that bad with you. Why, boy, you're—*alcoholic!*

BRICK: That's the truth, Big Daddy. I'm alcoholic.

BIG DADDY: This shows how I—let things go!

BRICK: I have to hear that little click in my head that makes me peaceful. Usually I hear it sooner than this, sometimes as early as—noon, but—
    —Today it's—dilatory. . . .
    —I just haven't got the right level of alcohol in my bloodstream yet!

(This last statement is made with energy as he freshens his drink.)

BIG DADDY: Uh—huh. Expecting death made me blind. I didn't have no idea that a son of mine was turning into a drunkard under my nose.

BRICK *(gently)*: Well, now you do, Big Daddy, the news has penetrated. . . .

BIG DADDY: Uh-huh, yes, now I do. The news has penetrated.

BRICK: And so if you'll excuse me—

BIG DADDY: No, I won't excuse you.

BRICK: —I'd better sit by myself till I hear that click in my head, it's just a mechanical thing but it don't happen except when I'm alone or talking to no one. . . .

BIG DADDY: You got a long, long time to sit still, boy, and talk to no one, but now you're talkin' to me. At least I'm talking to you. And you set there and listen until I tell you the conversation is over!

BRICK: But this talk is like all the others we've ever had together in our lives! It's nowhere, nowhere!—it's—it's *painful,* Big Daddy. . . .

BIG DADDY: All right, then let it be painful, but don't you move from that chair!—I'm going to remove that crutch. . . . *(He seizes the crutch and tosses it across room.)*

BRICK: I can hop on one foot, and if I fall, I can crawl!

BIG DADDY: If you ain't careful you're gonna crawl off this plantation and then, by Jesus, you'll have to hustle your drinks along Skid Row!

BRICK: That'll come, Big Daddy.

BIG DADDY: Naw, it won't. You're my son and I'm going to straighten you out; now that *I'm* straightened out, I'm going to straighten out you!

BRICK: Yeah?

BIG DADDY: Today the report come in from Ochsner Clinic. Y'know what they told me? *(His face glows with triumph.)* The only thing that they could detect with all the instruments of science in that great hospital is a little spastic condition of the colon! And nerves torn to pieces by all that worry about it.

(A little girl bursts into room with a sparkler clutched in each fist, hops and shrieks like a monkey gone mad and rushes back out again as BIG DADDY *strikes at her.)*
(Silence. The two men stare at each other. A woman laughs gaily outside.)

I want you to know I breathed a sigh of relief almost as powerful as the Vicksburg tornado!

(There is laughter outside, running footsteps, the soft, plushy sound and light of exploding rockets.)
*(*BRICK *stares at him soberly for a long moment; then makes a sort of startled sound in his nostrils and springs up on one foot and hops across the room to grab his crutch, swinging on the furniture for support. He gets the crutch and flees as if in horror for the gallery. His father seizes him by the sleeve of his white silk pajamas.)*

Stay here, you son of a bitch!—till I say go!

BRICK: I can't.

BIG DADDY: You sure in hell will, God damn it.

BRICK: No, I can't. We talk, you talk, in—circles! We get no where, no where! It's always the same, you say you want to talk to me and don't have a fuckin' thing to say to me!

BIG DADDY: Nothin' to say when I'm tellin' you I'm going to live when I thought I was dying?!

BRICK: Oh—*that*—Is that what you have to say to me?

BIG DADDY: Why, you son of a bitch! Ain't that, ain't that—*important?!*

BRICK: Well, you said that, that's said, and now *I*—

BIG DADDY: Now you set back down.

BRICK: You're all balled up, you—

BIG DADDY: I ain't balled up!

BRICK: You are, you're all balled up!

BIG DADDY: Don't tell me what I am, you drunken whelp! I'm going to tear this coat sleeve off you if you don't set down!

BRICK: Big Daddy—

BIG DADDY: Do what I tell you! I'm the boss here, now! I want you to know I'm back in the driver's seat now!

(BIG MAMA *rushes in, clutching her great heaving bosom.*)

BIG MAMA: Big Daddy!

BIG DADDY: What in hell do you want in here, Big Mama?

BIG MAMA: Oh, Big Daddy! Why are you shouting like that? I just cain't *stainnnnnnnd*—it. . . .

BIG DADDY (*raising the back of his hand above his head*): *GIT!*—outa here.

(*She rushes back out, sobbing.*)

BRICK (*softly, sadly*): *Christ.* . . .

BIG DADDY (*fiercely*): Yeah! Christ!—is right . . .

(BRICK *breaks loose and hobbles toward the gallery.*)
(BIG DADDY *jerks his crutch from under* BRICK *so he steps with the injured ankle. He utters a hissing cry of anguish, clutches a chair and pulls it over on top of him on the floor.*)

Son of a—tub of—hog fat. . . .

BRICK: Big Daddy! Give me my crutch.

(BIG DADDY *throws the crutch out of reach.*)

Give me that crutch, Big Daddy.

BIG DADDY: Why do you drink?

BRICK: Don't know, give me my crutch!

BIG DADDY: You better think why you drink or give up drinking!

BRICK: Will you please give me my crutch so I can get up off this floor?

BIG DADDY: First you answer my question. Why do you drink? Why are you throwing your life away, boy, like somethin' disgusting you picked up on the street?

BRICK (*getting onto his knees*): Big Daddy, I'm in pain, I stepped on that foot.

BIG DADDY: Good! I'm glad you're not too numb with the liquor in you to feel some pain!

BRICK: You—spilled my—drink . . .

BIG DADDY: I'll make a bargain with you. You tell me why you drink and I'll hand you one. I'll pour the liquor myself and hand it to you.

BRICK: Why do I drink?

BIG DADDY: Yea! Why?

BRICK: Give me a drink and I'll tell you.

BIG DADDY: Tell me first!

BRICK: I'll tell you in one word.

BIG DADDY: What word?

BRICK: DISGUST!

(*The clock chimes softly, sweetly.* BIG DADDY *gives it a short, outraged glance.*)

Now how about that drink?

BIG DADDY: What are you disgusted with? You got to tell me that, first. Otherwise being disgusted don't make no sense!

BRICK: Give me my crutch.

BIG DADDY: You heard me, you got to tell me what I asked you first.

BRICK: I told you, I said to kill my disgust!

BIG DADDY: DISGUST WITH WHAT!

BRICK: You strike a hard bargain.

BIG DADDY: What are you disgusted with?—an' I'll pass you the liquor.

BRICK: I can hop on one foot, and if I fall, I can crawl.

BIG DADDY: You want liquor that bad?

BRICK (*dragging himself up, clinging to bedstead*): Yeah, I want it that bad.

BIG DADDY: If I give you a drink, will you tell me what it is you're disgusted with, Brick?

BRICK: Yes, sir, I will try to.

(*The old man pours him a drink and solemnly passes it to him.*)
(*There is a silence as* BRICK *drinks.*)

Have you ever heard the word "mendacity"?

BIG DADDY: Sure. Mendacity is one of them five dollar words that cheap politicians throw back and forth at each other.

BRICK: You know what it means?

BIG DADDY: Don't it mean lying and liars?

BRICK: Yes, sir, lying and liars.

BIG DADDY: Has someone been lying to you?

CHILDREN (*chanting in chorus offstage*):
   We want Big Dad-dee!
   We want Big Dad-dee

(GOOPER *appears in the gallery door.*)

GOOPER: Big Daddy, the kiddies are shouting for you out there.

BIG DADDY (*fiercely*): Keep out, Gooper!

GOOPER: 'Scuse *me*!

(BIG DADDY *slams the doors after* GOOPER.)

BIG DADDY: Who's been lying to you, has Margaret been lying to you, has your wife been lying to you about something, Brick?

BRICK: Not her. That wouldn't matter.

BIG DADDY: Then who's been lying to you, and what about?

BRICK: No one single person and no one lie. . . .

BIG DADDY: Then what, what then, for Christ's sake?

BRICK: The whole, the whole—thing. . . .

BIG DADDY: Why are you rubbing your head? You got a headache?

BRICK: No, I'm tryin' to—

BIG DADDY: —Concentrate, but you can't because your brain's all soaked with liquor, is that the trouble? Wet brain! (*He snatches the glass from* BRICK's *hand.*) What do you know about this mendacity thing? Hell! I could write a book on it! Don't you know that? I could write a book on it and still not cover the subject. Well, I could, I could write a goddam book on it and still not cover the subject anywhere near enough!!—Think of all the lies I got to put up with!—Pretenses! Ain't that mendacity? Having to pretend stuff you don't think or feel or have any idea of? Having for instance to act like I care for Big Mama!—I haven't been able to stand the sight, sound, or smell of that woman for forty years now!—even when I *laid* her!—regular as a piston. . . .

Pretend to love that son of a bitch of a Gooper and his wife Mae and those five same screechers out there like parrots in a jungle? Jesus! Can't stand to look at 'em!

Church!—it bores the bejesus out of me but I go!—I go an' sit there and listen to the fool preacher!

Clubs!—Elks! Masons! Rotary!—*crap!*

(*A spasm of pain makes him clutch his belly. He sinks into a chair and his voice is softer and hoarser.*)

You I *do* like for some reason, did always have some kind of real feeling for—affection—respect—yes, always. . . .

You and being a success as a planter is all I ever had any devotion to in my whole life!—and that's the truth. . . .

I don't know why, but it is!

I've lived with mendacity!—Why can't *you* live with it? Hell, you *got* to live with it, there's nothing *else* to *live* with except mendacity, is there?

BRICK: Yes, sir. Yes, sir there is something else that you can live with!

BIG DADDY: What?

BRICK (*lifting his glass*): This!—Liquor. . . .

BIG DADDY: That's not living, that's dodging away from life.

BRICK: I want to dodge away from it.

BIG DADDY: Then why don't you kill yourself, man?

BRICK: I like to drink. . . .

BIG DADDY: Oh, God, I can't talk to you. . . .

BRICK: I'm sorry, Big Daddy.

BIG DADDY: Not as sorry as I am. I'll tell you something. A little while back when I thought my number was up—

(*This speech should have torrential pace and fury.*)

—before I found out it was just this—spastic—colon. I thought about you. Should I or should I not, if the jig was up, give you this place when I go—since I hate Gooper an' Mae an' know that they hate me, and since all five same monkeys are little Maes an' Goopers.—And I thought, No!—Then I thought, Yes!—I couldn't make up my mind. I hate Gooper and his five same monkeys and that bitch Mae! Why should I turn over twenty-eight thousand acres of the richest land this side of the valley Nile to not my kind?—But why in hell, on the other hand, Brick—should I subsidize a goddam fool on the bottle?—Liked or not liked, well, maybe even—*loved!*—Why should I do that?—Subsidize worthless behavior? Rot? Corruption?

BRICK (*smiling*): I understand.

BIG DADDY: Well, if you do, you're smarter than I am. God damn it, because I don't understand. And this I will tell you frankly. I didn't make up my mind at all on that question and still to this day I ain't made out no will!—Well, now I don't *have* to. The pressure is gone. I can just wait and see if you pull yourself together or if you don't.

BRICK: That's right, Big Daddy.

BIG DADDY: You sound like you thought I was kidding.

BRICK (*rising*): No, sir, I know you're not kidding.

BIG DADDY: But you don't care—?

BRICK (*hobbling toward the gallery door*): No, sir, I don't care. . . .

(*He stands in the gallery doorway as the night sky turns pink and green and gold with successive flashes of light.*)

BIG DADDY: WAIT!—Brick. . . .

(*His voice drops. Suddenly there is something shy, tender, in his restraining gesture.*)

Don't let's—leave it like this, like them other talks we've had, we've always—talked around things, we've—just talked around things for some fuckin' reason. I don't know what, it's always like something was left not spoken, something avoided because neither of us was honest enough with the—other. . . .

BRICK: I never lied to you, Big Daddy.

BIG DADDY: Did I ever to *you?*

BRICK: No, sir. . . .

BIG DADDY: Then there is at least two people that never lied to each other.

BRICK: But we've never *talked* to each other.

BIG DADDY: We can *now.*

BRICK: Big Daddy, there don't seem to be anything much to say.

BIG DADDY: You say that you drink to kill your disgust with lying.

BRICK: You said to give you a reason.

BIG DADDY: Is liquor the only thing that'll kill this disgust?

BRICK: Now. Yes.

BIG DADDY: But not once, huh?

BRICK: Not when I was still young an' believing. A drinking man's someone who wants to forget he isn't still young an' believing.

BIG DADDY: Believing what?

BRICK: Believing. . . .

BIG DADDY: Believing *what?*

BRICK *(stubbornly evasive):* Believing. . . .

BIG DADDY: I don't know what the hell you mean by believing and I don't think you know what you mean by believing, but if you still got sports in your blood, go back to sports announcing and—

BRICK: Sit in a glass box watching games I can't play? Describing what I can't do while players do it? Sweating out their disgust and confusion in contests I'm not fit for? Drinkin' a coke, half bourbon, so I can stand it? That's no goddam good any more, no help—time just outran me, Big Daddy—got there first . . .

BIG DADDY: I think you're passing the buck.

BRICK: You know many drinkin' men?

BIG DADDY *(with a slight, charming smile):* I have known a fair number of that species.

BRICK: Could any of them tell you why he drank?

BIG DADDY: Yep, you're passin' the buck to things like time and disgust with "mendacity" and—crap!—if you got to use that kind of language about a thing, it's ninety-proof bull, and I'm not buying any.

BRICK: I had to give you a reason to get a drink!

BIG DADDY: You started drinkin' when your friend Skipper died.

(Silence for five beats. Then BRICK *makes a startled movement, reaching for his crutch.)*

BRICK: What are you suggesting?

BIG DADDY: I'm suggesting nothing.

(The shuffle and clop of BRICK'S *rapid hobble away from*

his father's steady, grave attention.)

—But Gooper an' Mae suggested that there was something not right exactly in your—

BRICK *(stopping short downstage as if backed to a wall):* "Not right"?

BIG DADDY: Not, well, exactly *normal* in your friendship with—

BRICK: They suggested that, too? I thought that was Maggie's suggestion.

*(*BRICK'S *detachment is at last broken through. His heart is accelerated; his forehead sweat-beaded; his breath becomes more rapid and his voice hoarse. The thing they're discussin, timidly and painfully on the side of* BIG DADDY, *fiercely, violently on* BRICK'S *side, is the inadmissible thing that* SKIPPER *died to disavow between them. The fact that if it existed it had to be disavowed to "keep face" in the world they lived in, may be at the heart of the "mendacity" that* BRICK *drinks to kill his disgust with. It may be the root of his collapse. Or maybe it is only a single manifestation of it, not even the most important. The bird that I hope to catch in the net of this play is not the solution of one man's psychological problem. I'm trying to catch the true quality of experience in a group of people, that cloudy, flickering, evanescent—fiercely charged!—interplay of live human beings in the thundercloud of a common crisis. Some mystery should be left in the revelation of characters in a play, just as a great deal of mystery is always left in the revelation of character in life, even in one's own character to himself. This does not absolve the playwright of his duty to observe and probe as clearly and deeply as he legitimately can: but it should steer him away from "pat" conclusions, facile definitions which make a play just a play, not a snare for the truth of human experience.)*

(The following scene should be played with great concentration, with most of the power leashed but palpable in what is left unspoken.)

Who else's suggestion is it, is it *yours?* How many others thought that Skipper and I were—

BIG DADDY *(gently):* Now, hold on, hold on a minute, son.—I knocked around in my time.

BRICK: What's that got to do with—

BIG DADDY: I said "Hold on!"—I bummed, I bummed this country till I was—

BRICK: Whose suggestion, who else's suggestion is it?

BIG DADDY: Slept in hobo jungles and railroad Y's and flophouses in all cities before I—

BRICK: Oh, *you* think so, too, you call me your son and a queer. Oh! Maybe that's why you put Maggie and me in this room that was Jack Straw's and Peter Ochello's, in which that pair of old sisters slept in a double bed where both of 'em died!

BIG DADDY: *Now just don't go throwing rocks at—*

(Suddenly REVEREND TOOKER *appears in the gallery doors, his head slightly, playfully, fatuously cocked, with a*

practised clergyman's smile, sincere as a bird call blown on a hunter's whistle, the living embodiment of the pious, conventional lie.)

(BIG DADDY gasps a little at this perfectly timed, but incongruous, apparition.)

—What're you lookin' for, Preacher?

REVEREND TOOKER: The gentleman's lavatory, ha ha!—heh, heh . . .

BIG DADDY *(with strained courtesy)*: —Go back out and walk down to the other end of the gallery, Reverend Tooker, and use the bathroom connected with my bedroom, and if you can't find it, ask them where it is!

REVEREND TOOKER: Ah, thanks. *(He goes out with a deprecatory chuckle.)*

BIG DADDY: It's hard to talk in this place . . .

BRICK: Son of a—!

BIG DADDY *(leaving a lot unspoken)*: —I seen all things and understood a lot of them, till 1910. Christ, the year that—I had worn my shoes through, hocked my—I hopped off a yellow dog freight car half a mile down the road, slept in a wagon of cotton outside the gin—Jack Straw an' Peter Ochello took me in. Hired me to manage this place which grew into this one.—When Jack Straw died—why, old Peter Ochello quit eatin' like a dog does when its master's dead, and died, too!

BRICK: Christ!

BIG DADDY: I'm just saying I understand such—

BRICK *(violently)*: Skipper is dead. I have not quit eating!

BIG DADDY: No, but you started drinking.

(BRICK wheels on his crutch and hurls his glass across the room shouting.)

BRICK: YOU THINK SO, TOO?

(Footsteps run on the gallery. There are women's calls.)
(BIG DADDY goes toward the door.)
(BRICK is transformed, as if a quiet mountain blew suddenly up in volcanic flame.)

BRICK: You think so, too? You think so, too? You think me an' Skipper did, did, did!—sodomy!—together?

BIG DADDY: Hold—!

BRICK: That what you—

BIG DADDY: —ON—a minute!

BRICK: You think we did dirty things between us, Skipper an'—

BIG DADDY: Why are you shouting like that? Why are you—

BRICK: —Me, is that what you think of Skipper, is that—

BIG DADDY: —so excited? I don't think nothing. I don't know nothing. I'm simply telling you what—

BRICK: You think that Skipper and me were a pair of dirty old men?

BIG DADDY: Now that's—

BRICK: Straw? Ochello? A couple of—

BIG DADDY: Now just—

BRICK: —fucking sissies? Queers? Is that what you—

BIG DADDY: Shhh.

BRICK: —think?

(He loses his balance and pitches to his knees without noticing the pain. He grabs the bed and drags himself up.)

BIG DADDY: Jesus!—Whew. . . . Grab my hand!

BRICK: Naw, I don't want your hand. . . .

BIG DADDY: Well, I want yours. Git up!

(He draws him up, keeps an arm about him with concern and affection.)

You broken out in a sweat! You're panting like you'd run a race with—

BRICK *(freeing himself from his father's hold)*: Big Daddy, you shock me, Big Daddy, you, you—*shock* me! Talkin' so— *(He turns away from his father.)* —casually!—about a—thing like that . . .

—Don't you know how people *feel* about things like that? How, how *disgusted* they are by things like that? Why, at Ole Miss when it was discovered a pledge to our fraternity, Skipper's and mine, did a, *attempted* to do a, unnatural thing with—

We not only dropped him like a hot rock!—We told him to git off the campus, and he did, he got!—All the way to— *(He halts, breathless.)*

BIG DADDY: —Where?

BRICK: —North Africa, last I heard!

BIG DADDY: Well, I have come back from further away than that, I have just now returned from the other side of the moon, death's country, son, and I'm not easy to shock by anything here. *(He comes downstage and faces out.)* Always, anyhow, lived with too much space around me to be infected by ideas of other people. One thing you can grow on a big place more important than cotton!—is *tolerance!*—I grown it. *(He returns toward BRICK.)*

BRICK: Why can't exceptional friendship, *real, real, deep, deep friendship!* between two men be respected as something clean and decent without being thought of as—

BIG DADDY: It can, it is, for God's sake.

BRICK: —Fairies. . . .

(In his utterance of this word, we gauge the wide and profound reach of the conventional mores he got from the world that crowned him with early laurel.)

BIG DADDY: I told Mae an' Gooper—

BRICK: Frig Mae and Gooper, frig all dirty lies and liars!—Skipper and me had a clean, true thing between us!—had a clean friendship, practically all our lives, till Maggie got the idea you're talking about. Normal? No!—it was too rare to be normal, any true thing between two people is too rare to be normal. Oh, once in a while he put his hand on my shoulder or I'd put mine on his, oh, maybe even, when we were touring the country in pro-football an' shared hotel-rooms we'd reach across the space between the two beds and shake hands to say goodnight, yeah, one or two times we—

BIG DADDY: Brick, nobody thinks that that's not normal!

BRICK: Well, they're mistaken, it was! It was a pure an' true thing an' that's not normal.

MAE (off stage): Big Daddy, they're startin' the fireworks.

(They both stare straight at each other for a long moment. The tension breaks and both turn away as if tired.)

BIG DADDY: Yeah, it's—hard t'—talk. . . .

BRICK: All right, then, let's—let it go. . . .

BIG DADDY: Why did Skipper crack up? Why have you?

(BRICK looks back at his father again. He has already decided, without knowing that he has made this decision, that he is going to tell his father that he is dying of cancer. Only this could even the score between them: one inadmissible thing in return for another.)

BRICK (ominously): All right. You're asking for it, Big Daddy. We're finally going to have that real true talk you wanted. It's too late to stop it, now, we got to carry it through and cover every subject.

(He hobbles back to the liquor cabinet.)

Uh-huh.

(He opens the ice bucket and picks up the silver tongs with slow admiration of their frosty brightness.)

Maggie declares that Skipper and I went into pro-football after we left "Ole Miss" because we were scared to grow up . . .

(He moves downstage with the shuffle and clop of a cripple on a crutch. As MARGARET did when her speech became "recitative," he looks out into the house, commanding its attention by his direct, concentrated gaze—a broken, "tragically elegant" figure telling simply as much as he knows of "the Truth.")

—Wanted to—keep on tossing—those long, long!—high, high!—passes that—couldn't be intercepted except by time, the aerial attack that made us famous! And so we did, we did, we kept it up for one season, that aerial attack, we held it high!—Yeah, but—

—that summer, Maggie, she laid the law down to me, said, Now or never, and so I married Maggie. . . .

BIG DADDY: How was Maggie in bed?

BRICK (wryly): Great! the greatest!

(BIG DADDY nods as if he thought so.)

She went on the road that fall with the Dixie Stars. Oh, she made a great show of being the world's best sport. She wore a—wore a—tall bearskin cap! A shako, they call it, a dyed moleskin coat, a moleskin coat dyed red!—Cut up crazy! Rented hotel ballrooms for victory celebrations, wouldn't cancel them when it—turned out—defeat. . . .

MAGGIE THE CAT! Ha ha!

(BIG DADDY nods.)

—But Skipper, he had some fever which came back on him which doctors couldn't explain and I got that injury—turned out to be just a shadow on the X-ray plate—and a touch of bursitis. . . .

I lay in a hospital bed, watched our games on TV, saw Maggie on the bench next to Skipper when he was hauled out of a game for stumbles, fumbles!—Burned me up the way she hung on his arm!—Y'know, I think that Maggie had always felt sort of left out because she and me never got any closer together than two people just get in bed, which is not much closer than two cats on a—fence humping. . . .

So! She took this time to work on poor dumb Skipper. He was a less than average student at Ole Miss, you know that, don't you?!—Poured in his mind the dirty, false idea that what we were, him and me, was a frustrated case of that ole pair of sisters that lived in this room, Jack Straw and Peter Ochello!—He, poor Skipper, went to bed with Maggie to prove it wasn't true, and when it didn't work out, he thought it *was* true!—Skipper broke in two like a rotten stick—nobody ever turned so fast to a lush—or died of it so quick. . . .

—Now are you satisfied?

(BIG DADDY has listened to this story, dividing the grain from the chaff. Now he looks at his son.)

BIG DADDY: Are *you* satisfied?

BRICK: With what?

BIG DADDY: That half-ass story!

BRICK: What's half-ass about it?

BIG DADDY: Something's left out of that story. What did you leave out?

(The phone has started ringing in the hall.)

GOOPER *(off stage)*: Hello.

(As if it reminded him of something BRICK *glances suddenly toward the sound and says.)*

BRICK: Yes!—I left out a long-distance call which I had from Skipper—

GOOPER: Speaking, go ahead.

BRICK: —In which he made a drunken confession to me and on which I hung up!

GOOPER: No.

BRICK: Last time we spoke to each other in our lives . . .

GOOPER: No, sir.

BIG DADDY: You musta said something to him before you hung up.

BRICK: What could I say to him?

BIG DADDY: Anything. Something.

BRICK: Nothing.

BIG DADDY: Just hung up?

BRICK: Just hung up.

BIG DADDY: Uh-huh. Anyhow now!—we have tracked down the lie with which you're disgusted and which you are drinking to kill your disgust with, Brick. You been passing the buck. This disgust with mendacity is disgust with yourself.

　　You!—dug the grave of your friend and kicked him in it!—before you'd face truth with him!

BRICK: *His* truth, not *mine!*

BIG DADDY: His truth, okay! But you wouldn't face it with him!

BRICK: Who *can* face truth? Can *you?*

BIG DADDY: Now don't start passin' the rotten buck again, boy!

BRICK: *How about these birthday congratulations, these many, many happy returns of the day, when ev'rybody knows there won't be any except you!*

*(*GOOPER, *who has answered the hall phone, lets out a high, shrill laugh; the voice becomes audible saying: "No, no, you got it all wrong! Upside down. Are you crazy?")*
*(*BRICK *suddenly catches his breath as he realizes that he has made a shocking disclosure. He hobbles a few paces, then freezes, and without looking at his father's shocked face, says.)*

　　Let's, let's—go out, now, and—watch the fireworks. Come on, Big Daddy.

*(*BIG DADDY *moves suddenly forward and grabs hold of the boy's crutch like it was a weapon for which they were fighting for possession.)*

BIG DADDY: Oh, no, no! No one's going out! What did you start to say?

BRICK: I don't remember.

BIG DADDY: "Many happy returns when they know there won't be any"?

BRICK: Aw, hell, Big Daddy, forget it. Come on out on the gallery and look at the fireworks they're shooting off for your birthday. . . .

BIG DADDY: First you finish that remark you were makin' before you cut off. "Many happy returns when they know there won't be any"?—Ain't that what you just said?

BRICK: Look, now. I can get around without that crutch if I have to but it would be a lot easier on the furniture an' glassware if I didn' have to go swinging along like Tarzan of th'—

BIG DADDY: FINISH! WHAT YOU WAS SAYIN'!

(An eerie green glow shows in sky behind him.)

BRICK *(sucking the ice in his glass, speech becoming thick)*: Leave th' place to Gooper and Mae an' their five little same little monkeys. All I want is—

BIG DADDY: "LEAVE TH' PLACE," did you say?

BRICK *(vaguely)*: All twenty-eight thousand acres of the richest land this side of the valley Nile.

BIG DADDY: Who said I was "leaving the place" to Gooper or anybody? This is my sixty-fifth birthday! I got fifteen years or twenty years left in me! I'll outlive *you!* I'll bury you an' have to pay for your coffin!

BRICK: Sure. Many happy returns. Now let's go watch the fireworks, come on, let's—

BIG DADDY: Lying, have they been lying? About the report from th'—clinic? Did they, did they—find something—*Cancer.* Maybe?

BRICK: Mendacity is a system that we live in. Liquor is one way out an' death's the other. . . .

(He takes the crutch from BIG DADDY's *loose grip and swings out on the gallery leaving the doors open.)*
(A song, "Pick a Bale of Cotton," is heard.)

MAE *(appearing in door)*: Oh, Big Daddy, the field hands are singin' fo' you!

BRICK: I'm sorry, Big Daddy. My head don't work any more and it's hard for me to understand how anybody could care if he lived or died or was dying or cared about anything but whether or not there was liquor left in the bottle and so I said what I said without thinking. In some ways I'm no better than the others, in some ways worse because I'm less alive. Maybe it's being alive that makes them lie, and being almost *not* alive makes me sort of accidentally truthful—I don't know but—anyway—we've been friends . . .

　　—And being friends is telling each other the truth. . . .

(There is a pause.)

You told *me!* I told *you!*

BIG DADDY *(slowly and passionately)*: CHRIST—DAMN—

GOOPER *(off stage)*: Let her go!

(Fireworks off stage right.)

BIG DADDY: —ALL—LYING SONS OF—LYING BITCHES!

(He straightens at last and crosses to the inside door. At the door he turns and looks back as if he had some desperate question he couldn't put into words. Then he nods reflectively and says in a hoarse voice.)

Yes, all liars, all liars, all lying dying liars!

(This is said slowly, slowly, with a fierce revulsion. He goes on out.)

—Lying! Dying! Liars!

(BRICK remains motionless as the lights dim out and the curtain falls.)

ACT 3

(There is no lapse of time. BIG DADDY is seen leaving as at the end of ACT 2.)

BIG DADDY: ALL LYIN'—DYIN'!—LIARS!—LIARS!—LIARS!

(MARGARET enters.)

MARGARET: Brick, what in the name of God was goin' on in this room?

(DIXIE and TRIXIE enter through the doors and circle around MARGARET shouting. MAE enters from the lower gallery window.)

MAE: Dixie, Trixie, you quit that!

(GOOPER enters through the doors.)

Gooper, will y' please get these kiddies to bed right now!

GOOPER: Mae, you seen Big Mama?

MAE: Not yet.

(GOOPER and kids exit through the doors. REVEREND TOOKER enters through the windows.)

REVEREND TOOKER: Those kiddies are so full of vitality. I think I'll have to be starting back to town.

MAE: Not yet, Preacher. You know we regard you as a member of this family, one of our closest an' dearest, so you just got t' be with us when Doc Baugh gives Big Mama th' actual truth about th' report from the clinic.

MARGARET: Where do you think you're going?

BRICK: Out for some air.

MARGARET: Why'd Big Daddy shout "Liars"?

MAE: Has Big Daddy gone to bed, Brick?

GOOPER *(entering)*: Now where is that old lady?

REVEREND TOOKER: I'll look for her. *(He exits to the gallery.)*

MAE: Cain'tcha find her, Gooper?

GOOPER: She's avoidin' this talk.

MAE: I think she senses somethin'.

MARGARET *(going out to the gallery to BRICK)*: Brick, they're goin' to tell Big Mama the truth about Big Daddy and she's goin' to need you.

DOCTOR BAUGH: This is going to be painful.

MAE: Painful things cain't always be avoided.

REVEREND TOOKER: I see Big Mama.

GOOPER: Hey, Big Mama, come here.

MAE: Hush, Gooper, don't holler.

BIG MAMA *(entering)*: Too much smell of burnt fireworks makes me feel a little bit sick at my stomach.—Where is Big Daddy?

MAE: That's what I want to know, where has Big Daddy gone?

BIG MAMA: He must have turned in, I reckon he went to baid . . .

GOOPER: Well, then, now we can talk.

BIG MAMA: What *is* this talk, *what* talk?

(MARGARET appears on the gallery, talking to DOCTOR BAUGH.)

MARGARET *(musically)*: My family freed their slaves ten years before abolition. My great-great-grandfather gave his slaves their freedom five years before the War between the States started!

MAE: Oh, for God's sake! Maggie's climbed back up in her family tree!

MARGARET *(sweetly)*: What, Mae?

(The pace must be very quick: great Southern animation.)

BIG MAMA *(addressing them all)*: I think Big Daddy was just worn out. He loves his family, he loves to have them around him, but it's a strain on his nerves. He wasn't himself tonight, Big Daddy wasn't himself, I could tell he was all worked up.

REVEREND TOOKER: I think he's remarkable.

BIG MAMA: Yaisss! Just remarkable. Did you all notice the food he ate at that table? Did you all notice the supper he put away? Why he ate like a hawss!

GOOPER: I hope he doesn't regret it.

BIG MAMA: What? Why that man—ate a huge piece of cawn bread with molasses on it! Helped himself twice to hoppin' John.

MARGARET: Big Daddy loves hoppin' John.—We had a real country dinner.

BIG MAMA *(overlapping MARGARET)*: Yaiss, he simply adores it! an' candied yams? Son? That man put away enough food at that table to stuff a *field* hand!

GOOPER *(with grim relish)*: I hope he don't have to pay for it later on . . .

BIG MAMA (*fiercely*): What's *that*, Gooper?

MAE: Gooper says he hopes Big Daddy doesn't suffer tonight.

BIG MAMA: Oh, shoot, Gooper says, Gooper says! Why should Big Daddy suffer for satisfying a normal appetite? There's nothin' wrong with that man but nerves, he's sound as a dollar! And now he knows he is an' that's why he ate such a supper. He had a big load off his mind, knowin' he wasn't doomed t'—what he thought he was doomed to . . .

MARGARET (*sadly and sweetly*): Bless his old sweet soul . . .

BIG MAMA (*vaguely*): Yais, bless his heart, where's Brick?

MAE: Outside.

GOOPER: —Drinkin' . . .

BIG MAMA: I know he's drinkin'. Cain't I see he's drinkin' without you continually tellin' me that boy's drinkin'?

MARGARET: Good for you, Big Mama! (*She applauds.*)

BIG MAMA: Other people *drink* and *have* drunk an' will *drink*, as long as they make that stuff an' put it in bottles.

MARGARET: That's the truth. I never trusted a man that didn't drink.

BIG MAMA: *Brick? Brick!*

MARGARET: He's still on the gall'ry. I'll go bring him in so we can talk.

BIG MAMA (*worriedly*): I don't know what this mysterious family conference is about.

(*Awkward silence. BIG MAMA looks from face to face, then belches slightly and mutters, "Excuse me . . ." She opens an ornamental fan suspended about her throat. A black lace fan to go with her black lace gown, and fans her wilting corsage, sniffing nervously and looking from face to face in the uncomfortable silence as MARGARET calls "Brick?" and BRICK sings to the moon on the gallery.*)

MARGARET: Brick, they're gonna tell Big Mama the truth an' she's gonna need you.

BIG MAMA: I don't know what's wrong here, you all have such long faces! Open that door on the hall and let some air circulate through here, will you please, Gooper?

MAE: I think we'd better leave that door closed, Big Mama, till after the talk.

MARGARET: Brick!

BIG MAMA: Reveren' Tooker, will *you* please open that door?

REVEREND TOOKER: I sure will, Big Mama.

MAE: I just didn't think we ought t' take any chance of Big Daddy hearin' a word of this discussion.

BIG MAMA: *I swan!* Nothing's going to be said in Big Daddy's house that he cain't hear if he want to!

GOOPER: Well, Big Mama, it's—

(*MAE gives him a quick, hard poke to shut him up. He glares at her fiercely as she circles before him like a burlesque ballerina, raising her skinny bare arms over her head, jangling her bracelets, exclaiming.*)

MAE: *A breeze! A breeze!*

REVEREND TOOKER: I think this house is the coolest house in the Delta.—Did you all know that Halsey Bank's widow put air-conditioning units in the church and rectory at Friar's Point in memory of Halsey?

(*General conversation has resumed; everybody is chatting so that the stage sounds like a bird cage.*)

GOOPER: Too bad nobody cools your church off for you. I bet you sweat in that pulpit these hot Sundays, Reverend Tooker.

REVEREND TOOKER: Yes, my vestments are drenched. Last Sunday the gold in my chasuble faded into the purple.

GOOPER: Reveren', you musta been preachin' hell's fire last Sunday.

MAE (*at the same time to DOCTOR BAUGH*): You reckon those vitamin B12 injections are what they're cracked up t' be, Doc Baugh?

DOCTOR BAUGH: Well if you want to be stuck with something I guess they're as good to be stuck with as anything else.

BIG MAMA (*at the gallery door*): *Maggie, Maggie, aren't you comin' with Brick?*

MAE (*suddenly and loudly, creating a silence*): I have a strange feeling, I have a peculiar feeling!

BIG MAMA (*turning from the gallery*): What feeling?

MAE: That Brick said somethin' he shouldn't of said t' Big Daddy.

BIG MAMA: Now what on earth could Brick of said t' Big Daddy that he shouldn't say?

GOOPER: Big Mama, there's somethin'—

MAE: NOW, WAIT!

(*She rushes up to BIG MAMA and gives her a quick hug and kiss. BIG MAMA pushes her impatiently off.*)

DOCTOR BAUGH: In my day they had what they call the Keeley cure for heavy drinkers.

BIG MAMA: Shoot!

DOCTOR BAUGH: But now I understand they just take some kind of tablets.

GOOPER: They call them "Annie Bust" tablets.

BIG MAMA: *Brick* don't need to take *nothin'.*

(*BRICK and MARGARET appear in gallery doors. BIG MAMA unaware of his presence behind her.*)

That boy is just broken up over Skipper's death. You know how poor Skipper died. They gave him a big, big dose of that sodium amytal stuff at his home and then they called the ambulance and give him another big, big dose of it at the hospital and that and all of the alcohol in his system fo' months an' months just proved too much for his heart . . . I'm scared of needles! I'm more scared of a needle than the knife . . . I think more people have been needled out of this world than— (*She stops short and wheels about.*) Oh—here's Brick! My precious baby—

(*She turns upon* BRICK *with short, fat arms extended, at the same time uttering a loud, short sob, which is both comic and touching.* BRICK *smiles and bows slightly, making a burlesque gesture of gallantry for* MARGARET *to pass before him into the room. Then he hobbles on his crutch directly to the liquor cabinet and there is absolute silence, with everybody looking at* BRICK *as everybody has always looked at* BRICK *when he spoke or moved or appeared. One by one he drops ice cubes in his glass, then suddenly, but not quickly looks back over his shoulder with a wry, charming smile, and says.*)

BRICK: I'm sorry! Anyone else?

BIG MAMA (*sadly*): No, son, I *wish* you wouldn't!

BRICK: I wish I didn't have to, Big Mama, but I'm still waiting for that click in my head which makes it all smooth out!

BIG MAMA: Ow, Brick, you—BREAK MY HEART!

MARGARET (*at same time*): *Brick, go sit with Big Mama!*

BIG MAMA: I just cain't staiiiiiii-nnnnnnnd-it . . . (*She sobs.*)

MAE: Now that we're all assembled—

GOOPER: We kin talk . . .

BIG MAMA: Breaks my heart . . .

MARGARET: Sit with Big Mama, Brick, and hold her hand.

(BIG MAMA *sniffs very loudly three times, almost like three drumbeats in the pocket of silence.*)

BRICK: You do that, Maggie. I'm a restless cripple. I got to stay on my crutch.

(BRICK *hobbles to the gallery door; leans there as if waiting.*)

(MAE *sits beside* BIG MAMA, *while* GOOPER *moves in front and sits on the end of the couch, facing her.* REVEREND TOOKER *moves nervously into the space between them; on the other side,* DOCTOR BAUGH *stands looking at nothing in particular and lights a cigar.* MARGARET *turns away.*)

BIG MAMA: Why're you all *surroundin'* me—like this? Why're you all starin' at me like this an' makin' signs at each other?

(REVEREND TOOKER *steps back startled.*)

MAE: Calm yourself, Big Mama.

BIG MAMA: Calm you'self, *you'self*, Sister Woman. How could I calm myself with everyone starin' at me as if big drops of blood had broken out on m'face? What's this all about, annh! What?

(GOOPER *coughs and takes a center position.*)

GOOPER: Now, Doc Baugh.

MAE: Doc Baugh?

GOOPER: Big Mama wants to know the complete truth about the report we got from the Ochsner Clinic.

MAE (*eagerly*): —on Big Daddy's condition!

GOOPER: Yais, on Big Daddy's condition, we got to face it.

DOCTOR BAUGH: Well . . .

BIG MAMA (*terrified, rising*): Is there? Something? Something that I? Don't—know?

(*In these few words, this startled, very soft question,* BIG MAMA *reviews the history of her forty-five years with* BIG DADDY, *her great almost embarrassingly true-hearted and simple-minded devotion to* BIG DADDY, *who must have had something* BRICK *has, who made himself loved so much by the "simple expedient" of not loving enough to disturb his charming detachment, also once coupled, like* BRICK, *with virile beauty.*)

(BIG MAMA *has a dignity at this moment; she almost stops being fat.*)

DOCTOR BAUGH (*after a pause, uncomfortably*): Yes?— Well—

BIG MAMA: I!!!—want to—knowwwwww . . .

(*Immediately she thrusts her fist to her mouth as if to deny that statement. Then for some curious reason, she snatches the withered corsage from her breast and hurls it on the floor and steps on it with her short, fat feet.*)

Somebody must be lyin'!—I want to know!

MAE: Sit down, Big Mama, sit down on this sofa.

MARGARET: Brick, go sit with Big Mama.

BIG MAMA: *What is it, what is it?*

DOCTOR BAUGH: I never have seen a more thorough examination than Big Daddy Pollitt was given in all my experience with the Ochsner Clinic.

GOOPER: It's one of the best in the country.

MAE: It's THE best in the country—bar *none!*

(*For some reason she gives* GOOPER *a violent poke as she goes past him. He slaps at her hand without removing his eyes from his mother's face.*)

DOCTOR BAUGH: Of course they were ninety-nine and nine-tenths per cent sure before they even started.

BIG MAMA: Sure of what, sure of what, sure of— *what?—what?*

(*She catches her breath in a startled sob.* MAE *kisses her quickly. She thrusts* MAE *fiercely away from her, staring at the* DOCTOR.)

MAE: Mommy, be a brave girl!

BRICK (*in the doorway, softly*): "By the light, by the light, Of the sil-ve-ry mo-oo-n . . ."

GOOPER: Shut up!—Brick.

BRICK: Sorry . . . (*He wanders out on the gallery.*)

DOCTOR BAUGH: But, now, you see, Big Mama, they

cut a piece off this growth, a specimen of the tissue and—

BIG MAMA: Growth? You told Big Daddy—

DOCTOR BAUGH: Now wait.

BIG MAMA (*fiercely*): You told me and Big Daddy there wasn't a thing wrong with him but—

MAE: Big Mama, they always—

GOOPER: Let Doc Baugh talk, will yuh?

BIG MAMA: —little spastic condition of—(*Her breath gives out in a sob.*)

DOCTOR BAUGH: Yes, that's what we told Big Daddy. But we had this bit of tissue run through the laboratory and I'm sorry to say the test was positive on it. It's—well—malignant . . .

(*Pause.*)

BIG MAMA: Cancer?! Cancer?!

(DOCTOR BAUGH *nods gravely.* BIG MAMA *gives a long gasping cry.*)

MAE AND GOOPER: Now, now, now. Big Mama, you had to know . . .

BIG MAMA: WHY DIDN'T THEY CUT IT OUT OF HIM? HANH? HANH?

DOCTOR BAUGH: Involved too much, Big Mama, too many organs affected.

MAE: Big Mama, the liver's affected and so's the kidneys, both! It's gone way past what they call a—

GOOPER: A surgical risk.

MAE: —Uh-huh . . .

(BIG MAMA *draws a breath like a dying gasp.*)

REVEREND TOOKER: Tch, tch, tch, tch, tch!

DOCTOR BAUGH: Yes, it's gone past the knife.

MAE: *That's why he's turned yellow, Mommy!*

BIG MAMA: *Git away from me, git away from me, Mae!* (*She rises abruptly.*) *I want Brick! Where's Brick? Where is my only son?*

MAE: Mama! Did she say "only son"?

GOOPER: What does that make *me?*

MAE: A sober responsible man with five precious children!—*Six!*

BIG MAMA: I want Brick to tell me! Brick! Brick!

MARGARET (*rising from her reflections in a corner*): Brick was so upset he went back out.

BIG MAMA: *Brick!*

MARGARET: Mama, let *me* tell you!

BIG MAMA: No, no, leave me alone, you're not my blood!

GOOPER: *Mama, I'm your son!* Listen to *me!*

MAE: Gooper's your son, he's your first-born!

BIG MAMA: Gooper never liked Daddy.

MAE (*as if terribly shocked*): That's not TRUE!

(*There is a pause. The minister coughs and rises.*)

REVEREND TOOKER (*to* MAE): I think I'd better slip away at this point. (*Discreetly.*) Good night, good

night, everybody, and God bless you all . . . on this place . . .

(*He slips out.*)

(MAE *coughs and points at* BIG MAMA.)

DOCTOR BAUGH: Well, Big Mama . . . (*He sighs.*)

BIG MAMA: It's all a mistake, I know it's just a bad dream.

DOCTOR BAUGH: We're gonna keep Big Daddy as comfortable as we can.

BIG MAMA: Yes, it's just a bad dream, that's all it is, it's just an awful dream

GOOPER: In my opinion Big Daddy is having some pain but won't admit that he has it.

BIG MAMA: Just a dream, a bad dream.

DOCTOR BAUGH: That's what lots of them do, they think if they don't admit they're having the pain they can sort of escape the fact of it.

GOOPER (*with relish*): Yes, they get sly about it, they get real sly about it.

MAE: Gooper and I think—

GOOPER: Shut up, Mae! Big Mama, I think—Big Daddy ought to be started on morphine.

BIG MAMA: Nobody's going to give Big Daddy morphine.

DOCTOR BAUGH: Now, Big Mama, when that pain strikes it's going to strike mighty hard and Big Daddy's going to need the needle to bear it.

BIG MAMA: I tell you, nobody's going to give him morphine.

MAE: Big Mama, you don't want to see Big Daddy suffer, you know you—

(GOOPER, *standing beside her, gives her a savage poke.*)

DOCTOR BAUGH (*placing a package on the table*): I'm leaving this stuff here, so if there's a sudden attack you all won't have to send out for it.

MAE: I know how to give a hypo.

BIG MAMA: Nobody's gonna give Big Daddy morphine.

GOOPER: Mae took a course in nursing during the war.

MARGARET: Somehow I don't think Big Daddy would want Mae to give him a hypo.

MAE: You think he'd want *you* to do it?

DOCTOR BAUGH: Well . . .

(DOCTOR BAUGH *rises.*)

GOOPER: Doctor Baugh is goin'.

DOCTOR BAUGH: Yes, I got to be goin'. Well, keep your chin up, Big Mama.

GOOPER (*with jocularity*): She's gonna keep *both* chins up, aren't you, Big Mama?

(BIG MAMA *sobs.*)

Now stop that, Big Mama.

GOOPER (*at the door with* DOCTOR BAUGH): Well, Doc,

we sure do appreciate all you done. I'm telling you, we're surely obligated to you for—

(DOCTOR BAUGH *has gone out without a glance at him.*)

—I guess that doctor has got a lot on his mind but it wouldn't hurt him to act a little more human . . .

(BIG MAMA *sobs.*)

Now be a brave girl Mommy.

BIG MAMA: It's not true, I know that it's just not true!

GOOPER: Mama, those tests are infallible!

BIG MAMA: Why are you so determined to see your father daid?

MAE: Big Mama!

MARGARET (*gently*): I know what Big Mama means.

MAE (*fiercely*): Oh, do you?

MARGARET (*quietly and very sadly*): Yes, I think I do.

MAE: For a newcomer in the family you sure do show a lot of understanding.

MARGARET: Understanding is needed on this place.

MAE: I guess you must have needed a lot of it in your family, Maggie, with your father's liquor problem and now you've got Brick with his!

MARGARET: Brick does not have a liquor problem at all. Brick is devoted to Big Daddy. This thing is a terrible strain on him.

BIG MAMA: Brick is Big Daddy's boy, but he drinks too much and it worries me and Big Daddy, and, Margaret, you've got to cooperate with us, you've got to cooperate with Big Daddy and me in getting Brick straightened out. Because it will break Big Daddy's heart if Brick don't pull himself together and take hold of things.

MAE: Take hold of *what* things, Big Mama?

BIG MAMA: The place.

(*There is a quick violent look between* MAE *and* GOOPER.)

GOOPER: Big Mama, you've had a shock.

MAE: Yais, we've all had a shock, but . . .

GOOPER: Let's be realistic—

MAE: Big Daddy would never, would *never*, be foolish enough to—

GOOPER: —put this place in irresponsible hands!

BIG MAMA: Big Daddy ain't going to leave the place in anybody's hands; Big Daddy is *not* going to die. I want you to get that in your heads, all of you!

MAE: Mommy, Mommy, Big Mama, we're just as hopeful an' optimistic as you are about Big Daddy's prospects, we have faith in *prayer*—but nevertheless there are certain matters that have to be discussed an' dealt with, because otherwise—

GOOPER: Eventualities have to be considered and now's the time . . . Mae, will you please get my brief case out of our room?

MAE: Yes, honey. (*She rises and goes out through the hall door.*)

GOOPER (*standing over* BIG MAMA): Now, Big Mom. What you said just now was not at all true and you know it. I've always loved Big Daddy in my own quiet way. I never made a show of it, and I know that Big Daddy has always been fond of me in a quiet way, too, and he never made a show of it neither.

(MAE *returns with* GOOPER'S *brief case.*)

MAE: Here's your brief case, Gooper, honey.

GOOPER (*handing the brief case back to her*): Thank you . . . Of cou'se, my relationship with Big Daddy is different from Brick's.

MAE: You're eight years older'n Brick an' always had t' carry a bigger load of th' responsibilities than Brick ever had t' carry. He never carried a thing in his life but a football or a highball.

GOOPER: Mae, will y' let me talk, please?

MAE: Yes, honey.

GOOPER: Now, a twenty-eight-thousand-acre plantation's a mighty big thing t' run.

MAE: Almost singlehanded.

(MARGARET *has gone onto the gallery and can be heard calling softly to* BRICK.)

BIG MAMA: You never had to run this place! What are you talking about? As if Big Daddy was dead and in his grave, you had to run it? Why, you just helped him out with a few business details and had your law practice at the same time in Memphis!

MAE: Oh, Mommy, Mommy, Big Mommy! Let's be fair!

MARGARET: Brick!

MAE: Why, Gooper has given himself body and soul to keeping this place up for the past five years since Big Daddy's health started failing.

MARGARET: Brick!

MAE: Gooper won't say it, Gooper never thought of it as a duty, he just did it. And what did Brick do? Brick kept living in his past glory at college! Still a football player at twenty-seven!

MARGARET (*returning alone*): Who are you talking about now? Brick? A football player? He isn't a football player and you know it. Brick is a sports announcer on T.V. and one of the best-known ones in the country!

MAE: I'm talking about what he was.

MARGARET: Well, I wish you would just stop talking about my husband.

GOOPER: I've got a right to discuss my brother with other members of MY OWN family, which don't include *you.* Why don't you go out there and drink with Brick?

MARGARET: I've never seen such malice toward a brother.

GOOPER: How about his for me? Why, he can't stand to be in the same room with me!

MARGARET: This is a deliberate campaign of vilification for the most disgusting and sordid reason on earth, and I know what it is! It's *avarice, greed, greed!*

BIG MAMA: *Oh, I'll scream! I will scream in a moment unless this stops!*

(GOOPER *has stalked up to* MARGARET *with clenched fists at his sides as if he would strike her.* MAE *distorts her face again into a hideous grimace behind* MARGARET's *back.*)

BIG MAMA (*sobs*): Margaret. Child. Come here. Sit next to Big Mama.

MARGARET: Precious Mommy. I'm sorry, I'm, sorry, I—!

(*She bends her long graceful neck to press her forehead to* BIG MAMA's *bulging shoulder under its black chiffon.*)

MAE: How beautiful, how touching, this display of devotion! Do you know why she's childless? She's childless because that big beautiful athlete husband of hers won't go to bed with her!

GOOPER: You jest won't let me do this in a nice way, will yah? Aw right—I don't give a goddam if Big Daddy likes me or don't like me or did or never did or will or will never! I'm just appealing to a sense of common decency and fair play. I'll tell you the truth. I've resented Big Daddy's partiality to Brick ever since Brick was born, and the way I've been treated like I was just barely good enough to spit on and sometimes not even good enough for that. Big Daddy is dying of cancer, and it's spread all through him and it's attacked all his vital organs including the kidneys and right now he is sinking into uremia, and you all know what uremia is, it's poisoning of the whole system due to the failure of the body to eliminate its poisons.

MARGARET (*to herself, downstage, hissingly*): *Poisons, poisons! Venomous thoughts and words! In hearts and minds!—That's poisons!*

GOOPER (*overlapping her*): I am asking for a square deal, and by God, I expect to get one. But if I don't get one, if there's any peculiar shenanigans going on around here behind my back, well, I'm not a corporation lawyer for nothing, I know how to protect my own interests.

(BRICK *enters from the gallery with a tranquil, blurred smile, carrying an empty glass with him.*)

BRICK: Storm coming up.

GOOPER: Oh! A late arrival!

MAE: Behold the conquering hero comes!

GOOPER: The fabulous Brick Pollitt! Remember him?—Who could forget him!

MAE: He looks like he's been injured in a game!

GOOPER: Yep, I'm afraid you'll have to warm the bench at the Sugar Bowl this year, Brick!

(MAE *laughs shrilly.*)

Or was it the Rose Bowl that he made that famous run in?—

(*Thunder.*)

MAE: The punch bowl, honey. It was in the punch bowl, the cut-glass punch bowl!

GOOPER: Oh, that's right, I'm getting the bowls mixed up!

MARGARET: Why don't you stop venting your malice and envy on a sick boy?

BIG MAMA: *Now you two hush, I mean it, hush, all of you, hush!*

DAISY, SOOKEY: Storm! Storm comin'! Storm! Storm!

LACEY: Brightie, close them shutters.

GOOPER: Lacey, put the top up on my Cadillac, will yuh?

LACEY: Yes, suh, Mistah Pollitt!

GOOPER (*at the same time*): Big Mama, you know it's necessary for me t' go back to Memphis in th' mornin' t' represent the Parker estate in a lawsuit.

(MAE *sits on the bed and arranges papers she has taken from the brief case.*)

BIG MAMA: Is it, Gooper?

MAE: Yaiss.

GOOPER: That's why I'm forced to—to bring up a problem that—

MAE: Somethin' that's too important t' be put off!

GOOPER: If Brick was sober, he ought to be in on this.

MARGARET: Brick is present; we're present.

GOOPER: Well, good. I will now give you this outline my partner, Tom Bullitt, an' me have drawn up—a sort of dummy—trusteeship.

MARGARET: Oh, that's it! You'll be in charge an' dole out remittances, will you?

GOOPER: This we did as soon as we got the report on Big Daddy from th' Ochsner Laboratories. We did this thing, I mean we drew up this dummy outline with the advice and assistance of the Chairman of the Boa'd of Directors of th' Southern Plantahs Bank and Trust Company in Memphis, C. C. Bellowes, a man who handles estates for all th' prominent fam'lies in West Tennessee and th' Delta.

BIG MAMA: Gooper?

GOOPER (*crouching in front of* BIG MAMA): Now this is not—not final, or anything like it. This is just a preliminary outline. But it does provide a basis—a design—a—possible, feasible—*plan!*

MARGARET: Yes, I'll bet it's a plan.

(*Thunder.*)

MAE: It's a plan to protect the biggest estate in the Delta from irresponsibility an'—

BIG MAMA: Now you listen to me, all of you, you listen here? They's not goin' to be any more catty talk in my house! And Gooper, you put that away before I grab it out of your hand and tear it right up! I don't know what the hell's in it, and I don't want to know what the hell's in it. I'm talkin' in Big Daddy's language now; I'm his *wife* not his *widow*, I'm still his *wife!* And I'm talkin' to you in his language an'—

GOOPER: Big Mama, what I have here is—

MAE (*at the same time*): Gooper explained that it's just a plan . . .

BIG MAMA: I don't care what you got there. Just put it back where it came from, an' don't let me see it again, not even the outside of the envelope of it! Is that understood? Basis! Plan! Preliminary! Design! I say—what is it Big Daddy always says when he's disgusted?

BRICK (*from the bar*): Big Daddy says "crap" when he's disgusted.

BIG MAMA (*rising*): That's right!—CRAP! I say CRAP too, like Big Daddy!

(*Thunder.*)

MAE: Coarse language doesn't seem called for in this—

GOOPER: Somethin' in me is *deeply outraged* by hearin' you talk like this.

BIG MAMA: *Nobody's goin' to take nothin'!*—till Big Daddy lets go of it—maybe, just possibly, not—not even then! No, not even then!

(*Thunder.*)

MAE: Sookey, hurry up an' git that po'ch furniture covahed; want th' paint to come off?

GOOPER: Lacey, put mah car away!

LACEY: Caint, Mistah Pollitt, you got the keys!

GOOPER: Naw, you got 'em, man. Where th' keys to th' car, honey?

MAE: You got 'em in your pocket!

BRICK: "You can always hear me singin' this song, Show me the way to go home."

(*Thunder distantly.*)

BIG MAMA: Brick! Come here, Brick, I need you. Tonight Brick looks like he used to look when he was a little boy, just like he did when he played wild games and used to come home when I hollered myself hoarse for him, all sweaty and pink cheeked and sleepy, with his—red curls shining . . .

(BRICK *draws aside as he does from all physical contact and continues the song in a whisper, opening the ice bucket and dropping in the ice cubes one by one as if he were mixing some important chemical formula.*)

(*Distant thunder.*)

Time goes by so fast. Nothin' can outrun it. Death commences too early—almost before you're half acquainted with life—you meet the other . . . Oh, you know we just got to love each other an' stay together, all of us, just as close as we can, especially now that such a *black* thing has come and moved into this place without invitation.

(*Awkwardly embracing* BRICK, *she presses her head to his shoulder.*)

(*A dog howls off stage.*)

Oh, Brick, son of Big Daddy, Big Daddy does so love you. Y'know what would be his fondest dream come true? If before he passed on, if Big Daddy has to pass on . . .

(*A dog howls.*)

. . . you give him a child of yours, a grandson as much like his son as his son is like Big Daddy . . .

MARGARET: I know that's Big Daddy's dream.

BIG MAMA: That's his dream.

MAE: Such a pity that Maggie and Brick can't oblige.

BIG DADDY (*off down stage right on the gallery*): Looks like the wind was takin' liberties with this place.

SERVANT (*off stage*): Yes, sir, Mr. Pollitt.

MARGARET (*crossing to the right door*): Big Daddy's on the gall'ry.

(BIG MAMA *has turned toward the hall door at the sound of* BIG DADDY's *voice on the gallery.*)

BIG MAMA: I can't stay here. He'll see somethin' in my eyes.

(BIG DADDY *enters the room from up stage right.*)

BIG DADDY: Can I come in?

(*He puts his cigar in an ash tray.*)

MARGARET: Did the storm wake you up, Big Daddy?

BIG DADDY: Which stawm are you talkin' about—th' one outside or th' hullaballoo in here?

(GOOPER *squeezes past* BIG DADDY.)

GOOPER: 'Scuse me.

(MAE *tries to squeeze past* BIG DADDY *to join* GOOPER, *but* BIG DADDY *puts his arm firmly around her.*)

BIG DADDY: I heard some mighty loud talk. Sounded like somethin' important was bein' discussed. What was the powwow about?

MAE (*flustered*): Why—nothin', Big Daddy . . .

BIG DADDY (*crossing to extreme left center, taking* MAE *with him*): What is that pregnant-lookin' envelope you're puttin' back in your brief case, Gooper?

GOOPER (*at the foot of the bed, caught, as he stuffs papers into envelope*): That? Nothin', suh—nothin' much of anythin' at all . . .

BIG DADDY: Nothin'? It looks like a whole lot of nothin'!

(*He turns up stage to the group.*)

You all know th' story about th' young married couple—

GOOPER: Yes, sir!

BIG DADDY: Hello, Brick—

BRICK: Hello, Big Daddy.

(*The group is arranged in a semicircle above* BIG DADDY, MARGARET *at the extreme right, then* MAE *and* GOOPER, *then* BIG MAMA, *with* BRICK *at the left.*)

BIG DADDY: Young married couple took Junior out to th' zoo one Sunday, inspected all of God's creatures in their cages, with satisfaction.

GOOPER: Satisfaction.

BIG DADDY (*crossing to up stage center, facing front*): This afternoon was a warm afternoon in spring an' that ole elephant had somethin' else on his mind which was bigger'n peanuts. You know this story, Brick?

(GOOPER *nods.*)

BRICK: No, sir, I don't know it.

BIG DADDY: Y'see, in th' cage adjoinin' they was a young female elephant in heat!

BIG MAMA (*at* BIG DADDY's *shoulder*): Oh, Big Daddy!

BIG DADDY: What's the matter, preacher's gone, ain't he? All right. That female elephant in the next cage was permeatin' the atmosphere about her with a powerful and excitin' odor of female fertility! Huh! Ain't that a nice way to put it, Brick?

BRICK: Yes, sir, nothin' wrong with it!

BIG DADDY: Brick says th's nothin' wrong with it!

BIG MAMA: Oh, Big Daddy!

BIG DADDY (*crossing to down stage center*): So this ole bull elephant still had a couple of fornications left in him. He reared back his trunk an' got a whiff of that elephant lady next door!—began to paw at the dirt in his cage an' butt his head against the separatin' partition and, first thing y'know, there was a conspicuous change in his *profile*—very *conspicuous*! Ain't I tellin' this story in decent language, Brick?

BRICK: Yes, sir, too fuckin' decent!

BIG DADDY: So, the little boy pointed at it and said, "What's that?" His mama said, "Oh, that's—nothin'!"—His papa said, "She's spoiled!"

(BIG DADDY *crosses to* BRICK *at left.*)

You didn't laugh at that story, Brick.

(BIG MAMA *crosses to down stage right crying.* MARGARET *goes to her.* MAE *and* GOOPER *hold up stage right center.*)

BRICK: No, sir, I didn't laugh at that story.

BIG DADDY: What is the smell in this room? Don't you notice it, Brick? Don't you notice a powerful and obnoxious odor of mendacity in this room?

BRICK: Yes, sir, I think I do, sir.

GOOPER: Mae, Mae . . .

BIG DADDY: There is nothing more powerful. Is there, Brick?

BRICK: No, sir. No, sir there isn't, an' nothin' more obnoxious.

BIG DADDY: Brick agrees with me. The odor of mendacity is a powerful and obnoxious odor an' the stawm hasn't blown it away from this room yet. You notice it, Gooper?

GOOPER: What, sir?

BIG DADDY: How about you, Sister Woman? You notice the unpleasant odor of mendacity in this room?

MAE: Why, Big Daddy, I don't even know what that is.

BIG DADDY: You can smell it. Hell it smells like death!

(BIG MAMA *sobs.* BIG DADDY *looks toward her.*)

What's wrong with that fat woman over there, loaded with diamonds? Hey, what's-you-name, what's the matter with you?

MARGARET (*crossing toward* BIG DADDY): She had a slight dizzy spell, Big Daddy.

BIG DADDY: You better watch that, Big Mama. A stroke is a bad way to go.

MARGARET (*crossing to* BIG DADDY *at center*): Oh, Brick, Big Daddy has on your birthday present to him, Brick, he has on your cashmere robe, the softest material I have ever felt.

BIG DADDY: Yeah, this is my soft birthday, Maggie . . . Not my gold or my silver birthday, but my soft birthday, everything's got to be soft for Big Daddy on this soft birthday.

(MAGGIE *kneels before* BIG DADDY *at center.*)

MARGARET: Big Daddy's got on his Chinese slippers that I gave him, Brick. Big Daddy, I haven't given you my big present yet, but now I will, now's the time for me to present it to you! I have an announcement to make!

MAE: What? What kind of announcement?

GOOPER: A sports announcement, Maggie?

MARGARET: Announcement of life beginning! A child is coming, sired by Brick, and out of Maggie the

Cat! I have Brick's child in my body, an' that's my birthday present to Big Daddy on this birthday!

(BIG DADDY *looks at* BRICK *who crosses behind* BIG DADDY *to down stage portal, left.*)

BIG DADDY: Get up, girl, get up off your knees, girl.

(BIG DADDY *helps* MARGARET *to rise. He crosses above her, to her right, bites off the end of a fresh cigar, taken from his bathrobe pocket, as he studies* MARGARET.)

Uh-huh, this girl has life in her body, that's no lie!

BIG MAMA: BIG DADDY'S DREAM COME TRUE!

BRICK: JESUS!

BIG DADDY (*crossing right below wicker stand*): Gooper, I want my lawyer in the mornin'.

BRICK: Where are you goin', Big Daddy?

BIG DADDY: Son, I'm goin' up on the roof, to the belvedere on th' roof to look over my kingdom before I give up my kingdom—twenty-eight thousand acres of th' richest land this side of the valley Nile!

(*He exits through right doors, and down right on the gallery.*)

BIG MAMA (*following*): Sweetheart, sweetheart, sweetheart—can I come with you?

(*She exits down stage right.*)
(MARGARET *is down stage center in the mirror area.* MAE *has joined* GOOPER *and she gives him a fierce poke, making a low hissing sound and a grimace of fury.*)

GOOPER (*pushing her aside.*): Brick, could you possibly spare me one small shot of that liquor?

BRICK: Why, help yourself, Gooper boy.

GOOPER: I will.

MAE (*shrilly*): Of course we know that this is—a lie.

GOOPER: *Be still, Mae.*

MAE: I won't be still! I know she's made this up!

GOOPER: Goddam it, I said shut up!

MARGARET: Gracious! I didn't know that my little announcement was going to provoke such a storm!

MAE: *That* woman isn't *pregnant!*

GOOPER: Who said she was?

MAE: *She* did.

GOOPER: The doctor didn't. Doc Baugh didn't.

MARGARET: I haven't gone to Doc Baugh.

GOOPER: Then who'd you go to, Maggie?

MARGARET: One of the best gynecologists in the South.

GOOPER: Uh huh, uh huh!—I see ... (*He takes out a pencil and notebook.*) —May we have his name, please?

MARGARET: No, you may not, Mister Prosecuting Attorney!

MAE: He doesn't have any name, he doesn't exist!

MARGARET: Oh, he exists all right, and so does my child, Brick's baby!

MAE: You can't conceive a child by a man that won't sleep with you unless you think you're—

(BRICK *has turned on the phonograph. A scat song cuts* MAE's *speech.*)

GOOPER: *Turn that off!*

MAE: We know it's a lie because we hear you in here; he won't sleep with you, we hear you! So don't imagine you're going to put a trick over on us, to fool a dying man with a—

(*A long drawn cry of agony and rage fills the house.* MARGARET *turns the phonograph down to a whisper. The cry is repeated.*)

MAE: Did you hear that, Gooper, did you hear that?

GOOPER: Sounds like the pain has struck.

MAE: Go see, Gooper!

GOOPER: Come along and leave these lovebirds together in their nest!

(*He goes out first.* MAE *follows but turns at the door, contorting her face and hissing at* MARGARET.)

MAE: *Liar!*

(*She slams the door.*)
(MARGARET *exhales with relief and moves a little unsteadily to catch hold of* BRICK's *arm.*)

MARGARET: Thank you for—keeping still ...

BRICK: O.K., Maggie.

MARGARET: It was gallant of you to save my face!

(*He now pours down three shots in quick succession and stands waiting, silent. All at once he turns with a smile and says.*)

BRICK: *There!*

MARGARET: What?

BRICK: The *click* ...

(*His gratitude seems almost infinite as he hobbles out on the gallery with a drink. We hear his crutch as he swings out of sight. Then, at some distance, he begins singing to himself a peaceful song.* MARGARET *holds the big pillow forlornly as if it were her only companion, for a few moments, then throws it on the bed. She rushes to the liquor cabinet, gathers all the bottles in her arms, turns about undecidedly, then runs out of the room with them, leaving the door ajar on the dim yellow hall.* BRICK *is heard hobbling back along the gallery, singing his peaceful song. He comes back in, sees the pillow on the bed, laughs lightly, sadly, picks it up. He has it under his arm as* MARGARET *returns to the room.* MARGARET *softly shuts the door and leans against it, smiling softly at* BRICK.)

MARGARET: Brick, I used to think that you were stronger than me and I didn't want to be overpowered by you. But now, since you've taken to liquor—you know what?—I guess it's bad, but now I'm stronger than you and I can love you more truly! Don't move that pillow, I'll move it right back if you do!—Brick?

(She turns out all the lamps but a single rose-silk-shaded one by the bed.)

I really have been to a doctor and I know what to do and—Brick?—this is my time by the calendar to conceive?

BRICK: Yes, I understand, Maggie. But how are you going to conceive a child by a man in love with his liquor?

MARGARET: By locking his liquor up and making him satisfy my desire before I unlock it!

BRICK: Is that what you've done, Maggie?

MARGARET: Look and see. That cabinet's mighty empty compared to before!

BRICK: Well, I'll be a son of a—

(He reaches for his crutch but she beats him to it and rushes out on the gallery, hurls the crutch over the rail and comes back in, panting.)

MARGARET: And so tonight we're going to make the lie true, and when that's done, I'll bring the liquor back here and we'll get drunk together, here, tonight, in this place that death has come into . . . —What do you say?

BRICK: I don't say anything. I guess there's nothing to say.

MARGARET: Oh, you weak people, you weak, beautiful people who give up with such grace. What you want is someone to—

(She turns out the rose-silk lamp.)

—take hold of you.—Gently, gently with love hand your life back to you, like somethin' gold you let go of. I *do* love you, Brick, I *do!*

BRICK *(smiling with charming sadness)*: Wouldn't it be funny if that was true?

Figure 1. Maggie (Elizabeth Ashley) and Brick (Keir Dullea) in the American Shakespeare Theater production of *Cat on a Hot Tin Roof*, directed by Michael Kahn and designed by John Conklin, New York, 1974. (Photograph: Martha Swope.)

Figure 2. Brick (Keir Dullea) and Big Daddy (Fred Gwynne) in the American Shakespeare Theater production of *Cat on a Hot Tin Roof*, directed by Michael Kahn and designed by John Conklin, New York, 1974. (Photograph: Martha Swope.)

Figure 3. Mae (Joan Pape, *standing center*), Gooper (Charles Siebert), and their five children perform a musical chorus to celebrate the birthday of Big Daddy (Fred Gwynne), while *(left to right)* Reverend Tooker (Wyman Pendleton), Doctor Baugh (William Larsen), Big Mama (Kate Reid), Sookey (Sarallen), and Lacey look on in the American Shakespeare Theater production of *Cat on a Hot Tin Roof*, directed by Michael Kahn and designed by John Conklin, New York, 1974. This photograph also shows the realistic/expressionistic set with walls that "dissolve mysteriously into air," as Williams specified in his "Notes to the Designer." (Photograph: Martha Swope.)

Figure 4. Big Daddy (Fred Gwynne) tells the story of the "ole bull elephant" to Mae (Joan Pape), Big Mama (Kate Reid), and Maggie (Elizabeth Ashley) in the American Shakespeare Theater production of *Cat on a Hot Tin Roof*, directed by Michael Kahn and designed by John Conklin, New York, 1974. (Photograph: Martha Swope.)

Staging of *Cat on a Hot Tin Roof*

**REVIEW OF THE AMERICAN SHAKESPEARE
THEATER PRODUCTION, 1974, BY CLIVE BARNES**

People used to think that Tennessee Williams's plays were about sex and violence. How wrong they were—they are about love and survival. Mr. Williams's "Cat on a Hot Tin Roof" is now 20 years old, and in its first day it was regarded as something of a shocker. Now even though a certain four-letter word has been restored where a euphemism once reigned stupidly supreme, I doubt whether anyone is going to be shocked . . . . But I hope they will be affected. This is a gripping and intensely moving play, a play that can hold its own with anything written in the post-O'Neill American theater.

The Cat is Maggie—a Southern beauty of indefinite lineage. She is married to Brick, a handsome, former football player, now TV sportscaster. The marriage could be perfect, but Brick is an impotent alcoholic who fears that he failed his best friend, apparently a homosexual. Brick's father, Big Daddy, a self-made Southern millionaire, is dying of cancer. He doesn't know it. His wife doesn't know it. But the family, including Brick's brother and sister-in-law, they know it. It is Big Daddy's 65th, and last, birthday.

Michael Kahn's new staging, which opened at the ANTA Theater last night for a limited run, really is new. It originated at the American Shakespeare Theater in Connecticut this summer, and it offers a rewarding new variant on the original play.

As is well known, the Broadway version, directed by Elia Kazan, incorporated in its last act a number of Mr. Kazan's own ideas. Indeed in most printed versions of the play the last act exists in two versions, the so-called "Broadway" version, and the original. In the latter Big Daddy does not appear and Brick, faced with some faint prospect of fatherhood, changes somewhat in his character. Mr. Kahn, presumably with the playwright's permission, seems to have taken the best of both acts—following Mr. Kazan in his inclusion of Big Daddy in the last act (and Kazan was right in his thinking there), and yet following the original in its far more sensitive handling of the final relationship between Brick and Maggie. The result seems to be a definitive version of the play.

Twenty years ago everyone made much of the symbolism in Tennessee Williams, and undoubtedly the symbolism is here. The magnolia scented bedroom that used to belong to the old-maidish bachelors that once owned the plantation, the concept of the bed itself as Maggie's territory, or Brick's possible latent homosexuality symbolized by his hazy impotence—yes, all these are symbols of the sexual warfare that underlies the story. But the story itself, and the compassion Mr. Williams brings to the telling of it, is what really matters.

Mr. Williams has the one vital gift a playwright must possess—he holds the interest. He makes you care by showing you a world. His characters are drawn with rough strokes, for Mr. Williams always demonstrates by exaggeration. He is also a playwright who wants to be very popular (or, rather, very much loved) and this sometimes leads hin into cheapness. But he is a master. His plays have a time, a place, a development and ring true.

He is lucky with Mr. Kahn, whose direction seems directly aimed at lowering the play's hot-house temperature, and at making a domestic drama rather than an eternal triangle between a woman, a reluctant man and a bed. As a result Big Daddy becomes rather more important than before.

The imaginative setting by John Conklin, the cleverly evocative costumes by Jane Greenwood and the dappled lighting by Marc B. Weiss, are all splendid, but if Mr. Williams has been fortunate in Mr. Kahn and his collaborators, Mr. Kahn has been equally fortunate in his cast, or at least clever in his casting.

Elizabeth Ashley was much praised for her Maggie in Connecticut, but even then she was sold short. Sensuous, withdrawn, composed and determined, Miss Ashley's Maggie vibrantly combines charm with grit. She can stand outside a conversation like a cobra, or flutter in like a bird. Splendid.

Keir Dullea's ironic, embittered Brick makes her the perfect partner. He has precisely "the charm of the defeated," with his alcoholic eyes staring into the mid-distance of half-forgotten memory, still waiting for the click of oblivion. Both this Brick and this Maggie are oddly vulnerable, which is also the special quality of Fred Gwynne's blustering, hollowed out Big Daddy. These three performances are so right that they detract from the more shallow playing of the rest of the cast, including Kate Reid, slightly too shrill as a miscast Big Mama.

This is a glowing play, memorably staged. It gets Broadway's dramatic season off to a flying start.

CONTEMPORARY THEATER

Most periods in the history of drama are associated with distinctive theatrical structures—the classical Greek with outdoor amphitheaters; the middle ages with pageant wagons and platform stages; the renaissance English with multilevel open-air theaters; the neoclassical with indoor theaters, proscenium stages, and perspective backdrops; the modern with fan-shaped auditoriums and box sets. During the contemporary period, variety is the rule in theatrical structures and staging conventions. The fan-shaped auditorium and the box set of realistic theater (see pages 530 and 532) continue to flourish in many amateur and professional houses. Yet, in addition to this now common pattern, other theatrical arrangements have developed, reflecting a renewed interest in earlier methods of staging. In an attempt to reclaim and combine elements of the classical Greek and renaissance English theaters, mid-twentieth-century designers created the thrust stage (see Figure 1), in which the audience is seated on rising tiers around three sides of a platform, the fourth side being occupied by a permanent setting that contains multiple acting surfaces. And somewhat earlier in the century, designers reclaimed the medieval style of theater-in-the-round and turned it into the arena stage (see Figure 2), an arrangement placing the audience on all four sides of the actors and using the aisles for entrances and exits. The theatrical freedom of the arena stage has also prompted directors and producers to reclaim another medieval heritage by putting on plays in the street, in public squares, or any other open space that will bring actors and spectators closer to each other than is possible in the traditional theater.

Contemporary set design has been equally flexible, ranging from a total abandonment of settings, set pieces, and props to the use of highly elaborate set designs in a realistic or symbolic style. In part, of course, various styles in set design have been determined by the nature of the theatrical environment. Arena stages and thrust stages clearly do not invite the use of box sets or painted backdrops. But even in a conventional modern theater, where the realism of the box set has been readily accessible, designers have taken the liberty of blending and modifying a combination of styles to achieve unique dramatic effects. Harold Pinter's stage direction for *The Homecoming* (1965) asks for "An old house in North London. A large room, extending the width of the stage" but also specifies that "The back wall, which contained the door, has been removed. A square arch shape remains." Such a direction, and the resulting design by John Bury, clearly portrayed a house both real and unreal, familiar and strange, a setting in which individual props, such as the glass of water about which Lenny and Ruth talk, seem to take on symbolic weight far greater than they might have in a more conventional set.

The freedom in contemporary theater to choose among a variety of styles has also made it possible for dramatists to reject realistic conventions altogether, as did the playwrights of the most influential movement of the 1950s and 1960s,

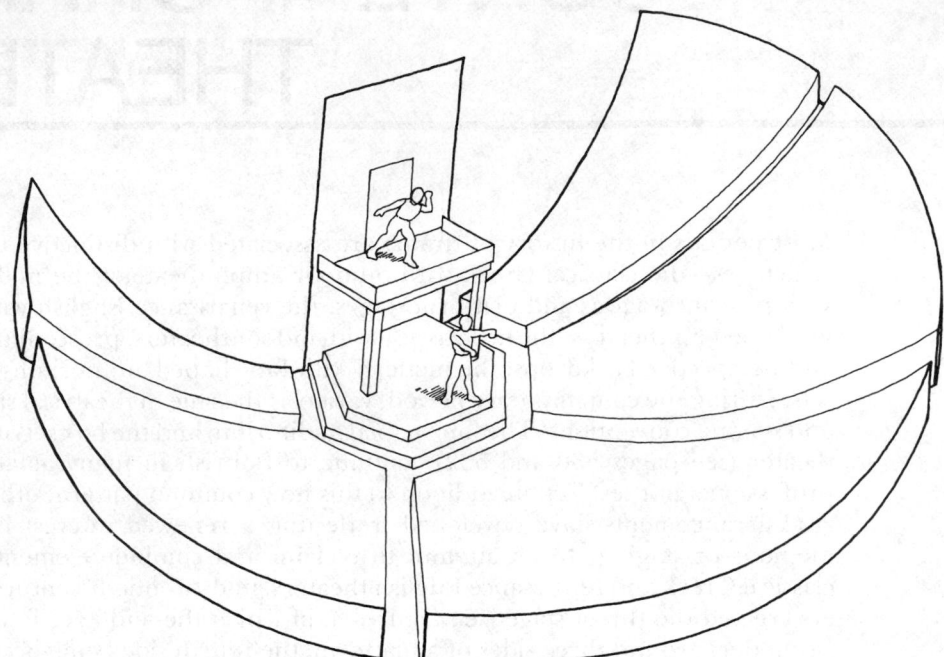

Figure 1. The contemporary thrust stage, showing the multiple acting surfaces adapted from the renaissance English theater, surrounded on three sides by the rising tiers of seats adapted from the classical Greek theater.

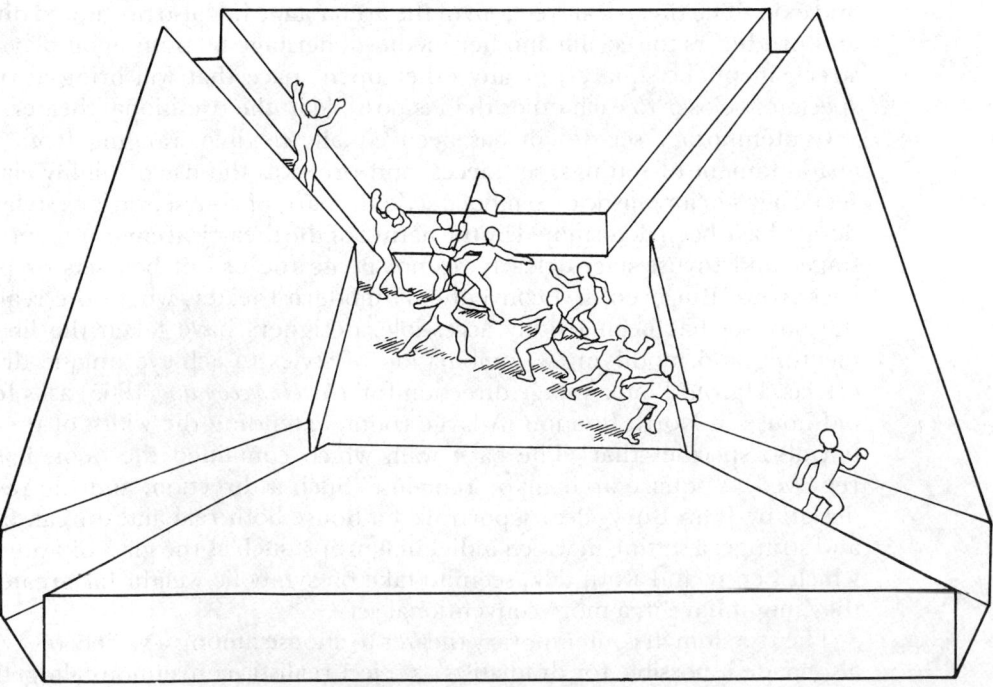

Figure 2. The contemporary arena stage.

the "Theater of the Absurd," a movement defined and named by the critic Martin Esslin. The absurdists—most notably Samuel Beckett, Eugène Ionesco, and Jean Genet—rejected such realistic conventions as psychologically motivated characters and plots, logically consistent dialogue, and familiar styles of presentation, for, as Esslin explained, "The Theatre of the Absurd has renounced arguing about the absurdity of the human condition; it merely presents it in being—that is, in terms of the concrete stage images of the absurdity of existence." Given their acute sense of the malignancy, or meaninglessness, or sterility of existence, the absurdists deliberately favor stage actions and images that will clearly evoke such a view of experience, whether it is the garbage can residents of Beckett's *Endgame* (1957) or the rhinoceros that takes over the world in Ionesco's *Rhinoceros* (1959). The drama that Esslin has labelled absurdist has its roots in avant-garde theater of the early twentieth century, in such plays as Alfred Jarry's *Ubu Roi* (1896), a scatological and seemingly nonsensical play about a brutal and whimsical ruler, or Guillaume Apollinaire's *The Breasts of Tiresias* (1917), which features a dancing news-kiosk and a woman turning into a man when her breasts float away as balloons. Absurdism derives as well from the radical ideas of Antonin Artaud, who in 1938 expounded a "theater of cruelty" which he based on the assumption that "Everything that acts is a cruelty. It is upon this idea of extreme action, pushed beyond all limits, that theatre must be rebuilt." Although absurdist drama, strictly speaking, does not exemplify the theater of cruelty, it does clearly push drama to extreme actions and images.

Not only is absurdist drama a striking instance of the stylistic freedom in contemporary theater, it has also been an influence nurturing even greater experimentation among playwrights, directors, actors, and set designers. After seeing Beckett's *Waiting for Godot* (1952), for example, the dramatist William Saroyan said, "It will make it easier for me and everyone else to write freely in the theatre." Unhampered by expectations about what drama should be, contemporary playwrights have constantly experimented with symbolic and image-centered drama, as indicated by the metaphoric titles of their plays, such as *Endgame, Dutchman, spell #7,* and *Fool for Love.* The dramatic inventions of the playwrights have, in turn, stimulated designers, such as Eiko Ishioka who created the curving ramp that swirls around the stage in *M. Butterfly.* And the actors themselves, of course, have been forced to develop nonrealistic styles of performance, a challenge that has provoked them to explore the arts of dance, mime, and vaudeville. How, after all, is it possible for an actor to portray "realistically" the process of a man turning into a rhinoceros, or of a mute, in *Waiting for Godot,* suddenly unleashing a torrent of speech? The need to find new acting styles and to make sense of these plays for an audience has ultimately led to a greatly increased emphasis on the imaginative leadership of the director.

Indeed, contemporary theater, whether it has taken the form of realism, modified realism, or absurdism, has often been determined not only by a playwright's script but also by a director's creative influence upon the script, especially when the director and the playwright work together on a regular basis. Max Stafford-Clark, artistic director of England's Royal Court Theatre, a nationally subsidized theater devoted to the production of new plays, has worked often and closely with Caryl Churchill. Most of David Mamet's plays were originally directed by Gregory Mosher of Chicago's Goodman Theatre, while August Wilson dedicated *Fences* to "Lloyd Richards, who adds to whatever he touches," publicly acknowledging his debt to the Yale Repertory Theatre director who has directed all of his major works.

Perhaps the most striking example of the creative director in contemporary theater is the Englishman, Peter Brook, whose productions of Shakespeare have moved critics to speak of "Brook's *King Lear*" and "Brook's *A Midsummer Night's Dream*," rather than Shakespeare's. Brook first came to public notice in the early 1940s and 1950s as a "boy genius" directing major productions of Shakespeare in London and Stratford. But his sensational reputation as a revolutionary director did not get established until 1962 when he produced *King Lear* in a style heavily influenced by the starkly expressionistic techniques of Brecht's epic theater. Brook was further influenced by Artaud's theater of cruelty, which led him to argue that cruelty is a necessary "form of self-discipline" for performers; he thus entered into an intense period of physical exercises and improvisations with a group of selected actors, a project culminating in his 1964 production of Peter Weiss's *Marat/Sade,* an elaborate play-within-a-play that features the inmates of a mental asylum staging the events of the French Revolution. Brook's highly disciplined actors kept the stage in a continuous state of theatrical disarray in order to convey the deranged experience of a mental asylum—the actors performing as inmates never stopped moving and drooling and acting out their fantasies. And at the play's conclusion, when the inmates begin attacking the onstage audience who have watched the play, Brook added a final inventive touch: as the audience applauded, the actors lined up and steadily, smirkingly, rhythmically applauded back. Since his work in the 1960s with the Royal Shakespeare Company, Brook has formed his own theater company and established himself in Paris, where he has presented productions as varied as *The Cherry Orchard* (see pages 642–643), a reworking of Bizet's opera *Carmen,* and a ten-hour adaptation of the great Indian epic, *The Mahabharata.*

The revolution in contemporary theater has been carried to its logical extreme by directors who have formed repertory groups committed to a radical alteration of virtually all the traditional conventions of drama. During the late 1960s, for example, the Living Theater of Julian Beck and Judith Malina staged a series of works stressing political activism—an activism they sought to dramatize by deliberately breaking the barrier that has traditionally separated actors from spectators. Members of the Living Theater routinely talked to, touched, and even invited the audience onstage during their performances, and one of their productions, *Paradise Now,* actually climaxed with a "love pile" or "group grope" for both actors and those members of the audience who still remained in the theater. By contrast, Jerzy Grotowski and the Polish Laboratory Theatre deliberately sought to isolate members of the audience, bringing each person in a forty- or fifty-person group into the acting space one by one, sometimes even seating them behind raised walls. Furthermore, by abandoning a permanent stage and choosing to redesign the acting space for each play, by discarding makeup, costumes, props, and music, Grotowski created what has been known as "poor theater," in order to focus on "the personal and scenic technique of the actor as the core of theater art." Other experimental groups of the 1960s and 1970s have applied the rituals of yoga and meditation to theatrical performance, and still others have staged productions in slow motion, creating barely moving visual images in works that run from three to twelve hours in length. Perhaps the most remarkable element in all these experimental groups is not their assault upon theatrical conventions, nor their intense fascination with sound and movement, but their abandonment of scripted plays in favor of improvisation—a phenomenon reminiscent of Artaud's manifesto calling for "No More Masterpieces!"

The 1980s may have brought about a closer working relationship between playwright, director, and actors, especially when one considers the plays of Caryl Churchill, the most notable of which grew out of workshops with actors and directors, or the productions of Ariane Mnouchkine in Paris, whose company of actors and musicians, like that of Peter Brook, has worked with established writers to create the script for productions such as an eight-hour play about Cambodia and Prince Sihanouk. Great Britain's long tradition of repertory companies has led to these groups either commissioning plays or sometimes creating elaborate adaptations, such as a two-part, eight-and-a-half-hour version of Dickens' *Nicholas Nickleby,* which grew out of a collaboration between directors Trevor Nunn and John Caird, playwright David Edgar, and forty-some actors of the Royal Shakespeare Company. In America, several regional theaters have been particularly important in developing new plays and playwrights. The Actors Theater of Louisville and its artistic director, Jon Jory, have been crucial in the development of Marsha Norman's work, just as the Yale Repertory Theatre and its director, Lloyd Richards, have been central to the career of August Wilson.

While contemporary drama has developed through a series of collaborative theatrical ventures, it also reflects and challenges the most popular art forms of our day, film and television. Because film and television can attract such large audiences, contemporary drama must contend with these popular forms of entertainment. One strategy is to create a strikingly different kind of theatrical experience: contemporary drama is often spare where film is lush, asbstract where television is realistic. In Beckett's *Endgame,* people live with only the barest remnants of ordinary life; in Shange's *spell #7,* the performers sometimes wear masks to reflect stereotypes; in Churchill's *Top Girls,* six of the seven actresses perform at least two different roles, forcing the audience to draw thematic connections as a result of the doubling. But contemporary drama also *uses* the realism associated with film and television. Neil Simon's phenomenally successful career reflects his particular talent for finding humor in details from domestic life and in his characters' inability to cope with such details. The same reliance on realistic detail appears in Marsha Norman's *'night, Mother,* though in this play Jessie's insistence on dealing with the minutiae of everyday life throws into horrifying relief her lack of control over everything else. Much as contemporary drama has drawn on the techniques of film and television, so contemporary dramatists often write for both stage and screen: Harold Pinter, Sam Shepard, and David Mamet are successful filmscript writers; Mamet has also written for the television series *Hill Street Blues.* Film and television scripts usually involve many short scenes, perhaps because the medium allows for such fast cutting from one place to another, while realistic stage scripts have often opted for a single set. Yet the blending of the two approaches is also frequent in contemporary drama, as in the many short scenes of *M. Butterfly*, scenes that shift the audience's focus not only from one group of characters to another but from one place to another.

Such "fragmentary" structures are not unique to film or television, as one can see just by looking at the early modern episodic plays of Büchner or of Brecht. And long before them, Elizabethan dramatists often juxtaposed short scenes, frequently contrasting social classes or geographic locales. Indeed, one might argue that what is new in contemporary theater is really an echo of what is old. Just as contemporary theatrical design reflects a variety of staging techniques from the classical, medieval, and renaissance periods, so the contemporary experimental fascination with sound and movement recalls the religious rituals from which drama first arose. In fact, contemporary drama often alludes to or revises plays, music, and dance from previous eras. Hamm in *Endgame* mimics Shakespearean characters; the South African waiters in *"Master Harold"* . . . *and the Boys* recreate ballroom dancing through their memories of Fred Astaire and Ginger Rogers; Hwang's *M. Butterfly* rewrites and directly quotes Puccini's opera, *Madame Butterfly*; and the last play in the collection, Mamet's *Oleanna*, takes up issues of domination through language and gender in ways that indirectly recall Shaw's *Pygmalion* and Ionesco's *The Lesson*. Thus the history of theater seems to follow a cyclical or echoic pattern, though perhaps it would be more accurate to say, as Peter Brook has, that the theater is not static or unchanging, that "truth in the theater is always on the move." Such movement is inherent in drama, on any stage, at any stage of history, for drama is a living form of art; it draws its life from live actors and a live audience coming together to create the performance.

EUGÈNE IONESCO

1912–1994

When Martin Esslin coined the phrase "the theatre of the absurd," he adopted Albert Camus's idea of the human being as a stranger, "an irremediable exile," caught in the absurd and painful predicament of having neither a past to remember nor a future to hope for. Eugène Ionesco, born in Bucharest, Rumania, to a Rumanian father and a French mother, was in a sense always an exile. When he was very young, his parents took him to France where he lived first in Paris, and then, because he developed anemia, they moved him to a farm in the country, a place he would later describe as his lost paradise. In 1925, the family returned to Rumania where, at the age of thirteen, Ionesco learned his native language for the first time. As a young literary critic, he published an attack on three Rumanian writers, only to bring out a second essay a few days later praising the very same authors; then under the title *No!*, he published the two essays together, a first glimpse of the confusing and often contradictory experience that his plays would later dramatize. Ionesco taught French for two years in Bucharest but then returned to France, planning to write a doctoral thesis on contemporary French poetry. Instead he wrote about his childhood, began a novel, and to support himself, worked in a publishing house. The outbreak of World War II in 1939 compelled him to remain in France, together with his wife and baby daughter.

How then did Ionesco become a playwright? Already fluent in both French and Rumanian, Ionesco decided in 1948 to learn English. Picking up a self-study course in dialogue form, "L'Anglais Sans Peine" ("English without difficulty"), he became fascinated by the conversation between the characters: "To my astonishment, Mrs. Smith informed her husband that they had several children, that they lived in the vicinity of London, that their name was Smith, that Mr. Smith was a clerk, that they had a servant, Mary—English, like themselves." As Ionesco copied out the sentences, he found a "tragedy of language" in this conversation so full of clichés as to be meaningless—and thus drafted his "anti-play," *La Cantatrice chauve* (*The Bald Soprano*). The friends to whom he read this play found it not tragic but very funny, so much so that one of them helped to get it produced at a small avant-garde theater. In Ionesco's exuberant adaptation of the English lessons, not only do the Smiths inform each other of facts that they must already know, but their dinner guests, Mr. and Mrs. Martin, begin by addressing each other as strangers but eventually discover that they are married to each other. After building to a crescendo of nonsense words and syllables, the play then begins again, this time with the Martins speaking the lines of the Smiths.

Though *The Bald Soprano* ran for only six weeks in 1950, Ionesco continued to write absurdist plays and to get them produced: *The Lesson* (1951), *The Chairs* (1952), *Amédée, or How to Get Rid of It* (1954), *Jack or the Submission* (1955). Most of these were one-acts, although *Amédée*, which features a corpse that keeps growing and finally floats away into space carrying Amédée with it, is a three-act play, as is *The Killer* (1959). In *The Killer*, whose French title, *Tueur sans gages*, implies that the killer works without payment and thus kills almost randomly, Ionesco presents a world clearly echoing the memories of his idyllic childhood in the French countryside, a "radiant city" where it is always springtime, but a city now deserted because of the mysterious killer. In the last act, the protagonist, Bérenger, tries to appeal to the killer, but hears only chuckling. The ineffectiveness of Bérenger's arguments against such meaningless murder represents Ionesco's most despairing view of humanity. Such helplessness also underlies his next major play, *Rhinoceros* (1960), in which Bérenger, again the protagonist, resists the forces of social/political conformity as represented by the rhinoceros. While *The Killer* shows Bérenger gradually succumbing both to the killer's inexorable chuckling and, in Ionesco's words, to "the vacuity of his own rather commonplace morality," *Rhinoceros* presents at least the possibility that an individual human being might triumph over the thundering menace of mass thinking. Two major productions of *Rhinoceros* in 1960 (the first in Paris, starring the great French actor-manager, Jean-Louis Barrault, the second in London, directed by Orson Welles and starring Laurence Olivier) both reflected and contributed to Ionesco's growing public stature.

To many critics, the take-over by the rhinoceroses and the willingness of everyone in the play, except for Bérenger, to change into a rhinoceros, was a parable about the success of the Nazi movement. Ionesco had seen the violence of the Nazis when he lived in Rumania, and had felt for himself the difficulty of challenging Fascist doctrine: "When you're twenty years old and you have teachers who offer you scientific or pseudo-scientific theories and explanations, when you have newspapers, when you have a whole atmosphere, doctrines, a whole movement against you, it's really very hard to resist, hard not to let yourself be convinced." And, as the reference to teachers suggests, Ionesco held major doubts about his own life both as a student and then as a teacher.

All of the major themes in Ionesco's plays—the meaningless aspect of language, the human being's tendency to violence, the destructive power of collective thinking—find chilling expression in *The Lesson*. At first, *The Lesson* seems a comedy about education as the young woman coming for a private tutorial with the Professor can hardly remember the capital of France but wishes to qualify for a doctorate in just three weeks. Comically, too, the tutorial begins with arithmetic (the Pupil can't subtract but she can multiply two ten-digit numbers correctly) and then moves to linguistics and comparative philology. Just as Ionesco delights in exposing linguistic clichés in *The Bald Soprano*, so in *The Lesson* the Professor explains how languages differ from one another through "something intangible that one is able to perceive only after very long study, with a great deal of trouble and after the broadest experience." The Professor's discussion of the names of countries, while ridiculous on one level, is also a painful echo of Ionesco's own confusion when he moved from France to Rumania: "At primary school, in France, I'd been taught that French—which was my language—was the most beautiful language in the world, that the French were the bravest people in the world. . . . When I got to Bucharest, my teachers explained that my language was Rumanian, that the most beautiful language in the world was not French but Rumanian. . . ."

By the end of the play, when the Professor attacks the Pupil not only with words but with a knife, Ionesco's perception of the world as one in which "the comic is terrifying, the comic is tragic," becomes frighteningly clear. The donning of an armband with a swastika implies political violence, just as the description of the attack on the Pupil implies not only murder but also rape. The explicit onstage attack, similar to the endings of Albee's *The Zoo Story* and Baraka's *Dutchman*, dramatizes the struggle for power in terms of sexual relationships. Indeed, more recent plays, such as Robert Athayde's *Miss Margarida's Way* (first American production, 1977) and David Mamet's highly controversial *Oleanna* (1992), have taken the teacher/student relationship and used it, as Ionesco does, as a metaphor for political, social, and sexual domination.

In performance, *The Lesson* has seemed both opaque and accessible, as reflected in reviews of the 1958 New York production. Brooks Atkinson, writing in the *New York Times*, seemed willing to accept *The Chairs* and *The Lesson* as "odd, elliptical fantastifications" and to enjoy a "diverting evening," without feeling bothered by the fact that he couldn't "explain the cosmic significance of M. Ionesco's theme." Walter Kerr, whose review is reprinted following the text, was bothered by the "defiant mindlessness" of both plays, and felt he had followed "a long, tortured, circuitous, pretentious road to a nice, round zero that might be drawn at once." Yet Kerr still responded to the power of the production, with most of his reservations coming afterwards when he thought about what he had seen. The theatrical energy of the performance, so strikingly evoked in Kerr's description of Max Adrian and Joan Plowright (see Figure 1), is thus balanced by the "black despair" of the playwright's vision, as the maid comforts the murderous Professor (see Figure 2) and then calmly ushers in the forty-first pupil and the forty-first victim.

THE LESSON
A Comic Drama

BY EUGÈNE IONESCO

THE CHARACTERS

THE PROFESSOR, *aged fifty to sixty*
THE YOUNG PUPIL, *aged eighteen*
THE MAID, *aged forty-five to fifty*

SCENE

The office of the old professor, which also serves as a dining room. To the left, a door opens onto the apartment stairs; upstage, to the right, another door opens onto a corridor of the apartment. Upstage, a little left of center, a window, not very large, with plain curtains; on the outside sill of the window are ordinary potted plants. The low buildings with red roofs of a small town can be seen in the distance. The sky is grayish-blue. On the right stands a provincial buffet. The table doubles as a desk, it stands at stage center. There are three chairs around the table, and two more stand on each side of the window. Light-colored wallpaper, some shelves with books.

(When the curtain rises the stage is empty, and it remains so for a few moments. Then we hear the doorbell ring.)

VOICE OF THE MAID *(from the corridor)*: Yes. I'm coming.

(The MAID *comes in, after having run down the stairs. She is stout, aged forty-five to fifty, red-faced, and wears a peasant woman's cap. She rushes in, slamming the door to the right behind her, and dries her hands on her apron as she runs towards the door on the left. Meanwhile we hear the doorbell ring again.)*

MAID: Just a moment, I'm coming.

(She opens the door. A young PUPIL, *aged eighteen, enters. She is wearing a gray student's smock, a small white collar, and carries a student's satchel under her arm.)*

MAID: Good morning, miss.
PUPIL: Good morning, madam. Is the Professor at home?
MAID: Have you come for the lesson?
PUPIL: Yes, I have.
MAID: He's expecting you. Sit down for a moment. I'll tell him you're here.
PUPIL: Thank you.

(She seats herself near the table, facing the audience; the hall door is to her left; her back is to the other door, through which the MAID *hurriedly exits, calling:)*

MAID: Professor, come down please, your pupil is here.
VOICE OF THE PROFESSOR *(rather reedy)*: Thank you. I'm coming . . . in just a moment . . .

(The MAID *exits; the* PUPIL *draws in her legs, holds her satchel on her lap, and waits demurely. She casts a glance or two around the room, at the furniture, at the ceiling too. Then she takes a notebook out of her satchel, leafs through it, and stops to look at a page for a moment as though reviewing a lesson, as though taking a last look at her homework. She seems to be a well-brought-up girl,* polite, but lively, gay, dynamic; a fresh smile is on her lips. During the course of the play she progressively loses the lively rhythm of her movement and her carriage, she becomes withdrawn. From gay and smiling she becomes progressively sad and morose; from very lively at the beginning, she becomes more and more fatigued and somnolent. Towards the end of the play her face must clearly express a nervous depression; her way of speaking shows the effects of this, her tongue becomes thick, words come to her memory with difficulty and emerge from her mouth with as much difficulty; she comes to have a manner vaguely paralyzed, the beginning of aphasia.° Firm and determined at the beginning, so much so as to appear to be almost aggressive, she becomes more and more passive, until she is almost a mute and inert object, seemingly inanimate in the PROFESSOR's hands, to such an extent that when he makes his final gesture, she no longer reacts. Insensible, her reflexes deadened, only her eyes in an expressionless face will show inexpressible astonishment and fear. The transition from one manner to the other must of course be made imperceptibly.)*

(The PROFESSOR *enters. He is a little old man with a little white beard. He wears pince-nez,° a black skull cap, a long black schoolmaster's coat, trousers and shoes of black, detachable white collar, a black tie. Excessively polite, very timid, his voice deadened by his timidity, very proper, very much the teacher. He rubs his hands together constantly; occasionally a lewd gleam comes into his eyes and is quickly repressed.)*

(During the course of the play his timidity will disappear progressively, imperceptibly; and the lewd gleams in his eyes will become a steady devouring flame in the end.

---

aphasia, loss of the power of using or understanding words. **pince-nez,** eyeglasses attached to the nose by a spring-clip.

From a manner that is inoffensive at the start, the PRO-FESSOR *becomes more and more sure of himself, more and more nervous, aggressive, dominating, until he is able to do as he pleases with the* PUPIL, *who has become, in his hands, a pitiful creature. Of course, the voice of the* PROFESSOR *must change too, from thin and reedy, to stronger and stronger, until at the end it is extremely powerful, ringing, sonorous, while the* PUPIL's *voice changes from the very clear and ringing tones that she has at the beginning of the play until it is almost inaudible. In these first scenes the* PROFESSOR *might stammer very slightly.)*

PROFESSOR: Good morning, young lady. You . . . I expect that you . . . that you are the new pupil?

PUPIL *(turns quickly with a lively and self-assured manner; she gets up, goes toward the* PROFESSOR, *and gives him her hand):* Yes, Professor. Good morning, Professor. As you see, I'm on time. I didn't want to be late.

PROFESSOR: That's fine, miss. Thank you, you didn't really need to hurry. I am very sorry to have kept you waiting . . . I was just finishing up . . . well . . . I'm sorry . . . You will excuse me, won't you?

PUPIL: Oh, certainly, Professor. It doesn't matter at all, Professor.

PROFESSOR: Please excuse me . . . Did you have any trouble finding the house?

PUPIL: No . . . Not at all. I just asked the way. Everybody knows you around here.

PROFESSOR: For thirty years I've lived in this town. You've not been here for long? How do you find it?

PUPIL: It's all right. The town is attractive and even agreeable, there's a nice park, a boarding school, a bishop, nice shops and streets . . .

PROFESSOR: That's very true, young lady. And yet, I'd just as soon live somewhere else. In Paris, or at least Bordeaux.

PUPIL: Do you like Bordeaux?

PROFESSOR: I don't know. I've never seen it.

PUPIL: But you know Paris?

PROFESSOR: No, I don't know it either, young lady, but if you'll permit me, can you tell me, Paris is the capital city of . . . miss?

PUPIL *(searching her memory for a moment, then, happily guessing):* Paris is the capital city of . . . France?

PROFESSOR: Yes, young lady, bravo, that's very good, that's perfect. My congratulations. You have your French geography at your finger tips. You know your chief cities.

PUPIL: Oh! I don't know them all yet, Professor, it's not quite that easy, I have trouble learning them.

PROFESSOR: Oh! it will come . . . you mustn't give up . . . young lady . . . I beg your pardon . . . have patience . . . little by little . . . You will see, it will come in time . . . What a nice day it is today . . . or rather, not so nice . . . Oh! but then yes it is nice. In short, it's not too bad a day, that's the main thing . . . ahem . . . ahem . . . it's not raining and it's not snowing either.

PUPIL: That would be most unusual, for it's summer now.

PROFESSOR: Excuse me, miss, I was just going to say so . . . but as you will learn, one must be ready for anything.

PUPIL: I guess so, Professor.

PROFESSOR: We can't be sure of anything, young lady, in this world.

PUPIL: The snow falls in the winter. Winter is one of the four seasons. The other three are . . . uh . . . spr . . .

PROFESSOR: Yes?

PUPIL: . . . ing, and then summer . . . and . . . uh . . .

PROFESSOR: It begins like "automobile," miss.

PUPIL: Ah, yes, autumn . . .

PROFESSOR: That's right, miss. That's a good answer, that's perfect. I am convinced that you will be a good pupil. You will make real progress. You are intelligent, you seem to me to be well informed, and you've a good memory.

PUPIL: I know my seasons, don't I, Professor?

PROFESSOR: Yes, indeed, miss . . . or almost. But it will come in time. In any case, you're coming along. Soon you'll know all the seasons, even with your eyes closed. Just as I do.

PUPIL: It's hard.

PROFESSOR: Oh, no. All it takes is a little effort, a little good will, miss. You will see. It will come, you may be sure of that.

PUPIL: Oh, I do hope so, Professor. I have a great thirst for knowledge. My parents also want me to get an education. They want me to specialize. They consider a little general culture, even if it is solid, is no longer enough, in these times.

PROFESSOR: Your parents, miss, are perfectly right. You must go on with your studies. Forgive me for saying so, but it is very necessary. Our contemporary life has become most complex.

PUPIL: And so very complicated too . . . My parents are fairly rich, I'm lucky. They can help me in my work, help me in my very advanced studies.

PROFESSOR: And you wish to qualify for . . . ?

PUPIL: Just as soon as possible, for the first doctor's orals. They're in three weeks' time.

PROFESSOR: You already have your high school diploma, if you'll pardon the question?

PUPIL: Yes, Professor, I have my science diploma and my arts diploma, too.

PROFESSOR: Ah, you're very far advanced, even perhaps too advanced for your age. And which doctorate do you wish to qualify for? In the physical sciences or in moral philosophy?

PUPIL: My parents are very much hoping—if you think it will be possible in such a short time—they very much hope that I can qualify for the total doctorate.

PROFESSOR: The total doctorate? . . . You have great courage, young lady, I congratulate you sincerely. We will try, miss, to do our best. In any case, you already know quite a bit, and at so young an age too.

PUPIL: Oh, Professor.

PROFESSOR: Then, if you'll permit me, pardon me, please, I do think that we ought to get to work. We have scarcely any time to lose.

PUPIL: Oh, but certainly, Professor, I want to. I beg you to.

PROFESSOR: Then, may I ask you to sit down . . . there . . . Will you permit me, miss, that is if you have no objections, to sit down opposite you?

PUPIL: Oh, of course, Professor, please do.

PROFESSOR: Thank you very much, miss. *(They sit down facing each other at the table, their profiles to the audience.)* There we are. Now have you brought your books and notebooks?

PUPIL *(taking notebooks and books out of her satchel)*: Yes, Professor. Certainly, I have brought all that we'll need.

PROFESSOR: Perfect, miss. This is perfect. Now, if this doesn't bore you . . . shall we begin?

PUPIL: Yes, indeed, Professor, I am at your disposal.

PROFESSOR: At my disposal? *(A gleam comes into his eyes and is quickly extinguished; he begins to make a gesture that he suppresses at once.)* Oh, miss, it is I who am at your disposal. I am only your humble servant.

PUPIL: Oh, Professor . . .

PROFESSOR: If you will . . . now . . . we . . . we . . . I . . . I will begin by making a brief examination of your knowledge, past and present, so that we may chart our future course . . . Good. How is your perception of plurality?

PUPIL: It's rather vague . . . confused.

PROFESSOR: Good. We shall see.

(He rubs his hands together. The MAID *enters, and this appears to irritate the* PROFESSOR. *She goes to the buffet and looks for something, lingering.)*

PROFESSOR: Now, miss, would you like to do a little arithmetic, that is if you want to . . .

PUPIL: Oh, yes, Professor. Certainly, I ask nothing better.

PROFESSOR: It is rather a new science, a modern science, properly speaking, it is more a method than a science . . . And it is also a therapy. *(To the* MAID:*)* Have you finished, Marie?

MAID: Yes, Professor, I've found the plate. I'm just going . . .

PROFESSOR: Hurry up then. Please go along to the kitchen, if you will.

MAID: Yes, Professor, I'm going. *(She starts to go out.)* Excuse me, Professor, but take care, I urge you to remain calm.

PROFESSOR: You're being ridiculous, Marie. Now, don't worry.

MAID: That's what you always say.

PROFESSOR: I will not stand for your insinuations. I know perfectly well how to comport myself. I am old enough for that.

MAID: Precisely, Professor. You will do better not to start the young lady on arithmetic. Arithmetic is tiring, exhausting.

PROFESSOR: Not at my age. And anyhow, what business is it of yours? This is my concern. And I know what I'm doing. This is not your department.

MAID: Very well, Professor. But you can't say that I didn't warn you.

PROFESSOR: Marie, I can get along without your advice.

MAID: As you wish, Professor. *(She exits.)*

PROFESSOR: Miss, I hope you'll pardon this absurd interruption . . . Excuse this woman . . . She is always afraid that I'll tire myself. She fusses over my health.

PUPIL: Oh, that's quite all right, Professor. It shows that she's very devoted. She loves you very much. Good servants are rare.

PROFESSOR: She exaggerates. Her fears are stupid. But let's return to our arithmetical knitting.

PUPIL: I'm following you, Professor.

PROFESSOR *(wittily)*: Without leaving your seat!

PUPIL *(appreciating his joke)*: Like you, Professor.

PROFESSOR: Good. Let us arithmetize a little now.

PUPIL: Yes, gladly, Professor.

PROFESSOR: It wouldn't be too tiresome for you to tell me . . .

PUPIL: Not at all, Professor, go on.

PROFESSOR: How much are one and one?

PUPIL: One and one make two.

PROFESSOR *(marveling at the* PUPIL's *knowledge)*: Oh, but that's very good. You appear to me to be well along in your studies. You should easily achieve the total doctorate, miss.

PUPIL: I'm so glad. Especially to have someone like you tell me this.

PROFESSOR: Let's push on: how much are two and one?

PUPIL: Three.

PROFESSOR: Three and one?

PUPIL: Four.

PROFESSOR: Four and one?

PUPIL: Five.

PROFESSOR: Five and one?

PUPIL: Six.

PROFESSOR: Six and one?

PUPIL: Seven.

PROFESSOR: Seven and one?

PUPIL: Eight.

PROFESSOR: Seven and one?

PUPIL: Eight again.

PROFESSOR: Very well answered. Seven and one?

PUPIL: Eight once more.

PROFESSOR: Perfect. Excellent. Seven and one?

PUPIL: Eight again. And sometimes nine.

PROFESSOR: Magnificent. You are magnificent. You are

exquisite. I congratulate you warmly, miss. There's scarcely any point in going on. At addition you are a past master. Now, let's look at subtraction. Tell me, if you are not exhausted, how many are four minus three?

PUPIL: Four minus three? . . . Four minus three?

PROFESSOR: Yes. I mean to say: subtract three from four.

PUPIL: That makes . . . seven?

PROFESSOR: I am sorry but I'm obliged to contradict you. Four minus three does not make seven. You are confused: four plus three makes seven, four minus three does not make seven . . . This is not addition anymore, we must subtract now.

PUPIL (trying to understand): Yes . . . yes . . .

PROFESSOR: Four minus three makes . . . How many? . . . How many?

PUPIL: Four?

PROFESSOR: No, miss, that's not it.

PUPIL: Three, then.

PROFESSOR: Not that either, miss . . . Pardon, I'm sorry . . . I ought to say, that's not it . . . excuse me.

PUPIL: Four minus three . . . Four minus three . . . Four minus three? . . . But now doesn't that make ten?

PROFESSOR: Oh, certainly not, miss. It's not a matter of guessing, you've got to think it out. Let's try to deduce it together. Would you like to count?

PUPIL: Yes, Professor. One . . . two . . . uh . . .

PROFESSOR: You know how to count? How far can you count up to?

PUPIL: I can count to . . . infinity.

PROFESSOR: That's not possible, miss.

PUPIL: Well then, let's say to sixteen.

PROFESSOR: That is enough. One must know one's limits. Count then, if you will, please.

PUPIL: One . . . two . . . and after two, comes three . . . then four . . .

PROFESSOR: Stop there, miss. Which number is larger? Three or four?

PUPIL: Uh . . . three or four? Which is the larger? The larger of three or four? In what sense larger?

PROFESSOR: Some numbers are smaller and others are larger. In the large numbers there are more units than in the small . . .

PUPIL: Than in the small numbers?

PROFESSOR: Unless the small ones have smaller units. If they are very small, then there might be more units in the small numbers than in the large . . . if it is a question of other units . . .

PUPIL: In that case, the small numbers can be larger than the large numbers?

PROFESSOR: Let's not go into that. That would take us much too far. You must realize simply that there are also magnitudes, totals, there are groups, there are heaps, heaps of such things as plums, trucks, geese, prune pits, etc. To facilitate our work, let's merely suppose that we have only equal numbers, then the bigger numbers will be those that have the most units.

PUPIL: The one that has the most is the biggest? Ah, I understand, Professor, you are identifying quality with quantity.

PROFESSOR: That is too theoretical, miss, too theoretical. You needn't concern yourself with that. Let us take an example and reason from a definite case. Let's leave the general conclusions for later. We have the number four and the number three, and each has always the same number of units. Which number will be larger, the smaller or the larger?

PUPIL: Excuse me, Professor . . . What do you mean by the larger number? Is it the one that is not so small as the other?

PROFESSOR: That's it, miss, perfect. You have understood me very well.

PUPIL: Then, it is four.

PROFESSOR: What is four—larger or smaller than three?

PUPIL: Smaller . . . no, larger.

PROFESSOR: Excellent answer. How many units are there between three and four? . . . Or between four and three, if you prefer?

PUPIL: There aren't any units, Professor, between three and four. Four comes immediately after three; there is nothing at all between three and four!

PROFESSOR: I haven't made myself very well understood. No doubt, it is my fault. I've not been sufficiently clear.

PUPIL: No, Professor, it's my fault.

PROFESSOR: Look here. Here are three matches. And here is another one, that makes four. Now watch carefully—we have four matches. I take one away, now how many are left?

(We don't see the matches, nor any of the objects that are mentioned. The PROFESSOR gets up from the table, writes on the imaginary blackboard with an imaginary piece of chalk, etc.)

PUPIL: Five. If three and one make four, four and one make five.

PROFESSOR: That's not it. That's not it at all. You always have a tendency to add. But one must be able to subtract too. It's not enough to integrate, you must also disintegrate. That's the way life is. That's philosophy. That's science. That's progress, civilization.

PUPIL: Yes, Professor.

PROFESSOR: Let's return to our matches. I have four of them. You see, there are really four. I take one away, and there remain only . . .

PUPIL: I don't know, Professor.

PROFESSOR: Come now, think. It's not easy, I admit. Nevertheless, you've had enough training to make the intellectual effort required to arrive at an understanding. So?

PUPIL: I can't get it, Professor. I don't know, Professor.

PROFESSOR: Let us take a simpler example. If you had

two noses, and I pulled one of them off . . . how many would you have left?

PUPIL: None.

PROFESSOR: What do you mean, none?

PUPIL: Yes, it's because you haven't pulled off any, that's why I have one now. If you had pulled it off, I wouldn't have it anymore.

PROFESSOR: You've not understood my example. Suppose that you have only one ear.

PUPIL: Yes, and then?

PROFESSOR: If I gave you another one, how many would you have then?

PUPIL: Two.

PROFESSOR: Good. And if I gave you still another ear. How many would you have then?

PUPIL: Three ears.

PROFESSOR: Now, I take one away . . . and there remain . . . how many ears?

PUPIL: Two.

PROFESSOR: Good. I take away still another one, how many do you have left?

PUPIL: Two.

PROFESSOR: No. You have two, I take one away, I eat one up, then how many do you have left?

PUPIL: Two.

PROFESSOR: I eat one of them . . . one.

PUPIL: Two.

PROFESSOR: One.

PUPIL: Two.

PROFESSOR: One!

PUPIL: Two!

PROFESSOR: One!!!

PUPIL: Two!!!

PROFESSOR: One!!!

PUPIL: Two!!!

PROFESSOR: One!!!

PUPIL: Two!!!

PROFESSOR: No. No. That's not right. The example is not . . . it's not convincing. Listen to me.

PUPIL: Yes, Professor.

PROFESSOR: You've got . . . you've got . . . you've got . . .

PUPIL: Ten fingers!

PROFESSOR: If you wish. Perfect. Good. You have then ten fingers.

PUPIL: Yes, Professor.

PROFESSOR: How many would you have if you had only five of them?

PUPIL: Ten, Professor.

PROFESSOR: That's not right!

PUPIL: But it is, Professor.

PROFESSOR: I tell you it's not!

PUPIL: You just told me that I had ten . . .

PROFESSOR: I also said, immediately afterwards, that you had five!

PUPIL: I don't have five, I've got ten!

PROFESSOR: Let's try another approach . . . for purposes of subtraction let's limit ourselves to the numbers

from one to five . . . Wait now, miss, you'll soon see. I'm going to make you understand.

(The PROFESSOR begins to write on the imaginary blackboard. He moves it closer to the PUPIL, who turns around in order to see it.)

PROFESSOR: Look here, miss . . . (He pretends to draw a stick on the blackboard and the number 1 below the stick; then two sticks and the number 2 below, then three sticks and the number 3 below, then four sticks with the number 4 below.) You see . . .

PUPIL: Yes, Professor.

PROFESSOR: These are sticks, miss, sticks. This is one stick, these are two sticks, and three sticks, then four sticks, then five sticks. One stick, two sticks, three sticks, four and five sticks, these are numbers. When we count the sticks, each stick is a unit, miss . . . What have I just said?

PUPIL: "A unit, miss! What have I just said?"

PROFESSOR: Or a figure! Or a number! One, two, three, four, five, these are the elements of numeration, miss.

PUPIL (hesitant): Yes, Professor. The elements, figures, which are sticks, units and numbers . . .

PROFESSOR: At the same time . . . that's to say, in short—the whole of arithmetic is there.

PUPIL: Yes, Professor. Good, Professor. Thanks, Professor.

PROFESSOR: Now, count, if you will please, using these elements . . . add and subtract . . .

PUPIL (as though trying to impress them on her memory): Sticks are really figures and numbers are units?

PROFESSOR: Hmm . . . so to speak. And then?

PUPIL: One could subtract two units from three units, but can one subtract two twos from three threes? And two figures from four numbers? And three numbers from one unit?

PROFESSOR: No, miss.

PUPIL: Why, Professor?

PROFESSOR: Because, miss.

PUPIL: Because why, Professor? Since one is the same as the other?

PROFESSOR: That's the way it is, miss. It can't be explained. This is only comprehensible through internal mathematical reasoning. Either you have it or you don't.

PUPIL: So much the worse for me.

PROFESSOR: Listen to me, miss, if you don't achieve a profound understanding of these principles, these arithmetical archetypes, you will never be able to perform correctly the functions of a polytechnician. Still less will you be able to teach a course in a polytechnical school . . . or the primary grades. I realize that this is not easy, it is very, very abstract . . . obviously . . . but unless you can comprehend the primary elements, how do you expect to be able to calculate mentally—and this is the least of the things that even an ordinary engineer must be able to do—how much, for example, are three billion seven hundred fifty-five million nine hundred ninety-eight thousand two hundred fifty one, multiplied by five billion one hundred sixty-two million three hundred and three thousand five hundred and eight?

PUPIL (*very quickly*): That makes nineteen quintillion three hundred ninety quadrillion two trillion eight hundred forty-four billion two hundred nineteen million one hundred sixty-four thousand five hundred and eight . . .

PROFESSOR (*astonished*): No. I don't think so. That must make nineteen quintillion three hundred ninety quadrillion two trillion eight hundred forty-four billion two hundred nineteen million one hundred sixty-four thousand five hundred and nine . . .

PUPIL: . . . No . . . five hundred and eight . . .

PROFESSOR (*more and more astonished, calculating mentally*): Yes . . . you are right . . . the result is indeed . . . (*He mumbles unintelligibly:*) . . . quintillion, quadrillion, trillion, billion, million . . . (*Clearly:*) one hundred sixty-four thousand five hundred and eight . . . (*Stupefied:*) But how did you know that, if you don't know the principles of arithmetical reasoning?

PUPIL: It's easy. Not being able to rely on my reasoning, I've memorized all the products of all possible multiplications.

PROFESSOR: That's pretty good . . . However, permit me to confess to you that that doesn't satisfy me, miss, and I do not congratulate you: in mathematics and in arithmetic especially, the thing that counts—for in arithmetic it is always necessary to count—the thing that counts is, above all, understanding . . . It is by mathematical reasoning, simultaneously inductive and deductive, that you ought to arrive at this result—as well as at any other result. Mathematics is the sworn enemy of memory, which is excellent otherwise, but disastrous, arithmetically speaking! . . . That's why I'm not happy with this . . . this won't do, not at all . . .

PUPIL (*desolated*): No, Professor.

PROFESSOR: Let's leave it for the moment. Let's go on to another exercise . . .

PUPIL: Yes, Professor.

MAID (*entering*): Hmm, hmm, Professor . . .

PROFESSOR (*who doesn't hear her*): It is unfortunate, miss, that you aren't further along in specialized mathematics . . .

MAID (*taking him by the sleeve*): Professor! Professor!

PROFESSOR: I hear that you will not be able to qualify for the total doctor's orals . . .

PUPIL: Yes, Professor, it's too bad!

PROFESSOR: Unless you . . . (*To the* MAID:) Let me be, Marie . . . Look here, why are you bothering me?

Go back to the kitchen! To your pots and pans! Go away! Go away! (*To the* PUPIL:) We will try to prepare you at least for the partial doctorate . . .

MAID: Professor! . . . Professor! . . . (*She pulls his sleeve.*)

PROFESSOR (*to the* MAID): Now leave me alone! Let me be! What's the meaning of this? . . . (*To the* PUPIL:) I must therefore teach you, if you really do insist on attempting the partial doctorate . . .

PUPIL: Yes, Professor.

PROFESSOR: . . . The elements of linguistics and of comparative philology° . . .

MAID: No, Professor, no! . . . You mustn't do that! . . .

PROFESSOR: Marie, you're going too far!

MAID: Professor, especially not philology, philology leads to calamity . . .

PUPIL (*astonished*): To calamity? (*Smiling, a little stupidly:*) That's hard to believe.

PROFESSOR (*to the* MAID): That's enough now! Get out of here!

MAID: All right, Professor, all right. But you can't say that I didn't warn you! Philology leads to calamity!

PROFESSOR: I'm an adult, Marie!

PUPIL: Yes, Professor.

MAID: As you wish.

(*She exits.*)

PROFESSOR: Let's continue, miss.

PUPIL: Yes, Professor.

PROFESSOR: I want you to listen now with the greatest possible attention to a lecture I have prepared . . .

PUPIL: Yes, Professor!

PROFESSOR: . . . Thanks to which, in fifteen minutes' time, you will be able to acquire the fundamental principles of the linguistic and comparative philology of the neo-Spanish languages.

PUPIL: Yes, Professor, oh good!

(*She claps her hands.*)

PROFESSOR (*with authority*): Quiet! What do you mean by that?

PUPIL: I'm sorry, Professor.

(*Slowly, she replaces her hands on the table.*)

PROFESSOR: Quiet! (*He gets up, walks up and down the room, his hands behind his back; from time to time he stops at stage center or near the* PUPIL, *and underlines his words with a gesture of his hand; he orates, but without being too emotional. The* PUPIL *follows him with her eyes, occasionally with some difficulty, for she has to turn her head far around; once or twice, not more, she turns around completely.*) And now, miss, Spanish is truly the mother tongue which gave birth to all the neo-Spanish languages, of which Spanish, Latin, Italian,

---

philology, study of language.

our own French, Portuguese, Romanian, Sardinian or Sardanapalian, Spanish and neo-Spanish—and also, in certain of its aspects, Turkish which is otherwise very close to Greek, which is only logical, since it is a fact that Turkey is a neighbor of Greece and Greece is even closer to Turkey than you are to me—this is only one more illustration of the very important linguistic law which states that geography and philology are twin sisters . . . You may take notes, miss.

PUPIL *(in a dull voice)*: Yes, Professor!

PROFESSOR: That which distinguishes the neo-Spanish languages from each other and their idioms from the other linguistic groups, such as the group of languages called Austrian and neo-Austrian or Hapsburgian, as well as the Esperanto, Helvetian, Monacan, Swiss, Andorran, Basque, and jai alai° groups, and also the groups of diplomatic and technical languages—that which distinguishes them, I repeat, is their striking resemblance which makes it so hard to distinguish them from each other— I'm speaking of the neo-Spanish languages which one is able to distinguish from each other, however, only thanks to their distinctive characteristics, absolutely indisputable proofs of their extraordinary resemblance, which renders indisputable their common origin, and which, at the same time, differentiates them profoundly—through the continuation of the distinctive traits which I've just cited.

PUPIL: Oooh! Ye-e-e-s-s-s, Professor!

PROFESSOR: But let's not linger over generalities . . .

PUPIL *(regretfully, but won over)*: Oh, Professor . . .

PROFESSOR: This appears to interest you. All the better, all the better.

PUPIL: Oh, yes, Professor . . .

PROFESSOR: Don't worry, miss. We will come back to it later . . . That is if we come back to it at all. Who can say?

PUPIL *(enchanted in spite of everything)*: Oh, yes, Professor.

PROFESSOR: Every tongue—you must know this, miss, and remember it *until the hour of your death* . . .

PUPIL: Oh! yes, Professor, until the hour of my death . . . Yes, Professor . . .

PROFESSOR: . . . And this, too, is a fundamental principle, every tongue is at bottom nothing but language, which necessarily implies that it is composed of sounds, or . . .

PUPIL: Phonemes . . .

PROFESSOR: Just what I was going to say. Don't parade your knowledge. You'd do better to listen.

PUPIL: All right, Professor. Yes, Professor.

PROFESSOR: The sounds, miss, must be seized on the wing as they fly so that they'll not fall on deaf ears. As a result, when you set out to articulate, it is recommended, insofar as possible, that you lift up your neck and chin very high, and rise up on the tips of your toes, you see, this way . . .

PUPIL: Yes, Professor.

PROFESSOR: Keep quiet. Remain seated, don't interrupt me . . . And project the sounds very loudly with all the force of your lungs in conjunction with that of your vocal cords. Like this, look: "Butterfly," "Eureka," "Trafalgar," "Papaya." This way, the sounds become filled with a warm air that is lighter than the surrounding air so that they can fly without danger of falling on deaf ears, which are veritable voids, tombs of sonorities. If you utter several sounds at an accelerated speed, they will automatically cling to each other, constituting thus syllables, words, even sentences, that is to say groupings of various importance, purely irrational assemblages of sounds, denuded of all sense, but for that very reason the more capable of maintaining themselves without danger at a high altitude in the air. By themselves, words charged with significance will fall, weighted down by their meaning, and in the end they always collapse, fall . . .

PUPIL: . . . On deaf ears.

PROFESSOR: That's it, but don't interrupt . . . and into the worst confusion . . . Or else burst like balloons. Therefore, miss . . . *(The* PUPIL *suddenly appears to be unwell.)* What's the matter?

PUPIL: I've got a toothache, Professor.

PROFESSOR: That's not important. We're not going to stop for anything so trivial. Let us go on . . .

PUPIL *(appearing to be in more and more pain)*: Yes, Professor.

PROFESSOR: I draw your attention in passing to the consonants that change their nature in combinations. In this case *f* becomes *v*, *d* becomes *t*, *g* becomes *k*, and vice versa, as in these examples that I will cite for you: "That's all right," "hens and chickens," "Welsh rabbit," "lots of nothing," "not at all."°

PUPIL: I've got a toothache.

PROFESSOR: Let's continue.

PUPIL: Yes.

PROFESSOR: To resume: it takes years and years to learn to pronounce. Thanks to science, we can achieve this in a few minutes. In order to project words, sounds and all the rest, you must realize that it is necessary to pitilessly expel air from the lungs, and make it pass delicately, caressingly, over the vocal cords, which, like harps or leaves in the wind, will suddenly shake, agitate, vibrate, vibrate, vibrate or uvulate, or fricate or jostle against each other, or sibilate, sibilate, placing everything in movement, the uvula, the tongue, the palate, the teeth . . .

PUPIL: I have a toothache.

---

jai alai, handball-like game.

All to be heavily elided.—Translator's note.

PROFESSOR: . . . And the lips . . . Finally the words come out through the nose, the mouth, the ears, the pores, drawing along with them all the organs that we have named, torn up by the roots, in a powerful, majestic flight, which is none other than what is called, improperly, the voice, whether modulated in singing or transformed into a terrible symphonic storm with a whole procession . . . of garlands of all kinds of flowers, of sonorous artifices: labials, dentals, occlusives, palatals, and others, some caressing, some bitter or violent.

PUPIL: Yes, Professor, I've got a toothache.

PROFESSOR: Let's go on, go on. As for the neo-Spanish languages, they are closely related, so closely to each other, that they can be considered as true second cousins. Moreover, they have the same mother: Spanishe, with a mute *e*. That is why it is so difficult to distinguish them from one another. That is why it is so useful to pronounce carefully, and to avoid errors in pronunciation. Pronunciation itself is worth a whole language. A bad pronunciation can get you into trouble. In this connection, permit me, parenthetically, to share a personal experience with you. (*Slight pause. The* PROFESSOR *goes over his memories for a moment; his features mellow, but he recovers at once.*) I was very young, little more than a child. It was during my military service. I had a friend in the regiment, a vicomte, who suffered from a rather serious defect in his pronunciation: he could not pronounce the letter *f*. Instead of *f*, he said *f*. Thus, instead of "Birds of a feather flock together," he said: "Birds of a feather flock together." He pronounced filly instead of filly, Firmin instead of Firmin, French bean instead of French bean, go frig yourself instead of go frig yourself, farrago instead of farrago, fee fi fo fum instead of fee fi fo fum, Philip instead of Philip, fictory instead of fictory, February instead of February, March-April instead of March-April, Gerard de Nerval and not as is correct—Gerard de Nerval, Mirabeau instead of Mirabeau, etc., instead of etc., and thus instead of etc., instead of etc., and thus and so forth. However, he managed to conceal his fault so effectively that, thanks to the hats he wore, no one ever noticed it.

PUPIL: Yes, I've got a toothache.

PROFESSOR (*abruptly changing his tone, his voice hardening*): Let's go on. We'll first consider the points of similarity in order the better to apprehend, later on, that which distinguishes all these languages from each other. The differences can scarcely be recognized by people who are not aware of them. Thus, all the words of all the languages . . .

PUPIL: Uh, yes? . . . I've got a toothache.

PROFESSOR: Let's continue . . . are always the same, just as all the suffixes, all the prefixes, all the terminations, all the roots . . .

PUPIL: Are the roots of words square?

PROFESSOR: Square or cube. That depends.

PUPIL: I've got a toothache.

PROFESSOR: Let's go on. Thus, to give you an example which is little more than an illustration, take the word "front" . . .

PUPIL: How do you want me to take it?

PROFESSOR: However you wish, so long as you take it, but above all do not interrupt.

PUPIL: I've got a toothache.

PROFESSOR: Let's continue . . . I said: Let's continue. Take now the word "front." Have you taken it?

PUPIL: Yes, yes, I've got it. My teeth, my teeth . . .

PROFESSOR: The word "front" is the root of "frontispiece." It is also to be found in "affronted." "Ispiece" is the suffix, and "af" the prefix. They are so called because they do not change. They don't want to.

PUPIL: I've got a toothache.

PROFESSOR: Let's go on (*Rapidly:*) These prefixes are of Spanish origin. I hope you noticed that, did you?

PUPIL: Oh, how my tooth aches.

PROFESSOR: Let's continue. You've surely also noticed that they've not changed in French. And now, young lady, nothing has succeeded in changing them in Latin either, nor in Italian, nor in Portuguese, nor in Sardanapalian, nor in Sardanapali, nor in Romanian, nor in neo-Spanish, nor in Spanish, nor even in the Oriental: front, frontispiece, affronted, always the same word, invariably with the same root, the same suffix, the same prefix, in all the languages I have named. And it is always the same for all words.

PUPIL: In all languages, these words mean the same thing? I've got a toothache.

PROFESSOR: Absolutely. Moreover, it's more a notion than a word. In any case, you have always the same signification, the same composition, the same sound structure, not only for this word, but for all conceivable words, in all languages. For one single notion is expressed by one and the same word, and its synonyms, in all countries. Forget about your teeth.

PUPIL: I've got a toothache. Yes, yes, yes.

PROFESSOR: Good, let's go on. I tell you, let's go on . . . How would you say, for example, in French: the roses of my grandmother are as yellow as my grandfather who was Asiatic?

PUPIL: My teeth ache, ache, ache.

PROFESSOR: Let's go on, let's go on, go ahead and answer, anyway.

PUPIL: In French?

PROFESSOR: In French.

PUPIL: Uhh . . . I should say in French: the roses of my grandmother are . . . ?

PROFESSOR: As yellow as my grandfather who was Asiatic . . .

PUPIL: Oh well, one would say, in French, I believe, the roses . . . of my . . . how do you say "grandmother" in French?

PROFESSOR: In French? Grandmother.

PUPIL: The roses of my grandmother are as yellow—in in French, is it "yellow"?

PROFESSOR: Yes, of course!

PUPIL: Are as yellow as my grandfather when he got angry.

PROFESSOR: No . . . who was A . . .

PUPIL: . . . siatic . . . I've got a toothache.

PROFESSOR: That's it.

PUPIL: I've got a tooth . . .

PROFESSOR: Ache . . . so what . . . let's continue! And now translate the same sentence into Spanish, then into neo-Spanish . . .

PUPIL: In Spanish . . . this would be: the roses of my grandmother are as yellow as my grandfather who was Asiatic.

PROFESSOR: No. That's wrong.

PUPIL: And in neo-Spanish: the roses of my grandmother are as yellow as my grandfather who was Asiatic.

PROFESSOR: That's wrong. That's wrong. That's wrong. You have inverted it, you've confused Spanish with neo-Spanish, and neo-Spanish with Spanish . . . Oh . . . no . . . it's the other way around . . .

PUPIL: I've got a toothache. You're getting mixed up.

PROFESSOR: You're the one who is mixing me up. Pay attention and take notes. I will say the sentence to you in Spanish, then in neo-Spanish, and finally, in Latin. You will repeat after me. Pay attention, for the resemblances are great. In fact, they are identical resemblances. Listen, follow carefully . . .

PUPIL: I've got a tooth . . .

PROFESSOR: . . . Ache.

PUPIL: Let us go on . . . Ah! . . .

PROFESSOR: . . . In Spanish: the roses of my grandmother are as yellow as my grandfather who was Asiatic; in Latin; the roses of my grandmother are as yellow as my grandfather who was Asiatic. Do you detect the differences? Translate this into . . . Romanian.

PUPIL: The . . . how do you say "roses" in Romanian?

PROFESSOR: But "roses," what else?

PUPIL: It's not "roses"? Oh, how my tooth aches!

PROFESSOR: Certainly not, certainly not, since "roses" is a translation in Oriental of the French word "roses," in Spanish "roses," do you get it? In Sardanapali, "roses" . . .

PUPIL: Excuse me, Professor, but . . . Oh, my toothache! . . . I don't get the difference.

PROFESSOR: But it's so simple! So simple! It's a matter of having a certain experience, a technical experience and practice in these diverse languages, which are so diverse in spite of the fact that they present wholly identical characteristics. I'm going to try to give you a key . . .

PUPIL: Toothache . . .

PROFESSOR: That which differentiates these languages, is neither the words, which are absolutely the same, nor the structure of the sentence which is everywhere the same, nor the intonation, which does not offer any differences, nor the rhythm of the language . . . that which differentiates them . . . are you listening?

PUPIL: I've got a toothache.

PROFESSOR: Are you listening to me, young lady? Aah! We're going to lose our temper.

PUPIL: You're bothering me, Professor. I've got a toothache.

PROFESSOR: Son of a cocker spaniel! Listen to me!

PUPIL: Oh well . . . yes . . . yes . . . go on . . .

PROFESSOR: That which distinguishes them from each other, on the one hand, and from their mother, Spanishe with its mute e, on the other hand . . . is . . .

PUPIL (grimacing): Is what?

PROFESSOR: Is an intangible thing. Something intangible that one is able to perceive only after very long study, with a great deal of trouble and after the broadest experience . . .

PUPIL: Ah?

PROFESSOR: Yes, young lady. I cannot give you any rule. One must have a feeling for it, and well, that's it. But in order to have it, one must study, study, and then study some more.

PUPIL: Toothache.

PROFESSOR: All the same, there are some specific cases where words differ from one language to another . . . but we cannot base our knowledge on these cases, which are, so to speak, exceptional.

PUPIL: Oh, yes? . . . Oh, Professor, I've got a toothache.

PROFESSOR: Don't interrupt! Don't make me lose my temper! I can't answer for what I'll do. I was saying, then . . . Ah, yes, the exceptional cases, the so-called easily distinguished . . . or facilely distinguished . . . or conveniently . . . if you prefer . . . I repeat, if you prefer, for I see that you're not listening to me . . .

PUPIL: I've got a toothache.

PROFESSOR: I say then: in certain expressions in current usage, certain words differ totally from one language to another, so much so that the language employed is, in this case, considerably easier to identify. I'll give you an example: the neo-Spanish expression, famous in Madrid: "My country is the new Spain," becomes in Italian: "My country is . . .

PUPIL: The new Spain.

PROFESSOR: No! "My country is Italy." Tell me now, by simple deduction, how do you say "Italy" in French?

PUPIL: I've got a toothache.

PROFESSOR: But it's so easy: for the word "Italy," in French we have the word "France," which is an exact translation of it. My country is France. And "France" in Oriental: "Orient!" My country is the Orient. And "Orient" in Portuguese: "Portugal!" The Oriental expression: My country is the Orient is translated then in the same fashion into Portuguese: My country is Portugal! And so on . . .

PUPIL: Oh, no more, no more. My teeth . . .

PROFESSOR: Ache! ache! ache! . . . I'm going to pull them out, I will! One more example. The word "capital"—it takes on, according to the language one speaks, a different meaning. That is to say that when a Spaniard says: "I reside in the capital," the word "capital" does not mean at all the same thing that a Portuguese means when he says: "I reside in the capital." All the more so in the case of a Frenchman, a neo-Spaniard, a Romanian, a Latin, a Sardanapali . . . Whenever you hear it, young lady— young lady, I'm saying this for you! Pooh! Whenever you hear the expression: "I reside in the capital," you will immediately and easily know whether this is Spanish or Spanish, neo-Spanish, French, Oriental, Romanian, or Latin, for it is enough to know which metropolis is referred to by the person who pronounces the sentence . . . at the very moment he pronounces it . . . But these are almost the only precise examples that I can give you . . .

PUPIL: Oh dear! My teeth . . .

PROFESSOR: Silence! Or I'll bash in your skull!

PUPIL: Just try to! Skulldugger!°

(The PROFESSOR seizes her wrist and twists it.)

PUPIL: Oww!

PROFESSOR: Keep quiet now! Not a word!

PUPIL (whimpering): Toothache . . .

PROFESSOR: One thing that is the most . . . how shall I say it? . . . the most paradoxical . . . yes . . . that's the word . . . the most paradoxical thing, is that a lot of people who are completely illiterate speak these different languages . . . do you understand? What did I just say?

PUPIL: . . . "Speak these different languages! What did I just say?"

PROFESSOR: You were lucky that time! . . . The common people speak a Spanish full of neo-Spanish words that they are entirely unaware of, all the while believing that they are speaking Latin . . . or they speak Latin, full of Oriental words, all the while believing that they're speaking Romanian . . . or Spanish, full of neo-Spanish, all the while believing that they're speaking Sardanapali, or Spanish . . . Do you understand?

PUPIL: Yes! yes! yes! yes! What more do you want . . . ?

PROFESSOR: No insolence, my pet, or you'll be sorry . . . (In a rage:) But the worst of all, young lady, is that certain people, for example, in a Latin that they suppose is Spanish, say: "Both my kidneys are of the same kidney," in addressing themselves to a Frenchman who does not know a word of Spanish, but the latter understands it as if it were his own language. For that matter he thinks it is his own language. And the Frenchman will reply, in French: "Me too, sir, mine are too," and this will be perfectly comprehensible to a Spaniard, who will feel certain that the reply is in pure Spanish and that Spanish is being spoken . . . when, in reality, it was neither Spanish nor French, but Latin in the neo-Spanish dialect . . . Sit still, young lady, don't fidget, stop tapping your feet . . .

PUPIL: I've got a toothache.

PROFESSOR: How do you account for the fact that, in speaking without knowing which language they speak, or even while each of them believes that he is speaking another, the common people understand each other at all?

PUPIL: I wonder.

PROFESSOR: It is simply one of the inexplicable curiosities of the vulgar empiricism of the common people—not to be confused with experience!—a paradox, a non-sense, one of the aberrations of human nature, it is purely and simply instinct—to put it in a nutshell . . . That's what is involved here.

PUPIL: Hah! hah!

PROFESSOR: Instead of staring at the flies while I'm going to all this trouble . . . you would do much better to try to be more attentive . . . it is not I who is going to qualify for the partial doctor's orals . . . I passed mine a long time ago . . . and I've won my total doctorate, too . . . and my super-total diploma . . . Don't you realize that what I'm saying is for your own good?

PUPIL: Toothache!

PROFESSOR: Ill-mannered . . . It can't go on like this, it won't do, it won't do, it won't do . . .

PUPIL: I'm . . . listening . . . to you . . .

PROFESSOR: Ahah! In order to learn to distinguish all the different languages, as I've told you, there is nothing better than practice . . . Let's take them up in order. I am going to try to teach you all the translations of the word "knife."

PUPIL: Well, all right . . . if you want . . .

PROFESSOR (calling the MAID): Marie! Marie! She's not there . . . Marie! Marie! . . . Marie, where are you? (He opens the door on the right.) Marie! . . .

(He exits. The PUPIL remains alone several minutes, staring into space, wearing a stupefied expression.)

PROFESSOR (offstage, in a shrill voice): Marie! What are you up to? Why don't you come! When I call you, you must come! (He re-enters, followed by MARIE.) It is I who gives the orders, do you hear? (He points at the PUPIL:) She doesn't understand anything, that girl. She doesn't understand!

MAID: Don't get into such a state, sir, you know where it'll end! You're going to go too far, you're going to go too far.

PROFESSOR: I'll be able to stop in time.

Skulldugger, contemptible person.

MAID: That's what you always say. I only wish I could see it.

PUPIL: I've got a toothache.

MAID: You see, it's starting, that's the symptom!

PROFESSOR: What symptom? Explain yourself? What do you mean?

PUPIL (in a spiritless voice): Yes, what do you mean? I've got a toothache.

MAID: The final symptom! The chief symptom!

PROFESSOR: Stupid! stupid! stupid! (The MAID starts to exit.) Don't go away like that! I called you to help me find the Spanish, neo-Spanish, Portuguese, French, Oriental, Romanian, Sardanapali, Latin and Spanish knives.

MAID (severely): Don't ask me. (She exits.)

PROFESSOR (makes a gesture as though to protest, then refrains, a little helpless. Suddenly, he remembers): Ah! (He goes quickly to the drawer where he finds a big knife, invisible or real according to the preference of the director. He seizes it and brandishes it happily.) Here is one, young lady, here is a knife. It's too bad that we only have this one, but we're going to try to make it serve for all the languages, anyway! It will be enough if you will pronounce the word "knife" in all the languages, while looking at the object, very closely, fixedly, and imagining that it is in the language that you are speaking.

PUPIL: I've got a toothache.

PROFESSOR (almost singing, chanting): Now, say "kni," like "kni," "fe," like "fe" . . . And look, look, look at it, watch it . . .

PUPIL: What is this one in? French, Italian or Spanish?

PROFESSOR: That doesn't matter now . . . That's not your concern. Say: "kni."

PUPIL: "Kni."

PROFESSOR: . . . "fe" . . . Look.

(He brandishes the knife under the PUPIL's eyes.)

PUPIL: "fe" . . .

PROFESSOR: Again . . . Look at it.

PUPIL: Oh, no! My God! I've had enough. And besides, I've got a toothache, my feet hurt me, I've got a headache.

PROFESSOR (abruptly): Knife . . . look . . . knife . . . look . . . knife . . . look . . .

PUPIL: You're giving me an earache, too. Oh, your voice! It's so piercing!

PROFESSOR: Say: knife . . . kni . . . fe . . .

PUPIL: No! My ears hurt, I hurt all over . . .

PROFESSOR: I'm going to tear them off, your ears, that's what I'm going to do to you, and then they won't hurt you anymore, my pet.

PUPIL: Oh . . . you're hurting me, oh, you're hurting me . . .

PROFESSOR: Look, come on, quickly, repeat after me: "kni" . . .

PUPIL: Oh, since you insist . . . knife . . . knife . . . (In a lucid moment, ironically:) Is that neo-Spanish . . . ?

PROFESSOR: If you like, yes, it's neo-Spanish, but hurry up . . . we haven't got time . . . And then, what do you mean by that insidious question? What are you up to?

PUPIL (becoming more and more exhausted, weeping, desperate, at the same time both exasperated and in a trance): Ah!

PROFESSOR: Repeat, watch. (He imitates a cuckoo:) Knife, knife . . . knife, knife . . . knife, knife . . . knife, knife . . .

PUPIL: Oh, my head . . . aches . . . (With her hand she caressingly touches the parts of her body as she names them:) . . . My eyes . . .

PROFESSOR (like a cuckoo): Knife, knife . . . knife, knife . . . (They are both standing. The PROFESSOR still brandishes his invisible knife, nearly beside himself, as he circles around her in a sort of scalp dance, but it is important that this not be exaggerated and that his dance steps be only suggested. The PUPIL stands facing the audience, then recoils in the direction of the window, sickly, languid, victimized.)

PROFESSOR: Repeat, repeat: knife . . . knife . . . knife . . .

PUPIL: I've got a pain . . . my throat, neck . . . oh, my shoulders . . . my breast . . . knife . . .

PROFESSOR: Knife . . . knife . . . knife . . .

PUPIL: My hips . . . knife . . . my thighs . . . kni . . .

PROFESSOR: Pronounce it carefully . . . knife . . . knife . . .

PUPIL: Knife . . . my throat . . .

PROFESSOR: Knife . . . knife . . .

PUPIL: Knife . . . my shoulders . . . my arms, my breast, my hips . . . knife . . . knife . . .

PROFESSOR: That's right . . . Now, you're pronouncing it well . . .

PUPIL: Knife . . . my breast . . . my stomach . . .

PROFESSOR (changing his voice): Pay attention . . . don't break my window . . . the knife kills . . .

PUPIL (in a weak voice): Yes, yes, . . . the knife kills?

PROFESSOR (striking the PUPIL with a very spectacular blow of the knife): Aaah! That'll teach you!

(PUPIL also cries "Aah!" then falls, flopping in an immodest position onto a chair which, as though by chance, is near the window. The murderer and his victim shout "Aaah!" at the same moment. After the first blow of the knife, the PUPIL flops onto the chair, her legs spread wide and hanging over both sides of the chair. The PROFESSOR remains standing in front of her, his back to the audience. After the first blow, he strikes her dead with a second slash of the knife, from bottom to top. After that blow a noticeable convulsion shakes his whole body.)

PROFESSOR (winded, mumbling): Bitch . . . Oh, that's good, that does me good . . . Ah! Ah! I'm exhausted . . . I can scarcely breathe . . . Aah! (He breathes with difficulty; he falls—fortunately a chair is there; he mops his brow, mumbles some incomprehensible words; his breathing becomes normal. He gets up, looks at the knife *in his hand, looks at the young girl, then as though he were waking up, in a panic:)* What have I done! What's going to happen to me now! What's going to happen! Oh! dear! Oh dear, I'm in trouble! Young lady, young lady, get up! *(He is agitated, still holding onto the invisible knife, which he doesn't know what to do with.)* Come now, young lady, the lesson is over . . . you may go . . . you can pay another time . . . Oh! she is dead . . . dea-ead . . . And by my knife . . . She is dea-ead . . . It's terrible. *(He calls the* MAID:*)* Marie! Marie! My good Marie, come here! Ah! Ah! *(The door on the right opens a little and* MARIE *appears.)* No . . . don't come in . . . I made a mistake . . . I don't need you, Marie . . . I don't need you anymore . . . do you understand? . . .

*(*MAID *enters wearing a stern expression, without saying a word. She sees the corpse.)*

PROFESSOR *(in a voice less and less assured)*: I don't need you, Marie . . .

MAID *(sarcastic)*: Then, you're satisfied with your pupil, she's profited by your lesson?

PROFESSOR *(holding the knife behind his back)*: Yes, the lesson is finished . . . but . . . she . . . she's still there . . . she doesn't want to leave . . .

MAID *(very harshly)*: Is that a fact? . . .

PROFESSOR *(trembling)*: It wasn't I . . . it wasn't I . . . Marie . . . No . . . I assure you . . . it wasn't I, my little Marie . . .

MAID: And who was it? Who was it then? Me?

PROFESSOR: I don't know . . . maybe . . .

MAID: Or the cat?

PROFESSOR: That's possible . . . I don't know . . .

MAID: And today makes it the fortieth time! . . . And every day it's the same thing! Every day! You should be ashamed, at your age . . . and you're going to make yourself sick! You won't have any pupils left. That will serve you right.

PROFESSOR *(irritated)*: It wasn't my fault! She didn't want to learn! She was disobedient! She was a bad pupil! She didn't want to learn!

MAID: Liar! . . .

PROFESSOR *(craftily approaching the* MAID, *holding the knife behind his back)*: It's none of your business! *(He tries to strike her with a great blow of the knife; the* MAID *seizes his wrist in mid-gesture and twists it; the* PROFESSOR *lets the knife fall to the floor):* . . . I'm sorry!

MAID *(gives him two loud, strong slaps; the* PROFESSOR *falls onto the floor, on his prat; he sobs)*: Little murderer! bastard! You're disgusting! You wanted to do that to me? I'm not one of your pupils, not me! *(She pulls him up by the collar, picks up his skullcap and puts it on his head; he's afraid she'll slap him again and holds his arm up to protect his face, like a child.)* Put the knife back where it belongs, go on! *(The* PROFESSOR *goes and puts it back in the drawer of the buffet, then comes back to her.)* Now didn't I warn you, just a little while

ago: arithmetic leads to philology, and philology leads to crime . . .

PROFESSOR: You said "to calamity"!

MAID: It's the same thing.

PROFESSOR: I didn't understand you. I thought that "calamity" was a city and that you meant that philology leads to the city of Calamity . . .

MAID: Liar! Old fox! An intellectual like you is not going to make a mistake in the meanings of words. Don't try to pull the wool over my eyes.

PROFESSOR *(sobbing)*: I didn't kill her on purpose!

MAID: Are you sorry at least?

PROFESSOR: Oh, yes, Marie, I swear it to you!

MAID: I can't help feeling sorry for you! Ah! you're a good boy in spite of everything! I'll try to fix this. But don't start it again . . . It could give you a heart attack . . .

PROFESSOR: Yes, Marie! What are we going to do, now?

MAID: We're going to bury her . . . along with the thirty-nine others . . . that will make forty coffins . . . I'll call the undertakers and my lover, Father Auguste . . . I'll order the wreaths . . .

PROFESSOR: Yes, Marie, thank you very much.

MAID: Well, that's that. And perhaps it won't be necessary to call Auguste, since you yourself are something of a priest at times, if one can believe the gossip.

PROFESSOR: In any case, don't spend too much on the wreaths. She didn't pay for her lesson.

MAID: Don't worry . . . The least you can do is cover her up with her smock, she's not decent that way. And then we'll carry her out . . .

PROFESSOR: Yes, Marie, yes. *(He covers up the body.)* There's a chance that we'll get pinched° . . . with forty coffins . . . Don't you think . . . people will be surprised . . . Suppose they ask us what's inside them?

MAID: Don't worry so much. We'll say that they're empty. And besides, people won't ask questions, they're used to it.

PROFESSOR: Even so . . .

MAID *(she takes out an armband with an insignia, perhaps the Nazi swastika)*: Wait, if you're afraid, wear this, then you won't have anything more to be afraid of. *(She puts the armband around his arm.)* . . . That's good politics.

PROFESSOR: Thanks, my little Marie. With this, I won't need to worry . . . You're a good girl, Marie . . . very loyal . . .

MAID: That's enough. Come on, sir. Are you all right?

PROFESSOR: Yes, my little Marie. *(The* MAID *and the* PROFESSOR *take the body of the young girl, one by the shoulders, the other by the legs, and move towards the door on the right.)* Be careful. We don't want to hurt her.

---

pinched, caught, or arrested.

(They exit. The stage remains empty for several moments. We hear the doorbell ring at the left.)

VOICE OF THE MAID: Just a moment, I'm coming!

(She appears as she was at the beginning of the play, and goes towards the door. The doorbell rings again.)

MAID *(aside)*: She's certainly in a hurry, this one! *(Aloud:)* Just a moment! *(She goes to the door on the left, and opens it.)* Good morning, miss! You are the new pupil? You have come for the lesson? The Professor is expecting you. I'll go tell him that you've come. He'll be right down. Come in, miss, come in!

Figure 1. The Professor (Max Adrian) begins to lecture the Pupil (Joan Plowright) on linguistics and comparative philology while the Maid (Paula Bauersmith) looks on with stern disapproval in the 1958 Phoenix Theatre production, directed by Tony Richardson. (Photograph: Yale Collection of American Literature. Beinecke Rare Book & Manuscript Library. Yale University.)

Figure 2. After killing the Pupil, the Professor (Max Adrian) clings "like a child" to the comforting Maid (Paula Bauersmith) in the 1958 Phoenix Theatre production, directed by Tony Richardson. (Photograph: Yale Collection of American Literature. Beinecke Rare Book & Manuscript Library. Yale University.)

Staging of *The Lesson*

**REVIEW OF THE PHOENIX THEATRE
PRODUCTION, NEW YORK, 1958,
BY WALTER KERR**

I once knew a man who wanted to write a play on the meaninglessness of meaning. I hope he isn't still working on it, for Eugène Ionesco has beaten him to the punch with at least two such treasures, "The Chairs" and "The Lesson," both of which were passionately and perhaps even properly produced at the Phoenix last night.

The first, and far more nerve-wracking, of the pair takes place in what I took to be a lighthouse, beyond which the waters of the sea ripple gently and vacantly. Two toothless and arthritic creatures, played with cackling enthusiasm and considerable skill by Joan Plowright and Eli Wallach, nurse each other's daydreams and blow each other's noses while they wait for a company of invisible friends to assemble so that the old fellow's terribly important "message to mankind" can be delivered by an Orator hired for the occasion.

Before the non-company comes, Mr. Wallach sits on Miss Plowright's lap: she is both his wife and his "mummy." Once the guests are not occupying the several dozens of chairs hurtled onto the stage for them, Miss Plowright explains to her portion of empty air that their only son left them at the age of seven ("the age of discretion"), while Mr. Wallach confides to his vacuum that they have never had any children. When all of the absent guests are assembled, the Orator—looking like Lon Chaney in the role of the Mad Hatter—appears. In a spastic grinding of teeth and tongue, the message is delivered: it is gibberish.

"The Lesson," which affords the extremely adaptable and really talented Miss Plowright an opportunity to wipe off the makeup and appear as a sunny little monster with a toothache, begins with a stoop-shouldered, feverishly intense tutor (Max Adrian, in brilliant form) opening the door to a student who can count to infinity or to 16, whichever is easier. The fact that the child can add but not subtract throws Mr. Adrian into a frenzy ("Integration alone is not enough—disintegration is necessary, too"). The pursuit of mathematics leads the increasingly shaken Adrian to the brink of some secret malaise; as they proceed to the study of words he is toppled over the brink, for "philology is the worst of all." He cuts Miss Plowright's throat, tidies the body away, and opens the door to the next pupil: Miss Plowright. (I wouldn't tell you this if I wasn't pretty certain you'd guess it).

In the course of these two calculated journeys into unreason, some astonishing theatrical effects are spun by director Tony Richardson's ingenious hand: a nightmare cyclone of flapping doors, spinning bodies (only two, it seems like twenty), and whining musical strings; a blur of purple color bleeding downward over the set; a red-and-green electrical storm while confetti uncoils from the heavens. The simple shock value of these violent images is enormous; and the players seem honestly to inherit the wind.

What bothers me about both these exercises, aside from a slight headache that is going away now, is their delicate, insistent assault upon form. I'm not thinking now of the arrogant and fanciful "irregularities" that dot the surface every inch of the way, but of the destiny to which we are being so ruthlessly led: to the defiant mindlessness that is the "answer" in each case. And is, inevitably, "nothing"—intellectual opposites mean the same thing, the only possible message is literally without content: if anything begins over again it is nothing that is beginning again. A philosophy of nihilism is perfectly possible to grasp. But its elaboration into theatrical nonsequiturs becomes a long, tortured, circuitous, pretentious road to a nice, round zero that might be drawn at once. Not the complexity, but the almost juvenile simplicity, of the evening's course is, I think, its undoing.

It is quite as though Lewis Carroll had gone about his work with no playfulness at all, but in black despair, believing hopelessly in every "Off with his head!"

SAMUEL BECKETT

1906–1989

Beckett did not start writing plays until his early forties, but by his mid-fifties he had become internationally recognized as one of the most revolutionary, influential, and philosophically significant dramatists of the contemporary period. Born near Dublin to a wealthy family, he was sent away at the age of fourteen to an Irish boarding school, and from there went on to Trinity College, Dublin, where he proved himself an exceptional student of French and Italian. In 1928, he went to Paris as an exchange teacher and there became acquainted with the most famous Irish author of his day, James Joyce, whose radically new fiction stimulated Beckett to experiment with avant-garde methods of poetry and fiction writing. He returned briefly to Dublin to serve as lecturer in French and to receive his master's degree in 1931 for a study of Marcel Proust, but by the mid-1930s he was on the move again in France and Germany, supporting himself at odd jobs, while he continued to write fiction and poetry. Then, in 1937, he settled in Paris, and when World War II began he worked for the French resistance movement. Shortly after the end of the war, having taken up permanent residence in Paris, he wrote his first play, *Waiting for Godot.* When it was produced in 1953, it quickly turned into an international sensation.

Waiting for Godot startled audiences and reviewers because it challenged most of their assumptions about the nature of dramatic form. It undercut their ideas of plot with its persistently illogical and purposeless activity; it questioned their ideas of dialogue with its endless contradictions between language and action; it defied their ideas of spectacle with its stage bare except for a tree that is also bare until the second act when it has somehow acquired "four or five leaves." And in all his subsequent plays, Beckett continued to challenge audiences by stripping away more and more of the conventions associated with theater, as if he were seeking to discover how much can be taken away from drama without forsaking the essence of dramatic experience.

In seeking to discover the limits of drama, Beckett progressively stripped away virtually all the elements of theater. Physical action decreased as Beckett's protagonists became less and less mobile. In *Waiting for Godot,* two of the characters are roped to one another, and though everyone can walk they frequently fall down. In *Endgame* (1957), Nagg and Nell are confined to ashbins, Hamm is confined to a wheelchair, and Clov, the only mobile character, hobbles around the stage. In *Happy Days,* Winnie is buried up to her waist in a mound, and by Act 2 the mound has reached her neck. In *Play* (1964), all three characters are immobilized in urns and speak only when a light shines upon them. And in *Not I* (1972), the only visible action is the mouth of a woman speaking. Characters likewise decrease from the five in *Waiting for Godot* to one (and his tape recorder) in *Krapp's Last Tape* (1958). Even language disappears in Beckett's shorter pieces. *Act without Words I* (1957) and *II* (1960) are mime pieces, and *Breath* (1970) lasts for one minute of cries and breaths. Consequently many audiences and reviewers have often been moved in witnessing Beckett's plays to echo the words of

Estragon in *Waiting for Godot*: "Nothing happens, nobody comes, nobody goes, it's awful."

Today, however, *Waiting for Godot* and *Endgame* are recognized as two of the most important plays in contemporary drama, and they have been performed throughout the world to appreciative audiences in Paris and London, on Broadway and off, at San Quentin Prison, and even in community churches. The two couples of *Waiting for Godot*—the tramps Vladimir and Estragon, and the master and his slave, Pozzo and Lucky—have been examined, annotated, and allegorized, yet they still survive. In fact, survival—or existence, to use a more neutral term—is the action of the play. Stranded on a bare stage, in a barren existence, Vladimir and Estragon "wait for Godot," and while they wait they tell stories to each other, they reminisce, they contemplate suicide, they munch carrots and radishes, they pull their boots on and off, and they go through many other routines that Beckett appears to have drawn from the vaudeville world of Charlie Chaplin, Buster Keaton, and the Marx brothers. Estragon sums up their existence when he says, "We always find something, eh Didi, to give us the impression we exist?" Although Godot does not arrive at the end of the first act, nor at the end of the second—though their world grows increasingly meaningless—they sustain themselves through their continued inventiveness. And in contrast to Pozzo and Lucky, who are tied to one another by a rope, Vladimir and Estragon are bound to each other by a friendship that survives repeated separations and quarrels. *Endgame* is a grimmer and tighter play. The two acts of *Godot* have shrunk to a single long act. The two pairs of characters are still present but the emphasis has been drastically changed; the master-slave pair, the blind Hamm and the hobbling Clov, dominate the play, while Nagg and Nell, who are reminiscent of Vladimir and Estragon in their exchanging of memories and food, are confined to ashbins and appear only occasionally. Instead of a road on which the characters might come and go, there is only a room, and the world outside does not appear to contain any sign of life, not even a tree with a few leaves on it.

Endgame has repeatedly tempted critics to define its meaning, in part because it so insistently appears to deny itself significance—Hamm, for example, says "We're not beginning to . . . to . . . mean something?" and Clov replies, "Mean something! You and I, mean something!"—in part because it implicitly alludes to so many interpretative contexts. The chess metaphor of the title is echoed in the physical action of Hamm, the king who can move only in limited ways, and in the "very red faces" of Hamm and Clov contrasted to the "very white faces" of Nagg and Nell. Allusions to Shakespeare abound throughout the play: Hamm's name seems to be a shortened form of Hamlet; he sees himself as a deposed king, like Lear and Richard II; he parodies Richard III's final words when he calls out "My kingdom for a nightman"; and he directly quotes Prospero, "Our revels now are ended," and then throws away his gaff, much as Prospero breaks his magic wand at the end of *The Tempest*. The theatrical metaphor running throughout the play provides another interpretative context. Hamm's first words, for example, are "Me—*(he yawns)*—to play." Clov looks out at the auditorium and comments, ironically, "I see . . . a multitude . . . in transports . . . of joy." Hamm speaks of the "dialogue," worries that the small boy may provide an "underplot," grumbles when Clov reacts to "an aside," and announces, "I'm warming up for my last soliloquy." Clov starts to leave the stage with the line, "This is what we call making an exit." Thus the stage is, it seems, the only place of life in a world Clov calls "corpsed." And that reference to death is only one of innumerable references to it from the title to the final tableau.

Yet in the theater, as indicated by the review of the Paris premiere following the text, *Endgame* also turns out to be a highly comic experience, in spite of, or perhaps because of, its grim situation. Clov may find his repeated taunting of Hamm amusing (see Figure 1), even if Hamm does not. Yet at moments Clov and Hamm join together in comic routines, as when Clov thinks he has discovered a flea; Hamm's fear that "humanity might start from there all over again" leads to Clov searching for the insecticide powder he winds up sprinkling in his trousers. Even the two old people in the ashbins take part in the vaudeville routines:

NAGG: Can you hear me?
NELL: Yes. And you?
NAGG: Yes.

(Pause)

Our hearing hasn't failed.
NELL: Our what?
NAGG: Our hearing.

Even moments that might well be solemn, such as Hamm's order, "Let us pray to God" (see Figure 2), are interrupted by Clov's interest in getting back to rat-extermination and Nagg's cry for "me sugar-plum." Nell seems to have the final word on the play's theatrical meaning when she says, "Nothing is funnier than unhappiness, I grant you that."

ENDGAME
A Play in One Act

BY SAMUEL BECKETT

CHARACTERS

NAGG
NELL
HAMM
CLOV

SCENE

Bare interior. Grey light. Left and right back, high up, two small windows, curtains drawn. Front right, a door.

Hanging near door, its face to wall, a picture. Front left, touching each other, covered with an old sheet, two ashbins. Center, in an armchair on castors, covered with an old sheet, HAMM. Motionless by the door, his eyes fixed on HAMM, CLOV. Very red face. Brief tableau.

(CLOV goes and stands under window left. Stiff, staggering walk. He looks up at window left. He turns and looks at window right. He goes and stands under window right. He looks up at window right. He turns and looks at window left. He goes out, comes back immediately with a small step-ladder, carries it over and sets it down under window left, gets up on it, draws back curtain. He gets down, takes six steps (for example) towards window right, goes back for ladder, carries it over and sets it down under window right, gets up on it, draws back curtain. He gets down, takes three steps towards window left, goes back for ladder, carries it over and sets it down under window left, gets up on it, looks out of window. Brief laugh. He gets down, goes with ladder towards ashbins, halts, turns, carries back ladder and sets it down under window right, goes to ashbins, removes sheet covering them, folds it over his arm. He raises one lid, stoops and looks into bin. Brief laugh. He closes lid. Same with other bin. He goes to HAMM, removes sheet covering him, folds it over his arm. In a dressing-gown, a stiff toque on his head, a large blood-stained handkerchief over his face, a whistle hanging from his neck, a rug over his knees, thick socks on his feet, HAMM seems to be asleep. CLOV looks him over. Brief laugh. He goes to door, halts, turns towards auditorium.)

CLOV (fixed gaze, tonelessly): Finished, it's finished, nearly finished, it must be nearly finished.

(Pause.)

Grain upon grain, one by one, and one day, suddenly, there's a heap, a little heap, the impossible heap.

(Pause.)

I can't be punished any more.

(Pause.)

I'll go now to my kitchen, ten feet by ten feet by ten feet, and wait for him to whistle me.

(Pause.)

Nice dimensions, nice proportions, I'll lean on the table, and look at the wall, and wait for him to whistle me.

(He remains a moment motionless, then goes out. He comes back immediately, goes to window right, takes up the ladder and carries it out. Pause. HAMM stirs. He yawns under the handkerchief. He removes the handkerchief from his face. Very red face. Black glasses.)

HAMM: Me—(He yawns.)—to play.

(He holds the handkerchief spread out before him.)

Old stancher!

(He takes off his glasses, wipes his eyes, his face, the glasses, puts them on again, folds the handkerchief and puts it back neatly in the breast-pocket of his dressing-gown. He clears his throat, joins the tips of his fingers.)

Can there be misery—(He yawns.)—loftier than mine? No doubt. Formerly. But now?

(Pause.)

My father?

(Pause.)

My mother?

(Pause.)

My . . . dog?

(Pause.)

Oh I am willing to believe they suffer as much as

such creatures can suffer. But does that mean their sufferings equal mine? No doubt.

(Pause.)

No, all is a—*(He yawns.)*—bsolute, *(Proudly.)* the bigger a man is the fuller he is.

(Pause. Gloomily.)

And the emptier.

(He sniffs.)

Clov!

(Pause.)

No, alone.

(Pause.)

What dreams! Those forests!

(Pause.)

Enough, it's time it ended, in the shelter too.

(Pause.)

And yet I hesitate, I hesitate to . . . to end. Yes, there it is, it's time it ended and yet I hesitate to—*(He yawns.)*—to end. *(Yawns.)*

God, I'm tired, I'd be better off in bed.

(He whistles. Enter CLOV *immediately. He halts beside the chair.)*

You pollute the air!

(Pause.)

Get me ready. I'm going to bed.

CLOV: I've just got you up.

HAMM: And what of it?

CLOV: I can't be getting you up and putting you to bed every five minutes, I have things to do.

(Pause.)

HAMM: Did you ever see my eyes?

CLOV: No.

HAMM: Did you never have the curiosity, while I was sleeping, to take off my glasses and look at my eyes?

CLOV: Pulling back the lids?

(Pause.)

No.

HAMM: One of these days I'll show them to you.

(Pause.)

It seems they've gone all white.

(Pause.)

What time is it?

CLOV: The same as usual.

HAMM *(gestures toward window right)*: Have you looked?

CLOV: Yes

HAMM: Well?

CLOV: Zero.

HAMM: It'd need to rain.

CLOV: It won't rain.

(Pause.)

HAMM: Apart from that, how do you feel?

CLOV: I don't complain.

HAMM: You feel normal?

CLOV *(irritably)*: I tell you I don't complain.

HAMM: I feel a little queer.

(Pause.)

Clov!

CLOV: Yes.

HAMM: Have you not had enough?

CLOV: Yes.

(Pause.)

Of what?

HAMM: Of this . . . this . . . thing.

CLOV: I always had.

(Pause)

Not you?

HAMM *(gloomily)*: Then there's no reason for it to change.

CLOV: It may end.

(Pause.)

All life long the same questions, the same answers.

HAMM: Get me ready.

*(*CLOV *does not move.)*

Go and get the sheet.

*(*CLOV *does not move.)*

Clov!

CLOV: Yes.

HAMM: I'll give you nothing more to eat.

CLOV: Then we'll die.

HAMM: I'll give you just enough to keep you from dying. You'll be hungry all the time.

CLOV: Then we won't die.

(Pause.)

I'll go and get the sheet.

(He goes toward the door.)

HAMM: No!

(CLOV halts.)

I'll give you one biscuit per day.

(Pause.)

One and a half.

(Pause.)

Why do you stay with me?
CLOV: Why do you keep me?
HAMM: There's no one else.
CLOV: There's nowhere else.

(Pause.)

HAMM: You're leaving me all the same.
CLOV: I'm trying.
HAMM: You don't love me.
CLOV: No.
HAMM: You loved me once.
CLOV: Once!
HAMM: I've made you suffer too much.

(Pause.)

Haven't I?
CLOV: It's not that.
HAMM *(shocked)*: I haven't made you suffer too much?
CLOV: Yes!
HAMM *(relieved)*: Ah you gave me a fright!

(Pause. Coldly.)

Forgive me.

(Pause. Louder.)

I said, Forgive me.
CLOV: I heard you.

(Pause.)

Have you bled?
HAMM: Less.

(Pause.)

Is it not time for my pain-killer?
CLOV: No.

(Pause.)

HAMM: How are your eyes?
CLOV: Bad.
HAMM: How are your legs?
CLOV: Bad.
HAMM: But you can move.
CLOV: Yes.
HAMM *(violently)*: Then move!

(CLOV goes to back wall, leans against it with his forehead and hands.)

Where are you?

CLOV: Here.
HAMM: Come back!

(CLOV returns to his place beside the chair.)

Where are you?
CLOV: Here.
HAMM: Why don't you kill me?
CLOV: I don't know the combination of the cupboard.

(Pause.)

HAMM: Go and get two bicycle-wheels.
CLOV: There are no more bicycle-wheels.
HAMM: What have you done with your bicycle?
CLOV: I never had a bicycle.
HAMM: The thing is impossible.
CLOV: When there were still bicycles I wept to have one. I crawled at your feet. You told me to go to hell. Now there are none.
HAMM: And your rounds? When you inspected my paupers. Always on foot?
CLOV: Sometimes on horse.

(The lid of one of the bins lifts and the hands of NAGG appear, gripping the rim. Then his head emerges. Night-cap. Very white face. NAGG yawns, then listens.)

I'll leave you, I have things to do.
HAMM: In your kitchen?
CLOV: Yes.
HAMM: Outside of here it's death.

(Pause.)

All right, be off.

(Exit CLOV. Pause.)

We're getting on.
NAGG: Me pap!
HAMM: Accursed progenitor!
NAGG: Me pap!
HAMM: The old folks at home! No decency left! Guzzle, guzzle, that's all they think of.

(He whistles. Enter CLOV. He halts beside the chair.)

Well! I thought you were leaving me.
CLOV: Oh not just yet, not just yet.
NAGG: Me pap!
HAMM: Give him his pap.
CLOV: There's no more pap.
HAMM *(to NAGG)*: Do you hear that? There's no more pap. You'll never get any more pap.
NAGG: I want me pap!
HAMM: Give him a biscuit.

(Exit CLOV.)

Accursed fornicator! How are your stumps?
NAGG: Never mind me stumps.

(Enter CLOV *with biscuit.)*

CLOV: I'm back again, with the biscuit.

(He gives biscuit to NAGG *who fingers it, sniffs it.)*

NAGG *(plaintively)*: What is it?

CLOV: Spratt's medium.

NAGG *(as before)*: It's hard! I can't!

HAMM: Bottle him!

*(*CLOV *pushes* NAGG *back into the bin, closes the lid.)*

CLOV *(returning to his place beside the chair)*: If age but knew!

HAMM: Sit on him!

CLOV: I can't sit.

HAMM: True. And I can't stand.

CLOV: So it is.

HAMM: Every man his specialty.

(Pause.)

No phone calls?

(Pause.)

Don't we laugh?

CLOV *(after reflection)*: I don't feel like it.

HAMM *(after reflection)*: Nor I.

(Pause.)

Clov!

CLOV: Yes.

HAMM: Nature has forgotten us.

CLOV: There's no more nature.

HAMM: No more nature! You exaggerate.

CLOV: In the vicinity.

HAMM: But we breathe, we change! We lose our hair, our teeth! Our bloom! Our ideals!

CLOV: Then she hasn't forgotten us.

HAMM: But you say there is none.

CLOV *(sadly)*: No one that ever lived ever thought so crooked as we.

HAMM: We do what we can.

CLOV: We shouldn't.

(Pause.)

HAMM: You're a bit of all right, aren't you?

CLOV: A smithereen.

(Pause.)

HAMM: This is slow work.

(Pause.)

Is it not time for my pain-killer?

CLOV: No.

(Pause.)

I'll leave you, I have things to do.

HAMM: In your kitchen?

CLOV: Yes.

HAMM: What, I'd like to know.

CLOV: I look at the wall.

HAMM: The wall! And what do you see on your wall? Mene, mene? Naked bodies?

CLOV: I see my light dying.

HAMM: Your light dying! Listen to that! Well, it can die just as well here, *your* light. Take a look at me and then come back and tell me what you think of *your* light.

(Pause.)

CLOV: You shouldn't speak to me like that.

(Pause.)

HAMM *(coldly)*: Forgive me.

(Pause. Louder.)

I said, Forgive me.

CLOV: I heard you.

(The lid of NAGG's *bin lifts. His hands appear, gripping the rim. Then his head emerges. In his mouth the biscuit. He listens.)*

HAMM: Did your seeds come up?

CLOV: No.

HAMM: Did you scratch round them to see if they had sprouted?

CLOV: They haven't sprouted.

HAMM: Perhaps it's still too early.

CLOV: If they were going to sprout they would have sprouted.

(Violently.)

They'll never sprout!

(Pause. NAGG *takes biscuit in his hand.)*

HAMM: This is not much fun.

(Pause.)

But that's always the way at the end of the day, isn't it, Clov?

CLOV: Always.

HAMM: It's the end of the day like any other day, isn't it, Clov?

CLOV: Looks like it.

(Pause.)

HAMM *(anguished)*: What's happening, what's happening?

CLOV: Something is taking its course.

(Pause.)

HAMM: All right, be off.

(He leans back in his chair, remains motionless. CLOV *does not move, heaves a great groaning sigh.* HAMM *sits up.)*

I thought I told you to be off.

CLOV: I'm trying.

(He goes to door, halts.)

Ever since I was whelped.

(Exit CLOV.*)*

HAMM: We're getting on.

(He leans back in his chair, remains motionless. NAGG *knocks on the lid of the other bin. Pause. He knocks harder. The lid lifts and the hands of* NELL *appear, gripping the rim. Then her head emerges. Lace cap. Very white face.)*

NELL: What is it, my pet?

(Pause.)

Time for love?

NAGG: Were you asleep?

NELL: Oh no!

NAGG: Kiss me.

NELL: We can't.

NAGG: Try.

(Their heads strain toward each other, fail to meet, fall apart again.)

NELL: Why this farce, day after day?

(Pause.)

NAGG: I've lost me tooth.

NELL: When?

NAGG: I had it yesterday.

NELL *(elegiac)*: Ah yesterday!

(They turn painfully toward each other.)

NAGG: Can you see me?

NELL: Hardly. And you?

NAGG: What?

NELL: Can you see me?

NAGG: Hardly.

NELL: So much the better, so much the better.

NAGG: Don't say that.

(Pause.)

Our sight has failed.

NELL: Yes.

(Pause. They turn away from each other.)

NAGG: Can you hear me?

NELL: Yes, And you?

NAGG: Yes.

(Pause.)

Our hearing hasn't failed.

NELL: Our what?

NAGG: Our hearing.

NELL: No.

(Pause.)

Have you anything else to say to me?

NAGG: Do you remember—

NELL: No.

NAGG: When we crashed on our tandem and lost our shanks.

(They laugh heartily.)

NELL: It was in the Ardennes.

(They laugh less heartily.)

NAGG: On the road to Sedan.

(They laugh still less heartily.)

Are you cold?

NELL: Yes, perished. And you?

NAGG *(pause)*: I'm freezing.

(Pause.)

Do you want to go in?

NELL: Yes.

NAGG: Then go in.

*(*NELL *does not move.)*

Why don't you go in?

NELL: I don't know.

(Pause.)

NAGG: Has he changed your sawdust?

NELL: It isn't sawdust.

(Pause. Wearily.)

Can you not be a little accurate, Nagg?

NAGG: Your sand then. It's not important.

NELL: It is important.

(Pause.)

NAGG: It was sawdust once.

NELL: Once!

NAGG: And now it's sand.

(Pause.)

From the shore.

(Pause. Impatiently.)

Now it's sand he fetches from the shore.

NELL: Now it's sand.

NAGG: Has he changed yours?

NELL: No.

NAGG: Nor mine.

(Pause.)

I won't have it!

(Pause. Holding up the biscuit.)

Do you want a bit?

NELL: No.

(Pause.)

Of what?

NAGG: Biscuit. I've kept you half.

(He looks at the biscuit. Proudly.)

Three quarters. For you. Here.

(He proffers the biscuit.)

No?

(Pause.)

Do you not feel well?

HAMM *(wearily)*: Quiet, quiet, you're keeping me awake.

(Pause.)

Talk softer.

(Pause.)

If I could sleep I might make love. I'd go into the woods. My eyes would see . . . the sky, the earth. I'd run, run, they wouldn't catch me.

(Pause.)

Nature!

(Pause.)

There's something dripping in my head.

(Pause.)

A heart, a heart in my head.

(Pause.)

NAGG *(softly)*: Do you hear him? A heart in his head!

(He chuckles cautiously.)

NELL: One mustn't laugh at those things, Nagg. Why must you always laugh at them?

NAGG: Not so loud!

NELL *(without lowering her voice)*: Nothing is funnier than unhappiness, I grant you that. But—

NAGG *(shocked)*: Oh!

NELL: Yes, yes, it's the most comical thing in the world. And we laugh, we laugh, with a will, in the beginning. But it's always the same thing. Yes, it's like the funny story we have heard too often, we still find it funny, but we don't laugh any more.

(Pause.)

Have you anything else to say to me?

NAGG: No.

NELL: Are you quite sure?

(Pause.)

Then I'll leave you.

NAGG: Do you not want your biscuit?

(Pause.)

I'll keep it for you.

(Pause.)

I thought you were going to leave me.

NELL: I am going to leave you.

NAGG: Could you give me a scratch before you go?

NELL: No.

(Pause.)

Where?

NAGG: In the back.

NELL: No.

(Pause.)

Rub yourself against the rim.

NAGG: It's lower down. In the hollow.

NELL: What hollow?

NAGG: The hollow!

(Pause.)

Could you not?

(Pause.)

Yesterday you scratched me there.

NELL *(elegaic)*: Ah yesterday!

NAGG: Could you not?

(Pause.)

Would you like me to scratch you?

(Pause.)

Are you crying again?

NELL: I was trying.

(Pause)

HAMM: Perhaps it's a little vein.

(Pause.)

NAGG: What was that he said?

NELL: Perhaps it's a little vein.

NAGG: What does that mean?

(Pause.)

That means nothing.

(Pause.)

Will I tell you the story of the tailor?

NELL: No.

(Pause.)

What for?

NAGG: To cheer you up.

NELL: It's not funny.

NAGG: It always made you laugh.

(Pause.)

The first time I thought you'd die.

NELL: It was on Lake Como.

(Pause.)

One April afternoon.

(Pause.)

Can you believe it?

NAGG: What?

NELL: That we once went out rowing on Lake Como.

(Pause.)

One April afternoon.

NAGG: We had got engaged the day before.

NELL: Engaged!

NAGG: You were in such fits that we capsized. By rights we should have been drowned.

NELL: It was because I felt happy.

NAGG *(indignant)*: It was not, it was not, it was my story and nothing else. Happy! Don't you laugh at it still? Every time I tell it. Happy!

NELL: It was deep, deep. And you could see down to the bottom. So white. So clean.

NAGG: Let me tell it again.

(Raconteur's voice.)

An Englishman, needing a pair of striped trousers in a hurry for the New Year festivities, goes to his tailor who takes his measurements.

(Tailor's voice.)

"That's the lot, come back in four days, I'll have it ready." Good. Four days later.

(Tailor's voice.)

"So sorry, come back in a week. I've made a mess of the seat." Good, that's all right, a neat seat can be very ticklish. A week later.

(Tailor's voice.)

"Frightfully sorry, come back in ten days, I've made a hash of the crotch." Good, can't be helped, a snug crotch is always a teaser. Ten days later.

(Tailor's voice.)

"Dreadfully sorry, come back in a fortnight, I've made a balls of the fly." Good, at a pinch, a smart fly is a stiff proposition.

(Pause. Normal voice.)

I never told it worse.

(Pause. Gloomy.)

I tell this story worse and worse.

(Pause. Raconteur's voice.)

Well, to make it short, the bluebells are blowing and he ballockses the buttonholes.

(Customer's voice.)

"God damn you to hell, Sir, no, it's indecent, there are limits! In six days, do you hear me, six days, God made the world. Yes Sir, no less Sir, the WORLD! And you are not bloody well capable of making me a pair of trousers in three months!"

(Tailor's voice, scandalized.)

"But my dear Sir, my dear Sir, look—

(Disdainful gesture, disgustedly.)

—at the world—

(Pause.)

and look—

(Loving gesture, proudly.)—at my TROUSERS!"

(Pause. He looks at NELL who has remained impassive, her eyes unseeing, breaks into a high forced laugh, cuts it short, pokes his head towards NELL, launches his laugh again.)

HAMM: Silence!

(NAGG starts, cuts short his laugh.)

NELL: You could see down to the bottom.

HAMM *(exasperated)*: Have you not finished? Will you never finish?

(With sudden fury.)

Will this never finish?

(NAGG disappears into his bin, closes the lid behind him. NELL does not move. Frenziedly.)

My kingdom for a nightman!

(He whistles. Enter CLOV.)

Clear away this muck! Chuck it in the sea!

(CLOV goes to bins, halts.)

NELL: So white.

HAMM: What? What's she blathering about?

(CLOV stoops, takes NELL's hand, feels her pulse.)

NELL *(to CLOV)*: Desert!

(CLOV lets go her hand, pushes her back in the bin, closes the lid.)

CLOV *(returning to his place beside the chair)*: She has no pulse.

HAMM: What was she drivelling about?

CLOV: She told me to go away, into the desert.

HAMM: Damn busybody! Is that all?

CLOV: No.
HAMM: What else?
CLOV: I didn't understand.
HAMM: Have you bottled her?
CLOV: Yes.
HAMM: Are they both bottled?
CLOV: Yes
HAMM: Screw down the lids.

(CLOV *goes toward door.*)

Time enough.

(CLOV *halts.*)

My anger subsides, I'd like to pee.
CLOV (*with alacrity*): I'll go and get the catheter.

(*He goes toward door.*)

HAMM: Time enough.

(CLOV *halts.*)

Give me my pain-killer.
CLOV: It's too soon.

(*Pause.*)

It's too soon on top of your tonic, it wouldn't act.
HAMM: In the morning they brace you up and in the evening they calm you down. Unless it's the other way round.

(*Pause.*)

That old doctor, he's dead naturally?
CLOV: He wasn't old.
HAMM: But he's dead?
CLOV: Naturally.

(*Pause.*)

You ask *me* that?

(*Pause.*)

HAMM: Take me for a little turn.

(CLOV *goes behind the chair and pushes it forward.*)

Not too fast!

(CLOV *pushes chair.*)

Right round the world!

(CLOV *pushes chair.*)

Hug the walls, then back to the center again.

(CLOV *pushes chair.*)

I was right in the center, wasn't I?
CLOV (*pushing*): Yes.
HAMM: We'd need a proper wheel-chair. With big wheels. Bicycle wheels!

(*Pause.*)

Are you hugging?
CLOV (*pushing*): Yes.
HAMM (*groping for wall*): It's a lie! Why do you lie to me?
CLOV (*bearing close to wall*): There! There!
HAMM: Stop!

(CLOV *stops chair close to back wall.* HAMM *lays his hand against the wall.*)

Old wall!

(*Pause.*)

Beyond is the . . . other hell.

(*Pause. Violently.*)

Closer! Closer! Up against!
CLOV: Take away your hand.

(HAMM *withdraws his hand.* CLOV *rams chair against wall.*)

There!

(HAMM *leans toward wall, applies his ear to it.*)

HAMM: Do you hear?

(*He strikes the wall with his knuckles.*)

Do you hear? Hollow bricks!

(*He strikes again.*)

All that's hollow!

(*Pause. He straightens up. Violently.*)

That's enough. Back!
CLOV: We haven't done the round.
HAMM: Back to my place!

(CLOV *pushes chair back to center.*)

Is that my place?
CLOV: Yes, that's your place.
HAMM: Am I right in the center?
CLOV: I'll measure it.
HAMM: More or less! More or less!
CLOV (*moving chair slightly*): There!
HAMM: I'm more or less in the center?
CLOV: I'd say so.
HAMM: You'd say so! Put me right in the center!
CLOV: I'll go and get the tape.
HAMM: Roughly! Roughly!

(CLOV *moves chair slightly.*)

Bang in the center!
CLOV: There!

(*Pause.*)

HAMM: I feel a little too far to the left.

(CLOV *moves chair slightly.*)

Now I feel a little too far to the right.

(CLOV *moves chair slightly.*)

I feel a little too far forward.

(CLOV *moves chair slightly.*)

Now I feel a little too far back.

(CLOV *moves chair slightly.*)

Don't stay there, (*i.e., behind the chair*) you give me the shivers.

(CLOV *returns to his place beside the chair.*)

CLOV: If I could kill him I'd die happy.

(*Pause.*)

HAMM: What's the weather like?
CLOV: As usual.
HAMM: Look at the earth.
CLOV: I've looked.
HAMM: With the glass?
HAMM: No need of the glass.
HAMM: Look at it with the glass.
CLOV: I'll go and get the glass.

(*Exit* CLOV.)

HAMM: No need of the glass!

(*Enter* CLOV *with telescope.*)

CLOV: I'm back again, with the glass.

(*He goes to window right, looks up at it.*)

I need the steps.
HAMM: Why? Have you shrunk?

(*Exit* CLOV *with telescope.*)

I don't like that, I don't like that.

(*Enter* CLOV *with ladder, but without telescope.*)

CLOV: I'm back again, with the steps.

(*He sets down ladder under window right, gets up on it, realizes he has not the telescope, gets down.*)

I need the glass.

(*He goes toward door.*)

HAMM (*violently*): But you have the glass!
CLOV (*halting, violently*): No, I haven't the glass!

(*Exit* CLOV.)

HAMM: This is deadly.

(*Enter* CLOV *with telescope. He goes toward ladder.*)

CLOV: Things are livening up.

(*He gets up on a ladder, raises the telescope, lets it fall.*)

I did it on purpose.

(*He gets down, picks up the telescope, turns it on auditorium.*)

I see . . . a multitude . . . in transports . . . of joy.

(*Pause.*)

That's what I call a magnifier.

(*He lowers the telescope, turns toward* HAMM.)

Well? Don't we laugh?
HAMM (*after reflection*): I don't.
CLOV (*after reflection*): Nor I.

(*He gets up on ladder, turns the telescope on the without.*)

Let's see.

(*He looks, moving the telescope.*)

Zero . . . (*He looks.*) . . . zero . . . (*He looks.*) . . . and zero.
HAMM: Nothing stirs. All is—
CLOV: Zer—
HAMM (*violently*): Wait till you're spoken to!

(*Normal voice.*)

All is . . . all is . . . all is what?

(*Violently.*)

All is what?
CLOV: What all is? In a word? Is that what you want to know? Just a moment.

(*He turns the telescope on the without, looks, lowers the telescope, turns toward* HAMM.)

Corpsed.

(*Pause.*)

Well? Content?
HAMM: Look at the sea.
CLOV: It's the same.
HAMM: Look at the ocean!

(CLOV *gets down, takes a few steps toward window left, goes back for ladder, carries it over and sets it down under window left, gets up on it, turns the telescope on the without, looks at length. He starts, lowers the telescope, examines it, turns it again on the without.*)

CLOV: Never seen anything like that!
HAMM (*anxiously*): What? A sail? A fin? Smoke?
CLOV (*looking*): The light is sunk.
HAMM (*relieved*): Pah! We all knew that.
CLOV (*looking*): There was a bit left.
HAMM: The base.
CLOV (*looking*): Yes.
HAMM: And now?
CLOV (*looking*): All gone.
HAMM: No gulls?
CLOV (*looking*): Gulls!

HAMM: And the horizon? Nothing on the horizon?

CLOV (*lowering the telescope, turning toward* HAMM, *exasperately*): What in God's name could there be on the horizon?

(*Pause.*)

HAMM: The waves, how are the waves?

CLOV: The waves?

(*He turns the telescope on the waves.*)

Lead.

HAMM: And the sun?

CLOV (*looking*): Zero.

HAMM: But it should be sinking. Look again.

CLOV (*looking*): Damn the sun.

HAMM: Is it night already then?

CLOV (*looking*): No.

HAMM: Then what is it?

CLOV (*looking*): Gray.

(*Lowering the telescope, turning toward* HAMM, *louder.*)

Gray!

(*Pause. Still louder.*)

GRRAY!

(*Pause. He gets down, approaches* HAMM *from behind, whispers in his ear.*)

HAMM (*starting*): Gray! Did I hear you say gray?

CLOV: Light black. From pole to pole.

HAMM: You exaggerate.

(*Pause.*)

Don't stay there, you give me the shivers.

(CLOV *returns to his place beside the chair.*)

CLOV: Why this farce, day after day?

HAMM: Routine. One never knows.

(*Pause.*)

Last night I saw inside my breast. There was a big sore.

CLOV: Pah! You saw your heart.

HAMM: No, it was living.

(*Pause. Anguished.*)

Clov!

CLOV: Yes.

HAMM: What's happening?

CLOV: Something is taking its course.

(*Pause.*)

HAMM: Clov!

CLOV (*impatiently*): What is it?

HAMM: We're not beginning to . . . to . . . mean something?

CLOV: Mean something! You and I, mean something!

(*Brief laugh.*)

Ah that's a good one!

HAMM: I wonder.

(*Pause.*)

Imagine if a rational being came back to earth, wouldn't he be liable to get ideas into his head if he observed us long enough.

(*Voice of rational being.*)

Ah, good, now I see what it is, yes, now I understand what they're at!

(CLOV *starts, drops the telescope and begins to scratch his belly with both hands. Normal voice.*)

And without going so far as that, we ourselves . . . (*With emotion.*) . . . we ourselves . . . at certain moments . . . (*Vehemently.*) To think perhaps it won't all have been for nothing!

CLOV (*anguished, scratching himself*): I have a flea!

HAMM: A flea! Are there still fleas?

CLOV: On me, there's one.

(*Scratching.*)

Unless it's a crablouse.

HAMM (*very perturbed*): But humanity might start from there all over again! Catch him, for the love of God!

CLOV: I'll go and get the powder.

(*Exit* CLOV.)

HAMM: A flea! This is awful! What a day!

(*Enter* CLOV *with a sprinkling-tin.*)

CLOV: I'm back again, with the insecticide.

HAMM: Let him have it!

(CLOV *loosens the top of his trousers, pulls it forward and shakes powder into the aperture. He stoops, looks, waits, starts, frenziedly shakes more powder, stoops, looks, waits.*)

CLOV: The bastard!

HAMM: Did you get him?

CLOV: Looks like it.

(*He drops the tin and adjusts his trousers.*)

Unless he's laying doggo.

HAMM: Laying! Lying you mean. Unless he's *lying* doggo.

CLOV: Ah? One says lying? One doesn't say laying?

HAMM: Use your head, can't you. If he was laying we'd be bitched.

CLOV: Ah.

(*Pause.*)

What about that pee?

HAMM: I'm having it.

CLOV: Ah that's the spirit, that's the spirit!

(Pause.)

HAMM *(with ardour)*: Let's go from here, the two of us! South! You can make a raft and the currents will carry us away, far away, to other . . . mammals!

CLOV: God forbid!

HAMM: Alone, I'll embark alone! Get working on that raft immediately. Tomorrow I'll be gone for ever.

CLOV *(hastening toward door)*: I'll start straight away.

HAMM: Wait!

(CLOV halts.)

Will there be sharks, do you think?

CLOV: Sharks? I don't know. If there are there will be.

(He goes toward door.)

HAMM: Wait!

(CLOV halts.)

Is it not yet time for my pain-killer?

CLOV *(violently)*: No!

(He goes toward door.)

HAMM: Wait!

(CLOV halts.)

How are your eyes?

CLOV: Bad.

HAMM: But you can see.

CLOV: All I want.

HAMM: How are your legs?

CLOV: Bad.

HAMM: But you can walk.

CLOV: I come . . . and go.

HAMM: In my house.

(Pause. With prophetic relish.)

One day you'll be blind, like me. You'll be sitting there, a speck in the void, in the dark, for ever, like me.

(Pause.)

One day you'll say to yourself, I'm tired. I'll sit down, and you'll go and sit down. Then you'll say, I'm hungry, I'll get up and get something to eat. But you won't get up. You'll say, I shouldn't have sat down, but since I have I'll sit on a little longer, then I'll get up and get something to eat. But you won't get up and you won't get anything to eat.

(Pause.)

You'll look at the wall a while, then you'll say, I'll close my eyes, perhaps have a little sleep, after that I'll feel better, and you'll close them. And when you open them again there'll be no wall any more.

(Pause.)

Infinite emptiness will be all around you, all the resurrected dead of all the ages wouldn't fill it, and there you'll be like a little bit of grit in the middle of the steppe.

(Pause.)

Yes, one day you'll know what it is, you'll be like me, except that you won't have anyone with you, because you won't have had pity on anyone and because there won't be anyone left to have pity on.

(Pause.)

CLOV: It's not certain.

(Pause.)

And there's one thing you forget.

HAMM: Ah?

CLOV: I can't sit down.

HAMM *(impatiently)*: Well you'll lie down then, what the hell! Or you'll come to a standstill, simply stop and stand still, the way you are now. One day you'll say, I'm tired, I'll stop. What does the attitude matter?

(Pause.)

CLOV: So you all want me to leave you.

HAMM: Naturally.

CLOV: Then I'll leave you.

HAMM: You can't leave us.

CLOV: Then I won't leave you.

(Pause.)

HAMM: Why don't you finish us?

(Pause.)

I'll tell you the combination of the cupboard if you promise to finish me.

CLOV: I couldn't finish you.

HAMM: Then you won't finish me.

(Pause.)

CLOV: I'll leave you, I have things to do.

HAMM: Do you remember when you came here?

CLOV: No. Too small, you told me.

HAMM: Do you remember your father?

CLOV *(wearily)*: Same answer.

(Pause.)

You've asked me these questions millions of times.

HAMM: I love the old questions.

(With fervour.)

Ah the old questions, the old answers, there's nothing like them!

(Pause.)

It was I was a father to you.

CLOV: Yes.

(He looks at HAMM *fixedly.)*

You were that to me.

HAMM: My house a home for you.

CLOV: Yes.

(He looks about him.)

This was that for me.

HAMM *(proudly)*: But for me, *(Gesture toward himself.)* no father. But for Hamm, *(Gesture toward surroundings.)* no home.

(Pause.)

CLOV: I'll leave you.

HAMM: Did you ever think of one thing?

CLOV: Never.

HAMM: That here we're down in a hole.

(Pause.)

But beyond the hills? Eh? Perhaps it's still green. Eh?

(Pause.)

Flora! Pomona!

(Ecstatically.)

Ceres!

(Pause.)

Perhaps you won't need to go very far.

CLOV: I can't go very far.

(Pause.)

I'll leave you.

HAMM: Is my dog ready?

CLOV: He lacks a leg.

HAMM: Is he silky?

CLOV: He's a kind of Pomeranian.

HAMM: Go and get him.

CLOV: He lacks a leg.

HAMM: Go and get him!

(Exit CLOV.*)*

We're getting on.

(Enter CLOV *holding by one of its three legs a black toy dog.)*

CLOV: Your dogs are here.

(He hands the dog to HAMM *who feels it, fondles it.)*

HAMM: He's white, isn't he?

CLOV: Nearly.

HAMM: What do you mean, nearly? Is he white or isn't he?

CLOV: He isn't.

(Pause.)

HAMM: You've forgotten the sex.

CLOV *(vexed)*: But he isn't finished. The sex goes at the end.

(Pause.)

HAMM: You haven't put on his ribbon.

CLOV *(angrily)*: But he isn't finished, I tell you! First you finish your dog and then you put on his ribbon!

(Pause.)

HAMM: Can he stand?

CLOV: I don't know.

HAMM: Try.

(He hands the dog to CLOV *who places it on the ground.)*

Well?

CLOV: Wait!

(He squats down and tries to get the dog to stand on its three legs, fails, lets it go. The dog falls on its side.)

HAMM *(impatiently)*: Well?

CLOV: He's standing.

HAMM *(groping for the dog)*: Where? Where is he?

*(*CLOV *holds up the dog in a standing position.)*

CLOV: There.

(He takes HAMM's *hand and guides it toward the dog's head.)*

HAMM *(his hand on the dog's head)*: Is he gazing at me?

CLOV: Yes.

HAMM *(proudly)*: As if he were asking me to take him for a walk?

CLOV: If you like.

HAMM *(as before)*: Or as if he were begging me for a bone.

(He withdraws his hand.)

Leave him like that, standing there imploring me.

*(*CLOV *straightens up. The dog falls on its side.)*

CLOV: I'll leave you.

HAMM: Have you had your visions?

CLOV: Less.

HAMM: Is Mother Pegg's light on?

CLOV: Light! How could anyone's light be on?

HAMM: Extinguished!

CLOV: Naturally it's extinguished. If it's not on it's extinguished.

HAMM: No, I mean Mother Pegg.

CLOV: But naturally she's extinguished!

(Pause.)

What's the matter with you today?

HAMM: I'm taking my course.

(Pause.)

Is she buried?

CLOV: Buried! Who would have buried her?

HAMM: You.

CLOV: Me! Haven't I enough to do without burying people?

HAMM: But you'll bury me.

CLOV: No I won't bury you.

(Pause.)

HAMM: She was bonny once, like a flower of the field.

(With reminiscent leer.)

And a great one for the men!

CLOV: We too were bonny—once. It's a rare thing not to have been bonny—once.

(Pause.)

HAMM: Go and get the gaff.

(CLOV goes to door, halts.)

CLOV: Do this, do that, and I do it. I never refuse. Why?

HAMM: You're not able to.

CLOV: Soon I won't do it any more.

HAMM: You won't be able to any more.

(Exit CLOV.)

Ah the creatures, the creatures, everything has to be explained to them.

(Enter CLOV with gaff.)

CLOV: Here's your gaff. Stick it up.

(He gives the gaff to HAMM who, wielding it like a puntpole, tries to move his chair.)

HAMM: Did I move?

CLOV: No.

(HAMM throws down the gaff.)

HAMM: Go and get the oilcan.

CLOV: What for?

HAMM: To oil the castors.

CLOV: I oiled them yesterday.

HAMM: Yesterday! What does that mean? Yesterday!

CLOV *(violently)*: That means that bloody awful day long ago, before this bloody awful day. I use the words you taught me. If they don't mean anything any more, teach me others. Or let me be silent.

(Pause.)

HAMM: I once knew a madman who thought the end of the world had come. He was a painter—and engraver. I had a great fondness for him. I used to go and see him, in the asylum. I'd take him by the hand and drag him to the window. Look! There! All that rising corn. And there! Look! The sails of the herring fleet! All that loveliness!

(Pause.)

He'd snatch away his hand and go back into his corner. Appalled. All he had seen was ashes.

(Pause.)

He alone had been spared.

(Pause.)

Forgotten.

(Pause.)

It appears the case is . . . was not so . . . so unusual.

CLOV: A madman? When was that?

HAMM: Oh way back, way back, you weren't in the land of the living.

CLOV: God be with the days!

(Pause. HAMM raises his toque.)

HAMM: I had a great fondness for him.

(Pause. He puts on his toque again.)

He was a painter—and engraver.

CLOV: There are so many terrible things.

HAMM: No, no, there are not so many now.

(Pause.)

Clov!

CLOV: Yes.

HAMM: Do you not think this has gone on long enough?

CLOV: Yes!

(Pause.)

What?

HAMM: This . . . this . . . thing.

CLOV: I've always thought so.

(Pause.)

You not?

HAMM *(gloomily)*: Then it's a day like any other day.

CLOV: As long as it lasts.

(Pause.)

All life long the same inanities.

HAMM: I can't leave you.

CLOV: I know. And you can't follow me.

(Pause.)

HAMM: If you leave me how shall I know?

CLOV *(briskly)*: Well you simply whistle me and if I don't come running it means I've left you.

(Pause.)

HAMM: You won't come and kiss me goodbye?

CLOV: Oh I shouldn't think so.

(Pause.)

HAMM: But you might be merely dead in your kitchen.

CLOV: The result would be the same.

HAMM: Yes, but how would I know, if you were merely dead in your kitchen?

CLOV: Well . . . sooner or later I'd start to stink.

HAMM: You stink already. The whole place stinks of corpses.

CLOV: The whole universe.

HAMM *(angrily)*: To hell with the universe.

(Pause.)

Think of something.

CLOV: What?

HAMM: An idea, have an idea.

(Angrily.)

A bright idea!

CLOV: Ah good.

(He starts pacing to and fro, his eyes fixed on the ground, his hands behind his back. He halts.)

The pains in my legs! It's unbelievable! Soon I won't be able to think any more.

HAMM: You won't be able to leave me.

(CLOV resumes his pacing.)

What are you doing?

CLOV: Having an idea.

(He paces.)

Ah!

(He halts.)

HAMM: What a brain!

(Pause.)

Well?

CLOV: Wait!

(He meditates. Not very convinced.)

Yes . . .

(Pause. More convinced.)

Yes!

(He raises his head.)

I have it! I set the alarm.

(Pause.)

HAMM: This is perhaps not one of my bright days, but frankly—

CLOV: You whistle me. I don't come. The alarm rings. I'm gone. It doesn't ring. I'm dead.

(Pause.)

HAMM: Is it working?

(Pause. Impatiently.)

The alarm, is it working?

CLOV: Why wouldn't it be working?

HAMM: Because it's worked too much.

CLOV: But it's hardly worked at all.

HAMM *(angrily)*: Then because it's worked too little!

CLOV: I'll go and see.

(Exit CLOV. Brief ring of alarm off. Enter CLOV with alarm-clock. He holds it against HAMM's ear and releases alarm. They listen to it ringing to the end. Pause.)

Fit to wake the dead! Did you hear it?

HAMM: Vaguely.

CLOV: The end is terrific!

HAMM: I prefer the middle.

(Pause.)

Is it not time for my pain-killer?

CLOV: No!

(He goes to door, turns.)

I'll leave you.

HAMM: It's time for my story. Do you want to listen to my story.

CLOV: No.

HAMM: Ask my father if he wants to listen to my story.

(CLOV goes to bins, raises the lid of NAGG's, stoops, looks into it. Pause. He straightens up.)

CLOV: He's asleep.

HAMM: Wake him.

(CLOV stoops, wakes NAGG with the alarm. Unintelligible words. CLOV straightens up.)

CLOV: He doesn't want to listen to your story.

HAMM: I'll give him a bon-bon.

(CLOV stoops. As before.)

CLOV: He wants a sugar-plum.

HAMM: He'll get a sugar-plum.

(CLOV stoops. As before.)

CLOV: It's a deal.

(*He goes toward door.* NAGG's *hands appear, gripping the rim. Then the head emerges.* CLOV *reaches door, turns.*)

Do you believe in the life to come?
HAMM: Mine was always that.

(*Exit* CLOV.)

Got him that time!
NAGG: I'm listening.
HAMM: Scoundrel! Why did you engender me?
NAGG: I didn't know.
HAMM: What? What didn't you know?
NAGG: That it'd be you.

(*Pause.*)

You'll give me a sugar-plum?
HAMM: After the audition.
NAGG: You swear?
HAMM: Yes.
NAGG: On what?
HAMM: My honor.

(*Pause. They laugh heartily.*)

NAGG: Two.
HAMM: One.
NAGG: One for me and one for—
HAMM: One! Silence!

(*Pause.*)

Where was I?

(*Pause. Gloomily.*)

It's finished, we're finished.

(*Pause.*)

Nearly finished.

(*Pause.*)

There'll be no more speech.

(*Pause.*)

Something dripping in my head, ever since the fontanelles.

(*Stifled hilarity of* NAGG.)

Splash, splash, always on the same spot.

(*Pause.*)

Perhaps it's a little vein.

(*Pause.*)

A little artery.

(*Pause. More animated.*)

Enough of that, it's story time, where was I?

(*Pause. Narrative tone.*)

The man came crawling towards me, on his belly. Pale, wonderfully pale and thin, he seemed on the point of—

(*Pause. Normal tone.*)

No, I've done that bit.

(*Pause. Narative tone.*)

I calmly filled my pipe—the meerschaum, lit it with . . . let us say a vesta, drew a few puffs. Aah!

(*Pause.*)

Well, what is it *you* want?

(*Pause.*)

It was an extra-ordinarily bitter day, I remember, zero by the thermometer. But considering it was Christmas Eve there was nothing . . . extra-ordinary about that. Seasonable weather, for once in a way.

(*Pause.*)

Well, what ill wind blows you my way? He raised his face to me, black with mingled dirt and tears.

(*Pause. Normal tone.*)

That should do it.

(*Narrative tone.*)

No, no, don't look at me, don't look at me. He dropped his eyes and mumbled something, apologies I presume.

(*Pause.*)

I'm a busy man, you know, the final touches, before the festivities. You know what it is.

(*Pause. Forcibly.*)

Come on now, what is the object of this invasion?

(*Pause.*)

It was a glorious bright day, I remember, fifty by the heliometer, but already the sun was sinking down into the . . . down among the dead.

(*Normal tone.*)

Nicely put, that.

(*Narrative tone.*)

Come on now, come on, present your petition and let me resume my labors.

(*Pause. Normal tone.*)

There's English for you. Ah well . . .

(*Narrative tone.*)

It was then he took the plunge. It's my little one, he said. Tsstss, a little one, that's bad. My little boy, he said, as if the sex mattered. Where did he come from? He named the hole. A good half-day, on horse. What are you insinuating? That the place is still inhabited? No, no, not a soul except himself and the child—assuming he existed. Good. I enquired about the situation at Kov, beyond the gulf. Not a sinner. Good. And you expect me to believe you have left your little one back there, all alone, and alive into the bargain? Come now!

(Pause.)

It was a howling wild day, I remember, a hundred by the anenometer. The wind was tearing up the dead pines and sweeping them . . . away.

(Pause. Normal tone.)

A bit feeble, that.

(Narrative tone.)

Come on, man, speak up, what is you want from me. I have to put up my holly.

(Pause.)

Well to make it short it finally transpired that what he wanted from me was . . . bread for his brat? Bread? But I have no bread, it doesn't agree with me. Good. Then perhaps a little corn?

(Pause. Normal tone.)

That should do it.

(Narrative tone.)

Corn, yes, I have corn, it's true, in my granaries. But use your head. I give you some corn, a pound, a pound and a half, you bring it back to your child and you make him—if he's still alive—a nice pot of porridge,

(NAGG reacts.)

a nice pot and a half of porridge, full of nourishment. Good. The colors come back into his little cheeks—perhaps. And then?

(Pause.)

I lost patience.

(Violently.)

Use your head, can't you, use your head, you're on earth, there's no cure for that!

(Pause.)

It was an exceedingly dry day, I remember, zero by the hygrometer. Ideal weather, for my lumbago.

(Pause. Violently.)

But what in God's name do you imagine? That the earth will awake in spring? That the rivers and seas will run with fish again? That there's manna in heaven still for imbeciles like you?

(Pause.)

Gradually I cooled down, sufficiently at least to ask him how long he had taken on the way. Three whole days. Good. In what condition he had left the child. Deep in sleep.

(Forcibly.)

But deep in what sleep, deep in what sleep already?

(Pause.)

Well to make it short I finally offered to take him into my service. He had touched a chord. And then I imagined already that I wasn't much longer for this world.

(He laughs. Pause.)

Well?

(Pause.)

Well? Here if you were careful you might die a nice natural death, in peace and comfort.

(Pause.)

Well?

(Pause.)

In the end he asked me would I consent to take in the child as well—if he were still alive.

(Pause.)

It was the moment I was waiting for.

(Pause.)

Would I consent to take the child . . .

(Pause.)

I can see him still, down on his knees, his hands flat on the ground, glaring at me with his mad eyes, in defiance of my wishes.

(Pause. Normal tone.)

I'll soon have finished with this story.

(Pause.)

Unless I bring in other characters.

(Pause.)

But where would I find them?

(Pause.)

Where would I look for them?

(Pause. He whistles. Enter CLOV.*)*

Let us pray to God.

NAGG: Me sugar-plum!

CLOV: There's a rat in the kitchen!

HAMM: A rat! Are there still rats?

CLOV: In the kitchen there's one.

HAMM: And you haven't exterminated him?

CLOV: Half. You disturbed us.

HAMM: He can't get away?

CLOV: No.

HAMM: You'll finish him later. Let us pray to God.

CLOV: Again!

NAGG: Me sugar-plum!

HAMM: God first!

(Pause.)

Are you right?

CLOV *(resigned)*: Off we go.

HAMM *(to* NAGG*)*: And you?

NAGG *(clasping his hands, closing his eyes, in a gabble)*: Our Father which art—

HAMM: Silence! In silence! Where are your manners?

(Pause.)

Off we go.

(Attitudes of prayer. Silence. Abandoning his attitude, discouraged.)

Well?

CLOV *(abandoning his attitude)*: What a hope! And you?

HAMM: Sweet damn all! *(to* NAGG*)* And you?

NAGG: Wait!

(Pause. Abandoning his attitude.)

Nothing doing!

HAMM: The bastard! He doesn't exist!

CLOV: Not yet.

NAGG: Me sugar-plum!

HAMM: There are no more sugar-plums!

(Pause.)

NAGG: It's natural. After all I'm your father. It's true if it hadn't been me it would have been someone else. But that's no excuse.

(Pause.)

Turkish Delight, for example, which no longer exists, we all know that, there is nothing in the world I love more. And one day I'll ask you for some, in return for a kindness, and you'll promise it to me. One must live with the times.

(Pause.)

Whom did you call when you were a tiny boy, and were frightened, in the dark? Your mother? No. Me. We let you cry. Then we moved you out of earshot, so that we might sleep in peace.

(Pause.)

I was asleep, as happy as a king, and you woke me up to have me listen to you. It wasn't indispensable, you didn't really need to have me listen to you.

(Pause.)

I hope the day will come when you'll really need to have me listen to you, and need to hear my voice, any voice.

(Pause.)

Yes, I hope I'll live till then, to hear you calling me like when you were a tiny boy, and were frightened, in the dark, and I was your only hope.

(Pause. NAGG *knocks on lid of* NELL's *bin. Pause.)*

Nell!

(Pause. He knocks louder. Pause. Louder.)

Nell!

(Pause. NAGG *sinks back into his bin, closes the lid behind him. Pause.)*

HAMM: Our revels now are ended.

(He gropes for the dog.)

The dog's gone.

CLOV: He's not a real dog, he can't go.

HAMM *(groping)*: He's not there.

CLOV: He's lain down.

HAMM: Give him to me.

(CLOV picks up the dog and gives it to HAMM. HAMM *holds it in his arms. Pause.* HAMM *throws away the dog.)*

Dirty brute!

(CLOV begins to pick up the objects lying on the ground.)

What are you doing?

CLOV: Putting things in order.

(He straightens up. Fervently.)

I'm going to clear everything away!

(He starts picking up again.)

HAMM: Order!

CLOV *(straightening up)*: I love order. It's my dream. A world where all would be silent and still and each thing in its last place, under the last dust.

(He starts picking up again.)

HAMM *(exasperated)*: What in God's name do you think you are doing?

CLOV *(straightening up)*: I'm doing my best to create a little order.

HAMM: Drop it!

(CLOV drops the objects he has picked up.)

CLOV: After all, there or elsewhere.

(He goes toward door.)

HAMM *(irritably)*: What's wrong with your feet?

CLOV: My feet?

HAMM: Tramp! Tramp!

CLOV: I must have put on my boots.

HAMM: Your slippers were hurting you?

(Pause.)

CLOV: I'll leave you.

HAMM: No!

CLOV: What is there to keep me here?

HAMM: The dialogue.

(Pause.)

I've got on with my story.

(Pause.)

I've got on with it well.

(Pause. Irritably.)

Ask me where I've got to.

CLOV: Oh, by the way, your story?

HAMM *(surprised)*: What story?

CLOV: The one you've been telling yourself all your days.

HAMM: Ah you mean my chronicle?

CLOV: That's the one.

(Pause.)

HAMM *(angrily)*: Keep going, can't you, keep going!

CLOV: You've got on with it, I hope.

HAMM *(modestly)*: Oh not very far, not very far.

(He sighs.)

There are days like that, one isn't inspired.

(Pause.)

Nothing you can do about it, just wait for it to come.

(Pause.)

No forcing, no forcing, it's fatal.

(Pause.)

I've got on with it a little all the same.

(Pause.)

Technique, you know.

(Pause. Irritably.)

I say I've got on with it a little all the same.

CLOV *(admiringly)*: Well I never! In spite of everything you were able to get on with it!

HAMM *(modestly)*: Oh not very far, you know, not very far, but nevertheless, better than nothing.

CLOV: Better than nothing! Is it possible?

HAMM: I'll tell you how it goes. He comes crawling on his belly—

CLOV: Who?

HAMM: What?

CLOV: Who do you mean, he?

HAMM: Who do I mean! Yet another.

CLOV: Ah him! I wasn't sure.

HAMM: Crawling on his belly, whining for bread for his brat. He's offered a job as gardener. Before—

(CLOV bursts out laughing.)

What is there so funny about that?

CLOV: A job as gardener!

HAMM: Is that what tickles you?

CLOV: It must be that.

HAMM: It wouldn't be the bread?

CLOV: Or the brat.

(Pause.)

HAMM: The whole thing is comical, I grant you that. What about having a good guffaw the two of us together?

CLOV *(after reflection)*: I couldn't guffaw again today.

HAMM *(after reflection)*: Nor I.

(Pause.)

I continue then. Before accepting with gratitude he asks if he may have his little boy with him.

CLOV: What age?

HAMM: Oh tiny.

CLOV: He would have climbed the trees.

HAMM: All the little odd jobs.

CLOV: And then he would have grown up.

HAMM: Very likely.

(Pause.)

CLOV: Keep going, can't you, keep going!

HAMM: That's all. I stopped there.

(Pause.)

CLOV: Do you see how it goes on.

HAMM: More or less.

CLOV: Will it not soon be the end?

HAMM: I'm afraid it will.

CLOV: Pah! You'll make up another.

HAMM: I don't know.

(Pause.)

I feel rather drained.

(Pause.)

The prolonged creative effort.

(Pause.)

If I could drag myself down to the sea! I'd make a pillow of sand for my head and the tide would come.

CLOV: There's no more tide.

(Pause.)

HAMM: Go and see is she dead.

(CLOV goes to bins, raises the lid of NELL's, stoops, looks into it. Pause.)

CLOV: Looks like it.

(He closes the lid, straightens up. HAMM raises his toque. Pause. He puts it on again.)

HAMM *(with his hand to his toque)*: And Nagg?

(CLOV raises lid of NAGG's bin, stoops, looks into it. Pause.)

CLOV: Doesn't look like it.

(He closes the lid, straightens up.)

HAMM *(letting go his toque)*: What's he doing?

(CLOV raises lid of NAGG's bin, stoops, looks into it. Pause.)

CLOV: He's crying.

(He closes lid, straightens up.)

HAMM: Then he's living.

(Pause.)

Did you ever have an instant of happiness?

CLOV: Not to my knowledge.

(Pause.)

HAMM: Bring me under the window.

(CLOV goes toward chair.)

I want to feel the light on my face.

(CLOV pushes chair.)

Do you remember, in the beginning, when you took me for a turn? You used to hold the chair too high. At every step you nearly tipped me out.

(With senile quaver.)

Ah great fun, we had, the two of us, great fun.

(Gloomily.)

And then we got into the way of it.

(CLOV stops the chair under window right.)

There already?

(Pause. He tilts back his head.)

Is it light?

CLOV: It isn't dark.

HAMM *(angrily)*: I'm asking you is it light.

CLOV: Yes.

(Pause.)

HAMM: The curtain isn't closed?

CLOV: No.

HAMM: What window is it?

CLOV: The earth.

HAMM: I knew it!

(Angrily.)

But there's no light there! The other!

(CLOV pushes the chair toward window left.)

The earth!

(CLOV stops the chair under window left. HAMM tilts back his head.)

That's what I call light!

(Pause.)

Feels like a ray of sunshine.

(Pause.)

No?

CLOV: No.

HAMM: It isn't a ray of sunshine I feel on my face?

CLOV: No.

(Pause.)

HAMM: Am I very white?

(Pause. Angrily.)

I'm asking you am I very white!

CLOV: Not more so than usual.

(Pause.)

HAMM: Open the window.

CLOV: What for?

HAMM: I want to hear the sea.

CLOV: You wouldn't hear it.

HAMM: Even if you opened the window?

CLOV: No.

HAMM: Then it's not worth while opening it?

CLOV: No.

HAMM *(violently)*: Then open it!

(CLOV gets up on the ladder, opens the window. Pause.)

Have you opened it?

CLOV: Yes.

(*Pause.*)

HAMM: You swear you've opened it?

CLOV: Yes.

(*Pause.*)

HAMM: Well . . . !

(*Pause.*)

It must be very calm.

(*Pause. Violently.*)

I'm asking you is it very calm!

CLOV: Yes.

HAMM: It's because there are no more navigators.

(*Pause.*)

You haven't much conversation all of a sudden. Do you not feel well?

CLOV: I'm cold.

HAMM: What month are we?

(*Pause.*)

Close the window, we're going back.

(CLOV *closes the window, gets down, pushes the chair back to its place, remains standing behind it, head bowed.*)

Don't stay there, you give me the shivers!

(CLOV *returns to his place beside the chair.*)

Father!

(*Pause. Louder.*)

Father!

(*Pause.*)

Go and see did he hear me.

(CLOV *goes to* NAGG's *bin, raises the lid, stoops. Unintelligible words.* CLOV *straightens up.*)

CLOV: Yes.

HAMM: Both times?

(CLOV *stops. As before.*)

CLOV: Once only.

HAMM: The first time or the second?

(CLOV *stoops. As before.*)

CLOV: He doesn't know.

HAMM: It must have been the second.

CLOV: We'll never know.

(*He closes lid.*)

HAMM: Is he still crying?

CLOV: No.

HAMM: The dead go fast.

(*Pause.*)

What's he doing?

CLOV: Sucking his biscuit.

HAMM: Life goes on.

(CLOV *returns to his place beside the chair.*)

Give me a rug, I'm freezing.

CLOV: There are no more rugs.

(*Pause.*)

HAMM: Kiss me.

(*Pause.*)

Will you not kiss me?

CLOV: No.

HAMM: On the forehead.

CLOV: I won't kiss you anywhere.

(*Pause.*)

HAMM (*holding out his hand*): Give me your hand at least.

(*Pause.*)

Will you not give me your hand?

CLOV: I won't touch you.

(*Pause.*)

HAMM: Give me the dog.

(CLOV *looks round for the dog.*)

No!

CLOV: Do you not want your dog?

HAMM: No.

CLOV: Then I'll leave you.

HAMM (*head bowed, absently*): That's right.

(CLOV *goes to door, turns.*)

CLOV: If I don't kill that rat he'll die.

HAMM (*as before*): That's right.

(*Exit* CLOV. *Pause.*)

Me to play.

(*He takes out his handkerchief, unfolds it, holds it spread out before him.*)

We're getting on.

(*Pause.*)

You weep, and weep, for nothing, so as not to laugh, and little by little . . . you begin to grieve.

(*He folds the handkerchief, he puts it back in his pocket, raises his head.*)

All those I might have helped.

(Pause.)

Helped!

(Pause.)

Saved.

(Pause.)

Saved!

(Pause.)

The place was crawling with them!

(Pause. Violently.)

Use your head, can't you, use your head, you're on earth, there's no cure for that!

(Pause.)

Get out of here and love one another! Lick your neighbor as yourself!

(Pause. Calmer.)

When it wasn't bread they wanted it was crumpets.

(Pause. Violently.)

Out of my sight and back to your petting parties!

(Pause.)

All that, all that!

(Pause.)

Not even a real dog!

(Calmer.)

The end is in the beginning and yet you go on.

(Pause.)

Perhaps I could go on with my story, end it and begin another.

(Pause.)

Perhaps I could throw myself out on the floor.

(He pushes himself painfully off his seat, falls back again.)

Dig my nails into the cracks and drag myself forward with my fingers.

(Pause.)

It will be the end and there I'll be, wondering what can have brought it on and wondering what can have . . . *(He hesitates.)* . . . why it was so long coming.

(Pause.)

There I'll be, in the old shelter, alone against the silence and . . . *(He hesitates.)* . . . the stillness. If I can hold my peace, and sit quiet, it will be all over with sound, and motion, all over and done with.

(Pause.)

I'll have called my father and I'll have called my . . . *(He hesitates.)* . . . my son. And even twice, or three times, in case they shouldn't have heard me, the first time, or the second.

(Pause.)

I'll say to myself. He'll come back.

(Pause.)

And then?

(Pause.)

And then?

(Pause.)

He couldn't, he has gone too far.

(Pause.)

And then?

(Pause. Very agitated.)

All kinds of fantasies! That I'm being watched! A rat! Steps! Breath held and then . . .

(He breathes out.)

Then babble, babble, words, like the solitary child who turns himself into children, two, three, so as to be together, and whisper together in the dark.

(Pause.)

Moment upon moment, pattering down, like the millet grains of . . . *(He hesitates.)* . . . that old Greek, and all life long you wait for that to mount up to a life.

(Pause. He opens his mouth to continue, renounces.)

Ah let's get it over!

(He whistles. Enter CLOV *with alarm-clock. He halts beside the chair.)*

What? Neither gone nor dead?

CLOV: In spirit only.

HAMM: Which?

CLOV: Both.

HAMM: Gone from me you'd be dead.

CLOV: And vice versa.

HAMM: Outside of here it's death!

(Pause.)

And the rat?

CLOV: He's got away.

HAMM: He can't go far.

(*Pause. Anxious.*)

Eh?

CLOV: He doesn't need to go far.

(*Pause.*)

HAMM: Is it not time for my pain-killer?

CLOV: Yes.

HAMM: Ah! At last! Give it to me! Quick!

(*Pause.*)

CLOV: There's no more pain-killer.

(*Pause.*)

HAMM (*appalled*): Good . . . !

(*Pause.*)

No more pain-killer!

CLOV: No more pain-killer. You'll never get any more pain-killer.

(*Pause.*)

HAMM: But the little round box. It was full!

CLOV: Yes. But now it's empty.

(*Pause.* CLOV *starts to move about the room. He is looking for a place to put down the alarm-clock.*)

HAMM (*soft*): What'll I do?

(*Pause. In a scream.*)

What'll I do?

(CLOV *sees the picture, takes it down, stands it on the floor with its face to the wall, hangs up the alarm-clock in its place.*)

What are you doing?

CLOV: Winding up.

HAMM: Look at the earth.

CLOV: Again!

HAMM: Since it's calling to you.

CLOV: Is your throat sore?

(*Pause.*)

Would you like a lozenge?

(*Pause.*)

No.

(*Pause.*)

Pity.

(CLOV *goes, humming, toward window right, halts before it, looks up at it.*)

HAMM: Don't sing.

CLOV (*turning toward* HAMM): One hasn't the right to sing any more?

HAMM: No.

CLOV: Then how can it end?

HAMM: You want it to end?

CLOV: I want to sing.

HAMM: I can't prevent you.

(*Pause.* CLOV *turns toward window right.*)

CLOV: What did I do with that steps?

(*He looks around for ladder.*)

You didn't see that steps?

(*He sees it.*)

Ah, about time.

(*He goes toward window left.*)

Sometimes I wonder if I'm in my right mind. Then it passes over and I'm as lucid as before.

(*He gets up on ladder, looks out of window.*)

Christ, she's under water!

(*He looks.*)

How can that be?

(*He pokes forward his head, his hand above his eyes.*)

It hasn't rained.

(*He wipes the pane, looks. Pause.*)

Ah what a fool I am! I'm on the wrong side!

(*He gets down, takes a few steps towards window right.*)

Under water!

(*He goes back for ladder.*)

What a fool I am!

(*He carries ladder toward window right.*)

Sometimes I wonder if I'm in my right senses. Then it passes off and I'm as intelligent as ever.

(*He sets down ladder under window right, gets up on it, looks out of window. He turns toward* HAMM.)

Any particular sector you fancy? Or merely the whole thing?

HAMM: Whole thing.

CLOV: The general effect? Just a moment.

(*He looks out of window. Pause.*)

HAMM: Clov.

CLOV (*absorbed*): Mmm.

HAMM: Do you know what it is?

CLOV (*as before*): Mmm.

HAMM: I was never there.

(*Pause.*)

Clov!

CLOV (*turning toward* HAMM, *exasperated*): What is it?
HAMM: I was never there.
CLOV: Lucky for you.

(*He looks out of window.*)

HAMM: Absent, always. It all happened without me. I don't know what's happened.

(*Pause.*)

Do you know what's happened?

(*Pause.*)

Clov!

CLOV (*turning toward* HAMM, *exasperated*): Do you want me to look at this muckheap, yes or no?
HAMM: Answer me first.
CLOV: What?
HAMM: Do you know what's happened?
CLOV: When? Where?
HAMM (*violently*): When! What's happened? Use your head, can't you? What has happened?
CLOV: What for Christ's sake does it matter?

(*He looks out of window.*)

HAMM: I don't know.

(*Pause.* CLOV *turns toward* HAMM.)

CLOV (*harshly*): When old Mother Pegg asked you for oil for her lamp and you told her to get out to hell, you knew what was happening then, no?

(*Pause.*)

You know what she died of, Mother Pegg? Of darkness.
HAMM (*feebly*): I hadn't any.
CLOV (*as before*): Yes, you had.

(*Pause.*)

HAMM: Have you the glass?
CLOV: No, it's clear enough as it is.
HAMM: Go and get it.

(*Pause.* CLOV *casts up his eyes, brandishes his fists. He loses balance, clutches on to the ladder. He starts to get down, halts.*)

CLOV: There's one thing I'll never understand.

(*He gets down.*)

Why I always obey you. Can you explain that to me?
HAMM: No. . . . Perhaps it's compassion.

(*Pause.*)

A kind of compassion.

(*Pause.*)

Oh you won't find it easy, you won't find it easy.

(*Pause.* CLOV *begins to move about the room in search of the telescope.*)

CLOV: I'm tired of our goings on, very tired.

(*He searches.*)

You're not sitting on it?

(*He moves the chair, looks at the place where it stood, resumes his search.*)

HAMM (*anguished*): Don't leave me there!

(*Angrily* CLOV *restores the chair to its place.*)

Am I right in the center?
CLOV: You'd need a microscope to find this—

(*He sees the telescope.*)

Ah, about time.

(*He picks up the telescope, gets up on the ladder, turns the telescope on the without.*)

HAMM: Give me the dog.
CLOV (*looking*): Quiet!
HAMM (*angrily*): Give me the dog!

(CLOV *drops the telescope, clasps his hands to his head. Pause. He gets down precipitately, looks for the dog, sees it, picks it up, hastens toward* HAMM *and strikes him violently on the head with the dog.*)

CLOV: There's your dog for you!

(*The dog falls to the ground. Pause.*)

HAMM: He hit me!
CLOV: You drive me mad, I'm mad!
HAMM: If you must hit me, hit me with the axe.

(*Pause.*)

Or with the gaff, hit me with the gaff. Not with the dog. With the gaff. Or with the axe.

(CLOV *picks up the dog and gives it to* HAMM *who takes it in his arms.*)

CLOV (*imploringly*): Let's stop playing!
HAMM: Never!

(*Pause.*)

Put me in my coffin.
CLOV: There are no more coffins.
HAMM: Then let it end!

(CLOV *goes toward ladder.*)

With a bang!

(CLOV *gets up on ladder, gets down again, looks for telescope, sees it, picks it up, gets up on ladder, raises telescope.*)

Of darkness! And me? Did anyone ever have pity on me?

CLOV (*lowering the telescope, turning toward* HAMM): What?

(*Pause.*)

Is it me you're referring to?

HAMM (*angrily*): An aside, ape! Did you never hear an aside before?

(*Pause.*)

I'm warming up for my last soliloquy.

CLOV: I warn you. I'm going to look at this filth since it's an order. But it's the last time.

(*He turns the telescope on the without.*)

Let's see.

(*He moves the telescope.*)

Nothing . . . nothing . . . good . . . good . . . nothing . . . goo—

(*He starts, lowers the telescope, examines it, turns it again on the without. Pause.*)

Bad luck to it!

HAMM: More complications!

(CLOV *gets down.*)

Not an underplot, I trust.

(CLOV *moves ladder nearer window, gets up on it, turns telescope on the without.*)

CLOVE (*dismayed*): Looks like a small boy!

HAMM (*sarcastic*): A small . . . boy!

CLOV: I'll go and see.

(*He gets down, drops the telescope, goes toward door, turns.*)

I'll take the gaff.

(*He looks for the gaff, sees it, picks it up, hastens toward door.*)

HAMM: No!

(CLOV *halts.*)

CLOV: No? A potential procreator?

HAMM: If he exists he'll die there or he'll come here. And if he doesn't . . .

(*Pause.*)

CLOV: You don't believe me? You think I'm inventing?

(*Pause.*)

HAMM: It's the end, Clov, we've come to the end. I don't need you any more.

(*Pause.*)

CLOV: Lucky for you.

(*He goes toward door.*)

HAMM: Leave me the gaff.

(CLOV *gives him the gaff, goes toward door, halts, looks at alarm-clock, takes it down, looks round for a better place to put it, goes to bins, puts it on lid of* NAGG's *bin. Pause.*)

CLOV: I'll leave you.

(*He goes toward door.*)

HAMM: Before you go . . .

(CLOV *halts near door.*)

. . . say something.

CLOV: There is nothing to say.

HAMM: A few words . . . to ponder . . . in my heart.

CLOV: Your heart!

HAMM: Yes.

(*Pause. Forcibly.*)

Yes!

(*Pause.*)

With the rest, in the end, the shadows, the murmurs, all the trouble, to end up with.

(*Pause.*)

Clov. . . . He never spoke to me. Then, in the end, before he went, without my having asked him, he spoke to me. He said . . .

CLOV (*despairingly*): Ah . . . !

HAMM: Something . . . from your heart.

CLOV: My heart!

HAMM: A few words . . . from your heart.

(*Pause.*)

CLOV (*fixed gaze, tonelessly, toward auditorium*): They said to me, That's love, yes, yes, not a doubt, now you see how—

HAMM: Articulate!

CLOV (*as before*): How easy it is. They said to me, That's friendship, yes, yes, no question, you've found it. They said to me, Here's the place, stop, raise your head and look at all that beauty. That order! They said to me, Come now, you're not a brute beast, think upon these things and you'll see how all becomes clear. And simple! They said to me, What skilled attention they get, all these dying of their wounds.

HAMM: Enough!

CLOV (*as before*): I say to myself—sometimes, Clov, you must learn to suffer better than that if you want them to weary of punishing you—one day. I say to myself—sometimes, Clov, you must be there better than that if you want them to let you go—one day. But I feel too old, and too far, to form new habits. Good, it'll never end, I'll never go.

(*Pause.*)

Then one day, suddenly, it ends, it changes, I don't understand, it dies, or it's me, I don't understand, that either. I ask the words that remain—sleeping, waking, morning, evening. They have nothing to say.

(*Pause.*)

I open the door of the cell and go. I am so bowed I only see my feet, if I open my eyes, and between my legs a little trail of black dust. I say to myself that the earth is extinguished, though I never saw it lit.

(*Pause.*)

It's easy going.

(*Pause.*)

When I fall I'll weep for happiness.

(*Pause. He goes toward door.*)

HAMM: Clov!

(CLOV *halts, without turning.*)

Nothing.

(CLOV *moves on.*)

Clov!

(CLOV *halts, without turning.*)

CLOV: This is what we call making an exit.
HAMM: I'm obliged to you, Clov. For your services.
CLOV (*turning, sharply*): Ah pardon, it's I am obliged to you.
HAMM: It's we are obliged to each other.

(*Pause.* CLOV *goes toward door.*)

One thing more.

(CLOV *halts.*)

A last favor.

(*Exit* CLOV.)

Cover me with the sheet.

(*Long pause.*)

No? Good.

(*Pause.*)

Me to play.

(*Pause. Wearily.*)

Old endgame lost of old, play and lose and have done with losing.

(*Pause. More animated.*)

Let me see.

(*Pause.*)

Ah yes!

(*He tries to move the chair, using the gaff as before. Enter* CLOV, *dressed for the road. Panama hat, tweed coat, raincoat over his arm, umbrella, bag. He halts by the door and stands there, impassive and motionless, his eyes are fixed on* HAMM, *till the end.* HAMM *gives up.*)

Good.

(*Pause.*)

Discard.

(*He throws away the gaff, makes to throw away the dog, thinks better of it.*)

Take it easy.

(*Pause.*)

And now?

(*Pause.*)

Raise hat.

(*He raises his toque.*)

Peace to our . . . arses.

(*Pause.*)

And put on again.

(*He puts on his toque.*)

Deuce.

(*Pauses. He takes off his glasses.*)

Wipe.

(*He takes out his handkerchief and, without unfolding it, wipes his glasses.*)

And put on again.

(*He puts on his glasses, puts back the handkerchief in his pocket.*)

We're coming. A few more squirms like that and I'll call.

(*Pause.*)

A little poetry.

(*Pause.*)

You prayed—

(*Pause. He corrects himself.*)

You CRIED for night; it comes—

(Pause, He corrects himself.)

It FALLS: now cry in darkness.

(He repeats, chanting.)

You cried for night; it falls; now cry in darkness.

(Pause.)

Nicely put, that.

(Pause.)

And now?

(Pause.)

Moments for nothing, now as always, time was never and time is over, reckoning closed and story ended.

(Pause. Narrative tone.)

If he could have his child with him. . . .

(Pause.)

It was the moment I was waiting for.

(Pause.)

You don't want to abandon him? You want him to bloom while you are withering? Be there to solace your last million last moments?

(Pause.)

He doesn't realize, all he knows is hunger, and cold, and death to crown it all. But you! You ought to know what the earth is like, nowadays. Oh I put him before his responsibilities!

(Pause. Normal tone.)

Well, there we are, there I am, that's enough.

(He raises the whistle to his lips, hesitates, drops it. Pause.)

Yes, truly!

(He whistles. Pause. Louder. Pause.)

Good.

(Pause.)

Father!

(Pause. Louder.)

Father!

(Pause.)

Good.

(Pause.)

We're coming.

(Pause.)

And to end up with?

(Pause.)

Discard.

(He throws away the dog. He tears the whistle from his neck.)

With my compliments.

(He throws whistle toward auditorium. Pause. He sniffs. Soft.)

Clov!

(Long pause.)

No? Good.

(He takes out the handkerchief.)

Since that's the way we're playing it . . . *(He unfolds handkerchief.)* . . . let's play it that way . . . *(He unfolds.)* . . . and speak no more about it . . . *(He finishes unfolding.)* . . . speak no more.

(He holds handkerchief spread out before him.)

Old stancher!

(Pause.)

You . . . remain.

(Pause. He covers his face with handkerchief, lowers his arms to armrests, remains motionless.)
(Brief tableau.)

CURTAIN

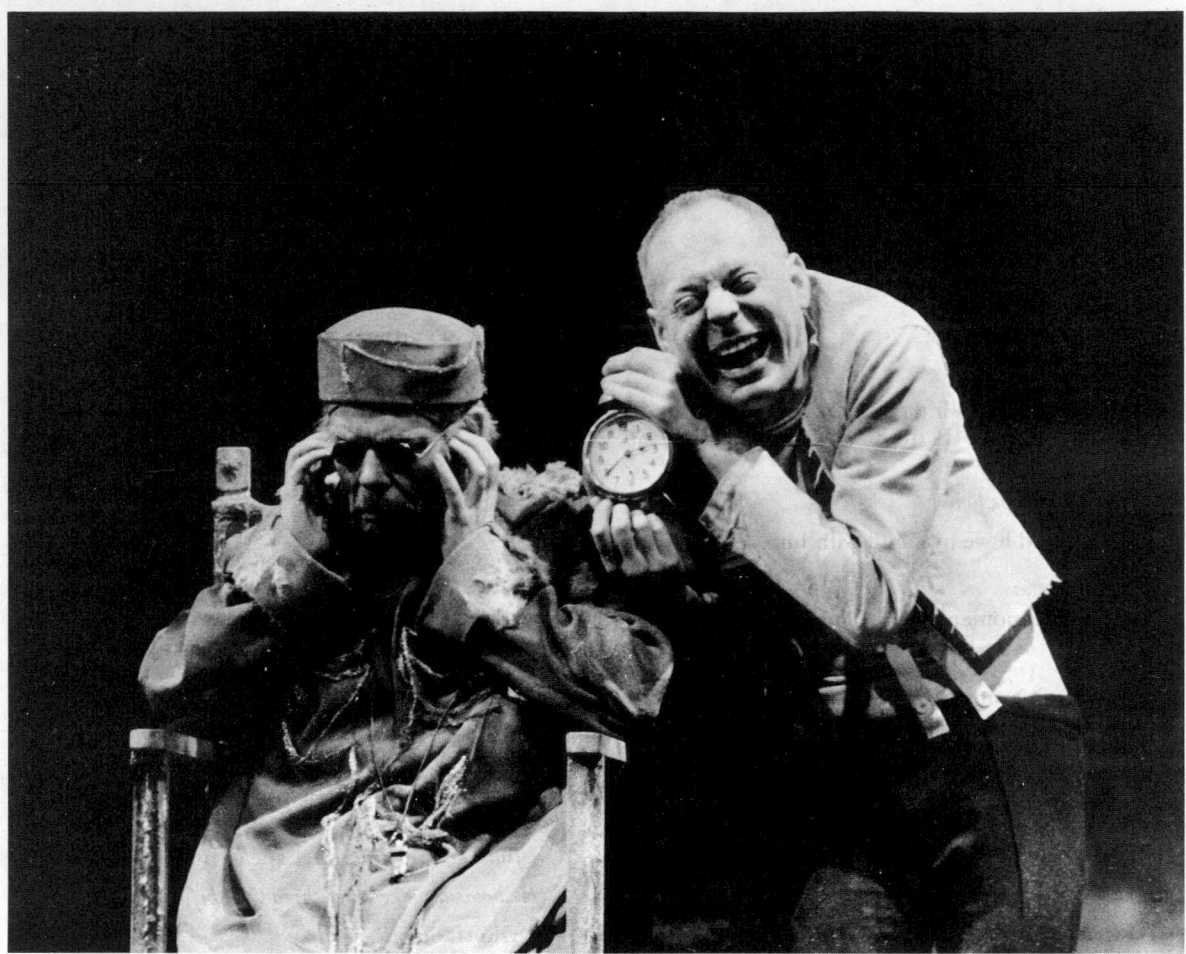

Figure 1. Hamm (Roger Blin) and Clov (Jean Martin) in the Studio des Champs-Élysées production of *Endgame,* directed by Roger Blin and designed by Jacques Noel, Paris, 1957. (Photograph: Roger PIC, Paris.)

Figure 2. Nagg (Georges Adet) asks for his sugar-plum while Hamm (Roger Blin) and Clov (Jean Martin) pray to God in the Studio des Champs-Élysées production of *Endgame*, directed by Roger Blin and designed by Jacques Noel, Paris, 1957. (Photograph: Roger PIC, Paris.)

Staging of *Endgame*

REVIEW OF THE STUDIO DES CHAMPS-ÉLYSÉES
PRODUCTION, 1957, BY JACQUES LEMARCHAND

"Endgame" by Samuel Beckett lends a theatrical reality, a frightening reality, to a certain daydream that I imagine we have all yielded to at one time or another: some day, it matters little under what conditions, there will no longer be any men on Earth; nor will there be any Earth then either. One short moment, no more, in the entire universe, when a single man, the very last man, will have the task of feeling the last emotion, the last sensation, of speaking the last word—and that word will not be historic. To young people this seems, if I remember correctly, frightening, dizzying. To those not so young it can seem more like a pleasant reassurance that one should not attach a great deal of importance to winning literary prizes, nor fret too much about honors granted to imbeciles. This is a rather peaceful daydream, blending a fair amount of humor into the inevitable terror that the end of *everything* arouses in man.

And this terror and comedy have never been presented on stage in a manner so immediately perceptible, and with so little rhetoric as well as so much persuasive power, as in this "Endgame," playing at the Studio des Champs-Élysées, to its infinite honor. It is easy, and legitimate, to seek and to find in "Endgame" some sort of sequel to, or echo of, "Waiting for Godot." In fact, Beckett's second play, although it bears the undeniable stamp of its author— that clown-like naiveté, with which the characters juggle, to all appearances innocently, our most secret and serious anxieties—is a play entirely different from "Waiting for Godot." Godot has absolutely refused to come, and no one is waiting for him any more; what they are waiting for is to "make an exit"; and words of waiting, hope, and desire have lost all meaning: the characters of "Endgame" simply consent to something they know is inevitable.

These protagonists have been criticized for not being very attractive young men. It is true that Beckett's play is lacking in young leads. One could just as well criticize them for having names that are rather uncommon in the boulevard theaters. They are called Hamm, Clov, Nagg and Nell, names reeking of the circus and lacking in distinction. But after all, this is the very last day of the human race, and it is permissible to imagine that the saints of the calendar have withdrawn. It is no less true that these characters are in poor health: Hamm is paralyzed and cannot leave his armchair; Clov, his slave, has difficulty walking and shakes with palsy; as for Nagg and his wife Nell, their situation is quite simple: they are legless cripples, and each lives in an ashbin, comfortably, it seems, considering their smaller size; these four characters are shut in a sort of bunker, in which they will certainly have to die. The two windows of the shelter look out upon a leaden sea and empty land, equally forsaken by humanity. This is hardly a pleasant situation, I admit, but it can surely be granted that is eminently dramatic.

Among these four human beings there is no other solidarity than that arising from self-interest. Nagg and Nell, who are Hamm's parents, depend on him for the last few mouthfuls of pap that will prolong their mediocre lives; Hamm depends on his servant-son, Clov, for the attentions required by his condition; and if Clov refrains from dispatching Hamm, it is simply because he does not have the "combination to the cupboard" where the last few biscuits are locked up. And yet there is not one of these human beings who does not have his dream, a dream he tries to make the others share, to communicate to them: and this need to communicate is as vital to their lives as is the diminishing store of biscuits. From one ashbin to the other, Nagg and Nell allusively exchange their memories: that of rowing a boat one April afternoon on Lake Como, or even the evocation of the accident that crippled them, draws them closer together; from time to time Hamm pursues the fabrication of a long drawn-out literary story, for which, like a true man of letters, he requires an audience. Clov announces his own imminent departure, though he knows it to be impossible, and does all he can to convince himself that his departure depends on his will alone.

It is the spectacle of a game that is coming to an end, of an endgame, that is presented to us in Beckett's play. The fact that this may be the very game we play all the time, without ever believing it to be as close as it is to its end, is made constantly apparent by the way relations among the four characters are stripped down and reduced to an elemental level. The humor of this grim play—vigorous, savage, never gratuitous, provoking brusque outbreaks of laughter—arises also from flashes of confrontation between the actual situation of these characters and the tremendous futility of their malice as well as of their moments of tenderness. It arises too from the frenzy we discover in these characters, which they reveal in their furious acceptance of their fate: the distant apparition of what they take to be a human figure, the discovery of a live rat or a live flea horrifies them. "But humanity might start from there all over again," says Hamm. "Catch him, for the love of God!" Black humor indeed, but of a kind that arises spontaneously from felicitous and unexpected phrases, from a latent tragicomicality that suddenly becomes enormously ludicrous. A humor whose power is in no way increased by one obscene pun and two or three instances of coarse language.

I have limited myself to describing only the exterior aspect of "Endgame": a poem in dialogue, full of surprises and verbal successes, a play that moves and progresses, despite its immobile protagonists and subtle repetitions, towards a poignant and beautiful ending. As for any metaphysical conclusions it may imply, naturally it is for each spectator to understand them to his own liking; the author leaves them complete latitude, and this is not the least of the reasons for the fascination one experiences at a performance of "Endgame."

Jacques Noel's set, that bare bunker in which the human race is coming to an end, is stifling; assuredly just as Beckett must have conceived it. Roger Blin (Hamm), who ensured the meticulous direction of the play, and Jean Martin (Clov) are its extremely impressive protagonists; Germane de France (Nell) and Georges Adet (Nagg), emerging from their Diogenesque ashbins, succeed in being at once ludicrous and pathetic.

The performance ends with an "Act Without Words," by Beckett—a pantomime for one actor, carried through to its termination with the sureness of a great artist by Deryk Mendel—who, amid silence punctuated by blasts from a whistle, shows the same qualities of humor and cruelty we enjoyed in "Endgame." (Translated by Jean M. Sommermeyer)

EDWARD ALBEE

1928–

Twice in *The Zoo Story*, Jerry asserts: "sometimes a person has to go a very long distance out of his way to come back a short distance correctly." Perhaps Jerry speaks for his creator, Edward Albee, whose first theatrical success, *The Zoo Story*, which he wrote in 1958, was originally turned down by various New York producers, then via a circuitous route of being sent from one friend to another was initially performed in Berlin in 1959 and only after its German success was finally produced in New York in January 1960. Before those two productions Albee's life itself seems to have been a complex blend of privilege and insecurity, of opportunity and failure, beginning with his adoption at two weeks old; he was thus a child both wanted and unwanted, a paradox he would return to in his plays. Young Albee attended, and was dismissed from, three different prep schools before he finally settled down at Choate, a prestigious Connecticut private school, where he published short stories, poems, and essays in the school literary magazine. He entered Trinity College in Connecticut in 1946 and took part in amateur theatrical groups, but was dismissed three semesters later. By 1948, Albee was living in New York City and working in a variety of jobs—office boy, sales clerk, luncheonette counterperson, and Western Union messenger. Yet, because he was supported by a trust fund from his grandmother, he was able to travel to Italy in 1952 and take time to write several unpublished plays, to visit the McDowell Colony for writers, and to study briefly at Columbia University.

In 1959, with the world premiere of *The Zoo Story*, which won the Berlin Festival Award, Albee's theatrical career began and moved swiftly from one striking success to another, resulting in the production of four new plays in one year. A double bill of Samuel Beckett's *Krapp's Last Tape* and Albee's *The Zoo Story* opened at the Provincetown Playhouse in New York's Greenwich Village; this combination of plays by the already well-known Beckett and the newly visible Albee ran for 582 performances. In April 1960, Albee had another premiere in Berlin, this time for *The Death of Bessie Smith*. In May, his fourteen-minute play, *The Sandbox*, opened at the Jazz Gallery in New York, and by the end of May. Albee received both the Obie (Off-Broadway) and the Vernon Rice awards for *The Zoo Story*. Later that year, in August, a sketch called *FAM and YAM*, a dialogue between a new playwright and a more established one, played in Connecticut and then off-Broadway. And just a year after *The Zoo Story* opened in New York, Albee's *The American Dream*, his bitterly funny attack on the American family and its cruelty towards both young and old, began a run of 360 performances at the York Theatre.

The capstone to this amazing record of successful new plays came with Albee's first full-length work, *Who's Afraid of Virginia Woolf?*, which opened on Broadway on October 13, 1962. In the savage marital battles that Albee dramatizes in this major work, he forces his four characters, hosts George and Martha, as well as guests Nick and Honey, to spend the early hours of the morning drinking themselves into a frightening recognition of the truths about themselves and their marriages. Thus an evening that begins with "Fun and Games" (the title of the first act), then turns into a "Walpurgisnacht" (the title of the second act, which refers to the orgiastic and nightmarish celebrations that once took place the evening before May Day), and concludes with "The Exorcism" (the title of the third and final act)—an exorcism fraught with social and psychological significance. But whether one considers *Who's Afraid of Virginia Woolf?* to be a study in truth and illusion, or an uncompromising analysis of the psychological and social games people play, or a veiled attack on American values (the names George and Martha recall the first president and his wife), the play's power derives from the combination of its biting humor, and, unforgettably, its seering and often vicious dialogue. In 1963, the play won almost every award possible, with the exception of the Pulitzer Prize; two members of the Pulitzer committee, the drama critic John Mason Brown, and the scholar John Gassner, resigned in protest when the Pulitzer trustees refused to award the prize to Albee because of the play's subject and its language. In London, the play won the *Evening Standard* Award in 1964, and in 1966, the film of the play starred a couple already famous for their own offstage brawls, Richard Burton and Elizabeth Taylor.

None of Albee's later plays (*Tiny Alice*, 1964; *A Delicate Balance*, 1966; *Box* and *Quotations from Chairman Mao Tse-tung*, 1968; *All Over*, 1971; *Seascape*, 1975; *Counting the Ways*, 1976; *The Man Who Had Three Arms*, 1983; *Marriage Play*, 1987; *Three Women*, 1991; *Fragments*, 1993) has ever achieved the popular dramatic success of his early ones, though the Pulitzer committee did award the drama prize to both *A Delicate Balance* and *Seascape*. Albee's most recent success (and his third Pulitzer Prize for drama) has come with the autobiographical *Three Women*, in which he portrays his adoptive mother as embodied by three different actresses. Characteristically, the play opened first abroad, coming to New York only in 1994. For many critics, Albee's later plays seem more abstract and detached, while the early ones, in George's words, "peel the labels," working through the emotional skin, muscle, bones, and marrow of the characters. And of the short early plays, it is *The Zoo Story* that accomplishes that process of dissection with the greatest urgency and pathos.

As Henry Hewes points out in his review following the text, *The Zoo Story* seems very simple: a park bench, two men, conversation. At first, Jerry's questions to Peter may seem merely annoying and only slightly threatening. The audience, like Peter, may think that Jerry is planning to rob Peter, or, given the number of references to homosexuals, attempting a sexual pickup. But while the continuing questions and the hesitant answers reveal Peter's life of compromise, it is Jerry's desperate longing to make contact that drives the play forward: "every once in a while I like to talk to somebody, really *talk*; like to get to know somebody, know all about him." Peter, sitting alone on a "sun-drenched Sunday afternoon," may not know that he is escaping from his conventional existence, but Jerry recognizes in him another lonely figure. Albee's awareness that relationships may be both mutually sustaining and mutually destructive underlies not only *Who's Afraid of Virginia Woolf?* but also *The Zoo Story*. Jerry and Peter, one a "permanent transient," the other with a wife, two daughters, two cats, and two parakeets, need each other, a need acted out in the gesture of violence and sexuality which ends the play.

When *The Zoo Story* was first performed, it attracted much praise as a first play, though a number of critics called the ending melodramatic and sentimental. Yet both Henry Hewes, in the accompanying review, and Harold Clurman, the noted director-critic, found the ending one of success, whether read as Jerry's achievement of connection, albeit in death (Clurman) or Jerry's ability to shake Peter out of his "deep modern lethargy" (Hewes). No matter how one interprets the ending, the central strength of the play still lies in the fascination/repulsion that flows between Jerry and Peter (see Figure 1). Whether Jerry is shocking Peter with his description of his "laughably small room" or tickling him into hysterical laughter (see Figure 2), he is always compelling. He may be the nightmare of the middle class brought to life as a nonstop talker, or he may be a parodic savior, or a demonic version of life imitating the violence reported on television news. Gradually he invades Peter's physical space and, in so doing, invades the audience's mental space. Peter's bench is no longer a refuge, and the theater is not a safe place; the animals have left their cages.

THE ZOO STORY

BY EDWARD ALBEE

THE PLAYERS

PETER, *A man in his early forties, neither fat nor gaunt, neither handsome nor homely. He wears tweeds, smokes a pipe, carries horn-rimmed glasses. Although he is moving into middle age, his dress and his manner would suggest a man younger.*

JERRY, *A man in his late thirties, not poorly dressed, but carelessly. What was once a trim and lightly muscled body has begun to go to fat; and while he is no longer handsome, it is evident that he once was. His fall from physical grace should not suggest debauchery; he has, to come closest to it, a great weariness.*

THE SCENE

It is Central Park; a Sunday afternoon in summer; the present. There are two park benches, one toward either side of the stage; they both face the audience. Behind them: foliage, trees, sky. At the beginning, PETER *is seated on one of the benches.*

STAGE DIRECTIONS

As the curtain rises, PETER *is seated on the bench stage-right. He is reading a book. He stops reading, cleans his glasses, goes back to reading.* JERRY *enters.*

JERRY: I've been to the zoo. (PETER *doesn't notice*) I said, I've been to the zoo. MISTER, I'VE BEEN TO THE ZOO!

PETER: Hm? . . . What? . . . I'm sorry, were you talking to me?

JERRY: I went to the zoo, and then I walked until I came here. Have I been walking north?

PETER (*Puzzled*): North? Why . . . I . . . I think so. Let me see.

JERRY (*Pointing past the audience*): Is that Fifth Avenue?

PETER: Why yes; yes, it is.

JERRY: And what is that cross street there; that one, to the right?

PETER: That? Oh, that's Seventy-fourth Street.

JERRY: And the zoo is around Sixty-fifth Street; so, I've been walking north.

PETER (*Anxious to get back to his reading*): Yes; it would seem so.

JERRY: Good old north.

PETER (*Lightly, by reflex*): Ha, ha.

JERRY (*After a slight pause*): But not due north.

PETER: I . . . well, no, not due north; but, we . . . call it north. It's northerly.

JERRY (*Watches as* PETER, *anxious to dismiss him, prepares his pipe*): Well, boy; *you're* not going to get lung cancer, are you?

PETER (*Looks up, a little annoyed, then smiles*): No, sir. Not from this.

JERRY: No, sir. What you'll probably get is cancer of the mouth, and then you'll have to wear one of those things Freud wore after they took one whole side of his jaw away. What do they call those things?

PETER (*Uncomfortable*): A prosthesis?

JERRY: The very thing! A prosthesis. You're an educated man, aren't you? Are you a doctor?

PETER: Oh, no; no. I read about it somewhere; *Time* magazine, I think. (*He turns to his book*)

JERRY: Well, *Time* magazine isn't for blockheads.

PETER: No, I suppose not.

JERRY (*After a pause*): Boy, I'm glad that's Fifth Avenue there.

PETER (*Vaguely*): Yes.

JERRY: I don't like the west side of the park much.

PETER: Oh? (*Then, slightly wary, but interested*) Why?

JERRY (*Offhand*): I don't know.

PETER: Oh. (*He returns to his book*)

JERRY (*He stands for a few seconds, looking at* PETER, *who finally looks up again, puzzled*): Do you mind if we talk?

PETER (*Obviously minding*): Why . . . no, no.

JERRY: Yes you do; you do.

PETER (*Puts his book down, his pipe out and away, smiling*): No, really; I don't mind.

JERRY: Yes you do.

PETER (*Finally decided*): No; I don't mind at all, really.

JERRY: It's . . . it's a nice day.

PETER (*Stares unnecessarily at the sky*): Yes. Yes, it is; lovely.

JERRY: I've been to the zoo.

PETER: Yes, I think you said so . . . didn't you?

JERRY: You'll read about it in the papers tomorrow, if you don't see it on your TV tonight. You have TV, haven't you?

PETER: Why yes, we have two; one for the children.

JERRY: You're married!

PETER (*With pleased emphasis*): Why, certainly.

JERRY: It isn't a law, for God's sake.

PETER: No . . . no, of course not.

JERRY: And you have a wife.

PETER (*Bewildered by the seeming lack of communication*): Yes!

JERRY: And you have children.

PETER: Yes; two.

JERRY: Boys?

PETER: No, girls . . . both girls.

JERRY: But you wanted boys.

PETER: Well . . . naturally, every man wants a son, but . . .

JERRY (*Lightly mocking*): But that's the way the cookie crumbles?

PETER (*Annoyed*): I wasn't going to say that.

JERRY: And you're not going to have any more kids, are you?

PETER (*A bit distantly*): No. No more. (*Then back, and irksome*) Why did you say that? How would you know about that?

JERRY: The way you cross your legs, perhaps; something in the voice. Or maybe I'm just guessing. Is it your wife?

PETER (*Furious*): That's none of your business! (*A silence*) Do you understand? (JERRY *nods.* PETER *is quiet now*) Well, you're right. We'll have no more children.

JERRY (*Softly*): That *is* the way the cookie crumbles.

PETER (*Forgiving*): Yes . . . I guess so.

JERRY: Well, now; what else?

PETER: What were you saying about the zoo . . . that I'd read about it, or see . . . ?

JERRY: I'll tell you about it, soon. Do you mind if I ask you questions?

PETER: Oh, not really.

JERRY: I'll tell you why I do it; I don't talk to many people—except to say like: give me a beer, or where's the john, or what time does the feature go on, or keep your hands to yourself, buddy. You know—things like that.

PETER: I must say I don't . . .

JERRY: But every once in a while I like to talk to somebody, really *talk;* like to get to know somebody, know all about him.

PETER (*Lightly laughing, still a little uncomfortable*): And am I the guinea pig for today?

JERRY: On a sun-drenched Sunday afternoon like this? Who better than a nice married man with two daughters and . . . uh . . . a dog? (PETER *shakes his head*) No? Two dogs? (PETER *shakes his head again*) Hm. No dogs? (PETER *shakes his head, sadly*) Oh, that's a shame. But you look like an animal man. CATS? (PETER *nods his head, ruefully*) Cats! But, that can't be your idea. No, sir. Your wife and daughters? (PETER *nods his head*) Is there anything else I should know?

PETER (*He has to clear his throat*): There are . . . there are two parakeets. One . . . uh . . . one for each of my daughters.

JERRY: Birds.

PETER: My daughters keep them in a cage in their bedroom.

JERRY: Do they carry disease? The birds.

PETER: I don't believe so.

JERRY: That's too bad. If they did you could set them loose in the house and the cats could eat them and die, maybe. (PETER *looks blank for a moment, then laughs*) And what else? What do you do to support your enormous household?

PETER: I . . . uh . . . I have an executive position with a . . . a small publishing house. We . . . uh . . . we publish textbooks.

JERRY: That sounds nice; very nice. What do you make?

PETER (*Still cheerful*): Now look here!

JERRY: Oh, come on.

PETER: Well, I make around eighteen thousand a year, but I don't carry more than forty dollars at any one time . . . in case you're a . . . a holdup man . . . ha, ha, ha.

JERRY (*Ignoring the above*): Where do you live? (PETER *is reluctant*) Oh, look; I'm not going to rob you, and I'm not going to kidnap your parakeets, your cats, or your daughters.

PETER (*Too loud*): I live between Lexington and Third Avenue, on Seventy-fourth Street.

JERRY: That wasn't so hard, was it?

PETER: I didn't mean to seem . . . ah . . . it's that you don't really carry on a conversation; you just ask questions. And I'm . . . I'm normally . . . uh . . . reticent. Why do you just stand there?

JERRY: I'll start walking around in a little while, and eventually I'll sit down. (*Recalling*) Wait until you see the expression on his face.

PETER: What? Whose face? Look here; is this something about the zoo?

JERRY (*Distantly*): The what?

PETER: The zoo; the zoo. Something about the zoo.

JERRY: The zoo?

PETER: You've mentioned it several times.

JERRY (*Still distant, but returning abruptly*): The zoo? Oh, yes; the zoo. I was there before I came here. I told you that. Say, what's the dividing line between upper-middle-middle-class and lower-upper-middle-class?

PETER: My dear fellow, I . . .

JERRY: Don't my dear fellow me.

PETER (*Unhappily*): Was I patronizing? I believe I was; I'm sorry. But, you see, your question about the classes bewildered me.

JERRY: And when you're bewildered you become patronizing?

PETER: I . . . I don't express myself too well, sometimes. (*He attempts a joke on himself*) I'm in publishing, not writing.

JERRY (*Amused, but not at the humor*): So be it. The truth *is: I* was being patronizing.

PETER: Oh, now; you needn't say that.

(It is at this point that JERRY *may begin to move about the stage with slowly increasing determination and authority, but pacing himself, so that the long speech about the dog comes at the high point of the arc)*

JERRY: All right. Who are your favorite writers? Baudelaire° and J. P. Marquand?°

PETER *(Wary)*: Well, I like a great many writers; I have a considerable . . . catholicity of taste, if I may say so. Those two men are fine, each in his way. *(Warming up)* Baudelaire, of course . . . uh . . . is by far the finer of the two, but Marquand has a place . . . in our . . . uh . . . national . . .

JERRY: Skip it.

PETER: I . . . sorry.

JERRY: Do you know what I did before I went to the zoo today? I walked all the way up Fifth Avenue from Washington Square; all the way.

PETER: Oh: you live in the Village!° *(This seems to enlighten* PETER*)*

JERRY: No, I don't. I took the subway down to the Village so I could walk all the way up Fifth Avenue to the zoo. It's one of those things a person has to do; sometimes a person has to go a very long distance out of his way to come back a short distance correctly.

PETER *(Almost pouting)*: Oh, I thought you lived in the Village.

JERRY: What were you trying to do? Make sense out of things? Bring order? The old pigeonhole bit? Well, that's easy; I'll tell you. I live in a four-story brownstone roominghouse on the upper West Side between Columbus Avenue and Central Park West. I live on the top floor; rear; west. It's a laughably small room, and one of my walls is made of beaverboard; this beaverboard separates my room from another laughably small room, so I assume that the two rooms were once one room, a small room, but not necessarily laughable. The room beyond my beaverboard wall is occupied by a colored queen who always keeps his door open; well, not always, but *always* when he's plucking his eyebrows, which he does with Buddhist concentration. This colored queen has rotten teeth, which is rare, and he has a Japanese kimono, which is also pretty rare; and he wears this kimono to and from the john in the hall, which is pretty frequent. I mean, he goes to the john a lot. He never bothers me, and he never brings anyone up to his room. All he does is pluck his eyebrows, wear his kimono and go to the john. Now, the two front rooms on my floor are a little larger, I guess; but they're pretty small, too. There's a Puerto Rican family in one of them, a husband, a

wife, and some kids; I don't know how many. These people entertain a lot. And in the other front room, there's somebody living there, but I don't know who it is. I've never seen who it is. Never. Never ever.

PETER *(Embarrassed)*: Why . . . why do you live there?

JERRY *(From a distance again)*: I don't know.

PETER: It doesn't sound like a very nice place . . . where you live.

JERRY: Well, no; it isn't an apartment in the East Seventies. But, then again, I don't have one wife, two daughters, two cats and two parakeets. What I do have, I have toilet articles, a few clothes, a hot plate that I'm not supposed to have, a can opener, one that works with a key, you know; a knife, two forks, and two spoons, one small, one large; three plates, a cup, a saucer, a drinking glass, two picture frames, both empty, eight or nine books, a pack of pornographic playing cards, regular deck, an old Western Union typewriter that prints nothing but capital letters, and a small strongbox without a lock which has in it . . . what? Rocks! Some rocks . . . sea-rounded rocks I picked up on the beach when I was a kid. Under which . . . weighed down . . . are some letters . . . please letters . . . please why don't you do this, and please when will you do that letters. And when letters, too. When will you write? When will you come? When? These letters are from more recent years.

PETER *(Stares glumly at his shoes, then)*: About those two empty picture frames . . . ?

JERRY: I don't see why they need any explanation at all. Isn't it clear? I don't have pictures of anyone to put in them.

PETER: Your parents . . . perhaps . . . a girl friend . . .

JERRY: You're a very sweet man, and you're possessed of a truly enviable innocence. But good old Mom and good old Pop are dead . . . you know? . . . I'm broken up about it, too . . . I mean really. BUT. That particular vaudeville act is playing the cloud circuit now, so I don't see how I can look at them, all neat and framed. Besides, or, rather, to be pointed about it, good old Mom walked out on good old Pop when I was ten and a half years old; she embarked on an adulterous turn of our southern states . . . a journey of a year's duration . . . and her most constant companion . . . among others, among many others . . . was a Mr. Barleycorn.° At least, that's what good old Pop told me after he went down . . . came back . . . brought her body north. We'd received the news between Christmas and New Year's, you see, that good old Mom had parted with the ghost in some dump in Alabama. And, without the ghost . . . she was less welcome. I mean, what was she? A stiff . . . a northern stiff. At any

---

Baudelaire, French poet and critic (1821–1867), best known for his poems published in *Les Fleurs du Mal (The Flowers of Evil);* some of the poems were condemned for obscenity. **J. P. Marquand,** American novelist (1893–1960), whose writing focused primarily on upper-class New England society. **Village,** Greenwich Village, residential area in New York City, associated with artistic and "bohemian" life.

Mr. Barleycorn, jocular name for whiskey.

rate, good old Pop celebrated the New Year for an even two weeks and then slapped into the front of a somewhat moving city omnibus, which sort of cleaned things out family-wise. Well no; then there was Mom's sister, who was given neither to sin nor the consolations of the bottle. I moved in on her, and my memory of her is slight excepting I remember still that she did all things dourly: sleeping, eating, working, praying. She dropped dead on the stairs to her apartment, my apartment then, too, on the afternoon of my high school graduation. A terribly middle-European joke, if you ask me.

PETER: Oh, my; oh, my.

JERRY: Oh, your what? But that was a long time ago, and I have no feeling about any of it that I care to admit to myself. Perhaps you can see, though, why good old Mom and good old Pop are frameless. What's your name? Your first name?

PETER: I'm Peter.

JERRY: I'd forgotten to ask you. I'm Jerry.

PETER (*With a slight, nervous laugh*): Hello, Jerry.

JERRY (*Nods his hello*): And let's see now; what's the point of having a girl's picture, especially in two frames? I have two picture frames, you remember. I never see the pretty little ladies more than once, and most of them wouldn't be caught in the same room with a camera. It's odd, and I wonder if it's sad.

PETER: The girls?

JERRY: No. I wonder if it's sad that I never see the little ladies more than once. I've never been able to have sex with, or how is it put? . . . make love to anybody more than once. Once; that's it. . . . Oh, wait; for a week and a half, when I was fifteen . . . and I hang my head in shame that puberty was late . . . I was a h-o-m-o-s-e-x-u-a-l. I mean, I was queer . . . (*Very fast*) . . . queer, queer, queer . . . with bells ringing, banners snapping in the wind. And for those eleven days, I met at least twice a day with the park superintendent's son . . . a Greek boy, whose birthday was the same as mine, except he was a year older. I think I was very much in love . . . maybe just with sex. But that was the jazz of a very special hotel, wasn't it? And now; oh, do I love the little ladies; really, I love them. For about an hour.

PETER: Well, it seems perfectly simple to me. . . .

JERRY (*Angry*): Look! Are you going to tell me to get married and have parakeets?

PETER (*Angry himself*): Forget the parakeets! And stay single if you want to. It's no business of mine. I didn't start this conversation in the . . .

JERRY: All right, all right. I'm sorry. All right? You're not angry?

PETER (*Laughing*): No, I'm not angry.

JERRY (*Relieved*): Good. (*Now back to his previous tone*) Interesting that you asked me about the picture frames. I would have thought that you would have asked me about the pornographic playing cards.

PETER (*With a knowing smile*): Oh, I've seen those cards.

JERRY: That's not the point. (*Laughs*) I suppose when you were a kid you and your pals passed them around, or you had a pack of your own.

PETER: Well, I guess a lot of us did.

JERRY: And you threw them away just before you got married.

PETER: Oh, now; look here. I didn't *need* anything like that when I got older.

JERRY: No?

PETER (*Embarrassed*): I'd rather not talk about these things.

JERRY: So? Don't. Besides, I wasn't trying to plumb your post-adolescent sexual life and hard times; what I wanted to get at is the value difference between pornographic playing cards when you're a kid, and pornographic playing cards when you're older. It's that when you're a kid you use the cards as a substitute for a real experience, and when you're older you use real experience as a substitute for the fantasy. But I imagine you'd rather hear about what happened at the zoo.

PETER (*Enthusiastic*): Oh, yes; the zoo. (*Then, awkward*) That is . . . if you. . . .

JERRY: Let me tell you about why I went . . . well, let me tell you some things. I've told you about the fourth floor of the roominghouse where I live. I think the rooms are better as you go down, floor by floor. I guess they are; I don't know. I don't know any of the people on the third and second floors. Oh, wait! I do know that there's a lady living on the third floor, in the front. I know because she cries all the time. Whenever I go out or come back in, whenever I pass her door, I always hear her crying, muffled, but . . . very determined. Very determined indeed. But the one I'm getting to, and all about the dog, is the landlady. I don't like to use words that are too harsh in describing people. I don't like to. But the landlady is a fat, ugly, mean, stupid, unwashed, misanthropic, cheap, drunken bag of garbage. And you may have noticed that I very seldom use profanity, so I can't describe her as well as I might.

PETER: You describe her . . . vividly.

JERRY: Well, thanks. Anyway, she has a dog, and I will tell you about the dog, and she and her dog are the gatekeepers of my dwelling. The woman is bad enough; she leans around in the entrance hall, spying to see that I don't bring in things or people, and when she's had her mid-afternoon pint of lemon-flavored gin she always stops me in the hall, and grabs ahold of my coat or my arm, and presses her disgusting body up against me to keep me in a corner so she can talk to me. The smell of her body and her breath . . . you can't imagine it . . . and somewhere, somewhere in the back of that pea-sized brain of hers, an organ developed just enough to let her eat, drink, and emit, she has some foul parody of sexual desire. And I, Peter, I am the object of her sweaty lust.

PETER: That's disgusting. That's . . . horrible.

JERRY: But I have found a way to keep her off. When she talks to me, when she presses herself to my body and mumbles about her room and how I should come there, I merely say: but, Love; wasn't yesterday enough for you, and the day before? Then she puzzles, she makes slits of her tiny eyes, she sways a little, and then, Peter . . . and it is at this moment that I think I might be doing some good in that tormented house . . . a simple-minded smile begins to form on her unthinkable face, and she giggles and groans as she thinks about yesterday and the day before; as she believes and relives what never happened. Then, she motions to that black monster of a dog she has, and she goes back to her room. And I am safe until our next meeting.

PETER: It's so . . . unthinkable. I find it hard to believe that people such as that really *are.*

JERRY (*Lightly mocking*): It's for reading about, isn't it?

PETER (*Seriously*): Yes.

JERRY: And fact is better left to fiction. You're right, Peter. Well, what I have been meaning to tell you about is the dog; I shall, now.

PETER (*Nervously*): Oh, yes; the dog.

JERRY: Don't go. You're not thinking of going, are you?

PETER: Well . . . no, I don't think so.

JERRY (*As if to a child*): Because after I tell you about the dog, do you know what then? Then . . . then I'll tell you about what happened at the zoo.

PETER (*Laughing faintly*): You're . . . you're full of stories, aren't you?

JERRY: You don't *have* to listen. Nobody is holding you here; remember that. Keep that in your mind.

PETER (*Irritably*): I know that.

JERRY: You do? Good.

(*The following long speech, it seems to me, should be done with a great deal of action, to achieve a hypnotic effect on* PETER, *and on the audience, too. Some specific actions have been suggested, but the director and the actor playing* JERRY *might best work it out for themselves*)

ALL RIGHT. (*As if reading from a huge billboard*) THE STORY OF JERRY AND THE DOG! (*Natural again*) What I am going to tell you has something to do with how sometimes it's necessary to go a long distance out of the way in order to come back a short distance correctly; or, maybe I only think that it has something to do with that. But, it's why I went to the zoo today, and why I walked north . . . northerly, rather . . . until I came here. All right. The dog, I think I told you, is a black monster of a beast: an oversized head, tiny, tiny ears, and eyes . . . bloodshot, infected, maybe; and a body you can see the ribs through the skin. The dog is black, all black; all black except for the blood-shot eyes, and . . . yes . . . and an open sore on its . . . *right* forepaw; that is red, too. And, oh yes; the poor monster, and I do believe it's an old dog . . .

it's certainly a misused one . . . almost always has an erection . . . of sorts. That's red, too. And . . . what else? . . . oh, yes; there's a gray-yellow-white color, too, when he bares his fangs. Like this: Grrrrrr! Which is what he did when he saw me for the first time . . . the day I moved in. I worried about that animal the very first minute I met him. Now, animals don't take to me like Saint Francis had birds hanging off him all the time. What I mean is: animals are indifferent to me . . . like people (*He smiles slightly*) . . . most of the time. But this dog wasn't indifferent. From the very beginning he'd snarl and then go for me, to get one of my legs. Not like he was rabid, you know; he was sort of a stumbly dog, but he wasn't half-assed, either. It was a good, stumbly run; but I always got away. He got a piece of my trouser leg, look, you can see right here, where it's mended; he got that the second day I lived there; but, I kicked free and got upstairs fast, so that was that. (*Puzzles*) I still don't know to this day how the other roomers manage it, but you know what I *think:* I think it had to do only with me. Cozy. So. Anyway, this went on for over a week, whenever I came in; but never when I went out. That's funny. Or, it *was* funny. I could pack up and live in the street for all the dog cared. Well, I thought about it up in my room one day, one of the times after I'd bolted upstairs, and I made up my mind. I decided: First, I'll kill the dog with kindness, and if that doesn't work . . . I'll just kill him. (PETER *winces*) Don't react, Peter; just listen. So, the next day I went out and bought a bag of hamburgers, medium rare, no catsup, no onion; and on the way home I threw away all the rolls and kept just the meat.

(*Action for the following, perhaps*)

When I got back to the roominghouse the dog was waiting for me. I half opened the door that led into the entrance hall, and there he was; waiting for me. It figured. I went in, very cautiously, and I had the hamburgers, you remember; I opened the bag, and I set the meat down about twelve feet from where the dog was snarling at me. Like so! He snarled; stopped snarling; sniffed; moved slowly; then faster; then faster toward the meat. Well, when he got to it he stopped, and he looked at me. I smiled; but tentatively, you understand. He turned his face back to the hamburgers, smelled, sniffed some more, and then . . . RRRAAAAGGGGGHHHH, like that . . . he tore into them. It was as if he had never eaten anything in his life before, except like garbage. Which might very well have been the truth. I don't think the landlady ever eats anything but garbage. But. He ate all the hamburgers, almost all at once, making sounds in his throat like a woman. *Then,* when he'd finished the meat, the hamburger, and tried to eat the paper, too, he sat down and smiled. I think he smiled; I know cats do. It was a very gratifying few moments. Then, BAM, he snarled and made for me again. He didn't get me this time, either. So, I got upstairs, and I lay down on my bed and started to think about the dog again. To be truthful, I was offended, and I was damn mad, too. It was six perfectly good hamburgers with not enough pork in them to make it disgusting. I was offended. But, after a while, I decided to try it for a few more days. If you think about it, this dog had what amounted to an antipathy toward me; really. And, I wondered if I mightn't overcome this antipathy. So, I tried it for five more days, but it was always the same: snarl; sniff; move; faster; stare; gobble; RAAGGGHHH; smile; snarl; BAM. Well, now; by this time Columbus Avenue was strewn with hamburger rolls and I was less offended than disgusted. So, I decided to kill the dog.

(PETER *raises a hand in protest*)

Oh, don't be so alarmed, Peter; I didn't succeed. The day I tried to kill the dog I bought only one hamburger and what I thought was a murderous portion of rat poison. When I bought the hamburger I asked the man not to bother with the roll, all I wanted was the meat. I expected some reaction from him, like: we don't sell no hamburgers without rolls; or, wha' d'ya wanna do, eat it out'a ya han's? But no; he smiled benignly, wrapped up the hamburger in waxed paper, and said: A bite for ya pussy-cat? I wanted to say: No, not really; it's part of a plan to poison a dog I know. But, you can't say "a dog I know" without sounding funny; so I said, a little too loud, I'm afraid, and too formally: YES, A BITE FOR MY PUSSY-CAT. People looked up. It always happens when I try to simplify things; people look up. But that's neither hither nor thither. So. On my way back to the roominghouse, I kneaded the hamburger and the rat poison together between my hands, at that point feeling as much sadness as disgust. I opened the door to the entrance hall, and there the monster was, waiting to take the offering and then jump me. Poor bastard; he never learned that the moment he took to smile before he went for me gave me time enough to get out of range. BUT, there he was; malevolence with an erection, waiting. I put the poison patty down, moved toward the stairs and watched. The poor animal gobbled the food down as usual, smiled, which made me almost sick, and then, BAM. But, I sprinted up the stairs, as usual, and the dog didn't get me, as usual. AND IT CAME TO PASS THAT THE BEAST WAS DEATHLY ILL. I knew this because he no longer attended me, and because the landlady sobered up. She stopped me in the hall the same evening of the attempted murder and confided the information that God had struck her puppy-dog a surely fatal blow. She had

forgotten her bewildered lust, and her eyes were wide open for the first time. They looked like the dog's eyes. She sniveled and implored me to pray for the animal. I wanted to say to her: Madam, I have myself to pray for, the colored queen, the Puerto Rican family, the person in the front room whom I've never seen, the woman who cries deliberately behind her closed door, and the rest of the people in all roominghouses, everywhere; besides, Madam, I don't understand how to pray. But . . . to simplify things . . . I told her I would pray. She looked up. She said that I was a liar, and that I probably wanted the dog to die. I told her, and there was so much truth here, that I didn't want the dog to die. I didn't, and not just because I'd poisoned him. I'm afraid that I must tell you I wanted the dog to live so that I could see what our new relationship might come to.

(PETER *indicates his increasing displeasure and slowly growing antagonism*)

Please understand, Peter; that sort of thing is important. You must believe me; it *is* important. We have to know the effect of our actions. (*Another deep sigh*) Well, anyway; the dog recovered. I have no idea why, unless he was a descendant of the puppy that guarded the gates of hell° or some such resort. I'm not up on my mythology. (*He pronounces the word myth-o-logy*) Are you?

(PETER *sets to thinking, but* JERRY *goes on*)

At any rate, and you've missed the eight-thousand-dollar question, Peter; at any rate, the dog recovered his health and the landlady recovered her thirst, in no way altered by the bow-wow's deliverance. When I came home from a movie that was playing on Forty-second Street, a movie I'd seen, or one that was very much like one or several I'd seen, after the landlady told me puppykins was better, I was so hoping for the dog to be waiting for me. I was . . . well, how would you put it . . . enticed? . . . fascinated? . . . no, I don't think so . . . heart-shatteringly anxious, that's it; I was heart-shatteringly anxious to confront my friend again.

(PETER *reacts scoffingly*)

Yes, Peter; friend. That's the only word for it. I was heart-shatteringly et cetera to confront my doggy friend again. I came in the door and advanced, unafraid, to the center of the entrance hall. The beast was there . . . looking at me. And, you know, he looked better for his scrape with the nevermind. I stopped; I looked at him; he looked at me. I think

---

puppy that guarded the gates of hell, Cerberus, a fierce, three-headed dog.

. . . I think we stayed a long time that way . . . still, stone-statue . . . just looking at one another. I looked more into his face than he looked into mine. I mean, I can concentrate longer at looking into a dog's face than a dog can concentrate at looking into mine, or into anybody else's face, for that matter. But during that twenty seconds or two hours that we looked into each other's face, we made contact. Now, here is what I had wanted to happen: I loved the dog now, and I wanted him to love me. I had tried to love, and I had tried to kill, and both had been unsuccessful by themselves. I hoped . . . and I don't really know why I expected the dog to understand anything, much less my motivations . . . I hoped that the dog would understand.

(PETER *seems to be hypnotized*)

It's just . . . it's just that . . . (JERRY *is abnormally tense, now*) . . . it's just that if you can't deal with people, you have to make a start somewhere. WITH ANIMALS! (*Much faster now, and like a conspirator*) Don't you see? A person has to have some way of dealing with SOMETHING. If not with people . . . if not with people . . . SOMETHING. With a bed, with a cockroach, with a mirror . . . no, that's too hard, that's one of the last steps. With a cockroach, with a . . . with a . . . with a carpet, a roll of toilet paper . . . no, not that, either . . . that's a mirror, too; always check bleeding. You see how hard it is to find things? With a street corner, and too many lights, all colors reflecting on the oily-wet streets . . . with a wisp of smoke, a wisp . . . of smoke . . . with . . . with pornographic playing cards, with a strongbox . . . WITHOUT A LOCK . . . with love, with vomiting, with crying, with fury because the pretty little ladies aren't pretty little ladies, with making money with your body which is an act of love and I could prove it, with howling because you're alive; with God. How about that? WITH GOD WHO IS A COLORED QUEEN WHO WEARS A KIMONO AND PLUCKS HIS EYEBROWS, WHO IS A WOMAN WHO CRIES WITH DETERMINATION BEHIND HER CLOSED DOOR . . . with God who, I'm told, turned his back on the whole thing some time ago . . . with . . . some day, with people. (JERRY *sighs the next word heavily*) People. With an idea; a concept. And where better, where ever better in this humiliating excuse for a jail, where better to communicate one single, simple-minded idea than in an entrance hall? Where? It would be A START! Where better to make a beginning . . . to understand and just possibly be understood . . . a beginning of an understanding, than with . . .

(Here JERRY *seems to fall into almost grotesque fatigue*)

. . . than with A DOG. Just that; a dog.

(*Here there is a silence that might be prolonged for a moment or so; then* JERRY *wearily finishes his story*)

A dog. It seemed like a perfectly sensible idea. Man is a dog's best friend, remember. So: the dog and I looked at each other. I longer than the dog. And what I saw then has been the same ever since. Whenever the dog and I see each other we both stop where we are. We regard each other with a mixture of sadness and suspicion, and then we feign indifference. We walk past each other safely; we have an understanding. It's very sad, but you'll have to admit that it is an understanding. We had made many attempts at contact, and we had failed. The dog has returned to garbage, and I to solitary but free passage. I have not returned. I mean to say, I have *gained* solitary free passage, if that much further loss can be said to be gain. I have learned that neither kindness nor cruelty by themselves, independent of each other, creates any effect beyond themselves; and I have learned that the two combined, together, at the same time, are the teaching emotion. And what is gained is loss. And what has been the result: the dog and I have attained a compromise; more of a bargain, really. We neither love nor hurt because we do not try to reach each other. And, *was* trying to feed the dog an act of love? And, perhaps, was the dog's attempt to bite me *not* an act of love? If we can so misunderstand, well then, why have we invented the word love in the first place?

(*There is silence.* JERRY *moves to* PETER's *bench and sits down beside him. This is the first time* JERRY *has sat down during the play*)

The Story of Jerry and the Dog: the end.

(PETER *is silent*)

Well, Peter? (JERRY *is suddenly cheerful*) Well, Peter? Do you think I could sell that story to the *Reader's Digest* and make a couple of hundred bucks for *The Most Unforgettable Character I've Ever Met*? Huh?

(JERRY *is animated, but* PETER *is disturbed*)

Oh, come on now, Peter; tell me what you think.
PETER (*Numb*): I . . . I don't understand what . . . I don't think I . . . (*Now, almost tearfully*) Why did you tell me all of this?
JERRY: Why not?
PETER: I DON'T UNDERSTAND!
JERRY (*Furious, but whispering*): That's a lie.
PETER: No. No, it's not.
JERRY (*Quietly*): I tried to explain it to you as I went along. I went slowly; it all has to do with . . .
PETER: I DON'T WANT TO HEAR ANY MORE. I don't understand you, or your landlady, or her dog . . .
JERRY: *Her* dog! I thought it was my . . . No. No, you're

right. It *is* her dog. (*Looks at* PETER *intently, shaking his head*) I don't know what I was thinking about; of course you don't understand. (*In a monotone, wearily*) I don't live in your block; I'm not married to two parakeets, or whatever your setup is. I am a *permanent transient,* and my home is the sickening roominghouses on the West Side of New York City, which is the greatest city in the world. Amen.

PETER: I'm . . . I'm sorry; I didn't mean to . . .

JERRY: Forget it. I suppose you don't quite know what to make of me, eh?

PETER (*A joke*): We get all kinds in publishing. (*Chuckles*)

JERRY: You're a funny man. (*He forces a laugh*) You know that? You're a very . . . a richly comic person.

PETER (*Modestly, but amused*): Oh, now, not really. (*Still chuckling*)

JERRY: Peter, do I annoy you, or confuse you?

PETER (*Lightly*): Well, I must confess that this wasn't the kind of afternoon I'd anticipated.

JERRY: You mean, I'm not the gentleman you were expecting.

PETER: I wasn't expecting anybody.

JERRY: No, I don't imagine you were. But I'm here, and I'm not leaving.

PETER (*Consulting his watch*): Well, you may not be, but I must be getting home soon.

JERRY: Oh, come on; stay a while longer.

PETER: I really should get home; you see . . .

JERRY (*Tickles* PETER's *ribs with his fingers*): Oh, come on.

PETER (*He is very ticklish; as* JERRY *continues to tickle him his voice becomes falsetto*): No, I . . . OHHHHH! Don't do that. Stop, Stop. Ohhh, no, no.

JERRY: Oh, come on.

PETER (*As* JERRY *tickles*): Oh, hee, hee, hee. I must go. I . . . hee, hee, hee. After all, stop, stop, hee, hee, hee, after all, the parakeets will be getting dinner ready soon. Hee, hee. And the cats are setting the table. Stop, stop, and, and . . . (PETER *is beside himself now*) . . . and we're having . . . hee, hee . . . uh . . . ho, ho, ho.

(JERRY *stops tickling* PETER, *but the combination of the tickling and his own mad whimsy has* PETER *laughing almost hysterically. As his laughter continues, then subsides,* JERRY *watches him, with a curious fixed smile*)

JERRY: Peter?

PETER: Oh, ha, ha, ha, ha, ha. What? What?

JERRY: Listen, now.

PETER: Oh, ho, ho. What . . . what is it, Jerry? Oh, my.

JERRY (*Mysteriously*): Peter, do you want to know what happened at the zoo?

PETER: Ah, ha, ha. The what? Oh, yes; the zoo. Oh, ho, ho. Well, I had my own zoo there for a moment with . . . hee, hee, the parakeets getting dinner ready, and the . . . ha, ha, whatever it was, the . . .

JERRY (*Calmly*): Yes, that was very funny, Peter. I wouldn't have expected it. But do you want to hear about what happened at the zoo, or not?

PETER: Yes. Yes, by all means; tell me what happened at the zoo. Oh, my. I don't know what happened to me.

JERRY: Now I'll let you in on what happened at the zoo; but first, I should tell you why I went to the zoo. I went to the zoo to find out more about the way people exist with animals, and the way animals exist with each other, and with people too. It probably wasn't a fair test, what with everyone separated by bars from everyone else, the animals for the most part from each other, and always the people from the animals. But, if it's a zoo, that's the way it is. (*He pokes* PETER *on the arm*) Move over.

PETER (*Friendly*): I'm sorry, haven't you enough room? (*He shifts a little*)

JERRY (*Smiling slightly*): Well, all the animals are there, and all the people are there, and it's Sunday and all the children are there. (*He pokes* PETER *again*) Move over.

PETER (*Patiently, still friendly*): All right.

(*He moves some more, and* JERRY *has all the room he might need*)

JERRY: And it's a hot day, so all the stench is there, too, and all the balloon sellers, and all the ice cream sellers, and all the seals are barking, and all the birds are screaming. (*Pokes* PETER *harder*) Move over!

PETER (*Beginning to be annoyed*): Look here, you have more than enough room! (*But he moves more, and is now fairly cramped at one end of the bench*)

JERRY: And I am there, and it's feeding time at the lions' house, and the lion keeper comes into the lion cage, one of the lion cages, to feed one of the lions. (*Punches* PETER *on the arm, hard*) MOVE OVER!

PETER (*Very annoyed*): I can't move over any more, and stop hitting me. What's the matter with you?

JERRY: Do you want to hear the story? (*Punches* PETER's *arm again*)

PETER (*Flabbergasted*): I'm not so sure! I certainly don't want to be punched in the arm.

JERRY (*Punches* PETER's *arm again*): Like that?

PETER: Stop it! What's the matter with you?

JERRY: I'm crazy, you bastard.

PETER: That isn't funny.

JERRY: Listen to me, Peter. I want this bench. You go sit on the bench over there, and if you're good I'll tell you the rest of the story.

PETER (*Flustered*): But . . . whatever for? What *is* the matter with you? Besides, I see no reason why I should give up this bench. I sit on this bench almost every Sunday afternoon, in good weather. It's secluded here; there's never anyone sitting here, so I have it all to myself.

JERRY (*Softly*): Get off this bench, Peter; I want it.

PETER (*Almost whining*): No.

JERRY: I said I want this bench, and I'm going to have it. Now get over there.

PETER: People can't have everything they want. You should know that; it's a rule; people can have some of the things they want, but they can't have everything.

JERRY (*Laughs*): Imbecile! You're slow-witted!

PETER: Stop that!

JERRY: You're a vegetable! Go lie down on the ground.

PETER (*Intense*): Now *you* listen to me. I've put up with you all afternoon.

JERRY: Not really.

PETER: LONG ENOUGH. I've put up with you long enough. I've listened to you because you seemed . . . well, because I thought you wanted to talk to somebody.

JERRY: You put things well; economically, and, yet . . . oh, what is the word I want to put justice to your . . . JESUS, you make me sick . . . get off here and give me my bench.

PETER: MY BENCH!

JERRY (*Pushes* PETER *almost, but not quite, off the bench*): Get out of my sight.

PETER (*Regaining his position*): God da . . . mn you. That's enough! I've had enough of you. I will not give up this bench; you can't have it, and that's that. Now, go away.

(JERRY *snorts but does not move*)

Go away, I said.

(JERRY *does not move*)

Get away from here. If you don't move on . . . you're a bum . . . that's what you are. . . . If you don't move on, I'll get a policeman here and make you go.

(JERRY *laughs, stays*)

I warn you, I'll call a policeman.

JERRY (*Softly*): You won't find a policeman around here; they're all over on the west side of the park chasing fairies down from trees or out of the bushes. That's all they do. That's their function. So scream your head off; it won't do you any good.

PETER: POLICE! I warn you, I'll have you arrested. POLICE! (*Pause*) I said POLICE! (*Pause*) I feel ridiculous.

JERRY: You look ridiculous: a grown man screaming for the police on a bright Sunday afternoon in the park with nobody harming you. If a policeman *did* fill his quota and come sludging over this way he'd probably take you in as a nut.

PETER (*With disgust and impotence*): Great God, I just came here to read, and now you want me to give up the bench. You're mad.

JERRY: Hey, I got news for you, as they say. I'm on your precious bench, and you're never going to have it for yourself again.

PETER (*Furious*): Look, you; get off my bench. I don't care if it makes any sense or not. I want this bench to myself; I want you OFF IT!

JERRY (*Mocking*): Aw . . . look who's mad.

PETER: GET OUT!

JERRY: No.

PETER: I WARN YOU!

JERRY: Do you know how ridiculous you look *now*?

PETER (*His fury and self-consciousness have possessed him*): It doesn't matter. (*He is almost crying*) GET AWAY FROM MY BENCH!

JERRY: Why? You have everything in the world you want; you've told me about your home, and your family, and *your own* little zoo. You have everything, and now you want this bench. Are these the things men fight for? Tell me, Peter, is this bench, this iron and this wood, is this your honor? Is this the thing in the world you'd fight for? Can you think of anything more absurd?

PETER: Absurd? Look, I'm not going to talk to you about honor, or even try to explain it to you. Besides, it isn't a question of honor; but even if it were, you wouldn't understand.

JERRY (*Contemptuously*): You don't even know what you're saying, do you? This is probably the first time in your life you've had anything more trying to face than changing your cats' toilet box. Stupid! Don't you have any idea, not even the slightest, what other people *need*?

PETER: Oh, boy, listen to you; well, you don't need this bench. That's for sure.

JERRY: Yes; yes, I do.

PETER (*Quivering*): I've come here for years; I have hours of great pleasure, great satisfaction, right here. And that's important to a man. I'm a responsible person, and I'm a GROWNUP. This is my bench, and you have no right to take it away from me.

JERRY: Fight for it, then. Defend yourself; defend your bench.

PETER: You've *pushed* me to it. Get up and fight.

JERRY: Like a man?

PETER (*Still angry*): Yes, like a man, if you insist on mocking me even further.

JERRY: I'll have to give you credit for one thing: you *are* a vegetable, and a slightly nearsighted one, I think . . .

PETER: THAT'S ENOUGH. . . .

JERRY: . . . but, you know, as they say on TV all the time—you know—and I mean this, Peter, you have a certain dignity; it surprises me. . . .

PETER: STOP!

JERRY (*Rises lazily*): Very well, Peter, we'll battle for the bench, but we're not evenly matched.

(*He takes out and clicks open an ugly-looking knife*)

PETER (*Suddenly awaking to the reality of the situation*): You *are* mad! You're stark raving mad! YOU'RE GOING TO KILL ME!

(*But before* PETER *has time to think what to do*, JERRY *tosses the knife at* PETER's *feet*)

JERRY: There you go. Pick it up. You have the knife and we'll be more evenly matched.

PETER (*Horrified*): No!

JERRY (*Rushes over to* PETER, *grabs him by the collar;* PETER *rises; their faces almost touch*): Now you pick up that knife and you fight with me. You fight for your self-respect; you fight for that goddamned bench.

PETER (*Struggling*): No! Let . . . let go of me! He . . . Help!

JERRY (*Slaps* PETER *on each* "*fight*"): You fight, you miserable bastard; fight for that bench; fight for your parakeets; fight for your cats, fight for your two daughters; fight for your wife; fight for your manhood, you pathetic little vegetable. (*Spits in* PETER*'s face*) You couldn't even get your wife with a male child.

PETER (*Breaks away, enraged*): It's a matter of genetics, not manhood, you . . . you monster.

(*He darts down, picks up the knife and backs off a little; he is breathing heavily*)

I'll give you one last chance; get out of here and leave me alone!

(*He holds the knife with a firm arm, but far in front of him, not to attack, but to defend*)

JERRY (*Sighs heavily*): So be it!

(*With a rush he charges* PETER *and impales himself on the knife. Tableau: For just a moment, complete silence,* JERRY *impaled on the knife at the end of* PETER*'s still firm arm. Then* PETER *screams, pulls away, leaving the knife in* JERRY. JERRY *is motionless, on point. Then he, too, screams, and it must be the sound of an infuriated and fatally wounded animal. With the knife in him, he stumbles back to the bench that* PETER *had vacated. He crumbles there, sitting, facing* PETER, *his eyes wide in agony, his mouth open*)

PETER (*Whispering*): Oh my God, oh my God, oh my God . . .

(*He repeats these words many times, very rapidly*)

JERRY (JERRY *is dying; but now his expression seems to change. His features relax, and while his voice varies, sometimes wrenched with pain, for the most part he seems removed from his dying. He smiles*): Thank you, Peter. I mean that, now; thank you very much.

(PETER*'s mouth drops open. He cannot move; he is transfixed*)

Oh, Peter, I was so afraid I'd drive you away. (*He laughs as best he can*) You don't know how afraid I was you'd go away and leave me. And now I'll tell you what happened at the zoo. I think . . . I think this is what happened at the zoo . . . I think. I think that while I was at the zoo I decided that I would walk north . . . northerly, rather . . . until I found

you . . . or somebody . . . and I decided that I would talk to you . . . I would tell you things . . . and things that I would tell you would . . . Well, here we are. You see? Here we *are*. But . . . I don't know . . . could I have planned all this? No . . . no, I couldn't have. But I think I did. And now I've told you what you wanted to know, haven't I? And now you know all about what happened at the zoo. And now you know what you'll see in your TV, and the face I told you about . . . you remember . . . the face I told you about . . . my face, the face you see right now. Peter . . . Peter? . . . Peter . . . thank you. I came unto you (*He laughs, so faintly*) and you have comforted me. Dear Peter.

PETER (*Almost fainting*): Oh my God!

JERRY: You'd better go now. Somebody might come by, and you don't want to be here when anyone comes.

PETER (*Does not move, but begins to weep*): Oh my God, oh my God.

JERRY (*Most faintly, now; he is very near death*): You won't be coming back here any more, Peter; you've been dispossessed. You've lost your bench, but you've defended your honor. And Peter, I'll tell you something now; you're not really a vegetable; it's all right, you're an animal. You're an animal, too. But you'd better hurry now, Peter. Hurry, you'd better go . . . see?

(JERRY *takes a handkerchief and with great effort and pain wipes the knife handle clean of fingerprints*)

Hurry away, Peter.

(PETER *begins to stagger away*)

Wait . . . wait, Peter. Take your book . . . book. Right here . . . beside me . . . on your bench . . . my bench, rather. Come . . . take your book.

(PETER *starts for the book, but retreats*)

Hurry . . . Peter.

(PETER *rushes to the bench, grabs the book, retreats*)

Very good, Peter . . . very good. Now . . . hurry away.

(PETER *hesitates for a moment, then flees, stage-left*)

Hurry away. . . . (*His eyes are closed now*) Hurry away, your parakeets are making the dinner . . . the cats . . . are setting the table . . .

PETER (*Off stage*): (*A pitiful howl*) OH MY GOD!

JERRY (*His eyes still closed, he shakes his head and speaks; a combination of scornful mimicry and supplication*): Oh . . . my . . . God.

(*He is dead*)

CURTAIN

Figure 1. Jerry (Mark Richman, who took over the role from George Maharis) questions a wary and reserved Peter (William Daniels) in the Provincetown Playhouse production of *The Zoo Story*, directed by Milton Katselas. (Photograph: Billy Rose Theatre Collection. The New York Public Library for the Performing Arts. Astor, Lenox, and Tilden Foundations.)

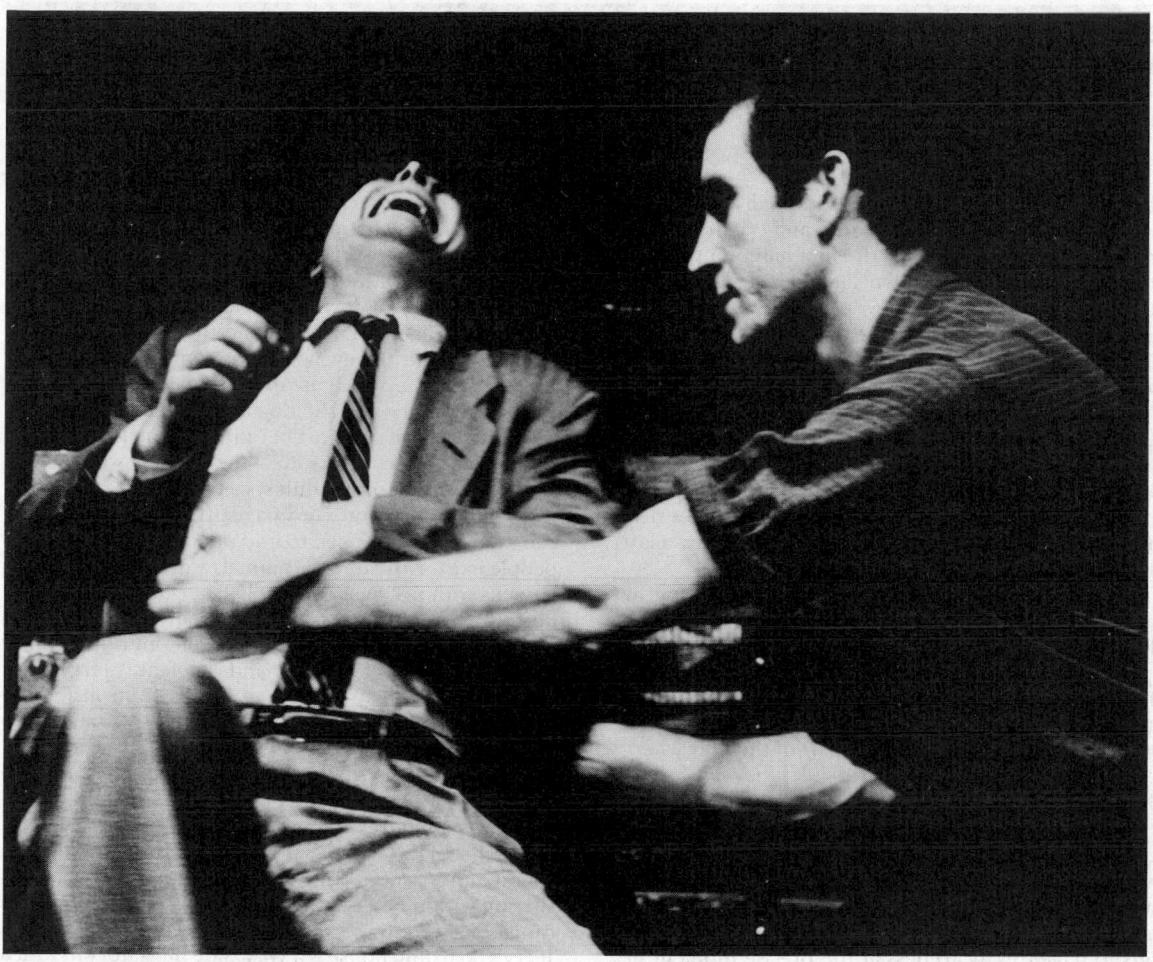

Figure 2. Peter (William Daniels) responds with hysterical laughter as Jerry (Mark Richman) calmly tickles him in the Provincetown Playhouse production of *The Zoo Story*, directed by Milton Katselas. (Photograph: Billy Rose Theatre Collection. The New York Public Library for the Performing Arts. Astor, Lenox, and Tilden Foundations.)

Staging of *The Zoo Story*

REVIEW OF THE PROVINCETOWN PLAYHOUSE
PRODUCTION, 1960, BY HENRY HEWES

Last week these columns were devoted mainly to a discussion of Samuel Beckett's rich and poetic playlet, *Krapp's Last Tape*. This play is the first half of a twin bill currently at the Provincetown Playhouse. The second play there, titled *The Zoo Story*, is equally exciting, not only because it is compelling theatre, but also because it introduces Edward Albee, a young (circa thirty) playwright of considerable potentiality.

Mr. Albee's play is quite simple in form. A dull, respectable man with that upper-middle-middle expression on his face is reading on a park bench when an obnoxious stranger approaches him with irritating personal questions and remarks. The stranger has a desperate need to make contact with someone, and as a last resort pushes his listener to violence.

The details of these events are made fascinating by the actors George Maharis and William Daniels. To the role of Jerry, the beatnik, Mr. Maharis brings a quietly hypnotic rhythm that comes across as theatrically colorful yet integrated with his own personality. And as Peter, the square, Mr. Daniels provides a genuine humor. He is at his best in the early part of the play where the tone *is* humorous, as Jerry ridicules the clichés he is able to smoke out of Peter's Madison Avenue existence. Of course, this ridicule has itself become a cliché, and if unimaginatively played would seem merely tired and predictable satire. But director Milton Katselas has permitted each actor an awareness of the situation and of what the dialogue means to one who speaks it. Jerry tends to have this awareness at the precise moment he speaks. And Peter has it a second or two after he has said his line. Even an ordinary interchange (JERRY: "Well, *Time* magazine isn't for blockheads." PETER: "No, I suppose not.") becomes subtly hilarious when given this particular treatment. And it is not just funny, for as he considers each random question, Peter becomes more and more aware of inadequacies not really faced before.

Jerry, on the other hand, seems compelled by an inner, not quite understood drive, an unwillingness to stop short of scraping out the last layer of truth. And even when he is using such colorful language as "But that was the jazz of a very special hotel," it is not done for effect, but rather because that is the best way he knows to express his nostalgia without oversentimentalization. The high point of his performance is reached when he tells "The Story of Jerry and the Dog." In the parable Jerry attempts first kindness and then cruelty to a dog that tries to bite him every time he comes into his boarding house. The result is an eventual compromise in which both Jerry and the dog arrive at a state in which they neither love nor hurt because they no longer try to reach each other. This state—the basis of so many relationships in modern adult society—is what has driven Jerry into his present pilgrimage up Fifth Avenue to the zoo where he had hoped to find out more about the way people exist with animals, animals with each other, and animals with people. As he tells Peter the story of what he saw at the zoo, Jerry attempts, through cruelty, to provoke some animal feeling in Peter, and though the ending is melodramatic and violent, Jerry—like Christ—succeeds at the cost of his life in arousing the human soul out of its deep modern lethargy to an awareness of its animal self.

The Zoo Story is done so well that we can afford to point out that Mr. Katselas might have made this production even more effective if he had been able to highlight some of the author's points more distinctly and had found a more interesting way of expressing the animal stirring within Peter at the play's melodramatic end. We can also afford to wonder if Mr. Albee's suggestion that Jerry's boarding house is a West Side purgatory in which God is a queen who plucks his eyebrows and goes to the john is not one that needs the fuller development he might give it in a longer play. And doesn't his description of Jerry's deceased mother ("She embarked on an adulterous turn of our Southern states . . . and her most constant companion among others, among many others, was a Mr. Barleycorn") owe something to Tennessee Williams? No matter. Mr. Albee has written an extraordinary first play, which, next to Jack Gelber's *The Connection*, constitutes the finest new achievement in the theatre this season. Thank God for Off-Broadway, and, I guess, thank God for beatniks.

IMAMU AMIRI BARAKA

1934–

Between March and December 1964, Baraka, who was then still writing under his original name of LeRoi Jones, had four one-act plays produced off-Broadway, one of which, *Dutchman*, won the Obie award for the best off-Broadway play of 1963–64. That production record would be considered astonishing for any playwright, particularly for a young African-American who until then was known only as a writer of essays and poems. Baraka was born in Newark, New Jersey, where he attended public school and then began college at Rutgers University, later transferring to Howard University, one of America's historically black colleges. Subsequently, he served in the United States Air Force, from 1954 to 1957, and then settled in New York City where, with Hettie Cohen, whom he married in 1958, he edited a literary magazine, publishing avant-garde writers such as William Burroughs, Gregory Corso, Allen Ginsburg, Jack Kerouac, Charles Olson, and himself. His sudden fame after the success of *Dutchman* led him to teaching positions at Columbia University and the New School for Social Research, as well as to the award of a Guggenheim Fellowship in 1965. It was also in 1965 that he changed his name to Imamu Amiri Baraka, roughly translatable as Priest-Warrior-Blessing, and wrote his well-known manifesto, "The Revolutionary Theater." In it he asserted that theater "should force change, it should be change," that it "must EXPOSE! Show up the insides of these humans, look into black skulls. White men will cower before this theater because it hates them." And in his subsequent plays, Baraka followed up on his manifesto, for they are all essentially political in purpose, aimed at stirring African-American audiences to radical action, and thus similar in intent to the "learning plays" that Brecht was writing during the late 1920s and early 1930s.

Although *Dutchman* was written before Baraka became explicitly associated with "revolutionary theater," it is clearly a revolutionary play, particularly when it is seen in the context of the African-American drama that had preceded it. African Americans had written plays during the nineteenth century, yet their works did not achieve prominence until the 1920s with the plays of Garland Anderson, Wallace Thurman, and Willis Richardson. The Federal Theater project of the 1930s gave special encouragement to African-American dramatists and led, in particular, to the plays of Langston Hughes, one of the leading figures of the Harlem Renaissance, whose works include *Mulatto* (1935), *Don't You Want to Be Free* (1936), a long-running historical panorama, and *Emperor of Haiti* (1938). In Chicago, the Federal Theater Unit sponsored the first production of Theodore Ward's *Big White Fog* (1938), a play that shows a family's struggle to attain a new life in the context of urban society through the political movement known as "back-to-Africa." Ward's later play, *Our Lan'* (1941), was even more successful with its depiction of newly freed blacks trying to live on an island off the Georgia coast. At the end of the 1950s, Lorraine Hansberry's *A Raisin in the Sun* (1959) became a major Broadway success by taking up once again the theme of the "new life," this time by showing a protagonist who maintains his individual and racial pride by moving out of the slums and into a white middle-class neighborhood, a neighborhood that had tried to buy him off to keep him from moving in.

All these plays concerned themselves with the social and political problems of African Americans, yet most concentrated almost exclusively on issues within that community, with only a few venturing to deal directly with confrontations between black and white characters. Not until the plays of Baraka did such confrontations become insistently—and violently—central. In *The Slave* (1964), Baraka shows a black leader, Walker Vessels, engaged in a long argument with two white liberals, Grace and Bradford Easley, about their conflicting ideologies. In *The Toilet* (1964), a group of African-American boys beat up a white boy, a Puerto Rican, who has sent a "love letter" to the leader of their group. And in *Dutchman*, Baraka dramatizes the ultimate confrontation in a sexual encounter between a black man and a white woman, a confrontation that leads to a violent conclusion, in which the black man becomes the victim. In *Dutchman*, too, Baraka moved away from the realistic style that had prevailed in earlier African-American plays toward a symbolic style, immediately announced by its title.

This title is meant to evoke the legend of the Flying Dutchman, the man doomed to sail the seas forever until he found a woman who would be faithful to him, and the subway in which the play is set reflects that ceaseless and meaningless voyaging. The title also alludes to the Dutch ships that brought black slaves to North America, and in this context Lula may be seen as a relentless traveler and destroyer, embodying the way that whites have always treated blacks. Baraka himself claimed that the situation rather than the characters was meant to be symbolic, an interpretation stressing the ceaselessness of racial violence. Apart from the title, the play's mythic quality is emphasized by Baraka's stage direction, "The subway heaped in modern myth," by the appearance of Lula eating an apple, by her later remark that "Eating apples is always the first step," and by Clay's name, which echoes Adam's formation "out of the dust of the ground." The interweaving of the realistic and the symbolic can also be seen in the dialogue of the play, which begins essentially with everyday conversation but quickly turns into metaphor, when Lula tells Clay that "You look like death eating a soda cracker." Lula then turns into a mock prophet in her litany at the end of the first scene, and finally a chanter of vicious and obscene litanies, meant to goad Clay into action.

When she does finally arouse him to the violent action and speech audiences yearn for after her relentless taunting, the effect is devastating, for he destroys any myths that whites may have about blacks, ending as he does with an explicit threat about what will happen when blacks are "accepted" by whites:

> They'll murder you, and have very rational explanations. Very much like your own. They'll cut your throats, and drag you out to the edge of your cities, so the flesh can fall away from your bones, in sanitary isolation.

But instead of the physical assault that might be expected from Clay after this speech, Baraka creates an even more frightening conclusion in Lula's stabbing of him, an act that grotesquely inverts and parodies the sexual act they have been discussing. Her comment, "Get this man off me!" continues the sexual subtext. And when a young African American of twenty next enters the subway car, her act of turning and giving him a long slow look clearly indicates that the destructive cycle will begin again, repeating itself endlessly like the travels of the subway and the flying Dutchman.

When the play was first produced, critics were both impressed and defensive, as revealed in the two reviews reprinted following the text. But they also noted the symbolic significance of the play, as indicated by Harold Clurman's remarks about Lula: "She is our neurosis. Not a neurosis in regard to the Negro, but the absolute neurosis of American society." Jennifer West's performance conveyed that neurosis in her move from demure sexuality (see Figure 1) to uncontrollable aggression. When the play was turned into a film in 1967, critics found it stagey and dull, for the real subway car seemed much less effective as a frame for the play's violence than the make-believe one. On stage, the play still shocks, still continues to explode, precisely because the subway car is only a set while the anger, the cruelty, and the hatred are real.

DUTCHMAN

BY IMAMU AMIRI BARAKA

CHARACTERS

CLAY, *twenty-year-old Negro*
LULA, *thirty-year-old white woman*
RIDERS OF COACH, *white and black*
YOUNG NEGRO
CONDUCTOR

SCENE

In the flying underbelly of the city. Steaming hot, and summer on top, outside. Underground. The subway heaped in modern myth.

Opening scene is a man sitting in a subway seat, holding a magazine but looking vacantly just above its wilting pages. Occasionally he looks blankly toward the window on his right. Dim lights and darkness whistling by against the glass. (Or paste the lights, as admitted props, right on the subway windows. Have them move, even dim and flicker. But give the sense of speed. Also stations, whether the train is stopped or the glitter and activity of these stations merely flashes by the windows.)

The man is sitting alone. That is, only his seat is visible, though the rest of the car is outfitted as a complete subway car. But only his seat is shown. There might be, for a time, as the play begins, a loud scream of the actual train. And it can recur throughout the play, or continue on a lower key once the dialogue starts.

The train slows after a time, pulling to a brief stop at one of the stations. The man looks idly up, until he sees a woman's face staring at him through the window; when it realizes that the man has noticed the face, it begins very premeditatedly to smile. The man smiles too, for a moment, without a trace of self-consciousness. Almost an instinctive though undesirable response. Then a kind of awkwardness or embarrassment sets in, and the man makes to look away, is further embarrassed, so he brings back his eyes to where the face was, but by now the train is moving again, and the face would seem to be left behind by the way the man turns his head to look back through the other windows at the slowly fading platform. He smiles then; more comfortably confident, hoping perhaps that his memory of this brief encounter will be pleasant. And then he is idle again.

SCENE 1

(Train roars. Lights flash outside the windows.

LULA *enters from the rear of the car in bright, skimpy summer clothes and sandals. She carries a net bag full of paper books, fruit, and other anonymous articles. She is wearing sunglasses, which she pushes up on her forehead from time to time.* LULA *is a tall, slender, beautiful woman with long red hair hanging straight down her back, wearing only loud lipstick in somebody's good taste. She is eating an apple, very daintily. Coming down the car toward* CLAY.

She stops beside CLAY'S *seat and hangs languidly from the strap, still managing to eat the apple. It is apparent that she is going to sit in the seat next to* CLAY, *and that she is only waiting for him to notice her before she sits.*

CLAY *sits as before, looking just beyond his magazine, now and again pulling the magazine slowly back and forth in front of his face in a hopeless effort to fan himself. Then he sees the woman hanging there beside him and he looks up into her face, smiling quizzically.)*

LULA: Hello.
CLAY: Uh, hi're you?
LULA: I'm going to sit down. . . . O.K.?
CLAY: Sure.
LULA *(swings down onto the seat, pushing her legs straight out as if she is very weary)*: Oooof! Too much weight.
CLAY: Ha, doesn't look like much to me.

(Leaning back against the window, a little surprised and maybe stiff.)

LULA: It's so anyway.

(And she moves her toes in the sandals, then pulls her right leg up on the left knee, better to inspect the bottoms of the sandals and the back of her heel. She appears for a second not to notice that CLAY *is sitting next to her or that she has spoken to him just a second before.* CLAY *looks at the magazine, then out the black window. As he does this, she turns very quickly toward him.)*

Weren't you staring at me through the window?
CLAY *(wheeling around and very much stiffened)*: What?
LULA: Weren't you staring at me through the window? At the last stop?
CLAY: Staring at you? What do you mean?
LULA: Don't you know what staring means?
CLAY: I saw you through the window . . . if that's what it means. I don't know if I was staring. Seems to me you were staring through the window at me.
LULA: I was. But only after I'd turned around and saw you staring through that window down in the vicinity of my ass and legs.
CLAY: Really?
LULA: Really. I guess you were just taking those idle

potshots. Nothing else to do. Run your mind over people's flesh.

CLAY: Oh boy. Wow, now I admit I was looking in your direction. But the rest of that weight is yours.

LULA: I suppose.

CLAY: Staring through train windows is weird business. Much weirder than staring very sedately at abstract asses.

LULA: That's why I came looking through the window . . . so you'd have more than that to go on. I even smiled at you.

CLAY: That's right.

LULA: I even got into this train, going some other way than mine. Walked down the aisle . . . searching you out.

CLAY: Really? That's pretty funny.

LULA: That's pretty funny. . . . God, you're dull.

CLAY: Well, I'm sorry, lady, but I really wasn't prepared for party talk.

LULA: No, you're not. What are you prepared for?

(Wrapping the apple core in a Kleenex and dropping it on the floor.)

CLAY *(takes her conversation as pure sex talk. He turns to confront her squarely with this idea)*: I'm prepared for anything. How about you?

LULA *(laughing loudly and cutting it off abruptly)*: What do you think you're doing?

CLAY: What?

LULA: You think I want to pick you up, get you to take me somewhere and screw me, huh?

CLAY: Is that the way I look?

LULA: You look like you been trying to grow a beard. That's exactly what you look like. You look like you live in New Jersey with your parents and are trying to grow a beard. That's what. You look like you've been reading Chinese poetry and drinking lukewarm sugarless tea. *(Laughs, uncrossing and recrossing her legs.)* You look like death eating a soda cracker.

CLAY: *(cocking his head from one side to the other, embarrassed and trying to make some comeback, but also intrigued by what the woman is saying . . . even the sharp city coarseness of her voice, which is still a kind of gentle sidewalk throb)*: Really? I look like all that?

LULA: Not all of it.

(She feints a seriousness to cover an actual somber tone.)

I lie a lot. *(Smiling.)* It helps me control the world.

CLAY *(relieved and laughing louder than the humor)*: Yeah, I bet.

LULA: But it's true, most of it, right? Jersey? Your bumpy neck?

CLAY: How'd you know all that? Huh? Really, I mean about Jersey . . . and even the beard. I met you

before? You know Warren Enright?

LULA: You tried to make it with your sister when you were ten. *(CLAY leans back hard against the back of the seat, his eyes opening now, still trying to look amused.)* But I succeeded a few weeks ago. *(She starts to laugh again.)*

CLAY: What're you talking about? Warren tell you that? You're a friend of Georgia's?

LULA: I told you I lie. I don't know your sister. I don't know Warren Enright.

CLAY: You mean you're just picking these things out of the air?

LULA: Is Warren Enright a tall skinny black black boy with a phony English accent?

CLAY: I figured you knew him.

LULA: But I don't. I just figured you would know somebody like that. *(Laughs.)*

CLAY: Yeah, yeah.

LULA: You're probably on your way to his house now.

CLAY: That's right.

LULA *(putting her hand on CLAY's closest knee, drawing it from the knee up to the thigh's hinge, then removing it, watching his face very closely, and continuing to laugh, perhaps more gently than before)*: Dull, dull, dull. I bet you think I'm exciting.

CLAY: You're O.K.

LULA: Am I exciting you now?

CLAY: Right. That's not what's supposed to happen?

LULA: How do I know? *(She returns her hand, without moving it, then takes it away and plunges it in her bag to draw out an apple.)* You want this?

CLAY: Sure.

LULA *(she gets one out of the bag for herself)*: Eating apples together is always the first step. Or walking up uninhabited Seventh Avenue in the twenties on weekends. *(Bites and giggles, glancing at CLAY and speaking in loose sing-song.)* Can get you involved . . . boy! Get us involved. Um-huh. *(Mock seriousness.)* Would you like to get involved with me, Mister Man?

CLAY *(trying to be as flippant as LULA, whacking happily at the apple)*: Sure. Why not? A beautiful woman like you. Huh, I'd be a fool not to.

LULA: And I bet you're sure you know what you're talking about. *(Taking him a little roughly by the wrist, so he cannot eat the apple, then shaking the wrist.)* I bet you're sure of almost everything anybody ever asked you . . . right? *(Shakes his wrist harder.)* Right?

CLAY: Yeah, right. . . . Wow, you're pretty strong, you know? Whatta you, a lady wrestler or something?

LULA: What's wrong with lady wrestlers? And don't answer because you never knew any. Huh. *(Cynically.)* That's for sure. They don't have any lady wrestlers in that part of Jersey. That's for sure.

CLAY: Hey, you still haven't told me how you know so much about me.

LULA: I told you I didn't know anything about *you* . . . you're a well-known type.

CLAY: Really?

LULA: Or at least I know the type very well. And your skinny English friend too.

CLAY: Anonymously?

LULA *(settles back in seat, single-mindedly finishing her apple and humming snatches of rhythm and blues song)*: What?

CLAY: Without knowing us specifically?

LULA: Oh boy. *(Looking quickly at* CLAY.*)* What a face. You know, you could be a handsome man.

CLAY: I can't argue with you.

LULA *(vague, off-center response)*: What?

CLAY *(raising his voice, thinking the train noise has drowned part of his sentence)*: I can't argue with you.

LULA: My hair is turning gray. A gray hair for each year and type I've come through.

CLAY: Why do you want to sound so old?

LULA: But it's always gentle when it starts. *(Attention drifting.)* Hugged against tenements, day or night.

CLAY: What?

LULA *(refocusing)*: Hey, why don't you take me to that party you're going to?

CLAY: You must be a friend of Warren's to know about the party.

LULA: Wouldn't you like to take me to the party? *(Imitates clinging vine.)* Oh, come on, ask me to your party.

CLAY: Of course I'll ask you to come with me to the party. And I'll bet you're a friend of Warren's.

LULA: Why not be a friend of Warren's? Why not? *(Taking his arm.)* Have you asked me yet?

CLAY: How can I ask you when I don't know your name?

LULA: Are you talking to my name?

CLAY: What is it, a secret?

LULA: I'm Lena the Hyena.

CLAY: The famous woman poet?

LULA: Poetess! the same!

CLAY: Well, you know so much about me . . . what's my name?

LULA: Morris the Hyena.

CLAY: The famous woman poet?

LULA: The same. *(Laughing and going into her bag.)* You want another apple?

CLAY: Can't make it, lady. I only have to keep one doctor away a day.

LULA: I bet your name is . . . something like . . . uh, Gerald or Walter. Huh?

CLAY: God, no.

LULA: Lloyd, Norman? One of those hopeless colored names creeping out of New Jersey. Leonard? Gag. . . .

CLAY: Like Warren?

LULA: Definitely. Just exactly like Warren. Or Everett.

CLAY: Gag. . . .

LULA: Well, for sure, it's not Willie.

CLAY: It's Clay.

LULA: Clay? Really? Clay what?

CLAY: Take your pick. Jackson, Johnson, or Williams.

LULA: Oh, really? Good for you. But it's got to be Williams. You're too pretentious to be a Jackson or Johnson.

CLAY: Thass right.

LULA: But Clay's O.K.

CLAY: So's Lena.

LULA: It's Lula.

CLAY: Oh?

LULA: Lula the Hyena.

CLAY: Very good.

LULA *(starts laughing again)*: Now you say to me, "Lula, Lula, why don't you go to this party with me tonight?" It's your turn, and let those be your lines.

CLAY: Lula, why don't you go to this party with me tonight, Huh?

LULA: Say my name twice before you ask, and no huh's.

CLAY: Lula, Lula, why don't you go to this party with me tonight?

LULA: I'd like to go, Clay, but how can you ask me to go when you barely know me?

CLAY: That is strange, isn't it?

LULA: What kind of reaction is that? You're supposed to say, "Aw, come on, we'll get to know each other better at the party."

CLAY: That's pretty corny.

LULA: What are you into anyway? *(Looking at him half sullenly but still amused.)* What thing are you playing at, Mister? Mister Clay Williams? *(Grabs his thigh, up near the crotch.)* What are *you* thinking about?

CLAY: Watch it now, you're gonna excite me for real.

LULA *(taking her hand away and throwing her apple core through the window)*: I bet. *(She slumps in the seat and is heavily silent.)*

CLAY: I thought you knew everything about me? What happened? *(*LULA *looks at him, then looks slowly away, then over where the other aisle would be. Noise of the train. She reaches in her bag and pulls out one of the paper books. She puts it on her leg and thumbs the pages listlessly.* CLAY *cocks his head to see the title of the book. Noise of the train.* LULA *flips pages and her eyes drift. Both remain silent.)* Are you going to the party with me, Lula?

LULA *(bored and not even looking)*: I don't even know you.

CLAY: You said you know my type.

LULA *(strangely irritated)*: Don't get smart with me,

Buster. I know you like the palm of my hand.

CLAY: The one you eat the apples with?

LULA: Yeh. And the one I open doors late Saturday evening with. That's my door. Up at the top of the stairs. Five flights. Above a lot of Italians and lying Americans. And scrape carrots with. Also . . . *(Looks at him.)* the same hand I unbutton my dress with, or let my skirt fall down. Same hand. Lover.

CLAY: Are you angry about something? Did I say something wrong?

LULA: Everything you say is wrong. *(Mock smile.)* That's what makes you so attractive. Ha. In that funnybook jacket with all the buttons. *(More animate, taking hold of his jacket.)* What've you got that jacket and tie on in all this heat for? And why're you wearing a jacket and tie like that? Did your people ever burn witches or start revolutions over the price of tea? Boy, those narrow-shoulder clothes come from a tradition you ought to feel oppressed by. A three-button suit. What right do you have to be wearing a three-button suit and striped tie? Your father was a slave, he didn't go to Harvard.

CLAY: My grandfather was a night watchman.

LULA: And you went to a colored college where everybody thought they were Averell Harriman.

CLAY: All except me.

LULA: And who did you think you were? Who do you think you are now?

CLAY *(laughs as if to make light of the whole trend of the conversation)*: Well, in college I thought I was Baudelaire. But I've slowed down since.

LULA: I bet you never once thought you were a black nigger. *(Mock serious, then she howls with laughter.* CLAY *is stunned but after initial reaction, he quickly tries to appreciate the humor.* LULA *almost shrieks.)* A black Baudelaire.

CLAY: That's right.

LULA: Boy, are you corny. I take back what I said before. Everything you say is not wrong. It's perfect. You should be on television.

CLAY: You act like you're on television already.

LULA: That's because I'm an actress.

CLAY: I thought so.

LULA: Well, you're wrong. I'm no actress. I told you I always lie. I'm nothing, honey, and don't you ever forget it. *(Lighter.)* Although my mother was a Communist. The only person in my family ever to amount to anything.

CLAY: My mother was a Republican.

LULA: And your father voted for the man rather than the party.

CLAY: Right!

LULA: Yea for him. Yea, yea for him.

CLAY: Yea!

LULA: And yea for America where he is free to vote for the mediocrity of his choice! Yea!

CLAY: Yea!

LULA: And yea for both your parents who even though they differ about so crucial a matter as the body politic still forged a union of love and sacrifice that was destined to flower at the birth of the noble Clay . . . what's your middle name?

CLAY: Clay.

LULA: A union of love and sacrifice that was destined to flower at the birth of the noble Clay Clay Williams. Yea! And most of all yea yea for you, Clay Clay. The Black Baudelaire! Yes! *(And with knifelike cynicism.)* My Christ. My Christ.

CLAY: Thank you, ma'am.

LULA: May the people accept you as a ghost of the future. And love you, that you might not kill them when you can.

CLAY: What?

LULA: You're a murderer, Clay, and you know it. *(Her voice darkening with significance.)* You know god-damn well what I mean.

CLAY: I do?

LULA: So we'll pretend the air is light and full of perfume.

CLAY *(sniffing at her blouse)*: It is.

LULA: And we'll pretend the people cannot see you. That is, the citizens. And that you are free of your own history. And I am free of my history. We'll pretend that we are both anonymous beauties smashing along through the city's entrails. *(She yells as loud as she can.)* GROOVE!

SCENE 2

(Scene is the same as before, though now there are other seats visible in the car. And throughout the scene other people get on the subway. There are maybe one or two seated in the car as the scene opens, though neither CLAY *or* LULA *notices them.* CLAY'S *tie is open.* LULA *is hugging his arm.)*

CLAY: The party!

LULA: I know it'll be something good. You can come in with me, looking casual and significant. I'll be strange, haughty, and silent, and walk with long slow strides.

CLAY: Right.

LULA: When you get drunk, pat me once, very lovingly on the flanks, and I'll look at you cryptically, licking my lips.

CLAY: It sounds like something we can do.

LULA: You'll go around talking to young men about your mind, and to old men about your plans. If you meet a very close friend who is also with someone like me, we can stand together, sipping our drinks and exchanging codes of lust. The atmosphere will be slithering in love and half-love and very open moral decision.

CLAY: Great. Great.

LULA: And everyone will pretend they don't know your name, and then ... (*She pauses heavily.*) later, when they have to, they'll claim a friendship that denies your sterling character.

CLAY (*kissing her neck and fingers*): And then what?

LULA: Then? Well, then we'll go down the street, late night, eating apples and winding very deliberately toward my house.

CLAY: Deliberately?

LULA: I mean, we'll look in all the shopwindows, and make fun of the queers. Maybe we'll meet a Jewish Buddhist and flatten his conceits over some very pretentious coffee.

CLAY: In honor of whose God?

LULA: Mine.

CLAY: Who is ... ?

LULA: Me ... and you?

CLAY: A corporate Godhead.

LULA: Exactly. Exactly. (*Notices one of the other people entering.*)

CLAY: Go on with the chronicle. Then what happens to us?

LULA (*a mild depression, but she still makes her description triumphant and increasingly direct*): To my house, of course.

CLAY: Of course.

LULA: And up the narrow steps of the tenement.

CLAY: You live in a tenement?

LULA: Wouldn't live anywhere else. Reminds me specifically of my novel form of insanity.

CLAY: Up the tenement stairs.

LULA: And with my apple-eating hand I push open the door and lead you, my tender big-eyed prey, into my ... God, what can I call it ... into my hovel.

CLAY: Then what happens?

LULA: After the dancing and games, after the long drinks and long walks, the real fun begins.

CLAY: Ah, the real fun. (*Embarrassed, in spite of himself.*) Which is ... ?

LULA (*laughs at him*): Real fun in the dark house. Hah! Real fun in the dark house, high up above the street and the ignorant cowboys. I lead you in, holding your wet hand gently in my hand ...

CLAY: Which is not wet?

LULA: Which is dry as ashes.

CLAY: And cold?

LULA: Don't think you'll get out of your responsibility that way. It's not cold at all. You Fascist! Into my dark living room. Where we'll sit and talk endlessly, endlessly.

CLAY: About what?

LULA: About what? About your manhood, what do you think? What do you think we've been talking about all this time?

CLAY: Well, I didn't know it was that. That's for sure. Every other thing in the world but that. (*Notices another person entering, looks quickly, almost involuntarily up and down the car, seeing the other people in the car.*) Hey, I didn't even notice when those people got on.

LULA: Yeah, I know.

CLAY: Man, this subway is slow.

LULA: Yeah, I know.

CLAY: Well, go on. We were talking about my manhood.

LULA: We still are. All the time.

CLAY: We were in your living room.

LULA: My dark living room. Talking endlessly.

CLAY: About my manhood.

LULA: I'll make you a map of it. Just as soon as we get to my house.

CLAY: Well, that's great.

LULA: One of the things we do while we talk. And screw.

CLAY (*trying to make his smile broader and less shaky*): We finally got there.

LULA: And you'll call my rooms black as a grave. You'll say, "This place is like Juliet's tomb."

CLAY (*laughs*): I might.

LULA: I know. You've probably said it before.

CLAY: And is that all? The whole grand tour?

LULA: Not all. You'll say to me very close to my face, many, many times, you'll say, even whisper, that you love me.

CLAY: Maybe I will.

LULA: And you'll be lying.

CLAY: I wouldn't lie about something like that.

LULA: Hah. It's the only kind of thing you will lie about. Especially if you think it'll keep me alive.

CLAY: Keep you alive? I don't understand.

LULA (*bursting out laughing, but too shrilly*): Don't understand? Well, don't look at me. It's the path I take, that's all. Where both feet take me when I set them down. One in front of the other.

CLAY: Morbid. Morbid. You sure you're not an actress? All that self-aggrandizement.

LULA: Well, I told you I wasn't an actress ... but I also told you I lie all the time. Draw your own conclusions.

CLAY: Morbid. Morbid. You sure you're not an actress. All scribed? There's no more?

LULA: I've told you all I know. Or almost all.

CLAY: There's no funny parts?

LULA: I thought it was all funny.

CLAY: But you mean peculiar, not ha-ha.

LULA: You don't know what I mean.

CLAY: Well, tell me the almost part then. You said almost all. What else? I want the whole story.

LULA (*searching aimlessly through her bag. She begins to talk breathlessly, with a light and silly tone*): All stories are whole stories. All of 'em. Our whole story . . . nothing but change. How could things go on like that forever? Huh? (*Slaps him on the shoulder, begins finding things in her bag, taking them out and throwing them over her shoulder into the aisle.*) Except I do go on as I do. Apples and long walks with deathless intelligent lovers. But you mix it up. Look out the window, all the time. Turning pages. Change change change. Till, shit, I don't know you. Wouldn't, for that matter. You're too serious. I bet you're even too serious to be psychoanalyzed. Like all those Jewish poets from Yonkers, who leave their mothers looking for other mothers, or others' mothers, on whose baggy tits they lay their fumbling heads. Their poems are always funny, and all about sex.

CLAY: They sound great. Like movies.

LULA: But you change. (*Blankly.*) And things work on you till you hate them.

(*More people come into the train. They come closer to the couple, some of them not sitting, but swinging drearily on the straps, staring at the two with uncertain interest.*)

CLAY: Wow. All these people, so suddenly. They must all come from the same place.

LULA: Right. That they do.

CLAY: Oh? You know about them too?

LULA: Oh yeah. About them more than I know about you. Do they frighten you?

CLAY: Frighten me? Why should they frighten me?

LULA: 'Cause you're an escaped nigger.

CLAY: Yeah?

LULA: 'Cause you crawled through the wire and made tracks to my side.

CLAY: Wire?

LULA: Don't they have wire around plantations?

CLAY: You must be Jewish. All you can think about is wire. Plantations didn't have any wire. Plantations were big open whitewashed places like heaven, and everybody on 'em was grooved to be there. Just strummin' and hummin' all day.

LULA: Yes, yes.

CLAY: And that's how the blues was born.

LULA: Yes, yes. And that's how the blues was born. (*Begins to make up a song that becomes quickly hysterical. As she sings she rises from her seat, still throwing things out of her bag into the aisle, beginning a rhythmical shudder and twistlike wiggle, which she continues up and down the aisle, bumping into many of the standing people and tripping over the feet of those sitting. Each time she runs into a person she lets out a very vicious piece of profanity, wiggling and stepping all the time.*) And that's how the blues was born. Yes. Yes. Son of a bitch, get out of the way. Yes.

Quack. Yes. Yes. And that's how the blues was born. Ten little niggers sitting on a limb, but none of them ever looked like him. (*Points to* CLAY, *returns toward the seat, with her hands extended for him to rise and dance with her.*) And that's how the blues was born. Yes. Come on, Clay. Let's do the nasty. Rub bellies. Rub bellies.

CLAY (*waves his hands to refuse. He is embarrassed, but determined to get a kick out of the proceedings*): Hey, what was in those apples? Mirror, mirror on the wall, who's the fairest one of all? Snow White, baby, and don't you forget it.

LULA (*grabbing for his hands, which he draws away*): Come on, Clay. Let's rub bellies on the train. The nasty. The nasty. Do the gritty grind, like your ol' rag-head mammy. Grind till you lose your mind. Shake it, shake it, shake it, shake it! OOOOweeee! Come on, Clay. Let's do the choo-choo train shuffle, the navel scratcher.

CLAY: Hey, you coming on like the lady who smoked up her grass skirt.

LULA (*becoming annoyed that he will not dance, and becoming more animated as if to embarrass him still further*): Come on, Clay . . . let's do the thing. Uhh! Uhh! Clay! Clay! You middle-class black bastard. Forget your social-working mother for a few seconds and let's knock stomachs. Clay, you liver-lipped white man. You would-be Christian. You ain't no nigger, you're just a dirty white man. Get up, Clay. Dance with me, Clay.

CLAY: Lula! Sit down, now. Be cool.

LULA (*mocking him, in wild dance*): Be cool. Be cool. That's all you know . . . shaking that wildroot cream-oil on your knotty head, jackets buttoning up to your chin, so full of white man's words. Christ. God. Get up and scream at these people. Like scream meaningless shit in these hopeless faces. (*She screams at people in train, still dancing.*) Red trains cough Jewish underwear for keeps! Expanding smells of silence. Gravy snot whistling like sea birds. Clay, Clay, you got to break out. Don't sit there dying the way they want you to die. Get up.

CLAY: Oh, sit the fuck down. (*He moves to restrain her.*) Sit down, goddamn it.

LULA (*twisting out of his reach*): Screw yourself, Uncle Tom. Thomas Woolly-head. (*Begins to dance a kind of jig, mocking* CLAY *with loud forced humor*) There is Uncle Tom . . . I mean, Uncle Thomas Woolly-Head. With old white matted mane. He hobbles on his wooden cane. Old Tom. Old Tom. Let the white man hump his ol' mama and he jes' shuffle off in the woods and hide his gentle gray head. Ol' Thomas Woolly-Head.

(*Some of the other riders are laughing now. A drunk gets*

up and joins LULA *in her dance, singing, as best he can, her "song."* CLAY *gets up out of his seat and visibly scans the faces of the other riders.)*

CLAY: Lula! Lula! *(She is dancing and turning, still shouting as loud as she can. The drunk too is shouting, and waving his hands wildly.)* Lula . . . you dumb bitch. Why don't you stop it? *(He rushes half stumbling from his seat, and grabs one of her flailing arms.)*

LULA: Let me go! You black son of a bitch. *(She struggles against him.)* Let me go! Help!

(CLAY is dragging her toward her seat, and the drunk seeks to interfere. He grabs CLAY around the shoulders and begins wrestling with him. CLAY clubs the drunk to the floor without releasing LULA, who is still screaming. CLAY finally gets her to the seat and throws her into it.)

CLAY: Now you shut the hell up. *(Grabbing her shoulders.)* Just shut up. You don't know what you're talking about. You don't know anything. So just keep your stupid mouth closed.

LULA: You're afraid of white people. And your father was. Uncle Tom Big Lip!

CLAY *(slaps her as hard as he can, across the mouth.* LULA's *head bangs against the back of the seat. When she raises it again,* CLAY *slaps her again)*: Now shut up and let me talk. *(He turns toward the other riders, some of whom are sitting on the edge of their seats. The drunk is on one knee, rubbing his head, and singing softly the same song. He shuts up too when he sees* CLAY *watching him. The others go back to newspapers or stare out the window)* Shit, you don't have any sense, Lula, nor feelings either. I could murder you now. Such a tiny ugly throat. I could squeeze it flat, and watch you turn blue, on a humble. For dull kicks. And all these weak-faced ofays squatting around here, staring over their papers at me. Murder them too. Even if they expected it. That man there . . . *(Points to well-dressed man.)* I could rip that *Times* right out of his hand, as skinny and middle-classed as I am, I could rip that paper out of his hand and just as easily rip out his throat. It takes no great effort. For what? To kill you soft idiots? You don't understand anything but luxury.

LULA: You fool!

CLAY *(pushing her against the seat)*: I'm not telling you again, Tallulah Bankhead! Luxury. In your face and your fingers. You telling me what I ought to do. *(Sudden scream frightening the whole coach.)* Well, don't! Don't you tell me anything! If I'm a middle-class fake white man . . . let me be. And let me be in the way I want. *(Through his teeth.)* I'll rip your lousy breasts off! Let me be who I feel like being. Uncle Tom. Thomas. Whoever. It's none of your business. You don't know anything except what's there for you to see. An act. Lies. Device. Not the pure heart, the pumping black heart. You don't ever know that. And I sit here, in this buttoned-up suit, to keep myself from cutting all your throats. I mean wantonly. You great liberated whore! You fuck some black man and right away you're an expert on black people. What a lotta shit that is. The only thing you know is that you come if he bangs you hard enough. And that's all. The belly rub? You wanted me to do the belly rub? Shit, you don't even know how. You don't know that. That ol' dipty-dip shit you do, rolling your ass like an elephant. That's not my kind of belly rub. Belly rub is not Queens. Belly rub is dark places, with big hats and overcoats held up with one arm. Belly rub hates you. Old bald-headed four-eyed ofays popping their fingers . . . and don't know yet what they're doing. They say, "I love Bessie Smith." And don't even understand that Bessie Smith is saying, "Kiss my ass, kiss my black unruly ass." Before love, suffering, desire, anything you can explain, she's saying, and very plainly, "Kiss my black ass." And if you don't know that, it's you that's doing the kissing.

Charlie Parker? Charlie Parker. All the hip white boys scream for Bird. And Bird saying, "Up your ass, feeble-minded ofay! Up your ass." And they sit there talking about the tortured genius of Charlie Parker. Bird would've played not a note of music if he just walked up to East Sixty-seventh Street and killed the first ten white people he saw. Not a note! And I'm the great would-be poet. Yes. That's right! Poet. Some kind of bastard literature . . . all it needs is a simple knife thrust. Just let me bleed you, you loud whore, and one poem vanished. A whole people of neurotics, struggling to keep from being sane. And the only thing that would cure the neurosis would be your murder. Simple as that. I mean if I murdered you, then other white people would begin to understand me. You understand? No. I guess not. If Bessie Smith had killed some white people she wouldn't have needed that music. She could have talked very straight and plain about the world. No metaphors. No grunts. No wiggles in the dark of her soul. Just straight two and two are four. Money. Power. Luxury. Like that. All of them. Crazy niggers turning their backs on sanity. When all it needs is that simple act. Murder. Just murder! Would make us all sane. *(Suddenly weary.)* Ahhh. Shit. But who needs it? I'd rather be a fool. Insane. Safe with my words, and no deaths, and clean, hard thoughts, urging me to new conquests. My people's madness. Hah! That's a laugh. My people. They don't need me to claim them. They got legs and arms of their own. Personal insanities. Mirrors. They don't need all those words. They don't need any defense. But listen, though, one more thing. And you tell this to your father, who's probably the kind of man who needs to know at once. So he can plan ahead. Tell him not to preach so much rationalism and cold logic to these niggers. Let them alone. Let them sing curses at you in code and see your filth as simple lack of style. Don't make the mistake, through some irresponsible surge of Christian charity, of talking too much about the advantages of Western rationalism, or the great intellectual legacy of the white man, or maybe they'll begin to listen. And then, maybe one day, you'll find they actually do understand exactly what you are talking about, all these fantasy people. All these blues people. And on that day, as sure as shit, when you really believe you can "accept" them into your fold, as half-white trusties late of the subject peoples. With no more blues, except the very old ones, and not a watermelon in sight, the great missionary heart will have triumphed, and all of those ex-coons will be stand-up Western men, with eyes for clean hard useful lives, sober, pious and sane, and they'll murder you. They'll murder you, and have very rational explanations. Very much like your own. They'll cut your throats, and drag you out to the edge of your cities so the flesh can fall away from your bones, in sanitary isolation.

LULA (*her voice takes on a different, more businesslike quality*): I've heard enough.

CLAY (*reaching for his books*): I bet you have. I guess I better collect my stuff and get off this train. Looks like we won't be acting out that little pageant you outlined before.

LULA: No. We won't. You're right about that, at least.

(*She turns to look quickly around the rest of the car.*) All right! (*The others respond.*)

CLAY (*bending across the girl to retrieve his belongings*): Sorry, baby, I don't think we could make it.

(*As he is bending over her, the girl brings up a small knife and plunges it into* CLAY's *chest. Twice. He slumps across her knees, his mouth working stupidly.*)

LULA: Sorry is right. (*Turning to the others in the car who have already gotten up from their seats.*) Sorry is the rightest thing you've said. Get this man off me! Hurry, now! (*The others come and drag* CLAY's *body down the aisle.*) Open the door and throw his body out. (*They throw him off.*) And all of you get off at the next stop.

(LULA *busies herself straightening her things. Getting everything in order. She takes out a notebook and makes a quick scribbling note. Drops it in her bag. The train apparently stops and all the others get off, leaving her alone in the coach. Very soon a young Negro of about twenty comes into the coach, with a couple of books under his arms. He sits a few seats in back of* LULA. *When he is seated she turns and gives him a long slow look. He looks up from his book and drops the book on his lap. Then an old Negro conductor comes into the car, doing a sort of restrained soft shoe, and half mumbling the words of some song. He looks at the young man, briefly, with a quick greeting.*)

CONDUCTOR: Hey, brother!
YOUNG MAN: Hey.

(*The conductor continues down the aisle with his little dance and the mumbled song.* LULA *turns to stare at him and follows his movements down the aisle. The conductor tips his hat when he reaches her seat, and continues out the car.*)

CURTAIN

Figure 1. Lula (Jennifer West) munches her apple and provocatively crosses her legs while Clay (Robert Hooks) looks at his magazine in the opening moments of the Cherry Lane Theater production of *Dutchman*, directed by Edward Parone, New York, 1964. (Photograph: Alix Jeffry. Billy Rose Theatre Collection. The New York Public Library for the Performing Arts. Astor, Lenox, and Tilden Foundations.)

Staging of *Dutchman*

It is altogether likely that the folk who go down to the Cherry Lane Theatre to see the three one-act plays now being given there are witnesses to a signal event: the emergence of an outstanding dramatist—LeRoi Jones.

His is a turbulent talent. While turbulence is not always a sign of power or of valuable meaning, I have a hunch that Leroi Jones's fire will burn ever higher and clearer if our theatre can furnish an adequate vessel to harbor his flame. We need it.

He is very angry. Anger alone may merely make a loud noise, confuse, sputter and die. For anger to burn to useful effect, it must be guided by an idea. With the "angry young men" of England one was not always certain of the source of dissatisfaction nor of its goal. With Leroi Jones it is easy to say that the plight of the Negro ignited the initial rage—justification enough—and that the rage will not be appeased until there is no more black and white, no more color except as differences in hue and accent are part of the world's splendid spectacle. But there is more to his ferocity than a protest against the horrors of racism.

Dutchman, the first of Jones's plays to reach the professional stage, is a stylized account of a subway episode. A white girl picks up a young Negro who at first is rather embarrassed and later piqued by her advances. There is a perversity in her approach which finally provokes him to a hymn of hate. With lyrical obscenity he declares that murder is in his and every Negro's heart and were it to reach the point of action there would be less "singin' of the blues," less of that delightful folk music and hot jazz which beguile the white man's fancy, more calm in the Negro soul. Meanwhile, it is the black man who is murdered.

What we must not overloook in seeing the play is that, while this explosion of fury is its rhetorical and emotional climax, the crux of its significance resides in the depiction of the white girl whose relevance to the play's situation does not lie in her whiteness but in her representative value as a token of our civilization. She is our neurosis. Not a neurosis in regard to the Negro, but the absolute neurosis of American society.

She is "hep": she has heard about everything, understands and feels nothing. She twitches, jangles, jitters with a thin but inexhaustible energy, propelled by the vibrations from millions of ads, television quiz programs, newspaper columns, intellectual jargon culled from countless digests, panel discussions, illustrated summaries, smatterings of gossip on every conceivable subject (respectable and illicit), epithets, wisecracks, formulas, slogans, cynicisms, cures and solutions. She is the most "informed" person in the world and the most ignorant. (The information feeds the ignorance.) She is the bubbling, boiling garbage cauldron newly produced by our progress. She is a calculating machine gone berserk; she is the real killer. What she destroys is not men of a certain race but mankind. She is the compendium in little of the universal mess.

If *Dutchman* (a title I don't understand) has a fault, it is its completeness. Its ending is somewhat too pat, too pointed in its symbolism. If one has caught the drift of the play's meaning before its final moment, the ending is supererogatory; if one has failed to do so, it is probably useless.

Dutchman is very well played by Jennifer West and Robert Hooks.

Everything about LeRoi Jones's "Dutchman" is designed to shock—its basic idea, its language and its murderous rage.

This half-hour-long piece, the last of three one-act plays being performed at the Cherry Lane Theater, is an explosion of hatred rather than a play. It puts into the mouth of its principal Negro character a scathing denunciation of all the white man's good works, pretensions and condescensions.

If this is the way the Negroes really feel about the

white world around them, there's more rancor buried in the breasts of colored conformists than anyone can imagine. If this is the way even one Negro feels, there is ample cause for guilt as well as alarm, and for a hastening of change.

As an extended metaphor of bitterness and fury, "Dutchman" is transparently simple in structure. Clay, a Negro who wears a three-button suit and is reserved and well-spoken, is accosted by a white female on a train. Lula is a liar, a slut, essentially an agent provocateur of a Caucasian society.

After she disarms Clay with her wild outbursts and sinuous attentions, she turns on him in challenging contempt. His answer is to drop the mask of conformity and to spew out all the anger that has built up in him and his fellow Negroes. When this outburst of violent resentment has finished and Clay has left the train, Lula notices that another Negro has boarded and she sets her slinky charms for him.

Mr. Jones writes with a kind of sustained frenzy. His little work is a mélange of sardonic images and undisciplined filth. The impact of his ferocity would be stronger if he did not work so hard and persistently to be shocking.

Jennifer West in a straight, tight-fitting dress striped like a prisoner's suit plays Lula with a rousing mixture of sultriness and insolence. Robert Hooks as Clay is impressive as he shifts from patient tolerance to savage wrath. Edward Parone's staging is mordant, and intense.

HAROLD PINTER

1930–

Pinter, whose drama has come to be internationally known by critics as the "comedy of menace," is the son of a Portuguese-Jewish tailor who emigrated to London by way of eastern Europe early in the twentieth century. Pinter was born and raised in London's East End, where he attended the local grammar school and during his teens began writing poems, short stories, and dialogues for little magazines, as well as taking part in school theatrical productions. During the late 1940s, he spent a couple of terms at the Royal Academy of Dramatic Art, but he was put off by the sophistication of his fellow students and thus withdrew to start a professional career in acting, first in radio work during 1950, then with a professional company touring Ireland during 1951 and 1952. On returning to England, he continued acting in London and the provinces, under the pseudonym of David Baron, until 1957, when he wrote his first play, *The Room,* a one-act piece he did at the suggestion of a friend who was then studying drama at Bristol University. This eerie little play, which depicts an old couple suddenly beset by menacing visits and messages, clearly anticipated the inexplicably threatening situations that Pinter has dramatized repeatedly in his subsequent plays. During 1957, Pinter also wrote his first full-length work for the stage, *The Birthday Party,* and this time the menacing situation took the form of humiliating physical and verbal games inflicted on a retired pianist by two sinister men who turn up at his room on the afternoon of his birthday, then subject him to their birthday party games that evening, and finally carry him off with them the next morning.

When *The Birthday Party* opened in London in 1958, most critics found it "opaque" and charged that the characters spoke "in non-sequiturs, half-gibberish, and lunatic ravings." Although it closed after one week, *The Birthday Party* was revived six years later by the Royal Shakespeare Company in a highly successful production directed by Pinter himself. By then, Pinter had already achieved his first popular success with *The Caretaker* (1960), which dramatizes the comic but convulsive quarrels and competition that develop in a run-down house among the owner, his brain-damaged brother, and a devious tramp whom the brother has befriended. Several of his shorter plays, including *The Room, The Dumb Waiter* (1957), and *A Slight Ache* (1961) had also been successfully staged, while others, such as *A Night Out* (1960), *Night School* (1960), *The Collection* (1961), and *The Lover* (1963) had been filmed for television. By the mid-1960s, Pinter's screenplays for *The Servant* (1962) and *The Pumpkin Eater* (1964) had received major awards, and in 1965, *The Homecoming* opened in London, again in a highly successful production by the Royal Shakespeare Company. Given these astonishing dramatic accomplishments, it is hardly surprising that in 1966, Pinter was awarded the C.B.E. (Commander of the Order of the British Empire) by the Queen, All of Pinter's major plays have now received major productions first in London, then in New York, and his work is now no longer regarded as being quite so baffling and frustrating as it seemed some thirty years ago.

Years of discerning criticism about other dramatists of the absurd, such as Beckett, Genet, and Ionesco, have helped readers and playgoers to recognize Pinter's work as part of a widespread movement in contemporary drama away from clearly motivated characters and plots, as well as from entirely logical dialogue and events, to a theater in which the actions and utterances of characters, however preposterous or alarming, are interesting, even fascinating, because they can and do take place on stage. Pinter himself has also talked openly and helpfully about this aspect of his plays. For the audiences who came to the Royal Court Theater in 1960 to see *The Room* and *The Dumb Waiter*, he offered this brief statement revealing his approach to characterization:

> A character on the stage who can present no convincing argument or information as to his past experience, his present behaviour or his aspirations, nor give a comprehensive analysis of his motives is as legitimate and as worthy of attention as one who, alarmingly, can do all these things.

Pinter's view of character and motive also accounts for his special view of dialogue, which he also announced in his program notes for the Royal Court Theater:

> The more acute the experience, the less articulate its expression.

Given this concept of inarticulateness in the theater, Pinter was naturally led to his famous statement about "the two silences," which he formulated in a speech to a student drama festival in Bristol, in 1962:

> There are two silences. One when no word is spoken. The other when perhaps a torrent of language is employed. This speech is speaking of a language locked beneath it. That is its continual reference. The speech we hear is an indication of that we don't hear. It is a necessary avoidance, a violent, shy, anguished, or mocking smoke-screen which keeps the other in its place. When true silence falls we are still left with echo but are nearer nakedness. One way of looking at speech is to say it is a constant stratagem to cover nakedness.

Both these kinds of silence are, of course, true to general human experience, as Chekhov had clearly recognized in the dialogue of his plays seventy years earlier, but only in drama of the absurd, particularly in the plays of Pinter, have they become a pervasive theatrical element.

Both these silences occur throughout *The Homecoming*, and thus a recognition of them will usually help to make sense of what is happening in the play and between the characters. For example, when Lenny tells Ruth, whom he has just met, about "a certain lady" and "a certain proposal," both of which he rejected, he is not only telling a long anecdote, but also letting her know of his involvement in the world of pimps and prostitutes, and thus of his capacity for violence. His "torrent of language" is not only a reference to something else about himself, but also a tacit assertion of his having recognized her own lascivious disposition, even before she has said or done anything to reveal it. And when Ruth responds by saying quietly, "Have a sip. Go on. Have a sip from my glass. Sit on my lap. Take a long cool sip. Put your head back and open your mouth," she is not really talking about a glass of water, but returning his implicit sexual proposal. The other kind of silence, "when no word is spoken," may be seen near the beginning of the play, when Teddy returns home after being away for six years and first encounters his younger brother Lenny:

TEDDY: Hullo, Lenny.
LENNY: Hullo, Teddy.
    (Pause.)

The brevity of their greeting followed by that pause, that silence, quickly reveals their indifference, even their hostility, to one another.

Pinter's plays are distinguished not only by his use of language and silence, but also by his fascination with the dramatic situation of "two people sitting in a room." His early works, particularly *The Room, The Birthday Party,* and *The Caretaker,* are all set in a single room and explore the tensions that explode in that closed place and the menace that can intrude without warning. In commenting on this basic situation, Pinter has clearly related its application to ordinary human experience:

> A door can open at any moment and someone will come in. We'd love to know who it is, we'd love to know exactly what he has on his mind and why he comes in, but how often do we know what someone has on his mind or who this somebody is, and what goes to make him and make him what he is, and what his relationship is to others?

And throughout *The Homecoming,* he dramatizes the unanswerability of such questions. Why, for example, do Teddy and his wife, Ruth, suddenly come home to his father's house? Why does his father, Max, not know about his marriage to Ruth, not to mention their children? How does Max really feel about the son he insults and then offers to "cuddle and kiss"? And how does he feel about Ruth whom he labels "a stinking pox-ridden slut" when he first meets her and later praises as a "charming woman," "an intelligent and sympathetic woman"? Why does Teddy stand by silently when his brother Joey proceeds to make love to Ruth on the couch? Indeed, as the play proceeds, the questions about motivation and human relationships become even more troublesome. Why, for example, does Ruth so calmly and in such a businesslike way proceed to negotiate for a position of being resident prostitute to her husband's family? Why does Teddy offer no resistance at all, no plea for her to change her mind? These questions, Pinter would say, cannot really be answered. What is important and dramatically unforgettable in *The Homecoming* is that the events, bizarre as they may seem, do happen. And, in happening, they reveal a disturbing aspect of human experience, or at least a disturbing possibility in human experience.

When *The Homecoming* opened in London and later in New York, critics and audiences alike struggled to find explanations for the behavior they witnessed. Reviews of the New York production, reprinted following the text, reflect two contrasting views of the play: one believes that Pinter is "simply cheating us," the other argues that if we are willing to follow Pinter's vision, "we will have overcome our deadly habit of wanting what we expect." Two of the play's unexpected situations are pictured in photographs of the New York production, one showing Ruth about to offer Lenny a sip of water (see Figure 1), the other of Max insulting Ruth during their first encounter (see Figure 2). Debate about these and the other unexpected situations in the play raged for several months after it came to New York, and the *New York Times* went so far as to print a symposium of opinions under the title "What does *The Homecoming* Mean?" (February 5, 1967). Pinter's reply to that question can be found, perhaps, in the words of Ruth, when she breaks into a pseudophilosophical argument that Lenny and Teddy are having about a table: "My lips move. Why don't you restrict . . . your observations to that? Perhaps the fact that they move is more significant . . . than the words which come through them. You must bear that . . . possibility . . . in mind."

THE HOMECOMING

BY HAROLD PINTER

CHARACTERS

MAX, *a man of seventy*
LENNY, *a man in his early thirties*
SAM, *a man of sixty-three*
JOEY, *a man in his middle twenties*
TEDDY, *a man in his middle thirties*
RUTH, *a woman in her early thirties*

SCENE

Summer. An old house in North London.
A large room, extending the width of the stage.

The back wall, which contained the door, has been removed. A square arch shape remains. Beyond it, the hall. In the hall a staircase ascending upper left, well in view. The front door upper right. A coatstand, hooks, etc.

In the room, a window, right. Odd tables, chairs. Two large armchairs. A large sofa, left. Against right wall a large sideboard, the upper half of which contains a mirror. Upper left, a radiogram.

ACT 1

(Evening.

LENNY *is sitting on the sofa with a newspaper, a pencil in his hand. He wears a dark suit. He makes occasional marks on the back page.*

MAX *comes in, from the direction of the kitchen. He goes to sideboard, opens top drawer, rummages in it, closes it.*

He wears an old cardigan and a cap, and carries a stick.

He walks downstage, stands, looks about the room.)

MAX: What have you done with the scissors?

(Pause.)

I said I'm looking for the scissors. What have you done with them?

(Pause.)

Did you hear me? I want to cut something out of the paper.
LENNY: I'm reading the paper.
MAX: Not that paper. I haven't read that paper. I'm talking about last Sunday's paper. I was just having a look at it in the kitchen.

(Pause.)

Do you hear what I'm saying? I'm talking to you! Where's the scissors?
LENNY *(looking up, quietly.)*: Why don't you shut up, you daft prat?

*(*MAX *lifts his stick and points it at him.)*

MAX: Don't you talk to me like that. I'm warning you.

(He sits in large armchair.)

There's an advertisement in the paper about

flannel vests. Cut price. Navy surplus. I could do with a few of them.

(Pause.)

I think I'll have a fag. Give me a fag.

(Pause.)

I just asked you to give me a cigarette.

(Pause.)

Look what I'm lumbered with.

(He takes a crumpled cigarette from his pocket.)

I'm getting old, my word of honour.

(He lights it.)

You think I wasn't a tearaway? I could have taken care of you, twice over. I'm still strong. You ask your Uncle Sam what I was. But at the same time I always had a kind heart. Always.

(Pause.)

I used to knock about with a man called Mac-Gregor. I called him Mac. You remember Mac? Eh?

(Pause.)

Huhh! We were two of the worst hated men in the West End of London. I tell you, I still got the scars. We'd walk into a place, the whole room'd stand up, they'd make way to let us pass. You never heard such silence. Mind you, he was a big man, he was over six foot tall. His family were all MacGregors, they came all the way from Aberdeen, but he was the only one they called Mac.

(Pause.)

1044

He was very fond of your mother, Mac was. Very fond. He always had a good word for her.

(Pause.)

Mind you, she wasn't such a bad woman. Even though it made me sick just to look at her rotten stinking face, she wasn't such a bad bitch. I gave her the best bleeding years of my life, anyway.

LENNY: Plug it, will you, you stupid sod, I'm trying to read the paper.

MAX: Listen! I'll chop your spine off, you talk to me like that! You understand? Talking to your lousy filthy father like that!

LENNY: You know what, you're getting demented.

(Pause.)

What do you think of Second Wind for the three-thirty?

MAX: Where?

LENNY: Sandown Park.

MAX: Don't stand a chance.

LENNY: Sure he does.

MAX: Not a chance.

LENNY: He's the winner.

*(*LENNY *ticks the paper.)*

MAX: He talks to me about horses.

(Pause.)

I used to live on the course. One of the loves of my life. Epsom? I knew it like the back of my hand. I was one of the best-known faces down at the paddock. What a marvellous open-air life.

(Pause.)

He talks to me about horses. You only read their names in the papers. But I've stroked their manes, I've held them, I've calmed them down before a big race. I was the one they used to call for. Max, they'd say, there's a horse here, he's highly strung, you're the only man on the course who can calm him. It was true. I had a . . . I had an instinctive understanding of animals. I should have been a trainer. Many times I was offered the job—you know, a proper post, by the Duke of . . . I forget his name . . . one of the Dukes. But I had family obligations, my family needed me at home.

(Pause.)

The times I've watched those animals thundering past the post. What an experience. Mind you, I didn't lose, I made a few bob out of it, and you know why? Because I always had the smell of a good horse. I could smell him. And not only the colts but the fillies. Because the fillies are more highly strung than the colts, they're more unreliable, did you know that? No, what do you know? Nothing. But I was always able to tell a good filly by one particular trick. I'd look her in the eye. You see? I'd stand in front of her and look her straight in the eye, it was a kind of hypnotism, and by the look deep down in her eye I could tell whether she was a stayer or not. It was a gift. I had a gift.

(Pause.)

And he talks to me about horses.

LENNY: Dad, do you mind if I change the subject?

(Pause.)

I want to ask you something. That dinner we had before, what was the name of it? What do you call it?

(Pause.)

Why don't you buy a dog? You're a dog cook. Honest. You think you're cooking for a lot of dogs.

MAX: If you don't like it get out.

LENNY: I am going out. I'm going out to buy myself a proper dinner.

MAX: Well, get out! What are you waiting for?

*(*LENNY *looks at him.)*

LENNY: What did you say?

MAX: I said shove off out of it, that's what I said.

LENNY: You'll go before me, Dad, if you talk to me in that tone of voice.

MAX: Will I, you bitch?

*(*MAX *grips his stick.)*

LENNY: Oh, Daddy, you're not going to use your stick on me, are you? Eh? Don't use your stick on me, Daddy. No, please. It wasn't my fault, it was one of the others. I haven't done anything wrong, Dad, honest. Don't clout me with that stick, Dad.

(Silence.
MAX *sits hunched.* LENNY *reads the paper.*
SAM *comes in the front door. He wears a chauffeur's uniform. He hangs his hat on a hook in the hall and comes into the room. He goes to a chair, sits in it and sighs.)*

Hullo, Uncle Sam.

SAM: Hullo.

LENNY: How are you, Uncle!

SAM: Not bad. A bit tired.

LENNY: Tired? I bet you're tired. Where you been?

SAM: I've been to London Airport.

LENNY: All the way up to London Airport? What, right up the M4?

SAM: Yes, all the way up there.

LENNY: Tch, tch, tch. Well, I think you're entitled to be tired, Uncle.

SAM: Well, it's the drivers.

LENNY: I know. That's what I'm talking about. I'm talking about the drivers.

SAM: Knocks you out.

(Pause.)

MAX: I'm here, too, you know.

(SAM looks at him.)

I said I'm here, too. I'm sitting here.

SAM: I know you're here.

(Pause.)

SAM: I took a Yankee out there today . . . to the Airport.

LENNY: Oh, a Yankee, was it?

SAM: Yes, I been with him all day. Picked him up at the Savoy at half past twelve, took him to the Caprice for his lunch. After lunch I picked him up again, took him down to a house in Eaton Square—he had to pay a visit to a friend there—and then round about tea-time I took him right the way out to the Airport.

LENNY: Had to catch a plane there, did he?

SAM: Yes. Look what he gave me. He gave me a box of cigars.

(SAM takes a box of cigars from his pocket.)

MAX: Come here. Let's have a look at them.

(SAM shows MAX the cigars. MAX takes one from the box, pinches it and sniffs it.)

It's a fair cigar.

SAM: Want to try one?

(MAX and SAM light cigars.)

You know what he said to me? He told me I was the best chauffeur he'd ever had. The best one.

MAX: From what point of view?

SAM: Eh?

MAX: From what point of view?

LENNY: From the point of view of his driving, Dad, and his general sense of courtesy, I should say.

MAX: Thought you were a good driver, did he, Sam? Well, he gave you a first-class cigar.

SAM: Yes, he thought I was the best he'd ever had. They all say that, you know. They won't have anyone else, they only ask for me. They say I'm the best chauffeur in the firm.

LENNY: I bet the other drivers tend to get jealous, don't they, Uncle?

SAM: They do get jealous. They get very jealous.

MAX: Why?

(Pause.)

SAM: I just told you.

MAX: No, I just can't get it clear, Sam. Why do the other drivers get jealous?

SAM: Because (a) I'm the best driver, and because . . . (b) I don't take liberties.

(Pause.)

I don't press myself on people, you see. These big businessmen, men of affairs, they don't want the driver jawing all the time, they like to sit in the back, have a bit of peace and quiet. After all, they're sitting in a Humber Super Snipe, they can afford to relax. At the same time, though, this is what really makes me special . . . I do know how to pass the time of day when required.

(Pause.)

For instance, I told this man today I was in the second world war. Not the first. I told him I was too young for the first. But I told him I fought in the second.

(Pause.)

So did he, it turned out.

(LENNY stands, goes to the mirror and straightens his tie.)

LENNY: He was probably a colonel or something in the American Air Force.

SAM: Yes.

LENNY: Probably a navigator, or something like that, in a Flying Fortress. Now he's most likely a high executive in a worldwide group of aeronautical engineers.

SAM: Yes.

LENNY: Yes, I know the kind of man you're talking about.

(LENNY goes out, turning to his right.)

SAM: After all, I'm experienced. I was driving a dust cart at the age of nineteen. Then I was in long-distance haulage. I had ten years as a taxi-driver and I've had five as a private chauffeur.

MAX: It's funny you never got married, isn't it? A man with all your gifts.

(Pause.)

Isn't it? A man like you?

SAM: There's still time.

MAX: Is there?

(Pause.)

SAM: You'd be surprised.

MAX: What you been doing, banging away at your lady customers, have you?

SAM: Not me.

MAX: In the back of the Snipe? Been having a few crafty reefs in a layby, have you?

SAM: Not me.

MAX: On the back seat? What about the armrest, was it up or down?

SAM: I've never done that kind of thing in my car.

MAX: Above all that kind of thing, are you, Sam?

SAM: Too true.

MAX: Above having a good bang on the back seat, are you?

SAM: Yes, I leave that to others.

MAX: You leave it to others? What others? You paralysed prat!

SAM: I don't mess up my car! Or my . . . my boss's car! Like other people.

MAX: Other people? What other people?

(Pause.)

What other people?

(Pause.)

SAM: Other people.

(Pause.)

MAX: When you find the right girl, Sam, let your family know, don't forget, we'll give you a number one send-off, I promise you. You can bring her to live here, she can keep us all happy. We'd take it in turns to give her a walk round the park.

SAM: I wouldn't bring her here.

MAX: Sam, it's your decision. You're welcome to bring your bride here, to the place where you live, or on the other hand you can take a suite at the Dorchester. It's entirely up to you.

SAM: I haven't got a bride.

(SAM stands, goes to the sideboard, takes an apple from the bowl, bites into it.)

Getting a bit peckish.

(He looks out of the window.)

Never get a bride like you had, anyway. Nothing like your bride . . . going about these days. Like Jessie.

(Pause.)

After all, I escorted her once or twice, didn't I? Drove her round once or twice in my cab. She was a charming woman.

(Pause.)

All the same, she was your wife. But still . . . they were some of the most delightful evenings I've ever had. Used to just drive her about. It was my pleasure.

MAX *(softly, closing his eyes)*: Christ.

SAM: I used to pull up at a stall and buy her a cup of coffee. She was a very nice companion to be with.

(Silence.
JOEY *comes in the front door. He walks into the room,* takes his jacket off, throws it on a chair and stands. Silence.)*

JOEY: Feel a bit hungry.

SAM: Me, too.

MAX: Who do you think I am, your mother? Eh? Honest. They walk in here every time of the day and night like bloody animals. Go and find yourself a mother.

(LENNY walks into the room, stands.)

JOEY: I've been training down at the gym.

SAM: Yes, the boy's been working all day and training all night.

MAX: What do you want, you bitch? You spend all the day sitting on your arse at London Airport, buy yourself a jamroll. You expect me to sit here waiting to rush into the kitchen the moment you step in the door? You've been living sixty-three years, why don't you learn to cook?

SAM: I can cook.

MAX: Well, go and cook!

LENNY: What the boys want, Dad, is your own special brand of cooking, Dad. That's what the boys look forward to. The special understanding of food, you know, that you've got.

MAX: Stop calling me Dad. Just stop all that calling me Dad, do you understand?

LENNY: But I'm your son. You used to tuck me up in bed every night. He tucked you up, too, didn't he, Joey?

(Pause.)

He used to like tucking up his sons.

(LENNY turns and goes toward the front door.)

MAX: Lenny.

LENNY *(turning)*: What?

MAX: I'll give you a proper tuck up one of these nights, son. You mark my word.

(They look at each other.
LENNY *opens the front door and goes out.*
Silence.)*

JOEY: I've been training with Bobby Dodd.

(Pause.)

And I had a good go at the bag as well.

(Pause.)

I wasn't in bad trim.

MAX: Boxing's a gentleman's game.

(Pause.)

I'll tell you what you've got to do. What you've got to do is you've got to learn how to defend yourself, and you've got to learn how to attack.

That's your only trouble as a boxer. You don't know how to defend yourself, and you don't know how to attack.

(*Pause.*)

Once you've mastered those arts you can go straight to the top.

(*Pause.*)

JOEY: I've got a pretty good idea . . . of how to do that.

(JOEY *looks round for his jacket, picks it up, goes out of the room and up the stairs.*
Pause.)

MAX: Sam . . . why don't you go, too, eh? Why don't you just go upstairs? Leave me quiet. Leave me alone.

SAM: I want to make something clear about Jessie, Max. I want to. I do. When I took her out in the cab, round the town, I was taking care of her, for you. I was looking after her for you, when you were busy, wasn't I? I was showing her the West End.

(*Pause.*)

You wouldn't have trusted any of your other brothers. You wouldn't have trusted Mac, would you? But you trusted me. I want to remind you.

(*Pause.*)

Old Mac died a few years ago, didn't he? Isn't he dead?

(*Pause.*)

He was a lousy stinking rotten loudmouth. A bastard uncouth sodding runt. Mind you, he was a good friend of yours.

(*Pause.*)

MAX: Eh, Sam . . .
SAM: What?
MAX: Why do I keep you here? You're just an old grub.
SAM: Am I?
MAX: You're a maggot.
SAM: Oh yes?
MAX: As soon as you stop paying your way here, I mean when you're too old to pay your way, you know what I'm going to do? I'm going to give you the boot.
SAM: You are, eh?
MAX: Sure. I mean, bring in the money and I'll put up with you. But when the firm gets rid of you—you can flake off.
SAM: This is my house as well, you know. This was our mother's house.

MAX: One lot after the other. One mess after the other.
SAM: Our father's house.
MAX: Look what I'm lumbered with. One cast-iron bunch of crap after another. One flow of stinking pus after another.

(*Pause.*)

Our father? I remember him. Don't worry. You kid yourself. He used to come over to me and look down at me. My old man did. He'd bend right over me, then he'd pick me up. I was only that big. Then he'd dandle me. Give me the bottle. Wipe me clean. Give me a smile. Pat me on the bum. Pass me around, pass me from hand to hand. Toss me up in the air. Catch me coming down. I remember my father.

(BLACKOUT.
LIGHTS UP.
Night.)
(TEDDY *and* RUTH *stand at the threshold of the room. They are both well dressed in light summer suits and light raincoats. Two suitcases are by their side. They look at the room.* TEDDY *tosses the key in his hand, smiles.*)

TEDDY: Well, the key worked.

(*Pause.*)

They haven't changed the lock.

(*Pause.*)

RUTH: No one's here.
TEDDY (*looking up*): They're asleep.

(*Pause.*)

RUTH: Can I sit down?
TEDDY: Of course.
RUTH: I'm tired.

(*Pause.*)

TEDDY: Then sit down.

(*She does not move.*)

That's my father's chair.
RUTH: That one?
TEDDY (*smiling*): Yes, that's it. Shall I go up and see if my room's still there?
RUTH: It can't have moved.
TEDDY: No, I mean if my bed's still there.
RUTH: Someone might be in it.
TEDDY: No. They've got their own beds.

(*Pause.*)

RUTH: Shouldn't you wake someone up? Tell them you're here?
TEDDY: Not at this time of night. It's too late.

(Pause.)

Shall I go up?

(He goes into the hall, looks up the stairs, comes back.)

Why don't you sit down?

(Pause.)

I'll just go up . . . have a look.

(He goes up the stairs, stealthily.
RUTH *stands, then slowly walks across the room.*
TEDDY *returns.)*

It's still there. My room. Empty. The bed's there. What are you doing?

(She looks at him.)

Blankets, no sheets. I'll find some sheets. I could hear snores. Really. They're all still here, I think. They're all snoring up there. Are you cold?
RUTH: No.
TEDDY: I'll make something to drink, if you like. Something hot.
RUTH: No, I don't want anything.

(TEDDY walks about.)

TEDDY: What do you think of the room? Big, isn't it? It's a big house. I mean, it's a fine room, don't you think? Actually there was a wall, across there . . . with a door. We knocked it down . . . years ago . . . to make an open living area. The structure wasn't affected, you see. My mother was dead.

(RUTH sits.)

Tired?
RUTH: Just a little.
TEDDY: We can go to bed if you like. No point in waking anyone up now. Just go to bed. See them all in the morning . . . see my father in the morning. . . .

(Pause.)

RUTH: Do you want to stay?
TEDDY: Stay?

(Pause.)

We've come to stay. We're bound to stay . . . for a few days.
RUTH: I think . . . the children . . . might be missing us.
TEDDY: Don't be silly.
RUTH: They might.
TEDDY: Look, we'll be back in a few days, won't we?

(He walks about the room.)

Nothing's changed. Still the same.

(Pause.)

Still, he'll get a surprise in the morning, won't he? The old man. I think you'll like him, very much. Honestly. He's a . . . well, he's old, of course. Getting on.

(Pause.)

I was born here, do you realize that?
RUTH: I know.

(Pause.)

TEDDY: Why don't you go to bed? I'll find some sheets. I feel . . . wide awake, isn't it odd? I think I'll stay up for a bit. Are you tired?
RUTH: No.
TEDDY: Go to bed. I'll show you the room.
RUTH: No, I don't want to.
TEDDY: You'll be perfectly all right up there without me. Really you will. I mean, I won't be long. Look, it's just up there. It's the first door on the landing. The bathroom's right next door. You . . . need some rest, you know.

(Pause.)

I just want to walk about for a few minutes. Do you mind?
RUTH: Of course I don't.
TEDDY: Well . . . Shall I show you the room?
RUTH: No, I'm happy at the moment.
TEDDY: You don't have to go to bed. I'm not saying you have to. I mean, you can stay up with me. Perhaps I'll make a cup of tea or something. The only thing is we don't want to make too much noise, we don't want to wake anyone up.
RUTH: I'm not making any noise.
TEDDY: I know you're not.

(He goes to her.)

(Gently.) Look, it's all right, really. I'm here. I mean . . . I'm with you. There's no need to be nervous. Are you nervous?
RUTH: No.
TEDDY: There's no need to be.

(Pause.)

They're very warm people, really. Very warm. They're my family. They're not ogres.

(Pause.)

Well, perhaps we should go to bed. After all, we have to be up early, see Dad. Wouldn't be quite right if he found us in bed, I think. *(He chuckles.)* Have to be up before six, come down, say hullo.

(Pause.)

RUTH: I think I'll have a breath of air.

TEDDY: Air?

(*Pause.*)

What do you mean?

RUTH (*standing*): Just a stroll.

TEDDY: At this time of night? But we've . . . only just got here. We've got to go to bed.

RUTH: I just feel like some air.

TEDDY: But I'm going to bed.

RUTH: That's all right.

TEDDY: But what am I going to do?

(*Pause.*)

The last thing I want is a breath of air. Why do you want a breath of air?

RUTH: I just do.

TEDDY: But it's late.

RUTH: I won't go far. I'll come back.

(*Pause.*)

TEDDY: I'll wait up for you.

RUTH: Why?

TEDDY: I'm not going to bed without you.

RUTH: Can I have the key?

(*He gives it to her.*)

Why don't you go to bed?

(*He puts his arms on her shoulders and kisses her. They look at each other, briefly. She smiles.*)

I won't be long.

(*She goes out of the front door.
TEDDY goes to the window, peers out after her, half turns from the window, stands, suddenly chews his knuckles.
LENNY walks into the room from upper left. He stands. He wears pyjamas and dressing-gown. He watches TEDDY. TEDDY turns and sees him.
Silence.*)

TEDDY: Hullo, Lenny.

LENNY: Hullo, Teddy.

(*Pause.*)

TEDDY: I didn't hear you come down the stairs.

LENNY: I didn't.

(*Pause.*)

I sleep down here now. Next door. I've got a kind of study, workroom cum bedroom next door now, you see.

TEDDY: Oh. Did I . . . wake you up?

LENNY: No. I just had an early night tonight. You know how it is. Can't sleep. Keep waking up.

(*Pause.*)

TEDDY: How are you?

LENNY: Well, just sleeping a bit restlessly, that's all. Tonight, anyway.

TEDDY: Bad dreams?

LENNY: No, I wouldn't say I was dreaming. It's not exactly a dream. It's just that something keeps waking me up. Some kind of tick.

TEDDY: A tick?

LENNY: Yes.

TEDDY: Well, what is it?

LENNY: I don't know.

(*Pause.*)

TEDDY: Have you got a clock in your room?

LENNY: Yes.

TEDDY: Well, maybe it's the clock.

LENNY: Yes, could be, I suppose.

(*Pause.*)

Well, if it's the clock I'd better do something about it. Stifle it in some way, or something.

(*Pause.*)

TEDDY: I've . . . just come back for a few days.

LENNY: Oh yes? Have you?

(*Pause.*)

TEDDY: How's the old man?

LENNY: He's in the pink.

(*Pause.*)

TEDDY: I've been keeping well.

LENNY: Oh, have you?

(*Pause.*)

Staying the night then, are you?

TEDDY: Yes.

LENNY: Well, you can sleep in your old room.

TEDDY: Yes, I've been up.

LENNY: Yes, you can sleep there.

(LENNY *yawns.*)

Oh well.

TEDDY: I'm going to bed.

LENNY: Are you?

TEDDY: Yes, I'll get some sleep.

LENNY: Yes, I'm going to bed, too.

(TEDDY *picks up the cases.*)

I'll give you a hand.

TEDDY: No, they're not heavy.

(TEDDY *goes into the hall with the cases.
LENNY turns out the light in the room.
The light in the hall remains on.
LENNY follows into the hall.*)

LENNY: Nothing you want?

TEDDY: Mmmm?

LENNY: Nothing you might want, for the night? Glass of water, anything like that?

TEDDY: Any sheets anywhere?

LENNY: In the sideboard in your room.

TEDDY: Oh, good.

LENNY: Friends of mine occasionally stay there, you know, in your room, when they're passing through this part of the world.

(LENNY *turns out the hall light and turns on the first landing light.*

TEDDY *begins to walk up the stairs.*)

TEDDY: Well, I'll see you at breakfast, then.

LENNY: Yes, that's it. Ta-ta.

(TEDDY *goes upstairs.*
LENNY *goes off left.*
Silence.
The landing light goes out.
Slight night light in the hall and room.
LENNY *comes back into the room, goes to the window and looks out.*
He leaves the window and turns on a lamp.
He is holding a small clock.
He sits, places the clock in front of him, lights a cigarette and sits.
RUTH *comes in the front door.*
She stands still. LENNY *turns his head, smiles. She walks slowly into the room.*)

LENNY: Good evening.

RUTH: Morning, I think.

LENNY: You're right there.

(Pause.)

My name's Lenny. What's yours?

RUTH: Ruth.

(*She sits, puts her coat collar around her.*)

LENNY: Cold?

RUTH: No.

LENNY: It's been a wonderful summer, hasn't it? Remarkable.

(Pause.)

Would you like something? Refreshment of some kind? An aperitif, anything like that?

RUTH: No, thanks.

LENNY: I'm glad you said that. We haven't got a drink in the house. Mind you, I'd soon get some in, if we had a party or something like that. Some kind of celebration . . . you know.

(Pause.)

You must be connected with my brother in some way. The one who's been abroad.

RUTH: I'm his wife.

LENNY: Eh listen, I wonder if you can advise me. I've been having a bit of a rough time with this clock. The tick's been keeping me up. The trouble is I'm not all that convinced it was the clock. I mean there are lots of things which tick in the night, don't you find that? All sorts of objects, which, in the day, you wouldn't call anything else but commonplace. They give you no trouble. But in the night any given one of a number of them is liable to start letting out a bit of a tick. Whereas you look at these objects in the day and they're just commonplace. They're as quiet as mice during the daytime. So . . . all things being equal . . . this question of me saying it was the clock that woke me up, well, that could very easily prove something of a false hypothesis.

(*He goes to the sideboard, pours from a jug into a glass, takes the glass to* RUTH.)

Here you are. I bet you could do with this.

RUTH: What is it?

LENNY: Water.

(*She takes it, sips, places the glass on a small table by her chair.*
LENNY *watches her.*)

Isn't it funny? I've got my pyjamas on and you're fully dressed?

(*He goes to the sideboard and pours another glass of water.*)

Mind if I have one? Yes, it's funny seeing my old brother again after all these years. It's just the sort of tonic my Dad needs, you know. He'll be chuffed to his bollocks in the morning, when he sees his eldest son. I was surprised myself when I saw Teddy, you know. Old Ted. I thought he was in America.

RUTH: We're on a visit to Europe.

LENNY: What, both of you?

RUTH: Yes.

LENNY: What, you sort of live with him over there, do you?

RUTH: We're married.

LENNY: On a visit to Europe, eh? Seen much of it?

RUTH: We've just come from Italy.

LENNY: Oh, you went to Italy first, did you? And then he brought you over here to meet the family, did he? Well, the old man'll be pleased to see you, I can tell you.

RUTH: Good.

LENNY: What did you say?

RUTH: Good.

(Pause.)

LENNY: Where'd you go to in Italy?

RUTH: Venice.

LENNY: Not dear old Venice? Eh? That's funny. You

know, I've always had a feeling that if I'd been a soldier in the last war—say in the Italian campaign—I'd probably have found myself in Venice. I've always had that feeling. The trouble was I was too young to serve, you see. I was only a child, I was too small, otherwise I've got a pretty shrewd idea I'd probably have gone through Venice. Yes, I'd almost certainly have gone through it with my battalion. Do you mind if I hold your hand?

RUTH: Why?

LENNY: Just a touch.

(He stands and goes to her.)

Just a tickle.

RUTH: Why?

(He looks down at her.)

LENNY: I'll tell you why.

(Slight pause.)

One night, not too long ago, one night down by the docks, I was standing alone under an arch, watching all the men jibbing the boom, out in the harbour, and playing about with the yardarm, when a certain lady came up to me and made me a certain proposal. This lady had been searching for me for days. She'd lost track of my where-abouts. However, the fact was she eventually caught up with me, and when she caught up with me she made me this certain proposal. Well, this proposal wasn't entirely out of order and nor-mally I would have subscribed to it. I mean I would have subscribed to it in the normal course of events. The only trouble was she was falling apart with the pox. So I turned it down. Well, this lady was very insistent and started taking liberties with me down under this arch, liberties which by any criterion I couldn't be expected to tolerate, the facts being what they were, so I clumped her one. It was on my mind at the time to do away with her, you know, to kill her, and the fact is, that as killings go, it would have been a simple matter, nothing to it. Her chauffeur, who had located me for her, he'd popped round the corner to have a drink, which just left this lady and myself, you see, alone, standing un-derneath this arch, watching all the steamers steaming up, no one about, all quiet on the Western Front, and there she was up against this wall—well, just sliding down the wall, following the blow I'd given her. Well, to sum up, every-thing was in my favour, for a killing. Don't worry about the chauffeur. The chauffeur would never have spoken. He was an old friend of the family. But . . . in the end I thought . . . Aaah, why go to all the bother . . . you know, getting rid of the corpse and all that, getting yourself into a state of tension. So I just gave her another belt in the nose and a couple of turns of the boot and sort of left it at that.

RUTH: How did you know she was diseased?

LENNY: How did I know?

(Pause.)

I decided she was.

(Silence.)

You and my brother are newly-weds, are you?

RUTH: We've been married six years.

LENNY: He's always been my favourite brother, old Teddy. Do you know that? And my goodness we are proud of him here, I can tell you. Doctor of Philosophy and all that . . . leaves quite an im-pression. Of course, he's a very sensitive man, isn't he? Ted. Very. I've often wished I was as sensitive as he is.

RUTH: Have you?

LENNY: Oh yes. Oh yes, very much so. I mean, I'm not saying I'm not sensitive. I am. I could just be a bit more so, that's all.

RUTH: Could you?

LENNY: Yes, just a bit more so, that's all.

(Pause.)

I mean, I am very sensitive to atmosphere, but I tend to get desensitized, if you know what I mean, when people make unreasonable de-mands on me. For instance, last Christmas I decided to do a bit of snow-clearing for the Borough Council, because we had a heavy snow over here that year in Europe. I didn't have to do this snow-clearing—I mean I wasn't financially embarrassed in any way—it just appealed to me, it appealed to something inside me. What I anticipated with a good deal of pleasure was the brisk cold bite in the air in the early morning. And I was right. I had to get my snowboots on and I had to stand on a corner, at about five-thirty in the morning, to wait for the lorry to pick me up, to take me to the allotted area. Bloody freezing. Well, the lorry came, I jumped on the tailboard, headlights on, dipped, and off we went. Got there, shovels up, fags on, and off we went, deep into the December snow, hours before cockcrow. Well, that morning, while I was having my mid-morning cup of tea in a neighbouring cafe, the shovel standing by my chair, an old lady approached me and asked me if I would give her a hand with her iron mangle. Her brother-in-law, she said, had left it for her, but he'd left it in the wrong room, he'd left it in the front room. Well, naturally, she wanted it in the back room. It was a present he'd given her, you see, a mangle, to iron out the washing. But he'd left it in the wrong room, he'd left it in the front room, well that was a silly place to leave it, it couldn't stay there. So I took time off to give her a hand. She only lived up the road. Well, the only trouble was when I got there I couldn't move this mangle. It must have weighed about half a ton. How this brother-in-law got it up there in the first place I can't even begin to envisage. So there I was, doing a bit of shoulders on with the mangle, risking a rupture, and this old lady just standing there, waving me on, not even lifting a little finger to give me a helping hand. So after a few minutes I said to her, now look here, why don't you stuff this iron mangle up your arse? Anyway, I said, they're out of date, you want to get a spin drier. I had a good mind to give her a workover there and then, but as I was feeling jubilant with the snow-clearing I just gave her a short-arm jab to the belly and jumped on a bus outside. Excuse me, shall I take this ashtray out of your way?

RUTH: It's not in my way.

LENNY: It seems to be in the way of your glass. The glass was about to fall. Or the ashtray. I'm rather worried about the carpet. It's not me, it's my father. He's obsessed with order and clarity. He doesn't like a mess. So, as I don't believe you're smoking at the moment, I'm sure you won't object if I move the ashtray.

(He does so.)

And now perhaps I'll relieve you of your glass.

RUTH: I haven't quite finished.

LENNY: You've consumed quite enough, in my opinion.

RUTH: No, I haven't.

LENNY: Quite sufficient, in my opinion.

RUTH: Not in mine, Leonard.

(Pause.)

LENNY: Don't call me that, please.

RUTH: Why not?

LENNY: That's the name my mother gave me.

(Pause.)

Just give me the glass.

RUTH: No.

(Pause.)

LENNY: I'll take it, then.

RUTH: If you take the glass . . . I'll take you.

(Pause.)

LENNY: How about me taking the glass without you taking me?

RUTH: Why don't I just take you?

(Pause.)

LENNY: You're joking.

(Pause.)

You're in love, anyway, with another man. You've had a secret liaison with another man. His family didn't even know. Then you come here without a word of warning and start to make trouble.

(She picks up the glass and lifts it toward him.)

RUTH: Have a sip. Go on. Have a sip from my glass.

(He is still.)

Sit on my lap. Take a long cool sip.

(She pats her lap. Pause.
She stands, moves to him with the glass.)

Put your head back and open your mouth.

LENNY: Take that glass away from me.

RUTH: Lie on the floor. Go on. I'll pour it down your throat.

LENNY: What are you doing, making me some kind of proposal?

(She laughs shortly, drains the glass.)

RUTH: Oh, I was thirsty.

(She smiles at him, puts the glass down, goes into the hall and up the stairs.
He follows into the hall and shouts up the stairs.)

LENNY: What was that supposed to be? Some kind of proposal?

(Silence.
He comes back into the room, goes to his own glass, drains it.
A door slams upstairs.
The landing light goes on.
MAX comes down the stairs, in pyjamas and cap. He comes into the room.)

MAX: What's going on here? You drunk?

(He stares at LENNY.)

What are you shouting about? You gone mad?

(LENNY pours another glass of water.)

Prancing about in the middle of the night shouting your head off. What are you, a raving lunatic?

LENNY: I was thinking aloud.

MAX: Is Joey down here? You been shouting at Joey?

LENNY: Didn't you hear what I said, Dad? I said I was thinking aloud.

MAX: You were thinking so loud you got me out of bed.

LENNY: Look, why don't you just . . . pop off, eh?

MAX: Pop off? He wakes me up in the middle of the night, I think we got burglars here, I think he's got a knife stuck in him, I come down here, he tells me to pop off.

(LENNY *sits down.*)

He was talking to someone. Who could he have been talking to? They're all asleep. He was having a conversation with someone. He won't tell me who it was. He pretends he was thinking aloud. What are you doing, hiding someone here?

LENNY: I was sleepwalking. Get out of it, leave me alone, will you?

MAX: I want an explanation, you understand? I asked you who you got hiding here.

(*Pause.*)

LENNY: I'll tell you what, Dad, since you're in the mood for a bit of a . . . chat, I'll ask you a question. It's a question I've been meaning to ask you for some time. That night . . . you know . . . the night you got me . . . that night with Mum, what was it like? Eh? When I was just a glint in your eye. What was it like? What was the background to it? I mean, I want to know the real facts about my background, I mean, for instance, is it a fact that you had me in mind all the time, or is it a fact that I was the last thing you had in mind?

(*Pause.*)

I'm only asking this in a spirit of inquiry, you understand that, don't you? I'm curious. And there's lots of people of my age share that curiosity, you know that, Dad? They often ruminate, sometimes singly, sometimes in groups, about the true facts of that particular night—the night they were made in the image of those two people *at it*. It's a question long overdue, from my point of view, but as we happen to be passing the time of day here tonight I thought I'd pop it to you.

(*Pause.*)

MAX: You'll drown in your own blood.

LENNY: If you prefer to answer the question in writing I've got no objection.

(MAX *stands.*)

I should have asked my dear mother. Why didn't I ask my dear mother? Now it's too late. She's passed over to the other side.

(MAX *spits at him.*
LENNY *looks down at the carpet.*)

Now look what you've done. I'll have to Hoover that in the morning, you know.

(MAX *turns and walks up the stairs.*
LENNY *sits still.*
BLACKOUT.
LIGHTS UP.
Morning.
JOEY *in front of the mirror. He is doing some slow limbering-up exercises. He stops, combs his hair, carefully. He then shadowboxes, heavily, watching himself in the mirror.*
MAX *comes in from upper left.*
Both MAX *and* JOEY *are dressed.* MAX *watches* JOEY *in silence.* JOEY *stops shadowboxing, picks up a newspaper and sits.*
Silence.)

MAX: I hate this room.

(*Pause.*)

It's the kitchen I like. It's nice in there. It's cosy.

(*Pause.*)

But I can't stay in there. You know why? Because he's always washing up in there, scraping the plates, driving me out of the kitchen, that's why.

JOEY: Why don't you bring your tea in here?

MAX: I don't want to bring my tea in here. I hate it here. I want to drink my tea in there.

(*He goes into the hall and looks toward the kitchen.*)

What's he doing in there?

(*He returns.*)

What's the time?

JOEY: Half past six.

MAX: Half past six.

(*Pause.*)

I'm going to see a game of football this afternoon. You want to come?

(*Pause.*)

I'm talking to you.

JOEY: I'm training this afternoon. I'm doing six rounds with Blackie.

MAX: That's not till five o'clock. You've got time to see a game of football before five o'clock. It's the first game of the season.

JOEY: No, I'm not going.

MAX: Why not?

(*Pause.*
MAX *goes into the hall.*)

Sam! Come here!

(MAX *comes back into the room.*

SAM *enters with a cloth.)*

SAM: What?

MAX: What are you doing in there?

SAM: Washing up.

MAX: What else?

SAM: Getting rid of your leavings.

MAX: Putting them in the bin, eh?

SAM: Right in.

MAX: What point you trying to prove?

SAM: No point.

MAX: Oh yes, you are. You resent making my break-fast, that's what it is, isn't it? That's why you bang round the kitchen like that, scraping the frying-pan, scraping all the leavings into the bin, scraping all the plates, scraping all the tea out of the teapot . . . that's why you do that, every single stinking morning. I know. Listen, Sam. I want to say something to you. From my heart.

(He moves closer.)

I want you to get rid of these feelings of resentment you've got towards me. I wish I could understand them. Honestly, have I ever given you cause? Never. When Dad died he said to me, Max, look after your brothers. That's exactly what he said to me.

SAM: How could he say that when he was dead?

MAX: What?

SAM: How could he speak if he was dead?

(Pause.)

MAX: Before he died, Sam. Just before. They were his last words. His last sacred words, Sammy. A split second after he said those words . . . he was a dead man. You think I'm joking? You think when my father spoke—on his death-bed—I wouldn't obey his words to the last letter? You hear that, Joey? He'll stop at nothing. He's even prepared to spit on the memory of our Dad. What kind of son were you, you wet wick? You spent half your time doing crossword puzzles! We took you into the butcher's shop, you couldn't even sweep the dust off the floor. We took MacGregor into the shop, he could run the place by the end of a week. Well, I'll tell you one thing. I respected my father not only as a man but as a number one butcher! And to prove it I followed him into the shop. I learned to carve a carcass at his knee. I commemorated his name in blood. I gave birth to three grown men! All on my own bat. What have you done?

(Pause.)

What have you done? You tit!

SAM: Do you want to finish the washing up? Look, here's the cloth.

MAX: So try to get rid of these feelings of resentment, Sam. After all, we are brothers.

SAM: Do you want the cloth? Here you are. Take it.

(TEDDY and RUTH come down the stairs. They walk across the hall and stop just inside the room. The others turn and look at them. JOEY stands. TEDDY and RUTH are wearing dressing-gowns. Silence.
TEDDY *smiles.)*

TEDDY: Hullo . . . Dad . . . We overslept.

(Pause.)

What's for breakfast?

(Silence.)
(TEDDY chuckles.)

Huh. We overslept.

(MAX turns to SAM.)

MAX: Did you know he was here?

SAM: No.

(MAX turns to JOEY.)

MAX: Did you know he was here?

(Pause.)

I asked you if you knew he was here.

JOEY: No.

MAX: Then who knew?

(Pause.)

Who knew?

(Pause.)

I didn't know.

TEDDY: I was going to come down, Dad, I was going to . . . be here, when you came down.

(Pause.)

How are you?

(Pause.)

Uh . . . look, I'd . . . like you to meet . . .

MAX: How long you been in this house?

TEDDY: All night.

MAX: All night? I'm a laughing-stock. How did you get in?

TEDDY: I had my key.

(MAX whistles and laughs.)

MAX: Who's this?

TEDDY: I was just going to introduce you.

MAX: Who asked you to bring tarts in here?

TEDDY: Tarts?

MAX: Who asked you to bring dirty tarts into this house?

TEDDY: Listen, don't be silly—

MAX: You been here all night?

TEDDY: Yes, we arrived from Venice—

MAX: We've had a smelly scrubber in my house all night. We've had a stinking pox-ridden slut in my house all night.

TEDDY: Stop it! What are you talking about?

MAX: I haven't seen the bitch for six years, he comes home without a word, he brings a filthy scrubber off the street, he shacks up in my house!

TEDDY: She's my wife! We're married!

(Pause.)

MAX: I've never had a whore under this roof before. Ever since your mother died. My word of honour. (to JOEY) Have you ever had a whore here? Has Lenny ever had a whore here. They come back from America, they bring the slopbucket with them. They bring the bedpan with them. *(to* TEDDY*)* Take that disease away from me. Get her away from me.

TEDDY: She's my wife.

MAX *(to* JOEY*)*: Chuck them out.

(Pause.)

A Doctor of Philosophy. Sam, you want to meet a Doctor of Philosophy? *(to* JOEY*)* I said chuck them out.

(Pause.)

What's the matter? You deaf?

JOEY: You're an old man. *(to* TEDDY*)* He's an old man.

*(*LENNY *walks into the room, in a dressing-gown.*
He stops.
They all look round.
MAX turns back, hits JOEY *in the stomach with all his might.*
JOEY contorts, staggers across the stage. MAX, *with the exertion of the blow, begins to collapse. His knees buckle. He clutches his stick.*
SAM moves forward to help him.
MAX hits him across the head with his stick. SAM *sits, head in hands.*
JOEY, hands pressed to his stomach, sinks down at the feet of RUTH.
She looks down at him.
LENNY and TEDDY are still.
JOEY slowly stands. He is close to RUTH. *He turns from* RUTH, *looks round at* MAX.
SAM clutches his head.
MAX breathes heavily, very slowly gets to his feet.
JOEY moves to him.
They look at each other.
Silence.
MAX moves past JOEY, *walks toward* RUTH. *He gestures with his stick.)*

MAX: Miss.

*(*RUTH *walks toward him.)*

RUTH: Yes?

(He looks at her.)

MAX: You a mother?

RUTH: Yes.

MAX: How many you got?

RUTH: Three.

(He turns to TEDDY.*)*

MAX: All yours, Ted?

(Pause.)

Teddy, why don't we have a nice cuddle and kiss, eh? Like the old days? What about a nice cuddle and kiss, eh?

TEDDY: Come on, then.

(Pause)

MAX: You want to kiss your old father? Want a cuddle with your old father?

TEDDY: Come on, then.

*(*TEDDY *moves a step toward him.)*

Come on.

(Pause.)

MAX: You still love your old Dad, eh?

(They face each other.)

TEDDY: Come on, Dad. I'm ready for the cuddle.

*(*MAX *begins to chuckle, gurgling.*
He turns to the family and addresses them.)

MAX: He still loves his father!

ACT 2

(Afternoon. MAX, TEDDY, LENNY *and* SAM *are about the stage, lighting cigars.*
  JOEY *comes in from upper left with a coffee tray, followed by* RUTH. *He puts the tray down.* RUTH *hands coffee to all the men. She sits with her cup.* MAX *smiles at her.)*

RUTH: That was a very good lunch.

MAX: I'm glad you liked it. (to the others) Did you hear that? *(to* RUTH*)* Well, I put my heart and soul into it, I can tell you. *(He sips.)* And this is a lovely cup of coffee.

RUTH: I'm glad.

(Pause.)

MAX: I've got the feeling you're a first-rate cook.

RUTH: I'm not bad.

MAX: No, I've got the feeling you're a number one cook. Am I right, Teddy?

TEDDY: Yes, she's a very good cook.

(Pause.)

MAX: Well, it's a long time since the whole family was together, eh? If only your mother was alive. Eh, what do you say, Sam? What would Jessie say if she was alive? Sitting here with her three sons. Three fine grown-up lads. And a lovely daughter-in-law. The only shame is her grandchildren aren't here. She'd have petted them and cooed over them, wouldn't she, Sam? She'd have fussed over them and played with them, told them stories, tickled them—I tell you she'd have been hysterical. *(to* RUTH*)* Mind you, she taught those boys everything they know. She taught them all the morality they know. I'm telling you. Every single bit of the moral code they live by—was taught to them by their mother. And she had a heart to go with it. What a heart. Eh, Sam? Listen, what's the use of beating round the bush? That woman was the backbone to this family. I mean, I was busy working twenty-four hours a day in the shop. I was going all over the country to find meat, I was making my way in the world, but I left a woman at home with a will of iron, a heart of gold and a mind. Right, Sam?

(Pause.)

What a mind.

(Pause.)

Mind you, I was a generous man to her. I never left her short of a few bob. I remember one year I entered into negotiations with a top-class group of butchers with continental connections. I was going into association with them. I remember the night I came home, I kept quiet. First of all I gave Lenny a bath, then Teddy a bath, then Joey a bath. What fun we used to have in the bath, eh, boys? Then I came downstairs and I made Jessie put her feet up on a pouffe—what happened to that pouffe, I haven't seen it for years—she put her feet up on the pouffe and I said to her, Jessie, I think our ship is going to come home, I'm going to treat you to a couple of items, I'm going to buy you a dress in pale corded blue silk, heavily encrusted in pearls, and for casual wear, a pair of pantaloons in lilac flowered taffeta. Then I gave her a drop of cherry brandy. I remember the boys came down, in their pyjamas, all their hair shining, their faces pink, it was before they started shaving, and they knelt down at our feet, Jessie's and mine. I tell you, it was like Christmas.

(Pause.)

RUTH: What happened to the group of butchers?

MAX: The group? They turned out to be a bunch of criminals like everyone else.

(Pause.)

This is a lousy cigar.

*(He stubs it out.
He turns to* SAM.*)*

What time you going to work?

SAM: Soon.

MAX: You've got a job on this afternoon, haven't you?

SAM: Yes, I know.

MAX: What do you mean, you know? You'll be late. You'll lose your job? What are you trying to do, humiliate me?

SAM: Don't worry about me.

MAX: It makes the bile come up in my mouth. The bile—you understand? *(to* RUTH*)* I worked as a butcher all my life, using the chopper and the slab, the slab, you know what I mean, the chopper and the slab! To keep my family in luxury. Two families! My mother was bedridden, my brothers were all invalids. I had to earn the money for the leading psychiatrists. I had to read books! I had to study the disease, so that I could cope with an emergency at every stage. A crippled family, three bastard sons, a slutbitch of a wife—don't talk to me about the pain of childbirth—I suffered the pain, I've still got the pangs—when I give a little cough my back collapses—and here I've got a lazy idle bugger of a brother won't even get to work on time. The best chauffeur in the world. All his life he's sat in the front seat giving lovely hand signals. You call that work? This man doesn't know his gearbox from his arse!

SAM: You go and ask my customers! I'm the only one they ever ask for.

MAX: What do the other drivers do, sleep all day?

SAM: I can only drive one car. They can't all have me at the same time.

MAX: Anyone could have you at the same time. You'd bend over for half a dollar on Blackfriars Bridge.

SAM: Me!

MAX: For two bob and a toffee apple.

SAM: He's insulting me. He's insulting his brother. I'm driving a man to Hampton Court at four forty-five.

MAX: Do you want to know who could drive? MacGregor! MacGregor was a driver.

SAM: Don't you believe it.

*(*MAX *points his stick at* SAM.*)*

MAX: He didn't even fight in the war. This man didn't even fight in the bloody war!

SAM: I did!

MAX: Who did you kill?

(Silence.
SAM gets up, goes to RUTH, shakes her hand and goes out
of the front door.
MAX turns to TEDDY.)

Well, how you been keeping, son?

TEDDY: I've been keeping very well, Dad.

MAX: It's nice to have you with us, son.

TEDDY: It's nice to be back, Dad.

(Pause.)

MAX: You should have told me you were married, Teddy. I'd have sent you a present. Where was the wedding, in America?

TEDDY: No. Here. The day before we left.

MAX: Did you have a big function?

TEDDY: No, there was no one there.

MAX: You're mad. I'd have given you a white wedding. We'd have had the cream of the cream here. I'd have been only too glad to bear the expense, my word of honour.

(Pause.)

TEDDY: You were busy at the time. I didn't want to bother you.

MAX: But you're my own flesh and blood. You're my first born. I'd have dropped everything. Sam would have driven you to the reception in the Snipe, Lenny would have been your best man, and then we'd have all seen you off on the boat. I mean, you don't think I disapprove of marriage, do you? Don't be daft. *(to RUTH)* I've been begging my two youngsters for years to find a nice feminine girl with proper credentials—it makes life worth living. *(to TEDDY)* Anyway, what's the difference, you did it, you made a wonderful choice, you've got a wonderful family, a marvellous career ... so why don't we let bygones be bygones?

(Pause.)

You know what I'm saying? I want you both to know that you have my blessing.

TEDDY: Thank you.

MAX: Don't mention it. How many other houses in the district have got a Doctor of Philosophy sitting down drinking a cup of coffee?

(Pause.)

RUTH: I'm sure Teddy's very happy ... to know that you're pleased with me.

(Pause.)

I think he wondered whether you would be pleased with me.

MAX: But you're a charming woman.

(Pause.)

RUTH: I was ...

MAX: What?

(Pause.)

What she say?

(They all look at her.)

RUTH: I was ... different ... when I met Teddy ... first.

TEDDY: No you weren't. You were the same.

RUTH: I wasn't.

MAX: Who cares? Listen, live in the present, what are you worrying about? I mean, don't forget the earth's about five thousand million years old, at least. Who can afford to live in the past?

(Pause.)

TEDDY: She's a great help to me over there. She's a wonderful wife and mother. She's a very popular woman. She's got lots of friends. It's a great life, at the University ... you know ... it's a very good life. We've got a lovely house ... we've got all ... we've got everything we want. It's a very stimulating environment.

(Pause.)

My department ... is highly successful.

(Pause.)

We've got three boys, you know.

MAX: All boys? Isn't that funny, eh? You've got three, I've got three. You've got three nephews, Joey. Joey! You're an uncle, do you hear? You could teach them how to box.

(Pause.)

JOEY *(to RUTH)*: I'm a boxer. In the evenings, after work. I'm in demolition in the daytime.

RUTH: Oh?

JOEY: Yes. I hope to be full time, when I get more bouts.

MAX *(to LENNY)*: He speaks so easily to his sister-in-law, do you notice. That's because she's an intelligent and sympathetic woman.

(He leans to her.)

Eh, tell me, do you think the children are missing their mother?

(She looks at him.)

TEDDY: Of course they are. They love her. We'll be seeing them soon.

(Pause.)

LENNY *(to* TEDDY): Your cigar's gone out.
TEDDY: Oh, yes.
LENNY: Want a light?
TEDDY: No. No.

(Pause.)

So has yours.
LENNY: Oh, yes.

(Pause.)

Eh, Teddy, you haven't told us much about your Doctorship of Philosophy. What do you teach?
TEDDY: Philosophy.
LENNY: Well, I want to ask you something. Do you detect a certain logical incoherence in the central affirmations of Christian theism?
TEDDY: That question doesn't fall within my province.
LENNY: Well, look at it this way . . . you don't mind my asking you some questions, do you?
TEDDY: If they're within my province.
LENNY: Well, look at it this way. How can the unknown merit reverence? In other words, how can you revere that of which you're ignorant? At the same time, it would be ridiculous to propose that what we *know* merits reverence. What we know merits any one of a number of things, but it stands to reason reverence isn't one of them. In other words, apart from the known and the unknown, what else is there?

(Pause.)

TEDDY: I'm afraid I'm the wrong person to ask.
LENNY: But you're a philosopher. Come on, be frank. What do you make of all this business of being and not-being?
TEDDY: What do you make of it?
LENNY: Well, for instance, take a table. Philosophically speaking. What is it?
TEDDY: A table.
LENNY: Ah. You mean it's nothing else but a table. Well, some people would envy your certainty, wouldn't they, Joey? For instance, I've got a couple of friends of mine, we often sit round the Ritz Bar having a few liqueurs, and they're always saying things like that, you know, things like: Take a table, take it. All right, I say, *take* it, *take* a table, but once you've taken it, what are you going to do with it? Once you've got hold of it, where you going to take it?
MAX: You'd probably sell it.
LENNY: You wouldn't get much for it.
JOEY: Chop it up for firewood.

*(*LENNY *looks at him and laughs.)*

RUTH: Don't be too sure though. You've forgotten something. Look at me. I . . . move my leg.

That's all it is. But I wear . . . underwear . . . which moves with me . . . it . . . captures your attention. Perhaps you misinterpret. The action is simple. It's a leg . . . moving. My lips move. Why don't you restrict . . . your observations to that? Perhaps the fact that they move is more significant . . . than the words which come through them. You must bear that . . . possibility . . . in mind.

(Silence.
TEDDY *stands.)*

I was born quite near here.

(Pause.)

Then . . . six years ago, I went to America.

(Pause.)

It's all rock. And sand. It stretches . . . so far . . . everywhere you look. And there's lots of insects there.

(Pause.)

And there's lots of insects there.

(Silence.
She is still.
MAX *stands.)*

MAX: Well, it's time to go to the gym. Time for your workout, Joey.
LENNY *(standing.)*: I'll come with you.

*(*JOEY *sits looking at* RUTH.)*

MAX: Joe.

*(*JOEY *stands. The three go out.*
TEDDY *sits by* RUTH, *holds her hand.*
She smiles at him.
Pause.)

TEDDY: I think we'll go back. Mmnn?

(Pause.)

Shall we go home?
RUTH: Why?
TEDDY: Well, we were only here for a few days, weren't we? We might as well . . . cut it short, I think.
RUTH: Why? Don't you like it here?
TEDDY: Of course I do. But I'd like to go back and see the boys now.

(Pause.)

RUTH: Don't you like your family?
TEDDY: Which family?
RUTH: Your family here.
TEDDY: Of course I like them. What are you talking about?

(Pause.)

RUTH: You don't like them as much as you thought you did?

TEDDY: Of course I do. Of course I . . . like them. I don't know what you're talking about.

(Pause.)

Listen. You know what time of the day it is there now, do you?

RUTH: What?

TEDDY: It's morning. It's about eleven o'clock.

RUTH: Is it?

TEDDY: Yes, they're about six hours behind us . . , I mean . . . behind the time here. The boys'll be at the pool . . . now . . . swimming. Think of it. Morning over there. Sun. We'll go anyway, mmnn? It's so clean there.

RUTH: Clean.

TEDDY: Yes.

RUTH: Is it dirty here?

TEDDY: No, of course not. But it's cleaner there.

(Pause.)

Look, I just brought you back to meet the family, didn't I? You've met them, we can go. The fall semester will be starting soon.

RUTH: You find it dirty here?

TEDDY: I didn't say I found it dirty here.

(Pause.)

I didn't say that.

(Pause.)

Look. I'll go and pack. You rest for a while. Will you? They won't be back for at least an hour. You can sleep. Rest. Please.

(She looks at him.)

You can help me with my lectures when we get back. I'd love that. I'd be so grateful for it, really. We can bathe till October. You know that. Here, there's nowhere to bathe, except the swimming bath down the road. You know what it's like? It's like a urinal. A filthy urinal!

(Pause.)

You liked Venice, didn't you? It was lovely, wasn't it? You had a good week. I mean . . . I took you there. I can speak Italian.

RUTH: But if I'd been a nurse in the Italian campaign I would have been there before.

(Pause.)

TEDDY: You just rest. I'll go and pack.

(TEDDY goes out and up the stairs.
(She closes her eyes.
LENNY appears from upper left.

He walks into the room and sits near her.
She opens her eyes.
Silence.)

LENNY: Well, the evenings are drawing in.

RUTH: Yes, it's getting dark.

(Pause.)

LENNY: Winter'll soon be upon us. Time to renew one's wardrobe.

(Pause.)

RUTH: That's a good thing to do.

LENNY: What?

(Pause.)

RUTH: I always . . .

(Pause.)

Do you like clothes?

LENNY: Oh, yes. Very fond of clothes.

(Pause.)

RUTH: I'm fond . . .

(Pause.)

What do you think of my shoes?

LENNY: They're very nice.

RUTH: No, I can't get the ones I want over there.

LENNY: Can't get them over there, eh?

RUTH: No . . . you don't get them there.

(Pause.)

I was a model before I went away.

LENNY: Hats?

(Pause.)

I bought a girl a hat once. We saw it in a glass case, in a shop. I tell you what it had. It had a bunch of daffodils on it, tied with a black satin bow, and then it was covered with a cloche of black veiling. A cloche. I'm telling you. She was made for it.

RUTH: No . . . I was a model for the body. A photographic model for the body.

LENNY: Indoor work?

RUTH: That was before I had . . . all my children.

(Pause.)

No, not always indoors.

(Pause.)

Once or twice we went to a place in the country, by train. Oh, six or seven times. We used to pass a . . . a large white water tower. This place . . . this house . . . was very big . . . the trees . . . there was a lake, you see . . . we used to change and walk down towards the lake . . . we went down a path . . . on stones . . . there were . . . on this path. Oh, just . . . wait . . . yes . . . when we changed in the house we had a drink. There was a cold buffet.

(Pause.)

Sometimes we stayed in the house but . . . most often . . . we walked down to the lake . . . and did our modelling there.

(Pause.)

Just before we went to America I went down there. I walked from the station to the gate and then I walked up the drive. There were lights on . . . I stood in the drive . . . the house was very light.

(TEDDY comes down the stairs with the cases. He puts them down, looks at LENNY.)

TEDDY: What have you been saying to her?

(He goes to RUTH.)

Here's your coat.

(LENNY goes to the radiogram and puts on a record of slow jazz.)

Ruth. Come on. Put it on.

LENNY *(to RUTH)*: What about one dance before you go?
TEDDY: We're going.
LENNY: Just one.
TEDDY: No. We're going.
LENNY: Just one dance, with her brother-in-law, before she goes.

(LENNY bends to her.)

Madam?

(RUTH stands. They dance, slowly.
TEDDY *stands, with RUTH's coat.*
MAX *and JOEY come in the front door and into the room. They stand.*
LENNY *kisses RUTH. They stand, kissing.)*

JOEY: Christ, she's wide open. Dad, look at that.

(Pause.)

She's a tart.

(Pause.)

Old Lenny's got a tart in here.

(JOEY goes to them. He takes RUTH's arm. He smiles at LENNY. He sits with RUTH on the sofa, embraces and kisses her.
He looks up at LENNY.)*

Just up my street.

(He leans her back until she lies beneath him. He kisses her.
He looks up at TEDDY and MAX.)*

It's better than a rubdown, this.

(LENNY sits on the arm of the sofa. He caresses RUTH's hair as JOEY embraces her.
MAX comes forward, looks at the cases.)*

MAX: You going, Teddy? Already?

(Pause.)

Well, when you coming over again, eh? Look, next time you come over, don't forget to let us know beforehand whether you're married or not. I'll always be glad to meet the wife. Honest. I'm telling you.

(JOEY lies heavily on RUTH.
They are almost still.*
LENNY caresses her hair.)*

Listen, you think I don't know why you didn't tell me you were married? I know why. You were ashamed. You thought I'd be annoyed because you married a woman beneath you. You should have known me better. I'm broadminded. I'm a broadminded man.

(He peers to see RUTH's face under JOEY, turns back to TEDDY.)

Mind you, she's a lovely girl. A beautiful woman. And a mother too. A mother of three. You've made a happy woman out of her. It's something to be proud of. I mean, we're talking about a woman of quality. We're talking about a woman of feeling.

(JOEY and RUTH roll off the sofa on to the floor.
JOEY clasps her. LENNY moves to stand above them. He looks down on them. He touches RUTH gently with his foot.*
RUTH suddenly pushes JOEY away.*
She stands up.*
JOEY gets to his feet, stares at her.)*

RUTH: I'd like something to eat. *(To LENNY.)* I'd like a drink. Did you get any drink?
LENNY: We've got drink.
RUTH: I'd like one, please.
LENNY: What drink?
RUTH: Whisky.
LENNY: I've got it.

(Pause.)

RUTH: Well, get it.

(LENNY goes to the sideboard, takes out bottle and glasses.
JOEY moves toward her.)*

Put the record off.

(*He looks at her, turns, puts the record off.*)

I want something to eat.

(*Pause.*)

JOEY: I can't cook. (*Pointing to* MAX.) He's the cook.

(LENNY *brings her a glass of whisky.*)

LENNY: Soda on the side?

RUTH: What's this glass? I can't drink out of this. Haven't you got a tumbler?

LENNY: Yes.

RUTH: Well, put it in a tumbler.

(*He takes the glass back, pours whisky into a tumbler, brings it to her.*)

LENNY: On the rocks. Or as it comes?

RUTH: Rocks? What do you know about rocks?

LENNY: We've got rocks. But they're frozen stiff in the fridge.

(RUTH *drinks.*
LENNY *looks round at the others.*)

Drinks all round?

(*He goes to the sideboard and pours drinks.*
JOEY *moves closer to* RUTH.)

JOEY: What food do you want?

(RUTH *walks round the room.*)

RUTH (*to* TEDDY): Have your family read your critical works?

MAX: That's one thing I've never done. I've never read one of his critical works.

TEDDY: You wouldn't understand them.

(LENNY *hands drinks all round.*)

JOEY: What sort of food do you want? I'm not the cook, anyway.

LENNY: Soda, Ted? Or as it comes?

TEDDY: You wouldn't understand my works. You wouldn't have the faintest idea of what they were about. You wouldn't appreciate the points of reference. You're way behind. All of you. There's no point in my sending you my works. You'd be lost. It's nothing to do with the question of intelligence. It's a way of being able to look at the world. It's a question of how far you can operate on things and not in things. I mean it's a question of your capacity to ally the two, to relate the two, to balance the two. To see, to be able to see! I'm the one who can see. That's why I can write my critical works. Might do you good . . . have a look at them . . . see how certain people can view . . . things . . . how certain people can maintain . . . intellectual equilibrium. Intellec-

tual equilibrium. You're just objects. You just . . . move about. I can observe it. I can see what you do. It's the same as I do. But you're lost in it. You won't get me being . . . I won't be lost in it.

(BLACKOUT.
LIGHTS UP.
Evening.
TEDDY *sitting, in his coat, the cases by him.* SAM. *Pause.*)

SAM: Do you remember MacGregor, Teddy?

TEDDY: Mac?

SAM: Yes.

TEDDY: Of course I do.

SAM: What did you think of him? Did you take to him?

TEDDY: Yes. I liked him. Why?

(*Pause.*)

SAM: You know, you were always my favourite, of the lads. Always.

(*Pause.*)

When you wrote to me from America I was very touched, you know. I mean you'd written to your father a few times but you'd never written to me. But then, when I got that letter from you . . . well, I was very touched. I never told him. I never told him I'd heard from you.

(*Pause.*)

(*Whispering.*) Teddy, shall I tell you something? You were always your mother's favourite. She told me. It's true. You were always the . . . you were always the main object of her love.

(*Pause.*)

Why don't you stay for a couple more weeks, eh? We could have a few laughs.

(LENNY *comes in the front door and into the room.*)

LENNY: Still here, Ted? You'll be late for your first seminar.

(*He goes to the sideboard, opens it, peers in it, to the right and the left, stands.*)

Where's my cheese-roll?

(*Pause.*)

Someone's taken my cheese-roll. I left it there. (*To* SAM.) You been thieving?

TEDDY: I took your cheese-roll, Lenny.

(*Silence.*
SAM *looks at them, picks up his hat and goes out of the front door.*
Silence.)

LENNY: You took my cheese-roll?

TEDDY: Yes.

LENNY: I made that roll myself. I cut it and put the butter on. I sliced a piece of cheese and put it in between. I put it on a plate and I put it in the sideboard. I did all that before I went out. Now I come back and you've eaten it.

TEDDY: Well, what are you going to do about it?

LENNY: I'm waiting for you to apologize.

TEDDY: But I took it deliberately, Lenny.

LENNY: You mean you didn't stumble on it by mistake?

TEDDY: No, I saw you put it there. I was hungry, so I ate it.

(Pause.)

LENNY: Barefaced audacity.

(Pause.)

What led you to be so . . . vindictive against your own brother? I'm bowled over.

(Pause.)

Well, Ted, I would say this is something approaching the naked truth, isn't it? It's a real cards on the table stunt. I mean, we're in the land of no holds barred now. Well, how else can you interpret it? To pinch your younger brother's specially made cheese-roll when he's out doing a spot of work, that's not equivocal, it's unequivocal.

(Pause.)

Mind you, I will say you do seem to have grown a bit sulky during the last six years. A bit sulky. A bit inner. A bit less forthcoming. It's funny, because I'd have thought that in the United States of America, I mean with the sun and all that, the open spaces, on the old campus, in your position, lecturing, in the centre of all the intellectual life out there, on the old campus, all the social whirl, all the stimulation of it all, all your kids and all that, to have fun with, down by the pool, the Greyhound buses and all that, tons of iced water, all the comfort of those Bermuda shorts and all that, on the old campus, no time of the day or night you can't get a cup of coffee or a Dutch gin, I'd have thought you'd have grown more forthcoming, not less. Because I want you to know that you set a standard for us, Teddy. Your family looks up to you, boy, and you know what it does? It does its best to follow the example you set. Because you're a great source of pride to us. That's why we were so glad to see you come back, to welcome you back to your birthplace. That's why.

(Pause.)

No, listen, Ted, there's no question that we live a less rich life here than you do over there. We live a closer life. We're busy, of course. Joey's busy with his boxing, I'm busy with my occupation, Dad still plays a good game of poker, and he does the cooking as well, well up to his old standard, and Uncle Sam's the best chauffeur in the firm. But nevertheless we do make up a unit, Teddy, and you're an integral part of it. When we all sit round the backyard having a quiet gander at the night sky, there's always an empty chair standing in the circle, which is in fact yours. And so when you at length return to us, we do expect a bit of grace, a bit of je ne sais quoi, a bit of generosity of mind, a bit of liberality of spirit, to reassure us. We do expect that. But do we get it? Have we got it? Is that what you've given us?

(Pause.)

TEDDY: Yes.

(JOEY comes down the stairs and into the room, with a newspaper.)

LENNY *(to JOEY)*: How'd you get on?

JOEY: Er . . . not bad.

LENNY: What do you mean?

(Pause.)

What do you mean?

JOEY: Not bad.

LENNY: I want to know what you *mean*—by not bad.

JOEY: What's it got to do with you?

LENNY: Joey, you tell your brother everything.

(Pause.)

JOEY: I didn't get all the way.

LENNY: You didn't get all the way?

(Pause.)

(With emphasis.) You didn't get all the way? But you've had her up there for two hours.

JOEY: Well?

LENNY: You didn't get all the way and you've had her up there for two hours!

JOEY: What about it?

(LENNY moves closer to him.)

LENNY: What are you telling me?

JOEY: What do you mean?

LENNY: Are you telling me she's a tease?

(Pause.)

She's a tease!

(Pause.)

What do you think of that, Ted? Your wife turns out to be a tease. He's had her up there for two hours and he didn't go the whole hog.

JOEY: I didn't say she was a tease.

LENNY: Are you joking? It sounds like a tease to me, don't it to you, Ted?

TEDDY: Perhaps he hasn't got the right touch.

LENNY: Joey? Not the right touch? Don't be ridiculous. He's had more dolly than you've had cream cakes. He's irresistible. He's one of the few and far between. Tell him about the last bird you had, Joey.

(Pause.)

JOEY: What bird?

LENNY: The last bird! When we stopped the car . . .

JOEY: Oh, that . . . yes . . . well, we were in Lenny's car one night last week . . .

LENNY: The Alfa.

JOEY: And er . . . bowling down the road . . .

LENNY: Up near the Scrubs.

JOEY: Yes, up over by the Scrubs . . .

LENNY: We were doing a little survey of North Paddington.

JOEY: And er . . . it was pretty late, wasn't it?

LENNY: Yes, it was late. Well?

(Pause.)

JOEY: And then we . . . well, by the kerb, we saw this parked car . . . with a couple of girls in it.

LENNY: And their escorts.

JOEY: Yes, there were two geezers in it. Anyway . . .

(Pause.)

What we do then?

LENNY: We stopped the car and got out!

JOEY: Yes . . . we got out . . . and we told the . . . two escorts . . . to go away . . . which they did . . . and then we . . . got the girls out of the car . . .

LENNY: We didn't take them over the Scrubs.

JOEY: Oh, no. Not over the Scrubs. Well, the police would have noticed us there . . . you see. We took them over a bombed site.

LENNY: Rubble. In the rubble.

JOEY: Yes, plenty of rubble.

(Pause.)

Well . . . you know . . . then we had them.

LENNY: You've missed out the best bit. He's missed out the best bit!

JOEY: What bit?

LENNY *(to TEDDY)*: His bird says to him, I don't mind, she says, but I've got to have some protection. I've got to have some contraceptive protection. I haven't got any contraceptive protection, old Joey says to her. In that case I won't do it, she says. Yes you will, says Joey, never mind about the contraceptive protection.

(LENNY laughs.)

Even my bird laughed when she heard that. Yes, even she gave out a bit of a laugh. So you can't say old Joey isn't a bit of a knockout when he gets going, can you? And here he is upstairs with your wife for two hours and he hasn't even been the whole hog. Well, your wife sounds like a bit of a tease to me, Ted. What do you make of it, Joey? You satisfied? Don't tell me you're satisfied without going the whole hog?

(Pause.)

JOEY: I've been the whole hog plenty of times. Sometimes . . . you can be happy . . . and not go the whole hog. Now and again . . . you can be happy . . . without going any hog.

(LENNY stares at him.
MAX and SAM come in the front door and into the room.)

MAX: Where's the whore? Still in bed? She'll make us all animals.

LENNY: The girl's a tease.

MAX: What?

LENNY: She's had Joey on a string.

MAX: What do you mean?

TEDDY: He had her up there for two hours and he didn't go the whole hog.

(Pause.)

MAX: My Joey? She did that to my boy?

(Pause.)

To my youngest son? Tch, tch, tch, tch. How you feeling, son? Are you all right?

JOEY: Sure I'm all right.

MAX *(to TEDDY)*: Does she do that to you, too?

TEDDY: No.

LENNY: He gets the gravy.

MAX: You think so?

JOEY: No he don't.

(Pause.)

SAM: He's her lawful husband. She's his lawful wife.

JOEY: No he don't! He don't get no gravy! I'm telling you. I'm telling all of you. I'll kill the next man who says he gets the gravy.

MAX: Joey . . . what are you getting so excited about? *(to LENNY)* It's because he's frustrated. You see what happens?

JOEY: Who is?

MAX: Joey. No one's saying you're wrong. In fact everyone's saying you're right.

(Pause.

MAX *turns to the others.)*

You know something? Perhaps it's not a bad idea to have a woman in the house. Perhaps it's a good thing. Who knows? Maybe we should keep her.

(Pause.)

Maybe we'll ask her if she wants to stay.

(Pause.)

TEDDY: I'm afraid not, Dad. She's not well, and we've got to get home to the children.

MAX: Not well? I told you, I'm used to looking after people who are not so well. Don't worry about that. Perhaps we'll keep her here.

(Pause.)

SAM: Don't be silly.

MAX: What's silly?

SAM: You're talking rubbish.

MAX: Me?

SAM: She's got three children.

MAX: She can have more! If she's so keen.

TEDDY: She doesn't want any more.

MAX: What do you know about what she wants, eh, Ted?

TEDDY *(smiling)*: The best thing for her is to come home with me, Dad. Really. We're married, you know.

(MAX walks about the room, clicks his fingers.)

MAX: We'd have to pay her, of course. You realize that? We can't leave her walking about without any pocket money. She'll have to have a little allowance.

JOEY: Of course we'll pay her. She's got to have some money in her pocket.

MAX: That's what I'm saying. You can't expect a woman to walk about without a few bob to spend on a pair of stockings.

(Pause.)

LENNY: Where's the money going to come from?

MAX: Well, how much is she worth? What we talking about three figures?

LENNY: I asked you where the money's going to come from. It'll be an extra mouth to feed. It'll be an extra body to clothe. You realize that?

JOEY: I'll buy her clothes.

LENNY: What with?

JOEY: I'll put in a certain amount out of my wages.

MAX: That's it. We'll pass the hat round. We'll make a donation. We're all grown-up people, we've got a sense of responsibility. We'll put a little in the hat. It's democratic.

LENNY: It'll come to a few quid, Dad.

(Pause.)

I mean, she's not a woman who likes walking around in second-hand goods. She's up to the latest fashion. You wouldn't want her walking about in clothes which don't show her off at her best, would you?

MAX: Lenny, do you mind if I make a little comment? It's not meant to be critical. But I think you're concentrating too much on the economic considerations. There are other considerations. There are the human considerations. You understand what I mean? There are the human considerations. Don't forget them.

LENNY: I won't.

MAX: Well don't.

(Pause.)

Listen, we're bound to treat her in something approximating, at least, to the manner in which she's accustomed. After all, she's not someone off the street, she's my daughter-in-law!

JOEY: That's right.

MAX: There you are, you see. Joey'll donate, Sam'll donate. . . .

(SAM looks at him.)

I'll put in a few bob out of my pension, Lenny'll cough up. We're laughing. What about you, Ted? How much you going to put in the kitty?

TEDDY: I'm not putting anything in the kitty.

MAX: What? You won't even help to support your own wife? I thought he was a son of mine. You lousy stinkpig. Your mother would drop dead if she heard you take that attitude.

LENNY: Eh, Dad.

(LENNY walks forward.)

I've got a better idea.

MAX: What?

LENNY: There's no need for us to go to all this expense. I know these women. Once they get started they ruin your budget. I've got a better idea. Why don't I take her up with me to Greek Street?

(Pause.)

MAX: You mean put her on the game?

(Pause.)

We'll put her on the game. That's a stroke of genius, that's a marvellous idea. You mean she can earn the money herself—on her back?

LENNY: Yes.

MAX: Wonderful. The only thing is, it'll have to be

short hours. We don't want her out of the house all night.

LENNY: I can limit the hours.

MAX: How many?

LENNY: Four hours a night.

MAX (*dubiously*): Is that enough?

LENNY: She'll bring in a good sum for four hours a night.

MAX: Well, you should know. After all, it's true, the last thing we want to do is wear the girl out. She's going to have her obligations this end as well. Where you going to put her in Greek Street?

LENNY: It doesn't have to be right in Greek Street, Dad. I've got a number of flats all around that area.

MAX: You have? Well, what about me? Why don't you give me one?

LENNY: You're sexless.

JOEY: Eh, wait a minute, what's all this?

MAX: I know what Lenny's saying. Lenny's saying she can pay her own way. What do you think, Teddy? That'll solve all our problems.

JOEY: Eh, wait a minute. I don't want to share her.

MAX: What did you say?

JOEY: I don't want to share her with a lot of yobs!

MAX: Yobs! You arrogant git! What arrogance. (*to* LENNY) Will you be supplying her with yobs?

LENNY: I've got a very distinguished clientèle, Joey. They're more distinguished than you'll ever be.

MAX: So you can count yourself lucky we're including you in.

JOEY: I didn't think I was going to have to share her!

MAX: Well, you *are* going to have to share her! Otherwise she goes straight back to America. You understand?

(*Pause.*)

It's tricky enough as it is, without you shoving your oar in. But there's something worrying me. Perhaps she's not so up to the mark. Eh? Teddy, you're the best judge. Do you think she'd be up to the mark?

(*Pause.*)

I mean what about all this teasing? Is she going to make a habit of it? That'll get us nowhere.

(*Pause.*)

TEDDY: It was just love play . . . I suppose . . . that's all I suppose it was.

MAX: Love play? Two bleeding hours? That's a bloody long time for love play!

LENNY: I don't think we've got anything to worry about on that score, Dad.

MAX: How do you know?

LENNY: I'm giving you a professional opinion.

(LENNY *goes to* TEDDY.)

LENNY: Listen, Teddy, you could help us, actually. If I were to send you some cards, over to America . . . you know, very nice ones, with a name on, and a telephone number, very discreet, well, you could distribute them . . . to various parties, who might be making a trip over here. Of course, you'd get a little percentage out of it.

MAX: I mean, you needn't tell them she's your wife.

LENNY: No, we'd call her something else. Dolores, or something.

MAX: Or Spanish Jacky.

LENNY: No, you've got to be reserved about it, Dad. We could call her something nice . . . like Cynthia . . . or Gillian.

(*Pause.*)

JOEY: Gillian.

(*Pause.*)

LENNY: No, what I mean, Teddy, you must know lots of professors, heads of departments, men like that. They pop over here for a week at the Savoy, they need somewhere they can go to have a nice quiet poke. And of course you'd be in a position to give them inside information.

MAX: Sure. You can give them proper data. You know, the kind of thing she's willing to do. How far she'd be prepared to go with their little whims and fancies. Eh, Lenny. To what extent she's various. I mean if you don't know, who does?

(*Pause.*)

I bet you before two months we'd have a waiting list.

LENNY: You could be our representative in the States.

MAX: Of course. We're talking in international terms! By the time we've finished Pan-American'll give us a discount.

(*Pause.*)

TEDDY: She'd get old . . . very quickly.

MAX: No . . . not in this day and age! With the health service? Old! How could she get old? She'll have the time of her life.

(RUTH *comes down the stairs, dressed.*
She comes into the room.
She smiles at the gathering, and sits.
Silence.)

TEDDY: Ruth . . . the family have invited you to stay, for a little while longer. As a . . . as a kind of guest. If you like the idea I don't mind. We can manage very easily at home . . . until you come back.

RUTH: How very nice of them.

(Pause.)

MAX: It's an offer from our heart.

RUTH: It's very sweet of you.

MAX: Listen . . . it would be our pleasure.

(Pause.)

RUTH: I think I'd be too much trouble.

MAX: Trouble? What are you talking about? What trouble? Listen, I'll tell you something. Since poor Jessie died, eh, Sam? we haven't had a woman in the house. Not one. Inside this house. And I'll tell you why. Because their mother's image was so dear any other woman would have . . . tarnished it. But you . . . Ruth . . . you're not only lovely and beautiful, but you're kin. You're kith. You belong here.

(Pause.)

RUTH: I'm very touched.

MAX: Of course you're touched. I'm touched.

(Pause.)

TEDDY: But Ruth, I should tell you . . . that you'll have to pull your weight a little, if you stay. Financially. My father isn't very well off.

RUTH (to MAX): Oh, I'm sorry.

MAX: No, you'd just have to bring in a little, that's all. A few pennies. Nothing much. It's just that we're waiting for Joey to hit the top as a boxer. When Joey hits the top . . . well . . .

(Pause.)

TEDDY: Or you can come home with me.

LENNY: We'd get you a flat.

(Pause.)

RUTH: A flat?

LENNY: Yes.

RUTH: Where?

LENNY: In town.

(Pause.)

But you'd live here, with us.

MAX: Of course you would. This would be your home. In the bosom of the family.

LENNY: You'd just pop up to the flat a couple of hours a night, that's all.

MAX: Just a couple of hours, that's all. That's all.

LENNY: And you make enough money to keep you going here.

(Pause.)

RUTH: How many rooms would this flat have?

LENNY: Not many.

RUTH: I would want at least three rooms and a bathroom.

LENNY: You wouldn't need three rooms and a bathroom.

MAX: She'd need a bathroom.

LENNY: But not three rooms.

(Pause.)

RUTH: Oh, I would. Really.

LENNY: Two would do.

RUTH: No. Two wouldn't be enough.

(Pause.)

I'd want a dressing-room, a rest-room, and a bedroom.

(Pause.)

LENNY: All right, we'll get you a flat with three rooms and a bathroom.

RUTH: With what kind of conveniences?

LENNY: All conveniences.

RUTH: A personal maid?

LENNY: Of course.

(Pause.)

We'd finance you, to begin with, and then, when you were established, you could pay us back, in instalments.

RUTH: Oh, no, I wouldn't agree to that.

LENNY: Oh, why not?

RUTH: You would have to regard your original outlay simply as a capital investment.

(Pause.)

LENNY: I see. All right.

RUTH: You'd supply my wardrobe, of course?

LENNY: We'd supply everything. Everything you need.

RUTH: I'd need an awful lot. Otherwise I wouldn't be content.

LENNY: You'd have everything.

RUTH: I would naturally want to draw up an inventory of everything I would need, which would require your signatures in the presence of witnesses.

LENNY: Naturally.

RUTH: All aspects of the agreement and conditions of employment would have to be clarified to our mutual satisfaction before we finalized the contract.

LENNY: Of course.

(Pause.)

RUTH: Well, it might prove a workable arrangement.

LENNY: I think so.

MAX: And you'd have the whole of your daytime free, of course. You could do a bit of cooking here if you wanted to.

LENNY: Make the beds.

MAX: Scrub the place out a bit.

TEDDY: Keep everyone company.

(SAM *comes forward.*)

SAM (*in one breath*): MacGregor had Jessie in the back of my cab as I drove them along.

(*He croaks and collapses.*
He lies still.
They look at him.)

MAX: What's he done? Dropped dead?

LENNY: Yes.

MAX: A corpse? A corpse on my floor? Get him out of here! Clear him out of here!

(JOEY *bends over* SAM.)

JOEY: He's not dead.

LENNY: He probably was dead, for about thirty seconds.

MAX: He's not even dead!

(LENNY *looks down at* SAM.)

LENNY: Yes, there's still some breath there.

MAX (*pointing at* SAM): You know what that man had?

LENNY: Has.

MAX: Has! A diseased imagination.

(*Pause.*)

RUTH: Yes, it sounds a very attractive idea.

MAX: Do you want to shake on it now, or do you want to leave it till later?

RUTH: Oh, we'll leave it till later.

(TEDDY *stands.*
He looks down at SAM.)

TEDDY: I was going to ask him to drive me to London Airport.

(*He goes to the cases, picks one up.*)

Well, I'll leave your case, Ruth. I'll just go up the road to the Underground.

MAX: Listen if you go the other way, first left, first right, you remember, you might find a cab passing there.

TEDDY: Yes, I might do that.

MAX: Or you can take the tube to Piccadilly Circus, won't take you ten minutes, and pick up a cab from there out to the Airport.

TEDDY: Yes, I'll probably do that.

MAX: Mind you, they'll charge you double fare. They'll charge you for the return trip. It's over the six-mile limit.

TEDDY: Yes. Well, bye-bye, Dad. Look after yourself.

(*They shake hands.*)

MAX: Thanks, son. Listen. I want to tell you something. It's been wonderful to see you.

(*Pause.*)

TEDDY: It's been wonderful to see you.

MAX: Do your boys know about me? Would they like to see a photo, do you think, of their grandfather?

TEDDY: I know they would.

(MAX *brings out his wallet.*)

MAX: I've got one on me. I've got one here. Just a minute. Here you are. Will they like that one?

TEDDY (*taking it*): They'll be thrilled.

(*He turns to* LENNY.)

Good-bye, Lenny.

(*They shake hands.*)

LENNY: Ta-ta, Ted. Good to see you. Have a good trip.

TEDDY: Bye-bye, Joey.

(JOEY *does not move.*)

JOEY: Ta-ta.

(TEDDY *goes to the front door.*)

RUTH: Eddie.

(TEDDY *turns.*
Pause.)

Don't become a stranger.

(TEDDY *goes, shuts the front door.*
Silence.
The three men stand.
RUTH *sits relaxed in her chair.*
SAM *lies still.*
JOEY *walks slowly across the room.*
He kneels at her chair.
She touches his head, lightly.
He puts his head in her lap.
MAX *begins to move above them, backwards and forwards.*
LENNY *stands still.*
MAX *turns to* LENNY.)

MAX: I'm too old, I suppose. She thinks I'm an old man.

(*Pause.*)

I'm not such an old man.

(*Pause.*)

(*To* RUTH) You think I'm too old for you?

(Pause.)

Listen. You think you're just going to get that big slag all the time? You think you're just going to have him . . . you're going to just have him all the time? You're going to have to work! You'll have to take them on, you understand?

(Pause.)

Does she realize that?

(Pause.)

Lenny, do you think she understands . . .

(He begins to stammer.)

What . . . what . . . what . . . we're getting at? What . . . we've got in mind? Do you think she's got it clear?

(Pause.)

I don't think she's got it clear.

(Pause.)

You understand what I mean? Listen, I've got a funny idea she'll do the dirty on us, you want to bet? She'll use us, she'll make use of us, I can tell you that! I can smell it! You want to bet?

(Pause.)

She won't . . . be adaptable!

(He falls to his knees, whimpers, begins to moan and sob. He stops sobbing, crawls past SAM's *body round her chair, to the other side of her.)*

I'm not an old man.

(He looks up at her.)

Do you hear me?

(He raises his face to her.)

Kiss me.

(She continues to touch JOEY's *head, lightly.* LENNY *stands, watching.)*

CURTAIN

Figure 1. Lenny (Ian Holm) offers Ruth (Vivien Merchant) a glass of water in the Royal Shakespeare Company production of *The Homecoming,* directed by Peter Hall, New York, 1967. (Photograph: Friedman-Abeles.)

Figure 2. Max (Paul Rogers, *left*) insults Ruth (Vivien Merchant) while *(left to right)* Joey (Terence Rigby), Sam (John Normington), Teddy (Michael Craig), and Lenny (Ian Holm) listen in the Royal Shakespeare Company production of *The Homecoming*, directed by Peter Hall, New York, 1967. (Photograph: Friedman-Abeles.)

Staging of *The Homecoming*

REVIEW OF THE ROYAL SHAKESPEARE COMPANY PRODUCTION, 1967, BY WALTER KERR

Harold Pinter's "The Homecoming" consists of a single situation that the author refuses to dramatize until he has dragged us all, aching, through a half-drugged dream.

The situation, when it is arrived at, is interesting in the way that Pinter's numbed fantasies are almost always interesting. A Doctor of Philosophy who actually teaches philosophy returns with his wife to the family home in North London, a home that looks like an emptied-out wing of the British Museum gone thoroughly to seed. (The few pieces of furniture are lonely in this cavern. The molding along the walls breaks off and gives up before it can reach the doorways, the carpet could be made of cement.)

A father and two brothers take one look at the wife and mistake (or do not mistake) her for a whore. She is silent, poised, leggy, self-contained. In due time the family decides that they would rather like to have a whore around, whatever about her husband and about the three children she has left behind in America. She might very well be kept available in a room at the top of the steep, forbidding staircase, and she could always pay her own keep by renting herself out a few nights a week.

They put the proposition to her, matter-of-factly, after she has obliged them by moving into trance-like dance with one of the brothers, brushing unfinished kisses across his lips and then obligingly draping herself to another brother's needs across a cold and impersonal sofa.

It is at this point that Mr. Pinter's most curious and most characteristic abilities as a diviner of unspecified demons come effectively into play. We are in an unconventional situation, and of course we know that. But our habits of mind—our compulsive attempts to try to deal with the world by slide rule—still continue to function, stubbornly. We expect even so bizarre a crisis to provoke logical responses: the husband will be humiliated or outraged, the wife will prove herself either a genuine wife or a genuine whore, and so on. We have the probabilities all ready in our heads.

But Mr. Pinter is not interested in the rational probabilities of the moment. He is interested in what *might* happen if our controlling expectations were suddenly junked, if flesh and heart and moving bone were freed from preconditioning and allowed simply to behave, existentially. The world might go another way—a surprising and ultimately unexplained way—if it went its own way, indifferent to philosophers.

Just how the tangle at the Music Box rearranges itself I won't say, because saying nails down what is meant to continue as movement. It's enough to report that for approximately 20 minutes during the final third of "The Homecoming" the erratic energies onstage display their own naked authority by forcing us to accept the unpredictable as though it were the natural shape of things.

During this time Vivien Merchant, as the wife who is hard-headed as she is enigmatic, cooly and with great reserve points out that her legs move, her underwear moves with her, her lips move. ("Perhaps the fact that they move is more significant than the words that come through them.") Husband Michael Craig draws on his donnish pipe with opaque detachment ("I won't be lost in it"), father Paul Rogers leers through sucked-in teeth that seem to have been borrowed from Bert Lahr, and poltergeist Iam Holm grins maliciously at the thought of all the tables that can be turned. The performing is cagey, studied, bristling with overtones. (A good half of Mr. Pinter's suspense invariably comes from the question that sticks in our heads: "What are these people *not* mentioning?").

Until the final moments of the evening, however, the playwright is simply cheating us, draining away our interest with his deliberate delay He has no more vital material to offer here than he had, say, in the very much shorter "A Slight Ache," to which "The Homecoming" bears a strong resemblance.

But he is determined that we shall have two hours worth of improvisational feinting, and it leads him into a good bit of coy teasing giggly echoes of Ionesco ("You liked Venice, didn't you? You had a good week. I mean, I took you there. I can speak Italian") and calculated incidental violence that is without cumulative effect (the father spits at one son, rams another in the gut, canes his own paraffin-coated dullard of a brother).

Because none of this is of any growing importance to the ultimate confrontation, *everything* must seem to have its own arbitrary and artificial importance: the clink of a sugar lump on a saucer, the stiff, ritual crossing of trousered legs, the huddled lighting of four cigars, the effortful pronunciation of so much as a single word.

Holding too much back for too long, the play comes to seem afflicted by an arthritic mind and tongue, and while Peter Hall has directed the visiting members of England's Royal Shakespeare Company to make sleep-walking and strangled speech constitute a theatrical effect in and for itself, we are not engrossed by the eternal hesitation waltz, but seriously put off by it. The play agonizes over finding its starting point, and we share the prolonged agony without being certain that the conundrum is approaching a real core.

Mr. Pinter is one of the most naturally gifted dramatists to have come out of England since the war. I think he is making the mistake, just now, of supposing that the elusive kernel of impulse that will do for a 40-minute play will serve just as handily and just as suspensefully for an all-day outing. "The Homecoming," to put the matter as simply as possible, needs a second situation: We could easily take an additional act if the author would only scrap the interminable first. The tide must come in at least twice if we are to be fascinated so long by the shoreline.

REVIEW OF THE ROYAL SHAKESPEARE COMPANY PRODUCTION, 1967, BY RICHARD GILMAN

In all his plays, from *The Room,* which was written in 1957 as a more or less naïve exercise in the kind of drama Beckett and Ionesco had already made known, to his latest work, *The Homecoming,* Harold Pinter has been engaged with the question of what drama really is. It might be thought that the playwright, of all people, would know; yet if twentieth-century aesthetic developments have taught us anything, it is that the artist, rather than the public—which knows what it knows—is in continuing doubt about the nature of art. And since the theatre is the most immovable of all the arts, the most resistant to change, it is the playwright who has had to struggle most strenuously for new forms, against the heavy, unyielding conviction of nearly everybody else that there is no mystery about what plays are.

Plays are sequences of imagined events, recognizable to one degree or another as analogous to the events of life, and these events are participated in by "characters," whose interest and credibility are also measured by their potential actuality, their being possible to imagine in one or another way as existing in the world outside the drama. Beyond that, plays must "develop," must move steadily along, generally to a "higher" or "deeper" level, and must not, on pain of murderous responses from the audience, stop at any point—to give opportunity for reflection to gather new kinds of momentum, to simply be still, circular, without linear progression. What plays must do (the last stronghold of realism) is to trace a parabola for which life is thought to have provided the model.

Such, tightly stated, are the sovereign notions that still rule audiences, reviewers and commonplace playwrights alike. They learn nothing from the fact that nearly all the interesting drama of any period has taken place outside the textbook definitions. The complaint is still made against a play like *The Homecoming* that it is slow, illogical, unlifelike, wasteful of its opportunities—which are to be fast, logical, lifelike—and that its characters are not the sort one would expect or want to meet on one's daily round. (Get me Ivan Karamazov: Ivan, baby, we're having a party and we'd love you to . . .)

In Pinter's growth as a dramatist, which in a central way means progress toward colonizing hitherto unconsidered territories of the dramatic, shaping a redefinition, *on the stage,* of character, plot, action, etc., he has come unevenly but significantly to redirect procedures and techniques that had early threatened to congeal into mere negatives. His capacity for extracting ranges of implication from the most conventional varieties of speech themselves—incantatory, often, dreamlike yet anchored in the sharpest accuracy about how people really talk—his use of the most commonplace objects to undermine our complacency about the material world: all this was for the most part unsupported by imposing intellectual structure, any more solid knowledge or intuition than that traditions of perception and experience were not to be relied on.

From his first impact here, by way of rumor and the published early plays and then through *The Caretaker* when it arrived, we spoke of Pinter as a new presence, the master of striking if not quite trustworthy, because seemingly autonomous, effects. The world, his plays announced, is arbitrary, everything menaces, nothing is what it seems; he had broken into a new universe of drama, one in which language seldom coheres with gesture, terror is the obverse of humor, and habits of action conceal other kinds of action we can sense but never know.

In this universe, he once wrote in a program note, "there are no hard distinctions between what is real and what is unreal, nor between what is true and what is false." It is precisely its tendency to assume at some point that it knows what is real and unreal (which means what has up to now been *considered* so) that compels every art including drama continually to remonstrate with its own past, to repudiate its own inertia. This is the least that so-called avant-garde art does—but it has to do more. The peculiar giddiness, the sensations of disequilibrium and disturbed orientation which Pinter induced through his dislocations of the familiar—these, while enormously valuable, were not fully satisfying. For what was being let in through the holes he had punched in conventional dramaturgy? Not what meaning but what new and substanceful drama of his own?

The Homecoming, though flawed and marked by aesthetic problems not yet overcome, is the impressive culmination of a subtle process of change that set in midway in Pinter's career. It was toward a seemingly greater realism, a filling in the vacancies, in which abstract menace and unspecific fear lurked, that had resulted from his abandonment of accepted thematic developments, of ordinary psychologies and sociologies and the sequential narratives in which the stage has traditionally encased them. But this realism had nothing to do with an imitation of life or the conventions of popular drama, except that, in the latter case, it made a canny and partly ironic use of them.

The shift can be studied through Pinter's changing *mises en scène*. Moving into domestic settings, usually middle- or upper-middle class, he largely withdrew from those alarming locales of his earlier plays—the basement room of *The Dumbwaiter*, the seedy rooming house of *The Birthday Party*, the dementedly cluttered room of *The Caretaker*.

These theatrical sites were objectively disturbing, menacing in their own right, physical metaphors of violence which meant that their atmospheres tended to carry a disproportionate share of the plays' effects, tended in fact to consolidate those effects as the very essence of the works.

The setting of *The Homecoming* still possesses disquieting features in its great gray sparsely furnished room. But something crucial has happened. This new Pinter room no longer largely dictates what is to happen to its inhabitants but only reflects what has happened and will happen to them; its walls and furnishings have soaked up their emanations, for the center of dramatic reality has passed to them.

Yet it doesn't lie in them now in any way which we can organically connect with what we think of as domestic drama. If you think during the opening moments that you are watching a familiar battle scene, on the order of *Virginia Woolf,* or *Cat on a Hot Tin Roof,* you will be unprepared for what is to come and you may grow disgruntled, having expected, in the second act, denouement, completion, some satisfying rich ripe finale. But the play moves to its own logic, and it is not a tale; its characters are only tactically engaged in representing potentially real people, their strategic task being to incarnate, along the lines of the "characters" in *The Brothers Karamazov,* certain human faculties, dividing among themselves fundamental possibilities of attitude and approach to existence. They are their figures in a drama of the mind, which is not to say an intellectual drama, but one which makes no pretense (or only a pretense) of being a replica of actuality.

The relationship of the four men who occupy the stage at first is savage, almost cannibalistic, at the same time that it is self-lacerating. "Mind you she wasn't such a bad woman," Max, the roaring foulmouthed old man, says of his dead wife, "even though it made me sick just to look at her rotten stinking face, she wasn't a bad bitch." And he berates his coldly ironic son Lenny, the master of a stable of prostitutes, for "talking to your lousy filthy father like that."

Yet however straightforward, if extreme, their dialogue seems at first, its purpose is not to frame character or psychology, not as an English critic has pointed out, to reveal "inner life or intentions." Pinter's marvelously funny, splendidly violent or consciously banal dialogue is a matter of *kinds* of speech and therefore archetypes of being, warring with one another—Max's scatology, Lenny's wit, Max's pallid brother Sam's pinched rhetoric—as the faculties incarnated by the personages of the play similarly war. And the dialogue is there to serve the play, to serve its mostly immobile, nonanecdotal, ritualistic vision, not its presumed thesis, its "story" or concatenation of events.

That there is to be no plausible story quickly becomes apparent with the entrance of Teddy, Max's oldest son; a philosophy professor at an American university, he is returning for the first time in six years, with his wife Ruth, whom the others do not know of. Cooly elegant, enigmatic, sensual, Ruth immediately shifts the play to a new dimension. In the most Pinteresque of scenes, where language, objects and gestures unite to reinforce one another's elliptical and mythic condition, Ruth and Lenny clash. "I'll take it [a glass of water he has given her]," Lenny says, unaccountably threatening, to which she replies with deadly calm, "If you take the glass . . . I'll take *you*."

From then on the play is about who takes whom,

that is to say, whose presence triumphs or yields, who, in the game of existence—not in that of society—are winners or losers. What loses most decisively is on-looking spectatorship, the propriety of consciousness when pitted against the absolutism of the physical self. In a world beyond morality, what is being sought for is a condition of authenticity, an immersion in what is. And to accomplish this, the play now leaves irrevocably behind it (the point at which the public grumbling starts) all verisimilitude, all pretense of being about a family, a social situation, people like you and me. Pinter is at the heart of his vision here, and if we follow him into it—attending to these characters who can no longer be mistaken for types or personalities but only seen as incarnations of possibility, of desire and refusal—we will have overcome our deadly habit of wanting what we expect.

When Ruth engages Lenny, and afterwards Joey, the naïve strongboy younger brother, in a sexual embrace which Teddy, her husband, watches with pipe-smoking professorial detachment, and when later the family proposes that Ruth stay with them, working for her keep as a prostitute—a proposal which leaves Teddy as unruffled as before—we are not in the presence of social behavior but of a dance of death—and life. Ruth's acceptance of the proposal is a movement toward the greater authenticity of the family, their closer proximity to genuine being. For Teddy is an abstract man, a figure of pure consciousness, an observer, while she is almost pure instinct and physicality.

In the key monologue of the play, the central speech which, as in all Pinter's work, offers the one irradiation of intention to light the rest of the play, Teddy tells the others:

"You wouldn't understand my works ... You wouldn't appreciate the points of reference. You're way behind ... It's nothing to do with the question of intelligence. It's a way of being able to look at the world. It's a question of how far you can operate on things and not in things ... To see, to be able to *see!* I'm the one who can see ... [I have] intellectual equilibrium ... You're just objects. You just ... move about. I can observe it. I can see what you do. It's the same as I do. But you're lost in it. You won't get me being ... I won't be lost in it."

It is a brilliant piece of writing, one almost no other English-speaking playwright would be capable of. Fusing the most exact and compressed meanings with the most intense feeling, colloquial at the same time that it stretches to a more inclusive and nonrealistic level of speech, it exemplifies what is never considered in our public chatter about the theatre: that language can itself be dramatic, can *be* the play, not merely the means of advancing an anecdote, a decoration, or the emblem of something thought to be realer than itself.

Teddy's speech is followed by a longer one of Lenny's, an equally masterly piece of writing, opposing another rhythm and another mode of language as action to its predecessor. In it Lenny, the wit, the implicated observer, moral consciousness corrupted but still alive, throws at Teddy an image of America which in the conditions of the play, entirely transcends social criticism to become the truest kind of poetic fact:

"I will say you do seem to have grown a bit sulky ... I'd have thought that in the United States of America, I mean with the sun and all that, the open spaces, on the old campus, in your position, lecturing, in the center of all the intellectual life out there, on the old campus, all the social whirl, all the stimulation of it all, all your kids and all that, to have fun with, down by the pool, the Greyhound buses and all that, tons of iced water, all the comforts of those Bermuda shorts and all that, on the old campus ... I'd have thought you'd have grown more forthcoming ... Listen, Ted, there's no question we lead a less rich life here than you do over there ... We lead a closer life."

In the final movement of the play, this closer life is revealed to be partly one of fantasy. There is something crowded, rushed into being, somewhat arbitrary about this last section. Ruth takes command, promising in the manner of a contemporary fairy godmother to be whatever the men want her to be: for Joey a madonna figure, for Lenny, a whore, for Max a young and rejuvenating wife. A whole allegorical structure now rises shadowily into view. But it is too late, it has not been fully prepared for and therefore comes as an afterthought. Yet the main action of the play has been completed with Ruth's move toward the family and Teddy's devastating acceptance of it; to wish to do more, to want his dense, specific, precisely nonallegorical vision to yield up such further tenuous meanings is evidence that Pinter has not yet solved his major problem. And that is how to fuse meaning so securely with language, gesture and setting that it cannot be extrapolated from them. The taints of the old worn-out dramatic procedures—characters who represent action that points to something else—are still discernible in his work.

Yet, they are taints, not major infections. A struggle for the new is always more interesting than a successful appropriation of the old. *The Homecoming* is such a struggle, and nothing on Broadway in recent years comes close to matching it for the kind of excitement that our debased ad-man's vocabulary of critical appreciation ("*The Odd Couple* is the funniest play ever!") has so thoroughly disillusioned us about. The play itself, Peter Hall's direction and the Royal Shakespeare Company's acting ensemble offer examples of work in a dimension beyond anything we have been accustomed to.

MARIA IRENE FORNES

1930–

For thirty years, Maria Irene Fornes has been a vital force in American drama as playwright, director, designer, teacher, and theatrical administrator. Born in Havana, Cuba, in 1930, she emigrated to the United States in 1945 and became a citizen in 1951. Her first artistic interest was in painting and textile design, an interest which led to work as a costume designer at the Judson Poets Theatre in New York, one of the most successful Off-Off Broadway production groups. Fornes's subsequent playwriting career may be divided roughly by decades: the 1960s, when she wrote and directed a series of nonrealistic and often light-hearted works; the 1970s, when she wrote fewer plays because of her work as president of New York Theatre Strategy, a playwrights' organization supporting the development of experimental work throughout the United States; and the 1980s, when her plays took on noticeably darker and more overtly political tones. Thus far Fornes has written some thirty plays and adaptations, working with material that ranges widely over styles and cultures: the ritual for a Vietnamese wedding served as the basis for a staged reading in 1967 protesting American involvement in Vietnam; the diary of a servant in New Hampshire became *Evelyn Brown: A Diary* (1980); and her own Cuban background informed her first play, *The Widow* (1961) as well as later plays such as *Sarita* (1984). She has won the Obie Award (Off-Broadway) six times, including a special Obie in 1982 for "Sustained Achievement," and she continues an active teaching, writing, and directing career, working both in professional repertory theaters around the country and on university campuses.

Commenting on her unusual creative process in *Drama Review* (December 1977), Fornes reveals her willingness to accept the accidental and her distrust of the deliberate: "When something happens by accident, I trust that the play is making its own point." So, too, she describes herself as a transmitter of messages rather than a creator of ideas: "Thoughts come to my mind at any point, anywhere—I could be on the subway—and if I am alert enough and I have a pencil and paper, I write these *messages* that come." And, like the painter she once was, Fornes talks about her work in visual terms, noting that as a play and its characters take shape, she sees the characters, the set, and, most importantly, the colors. At that point, the play exists, and Fornes sees herself as the reporter: "I just listen to it. I move along with it. I let it write itself." Yet once the first draft has "written itself," analysis and rewriting become central.

One of Fornes's earliest experimental successes, *Promenade* (1965), a play with music by Al Carmines of the Judson Poets Theatre, actually grew out of an exercise in seemingly random composition. Fornes wrote down a set of characters on one group of cards and a list of places on another, picked her first "character" card—which said "Aristocrats"—and her first place card—"The Prison"—and then tried to deal with the difficulty of writing about aristocrats in prison. Her solution was to have them dig their way out, and so the adventures of Prisoners 105 and 106 begin. Chased by their jailer, they gatecrash an elaborate society banquet, evade capture by putting their jackets on a man injured in a car accident, are reunited with their mother, take part in a military battle, and finally return to their jail cell. The ending blends social criticism and gentleness, for though the mother sings a lullaby that alludes to poverty and homelessness, the two aristocratic prisoners seem untouched by the pain they have witnessed.

Other plays from the 1960s, such as *The Successful Life of 3* (1965) and *Molly's Dream* (1968), use the movies as a constant point of reference, thus exploiting the popular clichés by which people imagine their lives, particularly their romantic relationships, and, thereby, revealing the emptiness of such clichés. The two men and one woman of *The Successful Life of 3* see themselves as figures from the movies (gangsters, Zorro-type romantic heroes, attractive sex objects) as they move through ten short scenes spread out over sixteen years, scenes that often have no transition but simply "cut" from one locale and time to another. *Molly's Dream* is set entirely in a stereotypical Hollywood saloon, and for much of the play Molly adopts a German accent and gestures reminiscent of Marlene Dietrich. But while all of these characters allude to, and even imitate, actual or fictional characters from Hollywood, they also can see that their lives are much less glamorous. In *Molly's Dream*, for example, when the lights dim and the music begins, a spotlight comes up on Molly, but she undercuts this theatrical cliché by saying, "No. I'm not breaking into song. The moment is too sad."

By contrast, the characters in Fornes's plays of the 1980s seem utterly trapped, unable to break out of the relationships and obsessions that imprison them. Susan Sontag, introducing the second published volume of Fornes's plays, aptly comments that *Mud* (1983) is "about the unsuccessful life of three," since *Mud*, like *The Successful Life of 3*, focuses on two men and the woman they both want. But whereas the earlier play ends with the three characters reunited and singing together, *Mud* ends with Mae's attempt to leave the bleak wooden room where both Henry and Lloyd compete for her, only to be brought back, bleeding and dying, after Lloyd shoots her. While *Molly's Dream* surrealistically depicts the notion of women obsessively clinging to men by surrounding the sexy young man, Jim, with a chorus of five "Hanging Women" who never let go of him, *Sarita* (1984) offers a much more frightening vision of sexual obsession. Sarita first appears as a schoolgirl of thirteen, staring at fortune-telling cards to find out if Julio loves her; eight years later, after a series of reunions and desertions, she can free herself only by stabbing Julio. *The Danube* (1982) and *The Conduct of Life* (1985) also focus on imprisoning worlds and relationships, fraught with disturbing political implications. *The Danube*, which begins in 1938 shortly before World War II, seems at first a rewriting of Ionesco's *The Bald Soprano*, with the "well-meaning American" Paul Green learning Hungarian by repeating phrases from an English/Hungarian language tape. But it turns increasingly sinister as the tyranny of stilted language evokes political repression, particularly when the central characters are replaced by puppets. Even more oppressive is *The Conduct of Life*, set in a Latin American country of the present, with its central character a military commander who imprisons a twelve-year-old girl, first in an empty warehouse, then in his cellar, and repeatedly rapes her. The sexual violence onstage embodies the political violence offstage, since the play's dialogue gradually reveals that the commander is in charge of torturing political prisoners.

Fefu and Her Friends (1977), Fornes's best-known and most widely performed play, is sometimes zanily surreal like her earlier plays, but like her later plays, it is also intensely serious. Fefu's opening line is meant to shake up both onstage and offstage listeners, "My husband married me to have a constant reminder of how loathsome women are," as is the moment soon after when she casually refers to her husband, Phillip, then aims a shotgun out the French doors and shoots at him (though it turns out that the shot was a blank). While Fefu's announced plan for the weekend is the rehearsal of a fund-raising program, with such apparently bland topics as "the stifling conditions of primary school education" or "Art as a Tool for Learning," the actual process of education is revealed to be more like turning over a smooth stone and finding underneath "another life that is parallel to the one we manifest," a life with "worms crawling on it." Thus the seemingly aimless dialogue reveals the disturbing quality of women's existence, particularly the extent to which men, though completely absent from the cast of eight women, still dominate their lives. Nowhere is the domination more evident than in Julia's soliloquy, in which she first speaks of herself as if she's being tortured and then, to save herself from further pain, recites a "prayer" defining men as human and women as not-human and evil. Julia's submission to such perverted thoughts is, Fornes suggests, literally as well as mentally paralyzing, since she must use a wheelchair because of a freak accident, though for an eerie moment in the final scene, she gets up and walks.

While Fefu and Julia are the women whose inner lives are most fully revealed, each of the eight gets a chance to present her feelings to the others and to the audience. Indeed, because of Fornes's unusual staging requirements, the audience is put into the position of snooping on a series of private conversations since the four middle scenes are set in four separate acting spaces, requiring the audience to move in separate groups from scene to scene, while the actors repeat each scene four times. The choice, Fornes explains, came about because she accidentally found the spaces in the process of writing the play and directing the play. Erika Munk, whose review is reprinted following the text, saw the repetition of scenes as a metaphor for "entire trapped lifetimes." But the physical involvement of the audience in its performance also creates a special kind of intimacy, mirroring the relationships found in the play. Those relationships embody or display both playfulness (Figures 1 and 3) and intensity (Figures 2 and 4), just as the play begins with a gunshot that is partially a joke and ends with a gunshot that forces the audience to question what is real and what is hallucination. In these and other boldly dramatic ways, *Fefu* disconcerts and startles us, asking us to rethink, or even re-imagine, our own conventional lives.

FEFU AND HER FRIENDS

BY MARIA IRENE FORNES

CHARACTERS

FEFU
CINDY
CHRISTINA
JULIA
EMMA
PAULA
SUE
CECILIA

New England, Spring 1935. The play is performed in five spaces: the theater proper, with a seating capacity for the whole audience, and four different spaces, each with a seating capacity of a quarter of the audience. The set on stage represents the living room.

Part 1: Noon. The living room. The entire audience watches from the main space.

Part 2: Afternoon. The lawn, the study, the bedroom, the kitchen. The audience is divided into four groups. Each group is led by ushers to the spaces. These scenes are performed simultaneously. When the scenes are completed the audience moves to the next space and the scenes are performed again. This is repeated four times until each group has seen all four scenes. Then they are led to the main space.

Part 3: Evening. The living room. The entire audience watches from the main space.

PART 1

(The living room of a country house in New England. The style is simple and although ample it resembles a farm house. To the left, French doors leading to a terrace, the lawn and a pond. Upstage right is the entrance to the foyer and main entrance. On the rear there is an entrance that leads to the kitchen and the yard (right) and to Julia's and the other rooms (left). At center there are stairs to the upper floor and a set of French doors leading to the lawn and pond. Upstage center there is a couch with a chair on each side, a coffee table downstage from the couch. Upstage left there is a piano. Against the right wall there is a liquor cabinet. Besides liquor bottles and glasses, there are an ice bucket and a siphon. On the couch there is a throw. A double barrel shotgun leans against the wall near the French doors. On the table there is a dish with chocolates. FEFU *stands on the landing.* CINDY *lies on the couch.* CHRISTINA *sits on the chair to the right.)*

FEFU: My husband married me to have a constant reminder of how loathsome women are.
CINDY: What?
FEFU: Yup.
CINDY: That's just awful.
FEFU: No, it isn't.
CINDY: It isn't awful?
FEFU: No.
CINDY: I don't tink anyone would marry for that reason.
FEFU: He did.
CINDY: Did he say so?
FEFU: He tells me constantly.
CINDY: Oh, dear.
FEFU: I don't mind. I laugh when he tells me.
CINDY: You laugh?

FEFU: I do.
CINDY: How can you?
FEFU: It's funny.—And it's true. That's why I laugh.
CINDY: What is true?
FEFU: That women are loathsome.
CINDY: . . . Fefu!
FEFU: That shocks you.
CINDY: It does. I don't feel loathsome.
FEFU: I don't mean that you are loathsome.
CINDY: You don't mean that I'm loathsome.
FEFU: No . . . It's something to think about. It's a thought.
CINDY: It's a hideous thought.
FEFU: I take it all back.
CINDY: Isn't she incredible?
FEFU: Cindy, I'm not talking about anyone in particular. It's something to think about.
CINDY: No one in particular, just women.
FEFU: Yes.
CINDY: In that case I am relieved. I thought you were referring to us.
FEFU: *(Affectionately.)* You are being stupid.
CINDY: Stupid and loathsome. *(To* CHRISTINA.*)* Have you ever heard anything so outrageous?
CHRISTINA: I am speechless.
FEFU: Why are you speechless?
CHRISTINA: I think you are outrageous.
FEFU: Don't be offended. I don't take enough care to be tactful. I know I don't. But don't be offended. Cindy is not offended. She pretends to be, but she isn't really. She understands what I mean.
CINDY: I do not.
FEFU: Yes, you do.—I like exciting ideas. They give me energy.
CHRISTINA: And how is women being loathsome an exciting idea?

FEFU: (With mischief.) It revolts me.

CHRISTINA: You find revulsion exciting?

FEFU: Don't you?

CHRISTINA: No.

FEFU: I do. It's something to grapple with.—What do you do with revulsion?

CHRISTINA: I avoid anything that's revolting to me.

FEFU: Hmmm. (To CINDY.) You too?

CINDY: Yes.

FEFU: Hmm. Have you ever turned a stone over in damp soil?

CHRISTINA: Ahm.

FEFU: And when you turn it there are worms crawling on it?

CHRISTINA: Ahm.

FEFU: And it's damp and full of fungus?

CHRISTINA: Ahm.

FEFU: Were you revolted?

CHRISTINA: Yes.

FEFU: Were you fascinated?

CHRISTINA: I was.

FEFU: There you have it! You too are fascinated with revulsion. You see, that which is exposed to the exterior . . . is smooth and dry and clean. That which is not . . . underneath, is slimy and filled with fungus and crawling with worms. It is another life that is parallel to the one we manifest. It's there. The way worms are underneath the stone. If you don't recognize it . . . (Whispering.) it eats you. That's my opinion. Well, who is ready for lunch?

CINDY: I'll have some raw fried worms with lots of pepper.

FEFU: (To CHRISTINA.) You?

CHRISTINA: I'll have mine in a sandwich with mayonnaise.

FEFU: And to drink?

CHRISTINA: Just some dirty dishwater in a tall glass with ice.

(FEFU looks at CINDY.)

CINDY: That sounds fine.

FEFU: I'll go dig them up. (FEFU walks to the doors. Beckoning CHRISTINA.) Pst! (Getting the gun.) You haven't met Phillip. Have you?

CHRISTINA: (Walking to her.) No.

FEFU: (Looking outside.) That's him.

CHRISTINA: Which one?

FEFU: (Aims and shoots outside.) That one!

(CHRISTINA and CINDY scream. FEFU smiles proudly. She blows on the mouth of the barrel. She puts down the gun and looks out again.)

CINDY: Christ, Fefu.

FEFU: There he goes. He's up. It's a game we play. I shoot and he falls. Whenever he hears the blast he falls. No matter where he is, he falls. One time he fell in a puddle of mud and his clothes were a mess. (She looks out.) It's not too bad. He's just dusting off some stuff. (She waves to PHILLIP and starts to go upstairs.) He's all right. Look.

(CHRISTINA looks out.)

CINDY: A drink?

CHRISTINA: Yes.

(CINDY goes to the liquor cabinet.)

CINDY: What would you like?

CHRISTINA: Bourbon and soda . . . (CINDY puts ice in a glass, opens a bottle of bourbon and pours it. She reaches for the soda.) lots of soda. (As CINDY starts to pour) Just soda. (CINDY takes another glass and starts to squirt soda in it just as CHRISTINA speaks.) Wait. (CINDY stops squirting.) I'll have an ice cube with a few drops of bourbon.

CINDY: (CINDY starts with a fresh glass.) One or two ice cubes?

CHRISTINA: One. (CINDY puts one ice cube in another glass, and pours in a few drops of bourbon.) Something to suck on. (CINDY gives the drink to CHRISTINA who is still behind the couch.) Thanks.

CINDY: She's unique. There's no one like her.

CHRISTINA: Thank God.

CINDY: But she is lovely you know. She really is.

CHRISTINA: She's crazy.

CINDY: A little. She has a strange marriage.

CHRISTINA: Strange? It's revolting.—What is he like?

CINDY: He's crazy too. They drive each other crazy. They are not crazy really. They drive each other crazy.

CHRISTINA: Why do they stay together?

CINDY: They love each other.

CHRISTINA: Love?

CINDY: It's love.

CHRISTINA: Who are the other two men?

CINDY: Fefu's nephew, John. And the gardener. His name is Tom.—The gun is not loaded.

CHRISTINA: How do you know?

CINDY: It's not. Why should it be loaded?

CHRISTINA: It seemed to be loaded a moment ago.

CINDY: That was just a blank.

CHRISTINA: It sounded like a cannon shot.

CINDY: That was just gun powder. There's no bullet in a blank.

CHRISTINA: The blast alone could kill you. One can die of fright, you know.

CINDY: True.

CHRISTINA: My heart is still beating.

CINDY: That's just fright. You're being a scaredy cat.

CHRISTINA: Of course it's just fright.

CINDY: You were just scared. You didn't get hurt.

CHRISTINA: I guess I was lucky I didn't get shot.

CINDY: Fefu won't shoot you. She only shoots Phillip.

CHRISTINA: That's nice of her. Put the gun away, I don't like looking at it.

FEFU: (As she appears on the landing.) I just fixed the toilet in your bathroom.

CINDY: You did?

FEFU: I did. The water stopper didn't work. It drained. I adjusted it. I'm waiting for the tank to fill up. Make sure it all works.

CHRISTINA: You do your own plumbing?

FEFU: I just had to bend the metal that supports the rubber stopper so it falls right over the hole. What happened was it fell to the side so the water wouldn't stop running into the bowl. (FEFU *sits near* CINDY.) He scared me this time, you know. He looked like he was really hurt.

CINDY: I thought the guns were not loaded.

FEFU: I'm never sure.

CHRISTINA: What?

CINDY: Fefu! What do you mean?

FEFU: He told me one day he'll put real bullets in the guns. He likes to make me nervous. (*There is a moment's silence.*) I have upset you . . . I don't mean to upset you. That's the way we are with each other. We always go to extremes but it's not anything to be upset about.

CHRISTINA: You scare me.

FEFU: That's all right. I scare myself too, sometimes. But there's nothing wrong with being scared . . . it makes you stronger.—It does me.—He won't put real bullets in the guns.—It suits our relationship . . . the game, I mean. If I didn't shoot him with blanks, I might shoot him for real. Do you see the sense of it?

CHRISTINA: I think you're crazy.

FEFU: I'm not. I'm sane.

CHRISTINA: (*Gently.*) You're very stupid.

FEFU: I'm not. I'm very bright.

CHRISTINA: (*Gently.*) You depress me.

FEFU: Don't be depressed. Laugh at me if you don't agree with me. Say I'm ridiculous. I know I'm ridiculous. Come on, laugh. I hate to think I'm depressing to you.

CHRISTINA: All right. I'll laugh.

FEFU: I'll make you a drink.

CHRISTINA: No, I'm just sucking on the ice.

FEFU: Don't you feel well?

CHRISTINA: I'm all right.

FEFU: What are you drinking?

CHRISTINA: Bourbon.

FEFU: (*Getting* CHRISTINA's *glass and going to the liquor cabinet.*) Would you like some more? I'll get you some.

CHRISTINA: Just a drop.

FEFU: (*With great care pours a single drop of bourbon on the ice cube.*) Like that?

CHRISTINA: Yes, thank you.

FEFU: (*Gives* CHRISTINA *the drink and watches her put the cube to her lips.*) That's the cutest thing I've ever seen. It's cold. (CHRISTINA *nods.*) You need a stick in the ice, like a popsicle stick. You hold the stick and your fingers won't get cold. I have some sticks. I'll do some for you.

CHRISTINA: Don't trouble yourself.

FEFU: It won't be any trouble.—I'm strange, Christina. But I am fortunate in that I don't mind being strange. It's hard on others sometimes. But not that hard. Is it, Cindy? Those who love me, love me precisely because I am the way I am. (*To* CINDY.) Isn't that so? (CINDY *smiles and nods at the same time.*)

CINDY: I would love you even if you weren't the way you are.

FEFU: You wouldn't know it was me if I weren't the way I am.

CINDY: I would still know it was you underneath.

FEFU: (*To* CHRISTINA.) You see?—There are some good things about me.—I'm never angry, for example.

CHRISTINA: But you make everyone else angry.

(FEFU *thinks a moment.*)

FEFU: No.

CHRISTINA: You've made me furious.

FEFU: I know. And I might make you angry again. Still I would like it if you liked me.—You think it's unlikely.

CHRISTINA: I don't know.

FEFU: . . . We'll see. (FEFU *goes to the doors. She stands there briefly and speaks reflectively.*) I still like men better than women.—I envy them. I like being like a man. Thinking like a man. Feeling like a man.—They are well together. Women are not. Look at them. They are checking the new grass mower. . . . Out in the fresh air and the sun, while we sit here in the dark. . . . Men have natural strength. Women have to find their strength, and when they do find it, it comes forth with bitterness and it's erratic. . . . Women are restless with each other. They are like live wires . . . either chattering to keep themselves from making contact, or else, if they don't chatter, they avert their eyes . . . like Orpheus° . . . as if a god once said "and if they shall recognize each other, the world will be blown apart." They are always eager for the men to arrive. When they do, they can put themselves at rest, tranquilized and in a mild stupor. With the men they feel safe. The danger is gone. That's the closest they can be to feeling wholesome. Men are muscle that cover the raw nerve. They are the insulators. The danger is gone, but the price is the mind and the spirit. . . . High price. Why?—What is feared? I've never understood it.—Hmm. Well . . .—Do you know? Perhaps the heavens would fall.—Have I offended you again?

CHRISTINA: No. I too have wished for that trust men have for each other. The faith the world puts in

---

Orpheus, mythic Greek musician who tried to bring his wife back from the underworld by leading her back to the living without looking at her.

them and they in turn put in the world. I know I
don't have it.

FEFU: Hmm. Well, I have to see how my toilet is doing.
(FEFU *goes up the stairs. She puts her head out. She smiles.*)
Plumbing is more important than you think.

(CHRISTINA *falls off her chair in a mock faint.* CINDY
goes to her.)

CINDY: What do you think?
CHRISTINA: Think? I hurt. I'm all shreds inside.
CINDY: Anything I can do?
CHRISTINA: Sing.

(CINDY *sings "Winter Wonderland."* CHRISTINA *har-
monizes. Lying on the floor, they do a dance with their
legs and hands. There is the sound of a horn.* FEFU
enters.)

FEFU: It's Julia. (*To* CHRISTINA, *who is on the floor.*) Are
you all right?
CHRISTINA: Yes. (FEFU *exits through the foyer.*) Darn it!
(CHRISTINA *starts to stand.*)
FEFU: (*Off-stage.*) Julia . . . let me help you.
JULIA: I can manage. I'm much stronger now.
FEFU: There you go.
JULIA: You have my bag.
FEFU: Yes.

(JULIA *and* FEFU *enter.* JULIA *is in a wheelchair.*)

JULIA: Hello Cindy.
CINDY: Hello darling. How are you?
JULIA: I'm very well now. I'm driving now. You must
see my car. It's very clever the way they worked it
all out. You might want to drive it. It's not hard at
all. (*Turning to* CHRISTINA.) Christina.
CHRISTINA: Hello Julia.
JULIA: I'm glad to see you.
FEFU: I'll take this to your room. You're down here, if
you want to wash up.

(FEFU *exits through the upstage exit.* JULIA *follows her.*)

CINDY: I can't get used to it.
CHRISTINA: She's better. Isn't she?
CINDY: Not really.
CHRISTINA: Was she actually hit by the bullet?
CINDY: No . . . I was with her.
CHRISTINA: I know.
CINDY: I thought the bullet hit her, but it didn't.—How
do you know if a person is hit by a bullet?
CHRISTINA: Cindy . . . there's a wound and . . . there's
a bullet.
CINDY: Well, the hunter aimed . . . at the deer. He shot.
CHRISTINA: He?
CINDY: Yes.
CHRISTINA: (*Pointing in the direction of* FEFU.) It wasn't
. . . ?
CINDY: Fefu? . . . No. She wasn't even there. She used
to hunt but she doesn't hunt any more. She loves
animals.

CHRISTINA: Go on.
CINDY: He shot. Julia and the deer fell. The deer was
dead . . . dying. Julia was unconscious. She had
convulsions . . . like the deer. He died and she
didn't. I screamed for help and the hunter came
and examined Julia. He said, "She is not hurt."
Julia's forehead was bleeding. He said, "It is a surface wound. I didn't hurt her." I know it wasn't he
who hurt her. It was someone else. He went for
help and Julia started talking. She was delirious.—
Apparently there was a spinal nerve injury. She hit
her head and she suffered a concussion. She blanks
out and that is caused by the blow on the head. It's
a scar in the brain. It's called the petit mal.°

(FEFU *enters.*)

CHRISTINA: What was it she said?
CINDY: Hmm? . . .
CHRISTINA: When she was delirious.
CINDY: When she was delirious? That she was perse-
cuted.—That they tortured her. . . . That they had
tried her and that the shot was her execution. That
she recanted because she wanted to live. . . . That
if she talked about it . . . to anyone . . . she would
be tortured further and killed. And I have not
mentioned this before because . . . I fear for her.
CHRISTINA: It doesn't make any sense, Cindy.
CINDY: It makes sense to me. You heard? (FEFU *goes to*
CINDY *and holds her.*)
FEFU: Who hurt her?
CINDY: I don't know.
FEFU: (*To* CHRISTINA.) Did you know her?
CHRISTINA: I met her once years ago.
FEFU: You remember her then as she was. . . . She was
afraid of nothing. . . . Have you ever met anyone
like that? . . . She knew so much. She was so young
and yet she knew so much. . . . How did she learn
all that? . . . (*To* CINDY.) Did you ever wonder?
(*Playfully.*) Well, I still haven't checked my toilet.
Can you believe that. I still haven't checked it. (FEFU
goes upstairs.)
CHRISTINA: How long ago was the accident?
CINDY: A year . . . a little over a year.
CHRISTINA: Is she in pain?
CINDY: I don't think so.
CHRISTINA: We are made of putty. Aren't we?

(*There is the sound of a car. Car doors opening and
closing. A house window opening.*)

FEFU: (*Off-stage.*) Emma! What is that you're wearing.
You look marvelous.
EMMA: (*Off-stage.*) I got it in Turkey.
FEFU: Hi Paula, Sue.
PAULA: Hi.
SUE: Hi.

---

petit mal, comparatively mild form of epilepsy.

(CINDY goes out to greet them. JULIA enters. She wheels herself to the downstage area.)

FEFU: I'll be right down! Hey, my toilet works.

EMMA: Mine does too.

FEFU: Don't be funny.

EMMA: Come down.

(FEFU enters as EMMA, SUE, and PAULA enter. EMMA and FEFU embrace.)

FEFU: How are you?

EMMA: Good . . . good . . . good . . . *(Still embracing FEFU, EMMA sees JULIA.)* Julia! *(She runs to JULIA and sits on her lap.)*

FEFU: Emma!

JULIA: It's all right.

EMMA: Take me for a ride. *(JULIA wheels the chair in a circle. EMMA waves as they ride.)* Hi, Cindy, Paula, Sue, Fefu.

JULIA: Do you know Christina?

EMMA: How do you do.

CHRISTINA: How do you do.

EMMA: *(Pointing.)* Sue . . . Paula . . .

SUE: Hello.

PAULA: Hello.

CHRISTINA: Hello.

PAULA: *(To FEFU.)* I liked your talk at Flossie Crit.

FEFU: Oh god, don't remind me. I thought I was awful. Come, I'll show you your rooms. *(She starts to go up.)*

PAULA: I thought you weren't. I found it very stimulating.

EMMA: When was that? . . . What was it on?

FEFU: Aviation.

PAULA: It wasn't on aviation. It was on Voltairine de Cleyre.°

JULIA: I wish I had known.

FEFU: It wasn't important.

JULIA: I would have gone, Fefu.

FEFU: Really, it wasn't worth the trouble.

EMMA: Now you'll have to tell Julia and me all about Voltairine de Cleyre.

FEFU: You know all about Voltairine de Cleyre.

EMMA: I don't.

FEFU: I'll tell you at lunch.

EMMA: I had lunch.

JULIA: You can sit and listen while we eat.

EMMA: I will. When do we start our meeting?

FEFU: After lunch. We'll have something to eat and then we'll have our meeting. Who's ready for lunch?

(The following lines are said almost simultaneously.)

CINDY: I am.

JULIA: I'm not really hungry.

CHRISTINA: I could eat now.

PAULA: I'm ready.

SUE: I'd rather wait.

EMMA: I'll have coffee.

FEFU: . . . Well . . . we'll take a vote later.

CINDY: What are we doing exactly?

FEFU: About lunch?

CINDY: That too, but I meant the agenda.

SUE: Well, I thought we should first discuss what each of us is going to talk about, so we don't duplicate what someone else is saying, and then we have a review of it, a sort of rehearsal, so we know in what order we should speak and how long it's going to take.

EMMA: We should do a rehearsal in costume. What color should each wear. It matters. Do you know what you're wearing?

PAULA: I haven't thought about it. What color should I wear?

EMMA: Red.

PAULA: Red!

EMMA: Cherry red or white.

SUE: And I?

EMMA: Dark green.

CINDY: The treasurer should wear green.

EMMA: It suits her too.

SUE: And then we'll speak in order of color.

EMMA: Right. Who else wants to know? *(CINDY and JULIA raise their hands. To CINDY.)* For you lavender. *(To JULIA.)* Purpura.° *(FEFU raises her hand.)* For you, all the gold in Persia.

FEFU: There is no gold in Persia.

EMMA: In Peru. I brought my costume. I'll put it on later.

FEFU: You're not in costume?

EMMA: No. This is just a dress. My costume is . . . dramatic. I won't tell you any more about it. You'll see it.

SUE: I had no idea we were going to do theatre.

EMMA: Life is theatre. Theatre is life. If we're showing what life is, can be, we must do theatre.

SUE: Will I have to act?

EMMA: It's not acting. It's being. It's springing forth with the powers of the spirit. It's breathing.

JULIA: I'll do a dance.

EMMA: I'll stage a dance for you.

JULIA: Sitting?

EMMA: On a settee.

JULIA: I'm game.

EMMA: *(Hums and walks through the French doors.)* Phillip! What are you doing?—Hello.—Hello, John. Glorious day, isn't it?—What?

Voltairine de Cleyre, American anarchist/feminist/poet (1866–1912).

Purpura, purple.

FEFU: We'll never see her again.—Come.

(FEFU, PAULA, and SUE *go upstairs.* JULIA *goes to the gun, takes it and smells the mouth of the barrel. She looks at* CINDY.)

CINDY: It's a blank.

(JULIA *takes the remaining slug out of the gun. She lets it fall on the floor.)*

JULIA: She's hurting herself. (JULIA *looks blank and is motionless.* CINDY *picks up the slug. She notices* JULIA's *condition.)*

CINDY: Julia. *(To* CHRISTINA.) She's absent.

CHRISTINA: What do we do?

CINDY: Nothing, she'll be all right in a moment. *(She takes the gun from* JULIA. JULIA *comes to.)*

JULIA: It's a blank . . .

CINDY: It is.

JULIA: She's hurting herself. (JULIA *lets out a strange whimper. She goes to the coffee table, takes a piece of chocolate, puts it in her mouth and goes toward her room. After she crosses the threshold, she stops without turning.)* I must lie down a while.

CINDY: Call me if you need anything.

JULIA: I will. *(She exits.* CINDY *tries to put the slug in the rifle. There is the sound of a car, a car door opening, closing.)*

CINDY: Do you know how to do this?

CHRISTINA: Of course not.

(CINDY *succeeds in putting the slug in the gun.* CECILIA *stands in the threshold of the foyer. There is a spot on her.)*

CECILIA: I am Cecilia Johnson. Do I have the right place?

CINDY: Yes.

(*The sound of* CINDY *locking the trigger is heard. Lights fade all around* CECILIA. *Only her head is lit. The spot fades.)*

PART 2

A path or loop going through each of the different locations of Part 2 has been established. This path should be as economical and practical as possible. The order in which the scenes are viewed is irrelevant.

Lights come up on the audience and on the down-stage area. One of four ushers steps on the stage. The others stand near exits. The ushers will behave in a non-assuming manner to allow the audience to stay with their own thoughts. The usher on stage will say something along these lines: "We will now go to different rooms in FEFU's *house. There will be four different groups. Each group will be lead by an usher. Please stay with your group. If you do, you will*

be able to see each one of the scenes. From this (indicate person, or aisle) to this (person or aisle), please follow the usher on (place) or (identifiable clothing)." Don't identify usher by name.

The group going to the furthest location should be selected first so they have a head-start. The group going the shortest distance should be selected last. As the last group is meeting the usher, '30s music starts playing.

The stage manager goes where he or she can see the last group reaching their destination and cue the music to stop. This will signal all scenes to start.

The longest running scene is usually the Kitchen. During the four-scene sequence the stage manager will be where he or she can see PAULA *and* CECILIA *exiting at the end of the scene. The stage manager will then cue the music to start again which is the cue for all other scenes to end and the audience to start their move to the next location in the loop. At the end of the fourth repeat the audience will be led back to the auditorium where Part 3 will start.*

On the Lawn

(The side of a shed or small barn. The door is open. As the audience approaches FEFU *and* EMMA *are criss-crossing each other while they take out crates of fruits and vegetables and put them in a cart.* FEFU *wears gardening gloves and a straw hat. The music stops.* FEFU *is by the cart.* EMMA *is coming out of the shed.)*

EMMA: Do you think about genitals all the time?

(FEFU *goes in the shed.)*

FEFU: Genitals? No, I don't think about genitals all the time.

EMMA: *(Putting a crate on the cart.)* I do, and it drives me crazy. *(Going to the shed.)* Each person I see in the street, anywhere at all . . . I keep thinking of their genitals; what they look like, what position they are in. I think it's odd that everyone has them. Don't you?

FEFU: *(They cross each other and continue to go back and forth to the shed.)* No, I think it'd be odder if they didn't have them.

(EMMA *laughs.)*

EMMA: I mean, people act as if they don't have genitals.

FEFU: How do people with genitals act?

EMMA: I mean, how can business men and women stand in a room and discuss business without even one reference to their genitals. I mean everybody has them. They just pretend they don't.

FEFU: I see. *(She moves her eyebrows and moves her eyes from side to side in appreciation of imaginary crotches.)* You mean they should do this all the time?

(EMMA *laughs.)*

EMMA: No, I don't mean that. Think of it. Don't you think I'm right?

FEFU: Yes, I think you're right. *(FEFU sits.)* Oh, Emma,

EmmaEmmaEmma.

EMMA: That's m'name.—Well, you see, it's generally believed that you go to heaven if you are good. If you
are bad you go to hell. That is correct. However, in
heaven they don't judge goodness the way we do
on earth. They don't. They have a divine registry
of sexual performance. In that registry they mark
down every little sexual activity in your life. If your
faith is not entirely in it, if you just perform as an
obligation and you don't feel the most profound
devotion, if your spirit, your heart, and your flesh
is not religiously delivered to it, you are condemned. They put you down in the black list and
you don't go to heaven. Heaven is populated with
divine lovers. And in hell live the duds.

FEFU: That's probably true.

EMMA: I knew you'd see it that way.

FEFU: Oh, I do. I do. You see, on earth we are judged
by public acts, and sex is a private act. The partner
cannot be said to be the public, since both partners
are engaged. So naturally, it stands to reason that
it's angels who judge our sexual life.

EMMA: Naturally.

(Pause.)

FEFU: You always bring joy to me.

EMMA: Thank you.

FEFU: I thank you. (FEFU becomes distressed. She takes off
her hat and gloves and sits.) I am in constant pain. I
don't want to give in to it. If I do I am afraid I will
never recover. . . . It's not physical, and it's not
sorrow. It's very strange Emma, I can't describe it,
and it's very frightening. . . . It is as if normally
there is a lubricant . . . not in the body . . . a spiritual
lubricant . . . it's hard to describe . . . and without
it, life is a nightmare, and everything is distorted.—
A black cat started coming to my kitchen. He's awfully mangled and big. He is missing an eye and his
skin is diseased. At first I was repelled by him, but
then, I thought, this is a monster that has been sent
to me and I must feed him. And I fed him. One
day he came and shat all over my kitchen. Foul
diarrhea. He still comes and I still feed him.—I am
afraid of him. (EMMA kisses FEFU.) How about a little
lemonade?

EMMA: Yes.

(FEFU exits leaving her hat and gloves behind. EMMA
makes an effigy of FEFU using her hat and gloves. She
recites the following sonnet to the effigy.)

Not from the stars do I my judgment pluck.
And yet methinks I have astronomy;
But not to tell of good or evil luck,
Of plagues, of dearths, or seasons' quality;
Nor can I fortune to brief minutes tell,
Pointing to each his thunder, rain, and wind,
Or say with princes if it shall go well

By oft predict that I in heaven find.
But from thine eyes my knowledge I derive.
And, constant stars, in them I read such art
As truth and beauty shall together thrive
If from thyself to store thou wouldst convert:
    Or else of thee this I prognosticate,
    Thy end is truth's and beauty's doom and date.°

(EMMA does a song and dance for the effigy until the
music cue is heard and the usher leads the audience to
the next space. At the end of the fourth repeat the audience
is led back to the auditorium.)

In the Study

(There are books on the walls, a desk, Victorian chairs,
a rug on the floor. CHRISTINA sits behind the desk. She
holds a French text book. When the music stops, she
mumbles French sentences. CINDY sits to the left of the
desk with her feet up on a chair. She looks at a magazine.)

CHRISTINA: (Practicing.) Etes-vous externe ou demi-
pensionnaire? La cuisine de votre cantine est-elle
bonne, passable ou mauvaise?° (She continues reading
almost inaudibly. A moment passes.)

CINDY: (Reading.) A lady in Africa divorced her husband because he was a cheetah.

CHRISTINA: Oh, dear. (They laugh. They go back to their
reading. A moment passes.) Est-ce que votre professeur interroge souvent les eleves?° (They go back to
their reading. A moment passes.)

CINDY: I suppose . . . when a person is swept off their
feet . . . the feet remain and the person goes off . . .
with the broom.

CHRISTINA: No . . . when a person is swept off their feet
. . . there is no broom.

CINDY: What does the sweeping?

CHRISTINA: An emotion . . . a feeling.

CINDY: Then emotions have bristles?

CHRISTINA: Yes.

CINDY: Now I understand. Do the feet remain?

CHRISTINA: No, the feet fly also . . . but separate from
the body. At the end of the leap, just before the
landing, they join the ankles and one is complete
again.

CINDY: Oh, that sounds nice.

CHRISTINA: It is. Being swept off your feet is nice. Anything else?

CINDY: Not for now. (They go back to their reading.)

Not from the stars . . . doom and date, Shakespeare's
Sonnet 14. **Etes-vous externe . . . mauvaise?** Do you eat all
your meals away or have lunch at school? The cooking of
your school cafeteria—is it good, fair, or bad? **Est-ce que
votre professeur . . . eleves?** Does your teacher often question
the students?

CHRISTINA: *(Questioning* CINDY.*)* Aimez-vous mieux le français ou l'anglais?°

CINDY: . . . Le français.°

CHRISTINA: Votre pere, est-il militaire, avocat, ou pharmacien?°

CINDY: Moi?°

CHRISTINA: Non, votre pere.°

CINDY: Oui.°

CHRISTINA: Bon.° *(They go back to their reading.)*

CINDY: A lady leopard in Africa divorced her husband because he was a cheetah. Huh huh huh huh. *(*CHRISTINA *smiles at* CINDY.*)* Are you having a good time?

CHRISTINA: Yes, I'm very glad I came.

CINDY: Do you like everybody?

CHRISTINA: Yes.

CINDY: Do you like Fefu?

CHRISTINA: I do . . . She confuses me a little.—I try to be honest . . . and I wonder if she is . . . I don't mean that she doesn't tell the truth. I know she does. I mean a kind of integrity. I know she has integrity too. . . . But I don't know if she's careful with life . . . something bigger than the self . . . I suppose I don't mean with life but more with convention. I think she is an adventurer in a way. Her mind is adventurous. I don't know if there is dishonesty in that. But in adventure there is taking chances and risks, and then one has to, somehow, have less regard or respect for things as they are. That is, regard for a kind of convention, I suppose. I am probably ultimately a conformist, I think. And I suppose I do hold back for fear of being disrespectful or destroying something—and I admire those who are not. But I also feel they are dangerous to me. I don't think they are dangerous to the world; they are more useful than I am, more important, but I feel some of my life is endangered by their way of thinking. Do you understand?

CINDY: Yes, I do.

CHRISTINA: I guess I am proud and I don't like thinking that I am thoughtful of things that have no value.— I like her.

CINDY: I had a terrible dream last night.

CHRISTINA: What was it?

CINDY: I was at a dance. And there was a young doctor I had seen in connection with my health. We all danced in a circle and he identified himself and said that he had spoken to Mike about me, but that it was all right, that he had put it so that it was all

---

Aimez-vous mieux le français ou l'anglais? Do you prefer French or English? ***Le français,*** French ***Votre pere . . . pharmacien?*** Your father, is he a soldier, lawyer, or pharmacist? ***Moi?*** Me? ***Non, votre pere,*** No, your father ***Oui,*** Yes ***Bon,*** Good.

right. I was puzzled as to why Mike would mind and why he had spoken to him. Then, suddenly everybody sat down on the floor and pretended they were having singing lessons and one person was practicing Italian. The singing professor was being tested by two secret policemen. They were having him correct the voice of someone they had brought. He apparently didn't know how to do it. Then, one of the policemen put his hands on his vocal cords and kicked him out the door. Then he grabbed me and felt my throat from behind with his thumbs while I rubbed my nipples with his pinkies. Then, he pushed me out the door. Then, the young doctor started cursing me. His mouth moved like the mouth of a horse. I was on an upper level with a railing and I said to him, "Stop and listen to me." I said it so strongly that he stopped. Everybody turned to me in admiration because I had made him stop. Then, I said to him, "Restrain yourself." I wanted to say respect me. I wasn't sure whether the words coming out of my mouth were what I wanted to say. I turned to ask my sister. The young man was bending over and trembling in mad rage. Another man told me to run before the young man tried to kill me. Meg and I ran downstairs. She asked me if I wanted to go to her place. We grabbed a taxi, but before the taxi got enough speed he came out and ran to the taxi and was on the verge of opening the door when I woke up.

(The door opens. FEFU *looks in. Her entrance may interrupt* CINDY's *speech at any point according to how long it takes her to reach the kitchen.)*

FEFU: Who's for a game of croquet?

CINDY: In a little while.

FEFU: See you outside.

CHRISTINA: That was quite a dream.

CINDY: What do you think it means?

CHRISTINA: I think it means you should go to a different doctor.

CINDY: He's not my doctor. I never saw him before.

CHRISTINA: Well good. I'm sure he's not a good doctor.

CINDY: It was just a dream.

*(*CINDY *will read sections of interest from her magazine out loud until the music cue is heard and the usher leads the audience to the next space. At the end of the fourth repeat, when* FEFU *invites them for croquet,* CINDY *says, "Oh let's play croquet" and they follow* FEFU. *The audience is led back to the auditorium.)*

In the Bedroom

(A plain unpainted room. Perhaps a room that was used for storage and was set up as a sleeping place for JULIA. *There is a mattress on the floor. To the right of the mattress there is a small table, to the left is* JULIA's *wheelchair. There is a sink on the wall. There are dry leaves on the*

floor although the time is not fall. The sheets are linen. JULIA *lies in bed covered to her shoulders. She wears a white hospital gown.* JULIA *hallucinates. However, her behavior should not be the usual behavior attributed to a mad person. It should be rather still and luminous. There will be aspects of her hallucinations that frighten her, but hallucinating itself does not.)*

JULIA: They clubbed me. They broke my head. They broke my will. They broke my hands. They tore my eyes out. They took my voice away. They didn't do anything to my heart because I didn't bring my heart with me. They clubbed me again, but my head did not fall off in pieces. That was because they were so good and they felt sorry for me. The judges. You didn't know the judges?—I was good and quiet. I never dropped my smile. I smiled to everyone. If I stopped smiling I would get clubbed because they love me. They say they love me. I go along with that because if I don't . . .

(With her finger she indicates her throat being cut and makes the sound that usually accompanies that gesture.)

I told them the stinking parts of the body are the important ones: the genitals, the anus, the mouth, the armpit. All important parts except the armpits. And who knows, maybe the armpits are important too. That's what I said. *(Her voice becomes tremulous and tight in imitation of the judges.)* He said "All those parts must be kept clean and put away." He said "Women's entrails are heavier than anything on earth and to see a woman running creates a disparate and incongruous image in the mind. It's anti-aesthetic. Therefore women should not run. Instead they should strike positions that take into account the weight of their entrails. Only if they do, can they be aesthetic." He said, "For example, Goya's Maja."° He said "Rubens'° women are not aesthetic. Flesh." He said that a woman's bottom should be in a cushion, otherwise it's revolting. He said there are exceptions. "Ballet dancers are exceptions. They can run and lift their legs because they have no entrails. Isadora Duncan° had entrails, that's why she should not have danced. But she danced and for this reason became crazy." *(Her voice is back to normal.)* She wasn't crazy.

(She moves her hand as if guarding from a blow.)

She was. He said that I had to be punished because

Goya's Maja, Spanish painter Francisco Goya (1746–1828); the painting is *The Naked Maja*. **Rubens,** Flemish painter Peter Paul Rubens (1577–1640), often featured heavily built women in his paintings. **Isadora Duncan,** American dancer (1878–1927), one of the great figures in modern dance.

I was getting too smart. I'm not smart. I never was. Neither is Fefu smart. They are after her too. Well, she's still walking!

(She guards from a blow. Her eyes close.)

Wait! I'll say my prayer. I'm saying it.

(She mumbles. She opens her eyes with caution.)

(An aside to the audience.) You don't think I'm going to argue with them, do you? I repented. I told them what they wanted to hear. They killed me. I was dead. The bullet didn't hit me. It hit the deer. But I died. He didn't. Then I repented and the deer died and I lived. *(With a gravelly voice.)* They said, "Live but crippled. And if you tell . . ."

(She repeats the throat cutting gesture.)

Why do you have to kill Fefu, for she's only a joker? *(With a gravelly voice.)* "Not kill, cure. Cure her." Will it hurt?

(She whimpers.)

Oh, dear, dear, my dear, they want your light. Your light my dear. Your precious light. Oh dear, my dear.

(Her head moves as if slapped. She is exhausted and cannot fight anymore.)

Not cry. I'll say my prayer. I'll say it. Right now. Look.

(She sits up as if pulled by an invisible force.)

The human being is of the masculine gender. The human being is a boy as a child and grown up he is a man. Everything on earth is for the human being, which is man. To nourish him.—There are evil things on earth, and noxious things. Evil and noxious things are on earth for man also. For him to fight with, and conquer and turn its evil into good. So that it too can nourish him.—There are Evil Plants, Evil Animals, Evil Minerals, and Women are Evil.—Woman is not a human being. She is: 1—A mystery. 2—Another species. 3—As yet undefined. 4—Unpredictable; therefore wicked and gentle and evil and good which is evil.—If a man commits an evil act, he must be pitied. The evil comes from outside him, through him and into the act. Woman generates the evil herself.—God gave man no other mate but woman. The oxen is good but it is not a mate for man. The sheep is good but it is not a mate for man. The mate for man is woman and that is the cross man must bear.—Man is not spiritually sexual, he therefore can enjoy sexuality. His sexuality is physical which means his spirit is pure. Women's spirit is sexual. That is why after coitus they dwell in nefarious feelings. Because that is their natural habitat. That is why it is difficult for them to return to the human world. Their sexual feelings remain with them till they die. And they take those feelings with them to the afterlife where they corrupt the heavens, and they are sent to hell where through suffering they may shed those feelings and return to earth as man.

(Her head moves as if slapped. She is weak.)

Don't hit me. Didn't I just say my prayer?

(A smaller slap.)

I believe it.

(She lies back.)

They say when I believe the prayer I will forget the judges. And when I forget the judges I will believe the prayer. They say both happen at once. And all women have done it. Why can't I?

(SUE enters with a bowl of soup on a tray.)

SUE: Julia, are you asleep?

(Short pause.)

JULIA: No.
SUE: I brought your soup.
JULIA: Put it down. I'm getting up in a moment.

(SUE puts the soup down.)

SUE: Do you want me to help you?
JULIA: No, I can manage. Thank you, Sue.

(SUE goes to the door.)

SUE: You're all right?
JULIA: Yes.
SUE: I'll see you later.
JULIA: Thank you, Sue.

(SUE exits. JULIA closes her eyes. When the music cue is heard the usher leads the audience to the next space. As soon as each audience group leaves, the tray is removed, if possible through a back door. After the fourth repeat the audience is led back to the auditorium.)

In the Kitchen

(A fully equipped kitchen. There is a table and chairs and a high cutting table. On a counter next to the stove there is a tray with a soup dish and a spoon. There is also a ladle. On the cutting table there are two empty glasses. Soup is heating on a burner. A kettle with water sits on an unlit burner. In the refrigerator there is an ice tray with wooden sticks in each cube. The sticks should rest on the edge of the tray forming two parallel rows, like a caterpillar lying on its back. In the refrigerator there are also two pitchers, one with water, one with lemonade. PAULA sits at the table. She is writing on a pad. SUE waits for the soup to heat.)

PAULA: I have it all figured out.
SUE: What?
PAULA: A love affair lasts seven years and three months.

SUE: It does?
PAULA: *(Reading.)* 3 months of love. 1 year saying: It's all right. This is just a passing disturbance. 1 year trying to understand what's wrong. 2 years knowing the end had come. 1 year finding the way to end it. After the separation, 2 years trying to understand what happened. 7 years, 3 months. *(No longer reading.)* At any point the sequence might be interrupted by another love affair that has the same sequence. That is, it's not really interrupted, the new love affair relegates the first one to a second plane and both continue their sequence at the same time.

(SUE looks over PAULA's shoulder.)

SUE: You really added it up.
PAULA: Sure.
SUE: What do you want to drink?
PAULA: Water. The old love affair may fade, so you are not aware the process goes on. A year later it may surface and you might find yourself figuring out what's wrong with the new one while trying to end the old one.
SUE: So how do you solve the problem?
PAULA: Celibacy?
SUE: *(Going to the refrigerator.)* Celibacy doesn't solve anything.
PAULA: That's true.
SUE: *(Taking out the ice tray with the sticks.)* What's this? *(PAULA shakes her head.)* Dessert. *(PAULA shrugs her shoulders. SUE takes an ice cube and places it against her forehead.)* For a headache. *(She takes another cube and moves her arms in a Judo style.)* Eskimo wrestling. *(She places one stick behind her ear.)* Brain cooler. That's when you're thinking too much. You could use one. *(She tries to put the ice cube behind PAULA's ear. They wrestle and laugh. She puts the stick in her own mouth. She takes it out to speak.)* This is when you want to keep chaste. No one will kiss you. *(She puts it back in to demonstrate. Then takes it out.)* That's good for celibacy. If you walk around with one of these in your mouth for seven years you can keep all your sequences straight. Finish one before you start the other. *(She puts the ice cube in the tray and looks at it.)* A frozen caterpillar. *(She puts the tray away.)*
PAULA: You're leaving that ice cube in there?
SUE: I'm clean. *(Looking at the soup.)* So what else do you have on love? *(SUE places a bowl and spoon on the table and sits as she waits for the soup to heat.)*
PAULA: Well, the break-up takes place in parts. The brain, the heart, the body, mutual things, shared things. The mind leaves but the heart is still there. The heart has left but the body wants to stay. The body leaves but the things are still at the apartment. You must come back. You move everything out of the apartment but the mind stays behind. Memory lingers in the place. Seven years later, perhaps seven years later, it doesn't matter any more. Per-

haps it takes longer. Perhaps it never ends.

SUE: It depends.

PAULA: Yup. It depends.

SUE: (*Pouring soup in the bowl.*) Something's bothering you.

PAULA: No.

SUE: (*Taking the tray.*) I'm going to take this to Julia.

PAULA: Go ahead.

(*As* SUE *exits,* CECILIA *enters.*)

CECILIA: May I come in?

PAULA: Yes . . . Would you like something to eat?

CECILIA: No, I ate lunch.

PAULA: I didn't eat lunch. I wasn't very hungry.

CECILIA: I know.

PAULA: Would you like some coffee?

CECILIA: I'll have tea.

PAULA: I'll make some.

CECILIA: No, you sit. I'll make it. (CECILIA *looks for tea.*)

PAULA: Here it is. (*She gets the tea and gives it to* CECILIA.)

CECILIA: (*As she lights the burner.*) I've been meaning to call you.

PAULA: It doesn't matter. I know you're busy.

CECILIA: Still I would have called you but I really didn't find the time.

PAULA: Don't worry.

CECILIA: I wanted to see you again. I want to see you often.

PAULA: There's no hurry. Now we know we can see each other.

CECILIA: Yes, I'm glad we can.

PAULA: I have thought a great deal about my life since I saw you. I have questioned my life. I can't help doing that. It's been many years and I wondered how you see me now.

CECILIA: You're the same.

PAULA: I felt small in your presence . . . I haven't done all that I could have. All I wanted to do. Our lives have gone in such different directions I cannot help but review what those years have been for me. I gave up, almost gave up. I have missed you in my life. . . . I became lazy. I lost the drive. You abandoned me and I kept going. But after a while I didn't know how to. I didn't know how to go on. I knew why when I was with you. To give you pleasure. So we could laugh together. So we could rejoice together. To bring beauty to the world. . . . Now we look at each other like strangers. We are guarded. I speak and you don't understand my words. I remember every day.

(FEFU *enters. She takes the lemonade pitcher from the refrigerator and two glasses from the top of the refrigerator.*)

FEFU: Emma and I are going to play croquet. You want to join us? . . . No. You're having a serious conversation.

PAULA: Very serious. (PAULA *smiles at* CECILIA *in a conciliatory manner.*) Too serious.

FEFU: (*As she exits.*) Come.

PAULA: I'm sorry. (*To* CECILIA.) Let's go play croquet.— I'm not reproaching you.

CECILIA: (*Reaching for* PAULA'S *hand.*) I know. I've missed you too.

(*They exit. As soon as the audience leaves the props are reset.*)

PART 3

(*The living room. It is dusk. There are flowers in the liquor cabinet. As the audience enters, two or three of the women stand around the piano playing and singing Schubert's "Who Is Silvia?"° They exit.* EMMA *enters, checks the lights in the room on her hand, looks around the room and goes upstairs. The rest enter through the rear.* CECILIA, SUE, *and* JULIA *are last.* CECILIA *enters speaking. She sits in the center of the couch. The others surround her and listen attentively.*)

CECILIA: Well, we each have our own system of receiving information, placing it, responding to it. That system can function with such a bias that it could take any situation and translate it into one formula. That is, I think, the main reason for stupidity or even madness, not being able to tell the difference between things.

SUE: Like?

CECILIA: Like . . . this person is screaming at me. He's a bully. I don't like being screamed at. Another person, or the same person, screams. But you know you have done something that provokes him to scream. He has a good reason. These are two different things, the screaming of one and the screaming of the other. Often that distinction is not made.

SUE: I see.

CECILIA: We cannot survive in a vacuum. We must be part of a community, perhaps 10, 100, 1000. It depends on how strong you are. But even the strongest will need a dozen, three, even one who sees, thinks, and feels as he does. The greater the need for that kind of reassurance, the greater the number that he needs to identify with. Some need to identify with the whole nation. Then, the greater the number the more limited the number of responses and thoughts. A common denominator must be reached. Thoughts, emotions that fit all, have to be limited to a small number. (FEFU *enters from the left. She stares at* JULIA. *She crosses to left slowly*

Schubert's "Who Is Silvia?" setting of famous song from Shakespeare's *The Two Gentlemen of Verona,* IV.ii.

behind them as she stares at JULIA.) That is, I feel, the concern of the educator—to teach how to be sensitive to the differences in ourselves as well as outside ourselves, not to supervise the memorization of facts. (EMMA *appears at the top of the stairs. She sits on a step and listens.*) Otherwise the unusual in us will perish. As we grow we feel we are strange and fear any thought that is not shared with everyone.

JULIA: As I feel I am perishing. My hallucinations are madness, of course, but I wish I could be with others who hallucinate also. I would still know I am mad but I would not feel so isolated.—Hallucinations are real, you know. They are not like dreams. They are as real as all of you here. I have actually asked to be hospitalized so I could be with other nuts. But the doctors don't want to. They can't diagnose me. That makes me even more isolated. *(There is a moment's silence.)* You see, right now, it's an awful moment because you don't know what to say or do. If I were with other people who hallucinate, they would say, "Oh yeah. Sure. It's awful. Those dummies, they don't see anything." *(The others begin to relax.)* It's not so bad, really. I can laugh at it. . . . Emma is ready. We should start. *(The others are hesitant.* JULIA *speaks to* FEFU.) Come on.

FEFU: Sure. (FEFU *begins to move the table. Others help move the table and enough furniture to clear a space in the center. They sit in a semicircle downstage on the floor facing upstage.* CECILIA *sits on a chair to the left of the semicircle.*) All right. I start. Right?

CINDY: Right.

(FEFU *goes to center and faces downstage.*)

FEFU: I talk about the stifling conditions of primary school education, etc. . . . etc. . . . The project . . . I know what I'm going to say but I don't want to bore you with it. We all know it by heart. Blah blah blah blah. And so on and so on. And so on and so on. Then I introduce Emma . . . And now Miss Emma Blake. *(They applaud.)*

EMMA: Paula goes next.

FEFU: Does it matter?

EMMA: Of course it matters. Dra-ma-tics. It has to build. I'm in costume.

FEFU: Oh. And now, ladies and gentlemen, Miss Paula Cori will speak on Art as a Tool for Learning. And I tell them the work you have done at the Institute, community centers, essays, etc. Miss Paula Cori.

(*They applaud.* PAULA *goes to center.*)

PAULA: Ladies and gentlemen, I, like my fellow educator and colleague, Stephany Beckmann . . .

FEFU: I am not an educator.

PAULA: What are you?

FEFU: . . . a do gooder. A girl scout.

PAULA: Well, I, like my fellow girl scout Stephany Beck-

mann say blah blah blah blah, blah blah blah and I offer the jewels of my wisdom and experience, which I will write down and memorize, otherwise I would just stand there and stammer and go blank. And even after I memorize it I'm sure I will just stand there and stammer and go blank.

EMMA: I'll work with you on it.

PAULA: However, after our other colleague Miss Emma Blake works with me on it . . . (*In imitation of* EMMA *she brings her hands together and opens her arms as she moves her head back and speaks.*) My impulses will burst forth through a symphony of eloquence.

EMMA: Breathe . . . in . . . (PAULA *inhales slowly.*) And bow. (PAULA *bows. They applaud.*)

PAULA: (*Coming up from the bow.*) Oh, I liked that. *(She sits.)*

EMMA: Good . . .

(*They applaud.*)

FEFU: And now, ladies and gentlemen, the one and only, the incomparable, our precious, dear Emma Blake.

(EMMA *walks to center. She wears a robe with sleeves that hang from her arms to the floor.*)

EMMA: From the prologue to "The Science of Educational Dramatics" by Emma Sheridan Fry.° (*She takes a dramatic pose and starts. The whole speech is dramatized by interpretive gestures and movements that cover the stage area.*)

Environment knocks at the gateway of the senses. A rain of summons beats upon us day and night. . . . We do not answer. Everything around us shouts against our deafness, struggles with our unwillingness, batters our walls, flashes into our blindness, strives to sieve through us at every pore, begging, fighting, insisting. It shouts, "Where are you? Where are you?" But we are deaf. The signals do not reach us.

Society restricts us, school straight jackets us, civilization submerges us, privation wrings us, luxury feather-beds us. The Divine Urge is checked. The Winged Horse balks on the road, and we, discouraged, defeated, dismount and burrow into ourselves. The gates are closed and Divine Urge is imprisoned at Center. Thus we are taken by indifference that is death.

Environment finding the gates closed tries to break in. Turned away, it comes another way. Kept back, it stretches its hands to us. Always scheming to reach us.

Emma Sheridan Fry, taught acting to children at the Educational Alliance in New York from 1903 to 1909. In 1917, her book *Educational Dramatics* was published by Lloyd Adams Noble. The text of Emma's speech is taken from the prologue.

Never was suitor more insistent than Environment, seeking admission, claiming recognition, signaling to be seen, shouting to be heard. And through the ages we sit inside ourselves deaf, dumb and blind, and will not stir. . . .

. . . Maybe you are not deaf. . . . Perhaps signals reach you. Maybe you stir. . . . The gates give. . . . Eternal Urge pushes through the stupor of our senses, making paths to meet the challenging suitor, windows through which to see him, ears through which to hear him. Environment shouting, "Where are you?" and Center battering at the inner side of the wall crying, "Here I am," and dragging down bars, wrenching gates, prying at port-holes. Listening at cracks, reaching everywhere, and demanding that sense gates be flung open. The gates are open! Eternal Urge stands at the threshold signaling with venturous flag. An imperious instinct lets us know that "all" is ours, and that whatever anyone has ever known, or may ever have or know, we will call and claim. A sense of life universal surges through our life individual. We attack the feast of this table with an insatiable appetite that cries for all.

What are we? A creation of God's consciousness coming now slowly and painfully into recognition of ourselves.

What is Personality? A small part of us. The whole of us is behind that hungry rush at the gates of Senses.

What is Civilization? A circumscribed order in which the whole has not entered.

What is Environment? Our mate, our true mate that clamors for our reunion.

We will meet him. We will seize all, learn all, know all here, that we may fare further on the great quest! The task of Now is only a step toward the task of the Whole! Let us then seek the laws governing real life forces, that coming into their own, they may create, develop and reconstruct. Let us awaken life dormant! Let us, boldly, seizing the star of our intent, lift it as the lantern of our necessity, and let it shine over the darkness of our compliance. Come! The light shines. Come! It brightens our way. Come! Don't let its glorious light pass you by! Come! The day has come!

(EMMA *throws herself on the couch.* PAULA *embraces her.*)

Oh, it's so beautiful.

JULIA: It is, Emma. It is.

(*They applaud.*)

CINDY: Encore! Encore!

(EMMA *stands.*)

EMMA: Environment knocks at the gateway . . . (*She laughs and joins the others in the semicircle.* PAULA *remains seated on the couch.*) What's next.

FEFU: (*Going center.*) I introduce Cecilia. I don't think I should introduce Cecilia. She should just come after Emma. Now things don't need introduction. (*Imitating* EMMA *as she goes to her seat.*) They are happening.

EMMA: Right!

(CECILIA *goes to center.*)

CECILIA: Well, as we say in the business, that's a very hard act to follow.

EMMA: Not *very* hard. It's a hard act to follow.

CECILIA: Right. I should say my name first.

FEFU: Yes.

CECILIA: I should breathe too. (*She takes a breath. All except* PAULA *start singing "Cecilia."* CECILIA *is flustered and walks backwards till she sits on the couch. She is next to* PAULA. *Unaware of who she is next to, she puts her hand on* PAULA's *leg. At the end of the song* CECILIA *realizes she is next to* PAULA *and stands.*) I should go before Emma. I don't think anyone should speak after Emma.

CINDY: Right. It should be Fefu, Paula, Cecilia, then Emma, and then Sue explaining the finances and asking for pledges. And the money should roll in. It's very good. (*They applaud.*) Sue . . . (SUE *goes to center.*)

SUE: Yes, blahblahblahblah, pledges and money. (*She does a few balletic moves and bows. They applaud.*)

FEFU: (*As* SUE *returns to her seat.*) Who's ready for coffee?

CINDY: (*As she stands.*) And dishes.

CHRISTINA: (*As she stands.*) I'll help.

EMMA: (*As she stands.*) Me too.

FEFU: Don't all come. Sit. Sit. You have done enough, relax.

(*They put the furniture back as* EMMA *and* SUE *jump over the couch to exit to the kitchen. All except* CINDY *and* JULIA *exit.*)

JULIA: I should go do the dishes. I haven't done anything.

CINDY: You can do them tomorrow.

JULIA: True.—So how have you been?

CINDY: Hmm.

JULIA: Let me see. I can tell by looking at your face. Not so bad.

CINDY: Not so bad.

(*There is the sound of laughter from the kitchen.* CHRISTINA *runs in.*)

CHRISTINA: They're having a water fight over who's going to do the dishes. (*She hides.*)

CINDY: Emma?

CHRISTINA: And Paula, and Sue, all of them. Fefu was getting into it when I left. Cecilia got out the back door.

(CHRISTINA *walks back to the kitchen with some caution.*

She runs back and lies on the couch covering her head with the throw. EMMA *enters with a pan of water in her hand. She is wet.* CINDY *and* JULIA *point to the lawn.* EMMA *runs to the lawn. There is the sound of knocking from upstairs. While the following conversation goes on,* EMMA, SUE, CINDY, *and* JULIA *engage in water fights in and out of the living room. The screams, laughter, and water splashing may drown the words.)*

PAULA: Open up.

FEFU: There's no one here.

PAULA: Open up you coward.

FEFU: I can't. I'm busy.

PAULA: What are you doing?

FEFU: I have a man here.

PAULA: O.K. I'll wait. Take your time.

FEFU: It's going to take quite a while.

PAULA: It's all right. I'll wait.

FEFU: Do me a favor?

PAULA: Sure. Open up and I'll do you a favor.

(There is the sound of a pot falling, a door slamming.)

FEFU: Fill it up for me.

PAULA: O.K.

FEFU: Thank you.

PAULA: Here's water. Open up.

FEFU: Leave it there. I'll come out in a minute.

PAULA: O.K. Here it is. I'm leaving now.

*(*PAULA *comes downstairs with a filled pan. She walks cautiously to the lawn. Water splashes. There is loud screaming.)*

EMMA: You missed!

*(*SUE *enters. She carries a filled pot.* PAULA *enters running. She sees* SUE.*)*

PAULA: Truce!

SUE: Who's the winner?

PAULA: You are.

*(*EMMA *enters. Both* EMMA *and* SUE *empty their pots on* PAULA.*)*

EMMA: I'm the winner.

SUE: Gotcha.

PAULA: Please don't.

*(*FEFU *appears on the landing with a pot.)*

PAULA: Truce. Truce.

FEFU: Back to the kitchen. Back to the kitchen. (PAULA *tries to run.)* Halt! (PAULA *stops.)* To the kitchen. *(They exit. A moment later they scream.)*

FEFU: (*Off-stage.)* O.K. Line up. Put that down. *(There is a moment's silence.)*

JULIA: It's over.

CINDY: We're safe.

JULIA: (*To* CHRISTINA.*)* You can come up now. (CHRISTINA *stays down.)* You rather wait a while. (CHRISTINA *nods.)*

CHRISTINA: (*Playful.)* I feel danger lurking.

CINDY: She's been hiding all day.

*(*FEFU *enters. She is wet.)*

FEFU: I won. I got them working.

JULIA: I thought the fight was over who'd do the dishes.

FEFU: Yes. (*Starting to go.)* I have to change. I'm soaked.

CHRISTINA: They forgot what the fight was about.

FEFU: We did?

JULIA: That's usually the way it is.

FEFU: (*Going to* CHRISTINA *and lifting the cover from her face.)* Are you ready for an ice cube?

*(*FEFU *exits upstairs.* CHRISTINA *runs upstairs. There is silence.)*

CINDY: So.—And how have you been?

JULIA: All right. I've been taking care of myself.

CINDY: You look well.

JULIA: I do not. . . . Have you seen Mike?

CINDY: No, not since Christmas.

JULIA: I'm sorry.

CINDY: I'm O.K.—And how's your love life?

JULIA: Far away. . . . I have no need for it.

CINDY: I'm sorry.

JULIA: Don't be. I'm very morbid these days. I think of death all the time.

PAULA: (*Standing in the doorway.)* Anyone for coffee? *(They raise their hands.)* Anyone take milk? *(They raise their hands.)*

JULIA: Should we go in?

PAULA: I'll bring it out. (PAULA *exits.)*

JULIA: I feel we are constantly threatened by death, every second, every instant, it's there. And every moment something rescues us. Something rescues us from death every moment of our lives. For every moment we live we have to thank something. We have to be grateful to something that fights for us and saves us. I have felt lifeless and in the face of death. Death is not anything. It's being lifeless and I have felt lifeless sometimes for a brief moment, but I have been rescued by these . . . guardians. I am not sure who these guardians are. I only know they exist because I have felt their absence. I think we have come to know them as life, and we have become familiar with certain forms they take. Our sight is a form they take. That is why we take pleasure in seeing things, and we find some things beautiful. The sun is a guardian. Those things we take pleasure in are usually guardians. We enjoy looking at the sunlight when it comes through the window. Don't we? We, as people, are guardians to each other when we give love. And then of course we have white cells and antibodies protecting us. Those moments when I feel lifeless have occurred, and I am afraid one day the guardians won't come in time and I will be defenseless. I will die . . . for no apparent reason.

(Pause. PAULA *stands in the doorway with a bottle of milk.)*

PAULA: *(In a low-keyed manner.)* Anyone take rotten milk? *(Pause.)* I'm kidding. This one is no good but there's more in there . . . *(Remaining in good spirits.)* Forget it. It's not a good joke.

JULIA: It's good.

PAULA: In there it seemed funny but here it isn't. *(As she exits and shrugging her shoulders.)* It's a kitchen joke. Bye.

JULIA: *(After her.)* It is funny, Paula. *(To* CINDY.*)* It was funny.

CINDY: It's all right, Paula doesn't mind.

JULIA: I'm sure she minds. I'll go see . . . *(*JULIA *starts to go.* PAULA *appears in the doorway.)*

PAULA: *(In a low-keyed manner.)* Hey, who was that lady I saw you with?—That was no lady. That was my rotten wife. That wasn't good either, was it? *(Exiting.)* Emma. . . . That one was no good either.

*(*SUE *starts to enter carrying a tray with sugar, milk, and two cups of coffee. She stops at the doorway to look at* PAULA *and* EMMA *who are behind the wall.)*

SUE: *(Whispering.)* What are you doing?—What?—O.K., O.K. *(She enters whispering.* SUE *puts the tray down.)* They're plotting something.

*(*PAULA *appears in the doorway.)*

PAULA: *(In a low-keyed manner.)* Ladies and gentlemen. Ladies, since our material is too shocking and avant-garde, we have decided to uplift our subject matter so it's more palatable to the sensitive public. *(*PAULA *takes a pose.* EMMA *enters. She lifts an imaginary camera to her face.)*

EMMA: Say cheese.

PAULA: Cheese. *(They both turn front and smile. The others applaud.)* Ah, success, success. Make it clean and you'll succeed.—Coffee's in the kitchen.

SUE: Oh, I brought theirs out.

PAULA: Oh, shall we have it here?

JULIA: We can all go in the kitchen. *(They each take their coffee and go to the kitchen.* SUE *takes the tray to the kitchen. The sugar remains on the table.)*

PAULA: Either here or there. *(She sits on the couch.)* I'm exhausted.

*(*CECILIA *enters from the lawn.)*

CECILIA: Is the war over?

PAULA: Yes.

CECILIA: It's nice out. *(*PAULA *nods in agreement.)* Where's everybody?

PAULA: In the kitchen, having coffee.

CECILIA: We must talk. *(*PAULA *starts to speak.)* Not now. I'll call you. *(*CECILIA *starts to go.)*

PAULA: When?

CECILIA: I don't know.

PAULA: I don't want you, you know.

CECILIA: I know.

PAULA: No, you don't. I'm not lusting after you.

CECILIA: I know that. *(She starts to go.)* I'll call you.

PAULA: When?

CECILIA: As soon as I can.

PAULA: I won't be home then.

CECILIA: When will you be home?

PAULA: I'll check my book and let you know.

CECILIA: Do that.—I'll be leaving after coffee. I'll say goodbye now.

PAULA: Goodbye. *(*CECILIA *goes towards the kitchen.* PAULA *starts towards the steps.* FEFU *comes down the steps.)*

FEFU: You're still wet.

PAULA: I'm going to change now.

FEFU: Do you need anything?

PAULA: No, I have something I can change to. Thank you.

*(*PAULA *goes upstairs.* FEFU *takes a few steps down and stops. The lights change to an eerie quality. There is a sense of mystery to suggest that what is about to happen is not real but that it is in* FEFU's *imagination.* FEFU *turns to look at the flowers. She walks to them. She smells one, then turns to look behind her.* JULIA *enters. She walks in a zombie-like manner. She walks to the coffee table, picks up the sugar bowl, lifts it in* FEFU's *direction, takes the cover off, puts it back on, puts the sugar bowl on the table and walks to the kitchen. As soon as* JULIA *exits as the lights go back to normal* SUE's *voice is heard from the kitchen moving into the hallway speaking the following lines. To confirm the fact that* FEFU *has hallucinated,* JULIA *should appear in the wheelchair with a throw over her legs and a tray with cups and a pitcher of coffee resting on the wheelchair as quickly as it could possibly be achieved. This should be executed so quickly as to appear that* JULIA *was walking into the hallway and being wheeled into the living room at the same time. Surrounding* JULIA *are* CINDY, CHRISTINA, EMMA, *and* CECILIA. *As they reach the couch they sit and take coffee.* FEFU *stares at* JULIA.*)*

SUE: I was terribly exhausted and run down. I lived on coffee so I could stay up all night and do my work. And they used to give us these medical check-ups all the time. But all they did was ask how we felt and we'd say "Fine," and they'd check us out. In the meantime I looked like a ghost. I was all bones. Remember Susan Austin? She was very naive and when they asked her how she felt, she said she was nervous and she wasn't sleeping well. So she had to see a psychiatrist from then on.

EMMA: Well, she was crazy.

*(*FEFU *exits.)*

SUE: No, she wasn't.—Oh god, those were awful days. . . . Remember Julie Brooks?

EMMA: Sure.

SUE: She was a beautiful girl.

EMMA: Ah yes, she was gorgeous.

(PAULA *comes down the stairs as soon as she has changed. She sits on the steps half way down.*)

SUE: At the end of the first semester they called her in because she had been out with 28 men and they thought that was awful. And the worst thing was that after that, she thought there was something wrong with her.

CINDY: (*Jokingly.*) She was a nymphomaniac, that's all.

SUE: She was not. She was just very beautiful so all the boys wanted to go out with her. And if a boy asked her to go have a cup of coffee she'd sign out and write in the name of the boy. None of us did of course. All she did was go for coffee or go to a movie. She was really very innocent.

EMMA: And Gloria Schuman? She wrote a psychology paper the faculty decided she didn't write and they called her in to try to make her admit she hadn't written it. She insisted she wrote it and they sent her to a psychiatrist also.

JULIA: Everybody ended going to the psychiatrist.

(FEFU *enters through the foyer.*)

EMMA: After a few visits the psychiatrist said: Don't you think you know me well enough now that you can tell me the truth about the paper? He almost drove her crazy. They just couldn't believe she was so smart.

SUE: Those were difficult times.

PAULA: We were young. That's why it was difficult. On my first year I thought you were all very happy. I had been so deprived in my childhood that I believed the rich were all happy. During the summer you spent your vacations in Europe or the Orient. I went to work and I resented that. But then I realized that many lives are ruined by poverty and many lives are ruined by wealth. I was always able to manage. And I think I enjoyed myself as much when I went to Revere Beach on my day off as you did when you visited the Taj Mahal. (CECILIA *enters from the foyer. She stands there and listens.* PAULA *doesn't acknowledge her.*) Then, when I stopped feeling envy, I started noticing the waste. I began feeling contempt for those who, having everything a person can ask for, make such a mess of it. I resented them because they were not better than the poor. If you have all you need you should be generous. If you can afford to go to school your mind should be better. If you didn't have to fight for your place on earth you should be nobler. But I saw them cheating and grabbing like the kids in the slums, or wasting away with self-indulgence. And I saw them be plain stupid. If there is a reason why some are rich while others starve it must be so they put everything they have at the service of others. They should take the responsibility of everything that happens in the world. They are the only ones who can influence things. The poor don't have the power to change things. I think we should teach the poor and let the rich take care of themselves. I'm sorry, I know that's what we're doing. That's what Emma has been doing. I'm sorry . . . I guess I feel it's not enough. (PAULA *sobs.*) I'll wash my face. I'll be right back. (*She starts to go towards the kitchen.*) I think highly of all of you. (CECILIA *follows her.* PAULA *turns.* CECILIA *opens her arms and puts them around* PAULA, *engulfing her. She kisses* PAULA *on the lips.* PAULA *steps back. She is fearful.* CECILIA *follows her.* FEFU *enters from the lawn.*)

FEFU: Have you been out? The sky is full of stars.

(EMMA, SUE, CHRISTINA, *and* CINDY *exit.*)

JULIA: What's the matter?

(FEFU *shakes her head.* JULIA *starts to go toward the door.*)

FEFU: Stay a moment, will you?

JULIA: Of course.

FEFU: Did you have enough coffee?

JULIA: Yes.

FEFU: Did you find the sugar?

JULIA: Yes. There was sugar in the kitchen. What's the matter?

FEFU: Can you walk? (JULIA *is hurt. She opens her arms implying she hides nothing.*) I am sorry, my dear.

JULIA: What is the matter?

FEFU: I don't know, Julia. Every breath is painful for me. I don't know. (FEFU *turns* JULIA's *head to look into her eyes.*) I think you know.

(JULIA *breaks away from* FEFU.)

JULIA: (*Avoiding* FEFU's *glance.*) No, I don't know. I haven't seen much of you lately. I have thought of you a great deal. I always think of you. Cindy tells me how you are. I always ask her. How is Phillip? Things are not well with Phillip?

FEFU: No.

JULIA: What's wrong?

FEFU: A lot is wrong.

JULIA: He loves you.

FEFU: He can't stand me.

JULIA: He loves you.

FEFU: He's left me. His body is here but the rest is gone. I exhaust him. I torment him and I torment myself. I need him, Julia.

JULIA: I know you do.

FEFU: I need his touch. I need his kiss. I need the person he is. I can't give him up. (*She looks into* JULIA's *eyes.*) I look into your eyes and I know what you see. (JULIA *closes her eyes.*) It's death. (JULIA *shakes her head.*) Fight!

JULIA: I can't.

FEFU: I saw you walking.

JULIA: No. I can't walk.

FEFU: You came for sugar, Julia. You came for sugar. Walk!

JULIA: You know I can't walk.

FEFU: Why not? Try! Get up! Stand up!

JULIA: What is wrong with you?

FEFU: You have given up!

JULIA: I get tired! I get exhausted! I am exhausted!

FEFU: What is it you see? (JULIA *doesn't answer.*) What is it you see! Where is it you go that tires you so?

JULIA: I can't spend time with others! I get tired!

FEFU: What is it you see!

JULIA: You want to see it too?

FEFU: No, I don't. You're nuts, and willingly so.

JULIA: You know I'm not.

FEFU: And you're contagious. I'm going mad too.

JULIA: I try to keep away from you.

FEFU: Why?

JULIA: I might be harmful to you.

FEFU: Why?

JULIA: I am contagious. I can't be what I used to be.

FEFU: You have no courage.

JULIA: You're being cruel.

FEFU: I want to rest, Julia. How does a person rest. I want to put my mind at rest. I am frightened. (JULIA *looks at* FEFU.) Don't look at me. (*She covers* JULIA'*s eyes with her hand.*) I lose my courage when you look at me.

JULIA: May no harm come to your head.

FEFU: Fight!

JULIA: May no harm come to your will.

FEFU: Fight, Julia!

(FEFU *starts shaking the wheelchair and pulling* JULIA *off the wheelchair.*)

JULIA: I have no life left.

FEFU: Fight, Julia!

JULIA: May no harm come to your hands.

FEFU: I need you to fight.

JULIA: May no harm come to your eyes.

FEFU: Fight with me!

JULIA: May no harm come to your voice.

FEFU: Fight with me!

JULIA: May no harm come to your heart.

(CHRISTINA *enters.* FEFU *sees* CHRISTINA, *releases* JULIA. *To* CHRISTINA.)

FEFU: Now I have done it. Haven't I. You think I'm a monster. (*She turns to* JULIA *and speaks to her with kindness.*) Forgive me if you can. (JULIA *nods.*)

JULIA: I forgive you.

(FEFU *gets the gun.*)

CHRISTINA: What in the world are you doing with that gun!

FEFU: I'm going to clean it!

CHRISTINA: I think you better not!

FEFU: You're silly!

(CECILIA *appears on the landing.*)

CHRISTINA: I don't care if you shoot yourself! I just don't like the mess you're making!

(FEFU *starts to go to the lawn and turns.*)

FEFU: I enjoy betting it won't be a real bullet! You want to bet!

CHRISTINA: No! (FEFU *exits.* CHRISTINA *goes to* JULIA.) Are you all right?

JULIA: Yes.

CHRISTINA: Can I get you anything?

JULIA: Water. (CECILIA *goes to the liquor cabinet for water.*) Put some sugar in it. Could I have a damp cloth for my forehead? (CHRISTINA *goes toward the kitchen.* JULIA *speaks front.*) I didn't tell her anything. Did I? I didn't.

CECILIA: (*Going to* JULIA *with the water.*) About what?

JULIA: She knew.

(*There is the sound of a shot.* CHRISTINA *and* CECILIA *run out.* JULIA *puts her hand to her forehead. Her hand goes down slowly. There is blood on her forehead. Her head falls back.* FEFU *enters holding a dead rabbit.*)

FEFU: I killed it . . . I just shot . . . and it died . . . I killed it. . . . Julia . . .

(*Dropping the rabbit,* FEFU *walks to* JULIA *and stands behind the chair as she looks at* JULIA. SUE *and* CINDY *enter from the foyer,* EMMA *and* PAULA *from the kitchen,* CHRISTINA *and* CECILIA *from the lawn. They surround* JULIA. *The lights fade.*)

Figure 1. Fefu (Rebecca Schull, *right*) pours one drop of bourbon "with great care" for Christina (Elizabeth Perry, *left*) while Cindy (Dorothy Lyman) watches in the 1978 American Place Theatre production of *Fefu and Her Friends*, directed by the author. (Photograph: Martha Holmes.)

Figure 2. Emma (Gordana Rashovich) holds Fefu's hand (Rebecca Schull) to comfort her in the 1978 American Place Theatre production of *Fefu and Her Friends*, directed by the author. (Photograph: Martha Holmes.)

Figure 3. Sue (Arleigh Richards) demonstrates possible ways of using an ice cube on a stick for Paula (Connie LoCurto Cicone, *seated*) in the 1978 American Place Theatre production of *Fefu and Her Friends*, directed by the author. (Photograph: Martha Holmes.)

Figure 4. Fefu (Rebecca Schull) confronts the tired Julia (Margaret Harrington) in the last act of the 1978 American Place Theatre production of *Fefu and Her Friends*, directed by the author. (Photograph: Martha Holmes.)

Staging of *Fefu and Her Friends*

**REVIEW OF THE AMERICAN PLACE THEATRE
PRODUCTION, 1977, BY ERIKA MUNK**

My reactions to Irene Fornes's new play and the Manhattan Theatre Club's evening of readings were peculiarly self-conscious because I had just received some disagreeable letters protesting an April review of Kay Carney's show about Off-Off-Broadway. The angriest was from a playwright, Judith Katz, who claimed that because I criticized Megan Terry's recent work as sentimental and said that Fornes had not developed into a "major" force while Sam Shepard has, I denied an entire American theatre movement and its audience, "trashed" Katz's artistic mothers, and worst of all, was a "male-identified" critic, unable to recognize that "women writers were like women which means that we write emotionally . . . what better place [than the theatre] to have your heart hugged!"

It was tempting to poke fun at this squishy image of blood and veins all tangled on stage as the poor pump tried to beat despite those encircling arms—but the basic indictment filled me with resentment and dismay. Feminism and socialism have made me suspicious of, while easily guilt-stricken by, accusations of bad faith and trafficking with the enemy. Sometimes "male-identified" seems, idiotically, to mean one collaborates through heterosexuality, or having children, or working with men: only the ghetto can be pure. At other times it applies to one's mental style and processes: that is, the degree to which heart-hugging is found inadequate as art or politics. But because reviewing is a profession easily suspect as a form of egotism and always wound about with self-doubt (why am I doing this of all things? am I doing it honestly? what *is* doing it honestly?) I saw the Fornes and heard the readings wary of smart-ass opinions, cute judgments, and simultaneously watching myself for sloppy identification and trashy uplifting of consciousness.

The MTC's evening turned out to be a celebration of Honor Moore's just-published anthology. *The New Women's Theatre*, which includes plays by 10 writers of whom six read from their work: Alice Childress, Tina Howe, Corinne Jacker, Myrna Lamb, Moore herself, and Ruth Wolff. Still brooding about the letters, I found it ironic that the basic premise of Moore's collection pretty well dismissed the eminent women playwrights of the '60s (Drexler, Kennedy, Yankowitz, Owens, as well as Terry and Fornes). Her introduction says: "During the '60s, much of the theatre did not touch real women in spite of the number of female dramatists. But in the '70s, with the shift away from 'absurdism' and back to a kind of realism, women have begun to write from their own experience." The assumption that a nonnaturalistic

style is less "real" or less reflective of experience than a naturalistic one is left unexamined. Moore gently criticizes Lillian Hellman's plays for containing no autobiographical characters or "expressions of need"; she says that Gertrude Stein is "not as important as a reinventor of language and syntax as she is as a woman writer who knew women profoundly and expressed that knowledge." Moore rightly calls for "woman-centered" plays, and then says Martha Graham is "perhaps the most important woman dramatist who ever lived," which gives up on words with a '60s-ish vengeance; oddly, from a poet.

The playwrights themselves were less confessional and didactic than this would lead one to expect, though none seemed deeply interested in formal experimentation. When they talked about their working lives and beliefs, Childress and Wolff were models of how to fight back and stay human: both had special battles, Childress because she is black, Wolff, less seriously (think of all the money!) because a major movie was made from the corpse of her play after its feminist heart had been cut out. I don't want to review the readings—you can look at the book. But when I read it in its entirety, Tina Howe's *Birth and After Birth*, a satiric and exterior play, moved me most, perhaps because it's rather coarse and mean, and deals with the pain we inflict on small children and they on us: a subject I have never seen written for stage so precisely (*not* naturalistically).

Yet I do not see how these plays, in all their various virtues and failings, are more woman-centered than those of the '60s; only that their realistic surfaces are more useful for consciousness-raising and television adaptations. I wonder at the historical perspective behind the claim that women have finally "begun" to write from their own experiences, and was bemused by the slight self-congratulatory aura of the event.

Irene Fornes's nuanced and mysterious play is about a middle-aged woman who has invited a group of friends to her country house; it is the '30s, and these women, each at some crucial point in the development of her spirit, are unconscious pioneers of feminism. The house itself, the sense of interior action its rooms engender, holds the play together.

The first scene is conventional enough: The audience sits on bleachers facing a living room. Fefu's friends gather slowly: a sophisticate amused at her hostess's strong eccentricities; a drinker, who finds a lurking sense of menace; a young lesbian couple; a spirited and beautiful but very actressy actress; a woman in a wheelchair, her face like a death's head, who phases in and out of paranoid hallucinations; finally, a chic woman in black—it is like the country house gatherings of a '30s' mystery story.

Fefu has a husband, whom we never see. Now and then she aims a gun into the garden and shoots at him: the game is that she doesn't know whether he has replaced the gun's blanks with bullets. Of this husband, she says: "He married me as a constant reminder how loathsome women are." And his role is strange but clear: "If women shall recognize each other, the world shall blow us apart. Men remove the danger, but the price is the mind and the spirit."

In the second scene the conventions disappear. The audience is divided into four groups, each of which goes to a different room. All end up seeing the same events, in different order. Mine was: (1) in a real kitchen—apparently a large living loft has been made over to accommodate the play—the lesbian couple have a wry conversation about affairs; one leaves; the woman in black comes in and talks with regret and subdued anger to the other, her former lover. (2) On the lawn Fefu and the actress play croquet and also talk of love, but wittily—the scene exists in a golden haze of deep friendship. (3) In the study, two guests talk desultorily, telling dreams, reading bits from magazines; there is a stifling sense of ennui and the unspoken. (4) In a bedroom the crippled woman lies under a sheet like a corpse, sunk in self-loathing visions of woman's evil and man's torture. One sees each scene knowing that another group has just seen it and a new one will see it next, and that the order of scenes does not matter; this enclosed repetitiveness sums up entire trapped lifetimes.

In the third scene, we return to the living room. The women are released into games and theatre. But suddenly we find out that the crippled woman can walk, though she herself does not seem to know she can. This self-deception leads to the end, in which, of course (for the author is mocking the conventions of three-act thinking), the gun is shot, and there's a real bullet. It kills an animal outside—but at the moment the animal is hit, blood streams from the crippled woman's head, and she dies. Fornes is a delicate writer and I reduce this event to a message at some risk—but: if you kill the external enemy the hysteric inside dies, too. For Fornes, at least here, such freedom comes at the price of women being only with women. Yet, however much I may disagree with this message, the play itself is not a polemic but a lovely piece of theatre.

NTOZAKE SHANGE

1948–

> sing a black girl's song
> bring her out
> to know herself
> to know you

How does an upper-middle-class "black girl" get to know herself? For Paulette Williams, whose father was a surgeon and mother a psychiatric social worker, the process involved continual exploration and an unwillingness to settle for a life of privilege or even for a given name. Though her family was wealthy enough to afford a live-in maid, young Paulette also experienced the frightening experience of being one of the first African Americans in St. Louis's previously all-white public school system. After a B.A. from Barnard and an M.A. from the University of Southern California, both in American Studies, she moved to San Francisco and taught humanities and women's studies at various colleges in the area. In San Francisco, she also found a series of artistic and literary communities that challenged and nurtured her: Third World Communications (The Woman's Collective), a group sponsoring poetry readings by women; the Women's Studies Program at Sonoma State College; dance classes with Raymond Sawyer and Ed Mock, who joined folk traditions of Africa and the Caribbean to American dance traditions; and finally the Spirit of Dance, a dance troupe incorporating Cuban, Caribbean, and African styles. "Knowing a woman's mind & spirit had been allowed me, with dance I discovered my body more intimately than I had imagined possible. With the acceptance of the ethnicity of my thighs & backside, came a clearer understanding of my voice as a woman & as a poet." Thus Shange explains how she came to know herself, from accepting her body to freeing her poetic voice.

Part of that liberating process came by embracing her African heritage, which she signified when she was still a graduate student by taking a new name: Ntozake Shange (pronounced "en-toe-zah-key" "shang-gay") meaning "she who brings her own things" and "one who walks with lions." She also freed herself by rejecting many of the grammatical and mechanical rules of writing. In her poems and plays, Shange deliberately uses abbreviations and phonetic spellings, avoids standard punctuation and capitalization, and forges her own distinctive style as a way of declaring her independence. To break the rules is for her a political act: "in murdering the King's English we free ourselves." Yet, as she makes clear, a writer should take such a step only from a position of complete control. "I insist that my students and my colleagues do master the King's English or the King's French, because then it becomes the same thing that you do in military combat: You know your enemy so well that you're able to do something with his weapon."

Shange's artistic liberation expresses itself not only in the mechanics of her sentences but also in the structure of her plays. Her first play, and still her best-known work, *for colored girls who have considered suicide/when the rainbow is enuf* (1975) began as a series of poems and dances that Shange created together with another dancer (Paula Moss), a horn trio, and a blues band. First performed in bars and cafés, as well as on campuses, "the show" moved from California to New York, expanding and refining itself through performance. Starting with seven poems, Shange developed what she calls a "choreopoem," with twenty poems for seven performers. Joseph Papp of the New York Shakespeare Festival produced this musical play first at the Public Theater and then on Broadway; it won both an Obie (Off-Broadway) award and the New York Drama Critics Circle Award.

Focusing on the experience of women, particularly "women of color"—a term Shange puns on in the title and in the identification of the seven performers only through their differently colored costumes—the play reflects both sexual and racial stereotyping, often with pain and anger but also with humor. The Lady in Brown speaks as a young girl who finds both her adult and racial identity simultaneously by rejecting the choices she finds in the children's room of the public library because they concern "only pioneer girls & magic rabbits/ & big city white boys." In the "ADULT READING ROOM" she finds a book about TOUSSAINT L'OUVERTURE:

TOUSSAINT waz a blk man a negro like my mama say
who refused to be a slave
& he spoke french
& didn't low no white man to tell him nothin

The child's delight in finding a person who represents black strength and independence leads her to read "15 books in three weeks." Other encounters in the play are less liberating, especially the climactic monologue in which the Lady in Red tells about the tortured relationship between Beau Willie Brown, the ex-Vietnam vet, and Crystal, the mother of his two children. This monologue builds to a frightening conclusion as Beau Willie's rage at Crystal's refusal to marry him leads him to dangle the children out the window. At that moment, the Lady in Red virtually identifies herself with the agonized mother in her story:

i stood by beau in the window/ with naomi reachin
for me/ & kwame screaming mommy mommy from the fifth
story/ but i cd only whisper/ & he dropped em

While public response to *for colored girls* was primarily positive, the harrowing effect of "beau willie brown," as well as the number of other violent male-female relationships described in the play raised questions about Shange's racial sensitivity: how could an African-American woman so thoroughly attack African-American men? Were they the only enemies? What about the dominant "other," the entire white community? Shange's 1979 play, *spell #7*, seems to answer those questions by looking not just at the experience of women of color, but of all persons of color ("technologically stressed third world people"), and especially those trapped by the stereotypes created by the white community. In addressing such issues, Shange joins writers such as Alice Childress (1920–), Lorraine Hansberry (1930–1965), and Adrienne Kennedy (1931–) all of whom see all African Americans as continually struggling with the problems of identity. In *Trouble in Mind* (1955), Childress, who worked as an actress and director, examines the problems of a black actress fighting against the degrading stereotype she is asked to play—a mother who would consciously allow her son to turn himself in and be lynched. In *Raisin in the Sun* (1959), Lorraine Hansberry focuses on the conflict between racial pride and the American dream of middle-class security; her protagonist, Walter Lee Younger, seems at first willing to play the subservient "black man" but finally rejects that role to move into a white neighborhood that has tried to exclude him and his family. And in *Funnyhouse of a Negro* (1964) and *The Owl Answers* (1965), Adrienne Kennedy uses surrealist theatrical images and language to explore the distorted views of the African-American culture confronted by her protagonists, "Negro-Sarah" and "She who is Clara Passmore."

Like Kennedy, who deliberately rejects the realistic drama of Childress and Hansberry, Shange begins *spell #7* with a striking theatrical image, "a huge black-face mask" and actors "in tattered fieldhand garb, blackface, and the countenance of stepan fetchit when he waz frightened" (see Figure 1). She thus shows the grinning lie of the minstrel show substituted for the truth of oppression. The opening monologue of Lou, the magician, promises both reality and transformation:

    & i'm fixin you up good/ fixin you up good & colored
    & you gonna be colored all yr life
    & you gonna love it/ bein colored/ all yr life/ colored & love It
    love it/ bein colored. SPELL #7!

Just as *for colored girls* moved through the despair of Crystal's loss to the final choral affirmation, "i found god in myself/ & i loved her/ i loved her fiercely," so *spell #7* progresses towards acceptance though the path to that acceptance is anything but easy. Natalie's first-act monologue about "sue-jean" who "always wanted to have a baby/ a lil boy/ named myself" indicates that bringing a child into the world seems not merely painful but self-destructive; the birth of the child is followed by the death of the child and the minstrel mask that had lifted for most of the act is slowly lowered into place. By the end of the second act, the difficulty of self-acceptance becomes even more pronounced with two bitterly disturbing monologues that explore the consequences of racial stereotyping and oppression.

Yet on stage, the unquenchable vitality of the performers who celebrate the heritage of artists of color make it possible to believe the final line, "colored & love it." The stage directions call for an opening dance drawn from "every period of afro-american entertainment: from acrobats, comedians, tap-dancers, calindy dancers, cotton club choruses, apollo theatre du-wop groups." The text constantly evokes the energetic creativity of popular artists—Tina Turner, Chuck Berry, Butch Morris, Bob Marley, Stevie Wonder. On one level, the nine actors must adopt the presentational style of singer-dancers, putting on a show, telling stories, entertaining each other as well as the audience. But though they begin as masked, stereotyped, imprisoned look-alikes (Figure 1), they gradually reveal the heartfelt reality of individuals caught in immensely personal human dramas (see Figure 2). The return of the minstrel mask at the end forces the audience to confront the contradictions. Shange does not suggest that stereotypes disappear, but she does argue for the possibility that they may be transformed.

spell #7

geechee jibara quik magic trance manual for technologically stressed third world people

A THEATER PIECE BY NTOZAKE SHANGE

CAST *(in order of appearance)*

LOU, *a practicing magician*
ALEC, *a frustrated, angry actor's actor*
DAHLIA, *young gypsy (singer/dancer)*
ELI, *a bartender who is also a poet*
BETTINA, DAHLIA'S *co-worker in a chorus*
LILY, *an unemployed actress working as a barmaid*

NATALIE, *a not too successful performer*
ROSS, *guitarist-singer with* NATALIE
MAXINE, *an experienced actress*

this show is dedicated to my great aunt marie, aunt lizzie, aunt jane and my grandma, viola benzena, and her buddy, aunt effie, and the lunar year.

ACT 1

(there is a huge black-face mask hanging from the ceiling of the theater as the audience enters. in a way the show has already begun, for the members of the audience must integrate this grotesque, larger-than-life misrepresentation of life into their preshow chatter. slowly the house lights fade, but the mask looms even larger in the darkness.

once the mask is all that can be seen, LOU, *the magician, enters. he is dressed in the traditional costume of Mr. Interlocutor: tuxedo, bow tie, top hat festooned with all kinds of whatnots that are obviously meant for good luck, he does a few catchy "soft-shoe" steps & begins singing a traditional version of a black play song)*

LOU: *(singing.)*

10 lil picaninnies all in bed
one fell out and the other nine said:
i sees yr hiney
all black & shiny
i see yr hiney
all black & shiny/ shiny

(as a greeting.)

yes/ yes/ yes   isnt life wonderful

(confidentially.)

my father is a retired magician
which accounts for my irregular behavior
everything comes outta magic hats
or bottles wit no bottoms & parakeets
   are as easy to get as a couple a rabbits
or 3 fifty-cent pieces/ 1958
my daddy retired from magic & took
up another trade cuz this friend of mine

from the 3rd grade/ asked to be made white
on the spot

what cd any self-respectin colored american magician
do wit such an outlandish request/ cept
put all them razzamatazz hocus pocus zippity-
   doo-dah
thingamajigs away   cuz
colored chirren believin in magic
waz becomin politically dangerous for the race
& waznt nobody gonna be made white
on the spot
from a clap of my daddy's hands
& the reason i'm so peculiar's
cuz i been studyin up on my daddy's technique
& everything i do is magic these days
& it's very colored/ very now you see it/ now you
dont mess with me

(boastfully.)

                    i come from a family of retired
sorcerers/ active houngans & pennyante fortune
   tellers
wit 41 million spirits/ critturs & celestial bodies
on our side
      i'll listen to yr problems
      help wit yr career/ yr lover/ yr wanderin
         spouse
      make yr grandma's stay in heaven more
gratifyin
      ease yr mother thru menopause &
         show yr son
      how to clean his room

(while LOU *has been easing the audience into acceptance of his appearance & the mask [his father, the ancestors, our magic], the rest of the company enters in tattered fieldhand garb, blackface, and the countenance of stepan fetchit when he waz frightened. their presence belies the magician's promise that "you'll be colored n love it," just as the minstrel shows were lies, but* LOU *continues.)*

> YES YES YES 3 wishes is all you get
> > scarlet ribbons for yr hair
> > a farm in mississippi
> > someone to love you madly
> all things are possible
> but aint no colored magician in his right mind
> gonna make you   white
> i mean
> > > this is blk magic
> you lookin at
> & i'm fixin you up good/ fixin you up good &
> > colored
> & you gonna be colored all yr life
> & you gonna love it/ bein colored/ all yr life/
> > colored & love it
> love it/ bein colored. SPELL #7!

*(*LOU *claps his hands, & the company which had been absolutely still til this moment/ jumps up. with a rhythm set on a washboard carried by one of them/ they begin a series of steps that identify every period of afro-american entertainment: from acrobats, comedians, tap-dancers, calindy dancers, cotton club choruses, apollo theatre du-wop groups, til they reach a frenzy in the midst of "ham-bone, hambone where ya been"/ & then take a bow à la bert williams/ the lights bump up abruptly.*

the magician, LOU, *walks through the black-faced fig-ures in their kneeling poses, arms outstretched as if they were going to sing "mammy." he speaks now [as a com-panion of the mask] to the same audience who fell so easily into his hands & who were so aroused by the way the black-faced figures "sang n danced.")*

LOU: why don't you go on & integrate a german-amer-ican school in st. louis mo./ 1955/ better yet why dont ya go on & be a red niggah in a blk school in 1954/ i got it/ try & make one friend at camp in the ozarks in 1957/ crawl thru one a jesse james' caves wit a class of white kids waitin outside to see the whites of yr eyes/ why dontcha invade a clique of working class italians trying to be protestant in a jewish community/ & come up a spade/ be a lil too dark/ lips a lil too full/ hair entirely too nappy/ to be beautiful/ be a smart child trying to be dumb/ you go meet somebody who wants/ always/ a lil less/ be cool when yr body says hot/ & more/ be a mistake in racial integrity/ an error in white folks' most absurd fantasies/ be a blk kid in 1954/ who's not blk enuf to lovingly ignore/ not beautiful enuf to leave alone/ not smart enuf to move outta the way/ not

bitter enuf to die at an early age/ why dontchu c'mon & live my life for me/ since the dreams aint enuf/ go on & live my life for me/ i didnt want certain moments at all/ i'd give em to anybody . . . awright. alec.

(the black-faced ALEC *gives his minstrel mask to* LOU *when he hears his name/* ALEC *rises. the rest of the com-pany is intimidated by this figure daring to talk without the protection of black-face. they move away from him/ or move in place as if in mourning.)*

ALEC: st. louis/ such a colored town/ a whiskey black space of history & neighborhood/ forever ours to lawrenceville/ where the only road open to me waz cleared by colonial slaves/ whose children never moved/ never seems like mended the torments of the Depression or the stains of demented spittle/ dropped from the lips of crystal women/ still makin independence flags/
> st. louis/ on a halloween's eve to the veiled prophet/ usurpin the mystery of mardi gras/ i made it mine tho the queen waz always fair/ that parade of pagan floats & tambourines/ commemorates me/ unlike the lonely walks wit liberal trick or treaters/ back to my front door/ bag half empty/
> my face enuf to scare anyone i passed/ gee/ a colored kid/ whatta gas. here/ a tree/ wanderin the horizon/ dipped in blues/ untended bones/ usedta hugs drawls rhythm & decency here a tree/ waitin to be hanged
> summer high school/ squat & pale on the corner/ like our vision waz to be vague/ our memory of the war/ that made us free/ to be forgotten/ becomin paler/ linear movement from sous' carolina to mis-souri/ freedmen/ landin in jackie wilson's yelp/ daughters of the manumitted swimmin in tina tur-ner's grinds/ this is chuck berry's town disavowin miscega-nation/ in any situation/ & they let us be/ electric blues & bo didley/ the rockin pneumonia & boogie-woogie flu/ the slop & short fried heads/ runnin always to the river chambersburg/ lil italy/ i passed everyday at the sweet shoppe/ & waz afraid/ the cops raided truants/ regularly/ & after dark i wd not be seen wit any other colored/ sane & lovin my life

(shouts n cries that are those of a white mob are heard, very loud . . . the still black-faced figures try to move away from the menacing voices & memories.)

VOICES: hey niggah/ over here
ALEC: behind the truck lay five hands claspin chains
VOICES: hey niggah/ over here
ALEC: round the trees/ 4 more sucklin steel
VOICES: hey niggah/ over here
ALEC: this is the borderline
VOICE: hey niggah/ over here
ALEC: a territorial dispute

VOICES: hey niggah/ over here
ALEC: *(crouched on floor.)*

> cars loaded with families/ fellas from the factory/
> one or two practical nurses/ become our
>   trenches/
> some dig into cement wit elbows/ under engines/
> do not be seen in yr hometown
> after sunset/ we suck up our shadows

(finally moved to tear off their "shadows," all but two of the company leave with their true faces bared to the audience. DAHLIA has, as if by some magical cause, shed not only her mask, but also her hideous overalls & pic-aninny-buckwheat wig, to reveal a finely laced unitard/ the body of a modern dancer. she throws her mask to ALEC, who tosses it away. DAHLIA begins a lyrical but pained solo as ALEC speaks for them.)

ALEC:

> we will stand here
> our shoulders embrace an enormous spirit
> my dreams waddle in my lap
> run round to miz bertha's
> where lil richard gets his process
> run backward to the rosebushes
> & a drunk man lyin
> down the block to the nuns
> in pink habits/ prayin in a pink chapel
> my dreams run to meet aunt marie
> my dreams haunt me like the little geechee river
> our dreams draw blood from old sores
> this is our space
> we are not movin

(DAHLIA finishes her movement/ ALEC is seen reaching for her/ lights out. in the blackout they exit as LOU enters. lights come up on LOU who repeats bitterly his challenge to the audience.)

LOU:

> why dontchu go on & live my life for me
> i didnt want certain moments at all
> i'd give them to anybody

(LOU waves his hand commanding the minstrel mask to disappear, which it does. he signals to his left & again by magic, the lights come up higher revealing the interior of a lower manhattan bar & its bartender, ELI, setting up for the night. ELI greets LOU as he continues to set up tables, chairs, candles, etc., for the night's activities. LOU goes over to the jukebox, & plays "we are family" by sister sledge. LOU starts to tell us exactly where we are, but ELI takes over as characters are liable to do. throughout ELI's poem, the other members of the company enter the bar in their street clothes, & doing steps reminiscent of their

solos during the minstrel sequence. as each enters, the audience is made aware that these ordinary people are the minstrels. the company continues to dance individually as ELI speaks.)

> this is . . .

ELI:

> MY kingdom
> there shall be no trespassers/ no marauders
> no tourists in my land
> you nurture these gardens   or   be shot on
>   sight
> carelessness & other priorities
> are not permitted within these walls
> i am mantling an array of strength & beauty
> no one shall interfere with this
> the construction of myself
> my city   my theater
> my bar   come to my poems
> but understand we speak english carefully
> & perfect antillean french
> our toilets are disinfected
> the plants here sing to me each morning
> come to my kitchen my parlor even my bed
> i sleep on satin   surrounded by hand made
> infants who bring me good luck & warmth
> come even to my door
> the burglar alarm/ armed guards vault from the
>   east side
> if i am in danger   a siren shouts
> you are welcome
> to my kingdom   my city   my self
> but yr presence must not disturb these inhabit-
>   ants
> leave nothing out of place/ push no dust under
>   my rugs
> leave not a crack in my wine glasses
> no finger prints
> clean up after yrself in the bathroom
> there are no maids here   no days off
> for healing   no insurance policies
> for dislocation of the psyche
> aliens/ foreigners/ are granted resident status
> we give them a little green card
> as they prove themselves non-injurious
> to the joy of my nation
> i sustain no intrusions/ no double-entendre ro-
>   mance
> no soliciting of sadness   in my life
> are those who love me well
> the rest are denied their visas . . .
> is everyone ready to boogie

(finally, when ELI calls for a boogie, the company does a dance that indicates these people have worked & played together a long time. as dance ends, the company sits &

*chats at the tables & at the bar. this is now a safe haven
for these "minstrels" off from work. here they are free to
be themselves, to reveal secrets, fantasies, nightmares, or
hope. it is safe because it is segregated & magic reigns.*

*LILI, the waitress, is continually moving abt the bar,
taking orders for drinks & generally staying on top of
things.)*

ALEC: gimme a triple bourbon/ & a glass of angel dust
these thursday nite audiences are abt to kill me

(ELI goes behind bar to get drinks.)

DAHLIA: why do i drink so much?

BETTINA, LILY, NATALIE. *(in unison.)*: who cares?

DAHLIA: but i'm an actress. i have to ask myself these
questions

LILY: that's a good reason to drink

DAHLIA: no/ i mean the character/ alec, you're a direc-
tor/ give me some motivation

ALEC: motivation/ if you didn't drink you wd remember
that you're not workin

LILY: i wish i cd get just one decent part

LOU: say as lady macbeth or mother courage

ELI: how the hell is she gonna play lady macbeth and
macbeth's a white dude?

LILY: ross & natalie/ why are you countin pennies like
that?

NATALIE: we had to wait on our money again

ROSS: and then we didnt get it

BETTINA: maybe they think we still accept beads & ribbons

NATALIE: i had to go around wit my tambourine just to
get subway fare

ELI: dont worry abt it/ have one on me

NATALIE: thank you eli

BETTINA: *(falling out of her chair.)* oh . . .

ALEC: cut her off eli/ dont give her no more

LILY: what's the matter bettina/ is yr show closin?

BETTINA: *(gets up, resets chair.)* no/ my show is not closin/
but if that director asks me to play it any blacker/
i'm gonna have to do it in a mammy dress

LOU: you know/ countin pennies/ looking for parts/
breakin tambourines/ we must be outta our minds
for doin this

BETTINA: no we're not outta our minds/ we're just sorta
outta our minds

LILY: no/ we're not outta our minds/ we've been doing
this shit a long time . . . ross/ captain theophilis
conneau/ in *a slaver's logbook/* says that "youths of
both sexes wear rings in the nose and lower lip and
stick porcupine quills thru the cartilage of the ear."
ross/ when ringlin' bros. comes to madison square
garden/ dontcha know the white people just go

ROSS: in their cb radios

DAHLIA: in their mcdonald's hats

ELI: with their save america t-shirts & those chirren who
score higher on IQ tests for the white chirren who
speak english

ALEC: when the hockey games absorb all america's attention in winter/ they go with their fists clenched
& their tongues battering their women who dont
know a puck from a 3-yr-old harness racer

BETTINA: they go & sweat in fierce anger

ROSS: these factories

NATALIE: these middle management positions

ROSS: make madison square garden

BETTINA: the temple of the primal scream

*(LILY gets money from cash register & heads toward
jukebox.)*

LILY: oh how they love blood

NATALIE: & how they dont even dress for the occasion/
all inconspicuous & pink

ELI: now if willie colon come there

BETTINA: if/ we say/ the fania all stars gonna be there in
that nasty fantasy of the city council

ROSS: where the hot dogs are not even hebrew national

LILY: and the bread is stale

ROSS: even in such a place where dance is an obscure
notion

BETTINA: where one's joy is good cause for a boring
chat with the pinkerton guard

DAHLIA: where the halls lead nowhere

ELI: & "back to yr seat/ folks"

LILY: when all one's budget for cruisin

LOU: one's budget for that special dinner with you know
who

LILY: the one you wd like to love you

BETTINA: when yr whole reasonable allowance for leisure activity/ buys you a seat where what's going on
dont matter

DAHLIA: cuz you so high up/ you might be in seattle

LILY: even in such a tawdry space

ELI: where vorster & his pals wd spit & expect black
folks to lick it up

ROSS: *(stands on chair.)* in such a place i've seen miracles

ALL: oh yeah/ aw/ ross

ROSS: the miracles

*("music for the love of it," by butch morris, comes up on
the jukebox/ this is a catchy uptempo rhythm & blues post
WW II. as they speak the company does a dance that
highlights their ease with one another & their familiarity
with "all the new dance steps.")*

LILY: the commodores

DAHLIA: muhammad ali

NATALIE: bob marley

ALEC: & these folks who upset alla 7th avenue with their
glow/ how the gold in their braids is new in this
world of hard hats & men with the grace of
wounded buffalo/ how these folks in silk & satin/ in
bodies reekin of good love comin/ these pretty mu-
thafuckahs

DAHLIA: make this barn

LILY: this insult to good taste

BETTINA: a foray into paradise

DAHLIA, LILY, ALEC, NATALIE, & ROSS: *(in unison.)* we dress up

BETTINA, ELI, & LOU: *(in unison.)* we dress up

DAHLIA: cuz we got good manners

ROSS: cd you really ask dr. funkenstein to come all that way & greet him in the clothes you sweep yr kitchen in?

ALL: NO!

BETTINA: cd you say to muhammad ali/ well/ i just didnt have a chance to change/ you see i have a job/ & then i went jogging & well, you know its just madison square garden

LOU: my dear/ you know that wont do

NATALIE: we honor our guests/ if it costs us all we got

DAHLIA: when stevie wonder sings/ he don't want us lookin like we ain't got no common sense/ he wants us to be as lovely as we really are/ so we strut & reggae

ELI: i seen some doing the jump up/ i myself just got happy/ but i'm tellin you one thing for sure

LILY: we fill up where we at

BETTINA: no police

NATALIE: no cheap beer

DAHLIA: no nasty smellin bano

ROSS: no hallways fulla derelicts & hustlers

NATALIE: gonna interfere wit alla this beauty

ALEC: if it wasnt for us/ in our latino chic/ our rasta-fare our outer space funk suits & all the rest i have never seen

BETTINA: tho my daddy cd tell you bout them fox furs & stacked heels/ the diamonds & marie antoinette wigs

ELI: it's not cuz we got money

NATALIE: it's not cuz if we had money we wd spend it on luxury

LILY: it's just when you gotta audience with the pope/ you look yr best

BETTINA: when you gonna see the queen of england/ you polish yr nails

NATALIE: when you gonna see one of them/ & you know who i mean

ALEC: they gotta really know

BETTINA: we gotta make em feel

ELI: we dont do this for any old body

LOU: we're doin this for you

NATALIE: we dress up

ALEC: is our way of sayin/ you getting the very best

DAHLIA: we cant do less/ we love too much to be stingy

ROSS: they give us too much to be loved ordinary

LILY: we simply have good manners

ROSS: & an addiction to joy

FEMALE CAST MEMBERS: *(in unison.)* WHEE . . .

DAHLIA: we dress up

MALE CAST MEMBERS: *(in unison.)* HEY . . .

BETTINA: we gotta show the world/ we gotta corner on the color

ROSS: happiness just jumped right outta us/ & we are lookin good

(everyone in the bar is having so much fun/ that MAXINE takes on an exaggerated character as she enters/ in order to bring them to attention. the company freezes, half in respect/ half in parody.)

MAXINE: cognac!

(the company relaxes, goes to tables or the bar. in the meantime, ROSS has remained in the spell of the character that MAXINE had introduced when she came in. he goes over to MAXINE who is having a drink/ & begins an improvisation.)

ROSS: she left the front gate open/ not quite knowing she wanted someone to walk on thru the wrought iron fence/ scrambled in whiskey bottles broken round old bike spokes/ some nice brown man to wind up in her bed/ she really didnt know/ the sombrero that enveloped her face was a lil too much for an april nite on the bowery/ & the silver halter dug out from summer cookouts near riis beach/ didnt sparkle with the intensity of her promise to have one good time/ before the children came back from carolina. brooklyn cd be such a drag. every street cept flatbush & nostrand/ reminiscent of europe during the plague/ seems like nobody but sickness waz out walkin/ drivels & hypes/ a few youngsters lookin for more than they cd handle/ & then there waz fay/

(MAXINE rises, begins acting the story out.)

waitin for a cab, anyone of the cars inchin along the boulevard cd see fay waznt no whore/ just a good clean woman out for the nite/ & tho her left titty jumped out from under her silver halter/ she didnt notice cuz she waz lookin for a cab. the dank air fondled her long saggin bosom like a possible companion/ she felt good. she stuck her tin-ringed hand on her waist & watched her own ankles dance in the nite. she waz gonna have a good time tonight/ she waz awright/ a whole lotta woman/ wit that special brooklyn bottom strut. knowin she waznt comin in til dawn/ fay covered herself/ sorta/ wit a light kacky jacket that just kept her titties from rompin in the wind/ & she pulled it closer to her/ the winds waz comin/ from nowhere jabbin/ & there waznt no cabs/ the winds waz beatin her behind/ whisperin/ gigglin/ you aint goin noplace/ you an ol bitch/ shd be at home wit ur kids. fay beat off the voices/ & an EBONY-TRUE-TO-YOU cab climbed the curb to get her. *(as cabdriver.)*

hope you aint plannin on stayin in brooklyn/ after 8:00 you dead in brooklyn. *(as narrator.)*

she let her titty shake like she thot her mouth oughtta bubble like/ wd she take off her panties/ i'd take her anywhere.

MAXINE: *(as in cab.)* i'm into havin a good time/ yr arms/ veins burstin/ like you usedta lift tobacco onto trucks or cut cane/ i want you to be happy/ long as we dont haveta stay in brooklyn

ROSS: & she made like she waz gypsy rose lee/ or the hotsy totsy girls in the carnival round from waycross/ when it waz segregated

MAXINE: what's yr name?

ROSS: my name is raphael

MAXINE: oh that's nice

ROSS: & fay moved where i cd see her out the rear view mirror/ waz tellin me all bout her children & big eddie who waz away/ while we crossed the manhattan bridge/ i kept smilin. *(as cabdriver.)* where exactly you going?

MAXINE: i dont really know. i just want to have a good time. take me where i can see famous people/ & act bizarre like sinatra at the kennedys/ maybe even go round & beat up folks like jim brown/ throw somebody offa balcony/ you know/ for a good time

ROSS: the only place i knew/ i took her/ after i kisst the spaces she'd been layin open to me. fay had alla her $17 cuz i hadn't charged her nothin/ turned the meter off/ said it waz wonderful to pick up a lady like her on atlantic avenue/ i saw nobody but those goddamn whores/ & fay

(MAXINE moves in to ROSS & gives him a very long kiss.)

now fay waz a gd clean woman/ & waz burstin with pride & enthusiasm when she walked into the place where I swore/ all the actresses & actors hung out

(the company joins in ROSS's story; responding to MAXINE as tho she waz entering their bar.)

oh yes/ there were actresses in braids & lipsticks/ wigs & winged tip pumps/ fay assumed the posture of someone she'd always admired/ etta james/ the waitress asked her to leave cuz she waz high/ & fay knew better than that

MAXINE: *(responding to LILY's indication of throwing her out.)* i aint high/ i'm enthusiastic/ and i'm gonna have me a goooooooood/ ol time

ROSS: she waz all dressed up/ she came all the way from brooklyn/ she must look high cuz i/ the taxi-man/ well i got her a lil excited/ that waz all/ but she waz gonna cool out/ cuz she waz gonna meet her friends/ at this place/ yes. she knew that/ & she pushed a bunch of rhododendrum/ outta her way so she cd get over to that table/ & stood over the man with the biggest niggah eyes & warmest smellin mouth

MAXINE: please/ let me join you/ i come all the way from brooklyn/ to have a good time/ you dont think i'm high do ya/ cd i please join ya/ i just wanna have a good ol time

ROSS: *(as BETTINA turns away.)* the woman sipped chablis & looked out the window hopin to see one of the

bowery drunks fall down somewhere/ fay's voice hoverin/ flirtin wit hope

LOU: *(turning to face MAXINE.)* why dont you go downstairs & put yr titty in yr shirt/ you cant have no good time lookin like that/ now go on down & then come up & join us

(BETTINA & LOU rise & move to another table.)

ROSS: fay tried to shove her flesh anywhere/ she took off her hat/ bummed a kool/ swallowed somebody's cognac/ & sat down/ waitin/ for a gd time

MAXINE: *(rises & hugs ROSS.)* aw ross/ when am i gonna get a chance to feel somethin like that/ i got into this business cuz i wanted to feel things all the time/ & all they want me to do is put my leg in my face/ smile/ &

LILY: you better knock on some wood/ maxine/ at least yr workin

BETTINA: & at least yr not playin a whore/ if some other woman comes in here & tells me she's playin a whore/ i think i might kill her

ELI: you'd kill her so you cd say/ oh dahlia died & i know all her lines

BETTINA: aw hush up eli/ dnt you know what i mean?

ELI: no miss/ i dont/ are you in the theater?

BETTINA: mr. bartender/ poet sir/ i am theater

DAHLIA: well miss theater/ that's a surprise/ especially since you fell all over the damn stage in the middle of my solo

LILY: she did

ELI: miss theater herself fell down?

DAHLIA: yeah/ she cant figure out how to get attention without makin somebody else look bad

MAXINE: now dahlia/ it waznt that bad/ i hardly noticed her

DAHLIA: it waz my solo/ you werent sposed to notice her at all!

BETTINA: you know dahlia/ i didnt do it on purpose/ i cda hurt myself

DAHLIA: that wd be unfortunate

BETTINA: well miss thing with those big ass hips you got/ i dont know why you think you do the ballet anyway

(the company breaks; they're expecting a fight.)

DAHLIA: *(crossing to BETTINA.)* i got this

(demonstrates her leg extension.)

& alla this

(DAHLIA turns her back to BETTINA/ & slaps her own backside. BETTINA grabs DAHLIA, turns her around & they begin a series of finger snaps that are a paraphrase of ailey choreography for very dangerous fights. ELI comes to break up the impending altercation.)

ELI: ladies ladies ladies

(ELI separates the two.)

ELI:

    people keep tellin me to put my feet on the
       ground
    i get mad & scream/ there is no ground
    only shit pieces from dogs horses & men who
       dont live
    anywhere/ they tell me think straight & make
       myself
    somethin/ i shout & sigh/ i am a poet/ i write
       poems
    i make words cartwheel & somersault down
       pages
    outta my mouth come visions distilled like boot-
       leg
    whiskey/ i am like a radio but i am a channel of
       my own
    i keep sayin i write poems/ & people keep askin
       me
    what do i do/ what in the hell is going on?
    people keep tellin me these are hard times/ what
       are
    you gonna be doin ten years from now/
    what in the hell do you think/ i am gonna be
       writin poems
    i will have poems inchin up the walls of the
       lincoln tunnel/
    i am gonna feed my children poems on rye bread
       with horseradish/
    i am gonna send my mailman off with a poem
       for his wagon/
    give my doctor a poem for his heart/ i am a poet/
    i am not a part-time poet/ i am not a amateur
       poet/
    i dont even know what that person cd be/
       whoever that is
    authorizing poetry as an avocation/ is a fraud/
    put yr own feet on the ground

BETTINA: i'm sorry eli/ i just dont want to be a gypsy
    all my life

*(the bar returns to normal humming & sipping. the lights
change to focus on* LILY/ *who begins to say what's really
been on her mind. the rest of the company is not aware
of* LILY's *private thoughts. only* BETTINA *responds to*
LILY, *but as a partner in fantasy, not as a voyeur.)*

LILY: *(illustrating her words with movement.)* i'm gonna
    simply brush my hair. rapunzel pull yr tresses back
    into the tower. & lady godiva give up horseback
    riding. i'm gonna alter my social & professional life
    dramatically. i will brush 100 strokes in the morn-
    ing/ 100 strokes midday & 100 strokes before retir-
    ing. i will have a very busy schedule. between the
    local trains & the express/ i'm gonna brush. i brush
    between telephone calls. at the disco i'm gonna
    brush on the slow songs/ i dont slow dance with

strangers. i'ma brush my hair before making love
& after. i'll brush my hair in taxis. while window-
shopping. when i have visitors over the kitchen
table/ i'ma brush. i brush my hair while thinking
abt anything. mostly i think abt how it will be when
i get my full heada hair. like lifting my head in the
morning will become a chore. i'll try to turn my
cheek & my hair will weigh me down

*(*LILY *falls to the floor.* BETTINA *helps lift her to her
knees, then begins to dance & mime as* LILY *speaks.)*

i dream of chaka khan/ chocolate from graham
central station with all seven wigs/ & medusa. i
brush & brush. i use olive oil hair food/ & posner's
vitamin E. but mostly i brush & brush. i may lose
contact with most of my friends. i cd lose my job/
but i'm on unemployment & brush while waiting
on line for my check. i'm sure i get good recom-
mendations from my social worker: such a fastidious woman/ that lily/ always brushing her hair.
nothing in my dreams suggests that hair brushing/
per se/ has anything to do with my particular heada
hair. a therapist might say that the head fulla hair
has to do with something else/ like: a symbol of lily's
unconscious desires. but i have no therapist

(she takes imaginary pen from BETTINA, *who was pretending to be a therapist/ & sits down at table across from
her.)*

& my dreams mean things to me/ like if you
dreamed abt tobias/ then something has happened
to tobias/ or he is gonna show up. if you dream abt
yr grandma who's dead/ then you must be doing
something she doesnt like/ or she wdnta gone to all
the trouble to leave heaven like that. if you dream
something red/ you shd stop. if you dream something green/ you shd keep doing it. if a blue person
appears in yr dreams/ then that person is yr true
friend

& that's how i see my dreams. & this head full
hair i have in my dreams is lavender & nappy as a
3-yr-old's in a apple tree. i can fry an egg & see the
white of the egg spreadin in the grease like my hair
is gonna spread in the air/ but i'm not egg-yolk
yellow/ i am brown & the egg white isnt white at all/
it is my actual hair/ & it wd go on & on forever/
irregular like a rasta-man's hair. irregular/ gargan-
tuan & lavender. nestled on blue satin pillows/ pillows like the sky. & so i fry my eggs. i buy daisies
dyed lavender & laced lavender tablemats & lavender nail polish. though i never admit it/ i really
do believe in magic/ & can do strange things when
something comes over me. soon everything around
me will be lavender/ fluffy & consuming. i will know
not a moment of bitterness/ through all the wrist
aching & tennis elbow from brushing/ i'll smile. no
regrets/ "je ne regrette rien" i'll sing like edith piaf.
when my friends want me to go see tina turner or

pacheco/ i'll croon "sorry/ i have to brush my hair."

i'll find ambrosia. my hair'll grow pomegranates & soil/ rich as round the aswan/ i wake in my bed to bananas/ avocados/ collard greens/ the tramps' latest disco hit/ fresh croissant/ pouilly fuissé/ ishmael reed's essays/ charlotte carter's stories/ all stream from my hair.

& with the bricks that plop from where a 9-year-old's top braid wd be/ i will brush myself a house with running water & a bidet. i'll have a closet full of clean bed linen & the lil girl from the castro convertible commercial will come & open the bed repeatedly & stay on as a helper to brush my hair. lily is the only person i know whose every word leaves a purple haze on the tip of yr tongue. when this happens i says clouds are forming/ & i has to close the windows. violet rain is hard to remove from blue satin pillows

(LOU, *the magician, gets up, he points to* LILY *sitting very still. he reminds us that it is only thru him that we are able to know these people without the "masks"/ the lies/ & he cautions that all their thoughts are not benign. they are not safe from what they remember or imagine.*)

LOU: you have t come with me/ to this place where magic is/ to hear my song/ some times i forget & leave my tune in the corner of the closet under all the dirty clothes/ in this place/ magic asks me where i've been/ how i've been singin/ lately i leave my self in all the wrong hands/ in this place where magic is involved in undoin our masks/ i am able to smile & answer that. in this place where magic always asks for me i discovered a lot of other people who talk without mouths who listen to what you say/ by watchin yr jewelry dance & in this place where magic stays you can let yrself in or out but when you leave yrself at home/ burglars & daylight thieves pounce on you & sell yr skin/ at cut-rates on tenth avenue

(ROSS *has been playing the acoustic guitar softly as* LOU *spoke.* ALEC *picks up on the train of* LOU's *thoughts & tells a story that in turn captures* NATALIE's *attention. slowly,* NATALIE *becomes the woman* ALEC *describes.*)

ALEC: she had always wanted a baby/ never a family/ never a man/ she had always wanted a baby/ who wd suckle & sleep a baby boy who wd wet/ & cry/ & smile suckle & sleep when she sat in bars/ on the stool/ near the door/ & cross from the juke box/ with her legs straddled & revealin red lace pants/ & lil hair smashed under the stockings/ she wd think how she wanted this baby & how she wd call the baby/ "myself" & as she thot/ bout this brown lil thing/ she ordered another bourbon/ double & tilted her head as if to cuddle some infant/ not present/ the men in the bar never imagined her as someone's mother/ she rarely tended her own self carefully/

(NATALIE *rises slowly, sits astride on the floor.*)

just enough to exude a languid sexuality that teased the men off work/ & the bartender/ ray who waz her only friend/ women didnt take to her/ so she spent her afternoons with ray/ in the bar round the corner from her lil house/ that shook winsomely in a hard wind/ surrounded by three weepin willows

NATALIE: my name is sue-jean & i grew here/ a ordinary colored girl with no claims to any thing/ or anyone/ i drink now/ bourbon/ in harder times/ beer/ but i always wanted to have a baby/ a lil boy/ named myself

ALEC: one time/ she made it with ray

NATALIE: & there waz nothin special there/ only a hot rough bangin/ a brusque barrelin throwin of torso/ legs & sweat/ ray wanted to kiss me/ but i screamed/ cuz i didnt like kissin/ only fuckin/ & we rolled round/ i waz a peculiar sorta woman/ wantin no kisses/ no caresses/ just power/ heat & no eaziness of thrust/ ray pulled himself outa me/ with no particular exclamation/ he smacked me on my behind/ i waz grinnin/ & he took that as a indication of his skill/ he believed he waz a good lover/ & a woman like me/ didnt never want nothin but a hard dick/ & everyone believed that/ tho no one in town really knew

ALEC: so ray/ went on behind the bar cuz he had got his

NATALIE: & i lay in the corner laughin/ with my drawers/ twisted round my ankles & my hair standin every which way/ i waz laughin/ knowin i wd have this child/ myself/ & no one wd ever claim him/ cept me cuz i waz a low-down thing/ layin in sawdust & whiskey stains/ i laughed & had a good time masturbatin in the shadows.

ALEC: sue-jean ate starch for good luck

NATALIE: like mamma kareena/ tol me

ALEC: & she planted five okras/ five collards/ & five tomatoes

NATALIE: for good luck too/ i waz gonna have this baby/ i even went over to the hospital to learn prenatal care/ & i kept myself clean

ALEC: sue-jean's lanky body got ta spreadin & her stomach waz taut & round high in her chest/ a high pregnancy is sure to be a boy/ & she smiled

NATALIE: i stopped goin to the bar

ALEC: started cannin food

NATALIE: knittin lil booties

ALEC: even goin to church wit the late nite radio evangelist

NATALIE: i gotta prayer cloth for the boy/ myself waz gonna be safe from all that his mama/ waz prey to

ALEC: sure/ sue-jean waz a scandal/ but that waz to be expected/ cuz she waz always a po criterish chile

NATALIE: & wont no man bout step my way/ ever/ just cuz i hadda bad omen on me/ from the very womb/ i waz bewitched is what the old women usedta say

ALEC: sue-jean waz born on a full moon/ the year of the flood/ the night the river raised her skirts & sat over alla the towns & settlements for 30 miles in each direction/ the nite the river waz in labor/ gruntin & groanin/ splittin trees & families/ spillin cupboards over the ground/ waz the nite sue-jean waz born

NATALIE: & my mother died/ drownin/ holdin me up over the mud crawlin in her mouth

ALEC: somebody took her & she lived to be the town's no one/ now with the boy achin & dancin in her belly/ sue-jean waz a gay & gracious woman/ she made pies/ she baked cakes & left them on the stoop of the church she had never entered just cuz she wanted/ & she grew plants & swept her floors/ she waz someone she had never known/ she waz herself with child/ & she waz a wonderful bulbous thing

NATALIE: the nite/ myself waz born/ ol mama kareena from the hills came down to see bout me/ i hollered & breathed/ i did exactly like mama kareena said/ & i pushed & pushed & there waz a earthquake up in my womb/ i wanted to sit up & pull the tons of logs trapped in my crotch out/ so i cd sleep/ but it wdnt go way/ i pushed & thot i saw 19 horses runnin in my pussy/ i waz sure there waz a locomotive stalled up in there burnin coal & steamin & pushin gainst a mountain

ALEC: finally the child's head waz within reach & mama kareena/ brought the boy into this world

NATALIE: & he waz awright/ with alla his toes & his fingers/ his lil dick & eyes/ elbows that bent/ & legs/ straight/ i wanted a big glassa bourbon/ & mama kareena brought it/ right away/ we sat drinkin the bourbon/ & lookin at the child whose name waz myself/ like i had wanted/ & the two of us ate placenta stew . . . i waznt really sure . . .

ALEC: sue-jean you werent really sure you wanted myself to wake up/ you always wanted him to sleep/ or at most to nurse/ the nites yr dreams were disturbed by his cryin

NATALIE: i had no one to help me

ALEC: so you were always with him/ & you didnt mind/ you knew this waz yr baby/ myself/ & you cuddled him/ carried him all over the house with you all day/ no matter/ what

NATALIE: everythin waz goin awright til/ myself wanted to crawl

ALEC: (moving closer to NATALIE.) & discover a world of his own/ then you became despondent/ & yr tits began to dry & you lost the fullness of yr womb/ where myself/ had lived

NATALIE: i wanted that back

ALEC: you wanted back the milk

NATALIE: & the tight gourd of a stomach i had when myself waz bein in me

ALEC: so you slit his wrists

NATALIE: he waz sleepin

ALEC: sucked the blood back into yrself/ & waited/ myself shriveled up in his crib

NATALIE: a dank lil blk thing/ i never touched him again

ALEC: you were always holdin yr womb/ feelin him kick & sing to you bout love/ & you wd hold yr tit in yr hand

NATALIE: like i always did when i fed him

ALEC: & you waited & waited/ for a new myself. tho there were labor pains

NATALIE: & i screamed in my bed

ALEC: yr legs pinnin to the air

NATALIE: spinnin sometimes like a ferris wheel/ i cd get no child to fall from me

ALEC: & she forgot abt the child bein born/ & waz heavy & full all her life/ with "myself"

NATALIE: who'll be out/ any day now

(ELI moves from behind the bar to help NATALIE/ or to clean tables, he doesnt really know. he stops suddenly.)

ELI: aint that a goddamn shame/ aint that a way to come into the world sometimes i really cant write sometimes i cant even talk

(the minstrel mask comes down very slowly. blackout, except for lights on the big minstrel mask which remains visible throughout intermission.)

ACT 2

(all players onstage are frozen, except LOU, who makes a motion for the big minstrel mask to disappear again. as the mask flies up, LOU begins.)

LOU: in this place where magic stays you can let yrself in or out

(he makes a magic motion. a samba is heard from the jukebox & activity is begun in the bar again. DAHLIA, NATALIE & LILY enter, apparently from the ladies room.)

NATALIE: i swear we went to that audition in good faith/ & that man asked us where we learned to speak english so well/ i swear this foreigner/ asked us/ from the city of new york/ where we learned to speak english.

LILY: all i did was say "bom dia/ como vai"/ and the englishman got red in the face.

LOU: (as the englishman.) yr from the states/ aren't you?

LILY: "sim"/ i said/ in good portuguese

LOU: but you speak portuguese

LILY: "sim" i said/ in good portuguese

LOU: how did you pick that up?

LILY: i hadda answer so simple/ i cdnt say i learned it/ cuz niggahs cant learn & that wda been too hard on the man/ so i said/ in good english: i held my ear to the ground & listened to the samba from bêlim

DAHLIA: you should have said: i make a lotta phone calls to cascais, portugao

BETTINA: i gotta bahiano boyfriend

NATALIE: how abt: i waz an angolan freedom fighter

MAXINE: no/ lily/ tell him: i'm a great admirer of zeza
motto & leci brandao
LILY: when the japanese red army invaded san juan/
they poisoned the papaya with portuguese. i eat a
lotta papaya. last week/ i developed a strange schizophrenic condition/ with 4 manifest personalities:
one spoke english & understood nothing/ one
spoke french & had access to the world/ one spoke
spanish & voted against statehood for puerto rico/
one spoke portuguese. "eu naõ falo ingles entaõ y
voce"/ i dont speak english anymore/ & you?

*(all the women in the company have been doing samba
steps as the others spoke/ now they all dance around a
table in their own ritual/ which stirs* ALEC *&* LOU *to
interrupt this female segregation. the women scatter to
different tables, leaving the two interlopers alone. so,*
ALEC *&* LOU *begin their conversation.)*

ALEC: not only waz she without a tan, but she held her
purse close to her hip like a new yorker. someone
who rode the paris métro or listened to mariachis
in plaza santa cecilia. she waz not from here

(he sits at table.)

LOU: *(following suit.)* but from there
ALEC: some there where coloureds/ mulattoes/ negroes/
blacks cd make a living big enough to leave there
to come here/ where no one went there much any
more for all sorts of reasons
LOU: the big reasons being immigration restrictions &
unemployment. nowadays, immigration restrictions of every kind apply to any non-european persons who want to go there from here
ALEC: some who want to go there from here risk fetching trouble with the customs authority there
LOU: or later with the police, who can tell who's not
from there cuz the shoes are pointed & laced
strange
ALEC: the pants be for august & yet it's january
LOU: the accent is patterned for pétionville, but working in crown heights
ALEC: what makes a person comfortably ordinary here
cd make him dangerously conspicuous there.
LOU: so some go to london or amsterdam or paris/
where they are so abounding no one tries to tell
who is from where
ALEC: still the far right wing of every there prints lil
pamphlets that say everyone from there shd leave
& go back where they came from
LOU: this is manifest legally thru immigration restrictions & personally thru unemployment
ALEC: anyway the yng woman waz from there/ & she
waz alone. that waz good. cuz if a person had no
big brother in gronigen/ no aunt in rouen
LOU: no sponsor in chicago
ALEC: this brown woman from there might be a good
idea. everybody in the world/ european & non-
european alike/ everybody knows that rich white

girls are hard to find. some of them joined the
weather underground/ some the baader-meinhof
gang.
LOU: a whole bunch of them gave up men entirely
ALEC: so the exotic lover in the sun routine becomes
more difficult to swing/ if she wants to talk abt
plastic explosives & the resistance of the black
masses to socialism/ instead of giving head as the
tide slips in or lending money
LOU: just for the next few days
ALEC: is hard to find a rich white girl who is so dumb/
too
LOU: anyway. the whole world knows/ european & non-
european alike/ the whole world knows that nobody
loves the black woman like they love farrah fawcett-
majors. the whole world dont turn out for a dead
black woman like they did for marilyn monroe.
ALEC: actually/ the demise of josephine baker waz an
international event
LOU: but she waz a war hero the worldwide un-beloved
black woman is a good idea/ if she is from there &
one is a young man with gd looks/ piercing eyes/ &
knowledge of several romantic languages

(throughout this conversation, ALEC *&* LOU *will make
attempts to seduce, cajole, & woo the women of the bar
as their narrative indicates. the women play the roles as
described, being so moved by romance.)*

ALEC: the best dancing spots/ the hill where one can see
the entire bay at twilight
LOU: the beach where the seals & pelicans run free/ the
hidden "local" restaurants
ALEC: "aw babee/ you so pretty" begins often in the
lobby of hotels where the bright handsome yng men
wd be loiterers
LOU: were they not needed to tend the needs of the
black women from there
ALEC: tourists are usually white people or asians who
didnt come all this way to meet a black woman who
isnt even foreign
LOU: so hotel managers wink an eye at the yng men in
the lobby or by the bar who wd be loitering/ but are
gonna help her have a gd time
ALEC: maybe help themselves too
LOU: everybody in the world/ european & non-european alike/ everybody knows the black woman from
there is not treated as a princess/ as a jewel/ a cherished lover
ALEC: that's not how sapphire got her reputation/ nor
how mrs. jefferson perceives the world
LOU: you know/ babee/ you dont act like them. aw ba-
bee/ you so pretty
ALEC: the yng man in the hotel watches the yng blk
woman sit & sit & sit/ while the european tourists
dance with each other/ & the dapper local fellas
mambo frenetically with secretaries from arizona/
in search of the missing rich white girl. our girl sits
&

FEMALE CAST MEMBERS: *(in unison.)* sits & sits & sits

ALEC: *(to* DAHLIA *&* NATALIE, *who move to the music.)* maybe she is courageous & taps her foot. maybe she is bold & enjoys the music/ smiling/ shaking shoulders. let her sit & let her know she is unwanted

LOU: she is not white & she is not from here

ALEC: let her know she is not pretty enuf to dance the next merengue. then appear/ mysteriously/ in the corner of the bar. stare at her. just stare. when stevie wonder's song/ "isnt she lovely"/ blares thru the red-tinted light/ ask her to dance & hold her as tyrone power wda. hold her & stare

*(*ROSS *&* ELI *sing the chorus to stevie wonder's "isn't she lovely.")*

LOU: dance yr ass off. she has been discovered by the non-european fred astaire

ALEC: let her know she is a surprise/ an event. by the look on yr face you've never seen anyone like this black woman from there. you say: "aw/ you not from here?"/ totally astonished. she murmurs that she is from there. as if to apologize for her unfortunate place of birth

LOU: you say

ALEC: aw babee/ you so pretty. & it's all over

LOU: a night in a pension near the sorbonne. pick her up from the mattress. throw her gainst the wall in a show of exotic temper & passion: "maintenant/ tu es ma femme. nous nous sommes mariés."° unions of this sort are common wherever the yng black women travel alone. a woman traveling alone is an affront to the non-european man who is known the world over/ to european & non-european alike/ for his way with women

ALEC: his sense of romance/ how he can say:

LOU: aw babee/ you so pretty . . . and even a beautiful woman will believe no one else ever recognized her loveliness

ELI: or else/ he comes to a cafe in willemstad in the height of the sunset. an able-bodied/ sinewy yng man who wants to buy one beer for the yng woman. after the first round/ he discovers he has run out of money/ so she must buy the next round/ when he discovers/ what beautiful legs you have/ how yr mouth is like the breath of tiger lilies. we shall make love in the/ how you call it/ yes in the earth/ in the dirt/ i will have you in my/ how you say/ where things grow/ aw/ yes/ i will have you in the soil. probably under the stars & smelling of wire/ an unforgettable international affair can be consummated

(the company sings "tara's theme" as ELI *ends his speech.* ELI *&* BETTINA *take a tango walk to the bar, while*

MAXINE *mimics a 1930s photographer, shooting them as they sail off into the sunset.)*

MAXINE: at 11:30 one evening i waz at the port authority/ new york/ united states/ myself. now i waz there & i spoke english & waz holding approximately $7 american currency/ when a yng man from there came up to me from the front of the line of people waiting for the princeton new jersey united states local bus. i mean to say/ he gave up his chance for a good seat to come say to me:

ROSS: i never saw a black woman reading nietzsche

MAXINE: i waz demure enough/ i said i have to for a philosophy class. but as the night went on i noticed this yng man waz so much like the other yng men from here/ who use their bodies as bait & their smiles as passport alternatives. anyway the night did go on. we were snuggled together in the rear of the bus going down the jersey turnpike. he told me in english/ that he had spoken all his life in st. louis/ where he waz raised:

ROSS: i've wanted all my life to meet someone like you. i want you to meet my family/ who haven't seen me in a long time/ since i left missouri looking for opportunity . . .

(he is lost for words.)

LOU: *(stage whisper.)* opportunity to sculpt

ROSS: thank you/ opportunity to sculpt

MAXINE: he had been everyplace/ he said

ROSS: you arent like any black woman i've ever met anywhere

MAXINE: here or there

ROSS: i had to come back to new york cuz of immigration restrictions & high unemployment among black american sculptors abroad

MAXINE: just as we got to princeton/ he picked my face up from his shoulder & said:

ROSS: aw babee/ you so pretty

MAXINE: aw babee/ you so pretty. i believe that night i must have looked beautiful for a black woman from there/ though i cd be asked at any moment to tour the universe/ to climb a 6-story walkup with a brilliant & starving painter/ to share kadushi/ to meet mama/ to getta kiss each time the swing falls toward the willow branch/ to imagine where he say he from/ & more. i cd/ i cd have all of it/ but i cd not be taken/ long as i don't let a stranger be the first to say:

LOU: aw babee/ you so pretty

MAXINE: after all/ immigration restrictions & unemployment cd drive a man to drink or to lie

(she breaks away from ROSS.*)*

so if you know yr beautiful & bright & cherishable awready/ when he say/ in whatever language:

ALEC: *(to* NATALIE.*)* aw babee/ you so pretty

MAXINE: you cd say:

NATALIE: i know. thank you

°**"maintenant . . . mariés,"** now/ you are my wife. we are married.

MAXINE: then he'll smile/ & you'll smile. he'll say:

ELI: *(stroking* BETTINA's *thigh.)* what nice legs you have

MAXINE: you can say:

BETTINA: *(removing his hand.)* yes. they run in the family

MAXINE: oh! whatta universe of beautiful & well traveled women!

MALE CAST MEMBERS: *(in unison.)* aw babee/ i've never met anyone like you

FEMALE CAST MEMBERS: *(in unison, pulling away from men to stage edges.)* that's strange/ there are millions of us!

(men all cluster after unsuccessful attempts to persuade their women to talk. ALEC *gets the idea to serenade the women;* ROSS *takes the first verse, with men singing backup. song is "ooh baby," by smokey robinson.)*

ROSS: *(singing.)*

> i did you wrong/ my heart went out to play/ but in the game
> i lost you/what a price to pay/ i'm cryin . . .

MALE PLAYERS: *(singing.)* oo oo oo/ baby baby. . . . oo oo oo/ baby baby

(this brings no response from the women; the men elect ELI *to lead the second verse.)*

ELI:

> mistakes i know i've made a few/ but i'm only human/ you've made mistakes too/ i'm cryin . . .
> oo oo oo/ baby baby . . . oo oo oo/ baby baby

(the women slowly forsake their staunch indignation/ returning to the arms of their partners. all that is except LILY, *who walks abt the room of couples awkwardly)*

MALE CAST MEMBERS & LILY: *(singing.)*

> i'm just about at the end of my rope
> but i can't stop trying/ i cant give up hope
> cause i/ i believe one day/ i'll hold you near
> whisper i love you/ until that day is here
> i'm cryin . . . oo oo oo/ baby baby

*(*LILY *begins as the company continues to sing.)*

LILY:

> unfortunately
> the most beautiful man in the world
> is unavailable
>   that's what he told me
> i saw him wandering abt/ said well this is one of a kind
> & i might be able to help him out
> so alone & pretty in all this ganja & bodies melting
> he danced with me & i cd become that

> a certain way to be held that's considered in advance
> a way a thoughtful man wd kiss a woman who cd be offended easily/ but waznt cuz
> of course the most beautiful man in the world knows exactly what to do
> with someone who knows that's who he is/
> these dreads fallin thru my dress
> so my nipples just stood up
> these hands playin the guitar on my back
> the lips somewhere between my neck
> & my forehead
> talking bout ocho rios & how i really must go
> marcus garvey cda come in the door & we/
> we wd still be dancin that dance
> the motion that has more to do with kinetic energy
> than shootin stars/ more to do with the impossibility
> of all this/ & how it waz awready bein too much
> our reason failed
> we tried to go away & be just together
> aside from the silence that weeped
> with greed/ we didnt need/ anything/ but one another
> for tonite
> but he is the most beautiful man in the world
>   says he's unavailable/
> & this man whose eyes made me
> half-naked & still & brazen/ was singin with me
> since we cd not talk/ we sang

*(*MALE PLAYERS *end their chorus with a flourish.)*

LILY:

> we sang with bob marley
> this man/ surely the most beautiful man in the world/ &
> i
> sang/ "i wanna love you & treat you right/

(the couples begin different kinds of reggae dances.)

> i wanna love you every day & every night"

THE COMPANY: *(dancing & singing.)*

> we'll be together with
> the roof right over our heads
> we'll share the shelter of my single bed
> we'll share the same room/ jah provide the bread

DAHLIA: *(stops dancing during conversation.)* i tell you it's not just the part that makes me love you so much

LOU: what is it/ wait/ i know/ you like my legs

DAHLIA: yes/ uh huh/ yr legs & yr arms/ & . . .

LOU: but that's just my body/ you started off saying you loved me & now i see it's just my body

DAHLIA: oh/ i didn't mean that/ it's just i dont know you/

except as the character i'm sposed to love/ & well i know rehearsal is over/ but i'm still in love with you

(they go to the bar to get drinks, then sit at a table.)

ROSS: but baby/ you have to go on the road. we need the money

NATALIE: i'm not going on the road so you can fuck all these aspiring actresses

ROSS: aw/ just some of them/ baby

NATALIE: that's why i'm not going

ROSS: if you dont go on the road i'll still be fuckin em/ but you & me/ we'll be in trouble/ you understand?

NATALIE: *(stops dancing.)* no i dont understand

ROSS: well let me break it down to you

NATALIE: please/ break it down to me

BETTINA: *(stops dancing.)* hey/ natalie/ why dont you make him go on the road/ they always want us to be so goddamned conscientious

ALEC: *(stops dancing.)* dont you think you shd mind yr own bizness?

NATALIE: yeah bettina/ mind yr own bizness

(she pulls ROSS to the table with her.)

BETTINA: *(to ALEC.)* no/ i'm tired of having to take any & every old job to support us/ & you get to have artistic integrity & refuse parts that are beneath you

ALEC: thats right/ i'm not playing the fool or the black buck pimp circus/ i'm an actor not a stereotype/ i've been trained. you know i'm a classically trained actor

BETTINA: & just what do you think we are?

MAXINE: well/ i got offered another whore part downtown

ELI: you gonna take it?

MAXINE: yeah

LILY: if you dont/ i know someone who will

ALEC: *(to BETTINA.)* i told you/ we arent gonna get anyplace/ by doin every bit part for a niggah that someone waves in fronta my face

BETTINA: & we arent gonna live long on nothin/ either/ cuz i'm quittin my job

ALEC: be in the real world for once & try to understand me

BETTINA: you mean/ i shd understand that you are the great artist & i'm the trouper.

ALEC: i'm not sayin that we cant be gigglin & laughin all the time dancin around/ but i cant stay in these "hate whitey" shows/ cuz they arent true

BETTINA: a failure of imagination on yr part/ i take it

ALEC: no/ an insult to my person

BETTINA: oh i see/ you wanna give the people some more make-believe

ALEC: i cd always black up again & do minstrel work/ wd that make you happy?

BETTINA: there is nothin niggardly abt a decent job. work is honorable/ work!

ALEC: well/ i got a problem. i got lots of problems/ but i got one i want you to fix & if you can fix it/ i'll do

anything you say. last spring this niggah from the midwest asked for president carter to say he waz sorry for that forgettable phenomenon/ slavery/ which brought us all together. i never did get it/ none of us ever got no apology from no white folks abt not bein considered human beings/ that makes me mad & tired. someone told me "roots" was the way white folks worked out their guilt/ the success of "roots" is the way white folks assuaged their consciences/ i dont know this/ this is what i waz told. i dont get any pleasure from nobody watchin me trying to be a slave i once waz/ who got away/ when we all know they had an emancipation proclamation/ that the civil war waz not fought over us. we all know that we/ actually dont exist unless we play football or basketball or baseball or soccer/ pélé/ see they still import a strong niggah to earn money. art here/ isnt like in the old country/ where we had some spare time & did what we liked to do/ i dont know this either/ this is also something i've been told. i just want to find out why no one has even been able to sound a gong & all the reporters recite that the gong is ringin/ while we watch all the white people/ immigrants & invaders/ conquistadors & relatives of london debtors from georgia/ kneel & apologize to us/ just for three or four minutes. now/ this is not impossible/ & someone shd make a day where a few minutes of the pain of our lives is acknowledged. i have never been very interested in what white people did/ cuz i waz able/ like most of us/ to have very lil to do with them/ but if i become a success that means i have to talk to white folks more than in high school/ they are everywhere/ you know how they talk abt a neighborhood changin/ we suddenly become all over the place/ they are now all over my life/ & i dont like it. i am not talkin abt poets & painters/ not abt women & lovers of beauty/ i am talkin abt that proverbial white person who is usually a man who just/ turns yr body around/ looks at yr teeth & yr ass/ who feels yr calves & back/ & agrees on a price. we are/ you see/ now able to sell ourselves/ & i am still a person who is tired/ a person who is not into his demise/ just three minutes for our lives/ just three minutes of silence & a gong in st. louis/ oakland/ in los angeles . . .

(the entire company looks at him as if he's crazy/ he tries to leave the bar/ but BETTINA stops him.)

BETTINA: you're still outta yr mind. ain't no apologies keeping us alive.

LOU: what are you gonna do with white folks kneeling all over the country anyway/ man

(LOU signals everyone to kneel.)

LILY: they say i'm too light to work/ but when i asked him what he meant/ he said i didnt actually look black. but/ i said/ my mama knows i'm black & my daddy/ damn sure knows i'm black/ & he is the only

one who has a problem thinkin i'm black/ i said so
let me play a white girl/ i'm a classically trained
actress & i need the work & i can do it/ he said that
wdnt be very ethical of him. can you imagine that
shit/ not ethical

NATALIE: as a red-blooded white woman/ i cant allow
you all to go on like that

(NATALIE *starts jocularly.*)

cuz today i'm gonna be a white girl/ i'll retroactively
wake myself up/ ah low & behold/ a white girl in
my bed/ but first i'll haveta call a white girl i know
to have some more accurate information/ what's the
first thing white girls think in the morning/ do they
get up being glad they aint niggahs/ do they remember mama/ or worry abt gettin to work/ do
they work?/ do they play isdora & wrap themselves
in sheets & go tip toeing to the kitchen to make
maxwell house coffee/ oh i know/ the first thing a
white girl does in the morning is fling her hair/

So now i'm done with that/ i'm gonna water my
plants/ but am i a po white trash white girl with a
old jellyjar/ or am i a sophisticated & protestant
suburbanite with 2 valiums slugged awready & a
porcelain water carrier leading me up the stairs
strewn with heads of dolls & nasty smellin white
husband person's underwear/ if i was really protected from the niggahs/ i might go to early morning mass & pick up a tomato pie on the way home/
so i cd eat it during the young & the restless. in
williams arizona as a white girl/ i cd push the navaho
women outta my way in the supermarket & push
my nose in the air so i wdnt haveta smell them.
coming from bay ridge on the train i cd smile at all
the black & puerto rican people/ & hope they cant
tell i want them to go back where they came from/
or at least be invisible.

i'm still in my kitchen/ so i guess i'll just have to
fling my hair again & sit down. i shd pinch my
cheeks to bring the color back/ i wonder why the
colored lady hasn't arrived to clean my house yet/
so i cd go to the beauty parlor & sit under a sunlamp
to get some more color back/ it's terrible how god
gave those colored women such clear complexions/
it take em years to develop wrinkles/ but beauty can
be bought & flattered into the world.

as a white girl on the street/ i can assume since i
am a white girl on the streets/ that everyone notices
how beautiful i am/ especially lil black & caribbean
boys/ they love to look at me/ i'm exotic/ no one in
their families looks like me/ poor things. if i waz
one of those white girls who loves one of those
grown black fellas/ i cd say with my eyes wide open/
totally sincere/ oh i didnt know that/ i cd say i didnt
know/ i cant/ i dont know how/ cuz i'ma white girl
& i dont have to do much of anything.

all of this is the fault of the white man's sexism/
oh how i loathe tight-assed-thin-lipped pink white

men/ even the football players lack a certain relaxed
virility. that's why my heroes are either just like my
father/ who while he still cdnt speak english knew
enough to tell me how the niggers shd go back
where they came from/ or my heroes are psychotic
faggots who are white/ or else they are/ oh/ you
know/ colored men.

being a white girl by dint of my will/ is much more
complicated than i thought it wd be/ but i wanted
to try it cuz so many men like white girls/ white
men/ black men/ latin men/ jewish men/ asians/
everybody. so i thought if i waz a white girl for a
day i might understand this better/ after all gertrude stein wanted to know abt the black women/
alice adams wrote *thinking abt billie*/ joyce carol oates
has three different black characters all with the
same name/ i guess cuz we are underdeveloped
individuals or cuz we are all the same/ at any rate
i'm gonna call this thinkin abt white girls/ cuz hel-
mut newton's awready gotta book called *white
women*/ see what i mean/ that's a best seller/ one
store i passed/ hadda sign said/

> WHITE WOMEN
> SOLD OUT

it's this kinda pressure that forces us white girls to
be so absolutely pathological abt the other women
in the world/ who now that they're not all servants
or peasants want to be considered beautiful too. we
simply krinkle our hair/ learn to dance the woogie
dances/ slant our eyes with make-up or surgery/
learn spanish & claim argentinian background/ or
as a real trump card/ show up looking like a real
white girl. you know all western civilization depends
on us/

i still havent left my house. i think i'll fling my
hair once more/ but this time with a pout/ cuz i
think i havent been fair to the sisterhood/ women's
movement faction of white girls/ although/ they
always ask what do you people really want. as if the
colored woman of the world were a strange sort of
neutered workhorse/ which isnt too far from real-
ity/ since i'm still waiting for my cleaning lady & the
lady who takes care of my children & the lady who
caters my parties & the lady who accepts quarters
at the bathroom in sardi's. those poor creatures shd
be sterilized/ no one shd have to live such a life. cd
you hand me a towel/ thank-you caroline. i've left
all of maxime's last winter clothes in a pile for you
by the back door. they have to be cleaned but i hope
yr girls can make gd use of them.

oh/ i'm still not being fair/ all the white women in

the world dont wake up being glad they aint nig-gahs/ only some of them/ the ones who dont/ wake up thinking how can i survive another day of this culturally condoned incompetence. i know i'll play a tenor horn & tell all the colored artists i meet/ that now i'm just like them/ i'm colored i'll say cuz i have a struggle too. or i cd punish this white beleaguered body of mine with the advances of a thousand ebony bodies/ all built like franco harris or peter tosh/ a thousand of them may take me & do what they want/ cuz i'm so sorry/ yes i'm so sorry they were born niggahs. but then if i cant punish myself to death for being white/ i certainly cant in good conscience keep waiting for the cleaning lady/ & everytime i attempt even the smallest venture into the world someone comes to help me/ like if i do anything/ anything at all i'm extending myself as a white girl/ cuz part of being a white girl is being absent/ like those women who are just with a man but whose names the black people never remember/ they just say oh yeah his white girl waz with him/. or a white girl got beat & killed today/ why someone will say/ cuz some niggah told her to give him her money & she said no/ cuz she thought he realized that she waz a white girl/ & he did know but he didnt care/ so he killed her & took the money/ but the cops knew she waz a white girl & cdnt be killed by a niggah especially/ when she had awready said no. the niggah was sposed to hop round the corner backwards/ you dig/ so the cops/ found the culprit within 24 hours/ cuz just like emmett till/ niggahs do not kill white girls.

i'm still in my house/ having flung my hair-do for the last time/ what with having to take 20 valium a day/ to consider the ERA/ & all the men in the world/ & my ignorance of the world/ it is over-whelming. i'm so glad i'm colored. boy i cd wake up in the morning & think abt anything. i can remember emmett till & not haveta smile at anybody.

MAXINE: (compelled to speak by NATALIE's pain.) whenever these things happened to me/ & i waz young/ i wd eat a lot/ or buy new fancy underwear with rhine-stones & lace/ or go to the movies/ maybe call a friend/ talk to made-up boyfriends till dawn. this waz when i waz under my parents' roof/ & trees that grew into my room had to be cut back once a year/ this waz when the birds sometimes flew thru the halls of the house as if the ceilings were sky & i/simply another winged creature. yet no one around me noticed me especially. no one around saw anything but a precocious brown girl with pe-culiar ideas. like during the polio epidemic/ i wanted to have a celebration/ which nobody cd un-derstand since iron lungs & not going swimming waznt nothing to celebrate. but i explained that i waz celebrating the bounty of the lord/ which more people didnt understand/ til i went on to say that/ it waz obvious that god had protected the colored

folks from polio/ nobody understood that. i did/ if god had made colored people susceptible to polio/ then we wd be on the pictures & the television with the white children. i knew only white folks cd get that particular disease/ & i celebrated. that's how come i always commemorated anything that af-fected me or the colored people. according to my history of the colored race/ not enough attention was paid to small victories or small personal defeats of the colored. i celebrated the colored trolley driver/ the colored basketball team/ the colored blues singer/ & the colored light heavy weight champion of the world. then too/ i had a baptist child's version of high mass for the slaves in new orleans whom i had read abt/ & i tried to grow watermelons & rice for the dead slaves from the east. as a child i took on the burden of easing the ghost-colored folks' souls & trying hard to keep up with the affairs of my own colored world.

when i became a woman, my world got smaller. my grandma closed up the windows/ so the birds wdnt fly in the house any more. waz bad luck for a girl so yng & in my condition to have the shadows of flying creatures over my head. i didn't celebrate the trolley driver anymore/ cuz he might know i waz in this condition. i didnt celebrate the basketball team anymore/ cuz they were yng & handsome/ & yng & handsome cd mean trouble. but trouble waz when white kids called you names or beat you up cuz you had no older brother/ trouble waz when someone died/ or the tornado hit yr house/ now trouble meant something abt yng & handsome/ & white or colored. if he waz yng & handsome that meant trouble. seemed like every one who didnt have this condition/ so birds cdnt fly over yr head/ waz trouble. as i understood it/ my mama & my grandma were sending me out to be with trouble/ but not to get into trouble. the yng & handsome cd dance with me & call for sunday supper/ the yng & handsome cd write my name on their notebooks/ cd carry my ribbons on the field for gd luck/ the uncles cd hug me & chat for hours abt my growing up/ so i counted all 492 times this condition wd make me victim to this trouble/ before i wd be im-mune to it/ the way colored folks were immune to polio.

i had discovered innumerable manifestations of trouble: jealousy/ fear/ indignation & recurring fits of vulnerability that lead me right back to the con-tradiction i had never understood/ even as a child/ how half the world's population cd be bad news/ be yng & handsome/ & later/ eligible & interested/ & trouble.

plus/ according to my own version of the history of the colored people/ only white people hurt little colored girls or grown colored women/ my mama told me only white people had social disease & mo-lested children/ and my grandma told me only white people committed unnatural acts. that's how come i knew only white folks got polio/ muscular dystrophy/ sclerosis/ & mental illness/ this waz all verified by the television. but i found out that the colored folks knew abt the same vicious & disease-ridden passions that the white folks knew.

the pain i succumbed to each time a colored person did something that i believed only white people did waz staggering. my entire life seems to be worthless/ if my own folks arent better than white folks/ then surely the sagas of slavery & the jim crow hadnt convinced anyone that we were better than them. i commenced to buying pieces of gold/ 14 carat/ 24 carat/ 18 carat gold/ every time some black person did something that waz beneath him as a black person & more like a white person. i bought gold cuz it came from the earth/ & more than likely it came from south africa/ where the black people are humiliated & oppressed like in slavery. i wear all these things at once/ to remind the black people that it cost a lot for us to be here/ our value/ can be known instinctively/ but since so many black people are having a hard time not being like white folks/ i wear these gold pieces to protest their ignorance/ their disconnect from history. i buy gold with a vengeance/ each time someone appropriates my space or my time without permission/ each time someone is discourteous or actually cruel to me/ if my mind is not respected/ my body toyed with/ i buy gold/ & weep. i weep as i fix the chains round my neck/ my wrists/ my ankles. i weep cuz all my childhood ceremonies for the ghost-slaves have been in vain. colored people can get polio & mental illness. slavery is not unfamiliar to me. no one on this planet knows/ what i know abt gold/ abt anything hard to get & beautiful/ anything lasting/ wrought from pain. no one understands that sur-viving the impossible is sposed to accentuate the positive aspects of a people.

(ALEC *is the only member of the company able to come immediately to* MAXINE. *when he reaches her,* LOU, *in his full magician's regalia, freezes the whole company*)

LOU:

    yes yes yes   3 wishes is all you get
       scarlet ribbons for yr hair
       a farm in mississippi
       someone to love you madly
    all things are possible
    but aint no colored magician in his right mind
    gonna make you white
    cuz this is blk magic you lookin at
    & i'm fixin you up good/ fixin you up good &
       colored
    & you gonna be colored all yr life
    & you gonna love it/ bein colored/ all yr life
    colored & love it/ love it/ bein colored

(LOU *beckons the others to join him in the chant,* "colored & love it." *it becomes a serious celebration, like church/ like home/ but then* LOU *freezes them suddenly.*)

LOU:

    crackers are born with the right to be
    alive/ i'm making ours up right here
    in yr face/ & we gonna be
    colored & love it

(*the huge minstrel mask comes down as company continues to sing* "colored & love it/ love it being colored." *blackout/ but the minstrel mask remains visible. the company is singing* "colored & love it being colored" *as audience exits*)

Figure 1. The opening tableau of *spell #7* shows all nine performers in exaggerated makeup representing the minstrel-show stereotype while the huge minstrel mask looms behind them in the 1979 New York Shakespeare Festival production, directed by Oz Scott. (Photograph: Martha Swope.)

Figure 2. Natalie (La Tanya Richardson, *foreground*) and Alec (Avery Brooks, *left*) tell the story of "sue-jean" and the baby "myself" while Ross (Reyno) strums his guitar. At the bar are Maxine (Mary Alice) and Eli (Ellis Williams) in the 1979 New York Shakespeare Festival production, directed by Oz Scott. (Photograph: Martha Swope.)

Staging of *spell #7*

**REVIEW OF THE NEW YORK SHAKESPEARE
FESTIVAL PRODUCTION, 1979,
BY RICHARD EDER**

Poetry is as contagious as poison ivy though less prevalent. Look at the response these days to the dramatic poems in Ntozake Shange's remarkable "Spell No. 7." When I went to see the new revised version at the Public Theater the other night, the sketches—lyrical, wry, painful and comically prosaic by turn—lapped over the Anspacher stage and invaded the audience. The place was alive with response, but it wasn't the ordinary applause or laughter of an audience that is pleased or moved. There was a kind of rumination, a repeating of lines, even a few tentative essays at embroidering them.

From two women sitting behind me there was an insistent whispering all through the evening. Sometimes it was one of those counter-accented phrases—"oh yes"—of a revival meeting. When Larry Marshall, as the gleeful *compere*, sets out the long line "you're going to be colored all your life, and you're going to love it being colored," the whispering took up with "and we *do* love it." When Mary Alice chanted references to South Africa, the whisper, in its use of the inconsequential to express strong emotion, could have been designed by Miss Shange herself. "Check it out," the whisper came back giddily, after each fierce line.

I mentioned a revival meeting, and sometimes the springy rhetoric and response of these poetic vignettes about how it feels to be black do have the liveliness and stem-winding buildup of first rate preaching. But if there is any event that Miss Shange's best work approaches, it is something more familiar in other countries—particularly the Soviet Union—than in this one. I am thinking of those highly charged poetry recitals in which a Voznesensky would advance toward the emotions of his audiences head-on, not merely giving words to what was buried or half-buried inside them, but providing them with the public emblem of a man speaking out.

Miss Shange's performers enter as if they were actors gathering in an after-hours bar, but under the tutelage of Mr. Marshall's *compere*, they hurl themselves into their poetic representations. Mr. Marshall has announced that he is the son of a magician who gave up his trade when a black child asked him to perform a spell to make him white. Mr. Marshall proposes a different kind of spell: setting his performers to speaking, he will demonstrate that there is pride and rejoicing in being black. Poetry, of course, demonstrates nothing, not even rejoicing; but it can transmit it. Miss Shange's does, and not only to the black members of the audience.

The bar is a naturalistic setting, a refuge where the performers rest, drink and talk while waiting to assume their roles and deliver their recitations. Although each performer speaks out several times, in different characters, there is little sense of separation between performer and poem. Ellis Williams, corpulent, bearded and bouncy, shifts imperceptibly from serving the drinks in his bar to becoming the particular voice of Miss Shange asserting the commitment to poetry. "I feed my children poems on rye bread."

Mary Alice can become a housewife on a hilarious spree, or the suffering protagonist in a search for black responsibility, but the effect is as if she were moving in and out of her own vision and memory. The visions, of course, are Miss Shange's, but when the performers are not embodying them they are listening to the others embody them. They are each other's audience, linking us, the real audience, to the transformations on the stage.

They speak out with a pyramiding effect. Miss Shange's vignettes proceed with excess, that of the classic tall story, an image is taken, worked up comically, exaggerated and blown up some more. Each vignette is a circus vehicle, clown after clown climbs out, past all reasonable capacity. First they are comic clowns, then ironic clowns, and finally their message is pure pain; or would be except that art redeems the burden it carries by the raffishness with which it carries it.

Take the skittish, wide-eyed swoop with which Mary Alice begins what may be the finest sketch in the play. Flapping her arms, her elbows close to her side, she is a dizzy parody of a skipping child but her beaming innocence is only the first step in a crooked, comical hopscotch into deepening anger.

As a child, she says, she thought that black people had a providential immunity to serious disease, since the handicapped children on the television appeals were always white. (This is certainly true no longer, and I don't know if it ever was, but there is a suggestive truth about the conceit.) She grew up convinced that black people enjoyed a natural edge on virtue and talent.

It was white men who did bad things, her grandmothers told her; and now Mary Alice's face grows heavy as a middle section of the poem explores the disillusioning realization of the hurt that blacks inflict upon each other. The heaviness gives way to a glittering wildness.

"I buy gold," she cries out, shaking her gold necklaces and bracelets. It is the most stunning image of the evening. Gold is mined in South Africa and so, whenever she hears of her own people doing bad things she flaunts the symbol of the country where blacks are most publicly cast down.

We have been angled, played along by Shange's bubbling images, her gift for sprightly ludicrousness; and suddenly we are harpooned right through the gills.

There is a similar power though not quite the same delicate, shifting complexity in the sketch of a young black woman killing her baby. But there is a moving, startling thought contained in it. The woman, suffering and abused, has loved the child to the point of ecstasy as long as she was carrying it in her womb. It is part of her, preserved from any part of the world that has meant so much pain. Once it is born and outside her, it becomes one of the enemy.

There is a great deal more: the lyrically ironic sketch of a black girl, a ferocious gamin played by Laurie Carlos, brushing her knotted hair and insisting that all the fabled rewards of the good life will come once she gets it long and silky. There is a comical, musical collage of black Lotharios and their skeptical and susceptible victims.

Since its first workshop production earlier this summer, a number of adjustments, both of script and cast, have been made. Many of them are improvements, others are not. Despite some convincing individual transitions, there is still awkwardness in relating the recitations, which are the heart of the piece, to the anecdotal mood of the barful of players.

It seems likely that the adjustments will continue. It will certainly be worth it. This is not only a triumph for Miss Shange, director Oz Scott and a splendid cast. It is the triumph of an uneven season for the New York Shakespeare Festival and it is even more than that. Miss Shange, after her success with "For Colored Girls," had a poorish time with her second Festival work, "Photograph." Nothing so justifies the Festival's policy or long-range nurturing of its artists as this lovely new advance for her.

ATHOL FUGARD

1932–

Although Fugard's plays deal almost exclusively with the world of South African experience, they have engaged and challenged audiences throughout the world, for in bearing witness to the inhumanity of his country's long-standing racist policy of "apartheid" (literally, separateness), Fugard persistently creates characters and situations that lamentably reflect an international condition. Even with the legal dismantling of "apartheid," South Africa is still a country divided, often violently, between the white minority and the black majority, as well as between political factions on both sides. Fugard himself grew up in a family that was sharply divided in its view of racial affairs: his father, a hard-drinking jazz pianist of English and Irish descent, was, as Fugard remembers him, "full of pointless, unthought-out prejudices," whereas his mother, an Afrikaner of Dutch colonial stock, had a limitless "capacity for rising above the South African situation and seeing people as people." Thus he speaks of his mother as having "paced my emancipation from prejudice and bigotry."

Born in Middleburg, a village in the semidesert region of South Africa, where his father once led a small band called the Orchestral Jazzonians, Fugard became so alcoholic and indolent that his mother was compelled to support the family, first by running a small boarding house, the Jubilee Hotel, then by operating a café, the St. George's Park Tea Room, which is the setting for Fugard's highly autobiographical play, "*Master Harold*" . . . *and the Boys* (1982). As an adolescent, Fugard, like the character Hally who is modelled on him (indeed, who bears his childhood nickname), developed a close friendship with one of his mother's black waiters, a man named Sam Semela. Despite the racial gulf and the difference of some twenty years in their ages, they became so close that Fugard thinks of Semela as "the most significant—the only—friend of my boyhood years." Like Hally in the play, Fugard vividly remembers a kite-flying experience with Sam as one of his most precious boyhood experiences. Similarly, Fugard shared his reading and academic learning with Sam, and Sam shared his worldly experience and wisdom with Fugard. And when he was ten years old, Fugard had an argument with his friend (the cause of which he does not remember), and as he bicycled past Sam shortly after the argument "spat in his face." Looking back upon that event years later in his notebooks, Fugard did not imagine he would "ever deal with the shame that overwhelmed me the second after I had done that."

Though the play reflects Fugard's overwhelming sense of shame about that incident, it does not show another prominent side of his adolescence, namely the fact that he was, like his friend Sam, a highly accomplished ballroom dancer. Indeed, he and his sister Glenda were junior ballroom dancing champions several times during his teenage years. As a teenager, he also attended the equivalent of technical high school, evidently planning to become a mechanic, but was so academically gifted that he won a scholarship to the University of Cape Town, where he majored in philosophy and did some lightweight boxing on the side. By the time of his senior year, however, he "had a sense of horizons *shrinking*," so he quit school before graduation and started hitchhiking north in the hopes of eventually reaching Cairo. But after running out of money in Port Sudan, he took a job as the only white seaman on a ship bound for Japan, and during the next two years developed several friendships with blacks and Asians that called into question the racial prejudices of his native land. In his spare time aboard ship, Fugard spent hundreds of hours working on a novel based on his mother's life—he "wanted to write the great South African novel"—but eventually became discouraged with the manuscript and threw it overboard. When he returned to South Africa, however, he could not imagine any other line of working than writing, so his mother bought him a typewriter, and he began writing articles for the local paper, then news bulletins for the national radio in Cape Town.

As a journalist, Fugard was evidently impatient with the task of objective reporting—"my work was always too colored by emotion." So, when in 1956 he met and married an actress, Sheila Meiring, he was naturally inclined to become "more and more involved in theater." He turned out a few highly artificial one-acts, but after witnessing the rebellious drama of the English playwright John Osborne, as well as reading the "*unashamedly* regional" fiction of William Faulkner, Fugard came to realize "how many bloody good South African stories there were to be told." Fugard's decision to focus his plays on South African life was also fuelled by his dismaying experience as a clerk in the Johannesburg office of the Native Commissioner's Court, where he witnessed firsthand the impersonal and oppressive imposition of South Africa's passbook laws, which severely restrict the lives and livelihood of black South Africans. Out of this experience and his encounters with several black South African writers in their segregated shantytowns, Fugard wrote his first full-length play, *No-Good Friday* (1958), which bears witness to both the idealistic impulses and the oppressed lives of black South Africans in the townships. As with many of his subsequent works, Fugard directed *No-Good Friday* and acted in it together with a cast of non-professional black actors, including Zakes Mokae, who has since come to assume a leading role in many of Fugard's plays.

After a brief and frustrating period in London, where Fugard and his wife had gone seeking further theatrical experience, they decided to return home in 1960, to be among friends and to lend support to the anti-apartheid movement after a massacre of peacefully protesting blacks took place in Sharpesville, South Africa. During 1961, drawing on a notebook of literary quotations, personal observations, and theatrical ideas that he had begun keeping in London, Fugard wrote his first highly successful play, *Blood Knot*, which explores the psychologically complex love-hate relationship between two "coloured" (the South African term for people of mixed race) half brothers—the light-skinned and guilt-ridden Morrie (performed by Fugard himself) and the dark-skinned, envious, and bitter Zach (performed by Zakes Mokae). Following their performance of the play for an enthusiastic audience of invited friends, critics, writers, and actors, Fugard and Mokae took the play throughout South Africa, segregated while on trains, but together on stage. A London production of *Blood Knot* did not fare so well, but in 1964 an off-Broadway production starring

James Earl Jones as Zach ran for seven months and established Fugard's reputation in America.

Like *Blood Knot* most of Fugard's subsequent plays have focused on two or three characters complexly related to each other not only by blood, friendship, or marriage, but also by the racially divided world of South African life. Among the most successful of these highly concentrated works are *Boesman and Lena* (1968), which details the wretched life and abusive marriage of a coloured husband and wife wandering across the veld; *The Island* (1972), which dramatizes the heroic effort of two black political prisoners to transcend the brutality of the prison by producing the Greek play *Antigone* in an adaptation that applies the civil disobedience of its heroine to the state of affairs in South Africa; *Sizwe Bansi Is Dead* (1972), which focuses on an unemployed black man whose fear of being arrested because his passbook is not in order drives him to steal the passbook, and thus the identity, of a dead man; *Statements after an Arrest under the Immorality Act* (1974), which explores the multifaceted relationship between a white female librarian and a coloured teacher to whom she first lends books secretly and with whom she then falls in love; *A Lesson from Aloes* (1978), which features the story of an activist white bus driver, suspected of being a political informer, his emotionally distressed wife, and the inspiration he draws from the endurance of his aloe plants to remain true to his own moral convictions; and *The Road to Mecca* (1984), which centers on several days in the life of an eccentric white sculptress as she faces the terror both of losing her artistic inspiration and of being committed to an old folks' rest home.

"Master Harold" . . . *and the Boys,* widely regarded as Fugard's finest play, also focuses intensely on just a few characters. But in this case, the focal relationship of the play does not involve racially identical persons—blacks, coloureds, or whites—as do most of Fugard's earlier works. Instead *"Master Harold,"* like *Statements after an Arrest,* centers on a relationship involving racially different persons, in particular the long-standing friendship between a black waiter and the white son of his employer. In this respect, it depicts a special relationship that seems to transcend the racial tension and conflict engendered by the South African policy of "apartheid." But as the play unfolds, we discover that loving relationship to be painfully, indeed shockingly, subverted by the complex familial and cultural situation within which it is deeply rooted. For just as Fugard drew on Sam Semela to create the play's Sam, so too he made Hally's offstage father, like his own father, an alcoholic and a cripple. Hally's rejection of his natural father, his turning to a black "father-figure," and his attack on both when he spits on Sam thus come not only out of Fugard's life, but also out of his understanding that racial hatred can be seen, in part, as each individual's own psychological choice. In this fundamental sense, *"Master Harold,"* as Frank Rich notes in the review following the text, is concerned not just with South African apartheid, but with the capacity for cruelty that divides human beings everywhere.

The two major insults of the play—Sam baring his rump to Hally and Hally spitting at Sam—are so arresting and intense, especially following upon the earlier warmth and camaraderie between the two characters (see Figure 1), that one can readily understand how difficult it is for actors to perform them, even in rehearsal. Indeed when Fugard was directing his play for the Yale Repertory Theatre premiere, he had to shock the actors into these insulting gestures by performing them himself, first baring his own backside to Zakes Mokae, the actor playing Sam, and then repeatedly spitting at him. The risk Fugard took in re-enacting the moment of shame—a moment that he thought he would never deal with—was ultimately liberating both for himself and for the actors. Political theater can ask for no greater success, and Fugard's plays, though written out of a specific political reality, nonetheless speak to audiences everywhere. Perhaps they do so because they root the political in the personal, as Sam eloquently displays when he sternly rebukes Hally for mocking his father (see Figure 2), or when he says to Hally, late in the play, "I've got no right to tell you what being a man means if I don't behave like one myself, and I'm not doing so well at that this afternoon. Should we try again, Hally?" Though Hally can't give him a positive answer, Sam's willingness to try again reflects Fugard's hope that solutions, both personal and political, may yet be found.

"MASTER HAROLD" . . . AND THE BOYS

BY ATHOL FUGARD

CHARACTERS

WILLIE
SAM
HALLY

The St. George's Park Tea Room on a wet and windy Port Elizabeth afternoon.

Tables and chairs have been cleared and are stacked on one side except for one which stands apart with a single chair. On this table a knife, fork, spoon and side plate in anticipation of a simple meal, together with a pile of comic books.

Other elements: a serving counter with a few stale cakes under glass and a not very impressive display of sweets, cigarettes and cool drinks, etc.; a few cardboard advertising handouts—Cadbury's Chocolate, Coca-Cola—and a black-board on which an untrained hand has chalked up the prices of Tea, Coffee, Scones, Milkshakes—all flavors—and Cool Drinks; a few sad ferns in pots; a telephone; an old-style jukebox.

There is an entrance on one side and an exit into a kitchen on the other.

Leaning on the solitary table, his head cupped in one hand as he pages through one of the comic books, is Sam. A black man in his mid-forties. He wears the white coat of a waiter. Behind him on his knees, mopping down the floor with a bucket of water and a rag, is Willie. Also black and about the same age as Sam. He has his sleeves and trousers rolled up.

The year: 1950.

WILLIE: (*Singing as he works*)

"She was scandalizin' my name,
She took my money
She called me honey
But she was scandalizin' my name.
Called it love but was playin' a game. . . ."

(*He gets up and moves the bucket. Stands thinking for a moment, then, raising his arms to hold an imaginary partner, he launches into an intricate ballroom dance step. Although a mildly comic figure, he reveals a reasonable degree of accomplishment.*)

Hey, Sam.

(SAM, *absorbed in the comic book, does not respond.*)

Hey, Boet Sam!

(SAM *looks up.*)

I'm getting it. The quickstep. Look now and tell me. (*He repeats the step.*) Well?

SAM: (*Encouragingly*) Show me again.

WILLIE: Okay, count for me.

SAM: Ready?

WILLIE: Ready.

SAM: Five, six, seven, eight. . . . (*Willie starts to dance.*) A-n-d one two three four . . . and one two three four. . . . (*Ad libbing as* WILLIE *dances.*) Your shoulders, Willie . . . your shoulders! Don't look down! Look happy, Willie! Relax, Willie!

WILLIE: (*Desperate but still dancing*) I am relax.

SAM: No, you're not.

WILLIE: (*He falters*) Ag no man, Sam! Mustn't talk. You make me make mistakes.

SAM: But you're stiff.

WILLIE: Yesterday I'm not straight . . . today I'm too stiff!

SAM: Well, you are. You asked me and I'm telling you.

WILLIE: Where?

SAM: Everywhere. Try to glide through it.

WILLIE: Glide?

SAM: Ja, make it smooth. And give it more style. It must look like you're enjoying yourself.

WILLIE: (*Emphatically*) I wasn't.

SAM: Exactly.

WILLIE: How can I enjoy myself? Not straight, too stiff and now it's also glide, give it more style, make it smooth. . . . Haai! Is hard to remember all those things, Boet Sam.

SAM: That's your trouble. You're trying too hard.

WILLIE: I try hard because it *is* hard.

SAM: But don't let me see it. The secret is to make it look easy. Ballroom must look happy, Willie, not like hard work. It must. . . . Ja! . . . it must look like romance.

WILLIE: Now another one! What's romance?

SAM: Love story with happy ending. A handsome man

in tails, and in his arms, smiling at him, a beautiful lady in evening dress!

WILLIE: Fred Astaire, Ginger Rogers.

SAM: You got it. Tapdance or ballroom, it's the same. Romance. In two weeks' time when the judges look at you and Hilda, they must see a man and a woman who are dancing their way to a happy ending. What I saw was you holding her like you were frightened she was going to run away.

WILLIE: Ja! Because that is what she wants to do! I got no romance left for Hilda anymore, Boet Sam.

SAM: Then pretend. When you put your arms around Hilda, imagine she is Ginger Rogers.

WILLIE: With no teeth? You try.

SAM: Well, just remember, there's only two weeks left.

WILLIE: I know, I know! (*To the jukebox.*) I do it better with music. You got sixpence for Sarah Vaughan?

SAM: That's a slow foxtrot. You're practicing the quick-step.

WILLIE: I'll practice slow foxtrot.

SAM: (*Shaking his head*) It's your turn to put money in the jukebox.

WILLIE: I only got bus fare to go home. (*He returns disconsolately to his work.*) Love story and happy ending! She's doing it all right, Boet Sam, but is not me she's giving happy endings. Fuckin' whore! Three nights now she doesn't come practice. I wind up gramophone, I get record ready and I sit and wait. What happens? Nothing. Ten o'clock I start dancing with my pillow. You try and practice romance by yourself, Boet Sam. Struesgod, she doesn't come tonight I take back my dress and ballroom shoes and I find me new partner. Size twenty-six. Shoes size seven. And now she's also making trouble for me with the baby again. Reports me to Child Wellfed, that I'm not giving her money. She lies! Every week I am giving her money for milk. And how do I know is my baby? Only his hair looks like me. She's fucking around all the time I turn my back. Hilda Samuels is a bitch! (*Pause.*) Hey, Sam!

SAM: Ja.

WILLIE: You listening?

SAM: Ja.

WILLIE: So what you say?

SAM: About Hilda?

WILLIE: Ja.

SAM: When did you last give her a hiding?

WILLIE: (*Reluctantly*) Sunday night.

SAM: And today is Thursday.

WILLIE: (*He knows what's coming*) Okay.

SAM: Hiding on Sunday night, then Monday, Tuesday, and Wednesday she doesn't come to practice . . . and you are asking me why?

WILLIE: I said okay, Boet Sam!

SAM: You hit her too much. One day she's going to leave you for good.

WILLIE: So? She makes me the hell-in too much.

SAM: (*Emphasizing his point*) Too much and *too* hard. You had the same trouble with Eunice.

WILLIE: Because she also make the hell-in, Boet Sam. She never got the steps right. Even the waltz.

SAM: Beating her up every time she makes a mistake in the waltz? (*Shaking his head.*) No, Willie! That takes the pleasure out of ballroom dancing.

WILLIE: Hilda is not too bad with the waltz, Boet Sam. Is the quickstep where the trouble starts.

SAM: (*Teasing him gently*) How's your pillow with the quickstep?

WILLIE: (*Ignoring the tease*) Good! And why? Because it got no legs. That's her trouble. She can't move them quick enough, Boet Sam. I start the record and before halfway Count Basie is already winning. Only time we catch up with him is when gramophone runs down. (*Sam laughs.*) Haaikona, Boet Sam, is not funny.

SAM: (*Snapping his fingers*) I got it! Give her a handicap.

WILLIE: What's that?

SAM: Give her a ten-second start and then let Count Basie go. Then I put my money on her. Hot favorite in the Ballroom Stakes: Hilda Samuels ridden by Willie Malopo.

WILLIE: (*Turning away*) I'm not talking to you no more.

SAM: (*Relenting*) Sorry, Willie. . . .

WILLIE: It's finish between us.

SAM: Okay, okay . . . I'll stop.

WILLIE: You can also fuck off.

SAM: Willie, listen! I want to help you!

WILLIE: No more jokes?

SAM: I promise.

WILLIE: Okay. Help me.

SAM: (*His turn to hold an imaginary partner*) Look and learn. Feet together. Back straight. Body relaxed. Right hand placed gently in the small of her back and wait for the music. Don't start worrying about making mistakes or the judges or the other competitors. It's just you, Hilda and the music, and you're going to have a good time. What Count Basie do you play?

WILLIE: "You the cream in my coffee, you the salt in my stew."

SAM: Right. Give it to me in strict tempo.

WILLIE: Ready?

SAM: Ready.

WILLIE: A-n-d . . . (*Singing.*)

"*You the cream in my coffee.*
You the salt in my stew.
You will always be my necessity.
I'd be lost without you. . . ." (*etc.*)

(SAM *launches into the quickstep. He is obviously a much more accomplished dancer than* WILLIE. HALLY *enters. A seventeen-year-old white boy. Wet raincoat and school case. He stops and watches* SAM. *The demonstration* comes to an end with a flourish. Applause from HALLY and WILLIE.)

HALLY: Bravo! No question about it. First place goes to Mr. Sam Semela.

WILLIE: (In total agreement) You was gliding with style, Boet Sam.

HALLY: (Cheerfully) How's it, chaps?

SAM: Okay, Hally.

WILLIE: (Springing to attention like a soldier and saluting) At your service, Master Harold!

HALLY: Not long to the big event, hey!

SAM: Two weeks.

HALLY: You nervous.

SAM: No.

HALLY: Think you stand a chance?

SAM: Let's just say I'm ready to go out there and dance.

HALLY: It looked like it. What about you, Willie?

(WILLIE groans.)

What's the matter?

SAM: He's got leg trouble.

HALLY: (Innocently) Oh, sorry to hear that, Willie.

WILLIE: Boet Sam! You promised. (WILLIE returns to his work.)

(HALLY deposits his school case and takes off his raincoat. His clothes are a little neglected and untidy: black blazer with school badge, gray flannel trousers in need of an ironing, khaki shirt and tie, black shoes. SAM has fetched a towel for HALLY to dry his hair.)

HALLY: God, what a lousy bloody day. It's coming down cats and dogs out there. Bad for business, chaps. . . . (Conspiratorial whisper.) . . . but it also means we're in for a nice quiet afternoon.

SAM: You can speak loud. Your Mom's not here.

HALLY: Out shopping?

SAM: No. The hospital.

HALLY: But it's Thursday. There's no visiting on Thursday afternoons. Is my Dad okay?

SAM: Sounds like it. In fact, I think he's going home.

HALLY: (Stopped short by SAM's remark) What do you mean?

SAM: The hospital phoned.

HALLY: To say what?

SAM: I don't know. I just heard your Mom talking.

HALLY: So what makes you say he's going home?

SAM: It sounded as if they were telling her to come and fetch him.

(HALLY thinks about what SAM has said for a few seconds.)

HALLY: When did she leave?

SAM: About an hour ago. She said she would phone you. Want to eat?

(HALLY doesn't respond.)

Hally, want your lunch?

HALLY: I suppose so. (His mood has changed.) What's on the menu? . . . as if I don't know.

SAM: Soup, followed by meat pie and gravy.

HALLY: Today's?

SAM: No.

HALLY: And the soup?

SAM: Nourishing pea soup.

HALLY: Just the soup. (The pile of comic books on the table.) And these?

SAM: For your Dad. Mr. Kempston brought them.

HALLY: You haven't been reading them, have you?

SAM: Just looking.

HALLY: (Examining the comics) Jungle Jim . . . Batman and Robin . . . Tarzan . . . God, what rubbish! Mental pollution. Take them away.

(SAM exits waltzing into the kitchen. HALLY turns to WILLIE.)

HALLY: Did you hear my Mom talking on the telephone, Willie?

WILLIE: No, Master Hally. I was at the back.

HALLY: And she didn't say anything to you before she left?

WILLIE: She said I must clean the floors.

HALLY: I mean about my Dad.

WILLIE: She didn't say nothing to me about him, Master Hally.

HALLY: (With conviction) No! It can't be. They said he needed at least another three weeks of treatment. Sam's definitely made a mistake. (Rummages through his school case, finds a book and settles down at the table to read.) So, Willie!

WILLIE: Yes, Master Hally! Schooling okay today?

HALLY: Yes, okay. . . . (He thinks about it.) . . . No, not really. Ag, what's the difference? I don't care. And Sam says you've got problems.

WILLIE: Big problems.

HALLY: Which leg is sore?

(WILLIE groans.)

Both legs.

WILLIE: There is nothing wrong with my legs. Sam is just making jokes.

HALLY: So then you will be in the competition.

WILLIE: Only if I can find a partner.

HALLY: But what about Hilda?

SAM: (Returning with a bowl of soup) She's the one who's got trouble with her legs.

HALLY: What sort of trouble, Willie?

SAM: From the way he describes it, I think the lady has gone a bit lame.

HALLY: Good God! Have you taken her to see a doctor?

SAM: I think a vet would be better.

HALLY: What do you mean?

SAM: What do you call it again when a racehorse goes very fast?

HALLY: Gallop?

SAM: That's it!

WILLIE: Boet Sam!

HALLY: "A gallop down the homestretch to the winning post." But what's that got to do with Hilda?

SAM: Count Basie always gets there first.

(WILLIE *lets fly with his slop rag. It misses* SAM *and hits* HALLY.)

HALLY: (*Furious*) For Christ's sake, Willie! What the hell do you think you're doing?

WILLIE: Sorry, Master Hally, but it's him. . . .

HALLY: Act your bloody age! (*Hurls the rag back at* WILLIE.) Cut out the nonsense now and get on with your work. And you too, Sam. Stop fooling around.

(SAM *moves away.*)

No. Hang on. I haven't finished! Tell me exactly what my Mom said.

SAM: I have. "When Hally comes, tell him I've gone to the hospital and I'll phone him."

HALLY: She didn't say anything about taking my Dad home?

SAM: No. It's just that when she was talking on the phone. . . .

HALLY: (*Interrupting him*) No, Sam. They can't be discharging him. She would have said so if they were. In any case, we saw him last night and he wasn't in good shape at all. Staff nurse even said there was talk about taking more X-rays. And now suddenly today he's better? If anything, it sounds more like a bad turn to me . . . which I sincerely hope it isn't. Hang on . . . how long ago did you say she left?

SAM: Just before two . . . (*His wrist watch.*) . . . hour and a half.

HALLY: I know how to settle it. (*Behind the counter to the telephone. Talking as he dials.*) Let's give her ten minutes to get to the hospital, ten minutes to load him up, another ten, at the most, to get home, and another ten to get him inside. Forty minutes. They should have been home for at least half an hour already. (*Pause—he waits with the receiver to his ear.*) No reply, chaps. And you know why? Because she's at his bedside in hospital helping him pull through a bad turn. You definitely heard wrong.

SAM: Okay.

(*As far as* HALLY *is concerned, the matter is settled. He returns to his table, sits down, and divides his attention between the book and his soup. Sam is at his school case and picks up a textbook.*)

Modern Graded Mathematics for Standards Nine and Ten.

(*Opens it at random and laughs at something he sees.*) Who is this supposed to be?

HALLY: Old fart-face Prentice.

SAM: Teacher?

HALLY: Thinks he is. And believe me, that is not a bad likeness.

SAM: Has he seen it?

HALLY: Yes.

SAM: What did he say?

HALLY: Tried to be clever, as usual. Said I was no Leonardo da Vinci and that bad art had to be punished. So, six of the best, and his are bloody good.

SAM: On your bum?

HALLY: Where else? The days when I got them on my hands are gone forever, Sam.

SAM: With your trousers down!

HALLY: No. He's not quite that barbaric.

SAM: That's the way they do it in jail.

HALLY: (*Flicker of morbid interest*) Really?

SAM: Ja. When the magistrate sentences you to "strokes with a light cane."

HALLY: Go on.

SAM: They make you lie down on a bench. One policeman pulls down your trousers and holds your ankles, another one pulls your shirt over your head and holds your arms. . . .

HALLY: Thank you! That's enough.

SAM: . . . and the one that gives you the strokes talks to you gently and for a long time between each one. (*He laughs.*)

HALLY: I've heard enough. Sam! Jesus! It's a bloody awful world when you come to think of it. People can be real bastards.

SAM: That's the way it is, Hally.

HALLY: It doesn't *have* to be that way. There is something called progress, you know. We don't exactly burn people at the stake anymore.

SAM: Like Joan of Arc.

HALLY: Correct. If she was captured today, she'd be given a fair trial.

SAM: And then the death sentence.

HALLY: (*A world-weary sigh*) I know, I know! I oscillate between hope and despair for this world as well, Sam. But things will change, you wait and see. One day somebody is going to get up and give history a kick up the backside and get it going again.

SAM: Like who?

HALLY: (*After thought*) They're called social reformers. Every age, Sam, has got its social reformer. My history book is full of them.

SAM: So where's ours?

HALLY: Good question. And I hate to say it, but the answer is: I don't know. Maybe he hasn't even been born yet. Or is still only a babe in arms at his mother's breast. God, what a thought.

SAM: So we just go on waiting.

HALLY: Ja, looks like it. (*Back to his soup and the book.*)

SAM: (*Reading from the textbook*) "Introduction: In some mathematical problems only the magnitude. . . ." (*He mispronounces the word "magnitude."*)

HALLY: (*Correcting him without looking up*) Magnitude.

SAM: What's it mean?

HALLY: How big it is. The size of the thing.

SAM: (*Reading*) ". . . magnitude of the quantities is of importance. In other problems we need to know whether these quantities are negative or positive. For example, whether there is a debit or credit bank balance . . ."

HALLY: Whether you're broke or not.

SAM: ". . . whether the temperature is above or below Zero. . . ."

HALLY: Naught degrees. Cheerful state of affairs! No cash and you're freezing to death. Mathematics won't get you out of that one.

SAM: "All these quantities are called . . ." (*Spelling the word*) . . . s-c-a-l . . .

HALLY: Scalars.

SAM: Scalars! (*Shaking his head with a laugh.*) You understand all that?

HALLY: (*Turning a page*) No. And I don't intend to try.

SAM: So what happens when the exams come?

HALLY: Failing a maths exam isn't the end of the world, Sam. How many times have I told you that examination results don't measure intelligence?

SAM: I would say about as many times as you've failed one of them.

HALLY: (*Mirthlessly*) Ha, ha, ha.

SAM: (*Simultaneously*) Ha, ha, ha.

HALLY: Just remember Winston Churchill didn't do particularly well at school.

SAM: You've also told me that one many times.

HALLY: Well, it just so happens to be the truth.

SAM: (*Enjoying the word*) Magnitude! Magnitude! Show me how to use it.

HALLY: (*After thought*) An intrepid social reformer will not be daunted by the magnitude of the task he has undertaken.

SAM: (*Impressed*) Couple of jaw-breakers in there!

HALLY: I gave you three for the price of one. Intrepid, daunted, and magnitude. I did that once in an exam. Put five of the words I had to explain in one sentence. It was half a page long.

SAM: Well, I'll put my money on you in the English exam.

HALLY: Piece of cake. Eighty percent without even trying.

SAM: (*Another textbook from Hally's case*) And history?

HALLY: So-so. I'll scrape through. In the fifties if I'm lucky.

SAM: You didn't do too badly last year.

HALLY: Because we had World War One. That at least has some action. You try to find that in the South African Parliamentary system.

SAM: (*Reading from the history textbook*) "Napoleon and the principle of equality." Hey! This sounds interesting. "After concluding peace with Britain in 1802, Napoleon used a brief period of calm to in-sti-tute . . ."

HALLY: Introduce.

SAM: ". . . many reforms. Napoleon regarded all people

as equal before the law and wanted them to have equal opportunities for advancement. All ves-ti-ges of the feu-dal sys-tem with its oppression of the poor were abol-ished." Vestiges, feudal system, and abolished. I'm all right on oppression.

HALLY: I'm thinking. He swept away . . . abolished . . . the last remains . . . vestiges . . . of the bad old days . . . feudal system.

SAM: Ha! There's the social reformer we're waiting for. He sounds like a man of some magnitude.

HALLY: I'm not so sure about that. It's a damn good title for a book, though. A man of magnitude!

SAM: He sounds pretty big to me, Hally.

HALLY: Don't confuse historical significance with greatness. But maybe I'm being a bit prejudiced. Have a look in there and you'll see he's two chapters long. And hell! . . . has he only got dates, Sam, all of which you've got to remember! This campaign and that campaign, and then, because of all the fighting, the next thing is we get Peace Treaties all over the place. And what's the end of the story? Battle of Waterloo, which he loses. Wasn't worth it. No, I don't know about him as a man of magnitude.

SAM: Then who would you say was?

HALLY: To answer that, we need a definition of greatness, and I suppose that would be somebody who . . . somebody who benefited all mankind.

SAM: Right. But like who?

HALLY: (*He speaks with total conviction*) Charles Darwin. Remember him? That big book from the library. *The Origin of the Species.*

SAM: Him?

HALLY: Yes. For his Theory of Evolution.

SAM: You didn't finish it.

HALLY: I ran out of time. I didn't finish it because my two weeks was up. But I'm going to take it out again after I've digested what I read. It's safe. I've hidden it away in the Theology section. Nobody ever goes in there. And anyway who are you to talk? You hardly even looked at it.

SAM: I tried. I looked at the chapters in the beginning and I saw one called "The Struggle for an Existence." Ah ha, I thought. At last! But what did I get? Something called the mistiltoe which needs the apple tree and there's too many seeds and all are going to die except one . . . ! No, Hally.

HALLY: (*Intellectually outraged*) What do you mean, No! The poor man had to start somewhere. For God's sake, Sam, he revolutionized science. Now we know.

SAM: What?

HALLY: Where we come from and what it all means.

SAM: And that's a benefit to mankind? Anyway, I still don't believe it.

HALLY: God, you're impossible. I showed it to you in black and white.

SAM: Doesn't mean I got to believe it.

HALLY: It's the likes of you that kept the Inquisition in

business. It's called bigotry. Anyway, that's my man of magnitude. Charles Darwin! Who's yours?

SAM: (*Without hesitation*) Abraham Lincoln.

HALLY: I might have guessed as much. Don't get sentimental, Sam. You've never been a slave, you know. And anyway we freed your ancestors here in South Africa long before the Americans. But if you want to thank somebody on their behalf, do it to Mr. William Wilberforce. Come on. Try again. I want a real genius.

(*Now enjoying himself, and so is* SAM. HALLY *goes behind the counter and helps himself to a chocolate.*)

SAM: William Shakespeare.

HALLY: (*No enthusiasm*) Oh. So you're also one of them, are you? You're basing that opinion on only one play, you know. You've only read my *Julius Caesar* and even I don't understand half of what they're talking about. They should do what they did with the old Bible: bring the language up to date.

SAM: That's all you've got. It's also the only one *you've* read.

HALLY: I know. I admit it. That's why I suggest we reserve our judgment until we've checked up on a few others. I've got a feeling, though, that by the end of this year one is going to be enough for me, and I can give you the names of twenty-nine other chaps in the Standard Nine class of the Port Elizabeth Technical College who feel the same. But if you want him, you can have him. My turn now. (*Pacing.*) This is a damned good exercise, you know! It started off looking like a simple question and here it's got us really probing into the intellectual heritage of our civilization.

SAM: So who is it going to be?

HALLY: My next man . . . and he gets the title on two scores: social reform and literary genius . . . is Leo Nikolaevich Tolstoy.

SAM: That Russian.

HALLY: Correct. Remember the picture of him I showed you?

SAM: With the long beard.

HALLY: (*Trying to look like Tolstoy*) And those burning, visionary eyes. My God, the face of a social prophet if ever I saw one! And remember my words when I showed it to you? Here's a *man*, Sam!

SAM: Those were words, Hally.

HALLY: Not many intellectuals are prepared to shovel manure with the peasants and then go home and write a "little book" called *War and Peace*. Incidentally, Sam, he was somebody else who, to quote, ". . . did not distinguish himself scholastically."

SAM: Meaning?

HALLY: He was also no good at school.

SAM: Like you and Winston Churchill.

HALLY: (*Mirthlessly*) Ha, ha, ha.

SAM: (*Simultaneously*) Ha, ha, ha.

HALLY: Don't get clever, Sam. That man freed his serfs of his own free will.

SAM: No argument. He was somebody, all right. I accept him.

HALLY: I'm sure Count Tolstoy will be very pleased to hear that. Your turn. Shoot. (*Another chocolate from behind the counter.*) I'm waiting, Sam.

SAM: I've got him.

HALLY: Good. Submit your candidate for examination.

SAM: Jesus.

HALLY: (*Stopped dead in his tracks*) Who?

SAM: Jesus Christ.

HALLY: Oh, come on, Sam!

SAM: The Messiah.

HALLY: Ja, but still . . . No, Sam. Don't let's get started on religion. We'll just spend the whole afternoon arguing again. Suppose I turn around and say Mohammed?

SAM: All right.

HALLY: You can't have them both on the same list!

SAM: Why not? You like Mohammed, I like Jesus.

HALLY: I *don't* like Mohammed. I never have. I was merely being hypothetical. As far as I'm concerned, the Koran is as bad as the Bible. No. Religion is out! I'm not going to waste my time again arguing with you about the existence of God. You know perfectly well I'm an atheist . . . and I've got homework to do.

SAM: Okay, I take him back.

HALLY: You've got time for one more name.

SAM: (*After thought*) I've got one I know we'll agree on. A simple straightforward great Man of Magnitude . . . and no arguments. And *he* really *did* benefit all mankind.

HALLY: I wonder. After your last contribution I'm beginning to doubt whether anything in the way of an intellectual agreement is possible between the two of us. Who is he?

SAM: Guess.

HALLY: Socrates? Alexandre Dumas? Karl Marx, Dostoevsky? Nietzsche?

(SAM *shakes his head after each name.*)

Give me a clue.

SAM: The letter *P* is important. . . .

HALLY: Plato!

SAM: . . . and his name begins with an *F*.

HALLY: I've got it. Freud and Psychology.

SAM: No. I didn't understand him.

HALLY: That makes two of us.

SAM: Think of moldy apricot jam.

HALLY: (*After a delighted laugh*) Penicillin and Sir Alexander Fleming! And the title of the book: *The Microbe Hunters*. (*Delighted.*) Splendid, Sam! Splendid. For once we are in total agreement. The major breakthrough in medical science in the Twentieth Century. If it wasn't for him, we might have lost the Second World War. It's deeply gratifying, Sam, to know that I haven't been wasting my time in talking to you. (*Strutting around proudly.*) Tolstoy may have educated his peasants, but I've educated you.

SAM: Standard Four to Standard Nine.

HALLY: Have we been at it as long as that?

SAM: Yep. And my first lesson was geography.

HALLY: (*Intrigued*) Really? I don't remember.

SAM: My room there at the back of the old Jubilee Boarding House. I had just started working for your Mom. Little boy in short trousers walks in one afternoon and asks me seriously: "Sam, do you want to see South Africa?" Hey man! Sure I wanted to see South Africa!

HALLY: Was that me?

SAM: . . . So the next thing I'm looking at a map you had just done for homework. It was your first one and you were very proud of yourself.

HALLY: Go on.

SAM: Then came my first lesson. "Repeat after me, Sam: Gold in the Transvaal, mealies in the Free State, sugar in Natal, and grapes in the Cape." I still know it!

HALLY: Well, I'll be buggered. So that's how it all started.

SAM: And your next map was one with all the rivers and the mountains they came from. The Orange, the Vaal, the Limpopo, the Zambezi. . . .

HALLY: You've got a phenomenal memory!

SAM: You should be grateful. That is why you started passing your exams. You tried to be better than me.

(*They laugh together.* WILLIE *is attracted by the laughter and joins them.*)

HALLY: The old Jubilee Boarding House. Sixteen rooms with board and lodging, rent in advance and one week's notice. I haven't thought about it for donkey's years . . . and I don't think that's an accident. God, was I glad when we sold it and moved out. Those years are not remembered as the happiest ones of an unhappy childhood.

WILLIE: (*Knocking on the table and trying to imitate a woman's voice*) "Hally, are you there?"

HALLY: Who's that supposed to be?

WILLIE: "What you doing in there, Hally? Come out at once!"

HALLY: (*To* SAM) What's he talking about?

SAM: Don't you remember?

WILLIE: "Sam, Willie . . . is he in there with you boys?"

SAM: Hiding away in our room when your mother was looking for you.

HALLY: (*Another good laugh*) Of course! I used to crawl and hide under your bed! But finish the story, Willie. Then what used to happen? You chaps would give the game away by telling her I was in there with you. So much for friendship.

SAM: We couldn't lie to her. She knew.

HALLY: Which meant I got another rowing for hanging around the "servants' quarters." I think I spent more time in there with you chaps than anywhere else in that dump. And do you blame me? Nothing but bloody misery wherever you went. Somebody was always complaining about the food, or my mother was having a fight with Micky Nash because she'd caught her with a petty officer in her room. Maud Meiring was another one. Remember those two? They were prostitutes, you know. Soldiers and sailors from the troopships. Bottom fell out of the business when the war ended. God, the flotsam and jetsam that life washed up on our shores! No joking, if it wasn't for your room, I would have been the first certified ten-year-old in medical history. Ja, the memories are coming back now. Walking home from school and thinking: "What can I do this afternoon?" Try out a few ideas, but sooner or later I'd end up in there with you fellows. I bet you I could still find my way to your room with my eyes closed. (*He does exactly that.*) Down the corridor . . . telephone on the right, which my Mom keeps locked because somebody is using it on the sly and not paying . . . past the kitchen and unappetizing cooking smells . . . around the corner into the backyard, hold my breath again because there are more smells coming when I pass your lavatory, then into that little passageway, first door on the right and into your room. How's that?

SAM: Good. But, as usual, you forgot to knock.

HALLY: Like that time I barged in and caught you and Cynthia . . . at it. Remember? God, was I embarrassed! I didn't know what was going on at first.

SAM: Ja, that taught you a lesson.

HALLY: And about a lot more than knocking on doors, I'll have you know, and I don't mean geography either. Hell, Sam, couldn't you have waited until it was dark?

SAM: No.

HALLY: Was it that urgent?

SAM: Yes, and if you don't believe me, wait until your time comes.

HALLY: No, thank you. I am not interested in girls. (*Back to his memories. . . . Using a few chairs he re-creates the room as he lists the items.*) A gray little room with a cold cement floor. Your bed against that wall . . . and I now know why the mattress sags so much! . . . Willie's bed . . . it's propped up on bricks because one leg is broken . . . that wobbly little table with the washbasin and jug of water . . . Yes! . . . stuck to the wall above it are some pin-up pictures from magazines. Joe Louis. . . .

WILLIE: Brown Bomber. World Title. (*Boxing pose.*) Three rounds and knockout.

HALLY: Against who?

SAM: Max Schmeling.

HALLY: Correct. I can also remember Fred Astaire and Ginger Rogers, and Rita Hayworth in a bathing costume which always made me hot and bothered when I looked at it. Under Willie's bed is an old suitcase with all his clothes in a mess, which is why I never hide there. Your things are neat and tidy in a trunk next to your bed, and on it there is a picture of you and Cynthia in your ballroom clothes, your first silver cup for third place in a competition and an old radio which doesn't work anymore. Have I left out anything?

SAM: No.

HALLY: Right, so much for the stage directions. Now the characters. (SAM *and* WILLIE *move to their appropriate positions in the bedroom.*) Willie is in bed, under his blankets with his clothes on, complaining nonstop about something, but we can't make out a word of what he's saying because he's got his head under the blankets as well. You're on your bed trimming your toenails with a knife—not a very edifying sight—and as for me. . . . What am I doing?

SAM: You're sitting on the floor giving Willie a lecture about being a good loser while you get the checkerboard and pieces ready for a game. Then you go to Willie's bed, pull off the blankets and make him play with you first because you know you're going to win, and that gives you the second game with me.

HALLY: And you certainly were a bad loser, Willie!

WILLIE: Haai!

HALLY: Wasn't he, Sam? And so slow! A game with you almost took the whole afternoon. Thank God I gave up trying to teach you how to play chess.

WILLIE: You and Sam cheated.

HALLY: I never saw Sam cheat, and mine were mostly the mistakes of youth.

WILLIE: Then how is it you two was always winning?

HALLY: Have you ever considered the possibility, Willie, that it was because we were better than you?

WILLIE: Every time better?

HALLY: Not every time. There were occasions when we deliberately let you win a game so that you would stop sulking and go on playing with us. Sam used to wink at me when you weren't looking to show me it was time to let you win.

WILLIE: So then you two didn't play fair.

HALLY: It was for your benefit, Mr. Malopo, which is more than being fair. It was an act of self-sacrifice. (*To* SAM.) But you know what my best memory is, don't you?

SAM: No.

HALLY: Come on, guess. If your memory is so good, you must remember it as well.

SAM: We got up to a lot of tricks in there, Hally.

HALLY: This one was special, Sam.

SAM: I'm listening.

HALLY: It started off looking like another of those useless nothing-to-do afternoons. I'd already been down to Main Street looking for adventure, but nothing had happened. I didn't feel like climbing trees in the Donkin Park or pretending I was a private eye and following a stranger . . . so as usual: See what's cooking in Sam's room. This time it was you on the floor. You had two thin pieces of wood and you were smoothing them down with a knife. It didn't look particularly interesting, but when I asked you what you were doing, you just said, "Wait and see, Hally. Wait . . . and see" . . . in that secret sort of way of yours, so I knew there was a surprise coming. You teased me, you bugger, by being deliberately slow and not answering my questions!

(SAM *laughs.*)

And whistling while you worked away! God, it was infuriating! I could have brained you! It was only when you tied them together in a cross and put that down on the brown paper that I realized what you were doing. "Sam is making a kite?" And when I asked you and you said "Yes" . . . ! (*Shaking his head with disbelief.*) The sheer audacity of it took my breath away. I mean, seriously, what the hell does a black man know about flying a kite? I'll be honest with you, Sam, I had no hopes for it. If you think I was excited and happy, you got another guess coming. In fact, I was shit-scared that we were going to make fools of ourselves. When we left the boarding house to go up onto the hill, I was praying quietly that there wouldn't be any other kids around to laugh at us.

SAM: (*Enjoying the memory as much as* HALLY) Ja, I could see that.

HALLY: I made it obvious, did I?

SAM: Ja. You refused to carry it.

HALLY: Do you blame me? Can you remember what the poor thing looked like? Tomato-box wood and brown paper! Flour and water for glue! Two of my mother's old stockings for a tail, and then all those bits and pieces of string you made me tie together so that we could fly it! Hell, no, that was now only asking for a miracle to happen.

SAM: Then the big argument when I told you to hold the string and run with it when I let go.

HALLY: I was prepared to run, all right, but straight back to the boarding house.

SAM: (*Knowing what's coming*) So what happened?

HALLY: Come on, Sam, you remember as well as I do.

SAM: I want to hear it from you.

(HALLY *pauses. He wants to be as accurate as possible.*)

HALLY: You went a little distance from me down the hill, you held it up ready to let it go. . . . "This is it," I thought. "Like everything else in my life, here comes another fiasco." Then you shouted, "Go, Hally!" and I started to run. (*Another pause.*) I don't know how to describe it, Sam. Ja! The miracle happened! I was running, waiting for it to crash to the ground, but instead suddenly there was something alive behind me at the end of the string, tugging at it as if it wanted to be free. I looked back . . . (*Shakes his head.*) . . . I still can't believe my eyes. It was flying! Looping around and trying to climb even higher into the sky. You shouted to me to let it have more string. I did, until there was none left and I was just holding that piece of wood we had tied it to. You came up and joined me. You were laughing.

SAM: So were you. And shouting, "It works, Sam! We've done it!"

HALLY: And we had! I was so proud of us! It was the most splendid thing I had ever seen. I wished there were hundreds of kids around to watch us. The part that scared me, though, was when you showed me how to make it dive down to the ground and then just when it was on the point of crashing, swoop up again!

SAM: You didn't want to try yourself.

HALLY: Of course not! I would have been suicidal if anything had happened to it. Watching you do it made me nervous enough. I was quite happy just to see it up there with its tail fluttering behind it. You left me after that, didn't you? You explained how to get it down, we tied it to the bench so that I could sit and watch it, and you went away. I wanted you to stay, you know. I was a little scared of having to look after it by myself.

SAM: (*Quietly*) I had work to do, Hally.

HALLY: It was sort of sad bringing it down, Sam. And it looked sad again when it was lying there on the ground. Like something that had lost its soul. Just tomato-box wood, brown paper and two of my mother's old stockings! But, hell, I'll never forget that first moment when I saw it up there. I had a stiff neck the next day from looking up so much.

(SAM *laughs.* HALLY *turns to him with a question he never thought of asking before.*)

Why did you make that kite, Sam?

SAM: (*Evenly*) I can't remember.

HALLY: Truly?

SAM: Too long ago, Hally.

HALLY: Ja, I suppose it was. It's time for another one, you know.

SAM: Why do you say that?

HALLY: Because it feels like that. Wouldn't be a good day to fly it, though.

SAM: No. You can't fly kites on rainy days.

HALLY: (*He studies* SAM. *Their memories have made him conscious of the man's presence in his life.*)

How old are you, Sam?

SAM: Two score and five.

HALLY: Strange, isn't it?

SAM: What?

HALLY: Me and you.

SAM: What's strange about it?

HALLY: Little white boy in short trousers and a black man old enough to be his father flying a kite. It's not every day you see that.

SAM: But why strange? Because the one is white and the other black?

HALLY: I don't know. Would have been just as strange, I suppose, if it had been me and my Dad . . . cripple man and a little boy! Nope! There's no chance of me flying a kite without it being strange. (*Simple statement of fact—no self-pity.*) There's a nice little short story there. "The Kite-Flyers." But we'd have to find a twist in the ending.

SAM: Twist?

HALLY: Yes. Something unexpected. The way it ended with us was too straightforward . . . me on the bench and you going back to work. There's no drama in that.

WILLIE: And me?

HALLY: You?

WILLIE: Yes me.

HALLY: You want to get into the story as well, do you? I got it! Change the title: "Afternoons in Sam's Room" . . . expand it and tell all the stories. It's on its way to being a novel. Our days in the old Jubilee. Sad in a way that they're over. I almost wish we were still in that little room.

SAM: We're still together.

HALLY: That's true. It's just that life felt the right size in there . . . not too big and not too small. Wasn't so hard to work up a bit of courage. It's got so bloody complicated since then.

(*The telephone rings.* SAM *answers it.*)

SAM: St. George's Park Tea Room . . . Hello, Madam . . . Yes, Madam, he's here. . . . Hally, it's your mother.

HALLY: Where is she phoning from?

SAM: Sounds like the hospital. It's a public telephone.

HALLY: (*Relieved*) You see! I told you. (*The telephone.*) Hello, Mom . . . Yes . . . Yes no fine. Everything's under control here. How's things with poor old Dad? . . . Has he had a bad turn? . . . What? . . . Oh, God! . . . Yes, Sam told me, but I was sure he'd made a mistake. But what's this all about, Mom? He didn't look at all good last night. How can he get better so quickly? . . . Then very obviously you must say no. Be firm with him. You're the boss. . . . You know what it's going to be like if he comes home. . . . Well then, don't blame me when I fail my exams at the end of the year. . . . Yes! How am I expected to be fresh for school when I spend half the night massaging his gammy leg? . . . So am I! . . . So tell him a white lie. Say Dr. Colley wants more X-rays of his stump. Or bribe him. We'll sneak in double tots of brandy in future. . . . What? . . . Order him to get back into bed at once! If he's going to behave like a child, treat him like one. . . . All right, Mom! I was just trying to . . . I'm sorry. . . . I said I'm sorry. . . . Quick, give me your number. I'll phone you back. (*He hangs up and waits a few seconds.*) Here we go again! (*He dials.*) I'm sorry, Mom. . . . Okay. . . . But now listen to me carefully. All it needs is for you to put your foot down. Don't take no for an answer. . . . Did you hear me? And whatever you do, don't discuss it with him. . . . Because I'm frightened you'll give in to him. . . . Yes, Sam gave me lunch. . . . I ate all of it! . . . No, Mom not a soul. It's still raining here. . . . Right, I'll tell them. I'll just do some homework and then lock up. . . . But remember now, Mom. Don't listen to anything he says. And phone me back and let me know what happens. . . . Okay. Bye, Mom. (*He hangs up. The men are staring at him.*) My Mom says that when you're finished with the floors you must do the windows. (*Pause.*) Don't misunderstand me, chaps. All I want is for him to get better. And if he was, I'd be the first person to say: "Bring him home." But he's not, and we can't give him the medical care and attention he needs at home. That's what hospitals are there for. (*Brusquely.*) So don't just stand there! Get on with it!

(*Sam clears Hally's table.*)

You heard right. My Dad wants to go home.

SAM: Is he better?

HALLY: (*Sharply*) No! How the hell can he be better when last night he was groaning with pain? This is not an age of miracles!

SAM: Then he should stay in hospital.

HALLY: (*Seething with irritation and frustration*) Tell me something I don't know, Sam. What the hell do you think I was saying to my Mom? All I can say is fuck-it-all.

SAM: I'm sure he'll listen to your Mom.

HALLY: You don't know what she's up against. He's already packed his shaving kit and pajamas and is sitting on his bed with his crutches, dressed and ready to go. I know him when he gets in that mood. If she tries to reason with him, we've had it. She's no match for him when it comes to a battle of words. He'll tie her up in knots. (*Trying to hide his true feelings.*)

SAM: I suppose it gets lonely for him in there.

HALLY: With all the patients and nurses around? Regular visits from the Salvation Army? Balls! It's ten times worse for him at home. I'm at school and my mother is here in the business all day.

SAM: He's at least got you at night.

HALLY: (*Before he can stop himself*) And we've got him! Please! I don't want to talk about it anymore. (*Unpacks his school case, slamming down books on the table.*) Life is just a plain bloody mess, that's all. And people are fools.

SAM: Come on, Hally.

HALLY: Yes, they are! They bloody well deserve what they get.

SAM: Then don't complain.

HALLY: Don't try to be clever, Sam. It doesn't suit you. Anybody who thinks there's nothing wrong with this world needs to have his head examined. Just when things are going along all right, without fail someone or something will come along and spoil everything. Somebody should write that down as a fundamental law of the Universe. The principle of perpetual disappointment. If there is a God who created this world, he should scrap it and try again.

SAM: All right, Hally, all right. What you got for homework?

HALLY: Bullshit, as usual. (*Opens an exercise book and reads.*) "Write five hundred words describing an annual event of cultural or historical significance."

SAM: That should be easy enough for you.

HALLY: And also plain bloody boring. You know what he wants, don't you? One of their useless old ceremonies. The commemoration of the landing of the 1820 Settlers, or if it's going to be culture, Carols by Candlelight every Christmas.

SAM: It's an impressive sight. Make a good description, Hally. All those candles glowing in the dark and the people singing hymns.

HALLY: And it's called religious hysteria. (*Intense irritation.*) Please, Sam! Just leave me alone and let me get on with it. I'm not in the mood for games this afternoon. And remember my Mom's orders . . . you're to help Willie with the windows. Come on now, I don't want any more nonsense in here.

SAM: Okay, Hally, okay.

(*HALLY settles down to his homework; determined preparations . . . pen, ruler, exercise book, dictionary, another cake . . . all of which will lead to nothing.*)

(*SAM waltzes over to WILLIE and starts to replace tables and chairs. He practices a ballroom step while doing so. WILLIE watches. When SAM is finished, WILLIE tries.*)

Good! But just a little bit quicker on the turn and only move in to her after she's crossed over. What about this one?

(*Another step. When SAM is finished, WILLIE again has a go.*)

Much better. See what happens when you just relax and enjoy yourself? Remember that in two weeks' time and you'll be all right.

WILLIE: But I haven't got partner, Boet Sam.

SAM: Maybe Hilda will turn up tonight.

WILLIE: No, Boet Sam. (*Reluctantly.*) I gave her a good hiding.

SAM: You mean a bad one.

WILLIE: Good bad one.

SAM: Then you mustn't complain either. Now you pay the price for losing your temper.

WILLIE: I also pay two pounds ten shilling entrance fee.

SAM: They'll refund you if you withdraw now.

WILLIE: (*Appalled*) You mean, don't dance?

SAM: Yes.

WILLIE: No! I wait too long and I practice too hard. If I find me new partner, you think I can be ready in two weeks? I ask Madam for my leave now and we practice every day.

SAM: Quickstep nonstop for two weeks. World record, Willie, but you'll be mad at the end.

WILLIE: No jokes, Boet Sam.

SAM: I'm not joking.

WILLIE: So then what?

SAM: Find Hilda. Say you're sorry and promise you won't beat her again.

WILLIE: No.

SAM: Then withdraw. Try again next year.

WILLIE: No.

SAM: Then I give up.

WILLIE: Haaikona, Boet Sam, you can't.

SAM: What do you mean, I can't? I'm telling you: I give up.

WILLIE: (*Adamant*) No! (*Accusingly.*) It was you who start me ballroom dancing.

SAM: So?

WILLIE: Before that I use to be happy. And is you and Miriam who bring me to Hilda and say here's partner for you.

SAM: What are you saying, Willie?

WILLIE: You!

SAM: But me what? To blame?

WILLIE: Yes.

SAM: Willie . . . ? (*Bursts into laughter.*)

WILLIE: And now all you do is make jokes at me. You wait. When Miriam leaves you is my turn to laugh. Ha! Ha! Ha!

SAM: (*He can't take* WILLIE *seriously any longer*) She can leave me tonight! I know what to do. (*Bowing before an imaginary partner.*) May I have the pleasure? (*He dances and sings.*)

"*Just a fellow with his pillow . . .*
Dancin' like a willow . . .
In an autumn breeze. . . ."

WILLIE: There you go again! (SAM *goes on dancing and singing.*) Boet Sam!

SAM: There's the answer to your problem! Judges' announcement in two weeks' time: "Ladies and gentlemen, the winner in the open section . . . Mr. Willie Malopo and his pillow!"

(*This is too much for a now really angry* WILLIE. *He goes for* SAM, *but the latter is too quick for him and puts* HALLY's *table between the two of them.*)

HALLY: (*Exploding*) For Christ's sake, you two!

WILLIE: (*Still trying to get at* SAM) I donner you, Sam! Struesgod!

SAM: (*Still laughing*) Sorry, Willie . . . Sorry. . . .

HALLY: Sam! Willie! (*Grabs his ruler and gives* WILLIE *a vicious whack on the bum.*) How the hell am I supposed to concentrate with the two of you behaving like bloody children!

WILLIE: Hit him too!

HALLY: Shut up, Willie.

WILLIE: He started jokes again.

HALLY: Get back to your work. You too, Sam. (*His ruler.*) Do you want another one, Willie?

(SAM *and* WILLIE *return to their work.* HALLY *uses the opportunity to escape from his unsuccessful attempt at homework. He struts around like a little despot, ruler in hand, giving vent to his anger and frustration.*)

Suppose a customer had walked in then? Or the Park Superintendent. And seen the two of you behaving like a pair of hooligans. That would have been the end of my mother's license, you know. And your jobs? Well, this is the end of it. From now on there will be no more of your ballroom nonsense in here. This is a business establishment, not a bloody New Brighton dancing school. I've been far too lenient with the two of you. (*Behind the counter for a green cool drink and a dollop of ice cream. He keeps up his tirade as he prepares it.*) But what really makes me bitter is that I allow you chaps a little freedom in here when business is bad and what do you do with it? The foxtrot! Specially you, Sam. There's more to life than trotting around a dance floor and I thought at least you knew it.

SAM: It's a harmless pleasure, Hally. It doesn't hurt anybody.

HALLY: It's also a rather simple one, you know.

SAM: You reckon so? Have you ever tried?

HALLY: Of course not.

SAM: Why don't you? Now.

HALLY: What do you mean? Me dance?

SAM: Yes. I'll show you a simple step—the waltz—then you try it.

HALLY: What will that prove?

SAM: That it might not be as easy as you think.

HALLY: I didn't say it was easy. I said it was simple—like in simple-minded, meaning mentally retarded. You can't exactly say it challenges the intellect.

SAM: It does other things.

HALLY: Such as?

SAM: Make people happy.

HALLY: (*The glass in his hand*) So do American cream sodas with ice cream. For God's sake, Sam, you're not asking me to take ballroom dancing serious, are you?

SAM: Yes.

HALLY: (*Sigh of defeat*) Oh, well, so much for trying to give you a decent education. I've obviously achieved nothing.

SAM: You still haven't told me what's wrong with admiring something that's beautiful and then trying to do it yourself.

HALLY: Nothing. But we happen to be talking about a foxtrot, not a thing of beauty.

SAM: But that is just what I'm saying. If you were to see two champions doing, two masters of the art . . . !

HALLY: Oh God, I give up. So now it's also art!

SAM: Ja.

HALLY: There's a limit, Sam. Don't confuse art and entertainment.

SAM: So then what is art?

HALLY: You want a definition?

SAM: Ja.

HALLY: (*He realizes he has got to be careful. He gives the matter a lot of thought before answering.*) Philosophers have been trying to do that for centuries. What is Art? What is Life? But basically I suppose it's . . . the giving of meaning to matter.

SAM: Nothing to do with beautiful?

HALLY: It goes beyond that. It's the giving of form to the formless.

SAM: Ja, well, maybe it's not art, then. But I still say it's beautiful.

HALLY: I'm sure the word you mean to use is entertaining.

SAM: (*Adamant*) No. Beautiful. And if you want proof come along to the Centenary Hall in New Brighton in two weeks' time.

(*The mention of the Centenary Hall draws* WILLIE *over to them.*)

HALLY: What for? I've seen the two of you prancing around in here often enough.

SAM: (*He laughs*) This isn't the real thing, Hally. We're just playing around in here.

HALLY: So? I can use my imagination.

SAM: And what do you get?

HALLY: A lot of people dancing around and having a so-called good time.

SAM: That all?

HALLY: Well, basically, it is that, surely.

SAM: No, it isn't. Your imagination hasn't helped you at all. There's a lot more to it than that. We're getting ready for the championships, Hally, not just another dance. There's going to be a lot of people, all right, and they're going to have a good time, but they'll only be spectators, sitting around and watching. It's just the competitors out there on the dance floor. Party decorations and fancy lights all around the walls! The ladies in beautiful evening dresses!

HALLY: My mother's got one of those, Sam, and, quite frankly, it's an embarrassment every time she wears it.

SAM: (*Undeterred*) Your imagination left out the excitement.

(HALLY *scoffs.*)

Oh, yes. The finalists are not going to be out there

just to have a good time. One of those couples will be the 1950 Eastern Province Champions. And your imagination left out the music.

WILLIE: Mr. Elijah Gladman Guzana and his Orchestral Jazzonions.

SAM: The sound of the big band, Hally. Trombone, trumpet, tenor and alto sax. And then, finally, your imagination also left out the climax of the evening when the dancing is finished, the judges have stopped whispering among themselves and the Master of Ceremonies collects their scorecards and goes up onto the stage to announce the winners.

HALLY: All right. So you make it sound like a bit of a do. It's an occasion. Satisfied?

SAM: (*Victory*) So you admit that!

HALLY: Emotionally yes, intellectually no.

SAM: Well, I don't know what you mean by that, all I'm telling you is that it is going to be *the* event of the year in New Brighton. It's been sold out for two weeks already. There's only standing room left. We've got competitors coming from Kingwilliamstown, East London, Port Alfred.

(HALLY *starts pacing thoughtfully.*)

HALLY: Tell me a bit more.

SAM: I thought you weren't interested . . . intellectually.

HALLY: (*Mysteriously*) I've got my reasons.

SAM: What do you want to know?

HALLY: It takes place every year?

SAM: Yes. But only every third year in New Brighton. It's East London's turn to have the championships next year.

HALLY: Which, I suppose, makes it an even more significant event.

SAM: Ah ha! We're getting somewhere. Our "occasion" is now a "significant event."

HALLY: I wonder.

SAM: What?

HALLY: I wonder if I would get away with it.

SAM: But what?

HALLY: (*To the table and his exercise book*) "Write five hundred words describing an annual event of cultural or historical significance." Would I be stretching poetic license a little too far if I called your ballroom championships a cultural event?

SAM: You mean . . . ?

HALLY: You think we could get five hundred words out of it, Sam?

SAM: Victor Sylvester has written a whole book on ballroom dancing.

WILLIE: You going to write about it, Master Hally?

HALLY: Yes, gentlemen, that is precisely what I am considering doing. Old Doc Bromely—he's my English teacher—is going to argue with me, of course. He doesn't like natives. But I'll point out to him that in strict anthropological terms the culture of a primitive black society includes its dancing and singing. To put my thesis in a nutshell: The war-dance has been replaced by the waltz. But it still amounts to the same thing: the release of primitive emotions through movement. Shall we give it a go?

SAM: I'm ready.

WILLIE: Me also.

HALLY: Ha! This will teach the old bugger a lesson. (*Decision taken.*) Right. Let's get ourselves organized. (*This means another cake on the table. He sits.*) I think you've given me enough general atmosphere, Sam, but to build the tension and suspense I need facts. (*Pencil poised.*)

WILLIE: Give him facts, Boet Sam.

HALLY: What you called the climax . . . how many finalists?

SAM: Six couples.

HALLY: (*Making notes*) Go on. Give me the picture.

SAM: Spectators seated right around the hall. (WILLIE *becomes a spectator.*)

HALLY: . . . and it's a full house.

SAM: At one end, on the stage, Gladman and his Orchestral Jazzonions. At the other end is a long table with the three judges. The six finalists go onto the dance floor and take up their positions. When they are ready and the spectators have settled down, the Master of Ceremonies goes to the microphone. To start with, he makes some jokes to get people laughing. . . .

HALLY: Good touch. (*As he writes.*) ". . . creating a relaxed atmosphere which will change to one of tension and drama as the climax is approached."

SAM: (*Onto a chair to act out the M.C.*) "Ladies and gentlemen, we come now to the great moment you have all been waiting for this evening. . . . The finals of the 1950 Eastern Province Open Ballroom Dancing Championships. But first let me introduce the finalists! Mr. and Mrs. Welcome Tchabalala from Kingwilliamstown . . ."

WILLIE: (*He applauds after every name*) Is when the people clap their hands and whistle and make a lot of noise, Master Hally.

SAM: "Mr. Mulligan Njikelane and Miss Nomhle Nkonyeni of Grahamstown; Mr. and Mrs. Norman Nchinga from Port Alfred; Mr. Fats Bokolane and Miss Dina Plaatjies from East London; Mr. Sipho Dugu and Mrs. Mable Magada from Peddie; and from New Brighton our very own Mr. Willie Malopo and Miss Hilda Samuels."

(WILLIE *can't believe his ears. He abandons his role as spectator and scrambles into position as a finalist.*)

WILLIE: Relaxed and ready to romance!

SAM: The applause dies down. When everybody is silent, Gladman lifts up his sax, nods at the Orchestral Jazzonions. . . .

WILLIE: Play the jukebox please, Boet Sam!

SAM: I also only got bus fare, Willie.

HALLY: Hold it, everybody. (*Heads for the cash register behind the counter.*) How much is in the till, Sam?

SAM: Three shillings. Hally . . . Your Mom counted it before she left.

(HALLY *hesitates.*)

HALLY: Sorry, Willie. You know how she carried on the last time I did it. We'll just have to pool our combined imaginations and hope for the best. (*Returns to the table.*) Back to work. How are the points scored, Sam?

SAM: Maximum of ten points each for individual style, deportment, rhythm, and general appearance.

WILLIE: Must I start?

HALLY: Hold it for a second, Willie. And penalties?

SAM: For what?

HALLY: For doing something wrong. Say you stumble or bump into somebody . . . do they take off any points?

SAM: (*Aghast*) Hally . . . !

HALLY: When you're dancing. If you and your partner collide into another couple.

(HALLY *can get no further.* SAM *has collapsed with laughter. He explains to* WILLIE.)

SAM: If me and Miriam bump into you and Hilda. . . .

(WILLIE *joins him in another good laugh.*)

Hally, Hally . . . !

HALLY: (*Perplexed*) Why? What did I say?

SAM: There's no collisions out there, Hally. Nobody trips or stumbles or bumps into anybody else. That's what that moment is all about. To be one of those finalists on that dance floor is like . . . like being in a dream about a world in which accidents don't happen.

HALLY: (*Genuinely moved by* SAM's *image*) Jesus, Sam! That's beautiful!

WILLIE: (*Can endure waiting no longer*) I'm starting!

(WILLIE *dances while* SAM *talks.*)

SAM: Of course it is. That's what I've been trying to say to you all afternoon. And it's beautiful because that is what we want life to be like. But instead, like you said, Hally, we're bumping into each other all the time. Look at the three of us this afternoon: I've bumped into Willie, the two of us have bumped into you, you've bumped into your mother, she bumping into your Dad. . . . None of us knows the steps and there's no music playing. And it doesn't stop with us. The whole world is doing it all the time. Open a newspaper and what do you read? America has bumped into Russia, England is bumping into India, rich man bumps into poor man. Those are big collisions, Hally. They make for a lot of bruises. People get hurt in all that bumping, and we're sick and tired of it now. It's been going on for too long. Are we never going to get it right? . . . Learn to dance life like champions instead of always being just a bunch of beginners at it?

HALLY: (*Deep and sincere admiration of the man*) You've got a vision, Sam!

SAM: Not just me. What I'm saying to you is that everybody's got it. That's why there's only standing room left for the Centenary Hall in two weeks' time. For as long as the music lasts, we are going to see six couples get it right, the way we want life to be.

HALLY: But is that the best we can do, Sam . . . watch six finalists dreaming about the way it should be?

SAM: I don't know. But it starts with that. Without the dream we won't know what we're going for. And anyway I reckon there are a few people who have got past just dreaming about it and are trying for something real. Remember that thing we read once in the paper about the Mahatma Gandhi? Going without food to stop those riots in India?

HALLY: You're right. He certainly was trying to teach people to get the steps right.

SAM: And the Pope.

HALLY: Yes, he's another one. Our old General Smuts as well, you know. He's also out there dancing. You know, Sam, when you come to think of it, that's what the United Nations boils down to . . . a dancing school for politicians!

SAM: And let's hope they learn.

HALLY: (*A little surge of hope*) You're right. We mustn't despair. Maybe there's some hope for mankind after all. Keep it up, Willie. (*Back to his table with determination.*) This is a lot bigger than I thought. So what have we got? Yes, our title: "A World Without Collisions."

SAM: That sounds good! "A World Without Collisions."

HALLY: Subtitle: "Global Politics on the Dance Floor." No. A bit too heavy, hey? What about "Ballroom Dancing as a Political Vision"?

(*The telephone rings. SAM answers it.*)

SAM: St. George's Park Tea Room . . . Yes, Madam . . . Hally, it's your Mom.

HALLY: (*Back to reality*) Oh, God, yes! I'd forgotten all about that. Shit! Remember my words, Sam? Just when you're enjoying yourself, someone or something will come along and wreck everything.

SAM: You haven't heard what she's got to say yet.

HALLY: Public telephone?

SAM: No.

HALLY: Does she sound happy or unhappy?

SAM: I couldn't tell. (*Pause.*) She's waiting, Hally.

HALLY: (*To the telephone*) Hello, Mom . . . No, everything is okay here. Just doing my homework. . . . What's your news? . . . You've what? . . . (*Pause. He takes the receiver away from his ear for a few seconds. In the course of HALLY's telephone conversation, SAM and WILLIE discreetly position the stacked tables and chairs. HALLY places the receiver back to his ear.*) Yes, I'm still here. Oh, well, I give up now. Why did you do it, Mom? . . . Well, I just hope you know what you've let us in for. . . . (*Loudly.*) I said I hope you know what you've let us in for! It's the end of the peace and quiet we've been having. (*Softly.*) Where is he? (*Normal voice.*) He can't hear us from in there. But for God's sake, Mom, what happened? I told you to be firm with him. . . . Then you and the nurses should have held him down, taken his crutches away. . . . I know only too well he's my father! . . . I'm not being disrespectful, but I'm sick and tired of emptying stinking chamber pots full of phlegm and piss. . . . Yes, I do! When you're not there, he asks *me* to do it. . . . If you really want to know the truth, that's why I've got no appetite for my food. . . . Yes! There's a lot of things you don't know about. For your information, I still haven't got that science textbook I need. And you know why? He borrowed the money you gave me for it. . . . Because I didn't want to start another fight between you two. . . . He says that every time. . . . All right, Mom! (*Viciously.*) Then just remember to start hiding your bag away again, because he'll be at your purse before long for money for booze. And when he's well enough to come down here, you better keep an eye on the till as well, because that is also going to develop a leak. . . . Then don't complain to me when he starts his old tricks. . . . Yes, you do. I get it from you on one side and from him on the other, and it makes life hell for me. I'm not going to be the peacemaker anymore. I'm warning you now: when the two of you start fighting again, I'm leaving home. . . . Mom, if you start crying, I'm going to put down the receiver. . . . Okay. . . . (*Lowering his voice to a vicious whisper.*) Okay, Mom. I heard you. (*Desperate.*) No. . . . Because I don't want to. I'll see him when I get home! Mom! . . . (*Pause. When he speaks again, his tone changes completely. It is not simply pretense. We sense a genuine emotional conflict.*) Welcome home, chum! . . . What's that? . . . Don't be silly, Dad. You being home is just about the best news in the world. . . . I bet you are. Bloody depressing there with everybody going on about their ailments, hey! . . . How you feeling? . . . Good. . . . Here as well, pal. Coming down cats and dogs. . . . That's right. Just the day for a kip and a toss in your old Uncle Ned. . . . Everything's just hunky-dory on my side, Dad. . . . Well, to start with, there's a nice pile of comics for you on the counter. . . . Yes, old Kemple brought them in. *Batman and Robin, Submariner* . . . just your cup of tea. . . . I will. . . . Yes, we'll spin a few yarns tonight. . . . Okay, chum, see you in a little while. . . . No, I promise. I'll come straight home. . . . (*Pause—his mother comes back on the phone.*) Mom? Okay. I'll lock up now. . . . What? . . . Oh, the brandy . . . Yes, I'll remember! . . . I'll put it in my suitcase now, for God's sake. I know well enough what will happen if he doesn't get it. . . . (*Places a bottle of brandy on the counter.*) I *was* kind to him, Mom. I didn't say anything nasty! . . . All right. Bye. (*End of telephone conversation. A desolate* HALLY *doesn't move. A strained silence.*)

SAM: (*Quietly*) That sounded like a bad bump, Hally.

HALLY: (*Having a hard time controlling his emotions. He speaks carefully.*) Mind your own business, Sam.

SAM: Sorry, I wasn't trying to interfere. Shall we carry on? Hally? (*He indicates the exercise book. No response from* HALLY.)

WILLIE: (*Also trying*) Tell him about when they give out the cups, Boet Sam.

SAM: Ja! That's another big moment. The presentation of the cups after the winners have been announced. You've got to put that in.

(*Still no response from* HALLY.)

WILLIE: A big silver one, Master Hally, called floating trophy for the champions.

SAM: We always invite some big-shot personality to hand them over. Guest of honor this year is going to be His Holiness Bishop Jabulani of the All African Free Zionist Church.

(HALLY *gets up abruptly, goes to his table, and tears up the page he was writing on.*)

HALLY: So much for a bloody world without collisions.

SAM: Too bad. It was on its way to being a good composition.

HALLY: Let's stop bullshitting ourselves, Sam.

SAM: Have we been doing that?

HALLY: Yes! That's what all our talk about a decent world has been . . . just so much bullshit.

SAM: We did say it was still only a dream.

HALLY: And a bloody useless one at that. Life's a fuckup and it's never going to change.

SAM: Ja, maybe that's true.

HALLY: There's no maybe about it. It's a blunt and brutal fact. All we've done this afternoon is waste our time.

SAM: Not if we'd got your homework done.

HALLY: I don't give a shit about my homework, so, for Christ's sake, just shut up about it. (*Slamming books viciously into his school case.*) Hurry up now and finish your work. I want to lock up and get out of here. (*Pause.*) And then go where? Home-sweet-fucking-home. Jesus, I hate that word.

(HALLY *goes to the counter to put the brandy bottle and comics in his school case. After a moment's hesitation, he smashes the bottle of brandy. He abandons all further attempts to hide his feelings.* SAM *and* WILLIE *work away as unobtrusively as possible.*)

Do you want to know what is really wrong with your lovely little dream, Sam? It's not just that we are all bad dancers. That does happen to be perfectly true, but there's more to it than just that. You left out the cripples.

SAM: Hally!

HALLY: (*Now totally reckless*) Ja! Can't leave them out, Sam. That's why we always end up on our backsides on the dance floor. They're also out there dancing . . . like a bunch of broken spiders trying to do the quickstep! (*An ugly attempt at laughter.*) When you come to think of it, it's a bloody comical sight. I mean, it's bad enough on two legs . . . but one and a pair of crutches! Hell, no, Sam. That's guaranteed to turn that dance floor into a shambles. Why you shaking your head? Picture it, man. For once this afternoon let's use our imaginations sensibly.

SAM: Be careful, Hally.

HALLY: Of what? The truth? I seem to be the only one around here who is prepared to face it. We've had the pretty dream, it's time now to wake up and have a good long look at the way things really are. Nobody knows the steps, there's no music, the cripples are also out there tripping up everybody and trying to get into the act, and it's all called the All-Comers-How-to-Make-a-Fuckup-of-Life Championships. (*Another ugly laugh.*) Hang on, Sam! The best bit is still coming. Do you know what the winner's trophy is? A beautiful big chamber pot with roses on the side, and it's full to the brim with piss. And guess who I think is going to be this year's winner.

SAM: (*Almost shouting*) Stop now!

HALLY: (*Suddenly appalled by how far he has gone*) Why?

SAM: Hally? It's your father you're talking about.

HALLY: So?

SAM: Do you know what you've been saying?

(HALLY *can't answer. He is rigid with shame.* SAM *speaks to him sternly.*)

No, Hally, you mustn't do it. Take back those words and ask for forgiveness! It's a terrible sin for a son to mock his father with jokes like that. You'll be punished if you carry on. Your father is your father, even if he is a . . . cripple man.

WILLIE: Yes, Master Hally. Is true what Sam say.

SAM: I understand how you are feeling, Hally, but even so. . . .

HALLY: No, you don't!

SAM: I think I do.

HALLY: And I'm telling you you don't. Nobody does. (*Speaking carefully as his shame turns to rage at* SAM.) It's your turn to be careful, Sam. Very careful! You're treading on dangerous ground. Leave me and my father alone.

SAM: I'm not the one who's been saying things about him.

HALLY: What goes on between me and my Dad is none of your business!

SAM: Then don't tell me about it. If that's all you've got to say about him, I don't want to hear.

(*For a moment* HALLY *is at loss for a response.*)

HALLY: Just get on with your bloody work and shut up.

SAM: Swearing at me won't help you.

HALLY: Yes, it does! Mind your own fucking business and shut up!

SAM: Okay. If that's the way you want it, I'll stop trying.

(*He turns away. This infuriates* HALLY *even more.*)

HALLY: Good. Because what you've been trying to do is meddle in something you know nothing about. All that concerns you in here, Sam, is to try and do what you get paid for—keep the place clean and serve the customers. In plain words, just get on with your job. My mother is right. She's always warning me about allowing you to get too familiar. Well, this time you've gone too far. It's going to stop right now.

(*No response from* SAM.)

You're only a servant in here, and don't forget it.

(*Still no response.* HALLY *is trying hard to get one.*)

And as far as my father is concerned, all you need to remember is that he is your boss.

SAM: (*Needled at last*) No, he isn't. I get paid by your mother.

HALLY: Don't argue with me, Sam!

SAM: Then don't say he's my boss.

HALLY: He's a white man and that's good enough for you.

SAM: I'll try to forget you said that.

HALLY: Don't! Because you won't be doing me a favor if you do. I'm telling you to remember it.

(*A pause.* SAM *pulls himself together and makes one last effort.*)

SAM: Hally, Hally . . . ! Come on now. Let's stop before it's too late. You're right. We *are* on dangerous ground. If we're not careful, somebody is going to get hurt.

HALLY: It won't be me.

SAM: Don't be so sure.

HALLY: I don't know what you're talking about, Sam.

SAM: Yes, you do.

HALLY: (*Furious*) Jesus, I wish you would stop trying to tell me what I do and what I don't know.

(SAM *gives up. He turns to* WILLIE.)

SAM: Let's finish up.

HALLY: Don't turn your back on me! I haven't finished talking.

(*He grabs* SAM *by the arm and tries to make him turn around.* SAM *reacts with a flash of anger.*)

SAM: Don't do that, Hally! (*Facing the boy.*) All right, I'm listening. Well? What do you want to say to me?

HALLY: (*Pause as* HALLY *looks for something to say*) To begin with, why don't you also start calling me Master Harold, like Willie.

SAM: Do you mean that?

HALLY: Why the hell do you think I said it?

SAM: And if I don't?

HALLY: You might just lose your job.

SAM: (*Quietly and very carefully*) If you make me say it once, I'll never call you anything else again.

HALLY: So? (*The boy confronts the man.*) Is that meant to be a threat?

SAM: Just telling you what will happen if you make me do that. You must decide what it means to you.

HALLY: Well, I have. It's good news. Because that is exactly what Master Harold wants from now on. Think of it as a little lesson in respect, Sam, that's long overdue, and I hope you remember it as well as you do your geography. I can tell you now that somebody who will be glad to hear I've finally given it to you will be my Dad. Yes! He agrees with my Mom. He's always going on about it as well. "You must teach the boys to show you more respect, my son."

SAM: So now you can stop complaining about going home. Everybody is going to be happy tonight.

HALLY: That's perfectly correct. You see, you mustn't get the wrong idea about me and my Dad, Sam. We also have our good times together. Some bloody good laughs. He's got a marvelous sense of humor. Want to know what our favorite joke is? He gives out a big groan, you see, and says: "It's not fair, is it, Hally?" Then I have to ask: "What, chum?" And then he says: "A nigger's arse" . . . and we both have a good laugh.

(*The men stare at him with disbelief.*)

What's the matter, Willie? Don't you catch the joke? You always were a bit slow on the uptake. It's what is called a pun. You see, fair means both light in color and to be just and decent. (*He turns to* SAM.) I thought *you* would catch it, Sam.

SAM: Oh ja, I catch it all right.

HALLY: But it doesn't appeal to your sense of humor.

SAM: Do you really laugh?

HALLY: Of course.

SAM: To please him? Make him feel good?

HALLY: No, for heaven's sake! I laugh because I think it's a bloody good joke.

SAM: You're really trying hard to be ugly, aren't you? And why drag poor old Willie into it? He's done nothing to you except show you the respect you want so badly. That's also not being fair, you know . . . and *I* mean just or decent.

WILLIE: It's all right, Sam. Leave it now.

SAM: It's me you're after. You should just have said "Sam's arse" . . . because that's the one you're trying to kick. Anyway, how do you know it's not fair? You've never seen it. Do you want to? (*He drops his trousers and underpants and presents his backside for* HALLY's *inspection.*) Have a good look. A real Basuto arse . . . which is about as nigger as they can come.

Satisfied? (*Trousers up.*) Now you can make your Dad even happier when you go home tonight. Tell him I showed you my arse and he is quite right. It's not fair. And if it will give him an even better laugh next time, I'll also let *him* have a look. Come, Willie, let's finish up and go.

(SAM *and* WILLIE *start to tidy up the tea room.* HALLY *doesn't move. He waits for a moment when* SAM *passes him.*)

HALLY: (*Quietly*) Sam ...

(SAM *stops and looks expectantly at the boy.* HALLY *spits in his face. A long and heartfelt groan from* WILLIE. *For a few seconds* SAM *doesn't move.*)

SAM: (*Taking out a handkerchief and wiping his face*) It's all right, Willie.

(*To* HALLY.)

Ja, well, you've done it ... Master Harold. Yes, I'll start calling you that from now on. It won't be difficult anymore. You've hurt yourself, Master Harold. I saw it coming. I warned you, but you wouldn't listen. You've just hurt yourself *bad.* And you're a coward, Master Harold. The face you should be spitting in is your father's ... but you used mine, because you think you're safe inside your fair skin ... and this time I don't mean just or decent. (*Pause, then moving violently toward* HALLY.) Should I hit him, Willie?

WILLIE: (*Stopping* SAM) No, Boet Sam.

SAM: (*Violently*) Why not?

WILLIE: It won't help, Boet Sam.

SAM: I don't want to help! I want to hurt him.

WILLIE: You also hurt yourself.

SAM: And if he had done it to you, Willie?

WILLIE: Me? Spit at me like I was a dog? (*A thought that had not occurred to him before. He looks at* HALLY.) Ja. Then I want to hit him. I want to hit him hard!

(*A dangerous few seconds as the men stand staring at the boy.* WILLIE *turns away, shaking his head.*)

But maybe all I do is go cry at the back. He's little boy, Boet Sam. Little *white* boy. Long trousers now, but he's still little boy.

SAM: (*His violence ebbing away into defeat as quickly as it flooded*) You're right. So go on, then: groan again, Willie. You do it better than me. (*To* HALLY.) You don't know all of what you've just done ... Master Harold. It's not just that you've made me feel dirtier than I've ever been in my life ... I mean, how do I wash off yours and your father's filth? ... I've also failed. A long time ago I promised myself I was going to try and do something, but you've just shown me ... Master Harold ... that I've failed. (*Pause.*) I've also got a memory of a little white boy when he was still wearing short trousers and a black man, but they're not flying a kite. It was the old

Jubilee days, after dinner one night. I was in my room. You came in and just stood against the wall, looking down at the ground, and only after I'd asked you what you wanted, what was wrong, I don't know how many times, did you speak and even then so softly I almost didn't hear you. "Sam, please help me to go and fetch my Dad." Remember? He was dead drunk on the floor of the Central Hotel Bar. They'd phoned for your Mom, but you were the only one at home. And do you remember how we did it? You went in first by yourself to ask permission for me to go into the bar. Then I loaded him onto my back like a baby and carried him back to the boarding house with you following behind carrying his crutches. (*Shaking his head as he remembers.*) A crowded Main Street with all the people watching a little white boy following his drunk father on a nigger's back! I felt for that little boy ... Master Harold. I felt for him. After that we still had to clean him up, remember? He'd messed in his trousers, so we had to clean him up and get him into bed.

HALLY: (*Great pain*) I love him, Sam.

SAM: I know you do. That's why I tried to stop you from saying these things about him. It would have been so simple if you could have just despised him for being a weak man. But he's your father. You love him and you're ashamed of him. You're ashamed of so much! ... And now that's going to include yourself. That was the promise I made to myself: to try and stop that happening. (*Pause.*) After we got him to bed you came back with me to my room and sat in a corner and carried on just looking down at the ground. And for two days after that! You hadn't done anything wrong, but you went around as if you owed the world an apology for being alive. I didn't like seeing that! That's not the way a boy grows up to be a man! ... But the one person who should have been teaching you what that means was the cause of your shame. If you really want to know, that's why I made you that kite. I wanted you to look up, be proud of something, of yourself ... (*Bitter smile at the memory*) ... and you certainly were that when I left you with it up there on the hill. Oh, ja ... something else! ... If you ever do write it as a short story, there *was* a twist in our ending. I couldn't sit down there and stay with you. It was a "Whites Only" bench. You were too young, too excited to notice then. But not anymore. If you're not careful ... Master Harold ... you're going to be sitting up there by yourself for a long time to come, and there won't be a kite in the sky. (SAM *has got nothing more to say. He exits into the kitchen, taking off his waiter's jacket.*)

WILLIE: Is bad. Is all bad in here now.

HALLY: (*Books into his school case, raincoat on*) Willie ... (*It is difficult to speak.*) Will you lock up for me and look after the keys?

WILLIE: Okay.

(SAM *returns.* HALLY *goes behind the counter and collects the few coins in the cash register. As he starts to leave.* . . .)

SAM: Don't forget the comic books.

(HALLY *returns to the counter and puts them in his case. He starts to leave again.*)

SAM: (*To the retreating back of the boy*) Stop . . . Hally. . . .

(HALLY *stops, but doesn't turn to face him.*)

Hally . . . I've got no right to tell you what being a man means if I don't behave like one myself, and I'm not doing so well at that this afternoon. Should we try again, Hally?

HALLY: Try what?

SAM: Fly another kite, I suppose. It worked once, and this time I need it as much as you do.

HALLY: It's still raining, Sam. You can't fly kites on rainy days, remember.

SAM: So what do we do? Hope for better weather tomorrow?

HALLY: (*Helpless gesture*) I don't know. I don't know anything anymore.

SAM: You sure of that, Hally? Because it would be pretty hopeless if that was true. It would mean nothing has been learnt in here this afternoon, and there was a hell of a lot of teaching going on . . . one way or the other. But anyway, I don't believe you. I reckon there's one thing you know. You don't *have* to sit up there by yourself. You know what that bench means now, and you can leave it any time you choose. All you've got to do is stand up and walk away from it.

(HALLY *leaves.* WILLIE *goes up quietly to* SAM.)

WILLIE: Is okay, Boet Sam. You see. Is . . . (*He can't find any better words*) . . . is going to be okay tomorrow. (*Changing his tone.*) Hey, Boet Sam! (*He is trying hard.*) You right. I think about it and you right. Tonight I find Hilda and say sorry. And make promise I won't beat her no more. You hear me, Boet Sam?

SAM: I hear you, Willie.

WILLIE: And when we practice I relax and romance with her from beginning to end. Nonstop! You watch! Two weeks' time: "First prize for promising newcomers: Mr. Willie Malopo and Miss Hilda Samuels." (*Sudden impulse.*) To hell with it! I walk home. (*He goes to the jukebox, puts in a coin and selects a record. The machine comes to life in the gray twilight, blushing its way through a spectrum of soft, romantic colors.*) How did you say it, Boet Sam? Let's dream. (WILLIE *sways with the music and gestures for* SAM *to dance.*)

(*Sarah Vaughan sings.*)

"*Little man you're crying,
I know why you're blue,
Someone took your kiddy car away;
Better go to sleep now,
Little man you've had a busy day.*" (*etc., etc.*)

You lead. I follow.

(*The men dance together.*)

"*Johnny won your marbles,
Tell you what we'll do;
Dad will get you new ones right away;
Better go to sleep now,
Little man you've had a busy day.*"

Figure 1. Hally (Lonny Price) and Willie (Danny Glover) listen to Sam (Zakes Mokae) describing the dancing championships in the Yale Repertory Theatre production of *"Master Harold" . . . and the Boys,* directed by Athol Fugard, 1982. (Photograph: Martha Swope.)

Figure 2. Sam (Zakes Mokae) rebukes Hally (Lonny Price) for mocking his father, while Willie (Danny Glover) looks on in surprise, in the Yale Repertory Theatre production of *"Master Harold" . . . and the Boys,* directed by Athol Fugard, 1982. (Photograph: Martha Swope.)

Staging of *"Master Harold" . . . and the Boys*

REVIEW OF THE YALE REPERTORY THEATRE PRODUCTION, 1982, FRANK RICH

There may be two or three living playwrights in the world who can write as well as Athol Fugard, but I'm not sure that any of them has written a recent play that can match *"Master Harold" . . . and the Boys*. Mr. Fugard's drama—lyrical in design, shattering in impact—is likely to be an enduring part of the theater long after most of this Broadway season has turned to dust.

"Master Harold," which opened at the Lyceum last night following its March premiere at the Yale Repertory Theater, may even outlast the society that spawned it—the racially divided South Africa of apartheid. Though Mr. Fugard's play is set there in 1950, it could take place nearly anywhere at any time. The word "apartheid" is never mentioned; the South African references are minimal. The question that Mr. Fugard raises—how can men of all kinds find the courage to love one another?—is dealt with at such a profound level that *"Master Harold"* sweeps quickly beyond the transitory specifics of any one nation. It's not for nothing that this is the first play Mr. Fugard has chosen to open away from home.

What's more, the author deals with his issue without attitudinizing, without sentimentality, without lecturing the audience. *"Master Harold"* isn't another problem play in which people stand for ideological positions. By turns funny and tragic, it uncovers its moral imperatives by burrowing deeply into the small, intimately observed details of its three characters' lives.

We meet those characters on a rainy afternoon, as they josh and chat in a fading tea room. Two of them, Sam (Zakes Mokae) and Willie (Danny Glover), are black waiters who rehearse for a coming ballroom dancing contest while tidying up the restaurant. Because they only have enough money for bus fare home, they can't put Sarah Vaughan on the jukebox: they imagine the music, as well as their Ginger Rogers–like partners, as they twirl about. Eventually they are joined by Hally (Lonny Price), who is the son of the tea room's owner. A precocious white prep-school student on the verge of manhood, Hally has stopped by to eat lunch and work on an English essay.

The black servants are the boy's second family: they have been employed by his parents since Hally was in short trousers. But, for all the easy camaraderie and tender memories that unite master and servants, there's a slight distance in their relationship, too. As the waiters practice their steps, Hally playfully but condescendingly calls them "a pair of hooligans." To the boy, such danc-

ing is a "simple-minded" reflection of "the culture of primitive black society"—only now "the war dance has been replaced by the waltz."

But the articulate Sam, an unacknowledged mentor to Hally since childhood, patiently sets the boy to thinking otherwise. Dancing, Sam contends, "is like being in a dream about a world where accidents don't happen"— where white and black, rich and poor, men and women don't bump into one another. Hally is so taken with this theory that he decides to write his essay about it. Maybe, he postulates, "the United Nations is a dancing school for politicians." Maybe "there is hope for mankind after all."

It's a lovely, idyllic metaphor, and there is much joy in *"Master Harold"* as the characters imagine their utopian "world without collisions." Yet the joy soon dissipates. Mr. Fugard has structured his intermissionless 100-minute play much as Sam describes a dance contest: "a relaxed atmosphere changes to one of tension and drama as the climax approaches." When the tension erupts in *"Master Harold,"* it rips through the audience so mercilessly that the Lyceum falls into an almost deathly hush.

The drama is catalyzed by a series of phone calls Hally receives from his real-life family offstage. Hally's father, we learn, is a drunk, a cripple and a racist; his mother is his long-suffering victim. Hally is caught between them, and, as old wounds are ripped open, the bitterness of his entire childhood comes raging to the surface. The boy is soon awash in tearful self-pity and, in the absence of his real father, takes out his anger on his surrogate father, Sam. What follows is an unstoppable, almost unwatchable outpouring of ugliness, in which Hally humiliates the black man he loves by insisting that he call him "Master Harold," by mocking their years of shared secrets, by spitting in his face.

Mr. Fugard's point is simple enough: Before we can practice compassion—before we can, as Sam says, "dance life like champions"—we must learn to respect ourselves. It is Hally's self-hatred that leads him to strike at the black man and his crippled Dad and, in this sense, the boy is typical of anyone who attacks the defenseless to bolster his own self-esteem.

But *"Master Harold,"* unlike many works that deal with the genesis of hatred, forces us to identify with the character who inflicts the cruelty. We like Hally so much in the play's early stages, and empathize with his familial sorrow so keenly later on, that it's impossible to pull back once he lashes out. And because we can't sever ourselves from Hally, we're forced to confront our own capacity for cruelty—and to see all too clearly just who it is we really hurt when we give in to it.

Mr. Fugard can achieve this effect because he has the guts to face his own shame: Hally, a fledgling artist who believes in social reform, is too richly drawn not to be a ruthlessly honest portrait of the playwright as a young man. But if Mr. Fugard's relentless conscience gives "*Master Harold*" its remarkable moral center, his brilliance as an artist gives the play its classic esthetic simplicity.

This work is totally without pretension. As Sam says that the trick of dancing is to "make it look easy," so Mr. Fugard understands that the same is true in the theater. The dialogue is light and easy, full of lilting images that gradually warp as the darkness descends. After Hally relives the exultant childhood experience of flying his first kite with Sam, the kite comes down to the ground, "like something that has lost its soul." Sam's description of graceful waltzers is usurped by the boy's vision of "cripples dancing like a bunch of broken spiders."

Like the script, the production has been deftly choreographed by the author: you don't know you're en-tering the center of a storm until you're there. The one newcomer to the cast since Yale, Mr. Price, will be at the level of his predecessor, Zeljko Ivanek, as soon as he tones down his overly cute youthful friskiness in Hally's early scenes. Once the protagonist falls apart, Mr. Price takes the audience right with him on his bottomless descent to self-immolation.

As the easygoing Willie, Mr. Glover is a paragon of sweet kindliness—until events leave him whipped and sobbing in a chair, his low moans serving as forlorn counterpoint to the play's main confrontation. Mr. Mokae's Sam is a transcendental force—an avuncular, hearty figure who slowly withdraws into dignified serenity as Hally taunts him. Though the boy has repaid the servant's lifelong instruction in tolerance by making him feel "dirty," Mr. Mokae still glows with his dream of a world of perfect dancers—one that's like "a love story with a happy ending."

The author doesn't provide that happy ending, of course—it's not his to confer. But if "*Master Harold*" finally lifts us all the way from pain to hope, it's because Mr. Fugard insists that that ending can be—must be—ours to write.

CARYL CHURCHILL

1938–

When asked if she thought there was a "female aesthetic," Caryl Churchill responded: "I don't see how you can tell until there are so many plays by women that you can begin to see what they have in common that's different from the way men have written, and there are still relatively so few." But among those "relatively few," the thirty-two dramas of Caryl Churchill, ranging from radio and television scripts to stage plays, have put her unquestionably into the ranks of major contemporary playwrights.

An only child, Churchill began writing stories at an early age, attended school in London and then in Montreal, and returned to England to study at Oxford University where she started writing plays for student productions. Marriage in 1961 to David Harter, a lawyer, took her to London and to her initial work on radio and television plays. As Churchill put it, she turned to radio plays in part because she liked radio but also because the process of bearing and raising children made it virtually impossible to do anything but shorter pieces. After her third child was born, Churchill felt she needed more time for her writing, and briefly hired a nanny to care for her youngest child—that "a woman must have money and a room of her own if she is to write fiction" seems just as true for Churchill as it was when Virginia Woolf issued her famous manifesto in 1929.

Churchill has said that her 1972 play *Owners* was the beginning of the second part of her career, since it marked the start of her almost total commitment to theater, instead of radio and television. That play, like *Objections to Sex and Violence* (1975) and *Traps* (1977), opened originally at London's Royal Court Theatre, the home since 1956 for many new British plays. Churchill's plays show men and women caught in social, political, gender-based, and personal "traps," from which they try to escape in a variety of ways, including through terrorism and suicide. Perhaps the major influence on Churchill's work came in 1976 when she began working with experimental theater groups in the process of conceiving and drafting her plays. For *Light Shining in Buckinghamshire* (1976), which she developed in collaboration with Joint Stock, Churchill and her director first decided on their subject—the millennial movement during the English Civil War, an essentially working-class movement based on the belief that fighting the king (Charles I) would lead to the second coming of Christ. Then the crucial part of the creative process was, according to Churchill, a three-week workshop with the Joint Stock actors where, "through talk, reading, games, and improvisation, we tried to get closer to the issues and the people." She next spent nine weeks writing a script and worked with the company for another six weeks of rehearsal. Given such extensive collaboration, she acknowledges that, while the actors did not write the lines, "many of the characters and scenes were based on ideas that came from improvisation at the workshop and during rehearsal."

Churchill's reading in seventeenth-century material also fostered her work with Monstrous Regiment, a feminist/socialist theater group with whom she had agreed to do a play about witches. Her research convinced her that she "wanted to write a play about witches with no witches in it; a play not about evil, hysteria, and possession by the devil but about poverty, humiliation, and prejudice, and how the women accused of witchcraft saw themselves." For this play, *Vinegar Tom* (1976), she first talked with the group, drafted the play in three days, went off to work with Joint Stock, came back to Monstrous Regiment in the autumn, and expanded the play to create a new character, in part because a new actress had joined the company, and in part because discussion with the actors indicated that a certain kind of character was needed. Not only did both of these plays come out of similar working conditions and deal with (roughly) the same historical period, but both show Churchill's move into a less realistic kind of drama than she had previously written. The plays call for large casts, yet each production uses only a small group of actors: twenty-five roles in *Light Shining in Buckinghamshire* were played by six actors, while fourteen roles in *Vinegar Tom* were played by nine actors. What may have started as a financial necessity—a limit on the number of actors the group could support—turns into a highly suggestive mode of staging, since, as Churchill points out, "When different actors play the parts what comes over is a large event involving many people, whose characters resonate in a way they wouldn't if they were more clearly defined." The events and their political significance become central rather than the psychology of the characters or the star quality of the actors.

Most of Churchill's major plays since the 1976 collaborative ventures show the influence of that experience, for *Cloud Nine* (1979), *Fen* (1983), and *Serious Money* (1987) have also been developed out of workshops with the original actors. These plays, as well as *Top Girls* (1982) and *Softcops* (1984), call for actors to play multiple roles, and increasingly Churchill stresses the connection of the actor with the role. Thus, in *Cloud Nine,* a black farce which examines the similarities between colonial and sexual repression, the casting of a man in the role of Betty, the wife of the white colonial administrator in Africa, represents for Churchill the idea that Betty "wants to be what men want her to be." Similarly, the black servant, Joshua, is played by a white man, and Edward, the young son whose homosexual tendencies are both repressed and revealed, by a woman. In the second act, which moves forward 100 years to contemporary London, with the characters only twenty-five years older, Churchill asks for different gender castings, again to make points about the changing self-perceptions of men and women; thus Betty "is now played by a woman, as she gradually becomes real to herself, " but Cathy, a child of five, is to be played by a man, "partly, as with Edward, to show more clearly the issues involved in learning what is considered correct behavior for a girl."

Churchill's preoccupation with the past and its relation to the present is most dazzlingly represented in the first scene of *Top Girls*. In a contemporary London restaurant, Marlene, the new managing director of the Top Girls Employment Agency, hosts a dinner to celebrate her promotion, and her dinner guests, who span centuries and continents, include both real women and women imagined by men. Thus, the Victorian traveler Isabella Bird, the Japanese-courtesan-turned-nun Lady Nijo, and the Italian Pope Joan join Marlene along with Dull

Gret, a woman in apron and armor from Brueghel's painting "Dulle Griet," and Patient Griselda, the much-abused heroine of Chaucer's "The Clerk's Tale" (see Figure 1). Not only does Churchill blend the real and the imaginary with the medieval, Renaissance, Victorian, and modern worlds, but she invents an overlapping style, so that characters speak over each other, or continue their speeches without noticing that another character has spoken on a seemingly different topic. Although these women from the past look unrelated, their stories link together in that they show the painful experiences women suffer in dealing with men, with children, and with their own sexual identity. Even Dull Gret, who speaks in monosyllables for most of the scene, suddenly bursts into a long speech which recounts the Brueghel painting from her own point of view, showing that her anger springs from a mother's outrage rather than from the plundering instincts of an unwomanly woman.

Churchill devotes the rest of the play to Marlene's story, gradually detailing what she has become in order to run Top Girls, and the price she has paid for her success. Marlene is the only role not switched or shared, a theatrical choice which may also suggest that she can't escape into another life. The fifteen other characters are played by only six actresses, often with ironic juxtapositions. The intrepid traveler Isabella Bird turns into Marlene's sister Joyce, who, unlike Marlene and Isabella, is trapped at home, visiting their sick mother once a week, and taking care of Angie, a "slow" sixteen-year-old, who turns out to be Marlene's daughter rather than her niece. Angie, less surprisingly, is played by the actress who played Dull Gret, both characters who seem to have little to say. And Patient Griselda, who has taken so much abuse from her husband, becomes a client interviewed by Marlene, showing the same vacuous adaptability as the character from the past.

When the play opened in 1982, reviews commented extensively on the play's elaborate dinner scene (see Figure 1), but also on the quality of the acting of the seven women taking the sixteen roles. While reactions to the play ranged widely ("articulate, eloquent, alive" or "predictable and, at times, rather trite" or "a strange play, disturbing and intriguing"), most reviewers agreed that Churchill had created a feast of acting opportunities, fully realized in performance. Though all of the actresses received praise, frequent attention went most often to Carole Hayman's "lovely, humane performance" of Angie, who is "a bit thick." Angie's existence, and Marlene's attempt to hide from her true relationship to the girl, posed the question for one reviewer: "What use is female emancipation, Churchill asks, if it transforms the clever women into predators and does nothing for the stupid, weak, and helpless?" Thus it seems especially appropriate that the exotic worlds conjured up in the play's first scene shrink to the rooms of the employment agency and Joyce's backyard, where Angie and her friend Kit play "squashed together" in "a shelter made of junk" (see Figure 2). No matter what dreams women have had, have enacted, have yet to dream, Churchill reminds us in the play's final lines of today's reality. Marlene comforts Angie, who has suddenly awakened: "Did you have a bad dream? What happened in it? Well you're awake now, aren't you pet?" Angie's answer may reflect Churchill's: "Frightening."

TOP GIRLS

BY CARYL CHURCHILL

CHARACTERS

MARLENE
WAITRESS/KIT/SHONA
ISABELLA BIRD/JOYCE/MRS. KIDD
LADY NIJO/WIN
DULL GRET/ANGIE
POPE JOAN/LOUISE
PATIENT GRISELDA/NELL/JEANINE

ACT 1

Scene 1: *A Restaurant.*
Scene 2: *Top Girls' Employment Agency, London.*
Scene 3: *Joyce's backyard in Suffolk.*

ACT 2

Scene 1: *Top Girls' Employment Agency.*
Scene 2: *A Year Earlier. Joyce's kitchen.*

Production Note: *The seating order for Act 1, Scene 1 in the original production at the Royal Court was (from right) Gret, Nijo, Marlene, Joan, Griselda, Isabella.*

THE CHARACTERS

ISABELLA BIRD (1831–1904): Lived in Edinburgh, traveled extensively between the ages of forty and seventy.
LADY NIJO (b. 1258): Japanese, was an Emperor's courtesan and later a Buddhist nun who traveled on foot through Japan.
DULL GRET: Is the subject of the Brueghel painting *Dulle Griet*, in which a woman in an apron and armor leads a crowd of women charging through hell and fighting the devils.
POPE JOAN: Disguised as a man, is thought to have been pope between 854 and 856.

PATIENT GRISELDA: Is the obedient wife whose story is told by Chaucer in "The Clerk's Tale" of *The Canterbury Tales*.

THE LAYOUT: *A speech usually follows the one immediately before it but: (1) When one character starts speaking before the other has finished, the point of interruption is marked "/." E.g.,*

ISABELLA: This is the Emperor of Japan? / I once met the Emperor of Morocco.
NIJO: In fact he was the ex-Emperor.

(2) A character sometimes continues speaking right through another's speech. E.g.,

ISABELLA: When I was forty I thought my life was over. / Oh I was pitiful. I was
NIJO: I didn't say I felt it for twenty years. Not every minute.
ISABELLA: sent on a cruise for my health and felt even worse. Pains in my bones, pins and needles . . . etc.

(3) Sometimes a speech follows on from a speech earlier than the one immediately before it, and continuity is marked *. E.g.,

GRISELDA: I'd seen him riding by, we all had. And he'd seen me in the fields with the sheep.*
ISABELLA: I would have been well suited to minding sheep.
NIJO: And Mr. Nugent went riding by.
ISABELLA: Of course not, Nijo, I mean a healthy life in the open air.
JOAN: *He just rode up while you were minding the sheep and asked you to marry him?

where "in the fields with the sheep" is the cue to both "I would have been" and "He just rode up."

ACT 1 / SCENE 1

(Restaurant. Saturday night. There is a table with a white cloth set for dinner with six places. The lights come up on MARLENE and the WAITRESS.)

MARLENE: Excellent, yes, table for six. One of them's going to be late but we won't wait. I'd like a bottle of Frascati straight away if you've got one really cold. *(The WAITRESS goes. ISABELLA BIRD arrives.)* Here we are. Isabella.
ISABELLA: Congratulations, my dear.
MARLENE: Well, it's a step. It makes for a party. I haven't time for a holiday. I'd like to go somewhere exotic

like you but I can't get away. I don't know how you could bear to leave Hawaii. / I'd like to lie
ISABELLA: I did think of settling.
MARLENE: in the sun forever, except of course I can't bear sitting still.
ISABELLA: I sent for my sister Hennie to come and join me. I said, Hennie we'll live here forever and help the natives. You can buy two sirloins of beef for what a pound of chops cost in Edinburgh. And Hennie wrote back, the dear, that yes, she would come to Hawaii if I wished, but I said she had far better stay where she was. Hennie was suited to life in Tobermory.
MARLENE: Poor Hennie.

ISABELLA: Do you have a sister?

MARLENE: Yes in fact.

ISABELLA: Hennie was happy. She was good. I did miss its face, my own pet. But I couldn't stay in Scotland. I loathed the constant murk.

(Lady NIJO *arrives.)*

MARLENE: *(Seeing her)* Ah! Nijo! *(The* WAITRESS *enters with the wine.)*

NIJO: Marlene! *(To* ISABELLA.*)* So excited when Marlene told me / you were coming.

ISABELLA: I'm delighted / to meet you.

MARLENE: I think a drink while we wait for the others. I think a drink anyway. What a week. *(*MARLENE *seats* NIJO. *The* WAITRESS *pours the wine.)*

NIJO: It was always the men who used to get so drunk. I'd be one of the maidens, passing the sake.

ISABELLA: I've had sake. Small hot drink. Quite fortifying after a day in the wet.

NIJO: One night my father proposed three rounds of three cups, which was normal, and then the Emperor should have said three rounds of three cups, but he said three rounds of nine cups, so you can imagine. Then the Emperor passed his sake cup to my father and said, "Let the wild goose come to me this spring."

MARLENE: Let the what?

NIJO: It's a literary allusion to a tenth-century epic, / His Majesty was very cultured.

ISABELLA: This is the Emperor of Japan? / I once met the Emperor of Morocco.

NIJO: In fact he was the ex-Emperor.

MARLENE: But he wasn't old? / Did you, Isabella?

NIJO: Twenty-nine.

ISABELLA: Oh it's a long story.

MARLENE: Twenty-nine's an excellent age.

NIJO: Well I was only fourteen and I knew he meant something but I didn't know what. He sent me an eight-layered gown and I sent it back. So when the time came I did nothing but cry. My thin gowns were badly ripped. But even that morning when he left / he'd a green

MARLENE: Are you saying he raped you?

NIJO: robe with a scarlet lining and very heavily embroidered trousers, I already felt different about him. It made me uneasy. No, of course not, Marlene, I belonged to him, it was what I was brought up for from a baby. I soon found I was sad if he stayed away. It was depressing day after day not knowing when he would come. I never enjoyed taking other women to him.

ISABELLA: I certainly never saw my father drunk. He was a clergyman. / And I didn't get married till I was fifty. *(The* WAITRESS *brings the menus.)*

NIJO: Oh, my father was a very religious man. Just before he died he said to me, "Serve His Majesty, be respectful, if you lose his favor enter holy orders."

MARLENE: But he meant stay in a convent, not go wandering round the country.

NIJO: Priests were often vagrants, so why not a nun? You think I shouldn't / I still did what my father wanted.

MARLENE: No no, I think you should. / I think it was wonderful.

*(*DULL GRET *arrives.)*

ISABELLA: I tried to do what my father wanted.

MARLENE: Gret, good. Nijo. Gret / I know Griselda's going to be late, but should we wait for Joan? / Let's get you a drink.

ISABELLA: Hello, Gret! *(She continues to* NIJO.*)* I tried to be a clergyman's daughter. Needlework, music, charitable schemes. I had a tumor removed from my spine and spent a great deal of time on the sofa. I studied the metaphysical poets and hymnology. / I thought I enjoyed intellectual pursuits.

NIJO: Ah, you like poetry. I come of a line of eight generations of poets. Father had a poem / in the anthology.

ISABELLA: My father taught me Latin although I was a girl. / But really I was

MARLENE: They didn't have Latin at my school.

ISABELLA: more suited to manual work. Cooking, washing, mending, riding horses. / Better than reading

NIJO: Oh but I'm sure you're very clever.

ISABELLA: books, eh Gret? A rough life in the open air.

NIJO: I can't say I enjoyed my rough life. What I enjoyed most was being the Emperor's favorite / and wearing thin silk.

ISABELLA: Did you have any horses, Gret?

GRET: Pig.

*(*POPE JOAN *arrives.)*

MARLENE: Oh Joan, thank God, we can order. Do you know everyone? We were just talking about learning Latin and being clever girls. Joan was by way of an infant prodigy. Of course you were. What excited you when you were ten?

JOAN: Because angels are without matter they are not individuals. Every angel is a species.

MARLENE: There you are. *(They laugh. They look at the menus.)*

ISABELLA: Yes, I forgot all my Latin. But my father was the mainspring of my life and when he died I was so grieved. I'll have the chicken, please, / and the soup.

NIJO: Of course you were grieved. My father was saying his prayers and he dozed off in the sun. So I touched his knee to rouse him. "I wonder what will happen," he said, and then he was dead before he finished the sentence. / If he'd

MARLENE: What a shock.

NIJO: died saying his prayers he would have gone straight to heaven. / Waldorf salad.

JOAN: Death is the return of all creatures to God.

NIJO: I shouldn't have woken him.

JOAN: Damnation only means ignorance of the truth. I was always attracted by the teachings of John the Scot, though he was inclined to confuse / God and the world.

ISABELLA: Grief always overwhelmed me at the time.

MARLENE: What I fancy is a rare steak. Gret?

ISABELLA: I am of course a member of the / Church of England.

MARLENE: Gret?

GRET: Potatoes.

MARLENE: I haven't been to church for years. / I like Christmas carols.

ISABELLA: Good works matter more than church attendance.

MARLENE: Make that two steaks and a lot of potatoes. Rare. But I don't do good works either.

JOAN: Canelloni, please, / and a salad.

ISABELLA: Well, I tried, but oh dear. Hennie did good works.

NIJO: The first half of my life was all sin and the second / all repentance.*

MARLENE: Oh what about starters?

GRET: Soup.

JOAN: *And which did you like best?

MARLENE: Were your travels just a penance? Avocado vinaigrette. Didn't you / enjoy yourself?

JOAN: Nothing to start with for me, thank you.

NIJO: Yes, but I was very unhappy. / It hurt to remember the past.

MARLENE: And the wine list.

NIJO: I think that was repentance.

MARLENE: Well I wonder.

NIJO: I might have just been homesick.

MARLENE: Or angry.

NIJO: Not angry, no, / why angry?

GRET: Can we have some more bread?

MARLENE: Don't you get angry? I get angry.

NIJO: But what about?

MARLENE: Yes let's have two more Frascati. And some more bread, please. (*The* WAITRESS *exits.*)

ISABELLA: I tried to understand Buddhism when I was in Japan but all this birth and death succeeding each other through eternities just filled me with the most profound melancholy. I do like something more active.

NIJO: You couldn't say I was inactive. I walked every day for twenty years.

ISABELLA: I don't mean walking. / I mean in the head.

NIJO: I vowed to copy five Mahayana sutras.° / Do you know how long they are?

MARLENE: I don't think religious beliefs are something we have in common. Activity yes. (GRET *empties the bread basket into her apron.*)

Mahayana sutras, Buddhist religious texts.

NIJO: My head was active. / My head ached.

JOAN: It's no good being active in heresy.

ISABELLA: What heresy? She's calling the Church of England / a heresy.

JOAN: There are some very attractive / heresies.

NIJO: I had never heard of Christianity. Never / heard of it. Barbarians.

MARLENE: Well I'm not a Christian. / And I'm not a Buddhist.

ISABELLA: You have heard of it?

MARLENE: We don't all have to believe the same.

ISABELLA: I knew coming to dinner with a Pope we should keep off religion.

JOAN: I always enjoy a theological argument. But I won't try to convert you, I'm not a missionary. Anyway I'm a heresy myself.

ISABELLA: There are some barbaric practices in the east.

NIJO: Barbaric?

ISABELLA: Among the lower classes.

NIJO: I wouldn't know.

ISABELLA: Well theology always made my head ache.

MARLENE: Oh good, some food. (*The* WAITRESS *brings the first course, serves it during the following, then exits.*)

NIJO: How else could I have left the court if I wasn't a nun? When father died I had only His Majesty. So when I fell out of favor I had nothing. Religion is a kind of nothing / and I dedicated what was left of me to nothing.

ISABELLA: That's what I mean about Buddhism. It doesn't brace.

MARLENE: Come on, Nijo, have some wine.

NIJO: Haven't you ever felt like that? You've all felt / like that. Nothing will ever happen again. I am dead already.

ISABELLA: You thought your life was over but it wasn't.

JOAN: You wish it was over.

GRET: Sad.

MARLENE: Yes, when I first came to London I sometimes . . . and when I got back from America I did. But only for a few hours. Not twenty years.

ISABELLA: When I was forty I thought my life was over. / Oh I was pitiful. I was sent

NIJO: I didn't say I felt it for twenty years. Not every minute.

ISABELLA: on a cruise for my health and I felt even worse. Pains in my bones, pins and needles in my hands, swelling behind the ears, and—oh, stupidity. I shook all over, indefinable terror. And Australia seemed to me a hideous country, the acacias stank like drains. / I

NIJO: You were homesick. (GRET *steals a bottle of wine.*)

ISABELLA: had a photograph taken for Hennie but I told her I wouldn't send it, my hair had fallen out and my clothes were crooked, I looked completely insane and suicidal.

NIJO: So did I, exactly, dressed as a nun. / I was wearing walking shoes for the first time.

ISABELLA: I longed to go home, / but home to what? Houses are so perfectly dismal.*

NIJO: I longed to go back ten years.

MARLENE: *I thought traveling cheered you both up.

ISABELLA: Oh it did / of course. It was on

NIJO: I'm not a cheerful person, Marlene. I just laugh a lot.

ISABELLA: the trip from Australia to the Sandwich Isles, I fell in love with the sea. There were rats in the cabin and ants in the food but suddenly it was like a new world. I woke up every morning happy, knowing there would be nothing to annoy me. No nervousness. No dressing.

NIJO: Don't you like getting dressed? I adored my clothes. / When I was chosen

MARLENE: You had prettier colors than Isabella.

NIJO: to give sake to His Majesty's brother, the Emperor Kameyana, on his formal visit, I wore raw silk pleated trousers and a seven-layered gown in shades of red, and two outer garments, / yellow lined with green

MARLENE: Yes, all that silk must have been very— (*The* WAITRESS *enters, clears the first course and exits.*)

JOAN: I dressed as a boy when I left home.*

NIJO: and a light green jacket. Lady Betto had a five-layered gown in shades of green and purple.

ISABELLA: *You dressed as a boy?

MARLENE: Of course, / for safety.

JOAN: It was easy, I was only twelve. / Also women weren't allowed in the library. We wanted to study in Athens.

MARLENE: You ran away alone?

JOAN: No, not alone, I went with my friend. / He was

NIJO: Ah, an elopement.

JOAN: sixteen but I thought I knew more science than he did and almost as much philosophy.

ISABELLA: Well I always traveled as a lady and I repudiated strongly any suggestion in the press that I was other than feminine.

MARLENE: I don't wear trousers in the office. / I could but I don't.

ISABELLA: There was no great danger to a woman of my age and appearance.

MARLENE: And you got away with it, Joan?

JOAN: I did then. (*The* WAITRESS *brings in the main course.*)

MARLENE: And nobody noticed anything?

JOAN: They noticed I was a very clever boy. / And

MARLENE: I couldn't have kept pretending for so long.

JOAN: when I shared a bed with my friend, that was ordinary—two poor students in a lodging house. I think I forgot I was pretending.

ISABELLA: Rocky Mountain Jim, Mr. Nugent, showed me no disrespect. He found it interesting, I think, that I could make scones and also lasso cattle. Indeed he declared his love for me, which was most distressing.

NIJO: What did he say? / We always sent poems first.

MARLENE: What did you say?

ISABELLA: I urged him to give up whiskey, / but he said it was too late.

MARLENE: Oh Isabella.

ISABELLA: He had lived alone in the mountains for many years.

MARLENE: But did you—? (*The* WAITRESS *goes.*)

ISABELLA: Mr. Nugent was a man that any woman might love but none could marry. I came back to England.

NIJO: Did you write him a poem when you left? / Snow on the mountains. My sleeves

MARLENE: Did you never see him again?

ISABELLA: No, never.

NIJO: are wet with tears. In England no tears, no snow.

ISABELLA: Well, I say never. One morning very early in Switzerland, it was a year later, I had a vision of him as I last saw him / in his trapper's clothes with his

NIJO: A ghost!

ISABELLA: hair round his face, and that was the day, / I learned later, he died with a

NIJO: Ah!

ISABELLA: bullet in his brain. / He just bowed to me and vanished.

MARLENE: Oh Isabella.

NIJO: When your lover dies—One of my lovers died. / The priest Ariake.

JOAN: My friend died. Have we all got dead lovers?

MARLENE: Not me, sorry.

NIJO: (*To* ISABELLA) I wasn't a nun, I was still at court, but he was a priest, and when he came to me he dedicated his whole life to hell. / He knew that when he died he would fall into one of the three lower realms. And he died, he did die.

JOAN: (*To* MARLENE) I'd quarreled with him over the teachings of John the Scot,° who held that our ignorance of God is the same as his ignorance of himself. He only knows what he creates because he creates everything he knows but he himself is above being—do you follow?

MARLENE: No, but go on.

NIJO: I couldn't bear to think / in what shape would he be reborn.*

JOAN: St. Augustine maintained that the Neo-Platonic Ideas are indivisible

ISABELLA: *Buddhism is really most uncomfortable.

JOAN: from God, but I agreed with John that the created world is essences derived from Ideas which derived from God. As Denys the Areopagite° said— the pseudo-Denys—first we give God a name, then deny it, / then reconcile the contradiction

---

John the Scot, John Scotus Erigena (c. 810–866), Irish scholastic philosopher. **Denys the Areopagite,** the "pseudo-Denys" is the author of influential Neoplatonic philosophical texts dating from the late fifth or early sixth century.

NIJO: In what shape would he return?

JOAN: by looking beyond / those terms—

MARLENE: Sorry, what? Denys said what?

JOAN: Well we disagreed about it, we quarreled. And next day he was ill, / I was so annoyed with him

NIJO: Misery in this life and worse in the next, all because of me.

JOAN: all the time I was nursing him I kept going over the arguments in my mind. Matter is not a means of knowing the essence. The source of the species is the Idea. But then I realized he'd never understand my arguments again, and that night he died. John the Scot held that the individual disintegrates / and there is no personal immortality.

ISABELLA: I wouldn't have you think I was in love with Jim Nugent. It was yearning to save him that I felt.

MARLENE: (To JOAN) So what did you do?

JOAN: First I decided to stay a man. I was used to it. And I wanted to devote my life to learning. Do you know why I went to Rome? Italian men didn't have beards.

ISABELLA: The loves of my life were Hennie, my own pet, and my dear husband the doctor, who nursed Hennie in her last illness. I knew it would be terrible when Hennie died but I didn't know how terrible. I felt half of myself had gone. How could I go on my travels without that sweet soul waiting at home for my letters? It was Doctor Bishop's devotion to her in her last illness that made me decide to marry him. He and Hennie had the same sweet character. I had not.

NIJO: I thought His Majesty had sweet character because when he found out about Ariake he was so kind. But really it was because he no longer cared for me. One night he even sent me out to a man who had been pursuing me. / He lay awake on the other side of the screens and listened.

ISABELLA: I did wish marriage had seemed more of a step. I tried very hard to cope with the ordinary drudgery of life. I was ill again with carbuncles on the spine and nervous prostration. I ordered a tricycle, that was my idea of adventure then. And John himself fell ill, with erysipelas and anemia. I began to love him with my whole heart but it was too late. He was a skeleton with transparent white hands. I wheeled him on various seafronts in a bathchair. And he faded and left me. There was nothing in my life. The doctors said I had gout / and my heart was much affected.

NIJO: There was nothing in my life, nothing, without the Emperor's favor. The Empress had always been my enemy, Marlene, she said I had no right to wear three-layered gowns. / But I was the adopted daughter of my grandfather the Prime Minister. I had been publicly granted permission to wear thin silk.

JOAN: There was nothing in my life except my studies. I was obsessed with pursuit of the truth. I taught

at the Greek School in Rome, which St. Augustine had made famous. I was poor, I worked hard, I spoke apparently brilliantly, I was still very young, I was a stranger, suddenly I was quite famous, I was everyone's favorite. Huge crowds came to hear me. The day after they made me cardinal I fell ill and lay two weeks without speaking, full of terror and regret. / But then I got up determined to

MARLENE: Yes, success is very . . .

JOAN: go on. I was seized again / with a desperate longing for the absolute.

ISABELLA: Yes, yes, to go on. I sat in Tobermory among Hennie's flowers and sewed a complete outfit in Jaeger flannel. / I was fifty-six years old.

NIJO: Out of favor but I didn't die. I left on foot, nobody saw me go. For the next twenty years I walked through Japan.

GRET: Walking is good. (*Meanwhile, the* WAITRESS *enters, pours lots of wine, then shows* MARLENE *the empty bottle.*)

JOAN: Pope Leo died and I was chosen. All right then. I would be Pope. I would know God. I would know everything.

ISABELLA: I determined to leave my grief behind and set off for Tibet.

MARLENE: Magnificent all of you. We need some more wine, please, two bottles I think, Griselda isn't even here yet, and I want to drink a toast to you all. (*The* WAITRESS *exits.*)

ISABELLA: To yourself surely, / we're here to celebrate your success.

NIJO: Yes, Marlene.

JOAN: Yes, what is it exactly, Marlene?

MARLENE: Well it's not Pope but it is managing director.*

JOAN: And you find work for people.

MARLENE: Yes, an employment agency.

NIJO: *Over all the women you work with. And the men.

ISABELLA: And very well deserved too. I'm sure it's just the beginning of something extraordinary.

MARLENE: Well it's worth a party.

ISABELLA: To Marlene.*

MARLENE: And all of us.

JOAN: *Marlene.

NIJO: Marlene.

GRET: Marlene.

MARLENE: We've all come a long way. To our courage and the way we changed our lives and our extraordinary achievements. (*They laugh and drink a toast.*)

ISABELLA: Such adventures. We were crossing a mountain pass at seven thousand feet, the cook was all to pieces, the muleteers suffered fever and snow blindness. But even though my spine was agony I managed very well.*

MARLENE: Wonderful.

NIJO: *Once I was ill for four months lying alone at an inn. Nobody to offer a horse to Buddha. I had to live for myself, and I did live.

ISABELLA: Of course you did. It was far worse returning

to Tobermory. I always felt dull when I was stationary. / That's why I could never stay anywhere.

NIJO: Yes, that's it exactly. New sights. The shrine by the beach, the moon shining on the sea. The goddess had vowed to save all living things. / She would even save the fishes. I was full of hope.

JOAN: I had thought the Pope would know everything. I thought God would speak to me directly. But of course he knew I was a woman.

MARLENE: But nobody else even suspected? (*The WAITRESS brings more wine and then exits.*)

JOAN: In the end I did take a lover again.*

ISABELLA: In the Vatican?

GRET: *Keep you warm.

NIJO: *Ah, lover.

MARLENE: *Good for you.

JOAN: He was one of my chamberlains. There are such a lot of servants when you're Pope. The food's very good. And I realized I did know the truth. Because whatever the Pope says, that's true.

NIJO: What was he like, the chamberlain?*

GRET: Big cock.

ISABELLA: Oh, Gret.

MARLENE: *Did he fancy you when he thought you were a fella?

NIJO: What was he like?

JOAN: He could keep a secret.

MARLENE: So you did know everything.

JOAN: Yes, I enjoyed being Pope. I consecrated bishops and let people kiss my feet. I received the King of England when he came to submit to the church. Unfortunately there were earthquakes, and some village reported it had rained blood, and in France there was a plague of giant grasshoppers, but I don't think that can have been my fault, do you?* (*Laughter.*) The grasshoppers fell on the English Channel / and were washed up on shore

NIJO: I once went to sea. It was very lonely. I realized it made very little difference where I went.

JOAN: and their bodies rotted and poisoned the air and everyone in those parts died. (*Laughter.*)

ISABELLA: *Such superstition! I was nearly murdered in China by a howling mob. They thought the barbarians ate babies and put them under railway sleepers to make the tracks steady, and ground up their eyes to make the lenses of cameras. / So they were shouting,

MARLENE: And you had a camera!

ISABELLA: "Child-eater, child-eater." Some people tried to sell girl babies to Europeans for cameras or stew! (*Laughter.*)

MARLENE: So apart from the grasshoppers it was a great success.

JOAN: Yes, if it hadn't been for the baby I expect I'd have lived to an old age like Theodora of Alexandria, who lived as a monk. She was accused by a girl / who fell in love with her of being the father of her child and—

NIJO: But tell us what happened to your baby. I had some babies.

MARLENE: Didn't you think of getting rid of it?

JOAN: Wouldn't that be a worse sin than having it? / But a Pope with a child was about as bad as possible.

MARLENE: I don't know, you're the Pope.

JOAN: But I wouldn't have known how to get rid of it.

MARLENE: Other Popes had children, surely.

JOAN: They didn't give birth to them.

NIJO: Well you were a woman.

JOAN: Exactly and I shouldn't have been a woman. Women, children, and lunatics can't be Pope.

MARLENE: So the only thing to do / was to get rid of it somehow.

NIJO: You had to have it adopted secretly.

JOAN: But I didn't know what was happening. I thought I was getting fatter, but then I was eating more and sitting about, the life of a Pope is quite luxurious. I don't think I'd spoken to a woman since I was twelve. The chamberlain was the one who realized.

MARLENE: And by then it was too late.

JOAN: Oh I didn't want to pay attention. It was easier to do nothing.

NIJO: But you had to plan for having it. You had to say you were ill and go away.

JOAN: That's what I should have done I suppose.

MARLENE: Did you want them to find out?

NIJO: I too was often in embarrassing situations, there's no need for a scandal. My first child was His Majesty's, which unfortunately died, but my second was Akebono's. I was seventeen. He was in love with me when I was thirteen, he was very upset when I had to go to the Emperor, it was very romantic, a lot of poems. Now His Majesty hadn't been near me for two months so he thought I was four months pregnant when I was really six, so when I reached the ninth month / I announced I was seriously ill,

JOAN: I never knew what month it was.

NIJO: and Akebono announced he had gone on a religious retreat. He held me round the waist and lifted me up as the baby was born. He cut the cord with a short sword, wrapped the baby in white and took it away. It was only a girl but I was sorry to lose it. Then I told the Emperor that the baby had miscarried because of my illness, and there you are. The danger was past.

JOAN: But, Nijo, I wasn't used to having a woman's body.

ISABELLA: So what happened?

JOAN: I didn't know of course that it was near the time. It was Rogation Day,° there was always a procession. I was on the horse dressed in my robes and a cross was carried in front of me, and all the cardinals

---

Rogation Day, day set aside for solemn procession to invoke God's mercy; the major Rogation Day was April 25.

were following, and all the clergy of Rome, and a huge crowd of people. / We set off from St. Peter's° to go

MARLENE: Total Pope. (GRET *pours the wine and steals the bottle.*)

JOAN: to St. John's.° I had felt a slight pain earlier, I thought it was something I'd eaten, and then it came back, and came back more often. I thought when this is over I'll go to bed. There were still long gaps when I felt perfectly all right and I didn't want to attract attention to myself and spoil the ceremony. Then I suddenly realized what it must be. I had to last out till I could get home and hide. Then something changed, my breath started to catch. I couldn't plan things properly anymore. We were in a little street that goes between St. Clement's° and the Colosseum, and I just had to get off the horse and sit down for a minute. Great waves of pressure were going through my body, I heard sounds like a cow lowing, they came out of my mouth. Far away I heard people screaming, "The Pope is ill, the Pope is dying." And the baby just slid out on to the road.*

MARLENE: The cardinals / won't have known where to put themselves.

NIJO: Oh dear, Joan, what a thing to do! In the street!

ISABELLA: *How embarrassing.

GRET: In a field, yah. (*They are laughing.*)

JOAN: One of the cardinals said, "The Antichrist!" and fell over in a faint. (*They all laugh.*)

MARLENE: So what did they do? They weren't best pleased.

JOAN: They took me by the feet and dragged me out of town and stoned me to death. (*They stop laughing.*)

MARLENE: Joan, how horrible.

JOAN: I don't really remember.

NIJO: And the child died too?

JOAN: Oh yes, I think so, yes. (*The* WAITRESS *enters to clear the plates. Pause. They start talking very quietly.*)

ISABELLA: (*To* JOAN) I never had any children. I was very fond of horses.

NIJO: (*To* MARLENE) I saw my daughter once. She was three years old. She wore a plum-red / small sleeved gown. Akebono's wife

ISABELLA: Birdie was my favorite. A little Indian bay mare I rode in the Rocky Mountains.

NIJO: had taken the child because her own died. Everyone thought I was just a visitor. She was being brought up carefully so she could be sent to the palace like I was. (GRET *steals her empty plate.*)

ISABELLA: Legs of iron and always cheerful, and such a pretty face. If a stranger led her she reared up like a bronco.

NIJO: I never saw my third child after he was born, the son of Ariake the priest. Ariake held him on his lap the day he was born and talked to him as if he could understand, and cried. My fourth child was Ariake's too. Ariake died before he was born. I didn't want to see anyone, I stayed alone in the hills. It was a boy again, my third son. But oddly enough I felt nothing for him.

MARLENE: How many children did you have, Gret?

GRET: Ten.

ISABELLA: Whenever I came back to England I felt I had so much to atone for. Hennie and John were so good. I did no good in my life. I spent years in self-gratification. So I hurled myself into committees, I nursed the people of Tobermory in the epidemic of influenza, I lectured the Young Women's Christian Association on Thrift. I talked and talked explaining how the East was corrupt and vicious. My travels must do good to someone besides myself. I wore myself out with good causes.

MARLENE: (*Pause*) Oh god, why are we all so miserable?

JOAN: (*Pause*) The procession never went down that street again.

MARLENE: They rerouted it specially?

JOAN: Yes they had to go all round to avoid it. And they introduced a pierced chair.

MARLENE: A pierced chair?

JOAN: Yes, a chair made out of solid marble with a hole in the seat / and it was

MARLENE: You're not serious.

JOAN: in the Chapel of the Savior, and after he was elected the Pope had to sit in it.

MARLENE: And someone looked up his skirts? / Not really!

ISABELLA: What an extraordinary thing.

JOAN: Two of the clergy / made sure he was a man.

NIJO: On their hands and knees!

MARLENE: A pierced chair!

GRET: Balls!

(GRISELDA *arrives unnoticed.*)

NIJO: Why couldn't he just pull up his robe?

JOAN: He had to sit there and look dignified.

MARLENE: You could have made all your chamberlains sit in it.*

GRET: Big one. Small one.

NIJO: Very useful chair at court.

ISABELLA: *Or the Laird of Tobermory in his kilt.

(*They are quite drunk. They get the giggles.* MARLENE *notices* GRISELDA *and gets up to welcome her. The others go on talking and laughing.* GRET *crosses to* JOAN *and* ISABELLA *and pours them wine from her stolen bottles. The* WAITRESS *gives out the menus.*)

MARLENE: Griselda! / There you are. Do you want to eat?

GRISELDA: I'm sorry I'm so late. No, no, don't bother.

MARLENE: Of course it's no bother. / Have you eaten?

St. Peter's, St. John's, major churches in Rome. **St. Clement's,** church in Rome.

GRISELDA: No really, I'm not hungry.

MARLENE: Well have some pudding.

GRISELDA: I never eat pudding.

MARLENE: Griselda, I hope you're not anorexic. We're having pudding, I am, and getting nice and fat.

GRISELDA: Oh if everyone is. I don't mind.

MARLENE: Now who do you know? This is Joan who was Pope in the ninth century, and Isabella Bird, the Victorian traveler, and Lady Nijo from Japan, Emperor's concubine and Buddhist nun, thirteenth century, nearer your own time, and Gret who was painted by Brueghel. Griselda's in Boccaccio and Petrarch and Chaucer because of her extraordinary marriage. I'd like profiteroles because they're disgusting.

JOAN: Zabaglione,° please.

ISABELLA: Apple pie / and cream.

NIJO: What's this?

MARLENE: Zabaglione, it's Italian, it's what Joan's having, / it's delicious.

NIJO: A Roman Catholic / dessert? Yes please.

MARLENE: Gret?

GRET: Cake.

GRISELDA: Just cheese and biscuits, thank you. (*The* WAITRESS *exits.*)

MARLENE: Yes, Griselda's life is like a fairy story, except it starts with marrying the prince.

GRISELDA: He's only a marquis, Marlene.

MARLENE: Well everyone for miles around is his liege and he's absolute lord of life and death and you were the poor but beautiful peasant girl and he whisked you off. / Near enough a prince.

NIJO: How old were you?

GRISELDA: Fifteen.

NIJO: I was brought up in court circles and it was still a shock. Had you ever seen him before?

GRISELDA: I'd seen him riding by, we all had. And he'd seen me in the fields with the sheep.*

ISABELLA: I would have been well suited to minding sheep.

NIJO: And Mr. Nugent riding by.

ISABELLA: Of course not, Nijo, I mean a healthy life in the open air.

JOAN: *He just rode up while you were minding the sheep and asked you to marry him?

GRISELDA: No, no, it was on the wedding day. I was waiting outside the door to see the procession. Everyone wanted him to get married so there'd be an heir to look after us when he died, / and at last he

MARLENE: I don't think Walter wanted to get married. It is Walter? Yes.

GRISELDA: announced a day for the wedding but nobody knew who the bride was, we thought it must

be a foreign princess, we were longing to see her. Then the carriage stopped outside our cottage and we couldn't see the bride anywhere. And he came and spoke to my father.

NIJO: And your father told you to serve the Prince.

GRISELDA: My father could hardly speak. The Marquis said it wasn't an order, I could say no, but if I said yes I must always obey him in everything.

MARLENE: That's when you should have suspected.

GRISELDA: But of course a wife must obey her husband. / And of course I must obey the Marquis.*

ISABELLA: I swore to obey dear John, of course, but it didn't seem to arise. Naturally I wouldn't have wanted to go abroad while I was married.

MARLENE: *Then why bother to mention it at all? He'd got a thing about it, that's why.

GRISELDA: I'd rather obey the Marquis than a boy from the village.

MARLENE: Yes, that's a point.

JOAN: I never obeyed anyone. They all obeyed me.

NIJO: And what did you wear? He didn't make you get married in your own clothes? That would be perverse.*

MARLENE: Oh, you wait.

GRISELDA: *He had ladies with him who undressed me and they had a white silk dress and jewels for my hair.

MARLENE: And at first he seemed perfectly normal?

GRISELDA: Marlene, you're always so critical of him. / Of course he was normal, he was very kind.

MARLENE: But, Griselda, come on, he took your baby.

GRISELDA: Walter found it hard to believe I loved him. He couldn't believe I would always obey him. He had to prove it.

MARLENE: I don't think Walter likes women.

GRISELDA: I'm sure he loved me, Marlene, all the time.

MARLENE: He just had a funny way / of showing it.

GRISELDA: It was hard for him too.

JOAN: How do you mean he took away your baby?

NIJO: Was it a boy?

GRISELDA: No, the first one was a girl.

NIJO: Even so it's hard when they take it away. Did you see it at all?

GRISELDA: Oh yes, she was six weeks old.

NIJO: Much better to do it straight away.

ISABELLA: But why did your husband take the child?

GRISELDA: He said all the people hated me because I was just one of them. And now I had a child they were restless. So he had to get rid of the child to keep them quiet. But he said he wouldn't snatch her, I had to agree and obey and give her up. So when I was feeding her a man came in and took her away. I thought he was going to kill her even before he was out of the room.

MARLENE: But you let him take her? You didn't struggle?

GRISELDA: I asked him to give her back so I could kiss her. And I asked him to bury her where no animals

---

Zabaglione, frothy dessert of beaten eggs, sugar, wine.

could dig her up. / It was Walter's child to do what he

ISABELLA: Oh, my dear.

GRISELDA: liked with.*

MARLENE: Walter was bonkers.°

GRET: Bastard.

ISABELLA: *But surely, murder.

GRISELDA: I had promised.

MARLENE: I can't stand this. I'm going for a pee.

(MARLENE *goes out. The* WAITRESS *brings the dessert, serves it during the following, then exits.*)

NIJO: No, I understand. Of course you had to, he was your life. And were you in favor after that?

GRISELDA: Oh yes, we were very happy together. We never spoke about what had happened.

ISABELLA: I can see you were doing what you thought was your duty. But didn't it make you ill?

GRISELDA: No, I was very well, thank you.

NIJO: And you had another child?

GRISELDA: Not for four years, but then I did, yes, a boy.

NIJO: Ah a boy. / So it all ended happily.

GRISELDA: Yes he was pleased. I kept my son till he was two years old. A peasant's grandson. It made the people angry. Walter explained.

ISABELLA: But surely he wouldn't kill his children / just because—

GRISELDA: Oh it wasn't true. Walter would never give in to the people. He wanted to see if I loved him enough.

JOAN: He killed his children / to see if you loved him enough?

NIJO: Was it easier the second time or harder?

GRISELDA: It was always easy because I always knew I would do what he said. (*Pause. They start to eat.*)

ISABELLA: I hope you didn't have any more children.

GRISELDA: Oh no, no more. It was twelve years till he tested me again.

ISABELLA: So whatever did he do this time? / My poor John, I never loved him enough, and he would never have dreamt . . .

GRISELDA: He sent me away. He said the people wanted him to marry someone else who'd give him an heir and he'd got special permission from the Pope. So I said I'd go home to my father. I came with nothing / so I went with nothing. I took

NIJO: Better to leave if your master doesn't want you.

GRISELDA: off my clothes. He let me keep a slip so he wouldn't be shamed. And I walked home barefoot. My father came out in tears. Everyone was crying except me.

NIJO: At least your father wasn't dead. / I had nobody.

ISABELLA: Well it can be a relief to come home. I loved to see Hennie's sweet face again.

GRISELDA: Oh yes, I was perfectly content. And quite soon he sent for me again.

JOAN: I don't think I would have gone.

GRISELDA: But he told me to come. I had to obey him. He wanted me to help prepare his wedding. He was getting married to a young girl from France / and nobody except me knew how to arrange things the way he liked them.

NIJO: It's always hard taking him another woman. (MARLENE *comes back.*)

JOAN: I didn't live a woman's life. I don't understand it.

GRISELDA: The girl was sixteen and far more beautiful than me. I could see why he loved her. / She had her younger brother with her as a page. (*The* WAITRESS *enters.*)

MARLENE: Oh God, I can't bear it. I want some coffee. Six coffees. Six brandies. / Double brandies. Straightaway. (*The* WAITRESS *exits.*)

GRISELDA: They all went into the feast I'd prepared. And he stayed behind and put his arms round me and kissed me. / I felt half asleep with the shock.

NIJO: Oh, like a dream.

MARLENE: And he said, "This is your daughter and your son."

GRISELDA: Yes.

JOAN: What?

NIJO: Oh. Oh I see. You got them back.

ISABELLA: I did think it was remarkably barbaric to kill them but you learn not to say anything. / So he had them brought up secretly I suppose.

MARLENE: Walter's a monster. Weren't you angry? What did you do?

GRISELDA: Well I fainted. Then I cried and kissed the children. / Everyone was making a fuss of me.

NIJO: But did you feel anything for them?

GRISELDA: What?

NIJO: Did you feel anything for the children?

GRISELDA: Of course, I loved them.

JOAN: So you forgave him and lived with him?

GRISELDA: He suffered so much all those years.

ISABELLA: Hennie had the same sweet nature.

NIJO: So they dressed you again?

GRISELDA: Cloth of gold.

JOAN: I can't forgive anything.

MARLENE: You really are exceptional, Griselda.

NIJO: Nobody gave me back my children. (*She cries.*)

(*The* WAITRESS *brings the brandies and then exits. During the following,* JOAN *goes to* NIJO.)

ISABELLA: I can never be like Hennie. I was always so busy in England, a kind of business I detested. The very presence of people exhausted my emotional reserves. I could not be like Hennie however I tried. I tried and was as ill as could be. The doctor suggested a steel net to support my head, the weight of my own head was too much for my diseased spine. It is dangerous to put oneself in depressing circumstances. Why should I do it?

---

bonkers, crazy.

JOAN: (*To* NIJO) Don't cry.

NIJO: My father and the Emperor both died in the autumn. So much pain.

JOAN: Yes, but don't cry.

NIJO: They wouldn't let me into the palace when he was dying. I hid in the room with his coffin, then I couldn't find where I'd left my shoes, I ran after the funeral procession in bare feet, I couldn't keep up. When I got there it was over, a few wisps of smoke in the sky, that's all that was left of him. What I want to know is, if I'd still been at court, would I have been allowed to wear full mourning?

MARLENE: I'm sure you would.

NIJO: Why do you say that? You don't know anything about it. Would I have been allowed to wear full mourning?

ISABELLA: How can people live in this dim pale island and wear our hideous clothes? I cannot and will not live the life of a lady.

NIJO: I'll tell you something that made me angry. I was eighteen, at the Full Moon Ceremony. They make a special rice gruel and stir it with their sticks, and then they beat their women across the loins so they'll have sons and not daughters. So the Emperor beat us all / very hard as

MARLENE: What a sod. (*The* WAITRESS *enters with the coffees.*)

NIJO: usual—that's not it, Marlene, that's normal, what made us angry he told his attendants they could beat us too. Well they had a wonderful time. / So Lady Genki and I made a plan, and the ladies

MARLENE: I'd like another brandy, please. Better make it six. (*The* WAITRESS *exits.*)

NIJO: all hid in his rooms, and Lady Mashimizu stood guard with a stick at the door, and when His Majesty came in Genki seized him and I beat him till he cried out and promised he would never order anyone to hit us again. Afterward there was a terrible fuss. The nobles were horrified. "We wouldn't even dream of stepping on Your Majesty's shadow." And I had hit him with a stick. Yes, I hit him with a stick.

(*The* WAITRESS *brings the brandy bottle and tops up the glasses.* JOAN *crosses in front of the table and back to her place while drunkenly reciting:*)

JOAN:

Suave, mari magno turantibus aequora ventis,
e terra magnum alterius spectare laborem;
non quia vexari quemquamst iucunda voluptas,
sed quibus ipse malis careas quia cernere suave est.
Suave etiam belli certamina magna tueri
per campos instructa tua sine parte pericli.
Sed nil dulcius est, bene quam munita tenere
edita doctrina sapientum templa serena, /

despicere unde queas alios passimque videre
errare atque viam palantis quaerere vitae,°

GRISELDA: I do think—I do wonder—it would have been nicer if Walter hadn't had to.

ISABELLA: Why should I? Why should I?

MARLENE: Of course not.

NIJO: I hit him with a stick.

JOAN:

certare ingenio, contendere nobilitate,
noctes atque dies niti praestante labore
ad summas emergere opes rerumque potiri.
O miseras hominum mentis, / o pectora caeca!°

ISABELLA: O miseras!

NIJO: *Pectora caeca!

JOAN:

qualibus in tenebris vitae quantisque periclis
degitur hoc aevi quodcumquest! / nonne videre
nil aliud sibi naturam latrare, nisi utqui
corpore seiunctus dolor absit, mente fruatur° . . .
(*She subsides.*)

GRET: We come to hell through a big mouth. Hell's black and red. / It's

MARLENE: (*To* JOAN) Shut up, pet.

GRISELDA: Hush, please.

Suave, . . . quaerere vitae, This passage opens the second book of the long poem, *De Rerum Natura* (*On the Nature of Things*) by the Roman stoic philosopher Lucretius (97?–54 BCE). The speaker begins by contrasting the privilege of calm observation with the turmoil of dangerous involvement. Translation by Rolfe Humphries. "How sweet it is, when whirlwinds roil great ocean, / To watch, from land, the danger of another, / Not that to see some other person suffer / Brings great enjoyment, but the sweetness lies / In watching evils you yourself are free from. / How sweet, again, to see the clash of battle / Across the plains, yourself immune to danger. / But nothing is more sweet than full possession / Of those calm heights, well built, well fortified / By wise men's teaching, to look down from here / At others wandering below, men lost, / Confused, in hectic search for the right road." ***certare . . . caeca!*** Lucretius continues: "The strife of wits, the wars for precedence / The everlasting struggle, night and day, / To win towards heights of wealth and power. O wretched, / O wretched minds of men! / O hearts in darkness!" ***qualibus . . . mente fruatur . . . ,*** "Under what shadows and among what dangers / Your lives are spent, such as they are. But look— / Your nature snarls, yaps, barks for nothing, really, / Except that pain be absent from the body / And mind enjoy delight. . . ."

ISABELLA: Listen, she's been to hell.

GRET: like the village where I come from. There's a river and a bridge and houses. There's places on fire like when the soldiers come. There's a big devil sat on a roof with a big hole in his arse and he's scooping stuff out of it with a big ladle and it's falling down on us, and it's money, so a lot of the women stop and get some. But most of us is fighting the devils. There's lots of little devils, our size, and we get them down all right and give them a beating. There's lots of funny creatures round your feet, you don't like to look, like rats and lizards, and nasty things, a bum° with a face, and fish with legs, and faces on things that don't have faces on. But they don't hurt, you just keep going. Well we'd had worse, you see, we'd had the Spanish. We'd all had family killed. My big son die on a wheel. Birds eat him. My baby, a soldier run her through with a sword. I'd had enough, I was mad, I hate the bastards. I come out of my front door that morning and shout till my neighbors come out and I said, "Come on, we're going where the evil come from and pay the bastards out." And they all come out just as they was / from baking or

NIJO: All the ladies come.

GRET: washing in their aprons, and we push down the street and the ground opens up and we go through a big mouth into a street just like ours but in hell. I've got a sword in my hand from somewhere and I fill a basket with gold cups they drink out of down there. You just keep running on and fighting, / you didn't stop for nothing. Oh we give them devils such a beating.*

NIJO: Take that, take that.

JOAN:

Something something something mortisque timores
tum vacuum pectus—damn.
Quod si ridicula—
something something on and on and on
and something splendorem purpureai.°

ISABELLA: I thought I would have a last jaunt up the west river in China. Why not? But the doctors were so very grave I just went to Morocco. The sea was so wild I had to be landed by ship's crane in a coal bucket. / My horse was a terror to me, a powerful black charger.

GRET: Coal bucket good.

JOAN:

nos in luce timemus
something
terrorem°

(NIJO *is laughing and crying.* JOAN *gets up and is sick.* GRISELDA *looks after her.*)

GRISELDA: Can I have some water, please? (*The* WAITRESS *exits.*)

ISABELLA: So off I went to visit the Berber sheikhs in full blue trousers and great brass spurs. I was the only European woman ever to have seen the Emperor of Morocco. I was (*The* WAITRESS *brings the water*) seventy years old. What lengths to go to for a last chance of joy. I knew my return of vigor was only temporary, but how marvelous while it lasted.

ACT 1 / SCENE 2

(*"Top Girls" Employment Agency. Monday morning. The lights come up on* MARLENE *and* JEANINE.)

MARLENE: Right, Jeanine, you are Jeanine aren't you? Let's have a look. O's and A's.° / No A's, all those

JEANINE: Six O's.

MARLENE: O's you probably could have got an A. / Speeds, not brilliant, not too bad.

JEANINE: I wanted to go to work.

MARLENE: Well, Jeanine, what's your present job like?

JEANINE: I'm a secretary.

MARLENE: Secretary or typist?

JEANINE: I did start as a typist but the last six months I've been a secretary.

MARLENE: To?

JEANINE: To three of them, really, they share me.

---

bum, buttocks. ***Something . . . splendorem purpureai,*** Joan is still quoting from Lucretius, this time in fragments. The passage she is attempting to remember is this: "And does all this frighten religious terror / In panic from your heart? does the great fear / Of death depart, and leave you comforted? / What vanity, what nonsense! If men's fears, / Anxieties, pursuing horrors, move, / Indifferent to any clash of arms, / Untroubled among lords and monarchs, bow / Before no gleam of gold, no crimson robe [*splendorem purpureai*], / Why do you hesitate, why doubt that reason / Alone has absolute power?"

nos in luce . . . terrorem, The passage Joan is trying to remember ends with an appeal to reason, though she gets only to the notion of "terrors": "As children tremble and fear everything / In their dark shadows, we, in the full light, / Fear things that really are not one bit more awful / Than what poor babies shudder at in darkness, / The horrors they imagine to be coming. / Our terrors and our darknesses of mind / Must be dispelled, then, not by sunshine's rays, / . . . / But by insight into nature, and a scheme / Of systematic contemplation." ***O's and A's,*** standardized exams in the British educational system. O-levels (Ordinary) are usually taken at sixteen and A-levels (Advanced) are usually taken at eighteen.

There's Mr. Ashford, he's the office manager, and Mr. Philby / is sales, and—

MARLENE: Quite a small place?

JEANINE: A bit small.

MARLENE: Friendly?

JEANINE: Oh it's friendly enough.

MARLENE: Prospects?

JEANINE: I don't think so, that's the trouble. Miss Lewis is secretary to the managing director and she's been there forever, and Mrs. Bradford / is—

MARLENE: So you want a job with better prospects?

JEANINE: I want a change.

MARLENE: So you'll take anything comparable?

JEANINE: No, I do want prospects. I want more money.

MARLENE: You're getting—?

JEANINE: Hundred.

MARLENE: It's not bad you know. You're what? Twenty?

JEANINE: I'm saving to get married.

MARLENE: Does that mean you don't want a long-term job, Jeanine?

JEANINE: I might do.

MARLENE: Because where do the prospects come in? No kids for a bit?

JEANINE: Oh no, not kids, not yet.

MARLENE: So you won't tell them you're getting married?

JEANINE: Had I better not?

MARLENE: It would probably help.

JEANINE: I'm not wearing a ring. We thought we wouldn't spend on a ring.

MARLENE: Saves taking it off.

JEANINE: I wouldn't take it off.

MARLENE: There's no need to mention it when you go for an interview. / Now, Jeanine, do you have a feel

JEANINE: But what if they ask?

MARLENE: for any particular kind of company?

JEANINE: I thought advertising.

MARLENE: People often do think advertising. I have got a few vacancies but I think they're looking for something glossier.

JEANINE: You mean how I dress? / I can

MARLENE: I mean experience.

JEANINE: dress different. I dress like this on purpose for where I am now.

MARLENE: I have a marketing department here of a knitwear manufacturer. / Marketing is near enough

JEANINE: Knitwear?

MARLENE: advertising. Secretary to the marketing manager, he's thirty-five, married, I've sent him a girl before and she was happy, left to have a baby, you won't want to mention marriage there. He's very fair I think, good at his job, you won't have to nurse him along. Hundred and ten, so that's better than you're doing now.

JEANINE: I don't know.

MARLENE: I've a fairly small concern here, father and two sons, you'd have more say potentially, secretarial and reception duties, only a hundred but the job's going to grow with the concern and then you'll be in at the top with new girls coming in underneath you.

JEANINE: What is it they do?

MARLENE: Lampshades. / This would be my first choice for you.

JEANINE: Just lampshades?

MARLENE: There's plenty of different kinds of lampshade. So we'll send you there, shall we, and the knitwear second choice. Are you free to go for an interview any day they call you?

JEANINE: I'd like to travel.

MARLENE: We don't have any foreign clients. You'd have to go elsewhere.

JEANINE: Yes I know. I don't really . . . I just mean . . .

MARLENE: Does your fiancé want to travel?

JEANINE: I'd like a job where I was here in London and with him and everything but now and then—I expect it's silly. Are there jobs like that?

MARLENE: There's personal assistant to a top executive in a multinational. If that's the idea you need to be planning ahead. Is that where you want to be in ten years?

JEANINE: I might not be alive in ten years.

MARLENE: Yes but you will be. You'll have children.

JEANINE: I can't think about ten years.

MARLENE: You haven't got the speeds anyway. So I'll send you to these two shall I? You haven't been to any other agency? Just so we don't get crossed wires. Now, Jeanine, I want you to get one of these jobs, all right? If I send you that means I'm putting myself on the line for you. Your presentation's OK, you look fine, just be confident and go in there convinced that this is the best job for you and you're the best person for the job. If you don't believe it they won't believe it.

JEANINE: Do you believe it?

MARLENE: I think you could make me believe it if you put your mind to it.

JEANINE: Yes, all right.

ACT 1 / SCENE 3

(JOYCE's *back yard. Sunday afternoon. The house with a back door is upstage. Downstage is a shelter made of junk, made by children. The lights come up on two girls,* ANGIE *and* KIT, *who are squashed together in the shelter.* ANGIE *is sixteen,* KIT *is twelve. They cannot be seen from the house.*)

JOYCE: (*Off, calling from the house*) Angie. Angie, are you out there?

(*Silence. They keep still and wait. When nothing else happens they relax.*)

ANGIE: Wish she was dead.

KIT: Wanna watch *The Exterminator*?

ANGIE: You're sitting on my leg.

KIT: There's nothing on telly. We can have an ice cream. Angie?

ANGIE: Shall I tell you something?

KIT: Do you wanna watch *The Exterminator*?

ANGIE: It's X, innit?

KIT: I can get into Xs.

ANGIE: Shall I tell you something?

KIT: We'll go to something else. We'll go to Ipswich. What's on the Odeon?°

ANGIE: She won't let me, will she?

KIT: Don't tell her.

ANGIE: I've no money.

KIT: I'll pay.

ANGIE: She'll moan though, won't she?

KIT: I'll ask her for you if you like.

ANGIE: I've no money, I don't want you to pay.

KIT: I'll ask her.

ANGIE: She don't like you.

KIT: I still got three pounds birthday money. Did she say she don't like me? I'll go by myself then.

ANGIE: Your mum don't let you. I got to take you.

KIT: She won't know.

ANGIE: You'd be scared who'd sit next to you.

KIT: No I wouldn't. She does like me anyway. Tell me then.

ANGIE: Tell you what?

KIT: It's you she doesn't like.

ANGIE: Well I don't like her so tough shit.

JOYCE: (*Off*) Angie. Angie. Angie. I know you're out there. I'm not coming out after you. You come in here. (*Silence. Nothing happens.*)

ANGIE: Last night when I was in bed. I been thinking yesterday could I make things move. You know, make things move by thinking about them without touching them. Last night I was in bed and suddenly a picture fell down off the wall.

KIT: What picture?

ANGIE: My gran, that picture. Not the poster. The photograph in the frame.

KIT: Had you done something to make it fall down?

ANGIE: I must have done.

KIT: But were you thinking about it?

ANGIE: Not about it, but about something.

KIT: I don't think that's very good.

ANGIE: You know the kitten?

KIT: Which one?

ANGIE: There only is one. The dead one.

KIT: What about it?

ANGIE: I heard it last night.

KIT: Where?

ANGIE: Out here. In the dark. What if I left you here in the dark all night?

KIT: You couldn't. I'd go home.

ANGIE: You couldn't.

KIT: I'd / go home.

ANGIE: No you couldn't, not if I said.

KIT: I could.

ANGIE: Then you wouldn't see anything. You'd just be ignorant.

KIT: I can see in the daytime.

ANGIE: No you can't. You can't hear it in the daytime.

KIT: I don't want to hear it.

ANGIE: You're scared that's all.

KIT: I'm not scared of anything.

ANGIE: You're scared of blood.

KIT: It's not the same kitten anyway. You just heard an old cat, / you just heard some old cat.

ANGIE: You don't know what I heard. Or what I saw. You don't know nothing because you're a baby.

KIT: You're sitting on me.

ANGIE: Mind my hair / you silly cunt.

KIT: Stupid fucking cow, I hate you.

ANGIE: I don't care if you do.

KIT: You're horrible.

ANGIE: I'm going to kill my mother and you're going to watch.

KIT: I'm not playing.

ANGIE: You're scared of blood. (KIT *puts her hand under dress, brings it out with blood on her finger.*)

KIT: There, see, I got my own blood, so. (ANGIE *takes* KIT's *hand and licks her finger.*)

ANGIE: Now I'm a cannibal. I might turn into a vampire now.

KIT: That picture wasn't nailed up right.

ANGIE: You'll have to do that when I get mine.

KIT: I don't have to.

ANGIE: You're scared.

KIT: I'll do it, I might do it. I don't have to just because you say. I'll be sick on you.

ANGIE: I don't care if you are sick on me, I don't mind sick. I don't mind blood. If I don't get away from here I'm going to die.

KIT: I'm going home.

ANGIE: You can't go through the house. She'll see you.

KIT: I won't tell her.

ANGIE: Oh great, fine.

KIT: I'll say I was by myself. I'll tell her you're at my house and I'm going there to get you.

ANGIE: She knows I'm here, stupid.

KIT: Then why can't I go through the house?

ANGIE: Because I said not.

KIT: My mum don't like you anyway.

ANGIE: I don't want her to like me. She's a slag.°

KIT: She is not.

ANGIE: She does it with everyone.

KIT: She does not.

ANGIE: You don't even know what it is.

KIT: Yes I do.

Odeon, popular chain of cinemas.

slag, slut.

ANGIE: Tell me then.

KIT: We get it all at school, cleverclogs. It's on television. You haven't done it.

ANGIE: How do you know?

KIT: Because I know you haven't.

ANGIE: You know wrong then because I have.

KIT: Who with?

ANGIE: I'm not telling you / who with.

KIT: You haven't anyway.

ANGIE: How do you know?

KIT: Who with?

ANGIE: I'm not telling you.

KIT: You said you told me everything.

ANGIE: I was lying wasn't I.

KIT: Who with? You can't tell me who with because / you never—

ANGIE: Sh.

(JOYCE *has come out of the house. She stops halfway across the yard and listens. They listen.*)

JOYCE: You there Angie? Kit? You there Kitty? Want a cup of tea? I've got some chocolate biscuits. Come on now I'll put the kettle on. Want a choccy biccy, Angie? (*They all listen and wait.*) Fucking rotten little cunt. You can stay there and die. I'll lock the door.

(*They all wait.* JOYCE *goes back to the house.* ANGIE *and* KIT *sit in silence for a while.*)

KIT: When there's a war, where's the safest place?

ANGIE: Nowhere.

KIT: New Zealand is, my mum said. Your skin's burned right off. Shall we go to New Zealand?

ANGIE: I'm not staying here.

KIT: Shall we go to New Zealand?

ANGIE: You're not old enough.

KIT: You're not old enough.

ANGIE: I'm old enough to get married.

KIT: You don't want to get married.

ANGIE: No but I'm old enough.

KIT: I'd find out where they were going to drop it and stand right in the place.

ANGIE: You couldn't find out.

KIT: Better than walking round with your skin dragging on the ground. Eugh. / Would you like walking round with your skin dragging on the ground?

ANGIE: You couldn't find out, stupid, it's a secret.

KIT: Where are you going?

ANGIE: I'm not telling you.

KIT: Why?

ANGIE: It's a secret.

KIT: But you tell me all your secrets.

ANGIE: Not the true secrets.

KIT: Yes you do.

ANGIE: No I don't.

KIT: I want to go somewhere away from the war.

ANGIE: Just forget the war.

KIT: I can't.

ANGIE: You have to. It's so boring.

KIT: I'll remember it at night.

ANGIE: I'm going to do something else anyway.

KIT: What? Angie, come on. Angie.

ANGIE: It's a true secret.

KIT: It can't be worse than the kitten. And killing your mother. And the war.

ANGIE: Well I'm not telling you so you can die for all I care.

KIT: My mother says there's something wrong with you playing with someone my age. She says why haven't you got friends your own age. People your own age know there's something funny about you. She says you're a bad influence. She says she's going to speak to your mother. (ANGIE *twists* KIT's *arm till she cries out.*)

ANGIE: Say you're a liar.

KIT: She said it not me.

ANGIE: Say you eat shit.

KIT: You can't make me. (ANGIE *lets go.*)

ANGIE: I don't care anyway. I'm leaving.

KIT: Go on then.

ANGIE: You'll all wake up one morning and find I've gone.

KIT: Good.

ANGIE: I'm not telling you when.

KIT: Go on then.

ANGIE: I'm sorry I hurt you.

KIT: I'm tired.

ANGIE: Do you like me?

KIT: I don't know.

ANGIE: You do like me.

KIT: I'm going home. (*She gets up.*)

ANGIE: No you're not.

KIT: I'm tired.

ANGIE: She'll see you.

KIT: She'll give me a chocolate biscuit.

ANGIE: Kitty.

KIT: Tell me where you're going.

ANGIE: Sit down.

KIT: (*Sitting down again*) Go on then.

ANGIE: Swear?

KIT: Swear.

ANGIE: I'm going to London. To see my aunt.

KIT: And what?

ANGIE: That's it.

KIT: I see my aunt all the time.

ANGIE: I don't see my aunt.

KIT: What's so special?

ANGIE: It is special. She's special.

KIT: Why?

ANGIE: She is.

KIT: Why?

ANGIE: She is.

KIT: Why?

ANGIE: My mother hates her.

KIT: Why?

ANGIE: Because she does.

KIT: Perhaps she's not very nice.

ANGIE: She is nice.

KIT: How do you know?

ANGIE: Because I know her.

KIT: You said you never see her.

ANGIE: I saw her last year. You saw her.

KIT: Did I?

ANGIE: Never mind.

KIT: I remember her. That aunt. What's so special?

ANGIE: She gets people jobs.

KIT: What's so special?

ANGIE: I think I'm my aunt's child. I think my mother's really my aunt.

KIT: Why?

ANGIE: Because she goes to America, now shut up.

KIT: I've been to London.

ANGIE: Now give us a cuddle and shut up because I'm sick.

KIT: You're sitting on my arm.

(They curl up in each other's arms. Silence. JOYCE *comes out of the house and comes up to them quietly.)*

JOYCE: Come on.

KIT: Oh hello.

JOYCE: Time you went home.

KIT: We want to go to the Odeon.

JOYCE: What time?

KIT: Don't know.

JOYCE: What's on?

KIT: Don't know.

JOYCE: Don't know much do you?

KIT: That all right then?

JOYCE: Angie's got to clean her room first.

ANGIE: No I don't.

JOYCE: Yes you do, it's a pigsty.

ANGIE: Well I'm not.

JOYCE: Then you're not going. I don't care.

ANGIE: Well I am going.

JOYCE: You've no money, have you?

ANGIE: Kit's paying anyway.

JOYCE: No she's not.

KIT: I'll help you with your room.

JOYCE: That's nice.

ANGIE: No you won't. You wait here.

KIT: Hurry then.

ANGIE: I'm not hurrying. You just wait. (ANGIE *goes slowly into the house. Silence.*)

JOYCE: I don't know. (*Silence.*) How's school then?

KIT: All right.

JOYCE: What are you now? Third year?

KIT: Second year.

JOYCE: Your mum says you're good at English. (*Silence.*) Maybe Angie should've stayed on.

KIT: She didn't like it.

JOYCE: I didn't like it. And look at me. If your face fits at school it's going to fit other places too. It wouldn't make no difference to Angie. She's not going to get a job when jobs are hard to get. I'd be sorry for anyone in charge of her. She'd better get married. I don't know who'd have her, mind. She's one of those girls might never leave home. What do you want to be when you grow up, Kit?

KIT: Physicist.

JOYCE: What?

KIT: Nuclear physicist.

JOYCE: Whatever for?

KIT: I could, I'm clever.

JOYCE: I know you're clever, pet. (*Silence.*) I'll make a cup of tea. (*Silence.*) Looks like it's going to rain. (*Silence.*) Don't you have friends your own age?

KIT: Yes.

JOYCE: Well then.

KIT: I'm old for my age.

JOYCE: And Angie's simple is she? She's not simple.

KIT: I love Angie.

JOYCE: She's clever in her own way.

KIT: You can't stop me.

JOYCE: I don't want to.

KIT: You can't, so.

JOYCE: Don't be cheeky, Kitty. She's always kind to little children.

KIT: She's coming so you better leave me alone.

*(*ANGIE *comes out. She has changed into an old best dress, slightly small for her.)*

JOYCE: What you put that on for? Have you done your room? You can't clean your room in that.

ANGIE: I looked in the cupboard and it was there.

JOYCE: Of course it was there, it's meant to be there. Is that why it was a surprise, finding something in the right place? I should think she's surprised, wouldn't you, Kit, to find something in her room in the right place.

ANGIE: I decided to wear it.

JOYCE: Not today, why? To clean your room? You're not going to the pictures till you've done your room. You can put your dress on after if you like. (ANGIE *picks up a brick.*) Have you done your room? You're not getting out of it, you know.

KIT: Angie, let's go.

JOYCE: She's not going till she's done her room.

KIT: It's starting to rain.

JOYCE: Come on, come on then. Hurry and do your room, Angie, and then you can go to the cinema with Kit. Oh it's wet, come on. We'll look up the time in the paper. Does your mother know, Kit, it's going to be a late night for you, isn't it? Hurry up, Angie. You'll spoil your dress. You make me sick. (JOYCE *and* KIT *run into the house.* ANGIE *stays where she is. There is the sound of rain.* KIT *comes out of the house.*)

KIT: (*Shouting*) Angie. Angie, come on, you'll get wet. (*She comes back to* ANGIE.)

ANGIE: I put on this dress to kill my mother.

KIT: I suppose you thought you'd do it with a brick.

ANGIE: You can kill people with a brick. (*She puts the brick down.*)

KIT: Well you didn't, so.

ACT 2 / SCENE 1

(*"Top Girls" Employment Agency. Monday morning. There are three desks in the main office and a separate small interviewing area. The lights come up in the main office on* WIN *and* NELL *who have just arrived for work.*)

NELL: Coffee coffee coffee coffee / coffee.

WIN: The roses were smashing. / Mermaid.

NELL: Ohhh.

WIN: Iceberg. He taught me all their names. (NELL *has some coffee now.*)

NELL: Ah. Now then.

WIN: He has one of the finest rose gardens in West Sussex. He exhibits.

NELL: He what?

WIN: His wife was visiting her mother. It was like living together.

NELL: Crafty, you never said.

WIN: He rang on Saturday morning.

NELL: Lucky you were free.

WIN: That's what I told him.

NELL: Did you hell.

WIN: Have you ever seen a really beautiful rose garden?

NELL: I don't like flowers. / I like swimming pools.

WIN: Marilyn. Esther's Baby. They're all called after birds.

NELL: Our friend's late. Celebrating all weekend I bet you.

WIN: I'd call a rose Elvis. Or John Conteh.°

NELL: Is Howard in yet?

WIN: If he is he'll be bleeping us with a problem.

NELL: Howard can just hang on to himself.

WIN: Howard's really cut up.

NELL: Howard thinks because he's a fella the job was his as of right. Our Marlene's got far more balls than Howard and that's that.

WIN: Poor little bugger.

NELL: He'll live.

WIN: He'll move on.

NELL: I wouldn't mind a change of air myself.

WIN: Serious?

NELL: I've never been a staying-put lady. Pastures new.

WIN: So who's the pirate?

NELL: There's nothing definite.

WIN: Inquiries?

NELL: There's always inquiries. I'd think I'd got bad breath if there stopped being inquiries. Most of them can't afford me. Or you.

WIN: I'm all right for the time being. Unless I go to Australia.

NELL: There's not a lot of room upward.

WIN: Marlene's filled it up.

NELL: Good luck to her. Unless there's some prospects moneywise.

WIN: You can but ask.

NELL: Can always but ask.

WIN: So what have we got? I've got a Mr. Holden I saw last week.

NELL: Any use?

WIN: Pushy. Bit of a cowboy.

NELL: Goodlooker?

WIN: Good dresser.

NELL: High flyer?°

WIN: That's his general idea certainly but I'm not sure he's got it up there.

NELL: Prestel° wants six flyers and I've only seen two and a half.

WIN: He's making a bomb on the road but he thinks it's time for an office. I sent him to IBM but he didn't get it.

NELL: Prestel's on the road.

WIN: He's not overbright.

NELL: Can he handle an office?

WIN: Provided his secretary can punctuate he should go far.

NELL: Bear Prestel in mind then, I might put my head round the door. I've got that poor little nerd I should never have said I could help. Tender heart me.

WIN: Tender like old boots. How old?

NELL: Yes well forty-five.

WIN: Say no more.

NELL: He knows his place, he's not after calling himself a manager, he's just a poor little bod wants a better commission and a bit of sunshine.

WIN: Don't we all.

NELL: He's just got to relocate. He's got a bungalow in Dymchurch.

WIN: And his wife says.

NELL: The lady wife wouldn't care to relocate. She's going through the change.

WIN: It's his funeral, don't waste your time.

NELL: I don't waste a lot.

WIN: Good weekend you?

NELL: You could say.

WIN: Which one?

NELL: One Friday, one Saturday.

WIN: Aye—aye.

NELL: Sunday night I watched telly.

WIN: Which of them do you like best really?

NELL: Sunday was best, I like the Ovaltine.°

John Conteh, popular boxer and model.

High flyer, someone who is succeeding by moving up in a chosen field. **Prestel,** television and computer stock market information service. **Ovaltine,** hot chocolate malt drink.

WIN: Holden, Barker, Gardner, Duke.

NELL: I've a lady here thinks she can sell.

WIN: Taking her on?

NELL: She's had some jobs.

WIN: Services?

NELL: No, quite heavy stuff, electric.

WIN: Tough bird like us.

NELL: We could do with a few more here.

WIN: There's nothing going here.

NELL: No but I always want the tough ones when I see them. Hang on to them.

WIN: I think we're plenty.

NELL: Derek asked me to marry him again.

WIN: He doesn't know when he's beaten.

NELL: I told him I'm not going to play house, not even in Ascot.

WIN: Mind you, you could play house.

NELL: If I chose to play house I would play house ace.°

WIN: You could marry him and go on working.

NELL: I could go on working and not marry him.

(MARLENE *arrives.*)

MARLENE: Morning ladies. (WIN *and* NELL *cheer and whistle.*) Mind my head.

NELL: Coffee coffee coffee.

WIN: We're tactfully not mentioning you're late.

MARLENE: Fucking tube.°

WIN: We've heard that one.

NELL: We've used that one.

WIN: It's the top executive doesn't come in as early as the poor working girl.

MARLENE: Pass the sugar and shut your face, pet.

WIN: Well I'm delighted.

NELL: Howard's looking sick.

WIN: Howard is sick. He's got ulcers and heart. He told me.

NELL: He'll have to stop then, won't he?

WIN: Stop what?

NELL: Smoking, drinking, shouting. Working.

WIN: Well, working.

NELL: We're just looking through the day.

MARLENE: I'm doing some of Pam's ladies. They've been piling up while she's away.

NELL: Half a dozen little girls and an arts graduate who can't type.

WIN: I spent the whole weekend at his place in Sussex.

NELL: She fancies his rose garden.

WIN: I had to lie down in the back of the car so the neighbors wouldn't see me go in.

NELL: You're kidding.

WIN: It was funny.

NELL: Fuck that for a joke.

WIN: It was funny.

MARLENE: Anyway they'd see you in the garden.

WIN: The garden has extremely high walls.

NELL: I think I'll tell the wife.

WIN: Like hell.

NELL: She might leave him and you could have the rose garden.

WIN: The minute it's not a secret I'm out on my ear.

NELL: Don't know why you bother.

WIN: Bit of fun.

NELL: I think it's time you went to Australia.

WIN: I think it's pushy Mr. Holden time.

NELL: If you've any really pretty bastards, Marlene, I want some for Prestel.

MARLENE: I might have one this afternoon. This morning it's all Pam's secretarial.

NELL: Not long now and you'll be upstairs watching over us all.

MARLENE: Do you feel bad about it?

NELL: I don't like coming second.

MARLENE: Who does?

WIN: We'd rather it was you than Howard. We're glad for you, aren't we, Nell?

NELL: Oh yes. Aces.

(LOUISE *enters the interviewing area. The lights crossfade to* WIN *and* LOUISE *in the interviewing area.* NELL *exits.*)

WIN: Now, Louise, hello, I have your details here. You've been very loyal to the one job I see.

LOUISE: Yes I have.

WIN: Twenty-one years is a long time in one place.

LOUISE: I feel it is. I feel it's time to move on.

WIN: And you are what age now?

LOUISE: I'm in my early forties.

WIN: Exactly?

LOUISE: Forty-six.

WIN: It's not necessarily a handicap, well it is of course we have to face that, but it's not necessarily a disabling handicap, experience does count for something.

LOUISE: I hope so.

WIN: Now between ourselves is there any trouble, any reason why you're leaving that wouldn't appear on the form?

LOUISE: Nothing like that.

WIN: Like what?

LOUISE: Nothing at all.

WIN: No long-term understandings come to a sudden end, making for an insupportable atmosphere?

LOUISE: I've always completely avoided anything like that at all.

WIN: No personality clashes with your immediate superiors or inferiors?

LOUISE: I've always taken care to get on very well with everyone.

WIN: I only ask because it can affect the reference and it also affects your motivation, I want to be quite clear why you're moving on. So I take it the job itself no longer satisfies you. Is it the money?

---

ace, slang for "first-class."   **tube,** London subway.

LOUISE: It's partly the money. It's not so much the money.

WIN: Nine thousand is very respectable. Have you dependants?

LOUISE: No, no dependants. My mother died.

WIN: So why are you making a change?

LOUISE: Other people make changes.

WIN: But why are you, now, after spending most of your life in the one place?

LOUISE: There you are, I've lived for that company, I've given my life really you could say because I haven't had a great deal of social life, I've worked in the evenings. I haven't had office entanglements for the very reason you just mentioned and if you are committed to your work you don't move in many other circles. I had management status from the age of twenty-seven and you'll appreciate what that means. I've built up a department. And there it is, it works extremely well, and I feel I'm stuck there. I've spent twenty years in middle management. I've seen young men who I trained go on, in my own company or elsewhere, to higher things. Nobody notices me, I don't expect it, I don't attract attention by making mistakes, everybody takes it for granted that my work is perfect. They will notice me when I go, they will be sorry I think to lose me, they will offer me more money of course, I will refuse. They will see when I've gone what I was doing for them.

WIN: If they offer you more money you won't stay?

LOUISE: No I won't.

WIN: Are you the only woman?

LOUISE: Apart from the girls of course, yes. There was one, she was my assistant, it was the only time I took on a young woman assistant, I always had my doubts. I don't care greatly for working with women, I think I pass as a man at work. But I did take on this young woman, her qualifications were excellent, and she did well, she got a department of her own, and left the company for a competitor where she's now on the board and good luck to her. She has a different style, she's a new kind of attractive well dressed—I don't mean I don't dress properly. But there is a kind of woman who is thirty now who grew up in a different climate. They are not so careful. They take themselves for granted. I have had to justify my existence every minute, and I have done so, I have proved—well.

WIN: Let's face it, vacancies are ones where you'll be in competition with younger men. And there are companies that will value your experience enough that you'll be in with a chance. There are also fields that are easier for a woman, there is a cosmetic company here where your experience might be relevant. It's eight and a half, I don't know if that appeals.

LOUISE: I've proved I can earn money. It's more important to get away. I feel it's now or never. I sometimes / think—

WIN: You shouldn't talk too much at an interview.

LOUISE: I don't. I don't normally talk about myself. I know very well how to handle myself in an office situation. I only talk to you because it seems to me this is different, it's your job to understand me, surely. You asked the questions.

WIN: I think I understand you sufficiently.

LOUISE: Well good, that's good.

WIN: Do you drink?

LOUISE: Certainly not. I'm not a teetotaler, I think that's very suspect, it's seen as being an alcoholic if you're teetotal. What do you mean? I don't drink. Why?

WIN: I drink.

LOUISE: I don't.

WIN: Good for you.

(The lights crossfade to the main office with MARLENE *sitting at her desk.* WIN *and* LOUISE *exit.* ANGIE *arrives in the main office.)*

ANGIE: Hello.

MARLENE: Have you an appointment?

ANGIE: It's me. I've come.

MARLENE: What? It's not Angie?

ANGIE: It was hard to find this place. I got lost.

MARLENE: How did you get past the receptionist? The girl on the desk, didn't she try to stop you?

ANGIE: What desk?

MARLENE: Never mind.

ANGIE: I just walked in. I was looking for you.

MARLENE: Well you found me.

ANGIE: Yes.

MARLENE: So where's your mum? Are you up in town for the day?

ANGIE: Not really.

MARLENE: Sit down. Do you feel all right?

ANGIE: Yes thank you.

MARLENE: So where's Joyce?

ANGIE: She's at home.

MARLENE: Did you come up on a school trip then?

ANGIE: I've left school.

MARLENE: Did you come up with a friend?

ANGIE: No. There's just me.

MARLENE: You came up by yourself, that's fun. What have you been doing? Shopping? Tower of London?

ANGIE: No, I just come here. I come to you.

MARLENE: That's very nice of you to think of paying your aunty a visit. There's not many nieces make that the first port of call. Would you like a cup of coffee?

ANGIE: No thank you.

MARLENE: Tea, orange?

ANGIE: No thank you.

MARLENE: Do you feel all right?

ANGIE: Yes thank you.

MARLENE: Are you tired from the journey?

ANGIE: Yes, I'm tired from the journey.

MARLENE: You sit there for a bit then. How's Joyce?

ANGIE: She's all right.

MARLENE: Same as ever.

ANGIE: Oh yes.

MARLENE: Unfortunately you've picked a day when I'm rather busy, if there's ever a day when I'm not, or I'd take you out to lunch and we'd go to Madame Tussaud's.° We could go shopping. What time do you have to be back? Have you got a day return?

ANGIE: No.

MARLENE: So what train are you going back on?

ANGIE: I came on the bus.

MARLENE: So what bus are you going back on? Are you staying the night?

ANGIE: Yes.

MARLENE: Who are you staying with? Do you want me to put you up for the night, is that it?

ANGIE: Yes please.

MARLENE: I haven't got a spare bed.

ANGIE: I can sleep on the floor.

MARLENE: You can sleep on the sofa.

ANGIE: Yes please.

MARLENE: I do think Joyce might have phoned me. It's like her.

ANGIE: This is where you work is it?

MARLENE: It's where I have been working the last two years but I'm going to move into another office.

ANGIE: It's lovely.

MARLENE: My new office is nicer than this. There's just the one big desk in it for me.

ANGIE: Can I see it?

MARLENE: Not now, no, there's someone else in it now. But he's leaving at the end of next week and I'm going to do his job.

ANGIE: Is that good?

MARLENE: Yes, it's very good.

ANGIE: Are you going to be in charge?

MARLENE: Yes I am.

ANGIE: I knew you would be.

MARLENE: How did you know?

ANGIE: I knew you'd be in charge of everything.

MARLENE: Not quite everything.

ANGIE: You will be.

MARLENE: Well we'll see.

ANGIE: Can I see it next week then?

MARLENE: Will you still be here next week?

ANGIE: Yes.

MARLENE: Don't you have to go home?

ANGIE: No.

MARLENE: Why not?

ANGIE: It's all right.

MARLENE: Is it all right?

ANGIE: Yes, don't worry about it.

MARLENE: Does Joyce know where you are?

ANGIE: Yes of course she does.

MARLENE: Well does she?

ANGIE: Don't worry about it.

MARLENE: How long are you planning to stay with me then?

ANGIE: You know when you came to see us last year?

MARLENE: Yes, that was nice wasn't it.

ANGIE: That was the best day of my whole life.

MARLENE: So how long are you planning to stay?

ANGIE: Don't you want me?

MARLENE: Yes yes, I just wondered.

ANGIE: I won't stay if you don't want me.

MARLENE: No, of course you can stay.

ANGIE: I'll sleep on the floor. I won't be any bother.

MARLENE: Don't get upset.

ANGIE: I'm not, I'm not. Don't worry about it.

(MRS. KIDD comes in.)

MRS. KIDD: Excuse me.

MARLENE: Yes.

MRS. KIDD: Excuse me.

MARLENE: Can I help you?

MRS. KIDD: Excuse me bursting in on you like this but I have to talk to you.

MARLENE: I am engaged at the moment. / If you could go to reception—

MRS. KIDD: I'm Rosemary Kidd, Howard's wife, you don't recognize me but we did meet, I remember you of course / but you wouldn't—

MARLENE: Yes of course, Mrs. Kidd, I'm sorry, we did meet. Howard's about somewhere I expect, have you looked in his office?

MRS. KIDD: Howard's not about, no. I'm afraid it's you I've come to see if I could have a minute or two.

MARLENE: I do have an appointment in five minutes.

MRS. KIDD: This won't take five minutes. I'm very sorry. It is a matter of some urgency.

MARLENE: Well of course. What can I do for you?

MRS. KIDD: I just wanted a chat, an informal chat. It's not something I can simply—I'm sorry if I'm interrupting your work. I know office work isn't like housework / which is all interruptions.

MARLENE: No no, this is my niece. Angie. Mrs. Kidd.

MRS. KIDD: Very pleased to meet you.

ANGIE: Very well thank you.

MRS. KIDD: Howard's not in today.

MARLENE: Isn't he?

MRS. KIDD: He's feeling poorly.

MARLENE: I didn't know. I'm sorry to hear that.

MRS. KIDD: The fact is he's in a state of shock. About what's happened.

MARLENE: What has happened?

MRS. KIDD: You should know if anyone. I'm referring to you being appointed managing director instead of Howard. He hasn't been at all well all weekend. He hasn't slept for three nights. I haven't slept.

MARLENE: I'm sorry to hear that, Mrs. Kidd. Has he thought of taking sleeping pills?

Madame Tussaud's, London waxworks museum.

MRS. KIDD: It's very hard when someone has worked all these years.

MARLENE: Business life is full of little setbacks. I'm sure Howard knows that. He'll bounce back in a day or two. We all bounce back.

MRS. KIDD: If you could see him you'd know what I'm talking about. What's it going to do to him working for a woman? I think if it was a man he'd get over it as something normal.

MARLENE: I think he's going to have to get over it.

MRS. KIDD: It's me that bears the brunt. I'm not the one that's been promoted. I put him first every inch of the way. And now what do I get? You women this, you women that. It's not my fault. You're going to have to be very careful how you handle him. He's very hurt.

MARLENE: Naturally I'll be tactful and pleasant to him, you don't start pushing someone around. I'll consult him over any decisions affecting his department. But that's no different, Mrs. Kidd, from any of my other colleagues.

MRS. KIDD: I think it is different, because he's a man.

MARLENE: I'm not quite sure why you came to see me.

MRS. KIDD: I had to do something.

MARLENE: Well you've done it, you've seen me. I think that's probably all we've time for. I'm sorry he's been taking it out on you. He really is a shit, Howard.

MRS. KIDD: But he's got a family to support. He's got three children. It's only fair.

MARLENE: Are you suggesting I give up the job to him then?

MRS. KIDD: It had crossed my mind if you were unavailable after all for some reason, he would be the natural second choice I think, don't you? I'm not asking.

MARLENE: Good.

MRS. KIDD: You mustn't tell him I came. He's very proud.

MARLENE: If he doesn't like what's happening here he can go and work somewhere else.

MRS. KIDD: Is that a threat?

MARLENE: I'm sorry but I do have some work to do.

MRS. KIDD: It's not that easy, a man of Howard's age. You don't care. I thought he was going too far but he's right. You're one of these ballbreakers, / that's what you

MARLENE: I'm sorry but I do have some work to do.

MRS. KIDD: are. You'll end up miserable and lonely. You're not natural.

MARLENE: Could you please piss off?

MRS. KIDD: I thought if I saw you at least I'd be doing something. (MRS. KIDD goes.)

MARLENE: I've got to go and do some work now. Will you come back later?

ANGIE: I think you were wonderful.

MARLENE: I've got to go and do some work now.

ANGIE: You told her to piss off.

MARLENE: Will you come back later?

ANGIE: Can't I stay here?

MARLENE: Don't you want to go sightseeing?

ANGIE: I'd rather stay here.

MARLENE: You can stay here I suppose, if it's not boring.

ANGIE: It's where I most want to be in the world.

MARLENE: I'll see you later then.

(MARLENE goes. SHONA and NELL enter the interviewing area. ANGIE sits at WIN's desk. The lights crossfade to NELL and SHONA in the interviewing area.)

NELL: Is this right? You are Shona?

SHONA: Yeh.

NELL: It says here you're twenty-nine.

SHONA: Yeh.

NELL: Too many late nights, me. So you've been where you are for four years, Shona, you're earning six basic and three commission. So what's the problem?

SHONA: No problem.

NELL: Why do you want a change?

SHONA: Just a change.

NELL: Change of product, change of area?

SHONA: Both.

NELL: But you're happy on the road?

SHONA: I like driving.

NELL: You're not after management status?

SHONA: I would like management status.

NELL: You'd be interested in titular management status but not come off the road?

SHONA: I want to be on the road, yeh.

NELL: So how many calls have you been making a day?

SHONA: Six.

NELL: And what proportion of those are successful?

SHONA: Six.

NELL: That's hard to believe.

SHONA: Four.

NELL: You find it easy to get the initial interest do you?

SHONA: Oh yeh, I get plenty of initial interest.

NELL: And what about closing?

SHONA: I close, don't I?

NELL: Because that's what an employer is going to have doubts about with a lady as I needn't tell you, whether she's got the guts to push through to a closing situation. They think we're too nice. They think we listen to the buyer's doubts. They think we consider his needs and his feelings.

SHONA: I never consider people's feelings.

NELL: I was selling for six years, I can sell anything, I've sold in three continents, and I'm jolly as they come but I'm not very nice.

SHONA: I'm not very nice.

NELL: What sort of time do you have on the road with the other reps? Get on all right? Handle the chat?

SHONA: I get on. Keep myself to myself.

NELL: Fairly much of a loner are you?

SHONA: Sometimes.

NELL: So what field are you interested in?

SHONA: Computers.

NELL: That's a top field as you know and you'll be up against some very slick fellas there, there's some very pretty boys in computers, it's an American-style field.

SHONA: That's why I want to do it.

NELL: Video systems appeal? That's a high-flying situation.

SHONA: Video systems appeal OK.

NELL: Because Prestel have half a dozen vacancies I'm looking to fill at the moment. We're talking in the area of ten to fifteen thousand here and upwards.

SHONA: Sounds OK.

NELL: I've half a mind to go for it myself. But it's good money here if you've got the top clients. Could you fancy it do you think?

SHONA: Work here?

NELL: I'm not in a position to offer, there's nothing officially going just now, but we're always on the lookout. There's not that many of us. We could keep in touch.

SHONA: I like driving.

NELL: So the Prestel appeals?

SHONA: Yeh.

NELL: What about ties?

SHONA: No ties.

NELL: So relocation wouldn't be a problem.

SHONA: No problem.

NELL: So just fill me in a bit more could you about what you've been doing.

SHONA: What I've been doing. It's all down there.

NELL: The bare facts are down here but I've got to present you to an employer.

SHONA: I'm twenty-nine years old.

NELL: So it says here.

SHONA: We look young. Youngness runs in the family in our family.

NELL: So just describe your present job for me.

SHONA: My present job at present. I have a car. I have a Porsche. I go up the M1° a lot. Burn up the M1 a lot. Straight up the M1 in the fast lane to where the clients are, Staffordshire, Yorkshire, I do a lot in Yorkshire. I'm selling electric things. Like dish-washers, washing machines, stainless steel tubs are a feature and the reliability of the program. After sales service, we offer a very good after sales service, spare parts, plenty of spare parts. And fridges, I sell a lot of fridges specially in the summer. People want to buy fridges in the summer because of the heat melting the butter and you get fed up standing the milk in a basin of cold water with a cloth over, stands to reason people don't want to do that in this day and age. So I sell a lot of them. Big ones with big freezers. Big freezers. And I stay in hotels at night when I'm away from home. On my expense

---

M1, expressway running from London to Yorkshire.

account. I stay in various hotels. They know me, the ones I go to. I check in, have a bath, have a shower. Then I go down to the bar, have a gin and tonic, have a chat. Then I go into the dining room and have dinner. I usually have fillet steak and mushrooms, I like mushrooms. I like smoked salmon very much. I like having a salad on the side. Green salad. I don't like tomatoes.

NELL: Christ what a waste of time.

SHONA: Beg your pardon?

NELL: Not a word of this is true, is it?

SHONA: How do you mean?

NELL: You just filled in the form with a pack of lies.

SHONA: Not exactly.

NELL: How old are you?

SHONA: Twenty-nine.

NELL: Nineteen?

SHONA: Twenty-one.

NELL: And what jobs have you done? Have you done any?

SHONA: I could though, I bet you.

(The lights crossfade to the main office with ANGIE *sitting as before.* WIN *comes in to the main office.* SHONA *and* NELL *exit.)*

WIN: Who's sitting in my chair?

ANGIE: What? Sorry.

WIN: Who's been eating my porridge?

ANGIE: What?

WIN: It's all right, I saw Marlene. Angie, isn't it? I'm Win. And I'm not going out for lunch because I'm knackered. I'm going to set me down here and have a yogurt. Do you like yogurt?

ANGIE: No.

WIN: That's good because I've only got one. Are you hungry?

ANGIE: No.

WIN: There's a café on the corner.

ANGIE: No thank you. Do you work here?

WIN: How did you guess?

ANGIE: Because you look as if you might work here and you're sitting at the desk. Have you always worked here?

WIN: No I was headhunted. That means I was working for another outfit like this and this lot came and offered me more money. I broke my contract, there was a hell of a stink. There's not many top ladies about. Your aunty's a smashing bird.

ANGIE: Yes I know.

MARLENE: Fan are you? Fan of your aunty's?

ANGIE: Do you think I could work here?

WIN: Not at the moment.

ANGIE: How do I start?

WIN: What can you do?

ANGIE: I don't know. Nothing.

WIN: Type?

ANGIE: Not very well. The letters jump up when I do

capitals. I was going to do a CSE° in commerce but I didn't.

WIN: What have you got?

ANGIE: What?

WIN: CSE's, O's.

ANGIE: Nothing, none of that. Did you do all that?

WIN: Oh yes, all that, and a science degree funnily enough. I started out doing medical research but there's no money in it. I thought I'd go abroad. Did you know they sell Coca Cola in Russia and Pepsi-Cola in China? You don't have to be qualified as much as you might think. Men are awful bullshitters, they like to make out jobs are harder than they are. Any job I ever did I started doing it better than the rest of the crowd and they didn't like it. So I'd get unpopular and I'd have a drink to cheer myself up. I lived with a fella and supported him for four years, he couldn't get work. After that I went to California. I like the sunshine. Americans know how to live. This country's too slow. Then I went to Mexico, still in sales, but it's no country for a single lady. I came home, went bonkers for a bit, thought I was five different people, got over that all right, the psychiatrist said I was perfectly sane and highly intelligent. Got married in a moment of weakness and he's inside° now, he's been inside four years, and I've not been to see him too much this last year. I like this better than sales, I'm not really that aggressive. I started thinking sales was a good job if you want to meet people, but you're meeting people that don't want to meet you. It's no good if you like being liked. Here your clients want to meet you because you're the one doing them some good. They hope. (ANGIE *has fallen asleep.* NELL *comes in.*)

NELL: You're talking to yourself, sunshine.

WIN: So what's new?

NELL: Who is this?

WIN: Marlene's little niece.

NELL: What's she got, brother, sister? She never talks about her family.

WIN: I was telling her my life story.

NELL: Violins?

WIN: No, success story.

NELL: You've heard Howard's had a heart attack?

WIN: No, when?

NELL: I heard just now. He hadn't come in, he was at home, he's gone to hospital. He's not dead. His wife was here, she rushed off in a cab.

WIN: Too much butter, too much smoke. We must send him some flowers. (MARLENE *comes in.*) You've heard about Howard?

MARLENE: Poor sod.

NELL: Lucky he didn't get the job if that's what his health's like.

MARLENE: Is she asleep?

WIN: She wants to work here.

MARLENE: Packer in Tesco° more like.

WIN: She's a nice kid. Isn't she?

MARLENE: She's a bit thick. She's a bit funny.

WIN: She thinks you're wonderful.

MARLENE: She's not going to make it.

ACT 2 / SCENE 2

(JOYCE's *kitchen. Sunday evening, a year earlier. The lights come up on* JOYCE, ANGIE, *and* MARLENE. MARLENE *is taking presents out of bright carrier bag.* ANGIE *has already opened a box of chocolates.*)

MARLENE: Just a few little things. / I've

JOYCE: There's no need.

MARLENE: no memory for birthdays have I, and Christmas seems to slip by. So I think I owe Angie a few presents.

JOYCE: What do you say?

ANGIE: Thank you very much. Thank you very much, Aunty Marlene. (*She opens a present. It is the dress from Act 1, new.*) Oh look, Mum, isn't it lovely?

MARLENE: I don't know if it's the right size. She's grown up since I saw her. / I knew she was always

ANGIE: Isn't it lovely?

MARLENE: tall for her age.

JOYCE: She's a big lump.

MARLENE: Hold it up, Angie, let's see.

ANGIE: I'll put it on, shall I?

MARLENE: Yes, try it on.

JOYCE: Go on to your room then, we don't want / a strip show thank you.

ANGIE: Of course I'm going to my room, what do you think. Look, Mum, here's something for you. Open it, go on. What is it? Can I open it for you?

JOYCE: Yes, you open it, pet.

ANGIE: Don't you want to open it yourself? / Go on.

JOYCE: I don't mind, you can do it.

ANGIE: It's something hard. It's—what is it? A bottle. Drink is it? No, it's what? Perfume, look. What a lot. Open it, look, let's smell it. Oh it's strong. It's lovely. Put it on me. How do you do it? Put it on me.

JOYCE: You're too young.

ANGIE: I can play wearing it like dressing up.

JOYCE: And you're too old for that. Here, give it here, I'll do it, you'll tip the whole bottle over yourself / and we'll have you smelling all summer.

CSE, Certificate of Secondary Education, similar to O-levels, but less prestigious. *inside,* in jail.

Packer in Tesco, shelf-stocker in major grocery store.

ANGIE: Put it on you. Do I smell? Put it on Aunty too. Put it on Aunty too. Let's all smell.

MARLENE: I didn't know what you'd like.

JOYCE: There's no danger I'd have it already, / that's one thing.

ANGIE: Now we all smell the same.

MARLENE: It's a bit of nonsense.

JOYCE: It's very kind of you Marlene, you shouldn't.

ANGIE: Now I'll put on the dress and then we'll see. (ANGIE *goes*.)

JOYCE: You've caught me on the hop with the place in a mess. / If you'd let me

MARLENE: That doesn't matter.

JOYCE: know you was coming I'd have got something in to eat. We had our dinner dinnertime. We're just going to have a cup of tea. You could have an egg.

MARLENE: No, I'm not hungry. Tea's fine.

JOYCE: I don't expect you take sugar.

MARLENE: Why not?

JOYCE: You take care of yourself.

MARLENE: How do you mean you didn't know I was coming?

JOYCE: You could have written. I know we're not on the phone but we're not completely in the dark ages, / we do have a postman.

MARLENE: But you asked me to come.

JOYCE: How did I ask you to come?

MARLENE: Angie said when she phoned up.

JOYCE: Angie phoned up, did she.

MARLENE: Was it just Angie's idea?

JOYCE: What did she say?

MARLENE: She said you wanted me to come and see you. / It was a couple of

JOYCE: Ha.

MARLENE: weeks ago. How was I to know that's a ridiculous idea? My diary's always full a couple of weeks ahead so we fixed it for this weekend. I was meant to get here earlier but I was held up. She gave me messages from you.

JOYCE: Didn't you wonder why I didn't phone you myself?

MARLENE: She said you didn't like using the phone. You're shy on the phone and can't use it. I don't know what you're like, do I?

JOYCE: Are there people who can't use the phone?

MARLENE: I expect so.

JOYCE: I haven't met any.

MARLENE: Why should I think she was lying?

JOYCE: Because she's like what she's like.

MARLENE: How do I know / what she's like?

JOYCE: It's not my fault you don't know what she's like. You never come and see her.

MARLENE: Well I have now / and you don't seem over the moon.*

JOYCE: Good. *Well I'd have got a cake if she'd told me. (*Pause*.)

MARLENE: I did wonder why you wanted to see me.

JOYCE: I didn't want to see you.

MARLENE: Yes, I know. Shall I go?

JOYCE: I don't mind seeing you.

MARLENE: Great, I feel really welcome.

JOYCE: You can come and see Angie any time you like, I'm not stopping you. / You

MARLENE: Ta ever so.°

JOYCE: know where we are. You're the one went away, not me. I'm right here where I was. And will be a few years yet I shouldn't wonder.

MARLENE: All right. All right. (JOYCE *gives* MARLENE *a cup of tea*.)

JOYCE: Tea.

MARLENE: Sugar? (JOYCE *passes* MARLENE *the sugar*.) It's very quiet down here.

JOYCE: I expect you'd notice it.

MARLENE: The air smells different too.

JOYCE: That's the scent.

MARLENE: No, I mean walking down the lane.

JOYCE: What sort of air you get in London then?

(ANGIE *comes in, wearing the dress. It fits*.)

MARLENE: Oh, very pretty. / You do look pretty, Angie.

JOYCE: That fits all right.

MARLENE: Do you like the color?

ANGIE: Beautiful. Beautiful.

JOYCE: You better take it off, / you'll get it dirty.

ANGIE: I want to wear it. I want to wear it.

MARLENE: It is for wearing after all. You can't just hang it up and look at it.

ANGIE: I love it.

JOYCE: Well if you must you must.

ANGIE: If someone asks me what's my favorite color I'll tell them it's this. Thank you very much, Aunty Marlene.

MARLENE: You didn't tell your mum you asked me down.

ANGIE: I wanted it to be a surprise.

JOYCE: I'll give you a surprise / one of these days.

ANGIE: I thought you'd like to see her. She hasn't been here since I was nine. People do see their aunts.

MARLENE: Is it that long? Doesn't time fly.

ANGIE: I wanted to.

JOYCE: I'm not cross.

ANGIE: Are you glad?

JOYCE: I smell nicer anyhow, don't I?

(KIT *comes in without saying anything, as if she lived there*.)

MARLENE: I think it was a good idea, Angie, about time. We are sisters after all. It's a pity to let that go.

JOYCE: This is Kitty, / who lives up the road. This is Angie's Aunty Marlene.

KIT: What's that?

ANGIE: It's a present. Do you like it?

Ta ever so, Thanks ever so much.

KIT: It's all right. / Are you coming out?*

MARLENE: Hello, Kitty.

ANGIE: *No.

KIT: What's that smell?

ANGIE: It's a present.

KIT: It's horrible. Come on.*

MARLENE: Have a chocolate.

ANGIE: *No, I'm busy.

KIT: Coming out later?

ANGIE: No.

KIT: (*To* MARLENE) Hello. (KIT *goes without a chocolate.*)

JOYCE: She's a little girl Angie sometimes plays with because she's the only child lives really close. She's like a little sister to her really. Angie's good with little children.

MARLENE: Do you want to work with children, Angie? / Be a teacher or a nursery nurse?

JOYCE: I don't think she's ever thought of it.

MARLENE: What do you want to do?

JOYCE: She hasn't an idea in her head what she wants to do. / Lucky to get anything.

MARLENE: Angie?

JOYCE: She's not clever like you. (*Pause.*)

MARLENE: I'm not clever, just pushy.

JOYCE: True enough. (MARLENE *takes a bottle of whiskey out of the bag.*) I don't drink spirits.

ANGIE: You do at Christmas.

JOYCE: It's not Christmas, is it?

ANGIE: It's better than Christmas.

MARLENE: Glasses?

JOYCE: Just a small one then.

MARLENE: Do you want some, Angie?

ANGIE: I can't, can I?

JOYCE: Taste it if you want. You won't like it. (ANGIE *tastes it.*)

ANGIE: Mmm.

MARLENE: We got drunk together the night your grandfather died.

JOYCE: We did not get drunk.

MARLENE: I got drunk. You were just overcome with grief.

JOYCE: I still keep up the grave with flowers.

MARLENE: Do you really?

JOYCE: Why wouldn't I?

MARLENE: Have you seen Mother?

JOYCE: Of course I've seen Mother.

MARLENE: I mean lately.

JOYCE: Of course I've seen her lately, I go every Thursday.

MARLENE: (*To* ANGIE) Do you remember your grandfather?

ANGIE: He got me out of the bath one night in a towel.

MARLENE: Did he? I don't think he ever gave me a bath. Did he give you a bath, Joyce? He probably got soft in his old age. Did you like him?

ANGIE: Yes of course.

MARLENE: Why?

ANGIE: What?

MARLENE: So what's the news? How's Mrs. Paisley? Still going crazily? / And Dorothy. What happened to Dorothy?*

ANGIE: Who's Mrs. Paisley?

JOYCE: *She went to Canada.

MARLENE: Did she? What to do?

JOYCE: I don't know. She just went to Canada.

MARLENE: Well / good for her.

ANGIE: Mr. Connolly killed his wife.

MARLENE: What, Connolly at Whitegates?

ANGIE: They found her body in the garden. / Under the cabbages.

MARLENE: He was always so proper.

JOYCE: Stuck up git,° Connolly. Best lawyer money could buy but he couldn't get out of it. She was carrying on with Matthew.

MARLENE: How old's Matthew then?

JOYCE: Twenty-one. / He's got a motorbike.

MARLENE: I think he's about six.

ANGIE: How can he be six? He's six years older than me. / If he was six I'd be nothing, I'd be just born this minute.

JOYCE: Your aunty knows that, she's just being silly. She means it's so long since she's been here she's forgotten about Matthew.

ANGIE: You were here for my birthday when I was nine. I had a pink cake. Kit was only five then, she was four, she hadn't started school yet. She could read already when she went to school. You remember my birthday? / You remember me?

MARLENE: Yes, I remember the cake.

ANGIE: You remember me?

MARLENE: Yes, I remember you.

ANGIE: And Mum and Dad was there, and Kit was.

MARLENE: Yes, how is your dad? Where is he tonight? Up the pub?

JOYCE: No, he's not here.

MARLENE: I can see he's not here.

JOYCE: He moved out.

MARLENE: What? When did he? / Just recently?*

ANGIE: Didn't you know that? You don't know much.

JOYCE: *No, it must be three years ago. Don't be rude, Angie.

ANGIE: I'm not, am I, Aunty? What else don't you know?

JOYCE: You was in America or somewhere. You sent a postcard.

ANGIE: I've got that in my room. It's the Grand Canyon. Do you want to see it? Shall I get it? I can get it for you.

MARLENE: Yes, all right. (ANGIE *goes.*)

JOYCE: You could be married with twins for all I know. You must have affairs and break up and I don't need to know about any of that so I don't see what the fuss is about.

---

git, idiot.

MARLENE: What fuss? (ANGIE *comes back with the postcard.*)

ANGIE: "Driving across the states for a new job in L.A. It's a long way but the car goes very fast. It's very hot. Wish you were here. Love from Aunty Marlene."

JOYCE: Did you make a lot of money?

MARLENE: I spent a lot.

ANGIE: I want to go to America. Will you take me?

JOYCE: She's not going to America, she's been to America, stupid.

ANGIE: She might go again, stupid. It's not something you do once. People who go keep going all the time, back and forth on jets. They go on Concorde and Laker and get jet lag. Will you take me?

MARLENE: I'm not planning a trip.

ANGIE: Will you let me know?

JOYCE: Angie, / you're getting silly.

ANGIE: I want to be American.

JOYCE: It's time you were in bed.

ANGIE: No it's not. / I don't have to go to bed at all tonight.

JOYCE: School in the morning.

ANGIE: I'll wake up.

JOYCE: Come on now, you know how you get.

ANGIE: How do I get? / I don't get anyhow.*

JOYCE: Angie. *Are you staying the night?

MARLENE: Yes, if that's all right. / I'll see you in the morning.

ANGIE: You can have my bed. I'll sleep on the sofa.

JOYCE: You will not, you'll sleep in your bed. / Think

ANGIE: Mum.

JOYCE: I can't see through that? I can just see you going to sleep / with us talking.

ANGIE: I would, I would go to sleep, I'd love that.

JOYCE: I'm going to get cross, Angie.

ANGIE: I want to show her something.

JOYCE: Then bed.

ANGIE: It's a secret.

JOYCE: Then I expect it's in your room so off you go. Give us a shout when you're ready for bed and your aunty'll be up and see you.

ANGIE: Will you?

MARLENE: Yes of course. (ANGIE *goes. Silence.*) It's cold tonight.

JOYCE: Will you be all right on the sofa? You can / have my bed.

MARLENE: The sofa's fine.

JOYCE: Yes the forecast said rain tonight but it's held off.

MARLENE: I was going to walk down to the estuary but I've left it a bit late. Is it just the same?

JOYCE: They cut down the hedges a few years back. Is that since you were here?

MARLENE: But it's not changed down the end, all the mud? And the reeds? We used to pick them up when they were bigger than us. Are there still lapwings?

JOYCE: You get strangers walking there on a Sunday. I expect they're looking at the mud and the lapwings, yes.

MARLENE: You could have left.

JOYCE: Who says I wanted to leave?

MARLENE: Stop getting at me then, you're really boring.

JOYCE: How could I have left?

MARLENE: Did you want to?

JOYCE: I said how, / how could I?

MARLENE: If you'd wanted to you'd have done it.

JOYCE: Christ.

MARLENE: Are we getting drunk?

JOYCE: Do you want something to eat?

MARLENE: No, I'm getting drunk.

JOYCE: Funny time to visit, Sunday evening.

MARLENE: I came this morning. I spent the day—

ANGIE: (*Off*) Aunty! Aunty Marlene!

MARLENE: I'd better go.

JOYCE: Go on then.

MARLENE: All right.

ANGIE: (*Off*) Aunty! Can you hear me? I'm ready.

(MARLENE *goes.* JOYCE *goes on sitting, clears up, sits again.* MARLENE *comes back.*)

JOYCE: So what's the secret?

MARLENE: It's a secret.

JOYCE: I know what it is anyway.

MARLENE: I bet you don't. You always said that.

JOYCE: It's her exercise book.

MARLENE: Yes, but you don't know what's in it.

JOYCE: It's some game, some secret society she has with Kit.

MARLENE: You don't know the password. You don't know the code.

JOYCE: You're really in it, aren't you. Can you do the handshake?

MARLENE: She didn't mention a handshake.

JOYCE: I thought they'd have a special handshake. She spends hours writing that but she's useless at school. She copies things out of books about black magic, and politicians out of the paper. It's a bit childish.

MARLENE: I think it's a plot to take over the world.

JOYCE: She's been in the remedial class the last two years.

MARLENE: I came up this morning and spent the day in Ipswich. I went to see Mother.

JOYCE: Did she recognize you?

MARLENE: Are you trying to be funny?

JOYCE: No, she does wander.

MARLENE: She wasn't wandering at all, she was very lucid thank you.

JOYCE: You were very lucky then.

MARLENE: Fucking awful life she's had.

JOYCE: Don't tell me.

MARLENE: Fucking waste.

JOYCE: Don't talk to me.

MARLENE: Why shouldn't I talk? Why shouldn't I talk to you? / Isn't she my mother too?

JOYCE: Look, you've left, you've gone away, / we can do without you.

MARLENE: I left home, so what, I left home. People do leave home / it is normal.

JOYCE: We understand that, we can do without you.

MARLENE: We weren't happy. Were you happy?

JOYCE: Don't come back.

MARLENE: So it's just your mother is it, your child, you never wanted me round, / you were jealous

JOYCE: Here we go.

MARLENE: of me because I was the little one and I was clever.

JOYCE: I'm not clever enough for all this psychology / if that's what it is.

MARLENE: Why can't I visit my own family / without

JOYCE: Aah.

MARLENE: all this?

JOYCE: Just don't go on about Mum's life when you haven't been to see her for how many years. / I go

MARLENE: It's up to me.

JOYCE: and see her every week.

MARLENE: Then don't go and see her every week.

JOYCE: Somebody has to.

MARLENE: No they don't. / Why do they?

JOYCE: How would I feel if I didn't go?

MARLENE: A lot better.

JOYCE: I hope you feel better.

MARLENE: It's up to me.

JOYCE: You couldn't get out of here fast enough. (*Pause.*)

MARLENE: Of course I couldn't get out of here fast enough. What was I going to do? Marry a dairyman who'd come home pissed? / Don't you fucking this

JOYCE: Christ.

MARLENE: fucking that fucking bitch fucking tell me what to fucking do fucking.

JOYCE: I don't know how you could leave your own child.

MARLENE: You were quick enough to take her.

JOYCE: What does that mean?

MARLENE: You were quick enough to take her.

JOYCE: Or what? Have her put in a home? Have some stranger / take her would you rather?

MARLENE: You couldn't have one so you took mine.

JOYCE: I didn't know that then.

MARLENE: Like hell, / married three years.

JOYCE: I didn't know that. Plenty of people / take that long.

MARLENE: Well it turned out lucky for you, didn't it?

JOYCE: Turned out all right for you by the look of you. You'd be getting a few less thousand a year.

MARLENE: Not necessarily.

JOYCE: You'd be stuck here / like you said.

MARLENE: I could have taken her with me.

JOYCE: You didn't want to take her with you. It's no good coming back now, Marlene, / and saying—

MARLENE: I know a managing director who's got two children, she breastfeeds in the board room, she pays a hundred pounds a week on domestic help alone and she can afford that because she's an extremely high-powered lady earning a great deal of money.

JOYCE: So what's that got to do with you at the age of seventeen?

MARLENE: Just because you were married and had somewhere to live—

JOYCE: You could have lived at home. / Or live

MARLENE: Don't be stupid.

JOYCE: with me and Frank. / You

MARLENE: You never suggested.

JOYCE: said you weren't keeping it. You shouldn't have had it / if you wasn't

MARLENE: Here we go.

JOYCE: going to keep it. You was the most stupid, / for someone so clever you was the most stupid, get yourself pregnant, not go to the doctor, not tell.

MARLENE: You wanted it, you said you were glad, I remember the day, you said I'm glad you never got rid of it, I'll look after it, you said that down by the river. So what are you saying, sunshine, you don't want her?

JOYCE: Course I'm not saying that.

MARLENE: Because I'll take her, / wake her up and pack now.

JOYCE: You wouldn't know how to begin to look after her.

MARLENE: Don't you want her?

JOYCE: Course I do, she's my child.

MARLENE: Then what are you going on about / why did I have her?

JOYCE: You said I got her off you / when you didn't—

MARLENE: I said you were lucky / the way it—

JOYCE: Have a child now if you want one. You're not old.

MARLENE: I might do.

JOYCE: Good. (*Pause.*)

MARLENE: I've been on the pill so long / I'm probably sterile.

JOYCE: Listen when Angie was six months I did get pregnant and I lost it because I was so tired looking after your fucking baby / because she cried so

MARLENE: You never told me.

JOYCE: much—yes I did tell you— / and the doctor

MARLENE: Well I forgot.

JOYCE: said if I'd sat down all day with my feet up I'd've kept it / and that's the only chance I ever had because after that—

MARLENE: I've had two abortions, are you interested? Shall I tell you about them? Well I won't, it's boring, it wasn't a problem. I don't like messy talk about blood / and what a bad time we all had. I

JOYCE: If I hadn't had your baby. The doctor said.

MARLENE: don't want a baby. I don't want to talk about gynecology.

JOYCE: Then stop trying to get Angie off of me.

MARLENE: I come down here after six years. All night you've been saying I don't come often enough. If I don't come for another six years she'll be twenty-one, will that be OK?

JOYCE: That'll be fine, yes, six years would suit me fine. (*Pause.*)

MARLENE: I was afraid of this. I only came because I thought you wanted . . . I just want . . . (*She cries.*)

JOYCE: Don't grizzle,° Marlene, for God's sake. Marly? Come on, pet. Love you really. Fucking stop it, will you? (*She goes to* MARLENE.)

MARLENE: No, let me cry. I like it. (*They laugh,* MARLENE *begins to stop crying.*) I knew I'd cry if I wasn't careful.

JOYCE: Everyone's always crying in this house. Nobody takes any notice.

MARLENE: You've been wonderful looking after Angie.

JOYCE: Don't get carried away.

MARLENE: I can't write letters but I do think of you.

JOYCE: You're getting drunk. I'm going to make some tea.

MARLENE: Love you. (JOYCE *goes to make tea.*)

JOYCE: I can see why you'd want to leave. It's a dump here.

MARLENE: So what's this about you and Frank?

JOYCE: He was always carrying on, wasn't he. And if I wanted to go out in the evening he'd go mad, even if it was nothing, a class, I was going to go to an evening class. So he had this girlfriend, only twenty-two poor cow, and I said go on, off you go, hoppit. I don't think he even likes her.

MARLENE: So what about money?

JOYCE: I've always said I don't want your money.

MARLENE: No, does he send you money?

JOYCE: I've got four different cleaning jobs. Adds up. There's not a lot round here.

MARLENE: Does Angie miss him?

JOYCE: She doesn't say.

MARLENE: Does she see him?

JOYCE: He was never that fond of her to be honest.

MARLENE: He tried to kiss me once. When you were engaged.

JOYCE: Did you fancy him?

MARLENE: No, he looked like a fish.

JOYCE: He was lovely then.

MARLENE: Ugh.

JOYCE: Well I fancied him. For about three years.

MARLENE: Have you got someone else?

JOYCE: There's not a lot round here. Mind you, the minute you're on your own, you'd be amazed how your friends' husbands drop by. I'd sooner do without.

MARLENE: I don't see why you couldn't take my money.

JOYCE: I do, so don't bother about it.

MARLENE: Only got to ask.

JOYCE: So what about you? Good job?

MARLENE: Good for a laugh. / Got back

JOYCE: Good for more than a laugh I should think.

MARLENE: from the US of A a bit wiped out and slotted into this speedy employment agency and still there.

JOYCE: You can always find yourself work then?

MARLENE: That's right.

JOYCE: And men?

MARLENE: Oh there's always men.

JOYCE: No one special?

MARLENE: There's fellas who like to be seen with a high-flying lady. Shows they've got something really good in their pants. But they can't take the day to day. They're waiting for me to turn into the little woman. Or maybe I'm just horrible of course.

JOYCE: Who needs them.

MARLENE: Who needs them. Well I do. But I need adventures more. So on on into the sunset. I think the eighties are going to be stupendous.

JOYCE: Who for?

MARLENE: For me. / I think I'm going up up up.

JOYCE: Oh for you. Yes, I'm sure they will.

MARLENE: And for the country, come to that. Get the economy back on its feet and whoosh. She's a tough lady, Maggie.° I'd give her a job. / She just needs to hang

JOYCE: You voted for them, did you?

MARLENE: in there. This country needs to stop whining. / Monetarism is not

JOYCE: Drink your tea and shut up, pet.

MARLENE: stupid. It takes time, determination. No more slop. / And

JOYCE: Well I think they're filthy bastards.

MARLENE: who's got to drive it on? First woman prime minister. Terrifico. Aces. Right on. / You must admit. Certainly gets my vote.

JOYCE: What good's first woman if it's her? I suppose you'd have liked Hitler if he was a woman. Ms. Hitler. Got a lot done, Hitlerina. / Great adventures.

MARLENE: Bosses still walking on the workers' faces? Still dadda's little parrot? Haven't you learned to think for yourself? I believe in the individual. Look at me.

JOYCE: I am looking at you.

MARLENE: Come on, Joyce, we're not going to quarrel over politics.

JOYCE: We are though.

MARLENE: Forget I mentioned it. Not a word about the slimy unions will cross my lips. (*Pause.*)

JOYCE: You say Mother had a wasted life.

MARLENE: Yes I do. Married to that bastard.

JOYCE: What sort of life did he have? /

---

grizzle, whine.

Maggie, Margaret Thatcher, former prime minister (1979–1991).

MARLENE: Violent life?

JOYCE: Working in the fields like an animal. / Why

MARLENE: Come off it.

JOYCE: wouldn't he want a drink? You want a drink. He couldn't afford whiskey.

MARLENE: I don't want to talk about him.

JOYCE: You started, I was talking about her. She had a rotten life because she had nothing. She went hungry.

MARLENE: She was hungry because he drank the money. / He used to hit her.

JOYCE: It's not all down to him. / Their

MARLENE: She didn't hit him.

JOYCE: lives were rubbish. They were treated like rubbish. He's dead and she'll die soon and what sort of life / did they have?

MARLENE: I saw him one night. I came down.

JOYCE: Do you think I didn't? / They

MARLENE: I still have dreams.

JOYCE: didn't get to America and drive across it in a fast car. / Bad nights, they had bad days.

MARLENE: America, America, you're jealous. / I had to get out, I knew when I

JOYCE: Jealous?

MARLENE: was thirteen, out of their house, out of them, never let that happen to me, / never let him, make my own way, out.

JOYCE: Jealous of what you've done, you'd be ashamed of me if I came to your office, your smart friends, wouldn't you, I'm ashamed of you, think of nothing but yourself, you've got on, nothing's changed for most people, / has it?

MARLENE: I hate the working class / which is what

JOYCE: Yes you do.

MARLENE: you're going to go on about now, it doesn't exist any more, it means lazy and stupid. / I don't

JOYCE: Come on, now we're getting it.

MARLENE: like the way they talk. I don't like beer guts and football vomit and saucy tits / and brothers and sisters—

JOYCE: I spit when I see a Rolls Royce, scratch it with my ring / Mercedes it was.

MARLENE: Oh very mature—

JOYCE: I hate the cows I work for / and their dirty dishes with blanquette of fucking veau.

MARLENE: and I will not be pulled down to their level by a flying picket and I won't be sent to Siberia / or a loony bin just because I'm original. And I support

JOYCE: No, you'll be on a yacht, you'll be head of Coca Cola and you wait, the eighties is going to be stupendous all right because we'll get you lot off our backs—

MARLENE: Reagan even if he is a lousy movie star because the reds are swarming up his map and I want to be free in a free world—

JOYCE: What? / What?

MARLENE: I know what I mean / by that—not shut up here.

JOYCE: So don't be round here when it happens because if someone's kicking you I'll just laugh. (*Silence.*)

MARLENE: I don't mean anything personal. I don't believe in class. Anyone can do anything if they've got what it takes.

JOYCE: And if they haven't?

MARLENE: If they're stupid or lazy or frightened, I'm not going to help them get a job, why should I?

JOYCE: What about Angie?

MARLENE: What about Angie?

JOYCE: She's stupid, lazy, and frightened, so what about her?

MARLENE: You run her down too much. She'll be all right.

JOYCE: I don't expect so, no. I expect her children will say what a wasted life she had. If she has children. Because nothing's changed and it won't with them in.

MARLENE: Them, them. / Us and them?

JOYCE: And you're one of them.

MARLENE: And you're us, wonderful us, and Angie's us / and Mum and Dad's us.

JOYCE: Yes, that's right, and you're them.

MARLENE: Come on, Joyce, what a night. You've got what it takes.

JOYCE: I know I have.

MARLENE: I didn't really mean all that.

JOYCE: I did.

MARLENE: But we're friends anyway.

JOYCE: I don't think so, no.

MARLENE: Well it's lovely to be out in the country. I really must make the effort to come more often. I want to go to sleep. I want to go to sleep. (JOYCE *gets blankets for the sofa.*)

JOYCE: Goodnight then. I hope you'll be warm enough.

MARLENE: Goodnight. Joyce—

JOYCE: No, pet. Sorry. (JOYCE *goes.* MARLENE *sits wrapped in a blanket and has another drink.* ANGIE *comes in.*)

ANGIE: Mum?

MARLENE: Angie? What's the matter?

ANGIE: Mum?

MARLENE: No, she's gone to bed. It's Aunty Marlene.

ANGIE: Frightening.

MARLENE: Did you have a bad dream? What happened in it? Well you're awake now, aren't you, pet?

ANGIE: Frightening.

Figure 1. Marlene (Gwen Taylor, *seated center*) hosts a dinner for her guests. They are (*left to right*): Lady Nijo (Lindsay Duncan), Dull Gret (Carole Hayman), Pope Joan (Selina Cadell), Patient Griselda (Lesley Manville), and Isabella Bird (Deborah Findlay). The Royal Court production of *Top Girls,* was directed by Max Stafford-Clark, 1982. (Photograph: Donald Cooper, Photostage Limited.)

Figure 2. Kit (Lou Wakefield) and Angie (Carole Hayman) share confidences in "a shelter made of junk, made by children" in the Royal Court production of *Top Girls,* directed by Max Stafford-Clark, 1982. (Photograph: Donald Cooper, Photostage Limited.)

Staging of *Top Girls*

REVIEW OF THE ROYAL COURT THEATRE
PREMIERE, 1982, BY ROBERT CUSHMAN

Last week Caryl Churchill's *Top Girls* opened on the Royal Court's main stage, while Louise Page's *Salonika* ended its run upstairs. For a short time the Court housed the two most interesting new plays of the year, both of them written by women. A chap has to take notice.

Miss Churchill's last play, *Cloud Nine,* had a complicated time-scheme, simplicity itself compared to what happens in *Top Girls.* In the first scene Marlene, who has just been made managing director of an employment agency, hosts a dinner party at a London restaurant called La Prima Donna. Her guests are various historical prima donnas: Isabella Bird, Scots Victorian lady traveler; Lady Nijo, thirteenth-century Japanese courtesan turned Buddhist nun, and also a traveler; Dull Gret, kitchenmaid in armor, centerpiece of a Bruegel painting depicting a female invasion of Hell; Pope Joan; Patient Griselda.

These are all ladies who have suffered. Joan, for example, may have been Pope, but she ended up stoned to death, having ill-advisedly given birth. On the other hand they are all, in some sense, successes. Even Griselda, as Marlene points out, made it into three bestsellers through the terrible psychological battering she took from her husband.

They all profess devotion to the men in their lives: fathers, emperors, lovers actual or platonic, even husbands. This shocks Marlene; she wants them all as her patron saints, but she can't stomach Griselda, who typically arrives late and will only order cheese and biscuits. At first we share her irritation; after all, she's modern and they're archaic. Then our feelings slide.

Dull Gret doesn't say much. She's the real subversive. She—if you except an even more silent waitress—is the only person present not, by birth or adoption, upper class. She is played by Carole Hayman, who appears in the rest of the play as a modern girl similarly disinherited: someone who has dreams but no prospects.

This girl is presented to us as Marlene's niece. The bulk of the play is split between Marlene's London office and her East Anglian roots. The office is revealing, since not only is Marlene a success herself, but she is in the business of sniffing out success in other people, and of mercilessly weeding out failure. The play here goes down intriguing side-turnings, showing us two of Marlene's juniors, both self-consciously tough, and a variety of their clients.

One of them is nervous and middle-aging, aware of having suppressed her sexuality to survive on men's terms in their world. She is played by Selina Cadell, who has already scored a booming success as Pope Joan. Another is differently androgynous, with salesman fantasies.

Meanwhile there is Marlene's sister, who stayed at home. (Isabella Bird's sister also stayed home, though I confess I failed to pick up this thread at the time.) She points out that Marlene's upward mobility has changed nothing for most women, or indeed most men. Marlene declares herself a Thatcherite, which we might have deduced for ourselves. Her sister's political stance comes as a surprise, and seems manufactured for the occasion.

But the play runs thin nowhere else. Thoroughly personal in tone and structure, it manages to be an amazingly full polygonal presentation of a feminist predicament: career women behaving like career men. The situation is (mostly) deplored, but sympathy is withheld from no one. Miss Churchill also does for overlapping dialogue on stage what Robert Altman has done in the movies.

The seven actresses are terrific. Gwen Taylor, in her third play on socially sundered sisters (she's also played Mrs. Thatcher), is Marlene; Lindsay Duncan is gorgeous as Lady Nijo, wrestling simultaneously with the ways of Western woman and her first zabaglione. Max Stafford-Clark directed; I congratulate him, and wonder how he felt at rehearsals.

SAM SHEPARD

1943–

Sam Shepard has always been on the move, beginning with his early days as an Air Force child: "By the time I was six I had lived or spent time in Illinois, Wisconsin, Florida, North and South Dakota, Iowa, Washington, Indiana, Idaho, Michigan, the Marianas Islands, and finally California, where I stayed more or less until the age of eighteen." After high school, a year at junior college, and a variety of jobs in California (stable hand, herdsman, orange picker, sheep shearer), Shepard joined the Bishop's Company Repertory Players and hit the road again, touring New England and finally ending up in New York City. There, in addition to the commercial theater on Broadway, and the lively world of Off-Broadway, a new movement was flourishing, financed by playwrights and actors, usually in nontheatrical settings (churches, restaurants, even a hardware store), known collectively as Off-Off-Broadway. Shepard made his way into that world by a happy coincidence of timing and employment. Working as a bus boy at the Village Gate, a nightclub specializing in jazz, he met the head waiter, Ralph Cook, just as Cook was planning a new Off-Off venture at St. Mark's Church (located in New York's Bowery). Prophetically named Theatre Genesis, the new company opened its doors with a double bill of Shepard's *Cowboys* and *The Rock Garden* (1964). Shepard's prolific output (six short plays in 1965 alone) found a highly supportive environment in Theatre Genesis. Not only did he drop his family name (he was originally named Samuel Shepard Rogers III) but he quickly established his theatrical identity.

Though many now well-known playwrights were associated with Off-Off Broadway in the 1960s—John Guare, Maria Irene Fornes, Megan Terry, Jean-Claude van Itallie, Leonard Melfi, Rochelle Owens, Lanford Wilson, to name a few—Shepard's astonishing output and his compellingly surrealist visions of America distinguished him as a playwright of extraordinary talent. His plays moved from Theatre Genesis to the American Place Theatre where *La Turista*, produced in 1967, won him the first of nine Obie awards; *The Unseen Hand* (1969) was produced at the La Mama Experimental Theatre Club, one of the still surviving venues of Off-Off Broadway; and in 1970, his most scenically complex and longest play to date, *Operation Sidewinder*, opened at Lincoln Center's Vivian Beaumont Theater, with a large cast, and, in the center of the stage, a six-foot sidewinder rattlesnake, which was also an Air Force computer. Such arresting theatrical images helped Shepard's plays gain recognition from audiences and critics alike, as well as support for himself from prestigious foundations; he won a Rockefeller grant in 1967 and a Guggenheim fellowship in 1968.

But the real turning point in Shepard's playwriting came during his extended stay in England from 1971 to 1974: "It wasn't until I came to England that I found out what it means to be an American." Having discovered his cultural roots, he immediately embodied them in *The Tooth of Crime* (1972), a recasting of the Western shoot-out as a confrontation between the established rock star, Hoss, and the "gypsy" challenger, Crow. Combining the mythology of the Western and popular music, the use of a referee and pom-pom–waving cheerleaders, Shepard drew not only on his own intermittent musical career (as a drummer), but even more on his fascination with language, since the climactic duel between Hoss and Crow involves a variety of linguistic styles, which in turn create striking physical gestures. Working in a similarly eclectic cultural vein, Shepard to date has written over forty plays—short pieces, full-length works, collaborative efforts, and film scripts. Not since Eugene O'Neill has an American playwright been so prolific. And, like O'Neill, who went through an extended period of experimenting with symbolic drama before turning in his last autobiographical plays to a much more realistic style, Shepard too has moved from symbolic settings such as the junkyard of Azusa ("Everything from 'A' to 'Z' in the USA") in *The Unseen Hand* or the snake-dominated desert of *Operation Sidewinder* to settings that people might actually live in. Thus, the stage directions in *Curse of the Starving Class* (1978) call for "a very plain breakfast table with a red oilcloth covering it" as well as "a working refrigerator and a small gas stove." In *Buried Child* (1979), the action takes place in an old farmhouse, sparsely furnished, but with realistic items such as a couch and a television set. In *True West* (1980), the set combines kitchen and living room, and Shepard insists in his stage directions that "the set should be constructed realistically" and that "the costumes should be exactly representative of who the characters are."

Though the worlds of these three plays—like those of *Fool for Love* (1983) and *A Lie of the Mind* (1985)—may seem more realistic than those depicted in his earlier work, certain thematic and structural motifs link them to the early plays. Drawing on his unrooted childhood and on his adolescence in California, a state that is literally the last frontier of America, Shepard constantly shows people living on the edge, sometimes physically, but always emotionally. *Curse of the Starving Class* takes place in Southern California, where the lushness of the surroundings throws into sharp relief the barrenness of family relationships ("I could smell the avocado blossoms" says one character while another later unloads a bagful of artichokes into a mostly empty refrigerator). *True West* also takes place in Southern California, where the smooth glittery world of Hollywood, both as a real place and as a world of dreams and fictions, is constantly threatened by the conflict between two brothers. And in *Fool for Love*, the setting is significantly a "stark, low-rent motel room *on the edge of the Mojave Desert*" [emphasis added]. All of these Western settings picture an America teetering on the verge of emotional and social annihilation. In the nineteenth century, the West lured adventurers, speculators, outcasts, and pioneers and thus became the mythic place for America to reinvent itself. In the twentieth century, Shepard evokes that myth as a way of showing how desperately America—and its people—need to find themselves again.

That need for self-definition and identity creates one of Shepard's most noticeable stylistic traits, the monologue. In one sense, Shepard's characters speak in monologue because they are isolated and, like Jerry in Edward Albee's *The Zoo Story*, can't easily make contact. Blue Morphan in *The Unseen Hand* sits in a junked Chevy convertible and talks to an imaginary driver because there is no one else for him to talk to. Halie, the mother in *Buried Child*, lives in emotional isolation, focusing on her dead son, Ansel, and imagining how different her barren life would have been if Ansel had lived, ignoring the two men on stage with her. And in *Fool for Love*, Eddie's monologue about his missing father and May's monologue about her mother lead finally to the revelation that they are half-brother and sister.

Repeatedly, Shepard sees his characters linked in mutual dependence and mutual estrangement or hostility. The story of the eagle who picked up a tomcat ends *Curse of the Starving Class* with a metaphoric statement that reverberates through many of Shepard's plays: "They fight like crazy in the middle of the sky. That cat's tearing his chest out, and the eagle's trying to drop him, but the cat won't let go because he knows if he falls he'll die." Usually the linkage is a violent one, as Shepard finds many ways to represent the violence that seems inherent in both people and places. There is literal violence, with offstage explosions such as the car blowing up at the end of *Curse of the Starving Class* and Eddie's horse trailer catching fire at the end of *Fool for Love*. There is symbolic violence when Bradley puts his fingers into Shelly's mouth in *Buried Child* or Eddie systematically ropes the bedposts in *Fool for Love*. There is the physical violence of a set turned from a neat apartment to "a desert junkyard" in *True West*. And in *Fool for Love*, Shepard requires that his actors not only slam doors (carefully miked so that the slam reverberates) but actually hit the walls with their bodies. Thus the motel room becomes a prison in which Eddie and May must confront feelings that both pull them together and drive them apart; they can't live with each other, but they also can't live without each other.

The insistent physicality of *Fool for Love* grows not only from Shepard's vision but also from the collaboration of the actors who first performed Eddie and May—namely, Ed Harris and Kathy Baker—with Shepard, who directed the first two productions in San Francisco and in New York. The actors' willingness to throw themselves—often literally—into their roles exemplifies the powerful hold this destructive relationship can create. After four performances on a weekend, said Ed Harris, "there's a desperation about it. The play is like that. It's the characters' last hour and a half together." May's clinging to Eddie in the opening moments (see Figure 1) powerfully embodies her need for him, while the violence that permeates their relationship is expressed not only through body language but through props such as the shotgun that Eddie carefully dismantles (see Figure 2). Though the motel room is bleakly empty (see Figure 3), such emptiness is filled with the desperation and energy of both characters and actors as they create what Shepard calls "a certain kind of emotional terrain that was true to itself," a territory not of land but of feeling.

FOOL FOR LOVE
for Billy Pearson

BY SAM SHEPARD

"The proper response to love is to accept it. There is nothing to do."

—Archbishop Anthony Bloom

This play is to be performed relentlessly without a break.

SCENE

Stark, low-rent motel room on the edge of the Mojave Desert. Faded green plaster walls. Dark brown linoleum floor. No rugs. Cast iron four poster single bed, slightly off center favoring stage right, set horizontally to audience. Bed covered with faded blue chenille bedspread. Metal table with well-worn yellow Formica top. Two matching metal chairs in the fifties "S" shape design with yellow plastic seats and backs, also well-worn. Table set extreme down left (from actor's p.o.v.). Chairs set upstage and down right of table. Nothing on the table. Faded yellow exterior door in the center of the stage-left wall. When this door is opened, a small orange porch light shines into room. Yellow bathroom door up right of the stage-right wall. This door slightly ajar to begin with, revealing part of an old style porcelain sink, white towels, a general clutter of female belongings and allowing a yellow light to bleed onto stage. Large picture window dead center of upstage wall, framed by dirty, long, dark green plastic curtains. Yellow-orange light from a streetlamp shines thru window.

Extreme down left, next to the table and chairs is a small extended platform on the same level as the stage. The floor is black and it's framed by black curtains. The only object on the platform is an old maple rocking chair facing upstage right. A pillow with no slipcover rests on the seat. An old horse blanket with holes is laced to the back of the rocker. The color of the blanket should be subdued—grays and blacks.

Lights fade to black on set. In the dark, Merle Haggard's tune "Wake Up" from his The Way I Am album is heard. Lights begin to rise slowly on stage in the tempo of the song. Volume swells with the lights until they arrive at their mark. The platform remains in darkness with only a slight spill from the stage lights. Three actors are revealed.

CHARACTERS

THE OLD MAN *sits in the rocker facing up right so he's just slightly profile to the audience. A bottle of whiskey sits on the floor beside him. He picks up bottle and pours whiskey into a Styrofoam cup and drinks. He has a scraggly red beard, wears an old stained "open-road" Stetson hat (the kind with the short brim), a sun-bleached, dark quilted jacket with the stuffing coming out at the elbows, black-and-white checkered slacks that are too short in the legs, beat up, dark western boots, an old vest and a pale green shirt. He exists only in the minds of* MAY *and* EDDIE, *even though they might talk to him directly and acknowledge his physical presence.* THE OLD MAN *treats them as though they all existed in the same time and place.*

MAY *sits on the edge of bed facing audience, feet on floor, legs apart, elbows on knees, hands hanging limp and crossed between her knees, head hanging forward, face staring at floor. She is absolutely still and maintains this attitude until she speaks. She wears a blue denim full skirt, baggy white T-shirt and bare feet with a silver ankle bracelet. She's in her early thirties.*

EDDIE *sits in the upstage chair by the table, facing* MAY. *He wears muddy, broken-down cowboy boots with silver gaffer's tape wrapped around them at the toe and instep, well-worn, faded, dirty jeans that smell like horse sweat. Brown western shirt with snaps. A pair of spurs dangles from his belt. When he walks, he limps slightly and gives the impression he's rarely off a horse. There's a peculiar broken-down quality about his body in general, as though he's aged long before his time. He's in his late thirties. On the floor, between his feet, is a leather bucking strap like bronc riders use. He wears a bucking glove on his right hand and works resin into the glove from a small white bag. He stares at* MAY *as he does this and ignores* THE OLD MAN. *As the song nears the end of its fade, he leans over, sticks his gloved hand into the handle of the bucking strap and twists it so that it makes a weird stretching sound from the friction of the resin and leather. The song ends, lights up full. He pulls his hand out and removes glove.*

EDDIE: *(seated, tossing glove on the table. Short pause)* May, look. May? I'm not goin' anywhere. See? I'm right here. I'm not gone. Look. *(she won't)* I don't know why you won't just look at me. You know it's me.

Who else do you think it is. *(pause)* You want some water or somethin'? Huh? *(he gets up slowly, goes cautiously to her, strokes her head softly, she stays still)* May? Come on. You can't just sit around here like this. How long you been sittin' here anyway? You want me to go outside and get you something? Some potato chips or something? *(she suddenly grabs his closest leg with both arms and holds tight burying her head between his knees)* I'm not gonna' leave. Don't worry. I'm not gonna' leave. I'm stayin' right here. I already told ya' that. *(she squeezes tighter to his leg, he just stands there, strokes her head softly)* May? Let go, okay? Honey? I'll put you back in bed. Okay? *(she grabs his other leg and holds on tight to both)* Come on. I'll put you in bed and make you some hot tea or somethin'. You want some tea? *(she shakes her head violently, keeps holding on)* With lemon? Some Ovaltine? May, you gotta' let go of me now, okay? *(pause, then she pushes him away and returns to her original position)* Now just lay back and try to relax. *(he starts to try to push her back gently on the bed as he pulls back the blankets. She erupts furiously, leaping off bed and lashing out at him with her fists. He backs off. She returns to bed and stares at him wild-eyed and angry, faces him squarely)*

EDDIE: *(after pause)* You want me to go?

(She shakes her head.)

MAY: No!
EDDIE: Well, what do you want then?
MAY: You smell.
EDDIE: I smell.
MAY: You do.
EDDIE: I been drivin' for days.
MAY: Your fingers smell.
EDDIE: Horses.
MAY: Pussy.
EDDIE: Come on, May.
MAY: They smell like metal.
EDDIE: I'm not gonna' start this shit.
MAY: Rich pussy. Very clean.
EDDIE: Yeah, sure.
MAY: You know it's true.
EDDIE: I came to see if you were all right.
MAY: I don't need you!
EDDIE: Okay. *(turns to go, collects his glove and bucking strap)* Fine.
MAY: Don't go!
EDDIE: I'm goin'.

(He exits stage-left door, slamming it behind him; the door booms.)

MAY: *(agonized scream)* Don't go!!!

(She grabs pillow, clutching it to her chest, then throws herself face down on bed, moaning and moving from one end of the bed to the other on her elbows and knees. EDDIE is heard returning to stage-left door outside. She leaps off bed clutching pillow, stands upstage right of bed, facing stage-left door. EDDIE enters stage-left door, banging it behind him. He's left the glove and bucking strap offstage. They stand there facing each other for a second. He makes a move toward her. MAY retreats to extreme upstage-right corner of room clutching pillow to her chest. EDDIE stays against left wall, facing her.)

EDDIE: What am I gonna' do? Huh? What am I supposed to do?
MAY: You know.
EDDIE: What.
MAY: You're gonna' erase me.
EDDIE: What're you talkin' about?
MAY: You're either gonna' erase me or have me erased.
EDDIE: Why would I want that? Are you kidding?
MAY: Because I'm in the way.
EDDIE: Don't be stupid.
MAY: I'm smarter than you are and you know it. I can smell your thoughts before you even think 'em.

(EDDIE moves along wall to upstage-left corner. MAY holds her ground in opposite corner.)

EDDIE: May, I'm tryin' to take care of you. All right?
MAY: No, you're not. You're just guilty. Gutless and guilty.
EDDIE: Great.

(He moves down left to table, sticking close to wall. Pause.)

MAY: *(quietly, staying in corner)* I'm gonna' kill her ya' know.
EDDIE: Who?
MAY: Who.
EDDIE: Don't talk like that.

(MAY slowly begins to move downstage right as EDDIE simultaneously moves up left. Both of them press the walls as they move.)

MAY: I am. I'm gonna' kill her and then I'm gonna' kill you. Systematically. With sharp knives. Two separate knives. One for her and one for you. *(she slams wall with her elbow. Wall resonates)* So the blood doesn't mix. I'm gonna' torture her first though. Not you. I'm just gonna' let you have it. Probably in the midst of a kiss. Right when you think everything's been healed up. Right in the moment when you're sure you've got me buffaloed. That's when you'll die.

(She arrives extreme down right at the very limits of the set. EDDIE in the extreme up left corner. Pause.)

EDDIE: You know how many miles I went outa' my way just to come here and see you? You got any idea?
MAY: Nobody asked you to come.
EDDIE: Two thousand, four hundred and eighty.
MAY: Yeah? Where were you, Katmandu or something?

EDDIE: Two thousand, four hundred and eighty miles.
MAY: So what!

(He drops his head, stares at floor. Pause. She stares at him. He begins to move slowly down left, sticking close to wall as he speaks.)

EDDIE: I missed you. I did. I missed you more than anything I ever missed in my whole life. I kept thinkin' about you the whole time I was driving. Kept seeing you. Sometimes just a part of you.
MAY: Which part?
EDDIE: Your neck.
MAY: My neck?
EDDIE: Yeah.
MAY: You missed my neck?
EDDIE: I missed all of you but your neck kept coming up for some reason. I kept crying about your neck.
MAY: Crying?
EDDIE: *(he stops by stage-left door. She stays down right)* Yeah. Weeping. Like a little baby. Uncontrollable. It would just start up and stop and then start up all over again. For miles. I couldn't stop it. Cars would pass me on the road. People would stare at me. My face was all twisted up. I couldn't stop my face.
MAY: Was this before or after your little fling with the Countess?
EDDIE: *(he bangs his head into the wall. Wall booms)* There wasn't any fling with any Countess!
MAY: You're a liar.
EDDIE: I took her out to dinner once, okay?
MAY: Ha!

(She moves upstage-right wall.)

EDDIE: Twice.
MAY: You were bumping her on a regular basis! Don't gimme that shit.
EDDIE: You can believe whatever you want.
MAY: *(she stops by bathroom door, opposite Eddie)* I'll believe the truth! It's less confusing.

(Pause.)

EDDIE: I'm takin' you back, May.

(She tosses pillow on bed and moves to upstage-right corner.)

MAY: I'm not going back to that idiot trailer if that's what you think.
EDDIE: I'm movin' it. I got a piece of ground up in Wyoming.
MAY: Wyoming? Are you crazy? I'm not moving to Wyoming. What's up there? Marlboro Men?
EDDIE: You can't stay here.
MAY: Why not? I got a job. I'm a regular citizen here now.
EDDIE: You got a job?
MAY: *(she moves back down to head of bed)* Yeah. What'd you think, I was helpless?

EDDIE: No. I mean—it's been a long time since you had a job.
MAY: I'm a cook.
EDDIE: A cook? You can't even flip an egg, can you?
MAY: I'm not talkin' to you anymore!

(She turns away from him, runs into the bathroom, slams door behind her. EDDIE goes after her, tries door, but she's locked it.)

EDDIE: *(at bathroom door)* May, I got everything worked out. I been thinkin' about this for weeks. I'm gonna' move the trailer. Build a little pipe corral to keep the horses. Have a big vegetable garden. Some chickens maybe.
MAY'S VOICE: *(unseen, behind bathroom door)* I hate chickens! I hate horses! I hate all that shit! You know that. You got me confused with somebody else. You keep comin' up here with this lame country dream life with chickens and vegetables and I can't stand any of it. It makes me puke to even think about it.
EDDIE: *(EDDIE has crossed stage left during this, stops at table)* You'll get used to it.
MAY: *(enters from bathroom)* You're unbelievable!

(She slams bathroom door, crosses upstage to window.)

EDDIE: I'm not lettin' go of you this time, May.

(He sits in chair upstage of table.)

MAY: You never had ahold of me to begin with. *(pause)* How many times have you done this to me?
EDDIE: What.
MAY: Suckered me into some dumb little fantasy and then dropped me like a hot rock. How many times has that happened?
EDDIE: It's no fantasy.
MAY: It's all a fantasy.
EDDIE: And I never dropped you either.
MAY: No, you just disappeared!
EDDIE: I'm here now aren't I?
MAY: Well, praise Jesus God!
EDDIE: I'm gonna' take care of you, May. I am. I'm gonna' stick with you no matter what. I promise.
MAY: Get outa' here.

(Pause.)

EDDIE: What'd you have to go and run off for anyway.
MAY: Run off? Me?
EDDIE: Yeah. Why couldn't you just stay put. You knew I was comin' back to get you.
MAY: *(crossing down to head of bed)* What do you think it's like sittin' in a tin trailer for weeks on end with the wind ripping through it? Waitin' around for the butane to arrive. Hiking down to the Laundromat in the rain. Do you think that's thrilling or some-thin'?
EDDIE: *(still sitting)* I bought you all those magazines.
MAY: What magazines?

EDDIE: I bought you a whole stack of those fashion magazines before I left. I thought you liked those. Those French kind.

MAY: Yeah, I especially liked the one with the Countess on the cover. That was real cute.

(*Pause.*)

EDDIE: All right.

(*He stands.*)

MAY: All right, what.

(*He turns to go out stage-left door.*)

MAY: Where are you going?

EDDIE: Just to get my stuff outa' the truck. I'll be right back.

MAY: What're you movin' in now or something?

EDDIE: Well, I thought I'd spend the night if that's okay.

MAY: Are you kidding?

EDDIE: (*opens door*) Then I'll just leave, I guess.

MAY: (*she stands*) Wait.

(*He closes door. They stand there facing each other for a while. She crosses slowly to him. She stops. He takes a few steps toward her. Stops. They both move closer. Stop. Pause as they look at each other. They embrace. Long, tender kiss. They are very soft with each other. She pulls away from him slightly. Smiles. She looks him straight in the eyes, then suddenly knees him in the groin with tremendous force. EDDIE doubles over and drops like a rock. She stands over him. Pause.*)

MAY: You can take it, right. You're a stunt man.

(*She exits into bathroom, stage right, slams the door behind her. The door is amplified with microphones and a bass drum hidden in the frame so that each time an actor slams it, the door booms loud and long. Same is true for the stage-left door. EDDIE remains on the floor holding his stomach in pain. Stage lights drop to half their intensity as a spot rises softly on THE OLD MAN. He speaks directly to EDDIE.*)

THE OLD MAN: I thought you were supposed to be a fantasist, right? Isn't that basically the deal with you? You dream things up. Isn't that true?

EDDIE: (*stays on floor*) I don't know.

THE OLD MAN: You don't know. Well, if you don't know I don't know who the hell else does. I wanna' show you somethin'. Somethin' real, okay? Somethin' actual.

EDDIE: Sure.

THE OLD MAN: Take a look at that picture on the wall over there. (*he points at wall stage-right. There is no picture but EDDIE stares at the wall.*) Ya' see that? Take a good look at that. Ya' see it?

EDDIE: (*staring at wall*) Yeah.

THE OLD MAN: Ya' know who that is?

EDDIE: I'm not sure.

THE OLD MAN: Barbara Mandrell. That's who that is. Barbara Mandrell. You heard a' her?

EDDIE: Sure.

THE OLD MAN: Well, would you believe me if I told ya' I was married to her?

EDDIE: (*pause*) No.

THE OLD MAN: Well, see, now that's the difference right there. That's realism. I am actually married to Barbara Mandrell in my mind. Can you understand that?

EDDIE: Sure.

THE OLD MAN: Good. I'm glad we have an understanding.

(*THE OLD MAN drinks from his cup. Spot slowly fades to black as stage lights come back up full. These light changes are cued to the opening and closing of doors. MAY enters from bathroom, closes door quietly. She is carrying a sleek red dress, panty hose, a pair of black high heels, a black shoulder purse and a hairbrush. She crosses to foot of bed and throws the clothes on it. Hangs the purse on a bedpost, sits on foot of bed her back to EDDIE and starts brushing her hair. EDDIE remains on floor. She finishes brushing her hair, throws brush on bed, then starts taking off her clothes and changing into the clothes she brought onstage. As she speaks to EDDIE and changes into the new clothes, she gradually transforms from her former tough drabness into a very sexy woman. This occurs almost unnoticeably in the course of her speech.*)

MAY: (*very cold, quick, almost monotone voice like she's writing him a letter*) I don't understand my feelings. I really don't. I don't understand how I could hate you so much after so much time. How, no matter how much I'd like to not hate you, I hate you even more. It grows. I can't even see you now. All I see is a picture of you. You and her. I don't even know if the picture's real anymore. I don't even care. It's a made-up picture. It invades my head. The two of you. And this picture stings even more than if I'd actually seen you with her. It cuts me. It cuts me so deep I'll never get over it. And I can't get rid of this picture either. It just comes. Uninvited. Kinda' like a little torture. And I blame you more for this little torture than I do for what you did.

EDDIE: (*standing slowly*) I'll go.

MAY: You better.

EDDIE: Why?

MAY: You just better.

EDDIE: I thought you wanted me to stay.

MAY: I got somebody coming to get me.

EDDIE: (*short pause, on his feet*) Here?

MAY: Yeah, here. Where else?

EDDIE: (*makes a move toward her upstage*) You been seeing somebody?

MAY: (*she moves quickly down left, crosses right*) When was the last time we were together, Eddie? Huh? Can you remember that far back?

EDDIE: Who've you been seeing?

(*He moves violently toward her.*)

MAY: Don't you touch me! Don't you even think about it.

EDDIE: How long have you been seeing him!

MAY: What difference does it make!

(*Short pause. He stares at her, then turns suddenly and exits out the stage-left door and slams it behind him. Door booms.*)

MAY: Eddie! Where are you going? Eddie!

(*Short pause. She looks after* EDDIE, *then turns fast, moves upstage to window. She parts the Venetian blinds, looks out window, turns back into room. She rushes to upstage side of bed, gets down on hands and knees, pulls a suitcase out from under bed, throws it on top of bed, opens it. She rushes into bathroom, disappears, leaving door open. She comes back in with various items of clothing, throws stuff into suitcase, turns as if to go back into bathroom. Stops. She hears* EDDIE *off left. She quickly shuts suitcase, slides it under bed again, rushes around to downstage side of bed. Sits on bed. Stands again. Rushes back into bathroom, returns with hairbrush, slams bathroom door. Starts brushing her hair as though that's what she's been doing all along. She sits on bed brushing her hair.* EDDIE *enters stage left, slams door behind him, door booms. He stands there holding a ten gauge shotgun in one hand and a bottle of tequila in the other. He moves toward bed, tosses shotgun on bed beside her.*)

MAY: (*she stands, moves upstage, stops brushing her hair*) Oh, wonderful. What're you gonna' do with that?

EDDIE: Clean it.

(*He opens the bottle.*)

EDDIE: You got any glasses?

MAY: In the bathroom.

EDDIE: What're they doin' in the bathroom?

(EDDIE *crosses toward bathroom door with bottle.*)

MAY: I keep everything in the bathroom. It's safer.

EDDIE: You want some a' this?

MAY: I'm on the wagon.

EDDIE: Good. 'Bout time.

(*He exits into bathroom.* MAY *moves back to bed, stares at shotgun.*)

MAY: Eddie, this is a very friendly person who's coming over here. He's not malicious in any way. (*pause*) Eddie?

EDDIE'S VOICE: (*off right*) Where's the damn glasses?

MAY: In the medicine cabinet!

EDDIE'S VOICE: What the hell're they doin' in the medicine cabinet!

(*Sound of medicine cabinet being opened and slammed shut off right.*)

MAY: There's no germs in the medicine cabinet!

EDDIE'S VOICE: Germs.

MAY: Eddie, did you hear me?

(EDDIE *enters with a glass, pouring tequila into it slowly until it's full as he crosses to table down left.*)

MAY: Did you hear what I said, Eddie?

EDDIE: About what?

MAY: About the man who's coming over here.

EDDIE: What man?

MAY: Oh, brother.

(EDDIE *sets bottle of tequila on table then sits in upstage chair. Takes a long drink from glass. He ignores* THE OLD MAN.)

EDDIE: First off, it can't be very serious.

MAY: Oh, really? And why is that?

EDDIE: Because you call him a "man."

MAY: What am I supposed to call him?

EDDIE: A "guy" or something. If you called him a "guy," I'd be worried about it but since you call him a "man" you give yourself away. You're in a dumb situation with this guy by calling him a "man." You put yourself below him.

MAY: What in the hell do you know about it.

EDDIE: This guy's gotta' be a twerp. He's gotta' be a punk chump in a two dollar suit or somethin'.

MAY: Anybody who doesn't half kill themselves falling off horses or jumping on steers is a twerp in your book.

EDDIE: That's right.

MAY: And what're you supposed to be, a "guy" or a "man"?

(EDDIE *lowers his glass slowly. Stares at her. Pause. He smiles then speaks low and deliberately.*)

EDDIE: I'll tell you what. We'll just wait for this "man" to come over here. The two of us. We'll just set right here and wait. Then I'll let you be the judge.

MAY: Why is everything a big contest with you? He's not competing with you. He doesn't even know you exist.

EDDIE: You can introduce me.

MAY: I'm not introducing you. I am definitely not introducing you. He'd be very embarrassed to find me here with somebody else. Besides, I've only just met him.

EDDIE: Embarrassed?

MAY: Yes! Embarrassed. He's a very gentle person.

EDDIE: Is that right. Well, I'm a very gentle person myself. My feelings get easily damaged.

MAY: What feelings.

(EDDIE *falls silent, takes a drink, then gets up slowly with glass, leaves bottle on table, crosses to bed, sits on bed, sets glass on floor, picks up shotgun and starts dismantling it.* MAY *watches him closely.*)

MAY: You can't keep messing me around like this. It's been going on too long. I can't take it anymore. I get sick everytime you come around. Then I get sick when you leave. You're like a disease to me. Besides, you got no right being jealous of me after all the bullshit I've been through with you.

(Pause. EDDIE keeps his attention on shotgun as he talks to her.)

EDDIE: We've got a pact.

MAY: Oh, God.

EDDIE: We made a pact.

MAY: There's nothing between us now!

EDDIE: Then what're you so excited about?

MAY: I'm not excited.

EDDIE: You're beside yourself.

MAY: You're driving me crazy. You're driving me totally crazy!

EDDIE: You know we're connected, May. We'll always be connected. That was decided a long time ago.

MAY: Nothing was decided! You made all that up.

EDDIE: You know what happened.

MAY: You promised me that was finished. You can't start that up all over again. You promised me.

EDDIE: A promise can't stop something like that. It happened.

MAY: Nothing happened! Nothing ever happened!

EDDIE: Innocent to the last drop.

MAY: (pause, controlled) Eddie—will you please leave? Now.

EDDIE: You're gonna' find out one way or the other.

MAY: I want you to leave.

EDDIE: You didn't want me to leave before.

MAY: I want you to leave now. And it's not because of this man. It's just—

EDDIE: What.

MAY: Stupid. You oughta' know that by now.

EDDIE: You think so, huh?

MAY: It'll be the same thing over and over again. We'll be together for a little while and then you'll be gone.

EDDIE: I'll be gone.

MAY: You will. You know it. You just want me now because I'm seeing somebody else. As soon as that's over, you'll be gone again.

EDDIE: I didn't come here because you were seein' somebody else! I don't give a damn who you're seeing! You'll never replace me and you know it!

MAY: Get outa' here!

(Long silence. EDDIE lifts his glass and toasts her, then slowly drinks it dry. He sets glass down softly on floor.)

EDDIE: (smiles at her) All right.

(He rises slowly, picks up the sections of his shotgun. He stands there looking down at the shotgun pieces for a second. MAY moves slightly toward him.)

MAY: Eddie—

(His head jerks up and stares at her. She stops cold.)

EDDIE: You're a traitor.

(He exits left with shotgun. Slams door. Door booms. MAY runs toward door.)

MAY: Eddie!!

(She throws herself against stage-left door. Her arms reach out and hug the walls. She weeps and slowly begins to move along the stage-left wall upstage to the corner, embracing the wall as she moves and weeps. THE OLD MAN begins to tell his story as MAY moves slowly along the wall. He tells it directly to her as though she's a child. MAY remains involved with her emotion of loss and keeps moving clear around the room, hugging the walls during the course of the story until she arrives in the extreme downstage-right corner of the room. She sinks to her knees.)

(Slowly, in the course of MAY's mourning, the spotlight softly rises on THE OLD MAN and the stage lights decrease to half again.)

THE OLD MAN: Ya' know, one thing I'll never forget. I'll never forget this as long as I live—and I don't even know why I remember it exactly. We were drivin' through southern Utah once, I think it was. Me, you and your mother—in that old Plymouth we had. You remember that Plymouth? Had a white plastic hood ornament on it. Replica of the Mayflower I think it was. Some kind a' ship. Anyway, we'd been drivin' all night and you were sound asleep in the front. And all of a sudden you woke up crying. Just bustin' a gut over somethin'. I don't know what it was. Nightmare or somethin'. Woke your mom right up and she climbed over the seat in back there with you to try to get you settled down. But you wouldn't shut up for hell or high water. Just kept wailing away. So I stopped the Plymouth by the side of the road. Middle a' nowhere. I can't even remember where it was exactly. Pitch black. I picked you up outa' the back seat there and carried you into this field. Thought the cold air might quiet you down a little bit. But you just kept on howling away. Then, all of a sudden, I saw somethin' move out there. Somethin' bigger than both of us put together. And it started to move toward us kinda' slow.

(MAY begins to crawl slowly on her hands and knees from down-right corner toward bed. When she reaches bed, she grabs pillow and embraces it, still on her knees. She rocks back and forth embracing pillow as THE OLD MAN continues.)

And then it started to get joined up by some other things just like it. Same shape and everything. It was so black out there I could hardly make out my own hand. But these things started to kinda' move in on us from all directions in a big circle. And I stopped dead still and turned back to the car to see if your mother was all right. But I couldn't see the car anymore. So I called out to her. I called her name loud and clear. And she answered me back from outa' the darkness. She yelled back to me. And just then these things started to "moo." They all started "mooing" away.

(He makes the sound of a cow.)

And it turns out, there we were, standin' smack in the middle of a goddamn herd of cattle. Well, you never heard a baby pipe down so fast in your life. You never made a peep after that. The whole rest of the trip.

(MAY stops rocking abruptly. Suddenly MAY hears EDDIE off left. Stage lights pop back up. Spot on THE OLD MAN cuts to black. She leaps to her feet, completely dropping her grief, hesitates a second, then rushes to chair upstage of table and sits. She takes a drink straight from the bottle, slams bottle down on table, leans back in the chair and stares at the bottle as though she's been sitting like that the whole time since he left. EDDIE enters fast from stage-left door carrying two steer ropes. He slams door. Door booms. He completely ignores MAY. She completely ignores him and keeps staring at the bottle. He crosses upstage of bed, throws one of the ropes on bed and starts building a loop in the other rope, feeding it with the left hand so that it makes a snakelike zipping sound as it passes through the honda. Now he begins to pay attention to MAY as he continues fooling with the rope. She remains staring at the bottle of tequila.)

EDDIE: Decided to jump off the wagon, huh?

(He spins the rope above his head in a flat horn-loop, then ropes one of the bedposts, taking up the slack with a sharp snap of the right hand. He takes the loop off the bedpost, rebuilds it, swings and ropes another bedpost. He continues this right around the bed, roping every post and never missing. MAY takes another drink and sets bottle down quietly.)

MAY: (still not looking at him) What're you doing?
EDDIE: Little practice. Gotta' stay in practice these days. There's kids out there ropin' calves in six seconds dead. Can you believe that? Six and no change. Flyin' off the saddle on the right hand side like a bunch a' Spider Monkeys. I'm tellin' ya', they got it down to a science.

(He continues roping bedposts, making his way around the bed in a circle.)

MAY: (flatly, staring at bottle) I thought you were leaving. Didn't you say you were leaving?
EDDIE: (as he ropes) Well, yeah, I was gonna'. But then it suddenly occurred to me in the middle of the parking lot out there that there probably isn't any man comin' over here at all. There probably isn't any

"guy" or any "man" or anybody comin' over here. You just made all that up.
MAY: Why would I do that?
EDDIE: Just to get even.

(She turns to him slowly in chair, takes a drink, stares at him, then sets bottle on table.)

MAY: I'll never get even with you.

(He laughs, crosses to table, takes a deep drink from bottle, cocks his head back, gargles, swallows, then does a back-flip across stage and crashes into stage-right wall.)

MAY: So, now we're gonna' get real mean and sloppy, is that it? Just like old times.
EDDIE: Well, I haven't dropped the reins in quite a while ya' know. I've been real good. I have. No hooch. No slammer. No women. No nothin'. I been a pretty boring kind of a guy actually. I figure I owe it to myself. Once a once.

(He returns to roping the bedposts. She just stares at him from the chair.)

MAY: Why are you doing this?
EDDIE: I already told ya'. I need the practice.
MAY: I don't mean that.
EDDIE: Well, say what ya' mean then, honey.
MAY: Why are you going through this whole thing again like you're trying to impress me or something. Like we just met. This is the same crap you laid on me in high school.
EDDIE: (still roping) Well, it's just a little testimony of my love, see, baby. I mean if I stopped trying to impress you, that'd mean it was all over, wouldn't it?
MAY: It is all over.
EDDIE: You're trying to impress me, too, aren't you?
MAY: You know me inside and out. I got nothing new to show you.
EDDIE: You got this guy comin' over. This new guy. That's very impressive. I woulda' thought you'd be hung out to dry by now.
MAY: Oh, thanks a lot.
EDDIE: What is he, a "younger man" or something?
MAY: It's none of your damn business.
EDDIE: Have you balled him yet?

(She throws him a mean glare and just pins him with her eyes.)

EDDIE: Have you? I'm just curious. (pause) You don't have to tell me. I already know.
MAY: You're just like a little kid, you know that? A jealous little snot-nosed kid.

(EDDIE laughs, spits, makes a snot-nosed-kid face, keeps roping bedposts.)

EDDIE: I hope this guy comes over. I really hope he does. I wanna' see him walk through that door.
MAY: What're you gonna' do?

(He stops roping, turns to her. He smiles.)

EDDIE: I'm gonna' nail his ass to the floor. Directly.

(He suddenly ropes chair downstage, right next to MAY. He takes up slack and drags chair violently back toward bed. Pause. They stare at each other. MAY suddenly stands, goes to bedpost, grabs her purse, slings it on her shoulder and heads for stage-left door.)

MAY: I'm not sticking around for this.

(She exits stage-left door, leaving it open. EDDIE runs offstage after her.)

EDDIE: Where're you goin'?

MAY: *(off left)* Take your hands offa' me!

EDDIE: *(off left)* Wait a second, wait a second. Just a second, okay?

(MAY screams. EDDIE carries her back onstage screaming and kicking. He sets her down, slams door shut. She walks away from him stage right, straightening her dress.)

EDDIE: Tell ya' what. I'll back off. I'll be real nice. I will. I promise. I'll be just like a little ole pussycat, okay? You can introduce me to him as your brother or something. Well—maybe not your brother.

MAY: Maybe not.

EDDIE: Your cousin. Okay? I'll be your cousin. I just wanna' meet him is all. Then I'll leave. Promise.

MAY: Why do you want to meet him? He's just a friend.

EDDIE: Just to see where you stand these days. You can tell a lot about a person by the company they keep.

MAY: Look. I'm going outside. I'm going to the pay phone across the street. I'm calling him up and I'm telling him to forget about the whole thing. Okay?

EDDIE: Good. I'll pack up your stuff while you're gone.

MAY: I'm not going with you, Eddie!

(Suddenly headlights arc across the stage from upstage right, through the window. They slash across the audience, then dissolve off left. These should be two intense beams of piercing white light and not "realistic" headlights.)

MAY: Oh, great.

(She rushes upstage to window, looks out. EDDIE laughs, takes a drink.)

EDDIE: Why don't ya' run out there. Go ahead. Run on out. Throw yourself into his arms or somethin'. Blow kisses in the moonlight.

(EDDIE laughs, moves to bed, pulls a pair of old spurs off his belt. Sits. Starts putting spurs on his boots. It's important these spurs look old and used, with small rowels—not cartoon "cowboy" spurs. MAY goes into bathroom, leaving door open.)

MAY: *(off right)* What're you doing?

EDDIE: Puttin' my hooks on. I wanna' look good for this "man." Give him the right impression. I'm yer cousin, after all.

MAY: *(entering from bathroom)* If you hurt him, Eddie—

EDDIE: I'm not gonna' hurt him. I'm a nice guy. Very sensitive, too. Very civilized.

MAY: He's just a date, you know. Just an ordinary date.

EDDIE: Yeah? Well, I'm gonna turn him into a fig.

(He starts laughing so hard at his own joke that he rolls off the bed and crashes to the floor. He goes into a fit of laughter, pounding his fists into the floor. MAY makes a move toward the door, then stops and turns to EDDIE.)

MAY: Eddie! Do me a favor. Just this once, okay?

EDDIE: *(laughing hard)* Anything you want, honey. Anything you want.

(He goes on laughing hysterically.)

MAY: *(turning away from him)* Shit.

(She goes to stage-left door and throws it open. Pitch black outside with only the porch light glowing. She stands in the doorway, staring out. Pause as EDDIE slowly gains control of himself and stops laughing. He stares at MAY.)

EDDIE: *(still on floor)* What're you doing? *(Pause. MAY keeps looking out)* May?

MAY: *(staring out open door)* It's not him.

EDDIE: It's not, huh?

MAY: No, it's not.

EDDIE: Well, who is it then?

MAY: Somebody else.

EDDIE: *(slowly getting up and sitting on bed)* Yeah. It's probably not ever gonna' be "him." What're you tryin' to make me jealous for? I know you've been livin' alone.

MAY: It's a big, huge, extra-long, black Mercedes-Benz.

EDDIE: *(pause)* Well, this is a motel, isn't it? People are allowed to park in front of a motel if they're stayin' here.

MAY: People who stay here don't drive a big, huge, extra-long, black Mercedes-Benz.

EDDIE: You don't, but somebody else might.

MAY: *(still at door)* This is not a black Mercedes-Benz type of motel.

EDDIE: Well, close the damn door then and get back inside.

MAY: Somebody's sitting out there in that car looking straight at me.

EDDIE: *(stands fast)* What're they doing?

MAY: It's not a "they," It's a "she."

(EDDIE drops to floor behind bed.)

EDDIE: Well, what's she doing, then?

MAY: Just sitting there. Staring at me.

EDDIE: Get away from the door, May.

MAY: *(turning toward him slowly)* You don't know anybody with a black Mercedes-Benz by any chance, do you?

EDDIE: Get away from the door!

(Suddenly the white headlight beams slash across the stage through the open door. EDDIE rushes to door, slams it

shut and pushes MAY *aside. Just as he slams the door the sound of a large caliber magnum pistol explodes off left, followed immediately by the sound of shattering glass, then a car horn blares and continues on one relentless note.)*

MAY: *(yelling over the sound of the horn)* Who is that! Who in the hell is that out there!

EDDIE: How should I know.

*(*EDDIE *flips the light switch off by stage-left door. Stage lights go black. Bathroom light stays on.)*

MAY: Eddie!

EDDIE: Just get down will ya'! Get down on the floor!

*(*EDDIE *grabs her and tries to pull her down on the floor beside the bed.* MAY *struggles in the dark with him. Car horn keeps blaring. Headlights start popping back and forth from high beam to low beam, slashing across stage through the window now.)*

MAY: Who is that? Did you bring her with you! You sonofabitch!

(She starts lashing out at EDDIE, *fighting with him as he tries to drag her down on the floor.)*

EDDIE: I didn't bring anybody with me! I don't know who she is! I don't know where she came from! Just get down on the floor, will ya'!

MAY: She followed you here! Didn't she! You told her where you were going and she followed you.

EDDIE: I didn't tell anybody where I was going. I didn't know where I was going till I got here.

MAY: You are gonna' pay for this! I swear to God. You are gonna' pay.

*(*EDDIE *finally pulls her down and rolls over on top of her so she can't get up. She slowly gives up struggling as he keeps her pinned to the floor. Car horn suddenly stops. Headlights snap off. Long pause. They listen in the dark.)*

MAY: What do you think she's doing?

EDDIE: How should I know.

MAY: Don't pretend you don't know her. That's the kind of car a Countess drives. That's the kind of car I always pictured her in. *(she starts struggling again)*

EDDIE: *(holding her down)* Just stay put.

MAY: I'm not gonna' lay here on my back with you on top of me and get shot by some dumb rich twat. Now lemme up, Eddie!

(Sound of tires burning rubber off left. Headlights arc back across the stage again from left to right. A car drives off. Sound fades.)

EDDIE: Just stay down!

MAY: I'm down!

(Long pause in the dark. They listen.)

MAY: How crazy is this chick anyway?

EDDIE: She's pretty crazy.

MAY: Have you balled her yet? *(pause)*

*(*EDDIE *gets up slowly, hunched over, crosses upstage to window cautiously, parts Venetian blinds and peeks outside.)*

EDDIE: *(looking out)* Shit, she's blown the windshield outa' my truck. Goddammit.

MAY: *(still on floor)* Eddie?

EDDIE: *(still looking out window)* What?

MAY: Is she gone?

EDDIE: I don't know. I can't see any headlights. *(pause)* I don't believe it.

MAY: *(gets up, crosses to light switch)* Yeah, you shoulda' thought of the consequences before you got in her pants.

(She switches the light back on. EDDIE *whirls around toward her. He stands.)*

EDDIE: *(moving toward her)* Turn the lights off! Keep the lights off!

(He rushes to light switch and turns lights back off. Stage goes back to darkness. MAY *shoves past him and turns the lights back on again. Stage lit.)*

MAY: This is my place!

EDDIE: Look, she's gonna' come back here. I know she's gonna' come back. We either have to get outa' here now or you have to keep the fuckin' lights off.

MAY: I thought you said you didn't know her!

EDDIE: Get your stuff! We're gettin' outa' here.

MAY: I'm not leaving! This is your mess, not mine.

EDDIE: I came here to get you! Whatsa' matter with you! I came all this way to get you! Do you think I'd do that if I didn't love you! Huh? That bitch doesn't mean anything to me! Nuthin'. I got no reason to be here but you.

MAY: I'm not goin', Eddie.

(Pause. EDDIE *stares at her.)*

(Spot rises on THE OLD MAN. *Stage lights stay the same.* EDDIE *and* MAY *just stand there staring at each other through the duration of* THE OLD MAN'*s words. They are not "frozen," they just stand there and face each other in a suspended moment of recognition.)*

THE OLD MAN: Amazing thing is, neither one a' you look a bit familiar to me. Can't figure that one out. I don't recognize myself in either one a' you. Never did. 'Course your mothers both put their stamp on ya'. That's plain to see. But my whole side a' the issue is absent, in my opinion. Totally unrecognizable. You could be anybody's. Probably are. I can't even remember the original circumstances. Been so long. Probably a lot a' things I forgot. Good thing I got out when I did though. Best thing I ever did.

(Spot fades on THE OLD MAN. *Stage lights come back up.* EDDIE *picks up his rope and starts to coil it up.* MAY *watches him.)*

EDDIE: I'm not leavin'. I don't care what you think anymore. I don't care what you feel. None a' that matters. I'm not leavin'. I'm stayin' right here. I don't
care if a hundred "dates" walk through that door—
I'll take every one of 'em on. I don't care if you hate
my guts. I don't care if you can't stand the sight of
me or the sound of me or the smell of me. I'm never
leavin'. You'll never get rid of me. You'll never
escape me either. I'll track you down no matter
where you go. I know exactly how your mind works.
I've been right every time. Every single time.

MAY: You've gotta' give this up, Eddie.

EDDIE: I'm not giving it up!

(Pause.)

MAY: *(calm)* Okay. Look. I don't understand what you've
got in your head anymore. I really don't. I don't
get it. *Now* you desperately need me. *Now* you can't
live without me. NOW you'll do anything for me.
Why should I believe it this time?

EDDIE: Because it's true.

MAY: It was supposed to have been true every time
before. Every other time. Now it's true again.
You've been jerking me off like this for fifteen
years. Fifteen years I've been a yo-yo for you. I've
never been split. I've never been two ways about
you. I've either loved you or not loved you. And
now I just plain don't love you. Understand? Do
you understand that? I don't love you. I don't need
you. I don't want you. Do you get that? Now if you
can still stay, then you're either crazy or pathetic.

*(She crosses down left to table, sits in upstage chair facing
audience, takes slug of tequila from bottle, slams it down
on table. Headlights again come slashing across the stage
from up right, across audience, then disappear off left.
EDDIE rushes to light switch, flips it off. Stage goes black.
Exterior lights shine through.)*

EDDIE: *(taking her by shoulder)* Get in the bathroom!

MAY: *(pulls away)* I'm not going in the bathroom! I'm
not gonna' hide in my own house! I'm gonna' go
out there. I'm gonna' go out there and tear her
damn head off! I'm gonna' wipe her out!

*(She moves toward stage-left door. EDDIE stops her. She
screams. They struggle as MAY yells at stage-left door.)*

MAY: *(yelling at door)* Come on in here! Come on in here
and bring your dumb gun! You hear me? Bring all
your weapons and your skinny silly self! I'll eat you
alive!

*(Suddenly the stage-left door bursts open and MARTIN
crashes onstage in the darkness. He's in his mid-thirties,
solidly built, wears a green plaid shirt, baggy work pants
with suspenders, heavy work boots. MAY and EDDIE pull
apart. MARTIN tackles EDDIE around the waist and the
two of them go crashing into the stage-right bathroom
door. The door booms. MAY rushes to light switch, flips it*

*on. Lights come back up onstage. MARTIN stands over
EDDIE who's crumpled up against the wall on the floor.
MARTIN is about to smash EDDIE in the face with his fist.
MAY stops him with her voice.)*

MAY: Martin, wait!

*(Pause. MARTIN turns and looks at MAY. EDDIE is dazed,
remains on floor. MAY goes to MARTIN and pulls him
away from EDDIE.)*

MAY: It's okay, Martin. It's uh—it's okay. We were just
having a kind of an argument. Really. Just take it
easy. All right?

*(MARTIN moves back away from EDDIE. EDDIE stays on
floor. Pause.)*

MARTIN: Oh. I heard you screaming when I drove up
and then all the lights went off. I thought somebody
was trying to—

MAY: It's okay. This is my uh—cousin. Eddie.

MARTIN: *(stares at EDDIE)* Oh. I'm sorry.

EDDIE: *(grins at MARTIN)* She's lying.

MARTIN: *(looks at MAY)* Oh.

MAY: *(moving to table)* Everything's okay, Martin. You
want a drink or something? Why don't you have a
drink.

MARTIN: Yeah. Sure.

EDDIE: *(stays on floor)* She's lying through her teeth.

MAY: I gotta' get some glasses.

*(MAY exits quickly into bathroom, stepping over EDDIE.
MARTIN stares at EDDIE. EDDIE grins back. Pause.)*

EDDIE: She keeps the glasses in the bathroom. Isn't that
weird?

*(MAY comes back on with two glasses. She goes to table,
pours two drinks from bottle.)*

MAY: I was starting to think you weren't going to show
up, Martin.

MARTIN: Yeah, I'm sorry. I had to water the football
field down at the high school. Forgot all about it.

EDDIE: Forgot all about what?

MARTIN: I mean I forgot all about watering. I was halfway here when I remembered. Had to go back.

EDDIE: Oh, I thought you meant you forgot all about
her.

MARTIN: Oh, no.

EDDIE: How far was halfway?

MARTIN: Excuse me?

EDDIE: How far were you when it was halfway here?

MARTIN: Oh—uh—I don't know. I guess a couple miles
or so.

EDDIE: Couple miles? That's all? Couple a' lousy little
miles? You wanna' know how many miles I came?
Huh?

MAY: We've been drinking a little bit, Martin.

EDDIE: She hasn't touched a drop.

(Pause.)

MAY: *(offering drink to* MARTIN*)* Here.

EDDIE: Yeah, that's my tequila, Martin.

MARTIN: Oh.

EDDIE: I don't care if you drink it. I just want you to know where it comes from.

MARTIN: Thanks.

EDDIE: You don't have to thank me. Thank the Mexicans. They made it.

MARTIN: Oh.

EDDIE: You should thank the entire Mexican nation in fact. We owe everything to Mexico down here. Do you realize that? You probably don't realize that, do ya'. We're sittin' on Mexican ground right now. It's only by chance that you and me aren't Mexican ourselves. What kinda' people do you hail from anyway, Martin?

MARTIN: Me? Uh—I don't know. I was adopted.

EDDIE: Oh. You must have a lotta' problems then, huh?

MARTIN: Well—not really, no.

EDDIE: No? You orphans are supposed to steal a lot aren't ya'? Shoplifting and stuff. You're also supposed to be the main group responsible for bumping off our Presidents.

MARTIN: Really? I never heard that.

EDDIE: Well, you oughta' read the papers, Martin.

(Pause.)

MARTIN: I'm really sorry I knocked you over. I mean, I thought she was in trouble or something.

EDDIE: She is in trouble.

MARTIN: *(looks at* MAY*)* Oh.

EDDIE: She's in big trouble.

MARTIN: What's the matter, May?

MAY: *(moves to bed with drink, sits)* Nothing.

MARTIN: How come you had the lights off?

MAY: We were uh—just about to go out.

MARTIN: You were?

MAY: Yeah—well, I mean, we were going to come back.

*(*MARTIN *stands there between them. He looks at* EDDIE*, then back to* MAY*. Pause.)*

EDDIE: *(laughs)* No, no, no. That's not what we were gonna' do. Your name's Martin, right?

MARTIN: Yeah, right.

EDDIE: That's not what we were gonna' do, Marty.

MARTIN: Oh.

EDDIE: Could you hand me that bottle, please?

MARTIN: *(crossing to bottle at table)* Sure.

EDDIE: Thanks.

*(*MARTIN *moves back to* EDDIE *with bottle and hands it to him.* EDDIE *drinks.)*

EDDIE: *(after drink)* We were actually having an argument about you. That's what we were doin'.

MARTIN: About me?

EDDIE: Yeah. We were actually in the middle of a big huge argument about you. It got so heated up we had to turn the lights off.

MARTIN: What was it about?

EDDIE: It was about whether or not you're actually a man or not. Ya' know? Whether you're a "man" or just a "guy."

(Pause. MARTIN *looks at* MAY*.* MAY *smiles politely.* MARTIN *looks back to* EDDIE*.)*

EDDIE: See, she says you're a man. That's what she calls you. A "man." Did you know that? That's what she calls you.

MARTIN: *(looks back to* MAY*)* No.

MAY: I never called you a man, Martin. Don't worry about it.

MARTIN: It's okay. I don't mind or anything.

EDDIE: No, but see I uh—told her she was fulla' shit. I mean I told her that way before I even saw you. And now that I see you I can't exactly take it back. Ya' see what I mean, Martin?

(Pause, MAY *stands.)*

MAY: Martin, do you want to go to the movies?

MARTIN: Well, yeah—I mean, that's what I thought we were going to do.

MAY: So let's go to the movies.

(She crosses fast to bathroom, steps over EDDIE*, goes into bathroom, slams door, door booms. Pause as* MARTIN *stares at bathroom door.* EDDIE *stays on floor, grins at* MARTIN*.)*

MARTIN: She's not mad or anything is she?

EDDIE: You got me, buddy.

MARTIN: I didn't mean to make her mad.

(Pause.)

EDDIE: What're you gonna' go see, Martin?

MARTIN: I can't decide.

EDDIE: What d'ya' mean you can't decide? You're supposed to have all that worked out ahead of time aren't ya'?

MARTIN: Yeah, but I'm not sure what she likes.

EDDIE: What's that got to do with it? You're takin' her out to the movies, right?

MARTIN: Yeah.

EDDIE: So you pick the movie, right? The guy picks the movie. The guy's always supposed to pick the movie.

MARTIN: Yeah, but I don't want to take her to see something she doesn't want to see.

EDDIE: How do you know what she wants to see?

MARTIN: I don't. That's the reason I can't decide. I mean what if I take her to something she's already seen before?

EDDIE: You miss the whole point, Martin. The reason you're taking her out to the movies isn't to see something she hasn't seen before.

MARTIN: Oh.

EDDIE: The reason you're taking her out to the movies is because you just want to be with her. Right? You just wanna' be close to her. I mean you could take her just about anywhere.

MARTIN: I guess.

EDDIE: I mean after a while you probably wouldn't have to take her out at all. You could just hang around here.

MARTIN: What would we do here?

EDDIE: Well, you could uh—tell each other stories.

MARTIN: Stories?

EDDIE: Yeah.

MARTIN: I don't know any stories.

EDDIE: Make 'em up.

MARTIN: That'd be lying wouldn't it?

EDDIE: No, no. Lying's when you believe it's true. If you already know it's a lie, then it's not lying.

MARTIN: (after pause) Do you want some help getting up off the floor?

EDDIE: I like it down here. Less tension. You notice how when you're standing up, there's a lot more tension?

MARTIN: Yeah. I've noticed that. A lot of times when I'm working, you know, I'm down on my hands and knees.

EDDIE: What line a' work do you follow, Martin?

MARTIN: Yard work mostly. Maintenance.

EDDIE: Oh, lawns and stuff?

MARTIN: Yeah.

EDDIE: You do lawns on your hands and knees?

MARTIN: Well—edging. You know, trimming around the edges.

EDDIE: Oh.

MARTIN: And weeding around the sprinkler heads. Stuff like that.

EDDIE: I get ya'.

MARTIN: But I've always noticed how much more relaxed I get when I'm down low to the ground like that.

EDDIE: Yeah. Well, you could get down on your hands and knees right now if you want to. I don't mind.

MARTIN: (grins, gets embarrassed, looks at bathroom door) Naw, I'll stand. Thanks.

EDDIE: Suit yourself. You're just gonna' get more and more tense.

(Pause.)

MARTIN: You're uh—May's cousin, huh?

EDDIE: See now, right there. Askin' me that. Right there. That's a result of tension. See what I mean?

MARTIN: What?

EDDIE: Askin' me if I'm her cousin. That's because you're tense you're askin' me that. You already know I'm not her cousin.

MARTIN: Well, how would I know that?

EDDIE: Do I look like her cousin.

MARTIN: Well, she said that you were.

EDDIE: (grins) She's lying.

(Pause.)

MARTIN: Well—what are you then?

EDDIE: (laughs) Now you're really gettin' tense, huh?

MARTIN: Look, maybe I should just go or something. I mean—

(MARTIN makes a move to exit stage left. EDDIE rushes to stage-left door and beats MARTIN to it. MARTIN freezes, then runs to window upstage, opens it and tries to escape. EDDIE runs to him and catches him by the back of the pants, pulls him out of the window, slams him up against stage-right wall, then pulls him slowly down the wall as he speaks. They arrive at down-right corner.)

EDDIE: No, no. Don't go, Martin. Don't go. You'll just get all blue and lonely out there in the black night. I know. I've wandered around lonely like that myself. Awful. Just eats away at ya'. (he puts his arm around MARTIN's shoulder and leads him to table down left) Now just come on over here and sit down and we'll have us a little drink. Okay?

MARTIN: (as he goes with EDDIE) Uh—do you think she's okay in there?

EDDIE: Sure she's okay. She's always okay. She just likes to take her time. Just to torture you.

MARTIN: Well—we were supposed to go to the movies.

EDDIE: She'll be out. Don't worry about it. She likes the movies.

(They sit at table, down left. EDDIE pulls out the down-right chair and seats MARTIN in it, then he goes to the upstage chair and sits so that he's now partially facing THE OLD MAN. Spot rises softly on THE OLD MAN but MARTIN does not acknowledge his presence. Stage lights stay the same. MARTIN sets his glass on table. EDDIE fills it up with the bottle. THE OLD MAN's left arm slowly descends and reaches across the table holding out his empty Styrofoam cup for a drink. EDDIE looks THE OLD MAN in the eye for a second, then pours him a drink, too. All three of them drink. EDDIE takes his from the bottle.)

MARTIN: What exactly's the matter with her anyway?

EDDIE: She's in a state a' shock.

(THE OLD MAN chuckles to himself. Drinks.)

MARTIN: Shock? How come?

EDDIE: Well, we haven't seen each other in a long time. I mean—me and her, we go back quite a ways, see. High school.

MARTIN: Oh. I didn't know that.

EDDIE: Yeah. Lotta' miles.

MARTIN: And you're not really cousins?

EDDIE: No. Not really. No.

MARTIN: You're—her husband?

EDDIE: No. She's my sister. (he and THE OLD MAN look at each other, then he turns back to MARTIN) My half-sister.

(Pause. EDDIE and THE OLD MAN drink.)

MARTIN: Your sister?

EDDIE: Yeah.

MARTIN: Oh. So—you knew each other even before high school then, huh?

EDDIE: No, see, I never knew I had a sister until it was too late.

MARTIN: How do you mean?

EDDIE: Well, by the time I found out we'd already—you know—fooled around.

(THE OLD MAN *shakes his head, drinks. Long pause.* MARTIN *just stares at* EDDIE.)

EDDIE: *(grins)* Whatsa' matter, Martin?

MARTIN: You fooled around?

EDDIE: Yeah.

MARTIN: Well—um—that's illegal, isn't it?

EDDIE: I suppose so.

THE OLD MAN: *(to* EDDIE*)* Who is this guy?

MARTIN: I mean—is that true? She's really your sister?

EDDIE: Half. Only half.

MARTIN: Which half?

EDDIE: Top half. In horses we call that the "topside."

THE OLD MAN: Yeah, and the mare's what? The mare's uh—"distaff," isn't it? Isn't that the bottom half? "Distaff." Funny I should remember that.

MARTIN: And you fooled around in high school together?

EDDIE: Yeah. Sure. Everybody fooled around in high school. Didn't you?

MARTIN: No. I never did.

EDDIE: Maybe you should have, Martin.

MARTIN: Well, not with my sister.

EDDIE: No, I wouldn't recommend that.

MARTIN: How could that happen? I mean—

EDDIE: Well, see—*(pause, he stares at* THE OLD MAN*)*—our daddy fell in love twice. That's basically how it happened. Once with my mother and once with her mother.

THE OLD MAN: It was the same love. Just got split in two, that's all.

MARTIN: Well, how come you didn't know each other until high school then?

EDDIE: He had two separate lives. That's how come. Two completely separate lives. He'd live with me and my mother for a while and then he'd disappear and go live with her and her mother for a while.

THE OLD MAN: Now don't be too hard on me, boy. It can happen to the best of us.

MARTIN: And you never knew what was going on?

EDDIE: Nope. Neither did my mother.

THE OLD MAN: She knew.

EDDIE: *(to* MARTIN*)* She never knew.

MARTIN: She must've suspected something was going on.

EDDIE: Well, if she did she never let on to me. Maybe she was afraid of finding out. Or maybe she just loved him. I don't know. He'd disappear for months at a time and she never once asked him where he went. She was always glad to see him when he came back. The two of us used to go running out of the house to meet him as soon as we saw the Studebaker coming across the field.

THE OLD MAN: *(to* EDDIE*)* That was no Studebaker, that was a Plymouth. I never owned a goddamn Studebaker.

EDDIE: This went on for years. He kept disappearing and reappearing. For years that went on. Then, suddenly, one day it stopped. He stayed home for a while. Just stayed in the house. Never went outside. Just sat in his chair. Staring. Then he started going on these long walks. He'd walk all day. Then he'd walk all night. He'd walk out across the fields. In the dark. I used to watch him from my bedroom window. He'd disappear in the dark with his overcoat on.

MARTIN: Where was he going?

EDDIE: Just walking.

THE OLD MAN: I was making a decision.

(EDDIE *gets* MARTIN *to his feet and takes him on a walk around the entire stage as he tells the story.* MARTIN *is reluctant but* EDDIE *keeps pulling him along.*)

EDDIE: But one night I asked him if I could go with him. And he took me. We walked straight out across the fields together. In the dark. And I remember it was just plowed and our feet sank down in the powder and the dirt came up over the tops of my shoes and weighed me down. I wanted to stop and empty my shoes out but he wouldn't stop. He kept walking straight ahead and I was afraid of losing him in the dark so I just kept up as best I could. And we were completely silent the whole time. Never said a word to each other. We could barely see a foot in front of us, it was so dark. And these white owls kept swooping down out of nowhere, hunting for jackrabbits. Diving right past our heads, then disappearing. And we just kept walking silent like that for miles until we got to town. I could see the drive-in movie way off in the distance. That was the first thing I saw. Just square patches of color shifting. Then vague faces began to appear. And, as we got closer, I could recognize one of the faces. It was Spencer Tracy. Spencer Tracy moving his mouth. Speaking without words. Speaking to a woman in a red dress. Then we stopped at a liquor store and he made me wait outside in the parking lot while he bought a bottle. And there were all these Mexican migrant workers standing around a pickup truck with red mud all over the tires. They were drinking beer and laughing and I remember being jealous of them and I didn't know why. And I remember seeing the old man through the glass door of the liquor store as he paid for the bottle. And I remember feeling sorry for him and I didn't know why. Then he came outside with the bottle wrapped in a brown paper sack and as soon as he came out, all the Mexican men stopped laughing. They just stared at us as we walked away.

(During the course of the story the lights shift down very slowly into blues and greens—moonlight.)

EDDIE: And we walked right through town. Past the donut shop, past the miniature golf course, past the Chevron station. And he opened the bottle up and offered it to me. Before he even took a drink, he offered it to me first. And I took it and drank it and handed it back to him. And we just kept passing it back and forth like that as we walked until we drank the whole thing dry. And we never said a word the whole time. Then, finally, we reached this little white house with a red awning, on the far side of town. I'll never forget the red awning because it flapped in the night breeze and the porch light made it glow. It was a hot, desert breeze and the air smelled like new-cut alfalfa. We walked right up to the front porch and he rang the bell and I remember getting real nervous because I wasn't expecting to visit anybody. I thought we were just out for a walk. And then this woman comes to the door. This real pretty woman with red hair. And she throws herself into his arms. And he starts crying. He just breaks down right there in front of me. And she's kissing him all over the face and holding him real tight and he's just crying like a baby. And then through the doorway, behind them both, I see this girl.

(The bathroom door very slowly and silently swings open revealing MAY, *standing in the doorframe backlit with yellow light in her red dress. She just watches* EDDIE *as he keeps telling story. He and* MARTIN *are unaware of her presence.)*

EDDIE: She just appears. She's just standing there, staring at me and I'm staring back at her and we can't take our eyes off each other. It was like we knew each other from somewhere but we couldn't place where. But the second we saw each other, that very second, we knew we'd never stop being in love.

*(*MAY *slams bathroom door behind her. Door booms. Lights bang back up to their previous setting.)*

MAY: *(to* EDDIE*)* Boy, you really are incredible! You're unbelievable! Martin comes over here. He doesn't know you from Adam and you start telling him a story like that. Are you crazy? None of it's true, Martin. He's had this weird, sick idea for years now and it's totally made up. He's nuts. I don't know where he got it from. He's completely nuts.

EDDIE: *(to* MARTIN*)* She's kinda' embarrassed about the whole deal, see. You can't blame her really.

MARTIN: I didn't even know you could hear us out here, May. I—

MAY: I heard every word. I followed it very carefully. He's told me that story a thousand times and it always changes.

EDDIE: I never repeat myself.

MAY: You do nothing but repeat yourself. That's all you do. You just go in a big circle.

MARTIN: *(standing)* Well, maybe I should leave.

EDDIE: NO! You sit down.

(Silence. MARTIN *slowly sits again.)*

EDDIE: *(quietly to* MARTIN, *leaning toward him)* Did you think that was a story, Martin? Did you think I made that whole thing up?

MARTIN: No. I mean, at the time you were telling it, it seemed real.

EDDIE: But now you're doubting it because she says it's a lie?

MARTIN: Well—

EDDIE: She suggests it's a lie to you and all of a sudden you change your mind? Is that it? You go from true to false like that, in a second?

MARTIN: I don't know.

MAY: Let's go to the movies, Martin.

*(*MARTIN *stands again.)*

EDDIE: Sit down!

*(*MARTIN *sits back down. Long pause.)*

MAY: Eddie—

(Pause.)

EDDIE: What?

MAY: We want to go to the movies.

Pause. EDDIE *just stares at her.)*

MAY: I want to go out to the movies with Martin. Right now.

EDDIE: Nobody's going to the movies. There's not a movie in this town that can match the story I'm gonna' tell. I'm gonna' finish this story.

MAY: Eddie—

EDDIE: You wanna' hear the rest of the story, don't ya', Martin?

MARTIN: *(pause. He looks at* MAY, *then back to* EDDIE*)* Sure.

MAY: Martin, let's go. Please.

MARTIN: I—

(Long pause. EDDIE *and* MARTIN *stare at each other.)*

EDDIE: You what?

MARTIN: I don't mind hearing the rest of it if you want to tell the rest of it.

THE OLD MAN: *(to himself)* I'm dyin' to hear it myself.

*(*EDDIE *leans back in his chair. Grins.)*

MAY: *(to* EDDIE*)* What do you think this is going to do? Do you think this is going to change something?

EDDIE: No.

MAY: Then what's the point?

EDDIE: It's absolutely pointless.

MAY: Then why put everybody through this. Martin doesn't want to hear this bullshit. *I* don't want to hear it.

EDDIE: I know *you* don't wanna' hear it.

MAY: Don't try to pass it off on me! You got it all turned around, Eddie. You got it all turned around. You don't even know which end is up anymore. Okay. Okay. I don't need either of you. I don't need any of it because I already know the rest of the story. I know the whole rest of the story, see (*she speaks directly to* EDDIE, *who remains sitting*) I know it just exactly the way it happened. Without any little tricks added onto it.

(THE OLD MAN *leans over to* EDDIE, *confidentially.*)

THE OLD MAN: What does she know?

EDDIE: (*to* THE OLD MAN) She's lying.

(*Lights begin to shift down again in the course of* MAY's *story. She moves very slowly downstage, then crosses toward* THE OLD MAN *as she tells it.*)

MAY: You want me to finish the story for you, Eddie? Huh? You want me to finish this story?

(*Pause as* MARTIN *sits again.*)

MAY: See, my mother—the pretty red-haired woman in the little white house with the red awning—was desperately in love with the old man. Wasn't she, Eddie? You could tell that right away. You could see it in her eyes. She was obsessed with him to the point where she couldn't stand being without him for even a second. She kept hunting for him from town to town. Following little clues that he left behind, like a postcard maybe, or a motel on the back of a matchbook. (*to* MARTIN) He never left her a phone number or an address or anything as simple as that because my mother was his secret, see. She hounded him for years and he kept trying to keep her at a distance because the closer these two separate lives drew together, these two separate women, these two separate kids, the more nervous he got. The more filled with terror that the two lives would find out about each other and devour him whole. That his secret would take him by the throat. But finally she caught up with him. Just by a process of elimination she dogged him down. I remember the day we discovered the town. She was on fire. "This is it!" she kept saying; "this is the place!" Her whole body was trembling as we walked through the streets, looking for the house where he lived. She kept squeezing my hand to the point where I thought she'd crush the bones in my fingers. She was terrified she'd come across him by accident on the street because she knew she was trespassing. She knew she was crossing this forbidden zone but she couldn't help herself. We walked all day through that stupid hick town. All day long. We went through every neighborhood, peering through every open window, looking in at every dumb family, until finally we found him.

(*Rest.*)

It was just exactly suppertime and they were all sitting down at the table and they were having fried chicken. That's how close we were to the window. We could see what they were eating. We could hear their voices but we couldn't make out what they were saying. Eddie and his mother were talking but the old man never said a word. Did he, Eddie? Just sat there eating his chicken in silence.

THE OLD MAN: (*to* EDDIE) Boy, is she ever off the wall with this one. You gotta' do somethin' about this.

MAY: The funny thing was, that almost as soon as we'd found him—he disappeared. She was only with him about two weeks before he just vanished. Nobody saw him after that. Ever. And my mother—just turned herself inside out. I never could understand that. I kept watching her grieve, as though somebody'd died. She'd pull herself up into a ball and just stare at the floor. And I couldn't understand that because I was feeling the exact opposite feeling. I was in love, see. I'd come home after school, after being with Eddie, and I was filled with this joy and there she'd be—standing in the middle of the kitchen staring at the sink. Her eyes looked like a funeral. And I didn't know what to say. I didn't even feel sorry for her. All I could think of was him.

THE OLD MAN: (*to* EDDIE) She's gettin' way outa' line, here.

MAY: And all he could think of was me. Isn't that right, Eddie. We couldn't take a breath without thinking of each other. We couldn't eat if we weren't together. We couldn't sleep. We got sick at night when we were apart. Violently sick. And my mother even took me to see a doctor. And Eddie's mother took him to see the same doctor but the doctor had no idea what was wrong with us. He thought it was the flu or something. And Eddie's mother had no idea what was wrong with him. But my mother—my mother knew exactly what was wrong. She knew it clear down to her bones. She recognized every symptom. And she begged me not to see him but I wouldn't listen. Then she begged Eddie not to see me but he wouldn't listen. Then she went to Eddie's mother and begged her. And Eddie's mother— (*pause. She looks straight at* EDDIE)—Eddie's mother blew her brains out. Didn't she, Eddie? Blew her brains right out.

THE OLD MAN: (*standing. He moves from the platform onto the stage, between* EDDIE *and* MAY) Now, wait a second! Wait a second. Just a goddamn second here. This story doesn't hold water. (*to* EDDIE, *who stays seated*) You're not gonna' let her off the hook with that one are ya'? That's the dumbest version I ever heard in my whole life. She never blew her brains out. Nobody ever told me that. Where the hell did that come from? (*to* EDDIE, *who remains seated*) Stand up!

Get on yer feet now goddammit! I wanna' hear the male side a' this thing. You gotta' represent me now. Speak on my behalf. There's no one to speak for me now! Stand up!

(EDDIE *stand slowly. Stares at* THE OLD MAN.)

THE OLD MAN: Now tell her. Tell her the way it happened. We've got a pact. Don't forget that.

EDDIE: *(calmly to* THE OLD MAN*)* It was your shotgun. Same one we used to duck-hunt with. Browning. She never fired a gun before in her life. That was her first time.

THE OLD MAN: Nobody told me any a' that. I was left completely in the dark.

EDDIE: You were gone.

THE OLD MAN: Somebody could've found me! Somebody could've hunted me down. I wasn't that impossible to find.

EDDIE: You were gone.

THE OLD MAN: That's right, I was gone! I was gone. You're right. But I wasn't disconnected. There was nothing cut off in me. Everything went on just the same as though I'd never left. *(to* MAY*)* But *your* mother—your mother wouldn't give it up, would she?

(THE OLD MAN *moves toward* MAY *and speaks directly to her.* MAY *keeps her eyes on* EDDIE, *who very slowly turns toward her in the course of* THE OLD MAN'S *speech. Once their eyes meet they never leave each other's gaze.)*

THE OLD MAN: *(to* MAY*)* She drew me to her. She went out of her way to draw me in. She was a force. I told her I'd never come across for her. I told her that right from the very start. But she opened up to me. She wouldn't listen. She kept opening up her heart to me. How could I turn her down when she loved me like that? How could I turn away from her? We were completely whole.

(EDDIE *and* MAY *just stand there staring at each other.* THE OLD MAN *moves back to* EDDIE. *Speaks to him directly.)*

THE OLD MAN: *(to* EDDIE*)* What're you doin'? Speak to her. Bring her around to our side. You gotta' make her see this thing in a clear light.

(*Very slowly* EDDIE *and* MAY *move toward each other.)*

THE OLD MAN: *(to* EDDIE*)* Stay away from her! What the hell are you doin'? Keep away from her! You two can't come together! You gotta' hold up my end a' this deal. I got nobody now! Nobody! You can't betray me! You gotta' represent me now! You're my son!

(EDDIE *and* MAY *come together center stage. They embrace. They kiss each other tenderly. Headlights suddenly arc across stage again from up right, cutting across the stage through window, then disappearing off left. Sound* of loud collision, shattering glass, an explosion. Bright orange and blue light of a gasoline fire suddenly illuminates upstage window. Then sounds of horses screaming wildly, hooves galloping on pavement, fading, then total silence. Light of gas fire continues now to end of play. EDDIE *and* MAY *never stop holding each other through all this. Long pause. No one moves. Then* MARTIN *stands and moves upstage to window, peers out through Venetian blinds. Pause.)*

MARTIN: *(upstage at window, looking out into flames)* Is that your truck with the horse trailer out there?

EDDIE: *(stays with* MAY*)* Yeah.

MARTIN: It's on fire.

EDDIE: Yeah.

MARTIN: All the horses are loose.

EDDIE: *(steps back away from* MAY*)* Yeah, I figured.

MAY: Eddie—

EDDIE: *(to* MAY*)* I'm just gonna' go out and take a look. I gotta' at least take a look, don't I?

MAY: What difference does it make?

EDDIE: Well, I can't just let her get away with that. What am I supposed to do? *(moves toward stage-left door)* I'll just be a second.

MAY: Eddie—

EDDIE: I'm only gonna' be a second. I'll just take a look at it and I'll come right back. Okay?

(EDDIE *exits stage-left door.* MAY *stares at door, stays where she is.* MARTIN *stays upstage.* MARTIN *turns slowly from window upstage and looks at* MAY. *Pause.* MAY *moves to bed, pulls suitcase out from underneath, throws it on bed and opens it. She goes into bathroom and comes out with clothes. She packs the clothes in suitcase.* MARTIN *watches her for a while, then moves slowly downstage to her as she continues.)*

MARTIN: May—

(MAY *goes back into bathroom and comes back out with more clothes. She packs them.)*

MARTIN: Do you need some help or anything? I got a car. I could drive you somewhere if you want. *(pause.* MAY *just keeps packing her clothes)* Are you going to go with him?

(*She stops. Straightens up. Stares at* MARTIN. *Pause.)*

MAY: He's gone.

MARTIN: He said he'd be back in a second.

MAY: *(pause)* He's gone.

(MAY *exits with suitcase out stage-left door. She leaves the door open behind her.* MARTIN *just stands there staring at open door for a while.* THE OLD MAN *looks stage left at his rocking chair, then a little above it, in blank space. Pause.* THE OLD MAN *starts moving slowly back to platform.)*

THE OLD MAN: *(pointing into space, stage left)* Ya' see that picture over there? Ya' see that? Ya' know who that is? That's the woman of my dreams. That's who that is. And she's mine. She's all mine. Forever.

(He reaches rocking chair, sits, but keeps staring at imaginary picture. He begins to rock very slowly in the chair. After THE OLD MAN sits in rocker, Merle Haggard's "I'm the One Who Loves You" starts playing as lights begin a very slow fade. MARTIN moves slowly upstage to window and stops. He stares out with his back to audience. The fire glows through window as stage lights fade. THE OLD MAN keeps rocking slowly. Stage lights keep fading slowly to black. Fire glows for a while in the dark, then cuts to black. Song continues in dark and swells in volume.)

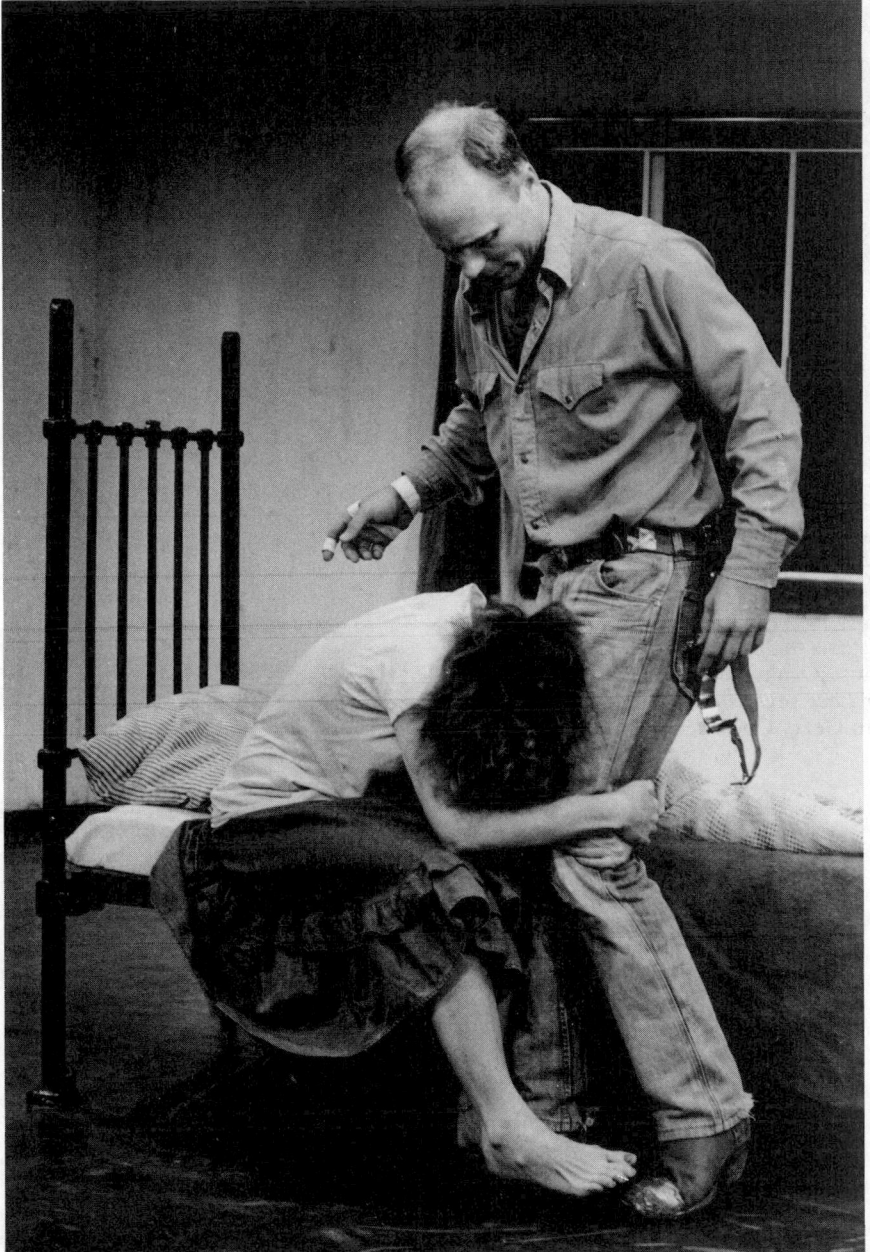

Figure 1. May (Kathy Baker) clings desperately to Eddie (Ed Harris) in the opening moments of *Fool for Love*, in the Magic Theater of San Francisco's Production presented at the Circle Repertory Company, 1983. (Photograph: Gerry Goodstein.)

Figure 2. Eddie (Ed Harris) starts to dismantle his shotgun while May (Kathy Baker) watches him closely, in the Magic Theater of San Francisco's Production of *Fool for Love* presented at the Circle Repertory Company, 1983. (Photograph: Gerry Goodstein.)

Figure 3. May (Kathy Baker) tries to explain to Martin (Dennis Ludlow) that "Everything's OK" after Martin has tackled Eddie (Ed Harris) to the floor in the Magic Theater of San Francisco's Production of *Fool for Love* presented at the Circle Repertory Company, 1983. (Photograph: Gerry Goodstein.)

Staging of *Fool for Love*

**REVIEW OF THE CIRCLE REPERTORY
COMPANY PRODUCTION, 1983,
BY FRANK RICH**

No one knows better than Sam Shepard that the true American West is gone forever, but there may be no writer alive more gifted at reinventing it out of pure literary air. Like so many Shepard plays, "Fool for Love," at the Circle Repertory Company, is a western for our time. We watch a pair of figurative gunslingers fight to the finish—not with bullets, but with piercing words that give ballast to the weight of a nation's buried dreams.

As theater, "Fool for Love" could be called an indoor rodeo. The setting is a present-day motel room on the edge of the Mojave Desert, where, for 90 minutes, May (Kathy Baker) and Eddie (Ed Harris) constantly batter one another against the walls. May and Eddie have been lovers for 15 years; they may even, like the fratricidal antagonists of "True West," be siblings. But May has had it: she'd now like nothing more than to "buffalo" Eddie by stabbing him in the middle of a passionate kiss.

Eddie is some sort of rancher, complete with saddle, rifle and lasso. Yet there's no more range—Marlboro men ride only on television—and he lives in a tin trailer. The motel room is May's most recent home. With its soiled green walls and a window facing black nothingness, it looks like a jail cell; its doors slam shut with a fierce metallic clang. When Eddie uses his rope, all he can snare is a bedpost. When the two lovers want to escape, they don't mount horses for a fast getaway—they merely run to the parking lot and back.

But if the West is now reduced to this—a blank empty room with an unmade bed—Mr. Shepard fills that space with reveries as big as all outdoors. When the play's fighting lets up, we hear monologues resembling crackling campfires tales. The characters—who also include May's new suitor (Dennis Ludlow) and a ghostly "old man" (Will Marchetti) sipping Jim Beam in a rocking chair—try to find who they are and where they are. Though the West has become but a figment of the movies, Eddie contends that "there's not a movie in this town that can match the story I can tell."

Laced with the floating images of cattle herds, old cars and even a spectral Spencer Tracy looming in the dark, these hallucinatory stories chart the Shepard vision. His characters are "disconnected"; they fear being "erased"; they hope to be "completely whole." In "Fool for Love," each story gives us a different "version" of who May, Eddie and the old man are, and the stories rarely mesh in terms of facts. Yet they do cohere as an expression of the author's consciousness: as Shepard's

people race verbally through the debris of the West, they search for the identities and familial roots that have disappeared with the landscape of legend.

Not finding what they seek, they use their dreams as weapons, to wipe each other out. The old man, a ghostly figure who may be May and Eddie's father, tells the couple that they could be "anybody's children"—"I don't recognize myself in either of you and never did." Eddie and May respond in kind, even as they obliterate their own shared past. "You got me confused with someone else," says May to her lover, vowing never again to be suckered into one of his "little fantasies." What remains of Eddie's fantastical West is ultimately destroyed, too: his few horses burn in the play's apocalyptic finale.

Mr. Shepard's conceits are arresting and funny. Eddie, in explaining his particular erotic fixation, tells May that her neck keeps "coming up for some reason." The old man contends that he's married to Barbara Mandrell and announces, without much fear of contradiction, that the singer's picture is hanging on an empty wall. There is a strange poignancy to May's suitor, a gentle maintenance man too lost even to dream of a self. Like a much talked-about "countess" of Eddie's supposed acquaintance, this sweet gentleman caller, intentionally or not, provides "Fool for Love" with an odd, unlikely echo of Tennessee Williams.

The production at the Circle Rep allows New York audiences to see the play in its native staging. "Fool for Love" has been transported here from Mr. Shepard's home base, the Magic Theater of San Francisco, complete with the original cast under the author's direction. The actors are all excellent: With utter directness, they create their own elusive yet robust world—feisty, muscular, sexually charged—and we either enter it or not.

"Fool for Love" isn't the fullest Shepard creation one ever hopes to encounter, but, at this point in this writer's prolific 20-year career, he almost demands we see his plays as a continuum: they bleed together. In the mode of his recent work, this play has a title and beat that's more redolent of country music than rock; the theatrical terms are somewhat more realistic than outright mythic (though reality is always in the eye of the beholder). The knockabout physical humor sometimes becomes excessive both in the writing and the playing; there are also, as usual, some duller riffs that invite us to drift away.

It could be argued, perhaps, that both the glory and failing of Mr. Shepard's art is its extraordinary afterlife: His works often play more feverishly in the mind after they're over than they do while they're before us in the theater. But that's the way he is, and who would or could change him? Like the visionary pioneers who once ruled the open geography of the West, Mr. Shepard rules his vast imaginative frontier by making his own, ironclad laws.

MARSHA NORMAN

1947–

Like Caryl Churchill and Maria Irene Fornes, Marsha Norman is among the most outstanding of the many women who have energized contemporary theater with plays that embody and explore female experience. Indeed, her best-known plays, *Getting Out* (1977) and *'night, Mother* (1983), focus on the psychic crises of women whose lives have been vexed by a complex array of disturbing and thwarting personal relationships, particularly their relationships with their mothers. In works such as these, Norman expresses her commitment "to a full, rich, and self-controlled life for the women on this planet." Her concern with the self-control of women is evidently rooted at least in part in her childhood experience of growing up in a highly repressive home, dominated by the moral strictures of her mother, who did not allow her to watch television, did not permit her to play with the neighborhood children because they were not "good enough," and did not let her "say anything that was in the least angry or that had any conflict in it at all."

Born and raised in a middle-class neighborhood in Louisville, Kentucky, Norman sought to escape the loneliness and solitude of her childhood through reading, through playing with an imaginary friend, and through writing stories. After graduating from high school, she attended Agnes Scott College in Decatur, Georgia, a liberal arts college for women, where she majored in philosophy and received her B.A. degree in 1969. Having returned to Louisville after graduation, she married one of her former English teachers (whom she divorced in 1974), studied for an M.A., which she received in 1971, and then went to work at the Kentucky Central State Hospital, as a teacher of disturbed adolescents. In her work at the hospital, she found herself confronted by "children who never talked at all," by others "who would just as soon stab you in the back as talk to you," but most of all by "violent kids," one of whom was so vicious that the memory of the terror she aroused in Norman provided the seminal idea for Norman's first play, *Getting Out,* which focuses on the psychic life of a recently rehabilitated woman parolee.

But Norman's work at the hospital school did not immediately lead her into playwriting. From 1973 to 1976, she worked at a school for gifted children, teaching filmmaking and developing a curriculum in the arts and humanities. It was during this period, evidently influenced by her creatively talented students, that she began to try her own hand at writing—mostly pieces for the local newspapers, but also a children's musical and scripts for a children's television program. During this time, she also first met Jon Jory, artistic director of the Actors Theatre of Louisville, one of several regional American theaters that has been particularly influential in the development of new plays and playwrights. Though she went to Jory seeking his advice about an arts program she was then developing to stimulate the interest of young people in the performing arts, he instead encouraged her to think about writing a play herself, in particular, a docu-drama about busing, which had recently hit Louisville and thus was a prominent local issue. But the subject of busing interested her less than Jory's subsequent suggestion that she think of writing a play about "a painful subject"—a suggestion that led her to think about the violent thirteen-year-old girl who had terrified her several years earlier at the hospital school.

Stimulated by that memory, Norman decided to write a play that would in some way incorporate a convulsively disturbed and disturbing young adolescent woman. But Norman was not content to focus just on someone like the violent young prisoner she had known, for in *Getting Out* she portrays two sides of a woman who has just been released from prison and is trying to make a new life for herself. In order to dramatize two sides of a single person, Norman created two distinctly different but clearly interrelated characters: Arlene Holsclaw, the protagonist, who, having served eight years in prison for robbery, kidnapping, and manslaughter, is shown during her first day out of prison, trying to fix up her apartment and in the process trying to deal with her past; and Arlie, the embodiment of her younger, vicious self, who suddenly appears at moments when Arlene's memory calls her into being, or when Arlene is cruelly reminded of her past by visits she receives from her former pimp, her former prison guard, and her mother. In working out the complex psychic drama of Arlene/Arlie, Norman drew not only on her memory of the vicious adolescent she had encountered in the hospital school, but also on extensive interviews with fifteen women prisoners who told her at length "exactly what it was like to be in prison and exactly what it was like to be out." She also drew on her own personal experience of feeling emotionally imprisoned, as she made clear in her forthright acknowledgment that "that person locked up was me" and that "the writing of *Getting Out* for me was my own opening of the door."

Though it was her first professionally staged play, *Getting Out* was produced not only at the Actors Theatre of Louisville in 1977, but also at the Mark Taper Forum in Los Angeles in 1978, and at the Phoenix Theater in Manhattan in 1978, where critics and audiences responded so enthusiastically that it was revived in 1979 for an eight-month run at the Theatre de Lys. *Getting Out* brought Norman several awards for the best new play by a new American playwright, and it evidently stimulated her to devote herself entirely to playwriting. During 1978 and 1979, she continued to work with the Actors Theatre of Louisville, though she moved to New York City at the end of 1978 with her new husband. As a playwright-in-residence during 1978, she completed a highly successful pair of one-acts: *The Laundromat,* which depicts the encounter of a widow and a woman involved in a failed marriage; and *The Pool Hall,* which portrays the owner of the hall in conversation with the son of a notorious pool shark. In these short naturalistic pieces, as in the less successful *Circus Valentine* (1979), which portrays the attempt of a woman aerialist to save a failing family circus, Norman continued to focus on the painful experience of "folks you wouldn't even notice in life."

Her next major success in dramatizing the lives of such people came with the Pulitzer Prize–winning *'night, Mother,* which was first staged in January 1983 at the American Repertory Theater in Cambridge before its Broadway opening in March 1983. In this spare and relentlessly worked-out study of a woman's decision to commit suicide, Norman creates a challengingly different kind of protagonist from the Arlene of *Getting Out,* for Jessie Cates, heroine of *'night,*

Mother, is by no means passive or emotionally imprisoned. In contrast to Arlene, she is vocally and actively concerned with regaining a significant measure of self-control in her life, so much so that she is willing to put an end to it, since she cannot imagine a tolerable future, afflicted as she is by the painful circumstances of her past. Given Jessie's clear-cut and reiterated announcement of her intention to commit suicide, the energy of *'night Mother* inevitably arises not out of whether (or when, or even how) she will go through with her decision, but rather out of how she attempts to make sense of such a momentous decision both for herself and for her mother.

Making sense of Jessie's decision is the work of the play for both characters and audience, and Norman deliberately chooses to emphasize the realistic world of the characters so as to contrast the abnormality of Jessie's decision, at first, with the setting in which it takes place. Her stage directions stress the "ordinary" quality of the house, and insist that "under no circumstances should the set and its dressing make a judgment about the intelligence or taste of Jessie and Mama. It should simply indicate that they are very specific real people who happen to live in a particular part of the country." Thus the kitchen so realistically presented in Heidi Landesman's set for the New York production at the John Golden Theater (see Figure 1) and the many details of stage properties create a world which seems familiar and "real" to the audience. At the same time, Jessie's list-making and deliberate handling of all the props, from the gun which she carefully cleans (see Figure 2) to the seemingly endless supply of candy for her mother, represents her attempt to control this world from which she feels alienated and which she can finally control only by "getting out" of it. The laughter which the play evokes in performance similarly functions as both protective and horrifying; the audience may laugh at familiar mother-daughter routines as well as at telling comments about the absent family members, and yet recoil from the laughter because it is inappropriate to the subject and situation.

Norman's combination of the ordinary and the extraordinary, of laughter and horror, has provoked equally contradictory reactions in critics, as suggested by the two reviews of the New York production reprinted following the text. Some reviewers, such as Douglas Watt, found the basic situation of the play to be "alien, pat, and unlikely," while others, such as Frank Rich, found themselves gradually drawn into Jessie's "inexorable logic." A further complication of the play is that it addresses not just the question of suicide, but the larger questions concerning a woman's identity in a world dominated by men. Though no men appear in the play, Jessie and Mama do, after all, talk constantly about Jessie's dead father, her brother, her husband, and her delinquent son. And shortly after the pistol shot, Mama seeks the counsel not of another woman, but of a man—"Loretta, let me talk to Dawson, honey." Norman's vision of the prison in which women find themselves, and put themselves, is unsparing. Readers and audiences will have to decide if it is also hopeless.

'NIGHT, MOTHER

BY MARSHA NORMAN

CHARACTERS

JESSIE CATES, *in her late thirties or early forties, is pale and vaguely unsteady physically. It is only in the last year that* JESSIE *has gained control of her mind and body, and tonight she is determined to hold on to that control. She wears pants and a long black sweater with deep pockets, which contain scraps of paper, and there may be a pencil behind her ear or a pen clipped to one of the pockets of the sweater.*

As a rule, JESSIE *doesn't feel much like talking. Other people have rarely found her quirky sense of humor amusing. She has a peaceful energy on this night, a sense of purpose, but is clearly aware of the time passing moment by moment. Oddly enough,* JESSIE *has never been as communicative or as enjoyable as she is on this evening, but we must know she has not always been this way. There is a familiarity between these two women that comes from having lived together for a long time. There is a shorthand to the talk and a sense of routine comfort in the way they relate to each other physically. Naturally, there are also routine aggravations.*

THELMA CATES, "MAMA," *is* JESSIE's *mother, in her late fifties or early sixties. She has begun to feel her age and so takes it easy when she can, or when it serves her purpose to let someone help her. But she speaks quickly and enjoys talking. She believes that things* are *what she says they are. Her sturdiness is more a mental quality than a physical one, finally. She is chatty and nosy, and this is* her *house.*

SCENE

The play takes place in a relatively new house built way out on a country road, with a living room and connecting kitchen, and a center hall that leads off to the bedrooms. A pull cord in the hall ceiling releases a ladder which leads to the attic. One of these bedrooms opens directly onto the hall, and its entry should be visible to everyone in the audience. It should be, in fact, the focal point of the entire set, and the lighting should make it disappear completely at times and draw the entire set into it at others. It is a point of both threat and promise. It is an ordinary door that opens onto absolute nothingness. That door is the point of all the action, and the utmost care should be given to its design and construction.

The living room is cluttered with magazines and needlework catalogues, ashtrays and candy dishes. Examples of MAMA's *needlework are everywhere—pillows, afghans, and quilts, doilies and rugs, and they are quite nice examples. The house is more comfortable than messy, but there is quite a lot to keep in place here. It is more personal than charming. It is not quaint. Under no circumstances should the set and its dressing make a judgment about the intelligence or taste of* JESSIE *and* MAMA. *It should simply indicate that they are very specific real people who happen to live in a particular part of the country. Heavy accents, which would further distance the audience from* JESSIE *and* MAMA, *are also wrong.*

The time is the present, with the action beginning about 8:15. Clocks onstage in the kitchen and on a table in the living room should run throughout the performance and be visible to the audience.

MAMA *stretches to reach the cupcakes in a cabinet in the kitchen. She can't see them, but she can feel around for them, and she's eager to have one, so she's working pretty hard at it. This may be the most serious exercise* MAMA *ever gets. She finds a cupcake, the coconut-covered, raspberry-and-marshmallow-filled kind known as a snowball, but sees that there's one missing from the package. She calls to* JESSIE, *who is apparently somewhere else in the house.*

MAMA: (*Unwrapping the cupcake*) Jessie, it's the last snow-ball, sugar. Put it on the list, O.K.? And we're out of Hershey bars, and where's that peanut brittle? I think maybe Dawson's been in it again. I ought to put a big mirror on the refrigerator door. That'll keep him out of my treats, won't it? You hear me, honey? (*Then more to herself.*) I hate it when the coconut falls off. Why does the coconut fall off?

(JESSIE *enters from her bedroom, carrying a stack of newspapers.*)

JESSIE: We got any old towels?

MAMA: There you are!

JESSIE: (*Holding a towel that was on the stack of newspapers*) Towels you don't want anymore. (*Picking up* MAMA's *snowball wrapper.*) How about this swimming towel Loretta gave us? Beach towel, that's the name of it. You want it? (MAMA *shakes her head no.*)

MAMA: What have you been doing in there?

JESSIE: And a big piece of plastic like a rubber sheet or something. Garbage bags would do if there's enough.

MAMA: Don't go making a big mess, Jessie. It's eight o'clock already.

JESSIE: Maybe an old blanket or towels we got in a soap box sometime?

MAMA: I said don't make a mess. You hair is black enough, hon.

JESSIE: (*Continuing to search the kitchen cabinets, finding two or three more towels to add to her stack*) It's not for my hair, Mama. What about some old pillows any-where, or a foam cushion out of a yard chair would be real good.

MAMA: You haven't forgot what night it is, have you? (*Holding up her fingernails.*) They're all chipped, see? I've been waiting all week, Jess. It's Saturday night, sugar.

JESSIE: I know. I got it on the schedule.

MAMA: (*Crossing to the living room*) You want me to wash 'em now or are you making your mess first? (*Looking at the snowball.*) We're out of these. Did I say that already?

JESSIE: There's more coming tomorrow. I ordered you a whole case.

MAMA: (*Checking the TV Guide*) A whole case will go stale, Jessie.

JESSIE: They can go in the freezer till you're ready for them. Where's Daddy's gun?

MAMA: In the attic.

JESSIE: Where in the attic? I looked your whole nap and couldn't find it anywhere.

MAMA: One of his shoeboxes, I think.

JESSIE: Full of shoes. I looked already.

MAMA: Well, you didn't look good enough, then. There's that box from the ones he wore to the hospital. When he died, they told me I could have them back, but I never did like those shoes.

JESSIE: (*Pulling them out of her pocket*) I found the bullets. They were in an old milk can.

MAMA: (*As* JESSIE *starts for the hall*) Dawson took the shot-gun, didn't he? Hand me that basket, hon.

JESSIE: (*Getting the basket for her*) Dawson better not've taken that pistol.

MAMA: (*Stopping her again*) Now my glasses, please. (JES-SIE *returns to get the glasses.*) I told him to take those rubber boots, too, but he said they were for fishing. I told him to take up fishing.

(JESSIE *reaches for the cleaning spray and cleans* MAMA's *glasses for her*)

JESSIE: He's just too lazy to climb up there, Mama. Or maybe he's just being smart. That floor's not very steady.

MAMA: (*Getting out a piece of knitting*) It's not a floor at all, hon, it's a board now and then. Measure this for me. I need six inches.

JESSIE: (*As she measures*) Dawson could probably use some of those clothes up there. Somebody should have them. You ought to call the Salvation Army before the whole thing falls in on you. Six inches exactly.

MAMA: It's plenty safe! As long as you don't go up there.

JESSIE: (*Turning to go again*) I'm careful.

MAMA: What do you want the gun for, Jess?

JESSIE: (*Not returning this time. Opening the ladder in the hall.*) Protection. (*She steadies the ladder as* MAMA *talks.*)

MAMA: You take the TV way too serious, hon. I've never seen a criminal in my life. This is way too far to come for what's out here to steal. Never seen a one.

JESSIE: (*Taking her first step up*) Except for Ricky.

MAMA: Ricky is mixed up. That's not a crime.

JESSIE: Get your hands washed. I'll be right back. And get 'em real dry. You dry your hands till I get back or it's no go, all right?

MAMA: I thought Dawson told you not to go up those stairs.

JESSIE: (*Going up*) He did.

MAMA: I don't like the idea of a gun, Jess.

JESSIE: (*Calling down from the attic*) Which shoebox, do you remember?

MAMA: Black.

JESSIE: The box was black?

MAMA: The shoes were black.

JESSIE: That doesn't help much, Mother.

MAMA: I'm not trying to help, sugar. (*No answer.*) We don't have anything anybody'd want, Jessie. I mean, I don't even want what we got, Jessie.

JESSIE: Neither do I. Wash your hands. (MAMA *gets up and crosses to stand under the ladder.*)

MAMA: You come down from there before you have a fit. I can't come up and get you, you know.

JESSIE: I know.

MAMA: We'll just hand it over to them when they come, how's that? Whatever they want, the criminals.

JESSIE: That's a good idea, Mama.

MAMA: Ricky will grow out of this and be a real fine boy, Jess. But I have to tell you, I wouldn't want Ricky to know we had a gun in the house.

JESSIE: Here it is. I found it.

MAMA: It's just something Ricky's going through. Maybe he's in with some bad people. He just needs some time, sugar. He'll get back in school or get a job or one day you'll get a call and he'll say he's sorry for all the trouble he's caused and invite you out for supper someplace dress-up.

JESSIE: (Coming back down the steps) Don't worry. It's not for him, it's for me.

MAMA: I didn't think you would shoot your own boy, Jessie. I know you've felt like it, well, we've all felt like shooting somebody, but we don't do it. I just don't think we need . . .

JESSIE: (Interrupting) Your hands aren't washed. Do you want a manicure or not?

MAMA: Yes, I do, but . . .

JESSIE: (Crossing to the chair) Then wash your hands and don't talk to me any more about Ricky. Those two rings he took were the last valuable things I had, so now he's started in on other people, door to door. I hope they put him away sometime. I'd turn him in myself if I knew where he was.

MAMA: You don't mean that.

JESSIE: Every word. Wash your hands and that's the last time I'm telling you.

(JESSIE sits down with the gun and starts cleaning it, pushing the cylinder out, checking to see that the chambers and barrel are empty, then putting some oil on a small patch of cloth and pushing it through the barrel with the push rod that was in the box. MAMA goes to the kitchen and washes her hands, as instructed, trying not to show her concern about the gun.)

MAMA: I shoulda got you to bring down that milk can. Agnes Fletcher sold hers to somebody with a flea market for forty dollars apiece.

JESSIE: I'll go back and get it in a minute. There's a wagon wheel up there, too. There's even a churn. I'll get it all if you want.

MAMA: (Coming over, now, taking over now) What are you doing?

JESSIE: The barrel has to be clean, Mama. Old powder, dust gets in it . . .

MAMA: What for?

JESSIE: I told you.

MAMA: (Reaching for the gun) And I told you, we don't get criminals out here.

JESSIE: (Quickly pulling it to her) And I told you . . . (Then trying to be calm.) The gun is for me.

MAMA: Well, you can have it if you want. When I die, you'll get it all, anyway.

JESSIE: I'm going to kill myself, Mama.

MAMA: (Returning to the sofa) Very funny. Very funny.

JESSIE: I am.

MAMA: You are not! Don't even say such a thing, Jessie.

JESSIE: How would you know if I didn't say it? You want it to be a surprise? You're lying there in your bed or maybe you're just brushing your teeth and you hear this . . . noise down the hall?

MAMA: Kill yourself.

JESSIE: Shoot myself. In a couple of hours.

MAMA: It must be time for your medicine.

JESSIE: Took it already.

MAMA: What's the matter with you?

JESSIE: Not a thing. Feel fine.

MAMA: You feel fine. You're just going to kill yourself.

JESSIE: Waited until I felt good enough, in fact.

MAMA: Don't make jokes, Jessie. I'm too old for jokes.

JESSIE: It's not a joke, Mama.

(MAMA watches for a moment in silence.)

MAMA: That gun's no good, you know. He broke it right before he died. He dropped it in the mud one day.

JESSIE: Seems O.K. (She spins the chamber, cocks the pistol, and pulls the trigger. The gun is not yet loaded, so all we hear is the click, but it will definitely work. It's also obvious that JESSIE knows her way around a gun. MAMA cannot speak.) I had Cecil's all ready in there, just in case I couldn't find this one, but I'd rather use Daddy's.

MAMA: Those bullets are at least fifteen years old.

JESSIE: (Pulling out another box) These are from last week.

MAMA: Where did you get those?

JESSIE: Feed store Dawson told me about.

MAMA: Dawson!

JESSIE: I told him I was worried about prowlers. He said he thought it was a good idea. He told me what kind to ask for.

MAMA: If he had any idea . . .

JESSIE: He took it as a compliment. He thought I might be taking an interest in things. He got through telling me all about the bullets and then he said we ought to talk like this more often.

MAMA: And where was I while this was going on?

JESSIE: On the phone with Agnes. About the milk can, I guess. Anyway, I asked Dawson if he thought they'd send me some bullets and he said he'd just call for me, because he knew they'd send them if he told them to. And he was absolutely right. Here they are.

MAMA: How could he do that?

JESSIE: Just trying to help, Mama.

MAMA: And then I told you where the gun was.

JESSIE: (Smiling, enjoying this joke) See? Everybody's doing what they can.

MAMA: You told me it was for protection!

JESSIE: It is! I'm still doing your nails, though. Want to try that new Chinaberry color?

MAMA: Well, I'm calling Dawson right now. We'll just see what he has to say about this little stunt.

JESSIE: Dawson doesn't have any more to do with this.

MAMA: He's your brother.

JESSIE: And that's all.

MAMA: (*Stands up, moves toward the phone*) Dawson will put a stop to this. Yes he will. He'll take the gun away.

JESSIE: If you call him, I'll just have to do it before he gets here. Soon as you hang up the phone, I'll just walk in the bedroom and lock the door. Dawson will get here just in time to help you clean up. Go ahead, call him. Then call the police. Then call the funeral home. Then call Loretta and see if *she'll* do your nails.

MAMA: You will not! This is crazy talk, Jessie!

(MAMA *goes directly to the telephone and starts to dial, but* JESSIE *is fast, coming up behind her and taking the receiver out of her hand, putting it back down.*)

JESSIE: (*Firm and quiet*) I said no. This is private. Dawson is not invited.

MAMA: Just me.

JESSIE: I don't want anybody else over here. Just you and me. If Dawson comes over, it'll make me feel stupid for not doing it ten years ago.

MAMA: I think we better call the doctor. Or how about the ambulance. You like that one driver, I know. What's his name, Timmy? Get you somebody to talk to.

JESSIE: (*Going back to her chair*) I'm through talking, Mama. You're it. No more.

MAMA: We're just going to sit around like every other night in the world and then you're going to kill yourself? (JESSIE *doesn't answer.*) You'll miss. (*Again there is no response.*) You'll just wind up a vegetable. How would you like that? Shoot your ear off? You know what the doctor said about getting excited. You'll cock the pistol and have a fit.

JESSIE: I think I can kill myself, Mama.

MAMA: You're not going to kill yourself, Jessie. You're not even upset! (JESSIE *smiles, or laughs quietly, and* MAMA *tries a different approach.*) People don't really kill themselves, Jessie. No, mam, doesn't make sense, unless you're retarded or deranged, and you're as normal as they come, Jessie, for the most part. We're all *afraid* to die.

JESSIE: I'm not, Mama. I'm cold all the time, anyway.

MAMA: That's ridiculous.

JESSIE: It's exactly what I want. It's dark and quiet.

MAMA: So is the back yard, Jessie! Close your eyes. Stuff cotton in your ears. Take a nap! It's quiet in your room. I'll leave the TV off all night.

JESSIE: So quiet I don't know it's quiet. So nobody can get me.

MAMA: You don't know what dead is like. It might not be quiet at all. What if it's like an alarm clock and you can't wake up so you can't shut it off. Ever.

JESSIE: Dead is everybody and everything I ever knew, gone. Dead is dead quiet.

MAMA: It's a sin. You'll go to hell.

JESSIE: Uh-huh.

MAMA: You will!

JESSIE: Jesus was a suicide, if you ask me.

MAMA: You'll go to hell just for saying that. Jessie!

JESSIE: (*With genuine surprise*) I didn't know I thought that.

MAMA: Jessie!

(JESSIE *doesn't answer. She puts the now-loaded gun back in the box and crosses to the kitchen. But* MAMA *is afraid she's headed for the bedroom.*)

MAMA: (*In a panic*) You can't use my towels! They're my towels. I've had them for a long time. I like my towels.

JESSIE: I asked you if you wanted that swimming towel and you said you didn't.

MAMA: And you can't use your father's gun, either. It's mine now, too. And you can't do it in my house.

JESSIE: Oh, come on.

MAMA: No. You can't do it. I won't let you. The house is in my name.

JESSIE: I have to go in the bedroom and lock the door behind me so they won't arrest you for killing me. They'll probably test your hands for gunpowder, anyway, but you'll pass.

MAMA: Not in my house!

JESSIE: If I'd known you were going to act like this, I wouldn't have told you.

MAMA: How am I supposed to act? Tell you to go ahead? O.K. by me, sugar? Might try it myself. What took you so long?

JESSIE: There's just no point in fighting me over it, that's all. Want some coffee?

MAMA: Your birthday's coming up, Jessie. Don't you want to know what we got you?

JESSIE: You got me dusting powder, Loretta got me a new housecoat, pink probably, and Dawson got me new slippers, too small, but they go with the robe, he'll say. (MAMA *cannot speak.*) Right? (*Apparently* JESSIE *is right.*) Be back in a minute.

(JESSIE *takes the gun box, puts it on top of the stack of towels and garbage bags, and takes them into her bedroom.* MAMA, *alone for a moment, goes to the phone, picks up the receiver, looks toward the bedroom, starts to dial, and then replaces the receiver in its cradle as* JESSIE *walks back into the room.* JESSIE *wonders, silently. They have lived together for so long there is very rarely any reason for one to ask what the other was about to do.*)

MAMA: I started to, but I didn't. I didn't call him.

JESSIE: Good. Thank you.

MAMA: (*Starting over, a new approach*) What's this all about, Jessie?

JESSIE: About?

(JESSIE *now begins the next task she had "on the schedule," which is refilling all the candy jars, taking the empty papers out of the boxes of chocolates, etc.* MAMA *generally snitches when* JESSIE *does this. Not tonight, though. Nevertheless,* JESSIE *offers.*)

MAMA: What did I do?

JESSIE: Nothing. Want a caramel?

MAMA: (*Ignoring the candy*) You're mad at me.

JESSIE: Not a bit. I am worried about you, but I'm going to do what I can before I go. We're not just going to sit around tonight. I made a list of things.

MAMA: What things?

JESSIE: How the washer works. Things like that.

MAMA: I know how the washer works. You put the clothes in. You put the soap in. You turn it on. You wait.

JESSIE: You do something else. You don't just wait.

MAMA: Whatever else you find to do, you're still mainly waiting. The waiting's the worst part of it. The waiting's what you pay somebody else to do, if you can.

JESSIE: (*Nodding*) O.K. Where do we keep the soap?

MAMA: I could find it.

JESSIE: See?

MAMA: If you're mad about doing the wash, we can get Loretta to do it.

JESSIE: Oh now, that might be worth staying to see.

MAMA: She'd never in her life, would she?

JESSIE: Nope.

MAMA: What's the matter with her?

JESSIE: She thinks she's better than we are. She's not.

MAMA: Maybe if she didn't wear that yellow all the time.

JESSIE: The washer repair number is on a little card taped to the side of the machine.

MAMA: Loretta doesn't ever have to come over here again. Dawson can just leave her at home when he comes. And we don't ever have to see Dawson either if he bothers you. Does he bother you?

JESSIE: Sure he does. Be sure you clean out the lint tray every time you use the dryer. But don't ever put your house shoes in, it'll melt the soles.

MAMA: What does Dawson do, that bothers you?

JESSIE: He just calls me Jess like he knows who he's talking to. He's always wondering what I do all day. I mean, I wonder that myself, but it's my day, so it's mine to wonder about, not his.

MAMA: Family is just accident, Jessie. It's nothing personal, hon. They don't mean to get on your nerves. They don't even mean to be your family, they just are.

JESSIE: They know too much.

MAMA: About what?

JESSIE: They know things about you, and they learned it before you had a chance to say whether you wanted them to know it or not. They were there

when it happened and it don't belong to them, it belongs to you, only they got it. Like my mail-order bra got delivered to their house.

MAMA: By accident!

JESSIE: All the same . . . they opened it. They saw the little rosebuds on it. (*Offering her another candy.*) Chewy mint?

MAMA: (*Shaking her head no*) What do they know about you? I'll tell them never to talk about it again. Is it Ricky or Cecil or your fits or your hair is falling out or you drink too much coffee or you never go out of the house or what?

JESSIE: I just don't like their talk. The account at the grocery is in Dawson's name when you call. The number's on a whole list of numbers on the back cover of the phone book.

MAMA: Well! Now we're getting somewhere. They're none of them ever setting foot in this house again.

JESSIE: It's not them, Mother. I wouldn't kill myself just to get away from them.

MAMA: You leave the room when they come over, anyway.

JESSIE: I stay as long as I can. Besides, it's you they come to see.

MAMA: That's because I stay in the room when they come.

JESSIE: It's not them.

MAMA: Then what is it?

JESSIE: (*Checking the list on her note pad*) The grocery won't deliver on Saturday anymore. And if you want your order the same day, you have to call before ten. And they won't deliver less than fifteen dollars' worth. What I do is tell them what we need and tell them to add on cigarettes until it gets to fifteen dollars.

MAMA: It's Ricky. You're trying to get through to him.

JESSIE: If I thought I could do that, I would stay.

MAMA: Make him sorry he hurt you, then. That's it, isn't it?

JESSIE: He's hurt me, I've hurt him. We're about even.

MAMA: You'll be telling him killing is O.K. with you, you know. Want him to start killing next? Nothing wrong with it. Mom did it.

JESSIE: Only a matter of time, anyway, Mama. When the call comes, you let Dawson handle it.

MAMA: Honey, nothing says those calls are always going to be some new trouble he's into. You could get one that he's got a job, that he's getting married, or how about he's joined the army, wouldn't that be nice?

JESSIE: If you call the Sweet Tooth before you call the grocery, that Susie will take your fudge next door to the grocery and it'll all come out together. Be sure you talk to Susie, though. She won't let them put it in the bottom of a sack like that one time, remember?

MAMA: Ricky could come over, you know. What if he calls us?

JESSIE: It's not Ricky, Mama.

MAMA: Or anybody could call us, Jessie.

JESSIE: Not on Saturday night, Mama.

MAMA: Then what is it? Are you sick? If your gums are swelling again, we can get you to the dentist in the morning.

JESSIE: No. Can you order your medicine or do you want Dawson to? I've got a note to him. I'll add that to it if you want.

MAMA: Your eyes don't look right. I thought so yesterday.

JESSIE: That was just the ragweed. I'm not sick.

MAMA: Epilepsy is sick, Jessie.

JESSIE: It won't kill me. (*A pause.*) If it would, I wouldn't have to.

MAMA: You don't *have* to.

JESSIE: No, I don't. That's what I like about it.

MAMA: Well, I won't let you!

JESSIE: It's not up to you.

MAMA: Jessie!

JESSIE: I want to hang a big sign around my neck, like Daddy's on the barn. GONE FISHING.

MAMA: You don't like it here.

JESSIE: (*Smiling*) Exactly.

MAMA: I meant here in my house.

JESSIE: I know you did.

MAMA: You never should have moved back in here with me. If you'd kept your little house or found another place when Cecil left you, you'd have made some new friends at least. Had a life to lead. Had your own things around you. Give Ricky a place to come see you. You never should've come here.

JESSIE: Maybe.

MAMA: But I didn't force you, did I?

JESSIE: If it was a mistake, we made it together. You took me in. I appreciate that.

MAMA: You didn't have any business being by yourself right then, but I can see how you might want a place of your own. A grown woman should . . .

JESSIE: Mama . . . I'm just not having a very good time and I don't have any reason to think it'll get anything but worse. I'm tired. I'm hurt. I'm sad. I feel used.

MAMA: Tired of what?

JESSIE: It all.

MAMA: What does that mean?

JESSIE: I can't say it any better.

MAMA: Well, you'll have to say it better because I'm not letting you alone till you do. What were those other things? Hurt . . . (*Before* JESSIE *can answer.*) You had this all ready to say to me, didn't you? Did you write this down? How long have you been thinking about this?

JESSIE: Off and on, ten years. On all the time, since Christmas.

MAMA: What happened at Christmas?

JESSIE: Nothing.

MAMA: So why Christmas?

JESSIE: That's it. On the nose.

(*A pause.* MAMA *knows exactly what* JESSIE *means. She was there, too, after all.*)

JESSIE: (*Putting the candy sacks away*) See where all this is? Red hots up front, sour balls and horehound mixed together in this one sack. New packages of toffee and licorice right in back there.

MAMA: Go back to your list. You're hurt by what?

JESSIE: (MAMA *knows perfectly well*) Mama . . .

MAMA: O.K. Sad about what? There's nothing real sad going on right now. If it was after your divorce or something, that would make sense.

JESSIE: (*Looking at her list, then opening the drawer*) Now, this drawer has everything in it that there's no better place for. Extension cords, batteries for the radio, extra lighters, sandpaper, masking tape, Elmer's glue, thumbtacks, that kind of stuff. The mousetraps are under the sink, but you call Dawson if you've got one and let him do it.

MAMA: Sad about what?

JESSIE: The way things are.

MAMA: Not good enough. What things?

JESSIE: Oh, everything from you and me to Red China.

MAMA: I think we can leave the Chinese out of this.

JESSIE: (*Crosses back into the living room*) There's extra light bulbs in a box in the hall closet. And we've got a couple of packages of fuses in the fuse box. There's candles and matches in the top of the broom closet, but if the lights go out, just call Dawson and sit tight. But don't open the refrigerator door. Things will stay cool in there as long as you keep the door shut.

MAMA: I asked you a question.

JESSIE: I read the paper. I don't like how things are. And they're not any better out there than they are in here.

MAMA: If you're doing this because of the newspapers, I can sure fix that!

JESSIE: There's just more of it on TV.

MAMA: (*Kicking the television set*) Take it out, then!

JESSIE: You wouldn't do that.

MAMA: Watch me.

JESSIE: What would you do all day?

MAMA: (*Desperately*) Sing. (JESSIE *laughs.*) I would, too. You want to watch? I'll sing till morning to keep you alive, Jessie, please!

JESSIE: No. (*Then affectionately.*) It's a funny idea, though. What do you sing?

MAMA: (*Has no idea how to answer this*) We've got a good life here!

JESSIE: (*Going back into the kitchen*) I called this morning and canceled the papers, except for Sunday, for your puzzles; you'll still get that one.

MAMA: Let's get another dog, Jessie! You liked a big dog, now, didn't you? That King dog, didn't you?

JESSIE: (*Washing her hands*) I did like that King dog, yes.

MAMA: I'm so dumb. He's the one run under the tractor.

JESSIE: That makes him dumb, not you.

MAMA: For bringing it up.

JESSIE: It's O.K. Handi-Wipes and sponges under the sink.

MAMA: We could get a new dog and keep him in the house. Dogs are cheap!

JESSIE: (Getting big pill jars out of the cabinet) No.

MAMA: Something for you to take care of.

JESSIE: I've had you, Mama.

MAMA: (Frantically starting to fill pill bottles) You do too much for me. I can fill pill bottles all day, Jessie, and change the shelf paper and wash the floor when I get through. You just watch me. You don't have to do another thing in this house if you don't want to. You don't have to take care of me, Jessie.

JESSIE: I know that. You've just been letting me do it so I'll have something to do, haven't you?

MAMA: (Realizing this was a mistake) I don't do it as well as you. I just meant if it tires you out or makes you feel used . . .

JESSIE: Mama, I know you used to ride the bus. Riding the bus and it's hot and bumpy and crowded and too noisy and more than anything in the world you want to get off and the only reason in the world you don't get off is it's still fifty blocks from where you're going? Well, I can get off right now if I want to, because even if I ride fifty more years and get off then, it's the same place when I step down to it. Whenever I feel like it, I can get off. As soon as I've had enough, it's my stop. I've had enough.

MAMA: You're feeling sorry for yourself!

JESSIE: The plumber's helper is under the sink, too.

MAMA: You're not having a good time! Whoever promised you a good time? Do you think I've had a good time?

JESSIE: I think you're pretty happy, yeah. You have things you like to do.

MAMA: Like what?

JESSIE: Like crochet.

MAMA: I'll teach you to crochet.

JESSIE: I can't do any of that nice work, Mama.

MAMA: Good time don't come looking for you, Jessie. You could work some puzzles or put in a garden or go to the store. Let's call a taxi and go to the A&P!

JESSIE: I shopped you up for about two weeks already. You're not going to need toilet paper till Thanksgiving.

MAMA: (Interrupting) You're acting like some little brat, Jessie. You're mad and everybody's boring and you don't have anything to do and you don't like me and you don't like going out and you don't like staying in and you never talk on the phone and you don't watch TV and you're miserable and it's your own sweet fault.

JESSIE: And it's time I did something about it.

MAMA: Not something like killing yourself. Something like . . . buying us all new dishes! I'd like that. Or maybe the doctor would let you get a driver's license now, or I know what let's do right this minute, let's rearrange the furniture.

JESSIE: I'll do that. If you want. I always thought if the TV was somewhere else, you wouldn't get such a glare on it during the day. I'll do whatever you want before I go.

MAMA: (Badly frightened by those words) You could get a job!

JESSIE: I took that telephone sales job and I didn't even make enough money to pay the phone bill, and I tried to work at the gift shop at the hospital and they said I made people real uncomfortable smiling at them the way I did.

MAMA: You could keep books. You kept your dad's books.

JESSIE: But nobody ever checked them.

MAMA: When he died, they checked them.

JESSIE: And that's when they took the books away from me.

MAMA: That's because without him there wasn't any business, Jessie!

JESSIE: (Putting the pill bottles away) You know I couldn't work. I can't do anything. I've never been around people my whole life except when I went to the hospital. I could have a seizure any time. What good would a job do? The kind of job I could get would make me feel worse.

MAMA: Jessie!

JESSIE: It's true!

MAMA: It's what you think is true!

JESSIE: (Struck by the clarity of that) That's right. It's what I think is true.

MAMA: (Hysterically) But I can't do anything about that!

JESSIE: (Quietly) No. You can't. (MAMA slumps, if not physically, at least emotionally.) And I can't do anything either, about my life, to change it, make it better, make me feel better about it. Like it better, make it work. But I can stop it. Shut it down, turn it off like the radio when there's nothing on I want to listen to. It's all I really have that belongs to me and I'm going to say what happens to it. And it's going to stop. And I'm going to stop it. So. Let's just have a good time.

MAMA: Have a good time.

JESSIE: We can't go on fussing all night. I mean, I could ask you things I always wanted to know and you could make me some hot chocolate. The old way.

MAMA: (In despair) It takes cocoa, Jessie.

JESSIE: (Gets it out of the cabinet) I bought cocoa, Mama. And I'd like to have a caramel apple and do your nails.

MAMA: You didn't eat a bite of supper.

JESSIE: Does that mean I can't have a caramel apple?

MAMA: Of course not. I mean . . . (Smiling a little.) Of course you can have a caramel apple.

JESSIE: I thought I could.

MAMA: I make the best caramel apples in the world.

JESSIE: I know you do.

MAMA: Or used to. And you don't get cocoa like mine anywhere anymore.

JESSIE: It takes time, I know, but . . .

MAMA: The salt is the trick.

JESSIE: Trouble and everything.

MAMA: (*Backing away toward the stove*) It's no trouble. What trouble? You put it in the pan and stir it up. All right. Fine. Caramel apples. Cocoa. O.K.

(JESSIE *walks to the counter to retrieve her cigarettes as* MAMA *looks for the right pan. There are brief near-smiles, and maybe* MAMA *clears her throat. We have a truce, for the moment. A genuine but nevertheless uneasy one.* JESSIE, *who has been in constant motion since the beginning, now seems content to sit.*)

(MAMA *starts looking for a pan to make the cocoa, getting out all the pans in the cabinets in the process. It looks like she's making a mess on purpose so* JESSIE *will have to put them all away again.* MAMA *is buying time, or trying to, and entertaining.*)

JESSIE: You talk to Agnes today?

MAMA: She's calling me from a pay phone this week. God only knows why. She has a perfectly good Trimline at home.

JESSIE: (*Laughing*) Well, how is she?

MAMA: How is she every day, Jessie? Nuts.

JESSIE: Is she really crazy or just silly?

MAMA: No, she's really crazy. She was probably using the pay phone because she had another little fire problem at home.

JESSIE: Mother . . .

MAMA: I'm serious! Agnes Fletcher's burned down every house she ever lived in. Eight fires, and she's due for a new one any day now.

JESSIE: (*Laughing*) No!

MAMA: Wouldn't surprise me a bit.

JESSIE: (*Laughing*) Why didn't you tell me this before? Why isn't she locked up somewhere?

MAMA: 'Cause nobody ever got hurt, I guess. Agnes woke everybody up to watch the fires as soon as she set 'em. One time she set out porch chairs and served lemonade.

JESSIE: (*Shaking her head*) Real lemonade?

MAMA: The houses they lived in, you knew they were going to fall down anyway, so why wait for it, is all I could ever make out about it. Agnes likes a feeling of accomplishment.

JESSIE: Good for her.

MAMA: (*Finding the pan she wants*) Why are you asking about Agnes? One cup or two?

JESSIE: One. She's your friend. No marshmallows.

MAMA: (*Getting the milk, etc.*) You have to have marshmallows. That's the old way, Jess. Two or three? Three is better.

JESSIE: Three, then. Her whole house burns up? Her clothes and pillows and everything? I'm not sure I believe this.

MAMA: When she was a girl, Jess, not now. Long time ago. But she's still got it in her, I'm sure of it.

JESSIE: She wouldn't burn her house down now. Where would she go? She can't get Buster to build her a new one, he's dead. How could she burn it up?

MAMA: Be exciting, though, if she did. You never know.

JESSIE: You do too know, Mama. She wouldn't do it.

MAMA: (*Forced to admit, but reluctant*) I guess not.

JESSIE: What else? Why does she wear all those whistles around her neck?

MAMA: Why does she have a house full of birds?

JESSIE: I didn't know she had a house full of birds!

MAMA: Well, she does. And she says they just follow her home. Well, I know for a fact she's still paying on the last parrot she bought. You gotta keep your life filled up, she says. She says a lot of stupid things. (JESSIE *laughs,* MAMA *continues, convinced she's getting somewhere.*) It's all that okra she eats. You can't just willy-nilly eat okra two meals a day and expect to get away with it. Made her crazy.

JESSIE: She really eats okra twice a day? Where does she get it in the winter?

MAMA: Well, she eats it a lot. Maybe not two meals, but . . .

JESSIE: More than the average person.

MAMA: (*Beginning to get irritated*) I don't know how much okra the average person eats.

JESSIE: Do you know how much okra Agnes eats?

MAMA: No.

JESSIE: How many birds does she have?

MAMA: Two.

JESSIE: Then what are the whistles for?

MAMA: They're not real whistles. Just little plastic ones on a necklace she won playing Bingo, and I only told you about it because I thought it might get a laugh out of you for once even if it wasn't the truth, Jessie. Things don't have to be true to talk about 'em, you know.

JESSIE: Why won't she come over here?

(MAMA *is suddenly quiet, but the cocoa and milk are in the pan now, so she lights the stove and starts stirring.*)

MAMA: Well now, what a good idea. We should've had more cocoa. Cocoa is perfect.

JESSIE: Except you don't like milk.

MAMA: (*Another attempt, but not as energetic*) I hate milk. Coats your throat as bad as okra. Something just downright disgusting about it.

JESSIE: It's because of me, isn't it?

MAMA: No, Jess.

JESSIE: Yes, Mama.

MAMA: O.K. Yes, then, but she's crazy. She's as crazy as they come. She's a lunatic.

JESSIE: What is it exactly? Did I say something, sometime? Or did she see me have a fit and's afraid I might have another one if she came over, or what?

MAMA: I guess.

JESSIE: You guess what? What's she ever said? She must've given you some reason.

MAMA: Your hands are cold.

JESSIE: What difference does that make?

MAMA: "Like a corpse," she says, "and I'm gonna be one soon enough as it is."

JESSIE: That's crazy.

MAMA: That's Agnes. "Jessie's shook the hand of death and I can't take the chance it's catching, Thelma, so I ain't comin' over, and you can understand or not, but I ain't comin'. I'll come up the driveway, but that's as far as I go."

JESSIE: (*Laughing, relieved*) I thought she didn't like me! She's scared of me! How about that! Scared of me.

MAMA: I could make her come over here, Jessie. I could call her up right now and she could bring the birds and come visit. I didn't know you ever thought about her at all. I'll tell her she just has to come and she'll come, all right. She owes me one.

JESSIE: No, that's all right. I just wondered about it. When I'm in the hospital, does she come over here?

MAMA: Her kitchen is just a tiny thing. When she comes over here, she feels like . . . (*Toning it down a little.*) Well, we all like a change of scene, don't we?

JESSIE: (*Playing along*) Sure we do. Plus there's no birds diving around.

MAMA: I hate those birds. She says I don't understand them. What's there to understand about birds?

JESSIE: Why Agnes likes them, for one thing. Why they stay with her when they could be outside with the other birds. What their singing means. How they fly. What they think Agnes is.

MAMA: Why do you have to know so much about things, Jessie? There's just not that much *to* things that I could ever see.

JESSIE: That you could ever *tell*, you mean. You didn't have to lie to me about Agnes.

MAMA: I didn't lie. You never asked before!

JESSIE: You lied about setting fire to all those houses and about how many birds she has and how much okra she eats and why she won't come over here. If I have to keep dragging the truth out of you, this is going to take all night.

MAMA: That's fine with me. I'm not a bit sleepy.

JESSIE: Mama . . .

MAMA: All right. Ask me whatever you want. Here.

(*They come to an awkward stop, as the cocoa is ready and* MAMA *pours it into the cups* JESSIE *has set on the table.*)

JESSIE: (*As* MAMA *takes her first sip*) Did you love Daddy?

MAMA: No.

JESSIE: (*Pleased that* MAMA *understands the rules better now*) I didn't think so. Were you really fifteen when you married him?

MAMA: The way he told it? I'm sitting in the mud, he comes along, drags me in the kitchen, "She's been there ever since"?

JESSIE: Yes.

MAMA: No. It was a big fat lie, the whole thing. He just thought it was funnier that way. God, this milk in here.

JESSIE: The cocoa helps.

MAMA: (*Pleased that they agree on this, at least*) Not enough, though, does it? You can still taste it, can't you?

JESSIE: Yeah, it's pretty bad. I thought it was my memory that was bad, but it's not. It's the milk, all right.

MAMA: It's a real waste of chocolate. You don't have to finish it.

JESSIE: (*Putting her cup down*) Thanks, though.

MAMA: I should've known not to make it. I knew you wouldn't like it. You never did like it.

JESSIE: You didn't ever love him, or he did something and you stopped loving him, or what?

MAMA: He felt sorry for me. He wanted a plain country woman and that's what he married, and then he held it against me the rest of my life like I was supposed to change and surprise him somehow. Like I remember this one day he was standing on the porch and I told him to get a shirt on and he went in and got one and then he said, real peaceful, but to the point, "You're right, Thelma. If God had meant for people to go around without any clothes on, they'd have been born that way."

JESSIE: (*Sees* MAMA's *hurt*) He didn't mean anything by that, Mama.

MAMA: He never said a word he didn't have to, Jessie. That was probably all he'd said to me all day, Jessie. So if he said it, there was something to it, but I never did figure that one out. What did that mean?

JESSIE: I don't know. I liked him better than you did, but I didn't know him any better.

MAMA: How could I love him, Jessie. I didn't have a thing he wanted. (JESSIE *doesn't answer.*) He got his share, though. You loved him enough for both of us. You followed him around like some . . . Jessie, all the man ever did was farm and sit . . . and try to think of somebody to sell the farm to.

JESSIE: Or make me a boyfriend out of pipe cleaners and sit back and smile like the stick man was about to dance and wasn't I going to get a kick out of that. Or sit up with a sick cow all night and leave me a chain of sleepy stick elephants on my bed in the morning.

MAMA: Or just sit.

JESSIE: I liked him sitting. Big old faded blue man in the chair. Quiet.

MAMA: Agnes gets more talk out of her birds than I got from the two of you. He could've had that GONE FISHING sign around his neck in that chair. I saw him stare off at the water. I saw him look at the weather rolling in. I got where I could practically see the boat myself. But you, you knew what he was thinking about and you're going to tell me.

JESSIE: I don't know, Mama! His life, I guess. His corn. His boots. Us. Things. You know.

MAMA: No, I don't know, Jessie! You had those quiet little conversations after supper every night. What were you whispering about?

JESSIE: We weren't whispering, you were just across the room.

MAMA: What did you talk about?

JESSIE: We talked about why black socks are warmer than blue socks. Is that something to go tell Mother? You were just jealous because I'd rather talk to him than wash the dishes with you.

MAMA: I was jealous because you'd rather talk to him than anything! (JESSIE *reaches across the table for the small clock and starts to wind it.*) If I had died instead of him, he wouldn't have taken you in like I did.

JESSIE: I wouldn't have expected him to.

MAMA: Then what would you have done?

JESSIE: Come visit.

MAMA: Oh, I see. He died and left you stuck with me and you're mad about it.

JESSIE: (*Getting up from the table*) Not anymore. He didn't mean to. I didn't have to come here. We've been through this.

MAMA: He felt sorry for you, too, Jessie, don't kid yourself about that. He said you were a runt and he said it from the day you were born and he said you didn't have a chance.

JESSIE: (*Getting the canister of sugar and starting to refill the sugar bowl*) I know he loved me.

MAMA: What if he did? It didn't change anything.

JESSIE: It didn't have to. I miss him.

MAMA: He never really went fishing, you know. Never once. His tackle box was full of chewing tobacco and all he ever did was drive out to the lake and sit in his car. Dawson told me. And Bennie at the bait shop, he told Dawson. They all laughed about it. And he'd come back from fishing and all he'd have to show for it was . . . a whole pipe-cleaner *family*—chickens, pigs, a dog with a bad leg—it was creepy strange. It made me sick to look at them and I hid his pipe cleaners a couple of times but he always had more somewhere.

JESSIE: I thought it might be better for you after he died. You'd get interested in things. Breathe better. Change somehow.

MAMA: Into what? The Queen? A clerk in a shoe store? Why should I? Because he said to? Because you said to? (JESSIE *shakes her head.*) Well I wasn't here for his entertainment and I'm not here for yours either, Jessie. I don't know what I'm here for, but then I don't think about it. (*Realizing what all this means.*) But I bet you wouldn't be killing yourself if he were still alive. That's a fine thing to figure out, isn't it?

JESSIE: (*Filling the honey jar now*) That's not true.

MAMA: Oh no? Then what were you asking about him for? Why did you want to know if I loved him?

JESSIE: I didn't think you did, that's all.

MAMA: Fine then. You were right. Do you feel better now?

JESSIE: (*Cleaning the honey jar carefully*) It feels good to be right about it.

MAMA: It didn't matter whether I loved him. It didn't matter to me and it didn't matter to him. And it didn't mean we didn't get along. It wasn't important. We didn't talk about it. (*Sweeping the pots off the cabinet.*) Take all these pots out to the porch!

JESSIE: What for?

MAMA: Just leave me this one pan. (*She jerks the silverware drawer open.*) Get me one knife, one fork, one big spoon, and the can opener, and put them out where I can get them. (*Starts throwing knives and forks in one of the pans.*)

JESSIE: Don't do that! I just straightened that drawer!

MAMA: (*Throwing the pan in the sink*) And throw out all the plates and cups. I'll use paper. Loretta can have what she wants and Dawson can sell the rest.

JESSIE: (*Calmly*) What are you doing?

MAMA: I'm not going to cook. I never liked it, anyway. I like candy. Wrapped in plastic or coming in sacks. And tuna. I like tuna. I'll eat tuna, thank you.

JESSIE: (*Taking the pan out of the sink*) What if you want to make apple butter? You can't make apple butter in that little pan. What if you leave carrots on cooking and burn up that pan?

MAMA: I don't like carrots.

JESSIE: What if the strawberries are good this year and you want to go picking with Agnes.

MAMA: I'll tell her to bring a pan. You said you would do whatever I wanted! I don't want a bunch of pans cluttering up my cabinets I can't get down to, anyway. Throw them out. Every last one.

JESSIE: (*Gathering up the pots*) I'm putting them all back in. I'm not taking them to the porch. If you want them, they'll be here. You'll bend down and get them, like you got the one for the cocoa. And if somebody else comes over here to cook, they'll have something to cook in, and that's the end of it!

MAMA: Who's going to come cook here?

JESSIE: Agnes.

MAMA: In my pots. Not on your life.

JESSIE: There's no reason why the two of you couldn't just live here together. Be cheaper for both of you and somebody to talk to. And if the birds bothered you, well, one day when Agnes is out getting her hair done, you could take them all for a walk!

MAMA: (*As* JESSIE *straightens the silverware*) So that's why you're pestering me about Agnes. You think you can rest easy if you get me a new babysitter? Well, I don't want to live with Agnes. I barely want to talk with Agnes. She's just around. We go back, that's all. I'm not letting Agnes near this place. You don't get off as easy as that, child.

JESSIE: O.K., then. It's just something to think about.

MAMA: I don't like things to think about. I like things to go on.

JESSIE: (*Closing the silverware drawer*) I want to know what Daddy said to you the night he died. You came storming out of his room and said I could wait it out with him if I wanted to, but you were going to watch *Gunsmoke*. What did he say to you?

MAMA: He didn't have *anything* to say to me, Jessie. That's why I left. He didn't say a thing. It was his last chance not to talk to me and he took full advantage of it.

JESSIE: (*After a moment*) I'm sorry you didn't love him. Sorry for you, I mean. He seemed like a nice man.

MAMA: (*As* JESSIE *walks to the refrigerator*) Ready for your apple now?

JESSIE: Soon as I'm through here, Mama.

MAMA: You won't like the apple, either. It'll be just like the cocoa. You never liked eating at all, did you? Any of it! What have you been living on all these years, toothpaste?

JESSIE: (*As she starts to clean out the refrigerator*) Now, you know the milkman comes on Wednesdays and Saturdays, and he leaves the order blank in an egg box, and you give the bills to Dawson once a month.

MAMA: Do they still make that orangeade?

JESSIE: It's not orangeade, it's just orange.

MAMA: I'm going to get some. I thought they stopped making it. You just stopped ordering it.

JESSIE: You should drink milk.

MAMA: Not anymore, I'm not. That hot chocolate was the last. Hooray.

JESSIE: (*Getting the garbage can from under the sink*) I told them to keep delivering a quart a week no matter what you said. I told them you'd run out of Cokes and you'd have to drink it. I told them I knew you wouldn't pour it on the ground . . .

MAMA: (*Finishing her sentence*) And you told them you weren't going to be ordering anymore?

JESSIE: I told them I was taking a little holiday and to look after you.

MAMA: And they didn't think something was funny about that? You who doesn't go to the front steps? You, who only sees the driveway looking down from a stretcher passed out cold?

JESSIE: (*Enjoying this, but not laughing*) They said it was about time, but why didn't I take you with me? And I said I didn't think you'd want to go, and they said, "Yeah, everybody's got their own idea of vacation."

MAMA: I guess you think that's funny.

JESSIE: (*Pulling jars out of the refrigerator*) You know there never was any reason to call the ambulance for me. All they ever did for me in the emergency room was let me wake up. I could've done that here. Now, I'll just call them out and you say yes or no. I know you like pickles. Ketchup?

MAMA: Keep it.

JESSIE: We've had this since last Fourth of July.

MAMA: Keep the ketchup. Keep it all.

JESSIE: Are you going to drink ketchup from the bottle or what? How can you want your food and not want your pots to cook it in? This stuff will all spoil in here, Mother.

MAMA: Nothing I ever did was good enough for you and I want to know why.

JESSIE: That's not true.

MAMA: And I want to know why you've lived here this long feeling the way you do.

JESSIE: You have no earthly idea how I feel.

MAMA: Well, how could I? You're real far back there, Jessie.

JESSIE: Back where?

MAMA: What's it like over there, where you are? Do people always say the right thing or get whatever they want, or what?

JESSIE: What are you talking about?

MAMA: Why do you read the newspaper? Why don't you wear that sweater I made for you? Do you remember how I used to look, or am I just any old woman now? When you have a fit, do you see stars or what? How did you fall off the horse, really? Why did Cecil leave you? Where did you put my old glasses?

JESSIE: (*Stunned by* MAMA's *intensity*) They're in the bottom drawer of your dresser in an old Milk of Magnesia box. Cecil left me because he made me choose between him and smoking.

MAMA: Jessie, I know he wasn't that dumb.

JESSIE: I never understood why he hated it so much when it's so good. Smoking is the only thing I know that's always just what you think it's going to be. Just like it was the last time, right there when you want it and real quiet.

MAMA: Your fits made him sick and you know it.

JESSIE: Say seizures, not fits. Seizures.

MAMA: It's the same thing. A seizure in the hospital is a fit at home.

JESSIE: They didn't bother him at all. Except he did feel responsible for it. It *was* his idea to go horseback riding that day. It was his idea I could do *anything* if I just made up my mind to. I fell off the horse because I didn't know how to hold on. Cecil left for pretty much the same reason.

MAMA: He had a girl, Jessie. I walked right in on them in the toolshed.

JESSIE: (*After a moment*) O.K. That's fair. (*Lighting another cigarette.*) Was she very pretty?

MAMA: She was Agnes's girl, Carlene. Judge for yourself.

JESSIE: (*As she walks to the living room*) I guess you and Agnes had a good talk about that, huh?

MAMA: I never thought he was good enough for you. They moved here from Tennessee, you know.

JESSIE: What are you talking about? You liked him better than I did. You flirted him out here to build your porch or I'd never even met him at all. You thought maybe he'd help you out around the place, come in and get some coffee and talk to you. God knows what you thought. All that curly hair.

MAMA: He's the best carpenter I ever saw. That little house of yours will still be standing at the end of the world, Jessie.

JESSIE: You didn't need a porch, Mama.

MAMA: All right! I wanted you to have a husband.

JESSIE: And I couldn't get one on my own, of course.

MAMA: How were you going to get a husband never opening your mouth to a living soul?

JESSIE: So I was quiet about it, so what?

MAMA: So I should have let you just sit here? Sit like your daddy? Sit here?

JESSIE: Maybe.

MAMA: Well, I didn't think so.

JESSIE: Well, what did you know?

MAMA: I never said I knew much. How was I supposed to learn anything living out here? I didn't know enough to do half the things I did in my life. Things happen. You do what you can about them and you see what happens next. I married you off to the wrong man, I admit that. So I took you in when he left. I'm sorry.

JESSIE: He wasn't the wrong man.

MAMA: He didn't love you, Jessie, or he wouldn't have left.

JESSIE: He wasn't the wrong man, Mama. I loved Cecil so much. And I tried to get more exercise and I tried to stay awake. I tried to learn to ride a horse. And I tried to stay outside with him, but he always knew I was trying, so it didn't work.

MAMA: He was a selfish man. He told me once he hated to see people move into his houses after he built them. He knew they'd mess them up.

JESSIE: I loved that bridge he built over the creek in back of the house. It didn't have to be anything special, a couple of boards would have been just fine, but he used that yellow pine and rubbed it so smooth . . .

MAMA: He had responsibilities here. He had a wife and son here and he failed you.

JESSIE: Or that baby bed he built for Ricky. I told him he didn't have to spend so much time on it, but he said it had to last, and the thing ended up weighing two hundred pounds and I couldn't move it. I said, "How long does a baby bed have to last, anyway?" But maybe he thought if it was strong enough, it might keep Ricky a baby.

MAMA: Ricky is too much like Cecil.

JESSIE: He is not. Ricky is as much like me as it's possible for any human to be. We even wear the same size pants. These are his, I think.

MAMA: That's just the same size. That's not you're the same person.

JESSIE: I see it on his face. I hear it when he talks. We look out at the world and we see the same thing: Not Fair. And the only difference between us is Ricky's out there trying to get even. And he knows not to trust anybody and he got it straight from me. And he knows not to try to get work, and guess where he got that. He walks around like there's loose boards in the floor, and you know who laid that floor, I did.

MAMA: Ricky isn't through yet. You don't know how he'll turn out!

JESSIE: (*Going back to the kitchen*) Yes I do and so did Cecil. Ricky is the two of us together for all time in too small a space. And we're tearing each other apart, like always, inside that boy, and if you don't see it, then you're just blind.

MAMA: Give him time, Jess.

JESSIE: Oh, he'll have plenty of that. Five years for forgery, ten years for armed assault . . .

MAMA: (*Furious*) Stop that! (*Then pleading.*) Jessie, Cecil might be ready to try it again, honey, that happens sometimes. Go downtown. Find him. Talk to him. He didn't know what he had in you. Maybe he sees things different now, but you're not going to know that till you go see him. Or call him up! Right now! He might be home.

JESSIE: And say what? Nothing's changed, Cecil, I'd just like to look at you, if you don't mind? No. He loved me, Mama. He just didn't know how things fall down around me like they do. I think he did the right thing. He gave himself another chance, that's all. But I did beg him to take me with him. I did tell him I would leave Ricky and you and everything I loved out here if only he would take me with him, but he couldn't and I understood that. (*Pause.*) I wrote that note I showed you. I wrote it. Not Cecil. I said "I'm sorry, Jessie, I can't fix it all for you." I said I'd always love me, not Cecil. But that's how he felt.

MAMA: Then he should've taken you with him!

JESSIE: (*Picking up the garbage bag she has filled*) Mama, you don't pack your garbage when you move.

MAMA: You will not call yourself garbage, Jessie.

JESSIE: (*Taking the bag to the big garbage can near the back door*) Just a way of saying it, Mama. Thinking about my list, that's all. (*Opening the can, putting the garbage in, then securing the lid.*) Well, a little more than that. I was trying to say it's all right that Cecil left. It was . . . a relief in a way. I never was what he wanted to see, so it was better when he wasn't looking at me all the time.

MAMA: I'll make your apple now.

JESSIE: No thanks. You get the manicure stuff and I'll be right there.

(JESSIE *ties up the big garbage bag in the can and replaces the small garbage bag under the sink, all the time trying desperately to regain her calm.* MAMA *watches, from a distance, her hand reaching unconsciously for the phone. Then she has a better idea. Or rather she thinks of the only other thing left and is willing to try it. Maybe she is even convinced it will work.)*

MAMA: Jessie, I think your daddy had little . . .

JESSIE: (*Interrupting her*) Garbage night is Tuesday. Put it out as late as you can. The Davis's dogs get in it if you don't. (*Replacing the garbage bag in the can under the sink.*) And keep ordering the heavy black bags. It doesn't pay to buy the cheap ones. And I've got all the ties here with the hammers and all. Take them out of the box as soon as you open a new one and put them in this drawer. They'll get lost if you don't, and rubber bands or something else won't work.

MAMA: I think your daddy had fits, too. I think he sat in his chair and had little fits. I read this a long time ago in a magazine, how little fits go, just little black-outs where maybe their eyes don't even close and people just call them "thinking spells."

JESSIE: (*Getting the slipcover out of the laundry basket*) I don't think you want this manicure we've been looking forward to. I washed this cover for the sofa, but it'll take both of us to get it back on.

MAMA: I watched his eyes. I know that's what it was. The magazine said some people don't even know they've had one.

JESSIE: Daddy would've known if he'd had fits, Mama.

MAMA: The lady in this story had kept track of hers and she'd had eighty thousand of them in the last eleven years.

JESSIE: Next time you wash this cover, it'll dry better if you put it on wet.

MAMA: Jessie, listen to what I'm telling you. This lady had anywhere between five and five hundred fits a day and they lasted maybe fifteen seconds apiece, so that out of her life, she'd only lost about two weeks altogether, and she had a full-time secretary job and an IQ of 120.

JESSIE: (*Amused by* MAMA's *approach*) You want to talk about fits, is that it?

MAMA: Yes. I do. I want to say . . .

JESSIE: (*Interrupting*) Most of the time I wouldn't even know I'd had one, except I wake up with different clothes on, feeling like I've been run over. Sometimes I feel my head start to turn around or hear myself scream. And sometimes there *is* this dizzy stupid feeling a little before it, but if the TV's on, well, it's easy to miss.

(*As* JESSIE *and* MAMA *replace the slipcover on the sofa and the afghan on the chair, the physical struggle somehow mirrors the emotional one in the conversation.*)

MAMA: I can tell when you're about to have one. Your eyes get this big! But, Jessie, you haven't . . .

JESSIE: (*Taking charge of this*) What do they look like? The seizures.

MAMA: (*Reluctant*) Different each time, Jess.

JESSIE: O.K. Pick one, then. A good one. I think I want to know now.

MAMA: There's not much to tell. You just . . . crumple, in a heap, like a puppet and somebody cut the strings all at once, or like the firing squad in some Mexican movie, you just slide down the wall, you know. You don't know what happens? How can you not know what happens?

JESSIE: I'm busy.

MAMA: That's not funny.

JESSIE: I'm not laughing. My head turns around and I fall down and then what?

MAMA: Well, your chest squeezes in and out, and you sound like you're gagging, sucking air in and out like you can't breathe.

JESSIE: Do it for me. Make the sound for me.

MAMA: I will not. It's awful-sounding.

JESSIE: Yeah. It felt like it might be. What's next?

MAMA: Your mouth bites down and I have to get your tongue out of the way fast, so you don't bite yourself.

JESSIE: Or you. I bite you, too, don't I?

MAMA: You got me once real good. I had to get a tetanus! But I know what to watch for now. And then you turn blue and the jerks start up. Like I'm standing there poking you with a cattle prod or you're sticking your finger in a light socket as fast as you can . . .

JESSIE: Foaming like a mad dog the whole time.

MAMA: It's bubbling, Jess, not foam like the washer overflowed, for God's sake; it's bubbling like a baby spitting up. I go get a wet washcloth, that's all. And then the jerks slow down and you wet yourself and it's over. Two minutes tops.

JESSIE: How do I get to the bed?

MAMA: How do you think?

JESSIE: I'm too heavy for you now. How do you do it?

MAMA: I call Dawson. But I get you cleaned up before he gets here and I make him leave before you wake up.

JESSIE: You could just leave me on the floor.

MAMA: I want you to wake up someplace nice, O.K.? (*Then making a real effort.*) But, Jessie, and this is the reason I even brought this up! You haven't had a seizure for a solid year. A whole year, do you realize that?

JESSIE: Yeah, the phenobarb's about right now, I guess.

MAMA: You bet it is. You might never have another one, ever! You might be through with it for all time!

JESSIE: Could be.

MAMA: You are. I know you are!

JESSIE: I sure am feeling good. I really am. The double vision's gone and my gums aren't swelling. No rashes or anything. I'm feeling as good as I ever felt in my life. I'm even feeling like worrying or getting mad and I'm not afraid it will start a fit if I do, I just go ahead.

MAMA: Of course you do! You can even scream at me, if you want to. I can take it. You don't have to act like you're just visiting here, Jessie. This is your house, too.

JESSIE: The best part is, my memory's back.

MAMA: Your memory's always been good. When couldn't you remember things? You're always reminding me what . . .

JESSIE: Because I've made lists for everything. But now I remember what things mean on my lists. I see "dish towels," and I used to wonder whether I was supposed to wash them, buy them, or look for them because I wouldn't remember where I put them after I washed them, but now I know it means wrap them up, they're a present for Loretta's birthday.

MAMA: (Finished with the sofa now) You used to go looking for your lists, too, I've noticed that. You always know where they are now! (Then suddenly worried.) Loretta's birthday isn't coming up, is it?

JESSIE: I made a list of all the birthdays for you. I even put yours on it. (A small smile.) So you can call Loretta and remind her.

MAMA: Let's take Loretta to Howard Johnson's and have those fried clams. I know you love that clam roll.

JESSIE: (Slight pause) I won't be here, Mama.

MAMA: What have we just been talking about? You'll be here. You're well, Jessie. You're starting all over. You said it yourself. You're remembering things and . . .

JESSIE: I won't be here. If I'd ever had a year like this, to think straight and all, before now, I'd be gone already.

MAMA: (Not pleading, commanding) No, Jessie.

JESSIE: (Folding the rest of the laundry) Yes, Mama. Once I started remembering, I could see what it all added up to.

MAMA: The fits are over!

JESSIE: It's not the fits, Mama.

MAMA: Then it's me for giving them to you, but I didn't do it!

JESSIE: It's not the fits! You said it yourself, the medicine takes care of the fits.

MAMA: (Interrupting) Your daddy gave you those fits, Jessie. He passed it down to you like your green eyes and your straight hair. It's not my fault!

JESSIE: So what if he had little fits? It's not inherited. I fell off the horse. It was an accident.

MAMA: The horse wasn't the first time, Jessie. You had a fit when you were five years old.

JESSIE: I did not.

MAMA: You did! You were eating a popsicle and down you went. He gave it to you. It's his fault, not mine.

JESSIE: Well, you took your time telling me.

MAMA: How do you tell that to a five-year-old?

JESSIE: What did the doctor say?

MAMA: He said kids have them all the time. He said there wasn't anything to do but wait for another one.

JESSIE: But I didn't have another one.

(Now there is a real silence.)

JESSIE: You mean to tell me I had fits all the time as a kid and you just told me I fell down or something and it wasn't till I had the fit when Cecil was looking that anybody bothered to find out what was the matter with me?

MAMA: It wasn't all the time, Jessie. And they changed when you started to school. More like your daddy's. Oh, that was some swell time, sitting here with the two of you turning off and on like light bulbs some nights.

JESSIE: How many fits did I have?

MAMA: You never hurt yourself. I never let you out of my sight. I caught you every time.

JESSIE: But you didn't tell anybody.

MAMA: It was none of their business.

JESSIE: You were ashamed.

MAMA: I didn't want anybody to know. Least of all you.

JESSIE: Least of all me. Oh, right. That was mine to know, Mama, not yours. Did Daddy know?

MAMA: He thought you were . . . you fell down a lot. That's what he thought. You were careless. Or maybe he thought I beat you. I don't know what he thought. He didn't think about it.

JESSIE: Because you didn't tell him!

MAMA: If I told him about you, I'd have to tell him about him!

JESSIE: I don't like this. I don't like this one bit.

MAMA: I didn't think you'd like it. That's why I didn't tell you.

JESSIE: If I'd known I was an epileptic, Mama, I wouldn't have ridden any horses.

MAMA: Make you feel like a freak, is that what I should have done?

JESSIE: Just get the manicure tray and sit down!

MAMA: (Throwing it to the floor) I don't want a manicure!

JESSIE: Doesn't look like you do, no.

MAMA: Maybe I did drop you, you don't know.

JESSIE: If you say you didn't, you didn't.

MAMA: (Beginning to break down) Maybe I fed you the wrong thing. Maybe you had a fever sometime and I didn't know it soon enough. Maybe it's a punishment.

JESSIE: For what?

MAMA: I don't know. Because of how I felt about your father. Because I didn't want any more children. Because I smoked too much or didn't eat right when I was carrying you. It has to be something I did.

JESSIE: It does not. It's just a sickness, not a curse. Epilepsy doesn't mean anything. It just is.

MAMA: I'm not talking about the fits here, Jessie! I'm talking about this killing yourself. It has to be me that's the matter here. You wouldn't be doing this if it wasn't. I didn't tell you things or I married you off to the wrong man or I took you in and let your life get away from you or all of it put together. I don't know what I did, but I did it, I know. This is all my fault, Jessie, but I don't know what to do about it now!

JESSIE: (*Exasperated at having to say this again*) It doesn't have anything to do with you!

MAMA: Everything you do has to do with me, Jessie. You can't do *anything*, wash your face or cut your finger, without doing it to me. That's right! You might as well kill me as you, Jessie, it's the same thing. This has to do with me, Jessie.

JESSIE: Then what if it does! What if it has everything to do with you! What if you are all I have and you're not enough? What if I could take all the rest of it if only I didn't have you here? What if the only way I can get away from you for good is to kill myself? What if it is? I can *still* do it!

MAMA: (*In desperate tears*) Don't leave me, Jessie! (JESSIE *stands for a moment, then turns for the bedroom.*) No! (*She grabs* JESSIE's *arm.*)

JESSIE: (*Carefully taking her arm away*) I have a box of things I want people to have. I'm just going to go get it for you. You . . . just rest a minute.

(JESSIE *is gone.* MAMA *heads for the telephone, but she can't even pick up the receiver this time and, instead, stoops to clean up the bottles that have spilled out of the manicure tray.*)

(JESSIE *returns, carrying a box that groceries were delivered in. It probably says Hershey Kisses or Starkist Tuna.* MAMA *is still down on the floor cleaning up, hoping that maybe if she just makes it look nice enough,* JESSIE *will stay.*)

MAMA: Jessie, how can I live here without you? I need you! You're supposed to tell me to stand up straight and say how nice I look in my pink dress, and drink my milk. You're supposed to go around and lock up so I know we're safe for the night, and when I wake up, you're supposed to be out there making the coffee and watching me get older every day, and you're supposed to help me die when the time comes. I can't do that by myself, Jessie. I'm not like you, Jessie. I hate the quiet and I don't want to die and I don't want you to go, Jessie. How can I . . . (*Has to stop a moment.*) How can I get up every day knowing you had to kill yourself to make it stop hurting and I was here all the time and I never even saw it. And then you gave me this chance to make it better, convince you to stay alive, and I couldn't do it. How can I live with myself after this, Jessie?

JESSIE: I only told you so I could explain it, so you wouldn't blame yourself, so you wouldn't feel bad. There wasn't anything you could say to change my mind. I didn't want you to save me. I just wanted you to know.

MAMA: Stay with me just a little longer. Just a few more years. I don't have that many more to go, Jessie. And as soon as I'm dead, you can do whatever you want. Maybe with me gone, you'll have all the quiet you want, right here in the house. And maybe one day you'll put in some begonias up the walk and get just the right rain for them all summer. And Ricky will be married by then and he'll bring your grandbabies over and you can sneak them a piece of candy when their daddy's not looking and then be real glad when they've gone home and left you to your quiet again.

JESSIE: Don't you see, Mama, everything I do winds up like this. How could I think you would understand? How could I think you would want a manicure? We could hold hands for an hour and then I could go shoot myself? I'm sorry about tonight, Mama, but it's exactly why I'm doing it.

MAMA: If you've got the guts to kill yourself, Jessie, you've got the guts to stay alive.

JESSIE: I know that. So it's really just a matter of where I'd rather be.

MAMA: Look, maybe I can't think of what you should do, but that doesn't mean there isn't something that would help. *You* find it. *You* think of it. You can keep trying. You can get brave and try some more. You don't have to give up!

JESSIE: I'm *not* giving up! This *is* the other thing I'm trying. And I'm sure there are some other things that might work, but *might* work isn't good enough anymore. I need something that *will* work. *This* will work. That's why I picked it.

MAMA: But something might happen. Something that could change everything. Who knows what it might be, but it might be worth waiting for! (JESSIE *doesn't respond.*) Try it for two more weeks. We could have more talks like tonight.

JESSIE: No, Mama.

MAMA: I'll pay more attention to you. Tell the truth when you ask me. Let you have your say.

JESSIE: No, Mama! We wouldn't have more talks like tonight, because it's this next part that's made this last part so good, Mama. No, Mama. *This* is how I have my say. This is how I say what I thought about it *all* and I say no. To Dawson and Loretta and the Red Chinese and epilepsy and Ricky and Cecil and you. And me. And hope. I say no! (*Then going to* MAMA *on the sofa.*) Just let me go easy, Mama.

MAMA: How can I let you go?

JESSIE: You can because you have to. It's what you've always done.

MAMA: You are my child!

JESSIE: I am what became of your child. (MAMA *cannot answer.*) I found an old baby picture of me. And it was somebody else, not me. It was somebody pink and fat who never heard of sick or lonely, somebody who cried and got fed, and reached up and got held and kicked but didn't hurt anybody, and slept whenever she wanted to, just by closing her eyes. Somebody who mainly just laid there and laughed at the colors waving around over her head and chewed on a polka-dot whale and woke up knowing some new trick nearly every day, and rolled over and drooled on the sheet and felt your hand pulling my quilt back up over me. That's who I started out and this is who is left. (*There is no self-pity here.*) That's what this is about. It's somebody I lost, all right, it's my own self. Who I never was. Or who I tried to be and never got there. Somebody I waited for who never came. And never will. So, see, it doesn't much matter what else happens in the world or in this house, even. I'm what was worth waiting for and I didn't make it. Me . . . who might have made a difference to me . . . I'm not going to show up, so there's no reason to stay, except to keep you company, and that's . . . not reason enough because I'm not . . . very good company. (*Pause.*) Am I.

MAMA: (*Knowing she must tell the truth*) No. And neither am I.

JESSIE: I had this strange little thought, well, maybe it's not so strange. Anyway, after Christmas, after I decided to do this, I would wonder, sometimes, what might keep me here, what might be worth staying for, and you know what it was? It was maybe if there was something I really liked, like maybe if I really liked rice pudding or cornflakes for breakfast or something, that might be enough.

MAMA: Rice pudding is good.

JESSIE: Not to me.

MAMA: And you're not afraid?

JESSIE: Afraid of what?

MAMA: I'm afraid of it, for me, I mean. When my time comes. I know it's coming, but . . .

JESSIE: You don't know when. Like in a scary movie.

MAMA: Yeah, sneaking up on me like some killer on the loose, hiding out in the back yard just waiting for me to have my hands full someday and how am I supposed to protect myself anyhow when I don't know what he looks like and I don't know how he sounds coming up behind me like that or if it will hurt or take very long or what I don't get done before it happens.

JESSIE: You've got plenty of time left.

MAMA: I forget what for, right now.

JESSIE: For whatever happens, I don't know. For the rest of your life. For Agnes burning down one more house or Dawson losing his hair or . . .

MAMA: (*Quickly*) Jessie, I can't just sit here and say O.K., kill yourself if you want to.

JESSIE: Sure you can. You just did. Say it again.

MAMA: (*Really startled*) Jessie! (*Quiet horror.*) How dare you! (*Furious.*) How dare you! You think you can just leave whenever you want, like you're watching television here? No, you can't, Jessie. You make me feel like a fool for being alive, child, and you are so wrong! I like it here, and I will stay here until they make me go, until they drag me screaming and I mean screeching into my grave, and you're real smart to get away before then because, I mean, honey, you've never heard noise like that in your life. (JESSIE *turns away.*) Who am I talking to? You're gone already, aren't you? I'm looking right through you! I can't stop you because you're already gone! I guess you think they'll all have to talk about you now! I guess you think this will really confuse them. Oh yes, ever since Christmas you've been laughing to yourself and thinking, "Boy, are they all in for a surprise." Well, nobody's going to be a bit surprised, sweetheart. This is just like you. Do it the hard way, that's my girl, all right. (JESSIE *gets up and goes into the kitchen, but* MAMA *follows her.*) You know who they're going to feel sorry for? Me! How about that! Not you, me! They're going to be *ashamed* of you. Yes. *Ashamed!* If somebody asks Dawson about it, he'll change the subject as fast as he can. He'll talk about how much he has to pay to park his car these days.

JESSIE: Leave me alone.

MAMA: It's the truth!

JESSIE: I should've just left you a note!

MAMA: (*Screaming*) Yes! (*Then suddenly understanding what she has said, nearly paralyzed by the thought of it, she turns slowly to face* JESSIE, *nearly whispering.*) No. No. I . . . might not have thought of all the things you've said.

JESSIE: It's O.K., Mama.

(MAMA *is nearly unconscious from the emotional devastation of these last few moments. She sits down at the kitchen table, hurt and angry and desperately afraid. But she looks almost numb. She is so far beyond what is known as pain that she is virtually unreachable and* JESSIE *knows this, and talks quietly, watching for signs of recovery.*)

JESSIE: (*Washes her hands in the sink*) I remember you liked that preacher who did Daddy's, so if you want to ask him to do the service, that's O.K. with me.

MAMA: (*Not an answer, just a word*) What.

JESSIE: (*Putting on hand lotion as she talks*) And pick some songs you like or let Agnes pick, she'll know exactly which ones. Oh, and I had your dress cleaned that you wore to Daddy's. You looked real good in that.

MAMA: I don't remember, hon.

JESSIE: And it won't be so bad once your friends start coming to the funeral home. You'll probably see people you haven't seen for years, but I thought about what you should say to get you over that nervous part when they first come in.

MAMA: (*Simply repeating*) Come in.

JESSIE: Take them up to see their flowers, they'd like that. And when they say, "I'm so sorry, Thelma," you just say, "I appreciate your coming, Connie." And then ask how their garden was this summer or what they're doing for Thanksgiving or how their children . . .

MAMA: I don't think I should ask about their children. I'll talk about what they have on, that's always good. And I'll have some crochet work with me.

JESSIE: And Agnes will be there, so you might not have to talk at all.

MAMA: Maybe if Connie Richards does come, I can get her to tell me where she gets that Irish yarn, she calls it. I know it doesn't come from Ireland. I think it just comes with a green wrapper.

JESSIE: And be sure to invite enough people home afterward so you get enough food to feed them all and have some left for you. But don't let anybody take anything home, especially Loretta.

MAMA: Loretta will get all the food set up, honey. It's only fair to let her have some macaroni or something.

JESSIE: No, Mama. You have to be more selfish from now on. (*Sitting at the table with* MAMA.) Now, somebody's bound to ask you why I did it and you just say you don't know. That you loved me and you know I loved you and we just sat around tonight like every other night of our lives, and then I came over and kissed you and said, "'night, Mother," and you heard me close my bedroom door and the next thing you heard was the shot. And whatever reasons I had, well, you guess I just took them with me.

MAMA: (*Quietly*) It was something personal.

JESSIE: Good. That's good, Mama.

MAMA: That's what I'll say, then.

JESSIE: Personal. Yeah.

MAMA: Is that what I tell Dawson and Loretta, too? We sat around, you kissed me, "'night, Mother"? They'll want to know more, Jessie. They won't believe it.

JESSIE: Well, then, tell them what we did. I filled up the candy jars. I cleaned out the refrigerator. We made some hot chocolate and put the cover back on the sofa. You had no idea. All right? I really think it's better that way. If they know we talked about it, they really won't understand how you let me go.

MAMA: I guess not.

JESSIE: It's private. Tonight is private, yours and mine, and I don't want anybody else to have any of it.

MAMA: O.K., then.

JESSIE: (*Standing behind* MAMA *now, holding her shoulders*) Now, when you hear the shot, I don't want you to come in. First of all, you won't be able to get in by yourself, but I don't want you trying. Call Dawson, then call the police, and then call Agnes. And then you'll need something to do till somebody gets here, so wash the hot-chocolate pan. You wash that pan till you hear the doorbell ring and I don't care if it's an hour, you keep washing that pan.

MAMA: I'll make my calls and then I'll just sit. I won't need something to do. What will the police say?

JESSIE: They'll do that gunpowder test, I guess, and ask you what happened, and by that time, the ambulance will be here and they'll come in and get me and you know how that goes. You stay out here with Dawson and Loretta. You keep Dawson out here. I want the police in the room first, not Dawson, O.K.?

MAMA: What if Dawson and Loretta want me to go home with them?

JESSIE: (*Returning to the living room*) That's up to you.

MAMA: I think I'll stay here. All they've got is Sanka.

JESSIE: Maybe Agnes could come stay with you for a few days.

MAMA: (*Standing up, looking into the living room*) I'd rather be by myself, I think. (*Walking toward the box* JESSIE *brought in earlier.*) You want me to give people those things?

JESSIE: (*They sit down on the sofa,* JESSIE *holding the box on her lap*) I want Loretta to have my little calculator. Dawson bought it for himself, you know, but then he saw one he liked better and he couldn't bring both of them home with Loretta counting every penny the way she does, so he gave the first one to me. Be funny for her to have it now, don't you think? And all my house slippers are in a sack for her in my closet. Tell her I know they'll fit and I've never worn any of them, and make sure Dawson hears you tell her that. I'm glad he loves Loretta so much, but I wish he knew not everybody has her size feet.

MAMA: (*Taking the calculator*) O.K.

JESSIE: (*Reaching into the box again*) This letter is for Dawson, but it's mostly about you, so read it if you want. There's a list of presents for you for at least twenty more Christmases and birthdays, so if you want anything special you better add it to this list before you give it to him. Or if you want to be surprised, just don't read that page. This Christmas, you're getting mostly stuff for the house, like a new rug in your bathroom and needlework, but next Christmas, you're really going to cost him next Christmas. I think you'll like it a lot and you'd never think of it.

MAMA: And you think he'll go for it?

JESSIE: I think he'll feel like a real jerk if he doesn't. Me telling him to, like this and all. Now, this number's where you call Cecil. I called it last week and he answered, so I know he still lives there.

MAMA: What do you want me to tell him?

JESSIE: Tell him we talked about him and I only had good things to say about him, but mainly tell him to find Ricky and tell him what I did, and tell Ricky you have something for him, out here, from me, and to come get it. (*Pulls a sack out of the box.*)

MAMA: (*The sack feels empty*) What is it?

JESSIE: (*Taking it off*) My watch. (*Putting it in the sack and taking a ribbon out of the sack to tie around the top of it.*)

MAMA: He'll sell it!

JESSIE: That's the idea. I appreciate him not stealing it already. I'd like to buy him a good meal.

MAMA: He'll buy dope with it!

JESSIE: Well, then, I hope he gets some good dope with it, Mama. And the rest of this is for you. (*Handing* MAMA *the box now.* MAMA *picks up the things and looks at them.*)

MAMA: (*Surprised and pleased*) When did you do all this? During my naps, I guess.

JESSIE: I guess. I tried to be quiet about it. (*As* MAMA *is puzzled by the presents.*) Those are just little presents. For whenever you need one. They're not bought presents, just things I thought you might like to look at, pictures or things you think you've lost. Things you didn't know you had, even. You'll see.

MAMA: I'm not sure I want them. They'll make me think of you.

JESSIE: No they won't. They're just things, like a free tube of toothpaste I found hanging on the door one day.

MAMA: Oh. All right, then.

JESSIE: Well, maybe there's one present in there somewhere. It's Granny's ring she gave me and I thought you might like to have it, but I didn't think you'd wear it if I gave it to you right now.

MAMA: (*Taking the box to a table nearby*) No. Probably not. (*Turning back to face her.*) I'm ready for my manicure, I guess. Want me to wash my hands again?

JESSIE: (*Standing up*) It's time for me to go, Mama.

MAMA: (*Starting for her*) No, Jessie, you've got all night!

JESSIE: (*As* MAMA *grabs her*) No, Mama.

MAMA: It's not even ten o'clock.

JESSIE: (*Very calm*) Let me go, Mama.

MAMA: I can't. You can't go. You can't do this. You didn't say it would be so soon, Jessie. I'm scared. I love you.

JESSIE: (*Takes her hands away*) Let go of me, Mama. I've said everything I had to say.

MAMA: (*Standing still a minute*) You said you wanted to do my nails.

JESSIE: (*Taking a small step backward*) I can't. It's too late.

MAMA: It's not too late!

JESSIE: I don't want you to wake Dawson and Loretta when you call. I want them to still be up and dressed so they can get right over.

MAMA: (*As* JESSIE *backs up,* MAMA *moves in on her, but carefully*) They wake up fast, Jessie, if they have to. They don't matter here, Jessie. You do. I do. We're not through yet. We've got a lot of things to take care of here. I don't know where my prescriptions are and you didn't tell me what to tell Dr. Davis when he calls or how much you want me to tell Ricky or who I call to rake the leaves or . . .

JESSIE: Don't try and stop me, Mama, you can't do it.

MAMA: (*Grabbing her again, this time hard*) I can too! I'll stand in front of this hall and you can't get past me. (*They struggle.*) You'll have to knock me down to get away from me, Jessie. I'm not about to let you . . .

(MAMA *struggles with* JESSIE *at the door and in the struggle* JESSIE *gets away from her and—*)

JESSIE: (*Almost a whisper*) 'night, Mother. (*She vanishes into her bedroom and we hear the door lock just as* MAMA *gets to it.*)

MAMA: (*Screams*) Jessie! (*Pounding on the door.*) Jessie, you let me in there. Don't you do this, Jessie. I'm not going to stop screaming until you open this door, Jessie. Jessie! Jessie! What if I don't do any of the things you told me to do! I'll tell Cecil what a miserable man he was to make you feel the way he did and I'll give Ricky's watch to Dawson if I feel like it and the only way you can make sure I do what you want is you come out here and make me, Jessie! (*Pounding again.*) Jessie! Stop this! I didn't know! I was here with you all the time. How could I know you were so alone?

(*And* MAMA *stops for a moment, breathless and frantic, putting her ear to the door, and when she doesn't hear anything, she stands up straight again and screams once more.*)

Jessie! Please!

(*And we hear the shot, and it sounds like an answer, it sounds like No.*)

(MAMA *collapses against the door, tears streaming down her face, but not screaming anymore. In shock now.*)

Jessie, Jessie, child . . . Forgive me. (*Pause.*) I thought you were mine.

(*And she leaves the door and makes her way through the living room, around the furniture, as though she didn't know where it was, not knowing what to do. Finally, she goes to the stove in the kitchen and picks up the hot-chocolate pan and carries it with her to the telephone and holds on to it while she dials the number. She looks down at the pan, holding it tight like her life depended on it. She hears Loretta answer.*)

MAMA: Loretta, let me talk to Dawson, honey.

Figure 1. Mama (Anne Pitoniak) shares her memories of Daddy with Jessie (Kathy Bates) in the John Golden Theater production of *'night, Mother,* directed by Tom Moore, 1983. (Photograph: Richard M. Feldman.)

Figure 2. Jessie (Kathy Bates) examines Daddy's gun, while Mama (Anne Pitoniak) tries to convince her that it's broken, in the John Golden Theater production of *'night, Mother,* directed by Tom Moore, 1983. (Photograph: Richard M. Feldman.)

Staging of 'night, Mother

**REVIEW OF THE JOHN GOLDEN THEATER
PRODUCTION, 1983, BY DOUGLAS WATT**

Marsha Norman doesn't fool around. In 'night, Mother, which came to the Golden last night, the author of the schizophrenic Getting Out of a few seasons back offers a clinical study of a suicide—of the last 85 minutes (the play's exact length) in the life of a hopeless young woman. It's a spellbinding idea, and one held in tight control by the playwright's spare, effective dialogue; but it is less involving than one might expect, even with that final offstage gunshot.

There are several reasons for this, not the least of them the fact that the act of suicide is, in its most profound sense, as mysterious as life itself. But then, there is the troublesome situation Norman has posed.

Jessie Cates lives with her mother, Thelma, in the latter's "relatively new house, built way out on a country road," someplace in the South, judging from speech patterns and the author's Louisville background. At the very start, Jessie asks where her late father's gun has been kept, then retrieves it from a shoebox in the storage space above the ceiling, starts cleaning and oiling it and, pushing bullets into the chambers, announces her intention of killing herself this very evening.

But not until she's polished her mother's fingernails (she never gets around to this, though), given instructions about milk and other deliveries, specified people to phone, bagged the garbage and relined the pail, attended to countless other details with cool efficiency, tidied up in general and resisted any attempt on Thelma's part to dissuade her from taking her life.

The way Jessie feels about it is that her life and her disposal of it is the one thing she has complete control over. The lonely and, until now, uncommunicative child of a loveless marriage (a married brother lives nearby), she has been divorced by her husband and has given up on a son who is already a common thief and who, she is certain, will end up in prison as a result of the coming together in him of the worst aspects of herself and her former husband.

That's not all, though. Jessie, as she learns now for the first time, has been subject to epileptic fits since childhood, manifestations that have been explained away by her mother as dizzy spells or "seizures." What with one thing and another, Jessie has decided that wherever her life might end (she compares it to riding on a bus and either getting off at will or continuing to a known and undesirable destination), it will never improve, so why not make a decisive move and end it right here instead of going on sinking deeper and deeper within herself in these tacky surroundings while looking after a mother who apparently is capable of caring for herself and, worse, listening to her endlessly foolish chatter.

So the evening is spent in watching the homely preparations made for the inevitable act and listening to the mundane, often joking, conversation. Norman's intent, somewhat akin to Hitchcock's frequent juxtaposition, is to build horror—though with much more deadly intensity than the film maker sought—within the familiar, commonplace, everyday world.

The troubling aspect of the play is that Jessie is not a truly tragic figure. Her self-containment as she busily sets things to order about the house suggests one dedicated to her awful purpose, true, but also suggests a congenitally deranged woman. And Thelma's actual acceptance of the situation, having at last given up arguing against it, has a surreal air about it, as strange in its way as Jessie's early announcement of her purpose and subsequent behavior, including a break to share cocoa with her mother. The final cap-pistol report from behind a bedroom door is as weak as the play's premise. The mother's faltering steps to the kitchen area following the gunshot and her near-blind dialing of the phone to call the brother is the evening's most real moment.

Kathy Bates holds our interest as the plump, tight-lipped, bustling Jessie, who breaks down briefly just once or twice, and Anne Pitoniak is a lanky flibbertigibbet of a vacant mother whose speech, sometimes a bit hard to understand, should have been cleared up by the director, Tom Moore, who otherwise has done a serviceable job. Heidi Landesman's set is, indeed, neat, new-looking and impersonal enough to drive any occupant to suicide sooner or later, given that secret urge to begin with.

Norman's writing is diamond-sharp and expressive, under the circumstances. It's just the circumstances that struck me as alien, pat, and unlikely.

"We've got a good life here," says Thelma Cates to her daughter, Jessie, in Marsha Norman's new play, *'night, Mother.* Many would agree. Thelma, who is a widow, and Jessie, who is divorced, live together in a spick-and-span house on a country road somewhere in the New South. There are no money problems. Nights are spent in such relaxed pursuits as crocheting and watching television.

But on the particular, ordinary Saturday night that we meet Thelma (Anne Pitoniak) and Jessie (Kathy Bates), we learn that the good life may not be so good after all. As the daughter prepares to perform her weekly ritual of giving her mother a manicure, she says calmly, almost as a throwaway line, "I'm going to kill myself, Mama." And, over the next 90 minutes, Mama—and the rest of us—must face the fact that Jessie is not kidding.

'night, Mother, which has traveled to Broadway's John Golden Theater from Harvard's American Repertory Theater, is a shattering evening, but it looks like simplicity itself. A totally realistic play, set in real time counted by onstage clocks, it shows us what happens after Jessie makes her announcement. What happens, unsurprisingly, is that the first skeptical and then terrified mother tries to cajole and talk her child out of suicide. "People don't really kill themselves," argues Thelma, "unless they're retarded or deranged."

But Jessie isn't deranged—she's never felt better in her life—and that's why *'night, Mother* is more complex than it looks, more harrowing than even its plot suggests. Miss Norman's play is simple only in the way that an Edward Hopper painting is simple. As she perfectly captures the intimate details of two individual, ordinary women, this playwright locates the emptiness that fills too many ordinary homes on too many faceless streets in the vast country we live in now.

Why does Jessie want to kill herself? There are many conceivable motives. She's a fat, lumpy, anonymous-looking woman in her thirties who spends her days indoors, eating junk food. Her son is a hoodlum. Her last job, working at a gift shop in a hospital, didn't work out. She misses her dead father, as well as the husband who left her. She suffers from epilepsy, though it's now been brought under control by medication.

As the play progresses, her mother enumerates all these disappointments, desperately offering to solve any of them she can. But Jessie will have none of it. She instead wants to use her last hours to help her mother get the house in order and to sit around chatting "like every other night of our lives." The daughter insists that they make cocoa, re-cover the couch and clean out the refrigerator.

Jessie is at peace about her decision because she has decided that nothing can change it. "It doesn't really matter what else happens in the world or in this house," she says, for the real problem is "nobody out there, but my own self." In Jessie's opinion, that self—her interior life—is something that she "lost" and that will "never show up." It is also the only "real" possession she has, and she claims the right to "stop it, shut it down, turn it off."

Although it is likely to kindle many debates about the subject, *'night, Mother* is not a message play about the choice to commit suicide. It's about contemporary life and what gives it—or fails to give it—value. We first get a sense of the Cates's existence before *'night, Mother* begins. Heidi Landesman's disturbing set, in view as we enter the theater, is an all-American living room and kitchen, right out of a television sitcom: homey, appointed with the right appliances, conventionally tasteful. But, when James F. Ingalls's cruelly bright lighting comes up, we see the house is colorless and dead—a pair of antiseptic model rooms, framed like a department-store window.

Miss Norman's dialogue maps the rest of the vacuum. When Thelma at first mistakes Jessie's preoccupation with guns for a fear of burglars, she says, "We don't have anything people would want." And we come to see that neither mother nor daughter do. Their lives are built on neighborhood gossip, ritualized familial obligations and housekeeping. Before tonight—when a gun is literally to their heads—they've never expressed their real feelings to one another or to anybody else. The more loneliness that is exposed the more we realize that the most horrifying aspect of *'night, Mother* is not Jessie's decision to end her life but her mother's gradual awakening—and ours—to the inexorable logic of that decision.

The play would never work, never make that logic real, if Miss Norman for a second condescended to her characters by painting them as fools—or if she stuck in authorial speeches that commented on or judged their predicament. As she previously demonstrated in *Getting Out,* Miss Norman is far too honest a writer to fall into those traps.

Jessie and Thelma are not caricatured as stupid yokels. They are not without wit. When the mother begs the daughter to stay around "for a few more years" until her own death, she uses every argument that the smartest member of the audience might muster. Jessie, meanwhile, knocks those arguments down with brutal, eloquent force.

The strongest argument, of course, is the blood tie. Miss Norman draws the mother-daughter relationship painfully, with all the guilt and anger and twisted passion it can contain. During the course of the play, Thelma and Jessie ask each other every question they've ever wanted to ask—from "Why did your husband leave you?" to "Why did you never wear the sweater I made you?" As they do, the women often switch roles, to the excruciating point at which Thelma becomes a tantrum-throwing infant, lashing out at Jessie any way she can.

At more tender times, we see the love between these women, but we also see that it's not enough to make a difference to Jessie, who has no self-love. "You are my child!" cries the mother, in a primal plea. "No," says the daughter. "I am what became of your child."

Under the brilliant, unerring choreographic hand of the director Tom Moore—who follows the playwright by refusing to gild or theatricalize any moment—the superb actresses, both veterans of Louisville's Actors Theater, circle each other in a grueling dance of death that ebbs and flows so naturally that every violent transition catches us by surprise. There are pockets of hu-

mor—the mother even gets a laugh describing her daughter's youthful epileptic fits—and there is warmth.

But there is also the sight of Miss Pitoniak's Thelma, a gabby "plain country woman," turning white and dumb with fear as she realizes that the daughter through whom she's lived by proxy is beyond her reach—"already gone," even though still alive. And there is the moment when the otherwise deliberate Miss Bates turns away from her whimpering mother to wail defiantly, "I say *no* to hope."

Does *'night, Mother* say no to hope? It's easy to feel that way after reeling from this play's crushing blow. But there *can* be hope if there is understanding, and it is Marsha Norman's profound achievement that she brings both understanding and dignity to forgotten and tragic American lives.

AUGUST WILSON

1945–

Though he has been preceded in the American theater by several well-known black playwrights and plays—Langston Hughes (*Don't You Want to Be Free,* 1936), Theodore Ward (*Our Lan',* 1941), Lorraine Hansberry (*A Raisin in the Sun,* (1959), Imamu Amiri Baraka (*Dutchman,* 1963), and Charles Fuller (*A Soldier's Story,* 1981)—August Wilson is unquestionably the most ambitious and likely to be the most widely produced and highly regarded black dramatist of the twentieth century. His ambitiousness may be seen in his intention to write a cycle of ten plays about the experience of African Americans, one for each decade of the twentieth century, each one focused on a distinctively different but emblematic set of characters and situations. The likelihood of his achieving that ambition is quite strong, given the fact that, since 1980, he has written six of the ten projected plays in the cycle. The quality of his accomplishments thus far may be judged from the fact that four of the most recent plays in the cycle have been widely produced and enthusiastically received: *Ma Rainey's Black Bottom* (1984), *Fences* (1985), and *Joe Turner's Come and Gone* (1986), all of which have won the prestigious New York Drama Critics Circle Award, and *The Piano Lesson* (1989), which, like *Fences,* won the Pulitzer Prize.

Wilson's probing drama of African-American experience is deeply rooted in his own quite complex personal experience of growing up in the Hill district of Pittsburgh, a black slum community, where he was raised in a two-room cold-water flat by his mother, after she had been abandoned by the white man who fathered all of her six children. Although he bears the name of his natural father, who died in 1965, Wilson knew him only from occasional visits and remembers him largely as a hard-drinking German baker who turned up intermittently with a bag of rolls in his hand. And though he acquired a stepfather, David Bedford, during his early adolescent years, Wilson found himself at odds with Bedford when, at the age of fifteen, he decided to quit his high school football team and drop out of school. Wilson's decision to quit school, as it turns out, was provoked largely by the racial harassment he suffered after his family moved into the heavily white community of Hazlewood, Pennsylvania.

Out of school, Wilson continued his education in the local library, where he discovered and read his way through a small section of some thirty "Negro" books by such eminent writers as Ralph Ellison, Langston Hughes, and Richard Wright—a discovery that he remembers as having been especially significant for him. "Those books were a comfort. Just the idea black people would write books. I wanted my book up there, too." From that point on, Wilson evidently read voraciously in the fiction, poetry, and drama of black and white writers alike, and then began to try his own hand at fiction and poetry writing. Looking back on that time, he recalls himself as having been heavily influenced by the theatricality of Dylan Thomas's verse, by the "psychic shorthand" of John Berryman's poetry, and by the jazzy street style of Baraka's poetry and plays.

But Wilson primarily describes himself as having been influenced by the extraordinary diversity of African-American culture—by the street talk and the

1235

street violence that he witnessed growing up in the black ghetto of Pittsburgh, by the Black Power movement that he became involved in during the late 1960s and early 1970s, and by the blues, which he regards as "a book of literature" that contains the "blacks' cultural response to the world" and which "influences everything I do." The Black Power movement initially attracted Wilson to the theater, for it led him to see drama as a powerful means to "politicize the community and raise consciousness." Indeed, during the 1960s, he co-founded a black activist theater in Pittsburgh, the Black Horizon on the Hill, which staged his earliest plays.

Paradoxically, however, Wilson did not really develop his unique talents as a dramatist of black experience until he moved away from the familiar world of his roots in Pittsburgh to the strikingly different community of St. Paul, Minnesota. There he became involved with the Playwrights Center of Minneapolis, and there, too, he began to remember in vivid detail the language and experience of the black ghetto, as well as to see the rich dramatic potentialities in the experience of that world. Thus during the late 1970s and early 1980s, Wilson began to write plays that aimed at a realistic evocation of African-American life as he had come to know it through his past experience in Pittsburgh. In *Jitney* (1982), for example, he focused attention on the lives that intersect in a Pittsburgh gypsy-cab station.

A similarly high degree of concentration is evident in his three best-known plays. *Ma Rainey's Black Bottom* is set in a Chicago recording studio in 1927; *Fences* in the front yard of a two-story brick house in Pittsburgh in 1957; and *Joe Turner's Come and Gone* in a Pittsburgh rooming house in 1911. Such highly localized settings enable Wilson to develop in each case an intensely focused human situation. *Ma Rainey's Black Bottom* relentlessly explores the tensions within an African-American musical group as well as between the musicians and the white men who manage and own the musical business. *Fences* documents the discord within a single family, in particular between Troy Maxson, the fifty-three-year-old protagonist; his wife Rose, whose love he betrays during the course of the play; and their son Cory, whose desire for fatherly affection Troy cannot fulfill. *Joe Turner's Come and Gone* follows the internal conflicts of black freedman Herald Loomis as he searches for his wife, who, during the period of her husband's enslavement by white bounty hunter Joe Turner, had fled to the North.

Ultimately such particularized situations enable Wilson to dramatize some of the most distinctive, significant, and complex aspects of African-American experience within the context of an authentically human predicament. The significance of *Fences*, for example, grows in part from Wilson's skillful manipulation of the myth of baseball as the all-American game and the game through which the color barrier was broken in professional sports—although too late for the play's protagonist, Troy Maxson, who thinks constantly of his batting record in the Negro leagues. For Troy, baseball provides a rich source of metaphors with which to express the frustrating conditions of his world, a world where "you born with two strikes on you before you come to the plate," and where Death is "the fastball in the outside corner." Thus, within the framework of family conflict, Wilson explores what it meant to be an African American in the 1950s.

Ma Rainey's Black Bottom is equally concerned with social issues, but draws its central image from the world of popular music, in particular from "singing the blues." Through its focus on this distinctive aspect of African-American culture, the play bears witness to the white exploitation of black performers in the racist world of Sturdyvant's recording studio. Ma Rainey (see Figure 1), the African-American singer known as "the Mother of the Blues" (1886–1939), never forgets that her manager is "always talking about sticking together," always treating her solicitously in public, but "the only time he had me in his house was to sing for some of his friends." The play's tension, however, is not just between white and black people but between blacks as well, a tension that is epitomized by the difference between the old-fashioned "jug-band music" favored by Ma as opposed to the newer "jazz" on which Levee hopes to make his name. Much of the first act, for example, concerns which version of Ma's signature song the band will play—Levee's, with an instrumental introduction, or Ma's, with a spoken one. But the real issue that fuels this conflict is what kind of identity and thus what kind of power is possible for an African-American person in the America of the 1920s.

Reviewers of the New York production (which originated at the Yale Repertory Theatre) recognized Wilson's broadly cultural concerns but disagreed about whether the political and social issues overwhelmed the dramatic experience. Some felt that nothing happens in the play until the final scene, whereas others, such as Frank Rich, whose review is reprinted following the text, perceived the play to be following a musical strategy in which the emphasis is placed on the "backup men" rather than on the lead singer. Each of the four African-American musicians (see Figure 2) does get a chance to solo, to have his say, in the true jazz tradition, and each of these extended speeches reveals the character of its speaker. While all of the speakers reflect an intense personal awareness of white oppression, no one is as angry or restless or ambitious as Levee, the brilliant trumpet player. So it is that each of the two acts in the play culminates in a scene focusing on the destructive (and self-destructive) rage of Levee. And while Levee's anger dominates the climax of *Ma Rainey*, the ending of *Fences* (produced the following year but dealing with a historical period thirty years later) is marked by another trumpet player, the war-wounded and mentally impaired Gabriel, blowing on a soundless trumpet and then dancing "a slow strange dance, eerie and life giving." Such strikingly different endings suggest the range of Wilson's vision, which embraces both the painfulness and the possibilities of twentieth-century African-American experience.

MA RAINEY'S BLACK BOTTOM

BY AUGUST WILSON

CHARACTERS

STURDYVANT, *studio owner*
IRVIN, *Ma Rainey's manager*
CUTLER, *guitar and trombone player*
TOLEDO, *piano player*
SLOW DRAG, *bass player*

LEVEE, *trumpet player*
MA RAINEY, *blues singer*
POLICEMAN
DUSSIE MAE, *Ma Rainey's companion*
SYLVESTER, *Ma Rainey's nephew*

They tore the railroad down
so the Sunshine Special can't run
I'm going away baby
build me a railroad of my own

—Blind Lemon Jefferson

THE SETTING

There are two playing areas: what is called the "band room," and the recording studio. The band room is at stage left and is in the basement of the building. It is entered through a door up left. There are benches and chairs scattered about, a piano, a row of lockers, and miscellaneous paraphernalia stacked in a corner and long since forgotten. A mirror hangs on a wall with various posters.

The studio is upstairs at stage right, and resembles a recording studio of the late 1920s. The entrance is from a hall on the right wall. A small control booth is at the rear and its access is gained by means of a spiral staircase. Against one wall there is a line of chairs, and a horn through which the control room communicates with the performers. A door in the rear wall allows access to the band room.

THE PLAY

It is early March in Chicago, 1927. There is a bit of a chill in the air. Winter has broken but the wind coming off the lake does not carry the promise of spring. The people of the city are bundled and brisk in their defense against such misfortunes as the weather, and the business of the city proceeds largely undisturbed.

Chicago in 1927 is a rough city, a bruising city, a city of millionaires and derelicts, gangsters and roughhouse dandies, whores and Irish grandmothers who move through its streets fingering long black rosaries. Somewhere a man is wrestling with the taste of a woman in his cheek. Somewhere a dog is barking. Somewhere the moon has fallen through a window and broken into thirty pieces of silver.

It is one o'clock in the afternoon. Secretaries are returning from their lunch, the noon Mass at St. Anthony's is over, and the priest is mumbling over his vestments while the altar boys practice their Latin. The procession of cattle cars through the stockyards continues unabated. The busboys in Mac's Place are cleaning away the last of the corned beef and cabbage, and on the city's Southside, sleepy-eyed negroes move lazily toward their small cold-water flats and rented rooms to await the onslaught of night, which will find them crowded in the bars and juke joints both dazed and dazzling in their rapport with life. It is with these negroes that our concern lies most heavily: their values, their attitudes, and particularly their music.

It is hard to define this music. Suffice it to say that it is music that breathes and touches. That connects. That is in itself a way of being, separate and distinct from any other. This music is called blues. Whether this music came from Alabama or Mississippi or other parts of the South doesn't matter anymore. The men and women who make this music have learned it from the narrow crooked streets of East St. Louis, or the streets of the city's Southside, and the Alabama or Mississippi roots have been strangled by the northern manners and customs of free men of definite and sincere worth, men for whom this music often lies at the forefront of their conscience and concerns. Thus they are laid open to be consumed by it; its warmth and redress, its braggadocio and roughly poignant comments, its vision and prayer, which would instruct and allow them to reconnect, to reassemble and gird up for the next battle in which they would be both victim and the ten thousand slain.

ACT 1

The lights come up in the studio. IRVIN enters, carrying a microphone. He is a tall, fleshy man who prides himself on his knowledge of blacks and his ability to deal with them. He hooks up the microphone, blows into it, taps it, etc. He crosses over to the piano, opens it, and fingers a few keys. STURDYVANT is visible in the control booth. Preoccupied *with money, he is insensitive to black performers and prefers to deal with them at arm's length. He puts on a pair of earphones.*

STURDYVANT: *(Over speaker)* Irv . . . let's crack that mike, huh? Let's do a check on it.

IRVIN: *(Crosses to mike, speaks into it)* Testing . . . one . . . two . . . three . . .

(There is a loud feedback. STURDYVANT *fiddles with the dials.)*

Testing . . . one . . . two . . . three . . . testing. How's that, Mel?

(STURDYVANT doesn't respond.)

Testing . . . one . . . two . . .

STURDYVANT: *(Taking off earphones)* Okay . . . that checks. We got a good reading. *(Pause.)* You got that list, Irv?

IRVIN: Yeah . . . yeah, I got it. Don't worry about nothing.

STURDYVANT: Listen, Irv . . . you keep her in line, okay? I'm holding you responsible for her . . . If she starts any of her . . .

IRVIN: Mel, what's with the goddamn horn? You wanna talk to me . . . okay! I can't talk to you over the goddamn horn . . . Christ!

STURDYVANT: I'm not putting up with any shenanigans. You hear, Irv?

(IRVIN crosses over to the piano and mindlessly runs his fingers over the keys.)

I'm just not gonna stand for it. I want you to keep her in line. Irv?

(STURDYVANT enters from the control booth.)

Listen, Irv . . . you're her manager . . . she's your responsibility . . .

IRVIN: Okay, okay, Mel . . . let me handle it.

STURDYVANT: She's your responsibility. I'm not putting up with any Royal Highness . . . Queen of the Blues bullshit!

IRVIN: Mother of the Blues, Mel. Mother of the Blues.

STURDYVANT: I don't care what she calls herself. I'm not putting up with it. I just want to get her in here . . . record those songs on that list . . . and get her out. Just like clockwork, huh?

IRVIN: Like clockwork, Mel. You just stay out of the way and let me handle it.

STURDYVANT: Yeah . . . yeah . . . you handled it last time. Remember? She marches in here like she owns the damn place . . . doesn't like the songs we picked out . . . says her throat is sore . . . doesn't want to do more than one take . . .

IRVIN: Okay . . . okay . . . I was here! I know all about it.

STURDYVANT: Complains about the building being cold

. . . and then . . . trips over the mike wire and threatens to sue me. That's taking care of it?

IRVIN: I've got it all worked out this time. I talked with her last night. Her throat is fine . . . We went over the songs together . . . I got everything straight, Mel.

STURDYVANT: Irv, that horn player . . . the one who gave me those songs . . . is he gonna be here today? Good. I want to hear more of that sound. Times are changing. This is a tricky business now. We've got to jazz it up . . . put in something different. You know, something wild . . . with a lot of rhythm. *(Pause.)* You know what we put out last time, Irv? We put out garbage last time. It was garbage. I don't even know why I bother with this anymore.

IRVIN: You did all right last time, Mel. Not as good as you did before, but you did all right.

STURDYVANT: You know how many records we sold in New York? You wanna see the sheet? And you know what's in New York, Irv? Harlem. Harlem's in New York, Irv.

IRVIN: Okay, so they didn't sell in New York. But look at Memphis . . . Birmingham . . . Atlanta. Christ, you made a bundle.

STURDYVANT: It's not the money, Irv. You know I couldn't sleep last night? This business is bad for my nerves. My wife is after me to slow down and take a vacation. Two more years and I'm gonna get out . . . get into something respectable. Textiles. That's a respectable business. You know what you could do with a shipload of textiles from Ireland?

(A buzzer is heard offstage.)

IRVIN: Why don't you go upstairs and let me handle it, Mel?

STURDYVANT: Remember . . . you're responsible for her.

(STURDYVANT exits to the control booth. IRVIN *crosses to get the door.* CUTLER, SLOW DRAG, *and* TOLEDO *enter.* CUTLER *is in his mid-fifties, as are most of the others. He plays guitar and trombone and is the leader of the group, possibly because he is the most sensible. His playing is solid and almost totally unembellished. His understanding of his music is limited to the chord he is playing at the time he is playing it. He has all the qualities of a loner except the introspection.* SLOW DRAG, *the bass player, is perhaps the one most bored by life. He resembles* CUTLER, *but lacks* CUTLER's *energy. He is deceptively intelligent, though, as his name implies, he appears to be slow. He is a rather large man with a wicked smile. Innate African rhythms underlie everything he plays, and he plays with an ease that is at times startling.* TOLEDO *is the piano player. In control of his instrument, he understands and recognizes that its limitations are an extension of himself. He is the only one in the group who can read. He is self-taught but misunderstands and misapplies his knowledge, though he is quick to penetrate to the core of a situation and his insights are thought-provoking. All*

of the men are dressed in a style of clothing befitting the members of a successful band of the era.)

IRVIN: How you boys doing, Cutler? Come on in. (*Pause.*) Where's Ma? Is she with you?

CUTLER: I don't know, Mr. Irvin. She told us to be here at one o'clock. That's all I know.

IRVIN: Where's . . . huh . . . the horn player? Is he coming with Ma?

CUTLER: Levee's supposed to be here same as we is. I reckon he'll be here in a minute. I can't rightly say.

IRVIN: Well, come on . . . I'll show you to the band room, let you get set up and rehearsed. You boys hungry? I'll call over to the deli and get some sandwiches. Get you fed and ready to make some music. Cutler . . . here's the list of songs we're gonna record.

STURDYVANT: (*Over speaker*) Irvin, what's happening? Where's Ma?

IRVIN: Everything under control, Mel. I got it under control.

STURDYVANT: Where's Ma? How come she isn't with the band?

IRVIN: She'll be here in a minute, Mel. Let me get these fellows down to the band room, huh?

(They exit the studio. The lights go down in the studio and up in the band room. IRVIN *opens the door and allows them to pass as they enter.)*

You boys go ahead and rehearse. I'll let you know when Ma comes.

*(*IRVIN *exits.* CUTLER *hands* TOLEDO *the list of songs.)*

CUTLER: What we got here, Toledo?

TOLEDO: (*Reading*) We got . . . "Prove It on Me" . . . "Hear Me Talking to You" . . . "Ma Rainey's Black Bottom" . . . and "Moonshine Blues."

CUTLER: Where Mr. Irvin go? Them ain't the songs Ma told me.

SLOW DRAG: I wouldn't worry about it if I were you, Cutler. They'll get it straightened out. Ma will get it straightened out.

CUTLER: I just don't want no trouble about these songs, that's all. Ma ain't told me them songs. She told me something else.

SLOW DRAG: What she tell you?

CUTLER: This "Moonshine Blues" wasn't in it. That's one of Bessie's songs.

TOLEDO: Slow Drag's right . . . I wouldn't worry about it. Let them straighten it up.

CUTLER: Levee know what time he supposed to be here?

SLOW DRAG: Levee gone out to spend your four dollars. He left the hotel this morning talking about he was gonna go buy some shoes. Say it's the first time he ever beat you shooting craps.

CUTLER: Do he know what time he supposed to be here? That's what I wanna know. I ain't thinking about no four dollars.

SLOW DRAG: Levee sure was thinking about it. That four dollars liked to burn a hole in his pocket.

CUTLER: Well, he's supposed to be here at one o'clock. That's what time Ma said. That nigger get out in the streets with that four dollars and ain't no telling when he's liable to show. You ought to have seen him at the club last night, Toledo. Trying to talk to some gal Ma had with her.

TOLEDO: You ain't got to tell me. I know how Levee do.

(Buzzer is heard offstage.)

SLOW DRAG: Levee tried to talk to that gal and got his feelings hurt. She didn't want no part of him. She told Levee he'd have to turn his money green before he could talk with her.

CUTLER: She out for what she can get. Anybody could see that.

SLOW DRAG: That's why Levee run out to buy some shoes. He's looking to make an impression on that gal.

CUTLER: What the hell she gonna do with his shoes? She can't do nothing with the nigger's shoes.

*(*SLOW DRAG *takes out a pint bottle and drinks.)*

TOLEDO: Let me hit that, Slow Drag.

SLOW DRAG: (*Handing him the bottle*) This some of that good Chicago bourbon!

(The door opens and LEVEE *enters, carrying a shoe box. In his early thirties,* LEVEE *is younger than the other men. His flamboyance is sometimes subtle and sneaks up on you. His temper is rakish and bright. He lacks fuel for himself and is somewhat of a buffoon. But it is an intelligent buffoonery, clearly calculated to shift control of the situation to where he can grasp it. He plays trumpet. His voice is strident and totally dependent on his manipulation of breath. He plays wrong notes frequently. He often gets his skill and talent confused with each other.)*

CUTLER: Levee . . . where Mr. Irvin go?

LEVEE: Hell, I don't know. I ain't none of his keeper.

SLOW DRAG: What you got there, Levee?

LEVEE: Look here, Cutler . . . I got me some shoes!

CUTLER: Nigger, I ain't studying you.

*(*LEVEE *takes the shoes out of the box and starts to put them on.)*

TOLEDO: How much you pay for something like that, Levee?

LEVEE: Eleven dollars. Four dollars of it belong to Cutler.

SLOW DRAG: Levee say if it wasn't for Cutler . . . he wouldn't have no new shoes.

CUTLER: I ain't thinking about Levee or his shoes. Come on . . . let's get ready to rehearse.

SLOW DRAG: I'm with you on that score, Cutler. I wanna get out of here. I don't want to be around here all night. When it comes time to go up there and re-

cord them songs . . . I just wanna go up there and
do it. Last time it took us all day and half the night.
TOLEDO: Ain't but four songs on the list. Last time we
recorded six songs.
SLOW DRAG: It felt like it was sixteen!
LEVEE: (*Finishes with his shoes*) Yeah! Now I'm ready! I
can play some good music now!

(*He goes to put up his old shoes and looks around the
room.*)

Damn! They done changed things around. Don't
never leave well enough alone.
TOLEDO: Everything changing all the time. Even the air
you breathing change. You got, monoxide, hydro-
gen . . . changing all the time. Skin changing . . .
different molecules and everything.
LEVEE: Nigger, what is you talking about? I'm talking
about the room. I ain't talking about no skin and
air. I'm talking about something I can see! Last time
the band room was upstairs. This time it's downstairs. Next time it be over there. I'm talking about
what I can see. I ain't talking about no molecules
or nothing.
TOLEDO: Hell, I know what you talking about. I just said
everything changin'. I know what you talking about,
but you don't know what I'm talking about.
LEVEE: That door! Nigger, you see that door? That's
what I'm talking about. That door wasn't there before.
CUTLER: Levee, you wouldn't know your right from
your left. This is where they used to keep the recording horns and things . . . and damn if that door
wasn't there. How in hell else you gonna get in
here? Now, if you talking about they done switched
rooms, you right. But don't go telling me that damn
door wasn't there!
SLOW DRAG: Damn the door and let's get set up. I wanna
get out of here.
LEVEE: Toledo started all that about the door. I'm just
saying that things change.
TOLEDO: What the hell you think I was saying? Things
change. The air and everything. Now you gonna
say you was saying it. You gonna fit two propositions
on the same track . . . run them into each other,
and because they crash, you gonna say it's the same
train.
LEVEE: Now this nigger talking about trains! We done
went from the air to the skin to the door . . . and
now trains. Toledo, I'd just like to be inside your
head for five minutes. Just to see how you think.
You done got more shit piled up and mixed up in
there than the devil got sinners. You been reading
too many goddamn books.
TOLEDO: What you care about how much I read? I'm
gonna ignore you 'cause you ignorant.

(LEVEE *takes off his coat and hangs it in the locker.*)

SLOW DRAG: Come on, let's rehearse the music.
LEVEE: You ain't gotta rehearse that . . . ain't nothing
but old jug-band music. They need one of them jug
bands for this.
SLOW DRAG: Don't make me no difference. Long as we
get paid.
LEVEE: That ain't what I'm talking about, nigger. I'm
talking about art!
SLOW DRAG: What's drawing got to do with it?
LEVEE: Where you get this nigger from, Cutler? He
sound like one of them Alabama niggers.
CUTLER: Slow Drag's all right. It's you talking all that
weird shit about art. Just play the piece, nigger. You
wanna be one of them . . . what you call . . . virtuoso
or something, you in the wrong place. You ain't no
Buddy Bolden or King Oliver . . . you just an old
trumpet player come a dime a dozen. Talking about
art.
LEVEE: What is you? I don't see your name in lights.
CUTLER: I just play the piece. Whatever they want. I
don't go talking about art and criticizing other people's music.
LEVEE: I ain't like you, Cutler. I got talent! Me and this
horn . . . we's tight. If my daddy knowed I was
gonna turn out like this, he would've named me
Gabriel. I'm gonna get me a band and make me
some records. I done give Mr. Sturdyvant some of
my songs I wrote and he say he's gonna let me
record them when I get my band together. (*Takes
some papers out of his pocket.*) I just gotta finish the
last part of this song. And Mr. Sturdyvant want me
to write another part to this song.
SLOW DRAG: How you learn to write music, Levee?
LEVEE: I just picked it up . . . like you pick up anything.
Miss Eula used to play the piano . . . she learned
me a lot. I knows how to play *real* music . . . not this
old jug-band shit. I got style!
TOLEDO: Everybody got style. Style ain't nothing but
keeping the same idea from beginning to end.
Everybody got it.
LEVEE: But everybody can't play like I do. Everybody
can't have their own band.
CUTLER: Well, until you get your own band where you
can play what you want, you just play the piece and
stop complaining. I told you when you came on
here, this ain't none of them hot bands. This is an
accompaniment band. You play Ma's music when
you here.
LEVEE: I got sense enough to know that. Hell, I can look
at you all and see what kind of band it is. I can look
at Toledo and see what kind of band it is.
TOLEDO: Toledo ain't said nothing to you now. Don't
let Toledo get started. You can't even spell music,
much less play it.
LEVEE: What you talking about? I can spell music. I got
a dollar say I can spell it! Put your dollar up. Where
your dollar?

(TOLEDO waves him away.)

Now come on. Put your dollar up. Talking about I can't spell music.

(LEVEE peels a dollar off his roll and slams it down on the bench beside TOLEDO.)

TOLEDO: All right, I'm gonna show you. Cutler. Slow Drag. You hear this? The nigger betting me a dollar he can spell music. I don't want no shit now!

(TOLEDO lays a dollar down beside LEVEE's.)

All right. Go ahead. Spell it.

LEVEE: It's a bet then. Talking about I can't spell music.

TOLEDO: Go ahead, then. Spell it. Music. Spell it.

LEVEE: I can spell it, nigger! M-U-S-I-K. There!

(He reaches for the money.)

TOLEDO: Naw! Naw! Leave that money alone! You ain't spelled it.

LEVEE: What you mean I ain't spelled it? I said M-U-S-I-K!

TOLEDO: That ain't how you spell it! That ain't how you spell it! It's M-U-S-I-C! C, nigger. Not K! C! M-U-S-I-C!

LEVEE: What you mean, C? Who say it's C?

TOLEDO: Cutler. Slow Drag. Tell this fool.

(They look at each other and then away.)

Well, I'll be a monkey's uncle!

(TOLEDO picks up the money and hands LEVEE his dollar back.)

Here's your dollar back, Levee. I done won it, you understand. I done won the dollar. But if don't nobody know but me, how am I gonna prove it to you?

LEVEE: You just mad 'cause I spelled it.

TOLEDO: Spelled what! M-U-S-I-K don't spell nothing. I just wish there was some way I could show you the right and wrong of it. How you gonna know something if the other fellow don't know if you're right or not? Now I can't even be sure that I'm spelling it right.

LEVEE: That's what I'm talking about. You don't know it. Talking about C. You ought to give me that dollar I won from you.

TOLEDO: All right. All right. I'm gonna show you how ridiculous you sound. You know the Lord's Prayer?

LEVEE: Why? You wanna bet a dollar on that?

TOLEDO: Just answer the question. Do you know the Lord's Prayer or don't you?

LEVEE: Yeah, I know it. What of it?

TOLEDO: Cutler?

CUTLER: What you Cutlering me for? I ain't got nothing to do with it.

TOLEDO: I just want to show the man how ridiculous he is.

CUTLER: Both of you all sound like damn fools. Arguing about something silly. Yeah, I know the Lord's Prayer. My daddy was a deacon in the church. Come asking me if I know the Lord's Prayer. Yeah, I know it.

TOLEDO: Slow Drag?

SLOW DRAG: Yeah.

TOLEDO: All right. Now I'm gonna tell you a story to show just how ridiculous he sound. There was these two fellows, see. So, the one of them go up to this church and commence to taking up the church learning. The other fellow see him out on the road and he say, "I done heard you taking up the church learning," say, "Is you learning anything up there?" The other one say, "Yeah, I done take up the church learning and I's learning all kinds of things about the Bible and what it say and all. Why you be asking?" The other one say, "Well, do you know the Lord's Prayer?" And he say, "Why, sure I know the Lord's Prayer, I'm taking up learning at the church ain't I? I know the Lord's Prayer backwards and forewards." And the other fellow says, "I bet you five dollars you don't know the Lord's Prayer, 'cause I don't think you knows it. I think you be going up to the church 'cause the Widow Jenkins be going up there and you just wanna be sitting in the same room with her when she cross them big, fine, pretty legs she got." And the other one say, "Well, I'm gonna prove you wrong and I'm gonna bet you that five dollars." So he say, "Well, go on and say it then." So he commenced to saying the Lord's Prayer. He say, "Now I lay me down to sleep, I pray the Lord my soul to keep." The other one say, "Here's your five dollars. I didn't think you knew it."

(They all laugh.)

Now, that's just how ridiculous Levee sound. Only 'cause I knowed how to spell music, I still got my dollar.

LEVEE: That don't prove nothing. What's that supposed to prove?

(TOLEDO takes a newspaper out of his back pocket and begins to read.)

TOLEDO: I'm through with it.

SLOW DRAG: Is you all gonna rehearse this music or ain't you?

(CUTLER takes out some papers and starts to roll a reefer.)

LEVEE: How many times you done played them songs? What you gotta rehearse for?

SLOW DRAG: This a recording session. I wanna get it right the first time and get on out of here.

CUTLER: Slow Drag's right. Let's go on and rehearse and get it over with.

LEVEE: You all go and rehearse, then. I got to finish this song for Mr. Sturdyvant.

CUTLER: Come on, Levee . . . I don't want no shit now.

You rehearse like everybody else. You in the band like everybody else. Mr. Sturdyvant just gonna have to wait. You got to do that on your own time. This is the band's time.

LEVEE: Well, what is you doing? You sitting there rolling a reefer talking about let's rehearse. Toledo reading a newspaper. Hell, I'm ready if you wanna rehearse. I just say there ain't no point in it. Ma ain't here. What's the point in it?

CUTLER: Nigger, why you gotta complain all the time?

TOLEDO: Levee would complain if a gal ain't laid across his bed just right.

CUTLER: That's what I know. That's why I try to tell him just play the music and forget about it. It ain't no big thing.

TOLEDO: Levee ain't got an eye for that. He wants to tie on to some abstract component and sit down on the elemental.

LEVEE: This is get-on-Levee time, huh? Levee ain't said nothing except this some old jug-band music.

TOLEDO: Under the right circumstances you'd play anything. If you know music, then you play it. Straight on or off to the side. Ain't nothing abstract about it.

LEVEE: Toledo, you sound like you got a mouth full of marbles. You the only cracker-talking nigger I know.

TOLEDO: You ought to have learned yourself to read . . . then you'd understand the basic understanding of everything.

SLOW DRAG: Both of you all gonna drive me crazy with that philosophy bullshit. Cutler, give me a reefer.

CUTLER: Ain't you got some reefer? Where's your reefer? Why you all the time asking me?

SLOW DRAG: Cutler, how long I done known you? How long we been together? Twenty-two years. We been doing this together for twenty-two years. All up and down the back roads, the side roads, the front roads . . . We done played the juke joints, the whorehouses, the barn dances, and city sit-downs . . . I done lied for you and lied with you . . . We done laughed together, fought together, slept in the same bed together, done sucked on the same titty . . . and now you don't wanna give me no reefer.

CUTLER: You see this nigger trying to talk me out of my reefer, Toledo? Running all that about how long he done knowed me and how we done sucked on the same titty. Nigger, you *still* ain't getting none of my reefer!

TOLEDO: That's African.

SLOW DRAG: What? What you talking about? What's African?

LEVEE: I know he ain't talking about me. You don't see me running around in no jungle with no bone between my nose.

TOLEDO: Levee, you worse than ignorant. You ignorant without a premise. (*Pauses.*) Now, what I was saying is what Slow Drag was doing is African. That's what

you call an African conceptualization. That's when you name the gods or call on the ancestors to achieve whatever your desires are.

SLOW DRAG: Nigger, I ain't no African! I ain't doing no African nothing!

TOLEDO: Naming all those things you and Cutler done together is like trying to solicit some reefer based on a bond of kinship. That's African. An ancestral retention. Only you forgot the name of the gods.

SLOW DRAG: I ain't forgot nothing, I was telling the nigger how cheap he is. Don't come talking that African nonsense to me.

TOLEDO: You just like Levee. No eye for taking an abstract and fixing it to a specific. There's so much that goes on around you and you can't even see it.

CUTLER: Wait a minute . . . wait a minute. Toledo, now when this nigger . . . when an African do all them things you say and name all the gods and whatnot . . . then what happens?

TOLEDO: Depends on if the gods is sympathetic with his cause for which he is calling them with the right names. Then his success comes with the right proportion of his naming. That's the way that go.

CUTLER: (*Taking out a reefer*) Here, Slow Drag. Here's a reefer. You done talked yourself up on that one.

SLOW DRAG: Thank you. You ought to have done that in the first place and saved me all the aggravation.

CUTLER: What I wants to know is . . . what's the same titty we done sucked on. That's what I want to know.

SLOW DRAG: Oh, I just threw that in there to make it sound good.

(*They all laugh.*)

CUTLER: Nigger, you ain't right.

SLOW DRAG: I knows it.

CUTLER: Well, come on . . . let's get it rehearsed. Time's wasting.

(*The musicians pick up their instruments.*)

Let's do it. "Ma Rainey's Black Bottom." One . . . two . . . You know what to do.

(*They begin to play.* LEVEE *is playing something different. He stops.*)

LEVEE: Naw! Naw! We ain't doing it that way.

(TOLEDO *stops playing, then* SLOW DRAG.)

We doing my version. It say so right there on that piece of paper you got. Ask Toledo. That's what Mr. Irvin told me . . . say it's on the list he gave you.

CUTLER: Let me worry about what's on the list and what ain't on the list. How you gonna tell me what's on the list?

LEVEE: 'Cause I know what Mr. Irvin told me! Ask Toledo!

CUTLER: Let me worry about what's on the list. You just play the song I say.

LEVEE: What kind of sense it make to rehearse the

wrong version of the song? That's what I wanna know. Why you wanna rehearse that version.

SLOW DRAG: You supposed to rehearse what you gonna play. That's the way they taught me. Now, *whatever* version we gonna play . . . let's go on and rehearse it.

LEVEE: That's what I'm trying to tell the man.

CUTLER: You trying to tell me what we is and ain't gonna play. And that ain't none of your business. Your business is to play what I say.

LEVEE: Oh, I see now. You done got jealous cause Mr. Irvin using my version. You done got jealous cause I proved I know something about music.

CUTLER: What the hell . . . nigger, you talk like a fool! What the hell I got to be jealous of you about? The day I get jealous of you I may as well lay down and die.

TOLEDO: Levee started all that 'cause he too lazy to rehearse. (*To* LEVEE.) You ought to just go on and play the song . . . What difference does it make?

LEVEE: Where's the paper? Look at the paper! Get the paper and look at it! See what it say. Gonna tell me I'm too lazy to rehearse.

CUTLER: We ain't talking about the paper. We talking about you understanding where you fit in when you around here. You just play what I say.

LEVEE: Look . . . I don't care what you play! All right? It don't matter to me. Mr. Irvin gonna straighten it up! I don't care what you play.

CUTLER: Thank you. (*Pauses.*) Let's play this "Hear Me Talking to You" till we find out what's happening with the "Black Bottom." Slow Drag, you sing Ma's part. (*Pauses.*) "Hear Me Talking to You." Let's do it. One . . . Two . . . You know what to do.

(*They play.*)

SLOW DRAG: (*Singing*)

> Rambling man makes no change in me
> I'm gonna ramble back to my used-to-be
> Ah, you hear me talking to you
> I don't bite my tongue
> You wants to be my man
> You got to fetch it with you when you come.
>
> Eve and Adam in the garden taking a chance
> Adam didn't take time to get his pants
> Ah, you hear me talking to you
> I don't bite my tongue
> You wants to be my man
> You got to fetch it with you when you come.
>
> Our old cat swallowed a ball of yarn
> When the kittens were born they had sweaters on
> Ah, you hear me talking to you
> I don't bite my tongue
> You wants to be my man
> You got to fetch it with you when you come.

(IRVIN *enters. The musicians stop playing.*)

IRVIN: Any of you boys know what's keeping Ma?

CUTLER: Can't say, Mr. Irvin. She'll be along directly, I reckon. I talked to her this morning, she say she'll be here in time to rehearse.

IRVIN: Well, you boys go ahead.

(*He starts to exit.*)

CUTLER: Mr. Irvin, about these songs . . . Levee say . . .

IRVIN: Whatever's on the list, Cutler. You got that list I gave you?

CUTLER: Yessir, I got it right here.

IRVIN: Whatever's on there. Whatever that says.

CUTLER: I'm asking about this "Black Bottom" piece . . . Levee say . . .

IRVIN: Oh, it's on the list. "Ma Rainey's Black Bottom" on the list.

CUTLER: I know it's on the list. I wanna know what version. We got two versions of that song.

IRVIN: Oh. Levee's arrangement. We're using Levee's arrangement.

CUTLER: Ok. I got that straight. Now, this "Moonshine Blues" . . .

IRVIN: We'll work it out with Ma, Cutler. Just rehearse whatever's on the list and use Levee's arrangement on that "Black Bottom" piece.

(*He exits.*)

LEVEE: See, I told you! It don't mean nothing when I say it. You got to wait for Mr. Irvin to say it. Well, I told you the way it is.

CUTLER: Levee, the sooner you understand it ain't what you say, or what Mr. Irvin say . . . it's what Ma say that counts.

SLOW DRAG: Don't nobody say when it come to Ma. She's gonna do what she wants to do. Ma says what happens with her.

LEVEE: Hell, the man's the one putting out the record! He's gonna put out what he wanna put out!

SLOW DRAG: He's gonna put out what Ma want him to put out.

LEVEE: You heard what the man told you . . . "Ma Rainey's Black Bottom," Levee's arrangement. There you go! That's what he told you.

SLOW DRAG: What you gonna do, Cutler?

CUTLER: Ma ain't told me what version. Let's go on and play it Levee's way.

TOLEDO: See, now . . . I'll tell you something. As long as the colored man look to white folks to put the crown on what he say . . . as long as he looks to white folks for approval . . . then he ain't never gonna find out who he is and what he's about. He's just gonna be about what white folks want him to be about. That's one sure thing.

LEVEE: I'm just trying to show Cutler where he's wrong.

CUTLER: Cutler don't need you to show him nothing.

SLOW DRAG: (*Irritated*) Come on, let's get this shit rehearsed! You all can bicker afterward!

CUTLER: Levee's confused about who the boss is. He don't know Ma's the boss.

LEVEE: Ma's the boss on the road! We at a recording session. Mr. Sturdyvant and Mr. Irvin say what's gonna be here! We's in Chicago, we ain't in Memphis! I don't know why you all wanna pick me about it, shit! I'm with Slow Drag . . . Let's go on and get it rehearsed.

CUTLER: All right. All right. I know how to solve this. "Ma Rainey's Black Bottom." Levee's version. Let's do it. Come on.

TOLEDO: How that first part go again, Levee?

LEVEE: It go like this. (*He plays.*) That's to get the people's attention to the song. That's when you and Slow Drag come in with the rhythm part. Me and Cutler play on the breaks. (*Becoming animated.*) Now we gonna dance it . . . but we ain't gonna countrify it. This ain't no barn dance. We gonna play it like . . .

CUTLER: The man ask you how the first part go. He don't wanna hear all that. Just tell him how the piece go.

TOLEDO: I got it. I got it. Let's go. I know how to do it.

CUTLER: "Ma Rainey's Black Bottom." One . . . two . . . You know what to do.

(*They begin to play.* LEVEE *stops.*)

LEVEE: You all got to keep up now. You playing in the wrong time. Ma come in over the top. She got to find her own way in.

CUTLER: Nigger, will you let us play this song? When you get your own band . . . then you tell them that nonsense. We know how to play the piece. I was playing music before you was born. Gonna tell me how to play . . . All right. Let's try it again.

SLOW DRAG: Cutler, wait till I fix this. This string started to unravel. (*Playfully.*) And you know I want to play Levee's music right.

LEVEE: If you was any kind of musician, you'd take care of your instrument. Keep it in tip-top order. If you was any kind of musician, I'd let you be in my band.

SLOW DRAG: Shhheeeeet!

(*He crosses to get his string and steps on* LEVEE'S *shoes.*)

LEVEE: Damn, Slow Drag! Watch them big-ass shoes you got.

SLOW DRAG: Boy, ain't nobody done nothing to you.

LEVEE: You done stepped on my shoes.

SLOW DRAG: Move them the hell out the way, then. You was in my way . . . I wasn't in your way.

(CUTLER *lights up another reefer.* SLOW DRAG *rummages around in his belongings for a string.* LEVEE *takes out a rag and begins to shine his shoes.*)

You can shine these when you get done, Levee.

CUTLER: If I had them shoes Levee got, I could buy me a whole suit of clothes.

LEVEE: What kind of difference it make what kind of shoes I got? Ain't nothing wrong with having nice shoes. I ain't said nothing about your shoes. Why you wanna talk about me and my Florsheims?

CUTLER: Any man who takes a whole week's pay and puts it on some shoes—you understand what I mean, what you walk around on the ground with— is a fool! And I don't mind telling you.

LEVEE: (*Irritated*) What difference it make to you, Cutler?

SLOW DRAG: The man ain't said nothing about your shoes. Ain't nothing wrong with having nice shoes. Look at Toledo.

TOLEDO: What about Toledo?

SLOW DRAG: I said ain't nothing wrong with having nice shoes.

LEVEE: Nigger got them clodhoppers! Old brogans! He ain't nothing but a sharecropper.

TOLEDO: You can make all the fun you want. It don't mean nothing. I'm satisfied with them and that's what counts.

LEVEE: Nigger, why don't you get some decent shoes? Got nerve to put on a suit and tie with them farming boots.

CUTLER: What you just tell me? It don't make no difference about the man's shoes. That's what you told me.

LEVEE: Aw, hell, I don't care what the nigger wear. I'll be honest with you. I don't care if he went barefoot. (SLOW DRAG *has put his string on the bass and is tuning it.*) Play something for me, Slow Drag. (SLOW DRAG *plays.*) A man got to have some shoes to dance like this! You can't dance like this with them clodhoppers Toledo got.

(LEVEE *sings.*)

Hello Central give me Doctor Jazz
He's got just what I need I'll say he has
When the world goes wrong and I have got the blues
He's the man who makes me get on my dancing shoes.

TOLEDO: That's the trouble with colored folks . . . always wanna have a good time. Good times done got more niggers killed than God got ways to count. What the hell having a good time mean? That's what I wanna know.

LEVEE: Hell, nigger . . . it don't need explaining. Ain't you never had no good time before?

TOLEDO: The more niggers get killed having a good time, the more good times niggers wanna have.

(SLOW DRAG *stops playing.*)

There's more to life than having a good time. If there ain't, then this is a piss-poor life we're having . . . if that's all there is to be got out of it.

SLOW DRAG: Toledo, just 'cause you like to read them books and study and whatnot . . . that's your good time. People get other things they likes to do to have a good time. Ain't no need you picking them about it.

CUTLER: Niggers been having a good time before you was born, and they gonna keep having a good time after you gone.

TOLEDO: Yeah, but what else they gonna do? Ain't nobody talking about making the lot of the colored man better for him here in America.

LEVEE: Now you gonna be Booker T. Washington.

TOLEDO: Everybody worried about having a good time. Ain't nobody thinking about what kind of world they gonna leave their youngens. "Just give me the good time, that's all I want." It just makes me sick.

SLOW DRAG: Well, the colored man's gonna be all right. He got through slavery, and he'll get through whatever else the white man put on him. I ain't worried about that. Good times is what makes life worth living. Now, you take the white man . . . The white man don't know how to have a good time. That's why he's troubled all the time. He don't know how to have a good time. He don't know how to laugh at life.

LEVEE: That's what the problem is with Toledo . . . reading all them books and things. He done got to the point where he forgot how to laugh and have a good time. Just like the white man.

TOLEDO: I know how to have a good time as well as the next man. I said, there's got to be more to life than having a good time. I said the colored man ought to be doing more than just trying to have a good time all the time.

LEVEE: Well, what is you doing, nigger? Talking all them highfalutin ideas about making a better world for the colored man. What is you doing to make it better? You playing the music and looking for your next piece of pussy same as we is. What is you doing? That's what I wanna know. Tell him, Cutler.

CUTLER: You all leave Cutler out of this. Cutler ain't got nothing to do with it.

TOLEDO: Levee, you just about the most ignorant nigger I know. Sometimes I wonder why I ever bother to try and talk with you.

LEVEE: Well, what is you doing? Talking that shit to me about I'm ignorant! What is you doing? You just a whole lot of mouth. A great big windbag. Thinking you smarter than everybody else. What is you doing, huh?

TOLEDO: It ain't just me, fool! It's everybody! What you think . . . I'm gonna solve the colored man's problems by myself? I said, we. You understand that? We. That's every living colored man in the world got to do his share. Got to do his part. I ain't talking about what I'm gonna do . . . or what you or Cutler or Slow Drag or anybody else. I'm talking about all of us together. What all of us is gonna do. That's what I'm talking about, nigger!

LEVEE: Well, why didn't you say that, then?

CUTLER: Toledo, I don't know why you waste your time on this fool.

TOLEDO: That's what I'm trying to figure out.

LEVEE: Now there go Cutler with his shit. Calling me a fool. You wasn't even in the conversation. Now you gonna take sides and call me a fool.

CUTLER: Hell, I was listening to the man. I got sense enough to know what he was saying. I could tell it straight back to you.

LEVEE: Well, you go on with it. But I'll tell you this . . . I ain't gonna be too many more of your fools. I'll tell you that. Now you put that in your pipe and smoke it.

CUTLER: Boy, ain't nobody studying you. Telling me what to put in my pipe. Who's you to tell me what to do?

LEVEE: All right, I ain't nobody. Don't pay me no mind. I ain't nobody.

TOLEDO: Levee, you ain't nothing but the devil.

LEVEE: There you go! That's who I am. I'm the devil. I ain't nothing but the devil.

CUTLER: I can see that. That's something you know about. You know all about the devil.

LEVEE: I ain't saying what I know. I know plenty. What you know about the devil? Telling me what I know. What you know?

SLOW DRAG: I know a man sold his soul to the devil.

LEVEE: There you go! That's the only thing I ask about the devil . . . to see him coming so I can sell him this one I got. 'Cause if there's a god up there, he done went to sleep.

SLOW DRAG: Sold his soul to the devil himself. Name of Eliza Cotter. Lived in Tuscaloosa County, Alabama. The devil came by and he done upped and sold him his soul.

CUTLER: How you know the man done sold his soul to the devil, nigger? You talking that old-woman foolishness.

SLOW DRAG: Everybody know. It wasn't no secret. He went around working for the devil and everybody knowed it. Carried him a bag . . . one of them carpetbags. Folks say he carried the devil's papers and whatnot where he put your fingerprint on the paper with blood.

LEVEE: Where he at now? That's what I want to know. He can put my whole handprint if he want to!

CUTLER: That's the damnedest thing I ever heard! Folks kill me with that talk.

TOLEDO: Oh, that's real enough, all right. Some folks go arm in arm with the devil, shoulder to shoulder, and talk to him all the time. That's real, ain't nothing wrong in believing that.

SLOW DRAG: That's what I'm saying. Eliza Cotter is one of them. All right. The man living up in an old shack on Ben Foster's place, shoeing mules and horses, making them charms and things in secret. He done hooked up with the devil, showed up one day all fancied out with just the finest clothes you ever seen on a colored man . . . dressed just like one of them crackers . . . and carrying this bag with them papers and things. All right. Had a pocketful of money, just living the life of a rich man. Ain't done no more work or nothing. Just had him a string of women he run around with and throw his money away on. Bought him a big fine house . . . Well, it wasn't all that big, but it did have one of them white picket fences around it. Used to hire a man once a week just to paint that fence. Messed around there and one of the fellows of them gals he was messing with got fixed on him wrong and Eliza killed him. And he laughed about it. Sheriff come and arrest him, and then let him go. And he went around in that town laughing about killing this fellow. Trial come up, and the judge cut him loose. He must have been in converse with the devil too . . . 'cause he cut him loose and give him a bottle of whiskey! Folks ask what done happened to make him change, and he'd tell them straight out he done sold his soul to the devil and ask them if they wanted to sell theirs 'cause he could arrange it for them. Preacher see him coming, used to cross on the other side of the road. He'd just stand there and laugh at the preacher and call him a fool to his face.

CUTLER: Well, whatever happened to this fellow? What come of him? A man who, as you say, done sold his soul to the devil is bound to come to a bad end.

TOLEDO: I don't know about that. The devil's strong. The devil ain't no pushover.

SLOW DRAG: Oh, the devil had him under his wing, all right. Took good care of him. He ain't wanted for nothing.

CUTLER: What happened to him? That's what I want to know.

SLOW DRAG: Last I heard, he headed north with that bag of his, handing out hundred-dollar bills on the spot to whoever wanted to sign on with the devil. That's what I hear tell of him.

CUTLER: That's a bunch of fool talk. I don't know how you fix your mouth to tell that story. I don't believe that.

SLOW DRAG: I ain't asking you to believe it. I'm just telling you the facts of it.

LEVEE: I sure wish I knew where he went. He wouldn't have to convince me long. Hell, I'd even help him sign people up.

CUTLER: Nigger, God's gonna strike you down with that blasphemy you talking.

LEVEE: Oh, shit! God don't mean nothing to me. Let him strike me! Here I am, standing right here. What you talking about he's gonna strike me? Here I am! Let him strike me! I ain't scared of him. Talking that stuff to me.

CUTLER: All right. You gonna be sorry. You gonna fix

yourself to have bad luck. Ain't nothing gonna work for you.

(Buzzer sounds offstage.)

LEVEE: Bad luck? What I care about some bad luck? You talking simple. I ain't knowed nothing but bad luck all my life. Couldn't get no worse. What the hell I care about some bad luck? Hell, I eat it everyday for breakfast! You dumber than I thought you was . . . talking about bad luck.

CUTLER: All right, nigger, you'll see! Can't tell a fool nothing. You'll see!

IRVIN: (IRVIN *enters the studio, checks his watch, and calls down the stairs*) Cutler . . . you boys' sandwiches are up here . . . Cutler?

CUTLER: Yessir, Mr. Irvin . . . be right there.

TOLEDO: I'll walk up there and get them.

(TOLEDO exits. The lights go down in the band room and up in the studio. IRVIN paces back and forth in an agitated manner. STURDYVANT enters.)

STURDYVANT: Irv, what's happening? Is she here yet? Was that her?

IRVIN: It's the sandwiches, Mel. I told you . . . I'll let you know when she comes, huh?

STURDYVANT: What's keeping her? Do you know what time it is? Have you looked at the clock? You told me she'd be here. You told me you'd take care of it.

IRVIN: Mel, for Chrissakes! What do you want from me? What do you want me to do?

STURDYVANT: Look what time it is, Irv. You told me she'd be here.

IRVIN: She'll be here, okay? I don't know what's keeping her. You know they're always late, Mel.

STURDYVANT: You should have went by the hotel and made sure she was on time. You should have taken care of this. That's what you told me, huh? "I'll take care of it."

IRVIN: Okay! Okay! I didn't go by the hotel! What do you want me to do? She'll be here, okay? The band's here . . . she'll be here.

STURDYVANT: Okay, Irv. I'll take your word. But if she doesn't come . . . if she doesn't come . . .

(STURDYVANT exits to the control booth as TOLEDO enters.)

TOLEDO: Mr. Irvin . . . I come up to get the sandwiches.

IRVIN: Say . . . uh . . . look . . . one o'clock, right? She said one o'clock.

TOLEDO: That's what time she told us. Say be here at one o'clock.

IRVIN: Do you know what's keeping her? Do you know why she ain't here?

TOLEDO: I can't say, Mr. Irvin. Told us one o'clock.

(The buzzer sounds. IRVIN *goes to the door. There is a flurry of commotion as* MA RAINEY *enters, followed closely by the* POLICEMAN, DUSSIE MAE, *and* SYLVESTER. MA RAINEY *is a short, heavy woman. She is dressed in a full-length fur coat with matching hat, an emerald-green dress, and several strands of pearls of varying lengths. Her hair is secured by a headband that matches her dress. Her manner is simple and direct, and she carries herself in a royal fashion.* DUSSIE MAE *is a young, dark-skinned woman whose greatest asset is the sensual energy which seems to flow from her. She is dressed in a fur jacket and a tight-fitting canary-yellow dress.* SYLVESTER *is an Arkansas country boy, the size of a fullback. He wears a new suit and coat, in which he is obviously uncomfortable. Most of the time, he stutters when he speaks.)*

MA RAINEY: Irvin . . . you better tell this man who I am! You better get him straight!

IRVIN: Ma, do you know what time it is? Do you have any idea? We've been waiting . . .

DUSSIE MAE: *(To* SYLVESTER*)* If you was watching where you was going . . .

SYLVESTER: I was watching . . . What you mean?

IRVIN: *(Notices* POLICEMAN*)* What's going on here? Officer, what's the matter?

MA RAINEY: Tell the man who he's messing with!

POLICEMAN: Do you know this lady?

MA RAINEY: Just tell the man who I am! That's all you gotta do.

POLICEMAN: Lady, will you let me talk, huh?

MA RAINEY: Tell the man who I am!

IRVIN: Wait a minute . . . wait a minute! Let me handle it. Ma, will you let me handle it?

MA RAINEY: Tell him who he's messing with!

IRVIN: Okay! Okay! Give me a chance! Officer, this is one of our recording artists . . . Ma Rainey.

MA RAINEY: Madame Rainey! Get it straight! Madame Rainey! Talking about taking me to jail!

IRVIN: Look, Ma . . . give me a chance, okay? Here . . . sit down. I'll take care of it. Officer, what's the problem?

DUSSIE MAE: *(To* SYLVESTER*)* It's all your fault.

SYLVESTER: I ain't done nothing . . . Ask Ma.

POLICEMAN: Well . . . when I walked up on the incident . . .

DUSSIE MAE: Sylvester wrecked Ma's car.

SYLVESTER: I d-d-did not! The m-m-man ran into me!

POLICEMAN: *(To* IRVIN*)* Look, buddy . . . if you want it in a nutshell, we got her charged with assault and battery.

MA RAINEY: Assault and what for what!

DUSSIE MAE: See . . . we was trying to get a cab . . . and so Ma . . .

MA RAINEY: Wait a minute! I'll tell you if you wanna know what happened. *(She points to* SYLVESTER*)* Now, that's Sylvester. That's my nephew. He was driving my car . . .

POLICEMAN: Lady, we don't know whose car he was driving.

MA RAINEY: That's my car!

DUSSIE MAE and SYLVESTER: That's Ma's car!

MA RAINEY: What you mean you don't know whose car it is? I bought and paid for that car.

POLICEMAN: That's what you say, lady . . . We still gotta check. *(To* IRVIN.*)* They hit a car on Market Street. The guy said the kid ran a stoplight.

SYLVESTER: What you mean? The man c-c-come around the corner and hit m-m-me!

POLICEMAN: While I was calling a paddy wagon to haul them to the station, they try to hop into a parked cab. The cabbie said he was waiting on a fare . . .

MA RAINEY: The man was just sitting there. Wasn't waiting for nobody. I don't know why he wanna tell that lie.

POLICEMAN: Look, lady . . . will you let me tell the story?

MA RAINEY: Go ahead and tell it then. But tell it right!

POLICEMAN: Like I say . . . she tries to get in this cab. The cabbie's waiting on a fare. She starts creating a disturbance. The cabbie gets out to try and explain the situation to her . . . and she knocks him down.

DUSSIE MAE: She ain't hit him! He just fell!

SYLVESTER: He just s-s-s-slipped!

POLICEMAN: He claims she knocked him down. We got her charged with assault and battery.

MA RAINEY: If that don't beat all to hell. I ain't touched the man! The man was trying to reach around me to keep his car door closed. I opened the door and it hit him and he fell down. I ain't touched the man!

IRVIN: Okay. Okay . . . I got it straight now, Ma. You didn't touch him. All right? Officer, can I see you for a minute?

DUSSIE MAE: Ma was just trying to open the door.

SYLVESTER: He j-j-just got in t-t-the way!

MA RAINEY: Said he wasn't gonna haul no colored folks . . . if you want to know the truth of it.

IRVIN: Okay, Ma . . . I got it straight now. Officer?

*(*IRVIN *pulls the* POLICEMAN *off to the side.)*

MA RAINEY: *(Noticing* TOLEDO*)* Toledo, Cutler and everybody here?

TOLEDO: Yeah, they down in the band room. What happened to your car?

STURDYVANT: *(Entering)* Irv, what's the problem? What's going on? Officer . . .

IRVIN: Mel, let me take care of it. I can handle it.

STURDYVANT: What's happening? What the hell's going on?

IRVIN: Let me handle it, Mel, huh?

*(*STURDYVANT *crosses over to* MA RAINEY.*)*

STURDYVANT: What's going on, Ma. What'd you do?

MA RAINEY: Sturdyvant, get on away from me! That's the last thing I need . . . to go through some of your shit!

IRVIN: Mel, I'll take care of it. I'll explain it all to you. Let me handle it, huh?

(STURDYVANT *reluctantly returns to the control booth.*)

POLICEMAN: Look, buddy, like I say . . . we got her charged with assault and battery . . . and the kid with threatening the cabbie.

SYLVESTER: I ain't done n-n-nothing!

MA RAINEY: You leave the boy out of it. He ain't done nothing. What's he supposed to have done?

POLICEMAN: He threatened the cabbie, lady! You just can't go around threatening people.

SYLVESTER: I ain't done nothing to him! He's the one talking about he g-g-gonna get a b-b-baseball bat on me! I just told him what I'd do with it. But I ain't done nothing 'cause he didn't get the b-b-bat!

IRVIN: (*Pulling the* POLICEMAN *aside*) Officer . . . look here . . .

POLICEMAN: We was on our way down to the precinct . . . but I figured I'd do you a favor and bring her by here. I mean, if she's as important as she says she is . . .

IRVIN: (*Slides a bill from his pocket*) Look, Officer . . . I'm Madame Rainey's manager . . . It's good to meet you. (*He shakes the* POLICEMAN'*s hand and passes him the bill.*) As soon as we're finished with the recording session, I'll personally stop by the precinct house and straighten up this misunderstanding.

POLICEMAN: Well . . . I guess that's all right. As long as someone is responsible for them.

(*He pockets the bill and winks at* IRVIN.)

No need to come down . . . I'll take care of it myself. Of course, we wouldn't want nothing like this to happen again.

IRVIN: Don't worry, Officer . . . I'll take care of everything. Thanks for your help.

(IRVIN *escorts the* POLICEMAN *to the door and returns. He crosses over to* MA RAINEY.)

Here, Ma . . . let me take your coat. (*To* SYLVESTER.) I don't believe I know you.

MA RAINEY: That's my nephew, Sylvester.

IRVIN: I'm very pleased to meet you. Here . . . you can give me your coat.

MA RAINEY: That there is Dussie Mae.

IRVIN: Hello . . .

(DUSSIE MAE *hands* IRVIN *her coat.*)

Listen, Ma, just sit there and relax. The boys are in the band room rehearsing. You just sit and relax a minute.

MA RAINEY: I ain't for no sitting. I ain't never heard of such. Talking about taking me to jail. Irvin, call down there and see about my car.

IRVIN: Okay, Ma . . . I'll take care of it. You just relax.

(IRVIN *exits with the coats.*)

MA RAINEY: Why you all keep it so cold in here? Sturdyvant try and pinch every penny he can. You all wanna make some records, you better put some heat on in here or give me back my coat.

IRVIN: (*Entering*) We got the heat turned up, Ma. It's warming up. It'll be warm in a minute.

DUSSIE MAE: (*Whispering to* MA RAINEY) Where's the bathroom?

MA RAINEY: It's in the back. Down the hall next to Sturdyvant's office. Come on, I'll show you where it is. Irvin, call down there and see about my car. I want my car fixed today.

IRVIN: I'll take care of everything, Ma.

(*He notices* TOLEDO.)

Say . . . uh . . . uh . . .

TOLEDO: Toledo.

IRVIN: Yeah . . . Toledo. I got the sandwiches, you can take down to the rest of the boys. We'll be ready to go in a minute. Give you boys a chance to eat and then we'll be ready to go.

(IRVIN *and* TOLEDO *exit. The lights go down in the studio and come up in the band room.*)

LEVEE: Slow Drag, you ever been to New Orleans?

SLOW DRAG: What's in New Orleans that I want?

LEVEE: How you call yourself a musician and ain't never been to New Orleans.

SLOW DRAG: You ever been to Fat Back, Arkansas? (*Pauses.*) All right, then. Ain't never been nothing in New Orleans that I couldn't get in Fat Back.

LEVEE: That's why you backwards. You just an old country boy talking about Fat Back, Arkansas, and New Orleans in the same breath.

CUTLER: I been to New Orleans. What about it?

LEVEE: You ever been to Lula White's?

CUTLER: Lula White's? I ain't never heard of it.

LEVEE: Man, they got some gals in there just won't wait! I seen a man get killed in there once. Got drunk and grabbed one of the gals wrong . . . I don't know what the matter of it was. But he grabbed her and she stuck a knife in him all the way up to the hilt. He ain't even fell. He just stood there and choked on his own blood. I was just asking Slow Drag 'cause I was gonna take him to Lula White's when we get down to New Orleans and show him a good time. Introduce him to one of them gals I know down there.

CUTLER: Slow Drag don't need you to find him no pussy. He can take care of his own self. Fact is . . . you better watch your gal when Slow Drag's around. They don't call him Slow Drag for nothing. (*He laughs.*) Tell him how you got your name Slow Drag.

SLOW DRAG: I ain't thinking about Levee.

CUTLER: Slow Drag break a woman's back when he dance. They had this contest one time in this little town called Bolingbroke about a hundred miles outside of Macon. We was playing for this dance and they was giving twenty dollars to the best slow draggers. Slow Drag looked over the competition, got down off the bandstand, grabbed hold of one of them gals, and stuck to her like a fly to jelly. Like wood to glue. Man had that gal whooping and hollering so . . . everybody stopped to watch. This fellow come in . . . this gal's fellow . . . and pulled a knife a foot long on Slow Drag. 'Member that, Slow Drag?

SLOW DRAG: Boy that mama was hot! The front of her dress was wet as a dishrag!

LEVEE: So what happened? What the man do?

CUTLER: Slow Drag ain't missed a stroke. The gal, she just look at her man with that sweet dizzy look in her eye. She ain't about to stop! Folks was clearing out, ducking and hiding under tables, figuring there's gonna be a fight. Slow Drag just looked over the gal's shoulder at the man and said, "Mister, if you'd quit hollering and wait a minute . . . you'll see I'm doing you a favor. I'm helping this gal win ten dollars so she can buy you a gold watch." The man just stood there and looked at him, all the while stroking that knife. Told Slow Drag, say, "All right, then, nigger. You just better make damn sure you win." That's when folks started calling him Slow Drag. The women got to hanging around him so bad after that, them fellows in that town ran us out of there.

(TOLEDO *enters, carrying a small cardboard box with the sandwiches.*)

LEVEE: Yeah . . . well, them gals in Lula White's will put a harness on his ass.

TOLEDO: Ma's up there. Some kind of commotion with the police.

CUTLER: Police? What the police up there for?

TOLEDO: I couldn't get it straight. Something about her car. They gone now . . . she's all right. Mr. Irvin sent some sandwiches.

(LEVEE *springs across the room.*)

LEVEE: Yeah, all right. What we got here?

(*He takes two sandwiches out of the box.*)

TOLEDO: What you doing grabbing two? There ain't but five in there . . . How you figure you get two?

LEVEE: 'Cause I grabbed them first. There's enough for everybody . . . What you talking about? It ain't like I'm taking food out of nobody's mouth.

CUTLER: That's all right. He can have mine too. I don't want none.

(LEVEE *starts toward the box to get another sandwich.*)

TOLEDO: Nigger, you better get out of here. Slow Drag, you want this?

SLOW DRAG: Naw, you can have it.

TOLEDO: With Levee around, you don't have to worry about no leftovers. I can see that.

LEVEE: What's the matter with you? Ain't you eating two sandwiches? Then why you wanna talk about me? Talking about there won't be no leftovers with Levee around. Look at your own self before you look at me.

TOLEDO: That's what you is. That's what we all is. A leftover from history. You see now, I'll show you.

LEVEE: Aw, shit . . . I done got the nigger started now.

TOLEDO: Now, I'm gonna show you how this goes . . . where you just a leftover from history. Everybody come from different places in Africa, right? Come from different tribes and things. Soonawhile they began to make one big stew. You had the carrots, the peas, and potatoes and whatnot over here. And over there you had the meat, the nuts, the okra, corn . . . and then you mix it up and let it cook right through to get the flavors flowing together . . . then you got one thing. You got a stew.

Now you take and eat the stew. You take and make your history with that stew. All right. Now it's over. Your history's over and you done ate the stew. But you look around and you see some carrots over here, some potatoes over there. That stew's still there. You done made your history and it's still there. You can't eat it all. So what you got? You got some leftovers. That's what it is. You got leftovers and you can't do nothing with it. You already making you another history . . . cooking you another meal, and you don't need them leftovers no more. What to do?

See, we's the leftovers. The colored man is the leftovers. Now, what's the colored man gonna do with himself? That's what we waiting to find out. But first we gotta know we the leftovers. Now, who knows that? You find me a nigger that knows that and I'll turn any whichaway you want me to. I'll bend over for you. You ain't gonna find that. And that's what the problem is. The problem ain't with the white man. The white man knows you just a leftover. 'Cause he the one who done the eating and he know what he done ate. But we don't know that we been took and made history out of. Done went and filled the white man's belly and now he's full and tired and wants you to get out the way and let him be by himself. Now, I know what I'm talking about. And if you wanna find out, you just ask Mr. Irvin what he had for supper yesterday. And if he's an honest white man . . . which is asking for a whole heap of a lot . . . he'll tell you he done ate your black ass and if you please I'm full up with you . . . so go on and get off the plate and let me eat something else.

SLOW DRAG: What that mean? What's eating got to do with how the white man treat you? He don't treat you no different according to what he ate.

TOLEDO: I ain't said it had nothing to do with how he treat you.

CUTLER: The man's trying to tell you something, fool!

SLOW DRAG: What he trying to tell me? Ain't you here. Why you say he was trying to tell *me* something? Wasn't he trying to tell you too?

LEVEE: He was trying all right. He was trying a whole heap. I'll say that for him. But trying ain't worth a damn. I got lost right there trying to figure out who puts nuts in their stew.

SLOW DRAG: I knowed that before. My grandpappy used to put nuts in his stew. He and my grandmama both. That ain't nothing new.

TOLEDO: They put nuts in their stew all over Africa. But the stew they eat, and the stew your grandpappy made, and all the stew that you and me eat, and the stew Mr. Irvin eats . . . ain't in no way the same stew. That's the way that go. I'm through with it. That's the last you know me to ever try and explain something to you.

CUTLER: (*After a pause*) Well, time's getting along . . . Come on, let's finish rehearsing.

LEVEE: (*Stretching out on a bench*) I don't feel like rehearsing. I ain't nothing but a leftover. You go and rehearse with Toledo . . . He's gonna teach you how to make a stew.

SLOW DRAG: Cutler, what you gonna do? I don't want to be around here all day.

LEVEE: I know my part. You all go on and rehearse your part. You all need some rehearsal.

CUTLER: Come on, Levee, get up off your ass and rehearse the songs.

LEVEE: I already know them songs . . . What I wanna rehearse them for?

SLOW DRAG: You in the band, ain't you? You supposed to rehearse when the band rehearse.

TOLEDO: Levee think he the king of the barnyard. He thinks he's the only rooster know how to crow.

LEVEE: All right! All right! Come on, I'm gonna show you I know them songs. Come on, let's rehearse. I bet you the first one mess be Toledo. Come on . . . I wanna see if he know how to crow.

CUTLER: "Ma Rainey's Black Bottom," Levee's version. Let's do it.

(*They begin to rehearse. The lights go down in the band room and up in the studio.* MA RAINEY *sits and takes off her shoe, rubs her feet.* DUSSIE MAE *wanders about looking at the studio.* SYLVESTER *is over by the piano.*)

MA RAINEY: (*Singing to herself*)

Oh, Lord, these dogs of mine
They sure do worry me all the time
The reason why I don't know
Lord, I beg to be excused
I can't wear me no sharp-toed shoes.
I went for a walk
I stopped to talk
Oh, how my corns did bark.

DUSSIE MAE: It feels kinda spooky in here. I ain't never been in no recording studio before. Where's the band at?

MA RAINEY: They off somewhere rehearsing. I don't know where Irvin went to. All this hurry up and he goes off back there with Sturdyvant. I know he better come on 'cause Ma ain't gonna be waiting. Come here . . . let me see that dress.

(DUSSIE MAE *crosses over.* MA RAINEY *tugs at the dress around the waist, appraising the fit.*)

That dress looks nice. I'm gonna take you tomorrow and get you some more things before I take you down to Memphis. They got clothes up here you can't get in Memphis. I want you to look nice for me. If you gonna travel with the show you got to look nice.

DUSSIE MAE: I need me some more shoes. These hurt my feet.

MA RAINEY: You get you some shoes that fit your feet. Don't you be messing around with no shoes that pinch your feet. Ma know something about bad feet. Hand me my slippers out my bag over yonder.

(DUSSIE MAE *brings the slippers.*)

DUSSIE MAE: I just want to get a pair of them yellow ones. About a half-size bigger.

MA RAINEY: We'll get you whatever you need. Sylvester, too . . . I'm gonna get him some more clothes. Sylvester, tuck your clothes in. Straighten them up and look nice. Look like a gentleman.

DUSSIE MAE: Look at Sylvester with that hat on.

MA RAINEY: Sylvester, take your hat off inside. Act like your mama taught you something. I know she taught you better than that.

(SYLVESTER *bangs on the piano.*)

Come on over here and leave that piano alone.

SYLVESTER: I ain't d-d-doing nothing to the p-p-piano. I'm just l-l-looking at it.

MA RAINEY: Well. Come on over here and sit down. As soon as Mr. Irvin comes back, I'll have him take you down and introduce you to the band.

(SYLVESTER *comes over.*)

He's gonna take you down there and introduce you in a minute . . . have Cutler show you how your part go. And when you get your money, you gonna send some of it home to your mama. Let her know you doing all right. Make her feel good to know you doing all right in the world.

(DUSSIE MAE *wanders about the studio and opens the door leading to the band room. The strains of* LEVEE's *version of "Ma Rainey's Black Bottom" can be heard.* IRVIN *enters.*)

IRVIN: Ma, I called down to the garage and checked on your car. It's just a scratch. They'll have it ready for you this afternoon. They're gonna send it over with one of their fellows.

MA RAINEY: They better have my car fixed right too. I ain't going for that. Brand-new car . . . they better fix it like new.

IRVIN: It was just a scratch on the fender, Ma . . . They'll take care of it . . . don't worry . . . they'll have it like new.

MA RAINEY: Irvin, what is that I hear? What is that the band's rehearsing? I know they ain't rehearsing Levee's "Black Bottom." I know I ain't hearing that?

IRVIN: Ma, listen . . . that's what I wanted to talk to you about. Levee's version of that song . . . it's got a nice arrangement . . . a nice horn intro . . . It really picks it up . . .

MA RAINEY: I ain't studying Levee nothing. I know what he done to that song and I don't like to sing it that way. I'm doing it the old way. That's why I brought my nephew to do the voice intro.

IRVIN: Ma, that's what the people want now. They want something they can dance to. Times are changing. Levee's arrangement gives the people what they want. It gets them excited . . . makes them forget about their troubles.

MA RAINEY: I don't care what you say, Irvin. Levee ain't messing up my song. If he got what the people want, let him take it somewhere else. I'm singing Ma Rainey's song. I ain't singing Levee's song. Now that's all there is to it. Carry my nephew on down there and introduce him to the band. I promised my sister I'd look out for him and he's gonna do the voice intro on the song my way.

IRVIN: Ma, we just figured that . . .

MA RAINEY: Who's this "we"? What you mean "we"? I ain't studying Levee nothing. Come talking this "we" stuff. Who's "we"?

IRVIN: Me and Sturdyvant. We decided that it would . . .

MA RAINEY: You decided, huh? I'm just a bump on the log. I'm gonna go which ever way the river drift. Is that it? You and Sturdyvant decided.

IRVIN: Ma, it was just that we thought it would be better.

MA RAINEY: I ain't got good sense. I don't know nothing about music. I don't know what's a good song and what ain't. You know more about my fans than I do.

IRVIN: It's not that, Ma. It would just be easier to do. It's more what the people want.

MA RAINEY: I'm gonna tell you something, Irvin . . . and you go on up there and tell Sturdyvant. What you all say don't count with me. You understand? Ma listens to her heart. Ma listens to the voice inside her. That's what counts with Ma. Now, you carry my nephew on down there . . . tell Cutler he's gonna do the voice intro on that "Black Bottom" song and that Levee ain't messing up my song with none of his music shit. Now, if that don't set right with you

and Sturdyvant . . . then I can carry my black bottom on back down South to my tour, 'cause I don't like it up here no ways.

IRVIN: Okay, Ma . . . I don't care. I just thought . . .

MA RAINEY: Damn what you thought! What you look like telling me how to sing my song? This Levee and Sturdyvant nonsense . . . I ain't going for it! Sylvester, go on down there and introduce yourself. I'm through playing with Irvin.

SYLVESTER: Which way you go? Where they at?

MA RAINEY: Here . . . I'll carry you down there myself.

DUSSIE MAE: Can I go? I wanna see the band.

MA RAINEY: You stay your behind up here. Ain't no cause in you being down there. Come on, Sylvester.

IRVIN: Okay, Ma. Have it your way. We'll be ready to go in fifteen minutes.

MA RAINEY: We'll be ready to go when Madame says we're ready. That's the way it goes around here.

(MA RAINEY *and* SYLVESTER *exit. The lights go down in the studio and up in the band room.* MA RAINEY *enters with* SYLVESTER.)

Cutler, this here is my nephew Sylvester. He's gonna do that voice intro on the "Black Bottom" song using the old version.

LEVEE: What you talking about? Mr. Irvin says he's using my version. What you talking about?

MA RAINEY: Levee, I ain't studying you or Mr. Irvin. Cutler, get him straightened out on how to do his part. I ain't thinking about Levee. These folks done messed with the wrong person this day. Sylvester, Cutler gonna teach you your part. You go ahead and get it straight. Don't worry about what nobody else say.

(MA RAINEY *exits.*)

CUTLER: Well, come on in, boy. I'm Cutler. You got Slow Drag . . . Levee . . . and that's Toledo over there. Sylvester, huh?

SYLVESTER: Sylvester Brown.

LEVEE: I done wrote a version of that song what picks it up and sets it down in the people's lap! Now she come talking this! You don't need that old circus bullshit! I know what I'm talking about. You gonna mess up the song Cutler and you know it.

CUTLER: I ain't gonna mess up nothing. Ma say . . .

LEVEE: I don't care what Ma say! I'm talking about what the intro gonna do to the song. The peoples in the North ain't gonna buy all that tent-show nonsense. They wanna hear some music!

CUTLER: Nigger, I done told you time and again . . . you just in the band. You plays the piece . . . whatever they want! Ma says what to play! Not you! You ain't here to be doing no creating. Your job is to play whatever Ma says!

LEVEE: I might not play nothing! I might quit!

CUTLER: Nigger, don't nobody care if you quit. Whose heart you gonna break?

TOLEDO: Levee ain't gonna quit. He got to make some money to keep him in shoe polish.

LEVEE: I done told you all . . . you all don't know me. You don't know what I'll do.

CUTLER: I don't think nobody too much give a damn! Sylvester, here's the way your part go. The band plays the intro . . . I'll tell you where to come in. The band plays the intro and then you say, "All right, boys, you done seen the rest . . . Now I'm gonna show you the best. Ma Rainey's gonna show you her black bottom." You got that? (SYLVESTER *nods.*) Let me hear you say it one time.

SYLVESTER: "All right, boys, you done s-s-seen the rest n-n-now I'm gonna show you the best. M-m-m-m-m-m-ma Rainey's gonna s-s-show you her black b-b-bottom."

LEVEE: What kind of . . . All right, Cutler! Let me see you fix that! You straighten that out! You hear that shit, Slow Drag? How in the hell the boy gonna do the part and he can't even talk!

SYLVESTER: W-w-w-who's you to tell me what to do, nigger! This ain't your band! Ma tell me to d-d-d-do it and I'm gonna do it. You can go to hell, n-n-n-nigger!

LEVEE: B-b-b-boy, ain't nobody studying you. You go on and fix that one, Cutler. You fix that one and I'll . . . I'll shine your shoes for you. You go on and fix that one!

TOLEDO: You say you Ma's nephew, huh?

SYLVESTER: Yeah. So w-w-what that mean?

TOLEDO: Oh, I ain't meant nothing . . . I was just asking.

SLOW DRAG: Well, come on and let's rehearse so the boy can get it right.

LEVEE: I ain't rehearsing nothing! You just wait till I get my band. I'm gonna record that song and show you how it supposed to go!

CUTLER: We can do it without Levee. Let him sit on over there. Sylvester, you remember your part?

SYLVESTER: I remember it pretty g-g-g-good.

CUTLER: Well, come on, let's do it, then.

(*The band begins to play.* LEVEE *sits and pouts.* STURDYVANT *enters the band room.*)

STURDYVANT: Good . . . you boys are rehearsing, I see.

LEVEE: (*Jumping up.*) Yessir! We rehearsing. We know them songs real good.

STURDYVANT: Good! Say, Levee, did you finish that song?

LEVEE: Yessir, Mr. Sturdyvant. I got it right here. I wrote that other part just like you say. It go like:

You can shake it, you can break it
You can dance at any hall
You can slide across the floor
You'll never have to stall

My jelly, my roll,
Sweet Mama, don't you let it fall.

Then I put that part in there for the people to dance, like you say, for them to forget about their troubles.

STURDYVANT: Good! Good! I'll just take this. I wanna see you about your songs as soon as I get the chance.

LEVEE: Yessir! As soon as you get the chance, Mr. Sturdyvant.

(STURDYVANT *exits.*)

CUTLER: You hear, Levee? You hear this nigger? "Yes-suh, we's rehearsing, boss."

SLOW DRAG: I heard him. Seen him too. Shuffling them feet.

TOLEDO: Aw, Levee can't help it none. He's like all of us. Spooked up with the white man.

LEVEE: I'm spooked up with him, all right. You let one of them crackers fix on me wrong. I'll show you how spooked up I am with him.

TOLEDO: That's the trouble of it. You wouldn't know if he was fixed on you wrong or not. You so spooked up by him you ain't had the time to study him.

LEVEE: I studies the white man. I got him studied good. The first time one fixes on me wrong, I'm gonna let him know just how much I studied. Come telling me I'm spooked up with the white man. You let one of them mess with me, I'll show you how spooked up I am.

CUTLER: You talking out your hat. The man come in here, call you a boy, tell you to get up off your ass and rehearse, and you ain't had nothing to say to him, except "Yessir!"

LEVEE: I can say "yessir" to whoever I please. What you got to do with it? I know how to handle white folks. I been handling them for thirty-two years, and now you gonna tell me how to do it. Just 'cause I say "yessir" don't mean I'm spooked up with him. I know what I'm doing. Let me handle him my way.

CUTLER: Well, go on and handle it, then.

LEVEE: Toledo, you always messing with somebody! Always agitating somebody with that old philosophy bullshit you be talking. You stay out of my way about what I do and say. I'm my own person. Just let me alone.

TOLEDO: You right, Levee. I apologize. It ain't none of my business that you spooked up by the white man.

LEVEE: All right! See! That's the shit I'm talking about. You all back up and leave Levee alone.

SLOW DRAG: Aw, Levee, we was all just having fun. Toledo ain't said nothing about you he ain't said about me. You just taking it all wrong.

TOLEDO: I ain't meant nothing by it Levee. (*Pauses.*) Cutler, you ready to rehearse?

LEVEE: Levee got to be Levee! And he don't need nobody messing with him about the white man—cause you don't know nothing about me. You don't know Levee. You don't know nothing about what kind of blood I got! What kind of heart I got beating here! (*He pounds his chest.*) I was eight years old when I watched a gang of white mens come into my daddy's house and have to do with my mama any way they wanted. (*Pauses.*) We was living in Jefferson County, about eighty miles outside of Natchez. My daddy's name was Memphis . . . Memphis Lee Green . . . had him near fifty acres of good farming land. I'm talking about good land! Grow anything you want! He done gone off of shares and bought this land from Mr. Hallie's widow woman after he done passed on. Folks called him an uppity nigger 'cause he done saved and borrowed to where he could buy this land and be independent. (*Pauses.*) It was coming on planting time and my daddy went into Natchez to get him some seed and fertilizer. Called me, say, "Levee you the man of the house now. Take care of your mama while I'm gone." I wasn't but a little boy, eight years old. (*Pauses.*) My mama was frying up some chicken when them mens come in that house. Must have been eight or nine of them. She standing there frying that chicken and them mens come and took hold of her just like you take hold of a mule and make him do what you want. (*Pauses.*) There was my mama with a gang of white mens. She tried to fight them off, but I could see where it wasn't gonna do her any good, I didn't know what they were doing to her . . . but I figured whatever it was they may as well do to me too. My daddy had a knife that he kept around there for hunting and working and whatnot. I knew where he kept it and I went and got it.

I'm gonna show you how spooked up I was by the white man. I tried my damndest to cut one of them's throat! I hit him on the shoulder with it. He reached back and grabbed hold of that knife and whacked me across the chest with it.

(LEVEE *raises his shirt to show a long ugly scar.*)

That's what made them stop. They was scared I was gonna bleed to death. My mama wrapped a sheet around me and carried me two miles down to the Furlow place and they drove me up to Doc Albans. He was waiting on a calf to be born, and say he ain't had time to see me. They carried me up to Miss Etta, the midwife, and she fixed me up.

My daddy came back and acted like he done accepted the facts of what happened. But he got the names of them mens from mama. He found out who they was and then we announced we was moving out of that county. Said good-bye to everybody . . . all the neighbors. My daddy went and smiled in the face of one of them crackers who had been with my mama. Smiled in his face and sold him our land. We moved over with relations in Caldwell. He got us settled in and then he took off one day. I ain't never seen him since. He sneaked back, hiding up in the woods, laying to get them eight or nine men. (*Pauses.*) He got four of them before they got him. They tracked him down in the woods. Caught up with him and hung him and set him afire. (*Pauses.*) My daddy wasn't spooked up by the white man. Nosir! And that taught me how to handle them. I seen my daddy go up and grin in this cracker's face . . . smile in his face and sell him his land. All the while he's planning how he's gonna get him and what he's gonna do to him. That taught me how to handle them. So you all just back up and leave Levee alone about the white man. I can smile and say yessir to whoever I please. I got time coming to me. You all just leave Levee alone about the white man.

(*There is a long pause.* SLOW DRAG *begins playing on the bass and sings.*)

SLOW DRAG: (*Singing*)

> If I had my way
> If I had my way
> If I had my way
> I would tear this old building down.

ACT 2

(*The lights come up in the studio. The musicians are setting up their instruments.* MA RAINEY *walks about shoeless, singing softly to herself.* LEVEE *stands near* DUSSIE MAE, *who hikes up her dress and crosses her leg.* CUTLER *speaks to* IRVIN *off to the side.*)

CUTLER: Mr. Irvin, I don't know what you gonna do. I ain't got nothing to do with it, but the boy can't do the part. He stutters. He can't get it right. He stutters right through it every time.

IRVIN: Christ! Okay. We'll . . . Shit! We'll just do it like we planned. We'll do Levee's version. I'll handle it, Cutler. Come on, let's go. I'll think of something.

(*He exits to the control booth.*)

MA RAINEY: (*Calling* CUTLER *over*) Levee's got his eyes in the wrong place. You better school him, Cutler.

CUTLER: Come on, Levee . . . let's get ready to play! Get your mind on your work!

IRVIN: (*Over speaker*) Okay, boys, we're gonna do "Moonshine Blues" first. "Moonshine Blues," Ma.

MA RAINEY: I ain't doing no "Moonshine" nothing. I'm doing the "Black Bottom" first. Come on, Sylvester. (*To* IRVIN.) Where's Sylvester's mike? You need a mike for Sylvester. Irvin . . . get him a mike.

IRVIN: Uh . . . Ma, the boys say he can't do it. We'll have to do Levee's version.

MA RAINEY: What you mean he can't do it? Who say he can't do it? What boys say he can't do it?

IRVIN: The band, Ma . . . the boys in the band.

MA RAINEY: What band? The band work for me! I say what goes! Cutler, what's he talking about? Levee, this some of your shit?

IRVIN: He stutters, Ma. They say he stutters.

MA RAINEY: I don't care if he do. I promised the boy he could do the part . . . and he's gonna do it! That's all there is to it. He don't stutter all the time. Get a microphone down here for him.

IRVIN: Ma, we don't have time. We can't . . .

MA RAINEY: If you wanna make a record, you gonna find time. I ain't playing with you, Irvin. I can walk out of here and go back to my tour. I got plenty fans. I don't need to go through all of this. Just go and get the boy a microphone.

(IRVIN and STURDYVANT consult in the booth, IRVIN exits.)

STURDYVANT: All right, Ma . . . we'll get him a microphone. But if he messes up . . . He's only getting one chance . . . The cost . . .

MA RAINEY: Damn the cost. You always talking about the cost. I make more money for this outfit than anybody else you got put together. If he messes up he'll just do it till he gets it right. Levee, I know you had something to do with this. You better watch yourself.

LEVEE: It was Cutler!

SYLVESTER: It was you! You the only one m-m-mad about it.

LEVEE: The boy stutter. He can't do the part. Everybody see that. I don't know why you want the boy to do the part no ways.

MA RAINEY: Well, can or can't . . . he's gonna do it! You ain't got nothing to do with it!

LEVEE: I don't care what you do! He can sing the whole goddamned song for all I care!

MA RAINEY: Well, all right. Thank you.

(IRVIN enters with a microphone and hooks it up. He exits to the control booth.)

MA RAINEY: Come on, Sylvester. You just stand here and hold your hands like I told you. Just remember the words and say them . . . That's all there is to it. Don't worry about messing up. If you mess up, we'll do it again. Now, let me hear you say it. Play for him, Cutler.

CUTLER: One . . . two . . . you know what to do.

(The band begins to play and SYLVESTER curls his fingers and clasps his hands together in front of his chest, pulling in opposite directions as he says his lines.)

SYLVESTER: "All right, boys, you d-d-d-done s-s-s-seen the best . . .

(LEVEE stops playing.)

Now I'm g-g-g-gonna show you the rest . . . Ma R-r-rainey's gonna show you her b-b-black b-b-b-bottom."

(The rest of the band stops playing.)

MA RAINEY: That's all right. That's real good. You take your time, you'll get it right.

STURDYVANT: (Over speaker) Listen, Ma . . . now, when you come in, don't wait so long to come in. Don't take so long on the intro, huh?

MA RAINEY: Sturdyvant, don't you go trying to tell me how to sing. You just take care of that up there and let me take care of this down here. Where's my Coke?

IRVIN: Okay, Ma. We're all set up to go up here. "Ma Rainey's Black Bottom," boys.

MA RAINEY: Where's my Coke? I need a Coke. You ain't got no Coke down here? Where's my Coke?

IRVIN: What's the matter, Ma? What's . . .

MA RAINEY: Where's my Coke? I need a Coca-Cola.

IRVIN: Uh . . . Ma, look, I forgot the Coke, huh? Let's do it without it, huh? Just this one song. What say, boys?

MA RAINEY: Damn what the band say! You know I don't sing nothing without my Coca-Cola!

STURDYVANT: We don't have any, Ma. There's no Coca-Cola here. We're all set up and we'll just go ahead and . . .

MA RAINEY: You supposed to have Coca-Cola. Irvin knew that. I ain't singing nothing without my Coca-Cola!

(She walks away from the mike, singing to herself. STURDYVANT enters from the control booth.)

STURDYVANT: Now, just a minute here, Ma. You come in an hour late . . . we're way behind schedule as it is . . . the band is set up and ready to go . . . I'm burning my lights . . . I've turned up the heat . . . We're ready to make a record and what? You decide you want a Coca-Cola?

MA RAINEY: Sturdyvant, get out of my face.

(IRVIN enters.)

Irvin . . . I told you keep him away from me.

IRVIN: Mel, I'll handle it.

STURDYVANT: I'm tired of her nonsense, Irv. I'm not gonna put up with this!

IRVIN: Let me handle it, Mel. I know how to handle her. (IRVIN to MA RAINEY.) Look, Ma . . . I'll call down to the deli and get you a Coke. But let's get started, huh? Sylvester's standing there ready to go . . . the band's set up . . . let's do this one song, huh?

MA RAINEY: If you too cheap to buy me a Coke, I'll buy my own. Slow Drag! Sylvester, go with Slow Drag and get me a Coca-Cola.

(SLOW DRAG *comes over.*)

Slow Drag, walk down to that store on the corner and get me three bottles of Coca-Cola. Get out my face, Irvin. You all just wait until I get my Coke. It ain't gonna kill you.

IRVIN: Okay, Ma. Get your Coke, for Chrissakes! Get your coke!

(IRVIN *and* STURDYVANT *exit into the hallway followed by* SLOW DRAG *and* SYLVESTER. TOLEDO, CUTLER *and* LEVEE *head for the band room.*)

MA RAINEY: Cutler, come here a minute. I want to talk to you.

(CUTLER *crosses over somewhat reluctantly.*)

What's all this about "the boys in the band say"? I tells you what to do. I says what the matter is with the band. I say who can and can't do what.

CUTLER: We just say 'cause the boy stutter . . .

MA RAINEY: I know he stutters. Don't you think I know he stutters. This is what's gonna help him.

CUTLER: Well, how can he do the part if he stutters? You want him to stutter through it? We just thought it be easier to go on and let Levee do it like we planned.

MA RAINEY: I don't care if he stutters or not! He's doing the part and I don't wanna hear any more of this shit about what the band says. And I want you to find somebody to replace Levee when we get to Memphis. Levee ain't nothing but trouble.

CUTLER: Levee's all right. He plays good music when he puts his mind to it. He knows how to write music too.

MA RAINEY: I don't care what he know. He ain't nothing but bad news. Find somebody else. I know it was his idea about who to say who can do what.

(DUSSIE MAE *wanders over to where they are sitting.*)

Dussie Mae, go sit your behind down somewhere and quit flaunting yourself around.

DUSSIE MAE: I ain't doing nothing.

MA RAINEY: Well, just go on somewhere and stay out of the way.

CUTLER: I been meaning to ask you, Ma . . . about these songs. This "Moonshine Blues" . . . that's one of them songs Bessie Smith sang, I believes.

MA RAINEY: Bessie what? Ain't nobody thinking about Bessie. I taught Bessie. She ain't doing nothing but imitating me. What I care about Bessie? I don't care if she sell a million records. She got her people and I got mine. I don't care what nobody else do. Ma was the *first* and don't you forget it!

CUTLER: Ain't nobody said nothing about that. I just said that's the same song she sang.

MA RAINEY: I been doing this a long time. Ever since I was a little girl. I don't care what nobody else do.

That's what gets me so mad with Irvin. White folks try to be put out with you all the time. Too cheap to buy me a Coca-Cola. I lets them know it, though. Ma don't stand for no shit. Wanna take my voice and trap it in them fancy boxes with all them buttons and dials . . . and then too cheap to buy me a Coca-Cola. And it don't cost but a nickle a bottle.

CUTLER: I knows what you mean about that.

MA RAINEY: They don't care nothing about me. All they want is my voice. Well, I done learned that, and they gonna treat me like I want to be treated no matter how much it hurt them. They back there now calling me all kinds of names . . . calling me everything but a child of god. But they can't do nothing else. They ain't got what they wanted yet. As soon as they get my voice down on them recording machines, then it's just like if I'd be some whore and they roll over and put their pants on. Ain't got no use for me then. I know what I'm talking about. You watch. Irvin right there with the rest of them. He don't care nothing about me either. He's been my manager for six years, always talking about sticking together, and the only time he had me in his house was to sing for some of his friends.

CUTLER: I know how they do.

MA RAINEY: If you colored and can make them some money, then you all right with them. Otherwise, you just a dog in the alley. I done made this company more money from my records than all the other recording artists they got put together. And they wanna balk about how much this session is costing them.

CUTLER: I don't see where it's costing them all what they say.

MA RAINEY: It ain't! I don't pay that kind of talk no mind.

(*The lights go down on the studio and come up on the band room.* TOLEDO *sits reading a newspaper.* LEVEE *sings and hums his song.*)

LEVEE: (*Singing*)

*You can shake it, you can break it
You can dance at any hall
You can slide across the floor
You'll never have to stall
My jelly, my roll,
Sweet Mama, don't you let it fall.*

Wait till Sturdyvant hear me play that! I'm talking about some real music, Toledo! I'm talking about *real* music!

(*The door opens and* DUSSIE MAE *enters.*)

Hey, mama! Come on in.

DUSSIE MAE: Oh, hi! I just wanted to see what it looks like down here.

LEVEE: Well, come on in . . . I don't bite.

DUSSIE MAE: I didn't know you could really write music. I thought you was just jiving me at the club last night.

LEVEE: Naw, baby . . . I knows how to write music. I done give Mr. Sturdyvant some of my songs and he says he's gonna let me record them. Ask Toledo. I'm gonna have my own band! Toledo, ain't I give Mr. Sturdyvant some of my songs I wrote?

TOLEDO: Don't get Toledo mixed up in nothing.

(He exits.)

DUSSIE MAE: You gonna get your own band sure enough?

LEVEE: That's right! Levee Green and his Footstompers.

DUSSIE MAE: That's real nice.

LEVEE: That's what I was trying to tell you last night. A man what's gonna get his own band need to have a woman like you.

DUSSIE MAE: A woman like me wants somebody to bring it and put it in my hand. I don't need nobody wanna get something for nothing and leave me standing in my door.

LEVEE: That ain't Levee's style, sugar. I got more style than that. I knows how to treat a woman. Buy her presents and things . . . treat her like she wants to be treated.

DUSSIE MAE: That's what they all say . . . till it come time to be buying the presents.

LEVEE: When we get down to Memphis, I'm gonna show you what I'm talking about. I'm gonna take you out and show you a good time. Show you Levee knows how to treat a woman.

DUSSIE MAE: When you getting your own band?

LEVEE: *(Moves closer to slip his arm around her)* Soon as Mr. Sturdyvant say. I done got my fellows already picked out. Getting me some good fellows know how to play real sweet music.

DUSSIE MAE: *(Moves away)* Go on now, I don't go for all that pawing and stuff. When you get your own band, maybe we can see about this stuff you talking.

LEVEE: *(Moving toward her)* I just wanna show you I know what the women like. They don't call me Sweet Lemonade for nothing.

(LEVEE takes her in his arms and attempts to kiss her.)

DUSSIE MAE: Stop it now. Somebody's gonna come in here.

LEVEE: Naw they ain't. Look here, sugar . . . what I wanna know is . . . can I introduce my red rooster to your brown hen?

DUSSIE MAE: You get your band, then we'll see if that rooster know how to crow.

(He grinds up against her and feels her buttocks.)

LEVEE: Now I know why my grandpappy sat on the back porch with his straight razor when grandma hung out the wash.

DUSSIE MAE: Nigger, you crazy!

LEVEE: I bet you sound like the midnight train from Alabama when it crosses the Mason-Dixon line.

DUSSIE MAE: How's you get so crazy?

LEVEE: It's women like you . . . drives me that way.

(He moves to kiss her as the lights go down in the band room and up in the studio. MA RAINEY sits with CUTLER and TOLEDO.)

MA RAINEY: It sure done got quiet in here. I never could stand no silence. I always got to have some music going on in my head somewhere. It keeps things balanced. Music will do that. It fills things up. The more music you got in the world, the fuller it is.

CUTLER: I can agree with that. I got to have my music too.

MA RAINEY: White folks don't understand about the blues. They hear it come out, but they don't know how it got there. They don't understand that's life's way of talking. You don't sing to feel better. You sing 'cause that's a way of understanding life.

CUTLER: That's right. You get that understanding and you done got a grip on life to where you can hold your head up and go on to see what else life got to offer.

MA RAINEY: The blues help you get out of bed in the morning. You get up knowing you ain't alone. There's something else in the world. Something's been added by that song. This be an empty world without the blues. I take that emptiness and try to fill it up with something.

TOLEDO: You fill it up with something the people can't be without, Ma. That's why they call you the Mother of the Blues. You fill up that emptiness in a way ain't nobody ever thought of doing before. And now they can't be without it.

MA RAINEY: I ain't started the blues way of singing. The blues always been here.

CUTLER: In the church sometimes you find that way of singing. They got blues in the church.

MA RAINEY: They say I started it . . . but I didn't. I just helped it out. Filled up that empty space a little bit. That's all. But if they wanna call me the Mother of the Blues, that's all right with me. It don't hurt none.

(SLOW DRAG and SYLVESTER enter with the Cokes.)

It sure took you long enough. That store ain't but on the corner.

SLOW DRAG: That one was closed. We had to find another one.

MA RAINEY: Sylvester, go and find Mr. Irvin and tell him we ready to go.

(SYLVESTER *exits. The lights in the band room come up while the lights in the studio stay on.* LEVEE *and* DUSSIE MAE *are kissing.* SLOW DRAG *enters. They break their embrace.* DUSSIE MAE *straightens up her clothes.*)

SLOW DRAG: Cold out. I just wanted to warm up with a little sip.

(*He goes to his locker, takes out his bottle and drinks.*)

Ma got her Coke, Levee. We about ready to start.

(SLOW DRAG *exits.* LEVEE *attempts to kiss* DUSSIE MAE *again.*)

DUSSIE MAE: No . . . Come on! I got to go. You gonna get me in trouble.

(*She pulls away and exits up the stairs.* LEVEE *watches after her.*)

LEVEE: Good God! Happy birthday to the lady with the cakes!

(*The lights go down in the band room and come up in the studio.* MA RAINEY *drinks her Coke.* LEVEE *enters from the band room. The musicians take their places.* SYLVESTER *stands by his mike.* IRVIN *and* STURDYVANT *look on from the control booth.*)

IRVIN: We're all set up here, Ma. We're all set to go. You ready down there?

MA RAINEY: Sylvester you just remember your part and say it. That's all there is to it. (*To* IRVIN.) Yeah, we ready.

IRVIN: Okay, boys. "Ma Rainey's Black Bottom." Take one.

CUTLER: One . . . two . . . You know what to do.

(*The band plays.*)

SYLVESTER: All right boys, you d-d-d-done s-s-seen the rest . . .

IRVIN: Hold it!

(*The band stops.* STURDYVANT *changes the recording disk and nods to* IRVIN.)

Okay. Take two.

CUTLER: One . . . two . . . You know what to do.

(*The band plays.*)

SYLVESTER: All right, boys, you done seen the rest . . . now I'm gonna show you the best. Ma Rainey's g-g-g-gonna s-s-show you her b-b-black bottom.

IRVIN: Hold it! Hold it!

(*The band stops.* STURDYVANT *changes the recording disk.*)

Okay. Take three. Ma, let's do it without the intro, huh? No voice intro . . . you just come in singing.

MA RAINEY: Irvin, I done told you . . . the boy's gonna do the part. He don't stutter all the time. Just give

him a chance. Sylvester, hold your hands like I told you and just relax. Just relax and concentrate.

IRVIN: All right. Take three.

CUTLER: One . . . two . . . You know what to do.

(*The band plays.*)

SYLVESTER: All right, boys, you done seen the rest . . . now, I'm gonna show you the best. Ma Rainey's gonna show you her black bottom.

MA RAINEY: (*Singing*)

> Way down south in Alabamy
> I got a friend they call dancing Sammy
> Who's crazy about all the latest dances
> Black Bottom stomping, two babies prancing
>
> The other night at a swell affair
> As soon as the boys found out that I was there
> They said, come on, Ma, let's go to the cabaret.
> When I got there, you ought to hear them say,
>
> I want to see the dance you call the black bottom
> I want to learn that dance
> I want to see the dance you call your big black bottom
> It'll put you in a trance.
>
> All the boys in the neighborhood
> They say your black bottom is really good
> Come on and show me your black bottom
> I want to learn that dance
>
> I want to see the dance you call the black bottom
> I want to learn that dance
> Come on and show the dance you call your big black bottom
> It puts you in a trance.
>
> Early last morning about the break of day
> Grandpa told my grandma, I heard him say,
> Get up and show your old man your black bottom
> I want to learn that dance.

(*Instrumental break.*)

> I done showed you all my black bottom
> You ought to learn that dance.

IRVIN: Okay, that's good, Ma. That sounded great! Good job, boys!

MA RAINEY: (*To* SYLVESTER) See! I told you. I knew you could do it. You just have to put your mind to it. Didn't he do good, Cutler? Sound real good. I told him he could do it.

CUTLER: He sure did. He did better than I thought he was gonna do.

IRVIN: (*Entering to remove* SYLVESTER's *mike*) Okay, boys

. . . Ma . . . let's do "Moonshine Blues" next, huh? "Moonshine Blues," boys.

STURDYVANT: (*Over speaker*) Irv! Something's wrong down there. We don't have it right.

IRVIN: What? What's the matter Mel . . .

STURDYVANT: We don't have it right. Something happened. We don't have the goddamn song recorded!

IRVIN: What's the matter? Mel, what happened? You sure you don't have nothing?

STURDYVANT: Check that mike, huh, Irv. It's the kid's mike. Something's wrong with the mike. We've got everything all screwed up here.

IRVIN: Christ almighty! Ma, we got to do it again. We don't have it. We didn't record the song.

MA RAINEY: What you mean you didn't record it? What was you and Sturdyvant doing up there?

IRVIN: (*Following the mike wire*) Here . . . Levee must have kicked the plug out.

LEVEE: I ain't done nothing. I ain't kicked nothing!

SLOW DRAG: If Levee had his mind on what he's doing . . .

MA RAINEY: Levee, if it ain't one thing, it's another. You better straighten yourself up!

LEVEE: Hell . . . it ain't my fault. I ain't done nothing!

STURDYVANT: What's the matter with that mike, Irv? What's the problem?

IRVIN: It's the cord, Mel. The cord's all chewed up. We need another cord.

MA RAINEY: This is the most disorganized . . . Irvin, I'm going home! Come on. Come on, Dussie.

(MA RAINEY *walks past* STURDYVANT *as he enters from the control booth. She exits offstage to get her coat.*)

STURDYVANT: (*To* IRVIN) Where's she going?

IRVIN: She said she's going home.

STURDYVANT: Irvin, you get her! If she walks out of here . . .

(MA RAINEY *enters carrying her and* DUSSIE MAE's *coat.*)

MA RAINEY: Come on, Sylvester.

IRVIN: (*Helping her with her coat*) Ma . . . Ma . . . listen. Fifteen minutes! All I ask is fifteen minutes!

MA RAINEY: Come on, Sylvester, get your coat.

STURDYVANT: Ma, if you walk out of this studio . . .

IRVIN: Fifteen minutes, Ma!

STURDYVANT: You'll be through . . . washed up! If you walk out on me . . .

IRVIN: Mel, for Chrissakes, shut up and let me handle it!

(He goes after MA RAINEY, *who has started for the door.*)

Ma, listen. These records are gonna be hits! They're gonna sell like crazy! Hell, even Sylvester will be a star. Fifteen minutes. That's all I'm asking! Fifteen minutes.

MA RAINEY: (*Crosses to a chair and sits with her coat on*) Fifteen minutes! You hear me, Irvin? Fifteen min-

utes . . . and then I'm gonna take my black bottom on back down to Georgia. Fifteen minutes. Then Madame Rainey is leaving!

IRVIN: (*Kisses her*) All right, Ma . . . fifteen minutes. I promise. (*To the band.*) You boys go ahead and take a break. Fifteen minutes and we'll be ready to go.

CUTLER: Slow Drag, you got any of that bourbon left?

SLOW DRAG: Yeah, there's some down there.

CUTLER: I could use a little nip.

(CUTLER *and* SLOW DRAG *exit to the band room, followed by* LEVEE *and* TOLEDO. *The lights go down in the studio and up in the band room.*)

SLOW DRAG: Don't make me no difference if she leave or not. I was kinda hoping she would leave.

CUTLER: I'm like Mr. Irvin . . . After all this time we done put in here, it's best to go ahead and get something out of it.

TOLEDO: Ma gonna do what she wanna do, that's for sure. If I was Mr. Irvin, I'd best go on and get them cords and things hooked up right. And I wouldn't take no longer than fifteen minutes doing it.

CUTLER: If Levee had his mind on his work, we wouldn't be in this fix. We'd be up there finishing up. Now we got to go back and see if that boy get that part right. Ain't no telling if he ever get that right again in his life.

LEVEE: Hey, Levee ain't done nothing!

SLOW DRAG: Levee up there got one eye on the gal and the other on his trumpet.

CUTLER: Nigger, don't you know that's Ma's gal?

LEVEE: I don't care whose gal it is. I ain't done nothing to her. I just talk to her like I talk to anybody else.

CUTLER: Well, that being Ma's gal, and that being that boy's gal, is one and two different things. The boy is liable to kill you . . . but you' ass gonna be out there scraping the concrete looking for a job if you messing with Ma's gal.

LEVEE: How am I messing with her? I ain't done nothing to the gal. I just asked her her name. Now, if you telling me I can't do that, then Ma will just have to go to hell.

CUTLER: All I can do is warn you.

SLOW DRAG: Let him hang himself, Cutler. Let him string his neck out.

LEVEE: I ain't done nothing to the gal! You all talk like I done went and done something to her. Leave me go with my business.

CUTLER: I'm through with it. Try and talk to a fool . . .

TOLEDO: Some mens got it worse than others . . . this foolishness I'm talking about. Some mens is excited to be fools. That excitement is something else. I know about it. I done experienced it. It makes you feel good to be a fool. But it don't last long. It's over in a minute. Then you got to tend with the consequences. You got to tend with what comes after.

That's when you wish you had learned something about it.

LEVEE: That's the best sense you made all day. Talking about being a fool. That's the only sensible thing you said today. Admitting you was a fool.

TOLEDO: I admits it, all right. Ain't nothing wrong with it. I done been a little bit of everything.

LEVEE: Now you're talking. You's as big a fool as they make.

TOLEDO: Gonna be a bit more things before I'm finished with it. Gonna be foolish again. But I ain't never been the same fool twice. I might be a different kind of fool, but I ain't gonna be the same fool twice. That's where we parts ways.

SLOW DRAG: Toledo, you done been a fool about a woman?

TOLEDO: Sure. Sure I have. Same as everybody.

SLOW DRAG: Hell, I ain't never seen you mess with no woman. I thought them books was your woman.

TOLEDO: Sure I messed with them. Done messed with a whole heap of them. And gonna mess with some more. But I ain't gonna be no fool about them. What you think? I done come in the world full-grown, with my head in a book? I done been young. Married. Got kids. I done been around and I done loved women to where you shake in your shoes just at the sight of them. Feel it all up and down your spine.

SLOW DRAG: I didn't know you was married.

TOLEDO: Sure. Legally. I been married legally. Got the papers and all. I done been through life. Made my marks. Followed some signs on the road. Ignored some others. I done been all through it. I touched and been touched by it. But I ain't never been the same fool twice. That's what I can say.

LEVEE: But you been a fool. That's what counts. Talking about I'm a fool for asking the gal her name and here you is one yourself.

TOLEDO: Now, I married a woman. A good woman. To this day I can't say she wasn't a good woman. I can't say nothing bad about her. I married that woman with all the good graces and intentions of being hooked up and bound to her for the rest of my life. I was looking for her to put me in my grave. But, you see . . . it ain't all the time what you' intentions and wishes are. She went out and joined the church. All right. There ain't nothing wrong with that. A good Christian woman going to church and wanna do right by her god. There ain't nothing wrong with that. But she got up there, got to seeing them good Christian mens and wondering why I ain't like that. Soon she figure she got a heathen on her hands. She figured she couldn't live like that. The church was more important than I was. So she left. Packed up one day and moved out. To this day I ain't never said another word to her. Come home one day and my house was empty! And I sat down

and figured out that I was a fool not to see that she needed something that I wasn't giving her. Else she wouldn't have been up there at the church in the first place. I ain't blaming her. I just said it wasn't gonna happen to me again. So, yeah, Toledo been a fool about a woman. That's part of making life.

CUTLER: Well, yeah, I been a fool too. Everybody done been a fool once or twice. But, you see, Toledo, what you call a fool and what I call a fool is two different things. I can't see where you was being a fool for that. You ain't done nothing foolish. You can't help what happened, and I wouldn't call you a fool for it. A fool is responsible for what happens to him. A fool cause it to happen. Like Levee . . . if he keeps messing with Ma's gal and his feet be out there scraping the ground. That's a fool.

LEVEE: Ain't nothing gonna happen to Levee. Levee ain't gonna let nothing happen to him. Now, I'm gonna say it again. I asked the gal her name. That's all I done. And if that's being a fool, then you looking at the biggest fool in the world . . . 'cause I sure as hell asked her.

SLOW DRAG: You just better not let Ma see you ask her. That's what the man's trying to tell you.

LEVEE: I don't need nobody to tell me nothing.

CUTLER: Well, Toledo, all I gots to say is that from the looks of it . . . from your story . . . I don't think life did you fair.

TOLEDO: Oh, life is fair. It's just in the taking what it gives you.

LEVEE: Life ain't shit. You can put it in a paper bag and carry it around with you. It ain't got no balls. Now, death . . . death got some style! Death will kick your ass and make you wish you never been born! That's how bad death is! But you can rule over life. Life ain't nothing.

TOLEDO: Cutler, how's your brother doing?

CUTLER: Who, Nevada? Oh, he's doing all right. Staying in St. Louis. Got a bunch of kids, last I heard.

TOLEDO: Me and him was all right with each other. Done a lot of farming together down in Plattsville.

CUTLER: Yeah, I know you all was tight. He in St. Louis now. Running an elevator, last I hear about it.

SLOW DRAG: That's better than stepping in muleshit.

TOLEDO: Oh, I don't know now. I liked farming. Get out there in the sun . . . smell that dirt. Be out there by yourself . . . nice and peaceful. Yeah, farming was all right by me. Sometimes I think I'd like to get me a little old place . . . but I done got too old to be following behind one of them balky mules now.

LEVEE: Nigger talking about life is fair. And ain't got a pot to piss in.

TOLEDO: See, now, I'm gonna tell you something. A nigger gonna be dissatisfied no matter what. Give a nigger some bread and butter . . . and he'll cry 'cause he ain't got no jelly. Give him some jelly, and he'll cry 'cause he ain't got no knife to put it on with. If there's one thing I done learned in this life, it's that you can't satisfy a nigger no matter what you do. A nigger's gonna make his own dissatisfaction.

LEVEE: Niggers got a right to be dissatisfied. Is you gonna be satisfied with a bone somebody done throwed you when you see them eating the whole hog?

TOLEDO: You lucky they let you be an entertainer. They ain't got to accept your way of entertaining. You lucky and don't even know it. You's entertaining and the rest of the people is hauling wood. That's the only kind of job for the colored man.

SLOW DRAG: Ain't nothing wrong with hauling wood. I done hauled plenty wood. My daddy used to haul wood. Ain't nothing wrong with that. That's honest work.

LEVEE: That ain't what I'm talking about. I ain't talking about hauling no wood. I'm talking about being satisfied with a bone somebody done throwed you. That's what's the matter with you all. You satisfied sitting in one place. You got to move on down the road from where you sitting . . . and all the time you got to keep an eye out for that devil who's looking to buy up souls. And hope you get lucky and find him!

CUTLER: I done told you about that blasphemy. Talking about selling your soul to the devil.

TOLEDO: We done the same thing, Cutler. There ain't no difference. We done sold Africa for the price of tomatoes. We done sold ourselves to the white man in order to be like him. Look at the way you dressed . . . That ain't African. That's the white man. We trying to be just like him. We done sold who we are in order to become someone else. We's imitation white men.

CUTLER: What else we gonna be, living over here?

LEVEE: I'm Levee. Just me. I ain't no imitation nothing!

SLOW DRAG: You can't change who you are by how you dress. That's what I got to say.

TOLEDO: It ain't all how you dress. It's how you act, how you see the world. It's how you follow life.

LEVEE: It don't matter what you talking about. I ain't no imitation white man. And I don't want to be no white man. As soon as I get my band together and make them records like Mr. Sturdyvant done told me I can make, I'm gonna be like Ma and tell the white man just what he can do. Ma tell Mr. Irvin she gonna leave . . . and Mr. Irvin get down on his knees and beg her to stay! That's the way I'm gonna be! Make the white man respect me!

CUTLER: The white man don't care nothing about Ma. The colored folks made Ma a star. White folks don't care nothing about who she is . . . what kind of music she make.

SLOW DRAG: That's the truth about that. You let her go down to one of them white-folks hotels and see how big she is.

CUTLER: Hell, she ain't got to do that. She can't even get a cab up here in the North. I'm gonna tell you something. Reverend Gates . . . you know Reverend Gates? . . . Slow Drag know who I'm talking about. Reverend Gates . . . now I'm gonna show you how this go where the white man don't care a thing about who you is. Reverend Gates was coming from Tallahassee to Atlanta, going to see his sister, who was sick at that time with the consumption. The train come up through Thomasville, then past Moultrie, and stopped in this little town called Sigsbee . . .

LEVEE: You can stop telling that right there! That train don't stop in Sigsbee. I know what train you talking about. That train got four stops before it reach Macon to go on to Atlanta. One in Thomasville, one in Moultrie, one in Cordele . . . and it stop in Centerville.

CUTLER: Nigger, I know what I'm talking about. You gonna tell me where the train stop?

LEVEE: Hell, yeah, if you talking about it stop in Sigsbee. I'm gonna tell you the truth.

CUTLER: I'm talking about *this* train! I don't know what train you been riding. I'm talking about *this* train!

LEVEE: Ain't but one train. Ain't but one train come out of Tallahassee heading north to Atlanta, and it don't stop at Sigsbee. Tell him, Toledo . . . that train don't stop at Sigsbee. The only train that stops at Sigsbee is the Yazoo Delta, and you have to transfer at Moultrie to get it!

CUTLER: Well, hell, maybe that what he done! I don't know. I'm just telling you the man got off the train at Sigsbee . . .

LEVEE: All right . . . you telling it. Tell it your way. Just make up anything.

SLOW DRAG: Levee, leave the man alone and let him finish.

CUTLER: I ain't paying Levee no never mind.

LEVEE: Go on and tell it your way.

CUTLER: Anyway . . . Reverend Gates got off this train in Sigsbee. The train done stopped there and he figured he'd get off and check the schedule to be sure he arrive in time for somebody to pick him up. All right. While he's there checking the schedule, it come upon him that he had to go to the bathroom. Now, they ain't had no colored rest rooms at the station. The only colored rest room is an outhouse they got sitting way back two hundred yards or so from the station. All right. He in the outhouse and the train go off and leave him there. He don't know nothing about this town. Ain't never been there before—in fact, ain't never even heard of it before.

LEVEE: I heard of it! I know just where it's at . . . and he ain't got off no train coming out of Tallahassee in Sigsbee!

CUTLER: The man standing there, trying to figure out what he's gonna do . . . where this train done left him in this strange town. It started getting dark. He see where the sun's getting low in the sky and he's trying to figure out what he's gonna do, when he noticed a couple of white fellows standing across the street from this station. Just standing there, watching him. And then two or three more come up and joined the other one. He look around, ain't seen no colored folks nowhere. He didn't know what was getting in these here fellows' minds, so he commence to walking. He ain't knowed where he was going. He just walking down the railroad tracks when he hear them call him. "Hey, nigger!" See, just like that. "Hey, nigger!" He kept on walking. They called him some more and he just keep walking. Just going down the tracks. And then he heard a gunshot where somebody done fired a gun in the air. He stopped then, you know.

TOLEDO: You don't even have to tell me no more. I know the facts of it. I done heard the same story a hundred times. It happened to me too. Same thing.

CUTLER: Naw, I'm gonna show you how the white folks don't care nothing about who or what you is. They crowded around him. These gang of mens made a circle around him. Now, he's standing there, you understand . . . got his cross around his neck like them preachers wear. Had his little Bible with him what he carry all the time. So they crowd on around him and one of them ask who he is. He told them he was Reverend Gates and that he was going to see his sister who was sick and the train left without him. And they said, "Yeah, nigger . . . but can you dance?" He looked at them and commenced to dancing. One of them reached up and tore his cross off his neck. Said he was committing a heresy by dancing with a cross and Bible. Took his Bible and tore it up and had him dancing till they got tired of watching him.

SLOW DRAG: White folks ain't never had no respect for the colored minister.

CUTLER: That's the only way he got out of there alive . . . was to dance. Ain't even had no respect for a man of God! Wanna make him into a clown. Reverend Gates sat right in my house and told me that story from his own mouth. So . . . the white folks don't care nothing about Ma Rainey. She's just another nigger who they can use to make some money.

LEVEE: What I wants to know is . . . if he's a man of God, then where the hell was God when all of this was going on? Why wasn't God looking out for him. Why didn't God strike down them crackers with some of this lightning you talk about to me?

CUTLER: Levee, you gonna burn in hell.

LEVEE: What I care about burning in hell? You talk like a fool . . . burning in hell. Why didn't God strike some of them crackers down? Tell me that! That's the question! Don't come telling me this burning-in-hell shit! He a man of God . . . why didn't God strike some of them crackers down? I'll tell you why! I'll tell you the truth! It's sitting out there as plain as day! 'Cause he a white man's God. That's why! God ain't never listened to no nigger's prayers. God take a nigger's prayers and throw them in the garbage. God don't pay niggers no mind. In fact . . . God hate niggers! Hate them with all the fury in his heart. Jesus don't love you, nigger! Jesus hate your black ass! Come talking that shit to me. Talking about burning in hell! God can kiss my ass.

(CUTLER can stand no more. He jumps up and punches LEVEE in the mouth. The force of the blow knocks LEVEE down and CUTLER jumps on him.)

CUTLER: You worthless . . . That's my God! That's my God! That's my God! You wanna blaspheme my God!

(TOLEDO and SLOW DRAG grab CUTLER and try to pull him off LEVEE.)

SLOW DRAG: Come on, Cutler . . . let it go! It don't mean nothing!

(CUTLER has LEVEE down on the floor and pounds on him with a fury.)

CUTLER: Wanna blaspheme my God! You worthless . . . talking about my God!

(TOLEDO and SLOW DRAG succeed in pulling CUTLER off LEVEE, who is bleeding at the nose and mouth.)

LEVEE: Naw, let him go! Let him go!

(He pulls out a knife.)

That's your God, huh? That's your God, huh? Is that right? Your God, huh? All right. I'm gonna give your God a chance. I'm gonna give your God a chance. I'm gonna give him a chance to save your black ass.

(LEVEE circles CUTLER with the knife. CUTLER picks up a chair to protect himself.)

TOLEDO: Come on, Levee . . . put the knife up!

LEVEE: Stay out of this, Toledo!

TOLEDO: That ain't no way to solve nothing.

(LEVEE alternately swipes at CUTLER during the following.)

LEVEE: I'm calling Cutler's God! I'm talking to Cutler's God! You hear me? Cutler's God! I'm calling Cutler's God. Come on and save this nigger! Strike me down before I cut his throat!

SLOW DRAG: Watch him, Cutler! Put that knife up, Levee!

LEVEE: (To CUTLER) I'm calling your God! I'm gonna

give him a chance to save you! I'm calling your God! We gonna find out whose God he is!

CUTLER: You gonna burn in hell, nigger!

LEVEE: Cutler's God! Come on and save this nigger! Come on and save him like you did my mama! Save him like you did my mama! I heard her when she called you! I heard her when she said, "Lord, have mercy! Jesus, help me! Please, God, have mercy on me, Lord Jesus, help me!" And did you turn your back? Did you turn your back, motherfucker? Did you turn your back?

(LEVEE *becomes so caught up in his dialogue with God that he forgets about* CUTLER *and begins to stab upward in the air, trying to reach God.*)

Come on! Come on and turn your back on me! Turn your back on me! Come on! Where is you? Come on and turn your back on me! Turn your back on me, motherfucker! I'll cut your heart out! Come on, turn your back on me! Come on! What's the matter? Where is you? Come on and turn your back on me! Come on, what you scared of? Turn your back on me! Come on! Coward, motherfucker!

(LEVEE *folds his knife and stands triumphantly.*)

Your God ain't shit, Cutler.

(*The lights fade to black.*)

MA RAINEY: (*Singing*)

Ah, you hear me talking to you
I don't bite my tongue
You wants to be my man
You got to fetch it with you when you come.

(*Lights come up in the studio. The last bars of the last song of the session are dying out.*)

IRVIN: (*Over speaker*) Good! Wonderful! We have that, boys. Good session. That's great, Ma. We've got ourselves some winners.

TOLEDO: Well, I'm glad that's over.

MA RAINEY: Slow Drag, where you learn to play the bass at? You had it singing! I heard you! Had that bass jumping all over the place.

SLOW DRAG: I was following Toledo. Nigger got them long fingers striding all over the piano. I was trying to keep up with him.

TOLEDO: That's what you supposed to do, ain't it? Play the music. Ain't nothing abstract about it.

MA RAINEY: Cutler, you hear Slow Drag on that bass? He make it do what he want it to do! Spank it just like you spank a baby.

CUTLER: Don't be telling him that. Nigger's head get so big his hat won't fit him.

SLOW DRAG: If Cutler tune that guitar up, we would really have something!

CUTLER: You wouldn't know what a tuned-up guitar sounded like if you heard one.

TOLEDO: Cutler was talking. I heard him moaning. He was all up in it.

MA RAINEY: Levee . . . what is that you doing? Why you playing all them notes? You play ten notes for every one you supposed to play. It don't call for that.

LEVEE: You supposed to improvise on the theme. That's what I was doing.

MA RAINEY: You supposed to play the song the way I sing it. The way everybody else play it. You ain't supposed to go off by yourself and play what you want.

LEVEE: I was playing the song. I was playing it the way I felt it.

MA RAINEY: I couldn't keep up with what was going on. I'm trying to sing the song and you up there messing up my ear. That's what you was doing. Call yourself playing music.

LEVEE: Hey . . . I know what I'm doing. I know what I'm doing, all right. I know how to play music. You all back up and leave me alone about my music.

CUTLER: I done told you . . . it ain't about *your* music. It's about *Ma's* music.

MA RAINEY: That's all right, Cutler. I done told you what to do.

LEVEE: I don't care what you do. You supposed to improvise on the theme. Not play note for note the same thing over and over again.

MA RAINEY: You just better watch yourself. You hear me?

LEVEE: What I care what you or Cutler do? Come telling me to watch myself. What's that supposed to mean?

MA RAINEY: All right . . . you gonna find out what it means.

LEVEE: Go ahead and fire me. I don't care. I'm gonna get my own band anyway.

MA RAINEY: You keep messing with me.

LEVEE: Ain't nobody studying you. You ain't gonna do nothing to me. Ain't nobody gonna do nothing to Levee.

MA RAINEY: All right, nigger . . . you fired!

LEVEE: You think I care about being fired? I don't care nothing about that. You doing me a favor.

MA RAINEY: Cutler, Levee's out! He don't play in my band no more.

LEVEE: I'm fired . . . Good! Best thing that ever happened to me. I don't need this shit!

(LEVEE *exits to the band room.* IRVIN *enters from the control booth.*)

MA RAINEY: Cutler, I'll see you back at the hotel.

IRVIN: Okay, boys . . . you can pack up. I'll get your money for you.

CUTLER: That's cash money, Mr. Irvin. I don't want no check.

IRVIN: I'll see what I can do. I can't promise you nothing.

CUTLER: As long as it ain't no check. I ain't got no use for a check.

IRVIN: I'll see what I can do, Cutler.

(CUTLER, TOLEDO, *and* SLOW DRAG *exit to the band room.*)

Oh, Ma, listen . . . I talked to Sturdyvant, and he said . . . Now, I tried to talk him out of it . . . He said the best he can do is to take your twenty-five dollars of your money and give it to Sylvester.

MA RAINEY: Take what and do what? If I wanted the boy to have twenty-five dollars of my money, I'd give it to him. He supposed to get his own money. He supposed to get paid like everybody else.

IRVIN: Ma, I talked to him . . . He said . . .

MA RAINEY: Go talk to him again! Tell him if he don't pay that boy, he'll never make another record of mine again. Tell him that. You supposed to be my manager. All this talk about sticking together. Start sticking! Go on up there and get that boy his money!

IRVIN: Okay, Ma . . . I'll talk to him again. I'll see what I can do.

MA RAINEY: Ain't no see about it! You bring that boy's money back here!

(IRVIN *exits. The lights stay on in the studio and come up in the band room. The men have their instruments packed and sit waiting for* IRVIN *to come and pay them.* SLOW DRAG *has a pack of cards.*)

SLOW DRAG: Come on, Levee, let me show you a card trick.

LEVEE: I don't want to see no card trick. What you wanna show me for? Why you wanna bother me with that?

SLOW DRAG: I was just trying to be nice.

LEVEE: I don't need you to be nice to me. What I need you to be nice to me for? I ain't gonna be nice to you. I ain't even gonna let you be in my band no more.

SLOW DRAG: Toledo, let me show you a card trick.

CUTLER: I just hope Mr. Irvin don't bring no check down here. What the hell I'm gonna do with a check?

SLOW DRAG: All right now . . . pick a card. Any card . . . go on . . . take any of them. I'm gonna show you something.

TOLEDO: I agrees with you, Cutler. I don't want no check either.

CUTLER: It don't make no sense to give a nigger a check.

SLOW DRAG: Okay, now. Remember your card. Remember which one you got. Now . . . put it back in the deck. Anywhere you want. I'm gonna show you something.

(TOLEDO *puts the card in the deck.*)

You remember your card? All right. Now I'm gonna shuffle the deck. Now . . . I'm gonna show you what card you picked. Don't say nothing now. I'm gonna tell you what card you picked.

CUTLER: Slow Drag, that trick is as old as my mama.

SLOW DRAG: Naw, naw . . . wait a minute! I'm gonna show him his card . . . There it go! The six of diamonds. Ain't that your card? Ain't that it?

TOLEDO: Yeah, that's it . . . the six of diamonds.

SLOW DRAG: Told you! Told you I'd show him what it was!

(*The lights fade in the band room and come up full on the studio.* STURDYVANT *enters with* IRVIN.)

STURDYVANT: Ma, is there something wrong? Is there a problem?

MA RAINEY: Sturdyvant, I want you to pay that boy his money.

STURDYVANT: Sure, Ma. I got it right here. Two hundred for you and twenty-five for the kid, right?

(STURDYVANT *hands the money to* IRVIN, *who hands it to* MA RAINEY *and* SYLVESTER.)

Irvin misunderstood me. It was all a mistake. Irv made a mistake.

MA RAINEY: A mistake, huh?

IRVIN: Sure, Ma. I made a mistake. He's paid, right? I straightened it out.

MA RAINEY: The only mistake was when you found out I hadn't signed the release forms. That was the mistake. Come on, Sylvester.

(*She starts to exit.*)

STURDYVANT: Hey, Ma . . . come on, sign the forms, huh?

IRVIN: Ma . . . come on now.

MA RAINEY: Get your coat, Sylvester. Irvin, where's my car?

IRVIN: It's right out front, Ma. Here . . . I got the keys right here. Come on, sign the forms, huh?

MA RAINEY: Irvin, give me my car keys!

IRVIN: Sure, Ma . . . just sign the forms, huh?

(*He gives her the keys, expecting a trade-off.*)

MA RAINEY: Send them to my address and I'll get around to them.

IRVIN: Come on, Ma . . . I took care of everything, right? I straightened everything out.

MA RAINEY: Give me the pen, Irvin.

(*She signs the forms.*)

You tell Sturdyvant . . . one more mistake like that and I can make my records someplace else.

(*She turns to exit.*)

Sylvester, straighten up your clothes. Come on, Dussie Mae.

(She exits, followed by DUSSIE MAE *and* SYLVESTER. *The lights go down in the studio and come up on the band room.)*

CUTLER: I know what's keeping him so long. He up there writing out checks. You watch. I ain't gonna stand for it. He ain't gonna bring me no check down here. If he do, he's gonna take it right back upstairs and get some cash.

TOLEDO: Don't get yourself all worked up about it. Wait and see. Think positive.

CUTLER: I am thinking positive. He positively gonna give me some cash. Man give me a check last time . . . you remember . . . we went all over Chicago trying to get it cashed. See a nigger with a check, the first thing they think is he done stole it someplace.

LEVEE: I ain't had no trouble cashing mine.

CUTLER: I don't visit no whorehouses.

LEVEE: You don't know about my business. So don't start nothing. I'm tired of you as it is. I ain't but two seconds off your ass no way.

TOLEDO: Don't you all start nothing now.

CUTLER: What the hell I care what you tired of. I wasn't even talking to you. I was talking to this man right here.

*(*IRVIN *and* STURDYVANT *enter.)*

IRVIN: Okay boys. Mr. Sturdyvant has your pay.

CUTLER: As long as it's cash money, Mr. Sturdyvant. 'Cause I have too much trouble trying to cash a check.

STURDYVANT: Oh, yes . . . I'm aware of that. Mr. Irvin told me you boys prefer cash, and that's what I have for you.

(He starts handing out the money.)

That was a good session you boys put in . . . That's twenty-five for you. Yessir, you boys really know your business and we are going to . . . Twenty-five for you . . . We are going to get you back in here real soon . . . twenty-five . . . and have another session so you can make some more money . . . and twenty-five for you. Okay, thank you, boys. You can get your things together and Mr. Irvin will make sure you find your way out.

IRVIN: I'll be out front when you get your things together, Cutler.

*(*IRVIN *exits.* STURDYVANT *starts to follow.)*

LEVEE: Mr. Sturdyvant, sir. About them songs I give you? . . .

STURDYVANT: Oh, yes, . . . uh . . . Levee. About them songs you gave me. I've thought about it and I just don't think the people will buy them. They're not the type of songs we're looking for.

LEVEE: Mr. Sturdyvant, sir . . . I done got my band

picked out and they's real good fellows. They knows how to play real good. I know if the peoples hear the music, they'll buy it.

STURDYVANT: Well, Levee, I'll be fair with you . . . but they're just not the right songs.

LEVEE: Mr. Sturdyvant, you got to understand about that music. That music is what the people is looking for. They's tired of jug-band music. They wants something that excites them. Something with some fire to it.

STURDYVANT: Okay, Levee. I'll tell you what I'll do. I'll give you five dollars a piece for them. Now that's the best I can do.

LEVEE: I don't want no five dollars, Mr. Sturdyvant. I wants to record them songs, like you say.

STURDYVANT: Well, Levee, like I say . . . they just aren't the kind of songs we're looking for.

LEVEE: Mr. Sturdyvant, you asked me to write them songs. Now, why didn't you tell me that before when I first give them to you? You told me you was gonna let me record them. What's the difference between then and now?

STURDYVANT: Well, look . . . I'll pay you for your trouble . . .

LEVEE: What's the difference, Mr. Sturdyvant? That's what I wanna know.

STURDYVANT: I had my fellows play your songs, and when I heard them, they just didn't sound like the kind of songs I'm looking for right now.

LEVEE: You got to hear *me* play them, Mr. Sturdyvant! You ain't heard *me* play them. That's what's gonna make them sound right.

STURDYVANT: Well, Levee, I don't doubt that really. It's just that . . . well, I don't thnk they'd sell like Ma's records. But I'll take them off your hands for you.

LEVEE: The people's tired of jug-band music, Mr. Sturdyvant. They wants something that's gonna excite them! They wants something with some fire! I don't know what fellows you had playing them songs . . . but if I could play them! I'd set them down in the people's lap! Now you told me I could record them songs!

STURDYVANT: Well, there's nothing I can do about that. Like I say, it's five dollars a piece. That's what I'll give you. I'm doing you a favor. Now, if you write any more, I'll help you out and take them off your hands. The price is five dollars apiece. Just like now.

(He attempts to hand LEVEE *the money, finally shoves it in* LEVEE's *coat pocket and is gone in a flash.* LEVEE *follows him to the door and it slams in his face. He takes the money from his pocket, balls it up and throws it on the floor. The other musicians silently gather up their belongings.* TOLEDO *walks past* LEVEE *and steps on his shoe.)*

LEVEE: Hey! Watch it . . . Shit Toledo! You stepped on my shoe!

TOLEDO: Excuse me there, Levee.

LEVEE: Look at that! Look at that! Nigger, you stepped on my shoe. What you do that for?

TOLEDO: I said I'm sorry.

LEVEE: Nigger gonna step on my goddamn shoe! You done fucked up my shoe! Look at that! Look at what you done to my shoe, nigger! I ain't stepped on your shoe! What you wanna step on my shoe for?

CUTLER: The man said he's sorry.

LEVEE: Sorry! How the hell he gonna be sorry after he gone ruin my shoe? Come talking about sorry!

(Turns his attention back to TOLEDO.*)*

Nigger, you stepped on my shoe! You know that!

*(*LEVEE *snatches his shoe off his foot and holds it up for* TOLEDO *to see.)*

See what you done done?

TOLEDO: What you want me to do about it? It's done now. I said excuse me.

LEVEE: Wanna go and fuck up my shoe like that. I ain't done nothing to your shoe. Look at this!

*(*TOLEDO *turns and continues to gather up his things.* LEVEE *spins him around by his shoulder.)*

LEVEE: Naw . . . naw . . . look what you done!

(He shoves the shoe in TOLEDO's *face.)*

Look at that! That's my shoe! Look at that! You did it! You did it! You fucked up my shoe! You stepped on my shoe with them raggedy-ass clodhoppers!

TOLEDO: Nigger, ain't nobody studying you and your shoe! I said excuse me. If you can't accept that, then the hell with it. What you want me to do?

*(*LEVEE *is in a near rage, breathing hard. He is trying to get a grip on himself, as even he senses, or perhaps only he senses, he is about to lose control. He looks around, uncertain of what to do.* TOLEDO *has gone back to packing, as have* CUTLER *and* SLOW DRAG. *They purposefully*

avoid looking at LEVEE *in hopes he'll calm down if he doesn't have an audience. All the weight in the world suddenly falls on* LEVEE *and he rushes at* TOLEDO *with his knife in his hand.)*

LEVEE: Nigger, you stepped on my shoe!

(He plunges the knife into TOLEDO's *back up to the hilt.* TOLEDO *lets out a sound of surprise and agony.* CUTLER *and* SLOW DRAG *freeze.* TOLEDO *falls backward with* LEVEE, *his hand still on the knife, holding him up.* LEVEE *is suddenly faced with the realization of what he has done. He shoves* TOLEDO *forward and takes a step back.* TOLEDO *slumps to the floor.)*

He . . . he stepped on my shoe. He did. Honest, Cutler, he stepped on my shoe. What he do that for? Toledo, what you do that for? Cutler, help me. He stepped on my shoe, Cutler.

(He turns his attention to TOLEDO.*)*

Toledo! Toledo, get up.

(He crosses to TOLEDO *and tries to pick him up.)*

It's okay, Toledo. Come on . . . I'll help you. Come on, stand up now. Levee'll help you.

*(*TOLEDO *is limp and heavy and awkward. He slumps back to the floor.* LEVEE *gets mad at him.)*

Don't look at me like that! Toledo! Nigger, don't look at me like that! I'm warning you, nigger! Close your eyes! Don't you look at me like that! (He turns to CUTLER) Tell him to close his eyes. Cutler. Tell him don't look at me like that.

CUTLER: Slow Drag, get Mr. Irvin down here.

(The sound of a trumpet is heard, LEVEE's *trumpet, a muted trumpet struggling for the highest of possibilities and blowing pain and warning.)*
(Black out.)

Figure 1. Irvin (Lou Criscuolo) cringingly tries to placate Ma Rainey (Theresa Merrit), while Toledo (Robert Judd), Cutler (Joe Seneca, *partly hidden*), and Sturdyvant (Richard M. Davidson) listen to Ma's complaints in the Yale Repertory Theatre production of *Ma Rainey's Black Bottom,* directed by Lloyd Richards, 1984. (Photograph: William B. Carter.)

Figure 2. Levee (Charles S. Dutton) dances and sings a jazz tune—"Hello Central give me Doctor Jazz"—accompanied by Slow Drag (Leonard Jackson), while Toledo (Robert Judd) tries to convince Cutler (Joe Seneca) that "Good times got more niggers killed than God got ways to count" in the Yale Repertory Theatre production of *Ma Rainey's Black Bottom,* directed by Lloyd Richards, 1984. (Photograph: William B. Carter.)

Staging of *Ma Rainey's Black Bottom*

**REVIEW OF THE YALE REPERTORY THEATRE
PRODUCTION, 1984, BY FRANK RICH**

Late in Act I of *Ma Rainey's Black Bottom,* a somber, aging band trombonist (Joe Seneca) tilts his head heavenward to sing the blues. The setting is a dilapidated Chicago recording studio of 1927, and the song sounds as old as time. "If I had my way," goes the lyric, "I would tear this old building down."

Once the play has ended, that lyric has almost become a prophecy. In *Ma Rainey's Black Bottom,* the writer August Wilson sends the entire history of black America crashing down upon our heads. This play is a searing inside account of what white racism does to its victims— and it floats on the same authentic artistry as the blues music it celebrates. Harrowing as *Ma Rainey's* can be, it is also funny, salty, carnal and lyrical. Like his real-life heroine, the legendary singer Gertrude (Ma) Rainey, Mr. Wilson articulates a legacy of unspeakable agony and rage in a spellbinding voice.

The play is Mr. Wilson's first to arrive in New York, and it reached here, via the Yale Repertory Theatre, under the sensitive hand of the man who was born to direct it, Lloyd Richards. On Broadway, Mr. Richards has honed *Ma Rainey's* to its finest form. What's more, the director brings us an exciting young actor—Charles S. Dutton—along with his extraordinary dramatist. One wonders if the electricity at the Cort is the same that audiences felt when Mr. Richards, Lorraine Hansberry and Sidney Poitier stormed into Broadway with *A Raisin in the Sun* a quarter-century ago.

As *Ma Rainey's* shares its director and Chicago setting with *Raisin,* so it builds on Hansberry's themes: Mr. Wilson's characters want to make it in white America. And, to a degree, they have. Ma Rainey (1886–1939) was among the first black singers to get a recording contract—albeit with a white company's "race" division. Mr. Wilson gives us Ma (Theresa Merritt) at the height of her fame. A mountain of glitter and feathers, she has become a despotic, temperamental star, complete with a retinue of flunkies, a fancy car and a kept young lesbian lover.

The evening's framework is a Paramount-label recording session that actually happened, but whose details and supporting players have been invented by the author. As the action swings between the studio and the band's warm-up room—designed by Charles Henry McClennahan as if they might be the festering last-chance saloon of *The Iceman Cometh*—Ma and her four accompanying musicians overcome various mishaps to record "Ma Rainey's Black Bottom" and other songs. During the delays, the band members smoke reefers, joke around and reminisce about past gigs on a well-

traveled road stretching through whorehouses and church socials from New Orleans to Fat Back, Ark.

The musicians' speeches are like improvised band solos—variously fizzy, haunting and mournful. We hear how the bassist Slow Drag (Leonard Jackson) got his nickname at a dance contest, but also about how a black preacher was tortured by being forced to "dance" by a white vigilante's gun. Gradually, we come to know these men, from their elusive pipe dreams to their hidden scars, but so deftly are the verbal riffs orchestrated that we don't immediately notice the incendiary drama boiling underneath.

That drama is ignited by a conflict between Ma and her young trumpeter Levee, played by Mr. Dutton. An ambitious sport eager to form his own jazz band, Levee mocks his employer's old "jugband music" and champions the new dance music that has just begun to usurp the blues among black audiences in the urban North. Already Levee has challenged Ma by writing a swinging version of "Ma Rainey's Black Bottom" that he expects the record company to use in place of the singer's traditional arrangement.

Yet even as the battle is joined between emblematic representatives of two generations of black music, we're thrust into a more profound war about identity. The African nationalist among the musicians, the pianist Toledo (Robert Judd), argues that, "We done sold ourselves to the white man in order to be like him." We soon realize that, while Ma's music is from the heart, her life has become a sad, ludicrous "imitation" of white stardom. Levee's music is soulful, too, but his ideal of success is having his "name in lights"; his pride is invested in the new shoes on which he's blown a week's pay.

Ma, at least, senses the limits of her success. Though she acts as if she owns the studio, she can't hail a cab in the white city beyond. She knows that her clout with the record company begins and ends with her viability as a commercial product: "When I've finished recording," she says, "it's just like I'd been some whore, and they roll over and put their pants on." Levee, by contrast, has yet to learn that a black man can't name his own terms if he's going to sell his music to a white world. As he plots his future career, he deceives himself into believing that a shoeshine and Uncle Tom smile will win white backers for his schemes.

Inevitably, the promised door of opportunity slams, quite literally, in Levee's face, and the sound has a violent ring that reverberates through the decades. Levee must confront not just the collapse of his hopes but the destruction of his dignity. Having played the white man's game and lost to its rigged rules, he is left with less than nothing: Even as he fails to sell himself to whites, Levee has sold out his own sense of self-worth.

Mr. Dutton's delineation of this tragic downfall is red-hot. A burly actor a year out of Yale, he is at first as jazzy as his music. With his boisterous wisecracks and jumpy sprinter's stance, he seems ready to leap into the stratosphere envisioned in his fantasies of glory. But once he crash lands, the poison of self-hatred ravages his massive body and distorts his thundering voice. No longer able to channel his anger into his music, he directs it to God, crying out that a black man's prayers are doomed to be tossed "into the garbage." As Mr. Dutton careens about with unchecked, ever escalating turbulence, he transforms an anonymous Chicago bandroom into a burial ground for a race's aspirations.

Mr. Dutton's fellow band members are a miraculous double-threat ensemble: They play their instruments nearly as convincingly as they spin their juicy monologues. Aleta Mitchell and Lou Criscuolo, as Ma's gum-chewing lover and harried white manager, are just right, and so is Scott Davenport-Richards, as Ma's erstwhile Little Lord Fauntleroy of a young nephew. It's one of the evening's more grotesquely amusing gags that Ma imperiously insists on having the boy, a chronic stutterer, recite a spoken introduction on her record.

Miss Merritt is Ma Rainey incarnate. A singing actress of both wit and power, she finds bitter humor in the character's distorted sense of self: When she barks her outrageous demands to her lackeys, we see a show business monster who's come a long way from her roots. Yet the roots can still be unearthed. In a rare reflective moment, she explains why she sings the blues. "You don't sing to feel better," Miss Merritt says tenderly. "You sing because that's a way of understanding life."

The lines might also apply to the play's author. Mr. Wilson can't mend the broken lives he unravels in *Ma Rainey's Black Bottom*. But, like his heroine, he makes their suffering into art that forces us to understand and won't allow us to forget.

DAVID HENRY HWANG

1957–

"Study your face and you will see—the shape of your face is the shape of faces back many generations—across an ocean, in another soil. You must become one with your family before you can hope to live away from it." In these haunting lines from David Henry Hwang's third play, a native Chinese character speaking to his Chinese-American great-nephew defines one of the central problems of identity that have perenially vexed immigrants and children of immigrants— the problem of how to honor one's ethnic heritage while at the same time making a new life in a new land. Hwang (pronounced "Wong"), a first-gener-ation Chinese-American, has explored such problems in a series of plays, each offering a slightly different perspective on the central question of constructing and maintaining one's identity, culminating in the award-winning *M. Butterfly* (1988). Hwang's parents were both born in China, his father emigrating to Los Angeles in the late 1940s to study business at the University of Southern California, his mother arriving in 1952 to study music. His father worked first as an accountant and then went into business for himself, eventually founding the first federally chartered Asian-American bank in the United States. Such notable business success led to almost complete assimilation for the children, all born in America; they studied Chinese for a while but then were withdrawn from those classes. Hwang took violin lessons, participated in debate competition at his private school, and entered Stanford University with plans to study law.

While at Stanford, Hwang became interested in writing plays, despite minimal theatrical experience, and switched his major to English. He saw Sam Shepard's new plays as they were produced at the San Francisco Magic Theater, spent the summer of 1977 working odd jobs in a theater, and in 1978, signed up for a playwriting workshop run by Sam Shepard. As a result, he drafted his first play, *FOB*, which was then produced by his Stanford dormitory as part of a campus festival of student-written plays. He also sent *FOB* to the 1979 Playwrights' Conference at the O'Neill Theater Center in Waterford, Connecticut, where it became one of the twelve selected for development. A year later, in June 1980, Joseph Papp produced *FOB* at the New York Shakespeare Festival Public Theater, thus beginning an association that would last for three years, during which Hwang saw five plays produced in New York.

FOB (the initials stand for "Fresh Off the Boat" in Hwang's play, as well as for "Free on Board" in standard shipping terminology) embodies many of the issues that dominate Hwang's writing. Most centrally, the play dramatizes the question of how Chinese-Americans cope with their various "faces." Each of the play's three characters represents a different stage in the process of cultural mixing and therefore a different balance of the dual heritage: Steve, the FOB, son of a wealthy Hong Kong souvenir manufacturer, has just arrived in Los Angeles; Grace, a first-generation Chinese-American, works in a Chinese res-taurant; and Dale, Grace's cousin, a second-generation American of Chinese descent, calls himself an ABC ("American Born Chinese") and despises all FOBs. Yet Hwang asks the audience to see that Dale's verbal attack on Steve is part of his desperate attempt to assimilate—"To not be a Chinese, a yellow, a slant, a gook." Faced with a heritage he cannot escape, in a world he wishes to join, Dale mocks Steve's accent, dumps a bottle of hot sauce all over Steve's food, and competes with Steve for Grace's attention. But in addition to the rivalry over Grace, which is depicted primarily in realistic confrontations, Hwang also presents a symbolic conflict between Grace and Steve staged as a ritual battle. Grace takes on the persona of Fa Mu Lan, the Chinese woman warrior, while Steve assumes the persona of Gwan Gung, the god of fighters and writers. Grace follows her victory over Steve with a peace-offering of Chinese food, the same food Steve asked for at the play's beginning, and then, in a swift return to the play's more realistic mode, invites Steve out for an evening of dancing.

While *FOB* ends with a staged battle, Hwang's second play, *The Dance and the Railroad* (1981), is concerned with performance as a way of accepting one's heritage. Set in 1867, on a mountaintop near the transcontinental railroad, the play presents just two characters: Lone, a dancer from the Chinese Opera, working as a railroad builder, and Ma, who has been in the country for four weeks and is also working on the railroad. By juxtaposing the highly disciplined and ritualistic world of Chinese opera with the unlikely setting of the American West, Hwang underscores Lone's intense commitment to his Chinese heritage. Ma, at first a naïve newcomer (another FOB), gradually wins Lone's respect, and in the play's final scene the two men stage their own "opera," with Ma as the hero.

Though Hwang's third play, *Family Devotions* (1981) also explores issues of Chinese and American identity, it draws much more directly on details from Hwang's own life: a prosperous Southern California setting, a Chinese-American banker, his violinist son, and elderly relations who, like Hwang's own family, are "born-again Christians." The vivid portrayal of the opulent California lifestyle, complete with sunroom, barbecue grill, and tennis courts, is replete with satiric detail, including an opening scene in which characters find the barbecue grill smoking and toss a series of burnt chickens all over the tennis court. As in his earlier plays, Hwang creates confrontations between figures who differ in their affiliation to their shared past. Di-Gou, a resident of the People's Republic of China, has come to California to bring his older sisters back to China. By exposing an unpleasant truth about their aunt See-Goh-Poh, who has become a legend through her status as a Christian missionary, Di-Gou tries to pull his sisters back to their common Chinese heritage, but the shock kills them. Perhaps there is hope only for the younger generation since, at the play's end, Chester, the violinist about to leave for Boston, stands in the same spotlight that singled out his great-uncle Di-Gou at the play's beginning. And, just as Di-Gou argued that "the shape of your face is the shape of faces back many generations," so Hwang's final stage direction reads "the shape of Chester's face begins to change."

Hwang's plays not only probe his own life as a Chinese-American but celebrate his rediscovery of the traditions of Oriental theater. While creating *The Dance and the Railroad*, Hwang drew on the extensive background in traditional Chinese dance and theater of his actors, John Lone (who appeared as Steve in the New York production of *FOB*) and Tzi Ma; so crucial was their special training that he named the characters for these actors. Likewise, in *The Sound of a Voice*, a one-act play about "a warrior who goes into the woods to kill a witch and winds up falling in love with her," Hwang originally imagined the Woman as an *onnagata* role, that is, to be played, as in Kabuki theater, by a man who specializes in playing women's roles. Although eventually an actress played the Woman, Hwang's intention creates double meanings throughout the text; the warrior's first line is "You are very kind to take me in" while near the end of the play the Woman demonstrates her ability to handle a sword and then apologizes by saying, "My skills—they're so—inappropriate. I look like a man."

So when Hwang heard what one might call a real-life *onnagata* story, involving a French diplomat and a performer from the Peking Opera, he found a situation that poignantly embodied many of his long-standing preoccupations with identity. In the Afterword to *M. Butterfly* (reprinted following the play), Hwang wonders "What did Bouriscot [the diplomat] think he was getting in this Chinese actress?" And his answer is "He probably thought he had found Madame Butterfly," or, as Hwang explains "the submissive Oriental number." In deconstructing the story that Puccini's opera has made world famous—the story of the ill-fated romance between Pinkerton, an American naval officer, and Butterfly, a young Japanese woman whom Pinkerton buys as a wife, impregnates, and then deserts—Hwang investigates yet again the question "What is the relationship between the Oriental and the Westerner?" But instead of working from the point of view of the Asian-American, who feels split between two worlds, Hwang suggests that the image of the Oriental is actually a deeply held cultural construction that reveals Western desires and fears. Gallimard (the renamed Bouriscot) falls in love with Song Liling as Butterfly—their first meeting comes after a performance of Butterfly's death scene—and tells his story to the audience in a desperate wish to rewrite the story, "always searching for a new ending . . . where she returns at last to my arms."

The unique theatricality of the play and its constant juxtaposing of "performance" and "reality" in the story of Gallimard were stunningly realized on stage in the original production directed by John Dexter. Eiko Ishioka's design surrounded the black rectangular central acting area with a curved ramp, swirling across and around the stage (see Figure 1). Clive Barnes, writing in the *New York Post*, called it "a runway equally fit for an Oriental queen or even Hollywood's Rita Hayworth," and indeed to many viewers, the ramp recalled the Japanese *hanamichi* (a long entrance platform in Kabuki theater) as well as the more Western version often used by strippers. The ornate costumes associated with Oriental theater and with Western opera (see Figure 2) made Song Liling a striking figure. In fact, even when not performing Butterfly, Song's attire seems to recall the suave elegance of Anna May Wong, a Chinese-American actress familiar to thousands of Americans through her appearance in Hollywood films (see Figure 3). By emphasizing the appealing exoticism of Song Liling's world, Hwang, Dexter, and Ishioka put the audience in the position of the protagonist, Gallimard. The gorgeous costumes, the choreographed movement, the music (both Oriental and Western) all work to seduce the audience so that Gallimard's surprising betrayal is ultimately ours as well.

M. BUTTERFLY

BY DAVID HENRY HWANG

CHARACTERS

RENE GALLIMARD
SONG LILING
MARC/MAN #2/CONSUL SHARPLESS
RENEE/WOMAN AT PARTY/GIRL IN MAGAZINE
COMRADE CHIN/SUZUKI/SHU FANG
HELGA
M. TOULON/MAN #1/JUDGE
KUROGO [dancers/stagehands]

PLAYWRIGHT'S NOTES

A former French diplomat and a Chinese opera singer have been sentenced to six years in jail for spying for China after a two-day trial that traced a story of clandestine love and mistaken sexual identity. . . . Mr. Bouriscot was accused of passing information to China after he fell in love with Mr. Shi, whom he believed for twenty years to be a woman.

—The New York Times, May 11, 1986

This play was suggested by international newspaper accounts of a recent espionage trial. For purposes of dramatization, names have been changed, characters created, and incidents devised or altered, and this play does not purport to be a factual record of real events or real people.

I could escape this feeling
With my China girl . . .

—David Bowie & Iggy Pop

SETTING

The action of the play takes place in a Paris prison in the present, and in recall, during the decade 1960 to 1970 in Beijing, and from 1966 to the present in Paris.

ACT 1 / SCENE 1

(M. GALLIMARD's prison cell. Paris. Present.)
(Lights fade up to reveal RENE GALLIMARD, 65, in a prison cell. He wears a comfortable bathrobe, and looks old and tired. The sparsely furnished cell contains a wooden crate upon which sits a hot plate with a kettle, and a portable tape recorder. GALLIMARD sits on the crate staring at the recorder, a sad smile on his face.

Upstage SONG, who appears as a beautiful woman in traditional Chinese garb, dances a traditional piece from the Peking Opera, surrounded by the percussive clatter of Chinese music.

Then, slowly, lights and sound cross-fade; the Chinese opera music dissolves into a Western opera, the "Love Duet" from Puccini's Madame Butterfly. SONG continues dancing, now to the Western accompaniment. Though her movements are the same, the difference in music now gives them a balletic quality.

GALLIMARD rises, and turns upstage towards the figure of SONG, who dances without acknowledging him.)

GALLIMARD: Butterfly, Butterfly . . .

(He forces himself to turn away, as the image of SONG fades out, and talks to us.)

GALLIMARD: The limits of my cell are as such: four-and-a-half meters by five. There's one window against the far wall; a door, very strong, to protect me from autograph hounds. I'm responsible for the tape recorder, the hot plate, and this charming coffee table.

When I want to eat, I'm marched off to the dining room—hot, steaming slop appears on my plate. When I want to sleep, the light bulb turns itself off—the work of fairies. It's an enchanted space I occupy. The French—we know how to run a prison.

But, to be honest, I'm not treated like an ordinary prisoner. Why? Because I'm a celebrity. You see, I make people laugh.

I never dreamed this day would arrive. I've never been considered witty or clever. In fact, as a young boy, in an informal poll among my grammar school classmates, I was voted "least likely to be invited to a party." It's a title I managed to hold on to for many years. Despite some stiff competition.

But now, how the tables turn! Look at me: the life of every social function in Paris. Paris? Why be modest? My fame has spread to Amsterdam, London, New York. Listen to them! In the world's smartest parlors. I'm the one who lifts their spirits!

(With a flourish, GALLIMARD directs our attention to another part of the stage.)

ACT 1 / SCENE 2

(A party. Present.)
(Lights go up on a chic-looking parlor, where a well-

dressed trio, two men and one woman, make conversation.
GALLIMARD *also remains lit; he observes them from his cell.*)

WOMAN: And what of Gallimard?
MAN 1: Gallimard?
MAN 2: Gallimard!
GALLIMARD (*To us*): You see? They're all determined to say my name, as if it were some new dance.
WOMAN: He still claims not to believe the truth.
MAN 1: What? Still? Even since the trial?
WOMAN: Yes. Isn't it mad?
MAN 2 (*Laughing*): He says . . . it was dark . . . and she was very modest!

(*The trio break into laughter.*)

MAN 1: So—what? He never touched her with his hands?
MAN 2: Perhaps he did, and simply misidentified the equipment. A compelling case for sex education in the schools.
WOMAN: To protect the National Security—the Church can't argue with that.
MAN 1: That's impossible! How could he not know?
MAN 2: Simple ignorance.
MAN 1: For twenty years?
MAN 2: Time flies when you're being stupid.
WOMAN: Well, I thought the French were ladies' men.
MAN 2: It seems Monsieur Gallimard was overly anxious to live up to his national reputation.
WOMAN: Well, he's not very good-looking.
MAN 1: No, he's not.
MAN 2: Certainly not.
WOMAN: Actually, I feel sorry for him.
MAN 2: A toast! To Monsieur Gallimard!
WOMAN: Yes! To Gallimard!
MAN 1: To Gallimard!
MAN 2: Vive la différence!

(*They toast, laughing. Lights down on them.*)

ACT 1 / SCENE 3

(M. GALLIMARD's *cell.*)

GALLIMARD (*Smiling*): You see? They toast me. I've become patron saint of the socially inept. Can they really be so foolish? Men like that—they should be scratching at my door, begging to learn my secrets! For I, Rene Gallimard, you see, I have known, and been loved by . . . the Perfect Woman.
     Alone in this cell, I sit night after night, watching our story play through my head, always searching for a new ending, one which redeems my honor, where she returns at last to my arms. And I imagine you—my ideal audience—who come to understand and even, perhaps just a little, to envy me.

(*He turns on his tape recorder. Over the house speakers, we hear the opening phrases of* Madame Butterfly.)

GALLIMARD: In order for you to understand what I did and why, I must introduce you to my favorite opera: *Madame Butterfly*. By Giacomo Puccini. First produced at La Scala, Milan, in 1904, it is now beloved throughout the Western world.

(*As* GALLIMARD *describes the opera, the tape segues in and out to sections he may be describing.*)

GALLIMARD: And why not? Its heroine, Cio-Cio-San, also known as Butterfly, is a feminine ideal, beautiful and brave. And its hero, the man for whom she gives up everything, is—(*He pulls out a naval officer's cap from under his crate, pops it on his head, and struts about*)—not very good-looking, not too bright, and pretty much a wimp: Benjamin Franklin Pinkerton of the U.S. Navy. As the curtain rises, he's just closed on two great bargains: one on a house, the other on a woman—call it a package deal.
     Pinkerton purchased the rights to Butterfly for one hundred yen—in modern currency, equivalent to about . . . sixty-six cents. So, he's feeling pretty pleased with himself as Sharpless, the American consul, arrives to witness the marriage.

(MARC, *wearing an official cap to designate* SHARPLESS, *enters and plays the character.*)

SHARPLESS/MARC: Pinkerton!
PINKERTON/GALLIMARD: Sharpless! How's it hangin'? It's a great day, just great. Between my house, my wife, and the rickshaw ride in from town, I've saved nineteen cents just this morning.
SHARPLESS: Wonderful. I can see the inscription on your tombstone already: "I saved a dollar, here I lie." (*He looks around*) Nice house.
PINKERTON: It's artistic. Artistic, don't you think? Like the way the shoji screens slide open to reveal the wet bar and disco mirror ball? Classy, huh? Great for impressing the chicks.
SHARPLESS: "Chicks"? Pinkerton, you're going to be a married man!
PINKERTON: Well, sort of.
SHARPLESS: What do you mean?
PINKERTON: This country—Sharpless, it is okay. You got all these geisha girls running around—
SHARPLESS: I know! I live here!
PINKERTON: Then, you know the marriage laws, right? I split for one month, it's annulled!
SHARPLESS: Leave it to you to read the fine print. Who's the lucky girl?
PINKERTON: Cio-Cio-San. Her friends call her Butterfly. Sharpless, she eats out of my hand!
SHARPLESS: She's probably very hungry.
PINKERTON: Not like American girls. It's true what they say about Oriental girls. They want to be treated bad!
SHARPLESS: Oh, please!
PINKERTON: It's true!
SHARPLESS: Are you serious about this girl?

PINKERTON: I'm marrying her, aren't I?

SHARPLESS: Yes—with generous trade-in terms.

PINKERTON: When I leave, she'll know what it's like to have loved a real man. And I'll even buy her a few nylons.

SHARPLESS: You aren't planning to take her with you?

PINKERTON: Huh? Where?

SHARPLESS: Home!

PINKERTON: You mean, America? Are you crazy? Can you see her trying to buy rice in St. Louis?

SHARPLESS: So, you're not serious.

(Pause.)

PINKERTON/GALLIMARD *(As* PINKERTON*)*: Consul, I am a sailor in port. *(As* GALLIMARD*)* They then proceed to sing the famous duet, "The Whole World Over."

(The duet plays on the speakers. GALLIMARD, *as* PINKERTON, *lip-syncs his lines from the opera.)*

GALLIMARD: To give a rough translation: "The whole world over, the Yankee travels, casting his anchor wherever he wants. Life's not worth living unless he can win the hearts of the fairest maidens, then hotfoot it off the premises ASAP." *(He turns towards* MARC*)* In the preceding scene, I played Pinkerton, the womanizing cad, and my friend Marc from school . . . *(*MARC *bows grandly for our benefit)* played Sharpless, the sensitive soul of reason. In life, however, our positions were usually—no, always—reversed.

ACT 1 / SCENE 4

(Ecole Nationale. Aix-en-Provence. 1947.)

GALLIMARD: No, Marc, I think I'd rather stay home.

MARC: Are you crazy?! We are going to Dad's condo in Marseilles! You know what happened last time?

GALLIMARD: Of course I do.

MARC: Of course you don't! You never know. . . . They stripped, Rene!

GALLIMARD: Who stripped?

MARC: The girls!

GALLIMARD: Girls? Who said anything about girls?

MARC: Rene, we're a buncha university guys goin' up to the woods. What are we gonna do—talk philosophy?

GALLIMARD: What girls? Where do you get them?

MARC: Who cares? The point is, they come. On trucks. Packed in like sardines. The back flips open, babes hop out, we're ready to roll.

GALLIMARD: You mean, they just—?

MARC: Before you know it, every last one of them—they're stripped and splashing around my pool. There's no moon out, they can't see what's going on, their boobs are flapping, right? You close your eyes, reach out—it's grab bag, get it? Doesn't matter whose ass is between whose legs, whose teeth are

sinking into who. You're just in there, going at it, eyes closed, on and on for as long as you can stand. *(Pause)* Some fun, huh?

GALLIMARD: What happens in the morning?

MARC: In the morning, you're ready to talk some philosophy. *(Beat)* So how 'bout it?

GALLIMARD: Marc, I can't . . . I'm afraid they'll say no—the girls. So I never ask.

MARC: You don't have to ask! That's the beauty—don't you see? They don't have to say yes. It's perfect for a guy like you, really.

GALLIMARD: You go ahead . . . I may come later.

MARC: Hey, Rene—it doesn't matter that you're clumsy and got zits—they're not looking!

GALLIMARD: Thank you very much.

MARC: Wimp.

*(*MARC *walks over to the other side of the stage, and starts waving and smiling at women in the audience.)*

GALLIMARD *(To us)*: We now return to my version of *Madame Butterfly* and the events leading to my recent conviction for treason.

*(*GALLIMARD *notices* MARC *making lewd gestures.)*

GALLIMARD: Marc, what are you doing?

MARC: Huh? *(Sotto voce)* Rene, there's a lotta great babes out there. They're probably lookin' at me and thinking, "What a dangerous guy."

GALLIMARD: Yes—how could they help but be impressed by your cool sophistication?

*(*GALLIMARD *pops the* SHARPLESS *cap on* MARC'S *head, and points him offstage.* MARC *exits, leering.)*

ACT 1 / SCENE 5

(M. GALLIMARD'S *cell.)*

GALLIMARD: Next, Butterfly makes her entrance. We learn her age—fifteen . . . but very mature for her years.

(Lights come up on the area where we saw SONG *dancing at the top of the play. She appears there again, now dressed as Madame Butterfly, moving to the "Love Duet."* GALLIMARD *turns upstage slightly to watch, transfixed.)*

GALLIMARD: But as she glides past him, beautiful, laughing softly behind her fan, don't we who are men sigh with hope? We, who are not handsome, nor brave, nor powerful, yet somehow believe, like Pinkerton, that we deserve a Butterfly. She arrives with all her possessions in the folds of her sleeves, lays them all out, for her man to do with as he pleases. Even her life itself—she bows her head as she whispers that she's not even worth the hundred yen he paid for her. He's already given too much, when we know he's really had to give nothing at all.

(Music and lights on SONG *out.* GALLIMARD *sits at his crate.)*

GALLIMARD: In real life, women who put their total worth at less than sixty-six cents are quite hard to find. The closest we come is in the pages of these magazines. *(He reaches into his crate, pulls out a stack of girlie magazines, and begins flipping through them)* Quite a necessity in prison. For three or four dollars, you get seven or eight women.

I first discovered these magazines at my uncle's house. One day, as a boy of twelve. The first time I saw them in his closet . . . all lined up—my body shook. Not with lust—no, with power. Here were women—a shelfful—who would do exactly as I wanted.

(The "Love Duet" creeps in over the speakers. Special comes up, revealing, not SONG *this time, but a pinup girl in a sexy negligee, her back to us.* GALLIMARD *turns upstage and looks at her.)*

GIRL: I know you're watching me.
GALLIMARD: My throat . . . it's dry.
GIRL: I leave my blinds open every night before I go to bed.
GALLIMARD: I can't move.
GIRL: I leave my blinds open and the lights on.
GALLIMARD: I'm shaking. My skin is hot, but my penis is soft. Why?
GIRL: I stand in front of the window.
GALLIMARD: What is she going to do?
GIRL: I toss my hair, and I let my lips part . . . barely.
GALLIMARD: I shouldn't be seeing this. It's so dirty. I'm so bad.
GIRL: Then, slowly, I lift off my nightdress.
GALLIMARD: Oh, god. I can't believe it. I can't—
GIRL: I toss it to the ground.
GALLIMARD: Now, she's going to walk away. She's going to—
GIRL: I stand there, in the light, displaying myself.
GALLIMARD: No. She's—why is she naked?
GIRL: To you.
GALLIMARD: In front of a window? This is wrong. No—
GIRL: Without shame.
GALLIMARD: No, she must . . . like it.
GIRL: I like it.
GALLIMARD: She . . . she wants me to see.
GIRL: I want you to see.
GALLIMARD: I can't believe it! She's getting excited!
GIRL: I can't see you. You can do whatever you want.
GALLIMARD: I can't do a thing. Why?
GIRL: What would you like me to do . . . next?

(Lights go down on her. Music off. Silence, as GALLIMARD *puts away his magazines. Then he resumes talking to us.)*

GALLIMARD: Act Two begins with Butterfly staring at the ocean. Pinkerton's been called back to the U.S., and he's given his wife a detailed schedule of his plans. In the column marked "return date," he's written "when the robins nest." This failed to ignite her suspicions. Now, three years have passed without a peep from him. Which brings a response from her faithful servant, Suzuki.

*(*COMRADE CHIN *enters, playing* SUZUKI.*)*

SUZUKI: Girl, he's a loser. What'd he ever give you? Nineteen cents and those ugly Day-Glo stockings? Look, it's finished! Kaput! Done! And you should be glad! I mean, the guy was a woofer! He tried before, you know—before he met you, he went down to geisha central and plunked down his spare change in front of the usual candidates—everyone else gagged! These are hungry prostitutes, and they were not interested, get the picture? Now, stop slathering when an American ship sails in, and let's make some bucks—I mean, yen! We are broke!

Now, what about Yamadori? Hey, hey—don't look away—the man is a prince—figuratively, and, what's even better, literally. He's rich, he's handsome, he says he'll die if you don't marry him—and he's even willing to overlook the little fact that you've been deflowered all over the place by a foreign devil. What do you mean, "But he's Japanese?" You're Japanese! You think you've been touched by the whitey god? He was a sailor with dirty hands!

*(*SUZUKI *stalks offstage.)*

GALLIMARD: She's also visited by Consul Sharpless, sent by Pinkerton on a minor errand.

*(*MARC *enters, as* SHARPLESS.*)*

SHARPLESS: I hate this job.
GALLIMARD: This Pinkerton—he doesn't show up personally to tell his wife he's abandoning her. No, he sends a government diplomat . . . at taxpayer's expense.
SHARPLESS: Butterfly? Butterfly? I have some bad—I'm going to be ill. Butterfly, I came to tell you—
GALLIMARD: Butterfly says she knows he'll return and if he doesn't she'll kill herself rather than go back to her own people. *(Beat)* This causes a lull in the conversation.
SHARPLESS: Let's put it this way . . .
GALLIMARD: Butterfly runs into the next room, and returns holding—

(Sound cue: a baby crying. SHARPLESS, *"seeing" this, backs away.)*

SHARPLESS: Well, good. Happy to see things going so well. I suppose I'll be going now. Ta ta. Ciao. *(He turns away. Sound cue out)* I hate this job. *(He exits)*
GALLIMARD: At that moment, Butterfly spots in the harbor an American ship—the *Abramo Lincoln!*

(*Music cue: "The Flower Duet."* SONG, *still dressed as Butterfly, changes into a wedding kimono, moving to the music.*)

GALLIMARD: This is the moment that redeems her years of waiting. With Suzuki's help, they cover the room with flowers—

(CHIN, *as* SUZUKI, *trudges onstage and drops a lone flower without much enthusiasm.*)

GALLIMARD: —and she changes into her wedding dress to prepare for Pinkerton's arrival.

(SUZUKI *helps Butterfly change.* HELGA *enters, and helps* GALLIMARD *change into a tuxedo.*)

GALLIMARD: I married a woman older than myself— Helga.
HELGA: My father was ambassador to Australia. I grew up among criminals and kangaroos.
GALLIMARD: Hearing that brought me to the altar—

(HELGA *exits.*)

GALLIMARD: —where I took a vow renouncing love. No fantasy woman would ever want me, so, yes, I would settle for a quick leap up the career ladder. Passion, I banish, and in its place—practicality!
  But my vows had long since lost their charm by the time we arrived in China. The sad truth is that all men want a beautiful woman, and the uglier the man, the greater the want.

(SUZUKI *makes final adjustments of Butterfly's costume, as does* GALLIMARD *of his tuxedo.*)

GALLIMARD: I married late, at age thirty-one. I was faithful to my marriage for eight years. Until the day when, as a junior-level diplomat in puritanical Peking, in a parlor at the German ambassador's house, during the "Reign of a Hundred Flowers," I first saw her . . . singing the death scene from *Madame Butterfly.*

(SUZUKI *runs offstage.*)

ACT 1 / SCENE 6

(*German ambassador's house. Beijing. 1960.*)
(*The upstage special area now becomes a stage. Several chairs face upstage, representing seating for some twenty guests in the parlor. A few "diplomats"—*RENEE, MARC, TOULON—*in formal dress enter and take seats.*
  GALLIMARD *also sits down, but turns towards us and continues to talk. Orchestral accompaniment on the tape is now replaced by a simple piano.* SONG *picks up the death scene from the point where Butterfly uncovers the hara-kiri knife.*)

GALLIMARD: The ending is pitiful. Pinkerton, in an act of great courage, stays home and sends his Amer-

ican wife to pick up Butterfly's child. The truth, long deferred, has come up to her door.

(SONG, *playing Butterfly, sings the lines from the opera in her own voice—which, though not classical, should be decent.*)

SONG: "Con onor muore/ chi non puo serbar/ vita con onore."
GALLIMARD (*Simultaneously*): "Death with honor/ Is better than life/ Life with dishonor."

(*The stage is illuminated; we are now completely within an elegant diplomat's residence.* SONG *proceeds to play out an abbreviated death scene. Everyone in the room applauds.* SONG, *shyly, takes her bows. Others in the room rush to congratulate her.* GALLIMARD *remains with us.*)

GALLIMARD: They say in opera the voice is everything. That's probably why I'd never before enjoyed opera. Here . . . here was a Butterfly with little or no voice—but she had the grace, the delicacy . . . I believed this girl. I believed her suffering. I wanted to take her in my arms—so delicate, even I could protect her, take her home, pamper her until she smiled.

(*Over the course of the preceding speech,* SONG *has broken from the upstage crowd and moved directly upstage of* GALLIMARD.)

SONG: Excuse me. Monsieur . . . ?

(GALLIMARD *turns upstage, shocked.*)

GALLIMARD: Oh! Gallimard. Mademoiselle . . . ? A beautiful . . .
SONG: Song Liling.
GALLIMARD: A beautiful performance.
SONG: Oh, please.
GALLIMARD: I usually—
SONG: You make me blush. I'm no opera singer at all.
GALLIMARD: I usually don't like *Butterfly.*
SONG: I can't blame you in the least.
GALLIMARD: I mean, the story—
SONG: Ridiculous.
GALLIMARD: I like the story, but . . . what?
SONG: Oh, you like it?
GALLIMARD: I . . . what I mean is, I've always seen it played by huge women in so much bad makeup.
SONG: Bad makeup is not unique to the West.
GALLIMARD: But, who can believe them?
SONG: And you believe me?
GALLIMARD: Absolutely. You were utterly convincing. It's the first time—
SONG: Convincing? As a Japanese woman? The Japanese used hundreds of our people for medical experiments during the war, you know. But I gather such an irony is lost on you.
GALLIMARD: No! I was about to say, it's the first time I've seen the beauty of the story.
SONG: Really?

GALLIMARD: Of her death. It's a . . . a pure sacrifice. He's unworthy, but what can she do? She loves him . . . so much. It's a very beautiful story.

SONG: Well, yes, to a Westerner.

GALLIMARD: Excuse me?

SONG: It's one of your favorite fantasies, isn't it? The submissive Oriental woman and the cruel white man.

GALLIMARD: Well, I didn't quite mean . . .

SONG: Consider it this way: what would you say if a blonde homecoming queen fell in love with a short Japanese businessman? He treats her cruelly, then goes home for three years, during which time she prays to his picture and turns down marriage from a young Kennedy. Then, when she learns he has remarried, she kills herself. Now, I believe you would consider this girl to be a deranged idiot, correct? But because it's an Oriental who kills herself for a Westerner—ah!—you find it beautiful.

(Silence.)

GALLIMARD: Yes . . . well . . . I see your point . . .

SONG: I will never do Butterfly again, Monsieur Gallimard. If you wish to see some real theatre come to the Peking Opera sometime. Expand your mind.

(SONG walks offstage.)

GALLIMARD *(To us)*: So much for protecting her in my big Western arms.

ACT 1 / SCENE 7

(M. GALLIMARD's apartment. Beijing. 1960.)
(GALLIMARD changes from his tux into a casual suit. HELGA enters.)

GALLIMARD: The Chinese are an incredibly arrogant people.

HELGA: They warned us about that in Paris, remember?

GALLIMARD: Even Parisians consider them arrogant. That's a switch.

HELGA: What is it that Madame Su says? "We are a very old civilization." I never know if she's talking about her country or herself.

GALLIMARD: I walk around here, all I hear every day, everywhere is how *old* this culture is. The fact that "old" may be synonymous with "senile" doesn't occur to them.

HELGA: You're not going to change them. "East is east, west is west, and . . ." whatever that guy said.

GALLIMARD: It's just that—silly. I met . . . at Ambassador Koening's tonight—you should've been there.

HELGA: Koening? Oh god, no. Did he enchant you all again with the history of Bavaria?

GALLIMARD: No. I met, I suppose, the Chinese equivalent of a diva. She's a singer in the Chinese opera.

HELGA: They have an opera, too? Do they sing in Chinese? Or maybe—in Italian?

GALLIMARD: Tonight, she did sing in Italian.

HELGA: How'd she manage that?

GALLIMARD: She must've been educated in the West before the Revolution. Her French is very good also. Anyway, she sang the death scene from *Madame Butterfly.*

HELGA: *Madame Butterfly!* Then I should have come. *(She begins humming, floating around the room as if dragging long kimono sleeves)* Did she have a nice costume? I think it's a classic piece of music.

GALLIMARD: That's what *I* thought, too. Don't let her hear you say that.

HELGA: What's wrong?

GALLIMARD: Evidently the Chinese hate it.

HELGA: She hated it, but she performed it anyway? Is she perverse?

GALLIMARD: They hate it because the white man gets the girl. Sour grapes if you ask me.

HELGA: Politics again? Why can't they just hear it as a piece of beautiful music? So, what's in their opera?

GALLIMARD: I don't know. But, whatever it is, I'm sure it must be *old.*

(HELGA exits.)

ACT 1 / SCENE 8

(Chinese opera house and the streets of Beijing. 1960.)
(The sound of gongs clanging fills the stage.)

GALLIMARD: My wife's innocent question kept ringing in my ears. I asked around, but no one knew anything about the Chinese opera. It took four weeks, but my curiosity overcame my cowardice. This Chinese diva—this unwilling Butterfly—what did she do to make her so proud?

The room was hot, and full of smoke. Wrinkled faces, old women, teeth missing—a man with a growth on his neck, like a human toad. All smiling, pipes falling from their mouths, cracking nuts between their teeth, a live chicken pecking at my foot—all looking, screaming, gawking . . . at her.

(The upstage area is suddenly hit with a harsh white light. It has become the stage for the Chinese opera performance. Two dancers enter, along with SONG. GALLIMARD stands apart, watching. SONG glides gracefully amidst the two dancers. Drums suddenly slam to a halt. SONG strikes a pose, looking straight at GALLIMARD. Dancers exit. Light change. Pause, then SONG walks right off the stage and straight up to GALLIMARD.)

SONG: Yes. You. White man. I'm looking straight at you.

GALLIMARD: Me?

SONG: You see any other white men? It was too easy to spot you. How often does a man in my audience come in a tie?

(SONG starts to remove her costume. Underneath, she wears simple baggy clothes. They are now backstage. The show is over.)

SONG: So, you are an adventurous imperialist?

GALLIMARD: I . . . thought it would further my education.

SONG: It took you four weeks. Why?

GALLIMARD: I've been busy.

SONG: Well, education has always been undervalued in the West, hasn't it?

GALLIMARD (Laughing): I don't think that's true.

SONG: No, you wouldn't. You're a Westerner. How can you objectively judge your own values?

GALLIMARD: I think it's possible to achieve some distance.

SONG: Do you? (Pause) It stinks in here. Let's go.

GALLIMARD: These are the smells of your loyal fans.

SONG: I love them for being my fans, I hate the smell .they leave behind. I too can distance myself from my people. (She looks around, then whispers in his ear) "Art for the masses" is a shitty excuse to keep artists poor. (She pops a cigarette in her mouth) Be a gentleman, will you? And light my cigarette.

(GALLIMARD fumbles for a match.)

GALLIMARD: I don't . . . smoke.

SONG (Lighting her own): Your loss. Had you lit my cigarette, I might have blown a puff of smoke right between your eyes. Come.

(They start to walk about the stage. It is a summer night on the Beijing streets. Sounds of the city play on the house speakers.)

SONG: How I wish there were even a tiny cafe to sit in. With cappuccinos, and men in tuxedos and bad expatriate jazz.

GALLIMARD: If my history serves me correctly, you weren't even allowed into the clubs in Shanghai before the Revolution.

SONG: Your history serves you poorly, Monsieur Gallimard. True, there were signs reading "No dogs and Chinamen." But a woman, especially a delicate Oriental woman—we always go where we please. Could you imagine it otherwise? Clubs in China filled with pasty, big-thighed white women, while thousands of slender lotus blossoms wait just outside the door? Never. The clubs would be empty. (Beat) We have always held a certain fascination for you Caucasian men, have we not?

GALLIMARD: But . . . that fascination is imperialist, or so you tell me.

SONG: Do you believe everything I tell you? Yes. It is always imperialist. But sometimes . . . sometimes, it is also mutual. Oh—this is my flat.

GALLIMARD: I didn't even—

SONG: Thank you. Come another time and we will further expand your mind.

(SONG exits. GALLIMARD continues roaming the streets as he speaks to us.)

GALLIMARD: What was that? What did she mean, "Sometimes . . . it is mutual"? Women do not flirt with me. And I normally can't talk to them. But tonight, I held up my end of the conversation.

ACT 1 / SCENE 9

(GALLIMARD's bedroom. Beijing. 1960.)
(HELGA enters.)

HELGA: You didn't tell me you'd be home late.

GALLIMARD: I didn't intend to. Something came up.

HELGA: Oh? Like what?

GALLIMARD: I went to the . . . to the Dutch ambassador's home.

HELGA: Again?

GALLIMARD: There was a reception for a visiting scholar. He's writing a six-volume treatise on the Chinese revolution. We all gathered that meant he'd have to live here long enough to actually write six volumes, and we all expressed our deepest sympathies.

HELGA: Well, I had a good night too. I went with the ladies to a martial arts demonstration. Some of those men—when they break those thick boards— (She mimes fanning herself) whoo-whoo!

(HELGA exits. Lights dim.)

GALLIMARD: I lied to my wife. Why? I've never had any reason to lie before. But what reason did I have tonight? I didn't do anything wrong. That night, I had a dream. Other people, I've been told, have dreams where angels appear. Or dragons, or Sophia Loren in a towel. In my dream, Marc from school appeared.

(MARC enters, in a nightshirt and cap.)

MARC: Rene! You met a girl!

(GALLIMARD and MARC stumble down the Beijing streets. Night sounds over the speakers.)

GALLIMARD: It's not that amazing, thank you.

MARC: No! It's so monumental, I heard about it halfway around the world in my sleep!

GALLIMARD: I've met girls before, you know.

MARC: Name one. I've come across time and space to congratulate you. (He hands GALLIMARD a bottle of wine)

GALLIMARD: Marc, this is expensive.

MARC: On those rare occasions when you become a formless spirit, why not steal the best?

(MARC pops open the bottle, begins to share it with GALLIMARD.)

GALLIMARD: You embarrass me. She . . . there's no reason to think she likes me.

MARC: "Sometimes, it is mutual"?

GALLIMARD: Oh.

MARC: "Mutual"? "Mutual"? What does that mean?

GALLIMARD: You heard?

MARC: It means the money is in the bank, you only have to write the check!

GALLIMARD: I am a married man!

MARC: And an excellent one too. I cheated after . . . six months. Then again and again, until now—three hundred girls in twelve years.

GALLIMARD: I don't think we should hold that up as a model.

MARC: Of course not! My life—it is disgusting! Phooey! Phooey! But, you—you are the model husband.

GALLIMARD: Anyway, it's impossible. I'm a foreigner.

MARC: Ah, yes. She cannot love you, it is taboo, but something deep inside her heart . . . she cannot help herself . . . she must surrender to you. It is her destiny.

GALLIMARD: How do you imagine all this?

MARC: The same way you do. It's an old story. It's in our blood. They fear us, Rene. Their women fear us. And their men—their men hate us. And, you know something? They are all correct.

(They spot a light in a window.)

MARC: There! There, Rene!

GALLIMARD: It's her window.

MARC: Late at night—it burns. The light—it burns for you.

GALLIMARD: I won't look. It's not respectful.

MARC: We don't have to be respectful. We're foreign devils.

(Enter SONG, in a sheer robe. The "One Fine Day"° aria creeps in over the speakers. With her back to us, SONG mimes attending to her toilette. Her robe comes loose, revealing her white shoulders.)

MARC: All your life you've waited for a beautiful girl who would lay down for you. All your life you've smiled like a saint when it's happened to every other man you know. And you see them in magazines and you see them in movies. And you wonder, what's wrong with me? Will anyone beautiful ever want me? As the years pass, your hair thins and you struggle to hold onto even your hopes. Stop struggling, Rene. The wait is over. *(He exits)*

GALLIMARD: Marc? Marc?

(At that moment, SONG, her back still towards us, drops her robe. A second of her naked back, then a sound cue: a phone ringing, very loud. Blackout, followed in the next beat by a special up on the bedroom area, where a phone now sits. GALLIMARD stumbles across the stage and picks up the phone. Sound cue out. Over the course of his conversation, area lights fill in the vicinity of his bed. It is the following morning.)

GALLIMARD: Yes? Hello?

SONG *(Offstage)*: Is it very early?

GALLIMARD: Why, yes.

SONG *(Offstage)*: How early?

GALLIMARD: It's . . . it's 5:30. Why are you—?

SONG *(Offstage)*: But it's light outside. Already.

GALLIMARD: It is. The sun must be in confusion today.

(Over the course of SONG's next speech, her upstage special comes up again. She sits in a chair, legs crossed, in a robe, telephone to her ear.)

SONG: I waited until I saw the sun. That was as much discipline as I could manage for one night. Do you forgive me?

GALLIMARD: Of course . . . for what?

SONG: Then I'll ask you quickly. Are you really interested in the opera?

GALLIMARD: Why, yes. Yes I am.

SONG: Then come again next Thursday. I am playing *The Drunken Beauty*. May I count on you?

GALLIMARD: Yes. You may.

SONG: Perfect. Well, I must be getting to bed. I'm exhausted. It's been a very long night for me.

(SONG hangs up; special on her goes off. GALLIMARD begins to dress for work.)

ACT 1 / SCENE 10

(SONG LILING's apartment. Beijing. 1960.)

GALLIMARD: I returned to the opera that next week, and the week after that . . . she keeps our meetings so short—perhaps fifteen, twenty minutes at most. So I am left each week with a thirst which is intensified. In this way, fifteen weeks have gone by. I am starting to doubt the words of my friend Marc. But no, not really. In my heart, I know she has . . . an interest in me. I suspect this is her way. She is outwardly bold and outspoken, yet her heart is shy and afraid. It is the Oriental in her at war with her Western education.

SONG *(Offstage)*: I will be out in an instant. Ask the servant for anything you want.

GALLIMARD: Tonight, I have finally been invited to enter her apartment. Though the idea is almost beyond belief, I believe she is afraid of me.

(GALLIMARD looks around the room. He picks up a picture in a frame, studies it. Without his noticing, SONG enters, dressed elegantly in a black gown from the twen-

---

"One Fine Day," the opera's most famous aria, "Un bel dì" ("One Fine Day"), in which Madame Butterfly rapturously describes the imagined return of Pinkerton.

ties. *She stands in the doorway looking like Anna May Wong.°*)

SONG: That is my father.
GALLIMARD (*Surprised*): Mademoiselle Song . . .

(*She glides up to him, snatches away the picture.*)

SONG: It is very good that he did not live to see the Revolution. They would, no doubt, have made him kneel on broken glass. Not that he didn't deserve such a punishment. But he is my father. I would've hated to see it happen.
GALLIMARD: I'm very honored that you've allowed me to visit your home.

(SONG *curtseys.*)

SONG: Thank you. Oh! Haven't you been poured any tea?
GALLIMARD: I'm really not—
SONG (*To her offstage servant*): Shu-Fang! Cha! Kwai-lah! (*To* GALLIMARD) I'm sorry. You want everything to be perfect—
GALLIMARD: Please.
SONG: —and before the evening even begins—
GALLIMARD: I'm really not thirsty.
SONG: —it's ruined.
GALLIMARD (*Sharply*): Mademoiselle Song!

(SONG *sits down.*)

SONG: I'm sorry.
GALLIMARD: What are you apologizing for now?

(*Pause;* SONG *starts to giggle.*)

SONG: I don't know!

(GALLIMARD *laughs.*)

GALLIMARD: Exactly my point.
SONG: Oh, I am silly. Lightheaded. I promise not to apologize for anything else tonight, do you hear me?
GALLIMARD: That's a good girl.

(SHU-FANG, *a servant girl, comes out with a tea tray and starts to pour.*)

SONG (*To* SHU-FANG): No! I'll pour myself for the gentleman!

(SHU-FANG, *staring at* GALLIMARD, *exits.*)

SONG: No, I . . . I don't even know why I invited you up.
GALLIMARD: Well, I'm glad you did.

(SONG *looks around the room.*)

Anna May Wong (1907–1961), Chinese-American actress, stereotyped as the "Oriental enchantress."

SONG: There is an element of danger to your presence.
GALLIMARD: Oh?
SONG: You must know.
GALLIMARD: It doesn't concern me. We both know why I'm here.
SONG: It doesn't concern me either. No . . . well perhaps . . .
GALLIMARD: What?
SONG: Perhaps I am slightly afraid of scandal.
GALLIMARD: What are we doing?
SONG: I'm entertaining you. In my parlor.
GALLIMARD: In France, that would hardly—
SONG: France. France is a country living in the modern era. Perhaps even ahead of it. China is a nation whose soul is firmly rooted two thousand years in the past. What I do, even pouring the tea for you now . . . it has . . . implications. The walls and windows say so. Even my own heart, strapped inside this Western dress . . . even it says things—things I don't care to hear.

(SONG *hands* GALLIMARD *a cup of tea.* GALLIMARD *puts his hand over both the teacup and* SONG's *hand.*)

GALLIMARD: This is a beautiful dress.
SONG: Don't.
GALLIMARD: What?
SONG: I don't even know if it looks right on me.
GALLIMARD: Believe me—
SONG: You are from France. You see so many beautiful women.
GALLIMARD: France? Since when are the European women—?
SONG: Oh! What am I trying to do, anyway?!

(SONG *runs to the door, composes herself, then turns towards* GALLIMARD.)

SONG: Monsieur Gallimard, perhaps you should go.
GALLIMARD: But . . . why?
SONG: There's something wrong about this.
GALLIMARD: I don't see what.
SONG: I feel . . . I am not myself.
GALLIMARD: No. You're nervous.
SONG: Please. Hard as I try to be modern, to speak like a man, to hold a Western woman's strong face up to my own . . . in the end, I fail. A small, frightened heart beats too quickly and gives me away. Monsieur Gallimard, I'm a Chinese girl. I've never . . . never invited a man up to my flat before. The forwardness of my actions makes my skin burn.
GALLIMARD: What are you afraid of? Certainly not me, I hope.
SONG: I'm a modest girl.
GALLIMARD: I know. And very beautiful. (*He touches her hair*)
SONG: Please—go now. The next time you see me, I shall again be myself.
GALLIMARD: I like you the way you are right now.
SONG: You are a cad.

GALLIMARD: What do you expect? I'm a foreign devil.

(GALLIMARD *walks downstage.* SONG *exits.*)

GALLIMARD (*To us*): Did you hear the way she talked about Western women? Much differently than the first night. She does—she feels inferior to them—and to me.

ACT 1 / SCENE 11

(*The French embassy. Beijing. 1960.*)
(GALLIMARD *moves towards a desk.*)

GALLIMARD: I determined to try an experiment. In *Madame Butterfly*, Cio-Cio-San fears that the Western man who catches a butterfly will pierce its heart with a needle, then leave it to perish. I began to wonder: had I, too, caught a butterfly who would writhe on a needle?

(MARC *enters, dressed as a bureaucrat, holding a stack of papers. As* GALLIMARD *speaks,* MARC *hands papers to him. He peruses, then signs, stamps, or rejects them.*)

GALLIMARD: Over the next five weeks, I worked like a dynamo. I stopped going to the opera, I didn't phone or write her. I knew this little flower was waiting for me to call, and, as I wickedly refused to do so, I felt for the first time that rush of power—the absolute power of a man.

(MARC *continues acting as the bureaucrat, but he now speaks as himself.*)

MARC: Rene! It's me!

GALLIMARD: Marc—I hear your voice everywhere now. Even in the midst of work.

MARC: That's because I'm watching you—all the time.

GALLIMARD: You were always the most popular guy in school.

MARC: Well, there's no guarantee of failure in life like happiness in high school. Somehow I knew I'd end up in the suburbs working for Renault and you'd be in the Orient picking exotic women off the trees. And they say there's no justice.

GALLIMARD: That's why you were my friend?

MARC: I gave you a little of my life, so that now you can give me some of yours. (*Pause*) Remember Isabelle?

GALLIMARD: Of course I remember! She was my first experience.

MARC: We all wanted to ball her. But she only wanted me.

GALLIMARD: I had her.

MARC: Right. You balled her.

GALLIMARD: You were the only one who ever believed me.

MARC: Well, there's a good reason for that. (*Beat*) C'mon. You must've guessed.

GALLIMARD: You told me to wait in the bushes by the cafeteria that night. The next thing I knew, she was on me. Dress up in the air.

MARC: She never wore underwear.

GALLIMARD: My arms were pinned to the dirt.

MARC: She loved the superior position. A girl ahead of her time.

GALLIMARD: I looked up, and there was this woman . . . bouncing up and down on my loins.

MARC: Screaming, right?

GALLIMARD: Screaming, and breaking off the branches all around me, and pounding my butt up and down into the dirt.

MARC: Huffing and puffing like a locomotive.

GALLIMARD: And in the middle of all this, the leaves were getting into my mouth, my legs were losing circulation, I thought, "God. So this is *it*?"

MARC: You thought that?

GALLIMARD: Well, I was worried about my legs falling off.

MARC: You didn't have a good time?

GALLIMARD: No, that's not what I—I had a great time!

MARC: You're sure?

GALLIMARD: Yeah. Really.

MARC: 'Cuz I wanted you to have a good time.

GALLIMARD: I did.

(*Pause.*)

MARC: Shit. (*Pause*) When all is said and done, she was kind of a lousy lay, wasn't she? I mean, there was a lot of energy there, but you never knew what she was doing with it. Like when she yelled "I'm coming!"—hell, it was so loud, you wanted to go, "Look, it's not that big a deal."

GALLIMARD: I got scared. I thought she meant someone was actually coming. (*Pause*) But, Marc?

MARC: What?

GALLIMARD: Thanks.

MARC: Oh, don't mention it.

GALLIMARD: It was my first experience.

MARC: Yeah. You got her.

GALLIMARD: I got her.

MARC: Wait! Look at that letter again!

(GALLIMARD *picks up one of the papers he's been stamping, and rereads it.*)

GALLIMARD (*To us*): After six weeks, they began to arrive. The letters.

(*Upstage special on* SONG, *as Madame Butterfly. The scene is underscored by the "Love Duet."*)

SONG: Did we fight? I do not know. Is the opera no longer of interest to you? Please come—my audiences miss the white devil in their midst.

(GALLIMARD *looks up from the letter, towards us.*)

GALLIMARD (*To us*): A concession, but much too dignified. (*Beat; he discards the letter*) I skipped the opera again that week to complete a position paper on trade.

(*The bureaucrat hands him another letter.*)

SONG: Six weeks have passed since last we met. Is this your practice—to leave friends in the lurch? Sometimes I hate you, sometimes I hate myself, but always I miss you.

GALLIMARD (*To us*): Better, but I don't like the way she calls me "friend." When a woman calls a man her "friend," she's calling him a eunuch or a homosexual. (*Beat; he discards the letter*) I was absent from the opera for the seventh week, feeling a sudden urge to clean out my files.

(*Bureaucrat hands him another letter.*)

SONG: Your rudeness is beyond belief. I don't deserve this cruelty. Don't bother to call. I'll have you turned away at the door.

GALLIMARD (*To us*): I didn't. (*He discards the letter; bureaucrat hands him another*) And then finally, the letter that concluded my experiment.

SONG: I am out of words. I can hide behind dignity no longer. What do you want? I have already given you my shame.

(GALLIMARD *gives the letter back to* MARC, *slowly. Special on* SONG *fades out.*)

GALLIMARD (*To us*): Reading it, I became suddenly ashamed. Yes, my experiment had been a success. She was turning on my needle. But the victory seemed hollow.

MARC: Hollow?! Are you crazy?

GALLIMARD: Nothing, Marc. Please go away.

MARC (*Exiting, with papers*): Haven't I taught you anything?

GALLIMARD: "I have already given you my shame." I had to attend a reception that evening. On the way, I felt sick. If there is a God, surely he would punish me now. I had finally gained power over a beautiful woman, only to abuse it cruelly. There must be justice in the world. I had the strange feeling that the ax would fall this very evening.

ACT 1 / SCENE 12

(AMBASSADOR TOULON's *residence. Beijing. 1960.*)
(*Sound cue: party noises. Light change. We are now in a spacious residence.* TOULON, *the French ambassador, enters and taps* GALLIMARD *on the shoulder.*)

TOULON: Gallimard? Can I have a word? Over here.

GALLIMARD (*To us*): Manuel Toulon. French ambassador to China. He likes to think of us all as his children. Rather like God.

TOULON: Look, Gallimard, there's not much to say. I've liked you. From the day you walked in. You were no leader, but you were tidy and efficient.

GALLIMARD: Thank you, sir.

TOULON: Don't jump the gun. Okay, our needs in China are changing. It's embarrassing that we lost Indochina. Someone just wasn't on the ball there. I don't mean you personally, of course.

GALLIMARD: Thank you, sir.

TOULON: We're going to be doing a lot more information-gathering in the future. The nature of our work here is changing. Some people are just going to have to go. It's nothing personal.

GALLIMARD: Oh.

TOULON: Want to know a secret? Vice-Consul LeBon is being transferred.

GALLIMARD (*To us*): My immediate superior!

TOULON: And most of his department.

GALLIMARD (*To us*): Just as I feared! God has seen my evil heart—

TOULON: But not you.

GALLIMARD (*To us*): —and he's taking her away just as . . . (*To* TOULON) Excuse me, sir?

TOULON: Scare you? I think I did. Cheer up, Gallimard. I want you to replace LeBon as vice-consul.

GALLIMARD: You—? Yes, well, thank you, sir.

TOULON: Anytime.

GALLIMARD: I . . . accept with great humility.

TOULON: Humility won't be part of the job. You're going to coordinate the revamped intelligence division. Want to know a secret? A year ago, you would've been out. But the past few months, I don't know how it happened, you've become this new aggressive confident . . . thing. And they also tell me you get along with the Chinese. So I think you're a lucky man, Gallimard. Congratulations.

(*They shake hands.* TOULON *exits. Party noises out.* GALLIMARD *stumbles across a darkened stage.*)

GALLIMARD: Vice-consul? Impossible! As I stumbled out of the party, I saw it written across the sky: There is no God. Or, no—say that there is a God. But that God . . . understands. Of course! God who creates Eve to serve Adam, who blesses Solomon with his harem but ties Jezebel to a burning bed— that God is a man. And he understands! At age thirty-nine, I was suddenly initiated into the way of the world.

ACT 1 / SCENE 13

(SONG LILING's *apartment. Beijing. 1960.*)
(SONG *enters, in a sheer dressing gown.*)

SONG: Are you crazy?

GALLIMARD: Mademoiselle Song—

SONG: To come here—at this hour? After . . . after eight weeks?

GALLIMARD: It's the most amazing—

SONG: You bang on my door? Scare my servants, scandalize the neighbors?

GALLIMARD: I've been promoted. To vice-consul.

(*Pause.*)

SONG: And what is that supposed to mean to me?

GALLIMARD: Are you my Butterfly?

SONG: What are you saying?

GALLIMARD: I've come tonight for an answer: are you my Butterfly?

SONG: Don't you know already?

GALLIMARD: I want you to say it.

SONG: I don't want to say it.

GALLIMARD: So, that is your answer?

SONG: You know how I feel about—

GALLIMARD: I do remember one thing.

SONG: What?

GALLIMARD: In the letter I received today.

SONG: Don't.

GALLIMARD: "I have already given you my shame."

SONG: It's enough that I even wrote it.

GALLIMARD: Well, then—

SONG: I shouldn't have it splashed across my face.

GALLIMARD: —if that's all true—

SONG: Stop!

GALLIMARD: Then what is one more short answer?

SONG: I don't want to!

GALLIMARD: Are you my Butterfly? (*Silence; he crosses the room and begins to touch her hair*) I want from you honesty. There should be nothing false between us. No false pride.

(*Pause.*)

SONG: Yes, I am. I am your Butterfly.

GALLIMARD: Then let me be honest with you. It is because of you that I was promoted tonight. You have changed my life forever. My little Butterfly, there should be no more secrets: I love you.

(*He starts to kiss her roughly. She resists slightly.*)

SONG: No . . . no . . . gently . . . please, I've never . . .

GALLIMARD: No?

SONG: I've tried to appear experienced, but . . . the truth is . . . no.

GALLIMARD: Are you cold?

SONG: Yes. Cold.

GALLIMARD: Then we will go very, very slowly.

(*He starts to caress her; her gown begins to open.*)

SONG: No . . . let me . . . keep my clothes . . .

GALLIMARD: But . . .

SONG: Please . . . it all frightens me. I'm a modest Chinese girl.

GALLIMARD: My poor little treasure.

SONG: I am your treasure. Though inexperienced, I am not . . . ignorant. They teach us things, our mothers, about pleasing a man.

GALLIMARD: Yes?

SONG: I'll do my best to make you happy. Turn off the lights.

(*GALLIMARD gets up and heads for a lamp. SONG, propped up on one elbow, tosses her hair back and smiles.*)

SONG: Monsieur Gallimard?

GALLIMARD: Yes, Butterfly?

SONG: "Vieni, vieni!"°

GALLIMARD: "Come, darling."

SONG: "Ah! Dolce notte!"

GALLIMARD: "Beautiful night."

SONG: "Tutto estatico d'amor ride il ciel!"

GALLIMARD: "All ecstatic with love, the heavens are filled with laughter."

(*He turns off the lamp. Blackout.*)

ACT 2 / SCENE 1

(*M. GALLIMARD's cell. Paris. Present.*)
(*Lights up on GALLIMARD. He sits in his cell, reading from a leaflet.*)

GALLIMARD: This, from a contemporary critic's commentary on *Madame Butterfly:* "Pinkerton suffers from . . . being an obnoxious bounder whom every man in the audience itches to kick." Bully for us men in the audience! Then, in the same note: "Butterfly is the most irresistibly appealing of Puccini's 'Little Women.' Watching the succession of her humiliations is like watching a child under torture." (*He tosses the pamphlet over his shoulder*) I suggest that, while we men may all want to kick Pinkerton, very few of us would pass up the opportunity to *be* Pinkerton.

(*GALLIMARD moves out of his cell.*)

ACT 2 / SCENE 2

(*GALLIMARD and Butterfly's flat. Beijing. 1960.*)
(*We are in a simple but well-decorated parlor. GALLIMARD moves to sit on a sofa, while SONG, dressed in a chong sam, enters and curls up at his feet.*)

GALLIMARD (*To us*): We secured a flat on the outskirts of Peking. Butterfly, as I was calling her now, decorated our "home" with Western furniture and Chinese antiques. And there, on a few stolen afternoons or evenings each week, Butterfly commenced her education.

SONG: The Chinese men—they keep us down.

GALLIMARD: Even in the "New Society"?

SONG: In the "New Society," we are all kept ignorant equally. That's one of the exciting things about loving a Western man. I know you are not threatened by a woman's education.

"Vieni, vieni," the words are from the love duet at the end of *Madame Butterfly's* first act.

GALLIMARD: I'm no saint, Butterfly.

SONG: But you come from a progressive society.

GALLIMARD: We're not always reminding each other how "old" we are, if that's what you mean.

SONG: Exactly. We Chinese—once, I suppose, it is true, we ruled the world. But so what? How much more exciting to be part of the society ruling the world today. Tell me—what's happening in Vietnam?

GALLIMARD: Oh, Butterfly—you want me to bring my work home?

SONG: I want to know what you know. To be impressed by my man. It's not the particulars so much as the fact that you're making decisions which change the shape of the world.

GALLIMARD: Not the world. At best, a small corner.

(TOULON *enters, and sits at a desk upstage.*)

ACT 2 / SCENE 3

(*French embassy. Beijing. 1961.*)
(GALLIMARD *moves downstage, to* TOULON'*s desk.* SONG *remains upstage, watching.*)

TOULON: And a more troublesome corner is hard to imagine.

GALLIMARD: So, the Americans plan to begin bombing?

TOULON: This is very secret, Gallimard: yes. The Americans don't have an embassy here. They're asking us to be their eyes and ears. Say Jack Kennedy signed an order to bomb North Vietnam, Laos. How would the Chinese react?

GALLIMARD: I think the Chinese will squawk—

TOULON: Uh-huh.

GALLIMARD: —but, in their hearts, they don't even like Ho Chi Minh.

(*Pause.*)

TOULON: What a bunch of jerks. Vietnam was *our* colony. Not only didn't the Americans help us fight to keep them, but now, seven years later, they've come back to grab the territory for themselves. It's very irritating.

GALLIMARD: With all due respect, sir, why should the Americans have won our war for us back in '54 if we didn't have the will to win it ourselves?

TOULON: You're kidding, aren't you?

(*Pause.*)

GALLIMARD: The Orientals simply want to be associated with whoever shows the most strength and power. You live with the Chinese, sir. Do you think they like Communism?

TOULON: I live in China. Not with the Chinese.

GALLIMARD: Well, I—

TOULON: *You* live with the Chinese.

GALLIMARD: Excuse me?

TOULON: I can't keep a secret.

GALLIMARD: What are you saying?

TOULON: Only that I'm not immune to gossip. So, you're keeping a native mistress? Don't answer. It's none of my business. (*Pause*) I'm sure she must be gorgeous.

GALLIMARD: Well . . .

TOULON: I'm impressed. You have the stamina to go out into the streets and hunt one down. Some of us have to be content with the wives of the expatriate community.

GALLIMARD: I do feel . . . fortunate.

TOULON: So, Gallimard, you've got the inside knowledge—what *do* the Chinese think?

GALLIMARD: Deep down, they miss the old days. You know, cappuccinos, men in tuxedos—

TOULON: So what do we tell the Americans about Vietnam?

GALLIMARD: Tell them there's a natural affinity between the West and the Orient.

TOULON: And that you speak from experience?

GALLIMARD: The Orientals are people too. They want the good things we can give them. If the Americans demonstrate the will to win, the Vietnamese will welcome them into a mutually beneficial union.

TOULON: I don't see how the Vietnamese can stand up to American firepower.

GALLIMARD: Orientals will always submit to a greater force.

TOULON: I'll note your opinions in my report. The Americans always love to hear how "welcome" they'll be. (*He starts to exit*)

GALLIMARD: Sir?

TOULON: Mmmm?

GALLIMARD: This . . . rumor you've heard.

TOULON: Uh-huh?

GALLIMARD: How . . . widespread do you think it is?

TOULON: It's only widespread within this embassy. Where nobody talks because everybody is guilty. We were worried about you, Gallimard. We thought you were the only one here without a secret. Now you go and find a lotus blossom . . . and top us all. (*He exits*)

GALLIMARD (*To us*): Toulon knows! And he approves! I was learning the benefits of being a man. We form our own clubs, sit behind thick doors, smoke—and celebrate the fact that we're still boys. (*He starts to move downstage, towards* SONG) So, over the—

(*Suddenly* COMRADE CHIN *enters.* GALLIMARD *backs away.*)

GALLIMARD (*To* SONG): No! Why does she have to come in?

SONG: Rene, be sensible. How can they understand the story without her? Now, don't embarrass yourself.

(GALLIMARD *moves down center.*)

GALLIMARD (*To us*): Now, you will see why my story is

so amusing to so many people. Why they snicker at parties in disbelief. Please—try to understand it from my point of view. We are all prisoners of our time and place. *(He exits)*

ACT 2 / SCENE 4

(GALLIMARD and Butterfly's flat. Beijing. 1961.)

SONG *(To us)*: 1961. The flat Monsieur Gallimard rented for us. An evening after he has gone.

CHIN: Okay, see if you can find out when the Americans plan to start bombing Vietnam. If you can find out what cities, even better.

SONG: I'll do my best, but I don't want to arouse his suspicions.

CHIN: Yeah, sure, of course. So, what else?

SONG: The Americans will increase troops in Vietnam to 170,000 soldiers with 120,000 militia and 11,000 American advisors.

CHIN *(Writing)*: Wait, wait. 120,000 militia and—

SONG: —11,000 American—

CHIN: —American advisors. *(Beat)* How do you remember so much?

SONG: I'm an actor.

CHIN: Yeah. *(Beat)* Is that how come you dress like that?

SONG: Like what, Miss Chin?

CHIN: Like that dress! You're wearing a dress. And every time I come here, you're wearing a dress. Is that because you're an actor? Or what?

SONG: It's a . . . disguise, Miss Chin.

CHIN: Actors, I think they're all weirdos. My mother tells me actors are like gamblers or prostitutes or—

SONG: It helps me in my assignment.

(Pause.)

CHIN: You're not gathering information in any way that violates Communist Party principles, are you?

SONG: Why would I do that?

CHIN: Just checking. Remember: when working for the Great Proletarian State, you represent our Chairman Mao in every position you take.

SONG: I'll try to imagine the Chairman taking my positions.

CHIN: We all think of him this way. Good-bye, comrade. *(She starts to exit)* Comrade?

SONG: Yes?

CHIN: Don't forget: there is no homosexuality in China!

SONG: Yes, I've heard.

CHIN: Just checking. *(She exits)*

SONG *(To us)*: What passes for a woman in modern China.

(GALLIMARD sticks his head out from the wings.)

GALLIMARD: Is she gone?

SONG: Yes, Rene. Please continue in your own fashion.

ACT 2 / SCENE 5

(Beijing. 1961–63.)

(GALLIMARD moves to the couch where SONG still sits. He lies down in her lap, and she strokes his forehead.)

GALLIMARD *(To us)*: And so, over the years 1961, '62, '63, we settled into our routine, Butterfly and I. She would always have prepared a light snack and then, ever so delicately, and only if I agreed, she would start to pleasure me. With her hands, her mouth . . . too many ways to explain, and too sad, given my present situation. But mostly we would talk. About my life. Perhaps there is nothing more rare than to find a woman who passionately listens.

(SONG remains upstage, listening, as HELGA enters and plays a scene downstage with GALLIMARD.)

HELGA: Rene, I visited Dr. Bolleart this morning.

GALLIMARD: Why? Are you ill?

HELGA: No, no. You see, I wanted to ask him . . . that question we've been discussing.

GALLIMARD: And I told you, it's only a matter of time. Why did you bring a doctor into this? We just have to keep trying—like a crapshoot, actually.

HELGA: I went, I'm sorry. But listen: he says there's nothing wrong with me.

GALLIMARD: You see? Now, will you stop—?

HELGA: Rene, he says he'd like you to go in and take some tests.

GALLIMARD: Why? So he can find there's nothing wrong with both of us?

HELGA: Rene, I don't ask for much. One trip! One visit! And then, whatever you want to do about it—you decide.

GALLIMARD: You're assuming he'll find something defective!

HELGA: No! Of course not! Whatever he finds—if he finds nothing, we decide what to do about nothing! But go!

GALLIMARD: If he finds nothing, we keep trying. Just like we do now.

HELGA: But at least we'll know! *(Pause)* I'm sorry. *(She starts to exit)*

GALLIMARD: Do you really want me to see Dr. Bolleart?

HELGA: Only if you want a child, Rene. We have to face the fact that time is running out. Only if you want a child. *(She exits)*

GALLIMARD *(To SONG)*: I'm a modern man, Butterfly. And yet, I don't want to go. It's the same old voodoo. I feel like God himself is laughing at me if I can't produce a child.

SONG: You men of the West—you're obsessed by your odd desire for equality. Your wife can't give you a child, and *you're* going to the doctor?

GALLIMARD: Well, you see, she's already gone.

SONG: And because this incompetent can't find the defect, you now have to subject yourself to him? It's unnatural.

GALLIMARD: Well, what is the "natural" solution?

SONG: In Imperial China, when a man found that one wife was inadequate, he turned to another—to give him his son.

GALLIMARD: What do you—? I can't . . . marry you, yet.

SONG: Please. I'm not asking you to be my husband. But I am already your wife.

GALLIMARD: Do you want to . . . have my child?

SONG: I thought you'd never ask.

GALLIMARD: But, your career . . . your—

SONG: Phooey on my career! That's your Western mind, twisting itself into strange shapes again. Of course I love my career. But what would I love most of all? To feel something inside me—day and night—something I know is yours. *(Pause)* Promise me . . . you won't go to this doctor. Who is this Western quack to set himself as judge over the man I love? I know who is a man, and who is not. *(She exits)*

GALLIMARD *(To us)*: Dr. Bolleart? Of course I didn't go. What man would?

ACT 2 / SCENE 6

(Beijing. 1963.)

(Party noises over the house speakers. RENEE enters, wearing a revealing gown.)

GALLIMARD: 1963. A party at the Austrian embassy. None of us could remember the Austrian ambassador's name, which seemed somehow appropriate. *(To RENEE)* So, I tell the Americans, Diem must go. The U.S. wants to be respected by the Vietnamese, and yet they're propping up this nobody seminarian as her president. A man whose claim to fame is his sister-in-law imposing fanatic "moral order" campaigns? Oriental women—when they're good, they're very good, but when they're bad, they're Christians.

RENEE: Yeah.

GALLIMARD: And what do you do?

RENEE: I'm a student. My father exports a lot of useless stuff to the Third World.

GALLIMARD: How useless?

RENEE: You know. Squirt guns, confectioner's sugar, hula hoops . . .

GALLIMARD: I'm sure they appreciate the sugar.

RENEE: I'm here for two years to study Chinese.

GALLIMARD: Two years?

RENEE: That's what everybody says.

GALLIMARD: When did you arrive?

RENEE: Three weeks ago.

GALLIMARD: And?

RENEE: I like it. It's primitive, but . . . well, this is the place to learn Chinese, so here I am.

GALLIMARD: Why Chinese?

RENEE: I think it'll be important someday.

GALLIMARD: You do?

RENEE: Don't ask me when, but . . . that's what I think.

GALLIMARD: Well, I agree with you. One hundred percent. That's very farsighted.

RENEE: Yeah. Well of course, my father thinks I'm a complete weirdo.

GALLIMARD: He'll thank you someday.

RENEE: Like when the Chinese start buying hula hoops?

GALLIMARD: There're a billion bellies out there.

RENEE: And if they end up taking over the world—well, then I'll be lucky to know Chinese too, right?

(Pause.)

GALLIMARD: At this point, I don't see how the Chinese can possibly take—

RENEE: You know what I *don't* like about China?

GALLIMARD: Excuse me? No—what?

RENEE: Nothing to do at night.

GALLIMARD: You come to parties at embassies like everyone else.

RENEE: Yeah, but they get out at ten. And then what?

GALLIMARD: I'm afraid the Chinese idea of a dance hall is a dirt floor and a man with a flute.

RENEE: Are you married?

GALLIMARD: Yes. Why?

RENEE: You wanna . . . fool around?

(Pause.)

GALLIMARD: Sure.

RENEE: I'll wait for you outside. What's your name?

GALLIMARD: Gallimard. Rene.

RENEE: Weird. I'm Renee too. *(She exits)*

GALLIMARD *(To us)*: And so, I embarked on my first extra-extramarital affair. Renee was picture perfect. With a body like those girls in the magazines. If I put a tissue paper over my eyes, I wouldn't have been able to tell the difference. And it was exciting to be with someone who wasn't afraid to be seen completely naked. But is it possible for a woman to be *too* uninhibited, *too* willing, so as to seem almost too . . . masculine?

(Chuck Berry blares from the house speakers, then comes down in volume as RENEE enters, toweling her hair.)

RENEE: You have a nice weenie.

GALLIMARD: What?

RENEE: Penis. You have a nice penis.

GALLIMARD: Oh. Well, thank you. That's very . . .

RENEE: What—can't take a compliment?

GALLIMARD: No, it's very . . . reassuring.

RENEE: But most girls don't come out and say it, huh?

GALLIMARD: And also . . . what did you call it?

RENEE: Oh. Most girls don't call it a "weenie," huh?

GALLIMARD: It sounds very—

RENEE: Small, I know.

GALLIMARD: I was going to say, "young."

RENEE: Yeah. Young, small, same thing. Most guys are

pretty, uh, sensitive about that. Like, you know, I had a boyfriend back home in Denmark. I got mad at him once and called him a little weeniehead. He got so mad! He said at least I should call him a great big weeniehead.

GALLIMARD: I suppose I just say "penis."

RENEE: Yeah. That's pretty clinical. There's "cock," but that sounds like a chicken. And "prick" is painful, and "dick" is like you're talking about someone who's not in the room.

GALLIMARD: Yes. It's a . . . bigger problem than I imagined.

RENEE: I—I think maybe it's because I really don't know what to do with them—that's why I call them "weenies."

GALLIMARD: Well, you did quite well with . . . mine.

RENEE: Thanks, but I mean, really *do* with them. Like, okay, have you ever looked at one? I mean, really?

GALLIMARD: No, I suppose when it's part of you, you sort of take it for granted.

RENEE: I guess. But, like, it just hangs there. This little . . . flap of flesh. And there's so much fuss that we make about it. Like, I think the reason we fight wars is because we wear clothes. Because no one knows—between the men, I mean—who has the bigger . . . weenie. So, if I'm a guy with a small one, I'm going to build a really big building or take over a really big piece of land or write a really long book so the other men don't know, right? But, see, it never really works, that's the problem. I mean, you conquer the country, or whatever, but you're still wearing clothes, so there's no way to prove absolutely whose is bigger or smaller. And that's what we call a civilized society. The whole world run by a bunch of men with pricks the size of pins. (*She exits*)

GALLIMARD (*To us*): This was simply not acceptable.

(*A high-pitched chime rings through the air.* SONG, *dressed as Butterfly, appears in the upstage special. She is obviously distressed. Her body swoons as she attempts to clip the stems of flowers she's arranging in a vase.*)

GALLIMARD: But I kept up our affair, wildly, for several months. Why? I believe because of Butterfly. She knew the secret I was trying to hide. But, unlike a Western woman, she didn't confront me, threaten, even pout. I remembered the words of Puccini's *Butterfly:*

SONG: "Noi siamo gente avvezza/ alle piccole cose/ umili e silenziose."

GALLIMARD: "I come from a people/ Who are accustomed to little/ Humble and silent." I saw Pinkerton and Butterfly, and what she would say if he were unfaithful . . . nothing. She would cry, alone, into those wildly soft sleeves, once full of possessions, now empty to collect her tears. It was her tears and her silence that excited me, every time I visited Renee.

TOULON (*Offstage*): Gallimard!

(TOULON *enters.* GALLIMARD *turns towards him. During the next section,* SONG, *up center, begins to dance with the flowers. It is a drunken dance, where she breaks small pieces off the stems.*)

TOULON: They're killing him.

GALLIMARD: Who? I'm sorry? What?

TOULON: Bother you to come over at this late hour?

GALLIMARD: No . . . of course not.

TOULON: Not after you hear my secret. Champagne?

GALLIMARD: Um . . . thank you.

TOULON: You're surprised. There's something that you've wanted, Gallimard. No, not a promotion. Next time. Something in the world. You're not aware of this, but there's an informal gossip circle among intelligence agents. And some of ours heard from some of the Americans—

GALLIMARD: Yes?

TOULON: That the U.S. will allow the Vietnamese generals to stage a coup . . . and assassinate President Diem.

(*The chime rings again.* TOULON *freezes.* GALLIMARD *turns upstage and looks at Butterfly, who slowly and deliberately clips a flower off its stem.* GALLIMARD *turns back towards* TOULON.)

GALLIMARD: I think . . . that's a very wise move!

(TOULON *unfreezes.*)

TOULON: It's what you've been advocating. A toast?

GALLIMARD: Sure. I consider this a vindication.

TOULON: Not exactly. "To the test. Let's hope you pass."

(*They drink. The chime rings again.* TOULON *freezes.* GALLIMARD *turns upstage, and* SONG *clips another flower.*)

GALLIMARD (*To* TOULON): The test?

TOULON (*Unfreezing*): It's a test of everything you've been saying. I personally think the generals probably will stop the Communists. And you'll be a hero. But if anything goes wrong, then your opinions won't be worth a pig's ear. I'm sure that won't happen. But sometimes it's easier when they don't listen to you.

GALLIMARD: They're your opinions too, aren't they?

TOULON: Personally, yes.

GALLIMARD: So we agree.

TOULON: But my opinions aren't on that report. Yours are. Cheers.

(TOULON *turns away from* GALLIMARD *and raises his glass. At that instant* SONG *picks up the vase and hurls it to the ground. It shatters.* SONG *sinks down amidst the shards of the vase, in a calm, childlike trance. She sings softly, as if reciting a child's nursery rhyme.*)

SONG (*Repeat as necessary*): "The whole world over, the white man travels, setting anchor, wherever he likes. Life's not worth living, unless he finds, the finest maidens, of every land . . ."

(GALLIMARD *turns downstage towards us.* SONG *continues singing.*)

GALLIMARD: I shook as I left his house. That coward! That worm! To put the burden for his decisions on my shoulders!

I started for Renee's. But no, that was all I needed. A schoolgirl who would question the role of the penis in modern society. What I wanted was revenge. A vessel to contain my humiliation. Though I hadn't seen her in several weeks, I headed for Butterfly's.

(GALLIMARD *enters* SONG's *apartment.*)

SONG: Oh! Rene . . . I was dreaming!

GALLIMARD: You've been drinking?

SONG: If I can't sleep, then yes, I drink. But then, it gives me these dreams which—Rene, it's been almost three weeks since you visited me last.

GALLIMARD: I know. There's been a lot going on in the world.

SONG: Fortunately I am drunk. So I can speak freely. It's not the world, it's you and me. And an old problem. Even the softest skin becomes like leather to a man who's touched it too often. I confess I don't know how to stop it. I don't know how to become another woman.

GALLIMARD: I have a request.

SONG: Is this a solution? Or are you ready to give up the flat?

GALLIMARD: It may be a solution. But I'm sure you won't like it.

SONG: Oh well, that's very important. "Like it?" Do you think I "like" lying here alone, waiting, always waiting for your return? Please—don't worry about what I may not "like."

GALLIMARD: I want to see you . . . naked.

(*Silence.*)

SONG: I thought you understood my modesty. So you want me to—what—strip? Like a big cowboy girl? Shiny pasties on my breasts? Shall I fling my kimono over my head and yell "ya-hoo" in the process? I thought you respected my shame!

GALLIMARD: I believe you gave me your shame many years ago.

SONG: Yes—and it is just like a white devil to use it against me. I can't believe it. I thought myself so repulsed by the passive Oriental and the cruel white man. Now I see—we are always most revolted by the things hidden within us.

GALLIMARD: I just mean—

SONG: Yes?

GALLIMARD: —that it will remove the only barrier left between us.

SONG: No, Rene. Don't couch your request in sweet words. Be yourself—a cad—and know that my love is enough, that I submit—submit to the worst you can give me. (*Pause*) Well, come. Strip me. Whatever happens, know that you have willed it. Our love, in your hands. I'm helpless before my man.

(GALLIMARD *starts to cross the room.*)

GALLIMARD: Did I not undress her because I knew, somewhere deep down, what I would find? Perhaps. Happiness is so rare that our mind can turn somersaults to protect it.

At the time, I only knew that I was seeing Pinkerton stalking towards his Butterfly, ready to reward her love with his lecherous hands. The image sickened me, pulled me to my knees, so I was crawling towards her like a worm. By the time I reached her, Pinkerton . . . had vanished from my heart. To be replaced by something new, something unnatural, that flew in the face of all I'd learned in the world—something very close to love.

(*He grabs her around the waist; she strokes his hair.*)

GALLIMARD: Butterfly, forgive me.

SONG: Rene . . .

GALLIMARD: For everything. From the start.

SONG: I'm . . .

GALLIMARD: I want to—

SONG: I'm pregnant. (*Beat*) I'm pregnant. (*Beat*) I'm pregnant.

(*Beat.*)

GALLIMARD: I want to marry you!

ACT 2 / SCENE 7

(GALLIMARD *and Butterfly's flat. Beijing. 1963.*)
(*Downstage,* SONG *paces as* COMRADE CHIN *reads from her notepad. Upstage,* GALLIMARD *is still kneeling. He remains on his knees throughout the scene, watching it.*)

SONG: I need a baby.

CHIN (*From pad*): He's been spotted going to a dorm.

SONG: I need a baby.

CHIN: At the Foreign Language Institute.

SONG: I need a baby.

CHIN: The room of a Danish girl . . . What do you mean, you need a baby?!

SONG: Tell Comrade Kang—last night, the entire mission, it could've ended.

CHIN: What do you mean?

SONG: Tell Kang—he told me to strip.

CHIN: *Strip?!*

SONG: Write!

CHIN: I tell you, I don't understand nothing about this case anymore. Nothing.

SONG: He told me to strip, and I took a chance. Oh, we Chinese, we know how to gamble.

CHIN *(Writing)*: ". . . told him to strip."

SONG: My palms were wet, I had to make a split-second decision.

CHIN: Hey! Can you slow down?!

(Pause.)

SONG: You write faster, I'm the artist here. Suddenly, it hit me—"All he wants is for her to submit. Once a woman submits, a man is always ready to become 'generous.'"

CHIN: You're just gonna end up with rough notes.

SONG: And it worked! He gave in! Now, if I can just present him with a baby. A Chinese baby with blond hair—he'll be mine for life!

CHIN: Kang will never agree! The trading of babies has to be a counterrevolutionary act!

SONG: Sometimes, a counterrevolutionary act is necessary to counter a counterrevolutionary act.

(Pause.)

CHIN: Wait.

SONG: I need one . . . in seven months. Make sure it's a boy.

CHIN: This doesn't sound like something the Chairman would do. Maybe you'd better talk to Comrade Kang yourself.

SONG: Good. I will.

(CHIN gets up to leave.)

SONG: Miss Chin? Why, in the Peking Opera, are women's roles played by men?

CHIN: I don't know. Maybe, a reactionary remnant of male—

SONG: No. *(Beat)* Because only a man knows how a woman is supposed to act.

(CHIN exits. SONG turns upstage, towards GALLIMARD.)

GALLIMARD *(Calling after* CHIN*)*: Good riddance! *(To* SONG*)* I could forget all that betrayal in an instant, you know. If you'd just come back and become Butterfly again.

SONG: Fat chance. You're here in prison, rotting in a cell. And I'm on a plane, winging my way back to China. Your President pardoned me of our treason, you know.

GALLIMARD: Yes, I read about that.

SONG: Must make you feel . . . lower than shit.

GALLIMARD: But don't you, even a little bit, wish you were here with me?

SONG: I'm an artist, Rene. You were my greatest . . . acting challenge. *(She laughs)* It doesn't matter how rotten I answer, does it? You still adore me. That's why I love you, Rene. *(She points to us)* So—you were telling your audience about the night I announced I was pregnant.

(GALLIMARD puts his arms around SONG's waist. He and SONG *are in the positions they were in at the end of Scene 6.)*

ACT 2 / SCENE 8

(Same.)

GALLIMARD: I'll divorce my wife. We'll live together here, and then later in France.

SONG: I feel so . . . ashamed.

GALLIMARD: Why?

SONG: I had begun to lose faith. And now, you shame me with your generosity.

GALLIMARD: Generosity? No, I'm proposing for very selfish reasons.

SONG: Your apologies only make me feel more ashamed. My outburst a moment ago!

GALLIMARD: Your outburst? What about my request?!

SONG: You've been very patient dealing with my . . . eccentricities. A Western man, used to women freer with their bodies—

GALLIMARD: It was sick! Don't make excuses for me.

SONG: I have to. You don't seem willing to make them for yourself.

(Pause.)

GALLIMARD: You're crazy.

SONG: I'm happy. Which often looks like crazy.

GALLIMARD: Then make me crazy. Marry me.

(Pause.)

SONG: No.

GALLIMARD: What?

SONG: Do I sound silly, a slave, if I say I'm not worthy?

GALLIMARD: Yes. In fact you do. No one has loved me like you.

SONG: Thank you. And no one ever will. I'll see to that.

GALLIMARD: So what is the problem?

SONG: Rene, we Chinese are realists. We understand rice, gold, and guns. You are a diplomat. Your career is skyrocketing. Now, what would happen if you divorced your wife to marry a Communist Chinese actress?

GALLIMARD: That's not being realistic. That's defeating yourself before you begin.

SONG: We conserve our strength for the battles we can win.

GALLIMARD: That sounds like a fortune cookie!

SONG: Where do you think fortune cookies come from!

GALLIMARD: I don't care.

SONG: You do. So do I. And we should. That is why I say I'm not worthy. I'm worthy to love and even to be loved by you. But I am not worthy to end the career of one of the West's most promising diplomats.

GALLIMARD: It's not that great a career! I made it sound like more than it is!

SONG: Modesty will get you nowhere. Flatter yourself, and you flatter me. I'm flattered to decline your offer. (She exits)

GALLIMARD (To us): Butterfly and I argued all night. And, in the end, I left, knowing I would never be her husband. She went away for several months— to the countryside, like a small animal. Until the night I received her call.

(A baby's cry from offstage. SONG enters, carrying a child.)

SONG: He looks like you.

GALLIMARD: Oh! (Beat; he approaches the baby) Well, babies are never very attractive at birth.

SONG: Stop!

GALLIMARD: I'm sure he'll grow more beautiful with age. More like his mother.

SONG: "Chi vide mai/ a bimbo del Giappon . . ."

GALLIMARD: "What baby, I wonder, was ever born in Japan"—or China, for that matter—

SONG: ". . . occhi azzurrini?"

GALLIMARD: "With azure eyes"—they're actually sort of brown, wouldn't you say?

SONG: "E il labbro."

GALLIMARD: "And such lips!" (He kisses SONG) And such lips.

SONG: "E i ricciolini d'oro schietto?"

GALLIMARD: "And such a head of golden"—if slightly patchy—"curls?"

SONG: I'm going to call him "Peepee."

GALLIMARD: Darling, could you repeat that because I'm sure a rickshaw just flew by overhead.

SONG: You heard me.

GALLIMARD: "Song Peepee"? May I suggest Michael, or Stephan, or Adolph?

SONG: You may, but I won't listen.

GALLIMARD: You can't be serious. Can you imagine the time this child will have in school?

SONG: In the West, yes.

GALLIMARD: It's worse than naming him Ping Pong or Long Dong or—

SONG: But he's never going to live in the West, is he?

(Pause.)

GALLIMARD: That wasn't my choice.

SONG: It is mine. And this is my promise to you: I will raise him, he will be our child, but he will never burden you outside of China.

GALLIMARD: Why do you make these promises? I want to be burdened! I want a scandal to cover the papers!

SONG (To us): Prophetic.

GALLIMARD: I'm serious.

SONG: So am I. His name is as I registered it. And he will never live in the West.

(SONG exits with the child.)

GALLIMARD (To us): Is it possible that her stubbornness only made me want her more. That drawing back at the moment of my capitulation was the most brilliant strategy she could have chosen. It is possible. But it is also possible that by this point she could have said, could have done . . . anything, and I would have adored her still.

ACT 2 / SCENE 9

(Beijing. 1966.)
(A driving rhythm of Chinese percussion fills the stage.)

GALLIMARD: And then, China began to change. Mao became very old, and his cult became very strong. And, like many old men, he entered his second childhood. So he handed over the reins of state to those with minds like his own. And children ruled the Middle Kingdom with complete caprice. The doctrine of the Cultural Revolution implied continuous anarchy. Contact between Chinese and foreigners became impossible. Our flat was confiscated. Her fame and my money now counted against us.

(Two dancers in Mao suits and red-starred caps enter, and begin crudely mimicking revolutionary violence, in an agitprop fashion.)

GALLIMARD: And somehow the American war went wrong too. Four hundred thousand dollars were being spent for every Viet Cong killed; so General Westmoreland's remark that the Oriental does not value life the way Americans do was oddly accurate. Why weren't the Vietnamese people giving in? Why were they content instead to die and die and die again?

(TOULON enters.)

TOULON: Congratulations, Gallimard.

GALLIMARD: Excuse me, sir?

TOULON: Not a promotion. That was last time. You're going home.

GALLIMARD: What?

TOULON: Don't say I didn't warn you.

GALLIMARD: I'm being transferred . . . because I was wrong about the American war?

TOULON: Of course not. We don't care about the Americans. We care about your mind. The quality of your analysis. In general, everything you've predicted here in the Orient . . . just hasn't happened.

GALLIMARD: I think that's premature.

TOULON: Don't force me to be blunt. Okay, you said China was ready to open to Western trade. The only thing they're trading out there are Western heads. And, yes, you said the Americans would succeed in Indochina. You were kidding, right?

GALLIMARD: I think the end is in sight.

TOULON: Don't be pathetic. And don't take this personally. You were wrong. It's not your fault.

GALLIMARD: But I'm going home.

TOULON: Right. Could I have the number of your mistress? (*Beat*) Joke! Joke! Eat a croissant for me.

(TOULON *exits.* SONG, *wearing a Mao suit, is dragged in from the wings as part of the upstage dance. They "beat" her, then lampoon the acrobatics of the Chinese opera, as she is made to kneel onstage.*)

GALLIMARD (*Simultaneously*): I don't care to recall how Butterfly and I said our hurried farewell. Perhaps it was better to end our affair before it killed her.

(GALLIMARD *exits.* COMRADE CHIN *walks across the stage with a banner reading: "The Actor Renounces His Decadent Profession!" She reaches the kneeling* SONG. *Percussion stops with a thud. Dancers strike poses.*)

CHIN: Actor-oppressor, for years you have lived above the common people and looked down on their labor. While the farmer ate millet—

SONG: I ate pastries from France and sweetmeats from silver trays.

CHIN: And how did you come to live in such an exalted position?

SONG: I was a plaything for the imperialists!

CHIN: What did you do?

SONG: I shamed China by allowing myself to be corrupted by a foreigner . . .

CHIN: What does this mean? The People demand a full confession!

SONG: I engaged in the lowest perversions with China's enemies!

CHIN: What perversions? Be more clear!

SONG: I let him put it up my ass!

(*Dancers look over, disgusted.*)

CHIN: Aaaa-ya! How can you use such sickening language?!

SONG: My language . . . is only as foul as the crimes I committed . . .

CHIN: Yeah. That's better. So—what do you want to do now?

SONG: I want to serve the people.

(*Percussion starts up, with Chinese strings.*)

CHIN: What?

SONG: I want to serve the people!

(*Dancers regain their revolutionary smiles, and begin a dance of victory.*)

CHIN: What?!

SONG: I want to serve the people!!

(*Dancers unveil a banner: "The Actor Is Rehabilitated!"* SONG *remains kneeling before* CHIN, *as the dancers bounce around them, then exit. Music out.*)

ACT 2 / SCENE 10

(*A commune. Hunan Province. 1970.*)

CHIN: How you planning to do that?

SONG: I've already worked four years in the fields of Hunan, Comrade Chin.

CHIN: So? Farmers work all their lives. Let me see your hands.

(SONG *holds them out for her inspection.*)

CHIN: Goddamn! Still so smooth! How long does it take to turn you actors into good anythings? Hunh. You've just spent too many years in luxury to be any good to the Revolution.

SONG: I served the Revolution.

CHIN: Serve the Revolution? Bullshit! You wore dresses! Don't tell me—I was there. I saw you! You and your white vice-consul! Stuck up there in your flat, living off the People's Treasury! Yeah, I knew what was going on! You two . . . homos! Homos! Homos! (*Pause; she composes herself*) Ah! Well . . . you will serve the people, all right. But not with the Revolution's money. This time, you use your own money.

SONG: I have no money.

CHIN: Shut up! And you won't stink up China anymore with your pervert stuff. You'll pollute the place where pollution begins—the West.

SONG: What do you mean?

CHIN: Shut up! You're going to France. Without a cent in your pocket. You find your consul's house, you make him pay your expenses—

SONG: No.

CHIN: And you give us weekly reports! Useful information!

SONG: That's crazy. It's been four years.

CHIN: Either that, or back to rehabilitation center!

SONG: Comrade Chin, he's not going to support me! Not in France! He's a white man! I was just his plaything—

CHIN: Oh yuck! Again with the sickening language? Where's my stick?

SONG: You don't understand the mind of a man.

(*Pause.*)

CHIN: Oh no? No I don't? Then how come I'm married, huh? How come I got a man? Five, six years ago, you always tell me those kind of things, I felt very bad. But not now! Because what does the Chairman say? He tells us *I'm* now the smart one, you're now the nincompoop! *You're* the blockhead, the harebrain, the nitwit! You think you're so smart? You understand "The Mind of a Man"? Good! Then *you* go to France and be a pervert for Chairman Mao!

(CHIN *and* SONG *exit in opposite directions.*)

ACT 2 / SCENE 11

(Paris. 1968–70.)
(GALLIMARD enters.)

GALLIMARD: And what was waiting for me back in Paris? Well, better Chinese food than I'd eaten in China. Friends and relatives. A little accounting, regular schedule, keeping track of traffic violations in the suburbs. . . . And the indignity of students shouting the slogans of Chairman Mao at me—in French.

HELGA: Rene? Rene? *(She enters, soaking wet)* I've had a . . . a problem. *(She sneezes)*

GALLIMARD: You're wet.

HELGA: Yes, I . . . coming back from the grocer's. A group of students, waving red flags, they—

(GALLIMARD fetches a towel.)

HELGA: — they ran by, I was caught up along with them. Before I knew what was happening—

(GALLIMARD gives her the towel.)

HELGA: Thank you. The police started firing water cannons at us. I tried to shout, to tell them I was the wife of a diplomat, but—you know how it is . . . *(Pause)* Needless to say, I lost the groceries. Rene, what's happening to France?

GALLIMARD: What's—? Well, nothing, really.

HELGA: Nothing?! The storefronts are in flames, there's glass in the streets, buildings are toppling—and I'm wet!

GALLIMARD: Nothing! . . . that I care to think about.

HELGA: And is that why you stay in this room?

GALLIMARD: Yes, in fact.

HELGA: With the incense burning? You know something? I hate incense. It smells so sickly sweet.

GALLIMARD: Well, I hate the French. Who just smell— period!

HELGA: And the Chinese were better?

GALLIMARD: Please—don't start.

HELGA: When we left, this exact same thing, the riots—

GALLIMARD: No, no . . .

HELGA: Students screaming slogans, smashing down doors—

GALLIMARD: Helga—

HELGA: It was all going on in China, too. Don't you remember?!

GALLIMARD: Helga! Please! *(Pause)* You have never understood China, have you? You walk in here with these ridiculous ideas, that the West is falling apart, that China was spitting in our faces. You come in, dripping of the streets, and you leave water all over my floor. *(He grabs HELGA's towel, begins mopping up the floor)*

HELGA: But it's the truth!

GALLIMARD: Helga, I want a divorce.

(Pause; GALLIMARD continues mopping the floor.)

HELGA: I take it back. China is . . . beautiful. Incense, I like incense.

GALLIMARD: I've had a mistress.

HELGA: So?

GALLIMARD: For eight years.

HELGA: I knew you would. I knew you would the day I married you. And now what? You want to marry her?

GALLIMARD: I can't. She's in China.

HELGA: I see. You want to leave. For someone who's not here, is that right?

GALLIMARD: That's right.

HELGA: You can't live with her, but still you don't want to live with me.

GALLIMARD: That's right.

(Pause.)

HELGA: Shit. How terrible that I can figure that out. *(Pause)* I never thought I'd say it. But, in China, I was happy. I knew, in my own way, I knew that you were not everything you pretended to be. But the pretense—going on your arm to the embassy ball, visiting your office and the guards saying, "Good morning, good morning, Madame Gallimard"— the pretense . . . was very good indeed. *(Pause)* I hope everyone is mean to you for the rest of your life. *(She exits)*

GALLIMARD *(To us)*: Prophetic.

(MARC enters with two drinks.)

GALLIMARD *(To MARC)*: In China, I was different from all other men.

MARC: Sure. You were white. Here's your drink.

GALLIMARD: I felt . . . touched.

MARC: In the head? Rene, I don't want to hear about the Oriental love goddess. Okay? One night—can we just drink and throw up without a lot of conversation?

GALLIMARD: You still don't believe me, do you?

MARC: Sure I do. She was the most beautiful, et cetera, et cetera, blasé blasé.

(Pause.)

GALLIMARD: My life in the West has been such a disappointment.

MARC: Life in the West is like that. You'll get used to it. Look, you're driving me away. I'm leaving. Happy, now? *(He exits, then returns)* Look, I have a date tomorrow night. You wanna come? I can fix you up with—

GALLIMARD: Of course. I would love to come.

(Pause.)

MARC: Uh—on second thought, no. You'd better get ahold of yourself first.

(He exits; GALLIMARD nurses his drink.)

GALLIMARD (*To us*): This is the ultimate cruelty, isn't it? That I can talk and talk and to anyone listening, it's only air—too rich a diet to be swallowed by a mundane world. Why can't anyone understand? That in China, I once loved, and was loved by, very simply, the Perfect Woman.

(SONG *enters, dressed as Butterfly in wedding dress.*)

GALLIMARD (*To* SONG): Not again. My imagination is hell. Am I asleep this time? Or did I drink too much?
SONG: Rene?
GALLIMARD: God, it's too painful! That you speak?
SONG: What are you talking about? Rene—touch me.
GALLIMARD: Why?
SONG: I'm real. Take my hand.
GALLIMARD: Why? So you can disappear again and leave me clutching at the air? For the entertainment of my neighbors who—?

(SONG *touches* GALLIMARD.)

SONG: Rene?

(GALLIMARD *takes* SONG's *hand. Silence.*)

GALLIMARD: Butterfly? I never doubted you'd return.
SONG: You hadn't . . . forgotten—?
GALLIMARD: Yes, actually, I've forgotten everything. My mind, you see—there wasn't enough room in this hard head—not for the world *and* for you. No, there was only room for one. (*Beat*) Come, look. See? Your bed has been waiting, with the Klimt poster you like, and—see? The xiang lu [incense burner] you gave me?
SONG: I . . . I don't know what to say.
GALLIMARD: There's nothing to say. Not at the end of a long trip. Can I make you some tea?
SONG: But where's your wife?
GALLIMARD: She's by my side. She's by my side at last.

(GALLIMARD *reaches to embrace* SONG. SONG *sidesteps, dodging him.*)

GALLIMARD: Why?!
SONG (*To us*): So I did return to Rene in Paris. Where I found—
GALLIMARD: Why do you run away? Can't we show them how we embraced that evening?
SONG: Please. I'm talking.
GALLIMARD: You have to do what I say! I'm conjuring you up in *my* mind!
SONG: Rene, I've never done what you've said. Why should it be any different in your mind? Now split— the story moves on, and I must change.
GALLIMARD: I welcomed you into my home! I didn't have to, you know! I could've left you penniless on the streets of Paris! But I took you in!
SONG: Thank you.
GALLIMARD: So . . . please . . . don't change.

SONG: You know I have to. You know I will. And anyway, what difference does it make? No matter what your eyes tell you, you can't ignore the truth. You already know too much.

(GALLIMARD *exits.* SONG *turns to us.*)

SONG: The change I'm going to make requires about five minutes. So I thought you might want to take this opportunity to stretch your legs, enjoy a drink, or listen to the musicians. I'll be here, when you return, right where you left me.

(SONG *goes to a mirror in front of which is a wash basin of water. She starts to remove her makeup as stagelights go to half and houselights come up.*)

ACT 3 / SCENE 1

(*A courthouse in Paris. 1986.*)
(*As he promised,* SONG *has completed the bulk of his transformation, onstage by the time the houselights go down and the stagelights come up full. He removes his wig and kimono, leaving them on the floor. Underneath, he wears a well-cut suit.*)

SONG: So I'd done my job better than I had a right to expect. Well, give him some credit, too. He's right— I was in a fix when I arrived in Paris. I walked from the airport into town, then I located, by blind groping, the Chinatown district. Let me make one thing clear: whatever else may be said about the Chinese, they are stingy! I slept in doorways three days until I could find a tailor who would make me this kimono on credit. As it turns out, maybe I didn't even need it. Maybe he would've been happy to see me in a simple shift and mascara. But . . . better safe than sorry.
   That was 1970, when I arrived in Paris. For the next fifteen years, yes, I lived a very comfy life. Some relief, believe me, after four years on a fucking commune in Nowheresville, China. Rene supported the boy and me, and I did some demonstrations around the country as part of my "cultural exchange" cover. And then there was the spying.

(SONG *moves upstage, to a chair.* TOULON *enters as a judge, wearing the appropriate wig and robes. He sits near* SONG. *It's 1986, and* SONG *is testifying in a courtroom.*)

SONG: Not much at first. Rene had lost all his high-level contacts. Comrade Chin wasn't very interested in parking-ticket statistics. But finally, at my urging, Rene got a job as a courier, handling sensitive documents. He'd photograph them for me, and I'd pass them on to the Chinese embassy.
JUDGE: Did he understand the extent of his activity?
SONG: He didn't ask. He knew that I needed those documents, and that was enough.

JUDGE: But he must've known he was passing classified information.

SONG: I can't say.

JUDGE: He never asked what you were going to do with them?

SONG: Nope.

(Pause.)

JUDGE: There is one thing that the court—indeed, that all of France—would like to know.

SONG: Fire away.

JUDGE: Did Monsieur Gallimard know you were a man?

SONG: Well, he never saw me completely naked. Ever.

JUDGE: But surely, he must've . . . how can I put this?

SONG: Put it however you like. I'm not shy. He must've felt around?

JUDGE: Mmmmm.

SONG: Not really. I did all the work. He just laid back. Of course we did enjoy more . . . complete union, and I suppose he *might* have wondered why I was always on my stomach, but. . . . But what you're thinking is, "Of course a wrist must've brushed . . . a hand hit . . . over twenty years!" Yeah. Well, Your Honor, it was my job to make him think I was a woman. And chew on this: it wasn't all that hard. See, my mother was a prostitute along the Bundt before the Revolution. And, uh, I think it's fair to say she learned a few things about Western men. So I borrowed her knowledge. In service to my country.

JUDGE: Would you care to enlighten the court with this secret knowledge? I'm sure we're all very curious.

SONG: I'm sure you are. (Pause) Okay, Rule One is: Men always believe what they want to hear. So a girl can tell the most obnoxious lies and the guys will believe them every time—"This is my first time"—"That's the biggest I've ever seen"—or *both,* which, if you really think about it, is not possible in a single lifetime. You've maybe heard those phrases a few times in your own life, yes, Your Honor?

JUDGE: It's not my life, Monsieur Song, which is on trial today.

SONG: Okay, okay, just trying to lighten up the proceedings. Tough room.

JUDGE: Go on.

SONG: Rule Two: As soon as a Western man comes into contact with the East—he's already confused. The West has sort of an international rape mentality towards the East. Do you know rape mentality?

JUDGE: Give us your definition, please.

SONG: Basically, "Her mouth says no, but her eyes say yes."

The West thinks of itself as masculine—big guns, big industry, big money—so the East is feminine—weak, delicate, poor . . . but good at art, and full of inscrutable wisdom—the feminine mystique.

Her mouth says no, but her eyes say yes. The West believes the East, deep down, *wants* to be dominated—because a woman can't think for herself.

JUDGE: What does this have to do with my question?

SONG: You expect Oriental countries to submit to your guns, and you expect Oriental women to be submissive to your men. That's why you say they make the best wives.

JUDGE: But why would that make it possible for you to fool Monsieur Gallimard? Please—get to the point.

SONG: One, because when he finally met his fantasy woman, he wanted more than anything to believe that she was, in fact, a woman. And second, I am an Oriental. And being an Oriental, I could never be completely a man.

(Pause.)

JUDGE: Your armchair political theory is tenuous, Monsieur Song.

SONG: You think so? That's why you'll lose in all your dealings with the East.

JUDGE: Just answer my question: did he know you were a man?

(Pause.)

SONG: You know, Your Honor, I never asked.

ACT 3 / SCENE 2

(Same.)

(Music from the "Death Scene" from Butterfly blares over the house speakers. It is the loudest thing we've heard in this play.

GALLIMARD enters, crawling towards SONG's wig and kimono.)

GALLIMARD: Butterfly? Butterfly?

(SONG remains a man, in the witness box, delivering a testimony we do not hear.)

GALLIMARD (To us): In my moment of greatest shame, here, in this courtroom—with that . . . person up there, telling the world. . . . What strikes me especially is how shallow he is, how glib and obsequious . . . completely . . . without substance! The type that prowls around discos with a gold medallion stinking of garlic. So little like my Butterfly.

Yet even in this moment my mind remains agile, flip-flopping like a man on a trampoline. Even now, my picture dissolves, and I see that . . . witness . . . talking to me.

(SONG suddenly stands straight up in his witness box, and looks at GALLIMARD.)

SONG: Yes. You. White man.

(SONG steps out of the witness box, and moves downstage towards GALLIMARD. Light change.)

GALLIMARD (To SONG): Who? Me?

SONG: Do you see any other white men?

GALLIMARD: Yes. There're white men all around. This is a French courtroom.

SONG: So you are an adventurous imperialist. Tell me, why did it take you so long? To come back to this place?

GALLIMARD: What place?

SONG: This theatre in China. Where we met many years ago.

GALLIMARD (To us): And once again, against my will, I am transported.

(Chinese opera music comes up on the speakers. SONG begins to do opera moves, as he did the night they met.)

SONG: Do you remember? The night you gave your heart?

GALLIMARD: It was a long time ago.

SONG: Not long enough. A night that turned your world upside down.

GALLIMARD: Perhaps.

SONG: Oh, be honest with me. What's another bit of flattery when you've already given me twenty years' worth? It's a wonder my head hasn't swollen to the size of China.

GALLIMARD: Who's to say it hasn't?

SONG: Who's to say? And what's the shame? In pride? You think I could've pulled this off if I wasn't already full of pride when we met? No, not just pride. Arrogance. It takes arrogance, really—to believe you can will, with your eyes and your lips, the destiny of another. (He dances) C'mon. Admit it. You still want me. Even in slacks and a button-down collar.

GALLIMARD: I don't see what the point of—

SONG: You don't? Well maybe, Rene, just maybe—I want you.

GALLIMARD: You do?

SONG: Then again, maybe I'm just playing with you. How can you tell? (Reprising his feminine character, he sidles up to GALLIMARD) "How I wish there were even a small cafe to sit in. With men in tuxedos, and cappuccinos, and bad expatriate jazz." Now you want to kiss me, don't you?

GALLIMARD (Pulling away): What makes you—?

SONG: —so sure? See? I take the words from your mouth. Then I wait for you to come and retrieve them. (He reclines on the floor)

GALLIMARD: Why?! Why do you treat me so cruelly?

SONG: Perhaps I was treating you cruelly. But now—I'm being nice. Come here, my little one.

GALLIMARD: I'm not your little one!

SONG: My mistake. It's I who am your little one, right?

GALLIMARD: Yes, I—

SONG: So come get your little one. If you like. I may even let you strip me.

GALLIMARD: I mean, you were! Before . . . but not like this!

SONG: I was? Then perhaps I still am. If you look hard enough. (He starts to remove his clothes)

GALLIMARD: What—what are you doing?

SONG: Helping you to see through my act.

GALLIMARD: Stop that! I don't want to! I don't—

SONG: Oh, but you asked me to strip, remember?

GALLIMARD: What? That was years ago! And I took it back!

SONG: No. You postponed it. Postponed the inevitable. Today, the inevitable has come calling.

(From the speakers, cacophony: Butterfly mixed in with Chinese gongs.)

GALLIMARD: No! Stop! I don't want to see!

SONG: Then look away.

GALLIMARD: You're only in my mind! All this is in my mind! I order you! To stop!

SONG: To what? To strip? That's just what I'm—

GALLIMARD: No! Stop! I want you—!

SONG: You want me?

GALLIMARD: To stop!

SONG: You know something, Rene? Your mouth says no, but your eyes say yes. Turn them away. I dare you.

GALLIMARD: I don't have to! Every night, you say you're going to strip, but then I beg you and you stop!

SONG: I guess tonight is different.

GALLIMARD: Why? Why should that be?

SONG: Maybe I've become frustrated. Maybe I'm saying "Look at me, you fool!" Or maybe I'm just feeling . . . sexy. (He is down to his briefs)

GALLIMARD: Please. This is unnecessary. I know what you are.

SONG: You do? What am I?

GALLIMARD: A—a man.

SONG: You don't really believe that.

GALLIMARD: Yes I do! I knew all the time somewhere that my happiness was temporary, my love a deception. But my mind kept the knowledge at bay. To make the wait bearable.

SONG: Monsieur Gallimard—the wait is over.

(SONG drops his briefs. He is naked. Sound cue out. Slowly, we and SONG come to the realization that what we had thought to be GALLIMARD's sobbing is actually his laughter.)

GALLIMARD: Oh god! What an idiot! Of course!

SONG: Rene—what?

GALLIMARD: Look at you! You're a man! (He bursts into laughter again)

SONG: I fail to see what's so funny!

GALLIMARD: "You fail to see—!" I mean, you never did have much of a sense of humor, did you? I just think it's ridiculously funny that I've wasted so much time on just a man!

SONG: Wait. I'm not "just a man."

GALLIMARD: No? Isn't that what you've been trying to convince me of?

SONG: Yes, but what I mean—

GALLIMARD: And now, I finally believe you, and you tell me it's not true? I think you must have some kind of identity problem.

SONG: Will you listen to me?

GALLIMARD: Why?! I've been listening to you for twenty years. Don't I deserve a vacation?

SONG: I'm not just any man!

GALLIMARD: Then, what exactly are you?

SONG: Rene, how can you ask—? Okay, what about this?

(He picks up Butterfly's robes, starts to dance around. No music.)

GALLIMARD: Yes, that's very nice. I have to admit.

(SONG holds out his arm to GALLIMARD.)

SONG: It's the same skin you've worshiped for years. Touch it.

GALLIMARD: Yes, it does feel the same.

SONG: Now—close your eyes.

(SONG covers GALLIMARD's eyes with one hand. With the other, SONG draws GALLIMARD's hand up to his face. GALLIMARD, like a blind man, lets his hands run over SONG's face.)

GALLIMARD: This skin, I remember. The curve of her face, the softness of her cheek, her hair against the back of my hand . . .

SONG: I'm your Butterfly. Under the robes, beneath everything, it was always me. Now, open your eyes and admit it—you adore me. *(He removes his hand from GALLIMARD's eyes)*

GALLIMARD: You, who knew every inch of my desires— how could you, of all people, have made such a mistake?

SONG: What?

GALLIMARD: You showed me your true self. When all I loved was the lie. A perfect lie, which you let fall to the ground—and now, it's old and soiled.

SONG: So—you never really loved me? Only when I was playing a part?

GALLIMARD: I'm a man who loved a woman created by a man. Everything else—simply falls short.

(Pause.)

SONG: What am I supposed to do now?

GALLIMARD: You were a fine spy, Monsieur Song, with an even finer accomplice. But now I believe you should go. Get out of my life!

SONG: Go where? Rene, you can't live without me. Not after twenty years.

GALLIMARD: I certainly can't live with you—not after twenty years of betrayal.

SONG: Don't be stubborn! Where will you go?

GALLIMARD: I have a date . . . with my Butterfly.

SONG: So, throw away your pride. And come . . .

GALLIMARD: Get away from me! Tonight, I've finally learned to tell fantasy from reality. And, knowing the difference, I choose fantasy.

SONG: I'm your fantasy!

GALLIMARD: You? You're as real as hamburger. Now get out! I have a date with my Butterfly and I don't want your body polluting the room! *(He tosses SONG's suit at him)* Look at these—you dress like a pimp.

SONG: Hey! These are Armani slacks and—! *(He puts on his briefs and slacks)* Let's just say . . . I'm disappointed in you, Rene. In the crush of your adoration, I thought you'd become something more. More like . . . a woman.

But no. Men. You're like the rest of them. It's all in the way we dress, and make up our faces, and bat our eyelashes. You really have so little imagination!

GALLIMARD: You, Monsieur Song? Accuse me of too little imagination? You, if anyone, should know—I am pure imagination. And in imagination I will remain. Now get out!

(GALLIMARD bodily removes SONG from the stage, taking his kimono.)

SONG: Rene! I'll never put on those robes again! You'll be sorry!

GALLIMARD *(To SONG)*: I'm already sorry! *(Looking at the kimono in his hands)* Exactly as sorry . . . as a Butterfly.

ACT 3 / SCENE 3

(M. GALLIMARD's prison cell. Paris. Present.)

GALLIMARD: I've played out the events of my life night after night, always searching for a new ending to my story, one where I leave this cell and return forever to my Butterfly's arms.

Tonight I realize my search is over. That I've looked all along in the wrong place. And now, to you, I will prove that my love was not in vain—by returning to the world of fantasy where I first met her.

(He picks up the kimono; dancers enter.)

GALLIMARD: There is a vision of the Orient that I have. Of slender women in chong sams and kimonos who die for the love of unworthy foreign devils. Who are born and raised to be the perfect women. Who take whatever punishment we give them, and bounce back, strengthened by love, unconditionally. It is a vision that has become my life.

(Dancers bring the wash basin to him and help him make up his face.)

GALLIMARD: In public, I have continued to deny that Song Liling is a man. This brings me headlines, and is a source of great embarrassment to my French colleagues, who can now be sent into a coughing fit by the mere mention of Chinese food. But alone, in my cell, I have long since faced the truth.

And the truth demands a sacrifice. For mistakes made over the course of a lifetime. My mistakes

were simple and absolute—the man I loved was a
cad, a bounder. He deserved nothing but a kick in
the behind, and instead I gave him . . . all my love.
    Yes—love. Why not admit it all? That was my
undoing, wasn't it? Love warped my judgment,
blinded my eyes, rearranged the very lines on my
face . . . until I could look in the mirror and see
nothing but . . . a woman.

(Dancers help him put on the Butterfly wig.)

GALLIMARD: I have a vision. Of the Orient. That, deep
    within its almond eyes, there are still women.
    Women willing to sacrifice themselves for the love
    of a man. Even a man whose love is completely
    without worth.

*(Dancers assist GALLIMARD in donning the kimono. They
hand him a knife.)*

GALLIMARD: Death with honor is better than life . . . life
    with dishonor. *(He sets himself center stage, in a seppuku
    position)* The love of a Butterfly can withstand many
    things—unfaithfulness, loss, even abandonment.
    But how can it face the one sin that implies all
    others? The devastating knowledge that, under-
    neath it all, the object of her love was nothing more,
    nothing less than . . . a man. *(He sets the tip of the
    knife against his body)* It is 19——. And I have found
    her at last. In a prison on the outskirts of Paris. My
    name is Rene Gallimard—also known as Madame
    Butterfly.

*(GALLIMARD turns upstage and plunges the knife into
his body, as music from the "Love Duet" blares over the
speakers. He collapses into the arms of the dancers, who
lay him reverently on the floor. The image holds for
several beats. Then a tight special up on SONG, who
stands as a man, staring at the dead GALLIMARD. He
smokes a cigarette; the smoke filters up through the lights.
Two words leave his lips.)*

SONG: Butterfly? Butterfly?

(Smoke rises as lights fade slowly to black.)

AFTERWORD

It all started in May of 1986, over casual dinner conversation. A friend asked, had I heard about the French
diplomat who'd fallen in love with a Chinese actress,
who subsequently turned out to be not only a spy, but a
man? I later found a two-paragraph story in *The New
York Times.* The diplomat, Bernard Bouriscot, attempting to account for the fact that he had never seen his
"girlfriend" naked, was quoted as saying, "I thought she
was very modest. I thought it was a Chinese custom."
    Now, I am aware that this is *not* a Chinese custom,
that Asian women are no more shy with their lovers
than are women of the West. I am also aware, however,
that Bouriscot's assumption was consistent with a certain

stereotyped view of Asians as bowing, blushing flowers.
I therefore concluded that the diplomat must have
fallen in love, not with a person, but with a fantasy
stereotype. I also inferred that, to the extent the Chinese
spy encouraged these misperceptions, he must have
played up to and exploited this image of the Oriental
woman as demure and submissive. (In general, by the
way, we prefer the term "Asian" to "Oriental," in the
same way "Black" is superior to "Negro." I use the term
"Oriental" specifically to denote an exotic or imperialis-
tic view of the East.)
    I suspected there was a play here. I purposely re-
frained from further research, for I was not interested
in writing docudrama. Frankly, I didn't want the "truth"
to interfere with my own speculations. I told Stuart
Ostrow, a producer with whom I'd worked before, that
I envisioned the story as a musical. I remember going
so far as to speculate that it could be some "great *Madame
Butterfly*–like tragedy." Stuart was very intrigued, and
encouraged me with some early funding.
    Before I can begin writing, I must "break the back of
the story," and find some angle which compels me to set
pen to paper. I was driving down Santa Monica Boulevard one afternoon, and asked myself, "What did Bouriscot think he was getting in this Chinese actress?" The
answer came to me clearly: "He probably thought he
had found Madame Butterfly."
    The idea of doing a deconstructivist *Madame Butterfly*
immediately appealed to me. This, despite the fact that
I didn't even know the plot of the opera! I knew Butterfly only as a cultural stereotype; speaking of an Asian
woman, we would sometimes say, "She's pulling a Butterfly," which meant playing the submissive Oriental
number. Yet, I felt convinced that the libretto would
include yet another lotus blossom pining away for a
cruel Caucasian man, and dying for her love. Such a
story has become too much of a cliché not to be included
in the archetypal East-West romance that started it all.
Sure enough, when I purchased the record, I discovered it contained a wealth of sexist and racist clichés,
reaffirming my faith in Western culture.
    Very soon after, I came up with the basic "arc" of my
play: the Frenchman fantasizes that he is Pinkerton and
his lover is Butterfly. By the end of the piece, he realizes
that it is he who has been Butterfly, in that the Frenchman has been duped by love; the Chinese spy, who
exploited that love, is therefore the real Pinkerton. I
wrote a proposal to Stuart Ostrow, who found it very
exciting. (On the night of the Tony Awards, Stuart
produced my original two-page treatment, and we were
gratified to see that it was, indeed, the play I eventually
wrote.)
    I wrote a play, rather than a musical, because, having
"broken the back" of the story, I wanted to start immediately and not be hampered by the lengthy process of
collaboration. I would like to think, however, that the
play has retained many of its musical roots. So *Monsieur
Butterfly* was completed in six weeks between September

and mid-October, 1986. My wife, Ophelia, thought *Monsieur Butterfly* too obvious a title, and suggested I abbreviate it in the French fashion. Hence, *M. Butterfly*, far more mysterious and ambiguous, was the result.

I sent the play to Stuart Ostrow as a courtesy, assuming he would not be interested in producing what had become a straight play. Instead, he flew out to Los Angeles immediately for script conferences. Coming from a background in the not-for-profit theater, I suggested that we develop the work at a regional institution. Stuart, nothing if not bold, argued for bringing it directly to Broadway.

It was also Stuart who suggested John Dexter to direct. I had known Dexter's work only by its formidable reputation. Stuart sent the script to John, who called back the next day, saying it was the best play he'd read in twenty years. Naturally, this predisposed me to like him a great deal. We met in December in New York. Not long after, we persuaded Eiko Ishioka to design our sets and costumes. I had admired her work from afar ever since, as a college student, I had seen her poster for *Apocalypse Now* in Japan. By January, 1987, Stuart had optioned *M. Butterfly*, Dexter was signed to direct, and the normally sloth-like pace of commercial theater had been given a considerable prod.

On January 4, 1988, we commenced rehearsals. I was very pleased that John Lithgow had agreed to play the French diplomat, whom I named Rene Gallimard. Throughout his tenure with us, Lithgow was every inch the center of our company, intelligent and professional, passionate and generous. B. D. Wong was forced to endure a five-month audition period before we selected him to play Song Liling. Watching B. D.'s growth was one of the joys of the rehearsal process, as he constantly attained higher levels of performance. It became clear that we had been fortunate enough to put together a company with not only great talent, but also wonderful camaraderie.

As for Dexter, I have never worked with a director more respectful of text and bold in the uses of theatricality. On the first day of rehearsal, the actors were given movement and speech drills. Then Dexter asked that everyone not required at rehearsal leave the room. A week later, we returned for an amazingly thorough runthrough. It was not until that day that I first heard my play read, a note I direct at many regional theaters who "develop" a script to death.

We opened in Washington, D.C., at the National Theatre, where *West Side Story* and *Amadeus* had premiered. On the morning after opening night, most of the reviews were glowing, except for *The Washington Post*. Throughout our run in Washington, Stuart never pressured us to make the play more "commercial" in reaction to that review. We all simply concluded that the gentleman was possibly insecure about his own sexual orientation and therefore found the play threatening. And we continued our work.

Once we opened in New York, the play found a life of its own. I suppose the most gratifying thing for me is that we had never compromised to be more "Broadway"; we simply did the work we thought best. That our endeavor should be rewarded to the degree it has is one of those all-too-rare instances when one's own perception and that of the world are in agreement.

Many people have subsequently asked me about the "ideas" behind the play. From our first preview in Washington, I have been pleased that people leaving the theater were talking not only about the sexual, but also the political, issues raised by the work.

From my point of view, the "impossible" story of a Frenchman duped by a Chinese man masquerading as a woman always seemed perfectly explicable; given the degree of misunderstanding between men and women and also between East and West, it seemed inevitable that a mistake of this magnitude would one day take place.

Gay friends have told me of a derogatory term used in their community: "Rice Queen"—a gay Caucasian man primarily attracted to Asians. In these relationships, the Asian virtually always plays the role of the "woman"; the Rice Queen, culturally and sexually, is the "man." This pattern of relationships had become so codified that, until recently, it was considered unnatural for gay Asians to date one another. Such men would be taunted with a phrase which implied they were lesbians.

Similarly, heterosexual Asians have long been aware of "Yellow Fever"—Caucasian men with a fetish for exotic Oriental women. I have often heard it said that "Oriental women make the best wives." (Rarely is this heard from the mouths of Asian men, incidentally.) This mythology is exploited by the Oriental mail-order bride trade which has flourished over the past decade. American men can now send away for catalogues of "obedient, domesticated" Asian women looking for husbands. Anyone who believes such stereotypes are a thing of the past need look no further than Manhattan cable television, which advertises call girls from "the exotic east, where men are king; obedient girls, trained in the art of pleasure."

In these appeals, we see issues of racism and sexism intersect. The catalogues and TV spots appeal to a strain in men which desires to reject Western women for what they have become—independent, assertive, self-possessed—in favor of a more reactionary model—the prefeminist, domesticated geisha girl.

That the Oriental woman is penultimately feminine does not of course imply that she is always "good." For every Madonna there is a whore; for every lotus blossom there is also a dragon lady. In popular culture, "good" Asian women are those who serve the White protagonist in his battle against her own people, often sleeping with him in the process. Stallone's *Rambo II*, Cimino's *Year of the Dragon*, Clavell's *Shogun*, Van Lustbader's *The Ninja* are all familiar examples.

Now our considerations of race and sex intersect the issue of imperialism. For this formula—good natives serve Whites, bad natives rebel—is consistent with the mentality of colonialism. Because they are submissive and obedient, good natives of both sexes necessarily take on "feminine" characteristics in a colonialist world. Gunga Din's unfailing devotion to his British master, for instance, is not so far removed from Butterfly's slavish faith in Pinkerton.

It is reasonable to assume that influences and attitudes so pervasively displayed in popular culture might also influence our policymakers as they consider the world. The neo-Colonialist notion that good elements of a native society, like a good woman, desire submission to the masculine West speaks precisely to the heart of our foreign policy blunders in Asia and elsewhere.

For instance, Frances Fitzgerald wrote in *Fire in the Lake*, "The idea that the United States could not master the problems of a country as small and underdeveloped as Vietnam did not occur to Johnson as a possibility." Here, as in so many other cases, by dehumanizing the enemy, we dehumanize ourselves. We become the Rice Queens of *realpolitik*.

M. Butterfly has sometimes been regarded as an anti-American play, a diatribe against the stereotyping of the East by the West, of women by men. Quite to the contrary, I consider it a plea to all sides to cut through our respective layers of cultural and sexual misperception, to deal with one another truthfully for our mutual good, from the common and equal ground we share as human beings.

For the myths of the East, the myths of the West, the myths of men, and the myths of women—these have so saturated our consciousness that truthful contact between nations and lovers can only be the result of heroic effort. Those who prefer to bypass the work involved will remain in a world of surfaces, misperceptions running rampant. This is, to me, the convenient world in which the French diplomat and the Chinese spy lived. This is why, after twenty years, he had learned nothing at all about his lover, not even the truth of his sex.

D. H. H.

*New York City
September, 1988*

Figure 1. At the opening of the play, Gallimard (John Lithgow) sits in his prison cell while Song Liling (B. D. Wong) poses above. The swirling ramp was designed by Eiko Ishioka for the 1988 production of *M. Butterfly* directed by John Dexter. (Photograph: Martha Swope.)

Figure 2. Song Liling (B. D. Wong) as Butterfly in the 1988 production of *M. Butterfly* directed by John Dexter. (Photograph: Martha Swope.)

Figure 3. Gallimard (John Lithgow) and Song Liling (B. D. Wong) in her Beijing apartment in the 1988 production of *M. Butterfly* directed by John Dexter. (Photograph: Martha Swope.)

Staging of *M. Butterfly*

**REVIEW OF THE NEW YORK PRODUCTION,
1988, BY FRANK RICH**

It didn't require genius for David Henry Hwang to see that there were the makings of a compelling play in the 1986 newspaper story that prompted him to write "M. Butterfly." Here was the incredible true-life tale of a career French foreign service officer brought to ruin— conviction for espionage—by a bizarre 20-year affair with a Beijing Opera diva. Not only had the French diplomat failed to recognize that his lover was a spy; he'd also failed to figure out that "she" was a he in drag. "It was dark, and she was very modest," says Gallimard (John Lithgow), Mr. Hwang's fictionalized protagonist, by half-joking way of explanation. When we meet him in the prison cell where he reviews his life, Gallimard has become, according to his own understatement, "the patron saint of the socially inept."

But if this story is a corker, what is it about, exactly? That's where Mr. Hwang's imagination, one of the most striking to emerge in the American theater in this decade, comes in, and his answer has nothing to do with journalism. This playwright, the author of "The Dance and the Railroad" and "Family Devotions," does not tease us with obvious questions such as is she or isn't she?, or does he know or doesn't he? Mr. Hwang isn't overly concerned with how the opera singer, named Song Liling (B. D. Wong), pulled his hocus-pocus in the boudoir, and he refuses to explain away Gallimard by making him a closeted, self-denying homosexual. An inversion of Puccini's "Madama Butterfly," "M. Butterfly" is also the inverse of most American plays. Instead of reducing the world to an easily digested cluster of sexual or familial relationships, Mr. Hwang cracks open a liaison to reveal a sweeping, universal meditation on two of the most heated conflicts—men versus women, East versus West—of this or any other time.

As a piece of playwriting that manages to encompass phenomena as diverse as the origins of the Vietnam War and the socio-economic code embedded in Giorgio Armani fashions, "M. Butterfly" is so singular that one hates to report that a visitor to the Eugene O'Neill Theater must overcome a number of obstacles to savor it. Because of some crucial and avoidable lapses—a winning yet emotionally bland performance from Mr. Lithgow and inept acting in some supporting roles—the experience of seeing the play isn't nearly as exciting as thinking about it after the curtain has gone down. The production only rises to full power in its final act, when the evening's triumphant performance, Mr. Wong's mesmerizing account of the transvestite diva, hits its own tragic high notes. Until then, one must settle for being grateful that a play of this ambition has made it to Broadway, and that the director, John Dexter, has

realized as much of Mr. Hwang's far-ranging theatricality as he has.

As usual, Mr. Hwang demands a lot from directors, actors and theatergoers. A 30-year-old Chinese-American writer from Los Angeles, he has always blended Oriental and Western theater in his work, and "M. Butterfly" does so on an epic scale beyond his previous plays, let alone such similarly minded Western hybrids as "Pacific Overtures" or "Nixon in China." While ostensibly constructed as a series of Peter Shafferesque flashbacks narrated by Gallimard from prison, the play is as intricate as an infinity of Chinese boxes. Even as we follow the narrative of the lovers' affair, it is being refracted through both overt and disguised burlesque deconstructions of "Madama Butterfly." As Puccini's music collides throughout with a percussive Eastern score by Lucia Hwong, so Western storytelling and sassy humor intermingle with flourishes of martial-arts ritual, Chinese opera (Cultural Revolution Maoist agitprop included) and Kabuki. Now and then, the entire mix is turned inside out, Genet and Pirandello style, to remind us that fantasy isn't always distinguishable from reality and that actors are not to be confused with their roles.

The play's form—whether the clashing and blending of Western and Eastern cultures or of male and female characters—is wedded to its content. It's Mr. Hwang's starting-off point that a cultural icon like "Madama Butterfly" bequeaths the sexist and racist roles that burden Western men: Gallimard believes he can become "a real man" only if he can exercise power over a beautiful and submissive woman, which is why he's so ripe to be duped by Song Liling's impersonation of a shrinking butterfly. Mr. Hwang broadens his message by making Gallimard an architect of the Western foreign policy in Vietnam. The diplomat disastrously reasons that a manly display of American might can bring the Viet Cong to submission as easily as he or Puccini's Pinkerton can overpower a Madama Butterfly.

Lest that ideological leap seem too didactic, the playwright shuffles the deck still more, suggesting that the roles played by Gallimard and Song Liling run so deep that they cross the boundaries of nations, cultures, revolutions and sexual orientations. That Gallimard was fated to love "a woman created by a man" proves to be figuratively as well as literally true: we see that the male culture that inspired his "perfect woman" is so entrenched that the attitudes of "Madama Butterfly" survive in his cherished present-day porno magazines. Nor is the third world, in Mr. Hwang's view, immune from adopting the roles it condemns in foreign devils. We're sarcastically told that men continue to play women in

Chinese opera because "only a man knows how a woman is supposed to act." When Song Liling reassumes his male "true self," he still must play a submissive Butterfly to Gallimard—whatever his or Gallimard's actual sexual persuasions—unless he chooses to play the role of aggressor to a Butterfly of his own.

Mr. Hwang's play is not without its repetitions and its overly explicit bouts of thesis mongering. When the playwright stops trusting his own instinct for the mysterious, the staging often helps out. Using Eiko Ishioka's towering, blood-red Oriental variant on the abstract sets Mr. Dexter has employed in "Equus" and the Metropolitan Opera "Dialogues of the Carmelites," the director stirs together Mr. Hwang's dramatic modes and settings until one floats to a purely theatrical imaginative space suspended in time and place. That same disorienting quality can be found in Mr. Wong's Song Liling—a performance that, like John Lone's in the early Hwang plays, finds even more surprises in the straddling of cultures than in the blurring of genders.

But Mr. Dexter's erratic handling of actors, also apparent in his Broadway "Glass Menagerie" revival, inflicts a serious toll. John Getz and Rose Gregorio, as Gallimard's oldest pal and wife, are wildly off-key, wrecking the intended high-style comedy of the all-Western scenes. Mr. Lithgow, onstage virtually throughout, projects intelligence and wit, and his unflagging energy drives and helps unify the evening. Yet this engaging, ironic Gallimard never seems completely consumed by passion, whether the eroticism of imperialism or of the flesh, and the performance seems to deepen more in pitch than despair from beginning to end. Though "M. Butterfly" presents us with a visionary work that bridges the history and culture of two worlds, the production stops crushingly short of finding the gripping human drama that merges Mr. Hwang's story with his brilliant play of ideas.

DAVID MAMET

1947–

Though he "kind of stumbled upon a career as a playwright," David Mamet during the past twenty years has clearly regained his footing—seven full-length plays, over a dozen one-acts, six screenplays, an Academy Award nomination, and a Pulitzer Prize. He grew up in Chicago and its suburbs, living first with his mother (his parents divorced when he was ten), then with his father. He got his first taste of theater through Chicago's famed center of improvisational sketches, Second City, where he worked as a busboy. As an undergraduate at Vermont's Goddard College, he spent his "junior year abroad" studying acting in New York City and then returned to Goddard where his senior thesis was the script of a revue. After graduation he worked in a variety of theatrical jobs (as an actor in Toronto, as a stage manager in New York) before moving back to Vermont as a teacher and director, first at Marlboro College, then at Goddard. At Marlboro, his students performed an early version of his first play, *Lakeboat* (1970), and at Goddard, he formed the St. Nicholas Theater Company, together with two students for whom he wrote *Duck Variations* (1972) and an early draft of *Sexual Perversity in Chicago* (1974). The memory of those early plays and student actors evidently gave rise to Mamet's deceptively simple explanation of his motive for playwriting: "I started writing because I was working with very young actors and there was nothing for them to do."

In 1972, Mamet returned to Chicago, and his hometown became the base of his artistic support. In 1974, those two student actors of the St. Nicholas Theater Company also moved to Chicago, and one of them, William H. Macy, continued to work with Mamet for years, appearing in the first production of *American Buffalo* (1975), then in *The Water Engine* (1977), in *Bobby Gould in Hell* (1989), and in *Oleanna* (1992). Another Chicago friend, Gregory Mosher, has directed most of Mamet's full-length plays, beginning with *American Buffalo* and continuing through the Pulitzer Prize-winning *Glengarry Glen Ross* (1984) and *Speed-the-Plow* (1988). With Macy and Mosher, as well as other close associates—stage designer Michael Merritt, actress Lindsay Crouse (Mamet's first wife), actor Joe Mantegna—Mamet has created a body of work marked by a uniquely harsh theatrical language and peopled by characters whose viciousness commands attention even as it repels.

Though Mamet's plays resound with his harsh voice and vision of experience, they also embody distinctive aspects of American life and drama. His early play, *Duck Variations,* came, as Mamet said, "from listening to a lot of old Jewish men all my life, particularly my grandfather," but it is also a cousin to Edward Albee's *The Zoo Story,* a kinship reflected in Mamet's comment, "You can count the playwrights who haven't written about two men sitting in a park on one hand. This is just another one." *A Life in the Theatre* (1977) extends and complicates the basic two-person conversation by having it take place between men of different ages (Robert, the older actor, and John, the younger one) and by alternating their backstage conversations with snippets from the plays they are performing. The set of *American Buffalo* is a junkshop, recalling the junkyard of Sam Shepard's *The Unseen Hand.* And *Glengarry Glen Ross* boldly takes up the commercial world of Arthur Miller's *Death of a Salesman* but populates it with a cast of tawdry and corrupt real estate salesmen, ready to steal, lie, and cheat, in order to "win."

Equally influential in Mamet's career is the playwright to whom he is most often compared, Harold Pinter. Both playwrights frequently dramatize enigmatic relationships and the sudden violence that can erupt in those relationships. Both playwrights also tend to create marginalized characters who speak in language that is simultaneously realistic yet poetic in its economy and spareness. And both playwrights are known for dialogue that often reveals character through what is *not* said or *not* acknowledged.

Yet what first attracted attention about Mamet's language was not just its fragmentary and elusive style but its obscenity and its comic rhythms. Jack Kroll, writing in *Newsweek,* called Mamet "the Aristophanes of the inarticulate," because of the "antiphonal exchanges, which dwindle to single words or even fragments of words and then explode into a crossfire of scatological buckshot." The repetition of phrases, the rush to finish other people's sentences or even to interrupt the speaker's own thoughts, and the limited vocabulary reflect the corrupted state of the characters' worlds from the macho posturing of Dan and Bernie in *Sexual Perversity* to the fake camaraderie of Hollywood producers in *Speed-the-Plow.* In such contexts, people who use polysyllabic words, such as the older actor Robert in *A Life in the Theatre* or the college professor John in *Oleanna,* seem pretentious and out of touch with their actual situations. Their language becomes defensive, covering up insecurity or unhappiness.

Though *Oleanna* shares similarities of language and structure with Mamet's preceding work, it is also the first of his plays to build directly on a specific contemporary event. Opening Off-Broadway in October, 1992, the play's conflict between a female college student and her male professor seemed to reflect the confirmation hearings for Clarence Thomas when his former assistant, Anita Hill, accused him of sexual harassment. The extensive media coverage of the hearings in the fall of 1991 for a prospective Supreme Court justice inevitably raised the question of who was really telling the truth. Mamet constructs a roughly parallel situation but makes the question even more intriguing by giving the audience direct access to the moments *before* the accusation has been made. Thus, when Carol first appears in John's office, she seems nervous and afraid, worried about her inability to understand John's lectures. John, trying to deal both with Carol's problems and with an impending house-closure, including repeated phone calls from his wife and their lawyer, alternates between irritation with Carol's presence and sympathetic attempts to allay her distress. The bombshell comes in the play's second act when John asks Carol to explain why she has filed a sexual harassment complaint against him with the committee reviewing him for tenure.

At this point, the audience must rethink the long first scene. Were John's actions indeed "sexist" and "elitist"? Did he really tell "a rambling, sexually explicit story"? Did he "embrace" Carol? The audience has seen everything, but now the question becomes, what did we actually see? And the more accusing Carol becomes, the more the audience must consider not only John's conscious motives but his unconscious ones as well. Is he, without realizing it, not merely pompous but condescending and invasive? Are his frequent interruptions of Carol genuine signs of his desire to help or indications of his unwillingness to actually listen to her? Most importantly, is the violence with which he attacks her in the play's final moments (Figure 3) a quality that has always been part of him and his attitude toward women or is it a response that her own accusation has created? Audience reaction to the attack has been audible and varied—expressions of shock but also applause.

Thus Mamet plays yet another variation on the theme of the domineering teacher and the submissive student, a theme explored in Shaw's *Pygmalion* and Ionesco's *The Lesson*. But Mamet complicates the problems of power and gender by relating them to recent discussions of feminism, censorship, and political correctness. The New York production, directed by Mamet, clearly portrayed the changing power relationships. In Figure 1, John is carefully dressed in suit and tie, his hair neatly combed, and he stands by his symbol of power, his desk; in Figure 2, Carol stands while *he* sits, his disheveled appearance reflecting how much power he has lost. Though the difference in the teacher/student relationship is clear, how one understands the motives and actions of the characters may still vary considerably. Therefore, we reprint not only a theatrical review but also a series of responses from six audience members, three women and three men. Their conflicting readings are evidence of *Oleanna*'s power to force audiences to confront their own prejudices and beliefs.

OLEANNA

BY DAVID MAMET

This play is dedicated to the memory of Michael Merritt

The want of fresh air does not seem much to affect the happiness of children in a London alley: the greater part of them sing and play as though they were on a moor in Scotland. So the absence of a genial mental atmosphere is not commonly recognized by children who have never known it. Young people have a marvelous faculty of either dying or adapting themselves to circumstances. Even if they are unhappy—very unhappy—it is astonishing how easily they can be prevented from finding it out, or at any rate from attributing it to any other cause than their own sinfulness.

The Way of All Flesh, SAMUEL BUTLER

"Oh, to be in *Oleanna,*
That's where I would rather be.
Than be bound in Norway
And drag the chains of slavery."
—folk song°

CHARACTERS

CAROL, *A woman of twenty*
JOHN, *A man in his forties*

The play takes place in John's office.

ACT 1

JOHN *is talking on the phone.* CAROL *is seated across the desk from him.*

JOHN *(on phone):* And what about the land. *(Pause)* The land. And what about the land? *(Pause)* What about it? *(Pause)* No. I don't understand. Well, yes, I'm I'm . . . no, I'm *sure* it's signif . . . I'm sure it's significant. *(Pause)* Because it's significant to mmmmmm . . . did you call Jerry? *(Pause)* Because . . . no, no, no, no, no. What did they say . . . ? Did you speak to the *real* estate . . . where *is* she . . . ? Well, well, all right. Where are her notes? Where are the notes we took with her. *(Pause)* I thought you were? No. No, I'm sorry, I didn't mean that, I just thought that I saw you, when we were there . . . what . . . ? I thought I saw you with a *pencil.* WHY NOW? is what I'm say . . . well, that's why I say "call Jerry." Well, I can't right now, be . . . no, I *didn't* schedule any . . . Grace: I *didn't* . . . I'm well aware . . . Look: Look. Did you call Jerry? Will you call Jerry . . . ? Because I can't now. I'll be there, I'm sure I'll be there in fifteen, in twenty. I intend to. No, we aren't *going* to lose the, we aren't *going* to lose the house. Look: Look, I'm not minimizing it. The "easement." Did she say "easement"? *(Pause)* What did she *say; is* it a "term of art," are we *bound* by it . . . I'm sorry . . . *(Pause)* are: we: yes. *Bound* by . . . Look: *(He checks his watch.)* before the other side *goes home,* all right? "a term of art." Because: that's right *(Pause)* The yard for the boy. Well, that's the whole . . . Look: I'm going to meet you there . . . *(He checks his watch.)* Is the realtor there? All right, tell her to show you the basement again. Look at the *this* because . . . Bec . . . I'm leaving in, I'm

leaving in ten or fifteen . . . Yes. No, no, I'll meet you at the new . . . That's a good. If he thinks it's necc . . . you tell Jerry to meet . . . All right? We *aren't* going to lose the deposit. All right? I'm sure it's going to be . . . *(Pause)* I hope so. *(Pause)* I love you, too. *(Pause)* I love you, too. As soon as . . . I will.

(He hangs up.) (He bends over the desk and makes a note.) (He looks up.) (To CAROL:) I'm sorry . . .

CAROL: *(Pause)* What is a "term of art"?

JOHN: *(Pause)* I'm sorry . . . ?

CAROL: *(Pause)* What is a "term of art"?

JOHN: Is that what you want to talk about?

CAROL: . . . to talk about . . . ?

JOHN: Let's take the mysticism out of it, shall we? Carol? *(Pause)* Don't you think? I'll tell you: when you have some "thing." Which must be broached. *(Pause)* Don't you think . . . ? *(Pause)*

CAROL: . . . don't I think . . . ?

JOHN: Mmm?

CAROL: . . . did I . . . ?

JOHN: . . . what?

CAROL: Did . . . did I . . . did I say something wr . . .

---

folk song, The Norwegian song, in a translation popularized by the folksinger Pete Seeger, refers to a nineteenth-century Norwegian colony founded in Pennsylvania by the violinist Ole Bull. But since Ole Bull mistakenly bought stony soil, the first colonists could plant no crops and the colony failed. The song's evocation of a place so bountiful that "the wheat and corn just plant themselves" and "the cows all like to milk themselves and hens lay eggs ten times a day" is thus simultaneously Utopian and satiric.

JOHN: *(Pause)* No. I'm sorry. No. You're right. I'm very sorry. I'm somewhat rushed. As you see. I'm sorry. You're right. *(Pause)* What is a "term of art"? It seems to mean a *term,* which has come, through its use, to mean something *more specific* than the words would, to someone *not acquainted* with them . . . indicate. That, I believe, is what a "term of art," would mean. *(Pause)*

CAROL: You don't know what it means . . . ?

JOHN: I'm not sure that I know what it means. It's one of those things, perhaps you've had them, that, you look them up, or have someone explain them to you, and you say "aha," and, you immediately *forget* what . . .

CAROL: You don't do that.

JOHN: . . . I . . . ?

CAROL: You don't do . . .

JOHN: . . . I don't, what . . . ?

CAROL: . . . for . . .

JOHN: . . . I don't for . . .

CAROL: . . . no . . .

JOHN: . . . forget things? Everybody does that.

CAROL: No, they don't.

JOHN: They don't . . .

CAROL: No.

JOHN: *(Pause)* No. Everybody does that.

CAROL: Why would they do that . . . ?

JOHN: Because. I don't know. Because it doesn't interest them.

CAROL: No.

JOHN: I think so, though. *(Pause)* I'm sorry that I was distracted.

CAROL: You don't have to say that to me.

JOHN: You paid me the compliment, or the "obeisance"—all right—of coming in here . . . All right. *Carol.* I find that I am at a *standstill.* I find that I . . .

CAROL: . . . what . . .

JOHN: . . . one moment. In regard to your . . . to your . . .

CAROL: Oh, oh. You're buying a new house!

JOHN: No, let's get on with it.

CAROL: "get on"? *(Pause)*

JOHN: I know how . . . *believe* me. I know how . . . potentially *humiliating* these . . . I have no desire to . . . I have no desire other than to help you. But: *(He picks up some papers on his desk.)* I won't even say "but." I'll say that as I go back over the . . .

CAROL: I'm just, I'm just trying to . . .

JOHN: . . . no, it will not do.

CAROL: . . . what? What will . . . ?

JOHN: No. I see, I see what you, it . . . *(He gestures to the papers.)* but your work . . .

CAROL: I'm just: I sit in class I . . . *(She holds up her notebook.)* I take notes . . .

JOHN *(simultaneously with* "notes"*)*: Yes. I understand. What I am trying to *tell* you is that some, some basic . . .

CAROL: . . . I . . .

JOHN: . . . one moment: some basic missed communi . . .

CAROL: I'm doing what I'm told. I bought your book, I read your . . .

JOHN: No, I'm sure you . . .

CAROL: No, no, no. I'm doing what I'm told. It's *difficult* for me. It's *difficult* . . .

JOHN: . . . but . . .

CAROL: I don't . . . lots of the *language* . . .

JOHN: . . . please . . .

CAROL: The *language,* the "things" that you say . . .

JOHN: I'm sorry. No. I don't think that that's true.

CAROL: It *is* true. I . . .

JOHN: I think . . .

CAROL: It *is* true.

JOHN: . . . I . . .

CAROL: Why would I . . . ?

JOHN: I'll tell you why: you're an incredibly bright girl.

CAROL: . . . I . . .

JOHN: You're an incredibly . . . you have no problem with the . . . Who's kidding who?

CAROL: . . . I . . .

JOHN: No. No. I'll tell you why. I'll tell. . . . I think you're *angry,* I . . .

CAROL: . . . why would I . . .

JOHN: . . . wait one moment. I . . .

CAROL: It *is* true. I have *problems* . . .

JOHN: . . . every . . .

CAROL: . . . I come from a different *social* . . .

JOHN: . . . ev . . .

CAROL: a different economic . . .

JOHN: . . . Look:

CAROL: No. I: when I *came* to this school:

JOHN: Yes. Quite . . . *(Pause)*

CAROL: . . . does that mean nothing . . . ?

JOHN: . . . but look: look . . .

CAROL: . . . I . . .

JOHN: *(Picks up paper.)* Here: Please: Sit down. *(Pause)* Sit down. *(Reads from her paper.)* "I think that the ideas contained in this work express the author's feelings in a way that he intended, based on his results." What can that mean? Do you see? What . . .

CAROL: I, the best that I . . .

JOHN: I'm saying, that perhaps this course . . .

CAROL: No, no, no, you can't, you can't . . . I have to . . .

JOHN: . . . how . . .

CAROL: . . . I have to pass it . . .

JOHN: Carol, I:

CAROL: I *have* to pass this course, I . . .

JOHN: Well.

CAROL: . . . don't you . . .

JOHN: Either the . . .

CAROL: . . . I . . .

JOHN: . . . either the, I . . . either the *criteria* for judging progress in the class are . . .

CAROL: No, no, no, no, I have to pass it.

JOHN: Now, look: I'm a human being, I . . .

CAROL: I did what you told me. I did, I did everything that, I read your *book,* you told me to buy your book and read it. Everything you *say* I . . . *(She gestures to her notebook.) (The phone rings.)* I do. . . . Ev . . .

JOHN: . . . look:

CAROL: . . . everything I'm told . . .

JOHN: Look. Look. I'm not your *father. (Pause)*

CAROL: What?

JOHN: I'm.

CAROL: Did I say you were my father?

JOHN: . . . no . . .

CAROL: Why did you say that . . . ?

JOHN: I . . .

CAROL: . . . why . . .?

JOHN: . . . in class I . . . *(He picks up the phone.) (Into phone:)* Hello. I can't talk now. Jerry? Yes? I underst . . . I can't talk now. I know . . . I know . . . Jerry. I can't *talk* now. Yes, I. Call me back in . . . Thank you. *(He hangs up.) (To* CAROL:*)* What do you want me to do? We are two people, all right? Both of whom have subscribed to . . .

CAROL: No, no . . .

JOHN: . . . certain arbitrary . . .

CAROL: No. You have to help me.

JOHN: Certain institutional . . . you tell me what you want me to do. . . . You tell me what you want me to . . .

CAROL: How can I go back and tell them the *grades* that I . . .

JOHN: . . . what can I do . . . ?

CAROL: *Teach* me. *Teach* me.

JOHN: . . . I'm trying to teach you.

CAROL: I read your book. I read it. I don't under . . .

JOHN: . . . you don't understand it.

CAROL: No.

JOHN: Well, perhaps it's not well *written* . . .

CAROL *(simultaneously with* "written"*)*: No. No. No. I want to *understand* it.

JOHN: What don't you understand? *(Pause)*

CAROL: *Any* of it. What you're trying to say. When you talk about . . .

JOHN: . . . yes . . . ? *(She consults her notes.)*

CAROL: "Virtual warehousing of the young" . . .

JOHN: "Virtual warehousing of the young." If we artificially prolong adolescence . . .

CAROL: . . . and about "The Curse of Modern Education."

JOHN: . . . well . . .

CAROL: I don't . . .

JOHN: Look. It's just a *course,* it's just a *book,* it's just a . . .

CAROL: No. No. There are *people* out there. People who came *here.* To know something they didn't *know.* Who *came* here. To be *helped.* To be *helped.* So someone would *help* them. To *do* something. To *know*

something. To get, what do they say? "To get on in the world." How can I do that if I don't, if I fail? But I don't *understand.* I don't *understand.* I don't understand what anything means . . . and I walk around. From morning 'til night: with this one thought in my head. I'm *stupid.*

JOHN: No one thinks you're stupid.

CAROL: No? What am I . . . ?

JOHN: I . . .

CAROL: . . . what am I, then?

JOHN: I think you're angry. Many people are. I have a *telephone* call that I have to make. And an *appointment,* which is rather *pressing;* though I sympathize with your concerns, and though I wish I had the time, this was not a previously scheduled meeting and I . . .

CAROL: . . . you think I'm nothing . . .

JOHN: . . . have an appointment with a *realtor,* and with my wife and . . .

CAROL: You think that I'm stupid.

JOHN: No. I certainly don't.

CAROL: You said it.

JOHN: No. I did not.

CAROL: You did.

JOHN: When?

CAROL: . . . you . . .

JOHN: No. I never did, or never would say that to a student, and . . .

CAROL: You said, "What can that mean?" *(Pause)* "What can that mean?" . . . *(Pause)*

JOHN: . . . and what did that mean to you . . . ?

CAROL: That meant I'm stupid. And I'll never learn. That's what that meant. And you're right.

JOHN: . . . I . . .

CAROL: But then. But then, what am I doing here . . . ?

JOHN: . . . if you thought that I . . .

CAROL: . . . when nobody wants me, and . . .

JOHN: . . . if you interpreted . . .

CAROL: Nobody *tells* me anything. And I *sit* there . . . in the *corner.* In the *back.* And everybody's talking about "this" all the time. And "concepts," and "precepts" and, and, and, and, and, WHAT IN THE WORLD ARE YOU *TALKING* ABOUT? And I read your book. And they said, "Fine, go in that class." Because you talked about responsibility to the young. I DON'T KNOW WHAT IT MEANS AND I'M *FAILING* . . .

JOHN: May . . .

CAROL: No, you're right. "Oh, hell." I failed. Flunk me out of it. It's garbage. Everything I do. "The ideas contained in this work express the author's feelings." That's right. That's right. I know I'm stupid. I know what I am. *(Pause)* I know what I am, Professor. You don't have to tell me. *(Pause)* It's pathetic. Isn't it?

JOHN: . . . Aha . . . *(Pause)* Sit down. Sit down. Please. *(Pause)* Please sit down.

CAROL: Why?

JOHN: I want to talk to you.

CAROL: Why?

JOHN: Just sit down. *(Pause)* Please. Sit down. Will you, please . . . ? *(Pause. She does so.)* Thank you.

CAROL: What?

JOHN: I want to tell you something.

CAROL: *(Pause)* What?

JOHN: Well, I know what you're talking about.

CAROL: No. You don't.

JOHN: I think I do. *(Pause)*

CAROL: How can you?

JOHN: I'll tell you a story about myself. *(Pause)* Do you mind? *(Pause)* I was raised to think myself stupid. That's what I want to tell you. *(Pause)*

CAROL: What do you mean?

JOHN: Just what I said. I was brought up, and my earliest, and most persistent memories are of being told that I was stupid. "You have such *intelligence.* Why must you behave so *stupidly?*" Or, "Can't you *understand?* Can't you *understand?*" And I could *not* understand. I could *not* understand.

CAROL: What?

JOHN: The simplest problem. Was beyond me. It was a mystery.

CAROL: What was a mystery?

JOHN: How people learn. How *I* could learn. Which is what I've been speaking of in class. And of *course* you can't hear it. Carol. Of *course* you can't. *(Pause)* I used to speak of "real people," and wonder what the *real* people did. The *real* people. Who were they? *They* were the people other than myself. The *good* people. The *capable* people. The people who could do the things, I could not do: learn, study, retain . . . all that *garbage*—which is what I have been talking of in class, and that's *exactly* what I have been talking of—If you are told. . . . Listen to this. If the young child is told he cannot understand. Then he takes it as a *description* of himself. What am I? I am *that which cannot understand.* And I saw you out there, when we were speaking of the concepts of . . .

CAROL: I can't understand any of them.

JOHN: Well, then, that's *my* fault. That's not your fault. And that is not verbiage. That's what I firmly hold to be the truth. And I am sorry, and I owe you an apology.

CAROL: Why?

JOHN: And I suppose that I have had some *things* on my mind. . . . We're buying a *house,* and . . .

CAROL: People said that you were stupid . . . ?

JOHN: Yes.

CAROL: When?

JOHN: I'll tell you when. Through my life. In my childhood; and, perhaps, they stopped. But I heard them continue.

CAROL: And what did they say?

JOHN: They said I was incompetent. Do you see? And when I'm tested the, the, the *feelings* of my youth about the *very subject of learning* come up. And I . . . I become, I feel "unworthy," and "unprepared." . . .

CAROL: . . . yes.

JOHN: . . . eh?

CAROL: . . . yes.

JOHN: And I feel that I must fail. *(Pause)*

CAROL: . . . but then you *do* fail. *(Pause)* You have to. *(Pause)* Don't you?

JOHN: *A pilot.* Flying a plane. The pilot is flying the plane. He thinks: Oh, my *God,* my mind's been drifting! Oh, my God! What kind of a cursed imbecile am I, that I, with this so precious cargo of *Life* in my charge, would allow my attention to wander. Why was I born? How deluded are those who put their trust in me, . . . et cetera, so on, and he crashes the plane.

CAROL: *(Pause)* He could just . . .

JOHN: That's right.

CAROL: He could say:

JOHN: My attention *wandered* for a moment . . .

CAROL: . . . uh huh . . .

JOHN: I had a *thought* I did not like . . . but now:

CAROL: . . . but now it's . . .

JOHN: That's what I'm telling you. It's time to put my attention . . . see: it is not: this is what I learned. It is Not Magic. Yes. Yes. *You.* You are going to be frightened. When faced with what may or may not be but which you are going to perceive as a test. You will become frightened. And you will say: "I am incapable of . . ." and everything *in* you will think these two things. "I must. But I can't." And you will think: Why was I born to be the laughingstock of a world in which everyone is better than I? In which I am entitled to nothing. Where I can not learn.

(Pause)

CAROL: Is that . . . *(Pause)* Is that what I have . . . ?

JOHN: Well. I don't know if I'd put it that way. Listen: I'm talking to you as I'd talk to my son. Because that's what I'd like him to have that I never had. I'm talking to you the way I wish that someone had talked to me. I don't know how to do it, other than to be *personal,* . . . but . . .

CAROL: Why would you want to be personal with me?

JOHN: Well, you see? That's what I'm saying. We can only interpret the behavior of others through the screen we . . . *(The phone rings.)* Through . . . *(To phone:)* Hello . . . ? *(To CAROL:)* Through the screen we create. *(To phone:)* Hello. *(To CAROL:)* Excuse me a moment. *(To phone:)* Hello? No, I can't talk nnn . . . I know I did. In a few . . . I'm . . . is he coming to the . . . yes. I talked to him. We'll meet you at the No, because I'm with a *student.* It's going to be fff . . . This is important, too. I'm with a *student,* Jerry's going to . . . Listen: the sooner I get off, the sooner I'll be down, all right. I love you. Listen, listen, I said "I love you," it's going to work *out* with the, because I feel that it is, I'll be right down. All right? Well, then it's going to take as long as it takes. *(He hangs up.) (To* CAROL.*)* I'm sorry.

CAROL: What was that?

JOHN: There are some problems, as there usually are, about the final agreements for the new house.

CAROL: You're buying a new house.

JOHN: That's right.

CAROL: Because of your promotion.

JOHN: Well, I suppose that that's right.

CAROL: Why did you stay here with me?

JOHN: Stay here.

CAROL: Yes. When you should have gone.

JOHN: Because I like you.

CAROL: You like me.

JOHN: Yes.

CAROL: Why?

JOHN: Why? Well? Perhaps we're similar. *(Pause)* Yes. *(Pause)*

CAROL: You said "everyone has problems."

JOHN: Everyone has problems.

CAROL: Do they?

JOHN: Certainly.

CAROL: You do?

JOHN: Yes.

CAROL: What are they?

JOHN: Well. *(Pause)* Well, you're perfectly right. *(Pause)* If we're going to take off the Artificial *Stricture,* of "Teacher," and "Student," why should *my* problems be any more a mystery than your own? Of *course* I have problems. As you saw.

CAROL: . . . with what?

JOHN: With my *wife* . . . with *work* . . .

CAROL: With work?

JOHN: Yes. And, and, perhaps my problems are, do you see? *Similar* to yours.

CAROL: Would you tell me?

JOHN: All right. *(Pause)* I came *late* to teaching. And I found it Artificial. The notion of "I know and you do not"; and I saw an *exploitation* in the education process. I told you. I hated school, I hated teachers. I hated everyone who was in the position of a "boss" because I *knew*—I didn't *think,* mind you, I *knew* I was going to fail. Because I was a fuckup. I was just no goddamned good. When I . . . late in life . . . *(Pause)* When I *got out from under* . . . when I worked my way out of the need to fail. When I . . .

CAROL: How do you do that? *(Pause)*

JOHN: You have to look at what you are, and what you feel, and how you act. And, finally, you have to look at how you act. And say: If that's what I *did,* that must be how I think of myself.

CAROL: I don't understand.

JOHN: If I fail all the time, it must be that I think of myself as a failure. If I do not want to think of myself as a failure, perhaps I should begin by *succeeding* now and again. Look. The tests, you see,

which you encounter, in school, in college, in life, were designed, in the most part, for idiots. *By* idiots. There is no need to fail at them. They are not a test of your worth. They are a test of your ability to retain and spout back misinformation. Of *course* you fail them. They're *nonsense.* And I . . .

CAROL: . . . no . . .

JOHN: Yes. They're *garbage.* They're a *joke.* Look at me. Look at me. The Tenure Committee. The Tenure Committee. Come to judge me. The Bad Tenure Committee.

The "Test." Do you see? They put me to the test. Why, they had people voting on me I wouldn't employ to wax my car. And yet, I go before the Great Tenure Committee, and I have an urge, to *vomit,* to, to, to puke my *badness* on the table, to show them: "I'm no good. Why would you pick *me?*"

CAROL: They granted you tenure.

JOHN: Oh no, they announced it, but they haven't *signed.* Do you see? "At any moment . . .

CAROL: . . . mmm . . .

JOHN: "They might not *sign*" . . . I might not . . . the *house* might not go through . . . Eh? Eh? They'll find out my "dark secret." *(Pause)*

CAROL: . . . what is it . . . ?

JOHN: There *isn't* one. But *they* will find an index of my badness . . .

CAROL: Index?

JOHN: A ". . . pointer." A "Pointer." You see? Do you see? I *understand* you. I. Know. That. Feeling. Am I entitled to my job, and my nice *home,* and my *wife,* and my *family,* and so on. This is what I'm saying: That theory of education which, that *theory:*

CAROL: I . . . I . . . *(Pause)*

JOHN: What?

CAROL: I . . .

JOHN: What?

CAROL: I want to know about my grade. *(Long pause)*

JOHN: Of course you do.

CAROL: Is that bad?

JOHN: No.

CAROL: Is it bad that I asked you that?

JOHN: No.

CAROL: Did I upset you?

JOHN: No. And I apologize. Of *course* you want to know about your grade. And, of course, you can't concentrate on anyth . . . *(The telephone starts to ring.)* Wait a moment.

CAROL: I should go.

JOHN: I'll make you a deal.

CAROL: No, you have to . . .

JOHN: Let it ring. I'll make you a deal. You stay here. We'll start the whole course over. I'm going to say it was not you, it was I who was not paying attention. We'll start the whole course over. Your grade is an "A." Your final grade is an "A." *(The phone stops ringing.)*

CAROL: But the class is only half over . . .

JOHN (*simultaneously with* "over"): Your grade for the whole term is an "A." If you will come back and meet with me. A few more times. Your grade's an "A." Forget about the paper. You didn't like it, you didn't like writing it. It's not important. What's important is that I awake your interest, if I can, and that I answer your questions. Let's start over. (*Pause*)

CAROL: Over. With what?

JOHN: Say this is the beginning.

CAROL: The beginning.

JOHN: Yes.

CAROL: Of what?

JOHN: Of the class.

CAROL: But we can't start over.

JOHN: I say we can. (*Pause*) I say we can.

CAROL: But I don't believe it.

JOHN: Yes, I know that. But it's true. What is The Class but you and me? (*Pause*)

CAROL: There are rules.

JOHN: Well. We'll break them.

CAROL: How can we?

JOHN: We won't tell anybody.

CAROL: Is that all right?

JOHN: I say that it's fine.

CAROL: Why would you do this for me?

JOHN: I like you. Is that so difficult for you to . . .

CAROL: Um . . .

JOHN: There's no one here but you and me. (*Pause*)

CAROL: All right. I did not understand. When you referred . . .

JOHN: All right, yes?

CAROL: When you referred to hazing.

JOHN: Hazing.

CAROL: You wrote, in your book. About the comparative . . . the comparative . . . (*She checks her notes.*)

JOHN: Are you checking your notes . . . ?

CAROL: Yes.

JOHN: Tell me in your own . . .

CAROL: I want to make sure that I have it right.

JOHN: No. Of course. You want to be exact.

CAROL: I want to know everything that went on.

JOHN: . . . that's good.

CAROL: . . . so I . . .

JOHN: That's very good. But I was suggesting, many times, that that which we wish to retain is retained oftentimes, I think, *better* with less expenditure of effort.

CAROL: (*Of notes*) Here it is: you wrote of *hazing*.

JOHN: . . . that's correct. Now: I said "hazing." It means ritualized annoyance. We shove this book at you, we say read it. Now, you say you've read it? I think that you're *lying*. I'll *grill* you, and when I find you've lied, you'll be disgraced, and your life will be ruined. It's a sick game. Why do we do it? Does it educate? In no sense. Well, then, what is higher education? It is something-other-than-useful.

CAROL: What is "something-other-than-useful?"

JOHN: It has become a ritual, it has become an article of faith. That all must be subjected to, or to put it differently, that all are entitled to Higher Education. And my point . . .

CAROL: You disagree with that?

JOHN: Well, let's address that. What do you think?

CAROL: I don't know.

JOHN: What do you think, though? (*Pause*)

CAROL: I don't know.

JOHN: I spoke of it in class. Do you remember my example?

CAROL: Justice.

JOHN: Yes. Can you repeat it to me? (*She looks down at her notebook.*) Without your notes? I ask you as a favor to me, so that I can see if my idea was interesting.

CAROL: You said "justice" . . .

JOHN: Yes?

CAROL: . . . that all are entitled . . . (*Pause*) I . . . I . . . I . . .

JOHN: Yes. To a speedy trial. To a fair trial. But they needn't be given a trial *at all* unless they stand accused. Eh? Justice is their right, should they choose to avail themselves of it, they should have a fair trial. It does not follow, of necessity, a person's life is incomplete without a trial in it. Do you see?

My point is a confusion between equity and *utility* arose. So we confound the *usefulness* of higher education with our, granted, right to equal access to the same. We, in effect, create a *prejudice* toward it, completely independent of . . .

CAROL: . . . that it is prejudice that we should go to school?

JOHN: Exactly. (*Pause*)

CAROL: How can you say that? How . . .

JOHN: Good. Good. *Good.* That's right! Speak up! What is a prejudice? An unreasoned belief. We are all subject to it. None of us is not. When it is threatened, or opposed, we feel anger, and feel, do we not? As you do now. Do you not? Good.

CAROL: . . . but how can you . . .

JOHN: . . . let us examine. Good.

CAROL: How . . .

JOHN: Good. Good. When . . .

CAROL: I'M SPEAKING . . . (*Pause*)

JOHN: I'm sorry.

CAROL: How can you . . .

JOHN: . . . I beg your pardon.

CAROL: That's all right.

JOHN: I beg your pardon.

CAROL: That's all right.

JOHN: I'm sorry I interrupted you.

CAROL: That's all right.

JOHN: You were saying?

CAROL: I was saying . . . I was saying . . . (*She checks her notes.*) How can you say in a class. Say in a college class, that college education is prejudice?

JOHN: I said that our predilection for it . . .

CAROL: Predilection . . .

JOHN: . . . you know what that means.

CAROL: Does it mean "liking"?

JOHN: Yes.

CAROL: But how can you say that? That College . . .

JOHN: . . . that's my *job,* don't you know.

CAROL: What is?

JOHN: To provoke you.

CAROL: No.

JOHN: Oh. Yes, though.

CAROL: To provoke me?

JOHN: That's right.

CAROL: To make me mad?

JOHN: That's right. To force you . . .

CAROL: . . . to make me mad is your job?

JOHN: To force you to . . . listen: *(Pause)* Ah. *(Pause)* When I was young somebody told me, are you ready, the rich copulate less often than the poor. But when they do, they take more of their clothes off. Years. Years, mind you, I would compare experiences of my own to this dictum, saying, aha, this fits the norm, or ah, this is a variation from it. What did it mean? Nothing. It was some jerk thing, some school kid told me that took up room inside my head. *(Pause)*

Somebody told *you,* and you hold it as an article of faith, that higher education is an unassailable good. This notion is so dear to you that when I question it you become angry. Good. Good, I say. Are not those the very things which we should question? I say college education, since the war, has become so a matter of course, and such a fashionable necessity, for those either of or aspiring *to* to the new vast middle class, that we *espouse* it, as a matter of right, and have ceased to ask, "What is it good for?" *(Pause)*

What might be some reasons for pursuit of higher education?

One: A love of learning.

Two: The wish for mastery of a skill.

Three: For economic betterment.

(Stops. Makes a note.)

CAROL: I'm keeping you.

JOHN: One moment. I have to make a note . . .

CAROL: It's something that I said?

JOHN: No, we're buying a house.

CAROL: You're buying the new house.

JOHN: To go with the tenure. That's right. Nice *house,* close to the *private school* . . . *(He continues making his note.)* . . . We were talking of economic *betterment* (CAROL *writes in her notebook.)* . . . I was thinking of the School Tax. *(He continues writing.) (To himself:)* . . . *where is it written* that I have to send my child to public school. . . . Is it a law that I have to improve the City Schools at the expense of my own interest? And, is this not simply *The White Man's Burden?*

Good. And *(Looks up to* CAROL*)* . . . does this interest you?

CAROL: No. I'm taking notes . . .

JOHN: You don't have to take notes, you know, you can just listen.

CAROL: I want to make sure I remember it. *(Pause)*

JOHN: I'm not lecturing you, I'm just trying to tell you some things I think.

CAROL: What do you think?

JOHN: Should all kids go to college? *Why* . . .

CAROL: *(Pause)* To learn.

JOHN: But if he does not learn.

CAROL: If the child does not learn?

JOHN: Then why is he in college? Because he was told it was his "right"?

CAROL: Some might find college instructive.

JOHN: I would hope so.

CAROL: But how do they feel? Being told they are wasting their time?

JOHN: I don't think I'm telling them that.

CAROL: You said that education was "prolonged and systematic hazing."

JOHN: Yes. It can be so.

CAROL: . . . if education is so *bad,* why do you do it?

JOHN: I do it because I love it. *(Pause)* Let's. . . . I suggest you look at the demographics, wage-earning capacity, college- and non-college-educated men and women, 1855 to 1980, and let's see if we can wring some worth from the statistics. Eh? And . . .

CAROL: No.

JOHN: What?

CAROL: I can't understand them.

JOHN: . . . you . . . ?

CAROL: . . . the "charts." The *Concepts,* the . . .

JOHN: "Charts" are simply . . .

CAROL: When I leave here . . .

JOHN: Charts, do you see . . .

CAROL: No, I can't . . .

JOHN: You can, though.

CAROL: NO, NO—I DON'T UNDERSTAND. DO YOU SEE??? I DON'T *UNDERSTAND* . . .

JOHN: What?

CAROL: *Any* of it. *Any* of it. I'm *smiling* in class, I'm *smiling,* the whole time. What are you *talking* about? What is everyone *talking* about? I don't *understand.* I don't know what it *means.* I don't know what it means to *be* here . . . you tell me I'm intelligent, and then you tell me I should not be *here,* what do you *want* with me? What does it *mean?* Who should I listen to . . . I . . .

(He goes over to her and puts his arm around her shoulder.)

No! *(She walks away from him.)*

JOHN: Sshhhh.

CAROL: No, I don't under . . .

JOHN: Sshhhhh.

CAROL: I don't know what you're *saying* . . .

JOHN: Sshhhhh. It's all right.

CAROL: . . . I have no . . .

JOHN: Sshhhhh. Sshhhhh. Let it go a moment. *(Pause)* Sshhhhh . . . let it go. *(Pause)* Just let it go. *(Pause)* Just let it go. It's all right. *(Pause)* Sshhhhh. *(Pause)* I understand . . . *(Pause)* What do you feel?

CAROL: I feel bad.

JOHN: I know. It's all right.

CAROL: I . . . *(Pause)*

JOHN: What?

CAROL: I . . .

JOHN: What? Tell me.

CAROL: I don't understand you.

JOHN: I know. It's all right.

CAROL: I . . .

JOHN: What? *(Pause)* What? *Tell* me.

CAROL: I can't tell you.

JOHN: No, you must.

CAROL: I can't.

JOHN: No. Tell me. *(Pause)*

CAROL: I'm bad. *(Pause)* Oh, God. *(Pause)*

JOHN: It's all right.

CAROL: I'm . . .

JOHN: It's all right.

CAROL: I can't talk about this.

JOHN: It's all right. Tell me.

CAROL: Why do you want to know this?

JOHN: I don't want to know. I want to know whatever you . . .

CAROL: I always . . .

JOHN: . . . good . . .

CAROL: I always . . . all my life . . . I have never told anyone this . . .

JOHN: Yes. Go on. *(Pause)* Go on.

CAROL: All of my life . . . *(The phone rings.)* *(Pause. JOHN goes to the phone and picks it up.)*

JOHN *(into phone):* I can't talk now. *(Pause)* What? *(Pause)* Hmm. *(Pause)* All right, I . . . I. Can't. Talk. Now. No, no, no, I *Know* I did, but . . . What? Hello. What? She *what?* She *can't,* she said the agreement is void? How, how is the agreement *void? That's Our House.*

I have the *paper;* when we come down, next week, with the payment, and the paper, that house is . . . wait, wait, wait, wait, wait, wait, wait: Did Jerry . . . is Jerry there? *(Pause)* Is *she* there . . . ? Does she have a *lawyer* . . . ? How the *hell,* how the *Hell.* That is . . . it's a question, you said, of the *easement.* I don't underst . . . it's not the *whole agreement.* It's just the *easement,* why would she? Put, put, put, *Jerry* on. *(Pause)* Jer, *Jerry:* What the *Hell* . . . that's my *house.* That's . . . Well, I'm, no, no, no, I'm *not* coming ddd . . . List, *Listen, screw* her. You *tell* her. You, listen: I want you to take *Grace,* you take Grace, and get out of that house. You *leave* her there. Her and her lawyer, and you *tell* them, we'll see them in court next . . . no. No. leave her there, leave her to *stew* in it: You tell her, we're *getting* that house, and we

are going to . . . No. I'm *not* coming down. I'll be damned if I'll sit in the same rrr . . . the next, you tell her the next time I *see* her is in court . . . I . . . *(Pause)* What? *(Pause)* What? I don't understand. *(Pause)* Well, what about the house? *(Pause)* There isn't any problem with the hhh . . . *(Pause)* No, no, no, that's all right. All ri . . . All right . . . *(Pause)* Of course. Tha . . . Thank you. No, I will. Right away. *(He hangs up.)* *(Pause)*

CAROL: What is it? *(Pause)*

JOHN: It's a surprise party.

CAROL: It is.

JOHN: Yes.

CAROL: A party for you.

JOHN: Yes.

CAROL: Is it your birthday?

JOHN: No.

CAROL: What is it?

JOHN: The tenure announcement.

CAROL: The tenure announcement.

JOHN: They're throwing a party for us in our new house.

CAROL: Your new house.

JOHN: The house that we're buying.

CAROL: You have to go.

JOHN: It seems that I do.

CAROL: *(Pause)* They're proud of you.

JOHN: Well, there are those who would say it's a form of aggression.

CAROL: What is?

JOHN: A surprise.

ACT 2

JOHN *and* CAROL *seated across the desk from each other.*

JOHN: You see, *(pause)* I love to teach. And flatter myself I am *skilled* at it. And I love the, the aspect of *performance.* I think I must confess that.

When I found I loved to teach I swore that I would not become that cold, rigid automaton of an instructor which I had encountered as a child.

Now, I was not unconscious that it was given me to err upon the other side. And, so, I asked and *ask* myself if I engaged in heterodoxy, I will not say "gratuitously" for I do not care to posit orthodoxy as a given good—but, "to the detriment of, of my students." *(Pause)*

As I said. When the possibility of tenure opened, and, of course, I'd long pursued it, I was, of course *happy,* and *covetous* of it.

I asked myself if I was wrong to covet it. And thought about it long, and, I hope, truthfully, and saw in myself several things in, I think, no particular order. *(Pause)*

That I *would* pursue it. That I *desired* it, that I was not pure of longing for security, and that that, perhaps, was not reprehensible in me. That I had duties *beyond* the school, and that my duty to my home, for instance, was, or should be, if it were not, of an equal weight. That tenure, and security, and yes, and *comfort,* were not, of themselves, to be scorned; and were even worthy of honorable pursuit. And that it was given me. Here, in this place, which I enjoy, and in which I find comfort, to assure myself of—as far as it rests in The Material—a continuation of that joy and comfort. In exchange for what? Teaching. Which I love.

What was the price of this security? To obtain *tenure.* Which tenure the committee is in the process of granting me. And on the basis of which I contracted to purchase a house. Now, as you don't have your own family, at this point, you may not know what that means. But to me it is important. A home. A Good Home. To raise my family. Now: The Tenure Committee will meet. This is the process, and a *good* process. Under which the school has functioned for quite a long time. They will meet, and hear your complaint—which you have the right to make; and they will dismiss it. They will *dismiss* your complaint; and, in the intervening period, I will lose my house. I will not be able to close on my house. I will lose my *deposit,* and the home I'd picked out for my wife and son will go by the boards. Now: I see I have angered you. I understand your anger at teachers. I was angry with mine. I felt hurt and humiliated by them. Which is one of the reasons that I went into education.

CAROL: What do you want of me?

JOHN: *(Pause)* I was hurt. When I received the report. Of the tenure committee. I was shocked. And I was hurt. No, I don't mean to subject you to my weak sensibilities. All right. Finally, I didn't understand. Then I thought: is it not always at those points at which we reckon ourselves unassailable that we are most vulnerable and . . . *(Pause)* Yes. All right. You find me pedantic. Yes. I am. By nature, by *birth,* by profession, I don't know . . . I'm always looking for a *paradigm* for . . .

CAROL: I don't know what a paradigm is.

JOHN: It's a model.

CAROL: Then why can't you use that word? *(Pause)*

JOHN: If it is important to you. Yes, all right. I was looking for a model. To continue: I feel that one point . . .

CAROL: I . . .

JOHN: One second . . . upon which I am unassailable is my unflinching concern for my students' dignity. I asked you here to . . . in the spirit of *investigation,* to ask you . . . to ask . . . *(Pause)* What have I done to you? *(Pause)* And, and, I suppose, how I can make amends. Can we not settle this now? It's pointless, really, and I want to know.

CAROL: What you can do to force me to retract?

JOHN: That is not what I meant at all.

CAROL: To bribe me, to convince me . . .

JOHN: . . . No.

CAROL: To retract . . .

JOHN: That is not what I meant at all. I think that you know it is not.

CAROL: That is not what I know. I *wish* I . . .

JOHN: I do not want to . . . you wish what?

CAROL: No, you said what amends can you make. To force me to retract.

JOHN: That is not what I said.

CAROL: I have my notes.

JOHN: Look. Look. The Stoics say . . .

CAROL: The Stoics?

JOHN: The Stoical Philosophers say if you remove the phrase "I have been injured," you have removed the injury. Now: Think: I know that you're upset. Just tell me. Literally. Literally: what wrong have I done you?

CAROL: Whatever you have done to me—to the extent that you've done it to *me,* do you know, rather than to me as a *student,* and, so, to the student body, is contained in my report. To the tenure committee.

JOHN: Well, all right. *(Pause)* Let's see. *(He reads.)* I find that I am sexist. That I am *elitist.* I'm not sure I know what that means, other than it's a derogatory word, meaning "bad." That I . . . That I insist on wasting time, in nonprescribed, in self-aggrandizing and theatrical *diversions* from the prescribed *text* . . . that these have taken both sexist and pornographic forms . . . here we find listed . . . *(Pause)* Here we find listed . . . instances ". . . closeted with a student" . . . "Told a rambling, sexually explicit story, in which the frequency and attitudes of fornication of the poor and rich are, it would seem, the central point . . . moved to *embrace* said student and . . . all part of a pattern . . ." *(Pause)*

(He reads.) That I used the phrase "The White Man's Burden" . . . that I told you how I'd asked you to my room because I quote like you. *(Pause)*

(He reads.) "He said he 'liked' me. That he 'liked being with me.' He'd let me write my examination paper over, if I could come back oftener to see him in his office." *(Pause)* *(To* CAROL:*)* It's *ludicrous.* Don't you know that? It's not *necessary.* It's going to humiliate you, and it's going to cost me my *house,* and . . .

CAROL: It's "*ludicrous* . . ."?

*(*JOHN *picks up the report and reads again.)*

JOHN: "He told me he had problems with his wife; and that he wanted to take off the artificial stricture of Teacher and Student. He put his arm around me . . ."

CAROL: Do you deny it? Can you deny it . . . ? Do you see? *(Pause)* Don't you see? You don't see, do you?

JOHN: I don't see . . .

CAROL: You think, you think you can deny that these things happened; or, if they *did,* if they *did,* that they meant what you *said* they meant. Don't you see? You drag me in here, you drag us, to listen to you "go on"; and "go on" about this, or that, or we don't "express" ourselves very well. We don't say what we mean. Don't we? Don't we? We *do* say what we mean. And you say that "I don't understand you . . .": Then *you* . . . *(Points.)*

JOHN: "Consult the Report"?

CAROL: . . . that's right.

JOHN: You see. You see. Can't you. . . . You see what I'm saying? Can't you tell me in your own words?

CAROL: Those are my own words. *(Pause)*

JOHN: *(He reads.)* "He told me that if I would stay alone with him in his office, he would change my grade to an A." *(To* CAROL:*)* What have I done to you? Oh. My God, are you so hurt?

CAROL: What I "feel" is irrelevant. *(Pause)*

JOHN: Do you know that I tried to help you?

CAROL: What I know I have reported.

JOHN: I would like to help you now. I would. Before this escalates.

CAROL *(simultaneously with* "escalates"*)*: You see. I don't think that I need your help. I don't think I need anything you have.

JOHN: I feel . . .

CAROL: I don't *care* what you feel. Do you see? DO YOU SEE? You can't *do* that anymore. You. Do. Not. Have. The. Power. Did you misuse it? *Someone* did. Are you part of that group? *Yes. Yes.* You Are. You've *done* these things. And to say, and to say, "Oh. Let me help you with your problem . . ."

JOHN: Yes. I understand. I understand. You're *hurt.* You're *angry.* Yes. I think your *anger* is *betraying* you. Down a path which helps no one.

CAROL: I don't *care* what you think.

JOHN: You don't? *(Pause)* But you talk of *rights.* Don't you see? *I* have rights too. Do you see? I have a *house* . . . part of the *real* world; and The Tenure Committee, Good Men and True . . .

CAROL: . . . Professor . . .

JOHN: . . . Please: *Also* part of that world: you understand? This is my *life.* I'm not a *bogeyman.* I don't "stand" for something, I . . .

CAROL: . . . Professor . . .

JOHN: . . . I . . .

CAROL: Professor. I came here as a *favor.* At your personal request. Perhaps I should not have done so. But I did. On my behalf, and on behalf of my group. And you speak of the tenure committee, one of whose members is a woman, as you know. And though you might call it Good Fun, or An Historical Phrase, or An Oversight, or, All of the Above, to refer to the committee as Good Men and True, it is a demeaning remark. It is a sexist remark, and to overlook it is to countenance continuation of that method of thought. It's a remark . . .

JOHN: OH COME ON. Come on. . . . Sufficient to deprive a family of . . .

CAROL: Sufficient? Sufficient? Sufficient? Yes. It is a *fact*

. . . and that story, which I quote, is *vile* and *classist,* and *manipulative* and *pornographic.* It . . .

JOHN: . . . it's pornographic . . . ?

CAROL: What gives you the *right.* Yes. To speak to a *woman* in your private . . . Yes. Yes. I'm sorry. I'm sorry. You feel yourself empowered . . . you say so yourself. To *strut.* To *posture.* To "perform." To "Call me in here . . ." Eh? You say that higher education is a joke. And treat it as such, you *treat* it as such. And *confess* to a taste to play the *patriarch* in your class. To grant *this.* To deny *that.* To embrace your students.

JOHN: How can you assert. How can you stand there and . . .

CAROL: How can you *deny* it. You did it to me. *Here.* You *did.* . . . You *confess.* You love the Power. To *deviate.* To *invent,* to transgress . . . to *transgress* whatever norms have been established for us. And you think it's charming to "question" in yourself this taste to mock and destroy. But you should question it. Professor. And you pick those things which you feel *advance* you: publication, *tenure,* and the steps to get them you call "harmless rituals." And you perform those steps. Although you say it is hypocrisy. But to the aspirations of your students. Of *hard-working students,* who come here, who *slave* to come here—you have no idea what it cost me to come to this school—you *mock* us. You call education "hazing," and from your so-protected, so-elitist seat you hold our confusion as a *joke,* and our hopes and efforts with it. Then you sit there and say "what have I done?" And ask me to understand that *you* have aspirations too. But I tell you. I tell you. That you are vile. And that you are exploitative. And if you possess one ounce of that inner honesty you describe in your book, you can look in yourself and see those things that I see. And you can find revulsion equal to my own. Good day. *(She prepares to leave the room.)*

JOHN: Wait a second, will you, just one moment. *(Pause)* Nice day today.

CAROL: What?

JOHN: You said "Good day." I think that it is a nice day today.

CAROL: *Is* it?

JOHN: Yes, I think it is.

CAROL: And why is that important?

JOHN: Because it is the essence of all human communication. I say something conventional, you respond, and the information we exchange is not about the "weather," but that we both agree to converse. In effect, we agree that we are both human. *(Pause)*

    I'm not a . . . "exploiter," and you're not a . . . "deranged," what? *Revolutionary* . . . that we may, that we may have . . . positions, and that we may have . . . desires, which are in *conflict,* but that we're just human. *(Pause)* That means that sometimes we're *imperfect. (Pause)* Often we're in conflict . . . *(Pause) Much* of what we do, you're right, in the name of "principles" is *self-serving* . . . much of what we do is *conventional. (Pause)* You're right. *(Pause)* You said you came in the class because you wanted to learn about *education.* I don't know what I can teach you about education. But I know that I can tell you what I *think* about education, and then *you* decide. And you don't have to fight with me. *I'm* not the subject. *(Pause)* And where I'm *wrong* . . . perhaps it's not your job to "fix" me. I don't want to fix *you.* I would like to tell you what I *think,* because that *is* my job, conventional as it is, and flawed as I may be. And then, if you can show me some better *form,* then we can proceed from there. But, just like "nice day, isn't it . . . ?" I don't think we can proceed until we accept that each of us is human. *(Pause)* And we still can have difficulties. We *will* have them . . . that's all right too. *(Pause)* Now:

CAROL: . . . wait . . .

JOHN: Yes. I want to hear it.

CAROL: . . . the . . .

JOHN: Yes. Tell me frankly.

CAROL: . . . my position . . .

JOHN: I want to hear it. In your own words. What you want. And what you feel.

CAROL: . . . I . . .

JOHN: . . . yes . . .

CAROL: My Group.

JOHN: Your "Group" . . . ? *(Pause)*

CAROL: The people I've been talking to . . .

JOHN: There's no shame in that. Everybody needs advisers. Everyone needs to expose themselves. To various points of view. It's not wrong. It's essential. Good. Good. Now: You and I . . . *(The phone rings.)* You and I . . .

(He hesitates for a moment, and then picks it up.) (Into phone) Hello. *(Pause)* Um . . . no, I know they do. *(Pause)* I know she does. Tell her that I . . . can I call you back? . . . Then tell her that I think it's going to be fine. *(Pause)* Tell her just, just hold on, I'll . . . can I get back to you? . . . Well . . . no, no, no, we're *taking* the house . . . no, no, nn . . . no, she will nnn, it's not a *question* of refunding the dep . . . no . . . it's not a *question* of the deposit . . . will you call Jerry? Babe, baby, will you just call Jerry? Tell him, nnn . . . tell him they, well, they're to keep the deposit, because the deal, be . . . because the deal is going to go *through* . . . because I know . . . be . . . will you please? Just *trust* me. Be . . . well, I'm dealing with the complaint. Yes. Right *Now.* Which is why I . . . yes, no, no, it's really, I can't *talk* about it now. Call Jerry, and I can't talk now. Ff . . . fine. Gg . . . good-bye. *(Hangs up.) (Pause)* I'm sorry we were interrupted.

CAROL: No . . .

JOHN: I . . . I was saying:

CAROL: You said that we should agree to talk about my complaint.

JOHN: That's correct.

CAROL: But we *are* talking about it.

JOHN: Well, that's correct too. You see? This is the *gist* of education.

CAROL: No, no. I mean, we're talking about it at the Tenure Committee Hearing. *(Pause)*

JOHN: Yes, but I'm saying: we can talk about it *now,* as easily as . . .

CAROL: No. I think that we should stick to the process . . .

JOHN: . . . wait a . . .

CAROL: . . . the "conventional" process. As you said. *(She gets up.)* And you're right, I'm sorry if I was, um, if I was "discourteous" to you. You're right.

JOHN: Wait, wait a . . .

CAROL: I really should go.

JOHN: Now, look, granted. I have an interest. In the status quo. All right? Everyone does. But what I'm saying is that the *committee* . . .

CAROL: Professor, you're right. Just don't impinge on me. We'll take our differences, and . . .

JOHN: You're going to make a . . . look, look, look, you're going to . . .

CAROL: I shouldn't have come here. They told me . . .

JOHN: One moment. No. No. There are *norms,* here, and there's no reason. Look: I'm trying to *save* you . . .

CAROL: No one *asked* you to . . . you're trying to save *me?* Do me the courtesy to . . .

JOHN: I *am* doing you the courtesy. I'm talking *straight* to you. We can settle this *now.* And I want you to sit *down* and . . .

CAROL: You must excuse me . . . *(She starts to leave the room.)*

JOHN: Sit down, it seems we each have a. . . . Wait one moment. Wait one moment . . . just do me the courtesy to . . .

(He restrains her from leaving.)

CAROL: LET ME GO.

JOHN: I have no desire to *hold* you, I just want to *talk* to you . . .

CAROL: LET ME GO. LET ME GO. WOULD SOMEBODY *HELP* ME? WOULD SOMEBODY *HELP* ME PLEASE . . .?

ACT 3

(At rise, CAROL *and* JOHN *are seated.)*

JOHN: I have asked you here. *(Pause)* I have asked you here against, against my . . .

CAROL: I was most surprised you asked me.

JOHN: . . . against my better *judgment,* against . . .

CAROL: I was most surprised . . .

JOHN: . . . against the . . . yes. I'm sure.

CAROL: . . . If you would like me to leave, I'll leave. I'll go right now . . . *(She rises.)*

JOHN: Let us begin *correctly*, may we? I feel . . .

CAROL: That is what I wished to do. That's why I came here, but now . . .

JOHN: . . . I feel . . .

CAROL: But now perhaps you'd like me to leave . . .

JOHN: I don't want you to leave. I asked you to come . . .

CAROL: I didn't have to come here.

JOHN: No. *(Pause)* Thank you.

CAROL: All right. *(Pause) (She sits down.)*

JOHN: Although I feel that it *profits*, it would *profit* you something to . . .

CAROL: . . . what I . . .

JOHN: If you would hear me out, if you would hear me out.

CAROL: I came here to, the court officers told me not to come.

JOHN: . . . the "court" officers . . . ?

CAROL: I was shocked that you asked.

JOHN: . . . wait . . .

CAROL: Yes. But I did *not* come here to hear what it "profits" me.

JOHN: The "court" officers . . .

CAROL: . . . no, no, perhaps I should leave . . . *(She gets up.)*

JOHN: Wait.

CAROL: No. I shouldn't have . . .

JOHN: . . . wait. Wait. Wait a moment.

CAROL: Yes? What is it you want? *(Pause)* What is it you want?

JOHN: I'd like you to stay.

CAROL: You want me to stay.

JOHN: Yes.

CAROL: You do.

JOHN: Yes. *(Pause)* Yes. I would like to have you hear me out. If you would. *(Pause)* Would you please? If you would do that I would be in your debt. *(Pause) (She sits.)* Thank You. *(Pause)*

CAROL: What is it you wish to tell me?

JOHN: All right. I cannot . . . *(Pause)* I cannot help but feel you are owed an apology. *(Pause) (Of papers in his hands)* I have read. *(Pause)* And reread these accusations.

CAROL: What "accusations"?

JOHN: The, the tenure comm . . . what other accusations . . ."

CAROL: The tenure committee . . . ?

JOHN: Yes.

CAROL: Excuse me, but those are not accusations. They have been *proved.* They are facts.

JOHN: . . . I . . .

CAROL: No. Those are not "accusations."

JOHN: . . . those?

CAROL: . . . the committee *(The phone starts to ring.)* the committee has . . .

JOHN: . . . All right . . .

CAROL: . . . those are not accusations. The Tenure Com-

mittee.

JOHN: ALL RIGHT, ALL RIGHT. ALL RIGHT. *(He picks up the phone.)* Hello. Yes. No. I'm here. Tell Mister . . . No, I can't talk to him now . . . I'm sure he has, but I'm fff . . . I know . . . No, I have no time t . . . tell Mister . . . tell Mist . . . tell Jerry that I'm *fine* and that I'll call him right aw . . . *(Pause)* My wife . . . Yes. I'm sure she has. Yes, thank you. Yes, I'll call her too. I cannot talk to you now. *(He hangs up.) (Pause)* All right. It was good of you to come. Thank you. I have studied. I have spent some time studying the indictment.

CAROL: You will have to explain that word to me.

JOHN: An "indictment" . . .

CAROL: Yes.

JOHN: Is a "bill of particulars." A . . .

CAROL: All right. Yes.

JOHN: In which is alleged . . .

CAROL: No. I cannot allow that. I cannot allow that. Nothing is alleged. Everything is proved . . .

JOHN: Please, wait a sec . . .

CAROL: I cannot *come* to allow . . .

JOHN: If I may . . . If I may, from whatever you feel is "established," by . . .

CAROL: The issue here is not what I "feel." It is not my "feelings," but the feelings of women. And men. Your superiors, who've been "polled," do you see? To whom *evidence* has been presented, who have *ruled*, do you see? Who have weighed the testimony and the evidence, and have *ruled*, do you see? That you are *negligent.* That you are *guilty*, that you are found *wanting,* and in *error;* and are *not,* for the reasons so-told, to be given tenure. That you are to be disciplined. For facts. For *facts.* Not "alleged," what is the word? But *proved.* Do you see? *By your own actions.*

That is what the tenure committee has said. That is what my lawyer said. For what you did in class. For what you did *in this office.*

JOHN: They're going to discharge me.

CAROL: As full well they should. You don't understand? You're angry? What has *led* you to this place? Not your sex. Not your race. Not your class. YOUR OWN ACTIONS. And you're *angry.* You *ask* me here. What *do* you want? You want to "charm" me. You want to "convince" me. You want me to recant. I will *not* recant. Why should I . . . ? What I say is right. You tell me, you are going to tell me that you have a wife and child. You are going to say that you have a career and that you've worked for twenty years for this. Do you know what you've *worked* for? *Power.* For *power.* Do you understand? And you sit there, and you tell me *stories.* About your *house,* about all the private *schools,* and about *privilege,* and how you are entitled. To *buy,* to *spend,* to *mock,* to *summon.* All your stories. All your silly weak *guilt,* it's all about *privilege;* and you won't know it. Don't you see? You worked twenty years for the right to *insult* me. And you feel entitled to be *paid* for it. Your Home. Your Wife . . . Your sweet "deposit" on your house.

JOHN: Don't you have feelings?

CAROL: That's my point. You see? Don't you have feelings? Your final argument. What is it that has no feelings. *Animals.* I don't take your side, you question if I'm Human.

JOHN: Don't you have feelings?

CAROL: I have a responsibility. I . . .

JOHN: . . . to . . . ?

CAROL: To? This institution. To the *students.* To my *group.*

JOHN: . . . your "group." . . .

CAROL: Because I speak, yes, not for myself. But for the group; for those who suffer what I suffer. On behalf of whom, even if I, were, inclined, to what, forgive? Forget? What? Overlook your . . .

JOHN: . . . my behavior?

CAROL: . . . it would be wrong.

JOHN: Even if you were inclined to "forgive" me.

CAROL: It would be wrong.

JOHN: And what would transpire.

CAROL: Transpire?

JOHN: Yes.

CAROL: "Happen?"

JOHN: Yes.

CAROL: Then *say* it. For Christ's sake. Who the *hell* do you think that you are? You want a post. You want unlimited power. To do and to say what you want. As it pleases you—Testing, Questioning, Flirting . . .

JOHN: I never . . .

CAROL: Excuse me, one moment, will you?

(She reads from her notes.)

The twelfth: "Have a good day, dear."
The fifteenth: "Now, don't *you* look fetching . . ."
April seventeenth: "If you girls would come over here . . . " I saw you. I saw you, Professor. For two semesters sit there, stand there and exploit our, as you thought, "paternal prerogative," and what is that but rape; I swear to God. You asked me in here to explain something to me, as a child, that I did not understand. But I came to explain something to you. You Are Not God. You ask me why I came? I came here to instruct you.

(She produces his book.)

And your book? You think you're going to show me some "light"? You "*maverick.*" Outside of tradition. No, no, *(She reads from the book's liner notes.)* "*Of* that fine tradition of *inquiry.* Of Polite *skepticism*" . . . and you say you believe in free intellectual discourse. YOU BELIEVE IN NOTHING. YOU BELIEVE IN NOTHING AT ALL.

JOHN: I believe in freedom of thought.

CAROL: Isn't that fine. *Do* you?

JOHN: Yes. I do.

CAROL: Then why do you question, for one moment, the committee's decision refusing your tenure? Why do you question your suspension? You believe in what *you call* freedom of thought. Then, fine. *You* believe in freedom-of-thought *and* a home, and, *and* prerogatives for your kid, *and* tenure. And I'm going to tell you. You believe *not* in "freedom of thought," but in an elitist, in, in a protected hierarchy which rewards you. And for whom you are the clown. And you mock and exploit the system which pays your rent. You're wrong. I'm not wrong. You're wrong. You think that I'm full of hatred. I know what you think I am.

JOHN: Do you?

CAROL: You think I'm a, of course I do. You think I am a frightened, repressed, confused, I don't know, abandoned young thing of some doubtful sexuality, who wants, power and revenge. *(Pause) Don't* you? *(Pause)*

JOHN: Yes. I do. *(Pause)*

CAROL: Isn't that better? And I feel that that is the first moment which you've treated me with respect. For you told me the truth. *(Pause)* I did not come here, as you are assured, to gloat. Why would I want to gloat? I've profited nothing from your, your, as you say, your "misfortune." I came here, as you did me the honor to *ask* me here, I came here to *tell* you something.

(Pause) That I think . . . that I think you've been wrong. That I think you've been terribly wrong. Do you hate me now? *(Pause)*

JOHN: Yes.

CAROL: Why do you hate me? Because you think me wrong? No. Because I have, you think, *power* over you. Listen to me. Listen to me, Professor. *(Pause)* It is the power that you hate. So deeply that, that any atmosphere of free discussion is impossible. It's not "unlikely." It's *impossible.* Isn't it?

JOHN: Yes.

CAROL: *Isn't* it . . . ?

JOHN: Yes. I suppose.

CAROL: Now. The thing which you find so cruel is the selfsame process of selection I, and my group, go through *every day of our lives.* In admittance to school. In our tests, in our class rankings. . . . Is it unfair? I can't tell you. But, if it is fair. Or even if it is "unfortunate but necessary" for us, then, by God, so must it be for you. *(Pause)* You write of your "responsibility to the young." Treat us with respect, and that will *show* you your responsibility. You write that education is just hazing. *(Pause)* But we worked to get to this school. *(Pause)* And some of us. *(Pause)* Overcame prejudices. Economic, sexual, you cannot begin to imagine. And endured humiliations I *pray* that you and those you love never will encounter. *(Pause)* To gain admittance here. To pursue that same dream of security *you* pursue. We, who, who are, at any moment, in danger of being deprived of it. By . . .

JOHN: . . . by . . . ?

CAROL: By the administration. By the teachers. By *you*.
By, say, one low grade, that keeps us out of graduate
school; by one, say, one capricious or inventive answer on our parts, which, perhaps, you don't find
amusing. Now you *know,* do you see? What it is to
be subject to that power. *(Pause)*

JOHN: I don't understand. *(Pause)*

CAROL: My charges are not trivial. You see that in the
haste, I think, with which they were accepted. A
joke you have told, with a sexist tinge. The language
you use, a verbal or physical caress, yes, yes, I know,
you say that it is meaningless. I understand. I differ
from you. To lay a hand on someone's shoulder.

JOHN: It was devoid of sexual content.

CAROL: I say it was not. I SAY IT WAS NOT. Don't you
begin to *see* . . . ? Don't you begin to understand?
IT'S NOT FOR YOU TO SAY.

JOHN: I take your point, and I see there is much good
in what you refer to.

CAROL: . . . do you think so . . . ?

JOHN: . . . but, and this is not to say that I cannot change,
in those things in which I am deficient . . . But, the
. . .

CAROL: Do you hold yourself harmless from the charge
of sexual exploitativeness . . . ? *(Pause)*

JOHN: Well, I . . . I . . . I . . . You know I, as I said. I . . .
think I am not too old to *learn,* and I *can* learn,
I . . .

CAROL: Do you hold yourself innocent of the charge
of . . .

JOHN: . . . wait, wait, wait . . . All right, let's go back
to . . .

CAROL: YOU FOOL. Who do you think I am? To come
here and be taken in by a *smile*. You little yapping
fool. You think I want "revenge." I don't want revenge. I WANT UNDERSTANDING.

JOHN: . . . *do* you?

CAROL: I do. *(Pause)*

JOHN: What's the use. It's over.

CAROL: Is it? What is?

JOHN: My job.

CAROL: Oh. Your job. That's what you want to talk
about. *(Pause) (She starts to leave the room. She steps
and turns back to him.)* All right. *(Pause)* What if it
were possible that my Group withdraws its complaint. *(Pause)*

JOHN: What?

CAROL: That's right. *(Pause)*

JOHN: Why.

CAROL: Well, let's say as an act of friendship.

JOHN: An act of friendship.

CAROL: Yes. *(Pause)*

JOHN: In exchange for what.

CAROL: Yes. But I don't think, "exchange." Not "in exchange." For what do we derive from it? *(Pause)*

JOHN: "Derive."

CAROL: Yes.

JOHN: *(Pause)* Nothing. *(Pause)*

CAROL: That's right. We derive nothing. *(Pause)* Do you
see that?

JOHN: Yes.

CAROL: That is a little word, Professor. "Yes." "I see
that." But you will.

JOHN: And you might speak to the committee . . . ?

CAROL: To the committee?

JOHN: Yes.

CAROL: Well. Of course. That's on your mind. We
might.

JOHN: "If" what?

CAROL: "Given" what. Perhaps. I think that that is more
friendly.

JOHN: GIVEN WHAT?

CAROL: And, believe me, I understand your rage. It is
not that I don't feel it. But I do not see that it is
deserved, so I do not resent it. . . . All right. I have
a list . . .

JOHN: . . . a list.

CAROL: Here is a list of books, which we . . .

JOHN: . . . a list of books . . . ?

CAROL: That's right. Which we find questionable.

JOHN: What?

CAROL: Is this so bizarre . . . ?

JOHN: I can't believe . . .

CAROL: It's not necessary you believe it.

JOHN: Academic freedom . . .

CAROL: Someone chooses the books. If you can choose
them, others can. What are you, "God"?

JOHN: . . . no, no, the "dangerous." . . .

CAROL: You have an agenda, we have an agenda. I am
not interested in your feelings or your motivation,
but your actions. If you would like me to speak to
the Tenure Committee, here is my list. You are a
Free Person, you decide. *(Pause)*

JOHN: Give me the list. *(She does so. He reads.)*

CAROL: I think you'll find . . .

JOHN: I'm capable of reading it. Thank you.

CAROL: We have a number of *texts* we need re . . .

JOHN: I see that.

CAROL: We're amenable to . . .

JOHN: Aha. Well, let me look over the . . . *(He reads.)*

CAROL: I think that . . .

JOHN: LOOK. I'm reading your demands. All right?!
(He reads) (Pause) You want to ban my book?

CAROL: We do not . . .

JOHN *(Of list)*: It says here . . .

CAROL: . . . We want it removed from inclusion as a
representative example of the university.

JOHN: Get out of here.

CAROL: If you put aside the issues of personalities.

JOHN: Get the fuck out of my office.

CAROL: No, I think I would reconsider.

JOHN: . . . you think you can.

CAROL: We can and we *will*. Do you want our support?
That is the only quest . . .

JOHN: . . . to ban my *book* . . . ?

CAROL: . . . that is correct . . .

JOHN: . . . this . . . this is a *university* . . . we . . .

CAROL: . . . and we have a statement . . . which we need you to . . . *(She hands him a sheet of paper.)*

JOHN: No, no. It's out of the question. I'm sorry. I don't know what I was thinking of. I want to tell you something. I'm a teacher. I am a teacher. Eh? It's my *name* on the door, and *I* teach the class, and that's what I do. I've got a book with my name on it. And my son will *see* that *book* someday. And I have a respon . . . No, I'm sorry I have a *responsibility* . . . to *myself,* to my *son,* to my *profession.* . . . I haven't been *home* for two days, do you know that? Thinking this out.

CAROL: . . . you haven't?

JOHN: I've been, no. If it's of interest to you. I've been in a *hotel. Thinking. (The phone starts ringing.) Think- ing* . . .

CAROL: . . . you haven't been home?

JOHN: . . . *thinking,* do you see.

CAROL: Oh.

JOHN: And, and, I owe you a debt, I see that now. *(Pause)* You're *dangerous,* you're *wrong* and it's my *job* . . . to say no to you. That's my job. You are absolutely right. You want to ban my book? Go to *hell,* and they can do whatever they want to me.

CAROL: . . . you haven't been home in two days . . .

JOHN: I think I told you that.

CAROL: . . . you'd better get that phone. *(Pause)* I think that you should pick up the phone. *(Pause)*

(JOHN picks up the phone.)

JOHN *(on phone):* Yes. *(Pause)* Yes. Wh . . . I. I. I had to be away. All ri . . . did they wor . . . did they worry ab . . . No. I'm all right, now, Jerry. I'm f . . . I got a little turned *around,* but I'm *sitting* here and . . . I've got it figured out. I'm fine. I'm fine don't worry about me. I got a little bit mixed up. But I am not sure that it's not a blessing. It cost me my job? Fine. Then the job was not worth having. Tell Grace that I'm coming home and everything is fff . . . *(Pause)* What? *(Pause)* What? *(Pause)* What do you *mean?* WHAT? Jerry . . . Jerry. They . . . Who, who, what can they do . . . ? *(Pause)* NO. *(Pause)* NO. They can't do th . . . What do you mean? *(Pause)* But how . . . *(Pause)* She's, she's, she's *here* with me. To . . . Jerry. I don't underst . . . *(Pause) (He hangs up.) (To* CAROL*:)* What does this mean?

CAROL: I thought you knew.

JOHN: What. *(Pause)* What does it mean. *(Pause)*

CAROL: You tried to rape me. *(Pause)* According to the law. *(Pause)*

JOHN: . . . what . . . ?

CAROL: You tried to rape me. I was leaving this office,

you "pressed" yourself into me. You "pressed" your body into me.

JOHN: . . . I . . .

CAROL: My Group has told your lawyer that we may pursue criminal charges.

JOHN: . . . no . . .

CAROL: . . . under the statute. I am told. It was battery.

JOHN: . . . no . . .

CAROL: Yes. And attempted rape. That's right. *(Pause)*

JOHN: I think that you should go.

CAROL: Of course. I thought you knew.

JOHN: I have to talk to my lawyer.

CAROL: Yes. Perhaps you should.

(The phone rings again.) (Pause)

JOHN: *(Picks up phone. Into phone:)* Hello? I . . . Hello . . . ? I . . . Yes, he just called. No . . . I. I can't talk to you now, Baby. *(To* CAROL*:)* Get out.

CAROL: . . . your wife . . . ?

JOHN: . . . who it is is no concern of yours. Get out. *(To phone:)* No, no, it's going to be all right. I. I can't talk now, Baby. *(To* CAROL*:)* Get out of here.

CAROL: I'm going.

JOHN: Good.

CAROL *(exiting):* . . . and don't call your wife "baby."

JOHN: What?

CAROL: Don't call your wife baby. You heard what I said.

*(*CAROL *starts to leave the room.* JOHN *grabs her and begins to beat her.)*

JOHN: You vicious little bitch. You think you can come in here with your political correctness and destroy my life?

(He knocks her to the floor.)

After how I treated you . . . ? You should be . . . *Rape you* . . . ? Are you kidding me . . . ?

(He picks up a chair, raises it above his head, and advances on her.)

I wouldn't touch you with a ten-foot pole. You little *cunt* . . .

(She cowers on the floor below him. Pause. He looks down at her. He lowers the chair. He moves to his desk, and arranges the papers on it. Pause. He looks over at her.)

. . . well . . .

(Pause. She looks at him.)

CAROL: Yes. That's right.

(She looks away from him, and lowers her head. To her- self:) . . . yes. That's right.

Figure 1. In the first scene of *Oleanna*, John (William H. Macy) looks quizzically at Carol (Rebecca Pidgeon) as she explains her confusion to him. The 1992 New York premiere was directed by David Mamet. (Photograph: Brigitte Lacombe, New York.)

Figure 2. In the last scene of *Oleanna*, Carol (Rebecca Pidgeon) demands that John (William H. Macy) accede to a list of demands, including removing his book from the reading list. The 1992 New York premiere was directed by David Mamet. (Photograph: Brigitte Lacombe, New York.)

Figure 3. In the last moments of *Oleanna*, John (William H. Macy) attacks Carol (Rebecca Pidgeon) both verbally and physically. The 1992 New York premiere was directed by David Mamet. (Photograph: Brigitte Lacombe, New York.)

Staging of *Oleanna*

REVIEW OF THE ORPHEUM THEATRE
PRODUCTION, 1992, BY JOHN LAHR

David Mamet understands that envy is the gasoline on which a competitive society runs, and no modern American playwright has been bolder or more brilliant in analyzing its corrosive social effects. In his most recent play, "Oleanna," at the Orpheum, Mamet returns to this theme but stages it in the upwardly mobile arena of university life. Here a sense of shaming humiliation at ignorance becomes the subtext of Mamet's powerful dissection of political correctness. John, a teacher with bona-fide intellectual credentials, tries to help Carol, a student who is paralyzed by her sense of inadequacy. "I don't *understand*. I don't *understand*. I don't understand what anything means. . . . I'm stupid," she says. Mamet is shrewdly setting the stage for the bracingly unfashionable notion of a woman harassing a man. What finally humiliates Carol is not so much her ignorance as his prowess. The battle that ensues brings the audience up against the awful spoiling power of envy disguised as political ideology. Carol ends up trashing the professor's life. To offer a story that risks the hue and cry of underclass ideologues is typical of Mamet's curmudgeonly brilliance. It's the theatrical equivalent of pulling to an inside straight, and Mamet, with his great narrative gifts, accomplishes it deftly, with a competent assist from two of his ever-expanding family of performers, William H. Macy and his new wife, the British-born Rebecca Pidgeon.

Mamet likes to jump the audience into the middle of a dramatic situation, and let it piece together the jigsaw of the story from the tantalizing chunks of speech his characters scatter around the stage. Here we encounter the professor on the phone, trying to close on the new house that is the first fruit of his tenure (newly granted but not yet confirmed). Across the stage, Carol, turned away from him, sits morosely on a bench. John is all orders and authority; Carol is subservience in a schmatte. Carol has arrived for an unscheduled appointment, and her professor is obviously in a rush. "Words are acts," Mamet has written, and when John and Carol finally talk to each other the authority both of John's position and of his knowledge makes the gap between them almost unbridgeable. John brusquely cuts through Carol's tentative opening questions. "Let's take the mysticism out of it," he says, sternly trying to teach Carol how to negotiate and to think like an adult. The line haunts the evening. Mystification of power is precisely the point on which John will be shafted. Carol has no apparent powers of analysis—something John demonstrates by reading a snatch of her failing essay. "'I think that the ideas contained in this work express the author's feelings in a way that he intended, based on his

results,'" he says, and breaks off in understandable professorial frustration. "What can that mean?" Carol asks the same question, not just about his lectures but about his language. Carol continually interrupts the discourse for definitions of John's educated vocabulary. Words like "predilection," "paradigm," "transpire" throw her. She demands meaning but hasn't the language to define her feelings to herself or to the world. Her adamant dimness is rightly interpreted by John as anger. In their stutter-speech, which Mamet orchestrates with overlapping rhythms, interjected phrases, emotional retreats, and attempted advances, the drama of their missed communication is made transparent and startling. No American playwright is more expert than Mamet at externalizing the sludge of consciousness and dramatizing both the meaning and the music in our stammerings:

CAROL: I'm just: I sit in class I . . . I take notes . . .
JOHN (*simultaneously with "notes"*): Yes. I understand. What I am trying to *tell* you is that some, some basic . . .
CAROL: . . . I . . .
JOHN: . . . one moment: some basic missed communi . . .
CAROL: No, no, no. I'm doing what I'm told. It's *difficult* . . .
JOHN: . . . but . . .
CAROL: I don't . . . lots of the *language* . . .
JOHN: . . . please . . .
CAROL: The *language*, the "things" that you say . . .
JOHN: I'm sorry. No. I don't think that that's true.
CAROL: It *is* true. I . . .
JOHN: I think . . .
CAROL: It *is* true.

By making Carol's situation so immediately poignant, Mamet sets a cunning trap for the sympathies of the audience. "*Teach* me. *Teach* me," she pleads, with that combination of fierce vacancy and ambition which distinguishes the American undergraduate. "I'm not your *father*," says John, who is nonetheless put in a parental role by her show of powerlessness. Carol literally calls out John's power. She has no command of language, no knowledge, no psychological understanding. But she has the pedigree of the underprivileged:

CAROL: It *is* true. I have problems.
JOHN: . . . every . . .
CAROL: . . . I come from a different *social* . . .
JOHN: . . . ev . . .
CAROL: a different . . .
JOHN: . . . Look:

CAROL: No. I: when I *came* to this school:
JOHN: Yes. quite . . .
CAROL: . . . does that mean nothing . . . ?

The issue of class does mean something to John. From their different positions in the pecking order, he has arrived at the secure place Carol wants a university education to get her to. After twenty years on the tenure track, John is now set to move into the upper middle class and to shift his son from public to private school. He interrupts their talk to make a note to himself about the school tax. "Is it a law that I have to improve the city schools at the expense of my own interest?" says John, whose liberality is confined to the classroom, and doesn't extend to society. "Is this not simply 'The White Man's Burden'?" John recognizes in Carol not only the same class struggle he underwent but the same educational struggle. His career in academe and his iconoclastic views on education are his revenge on early learning difficulties, which he spells out to Carol to assuage her panic. He immediately names her feeling of humiliation, and later shows her the dynamic of her terror, saying, "Why was I born to be the laughingstock of a world in which everyone is better than I? In which I am entitled to nothing. Where I can not learn." He is pedantic but decent. "Men are the puppydogs of the universe," Mamet wrote in his essay collection, "Some Freaks." And so John seems. He takes Carol's failure as his own, and in a rush of pedagogic vainglory he throws away the offending essay, takes up her educational challenge, and gives her a comradely hug. John becomes a latter-day Professor Higgins, offering to recap the course for her in private tutorials, and easing her anxiety about grades by promising her an A. When Carol asks why he's doing this for her, he replies, "I like you."

John, like Mamet, is a self-styled provocateur; he holds to the antique notion that education should encourage thought, and argues that the job of a teacher is to provoke. "To make me mad is your job?" says his incredulous, pragmatic pupil. John is a bit of a wag. He swaggers in speech, and the idioms that Carol finds impenetrable are metaphoric turns of phrase that intelligently tease received opinion about higher education. He talks of college as "warehousing of the young," as something that prolongs adolescence; refers to tests as "hazing"; and, like the American sociologist Thorstein Veblen, whose argument about higher learning Mamet cunningly glosses, characterizes university education as a "ritual" of "something-other-than-useful"—what Veblen called "a by-product of the priestly vicarious leisure class." Carol is a zealot who, having got educational religion, can't comprehend backsliders. As the audience soon discovers, John's skepticism about education marks him as a heretic.

When John and Carol square off in Act 2, John is no longer the master, although at first he fondly thinks he is. His power and his blocking have changed. He sits face to face with Carol, who is now dressed in greens and blacks that hint at the paramilitary, and tries to shortcut procedure by reasoning her out of her accusations of sexism, racism, and élitism before the Tenure Committee reconvenes, by which time he will have lost his new house and his deposit. "You think, you think you can deny that these things happened; or, if they *did,* if they *did,* that they meant what you *said* they meant," Carol says. Every gesture in Act 1, every exchange, every idea has been taken out of context and turned into an indictment. "What gives you the *right,*" she says, in highest dudgeon, "to speak to a woman in your private, yes. Yes. I'm sorry. I'm sorry. You feel yourself empowered. . . . To *strut.* To *posture.* . . . And *confess* to a taste to play the *Patriarch* in your class. To grant *this.* To deny *that.* To embrace—your students." Mamet puts the audience exactly where John sits: up against it. Such is the power of Mamet's storytelling that the audience receives each willful misinterpretation like a body blow, audibly catching its breath at Carol's argument. Carol, who lacked words before, has got educated in a hurry by what she refers to as her Group, and she speaks now with the righteous fervor of a woman whose day has come. This transition is jarring but intentional. She has acquired a new voice and a new vocabulary, whose authority precludes ambiguity. She adopts political correctness as an intellectual carapace that substitutes dogma for thought, mission for mastery. Naming is claiming, and since Carol won't work to master a world she can't comprehend, she changes the frame of reference to a world she can. She advocates a kind of linguistic affirmative action, forcing John to define "paradigm," for example. "It's a model," he says. Carol counters, sharpish, "Then why can't you use that word?" And later, when she requires a simpler definition for the word "transpire," she rounds on John with the full malice of her envy, offering "happen" as an alternative. "Then *say* it. For Christ's sake. Who the *hell* do you think that you are? You want a post. You want unlimited power. To do and to say what you want. As it pleases you—Testing, Questioning, Flirting." This policing of language leads inevitably to a policing of the curriculum. Carol holds out the possibility of reprieve from the Tenure Committee if he'll agree to a new reading list, from which his book, among many, has been banned. "If you can choose them, others can," Carol tells him. "What are you, God?" Here, in a series of exchanges, Mamet exposes the central paradox of political correctness, which demands diversity in everything but thought.

Carol remains staunch. She is the embodiment of Mamet's mischievous assertion that "women don't give a tinker's damn about being well-liked, which means they don't know how to compromise." Carol's rigidity is a sign of her insecurity. Her ruthless orthodoxy is skillfully shown as her means of controlling her enormous anxiety of ignorance. In this production, the intelligence of Rebecca Pidgeon, who plays Carol, makes it hard to suspend disbelief in her academic ineptness but also makes her puritan willfulness powerfully credible.

Dressed now, in the last of their three encounters, in a loose-fitting black jacket, green chinos, and sensible black shoes, and peering out from behind wire-rimmed glasses, Carol stands above John like some Maoist enforcer. By this last scene, it is the student who is dishing out the humiliation to the professor, calling him a "little yapping fool." William H. Macy plays John with droll liberal long-suffering. He's slow to kindle, but when Carol interprets as rape his attempt to keep her in the room to settle their disagreement ("I was leaving this office, you 'pressed' yourself into me. You 'pressed' your body into me") he finally ignites. A telephone call from his wife interrupts the final argument. "I can't talk now, baby," John says, and then orders Carol out of the office. "Don't call your wife 'baby,'" she says. It is Mamet's shrewdly placed parting shot. The throw-away line turns out to be the last straw. John belts Carol around the room. The explosion of violence sends both Carol and John's academic career crashing.

Because of the limits of the scope and intention in this short polemical play, "Oleanna" may not belong to the major part of Mamet's canon, but it's a powerful, exciting play that shows off his enormous skills as a writer. The production, however, reveals his limitations as a director. The actors' job, according to Mamet, "is to accomplish *beat by beat,* as simply as possible, the specific action set out for them by the script and the director." Both Mr. Macy and Ms. Pidgeon are a bit under wraps here, at once awed and cowed by Mamet's authority, which takes some of the acting oxygen out of the air. In this, Mamet joins the likes of Samuel Beckett and Harold Pinter, whose literary touch was always much surer than their directorial hand. Mamet keeps

his show clean and crisp, but leaves a lot of production values still to be explored in the many other versions that "Oleanna" will certainly have.

On the night I saw it, the play was already doing its work in the world as the audience filed out of the theatre; it was a drizzly evening, and people clustered under the Orpheum Theatre marquee to keep talking.

"Too bad he had to have a woman be the heavy," one matron said.

"He's a bit of a misogynist," her friend said, and then turned to a stooped man who was obviously her husband. "What do you think?"

"No one escaped sin in the Garden of Eden," the man said—an acid thought, in keeping with the evenhanded skepticism of the play, and one that echoed something Mamet had written elsewhere about corruption. "The corrupted person, politician, parent, doctor, and artist offer us two choices," he said in "Some Freaks." "To accept them and their presumption of power *totally,* or to reject them *totally* and, so, realize that we have been cruelly duped and accept the humiliation, anger, and despair that realization entails." "Oleanna" bravely makes the audience own the ambiguity of its idealism.

My friend Liz and I walked away talking about the play's title, which is never mentioned. Liz remembered the old Pete Seeger/Alan Lomax song about a world turned upside down—a song as oblique, and as knowing, as the play. The last stanza goes:

So if you'd like a happy life,
To Oleanna you must go,
The poorest man from the old country
Becomes a king in a year or so.

COMMENTARY ON THE ORPHEUM THEATRE PRODUCTION, 1992

A year after the Clarence Thomas–Anita Hill hearings, the issue of sexual harassment remains in the air. And not only in daily life. Take "Oleanna," a new play by David Mamet. Yet who is harassing whom in this two-character drama at the Orpheum? A man is targeted on half the playbill covers, a woman on the other half—both with a bull's-eye. The message, if there is one, seems to be: make up your own mind.

The college student Carol (played by Rebecca Pidgeon) and the professor John (W. H. Macy) meet in his office. She is doing badly in his course and can't understand the work. He, about to receive tenure and buy a new house, offers to tutor her.

The thwack of verbal exchange culminates in a physical struggle as the professor's career comes apart amid the student's charges of sexual harassment. Meanwhile, the playwright tosses additional incendiary topics on the

fire: censorship, political correctness (P.C.), the battle of the sexes. So what is "Oleanna" saying? And who wins? Six individuals offer their opinions.

SUSAN BROWNMILLER AUTHOR OF "AGAINST OUR WILL: MEN, WOMEN AND RAPE"

Since I'm one of those theater lovers who rushes to the box office whenever a new David Mamet play is announced, I scooped up eight tickets for the first preview of "Oleanna" and invited some friends who have a collective history of political activism that would do Rosa Luxemburg proud. A week before we convened, I heard the buzz that Mr. Mamet's new play was about sexual harassment. Uh-oh, I shuddered. He can't get it right. But with one exception, my feminist friends and

I had an exhilarating time. Our holdout, who could barely restrain herself from booing, favored a picket line to protest Mr. Mamet's "vicious misogyny" (her phrase).

I beg to differ. I found Mr. Mamet's two-character duel a welcome jolt of nervy political theater. No, he didn't get sexual harassment "right," but I gleefully appreciated his theatrical broadside against the stifling value system of "permissible" thinking.

Mr. Mamet is obviously aware that authoritarian thought control is not the exclusive province of young activists on a college campus. He creates a pompous professor of vague liberal persuasion, John, who is so entranced with his airy circumlocutions that he misunderstands, and underestimates, the failing student who comes to his office for help. Carol, the waiflike underachiever, egged on by her shadowy group, moves inexorably toward her villainous empowerment by latching on to the current catch phrases of radical dogma while the professor disintegrates before our eyes.

Still, I didn't have it in me to applaud at the end, although "Oleanna" had electrified me. Mr. Mamet makes cogent drama out of P.C. by hanging his play, and his professor's ruination, on an insupportable charge of sexual harassment and, worse, on a false charge of attempted rape. An insensitive word here, a brief touch on the shoulder there and, bingo, a list of charges, a set of demands, and tenure denied.

My friend who wishes to picket "Oleanna" argues that the play is a wicked denial of real rape and harassment, and says it is—ah—incorrect to make powerful theater out of the rare exception. I tend to believe that the feminist movement will survive David Mamet as it survived Arlen Specter and others who deny the validity of women's experiences as articulated by women themselves.

But by pinning P.C. on gender issues, the playwright is less brave than he thinks he is. Blaming women is a very old story and a conventional plot line. Would Mr. Mamet have had the guts to make his student a young black man or a ghetto Hispanic and engage the thornier P.C. issues of race and class? Too volatile, perhaps, and less commercially viable. Part of the strange power of this play, and why it appealed in a subliminal way to my feminist sensibilities, is the absolute lack of sexual involvement between the characters who are locked nonetheless in mortal struggle. Man against man and man against nature are typical themes in drama, but it is rare to see woman against man—much less the triumph of a female villain who is neither mother nor lover.

Come to think of it, any playwright's alleged misogyny poses a fascinating question. Was Strindberg guilty of misogyny in "Miss Julie" or Ibsen in "Hedda Gabler"? Absolutely. But can you name a half dozen better parts for female actors?

ENRIQUE FERNANDEZ EDITOR OF THE SPANISH-LANGUAGE MAGAZINE *MAS* AND A COMMENTATOR ON "CROSSROADS" ON NATIONAL PUBLIC RADIO

Does one root for Laertes or Hamlet? A play isn't a prizefight. Or is it? The audience at the performance of "Oleanna" I attended was clearly for either the male or female character; even when, after the show, some theatergoers (mostly men) strained to explain to their companions (mostly women) how they could see both sides of the story. "Oleanna" pushes rooting buttons. Teacher versus student. (About to be) tenured radical versus Shining Path-style ideologue. Thirtysomething versus twentysomething. Fuzzy humanism versus political correctness. And, of course, the battle of the sexes.

In "Teaneck Tanzi: The Venus Flytrap," which had a very short run on Broadway almost 10 years ago, the opposite-sex antagonists were wrestlers. The last act, nearly wordless, was a fierce wrestling match. I found it profoundly satisfying, for it dramatized the tensions between men and women in the most straightforward manner: let's see who kicks whom. In "Oleanna," as soon as the woman started raising politically correct issues, some audience members hissed. In the end, the female gets kicked and proves her argument. K.O.'d, she wins on points.

And that's my problem with "Oleanna." As a play, its structure is too pat, and as blood sport, it's not sporting enough. The structure: son of a bitch meets bitch. Unquestionably, the student deserves her whipping—which she must have anticipated and been willing to receive, for the good of her "group." The violence is perfectly logical and she, a kind of Maoist Mr. Spock, must accept it. And also unquestionably, the professor deserves his comeuppance. He is a puffed up, intellectually shallow petit bourgeois—a creature often spotted bathing in student adulation in elite liberal arts colleges. His flaws spill in spurts, like his stammering speech on the phone. Her only flaw is having none; she's as pure as a young ideologue in a 60s Godard film—without Godard's dry humor. They deserve each other.

But does the audience? I left the theater disappointed. Something about its perfect symmetry. It's the wild card, the offbeat rhythm, the off-center quirk that makes a performance meaningful. For example, as battle of the sexes, the Thomas–Hill televised confrontation was disturbing and provoking because both antagonists were black, thus obviating facile assumptions about victim and victimizer.

Supposedly that was life and this is theater, but, in fact, they are both spectacles. "Oleanna" has too many neat binary oppositions. Or perhaps the male-female confrontation is so rich and engaging in real life today that art cannot hold a candle to lived experience. I would have liked the pure young firebrand of

"Oleanna" to confront, say, a Camille Paglia character: an anti-P.C., self-aggrandizing academic of the same gender—with dangerously sharp teeth. Or the same play acted by two gay males; sexual harassment exists across gender lines. But, as it stands, "Oleanna" says very little, except: find out what college served as David Mamet's model, and don't send your kids there.

DEBORAH TANNEN AUTHOR OF "YOU JUST DON'T UNDERSTAND: WOMEN AND MEN IN CONVERSATION"

"Oleanna" isn't about sexual harassment. It is about the fear of witches: a woman lures a man by seeming helpless and feminine, then, after he becomes vulnerable by trying to help her, she destroys him.

There is no other way to understand the student Carol's unexplained transformation from the first half of "Oleanna" to the second. A soldier in a 17th-century play by Walter Carleton, "Ephesian Matron," addresses witches who "allure us with the fairness of your skins; and when folly hath brought us within your reach, you leap upon us and devour us."

There you have it: in the first act Carol is a shy, almost speechless young woman in a shapeless dress who wails that she sits smiling in a back corner in class but cannot understand anything because she's stupid. In the second she is an aggressively articulate, self-satisfied, theory-spouting caricature of a "feminist," dressed in man-styled trousers and vest. This witch turns the university into a dystopia where power relations are reversed and a woman student destroys an innocent man's life in the name of political correctness. Vagina dentata goes to college.

"Oleanna" would have us believe that Carol manipulated the professor by pretending to be vulnerable when she was really lying in wait to assault him. In fact, it is "Oleanna" that manipulates, pretending to be an honest play about the indeterminacy of language and abuse of power, then assaulting us with its simplistic and dehumanizing denouement.

Act 1 is Pinteresque, seemingly about the failure of communication, with endless repetitions of phrases like "I don't understand," unfinished sentences and broken-off words. Act 2 is Kafkaesque: the woman's unnamed "group," like a witches' coven, is out to get the lone professor, to pillory him for offenses he didn't know he committed, offenses the audience saw were minor.

Many men worry, "What would I do if someone brought a false charge against me? What remark have I made, in innocence, that could be misconstrued?" This tension could make a fascinating play—even a paranoid fantasy, for part of what art does is let us play out our nightmares, think through what we would do. But David Mamet doesn't touch these ambiguities. Carol is

all surface: just a stereotype that audiences can join in hating.

The most dangerous aspect of the play is its ending: the professor beats the young woman, punching her, hurling her to the floor, cursing at her and lifting a chair to break over her head as she crawls under a bench and huddles in fetal position. The evening I saw the play, the audience cheered and urged him on. All over the country, battered women's shelters fill up as quickly as they're opened. Yet many people feel, "She probably provoked it; she probably was asking for it." In "Oleanna," these cruel misconceptions are given weight: a woman is beaten because she provoked it, she deserved it. Right now, we don't need a play that helps anyone feel good about a man beating a woman.

MARK ALAN STAMATY CREATOR OF THE COMIC STRIP "WASHINGTOON"

In this era of political correctness, "Oleanna" is "'Rambo' Meets P.C." And "Rambo" wins for both sensitivity and humanity. On one level, the play can appear to be a kind of Lady-or-Tiger Rorschach test, intended to stir equal empathy and argument from "both sides." If so, maybe I'm about to take the bait and expose myself as an unconscious sexist. But I think not.

Despite the possibly equal justification that Carol and John are given for their individual behaviors, this play does take sides. With John, the man. Carol and John both struggle and suffer. But John suffers more, and his suffering is far more palpably articulated. Like "Rambo" or "Rocky," John is abused to a breaking point and finally explodes. When he does—like "Rambo" or "Rocky"—the audience is with him emotionally.

"Well," says John, who has just hit, kicked and thrown Carol around his office in the climax of "Oleanna." John appears sheepish and possibly shocked by his brief explosion of violent rage.

"Yes, that's right! . . ." says Carol twice in the last line of the play, seeming to imply: "Yes, you are a monster!"

Men should not be physically violent to women. And vice versa. If a man is violent toward a woman on stage without it being declared evil, is that a recommendation to society? Or can it simply be viewed as theater, as thought, but not suggested action?

John certainly is pompous, arrogant and self-absorbed. And he has power over the academic lives and destinies of students like Carol, which he somewhat unconsciously abuses. But John attempts always to see his flaws and change. He has tried to find truth and humanness beyond false structures, but finally decided on survival in a world of hollow rituals and institutions that he sees through but seems unable to change.

Carol's flaw is her fanaticism. Faced with John's power

and privilege, which she covets, and viewing his vulnerabilities simply as means by which to conquer, control and even destroy him, Carol increasingly exposes herself as single-mindedly obsessed with power. John's attitude toward power is more ambivalent. She becomes the villain, the automaton they both despise.

Despite Carol's effort in the play's last line to condemn John's final eruption, as if it were proof of his evil, John's attack against the automaton Carol has become is cathartic, an explosion of the humanness suffocating inside both of them.

ELLEN SCHWARTZMAN VICE PRESIDENT OF THE STUDENT GOVERNMENT ASSOCIATION AT BARNARD COLLEGE

"No—I don't understand. Do you see? I don't understand," says the student in "Oleanna," as she proclaims her view of academia. These words aptly describe my own amazement at David Mamet's new play.

As a woman in college, I'm concerned and disturbed by Mr. Mamet's Carol. Her sheer stupidity, marked in part by her inability to grasp basic ideas and vocabulary, such as "paradigm," or her constant whining reply, "I don't understand," combined with her ability to be swept away on a crusade for the destruction of a man's life (using twisted facts as evidence), provide a totally negative portrayal of women.

Carol is rapidly transformed from the imbecilic automaton of Act 1 to the vengeful calculating champion of female rights of Act 2, as the audience witnesses a new McCarthyism—that of sexual harassment.

In some quarters, "Oleanna" has been called the consummate rejoinder to the controversy surrounding the Thomas–Hill hearings. But it is not. Rather, Mr. Mamet's treatment of sexual harassment does a disservice to the subject's seriousness.

The audience's focus is shifted from the supposed ambiguity surrounding some cases of sexual harassment at the same time that the author funnels blame onto the alleged victim for her hateful actions. Furthermore, Mr. Mamet does nothing to create sympathy for this militant flat female character, leaving viewers to side with no other than the alleged harasser, John.

In his version of the Thomas–Hill hearings, Mr. Mamet presents a plot devoid of ambiguity, while perpetuating a myth prevalent in American culture: harassment exists in the mind of the victim alone.

LIONEL TIGER CHARLES DARWIN PROFESSOR OF ANTHROPOLOGY AT RUTGERS UNIVERSITY AND AUTHOR OF "MEN IN GROUPS" AND "THE PURSUIT OF PLEASURE"

"Oleanna" confronts two principal features of The New Improved American Puritanism. The Scarlet Letter is now affixed to men and women. And the univer-

sity, not the church, is the arena for the most dogmatic assertions about how to live and think.

The play also explores the transformation of even personal behavior into symptoms of contemporary political currents. Touching a person's shoulder, calling a spouse "baby," as in the play, cause mighty accusations of fiery guilt. Eternal vigilance and self-censorship are the price of moral purity.

University women and men in particular perch on platforms paved with eggshells. The situation can be forbidding. While good institutions may cope sensibly and fairly with this rectitudinous zeal, there is clearly a broad deadening of controversy and variety about hot-button issues, such as sex and race. One result is that ludicrous, flat-earther assertions—Andrea Dworkin's, for example, that all heterosexual sex is rape—are taken with undue seriousness because they fit into a larger picture of a world alive with chronic exploitation and harassment.

Of course exploitation and harassment exist. "Oleanna" describes one extreme of the response to advantage taken unfairly. A female student, coached by her "group," secures the dismissal of a male instructor for acts, attitudes and sentences about which many audience members appeared to have more than reasonable doubts. But the audience vote is not the point. The case made against the male is internally consistent and sturdy, given the assumptions of current discussion. The main one is that men are predatory and women potential victims. The scarlet letter is ready and waiting.

The problem is that the main assumption is broadly correct. Presumably both women and men display lively enthusiasm for sexual congress (and even reproduction—after all, those pleasure centers had to evolve for a reason). Nevertheless, it is characteristic that males will press their sexual case and females determine their own responses. As biologists know now, females are the evolutionary gatekeepers of any species. So there is a difference of sexual strategy that is rather hard-wired and affects not only sexual behavior directly but also how people talk.

This angular strategic difference is in part what animates the current legal turmoil. To solve the problem compassionately, the underlying biology has to be appreciated. Otherwise the dialogue will continue in two separate languages, translated by yet more lawyers who speak a common language, which they adore to operate for a fee.

Only one moment in "Oleanna"—the very last—suggests this central force field, perhaps inadvertently. The stage direction is not in the script; the dramatic impact is unexpected. The male has struck the female. She is huddled under a bench. She peers at him across the turmoiled air. Foul aggression has occurred. Her case about his malevolence appears to have been proved. Then she slowly removes her granny glasses and looks at him. The first sexuality in the play, after the first knockdown. One mean play ends and a harsher one begins.

APPENDIX A
Analyzing a Play: Close Reading for Writing

Writing about a play, like reading a play, requires close attention to the words in the text—both in the stage directions and in the dialogue. The dialogue is especially important not only because it contains the fundamental source of drama, both on stage and on the page, but also because it constitutes a basic source of information for discovering, developing, and documenting any thoughts you have about any aspect of the play. While a playwright can offer interpretative comments in stage directions, the playwright's voice is never heard directly on stage. Instead the dialogue is the primary means by which a play implies the total makeup of its imaginative world and describes the behavior of all the characters who populate that world. So, the more closely you examine the dialogue, the more ideas you will discover to write about and the more specific material you will have readily available to support your ideas when you begin to write. In the following section, we show how close reading and annotating is the preliminary "research" for any kind of writing about drama, whether that writing focuses on characters or scenes, in print or in production. We then discuss several different kinds of writing that can be developed from the process of questioning, analyzing, and annotating.

Analyzing and Annotating Dialogue

Whenever you annotate a passage of dialogue, the best way to proceed is by using a basic method of inquiry and discovery—that is, by asking yourself a series of key questions and jotting down your answers on a notepad, in a computer file, or in the margin next to the dialogue. These notes and annotations together with the dialogue become major source material for your writing.

What sections of the play might you choose for annotation? The obvious answer is "All of them" because the more information you gather, the more issues will present themselves as possible topics. Still, if you are trying to decide where to start, we offer some suggestions. Opening sequences are often important because from the play's first moments the playwright sends signals about the characters and the world they inhabit. The first entrance of a major character is crucial because the changes that a character undergoes are measured against those first impressions. In addition to looking at scenes that are obviously central, it is often helpful to look carefully at scenes that at first glance might seem unimportant or even irrelevant. And if a scene creates problems for you and you find yourself asking "What's going on here?" or "Why is this scene in the play?" you will want to work carefully with the scene so that its meaning becomes clear.

Once you've chosen a section of the play to annotate, you might ask the following questions.

• What happens during this dialogue and as a result of this dialogue?

• What does this passage reveal about the inner life and motives of each character?

• What does it reveal about the relationships of the characters to each other?

• What does it reveal about the plot or about any of the circumstances contributing to the complication or resolution of the plot?

• What are the most notable moments or statements in the passage?

• What implicit or unspoken matters are most important in this passage?

In addition to these questions, which focus on the imaginative world of the play, there are also questions pertaining to the play as a work meant to be acted and produced in a theater.

• How might each line be performed?

• What facial expressions, physical gestures, or bodily movements are implied by the dialogue?

• What props or set pieces are explicitly or implicitly called for in the dialogue?

• What vocal inflections or tone of voice does a line suggest?

• Where might the characters pause in delivering their lines?

• Where might the characters increase or decrease the volume or speed of their delivery?

• Where might the characters stand on stage and in relation to each other at the beginning of the passage and at later points in the passage?

As an example of how these questions can be applied to a particular piece of dialogue, we annotate a passage that occurs near the beginning of Eugène Ionesco's play *The Lesson,* namely the first meeting of a teacher and a young student who has come for a private tutoring session. The list of characters tells us that the professor is somewhere between fifty and sixty years old, and that the pupil is eighteen. We do not know their names and, although Ionesco does supply a description of each character in a stage direction, the theater audience doesn't read or hear the stage directions. Thus, as the professor and the pupil meet, their lines must reveal who they are.

The following annotation is deliberately suggestive in several ways. It represents the kind of thinking that actors and directors might do as they repeatedly comb every syllable for information about the characters—and thus it is more thorough than any single first reading would be. It is also suggestive in that it not only attempts to describe how the characters might respond to each other but also offers a range of possible choices. Thus, the annotation answers some of the questions we have raised and then poses more questions for further thought and exploration. We have put the dialogue of the characters in the left-hand column and our notes in the right-hand column.

PROFESSOR: Good morning, young lady.	Polite, but not very interested in her as an individual. Calling her "young lady" puts her in a role distinctly subservient to his.
You . . . I expect that you . . . that you are the new pupil?	He probably starts to say "You must be the new pupil"

PUPIL: Yes, Professor. Good morning, Professor.

As you see, I'm on time. I didn't want to be late.

PROFESSOR: That's fine, miss.

Thank you, you didn't really need to hurry. I am very sorry to have kept you waiting . . . I was just finishing up . . .

well . . . I'm sorry . . .

You will excuse me, won't you?

PUPIL: Oh, certainly, Professor.

It doesn't matter at all, Professor.

PROFESSOR: Please excuse me . . . Did you have any trouble finding the house?

but evidently finds it difficult to get that sentence spoken. What do those ellipses mean? Is he so absentminded that he can't remember what he was going to say? Or is he painfully shy?

She responds immediately, repeating his title twice. Is she flattering him by being so deferential? Does the repetition suggest nervousness? Her next lines similarly lend themselves to different readings.

Perhaps she's trying to impress him with her desire to learn and her punctuality. Or maybe she is one of those people who always explains every little thing.

Whatever her inflection, the professor may choose his response. He may wish to be equally polite, or he may try to cut off what could be a longer series of statements.

Here he seems genuinely reassuring and even moves into an apology of his own. Once again he doesn't quite finish the sentence. Does he feel that he somehow owes the pupil an explanation? That's what he seems to offer.

But then he decides not to continue the explanation. Perhaps she's not worth it. Perhaps the explanation would be too personal (was he in the bathroom?).

Still he apologizes. What is all this politeness about? "Why should he keep apologizing to me?" she may think. So she reassures him using his title, again repeating it. As before, she seems unable to say something only once. Now he's apologizing yet *again*. So the choices above are narrowing down; he seems, though we don't know

PUPIL: No . . . Not at all. I just asked the way.

Everybody knows you around here.

PROFESSOR: For thirty years I've lived in this town.

You've not been here for long?

How do you find it?
PUPIL: It's all right.

The town is attractive and even agreeable, there's a nice park, a boarding school, a bishop, nice shops and streets . . .

PROFESSOR: That's very true, young lady.

And yet, I'd just as soon live somewhere else. In Paris, or at least Bordeaux.

PUPIL: Do you like Bordeaux?

PROFESSOR: I don't know. I've never seen it.

PUPIL: But you know Paris?

PROFESSOR: No, I don't know it either, young lady,

why, anxious or insecure. And the pupil is eager to alleviate that insecurity. She thus throws in a reassuring and complimentary remark. Her compliment seems to work. He responds with a personal statement, rather than a worried apology. Perhaps he feels that he ought to find out something about her.
Polite small talk.
Hardly an enthusiastic response. He may look at her quizzically, and so she shifts to more extended—and more complimentary—statements. Her list reveals the average quality of her mind. The adjective she uses is the innocuous "nice" and she uses it twice. We note, almost in passing, that she seems to place the "bishop" in the list as if he's just another town feature, along with the park, the school, and the shops. Before she extends the list indefinitely, the professor hastily agrees with her.
Then, as if questioning what she's said, he adds reflectively, even wistfully—
Bordeaux is a less exciting town, but at least, his tone implies, it would be more exciting than *this* town.
She is slightly surprised by the turn the conversation has taken, but responds to the implied putdown of Bordeaux.
Not the remark we're expecting. Normally if someone prefers one place to another, we assume that he has seen both places.
The pupil shares our surprise and hurries to get back to what she expects, the praise of Paris from one who knows it well.
Is he embarrassed to admit

but if you'll permit me,

can you tell me, Paris is
the capital city of . . .
miss?

PUPIL: Paris is the capital city of . . .

France?

PROFESSOR: Yes, young lady,
bravo, that's very good, that's perfect. My congratulations.

You have your French geography at your finger
tips. You know your chief cities.

that he doesn't know Paris? How could anyone speaking French (the original language of the play) *not* know Paris? She gives him a questioning look and he hastens to take over the conversation. He returns to the overly polite tone of the first few lines. He phrases the question as a request; can this be a serious question? Is he testing her? She repeats the question and the pause indicated by . . . tells us that she is thinking of the answer. If we were surprised that the professor didn't know Paris, we're even more surprised that she hesitates over the capital of her own country.

He acknowledges the correct answer but *amazingly,* he keeps on congratulating her. Surely the pupil's trivial display of knowledge doesn't demand such a response. Perhaps, we wonder, he's being ironic. Or is this just a further manifestation of his own insecurity, one so great that he feels he has to compliment the student? Or do we have a situation in which *neither* the pupil (when she mentions the bishop) or the professor (at this point) recognize the incongruity of their remarks?

As you can see from our sample annotations, the process of close reading and analyzing dialogue can lead to richly detailed information, insights, and ideas about the characters, the plot, and the staging of the play; it is also a way to raise further questions, to see how a single line may suggest several interpretative choices. In our annotations, for instance, we raise questions about the Professor's politeness and whether that might imply shyness or nervousness. After seeing how the Professor behaves at the end of the play, we may want to come back to these questions and ask whether or not the nervousness is genuine. While the annotating process may help you to see certain patterns of behavior, it may also force you to realize that some moments are particularly problematic and do not fit easily into a consistent pattern. Don't ignore behaviors that don't seem to fit, but continue to look for other instances of such behavior.

Once you have used this process to examine a series of passages or scenes, you will then have an extensive body of material to draw on for any kind of piece you might wish to write about a play. You will have a wealth of material you can use to explain and support your ideas about the work, whether those ideas concern the play as it exists on the page or as it might be (or has been) produced on the stage.

Some Different Kinds of Writing: Staging Papers, Character or Scene Analyses, and Reviews

Once you've worked carefully on annotating a series of scenes, you may ask yourself "Where do I go from here?" The kinds of papers we suggest in this section are by no means the only possibilities. But they do suggest some approaches to writing about drama that not only grow out of careful analysis and annotation but also reflect the stage-oriented approach that this anthology embodies. While a play script may exist solely on the page, the play itself is most fully alive when it is produced—either on an actual stage or in the theater of the mind. Thus, we stress that your writing about a play, like your reading of a play, needs to recognize, and even imitate, the multifaceted experience of a play in performance. The types of papers that we outline suggest particular stage-oriented strategies.

Staging Papers   Your annotations can readily be turned into a staging paper, in which you imagine yourself as a director contemplating the production of a particular scene or segment of a scene, such as the one we considered from *The Lesson*. This kind of paper might begin with a brief discussion of the production problems and interpretative questions that you see as central to understanding the scene. In the annotated section of *The Lesson*, for example, one major interpretative question might be "What is the initial attitude of the pupil toward the professor?" A production question might deal with the set for the play. In many modern and contemporary plays, as in *The Lesson*, you often find stage directions for the characters provided by the playwright, but you will almost always need to be more detailed in your production notes. And even if the playwright provides a detailed set design, you may choose to create a different one to fit your own interpretation of the scene. At the beginning of *The Lesson*, for example, Ionesco's description of the professor's office calls for doors, a window, "ordinary potted plants," a buffet, a table, three chairs, and book-shelves, all of which suggest a fairly realistic setting against which the surprising behavior of the professor and pupil unfolds. But you might instead choose to design a setting that emphasizes the absurd world of these characters by showing a room with walls at strange angles (or no walls at all), decorated with unexpected colors and unusual furniture. Thus, one version of the staging paper would join questions about the play to annotations of the dialogue, together with notes on set design, costuming, props, and so on.

Another version of the staging paper, which focuses even more directly on visual and costume elements, might be built around the question, "What does the audience see and hear *before* the first line of the play?" For many readers, a play seems to begin with the first line, but in fact a production offers a great deal of information to the audience before any words are spoken: the set, the lighting, perhaps the music, and the physical appearance of the characters. In deciding what the audience will see, you will need to consider the set for the first scene (or, as in *The Lesson,* for the entire play), the clues for characterization that you have found in your annotations and how those might translate into casting and costume choices, as well as what the first speaking character is doing or has just done, which forms the basis for that character's first words.

Character or Scene Analyses   You can use the annotation technique to interpret the behavior of a major character or to explain the significance of a minor character in the play as a whole. Our sample annotations would be a useful point of departure for a detailed analysis, closely tracking the strange behavior of the professor or the pupil during the first third or first half of the play. Or, you might prefer instead to examine the behavior of the professor's maid, a third character who appears occasionally, but seems to have little if any influence on the behavior of the professor and the pupil. You might wonder if she is really necessary to the play. Using the annotation technique, you would look closely at the moments when she appears, considering her relationship to the professor and the pupil and noting in particular whom she speaks to and how she interacts with them. The same kind of analysis can be done for an apparently minor scene in a play. By imagining the play without the character or the scene and then examining the character or scene in detail, you will be able to show how seemingly insignificant elements in a play can help to shape a reader's or an audience's understanding of and response to the work.

Reviews   Once you've worked through scenes of a play in detail, you are then in a position to offer a judicious critique of the play in production. You should not expect that a production will necessarily correspond to the staging you've imagined, even though the director and actors working on a text during the weeks of rehearsal experiment with the same kind of possibilities that you do. But your process of thinking through the questions about staging the play and your search for a range of answers will make you more aware of the choices that a particular production has made. You then need to question a performance in the same way that you question a written text. If you watch a stage performance, which you only see once, you might want to jot down quick notes immediately after the performance and then, as soon as possible, try to remember more details about what you saw. If you watch a videotaped or filmed performance, you will be able to look back at particular moments, just as you would go back to a written text to find individual details. Thus you may write an analytical review of a production, including as much specific description as possible, so that you are both re-creating the performance for your reader and at the same time offering your reader a discriminating guide to the production.

Another way to write about a play in production is to gather together as many different reviews as possible from as many different productions as possible. Look for the topics that recur: characters who seem susceptible to different interpretations; major scenes or confrontations; the design of the production; unusual casting choices; or the impact of a particular actor on a particular role. While reviews are often evaluative rather than descriptive, they still can offer details that evoke the whole production. Look, for example, at Michael Billington's review of *The House of Bernarda Alba* (page 781) to see how a reviewer can vividly recreate a production, both in terms of setting and individual characterizations. Consider the conflicting reviews of *Juno and the Paycock* (pages 753–754) or of *'night, Mother* (pages 1232–1234) to see how reviewers can cite the same performance but offer very different judgments about it. Using the information (but not necessarily the judgments) from the reviews and your own detailed reading, you can then deduce a range of interpretative possibilities for the play.

All of these suggestions represent approaches to writing about plays which call on you to be both creator and spectator, both actor and audience. Thinking with the specificity of actors who must find a way to make sense of every word they speak and who must respond to what others do and say on stage leads you to discover more possibilities for interpreting those words. Writing about a play develops your understanding of the play and then allows you to communicate that understanding to others.

APPENDIX B
Film and Video Productions of Plays in
Stages of Drama

NOTE: DISTRIBUTORS' ADDRESSES, TELEPHONE NUMBERS, AND FAX NUMBERS FOLLOW THIS LIST OF FILM AND VIDEO PRODUCTIONS.

Aeschylus, *Agamemnon*
90 min.
VHS, Beta, 3/4 U.
Directed by Peter Hall.
Distributed by Films for the Humanities.

Aeschylus, *Agamemnon*
120 min., 1991.
VHS.
Directed by Peter Meineck.
Distributed by Insight Media.

Anonymous, *Everyman*
53 min., 1991.
VHS.
Produced in conjunction with Columbia University.
Distributed by Insight Media.

Anonymous, *Everyman*
55 min., 1971.
16 mm film.
Distributed by Paul Lewison.

Aristophanes, *Lysistrata*
97 min., 1987.
VHS.
Greek with English subtitles.
With Jenny Karezi and Costas Kazakos.
Directed by Yiannis Negrepontis.
Distributed by New York Film Annex and
     Insight Media.

Baraka, *Dutchman*
55 min., B/W, 1967.
With Shirley Knight, Al Freeman Jr.
Directed by Anthony Harvey.
Distributed by Insight Media.

Beckett, *Endgame*
96 min., 1992.
VHS.
Produced at University of Maryland.
Distributed by Insight Media.

Brecht, *Life of Galileo*
155 min., 1973.
16 mm film.
With Topol, Colin Blakely, Margaret Leighton, and
     John Gielgud.
Directed by Joseph Losey.
Distributed by Films, Inc.

Büchner, *Woyzeck*
82 min., 1978.
VHS, 3/4 U.
German with English subtitles.
Directed by Werner Herzog.
With Klaus Kinski, Eva Mattes and Wolfgang
     Reichmann.
Distributed by New Yorker Video.

Büchner, *Woyzeck*
60 min., 1978.
VHS, Beta, 3/4 U.
Hosted by José Ferrer.
Distributed by Films, Inc.

Chekhov, *The Cherry Orchard*
44 min., 1968.
VHS, Beta, 3/4 U.
Selected scenes.
Distributed by Encyclopedia Britannica
     Educational Corporation.

Fugard, *"Master Harold" . . . and the Boys*
90 min., 1984.
VHS, Beta.
With Matthew Broderick.
Directed by Michael Lindsay-Hogg.
Distributed by Lorimar Home Video, Warner
     Home Video Inc.

Hwang, *M. Butterfly*
101 min., 1993.
VHS, Laser.
With Jeremy Irons.
Directed by David Cronenberg.
Distributed by Warner Home Video Inc.

Ibsen, *A Doll's House*
89 min., B/W, 1959.
VHS, Beta.
With Julie Harris, Christopher Plummer, Jason
    Robards, Jr., Hume Cronyn, and Eileen
    Heckart.
Distributed by MGM/United Artists Home Video.

Ibsen, *A Doll's House*
63 min., 1968.
VHS, Beta, 3/4 U.
Distributed by Encyclopedia Britannica
    Educational Corporation.

Ibsen, *A Doll's House*
85 min., 1973.
VHS, Beta, Laser.
With Claire Bloom, Anthony Hopkins, Ralph
    Richardson, Denholm Elliott, Anna Massey,
    and Edith Evans.
Directed by Patrick Garland.
Distributed by Films, Inc.

Ibsen, *A Doll's House*
98 min., 1973.
VHS, Beta.
With Jane Fonda and Trevor Howard.
Directed by Joseph Losey.
Distributed by Starmaker Entertainment, Inc.,
    Prism Entertainment, and Insight Media.

Ibsen, *A Doll's House*
39 min., 1977.
VHS, Beta, 3/4 U.
With Claire Bloom.
Selected scenes.
Distributed by AIMS Media and Insight Media.

Jonson, *Volpone*
95 min., 1939.
VHS, Beta.
French with English subtitles.
With Harry Bauer and Louis Jouvet.
Directed by Maurice Tourneur.
Distributed by Budget Video.

Jonson, *Volpone*
90 min., B/W, 1967.
16 mm film.
A BBC Production.
Distributed by University of Michigan Media.

Lorca, *The House of Bernarda Alba*
1967.
Directed by Nuria Espert and Stuart Burge.
Holms Productions/Channel Four/WNET-13
    (British/US).
Not presently available for rental.

Marlowe, *Doctor Faustus*
93 min., 1968.
VHS, Beta.
With Richard Burton and Elizabeth Taylor.
Directed by Richard Burton and Nevill Coghill.
Distributed by Columbia Tristar Home Video and
    Insight Media.

Miller, *Death of a Salesman*
115 min., B/W, 1951.
16 mm film.
With Frederick March and Mildred Dunnock in
    their Broadway premiere roles.
Distributed by rental agencies throughout the
    United States.

Miller, *Death of a Salesman*
135 min., 1985.
VHS, Beta, 16 mm film.
With Dustin Hoffman, Kate Reid, John Malkovich,
    and Charles Durning.
Directed by Volker Schlondorff.
Produced by Dustin Hoffman and Arthur Miller.
Distributed by Lorimar Home Video.

Molière, *The Misanthrope*
52 min.
VHS, Beta, 3/4 U.
With Edward Petherbridge in the Richard Wilbur
    translation.
Distributed by Films for the Humanities.

Norman, *'night, Mother*
97 min., 1986.
VHS, Beta, Laser.
With Sissy Spacek and Anne Bancroft.
Directed by Tom Moore.
Distributed by MCA Home Video.

O'Casey, *Juno and the Paycock*
96 min., B/W, 1930.
VHS.
With Sara Allgood, Edward Chapman, and John
    Longden.
Directed by Alfred Hitchcock.
Distributed by Nostalgia Family Video, Valencia
    Entertainment Corporation, and Hollywood
    Home Theatre.

O'Casey, *Juno and the Paycock*
85 min., B/W, 1930.
16 mm film.
With Sara Allgood.
Directed by Alfred Hitchcock.
Distributed by Classic Films Museum.

Pinter, *The Homecoming*
111 min., 1973.
16 mm film.
With Cyril Cusack, Ian Holm, and Vivien
    Merchant.
Directed by Peter Hall.
An American Film Theatre Production.
Distributed by various rental agencies in the United
    States.

Pirandello, *Six Characters in Search of an Author*
60 min., 1978.
VHS, Beta, 3/4 U.
Hosted by José Ferrer and Ossie Davis.
Distributed by Films, Inc.

Pirandello, *Six Characters in Search of an Author*
52 min.
VHS, Beta, 3/4 U.
Large section of the play, but not the entire work.
Distributed by Films for the Humanities.

Shakespeare, *Othello*
92 min., B/W, 1952.
16 mm film.
With Orson Welles, Suzanne Cloutier, Michael
    MacLiammoir, and Fay Compton.
Directed by Orson Welles.
Distributed by Corinth Films.

Shakespeare, *Othello*
166 min., 1965.
16 mm film.
With Laurence Olivier, Maggie Smith, Frank
    Finlay, and Derek Jacobi.
Directed by Stuart Burge.
Distributed by Swank Motion Pictures.

Shakespeare, *Othello*
208 min., 1982.
VHS.
With Anthony Hopkins, Bob Hoskins, and
    Penelope Wilton.
Distributed by Ambrose Video Publishing, Inc. and
    Insight Media.

Shakespeare, *Othello*
198 min., 1987.
VHS, Beta, 3/4.
With John Kani and Joanna Weinberg.
Directed by Janet Suzman.
Distributed by Films for the Humanities.

Shakespeare, *Twelfth Night*
124 min., 1980.
VHS.
With Alec McCowen, Trevor Peacock, and Felicity
    Kendal.
Distributed by Ambrose Video Publishing, Inc. and
    Insight Media.

Shakespeare, *Twelfth Night*
165 min.
VHS, Beta, 3/4 U.
With Richard Briers, Frances Barber, Caroline
    Langrishe, and Christopher Ravenscroft.
Directed by Kenneth Branagh.
Distributed by Films for the Humanities.

Shaw, *Pygmalion*
96 min., B/W, 1938.
VHS.
With Wendy Hiller and Leslie Howard.
Directed by Gabriel Pascal.
Distributed by Zenger Video.

Shepard, *Fool for Love*
108 min., 1986.
VHS, Beta.
With Sam Shepard, Kim Basinger, Randy Quaid,
    and Harry Dean Stanton.
Directed by Robert Altman.
Distributed by Grapevine Video, Facets
    Multimedia, Inc.

Sheridan, *The School for Scandal*
100 min., 1965.
VHS, Beta, 3/4 U, 8 mm film.
With Joan Plowright and Felix Aylmer.
Distributed by Video Yesteryear and Insight
    Media.

Sophocles, *Oedipus Rex*
90 min., B/W, 1957.
VHS, Beta.
With Douglas Rain and Douglas Campbell.
Directed by Tyrone Guthrie.
Distributed by Insight Media.

Sophocles, *Oedipus the King*
110 min., 1967.
VHS, Beta, Cinemascope.
Italian with English subtitles.
With Franco Citti, Silvana Mangano and Alida
    Valli.
Directed by Pier Paolo Pasolini.
Distributed by Kino International Corp.

Sophocles, *Oedipus the King*
97 min., 1968.
16 mm film.
With Christopher Plummer, Orson Welles, Lilli
    Palmer, Cyril Cusack, and Donald Sutherland.
Directed by Philip Saville.
Distributed by Swank Motion Pictures.

Sophocles, *Oedipus the King*
120 min.
VHS, Beta, 3/4 U.
With Michael Pennington, John Gielgud, and
    Claire Bloom.
Distributed by Films for the Humanities.

Strindberg, *Miss Julie*
90 min., B/W, 1950.
VHS, Beta.
Swedish.
With Anita Bjork, Ulf Palme, and Anders
    Henrickson.
Directed by Alf Sjoberg.
Distributed by Sultan Entertainment.

Strindberg, *Miss Julie*
60 min., 1978.
VHS, Beta, 3/4 U.
With Patrick Stewart and Lisa Harrow.
Distributed by Films, Inc.

Wakefield Master, *The Second Shepherds' Play*
52 min.
VHS, Beta, 3/4 U.
Includes productions of *Quem quaeritis* and *Abraham
    and Isaac*.
Distributed by Films for the Humanities

Webster, *The Duchess of Malfi*
123 min.
VHS.
With Eileen Atkins, Michael Bryant, Charles Kay,
    T. P. McKenna, Gary Bond, and Sheila
    Ballantine.
Distributed by Time-Life Multimedia.

Williams, *Cat on a Hot Tin Roof*
108 min., color, 1958.
VHS, Beta, Laser.
With Elizabeth Taylor, Paul Newman, Burl Ives,
    and Jack Carson.
Directed by Richard Brooks.
Distributed by MGM/United Artists Home Video.

Williams, *Cat on a Hot Tin Roof*
1984.
VHS, Beta, Laser, 16 mm film.
With Jessica Lange, Tommy Lee Jones, and Rip
    Torn.
Distributed by Live Home Video.

DIRECTORY OF FILM AND VIDEO DISTRIBUTORS

AIMS Media
9710 De Soto Avenue
Chatsworth, CA 91311-9734
tel: (818) 773–4300
toll-free: (800) 367–2467
fax: (818) 341–6700

Ambrose Video Publishing, Inc.
381 Park Avenue South
New York, NY 10016
tel: (212) 696–4545
toll-free: (800) 526–4663
fax: (212) 865–5486

Budget Video
1540 N. Highland Avenue, No. 108
Los Angeles, CA 90028
tel: (213) 466–0121
toll-free: (800) 621–0849

Classic Films Museum
6 Union Square
Dover-Foxcroft, ME 04426
tel: (207) 564–8371

Columbia Tristar Home Video
3400 Riverside Drive
Burbank, CA 91505–4627
tel: (818) 972–8686
fax: (818) 972–0937

Corinth Films
410 East 62 Street
New York, NY 10021
tel: (212) 421–4770

Encyclopedia Britannica Educational Corporation
310 S. Michigan Avenue
Chicago, IL 60604
tel: (312) 347–7900
toll-free: (800) 554–9862
fax: (312) 347–7966

Facets Multimedia, Inc.
1517 W. Fullerton Avenue
Chicago, IL 60614
tel: (312) 281–9075

Film Forum
100 E. William Street
Carson City, NV 89701
tel: (213) 559–5033
toll-free: (800) 232–1006
toll-free: (800) 525–5216 (in California)

Films, Inc.
c/o Public Media, Inc.
5547 N. Ravenwood Avenue
Chicago, IL 60640
tel: (312) 898–2600
toll-free: (800) 323–4222
fax: (312) 878–8648

Films for the Humanities
P.O. Box 2053
Princeton, NJ 08543
tel: (609) 452–1128
toll-free: (800) 257–5126

Grapevine Video
P.O. Box 46161
Phoenix, AZ 85063
tel: (602) 245–0210

Hollywood Home Theatre
1540 N. Highland Avenue, Suite 110
Hollywood, CA 90028
tel: (213) 466–0127

Insight Media
2162 Broadway
New York, NY 10024
tel: (212) 721–6316
fax: (212) 799–5309

Kino International Corp.
338 W. 39th Street, Suite 503
New York, NY 10018–1410
tel: (212) 629–6880

Paul Lewison
8899 Beverly Boulevard, Suite 101
Los Angeles, CA 90048

Live Home Video
15400 Sherman Way
P.O. Box 10124
Van Nuys, CA 91406
tel: (818) 908–0303

Lorimar Home Video
4000 Warner Boulevard #19
Burbank, CA 91522
tel: (818) 954–6266
toll-free: (800) 626–9000
fax: (818) 954–6540

MCA Home Video
70 Universal City Plaza
Universal City, CA 91608
tel: (818) 777–4300
fax: (818) 777–6419

MGM/United Artists Home Video
10000 W. Washington Boulevard
Culver City, CA 90232
tel: (310) 280–6212
toll-free: (800) 443–5500, ext. 792

New York Film Annex
163 Joralemon Street, Suite 1282
Brooklyn, NY 11201
tel: (718) 499–1621

New Yorker Video
16 W. 61st Street
New York, NY 10023
tel: (212) 247–6100
toll-free: (800) 447–0196
fax: (212) 307–7855

Nostalgia Family Video
P.O. Box 606
Baker City, OR 97814
tel: (503) 523–9034

Prism Entertainment
1888 Century Park East, Suite 1000
Los Angeles, CA 90067
tel: (213) 277–3270
fax: (213) 203–8036

Starmaker Entertainment, Inc.
151 Industrial Way, E.
Eatontown, NJ 07724
tel: (908) 389–1020
toll-free: (800) 233–3738
fax: (908) 389–1021

Sultan Entertainment
335 N. Maple Drive, Suite 351
Beverly Hills, CA 90210–3899
tel: (310) 385–6000

Swank Motion Pictures
201 S. Jefferson Avenue
St. Louis, MO 63166
tel: (314) 534–6300

Time-Life Multimedia
1271 Avenue of the Americas
New York, NY 10020
tel: (212) 484–5940

University of Michigan Media
416 Fourth Street
Ann Arbor, MI 48109
tel: (313) 764–5360

Valencia Entertainment Corporation
28231 Avenue Crocker, Suite 120
Valencia, CA 91355
tel: (805) 257–6054
toll-free: (800) 323–2601
fax: (805) 949–3400

Video Yesteryear
Box C
Sandy Hook, CT 06482
tel: (203) 744–2476
toll-free: (800) 243–0987

Warner Home Video Inc.
4000 Warner Boulevard
Burbank, CA 91522
tel: (818) 954–6439
toll-free: (800) 626–9000
fax: (818) 954–6540

Zenger Video
10200 Jefferson Boulevard
P.O. Box 802
Culver City, CA 90232–0802
tel: (213) 839–2436
toll-free: (800) 421–4246
fax: (213) 839–2249

CREDITS